FOR THE GLORY ™

NOW & FOREVER

JUDE 24-25

MY NAME	**PHONE**
ADDRESS	**E-MAIL**

MY GROUP

Name _____

Address _____

City _____ State _____

Zip _____ Phone # _____

E-Mail _____

Name _____

Address _____

City _____ State _____

Zip _____ Phone # _____

E-Mail _____

Name _____

Address _____

City _____ State _____

Zip _____ Phone # _____

E-Mail _____

Name _____

Address _____

City _____ State _____

Zip _____ Phone # _____

E-Mail _____

Name _____

Address _____

City _____ State _____

Zip _____ Phone # _____

E-Mail _____

Name _____

Address _____

City _____ State _____

Zip _____ Phone # _____

E-Mail _____

Name _____

Address _____

City _____ State _____

Zip _____ Phone # _____

E-Mail _____

Name _____

Address _____

City _____ State _____

Zip _____ Phone # _____

E-Mail _____

FROM THE DESK OF
LES STECKEL
PRESIDENT

Dear Teammate –

You are holding in your hands the most powerful book in the world. It is God's Game Plan for your life, and everything you need as a competitor is right in front of you. Spending time in God's Word over the years has transformed my life, and the same life-change can happen to you!

The FCA theme this year is "For the Glory." In Jude 1:24-25, Jude wrote, **"Now to Him who is able to protect you from stumbling and to make you stand in the presence of His glory, blameless and with great joy, to the only God our Savior, through Jesus Christ our Lord, be glory, majesty, power, and authority before all time, now, and forever. Amen."**

The goal of life is to give God the glory in all we do. Competition is not about us, but about Him! We must die to ourselves and fully understand the power, majesty and authority of God. As competitors, we need to play for and live lives that will honor Him. We are to bring Him the praise in all that we do – on and off the field of competition. That is the challenge.

It is, however, hard to give glory where glory is due. Training, discipline, perseverance, and drive are all characteristics that can propel athletes to the next level and transform good athletes into great athletes. Often after achieving a goal, we feel that it is our hard work that got us to that point. We focus the praise, honor, and glory on ourselves as individual athletes. Part of FCA's Competitor's Creed states:

I do not trust in myself.
I do not boast in my abilities or believe in my own strength.
I rely solely on the power of God.
I compete for the pleasure of my Heavenly Father,
the honor of Christ and the reputation of the Holy Spirit.

Here's the bottom line: the results of our efforts must result in His glory. To accept it for ourselves would be to rob God of His glory.

Success means saying yes to a personal relationship with the ultimate Head Coach (Jesus Christ), and then allowing Him to live His life through you, giving Him glory every step of the way. In all of your life decisions, you are simply following the lead of Christ.

As you spend one-on-one time in God's Word, you will learn who you are as a competitor and also who Jesus Christ is as Lord and Savior. Let Him call the plays for your life. Be coachable. Allow your parents, Christian friends, and coaches to encourage you and challenge you in your walk with Christ. Have the desire to be in the middle of God's will. Accept the challenge to play and live for God's glory. There is no question that you were born for such a time as this – to serve the purposes of God in your own generation.

For the Glory,

Les Steckel

Les Steckel
President/CEO

FELLOWSHIP OF
CHRISTIAN ATHLETES

8701 Leeds Road | Kansas City, MO 64129-1680 | (816) 921-0909
www.fca.org | fca@fca.org

To see the world impacted for Jesus Christ through the influence of athletes and coaches.

GOD'S GAME PLAN

THE ATHLETES' BIBLE

FOR THE GLORY™

NOW & FOREVER

JUDE 24-25

Nashville, Tennessee

God's Game Plan: The Athlete's Bible 2006, HCSB
(Scripture notes and introductions, mini-study questionnaires, group warm-ups, and indices)
Copyright © 2006 by Serendipity House Publishers
Nashville, Tennessee. All rights reserved.

ISBN: 1-5749-4277-8

Dewey Decimal Classification: 220.52
Subject Headings: BIBLE \ ATHLETES—RELIGIOUS LIFE

Holman Christian Standard Bible® and Dictionary-Concordance
Copyright © 1999, 2000, 2002, 2003, 2005 by Holman Bible Publishers.

1-800-525-9563
www.SerendipityHouse.com

CONTRIBUTORS:

Serendipity House Writing and Editorial Team: Ben Colter (project manager), Kathy Bence, Greg Benoit, Steve Bond, LeAnne Constantine, Marilyn Duncan, Sarah Gant, John Glynn, Katharine Harris, Sarah Hogg, Ron Keck, George Knight, Derek Leman, Keith Madsen, Dan McArthur, Bethany McShurley, Lloyd Mullens, Reischa Feuerbacher, Joe Snider, and Cathy Tardif

Fellowship of Christian Athletes: Dave Kubal, Dan Britton, Danny Burns, Bethany Hermes, and the Devotional Writers: Josh Carter, Clay Elliott, David Hermes, Mike Hill, Jere Johnson, and Kyle Shultz

Design and Typesetting Team: Scott Lee (art director) of Scott Lee Designs, Alanna Cavanaugh, Garry and Trina Fulton of tfDesigns, John Nissen of Church Art Work, Jill Ewert, Carmen Foster, Rachel Koop, Scott Masters of FCA

Printed in the United States of America

08 07 06   1 2 3 4 5

TABLE OF CONTENTS

BOOKS OF THE BIBLE

Abbreviations Key:

v. – verse
vv. – verses

f – verse following
ff – verses following
ch. – chapter(s)
circa (C.). – about, around

e.g. – for example
i.e. – that is
NT – New Testament
OT – Old Testament

HOW TO USE THE FCA ATHLETE'S BIBLE

What is unique about this Bible?

This Bible is designed specifically for students. It is filled with discussion questions and exercises that help student athletes and coaches share every aspect of their lives in the context of God's Word.

How can groups use this Bible?

In lots of ways! For starters, look at the ready-made Study Plans on pages 15–28. Here you will find 330 relevant topics, grouped into 14 (8 Student and 6 Athlete) categories. After choosing a topic in the first eight categories, all you have to do is decide whether to use the questionnaire from a story passage or the questionnaire from a teaching passage. Each study includes a group Warm-Up beginning on page 1391 in the second tabbed section in the back of this Bible. There are nearly 25,000 combinations of small-group studies to help build community in your group.

CHOICES

TOPIC	WARM-UP	STORY PASSAGE	TEACHING PASSAGE
FAMILY TENSIONS	Parent Problems p. 1427	Family Feuds Genesis 21:1-21 (p. 60)	Parental Expectations Ephesians 6:1-4 (p. 1150)
SEEKING GOD'S GUIDANCE	Our Un-Calling p. 1416	Daring Escape Exodus 2:1-25 (p. 92)	One Day at a Time James 4:13-17 (p. 1221)
DANGER OF DISOBEDIENCE	Hallowed Inhibitions p. 1429	Israelite Spy Team Numbers 13:26–14:45 (p. 169)	Wrath and Rejoicing Revelation 14:1–15:8 (p. 1268)
TOUGH DECISIONS	What To Do? p. 1428	Mission Improbable Joshua 5:13–6:21 (p. 227)	Careful Choices 1 Corinthians 8:1-13 (p. 1104)
GOING YOUR OWN WAY	My Daily Routine p. 1401	Faith Under Fire Judges 14:1-20 (p. 259)	Letters of Warning Revelation 2:1–3:22 (p. 1257)
FINDING GOD'S STRENGTH	My Coat of Arms p. 1402	The Secret of Strength Judges 16:23-31 (p. 262)	The Question of Marriage 1 Corinthians 7:1-40 (p. 1102)
MOTIVES & CHOICES	Medical History p. 1405	Detrimental Desires 1 Samuel 8:1-22 (p. 278)	Walking by the Spirit Romans 8:1-17 (p. 1081)
LUST & SEXUAL PURITY	Some of My Feelings p. 1415	Adultery and Murder 2 Samuel 11:1-27 (p. 309)	Choosing the Best Way 1 Thessalonians 4:1-12 (p. 1171)
RISKING EVERYTHING	Assessing the Future p. 1413	A Beauty Contest Esther 2:1-18 (p. 466)	The Secret to Success Philippians 3:1-11 (p. 1157)
TAKING RESPONSIBILITY	Take Your Choice p. 1403	A Big Fish Story Jonah 2:1–3:10 (p. 834)	Who's Responsible? 2 Thessalonians 3:6-15 (p. 1176)
GOOD & BAD INFLUENCES	Who Influences You? p. 1418	Healing Forgiveness Mark 2:1-12 (p. 921)	You Will Be Assimilated! Romans 12:1-8 (p. 1087)
AVOIDING TROUBLE	Pick a Promise p. 1444	Losing Your Head Mark 6:14-29 (p. 927)	Follow the Light Ephesians 5:1-21 (p. 1149)
WHAT CONTROLS YOU?	Wallet Scavenger Hunt p. 1406	Perilous Possessions Mark 10:17-31 (p. 934)	The Perfect Offering Romans 6:15-23 (p. 1079)
MONEY & WEALTH	Money and Success p. 1421	Building True Wealth Luke 12:13-21 (p. 971)	Money Issues 1 Timothy 6:3-21 (p. 1184)
YOUR HEART FOCUS	My Favorite Things p. 1405	Where's Your Treasure? Luke 12:22-34 (p. 971)	Changing Priorities 1 Peter 4:1-11 (p. 1229)

PAGE 17

Are there any studies beyond those found in the Study Plans?

Yes. On page 32, you can see how the bonus mini-studies not covered in the 330 Study Plans can be used for other specific topics. You can also use the index of 150 favorite Bible stories on pages 29–31 to create your own course ... for example, stories about David, the miracles or parables of Jesus, and Jesus' last week.

TOPIC	PASSAGE	PAGE
Passover and Salvation	Exodus 12:1-30 – The Passover	101
Sin and Death of Son	2 Samuel 12:15-25 – Tragic Consequences	311
Hearing and Responding to Jesus	Matthew 13:1-23 – The Parable of the Four Soils	890
The Sabbath	Mark 2:23–3:6 – Remember the What?	921
Rejection of Jesus	Luke 4:14-30 – Get Out of Town	955
Communion, Eucharist	Luke 22:7-23 – Celebrating the Lord's Supper	986
God's Coworkers	1 Corinthians 3:1-23 – Building with Gold	1098
Christian Freedom	1 Corinthians 10:14–11:1 – Handling Our Freedom as Christians	1106
Spiritual Gifts	1 Corinthians 14:1-25 – Gifted and Talented	1110
Words of Life or Death	2 Corinthians 2:12–3:6 – Fragrant Letters	1120
Handling Foolish Teaching	2 Corinthians 11:16-33 – Tolerating Fools	1129
Hope in Jesus	Colossians 1:1-4 – The Lasting Hope	1162
Walking with Christ in Victory	Colossians 2:6-23 – Victory Over the Enemy	1164
Gifts from God	1 Thessalonians 5:12-28 – God's Incredible Gifts to Us	1172
Imitators of Jesus	2 Thessalonians 1:1-12 – Worthy of God's Kingdom	1175
End Times	2 Thessalonians 2:1-17 – The Man of Lawlessness	1175
Our Worth and Value	1 Timothy 2:1-15 – Finding Worth in Christ	1181
False Teachers	2 Timothy 3:1-9 – The Dark Side	1190
The Bible	2 Timothy 3:10–4:8 – The Living Word	1190

Can we use this Bible to do a book study?

Absolutely! There are mini-studies your group can use to study all the New Testament books from Matthew to Revelation, as well as several Old Testament books. Simply use the mini-study questionnaires where these gray boxes appear in the Scripture text. For some of the longer books, you may want to cover more than one questionnaire per meeting.

Calling Heaven's Number

1. When have you called on someone in authority for help? Did you get the help you needed? Why did you need it in the first place?

Romans 9:30-10:21
2. What is the only way to be saved, according to Paul in 10:9-10? How does this compare with other religious teachings? With the teachings of the world around you?
3. What does it mean to "call on the name of the Lord" (10:13)?
4. What does verse 14 suggest about the importance of sharing Jesus with others? How often do you tell others about Jesus? How can you do this more often?

What do the icons on some of the mini-study boxes mean?

They show that the mini-study is connected to a lesson plan in a particular topical category. However, all the mini-studies should be quite relevant to any group of students.
The 14 categories are listed below:

 You Will Be Assimilated!

1. When have you thought of yourself more highly than you should have? How did you discover your error?

Romans 12:1-8
2. What does Paul mean in verse 2 when he says, "Do not be conformed to this age, but be transformed by the renewing of your mind"?
3. How can you offer your body "as a living sacrifice" (v. 1)?
4. According to this passage, what is required of you to discover God's will for your life?
5. How much are you conforming to the world's standards? Are you working to transform your mind to God's way of thinking?

STUDENT STUDIES

 Awareness

 Relationships

 Choices

 Stress

 Issues

 Crisis

 Beliefs

 Discipleship

ATHLETE STUDIES

 Fundamentals

 Competition

 Teamwork

 Training

 Performance

 Game Plan

What is the purpose of the notes at the bottom of each Bible page?

These commentary notes help students understand key words and concepts of the Scripture passage covered by the questionnaire. In some cases, the notes also provide background information about what preceded the passage in that book of the Bible. Here is an example from Romans 12:3-11:

dom of choice and action, based on the inner renewing work of the Holy Spirit.

12:3 everyone among you. The truth about spiritual gifts applies to every believer. **think sensibly.** The command is to know oneself accurately rather than to have too high an opinion of oneself in comparison to others.

12:5 we who are many are one body in Christ. Paul is speaking here of believers in the church, the body of Christ. The church is like a family. Although individual members of the family are distinct and different, they belong to one another because of the common Lord whom they serve.

12:6 gifts. Those endowments given by God to every believer by grace (the words *grace* and *gifts* come from the same root word) to be used in God's service. The gifts listed here (or

elsewhere in the New Testament) are not meant to be exhaustive or absolute since no gift list overlaps completely. **prophecy.** Inspired utterances, distinguished from teaching by their immediacy and spontaneous nature, the source of which is direct revelation by God.

12:7 service. The special capacity for rendering practical service to the needy. **teaching.** In contrast to the prophet (with direct revelation from God), the teacher relied on the Old Testament Scriptures and the teachings of Jesus to instruct others.

12:8 exhorting. This is supporting and assisting others to live a life of obedience to God. **giving.** A person with this gift takes delight in giving away his or her possessions. **leading.** Those with special ability to guide a congregation are called upon to do so with zeal. **showing mercy.** Serving

those who need care with cheerfulness.

12:9 Love. The Greek word *agape*—self-giving love in action on behalf of others—which is made possible by God's Spirit. **without hypocrisy.** Genuine, not counterfeit or showy.

12:10 brotherly love. The word for love used here, *philadelphia*, denotes the tender affection expressed in families, now said to be appropriate to those in the church—which is the believer's new family. **honor.** Since other Christians are in union with Christ, they are to be honored.

12:11 be fervent. This Greek word is also used of water when it has been brought to a boil (or of metal, like copper, which glows red-hot in the refining or shaping process).

Is there a particular flow in the questions in the mini-studies?

Yes. The questions are arranged to move across the "Disclosure Scale" from NO RISK at the beginning of the mini-study to HIGH RISK at the end.

Can individuals use this Bible for daily devotions?

There is a Personal Reading Plan at the beginning of the Introduction to each book of the Bible. You can check off the passages as you read them. For your continued study, if you used all of the mini-studies in the gray boxes within the Bible text, there would be enough for every day of the year.

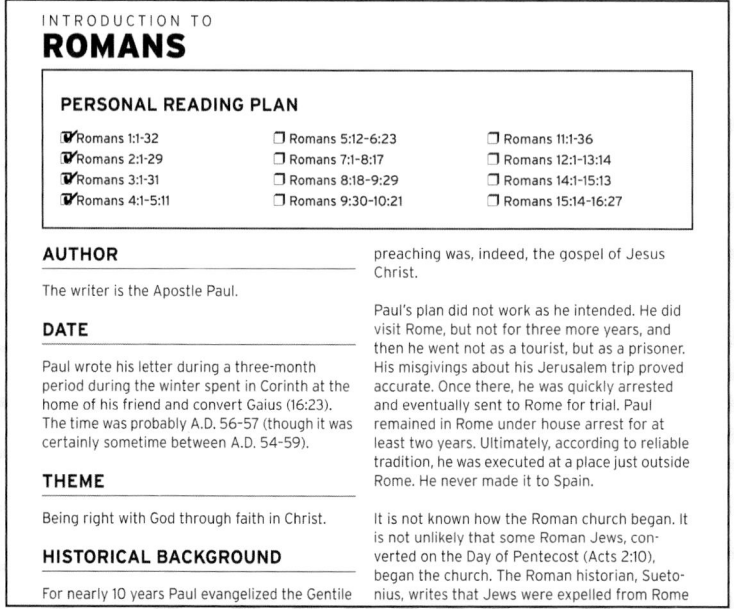

INTRODUCTION TO

ROMANS

PERSONAL READING PLAN

☑Romans 1:1-32	☐ Romans 5:12-6:23	☐ Romans 11:1-36
☑Romans 2:1-29	☐ Romans 7:1-8:17	☐ Romans 12:1-13:14
☑Romans 3:1-31	☐ Romans 8:18-9:29	☐ Romans 14:1-15:13
☑Romans 4:1-5:11	☐ Romans 9:30-10:21	☐ Romans 15:14-16:27

AUTHOR

The writer is the Apostle Paul.

DATE

Paul wrote his letter during a three-month period during the winter spent in Corinth at the home of his friend and convert Gaius (16:23). The time was probably A.D. 56-57 (though it was certainly sometime between A.D. 54-59).

THEME

Being right with God through faith in Christ.

HISTORICAL BACKGROUND

For nearly 10 years Paul evangelized the Gentile

preaching was, indeed, the gospel of Jesus Christ.

Paul's plan did not work as he intended. He did visit Rome, but not for three more years, and then he went not as a tourist, but as a prisoner. His misgivings about his Jerusalem trip proved accurate. Once there, he was quickly arrested and eventually sent to Rome for trial. Paul remained in Rome under house arrest for at least two years. Ultimately, according to reliable tradition, he was executed at a place just outside Rome. He never made it to Spain.

It is not known how the Roman church began. It is not unlikely that some Roman Jews, converted on the Day of Pentecost (Acts 2:10), began the church. The Roman historian, Suetonius, writes that Jews were expelled from Rome

What other information is found in the Introduction to each book of the Bible?

After the Personal Reading Plan, you will find helpful summaries about the author, date, theme, and characteristics of each book. For the books that contain mini-study question-naires, there is a chart, at the bottom of the Introduction page, listing those mini-studies. The passages that are used for the topical Study Plans (pages 15–22) are shown first, followed by the passages that are not specifically linked to a study plan (those without any icons).

How can our group use the Group Warm-Up section found in the second tabbed section of colored inserts (pages 1455–1502) of the Bible?

The first category—Warm-Ups—has numerous exercises designed to kick off meetings. The next three categories—Biblical Inventories, Special Topics, and Scripture Reflections—provide additional resources that groups can take advantage of as they desire. The final category—Affirmation—contains both fun and serious affirmation exercises, which can be used to close a meeting or special event. Lastly, this section offers an Evaluation for groups to use. The majority of these Group Warm-ups are integrated into the Study Plans on pages 15–28).

  LIFESTYLE CHECKUP

How healthy is your lifestyle? Taking one line at a time, mark an "X" where you would rate yourself for each of the areas. Share the results of your checkup with your group.

DIET / NUTRITION
health food _____ junk food

EXERCISE / PHYSICAL ACTIVITY
marathon runner _____ couch potato

SLEEPING HABITS
"Good morning, Lord!" _____ "O Lord, it's morning!"

TOBACCO
Mr. Clean _____ Joe Camel

STRESS / HYPERACTIVITY
Garfield _____ Tazmanian Devil

MENTAL ALERTNESS
Road Runner _____ Wile E. Coyote

OVERALL FITNESS / VITALITY
Energizer Bunny _____ dead battery

DESIGN A STUDY

365 STUDIES

STUDENT STUDIES

ATHLETE STUDIES

BIBLE STORY STUDIES

3 STEPS TO DESIGN A GREAT STUDY

1. READY

Pray! Ask the Lord to give you guidance.

2. SET

Choose a Group Workout from any of the study plans on pages 15-32 for Student Studies, Athlete Studies, or Bible Story Studies.

Choose a Warm-Up from the Group Warm-Ups section beginning on page 1391 (second set of tabs at the back of the Bible).

3. GO

Go expecting God to do great things!

Check out more resources at fca.org and look for Huddle eQuipment.

AWARENESS

TOPIC	WARM-UP	STORY PASSAGE	TEACHING PASSAGE
GOD'S LEADING & PURPOSES	Comfort Zones p. 1408	Strange but True Exodus 3:1-22 (p. 93)	Conflicting Spirits 1 Corinthians 2:6-16 (p. 1098)
YOUR HEART CONDITION	My Partner p. 1395	Heart Checkup Exodus 6:28–7:24 (p. 97)	Help for the Heart Hebrews 3:1-19 (p. 1201)
USING OUR BLESSINGS	Down Memory Lane p. 1411	Blessings to Remember Joshua 3:14–4:24 (p. 225)	Using What You Have 2 Corinthians 8:1-15 (p. 1125)
WEAKNESSES & STRENGTHS	Mr./Miss World Contest p. 1404	A Really Bad Hair Day Judges 16:1-22 (p. 261)	A Work in Process Philippians 1:1-11 (p. 1154)
WHAT'S INSIDE	My Temperament p. 1395	Seeing the Heart and Soul 1 Samuel 16:1-13 (p. 286)	Been Misjudged Lately? James 2:1-13 (p. 1218)
SUCCESS IN LIFE	Wild Predictions p. 1425	Overwhelmed by Temptation 1 Kings 10:23–11:13 (p. 340)	The Ultimate Reward Hebrews 4:1-13 (p. 1202)
STANDING STRONG	Robinson Crusoe p. 1417	Taking a Stand Mark 11:12-19 (p. 936)	The World's Garbage 1 Corinthians 4:1-21 (p. 1099)
CONNECTED WITH GOD	Childhood Supper Table p. 1412	In Dad's House Luke 2:41-52 (p. 952)	Picked for the Team Ephesians 1:3-14 (p. 1144)
THE MAIN THINGS	A Bunch of Bests p. 1406	Guilty as Charged Luke 7:36-50 (p. 961)	Doubtful Issues Romans 14:1–15:13 (p. 1089)
THANKFUL & CONTENT	Thanks a Bunch p. 1443	An Attitude of Gratitude Luke 17:11-19 (p. 978)	Carefree Contentment Philippians 4:10-20 (p. 1159)
SALVATION NOW & FOREVE	What is Your Dream? p. 1394	Out on a Limb Luke 19:1-10 (p. 981)	Heaven's Marriage Feast Revelation 18:1–19:10 (p. 1271)
GLORIFYING GOD	Preferences p. 1414	It's Alive! John 4:1-26 (p. 999)	Made for God 1 Peter 2:4-12 (p. 1235)
WALKING WITH GOD	This Little Light of Yours p. 1453	Walking in the Light John 8:12-20 (p. 1007)	God's Perpetual Presence Psalm 139 (p. 573)
CONFIDENCE & POWER	Automotive Affirmation p. 1451	Real Fire Power Acts 2:1-24,36-41 (p. 1030)	Confidence in Eternity 1 John 5:1-15 (p. 1245)
LOVE IN ACTION	The Giving Game p. 1453	A Loving Church Acts 2:42-47 (p. 1032)	God is My Dad 1 John 2:28–3:10 (p. 1242)

RELATIONSHIPS

TOPIC	WARM-UP	STORY PASSAGE	TEACHING PASSAGE
ANGER, HATRED, OR LOVE	Evil on the Prowl p. 1440	Murder One Genesis 4:1-16 (p. 47)	The Test of Faith 1 John 2:7-14 (p. 1241)
DATING & MARRIAGE	The Dating Game p. 1407	Love at First Sight Genesis 29:1-14 (p. 68)	Marriage Matters Ephesians 5:22-33 (p. 1149)
CAUTION IN TRUSTING	Four Facts ... One Lie p. 1402	In the Pits Genesis 37:12-36 (p. 77)	Favorable Friendship James 4:1-12 (p. 1220)
GETTING ALONG	Competition–Cooperation p. 1430	"Hey, It's Me!" Genesis 45:1-28 (p. 84)	Take Out the Trash Colossians 3:1-25 (p. 1165)
ROMANCE & MARRIAGE	Choosing Friends p. 1409	Love Song Songs 1:1–2:7 (p. 614)	Marriage that Works 1 Peter 3:1-7 (p. 1228)
MERCY OR PUNISHMENT	Good Stuff p. 1435	Forgive Him or Choke Him? Matthew 18:21-35 (p. 898)	Rage or Mercy? Romans 9:1-29 (p. 1083)
HELPING THE NEEDY	Obnoxious People p. 1417	The Good Samaritan Luke 10:25-37 (p. 967)	Truth or Consequences 2 John 1-14 (p. 1248)
FORGIVENESS	Parent Problems p. 1427	The Wasteful Son Luke 15:11-32 (p. 976)	Faithful Friendships Philemon 1-25 (p. 1197)
SELFLESS SERVICE	You Remind Me of Jesus p. 1449	Wedding Woes John 2:1-11 (p. 997)	The Power of Love Romans 13:8-14 (p. 1089)
CARING & HELPING	911 Phone Numbers p. 1404	What I Have is Yours! Acts 3:1-16 (p. 1033)	Love, Not Slavery Galatians 5:1-15 (p. 1140)
LOVE IN ACTION	How's Your Love Life? p. 1437	Glamour Ministry Acts 6:1-7 (p. 1037)	True Love (for Others) 1 Corinthians 13:1-13 (p. 1110)
SHARING GOD'S LOVE	The Old Neighborhood p. 1429	Sharing Good News Acts 8:26-40 (p. 1040)	True Love (for God) 1 John 3:11-24 (p. 1243)
CHOOSING FRIENDS	Friendship Survey p. 1409	Really? That Guy? Acts 9:1-19 (p. 1041)	Picking Your Friends 3 John 1-14 (p. 1249)
ACCEPTANCE	Family Expectations p. 1403	Accepting One Another Acts 10:1-23 (p. 1043)	Playing Judge Romans 2:1-16 (p. 1073)
SETTING BOUNDARIES	How's the Weather? p. 1408	Parting Company Acts 15:36-41 (p. 1051)	An Uneven Match 2 Corinthians 6:14-7:1 (p. 1124)

CHOICES

TOPIC	WARM-UP	STORY PASSAGE	TEACHING PASSAGE
FAMILY TENSIONS	Parent Problems p. 1427	Family Feuds Genesis 21:1-21 (p. 60)	Parental Expectations Ephesians 6:1-4 (p. 1150)
SEEKING GOD'S GUIDANCE	Our Un-Calling p. 1416	Daring Escape Exodus 2:1-25 (p. 92)	One Day at a Time James 4:13-17 (p. 1221)
DANGER OF DISOBEDIENCE	Hallowed Inhibitions p. 1429	Israelite Spy Team Numbers 13:26–14:45 (p. 169)	Wrath and Rejoicing Revelation 14:1–15:8 (p. 1268)
TOUGH DECISIONS	What to Do? p. 1428	Mission Improbable Joshua 5:13–6:21 (p. 227)	Careful Choices 1 Corinthians 8:1-13 (p. 1104)
GOING YOUR OWN WAY	My Daily Routine p. 1401	Faith Under Fire Judges 14:1-20 (p. 259)	Letters of Warning Revelation 2:1–3:22 (p. 1257)
FINDING GOD'S STRENGTH	My Coat of Arms p. 1402	The Secret of Strength Judges 16:23-31 (p. 262)	The Question of Marriage 1 Corinthians 7:1-40 (p. 1102)
MOTIVES & CHOICES	Medical History p. 1405	Detrimental Desires 1 Samuel 8:1-22 (p. 278)	Walking by the Spirit Romans 8:1-17 (p. 1081)
LUST & SEXUAL PURITY	Some of My Feelings p. 1415	Adultery and Murder 2 Samuel 11:1-27 (p. 309)	Choosing the Best Way 1 Thessalonians 4:1-12 (p. 1171)
RISKING EVERYTHING	Assessing the Future p. 1413	A Beauty Contest Esther 2:1-18 (p. 466)	The Secret to Success Philippians 3:1-11 (p. 1157)
TAKING RESPONSIBILITY	Take Your Choice p. 1403	A Big Fish Story Jonah 2:1–3:10 (p. 834)	Who's Responsible? 2 Thessalonians 3:6-15 (p. 1176)
GOOD & BAD INFLUENCES	Who Influences You? p. 1418	Healing Forgiveness Mark 2:1-12 (p. 921)	You Will Be Assimilated! Romans 12:1-8 (p. 1087)
AVOIDING TROUBLE	Pick a Promise p. 1444	Losing Your Head Mark 6:14-29 (p. 927)	Follow the Light Ephesians 5:1-21 (p. 1149)
WHAT CONTROLS YOU?	Wallet Scavenger Hunt p. 1406	Perilous Possessions Mark 10:17-31 (p. 934)	The Perfect Offering Romans 6:15-23 (p. 1079)
MONEY & WEALTH	Money and Success p. 1421	Building True Wealth Luke 12:13-21 (p. 971)	Money Issues 1 Timothy 6:3-21 (p. 1184)
YOUR HEART FOCUS	My Favorite Things p. 1405	Where's Your Treasure? Luke 12:22-34 (p. 971)	Changing Priorities 1 Peter 4:1-11 (p. 1229)

STRESS

TOPIC	WARM-UP	STORY PASSAGE	TEACHING PASSAGE
DIFFICULT OR SCARY TASKS	Stressing Me Out p. 1420	A Magical Staff Exodus 4:1-17 (p. 94)	The Power of Love Ephesians 3:14-21 (p. 1146)
TRUSTING GOD & WAITING	Things ... Drive You Crazy p. 1413	Survival Tactics Exodus 14:5-31 (p. 104)	It's Tough to Wait James 5:7-20 (p. 1222)
ATTITUDE IN TRIALS	Good Stuff p. 1435	Heavenly Food Exodus 16:1-35 (p. 106)	The Test of Faith 2 Corinthians 6:3-13 (p. 1123)
ASKING GOD FOR HELP	911 Phone Numbers p. 1404	Healing Phenomenon 2 Kings 5:1-16 (p. 360)	Enemy Outlook Psalm 17 (p. 506)
GOD IS IN CONTROL	How's the Weather? p. 1408	Struck Blind 2 Kings 6:8-23 (p. 361)	Finding Joy in Troubles Romans 5:1-11 (p. 1077)
PERSECUTION & HOPE	Headache Survey p. 1415	A Fiery Test Daniel 3:1-12,19-27 (p. 794)	The Point of Pain Romans 8:28-39 (p. 1082)
RECONNECT WITH GOD	Living Under the Influence p. 1414	Running Away Jonah 1:1-17 (p. 833)	A Ministry of Reconciliation 2 Corinthians 5:11–6:2 (p. 1122)
BOLD IN PRAYER	Life Signs p. 1433	Walking on Water Matthew 14:22-33 (p. 894)	Draw Near and Hold On Hebrews 10:19-39 (p. 1210)
RESENTMENT	Stress Test p. 1423	Hey—That's Not Fair! Matthew 20:1-16 (p. 901)	Carefree Contentment Philippians 4:10-20 (p. 1159)
BETRAYAL & SIN'S TRAP	You Are What You Eat p. 1401	Betrayed by a Kiss Matthew 26:47-56 (p. 912)	Enslaved Galatians 4:8-20 (p. 1138)
INSECURITY & FEAR	Medical History p. 1405	Calming the Storm Mark 4:35-41 (p. 925)	Fear vs. Love 1 John 4:7-21 (p. 1244)
FOLLOW GOD WHEN IT'S HARD	Comfort Zones p. 1408	Miracle Birth Luke 1:26-38 (p. 949)	Passing the Test 2 Corinthians 13:1-4 (p. 1131)
WORRY & ANXIETY	Emotional Dashboard p. 1431	One Necessary Thing Luke 10:38-42 (p. 968)	Don't Sweat It! Matthew 6:25-34 (p. 883)
SEEING GOD'S HAND	Pick a Promise p. 1444	Closed Doors Acts 16:6-10 (p. 1052)	Open Your Eyes! Ephesians 1:15-23 (p. 1144)
JOY IN TRIALS	Music in My Life p. 1434	Singing in Prison Acts 16:22-40 (p. 1053)	Don't Worry—Be Happy! Philippians 4:2-9 (p. 1158)

ISSUES

TOPIC	WARM-UP	STORY PASSAGE	TEACHING PASSAGE
CARING FOR CREATION & PEOPLE	My Temperament p. 1395	The Ultimate Garden Genesis 2:4-25 (p. 45)	Caring for All Galatians 2:1-10 (p. 1135)
ORDER & CHAOS	KWIZ p. 1396	Operation Recovery Genesis 8:1-22 (p. 50)	Order vs. Chaos 1 Corinthians 14:26-40 (p. 1111)
RADICAL OBEDIENCE	Comfort Zones p. 1408	Moving Out Genesis 12:1-9 (p. 52)	Gouge Out Your Eyes Matthew 5:27-30 (p. 880)
HOMOSEXUALITY	Hallowed Inhibitions p. 1429	Dangerous Values Genesis 19:1-29 (p. 58)	Homosexuality Romans 1:18-32 (p. 1072)
SEX STANDARDS	A Case Study on Sex p. 1442	"Everyone's Doing It" Genesis 39:1-23 (p. 78)	Sex and the Christian 1 Corinthians 5:1-13 (p. 1100)
SPEAKING OUT WITHOUT JUDGING	What Are Your Values? p. 1452	A Warning in the Night 1 Samuel 3:1-14 (p. 275)	Judging Others 1 Corinthians 6:1-11 (p. 1101)
FOLLOWING GOD & REBELLING	My Last Will & Testament p. 1427	Okay to Disobey 1 Samuel 20:1-42 (p. 291)	Maturing in the Faith 2 Peter 1:1-11 (p. 1234)
ROLES IN SOCIETY	Lay It On the Line p. 1416	Respecting Authority 1 Samuel 24:1-22 (p. 295)	Roles of Husbands and Wives 1 Corinthians 11:2-16 (p. 1107)
SUICIDE & DIVORCE	Live Like Your Were Dying p. 1441	Saul's Suicide 1 Samuel 31:1-13 (p. 300)	Divorce ... Life Shredder Matthew 19:1-12 (p. 899)
RAPE & SEX	Some of My Feelings p. 1415	Amnon's Rape of Tamar 2 Samuel 13:1-22 (p. 312)	Run From Sex 1 Corinthians 6:12-20 (p. 1101)
RESPONDING TO FALSE TEACHERS	Assessing the Future p. 1413	Fire from Heaven 1 Kings 18:16-40 (p. 348)	Watch Out for False Teachers! 1 Timothy 1:1-11 (p. 1180)
THE POOR & NEEDY	The Life Raft p. 1418	Sheep and Goats Matthew 25:31-46 (p. 910)	Lending a Helping Hand 1 Timothy 5:11–6:2 (p. 1183)
GIVING VS. EXTORTION	Fun Money p. 1412	Lying to Get in the Spotlight Acts 5:1-11 (p. 1035)	Generous Giving 2 Corinthians 8:16–9:5 (p. 1126)
CULTS, OCCULT, & FALSE PROPHETS	Power People p. 1432	False Prophets Acts 13:1-12 (p. 1047)	A Different Gospel Galatians 1:1-10 (p. 1134)
CULTS & ANTICHRISTS	Christian Basics p. 1426	Anger Over the Gospel Acts 19:23-41 (p. 1057)	Seeking Truth 1 John 4:1-6 (p. 1244)

CRISIS

TOPIC	WARM-UP	STORY PASSAGE	TEACHING PASSAGE
FAILURES & GRACE	My Roles p. 1434	Prayer Power Genesis 18:16-33 (p. 57)	Never Beyond God's Love 1 Timothy 1:12-20 (p. 1180)
WISDOM IN CRISES	Headache Survey p. 1415	Life and Death Crisis 1 Kings 3:16-28 (p. 330)	Living in the Light 1 John 1:5–2:6 (p. 1240)
TRAGEDY, LONELINESS & TRUSTING GOD	The Best of Times … p. 1398	Losing Everything Job 1:6-22 (p. 473)	Never Alone 2 Timothy 4:9-18 (p. 1191)
ACCUSATIONS & PERSECUTION	Competition - Cooperation p. 1430	Den of Lions Daniel 6:1-4 (p. 798)	Misunderstood 1 Thessalonians 2:1-16 (p. 1169)
SUFFERING LIKE JESUS	Things … Drive You Crazy p. 1413	A Crown of Thorns Matthew 27:26-31 (p. 914)	No Big Surprise 1 Peter 4:12-19 (p. 1230)
PERSEVERANCE & FAITH	A High Standard p. 1439	Miraculous Faith Mark 5:24-34 (p. 926)	Passing the Test James 1:2-18 (p. 1217)
WORRY & LACK OF FAITH	Stress Test p. 1423	Help My Unbelief Mark 9:14-29 (p. 932)	Stressed Out 1 Peter 5:1-11 (p. 1231)
OPPOSITION & VICTORY	The Armor of God p. 1438	Dealing with Demons Luke 8:26-39 (p. 963)	A Reason to Live Philippians 1:12-30 (p. 1154)
CHOOSING SIDES	Last Will and Testament p. 1427	Weeping for Others Luke 19:28-44 (p. 983)	The Last Battle Revelation 19:11–20:10 (p. 1274)
FACING OUR SINS	Medical History p. 1405	Anyone Without Sin? John 8:1-11 (p. 1006)	Godly Grief 2 Corinthians 7:2-16 (p. 1124)
GOD'S POWER & COMFORT	Emotional Dashboard p. 1431	Power in Weakness John 9:1-15,24-34 (p. 1009)	God's Comfort 2 Corinthians 1:3-11 (p. 1118)
ENDURANCE & POWER	Assessing the Future p. 1413	Raising the Dead John 11:17-44 (p. 1012)	Facing Hardship 1 Peter 2:13-25 (p. 1227)
JESUS' POWER & PROTECTION	Power People p. 1432	Tomb Raiders John 20:1-18 (p. 1024)	Sealed by Jesus from Wrath Revelation 6:1–7:17 (p. 1261)
GOD RESCUES US	Wallet Scavenger Hunt p. 1406	"Get Out of Jail Free" Card Acts 12:1-19 (p. 1046)	God, Our Refuge Psalm 46:1-11 (p. 525)
TRUST & HOPE	You and Me, Partner p. 1445	Singing in Prison Acts 16:22-40 (p. 1053)	Suffering and Hoping Romans 8:18-27 (p. 1081)

TOPIC	WARM-UP	STORY PASSAGE	TEACHING PASSAGE
FIRST ADAM & NEW PERFECT ADAM	Brain Food p. 1448	Extreme Creation Genesis 1:1–2:3 (p. 442)	Bold Confessions Hebrews 4:15–5:10 (p. 1203)
EVIL ENTERS PARADISE	Broadway Jobs p. 1447	Sin Enters Paradise Genesis 3:1-24 (p. 46)	Evil in Disguise 2 Corinthians 11:1-15 (p. 1128)
EXPERIENCING JESUS	Warm Memories p. 1423	God with Us Matthew 1:18-25 (p. 875)	The Greatest Gift Ephesians 2:1-10 (p. 1145)
FUTURE JUDGMENT	TV Game Show p. 1431	Baptized with Spirit and Fire Matthew 3:1-7 (p. 877)	Dragon Slayer Revelation 12:1–13:8 (p. 1266)
VALUE OF YOUR SOUL	Valued Values p. 1446	Deny Yourself Matthew 16:13-28 (p. 896)	Works vs. Faith Romans 11:1-36 (p. 1085)
PREPARING FOR JESUS' RETURN	A High Standard p. 1439	Be Prepared Matthew 25:1-13 (p. 908)	Heaven's Gonna be a Blast! 1 Thess. 4:13–5:11 (p. 1172)
JESUS DEFEATED DEATH	Life Signs p. 1433	He is Risen! Matthew 28:1-20 (p. 916)	Victory Over Death 1 Corinthians 15:35-58 (p. 1114)
SACRIFICING FOR US	You Remind Me of Jesus p. 1449	Sacrificing for Us! Mark 15:1-15 (p. 944)	The Suffering Servant Isaiah 52:13–53:12 (p. 664)
JESUS' KEY PURPOSE	What Are Your Values? p. 1452	Heavenly Purpose Luke 2:1-20 (p. 951)	Justified by Jesus Romans 5:12-21 (p. 1077)
ACCEPTING THE INVITATION	My Partner p. 1395	The Best Invitation Ever Luke 14:15-24 (p. 975)	Come! Revelation 22:7-21 (p. 1277)
FINAL DESTINATION	Preferences p. 1414	Heaven and Hell Luke 16:19-31 (p. 978)	Lake of Fire or Eternal Life? Revelation 20:11–21:8 (p. 1275)
JESUS VICTORIOUS	Down Memory Lane p. 1411	On the Cross Luke 23:26-49 (p. 990)	Lion and Lamb Revelation 4:1–5:14 (p. 1259)
EMBRACING GOD'S GRACE	Like Music to My Ears p. 1430	An Eye-Opening Experience Luke 24:13-35 (p. 991)	Grasping Grace Galatians 3:1-14 (p. 1136)
JESUS THE ONLY WAY	Christian Basics p. 1426	A Spiritual Birth John 3:1-21 (p. 998)	The Only Seed Galatians 3:15-25 (p. 1137)
BELIEVING THE EVIDENCE	Places in My Life p. 1407	You Gotta Believe John 20:24-31 (p. 1025)	The Old and New Covenants 2 Corinthians 3:7-18 (p. 1120)

TOPIC	WARM-UP	STORY PASSAGE	TEACHING PASSAGE
SELF EXAMINATION & TURNING TO GOD	Scouting Report p. 1399	Busted! 2 Samuel 12:1-4 (p. 310)	Evaluate Yourself 1 Corinthians 11:17-34 (p. 1107)
LOVING GOD & SERVING HIM	Dream Career p. 1450	Making a Profit Matthew 25:14-30 (p. 909)	Love is the Key 1 John 2:15-27 (p. 1241)
TIME WITH GOD (PRAYER)	Precious Time p. 1419	Perfect Priorities Mark 1:29-39 (p. 920)	Prayer Uplink Matthew 6:5-18 (p. 882)
GOD'S CARE FOR US	Old-Fashioned Auction p. 1424	Eternal Family Ties Mark 3:20-35 (p. 923)	The Great Shepherd Psalm 23:1-6 (p. 512)
PLEASING GOD	The Grand Total p. 1400	Rest and Refreshment Mark 6:30-44 (p. 928)	Health for Body and Mind Proverbs 3:1-8 (p. 580)
CONNECTION WITH GOD	Wow, So-So, or Ho-Hum p. 1411	Precious Time Mark 9:2-13 (p. 931)	Future Plans Romans 15:14-33 (p. 1091)
AUTHORITY	KWIZ p. 1396	Money Matters Mark 12:13-17 (p. 938)	Freedom vs. Obedience Galatians 4:21-31 (p. 1139)
GIVING FREELY	Money and Success p. 1421	Meaningful Giving Mark 12:41-44 (p. 939)	Cheerful Giving 2 Corinthians 9:6-15 (p. 1127)
TEMPTATION & SIN	Problem Survey p. 1422	That's Tempting Luke 4:1-13 (p. 954)	A New Way of Life Romans 6:1-14 (p. 1078)
COST OF FOLLOWING JESUS	I Dream of Genie p. 1432	Giving It All Up Luke 5:1-11 (p. 957)	Salt of the Earth Luke 14:25-35 (p. 975)
SPIRITUAL BATTLES & SIN	The Armor of God p. 1438	Confronting Sin Luke 22:54-62 (p. 988)	Weapons of War 2 Corinthians 10:1-18 (p. 1127)
LIVING BY FAITH	My Risk Quotient p. 1410	Cast Your Nets John 21:1-14 (p. 1026)	Not Ashamed Romans 1:8-17 (p. 1071)
EMPOWERED BY THE SPIRIT	Sharing Dreams p. 1422	Baptism of the Holy Spirit Acts 1:1-11 (p. 1029)	Do You Really Love Me? John 14:15-27 (p. 1017)
SERVING OTHERS; GOOD WORKS	A Slice of Life p. 1410	Glamour Ministry Acts 6:1-7 (p. 1037)	Talk is Cheap James 2:14-26 (p. 1219)
SHARING CHRIST	Lip Power p. 1436	Capable Christianity Acts 9:20-31 (p. 1042)	Serving Jesus Romans 1:1-7 (p. 1071)

FUNDAMENTALS

COMPETITION

TEAMWORK

TRAINING

PERFORMANCE

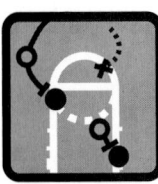

GAME PLAN

TOPIC	STUDY PAGE	PASSAGE	REFERENCE
GAME PLAN	page 1495	Escape Through the Red Sea	Exodus 13:17–14:31 (p. 103)
BLIND SPOTS	page 1496	Balaam's Donkey and the Angel	Numbers 22:21-41 (p. 178)
MIRACLE GAME	page 1496	The Day the Sun Stood Still	Joshua 10:1-14 (p. 231)
TEAMWORK	page 1497	David's Kindness to Mephibosheth	2 Samuel 9:1-13 (p. 308)
POWER GAME	page 1497	Pentecost	Acts 2:1-13 (p. 1030)
BROTHERS IN SPORT	page 1498	Peter's Vision (Gentile Conversion)	Acts 10:9-48 (p. 1044)
WEAKNESS	page 1498	Treasure in Clay Jars	2 Corinthians 4:1-18 (p. 1121)
GOD'S GAME PLAN	page 1499	God Warns Noah	Genesis 6:9-22 (p. 48)
TOUGH CHOICES	page 1499	Wisdom or Riches?	1 Kings 3:4-14 (p. 330)
RISK IT ALL	page 1500	Mordecai Appeals to Esther	Esther 4:1-17 (p. 467)
POWER OR SKILL?	page 1500	Not By Strength or Might	Zechariah 4:6-10 (p. 860)
TEAM PARTS	page 1501	Unity, Yet Diversity in the Body	1 Corinthians 12:12-31 (p. 1130)
TEAM UNITY	page 1501	Carry One Another's Burdens	Galatians 6:1-10 (p. 1141)
SWEAT OR HUMILITY	page 1502	Christian Humility	Philippians 2:1-18 (p. 1155)
OBEDIENCE	page 1502	Jonah's Flight	Jonah 1:1-17 (p. 833)

150 FAVORITE BIBLE STORY STUDIES - WITH QUESTIONNAIRES

OLD TESTAMENT

150 FAVORITE BIBLE STORY STUDIES

NEW TESTAMENT

Experiences of Jesus

Parables of Jesus

Jesus' Last Week

The Christian Church Begins

Paul's Missionary Journey

37 BONUS BIBLE STUDIES

The questionnaires for these stories, which are not part of the Study Plans on pages Study Index 13-28, can be used for the following topics:

INTRODUCTION TO THE
HOLMAN CHRISTIAN STANDARD BIBLE®

The Bible is God's revelation to man. It is the only book that gives us accurate information about God, man's need, and God's provision for that need. It provides us with guidance for life and tells us how to receive eternal life. The Bible can do these things because it is God's inspired Word, inerrant in the original manuscripts.

The Bible describes God's dealings with the ancient Jewish people and the early Christian church. It tells us about the great gift of God's Son, Jesus Christ, who fulfilled Jewish prophecies of the Messiah. It tells us about the salvation He accomplished through His death on the cross, His triumph over death in the resurrection, and His promised return to earth. It is the only book that gives us reliable information about the future, about what will happen to us when we die, and about where history is headed.

Bible translation is both a science and an art. It is a bridge that brings God's Word from the ancient world to the world today. In dependence on God to accomplish this sacred task, Holman Bible Publishers presents the Holman Christian Standard Bible, a new English translation of God's Word.

Textual base of the Holman CSB®

The textual base for the New Testament [NT] is the Nestle-Aland *Novum Testamentum Graece*, 27th edition, and the United Bible Societies' *Greek New Testament*, 4th corrected edition. The text for the Old Testament [OT] is the *Biblia Hebraica Stuttgartensia*, 5th edition. At times, however, the translators have followed an alternative manuscript tradition, disagreeing with the editors of these texts about the original reading.

Where there are significant differences among Hebrew [Hb] and Aramaic [Aram] manuscripts of the OT or among Greek [Gk] manuscripts of the NT, the translators have followed what they believe is the original reading and have indicated the main alternative(s) in footnotes. In a few places in the NT, large square brackets indicate texts that the translation team and most biblical scholars today believe were not part of the original text. However, these texts have been retained in brackets in the Holman CSB because of their undeniable antiquity and their value for tradition and the history of NT interpretation in the church. The Holman CSB uses traditional verse divisions found in most Protestant Bibles.

Goals of this translation

The goals of this translation are:

- to provide English-speaking people across the world with an accurate, readable Bible in contemporary English

- to equip serious Bible students with an accurate translation for personal study, private devotions, and memorization

- to give those who love God's Word a text that has numerous reader helps, is visually attractive on the page, and is appealing when heard

- to affirm the authority of Scripture as God's Word and to champion its absolute truth against social or cultural agendas that would compromise its accuracy

The name, Holman Christian Standard Bible, captures these goals: *Holman* Bible Publishers presents a new *Bible* translation, for *Christian* and English-speaking communities, which will be a *standard* in Bible translations for years to come.

Why is there a need for another English translation of the Bible?

There are several good reasons why Holman Bible publishers invested its resources in a modern language translation of the Bible:

1. Each generation needs a fresh translation of the Bible in its own language.

The Bible is the world's most important book, confronting each individual and each culture with issues that affect life, both now and forever. Since each new generation must be introduced to God's Word in its own language, there will always be a need for new translations such as the Holman Christian Standard Bible. The majority of Bible translations on the market today are revisions of translations from previous generations. The Holman CSB is a new translation for today's generation.

2. English, one of the world's greatest languages, is rapidly changing, and Bible translations must keep in step with those changes.

English is the first truly global language in history. It is the language of education, business, medicine, travel, research, and the Internet. More than 1.3 billion people around the world speak or read English as a primary or secondary language. The Holman CSB seeks to serve many of those people with a translation they can easily use and understand.

English is also the world's most rapidly changing language. The Holman CSB seeks to reflect recent changes in English by using modern punctuation, formatting, and vocabulary, while avoiding slang, regionalisms, or changes made specifically for the sake of political or social agendas. Modern linguistic and semantic advances have been incorporated into the Holman CSB, including modern grammar.

3. Rapid advances in biblical research provide new data for Bible translators.

This has been called the "information age," a term that accurately describes the field of biblical research. Never before in history has there been as much information about the Bible as there is today—from archaeological discoveries to analysis of ancient manuscripts to years of study and statistical research on individual Bible books. Translations made as recently as 10 or 20 years ago do not reflect many of these advances in biblical research. The translators have taken into consideration as much of this new data as possible.

4. Advances in computer technology have opened a new door for Bible translation.

The Holman CSB has used computer technology and telecommunications in its creation perhaps more than any Bible translation in history. Electronic mail was used daily and sometimes hourly for communication and transmission of manuscripts. An advanced Bible software program, Accordance®, was used to create and revise the translation at each step in its production. A developmental copy of the translation itself was used within Accordance to facilitate cross-checking during the translation process—something never done before with a Bible translation.

Translation Philosophy of the Holman CSB

Most discussions of Bible translations speak of two opposite approaches: formal equivalence and dynamic equivalence. Although this terminology is meaningful, Bible translations cannot be neatly sorted into these two categories any more than people can be neatly sorted into two categories according to height or weight. Holman Bible Publishers is convinced there is room for another category of translation philosophies that capitalizes on the strengths of the other two.

1. Formal Equivalence:

Often called "word-for-word" (or "literal") translation, the principle of formal equivalence seeks as nearly as possible to preserve the structure of the original language. It seeks to represent each word of the translated text with an exact equivalent word in the translation so that the reader can see word for word what the original human author wrote. The merits of this approach include its consistency with the conviction that the Holy Spirit did inspire the very words of Scripture in the original manuscripts. It also provides the English Bible student some access to the structure of the

34

text in the original language. Formal equivalence can achieve accuracy to the degree that English has an exact equivalent for each word and that the grammatical patterns of the original language can be reproduced in understandable English. However, it can sometimes result in awkward, if not incomprehensible, English or in a misunderstanding of the author's intent. The literal rendering of ancient idioms is especially difficult.

2. Dynamic Or Functional Equivalence:

Often called "thought-for-thought" translation, the principle of dynamic equivalence rejects as misguided the desire to preserve the structure of the original language. It proceeds by distinguishing the meaning of a text from its form and then translating the meaning so that it makes the same impact on modern readers that the ancient text made on its original readers. Strengths of this approach include a high degree of clarity and readability, especially in places where the original is difficult to render word for word. It also acknowledges that accurate and effective translation requires interpretation. However, the meaning of a text cannot always be neatly separated from its form, nor can it always be precisely determined. A biblical author may have intended multiple meanings. In striving for readability, dynamic equivalence also sometimes overlooks some of the less prominent elements of meaning. Furthermore, lack of formal correspondence to the original makes it difficult to verify accuracy and thus can affect the usefulness of the translation for in-depth Bible study.

3. Optimal Equivalence:

In practice, translations are seldom if ever purely formal or dynamic but favor one theory of Bible translation or the other to varying degrees. Optimal equivalence as a translation philosophy recognizes that form cannot be neatly separated from meaning and should not be changed (for example, nouns to verbs or third person "they" to second person "you") unless comprehension demands it. The primary goal of translation is to convey the sense of the original with as much clarity as the original text and the translation language permit. Optimal equivalence appreciates the goals of formal equivalence but also recognizes its limitations.

Optimal equivalence starts with an exhaustive analysis of the text at every level (word, phrase, clause, sentence, discourse) in the original language to determine its original meaning and intention (or purpose). Then relying on the latest and best language tools and experts, the nearest corresponding semantic and linguistic equivalents are used to convey as much of the information and intention of the original text with as much clarity and readability as possible. This process assures the maximum transfer of both the words and thoughts contained in the original.

The Holman CSB uses optimal equivalence as its translation philosophy. When a literal translation meets these criteria, it is used. When clarity and readability demand an idiomatic translation, the reader can still access the form of the original text by means of a footnote with the abbreviation "Lit."

The gender language policy in Bible translation

Some people today ignore the Bible's teachings on distinctive roles of men and women in family and church and have an agenda to eliminate those distinctions in every arena of life. These people have begun a program to engineer the removal of a perceived male bias in the English language. The targets of this program have been such traditional linguistic practices as the generic use of "man" or "men," as well as "he," "him," and "his."

A group of Bible scholars, translators, and other evangelical leaders met in 1997 to respond to this issue as it affects Bible translation. This group produced the "Guidelines for Translation of Gender-Related Language in Scripture" (adopted May 27, 1997 and revised Sept. 9, 1997). The Holman Christian Standard Bible was produced in accordance with these guidelines.

The goal of the translators has not been to promote a cultural ideology but to faithfully translate the Bible. While the Holman CSB avoids using "man" or "he" unnecessarily, the translation does

not restructure sentences to avoid them when they are in the text. For example, the translators have not changed "him" to "you" or to "them," neither have they avoided other masculine words such as "father" or "son" by translating them in generic terms such as "parent" or "child."

History of the *Holman Christian Standard Bible*

After several years of preliminary development, Holman Bible Publishers, the oldest Bible publisher in America, assembled an international, interdenominational team of 100 scholars, editors, stylists, and proofreaders, all of whom were committed to biblical inerrancy. Outside consultants and reviewers contributed valuable suggestions from their areas of expertise. An executive team then edited, polished, and reviewed the final manuscripts.

Traditional features found in the Holman CSB

In keeping with a long line of Bible publications, the Holman Christian Standard Bible has retained a number of features found in traditional Bibles:

1. Traditional theological vocabulary (such as justification, sanctification, redemption, etc.) has been retained since such terms have no translation equivalent that adequately communicates their exact meaning.
2. Traditional spellings of names and places found in most Bibles have been used to make the Holman CSB compatible with most Bible study tools.
3. Some editions of the Holman CSB will print the words of Christ in red letters to help readers easily locate the spoken words of the Lord Jesus Christ.
4. Nouns and personal pronouns that clearly refer to any person of the Trinity are capitalized.
5. Descriptive headings, printed above each section of Scripture, help readers quickly identify the contents of that section.
6. Small lower corner brackets: ⌊ ⌋ indicate words supplied for clarity by the translators (but see below, under <u>Substitution of words in sentences</u>, for supplied words that are not bracketed).
7. Two common forms of punctuation are used in the Holman CSB to help with clarity and ease of reading: em dashes (a long dash —) are used to indicate sudden breaks in thought or to help clarify long or difficult sentences. Parentheses are used infrequently to indicate words that are parenthetical in the original languages.

How certain names and terms are translated

The names of God

The Holman Christian Standard Bible OT consistently translates the Hebrew names for God as follows:

Holman CSB English:	Hebrew original:
God	*Elohim*
LORD	*YHWH (Yahweh)*
Lord	*Adonai*
Lord GOD	*Adonai Yahweh*
LORD of Hosts	*Yahweh Sabaoth*
God Almighty	*El Shaddai*

However, the Holman CSB OT uses Yahweh, the personal name of God in Hebrew, when a biblical text emphasizes Yahweh as a name: "His name is Yahweh" (Ps 68:4). Yahweh is used more often in the Holman CSB than in most Bible translations because the word LORD in English is a title of God and does not accurately convey to modern readers the emphasis on God's name in the original Hebrew.

The uses of Christ and Messiah

The Holman CSB translates the Greek word *Christos* ("anointed one") as either "Christ" or "Messiah" based on its use in different NT contexts. Where the NT emphasizes *Christos* as a name of our Lord or has a Gentile context, "Christ" is used (Eph 1:1 "Paul, an apostle of Christ Jesus..."). Where the NT *Christos* has a Jewish context, the title "Messiah" is used (Eph 1:12 "...we who had already put our hope in the Messiah"). The first use of "Messiah" in each chapter is also marked with a bullet referring readers to the Bullet Note at the back of most editions.

Place-names

In the original text of the Bible, particularly in the OT, a number of well-known places have names different from the ones familiar to contemporary readers. For example, "the Euphrates" often appears in the original text simply as "the River." In cases like this, the Holman Christian Standard Bible uses the modern name, "the Euphrates River," in the text without a footnote or lower corner brackets.

Substitution of words in sentences

A literal translation of the biblical text sometimes violates standard rules of English grammar, such as the agreement of subject and verb or person and number. In order to conform to standard usage, the Holman CSB has often made these kinds of grammatical constructions agree in English without footnotes or lower corner brackets.

In addition, the Greek or Hebrew texts sometimes seem redundant or ambiguous by repeating nouns where modern writing substitutes pronouns or by using pronouns where we would supply nouns for clarity and good style. When a literal translation of the original would make the English unclear, the Holman CSB sometimes changes a pronoun to its corresponding noun or a noun to its corresponding pronoun without a footnote or lower corner brackets. For example, Jn 1:42 reads: "And he brought Simon to Jesus . . ." The original Greek of this sentence reads: "And he brought him to Jesus."

Special Formatting Features

The Holman Christian Standard Bible has several distinctive formatting features:

1. OT passages quoted in the NT are set in boldface type. OT quotes consisting of two or more lines are block indented.

2. In dialogue, a new paragraph is used for each new speaker as in most modern publications.

3. Many passages, such as 1 Co 13, have been formatted as dynamic prose (separate block-indented lines like poetry) for ease in reading and comprehension. Special block-indented formatting has also been used extensively in both the OT and NT to increase readability and clarity in lists, series, genealogies and other parallel or repetitive texts.

4. Almost every Bible breaks lines in poetry using automatic typesetting programs with the result that words are haphazardly turned over to the next line. In the Holman CSB, special attention has been given to break every line in poetry and dynamic prose so that awkward or unsightly word wraps are avoided and complete units of thought turn over to the next line. The result is a Bible page that is much more readable and pleasing to the eye.

5. Certain foreign, geographical, cultural, or ancient words are preceded by a superscripted bullet (•Abba) at their first occurrence in each chapter. These words are listed in alphabetical order at the back of the Bible under the heading **Holman CSB Bullet Notes**. A few important or frequently misunderstood words (•slaves) are marked with a bullet more than one time per chapter.

6. Italics are used in the text for a transliteration of Greek and Hebrew words ("Hosanna!" in Jn 12:13) and in footnotes for direct quotations from the biblical text and for words in the

original languages (the footnote at Jn 1:1 reads: "The Word (Gk logos) is a title for Jesus...").

7. Since the majority of English readers do not need to have numbers and fractions spelled out in the text, the Holman CSB uses a similar style to that of modern newspapers in using Arabic numerals for the numbers 10 and above and in fractions, except in a small number of cases, such as when a number begins a sentence.

Footnotes

Footnotes are used to show readers how the original biblical language has been understood in the Holman Christian Standard Bible.

NT Textual Footnotes

NT textual notes indicate significant differences among Greek manuscripts (mss) and are normally indicated in one of three ways:

Other mss read _____
Other mss add _____
Other mss omit _____

In the NT, some textual footnotes that use the word "add" or "omit" also have square brackets before and after the corresponding verses in the biblical text (see the discussion above in the paragraph entitled "Textual base of the Holman CSB"). Examples of this use of square brackets are Mk 16:9-20, Jn 5:3-4, and Jn 7:53–18:11.

OT Textual Footnotes

OT textual notes show important differences among Hebrew manuscripts and among ancient OT versions, such as the Septuagint and the Vulgate. See the list of abbreviations on page 39 for a list of other ancient versions used.

Some OT textual notes (like NT textual notes) give only an alternate textual reading. However, other OT textual notes also give the support for the reading chosen by the editors as well as for the alternate textual reading. For example, the Holman CSB text of Ps 12:7 reads:

You will protect us[a] from this generation forever.

The textual footnote for this verse reads:

[a]**12:7** Some Hb mss, LXX; other Hb mss read *him*

The textual note in this example means that there are two different readings found in the Hebrew manuscripts: some manuscripts read *us* and others read *him*. The Holman CSB translators chose the reading *us*, which is also found in the Septuagint (LXX), and placed the other Hebrew reading *him* in the footnote.

Two other OT textual notes are:

| Alt Hb tradition reads _____ | a variation given by scribes in the Hebrew manuscript Tradition (known as *Kethiv/Qere* readings) |
| Hb uncertain | when it is uncertain what the original Hebrew text was |

Other Kinds of Footnotes

Lit _____	a more literal rendering in English of the Hebrew, Aramaic, or Greek text
Or _____	an alternate or less likely English translation of the same Hebrew, Aramaic, or Greek text
=	an abbreviation for "it means" or "it is equivalent to"
Hb, Aram, Gk	the actual Hebrew, Aramaic, or Greek word is given using English letters
Hb obscure	the existing Hebrew text is especially difficult to translate

38

emend(ed) to _____ the original Hebrew text is so difficult to translate that competent scholars have conjectured or inferred a restoration of the original text based on the context, probable root meanings of the words, and uses incomparative languages

In some editions of the Holman Christian Standard Bible, additional footnotes clarify the meaning of certain biblical texts or explain biblical history, persons, customs, places, activities, and measurements. Cross-references are given for parallel passages or passages with similar wording, and in the NT, for passages quoted from the OT.

Commonly Used Abbreviations in the Holman CSB

A.D.	in the year of our Lord
alt	alternate
a.m.	from midnight until noon
Aram	Aramaic
B.C.	before Christ
c.	circa
chap	chapter
DSS	Dead Sea Scrolls
Eng	English
Gk	Greek
Hb	Hebrew
Lat	Latin
Lit	Literally
LXX	Septuagint—an ancient translation of the Old Testament into Greek
MT	Masoretic Text
NT	New Testament
ms(s)	manuscript(s)
OT	Old Testament
p.m.	from noon until midnight
pl	plural
Ps(s)	psalm(s)
Sam	Samaritan Pentateuch
sg	singular
syn.	synonym
Sym	Symmachus
Syr	Syriac
Tg	Targum
Theod	Theodotian
v., vv.	verse, verses
Vg	Vulgate—an ancient translation of the Bible into Latin
vol(s).	volume(s)

PLAN OF SALVATION

What do you understand it takes for a person to go to Heaven?
Consider how the Bible answers this question: It's a matter of FAITH

F is for FORGIVENESS

We cannot have eternal life and heaven without God's forgiveness.—**Read Ephesians 1:7a.**

A is for AVAILABLE

Forgiveness is available. It is—

- Available for all.　　　—Read John 3:16.
- But not automatic.　　　—Read Matthew 7:21a.

I is for IMPOSSIBLE

It is impossible for God to allow sin into heaven.

- Because of who He is:
  God is loving and just.
  His judgment is
  against sin.　　　—Read James 2:13a.
- Because of who we are:
  Every person
  is a sinner.　　　—Read Romans 3:23.

But how can a sinful person enter heaven, when God allows no sin?

T is for TURN

Turn means to repent.

- Turn from something
  —sin and self.　　　—Read Luke 13:3b.
- Turn to Someone;
  trust Christ only.　　　—Read Romans 10:9.

H is for HEAVEN

Heaven is eternal life.

- Here　　　—Read John 10:10b.
- Hereafter　　　—Read John 14:3.

How can a person have God's forgiveness, heaven and eternal life, and Jesus as personal Savior and Lord? By trusting in Christ and asking Him for forgiveness. Take the step of faith described by another meaning of FAITH: Forsaking All I Trust Him.

Prayer:

Lord Jesus, I know I am a sinner and have displeased You in many ways. I believe You died for my sin and only through faith in Your death and resurrection can I be forgiven.

I want to turn from my sin and ask You to come into my life as my Savior and Lord. From this day on, I will follow You by living a life that pleases You. Thank You, Lord Jesus for saving me. Amen.

After you have received Jesus Christ into your life, tell a Christian friend about this important decision you have made. Follow Christ in believer's baptism and church membership. Grow in your faith and enjoy new friends in Christ by becoming part of His church. There, you'll find others who will love and support you.

THE OLD
TESTAMENT

THE OLD
TESTAMENT

INTRODUCTION TO
GENESIS

PERSONAL READING PLAN

AUTHOR

Moses is assumed to be the author and editor of most of the first five books of the Old Testament (the Pentateuch).

DATE

It is difficult to set a firm date for the writing of the Pentateuch. Conservative estimates place it in either the 15th or 13th century B.C., depending on when the Exodus occurred.

THEME

Everything begins with God, who elects a people of His own.

HISTORICAL BACKGROUND AND CHARACTERISTICS

Archaeological findings and ancient history have much in common with certain details of the Genesis narrative. The socio-cultural environment of the patriarchal narratives (Gen. 12-50) fits well within the context of the Middle Bronze Age (c. 1950-1550 B.C.) in Palestine. This "Book of Beginnings" is the origin for many of the major themes discussed in Scripture. Humanity's origin and mission, its fall and predicament, human responsibility and divine sovereignty, God's justice and mercy, His atonement for sin, the obedience of faith, the covenant of grace—all originate in Genesis. But Genesis is perhaps most often read for its vivid account of the pioneers of our faith—Abraham, Isaac, and Jacob—through whom God is known and can be trusted.

PASSAGES FOR TOPICAL GROUP STUDY

The Creation

1 In the beginning God created the heavens and the earth.

2 Now the earth was[a] formless and empty, darkness covered the surface of the watery depths, and the Spirit of God was hovering over the surface of the waters. 3 Then God said, "Let there be light," and there was light. 4 God saw that the light was good, and God separated the light from the darkness. 5 God called the light "day," and He called the darkness "night." Evening came, and then morning: the first day.

6 Then God said, "Let there be an expanse[b] between the waters, separating water from water." 7 So God made the expanse and separated the water under the expanse from the water above the expanse. And it was so. 8 God called the expanse "sky."[c] Evening came, and then morning: the second day.

Extreme Creation

1. What did you create when you were a kid? Mud pies? A tree house? Other?

Genesis 1:1-2:3

2. How does this account of creation compare with the theory of evolution?

3. Note the repetition of "God said .... And it was so." What does that tell us about God's word? About the creation of the world?

4. What does it mean by "God created man in His own image" (v. 27)? What is God's image?

5. Compare God's blessing on creatures (v. 22) and on man (v. 28).

6. What does it mean to "subdue" the earth and "rule" the creatures (v. 28)? How does this apply to your life?

9 Then God said, "Let the water under the sky be gathered into one place, and let the dry land appear." And it was so. 10 God called the dry land "earth," and He called the gathering of the water "seas." And God saw that it was good. 11 Then God said, "Let the earth produce vegetation: seed-bearing plants, and fruit trees on the earth bearing fruit with seed in it, according to their kinds." And it was so. 12 The earth brought forth vegetation: seed-bearing plants according to their kinds

and trees bearing fruit with seed in it, according to their kinds. And God saw that it was good. 13 Evening came, and then morning: the third day.

14 Then God said, "Let there be lights in the expanse of the sky to separate the day from the night. They will serve as signs for festivals and for days and years. 15 They will be lights in the expanse of the sky to provide light on the earth." And it was so. 16 God made the two great lights—the greater light to have dominion over the day and the lesser light to have dominion over the night—as well as the stars. 17 God placed them in the expanse of the sky to provide light on the earth, 18 to dominate the day and the night, and to separate light from darkness. And God saw that it was good. 19 Evening came, and then morning: the fourth day.

20 Then God said, "Let the water swarm with[d] living creatures, and let birds fly above the earth across the expanse of the sky." 21 So God created the large sea creatures[e] and every living creature that moves and swarms in the water, according to their kinds. ⌊He also created⌋ every winged bird according to its kind. And God saw that it was good. 22 So God blessed them, "Be fruitful, multiply, and fill the waters of the seas, and let the birds multiply on the earth." 23 Evening came, and then morning: the fifth day.

24 Then God said, "Let the earth produce living creatures according to their kinds: livestock, creatures that crawl, and the wildlife of the earth according to their kinds." And it was so. 25 So God made the wildlife of the earth according to their kinds, the livestock according to their kinds, and creatures that crawl on the ground according to their kinds. And God saw that it was good.

26 Then God said, "Let Us make man in Our image, according to Our likeness. They will rule the fish of the sea, the birds of the sky, the livestock, all the earth,[f] and the creatures that crawl[g] on the earth."

27 So God created man in His own image;
He created him in the image of God;
He created them male and female.

28 God blessed them, and God said to them, "Be fruitful, multiply, fill the earth, and subdue it. Rule the fish of the sea, the birds of the sky, and every creature that crawls[h] on the earth." 29 God also said, "Look, I have given you every seed-bearing plant on the surface of the entire earth, and every tree whose fruit contains seed. This food will be for you, 30 for all the wildlife of the earth, for every bird of the sky, and for every crea-

---

a1:1–2 Or When God began to create the sky and the earth, 2 the earth was b1:6 The Hb word for expanse is from a root meaning "to spread out, stamp, beat firmly," which suggests something like a dome; Jb 37:16–18; Is 40:22. c1:8 Or "heavens" d1:20 Lit with swarms of e1:21 Or created sea monsters f1:26 Syr reads sky, and over every animal of the land g1:26 Lit scurry h1:28 Lit and all scurrying animals that scurry

---

1:1 God created. This declaration means that God is, He created all things, and He brought us into being.

1:5 the first day. Either a literal day or a period of time. The phrase "morning and evening" suggests a literal day.

1:26 image ... likeness. God created people

to be like Him. Adam and Eve became unlike God only when they tried to be "like" Him in terms of authority (3:5).

1:27 male and female. Both men and women were created in the image of God and given the responsibility to take care of the earth.

1:28 Rule. Man's "rule" over the world carries

the idea of nurturing it with creativity and care.

2:3 He rested. "Rested" is the same Hebrew word as "Sabbath." Though His energy is unlimited, God rested on the seventh day from His creative work.

2:7 formed. While God "created" the physical world, He "formed" humankind. Man is the

ture that crawls on the earth—everything having the breath of life in it. ⌊I have given⌋ every green plant for food." And it was so. 31 God saw all that He had made, and it was very good. Evening came, and then morning: the sixth day.

2 So the heavens and the earth and everything in thema were completed. 2 By the seventhb day, God completed His work that He had done, and He restedc on the seventh day from all His work that He had done. 3 God blessed the seventh day and declared it holy, for on it He rested from His work of creation.d

Man and Woman in the Garden

4 These are the records of the heavens and the earth, concerning their creation at the timee that the LORD God made the earth and the heavens. 5 No shrub of the field had yet ⌊grown⌋ on the land,f and no plant of the field had yet sprouted, for the LORD God had not made it rain on the land, and there was no man to work the ground. 6 But water would come out of the ground and water the entire surface of the land. 7 Then the LORD God formed the man out of the dust from the ground and breathed the breath of life into his nostrils, and the man became a living being.

8 The LORD God planted a garden in Eden, in the east, and there He placed the man He had formed. 9 The LORD God caused to grow out of the ground every tree pleasing in appearance and good for food, including the tree of life in the midst of the garden, as well as the tree of the knowledge of good and evil.

10 A river wentg out from Eden to water the garden. From there it divided and became the source of four rivers.h 11 The name of the first is Pishon, which encircles the entire land of the Havilah, where there is gold. 12 Gold from that land is pure;i bdelliumj and onyxk are also there. 13 The name of the second river is Gihon, which encircles the entire land of •Cush. 14 The name of the third river is the Tigris, which flows to the east of Assyria. And the fourth river is the Euphrates.

15 The LORD God took the man and placed him in the garden of Eden to work it and watch over it. 16 And the LORD God commanded the man, "You are free to eat from any tree of the garden, 17 but you must not eatl from the tree of the knowledge of good and evil, for on the day you eat from it, you will certainly die." 18 Then the LORD God said, "It is not good for the man to be alone. I will make a helper who is like him." 19 So the LORD God formed out of the ground each wild animal and each bird of the sky, and brought each to the man

The Ultimate Garden

1. What pets have you had? What were their names?

Genesis 2:4-25

2. What was Adam's purpose in the Garden of Eden (v. 15)? How does this balance environmental responsibility ("watch over it") with the need to be productive ("work it")?

3. When Adam was lonely, God's solution was to create a woman (vv. 22-25). What does this say about modern views of homosexual "marriage"?

4. Death came to earth after Adam ate the forbidden fruit (v. 17). Evolution teaches that species evolve and adapt in order to avoid death. How does this prove that God could not have used "evolution" in creating humanity?

to see what he would call it. And whatever the man called a living creature, that was its name. 20 The man gave names to all the livestock, to the birds of the sky, and to every wild animal; but for the manm no helper was found who was like him. 21 So the LORD God caused a deep sleep to come over the man, and he slept. God took one of his ribs and closed the flesh at that place. 22 Then the LORD God made the rib He had taken from the man into a woman and brought her to the man. 23 And the man said:

This one, at last, is bone of my bone,
and flesh of my flesh;
this one will be called woman,
for she was taken from man.

24 This is why a man leaves his father and mother and bonds with his wife, and they become one flesh. 25 Both the man and his wife were naked, yet felt no shame.

The Temptation and the Fall

3 Now the serpent was the most cunning of all the wild animals that the LORD God had made. He said to the woman, "Did God really say, 'You can't eat from any tree in the garden'?"

2 The woman said to the serpent, "We may eat the fruit from the trees in the garden. 3 But about the fruit

---

a**2:1** Lit and all their host b**2:2** Sam, LXX, Syr read sixth c**2:2** Or ceased d**2:3** Lit work that God created to make e**2:4** Lit creation on the day f**2:5** Or earth g**2:10** Or goes h**2:10** Lit became four heads i**2:12** Lit good j**2:12** A yellowish, transparent gum resin k**2:12** Identity of this precious stone uncertain l**2:17** Lit eat from it m**2:20** Or for Adam

---

height of His creative artistry.

2:9 tree of the knowledge of good and evil. God had told Adam and Eve not to eat of the fruit of this tree (v. 17). They knew they had a choice to obey God or not.

2:15 work it and watch over it. God gave human beings the role of working and guard-

ing creation through their role as stewards.

2:18 not good for the man. God created a man and then a woman to bring children into the world. He also brought man a "helper like him" to provide support and companionship.

2:20 names to all the livestock. This was Adam's first act of stewardship over the

earth—naming the animals.

3:1 Did God really say, "You can't eat." The serpent tempted Eve to distrust God and her understanding of His word.

3:4 You will not die. Satan lied by telling Eve that God did not really mean what He had said.

3:8 they hid. Sin had disrupted Adam and

of the tree in the middle of the garden, God said, 'You must not eat it or touch it, or you will die.' "

4 "No! You will not die," the serpent said to the woman. 5 "In fact, God knows that whena you eat it your eyes will be opened and you will be like God,b knowing good and evil." 6 Then the woman saw that the tree was good for food and delightful to look at, and that it was desirable for obtaining wisdom. So she took some of its fruit and ate ⌊it⌋; she also gave ⌊some⌋ to her husband, ⌊who was⌋ with her, and he ate ⌊it⌋. 7 Then the eyes of both of them were opened, and they knew they were naked; so they sewed fig leaves together and made loincloths for themselves.

Sin Enters Paradise

1. What is your favorite food? What "junk food" is hardest for you to resist?

Genesis 3:1-24

2. Compare Eve's answer to the serpent (vv. 2-3) with God's command (2:16-17). What did she get wrong?

3. How did the serpent deceive Eve? How did he lure her into distrusting God?

4. How did God's questions (vv. 9,11) give Adam the opportunity to confess his sin and repent? What does this demonstrate about God's grace and forgiveness?

5. What was Adam's sin, according to God (v. 17)? To whom do you sometimes listen instead of God?

Sin's Consequences

8 Then the man and his wife heard the sound of the LORD God walking in the garden at the time of the evening breeze,c and they hid themselves from the LORD God among the trees of the garden. 9 So the LORD God called out to the man and said to him, "Where are you?"

10 And he said, "I heard Youd in the garden, and I was afraid because I was naked, so I hid."

11 Then He asked, "Who told you that you were naked? Did you eat from the tree that I had commanded you not to eat from?"

12 Then the man replied, "The woman You gave to be with me—she gave me ⌊some fruit⌋ from the tree, and I ate."

13 So the LORD God asked the woman, "What is this you have done?"

And the woman said, "It was the serpent. He deceived me, and I ate."

14 Then the LORD God said to the serpent:

Because you have done this,
you are cursed more than any livestock
and more than any wild animal.
You will move on your belly
and eat dust all the days of your life.

15 I will put hostility between you and the woman,
and between your •seed and her seed.
He will strike your head,
and you will strike his heel.

16 He said to the woman:

I will intensify your labor pains;
you will bear children in anguish.
Your desire will be for your husband,
yet he will dominate you.

17 And He said to Adam, "Because you listened to your wife's voice and ate from the tree about which I commanded you, 'Do not eat from it':

The ground is cursed because of you.
You will eat from it by means of painful labore
all the days of your life.

18 It will produce thorns and thistles for you,
and you will eat the plants of the field.

19 You will eat breadf by the sweat of your brow
until you return to the ground,
since you were taken from it.
For you are dust,
and you will return to dust."

20 Adam named his wife Eveg because she was the mother of all the living. 21 The LORD God made clothing out of skins for Adam and his wife, and He clothed them.

22 The LORD God said, "Since man has become like one of Us, knowing good and evil, he must not reach out, and also take from the tree of life, and eat, and live forever." 23 So the LORD God sent him away from the garden of Eden to work the ground from which he was taken. 24 He drove man out, and east of the garden of

---

a**3:5** Lit on the day   b**3:5** Or gods, or divine beings   c**3:8** Lit at the wind of the day   d**3:10** Lit the sound of You   e**3:17** Lit it through pain
f**3:19** Or food   g**3:20** Lit Living, or Life

Eve's relationship with God. It is impossible to hide from God, who knows everything about us.

3:12-13 Adam refused to take responsibility for his actions by blaming Eve for his disobedience. Eve then passed the blame on to the serpent.

3:15 strike your head ... strike his heel. This is the first prophecy of Christ's work in the Bible. In Adam's sin, Satan dealt a blow. But in Jesus' resurrection, He destroyed the work of Satan.

3:21 clothing out of skins. This killing of an animal for clothing for Adam and Eve fore-

shadowed the blood sacrifices that would be required to cleanse people from sin, as well as the eventual sacrifice of Christ.

3:22 good and evil. After their fall into sin, Adam and Eve discovered evil and its deadly consequences (Rom. 5:12; 6:23).

Eden He stationed •cherubim with a flaming, whirling sword to guard the way to the tree of life.

Cain Murders Abel

4 Adam knew his wife Eve intimately, and she conceived and gave birth to Cain. She said, "I have had a male child with the LORD's help."[a] 2 Then she also gave birth to his brother Abel. Now Abel became a shepherd of a flock, but Cain cultivated the land. 3 In the course of time Cain presented some of the land's produce as an offering to the LORD. 4 And Abel also presented ⌊an offering⌋—some of the firstborn of his flock and their fat portions. The LORD had regard for Abel and his offering, 5 but He did not have regard for Cain and his offering. Cain was furious, and he was downcast.[b]

6 Then the LORD said to Cain, "Why are you furious? And why are you downcast?[c] 7 If you do right, won't you be accepted? But if you do not do right, sin is crouching at the door. Its desire is for you, but you must master it."

8 Cain said to his brother Abel, "Let's go out to the field."[d] And while they were in the field, Cain attacked his brother Abel and killed him.

9 Then the LORD said to Cain, "Where is your brother Abel?"

"I don't know," he replied. "Am I my brother's guardian?"

10 Then He said, "What have you done? Your brother's blood cries out to Me from the ground! 11 So now you are cursed ⌊with alienation⌋ from the ground that opened its mouth to receive your brother's blood you have shed.[e] 12 If you work the land, it will never again give you its yield. You will be a restless wanderer on the earth."

13 But Cain answered the LORD, "My punishment[f] is too great to bear! 14 Since You are banishing me today from the soil, and I must hide myself from Your presence and become a restless wanderer on the earth, whoever finds me will kill me."

15 Then the LORD replied to him, "In that case,[g] whoever kills Cain will suffer vengeance seven times over."[h] And He placed a mark on Cain so that whoever found him would not kill him. 16 Then Cain went out from the LORD's presence and lived in the land of Nod, east of Eden.

The Line of Cain

17 Cain knew his wife intimately, and she conceived and gave birth to Enoch. Then Cain became the builder of a city, and he named the city Enoch after his son. 18 Irad was born to Enoch, Irad fathered Mehujael,

Murder One

1. Where are you in the birth order of your family—oldest, youngest, middle? What's the best and worst part about your birth order?

Genesis 4:1-16

2. Why did God accept Abel's offering but reject Cain's?

3. Cain was furious. What should his response have been (v. 7)?

4. Why did Cain murder Abel? Why did he blame Abel for his own sin?

5. What does Cain's answer to God (v. 9) reveal about his own selfishness? How was selfishness the root cause of Cain's murdering his own brother?

6. When has selfishness hurt your relationships with family and friends?

Mehujael fathered Methushael, and Methushael fathered Lamech. 19 Lamech took two wives for himself, one named Adah and the other named Zillah. 20 Adah bore Jabal; he was the father of the nomadic herdsmen.[i] 21 His brother was named Jubal; he was the father of all who play the lyre and the flute. 22 Zillah bore Tubal-cain, who made all kinds of bronze and iron tools. Tubal-cain's sister was Naamah.

23 Lamech said to his wives:

Adah and Zillah, hear my voice;
wives of Lamech, pay attention to my words.
For I killed a man for wounding me,
a boy for striking me.
24 If Cain is to be avenged seven times over,
then for Lamech it will be seventy-seven times!

25 Adam knew his wife intimately again, and she gave birth to a son and named him Seth, for ⌊she said,⌋ "God has given[j] me another child in place of Abel, since Cain killed him." 26 A son was born to Seth also, and he named him Enosh. At that time people began to call on the name of[k] the LORD.

The Line of Seth

5 These are the family[l] records of the descendants of Adam. On the day that God created man,[m] He

a4:1 Lit the LORD   b4:5 Lit and his face fell   c4:6 Lit why has your face fallen   d4:8 Sam, LXX, Syr, Vg; MT omits Let's go out to the field   e4:11 Lit blood from your hand   f4:13 Or sin   g4:15 LXX, Syr, Vg read Not so!   h4:15 Or suffer severely   i4:20 Lit the dweller of tent and livestock   j4:25 The Hb word translated given sounds like the name Seth.   k4:26 Or to worship, or to proclaim or invoke the name of   l5:1 Lit written family   m5:1 Or Adam

4:5–8 Cain got mad because God disapproved of his offering. The he killed his brother in a fit of jealous pride. Cain's concern was not for his relationship with God but for retribution and revenge because God had looked with favor on Abel's offering.

4:10 **Your brother's blood cries out.** The

horror of this first murder reveals the depths of evil to which people can sink.

4:12-15 Cain was driven from his home and from the Lord's presence (vv. 14,16). He would move from place to place as a restless wanderer. But God graciously placed on him some kind of identifiable sign that showed he

was under divine protection.

4:25 **another child.** Seth would carry on the line that would eventually result in the world's Savior (Luke 3:37).

5:3 **in his likeness.** Even after he sinned, Adam retained the image of God and passed it down to Seth.

made him in the likeness of God; 2 He created them male and female. When they were created, He blessed them and called them man.ᵃ

3 Adam was 130 years old when he fathered ⌊a child⌋ in his likeness, according to his image, and named him Seth. 4 Adam lived 800 years after the birth of Seth, and he fathered sons and daughters. 5 So Adam's life lasted 930 years; then he died.

6 Seth was 105 years old when he fathered Enosh. 7 Seth lived 807 years after the birth of Enosh, and he fathered sons and daughters. 8 So Seth's life lasted 912 years; then he died.

9 Enosh was 90 years old when he fathered Kenan. 10 Enosh lived 815 years after the birth of Kenan, and he fathered sons and daughters. 11 So Enosh's life lasted 905 years; then he died.

12 Kenan was 70 years old when he fathered Mahalalel. 13 Kenan lived 840 years after the birth of Mahalalel, and he fathered sons and daughters. 14 So Kenan's life lasted 910 years; then he died.

15 Mahalalel was 65 years old when he fathered Jared. 16 Mahalalel lived 830 years after the birth of Jared, and he fathered sons and daughters. 17 So Mahalalel's life lasted 895 years; then he died.

18 Jared was 162 years old when he fathered Enoch. 19 Jared lived 800 years after the birth of Enoch, and he fathered sons and daughters. 20 So Jared's life lasted 962 years; then he died.

21 Enoch was 65 years old when he fathered Methuselah. 22 And after the birth of Methuselah, Enoch walked with God 300 years and fathered sons and daughters. 23 So Enoch's life lasted 365 years. 24 Enoch walked with God, and he was not there, because God took him.

25 Methuselah was 187 years old when he fathered Lamech. 26 Methuselah lived 782 years after the birth of Lamech, and he fathered sons and daughters. 27 So Methuselah's life lasted 969 years; then he died.

28 Lamech was 182 years old when he fathered a son. 29 And he named him Noah, saying, "This one will bring us reliefᵇ from the agonizing labor of our hands, caused by the ground the LORD has cursed." 30 Lamech lived 595 years after Noah's birth, and he fathered sons and daughters. 31 So Lamech's life lasted 777 years; then he died.

32 Noah was 500 years old, and he fathered Shem, Ham, and Japheth.

Sons of God and Daughters of Men

6 When mankind began to multiply on the earth and daughters were born to them, 2 the sons of God saw that the daughters of manᶜ were beautiful, and they took any they chose as wivesᵈ for themselves. 3 And the LORD said, "My Spirit will not remaineᵉ withᶠ mankind forever, because they are corrupt.ᵍ Their days will be 120 years." 4 The Nephilimʰ were on the earth both in those days and afterwards, when the sons of God came to the daughters of man, who bore children to them. They were the powerful men of old, the famous men.

Weather Alert

1. If your house was about to be washed away in a flood, what three things would you quickly grab?

Genesis 6:5–7:12

2. What does 6:5 tell us about the human race? About our ability to find world peace?
3. Why did Noah find "favor in the eyes of the LORD" (6:8; see 6:22 and 7:5)?
4. Noah looked foolish building a huge boat. Why did he continue to build it? What happened when he finished?
5. How can obedience sometimes look foolish? What does this teach about obeying God? About obeying your coaches, teachers, parents, and other authorities?

Judgment Decreed

5 When the LORD saw that man's wickedness was widespread on the earth and that every scheme his mind thought of was nothing but evil all the time, 6 the LORD regretted that He had made man on the earth, and He was grieved in His heart. 7 Then the LORD said, "I will wipe off the face of the earth: man, whom I created, together with the animals, creatures that crawl, and birds of the sky—for I regret that I made them." 8 Noah, however, found favor in the eyes of the LORD.

God Warns Noah

9 These are the family records of Noah. Noah was a righteous man, blameless among his contemporaries; Noah walked with God. 10 And Noah fathered three sons: Shem, Ham, and Japheth.

11 Now the earth was corrupt in God's sight, and the earth was filled with violence.ⁱ 12 God saw how corrupt the earth was, for all flesh had corrupted its way on the

---

ᵃ5:2 Or Adam ᵇ5:29 The Hb word translated bring us relief sounds like the name of Noah. ᶜ6:2 Or the human women ᵈ6:2 Or women ᵉ6:3 Or strive ᶠ6:3 Or in ᵍ6:3 Lit flesh ʰ6:4 Possibly means "fallen ones"; traditionally giants; Nm 13:31–33 ⁱ6:11 Or injustice

---

5:22–24 Enoch is the only person listed in Genesis who did not die. He walked with God in a special way, and God simply took him away (Heb. 11:5).

6:6 the LORD regretted. God did not think He had made a mistake by creating man. But man's choice to turn from Him and His love

grieved Him deeply.

6:8–9 blameless among his contemporaries. Noah was the one person in the world at that time who followed the Lord.

6:14–16 God was concerned with the practical. Noah was to build a boat that had to last for 40 days of rain and 150 days of floating on

the flood waters.

6:17 destroy all flesh. The Bible is clear in saying that all life on earth was destroyed in the flood. Only Noah, his family, and the animals in the ark survived.

6:18 establish My covenant. God made an agreement with Noah to save his family if

---

earth. 13 Then God said to Noah, "I have decided to put an end to all flesh, for the earth is filled with violence[a] because of them; therefore I am going to destroy them along with the earth.

14 "Make yourself an ark of gofer[b] wood. Make rooms in the ark, and cover it with pitch inside and outside. 15 This is how you are to make it: The ark will be 450 feet long, 75 feet wide, and 45 feet high.[c] 16 You are to make a roof,[d] finishing ⌊the sides of the ark⌋ to within 18 inches[e] ⌊of the roof.⌋ You are to put a door in the side of the ark. Make it with lower, middle, and upper ⌊decks⌋.

17 "Understand that I am bringing a deluge—floodwaters on the earth to destroy all flesh under heaven with the breath of life in it. Everything on earth will die. 18 But I will establish My covenant with you, and you will enter the ark with your sons, your wife, and your sons' wives. 19 You are also to bring into the ark two of every living thing of all flesh, male and female, to keep them alive with you. 20 Two of everything—from the birds according to their kinds, from the livestock according to their kinds, and from every animal that crawls on the ground according to its kind—will come to you so that you can keep them alive. 21 Take with you every kind of food that is eaten; gather it as food for you and for them." 22 And Noah did this. He did everything that God had commanded him.

Entering the Ark

7 Then the LORD said to Noah, "Enter the ark, you and all your household, for I have seen that you ⌊alone⌋ are righteous before Me in this generation. 2 You are to take with you seven pairs, a male and its female, of all the clean animals, and two of the animals that are not clean, a male and its female, 3 and seven pairs, male and female, of the birds of the sky—in order to keep •offspring alive on the face of the whole earth. 4 Seven days from now I will make it rain on the earth 40 days and 40 nights, and I will wipe off the face of the earth every living thing I have made." 5 And Noah did everything that the LORD commanded him.

6 Noah was 600 years old when the deluge came ⌊and⌋ water covered the earth. 7 So Noah, his sons, his wife, and his sons' wives entered the ark because of the waters of the deluge. 8 From the clean animals, unclean animals, birds, and every creature that crawls on the ground, 9 two of each, male and female, entered the ark with Noah, just as God had commanded him. 10 Seven days later the waters of the deluge came on the earth.

The Deluge

11 In the six hundredth year of Noah's life, in the second month, on the seventeenth day of the month, on that day all the sources of the watery depths burst open, the floodgates of the sky were opened, 12 and the rain fell on the earth 40 days and 40 nights. 13 On that same day Noah along with his sons Shem, Ham, and Japheth, Noah's wife, and his three sons' wives entered the ark with him. 14 They ⌊entered it⌋ with all the wildlife according to their kinds, all livestock according to their kinds, every creature that crawls on the earth according to its kind, all birds, every fowl, and everything with wings according to their kinds. 15 Two of all flesh that has the breath of life in it entered the ark with Noah. 16 Those that entered, male and female of all flesh, entered just as God had commanded him. Then the LORD shut him in.

17 The deluge continued 40 days on the earth; the waters increased and lifted up the ark so that it rose above the earth. 18 The waters surged and increased greatly on the earth, and the ark floated on the surface of the water. 19 Then the waters surged even higher on the earth, and all the high mountains under the whole sky were covered. 20 The mountains were covered as the waters surged ⌊above them⌋ more than 20 feet.[f] 21 All flesh perished—creatures that crawl on the earth, birds, livestock, wildlife, and all creatures that swarm[g] on the earth, as well as all mankind. 22 Everything with the breath of the spirit of life in its nostrils—everything on dry land died. 23 He wiped out every living thing that was on the surface of the ground, from mankind to livestock, to creatures that crawl, to the birds of the sky, and they were wiped off the earth. Only Noah was left, and those that were with him in the ark. 24 And the waters surged on the earth 150 days.

The Flood Recedes

8 God remembered Noah, as well as all the wildlife and all the livestock that were with him in the ark. God caused a wind[h] to pass over the earth, and the water began to subside. 2 The sources of the watery depths and the floodgates of the sky were closed, and the rain from the sky stopped. 3 The water steadily receded from the earth, and by the end of 150 days the waters had decreased significantly. 4 The ark came to rest in the seventh month, on the seventeenth day of the month, on the mountains of Ararat.[i]

5 The waters continued to recede until the tenth month; in the tenth month, on the first day of the

---

[a]**6:13** Or *injustice* [b]**6:14** Unknown species of tree; perhaps pine or cypress [c]**6:15** Or *300 cubits long, 50 cubits wide, and 30 cubits high* [d]**6:16** Or *window,* or *hatch;* Hb uncertain [e]**6:16** Lit *to a cubit* [f]**7:20** Lit *surged 15 cubits* [g]**7:21** Lit *all the swarming swarms* [h]**8:1** Or *spirit;* Gn 1:2 [i]**8:4** Turkey or Armenia

---

Noah would build the ark and enter it by faith in God.

6:19 two of every living thing. A pair of each animal—male and female—was needed to replenish the earth after the flood. In addition, Noah took seven pairs of the kinds of animals that could be eaten and used for sacrifice (7:2).

7:20 mountains … more than 20 feet. Even the highest mountains in the area, the mountains of Ararat (8:4), which are about 17,000 feet high, were covered by the waters.

8:1 God remembered Noah. With floodwaters covering all the territory under judgment, the Lord kept Noah and his family safe and

prepared to return them to dry land.

8:17 multiply. As He had done at Creation (1:22), God gave His blessing to the creatures that would populate the planet.

8:20 burnt offerings. Noah had preserved and cared for the clean animals and birds on the ark for this purpose. He built an altar for

Operation Recovery

1. When you were a kid, what was something you used to do on a rainy day?

Genesis 8:1-22

2. Water rapidly covered the entire earth and then it dried suddenly (a little over a year total). How would this water movement have affected the earth's surface? How does this compare with the modern belief that the earth was shaped over millions of years?

3. Note verses 21 and 22. What does this tell us about modern fears that the earth will some-day become uninhabitable?

month, the tops of the mountains were visible. 6 After 40 days Noah opened the window of the ark that he had made, 7 and he sent out a raven. It went back and forth until the waters had dried up from the earth. 8 Then he sent out a dove to see whether the water on the earth's surface had gone down, 9 but the dove found no resting place for her foot. She returned to him in the ark because water covered the surface of the whole earth. He reached out and brought her into the ark to himself. 10 So Noah waited seven more days and sent out the dove from the ark again. 11 When the dove came to him at evening, there was a plucked olive leaf in her beak. So Noah knew that the water on the earth's surface had gone down. 12 After he had waited another seven days, he sent out the dove, but she did not return to him again. 13 In the six hundred and first year,[a] in the first month, on the first day of the month, the water ⌊that had covered⌋ the earth was dried up. Then Noah removed the ark's cover and saw that the surface of the ground was drying. 14 By the twenty-seventh day of the second month, the earth was dry.

The LORD's Promise

15 Then God spoke to Noah, 16 "Come out of the ark, you, your wife, your sons, and your sons' wives with you. 17 Bring out every living thing of all flesh that is with you—birds, livestock, creatures that crawl on the ground—and they will spread over the earth and be fruitful and multiply on the earth." 18 So Noah, along with his sons, his wife, and his sons' wives, came out. 19 All wildlife, all livestock, every bird, and every creature that crawls on the earth came out of the ark by their groups.

20 Then Noah built an altar to the LORD. He took some of every kind of clean animal and every kind of clean bird and offered •burnt offerings on the altar. 21 When the LORD smelled the pleasing aroma, He said to Himself, "I will never again curse the ground because of man, even though man's inclination is evil from his youth. And I will never again strike down every living thing as I have done.

> 22 As long as the earth endures,
> seedtime and harvest, cold and heat,
> summer and winter, and day and night
> will not cease."

God's Covenant with Noah

9 God blessed Noah and his sons and said to them, "Be fruitful and multiply and fill the earth. 2 The fear and terror of you will be in every living creature on the earth, every bird of the sky, every creature that crawls on the ground, and all the fish of the sea. They are placed under your authority.[b] 3 Every living creature will be food for you; as ⌊I gave⌋ the green plants, I have given you everything. 4 However, you must not eat meat with its lifeblood in it. 5 I will require the life of every animal and every man for your life and your blood. I will require the life of each man's brother for a man's life.

> 6 Whoever sheds man's blood,
> his blood will be shed by man,
> for God made man
> in His image.

7 But you, be fruitful and multiply; spread out over the earth and multiply on it."

8 Then God said to Noah and his sons with him, 9 "Understand that I am confirming My covenant with you and your descendants after you, 10 and with every living creature that is with you—birds, livestock, and all wildlife of the earth that are with you—all the animals of the earth that came out of the ark. 11 I confirm My covenant with you that never again will all flesh be wiped out by the waters of a deluge; there will never again be a deluge to destroy the earth."

12 And God said, "This is the sign of the covenant I am making between Me and you and every living creature with you, a covenant for all future generations: 13 I

---

[a] **8:13** Dating from the birth of Noah   [b] **9:2** Lit *are given in your hand*

---

sacrifice and worship of the Lord.

8:21 Never ... curse. God promised that He would never again destroy the earth by flood.

9:6 his blood will be shed. God gave humans the responsibility of carrying out justice for people who were found guilty of murder.

9:9 confirming My covenant. Noah was rewarded for his faithfulness with a personal promise from the Lord.

9:22 Ham. The reference is not simply to Ham's son, whose name was Canaan (10:6), but to the nation of Canaan, eventually settled by the Israelites.

10:1-2 Several nations in the Bible sprang from Noah's family members, including the Egyptians, Greeks, and Hebrews. Noah's oldest son, Japheth, represents many of the ancient nations in what is now known as Europe and Asia Minor. From Japheth, the Greeks became a small, but important nation.

have placed My bow in the clouds, and it will be a sign of the covenant between Me and the earth. [14] Whenever I form clouds over the earth and the bow appears in the clouds, [15] I will remember My covenant between Me and you and every living creature of all flesh: water will never again become a deluge to destroy all flesh. [16] The bow will be in the clouds, and I will look at it and remember the everlasting covenant between God and every living creature of all flesh on earth." [17] God said to Noah, "This is the sign of the covenant that I have confirmed between Me and all flesh on earth."

Prophecies about Noah's Family

[18] Noah's sons who came out of the ark were Shem, Ham, and Japheth. Ham was the father of Canaan. [19] These three were Noah's sons, and from them the whole earth was populated.

[20] Noah, a man of the soil, was the first to plant[a] a vineyard. [21] He drank some of the wine, became drunk, and uncovered himself inside his tent. [22] Ham, the father of Canaan, saw his father naked and told his two brothers outside. [23] Then Shem and Japheth took a cloak and placed it over both their shoulders, and walking backwards, they covered their father's nakedness. Their faces were turned away, and they did not see their father naked.

[24] When Noah awoke from his drinking and learned what his youngest son had done to him, [25] he said:

Canaan will be cursed.
He will be the lowest of slaves to his brothers.

[26] He also said:

Praise the LORD, the God of Shem;
Canaan will be[b] his slave.
[27] God will extend[c] Japheth;
he will dwell in the tents of Shem;
Canaan will be his slave.

[28] Now Noah lived 350 years after the flood. [29] So Noah's life lasted 950 years; then he died.

The Table of Nations

10 These are the family records of Noah's sons, Shem, Ham, and Japheth. They also had sons after the deluge.

[2] Japheth's sons: Gomer, Magog, Madai, Javan, Tubal, Meshech, and Tiras. [3] Gomer's sons: Ashkenaz, Riphath, and Togarmah. [4] And Javan's sons: Elishah,

Tarshish, Kittim, and Dodanim.[d] [5] The coastland peoples spread out into their lands. These are ⌊Japheth's sons⌋ by their clans, in their nations. Each ⌊group⌋ had its own language.

[6] Ham's sons: Cush, Egypt, Put, and Canaan. [7] Cush's sons: Seba, Havilah, Sabtah, Raamah, and Sabteca. And Raamah's sons: Sheba and Dedan.

[8] Cush fathered Nimrod, who was the first powerful man on earth. [9] He was a powerful hunter in the sight of the LORD. That is why it is said, "Like Nimrod, a powerful hunter in the sight of the LORD." [10] His kingdom started with Babylon, Erech,[e] Accad,[f] and Calneh,[g] in the land of •Shinar.[h] [11] From that land he went to Assyria and built Nineveh, Rehoboth-ir, Calah, [12] and Resen, between Nineveh and the great city Calah.

[13] Egypt fathered Ludim, Anamim, Lehabim, Naphtuhim, [14] Pathrusim, Casluhim (the Philistines came from them), and Caphtorim.

[15] Canaan fathered Sidon his firstborn, and the Hittites, [16] the Jebusites, the Amorites, the Girgashites, [17] the Hivites, the Arkites, the Sinites, [18] the Arvadites, the Zemarites, and the Hamathites. Afterwards the Canaanite clans scattered. [19] The Canaanite border went from Sidon going toward Gerar as far as Gaza, and going toward Sodom, Gomorrah, Admah, and Zeboiim, as far as Lasha.

[20] These are Ham's sons, by their clans, according to their languages, in their own lands and their nations.

[21] And Shem, Japheth's older brother, also had children. Shem was the father of all the children of Eber. [22] Shem's sons were Elam, Asshur,[i] Arpachshad, Lud, and Aram.

[23] Aram's sons: Uz, Hul, Gether, and Mash.

[24] Arpachshad fathered[j] Shelah, and Shelah fathered Eber. [25] Eber had two sons. One was named Peleg, for during his days the earth was divided; his brother was named Joktan. [26] And Joktan fathered Almodad, Sheleph, Hazarmaveth, Jerah, [27] Hadoram, Uzal, Diklah, [28] Obal, Abimael, Sheba, [29] Ophir, Havilah, and Jobab. All these were Joktan's sons. [30] Their settlements extended from Mesha to Sephar, the eastern hill country.

[31] These are Shem's sons by their clans, according to their languages, in their lands and their nations.

[32] These are the clans of Noah's sons, according to their family records, in their nations. The nations on earth spread out from these after the flood.

---

[a]**9:20** Or *Noah began to be a farmer and planted* [b]**9:26** As a prophecy; others interpret the verbs in vv. 26–27 as a wish or prayer: *let Canaan be . . .* [c]**9:27** The Hb word for *extend* sounds like *Japheth*. [d]**10:4** Some Hb mss, Sam, LXX read *Rodanim*; 1 Ch 1:7 [e]**10:10** Or *Uruk* [f]**10:10** Or *Akkad* [g]**10:10** Or *and all of them* [h]**10:10** Or *in Babylonia* [i]**10:22** Or *Assyria* [j]**10:24** LXX reads *fathered Cainan, and Cainan fathered*; Gn 11:12–13; Lk 3:35–36

10:12 great city. Nimrod was the great great grandson of Noah and the founder of the "great city" of Nineveh, Assyria.

10:16 Jebusites…Girgashites. These people groups were already settled in Canaan when the Israelites arrived in Joshua's time.

10:21 Shem. Shem is referred to as the "cho-sen line" because the Hebrews descended from him. In the Hebrew language, the name Eber (a descendant of Shem) is the origin of the word "Hebrew."

10:25 the earth was divided. This refers to the results of the next event in chapter 11—the Tower of Babel. God dispersed the peo-ple all across the earth as a result of their prideful behavior.

11:1-5 It was not long until sin and pride—demonstrated in the building of the Tower of Babel—resurfaced. The tower builders attempted to reach God by making a high building that would enable the gods to come

The Tower of Babylon

11 At one time the whole earth had the same language and vocabulary.[a] [2] As people[b] migrated from the east, they found a valley in the land of •Shinar and settled there. [3] They said to each other, "Come, let us make oven-fired bricks." They had brick for stone and asphalt for mortar. [4] And they said, "Come, let us build ourselves a city and a tower with its top in the sky. Let us make a name for ourselves; otherwise, we will be scattered over the face of the whole earth."

[5] Then the LORD came down to look over the city and the tower that the •men were building. [6] The LORD said, "If, as one people all having the same language, they have begun to do this, then nothing they plan to do will be impossible for them. [7] Come, let Us go down there and confuse[c] their language[d] so that they will not understand one another's speech."[e] [8] So the LORD scattered them from there over the face of the whole earth, and they stopped building the city. [9] Therefore its name is called Babylon,[f] for there the LORD confused the language of the whole earth, and from there the LORD scattered them over the face of the whole earth.

From Shem to Abram

[10] These are the family records of Shem. Shem lived 100 years and fathered Arpachshad two years after the deluge. [11] After he fathered Arpachshad, Shem lived 500 years and fathered ⌊other⌋ sons and daughters. [12] Arpachshad lived 35 years[g] and fathered Shelah. [13] After he fathered Shelah, Arpachshad lived 403 years and fathered ⌊other⌋ sons and daughters. [14] Shelah lived 30 years and fathered Eber. [15] After he fathered Eber, Shelah lived 403 years and fathered ⌊other⌋ sons and daughters. [16] Eber lived 34 years and fathered Peleg. [17] After he fathered Peleg, Eber lived 430 years and fathered ⌊other⌋ sons and daughters. [18] Peleg lived 30 years and fathered Reu. [19] After he fathered Reu, Peleg lived 209 years and fathered ⌊other⌋ sons and daughters. [20] Reu lived 32 years and fathered Serug. [21] After he fathered Serug, Reu lived 207 years and fathered ⌊other⌋ sons and daughters. [22] Serug lived 30 years and fathered Nahor. [23] After he fathered Nahor, Serug lived 200 years and fathered ⌊other⌋ sons and daughters. [24] Nahor lived 29 years and fathered Terah. [25] After he fathered Terah, Nahor lived 119 years and fathered ⌊other⌋ sons and daughters. [26] Terah lived 70 years and fathered Abram, Nahor, and Haran.

[27] These are the family records of Terah. Terah fathered Abram, Nahor, and Haran, and Haran fathered Lot. [28] Haran died in his native land, in Ur of the Chaldeans, during his father Terah's lifetime. [29] Abram and Nahor took wives: Abram's wife was named Sarai, and Nahor's wife was named Milcah. She was the daughter of Haran, the father of both Milcah and Iscah. [30] Sarai was barren; she had no child.

[31] Terah took his son Abram, his grandson Lot (Haran's son), and his daughter-in-law Sarai, his son Abram's wife, and they set out together from Ur of the Chaldeans to go to the land of Canaan. But when they came to Haran, they settled there. [32] Terah lived 205 years and died in Haran.

 Moving Out

1. What is the longest trip you have taken with your family in a car? How many times did you have to stop to use the bathroom?

Genesis 12:1-9

2. Abram was 75 years old when he moved his family far away from his homeland. Why did he do something so traumatic at that age? What does this highlight about Abram's character?

3. Abram was the father of the Jewish race, including modern Israel. What does God's promise to him (v. 3) suggest about modern tensions in the Middle East?

The Call of Abram

12 The LORD said to Abram:

Go out from your land,
your relatives,
and your father's house
to the land that I will show you.
[2] I will make you into a great nation,
I will bless you,
I will make your name great,
and you will be a blessing.[h]

---

[a]**11:1** Lit *one lip and the same words* [b]**11:2** Lit *they* [c]**11:7** Or *confound* [d]**11:7** Lit *lip* [e]**11:7** Lit *understand each man the lip of his companion* [f]**11:9** The Hb word for *confuse* sounds like *Babylon.* [g]**11:12–13** LXX reads *years and fathered Cainan.* [13] *After he fathered Cainan, Arphachshad lived 430 years and fathered [other] sons and daughters, and he died. Cainan lived 130 years and fathered Shelah. After he fathered Shelah, Cainan lived 330 years and fathered [other] sons and daughters, and he died;* Gn 10:24; Lk 3:35–36 [h]**12:2** Or *great. Be a blessing!*

---

down to man. But God intervened, and the tower project was abandoned.

11:10–26 In 10 generations, the line of Shem is traced to the beginning of Abram's story.

11:30 barren. Sarai, Abram's wife, was unable to have children. God would soon prom-

ise to make Abram the father of many nations by miraculously giving his wife a child.

12:1 Go out from your land. Abram had to leave the familiar in order to find his future. He left Ur to head to Haran and eventually settled in Canaan.

12:2–3 I will bless you. God's promise to

Abram assured him of a land, a nation, and a blessing. Out of his descendants the entire Jewish nation and, eventually, the Savior would arise.

12:10 Egypt. Abram found famine conditions when he arrived in Canaan. He continued on into Egypt, where the Nile River provided wa-

³ I will bless those who bless you,
   I will curse those who treat you with contempt,
   and all the peoplesᵃ on earth
   will be blessedᵇ through you.ᶜ

⁴ So Abram went, as the LORD had told him, and Lot went with him. Abram was 75 years old when he left Haran. ⁵ He took his wife Sarai, his nephew Lot, all the possessions they had accumulated, and the people he had acquired in Haran, and they set out for the land of Canaan. When they came to the land of Canaan, ⁶ Abram passed through the land to the site of Shechem, at the oak of Moreh. At that time the Canaanites were in the land. ⁷ But the LORD appeared to Abram and said, "I will give this land to your •offspring." So he built an altar there to the LORD who had appeared to him. ⁸ From there he moved on to the hill country east of Bethel and pitched his tent, with Bethel on the west and Ai on the east. There he built an altar to the LORD and worshipedᵈ Him. ⁹ Then Abram journeyed by stages to the •Negev.

Abram in Egypt

¹⁰ There was a famine in the land, so Abram went down to Egypt to live there for a while because the famine in the land was severe. ¹¹ When he was about to enter Egypt, he said to his wife Sarai, "Look, I know what a beautiful woman you are. ¹² When the Egyptians see you, they will say, 'This is his wife.' They will kill me but let you live. ¹³ Please say you're my sister so it will go well for me because of you, and my life will be spared on your account." ¹⁴ When Abram entered Egypt, the Egyptians saw that the woman was very beautiful. ¹⁵ Pharaoh's officials saw her and praised her to Pharaoh, so the woman was taken to Pharaoh's house. ¹⁶ He treated Abram well because of her, and Abram acquired flocks and herds, male and female donkeys, male and female slaves, and camels.

¹⁷ But the LORD struck Pharaoh and his house with severe plagues because of Abram's wife Sarai. ¹⁸ So Pharaoh sent for Abram and said, "What have you done to me? Why didn't you tell me she was your wife? ¹⁹ Why did you say, 'She's my sister,' so that I took her as my wife? Now, here's your wife. Take her and go!" ²⁰ Then Pharaoh gave ⌊his⌋ men orders about him, and they sent him away, with his wife and all he had.

Abram and Lot Separate

13 Then Abram went up from Egypt to the •Negev—he, his wife, and all he had, and Lot with him. ² Abram was very richᵉ in livestock, silver,

and gold. ³ He went by stages from the Negev to Bethel, to the place between Bethel and Ai where his tent had formerly been, ⁴ to the site where he had built the altar. And Abram worshipedᶠ the LORD there.

⁵ Now Lot, who was traveling with Abram, also had flocks, herds, and tents. ⁶ But the land was unable to support them as long as they stayed together, for they had so many possessions that they could not stay together, ⁷ and there was quarreling between the herdsmen of Abram's livestock and the herdsmen of Lot's livestock. At that time the Canaanites and the Perizzites were living in the land.

The Right Choice

1. Who is your favorite aunt, uncle, or cousin?

Genesis 13:1-18

2. Why did Lot choose "the entire Jordan Valley for himself" (vv. 10-11)? What does this reveal about Lot?

3. Abram allowed Lot to have first choice of where to live. What does this show about Abram? About God's choice to make Abram father of His chosen people?

4. The first thing Abram did when he settled was to build an altar to God (v. 18). How is this an example for you today?

5. How often do you put self-interests over doing what's right during training and practice in your sport or other team activities?

⁸ Then Abram said to Lot, "Please, let's not have quarreling between you and me, or between your herdsmen and my herdsmen, since we are relatives.ᵍ ⁹ Isn't the whole land before you? Separate from me: if ⌊you go⌋ to the left, I will go to the right; if ⌊you go⌋ to the right, I will go to the left."

¹⁰ Lot looked out and saw that the entire Jordan Valley as far asʰ Zoar was well-watered everywhere like the LORD's garden and the land of Egypt. This was before God destroyed Sodom and Gomorrah. ¹¹ So Lot chose the entire Jordan Valley for himself. Then Lot journeyed eastward, and they separated from each other. ¹² Abram lived in the land of Canaan, but Lot lived in the cities of the valley and set up his tent near

---

ᵃ**12:3** Lit *clans* ᵇ**12:3** Or *will find blessing* ᶜ**12:3** Or *will bless themselves by you* ᵈ**12:8** Or *proclaimed* or *invoked the name of*; lit *called on the name of* ᵉ**13:2** Lit *heavy* ᶠ**13:4** Or *proclaimed* or *invoked the name of*; lit *called on the name of* ᵍ**13:8** Lit *brothers* ʰ**13:10** Lit *Valley as you go to*

---

ter for the crops.

12:11–19 Abram feared his wife Sarai's beauty would impede their travel among potentially male suitors, so he lied to the Egyptian pharaoh by telling him she was his sister. Pharaoh took Sarai into his harem and rewarded Abram with livestock. When his lie

was exposed, Abram faced the pharaoh's anger.

13:1–11 After returning to Canaan from Egypt, Abram and Lot went their separate ways because the land would not support both their herds of livestock.

13:12 Lot ... near Sodom. By living so close

to the evil people of Sodom and Gomorrah, Lot soon joined with them and came under God's judgment.

13:16 dust of the earth. God promised Abram that he would become the father of many descendants—the nation of Israel.

14:12 Lot ... living in Sodom. Note Lot's pro-

Sodom. 13 Now the men of Sodom were evil, sinning greatly[a] against the LORD.

14 After Lot had separated from him, the LORD said to Abram, "Look from the place where you are. Look north and south, east and west, 15 for I will give you and your •offspring forever all the land that you see. 16 I will make your offspring like the dust of the earth, so that if one could count the dust of the earth, then your offspring could be counted. 17 Get up and walk from one end of the land to the other, for I will give it to you."

18 So Abram moved his tent and went to live beside the oaks of Mamre at Hebron, where he built an altar to the LORD.

Abram Rescues Lot

14 In those days Amraphel king of •Shinar, Arioch king of Ellasar, Chedorlaomer king of Elam,[b] and Tidal[c] king of Goiim[d] 2 waged war against Bera king of Sodom, Birsha king of Gomorrah, Shinab king of Admah, and Shemeber king of Zeboiim, as well as the king of Bela (that is, Zoar). 3 All of these came as allies to the Valley of Siddim (that is, the Dead Sea). 4 They were subject to Chedorlaomer for 12 years, but in the thirteenth year they rebelled. 5 In the fourteenth year Chedorlaomer and the kings who were with him came and defeated the Rephaim in Ashteroth-karnaim, the Zuzim in Ham, the Emim in Shaveh-kiriathaim, 6 and the Horites in the mountains of Seir, as far as El-paran by the wilderness. 7 Then they came back to invade En-mishpat (that is, Kadesh), and they defeated all the territory of the Amalekites, as well as the Amorites who lived in Hazazon-tamar.

8 Then the king of Sodom, the king of Gomorrah, the king of Admah, the king of Zeboiim, and the king of Bela (that is, Zoar) went out and lined up for battle in the Valley of Siddim 9 against Chedorlaomer king of Elam, Tidal king of Goiim, Amraphel king of Shinar, and Arioch king of Ellasar—four kings against five. 10 Now the Valley of Siddim contained many asphalt pits, and ⌊as⌋ the kings of Sodom and Gomorrah fled, ⌊some⌋ fell into them,[e] but the rest fled to the mountains. 11 The ⌊four kings⌋ took all the goods of Sodom and Gomorrah and all their food and went on. 12 They also took Abram's nephew Lot and his possessions, for he was living in Sodom, and they went on.

13 One of the survivors came and told Abram the Hebrew, who was at the oaks belonging to Mamre the Amorite, the brother of Eshcol and the brother of Aner. They were bound by a treaty with[f] Abram. 14 When Abram heard that his relative had been taken prisoner, he assembled[g] his 318 trained men, born in his household, and they went in pursuit as far as Dan. 15 And he and his servants deployed against them by night, attacked them, and pursued them as far as Hobah to the north of Damascus. 16 He brought back all the goods and also his relative Lot and his goods, as well as the women and the ⌊other⌋ people.

Melchizedek's Blessing

17 After Abram returned from defeating Chedorlaomer and the kings who were with him, the king of Sodom went out to meet him in the Valley of Shaveh (that is, the King's Valley). 18 Then Melchizedek, king of Salem, brought out bread and wine; he was a priest to God •Most High. 19 He blessed him and said:

Abram is blessed by God Most High,
Creator[h] of heaven and earth,
20 and give praise to[i] God Most High
who has handed over your enemies to you.

And Abram gave him a tenth of everything.

21 Then the king of Sodom said to Abram, "Give me the people, but take the possessions for yourself."

22 But Abram said to the king of Sodom, "I have raised my hand in an oath to the LORD, God Most High, Creator of heaven and earth, 23 that I will not take a thread or sandal strap or anything that belongs to you, so you can never say, 'I made Abram rich.' 24 I will take nothing[j] except what the servants have eaten. But as for the share of the men who came with me—Aner, Eshcol, and Mamre—they can take their share."

The Abrahamic Covenant

15 After these events, the word of the LORD came to Abram in a vision:

Do not be afraid, Abram.
I am your shield;
your reward will be very great.

2 But Abram said, "Lord GOD, what can You give me, since I am childless and the heir of my house is Eliezer of Damascus?"[k] 3 Abram continued, "Look, You have given me no •offspring, so a slave born in[l] my house will be my heir."

4 Now the word of the LORD came to him: "This one will not be your heir; instead, one who comes from your own body[m] will be your heir." 5 He took him out-

---

[a]13:13 Lit evil and sinful   [b]14:1 A region in southwest Iran   [c]14:1 The name Tidal may be related to the Hittite royal name Tudhaliya.   [d]14:1 Or nations   [e]14:10 Sam, LXX read fell there   [f]14:13 Lit were possessors of a covenant of   [g]14:14 Sam; MT reads poured out   [h]14:19 Or Possessor   [i]14:20 Or and blessed be   [j]14:24 Lit Nothing to me   [k]15:2 Hb obscure   [l]15:3 Lit a son of   [m]15:4 Lit loins

---

gression from having settled near the town (13:12) to living within its walls.

14:18 Melchizedek. This man was both a king and a priest in the city of Salem (Jerusalem). His appearance further exalts Abram as a recipient of God's blessing.

14:23 will not take. Abram saw no need for more earthly riches. His confidence was in God's provision.

15:1 your shield. Abram was reminded by God of His power and protection.

15:2 Eliezer. Since Abram had no heirs, he had made arrangements for his estate to go to one of his servants, Eliezer.

15:3–5 God promised Abram that he would have a son of his own who would become his heir. His descendants would be as numerous as the stars.

15:6 Abram believed the LORD. With this affirmation, Abram becomes the first person in the Bible to profess a faith relationship with

side and said, "Look at the sky and count the stars, if you are able to count them." Then He said to him, "Your offspring will be that ⌊numerous⌋."

6 Abram believed the LORD, and He credited it to him as righteousness.

7 He also said to him, "I am the LORD who brought you from Ur of the Chaldeans to give you this land to possess."

8 But he said, "Lord GOD, how can I know that I will possess it?"

9 He said to him, "Bring Me a three-year-old cow, a three-year-old female goat, a three-year-old ram, a turtledove, and a young pigeon."

10 So he brought all these to Him, split them down the middle, and laid the pieces opposite each other, but he did not cut up the birds. 11 Birds of prey came down on the carcasses, but Abram drove them away. 12 As the sun was setting, a deep sleep fell on Abram, and suddenly a terror and great darkness descended on him.

13 Then the LORD said to Abram, "Know this for certain: Your offspring will be strangers in a land that does not belong to them; they will be enslaved and oppressed[a] 400 years. 14 However, I will judge the nation they serve, and afterwards they will go out with many possessions. 15 But you will go to your fathers in peace and be buried at a ripe old age. 16 In the fourth generation they will return here, for the iniquity of the Amorites has not yet reached its full measure."[b]

17 When the sun had set and it was dark, a smoking fire pot and a flaming torch appeared and passed between the divided ⌊animals⌋. 18 On that day the LORD made a covenant with Abram, saying, "I give this land to your offspring, from the brook of Egypt to the Euphrates River:[c] 19 ⌊the land of⌋ the Kenites, Kenizzites, Kadmonites, 20 Hittites, Perizzites, Rephaim, 21 Amorites, Canaanites, Girgashites, and Jebusites."

Hagar and Ishmael

16 Abram's wife Sarai had not borne him children. She owned an Egyptian slave named Hagar. 2 Sarai said to Abram, "Since the LORD has prevented me from bearing children, go to my slave; perhaps I can have children[d] by her." And Abram agreed to what Sarai said.[e] 3 So Abram's wife Sarai took Hagar, her Egyptian slave, and gave her to her husband Abram as a wife for him. ⌊This happened⌋ after Abram had lived in the land of Canaan 10 years. 4 He

slept with[f] Hagar, and she became pregnant. When she realized that she was pregnant, she looked down on her mistress. 5 Then Sarai said to Abram, "You are responsible for my suffering![g] I put my slave in your arms,[h] and ever since she saw that she was pregnant, she has looked down on me. May the LORD judge between me and you."

6 Abram replied to Sarai, "Here, your slave is in your hands; do whatever you want with her."[i] Then Sarai mistreated her so much that she ran away from her.

7 The Angel of the LORD found her by a spring of water in the wilderness, the spring on the way to Shur. 8 He said, "Hagar, slave of Sarai, where have you come from, and where are you going?"

She replied, "I'm running away from my mistress Sarai."

9 Then the Angel of the LORD said to her, "You must go back to your mistress and submit to her mistreatment."[j] 10 The Angel of the LORD also said to her, "I greatly multiply your •offspring, and they will be too many to count."

11 Then the Angel of the LORD said to her:

You have conceived and will have a son.
You will name him Ishmael,[k]
for the LORD has heard your ⌊cry of⌋ affliction.
12 This man will be ⌊like⌋ a wild ass.
His hand will be against everyone,
and everyone's hand will be against him;
he will live at odds with all his brothers.

13 So she named the LORD who spoke to her: The God Who Sees,[l] for she said, "Have I really seen here the One who sees me?"[m] 14 That is why she named the spring, "A Well of the Living One Who Sees Me."[n] It is located[o] between Kadesh and Bered.

15 So Hagar gave birth to Abram's son, and Abram gave the name Ishmael to the son Hagar had. 16 Abram was 86 years old when Hagar bore Ishmael to him.

Covenant Circumcision

17 When Abram was 99 years old, the LORD appeared to him, saying, "I am •God Almighty. Live in My presence and be devout. 2 I will establish My covenant between Me and you, and I will multiply you greatly."

3 Then Abram fell to the ground,[p] and God spoke with him: 4 "As for Me, My covenant is with you, and you will become the father of many nations.[q] 5 Your

---

[a] **15:13** Lit *will serve them and they will oppress them*   [b] **15:16** Lit *Amorites is not yet complete*   [c] **15:18** Lit *the great river, the river Euphrates*   [d] **16:2** Lit *I will be built up*   [e] **16:2** Lit *Abram listened to the voice of Sarai*   [f] **16:4** Lit *He came to*   [g] **16:5** Or *May my suffering be on you*   [h] **16:5** Lit *bosom*   [i] **16:6** Lit *do to her what is good in your eyes*   [j] **16:9** Lit *to mistreatment under her hand*   [k] **16:11** = God Hears   [l] **16:13** Lit *her: You God Who Sees*   [m] **16:13** Hb obscure   [n] **16:14** Hb *Beer-lahai-roi*   [o] **16:14** Lit *Look*   [p] **17:3** Lit *fell on his face*   [q] **17:4** Abraham was father not only of the Israelites, but also of the Ishmaelites, the Edomites, and the Midianites. Spiritually, he is the father of all believers; Gl 3:7,29.

---

the Lord.

15:18 made a covenant. The animal sacrifice was a picture of God's promise to Abram. Through this act, God declared God's ownership of the land before him.

16:1–15 God had not delivered on his promise of an heir for Abram. So he agreed, at Sa-

rai's urging, to father a child by Sarai's Egyptian servant,

17:1 live in My presence. Abram had to wait patiently for God to fulfill His promise of a son and an heir. Trying to fulfill that promise in his own way (through Hagar) had resulted in disaster.

17:5 Abram … Abraham. God changed Abram's name to Abraham, meaning "father of nations." This was a sign of God's covenant promise.

17:8 eternal possession. The land of Canaan would belong to Abraham's descendants, as long as they obeyed the Lord.

name will no longer be Abram,[a] but your name will be Abraham,[b] for I will make you the father of many nations. 6 I will make you extremely fruitful and will make nations and kings come from you. 7 I will keep My covenant between Me and you, and your •offspring after you throughout their generations, as an everlasting covenant to be your God and the ⌊God⌋ of your offspring after you. 8 And to you and your offspring after you I will give the land where you are residing—all the land of Canaan—as an eternal possession, and I will be their God."

9 God also said to Abraham, "As for you, you and your offspring after you throughout their generations are to keep My covenant. 10 This is My covenant, which you are to keep, between Me and you and your offspring after you: Every one of your males must be circumcised. 11 You must circumcise the flesh of your foreskin to serve as a sign of the covenant between Me and you.[c] 12 Throughout your generations, every male among you at eight days old is to be circumcised. This includes a slave born in your house and one purchased with money from any foreigner. The one who is not your offspring, 13 a slave born in your house, as well as one purchased with money, must be circumcised. My covenant will be in your flesh as an everlasting covenant. 14 If any male is not circumcised in the flesh of his foreskin, that man will be cut off from his people; he has broken My covenant."

15 God said to Abraham, "As for your wife Sarai, do not call her Sarai, for Sarah[d] will be her name. 16 I will bless her; indeed, I will give you a son by her. I will bless her, and she will produce nations; kings of peoples will come from her."

17 Abraham fell to the ground,[e] laughed, and thought in his heart, "Can a child be born to a hundred-year-old man? Can Sarah, a ninety-year-old woman, give birth?" 18 So Abraham said to God, "If only Ishmael could live in Your presence!"

19 But God said, "No. Your wife Sarah will bear you a son, and you will name him Isaac.[f] I will confirm My covenant with him as an everlasting covenant for his offspring after him. 20 As for Ishmael, I have heard you. I will certainly bless him; I will make him fruitful and will multiply him greatly. He will father 12 tribal leaders, and I will make him into a great nation. 21 But I will confirm My covenant with Isaac, whom Sarah will bear to you at this time next year." 22 When He finished talking with him, God withdrew[g] from Abraham.

23 Then Abraham took his son Ishmael and all the slaves born in his house or purchased with his money—every male among the members of Abraham's household—and he circumcised the flesh of their foreskin on that very day, just as God had said to him. 24 Abraham was 99 years old when the flesh of his foreskin was circumcised, 25 and his son Ishmael was 13 years old when the flesh of his foreskin was circumcised. 26 On that same day Abraham and his son Ishmael were circumcised. 27 And all the men of his household—both slaves born in his house and those purchased with money from a foreigner—were circumcised with him.

Abraham's Three Visitors

18 Then the LORD appeared to Abraham at the oaks of Mamre while he was sitting in the entrance of his tent during the heat of the day. 2 He looked up, and he saw three men standing near him. When he saw them, he ran from the entrance of the tent to meet them and bowed to the ground. 3 Then he said, "My lord,[h] if I have found favor in your sight, please do not go on past your servant. 4 Let a little water be brought, that you may wash your feet and rest yourselves under the tree. 5 I will bring a bit of bread so that you may strengthen yourselves.[i] This is why you have passed your servant's ⌊way⌋. Later, you can continue on."

"Yes," they replied, "do as you have said."

6 So Abraham hurried into the tent and said to Sarah, "Quick! Knead three measures[j] of fine flour and make bread."[k] 7 Meanwhile, Abraham ran to the herd and got a tender, choice calf. He gave it to a young man, who hurried to prepare it. 8 Then Abraham took curds[l] and milk, and the calf that he had prepared, and set ⌊them⌋ before the men. He served[m] them as they ate under the tree.

Sarah Laughs

9 "Where is your wife Sarah?" they asked him.

"There, in the tent," he answered.

10 The LORD said, "I will certainly come back to you in about a year's time, and your wife Sarah will have a son!" Now Sarah was listening at the entrance of the tent behind him.

11 Abraham and Sarah were old and getting on in years.[n] Sarah had passed the age of childbearing.[o] 12 So she laughed to herself: "After I have become shriveled up and my lord is old, will I have delight?"

13 But the LORD asked Abraham, "Why did Sarah laugh, saying, 'Can I really have a baby when I'm old?'

---

a **17:5** = The Father Is Exalted b **17:5** = Father of a Multitude c **17:11** *You* in v. 11 is pl. d **17:15** = Princess e **17:17** Lit *fell on his face* f **17:19** = He Laughs g **17:22** Lit *went up, or ascended* h **18:3** Or *My Lord,* or *The Lord* i **18:5** Lit *may sustain your heart* j **18:6** Lit *three seahs;* about 21 quarts k **18:6** A round, thin, unleavened bread l **18:8** Or *butter* m **18:8** Lit *was standing by* n **18:11** Lit *days* o **18:11** Lit *The way of women had ceased for Sarah*

17:10–11 circumcised. God chose circumcision as the sign of His covenant with Abraham. This act was symbolic of God's rule over His people.

17:15 Sarai ... Sarah. Both these names mean "princess," but the change was a sign of God's His promise that she would be the mother of many descendants.

17:16 a son by her. Not through Hagar or any other person, but through Sarah this son would be born to Abraham.

17:17 Abraham ... laughed. This was his reaction to the seeming impossibility of the promise. God then named this son Isaac (v.

19), which means, "he laughs."

17:21 I will confirm My covenant with Isaac. God's covenant would be with the son born to Abraham and Sarah and not with Ishmael, Hagar's son.

18:18 nations ... blessed through him. The entire world would be invited to join God's

14 Is anything impossible for the LORD? At the appointed time I will come back to you, and in about a year she will have a son."

15 Sarah denied it. "I did not laugh," she said, because she was afraid.

But He replied, "No, you did laugh."

Abraham's Plea for Sodom

16 The men got up from there and looked out over Sodom, and Abraham was walking with them to see them off. 17 Then the LORD said, "Should I hide from Abraham what I am about to do? 18 Abraham is to become a great and powerful nation, and all the nations of the earth will be blessed through him. 19 For I have chosena him so that he will command his children and his house after him to keep the way of the LORD by doing what is right and just. This is how the LORD will fulfill to Abraham what He promised him." 20 Then the LORD said, "The outcry against Sodom and Gomorrah is immense, and their sin is extremely serious. 21 I will go down to see if what they have done justifies the cry that has come up to Me. If not, I will find out."

Prayer Power

1. When has persistence in asking for something paid off for you? When has it gotten you in trouble?

Genesis 18:16-33

2. Why did God choose to tell Abraham about His plans to destroy Sodom and Gomorrah?

3. How is Abraham's intercession for Sodom an example that we should follow today?

4. God chose to "go down to see if what they have done justifies the cry that has come up to Me" (v. 21). What does this illustrate about God's patience and grace?

5. How have you experienced God's grace in your life and relationships?

22 The men turned from there and went toward Sodom while Abraham remained standing before the LORD.b 23 Abraham stepped forward and said, "Will You really sweep away the righteous with the wicked? 24 What if there are 50 righteous people in the city? Will You really sweep it away instead of sparing the place for the sake of the 50 righteous people who are in it? 25 You could not possibly do such a thing: to kill the righteous with the wicked, treating the righteous and the wicked alike. You could not possibly do that! Won't the Judge of all the earth do what is just?"

26 The LORD said, "If at Sodom I find 50 righteous people in the city, I will spare the whole place for their sake."

27 Then Abraham answered, "Since I have ventured to speak to the Lord—even though I am dust and ashes— 28 suppose the 50 righteous lack five. Will you destroy the whole city for lack of five?"

He replied, "I will not destroy ⌊it⌋ if I find 45 there."

29 Then he spoke to Him again, "Suppose 40 are found there?"

He answered, "I will not do ⌊it⌋ on account of 40."

30 Then he said, "Let the Lord not be angry, and I will speak further. Suppose 30 are found there?"

He answered, "I will not do ⌊it⌋ if I find 30 there."

31 Then he said, "Since I have ventured to speak to the Lord, suppose 20 are found there?"

He replied, "I will not destroy ⌊it⌋ on account of 20."

32 Then he said, "Let the Lord not be angry, and I will speak one more time. Suppose 10 are found there?"

He answered, "I will not destroy ⌊it⌋ on account of 10." 33 When the LORD had finished speaking with Abraham, He departed, and Abraham returned to his place.

The Destruction of Sodom and Gomorrah

19 The two angels entered Sodom in the evening as Lot was sitting at Sodom's •gate. When Lot saw ⌊them⌋, he got up to meet them. He bowed ⌊with his⌋ face to the ground 2 and said, "My lords, turn aside to your servant's house, wash your feet, and spend the night. Then you can get up early and go on your way."

"No," they said. "We would rather spend the night in the square." 3 But he urged them so strongly that they followed him and went into his house. He prepared a feast and baked unleavened bread for them, and they ate.

4 Before they went to bed, the men of the city of Sodom, both young and old, the whole population, surrounded the house. 5 They called out to Lot and said, "Where are the men who came to you tonight? Send them out to us so we can have sex with them!"

6 Lot went out to them at the entrance and shut the door behind him. 7 He said, "Don't do ⌊this⌋ evil, my

---

a 18:19 Lit known b 18:22 One ancient Jewish tradition reads while the LORD remained standing before Abraham

---

covenant family through Jesus Christ, one of Abraham's descendants.

18:21 I will go down. God visited the earth for the purpose of judgment. His holiness would not tolerate the sin of Sodom and Gomorrah.

18:25 Judge of all the earth. Abraham be-

lieved that the Lord knows all, sees all, and always does what is just.

18:32 one more time. Abraham's repetition demonstrated his desire to save his relatives from Sodom and Gomorrah's destruction.

18:33 his place. Abraham went back to his campsite in Mamre (v. 1) to spend the night,

then returned the next day to the spot where he had talked with the Lord.

19:1 Sodom's gate. People who sat at the city gates were community leaders. Lot apparently had become a member of Sodom's city council.

19:13 destroy this place. Because 10 righ-

Dangerous Values

1. What's the closest you've come to rescuing someone or being rescued?

Genesis 19:1-29

2. What were the "sexual values" of Sodom? How do they compare with modern values?

3. God told Lot, "I cannot do anything until you get" to another town (v. 22). Why? How did Abraham's intercession help save this other town and Lot?

4. What happened to Lot's wife? How had living in Sodom affected her?

5. Is homosexuality a sin? What about sex before marriage?

6. How do you see the values of the world around you endangering your soul?

brothers. 8 Look, I've got two daughters who haven't had sexual relations with a man. I'll bring them out to you, and you can do whatever you want[a] to them. However, don't do anything to these men, because they have come under the protection of my roof."

9 "Get out of the way!" they said, adding, "This one came here as a foreigner, but he's acting like a judge! Now we'll do more harm to you than to them." They put pressure on Lot and came up to break down the door. 10 But the angels[b] reached out, brought Lot into the house with them, and shut the door. 11 They struck the men who were at the door of the house, both young and old, with a blinding light so that they were unable to find the door.

12 Then the angels[b] said to Lot, "Do you have anyone else here: a son-in-law, your sons and daughters, or anyone else in the city who belongs to you? Get them out of this place, 13 for we are about to destroy this place because the outcry against its people is great before the LORD, and the LORD has sent us to destroy it."

14 So Lot went out and spoke to his sons-in-law, who were going to marry[c] his daughters. "Get up," he said. "Get out of this place, for the LORD is about to destroy the city!" But his sons-in-law thought he was joking.

15 At the crack of dawn the angels urged Lot on: "Get up! Take your wife and your two daughters who are

here, or you will be swept away in the punishment[d] of the city." 16 But he hesitated, so because of the LORD's compassion for him, the men grabbed his hand, his wife's hand, and the hands of his two daughters. And they brought him out and left him outside the city.

17 As soon as the angels got them outside, one of them[e] said, "Run for your lives! Don't look back and don't stop anywhere on the plain! Run to the mountains, or you will be swept away!"

18 But Lot said to them, "No, Lord[f]—please. 19 Your servant has indeed found favor in Your sight, and You have shown me great kindness by saving my life. But I can't run to the mountains; the disaster will overtake me, and I will die. 20 Look, this town is close enough for me to run to. It is a small place. Please let me go there—it's only a small place, isn't it?—so that I can survive."

21 And he said to him, "All right,[g] I'll grant your request[h] about this matter too and will not overthrow the town you mentioned. 22 Hurry up! Run there, for I cannot do anything until you get there." Therefore the name of the city is Zoar.[i]

23 The sun had risen over the land when Lot reached Zoar. 24 Then the LORD rained burning sulfur on Sodom and Gomorrah from the LORD out of the sky. 25 He overthrew these cities, the entire plain, all the inhabitants of the cities, and whatever grew on the ground. 26 But his wife looked back and became a pillar of salt.

27 Early in the morning Abraham went to the place where he had stood before the LORD. 28 He looked down toward Sodom and Gomorrah and all the land of the plain, and he saw that smoke was going up from the land like the smoke of a furnace. 29 So it was, when God destroyed the cities of the plain, He remembered Abraham and brought Lot out of the middle of the upheaval when He overthrew the cities where Lot had lived.

The Origin of Moab and Ammon

30 Lot departed from Zoar and lived in the mountains along with his two daughters, because he was afraid to live in Zoar. Instead, he and his two daughters lived in a cave. 31 Then the firstborn said to the younger, "Our father is old, and there is no man in the land to sleep with us ⌊as is⌋ the custom of all the land. 32 Come, let's get our father to drink wine so that we can sleep with him and preserve our father's line." 33 So they got their father to drink wine that night, and the firstborn came and slept with her father; he did not know when she lay down or when she got up.

---

a**19:8** Lit *do what is good in your eyes* b**19:10,12** Lit *men* c**19:14** Lit *take* d**19:15** Or *iniquity,* or *guilt* e**19:17** LXX, Syr, Vg read *outside, they* f**19:18** Or *My Lord,* or *My lords* g**19:21** Or *Look!* h**19:21** Lit *I will lift up your face* i**19:22** *Zoar* is related to the word for *small place* in v. 20; its original name was Bela (Gn 14:2).

---

teous people could not be found in Sodom (18:32), the city would be destroyed.

19:14 thought he was joking. Even though Lot told the truth to his daughters' husbands, they did not believe him.

19:16 he hesitated. Perhaps Lot was having second thoughts about leaving his home, his

possessions, and his sons-in-law.

19:24 rained burning sulfur. Subterranean asphalt is located in this part of the world. It is possible that God caused an eruption that rained down black molten tar.

19:29 God ... remembered Abraham. Abraham had interceded for all the righteous in-

habitants of Sodom, but he was especially concerned for his nephew and his family. This is a reminder of the power of intercessory prayer (18:32).

19:36–38 Moabites ... Ammonites. The sons resulting from Lot's incest with his daughters were the ancestors of the Moab-

34 The next day the firstborn said to the younger, "Look, I slept with my father last night. Let's get him to drink wine again tonight so you can go sleep with him and we can preserve our father's line." 35 That night they again got their father to drink wine, and the younger went and slept with him; he did not know when she lay down or when she got up.

36 So both of Lot's daughters became pregnant by their father. 37 The firstborn gave birth to a son and named him Moab.a He is the father of the Moabites of today. 38 The younger also gave birth to a son, and she named him Ben-ammi.b He is the father of the Ammonites of today.

Sarah Rescued from Abimelech

20 From there Abraham traveled to the region of the •Negev and settled between Kadesh and Shur. While he lived in Gerar, 2 Abraham said about his wife Sarah, "She is my sister." So Abimelech king of Gerar had Sarah brought to him.

3 But God came to Abimelech in a dream by night and said to him, "You are about to die because of the woman you have taken, for she is a married woman."c

4 Now Abimelech had not approached her, so he said, "Lord, would you destroy a nation even though it is innocent? 5 Didn't he himself say to me, 'She is my sister'? And she herself said, 'He is my brother.' I did this with a clear conscienced and cleane hands."

6 Then God said to him in the dream, "Yes, I know that you did this with a clear conscience.f I have also kept you from sinning against Me. Therefore I have not let you touch her. 7 Now return the man's wife, for he is a prophet, and he will pray for you and you will live. But if you do not return her, know that you will certainly die, you and all who are yours."

8 Early in the morning Abimelech got up, called all his servants together, and personallyg told them all these things; and the men were terrified.

9 Then Abimelech called Abraham in and said to him, "What have you done to us? How did I sin against you that you have brought such enormous guilt on me and on my kingdom? You have done things to me that should never be done." 10 Abimelech also said to Abraham, "What did you intend when you did this thing?"

11 Abraham replied, "I thought, 'There is absolutely no •fear of God in this place. They will kill me because of my wife.' 12 Besides, she really is my sister, the daughter of my father though not the daughter of my mother, and she became my wife. 13 So when God had me wander from my father's house, I said to her: Show your loyalty to me wherever we go, and say about me: 'He's my brother.'"

14 Then Abimelech took sheep and cattle and male and female slaves, gave them to Abraham, and returned his wife Sarah to him. 15 Abimelech said, "Look, my land is before you. Settle wherever you want."h 16 And to Sarah he said, "Look, I am giving your brother 1,000 pieces of silver. It is a verification of your honori to all who are with you. You are fully vindicated."

17 Then Abraham prayed to God, and God healed Abimelech, his wife, and his female slaves so that they could bear children, 18 for the LORD had completely closed all the wombs in Abimelech's household on account of Sarah, Abraham's wife.

The Birth of Isaac

21 The LORD came to Sarah as He had said, and the LORD did for Sarah what He had promised. 2 Sarah became pregnant and bore a son to Abraham in his old age, at the appointed time God had told him. 3 Abraham named his son who was born to him—the one Sarah bore to him—Isaac. 4 When his son Isaac was eight days old, Abraham circumcised him, as God had commanded him. 5 Abraham was 100 years old when his son Isaac was born to him.

6 Sarah said, "God has made me laugh, and everyone who hears will laugh with me." 7 She also said, "Who would have told Abraham that Sarah would nurse children? Yet I have borne himj a son in his old age."

Hagar and Ishmael Sent Away

8 The child grew and was weaned, and Abraham held a great feast on the day Isaac was weaned. 9 But Sarah saw the son mockingk —the one Hagar the Egyptian had borne to Abraham. 10 So she said to Abraham, "Drive out this slave with her son, for the son of this slave will not be a co-heir with my son Isaac!"

11 Now this was a very difficult thing forl Abraham because of his son. 12 But God said to Abraham, "Do not be concernedm about the boy and your slave. Whatever Sarah says to you, listen to her, because your •offspring will be traced through Isaac. 13 But I will also make a nation of the slave's son because he is your offspring."

14 Early in the morning Abraham got up, took bread and a waterskin, ⌊put them⌋ on Hagar's shoulders, and sent her and the boy away.n She left and wandered in

a19:37 = From My Father   b19:38 = Son of My People   c20:3 Lit is possessed by a husband   d20:5 Lit with integrity of my heart   e20:5 Lit cleanness of my   f20:6 Lit with integrity of your heart   g20:8 Lit in their ears   h20:15 Lit Settle in the good in your eyes   i20:16 Lit a covering of the eyes   j21:7 Sam, Tg Jonathan; MT omits him   k21:9 LXX, Vg add Isaac her son   l21:11 Lit was very bad in the eyes of   m21:12 Lit Let it not be bad in your eyes   n21:14 To "send away" a woman = divorce her; Dt 24:1. To "send away" a slave = free her; Dt 15:13.

ites and Ammonites. These tribes plagued Abraham's descendants, the Hebrews, for centuries.

20:3 dream. God used a dream to offer caution to Abimelech, king of Gerar, about keeping Sarah in his harem. The Lord was preparing the way for her to bear the child He

had promised Abraham.

20:16 pieces of silver. The king felt obligated to compensate Abraham for the inconvenience he had caused by taking Sarah into his harem.

21:1 did ... what He had promised. Finally, God's promise came true—the birth of a son

to Abraham and Sarah (15:4; 17:15–19).

21:3 Isaac. The name means, "he laughs." Both Abraham and Sarah had once laughed, scoffing at the idea of fathering a son at their age (17:17; 18:12). This time, their laughter was filled with joy.

21:9–14 After Isaac was born, Sarah insisted

Family Feuds

1. Do you have any sibling rivalry in your family? With whom? Over what?

Genesis 21:1-21

2. Modern Jews and Israelis are descended from Isaac, while modern Arabic nations are descended from Ishmael. How does this passage help explain modern Middle East tensions?
3. Both Abraham and Sarah were around 100 years old when Isaac was born. What meaning does this give to Isaac's birth? How does this hint at the birth of Jesus?
4. Abraham had to give up his son born to his slave, Hagar. Why did he do this?
5. When have you had to give up something for God?

the Wilderness of Beer-sheba. ¹⁵ When the water in the skin was gone, she left the boy under one of the bushes. ¹⁶ Then she went and sat down nearby, about a bowshot away, for she said, "I can't ⌊bear to⌋ watch the boy die!" So as she sat nearby, she[a] wept loudly.

¹⁷ God heard the voice of the boy, and the[b] angel of God called to Hagar from heaven and said to her, "What's wrong, Hagar? Don't be afraid, for God has heard the voice of the boy from the place where he is. ¹⁸ Get up, help the boy up, and sustain him, for I will make him a great nation." ¹⁹ Then God opened her eyes, and she saw a well of water. So she went and filled the waterskin and gave the boy a drink. ²⁰ God was with the boy, and he grew; he settled in the wilderness and became an archer. ²¹ He settled in the Wilderness of Paran, and his mother got a wife for him from the land of Egypt.

Abraham's Covenant with Abimelech

²² At that time Abimelech, with Phicol the commander of his army, said to Abraham, "God is with you in everything you do. ²³ Now swear to me here by God that you will not break an agreement with me or with my children and descendants. As I have kept faith with you, so you will keep faith with me and with the country where you are a resident alien."

²⁴ And Abraham said, "I swear ⌊it⌋." ²⁵ But Abraham complained to Abimelech because of the water well that Abimelech's servants had seized. ²⁶ Abimelech replied, "I don't know who did this thing. You didn't report anything to me, so I hadn't heard about it until today."

²⁷ Then Abraham took sheep and cattle[c] and gave them to Abimelech, and the two of them made a covenant. ²⁸ But Abraham had set apart seven ewe lambs from the flock. ²⁹ And Abimelech said to Abraham, "Why have you set apart these seven ewe lambs?"

³⁰ He replied, "You are to accept the seven ewe lambs from my hand so that this act[d] will serve as my witness that I dug this well." ³¹ Therefore that place was called Beer-sheba[e] because it was there that the two of them swore an oath. ³² After they had made a covenant at Beer-sheba, Abimelech and Phicol, the commander of his army, left and returned to the land of the Philistines.

³³ Abraham planted a tamarisk tree in Beer-sheba, and there he worshiped[f] the LORD, the Everlasting God. ³⁴ And Abraham lived as a foreigner in the land of the Philistines for many days.

The Sacrifice of Isaac

22 After these things God tested Abraham and said to him, "Abraham!"

"Here I am," he answered.

² "Take your son," He said, "your only ⌊son⌋ Isaac, whom you love, go to the land of Moriah, and offer him there as a •burnt offering on one of the mountains I will tell you about."

³ So early in the morning Abraham got up, saddled his donkey, and took with him two of his young men and his son Isaac. He split wood for a burnt offering and set out to go to the place God had told him about. ⁴ On the third day Abraham looked up and saw the place in the distance. ⁵ Then Abraham said to his young men, "Stay here with the donkey. The boy and I will go over there to worship; then we'll come back to you." ⁶ Abraham took the wood for the burnt offering and laid it on his son Isaac. In his hand he took the fire and the sacrificial knife,[g] and the two of them walked on together.

⁷ Then Isaac spoke to his father Abraham and said, "My father."

And he replied, "Here I am, my son."

Isaac said, "The fire and the wood are here, but where is the lamb for the burnt offering?"

---

[a] **21:16** LXX reads *the boy* [b] **21:17** Or *an* [c] **21:27** A covenant or treaty was regularly ratified by animal sacrifice (Gn 8:20—9:9; 15:9-17; Ex 24:8) and often involved an exchange of gifts (1 Kg 15:19; Hs 12:1). The animals here could serve both purposes. [d] **21:30** Lit *that it* [e] **21:31** = Seven Wells, or Well of the Oath [f] **21:33** Or *proclaimed* or *invoked the name of*; lit *called on the name of* [g] **22:6** The same word is used in Jdg 19:29 and Pr 30:14.

---

that Ishmael and Hagar be driven away from their household.

21:17 God has heard. God heard Ishmael crying in the wilderness. His name means, "God hears."

21:19 God opened her eyes. God had to open Hagar's eyes so she could see the

spring of water that God had provided to save them.

22:2 Isaac, whom you love. Isaac was the only son of God's promise (21:12). God knew how much Abraham loved his son, so he wanted to see if Abraham was totally committed to Him.

22:4 third day. It took three days to journey the region of Moriah. These were agonizing days for Abraham as he contemplated that God had asked him to sacrifice his son.

22:11 Abraham, Abraham! Abraham was about to carry out the sacrifice, doing what he had been told by God to do. An angel called

The Supreme Sacrifice

1. What thing in your life would be the hardest for you to give up?

Genesis 22:1-19
2. Why did God ask Abraham to sacrifice his son? Why did Abraham obey?
3. How does this story illustrate the sacrifice made by God the Father and His Son, Jesus?
4. Is God calling you to make a large sacrifice for Him? What is it? How will you respond?
5. Does obedience to coaches or parents or other authorities sometimes require a big sacrifice on your part? How might God bless you when you make those sacrifices?

8 Abraham answered, "God Himself will provide[a] the lamb for the burnt offering, my son." Then the two of them walked on together.

9 When they arrived at the place that God had told him about, Abraham built the altar there and arranged the wood. He bound his son Isaac[b] and placed him on the altar, on top of the wood. 10 Then Abraham reached out and took the knife to slaughter his son.

11 But the Angel of the LORD called to him from heaven and said, "Abraham, Abraham!"

He replied, "Here I am."

12 Then He said, "Do not lay a hand on the boy or do anything to him. For now I know that you •fear God, since you have not withheld your only son from Me." 13 Abraham looked up and saw a ram[c] caught by its horns in the thicket. So Abraham went and took the ram and offered it as a burnt offering in place of his son. 14 And Abraham named that place The LORD Will Provide,[d] so today it is said: "It will be provided[e] on the LORD's mountain."

15 Then the Angel of the LORD called to Abraham a second time from heaven 16 and said, "By Myself I have sworn, says the LORD: Because you have done this thing and have not withheld your only son,[f] 17 I will indeed bless you and make your •offspring as numerous as the stars in the sky and the sand on the seashore. Your offspring will possess the gates of their enemies. 18 And all the nations of the earth will be blessed[g] by your offspring because you have obeyed My command."

19 Abraham went back to his young men, and they got up and went together to Beer-sheba. And Abraham settled in Beer-sheba.

Rebekah's Family

20 Now after these things Abraham was told, "Milcah also has borne sons to your brother Nahor: 21 Uz his firstborn, his brother Buz, Kemuel the father of Aram, 22 Chesed, Hazo, Pildash, Jidlaph, and Bethuel." 23 And Bethuel fathered Rebekah. Milcah bore these eight to Nahor, Abraham's brother. 24 His concubine, whose name was Reumah, also bore Tebah, Gaham, Tahash, and Maacah.

Sarah's Burial

23 Now Sarah lived 127 years; ⌊these were all⌋ the years of her life. 2 Sarah died in Kiriath-arba (that is, Hebron) in the land of Canaan, and Abraham went in to mourn for Sarah and to weep for her.

3 Then Abraham got up from beside his dead ⌊wife⌋ and spoke to the Hittites: 4 "I am a resident alien among you. Give me a burial site among you so that I can bury my dead."[h]

5 The Hittites replied to Abraham,[i] 6 "Listen to us, lord.[j] You are God's chosen one among us. Bury your dead in our finest burial place.[k] None of us will withhold from you his burial place for burying your dead."

7 Then Abraham rose and bowed down to the Hittites, the people of the land. 8 He said to them, "If you are willing ⌊for me⌋ to bury my dead, listen to me and ask Ephron son of Zohar on my behalf 9 to give me the cave of Machpelah that belongs to him; it is at the end of his field. Let him give it to me in your presence, for the full price, as a burial place."

10 Ephron was present with the Hittites. So in the presence[l] of all the Hittites who came to the •gate of his city, Ephron the Hittite answered Abraham: 11 "No, my lord. Listen to me. I give you the field, and I give you the cave that is in it. I give it to you in the presence[m] of my people. Bury your dead."

12 Abraham bowed down to the people of the land 13 and said to Ephron in the presence[l] of the people of the land, "Please listen to me. Let me pay the price of the field. Accept it from me, and let me bury my dead there."

[a]**22:8** Lit *see* [b]**22:9** Or perhaps *Isaac hand and foot* [c]**22:13** Some Hb mss, Sam, LXX, Syr, Tg; other Hb mss read *saw behind [him] a ram* [d]**22:14** Hb *Yahweh-yireh* [e]**22:14** Or *He will be seen* [f]**22:16** Sam, LXX, Syr, Vg add *from Me* [g]**22:18** Or *will bless themselves,* or *will find blessing* [h]**23:4** Lit *dead from before me* [i]**23:5** Lit *Abraham, saying to him* [j]**23:6** Lit *my lord* [k]**23:6** Or *finest graves* [l]**23:10,13** Lit *ears* [m]**23:11** Lit *in the eyes of the sons*

out to stop him.

22:13 burnt offering. This is the first time in the Bible that the concept of substituting a sacrifice is mentioned. The ram took Isaac's place on the altar, just as Christ did for us.

22:16 By Myself I have sworn. Oaths are made by calling upon someone to witness the oath; God swore by His own name.

23:4 resident alien among you. Abraham never owned any land in Canaan except the spot where he buried his beloved wife. But God had promised that all the surrounding territory would belong to his descendants one day.

23:9 cave of Machpelah. Although no one knows the exact location of this cave, according to tradition, it is beneath a Muslim shrine in Hebron.

23:10 who came to the gate. A city's main gateway through the defensive wall was the traditional place where important matters

[14] Ephron answered Abraham and said to him, [15] "My lord, listen to me. Land worth 400 •shekels of silver—what is that between you and me? Bury your dead." [16] Abraham agreed with Ephron, and Abraham weighed out to Ephron the silver that he had agreed to in the hearing of the Hittites: 400 shekels of silver at the current commercial rate. [17] So Ephron's field at Machpelah near Mamre—the field with its cave and all the trees anywhere within the boundaries of the field— became [18] Abraham's possession in the presence of all the Hittites who came to the gate of his city. [19] After this, Abraham buried his wife Sarah in the cave of the field at Machpelah near Mamre (that is, Hebron) in the land of Canaan. [20] The field with its cave passed from the Hittites to Abraham as a burial place.

A Wife for Isaac

24 Abraham was now old, getting on in years,[a] and the LORD had blessed him in everything. [2] Abraham said to his servant, the elder of his household who managed all he owned, "Place your hand under my thigh, [3] and I will have you swear by the LORD, God of heaven and God of earth, that you will not take a wife for my son from the daughters of the Canaanites among whom I live, [4] but will go to my land and my family to take a wife for my son Isaac."

[5] The servant said to him, "Suppose the woman is unwilling to follow me to this land? Should I have your son go back to the land you came from?"

[6] Abraham answered him, "Make sure that you don't take my son back there. [7] The LORD, the God of heaven, who took me from my father's house and from my native land, who spoke to me and swore to me, 'I will give this land to your •offspring'—He will send His angel before you, and you can take a wife for my son from there. [8] If the woman is unwilling to follow you, then you are free from this oath to me, but don't let my son go back there." [9] So the servant placed his hand under his master Abraham's thigh and swore an oath to him concerning this matter.

[10] The servant took 10 of his master's camels and departed with all kinds of his master's goods in hand. Then he set out for the town of Nahor, Aram-naharaim. [11] He made the camels kneel beside a well of water outside the town at evening. ⌊This was⌋ the time when the women went out to draw water.

[12] "LORD, God of my master Abraham," he prayed, "grant me success today, and show kindness to my master Abraham. [13] I am standing here at the spring where the daughters of the men of the town are coming out to draw water. [14] Let the girl to whom I say, 'Please lower your water jug so that I may drink,' and who responds, 'Drink, and I'll water your camels also'—let her be the one You have appointed for Your servant Isaac. By this I will know that You have shown kindness to my master."

[15] Before he had finished speaking, there was Rebekah—daughter of Bethuel son of Milcah, the wife of Abraham's brother Nahor—coming with a jug on her shoulder. [16] Now the girl was very beautiful, a young woman who had not known a man intimately. She went down to the spring, filled her jug, and came up. [17] Then the servant ran to meet her and said, "Please let me have a little water from your jug."

[18] She replied, "Drink, my lord." She quickly lowered her jug to her hand and gave him a drink. [19] When she had finished giving him a drink, she said, "I'll also draw water for your camels until they have had enough to drink."[b] [20] She quickly emptied her jug into the trough and hurried to the well again to draw water. She drew water for all his camels [21] while the man silently watched her to see whether or not the LORD had made his journey a success.

[22] After the camels had finished drinking, the man took a gold ring weighing half a •shekel, and for her wrists two bracelets weighing 10 shekels of gold. [23] "Whose daughter are you?" he asked. "Please tell me, is there room in your father's house for us to spend the night?"

[24] She answered him, "I am the daughter of Bethuel son of Milcah, whom she bore to Nahor." [25] She also said to him, "We have plenty of straw and feed, and a place to spend the night."

[26] Then the man bowed down, worshiped the LORD, [27] and said, "Praise the LORD, the God of my master Abraham, who has not withheld His kindness and faithfulness from my master. As for me, the LORD has led me on the journey to the house of my master's relatives."

[28] The girl ran and told her mother's household about these things. [29] Now Rebekah had a brother named Laban, and Laban ran out to the man at the spring. [30] As soon as he had seen the ring, and the bracelets on his sister's wrists, and when he had heard his sister Rebekah's words—"The man said this to me!"—he went to the man. He was standing there by the camels at the spring. [31] Laban said, "Come, you who are blessed by the LORD. Why are you standing out here? I have prepared the house and a place for the camels." [32] So the man came to the house, and the camels were unloaded. Straw and feed were given to the camels, and water was

---

[a] **24:1** Lit *days*   [b] **24:19** Lit *they are finished drinking*

---

were settled. The exchange between Ephron and Abraham took place before many witnesses (v. 16).

23:15 Land worth 400 shekels. Ephron acted as if his offer was generous, but 400 shekels was a high price for such a property.

23:17 field ... cave ... trees. Ephron negoti-

ated the sale of the entire field and its contents as well as the cave of Machpelah.

23:19 buried his wife. By establishing this "family plot" in Canaan, Abraham was expressing his deep faith in God's promise to give his descendants the land.

24:4 my land. Abraham sent his most trusted

servant back to where Abraham had come from to find a wife for his son, Isaac. Abraham did not want Isaac to intermarry with the Canaanites.

24:10 Aram-naharaim. An area in northern Syria between the Tigris and Euphrates Rivers, sometimes translated "Mesopotamia."

brought to wash his feet and the feet of the men with him.

³³ A meal was set before him, but he said, "I will not eat until I have said what I have to say."

So Laban said, "Speak on."

³⁴ "I am Abraham's servant," he said. ³⁵ "The LORD has greatly blessed my master, and he has become rich. He has given him sheep and cattle, silver and gold, male and female slaves, and camels and donkeys. ³⁶ Sarah, my master's wife, bore a son to my master in her^a old age, and he has given him everything he owns. ³⁷ My master put me under this oath: 'You will not take a wife for my son from the daughters of the Canaanites in whose land I live ³⁸ but will go to my father's household and to my family to take a wife for my son.' ³⁹ But I said to my master, 'Suppose the woman will not come back with me?' ⁴⁰ He said to me, 'The LORD before whom I have walked will send His angel with you and make your journey a success, and you will take a wife for my son from my family and from my father's household. ⁴¹ Then you will be free from my oath if you go to my family and they do not give ⌊her⌋ to you—you will be free from my oath.'

⁴² "Today when I came to the spring, I prayed: LORD, God of my master Abraham, if only You will make my journey successful! ⁴³ I am standing here at a spring. Let the virgin who comes out to draw water, and I say to her: Please let me drink a little water from your jug, ⁴⁴ and who responds to me, 'Drink, and I'll draw water for your camels also'—let her be the woman the LORD has appointed for my master's son.

⁴⁵ "Before I had finished praying in my heart, there was Rebekah coming with her jug on her shoulder, and she went down to the spring and drew water. So I said to her: Please let me have a drink. ⁴⁶ She quickly lowered her jug from her ⌊shoulder⌋ and said, 'Drink, and I'll water your camels also.' So I drank, and she also watered the camels. ⁴⁷ Then I asked her: Whose daughter are you? She responded, 'The daughter of Bethuel son of Nahor, whom Milcah bore to him.' So I put the ring on her nose and the bracelets on her wrists. ⁴⁸ Then I bowed down, worshiped the LORD, and praised the LORD, the God of my master Abraham, who guided me on the right way to take the daughter of my master's brother for his son. ⁴⁹ Now, if you are going to show kindness and faithfulness to my master, tell me; if not, tell me, and I will go elsewhere."^b

⁵⁰ Laban and Bethuel answered, "This is from the LORD; we have no choice in the matter.^c ⁵¹ Rebekah is here in front of you. Take ⌊her⌋ and go, and let her be a wife for your master's son, just as the LORD has spoken."

⁵² When Abraham's servant heard their words, he bowed to the ground before the LORD. ⁵³ Then he brought out objects of silver and gold, and garments, and gave ⌊them⌋ to Rebekah. He also gave precious gifts to her brother and her mother. ⁵⁴ Then he and the men with him ate and drank and spent the night.

When they got up in the morning, he said, "Send me to my master."

⁵⁵ But her brother and mother said, "Let the girl stay with us for about 10 days.^d Then she^e can go."

⁵⁶ But he responded to them, "Do not delay me, since the LORD has made my journey a success. Send me away so that I may go to my master."

⁵⁷ So they said, "Let's call the girl and ask her opinion."^f

⁵⁸ They called Rebekah and said to her, "Will you go with this man?"

She replied, "I will go." ⁵⁹ So they sent away their sister Rebekah and her nurse, and Abraham's servant and his men.

⁶⁰ They blessed Rebekah, saying to her:

> Our sister, may you become
> thousands upon ten thousands.
> May your offspring possess
> the gates of their^g enemies.

⁶¹ Then Rebekah and her young women got up, mounted the camels, and followed the man. So the servant took Rebekah and left.

⁶² Now Isaac was returning from Beer-lahai-roi,^h for he was living in the •Negev region. ⁶³ In the early evening, Isaac went out to walkⁱ in the field, and looking up, he saw camels coming. ⁶⁴ Rebekah looked up, and when she saw Isaac, she got down from her camel ⁶⁵ and asked the servant, "Who is that man in the field coming to meet us?"

The servant answered, "It is my master." So she took her veil and covered herself. ⁶⁶ Then the servant told Isaac everything he had done.

⁶⁷ And Isaac brought her into the tent of his mother Sarah and took Rebekah to be his wife. Isaac loved her, and he was comforted after his mother's ⌊death⌋.

Abraham's Other Wife and Sons

25 Now Abraham took another wife, whose name was Keturah, ² and she bore him Zimran,

---

^a**24:36** Sam, LXX read *his*   ^b**24:49** Lit *go to the right or to the left*   ^c**24:50** Lit *we cannot say to you anything bad or good*   ^d**24:55** Lit *us a few days or 10*   ^e**24:55** Or *you*   ^f**24:57** Lit *mouth*   ^g**24:60** Lit *his*   ^h**24:62** = A Well of the Living One Who Sees Me; Gn 16:13–14   ⁱ**24:63** Or *pray*, or *meditate*; Hb obscure

---

24:14 I will know. Eliezer prayed, asking God for a sign to discern the woman whom God had chosen for Isaac. Any woman might offer a drink to a weary traveler at the well, but for a woman to offer water for his camel would show a servant's spirit.

24:15 Rebekah. Isaac would be marrying within Abraham's extended family—Abraham's grandniece.

24:26 bowed down, worshiped the LORD. Abraham's servant was overwhelmed by God's gracious work in sending Rebekah.

24:53 gave them to Rebekah. The jewelry and clothing given to Rebekah and her family,

revealing the wealth of her new household, assured them that she would be provided for.

24:67 tent. After arriving in Canaan, Rebekah entered the family through marriage by entering the family through marriage and literally by intimacy with Isaac in one of the tents, which would be their home.

Jokshan, Medan, Midian, Ishbak, and Shuah. ³ Jokshan fathered Sheba and Dedan. Dedan's sons were the Asshurim, Letushim, and Leummim. ⁴ And Midian's sons were Ephah, Epher, Hanoch, Abida, and Eldaah. All these were sons of Keturah. ⁵ Abraham gave everything he owned to Isaac. ⁶ And Abraham gave gifts to the sons of his concubines, but while he was still alive he sent them eastward, away from his son Isaac, to the land of the East.

Abraham's Death

⁷ This is the length of Abraham's life:ᵃ 175 years. ⁸ He took his last breath and died at a ripe old age, old and contented,ᵇ and he was gathered to his people. ⁹ His sons Isaac and Ishmael buried him in the cave of Machpelah near Mamre, in the field of Ephron son of Zohar the Hittite. ¹⁰ This was the field that Abraham bought from the Hittites. Abraham was buried there with his wife Sarah. ¹¹ After Abraham's death, God blessed his son Isaac, who lived near Beer-lahai-roi.

Ishmael's Family Records

¹² These are the family records of Abraham's son Ishmael, whom Hagar the Egyptian, Sarah's slave, bore to Abraham. ¹³ These are the names of Ishmael's sons; their names according to the family records are: Nebaioth, Ishmael's firstborn, then Kedar, Adbeel, Mibsam, ¹⁴ Mishma, Dumah, Massa, ¹⁵ Hadad, Tema, Jetur, Naphish, and Kedemah. ¹⁶ These are Ishmael's sons, and these are their names by their villages and encampments: 12 leadersᶜ of their clans.ᵈ ¹⁷ This is the lengthᵉ of Ishmael's life: 137 years. He took his last breath and died, and was gathered to his people. ¹⁸ And theyᶠ settled from Havilah to Shur, which is opposite Egypt as you go toward Asshur. Heᵍ lived in opposition toʰ all his brothers.

The Birth of Jacob and Esau

¹⁹ These are the family records of Isaac son of Abraham. Abraham fathered Isaac. ²⁰ Isaac was 40 years old when he took as his wife Rebekah daughter of Bethuel the Aramean from Paddan-aram, and sister of Laban the Aramean. ²¹ Isaac prayed to the LORD on behalf of his wife because she was barren. The LORD heard his prayer, and his wife Rebekah conceived. ²² But the children inside her struggled with each other, and she said, "Why is this happening to me?"ⁱ So she went to inquire of the LORD. ²³ And the LORD said to her:

Two nations are in your womb;
two people will ⌊come⌋ from you
    and be separated.
One people will be stronger than the other,
and the older will serve the younger.

Honor and Privilege

1. What is the story behind your name? How did your parents come up with it? What does it mean?

Genesis 25:19-34

2. What did the Lord mean when He said to Rebekah, "Two nations are in your womb" (v. 23)?
3. What motivated Esau to sell his birthright? What were his top priorities?
4. What motivated Jacob to cheat his brother? What were his top priorities?
5. What is the "birthright" of every Christian? How do Christians sometimes "despise" their birthright as Esau did? How about you?
6. Does your attitude and behavior bring honor to your family, your school, and your team? How?

²⁴ When her time came to give birth, there were indeed twins in her womb. ²⁵ The first one came out reddish,ʲ covered with hairᵏ like a fur coat, and they named him Esau. ²⁶ After this, his brother came out grasping Esau's heel with his hand. So he was named Jacob.ˡ Isaac was 60 years old when they were born.

Esau Sells His Birthright

²⁷ When the boys grew up, Esau became an expert hunter, an outdoorsman,ᵐ but Jacob was a quiet man who stayed at home.ⁿ ²⁸ Isaac loved Esau because he had a taste for wild game, but Rebekah loved Jacob.

²⁹ Once when Jacob was cooking a stew, Esau came in from the field, exhausted. ³⁰ He said to Jacob, "Let me eat some of that red stuff, because I'm exhausted." That is why he was ⌊also⌋ named Edom.ᵒ

³¹ Jacob replied, "First sell me your birthright."

³² "Look," said Esau, "I'm about to die, so what good is a birthright to me?"

ᵃ**25:7** Lit *And these are the days of the years of the lives of Abraham that he lived*   ᵇ**25:8** Sam, LXX, Syr read *full of days*   ᶜ**25:16** Or *chieftains*   ᵈ**25:16** Or *peoples*   ᵉ**25:17** Lit *And these are the years*   ᶠ**25:18** LXX, Vg read *he*   ᵍ**25:18** Ishmael and his descendants   ʰ**25:18** Or *He settled down alongside of*   ⁱ**25:22** Lit *If thus, why this I*   ʲ**25:25** The Hb word for *reddish* sounds like the Hb word "Edom" (Gn 25:3).   ᵏ**25:25** The Hb word for *hair* sounds like the Hb word "Seir" (Gn 32:3).   ˡ**25:26** = He Grasps the Heel   ᵐ**25:27** Lit *a man of the field*   ⁿ**25:27** Lit *man living in tents*   ᵒ**25:30** = Red

---

25:1 another wife. Abraham had been married to Sarah, but apparently had many concubines, as noted in verse 6. Keturah may have been another concubine.

25:5 gave everything. Abraham left everything he owned to Isaac so all of God's promises would be kept within Isaac's line.

25:7–8 Abraham left Haran at age 75 (12:4) and died about 100 years later. God kept His promise to give him a long life (12:2; 15:15).

25:12–19 Ishmael's genealogy is followed by Isaac's. Ishmael's line includes many Arabic names, showing that he was the ancestor of that line of people.

25:23–25 Traditionally, the older son received the double portion of the inheritance. In this case, God's plan was to bless the younger son, Jacob, and continue the line of promise through him.

25:26 grasping Esau's heel. This is an early picture of the hostility that would develop be-

33 Jacob said, "Swear to me first." So he swore to Jacob and sold his birthright to him. 34 Then Jacob gave bread and lentil stew to Esau; he ate, drank, got up, and went away. So Esau despised his birthright.

The Promise Reaffirmed to Isaac

26 There was another famine in the land in addition to the one that had occurred in Abraham's time. And Isaac went to Abimelech, king of the Philistines, at Gerar. 2 The LORD appeared to him and said, "Do not go down to Egypt. Live in the land that I tell you about; 3 stay in this land as a foreigner, and I will be with you and bless you. For I will give all these lands to you and your •offspring, and I will confirm the oath that I swore to your father Abraham. 4 I will make your offspring as numerous as the stars of the sky, I will give your offspring all these lands, and all the nations of the earth will be blesseda by your offspring, 5 because Abraham listened to My voice and kept My mandate, My commands, My statutes, and My instructions." 6 So Isaac settled in Gerar.

Isaac's Deception

7 When the men of the place asked about his wife, he said, "She is my sister," for he was afraid to say "my wife," ⌊thinking⌋, "The men of the place will kill me on account of Rebekah, for she is a beautiful woman." 8 When Isaac had been there for some time, Abimelech king of the Philistines looked down from the window and was surprised to seeb Isaac caressing his wife Rebekah.

9 Abimelech sent for Isaac and said, "So she is really your wife! How could you say, 'She's my sister'?"

Isaac answered him, "Because I thought I might die on account of her."

10 Then Abimelech said, "What is this you've done to us? One of the people could easily have slept with your wife, and you would have brought guilt on us." 11 So Abimelech warned all the people with these words: "Whoever harms this man or his wife will certainly die."

Conflicts over Wells

12 Isaac sowed seed in that land, and in that year he reapedc a hundred times ⌊what was sown⌋. The LORD blessed him, 13 and the man became rich and kept getting richer until he was very wealthy. 14 He had flocks of sheep, herds of cattle, and many slaves, and the Philistines were envious of him. 15 The Philistines stopped up all the wells that his father's slaves had dug in the days of his father Abraham, filling them with dirt. 16 And Abimelech said to Isaac, "Leave us, for you are much too powerful for us."d

17 So Isaac left there, camped in the valley of Gerar, and lived there. 18 Isaac reopened the water wells that had been dug in the days of his father Abraham and that the Philistines had stopped up after Abraham died. He gave them the same names his father had given them. 19 Moreover, Isaac's slaves dug in the valley and found a well of springe water there. 20 But the herdsmen of Gerar quarreled with Isaac's herdsmen and said, "The water is ours!" So he named the well Quarrelf because they quarreled with him. 21 Then they dug another well and quarreled over that one also, so he named it Hostility.g 22 He moved from there and dug another, and they did not quarrel over it. He named it Open Spacesh and said, "For now the LORD has made room for us, and we will be fruitful in the land."

Theophany at Beer-sheba

23 From there he went up to Beer-sheba, 24 and the LORD appeared to him that night and said, "I am the God of your father Abraham. Do not be afraid, for I am with you. I will bless you and multiply your offspring because of My servant Abraham."

25 So he built an altar there, worshipedi the LORD, and pitched his tent there. Isaac's slaves also dug a well there.

Covenant with Abimelech

26 Then Abimelech came to him from Gerar with Ahuzzath his adviser and Phicol the commander of his army. 27 Isaac said to them, "Why have you come to me? You hated me and sent me away from you."

28 They replied, "We have clearly seen how the LORD has been with you. We think there should be an oath between two parties—between us and you. Let us make a covenant with you: 29 You will not harm us, just as we have not harmed you but have only done what was good to you, sending you away in peace. You are now blessed by the LORD."

30 So he prepared a banquet for them, and they ate and drank. 31 They got up early in the morning and swore an oath to each other.j Then Isaac sent them on their way, and they left him in peace. 32 On that same day Isaac's slaves came to tell him about the well they had dug, saying to him, "We have found water!" 33 He called it Oath.k Therefore the name of the city is Beer-shebal to this day.

---

a**26:4** Or will bless themselves   b**26:8** Or and he looked and behold—   c**26:12** Lit found   d**26:16** Or are more numerous than we are   e**26:19** Lit living   f**26:20** Hb Esek   g**26:21** Hb Sitnah   h**26:22** Hb Rehoboth   i**26:25** Or proclaimed or invoked the name of; lit called on the name of   j**26:31** Lit swore, each man to his brother   k**26:33** Hb Shibah   l**26:33** = Well of the Oath

---

tween Jacob's descendants (the Israelites) and Esau's descendants (the Edomites).

25:31 birthright. Jacob, a schemer from the day he was born, was determined to take away Esau's rights as the firstborn son.

25:34 lentil stew. Lentils, similar to beans, were an important source of nourishment.

26:2 The LORD appeared. God's first recorded appearance to Isaac. God repeated to Isaac the covenant He had made with his father Abraham (15:4–5).

26:16 too powerful for us. The presence of God's people in the land, worshiping their unseen God who blessed them, was a threat to the inhabitants of Canaan even at this early time.

26:20 The water is ours! Wells were greatly valued. Disagreements over the fresh water in a well were common.

26:25 built an altar. Isaac followed his father's practice of building an altar to worship

Esau's Wives

34 When Esau was 40 years old, he took as his wives Judith daughter of Beeri the Hittite, and Basemath daughter of Elon the Hittite. 35 They made life bitter[a] for Isaac and Rebekah.

The Stolen Blessing

27 When Isaac was old and his eyes were so weak that he could not see, he called his older son Esau and said to him, "My son."

And he answered, "Here I am."

2 He said, "Look, I am old and do not know the day of my death. 3 Take your ⌊hunting⌋ gear, your quiver and bow, and go out in the field to hunt some game for me. 4 Then make me the delicious food that I love and bring it to me to eat, so that I can bless you before I die."

5 Now Rebekah was listening to what Isaac said to his son Esau. So while Esau went to the field to hunt some game to bring in, 6 Rebekah said to her son Jacob, "Listen! I heard your father talking with your brother Esau. He said, 7 'Bring me some game and make some delicious food for me to eat so that I can bless you in the LORD's presence before I die.' 8 Now obey every order I give you, my son. 9 Go to the flock and bring me two choice young goats, and I will make them into a delicious meal for your father—the kind he loves. 10 Then take it to your father to eat so that he may bless you before he dies."

11 Jacob answered Rebekah his mother, "Look, my brother Esau is a hairy man, but I am a man with smooth skin. 12 Suppose my father touches me. Then I will seem to be deceiving him, and I will bring a curse rather than a blessing on myself."

13 His mother said to him, "Your curse be on me, my son. Just obey me and go get them for me."

14 So he went and got them and brought them to his mother, and his mother made the delicious food his father loved. 15 Then Rebekah took the best clothes of her older son Esau, which were there at the house, and had her younger son Jacob wear them. 16 She put the goatskins on his hands and the smooth part of his neck. 17 Then she handed the delicious food and the bread she had made to her son Jacob.

18 When he came to his father, he said, "My father." And he answered, "Here I am. Who are you, my son?"

19 Jacob replied to his father, "I am Esau, your firstborn. I have done as you told me. Please sit up and eat some of my game so that you may bless me."

20 But Isaac said to his son, "How did you ever find it so quickly, my son?"

He replied, "Because the LORD your God worked it out for me."

21 Then Isaac said to Jacob, "Please come closer so I can touch you, my son. Are you really my son Esau, or not?"

22 So Jacob came closer to his father Isaac. When he touched him, he said, "The voice is the voice of Jacob, but the hands are the hands of Esau." 23 He did not recognize him, because his hands were hairy like those of his brother Esau; so he blessed him. 24 Again he asked, "Are you really my son Esau?"

And he replied, "I am."

25 Then he said, "Serve me, and let me eat some of my son's game so that I can bless you." Jacob brought it to him, and he ate; he brought him wine, and he drank.

26 Then his father Isaac said to him, "Please come closer and kiss me, my son." 27 So he came closer and kissed him. When Isaac smelled[b] his clothes, he blessed him and said:

> Ah, the smell of my son
> is like the smell of a field
> that the LORD has blessed.
> 28 May God give to you—
> from the dew of the sky
> and from the richness of the land—
> an abundance of grain and new wine.
> 29 May peoples serve you
> and nations bow down to you.
> Be master over your brothers;
> may your mother's sons bow down to you.
> Those who curse you will be cursed,
> and those who bless you will be blessed.

30 As soon as Isaac had finished blessing Jacob and Jacob had left the presence of his father Isaac, his brother Esau arrived from the hunt. 31 He had also made some delicious food and brought it to his father. Then he said to his father, "Let my father get up and eat some of his son's game, so that you may bless me."

32 But his father Isaac said to him, "Who are you?"

He answered, "I am Esau your firstborn son."

33 Isaac began to tremble uncontrollably. "Who was it then," he said, "who hunted game and brought it to me? I ate it all before you came in, and I blessed him. Indeed, he will be blessed!"

34 When Esau heard his father's words, he cried out with a loud and bitter cry and said to his father, "Bless me—me too, my father!"

35 But he replied, "Your brother came deceitfully and took your blessing."

---

[a] **26:35** Lit *And they became bitterness of spirit* [b] **27:27** Lit *smelled the smell of*

God in a place where God appeared to him (12:7–8; 13:18).

26:30 banquet. To eat together signified friendship and peace. This bound the two parties to the oath they had sworn.

27:1–4 Isaac asked his son Esau to prepare a special meal of wild game so he could pronounce his blessing upon him.

27:5 Rebekah was listening. God had already told Rebekah that the inheritance would go to her younger son, Jacob (25:23). She eavesdropped and schemed to make sure this would happen.

27:29 over your brothers. The customary blessing included the fact that the elder son would be "lord over" his brothers. As Isaac spoke these words to his younger son, Jacob, he fulfilled what God had promised (25:23). Once spoken, these words could not be taken back.

36 So he said, "Isn't he rightly named Jacob?a For he has cheated me twice now. He took my birthright, and look, now he has taken my blessing." Then he asked, "Haven't you saved a blessing for me?"

37 But Isaac answered Esau: "Look, I have made him a master over you, have given him all of his relatives as his servants, and have sustained him with grain and new wine. What then can I do for you, my son?"

38 Esau said to his father, "Do you only have one blessing, my father? Bless me—me too, my father!" And Esau wept loudly.b

39 Then his father Isaac answered him:

Look, your dwelling place will be
away from the richness of the land,
away from the dew of the sky above.
40 You will live by your sword,
and you will serve your brother.
But when you rebel,c
you will break his yoke from your neck.

Esau's Anger

41 Esau held a grudge against Jacob because of the blessing his father had given him. And Esau determined in his heart: "The days of mourning for my father are approaching; then I will kill my brother Jacob."

42 When the words of her older son Esau were reported to Rebekah, she summoned her younger son Jacob and said to him, "Listen, your brother Esau is consoling himself by planning to kill you. 43 So now, my son, listen to me. Flee at once to my brother Laban in Haran, 44 and stay with him for a few days until your brother's anger subsides— 45 until your brother's rage turns away from you and he forgets what you have done to him. Then I will send for you and bring you back from there. Why should I lose you both in one day?"

46 So Rebekah said to Isaac, "I'm sick of my life because of these Hittite women. If Jacob marries a Hittite woman like one of them,d what good is my life?"

Jacob's Departure

28 Isaac summoned Jacob, blessed him, and commanded him: "Don't take a wife from the Canaanite women. 2 Go at once to Paddan-aram, to the house of Bethuel, your mother's father. Marry one of the daughters of Laban, your mother's brother. 3 May •God Almighty bless you and make you fruitful and multiply you so that you become an assembly of peoples. 4 May God give you and your •offspring the blessing of Abraham so that you may possess the land where you live as an alien, the land God gave to Abra-

ham." 5 So Isaac sent Jacob to Paddan-aram, to Laban son of Bethuel the Aramean, the brother of Rebekah, the mother of Jacob and Esau.

6 Esau noticed that Isaac blessed Jacob and sent him to Paddan-aram to get a wife there. When he blessed him, Isaac commanded Jacob not to marry a Canaanite woman. 7 And Jacob listened to his father and mother and went to Paddan-aram. 8 Esau realized that his father Isaac disapproved of the Canaanite women, 9 so Esau went to Ishmael and married, in addition to his other wives, Mahalath daughter of Ishmael, Abraham's son. She was the sister of Nebaioth.

Jacob at Bethel

10 Jacob left Beer-sheba and went toward Haran. 11 He reached a certain place and spent the night there because the sun had set. He took one of the stones from the place, put it there at his head, and lay down in that place. 12 And he dreamed: A stairway was set on the ground with its top reaching heaven, and God's angels were going up and down on it. 13 The LORD was standing there beside him, saying, "I am the LORD, the God of your father Abraham and the God of Isaac. I will give you and your offspring the land that you are now sleeping on. 14 Your offspring will be like the dust of the earth, and you will spread out toward the west, the east, the north, and the south. All the peoples on earth will be blessed through you and your offspring. 15 Look, I am with you and will watch over you wherever you go. I will bring you back to this land, for I will not leave you until I have done what I have promised you."

16 When Jacob awoke from his sleep, he said, "Surely the LORD is in this place, and I did not know it." 17 He was afraid and said, "What an awesome place this is! This is none other than the house of God. This is the gate of heaven."

18 Early in the morning Jacob took the stone that was near his head and set it up as a marker. He poured oil on top of it 19 and named the place Bethel,e though previously the city was named Luz. 20 Then Jacob made a vow: "If God will be with me and watch over me on this journey, if He provides me with food to eat and clothing to wear, 21 and if I return safely to my father's house, then the LORD will be my God. 22 This stone that I have set up as a marker will be God's house, and I will give to You a tenth of all that You give me."

Jacob Meets Rachel

29 Jacob resumed his journeyf and went to the eastern country.g 2 He looked and saw a well in

---

a**27:36** = He Grasps the Heel b**27:38** Lit *Esau lifted up his voice and wept* c**27:40** Hb obscure d**27:46** Lit *of these daughters of the land*
e**28:19** = House of God f**29:1** Lit *Jacob picked up his feet* g**29:1** Lit *the land of the children of the east*

27:34 loud and bitter cry. The gravity of the loss of his father's blessing overwhelmed Esau.

27:43–45 Because of the deceit of Jacob and his mother, he was forced to flee to escape Esau's wrath. Rebekah would never see him again.

28:11 one of the stones. Traditionally seen as a pillow, this stone may actually have been a sort of good luck charm in Jacob's thinking. The text does not say he put the stone under his head.

28:12–13 In Jacob's dream, God used a familiar picture from pagan religion, a stairway

linking heaven and earth, to invite Jacob into a relationship with Him.

28:15 I will not leave you. It did not matter where Jacob went; the one true God would be with him.

28:18 marker. At this location, Jacob's grandfather, Abraham, had built an altar and

a field. Three flocks of sheep were lying there beside it because the sheep were watered from this well. A large stone covered the opening of the well. 3 When all the flocks[a] were gathered there, the ⌊shepherds⌋ would roll the stone from the opening of the well and water the sheep. The stone was then placed back on the well's opening.

Love at First Sight

1. What do you know about how your parents met and fell in love?

Genesis 29:1-14

2. Why was it important to Jacob to meet a woman who was his relative? What does this suggest about Christians dating non-Christians?

3. How was Jacob's kindness to Rachel costly and extraordinary? Why would that kindness earn him favor from Rachel?

4. What are you looking for in a potential husband or wife? What principles can you learn from Jacob's actions? From Rachel's actions?

4 Jacob asked the men at the well, "My brothers! Where are you from?"

"We're from Haran," they answered.

5 "Do you know Laban son of Nahor?" Jacob asked them.

They answered, "We know ⌊him⌋."

6 "Is he well?" Jacob asked.

"Yes," they said, "and here is his daughter Rachel, coming with his sheep."

7 Then Jacob said, "Look, it is still broad daylight. It's not time for the animals to be gathered. Water the flock, then go out and let them graze."

8 But they replied, "We can't, until all the flocks have been gathered and the stone is rolled from the well's opening. Then we will water the sheep."

9 While he was still speaking with them, Rachel came with her father's sheep, for she was a shepherdess. 10 As soon as Jacob saw his uncle Laban's daughter Rachel with his sheep,[b] he went up and rolled the stone from the opening and watered his uncle Laban's sheep. 11 Then Jacob kissed Rachel and wept loudly.[c] 12 He told Rachel that he was her father's relative, Rebekah's son. She ran and told her father.

Jacob Deceived

13 When Laban heard the news about his sister's son Jacob, he ran to meet him, hugged him, and kissed him. Then he took him to his house, and Jacob told him all that had happened.

14 Laban said to him, "Yes, you are my own flesh and blood."[d]

After Jacob had stayed with him a month, 15 Laban said to him, "Just because you're my relative, should you work for me for nothing? Tell me what your wages should be."

16 Now Laban had two daughters: the older was named Leah, and the younger was named Rachel. 17 Leah had delicate[e] eyes, but Rachel was shapely and beautiful. 18 Jacob loved Rachel, so he answered Laban, "I'll work for you seven years for your younger daughter Rachel."

19 Laban replied, "Better that I give her to you than to some other man. Stay with me." 20 So Jacob worked seven years for Rachel, and they seemed like only a few days to him because of his love for her.

21 Then Jacob said to Laban, "Give me my wife, for my time is completed. I want to sleep with[f] her." 22 So Laban invited all the men of the place to a feast. 23 That evening, Laban took his daughter Leah and gave her to Jacob, and he slept with her. 24 And Laban gave his slave Zilpah to his daughter Leah as her slave.

25 When morning came, there was Leah! So he said to Laban, "What is this you have done to me? Wasn't it for Rachel that I worked for you? Why have you deceived me?"

26 Laban answered, "It is not the custom in this place to give the younger ⌊daughter in marriage⌋ before the firstborn. 27 Complete this week ⌊of wedding celebration⌋, and we will also give you this ⌊younger⌋ one in return for working yet another seven years for me."

28 And Jacob did just that. He finished the week ⌊of celebration⌋, and Laban gave him his daughter Rachel as his wife. 29 And Laban gave his slave Bilhah to his daughter Rachel as her slave. 30 Jacob slept with Rachel also, and indeed, he loved Rachel more than Leah. And he worked for Laban another seven years.

Jacob's Sons

31 When the LORD saw that Leah was unloved, He opened her womb; but Rachel was barren. 32 Leah con-

---

[a] **29:3** Sam, some LXX mss read *flocks and the shepherds* [b] **29:10** Lit *with the sheep of Laban his mother's brother* [c] **29:11** Lit *and he lifted his voice and wept* [d] **29:14** Lit *my bone and my flesh* [e] **29:17** Or *tender* [f] **29:21** Lit *to go to*

---

called on the name of the Lord (12:8). Jacob took the stone that he had placed near his head and consecrated it with oil as a memorial.

28:22 This stone. The stone would be a reminder of Jacob's meeting with God at Bethel. He never forgot this meeting and its significance.

29:21-25 Jacob did not specify that it was Rachel, the younger daughter, whom he wanted to marry, and Laban took advantage of him. In an ironic twist, the rights of the firstborn were turned on Jacob, and he received Laban's firstborn daughter, Leah, as his wife.

29:28 Laban gave ... Rachel. At least Jacob did not have to wait another seven years before taking Rachel as his wife. But he had to pay her bride price by working for Laban for seven more years (v. 30).

29:32 Reuben ... affliction. Leah was unloved by Jacob, so she lived a difficult life.

ceived, gave birth to a son, and named him Reuben,[a] for she said, "The LORD has seen my affliction; surely my husband will love me now."

[33] She conceived again, gave birth to a son, and said, "The LORD heard that I am unloved and has given me this ⌊son⌋ also." So she named him Simeon.[b]

[34] She conceived again, gave birth to a son, and said, "At last, my husband will become attached to me because I have borne him three sons." Therefore he was named Levi.[c]

[35] And she conceived again, gave birth to a son, and said, "This time I will praise the LORD." Therefore she named him Judah.[d] Then Leah stopped having children.

30

When Rachel saw that she was not bearing Jacob ⌊any children⌋, she envied her sister. "Give me sons, or I will die!" she said to Jacob.

[2] Jacob became angry with Rachel and said, "Am I in God's place, who has withheld children[e] from you?"

[3] Then she said, "Here is my slave Bilhah. Go sleep with her, and she'll bear ⌊children⌋ for me[f] so that through her I too can build ⌊a family⌋." [4] So Rachel gave her slave Bilhah to Jacob as a wife, and he slept with her. [5] Bilhah conceived and bore Jacob a son. [6] Rachel said, "God has vindicated me; yes, He has heard me and given me a son," and she named him Dan.[g]

[7] Rachel's slave Bilhah conceived again and bore Jacob a second son. [8] Rachel said, "In ⌊my⌋ wrestlings with God,[h] I have wrestled with my sister and won," and she named him Naphtali.[i]

[9] When Leah saw that she had stopped having children, she took her slave Zilpah and gave her to Jacob as a wife. [10] Leah's slave Zilpah bore Jacob a son. [11] Then Leah said, "What good fortune!"[j] and she named him Gad.[k]

[12] When Leah's slave Zilpah bore Jacob a second son, [13] Leah said, "I am happy that the women call me happy," so she named him Asher.[l]

[14] Reuben went out during the wheat harvest and found some mandrakes in the field. When he brought them to his mother Leah, Rachel asked, "Please give me some of your son's mandrakes."

[15] But Leah replied to her, "Isn't it enough that you have taken my husband? Now you also want to take my son's mandrakes?"

"Well," Rachel said, "you can sleep with him tonight in exchange for your son's mandrakes."

[16] When Jacob came in from the field that evening, Leah went out to meet him and said, "You must come with me, for I have hired you with my son's mandrakes." So Jacob slept with her that night.

[17] God listened to Leah, and she conceived and bore Jacob a fifth son. [18] Leah said, "God has rewarded me for giving my slave to my husband," and she named him Issachar.[m]

[19] Then Leah conceived again and bore Jacob a sixth son. [20] "God has given me a good gift," Leah said. "This time my husband will honor me because I have borne him six sons," and she named him Zebulun.[n] [21] Later, Leah bore a daughter and named her Dinah.

[22] Then God remembered Rachel. He listened to her and opened her womb. [23] She conceived and bore a son, and said, "God has taken away my shame." [24] She named him Joseph:[o] "May the LORD add another son to me."

Jacob's Flocks Multiply

[25] After Rachel gave birth to Joseph, Jacob said to Laban, "Send me on my way so that I can return to my homeland. [26] Give me my wives and my children that I have worked for, and let me go. You know how hard I have worked for you."

[27] But Laban said to him, "If I have found favor in your sight, ⌊stay.⌋ I have learned by •divination that the LORD has blessed me because of you." [28] Then Laban said, "Name your wages, and I will pay them."

[29] So Jacob said to him, "You know what I have done for you and your herds. [30] For you had very little before I came, but now your wealth has increased. The LORD has blessed you because of me. And now, when will I also do something for my own family?"

[31] Laban asked, "What should I give you?"

And Jacob said, "You don't need to give me anything. If you do this one thing for me, I will continue to shepherd and keep your flock. [32] Let me go through all your sheep today and remove every sheep that is speckled or spotted, every dark-colored sheep among the lambs, and the spotted and speckled among the female goats. ⌊Such⌋ will be my wages. [33] In the future when you come to check on my wages, my honesty will testify for me. ⌊If I have⌋ any female goats that are not speckled or spotted, or any lambs that are not black, they will be considered stolen."

[34] "Good," said Laban. "Let it be as you have said."

---

[a]**29:32** = See, a Son; but sounds like Hb "has seen my affliction" [b]**29:33** The name *Simeon* sounds like Hb "has heard." [c]**29:34** The name *Levi* sounds like Hb "attached to." [d]**29:35** The name *Judah* sounds like Hb "praise." [e]**30:2** Lit *the fruit of the womb* [f]**30:3** Lit *bear on my knees* [g]**30:6** The name *Dan* sounds like Hb "has vindicated," or "has judged." [h]**30:8** Or *With mighty wrestlings* [i]**30:8** The name *Naphtali* sounds like Hb "my wrestling." [j]**30:11** Alt Hb tradition, LXX, Vg read *Good fortune has come* [k]**30:11** = Good Fortune [l]**30:13** = Happy [m]**30:18** *Issachar* sounds like Hb "reward." [n]**30:20** The name *Zebulun* sounds like Hb "honored." [o]**30:24** = He Adds

---

Reuben's name reflected that.

30:1 I will die! Despite enjoying Jacob's favor, Rachel felt that she needed to have children or her life would not be worth living.

30:2 in God's place. Jacob, the schemer and manipulator, could do nothing to bring about the blessing of children. That gift was in God's hands.

30:3-4 If a man's wife could not conceive, it was an ancient custom for him to sleep with her female servant to ensure the birth of a male heir. Jacob did not actually marry Bilhah; she was a concubine through whom Rachel presented Jacob with children.

30:22-23 Children were a sign of God's favor; a woman who could not have children was disgraced. For Rachel to finally give birth was a time of great joy.

30:26 let me go. Jacob wanted to return to his homeland and his father's house, from which he had fled many years before (28:21; 31:13).

35 That day Laban removed the streaked and spotted male goats and all the speckled and spotted female goats— every one that had any white on it—and every dark-colored sheep among the lambs, and he placed his sons in charge of them. 36 He put a three-day journey between himself and Jacob. Jacob, meanwhile, was shepherding the rest of Laban's flock.

37 Jacob then took branches of fresh poplar, almond, and plane wood, and peeled ⌊the bark⌋, exposing white stripes on the branches. 38 He set the peeled branches in the troughs in front of the sheep—in the water channels where the sheep came to drink. And the sheep bred when they came to drink. 39 The flocks bred in front of the branches and bore streaked, speckled, and spotted young. 40 Jacob separated the lambs and made the flocks face the streaked and the completely dark sheep in Laban's flocks. Then he set his own stock apart and didn't put them with Laban's sheep.

41 Whenever the stronger of the flock were breeding, Jacob placed the branches in the troughs, in full view of the flocks, and they would breed in front of the branches. 42 As for the weaklings of the flocks, he did not put out the branches. So it turned out that the weak sheep belonged to Laban and the stronger ones to Jacob. 43 And the man became very rich.a He had many flocks, male and female slaves, and camels and donkeys.

Jacob Separates from Laban

31 Now Jacob heard what Laban's sons were saying: "Jacob has taken all that was our father's and has built this wealth from what belonged to our father." 2 And Jacob saw from Laban's face that his attitude toward him was not the same.

3 Then the LORD said to him, "Go back to the land of your fathers and to your family, and I will be with you." 4 Jacob had Rachel and Leah called to the field ⌊where⌋ his flocks were. 5 He said to them, "I can see from your father's face that his attitude toward me is not the same, but the God of my father has been with me. 6 You know that I've worked hard for your father 7 and that he has cheated me and changed my wages 10 times. But God has not let him harm me. 8 If he said, 'The spotted sheep will be your wages,' then all the sheep were born spotted. If he said, 'The streaked sheep will be your wages,' then all the sheep were born streaked. 9 God has taken your father's herds and given them to me.

10 "When the flocks were breeding, I saw in a dream that the streaked, spotted, and speckled males were mating with the females. 11 In that dream the Angel of God said to me, 'Jacob!' and I said: Here I am. 12 And He said, 'Look up and see: all the males that are mating with the flocks are streaked, spotted, and speckled, for I have seen all that Laban has been doing to you. 13 I am the God of Bethel, where you poured oil on the stone marker and made a solemn vow to Me. Get up, leave this land, and return to your native land.' "

14 Then Rachel and Leah answered him, "Do we have any portion or inheritance in our father's household? 15 Are we not regarded by him as outsiders? For he has sold us and has certainly spent our money. 16 In fact, all the wealth that God has taken from our father belongs to us and to our children. So do whatever God has said to you."

17 Then Jacob got up and put his children and wives on the camels. 18 He took all the livestock and possessions he had acquired in Paddan-aram, and he drove his herds to go to the land of his father Isaac in Canaan. 19 When Laban had gone to shear his sheep, Rachel stole her father's household idols. 20 And Jacob deceivedb Laban the Aramean, not telling him that he was fleeing. 21 He fled with all his possessions, crossed the Euphrates, and headed forc the hill country of Gilead.

Laban Overtakes Jacob

22 On the third day Laban was told that Jacob had fled. 23 So he took his relatives with him, pursued Jacob for seven days, and overtook him at Mount Gilead. 24 But God came to Laban the Aramean in a dream at night. "Watch yourself!" God warned him. "Don't say anything to Jacob, either good or bad."

25 When Laban overtook Jacob, Jacob had pitched his tent in the hill country, and Laban and his brothers also pitched ⌊their tents⌋ in the hill country of Gilead. 26 Then Laban said to Jacob, "What have you done? You have deceived me and taken my daughters away like prisoners of war! 27 Why did you secretly flee from me, deceive me, and not tell me? I would have sent you away with joy and singing, with tambourines and lyres, 28 but you didn't even let me kiss my grandchildren and my daughters. You have acted foolishly. 29 I could do you great harm, but last night the God of your father said to me: 'Watch yourself. Don't say anything to Jacob, either good or bad.' 30 Now you have gone off because you long for your father—but why have you stolen my gods?"

31 Jacob answered, "I was afraid, for I thought you would take your daughters from me by force. 32 If you find your gods with anyone ⌊here⌋, he will not live! Before our relatives, point out anything that is yours

---

a 30:43 Lit The man spread out very much, very much   b 31:20 Lit And he stole the heart of   c 31:21 Lit and set his face to

30:27 blessed me because of you. Jacob's hard work, marriage to Laban's daughters, and their many offspring had been a source of great blessing to Laban. This may also refer to the prophecy of 12:3.

30:35–39 Jacob agreed to stay on with Laban if he would let him keep some of the sheep and goats in his flock. Jacob selectively bred the livestock to increase his holdings.

31:3 Go back. After he had been away for 20 years (31:41), Jacob was told by the Lord that it was time to return to Canaan.

31:19 household idols. People kept small images of idols in their homes for protection. The gods Rachel stole from her father were objects of trust for the journey.

31:34 in the saddlebag. These "gods" that Rachel had taken were mere trinkets.

31:35 I cannot stand up. Rachel used the excuse of menstruation (considered unclean)

and take it." Jacob did not know that Rachel had stolen ⌊the idols⌋.

33 So Laban went into Jacob's tent, then Leah's tent, and then the tents of the two female slaves, but he found nothing. Then he left Leah's tent and entered Rachel's. 34 Now Rachel had taken Laban's household idols, put them in the saddlebag of the camel, and sat on them. Laban searched the whole tent but found nothing.

35 She said to her father, "Sir, don't be angry that I cannot stand up in your presence; I am having my monthly period." So Laban searched, but could not find the household idols.

Jacob's Covenant with Laban

36 Then Jacob became incensed and brought charges against Laban. "What is my crime?" he said to Laban. "What is my sin, that you have pursued me? 37 You've searched all my possessions! Have you found anything of yours? Put it here before my relatives and yours, and let them decide between the two of us. 38 I've been with you these 20 years. Your ewes and female goats have not miscarried, and I have not eaten the rams from your flock. 39 I did not bring you any of the flock torn by wild beasts; I myself bore the loss. You demanded ⌊payment⌋ from me for what was stolen by day or by night. 40 There I was—the heat consumed me by day and the frost by night, and sleep fled from my eyes. 41 For 20 years I have worked in your household—14 years for your two daughters and six years for your flocks—and you have changed my wages 10 times! 42 If the God of my father, the God of Abraham, the Fear of Isaac, had not been with me, certainly now you would have sent me off empty-handed. But God has seen my affliction and my hard work,[a] and He issued His verdict last night."

43 Then Laban answered Jacob, "The daughters are my daughters; the sons, my sons; and the flocks, my flocks! Everything you see is mine! But what can I do today for these daughters of mine or for the children they have borne? 44 Come now, let's make a covenant, you and I. Let it be a witness between the two of us."

45 So Jacob picked out a stone and set it up as a marker. 46 Then Jacob said to his relatives, "Gather stones." And they took stones and made a mound, then ate there by the mound. 47 Laban named the mound Jegar-sahadutha, but Jacob named it Galeed.[b]

48 Then Laban said, "This mound is a witness between me and you today." Therefore the place was called Galeed, 49 and ⌊also⌋ Mizpah,[b] for he said, "May the LORD watch between you and me when we are out of each other's sight. 50 If you mistreat my daughters or take other wives, though no one is with us, understand that God will be a witness between you and me." 51 Laban also said to Jacob, "Look at this mound and the marker I have set up between you and me. 52 This mound is a witness and the marker is a witness that I will not pass beyond this mound to you, and you will not pass beyond this mound and this marker to do me harm. 53 The God of Abraham, and the gods of Nahor—the gods of their father[c]—will judge between us." And Jacob swore by the Fear of his father Isaac. 54 Then Jacob offered a sacrifice on the mountain and invited his relatives to eat a meal. So they ate a meal and spent the night on the mountain. 55[d] Laban got up early in the morning, kissed his grandsons and daughters, and blessed them. Then Laban left to return home.

Preparing to Meet Esau

32 Jacob went on his way, and God's angels met him. 2 When he saw them, Jacob said, "This is God's camp." So he called that place Mahanaim.[e]

3 Jacob sent messengers ahead of him to his brother Esau in the land of Seir, the country of Edom. 4 He commanded them, "You are to say to my lord Esau, 'This is what your servant Jacob says. I have been staying with Laban and have been delayed until now. 5 I have oxen, donkeys, flocks, male and female slaves. I have sent ⌊this message⌋ to inform my lord, in order to seek your favor.'"

6 When the messengers returned to Jacob, they said, "We went to your brother Esau; he is coming to meet you—and he has 400 men with him." 7 Jacob was greatly afraid and distressed; he divided the people with him into two camps, along with the flocks, cattle, and camels. 8 He thought, "If Esau comes to one camp and attacks it, the remaining one can escape."

9 Then Jacob said, "God of my father Abraham and God of my father Isaac, the LORD who said to me, 'Go back to your land and to your family, and I will cause you to prosper,' 10 I am unworthy of all the kindness and faithfulness You have shown Your servant. Indeed, I crossed over this Jordan with my staff, and now I have become two camps. 11 Please rescue me from the hand of my brother Esau, for I am afraid of him; otherwise, he may come and attack me, the mothers, and their children. 12 You have said, 'I will cause you to prosper, and I will make your •offspring like the sand of the sea, which cannot be counted.'"

---

[a] 31:42 Lit and the work of my hands   [b] 31:47 Jegar-sahadutha is Aram, and Galeed is Hb; both names = Mound of Witness 31:49 = Watchtower
[c] 31:53 Two Hb mss, LXX omit the gods of their father   [d] 31:55 Gn 32:1 in Hb   [e] 32:2 = Two Camps

---

as a way of keeping her father from looking through the saddle on which she was sitting.

31:51–52 mound … marker. Jacob and Laban made a pile of stones to symbolize their agreement.

31:54 sacrifice … meal. Covenants (or agreements) in Old Testament days were sealed with a sacrifice and a shared meal (Ex. 24:5–8,11).

32:2 Mahanaim. The name Jacob gave this place means "two camps." He knew he would soon meet his brother, Esau, who had wanted to kill him many years before (27:41–45).

32:6 coming to meet you. The word that Esau was headed his way with 400 men must have been a source of anxiety to Jacob.

32:9 Jacob said. Jacob sought God's help. This is the first time we have seen him in a posture of prayer since he left Bethel (28:20–22).

13 He spent the night there and took part of what he had brought with him as a gift for his brother Esau: 14 200 female goats, 20 male goats, 200 ewes, 20 rams, 15 30 milk camels with their young, 40 cows, 10 bulls, 20 female donkeys, and 10 male donkeys. 16 He entrusted them to his slaves as separate herds and said to them, "Go on ahead of me, and leave some distance between the herds."

17 And he told the first one: "When my brother Esau meets you and asks, 'Who do you belong to? Where are you going? And whose ⌊animals⌋ are these ahead of you?' 18 then tell him, 'They belong to your servant Jacob. They are a gift sent to my lord Esau. And look, he is behind us.' "

19 He also told the second one, the third, and everyone who was walking behind the animals, "Say the same thing to Esau when you find him. 20 You are to also say, 'Look, your servant Jacob is right behind us.' " For he thought, "I want to appease Esau with the gift that is going ahead of me. After that, I can face him, and perhaps he will forgive me."

21 So the gift was sent on ahead of him while he remained in the camp that night. 22 During the night Jacob got up and took his two wives, his two female slaves, and his 11 sons, and crossed the ford of Jabbok. 23 He took them and brought them across the stream, along with all his possessions.

Wrestling with God

1. What is your nickname? How did you get it? Do you like it?

Genesis 32:22-32

2. Why did Jacob wrestle with God? Why did God wrestle with Jacob?
3. God could have destroyed Jacob, but He chose to let him go. What does this show us about God?
4. Jacob sought God's blessing. How did God bless him?
5. Are you wrestling with God? About what?
6. How does Jacob's perseverance in seeking God's blessing give you an example to follow in your own life?

Jacob Wrestles with an Angel

24 Jacob was left alone, and a man wrestled with him until daybreak. 25 When the man saw that He could not defeat him, He struck Jacob's hip as they wrestled and dislocated his hip socket. 26 Then He said to Jacob, "Let Me go, for it is daybreak."

But Jacob said, "I will not let You go unless You bless me."

27 "What is your name?" the man asked.

"Jacob!" he replied.

28 "Your name will no longer be Jacob," He said. "It will be Israel[a] because you have struggled with God and with men and have prevailed."

29 Then Jacob asked Him, "Please tell me Your name."

But He answered, "Why do you ask My name?" And He blessed him there.

30 Jacob then named the place Peniel,[b] "For," ⌊he said,⌋ "I have seen God face to face, and I have been delivered." 31 The sun shone on him as he passed by Penuel[c]—limping on his hip. 32 That is why, to this day, the Israelites don't eat the thigh muscle that is at the hip socket: because He struck Jacob's hip socket at the thigh muscle.[d]

Jacob Meets Esau

33 Now Jacob looked up and saw Esau coming toward him with 400 men. So he divided the children among Leah, Rachel, and the two female slaves. 2 He put the female slaves first, Leah and her sons next, and Rachel and Joseph last. 3 He himself went on ahead and bowed to the ground seven times until he approached his brother.

4 But Esau ran to meet him, hugged him, threw his arms around him, and kissed him. Then they wept. 5 When Esau looked up and saw the women and children, he asked, "Who are these with you?"

He answered, "The children God has graciously given your servant." 6 Then the female slaves and their children approached ⌊him⌋ and bowed down. 7 Leah and her children also approached and bowed down, and then Joseph and Rachel approached and bowed down.

8 So Esau said, "What do you mean by this whole procession[e] I met?"

"To find favor with you, my lord," he answered.

9 "I have enough, my brother," Esau replied. "Keep what you have."

10 But Jacob said, "No, please! If I have found favor with you, take this gift from my hand. For indeed, I

---

a **32:28** The name *Israel* sounds like Hb "he struggled (with) God." b **32:30** = Face of God c **32:31** Variant of *Peniel* d **32:32** Or *tendon*
e **33:8** Lit *camp*

32:12 like the sand of the sea. God had promised Abraham, Isaac, and Jacob that they would have descendants too numerous to count (22:17; 26:4). Jacob was remembering God's promise to him as well (28:14).

32:24–25 Jacob was known as a "heel grabber." Now he attempted to twist God's arm.

But God revealed that He had the ultimate power.

32:28 Israel. Not only was Jacob given a new walk (his limp reminded him of God's power, v. 31); he was given a new name, Israel, signifying the nation that would spring from his descendants.

32:30 Peniel. The name of the place where Jacob wrestled with God means "face of God." He had been graced with God's presence and blessing.

33:3 bowed. Jacob's show of honor was to cool his brother's anger.

33:4 Esau ran to meet him. All Jacob's ac-

have seen your face, ⌊and it is⌋ like seeing God's face, since you have accepted me. 11 Please take my present that was brought to you, because God has been gracious to me and I have everything I need." So Jacob urged him until he accepted.

12 Then Esau said, "Let's move on, and I'll go ahead of you."

13 Jacob replied, "My lord knows that the children are weak, and I have nursing sheep and cattle. If they are driven hard for one day, the whole herd will die. 14 Let my lord go ahead of his servant. I will continue on slowly, at a pace suited to the livestock and the children, until I come to my lord at Seir."

15 Esau said, "Let me leave some of my people with you."

But he replied, "Why do that? Please indulge me,ᵃ my lord."

16 On that day Esau started on his way back to Seir, 17 but Jacob went on to Succoth. He built a house for himself and stalls for his cattle; that is why the place was called Succoth.ᵇ 18 After Jacob came from Paddan-aram, he arrived safely at the Canaanite city of Shechem and camped in front of the city. 19 He purchased a section of the field from the sons of Hamor, Shechem's father, for 100 qesitahs,ᶜ where he had pitched his tent. 20 And he set up an altar there and called it "God, the God of Israel."ᵈ

Dinah Defiled

34 Dinah, Leah's daughter whom she bore to Jacob, went out to see some of the young women of the area. 2 When Shechem son of Hamor the Hivite, a prince of the region, saw her, he took her and raped her. 3 He became infatuated with Dinah, daughter of Jacob. He loved the young girl and spoke tenderly to her.ᵉ 4 "Get me this girl as a wife," he told his father Hamor.

5 Jacob heard that Shechem had defiled his daughter Dinah, but since his sons were with his cattle in the field, he remained silent until they returned. 6 Meanwhile, Shechem's father Hamor came to speak with Jacob. 7 Jacob's sons returned from the field when they heard ⌊about the incident⌋ and were deeply grieved and angry. For Shechem had committed an outrage against Israel by sleeping with Jacob's daughter, and such a thing should not be done.

8 Hamor said to Jacob's sons, "My son Shechem is strongly attracted to yourᶠ daughter. Please give her to him as a wife. 9 Intermarry with us; give your daughters

to us, and take our daughters for yourselves. 10 Live with us. The land is before you. Settle here, move about, and acquire property in it."

11 Then Shechem said to Dinah's father and brothers, "Grant me this favor,ᵍ and I'll give you whatever you say. 12 Set for me the compensationʰ and the gift; I'll give you whatever you ask me. Just give the girl to be my wife!"

13 But Jacob's sons answered Shechem and his father Hamor deceitfully because he had defiled their sister Dinah. 14 "We cannot do this thing," they said to them. "Giving our sister to an uncircumcised man is a disgrace to us. 15 We will agree with you only on this condition: if all your males are circumcised as we are. 16 Then we will give you our daughters, take your daughters for ourselves, live with you, and become one people. 17 But if you will not listen to us and be circumcised, then we will take our daughter and go."

18 Their words seemed good in the eyes of Hamor and his son Shechem. 19 The young man did not delay doing this, because he was delighted with Jacob's daughter. Now he was the most important in all his father's house. 20 So Hamor and his son Shechem went to the •gate of their city and spoke to the men there.

21 "These men are peaceful toward us," they said. "Let them live in our land and move about in it, for indeed, the region is large enough for them. Let us take their daughters as our wives and give our daughters to them. 22 But the men will agree to live with us and be one people only on this condition: if all our men are circumcised as they are. 23 Won't their herds, their possessions, and all their livestock become ours? Only let us agree with them, and they will live with us."

24 All the able-bodied menⁱ listened to Hamor and his son Shechem, and all the able-bodied menʲ were circumcised. 25 On the third day, when they were still in pain, two of Jacob's sons, Simeon and Levi, Dinah's brothers, took their swords, went into the unsuspecting city, and killed every male. 26 They killed Hamor and his son Shechem with their swords, took Dinah from Shechem's house, and went away. 27 Jacob's ⌊other⌋ sons came to the slaughter and plundered the city because their sister had been defiled. 28 They took their sheep, cattle, donkeys, and whatever was in the city and in the field. 29 They captured all their possessions, children, and wives, and plundered everything in the houses.

30 Then Jacob said to Simeon and Levi, "You have brought trouble on me, making me odious to the

---

ᵃ**33:15** Lit May I find favor in your eyes   ᵇ**33:17** = Stalls, or Huts   ᶜ**33:19** The value of this currency is unknown.   ᵈ**33:20** Hb El-Elohe-Israel
ᵉ**34:3** Lit spoke to her heart   ᶠ**34:8** Hb your is pl, showing that Hamor is speaking to Jacob and his sons.   ᵍ**34:11** Lit May I find favor in your eyes
ʰ**34:12** Or bride-price, or betrothal present   ⁱ**34:24** Lit All who went out of the city gate   ʲ**34:24** Lit all the males who went out of the city gate

---

tions to pacify Esau were not needed. Esau threw his arms around the brother who had wronged him.
34:7 grieved and angry. Dinah's brothers responded like this because their entire family had been violated by Shechem's actions.
34:9 intermarry. Rather than fight with the

clan of Israel, Hamor proposed a diplomatic solution—intermarriage between his clan and the Israelites.
34:12 I'll give you whatever you ask. In this culture, fathers received gifts in exchange for the hands of their daughters.
34:15 all your males are circumcised. The

demands of Dinah's brothers seemed reasonable. To these Canaanites, circumcision was just a way to close a lucrative business deal.
34:24 all the able-bodied men. All the men of the city were willing to undergo this painful ritual in order to get their hands on the prop-

inhabitants of the land, the Canaanites and the Perizzites. We are few in number; if they unite against me and attack me, I and my household will be destroyed." [31] But they answered, "Should he have treated our sister like a prostitute?"

Return to Bethel

35 God said to Jacob, "Get up! Go to Bethel and settle there. Build an altar there to the God who appeared to you when you fled from your brother Esau."

[2] So Jacob said to his family and all who were with him, "Get rid of the foreign gods that are among you. Purify yourselves and change your clothes. [3] We must get up and go to Bethel. I will build an altar there to the God who answered me in my day of distress. He has been with me everywhere I have gone."

[4] Then they gave Jacob all their foreign gods and their earrings, and Jacob hid them under the oak near Shechem. [5] When they set out, a terror from God came over the cities around them, and they did not pursue Jacob's sons. [6] So Jacob and all who were with him came to Luz (that is, Bethel) in the land of Canaan. [7] Jacob built an altar there and called the place God of Bethel[a] because it was there that God had revealed Himself to him when he was fleeing from his brother.

[8] Deborah, Rebekah's nurse, died and was buried under the oak south of Bethel. So Jacob named it Oak of Weeping.[b]

[9] God appeared to Jacob again after he returned from Paddan-aram, and He blessed him. [10] God said to him:

Your name is Jacob;
you will no longer be named Jacob,
but Israel will be your name.

So He named him Israel. [11] God also said to him:

I am •God Almighty.
Be fruitful and multiply.
A nation, indeed an assembly of nations,
will come from you,
and kings will descend from you.[c]

[12]   The land that I gave to Abraham and Isaac
I will give to you.
And I will give the land
to your descendants after you.

[13] Then God withdrew[d] from him at the place where He had spoken to him.

[14] Jacob set up a marker at the place where He had spoken to him—a stone marker. He poured a drink offering on it and anointed it with oil. [15] Jacob named the place where God had spoken with him Bethel.

Rachel's Death

[16] They set out from Bethel. When they were still some distance from Ephrath, Rachel began to give birth, and her labor was difficult. [17] During her difficult labor, the midwife said to her, "Don't be afraid, for this is another son for you." [18] With her last breath—for she was dying—she named him Ben-oni,[e] but his father called him Benjamin.[f] [19] So Rachel died and was buried on the way to Ephrath (that is, Bethlehem). [20] Jacob set up a marker on her grave; it is the marker at Rachel's grave to this day.

Israel's Sons

[21] Israel set out again and pitched his tent beyond the tower at Eder.[g] [22] While Israel was living in that region, Reuben went in and slept with his father's concubine Bilhah, and Israel heard about it.

Jacob had 12 sons:

[23]   Leah's sons were Reuben (Jacob's firstborn),
Simeon, Levi, Judah,
Issachar, and Zebulun.
[24]   Rachel's sons were
Joseph and Benjamin.
[25]   The sons of Rachel's slave Bilhah
were Dan and Naphtali.
[26]   The sons of Leah's slave Zilpah
were Gad and Asher.

These are the sons of Jacob, who were born to him in Paddan-aram.

Isaac's Death

[27] Jacob came to his father Isaac at Mamre in Kiriath-arba (that is, Hebron), where Abraham and Isaac had stayed. [28] Isaac lived 180 years. [29] He took his last breath and died, and was gathered to his people, old and full of days. His sons Esau and Jacob buried him.

Esau's Family

36 These are the family records of Esau (that is, Edom). [2] Esau took his wives from the Canaanite women: Adah daughter of Elon the Hittite, Oholibamah daughter of Anah and granddaughter[h] of Zibeon the Hivite; [3] and Basemath daughter of Ishmael and sister of Nebaioth. [4] Adah bore Eliphaz to Esau, Basemath bore Reuel, [5] and Oholibamah bore Jeush, Jalam, and Korah. These were Esau's sons, who were born to him in the land of Canaan.

---

[a]**35:7** Hb El-bethel   [b]**35:8** Hb Allon-bacuth   [c]**35:11** Lit will come from your loins   [d]**35:13** Lit went up   [e]**35:18** = Son of My Sorrow   [f]**35:18** = Son of the Right Hand   [g]**35:21** Or beyond Migdal-eder   [h]**36:2** Sam, LXX read Anah son

---

erty of the Israelites.

34:25 When Simeon and Levi slaughtered the males of Shechem, they were avenging the violation of their entire family, not just of their sister. Simeon and Levi paid for this in later years when their father Jacob cursed their descendants because of this horrible act

(49:5–7).

35:1 Bethel. This had been the site of Jacob's dream and his covenant with God (28:10–22).
35:3 God who answered me. After the terrible events at Shechem, God gave Jacob the opportunity to remember God's constant love

and presence.

35:10 Israel will be your name. This new name had been promised in 32:28, and the promise was fulfilled here.
35:11–13 I will give. God proclaimed a blessing on Jacob and his descendants and confirmed His promises to them. These were

⁶ Esau took his wives, sons, daughters, and all the people of his household, as well as his herds, all his livestock, and all the property he had acquired in Canaan; he went to a land away from his brother Jacob. ⁷ For their possessions were too many [for them] to live together, and because of their herds, the land where they stayed could not support them. ⁸ So Esau (that is, Edom) lived in the mountains of Seir.

⁹ These are the family records of Esau, father of the Edomites in the mountains of Seir.

10 These are the names of Esau's sons:
Eliphaz son of Esau's wife Adah,
and Reuel son of Esau's wife Basemath.

11 The sons of Eliphaz were
Teman, Omar, Zepho, Gatam, and Kenaz.

12 Timna, a concubine of Esau's son Eliphaz,
bore Amalek to Eliphaz.
These were the sons of Esau's wife Adah.

13 These are Reuel's sons:
Nahath, Zerah, Shammah, and Mizzah.
These were the sons of Esau's wife Basemath.

14 These are the sons of Esau's wife Oholibamah
daughter of Anah and granddaughterᵃ of Zibeon:
She bore Jeush, Jalam, and Korah to Edom.

15 These are the chiefs of Esau's sons:
the sons of Eliphaz, Esau's firstborn:
Chiefs Teman, Omar, Zepho, Kenaz,

16 Korah,ᵇ Gatam, and Amalek.
These are the chiefs of Eliphaz
in the land of Edom.
These are the sons of Adah.

17 These are the sons of Reuel, Esau's son:
Chiefs Nahath, Zerah, Shammah, and Mizzah.
These are the chiefs of Reuel
in the land of Edom.
These are the sons of Esau's wife Basemath.

18 These are the sons of Esau's wife Oholibamah:
Chiefs Jeush, Jalam, and Korah.
These are the chiefs of Esau's wife Oholibamah
daughter of Anah.

19 These are the sons of Esau (that is, Edom),
and these are their chiefs.

Seir's Family

20 These are the sons of Seir the Horite,
the inhabitants of the land:
Lotan, Shobal, Zibeon, Anah,

21 Dishon, Ezer, and Dishan.
These are the chiefs of the Horites,
the sons of Seir, in the land of Edom.

22 The sons of Lotan were Hori and Heman.
Timna was Lotan's sister.

23 These are Shobal's sons:
Alvan, Manahath, Ebal, Shepho, and Onam.

24 These are Zibeon's sons: Aiah and Anah.
This was the Anah who found the hot springsᶜ
in the wilderness
while he was pasturing the donkeys of his father
Zibeon.

25 These are the children of Anah:
Dishon and Oholibamah daughter of Anah.

26 These are Dishon's sons:
Hemdan, Eshban, Ithran, and Cheran.

27 These are Ezer's sons:
Bilhan, Zaavan, and Akan.

28 These are Dishan's sons: Uz and Aran.

29 These are the chiefs of the Horites:
Chiefs Lotan, Shobal, Zibeon, Anah,

30 Dishon, Ezer, and Dishan.
These are the chiefs of the Horites,
according to their divisions, in the land of Seir.

Rulers of Edom

31 These are the kings who ruled in the land
of Edom
before any king ruled over the Israelites:

32 Bela son of Beor ruled in Edom;
the name of his city was Dinhabah.

33 When Bela died, Jobab son of Zerah from Bozrah
ruled in his place.

34 When Jobab died, Husham from the land
of the Temanites ruled in his place.

35 When Husham died, Hadad son of Bedad ruled
in his place.
He defeated Midian in the field of Moab;
the name of his city was Avith.

36 When Hadad died, Samlah from Masrekah ruled
in his place.

37 When Samlah died, Shaul from Rehoboth-on-the-
River ruled in his place.

38 When Shaul died, Baal-hanan son of Achbor
ruled in his place.

39 When Baal-hanan son of Achbor died,
Hadarᵈ ruled in his place.
His city was Pau, and his wife's name
was Mehetabel
daughter of Matred daughter of Me-zahab.

ᵃ36:14 Sam, LXX read *Anah son*   ᵇ36:16 Sam omits *Korah*   ᶜ36:24 Syr, Vg; Tg reads *the mules*; Hb obscure   ᵈ36:39 Many Hb mss, Sam, Syr read *Hadad*

the covenant promises made to Abraham and passed through Isaac to Jacob.
35:17 another son for you. At Joseph's birth, Rachel had asked for another son (30:24).
35:18 Ben-oni ... Benjamin. Rachel's name for her son means "son of my trouble," a logi-

cal name for a son born with such difficulty. The name Benjamin means "son of my right hand."
35:19 Rachel died. Rachel died giving birth to Benjamin. Death in childbirth was not uncommon in that time (1 Sam. 4:20).
35:22 slept with his father's concubine. By

this action, Reuben claimed the rights to his inheritance as the firstborn—specifically the right to inherit his father's concubine.
35:29 Esau and Jacob buried him. The two brothers put the past aside and buried their father peacefully.
36:1 Esau. Esau was called Edom (meaning

40 These are the names of Esau's chiefs,
   according to their families and their localities,
   by their names:
   Chiefs Timna, Alvah, Jetheth,
41 Oholibamah, Elah, Pinon,
42 Kenaz, Teman, Mibzar,
43 Magdiel, and Iram.
   These are Edom's chiefs,
   according to their settlements in the land
      they possessed.
   Esau[a] was father of the Edomites.

Joseph's Dreams

37 Jacob lived in the land where his father had stayed, the land of Canaan. 2 These are the family records of Jacob.

At 17 years of age, Joseph tended sheep with his brothers. The young man ⌊was working⌋ with the sons of Bilhah and Zilpah, his father's wives, and he brought a bad report about them to their father.

Dream On

1. What's the strangest dream you've ever had? Did it have some deep meaning?

Genesis 37:1-11

2. Why did Joseph's brothers hate him? Who was at fault: Jacob? Joseph? The brothers?

3. What did Joseph's dreams mean? Why would the dreams have enraged his brothers even more?

4. Are you jealous of another person in your school or team? Why? Who is to blame for your jealousy?

5. Do you have dreams of becoming someone great one day? Are those dreams the same ones that God might have for you?

3 Now Israel loved Joseph more than his other sons because Joseph was a son ⌊born to him⌋ in his old age, and he made a robe of many colors[b] for him. 4 When his brothers saw that their father loved him more than all his brothers, they hated him and could not bring themselves to speak peaceably to him.

5 Then Joseph had a dream. When he told it to his brothers, they hated him even more. 6 He said to them, "Listen to this dream I had: 7 There we were, binding sheaves of grain in the field. Suddenly my sheaf stood up, and your sheaves gathered around it and bowed down to my sheaf."

8 "Are you really going to reign over us?" his brothers asked him. "Are you really going to rule us?" So they hated him even more because of his dream and what he had said.

9 Then he had another dream and told it to his brothers. "Look," he said, "I had another dream, and this time the sun, moon, and 11 stars were bowing down to me."

10 He told his father and brothers, but his father rebuked him. "What kind of dream is this that you have had?" he said. "Are your mother and brothers and I going to bow down to the ground before you?" 11 His brothers were jealous of him, but his father kept the matter ⌊in mind⌋.

Joseph Sold into Slavery

12 His brothers had gone to pasture their father's flocks at Shechem. 13 Israel said to Joseph, "Your brothers, you know, are pasturing ⌊the flocks⌋ at Shechem. Get ready. I'm sending you to them."

"I'm ready," Joseph replied.

14 Then Israel said to him, "Go and see how your brothers and the flocks are doing, and bring word back to me." So he sent him from the valley of Hebron, and he went to Shechem.

15 A man found him there, wandering in the field, and asked him, "What are you looking for?"

16 "I'm looking for my brothers," Joseph said. "Can you tell me where they are pasturing ⌊their flocks⌋?"

17 "They've moved on from here," the man said. "I heard them say, 'Let's go to Dothan.'" So Joseph set out after his brothers and found them at Dothan.

18 They saw him in the distance, and before he had reached them, they plotted to kill him. 19 They said to one another, "Here comes that dreamer![c] 20 Come on, let's kill him and throw him into one of the pits. We can say that a vicious animal ate him. Then we'll see what becomes of his dreams!"

21 When Reuben heard this, he tried to save him from them.[d] He said, "Let's not take his life." 22 Reuben also said to them, "Don't shed blood. Throw him into this pit in the wilderness, but don't lay a hand on him"—intending to rescue him from their hands and return him to his father.

---

[a]36:43 Lit He Esau   [b]37:3 Or robe with long sleeves   [c]37:19 Lit comes the lord of the dreams   [d]37:21 Lit their hands

---

"red") because of the red lentil stew he had traded for his birthright (25:30).

36:11 Eliphaz ... Teman. The appearance of this Edomite name helps clarify some of Job's story. Eliphaz the Temanite was a friend of Job (Job 2:11).

36:31 These are the kings. This verse implies that the reader knows about the Israelite kingship established hundreds of years after these events. This notation was probably added many years later.

37:3 robe. This robe was not only a gift of love from Joseph's father, Jacob, but of favoritism as well.

37:8 reign over us? There is no indication that Joseph actually intended to rule over his brothers. His mistake was telling them about these dreams in the first place.

37:21–22 Reuben. As the oldest brother, Reuben should have been able to protect Joseph. But Joseph had lost his brothers' re-

In the Pits

1. What kind of pranks have you pulled? Did your pranks ever go too far? If so, when?

Genesis 37:12-36

2. Why did Joseph's brothers want to kill him?
3. Why did Reuben try to save Joseph? Why did he say, "What am I going to do?" (v. 30) instead of "What are we going to do?"
4. What was Judah's motivation in not killing Joseph: Greed (v. 26)? Concern for his brother (v. 27)? Other?
5. Are you more concerned for the welfare of others or for how others can help you?

23 When Joseph came to his brothers, they stripped off his robe, the robe of many colors that he had on. 24 Then they took him and threw him into the pit. The pit was empty; there was no water in it.

25 Then they sat down to eat a meal. They looked up, and there was a caravan of Ishmaelites coming from Gilead. Their camels were carrying aromatic gum, balsam, and resin, going down to Egypt.

26 Then Judah said to his brothers, "What do we gain if we kill our brother and cover up his blood? 27 Come, let's sell him to the Ishmaelites and not lay a hand on him, for he is our brother, our ⌊own⌋ flesh." His brothers agreed. 28 When Midianite traders passed by, they pulled Joseph out of the pit and sold him for 20 pieces of silver to the Ishmaelites, who took Joseph to Egypt.

29 When Reuben returned to the pit and saw that Joseph was not there, he tore his clothes. 30 He went back to his brothers and said, "The boy is gone! What am I going to do?"a 31 So they took Joseph's robe, slaughtered a young goat, and dipped the robe in its blood. 32 They sent the robe of many colors to their father and said, "We found this. Examine it. Is it your son's robe or not?"

33 His father recognized it. "It is my son's robe," he said. "A vicious animal has devoured him. Joseph has been torn to pieces!" 34 Then Jacob tore his clothes, put •sackcloth around his waist, and mourned for his son

many days. 35 All his sons and daughters tried to comfort him, but he refused to be comforted. "No," he said. "I will go down to •Sheol to my son, mourning." And his father wept for him.

36 Meanwhile, the Midianites sold Joseph in Egypt to Potiphar, an officer of Pharaoh and the captain of the guard.

Judah and Tamar

38 At that time Judah left his brothers and settled near an Adullamite named Hirah. 2 There Judah saw the daughter of a Canaanite named Shua; he took her as a wife and slept with her. 3 She conceived and gave birth to a son, and he named him Er. 4 She conceived again, gave birth to a son, and named him Onan. 5 She gave birth to another son and named him Shelah. It was at Chezib thatb c she gave birth to him.

6 Judah got a wife for Er, his firstborn, and her name was Tamar. 7 Now Er, Judah's firstborn, was evil in the LORD's sight, and the LORD put him to death. 8 Then Judah said to Onan, "Sleep with your brother's wife. Perform your duty as her brother-in-law and produce •offspring for your brother." 9 But Onan knew that the offspring would not be his; so whenever he slept with his brother's wife, he released his semen on the ground so that he would not produce offspring for his brother. 10 What he did was evil in the LORD's sight, so He put him to death also.

11 Then Judah said to his daughter-in-law Tamar, "Remain a widow in your father's house until my son Shelah grows up." For he thought, "He might die too, like his brother." So Tamar went to live in her father's house.

12 After a long timed Judah's wife, the daughter of Shua, died. When Judah had finished mourning, he and his friend Hirah the Adullamite went up to Timnah to the sheepshearers. 13 Tamar was told, "Your father-in-law is going up to Timnah to shear his sheep." 14 So she took off her widow's clothes, veiled ⌊her face⌋, covered herself, and sat at the entrance to Enaim,e which is on the way to Timnah. For she saw that, though Shelah had grown up, she had not been given to him as a wife. 15 When Judah saw her, he thought she was a prostitute, for she had covered her face. 16 He went over to her and said, "Come, let me sleep with you," for he did not know that she was his daughter-in-law.

She said, "What will you give me for sleeping with me?"

a37:30 Lit And I, where am I going b38:5 LXX reads She was at Chezib when c38:5 Or He was at Chezib when d38:12 Lit And there were many days e38:14 Or sat by the mouth of the springs

spect, and they showed him no mercy.
37:23 stripped off his robe. This robe was a symbol to Joseph's brothers of their father's favoritism. They threw him in a cistern to die.
37:28 sold him for 20 pieces of silver. The brothers received from a traveling band of merchants what was considered a fair price

for Joseph, who was now a slave.
37:34 tore his clothes. Tearing one's clothes was a sign of loss. Jacob was heartbroken over the death of his favorite son.
37:36 Midianites sold Joseph. Joseph went quickly from the nomadic life of a shepherd to the greatest civilization of his day, and from

freedom to a life of bondage.
38:1 left his brothers. Joseph was forcibly removed from his family, but Judah was left to try his own way in the world. He seemed to have no sense of building up his family's position, just his own.
38:8-9 Without children, Tamar had no means

17 "I will send you a young goat from my flock," he replied.

But she said, "Only if you leave something ⌊with me⌋ until you send it."

18 "What should I give you?" he asked.

She answered, "Your signet ring, your cord, and the staff in your hand." So he gave them to her and slept with her, and she got pregnant by him. 19 She got up and left, then removed her veil and put her widow's clothes back on.

20 When Judah sent the young goat by his friend the Adullamite in order to get back the items he had left with the woman, he could not find her. 21 He asked the men of the place, "Where is the cult prostitute who was beside the road at Enaim?"

"There has been no cult prostitute here," they answered.

22 So the Adullamite returned to Judah, saying, "I couldn't find her, and furthermore, the men of the place said, 'There has been no cult prostitute here.'"

23 Judah replied, "Let her keep ⌊the items⌋ for herself; otherwise we will become a laughingstock. After all, I did send this young goat, but you couldn't find ⌊her⌋."

24 About three months later Judah was told, "Your daughter-in-law has been acting like a prostitute, and now she is pregnant."

"Bring her out!" Judah said. "Let her be burned ⌊to death⌋!"

25 As she was being brought out, she sent her father-in-law ⌊this message⌋: "I am pregnant by the man to whom these items belong." And she added, "Examine them. Whose signet ring, cord, and staff are these?"

26 Judah recognized ⌊them⌋ and said, "She is more in the right[a] than I, since I did not give her to my son Shelah." And he did not know her intimately again.

27 When the time came for her to give birth, there were twins in her womb. 28 As she was giving birth, one of them put out his hand, and the midwife took it and tied a scarlet ⌊thread⌋ around it, announcing, "This one came out first." 29 But then he pulled his hand back, and his brother came out. Then she said, "You have broken out ⌊first⌋!" So he was named Perez.[b] 30 Then his brother, who had the scarlet ⌊thread⌋ tied to his hand, came out, and was named Zerah.[c]

Joseph in Potiphar's House

39 Now Joseph had been taken to Egypt. An Egyptian ⌊named⌋ Potiphar, an officer of Pharaoh and the captain of the guard, bought him from the Ishmaelites who had brought him there. 2 The LORD was with Joseph, and he became a successful man, serving[d] in the household of his Egyptian master. 3 When his master saw that the LORD was with him and that the LORD made everything he did successful, 4 Joseph found favor in his master's sight and became his personal attendant. Potiphar also put him in charge of his household and placed all that he owned under his authority.[e] 5 From the time that he put him in charge of his household and of all that he owned, the LORD blessed the Egyptian's house because of Joseph. The LORD's blessing was on all that he owned, in his house and in his fields. 6 He left all that he owned under Joseph's authority;[f] he did not concern himself with anything except the food he ate.

"Everyone's Doing It"

1. Have you ever been accused of something you didn't do? What happened?

Genesis 39:1-23

2. Why did Joseph refuse to have sex with Potiphar's wife?

3. According to Joseph, who are we sinning against when we have sex outside of marriage?

4. How did Joseph resist the temptation of Potiphar's wife? How can we imitate his example?

5. Joseph was tempted "day after day" (v. 10). What excuses could he have made to justify giving in?

6. What is the best way to respond when someone coaxes you into compromising your sexual standards?

Now Joseph was well-built and handsome. 7 After some time[g] his master's wife looked longingly at Joseph and said, "Sleep with me."

8 But he refused and said to his master's wife, "Look, my master does not concern himself with anything in his house, and he has put all that he owns under my authority.[h] 9 No one in this house is greater than I am. He has withheld nothing from me except you, because you are his wife. So how could I do such a great evil and sin against God?"

10 Although she spoke to Joseph day after day, he refused[i] to go to bed with her. 11 Now one day he went

---

a**38:26** Or *more righteous*   b**38:29** = Breaking Out   c**38:30** = Brightness of Sunrise; perhaps related to the scarlet thread   d**39:2** Lit *and he was*   e**39:4** Lit *owned in his hand*   f**39:6** Lit *owned in Joseph's hand*   g**39:7** Lit *And after these things*   h**39:8** Lit *owns in my hand*   i**39:10** Lit *did not listen to her*

---

of support. The purpose of this custom (called "levirate marriage") was to give her an heir who could take care of her. By short-circuiting his levirate duties, Onan was condemning Tamar to a life of hardship.

38:14 Shelah … wife. Tamar had decided that Judah had no intention of honoring his

duty. Tamar had been deceived, so she decided to deceive Judah.

38:18 What should I give you? Tamar wanted proof of her act with Judah. If she became pregnant, she could claim that her child had inheritance rights.

38:24 bring her out. Judah was ready to

"cast the first stone" when he was told that Tamar had brought dishonor on his family.

38:29 Perez. Perez, one of the twin sons born of the union of Judah with Tamar, became head of the most important tribe in Judah and an ancestor of Jesus (Matt. 1:3).

39:1 Joseph … taken to Egypt. The scene

into the house to do his work, and none of the household servants was there.ᵃ ¹² She grabbed him by his garment and said, "Sleep with me!" But leaving his garment in her hand, he escaped and ran outside. ¹³ When she realized that he had left his garment with her and had run outside, ¹⁴ she called the household servants. "Look," she said to them, "my husband brought a Hebrew man to us to make fun of us. He came to me so he could sleep with me, and I screamed as loud as I could. ¹⁵ When he heard me screaming for help,ᵇ he left his garment with me and ran outside."

¹⁶ She put Joseph's garment beside her until his master came home. ¹⁷ Then she told him the same story: "The Hebrew slave you brought to us came to me to make fun of me, ¹⁸ but when I screamed for help,ᶜ he left his garment with me and ran outside."

¹⁹ When his master heard the story his wife told him—"These are the things your slave did to me"—he was furious ²⁰ and had him thrown into prison, where the king's prisoners were confined. So Joseph was there in prison.

Joseph in Prison

²¹ But the LORD was with Joseph and extended kindness to him. He granted him favor in the eyes of the prison warden. ²² The warden put all the prisoners who were in the prison under Joseph's authority,ᵈ and he was responsible for everything that was done there. ²³ The warden did not bother with anything under Joseph's authority,ᵉ because the LORD was with him, and the LORD made everything that he did successful.

Joseph Interprets Two Prisoners' Dreams

40 After this, the king of Egypt's cupbearer and his baker offended their master, the king of Egypt. ² Pharaoh was angry with his two officers, the chief cupbearer and the chief baker, ³ and put them in custody in the house of the captain of the guard, in the prison where Joseph was confined. ⁴ The captain of the guard assigned Joseph to them, and he became their personal attendant. And they were in custody for some time.ᶠ

⁵ The cupbearer and the baker of the king of Egypt, who were confined in the prison, each had a dream. Both had a dream on the same night, and each dream had its own meaning. ⁶ When Joseph came to them in the morning, he saw that they looked distraught. ⁷ So he asked Pharaoh's officers who were in custody with him in his master's house, "Why are your faces sad today?"

⁸ "We had dreams," they said to him, "but there is no one to interpret them."

Then Joseph said to them, "Don't interpretations belong to God? Tell me ⌊your dreams⌋."

⁹ So the chief cupbearer told his dream to Joseph: "In my dream there was a vine in front of me. ¹⁰ On the vine were three branches. As soon as it budded, its blossoms came out and its clusters ripened into grapes. ¹¹ Pharaoh's cup was in my hand, and I took the grapes, squeezed them into Pharaoh's cup, and placed the cup in Pharaoh's hand."

¹² "This is its interpretation," Joseph said to him. "The three branches are three days. ¹³ In just three days Pharaoh will lift up your head and restore you to your position. You will put Pharaoh's cup in his hand the way you used to when you were his cupbearer. ¹⁴ But when all goes well for you, remember that I was with you. Please show kindness to me by mentioning me to Pharaoh, and get me out of this prison. ¹⁵ For I was kidnapped from the land of the Hebrews, and even here I have done nothing that they should put me in the dungeon."

¹⁶ When the chief baker saw that the interpretation was positive, he said to Joseph, "I also had a dream. Three baskets of white bread were on my head. ¹⁷ In the top basket were all sorts of baked goods for Pharaoh, but the birds were eating them out of the basket on my head."

¹⁸ "This is its interpretation," Joseph replied. "The three baskets are three days. ¹⁹ In just three days Pharaoh will lift up your head—from off you—and hang you on a tree.ᵍ Then the birds will eat the flesh from your body."ʰ

²⁰ On the third day, which was Pharaoh's birthday, he gave a feast for all his servants. He lifted up the heads of the chief cupbearer and the chief baker: ²¹ he restored the chief cupbearer to his position as cupbearer, and he placed the cup in Pharaoh's hand; ²² but he hangedⁱ the chief baker, just as Joseph had explained to them. ²³ Yet the chief cupbearer did not remember Joseph; he forgot him.

Joseph Interprets Pharaoh's Dreams

41 Two years later Pharaoh had a dream: He was standing beside the Nile, ² when seven healthy-looking, well-fed cows came up from the Nile and began to graze among the reeds. ³ After them, seven other cows, sickly and thin, came up from the Nile and stood beside those cows along the bank of the

---

ᵃ**39:11** Lit there in the house ᵇ**39:15** Lit me raise my voice and scream ᶜ**39:18** Lit I raised my voice and screamed ᵈ**39:22** Lit prison in the hand of Joseph ᵉ**39:23** Lit anything in his hand ᶠ**40:4** Lit custody days ᵍ**40:19** Or and impale you on a pole ʰ**40:19** Lit eat your flesh from upon you ⁱ**40:22** Or impaled

---

shifts back to Egypt and to intrigue at the highest levels of Egyptian culture.

39:5 the LORD blessed … because of Joseph. When God called Abram (12:2–3), he promised him that the nations of the earth would be blessed through him. Joseph's success was part of the fulfillment of that promise.

39:6 under Joseph's authority. Joseph was a person whom people trusted. It was the way God worked through him that made him so effective.

39:7-9 Potiphar's wife lusted after Joseph. But Joseph would not hurt his master who trusted him, nor would he sin against God.

39:10,12 refused … escaped. Joseph knew how to deal with temptation. When the problem with his owner's wife reached the boiling point, he ran from her.

40:2 cupbearer. The cupbearer presided in Pharaoh's household and acted as a taster of his food.

Nile. 4 The sickly, thin cows ate the healthy, well-fed cows. Then Pharaoh woke up. 5 He fell asleep and dreamed a second time: Seven heads of grain, full and good, came up on one stalk. 6 After them, seven heads of grain, thin and scorched by the east wind, sprouted up. 7 The thin heads of grain swallowed up the seven full, good ones. Then Pharaoh woke up, and it was only a dream.

An Awesome Performance

1. If the president of the United States suddenly summoned you to the White House, what would your first thought be?

Genesis 41:1-40

2. Why did Pharaoh send for Joseph? How did he even hear of Joseph? What does this say about Joseph's faithfulness to God?

3. Why did Joseph say that he was not able to interpret Pharaoh's dreams (v. 16)?

4. How did Pharaoh know that Joseph had "the spirit of God in him" (v. 38)?

5. Who received glory for Joseph's interpretations: God? Joseph? Other?

6. Who receives glory when you perform well in school, athletics, or other visible activities?

8 When morning came, he was troubled, so he summoned all the magicians of Egypt and all its wise men. Pharaoh told them his dreams, but no one could interpret them for him.

9 Then the chief cupbearer said to Pharaoh, "Today I remember my faults. 10 Pharaoh had been angry with his servants, and he put me and the chief baker in the custody of the captain of the guard. 11 He and I had dreams on the same night; each dream had its own meaning. 12 Now a young Hebrew, a slave of the captain of the guards, was with us there. We told him our dreams, he interpreted our dreams for us, and each had its own interpretation. 13 It turned out just the way he interpreted them to us: I was restored to my position, and the other man was hanged."

14 Then Pharaoh sent for Joseph, and they quickly brought him from the dungeon. He shaved, changed his clothes, and went to Pharaoh.

15 Pharaoh said to Joseph, "I have had a dream, and no one can interpret it. But I have heard it said about you that you can hear a dream and interpret it."

16 "I am not able to," Joseph answered Pharaoh. "It is God who will give Pharaoh a favorable answer."a

17 So Pharaoh said to Joseph: "In my dream I was standing on the bank of the Nile, 18 when seven well-fed, healthy-looking cows came up from the Nile and began to graze among the reeds. 19 After them, seven other cows—ugly, very sickly, and thin—came up. I've never seen such ugly ones as these in all the land of Egypt. 20 Then the thin, ugly cows ate the first seven well-fed cows. 21 When they had devoured them, you could not tell that they had devoured them; their appearance was as bad as it had been before. Then I woke up. 22 In my dream I had also seen seven heads of grain, full and good, coming up on one stalk. 23 After them, seven heads of grain—withered, thin, and scorched by the east wind—sprouted up. 24 The thin heads of grain swallowed the seven full ones. I told this to the magicians, but no one can tell me what it means."

25 Then Joseph said to Pharaoh, "Pharaoh's dreams mean the same thing. God has revealed to Pharaoh what He is about to do. 26 The seven good cows are seven years, and the seven good heads are seven years. The dreams mean the same thing. 27 The seven thin, ugly cows that came up after them are seven years, and the seven worthless, scorched heads of grain are seven years of famine.

28 "It is just as I told Pharaoh: God has shown Pharaoh what He is about to do. 29 Sevenb years of great abundance are coming throughout the land of Egypt. 30 After them, seven years of famine will take place, and all the abundance in the land of Egypt will be forgotten. The famine will devastate the land. 31 The abundance in the land will not be remembered because of the famine that follows it, for the famine will be very severe. 32 Because the dream was given twice to Pharaoh, it means that the matter has been determined by God, and He will soon carry it out.

33 "So now, let Pharaoh look for a discerning and wise man and set him over the land of Egypt. 34 Let Pharaoh do this: Let him appoint overseers over the land and take one-fifth [of the harvest] of the land of Egypt during the seven years of abundance. 35 Let them gather all the [excess] food during these good years that are coming, store the grain under Pharaoh's authority as food in the cities, and preserve [it]. 36 The food will be a reserve for the land during the seven years of fam-

---

a **41:16** Or *"God will answer Pharaoh with peace [of mind]."* b **41:29** Lit *Look! Seven*

40:5 each had a dream. Pharaoh's dreams were the beginning of Joseph's rise to power.
40:8 interpretations belong to God. Although Joseph had the gift of dream interpretation, the truth he spoke was God's truth.
40:14 mentioning me to Pharaoh. Though the chief cupbearer forgot about Joseph for

two years, Joseph was eventually remembered and rescued.
41:13 just the way. The testimony of the cupbearer to Pharaoh was that Joseph's interpretation of dreams was exactly correct. His ability was a gift from God.
41:16 give Pharaoh ... answer. Pharaoh

sent for Joseph to interpret his dream. Joseph reminded the pharaoh that God's power, not his own, made all the difference.
41:27 famine. Seven years of famine in Egypt would be devastating.
41:40 Only ... will I be greater. Pharaoh gave Joseph an important leadership role in

ine that will take place in the land of Egypt. Then the country will not be wiped out by the famine."

Joseph Exalted

37 The proposal pleased Pharaoh and all his servants. 38 Then Pharaoh said to his servants, "Can we find anyone like this, a man who has the spirit of God[a] in him?" 39 So Pharaoh said to Joseph, "Since God has made all this known to you, there is no one as intelligent and wise as you. 40 You will be over my house, and all my people will obey your commands.[b] Only with regard to the throne will I be greater than you." 41 Pharaoh also said to Joseph, "See, I am placing you over all the land of Egypt." 42 Pharaoh removed his signet ring from his hand and put it on Joseph's hand, clothed him with fine linen garments, and placed a gold chain around his neck. 43 He had Joseph ride in his second chariot, and ⌊servants⌋ called out before him, "*Abrek!*"[c] So he placed him over all the land of Egypt. 44 Pharaoh said to Joseph, "I am Pharaoh, but without your permission no one will be able to raise his hand or foot in all the land of Egypt." 45 Pharaoh gave Joseph the name Zaphenath-paneah and gave him a wife, Asenath daughter of Potiphera, priest at On.[d] And Joseph went throughout[e] the land of Egypt.

Joseph's Administration

46 Joseph was 30 years old when he entered the service of Pharaoh king of Egypt. Joseph left Pharaoh's presence and traveled throughout the land of Egypt. 47 During the seven years of abundance the land produced outstanding harvests. 48 Joseph gathered all the ⌊excess⌋ food in the land of Egypt during the seven years and placed it in the cities. He placed the food in every city from the fields around it. 49 So Joseph stored up grain in such abundance—like the sand of the sea—that he stopped measuring it because it was beyond measure.

50 Two sons were born to Joseph before the years of famine arrived. Asenath daughter of Potiphera, priest at On,[d] bore ⌊them⌋ to him. 51 Joseph named the firstborn Manasseh, meaning, "God has made me forget all my hardship in my father's house." 52 And the second son he named Ephraim, meaning, "God has made me fruitful in the land of my affliction."

53 Then the seven years of abundance in the land of Egypt came to an end, 54 and the seven years of famine began, just as Joseph had said. There was famine in every country, but throughout the land of Egypt there was food. 55 Extreme hunger came to all the land of Egypt, and the people cried out to Pharaoh for food.

Pharaoh told all Egypt, "Go to Joseph and do whatever he tells you." 56 Because the famine had spread across the whole country, Joseph opened up ⌊all the storehouses⌋ and sold grain to the Egyptians, for the famine was severe in the land of Egypt. 57 The whole world came to Joseph in Egypt to buy grain, for the famine was severe all over the earth.

Joseph's Brothers in Egypt

42 When Jacob learned that there was grain in Egypt, he said to his sons, "Why do you keep looking at each other? 2 Listen," he went on, "I have heard there is grain in Egypt. Go down there and buy some for us so that we will live and not die." 3 So 10 of Joseph's brothers went down to buy grain from Egypt. 4 But Jacob did not send Joseph's brother Benjamin with his brothers, for he thought, "Something might happen to him."

5 The sons of Israel were among those who came to buy grain, for the famine was in the land of Canaan. 6 Joseph was in charge of the country; he sold grain to all its people. His brothers came and bowed down before him with their faces to the ground. 7 When Joseph saw his brothers, he recognized them, but he treated them like strangers and spoke harshly to them.

"Where do you come from?" he asked.

"From the land of Canaan to buy food," they replied.

8 Although Joseph recognized his brothers, they did not recognize him. 9 Joseph remembered his dreams about them and said to them, "You are spies. You have come to see the weakness[f] of the land."

10 "No, my lord. Your servants have come to buy food," they said. 11 "We are all sons of one man. We are honest; your servants are not spies."

12 "No," he said to them. "You have come to see the weakness of the land."

13 But they replied, "We, your servants, were 12 brothers, the sons of one man in the land of Canaan. The youngest is now[g] with our father, and one is no longer living."

14 Then Joseph said to them, "I have spoken:[h] 'You are spies!' 15 This is how you will be tested: As surely as Pharaoh lives, you will not leave this place unless your youngest brother comes here. 16 Send one of your number to get your brother. The rest of you will be imprisoned so that your words can be tested to see if they are true. If they are not, then as surely as Pharaoh lives, you are spies!" 17 So Joseph imprisoned them together for three days.

---

[a]41:38 Or *Spirit of God,* or *spirit of the gods*   [b]41:40 Lit *will kiss your mouth*   [c]41:43 Perhaps an Egyptian word meaning *Attention!*; others see it as a Hb word meaning *Kneel!*   [d]41:45,50 Or *Heliopolis*   [e]41:45 Or *Joseph gained authority over*   [f]42:9 Lit *nakedness*   [g]42:13 Or *today*
[h]42:14 Lit *"That which I spoke to you saying*

Egypt, making him his highest-ranking advisor.

41:45 name ... wife. Joseph got a new job, new status, a new name, and a new wife—even the daughter of a priest.

41:49 stopped measuring it. Joseph's preparation for the coming crisis in Egypt was so

thorough that no one could keep track of it.

41:51–52 Manasseh ... Ephraim. Joseph gave both his sons Hebrew names. He brought his Hebrew heritage into his Egyptian world, honoring God's promise to His people.

41:57 whole world came to Joseph. Egypt survived the famine, and Pharaoh's kingdom

multiplied. As Egypt prospered, surrounding nations sought its help.

42:4 Benjamin. Joseph and Benjamin were Jacob's only sons by his wife Rachel. After losing Joseph, Jacob was protective of Benjamin and would not allow him to travel with his brothers to Egypt.

18 On the third day Joseph said to them, "I •fear God—do this and you will live. 19 If you are honest men, let one of you[a] be confined to the guardhouse, while the rest of you go and take grain ⌊to relieve⌋ the hunger of your households. 20 Bring your youngest brother to me so that your words can be confirmed; then you won't die." And they consented to this.

21 Then they said to each other, "It is plain that we are being punished for what we did to our brother. We saw his deep distress when he pleaded with us, but we would not listen. That is why this trouble has come to us."

22 But Reuben replied: "Didn't I tell you not to harm the boy? But you wouldn't listen. Now we must account for his blood!"[b]

23 They did not realize that Joseph understood them, since there was an interpreter between them. 24 He turned away from them and wept. Then he turned back and spoke to them. He took Simeon from them and had him bound before their eyes. 25 Joseph then gave orders to fill their containers with grain, return each man's money to his sack, and give them provisions for their journey. This order was carried out. 26 They loaded the grain on their donkeys and left there.

The Brothers Return Home

27 At the place where they lodged for the night, one of them opened his sack to get feed for his donkey, and he saw his money there at the top of the bag. 28 He said to his brothers, "My money has been returned! It's here in my bag." Their hearts sank. Trembling, they turned to one another and said, "What is this that God has done to us?"

29 When they reached their father Jacob in the land of Canaan, they told him all that had happened to them: 30 "The man who is the lord of the country spoke harshly to us and accused us of spying on the country. 31 But we told him: We are honest men and not spies. 32 We were 12 brothers, sons of the same[c] father. One is no longer living, and the youngest is now[d] with our father in the land of Canaan. 33 The man who is the lord of the country said to us, 'This is how I will know if you are honest men: Leave one brother with me, take ⌊food to relieve⌋ the hunger of your households, and go. 34 Bring back your youngest brother to me, and I will know that you are not spies but honest men. I will then give your brother back to you, and you can trade in the country.'"

35 As they began emptying their sacks, there in each man's sack was his bag of money! When they and their father saw their bags of money, they were afraid.

36 Their father Jacob said to them, "You have deprived me of my sons. Joseph is gone and Simeon is gone. Now you want to take Benjamin. Everything happens to me!"

37 Then Reuben said to his father, "You can kill my two sons if I don't bring him back to you. Put him in my care,[e] and I will return him to you."

38 But Jacob answered, "My son will not go down with you, for his brother is dead and he alone is left. If anything happens to him on your journey, you will bring my gray hairs down to •Sheol in sorrow."

Decision to Return to Egypt

43 Now the famine in the land was severe. 2 When they had used up the grain they had brought back from Egypt, their father said to them, "Go back and buy us some food."

3 But Judah said to him, "The man specifically warned us: 'You will not see me again unless your brother is with you.' 4 If you will send our brother with us, we will go down and buy food for you. 5 But if you will not send him, we will not go, for the man said to us, 'You will not see me again unless your brother is with you.'"

6 "Why did you cause me so much trouble?" Israel asked. "Why did you tell the man that you had another brother?"

7 They answered, "The man kept asking about us and our family: 'Is your father still alive? Do you have ⌊another⌋ brother?' And we answered him accordingly. How could we know that he would say, 'Bring your brother here'?"

8 Then Judah said to his father Israel, "Send the boy with me. We will be on our way so that we may live, and not die—neither we, nor you, nor our children. 9 I will be responsible for him. You can hold me personally accountable![f] If I do not bring him back to you and set him before you, I will be guilty before you forever. 10 If we had not wasted time, we could have come back twice by now."

11 Then their father Israel said to them, "If it must be so, then do this: Put some of the best products of the land in your packs and take them down to the man as a gift—some balsam and some honey, aromatic gum and resin, pistachios and almonds. 12 Take twice as much money with you. Return the money that was returned ⌊to you⌋ in the top of your bags. Perhaps it was a mistake. 13 Take your brother also, and go back at once to the man. 14 May •God Almighty cause the man to be merciful to you so that he will release your other

---

[a] 42:19 Lit your brothers [b] 42:22 Lit Even his blood is being sought [c] 42:32 Lit of our [d] 42:32 Or today [e] 42:37 Lit hand [f] 43:9 Lit can seek him from my hand

---

42:6 bowed down before him. This is the first step in the fulfillment of Joseph's dream as a teenager that his brothers would bow down to him (37:5–8).
42:8 they did not recognize him. Joseph was dressed in Egyptian clothes and spoke a foreign language, communicating through an

interpreter.
42:15 your youngest brother. Joseph could not have asked his brothers to do a more difficult thing than to bring Benjamin with them to Egypt.
42:21 deep distress. Joseph's brothers immediately made the connection between their

actions and the consequences they were facing.
42:24 He took Simeon from them. It seems unusual that Joseph would have kept Simeon as a hostage, since Reuben, the oldest, had saved his life (37:21–22).

brother and Benjamin to you. As for me, if I am deprived of my sons, then I am deprived."

The Return to Egypt

15 The men took this gift, double the amount of money, and Benjamin. They made their way down to Egypt and stood before Joseph.

16 When Joseph saw Benjamin with them, he said to his steward,a "Take the men to ⌊my⌋ house. Slaughter an animal and prepare it, for they will eat with me at noon." 17 The man did as Joseph had said and brought them to Joseph's house.

18 But the men were afraid because they were taken to Joseph's house. They said, "We have been brought here because of the money that was returned in our bags the first time. They intend to overpower us, seize us, make us slaves, and take our donkeys." 19 So they approached Joseph's stewardb and spoke to him at the doorway of the house.

20 They said, "Sir, we really did come down here the first time only to buy food. 21 When we came to the place where we lodged for the night and opened our bags of grain, each one's money was at the top of his bag! It was the full amount of our money, and we have brought it back with us. 22 We have brought additional money with us to buy food. We don't know who put our money in the bags."

23 Then the steward said, "May you be well. Don't be afraid. Your God and the God of your father must have put treasure in your bags. I received your money." Then he brought Simeon out to them. 24 The man brought the men into Joseph's house, gave them water to wash their feet, and got feed for their donkeys. 25 Since the men had heard that they were going to eat a meal there, they prepared their gift for Joseph's arrival at noon. 26 When Joseph came home, they brought him the gift they had carried into the house, and they bowed to the ground before him.

27 He asked if they were well, and he said, "How is your elderly father that you told me about? Is he still alive?"

28 They answered, "Your servant our father is well. He is still alive." And they bowed down to honor him.

29 When he looked up and saw his brother Benjamin, his mother's son, he asked, "Is this your youngest brother that you told me about?" Then he said, "May God be gracious to you, my son." 30 Joseph hurried out because he was overcome with emotion for his brother, and he was about to weep. He went into an inner room

to weep. 31 Then he washed his face and came out. Regaining his composure, he said, "Serve the meal."

32 They served him by himself, his brothers by themselves, and the Egyptians who were eating with him by themselves, because Egyptians could not eat with Hebrews, since that is abhorrent to them. 33 They were seated before him in order by age, from the firstborn to the youngest. The men looked at each other in astonishment. 34 Portions were served to them from Joseph's table, and Benjamin's portion was five times larger than any of theirs. They drank, and they got drunk with Joseph.

Joseph's Final Test

44 Then Joseph commanded his steward: "Fill the men's bags with as much food as they can carry, and put each one's money at the top of his bag. 2 Put my cup, the silver one, at the top of the youngest one's bag, along with his grain money." So he did as Joseph told him.

3 At morning light, the men were sent off with their donkeys. 4 They had not gone very far from the city when Joseph said to his steward, "Get up. Pursue the men, and when you overtake them, say to them, 'Why have you repaid evil for good?c 5 Isn't this the cup that my master drinks from and uses for •divination? What you have done is wrong!' "

6 When he overtook them, he said these words to them. 7 They said to him, "Why does my lord say these things? Your servants could not possibly do such a thing. 8 We even brought back to you from the land of Canaan the money we found at the top of our bags. How could we steal gold and silver from your master's house? 9 If any of us isd found to have it, he must die, and we also will become my lord's slaves."

10 The steward replied, "What you have said is proper, but only the one who is found to have it will be my slave, and the rest of you will be blameless."

11 So each one quickly lowered his sack to the ground and opened it. 12 The steward searched, beginning with the oldest and ending with the youngest, and the cup was found in Benjamin's sack. 13 Then they tore their clothes, and each one loaded his donkey and returned to the city.

14 When Judah and his brothers reached Joseph's house, he was still there. They fell to the ground before him. 15 "What is this you have done?" Joseph said to them. "Didn't you know that a man like me could uncover the truth by divination?"

---

a43:16 Lit to the one who was over his house   b43:19 Lit approached the one who was over the house   c44:4 LXX adds Why have you stolen my silver cup?   d44:9 Lit If your servants are

---

42:37 my two sons. Reuben's offer of laying down the lives of both his sons to secure Benjamin's safety brought little relief to Jacob. God had promised his family a host of descendants, yet he was losing sons one at a time.

43:9 I will be responsible for him. While Reuben had offered the lives of his sons (42:37), Judah offered his own life in exchange for Benjamin.

43:11 do this. Jacob came up with a strategy of gift-giving to buy Joseph's favor.

43:26 they bowed to the ground. Imagine the pressure Joseph's brothers were under to make sure Benjamin came back home safely.

43:29 his brother Benjamin. Benjamin was Joseph's only full brother. Thus, the bond between him and Benjamin was much stronger than that with his other brothers.

43:33–34 in order by age. This unknown ruler seated the brothers in the exact order of

16 "What can we say to my lord?" Judah replied. "How can we plead? How can we justify ourselves? God has exposed your servants' iniquity. We are now my lord's slaves—both we and the one in whose possession the cup was found."

17 Then Joseph said, "I swear that I will not do this. The man in whose possession the cup was found will be my slave. The rest of you can go in peace to your father."

Judah's Plea for Benjamin

18 But Judah approached him and said, "Sir, please let your servant speak personally to my lord.[a] Do not be angry with your servant, for you are like Pharaoh. 19 My lord asked his servants, 'Do you have a father or a brother?' 20 and we answered my lord, 'We have an elderly father and a young brother, the child of his old age. The boy's[b] brother is dead. He is the only one of his mother's sons left, and his father loves him.' 21 Then you said to your servants, 'Bring him to me so that I can see him.' 22 But we said to my lord, 'The boy cannot leave his father. If he were to leave, his father would die.' 23 Then you said to your servants, 'If your younger brother does not come down with you, you will not see me again.'

24 "This is what happened when we went back to your servant my father: We reported your words to him. 25 But our father said, 'Go again, and buy us some food.' 26 We told him, 'We cannot go down unless our younger brother goes with us. But if our younger brother isn't with us, we cannot see the man.' 27 Your servant my father said to us, 'You know that my wife bore me two sons. 28 One left—I said that he must have been torn to pieces—and I have never seen him again. 29 If you also take this one from me and anything happens to him, you will bring my gray hairs down to •Sheol in sorrow.'

30 "So, if I come to your servant my father and the boy is not with us—his life is wrapped up with the boy's life— 31 when he sees that the boy is not with us, he will die. Then your servants will have brought the gray hairs of your servant our father down to Sheol in sorrow. 32 Your servant became accountable to my father for the boy, saying, 'If I do not return him to you, I will always bear the guilt for sinning against ⌊you,⌋ my father.' 33 Now please let your servant remain here as my lord's slave, in place of the boy. Let him go back with his brothers. 34 For how can I go back to my father without the boy? I could not bear to see[c] the grief that would overwhelm my father."

Joseph Reveals His Identity

45 Joseph could no longer keep his composure in front of all his attendants,[d] so he called out, "Send everyone away from me!" No one was with him when he revealed his identity to his brothers. 2 But he wept so loudly that the Egyptians heard it, and also Pharaoh's household heard it. 3 Joseph said to his brothers, "I am Joseph! Is my father still living?" But his brothers were too terrified to answer him.

4 Then Joseph said to his brothers, "Please, come near me," and they came near. "I am Joseph, your brother," he said, "the one you sold into Egypt. 5 And now don't be worried or angry with yourselves for selling me here, because God sent me ahead of you to preserve life. 6 For the famine has been in the land these two years, and there will be five more years without plowing or harvesting. 7 God sent me ahead of you to establish you as a remnant within the land and to keep you alive by a great deliverance.[e] 8 Therefore it was not you who sent me here, but God. He has made me a father to Pharaoh, lord of his entire household, and ruler over all the land of Egypt.

 "Hey, It's Me!"

1. Is there anyone you haven't seen in a long time that you would like to see again?

Genesis 45:1-28
2. Why did Joseph tell his brothers, "don't be worried or angry with yourselves for selling me here" (v. 5)?
3. How do you think Joseph was able to forgive his brothers for selling him as a slave? What's the lesson here for us?
4. Why did Joseph tell his brothers, as they were leaving, "Don't argue on the way" (v. 24)?
5. Is there someone you need to forgive? Is there someone with whom you need to stop arguing?

9 "Return quickly to my father and say to him, 'This is what your son Joseph says: "God has made me lord of all Egypt. Come down to me without delay. 10 You can settle in the land of Goshen and be near me—you, your chil-

---

[a]44:18 Lit *speak a word in my lord's ears*   [b]44:20 Lit *His*   [c]44:34 Lit *boy lest I see*   [d]45:1 Lit *all those standing about him*   [e]45:7 Or *keep alive for you many survivors*

---

their ages and then gave the youngest brother special treatment.

44:9 he must die. The brothers proclaimed that whoever had stolen Joseph's silver cup would lose his life, and the rest would lose their freedom.

44:10 will be my slave. Joseph's servant

proposed that the guilty party be enslaved and the others go free. This would create a great dilemma for the brothers—returning to their father without his youngest son.

44:14 fell to the ground. Joseph was testing his brothers. Were they still heartless? Would they treat Benjamin as they had treated him?

44:18 let your servant speak. Judah begged Joseph for the life of Benjamin.

44:30 wrapped up. Judah described Jacob's relationship to Benjamin as "tied together." In begging for Benjamin's life, Judah was also begging for his father's life.

44:33 let your servant remain. Then Judah

dren, and grandchildren, your sheep, cattle, and all you have. [11] There I will sustain you, for there will be five more years of famine. Otherwise, you, your household, and everything you have will become destitute." ' [12] Look! Your eyes and my brother Benjamin's eyes can see that it is I [, Joseph,] who am[a] speaking to you. [13] Tell my father all about my glory in Egypt and about all you have seen. And bring my father here quickly."

[14] Then Joseph threw his arms around Benjamin and wept, and Benjamin wept on his shoulder. [15] Joseph kissed each of his brothers as he wept,[b] and afterward his brothers talked with him.

The Return for Jacob

[16] When the news reached Pharaoh's house, "Joseph's brothers have come," Pharaoh and his servants were pleased. [17] Pharaoh said to Joseph, "Tell your brothers, 'Do this: Load your animals and go on back to the land of Canaan. [18] Get your father and your households, and come back to me. I will give you the best of the land of Egypt, and you can eat from the richness of the land.' [19] You are also commanded, 'Do this: Take wagons from the land of Egypt for your young children, your wives, and bring your father here. [20] Do not be concerned about your belongings, for the best of all the land of Egypt is yours.' "

[21] The sons of Israel did this. Joseph gave them wagons as Pharaoh had commanded, and he gave them provisions for the journey. [22] He gave each of the brothers changes of clothes, but he gave Benjamin 300 pieces of silver and five changes of clothes. [23] He sent his father the following: 10 donkeys carrying the best products of Egypt, and 10 female donkeys carrying grain, food, and provisions for his father on the journey. [24] So Joseph sent his brothers on their way, and as they were leaving, he said to them, "Don't argue on the way."

[25] So they went up from Egypt and came to their father Jacob in the land of Canaan. [26] They said, "Joseph is still alive, and he is ruler over all the land of Egypt!" Jacob was stunned,[c] for he did not believe them. [27] But when they told Jacob all that Joseph had said to them, and when he saw the wagons that Joseph had sent to transport him, the spirit of their father Jacob revived.

[28] Then Israel said, "Enough! My son Joseph is still alive. I will go to see him before I die."

Jacob Leaves for Egypt

46 Israel set out with all that he had and came to Beer-sheba, and he offered sacrifices to the God of his father Isaac. [2] That night God spoke to Israel in a vision: "Jacob, Jacob!" He said.

And Jacob replied, "Here I am."

[3] God said, "I am God, the God of your father. Do not be afraid to go down to Egypt, for I will make you a great nation there. [4] I will go down with you to Egypt, and I will also bring you back. Joseph will put his hands on your eyes."[d]

[5] Jacob left Beer-sheba. The sons of Israel took their father Jacob in the wagons Pharaoh had sent to carry him, along with their children and their wives. [6] They also took their cattle and possessions they had acquired in the land of Canaan. Then Jacob and all his children with him went to Egypt. [7] His sons and grandsons, his daughters and granddaughters, indeed all his •offspring, he brought with him to Egypt.

Jacob's Family

[8] These are the names of the Israelites, Jacob and his descendants, who went to Egypt:

Jacob's firstborn: Reuben.
[9] Reuben's sons: Hanoch, Pallu, Hezron,
 and Carmi.
[10] Simeon's sons: Jemuel, Jamin, Ohad, Jachin,
 Zohar, and Shaul, the son
 of a Canaanite woman.
[11] Levi's sons: Gershon, Kohath, and Merari.
[12] Judah's sons: Er, Onan, Shelah, Perez,
 and Zerah; but Er and Onan died in the land
 of Canaan.
 Perez's sons: Hezron and Hamul.
[13] Issachar's sons: Tola, Puvah,[e] Jashub,[f]
 and Shimron.
[14] Zebulun's sons: Sered, Elon, and Jahleel.
[15] These were Leah's sons born to Jacob in Paddan-
 aram, as well as his daughter Dinah.
 The total number of persons:[g] 33.
[16] Gad's sons: Ziphion, Haggi, Shuni, Ezbon, Eri,
 Arodi, and Areli.
[17] Asher's sons: Imnah, Ishvah, Ishvi, Beriah,
 and their sister Serah.
 Beriah's sons were Heber and Malchiel.
[18] These were the sons of Zilpah—whom Laban
 gave to his daughter Leah—that she bore
 to Jacob: 16 persons.
[19] The sons of Jacob's wife Rachel:
 Joseph and Benjamin.
[20] Manasseh and Ephraim were born to Joseph
 in the land of Egypt. They were born to him

---

[a]**45:12** Lit *that my mouth is* [b]**45:15** Lit *brothers, and he wept over them* [c]**45:26** Lit *Jacob's heart was numb* [d]**46:4** = Joseph will close your eyes after you die [e]**46:13** Sam, Syr read *Puah*; 1 Ch 7:1 [f]**46:13** Sam, LXX; MT reads *Iob* [g]**46:15** Lit *All persons his sons and his daughters*

---

offered himself in the place of his brother. There could be no doubt in Joseph's mind that this brother, who had once sold him into slavery, had changed.

45:1 could no longer keep his composure. Joseph had controlled himself as long as he could. He was ready to reveal himself

to his brothers.

45:3 terrified. These brothers were now face-to-face with the brother they had wronged and an Egyptian official who had total power over them.

45:5 don't be worried. Joseph told his brothers that everything had worked out for the

best because God had used him as part of His plan.

45:9 God has made me lord of all Egypt. Note that Joseph does not say, "Pharaoh has made me lord of all Egypt." He gives God the glory. **without delay.** Joseph wants his brothers to hurry home to their father Ja-

by Asenath daughter of Potiphera, a priest at On.ᵃ

21 Benjamin's sons: Bela, Becher, Ashbel, Gera, Naaman, Ehi, Rosh, Muppim, Huppim, and Ard.

22 These were Rachel's sons who were born to Jacob: 14 persons.

23 Dan's son:ᵇ Hashum.

24 Naphtali's sons: Jahzeel, Guni, Jezer, and Shillem.

25 These were the sons of Bilhah, whom Laban gave to his daughter Rachel. She bore to Jacob: seven persons.

26 The total number of persons belonging to Jacob—his direct descendants,ᶜ not including the wives of Jacob's sons— who came to Egypt: 66.

27 And Joseph's sons who were born to him in Egypt: two persons.

All those of Jacob's household who had come to Egypt: 70ᵈ persons.

Jacob Arrives in Egypt

28 Now Jacob had sent Judah ahead of him to Joseph to prepare for his arrivalᵉ at Goshen. When they came to the land of Goshen, 29 Joseph hitched ⌊the horses to⌋ his chariot and went up to Goshen to meet his father Israel. Joseph presented himself to him, threw his arms around him, and wept for a long time.

30 Then Israel said to Joseph, "At last I can die, now that I have seen your face ⌊and know⌋ you are still alive!"

31 Joseph said to his brothers and to his father's household, "I will go up and inform Pharaoh, telling him: My brothers and my father's household, who were in the land of Canaan, have come to me. 32 The men are shepherds; indeed they raise livestock. They have brought their sheep and cattle and all that they have. 33 When Pharaoh addresses you and asks, 'What is your occupation?' 34 you are to say, 'Your servants, both we and our fathers, have raised livestockᶠ from our youth until now.' Then you will be allowed to settle in the land of Goshen, since all shepherds are abhorrent to Egyptians."

Pharaoh Welcomes Jacob

47 So Joseph went and informed Pharaoh: "My father and my brothers, with their sheep and cattle and all that they have, have come from the land of Canaan and are now in the land of Goshen."

2 He took five of his brothers and presented them before Pharaoh. 3 Then Pharaoh asked his brothers, "What is your occupation?"

And they said to Pharaoh, "Your servants, both we and our fathers, are shepherds." 4 Then they said to Pharaoh, "We have come to live in the land for a while because there is no grazing land for your servants' sheep, since the famine in the land of Canaan has been severe. So now, please let your servants settle in the land of Goshen."

5 Then Pharaoh said to Joseph, "⌊Now that⌋ your father and brothers have come to you, 6 the land of Egypt is open before you; settle your father and brothers in the best part of the land. They can live in the land of Goshen. If you know of any capable men among them, put them in charge of my livestock."

7 Joseph then brought his father Jacob and presented him before Pharaoh, and Jacob blessed Pharaoh. 8 Then Pharaoh said to Jacob, "How many years have you lived?"ᵍ

9 Jacob said to Pharaoh, "My pilgrimage has lasted 130 years. My years have been few and hard, and they have not surpassed the years of my fathers during their pilgrimages." 10 So Jacob blessed Pharaoh and departed from Pharaoh's presence.

11 Then Joseph settled his father and brothers in the land of Egypt and gave them property in the best part of the land, the land of Rameses, as Pharaoh had commanded. 12 And Joseph provided his father, his brothers, and all his father's household with food for their dependents.

The Land Becomes Pharaoh's

13 But there was no food in that entire region, for the famine was very severe. The land of Egypt and the land of Canaan were exhausted by the famine. 14 Joseph collected all the money to be found in the land of Egypt and the land of Canaan in exchange for the grain they were purchasing, and he brought the money to Pharaoh's house. 15 When the money from the land of Egypt and the land of Canaan was gone, all the Egyptians came to Joseph and said, "Give us food. Why should we die here in front of you? The money is gone!"

16 But Joseph said, "Give me your livestock. Since the money is gone, I will give you food in exchange for your livestock." 17 So they brought their livestock to Joseph, and he gave them food in exchange for the horses, the herds of sheep, the herds of cattle, and the donkeys. That year he provided them with food in exchange for all their livestock.

ᵃ46:20 Or Heliopolis ᵇ46:23 Alt Hb tradition reads sons ᶜ46:26 Lit Jacob who came out from his loins ᵈ46:27 LXX reads 75; Ac 7:14
ᵉ46:28 Lit to give directions before him ᶠ46:34 Lit fathers, are men of livestock ᵍ47:8 Lit many are the days of the years

---

cob with the news.
46:2 Israel in a vision. God spoke to Jacob (Israel) in this same place where he had also spoken to Isaac, Jacob's father (26:4).
46:3 Do not be afraid to go down. God told Jacob to trust Him by traveling to Egypt. **I will make you a great nation.** This echoes God's

promise to Abraham passed down to Isaac and then to Jacob.
46:8 names of the Israelites. These names are the 12 tribes of the Old Testament. The rest of the Bible describes God's people in terms of the sons of Jacob, or Israel, from whom they descended.

46:27 Jacob's household. From this small number grew a great nation (Ex. 1:5; 12:37).
46:29 Goshen. Joseph's family settled in some of the most fertile land in Egypt.
46:34 shepherds. When Joseph's brothers told Pharaoh they were shepherds, he gave them land in the Egyptian back country. This

18 When that year was over, they came the next year and said to him, "We cannot hide from our lord that the money is gone and that all our livestock belongs to our lord. There is nothing left for our lord except our bodies and our land. 19 Why should we perish here in front of you—both us and our land? Buy us and our land in exchange for food. Then we with our land will become Pharaoh's slaves. Give us seed so that we can live and not die, and so that the land won't become desolate."

20 In this way, Joseph acquired all the land in Egypt for Pharaoh, because every Egyptian sold his field since the famine was so severe for them. The land became Pharaoh's, 21 and Joseph moved the people to the citiesa from one end of Egypt to the other. 22 The only land he didn't acquire was that of the priests, for it was their allotment from Pharaoh. They lived offb the allotment Pharaoh had given them; therefore they did not sell their land.

23 Then Joseph said to the people, "Understand today that I have acquired you and your land for Pharaoh. Here is seed for you. Sow it in the land. 24 At harvest, you are to give a fifth of it to Pharaoh, and four-fifths will be yours as seed for the field and as food for yourselves, your households, and your dependents."

25 And they said, "You have saved our lives. We have found favor in our lord's eyes and will be Pharaoh's slaves." 26 So Joseph made it a law, still in effect today in the land of Egypt, that a fifth ⌊of the produce⌋ belongs to Pharaoh. Only the priests' land does not belong to Pharaoh.

Israel Settles in Goshen

27 Israel settled in the land of Egypt, in the region of Goshen. They acquired property in it and became fruitful and very numerous. 28 Now Jacob lived in the land of Egypt 17 years, and his life span was 147 years. 29 When the time drew near for him to die, he called his son Joseph and said to him, "If I have found favor in your eyes, put your hand under my thigh ⌊and promise me⌋ that you will deal with me in faithful love. Do not bury me in Egypt. 30 When I lie down with my fathers, carry me away from Egypt and bury me in their burial place."

Joseph answered, "I will do what you have asked."

31 And Jacob said, "Swear to me." So Joseph swore to him. Then Israel bowed ⌊in thanks⌋ at the head of his bed.c

Jacob Blesses Ephraim and Manasseh

48 Some time after this, Joseph was told, "Your father is weaker." So he set out with his two sons, Manasseh and Ephraim. 2 When Jacob was told, "Your son Joseph has come to you," Israel summoned his strength and sat up in bed.

3 Jacob said to Joseph, "•God Almighty appeared to me at Luz in the land of Canaan and blessed me. 4 He said to me, 'I will make you fruitful and numerous; I will make many nations ⌊come from⌋ you, and I will give this land as an eternal possession to your descendants to come.' 5 Your two sons born to you in the land of Egypt before I came to you in Egypt are now mine. Ephraim and Manasseh belong to me just as Reuben and Simeon do. 6 Children born to you after them will be yours and will be recorded under the names of their brothers with regard to their inheritance. 7 When I was returning from Paddan, to my sorrow Rachel died along the way, some distance from Ephrath in the land of Canaan. I buried her there along the way to Ephrath," (that is, Bethlehem).

8 When Israel saw Joseph's sons, he said, "Who are these?"

9 And Joseph said to his father, "They are my sons God has given me here."

So Jacob said, "Bring them to me and I will bless them." 10 Now Jacob's eyesight was poor because of old age; he could hardlyd see. Joseph brought them to him, and he kissed and embraced them. 11 Israel said to Joseph, "I never expected to see your face ⌊again⌋, but now God has even let me see your •offspring." 12 Then Joseph took them from his ⌊father's⌋ knees and bowed with his face to the ground.

Ephraim's Greater Blessing

13 Then Joseph took them both—with his right hand Ephraim toward Israel's left, and with his left hand Manasseh toward Israel's right—and brought them to Israel. 14 But Israel stretched out his right hand and put it on the head of Ephraim, the younger, and crossing his hands, put his left on Manasseh's head, although Manasseh was the firstborn. 15 Then he blessed Joseph and said:

The God before whom my fathers Abraham
  and Isaac walked,
the God who has been my shepherd all my life
  to this day,
16 the Angel who has redeemed me
  from all harm—
may He bless these boys.
And may they be called by my name
and the names of my fathers Abraham and Isaac,

---

a 47:21 Sam, LXX, Vg read *and he made the people servants* b 47:22 Lit *They ate* c 47:31 Or *Israel worshiped while leaning on the top of his staff* d 48:10 Lit *he was not able to*

helped Jacob's family maintain their identity as a distinct people.

47:16 in exchange. By the end of the famine, the people had sold all they owned to the government, including themselves as slaves.

47:27 acquired property. Amazingly, while the Egyptian population was selling their land, the Israelites were acquiring property.

47:29 Do not bury me in Egypt. Jacob's body would find its rest in the manner of Jacob's life—on a journey.

47:30 bury me in their burial place. Jacob was referring to the family burial plot—the cave of Machpelah (23:14–20)—purchased by Abraham to bury Sarah,

47:31 Israel bowed [in thanks]. Jacob (Israel) was finished with his funeral and burial arrangements. Now he waited for life to end.

48:5 are now mine. When Jacob's descendants settled in Canaan, territory was apportioned not to the tribe of Joseph, but to the

and may they grow to be numerous
within the land.

¹⁷ When Joseph saw that his father had placed his right hand on Ephraim's head, he thought it was a mistakeᵃ and took his father's hand to move it from Ephraim's head to Manasseh's. ¹⁸ Joseph said to his father, "Not that way, my father! This one is the firstborn. Put your right hand on his head."

¹⁹ But his father refused and said, "I know, my son, I know! He too will become a tribe,ᵇ and he too will be great; nevertheless, his younger brother will be greater than he, and his offspring will become a populous nation."ᶜ ²⁰ So he blessed them that day with these words:

Israel will invoke blessings by you, saying,
"May God make you like Ephraim
and Manasseh,"

putting Ephraim before Manasseh.

²¹ Then Israel said to Joseph, "Look! I am about to die, but God will be with you and will bring you back to the land of your fathers. ²² Over and above what I am giving your brothers, I am giving you the one mountain slopeᵈ that I took from the hand of the Amorites with my sword and bow."

Jacob's Last Words

49 Then Jacob called his sons and said, "Gather around, and I will tell you what will happen to you in the days to come.ᵉ

² Come together and listen, sons of Jacob;
listen to your father Israel:

³ Reuben, you are my firstborn,
my strength and the firstfruits of my virility,
excelling in prominence, excelling in power.
⁴ Turbulent as water, you will no longer excel,
because you got into your father's bed
and you defiled it—heᶠ got into my bed.

⁵ Simeon and Levi are brothers;
their knives are vicious weapons.
⁶ May I never enter their council;
may I never join their assembly.
For in their anger they kill men,
and on a whim they hamstring oxen.
⁷ Their anger is cursed, for it is strong,
and their fury, for it is cruel!

I will disperse them throughout Jacob
and scatter them throughout Israel.

⁸ Judah, your brothers will praise you.
Your hand will be on the necks
of your enemies;
your father's sons will bow down to you.
⁹ Judah is a young lion—
my son, you return from the kill—
he crouches; he lies down like a lion
and like a lioness—who wants to rouse him?
¹⁰ The scepter will not depart from Judah,
or the staff from between his feet,
until He whose right it is comesᵍ
and the obedience of the peoples belongs
to Him.
¹¹ He ties his donkey to a vine,
and the colt of his donkey to the choice vine.
He washes his clothes in wine,
and his robes in the blood of grapes.
¹² His eyes are darker than wine,
and his teeth are whiter than milk.

¹³ Zebulun will live by the seashore
and will be a harbor for ships,
and his territory will be next to Sidon.

¹⁴ Issachar is a strong donkey
lying down between the saddlebags.ʰ
¹⁵ He saw that his resting place was good
and that the land was pleasant,
so he leaned his shoulder to bear a load
and became a forced laborer.

¹⁶ Dan will judge his people
as one of the tribes of Israel.
¹⁷ He will be a snake by the road,
a viper beside the path,
that bites the horses' heels
so that its rider falls backwards.

¹⁸ I wait for Your salvation, LORD.

¹⁹ Gad will be attacked by ⌊marauding⌋ bands,
but he will attack their heels.

²⁰ Asher'sⁱ food will be rich,
and he will produce royal delicacies.

²¹ Naphtali is a doe set free
that bears beautiful fawns.

ᵃ**48:17** Or *he was displeased*; lit *head, it was bad in his eyes* ᵇ**48:19** Lit *people* ᶜ**48:19** Lit *a fullness of nations*; perhaps *a multitude of nations* ᵈ**48:22** Lit *one shoulder*; Hb *Shechem*, Joseph's burial place ᵉ**49:1** Or *in the last days* ᶠ**49:4** LXX, Syr, Tg read *you* ᵍ**49:10** Or *until tribute comes to him*, or *until Shiloh comes*, or *until He comes to Shiloh* ʰ**49:14** Or *sheepfolds* ⁱ**49:19–20** LXX, Syr, Vg; MT reads *their heel.* ²⁰ From Asher

---

tribes named for his sons, Ephraim and Manasseh.

48:7 Rachel died. As Jacob passed on his blessing to Joseph's son, he reminisced about his beloved wife Rachel.

48:8 Who are these? Perhaps Jacob's eyesight was so dim he did not know who Jo-

seph's sons were.

48:15 Joseph. Joseph's name is used here as head of the family. When Jacob gave his blessing to Joseph's children, he was actually blessing Joseph.

48:16 the Angel who has redeemed me. This could refer to Jacob's wrestling all night

with God and then receiving a blessing and a new name (32:24–30).

49:2 listen to your father. Jacob blessed his sons by describing their traits.

49:4 Turbulent as water. The tribe of Reuben came to be known for its indecision (Judg. 5:16).

22 Joseph is a fruitful vine,
a fruitful vine beside a spring;
its branchesa climb over the wall.b
23 The archers attacked him,
shot at him, and were hostile toward him.
24 Yet his bow remained steady,
and his strongc arms were made agile
by the hands of the Mighty One of Jacob,
by the name ofd the Shepherd, the Rock
of Israel,
25 by the God of your father who helps you,
and by the •Almighty who blesses you
with blessings of the heavens above,
blessings of the deep that lies below,
and blessings of the breasts and the womb.
26 The blessings of your father excel
the blessings of my ancestorse
andf the bounty of the eternal hills.b
May they rest on the head of Joseph,
on the crown of the prince of his brothers.

27 Benjamin is a wolf; he tears ⌊his prey⌋.
In the morning he devours the prey,
and in the evening he divides the plunder."

28 These are the tribes of Israel, 12 in all, and this was what their father said to them. He blessed them, and he blessed each one with a suitable blessing.

Jacob's Burial Instructions

29 Then he commanded them: "I am about to be gathered to my people. Bury me with my fathers in the cave in the field of Ephron the Hittite. 30 The cave is in the field of Machpelah, near Mamre, in the land of Canaan. This is the field Abraham purchased from Ephron the Hittite as a burial site. 31 Abraham and his wife Sarah are buried there, Isaac and his wife Rebekah are buried there, and I buried Leah there. 32 The field and the cave in it ⌊were purchased⌋ from the Hittites." 33 When Jacob had finished instructing his sons, he drew his feet into the bed and died. He was gathered to his people.

Jacob's Burial

50 Then Joseph, leaning over his father's face, wept and kissed him. 2 He commanded his servants who were physicians to embalm his father. So they embalmed Israel. 3 They took 40 days to complete this, for embalming takes that long, and the Egyptians mourned for him 70 days.

4 When the days of mourning were over, Joseph said to Pharaoh's household, "If I have found favor with you, please tellg Pharaoh that 5 my father made me take an oath, saying, 'I am about to die. You must bury me there in the tomb that I hewed out for myself in the land of Canaan.' Now let me go and bury my father. Then I will return."

6 So Pharaoh said, "Go and bury your father in keeping with your oath."

7 Then Joseph went to bury his father, and all Pharaoh's servants, the elders of his household, and all the elders of the land of Egypt went with him, 8 along with all Joseph's household, his brothers, and his father's household. Only their children, their sheep, and their cattle were left in the land of Goshen. 9 Horses and chariots went up with him; it was a very impressive procession. 10 When they reached the threshing floor of Atad, which is across the Jordan, they lamented and wept loudly, and Joseph mourned seven days for his father. 11 When the Canaanite inhabitants of the land saw the mourning at the threshing floor of Atad, they said, "This is a solemn mourning on the part of the Egyptians." Therefore the place is named Abel-mizraim.h It is across the Jordan.

12 So Jacob's sons did for him what he had commanded them. 13 They carried him to the land of Canaan and buried him in the cave at Machpelah in the field near Mamre, which Abraham had purchased as a burial site from Ephron the Hittite. 14 After Joseph buried his father, he returned to Egypt with his brothers and all who had gone with him to bury his father.

Joseph's Kindness

15 When Joseph's brothers saw that their father was dead, they said to one another, "If Joseph is holding a grudge against us, he will certainly repay us for all the wrong we caused him."

16 So they sent this message to Joseph, "Before he died your father gave a command: 17 'Say this to Joseph: Please forgive your brothers' transgression and their sin—the wrong they caused you.' Therefore, please forgive the transgression of the servants of the God of your father." Joseph wept when their message came to him. 18 Then his brothers also came to him, bowed down before him, and said, "We are your slaves!"

19 But Joseph said to them, "Don't be afraid. Am I in the place of God? 20 You planned evil against me; God planned it for good to bring about the present result—the survival of many people. 21 Therefore don't be afraid. I will take care of you and your little ones." And he comforted them and spoke kindly to them.i

---

a49:22 Lit daughters   b49:22,26 Hb obscure   c49:24 Lit and the hands of his   d49:24 Syr, Tg; MT reads Jacob, from there   e49:26 Or of the mountains   f49:26 Lit to   g50:4 Lit please speak in the ears of   h50:11 = Mourning of Egypt   i50:21 Lit spoke to their hearts

---

49:5 vicious weapons. Jacob identified violence as the trait of Simeon and Levi. They had destroyed the Shechemites to avenge their sister's rape (34:25–29).

49:8 your brothers will praise you. Through Judah, King David descended. Also through Judah's line Jesus was born.

49:22 fruitful. The name Ephraim (Joseph's younger son who received the greater blessing) means "fruitful."

49:27 devours the prey. This trait of savagery is borne out in Benjamin's tribe. King Saul, a mighty warrior, was from this tribe (1 Sam. 10).

49:29 gathered to my people. This was Jacob's way of saying he was about to die.

50:2 embalm. Joseph directed the Egyptian physicians to embalm Jacob. They removed the organs of the body and filled it with salts and preservatives.

50:3 40 days … 70 days. Forty days was the

Joseph's Death

22 Joseph and his father's household remained in Egypt. Joseph lived 110 years. 23 He saw Ephraim's sons to the third generation; the sons of Manasseh's son Machir were recognized by[a] Joseph.

24 Joseph said to his brothers, "I am about to die, but God will certainly come to your aid and bring you up from this land to the land He promised Abraham, Isaac, and Jacob." 25 So Joseph made the Israelites take an oath: "When God comes to your aid, you are to carry my bones up from here."

26 Joseph died at the age of 110. They embalmed him and placed him in a coffin in Egypt.

a **50:23** Lit *were born on the knees of*; referring to a ritual of adoption or of legitimation; Gn 30:3

typical time for an Egyptian embalming. In the meantime, Jacob's family and Joseph's nation were grieving for Jacob. Seventy days to mourn was just two days shorter than the mourning period for an Egyptian Pharaoh—an indication of the respect of the Egyptians for Joseph.

50:5 let me go. Joseph faced the same journey to Canaan that his descendants would make 400 years later. When those descendants made that journey, they would carry Joseph's bones for burial in the promised land (Ex. 13:19).

50:15 repay us. With their father gone, Joseph's brothers were afraid that he would take revenge against them.

50:20 You planned evil against me. Joseph's ability to forgive his brothers was grounded in his belief that God worked his will through human events.

50:23 were recognized by Joseph. Joseph lived to see great great grandchildren. The custom was to place the babies on his knees, signifying that they belonged to him.

50:24 promised Abraham, Isaac, and Jacob. The legacy of God's promise to Abraham was so strong that even on Joseph's deathbed, after relocating his family to the farmlands of Goshen, he held on to the promise of another place. Hundreds of years later, that legacy began to be fulfilled in the exodus of Israel from Egypt slavery (Ex. 1:5–8).

50:25 carry my bones up. Joseph's desire was the same as his father's. He wanted to be buried in the home God had promised his family. His bones were eventually buried at Shechem (Ex. 13:19; Josh. 24:32).

INTRODUCTION TO
EXODUS

AUTHOR

Moses is assumed to be the author and editor of most of the first five books of the Old Testament (the Pentateuch).

DATE

It is difficult to set a firm date for the writing of the Pentateuch. Conservative estimates place it in either the 15th or 13th century B.C., depending on when the Exodus occurred.

THEME

Deliverance from Egypt; giving the Law; building the Tabernacle.

HISTORICAL BACKGROUND

No direct evidence fixes the events of this book within a specifically dated historical context. The Bible does not provide the name of the pharaoh of the Exodus, and extra-biblical texts and archaeology are silent concerning the Israelites' sojourn in and escape from Egypt. Indirect evidence present throughout the Bible can be used to support a wide range of dates. Certain recent archaeological evidence from Palestine suggests a late 13th century date for the appearance of the Israelites in Canaan. If we accept this date, then Moses and the events of this book may date earlier in this same century, sometime between 1300 and 1250 B.C.

CHARACTERISTICS

The Book of Exodus is dominated by the life and actions of Moses and arranged around two outstanding redemptive acts: the Exodus from Egypt and the establishment of the Covenant at Sinai. Moses and these events are fundamental to an understanding of God's plan for human redemption. It could be argued that much of the Bible is a dialogue that reacts to, explains, and completes the redemptive plan of God as it is revealed in this book.

PASSAGES FOR TOPICAL GROUP STUDY

PASSAGES FOR GENERAL GROUP STUDY

Israel Oppressed in Egypt

1 These are the names of the sons of Israel who came to Egypt with Jacob; each came with his family:

2 Reuben, Simeon, Levi, and Judah;
3 Issachar, Zebulun, and Benjamin;
4 Dan and Naphtali; Gad and Asher.

5 The total number of Jacob's descendants[a] was 70;[b] Joseph was already in Egypt.

6 Then Joseph and all his brothers and all that generation died. 7 But the Israelites were fruitful, increased rapidly, multiplied, and became extremely numerous so that the land was filled with them.

8 A new king, who had not known Joseph, came to power in Egypt. 9 He said to his people, "Look, the Israelite people are more numerous and powerful than we are. 10 Let us deal shrewdly with them; otherwise they will multiply ⌊further⌋, and if war breaks out, they may join our enemies, fight against us, and leave the country." 11 So the Egyptians assigned taskmasters over the Israelites to oppress them with forced labor. They built Pithom and Rameses as supply cities for Pharaoh. 12 But the more they oppressed them, the more they multiplied and spread so that the Egyptians came to dread[c] the Israelites. 13 They worked the Israelites ruthlessly 14 and made their lives bitter with difficult labor in brick and mortar, and in all kinds of fieldwork. They ruthlessly imposed all this work on them.

15 Then the king of Egypt said to the Hebrew midwives, one of whom was named Shiphrah and the other Puah, 16 "When you help the Hebrew women give birth, observe them as they deliver.[d] If the child is a son, kill him, but if it's a daughter, she may live." 17 The Hebrew midwives, however, •feared God and did not do as the king of Egypt had told them; they let the boys live. 18 So the king of Egypt summoned the midwives and asked them, "Why have you done this and let the boys live?"

19 The midwives said to Pharaoh, "The Hebrew women are not like the Egyptian women, for they are vigorous and give birth before a midwife can get to them."

20 So God was good to the midwives, and the people multiplied and became very numerous. 21 Since the midwives feared God, He gave them families. 22 Pharaoh then commanded all his people: "You must throw every son born to the Hebrews[e] into the Nile, but let every daughter live."

Daring Escape

1. How much do you know about your birth: Time? Place? Weight? Anything else?

Exodus 2:1-25
2. Why did Moses' mother hide her baby among reeds on the Nile (Ex. 1:22)? What does this show about her faith in God?
3. How did God honor the faith of Moses' family?
4. Why did Moses give up life in the palace to fight for the Jews? Did he do the right thing in killing the Egyptian, or might God have had another path for him to follow?
5. Is there a choice you need God's guidance for at this time?

Moses' Birth and Adoption

2 Now a man from the family of Levi married a Levite woman. 2 The woman became pregnant and gave birth to a son; when she saw that he was beautiful,[f] she hid him for three months. 3 But when she could no longer hide him, she got a papyrus basket for him and coated it with asphalt and pitch. She placed the child in it and set it among the reeds by the bank of the Nile. 4 Then his sister stood at a distance in order to see what would happen to him.

5 Pharaoh's daughter went down to bathe at the Nile while her servant girls walked along the riverbank. Seeing the basket among the reeds, she sent her slave girl to get it. 6 When she opened it, she saw the child—a little boy, crying. She felt sorry for him and said, "This is one of the Hebrew boys."

7 Then his sister said to Pharaoh's daughter, "Should I go and call a woman from the Hebrews to nurse the boy for you?"

8 "Go." Pharaoh's daughter told her. So the girl went and called the boy's mother. 9 Then Pharaoh's daughter said to her, "Take this child and nurse him for me, and I will pay your wages." So the woman took the boy and nursed him. 10 When the child grew older, she brought him to Pharaoh's daughter, and he became her son. She

---

[a]**1:5** Lit *of people issuing from Jacob's loins*   [b]**1:5** LXX, DSS read *75*; Gn 46:27; Ac 7:14   [c]**1:12** Or *Egyptians loathed*   [d]**1:16** Lit *birth, look at the stones*   [e]**1:22** Sam, LXX, Tg; MT omits *to the Hebrews*   [f]**2:2** Or *healthy*

1:1-5 sons of Israel who came to Egypt. Jacob (also called Israel, Gen. 32:28) and his sons had traveled to Egypt at the invitation of his son, Joseph, who had risen to prominence in Egypt (Gen. 46:1-7). Only 70 people had arrived in Egypt (Gen. 46:27); settling in the land of Goshen, separate from the Egyptians

(Gen. 46:31-34). When the Israelites left Egypt they numbered about 600,000 men plus women and children (12:37). The Israelites lived in Egypt for 430 years. **2:2 beautiful.** Moses was an exceptional baby (see Acts 7:20; Hebrews 11:23). He had two older siblings—Miriam (v. 4) and

Aaron (4:14; 7:7).

2:6-8 This is one of the Hebrew boys. When she unwrapped the baby, Pharaoh's daughter no doubt noticed he had been circumcised, since Israelites performed that rite on the eighth day after birth. Egyptians practiced circumcision but not on infants.

named him Moses, "Because," she said, "I drew him out of the water."[a]

Moses in Midian

[11] Years later,[b] after Moses had grown up, he went out to his own people[c] and observed their forced labor. He saw an Egyptian beating a Hebrew, one of his people. [12] Looking all around and seeing no one, he struck the Egyptian dead and hid him in the sand. [13] The next day he went out and saw two Hebrews fighting. He asked the one in the wrong, "Why are you attacking your neighbor?"[d]

[14] "Who made you a leader and judge over us?" the man replied. "Are you planning to kill me as you killed the Egyptian?"

Then Moses became afraid and thought: What I did is certainly known. [15] When Pharaoh heard about this, he tried to kill Moses. But Moses fled from Pharaoh and went to live in the land of Midian, and sat down by a well.

[16] Now the priest of Midian had seven daughters. They came to draw water and filled the troughs to water their father's flock. [17] Then some shepherds arrived and drove them away, but Moses came to their rescue and watered their flock. [18] When they returned to their father Reuel[e] he asked, "Why have you come back so quickly today?"

[19] They answered, "An Egyptian rescued us from the shepherds. He even drew water for us and watered the flock."

[20] "So where is he?" he asked his daughters. "Why then did you leave the man behind? Invite him to eat dinner."

[21] Moses agreed to stay with the man, and he gave his daughter Zipporah to Moses ⌊in marriage⌋. [22] She gave birth to a son whom he named Gershom, for he said, "I have become a stranger in a foreign land."[f]

[23] After a long time, the king of Egypt died. The Israelites groaned because of their difficult labor, and they cried out; and their cry for help ascended to God because of the difficult labor. [24] So God heard their groaning, and He remembered His covenant with Abraham, Isaac, and Jacob. [25] God saw the Israelites, and He took notice.

Moses and the Burning Bush

3 Meanwhile Moses was shepherding the flock of his father-in-law Jethro,[g] the priest of Midian. He led the flock to the far side of the wilderness and came

Strange but True

1. Have you ever seen anything strange or experienced something that defied common sense? What was it?

Exodus 3:1-22

2. Why did God appear in a burning bush? What might fire symbolize?

3. Why does God say that His name is "I AM WHO I AM" (v. 14)? What does that mean? What does it tell us about God's character?

4. Why did God tell Moses to ask Pharaoh to let the Israelites go, when He knew that Pharaoh would say no? What does this illustrate about God's purpose for our lives?

5. What is God's purpose for your life?

to Horeb,[h] the mountain of God. [2] Then the Angel of the LORD appeared to him in a flame of fire within a bush. As Moses looked, he saw that the bush was on fire but was not consumed. [3] So Moses thought: I must go over and look at this remarkable sight. Why isn't the bush burning up?

[4] When the LORD saw that he had gone over to look, God called out to him from the bush, "Moses, Moses!"

"Here I am," he answered.

[5] "Do not come closer," He said. "Take your sandals off your feet, for the place where you are standing is holy ground." [6] Then He continued, "I am the God of your father,[i] the God of Abraham, the God of Isaac, and the God of Jacob." Moses hid his face because he was afraid to look at God.

[7] Then the LORD said, "I have observed the misery of My people in Egypt, and have heard them crying out because of their oppressors, and I know about their sufferings. [8] I have come down to rescue them from the power of the Egyptians and to bring them from that land to a good and spacious land, a land flowing with milk and honey—the territory of the Canaanites, Hittites, Amorites, Perizzites, Hivites, and Jebusites. [9] The Israelites' cry for help has come to Me, and I have also seen the way the Egyptians are oppressing them.

---

[a]**2:10** *Moses* sounds like a Hb word meaning "drawing out" and an Egyptian word meaning "born." [b]**2:11** Lit *And it was in those days* [c]**2:11** Lit *his brothers* [d]**2:13** Or *fellow Hebrew* [e]**2:18** Jethro's clan or last name was *Reuel*; Ex 3:1 [f]**2:22** In Hb the name *Gershom* sounds like "a stranger there." [g]**3:1** Moses' father-in-law's first name was *Jethro*; Ex 2:18 [h]**3:1** = Desolation; another name for Mount Sinai; Dt 4:10,15; 18:16; Mal 4:4. [i]**3:6** Sam, some LXX mss read *fathers*; Ac 7:32

2:11 Moses had grown up. At this point, Moses is 40 years old (Acts 7:23).

2:15 Pharaoh. Possibly Thutmose III (1479-1425 B.C.). **Midian.** A dry wilderness quite different than Moses' sumptuous home in Egypt. He would remain here for 40 years (Acts 7:29-30).

2:24 remembered His covenant. God had promised Abraham, Isaac, and Jacob, that He would give the promised land to their descendants (Gen. 15:18-21; 26:2-6; 28:13-15). Abraham had also been told, however, that his descendants would "be strangers in a land that does not belong to them; they will be

enslaved and oppressed 400 years" (Gen. 15:13).

3:1 Horeb. Mount Sinai.

3:6 afraid to look at God. To see God's face, Israelites believed, was to die (Gen. 16:13; 32:30). Moses discovered a relationship with God that made him unafraid (19:3; 33:11),

10 Therefore, go. I am sending you to Pharaoh so that you may lead My people, the Israelites, out of Egypt."

11 But Moses asked God, "Who am I that I should go to Pharaoh and that I should bring the Israelites out of Egypt?"

12 He answered, "I will certainly be with you, and this will be the sign to you that I have sent you: when you bring the people out of Egypt, you will all worshipa God at this mountain."

13 Then Moses asked God, "If I go to the Israelites and say to them: The God of your fathers has sent me to you, and they ask me, 'What is His name?' what should I tell them?"

14 God replied to Moses, "I AM WHO I AM.b This is what you are to say to the Israelites: I AM has sent me to you." 15 God also said to Moses, "Say this to the Israelites: •Yahweh, the God of your fathers, the God of Abraham, the God of Isaac, and the God of Jacob, has sent me to you. This is My name forever; this is how I am to be remembered in every generation.

16 "Go and assemble the elders of Israel and say to them: Yahweh, the God of your fathers, the God of Abraham, Isaac, and Jacob, has appeared to me and said: I have paid close attention to you and to what has been done to you in Egypt. 17 And I have promised you that I will bring you up from the misery of Egypt to the land of the Canaanites, Hittites, Amorites, Perizzites, Hivites, and Jebusites—a land flowing with milk and honey. 18 They will listen to what you say. Then you, along with the elders of Israel, must go to the king of Egypt and say to him: The LORD, the God of the Hebrews, has met with us. Now please let us go on a three-day trip into the wilderness so that we may sacrifice to the LORD our God.

19 "However, I know that the king of Egypt will not allow you to go, unless ⌊he is forced⌋ by a strong hand. 20 I will stretch out My hand and strike Egypt with all My miracles that I will perform in it. After that, he will let you go. 21 And I will give this people such favor in the sight of the Egyptians that when you go, you will not go empty-handed. 22 Each woman will ask her neighbor and any woman staying in her house for silver and gold jewelry, and clothing, and you will put them on your sons and daughters. So you will plunder the Egyptians."

Miraculous Signs for Moses

4 Then Moses answered, "What if they won't believe me and will not obey me but say, 'The LORD did not appear to you'?"

A Magical Staff

1. Are you afraid of snakes? What's the most interesting "snake story" you know?

Exodus 4:1-17

2. Why did God make Moses' staff turn into a snake? Why did He have him pick it up by the tail, instead of near the head? What might the snake symbolize?

3. What did the miraculous healing of Moses' hand represent?

4. Why is Moses still hesitant to lead the people? Summarize God's answer (vv. 14-17) in your own words.

5. Has God asked you to do something that seems hard or scary? How might His words to Moses apply to you?

2 The LORD asked him, "What is that in your hand?"

"A staff," he replied.

3 Then He said, "Throw it on the ground." He threw it on the ground, and it became a snake. Moses ran from it, 4 but the LORD told him, "Stretch out your hand and grab it by the tail." So he stretched out his hand and caught it, and it became a staff in his hand. 5 "This will take place," He continued, "so they will believe that the LORD, the God of their fathers, the God of Abraham, the God of Isaac, and the God of Jacob, has appeared to you."

6 In addition the LORD said to him, "Put your hand inside your cloak." So he put his hand inside his cloak, and when he took it out, his hand was diseased, like snow.c 7 Then He said, "Put your hand back inside your cloak." He put his hand back inside his cloak, and when he took it out,d it had again become like the rest of his skin. 8 "If they will not believe you and will not respond to the evidence of the first sign, they may believe the evidence of the second sign. 9 And if they don't believe even these two signs or listen to what you say, take some water from the Nile and pour it on the dry ground. The water you take from the Nile will become blood on the ground."

10 But Moses replied to the LORD, "Please, Lord, I have never been eloquent—either in the past or

a3:12 Or *serve*   b3:14 Or *I AM BECAUSE I AM*, or *I WILL BE WHO I WILL BE*   c4:6 A reference to whiteness or flakiness of the skin   d4:7 Lit *out of his cloak*

and would even call on God to "let me see Your glory" (33:18).

3:14 I AM WHO I AM. The name Israel would call Him expresses God's eternal, dependable, and faithful character. **I AM.** Jesus used this phrase to describe Himself, in effect, as God (John 8:53-58). The power behind the

words "I am He," caused His captors to collapse (John 18:6).

3:15 Yahweh. Yahweh, translated LORD, is related to the verb "I am."

3:21 such favor. God had promised Abraham that Israel would leave Egypt "with many possessions" (Gen. 15:14). Indeed, when the

Israelites departed, the Egyptians gladly gave them whatever they asked for (12:35-36). Later the Israelites gave these same treasures for use in God's tabernacle (chapter 35).

4:3 snake. Making a staff turn into a snake showed Pharaoh's powerlessness, who used

recently or since You have been speaking to Your servant[a]—because I am slow and hesitant in speech."

[11] The LORD said to him, "Who made the human mouth? Who makes him mute or deaf, seeing or blind? Is it not I, the LORD? [12] Now go! I will help you speak and I will teach you what to say."

[13] Moses said, "Please, Lord, send someone else."[b]

[14] Then the LORD's anger burned against Moses, and He said, "Isn't Aaron the Levite your brother? I know that he can speak well. And also, he is on his way now to meet you. When he sees you, his heart will rejoice. [15] You will speak with him and tell him what to say. I will help[c] both you and him ⌊to speak⌋, and will teach you both what to do. [16] He will speak to the people for you. He will be your spokesman, and you will serve as God to him. [17] And take this staff in your hand that you will perform the signs with."

Moses' Return to Egypt

[18] Then Moses went back to his father-in-law Jethro and said to him, "Please let me return to my relatives in Egypt and see if they are still living."

Jethro said to Moses, "Go in peace."

[19] Now in Midian the LORD told Moses, "Return to Egypt, for all the men who wanted to kill you are dead." [20] So Moses took his wife and sons, put them on a donkey, and set out for the land of Egypt. And Moses took God's staff in his hand.

[21] The LORD instructed Moses, "When you go back to Egypt, make sure you do in front of Pharaoh all the wonders I have put within your power. But I will harden his heart[d] so that he won't let the people go. [22] Then you will say to Pharaoh: This is what the LORD says: Israel is My firstborn son. [23] I told you: Let My son go so that he may worship Me, but you refused to let him go. Now I will kill your firstborn son!"

[24] On the trip, at an overnight campsite, it happened that the LORD confronted him and sought to put him to death. [25] So Zipporah took a flint, cut off her son's foreskin, and threw it at Moses' feet.[e] Then she said, "You are a bridegroom of blood to me!" [26] So He let him alone. At that time she said, "You are a bridegroom of blood," referring to the circumcision.[f]

Reunion of Moses and Aaron

[27] Now the LORD had said to Aaron, "Go and meet Moses in the wilderness." So he went and met him at the mountain of God and kissed him. [28] Moses told Aaron everything the LORD had sent him to say, and about all the signs He had commanded him ⌊to do⌋.

[29] Then Moses and Aaron went and assembled all the elders of the Israelites. [30] Aaron repeated everything the LORD had said to Moses and performed the signs before the people. [31] The people believed, and when they heard that the LORD had paid attention to them and that He had seen their misery, they bowed down and worshiped.

Popularity Jeopardy

1. Have you ever worked with bricks? If so, what did you build? If not, what sort of construction projects have you worked on?

Exodus 5:1-21

2. Why did Pharaoh react to Moses' request by making life harder for the Israelites? What did this do to Moses' relationship with the Israelites?

3. In what ways might God's words to Moses at the burning bush (chap. 3) have encouraged him at this point?

4. How can obeying God sometimes make you unpopular in school or on your team? Is it more important to you to be obedient or popular, and why?

Moses Confronts Pharaoh

5 Later, Moses and Aaron went in and said to Pharaoh, "This is what the LORD, the God of Israel, says: Let My people go, so that they may hold a festival for Me in the wilderness."

[2] But Pharaoh responded, "Who is the LORD that I should obey Him by letting Israel go? I do not know the LORD, and what's more, I will not let Israel go."

[3] Then they answered, "The God of the Hebrews has met with us. Please let us go on a three-day trip into the wilderness so that we may sacrifice to the LORD our God, or else He may strike us with plague or sword."

[4] The king of Egypt said to them, "Moses and Aaron, why are you causing the people to neglect their work? Get to your labors!" [5] Pharaoh also said, "Look, the people of the land are so numerous, and you would stop them from working."

---

a **4:10** Moses   b **4:13** Lit *send by the hand of whom You will send*   c **4:15** Lit *be with*   d **4:21** Or *will make him stubborn*   e **4:25** Lit *his feet*; some interpret "feet" as a euphemism for genitals   f **4:25–26** Perhaps Zipporah appeased God on Moses' behalf by circumcising Gershom.

---

a cobra to symbolize his authority.

4:10 slow and hesitant in speech. A speech impediment? Stephen described Moses as "powerful in his speech" (Acts 7:22).

4:14 Levite. Aaron, Moses, and Miriam were from the tribe of Levi (6:16-20). Through Aaron the Levites would serve as priests in

God's tabernacle and temple (Num. 1:50-51).

4:21 I will harden his heart. Not until the sixth plague did God confirm Pharaoh's act of will against Him.

4:24 The LORD confronted him. Apparently God was angry because Moses had not obeyed Him in the matter of circumcising his

son (Gen. 17:9-14). Moses may have withheld circumcision of his son in order to please his Midianite family.

4:25-26 Zipporah ... cut off her son's foreskin. Moses' wife realized that God was displeased with her husband and quickly performed the young son's circumcision.

Further Oppression of Israel

6 That day Pharaoh commanded the overseers of the people as well as their foremen: 7 "Don't continue to supply the people with straw for making bricks, as before. They must go and gather straw for themselves. 8 But require the same quota of bricks from them as they were making before; do not reduce it. For they are slackers—that is why they are crying out, 'Let us go and sacrifice to our God.' 9 Impose heavier work on the men. Then they will be occupied with it and not pay attention to deceptive words."

10 So the overseers and foremen of the people went out and said to them, "This is what Pharaoh says: 'I am not giving you straw. 11 Go get straw yourselves wherever you can find it, but there will be no reduction at all in your workload.'" 12 So the people scattered throughout the land of Egypt to gather stubble for straw. 13 The overseers insisted, "Finish your assigned work each day, just as ⌊you did⌋ when straw was ⌊provided⌋." 14 Then the Israelite foremen, whom Pharaoh's slave drivers had set over the people, were beaten and asked, "Why haven't you finished making your prescribed number of bricks yesterday or today, as ⌊you did⌋ before?"

15 So the Israelite foremen went in and cried for help to Pharaoh: "Why are you treating your servants this way? 16 No straw has been given to your servants, yet they say to us, 'Make bricks!' Look, your servants are being beaten, but it is your own people who are at fault."

17 But he said, "You are slackers. Slackers! That is why you are saying, 'Let us go sacrifice to the LORD.' 18 Now get to work. No straw will be given to you, but you must produce the same quantity of bricks."

19 The Israelite foremen saw that they were in trouble when they were told, "You cannot reduce your daily quota of bricks." 20 When they left Pharaoh, they confronted Moses and Aaron, who stood ⌊waiting⌋ to meet them.

21 "May the LORD take note of you and judge," they said to them, "because you have made us reek in front of Pharaoh and his officials—putting a sword in their hand to kill us!"

22 So Moses went back to the LORD and asked, "Lord, why have You caused trouble for this people? And why did You ever send me? 23 Ever since I went in to Pharaoh to speak in Your name he has caused trouble for this people, and You haven't delivered Your people at all." 1 But the LORD replied to Moses, "Now you are going to see what I will do to Pharaoh: he will let them go because of My strong hand; he will drive them out of his land because of My strong hand."

God Promises Freedom

2 Then God spoke to Moses, telling him, "I am •Yahweh. 3 I appeared to Abraham, Isaac, and Jacob as •God Almighty, but I did not make My name Yahweh known to them. 4 I also established My covenant with them to give them the land of Canaan, the land they lived in as foreigners. 5 Furthermore, I have heard the groaning of the Israelites, whom the Egyptians are forcing to work as slaves, and I have remembered My covenant.

6 "Therefore tell the Israelites: I am Yahweh, and I will deliver you from the forced labor of the Egyptians and free you from slavery to them. I will redeem you with an outstretched arm and great acts of judgment. 7 I will take you as My people, and I will be your God. You will know that I am Yahweh your God, who delivered you from the forced labor of the Egyptians. 8 I will bring you to the land that I swore[a] to give to Abraham, Isaac, and Jacob, and I will give it to you as a possession. I am the LORD." 9 Moses told this to the Israelites, but they did not listen to him because of their broken spirit and hard labor.

10 Then the LORD spoke to Moses, 11 "Go and tell Pharaoh king of Egypt to let the Israelites go from his land."

12 But Moses said in the LORD's presence: "If the Israelites will not listen to me, then how will Pharaoh listen to me, since I am such a poor speaker?"[b] 13 Then the LORD spoke to Moses and Aaron and gave them commands concerning both the Israelites and Pharaoh king of Egypt to bring the Israelites out of the land of Egypt.

Genealogy of Moses and Aaron

14 These are the heads of their fathers' families:

The sons of Reuben, the firstborn of Israel:
Hanoch and Pallu, Hezron and Carmi.
These are the clans of Reuben.

15 The sons of Simeon:
Jemuel, Jamin, Ohad, Jachin,
Zohar, and Shaul, the son
of a Canaanite woman.
These are the clans of Simeon.

16 These are the names of the sons of Levi
according to their genealogy:
Gershon, Kohath, and Merari.
Levi lived 137 years.

17 The sons of Gershon:

---

a 6:8 Lit raised My hand   b 6:12 Lit I have uncircumcised lips

---

bridegroom of blood. Zipporah was shocked and angry that God would require circumcision.

4:27 at the mountain of God. It's fitting that the brothers reunited where they would minister together later (19:1-25).

5:23 You haven't delivered Your people. Moses expected Pharaoh to let the Israelites go immediately, even though God had warned him otherwise (3:19; 4:21).

6:4-7 remembered My covenant. These words fulfilled the covenant to Abraham, that God would choose his descendants to be a nation special to Him (Gen. 17:7).

6:12 will not listen to me. Moses was facing exactly what he had feared (4:1). In fact, he had made matters worse. In addition, his bumbling conversation with Pharaoh proved his other previous argument that he could not speak well (4:11). In essence, he was telling God, "I told you so ..." This is repeated in verses 29-30, with God's answer in 7:1-5.

18 The sons of Kohath:
Amram, Izhar, Hebron, and Uzziel.
Kohath lived 133 years.
19 The sons of Merari:
Mahli and Mushi.
These are the clans of the Levites
according to their genealogy.
20 Amram married his father's sister Jochebed,
and she bore him Aaron and Moses.
Amram lived 137 years.
21 The sons of Izhar:
Korah, Nepheg, and Zichri.
22 The sons of Uzziel:
Mishael, Elzaphan, and Sithri.
23 Aaron married Elisheba,
daughter of Amminadab and sister of Nahshon.
She bore him Nadab and Abihu, Eleazar
and Ithamar.
24 The sons of Korah:
Assir, Elkanah, and Abiasaph.
These are the clans of the Korahites.
25 Aaron's son Eleazar married
one of the daughters of Putiel
and she bore him Phinehas.
These are the heads of the Levite families
by their clans.

26 It was this Aaron and Moses whom the LORD told, "Bring the Israelites out of the land of Egypt according to their divisions." 27 Moses and Aaron were the ones who spoke to Pharaoh king of Egypt in order to bring the Israelites out of Egypt.

Moses and Aaron before Pharaoh

28 On the day the LORD spoke to Moses in the land of Egypt, 29 He said to him, "I am the LORD; tell Pharaoh king of Egypt everything I am telling you."

30 But Moses replied in the LORD's presence, "Since I am such a poor speaker,ᵃ how will Pharaoh listen to me?"

7 The LORD answered Moses, "See, I have made you like God to Pharaoh, and Aaron your brother will be your prophet. 2 You must say whatever I command you; then Aaron your brother must declare it to Pharaoh so that he will let the Israelites go from his land. 3 But I will harden Pharaoh's heart and multiply My signs and wonders in the land of Egypt. 4 Pharaoh will not listen to you, but I will put My hand on Egypt and bring out the ranks of My people the Israelites, out of the land of Egypt by great acts of judgment. 5 The Egyptians will know that I am the LORD when I stretch

Heart Checkup

1. Have you ever seen a magician perform? Which tricks were you able to figure out?

Exodus 6:28–7:24

2. What did God mean when He told Moses, "I have made you like God to Pharaoh, and Aaron your brother will be your prophet" (v. 1)?

3. How do you think the "magicians of Egypt" accomplished the same miracles as Moses? How can Satan or the world sometimes imitate God's miracles?

4. What does it mean that "Pharaoh's heart hardened" (v. 22)?

5. When have you hardened your heart toward God? Is it hard or soft right now, and why?

out My hand against Egypt, and bring out the Israelites from among them."

6 So Moses and Aaron did ⌊this⌋; they did just as the LORD commanded them. 7 Moses was 80 years old and Aaron 83 when they spoke to Pharaoh.

8 The LORD said to Moses and Aaron, 9 "When Pharaoh tells you: Perform a miracle, tell Aaron: Take your staff and throw it down before Pharaoh. It will become a serpent." 10 So Moses and Aaron went in to Pharaoh and did just as the LORD had commanded. Aaron threw down his staff before Pharaoh and his officials, and it became a serpent. 11 But then Pharaoh called the wise men and sorcerers—the magicians of Egypt, and they also did the same thing by their occult practices. 12 Each one threw down his staff, and it became a serpent. But Aaron's staff swallowed their staffs. 13 However, Pharaoh's heart hardened, and he did not listen to them, as the LORD had said.

The First Plague: Water Turned to Blood

14 Then the LORD said to Moses, "Pharaoh is unresponsive: he refuses to let the people go. 15 Go to Pharaoh in the morning. When you see him walking out to the water, stand ready to meet him by the bank of the Nile. Take in your hand the staff that turned into a snake. 16 Tell him: The LORD, the God of the Hebrews, has sent me to tell you: Let My people go, so that they may worshipᵇ Me in the wilderness, but so far you have

---

ᵃ6:30 Lit I have uncircumcised lips   ᵇ7:16 Or serve; Ex 4:23

6:13 Moses and Aaron. To assuage Israelite doubts concerning their authority (5:21), a partial genealogy is given to establish that Moses and Aaron both came from the tribe of Levi (4:14).

7:3-4 I will harden. As in 4:21, Pharaoh's heart is hardened by God only after Pharaoh

hardened his own heart. Pharaoh's hardening would give God the opportunity to unleash miraculous signs and wonders upon the land.

7:5 the Egyptians will know. With the first nine plagues, God used supernatural forces of nature to bring judgment, but in the tenth God would personally bring judg-

ment upon Egypt.

7:11 occult practices. The wise men were learned counselors. Sorcerers practiced divination, which God condemned (Lev. 19:26). Magicians were thought to possess occult knowledge. They were able to duplicate Moses' and Aaron's miracle—something God

not listened. 17 This is what the LORD says: Here is how you will know that I am the LORD. Watch. I will strike the water in the Nile with the staff in my hand, and it will turn to blood. 18 The fish in the Nile will die, the river will stink, and the Egyptians will be unable to drink water from it."

19 So the LORD said to Moses, "Tell Aaron: Take your staff and stretch out your hand over the waters of Egypt—over their rivers, canals,ª ponds, and all their water reservoirs—and they will become blood. There will be blood throughout the land of Egypt, even in wooden and stone ⌊containers⌋."

20 Moses and Aaron did just as the LORD had commanded; in the sight of Pharaoh and his officials, he raised the staff and struck the water in the Nile, and all the water in the Nile was turned to blood. 21 The fish in the Nile died, and the river smelled so bad the Egyptians could not drink water from it. There was blood throughout the land of Egypt.

22 But the magicians of Egypt did the same thing by their occult practices. So Pharaoh's heart hardened, and he would not listen to them, as the LORD had said. 23 Pharaoh turned around, went into his palace, and didn't even take this to heart. 24 All the Egyptians dug around the Nile for water to drink because they could not drink the water from the river. 25 Seven days passed after the LORD struck the Nile.

The Second Plague: Frogs

8 b Then the LORD said to Moses, "Go in to Pharaoh and tell him: This is what the LORD says: Let My people go, so that they may worship Me. 2 But if you refuse to let them go, then I will plague all your territory with frogs. 3 The Nile will swarm with frogs; they will come up and go into your palace, into your bedroom and on your bed, into the houses of your officials and your people, and into your ovens and kneading bowls. 4 The frogs will come up on you, your people, and all your officials."

5c The LORD then said to Moses, "Tell Aaron: Stretch out your hand with your staff over the rivers, canals, and ponds, and cause the frogs to come up onto the land of Egypt." 6 When Aaron stretched out his hand over the waters of Egypt, the frogs came up and covered the land of Egypt. 7 But the magicians did the same thing by their occult practices and brought frogs up onto the land of Egypt.

8 Pharaoh summoned Moses and Aaron and said, "Ask the LORD that He remove the frogs from me and

my people. Then I will let the people go and they can sacrifice to the LORD."

9 Moses said to Pharaoh, "Make the choice rather than me ⌊by saying⌋ when I should ask for you, your officials, and your people, that the frogs be taken away from you and your houses, and remain only in the Nile."

10 "Tomorrow," he answered.

Moses replied, "As you have said, so you may know there is no one like the LORD our God, 11 the frogs will go away from you, your houses, your officials, and your people. The frogs will remain only in the Nile." 12 After Moses and Aaron went out from Pharaoh, Moses cried out to the LORD for help concerning the frogs that He had brought againstd Pharaoh. 13 The LORD did as Moses had said: the frogs in the houses, courtyards, and fields died. 14 They piled them in countless heaps, and there was a terrible odor in the land. 15 But when Pharaoh saw there was relief, he hardened his heart and would not listen to them, as the LORD had said.

The Third Plague: Gnats

16 Then the LORD said to Moses, "Tell Aaron: Stretch out your staff and strike the dust of the earth, and it will become gnatse throughout the land of Egypt." 17 And they did this. Aaron stretched out his hand with his staff, and when he struck the dust of the earth, gnats were on the people and animals. All the dust of the earth became gnats throughout the land of Egypt. 18 The magicians tried to produce gnats using their occult practices, but they could not. The gnats remained on the people and animals.

19 "This is the finger of God," the magicians said to Pharaoh. But Pharaoh's heart hardened, and he would not listen to them, as the LORD had said.

The Fourth Plague: Swarms of Flies

20 The LORD said to Moses, "Get up early in the morning and present yourself to Pharaoh when you see him going out to the water. Tell him: This is what the LORD says: Let My people go, so that they may worshipf Me. 21 But if you will not let My people go, then I will send swarms of fliesg against you, your officials, your people, and your houses. The Egyptians' houses will swarm with flies, and so will the land where they live.h 22 But on that day I will give special treatment to the land of Goshen, where My people are living; no flies will be there. This way you will know that I, the LORD, am in the land. 23 I will make a distinctioni between My

---

a7:19 The Hb word refers specifically to the various branches and canals of the Nile River; Ex 8:5.   b8:1 Ex 7:26 in Hb   c8:5 Ex 8:1 in Hb
d8:12 Or frogs, as he had agreed with   e8:16 Perhaps sand fleas or mosquitoes   f8:20 Or serve   g8:21 Or insects   h8:21 Lit are   i8:23 LXX, Syr, Vg; MT reads will place deliverance

---

had not prepared them for. However, occult power is very real. These men used either tricks or demonic power to duplicate this and two other miracles (v. 22; 8:7). Finally, even they would have to admit to a power greater than their own (8:18-19).

7:17-20 water in the Nile. The Egyptians

worshiped Hopi, the god of the Nile, who would kindly irrigate the fields when pleased. But even Hopi could not keep water, even water in wooden buckets and stone jars, from becoming blood at Moses' command.

7:24 dug around the Nile. Fouled water would have been safer for drinking after be-

ing flushed through the riverbank. After this God allowed some time between plagues for the Egyptians to reflect.

8:2 plague ... with frogs. Heqt, a frog goddess who allegedly helped women deliver babies, had no luck delivering from frogs.

8:7 the magicians did the same thing. Ap-

people and your people. This sign will take place tomorrow."

24 And the LORD did this. Thick swarms of flies went into Pharaoh's palace and his officials' houses. Throughout Egypt the land was ruined because of the swarms of flies. 25 Then Pharaoh summoned Moses and Aaron and said, "Go sacrifice to your God within the country."

26 But Moses said, "It would not be righta to do that, because what we will sacrifice to the LORD our God is detestable to the Egyptians. If we sacrifice what the Egyptians detest in front of them, won't they stone us? 27 We must go a distance of three days into the wilderness and sacrifice to the LORD our God as He instructs us."

28 Pharaoh responded, "I will let you go and sacrifice to the LORD your God in the wilderness, but don't go very far. Make an appeal for me."

29 "As soon as I leave you," Moses said, "I will appeal to the LORD, and tomorrow the swarms of flies will depart from Pharaoh, his officials, and his people. But Pharaoh must not act deceptively again by refusing to let the people go and sacrifice to the LORD." 30 Then Moses left Pharaoh's presence and appealed to the LORD. 31 The LORD did as Moses had said: He removed the swarms of flies from Pharaoh, his officials, and his people; not one was left. 32 But Pharaoh hardened his heart this time also and did not let the people go.

The Fifth Plague: Death of Livestock

9 Then the LORD said to Moses, "Go in to Pharaoh and say to him: This is what the LORD, the God of the Hebrews, says: Let My people go, so that they may worship Me. 2 But if you refuse to let ⌊them⌋ go and keep holding them, 3 then the LORD's hand will bring a severe plague against your livestock in the field—the horses, donkeys, camels, herds, and flocks. 4 But the LORD will make a distinction between the livestock of Israel and the livestock of Egypt, so that nothing of all that the Israelites own will die." 5 And the LORD set a time, saying, "Tomorrow the LORD will do this thing in the land." 6 The LORD did this the next day. All the Egyptian livestock died, but none among the Israelite livestock died. 7 Pharaoh sent ⌊messengers⌋ who saw that not a single one of the Israelite livestock was dead. But Pharaoh's heart was hardened, and he did not let the people go.

The Sixth Plague: Boils

8 Then the LORD said to Moses and Aaron, "Take handfuls of furnace soot, and Moses is to throw it toward heaven in the sight of Pharaoh. 9 It will become fine dust over the entire land of Egypt. It will become festering boils on people and animals throughout the land of Egypt." 10 So they took furnace soot and stood before Pharaoh. Moses threw it toward heaven, and it became festering boils on man and beast. 11 The magicians could not stand before Moses because of the boils, for the boils were on the magicians as well as on all the Egyptians. 12 But the LORD hardened Pharaoh's heart and he did not listen to them, as the LORD had told Moses.

The Seventh Plague: Hail

13 Then the LORD said to Moses, "Get up early in the morning and present yourself to Pharaoh. Tell him: This is what the LORD, the God of the Hebrews says: Let My people go, so that they may worship Me. 14 Otherwise, I am going to send all My plagues against you, your officials, and your people. Then you will know there is no one like Me in all the earth. 15 By now I could have stretched out My hand and struck you and your people with a plague, and you would have been obliterated from the earth. 16 However, I have let you live for this purpose: to show you My power and to make My name known in all the earth. 17 You are still acting arrogantly againstb My people by not letting them go. 18 Tomorrow at this time I will rain down the worst hail that has ever occurred in Egypt from the day it was founded until now. 19 Therefore give orders to bring your livestock and all that you have in the field into shelters. Every person and animal that is in the field and not brought inside will die when the hail falls on them." 20 Those among Pharaoh's officials who •feared the word of the LORD made their servants and livestock flee to shelters, 21 but those who didn't take the LORD's word seriously left their servants and livestock in the field.

22 Then the LORD said to Moses, "Stretch out your hand toward heaven and let there be hail throughout the land of Egypt—on man and beast and every plant of the field in the land of Egypt." 23 So Moses stretched out his staff toward heaven, and the LORD sent thunder and hail. Lightning struck the earth, and the LORD rained hail on the land of Egypt. 24 The hail, with lightning flashing through it, was so severe that nothing like it had occurred in the land of Egypt since it had become a nation. 25 Throughout the land of Egypt, the hail struck down everything in the field, both man and beast. The hail beat down every plant of the field and shattered every tree in the field. 26 The only place it

---

a8:26 Or allowable   b9:17 Or still obstructing

---

parently, they could duplicate the problem, but not reverse it. For that, Pharaoh had to call Moses and Aaron (v. 8).

8:19 finger of God. The magicians' powers stopped and they could no longer duplicate Moses' acts as before (v. 7; 7:11, 22).

9:3 plague against your livestock. The Egyptians worshiped a number of animal-headed gods including Apis and Mnevis (bull gods), Hathor (cow god) and Khnum (ram god). This plague revealed that their gods had no power to protect livestock.

9:8 handfuls of furnace soot. Just as Moses had struck dust to begin the plague of gnats (8:16), here he took soot and tossed it into the air in Pharaoh's presence to make God's point about the effects of this coming plague.

9:16 I have let you live for this very purpose. God is in complete control of all nations and leaders (Ps. 2). God had given Pharaoh

didn't hail was in the land of Goshen where the Israelites were.

27 Pharaoh sent for Moses and Aaron. "I have sinned this time," he said to them. "The LORD is the Righteous One, and I and my people are the guilty ones. 28 Make an appeal to the LORD. There has been enough of God's thunder and hail. I will let you go; you don't need to stay any longer."

29 Moses said to him, "When I have left the city, I will extend my hands to the LORD. The thunder will cease, and there will be no more hail, so that you may know the earth is the LORD's. 30 But as for you and your officials, I know that you still do not fear the LORD God."

31 The flax and the barley were destroyed because the barley was ripea and the flax was budding, 32 but the wheat and the spelt were not destroyed since they are later crops.b

33 Moses went out from Pharaoh and the city, and extended his hands to the LORD. Then the thunder and hail ceased, and rain no longer poured down on the land. 34 When Pharaoh saw that the rain, hail, and thunder had ceased, he sinned again and hardened his heart, he and his officials. 35 So Pharaoh's heart hardened, and he did not let the Israelites go, as the LORD had said through Moses.

The Eighth Plague: Locusts

10 Then the LORD said to Moses, "Go to Pharaoh, for I have hardened his heart and the hearts of his officials so that I may do these miraculous signs of Mine among them,c 2 and so that you may telld your son and grandson how severely I dealt with the Egyptians and performed miraculous signs among them, and you will know that I am the LORD."

3 So Moses and Aaron went in to Pharaoh and told him, "This is what the LORD, the God of the Hebrews, says: How long will you refuse to humble yourself before Me? Let My people go, that they may worship Me. 4 But if you refuse to let My people go, then tomorrow I will bring locusts into your territory. 5 They will cover the surface of the land so that no one will be able to see the land. They will eat the remainder left to you that escaped the hail; they will eat every tree you have growing in the fields. 6 They will fill your houses, all your officials' houses, and the houses of all the Egyptians—something your fathers and ancestors never saw since the time they occupied the land until today." Then he turned and left Pharaoh's presence.

7 Pharaoh's officials asked him, "How long must this man be a snare to us? Let the men go, so that they may worship the LORD their God. Don't you realize yet that Egypt is devastated?"

8 So Moses and Aaron were brought back to Pharaoh. "Go, worship the LORD your God," Pharaoh said. "But exactly who will be going?"

9 Moses replied, "We will go with our young and our old; we will go with our sons and daughters and with our flocks and herds because we must hold the LORD's festival."

10 He said to them, "May the LORD be with you if I ⌊ever⌋ let you and your families go!e Look out—you are planning evil. 11 No, only the men may go and worship the LORD, for that is what you have been asking for." And they were driven from Pharaoh's presence.

12 The LORD then said to Moses, "Stretch out your hand over the land of Egypt and the locusts will come up over it and eat every plant in the land, everything that the hail left." 13 So Moses stretched out his staff over the land of Egypt, and the LORD sent an east wind over the land all that day and through the night. By morning the east wind had brought in the locusts. 14 The locusts went up over the entire land of Egypt and settled on the whole territory of Egypt. Never before had there been such a large number of locusts, and there will never be again. 15 They covered the surface of the whole land so that the land was black, and they consumed all the plants on the ground and all the fruit on the trees that the hail had left. Nothing green was left on the trees or the plants in the field throughout the land of Egypt.

16 Pharaoh urgently sent for Moses and Aaron and said, "I have sinned against the LORD your God and against you. 17 Please forgive my sin once more and make an appeal to the LORD your God, so that He will take this death away from me." 18 Moses left Pharaoh's presence and appealed to the LORD. 19 Then the LORD changed the wind to a strong westf wind, and it carried off the locusts and blew them into the •Red Sea. Not a single locust was left in all the territory of Egypt. 20 But the LORD hardened Pharaoh's heart, and he did not let the Israelites go.

The Ninth Plague: Darkness

21 Then the LORD said to Moses, "Stretch out your hand toward heaven, and there will be darkness over the land of Egypt, a darkness that can be felt." 22 So Moses stretched out his hand toward heaven, and there was thick darkness throughout the land of Egypt for

---

a9:31 Lit was ears of grain   b9:32 Lit are late   c10:1 Lit Mine in his midst   d10:2 Lit tell in the ears of   e10:10 Pharaoh's reply is sarcastic.
f10:19 Lit sea

---

power in order to make His name known throughout the earth. Suitably, the Exodus miracle story spread far and wide. The people of Jericho had heard it and were frightened of the Israelites as a result (Josh. 2:8-12).

9:27 I have sinned this time. Pharaoh con-

fessed his sinfulness, but Moses knew better (v. 30). Nevertheless, Moses stopped the plague at Pharaoh's request. Unfortunately, Pharoah would take these words back in his stubbornness (v. 34).

10:7 Egypt is devastated. The devastation of their livestock and fields had already ru-

ined the nation; a locust plague would be completely devastating. The officials perceived what Pharaoh would not, but in his pride, he would not be convinced.

10:11 only the men may go. Pharaoh obviously feared that the Israelites were planning to escape slavery. So Pharaoh attempted to

three days. 23 One person could not see another, and for three days they did not move from where they were. Yet all the Israelites had light where they lived.

24 Pharaoh summoned Moses and said, "Go, worship the LORD. Even your families may go with you; only your flocks and your herds must stay behind."

25 Moses responded, "You must also let us havea sacrifices and •burnt offerings to prepare for the LORD our God. 26 Even our livestock must go with us; not a hoof will be left behind because we will take some of them to worship the LORD our God. We will not know what we will use to worship the LORD until we get there."

27 But the LORD hardened Pharaoh's heart, and he was unwilling to let them go. 28 Pharaoh said to him, "Leave me! Make sure you never see my face again, for on the day you see my face, you will die."

29 "As you've said," Moses replied, "I will never see your face again."

The Tenth Plague: Death of the Firstborn

11 The LORD saidb to Moses, "I will bring one more plague on Pharaoh and on Egypt. After that, he will let you go from here. When he lets ⌊you⌋ go,c he will drive you out of here. 2 Now announce to the people that both men and women should ask their neighbors for gold and silver jewelry." 3 The LORD gaved the people favor in the sight of the Egyptians. And the man Moses was fearede in the land of Egypt, byf Pharaoh's officials and the people.

4 So Moses said, "This is what the LORD says: 'About midnight I will go throughout Egypt 5 and every firstborn ⌊male⌋ in the land of Egypt will die, from the firstborn of Pharaoh who sits on his throne to the firstborn of the servant girl who is behind the millstones, as well as every firstborn of the livestock. 6 Then there will be a great cry of anguish through all the land of Egypt such as never was before, or ever will be again. 7 But against all the Israelites, whether man or beast, not ⌊even⌋ a dog will snarl,g so that you may know that the LORD makes a distinction between Egypt and Israel. 8 All these officials of yours will come down to me and bow before me, saying: Leave, you and all the people who follow you.h After that, I will leave.' " And he left Pharaoh's presence in fierce anger.

9 The LORD said to Moses, "Pharaoh will not listen to you, so that My wonders may be multiplied in the land of Egypt." 10 Moses and Aaron did all these wonders before Pharaoh, but the LORD hardened Pharaoh's heart, and he would not let the Israelites go out of his land.

The Passover

1. What's your favorite food for special meals or banquets?

Exodus 12:1-30

2. Why did God name this "the Passover" (v. 27)?
3. Why did God command the people to put blood on the doorposts of their houses? How did this symbol distinguish them from the Egyptians when God's judgment came?
4. How does the sacrifice of the lamb in this story compare with the Lamb of God in the New Testament?
5. In what way does Jesus' blood protect His people from God's judgment?

Instructions for the Passover

12 The LORD said to Moses and Aaron in the land of Egypt: 2 "This month is to be the beginning of months for you; it is the first month of your year. 3 Tell the whole community of Israel that on the tenth day of this month they must each select an animal of the flock according to ⌊their⌋ fathers' households, one animal per household. 4 If the household is too small for a ⌊whole⌋ animal, that person and the neighbor nearest his house are to select one based on the combined number of people; you should apportion the animal according to what each personi will eat. 5 You must have an unblemished animal, a year-old male; you may take it from either the sheep or the goats. 6 You are to keep it until the fourteenth day of this month; then the whole assembly of the community of Israel will slaughter the animals at twilight. 7 They must take some of the blood and put it on the two doorposts and the lintel of the houses in which they eat them. 8 They are to eat the meat that night; they should eat it, roasted over the fire along with unleavened bread and bitter herbs. 9 Do not eat any of it raw or cooked in boilingj water, but only roasted over fire—its head as well as its legs and inner organs. 10 Do not let any of it remain until morning; you must burn up any part of it that does remain until morning. 11 Here is how you must eat it: dressed

---

a**10:25** Lit *also give in our hand*   b**11:1** Or *had said*   c**11:1** Or *go, it will be finished*—   d**11:3** Or *had given*   e**11:3** Or *was very great*   f**11:3** Or *in the eyes of*   g**11:7** Lit *point its tongue*   h**11:8** Lit *people at your feet*   i**12:4** Or *household*   j**12:9** Or *or boiled at all in*

---

compromise by keeping the women and children behind to insure that the men would return.

10:21 darkness that can be felt. One of Egypt's chief gods was Ra, the sun god. The darkness ridiculed Ra, revealing his complete powerlessness to keep darkness from covering Egypt for three full days.

12:5 unblemished animal. The sacrificed lambs or goats had to be chosen from the best of the herd.

12:6-7 take some of the blood. The animal's blood was a visible sign that a sacrifice had taken place on behalf of each household, and

would be their only means of escaping the coming plague. Four days after selection, the lamb was to be killed and eaten.

12:8 bitter herbs. Eating bitter herbs found in Egypt would remind the Israelites of their years of bitter slavery every year when they sat down to eat the Passover meal (Num. 9:11).

for travel,[a] your sandals on your feet, and your staff in your hand. You are to eat it in a hurry; it is the LORD's •Passover.

12 "I will pass through the land of Egypt on that night and strike every firstborn ⌊male⌋ in the land of Egypt, both man and beast. I am the LORD; I will execute judgments against all the gods of Egypt. 13 The blood on the houses where you are staying will be a distinguishing mark for you; when I see the blood, I will pass over you. No plague will be among you to destroy ⌊you⌋ when I strike the land of Egypt.

14 "This day is to be a memorial for you, and you must celebrate it as a festival to the LORD. You are to celebrate it throughout your generations as a permanent statute. 15 You must eat unleavened bread for seven days. On the first day you must remove yeast from your houses. Whoever eats what is leavened from the first day through the seventh day must be cut off from Israel. 16 You are to hold a sacred assembly on the first day and another sacred assembly on the seventh day. No work may be done on those ⌊days⌋ except for preparing what people need to eat—you may do only that.

17 "You are to observe the ⌊Festival of⌋ •Unleavened Bread because on this very day I brought your ranks out of the land of Egypt. You must observe this day throughout your generations as a permanent statute. 18 You are to eat unleavened bread in the first ⌊month⌋, from the evening of the fourteenth day of the month until the evening of the twenty-first day. 19 Yeast must not be found in your houses for seven days. If anyone eats something leavened, that person, whether a foreign resident or native of the land, must be cut off from the community of Israel. 20 Do not eat anything leavened; eat unleavened bread in all your homes."[b]

21 Then Moses summoned all the elders of Israel and said to them, "Go, select an animal from the flock according to your families, and slaughter the Passover lamb. 22 Take a cluster of hyssop, dip it in the blood that is in the basin, and brush the lintel and the two doorposts with some of the blood in the basin. None of you may go out the door of his house until morning. 23 When the LORD passes through to strike Egypt and sees the blood on the lintel and the two doorposts, He will pass over the door and not let the destroyer enter your houses to strike ⌊you⌋.

24 "Keep this command permanently as a statute for you and your descendants. 25 When you enter the land that the LORD will give you as He promised, you are to observe this ritual. 26 When your children ask you, 'What does this ritual mean to you?' 27 you are to reply,

'It is the Passover sacrifice to the LORD, for He passed over the houses of the Israelites in Egypt when He struck the Egyptians and spared our homes.' " So the people bowed down and worshiped. 28 Then the Israelites went and did ⌊this⌋; they did just as the LORD had commanded Moses and Aaron.

The Exodus

29 Now at midnight the LORD struck every firstborn ⌊male⌋ in the land of Egypt, from the firstborn of Pharaoh who sat on his throne to the firstborn of the prisoner who was in the dungeon, and every firstborn of the livestock. 30 During the night Pharaoh got up, he along with all his officials and all the Egyptians, and there was a loud wailing throughout Egypt because there wasn't a house without someone dead. 31 He summoned Moses and Aaron during the night and said, "Get up, leave my people, both you and the Israelites, and go, worship the LORD as you have asked. 32 Take even your flocks and your herds as you asked, and leave, and this will also be a blessing to me."

33 Now the Egyptians pressured the people in order to send them quickly out of the country, for they said, "We're all going to die!" 34 So the people took their dough before it was leavened, with their kneading bowls wrapped up in their clothes on their shoulders.

35 The Israelites acted on Moses' word and asked the Egyptians for silver and gold jewelry and for clothing. 36 And the LORD gave the people such favor in the Egyptians' sight that they gave them what they requested. In this way they plundered the Egyptians.

37 The Israelites traveled from Rameses to Succoth, about 600,000 soldiers on foot, besides their families. 38 An ethnically diverse crowd also went up with them, along with a huge number of livestock, both flocks and herds. 39 The people baked the dough they had brought out of Egypt into unleavened loaves, since it had no yeast; for when they had been driven out of Egypt they could not delay and had not prepared any provisions for themselves.

40 The time that the Israelites lived in Egypt[c] was 430 years. 41 At the end of 430 years, on that same day, all the divisions of the LORD went out from the land of Egypt. 42 It was a night of vigil in honor of the LORD, because He would bring them out of the land of Egypt. This same night is in honor of the LORD, a night vigil for all the Israelites throughout their generations.

Passover Instruction

43 The LORD said to Moses and Aaron, "This is the statute of the Passover: no foreigner may eat it. 44 But

---

[a] 12:11 Lit it: with your loins girded   [b] 12:20 Or settlements   [c] 12:40 LXX, Sam add and in Canaan

---

12:11 eat it in a hurry. The phrase "eat and run" could have been coined for this meal. The Israelites were to be already dressed for their deliverance at hand. **the LORD's Passover.** God's messenger of death would only pass over the homes that had blood on the doorframes.

12:14 a permanent statute. The Last Supper was a Passover (Matt. 26:17-19). In this sense, so is communion (1 Cor. 11:20).

12:17 [Festival of] Unleavened Bread. This seven-day festival, beginning with the Passover meal, commemorated Israel's deliverance from Egypt (Matt. 26:17; Acts 12:3;

20:6). Unleavened bread had made on the night when the people had no time to wait for bread to rise.

12:22 Take a cluster of hyssop. Hyssop, a strongly scented flowering plant of the mint family found in Egypt and Palestine, was used to raise a sponge soaked in wine vinegar to

any slave a man has purchased may eat it, after you have circumcised him. ⁴⁵ A temporary resident or hired hand may not eat the Passover. ⁴⁶ It is to be eaten in one house. You may not take any of the meat outside the house, and you may not break any of its bones. ⁴⁷ The whole community of Israel must celebrateᵃ it. ⁴⁸ If a foreigner resides with you and wants to celebrate the LORD's Passover, every male in his household must be circumcised, and then he may participate;ᵇ he will become like a native of the land. But no uncircumcised person may eat it. ⁴⁹ The same law will apply to both the native and the foreigner who resides among you."

⁵⁰ Then all the Israelites did ⌊this⌋; they did just as the LORD had commanded Moses and Aaron. ⁵¹ On that same day the LORD brought the Israelites out of the land of Egypt according to their military divisions.

13 The LORD spoke to Moses: ² "Consecrate every firstborn male to Me, the firstborn from every womb among the Israelites, both man and animal; it is Mine."

³ Then Moses said to the people, "Remember this day when you came out of Egypt, out of the place of slavery, for the LORD brought you out of here by the strength of ⌊His⌋ hand. Nothing leavened may be eaten. ⁴ Today, in the month of Abib,ᶜ you are leaving. ⁵ When the LORD brings you into the land of the Canaanites, Hittites, Amorites, Hivites, and Jebusites,ᵈ which He swore to your fathers that He would give you, a land flowing with milk and honey, you must carry out this ritual in this month. ⁶ For seven days you must eat unleavened bread, and on the seventh day there is to be a festival to the LORD. ⁷ Unleavened bread is to be eaten for those seven days. Nothing leavened may be found among you, and no yeast may be found among you in all your territory. ⁸ On that day explain to your son, 'This is because of what the LORD did for me when I came out of Egypt.' ⁹ Let it serve as a sign for you on your hand and as a reminder on your forehead,ᵉ so that the law of the LORD may be in your mouth; for the LORD brought you out of Egypt with a strong hand. ¹⁰ Keep this statute at its appointed time from year to year.

¹¹ "When the LORD brings you into the land of the Canaanites, as He swore to you and your fathers, and gives it to you, ¹² you are to present to the LORD every firstborn male of the womb. All firstborn offspring of the livestock you own that are males will be the LORD's. ¹³ You must redeem every firstborn of a donkey with a flock animal, but if you do not redeem it, break its neck. However, you must redeem every firstborn among your sons.

¹⁴ "In the future, when your son asks you, 'What does this mean?' say to him, 'By the strength of ⌊His⌋ hand the LORD brought us out of Egypt, out of the place of slavery. ¹⁵ When Pharaoh stubbornly refused to let us go, the LORD killed every firstborn ⌊male⌋ in the land of Egypt, from the firstborn of man to the firstborn of livestock. That is why I sacrifice to the LORD all the firstborn of the womb that are males, but I redeem all the firstborn of my sons.' ¹⁶ So let it be a sign on your hand and a symbolᶠ on your forehead, for the LORD brought us out of Egypt by the strength of His hand."

The Route of the Exodus

¹⁷ When Pharaoh let the people go, God did not lead them along the road to the land of the Philistines, even though it was nearby; for God said, "The people will change their minds and return to Egypt if they face war." ¹⁸ So He led the people around toward the •Red Sea along the road of the wilderness. And the Israelites left the land of Egypt in battle formation.

¹⁹ Moses took the bones of Joseph with him, because Joseph had made the Israelites swear a solemn oath, saying, "God will certainly come to your aid; then you must take my bones with you from this place."

²⁰ They set out from Succoth and camped at Etham on the edge of the wilderness. ²¹ The LORD went ahead of them in a pillar of cloud to lead them on their way during the day and in a pillar of fire to give them light at night, so that they could travel day or night. ²² The pillar of cloud by day and the pillar of fire by night never left its place in front of the people.

14 Then the LORD spoke to Moses: ² "Tell the Israelites to turn back and camp in front of Pi-hahiroth, between Migdol and the sea; you must camp in front of Baal-zephon, facing it by the sea. ³ Pharaoh will say of the Israelites: They are wandering around the land in confusion; the wilderness has boxed them in. ⁴ I will harden Pharaoh's heart so that he will pursue them. Then I will receive glory by means of Pharaoh and all his army, and the Egyptians will know that I am the LORD." So the Israelites did this.

The Egyptian Pursuit

⁵ When the king of Egypt was told that the people had fled, Pharaoh and his officials changed their minds

---

ᵃ**12:47** Lit *do* ᵇ**12:48** Lit *may come near to do it* ᶜ**13:4** March–April; called Nisan in the post-exilic period; Neh 2:1; Est 3:7 ᵈ**13:5** DSS, Sam, LXX, Syr include *Girgashites* and *Perizzites*; Jos 3:10 ᵉ**13:9** Lit *reminder between your eyes* ᶠ**13:16** Or *phylactery*

Jesus' lips while he hung on the cross.

12:36 plundered the Egyptians. God had promised this (3:21; Gen. 15:14).

12:37 about 600,000. The count for men only, the actual number was around two million.

12:41 430 years. God had foretold this number of Israel's years in Egypt to Abraham (Gen. 15:13).

12:46 any of its bones. The Passover lamb was not to have any bones broken. At the crucifixion, a similar decision was made to avoid breaking any of Jesus' bones. The Apostle John considered this action a fulfillment of God's commandment (Ps. 34:20; John 19:36).

13:9 a reminder on your forehead. Some of the religious leaders in Jesus' day had taken this commandment literally by tying little boxes, called phylacteries with parchment inside, across their foreheads. Jesus con-

Survival Tactics

1. Have you ever been chased? What happened?

Exodus 14:5-31

2. What does it mean to "stand firm and see the LORD's salvation" (v. 13)?

3. What would it be like to be told, "The LORD will fight for you; you must be quiet" (v. 14), when your enemy is bearing down on top of you?

4. How are you doing with standing firm in the Lord?

5. In what area of your life do you need faith that the Lord will fight for you?

about the people and said: "What have we done? We have released Israel from serving us." 6 So he got his chariot ready and took his troops[a] with him; 7 he took 600 of the best chariots and all the rest of the chariots of Egypt, with officers in each one. 8 The LORD hardened the heart of Pharaoh king of Egypt, and he pursued the Israelites, who were going out triumphantly.[b] 9 The Egyptians—all Pharaoh's horses and chariots, his horsemen,[c] and his army—chased after them and caught up with them as they camped by the sea beside Pi-hahiroth, in front of Baal-zephon.

10 As Pharaoh approached, the Israelites looked up and saw the Egyptians coming after them. Then the Israelites were terrified and cried out to the LORD for help. 11 They said to Moses: "Is it because there are no graves in Egypt that you took us to die in the wilderness? What have you done to us by bringing us out of Egypt? 12 Isn't this what we told you in Egypt: Leave us alone so that we may serve the Egyptians? It would have been better for us to serve the Egyptians than to die in the wilderness."

13 But Moses said to the people, "Don't be afraid. Stand firm and see the LORD's salvation He will provide for you today; for the Egyptians you see today, you will never see again. 14 The LORD will fight for you; you must be quiet."

Escape through the Red Sea

15 The LORD said to Moses, "Why are you crying out to Me? Tell the Israelites to break camp. 16 As for you, lift up your staff, stretch out your hand over the sea, and divide it so that the Israelites can go through the sea on dry ground. 17 I am going to harden the hearts of the Egyptians so that they will go in after them, and I will receive glory by means of Pharaoh, all his army, and his chariots and horsemen. 18 The Egyptians will know that I am the LORD when I receive glory through Pharaoh, his chariots, and his horsemen."

19 Then the Angel of God, who was going in front of the Israelite forces, moved and went behind them. The pillar of cloud moved from in front of them and stood behind them. 20 It came between the Egyptian and Israelite forces. The cloud was there ⌊in⌋ the darkness, yet it lit up the night.[d] So neither group came near the other all night long.

21 Then Moses stretched out his hand over the sea. The LORD drove the sea ⌊back⌋ with a powerful east wind all that night and turned the sea into dry land. So the waters were divided, 22 and the Israelites went through the sea on dry ground, with the waters ⌊like⌋ a wall to them on their right and their left.

23 The Egyptians set out in pursuit—all Pharaoh's horses, his chariots, and his horsemen—and went into the sea after them. 24 Then during the morning watch, the LORD looked down on the Egyptian forces from the pillar of fire and cloud, and threw them into confusion. 25 He caused their chariot wheels to swerve[e] [f] and made them drive[g] with difficulty. "Let's get away from Israel," the Egyptians said, "because the LORD is fighting for them against Egypt!"

26 Then the LORD said to Moses, "Stretch out your hand over the sea so that the waters may come back on the Egyptians, on their chariots and horsemen." 27 So Moses stretched out his hand over the sea, and at daybreak the sea returned to its normal depth. While the Egyptians were trying to escape from it, the LORD overthrew them in the sea. 28 The waters came back and covered the chariots and horsemen, the entire army of Pharaoh, that had gone after them into the sea. None of them survived.

29 But the Israelites had walked through the sea on dry ground, with the waters ⌊like⌋ a wall to them on their right and their left. 30 That day the LORD saved Israel from the power of the Egyptians, and Israel saw the Egyptians dead on the seashore. 31 When Israel saw the great power that the LORD used against the Egyp-

---

[a]**14:6** Lit *people*   [b]**14:8** Lit *with a raised hand*   [c]**14:9** Or *chariot drivers*   [d]**14:20** Perhaps the cloud brought darkness to the Egyptians but light to the Israelites; Ex 10:22–23; Ps 105:39   [e]**14:25** Sam, LXX, Syr read *He bound their chariot wheels*   [f]**14:25** Or *fall off*   [g]**14:25** Or *and they drove them*

---

demned the act of enlarging the phylacteries for show (Matt. 23:5).

13:19 bones of Joseph. Joseph, a ruler in Egypt well before the Hebrews became slaves, believed that God would one day return his people to Canaan. He had requested that they take his bones with them (Gen.

50:24-25).

14:2 turn back. Like a commander, God misled the enemy (v. 3) and planned their destruction (v. 4).

14:14 The LORD will fight. Both the victory and the glory belonged to God. The people were to proceed in faith.

14:20 darkness, yet it lit up the night. The pillar of cloud, which cloaked God's presence, stood between His people and their enemies. The fire representing God's glory, hidden in the cloud for protection, shone through at night.

14:21 The LORD drove the sea [back]. Many

tians, the people •feared the LORD and believed in Him and in His servant Moses.

Israel's Song

15 Then Moses and the Israelites sang this song to the LORD. They said:

I will sing to the LORD,
for He is highly exalted;
He has thrown the horse
and its rider into the sea.
2 The LORD is my strength and my song;[a]
He has become my salvation.
This is my God, and I will praise Him,
my father's God, and I will exalt Him.
3 The LORD is a warrior;
•Yahweh is His name.

4 He threw Pharaoh's chariots
and his army into the sea;
the elite of his officers
were drowned in the •Red Sea.
5 The floods covered them;
they sank to the depths like a stone.
6 LORD, Your right hand is glorious in power.
LORD, Your right hand shattered the enemy.
7 You overthrew Your adversaries
by Your great majesty.
You unleashed Your burning wrath;
it consumed them like stubble.
8 The waters heaped up at the blast
of Your nostrils;
the currents stood firm like a dam.
The watery depths congealed in the heart
of the sea.
9 The enemy said:
"I will pursue, I will overtake,
I will divide the spoil.
My desire will be gratified at their expense.
I will draw my sword;
my hand will destroy[b] them."
10 But You blew with Your breath,
and the sea covered them.
They sank like lead
in the mighty waters.

11 LORD, who is like You among the gods?
Who is like You, glorious in holiness,
revered with praises, performing wonders?
12 You stretched out Your right hand,
and the earth swallowed them.

13 You will lead the people
You have redeemed
with Your faithful love;
You will guide ⌊them⌋ to Your holy dwelling
with Your strength.

14 When the peoples hear, they will shudder;
anguish will seize the inhabitants of Philistia.
15 Then the chiefs of Edom will be terrified;
trembling will seize the leaders of Moab;
the inhabitants of Canaan will panic;
16 and terror and dread will fall on them.
They will be as still[c] as a stone
because of Your powerful arm
until Your people pass by, LORD,
until the people whom You purchased[d] pass by.

17 You will bring them in and plant them
on the mountain of Your possession;
LORD, You have prepared the place
for Your dwelling;
Lord,[e] Your hands have established
the sanctuary.
18 The LORD will reign forever and ever!

19 When Pharaoh's horses with his chariots and horsemen went into the sea, the LORD brought the waters of the sea back over them. But the Israelites walked through the sea on dry ground. 20 Then Miriam the prophetess, Aaron's sister, took a tambourine in her hand, and all the women followed her with tambourines and dancing. 21 Miriam sang to them:

Sing to the LORD,
for He is highly exalted;
He has thrown the horse
and its rider into the sea.

Water Provided

22 Then Moses led Israel on from the Red Sea, and they went out to the Wilderness of Shur. They journeyed for three days in the wilderness without finding water. 23 They came to Marah, but they could not drink the water at Marah because it was bitter—that is why it was named Marah.[f] 24 The people grumbled to Moses, "What are we going to drink?" 25 So he cried out to the LORD, and the LORD showed him a tree. When he threw it into the water, the water became drinkable.

He made a statute and ordinance for them at Marah and He tested them there. 26 He said, "If you will carefully obey the LORD your God, do what is right in His

---

[a]**15:2** Or *might*　[b]**15:9** Or *conquer*　[c]**15:16** Or *silent*　[d]**15:16** Or *created*　[e]**15:17** Other Hb mss, DSS, Sam, Tg read *LORD*　[f]**15:23** = bitter, or bitterness

---

differing opinions make the exact location of this sea impossible to determine. Nonetheless, God controlled nature to produce a strong east wind to divide the waters and deliver His people. The Lord had used the east wind previously to bring in the locust plague (10:13).

14:25 the LORD is fighting. Even the Egyptian soldiers realized that God was fighting for the Israelites (v. 14). They panicked and fled as God showed His power, just as God predicted (v. 4).

15:1-18 The Hebrews' despair and fear (14:12) has turned to joy and confidence in

God. His name appears 10 times.

15:14-15 Philistia … Edom … Moab … Canaan. News of the miraculous deliverance at the Red Sea would travel along this route, as would the Israelites after they left Mount Sinai. As God predicted (9:16; 14:4), His glory among the nations increased.

eyes, pay attention to His commands, and keep all His statutes, I will not inflict any illness on you I inflicted on the Egyptians. For I am the LORD who heals you."

27 Then they came to Elim, where there were 12 springs of water and 70 date palms, and they camped there by the waters.

Manna and Quail Provided

16 The entire Israelite community departed from Elim and came to the Wilderness of Sin, which is between Elim and Sinai, on the fifteenth day of the second month after they had left the land of Egypt. 2 The entire Israelite community grumbled against Moses and Aaron in the wilderness. 3 The Israelites said to them, "If only we had died by the LORD's hand in the land of Egypt, when we sat by pots of meat and ate all the bread we wanted. Instead, you brought us into this wilderness to make this whole assembly die of hunger!"

4 Then the LORD said to Moses, "I am going to rain bread from heaven for you. The people are to go out each day and gather enough for that day. This way I will test them to see whether or not they will follow My instructions. 5 On the sixth day, when they prepare what they bring in, it will be twice as much as they gather on other days."ᵃ

6 So Moses and Aaron said to all the Israelites: "This evening you will know that it was the LORD who brought you out of the land of Egypt; 7 in the morning you will see the LORD's glory because He has heard your complaints about Him. For who are we that you complain about us?" 8 Moses continued, "The LORD will give you meat to eat this evening and abundant bread in the morning, for He has heard the complaints that you are raising against Him. Who are we? Your complaints are not against us but against the LORD."

9 Then Moses told Aaron, "Say to the entire Israelite community, 'Come before the LORD, for He has heard your complaints.'" 10 As Aaron was speaking to the entire Israelite community, they turned toward the wilderness, and there, in a cloud, the LORD's glory appeared.

11 The LORD spoke to Moses, 12 "I have heard the complaints of the Israelites. Tell them: At twilight you will eat meat, and in the morning you will eat bread until you are full. Then you will know that I am the LORD your God."

13 So at evening quail came and covered the camp. In the morning there was a layer of dew all around the camp. 14 When the layer of dew evaporated, there on the desert surface were fine flakes, as fine as frost on

Heavenly Food

1. What is the strangest thing you have ever eaten?

Exodus 16:1-35

2. Why did the Israelites start to complain? How accurate is their memory of life in Egypt?
3. Why was there no manna on the Sabbath day? Why did God command the people to rest on the Sabbath?
4. Notice the sins of the Israelites in this passage (vv. 2,20,27). What does this show you about human nature?
5. How are you like the Israelites in your own life? Which of God's commands are you having difficulty obeying?

the ground. 15 When the Israelites saw it, they asked one another, "What is it?" because they didn't know what it was.

Moses told them, "It is the bread the LORD has given you to eat. 16 This is what the LORD has commanded: 'Gather as much of it as each person needs to eat. You may take two quartsᵇ per individual, according to the number of people each of you has in his tent.'"

17 So the Israelites did this. Some gathered a lot, some a little. 18 When they measured it by quarts,ᶜ the person who gathered a lot had no surplus, and the person who gathered a little had no shortage. Each gathered as much as he needed to eat. 19 Moses said to them, "No one is to let any of it remain until morning." 20 But they didn't listen to Moses; some people left part of it until morning, and it bred worms and smelled. Therefore Moses was angry with them.

21 They gathered it every morning. Each gathered as much as he needed to eat, but when the sun grew hot, it melted. 22 On the sixth day they gathered twice as much food, four quartsᵈ apiece, and all the leaders of the community came and reported [this] to Moses. 23 He told them, "This is what the LORD has said: 'Tomorrow is a day of complete rest, a holy Sabbath to the LORD. Bake what you want to bake, and boil what you want to boil, and everything left over set aside to be kept until morning.'"

ᵃ**16:5** Lit as gathering day to day   ᵇ**16:16** Lit an omer   ᶜ**16:18** Lit by an omer   ᵈ**16:22** Lit two omers

---

15:21 Miriam. The sister of Moses and Aaron (2:4).

15:24 grumbled to Moses. Only three days into the journey, there was already discontent. The Israelites changed quickly from being joyful and trusting (vv. 1-18) to fearful and questioning. This pattern would

continue for many years.

15:25 He tested them. God did not give the Israelites water because they passed the test. He provided it, then took the opportunity (while His gift was fresh in their minds) to declare a test of their obedience.

16:4 gather enough for that day. The food

God provided would keep the Israelites alive. He would provide, but they would have to trust Him. The fact that they were to gather only enough for one day meant they were to trust God to provide daily.

16:13 quail came. The meat that the Lord had promised arrived right on schedule. Later

24 So they set it aside until morning as Moses commanded, and it didn't smell or have any maggots in it. 25 "Eat it today," Moses said, "because today is a Sabbath to the LORD. Today you won't find any in the field. 26 For six days you may gather it, but on the seventh day, the Sabbath, there will be none."

27 Yet on the seventh day some of the people went out to gather, but they did not find any. 28 Then the LORD said to Moses, "How long will youa refuse to keep My commands and instructions? 29 Understand that the LORD has given you the Sabbath; therefore on the sixth day He will give you two days' worth of bread. Each of you stay where you are; no one is to leave his place on the seventh day." 30 So the people rested on the seventh day.

31 The house of Israel named the substance manna.b It resembled coriander seed, was white, and tasted like wafers ⌊made⌋ with honey. 32 Moses said, "This is what the LORD has commanded: 'Two quartsc of it are to be preserved throughout your generations, so that they may see the bread I fed you in the wilderness when I brought you out of the land of Egypt.' "

33 Moses told Aaron, "Take a container and put two quartsd of manna in it. Then place it before the LORD to be preserved throughout your generations." 34 As the LORD commanded Moses, Aaron placed it before the •testimony to be preserved.

35 The Israelites ate manna for 40 years, until they came to an inhabited land. They ate manna until they reached the border of the land of Canaan. 36 (Two quartse are a tenth of an ephah.)

Water from the Rock

17 The entire Israelite community left the Wilderness of Sin, moving from one place to the next according to the LORD's command. They camped at Rephidim, but there was no water for the people to drink. 2 So the people complained to Moses: "Give us water to drink."

"Why are you complaining to me?" Moses replied to them. "Why are you testing the LORD?"

3 But the people thirsted there for water, and grumbled against Moses. They said, "Why did you ever bring us out of Egypt to kill us and our children and our livestock with thirst?"

4 Then Moses cried out to the LORD, "What should I do with these people? In a little while they will stone me!"

5 The LORD answered Moses, "Go on ahead of the people and take some of the elders of Israel with you. Take the rod you struck the Nile with in your hand and go. 6 I am going to stand there in front of you on the rock at Horeb; when you hit the rock, water will come out of it and the people will drink." Moses did this in the sight of the elders of Israel. 7 He named the place Massahf and Meribahg because the Israelites complained, and because they tested the LORD, saying, "Is the LORD among us or not?"

The Amalekites Attack

8 At Rephidim, Amalekh came and fought against Israel. 9 Moses said to Joshua, "Select some men for us, and go fight against Amalek. Tomorrow I will stand on the hilltop with God's staff in my hand."

10 Joshua did as Moses had told him, and fought against Amalek, while Moses, Aaron, and Hur went up to the top of the hill. 11 While Moses held up his hand,i Israel prevailed, but whenever he put his handi down, Amalek prevailed. 12 When Moses' hands grew heavy, they took a stone and put ⌊it⌋ under him, and he sat down on it. Then Aaron and Hur supported his hands, one on one side and one on the other so that his hands remained steady until the sun went down. 13 So Joshua defeated Amalek and his armyj with the sword.

14 The LORD then said to Moses, "Write this down on a scroll as a reminder and recite it to Joshua: I will completely blot out the memory of Amalek under heaven."

15 And Moses built an altar and named it, "The LORD Is My Banner."k 16 He said, "Indeed, ⌊my⌋ hand is ⌊lifted up⌋ towardl the LORD's throne. The LORD will be at war with Amalek from generation to generation."

Jethro's Visit

18 Moses' father-in-law Jethro, the priest of Midian, heard about everything that God had done for Moses and His people Israel, and how the LORD had brought Israel out of Egypt.

2 Now Jethro, Moses' father-in-law, had taken in Zipporah, Moses' wife, after he had sent her back, 3 along with her two sons, one of whom was named Gershom (because Moses had said, "I have been a stranger in a foreign land")m 4 and the other Eliezer (because ⌊he had said,⌋ "The God of my father was my helper and delivered me from Pharaoh's sword").n

5 Moses' father-in-law Jethro, along with Moses' wife and sons, came to him in the wilderness where he was camped at the mountain of God. 6 He sent word to

a16:28 In Hb you is pl, referring to the whole nation.   b16:31 = What?; Ex 16:15   c16:32 Lit A full omer   d16:33 Lit a full omer   e16:36 Lit The omer is   f17:7 = testing   g17:7 = arguing   h17:8 A semi-nomadic people descended from Amalek, a grandson of Esau; Gn 36:12   i17:11 Sam, LXX, Syr, Tg, Vg read hands   j17:13 Or people   k17:15 Or Yahweh-nissi   l17:16 Or hand was on, or hand was against; Hb obscure   m18:3 The name Gershom sounds like Hb "a stranger there"   n18:4 = My God Is Help

in the journey God provided quail once again, but with less satisfying results (Num. 11:31-34).

16:14 flakes, as fine as frost. Like the quail, this food came from God in an unexpected way. It came with the dew, appeared when the dew evaporated and melted in the sun.

16:23 a day of complete rest. This is the first occurrence of the word "Sabbath" in Scripture. However, the idea of a seventh day of rest and holiness is presented in the creation account (Gen. 2:2).

16:34 placed it before the testimony. A jar of manna was placed in the ark with the 10

commandments (31:18).

17:4 Moses cried out to the LORD. Previously, the people had complained that Moses meant for them to starve (16:3). Here they grumbled that Moses meant for them to die of thirst even though God had always met their needs (15:23-25). Since they were ready to

your father-in-law Jethro, am coming to you
wife and her two sons."

So Moses went out to meet his father-in-law,
bowed down, and then kissed him. They asked each
other how they had been[a] and went into the tent.
8 Moses recounted to his father-in-law all that the LORD
had done to Pharaoh and the Egyptians for Israel's sake,
all the hardships that confronted them on the way, and
how the LORD delivered them.

9 Jethro rejoiced over all the good things the LORD
had done for Israel when He rescued them from the
Egyptians. 10 "Blessed is the LORD," Jethro exclaimed,
"who rescued you from Pharaoh and the power of the
Egyptians, and snatched the people from the power of
the Egyptians. 11 Now I know that the LORD is greater
than all gods, because He ⌊did wonders⌋ at the time the
Egyptians acted arrogantly against Israel."[b]

12 Then Jethro, Moses' father-in-law, brought a
•burnt offering and sacrifices to God, and Aaron came
with all the elders of Israel to eat a meal with Moses'
father-in-law in God's presence.

13 The next day Moses sat down to judge the people,
and they stood around Moses from morning until
evening. 14 When Moses' father-in-law saw everything
he was doing for them he asked, "What is this thing
you're doing for the people? Why are you alone sitting
as judge, while all the people stand around you from
morning until evening?"

15 Moses replied to his father-in-law, "Because the
people come to me to inquire of God. 16 Whenever they
have a dispute, it comes to me, and I make a decision
between one man and another. I teach ⌊them⌋ God's
statutes and laws."

17 "What you're doing is not good," Moses' father-in-
law said to him. 18 "You will certainly wear out both
yourself and these people who are with you, because
the task is too heavy for you. You can't do it alone.
19 Now listen to me; I will give you some advice, and
God be with you. You be the one to represent the people before God and bring their cases to Him. 20 Instruct
them about the statutes and laws, and teach them the
way to live and what they must do. 21 But you should
select from all the people able men, God-fearing, trustworthy, and hating bribes. Place ⌊them⌋ over the people
as officials of thousands, hundreds, fifties, and tens.
22 They should judge the people at all times. Then they
can bring you every important case but judge every
minor case themselves. In this way you will lighten
your load,[c] and they will bear ⌊it⌋ with you. 23 If you do
this, and God ⌊so⌋ directs you, you will be able to

endure, and also all these people will be able to go
home satisfied."[d]

24 Moses listened to his father-in-law and did everything he said. 25 So Moses chose able men from all
Israel and made them leaders over the people ⌊as⌋ officials of thousands, hundreds, fifties, and tens. 26 They
judged the people at all times; the hard cases they
would bring to Moses, but every minor case they would
judge themselves.

27 Then Moses said goodbye to his father-in-law, and
he journeyed to his own land.

Israel at Sinai

19 In the third month, on the same day ⌊of the
month⌋ that the Israelites had left the land of
Egypt, they entered the Wilderness of Sinai. 2 After
they departed from Rephidim, they entered the Wilderness of Sinai and camped in the wilderness, and
Israel camped there in front of the mountain.

3 Moses went up ⌊the mountain⌋ to God, and the
LORD called to him from the mountain: "This is what
you must say to the house of Jacob, and explain to the
Israelites: 4 You have seen what I did to the Egyptians
and how I carried you on eagles' wings and brought you
to Me. 5 Now if you will listen to Me and carefully keep
My covenant, you will be My own possession out of all
the peoples, although all the earth is Mine, 6 and you
will be My kingdom of priests and My holy nation.
These are the words that you are to say to the Israelites."

7 After Moses came back, He summoned the elders
of the people, and put before them all these words that
the LORD had commanded him. 8 Then all the people
responded together, "We will do all that the LORD has
spoken." So Moses brought the people's words back to
the LORD.

9 The LORD said to Moses, "I am going to come to you
in a dense cloud, so that the people will hear when I
speak with you and will always believe you." Then
Moses reported the people's words to the LORD. 10 And
the LORD told Moses, "Go to the people and purify them
today and tomorrow. They must wash their clothes
11 and be prepared by the third day, for on the third day
the LORD will come down on Mount Sinai in the sight
of all the people. 12 Put boundaries for the people all
around the ⌊mountain⌋ and say: Be careful that you
don't go up on the mountain or touch its base. Anyone
who touches the mountain will be put to death. 13 No
hand may touch him; instead he will be stoned or shot
⌊with arrows⌋, neither animal or man will live. When

---

a **18:7** Lit other about well-being   b **18:11** Hb obscure   c **18:22** Lit lighten from on you   d **18:23** Lit go to their place in peace

---

kill him, Moses referred to them as "these
people" instead of "My people."

17:7 Massah and Meribah. Psalm 95:7-8
and Hebrews 3:7-8,15 refer to the events of
verses 1-7. The names "Massah" (testing)
and "Meribah" (arguing) carry ominous connotations and are reminders of the Israelites'

lack of faith and obedience.
17:9 Joshua. Picking a man of wisdom (Deut.
34:9) with military prowess demonstrated
Moses' ability to pick the right man, as the
conquest of Canaan 40 years later would
show.
18:11 Now I know. God's victory over the

Egyptians brought Him glory as He predicted
(14:4). Whether Jethro was a true convert or
simply a well-meaning Midianite priest is not
explained. Some Samaritans had a similar response to Jesus (John 4:42).

18:16 God's statutes and laws. Moses' authority by divine sanction extended to even

The Ten Commandments

1. What is your coach's favorite "command-ment"? What rule does he or she repeat often? Do you follow it?

Exodus 19:10-20:21

2. What are some idols or false gods seen today? How can we avoid "bowing down" to them?
3. What does it mean to "misuse the name of the LORD your God" (20:7)?
4. What does it mean to "honor your father and your mother" (20:12)?
5. What does it mean to "covet your neighbor's house" and possessions (20:17)?
6. Which commandments do you need to work on most in your home life? Your athletic life?

the ram's horn sounds a long blast, they may go up the mountain."

14 Then Moses came down from the mountain to the people and consecrated them, and they washed their clothes. 15 He said to the people, "Be prepared by the third day. Do not have sexual relations with women."

16 On the third day, when morning came, there was thunder and lightning, a thick cloud on the mountain, and a loud trumpet sound, so that all the people in the camp shuddered. 17 Then Moses brought the people out of the camp to meet God, and they stood at the foot of the mountain. 18 Mount Sinai was completely envel-oped in smoke because the LORD came down on it in fire. Its smoke went up like the smoke of a furnace, and the whole mountain shook violently. 19 As the sound of the trumpet grew louder and louder, Moses spoke and God answered him in the thunder.

20 The LORD came down on Mount Sinai, at the top of the mountain. Then the LORD summoned Moses to the top of the mountain, and he went up. 21 The LORD directed Moses, "Go down and warn the people not to break through to see the LORD; otherwise many of them will die. 22 Even the priests who come near the LORD must purify themselves or the LORD will break out ⌊in anger⌋ against them."

23 But Moses responded to the LORD, "The people cannot come up Mount Sinai, since You warned us: Put a boundary around the mountain and consider it holy." 24 And the LORD replied to him, "Go down and come back with Aaron. But the priests and the people must not break through to come up to the LORD, or He will break out ⌊in anger⌋ against them." 25 So Moses went down to the people and told them.

The Ten Commandments

20 Then God spoke all these words:

2 I am the LORD your God, who brought you out of the land of Egypt, out of the place of slavery.

3 Do not have other gods besides Me.

4 Do not make an idol for yourself, whether in the shape of anything in the heavens above or on the earth below or in the waters under the earth. 5 You must not bow down to them or wor-ship them; for I, the LORD your God, am a jeal-ous God, punishing the children for the fathers' sin, to the third and fourth ⌊generations⌋ of those who hate Me, 6 but showing faithful love to a thousand ⌊generations⌋ of those who love Me and keep My commands.

7 Do not misuse the name of the LORD your God, because the LORD will punish anyone who mis-uses His name.

8 Remember to dedicate the Sabbath day: 9 You are to labor six days and do all your work, 10 but the seventh day is a Sabbath to the LORD your God. You must not do any work—you, your son or daughter, your male or female slave, your livestock, or the foreigner who is within your gates. 11 For the LORD made the heavens and the earth, the sea, and everything in them in six days; then He rested on the sev-enth day. Therefore the LORD blessed the Sab-bath day and declared it holy.

12 Honor your father and your mother so that you may have a long life in the land that the LORD your God is giving you.

13 Do not murder.

14 Do not commit adultery.

15 Do not steal.

16 Do not give false testimony against your neigh-bor.

17 Do not covet your neighbor's house. Do not covet your neighbor's wife, his male or female slave, his ox or donkey, or anything that belongs to your neighbor.

practical matters.

19:4 eagles' wings. The strength and maj-esty of the eagle is used as a recurring image of God in His role as Savior to those who "trust in the LORD." (Isaiah 40:31).

19:5 listen to Me and carefully keep My

covenant. God made a covenant with Israel at Mount Sinai based on obedience. This cov-enant was an extension of the one made with Abraham hundreds of years before. Accord-ing to the covenant, Israel's obedience would result in being favored by God and given a special role in His kingdom.

19:15 sexual relations. This was a tempo-rary abstinence so that they would be ritually clean, since sexual discharges made one un-clean (Lev. 15:18).

20:7 name of the LORD. Making an oath us-ing the name of God and then failing to keep it (22:10,11; Lev. 19:12) was to question His

The People's Reaction

18 All the people witnessed[a] the thunder and lightning, the sound of the trumpet, and the mountain ⌊surrounded by⌋ smoke. When the people saw ⌊it⌋[b] they trembled and stood at a distance. 19 "You speak to us, and we will listen," they said to Moses, "but don't let God speak to us, or we will die."

20 Moses responded to the people, "Don't be afraid, for God has come to test you, so that you will •fear Him and will not[c] sin." 21 And the people remained standing at a distance as Moses approached the thick darkness where God was.

Moses Receives Additional Laws

22 Then the LORD told Moses, "This is what you are to say to the Israelites: You have seen that I have spoken to you from heaven. 23 You must not make gods of silver to rival Me; you must not make ⌊gods of gold⌋ for yourselves.[d]

24 "You must make an earthen altar for Me and sacrifice on it your •burnt offerings and •fellowship offerings, your sheep and goats, as well as your cattle. I will come to you and bless you in every place where I cause My name to be remembered. 25 If you make a stone altar for Me, you must not build it out of cut stones. If you use your chisel on it, you will defile it. 26 You must not go up to My altar on steps, so that your nakedness is not exposed on it.

21 "These are the ordinances that you must set before them:

Laws about Slaves

2 "When you buy a Hebrew slave, he is to serve for six years; then in the seventh he is to leave as a free man[e] without paying anything. 3 If he arrives alone, he is to leave alone; if he arrives with[f] a wife, his wife is to leave with him. 4 If his master gives him a wife and she bears him sons or daughters, the wife and her children belong to her master, and the man must leave alone.

5 "But if the slave declares: 'I love my master, my wife, and my children; I do not want to leave as a free man,' 6 his master is to bring him to the judges[g] and then bring him to the door or doorpost. His master must pierce his ear with an awl, and he will serve his master for life.

7 "When a man sells his daughter as a slave,[h] she is not to leave as the male slaves do. 8 If she is displeasing to her master, who chose her for himself, then he must let her be redeemed. He has no right to sell her to foreigners because he has acted treacherously toward her. 9 Or if he chooses her for his son, he must deal with her according to the customary treatment of daughters. 10 If he takes an additional wife, he must not reduce the food, clothing, or marital rights of the first wife. 11 And if he does not do these three things for her, she may leave free of charge, without any exchange of money.[i]

Laws about Personal Injury

12 "Whoever strikes a person so that he dies must be put to death. 13 But if he didn't intend any harm,[j] and yet God caused it to happen by his hand, I will appoint a place for you where he may flee. 14 If a person willfully[k] acts against his neighbor to murder him by scheming, you must take him from My altar to be put to death.

15 "Whoever strikes his father or his mother must be put to death.

16 "Whoever kidnaps a person must be put to death, whether he sells him or the person is found in his possession.

17 "Whoever curses his father or his mother must be put to death.

18 "When men quarrel and one strikes the other with a stone or fist, and the injured man does not die but is confined to bed, 19 if he can ⌊later⌋ get up and walk around outside ⌊leaning⌋ on his staff, then the one who struck ⌊him⌋ will be exempt from punishment. Nevertheless, he must pay for his lost work time[l] and provide for ⌊his⌋ complete recovery.

20 "When a man strikes his male or female slave with a rod, and the slave dies under his abuse,[m] the owner must be punished.[n] 21 However, if the slave can stand up after a day or two, the owner should not be punished[o] because he is his ⌊owner's⌋ property.[p]

22 "When men get in a fight, and hit a pregnant woman so that her children are born ⌊prematurely⌋,[q] but there is no injury, the one who hit her must be fined as the woman's husband demands from him, and he must pay according to judicial assessment. 23 If there is an injury, then you must give life for life, 24 eye for eye, tooth for tooth, hand for hand, foot for foot, 25 burn for burn, bruise for bruise, wound for wound.

26 "When a man strikes the eye of his male or female slave and destroys it, he must let the slave go free in compensation for his eye. 27 If he knocks out the tooth of his male or female slave, he must let the slave go free in compensation for his tooth.

---

[a] **20:18** Lit *saw*   [b] **20:18** Sam, LXX, Syr, Tg, Vg read *smoking; the people* (or *they*) *were afraid*   [c] **20:20** Lit *that the fear of Him may be in you, and you do not*   [d] **20:23** Hb obscure   [e] **21:2** Lit *to go forth*   [f] **21:3** Lit *he is the husband of*   [g] **21:6** Or *to God;* that is, to His sanctuary or court   [h] **21:7** Or *concubine*   [i] **21:11** Without paying a redemption price for her   [j] **21:13** Lit *he was not lying in wait*   [k] **21:14** Or *maliciously*   [l] **21:19** Lit *his inactivity*   [m] **21:20** Lit *hand*   [n] **21:20** Or *must suffer vengeance*   [o] **21:21** Or *not suffer vengeance*   [p] **21:21** Lit *money*   [q] **21:22** Either a live birth or a miscarriage

---

existence. God's name is holy and should never be used to suit our own needs.

20:8 Remember to dedicate the Sabbath day. God had rested on the seventh day of creation. He commanded that all work stop so that everyone, including servants, could participate in a day of rest and renewal.

20:12 Honor your father and your mother. After defining the proper relationship between people (vv. 2–11), the Law declares that Israelite sons and daughters are to treat their parents with adoration, respect, and obedience—exactly what He demanded of parents themselves in their relationship with Him.

21:2 Hebrew slave. Voluntary slavery was a way to work out of debt. Servitude was never perpetual, except by the slave's own choice (v. 6). The period of seven years is still a part of modern bankruptcy law.

21:12-14 didn't intend ... willfully acts. Murder (intentional killing) was an evil act (20:13).

28 "When an ox[a] gores a man or a woman to death, the ox must be stoned, and its meat may not be eaten, but the ox's owner is innocent. 29 However, if the ox was in the habit of goring, and its owner has been warned yet does not restrain it, and it kills a man or a woman, the ox must be stoned, and its owner must also be put to death. 30 If instead a ransom is demanded of him, he can pay a redemption price for his life in the full amount demanded from him. 31 If it gores a son or a daughter, he is to be dealt with according to this same law. 32 If the ox gores a male or female slave, he must give 30 •shekels of silver[b] to the slave's master, and the ox must be stoned.

33 "When a man uncovers a pit or digs a pit, and does not cover it, and an ox or a donkey falls into it, 34 the owner of the pit must give compensation; he must pay money to its owner, but the dead animal will become his.

35 "When a man's ox injures his neighbor's ox and it dies, they must sell the live ox and divide its proceeds; they must also divide the dead animal. 36 If, however, it is known that the ox was in the habit of goring, yet its owner has not restrained it, he must compensate fully, ox for ox; the dead animal will become his.

Laws about Theft

22 c "When a man steals an ox or a sheep[d] and butchers it or sells it, he must repay five cattle for the ox or four sheep for the sheep. 2e If a thief is caught in the act of breaking in, and he is beaten to death, no one is guilty of bloodshed. 3 But if this happens after sunrise,[f] there is guilt of bloodshed. A thief must make full restitution. If he is unable, he is to be sold because of his theft. 4 If what was stolen—whether ox, donkey, or sheep—is actually found alive in his possession, he must repay double.

Laws about Crop Protection

5 "When a man lets a field or vineyard be grazed in, and then allows his animals to go and graze in someone else's field, he must repay[g] with the best of his own field or vineyard.

6 "When a fire gets out of control, spreads to thornbushes, and consumes stacks of cut grain, standing grain, or a field, the one who started the fire must make full restitution for what was burned.

Laws about Personal Property

7 "When a man gives his neighbor money or goods to keep, but they are stolen from that person's house, the thief, if caught, must repay double. 8 If the thief is not caught, the owner of the house must present himself to the judges[h] to determine[i] whether or not he has taken his neighbor's property. 9 In any case of wrongdoing involving an ox, a donkey, a sheep, a garment, or anything [else] lost, and someone claims: That's mine,[j] the case between the two parties is to come before the judges.[k] The one the judges condemn[l] must repay double to his neighbor.

10 "When a man gives his neighbor a donkey, an ox, a sheep, or any [other] animal to care for, but it dies, is injured, or is stolen, while no one is watching, 11 there must be an oath before the LORD between the two of them to determine whether or not he has taken his neighbor's property. Its owner must accept [the oath],[i] and the other man does not have to make restitution. 12 But if, in fact, the animal was stolen from his custody, he must make restitution to its owner. 13 If it was actually torn apart [by a wild animal], he is to bring it as evidence; he does not have to make restitution for the torn carcass.

14 "When a man borrows [an animal] from his neighbor, and it is injured or dies while its owner is not there with it, the man must make full restitution. 15 If its owner is there with it, the man does not have to make restitution. If it was rented, the loss is covered by[m] its rental price.

Laws about Seduction

16 "When a man seduces a virgin who was not promised in marriage, and he has sexual relations with her, he must certainly pay the bridal price for her to be his wife. 17 If her father absolutely refuses to give her to him, he must pay an amount in silver equal to the bridal price for virgins.

Capital Offenses

18 "You must not allow a sorceress to live.

19 "Whoever has sexual intercourse with an animal must be put to death.

20 "Whoever sacrifices to any gods, except the LORD alone, is to be •set apart for destruction.

Laws Protecting the Vulnerable

21 "You must not exploit a foreign resident or oppress him, since you were foreigners in the land of Egypt.

22 "You must not mistreat any widow or fatherless child. 23 If you do mistreat them, they will no doubt cry

---

a21:28 Or a bull, or a steer   b21:32 About 1 pound of silver   c22:1 Ex 21:37 in Hb   d22:1 The Hb word can refer to sheep or goats.
e22:2 Ex 22:1 in Hb   f22:3 Lit if the sun has risen over him   g22:5 LXX adds from his field according to its produce. But if someone lets his animals graze an entire field, he must repay; DSS, Sam also support this reading.   h22:8 Or to God   i22:8 LXX, Tg, Vg read swear   j22:9 Lit That is it
k22:9 Or before God   l22:9 Or one whom God condemns   m22:15 Lit rented, it comes with

---

Accidental manslaughter was terrible, but the punishment was not as severe and allowed for escape to a city of refuge (Num. 35:9-34).

21:23 injury. This fact weakens the case for rigid application of the law of retaliation; a person killing mother and child would have only one life to give up as punishment.

21:23-24 life for life, eye for eye. The punishment should fit the crime—not put out people's eyes. By contrast, in Hammurabi's law code, a person of low class who injured one of high class was to be put to death.

21:32 30 shekels of silver. The price had gone up since Joseph was sold for twenty

shekels 400 years earlier (Gen. 37:28). Judas' payment to betray Jesus was 30 shekels (Matt. 26:14; cf. Jer. 32:6-9) or four month's wages, still a princely sum in New Testament times. Yet, Judas assumed the price of slave compensation for Jesus was preferable to the cost of discipleship to Jesus. It wasn't the first time

will certainly hear their cry. 24 My anger ... and I will kill you with the sword; then your ... will be widows and your children fatherless.

25 "If you lend money to My people—to the poor person among you, you must not be like a moneylender to him; you must not charge him interest.

26 "If you ever take your neighbor's cloak as collateral, return it to him before sunset. 27 For it is his only covering; it is the clothing for his body.a What will he sleep in? And if he cries out to Me, I will listen because I am compassionate.

Respect for God

28 "You must not blaspheme Godb or curse a leader among your people.

29 "You must not hold back ⌊offerings from⌋ your harvest or your vats. Give Me the firstborn of your sons. 30 Do the same with your cattle and your flock. Let them stay with their mothers for seven days, but on the eighth day you are to give them to Me.

31 "Be My holy people. You must not eat the meat of a mauled animal ⌊found⌋ in the field; throw it to the dogs.

Laws about Honesty and Justice

23 "You must not spread a false report. Do not joinc the wicked to be a malicious witness. 2 "You must not follow a crowd in wrongdoing. Do not testify in a lawsuit and go along with a crowd to pervert ⌊justice⌋. 3 Do not show favoritism to a poor person in his lawsuit.

4 "If you come across your enemy's stray ox or donkey, you must return it to him.

5 "If you see the donkey of someone who hates you lying ⌊helpless⌋ under its load, and you want to refrain from helping it, you must help with it.d

6 "You must not deny justice to the poor among you in his lawsuit. 7 Stay far away from a false accusation. Do not kill the innocent and the just, because I will not justify the guilty. 8 You must not take a bribe, for a bribe blinds the clear-sighted and corrupts the wordse of the righteous. 9 You must not oppress a foreign resident; you yourselves know how it feels to be a foreigner because you were foreigners in the land of Egypt.

Sabbaths and Festivals

10 "Sow your land for six years and gather its produce. 11 But during the seventh year you are to let it rest and leave it uncultivated, so that the poor among

your people may eat ⌊from it⌋ and the wild animals may consume what they leave. Do the same with your vineyard and your olive grove.

12 "Do your work for six days but rest on the seventh day so that your ox and your donkey may rest, and the son of your female slave as well as the foreign resident may be refreshed.

13 "Pay strict attention to everything I have said to you. You must not invoke the names of other gods; they must not be heard on your lips.f

14 "Celebrate a festival in My honor three times a year. 15 Observe the Festival of •Unleavened Bread. As I commanded you, you are to eat unleavened bread for seven days at the appointed time in the month of Abib, because you came out of Egypt in that month. No one is to appear before Me empty-handed. 16 Also ⌊observe⌋ the Festival of Harvestg with the •firstfruits of your produce from what you sow in the field, and ⌊observe⌋ the Festival of Ingatheringh at the end of the year, when you gather your producei from the field. 17 Three times a year all your males are to appear before the Lord GOD.

18 "You must not offer the blood of My sacrifices with anything leavened. The fat of My festival offering must not remain until morning.

19 "Bring the best of the firstfruits of your land to the house of the LORD your God.

"You must not boil a young goat in its mother's milk.

Promises and Warnings

20 "I am going to send an Angel before you to protect you on the way and bring you to the place I have prepared. 21 Be attentive to Him and listen to His voice. Do not defyj Him, because He will not forgive your acts of rebellion, for My name is in Him. 22 But if you will carefully obey Him and do everything I say, then I will be an enemy to your enemies and a foe to your foes. 23 For My Angel will go before you and bring you to ⌊the land of⌋ the Amorites, Hittites, Perizzites, Canaanites, Hivites, and Jebusites, and I will wipe them out. 24 You must not bow down to their gods or worship them. Do not imitate their practices. Instead, demolish themk and smash their sacred pillars to pieces. 25 Worship the LORD your God, and Hel will bless your bread and your water. I will take away your illnesses.m 26 No woman will miscarry or be barren in your land. I will give ⌊you⌋ the full number of your days.

27 "I will cause the people ahead of you to feel terrorn and throw into confusion all the nations you come

a 22:27 Lit skin b 22:28 Or judges c 23:1 Lit join hands with d 23:5 Or load, you must refrain from leaving it to him; you must set it free with him e 23:8 Or and subverts the cause f 23:13 Lit mouth g 23:16 The Festival of Harvest is called Festival of Weeks elsewhere in the OT; Ex 34:22. In the NT it is called Pentecost; Ac 2:1. h 23:16 The Festival of Ingathering is called Festival of Booths elsewhere; Lv 23:34–36. i 23:16 Lit labors j 23:21 Or embitter k 23:24 Probably the idols l 23:25 LXX, Vg read I m 23:25 Lit away illnesses from among you n 23:27 Lit will send terror of Me ahead of you

---

the Shepherd was ill-regarded (Zech. 11:12).
22:3 after sunrise, there is guilt of bloodshed. It was not permitted to kill a prowler during the day, since an assailant's vision indicated some level of premeditation.
22:16 bridal price. In order to get a wife, a man was required to pay his future father-in-

law for the privilege. In this case, the man who has violated the daughter must satisfy the father. A high price could be expected.

23:4-5 enemy's stray ox. A person's enemies must be treated with the same regard as friends, returning hostility with kindness. Here the enemy is a Hebrew.

23:15 Festival of Unleavened Bread. Passover week was celebrated from around mid-March to mid-April. It was in memory of the Israelites' rapid escape from Egypt (12:17-20).

23:16 Festival of Harvest. Pentecost (Hebrew Shavuot) was celebrated seven weeks after the Feast of Unleavened Bread during

to. I will make all your enemies turn their backs to you in retreat. 28 I will send the horneta in front of you, and it will drive the Hivites, Canaanites, and Hittites away from you. 29 I will not drive them out ahead of you in a single year; otherwise, the land would become desolate, and wild animals would multiply against you. 30 I will drive them out little by little ahead of you until you have become numerousb and take possession of the land. 31 I will set your borders from the •Red Sea to the Mediterranean Sea,c and from the wilderness to the Euphrates River.d For I will place the inhabitants of the land under your control, and you will drive them out ahead of you. 32 You must not make a covenant with them or their gods. 33 They must not remain in your land, or else they will make you sin against Me. If you worship their gods, it will be a snare for you."

The Covenant Ceremony

24 Then He said to Moses, "Go up to the LORD, you and Aaron, Nadab, and Abihu, and 70 of Israel's elders, and bow in worship at a distance. 2 Moses alone is to approach the LORD, but the others are not to approach, and the people are not to go up with him."

3 Moses came and told the people all the commands of the LORD and all the ordinances. Then all the people responded with a single voice, "We will do everything that the LORD has commanded." 4 And Moses wrote down all the words of the LORD. He rose early the next morning and set up an altar and 12 pillars for the 12 tribes of Israel at the base of the mountain. 5 Then he sent out young Israelite men, and they offered •burnt offerings and sacrificed bulls as •fellowship offerings to the LORD. 6 Moses took half the blood and set it in basins; the ⌊other⌋ half of the blood he sprinkled on the altar. 7 He then took the covenant scroll and read ⌊it⌋ aloud to the people. They responded, "We will do and obey everything that the LORD has commanded."

8 Moses took the blood, sprinkled it on the people, and said, "This is the blood of the covenant that the LORD has made with you concerning all these words."

9 Then Moses went up with Aaron, Nadab, and Abihu, and 70 of Israel's elders, 10 and they saw the God of Israel. Beneath His feet was something like a pavement made of sapphiree stone, as clear as the sky itself. 11 God did not harmf the Israelite nobles; they saw Him, and they ate and drank.

12 The LORD said to Moses, "Come up to Me on the mountain and stay there so that I may give you the stone tablets with the law and commands I have written for their instruction."

13 So Moses arose with his assistant Joshua, and went up the mountain of God. 14 He told the elders, "Wait here for us until we return to you. Aaron and Hur are here with you. Whoever has a dispute should go to them." 15 When Moses went up the mountain, the cloud covered it. 16 The glory of the LORD settled on Mount Sinai, and the cloud covered it for six days. On the seventh day He called to Moses from the cloud. 17 The appearance of the LORD's glory to the Israelites was like a consuming fire on the mountaintop. 18 Moses entered the cloud as he went up the mountain, and he remained on the mountain 40 days and 40 nights.

Offerings to Build the Tabernacle

25 The LORD spoke to Moses: 2 "Tell the Israelites to take an offering for Me. You are to take My offering from everyone whose heart stirs him ⌊to give⌋. 3 This is the offering you are to receive from them: gold, silver, and bronze; 4 blue, purple, and scarlet yarn; fine linen and goat hair; 5 ram skins dyed red and manatee skins;g acacia wood; 6 oil for the light; spices for the anointing oil and for the fragrant incense; 7 and onyxh along with ⌊other⌋ gemstones for mounting on the •ephod and breastpiece.i

8 "They are to make a sanctuary for Me so that I may dwell among them. 9 You must make ⌊it⌋ according to all that I show you—the design of the tabernacle as well as the design of all its furnishings."

The Ark

10 "They are to make an ark of acacia wood, 45 inches long, 27 inches wide, and 27 inches high.j 11 Overlay it with pure gold; overlay it both inside and out. Also make a gold molding all around it. 12 Cast four gold rings for it and place ⌊them⌋ on its four feet, two rings on one side and two rings on the other side. 13 Make poles of acacia wood and overlay them with gold. 14 Insert the poles into the rings on the sides of the ark in order to carry the ark with them. 15 The poles are to remain in the rings of the ark; they must not be removed from it. 16 Put the ⌊tablets of the⌋ •testimony that I will give you into the ark. 17 Make a •mercy seat of pure gold, 45 inches long and 27 inches wide.k 18 Make two •cherubim of gold; make them of

---

a23:28 Or send panic   b23:30 Lit fruitful   c23:31 Lit the Sea of the Philistines   d23:31 Lit the River   e24:10 Or lapis lazuli   f24:11 Lit not stretch out His hand against   g25:5 Or and dolphin skins, or and fine leather; Hb obscure   h25:7 Or carnelian   i25:7 Traditionally, breastplate   j25:10 Lit two and a half cubits its length, one and a half cubits its width, and one and a half cubits its height   k25:17 Lit two and a half cubits its length, one and a half cubits its width

---

the time of the wheat harvest. At this feast, the Israelites made offerings to God of the harvest's firstfruits.

23:18 anything leavened. In His instructions for the Passover, God prohibited yeast, a symbol of sin and impurity, from even being in the home during that festival (12:14-16).

Jesus refers to this symbol (Matt. 16:5-12).

23:20 place I have prepared. The words Jesus used to describe our place in heaven echoes the language here (John 14:2-4).

24:2 Moses alone. Only the mediator Moses is allowed direct access. Jesus, a greater

middleman than Moses (v. 8; Heb. 3:3; 9:15), becomes the "mediator of a new covenant" with God (Heb. 12:24); bridging the gulf between human and divine.

24:8 sprinkled it on the people. A symbol of covenant acceptance, it is also a reminder of the first Passover when blood above and be-

hammered work at the two ends of the mercy seat. [19] Make one cherub at one end and one cherub at the other end. Make the cherubim of one piece with the mercy seat at its two ends. [20] The cherubim are to have wings spread out above, covering the mercy seat with their wings, and are to face one another. The faces of the cherubim should be toward the mercy seat. [21] Set the mercy seat on top of the ark and put the testimony that I will give you into the ark. [22] I will meet with you there above the mercy seat, between the two cherubim that are over the ark of the testimony; I will speak with you from there about all that I command you regarding the Israelites.

The Table

[23] "You are to construct a table of acacia wood, 36 inches long, 18 inches wide, and 27 inches high.[a] [24] Overlay it with pure gold and make a gold molding all around it. [25] Make a three-inch[b] frame all around it and make a gold molding for it all around its frame. [26] Make four gold rings for it, and attach the rings to the four corners at its four legs. [27] The rings should be next to the frame as holders for the poles to carry the table. [28] Make the poles of acacia wood and overlay them with gold so that the table can be carried by them. [29] You are also to make its plates and cups, as well as its pitchers and bowls for pouring drink offerings. Make them out of pure gold. [30] Put the bread of the Presence[c] on the table before Me at all times.

The Lampstand

[31] "You are to make a lampstand out of pure, hammered gold. It is to be made of one piece: its base and shaft, its ornamental cups, and its calyxes[d] and petals. [32] Six branches are to extend from its sides, three branches of the lampstand from one side and three branches of the lampstand from the other side. [33] There are to be three cups shaped like almond blossoms, each with a calyx and petals, on the first branch, and three cups shaped like almond blossoms, each with a calyx and petals, on the next branch. It is to be this way for the six branches that extend from the lampstand. [34] There are to be four cups shaped like almond blossoms on the lampstand shaft along with its calyxes and petals. [35] For the six branches that extend from the lampstand, a calyx must be under the first pair of branches from it, a calyx under the second pair of branches from it, and a calyx under the third pair of branches from it. [36] Their calyxes and branches are to

be of one piece.[e] All of it is to be a single hammered piece of pure gold.

[37] "Make seven lamps on it. Its lamps are to be set up so they illuminate the area in front of it. [38] Its snuffers and firepans must be of pure gold. [39] The lampstand[f] with all these utensils is to be made from 75 pounds[g] of pure gold. [40] Be careful to make everything according to the model of them you have been shown on the mountain.

The Tabernacle

26 "You are to construct the tabernacle itself with 10 curtains. You must make them of finely spun linen, and blue, purple, and scarlet yarn, with a design of •cherubim worked into them. [2] The length of each curtain should be 42 feet,[h] and the width of each curtain six feet;[i] all the curtains are to have the same measurements. [3] Five of the curtains should be joined together, and the other five curtains joined together. [4] Make loops of blue yarn on the edge of the last curtain[j] in the first set, and do the same on the edge of the outermost curtain in the second set. [5] Make 50 loops on the one curtain and make 50 loops on the edge of the curtain in the second set, so that the loops line up together. [6] Also make 50 gold clasps and join the curtains together with the clasps, so that the tabernacle may be a single unit.

[7] "You are to make curtains of goat hair for a tent over the tabernacle; make 11 of these curtains. [8] The length of each curtain should be 45 feet[k] and the width of each curtain six feet.[i] All 11 curtains are to have the same measurements. [9] Join five of the curtains by themselves, and the other six curtains by themselves. Then fold the sixth curtain double at the front of the tent. [10] Make 50 loops on the edge of the one curtain, the outermost in the first set, and make 50 loops on the edge of the corresponding curtain of the second set. [11] Make 50 bronze clasps; put the clasps through the loops and join the tent together so that it is a single unit. [12] As for the flap that is left over from the tent curtains, the leftover half curtain is to hang down over the back of the tabernacle. [13] The half yard[l] on one side and the half yard[m] on the other of what is left over along the length of the tent curtains should be hanging down over the sides of the tabernacle on either side to cover it. [14] Make a covering for the tent from ram skins dyed red, and a covering of manatee skins[n] on top of that.

---

[a]25:23 Lit two cubits its length, one cubit its width, and one and a half cubits its height   [b]25:25 Lit Make it a handbreadth   [c]25:30 Or of presentation   [d]25:31 The outer covering of a flower   [e]25:36 Lit piece with it   [f]25:39 Lit It   [g]25:39 Lit a talent   [h]26:2 Lit 28 cubits   [i]26:2,8 Lit four cubits   [j]26:4 Lit the one curtain on the end   [k]26:8 Lit 30 cubits   [l]26:13 Lit The cubit   [m]26:13 Lit the cubit   [n]26:14 Or of dolphin skins, or of fine leather; Hb obscure

---

side the door marked an Israelite home for salvation. Christ's blood seals the New covenant of forgiveness.

24:11 ate and drank. After a wedding it is traditional to celebrate. The Lord's Supper celebrates the New Covenant wedding of Christ and the church (v. 8; Matt. 26:26-29).

24:18 40 days and 40 nights. The length of Noah's flood (Gen. 7:12) and Christ's fast (Matt. 4:2).

25:5 manatee skins. Manatees (sea cows) were present in the Red Sea, and their leather skin was precious.

25:30 bread of the Presence. Twelve loaves

of (show)bread, one for each tribe of Israel, were kept on this table as a perpetual sacrifice and reminder that all blessings come from God.

25:37 illuminate the area in front. Priests later insured that these lamps burned all night (27:20-21). The lighted lamps are the Israel-

15 "You are to make upright planks[a] of acacia wood for the tabernacle. 16 The length of each plank is to be 15 feet,[b] and the width of each plank 27 inches.[c] 17 Each plank must be connected together with two tenons. Do the same for all the planks of the tabernacle. 18 Make the planks for the tabernacle as follows: 20 planks for the south side, 19 and make 40 silver bases under the 20 planks, two bases under the first plank for its two tenons, and two bases under the next plank for its two tenons; 20 20 planks for the second side of the tabernacle, the north side, 21 along with their 40 silver bases, two bases under the first plank and two bases under each plank; 22 and make six planks for the west side of the tabernacle. 23 Make two additional planks for the two back corners of the tabernacle. 24 They are to be paired at the bottom, and joined together[d] at the[e] top in a single ring. So it should be for both of them; they will serve as the two corners. 25 There are to be eight planks with their silver bases: 16 bases; two bases under the first plank and two bases under each plank.

26 "You are to make five crossbars of acacia wood for the planks on one side of the tabernacle, 27 five crossbars for the planks on the other side of the tabernacle, and five crossbars for the planks of the back side of the tabernacle on the west. 28 The central crossbar is to run through the middle of the planks from one end to the other. 29 Then overlay the planks with gold, and make their rings of gold as the holders for the crossbars. Also overlay the crossbars with gold. 30 You are to set up the tabernacle according to the plan for it that you have been shown on the mountain.

31 "You are to make a veil of blue, purple, and scarlet yarn, and finely spun linen with a design of cherubim worked into it. 32 Hang it on four gold-plated posts of acacia wood that have gold hooks ⌊and that stand⌋ on four silver bases. 33 Hang the veil under the clasps[f] and bring the ark of the •testimony there behind the veil, so the veil will make a separation for you between the holy place and the most holy place. 34 Put the •mercy seat on the ark of the testimony in the most holy place. 35 Place the table outside the veil and the lampstand on the south side of the tabernacle, opposite the table; put the table on the north side.

36 "For the entrance to the tent you are to make a screen embroidered with blue, purple, and scarlet yarn, and finely spun linen. 37 Make five posts of acacia wood for the screen and overlay them with gold; their hooks are to be gold, and you are to cast five bronze bases for them.

The Altar of Burnt Offering

27 "You are to construct the altar of acacia wood. The altar must be square, seven and a half feet long, and seven and a half feet wide;[g] it must be four and a half feet high.[h] 2 Make horns for it on its four corners; the horns are to be of one piece.[i] Overlay it with bronze. 3 Make its pots for removing ashes, and its shovels, basins, meat forks, and firepans; make all its utensils of bronze. 4 Construct a grate for it of bronze mesh, and make four bronze rings on the mesh at its four corners. 5 Set it below, under the altar's ledge,[j] so that the mesh comes halfway up[k] the altar. 6 Then make poles for the altar, poles of acacia wood, and overlay them with bronze. 7 The poles are to be inserted into the rings, so that the poles are on two sides of the altar when it is carried. 8 Construct the altar with boards so that it is hollow. They are to make it just as it was shown to you on the mountain.

The Courtyard

9 "You are to make the courtyard for the tabernacle. ⌊Make the hangings⌋ on the south of the courtyard out of finely spun linen, 150 feet[l] long on that side. 10 There are to be 20 posts and 20 bronze bases. The hooks and bands[m] of the posts must be silver. 11 Then ⌊make the hangings⌋ on the north side 150 ⌊feet⌋[n] long. There are to be 20 posts and 20 bronze bases. The hooks and bands[m] of the posts must be silver. 12 ⌊Make⌋ the hangings of the courtyard on the west side 75 feet[o] long, including their 10 posts and 10 bases. 13 Make the hangings of the courtyard on the east side toward the sunrise 75 feet.[o] 14 ⌊Make⌋ the hangings on one side ⌊of the gate⌋ 22 and a half feet,[p] including their three posts and their three bases. 15 And make the hangings on the other side 22 and a half ⌊feet⌋,[q] including their three posts and their three bases. 16 The gate of the courtyard is to have a thirty-foot[r] screen embroidered with blue, purple, and scarlet yarn, and finely spun linen. It is to have four posts including their four bases.

17 "All the posts around the courtyard are to be banded with silver and have silver hooks and bronze bases. 18 The length of the courtyard is to be 150 feet, the width 75 ⌊feet⌋ at each end, and the height seven and a half feet,[s] ⌊all of it made⌋ of finely spun linen. The bases of the posts must be bronze. 19 All the tools of the

---

[a] **26:15** Or *frames, or beams* [b] **26:16** Lit *10 cubits* [c] **26:16** Lit *a cubit and a half* [d] **26:24** Lit *and together they are to be complete* [e] **26:24** Lit *its*
[f] **26:33** The clasps that join the 10 curtains of the tabernacle; Ex 26:6 [g] **27:1** Lit *five cubits in length and five cubits in width* [h] **27:1** Lit *wide; and its height three cubits* [i] **27:2** Lit *piece with it* [j] **27:5** Perhaps a ledge around the altar on which the priests could stand; Lv 9:22 [k] **27:5** Or *altar's rim, so that the grid comes halfway down* [l] **27:9** Lit *100 cubits* [m] **27:10,11** Or *connecting rods* [n] **27:11** Lit *100 [cubits]* [o] **27:12,13** Lit *50 cubits*
[p] **27:14** Lit *15 cubits* [q] **27:15** Lit *15 [cubits]* [r] **27:16** Lit *twenty-cubit* [s] **27:18** Lit *be 100 by the cubit, and the width 50 by 50, and the height five cubits*

---

ites' response to the light of God's glory (29:43).

25:40 model ... shown on the mountain. God had specific designs for items in the tabernacle (27:8). Stephen said that these designs were made by God as He directed Moses (Acts 7:44).

26:1 tabernacle. The tabernacle was a rectangular tent covered by several layers. The inner layer was made of linen embroidered with images of cherubim. The three other layers were made of woven goat hair, dyed ram skins and manatee hides. All of its construction material was fit for a royal chamber.

26:31 veil. An embroidered curtain divided The Holy Place from the Most Holy Place. The Most Holy Place, representing God's throne room, contained only the ark. The Holy Place contained the table for the bread of the Presence, the lampstand and the altar of incense.

27:1 altar. This altar, outside the Holy Place in

tabernacle for every use and all its tent pegs as well as all the tent pegs of the courtyard are to be made of bronze.

The Lampstand Oil

20 "You are to command the Israelites to bring you pure oil from crushed olives for the light, in order to keep the lamp burning continually. 21 In the tent of meeting outside the veil that is in front of the •testimony, Aaron and his sons are to tend the lamp from evening until morning before the LORD. This is to be a permanent statute for the Israelites throughout their generations.

The Priestly Garments

28 "Have your brother Aaron, with his sons, come to you from the Israelites to serve Me as priest—Aaron, his sons Nadab and Abihu, Eleazar and Ithamar. 2 Make holy garments for your brother Aaron, for glory and beauty. 3 You are to instruct all the skilled craftsmen,a whom I have filled with a spirit of wisdom, to make Aaron's garments for consecrating him to serve Me as priest. 4 These are the garments that they must make: a breastpiece, an •ephod, a robe, a specially woven tunic,b a turban, and a sash. They are to make holy garments for your brother Aaron and his sons so that they may serve Me as priests. 5 They should usec gold; blue, purple, and scarlet yarn; and fine linen.

The Ephod

6 "They are to make the ephod of finely spun linen embroidered with gold, and with blue, purple, and scarlet yarn. 7 It must have two shoulder pieces attached to its two edges so that it can be joined together. 8 The artistically woven waistband that is on the ephodd must be of one piece,e according to the same workmanship of gold, of blue, purple, and scarlet yarn, and of finely spun linen.

9 "Take two onyx stones and engrave on them the names of Israel's sons: 10 six of their names on the first stone and the remaining six names on the second stone, in the order of their birth. 11 Engrave the two stones with the names of Israel's sons as a gem cutter engraves a seal. Mount them, surrounded with gold filigree settings. 12 Fasten both stones on the shoulder pieces of the ephod as memorial stones for the Israelites. Aaron will carry their names on his two shoulders before the LORD as a reminder. 13 Fashion gold filigree settings 14 and two chains of pure gold; you will make them of braided cord work, and attach the cord chains to the settings.

The Breastpiece

15 "You are to make an embroidered breastpiece for decisions.f Make it with the same workmanship as the ephod; make it of gold, of blue, purple, and scarlet yarn, and of finely spun linen. 16 It must be square and folded double, nine inches long and nine inches wide.g 17 Place a setting of gemstonesh on it, four rows of stones:

> The first row should be
> a row of carnelian, topaz, and emerald;i
> 18 the second row,
> a turquoise,j a sapphire,k and a diamond;l
> 19 the third row,
> a jacinth,b an agate, and an amethyst;
> 20 and the fourth row,
> a beryl, an onyx, and a jasper.

They should be adorned with gold filigree in their settings. 21 The 12 stones are to correspond to the names of Israel's sons. Each stone must be engraved like a seal, with one of the names of the 12 tribes.

22 "You are to make braided chainsm of pure gold cord work for the breastpiece. 23 Fashion two gold rings for the breastpiece and attach them to its two corners. 24 Then attach the two gold cords to the two gold rings at the corners of the breastpiece. 25 Attach the other ends of the two cords to the two filigree settings and in this way attach ⌊them⌋ to the ephod's shoulder pieces in the front. 26 Make two ⌊other⌋ gold rings and put them at the two other corners of the breastpiece on the edge that is next to the inner border of the ephod. 27 Make two ⌊more⌋ gold rings and attach them to the bottom of the ephod's two shoulder pieces on its front, close to its seam,n and above the ephod's woven waistband. 28 The craftsmen are to tie the breastpiece from its rings to the rings of the ephod with a cord of blue yarn, so that the breastpiece is above the ephod's waistband and does not come loose from the ephod.

29 "Whenever he enters the sanctuary, Aaron is to carry the names of Israel's sons over his heart on the breastpiece for decisions, as a continual reminder before the LORD. 30 Place the •Urim and Thummim in the breastpiece for decisions, so that they will also be over Aaron's heart whenever he comes before the LORD. Aaron will continually carry the ⌊means of⌋ decisions for the Israelites over his heart before the LORD.

---

a28:3 Lit all wise of heart   b28:4,19 Hb obscure   c28:5 Lit receive   d28:8 Lit waistband of its ephod, which is on it   e28:8 Lit piece with the ephod   f28:15 Used for determining God's will; Nm 27:21   g28:16 Lit a span its length and a span its width   h28:17 Many of these stones cannot be identified with certainty.   i28:17 Or beryl   j28:18 Or malachite, or garnet   k28:18 Or lapis lazuli   l28:18 Hb obscure; LXX, Vg read jasper   m28:22 The same chains mentioned in v. 14   n28:27 The place where the shoulder pieces join the front of the ephod

---

the courtyard, is known as the bronze altar or the altar of burnt offering.

27:9-18 courtyard. The entire tabernacle area was a rectangle with its long sides aligned east to west and surrounded by a seven and a half foot curtain. The tent containing the Holy Place and Most Holy Place

was in the western half; and the bronze altar, about seven and a half feet square, was in the eastern courtyard, which measured 150 by 75 feet. The entrance lay on the east end and was about thirty feet square.

27:20 pure oil from crushed olives. Olive oil was a versatile resource—a staple for cook-

ing and eating, and a fuel that produced almost no smoke. Pure oil would have comes from the initial extraction generally used for foods, while fatty lampstand oil usually came from the second and third pressings.

28:2 holy garments. The special garments worn by priests gave them a certain status

The Robe

31 "You are to make the robe of the ephod entirely of blue yarn. 32 There should be an opening at its top in the center of it. Around the opening, there should be a woven collar with an opening like that for body armor[a] so that it does not tear. 33 Make pomegranates of blue, purple, and scarlet yarn[b] on its lower hem and all around it. Put gold bells between them all the way around, 34 ⌊so that⌋ gold bells and pomegranates alternate around the lower hem of the robe. 35 The robe must be ⌊worn by⌋ Aaron whenever he ministers, and its sound will be heard when he enters the sanctuary before the LORD and when he exits, so that he does not die.

The Turban

36 "You are to make a plate[c] of pure gold and engrave it, like the engraving of a seal:

> **HOLY TO THE LORD**

37 Fasten it to a cord of blue yarn so it can be placed on the turban; the plate is to be on the front of the turban. 38 It will be on Aaron's forehead so that Aaron may bear the guilt connected with the holy offerings that the Israelites consecrate as all their holy gifts. It is always to be on his forehead, so that they may find acceptance with the LORD.

Other Priestly Garments

39 "You are to weave the tunic from fine linen, make a turban of fine linen, and make an embroidered sash. 40 Make tunics, sashes, and headbands for Aaron's sons to ⌊give them⌋ glory and beauty. 41 Put these on your brother Aaron and his sons; then anoint, ordain,[d] and consecrate them, so that they may serve Me as priests. 42 Make them linen undergarments to cover ⌊their⌋ naked bodies; they must extend from the waist[e] to the thighs. 43 These must be ⌊worn by⌋ Aaron and his sons whenever they enter the tent of meeting or approach the altar to minister in the sanctuary ⌊area⌋, so that they do not incur guilt and die. This is to be a permanent statute for Aaron and for his descendants after him.

Instructions about Consecration

29 "This is what you are to do for them to consecrate them to serve Me as priests. Take a young bull and two unblemished rams, 2 with unleavened bread, unleavened cakes mixed with oil, and unleavened wafers coated with oil. Make them out of

fine wheat flour, 3 put them in a basket, and bring them in the basket, along with the bull and two rams. 4 Bring Aaron and his sons to the entrance to the tent of meeting and wash them with water. 5 Then take the garments and clothe Aaron with the tunic, the robe for the •ephod, the ephod itself, and the breastpiece; fasten the ephod on him with its woven waistband. 6 Put the turban on his head and place the holy diadem on the turban. 7 Take the anointing oil, pour ⌊it⌋ on his head, and anoint him. 8 You must also bring his sons, clothe them with tunics, 9 fasten headbands on them, and tie sashes around both Aaron and his sons. The priesthood is to be theirs by a permanent statute. This is the way you will ordain Aaron and[f] his sons.

10 "You are to bring the bull to the front of the tent of meeting, and Aaron and his sons must lay their hands on the bull's head. 11 Slaughter the bull before the LORD at the entrance to the tent of meeting. 12 Take some of the bull's blood and apply ⌊it⌋ to the horns of the altar with your finger; then pour out all the ⌊rest⌋ of the blood at the base of the altar. 13 Take all the fat that covers the entrails, the fatty lobe of the liver, and the two kidneys with the fat on them, and burn ⌊them⌋ on the altar. 14 But burn up the bull's flesh, its hide, and its dung outside the camp; it is a •sin offering.

15 "Take one ram, and Aaron and his sons are to lay their hands on the ram's head. 16 You are to slaughter the ram, take its blood, and sprinkle ⌊it⌋ on all sides of the altar. 17 Cut the ram into pieces. Wash its entrails and shanks, and place ⌊them⌋ with its head and its pieces ⌊on the altar⌋. 18 Then burn the whole ram on the altar; it is a •burnt offering to the LORD. It is a pleasing aroma, a fire offering to the LORD.

19 "You are to take the second ram, and Aaron and his sons must lay their hands on the ram's head. 20 Slaughter the ram, take some of its blood, and put it on Aaron's right earlobe, on his sons' right earlobes, on the thumbs of their right hands, and on the big toes of their right feet. Sprinkle the ⌊remaining⌋ blood on all sides of the altar. 21 Take some of the blood that is on the altar and some of the anointing oil, and sprinkle ⌊them⌋ on Aaron and his garments, as well as on his sons and their garments. In this way, he and his garments will become holy, as well as his sons and their garments.

22 "Take the fat from the ram, the fat tail, the fat covering the entrails, the fatty lobe of the liver, the two kidneys and the fat on them, and the right thigh (since this is a ram for ordination[g]); 23 take one loaf of bread, one

---

[a] **28:32** Hb obscure [b] **28:33** Sam, LXX add *of finely spun linen* [c] **28:36** Or *medallion* [d] **28:41** Lit *anoint them, fill their hand* [e] **28:42** Lit *loins*
[f] **29:9** Lit *you will fill the hand of Aaron and the hand of*; Ex 29:23–24 [g] **29:22** Normally the priest would receive the right thigh to be eaten, but here it is burned; Lv 7:32–34

---

among the people and insured that those they were dressed in a manner appropriate to their proximity to the divine.
28:6 ephod. A sleeveless overgarment made of fine linen.
28:15 breastpiece for decisions. The high priest wore the fabric breastpiece or pouch

whenever he entered the Holy Place (v. 29). Within the breastpiece, the Urim and Thummim were held.
28:30 Urim and Thummim. Urim ("lights") and Thummim ("perfections") were sacred lots cast to ascertain the "yes" or "no" will of God.
28:35 sound will be heard. The bells on the

robe acted like the bird that miners would take with them into a mine. If the bird died, the miners knew something was wrong.
29:7 anoint him. Aaron was anointed with fragrant oil to serve God as Christ would later be anointed (John 12:3).
29:10 lay their hands on the bull's head. In

cake of bread ⌊made⌋ with oil, and one wafer from the basket of unleavened bread that is before the LORD; 24 and put all of them in the hands of Aaron and his[a] sons and wave them as a presentation offering before the LORD. 25 Take them from their hands and burn ⌊them⌋ on the altar on top of the burnt offering, as a pleasing aroma before the LORD; it is a fire offering to the LORD.

26 "Take the breast from the ram of Aaron's ordination and wave it as a presentation offering before the LORD; it is to be your portion. 27 Consecrate for Aaron and his sons the breast of the presentation offering that is waved and the thigh of the contribution that is lifted up from the ram of ordination. 28 This will belong to Aaron and his sons as a regular portion from the Israelites, for it is a contribution. It will be the Israelites' contribution from their •fellowship sacrifices, their contribution to the LORD.

29 "The holy garments that belong to Aaron are to belong to his sons after him, so that they can be anointed and ordained[b] in them. 30 Any priest who is one of his sons and who succeeds him and enters the tent of meeting to minister in the sanctuary must wear them for seven days.

31 "You are to take the ram of ordination and boil its flesh in a holy place. 32 Aaron and his sons are to eat the meat of the ram and the bread that is in the basket at the entrance to the tent of meeting. 33 They must eat those things by which •atonement was made at ⌊the time of⌋ their ordination[c] and consecration. An unauthorized person must not eat ⌊them⌋, for these things are holy. 34 If any of the meat of ordination or any of the bread is left until morning, burn up what is left over. It must not be eaten because it is holy.

35 "This is what you are to do for Aaron and his sons based on all I have commanded you. Ordain them for seven days. 36 Sacrifice a bull as a sin offering each day for atonement. Purify[d] the altar when you make atonement for it, and anoint it in order to consecrate it. 37 For seven days you must make atonement for the altar and consecrate it. The altar will become especially holy; whatever touches the altar will become holy.

38 "This is what you are to offer regularly on the altar every day: two year-old lambs. 39 In the morning offer one lamb, and at twilight offer the other lamb. 40 With the first lamb offer two quarts[e] of fine flour mixed with one quart[f] of crushed olive oil, and a drink offering of one quart[f] of wine. 41 You are to offer the second lamb at twilight. Offer a •grain offering and a drink offering

with it, like the one in the morning, as a pleasing aroma, a fire offering to the LORD. 42 This will be a regular burnt offering throughout your generations at the entrance to the tent of meeting before the LORD, where I will meet you[g] to speak with you. 43 I will also meet with the Israelites there, and that place will be consecrated by My glory. 44 I will consecrate the tent of meeting and the altar; I will also consecrate Aaron and his sons to serve Me as priests. 45 I will dwell among the Israelites and be their God. 46 And they will know that I am the LORD their God, who brought them out of the land of Egypt, so that I might dwell among them. I am the LORD their God.

The Incense Altar

30 "You are to make an altar for the burning of incense; make it of acacia wood. 2 It must be square, 18 inches long and 18 inches wide;[h] it must be 36 inches high.[i] Its horns must be of one piece.[j] 3 Overlay its top, all around its sides, and its horns with pure gold; make a gold molding all around it. 4 Make two gold rings for it under the molding on two of its sides; put these on opposite sides of it to be holders for the poles to carry it with. 5 Make the poles of acacia wood and overlay them with gold.

6 "You are to place the altar in front of the veil by the ark of the •testimony—in front of the •mercy seat that is over the testimony—where I will meet with you. 7 Aaron must burn fragrant incense on it; he must burn it every morning when he tends the lamps. 8 When Aaron sets up the lamps at twilight, he must burn incense. There is to be an incense ⌊offering⌋ before the LORD throughout your generations. 9 You must not offer unauthorized incense on it, or a •burnt or •grain offering; you are not to pour a drink offering on it.

10 "Once a year Aaron is to perform the purification rite[k] on the horns of the altar. Throughout your generations he is to perform the purification rite[k] for[l] it once a year, with the blood of the •sin offering for •atonement. The altar is especially holy to the LORD."

The Atonement Money

11 The LORD spoke to Moses: 12 "When you take a census of the Israelites to register them, each of the men must pay a ransom for himself to the LORD as they are registered. Then no plague will come on them as they are registered. 13 Everyone who is registered must pay half a shekel[m] according to the sanctuary •shekel (20 gerahs to the shekel). This half shekel is a contribution to the LORD. 14 Each man who is registered, 20 years old or

---

a 29:24 Lit in the hands of his   b 29:29 Lit him for anointing in them and for filling their hand   c 29:33 Lit made to fill their hand   d 29:36 Or Make a sin offering on   e 29:40 Lit offer a tenth   f 29:40 Lit a fourth of a hin   g 29:42 Moses   h 30:2 Lit one cubit its length and one cubit its width   i 30:2 Lit wide; and two cubits its height   j 30:2 Lit piece with it   k 30:10 Or to make atonement   l 30:10 Or on   m 30:13 About ⅖ of an ounce of silver

---

order for priests to make atonement, a special sacrifice was needed. Laying on hands signified the declaration of ownership for the animal to which the sin of the priest was transferred.

29:13 fat that covers the entrails. The richest part of the bull is offered to God. Its fat and organ meats are burned on the bronze altar.

29:18 a pleasing aroma. Burning meat is not a pleasant smell like grilled meat. The pleasing aroma is the obedience and cleansing, which pleases God.

29:24 presentation offering. A presentation offering involved waving sacrifices before the

Lord as a means of presenting them to Him. Sometimes the wave offering was followed by a burnt offering (vv. 24-26). A presentation offering was also made for that portion of the sacrificial meat that was reserved for the priests to eat (Lev. 7:30-31; 10:14).

29:38 regularly … every day. Although the

more, must give this contribution to the LORD. ¹⁵ The wealthy may not give more, and the poor may not give less, than half a shekel when giving the contribution to the LORD to atone for ͣ your lives. ¹⁶ Take the atonement money ͨ from the Israelites and use it for the service of the tent of meeting. It will serve as a reminder for the Israelites before the LORD to atone for ͣ your lives."

The Bronze Basin

¹⁷ The LORD spoke to Moses: ¹⁸ "Make a bronze basin for washing and a bronze stand for it. Set it between the tent of meeting and the altar, and put water in it. ¹⁹ Aaron and his sons must wash their hands and feet from the basin. ²⁰ Whenever they enter the tent of meeting or approach the altar to minister by burning up an offering to the LORD, they must wash with water so that they will not die. ²¹ They must wash their hands and feet so that they will not die; this is to be a permanent statute for them, for Aaron and his descendants throughout their generations."

The Anointing Oil

²² The LORD spoke to Moses: ²³ "Take for yourself the finest spices: 12 and a half pounds ͨ of liquid myrrh, half as much (six and a quarter pounds ͩ) of fragrant cinnamon, six and a quarter pounds ͩ of fragrant cane, ²⁴ 12 and a half pounds ͨ of cassia (by the sanctuary shekel), and one gallon ͤ of olive oil. ²⁵ Prepare from these a holy anointing oil, a scented blend, the work of a perfumer; it will be holy anointing oil.

²⁶ "With it you are to anoint the tent of meeting, the ark of the testimony, ²⁷ the table with all its utensils, the lampstand with its utensils, the altar of incense, ²⁸ the altar of burnt offering with all its utensils, and the basin with its stand. ²⁹ Consecrate them and they will be especially holy. Whatever touches them will be consecrated. ³⁰ Anoint Aaron and his sons and consecrate them to serve Me as priests.

³¹ "Tell the Israelites: This will be My holy anointing oil throughout your generations. ³² It must not be used for ⌊ordinary⌋ anointing on a person's body, and you must not make anything like it using its formula. It is holy, and it must be holy to you. ³³ Anyone who blends something like it or puts some of it on an unauthorized person must be cut off from his people."

The Sacred Incense

³⁴ The LORD said to Moses: "Take fragrant spices: stacte, onycha, and galbanum; the spices and pure frankincense are to be in equal measures. ³⁵ Prepare expertly blended incense from these; it is to be sea-soned with salt, pure and holy. ³⁶ Grind some of it into a fine powder and put some in front of the testimony in the tent of meeting, where I will meet with you. It must be especially holy to you. ³⁷ As for the incense you are making, you must not make ⌊any⌋ for yourselves using its formula. It is to be regarded by you as sacred to the LORD. ³⁸ Anyone who makes something like it to smell its fragrance must be cut off from his people."

God's Provision of the Skilled Workers

31 The LORD also spoke to Moses: ² "Look, I have appointed by name Bezalel son of Uri, son of Hur, of the tribe of Judah. ³ I have filled him with God's Spirit, with wisdom, understanding, and ability in every craft ⁴ to design artistic works in gold, silver, and bronze, ⁵ to cut gemstones for mounting, and to carve wood for work in every craft. ⁶ I have also selected Oholiab ͠ son of Ahisamach, of the tribe of Dan, to be with him. I have placed wisdom within every skilled craftsman ͡ in order to make all that I have commanded you: ⁷ the tent of meeting, the ark of the •testimony, the •mercy seat that is on top of it, and all the ⌊other⌋ furnishings of the tent—⁸ the table with its utensils, the pure ⌊gold⌋ lampstand with all its utensils, the altar of incense, ⁹ the altar of •burnt offering with all its utensils, the basin with its stand—¹⁰ the specially woven ͪ garments, both the holy garments for Aaron the priest and the garments for his sons to serve as priests, ¹¹ the anointing oil, and the fragrant incense for the sanctuary. They must make ⌊them⌋ according to all that I have commanded you."

Observing the Sabbath

¹² The LORD said to Moses: ¹³ "Tell the Israelites: You must observe My Sabbaths, for it is a sign between Me and you throughout your generations, so that you will know that I am the LORD who sets you apart. ¹⁴ Observe the Sabbath, for it is holy to you. Whoever profanes it must be put to death. If anyone does work on it, that person must be cut off from his people. ¹⁵ For six days work may be done, but on the seventh day there must be a Sabbath of complete rest, dedicated to the LORD. Anyone who does work on the Sabbath day must be put to death. ¹⁶ The Israelites must observe the Sabbath, celebrating it throughout their generations as a perpetual covenant. ¹⁷ It is a sign forever between Me and the Israelites, for in six days the LORD made the heavens and the earth, but on the seventh day He rested and was refreshed."

ͣ**30:15,16** Or *to ransom*   ͨ**30:16** Lit *the silver of the atonement*   ͨ**30:23,24** Lit *500* (shekels)   ͩ**30:23** Lit *250* (shekels)   ͤ**30:24** Lit *a hin*
ͦ**31:6** LXX, Syr read *Eliab*   ͡**31:6** Lit *every person skilled of heart*   ͪ**31:10** Hb obscure

---

Law commanded certain special ceremonies where offerings were made (23:15-16), God also commanded a daily sacrifice of "two lambs a year old."

29:45 dwell among the Israelites and be their God. God's presence with them in the tabernacle—even more tangible than the pil-lars of cloud and fire—fulfilled the covenant promise (19:5-6; 29:43).

30:12 take a census. The census could be used to select Israelites for particular service—such as the army (Num. 26:2), and was a form of state revenue (21:30).

30:34 fragrant spices: stacte, onycha, and galbanum ... pure frankincense. Except for frankincense, the same spices used in the anointing oil.

31:2 Hur. This man was with Aaron and Moses at Rephidim when the Israelites defeated the Amalekites (17:10-12).

31:3 with wisdom, understanding, and

The Two Stone Tablets

18 When He finished speaking with Moses on Mount Sinai, He gave him the two tablets of the testimony, stone tablets inscribed by the finger of God.

The Golden Calf

32 When the people saw that Moses delayed in coming down from the mountain, they gathered around Aaron and said to him, "Come, make us a god[a] who will go before us because this Moses, the man who brought us up from the land of Egypt—we don't know what has happened to him!"

2 Then Aaron replied to them, "Take off the gold rings that are on the ears of your wives, your sons, and your daughters and bring ⌊them⌋ to me." 3 So all the people took off the gold rings that were on their ears and brought ⌊them⌋ to Aaron. 4 He took ⌊the gold⌋ from their hands, fashioned it with an engraving tool, and made it into an image of a calf.

Then they said, "Israel, this is your God,[b] who brought you up from the land of Egypt!"

Prayer Changes Things

1. What is the most memorable statue you've seen? Why was it so memorable?

Exodus 32:1-35

2. Why do you think the Hebrews made a false idol right after all the miracles they had already seen? What does this teach us about human nature?

3. Why did God refer to the Israelites as "your people" to Moses (v. 7), instead of "My people"? How might this have encouraged Moses to intercede for them?

4. Why did Moses intercede by telling God that they are "Your people" (v. 11)?

5. How can you apply Moses' example to your prayers for others on your team or in your circle of friends?

---

5 When Aaron saw ⌊this⌋, he built an altar before it; then he made an announcement: "There will be a festival to the LORD tomorrow." 6 Early the next morning they arose, offered •burnt offerings, and presented •fellowship offerings. The people sat down to eat and drink, then got up to revel.

7 The LORD spoke to Moses: "Go down at once! For your people you brought up from the land of Egypt have acted corruptly. 8 They have quickly turned from the way I commanded them; they have made for themselves an image of a calf. They have bowed down to it, sacrificed to it, and said, 'Israel, this is your God,[b] who brought you up from the land of Egypt.'" 9 The LORD also said to Moses: "I have seen this people, and they are indeed a stiff-necked people. 10 Now leave Me alone, so that My anger can burn against them and I can destroy them. Then I will make you into a great nation."

11 But Moses interceded with the LORD his God: "LORD, why does Your anger burn against Your people You brought out of the land of Egypt with great power and a strong hand? 12 Why should the Egyptians say, 'He brought them out with an evil intent to kill them in the mountains and wipe them off the face of the earth'? Turn from Your great anger and change Your mind about this disaster ⌊planned⌋ for Your people. 13 Remember that You swore to Your servants Abraham, Isaac, and Israel by Yourself and declared to them, 'I will make your •offspring as numerous as the stars of the sky and will give your offspring all this land that I have promised, and they will inherit ⌊it⌋ forever.'" 14 So the LORD changed His mind about the disaster He said He would bring on His people.

15 Then Moses turned and went down the mountain with the two tablets of the •testimony in his hands. They were inscribed on both sides—inscribed front and back. 16 The tablets were the work of God, and the writing was God's writing, engraved on the tablets.

17 When Joshua heard the sound of the people as they shouted, he said to Moses, "There is a sound of war in the camp."

18 But Moses replied:

> It's not the sound of a victory cry
> and not the sound of a cry of defeat;
> I hear the sound of singing!

19 As he approached the camp and saw the calf and the dancing, Moses became enraged and threw the tablets out of his hands, smashing them at the base of the mountain. 20 Then he took the calf they had made, burned ⌊it⌋ up, and ground ⌊it⌋ to powder. He scattered ⌊the powder⌋ over the surface of the water and forced the Israelites to drink ⌊the water⌋.

21 Then Moses asked Aaron, "What did this people do to you that you have led them into ⌊such⌋ a grave sin?"

---

[a]**32:1** Or *us gods* [b]**32:4,8** Or *Israel, this is your god*, or *Israel, these are your gods*

---

ability. God prepared Bezalel for the work of the tabernacle by giving him the skills and inspiration he needed. God chooses the right person for a job (like Moses), then gives them the talents, experiences and inspiration needed to do it.

31:16-17 Sabbath ... sign. The observance

of the Sabbath was not only a command but also a symbolic act. Since God created the world in six days, then rested (Gen. 1:1–2:3), the observance of the Sabbath put Israel in the same pattern that God created. This pattern was a sign of the covenant relationship between them.

32:2 gold rings. The supreme irony is that the gold here, the result of a promise made by God (3:21-22; 12:35-36) and intended for the tabernacle (25:1-7; 35:4-9), is instead co-opted by the Israelites and made into what even Aaron considered to be a proper representation of Yahweh. Thus, they directly con-

22 "Don't be enraged, my lord," Aaron replied. "You yourself know that the people are ⌊intent⌋ on evil. 23 They said to me, 'Make us a godᵃ who will go before us because this Moses, the man who brought us up from the land of Egypt—we don't know what has happened to him!' 24 So I said to them, 'Whoever has gold, take it off,' and they gave ⌊it⌋ to me. When I threw it into the fire, out came this calf!"

25 Moses saw that the people were out of control, for Aaron had let them get out of control, so that they would be vulnerable to their enemies. 26 And Moses stood at the camp's entrance and said, "Whoever is for the LORD, ⌊come⌋ to me." And all the Levites gathered around him. 27 He told them, "This is what the LORD, the God of Israel, says, 'Every man fasten his sword to his side; go back and forth through the camp from entrance to entrance, and each of you kill his brother, his friend, and his neighbor.'" 28 The Levites did as Moses commanded, and about 3,000 men fell dead that day among the people. 29 Afterwards Moses said, "Today you have been dedicatedᵇ to the LORD, since each man went against his son and his brother. Therefore you have brought a blessing on yourselves today."

30 The following day Moses said to the people, "You have committed a great sin. Now I will go up to the LORD; perhaps I will be able to payᶜ for your sin."

31 So Moses returned to the LORD and said, "Oh, this people has committed a great sin; they have made for themselves a god of gold. 32 Now if You would only forgive their sin. But if not, please erase me from the book You have written."

33 The LORD replied to Moses: "Whoever has sinned against Me I will erase from My book. 34 Now go, lead the people to the place I told you about; see, My angel will go before you. But on the day I settle accounts, I will hold them accountable for their sin." 35 And the LORD inflicted a plague on the people for what they did with the calf Aaron had made.

The Tent Outside the Camp

33 The LORD spoke to Moses: "Go, leave here, you and the people you brought up from the land of Egypt, to the land I promised to Abraham, Isaac, and Jacob, saying: I will give it to your •offspring. 2 I will send an angel ahead of you and will drive out the Canaanites, Amorites, Hittites, Perizzites,ᵈ Hivites, and Jebusites. 3 ⌊Go up⌋ to a land flowing with milk and honey. But I will not go with

you because you are a stiff-necked people; otherwise, I might destroy you on the way." 4 When the people heard this bad news, they mourned and didn't put on their jewelry.

5 For the LORD said to Moses: "Tell the Israelites: You are a stiff-necked people. If I went with you for a single moment, I would destroy you. Now take off your jewelry, and I will decide what to do with you." 6 So the Israelites ⌊remained⌋ stripped of their jewelry from Mount Horeb ⌊onward⌋.

7 Now Moses took a tent and set it up outside the camp, far away from the camp; he called it the tent of meeting. Anyone who wanted to consult the LORD would go to the tent of meeting that was outside the camp. 8 Whenever Moses went out to the tent, all the people would stand up, each one at the door of his tent, and they would watch Moses until he entered the tent. 9 When Moses entered the tent, the pillar of cloud would come down and remain at the entrance to the tent, and ⌊the LORD⌋ would speak with Moses. 10 As all the people saw the pillar of cloud remaining at the entrance to the tent, they would stand up, then bow in worship, each one at the door of his tent. 11 The LORD spoke with Moses face to face, just as a man speaks with his friend. Then Moses would return to the camp, but his assistant, the young man Joshua son of Nun, would not leave the inside of the tent.

The LORD's Glory

12 Moses said to the LORD, "Look, You have told me, 'Lead this people up,' but You have not let me know whom You will send with me. You said, 'I know you by name, and you have also found favor in My sight.' 13 Now if I have indeed found favor in Your sight, please teach me Your ways, and I will know You and find favor in Your sight. Now consider that this nation is Your people."

14 Then He replied, "My presence will go ⌊with you⌋, and I will give you rest."

15 "If Your presence does not go," Moses responded to Him, "don't make us go up from here. 16 How will it be known that I and Your people have found favor in Your sight unless You go with us? I and Your people will be distinguished ⌊by this⌋ from all the other people on the face of the earth."

17 The LORD answered Moses, "I will do this very thing you have asked, for you have found favor in My sight, and I know you by name."

18 Then Moses said, "Please, let me see Your glory."

ᵃ 32:23 Or us gods   ᵇ 32:29 Text emended; MT reads Today dedicate yourselves; LXX, Vg read Today you have dedicated yourselves   ᶜ 32:30 Traditionally, make atonement   ᵈ 33:2 Sam, LXX include Girgashites

---

tradicted how God would use the gold to represent Himself in the sanctuary.

32:7 you brought up from the land of Egypt. The phrase is thick with irony. It was God who brought Israel out of Egypt. Contrast this verse with 15:1-12 and 19:4.

32:11 You brought out of …Egypt. Moses turns God's words back at Him (v. 7) by praising His deliverance of Israel.

32:14 the LORD changed His mind. It is inherent in God's character to execute justice within the context of mercy by giving everyone a second chance (see Jer. 18:7-8).

32:24 out came this calf. Aaron's explanation sounds like a six-year-old child's excuse for bad behavior.

32:33 Whoever has sinned against Me. This sin could not be atoned for because the people sinned defiantly (Num. 15:30) and not merely as faithful believers who strayed (Num. 15:22).

19 He said, "I will cause all My goodness to pass in front of you, and I will proclaim the name •Yahweh before you. I will be gracious to whom I will be gracious, and I will have compassion on whom I will have compassion." 20 But He answered, "You cannot see My face, for no one can see Me and live." 21 The LORD said, "Here is a place near Me. You are to stand on the rock, 22 and when My glory passes by, I will put you in the crevice of the rock and cover you with My hand until I have passed by. 23 Then I will take My hand away, and you will see My back, but My face will not be seen."

New Stone Tablets

34 The LORD said to Moses, "Cut two stone tablets like the first ones, and I will write on them the words that were on the first tablets, which you broke. 2 Be prepared by morning. Come up Mount Sinai in the morning and stand before Me on the mountaintop. 3 No one may go up with you; in fact, no one must be seen anywhere on the mountain. Even the flocks and herds are not to graze in front of that mountain."

4 Moses cut two stone tablets like the first ones. He got up early in the morning, and taking the two stone tablets in his hand, he climbed Mount Sinai, just as the LORD had commanded him.

5 The LORD came down in a cloud, stood with him there, and proclaimed ⌊His⌋ name •Yahweh. 6 Then the LORD passed in front of him and proclaimed:

Yahweh—Yahweh is a compassionate and gracious God, slow to anger and rich in faithful love and truth, 7 maintaining faithful love to a thousand ⌊generations⌋, forgiving wrongdoing, rebellion, and sin. But He will not leave ⌊the guilty⌋ unpunished, bringing the consequences of the fathers' wrongdoing on the children and grandchildren to the third and fourth generation.

8 Moses immediately bowed down to the ground and worshiped. 9 Then he said, "My Lord, if I have indeed found favor in Your sight, my Lord, please go with us. Even though this is a stiff-necked people, forgive our wrongdoing and sin, and accept us as Your own possession."

Covenant Obligations

10 And the LORD responded: "Look, I am making a covenant. I will perform wonders in the presence of all your peoplea that have never been doneb in all the earth or in any nation. All the people you live among will see the LORD's work, for what I am doing with you is awe-inspiring. 11 Observe what I command you today. I am going to drive out before you the Amorites, Canaanites, Hittites, Perizzites, Hivites,c and Jebusites. 12 Be careful not to make a treaty with the inhabitants of the land that you are going to enter; otherwise, they will become a snare among you. 13 Instead, you must tear down their altars, smash their sacred pillars, and chop down their •Asherah poles. 14 You are to never bow down to another god because the LORD, being jealous by nature, is a jealous God.

15 "Do not make a treaty with the inhabitants of the land, or else when they prostitute themselves with their gods and sacrifice to their gods, they will invite you, and you will eat of their sacrifice. 16 Then you will take some of their daughters ⌊as brides⌋ for your sons. Their daughters will prostitute themselves with their gods and cause your sons to prostitute themselves with their gods.

17 "Do not make cast images of gods for yourselves.

18 "Observe the Festival of •Unleavened Bread. You are to eat unleavened bread for seven days at the appointed time in the month of Abib as I commanded you. For you came out of Egypt in the month of Abib.

19 "The firstborn male from every womb belongs to Me, including all your maled e livestock, the firstborn of cattle or sheep. 20 You must redeem the firstborn of a donkey with a sheep, but if you do not redeem ⌊it⌋, break its neck. You must redeem all the firstborn of your sons. No one is to appear before Me empty-handed.

21 "You are to labor six days but you must rest on the seventh day; you must even rest during plowing and harvesting times.

22 "Observe the Festival of Weeks with the •firstfruits of the wheat harvest, and the Festival of Ingatheringf at the turn of the ⌊agricultural⌋ year. 23 Three times a year all your males are to appear before the Lord GOD, the God of Israel. 24 For I will drive out nations before you and enlarge your territory. No one will covet your land when you go up three times a year to appear before the LORD your God.

25 "Do not presentg the blood for My sacrifice with anything leavened. The sacrifice of the •Passover Festival must not remain until morning.

26 "Bring the best firstfruits of your land to the house of the LORD your God.

"You must not boil a young goat in its mother's milk."

---

a34:10 Lit in all nations   b34:10 Lit created   c34:11 DSS, Sam, LXX include Girgashites   d34:19 LXX, Theod, Vg, Tg read males   e34:19 Hb obscure   f34:22 The Festival of Ingathering is called Festival of Booths elsewhere in the OT; Lv 23:34–36   g34:25 Lit slaughter

---

33:3-5 stiff-necked. Stubborn and unyielding. might destroy you. God had expressed similar frustration only once before—just prior to Noah's flood (Gen. 6:6-8).

33:11 as a man speaks with his friend. Moses had seen God in a burning bush, a cloud, a still small voice, and a pillar of fire. He had met God on a mountain, in a desert and in the middle of a miraculously dry riverbed. Moses intimately knew God.

33:12 you have also found favor. Moses does not recall a contract or an agreement but the call of God that changed his life (chapters 3–4).

33:19 name. In ancient days, someone's name revealed his or her character. In proclaiming His name, God proclaimed His character.

34:6-7 the LORD. God's snapshot explanation of Himself is cited many other times in Scripture (Num. 14:17-18; Neh. 9:17; Ps. 86:15;

27 The LORD also said to Moses, "Write down these words, for I have made a covenant with you and with Israel based on these words."

28 Moses was there with the LORD 40 days and 40 nights; he did not eat bread or drink water. He wrote down on the tablets the words of the covenant—the Ten Commandments.

Moses' Radiant Face

29 As Moses descended from Mount Sinai—with the two tablets of the •testimony in his hands as he descended the mountain—he did not realize that the skin of his face shone as a result of his speaking with the LORD.a 30 When Aaron and all the Israelites saw Moses, the skin of his face shone! They were afraid to come near him. 31 But Moses called out to them, so Aaron and all the leaders of the community returned to him, and Moses spoke to them. 32 Afterwards all the Israelites came near, and he commanded them everything the LORD had told him on Mount Sinai. 33 When Moses had finished speaking with them, he put a veil over his face. 34 But whenever Moses went before the LORD to speak with Him, he would remove the veil until he came out. After he came out, he would tell the Israelites what he had been commanded, 35 and the Israelites would see that Moses' faceb was radiant. Then Moses would put the veil over his face again until he went to speak with the LORD.

The Sabbath Command

35 Moses assembled the entire Israelite community and said to them, "These are the things that the LORD has commanded you to do: 2 For six days work is to be done, but on the seventh day you are to have a holy day, a Sabbath of complete rest to the LORD. Anyone who does work on it must be executed. 3 Do not light a fire in any of your homes on the Sabbath day."

Building the Tabernacle

4 Then Moses said to the entire Israelite community, "This is what the LORD has commanded: 5 Take up an offering for the LORD among you. Let everyone whose heart is willing bring this as the LORD's offering: gold, silver, and bronze; 6 blue, purple, and scarlet yarn; fine linen and goat hair; 7 ram skins dyed red and manatee skins;c acacia wood; 8 oil for the light; spices for the anointing oil and for the fragrant incense; 9 and onyx with gemstones to mount on the •ephod and breastpiece.

10 "Let all the skilled craftsmend among you come and make everything that the LORD has commanded: 11 the tabernacle—its tent and covering, its clasps and planks, its crossbars, its posts and bases; 12 the ark with its poles, the •mercy seat, and the veil for the screen; 13 the table with its poles, all its utensils, and the bread of the Presence;e 14 the lampstand for light with its utensils and lamps as well as the oil for the light; 15 the altar of incense with its poles; the anointing oil and the fragrant incense; the entryway screen for the entrance to the tabernacle; 16 the altar of •burnt offering with its bronze grate, its poles, and all its utensils; the basin with its stand; 17 the hangings of the courtyard, its posts and bases, and the screen for the gate of the courtyard; 18 the tent pegs for the tabernacle and the tent pegs for the courtyard, along with their ropes; 19 and the specially wovenf garments for ministering in the sanctuary—the holy garments for Aaron the priest and the garments for his sons to serve as priests."

20 Then the entire Israelite community left Moses' presence. 21 Everyone whose heart was moved and whose spirit prompted him came and brought an offering to the LORD to construct the tent of meeting for every use, and ⌊to make⌋ the holy garments. 22 Both men and women came; all who had willing hearts brought brooches, earrings, rings, necklaces, and all kinds of gold jewelry—everyone who waved a presentation offering of gold to the LORD. 23 Everyone who had in his possession blue, purple, or scarlet yarn, fine linen or goat hair, ram skins dyed red or manatee skins,g brought ⌊them⌋. 24 Everyone who offered a contribution of silver or bronze brought it to the LORD. Everyone who possessed acacia wood useful for any task in the work brought ⌊it⌋. 25 Every skilledh woman spun ⌊yarn⌋ with her hands and brought it: blue, purple, and scarlet yarn, and fine linen. 26 And all the women whose hearts were moved spun the goat hair by virtue of ⌊their⌋ skill. 27 The leaders brought onyx and gemstones to mount on the ephod and breastpiece, 28 as well as the spice and oil for the light, for the anointing oil, and for the fragrant incense. 29 So the Israelites brought a freewill offering to the LORD, all the men and women whose hearts prompted them to bring ⌊something⌋ for all the work that the LORD, through Moses, had commanded to be done.

Bezalel and Oholiab

30 Moses then said to the Israelites: "Look, the LORD has appointed by name Bezalel son of Uri, son of Hur,

---

a34:29 Lit with Him   b34:35 Lit see Moses' face, that the skin of his face   c35:7 Or and dolphin skins, or and fine leather; Hb obscure   d35:10 Lit the skilled of heart   e35:13 Or of presentation   f35:19 Hb obscure   g35:23 Or or dolphin skins, or or fine leather; Hb obscure   h35:25 Lit wise of heart

---

Joel 2:13; Jonah 4:2).

34:10 covenant. A covenant can be a simple promise or as complex as a fine-print contract. With God, though, a covenant is not like a contract where both parties are bound equally to their obligations. In ancient days, God did make promises to people, some-

times based on how they might respond. God made a covenant with Noah (Gen. 6:18), Abraham (Gen. 17:3-4), Abraham's heirs, the Hebrews (6:3-4), and others.

34:15 you will eat. Certain portions of the meat were burned up or offered to the priests. In some cases, though, the worshiper's family

and friends ate part of the meat.

34:29 his face shone. Moses' shining countenance disturbed those around him. The miracle of God's glory lingering on Moses' face shows how magnificent that glory is.

34:33 veil. This word for "veil" is used only here in the Old Testament. Its only other oc-

123

of the tribe of Judah. [31] He has filled him with God's Spirit, with wisdom, understanding, and ability in every kind of craft [32] to design artistic works in gold, silver, and bronze, [33] to cut gemstones for mounting, and to carve wood for work in every kind of artistic craft. [34] He has also given both him and Oholiab son of Ahisamach, of the tribe of Dan, ⌊the ability⌋ to teach ⌊others⌋. [35] He has filled them with skill to do all the work of a gem cutter; a designer; an embroiderer in blue, purple, and scarlet yarn and fine linen; and a weaver. They can do every kind of craft and design artistic designs.

36 [1] Bezalel, Oholiab, and all the skilled[a] people are to work based on everything the LORD has commanded. The LORD has given them wisdom and understanding to know how to do all the work of constructing the sanctuary."

[2] So Moses summoned Bezalel, Oholiab, and every skilled[a] person in whose heart the LORD had placed wisdom, everyone whose heart moved him, to come to the work and do it. [3] They took from Moses' presence all the contributions that the Israelites had brought for the task of making the sanctuary. Meanwhile, the people continued to bring freewill offerings morning after morning.

[4] Then all the craftsmen who were doing all the work for the sanctuary came one by one from the work they were doing [5] and said to Moses, "The people are bringing more than is needed for the construction of the work the LORD commanded to be done."

[6] After Moses gave an order, they sent a proclamation throughout the camp: "Let no man or woman make anything else as an offering for the sanctuary." So the people stopped. [7] The materials were sufficient for them to do all the work. There was more than enough.

Building the Tabernacle

[8] All the skilled craftsmen[b] among those doing the work made the tabernacle with 10 curtains. Bezalel made them of finely spun linen, as well as blue, purple, and scarlet yarn, with a design of •cherubim worked into them. [9] The length of each curtain was 42 feet,[c] and the width of each curtain six feet;[d] all the curtains had the same measurements. [10] He joined five of the curtains to each other, and the ⌊other⌋ five curtains he joined to each other. [11] He made loops of blue yarn on the edge of the last curtain in the first set and did the same on the edge of the outermost curtain in the second set. [12] He made 50 loops on the one curtain and 50 loops on the edge of the curtain in the second set, so that the loops lined up with each other. [13] He also made 50 gold clasps and joined the curtains to each other, so that the tabernacle became a single unit.

[14] He made curtains of goat hair for a tent over the tabernacle; he also made 11 of them. [15] The length of each curtain was 45 feet,[e] and the width of each curtain six feet.[d] All 11 curtains had the same measurements. [16] He joined five of the curtains together, and ⌊the other⌋ six together. [17] He made 50 loops on the edge of the outermost curtain in the ⌊first⌋ set and 50 loops on the edge of the ⌊corresponding⌋ curtain in the second set. [18] He made 50 bronze clasps to join the tent together as a single unit. [19] He also made a covering for the tent from ram skins dyed red and a covering of manatee skins[f] on top of it.

[20] He made upright planks[g] of acacia wood for the tabernacle. [21] The length of each plank was 15 feet,[h] and the width of each was 27 inches.[i] [22] There were two tenons connected to each other for each plank. He did the same for all the planks of the tabernacle. [23] He made planks for the tabernacle as follows: 20 for the south side, [24] and he made 40 silver bases to put under the 20 planks, two bases under the first plank for its two tenons, and two bases under each of the following planks for their two tenons; [25] for the second side of the tabernacle, the north side, he made 20 planks, [26] with their 40 silver bases, two bases under the first plank and two bases under each of the following ones; [27] and for the west side of the tabernacle he made six planks. [28] He also made two additional planks for the two back corners of the tabernacle. [29] They were paired at the bottom and joined together[j] at the[k] top in a single ring. This is what he did with both of them for the two corners. [30] So there were eight planks with their 16 silver bases, two bases under each one.

[31] He made five crossbars of acacia wood for the planks on one side of the tabernacle, [32] five crossbars for the planks on the other side of the tabernacle, and five crossbars for those at the back of the tabernacle on the west. [33] He made the central crossbar run through the middle of the planks from one end to the other. [34] He overlaid them with gold and made their rings and holders for the crossbars out of gold. He also overlaid the crossbars with gold.

[35] Then he made the veil with blue, purple, and scarlet yarn, and finely spun linen. He made it with a design of cherubim worked into it. [36] For it he made four posts of acacia wood and overlaid them with gold; their hooks were of gold. And he cast four silver bases for the posts.

---

[a]**36:1,2** Lit *wise of heart* [b]**36:8** Lit *the wise of heart* [c]**36:9** Lit *28 cubits* [d]**36:9,15** Lit *four cubits* [e]**36:15** Lit *30 cubits* [f]**36:19** Or *of dolphin skins, or of fine leather;* Hb obscure [g]**36:20** Or *made frames* [h]**36:21** Lit *10 cubits* [i]**36:21** Lit *a cubit and a half* [j]**36:29** Lit *and together they are to be complete* [k]**36:29** Lit *its*

---

currence is in 2 Corinthians 3:13, which adds that Moses continued to wear the veil even after the glow began to fade.

35:2 holy day, a Sabbath of complete rest. The Sabbath was serious business to God. It was an extremely important custom directly related to God's resting from creation. By

Jesus' time, some had made the Sabbath into a legalistic set of rules, a development the Lord corrected (Matt. 12:1-14).

35:30 Hur. Hur, Bezalel's grandfather, is mentioned elsewhere (17:10; 24:14; 31:2; 38:32; 1 Chron. 2:19-20), perhaps as a point of exclamation to underscore Bezalel's impor-

tance to the building of the tabernacle.

36:8-39:31 Repetition was an ancient form that placed special emphasis on the topics discussed, and the description in the following chapters of the fulfillment of the instructions given to Moses regarding the tabernacle (25:1–31:18) heightens not only

37 He made a screen embroidered with blue, purple, and scarlet yarn, and finely spun linen for the entrance to the tent, 38 together with its five posts and their hooks. He overlaid the tops of the posts and their bands with gold, but their five bases were bronze.

Making the Ark

37 Bezalel made the ark of acacia wood, 45 inches long, 27 inches wide, and 27 inches high.ᵃ 2 He overlaid it with pure gold inside and out and made a gold molding all around it. 3 He cast four gold rings for it to be on its four feet, two rings on one side and two rings on the other side. 4 He made poles of acacia wood and overlaid them with gold. 5 He inserted the poles into the rings on the sides of the ark for carrying the ark.

6 He made a •mercy seat of pure gold, 45 inches long and 27 inches wide.ᵇ 7 He made two •cherubim of gold; he made them of hammered work at the two ends of the mercy seat, 8 one cherub at one end and one cherub at the other end. He made the cherubim ⌊of one piece⌋ with the mercy seat, ⌊a cherub⌋ at each end. 9 They had wings spread out, covering the mercy seat with their wings and facing each other. The faces of the cherubim were looking toward the mercy seat.

Making the Table

10 He constructed the table of acacia wood, 36 inches long, 18 inches wide, and 27 inches high.ᶜ 11 He overlaid it with pure gold and made a gold molding all around it. 12 He made a three-inchᵈ frame all around it and made a gold molding all around its frame. 13 He cast four gold rings for it and attached the rings to the four corners at its four legs. 14 The rings were next to the frame as holders for the poles to carry the table. 15 He made the poles for carrying the table from acacia wood and overlaid them with gold. 16 He also made the utensils that would be on the table out of pure gold: its plates and cups, as well as its bowls and pitchers for pouring drink offerings.

Making the Lampstand

17 Then he made the lampstand out of pure hammered gold. He made it ⌊all⌋ of one piece: its base and shaft, its ⌊ornamental⌋ cups, and its calyxesᵉ and petals. 18 Six branches extended from its sides, three branches of the lampstand from one side and three branches of the lampstand from the other side. 19 There were three cups shaped like almond blos-soms, each with a calyx and petals, on the first branch, and three cups shaped like almond blossoms, each with a calyx and petals, on the next branch. It was this way for the six branches that extended from the lamp-stand. 20 On the lampstand shaft there were four cups shaped like almond blossoms with its calyxes and pet-als. 21 For the six branches that extended from it, a calyx was under the first pair of branches from it, a calyx under the second pair of branches from it, and a calyx under the third pair of branches from it. 22 Their calyxes and branches were of one piece.ᶠ All of it was a single hammered piece of pure gold. 23 He also made its seven lamps, snuffers, and firepans of pure gold. 24 He made it and all its utensils of 75 poundsᵍ of pure gold.

Making the Altar of Incense

25 He made the altar of incense out of acacia wood. It was square, 18 inches long and 18 inches wide; it was 36 inches high.ʰ Its horns were of one piece.ᶠ 26 He overlaid it, its top, all around its sides, and its horns with pure gold. Then he made a gold molding all around it. 27 He made two gold rings for it under the molding on two of its sides; ⌊he put these⌋ on opposite sides of it to be holders for the poles to carry it with. 28 He made the poles of acacia wood and overlaid them with gold.

29 He also made the holy anointing oil and the pure, fragrant, and expertly blended incense.

Making the Altar of Burnt Offering

38 Bezalel constructed the altar of •burnt offering from acacia wood. It was square, seven and a half feet long and seven and a half feet wide,ⁱ and was four and a half feetʲ high. 2 He made horns for it on its four corners; the horns were of one piece.ᶠ Then he overlaid it with bronze.

3 He made all the altar's utensils: the pots, shovels, basins, meat forks, and firepans; he made all its uten-sils of bronze. 4 He constructed for the altar a grate of bronze mesh under its ledge,ᵏ halfway up from the bottom. 5 At the four corners of the bronze grate he cast four rings as holders for the poles. 6 He also made the poles of acacia wood and overlaid them with bronze. 7 Then he inserted the poles into the rings on the sides of the altar in order to carry it with them. He constructed the altar with boards so that it was hollow.

ᵃ**37:1** Lit *two and a half cubits its length, one and a half cubits its width, and one and a half cubits its height*   ᵇ**37:6** Lit *two and a half cubits its length and one and a half cubits its width*   ᶜ**37:10** Lit *two cubits its length, one cubit its width, and one and a half cubits its height*   ᵈ**37:12** Lit *a handbreadth*   ᵉ**37:17** = the outer covering of a flower   ᶠ**37:22,25; 38:2** Lit *piece with it*   ᵍ**37:24** Lit *a talent*   ʰ**37:25** Lit *a cubit its length, a cubit its width, and two cubits its height*   ⁱ**38:1** Lit *five cubits its length and five cubits its width*   ʲ**38:1** Lit *three cubits*   ᵏ**38:4** Or *rim*

---

the importance of the specific items being re-ferred to, but the absolute significance of the tabernacle itself as the dwelling place of God's Presence. The people obeyed God to the letter.

36:8-38 Here the tabernacle precedes the ark in proper order of construction, but the in-structions for its building (26:1-37) followed the ark's instructions (25:10-22) to emphasize the central importance of the ark; upon which resided God's spiritual presence on earth. The later filling of the Most Holy Place with God's glory (40:34) mirrors the descent of the Holy Spirit on Christ (Luke 3:22), and the sub-sequent descent of the Spirit on Christ's church (Acts 2:2).

37:1 the ark. The ark of the covenant (or ark of the testimony) was located in the Most Holy Place of the tabernacle. The ark was covered by the atonement seat. The Lord had told Moses "I will appear in the cloud over the

Making the Bronze Basin

8 He made the bronze basin and its stand from the ⌊bronze⌋ mirrors of the women who served at the entrance to the tent of meeting.

Making the Courtyard

9 Then he made the courtyard. The hangings on the south side of the courtyard were of finely spun linen, 150 feet in length,[a] 10 including their 20 posts and 20 bronze bases. The hooks and bands[b] of the posts were silver. 11 ⌊The hangings⌋ on the north side were also 150 feet in length,[a] including their 20 posts and 20 bronze bases. The hooks and bands[b] of the posts were silver. 12 The hangings on the west side were 75 feet in length,[c] including their 10 posts and 10 bases. The hooks and bands of the posts were silver. 13 ⌊The hangings⌋ on the east toward the sunrise were also 75 feet in length.[c] 14 The hangings on one side ⌊of the gate⌋ were 22 and a half feet,[d] including their three posts and three bases. 15 It was the same for the other side. The hangings were 22 and a half feet,[d] including their three posts and three bases on both sides of the courtyard gate. 16 All the hangings around the courtyard were of finely spun linen. 17 The bases for the posts were bronze; the hooks and bands[b] of the posts were silver; and the plating for the tops of the posts was silver. All the posts of the courtyard were banded with silver.

18 The screen for the gate of the courtyard was embroidered with blue, purple, and scarlet yarn, and finely spun linen. It was 30 feet[e] long, and like the hangings of the courtyard, seven and a half feet[f] high.[g] 19 It had four posts, including their four bronze bases. Their hooks were silver, and the bands[b] as well as the plating of their tops were silver. 20 All the tent pegs for the tabernacle and for the surrounding courtyard were bronze.

Inventory of Materials

21 This is the inventory for the tabernacle, the tabernacle of the •testimony, that was recorded at Moses' command. It was the work of the Levites under the direction of[h] Ithamar son of Aaron the priest. 22 Bezalel son of Uri, son of Hur, of the tribe of Judah, made everything that the LORD commanded Moses. 23 With him was Oholiab son of Ahisamach, of the tribe of Dan, a gem cutter, a designer, and an embroiderer with blue, purple, and scarlet yarn, and fine linen.

24 All the gold of the presentation offering that was used for the project in all the work on the sanctuary, was 2,193 pounds,[i] according to the sanctuary •shekel. 25 The silver from those of the community who were registered was 7,544 pounds,[j] according to the sanctuary shekel—26 two-fifths of an ounce[k] per man, that is, half a shekel according to the sanctuary shekel, from everyone 20 years old or more who had crossed over to the registered group, 603,550 men. 27 There were 7,500 pounds[l] of silver ⌊used⌋ to cast the bases of the sanctuary and the bases of the veil—100 bases from 7,500 pounds,[l] 75 pounds[m] for each base. 28 With the ⌊remaining⌋ 44 pounds[n] he made the hooks for the posts, overlaid their tops, and supplied bands[b] for them.

29 The bronze of the presentation offering totaled 5,310 pounds.[o] 30 He made with it the bases for the entrance to the tent of meeting, the bronze altar and its bronze grate, all the utensils for the altar, 31 the bases for the surrounding courtyard, the bases for the gate of the courtyard, all the tent pegs for the tabernacle, and all the tent pegs for the surrounding courtyard.

Making the Priestly Garments

39 They made specially woven[p] garments for ministry in the sanctuary, and the holy garments for Aaron from the blue, purple, and scarlet yarn, just as the LORD had commanded Moses.

Making the Ephod

2 Bezalel made the •ephod of gold, of blue, purple, and scarlet yarn, and of finely spun linen. 3 They hammered out thin sheets of gold, and he[q] cut threads ⌊from them⌋ to interweave with the blue, purple, and scarlet yarn, and the fine linen in a skillful design. 4 They made shoulder pieces for attaching it; it was joined together at its two edges. 5 The artistically woven waistband that was on the ephod was of one piece with the ephod, according to the same workmanship of gold, of blue, purple, and scarlet yarn, and of finely spun linen, just as the LORD had commanded Moses.

6 Then they mounted the onyx stones surrounded with gold filigree settings, engraved with the names of Israel's sons as a gem cutter engraves a seal. 7 He fastened them on the shoulder pieces of the ephod as memorial stones for the Israelites, just as the LORD had commanded Moses.

---

a 38:9,11 Lit 100 cubits b 38:10,11,17,19,28 Or connecting rods c 38:12,13 Lit 50 cubits d 38:14,15 Lit 15 cubits e 38:18 Lit 20 cubits f 38:18 Lit five cubits g 38:18 Lit high in width h 38:21 Lit Levites by the hand of i 38:24 Lit 29 talents and 730 shekels j 38:25 Lit 100 talents and 1,775 shekels k 38:26 Lit a beka l 38:27 Lit 100 talents m 38:27 Lit one talent n 38:28 Lit 1,775 (shekels) o 38:29 Lit 70 talents and 2,400 shekels p 39:1 Hb obscure q 39:3 Sam, Syr, Tg read they

---

atonement seat" (Lev. 16:2). Though the high priest could only appear there once a year on the day of atonement, Moses met there regularly with God to receive instructions for the Israelites (25:22). The ark was also a holy time capsule that held precious reminders of the Hebrews' journey from Egypt, such as the two

tablets of the Law (40:20), Aaron's rod (Num 17:1-11), and the golden jar of manna (16:33-34). Later the ark would prove to be a visible token of God's presence in Israelite military campaigns (Josh. 6:6), and at other times just a superstitious token (1 Sam. 4).

38:24-31 An enormous amount of gold, silver,

and bronze went into the construction, a little more than eight and a half tons. The gold and bronze had been acquired by means of a massive contribution of freewill offerings (36:3), but the nearly four tons of silver had come directly from the collection taken on behalf of the tabernacle (vv. 25-26). Each man

Making the Breastpiece

8 He also made the embroidered breastpiece with the same workmanship as the ephod of gold, of blue, purple, and scarlet yarn, and of finely spun linen. **9** They made the breastpiece square and folded double, nine inches long and nine inches wide.[a] **10** They mounted four rows of gemstones[b] on it. The first row was a row of carnelian, topaz, and emerald;[c] **11** the second row, a turquoise,[d] a sapphire,[e] and a diamond;[f] **12** the third row, a jacinth,[g] an agate, and an amethyst; **13** and the fourth row, a beryl, an onyx, and a jasper. They were surrounded with gold filigree in their settings.

14 The 12 stones corresponded to the names of Israel's sons. Each stone was engraved like a seal with one of the names of the 12 tribes.

15 They made braided chains of pure gold cord for the breastpiece. **16** They also fashioned two gold filigree settings and two gold rings and attached the two rings to its two corners. **17** Then they attached the two gold cords to the two gold rings on the corners of the breastpiece. **18** They attached the other ends of the two cords to the two filigree settings and, in this way, attached ⌊them⌋ to the ephod's shoulder pieces in front. **19** They made two ⌊other⌋ gold rings and put ⌊them⌋ at the two other corners of the breastpiece on the edge that is next to the inner border of the ephod. **20** They made two ⌊more⌋ gold rings and attached them to the bottom of the ephod's two shoulder pieces on its front, close to its seam,[h] above the ephod's woven waistband. **21** Then they tied the breastpiece from its rings to the rings of the ephod with a cord of blue yarn, so that the breastpiece was above the ephod's waistband and did not come loose from the ephod. ⌊They did⌋ just as the LORD had commanded Moses.

Making the Robe

22 They made the woven robe of the ephod entirely of blue yarn. **23** There was an opening in the center of the robe like that for body armor[g] with a collar around the opening so that it would not tear. **24** They made pomegranates of finely spun blue, purple, and scarlet yarn[i] on the lower hem of the robe. **25** They made bells of pure gold and attached the bells between the pomegranates, all around the hem of the robe between the pomegranates, **26** a bell and a pomegranate alternating all around the lower hem of the robe.[j] It is to be used for ministry, just as the LORD had commanded Moses.

The Other Priestly Garments

27 They made the tunics of fine woven linen for Aaron and his sons. **28** ⌊They also made⌋ the turban and the ornate headbands[k] of fine linen, the undergarments, **29** and the sash of finely spun linen of embroidered blue, purple, and scarlet yarn. ⌊They did⌋ just as the LORD had commanded Moses.

Making the Holy Diadem

30 They also made a plate,[l] the holy diadem, out of pure gold, and wrote on it an inscription like the engraving on a seal:

> **HOLY TO THE LORD**

31 Then they attached a cord of blue yarn to it in order to mount ⌊it⌋ on the turban, just as the LORD had commanded Moses.

Moses' Inspection of the Tabernacle

32 So all the work for the tabernacle, the tent of meeting, was finished. The Israelites did everything just as the LORD had commanded Moses. **33** Then they brought the tabernacle to Moses: the tent with all its furnishings, its clasps, its planks, its crossbars, and its posts and bases; **34** the covering of ram skins dyed red and the covering of manatee skins;[m] the veil for the screen; **35** the ark of the •testimony with its poles and the •mercy seat; **36** the table, all its utensils, and the bread of the Presence;[n] **37** the pure ⌊gold⌋ lampstand, with its lamps arranged and all its utensils, as well as the oil for the light; **38** the gold altar; the anointing oil; the fragrant incense; the screen for the entrance to the tent; **39** the bronze altar with its bronze grate, its poles, and all its utensils; the basin with its stand; **40** the hangings of the courtyard, its posts and bases, the screen for the gate of the courtyard, its ropes and tent pegs, and all the equipment for the service of the tabernacle, the tent of meeting; **41** and the specially woven[g] garments for ministering in the sanctuary, the holy garments for Aaron the priest and the garments for his sons to serve as priests. **42** The Israelites had done all the work according to everything the LORD had commanded Moses. **43** Moses inspected all the work they had accomplished. They had done just as the LORD commanded. Then Moses blessed them.

---

[a]**39:9** Lit *a span its length and a span its width* [b]**39:10** Many of these stones cannot be identified with certainty. [c]**39:10** Or *beryl* [d]**39:11** Or *malachite*, or *garnet* [e]**39:11** Or *lapis lazuli* [f]**39:11** Hb uncertain; LXX, Vg read *jasper* [g]**39:12,23,41** Hb obscure [h]**39:20** The place where the shoulder pieces join the front of the ephod [i]**39:24** Sam, LXX, Vg add *and linen* [j]**39:26** Lit *bell and pomegranate, bell and pomegranate, on the hem of the robe around* [k]**39:28** Lit *and the headdresses of headbands* [l]**39:30** Or *medallion* [m]**39:34** Or *of dolphin skins*, or *of fine leather*; Hb obscure [n]**39:36** Traditionally, *showbread*

---

over 20 had been required to pay a half-shekel for the census offering (30:11-16).

The number of half-shekels multiplied by the 603,550 men who took part in the census (cf. 12:37; Num. 1:46) exactly equals the weight of silver listed here.

38:25 pounds ... shekel. Often the coins were actually weights that would be placed on scales to buy that same weight of flour or grain. A shekel was about 1/5 of an ounce, and there were 75 pounds to a talent.

39:32 as the LORD had commanded. Throughout the Bible, people fail God. But here the Israelites obey Him to the letter.

Noah did the same with plans for the ark (Gen. 6:22). Moses and Aaron did it in their standoff with Pharaoh (7:10). David did it in battle (2 Sam. 5:25).

39:43 Moses inspected all the work. Moses had a difficult role to play in the lives of his people. He had to rally them as well as

Setting up the Tabernacle

40 The LORD spoke to Moses: 2 "You are to set up the tabernacle, the tent of meeting, on the first day of the first month.ᵃ 3 Put the ark of the •testimony there, and screen off the ark with the veil. 4 Then bring in the table and lay out its arrangement; also bring in the lampstand and set up its lamps. 5 Place the gold altar for incense in front of the ark of the testimony. Put up the screen for the entrance to the tabernacle. 6 Position the altar of burnt offering in front of the entrance to the tabernacle, the tent of meeting. 7 Place the basin between the tent of meeting and the altar, and put water in it. 8 Assemble the surrounding courtyard and hang the screen for the gate of the courtyard.

9 "Take the anointing oil, and anoint the tabernacle and everything in it; consecrate it along with all its furnishings so that it will be holy. 10 Anoint the altar of burnt offering and all its utensils; consecrate the altar so that it will be especially holy. 11 Anoint the basin and its stand, and consecrate it.

12 "Then bring Aaron and his sons to the entrance to the tent of meeting and wash them with water. 13 Clothe Aaron with the holy garments, anoint him, and consecrate him, so that he can serve Me as a priest. 14 Have his sons come forward and clothe them in tunics. 15 Anoint them just as you anointed their father, so that they may also serve Me as priests. Their anointing will serve to inaugurate a permanent priesthood for them throughout their generations."

16 Moses did everything just as the LORD had commanded him. 17 The tabernacle was set up in the first month of the second year, on the first ⌊day⌋ of the month.ᵇ 18 Moses set up the tabernacle: he laid its bases, positioned its planks, inserted its crossbars, and set up its posts. 19 Then he spread the tent over the tabernacle and put the covering of the tent on top of it, just as the LORD had commanded Moses.

20 Moses took the testimony and placed ⌊it⌋ in the ark, and attached the poles to the ark. He set the •mercy seat on top of the ark. 21 He brought the ark into the tabernacle, put up the veil for the screen, and screened off the ark of the testimony, just as the LORD had commanded him.

22 Moses placed the table in the tent of meeting on the north side of the tabernacle, outside the veil. 23 He arranged the bread on it before the LORD, just as the LORD had commanded him. 24 He also put the lampstand in the tent of meeting opposite the table on the south side of the tabernacle 25 and set up the lamps before the LORD, just as the LORD had commanded him.

26 Moses also installed the gold altar in the tent of meeting, in front of the veil, 27 and burned fragrant incense on it, just as the LORD had commanded him. 28 He put up the screen at the entrance to the tabernacle. 29 Then he placed the altar of burnt offering at the entrance to the tabernacle, the tent of meeting, and offered the •burnt offering and the •grain offering on it, just as the LORD had commanded him.

30 He set the basin between the tent of meeting and the altar and put water in it for washing. 31 Moses, Aaron, and his sons washed their hands and feet from it. 32 They washed whenever they came to the tent of meeting and approached the altar, just as the LORD had commanded Moses.

33 Next Moses set up the surrounding courtyard for the tabernacle and the altar and hung a screen for the gate of the courtyard. So Moses finished the work.

The LORD's Glory

34 The cloud covered the tent of meeting, and the glory of the LORD filled the tabernacle. 35 Moses was unable to enter the tent of meeting because the cloud rested on it, and the glory of the LORD filled the tabernacle.

36 The Israelites set out whenever the cloud was taken up from the tabernacle throughout all the stages of their journey. 37 If the cloud was not taken up, they did not set out until the day it was taken up. 38 For the cloud of the LORD was over the tabernacle by day, and there was a fire inside the cloud by night, visible to the entire house of Israel throughout all the stages of their journey.

ᵃ **40:2** Lit *on the day of the first month, on the first of the month*   ᵇ **40:17** DSS, Sam, LXX add *of their coming out of Egypt*

---

chastise them, confront them and mitigate their differences. Here is a rare moment when Moses gets to observe their work and offer them congratulations and blessings. **accomplished.** The same word was used for God's completed work of creation (Gen. 2:2). Likewise, Moses blessed as God had blessed (Gen. 1:22, 28; 2:3). Like the earth, God had designed the tabernacle and allowed His people to participate in its creation.

40:3 screen off the ark. As the seat of God's glory, it was important to read the ark's user manual. Once seventy men died from looking into it (1 Sam. 6:19). Another time, the ark was improperly transported in a cart that predictably tipped —into Uzzah's unfortunate hand (2 Sam. 6:6-7).

40:16 Moses did everything. God called Moses the earth's most humble man (Num. 12:3). He did not presume to know more than God.

40:36 whenever the cloud was taken up. Just as God led them with a cloud by day and a pillar of fire by night (13:21), now the cloud settled on the tabernacle and lifted when it was time to pack up.

40:38 fire inside the cloud. God's glory was the fire. The cloud covered the glory so that people could see it and live. At night, the glory showed through the cloud.

INTRODUCTION TO
LEVITICUS

AUTHOR

Moses is assumed to be the author and editor of most of the first five books of the Old Testament (the Pentateuch).

DATE

It is difficult to set a firm date for the writing of the Pentateuch. Conservative estimates place it in either the 15th or 13th century B.C., depending on when the Exodus occurred.

THEME

God's reconciliation and sanctification of His people.

HISTORICAL BACKGROUND

The name of this book, from the Greek and Latin versions, comes from its emphasis on the Levitical priesthood. The ministry of the tabernacle was conducted by the sons of Aaron (Moses' brother). These newly appointed priests were assisted by many of their relatives from the tribe of Levi. The events in Leviticus take place after the Exodus from Egypt and the giving of the Law at Sinai, and concern the formalizing of

Israelite religious practice. In Exodus, instructions were given for the building of the tabernacle; here in Leviticus, regulations are given for how to worship there.

CHARACTERISTICS

After the covenant at Sinai, Israel was the earthly representation of God's kingdom and, as her King, the Lord established His administration over all of Israel's life. Her religious, communal, and personal life were so regulated to establish her as God's holy people and to instruct her in holiness. To the modern reader, Leviticus may appear hopelessly outdated with its strange economic practices, and the blood of animal sacrifice, yet the questions it seeks to answer are as important for us as they were for the Israelites. How do we remain reconciled to God? What is the proper way to worship a holy God? How are we to act toward each other within the context of God's covenant? Leviticus answers these and other questions faced by the Israelites using symbols familiar to them. For us, the key to understanding Leviticus is looking beyond these strange symbols to the underlying principles describing God's way of holiness and reconciliation.

The Burnt Offering

1 Then the LORD summoned Moses and spoke to him from the tent of meeting: 2 "Speak to the Israelites and tell them: When any of you brings an offering to the LORD from the livestock, you[a] may bring your offering from the herd or the flock.

3 "If his gift is a •burnt offering from the herd, he is to bring an unblemished male. He must bring it to the entrance to the tent of meeting so that he[b] may be accepted by the LORD. 4 He is to lay his hand on the head of the burnt offering so it can be accepted on his behalf to make •atonement for him. 5 He is to slaughter the bull before the LORD; Aaron's sons the priests are to present the blood and sprinkle it on all sides of the altar that is at the entrance to the tent of meeting. 6 Then he must skin the burnt offering and cut it into pieces.[c] 7 The sons of Aaron the priest will prepare a fire on the altar and arrange wood on the fire. 8 Aaron's sons the priests are to arrange the pieces, the head, and the suet on top of the burning wood on the altar. 9 The offerer must wash its entrails and shanks with water. Then the priest will burn all of it on the altar as a burnt offering, a fire offering of a pleasing aroma to the LORD.

10 "But if his gift for a burnt offering is from the flock, from sheep or goats, he is to present an unblemished male. 11 He will slaughter it on the north side of the altar before the LORD. Aaron's sons the priests will sprinkle its blood against the altar on all sides. 12 He will cut it into pieces[c] with its head and its suet, and the priest will arrange them on top of the burning wood on the altar. 13 But he is to wash the entrails and shanks with water. The priest will then present all of it and burn ⌊it⌋ on the altar; it is a burnt offering, a fire offering of a pleasing aroma to the LORD.

14 "If his gift to the LORD is a burnt offering of birds, he is to present his offering from the turtledoves or young pigeons.[d] 15 Then the priest must bring it to the altar, and must twist off its head and burn ⌊it⌋ on the altar; its blood should be drained at the side of the altar. 16 He will remove its digestive tract,[e] cutting off the tail feathers, and throw it on the east side of the altar at the place for ashes. 17 He will tear it open by its wings without dividing ⌊the bird⌋. Then the priest is to burn it on the altar on top of the burning wood. It is a burnt offering, a fire offering of a pleasing aroma to the LORD.

The Grain Offering

2 "When anyone presents a •grain offering as a gift to the LORD, his gift must consist of fine flour.[f] He is to pour olive oil on it, put frankincense on it,[g] 2 and bring it to Aaron's sons the priests. The priest will take a handful of fine flour and oil from it, along with all its frankincense, and will burn this memorial portion of it on the altar, a fire offering of a pleasing aroma to the LORD. 3 But the rest of the grain offering will belong to Aaron and his sons, the holiest part of the fire offerings to the LORD.

4 "When you present a grain offering baked in an oven, it must be ⌊made⌋ of fine flour, either unleavened cakes mixed with oil or unleavened wafers coated with oil. 5 If your gift is a grain offering prepared on the griddle, it must be unleavened bread ⌊made⌋ of fine flour mixed with oil. 6 Break it into pieces and pour oil on it; it is a grain offering. 7 If your gift is a grain offering ⌊prepared⌋[h] in a pan, it must be made of fine flour with oil. 8 When you bring[i] to the LORD the grain offering made in any of these ways, it is to be presented to the priest, and he will take it to the altar. 9 The priest will remove the memorial portion[j] from the grain offering and burn it on the altar, a fire offering of a pleasing aroma to the LORD. 10 But the rest of the grain offering will belong to Aaron and his sons, the holiest part of the fire offerings to the LORD.

11 "No grain offering that you present to the LORD is to be made with yeast, for you are not to burn[k] any yeast or honey as a fire offering to the LORD. 12 You may present them to the LORD as an offering of •firstfruits, but they are not to be offered on the altar as a pleasing aroma. 13 You are to season each of your grain offerings with salt; you must not omit from your grain offering the salt of the covenant with your God. You are to present salt[l] with each of your offerings.

14 "If you present a grain offering of firstfruits to the LORD, you must present fresh heads of grain, crushed kernels, roasted on the fire, for your grain offering of firstfruits. 15 You are to put oil and frankincense on it; it is a grain offering. 16 The priest will then burn some of its crushed kernels and oil with all its frankincense as a fire offering to the LORD.

The Fellowship Offering

3 "If his offering is a •fellowship sacrifice, and he is presenting ⌊an animal⌋ from the herd, whether male or female, he must present one without blemish before the LORD. 2 He is to lay his hand on the head of his offering and slaughter it at the entrance to the tent of meeting. Then Aaron's sons the priests will sprinkle the blood on all sides of the altar. 3 He will present part

---

a 1:2 Or LORD, from the livestock you   b 1:3 Or it   c 1:6,12 Lit its pieces   d 1:14 Or or pigeons   e 1:16 Or its crop, or its crissum   f 2:1 Wheat flour; Ex 29:2   g 2:1 DSS, Sam, LXX add it is a grain offering   h 2:7 Or [fried]   i 2:8 DSS, LXX read When he brings   j 2:9 Lit portion of it   k 2:11 Some Hb mss, Sam, LXX, Tg read present   l 2:13 Salt, used as a preservative, is a symbol of the permanence of the covenant.

1:3 unblemished. The people were to bring the best animals from their herds as offerings to the Lord.

1:5 he is to slaughter. The sin offering required that a person kill his own animal, symbolically taking an innocent life for his own sins.

2:1 grain offering. These offerings were of flour, oil, and incense.

2:11–13 yeast or honey … salt. While yeast and honey were not allowed as part of the grain offering, honey was a part of the first-fruits offering. Salt was always a part of the offerings.

3:1–4 fellowship sacrifice. This sacrifice, also called a peace offering, was motivated by a person's gratitude rather than remorse over his sin.

3:17 fat … blood. God's prohibition against eating blood is universal (Gen. 9:4). The fat referred to is suet, or fat surrounding the animal's organs.

of the fellowship sacrifice as a fire offering to the LORD: the fat surrounding the entrails, all the fat that is on the entrails, 4 and the two kidneys with the fat on them at the loins; he will also remove the fatty lobe of the liver with the kidneys. 5 Aaron's sons will burn it on the altar along with the •burnt offering that is on the burning wood, a fire offering of a pleasing aroma to the LORD.

6 "If his offering as a fellowship sacrifice to the LORD is from the flock, he must present a male or female without blemish. 7 If he is presenting a lamb for his offering, he is to present it before the LORD. 8 He must lay his hand on the head of his offering, then slaughter it before the tent of meeting. Aaron's sons will sprinkle its blood on all sides of the altar. 9 He will then present part of the fellowship sacrifice as a fire offering to the LORD ⌊consisting of⌋ its fat and the entire fat tail, which he is to remove close to the backbone. He will also remove the fat surrounding the entrails, all the fat on the entrails, 10 the two kidneys with the fat on them at the loins, and the fatty lobe of the liver above the kidneys. 11 Then the priest will burn it on the altar as food, a fire offering to the LORD.

12 "If his offering is a goat, he is to present it before the LORD. 13 He must lay his hand on its head and slaughter it before the tent of meeting. Aaron's sons will sprinkle[a] its blood on all sides of the altar. 14 He will present part of his offering as a fire offering to the LORD: the fat surrounding the entrails, all the fat that is on the entrails, 15 and the two kidneys with the fat on them at the loins; he will also remove the fatty lobe of the liver with the kidneys. 16 Then the priest will burn them on the altar as food, a fire offering for a pleasing aroma.[b]

"All fat belongs to the LORD. 17 This is a permanent statute throughout your generations, wherever you live: you must not eat any fat or any blood."

The Sin Offering

4 Then the LORD spoke to Moses: 2 "Tell the Israelites: When someone sins unintentionally against any of the LORD's commands and does anything prohibited by them—

3 "If the anointed priest[c] sins, bringing guilt on the people, he is to present to the LORD a young, unblemished bull as a •sin[d] offering for the sin he has committed. 4 He must bring the bull to the entrance to the tent of meeting before the LORD, lay his hand on the bull's head, and slaughter it before the LORD. 5 The anointed priest must then take some of the bull's blood and bring

it into the tent of meeting. 6 The priest is to dip his finger in the blood and sprinkle some of it seven times before the LORD in front of the veil of the sanctuary. 7 The priest must apply some of the blood to the horns of the altar of fragrant incense that is before the LORD in the tent of meeting. He must pour out the rest of the bull's blood at the base of the altar of burnt offering that is at the entrance to the tent of meeting. 8 He is to remove all the fat from the bull of the sin offering: the fat surrounding the entrails; all the fat that is on the entrails; 9 and the two kidneys with the fat on them at the loins. He will also remove the fatty lobe of the liver with the kidneys, 10 just as the fat is removed from the ox of the •fellowship sacrifice. The priest is to burn them on the altar of burnt offering. 11 But the hide of the bull and all its flesh, with its head and shanks, and its entrails and dung— 12 all ⌊the rest⌋ of the bull—he must bring to a ceremonially clean place outside the camp to the ash heap, and must burn it on a wood fire. It is to be burned at the ash heap.

13 "Now if the whole community of Israel errs, and the matter escapes the notice of the assembly, so that they violate any of the LORD's commands and incur guilt by doing what is prohibited, 14 then the assembly must present a young bull as a sin offering. When the sin they have committed in regard to the command becomes known, they are to bring it before the tent of meeting. 15 The elders of the assembly are to lay their hands on the bull's head before the LORD and it is to be slaughtered before the LORD. 16 The anointed priest will bring some of the bull's blood into the tent of meeting. 17 The priest is to dip his finger in the blood and sprinkle ⌊it⌋ seven times before the LORD in front of the veil. 18 He is to apply some of the blood to the horns of the altar that is before the LORD in the tent of meeting. He must pour out the rest of the blood at the base of the altar of burnt offering that is at the entrance to the tent of meeting. 19 He is to remove all the fat from it and burn it on the altar. 20 He is to offer this bull just as he did with the bull in the sin offering; he will offer it the same way. So the priest will make •atonement on their behalf, and they will be forgiven. 21 Then he will bring the bull outside the camp and burn it just as he burned the first bull. It is the sin offering for the assembly.

22 "When a leader[e] sins and unintentionally violates any of the commands of the LORD his God by doing what is prohibited, and incurs guilt, 23 or someone informs him about the sin he has committed, he is to bring an unblemished male goat as his offering. 24 He is to lay his hand on the head of the goat and slaughter it

---

[a]3:13 Or dash   [b]3:16 Sam, LXX add to the LORD   [c]4:3 Probably the high priest; Lv 6:22   [d]4:3 Or purification   [e]4:22 Or ruler

---

4:3 bringing guilt on the people. When the high priest sinned, it made Israel a sinful nation.

4:5 the bull's blood. The blood cleansed the stains of sin from the altar and kept the nation ceremonially clean.

4:12 [the rest] of the bull … outside the camp. Since the bull had been a substitute for the priest, the entire carcass was disposed of outside of the camp. The carcass became holy and needed to be destroyed so it would not be defiled.

4:20 atonement. To atone is to cleanse sin so forgiveness is possible. The dead animals did

not change the sinful state of humanity. But the sacrifice as an act of faith—the holy God's revulsion at sin—connected the people with God's forgiveness.

4:23 goat. When a leader sinned, he brought a goat. Since he was in a responsible position, he had to pay a greater price for his sin.

at the place where the •burnt offering is slaughtered before the LORD. It is a sin offering. 25 Then the priest must take some of the blood from the sin offering with his finger and apply it to the horns of the altar of burnt offering. The rest of its blood he must pour out at the base of the altar of burnt offering. 26 He must burn all its fat on the altar, like the fat of the fellowship sacrifice. In this way the priest will make atonement on his behalf for that person's sin, and he will be forgiven.

27 "Now if any of the common people[a] sins unintentionally by violating one of the LORD's commands, does what is prohibited, and incurs guilt, 28 or if someone informs him about the sin he has committed, then he is to bring an unblemished female goat as his offering for the sin that he has committed. 29 He is to lay his hand on the head of the sin offering and slaughter it at the place of the burnt offering. 30 Then the priest must take some of its blood with his finger and apply it to the horns of the altar of burnt offering. He must pour out the rest of its blood at the base of the altar. 31 He is to remove all its fat just as the fat is removed from the fellowship sacrifice. The priest is to burn ⌊it⌋ on the altar as a pleasing aroma to the LORD. In this way the priest will make atonement on his behalf, and he will be forgiven.

32 "Or if the offering that he brings as a sin offering is a lamb, he is to bring an unblemished female. 33 He is to lay his hand on the head of the sin offering and slaughter it as a sin offering at the place where the burnt offering is slaughtered. 34 Then the priest must take some of the blood of the sin offering with his finger and apply it to the horns of the altar of burnt offering. He must pour out the rest of its blood at the base of the altar. 35 He is to remove all its fat just as the fat of the lamb is removed from the fellowship sacrifice. The priest will burn it on the altar along with the fire offerings to the LORD. In this way the priest will make atonement on his behalf for the sin he has committed, and he will be forgiven.

Cases Requiring Sin Offerings

5 "When someone sins ⌊in any of these ways⌋:

⌊If⌋ he has seen, heard, or known about something he has witnessed, and did not respond to a public call to testify, he is guilty.
2 Or ⌊if⌋ someone touches anything unclean—a carcass of an unclean wild animal, or unclean livestock, or an unclean swarming creature[b] —

without being aware of it, he is unclean and guilty.
3 Or ⌊if⌋ he touches human uncleanness—any uncleanness by which one can become defiled—without being aware of it, but ⌊later⌋ recognizes ⌊it⌋, he is guilty.
4 Or ⌊if⌋ someone swears rashly to do what is good or evil—concerning anything a person may speak rashly in an oath—without being aware of it, but ⌊later⌋ recognizes it, he incurs guilt in such an instance.[c]

5 If someone incurs guilt in one of these cases, he is to confess he has committed that sin. 6 He must bring his restitution for the sin he has committed to the LORD: a female lamb or goat from the flock as a •sin offering. In this way the priest will make •atonement on his behalf for his sin.

7 "But if he cannot afford an animal from the flock, then he may bring to the LORD two turtledoves or two young pigeons as restitution for his sin—one as a sin offering and the other as a •burnt offering. 8 He is to bring them to the priest, who will first present the one for the sin offering. He must twist its head at the back of the neck without severing ⌊it⌋. 9 Then he will sprinkle some of the blood of the sin offering on the side of the altar, while the rest of the blood is to be drained out at the base of the altar; it is a sin offering. 10 He must prepare the second ⌊bird⌋ as a burnt offering according to the regulation. In this way the priest will make atonement on his behalf for the sin he has committed, and he will be forgiven.

11 "But if he cannot afford[d] two turtledoves or two young pigeons, he may bring two quarts[e] of fine[f] flour[g] as an offering for his sin. He must not put olive oil or frankincense on it, for it is a sin offering. 12 He is to bring it to the priest, who will take a handful from it as its memorial portion and burn ⌊it⌋ on the altar along with the fire offerings to the LORD; it is a sin offering. 13 In this way the priest will make atonement on his behalf concerning the sin he has committed in any of these cases, and he will be forgiven. The rest will belong to the priest, like the •grain offering."

The Restitution Offering

14 Then the LORD spoke to Moses: 15 "If someone offends by sinning unintentionally in regard to any of the LORD's holy things,[h] he must bring his •restitution offering to the LORD: an unblemished ram from the flock by your valuation in silver •shekels, according to

---

[a] 4:27 Lit the people of the land   [b] 5:2 = a fish, insect, rodent, or reptile; Lv 11:20–23,29–31; Gn 1:20   [c] 5:4 Lit in one of such things   [d] 5:11 Lit if his hand is not sufficient for   [e] 5:11 Lit one-tenth of an ephah   [f] 5:11 Or wheat; Ex 29:2   [g] 5:11 Lit flour as a sin offering   [h] 5:15 Things dedicated to the LORD such as tabernacle furnishings, priestly portions of the sacrifices, tenths, firstfruits, and firstborn livestock

---

5:5 he is to confess. Just offering a sacrifice did not bring about forgiveness. God wants the heart of the sinner to repent in remorse and determine to follow God. Any genuine conversion or growth in faith requires this step.

5:7 cannot afford an animal. A poor person

was allowed to bring two turtledoves as a sacrifice instead of a more valuable cow, sheep, or goat. Jesus' family offered turtledoves at Mary's purification ceremony after Jesus was born (Luke 2:24).

5:15–17 restitution offering. When a person committed a sin that required restitution, he

brought an offering and was required to replace whatever loss he had caused plus 20 percent of its worth in silver.

6:2–7 The list of offenses here proves that "unintentional" sins are not unwitting sins only, but also sins of straying and giving in to temptation. Remorse and repentance dem-

the sanctuary shekel, as a restitution offering. ¹⁶ He must make restitution for his sin regarding any holy thing, adding a fifth of its value to it, and give it to the priest. Then the priest will make atonement on his behalf with the ram of the restitution offering, and he will be forgiven.

¹⁷ "If someone sins and without knowing ⌊it⌋ violates any of the LORD's commands concerning anything prohibited, he bears the consequences of his guilt. ¹⁸ He must bring an unblemished ram from the flock according to your valuation as a restitution offering to the priest. Then the priest will make atonement on his behalf for the error he has committed unintentionally, and he will be forgiven. ¹⁹ It is a restitution offering; he is indeed guilty before the LORD."

6 ᵃ The LORD spoke to Moses: ² "When someone sins and offends the LORD by deceiving his neighbor in regard to a deposit, a security,ᵇ or a robbery; or defrauds his neighbor; ³ or finds something lost and lies about it; or swears falsely about any of the sinful things a person may do— ⁴ once he has sinned and acknowledged ⌊his⌋ guilt—he must return what he stole or defrauded, or the deposit entrusted to him, or the lost item he found, ⁵ or anything else about which he swore falsely. He must make full restitution for it and add a fifth of its value to it. He is to pay it to its owner on the day he acknowledges ⌊his⌋ guilt. ⁶ Then he must bring his •restitution offering to the LORD: an unblemished ram from the flock, according to your valuation, as a restitution offering to the priest. ⁷ In this way the priest will make •atonement on his behalf before the LORD, and he will be forgiven for anything he may have done to incur guilt."

The Burnt Offering

⁸ᶜ The LORD spoke to Moses: ⁹ "Command Aaron and his sons: This is the law of the •burnt offering; the burnt offering itself must remain on the altar's hearth all night until morning, while the fire of the altar is kept burning on it. ¹⁰ The priest is to put on his linen robe and linen undergarments.ᵈ He is to remove the ashes of the burnt offering the fire has consumed on the altar, and place them beside the altar. ¹¹ Then he must take off his garments, put on other clothes, and bring the ashes outside the camp to a ceremonially clean place. ¹² The fire on the altar is to be kept burning; it must not go out. Every morning the priest will burn wood on the fire. He is to arrange the burnt offering on the fire and burn the fat portions from the •fellowship offerings on it. ¹³ Fire

must be kept burning on the altar continually; it must not go out.

The Grain Offering

¹⁴ "Now this is the law of the •grain offering: Aaron's sons will present it before the LORD in front of the altar. ¹⁵ The priest is to remove a handful of fine flour and olive oil from the grain offering, with all the frankincense that is on the offering, and burn its memorial portion on the altar as a pleasing aroma to the LORD. ¹⁶ Aaron and his sons may eat the rest of it. It is to be eaten as unleavened bread in a holy place; they are to eat it in the courtyard of the tent of meeting. ¹⁷ It must not be baked with yeast; I have assigned it as their portion from My fire offerings. It is especially holy, like the •sin offering and the restitution offering. ¹⁸ Any male among Aaron's descendants may eat it. It is a permanent portionᵉ throughout your generations from the fire offerings to the LORD. Anything that touches the offerings will become holy."

¹⁹ The LORD spoke to Moses: ²⁰ "This is the offering that Aaron and his sons must present to the LORD on the day that he is anointed: two quartsᶠ of fine flour as a regularᵍ grain offering, half of it in the morning and half in the evening. ²¹ It is to be prepared with oil on a griddle; you are to bring it well-kneaded. You must present it as a grain offering of baked pieces,ʰ a pleasing aroma to the LORD. ²² The priest, who is of Aaron's sons and will be anointed to take his place, is to prepare it. It must be completely burned as a permanent portion for the LORD. ²³ Every grain offering for a priest will be a whole burnt offering; it is not to be eaten."

The Sin Offering

²⁴ The LORD spoke to Moses: ²⁵ "Tell Aaron and his sons: This is the law of the sin offering. The sin offering is most holy and must be slaughtered before the LORD at the place where the burnt offering is slaughtered. ²⁶ The priest who offers it as a sin offering is to eat it. It must be eaten in a holy place, in the courtyard of the tent of meeting. ²⁷ Anything that touches its flesh will become holy, and if any of its blood spatters on a garment, then you must wash that garmentⁱ in a holy place. ²⁸ A clay pot in which the sin offering is boiled must be broken; if it is boiled in a bronze vessel, it must be scoured and rinsed with water. ²⁹ Any male among the priests may eat it; it is especially holy. ³⁰ But no sin offering may be eaten if its blood has been brought into the tent of meeting to make atonement in the holy place; it must be burned up.

ᵃ**6:1** Lv 5:20 in Hb   ᵇ**6:2** Or *an investment*   ᶜ**6:8** Lv 6:1 in Hb   ᵈ**6:10** Lit *undergarments on his flesh*   ᵉ**6:18** Or *statute*   ᶠ**6:20** Lit *a tenth of an ephah*   ᵍ**6:20** Daily   ʰ**6:21** Hb obscure   ⁱ**6:27** Lit *wash what it spattered on*

---

onstrate that a sin, even fraud or theft, was not defiant (Num. 15:30).

6:6 the LORD … the priest. In ancient days the worshipper brought his offering to the priest and by that action brought it also to the Lord. So it is today. When we bring our money or gifts to the ministries of our churches, we

bring them to God.

6:9 Aaron and his sons. Only God's authorized priests could prepare and present the people's sacrificial offerings to the Lord.

6:13 it must not go out. The fire on the altar never went out. It was started by God and was maintained continually (Lev. 9:24).

6:26 a holy place. Priests and their families could eat some of the remains of the sacrifices. This is how they were provided for. The remains of the sin offering could be eaten only at the tabernacle.

7:12–15 The fellowship sacrifice combined meat and grain sacrifices.

The Restitution Offering

7 "Now this is the law of the •restitution offering; it is especially holy. ² The restitution offering must be slaughtered at the place where the •burnt offering is slaughtered, and the priest is to sprinkle its blood on all sides of the altar. ³ The offerer must present all the fat from it: the fat tail, the fat surrounding the entrails,ᵃ ⁴ and the two kidneys with the fat on them at the loins; he will also remove the fatty lobe of the liver with the kidneys. ⁵ The priest will burn them on the altar as a fire offering to the LORD; it is a restitution offering. ⁶ Any male among the priests may eat it. It is to be eaten in a holy place; it is especially holy.

⁷ "The restitution offering is like the •sin offering; the law is the same for both. It belongs to the priest who makes •atonement with it. ⁸ As for the priest who presents someone's burnt offering, the hide of the burnt offering he has presented belongs to him; it is the priest's. ⁹ Any •grain offering that is baked in an oven, or prepared in a pan or on a griddle, belongs to the priest who presents it; it is his. ¹⁰ But any grain offering, whether dry or mixed with oil, belongs equallyᵇ to all of Aaron's sons.

The Fellowship Sacrifice

¹¹ "Now this is the law of the •fellowship sacrifice that someone may present to the LORD: ¹² If he presents it for thanksgiving, in addition to the thanksgiving sacrifice,ᶜ he is to present unleavened cakes mixed with olive oil, unleavened wafers coated with oil, and well-kneaded cakes of fine flour mixed with oil. ¹³ He is to present as his offering cakes of leavened bread,ᵈ with his thanksgiving sacrifice of fellowship. ¹⁴ From the cakes he must present one ⌊portion⌋ of each offering as a contribution to the LORD. It will belong to the priest who sprinkles the blood of the fellowship offering; it is his. ¹⁵ The meat of his thanksgiving sacrifice of fellowship must be eaten on the day he offers it; he may not leave any of it until morning.

¹⁶ "If the sacrifice he offers is a vowᵉ or a freewill offering,ᶠ it is to be eaten on the day he presents his sacrifice, and what is left over may be eaten on the next day. ¹⁷ But what remains of the sacrificial meat by the third day must be burned up. ¹⁸ If any of the meat of his fellowship sacrifice is eaten on the third day, it will not be accepted. It will not be credited to the one who pre-

sents it; it is repulsive. The person who eats any of it will be guilty.ᵍ

¹⁹ "Meat that touches anything unclean must not be eaten; it is to be burned up. Everyone who is clean may eat any ⌊other⌋ meat. ²⁰ But the one who eats meat from the LORD's fellowship sacrifice while he is unclean,ʰ that person must be cut off from his people. ²¹ If someone touches anything unclean, whether human uncleanness, an unclean animal, or any unclean, detestableⁱ creature, and eats meat from the LORD's fellowship sacrifice, that person must be cut off from his people."

Fat and Blood Prohibited

²² The LORD spoke to Moses: ²³ "Tell the Israelites: You are not to eat any fat of an ox, a sheep, or a goat. ²⁴ The fat of an animal that dies naturally or is mauled by wild beastsʲ may be used for any purpose, but you must not eat it. ²⁵ If anyone eats animal fat from a fire offering presented to the LORD, the person who eats ⌊it⌋ must be cut off from his people. ²⁶ Wherever you live, you must not eat the blood of any bird or animal. ²⁷ Whoever eats any blood, that person must be cut off from his people."

The Portion for the Priests

²⁸ The LORD spoke to Moses: ²⁹ "Tell the Israelites: The one who presents a fellowship sacrifice to the LORD must bring an offering to the LORD from his sacrifice. ³⁰ His own hands will bring the fire offerings to the LORD. He will bring the fat together with the breast. The breast is to be waved as a presentation offering before the LORD. ³¹ The priest is to burn the fat on the altar, but the breast belongs to Aaron and his sons. ³² You are to give the right thigh to the priest as a contribution from your fellowship sacrifices. ³³ The son of Aaron who presents the blood of the fellowship offering and the fat will have the right thigh as a portion. ³⁴ I have taken from the Israelites the breast of the presentation offering and the thigh of the contribution from their fellowship sacrifices, and have assigned them to Aaron the priest and his sons as a permanent portionᵏ from the Israelites."

³⁵ This is the portion from the fire offerings to the LORD for Aaron and his sons since the day they were presented to serve the LORD as priests. ³⁶ The LORD commanded this to be given to them by the Israelites

---

ᵃ**7:3** LXX, Sam add *and all the fat that is on the entrails;* Lv 3:3,9,14; 4:8 ᵇ**7:10** Lit *oil, will be a man like his brother* ᶜ**7:12** The *thanksgiving sacrifice* is the first of three kinds of fellowship sacrifices. It was given to express gratitude to God (Jr 33:11) in circumstances such as answered prayer (Ps 50:14–15) or safe travel (Ps 107:22–25). ᵈ**7:13** Although yeast was prohibited from being burned on the altar (Lv 2:11), *leavened bread* could still be an offering (Lv 23:17–20) to be eaten by the priests and their families. ᵉ**7:16** The *vow offering,* the second category of fellowship sacrifice, was brought as an expression of gratitude to fulfill a vow; Gn 28:20; 2 Sm 15:7–8; Pr 7:14. ᶠ**7:16** The *freewill offering,* the third category of fellowship sacrifice, was a voluntary expression of gratitude toward God for any reason; Dt 16:10; Ps 54:6. ᵍ**7:18** Or *will bear his guilt* ʰ**7:20** Lit *while his uncleanness is upon him* ⁱ**7:21** Some Hb mss, Sam, Syr, Tg read *swarming* ʲ**7:24** Lit *fat of a carcass or the fat of a mauled beast* ᵏ**7:34** Or *statute*

7:15–18 left over. The meat became holy because it was offered on the altar. Therefore, no remains could be left, lest they be defiled.

7:16 a vow or a freewill offering. This fellowship sacrifice was to thank God for help in some difficult situation.

7:20–21 cut off from his people. This was

more similar to execution than excommunication. The holiness of God was at stake.

7:30–34 waved. The breast and thigh of the sacrificial animal were waved back and forth before being offered to the priests. This was referred to as a wave offering and a heave offering.

8:2 anointing oil. Olive oil was used for appointing people to special offices.

8:6 washed them. Moses probably washed the priests at the bronze laver that stood at the entrance of the tent to prepare them for service as mediators between God and people.

on the day He anointed them. It is a permanent portion[a] throughout their generations.

37 This is the law for the burnt offering, the grain offering, the sin offering, the restitution offering, the ordination offering, and the fellowship sacrifice, 38 which the LORD commanded Moses on Mount Sinai on the day He[b] commanded the Israelites to present their offerings to the LORD in the Wilderness of Sinai.

Ordination of Aaron and His Sons

8 The LORD spoke to Moses: 2 "Take Aaron, his sons with him, the garments, the anointing oil, the bull of the •sin[c] offering, the two rams, and the basket of unleavened bread, 3 and assemble the whole community at the entrance to the tent of meeting." 4 So Moses did as the LORD commanded him, and the community assembled at the entrance to the tent of meeting. 5 Moses said to them, "This is what the LORD has commanded to be done."

6 Then Moses presented Aaron and his sons and washed them with water. 7 He put the tunic on Aaron, wrapped the sash around him, clothed him with the robe, and put the •ephod on him. He put the woven band of the ephod around him and fastened it to him. 8 Then he put the breastpiece on him and placed the •Urim and Thummim[d] into the breastpiece. 9 He also put the turban on his head and placed the plate[e] of gold, the holy diadem, on the front of the turban, as the LORD had commanded Moses.

10 Then Moses took the anointing oil and anointed the tabernacle and everything in it to consecrate them. 11 He sprinkled some of the oil on the altar seven times, anointing the altar with all its utensils, and the basin with its stand, to consecrate them. 12 He poured some of the anointing oil on Aaron's head and anointed and consecrated him. 13 Then Moses presented Aaron's sons, clothed them with tunics, wrapped sashes around them, and fastened headbands on them, as the LORD had commanded Moses.

14 Then he brought the bull near for the sin offering, and Aaron and his sons laid their hands on the head of the bull for the sin offering. 15 Then Moses slaughtered ⌊it⌋,[f] took the blood, and applied it with his finger to the horns of the altar on all sides, purifying the altar. He poured out the blood at the base of the altar and consecrated it by making •atonement for it. 16 Moses took all the fat that was on the entrails, the fatty lobe of the liver, and the two kidneys with their fat, and he burned them on the altar. 17 He burned up the bull with its

hide, flesh, and dung outside the camp, as the LORD had commanded Moses.

18 Then he presented the ram for the •burnt offering, and Aaron and his sons laid their hands on the head of the ram. 19 Moses slaughtered it and[g] sprinkled the blood on all sides of the altar. 20 Moses cut the ram into pieces and burned the head, the pieces, and the suet, 21 but he washed the entrails and shanks with water. He then burned the entire ram on the altar. It was a burnt offering for a pleasing aroma, a fire offering to the LORD as He had commanded Moses.

22 Next he presented the second ram, the ram of ordination, and Aaron and his sons laid their hands on the head of the ram. 23 Moses slaughtered ⌊it⌋,[h] took some of its blood, and put ⌊it⌋ on Aaron's right earlobe, on the thumb of his right hand, and on the big toe of his right foot. 24 Moses also presented Aaron's sons and put some of the blood on their right earlobes, on the thumbs of their right hands, and on the big toes of their right feet. Then Moses sprinkled the blood on all sides of the altar. 25 He took the fat—the fat tail, all the fat that was on the entrails, the fatty lobe of the liver, and the two kidneys with their fat—as well as the right thigh. 26 From the basket of unleavened bread that was before the LORD he took one cake of unleavened bread, one cake of bread ⌊made⌋ with oil, and one wafer, and placed ⌊them⌋ on the fat portions and the right thigh. 27 He put all ⌊these⌋ in the hands of Aaron and his sons and waved them before the LORD as a presentation offering. 28 Then Moses took them from their hands and burned ⌊them⌋ on the altar with the burnt offering. This was an ordination offering for a pleasing aroma, a fire offering to the LORD. 29 He also took the breast and waved it before the LORD as a presentation offering; it was Moses' portion of the ordination ram as the LORD had commanded him.

30 Then Moses took some of the anointing oil and some of the blood that was on the altar and sprinkled ⌊them⌋ on Aaron and his garments, as well as on his sons and their garments. In this way he consecrated Aaron and his garments, as well as his sons and their garments.

31 Moses said to Aaron and his sons, "Boil the meat at the entrance to the tent of meeting and eat it there with the bread that is in the basket for the ordination offering as I commanded:[i] Aaron and his sons are to eat it. 32 You must burn up what remains of the meat and bread. 33 You must not go outside the entrance to the tent of meeting for seven days, until the time your days

---

a7:36 Or statute b7:38 Or he c8:2 Or purification d8:8 Two objects used to determine God's will e8:9 Or medallion f8:14–15 Or offering, and he slaughtered [it]. 15 Then Moses g8:18–19 Or ram, 19 and he slaughtered it. Moses h8:22–23 Or ram, 23 and he slaughtered [it]. Moses i8:31 LXX, Syr, Tg read was commanded; Ex 29:31–32

8:7 clothed him. With pomp and ceremony, Moses and his brother Aaron were organizing the worship of God, and Aaron was being vested with leadership.

8:8 Urim and Thummim. The Urim and Thummim, two onyx stones, functioned like dice, though determining God's will was no

game. God gave the priests answers through the use of these stones.

8:11 seven. This was considered the perfect number in Bible times. Dashing blood seven times was a way of saying that sins were totally cleansed.

8:12 anointed and consecrated him.

Anointing a person with oil set him apart for some special task. All Christians have received the anointing of the Holy Spirit (1 John 2:20).

8:14 Aaron and his sons. Since Aaron and his sons were being consecrated, all of them were purified with a sin offering.

of ordination are completed, because it will take seven days to ordain you.[a] 34 The LORD commanded what has been done today in order to make atonement for you. 35 You must remain at the entrance to the tent of meeting day and night for seven days and keep the LORD's charge so that you will not die, for this is what I was commanded." 36 So Aaron and his sons did everything the LORD had commanded through Moses.

The Priestly Ministry Inaugurated

9 On the eighth day Moses summoned Aaron, his sons, and the elders of Israel. 2 He said to Aaron, "Take a young bull for a •sin[b] offering and a ram for a •burnt offering, both without blemish, and present ⌊them⌋ before the LORD. 3 And tell the Israelites:[c] 'Take a male goat for a sin offering; a calf and a lamb, male yearlings without blemish, for a burnt offering; 4 an ox and a ram for a •fellowship offering to sacrifice before the LORD; and a •grain offering mixed with oil. For today the LORD is going to appear to you.'"

5 They brought what Moses had commanded to the front of the tent of meeting, and the whole community came forward and stood before the LORD. 6 Moses said, "This is what the LORD commanded you to do, that the glory of the LORD may appear to you." 7 Then Moses said to Aaron, "Approach the altar and sacrifice your sin offering and your burnt offering; make •atonement for yourself and the people.[d] Sacrifice the people's offering and make atonement for them, as the LORD commanded."

8 So Aaron approached the altar and slaughtered the calf as a sin offering for himself. 9 Aaron's sons brought the blood to him, and he dipped his finger in the blood and applied it to the horns of the altar. He poured out the blood at the base of the altar. 10 He burned the fat, the kidneys, and the fatty lobe of the liver from the sin offering on the altar, as the LORD had commanded Moses. 11 He burned up the flesh and the hide outside the camp.

12 Then he slaughtered the burnt offering. Aaron's sons brought him the blood, and he sprinkled it on all sides of the altar. 13 They brought him the burnt offering piece by piece, along with the head, and he burned ⌊them⌋ on the altar. 14 He washed the entrails and the shanks and burned them with the burnt offering on the altar.

15 Aaron presented the people's offering. He took the male goat for the people's sin offering, slaughtered it, and made a sin offering with it as he did before. 16 He presented the burnt offering and sacrificed it according to the regulation. 17 Next he presented the grain offering, took a handful of it, and burned it on the altar in addition to the morning burnt offering.

18 Finally, he slaughtered the ox and the ram as the people's fellowship sacrifice. Aaron's sons brought him the blood, and he sprinkled it on all sides of the altar. 19 They also brought the fat portions from the ox and the ram—the fat tail, the ⌊fat⌋ surrounding ⌊the entrails⌋, the kidneys, and the fatty lobe of the liver— 20 and placed these on the breasts. Aaron burned the fat portions on the altar, 21 but he waved the breasts and the right thigh as a presentation offering before the LORD, as Moses had commanded.[e]

22 Aaron lifted up his hands toward the people and blessed them. He came down after sacrificing the sin offering, the burnt offering, and the fellowship offering. 23 Moses and Aaron then entered the tent of meeting. When they came out, they blessed the people, and the glory of the LORD appeared to all the people. 24 Fire came out from the LORD and consumed the burnt offering and the fat portions on the altar. And when all the people saw it, they shouted and fell facedown ⌊on the ground⌋.

Nadab and Abihu

10 Aaron's sons Nadab and Abihu each took his own firepan, put fire in it, placed incense on it, and presented unauthorized fire before the LORD, which He had not commanded them ⌊to do⌋. 2 Then flames leaped from the LORD's presence and burned them to death before the LORD. 3 So Moses said to Aaron, "This is what the LORD meant when He said:

I will show My holiness[f]
to those who are near Me,
and I will reveal My glory[g]
before all the people."

But Aaron remained silent.

4 Moses summoned Mishael and Elzaphan, sons of Aaron's uncle Uzziel, and said to them, "Come here and carry your relatives away from the front of the sanctuary to ⌊a place⌋ outside the camp." 5 So they came forward and carried them in their tunics outside the camp, as Moses had said.

6 Then Moses said to Aaron and his sons Eleazar and Ithamar, "Do not let your hair hang loose and do not tear your garments, or else you will die, and the LORD will become angry with the whole community. However, your brothers, the whole house of Israel, may mourn over that tragedy when the LORD sent the fire.

---

[a]8:33 Lit because he will fill your hands for seven days [b]9:2 Or purification [c]9:3 Sam, LXX read elders of Israel [d]9:7 LXX reads and your household [e]9:21 Some Hb mss, LXX, Sam read as the LORD commanded Moses [f]10:3 Or will be treated as holy [g]10:3 Or will be glorified

---

9:2 present [them] before the Lord. The first official act of the high priest was to admit his own sinfulness.

9:4 the LORD is going to appear. Moses' instructions—first a sin offering (repentance), then a burnt offering (dedication), and then a fellowship offering (open hand of fellowship)—prepared priests for God's appearance.

9:21 waved. The part of the animal that the priest was to eat was first presented to the Lord, probably by waving it in the air.

9:23–24 glory of the Lord. God's glory generally appears as a fire. God lit the altar fire with His own glorious appearance.

9:24 fell facedown. These people felt joy as well as fear that God appeared to them, and they expressed this by falling to the ground.

10:1 unauthorized. Nadab and Abihu were killed because they offered incense contrary to God's command (Lev. 16:13).

7 You must not go outside the entrance to the tent of meeting or you will die, for the LORD's anointing oil is on you." So they did as Moses said.

Regulations for Priests

8 The LORD spoke to Aaron: 9 "You and your sons are not to drink wine or beer when you enter the tent of meeting, or else you will die; this is a permanent statute throughout your generations. 10 You must distinguish between the holy and the common, and the clean and the unclean, 11 and teach the Israelites all the statutes that the LORD has given to them through Moses."

12 Moses spoke to Aaron and his remaining sons, Eleazar and Ithamar: "Take the •grain offering that is left over from the fire offerings to the LORD, and eat it prepared without yeast beside the altar, because it is especially holy. 13 You must eat it in a holy place because it is your portion[a] and your sons' from the fire offerings to the LORD, for this is what I was commanded. 14 But you and your sons and your daughters may eat the breast of the presentation offering and the thigh of the contribution in any ceremonially clean place, because these portions have been assigned to you and your children from the Israelites' •fellowship sacrifices. 15 They are to bring the thigh of the contribution and the breast of the presentation offering, together with the offerings of fat portions made by fire, to wave as a presentation offering before the LORD. It will belong permanently to you and your children, as the LORD commanded."

16 Later, Moses inquired about the male goat of the •sin offering, but it had already been burned up. He was angry with Eleazar and Ithamar, Aaron's surviving sons, and asked, 17 "Why didn't you eat the sin offering in the sanctuary area? For it is especially holy, and He has assigned it to you to take away the guilt of the community and make •atonement for them before the LORD. 18 Since its blood was not brought inside the sanctuary, you should have eaten it in the sanctuary ⌊area⌋, as I commanded."

19 But Aaron replied to Moses, "See, today they presented their sin offering and their •burnt offering before the LORD. Since these things have happened to me, if I had eaten the sin offering today, would it have been acceptable in the LORD's sight?" 20 When Moses heard this, it was acceptable to him.[b]

Clean and Unclean Land Animals

11 The LORD spoke to Moses and Aaron: 2 "Tell the Israelites: You may eat all these ⌊kinds⌋ of land animals. 3 You may eat any animal with divided hooves and that chews the cud. 4 But among the ones that chew the cud or have hooves you are not to eat ⌊these⌋:

> the camel, though it chews the cud,
> does not have hooves—it is unclean for you;
> 5 the hyrax,[c] though it chews the cud,
> does not have hooves—it is unclean for you;
> 6 the hare, though it chews the cud,
> does not have hooves—it is unclean for you;
> 7 the pig, though it has divided hooves,
> does not chew the cud—it is unclean for you.

8 Do not eat any of their meat or touch their carcasses—they are unclean for you.

Clean and Unclean Aquatic Animals

9 "This ⌊is what⌋ you may eat from all that is in the water: You may eat everything in the water that has fins and scales, whether in the seas or streams. 10 But these are to be detestable to you: everything that does not have fins and scales in the seas or streams, among all the swarming things and ⌊other⌋ living creatures in the water. 11 They are to remain detestable to you; you must not eat any of their meat, and you must detest their carcasses. 12 Everything in the water that does not have fins and scales will be detestable to you.

Unclean Birds

13 "You are to detest these birds. They must not be eaten because they are detestable:

> the eagle,[d] the bearded[e] vulture,
> the black vulture,[f] 14 the kite,[g]
> the various kinds of falcon,[h]
> 15 every kind of raven, 16 the ostrich,[i]
> the short-eared owl,[j] the gull,[k]
> the various kinds of hawk,
> 17 the little[l] owl, the cormorant,[m]
> the long-eared owl,[n]
> 18 the white[o] owl, the desert owl,[p]
> the osprey,[q] 19 the stork,[r]
> the various kinds of heron,[s]
> the hoopoe, and the bat.

Clean and Unclean Flying Insects

20 "All winged insects that walk on all fours are to be detestable to you. 21 But you may eat these kinds of all the winged insects that walk on all fours: those that have jointed legs above their feet for hopping on the ground. 22 You may eat these:

---

[a]10:13 Or statute   [b]10:20 Lit acceptable in his sight   [c]11:5 A rabbit-like animal   [d]11:13 Or griffon-vulture   [e]11:13 Or black   [f]11:13 Or the osprey, or the bearded vulture   [g]11:14 Or hawk   [h]11:14 Or buzzards, or hawks   [i]11:16 Or eagle owl   [j]11:16 Or the night hawk, or the screech owl   [k]11:16 Or long-eared owl   [l]11:17 Or tawny   [m]11:17 Or fisher owl, or pelican   [n]11:17 Or the ibis   [o]11:18 Or little   [p]11:18 Or the pelican, or the horned owl   [q]11:18 Or Egyptian vulture   [r]11:19 Or heron   [s]11:19 Or cormorant, or hawk

---

10:10 unclean. God created a symbolic system by which certain meats were unclean, as well as skin disease, menstruation, genital discharges, and corpses.

10:19–20 it was acceptable to him. Moses was content with Aaron's explanation; it did not seem to be a matter of open rebellion.

11:2–3 divided hooves ... chews the cud. The Israelites could eat beef because cows chewed the cud and had split hooves. Camels were out because they chewed their cud but didn't have split hooves. Horses were out on both counts. Pigs were the only animals that had the right hooves but didn't chew the cud.

11:6 hare. Rabbits do not actually chew the cud, but they appear to, because of repetitive chewing movements.

11:20–21 legs ... for hopping. Locusts and grasshoppers, not normally in the four food groups, were the only flying insects considered suitable for eating.

the various kinds of locust,
the various kinds of katydid,
the various kinds of cricket,
and the various kinds of grasshopper.

23 All ⌊other⌋ winged insects that have four feet are to be detestable to you.

Purification after Touching Dead Animals

24 "These will make you unclean. Whoever touches their carcasses will be unclean until evening, 25 and whoever carries any of their carcasses must wash his clothes and will be unclean until evening. 26 All animals that have hooves but do not have a divided hoof and do not chew the cud are unclean for you. Whoever touches them becomes unclean. 27 All the four-footed animals that walk on their paws are unclean for you. Whoever touches their carcasses will be unclean until evening, 28 and anyone who carries their carcasses must wash his clothes and will be unclean until evening. They are unclean for you.

29 "These creatures that swarm on the ground are unclean for you:

the weasel,ᵃ the mouse,
the various kinds of large lizard,ᵇ
30   the gecko, the monitor lizard,ᶜ
the common lizard,ᵈ the skink,ᵉ
and the chameleon.ᶠ

31 These are unclean for you among all the swarming creatures. Whoever touches them when they are dead will be unclean until evening. 32 When any one of them dies and falls on anything it becomes unclean—any item of wood, clothing, leather, •sackcloth, or any implement used for work. It is to be rinsed with water and will remain unclean until evening; then it will be clean. 33 If any of them falls into any clay pot, everything in it will become unclean; you must break it. 34 Any edible food coming into contact with ⌊that unclean⌋ water will become unclean, and any drinkable liquid in any container will become unclean. 35 Anything one of their carcasses falls on will become unclean. If it is an oven or stove, it must be smashed; it is unclean and will remain unclean for you. 36 A spring or cistern containing water will remain clean, but someone who touches a carcass ⌊in it⌋ will become unclean. 37 If one of their carcasses falls on any seed that is to be sown, it is clean; 38 but if water has been put on the seed and one of their carcasses falls on it, it is unclean for you.

39 "If one of the animals that you use for food dies,ᵍ anyone who touches its carcass will be unclean until evening. 40 Anyone who eats some of its carcass must wash his clothes and will be unclean until evening. Anyone who carries its carcass must wash his clothes and will be unclean until evening.

Unclean Swarming Creatures

41 "All the creatures that swarm on the earth are detestable; they must not be eaten. 42 Do not eat any of the creatures that swarm on the earth, anything that moves on its belly or walks on all fours or on many feet,ʰ for they are detestable. 43 Do not become contaminated by any creature that swarms; do not become unclean or defiled by them. 44 For I am the LORD your God, so you must consecrate yourselves and be holy because I am holy. You must not defile yourselves by any swarming creature that crawls on the ground. 45 For I am the LORD, who brought you up from the land of Egypt to be your God, so you must be holy because I am holy.

46 "This is the law concerning animals, birds, all living creatures that move in the water, and all creatures that swarm on the ground, 47 in order to distinguish between the unclean and the clean, between the animals that may be eaten and those that may not be eaten."

Purification after Childbirth

12 The LORD spoke to Moses: 2 "Tell the Israelites: When a woman becomes pregnant and gives birth to a male child, she will be unclean seven days, as she is during the days of her menstrual impurity. 3 The flesh of his foreskin must be circumcised on the eighth day. 4 She will continue in purification from her bleeding for 33 days. She must not touch any holy thing or go into the sanctuary until completing her days of purification. 5 But if she gives birth to a female child, she will be unclean for two weeks ⌊she is⌋ during her ⌊menstrual⌋ impurity. She will continue in purification from her bleeding for 66 days.

6 "When her days of purification are complete, whether for a son or daughter, she is to bring to the priest at the entrance to the tent of meeting a year-old male lamb for a •burnt offering, and a young pigeon or a turtledove for a •sinⁱ offering. 7 He will present them before the LORD and make •atonement on her behalf; she will be clean from her discharge of blood. This is the law for a woman giving birth, whether to a male or female. 8 But if she doesn't have sufficient

---

ᵃ11:29 Or mole rat, or rat   ᵇ11:29 Or of thorn-tailed or dabb lizard, or of crocodile   ᶜ11:30 Or the spotted lizard, or the chameleon   ᵈ11:30 Or the gecko, or the newt, or the salamander   ᵉ11:30 Or sand lizard, or newt, or snail   ᶠ11:30 Or salamander, or mole   ᵍ11:39 Dies of itself or by predators; this does not apply to animals slaughtered for food.   ʰ11:42 Lit fours, to anything multiplying pairs of feet   ⁱ12:6 Or purification

---

11:36 cistern. When something was discovered to be unclean, there were only two options: destroy it or purify it. Here the practical nature of the law takes over. The practical reality was that people could not destroy or purify their cisterns (holding tanks for water), because cisterns were needed for survival.

11:44 be holy. Leviticus is all about God's holiness and the holiness He desires from His people. Imagine being a people whose dietary and social customs issued from the understanding that God and His people were to be special, set apart to His service and spiritually clean.

11:45 up from the land of Egypt. The history of the Hebrews was always with them. The fact that God miraculously delivered them from Egypt was the starting point for every national policy after that. At a point in time they had been chosen and delivered. Now each day they had to decide how to live.

means[a] for a sheep, she may take two turtledoves or two young pigeons, one for a burnt offering and the other for a sin[b] offering. Then the priest will make atonement on her behalf, and she will be clean."

Skin Diseases

13 The LORD spoke to Moses and Aaron: [2] "When a person has a swelling,[c] scab,[d] or spot on the skin of his body, and it becomes a disease on the skin of his body, he is to be brought to Aaron the priest or to one of his sons, the priests. [3] The priest will examine the infection on the skin of his body. If the hair in the infection has turned white and the infection appears to be deeper than the skin of his body, it is a skin disease. After the priest examines him, he must pronounce him unclean. [4] But if the spot on the skin of his body is white and does not appear to be deeper than the skin, and the hair in it has not turned white, the priest must quarantine the infected person for seven days. [5] The priest will then reexamine him on the seventh day. If the infection remains unchanged in his sight and has not spread on the skin, the priest must quarantine him for another seven days. [6] The priest will examine him again on the seventh day. If the infection has faded and has not spread on the skin, the priest is to pronounce him clean; it is a scab. The person is to wash his clothes and will become clean. [7] But if the scab spreads further on his skin after he has presented himself to the priest for his cleansing, he must present himself again to the priest. [8] The priest will examine him, and if the scab has spread on the skin, then the priest must pronounce him unclean; he has a skin disease.

[9] "When a skin disease develops on a person, he is to be brought to the priest. [10] The priest will examine him. If there is a white swelling on the skin that has turned the hair white, and there is a patch of raw flesh in the swelling, [11] it is a chronic disease on the skin of his body, and the priest must pronounce him unclean. He need not quarantine him, for he is unclean. [12] But if the skin disease breaks out completely over the skin so that it covers all the skin of the infected person from his head to his feet so far as the priest can see, [13] the priest will look, and if the skin disease has covered his entire body, he is to pronounce the infected person clean. Since he has turned totally white, he is clean. [14] But whenever raw flesh appears on him, he will be unclean. [15] When the priest examines the raw flesh, he must pronounce him unclean. Raw flesh is unclean; it is a skin disease. [16] But if the raw flesh changes[e] and[f]

turns white, he must go to the priest. [17] The priest will examine him, and if the infection has turned white, the priest must pronounce the infected person clean; he is clean.

[18] "When a boil appears on the skin of one's body and it heals, [19] and a white swelling or a reddish-white spot develops where the boil was, the person must present himself to the priest. [20] The priest will make an examination, and if the spot seems to be beneath the skin and the hair in it has turned white, the priest must pronounce him unclean; it is a skin disease that has broken out in the boil. [21] But when the priest examines it, if there is no white hair in it, and it is not beneath the skin but is faded, the priest must quarantine him seven days. [22] If it spreads further on the skin, the priest must pronounce him unclean; it is an infection. [23] But if the spot remains where it is and does not spread, it is ⌊only⌋ the scar from the boil. The priest is to pronounce him clean.

[24] "When there is a burn on the skin of one's body produced by fire, and the patch made raw by the burn becomes a reddish-white or white spot, [25] the priest is to examine it. If the hair in the spot has turned white and the spot appears to be deeper than the skin, it is a skin disease that has broken out in the burn. The priest must pronounce him unclean; it is a skin disease. [26] But when the priest examines it, if there is no white hair in the spot and it is not beneath the skin but is faded, the priest must quarantine him seven days. [27] The priest will reexamine him on the seventh day. If it has spread further on the skin, the priest must pronounce him unclean; it is a skin disease. [28] But if the spot has remained where it was and has not spread on the skin but is faded, it is the swelling from the burn. The priest is to pronounce him clean, for it is ⌊only⌋ the scar from the burn.

[29] "When a man or woman has an infection on the head or chin, [30] the priest must examine the infection. If it appears to be deeper than the skin, and the hair in it is yellow and sparse, the priest must pronounce the person unclean. It is a scaly outbreak,[g] a skin disease of the head or chin. [31] When the priest examines the scaly infection, if it does not appear to be deeper than the skin, and there is no black hair in it, the priest must quarantine the person with the scaly infection for seven days. [32] The priest will reexamine the infection on the seventh day. If the scaly outbreak has not spread and there is no yellow hair in it and it does not appear to be deeper than the skin, [33] the person must shave himself

---

[a]**12:8** Lit *if her hand cannot obtain what is sufficient*   [b]**12:8** Or *purification recedes*   [f]**13:16** Or *flesh again*   [c]**13:2** Or *discoloration*   [d]**13:2** Or *rash,* or *eruption*   [e]**13:16** Or   [g]**13:30** Or *is scall;* Hb obscure

---

12:2–5 The act of childbirth did not cause a mother to be unclean. This uncleanness was a result of the blood and other body fluids that were secreted during the birth process.

13:1–46 The skin disease referred to here is not known, but it is not the same as leprosy (Hansen's disease), which is a condition of

the nerve endings. Biblical skin disease involves white, hard patches of skin. This disease made a person look like a corpse, and all uncleanness related in some way to death. This passage is almost pharmaceutical in its description of symptoms and treatments.

13:2 skin. Aaron would decide whether a

person's ailment was dangerous to others. The issue was not whether a person was contagious with a disease, but the ceremonial uncleanness he could pass on to others.

13:45–46 unclean. It was up to the infected person to guard the ceremonial purity of others by dressing appropriately and giving a

but not shave the scaly area. Then the priest must quarantine the person who has the scaly outbreak for another seven days. 34 The priest will examine the scaly outbreak on the seventh day, and if it has not spread on the skin and does not appear to be deeper than the skin, the priest is to pronounce the person clean. He is to wash his clothes, and he will be clean. 35 But if the scaly outbreak spreads further on the skin after his cleansing, 36 the priest is to examine the person. If the scaly outbreak has spread on the skin, the priest does not need to look for yellow hair; the person is unclean. 37 But if as far as he can see, the scaly outbreak remains unchanged and black hair has grown in it, then it has healed; he is clean. The priest is to pronounce the person clean.

38 "When a man or a woman has white spots on the skin of the body, 39 the priest is to make an examination. If the spots on the skin of the body are dull white, it is ⌊only⌋ a rash[a] that has broken out on the skin; the person is clean.

40 "If a man loses the hair of his head, he is bald, but he is clean. 41 Or if he loses the hair at his hairline, he is bald on his forehead, but he is clean. 42 But if there is a reddish-white infection on the bald head or forehead, it is a skin disease breaking out on his head or forehead. 43 The priest is to examine him, and if the swelling of the infection on his bald head or forehead is reddish-white, like the appearance of a skin disease on his body, 44 the man is afflicted with a skin disease; he is unclean. The priest must pronounce him unclean; the infection is on his head.

45 "The person afflicted with an infectious skin disease is to have his clothes torn and his hair hanging loose, and he must cover his mouth and cry out, 'Unclean, unclean!' 46 He will remain unclean as long as he has the infection; he is unclean. He must live alone in a place outside the camp.

Contaminated Fabrics

47 "If a fabric is contaminated with mildew—in wool or linen fabric, 48 in the warp or woof of linen or wool, or in leather or anything made of leather— 49 and if the contamination is green or red in the fabric, the leather, the warp, the woof, or any leather article, it is a mildew contamination and is to be shown to the priest. 50 The priest is to examine the contamination and quarantine the contaminated fabric for seven days. 51 The priest is to reexamine the contamination on the seventh day. If it has spread in the fabric, the warp, the woof, or the leather, regardless of how it is used, the contamination is harmful mildew; it is unclean. 52 He is to burn the

fabric, the warp or woof in wool or linen, or any leather article, which is contaminated. Since it is harmful mildew it must be burned up.

53 "When the priest examines ⌊it⌋, if the contamination has not spread in the fabric, the warp or woof, or any leather article, 54 the priest is to order whatever is contaminated to be washed and quarantined for another seven days. 55 After it has been washed, the priest is to reexamine the contamination. If the appearance of the contaminated article has not changed, it is unclean. Even though the contamination has not spread, you must burn up the fabric. It is a fungus[a] on the front or back ⌊of the fabric⌋.

56 "If the priest examines ⌊it⌋, and the contamination has faded after it has been washed, he must cut the contaminated section out of the fabric, the leather, or the warp or woof. 57 But if it reappears in the fabric, the warp or woof, or any leather article, it has broken out again. You must burn up whatever is contaminated. 58 But if the contamination disappears from the fabric, the warp or woof, or any leather article, which have been washed, it is to be washed again, and it will be clean.

59 "This is the law concerning a mildew contamination in wool or linen fabric, warp or woof, or any leather article, in order to pronounce it clean or unclean."

Cleansing Skin Diseases

14 The LORD spoke to Moses: 2 "This is the law concerning the person afflicted with a skin disease on the day of his cleansing. He is to be brought to the priest, 3 who will go outside the camp and examine ⌊him⌋. If the skin disease has disappeared from the afflicted person,[b] 4 the priest will order that two live clean birds, cedar wood, scarlet yarn, and hyssop be brought for the one who is to be cleansed. 5 Then the priest will order that one of the birds be slaughtered over fresh water in a clay pot. 6 He is to take the live bird together with the cedar wood, scarlet yarn, and hyssop, and dip them all into the blood of the bird that was slaughtered over the fresh water. 7 He will then sprinkle ⌊the blood⌋ seven times on the one who is to be cleansed from the skin disease. He is to pronounce him clean and release the live bird over the open countryside. 8 The one who is to be cleansed must wash his clothes, shave off all his hair, and bathe with water; he is clean. Afterwards he may enter the camp, but he must remain outside his tent for seven days. 9 He is to shave off all his hair ⌊again⌋ on the seventh day: his head, his beard, his eyebrows, and the rest of his hair.

---

a 13:39,55 Hb obscure   b 14:3 Lit the person afflicted with skin disease

---

verbal warning about his uncleanness

13:47 mildew. The mildew mentioned here has some similarities to the mildew of today. It was a pale fungus that grew on damp objects. Priests decided how to clean the item of mildew or whether to destroy it. Mildew was unclean because it grew on dead things.

14:4 the priest will order … hyssop. While the use of cedar wood, scarlet yarn, and hyssop is not explained here, these items are associated with cleansing in other passages in the Bible (Num. 19:6; Ps. 51:7). Hyssop was an herb used for medicine and as a seasoning in food.

14:5 one of the birds be slaughtered. The bird might have symbolized the death that the person had escaped when he was sick.

14:6 live bird. This bird probably symbolized the new life offered in cleansing from uncleanness. The person who had looked like a corpse because of his serious illness now

He is to wash his clothes and bathe himself with water; he is clean.

[10] "On the eighth day he must take two unblemished male lambs, an unblemished year-old ewe lamb, a •grain offering of three quarts[a] of fine flour mixed with olive oil, and one-third of a quart[b] of olive oil. [11] The priest who performs the cleansing will place the person who is to be cleansed, together with these offerings, before the LORD at the entrance to the tent of meeting. [12] The priest is to take one male lamb and present it as a •restitution offering, along with the one-third quart[b] of olive oil, and he must wave them as a presentation offering before the LORD. [13] He is to slaughter the male lamb at the place in the sanctuary area where the •sin offering and •burnt offering are slaughtered, for like the sin offering, the restitution offering belongs to the priest; it is especially holy. [14] The priest is to take some of the blood from the restitution offering and put ⌊it⌋ on the lobe of the right ear of the one to be cleansed, on the thumb of his right hand, and on the big toe of his right foot. [15] Then the priest will take some of the one-third of a quart[b] of olive oil and pour it into his left palm. [16] The priest will dip his right finger into the oil in his left palm and sprinkle some of the oil with his finger seven times before the LORD. [17] From the oil remaining in his palm the priest will put some on the lobe of the right ear of the one to be cleansed, on the thumb of his right hand, and on the big toe of his right foot, on top of the blood of the restitution offering. [18] What is left of the oil in the priest's palm he is to put on the head of the one to be cleansed. In this way the priest will make •atonement for him before the LORD. [19] The priest must sacrifice the sin offering and make atonement for the one to be purified from his uncleanness. Afterwards he will slaughter the burnt offering. [20] The priest is to offer the burnt offering and the grain offering on the altar. The priest will make atonement for him, and he will be clean.

[21] "But if he is poor and cannot afford ⌊these⌋,[c] he is to take one male lamb for a restitution offering to be waved in order to make atonement for him, along with two quarts[d] of fine flour mixed with olive oil for a grain offering, one-third of a quart[b] of olive oil, [22] and two turtledoves or two young pigeons, whatever he can afford,[e] one to be a sin offering and the other a burnt offering. [23] On the eighth day he is to bring these things for his cleansing to the priest at the entrance to the tent of meeting before the LORD. [24] The priest will take the male lamb for the restitution offering and the one-third of a quart[b] of olive oil, and wave them as a presentation offering before the LORD. [25] After he slaughters the male lamb for the restitution offering, the priest is to take some of the blood of the restitution offering and put ⌊it⌋ on the right earlobe of the one to be cleansed, on the thumb of his right hand, and on the big toe of his right foot. [26] Then the priest will pour some of the oil into his left palm. [27] With his right finger the priest will sprinkle some of the oil in his left palm seven times before the LORD. [28] The priest will also put some of the oil in his palm on the right earlobe of the one to be cleansed, on the thumb of his right hand, and on the big toe of his right foot, on the ⌊same⌋ place as the blood of the restitution offering. [29] What is left of the oil in the priest's palm he is to put on the head of the one to be cleansed to make atonement for him before the LORD. [30] He must then sacrifice one type of what he can afford,[f] either the turtledoves or young pigeons, [31] one as a sin offering and the other as a burnt offering, ⌊sacrificing⌋ what he can afford[g][h] together with the grain offering. In this way the priest will make atonement before the LORD for the one to be cleansed. [32] This is the law for someone who has[i] a skin disease and cannot afford[j] the cost of his cleansing."

Cleansing Contaminated Objects

[33] The LORD spoke to Moses and Aaron: [34] "When you enter the land of Canaan that I am giving you as a possession, and I place a mildew contamination in a house in the land you possess,[k] [35] the owner of the house is to come and tell the priest: Something like mildew contamination has appeared[l] in my house. [36] The priest must order them to clear the house before he enters to examine the contamination, so that nothing in the house becomes unclean. Afterwards the priest will come to examine the house. [37] He will examine it, and if the contamination in the walls of the house consists of green or red indentations[m] that appear to be beneath the surface of the wall, [38] the priest is to go outside the house to its doorway and quarantine the house for seven days. [39] The priest is to return on the seventh day and examine it. If the contamination has spread on the walls of the house, [40] the priest must order that the stones with the contamination be pulled out and thrown into an unclean place outside the city. [41] He is to have the inside of the house completely scraped, and the plaster[n] that is scraped off

---

[a]**14:10** Lit *three-tenths*; probably of an ephah   [b]**14:10,12,15,21,24** Lit *one log*   [c]**14:21** Lit *and his hand is not*   [d]**14:21** Lit *him, and one-tenth*; probably 1/10 of an ephah   [e]**14:22** Lit *pigeons, for which his hand is sufficient*   [f]**14:30** Lit *of that for which his hand is sufficient*   [g]**14:31** LXX, Syr, Vg omit *what he can afford*   [h]**14:31** Lit *[sacrificing] that for which his hand is sufficient*   [i]**14:32** Lit *someone on whom there is*   [j]**14:32** Lit *disease whose hand is not sufficient for*   [k]**14:34** Lit *land of your possession*   [l]**14:35** Lit *appeared to me*   [m]**14:37** Or *eruptions*; Hb obscure   [n]**14:41** Lit *dust*

---

looks alive.

14:7,16,51 seven. Throughout the Bible, seven is considered the number of completion and the perfect number.

14:7 release the live bird. This is a beautiful image of recovery and new life. The recovered person, like a bird, was set free to live among his own people.

14:14–18 These rites bear a resemblance to those Moses used in consecrating Aaron and his sons to the priesthood (8:23).

14:33–53 The ceremonial cleansing from mildew was similar to cleansing from skin diseases. The ritual focused on the atonement of a person or the place where he lived. The priest would examine the dwelling to determine if it was clean or unclean.

14:45 torn down. If the mildew continued to grow, the structure must be destroyed. In a society without disinfectants, there was no other choice.

must be dumped in an unclean place outside the city. [42] Then they must take different stones to replace the ⌊former⌋ ones and take additional plaster[n] to replaster the house.

[43] "If the contamination reappears in the house after the stones have been pulled out, and after the house has been scraped and replastered, [44] the priest must come and examine it. If the contamination has spread in the house, it is harmful mildew; the house is unclean. [45] It must be torn down with its stones, its beams, and all its plaster, and taken outside the city to an unclean place. [46] Whoever enters the house during any of the days the priest quarantines it will be unclean until evening. [47] Whoever lies down in the house is to wash his clothes, and whoever eats in it is to wash his clothes.

[48] "But when the priest comes and examines it, if the contamination has not spread in the house after it was replastered, he is to pronounce the house clean because the contamination has disappeared.[a] [49] He is to take two birds, cedar wood, scarlet yarn, and hyssop to purify the house, [50] and he is to slaughter one of the birds over a clay pot containing fresh water. [51] He will take the cedar wood, the hyssop, the scarlet yarn, and the live bird, dip them in the blood of the slaughtered bird and the fresh water, and sprinkle the house seven times. [52] He will purify the house with the blood of the bird, the fresh water, the live bird, the cedar wood, the hyssop, and the scarlet yarn. [53] Then he is to release the live bird into the open countryside outside the city. In this way he will make atonement for the house, and it will be clean.

[54] "This is the law for any skin disease or mildew, for a scaly outbreak,[c] [55] for mildew in clothing or on a house, [56] and for a swelling, scab, or spot, [57] to determine when something is unclean or clean. This is the law regarding skin disease and mildew."

Bodily Discharges

15 The LORD spoke to Moses and Aaron: [2] "Speak to the Israelites and tell them: When any man has a discharge from his body, he is unclean. [3] This is uncleanness of his discharge: Whether his body secretes the discharge or retains it, he is unclean. All the days that his body secretes or retains anything because of his discharge,[d] he is unclean.[e] [4] Any bed the man with the discharge lies on will be unclean, and any furniture he sits on will be unclean. [5] Anyone who touches his bed is to wash his clothes and bathe with water, and he will remain unclean until evening. [6] Whoever sits on furniture that the man with the discharge was sitting on is to wash his clothes and bathe with water, and he will remain unclean until evening. [7] Whoever touches the body of the man with a discharge is to wash his clothes and bathe with water, and he will remain unclean until evening. [8] If the man with the discharge spits on anyone who is clean, he is to wash his clothes and bathe with water, and he will remain unclean until evening. [9] Any saddle the man with the discharge rides on will be unclean. [10] Whoever touches anything that was under him will be unclean until evening, and whoever carries such things is to wash his clothes and bathe with water, and he will remain unclean until evening. [11] If the man with the discharge touches anyone without ⌊first⌋ rinsing his hands in water, the person who was touched is to wash his clothes and bathe with water, and he will remain unclean until evening. [12] Any clay pot that the man with the discharge touches must be broken, while any wooden utensil must be rinsed with water.

[13] "When the man with the discharge has been cured of it, he is to count seven days for his cleansing, wash his clothes, and bathe his body in fresh water; he will be clean. [14] He must take two turtledoves or two young pigeons on the eighth day, come before the LORD at the entrance to the tent of meeting, and give them to the priest. [15] The priest is to sacrifice them, one as a •sin offering and the other as a •burnt offering. In this way the priest will make •atonement for him before the LORD because of his discharge.

[16] "When a man has an emission of semen, he is to bathe himself completely with water, and he will remain unclean until evening. [17] Any clothing or leather on which there is an emission of semen must be washed with water, and it will remain unclean until evening. [18] If a man sleeps with a woman and has an emission of semen, both of them are to bathe with water, and they will remain unclean until evening.

[19] "When a woman has a discharge, and it consists of blood from her body, she will be unclean because of her menstruation for seven days. Everyone who touches her will be unclean until evening. [20] Anything she lies on during her menstruation will become unclean, and anything she sits on will become unclean. [21] Everyone who touches her bed is to wash his clothes and bathe with water, and he will remain unclean until evening. [22] Everyone who touches any furniture she was sitting on is to wash his clothes and bathe with water, and he will remain unclean until evening. [23] If discharge is on

---

[a]**14:42** Lit *dust* [b]**14:48** Lit *healed* [c]**14:54** Or *for a scall* [d]**15:3** DSS, Sam, LXX; MT omits *he is unclean. All the days that his body secretes or retains anything because of his discharge* [e]**15:3** A urinary tract infection

---

15:2 discharge. Some think this discharge was related to gonorrhea or some other sexually transmitted disease.

15:16 emission. An emission of semen, whether or not it was part of the sex act, was not necessarily the result of sin. Uncleanness is not identical with sin.

15:19 menstruation. A woman was considered untouchable during her monthly menstrual period.

15:25 if she has a discharge beyond her period. This commandment concerns blood flow beyond or at a different time than menstruation. It required more serious purifica-

tion, including an offering at the sanctuary.

15:31 among them. The people's uncleanness, as well as their sins, polluted the tabernacle and required offerings to cleanse it. God graciously provided sacrifices as a way for God and man to have fellowship together.

the bed or the furniture she was sitting on, when he touches it he will be unclean until evening. 24 If a man sleeps with her, and ⌊blood from⌋ her menstruation gets on him, he will be unclean for seven days, and every bed he lies on will become unclean.

25 "When a woman has a discharge of her blood for many days, though it is not the time of her menstruation, or if she has a discharge beyond her period, she will be unclean all the days of her unclean discharge, as ⌊she is⌋ during the days of her menstruation. 26 Any bed she lies on during the days of her discharge will be like her bed during menstrual impurity; any furniture she sits on will be unclean as in her menstrual period. 27 Everyone who touches them will be unclean; he must wash his clothes and bathe with water, and he will remain unclean until evening. 28 When she is cured of her discharge, she is to count seven days, and after that she will be clean. 29 On the eighth day she must take two turtledoves or two young pigeons and bring them to the priest at the entrance to the tent of meeting. 30 The priest is to sacrifice one as a sin offering and the other as a burnt offering. In this way the priest will make atonement for her before the LORD because of her unclean discharge.

31 "You must keep the Israelites from their uncleanness, so that they do not die by defiling My tabernacle that is among them. 32 This is the law for someone with a discharge: a man who has an emission of semen, becoming unclean by it; 33 a woman who is in her menstrual period; anyone who has a discharge, whether male or female; and a man who sleeps with an unclean woman."

The Day of Atonement

16 The LORD spoke to Moses after the death of two of Aaron's sons when they approached the presence of a the LORD and died. 2 The LORD said to Moses: "Tell your brother Aaron that he may not come whenever he wants into the holy place behind the veil in front of the •mercy seat on the ark or else he will die, because I appear in the cloud above the mercy seat.

3 "Aaron is to enter the ⌊most⌋ holy place in this way: with a young bull for a •sin offering and a ram for a •burnt offering. 4 He is to wear a holy linen tunic, and linen undergarments are to be on his body. He must tie a linen sash ⌊around him⌋ and wrap his head with a linen turban. These are holy garments; he must bathe his body with water before he wears them. 5 He is to take from the Israelite community two male goats for a sin offering and one ram for a burnt offering.

6 "Aaron will present the bull for his sin offering and make •atonement for himself and his household. 7 Next he will take the two goats and place them before the LORD at the entrance to the tent of meeting. 8 After Aaron casts lots for the two goats, one lot for the LORD and the other for Azazel,b 9 he is to present the goat chosen by lot for the LORD and sacrifice it as a sin offering. 10 But the goat chosen by lot for Azazel is to be presented alive before the LORD to make purification with it by sending it into the wilderness for Azazel.

11 "When Aaron presents the bull for his sin offering and makes atonement for himself and his household, he will slaughter the bull for his sin offering. 12 Then he must take a firepan full of fiery coals from the altar before the LORD and two handfuls of finely ground fragrant incense, and bring ⌊them⌋ inside the veil. 13 He is to put the incense on the fire before the LORD, so that the cloud of incense covers the mercy seat that is over the •testimony, or else he will die. 14 He is to take some of the bull's blood and sprinkle ⌊it⌋ with his finger against the east side of the mercy seat; then he will sprinkle some of the blood with his finger before the mercy seat seven times.

15 "When he slaughters the male goat for the people's sin offering and brings its blood inside the veil, he must do the same with its blood as he did with the bull's blood: he is to sprinkle it against the mercy seat and in front of it. 16 He will purify the ⌊most⌋ holy place in this way for all their sins because of the Israelites' impurities and rebellious acts. He will do the same for the tent of meeting that remains among them, because it is surrounded by their impurities. 17 No one may be in the tent of meeting from the time he enters to make atonement in the ⌊most⌋ holy place until he leaves after he has made atonement for himself, his household, and the whole assembly of Israel. 18 Then he will go out to the altar that is before the LORD and make atonement for it. He is to take some of the bull's blood and some of the goat's blood and put ⌊it⌋ on the horns on all sides of the altar. 19 He is to sprinkle some of the blood on it with his finger seven times to cleanse and set it apart from the Israelites' impurities.

20 "When he has finished purifying the ⌊most⌋ holy place, the tent of meeting, and the altar, he is to present the live male goat. 21 Aaron will lay both his hands on the head of the live goat and confess over it all the Israelites' wrongdoings and rebellious acts—all their sins. He is to put them on the goat's head and send ⌊it⌋ away into the wilderness by the man appointed for the task.c

---

a16:1 LXX, Tg, Syr, Vg read they brought strange fire before; Nm 3:4   b16:8 Azazel may be the name of a demon; traditionally, scapegoat
c16:21 Lit wilderness in the hand of a ready man

16:2 whenever he wants. God's presence was in the Holy Place of the tabernacle. Aaron was not to come and go there at will. Instead there was one special time when he was required to enter this special place.

16:3 enter the most holy place in this way. On the Day of Atonement, Aaron was to come

prepared with a burnt offering to express devotion to God and a sin offering to ask for God's forgiveness.

16:13 or else he will die. On several occasions God protected His people from seeing His presence, which would have brought death. The incense smoke at the ark func-

tioned the same way for Aaron.

16:20–22 goat will carry on it all their wrongdoings. The goat carried the pollution of the people's sins outside the camp. Jesus took our sins away forever (Isa. 53:5–6).

16:30 you will be clean. The Day of Atone-

22 The goat will carry on it all their wrongdoings into a desolate land, and he will release it there.

23 "Then Aaron is to enter the tent of meeting, take off the linen garments he wore when he entered the ⌊most⌋ holy place, and leave them there. 24 He will bathe his body with water in a holy place and put on his clothes. Then he must go out and sacrifice his burnt offering and the people's burnt offering; he will make atonement for himself and for the people. 25 He is to burn the fat of the sin offering on the altar. 26 The man who released the goat for Azazel is to wash his clothes and bathe his body with water; afterwards he may reenter the camp. 27 The bull for the sin offering and the goat for the sin offering, whose blood was brought into the ⌊most⌋ holy place to make atonement, must be brought outside the camp and their hide, flesh, and dung burned up. 28 The one who burns them is to wash his clothes and bathe himself with water; afterwards he may reenter the camp.

29 "This is to be a permanent statute for you: In the seventh month, on the tenth ⌊day⌋ of the month you are to practice self-denial[a] and do no work, both the native and the foreigner who resides among you. 30 Atonement will be made for you on this day to cleanse you, and you will be clean from all your sins before the LORD. 31 It is a Sabbath of complete rest for you, and you must practice self-denial; it is a permanent statute. 32 The priest who is anointed and ordained[b] to serve as ⌊high⌋ priest in place of his father will make atonement. He will put on the linen garments, the holy garments, 33 and purify the most holy place. He will purify the tent of meeting and the altar and will make atonement for the priests and all the people of the assembly. 34 This is to be a permanent statute for you, to make atonement for the Israelites once a year because of all their sins." And all this was done as the LORD commanded Moses.

Forbidden Sacrifices

17 The LORD spoke to Moses: 2 "Speak to Aaron, his sons, and all the Israelites and tell them: This is what the LORD has commanded: 3 Anyone from the house of Israel who slaughters an ox, sheep, or goat in the camp, or slaughters ⌊it⌋ outside the camp, 4 instead of bringing it to the entrance to the tent of meeting to present ⌊it⌋ as an offering to the LORD before His tabernacle—that person will be charged with murder.[c] He has shed blood and must be cut off from his people. 5 This is so the Israelites will bring to the LORD the sacrifices they have been offering in the open country. They are to bring them to the priest at the entrance to the tent of meeting and offer them as •fellowship sacrifices to the LORD. 6 The priest will then sprinkle the blood on the LORD's altar at the entrance to the tent of meeting and burn the fat as a pleasing aroma to the LORD. 7 They must no longer offer their sacrifices to the goat-demons that they have prostituted themselves with. This will be a permanent statute for them throughout their generations.

8 "Say to them: Anyone from the house of Israel or from the foreigners who live among them who offers a •burnt offering or a sacrifice 9 but does not bring it to the entrance to the tent of meeting to sacrifice it to the LORD, that person must be cut off from his people.

Eating Blood and Carcasses Prohibited

10 "Anyone from the house of Israel or from the foreigners who live among them who eats any blood, I will turn[d] against that person who eats blood and cut him off from his people. 11 For the life of a creature is in the blood, and I have appointed it to you to make •atonement on the altar for[e] your lives, since it is the lifeblood that makes atonement. 12 Therefore I say to the Israelites: None of you and no foreigner who lives among you may eat blood.

13 "Any Israelite or foreigner living among them, who hunts down a wild animal or bird that may be eaten must drain its blood and cover it with dirt. 14 Since the life of every creature is its blood, I have told the Israelites: You must not eat the blood of any creature, because the life of every creature is its blood; whoever eats it must be cut off.

15 "Every person, whether the native or the foreigner, who eats an animal that died a natural death or was mauled by wild beasts is to wash his clothes and bathe with water, and he will remain unclean until evening; he will be clean. 16 But if he does not wash ⌊his clothes⌋ and bathe himself, he will bear his punishment."

Prohibited Pagan Practices

18 The LORD spoke to Moses: 2 "Speak to the Israelites and tell them: I am the LORD your God. 3 Do not follow the practices of the land of Egypt, where you used to live, or follow the practices of the land of Canaan, where I am bringing you. You must not follow their customs. 4 You are to practice My ordinances and you are to keep My statutes by following them; I am the LORD your God. 5 Keep My statutes and ordinances; a person will live if he does them. I am the LORD.

ment was a start-over place, a renewal of God's forgiveness.

17:1–6 The Israelites apparently were offering sacrifices to idols outside the camp, then claiming they were slaughtering animals for food. To stop this practice, God required that all animals be slaughtered at the temple.

17:11 it is the lifeblood. The reason for animal sacrifices is because blood is life. Death is required for cleansing, since sin carries the death penalty.

18:2 I am the LORD. This phrase states the authority by which God demanded purity from His people.

18:3 not follow their customs. God was calling His people not to give in to the pagan culture around them.

18:16 your brother's wife. An exception to this law was Levirate marriage, which specified that a man should marry his brother's widow so she would not be destitute.

6 "You are not to come near any close relative[a] for sexual intercourse; I am the LORD. 7 You are not to shame your father by having sex with your mother. She is your mother; you must not have sexual intercourse with her. 8 You are not to have sex with your father's wife; it will shame your father. 9 You are not to have sexual intercourse with your sister, either your father's daughter or your mother's, whether born at home or born elsewhere. You are not to have sex with her. 10 You are not to have sexual intercourse with your son's daughter or your daughter's daughter, because it will shame your family.[b] 11 You are not to have sexual intercourse with your father's wife's daughter,[c] who is adopted by[d] your father; she is your sister. 12 You are not to have sexual intercourse with your father's sister; she is your father's close relative. 13 You are not to have sexual intercourse with your mother's sister, for she is your mother's close relative. 14 You are not to shame your father's brother by coming near his wife to have sexual intercourse; she is your aunt. 15 You are not to have sexual intercourse with your daughter-in-law. She is your son's wife; you are not to have sex with her. 16 You are not to have sexual intercourse with your brother's wife; it will shame your brother. 17 You are not to have sexual intercourse with a woman and her daughter. You are not to marry her son's daughter or her daughter's daughter and have sex with her. They are close relatives; it is depraved. 18 You are not to marry a woman as a rival to her sister and have sexual intercourse with her during her ⌊sister's⌋ lifetime.

19 "You are not to come near a woman during her menstrual impurity to have sexual intercourse with her. 20 You are not to have sexual intercourse with[e] your neighbor's wife, defiling yourself with her.

21 "You are not to make any of your children pass through ⌊the fire⌋ to •Molech.[f] Do not profane the name of your God; I am the LORD. 22 You are not to sleep with a man as with a woman; it is detestable. 23 You are not to have sexual intercourse with[g] any animal, defiling yourself with it; a woman is not to present herself to an animal to mate with it; it is a perversion.

24 "Do not defile yourselves by any of these ⌊practices⌋, for the nations I am driving out before you have defiled themselves by all these things. 25 The land has become defiled, so I am punishing it for its sin, and the land will vomit out its inhabitants. 26 But you are to keep My statutes and ordinances. You must not commit any of these abominations—not the native or the for-eigner who lives among you. 27 For the men who were in the land prior to you have committed all these abominations, and the land has become defiled. 28 If you defile the land, it will vomit you out as it has vomited out the nations that were before you. 29 Any person who does any of these abominations must be cut off from his people. 30 You must keep My instruction to not do any of the detestable customs that were practiced before you, so that you do not defile yourselves by them; I am the LORD your God."

Laws of Holiness

19 The LORD spoke to Moses: 2 "Speak to the entire Israelite community and tell them: Be holy because I, the LORD your God, am holy.

3 "Each of you is to respect his mother and father. You are to keep My Sabbaths; I am the LORD your God. 4 Do not turn to idols or make cast images of gods for yourselves; I am the LORD your God.

5 "When you offer a •fellowship sacrifice to the LORD, sacrifice it that you may be accepted. 6 It is to be eaten on the day you sacrifice ⌊it⌋ or on the next day, but what remains on the third day must be burned up. 7 If any is eaten on the third day, it is a repulsive thing; it will not be accepted. 8 Anyone who eats it will bear his punishment, for he has profaned what is holy to the LORD. That person must be cut off from his people.

9 "When you reap the harvest of your land, you are not to reap to the very edge of your field or gather the gleanings of your harvest. 10 You must not strip your vineyard bare or gather its fallen grapes. Leave them for the poor and the foreign resident; I am the LORD your God.

11 "You must not steal. You must not act deceptively or lie to one another. 12 You must not swear falsely by My name, profaning the name of your God; I am the LORD.

13 "You must not oppress your neighbor or rob ⌊him⌋. The wages due a hired hand must not remain with you until morning. 14 You must not curse the deaf or put a stumbling block in front of the blind, but you are to •fear your God; I am the LORD.

15 "You must not act unjustly when rendering judgment. Do not be partial to the poor or give preference to the rich; judge your neighbor fairly. 16 You must not go about spreading slander among your people; you must not jeopardize[h] your neighbor's life; I am the LORD.

17 "You must not hate your brother[i] in your heart. Rebuke your neighbor directly, and you will not incur guilt because of him. 18 Do not take revenge or bear a

---

a18:6 Lit any flesh of his flesh b18:10 Lit because they are your nakedness c18:11 This must refer to a daughter from a previous marriage. d18:11 Lit daughter, a relative of e18:20 Lit to give your emission of semen to f18:21 An ancient Near Eastern god to whom child sacrifices were offered by fire; Lv 20:2–5; Dt 18:10; 1 Kg 11:7; 2 Kg 23:10 g18:23 Lit to give your emission to h19:16 Lit not stand against i19:17 Or your fellow Israelite

---

18:17 depraved. This verse outlines boundaries of decency. Much wickedness is simply the violation of decency.

18:21 Molech. Molech was the national god of the Ammonites. Children were offered to Molech as temple prostitutes and as burnt sacrifices.

18:22 homosexuality. Later in Leviticus, acts of homosexuality are listed as punishable by death.

18:28–29 vomited. God used strong imagery to describe the reaction of the earth to the indecency described in the previous verses.

19:8 profaned. Profaning holy things is bring-ing them into contact with uncleanness.

19:9–10 gleanings. This practice of leaving leftover grain when gathering the harvest provided for the less fortunate.

19:17 Rebuke your neighbor directly. Talk directly to someone who has offended you rather than gossiping about him (Matt. 18:15).

grudge against members of your community, but love your neighbor as yourself; I am the LORD.

19 "You are to keep My statutes. You must not cross-breed two different kinds of your livestock, sow your fields with two kinds of seed, or put on a garment made of two kinds of material.

20 "If a man has sexual intercourse with a woman who is a slave designated for ⌊another⌋ man, but she has not been redeemed or given her freedom, there must be punishment.a They are not to be put to death, because she had not been freed. 21 However, he must bring his ram as a •restitution offering to the LORD at the entrance to the tent of meeting. 22 The priest will make •atonement on his behalf before the LORD with the ram of the restitution offering for the sin he has committed, and he will be forgiven for the sin he committed.

23 "When you come into the land and plant any kind of tree for food, you are to consider the fruit forbidden.b It will be forbidden to you for three years; it is not to be eaten. 24 In the fourth year all its fruit must be consecrated as a praise offering to the LORD. 25 But in the fifth year you may eat its fruit. In this way its yield will increase for you; I am the LORD your God.

26 "You are not to eat ⌊anything⌋ with blood ⌊in it⌋.c You are not to practice •divination or sorcery. 27 You are not to cut off the hair at the sides of your head or mar the edge of your beard. 28 You are not to make gashes on your bodies for the dead or put tattoo marks on yourselves; I am the LORD.

29 "Do not debased your daughter by making her a prostitute, or the land will be prostituted and filled with depravity. 30 You must keep My Sabbaths and revere My sanctuary; I am the LORD.

31 "Do not turn to mediumse or consult spiritists,f or you will be defiled by them; I am the LORD your God.

32 "You are to rise in the presence of the elderly and honor the old. Fear your God; I am the LORD.

33 "When a foreigner lives with you in your land, you must not oppress him. 34 You must regard the foreigner who lives with you as the native-born among you. You are to love him as yourself, for you were foreigners in the land of Egypt; I am the LORD your God.

35 "You must not act unfairly in measurements of length, weight, or volume. 36 You are to have honest balances, honest weights, an honest dry measure,g and an honest liquid measure;h I am the LORD your God,

who brought you out of the land of Egypt. 37 You must keep all My statutes and all My ordinances and do them; I am the LORD."

Molech Worship and Spiritism

20 The LORD spoke to Moses: 2 "Say to the Israelites: Any Israelite or foreigner living in Israel who gives any of his children to •Molech must be put to death; the people of the country are to stone him. 3 I will turni against that man and cut him off from his people, because he gave his •offspring to Molech, defiling My sanctuary and profaning My holy name. 4 But if the people of the country look the other way when that manj gives any of his children to Molech, and do not put him to death, 5 then I will turni against that man and his family, and cut off from their people both him and all who followk him, prostituting themselves with Molech.

6 "Whoever turns to mediumse or spiritistsf and prostitutes himself with them, I will turni against that person and cut him off from his people. 7 Consecrate yourselves and be holy, for I am the LORD your God. 8 Keep My statutes and do them; I am the LORD who sets you apart.

Family and Sexual Offenses

9 "If anyone curses his father or mother, he must be put to death. He has cursed his father or mother; his blood is on his own hands.l 10 If a man commits adultery with a married woman—if he commits adultery with his neighbor's wife—both the adulterer and the adulteress must be put to death. 11 If a man sleeps with his father's wife, he has shamed his father. Both of them must be put to death; their blood is on their own hands.m 12 If a man sleeps with his daughter-in-law, both of them must be put to death. They have acted perversely; their blood is on their own hands.m 13 If a man sleeps with a man as with a woman, they have both committed an abomination. They must be put to death; their blood is on their own hands.m 14 If a man marries a woman and her mother, it is depraved. Both he and they must be burned with fire, so that there will be no depravity among you. 15 If a man has sexual intercourse withn an animal, he must be put to death; you are also to kill the animal. 16 If a woman comes near any animal and mates with it, you are to kill the woman and the animal. They must be put to death; their ⌊own⌋ blood is on them. 17 If a man marries his sister, whether his father's daughter or his mother's daughter, and they

---

a 19:20 Or compensation   b 19:23 Lit uncircumcised   c 19:26 Or [anything] over its blood   d 19:29 Lit profane   e 19:31; 20:6 Or spirits of the dead   f 19:31; 20:6 Or familiar spirits   g 19:36 Lit honest ephah; an ephah is a dry measure of grain equivalent to 22 liters.   h 19:36 Lit honest hin; a hin is a liquid measure of about 4 liters or 1 gallon.   i 20:3,5,6 Lit will set My face   j 20:4 Lit country ever close their eyes from that man when he   k 20:5 Lit prostitute themselves with   l 20:9 Lit on him   m 20:11,12,13 Lit on them   n 20:15 Lit man gives his emission to

---

19:18 love your neighbor. This sums up all the laws on how to treat other people (Rom. 13:9).

19:26 blood. Leviticus 17:13–14 explains that the life of an animal is in its blood. This is why God commands His people not to eat blood (Gen. 9:4).

19:28 not to make gashes … tattoo marks. The purpose of this commands was to keep the Hebrews separate from the surrounding pagan cultures.

19:33–34 foreigner. The generosity of God would be reflected in the people's treatment of strangers in their midst.

19:35–36 honest balances. The ancient world had no standardized weights and measures. Cheating was easy, but integrity was still measured by the same standard.

20:3 profaning My holy name. God makes it clear that to offer a child to the false god Molech was a personal affront to Him.

have sexual relations,[a] it is a disgrace. They must be cut off publicly from their people. He has had sexual intercourse with his sister; he will bear his punishment. [18] If a man sleeps with a menstruating woman and has sexual intercourse with her, he has exposed the source of her [flow], and she has uncovered the source of her blood. Both of them must be cut off from their people. [19] You must not have sexual intercourse with your mother's sister or your father's sister, for it is exposing one's own blood relative; both people will bear their punishment. [20] If a man sleeps with his aunt, he has shamed his uncle; they will bear their guilt and die childless. [21] If a man marries his brother's wife, it is impurity. He has shamed his brother; they will be childless.

Holiness in the Land

[22] "You are to keep all My statutes and all My ordinances, and do them, so that the land where I am bringing you to live will not vomit you out. [23] You must not follow the statutes of the nations I am driving out before you, for they did all these things, and I abhorred them. [24] And I promised you: You will inherit their land, since I will give it to you to possess, a land flowing with milk and honey. I am the LORD your God who set you apart from the peoples. [25] Therefore you must distinguish the clean animal from the unclean one, and the unclean bird from the clean one. You are not to make yourselves detestable by any land animal, bird, or whatever crawls on the ground; I have set these apart as unclean for you. [26] You are to be holy to Me because I, the LORD, am holy, and I have set you apart from the nations to be Mine. [27] A man or a woman who is[b] a medium or a spiritist must be put to death. They are to be stoned; their blood is on their own hands."[c]

The Holiness of the Priests

21 The LORD said to Moses: "Speak to Aaron's sons, the priests, and tell them: A priest is not to make himself ceremonially unclean for a [dead] person among his relatives, [2] except for his immediate family: his mother, father, son, daughter, or brother. [3] He may make himself unclean for his young unmarried sister in his immediate family. [4] He is not to make himself unclean for those related to him by marriage[d] and so defile himself.

[5] "Priests may not make bald spots on their heads, shave the edge of their beards, or make gashes on their bodies. [6] They are to be holy to their God and not profane the name of their God, because they present the fire offerings to the LORD, the food of their God. They must be holy. [7] They are not to marry a woman defiled by prostitution[e] or divorced by her husband, for the priest is holy to his God. [8] You are to consider him holy since he presents the food of your God. He will be holy to you because I, the LORD who sets you apart, am holy. [9] If a priest's daughter defiles herself by promiscuity,[f] she defiles her father; she must be burned up.

[10] "The priest who is highest among his brothers, who has had the anointing oil poured on his head and has been ordained[g] to wear the garments, must not dishevel his hair[h] or tear his garments. [11] He must not go near any dead person or make himself unclean [even] for his father or mother. [12] He must not leave the sanctuary or he will desecrate the sanctuary of his God, for the consecration of the anointing oil of his God is on him; I am the LORD.

[13] "He is to marry a woman who is a virgin. [14] He is not to marry a widow, a divorced woman, or one defiled by prostitution. He is to marry a virgin from his own people, [15] so that he does not corrupt his bloodline[i] among his people, for I am the LORD who sets him apart."

Physical Defects and Priests

[16] The LORD spoke to Moses: [17] "Tell Aaron: None of your descendants throughout your generations who has a physical defect is to come near to present the food of his God. [18] No man who has any defect is to come near: no man who is blind, lame, facially disfigured, or deformed; [19] no man who has a broken foot or hand, [20] or who is a hunchback or a dwarf,[j] or who has an eye defect, a festering rash, scabs, or a crushed testicle. [21] No descendant of Aaron the priest who has a defect is to come near to present the fire offerings to the LORD. He has a defect and is not to come near to present the food of his God. [22] He may eat the food of his God from what is especially holy as well as from what is holy. [23] But because he has a defect, he must not go near the curtain or approach the altar. He is not to desecrate My sanctuaries, for I am the LORD who sets them apart." [24] Moses said [this] to Aaron and his sons and to all the Israelites.

Priests and Their Food

22 The LORD spoke to Moses: [2] "Tell Aaron and his sons to deal respectfully with the holy offerings of the Israelites that they have consecrated to Me, so they do not profane My holy name; I am the LORD. [3] Say to them: If any man from any of your descendants

---

[a]**20:17** Lit and he sees her nakedness and she sees his nakedness [b]**20:27** Lit is in them [c]**20:27** Lit on them [d]**21:4** Lit unclean a husband among his people [e]**21:7** Or a woman who has been deflowered [f]**21:9** Or prostitution [g]**21:10** Lit and one has filled his hand [h]**21:10** Or not uncover his head [i]**21:15** Lit not profane his seed [j]**21:20** Or or emaciated

---

20:6 mediums or spiritists. To consult a medium or spiritist was to trust someone besides God to direct one's future. This was a form of idolatry.

20:7 Consecrate. To keep oneself separate from sin in order to honor God.

20:8 statutes. The statutes listed here were

actually capital crimes. For God, holiness is a life-or-death issue.

21:1 a [dead] person among his relatives. Priests were not to touch a corpse unless it was that of an immediate family member.

21:5 bald spots on their heads. Some pagan priests shaved part or all of their heads.

The Nazarite vow included not cutting the hair at all.

21:8 who sets you apart. God gives us two foundations in this verse: He is holy, and He makes us holy.

21:16–23 a physical defect. In Aaron's day, handicapped priests received their share of

throughout your generations is in a state of uncleanness yet approaches the holy offerings that the Israelites consecrate to the LORD, that person will be cut off from My presence; I am the LORD. [4] No man of Aaron's descendants who has a skin disease[a] or a discharge is to eat from the holy offerings until he is clean. Whoever touches anything made unclean by a dead person or by a man who has an emission of semen, [5] or whoever touches any swarming creature that makes him unclean or any person who makes him unclean—whatever his uncleanness— [6] the man who touches any of these will remain unclean until evening and is not to eat from the holy offerings unless he has bathed his body with water. [7] When the sun has set, he will become clean, and then he may eat from the holy offerings, for that is his food. [8] He must not eat an animal that died naturally or was mauled by wild beasts,[b] making himself unclean by it; I am the LORD. [9] They must keep My instruction, or they will be guilty and die because they profane it; I am the LORD who sets them apart.

[10] "No one outside a priest's family[c] is to eat the holy offering. A foreigner staying with a priest or a hired hand is not to eat the holy offering. [11] But if a priest purchases someone with his money, that person may eat it, and those born in his house may eat his food. [12] If the priest's daughter is married to a man outside a priest's family,[d] she is not to eat from the holy contributions.[e] [13] But if the priest's daughter becomes widowed or divorced, has no children, and returns to her father's house as in her youth, she may share her father's food. But no outsider may share it. [14] If anyone eats a holy offering in error, he must add a fifth to its value and give the holy offering to the priest. [15] The priests must not profane the holy offerings the Israelites give to the LORD [16] and have them bear the penalty of restitution if the people eat their holy offerings. For I am the LORD who sets them apart."

Acceptable Sacrifices

[17] The LORD spoke to Moses: [18] "Speak to Aaron, his sons, and all the Israelites and tell them: Any man of the house of Israel or of the foreign residents in Israel who presents his offering—whether they present freewill gifts or payment of vows to the LORD as •burnt offerings— [19] must offer an unblemished male from the cattle, sheep, or goats in order for you to be accepted. [20] You are not to present anything that has a defect, because it will not be accepted on your behalf.

[21] "When a man presents a •fellowship sacrifice to the LORD to fulfill a vow or as a freewill offering from the herd or flock, it has to be unblemished to be acceptable; there must be no defect in it. [22] You are not to present any ⌊animal⌋ to the LORD that is blind, injured, maimed, or has a running sore, festering rash, or scabs; you may not put any of them on the altar as a fire offering to the LORD. [23] You may sacrifice as a freewill offering any animal from the herd or flock that has an elongated or stunted limb, but it is not acceptable as a vow offering. [24] You are not to present to the LORD anything that has bruised, crushed, torn, or severed ⌊testicles⌋; you must not sacrifice ⌊them⌋ in your land. [25] Neither you nor[f] a foreigner are to present food to your God from any of these animals. They will not be accepted for you because they are deformed and have a defect."

[26] The LORD spoke to Moses: [27] "When an ox, sheep, or goat is born, it must remain with[g] its mother for seven days; from the eighth day on, it will be acceptable as a gift, a fire offering to the LORD. [28] But you are not to slaughter an animal from the herd or flock on the same day as its young. [29] When you sacrifice a thank offering to the LORD, sacrifice it so that you may be accepted. [30] It is to be eaten on the same day. Do not let any of it remain until morning; I am the LORD.

[31] "You are to keep My commands and do them; I am the LORD. [32] You must not profane My holy name; I must be treated as holy among the Israelites. I am the LORD who sets you apart, [33] the One who brought you out of the land of Egypt to be your God; I am the LORD."

Holy Days

23 The LORD spoke to Moses: [2] "Speak to the Israelites and tell them: These are My appointed times, the times of the LORD that you will proclaim as sacred assemblies.

[3] "For six days work may be done, but on the seventh day there must be a Sabbath of complete rest, a sacred assembly. You are not to do any work; it is a Sabbath to the LORD wherever you live.

[4] "These are the LORD's appointed times, the sacred assemblies you are to proclaim at their appointed times. [5] The •Passover to the LORD comes in the first month, at twilight on the fourteenth day of the month. [6] The Festival of •Unleavened Bread to the LORD is on the fifteenth day of the same month. For seven days you must eat unleavened bread. [7] On the first day you are to hold a sacred assembly; you are not to do any daily work. [8] You are to present a fire offering to the LORD for seven days. On the seventh day there will be a sacred assembly; you must not do any daily work."

---

[a]**22:4** Or *has leprosy* or *scale disease*   [b]**22:8** Lit *eat a carcass* or *a mauled beast*   [c]**22:10** Lit *No stranger*   [d]**22:12** Lit *man, a stranger*   [e]**22:12** Lit *the contribution of holy offerings*   [f]**22:25** Lit *nor from the hand of*   [g]**22:27** Lit *under*

---

provisions for the priesthood, but they could not receive sacrifices and could not be high priests.
21:23 the curtain. This curtain was at the entrance of the tabernacle.
22:16 who sets them apart. When God gave instructions to the worshippers, it was enough

to say, "I am the LORD." Because of the role of the priests, it was equally important that they acknowledge God's holiness as well as His desire to make His people holy.
22:21 unblemished. While the fellowship offerings (7:11–36) were not for sin or guilt, they required the same standards of holiness.

23:2 appointed times. The biblical feasts of the Hebrews commemorated historical events and were timed to coordinate with the three annual harvests.
23:3 Sabbath. The Sabbath was a day of remembering that God created and God rested, that He is the one true God.

⁹ The LORD spoke to Moses: ¹⁰ "Speak to the Israelites and tell them: When you enter the land I am giving you and reap its harvest,ª you are to bring the first sheaf of your harvest to the priest. ¹¹ He will wave the sheaf before the LORD so that you may be accepted; the priest is to wave it on the day after the Sabbath. ¹² On the day you wave the sheaf, you are to offer a year-old male lambᵇ without blemish as a •burnt offering to the LORD. ¹³ Its •grain offering is to be four quartsᶜ of fine flour mixed with oil as a fire offering to the LORD, a pleasing aroma, and its drink offering will be one quartᵈ of wine. ¹⁴ You must not eat bread, roasted grain, or ⌊any⌋ new grainᵉ until this very day, and you have brought the offering of your God. This is to be a permanent statute throughout your generations wherever you live.

¹⁵ "You are to count sevenᶠ complete weeksᵍ starting from the day after the Sabbath, the day you brought the sheaf of the presentation offering. ¹⁶ You are to count 50 days until the day after the seventh Sabbath and then present an offering of new grainʰ to the LORD. ¹⁷ Bring two loaves of bread from your settlements as a presentation offering, each of them made from four quartsᶜ of fine flour, baked with yeast, as •firstfruits to the LORD. ¹⁸ You are to present with the bread seven unblemished male lambs a year old, one young bull, and two rams. They will be a burnt offering to the LORD, with their grain offerings and drink offerings, a fire offering of a pleasing aroma to the LORD. ¹⁹ You are also to prepare one male goat as a •sin offering, and two male lambs a year old as a •fellowship sacrifice. ²⁰ The priest will wave the lambs with the bread of firstfruits as a presentation offering before the LORD; the bread and the two lambs will be holy to the LORD for the priest. ²¹ On that same day you are to make a proclamation and hold a sacred assembly. You are not to do any daily work. This is to be a permanent statute wherever you live throughout your generations. ²² When you reap the harvest of your land, you are not to reap all the way to the edge of your field or gather the gleanings of your harvest. Leave them for the poor and the foreign resident; I am the LORD your God."

²³ The LORD spoke to Moses: ²⁴ "Tell the Israelites: In the seventh month, on the first ⌊day⌋ of the month, you are to have a day of complete rest, commemoration and jubilationⁱ —a sacred assembly. ²⁵ You must not do any daily work, but you must present a fire offering to the LORD."

²⁶ The LORD again spoke to Moses: ²⁷ "The tenth ⌊day⌋ of this seventh month is the Day of •Atonement. You are to hold a sacred assembly and practice self-denial;ʲ you are to present a fire offering to the LORD. ²⁸ On this particular day you are not to do any work, for it is a Day of Atonement to make atonement for yourselves before the LORD your God. ²⁹ If any person does not practice self-denial on this particular day, he must be cut off from his people. ³⁰ I will destroy among his people anyone who does any work on this same day. ³¹ You are not to do any work. This is a permanent statute throughout your generations wherever you live. ³² It will be a Sabbath of complete rest for you, and you must practice self-denial. You are to observe your Sabbath from the evening of the ninth ⌊day⌋ of the month until the ⌊following⌋ evening."

³³ The LORD spoke to Moses: ³⁴ "Tell the Israelites: The Festival of Boothsᵏ to the LORD begins on the fifteenth day of this seventh month and continues for seven days. ³⁵ There is to be a sacred assembly on the first day; you are not to do any daily work. ³⁶ You are to present a fire offering to the LORD for seven days. On the eighth day you are to hold a sacred assembly and present a fire offering to the LORD. It is a solemn gathering; you are not to do any daily work.

³⁷ "These are the LORD's appointed times that you are to proclaim as sacred assemblies for presenting fire offerings to the LORD, burnt offerings and grain offerings, sacrifices and drink offerings, each on its ⌊designated⌋ day. ³⁸ These are in addition to the offerings for the LORD's Sabbaths, your gifts, all your vow offerings, and all your freewill offerings that you give to the LORD.

³⁹ "You are to celebrate the LORD's festival on the fifteenth day of the seventh month for seven days after you have gathered the produce of the land. There will be complete rest on the first day and complete rest on the eighth day. ⁴⁰ On the first day you are to take the product of majestic trees—palm fronds, boughs of leafy trees, and willows of the brook—and rejoice before the LORD your God for seven days. ⁴¹ You are to celebrate it as a festival to the LORD seven days each year. This is a permanent statute for you throughout your generations; you must celebrate it in the seventh month. ⁴² You are to live in booths for seven days. All the native-born of Israel must live in booths, ⁴³ so that your generations may know that I made the Israelites live in booths when I brought them out of the land of Egypt; I

ª**23:10** The barley harvest   ᵇ**23:12** Or *a male lamb in its first year*   ᶜ**23:13,17** Lit *two-tenths [of an ephah]*   ᵈ**23:13** Lit *one-fourth of a hin*
ᵉ**23:14** *Grain* or *bread from the new* harvest   ᶠ**23:15** Lit *count; they will be seven*   ᵍ**23:15** Or *Sabbaths*   ʰ**23:16** From the wheat harvest; Ex 34:22
ⁱ**23:24** Lit *shout,* or *blast;* traditionally *trumpet blasts*   ʲ**23:27** Traditionally, fasting, abstinence from sex, and refraining from personal grooming
ᵏ**23:34** Or *Feast of Tabernacles*

23:5 Passover. This feast commemorated the night in Egypt when the firstborn of each household died unless blood had been sprinkled on the doorpost of one's house (Ex. 12).

23:6 The Festival of Unleavened Bread. This feast coincided with the barley harvest (March/April).

23:15–22 This feast, known as the Feast of Weeks, or Pentecost, celebrated the end of the wheat harvest and the giving of the Ten Commandments. Later, God gave the Holy Spirit during this feast (Acts 2).

23:16 count 50 days. The feast of Pentecost occurred 50 days after the Passover

observance.

23:24 seventh month ... first day. Today this is the traditional Jewish New Year, Rosh Hashanah. In the Bible it was a day to blow ram's horns (*shofars*) in preparation for the Day of Atonement.

23:27 Day of Atonement. This was the yearly

am the LORD your God." ⁴⁴ So Moses declared the LORD's appointed times to the Israelites.

Tabernacle Oil and Bread

24 The LORD spoke to Moses: ² "Command the Israelites to bring you pure oil of beaten olives for the light, so that the lamp will burn regularly. ³ Aaron is to tend it regularly from evening until morning before the LORD outside the veil of the •testimony in the tent of meeting. This is a permanent statute throughout your generations. ⁴ He must regularly tend the lamps on the pure ⌊gold⌋ lampstand in the LORD's presence.

⁵ "Take fine flour and bake it into 12 loaves; each loaf is to be made with four quarts.^a ⁶ Arrange them in two rows, six to a row, on the pure ⌊gold⌋ table before the LORD. ⁷ Place pure frankincense near each row, so that it may serve as a memorial portion for the bread and a fire offering to the LORD. ⁸ The bread is to be set out before the LORD every Sabbath day as a perpetual covenant obligation on the part of the Israelites. ⁹ It belongs to Aaron and his sons, who are to eat it in a holy place, for it is the holiest portion for him from the fire offerings to the LORD; this is a permanent rule."

A Case of Blasphemy

¹⁰ Now the son of an Israelite mother and an Egyptian father was^b among the Israelites. A fight broke out in the camp between the Israelite woman's son and an Israelite man. ¹¹ Her son cursed and blasphemed the Name, and they brought him to Moses. (His mother's name was Shelomith, a daughter of Dibri of the tribe of Dan.) ¹² They put him in custody until the LORD's decision could be made clear to them.

¹³ Then the LORD spoke to Moses: ¹⁴ "Bring the one who has cursed to the outside of the camp and have all who heard ⌊him⌋ lay their hands on his head; then have the whole community stone him. ¹⁵ And tell the Israelites: If anyone curses his God, he will bear the consequences of his sin. ¹⁶ Whoever blasphemes the name of the LORD is to be put to death; the whole community must stone him. If he blasphemes the Name, he is to be put to death, whether the foreign resident or the native.

¹⁷ "If a man kills anyone, he must be put to death. ¹⁸ Whoever kills an animal is to make restitution for it, life for life. ¹⁹ If any man inflicts a permanent injury on his neighbor, whatever he has done is to be done to him: ²⁰ fracture for fracture, eye for eye, tooth for tooth. Whatever injury he inflicted on the person, the same is to be inflicted on him. ²¹ Whoever kills an animal is to

make restitution for it, but whoever kills a person is to be put to death. ²² You are to have the same law for the foreign resident and the native, because I am the LORD your God."

²³ After Moses spoke to the Israelites, they brought the one who had cursed to the outside of the camp and stoned him. So the Israelites did as the LORD had commanded Moses.

Sabbath Years and Jubilee

25 The LORD spoke to Moses on Mount Sinai: ² "Speak to the Israelites and tell them: When you enter the land I am giving you, the land will observe a Sabbath to the LORD. ³ You may sow your field for six years, and you may prune your vineyard and gather its produce for six years. ⁴ But there will be a Sabbath of complete rest for the land in the seventh year, a Sabbath to the LORD: you are not to sow your field or prune your vineyard. ⁵ You are not to reap what grows by itself from your crop, or harvest the grapes of your untended vines. It must be a year of complete rest for the land. ⁶ ⌊Whatever⌋ the land ⌊produces during⌋ the Sabbath year can be food for you; for yourself, your male or female slave, and the hired hand or foreigner who stays with you. ⁷ All of its growth may serve as food for your livestock and the wild animals in your land.

⁸ "You are to count seven sabbatic years, seven times seven years, so that the time period of the seven sabbatic years amounts to 49. ⁹ Then you are to sound a trumpet loudly in the seventh month, on the tenth ⌊day⌋ of the month; you will sound it throughout your land on the Day of •Atonement. ¹⁰ You are to consecrate the fiftieth year and proclaim freedom in the land for all its inhabitants. It will be your Jubilee, when each of you is to return to his property and each of you to his clan. ¹¹ The fiftieth year will be your Jubilee; you are not to sow, reap what grows by itself, or harvest its untended vines. ¹² It is to be holy to you because it is the Jubilee; you may ⌊only⌋ eat its produce ⌊directly⌋ from the field.

¹³ "In this Year of Jubilee, each of you will return to his property. ¹⁴ If you make a sale to your neighbor or a purchase from him, do not cheat one another. ¹⁵ You are to make the purchase from your neighbor based on the number of years since the last Jubilee. He is to sell to you based on the number of ⌊remaining⌋ harvest years. ¹⁶ You are to increase its price in proportion to a greater amount of years, and decrease its price in proportion to a lesser amount of years, because what he is selling to you is a number of harvests. ¹⁷ You are not to

---

^a**24:5** Lit *two-tenths [of an ephah]*   ^b**24:10** Lit *went out*

---

sacrifice made by the high priest for the sins of the people.
23:34 The Festival of Booths (or Tabernacles) commemorated the nomadic journey of the people of Israel after they left Egypt and began making their way across the wilderness.
24:5 loaves. In Exodus these 12 loaves are

called the "bread of the Presence." Twelve loaves for the 12 tribes.
24:8–9 portion. The priests shared in this bread each week. It was part of the food provided for their support by the people.
25:4 Sabbath … for the land. Every seventh year the land was allowed to go uncultivated.

This had the same effect as our modern system of crop rotation—to keep the land productive.

25:10 Jubilee. The year of Jubilee was a time for reestablishing homelands and ownership. Land that had been sold since the last Jubilee reverted to the original owners.

cheat one another, but •fear your God, for I am the LORD your God.

18 "You are to observe My statutes and ordinances and carefully observe them, so that you may live securely in the land. 19 Then the land will yield its fruit, so that you can eat, be satisfied, and live securely in the land. 20 If you wonder: 'What will we eat in the seventh year if we don't sow or gather our produce?' 21 I will appoint My blessing for you in the sixth year, so that it will produce a crop sufficient for three years. 22 When you sow in the eighth year, you will be eating from the previous harvest. You will be eating this until the ninth year when its harvest comes in.

23 "The land is not to be permanently sold because it is Mine, and you are only foreigners and temporary residents on My land.a 24 You are to allow the redemption of any land you occupy. 25 If your brother becomes destitute and sells part of his property, his nearest relative may come and redeem what his brother has sold. 26 If a man has no •family redeemer, but he prospersb and obtains enough to redeem his land, 27 he may calculate the years since its sale, repay the balance to the man he sold it to, and return to his property. 28 But if he cannot obtain enough to repay him, what he sold will remain in the possession of its purchaser until the Year of Jubilee. It is to be released at the Jubilee, so that he may return to his property.

29 "If a man sells a residence in a walled city, his right of redemption will last until a year has passed after its sale; his right of redemption will last a year. 30 If it is not redeemed by the end of a full year, then the house in the walled city is permanently transferred to its purchaser throughout his generations. It is not to be released on the Jubilee. 31 But houses in villages that have no walls around them are to be classified as open fields. The right to redeem ⌊such⌋ houses stays in effect, and they are to be released at the Jubilee.

32 "Concerning the Levitical cities, the Levites always have the right to redeem houses in the cities they possess. 33 Whatever ⌊property⌋ one of the Levites can redeemc —a house sold in a city they possess— must be released at the Jubilee, because the houses in the Levitical cities are their possession among the Israelites. 34 The open pastureland around their cities may not be sold, for it is their permanent possession.

35 "If your brother becomes destitute and cannot sustain himself amongd you, you are to support him as a foreigner or temporary resident, so that he can continue to live among you. 36 Do not profit or take interest

from him, but fear your God and let your brother live among you. 37 You are not to lend him your silver with interest or sell ⌊him⌋ your food for profit. 38 I am the LORD your God, who brought you out of the land of Egypt to give you the land of Canaan and to be your God.

39 "If your brother among you becomes destitute and sells himself to you, you must not force him to do slave labor. 40 Let him stay with you as a hired hand or temporary resident; he may work for you until the Year of Jubilee. 41 Then he and his children are to be released from you, and he may return to his clan and his ancestral property. 42 They are not to be sold as slaves,e because they are My slaves I brought out of the land of Egypt. 43 You are not to rule over them harshly but fear your God. 44 Your male and female slaves are to be from the nations around you; you may purchase male and female slaves. 45 You may also purchase them from the foreigners staying with you, or from their families living among you—those born in your land. These may become your property. 46 You may leave them to your sons after you to inherit as property; you can make them slaves for life. But concerning your brothers, the Israelites, you must not rule over one another harshly.

47 "If a foreigner or temporary resident ⌊living⌋ among you prospers, but your brother ⌊living⌋ near him becomes destitute and sells himself to the foreigner living among you, or to a member of the foreigner's clan, 48 he has the right of redemption after he has been sold. One of his brothers may redeem him. 49 His uncle or cousin may redeem him, or any of his close relatives from his clan may redeem him. If he prospers, he may redeem himself. 50 The one who purchased him is to calculate ⌊the time⌋ from the year he sold himself to him until the Year of Jubilee. The price of his sale will be ⌊determined⌋ by the number of years. It will be ⌊set⌋ for him like the daily wages of a hired hand. 51 If many years are still left, he must pay his redemption price in proportion to them based on his purchase price. 52 If only a few years remain until the Year of Jubilee, he will calculate and pay the price of his redemption in proportion to his ⌊remaining⌋ years. 53 He will stay with him like a man hired year by year. A foreign owner is not to rule over him harshly in your sight. 54 If he is not redeemed in any of these ⌊ways⌋, he and his children are to be released at the Year of Jubilee. 55 For the Israelites are My slaves. They are My slaves I brought out of the land of Egypt; I am the LORD your God.

---

a 25:23 Lit residents with Me   b 25:26 Lit but his hand reaches   c 25:33 Hb obscure   d 25:35 Lit and his hand falters with   e 25:42 Lit sold with a sale of a slave

---

25:13 return to his property. God was evening things out in terms of accumulation of wealth.

25:15 based on. If the year of Jubilee was observed regularly, land sales would work as leases. When a land deal was struck, the buyer and seller would know the number of

years for which the deal was valid.
25:24 redemption of any land. The families who first received the allotment of the land would have the right to take possession of the land again.
25:25 redeem what his brother has sold. The land represented God's promise, His in-

heritance. If someone had sold his land because of financial difficulty, it was a relative's responsibility to make sure the land remained in the family.

25:35–36 live among you. It was easier at times to help a wandering foreigner than a down-and-out fellow citizen. The purpose of

Covenant Blessings and Discipline

26 "Do not make idols for yourselves, set up a carved image or sacred pillar for yourselves, or place a sculpted stone in your land to bow down to it, for I am the LORD your God. 2 You must keep My Sabbaths and honor My sanctuary; I am the LORD.

3 "If you follow My statutes and faithfully observe My commands, 4 I will give you rain at the right time, and the land will yield its produce, and the trees of the field will bear their fruit. 5 Your threshing will continue until grape harvest, and the grape harvest will continue until sowing time; you will have plenty of food to eat and live securely in your land. 6 I will give peace to the land, and you will lie down with nothing to frighten ⌊you⌋. I will remove dangerous animals from the land, and no sword will pass through your land. 7 You will pursue your enemies, and they will fall before you by the sword. 8 Five of you will pursue 100, and 100 of you will pursue 10,000; your enemies will fall before you by the sword.

9 "I will turn to you, make you fruitful and multiply you, and confirm My covenant with you. 10 You will eat the old grain of the previous year and will clear out the old to make room for the new. 11 I will place My residence[a] among you, and I will not reject you. 12 I will walk among you and be your God, and you will be My people. 13 I am the LORD your God, who brought you out of the land of Egypt, so that you would no longer be their slaves. I broke the bars of your yoke and enabled you to live in freedom.[b]

14 "But if you do not obey Me and observe all these commands— 15 if you reject My statutes and despise My ordinances, and do not observe all My commands— and break My covenant, 16 then I will do this to you: I will bring terror on you—wasting disease and fever that will cause your eyes to fail and your life to ebb away. You will sow your seed in vain because your enemies will eat it. 17 I will turn[c] against you, so that you will be defeated by your enemies. Those who hate you will rule over you, and you will flee even though no one is pursuing you.

18 "But if after these things you will not obey Me, I will proceed to discipline you seven times for your sins. 19 I will break down your strong pride. I will make your sky like iron and your land like bronze, 20 and your strength will be used up for nothing. Your land will not yield its produce, and the trees of the land will not bear their fruit.

21 "If you act with hostility toward Me and are unwilling to obey Me, I will multiply your plagues seven times for your sins. 22 I will send wild animals against you that will deprive you of your children, ravage your livestock, and reduce your numbers until your roads are deserted.

23 "If in spite of these things you do not accept My discipline, but act with hostility toward Me, 24 then I will act with hostility toward you; I also will strike you seven times for your sins. 25 I will bring a sword against you to execute the vengeance of the covenant. Though you withdraw into your cities, I will send a pestilence among you, and you will be delivered into enemy hands. 26 When I cut off your supply of bread, 10 women will bake your bread in a single oven and ration out your bread by weight, so that you will eat but not be satisfied.

27 "And if in spite of this you do not obey Me but act with hostility toward Me, 28 I will act with furious hostility toward you; I will also discipline you seven times for your sins. 29 You will eat the flesh of your sons; you will eat the flesh of your daughters. 30 I will destroy your •high places, cut down your incense altars, and heap your dead bodies on the lifeless bodies of your idols; I will reject you. 31 I will reduce your cities to ruins and devastate your sanctuaries. I will not smell the pleasing aroma of your ⌊sacrifices⌋. 32 I also will devastate the land, so that your enemies who come to live there will be appalled by it. 33 But I will scatter you among the nations, and I will draw a sword ⌊to chase⌋ after you. So your land will become desolate, and your cities will become ruins.

34 "Then the land will make up for its Sabbath ⌊years⌋ during the time it lies desolate, while you are in the land of your enemies. At that time the land will rest and make up for its Sabbaths. 35 As long as it lies desolate, it will have the rest it did not have during your Sabbaths when you lived there.

36 "I will put anxiety in the hearts of those of you who survive in the lands of their enemies. The sound of a wind-driven leaf will put them to flight, and they will flee as one flees from a sword, and fall though no one is pursuing ⌊them⌋. 37 They will stumble over one another as if ⌊fleeing⌋ from a sword though no one is pursuing ⌊them⌋. You will not be able to stand against your enemies. 38 You will perish among the nations; the land of your enemies will devour you. 39 Those[d] who survive in the lands of your enemies will waste away because of their sin; they will also waste away because of their fathers' sins along with theirs.

40 "But if they will confess their sin and the sin of their fathers—their unfaithfulness that they practiced against Me, and how they acted with hostility toward

---

---

this passage was not to forbid interest but to remind the people that making money from another person's misfortune was improper.
25:55 are My slaves. The year of Jubilee was a way for God to reclaim His people and His promise to them.
26:1 bow down. It was not just the image or

idol that was forbidden. It was the attitude of the heart that mattered. An idol is anything that takes the place of God in our commitment.
26:3–13 if you follow. This passage outlines the blessing that God promised His People if they obeyed Him.

26:14–39 if you do not obey Me. God couldn't have spelled out these curses any more clearly. Yet Israel often failed to follow the Lord.
26:41 uncircumcised hearts. Circumcision showed that the Israelites belonged to God. A person with an uncircumcised heart did not

Me, [41] and I acted with hostility toward them and brought them into the land of their enemies—and if their uncircumcised hearts will be humbled, and if they will pay the penalty for their sin, [42] then I will remember My covenant with Jacob. I will also remember My covenant with Isaac and My covenant with Abraham, and I will remember the land. [43] For the land abandoned by them will make up for its Sabbaths by lying desolate without the people, while they pay the penalty for their sin, because they rejected My ordinances and abhorred My statutes. [44] Yet in spite of this, while they are in the land of their enemies, I will not reject or abhor them so as to destroy them and break My covenant with them, since I am the LORD their God. [45] For their sake I will remember the covenant with their fathers, whom I brought out of the land of Egypt in the sight of the nations to be their God; I am the LORD."

[46] These are the statutes, ordinances, and laws the LORD established between Himself and the Israelites through Moses on Mount Sinai.

Funding the Sanctuary

27 The LORD spoke to Moses: [2] "Speak to the Israelites and tell them: When someone makes a special vow to the LORD that involves the valuation of people, [3] if the valuation concerns a male from 20 to 60 years old, your valuation is 50 silver •shekels ⌊measured⌋ by the standard sanctuary shekel. [4] If the person is a female, your valuation is 30 shekels. [5] If the person is from five to 20 years old, your valuation for a male is 20 shekels and for a female 10 shekels. [6] If the person is from one month to five years old, your valuation for a male is five silver shekels, and for a female your valuation is three shekels of silver. [7] If the person is 60 years or more, your valuation is 15 shekels for a male and 10 shekels for a female. [8] But if one is too poor to pay the valuation, he must present the person before the priest and the priest will set a value for him. The priest will set a value for him according to what the one making the vow can afford.

[9] "If the vow involves one of the animals that may be brought as an offering to the LORD, any of these he gives to the LORD will be holy. [10] He may not replace it or make a substitution for it, either good for bad, or bad for good. But if he does substitute one animal for another, both that animal and its substitute will be holy.

[11] "If the vow involves any of the unclean animals that may not be brought as an offering to the LORD, the animal must be presented before the priest. [12] The priest will set its value, whether high or low; the price

will be set as the priest makes the valuation for you. [13] If the one who brought it decides to redeem it, he must add a fifth to the[a] valuation.

[14] "When a man consecrates his house as holy to the LORD, the priest will assess its value, whether high or low. The price will stand just as the priest assesses it. [15] But if the one who consecrated his house redeems ⌊it⌋, he must add a fifth to the[a] valuation price, and it will be his.

[16] "If a man consecrates to the LORD any part of a field that he possesses, your valuation will be proportional to the seed needed to sow it, at the rate of 50 silver shekels for ⌊every⌋ five bushels[b] of barley seed.[c] [17] If he consecrates his field during the Year of Jubilee, the price will stand according to your valuation. [18] But if he consecrates his field after the Jubilee, the priest will calculate the price for him in proportion to the years left until the ⌊next⌋ Year of Jubilee, so that your valuation will be reduced. [19] If the one who consecrated the field decides to redeem it, he must add a fifth to the[a] valuation price, and the field will transfer back to him. [20] But if he does not redeem the field or if he has sold it to another man, it is no longer redeemable. [21] When the field is released in the Jubilee, it will be holy to the LORD like a field permanently set apart; it becomes the priest's property.

[22] "If a person consecrates to the LORD a field he has purchased that is not part of his inherited landholding, [23] then the priest will calculate for him the amount of the[a] valuation up to the Year of Jubilee, and the person will pay the valuation on that day as a holy offering to the LORD. [24] In the Year of Jubilee the field will return to the one he bought it from, the original owner. [25] All your valuations will be ⌊measured⌋ by the standard sanctuary shekel, 20 gerahs to the shekel.

[26] "But no one can consecrate a firstborn of the livestock, whether an animal from the herd or flock, to the LORD, because a firstborn ⌊already⌋ belongs to the LORD. [27] If it is one of the unclean livestock, it must be ransomed according to your valuation by adding a fifth of its value to it. If it is not redeemed, it can be sold according to your valuation.

[28] "Nothing that a man permanently sets apart to the LORD from all he owns, whether a person, an animal, or his inherited landholding, can be sold or redeemed; everything set apart is especially holy to the LORD. [29] No person who has been set apart ⌊for destruction⌋ is to be ransomed; he must be put to death.

[30] "Every tenth of the land's produce, grain from the soil or fruit from the trees, belongs to the LORD; it is

---

[a] **27:13,15,19,23** Lit *your* [b] **27:16** Lit *for a homer* [c] **27:16** Or *grain*

---

give evidence that he was a part of God's people.

26:44 as to destroy them. God has been true to this promise throughout history. The Israelites have been subjected to blow after blow, yet they have never been destroyed.

27:2 special vow. Vows were like a special offering, over and above the tithe. People made vows to God out of gratitude or to please Him and receive His favor. Parents could not give daughters to God's service, but they could give money dedicating a daughter in a vow.

27:10 substitute. The prophet Malachi cited this abuse (Mal. 1:13–14). The people were dedicating healthy, acceptable animals for sacrifice to God but then switching them for sick and blemished animals.

27:28 sets apart. People devoting themselves with a vow were accountable for the

holy to the LORD. 31 If a man decides to redeem any part of this tenth, he must add one-fifth to its value. 32 Every tenth animal from the herd or flock, which passes under the ⌊shepherd's⌋ rod, will be holy to the LORD. 33 He is not to inspect whether it is good or bad, and he is not to make a substitution for it. But if he does make a substitution, both the animal and its substitute will be holy; they cannot be redeemed."

34 These are the commands the LORD gave Moses for the Israelites on Mount Sinai.

---

outcome of their vow.

27:29 set apart [for destruction]. When the Israelites conquered Jericho, they were instructed to destroy people and property. But Achan, disobeyed this command from God.

Until he was found out, God held the nation accountable for Achan's sin (Josh. 7:1–20).

27:30 Every tenth. All crops and animals were tithed (a tenth set apart).

27:34 These are the commands. This verse functioned as a kind of sign-off, giving the source (God), the author (Moses), and the place (Mount Sinai).

INTRODUCTION TO
NUMBERS

AUTHOR

Moses is assumed to be the author and editor of most of the first five books of the Old Testament (the Pentateuch).

DATE

It is difficult to set a firm date for the writing of the Pentateuch. Conservative estimates place it in either the 15th century or 13th century B.C., depending on when the Exodus occurred.

THEME

God's faithfulness despite Israel's rebellion, resulting in 40 years of misery and mercy.

HISTORICAL BACKGROUND

The name of this book in the English Bible is derived from the census taking and the mustering of the Israelite army in preparation for invading the promised land. This is detailed in chapters 1-4 and 26. The title of the book in the Hebrew Bible, meaning "in the desert" or "in the wilderness" is actually much more descriptive. The Book of Numbers relates the story of the 40 years during which Israel journeyed from Mount

Sinai to the edge of Canaan. This was a time of great turmoil for Israel in which the people expressed not gratitude for deliverance from Egypt, but rebellion against God. Consequently, they lived out their lives in the desert.

CHARACTERISTICS

Arranged around the Israelites' wilderness wanderings, the book chronicles God's actions in leading his people toward the land of promise. What makes these actions truly remarkable is that they establish God's faithfulness in spite of the people's rebellious nature. The central human figure is Moses. He combines his many talents with a humble spirit to act as intermediary between his God and His people. The Book of Numbers provides us with a dramatic portrait of Moses, the Israelites, and God as they struggle to turn the disaster of the wilderness wanderings into success.

PASSAGES FOR
TOPICAL GROUP STUDY

12:1-15 . . . . REBELLION . . . . Rebelling Against Authority

13:26-14:10,26-45 . . . . LACK OF FAITH . . . . . Israelite Spy Team

The Census of Israel

1 The LORD spoke to Moses in the tent of meeting in the Wilderness of Sinai, on the first ⌊day⌋ of the second month of the second year after Israel's departure from the land of Egypt: 2 "Take a census of the entire Israelite community by their clans and their ancestral houses, counting the names of every male one by one. 3 You and Aaron are to register those who are 20 years old or more by their military divisions—everyone who can serve in Israel's army.a 4 A man from each tribe is to be with you, each one the head of his ancestral house. 5 These are the names of the men who are to assist you:

Elizur son of Shedeur from Reuben;
6 Shelumiel son of Zurishaddai from Simeon;
7 Nahshon son of Amminadab from Judah;
8 Nethanel son of Zuar from Issachar;
9 Eliab son of Helon from Zebulun;
10 from the sons of Joseph:
Elishama son of Ammihud from Ephraim,
Gamaliel son of Pedahzur from Manasseh;
11 Abidan son of Gideoni from Benjamin;
12 Ahiezer son of Ammishaddai from Dan;
13 Pagiel son of Ochran from Asher;
14 Eliasaph son of Deuelb from Gad;
15 Ahira son of Enan from Naphtali.

16 These are the men called from the community; they are leaders of their ancestral tribes, the heads of Israel's clans."

17 So Moses and Aaron took these men who had been designated by name, 18 and they assembled the whole community on the first day of the second month. They recorded their ancestry by their clans and their ancestral houses, counting one by one the names of those 20 years old or more, 19 just as the LORD commanded Moses. He registered them in the Wilderness of Sinai:

20 The descendants of Reuben, the firstborn of Israel: according to their family records by their clans and their ancestral houses, counting one by one the names of every male 20 years old or more, everyone who could serve in the army, 21 those registered for the tribe of Reuben numbered 46,500.

22 The descendants of Simeon: according to their family records by their clans and their ancestral houses, those registered counting one by one the names of every male 20 years old or more, everyone who could serve in the army, 23 those registered for the tribe of Simeon numbered 59,300.

24 The descendants of Gad: according to their family records by their clans and their ancestral houses, counting the names of those 20 years old or more, everyone who could serve in the army, 25 those registered for the tribe of Gad numbered 45,650.

26 The descendants of Judah: according to their family records by their clans and their ancestral houses, counting the names of those 20 years old or more, everyone who could serve in the army, 27 those registered for the tribe of Judah numbered 74,600.

28 The descendants of Issachar: according to their family records by their clans and their ancestral houses, counting the names of those 20 years old or more, everyone who could serve in the army, 29 those registered for the tribe of Issachar numbered 54,400.

30 The descendants of Zebulun: according to their family records by their clans and their ancestral houses, counting the names of those 20 years old or more, everyone who could serve in the army, 31 those registered for the tribe of Zebulun numbered 57,400.

32 The descendants of Joseph:

The descendants of Ephraim: according to their family records by their clans and their ancestral houses, counting the names of those 20 years old or more, everyone who could serve in the army, 33 those registered for the tribe of Ephraim numbered 40,500.

34 The descendants of Manasseh: according to their family records by their clans and their ancestral houses, counting the names of those 20 years old or more, everyone who could serve in the army, 35 those registered for the tribe of Manasseh numbered 32,200.

36 The descendants of Benjamin: according to their family records by their clans and their ancestral houses, counting the names of those 20 years old or more, everyone who could serve in the army, 37 those registered for the tribe of Benjamin numbered 35,400.

38 The descendants of Dan: according to their family records by their clans and their ancestral houses, counting the names of those 20 years old or more, everyone who could serve in the army,

---

a1:3 Lit everyone going out to war in Israel   b1:14 LXX, Syr read Reuel

---

1:2 census. This is the first census mentioned in the Bible. (See also ch. 26; 2 Sam. 24:1-9; and Luke 2.)
1:3 army. This census was to form an army, so it counted only fit males.
1:4 A man from each tribe. This smart move reduced competition among the tribes, and it allowed minor issues to be settled by tribal representatives.
1:5-16 Ten tribes represented sons of Jacob (Israel). The other two names were the sons of Joseph.
1:32-35 Joseph. Joseph's sons, rather than Joseph, were heads of tribes. This gave Joseph's family a double portion.
1:46 all those registered. Just 70 people moved to Egypt as part of Jacob's family; the total of 600,000 men was phenomenal.
1:47-50 Levi. The Levites were not counted in the military census because they were responsible for maintaining and moving the

39 those registered for the tribe of Dan numbered 62,700.

40 The descendants of Asher: according to their family records by their clans and their ancestral houses, counting the names of those 20 years old or more, everyone who could serve in the army, 41 those registered for the tribe of Asher numbered 41,500.

42 The descendants of Naphtali: according to their family records by their clans and their ancestral houses, counting the names of those 20 years old or more, everyone who could serve in the army, 43 those registered for the tribe of Naphtali numbered 53,400.

44 These are the men Moses and Aaron registered, with ⌊the assistance of⌋ the 12 leaders of Israel; each represented his ancestral house. 45 So all the Israelites 20 years old or more, everyone who could serve in Israel's army, were registered by their ancestral houses. 46 All those registered numbered 603,550.

Duties of the Levites

47 But the Levites were not registered with them by their ancestral tribe. 48 For the LORD had told Moses: 49 "Do not register or take a census of the tribe of Levi with the ⌊other⌋ Israelites. 50 Appoint the Levites over the tabernacle of the •testimony, all its furnishings, and everything in it. They are to transport the tabernacle and all its articles, take care of it, and camp around it. 51 Whenever the tabernacle is to move, the Levites are to take it down, and whenever it is to stop at a campsite, the Levites are to set it up. Any unauthorized person who comes near ⌊it⌋ must be put to death. 52 "The Israelites are to camp by their military divisions, each man with his encampment and under his banner. 53 The Levites are to camp around the tabernacle of the testimony and watch over it, so that no wrath will fall on the Israelite community." 54 The Israelites did everything just as the LORD had commanded Moses.

Organization of the Camps

2 The LORD spoke to Moses and Aaron: 2 "The Israelites are to camp under their respective banners beside the flags of their ancestral houses. They are to camp around the tent of meeting at a distance ⌊from it⌋:

3 Judah's military divisions will camp on the east side toward the sunrise under their banner. The leader of the descendants of Judah is Nahshon son of Amminadab. 4 His military division numbers 74,600. 5 The tribe of Issachar will camp next to it. The leader of the Issacharites is Nethanel son of Zuar. 6 His military division numbers 54,400. 7 The tribe of Zebulun ⌊will be next⌋. The leader of the Zebulunites is Eliab son of Helon. 8 His military division numbers 57,400. 9 The total number in their military divisions who belong to Judah's encampment is 186,400; they will move out first.

10 Reuben's military divisions will camp on the south side under their banner. The leader of the Reubenites is Elizur son of Shedeur. 11 His military division numbers 46,500. 12 The tribe of Simeon will camp next to it. The leader of the Simeonites is Shelumiel son of Zurishaddai. 13 His military division numbers 59,300. 14 The tribe of Gad ⌊will be next⌋. The leader of the Gadites is Eliasaph son of Deuel.a 15 His military division numbers 45,650. 16 The total number in their military divisions who belong to Reuben's encampment is 151,450; they will move out second.

17 The tent of meeting is to move out with the Levites' camp, which is in the middle of the camps. They are to move out just as they camp, each in his place,b with their banners.

18 Ephraim's military divisions will camp on the west side under their banner. The leader of the Ephraimites is Elishama son of Ammihud. 19 His military division numbers 40,500. 20 The tribe of Manasseh will be next to it. The leader of the Manassites is Gamaliel son of Pedahzur. 21 His military division numbers 32,200. 22 The tribe of Benjamin ⌊will be next⌋. The leader of the Benjaminites is Abidan son of Gideoni. 23 His military division numbers 35,400. 24 The total in their military divisions who belong to Ephraim's encampment number 108,100; they will move out third.

25 Dan's military divisions will camp on the north side under their banner. The leader of the Danites is Ahiezer son of Ammishaddai. 26 His military division numbers 62,700. 27 The tribe of Asher will camp next to it. The leader of the Asherites is Pagiel son of Ochran. 28 His military division numbers 41,500. 29 The tribe of Naphtali ⌊will be next⌋. The leader of the Naphtalites is Ahira son of Enan. 30 His military division numbers 53,400. 31 The total number who belong to Dan's encampment is

---

a2:14 Some Hb mss, Sam, Vg; other Hb mss read Reuel   b2:17 Lit each on his hand

---

tabernacle.

1:53 Levites ... around the tabernacle. The Levites served in the tabernacle; naturally they would set up their tents in a protective circle around it.

2:2 distance. Tribes kept their distance out of respect for the presence of God in the tabernacle.

2:3-4 Judah. Judah was not the firstborn, yet his tribe was listed first here. Jesus was born in his family line.

2:10 Reubenites. Jacob had predicted that Reuben's tribe would be known for indecision.

2:12-13 Simeon. Jacob had predicted that Simeon's tribe would eventually be scattered.

2:14 Gad. Jacob had predicted that Gad's tribe would have a history of being attacked.

2:18-22 Ephraimites, Manassites, Benjaminites. Ephraim and Manasseh were sons of Joseph. Joseph and Benjamin were Jacob's favorite sons.

157,600; they are to move out last, with their banners."

32 These are the Israelites registered by their ancestral houses. The total number in the camps by their military divisions is 603,550. 33 But the Levites were not registered among the Israelites, just as the LORD had commanded Moses.

34 The Israelites did everything the LORD commanded Moses; they camped by their banners in this way and moved out the same way, each man by his clan and by his ancestral house.

Aaron's Sons and the Levites

3 These are the family records of Aaron and Moses at the time the LORD spoke with Moses on Mount Sinai. 2 These are the names of Aaron's sons: Nadab, the firstborn, and Abihu, Eleazar, and Ithamar. 3 These are the names of Aaron's sons, the anointed priests, who were ordained to serve as priests. 4 But Nadab and Abihu died in the LORD's presence when they presented unauthorized fire before the LORD in the Wilderness of Sinai, and they had no sons. So Eleazar and Ithamar served as priests under the direction of Aaron their father.

5 The LORD spoke to Moses: 6 "Bring the tribe of Levi near and present them to Aaron the priest to assist him. 7 They are to perform duties for[a] him and the entire community before the tent of meeting by attending to the service of the tabernacle. 8 They are to take care of[a] all the furnishings of the tent of meeting and perform duties for[b] the Israelites by attending to the service of the tabernacle. 9 Assign the Levites to Aaron and his sons; they have been assigned exclusively to him[c] from the Israelites. 10 You are to appoint Aaron and his sons to carry out their priestly responsibilities, but any unauthorized person who comes near ⌊the sanctuary⌋ must be put to death."

11 The LORD spoke to Moses: 12 "See, I have taken the Levites from the Israelites in place of every firstborn Israelite from the womb. The Levites belong to Me, 13 because every firstborn belongs to Me. At the time I struck down every firstborn in the land of Egypt, I consecrated every firstborn in Israel to Myself, both man and animal; they are Mine; I am the LORD."

The Levitical Census

14 The LORD spoke to Moses in the Wilderness of Sinai: 15 "Register the Levites by their ancestral houses and their clans. You are to register every male one

month old or more." 16 So Moses registered them in obedience to the LORD as he had been commanded:

17 These were Levi's sons by name: Gershon, Kohath, and Merari. 18 These were the names of Gershon's sons by their clans: Libni and Shimei. 19 Kohath's sons by their clans were Amram, Izhar, Hebron, and Uzziel. 20 Merari's sons by their clans were Mahli and Mushi. These were the Levite clans by their ancestral houses.

21 The Libnite clan and the Shimeite clan came from Gershon; these were the Gershonite clans. 22 Those registered, counting every male one month old or more, numbered 7,500. 23 The Gershonite clans camped behind the tabernacle on the west side, 24 and the leader of the Gershonite family was Eliasaph son of Lael. 25 The Gershonites' duties at the tent of meeting involved the tabernacle, the tent, its covering, the screen for the entrance to the tent of meeting, 26 the hangings of the courtyard, the screen for the entrance to the courtyard that surrounds the tabernacle and the altar, and the tent ropes—all the work relating to these.

27 The Amramite clan, the Izharite clan, the Hebronite clan, and the Uzzielite clan came from Kohath; these were the Kohathites. 28 Counting every male one month old or more, there were 8,600[d] responsible for the duties of[e] the sanctuary. 29 The clans of the Kohathites camped on the south side of the tabernacle, 30 and the leader of the family of the Kohathite clans was Elizaphan son of Uzziel. 31 Their duties involved the ark, the table, the lampstand, the altars, the sanctuary utensils that were used with these, and the screen[f]—and all the work relating to them. 32 The chief of the Levite leaders was Eleazar son of Aaron the priest; he had oversight of those responsible for the duties of[e] the sanctuary.

33 The Mahlite clan and the Mushite clan came from Merari; these were the Merarite clans. 34 Those registered, counting every male one month old or more, numbered 6,200. 35 The leader of the family of the Merarite clans was Zuriel son of Abihail; they camped on the north side of the tabernacle. 36 The assigned duties of Merari's descendants involved the tabernacle's supports, crossbars, posts, bases, all its equip-

---

[a]3:7,8 Or to guard   [b]3:8 Or and guard   [c]3:9 Some Hb mss, LXX, Sam read Me; Nm 8:16   [d]3:28 LXX reads 8,300   [e]3:28,32 Or for guarding
[f]3:31 The screen between the holy of holies and the holy place; Ex 35:12

2:25 Danites. Jacob once described Dan's tribe as a serpent and a viper.

2:27 Asher. Jacob foretold wealth for Asher.

2:29 Naphtali. Jacob described Naphtali's tribe as mountain people.

2:32 603,550. This counted only the able-

bodied men aged 20 and over.

2:34 everything the LORD commanded Moses. Moses was God's mouthpiece for the Hebrews.

3:4 unauthorized. See Leviticus 22:9.

3:5-10 tribe of Levi ... Aaron. Aaron's de-

scendants were priests. All other Levites were tabernacle workers.

3:9 assigned exclusively to him. Aaron oversaw the tabernacle service of all Levites.

3:10 put to death. The tabernacle was the place of God's presence. No one besides Aaron and his descendants and Aaron's tribe

ment, and all the work related to these, [37] in addition to the posts of the surrounding courtyard with their bases, tent pegs, and ropes.

[38] Moses, Aaron, and his sons, who performed the duties of[a] the sanctuary as a service on behalf of the Israelites, camped in front of the tabernacle on the east, in front of the tent of meeting toward the sunrise. Any unauthorized person who came near ⌊it⌋ was to be put to death.

[39] The total number of all the Levite males one month old or more that Moses and Aaron[b] registered by their clans at the LORD's command was 22,000.

Redemption of the Firstborn

[40] The LORD told Moses: "Register every firstborn male of the Israelites one month old or more, and list their names. [41] You are to take the Levites for Me—I am the LORD—in place of every firstborn among the Israelites, and the Levites' cattle in place of every firstborn among the Israelites' cattle." [42] So Moses registered every firstborn among the Israelites, as the LORD commanded him. [43] The total number of the firstborn males one month old or more listed by name was 22,273.

[44] The LORD spoke to Moses again: [45] "Take the Levites in place of every firstborn among the Israelites, and the Levites' cattle in place of their cattle. The Levites belong to Me; I am the LORD. [46] As the redemption price for the 273 firstborn Israelites who outnumber the Levites, [47] collect five •shekels for each person, according to the standard sanctuary shekel—20 gerahs to the shekel. [48] Give the money to Aaron and his sons as the redemption price for those who are in excess among the Israelites."

[49] So Moses collected the redemption money from those in excess of the ones redeemed by the Levites. [50] He collected the money from the firstborn Israelites: 1,365 ⌊shekels[c] measured⌋ by the standard sanctuary shekel. [51] He gave the redemption money to Aaron and his sons in obedience to the LORD, just as the LORD commanded Moses.

Duties of the Kohathites

4 The LORD spoke to Moses and Aaron: [2] "Among the Levites, take a census of the Kohathites by their clans and their ancestral houses, [3] men from 30 years old to 50 years old—everyone who is qualified[d] to do work at the tent of meeting.

[4] "The service of the Kohathites at the tent of meeting concerns the most holy objects. [5] Whenever the camp is about to move on, Aaron and his sons are to go in, take down the screening veil, and cover the ark of the •testimony with it. [6] They are to place over this a covering made of manatee skin,[e] spread a solid blue cloth on top, and insert its poles.

[7] "They are to spread a blue cloth over the table of the Presence and place the plates and cups on it, as well as the bowls and pitchers for the drink offering. The regular bread ⌊offering⌋ is to be on it. [8] They are to spread a scarlet cloth over them, cover them with a covering made of manatee skin,[e] and insert the poles ⌊in the table⌋.

[9] "They are to take a blue cloth and cover the lampstand used for light, with its lamps, snuffers, and firepans, as well as its jars of oil by which they service it. [10] Then they must place it with all its utensils inside a covering made of manatee skin[e] and put ⌊them⌋ on the carrying frame.

[11] "They are to spread a blue cloth over the gold altar, cover it with a covering made of manatee skin,[e] and insert its poles. [12] They are to take all the serving utensils they use in the sanctuary, place ⌊them⌋ in a blue cloth, cover them with a covering made of manatee skin,[e] and put ⌊them⌋ on a carrying frame.

[13] "They are to remove the ashes from the ⌊bronze⌋ altar, spread a purple cloth over it, [14] and place all the equipment on it that they use in serving: the firepans, meatforks, shovels, and basins—all the equipment of the altar. They are to spread a covering made of manatee skin[e] over it and insert its poles.[f]

[15] "Aaron and his sons are to finish covering the holy objects and all their equipment whenever the camp is to move on. The Kohathites will come and carry them, but they are not to touch the holy objects or they will die. These are the transportation duties of the Kohathites regarding the tent of meeting.

[16] "Eleazar, son of Aaron the priest, has oversight of the lamp oil, the fragrant incense, the daily •grain offering, and the anointing oil. ⌊He has⌋ oversight of the entire tabernacle and everything in it, the holy objects and their utensils."[g]

[17] Then the LORD spoke to Moses and Aaron: [18] "Do not allow the Kohathite tribal clans to be wiped out from the Levites. [19] Do this for them so that they may live and not die when they come near the most holy objects: Aaron and his sons are to go in and assign each

---

[a] 3:38 Or who guarded   [b] 3:39 Some Hb mss, Sam, Syr omit and Aaron   [c] 3:50 Over 34 pounds of silver   [d] 4:3 Lit everyone entering the service   [e] 4:6,8,10,11,12,14 Or of dolphin skin, or of fine leather; Hb obscure   [f] 4:14 Sam, LXX add They are to take a purple cloth and cover the wash basin and its base. They are to place them in a covering made of manatee skin and put them on the carrying frame.   [g] 4:16 Or the sanctuary and its furnishings

---

(the Levites) was allowed to work in the tabernacle or offer sacrifices or enter the Holy Place or Most Holy Place, under penalty of death.

3:12-13 every firstborn Israelite. God had spared the firstborn sons of Israel when He killed all the firstborn sons of Egypt (Ex.

12:12-13). Thus, God had a right to the firstborn sons as His own. Instead, God claimed the Levite tribe to serve before Him and lead the worship.

3:15 Register. The Levites, not counted in the census, were counted here.

3:21-38 These people were to see to it that

God was welcomed, honored, and obeyed among the people.

3:25-26 screen. The tabernacle was a tent made of cloth or animal hide curtains held up by stakes.

3:28 sanctuary. The sanctuary of the tabernacle or temple usually meant the Holy Place,

man his task and transportation duty. 20 The Kohathites are not to go in and look at the holy objects, even for a moment,a or they will die."

Duties of the Gershonites

21 The LORD spoke to Moses: 22 "Take a census of the Gershonites also, by their ancestral houses and their clans. 23 Register men from 30 years old to 50 years old, everyone who is qualified to perform service, to do work at the tent of meeting. 24 This is the service of the Gershonite clans regarding work and transportation duties: 25 They are to transport the tabernacle curtains, the tent of meeting with its covering and the covering made of manatee skinb on top of it, the screen for the entrance to the tent of meeting, 26 the hangings of the courtyard, the screen for the entrance at the gate of the courtyard that surrounds the tabernacle and the altar, along with their ropes and all the equipment for their service. They will carry out everything that needs to be done with these items.

27 "All the service of the Gershonites, all their transportation duties and all their ⌊other⌋ work, is to be ⌊done⌋ at the command of Aaron and his sons; you are to assign to them all that they are responsible to carry. 28 This is the service of the Gershonite clans at the tent of meeting, and their duties will be under the direction of Ithamar son of Aaron the priest.

Duties of the Merarites

29 "As for the Merarites, you are to register them by their clans and their ancestral houses. 30 Register men from 30 years old to 50 years old, everyone who is qualified to do the work of the tent of meeting. 31 This is what they are responsible to carry as the whole of their service at the tent of meeting: the supports of the tabernacle, with its crossbars, posts, and bases, 32 the posts of the surrounding courtyard with their bases, tent pegs, and ropes, including all their equipment and all the work related to them. You are to assign by name the items that they are responsible to carry. 33 This is the service of the Merarite clans regarding all their work at the tent of meeting, under the direction of Ithamar son of Aaron the priest."

Census of the Levites

34 So Moses, Aaron, and the leaders of the community registered the Kohathites by their clans and their ancestral houses, 35 men from 30 years old to 50 years old, everyone who was qualified for work at the tent of meeting. 36 The men registered by their clans numbered 2,750. 37 These were the registered men of the Kohathite clans, everyone who could serve at the tent

of meeting. Moses and Aaron registered them at the LORD's command through Moses.

38 The Gershonites were registered by their clans and their ancestral houses, 39 men from 30 years old to 50 years old, everyone who was qualified for work at the tent of meeting. 40 The men registered by their clans and their ancestral houses numbered 2,630. 41 These were the registered men of the Gershonite clans. At the LORD's command Moses and Aaron registered everyone who could serve at the tent of meeting.

42 The men of the Merarite clans were registered by their clans and their ancestral houses, 43 those from 30 years old to 50 years old, everyone who was qualified for work at the tent of meeting. 44 The men registered by their clans numbered 3,200. 45 These were the registered men of the Merarite clans; Moses and Aaron registered them at the LORD's command through Moses.

46 Moses, Aaron, and the leaders of Israel registered all the Levites by their clans and their ancestral houses, 47 from 30 years old to 50 years old, everyone who was qualified to do the work of serving at the tent of meeting and transporting ⌊it⌋. 48 Their registered men numbered 8,580. 49 At the LORD's command they were registered under the direction of Moses, each one according to his work and transportation duty, and his assignment was as the LORD commanded Moses.

Isolation of the Unclean

5 The LORD instructed Moses: 2 "Command the Israelites to send away anyone from the camp who is afflicted with a skin disease, anyone who has a ⌊bodily⌋ discharge, or anyone who is defiled because of a corpse. 3 You must send away both male or female; send them outside the camp, so that they will not defile their camps where I dwell among them." 4 The Israelites did this, sending them outside the camp. The Israelites did as the LORD instructed Moses.

Compensation for Wrongdoing

5 The LORD spoke to Moses: 6 "Tell the Israelites: When a man or woman commits any sin against another, that person acts unfaithfully toward the LORD and is guilty. 7 The person is to confess the sin he has committed. He is to pay full compensation, add a fifth of its value to it, and give ⌊it⌋ to the individual he has wronged. 8 But if that individual has no relative to receive compensation,c the compensation goes to the LORD for the priest, along with the •atonement ram by which the priest will make atonement for the ⌊guilty⌋ person. 9 Every holy contribution the Israelites present

---

a4:20 Or at the covering of the holy objects   b4:25 Or of dolphin skin, or of fine leather; Hb obscure   c5:8 In the case of the individual's death

---

a highly restricted part of the structure.

3:31 the ark. Misuse of the ark, even if the person intended to be helpful, meant death (see 2 Sam. 6:1-7).

3:41 firstborn. See note at 3:12-13.

4:3 30 years old to 50. These were the prime years of service in the tabernacle. A Levite's

official duties began at 30.

4:16 Eleazar. It was no small job for Eleazar to oversee the whole process.

4:22-33 Specific duties were clearly assigned.

4:34-59 This census focused on Levite men ages 30 to 50.

5:2 disease ... discharge. Strict instructions were given to the people in Leviticus 13–15 about diagnosing, treating, and dealing with conditions that God defined as "unclean." Conditions deemed unclean all related to death—loss of blood or semen, skin white like a corpse, or touching a corpse. God taught separation from sin and death.

to the priest will be his. [10] Each one's holy contribution is his ⌊to give⌋; what each one gives to the priest will be his."

The Jealousy Ritual

[11] The LORD spoke to Moses: [12] "Speak to the Israelites and tell them: If any man's wife goes astray, is unfaithful to him, [13] and sleeps with another,[a] but it is concealed from her husband, and she is undetected, even though she has defiled herself, since there is no witness against her, and she wasn't caught ⌊in the act⌋, [14] and if a feeling of jealousy comes over the husband and he becomes jealous because of his wife who has defiled herself—or if a feeling of jealousy comes over him and he becomes jealous of her though she has not defiled herself— [15] then the man is to bring his wife to the priest. He is also to bring an offering for her of two quarts[b] of barley flour. He is not to pour oil over it or put frankincense on it because it is a •grain offering of jealousy, a grain offering for remembrance that brings sin to mind.

[16] "The priest is to bring her forward and have her stand before the LORD. [17] Then the priest is to take holy water in a clay bowl, and take some of the dust from the tabernacle floor and put ⌊it⌋ in the water. [18] After the priest has the woman stand before the LORD, he is to let down her hair[c] and place in her hands the grain offering for remembrance, which is the grain offering of jealousy. The priest is to hold the bitter water that brings a curse. [19] The priest will require the woman to take an oath and will say to her, 'If no man has slept with you, if you have not gone astray and become defiled while under your husband's authority, be unaffected by this bitter water that brings a curse. [20] But if you have gone astray while under your husband's authority, if you have defiled yourself and a man other than your husband has slept with you'— [21] at this point the priest must make the woman take the oath with the sworn curse, and he is to say to her— 'May the LORD make you into an object of your people's cursing and swearing when He makes your thigh[d] shrivel and your belly swell.[e] [22] May this water that brings a curse enter your stomach, causing ⌊your⌋ belly to swell and ⌊your⌋ thigh to shrivel.'

"And the woman must reply, '•Amen, Amen.'

[23] "Then the priest is to write these curses on a scroll and wash ⌊them⌋ off into the bitter water. [24] He will require the woman to drink the bitter water that brings a curse, and it will enter her and cause bitter suffering. [25] The priest is to take the grain offering of jealousy from the woman's hand, wave the offering before the LORD, and bring it to the altar. [26] The priest is to take a handful of the grain offering as a memorial portion and burn it on the altar. Then he will require the woman to drink the water.

[27] "When he makes her drink the water, if she has defiled herself and been unfaithful to her husband, the water that brings a curse will enter her and cause bitter suffering; her belly will swell, and her thigh will shrivel. She will become a curse among her people. [28] But if the woman has not defiled herself and is pure, she will be unaffected and will be able to conceive children.

[29] "This is the law regarding jealousy when a wife goes astray and defiles herself while under her husband's authority, [30] or when a feeling of jealousy comes over a husband and he becomes jealous of his wife. He is to have the woman stand before the LORD, and the priest will apply this entire ritual to her. [31] The husband will be free of guilt, but that woman will bear the consequences of her guilt."

The Nazirite Vow

6 The LORD instructed Moses: [2] "Speak to the Israelites and tell them: When a man or woman makes a special vow, a Nazirite vow, to consecrate himself to[f] the LORD, [3] he is to abstain[g] from wine and beer. He must not drink vinegar made from wine or from beer. He must not drink any grape juice or eat fresh grapes or raisins. [4] He is not to eat anything produced by the grapevine, from seeds to skin,[h] during his vow.

[5] "You must not cut his hair[i] throughout the time of his vow of consecration. He must be holy until the time is completed during which he consecrates himself to the LORD; he is to let the hair of his head grow long. [6] He must not go near a dead body during the time he consecrates himself to the LORD. [7] He is not to defile himself for his father or mother, or his brother or sister, when they die, because the hair consecrated to his God is on his head. [8] He is holy to the LORD during the time of consecration.

[9] "If someone suddenly dies near him, defiling his consecrated head of hair, he must shave his head on the day of his purification; he is to shave it on the seventh day. [10] On the eighth day he is to bring two turtledoves

---

[a]**5:13** Lit *and man lies with her [and has] an emission of semen* [b]**5:15** Lit *a tenth of an ephah* [c]**5:18** Or *to uncover her head* [d]**5:21–22** Possibly a euphemism for the reproductive organs [e]**5:21** Or *flood* [f]**6:2** Or *vow, to live as a Nazirite for* [g]**6:3** The words *Nazirite, consecrate,* and *abstain* come from the same Hb word, which involves the idea of separation. [h]**6:4** Or *from unripe grapes to hulls* [i]**6:5** Lit *A razor is not to pass over his head*

5:5-10 These verses focus on restitution. Preceding verses address cleanliness of the body and the holiness of God. These verses approach cleanliness in terms of human relationships and holiness of heart.

5:11-31 Now this chapter turns to marital relations. The Bible often uses marriage as a met-aphor for our relationship with God. It is not surprising then that marital unfaithfulness carried severe penalties.

5:14 jealousy. A husband was responsible to deal with his marriage even if his concern was not fully substantiated. He was not free to wait and see or to look the other way.

5:15-28 Unlike infamous witch trials in early American history, the trial described here is not deadly in and of itself. If a woman was cursed after drinking dusty water, this was a miracle showing God's judgment.

5:21 the oath with the sworn curse. Ultimately this curse was sterility.

or two young pigeons to the priest at the entrance to the tent of meeting. 11 The priest is to offer one as a •sin offering and the other as a •burnt offering to make •atonement on behalf of the Nazirite, since he sinned because of the corpse. On that day he must consecrate[a] his head ⌊again⌋. 12 He is to rededicate his time of consecration to the LORD and to bring a year-old male lamb as a •restitution offering. But do not count the previous period, because his consecrated hair became defiled.

13 "This is the law of the Nazirite: On the day his time of consecration is completed, he must be brought to the entrance to the tent of meeting. 14 He is to present an offering to the LORD of one unblemished year-old male lamb as a burnt offering, one unblemished year-old female lamb as a sin offering, one unblemished ram as a •fellowship offering, 15 along with their •grain offerings and drink offerings, and a basket of unleavened cakes made from fine flour mixed with oil, and unleavened wafers coated with oil.

16 "The priest is to present ⌊these⌋ before the LORD and sacrifice the Nazirite's sin offering and burnt offering. 17 He will also offer the ram as a fellowship sacrifice to the LORD, together with the basket of unleavened bread. Then the priest will offer the accompanying grain offering and drink offering.

18 "The Nazirite is to shave his consecrated head at the entrance to the tent of meeting, take the hair from his head, and put ⌊it⌋ on the fire under the fellowship sacrifice. 19 The priest is to take the boiled shoulder from the ram, one unleavened cake from the basket, and one unleavened wafer, and put ⌊them⌋ into the hands of the Nazirite after he has shaved his consecrated head. 20 The priest is to wave them as a presentation offering before the LORD. It is a holy portion for the priest, in addition to the breast of the presentation offering and the thigh of the contribution. After that, the Nazirite may drink wine.

21 "This is the ritual of the Nazirite who vows his offering to the LORD for his consecration, in addition to whatever else he can afford; he must fulfill whatever vow he makes in keeping with the ritual for his consecration."

The Priestly Blessing

22 The LORD spoke to Moses: 23 "Tell Aaron and his sons how you are to bless the Israelites. Say to them:

24 The LORD bless you and protect you;
25 the LORD make His face shine on you,
   and be gracious to you;

26 the LORD look with favor on you[b]
   and give you peace.[c]

27 In this way they will put[d] My name on the Israelites, and I will bless them."

Offerings from the Leaders

7 On the day Moses finished setting up the tabernacle, he anointed and consecrated it and all its furnishings, along with the altar and all its utensils. After he anointed and consecrated these things, 2 the leaders of Israel, the heads of their ancestral houses, presented ⌊an offering⌋. They were the tribal leaders who supervised the registration. 3 They brought as their offering before the LORD six covered carts and 12 oxen, a cart from every two leaders and an ox from each one, and presented them in front of the tabernacle.

4 The LORD said to Moses, 5 "Accept ⌊these⌋ from them to be used in the work of the tent of meeting, and give this offering to the Levites, to each ⌊division⌋ according to their service."

6 So Moses took the carts and oxen and gave them to the Levites. 7 He gave the Gershonites two carts and four oxen corresponding to their service, 8 and gave the Merarites four carts and eight oxen corresponding to their service, under the direction of Ithamar son of Aaron the priest. 9 But he did not give ⌊any⌋ to the Kohathites, since their responsibility was service related to the holy objects carried on their shoulders.

10 The leaders also presented the dedication gift for the altar when it was anointed. The leaders presented their offerings in front of the altar. 11 The LORD told Moses, "Each day have one leader present his offering for the dedication of the altar."

12 The one who presented his offering on the first day was Nahshon son of Amminadab from the tribe of Judah. 13 His offering was one silver dish weighing three and a quarter pounds[e] and one silver basin weighing one and three-quarter pounds,[f] ⌊measured⌋ by the standard sanctuary •shekel, both of them full of fine flour mixed with oil for a •grain offering; 14 one gold bowl weighing four ounces,[g] full of incense; 15 one young bull, one ram, and one male lamb a year old, for a •burnt offering; 16 one male goat for a •sin offering; 17 and two bulls, five rams, five male breeding goats, and five male lambs a year old, for the •fellowship sacrifice. This was the offering of Nahshon son of Amminadab.

---

a6:11 Lit set apart   b6:26 Lit LORD lift His face to you   c6:26 Or prosperity   d6:27 Or invoke   e7:13 Lit dish, 130 its shekel-weight   f7:13 Lit 70 shekels   g7:14 Lit 10 (shekels)

6:2 Nazirite. Other lifetime Nazirites in the Bible included John the Baptist (Luke 1:15), Samuel (1 Sam. 1:11), and probably the most famous, Samson (Judg. 13:1-7; 16:17). For most people, the Nazirite vow was only for a period of time.

6:6-7 dead body. Touching a corpse caused

uncleanness (Lev. 15) even though it was often necessary. Priests and Nazirites were forbidden to touch a corpse at all. God taught separation from sin and death.

6:9-12 This is one of the cases where the Bible demands perfection but makes practical provision for real life. Even though the Nazirite

was forbidden to be around a dead body, there are provisions for resuming his vow if his proximity to death was outside his control.

6:13-20 Only a few Nazirites-for-life are mentioned in the Bible, but many took the vow for a certain period of time. This was a special time to show dedication to God.

18 On the second day Nethanel son of Zuar, leader of Issachar, presented ⌊an offering⌋. 19 As his offering, he presented one silver dish weighing three and a quarter pounds[a] and one silver basin weighing one and three-quarter pounds,[b] ⌊measured⌋ by the standard sanctuary shekel, both of them full of fine flour mixed with oil for a grain offering; 20 one gold bowl weighing four ounces,[c] full of incense; 21 one young bull, one ram, and one male lamb a year old, for a burnt offering; 22 one male goat for a sin offering; 23 and two bulls, five rams, five male breeding goats, and five male lambs a year old, for the fellowship sacrifice. This was the offering of Nethanel son of Zuar.

24 On the third day Eliab son of Helon, leader of the Zebulunites, ⌊presented an offering⌋. 25 His offering was one silver dish weighing three and a quarter pounds[a] and one silver basin weighing one and three-quarter pounds,[b] ⌊measured⌋ by the standard sanctuary shekel, both of them full of fine flour mixed with oil for a grain offering; 26 one gold bowl weighing four ounces,[c] full of incense; 27 one young bull, one ram, and one male lamb a year old, for a burnt offering; 28 one male goat for a sin offering; 29 and two bulls, five rams, five male breeding goats, and five male lambs a year old, for the fellowship sacrifice. This was the offering of Eliab son of Helon.

30 On the fourth day Elizur son of Shedeur, leader of the Reubenites, ⌊presented an offering⌋. 31 His offering was one silver dish weighing three and a quarter pounds[a] and one silver basin weighing one and three-quarter pounds,[b] ⌊measured⌋ by the standard sanctuary shekel, both of them full of fine flour mixed with oil for a grain offering; 32 one gold bowl weighing four ounces,[c] full of incense; 33 one young bull, one ram, and one male lamb a year old, for a burnt offering; 34 one male goat for a sin offering; 35 and two bulls, five rams, five male breeding goats, and five male lambs a year old, for the fellowship sacrifice. This was the offering of Elizur son of Shedeur.

36 On the fifth day Shelumiel son of Zurishaddai, leader of the Simeonites, ⌊presented an offering⌋. 37 His offering was one silver dish weighing three and a quarter pounds[a] and one silver basin weighing one and three-quarter pounds,[b] ⌊measured⌋ by the standard sanctuary shekel, both of them full of fine flour mixed with oil for a grain offering; 38 one gold bowl weighing four ounces,[c] full of incense; 39 one young bull, one ram, and one male lamb a year old, for a burnt offering; 40 one male goat for a sin offering; 41 and two bulls, five rams, five male breeding goats, and five male lambs a year old, for the fellowship sacrifice. This was the offering of Shelumiel son of Zurishaddai.

42 On the sixth day Eliasaph son of Deuel,[d] leader of the Gadites, ⌊presented an offering⌋. 43 His offering was one silver dish weighing three and a quarter pounds[a] and one silver basin weighing one and three-quarter pounds,[b] ⌊measured⌋ by the standard sanctuary shekel, both of them full of fine flour mixed with oil for a grain offering; 44 one gold bowl weighing four ounces,[c] full of incense; 45 one young bull, one ram, and one male lamb a year old, for a burnt offering; 46 one male goat for a sin offering; 47 and two bulls, five rams, five male breeding goats, and five male lambs a year old, for the fellowship sacrifice. This was the offering of Eliasaph son of Deuel.[d]

48 On the seventh day Elishama son of Ammihud, leader of the Ephraimites, ⌊presented an offering⌋. 49 His offering was one silver dish weighing three and a quarter pounds[a] and one silver basin weighing one and three-quarter pounds,[b] ⌊measured⌋ by the standard sanctuary shekel, both of them full of fine flour mixed with oil for a grain offering; 50 one gold bowl weighing four ounces,[c] full of incense; 51 one young bull, one ram, and one male lamb a year old, for a burnt offering; 52 one male goat for a sin offering; 53 and two bulls, five rams, five male breeding goats, and five male lambs a year old, for the fellowship sacrifice. This was the offering of Elishama son of Ammihud.

54 On the eighth day Gamaliel son of Pedahzur, leader of the Manassites, ⌊presented an offering⌋. 55 His offering was one silver dish weighing three and a quarter pounds[a] and one silver basin weighing one and three-quarter pounds,[b] ⌊measured⌋ by the standard sanctuary shekel, both of them full of fine flour mixed with oil for a grain offering; 56 one gold bowl weighing four ounces,[c] full of incense; 57 one young bull, one ram, and one male lamb a year old, for a burnt offering; 58 one male goat for a sin offering; 59 and two bulls, five

---

[a]**7:19,25,31,37,43,49,55** Lit *dish, 130 its shekel-weight*   [b]**7:19,25,31,37,43,49,55** Lit *70 shekels*   [c]**7:20,26,32,38,44,50,56** Lit *10* (shekels)
[d]**7:42,47** LXX, Syr read *Reuel*

6:14-15 burnt ... sin ... fellowship ... grain ... drink offerings. A Nazirite vow was expensive and involved almost every kind of sacrifice. Paul took a Nazirite vow and offered sacrifices as a Christian (Acts 18:18; 21:23-26).

6:24-26 Lord bless you. This benediction

has journeyed through the history of the church. Many worship services today conclude with it. **look with favor upon you.** Literally "turn His face toward you." When God turns His face toward His people He gives them His presence and attention. This may be the benediction Jesus gave when He ascended (Luke 24:50).

6:25 make His face shine. This has the connotation of God's pleasure in His people. Even today we describe parents watching their children as "beaming" with pride.

6:27 put My name on the Israelites God intended for them to be His special people, blessed by Him, and through them a blessing

rams, five male breeding goats, and five male lambs a year old, for the fellowship sacrifice. This was the offering of Gamaliel son of Pedahzur.

60 On the ninth day Abidan son of Gideoni, leader of the Benjaminites, ⌊presented an offering⌋. 61 His offering was one silver dish weighing three and a quarter pounds[a] and one silver basin weighing one and three-quarter pounds,[b] ⌊measured⌋ by the standard sanctuary shekel, both of them full of fine flour mixed with oil for a grain offering; 62 one gold bowl weighing four ounces,[c] full of incense; 63 one young bull, one ram, and one male lamb a year old, for a burnt offering; 64 one male goat for a sin offering; 65 and two bulls, five rams, five male breeding goats, and five male lambs a year old, for the fellowship sacrifice. This was the offering of Abidan son of Gideoni.

66 On the tenth day Ahiezer son of Ammishaddai, leader of the Danites, ⌊presented an offering⌋. 67 His offering was one silver dish weighing three and a quarter pounds[a] and one silver basin weighing one and three-quarter pounds,[b] ⌊measured⌋ by the standard sanctuary shekel, both of them full of fine flour mixed with oil for a grain offering; 68 one gold bowl weighing four ounces,[c] full of incense; 69 one young bull, one ram, and one male lamb a year old, for a burnt offering; 70 one male goat for a sin offering; 71 and two bulls, five rams, five male breeding goats, and five male lambs a year old, for the fellowship sacrifice. This was the offering of Ahiezer son of Ammishaddai.

72 On the eleventh day Pagiel son of Ochran, leader of the Asherites, ⌊presented an offering⌋. 73 His offering was one silver dish weighing three and a quarter pounds[a] and one silver basin weighing one and three-quarter pounds,[b] ⌊measured⌋ by the standard sanctuary shekel, both of them full of fine flour mixed with oil for a grain offering; 74 one gold bowl weighing four ounces,[c] full of incense; 75 one young bull, one ram, and one male lamb a year old, for a burnt offering; 76 one male goat for a sin offering; 77 and two bulls, five rams, five male breeding goats, and five male lambs a year old, for the fellowship sacrifice. This was the offering of Pagiel son of Ochran.

78 On the twelfth day Ahira son of Enan, leader of the Naphtalites, ⌊presented an offering⌋. 79 His offering was one silver dish weighing three and a quarter pounds[a] and one silver basin weighing one and three-quarter pounds,[b] ⌊measured⌋ by the standard sanctuary shekel, both of them full of fine flour mixed with oil for a grain offering; 80 one gold bowl weighing four ounces,[c] full of incense; 81 one young bull, one ram, and one male lamb a year old, for a burnt offering; 82 one male goat for a sin offering; 83 and two bulls, five rams, five male breeding goats, and five male lambs a year old, for the fellowship sacrifice. This was the offering of Ahira son of Enan.

84 This was the dedication gift from the leaders of Israel for the altar when it was anointed: 12 silver dishes, 12 silver basins, and 12 gold bowls. 85 Each silver dish ⌊weighed⌋ three and a quarter pounds,[d] and each basin one and three-quarter pounds.[e] The total ⌊weight⌋ of the silver articles was 60 pounds[f] ⌊measured⌋ by the standard sanctuary shekel. 86 The 12 gold bowls full of incense each ⌊weighed⌋ four ounces[c] ⌊measured⌋ by the standard sanctuary shekel. The total ⌊weight⌋ of the gold bowls was three pounds.[g] 87 All the livestock for the burnt offering totaled 12 bulls, 12 rams, and 12 male lambs a year old, with their grain offerings, and 12 male goats for the sin offering. 88 All the livestock for the fellowship sacrifice totaled 24 bulls, 60 rams, 60 male breeding goats, and 60 male lambs a year old. This was the dedication gift for the altar after it was anointed.

89 When Moses entered the tent of meeting to speak with the LORD, he heard the voice speaking to him from above the •mercy seat that was on the ark of the •testimony, from between the two •cherubim. He spoke to him ⌊that way⌋.

The Lighting in the Tabernacle

8 The LORD spoke to Moses: 2 "Speak to Aaron and tell him: When you set up the lamps, the seven lamps are to give light in front of the lampstand." 3 So Aaron did this; he set up its lamps ⌊to give light⌋ in front of the lampstand just as the LORD had commanded Moses. 4 This is the way the lampstand was made: it was a hammered work of gold, hammered from its base to its flower petals. The lampstand was made according to the pattern the LORD had shown Moses.

Consecration of the Levites

5 The LORD spoke to Moses: 6 "Take the Levites from among the Israelites and ceremonially cleanse them. 7 This is what you must do to them for their purifica-

[a]7:61,67,73,79 Lit dish, 130 its shekel-weight   [b]7:61,67,73,79 Lit 70 shekels   [c]7:62,68,74,80,86 Lit 10 (shekels)   [d]7:85 Lit 130 (shekels)
[e]7:85 Lit 70 (shekels)   [f]7:85 Lit 2,400 (shekels)   [g]7:86 Lit 120 (shekels)

---

to other nations.

7:1-89 While the people had already received many instructions about the tabernacle, this passage describes the actual dedication of the tabernacle. The people brought gifts to be used in transporting the tabernacle from Mount Sinai on the journey to the Promised land.

7:12-83 As with the rest of community life, the people gave their gifts according to tribe, in an orderly fashion.

7:84-88 12. Indicates the 12 tribes of Israel.

7:89 He spoke to him [that way]. The tabernacle intended as a visual reminder of God's presence and a place for God to communi-

cate with His people.

8:10 lay their hands. This action was a symbol that the priests represented the Israelites before the Lord.

8:20 the LORD commanded. So far so good in terms of the Hebrews' obedience. Throughout Numbers, though, we see God's people

tion: Sprinkle them with the purification water. Have them shave their entire bodies and wash their clothes, and so purify themselves.

8 "They are to take a young bull and its •grain offering of fine flour mixed with oil, and you are to take a second young bull for a •sin offering. 9 Bring the Levites before the tent of meeting and assemble the entire Israelite community. 10 Then present the Levites before the LORD, and have the Israelites lay their hands on them. 11 Aaron is to present the Levites before the LORD as a presentation offering from the Israelites, so that they may perform the LORD's work. 12 Next the Levites are to lay their hands on the heads of the bulls. Sacrifice one as a sin offering and the other as a •burnt offering to the LORD, to make •atonement for the Levites.

13 "You are to have the Levites stand before Aaron and his sons, and you are to present them before the LORD as a presentation offering. 14 In this way you are to separate the Levites from the rest of the Israelites so that the Levites will belong to Me. 15 After that the Levites may come to serve ⌊at⌋ the tent of meeting, once you have ceremonially cleansed them and presented them as a presentation offering. 16 For they have been exclusively assigned to Me from the Israelites. I have taken them for Myself in place of all who come first from the womb, every Israelite firstborn. 17 For every firstborn among the Israelites is Mine, both man and animal. I consecrated them to Myself on the day I struck down every firstborn in the land of Egypt. 18 But I have taken the Levites in place of every firstborn among the Israelites. 19 From the Israelites, I have given the Levites exclusively to Aaron and his sons to perform the work for the Israelites at the tent of meeting and to make atonement on their behalf, so that no plague will come against the Israelites when they approach the sanctuary."

20 Moses, Aaron, and the entire Israelite community did ⌊this⌋ to the Levites. The Israelites did everything to them the LORD commanded Moses regarding the Levites. 21 The Levites purified themselves and washed their clothes; then Aaron presented[a] them before the LORD as a presentation offering. Aaron also made atonement for them to ceremonially cleanse them. 22 After that, the Levites came to do their work at the tent of meeting in the presence of Aaron and his sons. So they did to them as the LORD had commanded Moses concerning the Levites.

23 The LORD spoke to Moses: 24 "In regard to the Levites: From 25 years old or more, a man enters the service in the work at the tent of meeting. 25 But at 50

years old he is to retire from his service in the work and no longer serve. 26 He may assist his brothers to fulfill responsibilities[b] at the tent of meeting, but he must not do the work. This is how you are to deal with the Levites regarding their duties."

The Second Passover

9 In the first month of the second year after their departure from the land of Egypt, the LORD told Moses in the Wilderness of Sinai: 2 "The Israelites are to observe the •Passover at its appointed time. 3 You must observe it at its appointed time on the fourteenth day of this month at twilight; you are to observe it according to all its statutes and ordinances." 4 So Moses told the Israelites to observe the Passover, 5 and they observed it in the first month on the fourteenth day at twilight in the Wilderness of Sinai. The Israelites did everything as the LORD had commanded Moses.

6 But there were ⌊some⌋ men who were unclean because of a human corpse, so they could not observe the Passover on that day. These men came before Moses and Aaron the same day 7 and said to him, "We are unclean because of a human corpse. Why should we be excluded from presenting the LORD's offering at its appointed time with the ⌊other⌋ Israelites?"

8 Moses replied to them, "Wait here until I hear what the LORD commands for you."

9 Then the LORD spoke to Moses: 10 "Tell the Israelites: When any one of you or your descendants is unclean because of a corpse or is on a distant journey, he may still observe the Passover to the LORD. 11 Such people are to observe it in the second month, on the fourteenth day at twilight. They are to eat the animal with unleavened bread and bitter herbs; 12 they may not leave any of it until morning or break any of its bones. They must observe the Passover according to all its statutes.

13 "But the man who is ceremonially clean, is not on a journey, and yet fails to observe the Passover is to be cut off from his people, because he did not present the LORD's offering at its appointed time. That man will bear the consequences of his sin.

14 "If a foreigner resides with you and wants to observe the Passover to the LORD, he is to do so according to the Passover statute and its ordinances. You are to apply the same statute to both the foreign resident and the native of the land."

Guidance by the Cloud

15 On the day the tabernacle was set up, the cloud covered the tabernacle, the tent of the •testimony, and

---

a **8:21** Lit *waved*   b **8:26** Or *to keep guard*

---

not honoring God or His commands.

8:24-25 retire. This forced retirement system insured that the Levites gave God their prime years of service.

8:26 assist. The older Levites could mentor younger men.

9:7 excluded from presenting. The Israel-

ites considered the Passover an honor and a joy, not a burden.

9:10 he may still observe the Passover. God wanted holiness without compromise from His people, but on day-to-day matters, God's mercy and flexibility were evident.

9:12 break any of its bones. When Moses

prepared the people for the first Passover, he instructed them to roast a lamb, but not to break any of its bones (Ex. 12:43-51). The instruction was repeated here as a reminder to the people. Consider Jesus, the sacrificial Lamb of God (John 1:29), whose bones were not broken (John 19:36).

it appeared like fire above the tabernacle from evening until morning. 16 It remained that way continuously: the cloud would cover it,[a] appearing like fire at night. 17 Whenever the cloud was lifted up above the tent, the Israelites would set out; at the place where the cloud stopped, there the Israelites camped. 18 At the LORD's command the Israelites set out, and at the LORD's command they camped. As long as the cloud stayed over the tabernacle, they camped.

19 Even when the cloud stayed over the tabernacle many days, the Israelites carried out the LORD's requirement and did not set out. 20 Sometimes the cloud remained over the tabernacle for ⌊only⌋ a few days. They would camp at the LORD's command and set out at the LORD's command. 21 Sometimes the cloud remained ⌊only⌋ from evening until morning; when the cloud lifted in the morning, they set out. Or if it remained a day and a night, they moved out when the cloud lifted. 22 Whether it was two days, a month, or longer,[b] the Israelites camped and did not set out as long as the cloud stayed over the tabernacle. But when it was lifted, they set out. 23 They camped at the LORD's command, and they set out at the LORD's command. They carried out the LORD's requirement according to His command through Moses.

Two Silver Trumpets

10 The LORD spoke to Moses: 2 "Make two trumpets of hammered silver to summon the community and have the camps set out. 3 When both are sounded in long blasts, the entire community is to gather before you at the entrance to the tent of meeting. 4 However, if one is sounded, only the leaders, the heads of Israel's clans, are to gather before you.

5 "When you sound short blasts, the camps pitched on the east are to set out. 6 When you sound short blasts a second time, the camps pitched on the south are to set out. Short blasts are to be sounded for them to set out. 7 When calling the assembly together, you are to sound long blasts, not short ones. 8 The sons of Aaron, the priests, are to sound the trumpets. Your use of these is a permanent statute throughout your generations.

9 "When you enter into battle in your land against an adversary who is attacking you, sound short blasts on the trumpets, and you will be remembered before the LORD your God and be delivered from your enemies. 10 You are to sound the trumpets over your •burnt offerings and your •fellowship sacrifices and on your joyous occasions, your appointed festivals, and the beginning of each of your months. They will serve

as a reminder for you before your God: I am the LORD your God."

From Sinai to Paran

11 During the second year, in the second month on the twentieth ⌊day⌋ of the month, the cloud was lifted up above the tabernacle of the •testimony. 12 The Israelites traveled on from the Wilderness of Sinai, moving from one place to the next until the cloud stopped in the Wilderness of Paran. 13 They set out for the first time according to the LORD's command through Moses.

14 The military divisions of the camp of Judah with their banner set out first, and Nahshon son of Amminadab was over Judah's divisions. 15 Nethanel son of Zuar was over the division of the Issachar tribe, 16 and Eliab son of Helon was over the division of the Zebulun tribe. 17 The tabernacle was then taken down, and the Gershonites and the Merarites set out, transporting the tabernacle.

18 The military divisions of the camp of Reuben with their banner set out, and Elizur son of Shedeur was over Reuben's division. 19 Shelumiel son of Zurishaddai was over the division of Simeon's tribe, 20 and Eliasaph son of Deuel was over the division of the tribe of Gad. 21 The Kohathites then set out, transporting the holy objects; the tabernacle was to be set up before their arrival.

22 Next the military divisions of the camp of Ephraim with their banner set out, and Elishama son of Ammihud was over Ephraim's division. 23 Gamaliel son of Pedahzur was over the division of the tribe of Manasseh, 24 and Abidan son of Gideoni was over the division of the tribe of Benjamin.

25 The military divisions of the camp of Dan with their banner set out, serving as rear guard for all the camps, and Ahiezer son of Ammishaddai was over Dan's division. 26 Pagiel son of Ochran was over the division of the tribe of Asher, 27 and Ahira son of Enan was over the division of the tribe of Naphtali. 28 This was the order of march for the Israelites by their military divisions as they set out.

29 Moses said to Hobab, son of Moses' father-in-law[c] Reuel[d] the Midianite: "We're setting out for the place the LORD promised: 'I will give it to you.' Come with us, and we will treat you well, for the LORD has promised good things to Israel."

30 But he replied to him, "I don't want to go. Instead, I will go to my own land and my relatives."

31 "Please don't leave us," Moses said, "since you know where we should camp in the wilderness, and

---

a9:16 LXX, Vg, Syr, Tg read it by day   b9:22 Or a year   c10:29 Or said to Hobab's brother-in-law   d10:29 Also known as Jethro; Ex 2:16–18; 3:1; 4:18

9:13 fails to observe. If someone did not take part in the Passover, he was, in effect, spitting on God's provision for His people.

9:14 foreigner resides with you. A non-Hebrew must not only submit to dietary rules and daily rituals but must convert and be circumcised before observing the Passover.

9:15 the cloud. The cloud had been God's signal to move camp. Now at the completion of the tabernacle, the cloud hovered over it.

9:18 At the LORD's command. The Hebrews followed a personal God who provided daily guidance.

10:3-7 sounded. Using different trumpets

sounds, Moses could coordinate the movements of the people.

10:11 second year. It should have taken them only a few months to get from Mount Sinai to the promised land. The Book of Numbers tells why it took 40 years.

10:14 banner. A banner or flag represented

you can serve as our eyes. 32 If you come with us, whatever good the LORD does for us we will do for you."

33 They set out from the mountain of the LORD on a three-day journey to seek a resting place for them, with the ark of the LORD's covenant traveling ahead of them for the three days. 34 Meanwhile, the cloud of the LORD was over them by day when they set out from the camp.

35 Whenever the ark set out, Moses would say:

Arise, LORD!
Let Your enemies be scattered,
and those who hate You flee
from Your presence.

36 When it came to rest, he would say:

Return, LORD,
to the countless thousands of Israel.

Complaints about Hardship

11 Now the people began complaining openly before[a] the LORD about hardship. When the LORD heard, His anger burned, and the fire from the LORD blazed among them and consumed the outskirts of the camp. 2 Then the people cried out to Moses, and he prayed to the LORD, and the fire died down. 3 So that place was named Taberah,[b] because the LORD's fire had blazed among them.

Complaints about Food

4 Contemptible people[c] among them had a strong craving [for other food]. The Israelites cried again and said, "Who will feed us meat? 5 We remember the free fish we ate in Egypt, along with the cucumbers, melons, leeks, onions, and garlic. 6 But now our appetite is gone;[d] there's nothing to look at but this manna!"

7 The manna resembled coriander seed, and its appearance was like that of bdellium.[e] 8 The people walked around and gathered [it]. They ground [it] on a pair of grinding stones or crushed [it] in a mortar, then boiled [it] in a cooking pot and shaped it into cakes. It tasted like a pastry cooked with the finest oil. 9 When the dew fell on the camp at night, the manna would fall with it.

10 Moses heard the people, family after family, crying at the entrance of their tents. The LORD was very angry; Moses was also provoked.[f] 11 So Moses asked the LORD, "Why have You brought such trouble on Your servant? Why are You angry with me, and why do You burden me with all these people? 12 Did I conceive all these

people? Did I give them birth so You should tell me, 'Carry them at your breast, as a nursing woman carries a baby,' to the land that You[g] swore to [give] their fathers? 13 Where can I get meat to give all these people? For they are crying to me: 'Give us meat to eat!'

14 "I can't carry all these people by myself. They are too much for me. 15 If You are going to treat me like this, please kill me right now. If You are pleased with me, don't let me see my misery [any more]."

Seventy Elders Anointed

16 The LORD answered Moses, "Bring Me 70 men from Israel known to you as elders and officers of the people. Take them to the tent of meeting and have them stand there with you. 17 Then I will come down and speak with you there. I will take some of the Spirit who is on you and put [the Spirit] on them. They will help you bear the burden of the people, so that you do not have to bear it by yourself.

18 "Tell the people: Purify yourselves [in readiness] for tomorrow, and you will eat meat because you cried before the LORD: 'Who will feed us meat? We really had it good in Egypt.' The LORD will give you meat and you will eat. 19 You will eat, not for one day, or two days, or five days, or 10 days, or 20 days, 20 but for a whole month—until it comes out of your nostrils and becomes nauseating to you—because you have rejected the LORD who is among you, and cried to Him: 'Why did we ever leave Egypt?'"

21 But Moses replied, "I'm in the middle of a people with 600,000 foot soldiers, yet You say, 'I will give them meat, and they will eat for a month.' 22 If flocks and herds were slaughtered for them, would they have enough? Or if all the fish in the sea were caught for them, would they have enough?"

23 The LORD answered Moses, "Is the LORD's power limited?[h] You will see whether or not what I have promised will happen to you."

24 Moses went out and told the people the words of the LORD. He brought 70 men from the elders of the people and had them stand around the tent. 25 Then the LORD descended in the cloud and spoke to him. He took some of the Spirit that was on Moses and placed [the Spirit] on the 70 elders. As the Spirit rested on them, they prophesied, but they never did it again. 26 Two men had remained in the camp, one named Eldad and the other Medad; the Spirit rested on them—they were among those listed, but had not gone out to the tent— and they prophesied in the camp. 27 A young man ran

---

a**11:1** Lit *in the ears of*   b**11:3** = blaze   c**11:4** Or *The mixed multitude*; Hb obscure   d**11:6** Or *our lives are wasting away,* or *our throat is dry*   e**11:7** Probably a gum resin of yellowish, transparent color   f**11:10** Lit *and it was evil in the eyes of Moses*   g**11:12** One Hb ms, Sam, LXX, Syr, Tg read *I*   h**11:23** Lit *LORD's arm too short*

---

a family and helped keep the people marching in organized groups.

10:29 Hobab. Moses' brother-in-law (his wife, Zipporah's, brother). **Reuel.** Another name for Jethro, Moses' father-in-law (Ex. 18).

10:31 you know. Evidently Hobab knew the desert and could help the Hebrews in their

crossing. He did indeed travel with them, because his descendants were listed among those in the promised land (Judg. 1:16).

11:4 Contemptible people. The phrase means "mixed company." It probably applies to non-Hebrews who came out of Egypt in the Exodus—perhaps servants or in-laws.

11:7 manna. "Manna" means "What is it?" **coriander seed.** An herb in the carrot family used for cooking and for medicine. **bdellium.** A yellow, transparent resin (like powder of hardened tree sap).

11:12 Did I conceive all these people? In his frustration Moses wanted to pass the buck

and reported to Moses, "Eldad and Medad are prophesying in the camp."

28 Joshua son of Nun, assistant to Moses since his youth,ᵃ responded, "Moses, my lord, stop them!"

29 But Moses asked him, "Are you jealous on my account? If only all the LORD's people were prophets, and the LORD would place His Spirit on them." 30 Then Moses returned to the camp along with the elders of Israel.

Quail in the Camp

31 A wind sent by the LORD came up and blew quail in from the sea; it dropped ⌊them⌋ at the camp all around, three feetᵇ offᶜ the ground, about a day's journey in every direction. 32 The people were up all that day and night and all the next day gathering the quail—the one who took the least gathered 33 bushelsᵈ—and they spread them out all around the camp.ᵉ

33 While the meat was still between their teeth, before it was chewed, the LORD's anger burned against the people, and the LORD struck them with a very severe plague. 34 So they named that place Kibroth-hattaavah,ᶠ because there they buried the people who had craved ⌊the meat⌋.

35 From Kibroth-hattaavah the people moved on to Hazerothᵍ and remained there.

Miriam and Aaron Rebel

12 Miriam and Aaron criticized Moses because of the •Cushiteʰ ⁱ woman he married (for he had married a Cushite woman). 2 They said, "Does the LORD speak only through Moses? Does He not also speak through us?" And the LORD heard ⌊it⌋. 3 Moses was a very humble man, more so than any man on the face of the earth.

4 Suddenly the LORD said to Moses, Aaron, and Miriam, "You three come out to the tent of meeting." So the three of them went out. 5 Then the LORD descended in a pillar of cloud, stood at the entrance to the tent, and summoned Aaron and Miriam. When the two of them came forward, 6 He said:

"Listen to what I say:
If there is a prophet among you from the LORD,
I make Myself known to him in a vision;
I speak with him in a dream.
7 Not so with My servant Moses;
he is faithful inʲ all My household.
8 I speak with him directly,ᵏ
openly, and not in riddles;
he sees the form of the LORD.

So why were you not afraid to speak against My servant Moses?" 9 The LORD's anger burned against them, and He left.

10 As the cloud moved away from the tent, Miriam's ⌊skin⌋ suddenly became diseased, as ⌊white⌋ as snow. When Aaron turned toward her, he saw that she was diseased 11 and said to Moses, "My lord, please don't hold against us this sin we have so foolishly committed. 12 Please don't let her be like a dead ⌊baby⌋ whose flesh is half eaten away when he comes out of his mother's womb."

13 Then Moses cried out to the LORD, "God, please heal her!"

14 The LORD answered Moses, "If her father had merely spit in her face, wouldn't she remain in disgrace for seven days? Let her be confined outside the camp for seven days; after that she may be brought back in." 15 So Miriam was confined outside the camp for seven days, and the people did not move on until Miriam was brought back in. 16 After that, the people set out from Hazeroth and camped in the Wilderness of Paran.

Rebelling Against Authority

1. What's the most embarrassing situation you've ever experienced because of something you blurted out? What happened?

Numbers 12:1-15
2. Why do you think Miriam and Aaron were jealous of Moses? Were they right or wrong in complaining that others were allowed to speak on behalf of God? What did God say about it?
3. What is the lesson here about rebelling against God-given authorities?
4. How do people today rebel against authority on your team? At your school? In society? In the church?
5. Do you rebel against the authority of your parents? Your coach? Your teachers? Others? What are the consequences?

Scouting Out Canaan

13 The LORD spoke to Moses: 2 "Send men to scout out the land of Canaan I am giving to the

---

ᵃ**11:28** LXX, some Sam mss read *Moses, from his chosen ones*   ᵇ**11:31** Lit *two cubits*   ᶜ**11:31** Or *on,* or *above*   ᵈ**11:32** Lit *10 homers*   ᵉ**11:32** To dry or cure the meat; 2 Sm 17:19; Ezk 26:5,14   ᶠ**11:34** = Graves of Craving   ᵍ**11:35** = settlements; Nm 12:16; 33:16–17   ʰ**12:1** LXX reads *Ethiopian*   ⁱ**12:1** = Sudan and Ethiopia   ʲ**12:7** Or *is entrusted with*   ᵏ**12:8** Lit *mouth to mouth*

11:16-34 God helped Moses organize administratively, much like Jethro did earlier (Ex. 18:13-27).

11:20 rejected the LORD. Moses spoke bluntly. Their sin had to do with ingratitude and a lack of faith, not just an appetite for meat.

11:21 Moses replied. Compare the disciples' response when Jesus told them to feed 5,000 people (John 6:5-9).

11:23 the LORD's power. God asked Moses, in effect, "Do you not think I am able to produce so much meat?"

12:1 Miriam and Aaron. Moses' sister and

to God, the ultimate Father of "these people."

brother. **Cushite.** Cush was located in what is now southern Egypt, Sudan, and northern Ethiopia.

12:2 only through Moses. Miriam and Aaron felt insecure and displaced, perhaps by the 70 new elders, Moses' new wife, or simple jealousy.

Israelites. Send one man who is a leader among them from each of their ancestral tribes." ³ Moses sent them from the Wilderness of Paran at the LORD's command. All the men were leaders in Israel. ⁴ These were their names:

Shammua son of Zaccur from the tribe
   of Reuben;
⁵ Shaphat son of Hori from the tribe of Simeon;
⁶ Caleb son of Jephunneh from the tribe of Judah;
⁷ Igal son of Joseph from the tribe of Issachar;
⁸ Hoshea son of Nun from the tribe of Ephraim;
⁹ Palti son of Raphu from the tribe of Benjamin;
¹⁰ Gaddiel son of Sodi from the tribe of Zebulun;
¹¹ Gaddi son of Susi from the tribe of Manasseh
   (from the tribe of Joseph);
¹² Ammiel son of Gemalli from the tribe of Dan;
¹³ Sethur son of Michael from the tribe of Asher;
¹⁴ Nahbi son of Vophsi from the tribe of Naphtali;
¹⁵ Geuel son of Machi from the tribe of Gad.

¹⁶ These were the names of the men Moses sent to scout out the land, and Moses renamed Hoshea son of Nun, Joshua.

¹⁷ When Moses sent them to scout out the land of Canaan, he told them, "Go up this way to the •Negev, then go up into the hill country. ¹⁸ See what the land is like, and whether the people who live there are strong or weak, few or many. ¹⁹ Is the land they live in good or bad? Are the cities they live in encampments or fortifications? ²⁰ Is the land fertile or unproductive? Are there trees in it or not? Be courageous. Bring back some fruit from the land." It was the season for the first ripe grapes.

²¹ So they went up and scouted out the land from the Wilderness of Zinᵃ as far as Rehobᵇ near the entrance to Hamath.ᶜ ²² They went up through the Negev and came to Hebron, where Ahiman, Sheshai, and Talmai, the descendants of Anak, were living. Hebron was built seven years before Zoan in Egypt. ²³ When they came to the Valley of Eshcol, they cut down a branch with a single cluster of grapes, which was carried on a pole by two men. ⌊They⌋ also ⌊took⌋ some pomegranates and figs. ²⁴ That place was called the Valley of Eshcolᵈ because of the cluster ⌊of grapes⌋ the Israelites cut there. ²⁵ At the end of 40 days they returned from scouting out the land.

Report about Canaan

²⁶ The men went back to Moses, Aaron, and the entire Israelite community in the Wilderness of Paran

at Kadesh. They brought back a report for them and the whole community, and they showed them the fruit of the land. ²⁷ They reported to Moses: "We went into the land where you sent us. Indeed it is flowing with milk and honey, and here is some of its fruit. ²⁸ However, the people living in the land are strong, and the cities are large and fortified. We also saw the descendants of Anak there. ²⁹ The Amalekites are living in the land of the Negev; the Hittites, Jebusites, and Amorites live in the hill country; and the Canaanites live by the sea and along the Jordan."

 Israelite Spy Team

1. Are you more likely to stop and ask directions if you are lost or drive around until you find your way?

Numbers 13:26-14:10,26-45

2. Why did 10 spies recommend running away, while Joshua and Caleb recommended going in to the land of Canaan?
3. Why did the Israelites rebel against Moses and say that Egypt was better?
4. What was the result of the people's lack of faith? What does this teach about the very real danger of disobedience?

³⁰ Then Caleb quieted the people in the presence of Moses and said, "We must go up and take possession of the land because we can certainly conquer it!"

³¹ But the men who had gone up with him responded, "We can't go up against the people because they are stronger than we are!" ³² So they gave a negative report to the Israelites about the land they had scouted: "The land we passed through to explore is one that devours its inhabitants, and all the people we saw in it are men of great size. ³³ We even saw the Nephilimᵉ there." (The offspring of Anak were descended from the Nephilim.) "To ourselves we seemed like grasshoppers, and we must have seemed the same to them."

ᵃ**13:21** Southern border of the promised land   ᵇ**13:21** Northern border of the promised land   ᶜ**13:21** Or *near Lebo-hamath*   ᵈ**13:24** = cluster
ᵉ**13:33** Possibly means "fallen ones"; traditionally, *giants*; Gn 6:4

12:4 Suddenly. The Lord knows and deals with the sin that takes place on earth. God called a meeting to address the dispute that Moses' brother and sister had with him.
12:8 why were you not afraid? To question Moses is to question God.
12:10 diseased. Miriam's disease forced her

to live outside the community, without prestige or position.
12:14-15 confined. God responded to Aaron and Moses' appeal, but Miriam still had to endure a time of illness and separation.
13:2 each of their ancestral tribes. As with the earlier census, selecting one from each

tribe gave credibility and unity to their report.
13:17-20 strong or weak, few or many. Moses told the spies to report not only on the land of Canaan itself but also on the people who lived there.
13:21 scouted out the land. This journey of 250 miles each way probably also involved

Israel's Refusal to Enter Canaan

14 Then the whole community broke into loud cries, and the people wept that night. ² All the Israelites complained about Moses and Aaron, and the whole community told them, "If only we had died in the land of Egypt, or if only we had died in this wilderness! ³ Why is the LORD bringing us into this land to die by the sword? Our wives and little children will become plunder. Wouldn't it be better for us to go back to Egypt?" ⁴ So they said to one another, "Let's appoint a leader and go back to Egypt."

⁵ Then Moses and Aaron fell down with their faces ⌊to the ground⌋ in front of the whole assembly of the Israelite community. ⁶ Joshua son of Nun and Caleb son of Jephunneh, who were among those who scouted out the land, tore their clothes ⁷ and said to the entire Israelite community: "The land we passed through and explored is an extremely good land. ⁸ If the LORD is pleased with us, He will bring us into this land, a land flowing with milk and honey, and give it to us. ⁹ Only don't rebel against the LORD, and don't be afraid of the people of the land, for we will devour them. Their protection has been removed from them, and the LORD is with us. Don't be afraid of them!"

¹⁰ While the whole community threatened to stone them, the glory of the LORD appeared to all the Israelites at the tent of meeting.

God's Judgment of Israel's Rebellion

¹¹ The LORD said to Moses, "How long will these people despise Me? How long will they not trust in Me despite all the signs I have performed among them? ¹² I will strike them with a plague and destroy them. Then I will make you into a greater and mightier nation than they are."

¹³ But Moses replied to the LORD, "The Egyptians will hear about it, for by Your strength You brought up this people from them. ¹⁴ They will tell ⌊it to⌋ the inhabitants of this land. They have heard that You, LORD, are among these people, how You, LORD, are seen face to face, how Your cloud stands over them, and how You go before them in a pillar of cloud by day and in a pillar of fire by night. ¹⁵ If You kill this people with a single blow,[a] the nations that have heard of Your fame will declare, ¹⁶ 'Since the LORD wasn't able to bring this people into the land He swore to ⌊give⌋ them, He has slaughtered them in the wilderness.'

¹⁷ "So now, may My Lord's power be magnified just as You have spoken: ¹⁸ The LORD is slow to anger and rich in faithful love, forgiving wrongdoing and rebel-lion. But He will not leave ⌊the guilty⌋ unpunished, bringing the consequences of the fathers' wrongdoing on the children to the third and fourth generation. ¹⁹ Please pardon the wrongdoing of this people in keeping with the greatness of Your faithful love, just as You have forgiven them from Egypt until now."

²⁰ The LORD responded, "I have pardoned ⌊them⌋ as you requested. ²¹ Yet as surely as I live and as the whole earth is filled with the LORD's glory, ²² none of the men who have seen My glory and the signs I performed in Egypt and in the wilderness, and have tested Me these 10 times and did not obey Me, ²³ will ever see the land I swore to ⌊give⌋ their fathers. None of those who have despised Me will see it. ²⁴ But since My servant Caleb has a different spirit and has followed Me completely, I will bring him into the land where he has gone, and his descendants will inherit it. ²⁵ Since the Amalekites and Canaanites are living in the lowlands,[b] turn back tomorrow and head for the wilderness in the direction of the •Red Sea."

²⁶ Then the LORD spoke to Moses and Aaron: ²⁷ "How long ⌊must I endure⌋ this evil community that keeps complaining about Me? I have heard the Israelites' complaints that they make against Me. ²⁸ Tell them: As surely as I live, declares the LORD, I will do to you exactly as I heard you say. ²⁹ Your corpses will fall in this wilderness—all of you who were registered ⌊in the census⌋, the entire number of you 20 years old or more—because you have complained about Me. ³⁰ I swear that none of you will enter the land I promised[c] to settle you in, except Caleb son of Jephunneh and Joshua son of Nun. ³¹ I will bring your children whom you said would become plunder into the land you rejected, and they will enjoy it. ³² But as for you, your corpses will fall in this wilderness. ³³ Your children will be shepherds in the wilderness for 40 years and bear the penalty for your acts of unfaithfulness until all your corpses lie ⌊scattered⌋ in the wilderness. ³⁴ You will bear the consequences of your sins 40 years based on the number of the 40 days that you scouted the land, a year for each day.[d] You will know My displeasure.[e] ³⁵ I, the LORD, have spoken. I swear that I will do this to the entire evil community that has conspired against Me. They will come to an end in the wilderness, and there they will die."

³⁶ So the men Moses sent to scout out the land, and who returned and incited the entire community to complain about him by spreading a bad report about the land— ³⁷ those men who spread the report about the

---

[a] **14:15** Lit *people as one man*   [b] **14:25** Lit *valley*   [c] **14:30** Lit *I raised My hand*   [d] **14:34** Lit *a day for the year, a day for the year*   [e] **14:34** Or *My opposition*

---

tracing a possible line of attack.

13:23 cluster of grapes. The fact that the explorers needed a pole to carry the grapes showed the bounty of the land.

13:26-29 The spies were right to give an accurate report of both the prosperity and the dangers ahead. They sinned by not trusting

God to carry Israel through difficulties.

13:30 Caleb. Only Caleb is mentioned here, but Joshua also felt they should trust God and enter the land of Canaan (see 14:6-9).

13:32 a negative report. The spies' cynical report filled the people with doubt and dismay.

14:1-2 the people wept. The people succumbed to fear of the unknown instead of trusting in the power of God.

14:3-4 appoint a leader … go back. The obstacles ahead seemed too great, so the people were ready to return to Egypt.

14:9 the LORD is with us. Joshua and Caleb

land were struck down by the LORD. 38 Only Joshua son of Nun and Caleb son of Jephunneh remained alive of those men who went to scout out the land.

Israel Routed

39 When Moses reported these words to all the Israelites, the people were overcome with grief. 40 They got up early the next morning and went up the ridge of the hill country, saying, "Let's go to the place the LORD promised, for we were wrong."

41 But Moses responded, "Why are you going against the LORD's command? It won't succeed. 42 Don't go, because the LORD is not among you and you will be defeated by your enemies. 43 The Amalekites and Canaanites are right in front of you, and you will fall by the sword. The LORD won't be with you, since you have turned from following Him."

44 But they dared to go up the ridge of the hill country, even though the ark of the LORD's covenant and Moses did not leave the camp. 45 Then the Amalekites and Canaanites who lived in that ⌊part of the⌋ hill country came down, attacked them, and routed them as far as Hormah.

Laws About Offerings

15 The LORD instructed Moses: 2 "Speak to the Israelites and tell them: When you enter the land I am giving you to settle in, 3 and you make a fire offering to the LORD from the herd or flock—either a •burnt offering or a sacrifice, to fulfill a vow, or as a freewill offering, or at your appointed festivals—to produce a pleasing aroma for the LORD, 4 the one presenting his offering to the LORD must also present a •grain offering of two quarts^a of fine flour mixed with a quart^b of oil. 5 Prepare a quart^b of wine as a drink offering with the burnt offering or sacrifice of each lamb.

6 "If you prepare a grain offering with a ram, it must be four quarts^c of fine flour mixed with a third of a gallon^d of oil. 7 Also present a third of a gallon^d of wine for a drink offering as a pleasing aroma to the LORD.

8 "If you prepare a young bull as a burnt offering or as a sacrifice, to fulfill a vow, or as a •fellowship offering to the LORD, 9 a grain offering of six quarts^e of fine flour mixed with two quarts^f of oil must be presented with the bull. 10 Also present two quarts^f of wine as a drink offering. It is a fire offering of pleasing aroma to the LORD. 11 This is to be done for each ox, ram, lamb, or goat. 12 This is how you must prepare each of them, no matter how many.

13 "Every Israelite is to prepare these things in this way when he presents a fire offering as a pleasing aroma to the LORD. 14 When a foreigner resides with you or someone else is among you and wants to prepare a fire offering as a pleasing aroma to the LORD, he is to do exactly as you do throughout your generations. 15 The assembly is to have the same statute for^g both you and the foreign resident as a permanent statute throughout your generations. You and the foreigner will be alike before the LORD. 16 The same law and the same ordinance will apply to both you and the foreigner who resides with you."

17 The LORD instructed Moses: 18 "Speak to the Israelites and tell them: After you enter the land where I am bringing you, 19 you are to offer a contribution to the LORD when you eat from the food of the land. 20 You are to offer a loaf from your first batch of dough as a contribution; offer it just like a contribution from the threshing floor. 21 Throughout your generations, you are to give the LORD a contribution from the first batch of your dough.

22 "When you sin unintentionally and do not obey all these commands that the LORD spoke to Moses— 23 all that the LORD has commanded you through Moses, from the day the LORD issued the commands and onward throughout your generations— 24 and if it was done unintentionally without the community's awareness, the entire community is to prepare one young bull for a burnt offering as a pleasing aroma to the LORD, with its grain offering and drink offering according to the regulation, and one male goat as a •sin offering. 25 The priest must then make •atonement for the entire Israelite community so that they may be forgiven, for the sin was unintentional. They are to bring their offering, one made by fire to the LORD, and their sin offering before the LORD for their unintentional sin. 26 The entire Israelite community and the foreigner who resides among them will be forgiven, since it happened to all the people unintentionally.

27 "If one person sins unintentionally, he is to present a year-old female goat as a sin offering. 28 The priest must then make atonement before the LORD on behalf of the person who acts in error sinning unintentionally, and when he makes atonement for him, he will be forgiven. 29 You are to have the same law for the person who acts in error, whether he is an Israelite or a foreigner who lives among you.

30 "But the person who acts defiantly,^{h} whether native or foreign resident, blasphemes the LORD. That

^{a} 15:4 Lit a tenth (of an ephah) ^{b} 15:4,5 Lit a fourth hin ^{c} 15:6 Lit two-tenths (of an ephah) ^{d} 15:6,7 Lit a third hin ^{e} 15:9 Lit three-tenths (of an ephah) ^{f} 15:9,10 Lit a half hin ^{g} 15:14–15 Sam, LXX join The assembly to v. 14, reading LORD, the assembly must do exactly as you do. 15 The same statute will apply to ^{h} 15:30 Lit with a high hand

---

affirmed the truth that should have blotted out all objections: God's power would make the difference in the struggle.

14:11 the signs. In spite of many powerful signs, Israel demonstrated almost no faith.

14:17-19 In keeping with the greatness of Your faithful love. Moses knew God, so he

trusted God to be true to His character.

14:22 10 times. The people had been unfaithful over and over. (See Ex. 14:10-12; 15:22-24; 16:1-3; 16:19-20; 16:27-30; 17:1-4; 32:1-35; Num. 11:1-3, 4-34; and 14:3.)

14:24 Caleb. Caleb worshiped the Lord wholeheartedly (Josh. 14:13-14). Only he and

Joshua believed God would give the people the land (v. 9).

14:28 exactly as I heard you say. The people wished that they had died in the desert (v. 2), so God said, "So be it."

14:39-45 the LORD is not among you. The people tried to enter the promised land with-

person is to be cut off from his people. 31 He will certainly be cut off, because he has despised the LORD's word and broken His command; his guilt remains on him."

Sabbath Violation

32 While the Israelites were in the wilderness, they found a man gathering wood on the Sabbath day. 33 Those who found him gathering wood brought him to Moses, Aaron, and the entire community. 34 They placed him in custody, because it had not been decided what should be done to him. 35 Then the LORD told Moses, "The man is to be put to death. The entire community is to stone him outside the camp." 36 So the entire community brought him outside the camp and stoned him to death, as the LORD had commanded Moses.

Tassels for Remembrance

37 The LORD said to Moses, 38 "Speak to the Israelites and tell them that throughout their generations they are to make tassels for the corners of their garments, and put a blue cord on the tassel at ⌊each⌋ corner. 39 These will serve as tassels for you to look at, so that you may remember all the LORD's commands and obey them and not become unfaithful by following your own heart and your own eyes. 40 This way you will remember and obey all My commands and be holy to your God. 41 I am the LORD your God who brought you out of the land of Egypt to be your God; I am the LORD your God."

Korah Incites Rebellion

16 Now Korah son of Izhar, son of Kohath, son of Levi, with Dathan and Abiram, sons of Eliab, and On son of Peleth, sons of Reuben, took 2 250 prominent Israelite men who were leaders of the community and representatives in the assembly, and they rebelled against Moses. 3 They came together against Moses and Aaron and told them, "You have gone too far!a Everyone in the entire community is holy, and the LORD is among them. Why then do you exalt yourselves above the LORD's assembly?"

4 When Moses heard ⌊this⌋, he fell facedown. 5 Then he said to Korah and all his followers, "Tomorrow morning the LORD will reveal who belongs to Him, who is set apart, and ⌊the one⌋ He will let come near Him. He will let the one He chooses come near Him. 6 Korah, you and all your followers are to do this: take firepans, and tomorrow 7 place fire in them and put incense on them before the LORD. Then the man the LORD chooses

will be the one who is set apart. It is you Levites who have gone too far!"b

8 Moses also told Korah, "Now listen, Levites! 9 Isn't it enough for you that the God of Israel has separated you from the Israelite community to bring you near to Himself, to perform the work at the LORD's tabernacle, and to stand before the community to minister to them? 10 He has brought you near, and all your fellow Levites who are with you, but you are seeking the priesthood as well. 11 Therefore, it is you and all your followers who have conspired against the LORD! As for Aaron, who is hec that you should complain about him?"

12 Moses sent for Dathan and Abiram, the sons of Eliab, but they said, "We will not come! 13 Is it not enough that you brought us up from a land flowing with milk and honey to kill us in the wilderness? Do you also have to appoint yourself as ruler over us? 14 Furthermore, you didn't bring us to a land flowing with milk and honey or give us an inheritance of fields and vineyards. Will you gouge out the eyes of these men? We will not come!"

15 Then Moses became angry and said to the LORD, "Don't respect their offering. I have not taken one donkey from them or mistreated a single one of them." 16 So Moses told Korah, "You and all your followers are to appear before the LORD tomorrow—you, they, and Aaron. 17 Each of you is to take his firepan, place incense on it, and present his firepan before the LORD—250 firepans. You and Aaron ⌊are⌋ each ⌊to present⌋ your firepan also."

18 Each man took his firepan, placed fire in it, put incense on it, and stood at the entrance to the tent of meeting along with Moses and Aaron. 19 After Korah assembled the whole community against them at the entrance to the tent of meeting, the glory of the LORD appeared to the whole community. 20 The LORD spoke to Moses and Aaron, 21 "Separate yourselves from this community so I may consume them instantly."

22 But Moses and Aaron fell facedown and said, "God, God of the spiritsd of all flesh, when one man sins, will you vent Your wrath on the whole community?"

23 The LORD replied to Moses, 24 "Tell the community: Get away from the dwellings of Korah, Dathan, and Abiram."

25 Moses got up and went to Dathan and Abiram, and the elders of Israel followed him. 26 He warned the community, "Get away now from the tents of these wicked men. Don't touch anything that belongs to them, or you will be swept away because of all their

---

a16:3 Lit Enough of you   b16:7 Lit Enough of you, sons of Levi   c16:11 Or Aaron, what has he done   d16:22 Or breath; Nm 27:16

---

out putting their faith in God, so they were defeated.

15:1-41 Because of God's judgment, the older generation would never settle the promised land. It was time to pass down traditions to the younger crowd.

15:3-12 Most of these offerings were a review

of earlier teachings from Leviticus.

15:24 unintentionally. The Bible categorizes sins as either defiant (see v. 30) or sins of straying (unintentional). People who love God may sin, but they do not do so in defiance of God.

15:30 defiantly. No sacrifice covered defiant

sin until the cross.

15:41 I am. The people had wavered throughout the journey, but God was still the One who had delivered them.

16:1-7 Leaders of the tribes of Levi (the priests) and Reuben challenged Moses and Aaron's leadership but missed the key

sins." 27 So they got away from the dwellings of Korah, Dathan, and Abiram. Meanwhile, Dathan and Abiram came out and stood at the entrance of their tents with their wives, children, and infants.

28 Then Moses said, "This is how you will know that the LORD sent me to do all these things and that it was not of my own will: 29 If these men die ⌊naturally⌋ as all people would, and suffer the fate of all, then the LORD has not sent me. 30 But if the LORD brings about something unprecedented, and the ground opens its mouth and swallows them along with all that belongs to them so that they go down alive into •Sheol, then you will know that these men have despised the LORD."

31 Just as he finished speaking all these words, the ground beneath them split open. 32 The earth opened its mouth and swallowed them and their households, all Korah's people, and all ⌊their⌋ possessions. 33 They went down alive into Sheol with all that belonged to them. The earth closed over them, and they vanished from the assembly. 34 At their cries, all ⌊the people of Israel⌋ who were around them fled because they thought, "The earth may swallow us too!" 35 Fire also came out from the LORD and consumed the 250 men who were presenting the incense.

36a Then the LORD spoke to Moses: 37 "Tell Eleazar son of Aaron the priest to remove the firepans from the burning debris, because they are holy, and scatter the fire far away. 38 As for the firepans of those who sinned at the cost of their own lives, make them into hammered sheets as plating for the altar, for they presented them before the LORD, and the firepans are holy. They will be a sign to the Israelites."

39 So Eleazar the priest took the bronze firepans that those who were burned had presented, and they were hammered into plating for the altar, 40 just as the LORD commanded him through Moses. It was to be a reminder for the Israelites that no unauthorized person outside the lineage of Aaron should approach to offer incense before the LORD and become like Korah and his followers.

41 The next day the entire Israelite community complained about Moses and Aaron, saying, "You have killed the LORD's people!" 42 When the community assembled against them, Moses and Aaron turned toward the tent of meeting, and suddenly the cloud covered it, and the LORD's glory appeared.

43 Moses and Aaron went to the front of the tent of meeting, 44 and the LORD said to Moses, 45 "Get away from this community so that I may consume them instantly." But they fell facedown.

46 Then Moses told Aaron, "Take your firepan, place fire from the altar in it, and add incense. Go quickly to the community and make •atonement for them, because wrath has come from the LORD; the plague has begun." 47 So Aaron took his firepan as Moses had ordered, ran into the middle of the assembly, and saw that the plague had begun among the people. After he added incense, he made atonement for the people. 48 He stood between the dead and the living, and the plague was halted. 49 But those who died from the plague numbered 14,700, in addition to those who died because of the Korah incident. 50 Aaron then returned to Moses at the entrance to the tent of meeting, since the plague had been halted.

Aaron's Staff Chosen

17 [b] The LORD instructed Moses: 2 "Speak to the Israelites and take one staff from them for each ancestral house, 12 staffs from all the leaders of their ancestral houses. Write each man's name on his staff. 3 Write Aaron's name on Levi's staff, because there must be one staff for the head of each ancestral house. 4 Then place them in the tent of meeting in front of the •testimony where I meet with you. 5 The staff of the man I choose will sprout, and I will rid Myself of the Israelites' complaints that they have been making about you."

6 So Moses spoke to the Israelites, and each of their leaders gave him a staff, one for each of the leaders of their ancestral houses, 12 staffs ⌊in all⌋. Aaron's staff was among them. 7 Moses placed the staffs before the LORD in the tent of the testimony.

8 The next day Moses entered the tent of the testimony and saw that Aaron's staff, representing the house of Levi, had sprouted, formed buds, blossomed, and produced almonds! 9 Moses then brought out all the staffs from the LORD's presence to all the Israelites. They saw ⌊them⌋, and each man took his own staff. 10 The LORD told Moses, "Put Aaron's rod back in front of the testimony to be kept as a sign for the rebels, so that you may put an end to their complaints before Me, or else they will die." 11 So Moses did as the LORD commanded him.

12 Then the Israelites declared to Moses, "Look, we're perishing! We're lost; we're all lost! 13 Anyone who comes near the LORD's tabernacle will die. Will we all perish?"

Provision for the Priesthood

18 The LORD said to Aaron, "You, your sons, and your ancestral house will be responsible for sin

---

[a] 16:36 Nm 17:1 in Hb   [b] 17:1 Nm 17:16 in Hb

---

point—that God had chosen them.

16:12-13 milk and honey. Now this phrase is used to describe Egypt, the land where they had been enslaved.

16:15 taken one donkey. The complainers accused Moses of abusing his authority and misleading his people. Moses contended He

had taken nothing from them, but he had delivered them.

16:22 Moses and Aaron fell facedown. Once again, Moses and his brother prayed for God to spare the people.

16:30 the LORD brings about. Like Elijah on Mount Carmel (1 Kings 18), Moses asked

God to demonstrate that He was in charge.

16:41 entire Israelite community complained about Moses. As mediator between God and Israel, Moses endured constant complaints for God's decisions.

17:1-13 This chapter tells the story of Aaron's budding staff, which confirmed the Levites'

against the sanctuary. You and your sons will be responsible for sin involving your priesthood. 2 But also bring your brothers with you from the tribe of Levi, your ancestral tribe, so they may join you and serve with you and your sons in front of the tent of the •testimony. 3 They are to perform duties for you and for the whole tent. They must not come near the sanctuary equipment or the altar; otherwise, both they and you will die. 4 They are to join you and guard the tent of meeting, doing all the work at the tent, but no unauthorized person may come near you.

5 "You are to guard the sanctuary and the altar so that wrath may not fall on the Israelites again. 6 Look, I have selected your fellow Levites from the Israelites as a gift for you,[a] assigned by the LORD to work at the tent of meeting. 7 But you and your sons will carry out your priestly responsibilities for everything concerning the altar and for what is inside the veil, and you will do that work. I am giving you the work of the priesthood as a gift,[b] but an unauthorized person who comes near ⌊the sanctuary⌋ will be put to death."

Support for the Priests and Levites

8 Then the LORD spoke to Aaron, "Look, I have put you in charge of the contributions brought to Me. As for all the holy offerings of the Israelites, I have given them to you and your sons as a portion and a perpetual statute. 9 A portion of the holiest offerings ⌊kept⌋ from the fire will be yours; every one of their offerings that they give Me, whether the •grain offering, •sin offering, or •restitution offering will be most holy for you and your sons. 10 You are to eat it as a most holy offering.[c] Every male may eat it; it is to be holy to you.

11 "The contribution of their gifts also belongs to you. I have given all the Israelites' presentation offerings to you and to your sons and daughters as a perpetual statute. Every ceremonially clean person in your house may eat it. 12 I am giving you all the best of the fresh olive oil, new wine, and grain, which the Israelites give to the LORD as their •firstfruits. 13 The firstfruits of all that is in their land, which they bring to the LORD, belong to you. Every clean person in your house may eat them.

14 "Everything in Israel that is permanently dedicated ⌊to the LORD⌋ belongs to you. 15 The firstborn of every living thing, man or animal, presented to the LORD belongs to you. But you must certainly redeem the firstborn of man, and redeem the firstborn of an unclean animal. 16 You will pay the redemption price for a month-old male according to your valuation: five

•shekels of silver by the standard sanctuary shekel, which is 20 gerahs.

17 "However, you must not redeem the firstborn of an ox, a sheep, or a goat; they are holy. You are to sprinkle their blood on the altar and burn their fat as a fire offering for a pleasing aroma to the LORD. 18 But their meat belongs to you. It belongs to you like the breast of the presentation offering and the right thigh.

19 "I give to you and to your sons and daughters all the holy contributions that the Israelites present to the LORD as a perpetual statute. It is a perpetual covenant of salt before the LORD for you as well as your •offspring."

20 The LORD told Aaron, "You will not have an inheritance in their land; there will be no portion among them for you. I am your portion and your inheritance among the Israelites.

21 "Look, I have given the Levites every tenth in Israel as an inheritance in return for the work they do, the work of the tent of meeting. 22 The Israelites must never again come near the tent of meeting, or they will incur guilt and die. 23 The Levites will do the work of the tent of meeting, and they will bear the ⌊consequences⌋ of their sin. The Levites will not receive an inheritance among the Israelites; this is a perpetual statute throughout your generations. 24 For I have given them the tenth that the Israelites present to the LORD as a contribution for ⌊their⌋ inheritance. That is why I told them that they would not receive an inheritance among the Israelites."

25 The LORD instructed Moses, 26 "Speak to the Levites and tell them: When you receive from the Israelites the tenth that I have given you as your inheritance, you must present part of it as an offering to the LORD—a tenth of the tenth. 27 Your offering will be credited to you as if ⌊it were your⌋ grain from the threshing floor or the full harvest from the winepress. 28 You are to present an offering to the LORD from every tenth you receive from the Israelites. Give some of it to Aaron the priest as an offering to the LORD. 29 You must present the entire offering due the LORD from all your gifts. The best part of the tenth is to be consecrated.

30 "Tell them further: Once you have presented the best part of the tenth, and it is credited to you Levites as the produce of the threshing floor or the winepress, 31 then you and your household may eat it anywhere. It is your wage in return for your work at the tent of meeting. 32 You will not incur guilt because of it once you have presented the best part of it, but you must not defile the Israelites' holy offerings, so that you will not die."

---

[a]18:6 LXX, Syr, Vg omit for you   [b]18:7 Or veil. So you are to perform the service; a gift of your priesthood I grant   [c]18:10 Or it in a most holy place

---

preeminent role in the priesthood.
17:3 one staff for the head of each ancestral house. The demonstration had to show that the Levites' power surpassed that of any other tribal head.
17:4 in front of the testimony. The staffs were placed in front of the ark. If a staff

sprouted, the tribe represented by that staff was God's choice to serve in the tabernacle.
17:8 sprouted, formed buds, blossomed, and produced. Aaron's staff far exceeded the demands of the test. God's choice was very clear.
18:1-7 so that wrath may not fall on the Is-

raelites again. God, in grace and love, made Aaron's priesthood responsible for the sanctuary and the altar, and thus for the spiritual welfare of Israel.

18:8 portion. Since the Levites were not given any land or property, the other 11 tribes would share the task of supporting them.

Purification Ritual

19 The LORD spoke to Moses and Aaron, 2 "This is the legal statute that the LORD has commanded: Instruct the Israelites to bring you an unblemished red cow that has no defect and has never been yoked. 3 Give it to Eleazar the priest, and he will have it brought outside the camp and slaughtered in his presence. 4 Eleazar the priest is to take some of its blood with his finger and sprinkle it seven times toward the front of the tent of meeting. 5 The cow must be burned in his sight. Its hide, flesh, and blood, are to be burned along with its dung. 6 The priest is to take cedar wood, hyssop, and crimson yarn, and throw ⌊them⌋ onto the fire where the cow is burning. 7 Then the priest must wash his clothes and bathe his body in water; after that he may enter the camp, but he will remain ceremonially unclean until evening. 8 The one who burned the cow must also wash his clothes and bathe his body in water, and he will remain unclean until evening.

9 "A man who is clean is to gather up the cow's ashes and deposit them outside the camp in a ceremonially clean place. The ashes must be kept by the Israelite community for ⌊preparing⌋ the water ⌊to remove⌋ impurity; it is a •sin offering. 10 Then the one who gathers up the cow's ashes must wash his clothes, and he will remain unclean until evening. This is a perpetual statute for the Israelites and for the foreigner who resides among them.

11 "The person who touches any human corpse will be unclean for seven days. 12 He is to purify himself with the water[a] on the third day and the seventh day; then he will be clean. But if he does not purify himself on the third and seventh days, he will not be clean. 13 Anyone who touches a body of a person who has died, and does not purify himself, defiles the tabernacle of the LORD. That person will be cut off from Israel. He remains unclean because the water for impurity has not been sprinkled on him, and his uncleanness is still on him.

14 "This is the law when a person dies in a tent: everyone who enters the tent and everyone who is ⌊already⌋ in the tent will be unclean for seven days, 15 and any open container without a lid tied on it is unclean. 16 Anyone in the open field who touches a person who has been killed by the sword or has died, or a human bone, or a grave, will be unclean for seven days. 17 For ⌊the purification of⌋ the unclean person, they are to take some of the ashes of the burnt sin offering, ⌊put them⌋ in a jar, and add fresh water to them. 18 A person who is clean is to take hyssop, dip ⌊it⌋ in the water, and sprin-

kle the tent, all the furnishings, and the people who were there. He is also to sprinkle the one who touched a bone, a grave, a corpse, or a person who had been killed. 19 "The one who is clean is to sprinkle the unclean person on the third day and the seventh day. After he purifies the unclean person on the seventh day, the one being purified must wash his clothes and bathe in water, and he will be clean by evening. 20 But a person who is unclean and does not purify himself, that person will be cut off from the assembly because he has defiled the sanctuary of the LORD. The water for impurity has not been sprinkled on him; he is unclean. 21 This is a perpetual statute for them. The person who sprinkles the water for impurity is to wash his clothes, and whoever touches the water for impurity will be unclean until evening. 22 Anything the unclean person touches will become unclean, and anyone who touches ⌊it⌋[b] will be unclean until evening."

Water from the Rock

20 The entire Israelite community entered the Wilderness of Zin in the first month, and they[c] settled in Kadesh. Miriam died and was buried there.

2 There was no water for the community, so they assembled against Moses and Aaron. 3 The people quarreled with Moses and said, "If only we had perished when our brothers perished before the LORD. 4 Why have you brought the LORD's assembly into this wilderness for us and our livestock to die here? 5 Why have you led us up from Egypt to bring us to this evil place? It's not a place of grain, figs, vines, and pomegranates, and there is no water to drink!"

6 Then Moses and Aaron went from the presence of the assembly to the doorway of the tent of meeting. They fell down with their faces ⌊to the ground⌋, and the glory of the LORD appeared to them. 7 The LORD spoke to Moses, 8 "Take the staff and assemble the community. You and your brother Aaron are to speak to the rock while they watch, and it will yield its water. You will bring out water for them from the rock and provide drink for the community and their livestock."

9 So Moses took the staff from the LORD's presence just as He had commanded him. 10 Moses and Aaron summoned the assembly in front of the rock, and Moses said to them, "Listen, you rebels! Must we bring water out of this rock for you?" 11 Then Moses raised his hand and struck the rock twice with his staff, so that a great amount of water gushed out, and the community and their livestock drank.

---

a **19:12** Or ashes; lit with it　b **19:22** Or [him]　c **20:1** Lit the people

---

18:11 Every ceremonially clean person. Families of priests were included in the "regular share" of the offerings, provided they were ceremonially clean (see Leviticus 22:4-8).

18:12 olive oil … wine … grain. The Law required the offering of the firstfruits and the best of everything to the Lord. The priests would receive their share from this bounty.

19:12 purify himself with the water. A person who touched a dead body was considered unclean and required a purification ritual.

19:13 defiles the tabernacle of the LORD …

cut off. Failure to become ceremonially clean was an affront to the Law and to the tabernacle, a serious sin.

19:14 in the tent … unclean. All the causes of uncleanness relate to death (corpses, mildew, skin disease like a corpse) or loss of life (loss of blood, loss of semen).

12 But the LORD said to Moses and Aaron, "Because you did not trust Me to show My holiness in the sight of the Israelites, you will not bring this assembly into the land I have given them." 13 These are the waters of Meribah,a where the Israelites quarreled with the LORD, and He showed His holiness to them.

Edom Denies Passage

14 Moses sent messengers from Kadesh to the king of Edom, "This is what your brother Israel says, 'You know all the hardships that have overtaken us. 15 Our fathers went down to Egypt, and we lived in Egypt many years, but the Egyptians treated us and our fathers badly. 16 When we cried out to the LORD, He heard our voice, sent an Angel,b and brought us out of Egypt. Now look, we are in Kadesh, a city on the border of your territory. 17 Please let us travel through your land. We won't travel through ⌊any⌋ field or vineyard, or drink ⌊any⌋ well water. We will travel the King's Highway; we won't turn to the right or the left until we have traveled through your territory.' "

18 But Edom answered him, "You must not travel through our land, or we will come out and confront you with the sword."

19 "We will go on the main road," the Israelites replied to them, "and if we or our herds drink your water, we will pay its price. There will be no problem; only let us travel through on foot."

20 Yet Edom insisted, "You must not travel through." And they came out to confront them with a large force of heavily-armed people.c 21 Edom refused to allow Israel to travel through their territory, and Israel turned away from them.

Aaron's Death

22 After they set out from Kadesh, the entire Israelite community came to Mount Hor. 23 The LORD said to Moses and Aaron at Mount Hor on the border of the land of Edom, 24 "Aaron will be gathered to his people; he will not enter the land I have given the Israelites, because you both rebelled against My command at the waters of Meribah. 25 Take Aaron and his son Eleazar and bring them up Mount Hor. 26 Remove Aaron's garments and put them on his son Eleazar. Aaron will be gathered ⌊to his people⌋ and die there."

27 So Moses did as the LORD commanded, and they climbed Mount Hor in the sight of the whole community. 28 After Moses removed Aaron's garments and put them on his son Eleazar, Aaron died there on top of the mountain. Then Moses and Eleazar came down from the mountain. 29 When the whole community saw that Aaron had passed away, the entire house of Israel mourned for him 30 days.

Canaanite King Defeated

21 When the Canaanite king of Arad, who lived in the •Negev, heard that Israel was coming on the Atharim road, he fought against Israel and captured some prisoners. 2 Then Israel made a vow to the LORD, "If You will deliver this people into our hands, we will •completely destroy their cities." 3 The LORD listened to Israel's request, the Canaanites were defeated, and Israel completely destroyed them and their cities. So they named the place Hormah.d

The Bronze Serpent

4 Then they set out from Mount Hor by way of the •Red Sea to bypass the land of Edom, but the peoplee became impatient because of the journey. 5 The people spoke against God and Moses: "Why have you led us up from Egypt to die in the wilderness? There is no bread or water, and we detest this wretched food!" 6 Then the LORD sent poisonousf snakes among the people, and they bit them so that many Israelites died.

7 The people then came to Moses and said, "We have sinned by speaking against the LORD and against you. Intercede with the LORD so that He will take the snakes away from us." And Moses interceded for the people.

8 Then the LORD said to Moses, "Make a snake ⌊image⌋ and mount it on a pole. When anyone who is bitten looks at it, he will recover. 9 So Moses made a bronze snake and mounted it on a pole. Whenever someone was bitten, and he looked at the bronze snake, he recovered.

Journey around Moab

10 The Israelites set out and camped at Oboth. 11 They set out from Oboth and camped at Iye-abarim in the wilderness that borders Moab on the east. 12 From there they went and camped at Zered Valley. 13 They set out from there and camped on the other side of the Arnon ⌊River⌋, in the wilderness that extends from the Amorite border, because the Arnon was the Moabite border between Moab and the Amorites. 14 Therefore it is stated in the Book of the LORD's Wars:

> Wahebg in Suphah
> and the ravines of the Arnon,
> 15 even the slopes of the ravines
> that extend to the site of Arh
> and lie along the border of Moab.

a20:13 = quarreling b20:16 Or a messenger c20:20 Lit with numerous people and a strong hand d21:3 = destruction e21:4 Lit soul of the people f21:6 Lit burning; LXX reads deadly; Syr reads cruel; Vg reads fiery g21:14 The source of the Arnon River h21:15 A city in Moab; Nm 21:28; Dt 2:9,18,29; Is 15:1

19:18 dip [it] in the water, and sprinkle. Some of the cleansing water, made with the ashes of the red heifer, was sprinkled on everything that had some contact with the dead body.

20:2 no water for the community. Forty years earlier, God had Moses strike a rock with his staff, and water flowed out (Ex. 17:5-7). Now He gave Moses different instructions for getting water.

20:10 Must we bring water out of this rock for you? Moses spoke in anger and frustration, and implied he had some part in the miracle of water coming from the rock.

20:11 raised his hand and struck the rock ... staff. God's direct command to Moses was to speak to the rock, not strike it. Instead, Moses used his staff in anger.

20:12 did not trust ... you will not bring this assembly into the land. God's punishment was quick and severe. Israel's leaders for 40

16 From there ⌊they went⌋ to Beer,a the well the LORD told Moses about, "Gather the people so I may give them water." 17 Then Israel sang this song:

Spring up, well—sing to it!
18 The princes dug the well;
The nobles of the people hollowed it out
with a scepter and with their staffs.

⌊They went⌋ from the wilderness to Mattanah, 19 from Mattanah to Nahaliel, from Nahaliel to Bamoth, 20 from Bamoth to the valley in the territory of Moab near the Pisgah highlandsb that overlook the wasteland.c

Amorite Kings Defeated

21 Israel sent messengers to say to Sihon king of the Amorites: 22 "Let us travel through your land. We won't go into the fields or vineyards. We won't drink ⌊any⌋ well water. We will travel the King's Highway until we have traveled through your territory." 23 But Sihon would not let Israel travel through his territory. Instead, he gathered his whole army and went out to confront Israel in the wilderness. When he came to Jahaz, he fought against Israel. 24 Israel struck him with the sword and took possession of his land from the Arnon to the Jabbok, ⌊but only up⌋ to the Ammonite border, because it was fortified.d

25 Israel took all the cities and lived in all these Amorite cities, including Heshbon and all its villages. 26 Heshbon was the city of Sihon king of the Amorites, who had fought against the former king of Moab and had taken control of all his land as far as the Arnon. 27 Therefore the poetse say:

Come to Heshbon, let it be rebuilt;
let the city of Sihon be restored.f
28 For fire came out of Heshbon,
a flame from the city of Sihon.
It consumed Ar of Moab,
the lords ofg Arnon's heights.
29 Woe to you, Moab!
You have been destroyed, people of Chemosh!
He gave up his sons as refugees,
and his daughters into captivity
to Sihon the Amorite king.
30 We threw them down;
Heshbon has been destroyed as far as Dibon.h
We caused desolation as far as Nophah,
which reaches as far as Medeba.i

31 So Israel lived in the Amorites' land. 32 After Moses sent spies to Jazer, Israel captured its villages and drove out the Amorites who were there.

33 Then they turned and went up the road to Bashan, and Og king of Bashan came out against them with his whole army to do battle at Edrei. 34 But the LORD said to Moses, "Do not fear him, for I have handed him over to you along with his whole army and his land. Do to him as you did to Sihon king of the Amorites, who lived in Heshbon." 35 So they struck him, his sons, and his whole army until no one was left,j and they took possession of his land.

Balak Hires Balaam

22 The Israelites traveled on and camped in the plains of Moab near the Jordan across from Jericho. 2 Now Balak son of Zippor saw all that Israel had done to the Amorites. 3 Moab was terrified of the people because they were numerous, and dreaded the Israelites. 4 So the Moabites said to the elders of Midian, "This horde will devour everything around us like an ox eats up the green plants in the field."

Since Balak son of Zippor was Moab's king at that time, 5 he sent messengers to Balaam son of Beor at Pethor, which is by the Euphrates in the land of his people.k 1 Balak said to him: "Look, a people has come out of Egypt; they cover the surface of the land and are living right across from me. 6 Please come and put a curse on these people for me because they are more powerful than I am. I may be able to defeat them and drive them out of the land, for I know that those you bless are blessed and those you curse are cursed."

7 The elders of Moab and Midian departed with fees for •divination in hand. They came to Balaam and reported Balak's words to him. 8 He said to them, "Spend the night here, and I will give you the answer the LORD tells me." So the officials of Moab stayed with Balaam.

9 Then God came to Balaam and asked, "Who are these men with you?"

10 Balaam replied to God, "Balak son of Zippor, king of Moab, sent ⌊this message⌋ to me: 11 'Look, a people has come out of Egypt, and they cover the surface of the land. Now come and put a curse on them for me. I may be able to fight against them and drive them away.'"

12 Then God said to Balaam, "You are not to go with them. You are not to curse this people, for they are blessed."

a21:16 = well b21:20 Moabite mountain plateau; Nm 23:14; Dt 3:17,27; 4:49; 34:1; Jos 12:3; 13:20 c21:20 Or overlook Jeshimon d21:24 Or was at Az; LXX reads was Jazer e21:27 Lit ones who speak proverbs f21:27 Or firmly founded g21:28 LXX reads Moab, and swallowed h21:30 LXX reads Their seed will perish from Heshbon; Vg reads Their yoke has perished from Heshbon i21:30 LXX reads Dibon. And their women have further kindled a fire against Moab; Hb uncertain j21:35 Lit left to him k22:5 Sam, Vg, Syr read of the Ammonites l22:5 Or of the Amawites

years would not enter Canaan.

20:14-21 Please let us travel through your land. Moses tried a diplomatic approach with the Edomites, distant relatives of the Israelites.

20:20 large force of heavily-armed people. The Edomites probably feared this huge migration passing through their land.

20:25-28 Aaron and his son Eleazar ... Mount Hor ... put them on his son The mantle of family leadership passed from father to son through Aaron's priestly garments.

21:5 no bread or water ... we detest this wretched food. Certainly the Israelites were tired of manna after 40 years. Rejecting God's provision of food, however, amounted to rejecting His provision of grace.

21:8-9 snake [image]. The bronze snake was not an idol but a symbol of God's deliverance. The snake did not save the Israelites from the snakebite, but from its consequences.

13 So Balaam got up the next morning and said to Balak's officials, "Go back to your land, because the LORD has refused to let me go with you."

14 The officials of Moab arose, returned to Balak, and reported, "Balaam refused to come with us."

15 Balak sent officials again who were more numerous and higher in rank than the others. 16 They came to Balaam and said to him, "This is what Balak son of Zippor says: 'Let nothing keep you from coming to me, 17 for I will greatly honor you and do whatever you ask me. So please come and put a curse on these people for me!'"

18 But Balaam responded to the servants of Balak, "If Balak were to give me his house full of silver and gold, I could not go against the command of the LORD my God to do ⌊anything⌋ small or great. 19 Please stay here overnight as the others did, so that I may find out what else the LORD has to tell me."

20 God came to Balaam at night and said to him, "Since these men have come to summon you, get up and go with them, but you must only do what I tell you." 21 When he got up in the morning, Balaam saddled his donkey and went with the officials of Moab.

Balaam's Donkey and the Angel

22 But God was incensed that Balaam was going, and the Angel of the LORD took His stand on the path to oppose him. Balaam was riding his donkey, and his two servants were with him. 23 When the donkey saw the Angel of the LORD standing on the path with a drawn sword in His hand, she turned off the path and went into the field. So Balaam hit her to return her to the path. 24 Then the Angel of the LORD stood in a narrow passage between the vineyards, with a stone wall on either side. 25 The donkey saw the Angel of the LORD and pressed herself against the wall, squeezing Balaam's foot against it. So he hit her once again. 26 The Angel of the LORD went ahead and stood in a narrow place where there was no room to turn to the right or the left. 27 When the donkey saw the Angel of the LORD, she crouched down under Balaam. So he became furious and beat the donkey with his stick.

28 Then the LORD opened the donkey's mouth, and she asked Balaam, "What have I done to you that you have beaten me these three times?"

29 Balaam answered the donkey, "You made me look like a fool. If I had a sword in my hand, I'd kill you now!"

30 But the donkey said, "Am I not the donkey you've ridden all your life until today? Have I ever treated you this way before?"

"No," he replied.

31 Then the LORD opened Balaam's eyes, and he saw the Angel of the LORD standing in the path with a drawn sword in His hand. Balaam knelt and bowed with his face ⌊to the ground⌋. 32 The Angel of the LORD asked him, "Why have you beaten your donkey these three times? Look, I came out to oppose you, because what you are doing is evil in My sight. 33 The donkey saw Me and turned away from Me these three times. If she had not turned away from Me, I would have killed you by now and let her live."

34 Balaam said to the Angel of the LORD, "I have sinned, for I did not know that You were standing in the path to confront me. And now, if it is evil in Your sight, I will go back."

35 Then the Angel of the LORD said to Balaam, "Go with the men, but you are to say only what I tell you." So Balaam went with Balak's officials.

36 When Balak heard that Balaam was coming, he went out to meet him at the Moabite city[a] on the Arnon border at the edge of his territory. 37 Balak asked Balaam, "Did I not send you an urgent summons? Why didn't you come to me? Am I really not able to reward you?"

38 Balaam said to him, "Look, I have come to you, but can I say anything I want? I must speak only the message God puts in my mouth." 39 So Balaam went with Balak, and they came to Kiriath-huzoth.[b] 40 Balak sacrificed cattle and sheep, and sent for Balaam and the officials who were with him.

41 In the morning, Balak took Balaam and brought him to Bamoth-baal.[c] From there he saw the outskirts of the people's camp.

Balaam's Oracles

23 Then Balaam said to Balak, "Build me seven altars here and prepare seven bulls and seven rams for me." 2 So Balak did as Balaam directed, and they offered a bull and a ram on each altar. 3 Balaam said to Balak, "Stay here by your •burnt offering while I am gone. Maybe the LORD[d] will meet with me. I will tell you whatever He reveals to me." So he went to a barren hill.

4 God[e] met with him and Balaam said to Him, "I have arranged seven altars and offered a bull and a ram on each altar." 5 Then the LORD put a message in Balaam's mouth and said, "Return to Balak and say what I tell you."

6 So he returned to Balak, who was standing there by his burnt offering with all the officials of Moab.

---

a**22:36** Or at Ir-moab, or at Ar of Moab   b**22:39** = The City of Streets   c**22:41** = The High Places of Baal   d**23:3** DSS, LXX, Sam read Maybe God   e**23:4** DSS, Sam read The Angel of God

---

21:21-26 Let us travel through your land. Again the Israelites requested permission to travel through the territory of another tribe. The Amorites resisted, and Israel won a crushing victory.

21:35 took possession of his land. Israel's victory over Og and his armies gave them possession of the entire Transjordan.

22:1 camped in the plains of Moab ... across from Jericho. Israel moved into position to invade Canaan from the east, with Jericho the first target.

22:5 Balaam son of Beor. Balak felt pagan divination was his one chance to save his people.

22:8 give you the answer the LORD tells me. Balaam believed in many gods, but apparently he feared Israel's God. He would not give a false prophecy for money in the name of Israel's God.

22:20 go with them, but. God allowed Ba-

Balaam's First Oracle

7 Balaam proclaimed his poem:

Balak brought me from Aram;
the king of Moab, from the eastern mountains:
"Come, put a curse on Jacob for me;
come, denounce Israel!"

8 How can I curse someone God has not cursed?
How can I denounce someone
the LORD has not denounced?

9 I see them from the top of rocky cliffs,
and I watch them from the hills.
There is a people living alone;
it does not consider itself among the nations.

10 Who has counted the dust of Jacob
or numbered the dust clouds[a] of Israel?
Let me die the death of the upright;
let the end of my ⌊life⌋ be like theirs.

11 "What have you done to me?" Balak asked Balaam. "I brought you to curse my enemies, but look, you have only blessed ⌊them⌋!"

12 He answered, "Shouldn't I say exactly what the LORD puts in my mouth?"

Balaam's Second Oracle

13 Then Balak said to him, "Please come with me to another place where you can see them. You will only see the outskirts of their camp; you won't see all of them. From there, put a curse on them for me." 14 So Balak took him to Lookout Field[b] on top of Pisgah, built seven altars, and offered a bull and a ram on each altar.

15 Balaam said to Balak, "Stay here by your burnt offering while I seek ⌊the LORD⌋ over there."

16 The LORD met with Balaam and put a message in his mouth. Then He said, "Return to Balak and say what I tell you."

17 So he returned to Balak, who was standing there by his burnt offering with the officials of Moab. Balak asked him, "What did the LORD say?"

18 Balaam proclaimed his poem:

Balak, get up and listen;
son of Zippor, pay attention to what I say!

19 God is not a man who lies,
or a son of man who changes His mind.
Does He speak and not act,
or promise and not fulfill?

20 I have indeed received ⌊a command⌋ to bless;
since He has blessed,[c] I cannot change it.

21 He considers no disaster for Jacob;
He sees no trouble for Israel.[d]
The LORD their God is with them,
and there is rejoicing over the King
among them.

22 God brought them out of Egypt;
He is like the horns of a wild ox for them.[e]

23 There is no magic curse against Jacob
and no •divination against Israel.
It will now be said about Jacob and Israel,
"What ⌊great things⌋ God has done!"

24 A people rise up like a lioness;
They rouse themselves like a lion.
They will not lie down until they devour
the prey
and drink the blood of the slain.

25 Then Balak told Balaam, "Don't curse them and don't bless them!"

26 But Balaam answered him, "Didn't I tell you: Whatever the LORD says, I must do?"

Balaam's Third Oracle

27 Again Balak said to Balaam, "Please come. I will take you to another place. Maybe it will be agreeable to God that you can put a curse on them for me there." 28 So Balak took Balaam to the top of Peor, which overlooks the wasteland.[f]

29 Balaam told Balak, "Build me seven altars here and prepare seven bulls and seven rams for me." 30 So Balak did as Balaam said and offered a bull and a ram on each altar.

24 Since Balaam saw that it pleased the LORD to bless Israel, he did not go to seek omens as on previous occasions, but turned[g] toward the wilderness. 2 When Balaam looked up and saw Israel encamped tribe by tribe, the Spirit of God descended on him, 3 and he proclaimed his poem:

The •oracle of Balaam son of Beor,
the oracle of the man whose eyes are opened,[h]

4 the oracle of one who hears the sayings of God,
who sees a vision from the •Almighty,
who falls ⌊into a trance⌋ with ⌊his⌋ eyes
uncovered:

5 How beautiful are your tents, Jacob,
your dwellings, Israel.

6 they stretch out like river valleys,[i]
like gardens beside a stream,
like aloes the LORD has planted,

---

a 23:10 Or numbered a fourth   b 23:14 Or to the field of Zophim   c 23:20 Sam, LXX read since I will bless   d 23:21 Or He does not observe sin in Jacob; He does not see wrongdoing in Israel, or Disaster is not observed in Jacob; trouble is not seen in Israel   e 23:22 Or Egypt; they have the horns of a wild ox   f 23:28 Or overlooks Jeshimon   g 24:1 Lit set his face   h 24:3 LXX reads true; Vg reads closed   i 24:6 Or like date palms

---

laam to go, but only to do His will.

22:31 Then the LORD opened Balaam's eyes ... the Angel of the LORD. Two miracles in three verses: First, a donkey spoke—and spoke the truth. Then, Balaam's eyes were opened and he saw the truth.
22:35 Go with the men, but you are to say

only what I tell you. God amended His command to include the words Balaam could speak.
23:1 seven altars ... bulls ... rams. Balaam may have used seven because this number was significant to God.
23:2 they offered. Balak didn't care about

God's will; he just wanted the Israelites cursed so he could drive them out of his land (22:6).
23:8 How can I curse ... How can I denounce? If Balaam did the divine will, then he could not curse those whom God did not curse. If he went against God's will, he would

like cedars beside the water.

7 Water will flow from his buckets,
and his seed will be by abundant water.
His king will be greater than Agag,[a]
and his kingdom will be exalted.

8 God brought him out of Egypt;
He is like[b] the horns of a wild ox for them.
He will feed on enemy nations
and gnaw their bones;
he will strike ⌊them⌋ with his arrows.

9 He crouches, he lies down like a lion
or a lioness—who dares to rouse him?
Those who bless you will be blessed,
and those who curse you will be cursed.

10 Then Balak became furious with Balaam, struck his hands together, and said to him, "I summoned you to put a curse on my enemies, but instead, you have blessed ⌊them these three times⌋. 11 Now go to your home! I said I would reward you richly, but look, the LORD has denied you a reward."

12 Balaam answered Balak, "Didn't I previously tell the messengers you sent me: 13 If Balak were to give me his house full of silver and gold, I could not go against the LORD's command, to do ⌊anything⌋ good or bad of my own will? I will say whatever the LORD says. 14 Now I am going back to my people, but first, let me warn you what these people will do to your people in the future."

Balaam's Fourth Oracle

15 Then he proclaimed his poem:

The oracle of Balaam son of Beor,
the oracle of the man whose eyes are opened;[c]
16 the oracle of one who hears the sayings of God
and has knowledge from the •Most High,
who sees a vision from the Almighty,
who falls ⌊into a trance⌋ with ⌊his⌋ eyes
uncovered:
17 I see him,[d] but not now;
I perceive him,[d] but not near.
A star will come from Jacob,
and a scepter will arise from Israel.
He will smash the forehead[e] of Moab
and strike down[f] all the Shethites.[g]
18 Edom will become a possession;
Seir will become a possession of its enemies,
but Israel will be triumphant.
19 One who comes from Jacob will rule;
he will destroy the city's survivors.

20 Then Balaam saw Amalek and proclaimed his poem:

Amalek was first among the nations,
but his future is destruction.

21 Next he saw the Kenites and proclaimed his poem:

Your dwelling place is enduring;
your nest is set in the cliffs.
22 Kain will be destroyed
when Asshur takes you captive.

23 Once more he proclaimed his poem:

Ah, who can live when God does this?
24 Ships will come from the coast of Kittim;
they will afflict Asshur and Eber,
but they too will come to destruction.

25 Balaam then arose and went back to his homeland, and Balak also went his way.

Israel Worships Baal

25 While Israel was staying in Acacia Grove,[h] the people began to have sexual relations with the women of Moab. 2 The women invited them to the sacrifices for their gods, and the people ate and bowed in worship to their gods. 3 So Israel aligned itself with •Baal of Peor, and the LORD's anger burned against Israel. 4 The LORD said to Moses, "Take all the leaders of the people and execute[i] them in broad daylight before the LORD so that His burning anger may turn away from Israel."

5 So Moses told Israel's judges, "Kill each of the men who aligned themselves with Baal of Peor."

Phinehas Intervenes

6 An Israelite man came bringing a Midianite woman to his relatives in the sight of Moses and the whole Israelite community while they were weeping at the entrance to the tent of meeting. 7 When Phinehas son of Eleazar, son of Aaron the priest, saw ⌊this⌋, he got up from the assembly, took a spear in his hand, 8 followed the Israelite man into the tent,[j] and drove it through both the Israelite man and the woman—through her belly. Then the plague on the Israelites was stopped, 9 but those who died in the plague numbered 24,000.

10 The LORD spoke to Moses, 11 "Phinehas son of Eleazar, son of Aaron the priest, has turned back My wrath from the Israelites because he was zealous among them with My zeal,[k] so that I did not destroy the Israelites in

---

[a]**24:7** Sam, LXX, Sym, Theod read *Gog* [b]**24:8** Or *He has* [c]**24:15** LXX reads *true*; Vg reads *closed* [d]**24:17** Or *Him* [e]**24:17** Or *frontiers*
[f]**24:17** Sam reads *and the skulls of*; Jr 48:45 [g]**24:17** Or *Sethites* [h]**25:1** Or *in Shittim* [i]**25:4** Or *impale*, or *hang*, or *expose*; Hb obscure
[j]**25:8** Perhaps a tent shrine or bridal tent [k]**25:11** Or *jealousy*

---

be powerless to curse those whom God had blessed.
23:19 God is not a man who lies. As someone who gave "prophecies" to the highest bidder, Balaam knew plenty about lies.
23:21 The LORD their God is with them ... rejoicing over the King among them. The

first declaration of God's kingship was spoken by a pagan.
23:24 rise up like a lioness. From the outside, Israel's campaign to capture Canaan appeared to be like that of a hunting lioness: stalking the enemy, striking suddenly with great force, and devouring everything.

24:2 the spirit of God descended on him ... poem. In sharp contrast with Balaam's usual "sorcery," God caused Balaam to prophesy favorably toward Israel by overcoming him by the power of the Spirit.
24:11 I would reward ... the LORD has denied you a reward. Balak wanted Balaam to

My zeal. 12 Therefore declare: I grant him My covenant of peace. 13 It will be a covenant of perpetual priesthood for him and his descendants, because he was zealous for his God and made •atonement for the Israelites."

14 The name of the slain Israelite man, who was struck dead with the Midianite woman, was Zimri son of Salu, the leader of a Simeonite ancestral house. 15 The name of the slain Midianite woman was Cozbi, the daughter of Zur, a tribal head of an ancestral house in Midian.

Vengeance against the Midianites

16 The LORD told Moses: 17 "Attack the Midianites and strike them dead. 18 For they attacked you with the treachery that they used against you in the Peor incident. They did the same in the case involving their sister Cozbi, daughter of the Midianite leader who was killed the day the plague came at Peor."

The Second Census

26 After the plague, the LORD said to Moses and Eleazar son of Aaron the priest, 2 "Take a census of the entire Israelite community by their ancestral houses of those 20 years old or more who can serve in Israel's army."

3 So Moses and Eleazar the priest said to them in the plains of Moab by the Jordan ⌊across from⌋ Jericho, 4 "⌊Take a census of⌋ those 20 years old or more, as the LORD had commanded Moses and the Israelites who came out of the land of Egypt."

5 Reuben was the firstborn of Israel.
Reuben's descendants:
the Hanochite clan ⌊from⌋ Hanoch;
the Palluite clan from Pallu;
6 the Hezronite clan from Hezron;
the Carmite clan from Carmi.
7 These were the Reubenite clans,
and their registered men numbered 43,730.
8 The son of Pallu was Eliab.
9 The sons of Eliab were Nemuel, Dathan,
and Abiram.
(It was Dathan and Abiram, chosen by the community, who fought against Moses and Aaron; they and Korah's followers fought against the LORD. 10 The earth opened its mouth and swallowed them with Korah, when his followers died and the fire consumed 250 men. They ⌊serve as⌋ a warning sign. 11 The sons of Korah, however, did not die.)

12 Simeon's descendants by their clans:
the Nemuelite clan from Nemuel;[a]
the Jaminite clan from Jamin;
the Jachinite clan from Jachin;
13 the Zerahite clan from Zerah;
the Shaulite clan from Shaul.
14 These were the Simeonite clans, numbering 22,200 men.

15 Gad's descendants by their clans:
the Zephonite clan from Zephon;
the Haggite clan from Haggi;
the Shunite clan from Shuni;
16 the Oznite clan from Ozni;
the Erite clan from Eri;
17 the Arodite clan from Arod;
the Arelite clan from Areli.
18 These were the Gadite clans ⌊numbered⌋ by their registered men: 40,500.

19 Judah's sons included Er and Onan, but they died in the land of Canaan. 20 Judah's descendants by their clans:
the Shelanite clan from Shelah;
the Perezite clan from Perez;
the Zerahite clan from Zerah.
21 The descendants of Perez:
the Hezronite clan from Hezron;
the Hamulite clan from Hamul.
22 These were Judah's clans ⌊numbered⌋ by their registered men: 76,500.

23 Issachar's descendants by their clans:
the Tolaite clan from Tola;
the Punite clan from Puvah;[b]
24 the Jashubite clan from Jashub;
the Shimronite clan from Shimron.
25 These were Issachar's clans ⌊numbered⌋ by their registered men: 64,300.

26 Zebulun's descendants by their clans:
the Seredite clan from Sered;
the Elonite clan from Elon;
the Jahleelite clan from Jahleel.
27 These were the Zebulunite clans ⌊numbered⌋ by their registered men: 60,500.

28 Joseph's descendants by their clans ⌊from⌋ Manasseh and Ephraim:
29 Manasseh's descendants:
the Machirite clan from Machir.
Machir fathered Gilead;

---

[a]26:12 Syr reads *Jemuel* (Gn 46:10; Ex 6:15); 1 Ch 4:24 reads *Nemuel* [b]26:23 Sam, LXX, Vg, Syr read *Puite clan from Puah*; 1 Ch 7:1

---

pronounce only curses. He refused to pay for blessings.

24:15-16 knowledge from the Most High. The fourth oracle went beyond the third's claim of "visions" to "knowledge." Balaam felt his visions had given him a special understanding of the future.

24:17 star ... scepter. This oracle predicts the rise of David and his consolidation of power over the region. Its imagery even suggests the coming of a Messiah (Rev. 2:27-28; 22:16).

25:1-18 On the very doorstep of Canaan, Israelite men were the victims of sexual seduc-

tion (v. 2) that led to Baal worship.

25:1 Acacia Grove ... have sexual relations. Temple prostitutes sent by Balaam (Num. 31:16) lured Israelites into sexual sin as well as pagan practices.

25:4 Take all the leaders ... execute them in broad daylight. This punishment was se-

the Gileadite clan from Gilead.

30 These were Gilead's descendants:
the Iezerite clan ⌊from⌋ Iezer;
the Helekite clan from Helek;
31 The Asrielite clan ⌊from⌋ Asriel;
the Shechemite clan ⌊from⌋ Shechem;
32 the Shemidaite clan ⌊from⌋ Shemida;
the Hepherite clan ⌊from⌋ Hepher;
33 Zelophehad son of Hepher had no sons—only daughters. The names of Zelophehad's daughters were Mahlah, Noah, Hoglah, Milcah, and Tirzah.
34 These were Manasseh's clans, numbered by their registered men: 52,700.
35 These were Ephraim's descendants by their clans:
the Shuthelahite clan from Shuthelah;
the Becherite clan from Becher;
the Tahanite clan from Tahan.
36 These were Shuthelah's descendants:
the Eranite clan from Eran.
37 These were the Ephraimite clans ⌊numbered⌋ by their registered men: 32,500.
These were Joseph's descendants by their clans.

38 Benjamin's descendants by their clans:
the Belaite clan from Bela;
the Ashbelite clan from Ashbel;
the Ahiramite clan from Ahiram;
39 the Shuphamite clan from Shupham;[a]
the Huphamite clan from Hupham.
40 Bela's descendants ⌊from⌋ Ard and Naaman:
the Ardite clan ⌊from⌋ Ard;
the Naamite clan from Naaman.
41 These were the Benjaminite clans numbered by their registered men: 45,600.

42 These were Dan's descendants by their clans:
the Shuhamite clan from Shuham.
These were the clans of Dan by their clans.
43 All the Shuhamite clans ⌊numbered⌋ by their registered men were 64,400.

44 Asher's descendants by their clans:
the Imnite clan from Imnah;
the Ishvite clan from Ishvi;
the Beriite clan from Beriah.
45 From Beriah's descendants:
the Heberite clan from Heber;
the Malchielite clan from Malchiel.
46 And the name of Asher's daughter was Serah.
47 These were the Asherite clans ⌊numbered⌋ by their registered men: 53,400.

48 Naphtali's descendants by their clans:
the Jahzeelite clan from Jahzeel;
the Gunite clan from Guni;
49 the Jezerite clan from Jezer;
the Shillemite clan from Shillem.
50 These were the Naphtali clans numbered by their registered men: 45,400.

51 These registered Israelite men numbered 601,730.

52 The LORD spoke to Moses, 53 "The land is to be divided among them as an inheritance based on the number of names. 54 Increase the inheritance for a large ⌊tribe⌋, and decrease it for a small one. Each is to be given its inheritance according to those who were registered in it. 55 The land must be divided by lot; they will receive an inheritance according to the names of their ancestral tribes. 56 Each inheritance will be divided by lot among the larger and smaller ⌊tribes⌋."

57 These were the Levites registered by their clans:
the Gershonite clan from Gershon;
the Kohathite clan from Kohath;
the Merarite clan from Merari.
58 These were the Levite family groups:
the Libnite clan,
the Hebronite clan,
the Mahlite clan,
the Mushite clan,
and the Korahite clan.

Kohath was the ancestor of Amram. 59 The name of Amram's wife was Jochebed, a descendant of Levi, born to Levi in Egypt. She bore to Amram: Aaron, Moses, and their sister Miriam. 60 Nadab, Abihu, Eleazar, and Ithamar were born to Aaron, 61 but Nadab and Abihu died when they presented unauthorized fire before the LORD. 62 Those registered were 23,000, every male one month old or more; they were not registered among the ⌊other⌋ Israelites, because no inheritance was given to them among the Israelites.

63 These were the ones registered by Moses and Eleazar the priest when they registered the Israelites on the plains of Moab by the Jordan ⌊across from⌋ Jericho. 64 But among them there was not one of those who had been registered by Moses and Aaron the priest when they registered the Israelites in the Wilderness of Sinai. 65 For the LORD had said to them that they would all die in the wilderness. None of them was left except Caleb son of Jephunneh and Joshua son of Nun.

a 26:39 Some Hb mss, Sam, LXX, Syr, Tg, Vg; other Hb mss read Shephupham

---

vere. Execution and public display of the corpses would punish the guilty, but also humiliate their families and frighten everyone.

25:6 An Israelite man came bringing a Midianite woman. The man who did this, Zimri (v. 14), was insulting his family and defying the laws against fornication. His action also was

insensitive to the many deaths already caused by the plague (24,000, according to v. 9).

25:17 Attack the Midianites. Midian had been conspiring with Balak since Israel assumed the dominant position in the Transjordan (22:1-7). The Midianite women had

seduced Israelite men into Baal worship.

26:1-51 The first census had been taken over 38 years before, and nearly all the men 20 years old or older then were now dead. The new census would give the tribal leaders an idea of how many soldiers were ready to fight.

26:51 601,730. The first census, 38 years ear-

A Case of Daughters' Inheritance

27 The daughters of Zelophehad approached; ⌊Zelophehad was the⌋ son of Hepher, son of Gilead, son of Machir, son of Manasseh from the clans of Manasseh, the son of Joseph. These were the names of his daughters: Mahlah, Noah, Hoglah, Milcah, and Tirzah. ² They stood before Moses, Eleazar the priest, the leaders, and the entire community at the entrance to the tent of meeting and said, ³ "Our father died in the wilderness, but he was not among Korah's followers, who gathered together against the LORD. Instead, he died because of his own sin, and he had no sons. ⁴ Why should the name of our father be taken away from his clan? Since he had no son, give us property among our father's brothers."

⁵ Moses brought their case before the LORD, ⁶ and the LORD answered him, ⁷ "What Zelophehad's daughters say is correct. You are to give them hereditary property among their father's brothers and transfer their father's inheritance to them. ⁸ Tell the Israelites: When a man dies without having a son, transfer his inheritance to his daughter. ⁹ If he has no daughter, give his inheritance to his brothers. ¹⁰ If he has no brothers, give his inheritance to his father's brothers. ¹¹ If his father has no brothers, give his inheritance to the nearest relative of his clan, and he will take possession of it. This is to be a statutory ordinance for the Israelites as the LORD commanded Moses."

Joshua Commissioned to Succeed Moses

¹² Then the LORD said to Moses, "Go up this mountain of the Abarim ⌊range⌋[a] and see the land that I have given the Israelites. ¹³ After you have seen it, you will also be gathered to your people, as Aaron your brother was. ¹⁴ When the community quarreled in the Wilderness of Zin, both of you rebelled against My command to show My holiness in their sight at the waters." Those were the waters of Meribah[b] of Kadesh in the Wilderness of Zin.

¹⁵ So Moses appealed to the LORD, ¹⁶ "May the LORD, the God of the spirits of all flesh, appoint a man over the community ¹⁷ who will go out before them and come back in before them, and who will bring them out and bring them in, so that the LORD's community won't be like sheep without a shepherd."

¹⁸ The LORD replied to Moses, "Take Joshua son of Nun, a man who has the Spirit in him, and lay your hands on him. ¹⁹ Have him stand before Eleazar the priest and the whole community, and commission him

in their sight. ²⁰ Confer some of your authority on him so that the entire Israelite community will obey ⌊him⌋. ²¹ He will stand before Eleazar who will consult the LORD for him with the decision of the •Urim.[c] He and all the Israelites with him, even the entire community, will go out and come back in at his command."

²² Moses did as the LORD commanded him. He took Joshua, had him stand before Eleazar the priest and the entire community, ²³ laid his hands on him, and commissioned him, as the LORD had spoken through Moses.

Prescribed Offerings

28 The LORD spoke to Moses, ² "Command the Israelites and say to them: Be sure to present to Me at its appointed time My offering and My food as My fire offering, a pleasing aroma to Me. ³ And say to them: This is the fire offering you are to present to the LORD:

Daily Offerings

"Each day ⌊present⌋ two unblemished year-old male lambs as a regular •burnt offering. ⁴ Offer one lamb in the morning and the other lamb at twilight, ⁵ along with two quarts[d] of fine flour for a •grain offering mixed with a quart[e] of beaten olive oil. ⁶ It is a regular burnt offering established at Mount Sinai for a pleasing aroma, a fire offering to the LORD. ⁷ The drink offering is to be a quart[e] with each lamb. Pour out the offering of beer to the LORD in the sanctuary area. ⁸ Offer the second lamb at twilight, along with the same kind of grain offering and drink offering as in the morning. It is a fire offering, a pleasing aroma to the LORD.

Sabbath Offerings

⁹ "On the Sabbath day ⌊present⌋ two unblemished year-old male lambs, four quarts[f] of fine flour mixed with oil as a grain offering, and its drink offering. ¹⁰ It is the burnt offering for every Sabbath, in addition to the regular burnt offering and its drink offering.

Monthly Offerings

¹¹ "At the beginning of each of your months present a burnt offering to the LORD: two young bulls, one ram, seven male lambs a year old—⌊all⌋ unblemished— ¹² with six quarts[g] of fine flour mixed with oil as a grain offering for each bull, four quarts[f] of fine flour mixed with oil as a grain offering for the ram, ¹³ and two quarts[h] of fine flour mixed with oil as a grain offering for each lamb. It is a burnt offering, a pleasing aroma, a fire offering to the LORD. ¹⁴ Their drink offerings are to be two quarts[i] of wine with each bull, one and a third

---

[a]**27:12** Mount Nebo; Nm 33:47-48; Dt 32:49; Jr 22:20 [b]**27:14** = quarreling [c]**27:21** The *Urim* and Thummim were 2 objects used to determine God's will; Ex 28:30. [d]**28:5** Lit *one-tenth of an ephah* [e]**28:5,7** Lit *a fourth of a hin* [f]**28:9,12** Lit *two-tenths* (of an ephah) [g]**28:12** Lit *three-tenths* (of an ephah) [h]**28:13** Lit *one-tenth* (of an ephah) [i]**28:14** Lit *a half hin*

---

lier, had counted 603,550 males. Despite deaths from battles, disease, old age, and disobedience, Israel had remained strong.

26:53 based on the number of names. Each tribe was allotted land based on population. Locations would be determined later by lot (v. 55).

27:1-11 Zelophehad's daughters' appeal for an inheritance was an unprecedented act of courage. God's "ruling" changed the male-dominated rules that had long governed property.

27:4-5 name of our father . . . Moses brought their case before the LORD. Israel-

ite justice looked to its source: The Lord had written the Law, and He sat as the highest judge in its application.

27:12-23 Zelophehad's daughters got their justice, but God would not bend His justice to allow Moses to enter Canaan.

27:16 appoint a man over the community.

183

quarts[a] with the ram, and one quart[b] with each male lamb. This is the monthly burnt offering for all the months of the year. 15 And one male goat is to be offered as a •sin offering to the LORD, in addition to the regular burnt offering with its drink offering.

Offerings for Passover

16 "The •Passover to the LORD comes in the first month, on the fourteenth day of the month. 17 On the fifteenth day of this month there will be a festival; unleavened bread is to be eaten for seven days. 18 On the first day there is to be a sacred assembly; you are not to do any daily work. 19 Present a fire offering, a burnt offering to the LORD: two young bulls, one ram, and seven male lambs a year old. Your animals are to be unblemished. 20 The grain offering with them is to be of fine flour mixed with oil; offer six quarts[c] with each bull and four quarts[d] with the ram. 21 Offer two quarts[e] with each of the seven lambs 22 and one male goat for a sin offering to make •atonement for yourselves. 23 Offer these with the morning burnt offering that is part of the regular burnt offering. 24 You are to offer the same food each day for seven days as a fire offering, a pleasing aroma to the LORD. It is to be offered with its drink offering and the regular burnt offering. 25 On the seventh day you are to hold a sacred assembly; you are not to do any daily work.

Offerings for the Festival of Weeks

26 "On the day of •firstfruits, you are to hold a sacred assembly when you present an offering of new grain to the LORD at your ⌊Festival of⌋ Weeks; you are not to do any daily work. 27 Present a burnt offering for a pleasing aroma to the LORD: two young bulls, one ram, and seven male lambs a year old, 28 with their grain offering of fine flour mixed with oil, six quarts[c] with each bull, four quarts[d] with the ram, 29 and two quarts[e] with each of the seven lambs 30 and one male goat to make atonement for yourselves. 31 Offer ⌊them⌋ with their drink offerings in addition to the regular burnt offering and its grain offering. Your animals are to be unblemished.

New Year's Day Offerings

29 "You are to hold a sacred assembly in the seventh month, on the first ⌊day⌋ of the month, and you are not to do any daily work. This will be a day of jubilation[f] for you. 2 Offer a •burnt offering as a pleasing aroma to the LORD: one young bull, one ram, seven male lambs a year old—⌊all⌋ unblemished— 3 with their •grain offering of fine flour mixed with oil,

six quarts[c] with the bull, four quarts[d] with the ram, 4 and two quarts[e] with each of the seven male lambs. 5 Also ⌊offer⌋ one male goat as a •sin offering to make •atonement for yourselves. 6 These are in addition to the monthly and regular burnt offerings with their grain offerings and drink offerings. They are a pleasing aroma, a fire offering to the LORD.

Offerings for the Day of Atonement

7 "You are to hold a sacred assembly on the tenth ⌊day⌋ of this seventh month and practice self-denial;[g] you must not do any work. 8 Present a burnt offering to the LORD, a pleasing aroma: one young bull, one ram, and seven male lambs a year old. ⌊All⌋ your animals are to be unblemished. 9 Their grain offering is to be of fine flour mixed with oil, six quarts[c] with the bull, four quarts[d] with the ram, 10 and two quarts[e] with each of the seven lambs. 11 ⌊Offer⌋ one male goat for a sin offering. The regular burnt offering with its grain offering and drink offerings are in addition to the sin offering of atonement.

Offerings for the Festival of Booths

12 "You are to hold a sacred assembly on the fifteenth day of the seventh month; you must not do any daily work. You are to celebrate a seven-day festival for the LORD. 13 Present a burnt offering, a fire offering as a pleasing aroma to the LORD: 13 young bulls, two rams, and 14 male lambs a year old. They are to be unblemished. 14 Their grain offering is to be of fine flour mixed with oil, six quarts[c] with each of the 13 bulls, four quarts[d] with each of the two rams, 15 and two quarts[e] with each of the 14 lambs. 16 Also ⌊offer⌋ one male goat as a sin offering. These are in addition to the regular burnt offering with its grain and drink offerings.

17 "On the second day ⌊present⌋ 12 young bulls, two rams, and 14 male lambs a year old—⌊all⌋ unblemished— 18 with their grain and drink offerings for the bulls, rams, and lambs, in proportion to their number. 19 Also ⌊offer⌋ one male goat as a sin offering. These are in addition to the regular burnt offering with its grain and drink[h] offerings.

20 "On the third day ⌊present⌋ 11 bulls, two rams, 14 male lambs a year old—⌊all⌋ unblemished— 21 with their grain and drink offerings for the bulls, rams, and lambs, in proportion to their number. 22 Also ⌊offer⌋ one male goat as a sin offering. These are in addition to the regular burnt offering with its grain and drink offerings.

---

a 28:14 Lit bull, a third hin   b 28:14 Lit a fourth hin   c 28:20,28; 29:3,9,14 Lit three-tenths (of an ephah)   d 28:20,28; 29:3,9,14 Lit two-tenths (of an ephah)   e 28:21,29; 29:4,10,15 Lit one-tenth (of an ephah)   f 29:1 Lit shout, or blast; traditionally, trumpet blasts   g 29:7 Traditionally, this involved fasting, abstinence from sex, and refraining from personal grooming   h 29:19 Some Hb mss, Syr, Vg, Sam; other Hb mss, LXX read and their drink

---

Moses' first concern was for his people, and for a smooth leadership transition.

27:18 Take Joshua son of Nun. It was important that Joshua be made Moses' successor before Moses died. One of the original spies into Canaan (13:8, 16), Joshua had shown courage and willingness to lead (13:1–

14:38). He would need all his courage and fortitude as Israel's leader.

27:20 Confer some of your authority. Moses' authority over the nation of Israel came through God's miracles, his own fortitude, and by being the mediator between God and Israel. That role would be hard for a

successor to attain, so God commanded a transition period between Moses and Joshua.

28:1–29:40 During this interlude before Joshua leads them into the promised land, Israel is reminded of their proper response to their God.

28:1-8 Each day. These verses restated the

23 "On the fourth day ⌊present⌋ 10 bulls, two rams, 14 male lambs a year old—⌊all⌋ unblemished— 24 with their grain and drink offerings for the bulls, rams, and lambs, in proportion to their number. 25 Also ⌊offer⌋ one male goat as a sin offering. These are in addition to the regular burnt offering with its grain and drink offerings.

26 "On the fifth day ⌊present⌋ nine bulls, two rams, 14 male lambs a year old—⌊all⌋ unblemished— 27 with their grain and drink offerings for the bulls, rams, and lambs, in proportion to their number. 28 Also ⌊offer⌋ one male goat as a sin offering. These are in addition to the regular burnt offering with its grain and drink offerings.

29 "On the sixth day ⌊present⌋ eight bulls, two rams, 14 male lambs a year old—⌊all⌋ unblemished— 30 with their grain and drink offerings for the bulls, rams, and lambs, in proportion to their number. 31 Also ⌊offer⌋ one male goat as a sin offering. These are in addition to the regular burnt offering with its grain and drinkª offerings.

32 "On the seventh day ⌊present⌋ seven bulls, two rams, and 14 male lambs a year old—⌊all⌋ unblemished— 33 with their grain and drink offerings for the bulls, rams, and lambs, in proportion to their number. 34 Also ⌊offer⌋ one male goat as a sin offering. These are in addition to the regular burnt offering with its grain and drink offerings.

35 "On the eighth day you are to hold a solemn assembly; you are not to do any daily work. 36 Present a burnt offering, a fire offering as a pleasing aroma to the LORD: one bull, one ram, seven male lambs a year old—⌊all⌋ unblemished— 37 with their grain and drink offerings for the bulls, rams, and lambs, in proportion to their number. 38 Also ⌊offer⌋ one male goat as a sin offering. These are in addition to the regular burnt offering with its grain and drink offerings.

39 "You must offer these to the LORD at your appointed times in addition to your vow and freewill offerings, whether burnt, grain, drink, or •fellowship offerings." 40b So Moses told the Israelites everything the LORD had commanded him.

Regulations about Vows

30 Moses told the leaders of the Israelite tribes, "This is what the LORD has commanded: 2 When a man makes a vow to the LORD or swears an oath to put himself under an obligation, he must not break his word; he must do whatever he has promised.

3 "When a woman in her father's house during her youth makes a vow to the LORD or puts ⌊herself⌋ under an obligation, 4 and her father hears about her vow or the obligation she put herself under, and he says nothing to her, all her vows and every obligation she put herself under are binding. 5 But if her father prohibits her on the day he hears ⌊about it⌋, none of her vows and none of the obligations she put herself under are binding. The LORD will absolve her because her father has prohibited her.

6 "If a woman marries while her vows or the rash commitment she herself made are binding, 7 and her husband hears ⌊about it⌋ and says nothing to her when he finds out, her vows are binding, and the obligations she put herself under are binding. 8 But if her husband prohibits her when he hears ⌊about it⌋, he will cancel her vow that is binding or the rash commitment she herself made, and the LORD will forgive her.

9 "Every vow a widow or divorcée puts herself under is binding on her.

10 "If a woman in her husband's house has made a vow or put herself under an obligation with an oath, 11 and her husband hears ⌊about it⌋, says nothing to her, and does not prohibit her, all her vows are binding, and every obligation she put herself under is binding. 12 But if her husband cancels them on the day he hears ⌊about it⌋, nothing that came from her lips, whether her vows or her obligation, is binding. Her husband has canceled them, and the LORD will absolve her. 13 Her husband may confirm or cancel any vow or any sworn obligation to deny herself. 14 If her husband says nothing at all to her from day to day, he confirms all her vows and obligations, which are binding. He has confirmed them because he said nothing to her when he heard ⌊about them⌋. 15 But if he cancels them after he hears ⌊about them⌋, he will be responsible for herᶜ commitment."ᵈ

16 These are the statutes that the LORD commanded Moses concerning ⌊the relationship⌋ between a man and his wife, or between a father and his daughter in his house during her youth.

War with Midian

31 The LORD spoke to Moses, 2 "Execute vengeance for the Israelites against the Midianites. After that, you will be gathered to your people."

3 So Moses spoke to the people, "Equip some of your men for war. They will go against Midian to inflict the LORD's vengeance on them. 4 Send 1,000 men to war from each Israelite tribe." 5 So 1,000 were recruited from each Israelite tribe out of the thousandsᵉ in Israel—12,000 equipped for war. 6 Moses sent 1,000 from each tribe to war. They went with Phinehas son

---

ª29:31 Some Hb mss, Syr, Tg, Vg; other Hb mss, Sam read *and their drink* ᵇ29:40 Nm 30:1 in Hb ᶜ30:15 Sam, LXX, some Syr mss read *his*
ᵈ30:15 Or *will bear her guilt* ᵉ31:5 Or *clans*

Law concerning the required daily sacrifices, morning and evening. (Ex. 29:38-43.)

28:16-25 These verses restated the Law concerning the observance of Passover (Lev. 23:4-8).

28:26-31 [Festival of] Weeks. This festival, for the offering of firstfruits of wheat, was ob-

served 50 days after Passover. Thus, Pentecost (meaning "50") is the Greek name.

29:1-6 jubilation. Possibly the blast of a ram's horn. The Feast of Trumpets was celebrated on the first of the seventh month. Today it is called *Rosh Hashanah* and is a New Year's celebration.

29:7-11 a sacred assembly. Observed shortly after the Feast of Trumpets, this festival turned Israel's attentions inward. The high priest entered the Most Holy Place alone to make "atonement for himself, his household, and the whole community of Israel" (Lev. 16:17).

of Eleazar the priest, in whose care were the holy objects and signal trumpets.

7 They waged war against Midian, as the LORD had commanded Moses, and killed every male. 8 Along with the others slain by them, they killed the Midianite kings—Evi, Rekem, Zur, Hur, and Reba, the five kings of Midian. They also killed Balaam son of Beor with the sword. 9 The Israelites took the Midianite women and their children captive, and they plundered all their cattle, flocks, and property. 10 Then they burned all the cities where the Midianites lived, as well as all their encampments, 11 and took away all the spoils of war and the captives, both human and animal. 12 They brought the prisoners, animals, and spoils of war to Moses, Eleazar the priest, and the Israelite community at the camp on the plains of Moab by the Jordan ⌊across from⌋ Jericho.

13 Moses, Eleazar the priest, and all the leaders of the community went to meet them outside the camp. 14 But Moses became furious with the officers, the commanders of thousands and commanders of hundreds, who were returning from the military campaign. 15 "Have[a] you let every female live?" he asked them. 16 "Yet they are the ones who, at Balaam's advice, incited the Israelites to unfaithfulness against the LORD in the Peor incident, so that the plague came against the LORD's community. 17 So now, kill all the male children and kill every woman who has had sexual relations with a man, 18 but keep alive for yourselves all the young females who have not had sexual relations.

19 "You are to remain outside the camp for seven days. All of you and your prisoners who have killed a person or touched the dead are to purify yourselves on the third day and the seventh day. 20 Also purify everything: garments, leather goods, things made of goat hair, and every article of wood."

21 Then Eleazar the priest said to the soldiers who had gone to battle, "This is the legal statute the LORD commanded Moses: 22 Only the gold, silver, bronze, iron, tin, and lead— 23 everything that can withstand fire—put through fire, and it will be clean. It must still be purified with the purification water. Anything that cannot withstand fire, put through the water. 24 On the seventh day wash your clothes, and you will be clean. After that you may enter the camp."

25 The LORD told Moses, 26 "You, Eleazar the priest, and the family leaders of the community are to take a count of what was captured, human and animal. 27 Then divide the captives between the troops who went out to war and the entire community. 28 Set aside

a tribute for the LORD from what belongs to the fighting men who went out to war: one out of ⌊every⌋ 500 humans, cattle, donkeys, sheep, and goats. 29 Take ⌊the tribute⌋ from their half and give ⌊it⌋ to Eleazar the priest as a contribution to the LORD. 30 From the Israelites' half, take one out of every 50 from the people, cattle, donkeys, sheep, and goats, all the livestock, and give them to the Levites who perform the duties of[b] the LORD's tabernacle."

31 So Moses and Eleazar the priest did as the LORD commanded Moses. 32 The captives remaining from the plunder the army had taken totaled:

    675,000 sheep and goats,
33   72,000 cattle,
34   61,000 donkeys,
35   and 32,000 people, all the females
    who had not had sexual relations with a man.

36 The half portion for those who went out to war numbered:

    337,500 sheep and goats,
37   and the tribute to the LORD was 675
    from the sheep and goats;
38   from the 36,000 cattle,
    the tribute to the LORD was 72;
39   from the 30,500 donkeys,
    the tribute to the LORD was 61;
40   and from the 16,000 people,
    the tribute to the LORD was 32 people.

41 Moses gave the tribute to Eleazar the priest as a contribution for the LORD, as the LORD had commanded Moses.

42 From the Israelites' half, which Moses separated from the men who fought, 43 the community's half was:

    337,500 sheep and goats,
44   36,000 cattle,
45   30,500 donkeys,
46   and 16,000 people.

47 Moses took one out of ⌊every⌋ 50, selected from the people and the livestock from the Israelites' half. He gave them to the Levites who perform the duties of the LORD's tabernacle, as the LORD had commanded him.

48 The officers who were over the thousands of the army, the commanders of thousands and of hundreds, approached Moses 49 and told him, "Your servants have taken a census of the fighting men under our command, and not one of us is missing. 50 So we have presented to the LORD an offering of the gold articles each man

---

a 31:15 Sam, LXX, Syr, Vg read Why have   b 31:30 Or who protect

---

29:12-39 celebrate a seven-day festival. The festival called *Sukkot*, meaning "tabernacles" or "booths," recalled the time after the Exodus when the Israelites lived in small "booths" (Lev. 23:42-43). The festival also celebrated the end of the yearly harvest.

30:1-16 When a man makes a vow. Moses

stressed the seriousness of a vow or oath. He pointed out three exceptions related to women.

30:3-5 a woman in her father's house. An unmarried woman could be released from a vow by her father's actions. If he knew of the vow and did nothing, however, the vow was

binding.

30:6-8 If a woman marries. A husband could nullify a vow made by his wife, even if she had made it before they were married. If he knew of the vow and did nothing, however, the vow stood.

30:10-15 a woman in her husband's house.

found—armlets, bracelets, rings, earrings, and necklaces—to make •atonement for ourselves before the LORD."

51 Moses and Eleazar the priest received from them all the articles made out of gold. 52 All the gold of the contribution they offered to the LORD, from the commanders of thousands and of hundreds, was 420 pounds.a 53 Each of the soldiers had taken plunder for himself. 54 Moses and Eleazar the priest received the gold from the commanders of thousands and of hundreds and brought it into the tent of meeting as a memorial for the Israelites before the LORD.

Transjordan Settlements

32 The Reubenites and Gadites had a very large number of livestock. When they surveyed the lands of Jazer and Gilead, they saw that the region was a ⌊good⌋ one for livestock. 2 So the Gadites and Reubenites came to Moses, Eleazar the priest, and the leaders of the community and said: 3 "⌊The territory of⌋ Ataroth, Dibon, Jazer, Nimrah, Heshbon, Elealeh, Sebam,b Nebo, and Beon, 4 which the LORD struck down before the community of Israel, is ⌊good⌋ land for livestock, and your servants own livestock." 5 They said, "If we have found favor in your sight, let this land be given to your servants as a possession. Don't make us cross the Jordan."

6 But Moses asked the Gadites and Reubenites, "Should your brothers go to war while you stay here? 7 Why are you discouragingc the Israelites from crossing into the land the LORD has given them? 8 That's what your fathers did when I sent them from Kadesh-barnea to see the land. 9 After they went up as far as Eshcol Valley and saw the land, they discouraged the Israelites from entering the land the LORD had given them. 10 So the LORD's anger burned that day, and He swore an oath: 11 'Because they did not follow Me completely, none of the men 20 years old or more who came up from Egypt will see the land I swore ⌊to give⌋ Abraham, Isaac, and Jacob— 12 none except Caleb son of Jephunneh the Kenizzite and Joshua son of Nun, because they did follow the LORD completely.' 13 The LORD's anger burned against Israel, and He made them wander in the wilderness 40 years until the whole generation that had done what was evil in the LORD's sight was gone. 14 And here you, a brood of sinners, stand in your fathers' place adding even more to the LORD's burning anger against Israel. 15 If you turn back from following Him, He will once again leave this people in the wilderness, and you will destroy all of them."

16 Then they approached him and said, "We want to build sheepfolds here for our livestock and cities for our dependents. 17 But we will arm ourselves and be ready ⌊to go⌋ ahead of the Israelites until we have brought them into their place. Meanwhile, our dependents will remain in the fortified cities because of the inhabitants of the land. 18 We will not return to our homes until each of the Israelites has taken possession of his inheritance. 19 Yet we will not have an inheritance with them across the Jordan and beyond, because our inheritance will be across the Jordan to the east."

20 Moses replied to them, "If you do this—if you arm yourselves for battle before the LORD, 21 and every one of your armed men crosses the Jordan before the LORD until He has driven His enemies from His presence, 22 and the land is subdued before the LORD—afterwards you may return and be free from obligation to the LORD and to Israel. And this land will belong to you as a possession before the LORD. 23 But if you don't do this, you will certainly sin against the LORD; be sure your sin will catch up with you. 24 Build cities for your dependents and folds for your flocks, but do what you have promised."

25 The Gadites and Reubenites answered Moses, "Your servants will do just as my lord commands. 26 Our little children, wives, livestock, and all our animals will remain here in the cities of Gilead, 27 but your servants are equipped for war before the LORD and will go across to the battle as my lord orders."

28 So Moses gave orders about them to Eleazar the priest, Joshua son of Nun, and the family leaders of the Israelite tribes. 29 Moses told them, "If the Gadites and Reubenites cross the Jordan with you, every man in battle formation before the LORD, and the land is subdued before you, you are to give them the land of Gilead as a possession. 30 But if they don't go across with you in battle formation, they must accept land in Canaan with you."

31 The Gadites and Reubenites replied, "What the LORD has spoken to your servants is what we will do. 32 We will cross over in battle formation before the LORD into the land of Canaan, but we will keep our hereditary possession across the Jordan."

33 So Moses gave them—the Gadites, Reubenites, and half the tribe of Manasseh son of Joseph—the kingdom of Sihon king of the Amorites and the kingdom of Og king of Bashan, the land including its cities with the territories surrounding them. 34 The Gadites rebuilt Dibon, Ataroth, Aroer, 35 Atroth-shophan, Jazer,

---

a31:52 Lit *16,750 shekels* b32:3 Sam, LXX read *Sibmah* (as in v. 38); Syr reads *Sebah* c32:7 Lit *discouraging the hearts of*

A husband had the right to nullify a vow his wife had made without his knowledge.

31:1-24 As a final official act, Moses was commanded to wage war against the Midianites.

31:7 waged war against Midian, as the LORD had commanded Moses. Choosing to fight against the Midianites was God's idea, and God would determine the outcome.

31:8 killed Balaam son of Beor. Balaam's deception nearly toppled the Israelites.

31:9-18 The Israelites took the Midianite women and their children captive. God had commanded that all but the virgin women be annihilated. The others would jeopardize Israel's moral attitudes. Nonetheless, the Israelites let all the women and children live.

31:19-24 purify yourselves. In the process of wiping out Midian, the Israelites had contaminated themselves. When contact was made with a dead human or animal, a quar-

Jogbehah, ³⁶ Beth-nimrah, and Beth-haran as fortified cities, and ⌊built⌋ sheepfolds. ³⁷ The Reubenites rebuilt Heshbon, Elealeh, Kiriathaim, ³⁸ as well as Nebo and Baal-meon (whose names were changed), and Sibmah. They gave names to the cities they rebuilt.

³⁹ The descendants of Machir son of Manasseh went to Gilead, captured it, and drove out the Amorites who were there. ⁴⁰ So Moses gave Gilead to ⌊the clan of⌋ Machir son of Manasseh, and they settled in it. ⁴¹ Jair, a descendant of Manasseh, went and captured their villages, which he renamed Jair's Villages.ᵃ ⁴² Nobah went and captured Kenath with its villages and called it Nobah after his own name.

Wilderness Travels Reviewed

33 These were the stages of the Israelites' journey when they went out of the land of Egypt by their military divisions under the leadership of Moses and Aaron. ² At the LORD's command, Moses wrote down the starting points for the stages of their journey; these are the stages ⌊listed⌋ by their starting points:

³ They departed from Rameses in the first month, on the fifteenth day of the month. On the day after the •Passover the Israelites went out triumphantlyᵇ in the sight of all the Egyptians. ⁴ Meanwhile, the Egyptians were burying every firstborn male the LORD had struck down among them, for the LORD had executed judgment against their gods. ⁵ The Israelites departed from Rameses and camped at Succoth.

⁶ They departed from Succoth and camped at Etham, which is on the edge of the wilderness.

⁷ They departed from Etham and turned back to Pi-hahiroth, which faces Baal-zephon, and they camped before Migdol.

⁸ They departed from Pi-hahirothᶜ and crossed through the middle of the sea into the wilderness. They took a three-day journey into the Wilderness of Etham and camped at Marah.

⁹ They departed from Marah and came to Elim. There were 12 springs of water and 70 date palms at Elim, so they camped there.

¹⁰ They departed from Elim and camped by the •Red Sea.

¹¹ They departed from the Red Sea and camped in the Wilderness of Sin.

¹² They departed from the Wilderness of Sin and camped in Dophkah.

¹³ They departed from Dophkah and camped at Alush.

¹⁴ They departed from Alush and camped at Rephidim, where there was no water for the people to drink.

¹⁵ They departed from Rephidim and camped in the Wilderness of Sinai.

¹⁶ They departed from the Wilderness of Sinai and camped at Kibroth-hattaavah.

¹⁷ They departed from Kibroth-hattaavah and camped at Hazeroth.

¹⁸ They departed from Hazeroth and camped at Rithmah.

¹⁹ They departed from Rithmah and camped at Rimmon-perez.

²⁰ They departed from Rimmon-perez and camped at Libnah.

²¹ They departed from Libnah and camped at Rissah.

²² They departed from Rissah and camped at Kehelathah.

²³ They departed from Kehelathah and camped at Mount Shepher.

²⁴ They departed from Mount Shepher and camped at Haradah.

²⁵ They departed from Haradah and camped at Makheloth.

²⁶ They departed from Makheloth and camped at Tahath.

²⁷ They departed from Tahath and camped at Terah.

²⁸ They departed from Terah and camped at Mithkah.

²⁹ They departed from Mithkah and camped at Hashmonah.

³⁰ They departed from Hashmonah and camped at Moseroth.

³¹ They departed from Moseroth and camped at Bene-jaakan.

³² They departed from Bene-jaakan and camped at Hor-haggidgad.

³³ They departed from Hor-haggidgad and camped at Jotbathah.

³⁴ They departed from Jotbathah and camped at Abronah.

³⁵ They departed from Abronah and camped at Ezion-geber.

³⁶ They departed from Ezion-geber and camped in the Wilderness of Zin (that is, Kadesh).

ᵃ 32:41 Or renamed Havvoth-jair ᵇ 33:3 Lit with a raised hand; Ex 14:8 ᶜ 33:8 Some Hb mss, Sam, Syr, Vg; other Hb mss read from before Hahiroth

---

antine of sorts was required. These ceremonial laws of purification were a way of emphasizing the holiness of God.

31:26-35 take a count of what was captured. In these wars of the Old Testament, a portion of the spoils was to be offered to God in recognition that He was the commander-in-chief. The rest was distributed fairly among the soldiers and the community.

32:8 what your fathers did when I sent them. Moses was suspicious when the two tribes wanted to stay on the east side of the Jordan. It reminded him of the 10 spies who refused to conquer Canaan (chs. 13–14).

32:17 we will arm ourselves and be ready [to] go ahead. Moses was wrong. The two tribes quickly offered to fight with their brothers beyond the Jordan. Their wives and children would remain behind to stake out the land they wanted to claim.

32:33 and half the tribe of Manasseh son of

37 They departed from Kadesh and camped at Mount Hor on the edge of the land of Edom. 38 At the LORD's command, Aaron the priest climbed Mount Hor and died there on the first ⌊day⌋ of the fifth month in the fortieth year after the Israelites went out of the land of Egypt. 39 Aaron was 123 years old when he died on Mount Hor. 40 At that time the Canaanite king of Arad, who lived in the •Negev in the land of Canaan, heard the Israelites were coming.

41 They departed from Mount Hor and camped at Zalmonah.

42 They departed from Zalmonah and camped at Punon.

43 They departed from Punon and camped at Oboth.

44 They departed from Oboth and camped at Iye-abarim on the border of Moab.

45 They departed from Iyima and camped at Dibon-gad.

46 They departed from Dibon-gad and camped at Almon-diblathaim.

47 They departed from Almon-diblathaim and camped in the Abarim ⌊range⌋ facing Nebo.

48 They departed from the Abarim ⌊range⌋ and camped on the plains of Moab by the Jordan ⌊across from⌋ Jericho. 49 They camped by the Jordan from Beth-jeshimoth to Acacia Meadowsb on the plains of Moab.

Instructions for Occupying Canaan

50 The LORD spoke to Moses in the plains of Moab by the Jordan ⌊across from⌋ Jericho, 51 "Tell the Israelites: When you cross the Jordan into the land of Canaan, 52 you must drive out all the inhabitants of the land before you, destroy all their stone images and cast images, and demolish all their •high places. 53 You are to take possession of the land and settle in it because I have given you the land to possess. 54 You are to receive the land as an inheritance by lot according to your clans. Increase the inheritance for a large clan and decrease it for a small one. Whatever place the lot indicates for someone will be his. You will receive an inheritance according to your ancestral tribes. 55 But if you don't drive out the inhabitants of the land before you, those you allow to remain will become thorns in your eyes and in your sides; they will harass you in the land where you will live. 56 And what I had planned to do to them, I will do to you."

Boundaries of the Promised Land

34 The LORD spoke to Moses, 2 "Command the Israelites and say to them: When you enter the land of Canaan, it will be allotted to you as an inheritancec with these borders:

3 Your southern side will be from the Wilderness of Zin along the boundary of Edom. Your southern border on the east will begin at the east end of the Dead Sea. 4 Your border will turn south of the Ascent of Akrabbim,d proceed to Zin, and end south of Kadesh-barnea. It will go to Hazar-addar and proceed to Azmon. 5 The border will turn from Azmon to the Brook of Egypt, where it will end at the Mediterranean Sea.

6 Your western border will be the coastline of the Mediterranean Sea; this will be your western border.

7 This will be your northern border: From the Mediterranean Sea draw a line to Mount Hor;e 8 from Mount Hor draw a line to the entrance of Hamath,f and the border will reach Zedad. 9 Then the border will go to Ziphron and end at Hazar-enan. This will be your northern border.

10 For your eastern border, draw a line from Hazar-enan to Shepham. 11 The border will go down from Shepham to Riblah east of Ain. It will continue down and reach the eastern slope of the Sea of Chinnereth.g 12 Then the border will go down to the Jordan and end at the Dead Sea. This will be your land ⌊defined⌋ by its borders on all sides."

13 So Moses commanded the Israelites, "This is the land you are to receive by lot as an inheritance, which the LORD commanded to be given to the nine and a half tribes. 14 For the tribe of the Reubenites and the tribe of the Gadites have received ⌊their inheritance⌋ according to their ancestral houses, and half the tribe of Manasseh has received its inheritance. 15 The two and a half tribes have received their inheritance across the Jordan from Jericho, eastward toward the sunrise."

Leaders for Distributing the Land

16 The LORD spoke to Moses, 17 "These are the names of the men who are to distribute the land as an inheritance for you: Eleazar the priest and Joshua son of Nun. 18 Take one leader from each tribe to distribute the land. 19 These are the names of the men:

---

a33:45 A contraction of Iye-abarim   b33:49 Or Abel-shittim   c34:2 Lit inheritance the land of Canaan   d34:4 Lit of Scorpions; Jos 15:3; Jdg 1:36
e34:7 In Lebanon; Nm 20:22–28; 33:37–56   f34:8 Or to Lebo-hamath   g34:11 The Sea of Galilee; Jos 12:3; 13:27; Lk 5:1

Joseph. After Moses agreed to the arrangement with Gad and Reuben, half of another tribe decided to join the party. They too agreed to help with the conquest of Canaan. **33:1-49** Like the route on a road atlas traced with a highlighter, we can follow the progress God's people made en route to the land of

promise. The number 40 is an important biblical number. When God flooded the earth it rained for 40 days. When Jesus was tempted in the wilderness He fasted for 40 days. What is recorded here is most likely a general (rather than exhaustive) summary of the rest stops during 40 years. It was compiled to give

the Israelites a sacred history of God's leading.

33:51 When you cross the Jordan into the land of Canaan. When you are dealing with the promises of God, it is not a question of if but when. God would be faithful to bring His people into the promised land. Because of

Caleb son of Jephunneh from the tribe
of Judah;

20 Shemuel son of Ammihud from the tribe
of Simeon;

21 Elidad son of Chislon from the tribe
of Benjamin;

22 Bukki son of Jogli, a leader from the tribe
of Dan;

23 from the sons of Joseph:
Hanniel son of Ephod, a leader from the tribe
of Manasseh,

24 Kemuel son of Shiphtan, a leader from the tribe
of Ephraim;

25 Eli-zaphan son of Parnach, a leader
from the tribe of Zebulun;

26 Paltiel son of Azzan, a leader from the tribe
of Issachar;

27 Ahihud son of Shelomi, a leader from the tribe
of Asher;

28 Pedahel son of Ammihud, a leader
from the tribe of Naphtali."

29 These are the ones the LORD commanded to distribute the inheritance to the Israelites in the land of
Canaan.

Cities for the Levites

35 The LORD again spoke to Moses in the plains of
Moab by the Jordan ⌊across from⌋ Jericho:
2 "Command the Israelites to give cities out of their
hereditary property for the Levites to live in and pastureland around the cities. 3 The cities will be for them
to live in, and their pasturelands will be for their
herds, flocks, and all their ⌊other⌋ animals. 4 The pasturelands of the cities you are to give the Levites ⌊will
extend⌋ from the city wall 500 yards[a] on every side.
5 Measure 1,000 yards[b] outside the city for the east
side, 1,000 yards[b] for the south side, 1,000 yards[b] for
the west side, and 1,000 yards[b] for the north side,
with the city in the center. This will belong to them as
pasturelands for the cities.

6 "The cities you give the Levites will include six cities of refuge, which you must provide so that the one
who kills someone may flee there; in addition to these,
give 42 ⌊other⌋ cities. 7 The total number of cities you
give the Levites will be 48, along with their pasturelands. 8 Of the cities that you give from the Israelites'
territory, you should take more from a larger ⌊tribe⌋ and
less from a smaller one. Each ⌊tribe⌋ is to give some of
its cities to the Levites in proportion to the inheritance
it receives."

[a] 35:4 Lit 1,000 cubits   [b] 35:5 Lit 2,000 cubits

Cities of Refuge

9 The LORD said to Moses, 10 "Speak to the Israelites
and tell them: When you cross the Jordan into the land
of Canaan, 11 designate cities to serve as cities of refuge
for you, so that a person who kills someone unintentionally may flee there. 12 You will have the cities as a
refuge from the avenger, so that the one who kills
someone will not die until he stands trial before the
assembly. 13 The cities you select will be your six cities
of refuge. 14 Select three cities across the Jordan and
three cities in the land of Canaan to be cities of refuge.
15 These six cities will serve as a refuge for the Israelites and for the foreigner or temporary resident among
them, so that anyone who kills a person unintentionally may flee there.

16 "If anyone strikes a person with an iron object and
death results, he is a murderer; the murderer must be
put to death. 17 If a man has in his hand a stone capable
of causing death and strikes another man and he dies,
the murderer must be put to death. 18 If a man has in
his hand a wooden object capable of causing death and
he dies, the murderer must be put to death. 19 The
avenger of blood himself is to kill the murderer; when
he finds him, he is to kill him. 20 Likewise, if anyone in
hatred pushes a person or throws ⌊an object⌋ at him
with malicious intent and he dies, 21 or if in hostility he
strikes him with his hand and he dies, the one who
struck him must be put to death; he is a murderer. The
avenger of blood is to kill the murderer when he finds
him.

22 "But if anyone suddenly pushes a person without
hostility or throws any object at him without malicious
intent 23 or drops a stone without looking that could kill
a person and he dies, but he was not his enemy and
wasn't trying to harm him, 24 the assembly is to judge
between the slayer and the avenger of blood according
to these ordinances. 25 The assembly is to protect the
one who kills someone from the hand of the avenger of
blood. Then the assembly will return him to the city of
refuge he fled to, and he must live there until the death
of the high priest who was anointed with the holy oil.

26 "If the one who kills someone ever goes outside
the border of the city of refuge he fled to, 27 and the
avenger of blood finds him outside the border of his city
of refuge and kills him, the avenger will not be guilty of
bloodshed, 28 for the one who killed a person was supposed to live in his city of refuge until the death of the
high priest. Only after the death of the high priest may
the one who has killed a person return to the land he
possesses. 29 These ⌊instructions⌋ will be a statutory

---

disobedience and unbelief, the Israelites arrived in "the Land" 40 years late. But at last
the time had come.

34:3-12 The tribes did not choose their own
territory. Each tribe was given a specific plot
of real estate according to God's map. The
boundaries listed are actually larger than the

land occupied by each of the tribes.

34:13-15 The land you are to receive. Since
Gad, Reuben and half the tribe of Manasseh
had opted to pitch their permanent tents east
of the river, the land west of the Jordan was to
be distributed among only nine and a half
tribes.

34:16-29 Now that the land was to be settled,
Moses quickly acted on God's instruction to
put reliable leaders over the task of land allocation. Here is a great formula for getting a
job done. First, determine what needs to be
done. Then give clear instructions to those
specifically selected to oversee each part of

ordinance for you throughout your generations wherever you live.

30 "If anyone kills a person, the murderer is to be put to death based on the word of witnesses. But no one is to be put to death based on the testimony of one witness. 31 You are not to accept a ransom for the life of a murderer who is guilty of killing someone; he must be put to death. 32 Neither should you accept a ransom for the person who flees to his city of refuge, allowing him to return and live in the land before the death of the ⌊high⌋ priest.ᵃ

33 "Do not defile the land where you are,ᵇ for bloodshed defiles the land, and there can be no •atonement for the land because of the blood that is shed on it, except by the blood of the person who shed it. 34 Do not make the land unclean where you live and where I reside; for I, the LORD, reside among the Israelites."

The Inheritance of Zelophehad's Daughters

36 The family leaders from the clan of the descendants of Gilead—the son of Machir, son of Manasseh—one of the clans of the sons of Joseph approached and addressed Moses and the leaders who were over the Israelite families. 2 They said, "The LORD commanded my lord to give the land as an inheritance by lot to the Israelites. My lord was further commanded by the LORD to give our brother Zelophehad's inheritance to his daughters. 3 If they marry any of the men from the ⌊other⌋ Israelite tribes, their inheritance will be taken away from our fathers' inheritance and added to that of the tribe into which they marry.

Therefore, part of our allotted inheritance would be taken away. 4 When the Jubilee comes for the Israelites, their inheritance will be added to that of the tribe into which they marry, and their inheritance will be taken away from the inheritance of our ancestral tribe."

5 So Moses commanded the Israelites at the word of the LORD, "What the tribe of Joseph's descendants says is right. 6 This is what the LORD has commanded concerning Zelophehad's daughters: They may marry anyone they like provided they marry within a clan of their ancestral tribe. 7 An inheritance belonging to the Israelites must not transfer from tribe to tribe, because each of the Israelites is to retain the inheritance of his ancestral tribe. 8 Any daughter who possesses an inheritance from an Israelite tribe must marry someone from the clan of her ancestral tribe, so that each of the Israelites will possess the inheritance of his fathers. 9 No inheritance is to transfer from one tribe to another, because each of the Israelite tribes is to retain its inheritance."

10 The daughters of Zelophehad did as the LORD commanded Moses. 11 Mahlah, Tirzah, Hoglah, Milcah, and Noah, the daughters of Zelophehad, married cousins on their father's side. 12 They married ⌊men⌋ from the clans of the descendants of Manasseh son of Joseph, and their inheritance remained within the tribe of their father's clan.

13 These are the commands and ordinances the LORD commanded the Israelites through Moses in the plains of Moab by the Jordan ⌊across from⌋ Jericho.

ᵃ35:32 Sam, LXX, Syr read high priest ᵇ35:33 Sam, LXX, Syr, Vg, Tg read live

the project.

35:1-5 Although they were not eligible for large sections of land like the other tribes (1:47-53), God wanted the Levites to have specific locations to call home. "Levite" towns were to be scattered throughout the other tribes' lands.

35:6-15 Six of the Levite towns were designated as cities of refuge. Individuals who unintentionally caused the death of another could seek protection there from those seeking revenge. Three such cities were on the west side of the Jordan, and three were on the east.

35:16-21 In contrast to situations of acciden-

tal manslaughter, listed here are crimes judged to be murder.

35:22 without hostility. Crimes that were not premeditated or did not result from anger would not be judged on the same scale as those that were. This is the basis for our laws on manslaughter.

35:24 according to these ordinances. In order to maintain the integrity of the cities of refuge, a jury of sorts determined whether a candidate for sanctuary was truly deserving. Amnesty applied only as long as the refugee remained within the city limits.

36:1-13 This passage dealt with a specific in-

heritance question: a man with five daughters. Upon his death his land passed to his daughters. What would happen to the land if the daughters married outside of the tribe? After all, the land was each tribe's inheritance from God. The answer proposed was that daughters marry only within their tribe.

36:10 The daughters of Zelophehad. This act of obedience seems odd in today's world, where individual choice is valued above community. However, these women belonged to a tribe that was much larger than an extended family—more than 32,000 men over 20 years old. Also, remember that the family land was at stake.

INTRODUCTION TO
DEUTERONOMY

AUTHOR

Moses is assumed to be the author and editor of most of the first five books of the Old Testament (the Pentateuch).

DATE

It is difficult to form a firm date for the writing of the Pentateuch. Conservative estimates place it in either the 15th or 13th century B.C., depending on when the Exodus occurred.

THEME

God's covenant and Moses' personal plea with Israel.

HISTORICAL BACKGROUND

The events of this book take place on the plains of Moab as the Israelites are poised to enter the promised land. Moses oversees the important task of transferring his leadership to Joshua. At this important juncture in Israel's history, Moses gives his final instructions to the people. Moses' speeches in Deuteronomy actually were a renewal of Israel's covenant with the Lord. Much like a sermon, Moses emphasized laws that were particularly

appropriate at the time. The Book of Deuteronomy ends with an account of Moses' death.

CHARACTERISTICS

Arranged around three sermons given by Moses (1:1-4:43; 4:44-26:19; 29:1-32:47), the Book of Deuteronomy introduces the reader to the great theological themes of Judaism. Hence, we read of a God who acts in history for the redemption of his elect; we confront the Israelite concepts of sin, punishment and reward; and we are introduced to the essential creed of Judaism, "Hear, O Israel: The LORD our God, the LORD is one" (6:4). Behind these themes, and binding them together, is the covenant between God and Israel. It is this covenant that provides the driving force of the message of Deuteronomy, leaving no doubt as to the responsibilities, rewards, and punishments inherent in the covenant. Deuteronomy's spiritual emphasis and its call to total commitment to the Lord inspired references to its message throughout the rest of Scripture.

PASSAGES FOR TOPICAL GROUP STUDY

10:12-22 . . . . . WALKING WITH GOD . . . . Circumcised Hearts

Introduction

1 These are the words Moses spoke to all Israel across the Jordan in the wilderness, in the •Arabah opposite Suph,[a] between Paran and Tophel, Laban, Hazeroth, and Di-zahab. ² It is an eleven-day journey from Horeb to Kadesh-barnea by way of Mount Seir. ³ In the fortieth year, in the eleventh month, on the first of the month, Moses told the Israelites everything the LORD had commanded him ⌊to say⌋ to them. ⁴ This was after he had defeated Sihon king of the Amorites, who lived in Heshbon, and Og king of Bashan, who lived in Ashtaroth, at Edrei. ⁵ Across the Jordan in the land of Moab, Moses began to explain this law, saying:

Departure from Horeb

⁶ "The LORD our God spoke to us at Horeb, 'You have stayed at this mountain long enough. ⁷ Resume your journey and go to the hill country of the Amorites and their neighbors in the Arabah, the hill country, the lowlands, the •Negev and the sea coast—to the land of the Canaanites and to Lebanon as far as the Euphrates River.[b] ⁸ See, I have set the land before you. Enter and take possession of the land the LORD swore to give to your fathers Abraham, Isaac, and Jacob and their descendants after them.'

Leaders for the Tribes

⁹ "I said to you at that time: I can't bear ⌊the responsibility for⌋ you on my own. ¹⁰ The LORD your God has so multiplied you that today you are as numerous as the stars of the sky. ¹¹ May the LORD, the God of your fathers, increase you a thousand times more, and bless you as He promised you. ¹² But how can I bear your troubles, burdens, and disputes by myself? ¹³ Appoint for yourselves wise, understanding, and respected men from each of your tribes, and I will make them your leaders.

¹⁴ "You replied to me, 'What you propose to do is good.'

¹⁵ "So I took the leaders of your tribes, wise and respected men, and set them over you as leaders: officials for thousands, hundreds, fifties, and tens, and officers for your tribes. ¹⁶ I commanded your judges at that time: Hear ⌊the cases⌋ between your brothers, and judge rightly between a man and his brother or a foreign resident. ¹⁷ Do not show partiality when rendering judgment; listen to small and great alike. Do not be intimidated by anyone, for judgment belongs to God. Bring me any case too difficult for you, and I will hear it. ¹⁸ At that time I commanded you about all the things you were to do.

Israel's Disobedience at Kadesh-barnea

¹⁹ "We then set out from Horeb and went across all the great and terrible wilderness you saw on the way to the hill country of the Amorites, just as the LORD our God had commanded us. When we reached Kadesh-barnea, ²⁰ I said to you: You have reached the hill country of the Amorites, which the LORD our God is giving us. ²¹ See, the LORD your God has set the land before you. Go up and take possession of it as the LORD, the God of your fathers, has told you. Do not be afraid or discouraged.

²² "Then all of you approached me and said, 'Let's send men ahead of us, so that they may explore the land for us and bring us back a report about the route we should go up and the cities we will come to.' ²³ The plan seemed good to me, so I selected 12 men from among you, one man for each tribe. ²⁴ They left and went up into the hill country and came to the Valley of Eshcol, scouting the land. ²⁵ They took some of the fruit from the land in their hands, carried ⌊it⌋ down to us, and brought us back a report: 'The land the LORD our God is giving us is good.'

²⁶ "But you were not willing to go up, rebelling against the command of the LORD your God. ²⁷ You grumbled in your tents and said, 'The LORD brought us out of the land of Egypt to deliver us into the hands of the Amorites so they would destroy us, because He hated us. ²⁸ Where can we go? Our brothers have discouraged us, saying: The people are larger and taller than we are; the cities are large, fortified to the heavens. We also saw the descendants of the Anakim there.'

²⁹ "So I said to you: Don't be terrified or afraid of them! ³⁰ The LORD your God who goes before you will fight for you, just as you saw Him do for you in Egypt. ³¹ And you saw in the wilderness how the LORD your God carried you as a man carries his son all along the way you traveled until you reached this place. ³² But in spite of this you did not trust the LORD your God, ³³ who went before you on the journey to seek out a place for you to camp. He went in the fire by night and in the cloud by day to guide you on the road you were to travel.

³⁴ "When the LORD heard your[c] words, He grew angry and swore an oath: ³⁵ 'None of these men in this evil generation will see the good land I swore to give your fathers, ³⁶ except Caleb the son of Jephunneh. He will see it, and I will give him and his descendants the land on which he has set foot, because he followed the LORD completely.'

---

[a]**1:1** LXX, Tg, Vg read *the Red Sea*   [b]**1:7** Lit *the great river, the river Euphrates*   [c]**1:34** Lit *the sound of your*

1:1-5 Moses is speaking to those who were children at the Exodus or who were born in the wilderness period. The people are about to enter the land, so Moses summarizes the Law for them and calls for faithful obedience to the God who saved them.

1:2 Horeb. Another name for Mount Sinai (Ex.

19:20; 20:1-21). **Kadesh-barnea.** Where the Israelites camped while spying out Canaan (Num. 13:26).

1:21 as the LORD ... has told you. God's Word is the ultimate point of reference, whether spoken (to Abraham and Moses) or written (to us).

1:26 you. Moses' audience had not rebelled, their parents and grandparents had. Moses was referring to the nation as a group, past and present.

1:30 as you saw ... in Egypt. The character of the Lord is consistent. God led the Israelites to escape the Egyptian army and would

37 "The LORD was angry with me also because of you and said: 'You will not enter there either. 38 Joshua son of Nun, who attends you, will enter it. Encourage him, for he will enable Israel to inherit it. 39 Your little children whom you said would be plunder, your sons who[a] don't know good from evil, will enter there. I will give them the land, and they will take possession of it. 40 But you are to turn back and head for the wilderness by way of the •Red Sea.'

41 "You answered me, 'We have sinned against the LORD. We will go up and fight just as the LORD our God commanded us.' Then each of you put on his weapons of war and thought it would be easy to go up into the hill country.

42 "But the LORD said to me, 'Tell them: Don't go up and fight, for I am not with you to keep you from being defeated by your enemies.' 43 So I spoke to you, but you didn't listen. You rebelled against the LORD's command and defiantly went up into the hill country. 44 Then the Amorites who lived there came out against you and chased you like a swarm of bees. They routed you from Seir as far as Hormah. 45 When you returned, you wept before the LORD, but He didn't listen to your requests or pay attention to you. 46 For this reason you stayed in Kadesh as long as you did.[b]

Journey past Seir

2 "Then we turned back and headed for the wilderness by way of the •Red Sea, as the LORD had told me, and we traveled around the hill country of Seir for many days. 2 The LORD then said to me, 3 'You've been traveling around this hill country long enough; turn north. 4 Command the people: You are about to travel through the territory of your brothers, the descendants of Esau, who live in Seir. They will be afraid of you, so you must be very careful. 5 Don't fight with them, for I will not give you any of their land, not even an inch of it,[c] because I have given Esau the hill country of Seir as ⌊his⌋ possession. 6 You may purchase food from them with silver, so that you may eat, and buy water from them to drink. 7 For the LORD your God has blessed you in all the work of your hands. He has watched over your journey through this immense wilderness. The LORD your God has been with you this past 40 years, and you have lacked nothing.'

Journey past Moab

8 "So we bypassed our brothers, the descendants of Esau, who live in Seir. ⌊We turned⌋ away from the •Arabah road and from Elath and Ezion-geber. We traveled

along the road to the Wilderness of Moab. 9 The LORD said to me, 'Show no hostility toward Moab, and do not provoke them to battle, for I will not give you any of their land as a possession, since I have given Ar as a possession to the descendants of Lot.'"

10 The Emim, a great and numerous people as tall as the Anakim, had previously lived there. 11 They were also regarded as Rephaim, like the Anakim, though the Moabites called them Emim. 12 The Horites had previously lived in Seir, but the descendants of Esau drove them out, destroying them completely[d] and settling in their place, just as Israel did in the land of its possession the LORD gave them.

13 "⌊The LORD said,⌋ 'Now get up and cross the Zered Valley.' So we crossed the Zered Valley. 14 The time we spent traveling from Kadesh-barnea until we crossed the Zered Valley was 38 years until the entire generation of fighting men had perished from the camp, as the LORD had sworn to them. 15 Indeed, the LORD's hand was against them, to eliminate them from the camp until they had all perished.

Journey past Ammon

16 "When all the fighting men had died among the people, 17 the LORD spoke to me, 18 'Today you are going to cross the border of Moab at Ar. 19 When you get close to the Ammonites, don't show any hostility to them or fight with them, for I will not give you any of the Ammonites' land as a possession; I have given it as a possession to the descendants of Lot.'"

20 This too used to be regarded as the land of the Rephaim. The Rephaim lived there previously, though the Ammonites called them Zamzummim, 21 a great and numerous people, tall as the Anakim. The LORD destroyed the Rephaim at the advance of the Ammonites, so that they drove them out and settled in their place. 22 This was just as He had done for the descendants of Esau who lived in Seir, when He destroyed the Horites before them; they drove them out and have lived in their place until now. 23 The Caphtorim, who came from Caphtor,[e] destroyed the Avvim, who lived in villages as far as Gaza, and settled in their place.

Defeat of Sihon the Amorite

24 "⌊The LORD also said,⌋ 'Get up, move out, and cross the Arnon Valley. See, I have handed Sihon the Amorite, king of Heshbon, and his land over to you. Begin to take possession ⌊of it⌋; engage him in battle. 25 Today I will begin to put the fear and dread of you on the peoples everywhere under heaven. They will hear the

---

[a]1:39 Lit who today   [b]1:46 Lit Kadesh for many days, according to the days you stayed   [c]2:5 Lit land as far as the width of a sole of a foot   [d]2:12 Lit them before them   [e]2:23 Probably Crete

---

lead them to conquer Canaan.

1:37 angry ... because of you. Moses blamed the people, but his sin of striking the rock in anger disqualified him from entering the land.

1:43 I spoke to you, but you didn't listen. Here is what's wrong with the human race! It

was true of the wandering nation in the wilderness. It was true of the man and woman in the garden. It is true of us.

2:5,9 their land. God had given the land of Edom to Esau's descendants and the land of Moab to Lot's descendants as surely as He had promised the land of Canaan to the de-

scendants of Jacob (see Gen. 19:30-38; Am. 9:7).

2:10 Anakim. This was the tribe of giants that scared the spies sent by Moses (1:28).

2:11 Rephaim. The Moabites might have referred to these tall people as Emites (terrors).

2:12 Horites. The Horites ruled the area of

report about you, tremble, and be in anguish because of you.'

26 "So I sent messengers with an offer of peace to Sihon king of Heshbon from the Wilderness of Kedemoth, saying, 27 'Let us travel through your land; we will keep strictly to the highway. We will not turn to the right or the left. 28 You can sell us food in exchange for silver so we may eat, and give us water for silver so we may drink. Only let us travel through on foot, 29 just as the descendants of Esau who live in Seir did for us, and the Moabites who live in Ar, until we cross the Jordan into the land the LORD our God is giving us.' 30 But Sihon king of Heshbon would not let us travel through his land, for the LORD your God made his spirit stubborn and his heart obstinate in order to hand him over to you, as has now taken place.

31 "Then the LORD said to me, 'See, I have begun to give Sihon and his land to you. Begin to take possession of it.' 32 So Sihon and his whole army came out against us for battle at Jahaz. 33 The LORD our God handed him over to us, and we defeated him, his sons, and his whole army. 34 At that time we captured all his cities and •completely destroyed the people of every city, including the women and children. We left no survivors. 35 We took only the livestock and the spoil from the cities we captured as plunder for ourselves. 36 There was no city that was inaccessible to[a] us, from Aroer on the rim of the Arnon Valley, along with the city in the valley, even as far as Gilead. The LORD our God gave everything to us. 37 But you did not go near the Ammonites' land, all along the bank of the Jabbok River and the cities of the hill country, everything that the LORD our God had commanded.

Defeat of Og of Bashan

3 "Then we turned and went up the road to Bashan, and Og king of Bashan, with his whole army, came out against us for battle at Edrei. 2 But the LORD said to me, 'Do not fear him, for I have handed him over to you, along with his whole army and his land. Do to him as you did to Sihon king of the Amorites, who lived in Heshbon.' 3 So the LORD our God also handed over Og king of Bashan and his whole army to us. We struck him until there was no survivor left. 4 We captured all his cities at that time. There wasn't a city that we didn't take from them: 60 cities, the entire region of Argob, the kingdom of Og in Bashan. 5 All these were fortified with high walls, gates, and bars, besides a large number of rural villages. 6 We •completely destroyed them, as we had

done to Sihon king of Heshbon, destroying the men, women, and children of every city. 7 But we took all the livestock and the spoil from the cities as plunder for ourselves.

The Land of the Transjordan Tribes

8 "At that time we took the land from the two Amorite kings across the Jordan, from the Arnon Valley as far as Mount Hermon, 9 which the Sidonians call Sirion, but the Amorites call Senir, 10 all the cities of the plateau, Gilead, and Bashan as far as Salecah and Edrei, cities of Og's kingdom in Bashan. 11 (Only Og king of Bashan was left of the remnant of the Rephaim. His bed was made of iron.[b] Isn't it in Rabbah of the Ammonites? It is 13 feet six inches long and six feet wide by a standard measure.[c])

12 "At that time we took possession of this land. I gave to the Reubenites and Gadites ⌊the area extending⌋ from Aroer by the Arnon Valley, and half the hill country of Gilead along with its cities. 13 I gave to half the tribe of Manasseh the rest of Gilead and all Bashan, the kingdom of Og. The entire region of Argob, the whole territory of Bashan, used to be called the land of the Rephaim. 14 Jair, a descendant of Manasseh, took over the entire region of Argob as far as the border of the Geshurites and Maacathites. He called Bashan by his own name, Jair's Villages,[d] as it is today. 15 I gave Gilead to Machir, 16 and I gave to the Reubenites and Gadites ⌊the area extending⌋ from Gilead to the Arnon Valley (the middle of the valley was the border) and up to the Jabbok River, the border of the Ammonites. 17 The •Arabah and Jordan are also borders from Chinnereth[e] as far as the Sea of the Arabah, the Dead Sea, under the slopes of Pisgah on the east.

18 "I commanded you at that time: The LORD your God has given you this land to possess. All your fighting men will cross over in battle formation ahead of your brothers the Israelites. 19 But your wives, young children, and livestock—I know that you have a lot of livestock—will remain in the cities I have given you 20 until the LORD gives rest to your brothers as He has to you, and they also take possession of the land the LORD your God is giving them across the Jordan. Then each of you may return to his possession that I have given you.

The Transfer of Israel's Leadership

21 "I commanded Joshua at that time: Your own eyes have seen everything the LORD your God has done to these two kings. The LORD will do the same to all the

---

[a]**2:36** Or *was too high for*   [b]**3:11** Or *His sarcophagus was made of basalt*   [c]**3:11** Lit *Nine cubits its length and four cubits its width, by a man's cubit*   [d]**3:14** Or *Havvoth-jair*   [e]**3:17** The Sea of Galilee; Jos 12:3; 13:27; Lk 5:1

Edom before Esau settled there. Esau (later named Edom) either defeated the Horites or his tribe absorbed them.

2:23 Avvim. A remnant survived (Josh. 13:3). **Caphtorim.** Caphtor was where the Philistines originated, probably modern Crete. **2:24 Arnon.** The Arnon River flowed to the

east of the Dead Sea, about halfway between the north and south ends. **2:30 God made.** The language of the Old Testament sometimes subordinates a person's will to God's control (Ex. 7:3; see Rom. 9:18). **2:34 no survivors.** This was the way to rid the

land of idolatry. God put off giving Israel the land for many centuries waiting for the Canaanites to deserve this judgment (Gen. 15:16). God always gave people the opportunity to repent (see Jonah).

3:17 Chinnereth. Later called the Sea of Galilee (Josh. 12:2; Mark 1:16). **Pisgah.** Mount

kingdoms you are about to enter. 22 Don't be afraid of them, for the LORD your God fights for you.

23 "At that time I begged the LORD: 24 Lord GOD, You have begun to show Your greatness and power to Your servant, for what god is there in heaven or on earth who can perform deeds and mighty acts like Yours? 25 Please let me cross over and see the beautiful land on the other side of the Jordan, that good hill country and Lebanon.

26 "But the LORD was angry with me on account of you and would not listen to me. The LORD said to me, 'That's enough! Do not speak to Me again about this matter. 27 Go to the top of Pisgah and look to the west, north, south, and east, and see ⌊it⌋ with your own eyes, for you will not cross this Jordan. 28 But commission Joshua and encourage and strengthen him, for he will cross over ahead of the people and enable them to inherit this land that you will see.' 29 So we stayed in the valley facing Beth-peor.

Call to Obedience

4 "Now, Israel, listen to the statutes and ordinances I am teaching you to follow, so that you may live, enter, and take possession of the land the LORD, the God of your fathers, is giving you. 2 You must not add anything to what I command you or take anything away from it, so that you may keep the commands of the LORD your God I am giving you. 3 Your eyes have seen what the LORD did at Baal-peor, for the LORD your God destroyed every one of you who followed •Baal of Peor. 4 But you who have remained faithfula to the LORD your God are all alive today. 5 Look, I have taught you statutes and ordinances as the LORD my God has commanded me, so that you may follow them in the land you are entering to possess. 6 Carefully follow ⌊them⌋, for this will ⌊show⌋ your wisdom and understanding in the eyes of the peoples. When they hear about all these statutes, they will say, 'This great nation is indeed a wise and understanding people.' 7 For what great nation is there that has a god near to it as the LORD our God is ⌊to us⌋ whenever we call to Him? 8 And what great nation has righteous statutes and ordinances like this entire law I set before you today?

9 "Only be on your guard and diligently watch yourselves, so that you don't forget the things your eyes have seen and so that they don't slip from your mind as long as you live. Teach them to your children and your grandchildren. 10 The day you stood before the LORD your God at Horeb, the LORD said to me, 'Assemble the people before Me, and I will let them hear My words,

so that they may learn to •fear Me all the days they live on the earth and may instruct their children.' 11 You came near and stood at the base of the mountain, a mountain blazing with fire into the heavens and enveloped in a dense, black cloud. 12 Then the LORD spoke to you from the fire. You kept hearing the sound of the words, but didn't see a form; there was only a voice. 13 He declared His covenant to you. He commanded you to follow the Ten Commandments, which He wrote on two stone tablets. 14 At that time the LORD commanded me to teach you statutes and ordinances for you to follow in the land you are about to cross into and possess.

Worshiping the True God

15 "Be extremely careful for your own good—because you did not see any form on the day the LORD spoke to you at Horeb out of the fire— 16 not to act corruptly and make an idol for yourselves in the shape of any figure: a male or female form, 17 or the form of any beast on the earth, any winged creature that flies in the sky, 18 any creature that crawls on the ground, or any fish in the waters under the earth. 19 When you look to the heavens and see the sun, moon, and stars—all the array of heaven—do not be led astray to bow down and worship them. The LORD your God has provided them for all people everywhere under heaven. 20 But the LORD selected you and brought you out of Egypt's iron furnace to be a people for His inheritance, as you are today.

21 "The LORD was angry with me on your account. He swore that I would not cross the Jordan and enter the good land the LORD your God is giving you as an inheritance. 22 I won't be crossing the Jordan because I am going to die in this land. But you are about to cross over and take possession of this good land. 23 Be careful not to forget the covenant of the LORD your God that He made with you, and make an idol for yourselves in the shape of anything He has forbidden you. 24 For the LORD your God is a consuming fire, a jealous God.

25 "When you have children and grandchildren and have been in the land a long time, and if you act corruptly, make an idol in the form of anything, and do what is evil in the sight of the LORD your God, provoking Him to anger, 26 I call heaven and earth as witnesses against you today that you will quickly perish from the land you are about to cross the Jordan to possess. You will not live long there, but you will certainly be destroyed. 27 The LORD will scatter you among the peoples, and you will be reduced to a few survivorsb among the nations where the LORD your God will drive

---

a4:4 Lit have held on   b4:27 Lit be left few in number

Pisgah was near Mount Nebo (34:1).

3:22 God fights for you. The Hebrew spies compared themselves to the Canaanites (Num. 13), rather than comparing the strength of the Canaanites to the strength of God.

3:28 commission ... encourage ...

strengthen. Joshua was ordained by Moses like Elisha by Elijah (1 Kings 19:19-21) and Timothy by Paul (2 Tim. 1:5-7).

4:8 what ... nation. Pagans never knew how to please their gods (6:25).

4:19 do not be led astray. Today we face the same enticement to worship the created

world more than the Creator of the world.

4:21 LORD was angry. God commanded Moses to speak to a rock, but he struck it instead (Num. 20:5-12).

4:24 fire. God's anger is like fire (Ex. 24:7; 2 Sam. 22:9; Isa. 29:6; Heb. 12:29).

4:27 LORD will scatter you. God tells the fu-

you. ²⁸ There you will worship man-made gods of wood and stone, which cannot see, hear, eat, or smell. ²⁹ But from there, you will search for the LORD your God, and you will find ⌊Him⌋ when you seek Him with all your heart and all your soul. ³⁰ When you are in distress and all these things have happened to you, you will return to the LORD your God in later days and obey Him. ³¹ He will not leave you, destroy you, or forget the covenant with your fathers that He swore to them by oath, because the LORD your God is a compassionate God.

³² "Indeed, ask about the earlier days that preceded you, from the day God created man on the earth and from one end of the heavens to the other: Has anything like this great event ⌊ever⌋ happened, or has anything like it been heard of? ³³ Has a people ever heard God's voice speaking from the fire as you have, and lived? ³⁴ Or has a god ⌊ever⌋ attempted to go and take a nation as his own out of ⌊another⌋ nation, by trials, signs, wonders, and war, by a strong hand and an outstretched arm, by great terrors, as the LORD your God did for you in Egypt before your eyes? ³⁵ You were shown ⌊these things⌋ so that you would know that the LORD is God; there is no other besides Him. ³⁶ He let you hear His voice from heaven to instruct you. He showed you His great fire on earth, and you heard His words from the fire. ³⁷ Because He loved your fathers, He chose their descendants after them and brought you out of Egypt by His presence and great power, ³⁸ to drive out before you nations greater and stronger than you and to bring you in and give you their land as an inheritance, as is now taking place. ³⁹ Today, recognize and keep in mind that the LORD is God in heaven above and on earth below; there is no other. ⁴⁰ Keep His statutes and commands, which I am giving you today, so that you and your children after you may prosper and so that you may live long in the land the LORD your God is giving you for all time."

Cities of Refuge

⁴¹ Then Moses set apart three cities across the Jordan to the east, ⁴² where one could flee who committed manslaughter and killed his neighbor accidentally without previously hating him. He could flee to one of these cities and stay alive: ⁴³ Bezer in the wilderness on the plateau land, belonging to the Reubenites; Ramoth in Gilead, belonging to the Gadites; or Golan in Bashan, belonging to the Manassites.

Introduction to the Law

⁴⁴ This is the law Moses gave the Israelites. ⁴⁵ These are the decrees, statutes, and ordinances Moses proclaimed to them after they came out of Egypt, ⁴⁶ across the Jordan in the valley facing Beth-peor in the land of Sihon king of the Amorites. He lived in Heshbon, and Moses and the Israelites defeated him after they came out of Egypt. ⁴⁷ They took possession of his land and the land of Og king of Bashan, the two Amorite kings who were across the Jordan to the east, ⁴⁸ from Aroer on the rim of the Arnon Valley as far as Mount Sion (that is, Hermon) ⁴⁹ and all the •Arabah on the east side of the Jordan as far as the Dead Sea below the slopes of Pisgah.

The Ten Commandments

5 Moses summoned all Israel and said to them, "Israel, listen to the statutes and ordinances I am proclaiming as you hear them today. Learn and follow them carefully. ² The LORD our God made a covenant with us at Horeb. ³ He did not make this covenant with our fathers, but with all of us who are alive here today. ⁴ The LORD spoke to you face to face from the fire on the mountain. ⁵ At that time I was standing between the LORD and you to report the wordª of the LORD to you, because you were afraid of the fire and did not go up the mountain. And He said:

⁶ I am the LORD your God, who brought you out of the land of Egypt, out of the place of slavery.

⁷ Do not have other gods besides Me.

⁸ Do not make an idol for yourself in the shape of anything in the heavens above or on the earth below or in the waters under the earth. ⁹ You must not bow down to them or worship them, because I, the LORD your God, am a jealous God, punishing the children for the fathers' sin to the third and fourth ⌊generations⌋ of those who hate Me, ¹⁰ but showing faithful love to a thousand ⌊generations⌋ of those who love Me and keep My commands.

¹¹ Do not misuse the name of the LORD your God, because the LORD will punish anyone who misuses His name.

¹² Be careful to dedicate the Sabbath day, as the LORD your God has commanded you. ¹³ You are to labor six days and do all your work, ¹⁴ but the seventh day is a Sabbath to the LORD your God. You must not do any work—you, your son or daughter, your male or female slave, your ox or donkey, any of your livestock, or the foreigner who lives within your gates, so that your male and female slaves may rest as you do. ¹⁵ Remember that you were a slave in the land of Egypt, and the LORD your God brought you out of there with a strong hand and an outstretched

---

ª**5:5** One Hb ms, DSS, Sam, LXX, Syr, Vg read *words*

---

ture: Israel will disobey and be scattered to every nation, as they are still today.

4:29 you will find [Him]. There is a day (still future) when Israel will return to God (Rom. 11:26). Also, individual Jews today can find God if they seek Him.

4:37 He loved. God's motivation in covenant-

ing with Abraham is the same as in John 3:16: "God loved the world."

4:39 recognize and keep in mind. God expects us to show faith by recognizing that He is the one true God.

5:2 Horeb. Same as Sinai.

5:6 I am the LORD. This is the basis of the Ten

Commandments. When we understand who God is, what He speaks becomes priority.

5:12 Be careful to dedicate the Sabbath. Observing the Sabbath is not just about rest, but also about honoring God.

5:15 Remember. Before the printing press, the history of God's presence, guidance, and

arm. That is why the LORD your God has commanded you to keep the Sabbath day.

16 Honor your father and your mother, as the LORD your God has commanded you, so that you may live long and so that you may prosper in the land the LORD your God is giving you.

17 Do not murder.

18 Do not commit adultery.

19 Do not steal.

20 Do not give dishonest testimony against your neighbor.

21 Do not desire your neighbor's wife or covet your neighbor's house, his field, his male or female slave, his ox or donkey, or anything that belongs to your neighbor.

The People's Response

22 "The LORD spoke these commands in a loud voice to your entire assembly from the fire, cloud, and thick darkness on the mountain; He added nothing more. He wrote them on two stone tablets and gave them to me. 23 All of you approached me with your tribal leaders and elders when you heard the voice from the darkness and while the mountain was blazing with fire. 24 You said, 'Look, the LORD our God has shown us His glory and greatness, and we have heard His voice from the fire. Today we have seen that God speaks with a person, yet he still lives. 25 But now, why should we die? This great fire will consume us and we will die if we hear the voice of the LORD our God any longer. 26 For who out of all mankind has heard the voice of the living God speaking from the fire, as we have, and lived? 27 Go near and listen to everything the LORD our God says. Then you can tell us everything the LORD our God tells you; we will listen and obey.'

28 "The LORD heard your[a] words when you spoke to me. He said to me, 'I have heard the words that these people have spoken to you. Everything they have said is right. 29 If only they had such a heart to •fear Me and keep all My commands, so that they and their children will prosper forever. 30 Go and tell them: Return to your tents. 31 But you stand here with Me, and I will tell you every command—the statutes and ordinances—you are to teach them, so that they may follow ⌊them⌋ in the land I am giving them to possess.'

32 "Be careful to do as the LORD your God has commanded you; you are not to turn aside to the right or the left. 33 Follow the whole instruction the LORD your God has commanded you, so that you may live, prosper, and have a long life in the land you will possess.

The Greatest Commandment

6 "This is the command—the statutes and ordinances—the LORD your God has instructed ⌊me⌋ to teach you, so that you may follow ⌊them⌋ in the land you are about to enter and possess. 2 ⌊Do this⌋ so that you may •fear the LORD your God all the days of your life by keeping all His statutes and commands I am giving you, your son, and your grandson, and so that you may have a long life. 3 Listen, Israel, and be careful to follow ⌊them⌋, so that you may prosper and multiply greatly, because the LORD, the God of your fathers, has promised you a land flowing with milk and honey.

4 "Listen, Israel: The LORD our God, the LORD is One.[b] 5 Love the LORD your God with all your heart, with all your soul, and with all your strength. 6 These words that I am giving you today are to be in your heart. 7 Repeat them to your children. Talk about them when you sit in your house and when you walk along the road, when you lie down and when you get up. 8 Bind them as a sign on your hand and let them be a symbol[c] on your forehead.[d] 9 Write them on the doorposts of your house and on your gates.

Remembering God through Obedience

10 "When the LORD your God brings you into the land He swore to your fathers Abraham, Isaac, and Jacob that He would give you—a ⌊land with⌋ large and beautiful cities that you did not build, 11 houses full of every good thing that you did not fill ⌊them with⌋, wells dug that you did not dig, and vineyards and olive groves that you did not plant—and when you eat and are satisfied, 12 be careful not to forget the LORD who brought you out of the land of Egypt, out of the place of slavery. 13 Fear the LORD your God, worship Him, and take ⌊your⌋ oaths in His name. 14 Do not follow other gods, the gods of the peoples around you, 15 for the LORD your God, who is among you, is a jealous God. Otherwise, the LORD your God will become angry with you and wipe you off the face of the earth. 16 Do not test the LORD your God as you tested ⌊Him⌋ at Massah. 17 Carefully observe the commands of the LORD your God, the decrees and statutes He has commanded you. 18 Do what is right and good in the LORD's sight, so that you may prosper and so that you may enter and possess the good land the LORD your God swore to ⌊give⌋ your fathers, 19 by driving out all your enemies before you, as the LORD has said.

20 "When your son asks you in the future, 'What is the meaning of the decrees, statutes, and ordinances, which the LORD our God has commanded you?' 21 tell

---

a 5:28 Lit the sound of your   b 6:4 Or Yahweh is our God; Yahweh is One, or The LORD is our God, the LORD alone, or The LORD our God is one LORD
c 6:8 Or phylactery; Mt 23:5   d 6:8 Lit symbol between your eyes

---

holiness was passed down through customs, feasts, and stories.

5:16-21 This is summed up in the command to love our neighbor as ourselves (Rom. 13:9).

5:20 dishonest testimony. This applies to perjury, slander, and gossip.

6:2 fear the LORD ... by keeping. The essence of fearing God is obeying Him, recognizing His authority.

6:4-9 Listen, Israel. This passage is called the *Shema* (shuh-MAH), "listen." It is repeated daily in Jewish prayers. Jesus said this was the greatest commandment (Mark 12:29).

6:4 the LORD is One. This means that God is a unity, the only deity who exists and the only one to be worshiped (leaving open the later revelation of His three-in-one nature).

6:5 heart ... soul. "Heart" is the seat of emotions and thoughts. "Soul" means our whole being, including our body.

him, 'We were slaves of Pharaoh in Egypt, but the LORD brought us out of Egypt with a strong hand. 22 Before our eyes the LORD inflicted great and devastating signs and wonders on Egypt, on Pharaoh and all his household, 23 but He brought us from there in order to lead us in and give us the land that He swore to our fathers. 24 The LORD commanded us to follow all these statutes and to fear the LORD our God for our prosperity always and for our preservation, as it is today. 25 Righteousness will be ours if we are careful to follow every one of these commands before the LORD our God, as He has commanded us.'

Israel to Destroy Idolatrous Nations

7 "When the LORD your God brings you into the land you are entering to possess, and He drives out many nations before you—the Hittites, Girgashites, Amorites, Canaanites, Perizzites, Hivites and Jebusites, seven nations more numerous and powerful than you— 2 and when the LORD your God delivers them over to you and you defeat them, you must •completely destroy them. Make no treaty with them and show them no mercy. 3 Do not intermarry with them. Do not give your daughters to their sons or take their daughters for your sons, 4 because they will turn your sons away from Me to worship other gods. Then the LORD's anger will burn against you, and He will swiftly destroy you. 5 Instead, this is what you are to do to them: tear down their altars, smash their standing pillars, cut down their •Asherah poles, and burn up their carved images. 6 For you are a holy people belonging to the LORD your God. The LORD your God has chosen you to be His own possession out of all the peoples on the face of the earth.

7 "The LORD was devoted to you and chose you, not because you were more numerous than all peoples, for you were the fewest of all peoples. 8 But because the LORD loved you and kept the oath He swore to your fathers, He brought you out with a strong hand and redeemed you from the place of slavery, from the power of Pharaoh king of Egypt. 9 Know that •Yahweh your God is God, the faithful God who keeps His gracious covenant loyalty for a thousand generations with those who love Him and keep His commands. 10 But He directly pays back[a] and destroys those who hate Him. He will not hesitate to directly pay back[b] the one who hates Him. 11 So keep the command—the statutes and ordinances—that I am giving you to follow today.

12 "If you listen to and are careful to keep these ordinances, the LORD your God will keep His covenant loyalty with you, as He swore to your fathers. 13 He will

love you, bless you, and multiply you. He will bless your descendants,[c] and the produce of your soil—your grain, new wine, and oil—the young of your herds, and the newborn of your flocks, in the land He swore to your fathers that He would give you. 14 You will be blessed above all peoples; there will be no infertile male or female among you or your livestock. 15 The LORD will remove all sickness from you; He will not put on you all the terrible diseases of Egypt that you know about, but He will inflict them on all who hate you. 16 You must destroy all the peoples the LORD your God is delivering over to you and not look on them with pity. Do not worship their gods, for that will be a snare to you.

17 "If you say to yourself, 'These nations are greater than I; how can I drive them out?' 18 do not be afraid of them. Be sure to remember what the LORD your God did to Pharaoh and all Egypt: 19 the great trials that you saw, the signs and wonders, the strong hand and outstretched arm, by which the LORD your God brought you out. The LORD your God will do the same to all the peoples you fear. 20 The LORD your God will also send the hornet against them until all the survivors and those hiding from you perish. 21 Don't be terrified of them, for the LORD your God, a great and awesome God, is among you. 22 The LORD your God will drive out these nations before you little by little. You will not be able to destroy them all at once; otherwise, the wild animals will become too numerous for you. 23 The LORD your God will give them over to you and throw them into great confusion until they are destroyed. 24 He will hand their kings over to you, and you will wipe out their names under heaven. No one will be able to stand against you; you will annihilate them. 25 You must burn up the carved images of their gods. Don't covet the silver and gold on the images and take it for yourself, or else you will be ensnared by it, for it is abhorrent to the LORD your God. 26 You must not bring any abhorrent thing into your house, or you will be •set apart for destruction like it. You are to utterly detest and abhor it, because it is set apart for destruction.

Remember the LORD

8 "You must carefully follow every command I am giving you today, so that you may live and increase, and may enter and take possession of the land the LORD swore to your fathers. 2 Remember that the LORD your God led you on the entire journey these 40 years in the wilderness, so that He might humble you and test you to know what was in your heart, whether or not you would keep His commands. 3 He

---

[a]7:10 Lit He pays back to their faces   [b]7:10 Lit to pay back to their faces   [c]7:13 Lit bless the fruit of your womb

---

6:6 in your heart. This can be done by memorizing and meditating on God's truth.

6:12 be careful not to forget. People tend to turn to God in bad times and forget Him in easy times.

7:2-5 completely destroy them. God had given the Canaanites centuries to repent

(Gen. 15:16).

7:3 Do not intermarry. Jews were not forbidden to marry non-Jews but were forbidden to marry Canaanites. Many intercultural marriages occurred, including Joseph to an Egyptian priestess, Moses to Zipporah, a Midianite, and Boaz to Ruth, a Moabite. The

important point was that the non-Israelite followed the one true God.

7:7-8 The LORD ... chose you. The great truth here is that God did not love the Hebrews because they were valuable; they were valuable because He loved them.

7:26 detest and abhor. They were abhorrent

humbled you by letting you go hungry; then He gave you manna to eat, which you and your fathers had not known, so that you might learn that man does not live on bread alone but on every word that comes from the mouth of the LORD. [4] Your clothing did not wear out, and your feet did not swell these 40 years. [5] Keep in mind that the LORD your God has been disciplining you just as a man disciplines his son. [6] So keep the commands of the LORD your God by walking in His ways and •fearing Him. [7] For the LORD your God is bringing you into a good land, a land with streams of water, springs, and deep water sources, flowing in both valleys and hills; [8] a land of wheat, barley, vines, figs, and pomegranates; a land of olive oil and honey; [9] a land where you will eat food without shortage, where you will lack nothing; a land whose rocks are iron and from whose hills you will mine copper. [10] When you eat and are full, you will praise the LORD your God for the good land He has given you.

[11] "Be careful that you don't forget the LORD your God by failing to keep His command—the ordinances and statutes—I am giving you today. [12] When you eat and are full, and build beautiful houses to live in, [13] and your herds and flocks grow large, and your silver and gold multiply, and everything else you have increases, [14] ⌊be careful⌋ that your heart doesn't become proud and you forget the LORD your God who brought you out of the land of Egypt, out of the place of slavery. [15] He led you through the great and terrible wilderness with its poisonous snakes and scorpions, a thirsty land where there was no water. He brought water out of the flintlike rock for you. [16] He fed you in the wilderness with manna that your fathers had not known, in order to humble and test you, so that in the end He might cause you to prosper. [17] You may say to yourself, 'My power and my own ability have gained this wealth for me,' [18] but remember that the LORD your God gives you the power to gain wealth, in order to confirm His covenant He swore to your fathers, as it is today. [19] If you ever forget the LORD your God and go after other gods to worship and bow down to them, I testify against you today that you will perish. [20] Like the nations the LORD is about to destroy before you, you will perish if you do not obey the LORD your God.

Warning against Self-Righteousness

9 "Listen, Israel: Today you are about to cross the Jordan to go and drive out nations greater and stronger than you ⌊with⌋ large cities fortified to the heavens. [2] The people are strong and tall, the descendants of the Anakim. You know about them and you have heard it said about them, 'Who can stand up to

the sons of Anak?' [3] But understand that today the LORD your God will cross over ahead of you as a consuming fire; He will devastate and subdue them before you. You will drive them out and destroy them swiftly, as the LORD has told you. [4] When the LORD your God drives them out before you, do not say to yourself, 'The LORD brought me in to take possession of this land because of my righteousness.' Instead, the LORD will drive out these nations before you because of their wickedness. [5] You are not going to take possession of their land because of your righteousness or your integrity. Instead, the LORD your God will drive out these nations before you because of their wickedness, in order to keep the promise He swore to your fathers, Abraham, Isaac, and Jacob. [6] Understand that the LORD your God is not giving you this good land to possess because of your righteousness, for you are a stiff-necked people.

Israel's Rebellion and Moses' Intercession

[7] "Remember and do not forget how you provoked the LORD your God in the wilderness. You have been rebelling against the LORD from the day you left the land of Egypt until you reached this place. [8] You provoked the LORD at Horeb, and He was angry enough with you to destroy you. [9] When I went up the mountain to receive the stone tablets, the tablets of the covenant the LORD made with you, I stayed on the mountain 40 days and 40 nights. I did not eat bread or drink water. [10] On the day of the assembly the LORD gave me the two stone tablets, inscribed by God's finger. The exact words were on them, which the LORD spoke to you from the fire on the mountain. [11] The LORD gave me the two stone tablets, the tablets of the covenant, at the end of the 40 days and 40 nights.

[12] "The LORD said to me, 'Get up and go down immediately from here. For your people you brought out of Egypt have acted corruptly. They have quickly turned from the way that I commanded them; they have made a cast image for themselves.' [13] The LORD also said to me, 'I have seen this people, and indeed, they are a stiff-necked people. [14] Leave Me alone, and I will destroy them and blot out their name under heaven. Then I will make you into a nation stronger and more numerous than they.'

[15] "So I went back down the mountain, while it was blazing with fire, and the two tablets of the covenant were in my hands. [16] I saw how you had sinned against the LORD your God; you had made a calf image for yourselves. You had quickly turned from the way the LORD had commanded for you. [17] So I took hold of the tablets and threw them from my hands, shattering them before

---

if they represented other gods or even if the people worshipped God through them. God cannot be manipulated by an idol but can be prayed to with faith.

8:3 manna. See Exodus 16:31. Jesus quoted this verse when tempted by Satan (Matt. 4:4).

8:16 test you. The manna tested the people

to see if they would trust God every day and obey Him by handling the manna as He asked them to.

9:4 because of their wickedness. The Hebrews would not receive the land because of their own righteousness; their victories would be as much about God judging Canaanite sin.

9:6,13 stiff-necked. This means stubborn and defiant, inflexible and unwilling to follow where they were guided, like a horse that refuses to turn according to a rider's commands.

9:19 again, the LORD listened. As mediator, Moses appealed to God on behalf of

your eyes. [18] Then I fell down like the first time in the presence of the LORD for 40 days and 40 nights; I did not eat bread or drink water because of all the sin you committed, doing what was evil in the LORD's sight and provoking Him to anger. [19] I was afraid of the fierce anger the LORD had directed against you, because He was about to destroy you. But again, the LORD listened to me on that occasion. [20] The LORD was angry enough with Aaron to destroy him. But I prayed for Aaron at that time also. [21] I took the sinful calf you had made, burned it up, and crushed it, thoroughly grinding it to powder as ⌊fine as⌋ dust. Then I threw it into the stream that came down from the mountain.

[22] "You continued to provoke the LORD at Taberah, Massah, and Kibroth-hattaavah. [23] When the LORD sent you from Kadesh-barnea, He said, 'Go up and possess the land I have given you'; you rebelled against the command of the LORD your God. You did not believe or obey Him. [24] You have been rebelling against the LORD ever since I have[a] known you.

[25] "I fell down in the presence of the LORD 40 days and 40 nights because the LORD had threatened to destroy you. [26] I prayed to the LORD:

Lord GOD, do not annihilate Your people, Your inheritance, whom You redeemed through Your greatness and brought out of Egypt with a strong hand. [27] Remember Your servants Abraham, Isaac, and Jacob. Disregard this people's stubbornness, and their wickedness and sin. [28] Otherwise, those in the land you brought us from will say, 'Because the LORD wasn't able to bring them into the land He had promised them, and because He hated them, He brought them out to kill them in the wilderness.' [29] But they are Your people, Your inheritance, whom You brought out by Your great power and outstretched arm.

The Covenant Renewed

10 "The LORD said to me at that time, 'Cut two stone tablets like the first ones and come to Me on the mountain and make a wooden ark. [2] I will write on the tablets the words that were on the first tablets you broke, and you are to place them in the ark.' [3] So I made an ark of acacia wood, cut two stone tablets like the first ones, and climbed the mountain with the two tablets in my hand. [4] Then, on the day of the assembly, the LORD wrote on the tablets what had been written previously, the Ten Commandments that He had spoken to you on the mountain from the fire. The LORD gave them to me, [5] and I went back down the moun-

tain and placed the tablets in the ark I had made. And they have remained there, as the LORD commanded me."

[6] The Israelites traveled from Beeroth Bene-jaakan[b] to Moserah. Aaron died and was buried there, and Eleazar his son became priest in his place. [7] They traveled from there to Gudgodah, and from Gudgodah to Jotbathah, a land with streams of water.

[8] "At that time the LORD set apart the tribe of Levi to carry the ark of the LORD's covenant, to stand before the LORD to serve Him, and to bless in His name, as it is today. [9] For this reason, Levi does not have a portion or inheritance like his brothers; the LORD is his inheritance, as the LORD your God told him.

[10] "I stayed on the mountain 40 days and 40 nights like the first time. The LORD also listened to me on this occasion; He agreed not to annihilate you. [11] Then the LORD said to me, 'Get up. Continue your journey ahead of the people, so that they may enter and possess the land I swore to give their fathers.'

Circumcised Hearts

1. What is the hardest class you've ever taken? What were the toughest requirements, and how did you meet them?

Deuteronomy 10:12-22

2. What is God's basic requirement for His people (v. 12)?
3. What does it mean to "circumcise your hearts" (v. 16)? In what ways can we be "stiffnecked"?
4. Who is a "foreigner" in your group or school? How could you show love to that person?
5. Do you fear God and walk in all of His ways whether at home, school, or a sports event? How can you worship Him "with all your heart and all your soul"?

What God Requires

[12] "And now, Israel, what does the LORD your God ask of you except to •fear the LORD your God by walking

---

[a]9:24 Sam, LXX read since He has   [b]10:6 Or from the wells of Bene-jaakan, or from the wells of the Jaakanites

---

His people.
9:22 Taberah. The people complained, and fire destroyed part of the camp (Num. 11:1-3). **Massah.** Moses struck the rock to get water for the discontented people (Ex. 17: 6-7). **Kibroth-hattaavah.** The people craved other foods and made themselves

sick on quail (Num. 11:33-34).
10:6 Eleazar. Aaron's two older sons died when they administered their duties inappropriately (Lev. 10:1-2).
10:8 carry. Only certain people were to carry the ark. There were rings on each side so that poles could be inserted without any-

one actually touching it (Ex. 25:12-15).
10:9 Levi. The Levites were treated as a distinct class of people. They were not given any land because they received their sustenance from the sacrifices of the people. They were set apart completely to administer God's worship.

in all His ways, to love Him, and to worship the LORD your God with all your heart and all your soul? 13 Keep the LORD's commands and statutes I am giving you today, for your own good. 14 The heavens, indeed the highest heavens, belong to the LORD your God, as does the earth and everything in it. 15 Yet the LORD was devoted to your fathers and loved them. He chose their descendants after them—⌊He chose⌋ you out of all the peoples, as it is today. 16 Therefore, circumcise your hearts and don't be stiff-necked any longer. 17 For the LORD your God is the God of gods and Lord of lords, the great, mighty, and awesome God, showing no partiality and taking no bribe. 18 He executes justice for the fatherless and the widow, and loves the foreign resident, giving him food and clothing. 19 You also must love the foreigner, since you were foreigners in the land of Egypt. 20 You are to fear the LORD your God and worship Him. Remain faithfula to Him and take oaths in His name. 21 He is your praise and He is your God, who has done for you these great and awesome works your eyes have seen. 22 Your fathers went down to Egypt, 70 people in all, and now the LORD your God has made you as numerous as the stars of the sky.

Remember and Obey

11 "Therefore, love the LORD your God and always keep His mandate and His statutes, ordinances, and commands. 2 You must understand today that it is not your children who experienced or saw the discipline of the LORD your God:

His greatness, strong hand, and outstretched arm; 3 His signs and the works He did in Egypt to Pharaoh king of Egypt and all his land; 4 what He did to Egypt's army, its horses and chariots, when He made the waters of the •Red Sea flow over them as they pursued you, and He destroyed them completely;b 5 what He did to you in the wilderness until you reached this place; 6 and what He did to Dathan and Abiram, the sons of Eliab the Reubenite, when in the middle of the whole Israelite ⌊camp⌋ the earth opened its mouth and swallowed them, their households, their tents, and every living thing with them.

7 Your ⌊own⌋ eyes have seen every great work the LORD has done.

8 "Keep every command I am giving you today, so that you may have the strength to cross into and possess the land you are to inherit, 9 and so that you may live long in the land the LORD swore to your fathers to give them and their descendants, a land flowing with milk and honey. 10 For the land you are entering to possess is not like the land of Egypt, from which you have come, where you sowed your seed and irrigated by handc as in a vegetable garden. 11 But the land you are entering to possess is a land of mountains and valleys, watered by rain from the sky. 12 It is a land the LORD your God cares for. He is always watching over it from the beginning to the end of the year.

13 "If you carefully obey My commands I am giving you today, to love the LORD your God and worship Him with all your heart and all your soul, 14 Id will provide rain for your land in season, the early and late rains, and you will harvest your grain, new wine, and oil. 15 Id will provide grass in your fields for your livestock. You will eat and be satisfied. 16 Be careful that you are not enticed to turn aside, worship, and bow down to other gods. 17 Then the LORD's anger will burn against you. He will close the sky, and there will be no rain; the land will not yield its produce, and you will perish quickly from the good land the LORD is giving you.

18 "Impress these words of Mine on your hearts and souls, bind them as a sign on your hands, and let them be a symbole on your foreheads.f 19 Teach them to your children, talking about them when you sit in your house and when you walk along the road, when you lie down and when you get up. 20 Write them on the doorposts of your house and on your gates, 21 so that as long as the heavens are above the earth, your days and those of your children may be many in the land the LORD swore to give your fathers. 22 For if you carefully observe every one of these commands I am giving you to follow—to love the LORD your God, walk in all His ways, and remain faithfulg to Him— 23 the LORD will drive out all these nations before you, and you will drive out nations greater and stronger than you are. 24 Every place the sole of your foot treads will be yours. Your territory will extend from the wilderness to Lebanon and from the Euphrates Riverh to the Mediterranean Sea. 25 No one will be able to stand against you; the LORD your God will put fear and dread of you in all the land where you set foot, as He has promised you.

A Blessing and a Curse

26 "Look, today I set before you a blessing and a curse: 27 ⌊there will be⌋ a blessing, if you obey the commands of the LORD your God I am giving you today, 28 and a curse, if you do not obey the commands of the LORD your God, and you turn aside from the path I command you today by following other gods you have not

---

a10:20 Lit Hold on b11:4 Lit to this day c11:10 Lit foot d11:14,15 DSS, Sam, LXX read He e11:18 Or phylactery; Mt 23:5 f11:18 Lit symbol between your eyes; Dt 6:8; Ex 13:16 g11:22 Lit and hold on h11:24 Some Hb mss, LXX, Tg, Vg read the great river, the river Euphrates

---

10:12 And now. Moses had reviewed the history and was ready to answer the question, "Now what?" He called for the people to be totally committed to God. He was preparing the people to receive their inheritance and live in a manner worthy of it.

10:16 circumcise your hearts. Hebrew men were "marked" with God's ownership (Gen. 17:10-14). To circumcise their hearts would be to mark their hearts as owned by God (Deut. 30:6, Jer. 4:4; Rom. 2:29).

11:13 heart ... soul. See 6:4-5.

11:14 rain. The irrigation system in Egypt was man-made (v. 10), but in Israel God would control the rains.

11:16-17 other gods. The Canaanites believed that their gods controlled the rain.

11:18-20 talking about them. Moses expected that God's ways and instructions would be a daily topic of conversation (see 6:20).

known. 29 When the LORD your God brings you into the land you are entering to possess, you are to proclaim the blessing at Mount Gerizim and the curse at Mount Ebal. 30 Aren't these mountains across the Jordan, beyond the western road in the land of the Canaanites, who live in the •Arabah, opposite Gilgal, near the oaks[a] of Moreh? 31 For you are about to cross the Jordan to enter and take possession of the land the LORD your God is giving you. When you possess it and settle in it, 32 be careful to follow all the statutes and ordinances I set before you today.

The Chosen Place of Worship

12 "Be careful to follow these statutes and ordinances in the land that the LORD, the God of your fathers, has given you to possess all the days you live on the earth. 2 Destroy completely all the places where the nations you are driving out worship their gods—on the high mountains, on the hills, and under every flourishing tree. 3 Tear down their altars, smash their sacred pillars, burn up their •Asherah poles, cut down the carved images of their gods, and wipe out their names from every[b] place. 4 Don't worship the LORD your God this way. 5 Instead, you must go to the place the LORD your God chooses from all your tribes to put His name for His dwelling. 6 You are to bring there your •burnt offerings and sacrifices, your tenths and personal contributions,[c] your vow offerings and freewill offerings, and the firstborn of your herds and flocks. 7 You will eat there in the presence of the LORD your God and rejoice with your household in everything you do,[d] because the LORD your God has blessed you.

8 "You are not to do as we are doing here today; everyone ⌊is doing⌋ whatever seems right in his own eyes. 9 Indeed, you have not yet come into the resting place and the inheritance the LORD your God is giving you. 10 When you cross the Jordan and live in the land the LORD your God is giving you to inherit, and He gives you rest from all the enemies around you and you live in security, 11 then the LORD your God will choose the place to have His name dwell. Bring there everything I command you: your burnt offerings, sacrifices, offerings of the tenth, personal contributions,[e] and all your choice offerings you vow to the LORD. 12 You will rejoice before the LORD your God—you, your sons and daughters, your male and female slaves, and the Levite who is within your gates, since he has no portion or inheritance among you. 13 Be careful not to offer your burnt offerings in all the ⌊sacred⌋ places you see. 14 You

must offer your burnt offerings only in the place the LORD chooses in one of your tribes, and there you must do everything I command you.

Slaughtering Animals to Eat

15 "But whenever you want, you may slaughter and eat meat within any of your gates, according to the blessing the LORD your God has given you. Those who are clean or unclean may eat it, as they would a gazelle or deer, 16 but you must not eat the blood; pour it on the ground like water. 17 Within your gates you may not eat: the tenth of your grain, new wine, or oil; the first-born of your herd or flock; any of your vow offerings that you pledge; your freewill offerings; or your personal contributions.[f] 18 You must eat them in the presence of the LORD your God at the place the LORD your God chooses—you, your son and daughter, your male and female slave, and the Levite who is within your gates. Rejoice before the LORD your God in everything you do,[d] 19 and be careful not to neglect the Levite, as long as you live in your land.

20 "When the LORD your God enlarges your territory as He has promised you, and you say, 'I want to eat meat' because you have a strong desire to eat meat, you may eat it whenever you want. 21 If the place where the LORD your God chooses to put His name is too far from you, you may slaughter any of your herd or flock He has given you, as I have commanded you, and you may eat it within your gates whenever you want. 22 Indeed, you may eat it as the gazelle and deer are eaten; both the clean and the unclean may eat it. 23 But don't eat the blood, since the blood is the life, and you must not eat the life with the meat. 24 Do not eat blood; pour it on the ground like water. 25 Do not eat it, so that you and your children after you will prosper, because you will be doing what is right in the LORD's sight.

26 "But you are to take the holy offerings you have and your vow offerings and go to the place the LORD chooses. 27 Present the meat and blood of your burnt offerings on the altar of the LORD your God. The blood of your ⌊other⌋ sacrifices is to be poured out beside the altar of the LORD your God, but you may eat the meat. 28 Be careful to obey all these things I command you, so that you and your children after you may prosper forever, because you will be doing what is good and right in the sight of the LORD your God.

29 "When the LORD your God annihilates the nations before you, which you are entering to take possession of, and you drive them out and live in their land, 30 be careful not to be ensnared by their ways after they have

---

a 11:30 Sam, LXX, Syr, Aq, Sym read oak; Gn 12:6   b 12:3 Lit that   c 12:6 Lit and the contributions from your hands   d 12:7,18 Lit you put your hand to   e 12:11 Lit tenth, the contributions from your hands   f 12:17 Lit or the contributions from your hands

---

11:22-23 if you carefully observe ... the LORD will drive out. The people's relationship to God and their success in the land were deeply connected.

11:25 fear and dread. Rahab confirmed this (Josh. 2:8-10).

12:3 Tear down ... smash ... burn ... cut

down ... wipe out. It was very clear that the Hebrews were to allow no idol worship in the land. (7:5-6).

12:4 Don't worship the LORD your God this way. God forbade not only worshiping other gods, but even worshiping Him through statues and images.

12:5 to put His name. This referred to the place where the tabernacle would reside. Names were more symbolic in ancient days. God's name was His presence.

12:8 everyone [is doing] whatever seems right. In the wilderness and earlier, God had permitted altars to be built in many places,

been destroyed before you. Do not inquire about their gods, asking, 'How did these nations worship their gods? I'll also do the same.' 31 You must not do the same to the LORD your God, because they practice for their gods every detestable thing the LORD hates. They even burn their sons and daughters in the fire to their gods. 32a You must be careful to do everything I command you; do not add anything to it or take anything away from it.

The False Prophet

13 "If a prophet or someone who has dreams arises among you and proclaims a sign or wonder to you, 2 and that sign or wonder he has promised you comes about, but he says, 'Let us follow other gods,' which you have not known, 'and let us worship them,' 3 do not listen to that prophet's words or to that dreamer. For the LORD your God is testing you to know whether you love the LORD your God with all your heart and all your soul. 4 You must follow the LORD your God and •fear Him. You must keep His commands and listen to His voice; you must worship Him and remain faithfulb to Him. 5 That prophet or dreamer must be put to death, because he has urged rebellion against the LORD your God who brought you out of the land of Egypt and redeemed you from the place of slavery, to turn you from the way the LORD your God has commanded you to walk. You must purge the evil from you.

Don't Tolerate Idolatry

6 "If your brother, the son of your mother,c or your son or daughter, or the wife you embrace, or your closest friend secretly entices you, saying, 'Let us go and worship other gods'—which neither you nor your fathers have known, 7 any of the gods of the peoples around you, near you or far from you, from one end of the earth to the other— 8 you must not yield to him or listen to him. Show him no pity,d and do not spare ⌊him⌋ or shield him. 9 Instead, you must kill him. Your hand is to be the first against him to put him to death, and then the hands of all the people. 10 Stone him to death for trying to turn you away from the LORD your God who brought you out of the land of Egypt, out of the place of slavery. 11 All Israel will hear and be afraid, and they will no longer do anything evil like this among you.

12 "If you hear it said about one of your cities the LORD your God is giving you to live in, 13 that •wicked men have sprung up among you, led the inhabitants of their city astray, and said, 'Let us go and worship other gods,' which you have not known, 14 you are to inquire, investigate, and interrogate thoroughly. If the report turns out to be true that this detestable thing has happened among you, 15 you must strike down the inhabitants of that city with the sword. •Completely destroy everyone in it as well as its livestock with the sword. 16 You are to gather all its spoil in the middle of the city square and completely burn up the city and all its spoil for the LORD your God. The city must remain a mound of ruins forever; it is not to be rebuilt. 17 Nothing •set apart for destruction is to remain in your hand, so that the LORD will turn from His burning anger and grant you mercy, show you compassion, and multiply you as He swore to your fathers. 18 This ⌊will occur⌋ if you obey the LORD your God, keeping all His commands I am giving you today, doing what is right in the sight of the LORD your God.

Forbidden Practices

14 "You are sons of the LORD your God; do not cut yourselves or make a bald spot on your heade on behalf of the dead, 2 for you are a holy people belonging to the LORD your God. The LORD has chosen you to be His special people out of all the peoples on the face of the earth.

Clean and Unclean Foods

3 "You must not eat any detestable thing. 4 These are the animals you may eat:

> the ox, the sheep, the goat,
> 5   the deer, the gazelle, the roe deer,
>   the wild goat, the ibex, the antelope,
>   and the mountain sheep.

6 You may eat any animal that has hooves divided in two and chews the cud. 7 But among the ones that chew the cud or have divided hooves, you are not to eat these:

> the camel, the hare, and the hyrax,
> though they chew the cud, they do not
>   have hooves—
> they are unclean for you;
> 8   and the pig, though it has hooves, it does not
>   ⌊chew⌋ the cud—
>   it is unclean for you.

You must not eat their meat or touch their carcasses.

9 "You may eat everything from the water that has fins and scales, 10 but you may not eat anything that does not have fins and scales—it is unclean for you.

---

a 12:32 Dt 13:1 in Hb   b 13:4 Lit and hold on   c 13:6 DSS, Sam, LXX read If the son of your father or the son of your mother   d 13:8 Lit Your eye must not pity him   e 14:1 Or forehead

---

but once in the land, God would only have one altar.

12:9 resting place. The writer of Hebrews encouraged his readers to continue toward God's "rest"—a life of peace and faith.

12:12 rejoice. The church today sometimes treats worship as a solemn event. Certainly in

these ancient days there was a solemnity to the sacrifices and yet great joy when God was worshiped.

13:3 testing. To see miracles performed in the name of another god was a test of faith for the people.

13:5 he has urged rebellion. The prophet's

encouragement to worship other gods, coupled with his power to astonish the people, made him a dangerous man.

14:1 cut yourselves. This was an ancient custom of idol worship (1 Kings 18:28). **make a bald spot.** This was a way pagan priests marked themselves.

11 "You may eat every clean bird, 12 but these are the ones you may not eat:

the eagle, the bearded vulture,
the black vulture, 13 the kite,
the various kinds of falcon,[a]
14 every kind of raven, 15 the ostrich,
the short-eared owl, the gull,
the various kinds of hawk,
16 the little owl, the long-eared owl,
the white owl, 17 the desert owl,
the osprey, the cormorant, 18 the stork,
the various kinds of heron,
the hoopoe, and the bat.[b]

19 All winged insects are unclean for you; they may not be eaten. 20 But you may eat every clean flying creature.

21 "You are not to eat any carcass; you may give it to a resident alien within your gates, and he may eat it, or you may sell it to a foreigner. For you are a holy people belonging to the LORD your God. You must not boil a young goat in its mother's milk.

A Tenth for the LORD

22 "Each year you are to set aside a tenth of all the produce grown in your fields. 23 You are to eat a tenth of your grain, new wine, and oil, and the firstborn of your herd and flock, in the presence of the LORD your God at the place where He chooses to have His name dwell, so that you will always learn to •fear the LORD your God. 24 But if the distance is too great for you to carry it, since the place where the LORD your God chooses to put His name is too far away from you and since the LORD your God has blessed you, 25 then exchange it for money, take the money in your hand, and go to the place the LORD your God chooses. 26 You may spend the money on anything you want: cattle, sheep, wine, beer, or anything you desire. You are to feast there in the presence of the LORD your God and rejoice with your family. 27 Do not forget the Levite within your gates, since he has no portion or inheritance among you.

28 "At the end of ⌊every⌋ three years, bring a tenth of all your produce for that year and store ⌊it⌋ within your gates. 29 Then the Levite, who has no portion or inheritance among you, the foreign resident, fatherless, and widow within your gates may come, eat, and be satisfied. And the LORD your God will bless you in all the work of your hands that you do.

Debts Canceled

15 "At the end of ⌊every⌋ seven years you must cancel debts. 2 This is how to cancel debt: Every creditor[c] is to cancel what he has lent his neighbor. He is not to collect ⌊anything⌋ from his neighbor or brother, because the LORD's release of debts has been proclaimed. 3 You may collect ⌊something⌋ from a foreigner, but you must forgive whatever your brother owes you.

4 "There will be no poor among you, however, because the LORD is certain to bless you in the land the LORD your God is giving you to possess as an inheritance— 5 if only you obey the LORD your God and are careful to follow every one of these commands I am giving you today. 6 When the LORD your God blesses you as He has promised you, you will lend to many nations but not borrow; you will rule over many nations, but they will not rule over you.

Lending to the Poor

7 "If there is a poor person among you, one of your brothers within any of your gates in the land the LORD your God is giving you, you must not be hardhearted or tightfisted toward your poor brother. 8 Instead, you are to open your hand to him and freely loan him enough for whatever need he has. 9 Be careful that there isn't this wicked thought in your heart, 'The seventh year, the year of canceling debts, is near,' and you are stingy toward your poor brother and give him ⌊nothing⌋. He will cry out to the LORD against you, and you will be guilty. 10 Give to him, and don't have a stingy heart[d] when you give, and because of this the LORD your God will bless you in all your work and in everything you do.[e] 11 For there will never cease to be poor people in the land; that is why I am commanding you, 'You must willingly open your hand to your afflicted and poor brother in your land.'

Release of Slaves

12 "If your fellow Hebrew, a man or woman, is sold to you and serves you six years, you must set him free in the seventh year. 13 When you set him free, do not send him away empty-handed. 14 Give generously to him from your flock, your threshing floor, and your winepress. You are to give him whatever the LORD your God has blessed you with. 15 Remember that you were a slave in the land of Egypt and the LORD your God redeemed you; that is why I am giving you this command today. 16 But if your slave says to you, 'I don't want to leave you,' because he loves you and your

---

a**14:13** Some Hb mss, Sam, LXX; other Hb mss, Vg read *the falcon, the various kinds of kite*   b**14:5–18** The identification of some of these birds or animals is uncertain.   c**15:2** Lit *owner of a loan of his hand*   d**15:10** Lit *and let not your heart be grudging*   e**15:10** Lit *you put your hand to*

14:2 special people. God chose Israel to reveal Himself to the world. The Bible and the Messiah came from Israel (Rom. 9:4-5). God still has plans to restore and save Israel (Rom. 11:26).

14:3-21 The diet of the Hebrews set them apart from other nations. Keeping kosher was

an act of faith and obedience, and a mark of God's ownership.

14:21 carcass. This involved the prohibition on eating blood. When the animals were prepared properly, their blood was drained.

14:22-29 tenth. Also called a tithe, it provided for the priests and the community. It was an

act of faith on the part of the giver that God was the source of provision.

14:23 the place where He chooses to have His name dwell. The tabernacle and later the temple.

15:3 foreigner. Israelites had to let their crops lie fallow every seventh year, so all pay-

family, and is well off with you, [17] take an awl and pierce through his ear into the door, and he will become your slave for life. Also treat your female slave the same way. [18] Do not regard it as a hardship[a] when you set him free, because he worked for you six years— worth twice the wages of a hired hand. Then the LORD your God will bless you in everything you do.

Consecration of Firstborn Animals

[19] "You must consecrate to the LORD your God every firstborn male produced by your herd and flock. You are not to put the firstborn of your oxen to work or shear the firstborn of your flock. [20] Each year you and your family are to eat it before the LORD your God in the place the LORD chooses. [21] But if there is a defect in the animal, if it is lame or blind or has any serious defect, you must not sacrifice it to the LORD your God. [22] Eat it within your gates; both the unclean person and the clean ⌊may eat it⌋, as though it were a gazelle or deer. [23] But you must not eat its blood; pour it on the ground like water.

The Festival of Passover

16 "Observe the month of Abib[b] and celebrate the •Passover to the LORD your God, because the LORD your God brought you out of Egypt by night in the month of Abib. [2] Sacrifice to the LORD your God a Passover animal from the herd or flock in the place where the LORD chooses to have His name dwell. [3] You must not eat leavened bread with it. For seven days you are to eat unleavened bread with it, the bread of hardship—because you left the land of Egypt in a hurry—so that you may remember for the rest of your life the day you left the land of Egypt. [4] No yeast is to be found anywhere in your territory for seven days, and none of the meat you sacrifice in the evening of the first day is to remain until morning. [5] You are not to sacrifice the Passover animal in any of the towns the LORD your God is giving you. [6] You must only sacrifice the Passover animal at the place where the LORD your God chooses to have His name dwell. ⌊Do this⌋ in the evening as the sun sets at the ⌊same⌋ time ⌊of day⌋ you departed from Egypt. [7] You are to cook and eat ⌊it⌋ in the place the LORD your God chooses, and you are to return to your tents in the morning. [8] You must eat unleavened bread for six days. On the seventh day there is to be a solemn assembly to the LORD your God, and you must not do any work.

The Festival of Weeks

[9] "You are to count seven weeks, counting the weeks from the time the sickle is first ⌊put⌋ to the standing grain. [10] You are to celebrate the Festival of Weeks to the LORD your God with a freewill offering that you give in proportion to how the LORD your God has blessed you. [11] Rejoice before the LORD your God in the place where He chooses to have His name dwell—you, your son and daughter, your male and female slave, the Levite within your gates, as well as the foreign resident, the fatherless, and the widow among you. [12] Remember that you were slaves in Egypt; carefully follow these statutes.

The Festival of Booths

[13] "You are to celebrate the Festival of Booths for seven days when you have gathered in ⌊everything⌋ from your threshing floor and winepress. [14] Rejoice during your festival—you, your son and daughter, your male and female slave, as well as the Levite, the foreign resident, the fatherless, and the widow within your gates. [15] You are to hold a seven-day festival for the LORD your God in the place He chooses, because the LORD your God will bless you in all your produce and in all the work of your hands, and you will have abundant joy.

[16] "All your males are to appear three times a year before the LORD your God in the place He chooses: at the Festival of •Unleavened Bread, the Festival of Weeks, and the Festival of Booths. No one is to appear before the LORD empty-handed. [17] Everyone ⌊must appear⌋ with a gift suited to his means, according to the blessing the LORD your God has given you.

Appointing Judges and Officials

[18] "Appoint judges and officials for your tribes in all your towns the LORD your God is giving you. They are to judge the people with righteous judgment. [19] Do not deny justice or show partiality ⌊to anyone⌋. Do not accept a bribe, for it blinds the eyes of the wise and twists the words of the righteous. [20] Pursue justice and justice alone, so that you will live and possess the land the LORD your God is giving you.

Forbidden Worship

[21] "Do not set up an •Asherah of any kind of wood next to the altar you will build for the LORD your God, [22] and do not set up a sacred pillar; the LORD your God hates them.

17 "You must not sacrifice to the LORD your God an ox or sheep with a defect or any serious flaw, for that is detestable to the LORD your God.

The Judicial Procedure for Idolatry

[2] "If a man or woman among you in one of your towns that the LORD your God will give you is discov-

---

[a] **15:18** Lit *Let it not be hard in your sight*   [b] **16:1** March–April; called Nisan in the post-exilic period; Neh 2:1; Est 3:7

---

ments on debts were suspended. Since a foreigner would not have done this, he could continue to make payments on his debts.
15:4 no poor among you. If the people obeyed, their land would produce wealth, and there would not have been poverty.
15:11 there will never cease to be poor

people. Jesus made this same statement (Matt. 26:11). This does not contradict v. 4, which was the ideal if people obeyed (1 John 2:1).

15:19 firstborn. The first and best always belonged to God as a reminder that everything ultimately is His.

15:21 defect. Some people offered animals that were imperfect and unusable (Mal. 1:14).
16:6 Passover. This feast commemorated the last plague in Egypt (death of the firstborn). Jesus celebrated Passover at the Last Supper.
16:9 seven weeks. This was also called the

ered doing evil in the sight of the LORD your God and violating His covenant ³ and has gone to worship other gods by bowing down to the sun, moon, or all the stars in the sky—which I have forbidden— ⁴ and if you are told or hear ⌊about it⌋, you must investigate it thoroughly. If the report turns out to be true that this detestable thing has happened in Israel, ⁵ you must bring out to your •gates that man or woman who has done this evil thing and stone them to death. ⁶ The one condemned to die is to be executed on the testimony of two or three witnesses. No one is to be executed on the testimony of a single witness. ⁷ The witnesses' hands are to be the first in putting him to death, and after that, the hands of all the people. You must purge the evil from you.

Difficult Cases

⁸ "If a case is too difficult for you—concerning bloodshed, lawsuits, or assaults—cases disputed at your gates, you must go up to the place the LORD your God chooses. ⁹ You are to go to the Levitical priests and to the judge who presides at that time. Ask, and they will give you a verdict in the case. ¹⁰ You must abide by the verdict they give you at the place the LORD chooses. Be careful to do exactly as they instruct you. ¹¹ You must abide by the instruction they give you and the verdict they announce to you. Do not turn to the right or the left from the decision they declare to you. ¹² The person who acts arrogantly, refusing to listen either to the priest who stands there serving the LORD your God or to the judge, must die. You must purge the evil from Israel. ¹³ Then all the people will hear ⌊about it⌋, be afraid, and no longer behave arrogantly.

Appointing a King

¹⁴ "When you enter the land the LORD your God is giving you, take possession of it, live in it, and say, 'We want to appoint a king over us like all the nations around us,' ¹⁵ you are to appoint over you the king the LORD your God chooses. Appoint a king from your brothers. You are not to set a foreigner over you, or one who is not of your people. ¹⁶ However, he must not acquire many horses for himself or send the people back to Egypt to acquire many horses, for the LORD has told you, 'You are never to go back that way again.' ¹⁷ He must not acquire many wives for himself so that his heart won't go astray. He must not acquire very large amounts of silver and gold for himself. ¹⁸ When he is seated on his royal throne, he is to write a copy of this instruction for himself on a scroll in the presence of the

Levitical priests. ¹⁹ It is to remain with him, and he is to read from it all the days of his life, so that he may learn to •fear the LORD his God, to observe all the words of this instruction, and to do these statutes. ²⁰ Then his heart will not be exalted above his countrymen, he will not turn from this command to the right or the left, and he and his sons will continue ruling many yearsᵃ over Israel.

Provisions for the Levites

18 "The Levitical priests, the whole tribe of Levi, will have no portion or inheritance with Israel. They will eat the LORD's fire offerings; that is theirᵇ ᶜ inheritance. ² Although Levi has no inheritance among his brothers, the LORD is his inheritance, as He promised him. ³ This is the priests' share from the people who offer a sacrifice, whether it is an ox, a sheep, or a goat; the priests are to be given the shoulder, jaws, and stomach. ⁴ You are to give him the •firstfruits of your grain, new wine, and oil, and the first sheared ⌊wool⌋ of your flock. ⁵ For the LORD your God has chosen him and his sons from all your tribes to stand and minister in the LORD's name from now on.ᵈ ⁶ When a Levite leaves one of your towns where he lives in Israel and wants to go to the place the LORD chooses, ⁷ he may serve in the name of the LORD his God like all his fellow Levites who minister there in the presence of the LORD. ⁸ They will eat equal portions besides what he has received from the sale of the family estate.ᵉ

Occult Practices versus Prophetic Revelation

⁹ "When you enter the land the LORD your God is giving you, do not imitate the detestable customs of those nations. ¹⁰ No one among you is to make his son or daughter pass through the fire,ᶠ practice •divination, tell fortunes, interpret omens, practice sorcery, ¹¹ cast spells, consult a medium or a familiar spirit, or inquire of the dead. ¹² Everyone who does these things is detestable to the LORD, and the LORD your God is driving out the nations before you because of these detestable things. ¹³ You must be blameless before the LORD your God. ¹⁴ Though these nations you are about to drive out listen to fortune-tellers and diviners, the LORD your God has not permitted you to do this.

¹⁵ "The LORD your God will raise up for you a prophet like me from among your own brothers. You must listen to him. ¹⁶ This is what you requested from the LORD your God at Horeb on the day of the assembly when you said, 'Let us not continue to hear the voice of the LORD our God or see this great fire any longer, so

---

ᵃ**17:20** Lit *will lengthen days on his kingdom*   ᵇ**18:1** LXX; MT reads *his*   ᶜ**18:1** Or *His*   ᵈ**18:5** Lit *name all the days*   ᵉ**18:8** Hb obscure
ᶠ**18:10** Either a Canaanite cult practice or child sacrifice

---

Feast of the Harvest and later Pentecost (*pent* refers to the 50 days in the seven weeks). This was being celebrated when the Holy Spirit came (Acts 2:1-4).
16:13-15 Festival of Booths. The people camped out to commemorate the journey through the desert.

17:1 defect or any serious flaw. Jesus was the "lamb without defect or blemish" (1 Pet. 1:19).
17:3 sun, moon, or all the stars. God warned the people about worshiping creation over the Creator (4:19). The Israelites began this pagan practice in Egypt and often fell

back into it (2 Kings 17:16; 21:3-5).
17:7 The witnesses' hands. Perjury would be a much different experience if a lying witness had to participate in putting the accused to death.
17:14 like all the nations. God was not against a king but against them wanting one

that we will not die!' 17 Then the LORD said to me, 'They have spoken well. 18 I will raise up for them a prophet like you from among their brothers. I will put My words in his mouth, and he will tell them everything I command him. 19 I will hold accountable whoever does not listen to My words that he speaks in My name. 20 But the prophet who dares to speak in My name a message I have not commanded him to speak, or who speaks in the name of other gods—that prophet must die.' 21 You may say to yourself, 'How can we recognize a message the LORD has not spoken?' 22 When a prophet speaks in the LORD's name, and the message does not come true or is not fulfilled, that is a message the LORD has not spoken. The prophet has spoken it presumptuously. Do not be afraid of him.

Cities of Refuge

19 "When the LORD your God annihilates the nations whose land He is giving you, so that you drive them out and live in their cities and houses, 2 you are to set apart three cities for yourselves within the land the LORD your God is giving you to possess. 3 You are to determine the distances[a] and divide the land the LORD your God is granting you as an inheritance into three regions, so that anyone who commits manslaughter can flee to these cities.[b]

4 "Here is the law concerning a case of someone who kills a person and flees there to save his life, having killed his neighbor accidentally without previously hating him: 5 If he goes into the forest with his neighbor to cut timber, and his hand swings the ax to chop down a tree, but the blade flies off the handle and strikes his neighbor so that he dies, that person may flee to one of these cities and live. 6 Otherwise, the avenger of blood in the heat of his anger[c] might pursue the one who committed manslaughter, overtake him because the distance is great, and strike him dead. Yet he did not deserve to die,[d] since he did not previously hate his neighbor. 7 This is why I am commanding you to set apart three cities for yourselves. 8 If the LORD your God enlarges your territory as He swore to your fathers, and gives you all the land He promised to give them— 9 provided you keep every one of these commands I am giving you today and follow them, loving the LORD your God and walking in His ways at all times—you are to add three more cities to these three. 10 In this way, innocent blood will not be shed, and you will not become guilty of bloodshed in the land the LORD your God is giving you as an inheritance. 11 But if someone hates his neighbor, lies in ambush for him, attacks him,

and strikes him fatally, and flees to one of these cities, 12 the elders of his city must send ⌊for him⌋, take him from there, and hand him over to the avenger of blood and he will die. 13 You must not look on him with pity but purge from Israel the guilt of shedding innocent blood, and you will prosper.

Boundary Markers

14 "You must not move your neighbor's boundary marker, established at the start in the inheritance you will receive in the land the LORD your God is giving you to possess.

Witnesses in Court

15 "One witness cannot establish any wrongdoing or sin against a person, whatever that person has done. A fact must be established by the testimony of two or three witnesses.

16 "If a malicious witness testifies against someone accusing him of a crime, 17 the two people in the dispute must stand in the presence of the LORD before the priests and judges in authority at the time. 18 The judges are to make a careful investigation, and if the witness turns out to be a liar who has falsely accused his brother, 19 you must do to him as he intended to do to his brother. You must purge the evil from you. 20 Then everyone else will hear and be afraid, and they will never again do anything evil like this among you. 21 You must not show pity: life for life, eye for eye, tooth for tooth, hand for hand, and foot for foot.

Rules for War

20 "When you go out to war against your enemies and see horses, chariots, and an army larger than yours, do not be afraid of them, for the LORD your God, who brought you out of the land of Egypt, is with you. 2 When you are about to engage in battle, the priest is to come forward and address the army. 3 He is to say to them: 'Listen, Israel: Today you are about to engage in battle with your enemies. Do not be fainthearted. Do not be afraid, alarmed, or terrified because of them. 4 For the LORD your God is the One who goes with you to fight for you against your enemies to give you victory.'

5 "The officers are to address the army, 'Has any man built a new house and not dedicated it? Let him leave and return home. Otherwise, he may die in battle and another man dedicate it. 6 Has any man planted a vineyard and not begun to enjoy its fruit?[e] Let him leave and return home. Otherwise he may die in battle and another man enjoy its fruit.[f] 7 Has any man become

---

[a] **19:3** Or to prepare the roads [b] **19:3** Lit flee there [c] **19:6** Lit heart [d] **19:6** Lit did not have a judgment of death [e] **20:6** Lit not put it to use
[f] **20:6** Lit man put it to use

---

for the wrong reasons. Later, the people asked for a king who could raise an army to protect them, instead of relying on God their ultimate King (1 Sam. 8:5).

17:16 must not acquire. To assure that his people remained dependent upon God, they were instructed to not upgrade their military.

18:10 make his son or daughter pass through the fire. People who practice these things think that God is hidden and must be found by strange devices. Paul said that God "is not far from each one of us" (Acts 17:27).

18:21 How can we recognize. We must search the Bible to see if things people say

about God are true (Acts 17:11).

19:14 boundary marker. These were like a surveyor's stake. A person might move them secretly, but God knows all secrets.

19:15 two or three witnesses. By requiring more than one witness, God protected the accused from a false claim.

•engaged to a woman and not married her? Let him leave and return home. Otherwise he may die in battle and another man marry her.' ⁸ The officers will continue to address the army and say, 'Is there any man who is afraid or fainthearted? Let him leave and return home, so that his brothers' hearts won't melt like his own.' ⁹ When the officers have finished addressing the army, they will appoint military commanders to lead it.

¹⁰ "When you approach a city to fight against it, you must make an offer of peace. ¹¹ If it accepts your offer of peace and opens ⌊its gates⌋ to you, all the people found in it will become forced laborers for you and serve you. ¹² However, if it does not make peace with you but wages war against you, lay siege to it. ¹³ When the LORD your God hands it over to you, you must strike down all its males with the sword. ¹⁴ But you may take the women, children, animals, and whatever else is in the city—all its spoil—as plunder. You may enjoy the spoil of your enemies that the LORD your God has given you. ¹⁵ This is how you are to treat all the cities that are far away from you and are not among the cities of these nations. ¹⁶ However, you must not let any living thing survive among the cities of these people the LORD your God is giving you as an inheritance. ¹⁷ You must •completely destroy them—the Hittite, Amorite, Canaanite, Perizzite, Hivite, and Jebusite—as the LORD your God has commanded you, ¹⁸ so that they won't teach you to do all the detestable things they do for their gods, and you sin against the LORD your God.

¹⁹ "When you lay siege to a city for a long time, fighting against it in order to capture it, you must not destroy its trees by putting an ax to them, because you can get food from them. You must not cut them down. Are trees of the field human, to come under siege by you? ²⁰ But you may destroy the trees that you know do not produce food. You may cut them down to build siege works against the city that is waging war with you, until it falls.

Unsolved Murders

21 "If a murder victim is found lying in a field in the land the LORD your God is giving you to possess, and it is not known who killed him, ² your elders and judges must come out and measure ⌊the distance⌋ from the victim to the nearby cities. ³ The elders of the city nearest to the victim are to get a cow that has not been yoked or used for work. ⁴ The elders of that city will bring the cow down to a continually flowing stream, to a place not tilled or sown, and they will break the cow's neck there by the stream. ⁵ Then the priests, the sons of Levi, will come forward, for the

LORD your God has chosen them to serve Him and pronounce blessings in the LORD's name, and they are to give a ruling inª every dispute and ⌊case of⌋ assault. ⁶ All the elders of the city nearest to the victim will wash their hands by the stream over the heifer whose neck has been broken. ⁷ They will declare, 'Our hands did not shed this blood; our eyes did not see ⌊it⌋. ⁸ LORD, forgive Your people Israel You redeemed, and do not hold the shedding of innocent blood against them.' Then they will be absolved of responsibility for bloodshed. ⁹ You must purge from yourselves the guilt of shedding innocent blood, for you will be doing what is right in the LORD's sight.

Fair Treatment of Captured Women

¹⁰ "When you go to war against your enemies and the LORD your God hands them over to you and you take some of them prisoner, and ¹¹ if you see a beautiful woman among the captives, desire her, and want to take her as your wife, ¹² you are to bring her into your house. She must shave her head, trim her nails, ¹³ remove the clothes she was wearing when she was taken prisoner, live in your house, and mourn for her father and mother a full month. After that, you may have sexual relations with her and be her husband, and she will be your wife. ¹⁴ Then if you are not satisfied with her, you are to let her go where she wants, but you must not sell her for money or treat her as merchandise,ᵇ because you have humiliated her.

The Right of the Firstborn

¹⁵ "If a man has two wives, one loved and the other unloved, and both the loved and the unloved bear him sons, and if the unloved wife has the firstborn son, ¹⁶ when that man gives what he has to his sons as an inheritance, he is not to show favoritism to the son of the loved ⌊wife⌋ as his firstborn over the firstborn of the unloved wife. ¹⁷ He must acknowledge the firstborn, the son of the unloved wife, by giving him a double portion of everything that belongs to him, for he is the firstfruits of his virility; he has the rights of the firstborn.

A Rebellious Son

¹⁸ "If a man has a stubborn and rebellious son who does not obey his father or mother and doesn't listen to them even after they discipline him, ¹⁹ his father and mother must take hold of him and bring him to the elders of his city, to the •gate of his hometown. ²⁰ They will say to the elders of his city, 'This son of ours is stubborn and rebellious; he doesn't obey us. He's a glutton and a drunkard.' ²¹ Then all the men of his city will

---

ª**21:5** Lit and according to their mouth will be   ᵇ**21:14** Hb obscure

---

19:21 life for life. This law of retaliation limited vengeance by the victim and prevented cruel and unusual punishment by the judge. Though it may seem harsh, it reveals the goodness of God in protecting His people. Jesus rebuked the misuse of this law and the lack of mercy (Matt. 5:38-42).

20:10-15 a city. There were two sets of rules of engagement, one for taking the Promised Land and another for fighting neighbors. This refers to the latter.

20:11 serve you. Noah prophesied that Canaan would serve Shem (Gen. 9:25-26).

21:6 wash their hands. By this action they

claim to be innocent. Pilate intended the same message regarding Christ's death (Matt. 27:24).

21:10-11 against your enemies. These are enemies outside Canaan (20:14-16).

21:12 shave her head. This act symbolizes mourning, humiliation, and leaving an old way

stone him to death. You must purge the evil from you, and all Israel will hear and be afraid.

Display of Executed People

22 "If anyone is found guilty of an offense deserving the death penalty and is executed, and you hang his body on a tree, 23 you are not to leave his corpse on the tree overnight but are to bury him that day, for anyone hung ⌊on a tree⌋ is under God's curse. You must not defile the land the LORD your God is giving you as an inheritance.

Caring for Your Brother's Property

22 "If you see your brother's ox or sheep straying, you must not ignore it; make sure you return it to your brother. 2 If your brother does not live near you or you don't know him, you are to bring the animal to your home to remain with you until your brother comes looking for it; then you can return it to him. 3 Do the same for his donkey, his garment, or anything your brother has lost and you have found. You must not ignore ⌊it⌋. 4 If you see your brother's donkey or ox fallen down on the road, you must not ignore it; you must help him lift it up.

Preserving Natural Distinctions

5 "A woman is not to wear male clothing, and a man is not to put on a woman's garment, for everyone who does these things is detestable to the LORD your God.

6 "If you come across a bird's nest with chicks or eggs, either in a tree or on the ground along the road, and the mother is sitting on the chicks or eggs, you must not take the mother along with the young. 7 You may take the young for yourself, but be sure to let the mother go free, so that you may prosper and live long. 8 If you build a new house, make a railing around your roof, so that you don't bring bloodguilt on your house if someone falls from it. 9 Do not plant your vineyard with two types of seed; otherwise, the entire harvest, both the crop you plant and the produce of the vineyard, will be defiled. 10 Do not plow with an ox and a donkey together. 11 Do not wear clothes made of both wool and linen. 12 Make tassels on the four corners of the outer garment you wear.

Violations of Proper Sexual Conduct

13 "If a man marries a woman, has sexual relations with her, and comes to hate her, 14 and accuses ⌊her⌋ of shameful conduct, and gives her a bad name, saying, 'I married this woman and was intimate with her, but I didn't find ⌊any⌋ evidence of her virginity,' 15 the young woman's father and mother will take the evidence of her virginity and bring ⌊it⌋ to the city elders at the •gate. 16 The young woman's father will say to the elders, 'I gave my daughter to this man as a wife, but he hates her. 17 He has accused her of shameful conduct, saying: "I didn't find ⌊any⌋ evidence of your daughter's virginity, but here is the evidence of my daughter's virginity.'" They will spread out the cloth before the city elders. 18 Then the elders of that city will take the man and punish him. 19 They will also fine him 100 silver ⌊shekels⌋ and give ⌊them⌋ to the young woman's father, because that man gave an Israelite virgin a bad name. She will remain his wife; he cannot divorce her as long as he lives. 20 But if this accusation is true and no evidence of the young woman's virginity is found, 21 they will bring the woman to the door of her father's house, and the men of her city will stone her to death. For she has committed an outrage in Israel by being promiscuous in her father's house. You must purge the evil from you.

22 "If a man is discovered having sexual relations with ⌊another⌋ man's wife, both the man who had sex with the woman and the woman must die. You must purge the evil from Israel. 23 If there is a young woman who is a virgin •engaged to a man, and ⌊another⌋ man encounters her in the city and has sex with her, 24 you must take the two of them out to the gate of that city and stone them to death—the young woman because she did not cry out in the city and the man because he has violated his neighbor's fiancée. You must purge the evil from you. 25 But if the man encounters the engaged woman in the open country, and he seizes and rapes her, only the man who raped her must die. 26 Do nothing to the young woman, because she is not guilty of an offense deserving death. This case is just like one in which a man attacks his neighbor and murders him. 27 When he found her in the field, the engaged woman cried out, but there was no one to rescue her. 28 If a man encounters a young woman, a virgin who is not engaged, takes hold of her and rapes her, and they are discovered, 29 the man who raped her must give the young woman's father 50 silver ⌊shekels⌋, and she must become his wife because he violated her. He cannot divorce her as long as he lives.

30 "A man is not to marry his father's wife; he must not violate his father's marriage bed.[a] [b]

Exclusion and Inclusion

23 "No man whose ⌊testicles⌋ have been crushed[c] or whose penis has been cut off may enter the LORD's assembly. 2 No one of illegitimate birth may enter the LORD's assembly; none of his descendants,

---

[a]22:30 Dt 23:1 in Hb   [b]22:30 Lit *not uncover the edge of his father's garment*; Ru 3:9; Ezk 16:8   [c]23:1 Lit *man bruised by crushing*

21:14 humiliated. The divorcing husband is to treat his foreign wife with dignity.

21:15 two wives. Though God's original intention was one man and one woman (Gen. 2:23-25), polygamy became common.

21:17 double portion. The first son is to receive a double portion—and thus control over the estate—no matter what the father prefers.

21:18 stubborn and rebellious. This type of son dishonors his parents (5:16) in evil, audacious ways over a long period.

21:19 his father and mother. While elders oversaw the entire community, parents were ultimately responsible for their children.

21:21 stone him to death. See Ex. 21:15,17. **purge the evil**. God intended to protect His people from evil (13:6; 17:7,12; 19:19; 22:21,22,24; 24:7).

21:22 on a tree. The executed person was impaled on a pole (Josh. 10:26; 1 Sam. 31:10).

even to the tenth generation, may enter the LORD's assembly. 3 No Ammonite or Moabite may enter the LORD's assembly; none of their descendants, even to the tenth generation, may ever enter the LORD's assembly. 4 This is because they did not meet you with food and water on the journey after you came out of Egypt, and because Balaam son of Beor from Pethor in Aram-naharaim was hired to curse you. 5 Yet the LORD your God would not listen to Balaam, but He turned the curse into a blessing for you because the LORD your God loves you. 6 Never seek peace or friendship with them as long as you live. 7 Do not despise an Edomite, because he is your brother. Do not despise an Egyptian, because you were a foreign resident in his land. 8 The children born to them in the third generation may enter the LORD's assembly.

Cleanliness of the Camp

9 "When you are encamped against your enemies, be careful to avoid anything offensive. 10 If there is a man among you who is unclean because of a bodily emission during the night, he must go outside the camp; he may not come anywhere inside the camp. 11 When evening approaches, he must wash with water, and when the sun sets he may come inside the camp. 12 You must have a place outside the camp and go there ⌊to relieve yourself⌋. 13 You must have a digging tool in your equipment; when you relieve yourself, dig a hole with it and cover up your excrement. 14 For the LORD your God walks throughout your camp to protect you and deliver your enemies to you; so your encampments must be holy. He must not see anything improper among you or He will turn away from you.

Fugitive Slaves

15 "Do not return a slave to his master when he has escaped from his master to you. 16 Let him live among you wherever he wants within your gates. Do not mistreat him.

Cult Prostitution Forbidden

17 "No Israelite woman is to be a cult prostitute, and no Israelite man is to be a cult prostitute. 18 Do not bring a female prostitute's wages or a male prostitute's[a] earnings into the house of the LORD your God to fulfill any vow, because both are detestable to the LORD your God.

Interest on Loans

19 "Do not charge your brother interest on money, food, or anything that can earn interest. 20 You may charge a foreigner interest, but you must not charge your brother interest, so that the LORD your God may bless you in everything you do[b] in the land you are entering to possess.

Keeping Vows

21 "If you make a vow to the LORD your God, do not be slow to keep it, because He will require it of you, and it will be counted against you as sin. 22 But if you refrain from making a vow, it will not be counted against you as sin. 23 Be careful to do whatever comes from your lips, because you have freely vowed what you promised[c] to the LORD your God.

Neighbor's Crops

24 "When you enter your neighbor's vineyard, you may eat as many grapes as you want until you are full, but you must not put ⌊any⌋ in your container. 25 When you enter your neighbor's standing grain, you may pluck heads of grain with your hand, but you must not put a sickle to your neighbor's grain.

Marriage and Divorce Laws

24 "If a man marries a woman, but she becomes displeasing to him because he finds something improper about her, he may write her a divorce certificate, hand it to her, and send her away from his house. 2 If after leaving his house she goes and becomes another man's wife, 3 and the second man hates her, writes her a divorce certificate, hands it to her, and sends her away from his house or if he[d] dies, 4 the first husband who sent her away may not marry her again after she has been defiled, because that would be detestable to the LORD. You must not bring guilt on the land the LORD your God is giving you as an inheritance.

5 "When a man takes a bride, he must not go out with the army or be liable for any duty. He is free ⌊to stay⌋ at home for one year, so that he can bring joy to the wife he has married.

Safeguarding Life

6 "Do not take a pair of millstones or an upper millstone as security for a debt, because that is like taking a life as security.

7 "If a man is discovered kidnapping one of his Israelite brothers, whether he treats him as a slave or sells him, the kidnapper must die. You must purge the evil from you.

8 "Be careful in a case of infectious skin disease, following carefully everything the Levitical priests instruct

a 23:18 Lit a dog's   b 23:20 Lit you put your hand to   c 23:23 Lit promised with your mouth   d 24:3 Lit if the second man who has taken her as his wife

21:23 under God's curse. This was a symbol of God's righteous judgment and rejection. By taking the total judgment for the sins of the world, Christ became "a curse for us" (Gal. 3:13).

22:5 woman is not to wear. This rule is related to prohibitions against abnormal sexual practices (Lev. 18:22; 20:13).

22:8 railing ... roof. This commandment calls for reasonable safety measures on property.

22:29 50 silver [shekels]. This was the bride price.

23:1 [testicles] have been crushed. The removal of all or part of the sexual organs was a pagan practice forbidden in Israel.

23:3 Moabite. What about David, grandson of a Moabite woman? Some say that this prohibition was only for Moabite men, others that the prohibition was only for the first 10 generations after the tabernacle was built.

you to do. Be careful to do as I have commanded them. ⁹ Remember what the LORD your God did to Miriam on the journey after you left Egypt.

Consideration for People in Need

¹⁰ "When you make a loan of any kind to your neighbor, do not enter his house to collect what he offers as security. ¹¹ You must stand outside while the man you are making the loan to brings the security out to you. ¹² If he is a poor man, you must not sleep in ⌊the garment⌋ he has given as security. ¹³ Be sure to return it[a] to him at sunset. Then he will sleep in it and bless you, and this will be counted as righteousness to you before the LORD your God.

¹⁴ "Do not oppress a hired hand who is poor and needy, whether one of your brothers or one of the foreigners residing within a town[b] in your land. ¹⁵ You are to pay him his wages each day before the sun sets, because he is poor and depends on them. Otherwise he will cry out to the LORD against you, and you will be held guilty.

¹⁶ "Fathers are not to be put to death for ⌊their⌋ children or children for ⌊their⌋ fathers; each person will be put to death for his own sin. ¹⁷ Do not deny justice to a foreign resident ⌊or⌋ fatherless child, and do not take a widow's garment as security. ¹⁸ Remember that you were a slave in Egypt, and the LORD your God redeemed you from there. Therefore I am commanding you to do this.

¹⁹ "When you reap the harvest in your field, and you forget a sheaf in the field, do not go back to get it. It is to be left for the foreign resident, the fatherless, and the widow, so that the LORD your God may bless you in all the work of your hands. ²⁰ When you knock down the fruit from your olive tree, you must not go over the branches again. What remains will be for the foreign resident, the fatherless, and the widow. ²¹ When you gather the grapes of your vineyard, you must not glean what is left. What remains will be for the foreign resident, the fatherless, and the widow. ²² Remember that you were a slave in the land of Egypt. Therefore I am commanding you to do this.

Fairness and Mercy

25 "If there is a dispute between men, they are to go to court, and the judges will hear their case. They will clear the innocent and condemn the guilty. ² If the guilty party deserves to be flogged, the judge will make him lie down and be flogged in his presence with the number ⌊of lashes⌋ appropriate for his crime. ³ He may be flogged with 40 lashes, but no more. Oth-

erwise, if he is flogged with more lashes than these, your brother will be degraded in your sight.

⁴ "Do not muzzle an ox while it treads out grain.

Preserving the Family Line

⁵ "When brothers live on the same property[c] and one of them dies without a son, the wife of the dead man may not marry a stranger outside ⌊the family⌋. Her brother-in-law is to take her as his wife, have sexual relations with her, and perform the duty of a brother-in-law for her. ⁶ The first son she bears will carry on the name of the dead brother, so his name will not be blotted out from Israel. ⁷ But if the man doesn't want to marry his sister-in-law, she must go to the elders at the ⌊city⌋ •gate and say, 'My brother-in-law refuses to preserve his brother's name in Israel. He isn't willing to perform the duty of a brother-in-law for me.' ⁸ The elders of his city will summon him and speak with him. If he persists and says, 'I don't want to marry her,' ⁹ then his sister-in-law will go up to him in the sight of the elders, remove his sandal from his foot, and spit in his face. Then she will declare, 'This is what is done to a man who will not build up his brother's house.' ¹⁰ And his ⌊family⌋ name in Israel will be called 'The house of the man whose sandal was removed.'

¹¹ "If two men are fighting with each other, and the wife of one steps in to rescue her husband from the one striking him, and she puts out her hand and grabs his genitals, ¹² you are to cut off her hand. You must not show pity.

Honest Weights and Measures

¹³ "You must not have two different weights[d] in your bag, one heavy and one light. ¹⁴ You must not have two differing dry measures in your house, a larger and a smaller. ¹⁵ You must have a full and honest weight, a full and honest dry measure, so that you may live long in the land the LORD your God is giving you. ¹⁶ For everyone who does such things and acts unfairly is detestable to the LORD your God.

Revenge on the Amalekites

¹⁷ "Remember what the Amalekites did to you on the journey after you left Egypt. ¹⁸ They met you along the way and attacked all your stragglers from behind when you were tired and weary. They did not •fear God. ¹⁹ When the LORD your God gives you rest from all the enemies around you in the land the LORD your God is giving you to possess as an inheritance, blot out the memory of Amalek from under heaven. Do not forget.

---

[a]**24:13** Lit *return what he has given as security*   [b]**24:14** Lit *within the gates*   [c]**25:5** Lit *live together*   [d]**25:13** Lit *have a stone and a stone*

23:17 cult prostitute. In Canaanite religion, men had sexual relations with cultic prostitutes thinking it brought fertility and prosperity.

23:19 interest. Exodus 22:25-27 outlines God's thinking on interest. Jesus would encourage even greater generosity in Luke 6:34-35.

23:24-25 enter your neighbor's vineyard ... standing grain. Travelers were allowed to pick grapes or grain to eat (Mark 2:23-28), but harvesting or stockpiling was prohibited.

24:1 a divorce certificate. Here divorce is allowed. Later Jesus added a condition (Matt. 5:31-32), pointing to the precedent set by

creation (Matt. 19:3-9).

24:8 infectious skin disease. Not leprosy but a disease that whitened and hardened the skin (Lev. 13). It was not infectious but did cause ritual uncleanness.

24:16 for his own sin. In Ezekiel 18:4-24 the prophet addresses this issue, which may

Giving the Firstfruits

26 "When you enter the land the LORD your God is giving you as an inheritance, and you take possession of it and live in it, ² you must take some of the first of all the soil's produce that you harvest from the land the LORD your God is giving you and put ⌊it⌋ in a container. Then go to the place where the LORD your God chooses to have His name dwell. ³ When you come before the priest who is serving at that time, you must say to him, 'Today I acknowledge to the LORD yourᵃ God that I have entered the land the LORD swore to our fathers to give us.'

⁴ "Then the priest will take the container from your hand and place it before the altar of the LORD your God. ⁵ You are to respond by saying in the presence of the LORD your God:

My father was a wandering Aramean. He went down to Egypt with a few people and lived there. There he became a great, powerful, and populous nation. ⁶ But the Egyptians mistreated and afflicted us, and forced us to do hard labor. ⁷ So we called out to the LORD, the God of our fathers, and the LORD heard our cry and saw our misery, hardship, and oppression. ⁸ Then the LORD brought us out of Egypt with a strong hand and an outstretched arm, with terrifying power, and with signs and wonders. ⁹ He led us to this place and gave us this land, a land flowing with milk and honey. ¹⁰ I have now brought the first of the land's produce that You, LORD, have given me.

You will then place the container before the LORD your God and bow down to Him. ¹¹ You, the Levite, and the foreign resident among you will rejoice in all the good things the LORD your God has given you and your household.

The Tenth in the Third Year

¹² "When you have finished paying all the tenth of your produce in the third year, the year of the tenth, you are to give ⌊it⌋ to the Levite, the foreign resident, the fatherless, and the widow, so that they may eat in your towns and be satisfied. ¹³ Then you will say in the presence of the LORD your God:

I have taken the consecrated portion out of my house; I have also given it to the Levite, the foreign resident, the fatherless, and the widow, according to all the commands You gave me. I have not violated or forgotten Your commands. ¹⁴ I have not eaten any of it while in mourning, or

removed any of it while unclean, or offered any of it for the dead. I have obeyed the LORD my God; I have done all You commanded me. ¹⁵ Look down from Your holy dwelling, from heaven, and bless Your people Israel and the land You have given us as You swore to our fathers, a land flowing with milk and honey.

Covenant Summary

¹⁶ "The LORD your God is commanding you this day to follow these statutes and ordinances. You must be careful to follow them with all your heart and all your soul. ¹⁷ Today you have affirmed that the LORD is your God and that you will walk in His ways, keep His statutes, commands, and ordinances, and obey Him. ¹⁸ And today the LORD has affirmed that you are His special people as He promised you, that you are to keep all His commands, ¹⁹ that He will put you far above all the nations He has made in praise, fame, and glory, and that you will be a holy people to the LORD your God as He promised."

The Law Written on Stones

27 Moses and the elders of Israel commanded the people, "Keep every command I am giving you today. ² At the time you cross the Jordan into the land the LORD your God is giving you, you must set up large stones and cover them with plaster. ³ Write all the words of this law on the stones after you cross to enter the land the LORD your God is giving you, a land flowing with milk and honey, as the LORD, the God of your fathers, has promised you. ⁴ When you have crossed the Jordan, you are to set up these stones on Mount Ebal, as I am commanding you today, and you are to cover them with plaster. ⁵ Build an altar of stones there to the LORD your God—you must not use any iron tool on them. ⁶ Use uncut stones to build the altar of the LORD your God and offer •burnt offerings to the LORD your God on it. ⁷ There you are to sacrifice •fellowship offerings, eat, and rejoice in the presence of the LORD your God. ⁸ Write clearly all the words of this law on the ⌊plastered⌋ stones."

The Covenant Curses

⁹ Moses and the Levitical priests spoke to all Israel, "Be silent, Israel, and listen! This day you have become the people of the LORD your God. ¹⁰ Obey the LORD your God and follow His commands and statutes I am giving you today."

¹¹ On that day Moses commanded the people, ¹² "When you have crossed the Jordan, these ⌊tribes⌋ will

---

ᵃ **26:3** LXX reads *my*

25:3 **40 lashes.** A limit is imposed on beatings so they are not inhumane.

25:4 **muzzle an ox.** Muzzling prevented the animal from eating while working. Paul applies this verse to ministers (1 Cor. 9:9-10 and

have arisen from a faulty understanding of Exodus 20:5; 34:6-7.

1 Tim. 5:17-18). **treads out grain.** The ox walks on the grain that is spread over a hard, flat surface.

25:5-6 These practices were instituted to provide family heirs.

25:9 **remove his sandal.** This signifies a loss of rights.

25:17 **Amalekites.** See Ex. 17:8-16; Num. 14:45.

26:2 **first of all the soil's produce.** This is a one-time offering upon entering the land, distinct from the yearly offering of firstfruits (18:4).

26:5 **wandering Aramean.** Jacob journeyed

stand on Mount Gerizim to bless the people: Simeon, Levi, Judah, Issachar, Joseph, and Benjamin. ¹³ And these ⌊tribes⌋ will stand on Mount Ebal to deliver the curse: Reuben, Gad, Asher, Zebulun, Dan, and Naphtali. ¹⁴ The Levites will proclaim in a loud voice to every Israelite:

¹⁵ 'Cursed is the person who makes a carved idol or cast image, which is detestable to the LORD, the work of a craftsman, and sets ⌊it⌋ up in secret.'

And all the people will reply, '•Amen!'

¹⁶ 'Cursed is the one who dishonors his father or mother.'

And all the people will say, 'Amen!'

¹⁷ 'Cursed is the one who moves his neighbor's boundary marker.'

And all the people will say, 'Amen!'

¹⁸ 'Cursed is the one who leads a blind person astray on the road.'

And all the people will say, 'Amen!'

¹⁹ 'Cursed is the one who denies justice to a foreign resident, a fatherless child, or a widow.'

And all the people will say, 'Amen!'

²⁰ 'Cursed is the one who sleeps with his father's wife, for he has violated his father's marriage bed.'ᵃ

And all the people will say, 'Amen!'

²¹ 'Cursed is the one who has sexual intercourse with any animal.'

And all the people will say, 'Amen!'

²² 'Cursed is the one who sleeps with his sister, whether his father's daughter or his mother's daughter.'

And all the people will say, 'Amen!'

²³ 'Cursed is the one who sleeps with his mother-in-law.'

And all the people will say, 'Amen!'

²⁴ 'Cursed is the one who kills his neighbor in secret.'

And all the people will say, 'Amen!'

²⁵ 'Cursed is the one who accepts a bribe to kill an innocent person.'

And all the people will say, 'Amen!'

²⁶ 'Cursed is anyone who does not put the words of this law into practice.'

And all the people will say, 'Amen!'

Blessings for Obedience

28 "Now if you faithfully obey the LORD your God and are careful to follow all His commands I

am giving you today, the LORD your God will put you far above all the nations of the earth. ² All these blessings will come and overtake you, because you obey the LORD your God:

³ You will be blessed in the city
and blessed in the country.
⁴ Your descendantsᵇ will be blessed,
and your soil's produce,
and the offspring of your livestock,
including the young of your herds
and the newborn of your flocks.
⁵ Your basket and kneading bowl will be blessed.
⁶ You will be blessed when you come in
and blessed when you go out.

⁷ "The LORD will cause the enemies who rise up against you to be defeated before you. They will march out against you from one direction but flee from you in seven directions. ⁸ The LORD will grant you a blessing on your storehouses and on everything you do;ᶜ He will bless you in the land the LORD your God is giving you. ⁹ The LORD will establish you as His holy people, as He swore to you, if you obey the commands of the LORD your God and walk in His ways. ¹⁰ Then all the peoples of the earth will see that you are called by the LORD's name, and they will stand in awe of you. ¹¹ The LORD will make you prosper abundantly with children,ᵈ the offspring of your livestock, and your soil's produce in the land the LORD swore to your fathers to give you. ¹² The LORD will open for you His abundant storehouse, the sky, to give your land rain in its season and to bless all the work of your hands. You will lend to many nations, but you will not borrow. ¹³ The LORD will make you the head and not the tail; you will only move upward and never downward if you listen to the LORD your God's commands I am giving you today and are careful to follow ⌊them⌋. ¹⁴ Do not turn aside to the right or the left from all the things I am commanding you today, and do not go after other gods to worship them.

Curses for Disobedience

¹⁵ "But if you do not obey the LORD your God by carefully following all His commands and statutes I am giving you today, all these curses will come and overtake you:

¹⁶ You will be cursed in the city
and cursed in the country.
¹⁷ Your basket and kneading bowl will be cursed.

ᵃ**27:20** Lit has uncovered the edge of his father's garment; Ru 3:9; Ezk 16:8 ᵇ**28:4** Lit The fruit of your womb ᶜ**28:8** Lit you put your hand to
ᵈ**28:11** Lit abundantly in the fruit of your womb

---

from southern Canaan to Haran, then returned (Gen. 27–35). He also moved to Egypt with his family (Gen. 46:3-7). Two of his wives were Aramean (Gen. 28:5; 29:16,28). **populous nation.** While the Israelites lived in Egypt they grew from 70 people to over 600,000 men, plus women and children (Ex. 1:5,7).

26:12 the tenth. See 14:22-29.

26:15 holy dwelling. God is everywhere (Isa. 66:1-2), but heaven is seen as the place from which He reigns and answers prayer.

26:17 you have affirmed. This wording is found in treaties and covenants.

26:18 special people. This same idea is captured in New Testament phrases such as "chosen race" and "people for His possession" (1 Pet. 2:9). God clearly has authority over His people—and He lovingly treasures them.

27:2 large stones. It was common to com-

18 Your descendants[a] will be cursed,
    and your soil's produce,
    the young of your herds,
    and the newborn of your flocks.
19 You will be cursed when you come in
    and cursed when you go out.

20 The LORD will send against you curses, confusion, and rebuke in everything you do[b] until you are destroyed and quickly perish, because of the wickedness of your actions in abandoning Me. 21 The LORD will make pestilence cling to you until He has exterminated you from the land you are entering to possess. 22 The LORD will afflict you with wasting disease, fever, inflammation, burning heat, drought,[c] blight, and mildew; these will pursue you until you perish. 23 The sky above you will be bronze, and the earth beneath you iron. 24 The LORD will turn the rain of your land into falling[d] dust; it will descend on you from the sky until you are destroyed. 25 The LORD will cause you to be defeated before your enemies. You will march out against them from one direction but flee from them in seven directions. You will be an object of horror to all the kingdoms of the earth. 26 Your corpses will be food for all the birds of the sky and the wild animals of the land, and no one will scare them away.

27 "The LORD will afflict you with the boils of Egypt, tumors, a festering rash, and scabies, from which you cannot be cured. 28 The LORD will afflict you with madness, blindness, and mental confusion, 29 so that at noon you will grope as a blind man gropes in the dark. You will not be successful in anything you do. You will only be oppressed and robbed continually, and no one will help ⌊you⌋. 30 You will become •engaged to a woman, but another man will rape her. You will build a house but not live in it. You will plant a vineyard but not enjoy its fruit. 31 Your ox will be slaughtered before your eyes, but you will not eat any of it. Your donkey will be taken away from you and not returned to you. Your flock will be given to your enemies, and no one will help you. 32 Your sons and daughters will be given to another people, while your eyes grow weary looking for them every day. But you will be powerless to do anything.[e] 33 A people you don't know will eat your soil's produce and everything you have labored for. You will only be oppressed and crushed continually. 34 You will be driven mad by what you see. 35 The LORD will afflict you on your knees and thighs with painful and incurable boils from the sole of your foot to the top of your head.

36 "The LORD will bring you and your king that you have appointed to a nation neither you nor your fathers have known, and there you will worship other gods, of wood and stone. 37 You will become an object of horror, scorn, and ridicule among all the peoples where the LORD will drive you.

38 "You will sow much seed in the field but harvest little, because locusts will devour it. 39 You will plant and cultivate vineyards but not drink the wine or gather ⌊the grapes⌋, because worms will eat them. 40 You will have olive trees throughout your territory but not anoint yourself with oil, because your olives will drop off. 41 You will father sons and daughters, but they will not remain yours, because they will be taken prisoner. 42 Whirring insects will take possession of all your trees and your land's produce. 43 The foreign resident among you will rise higher and higher above you, while you sink lower and lower. 44 He will lend to you, but you won't lend to him. He will be the head, and you will be the tail.

45 "All these curses will come, pursue, and overtake you until you are destroyed, since you did not obey the LORD your God and keep the commands and statutes He gave you. 46 These curses will be a sign and a wonder against you and your descendants forever. 47 Because you didn't serve the LORD your God with joy and a cheerful heart, even though ⌊you had⌋ an abundance of everything, 48 you will serve your enemies the LORD will send against you, in famine, thirst, nakedness, and a lack of everything. He will place an iron yoke on your neck until He has destroyed you. 49 The LORD will bring a nation from far away, from the ends of the earth, to swoop down on you like an eagle, a nation whose language you don't understand, 50 a ruthless nation,[f] showing no respect for the old and not sparing the young. 51 They will eat the offspring of your livestock and your soil's produce until you are destroyed. They will leave you no grain, new wine, oil, young of your herds, or newborn of your flocks until they cause you to perish. 52 They will besiege you within all your gates until your high and fortified walls, that you trust in, come down throughout your land. They will besiege you within all your gates throughout the land the LORD your God has given you.

53 "You will eat your children,[g] the flesh of your sons and daughters the LORD your God has given you during the siege and hardship your enemy imposes on you. 54 The most sensitive and refined man among you will look grudgingly[h] at his brother, the wife he embraces,[i]

---

[a] 28:18 Lit The fruit of your womb   [b] 28:20 Lit you put your hand to   [c] 28:22 Or sword   [d] 28:24 Lit powder and   [e] 28:32 Lit day, and not for power your hand   [f] 28:50 Lit a nation strong of face   [g] 28:53 Lit eat the fruit of your womb   [h] 28:54 Lit you his eye will be evil   [i] 28:54 Lit wife of his bosom

---

memorate important events by setting up stones and writing messages on them for people to see and remember.
27:12-13 Gerizim ... Ebal. These mountains were on the south and north sides of Shechem.
27:15 carved idol ... cast image. This activity

would break the first two commandments (5:7-10). **Amen!** The people formally declare their acceptance of the covenant.
27:19 foreign resident, a fatherless child, or a widow. Such people had no resources to protect themselves.
27:26 Cursed. This comprehensive curse fell

on anyone who broke any part of the Law (Jms 2:10). Since not a single human fully obeys God's Law, humanity is under a curse (Gal. 3:10).
28:1-14 The terminology of the blessings parallels the terminology of the curses in verses 15-44.

and the rest of his children, 55 refusing to share with any of them his children's flesh that he will eat because he has nothing left during the siege and hardship your enemy imposes on you in all your towns. 56 The most sensitive and refined woman among you, who would not venture to set the sole of her foot on the ground because of her refinement and sensitivity, will begrudge the husband she embraces, her son, and her daughter, 57 the afterbirth that comes out from between her legs and the children she bears, because she will secretly eat them for lack of anything ⌊else⌋ during the siege and hardship your enemy imposes on you within your gates.

58 "If you are not careful to obey all the words of this law, which are written in this scroll, by •fearing this glorious and awesome name—•Yahweh, your God— 59 He will bring extraordinary plagues on you and your descendants, severe and lasting plagues, and terrible and chronic sicknesses. 60 He will afflict you again with all the diseases of Egypt, which you dreaded, and they will cling to you. 61 The LORD will also inflict you with every sickness and plague not recorded in the book of this law, until you are destroyed. 62 Though you were as numerous as the stars of the sky, you will be left with only a few people, because you did not obey the LORD your God. 63 Just as the LORD was glad to cause you to prosper and to multiply you, so He will also be glad to cause you to perish and to destroy you. You will be deported from the land you are entering to possess. 64 Then the LORD will scatter you among all peoples from one end of the earth to the other, and there you will worship other gods of wood and stone, which neither you nor your fathers have known. 65 You will find no peace among those nations, and there will be no resting place for the sole of your foot. There the LORD will give you a trembling heart, failing eyes, and a despondent spirit. 66 Your life will hang in doubt before you. You will be in dread night and day, never certain of survival. 67 In the morning you will say, 'If only it were evening!' and in the evening you will say, 'If only it were morning!'—because of the dread you will have in your heart and because of what you will see. 68 The LORD will take you back in ships to Egypt by a route that I said you would never see again. There you will sell yourselves to your enemies as male and female slaves, but no one will buy ⌊you⌋."

Renewing the Covenant

29 [a] These are the words of the covenant the LORD commanded Moses to make with the Israelites in the land of Moab, in addition to the covenant He had made with them at Horeb. 2[b] Moses summoned all Israel and said to them, "You have seen with your own eyes everything the LORD did in Egypt to Pharaoh, to all his officials, and to his entire land. 3 You saw with your own eyes the great trials and those great signs and wonders. 4 Yet to this day the LORD has not given you a mind to understand, eyes to see, or ears to hear. 5 I led you 40 years in the wilderness; your clothes and the sandals on your feet did not wear out; 6 you did not eat bread or drink wine or beer—so that you might know that I am the LORD your God. 7 When you reached this place, Sihon king of Heshbon and Og king of Bashan came out against us in battle, but we defeated them. 8 We took their land and gave it as an inheritance to the Reubenites, the Gadites, and half the tribe of Manasseh. 9 Therefore, observe the words of this covenant and follow them, so that you will succeed in everything you do.

10 "All of you are standing today before the LORD your God—your leaders, tribes, elders, officials, all the men of Israel, 11 your children, your wives, and the foreigners in your camps who cut your wood and draw your water— 12 so that you may enter into the covenant of the LORD your God, which He is making with you today, so that you may enter into His oath 13 and so that He may establish you today as His people and He may be your God as He promised you and as He swore to your fathers Abraham, Isaac, and Jacob. 14 I am making this covenant and this oath not only with you, 15 but also with those who are standing here with us today in the presence of the LORD our God and with those who are not here today.

Abandoning the Covenant

16 "Indeed, you know how we lived in the land of Egypt and passed through the nations where you traveled. 17 You saw their detestable images and idols ⌊made⌋ of wood, stone, silver, and gold, which were among them. 18 Be sure there is no man, woman, clan, or tribe among you today whose heart turns away from the LORD our God to go and worship the gods of those nations. Be sure there is no root among you bearing poisonous and bitter fruit. 19 When someone hears the words of this oath, he may bless himself in his mind, thinking, 'I will have peace even though I follow my ⌊own⌋ stubborn heart.' This will lead to the destruction of the well-watered ⌊land⌋ as well as the dry ⌊land⌋. 20 The LORD will not be willing to forgive him. Instead, His anger and jealousy will burn against that person, and every curse written in this scroll will descend on him. The LORD will blot out his name under heaven,

a **29:1** Dt 28:69 in Hb   b **29:2** Dt 29:1 in Hb

28:5 basket ... blessed. In other words, there will be plenty to eat.

28:12 His abundant storehouse. Heaven is pictured as a gigantic treasury of all good things that God dispenses to the blessed. **You will lend.** Israel will be so blessed by God it will have more than enough.

28:13 the head and not the tail. Israel would be preeminent, honored among the nations.

28:26 Your corpses will be food. Not being properly buried showed extreme disrespect for the deceased.

28:35 painful and incurable boils. This plague also infested the Egyptians (Ex. 9:11).

28:47 serve ... with joy. God expects His people to respond positively and naturally to His gracious provision.

28:49 ends of the earth. This is a poetic way of saying "very far away." **like an eagle.** This word picture is applied to the foreign nations of Assyria and Babylonia, who attacked

21 and single him out for harm from all the tribes of Israel, according to all the curses of the covenant written in this book of the law.

22 "Future generations of your children who follow you and the foreigner who comes from a distant country will see the plagues of the land and the sicknesses the LORD has inflicted on it. 23 All its soil will be a burning waste of sulfur and salt, unsown, producing nothing, with no plant growing on it, just like the fall of Sodom and Gomorrah, Admah and Zeboiim, which the LORD demolished in His fierce anger. 24 All the nations will ask, 'Why has the LORD done this to this land? Why this great outburst of anger?' 25 Then people will answer, 'It is because they abandoned the covenant of the LORD, the God of their fathers, which He had made with them when He brought them out of the land of Egypt. 26 They began to worship other gods, bowing down to gods they had not known—gods that the LORD had not permitted them ⌊to worship⌋. 27 Therefore the LORD's anger burned against this land, and He brought every curse written in this book on it. 28 The LORD uprooted them from their land in ⌊His⌋ anger, fury, and great wrath, and threw them into another land where they are today.' 29 The hidden things belong to the LORD our God, but the revealed things belong to us and our children forever, so that we may follow all the words of this law.

Returning to the LORD

30 "When all these things happen to you—the blessings and curses I have set before you—and you come to your senses ⌊while you are⌋ in all the nations where the LORD your God has driven you, 2 and you and your children return to the LORD your God and obey Him with all your heart and all your soul by doing[a] everything I am giving you today, 3 then He will restore your fortunes,[b] have compassion on you, and gather you again from all the peoples where the LORD your God has scattered you. 4 Even if your exiles are at the ends of the earth,[c] He will gather you and bring you back from there. 5 The LORD your God will bring you into the land your fathers possessed, and you will take possession of it. He will cause you to prosper and multiply you more than ⌊He did⌋ your fathers. 6 The LORD your God will circumcise your heart and the hearts of your descendants, and you will love Him with all your heart and all your soul, so that you will live. 7 The LORD your God will put all these curses on your enemies who hate and persecute you. 8 Then you

will again obey Him and follow all His commands I am giving you today. 9 The LORD your God will make you prosper abundantly in all the work of your hands with children,[d] the offspring of your livestock, and your soil's produce. Indeed, the LORD will again delight in your prosperity, as He delighted in that of your fathers, 10 when you obey the LORD your God by keeping His commands and statutes that are written in this book of the law and return to Him with all your heart and all your soul.

Choose Life

11 "This command that I give you today is certainly not too difficult or beyond your reach. 12 It is not in heaven, so that you have to ask, 'Who will go up to heaven, get it for us, and proclaim it to us so that we may follow it?' 13 And it is not across the sea, so that you have to ask, 'Who will cross the sea, get it for us, and proclaim it to us so that we may follow it?' 14 But the message is very near you, in your mouth and in your heart, so that you may follow it. 15 See, today I have set before you life and prosperity, death and adversity. 16 For[e] I am commanding you today to love the LORD your God, to walk in His ways, and to keep His commands, statutes, and ordinances, so that you may live[f] and multiply, and the LORD your God may bless you in the land you are entering to possess. 17 But if your heart turns away and you do not listen and you are led astray to bow down to other gods and worship them, 18 I tell you today that you will certainly perish and will not live long in the land you are entering to possess across the Jordan. 19 I call heaven and earth as witnesses against you today that I have set before you life and death, blessing and curse. Choose life so that you and your descendants may live, 20 love the LORD your God, obey Him, and remain faithful[g] to Him. For He is your life, and He will prolong your life in the land the LORD swore to give to your fathers Abraham, Isaac, and Jacob."

Joshua Takes Moses' Place

31 Then Moses continued to speak these[h] words to all Israel, 2 saying, "I am now 120 years old; I can no longer act as your leader.[i] The LORD has told me, 'You will not cross this Jordan.' 3 The LORD your God is the One who will cross ahead of you. He will destroy these nations before you, and you will drive them out. Joshua is the one who will cross ahead of you, as the LORD has said. 4 The LORD will deal with them as He did Sihon and Og, the kings of the Amorites, and their land when He destroyed them. 5 The

---

a**30:2** Lit *soul according to* b**30:3** Or *will end your captivity* c**30:4** Lit *skies* d**30:9** Lit *hands in the fruit of your womb* e**30:16** LXX reads *If you obey the commands of the LORD your God that* f**30:16** LXX reads *ordinances, then you will live* g**30:20** Lit *and hold on* h**31:1** Other Hb mss, DSS, LXX, Syr, Vg read *all these* i**31:2** Lit *no longer go out or come in*

---

swiftly and powerfully (Jer. 48:40; 49:22).

28:53 You will eat your children. The curse is that parents would eat the dead bodies of their children in order to stay alive during a siege (see 2 Kings 6:24-29; Lam. 2:20; 4:10).

28:58 this law. This could refer to Deuteronomy or all five books of Moses.

29:1 These are the words of the covenant. This is either a conclusion to the previous chapters or a preamble to chapters 29–32.

29:2 with your own eyes. This refers to the national experience of Israel, not to literal eyewitnesses.

29:4 eyes to see ... ears to hear. Paul de-

scribes a stubborn, hardened Israel (Rom. 11:8).

29:18 poisonous and bitter fruit. Idolatry spreads if not removed and destroyed completely.

29:19 bless himself. For one who merely pays lip service to God, the only blessing he

LORD will deliver them over to you, and you must do to them exactly as I have commanded you. ⁶ Be strong and courageous; don't be terrified or afraid of them. For it is the LORD your God who goes with you; He will not leave you or forsake you."

⁷ Moses then summoned Joshua and said to him in the sight of all Israel, "Be strong and courageous, for you will go with^a this people into the land the LORD swore to give to their fathers. You will enable them to take possession of it. ⁸ The LORD is the One who will go before you. He will be with you; He will not leave you or forsake you. Do not be afraid or discouraged."

⁹ Moses wrote down this law and gave it to the priests, the sons of Levi, who carried the ark of the LORD's covenant, and to all the elders of Israel. ¹⁰ Moses commanded them, "At the end of ⌊every⌋ seven years, at the appointed time in the year of debt cancellation, during the Festival of Booths, ¹¹ when all Israel assembles^b in the presence of the LORD your God at the place He chooses, you are to read this law aloud before all Israel. ¹² Gather the people—men, women, children, and foreigners living within your gates—so that they may listen and learn to •fear the LORD your God and be careful to follow all the words of this law. ¹³ Then their children who do not know ⌊the law⌋ will listen and learn to fear the LORD your God as long as you live in the land you are crossing the Jordan to possess."

¹⁴ The LORD said to Moses, "The time of your death is now approaching. Call Joshua and present yourselves at the tent of meeting, so that I may commission him." When Moses and Joshua went and presented themselves at the tent of meeting, ¹⁵ the LORD appeared at the tent in a pillar of cloud, and the cloud stood at the entrance to the tent.

¹⁶ The LORD said to Moses, "You are about to rest with your fathers, and this people will soon commit adultery with the foreign gods of the land they are entering. They will abandon Me and break the covenant I have made with them. ¹⁷ My anger will burn against them on that day; I will abandon them and hide My face from them so that they will become easy prey.^c Many troubles and afflictions will come to them. On that day they will say, 'Haven't these troubles come to us because our God is no longer with us?' ¹⁸ I will certainly hide My face on that day because of all the evil they have done by turning to other gods. ¹⁹ Therefore write down this song for yourselves and teach it to the Israelites; have them recite it,^d so that

this song may be a witness for Me against the Israelites. ²⁰ When I bring them into the land I swore to ⌊give⌋ their fathers, ⌊a land⌋ flowing with milk and honey, they will eat their fill and prosper.^e They will turn to other gods and worship them, despising Me and breaking My covenant. ²¹ And when many troubles and afflictions come to them, this song will testify against them, because^f their descendants will not have forgotten it. For I know what they are prone to do,^g even before I bring them into the land I swore ⌊to give them⌋." ²² So Moses wrote down this song on that day and taught it to the Israelites.

²³ The LORD commissioned Joshua son of Nun, "Be strong and courageous, for you will bring the Israelites into the land I swore to them, and I will be with you."

Moses Warns the People

²⁴ When Moses had finished writing down on a scroll every single word^h of this law, ²⁵ he commanded the Levites who carried the ark of the LORD's covenant, ²⁶ "Take this book of the law and place it beside the ark of the covenant of the LORD your God, so that it may remain there as a witness against you. ²⁷ For I know how rebellious and stiff-necked you are. If you are rebelling against the LORD now, while I am still alive, how much more ⌊will you rebel⌋ after I am dead! ²⁸ Assemble all your tribal elders and officers before me, so that I may speak these words directly to them and call heaven and earth as witnesses against them. ²⁹ For I know that after my death you will become completely corrupt and turn from the path I have commanded you. Disaster will come to you in the future, because you will do what is evil in the LORD's sight, infuriating Him with what your hands have made." ³⁰ Then Moses recited aloud every single word^i of this song to the entire assembly of Israel:

Song of Moses

32 Pay attention, heavens, and I will speak;
  listen, earth, to the words of my mouth.
² Let my teaching fall like rain
  and my word settle like dew,
  like gentle rain on new grass
  and showers on tender plants.
³ For I will proclaim the LORD's name.
  Declare the greatness of our God!
⁴ The Rock—His work is perfect;
  all His ways are entirely just.
A faithful God, without prejudice,
He is righteous and true.

---

^a**31:7** Other Hb mss, Sam, Syr, Vg read *you will bring* ^b**31:11** Lit *comes to appear* ^c**31:17** Lit *will be for devouring* ^d**31:19** Lit *Israelites; put it in their mouths* ^e**31:20** Lit *be fat* ^f**31:21** Lit *because the mouths of* ^g**31:21** Or *know the plans they are devising* ^h**31:24** Lit *scroll the words to their completion* ^i**31:30** Lit *recited the words to their completion*

---

will ever get is the one he gives himself.

30:1-10 God foretold that Israel would not keep the Law, yet He would not reject them but restore them physically and spiritually. The return from exile did not fulfill the promise to circumcise their hearts (v. 6), suggesting that God will yet do this in the future.

30:3 restore your fortunes. This could also be translated "bring you back from captivity."
30:6 circumcise your heart. See 10:16; see also Rom. 2:25-29; Gal. 5:6-11; 6:15; Phil. 3:3; Col. 2:11.
30:10 book of the law. See 28:58.
30:12 not in heaven. God's word is within ev-

eryone's grasp. All are able to hear it, comprehend it, believe it, and obey it (Rom. 10:6-10).

30:15 I have set before you life. This is the choice: obedience, which brings life and blessings; or disobedience, which brings death and curses.

5 His people have acted corruptly toward Him;
this is their defect[a]—they are not His children
but a devious and crooked generation.
6 Is this how you repay the LORD,
you foolish and senseless people?
Isn't He your Father and Creator?
Didn't He make you and sustain you?
7 Remember the days of old;
consider the years long past.
Ask your father, and he will tell you,
your elders, and they will teach you.
8 When the •Most High gave the nations
their inheritance[b]
and divided the •human race,
He set the boundaries of the peoples
according to the number of the people of Israel.[c]
9 But the LORD's portion is His people,
Jacob, His own inheritance.
10 He found him in a desolate land,
in a barren, howling wilderness;
He surrounded him, cared for him,
and guarded him as the pupil of His eye.
11 He watches over His nest like an eagle
and hovers over His young;
He spreads His wings, catches him,
and lifts him up on His pinions.
12 The LORD alone led him,
with no help from a foreign god.[d]
13 He made him ride on the heights of the land
and eat the produce of the field.
He nourished him with honey from the rock
and oil from flintlike rock,
14 cream from the herd and milk from the flock,
with the fat of lambs,
rams from Bashan, and goats,
with the choicest grains of wheat;
you drank wine from the finest grapes.[e]
15 Then[f] Jeshurun[g] became fat and rebelled—
you became fat, bloated, and gorged.
He abandoned the God who made him
and scorned the Rock of his salvation.
16 They provoked His jealousy with foreign gods;
they enraged Him with detestable practices.
17 They sacrificed to demons, not God,
to gods they had not known,
new gods that had just arrived,
which your fathers did not fear.

18 You ignored the Rock who gave you birth;
you forgot the God who brought you forth.
19 When the LORD saw ⌊this⌋, He despised ⌊them⌋,
provoked ⌊to anger⌋ by His sons and daughters.
20 He said: "I will hide My face from them;
I will see what will become of them,
for they are a perverse generation—
unfaithful children.
21 They have provoked My jealousy
with ⌊their⌋ so-called gods;[h]
they have enraged Me with their worthless
idols.
So I will provoke their jealousy
with an inferior people;[i]
I will enrage them with a foolish nation.
22 For fire has been kindled because of My anger
and burns to the depths of •Sheol;
it devours the land and its produce,
and scorches the foundations of the mountains.
23 I will pile disasters on them;
I will use up My arrows against them.
24 They will be weak from hunger,
ravaged by pestilence and bitter plague;
I will unleash on them wild beasts with fangs,
as well as venomous snakes that slither
in the dust.
25 Outside, the sword will take their children,
and inside, there will be terror;
the young man and the virgin ⌊will be killed⌋,
the infant and the gray-haired man.
26 I would have said: I will cut them to pieces[j]
and blot out the memory of them from mankind,
27 if I had not feared insult from the enemy,
⌊or feared⌋ that these foes might misunderstand
and say: Our own hand has prevailed;
it wasn't the LORD who did all this."
28 Israel is a nation lacking sense
with no understanding at all.[k]
29 If only they were wise, they would figure it out;
they would understand their fate.
30 How could one man pursue a thousand,
or two put ten thousand to flight,
unless their Rock had sold them,
unless the LORD had given them up?
31 But their "rock" is not like our Rock;
even our enemies concede.

---

[a]**32:5** Or *Him; through their fault*; Hb obscure [b]**32:8** Or *Most High divided the nations* [c]**32:8** One DSS reads *number of the sons of God*; LXX reads *number of the angels of God* [d]**32:12** Lit *him, and no foreign god with Him* [e]**32:14** Lit *the blood of grapes* [f]**32:15** DSS, Sam, LXX add *Jacob ate his fill*. [g]**32:15** = Upright One, referring to Israel [h]**32:21** Lit *with no gods* [i]**32:21** Lit *with no people* [j]**32:26** LXX reads *will scatter them* [k]**32:28** Lit *understanding in them*

30:20 remain faithful. This means to bond with (Gen. 2:24) or cling to (Ruth 1:14). **He is your life.** This means a full and blessed life.
31:2 You will not cross this Jordan. See Num. 20:2-13.
31:4 as He did Sihon and Og. See 2:26–3:22.

31:9 wrote ... this law and gave ... priests. Copies of a covenant, like a contract, are kept in order to be followed.

31:12 men, women, children, and foreigners. God's Word is for all the people, including children and non-Israelites living in the land. God intended for His Word to go out from Israel to the nations.

31:19 write down ... teach it. Moses obeys this command in verse 22. The song itself is recorded in 31:30–32:43. The use of poetic songs, sung in public worship meetings, was a way that Israel remembered what was important and worshiped the living God.

32 For their vine is from the vine of Sodom
and from the fields of Gomorrah.
Their grapes are poisonous;
their clusters are bitter.
33 Their wine is serpents' venom,
the deadly poison of cobras.

34 "Is it not stored up with Me,
sealed up in My vaults?
35 Vengeance[a] belongs to Me; I will repay.[b]
In time their foot will slip,
for their day of disaster is near,
and their doom is coming quickly."
36 The LORD will indeed vindicate His people
and have compassion on His servants
when He sees that ⌊their⌋ strength is gone
and no one is left—slave or free.
37 He will say: "Where are their gods,
the 'rock' they found refuge in?
38 Who ate the fat of their sacrifices
and drank the wine of their drink offerings?
Let them rise up and help you;
let it[c] be a shelter for you.
39 See now that I alone am He;
there is no God but Me.
I bring death and I give life;
I wound and I heal.
No one can rescue ⌊anyone⌋ from My hand.
40 I raise My hand to heaven and declare:
As surely as I live forever,
41 when I sharpen My flashing sword,
and My hand takes hold of judgment,
I will take vengeance on My adversaries
and repay those who hate Me.
42 I will make My arrows drunk with blood
while My sword devours flesh—
the blood of the slain and the captives,
the heads of the enemy leaders."[d]

43 Rejoice, you nations, over His people,[e]
for He will avenge the blood of His servants.[f]
He will take vengeance on His adversaries;[g]
He will purify His land and His people.[h]

44 Moses came with Joshua[i] son of Nun and recited
all the words of this song in the presence of the people.
45 After Moses finished reciting all these words to all

Israel, 46 he said to them, "Take to heart all these words
I am giving as a warning to you today, so that you may
command your children to carefully follow all the words
of this law. 47 For they are not meaningless words to
you but they are your life, and by them you will live
long in the land you are crossing the Jordan to possess."

Moses' Impending Death

48 On that same day the LORD spoke to Moses, 49 "Go
up Mount Nebo in the Abarim ⌊range⌋ in the land of
Moab, across from Jericho, and view the land of Canaan
I am giving the Israelites as a possession. 50 Then you
will die on the mountain that you go up, and you will
be gathered to your people, just as your brother Aaron
died on Mount Hor and was gathered to his people.
51 For ⌊both of⌋ you broke faith with Me among the Israelites at the waters of Meribath-kadesh in the Wilderness of Zin by failing to treat Me as holy in their
presence. 52 Although you will view the land from a distance, which I am giving the Israelites, you will not go
there."

Moses' Blessings

33 This is the blessing that Moses, the man of
God, gave the Israelites before his death. 2 He
said:

The LORD came from Sinai
and appeared to them from Seir;
He shone ⌊on them⌋ from Mount Paran
and came with ten thousand holy ones,[j]
with lightning[k] from His right hand[l] for them.
3 Indeed He loves the people.[m]
All Your[n] holy ones[o] are in Your hand,
and they assemble[p] at Your feet.
Each receives Your words.
4 Moses gave us instruction,
a possession for the assembly of Jacob.
5 So He became King in Jeshurun[q]
when the leaders of the people gathered
with the tribes of Israel.

6 Let Reuben live and not die
though his people become few.

7 He said this about Judah:

LORD, hear Judah's cry and bring him
to his people.

a 32:35 Sam, LXX read On a day of vengeance b 32:35 LXX, Tg, Vg read Me; and recompense I will recompense c 32:38 Sam, LXX, Tg, Vg read them d 32:42 Lit the long-haired heads of the enemy e 32:43 LXX reads Rejoice, you heavens, along with Him, and let all the sons of God worship Him; rejoice, you nations, with His people, and let all the angels of God strengthen themselves in Him; DSS reads Rejoice, you heavens, along with Him, and let all the angels worship Him; Heb 1:6 f 32:43 DSS, LXX read sons g 32:43 DSS, LXX add and He will recompense those who hate Him; v. 41 h 32:43 Syr, Tg; DSS, Sam, LXX, Vg read His people's land i 32:44 LXX, Syr, Vg; MT reads Hoshea; Nm 13:8,16 j 33:2 LXX reads Mount Paran with ten thousands from Kadesh k 33:2 Or fiery law; Hb obscure l 33:2 Or ones, from His southland to the mountain slopes m 33:3 Or peoples n 33:3 Lit His, or its o 33:3 Either the saints of Israel or angels p 33:3 Hb obscure q 33:5 = Upright One, referring to Israel

31:24 every single word. Perhaps just Deuteronomy or the whole of Genesis through
Deuteronomy.
31:26 place it beside the ark. It was standard practice to keep a copy of a covenant in
a nation's holiest place.
32:1 Pay attention, heavens. See Isa. 1:2;

34:1; Mic. 1:2; 6:1-2.
32:4 The Rock. A rock symbolizes strength
and stability, and speaks of God's protection
and power (see vv. 15,18,30-31).
32:6 Father. This title was used by the prophets (Isa. 9:6; 63:16; Jer. 3:4; Mal. 2:10), Jesus
(John 6:27), Paul (Rom. 1:7; 1 Cor. 8:6; 15:24;

Gal. 1:1; Eph. 5:20; 6:23; Phil. 2:11; Col. 1:3;
3:17), Peter (1 Pet. 1:2; 2 Pet. 1:17), and John
(2 John 3).
32:8 Most High. Elyon, a title that speaks of
God's sovereign power over all the earth.
32:15 Jeshurun. An ironic reference to Israel
as the "upright one" (Isa. 44:2).

He fights for his cause^a with his own hands,
but may You be a help against his foes.

8 He said about Levi:

Your Thummim and Urim^b belong to
  Your faithful one;^c
You tested him at Massah
and contended with him at the waters
  of Meribah.
9 He said about his father and mother,
"I do not regard them."
He disregarded his brothers
and didn't acknowledge his sons,
for they kept Your word
and maintained Your covenant.
10 They will teach Your ordinances to Jacob
and Your instruction to Israel;
they will set incense before You
and whole •burnt offerings on Your altar.
11 Lord, bless his possessions,^d
and accept the work of his hands.
Smash the loins of his adversaries and enemies,
so that they cannot rise again.

12 He said about Benjamin:

The Lord's beloved rests^e securely on Him.
He^f shields him all day long,
and he rests on His shoulders.^g

13 He said about Joseph:

May his land be blessed by the Lord
with the dew of heaven's bounty
and the watery depths that lie beneath;
14 with the bountiful harvest from the sun
and the abundant yield of the seasons;
15 with the best products of the ancient mountains
and the bounty of the eternal hills;
16 with the choice gifts of the land
and everything in it;
and with the favor of Him
who appeared^h in the ⌊burning⌋ bush.
May these rest on the head of Joseph,
on the crown of the prince of his brothers.
17 His firstborn bull hasⁱ splendor,
and horns like^j those of a wild ox;
he gores all the peoples with them
to the ends of the earth.

Such are the ten thousands of Ephraim,
and such are the thousands of Manasseh.

18 He said about Zebulun:

Rejoice, Zebulun, in your journeys,
and Issachar, in your tents.
19 They summon the peoples to a mountain;
there they offer acceptable sacrifices.
For they draw from the wealth of the seas
and the hidden treasures of the sand.

20 He said about Gad:

The one who enlarges Gad's ⌊territory⌋
will be blessed.
He lies down like a lion
and tears off an arm or even a head.
21 He chose the best ⌊part⌋ for himself,
because a ruler's portion was assigned there
  for him.
He came ⌊with⌋ the leaders of the people;
he carried out the Lord's justice
and His ordinances for Israel.

22 He said about Dan:

Dan is a young lion,
leaping out of Bashan.

23 He said about Naphtali:

Naphtali, enjoying approval,
full of the Lord's blessing,
take^k possession to the west and the south.

24 He said about Asher:

May Asher^l be the most blessed of the sons;
may he be the most favored among his brothers
and dip his foot in ⌊olive⌋ oil.^m
25 May the bolts of your gate be iron and bronze,
and your strength last as long as you live.

26 There is none like the God of Jeshurun,ⁿ
who rides the heavens to your aid
on the clouds in His majesty.
27 The God of old is ⌊your⌋ dwelling place,
and underneath are the everlasting arms.
He drives out the enemy before you,
and commands, "Destroy!"
28 So Israel dwells securely;
Jacob lives untroubled^o

a 33:7 Or He contends for them b 33:8 Two objects used to determine God's will c 33:8 DSS, LXX read Give to Levi Your Thummim, Your Urim to Your favored one d 33:11 Or abilities e 33:12 Or Let the Lord's beloved rest f 33:12 LXX reads The Most High g 33:12 Or and He dwells among his mountain slopes h 33:16 Lit dwelt i 33:17 Some DSS, Sam, LXX, Syr, Vg read A firstborn bull—he has j 33:17 Lit and his horns are k 33:23 Sam, LXX, Syr, Vg, Tg read he will take l 33:24 = Happy or Blessed; Gn 30:13 m 33:24 A symbol for prosperity n 33:26 = Upright One, referring to Israel o 33:28 Text emended; MT reads Jacob's fountain is alone

32:17 demons. Pagan gods were actually demonic powers (Ps. 106:37).

32:21 an inferior people. Literally "not a people," a nation not chosen as Israel was. Paul sees the fulfillment of this in Romans 10:19; 11:11.

32:22 depths of Sheol. The grave, or the realm of the dead.

32:34 sealed up in My vaults. God's sovereign will for the future has been established and will surely unfold.

32:35 Vengeance belongs to Me. The writer of Hebrews warns against ignoring the claims of Christ (Heb. 10:30).

32:35 I will repay. God alone has the right to punish evildoers (Rom. 12:19).

32:50 gathered to your people. Moses would join his deceased family members in death (Gen. 25:8).

32:51 you broke faith with Me. This incident is referred to in 1:37; 3:23-26; 4:21-22; 31:2;

in a land of grain and new wine;
even his skies drip with dew.
29 How happy you are, Israel!
Who is like you,
a people saved by the LORD?
He is the shield that protects you,
the sword you boast in.
Your enemies will cringe before you,
and you will tread on their backs.ᵃ

Moses' Death

34 Then Moses went up from the plains of Moab to Mount Nebo, to the top of Pisgah, which faces Jericho, and the LORD showed him all the land: Gilead as far as Dan, 2 all of Naphtali, the land of Ephraim and Manasseh, all the land of Judah as far as the Mediterraneanᵇ Sea, 3 the •Negev, and the region from the Valley of Jericho, the City of Palms, as far as Zoar. 4 The LORD then said to him, "This is the land I promised Abraham, Isaac, and Jacob, 'I will give it to your descendants.' I have let you see it with your own eyes, but you will not cross into it."

5 So Moses the servant of the LORD died there in the land of Moab, as the LORD had said. 6 He buried himᶜ in the valley in the land of Moab facing Beth-peor, and no one to this day knows where his grave is. 7 Moses was 120 years old when he died; his eyes were not weak, and his vitality had not left ⌊him⌋. 8 The Israelites wept for Moses in the plains of Moab 30 days. Then the days of weeping and mourning for Moses came to an end.

9 Joshua son of Nun was filled with the spirit of wisdom, because Moses had laid his hands on him. So the Israelites obeyed him and did as the LORD had commanded Moses. 10 No prophet has arisen again in Israel like Moses, whom the LORD knew face to face. 11 ⌊He was unparalleled⌋ for all the signs and wonders the LORD sent him to do against the land of Egypt—to Pharaoh, to all his officials, and to all his land, 12 and for all the mighty ⌊acts of⌋ power and terrifying deeds that Moses performed in the sight of all Israel.

ᵃ**33:29** Or *high places* ᵇ**34:2** Lit *Western* ᶜ**34:6** Or *He was buried*

---

and Numbers 20:10-13.

33:1 blessing. Moses' blessing of the tribes (verses 6-25) is similar to Jacob's blessing of his sons (Gen. 49:1-28). **man of God.** This is the first time this is used of Moses (Josh. 14:6; 1 Chron. 23:14; 2 Chron. 30:16; Ezra 3:2; Ps. 90, title).

33:5 King. God Himself was to rule Israel (Judg. 8:23). **Jeshurun.** A reference to Israel (Isa. 44:2).

33:8 Thummim and Urim. The sacred lots used to make decisions under the direction of God (Ex. 28:30). **Your faithful one.** The High Priest. **Massah ... Meribah.** "Testing" and "rebellion" (Exod. 17:7; Ps. 95:8)—the place where Israel stubbornly resisted God's will.

33:13 Joseph. That is, Ephraim and Manasseh. **dew ... watery depths.** A reference to

rain and springs or wells.

33:19 wealth of the seas. These tribes would enjoy success in maritime trade (Gen. 49:13).

33:21 the best [part]. Good land was required to maintain livestock, and livestock signified wealth.

33:24 dip his foot in [olive] oil. Asher would enjoy God's rich blessing.

33:26 on the clouds. This description has been found in Canaanite literature in reference to Baal. Its use here (and in Ps. 68:4) indicates that Yahweh is the true God who dwells in the heavens and is sovereign over creation.

34:6 no one to this day knows where his grave is. God kept Moses' burial plot a secret, no doubt to prevent it from becoming a shrine. This note was obviously added by

someone later with God's inspiration.

34:8 wept ... 30 days. This was the traditional time period for mourning. Moses had made an inestimable impact on the nation, which now had to say goodbye to its beloved leader.

34:10 No prophet has arisen again in Israel like Moses. Moses promised that other prophets would come who spoke for God just like him (18:15). Yet Moses stood out from other prophets by his privileged relationship with God, who spoke face to face with Moses.

34:11 [He was unparalleled]. Moses was the supreme example of the Old Testament servant of God. The writer of Hebrews contrasts Moses with Christ, the "servant" and the "Son," in Hebrews 3:1-6.

INTRODUCTION TO
JOSHUA

AUTHOR

The author is not identified. The book is named for its main character, Joshua, successor to Moses.

DATE

Suggested dates for Joshua range from circa 1405 to 1250 B.C.

THEME

Obedience brings long-awaited victory in the promised land.

HISTORICAL BACKGROUND

Having led the children of Israel to the entrance of the promised land, Moses is forbidden to guide them in. His servant and aide, Joshua, is chosen by God to take the people in, lead them to victory, and divide the land among them. Joshua's training has included accompanying Moses partially up Mount Sinai, being the captain of the army, and being sent as a spy into Canaan. He was one of only two spies who believed Israel could possess the land by God's

enablement. The Book of Joshua opens with the Israelites camped on the east side of the Jordan River. Through Joshua, the Lord commands the people to pass through the Jordan on dry ground. After recounting the series of military victories and allotments of land for the 12 tribes, the book concludes with Joshua's charge to the people before his death.

CHARACTERISTICS

This book highlights Joshua's successful leadership of Israel, and God's active involvement in history. We see this most obviously in the "book of war" (chapters 1–11), which chronicles a series of battles, with victory going to the 'strong and courageous' (a theme repeated at least eight times in God's call to Joshua). When the Israelites do what God calls them to do, they defeat the enemy. When they disobey, they are unable to win.

PASSAGES FOR
TOPICAL GROUP STUDY

3:14-4:24 . . . IMPORTANCE OF REMEMBERING. . . Blessings to Remember

5:13-6:21 . . . OBEYING GOD and WAR. . . .Mission Improbable

Encouragement of Joshua

1 After the death of Moses the LORD's servant, the LORD spoke to Joshua[a] son of Nun, who had served Moses: 2 "Moses My servant is dead. Now you and all the people prepare to cross over the Jordan to the land I am giving the Israelites. 3 I have given you every place where the sole of your foot treads, just as I promised Moses. 4 Your territory will be from the wilderness and Lebanon to the great Euphrates River—all the land of the Hittites—and west to the Mediterranean Sea.[b] 5 No one will be able to stand against you as long as you live. I will be with you, just as I was with Moses. I will not leave you or forsake you.

6 "Be strong and courageous, for you will distribute the land I swore to their fathers to give them as an inheritance. 7 Above all, be strong and very courageous to carefully observe the whole instruction My servant Moses commanded you. Do not turn from it to the right or the left, so that you will have success wherever you go. 8 This book of instruction must not depart from your mouth; you are to recite it day and night, so that you may carefully observe everything written in it. For then you will prosper and succeed in whatever you do. 9 Haven't I commanded you: be strong and courageous? Do not be afraid or discouraged, for the LORD your God is with you wherever you go."

Joshua Prepares the People

10 Then Joshua commanded the officers of the people: 11 "Go through the camp and tell the people, 'Get provisions ready for yourselves, for within three days you will be crossing the Jordan to go in and take possession of the land the LORD your God is giving you to inherit.'"

12 Joshua said to the Reubenites, the Gadites, and half the tribe of Manasseh: 13 "Remember what Moses the LORD's servant commanded you when he said, 'The LORD your God will give you rest, and He will give you this land.' 14 Your wives, young children, and livestock may remain in the land Moses gave you on this side of the Jordan.[c] But your fighting men must cross over in battle formation[d] ahead of your brothers[e] and help them 15 until the LORD gives our brothers rest, as ⌊He has given⌋ you, and they too possess the land the LORD your God is giving them. You may then return to the land of your inheritance and take possession of what Moses the LORD's servant gave you on the east side of the Jordan."

16 They answered Joshua, "Everything you have commanded us we will do, and everywhere you send us we will go. 17 We will obey you, just as we obeyed Moses in everything. And may the LORD your God be with you, as He was with Moses. 18 Anyone who rebels against your order and does not obey your words in all that you command him, will be put to death. Above all, be strong and courageous!"

Spies Sent to Jericho

2 Joshua son of Nun secretly sent two men as spies from Acacia Grove,[f] saying, "Go and scout the land, especially Jericho." So they left, and they came to the house of a woman, a prostitute named Rahab, and stayed there.

2 The king of Jericho was told, "Look, some of the Israelite men have come here tonight to investigate the land." 3 Then the king of Jericho sent ⌊word⌋ to Rahab and said, "Bring out the men who came to you and entered your house, for they came to investigate the entire land."

4 But the woman had taken the two men and hidden them. So she said, "Yes, the men did come to me, but I didn't know where they were from. 5 At nightfall, when the gate was about to close, the men went out, and I don't know where they were going. Chase after them quickly, and you can catch up with them!" 6 But she had taken them up to the roof and hidden them among the stalks of flax that she had arranged on the roof. 7 The men pursued them along the road to the fords of the Jordan, and as soon as they left to pursue them, the gate was shut.

The Promise to Rahab

8 Before the men fell asleep, she went up on the roof 9 and said to them, "I know that the LORD has given you this land and that dread of you has fallen on us, and everyone who lives in the land is panicking because of you.[g] 10 For we have heard how the LORD dried up the waters of the •Red Sea before you when you came out of Egypt, and what you did to Sihon and Og, the two Amorite kings you •completely destroyed across the Jordan. 11 When we heard this, we lost heart, and everyone's courage failed[h] because of you, for the LORD your God is God in heaven above and on earth below. 12 Now please swear to me by the LORD that you will also show kindness to my family, because I showed kindness to you.[i] Give me a sure sign[j] 13 that you will spare the lives of my father, mother, brothers, sisters, and all who belong to them, and save us from death."

14 The men answered her, "⌊We will give⌋ our lives for yours. If you don't report our mission, we will show

---

a**1:1** = The LORD Will Save, or The LORD Is Salvation; *Joshua* is related to the name *Jesus*. b**1:4** Lit *and to the Great Sea, the going down of the sun* c**1:14** East of the Jordan River d**1:14** Or *over armed* e**1:14** Fellow Israelites f**2:1** Or *from Shittim* g**2:9** Or *land panics at your approach* h**2:11** Lit *and spirit no longer remained in anyone* i**2:12** Lit *to your father's house* j**2:12** Or *a sign of truth*

1:1 Joshua ... who had served Moses. Joshua had served as captain of Moses' army and was one of the spies sent into the land of Canaan (Num. 14:38).

1:5 I will not leave you. God calmed Joshua's concerns about assuming leadership by assuring him of His presence.

1:10 Joshua commanded. The inauguration was over. It was time for this new leader to take charge and lead his people into the land.

2:1 came to the house of ... a prostitute. Prostitutes in the ancient world often operated inns. The spies were seeking lodging in a public house where information about Jericho could be gathered.

2:8-12 Rahab had heard about the wonders the Lord had performed for Israel, and she apparently believed in Him. But she wanted assurance that her family would be protected when the Israelites invaded Jericho.

kindness and faithfulness to you when the LORD gives us the land."

15 Then she let them down by a rope through the window, since she lived in a house that was ⌊built⌋ into the wall of the city. 16 "Go to the hill country so that the men pursuing you won't find you," she said to them. "Hide yourselves there for three days until they return; afterwards, go on your way."

17 The men said to her, "We will be free from this oath you made us swear, 18 unless, when we enter the land, you tie this scarlet cord to the window through which you let us down. Bring your father, mother, brothers, and all your father's family into your house. 19 If anyone goes out the doors of your house, his blood will be on his own head, and we will be innocent. But if anyone with you in the house should be harmed,a his blood will be on our heads. 20 And if you report our mission, we are free from the oath you made us swear."

21 "Let it be as you say," she replied, and she sent them away. After they had gone, she tied the scarlet cord to the window.

22 So the two men went into the hill country and stayed there three days until the pursuers had returned. They searched all along the way, but did not find them. 23 Then the men returned, came down from the hill country, and crossed ⌊the Jordan⌋. They went to Joshua son of Nun and reported everything that had happened to them. 24 They told Joshua, "The LORD has handed over the entire land to us. Everyone who lives in the land is also panicking because of us."b

Crossing the Jordan

3 Joshua started early the next morning and left Acacia Grovec with all the Israelites. They went as far as the Jordan and stayed there before crossing. 2 After three days the officers went through the camp 3 and commanded the people: "When you see the ark of the covenant of the LORD your God carried by the Levitical priests, you must break camp and follow it. 4 But keep a distance of about 1,000 yardsd between yourselves and the ark. Don't go near it, so that you can see the way to go, for you haven't traveled this way before."e

5 Joshua told the people, "Consecrate yourselves, because the LORD will do wonders among you tomorrow." 6 Then he said to the priests, "Take the ark of the covenant and go on ahead of the people." So they carried the ark of the covenant and went ahead of them.

7 The LORD spoke to Joshua: "Today I will begin to exalt you in the sight of all Israel, so they will know that I will be with you just as I was with Moses. 8 Command the priests carrying the ark of the covenant: 'When you reach the edge of the waters,f stand in the Jordan.' "

9 Then Joshua told the Israelites, "Come closer and listen to the words of the LORD your God." 10 He said, "You will know that the living God is among you and that He will certainly dispossess before you the Canaanites, Hittites, Hivites, Perizzites, Girgashites, Amorites, and Jebusites 11 when the ark of the covenant of the Lord of all the earth goes ahead of you into the Jordan. 12 Now choose 12 men from the tribes of Israel, one man for each tribe. 13 When the feetg of the priests who carry the ark of the LORD, the Lord of all the earth, come to rest in the Jordan's waters, its waters will be cut off. The water flowing downstream will stand up ⌊in⌋ a mass."

Blessings to Remember

1. What kind of souvenir do you collect to remember special times: T-shirt? Postcards? Some other kind of keepsake?

Joshua 3:14-4:24

2. Why did God command the people to set up a pile of stones (4:21-24)? Why was Joshua concerned about answering the children's questions?

3. Why is it important to remember God's miracles and blessings? How can remembering His blessings in your life help you in the future?

4. What is something God has done for you that's worth commemorating?

14 When the people broke camp to cross the Jordan, the priests carried the ark of the covenant ahead of the people. 15 Now the Jordan overflows its banks throughout the harvest season. But as soon as the priests carrying the ark reached the Jordan, their feet touched the water at its edge 16 and the water flowing downstream stood still, rising up ⌊in⌋ a mass that extended as far ash Adam, a city next to Zarethan. The water flowing downstream into the Sea of the •Arabah (the Dead Sea) was completely cut off, and the people crossed opposite

---

a2:19 Lit if a hand should be on him   b2:24 Or also panics at our approach   c3:1 Or left Shittim   d3:4 Lit 2,000 cubits   e3:4 Lit yesterday and the day before   f3:8 Lit waters of the Jordan   g3:13 Lit soles of the feet   h3:16 Alt Hb tradition reads mass at

---

2:18 scarlet cord. To identify Rahab's house, the invading Israelites would look for a dyed cord dangling from her window. This would signify that her household should be spared.

3:3 ark of the covenant. The people stepped into the Jordan River at the first sign of the ark's appearance. The ark of the covenant represented the Lord's presence.

3:7 I will be with you. God's assuring presence was as much to encourage Joshua as it was to spur the people on to battle.

3:12 choose 12 men. These men were to gather 12 large stones from the riverbed for a monument to be built on the other side of the river (4:2-3).

3:15 Jordan overflows its banks. God arranged for the Israelites to cross the Jordan River during the spring flood stage. The river would have been much less intimidating without the melting snow from Mt. Hermon far to the north.

Jericho. [17] The priests carrying the ark of the LORD's covenant stood firmly on dry ground in the middle of the Jordan, while all Israel crossed on dry ground until the entire nation had finished crossing the Jordan.

The Memorial Stones

4 After the entire nation had finished crossing the Jordan, the LORD spoke to Joshua, [2] "Choose 12 men from the people, one man for each tribe, [3] and command them, 'Take 12 stones from this place in the middle of the Jordan where the priests' feet are standing, carry them with you, and set them down at the place where you spend the night.' "

[4] So Joshua summoned the 12 men selected from the Israelites, one man for each tribe, [5] and said to them, "Go across to the ark of the LORD your God in the middle of the Jordan. Each of you lift a stone onto his shoulder, one for each[a] of the Israelite tribes, [6] so that this will be a sign among you. In the future, when your children ask you, 'What do these stones mean to you?' [7] you should tell them, 'The waters of the Jordan were cut off in front of the ark of the LORD's covenant. When it crossed the Jordan, the Jordan's waters were cut off.' Therefore these stones will always be a memorial for the Israelites."

[8] The Israelites did just as Joshua had commanded them. The 12 men took stones from the middle of the Jordan, one for each[b] of the Israelite tribes, just as the LORD had told Joshua. They carried them to the camp and set them down there. [9] Joshua also set up 12 stones in the middle of the Jordan where the priests[c] who carried the ark of the covenant were standing. The stones are there to this day.

[10] The priests carrying the ark continued standing in the middle of the Jordan until everything was completed that the LORD had commanded Joshua to tell the people, in keeping with all that Moses had commanded Joshua. The people hurried across, [11] and after everyone had finished crossing, the priests with the ark of the LORD crossed in the sight of the people. [12] The Reubenites, Gadites, and half the tribe of Manasseh went in battle formation in front of the Israelites, as Moses had instructed them. [13] About 40,000 equipped for war crossed to the plains of Jericho in the LORD's presence.

[14] On that day the LORD exalted Joshua in the sight of all Israel, and they revered him throughout his life, as they had revered Moses. [15] The LORD told Joshua, [16] "Command the priests who carry the ark of the •testimony[d] to come up from the Jordan."

[17] So Joshua commanded the priests, "Come up from the Jordan." [18] When the priests carrying the ark of the LORD's covenant came up from the middle of the Jordan, and their feet[e] stepped out on solid ground, the waters of the Jordan resumed their course, flowing over all the banks as before.

[19] The people came up from the Jordan on the tenth day of the first month,[f] and camped at Gilgal on the eastern limits of Jericho. [20] Then Joshua set up in Gilgal the 12 stones they had taken from the Jordan, [21] and he said to the Israelites, "When your children ask their fathers in the future, 'What is the meaning of these stones?' [22] you should tell your children, 'Israel crossed the Jordan on dry ground.' [23] For the LORD your God dried up the waters of the Jordan before you until you had crossed over, just as the LORD your God did to the •Red Sea, which He dried up before us until we had crossed over. [24] This is so that all the people of the earth may know that the LORD's hand is mighty, and so that you may always •fear the LORD your God."

Circumcision of the Israelites

5 When all the Amorite kings across the Jordan to the west and all the Canaanite kings near the sea heard how the LORD had dried up the waters of the Jordan before the Israelites until they had crossed over, they lost heart and their courage failed[g] because of the Israelites.

[2] At that time the LORD said to Joshua, "Make flint knives and circumcise the Israelite men again." [3] So Joshua made flint knives and circumcised the Israelite men at Gibeath-haaraloth.[h] [4] This is the reason Joshua circumcised ⌊them⌋: All the people who came out of Egypt who were males—all the men of war—had died in the wilderness along the way after they had come out of Egypt. [5] Though all the people who came out were circumcised, none of the people born in the wilderness along the way were circumcised after they had come out of Egypt. [6] For the Israelites wandered in the wilderness 40 years until all the nation's men of war who came out of Egypt had died off because they did not obey the LORD. So the LORD vowed never to let them see the land He had sworn to their fathers to give us, a land flowing with milk and honey. [7] Joshua raised up their sons in their place; it was these he circumcised. They were still uncircumcised, since they had not been circumcised along the way. [8] After the entire nation had been circumcised, they stayed where they were in the camp until they recovered. [9] The LORD then said to

---

[a]**4:5** Lit *shoulder according to the number*   [b]**4:8** Lit *Jordan according to the number*   [c]**4:9** Lit *feet of the priests*   [d]**4:16** The ark of the covenant
[e]**4:18** Lit *and the soles of the feet of the priests*   [f]**4:19** = Nisan (March–April)   [g]**5:1** Lit *and they did not have spirit in them any more*   [h]**5:3** Or *The Hill of Foreskins*

But less water would have required less faith.

3:17 firmly on dry ground. The priests stood in the middle of the river "on dry ground" and directed the people across.

4:6 a sign among you. This monument of stones taken from the Jordan River would

help the Israelites remember God's faithfulness for generations to come.

4:24 all the people of the earth. Although the miracle of the parting of Jordan's waters was specific to the Israelites at that time, God's fame would be spread throughout the world as a result.

5:6 wandered in the wilderness 40 years. The Lord waited for an entire disobedient generation to die off before bringing His people to the promised land.

5:11-12 For the first time, the Israelites would be able to enjoy the bounty of their new land. They would no longer have to eat manna, the

Joshua, "Today I have rolled away the disgrace of Egypt from you." Therefore, that place has been called Gilgal[a] to this day.

Food from the Land

10 While the Israelites camped at Gilgal on the plains of Jericho, they kept the •Passover on the evening of the fourteenth day of the month.[b] 11 The day after Passover they ate unleavened bread and roasted grain from the produce of the land. 12 And the day after they ate from the produce of the land, the manna ceased. Since there was no more manna for the Israelites, they ate from the crops of the land of Canaan that year.

Commander of the LORD's Army

13 When Joshua was near Jericho, he looked up and saw a man standing in front of him with a drawn sword in His hand. Joshua approached Him and asked, "Are You for us or for our enemies?"

14 "Neither," He replied. "I have now come as commander of the LORD's army."

Then Joshua bowed with his face to the ground in worship and asked Him, "What does my Lord want to say to His servant?"

15 The commander of the Lord's army said to Joshua, "Remove the sandals from your feet, for the place where you are standing is holy." And Joshua did so.

The Conquest of Jericho

6 Now Jericho was strongly fortified because of the Israelites—no one leaving or entering. 2 The LORD said to Joshua, "Look, I have handed Jericho, its king, and its fighting men over to you. 3 March around the city with all the men of war, circling the city one time. Do this for six days. 4 Have seven priests carry seven ram's-horn trumpets in front of the ark. But on the seventh day, march around the city seven times, while the priests blow the trumpets. 5 When there is a prolonged blast of the horn and you hear its sound, have all the people give a mighty shout. Then the city wall will collapse, and the people will advance, each man straight ahead."

6 So Joshua son of Nun summoned the priests and said to them, "Take up the ark of the covenant and have seven priests carry seven trumpets in front of the ark of the LORD." 7 He said to the people, "Move forward, march around the city, and have the armed troops go ahead of the ark of the LORD."

8 After Joshua had spoken to the people, seven priests carrying seven trumpets before the LORD moved forward and blew the trumpets; the ark of the LORD's covenant followed them. 9 While the trumpets were blowing, the armed troops went in front of the priests who blew the trumpets, and the rear guard went behind the ark. 10 But Joshua had commanded the people: "Do not shout or let your voice be heard. Don't let one word come out of your mouth until the time I say, 'Shout!' Then you are to shout." 11 So the ark of the LORD was carried around the city, circling it once. They returned to the camp and spent the night there.[c]

Mission Improbable

1. What's the biggest city you've visited?

Joshua 5:13-6:21

2. If you were Joshua, the military commander of Israel, how would you expect to conquer a walled city? How did God choose to do it? Why?

3. Why did God forbid the Israelites to keep any of the plunder from Jericho? Why did they have to kill everyone in the city?

4. Why did God command that a prostitute should be saved, out of all the people in Jericho (6:17)?

5. How do God's commands sometimes seem odd, harsh, or demanding? Do you strive to obey, even when His commands are difficult?

12 Joshua got up early the next morning. The priests took the ark of the LORD, 13 and the seven priests carrying seven trumpets marched in front of the ark of the LORD. While the trumpets were blowing, the armed troops went in front of them, and the rear guard went behind the ark of the LORD. 14 On the second day they marched around the city once and returned to the camp. They did this for six days.

15 Early on the seventh day, they started at dawn and marched around the city seven times in the same way. That was the only day they marched around the city seven times. 16 After the seventh time, the priests blew the trumpets, and Joshua said to the people, "Shout! For the LORD has given you the city. 17 But the city and everything in it are •set apart to the LORD for destruction. Only Rahab the prostitute and everyone with her in the house will live, because she hid the men[d] we sent. 18 But keep yourselves from the things set apart,

---

a **5:9** = to roll b **5:10** = Nisan (March–April) c **6:11** Lit *at the camp* d **6:17** Lit *messengers*

---

substance that had sustained them in the wilderness.

5:13 a man standing in front. Joshua's encounter with this man was an inspiring experience for the Israelites. A supernatural army's presence, in addition to his faithful men, also bolstered Joshua's confidence.

6:1 Jericho was strongly fortified. News of Israel's miraculous crossing of the Jordan River apparently preceded them and terrified the inhabitants of Jericho, although they were protected by two thick walls.

6:3 March around the city ... one time. Joshua's battle checklist surely never in-

cluded just marching around the walls of Jericho. But he obeyed God's orders without question.

6:4 ram's-horn trumpets. Priests used these "jubilee trumpets" in religious ceremonies to announce the presence of the Lord.

or you will be set apart for destruction. If you[a] take any of those things, you will set apart the camp of Israel for destruction and bring disaster on it. 19 For all the silver and gold, and the articles of bronze and iron, are dedicated to the LORD and must go into the LORD's treasury."

20 So the people shouted, and the trumpets sounded. When they heard the blast of the trumpet, the people gave a great shout, and the wall collapsed. The people advanced into the city, each man straight ahead, and they captured the city. 21 They •completely destroyed everything in the city with the sword—every man and woman, both young and old, and every ox, sheep, and donkey.

Rahab and Her Family Spared

22 Joshua said to the two men who had scouted the land, "Go to the prostitute's house and bring the woman out of there, and all who are with her, just as you promised her." 23 So the young men who had scouted went in and brought out Rahab and her father, mother, brothers, and all who belonged to her. They brought out her whole family and settled them outside the camp of Israel.

24 They burned up the city and everything in it, but they put the silver and gold and the articles of bronze and iron into the treasury of the LORD's house. 25 But Joshua spared Rahab the prostitute, her father's household, and all who belonged to her, because she hid the men Joshua had sent to spy on Jericho, and she lives in Israel to this day.

26 At that time Joshua imposed this curse:

> Cursed before the LORD is the man
> who undertakes the rebuilding of this city,
> Jericho.
> He will lay its foundation ⌊at the cost of⌋
> his firstborn;
> He will set up its gates ⌊at the cost of⌋
> his youngest.

27 And the LORD was with Joshua, and his fame spread throughout the land.

Defeat at Ai

7 The Israelites, however, were unfaithful regarding the things •set apart for destruction. Achan son of Carmi, son of Zabdi, son of Zerah, of the tribe of Judah, took some of what was set apart, and the LORD's anger burned against the Israelites.

2 Joshua sent men from Jericho to Ai, which is near Beth-aven, east of Bethel, and told them, "Go up and scout the land." So the men went up and scouted Ai.

3 After returning to Joshua they reported to him, "Don't send all the people, but send about 2,000 or 3,000[b] men to attack Ai. Since the people of Ai are so few, don't wear out all our people there." 4 So about 3,000 men[c] went up there, but they fled from the men of Ai. 5 The men of Ai struck down about 36 of them and chased them from outside the gate to the quarries,[d] striking them down on the descent. As a result, the people's hearts melted and became like water.

6 Then Joshua tore his clothes and fell before the ark of the LORD with his face to the ground until evening, as did the elders of Israel; they all put dust on their heads. 7 "Oh, Lord GOD," Joshua said, "why did You ever bring these people across the Jordan to hand us over to the Amorites for our destruction? If only we had been content to remain on the other side of the Jordan! 8 What can I say, Lord, now that Israel has turned its back ⌊and run⌋ from its enemies? 9 When the Canaanites and all who live in the land hear about this, they will surround us and wipe out our name from the earth. Then what will You do about Your great name?"

10 The LORD then said to Joshua, "Stand up! Why are you on the ground?[e] 11 Israel has sinned. They have violated My covenant that I appointed for them. They have taken some of what was set apart. They have stolen, deceived, and put ⌊the things⌋ with their own belongings. 12 This is why the Israelites cannot stand against their enemies. They will turn their backs ⌊and run⌋ from their enemies, because they have been set apart for destruction. I will no longer be with you unless you remove from you what is set apart.

13 "Go and consecrate the people. Tell them to consecrate themselves tomorrow, for this is what the LORD, the God of Israel, says, 'There are among you, Israel, things set apart. You will not be able to stand against your enemies until you remove what is set apart. 14 In the morning you must present yourselves tribe by tribe. The tribe the LORD selects is to come forward clan by clan. The clan the LORD selects is to come forward family by family. The family the LORD selects is to come forward man by man. 15 The one who is caught with the things set apart must be burned,[f] along with everything he has, because he has violated the LORD's covenant and committed an outrage in Israel.' "

Achan Judged

16 Joshua got up early the next morning. He had Israel come forward tribe by tribe, and the tribe of Judah was selected. 17 He had the clans of Judah come forward, and the Zerahite clan was selected. He had the

---

[a]6:18 LXX reads you covet and; Jos 7:21   [b]7:3 Or send two or three military units of   [c]7:4 Lit men from the people   [d]7:5 Or to Shebarim
[e]7:10 Lit Why have you fallen on your face?   [f]7:15 Lit burned with fire

---

6:5 give a mighty shout. The confused inhabitants inside Jericho would be stunned by the voices of thousands of warriors.

6:17 set apart to the LORD for destruction. For a city to be "set apart" under God's judgment meant that it was to be totally destroyed.

6:25 Rahab ... lives in Israel to this day. Rahab's family was saved due to her fateful encounter with the Israelite spies when they visited Jericho.

6:26 the rebuilding of this city. As a conquered city belonging to God, Jericho would never again be restored to its former glory.

7:6 Joshua tore his clothes and fell. After their easy victory over Jericho, Israel suffered a humiliating defeat by the defenders of the city of Ai.

7:11 some of what was set apart. All living things in Jericho were to be destroyed and burned. Anything of value was supposed to

Zerahite clan come forward by heads of families,[a] and Zabdi was selected. [18] He then had Zabdi's family come forward man by man, and Achan son of Carmi, son of Zabdi, son of Zerah, of the tribe of Judah, was selected.

[19] So Joshua said to Achan, "My son, give glory to the LORD, the God of Israel, and make a confession to Him.[b] I urge you, tell me what you have done. Don't hide anything from me."

[20] Achan replied to Joshua, "It is true. I have sinned against the LORD, the God of Israel. This is what I did: [21] When I saw among the spoils a beautiful cloak from Babylon,[c] 200 silver •shekels,[d] and a bar of gold weighing 50 shekels,[e] I coveted them and took them. You can see for yourself. They are concealed in the ground inside my tent, with the money under the cloak." [22] So Joshua sent messengers who ran to the tent, and there was the cloak, concealed in his tent, with the money underneath. [23] They took the things from inside the tent, brought them to Joshua and all the Israelites, and spread them out in the LORD's presence.

[24] Then Joshua and all Israel with him took Achan son of Zerah, the silver, the cloak, and the bar of gold, his sons and daughters, his ox, donkey, and sheep, his tent, and all that he had, and brought them up to the Valley of Achor. [25] Joshua said, "Why have you troubled us? Today the LORD will trouble you!" So all Israel stoned him to death. They burned their bodies,[f] threw stones on them, [26] and raised over him a large pile of rocks that remains to this day. Then the LORD turned from His burning anger. Therefore that place has been called the Valley of Achor[g] to this day.

Conquest of Ai

8 The LORD said to Joshua, "Do not be afraid or discouraged. Take the whole military force with you and go attack Ai. Look, I have handed over to you the king of Ai, his people, city, and land. [2] Treat Ai and its king as you did Jericho and its king; you may plunder its spoil and livestock for yourselves. Set an ambush behind the city."

[3] So Joshua and the whole military force set out to attack Ai. Joshua selected 30,000 fighting men and sent them out at night. [4] He commanded them: "Pay attention. Lie in ambush behind the city, not too far from it, and all of you be ready. [5] Then I and all the people who are with me will approach the city. When they come out against us as they did the first time, we will flee from them. [6] They will come after us until we have drawn them away from the city, for they will say, 'They are fleeing from us as before.' While we are fleeing from them, [7] you are to come out of your ambush and seize the city, for the LORD your God has handed it over to you. [8] After taking the city, set it on fire. Follow the LORD's command—see ⌊that you do⌋ as I have ordered you." [9] So Joshua sent them out, and they went to the ambush site and waited between Bethel and Ai, to the west of Ai. But he spent that night with the troops.

[10] Joshua started early the next morning and mobilized them. Then he and the elders of Israel led the troops up to Ai. [11] All those[h] who were with him went up and approached the city, arriving opposite Ai, and camped to the north of it, with a valley between them and the city. [12] Now Joshua had taken about 5,000 men and set them in ambush between Bethel and Ai, to the west of the city. [13] The military force was stationed in this way: the main[i] camp to the north of the city and its rear guard to the west of the city. And that night Joshua went into the valley.

[14] When the king of Ai saw ⌊the Israelites⌋, the men of the city hurried and went out early in the morning, so that he and all his people could engage Israel in battle at a suitable place facing the plain[j] ⌊of the Jordan⌋. But he did not know there was an ambush ⌊waiting⌋ for him behind the city. [15] Joshua and all Israel pretended to be beaten back by them and fled toward the wilderness. [16] Then all the troops of Ai were summoned to pursue them, and they pursued Joshua and were drawn away from the city. [17] Not a man was left in Ai or Bethel who did not go out after Israel, leaving the city exposed while they pursued Israel.

[18] Then the LORD said to Joshua, "Hold out the sword in your hand toward Ai, for I will hand the city over to you." So Joshua held out his sword toward it. [19] When he held out his hand, the men in ambush rose quickly from their position. They ran, entered the city, captured it, and immediately set it on fire.

[20] The men of Ai turned and looked back, and smoke from the city was rising to the sky! They could not escape in any direction, and the troops who had fled to the wilderness now became the pursuers. [21] When Joshua and all Israel saw that the ⌊men in⌋ ambush had captured the city and that smoke was rising from it, they turned back and struck down the men of Ai. [22] The men in the ambush came out of the city against them, and the men of Ai were ⌊trapped⌋ between the Israelite forces, some on one side and some on the other. They struck them down until no survivor or fugitive remained, [23] but they captured the king of Ai alive and brought him to Joshua.

---

[a]**7:17** Lit forward man by man   [b]**7:19** Or and praise Him   [c]**7:21** Lit Shinar   [d]**7:21** About 5 pounds of silver   [e]**7:21** About 1 pound of gold   [f]**7:25** Lit burned them with fire   [g]**7:26** Or of Trouble   [h]**8:11** Lit the people of war   [i]**8:13** Lit way: all the   [j]**8:14** Or the Arabah

---

be brought into the Lord's treasury.

7:13 You will not be able to stand against your enemies. Israel's potential for victory was based on obedience. A perfectly obedient army of ten could defeat thousands of the enemy. But one disobedient Israelite would bring defeat by even the weakest nation.

7:21 200 silver shekels … gold weighing 50 shekels. Achan kept for himself about five pounds of silver and one pound of gold from the spoils of war taken in the battle against Jericho.

7:25 They burned their bodies. Because of his disobedience of the Lord's command,

Achan was stoned to death, then his body was burned. This was supposed to be the destiny of every living thing in Jericho (6:18-19,24).

7:26 Then the LORD turned from His burning anger. Once the sin was removed from their midst, the Lord again walked with the Israelites.

24 When Israel had finished killing everyone living in Ai who had pursued them into the open country, and when every last one of them had fallen by the sword, all Israel returned to Ai and struck it down with the sword. 25 The total of those who fell that day, both men and women, was 12,000—all the people of Ai. 26 Joshua did not draw back his hand that was holding the sword until all the inhabitants of Ai were •completely destroyed. 27 Israel plundered only the cattle and spoil of that city for themselves, according to the LORD's command that He had given Joshua.

28 Joshua burned Ai and left it a permanent ruin, desolate to this day. 29 He hung[a] ⌊the body of⌋ the king of Ai on a tree[b] until evening, and at sunset Joshua commanded that they take his body down from the tree. They threw it down at the entrance of the city gate and put a large pile of rocks over it, which remains to this day.

Renewed Commitment to the Law

30 At that time Joshua built an altar on Mount Ebal to the LORD, the God of Israel, 31 just as Moses the LORD's servant had commanded the Israelites. He built it according to what is written in the book of the law of Moses: an altar of uncut stones on which no iron tool has been used. Then they offered •burnt offerings to the LORD and sacrificed •fellowship offerings on it. 32 There on the stones, Joshua copied the law of Moses, which he had written in the presence of the Israelites. 33 All Israel, foreigner and citizen alike, with their elders, officers, and judges, stood on either side of the ark of the LORD's covenant facing the Levitical priests who carried it. As Moses the LORD's servant had commanded earlier, half of them were in front of Mount Gerizim and half in front of Mount Ebal, to bless the people of Israel. 34 Afterwards, Joshua read aloud all the words of the law—the blessings as well as the curses—according to all that is written in the book of the law. 35 There was not a word of all that Moses had commanded that Joshua did not read before the entire assembly of Israel, including the women, little children, and foreigners who were with them.

Deception by Gibeon

9 When all the kings heard ⌊about Jericho and Ai⌋, those who were west of the Jordan in the hill country, in the Judean foothills,[c] and all along the coast of the Mediterranean Sea toward Lebanon—the Hittites, Amorites, Canaanites, Perizzites, Hivites, and Jebusites— 2 they formed a unified alliance to fight against Joshua and Israel.

3 When the inhabitants of Gibeon heard what Joshua had done to Jericho and Ai, 4 they acted deceptively. They gathered provisions[d] and took worn-out sacks on their donkeys and old wineskins, cracked and mended. 5 ⌊They wore⌋ old, patched sandals on their feet and threadbare clothing on their bodies. Their entire provision of bread was dry and crumbly. 6 They went to Joshua in the camp at Gilgal and said to him and the men of Israel, "We have come from a distant land. Please make a treaty with us."

7 The men of Israel replied to the Hivites,[e] "Perhaps you live among us. How can we make a treaty with you?"

8 They said to Joshua, "We are your servants."

Then Joshua asked them, "Who are you and where do you come from?"

9 They replied to him, "Your servants have come from a far away land because of the reputation of the LORD your God. For we have heard of His fame, and all that He did in Egypt, 10 and all that He did to the two Amorite kings beyond the Jordan—Sihon king of Heshbon and Og king of Bashan, who was in Ashtaroth. 11 So our elders and all the inhabitants of our land told us, 'Take provisions with you for the journey; go and meet them and say, "We are your servants. Please make a treaty with us." ' 12 This bread of ours was warm when we took it from our houses as food on the day we left to come to you. But take a look, it is now dry and crumbly. 13 These wineskins were new when we filled them, but look, they are cracked. And these clothes and sandals of ours are worn out from the extremely long journey." 14 Then the men ⌊of Israel⌋ took some of their provisions, but did not seek the LORD's counsel. 15 So Joshua established peace with them and made a treaty to let them live, and the leaders of the community swore an oath to them.

Gibeon's Deception Discovered

16 Three days after making the treaty with them, they heard that the Gibeonites were their neighbors, living among them. 17 So the Israelites set out and reached the Gibeonite cities on the third day. Now their cities were Gibeon, Chephirah, Beeroth, and Kiriath-jearim. 18 But the Israelites did not attack them, because the leaders of the community had sworn an oath to them by the LORD, the God of Israel. Then the whole community grumbled against the leaders.

19 All the leaders answered them, "We have sworn an oath to them by the LORD, the God of Israel, and now we cannot touch them. 20 This is how we will treat

---

[a]8:29 Or impaled [b]8:29 Or wooden stake [c]9:1 Or the Shephelah [d]9:4 Some Hb mss, LXX, Syr, Vg; MT reads They went disguised as ambassadors [e]9:7 = the men of Gibeon

---

8:1 Joshua, "Do not be afraid." God addressed Joshua's fears about returning to a city where Israel had suffered defeat. He promised to direct him in the battle.

8:13 stationed in this way. Israel's strategy was to exploit Ai's over-confidence. Joshua planned to lure the fighting men away from the city, then ambush them.

8:26 all … were completely destroyed. It was important that the army of Israel become known for total victory in its initial battles for control of the land of Canaan.

8:30-31 Joshua led the people to Mount Ebal for a spiritual event. Moses had spelled out the location and details of this covenant renewal ceremony before he died on the other side of the Jordan River (Deut. 27–28).

8:33 half … in front of Mount Gerizim and half in front of Mount Ebal. The two congregations of Israel faced each other

them: we will let them live, so that no wrath will fall on us because of the oath we swore to them." 21 They also said, "Let them live." So the Gibeonites became wood-cutters and water carriers for the whole community, as the leaders had promised them.

22 Joshua summoned the Gibeonites and said to them, "Why did you deceive us by telling us you live far away from us, when in fact you live among us? 23 Therefore you are cursed and will always be slaves—woodcutters and water carriers for the house of my God."

24 The Gibeonites answered him, "It was clearly reported to your servants that the LORD your God had commanded His servant Moses to give you all the land and to destroy all the inhabitants of the land before you. We greatly feared for our lives because of you, and that is why we did this. 25 Now we are in your hands. Do to us whatever you think is right."a 26 This is what Joshua did to them: he delivered them from the hands of the Israelites, and they did not kill them. 27 On that day he made them woodcutters and water carriers—as they are today—for the community and for the LORD's altar at the place He would choose.

The Day the Sun Stood Still

10 Now Adoni-zedek king of Jerusalem heard that Joshua had captured Ai and •completely de-stroyed it, doing to Ai and its king as he had done to Jericho and its king, and that the inhabitants of Gibeon had made peace with Israel and were ⌊living⌋ among them. 2 So Adoni-zedek and his people wereb greatly alarmed because Gibeon was a large city like one of the royal cities; it was larger than Ai, and all its men were warriors. 3 Therefore Adoni-zedek king of Jerusa-lem sent ⌊word⌋ to Hoham king of Hebron, Piram king of Jarmuth, Japhia king of Lachish, and Debir king of Eglon, saying, 4 "Come up and help me. We will attack Gibeon, because they have made peace with Joshua and the Israelites." 5 So the five Amorite kings—the kings of Jerusalem, Hebron, Jarmuth, Lachish, and Eglon—joined forces, advanced with all their armies, besieged Gibeon, and fought against it.

6 Then the men of Gibeon sent ⌊word⌋ to Joshua in the camp at Gilgal: "Don't abandonc your servants. Come quickly and save us! Help us, for all the Amorite kings living in the hill country have joined forces against us." 7 So Joshua and his whole military force, including all the fighting men, came from Gilgal.

8 The LORD said to Joshua, "Do not be afraid of them, for I have handed them over to you. Not one of them will be able to stand against you."

9 So Joshua caught them by surprise, after marching all night from Gilgal. 10 The LORD threw them into con-fusion before Israel. He defeated them in a great slaugh-ter at Gibeon, chased them through the ascent of Beth-horon, and struck them down as far as Azekah and Makkedah. 11 As they fled before Israel, the LORD threw large hailstones on them from the sky along the descent of Beth-horon all the way to Azekah, and they died. More of them died from the hail than the Israelites killed with the sword.

12 On the day the LORD gave the Amorites over to the Israelites, Joshua spoke to the LORD in the presence of Israel:

> "Sun, stand still over Gibeon,
>   and moon, over the valley of Aijalon."
13 And the sun stood still
>   and the moon stopped,
>   until the nation took vengeance on its enemies.

Isn't this written in the Book of Jashar?d

> So the sun stopped
> in the middle of the sky
> and delayed its setting
> almost a full day.

14 There has been no day like it before or since, when the LORD listened to the voice of a man, because the LORD fought for Israel. 15 Then Joshua and all Israel with him returned to the camp at Gilgal.

Execution of the Five Kings

16 Now the five ⌊defeated⌋ kings had fled and hidden themselves in the cave at Makkedah. 17 It was reported to Joshua: "The five kings have been found; they are hiding in the cave at Makkedah."

18 Joshua said, "Roll large stones against the mouth of the cave, and station men by it to guard the kings. 19 But as for the rest of you, don't stay there. Pursue your enemies and attack them from behind. Don't let them enter their cities, for the LORD your God has handed them over to you." 20 So Joshua and the Israel-ites finished inflicting a terrible slaughter on them until they were destroyed, although a few survivors ran away to the fortified cities. 21 The people returned safely to Joshua in the camp at Makkedah. No one could say a thinge against the Israelites.

22 Then Joshua said, "Open the mouth of the cave, and bring those five kings to me out of there." 23 That is what they did. They brought the five kings of Jerusa-lem, Hebron, Jarmuth, Lachish, and Eglon to Joshua out

---

a9:25 Lit us as is good and as is right in your eyes do b10:2 One Hb ms, Syr, Vg read So he was c10:6 Lit Don't let your hand go from
d10:13 Or of the Upright e10:21 Lit No one sharpened his tongue

---

across the valley between these two moun-tains. The Gerizim tribes called out "Amen" when the Levites read the blessings that would accompany covenant obedience (vv. 14-26). The Ebal tribes called out "Amen" when the curses that would accompany covenant disobedience were read.

9:3-6 Not willing to risk defeat by the Israel-ites, the leaders of the city of Gibeon lied to Joshua and succeeded in making a deal that assured them of Israel's protection.

9:14 men [of Israel] ... did not seek the LORD's counsel. The officers who in-spected the claims of the Gibeonites did

not seek God's direction in this matter.
9:18 community grumbled against the leaders. It was too late for complaining. A vow had been made. The honorable thing for Israel to do was uphold their agreement with the Gibeonites.
10:2-19 Several Canaanite kings formed a

of the cave. 24 When they had brought the kings to him, Joshua summoned all the men of Israel and said to the military commanders who had accompanied him, "Come here and put your feet on the necks of these kings." So the commanders came forward and put their feet on their necks. 25 Joshua said to them, "Do not be afraid or discouraged. Be strong and courageous, for the LORD will do this to all the enemies you fight."

26 After this, Joshua struck them down and executed them. He hung[a] their bodies on five trees[b] and they were there until evening. 27 At sunset Joshua commanded that they be taken down from the trees[b] and thrown into the cave where they had hidden. Then large stones were placed against the mouth of the cave, and the stones are there to this day.

Conquest of Southern Cities

28 On that day Joshua captured Makkedah and struck it down with the sword, including its king. He completely destroyed it[c] and everyone in it, leaving no survivors. So he treated the king of Makkedah as he had the king of Jericho.

29 Joshua and all Israel with him crossed from Makkedah to Libnah and fought against Libnah. 30 The LORD also handed it and its king over to Israel. He struck it down, putting everyone in it to the sword, and left no survivors in it. He treated Libnah's king as he had the king of Jericho.

31 From Libnah, Joshua and all Israel with him crossed to Lachish. They laid siege to it and attacked it. 32 The LORD handed Lachish over to Israel, and Joshua captured it on the second day. He struck it down, putting everyone in it to the sword, just as he had done to Libnah. 33 At that time Horam king of Gezer went to help Lachish, but Joshua struck him down along with his people, leaving no survivors in it.

34 Then Joshua crossed from Lachish to Eglon and all Israel with him. They laid siege to it and attacked it. 35 On that day they captured it and struck it down, putting everyone in it to the sword. He completely destroyed it that day, just as he had done to Lachish.

36 Next, Joshua and all Israel with him went up from Eglon to Hebron and attacked it. 37 They captured it and struck down its king, all its villages, and everyone in it with the sword. Just as he had done at Eglon, he left no survivors. He completely destroyed Hebron and everyone in it.

38 Finally, Joshua turned toward Debir and attacked it. And all Israel was with him. 39 He captured it—its king and all its villages. They struck them down with the sword and completely destroyed everyone in it, leaving no survivors. He treated Debir and its king as he had treated Hebron and as he had treated Libnah and its king.

40 So Joshua conquered the whole region—the hill country, the •Negev, the Judean foothills,[d] and the slopes—with all their kings, leaving no survivors. He completely destroyed every living being, as the LORD, the God of Israel, had commanded. 41 Joshua conquered everyone from Kadesh-barnea to Gaza, and all the land of Goshen as far as Gibeon. 42 Joshua captured all these kings and their land in one campaign,[e] because the LORD, the God of Israel, fought for Israel. 43 Then Joshua returned with all Israel to the camp at Gilgal.

Conquest of Northern Cities

11 When Jabin king of Hazor heard ⌊this news⌋, he sent ⌊a message⌋ to:

Jobab king of Madon,
the kings of Shimron and Achshaph,
2 and the kings of the north in the hill country,
the plain[f] south of Chinnereth,
the Judean foothills,[d]
and the Slopes of Dor[g] to the west,
3 the Canaanites in the east and west,
the Amorites, Hittites, Perizzites,
and Jebusites in the hill country,
and the Hivites at the foot of Hermon
in the land of Mizpah.

4 They went out with all their armies—a multitude as numerous as the sand on the seashore—along with a vast number of horses and chariots. 5 All these kings joined forces; they came together and camped at the waters of Merom to attack Israel.

6 The LORD said to Joshua, "Do not be afraid of them, for at this time tomorrow I will hand all of them over dead to Israel. You are to hamstring their horses and burn up their chariots." 7 So Joshua and his whole military force surprised them at the waters of Merom and attacked them. 8 The LORD handed them over to Israel, and they struck them down, pursuing them as far as Great Sidon and Misrephoth-maim, and to the east as far as the valley of Mizpeh.[h] They struck them down, leaving no survivors. 9 Joshua treated them as the LORD had told him; he hamstrung their horses and burned up their chariots.

10 At that time Joshua turned back, captured Hazor, and struck down its king with the sword, because Hazor had formerly been the leader of all these king-

---

[a]**10:26** Or *impaled* [b]**10:26,27** Or *wooden stakes* [c]**10:28** Other Hb mss read *them* [d]**10:40; 11:2** Or *the Shephelah* [e]**10:42** Lit *land at one time* [f]**11:2** Or *the Arabah* [g]**11:2** Or *and in Naphoth-dor* [h]**11:8** = *Mizpah*; Jos 11:3; 18:26

---

coalition and challenged Israel to a contest for control of the city of Gibeon. God fought for His people, and the Canaanite kings were defeated.

10:21 people returned ... No one could say a thing. If one Canaanite city grumbled against Israel often enough, other cities would soon become hostile against them. Silencing its foes quickly proved to be a powerful tactic used by Joshua.

10:28 Joshua ... destroyed ... everyone in it. Israel's destruction of its enemies portrayed God's intolerance for sin. When God destroyed sin, He also protected His peo-ple from idolatry and impurity.

10:41 Kadesh-barnea to Gaza. From Ai in the central highlands to the Negev desert, the Israelites' string of victories secured the southern half of the promised land.

11:1 Jabin king of Hazor. A brilliant military

doms. 11 They struck down everyone in it with the sword, •completely destroying them; he left no one alive. Then he burned down Hazor.

12 Joshua captured all these kings and their cities and struck them down with the sword. He completely destroyed them, as Moses the LORD's servant had commanded. 13 However, Israel did not burn any of the cities that stood on its mounds except Hazor, which Joshua burned. 14 The Israelites plundered all the spoils and cattle of these cities for themselves. But they struck down every person with the sword until they had annihilated them, leaving no one alive. 15 Just as the LORD had commanded His servant Moses, Moses commanded Joshua. That is what Joshua did, leaving nothing undone of all that the LORD had commanded Moses.

Summary of Conquests

16 So Joshua took all this land—the hill country, all the •Negev, all the land of Goshen, the Judean foothills,a the plain,b and the hill country of Israel with its Judean foothillsc — 17 from Mount Halak, which ascends to Seir, as far as Baal-gad in the Valley of Lebanon at the foot of Mount Hermon. He captured all their kings and struck them down, putting them to death. 18 Joshua waged war with all these kings for a long time. 19 No city made peace with the Israelites except the Hivites who inhabited Gibeon; all of them were taken in battle. 20 For it was the LORD's intention to harden their hearts, so that they would engage Israel in battle, be completely destroyed without mercy, and be annihilated, just as the LORD had commanded Moses.

21 At that time Joshua proceeded to exterminate the Anakim from the hill country—Hebron, Debir, Anab—all the hill country of Judah and of Israel. Joshua completely destroyed them with their cities. 22 No Anakim were left in the land of the Israelites, except for some remaining in Gaza, Gath, and Ashdod.

23 So Joshua took the entire land, in keeping with all that the LORD had told Moses. Joshua then gave it as an inheritance to Israel according to their tribal allotments. After this, the land had rest from war.

Territory East of the Jordan

12 The Israelites struck down the following kings of the land and took possession of their land beyond the Jordan to the east and from the Arnon Valley to Mount Hermon, including all the •Arabah eastward:

2 Sihon king of the Amorites lived in Heshbon. He ruled ⌊over the territory⌋ from Aroer on the rim of the Arnon Valley, along the middle of the valley,

and half of Gilead up to the Jabbok River (the border of the Ammonites), 3 the Arabah east of the Sea of Chinnerethd to the Sea of the Arabah (that is, the Dead Sea), eastward through Beth-jeshimoth and southwarde below the slopes of Pisgah.

4 Ogf king of Bashan, of the remnant of the Rephaim, lived in Ashtaroth and Edrei. 5 He ruled over Mount Hermon, Salecah, all Bashan up to the Geshurite and Maacathite border, and half of Gilead to the border of Sihon, king of Heshbon.

6 Moses the LORD's servant and the Israelites struck them down. And Moses the LORD's servant gave their land as an inheritance to the Reubenites, Gadites, and half the tribe of Manasseh.

Territory West of the Jordan

7 Joshua and the Israelites struck down the following kings of the land beyond the Jordan to the west, from Baal-gad in the valley of Lebanon to Mount Halak, which ascends toward Seir (Joshua gave their land as an inheritance to the tribes of Israel according to their allotments: 8 the hill country, the Judean foothills,a the plain,b the slopes, the desert, and the •Negev of the Hittites, Amorites, Canaanites, Perizzites, Hivites, and Jebusites):

9	the king of Jericho	one
	the king of Ai, which is next to Bethel	one
10	the king of Jerusalem	one
	the king of Hebron	one
11	the king of Jarmuth	one
	the king of Lachish	one
12	the king of Eglon	one
	the king of Gezer	one
13	the king of Debir	one
	the king of Geder	one
14	the king of Hormah	one
	the king of Arad	one
15	the king of Libnah	one
	the king of Adullam	one
16	the king of Makkedah	one
	the king of Bethel	one
17	the king of Tappuah	one
	the king of Hepher	one
18	the king of Aphek	one
	the king of Lasharon	one
19	the king of Madon	one
	the king of Hazor	one
20	the king of Shimron-meron	one

a11:16; 12:8 Or the Shephelah   b11:16; 12:8 Or the Arabah   c11:16 Or its Shephelah   d12:3 The Sea of Galilee   e12:3 Or and from Teman
f12:4 LXX; MT reads The territory of Og

---

strategist, this king convinced several nearby cities to amass their troops for one major offensive against the Israelites.

11:6 at this time tomorrow. Considering the size of the combined armies and their mounted chariots, this 24-hour promise seemed almost too good to be true. **horses**

... chariots. God wanted Israel to rely on Him rather than the "high-powered" weapons of that day (Deut. 17:16; Isa. 31:1).

11:10 Hazor. A large, powerful city that controlled the caravan route from Damascus to the coast of the Mediterranean Sea and on to Egypt.

11:12 as Moses the LORD's servant had commanded. Joshua destroyed the Canaanite cities and their population to purify the land of pagan idolatry and moral and spiritual pollution (Deut. 7:1-6).

11:18 Joshua waged war ... for a long time. Although he was outnumbered and in unfa-

the king of Achshaph	one
21 the king of Taanach	one
the king of Megiddo	one
22 the king of Kedesh	one
the king of Jokneam in Carmel	one
23 the king of Dor in Naphoth-dor[a]	one
the king of Goiim in Gilgal[b]	one
24 the king of Tirzah	one
⌊the total number of⌋ all kings:	31

Unconquered Lands

13 Joshua was now old, advanced in years, and the LORD said to him, "You have become old, advanced in years, but a great deal of the land remains to be possessed. 2 This is the land that remains:

All the districts of the Philistines and the Geshurites: 3 from the Shihor east of Egypt to the border of Ekron on the north (considered to be Canaanite territory)—the five Philistine rulers of Gaza, Ashdod, Ashkelon, Gath, and Ekron, as well as the Avvites 4 in the south; all the land of the Canaanites: from Arah of the Sidonians to Aphek and as far as the border of the Amorites; 5 the land of the Gebalites; and all Lebanon east from Baal-gad below Mount Hermon to the entrance of Hamath[c]—6 all the inhabitants of the hill country from Lebanon to Misrephoth-maim, all the Sidonians.

I will drive them out before the Israelites, only distribute the land as an inheritance for Israel, as I have commanded you. 7 Therefore, divide this land as an inheritance to the nine tribes and half the tribe of Manasseh."

The Inheritance East of the Jordan

8 With the other half of the tribe, the Reubenites and Gadites had received the inheritance Moses gave them beyond the Jordan to the east, just as Moses the LORD's servant had given them:

9 From Aroer on the rim of the Arnon Valley, along with the city in the middle of the valley, all the Medeba plateau as far as Dibon, 10 and all the cities of Sihon king of the Amorites, who reigned in Heshbon, to the border of the Ammonites; 11 also Gilead and the territory of the Geshurites and Maacathites, all Mount Hermon, and all Bashan to Salecah— 12 the whole kingdom of Og in Bashan, who reigned in Ashtaroth and Edrei; he was one of the remaining Rephaim.

Moses struck them down and drove them out, 13 but the Israelites did not drive out the Geshurites and Maacathites. So Geshur and Maacath live in Israel to this day.

14 He did not give any inheritance to the tribe of Levi. This was its inheritance, just as He had promised: the offerings made by fire to the LORD, the God of Israel.

Reuben's Inheritance

15 To the tribe of the Reubenites by their clans, Moses gave 16 this as their territory:

From Aroer on the rim of the Arnon Valley, along with the city in the middle of the valley, to the whole plateau as far as[d] Medeba, 17 with Heshbon and all its cities on the plateau—Dibon, Bamoth-baal, Beth-baal-meon, 18 Jahaz, Kedemoth, Mephaath, 19 Kiriathaim, Sibmah, Zereth-shahar on the hill in the valley, 20 Beth-peor, the slopes of Pisgah, and Beth-jeshimoth— 21 all the cities of the plateau, and all the kingdom of Sihon king of the Amorites, who reigned in Heshbon. Moses had killed him and the chiefs of Midian—Evi, Rekem, Zur, Hur, and Reba—the princes of Sihon who lived in the land. 22 Along with those the Israelites put to death, they also killed the diviner, Balaam son of Beor, with the sword.

23 The border of the Reubenites was the Jordan and its plain. This was the inheritance of the Reubenites by their clans, with the cities and their villages.

Gad's Inheritance

24 To the tribe of the Gadites by their clans, Moses gave 25 this as their territory:

Jazer and all the cities of Gilead, and half the land of the Ammonites to Aroer, near Rabbah; 26 from Heshbon to Ramath-mizpeh and Betonim, and from Mahanaim to the border of Debir;[e] 27 in the valley:[f] Beth-haram, Beth-nimrah, Succoth, and Zaphon—the rest of the kingdom of Sihon king of Heshbon. ⌊Their land also included⌋ the Jordan and its territory as far as the edge of the Sea of Chinnereth[g] on the east side of the Jordan.[h]

28 This was the inheritance of the Gadites by their clans, with the cities and their villages.

East Manasseh's Inheritance

29 And to half the tribe of Manasseh, that is, to half the tribe of Manasseh's descendants by their clans, Moses gave 30 this as their territory:

---

a**12:23** Or *in the Slopes of Dor* b**12:23** LXX reads *Galilee* c**13:5** Or *to Lebo-hamath* d**13:16** Other Hb mss read *plateau near* e**13:26** Or *Lidbir*, or *Lo-debar* f**13:27** = the Jordan River Valley g**13:27** = the Sea of Galilee h**13:27** Lit *Chinnereth beyond the Jordan to the east*

---

miliar territory, Joshua did not give up. He stayed at the task he had been assigned by the Lord.

11:20 harden their hearts. God confirmed that the Canaanites stubbornly resisted His grace. But Rahab showed his willingness to give these pagan people the opportunity to repent (6:25).

12:12 king of Gezer. Although Joshua defeated many Canaanite kings, the record does not necessarily mean their cities were captured as well. The king of Gezer is one example (10:33). With his limited army, Joshua was not able to station troops at all the cities of the Canaanites.

13:1 Joshua was now old. At the time of these events, Joshua was about 100 years old.

13:2-6 the land that remains. At the end of Joshua's conquest of Canaan, two primary territories remained in enemy hands: (1) the southwest coastal strip controlled by the Phi-

From Mahanaim through all Bashan—all the kingdom of Og king of Bashan, including all of Jair's Villages[a] that are in Bashan—60 cities. 31 But half of Gilead, and Og's royal cities in Bashan—Ashtaroth and Edrei—are for the descendants of Machir son of Manasseh, that is, half the descendants of Machir by their clans.

32 These were the portions Moses gave ⌊them⌋ on the plains of Moab beyond the Jordan east of Jericho. 33 But Moses did not give a portion to the tribe of Levi. The LORD, the God of Israel, was their inheritance, just as He had promised them.

Israel's Inheritance in Canaan

14 The Israelites received these portions that Eleazar the priest, Joshua son of Nun, and the heads of the families of the Israelite tribes gave them in the land of Canaan. 2 Their inheritance was by lot as the LORD commanded through Moses for the nine and a half tribes, 3 because Moses had given the inheritance to the two and a half tribes beyond the Jordan.[b] But he gave no inheritance among them to the Levites. 4 The descendants of Joseph became two tribes, Manasseh and Ephraim. No portion of the land was given to the Levites except cities to live in, along with pasturelands for their cattle and livestock. 5 So the Israelites did as the LORD commanded Moses, and they divided the land.

Caleb's Inheritance

6 The descendants of Judah approached Joshua at Gilgal, and Caleb son of Jephunneh the Kenizzite said to him, "You know what the LORD promised Moses the man of God at Kadesh-barnea about you and me. 7 I was 40 years old when Moses the LORD's servant sent me from Kadesh-barnea to scout the land, and I brought back an honest report. 8 My brothers who went with me caused the people's hearts to melt with fear, but I remained loyal to the LORD my God. 9 On that day Moses promised me, 'The land where you have set foot will be an inheritance for you and your descendants forever, because you have remained loyal to the LORD my God.'

10 "As you see, the LORD has kept me alive ⌊these⌋ 45 years as He promised, since the LORD spoke this word to Moses while Israel was journeying in the wilderness. Here I am today, 85 years old. 11 I am still as strong today as I was the day Moses sent me out. My strength for battle and for daily tasks[c] is now as it was then. 12 Now give me this hill country the LORD promised

⌊me⌋ on that day, because you heard then that the Anakim are there, as well as large fortified cities. Perhaps the LORD will be with me and I will drive them out as the LORD promised."

13 Then Joshua blessed Caleb son of Jephunneh and gave him Hebron as an inheritance. 14 Therefore, Hebron has belonged to Caleb son of Jephunneh the Kenizzite as an inheritance to this day, because he remained loyal to the LORD, the God of Israel. 15 Hebron's name used to be Kiriath-arba; Arba was the greatest man among the Anakim. After this, the land had rest from war.

Judah's Inheritance

15 Now the allotment for the tribe of the descendants of Judah by their clans was in the southernmost region, south of the wilderness of Zin to the border of Edom.

2 Their southern border began at the tip of the Dead Sea on the south bay[d] 3 and went south of the ascent of Akrabbim,[e] proceeded to Zin, ascended to the south of Kadesh-barnea, passed Hezron, ascended to Addar, and turned to Karka. 4 It proceeded to Azmon and to the Brook of Egypt and so the border ended at the Mediterranean Sea. This is your[f] southern border.

5 Now the eastern border was along the Dead Sea to the mouth of the Jordan.[g]

The border on the north side was from the bay of the sea at the mouth of the Jordan. 6 It ascended to Beth-hoglah, proceeded north of Beth-arabah, and ascended to the stone of Bohan son of Reuben. 7 Then the border ascended to Debir from the Valley of Achor, turning north to the Gilgal that is opposite the ascent of Adummim, which is south of the ravine. The border proceeded to the waters of En-shemesh and ended at En-rogel. 8 From there the border ascended the Valley of Hinnom to the southern Jebusite slope (that is, Jerusalem) and ascended to the top of the hill that faces the Valley of Hinnom on the west, at the northern end of the Valley of Rephaim. 9 From the top of the hill the border curved to the spring of the Waters of Nephtoah, went to the cities of Mount Ephron, and then curved to Baalah (that is, Kiriath-jearim). 10 The border turned westward from Baalah to Mount Seir, went to the northern slope of Mount Jearim (that is, Chesalon),

---

a**13:30** Or *all of Havvoth-jair*   b**14:3** = east of the Jordan River   c**14:11** Lit *for going out and coming in*   d**15:2** Lit *Sea at the tongue that turns southward*   e**15:3** Lit *of scorpions*   f**15:4** LXX reads *their*   g**15:5** The southern end of the *Jordan* River at the *Dead Sea*

---

listines and Geshurites and (2) the far northern plains associated with Sidon on the coast and Mt. Hermon in the interior.

13:15 tribe of the Reubenites. These Israelites were cattle herders, and they anxiously awaited possession of the rich grazing land southeast of the Jordan River.

13:24 tribe of the Gadites. Members of this tribe had settled in the central region east of the Jordan River.

13:29 to half the tribe of Manasseh. Although the land northeast of the Jordan River was beautiful, neither Manasseh, Gad, or Reuben had a natural protective border to the east.

14:1 Eleazar. Using the priest Eleazar to divide the land according to lots reemphasized God's role in each tribe's inheritance.

14:4 two tribes, Manasseh and Ephraim. These were actually Joseph's children, whom Jacob had adopted to form the twelve tribes. They shared full legal rights of inheritance.

descended to Beth-shemesh, and proceeded to Timnah. 11 Then the border reached to the slope north of Ekron, curved to Shikkeron, proceeded to Mount Baalah, went to Jabneel, and ended at the Mediterranean Sea.

12 Now the western border was the coastline of the Mediterranean Sea.

This was the boundary of the descendants of Judah around their clans.

Caleb and Othniel

13 He gave Caleb son of Jephunneh ⌊the following⌋ portion among the descendants of Judah based on the LORD's instruction to Joshua: Kiriath-arba (that is, Hebron; Arba was the father of Anak). 14 Caleb drove out from there the three sons of Anak: Sheshai, Ahiman, and Talmai, descendants of Anak. 15 From there he marched against the inhabitants of Debir whose name used to be Kiriath-sepher, 16 and Caleb said, "I will give my daughter Achsah as a wife to the one who strikes down and captures Kiriath-sepher." 17 So Othniel son of Caleb's brother, Kenaz, captured it, and Caleb gave his daughter Achsah to him as a wife. 18 When she arrived, she persuaded Othniel to ask her father for a field. As she got off her donkey, Caleb asked her, "What do you want?" 19 She replied, "Give me a blessing. Since you have given me land in the •Negev, give me the springs of water also." So he gave her the upper and lower springs.

Judah's Cities

20 This was the inheritance of the tribe of the descendants of Judah by their clans.

21 These were the outermost cities of the tribe of the descendants of Judah toward the border of Edom in the Negev: Kabzeel, Eder, Jagur, 22 Kinah, Dimonah, Adadah, 23 Kedesh, Hazor, Ithnan, 24 Ziph, Telem, Bealoth, 25 Hazor-hadattah, Keri-oth-hezron (that is, Hazor), 26 Amam, Shema, Moladah, 27 Hazar-gaddah, Heshmon, Beth-pelet, 28 Hazar-shual, Beer-sheba, Biziothiah, 29 Baalah, Iim, Ezem, 30 Eltolad, Chesil, Hormah, 31 Ziklag, Madmannah, Sansannah, 32 Lebaoth, Shilhim, Ain, and Rimmon—29 cities in all, with their villages.

33 In the Judean foothills:a Eshtaol, Zorah, Ashnah, 34 Zanoah, En-gannim, Tappuah,b Enam, 35 Jarmuth, Adullam, Socoh,c Azekah, 36 Shaaraim, Adithaim, Gederah, and Gederothaim—14 cities, with their villages; 37 Zenan, Hadashah, Migdal-gad, 38 Dilan, Mizpeh, Jokthe-el, 39 Lachish, Bozkath, Eglon, 40 Cabbon, Lahmam, Chitlish, 41 Gederoth, Beth-dagon, Naamah, and Makkedah—16 cities, with their villages; 42 Libnah, Ether, Ashan, 43 Iphtah, Ashnah, Nezib, 44 Keilah, Achzib, and Mareshah—nine cities, with their villages; 45 Ekron, with its towns and villages; 46 from Ekron to the sea, all ⌊the cities⌋ near Ashdod, with their villages; 47 Ashdod, with its towns and villages; Gaza, with its towns and villages, to the Brook of Egypt and the coastline of the Mediterranean Sea.

48 In the hill country: Shamir, Jattir, Socoh, 49 Dannah, Kiriath-sannah (that is, Debir), 50 Anab, Eshtemoh, Anim, 51 Goshen, Holon, and Giloh—11 cities, with their villages; 52 Arab, Dumah,d Eshan, 53 Janim, Beth-tappuah, Aphekah, 54 Humtah, Kiriath-arba (that is, Hebron), and Zior—nine cities, with their villages; 55 Maon, Carmel, Ziph, Juttah, 56 Jezreel, Jokdeam, Zanoah, 57 Kain, Gibeah, and Timnah—10 cities, with their villages; 58 Halhul, Beth-zur, Gedor, 59 Maarath, Beth-anoth, and Eltekon—six cities, with their villages;e 60 Kiriath-baal (that is, Kiriath-jearim), and Rabbah—two cities, with their villages.

61 In the wilderness: Beth-arabah, Middin, Secacah, 62 Nibshan, the City of Salt,f and En-gedi—six cities, with their villages.

63 But the descendants of Judah could not drive out the Jebusites who lived in Jerusalem. So the Jebusites live in Jerusalem among the descendants of Judah to this day.

Joseph's Inheritance

16 The allotment for the descendants of Josephg went from the Jordan at Jericho to the waters of Jericho on the east, through the wilderness ascending from Jericho into the hill country of Bethel. 2 From Bethel it went to Luz and proceeded to the border of the Archites by Ataroth. 3 It then descended westward to the border of the Japhletites as far as the border of lower Beth-horon, then to Gezer, and ended at the Mediterranean Sea. 4 So Ephraim and Manasseh, the sons of Joseph, received their inheritance.

---

a15:33 Or the Shephelah   b15:34 Or possibly 1 name: En-gannim-tappuah   c15:35 Or possibly 1 name: Adullam-socoh   d15:52 Other Hb mss read Rumah   e15:59 LXX adds Tekoa, Ephrathah (that is, Bethlehem), Peor, Etam, Culom, Tatam, Sores, Carem, Gallim, Baither, and Manach—11 cities, with their villages   f15:62 Or Ir-hamelach   g16:1 The tribes of Ephraim and Manasseh

---

Half of Manasseh had already received an allotment of land east of the Jordan River.

14:6-13 Caleb son of Jephunneh. Caleb, one of the original spies sent into Canaan, revealed his plans for securing his inheritance in Hebron. This had been the favored city of Abraham (Gen. 13:18) and the burial place of the patriarchs (Gen. 25:9; 35:27-29; 50:12-13). The 12 spies had visited Hebron (Num. 13:22).

15:1 descendants of Judah. From this tribe sprang powerful rulers like David and eventually the Messiah.

15:2 Their southern border. The great detail provided here (vv. 1-12) reveals the importance of the land inheritance to the people and God.

15:63 could not drive out the Jebusites ... in Jerusalem. Joshua had conquered Jerusalem (10:1-27; 12:10), but the Jebusites apparently reoccupied the city.

16:1–17:18 Not only did Joseph's tribes, Ma-

Ephraim's Inheritance

5 This was the territory of the descendants of Ephraim by their clans:

The border of their inheritance went from Ataroth-addar on the east of Upper Beth-horon. 6 In the north the border went westward from Mich-methath; it turned eastward from Taanath-shiloh and passed it east of Janoah. 7 From Janoah it descended to Ataroth and Naarah, and then reached Jericho and went to the Jordan. 8 From Tappuah the border[a] went westward along the Brook of Kanah and ended at the Mediterranean Sea.

This was the inheritance of the tribe of the descendants of Ephraim by their clans, together with 9 the cities set apart for the descendants of Ephraim within the inheritance of the descendants of Manasseh—all these cities with their villages. 10 But, they did not drive out the Canaanites who lived in Gezer. So the Canaanites live in Ephraim to this day, but they are forced laborers.

West Manasseh's Inheritance

17 This was the allotment for the tribe of Manasseh as Joseph's firstborn. Gilead and Bashan came to Machir, the firstborn of Manasseh and the father of Gilead, who was a man of war. 2 So the allotment was for the rest of Manasseh's descendants by their clans, for the sons of Abiezer, Helek, Asriel, Shechem, Hepher, and Shemida. These are the male descendants of Manasseh son of Joseph, by their clans.

3 Now Zelophehad son of Hepher, son of Gilead, son of Machir, son of Manasseh, had no sons, only daughters. These are the names of his daughters: Mahlah, Noah, Hoglah, Milcah, and Tirzah. 4 They came before Eleazar the priest, Joshua son of Nun, and the leaders, saying, "The LORD commanded Moses to give us an inheritance among our male relatives."[b] So they gave them an inheritance among their father's brothers, in keeping with the LORD's instruction. 5 As a result, 10 tracts fell to Manasseh, besides the land of Gilead and Bashan, which are beyond the Jordan,[c] 6 because Manasseh's daughters received an inheritance among his sons. The land of Gilead belonged to the rest of Manasseh's sons.

7 The border of Manasseh went from Asher to Michmethath near Shechem. It then went southward toward the inhabitants of En-tappuah. 8 The region of Tappuah belonged to Manasseh, but Tappuah [itself] on Manasseh's border belonged

to the descendants of Ephraim. 9 From there the border descended to the Brook of Kanah; south of the brook, cities belonged to Ephraim among Manasseh's cities. Manasseh's border was on the north side of the brook and ended at the Mediterranean Sea. 10 Ephraim's [territory] was to the south and Manasseh's to the north, with the Sea as its border. They[d] reached Asher on the north and Issachar on the east. 11 Within Issachar and Asher, Manasseh had Beth-shean with its towns, Ibleam with its towns, and the inhabitants of Dor with its towns; the inhabitants of En-dor with its towns, the inhabitants of Taanach with its towns, and the inhabitants of Megiddo with its towns—the three [cities] of[e] Naphath.

12 The descendants of Manasseh could not possess these cities, because the Canaanites were determined to stay in this land. 13 However, when the Israelites grew stronger, they imposed forced labor on the Canaanites but did not drive them out completely.

Joseph's Additional Inheritance

14 Joseph's descendants said to Joshua: "Why did you give us only one tribal allotment[f] as an inheritance? We have many people, because the LORD has greatly blessed us."

15 "If you have so many people," Joshua replied to them, "go to the forest and clear [an area] for yourselves there in the land of the Perizzites and the Rephaim, because Ephraim's hill country is too small for you."

16 But the descendants of Joseph said, "The hill country is not enough for us, and all the Canaanites who inhabit the valley area have iron chariots, both at Beth-shean with its towns and in the Jezreel Valley."

17 So Joshua replied to Joseph's family (that is, Ephraim and Manasseh), "You have many people and great strength. You will not have just one lot, 18 because the hill country will be yours also. It is a forest; clear it and its outlying areas will be yours. You can also drive out the Canaanites, even though they have iron chariots and are strong."

Land Distribution at Shiloh

18 The entire Israelite community assembled at Shiloh where it set up the tent of meeting there; the land had been subdued by them. 2 Seven tribes among the Israelites were left who had not divided up their inheritance. 3 So Joshua said to the Israelites, "How long will you delay going out to take possession of the land that the LORD, the God of your

---

a 16:8 Ephraim's northern border   b 17:4 Lit our brothers   c 17:5 East of the Jordan River   d 17:10 The people of Manasseh, or Manasseh's borders   e 17:11 LXX, Vg read the third is   f 17:14 Lit one lot and one territory

---

nasseh and Ephraim, follow Judah in priority; they were also given the beautiful central corridor of Canaan.

16:1 Joseph. Since Joseph played such a key role in the survival of the Israelites during a famine, it was fitting that his sons should be given such prominence.

16:5 Ephraim. His territory became well known because of Shiloh's role as the early location for the tabernacle.

17:1 Manasseh. The tribe of Manasseh would become Ephraim's northern neighbor and would receive a territory a little smaller than that of Judah.

17:3 Zelophehad. The great-great grandson of Manasseh.

17:5-10 tracts fell to Manasseh. Zelophehad's daughters received shares of land along with the male descendants of Manasseh.

17:14 only one tribal allotment. One of the

237

fathers, gave you? [4] Appoint for yourselves three men from each tribe, and I will send them out. They are to go and survey the land, write a description of it for the purpose of their inheritance, and return to me. [5] Then they are to divide it into seven portions. Judah is to remain in its territory in the south, and Joseph's family in their[a] territory in the north. [6] When you have written a description of the seven portions of land and brought it to me, I will cast lots for you here in the presence of the LORD our God. [7] But the Levites among you do not get a portion, because their inheritance is the priesthood of the LORD. Gad, Reuben, and half the tribe of Manasseh have taken their inheritance beyond the Jordan to the east, which Moses the LORD's servant gave them."

[8] As the men prepared to go, Joshua commanded them[b] to write down a description of the land, saying, "Go and survey the land, write a description of it, and return to me. I will then cast lots for you here in Shiloh in the presence of the LORD." [9] So the men left, went through the land, and described it by towns in a document of seven sections. They returned to Joshua at the camp in Shiloh. [10] Joshua cast lots for them at Shiloh in the presence of the LORD where he distributed the land to the Israelites according to their divisions.

Benjamin's Inheritance

[11] The lot came up for the tribe of Benjamin's descendants by their clans, and their allotted territory lay between Judah's descendants and Joseph's descendants.

[12] Their border on the north side began at the Jordan, ascended to the slope of Jericho on the north, through the hill country westward, and ended at the wilderness of Beth-aven. [13] From there the border went toward Luz, to the southern slope of Luz (that is, Bethel); it then went down by Ataroth-addar, over the hill south of Lower Beth-horon.

[14] On the west side, from the hill facing Beth-horon on the south, the border curved, turning southward, and ended at Kiriath-baal (that is, Kiriath-jearim), a city of the descendants of Judah. This was the west side [of their border].

[15] The south side began at the edge of Kiriath-jearim, and the border extended westward; it went to the spring at the Waters of Nephtoah. [16] The border descended to the foot of the hill that faces the Valley of Hinnom at the northern end of the Valley of Rephaim. It ran down the Valley of Hinnom toward the south Jebusite slope and downward to En-rogel. [17] It curved northward and went to En-shemesh and on to Geliloth, which is opposite the ascent of Adummim, and continued down to the Stone of Bohan, Reuben's son. [18] Then it went north to the slope opposite the Jordan Valley[c] [d] and proceeded into the valley.[d] [19] The border continued to the north slope of Beth-hoglah and ended at the northern bay of the Dead Sea, at the southern end of the Jordan. This was the southern border.

[20] The Jordan formed the border on the east side.

This was the inheritance of Benjamin's descendants, by their clans, according to its surrounding borders.

Benjamin's Cities

[21] These were the cities of the tribe of Benjamin's descendants by their clans:

Jericho, Beth-hoglah, Emek-keziz, [22] Beth-arabah, Zemaraim, Bethel, [23] Avvim, Parah, Ophrah, [24] Chephar-ammoni, Ophni, and Geba—12 cities, with their villages; [25] Gibeon, Ramah, Beeroth, [26] Mizpeh,[e] Chephirah, Mozah, [27] Rekem, Irpeel, Taralah, [28] Zela, Haeleph, Jebus[f] (that is, Jerusalem), Gibeah, and Kiriath[g]—14 cities, with their villages.

This was the inheritance for Benjamin's descendants by their clans.

Simeon's Inheritance

19 The second lot came out for Simeon, for the tribe of his descendants by their clans, but their inheritance was within the portion of Judah's descendants. [2] Their inheritance included:

Beer-sheba (or Sheba), Moladah, [3] Hazar-shual, Balah, Ezem, [4] Eltolad, Bethul, Hormah, [5] Ziklag, Beth-marcaboth, Hazar-susah, [6] Beth-lebaoth, and Sharuhen—13 cities, with their villages; [7] Ain, Rimmon, Ether, and Ashan—four cities, with their villages; [8] and all the villages surrounding these cities as far as Baalath-beer (Ramah of the south[h]).

This was the inheritance of the tribe of Simeon's descendants by their clans. [9] The inheritance of Simeon's descendants was within the territory of Judah's

---

[a]**18:5** = the tribes of Ephraim and Manasseh   [b]**18:8** Lit the ones going around   [c]**18:18** LXX reads went northward to Beth-arabah   [d]**18:18** Or the Arabah   [e]**18:26** Alt spelling of Mizpah; Jos 11:3,8   [f]**18:28** Lit Jebusite   [g]**18:28** LXX, Syr read Kiriath-jearim   [h]**19:8** Or the Negev

---

larger tribes felt too crowded in its current allotment.

17:15 go to the forest and clear [an area]. Joshua instructed this tribe to leverage their size, dominate their enemies, and expand beyond their hill country to gain more territory.

18:1–19:51 Joshua gathered the tribes at the tabernacle in Shiloh for the final divisions of the land. Lots were cast and a special allotment of land was set aside for Joshua.

18:1 Israelite community assembled at Shiloh. The tabernacle was located at Shiloh—a perfect spot for group decisions about what was important in Israel's priorities. Shiloh was in the hill country of Ephraim roughly 15 miles northwest of Jericho and 10 miles north of Bethel.

18:3 take possession of the land. It was one thing to conquer a rival king. It was quite another to move in and take over—as the tribes would soon find out.

descendants, because the share for Judah's descendants was too large for them. So Simeon's descendants received an inheritance within Judah's portion.

Zebulun's Inheritance

10 The third lot came up for Zebulun's descendants by their clans.

The territory of their inheritance stretched as far as Sarid; 11 their border went up westward to Maralah, reached Dabbesheth, and met the brook east of Jokneam. 12 From Sarid, it turned east toward the sunrise along the border of Chisloth-tabor, went to Daberath, and went up to Japhia. 13 From there, it went east toward the sunrise to Gath-hepher and to Eth-kazin; it extended to Rimmon, curving around to Neah. 14 The border then circled around Neah on the north to Hannathon and ended at the valley of Iphtah-el, 15 along with Kattath, Nahalal, Shimron, Idalah, and Bethlehem—12 cities, with their villages.

16 This was the inheritance of Zebulun's descendants by their clans, these cities, with their villages.

Issachar's Inheritance

17 The fourth lot came out for the tribe of Issachar's descendants by their clans.

18 Their territory went to Jezreel, and [included] Chesulloth, Shunem, 19 Hapharaim, Shion, Anaharath, 20 Rabbith, Kishion, Ebez, 21 Remeth, Engannim, En-haddah, Beth-pazzez. 22 The border reached Tabor, Shahazumah, and Beth-shemesh, and ended at the Jordan—16 cities, with their villages.

23 This was the inheritance of the tribe of Issachar's descendants by their clans, the cities, with their villages.

Asher's Inheritance

24 The fifth lot came out for the tribe of Asher's descendants by their clans.

25 Their boundary included Helkath, Hali, Beten, Achshaph, 26 Allammelech, Amad, and Mishal and reached westward to Carmel and Shihor-libnath. 27 It turned eastward to Beth-dagon, passed Zebulun and the valley of Iphtah-el, north toward Beth-emek and Neiel, and went north to Cabul, 28 Ebron, Rehob, Hammon, and Kanah, as far as Great Sidon. 29 The boundary then turned to

Ramah as far as the fortified city of Tyre; it turned back to Hosah and ended at the sea, including Mahalab, Achzib,[a] 30 Ummah, Aphek, and Rehob—22 cities, with their villages.

31 This was the inheritance of the tribe of Asher's descendants by their clans, these cities with their villages.

Naphtali's Inheritance

32 The sixth lot came out for Naphtali's descendants by their clans.

33 Their boundary went from Heleph and from the oak in Zaanannim, including Adami-nekeb and Jabneel, as far as Lakkum, and ended at the Jordan. 34 To the west, the boundary turned to Aznoth-tabor and went from there to Hukkok, reaching Zebulun on the south, Asher on the west, and Judah[b] at the Jordan on the east. 35 The fortified cities were Ziddim, Zer, Hammath, Rakkath, Chinnereth,[c] 36 Adamah, Ramah, Hazor, 37 Kedesh, Edrei, En-hazor, 38 Iron, Migdal-el, Horem, Beth-anath, and Beth-shemesh—19 cities, with their villages.

39 This was the inheritance of the tribe of Naphtali's descendants by their clans, the cities with their villages.

Dan's Inheritance

40 The seventh lot came out for the Danite tribe by its clans.

41 The territory of their inheritance included Zorah, Eshtaol, Ir-shemesh, 42 Shaalabbin, Aijalon, Ithlah, 43 Elon, Timnah, Ekron, 44 Eltekeh, Gibbethon, Baalath, 45 Jehud, Bene-berak, Gathrimmon, 46 Me-jarkon, and Rakkon, with the territory facing Joppa.

47 When the territory of the Danites slipped out of their control,[d] they went up and fought against Leshem, captured it, and struck it down with the sword. So they took possession of it, lived there, and renamed Leshem after[e] their ancestor Dan. 48 This was the inheritance of the Danite tribe by its clans, these cities with their villages.

Joshua's Inheritance

49 When they had finished distributing the land into its territories, the Israelites gave Joshua son of Nun an inheritance among them. 50 By the LORD's command, they gave him the city Timnath-serah in the hill country

---

a 19:29 Or sea, in the region of Achzib   b 19:34 LXX omits Judah   c 19:35 A town near the Sea of Galilee   d 19:47 Lit territory of the sons of Dan went out from them   e 19:47 Lit and called Leshem, Dan, after the name of

---

18:6 I will cast lots. The Lord distributed the portions of land to the various tribes by means of lots. No politicking, favoritism, or pressure tactics played any role in who got what territory.

18:11 Benjamin's … allotted territory. The territory settled by this tribe was squeezed between the two dominant tribes, Judah and

Ephraim and served as an important link between these two tribes. In the years to come, Benjamin would exert an influence in Israel far beyond its territorial and population size . The following key cities fell within the boundaries of Benjamin: Jericho, Bethel, Gibeon, Mizpah, Ai and Jerusalem. The temple would be built in

the territory of Benjamin. Israel's first king, Saul, would come from the tribe of Benjamin as would another Saul (of Tarsus, Paul), Christ's foremost representative to the Gentile world.

19:47 went up … took possession. Joshua assigned Dan tribal land between Judah and Benjamin to the east and the Amorites and

of Ephraim, which he requested. He rebuilt the city and lived in it.

51 These were the portions that Eleazar the priest, Joshua son of Nun, and the heads of the families distributed to the Israelite tribes by lot at Shiloh in the LORD's presence at the entrance to the tent of meeting. So they finished dividing up the land.

Cities of Refuge

20 Then the LORD spoke to Joshua, 2 "Tell the Israelites: 'Select your cities of refuge, as I instructed you through Moses, 3 so that a person who kills someone unintentionally or accidentally may flee there. These will be your refuge from the avenger of blood. 4 When someone flees to one of these cities, stands at the entrance of the city ·gate, and states his case before[a] the elders of that city, they are to bring him into the city and give him a place to live among them. 5 And if the avenger of blood pursues him, they must not hand the one who committed manslaughter over to him, for he killed his neighbor accidentally and did not hate him beforehand. 6 He is to stay in that city until he stands trial before the assembly and until the death of the high priest serving at that time. Then the one who committed manslaughter may return home to his own city from which he fled.'"

7 So they designated Kedesh in the hill country of Naphtali in Galilee, Shechem in the hill country of Ephraim, and Kiriath-arba (that is, Hebron) in the hill country of Judah. 8 Across the Jordan east of Jericho, they selected Bezer on the wilderness plateau from Reuben's tribe, Ramoth in Gilead from Gad's tribe, and Golan in Bashan from Manasseh's tribe. 9 These are the cities appointed for all the Israelites and foreigners among them, so that anyone who kills a person unintentionally may flee there and not die at the hand of the avenger of blood until he stands before the assembly.

Cities of the Levites

21 The heads of the Levite families approached Eleazar the priest, Joshua son of Nun, and the heads of the families of the Israelite tribes. 2 They told them at Shiloh in the land of Canaan: "The LORD commanded through Moses that we be given cities to live in, with their pasturelands for our livestock." 3 So the Israelites, by the LORD's command, gave the Levites these cities with their pasturelands from their inheritance.

4 The lot came out for the Kohathite clans: The Levites who were the descendants of Aaron the

priest received 13 cities by lot from the tribes of Judah, Simeon, and Benjamin. 5 The remaining descendants of Kohath[b] received 10 cities by lot from the clans of the tribes of Ephraim, Dan, and half the tribe of Manasseh.

6 Gershon's descendants received 13 cities by lot from the clans of the tribes of Issachar, Asher, Naphtali, and half the tribe of Manasseh in Bashan.

7 Merari's descendants received 12 cities for their clans from the tribes of Reuben, Gad, and Zebulun.

8 The Israelites gave these cities with their pasturelands around them to the Levites by lot, as the LORD had commanded through Moses.

Cities of Aaron's Descendants

9 The Israelites gave these cities by name from the tribes of the descendants of Judah and Simeon 10 to the descendants of Aaron from the Kohathite clans of the Levites, because they received the first lot. 11 They gave them Kiriath-arba (that is, Hebron) with its surrounding pasturelands in the hill country of Judah. Arba was the father of Anak. 12 But they gave the fields and villages of the city to Caleb son of Jephunneh as his possession.

13 They gave to the descendants of Aaron the priest:

Hebron, the city of refuge for the one who commits manslaughter, with its pasturelands, Libnah with its pasturelands, 14 Jattir with its pasturelands, Eshtemoa with its pasturelands, 15 Holon with its pasturelands, Debir with its pasturelands, 16 Ain with its pasturelands, Juttah with its pasturelands, and Beth-shemesh with its pasturelands—nine cities from these two tribes.

17 From the tribe of Benjamin ⌊they gave⌋:

Gibeon with its pasturelands, Geba with its pasturelands, 18 Anathoth with its pasturelands, and Almon with its pasturelands—four cities. 19 All 13 cities with their pasturelands were for the priests, the descendants of Aaron.

Cities of Kohath's Other Descendants

20 The allotted cities to the remaining clans of Kohath's descendants, who were Levites, came from the tribe of Ephraim. 21 The Israelites gave them:

Shechem, the city of refuge for the one who commits manslaughter, with its pasturelands in the

---

a 20:4 Lit in the ears of   b 21:5 = descendants not in Aaron's priestly line

---

Philistines to the west. Dan could not conquer its assigned territory (Judg. 1:34; 18:1). Eventually most of the tribe migrated about 100 miles to the far north of Israel and seized undefended towns and land (18:2-31).

19:49 an inheritance among them. A true leader, Joshua served his people first. At last,

he was rewarded with a land allotment that he wanted and deserved.

20:1-9 Now that Israel was settled in the land, the crime of manslaughter was the first issue addressed. A city of refuge under the supervision of the Levites would provide justice for people accused of this crime.

20:3 refuge from the avenger of blood. A relative of the person who had been killed was responsible for killing the criminal in a murder case.

20:4 entrance of the city gate. The city gate was a place where commerce and trials took place. This gate was more than a doorway. It

hill country of Ephraim, Gezer with its pasture-lands, ²² Kibzaim with its pasturelands, and Beth-horon with its pasturelands—four cities.

²³ From the tribe of Dan ⌊they gave⌋:

Elteke with its pasturelands, Gibbethon with its pasturelands, ²⁴ Aijalon with its pasturelands, and Gath-rimmon with its pasturelands—four cities.

²⁵ From half the tribe of Manasseh ⌊they gave⌋:

Taanach with its pasturelands and Gath-rimmon^a with its pasturelands—two cities.

²⁶ All 10 cities with their pasturelands were for the clans of Kohath's other descendants.

Cities of Gershon's Descendants

²⁷ From half the tribe of Manasseh, ⌊they gave⌋ to the descendants of Gershon, who were one of the Levite clans:

Golan, the city of refuge for the one who commits manslaughter, with its pasturelands in Bashan, and Beeshterah with its pasturelands—two cities.

²⁸ From the tribe of Issachar ⌊they gave⌋:

Kishion with its pasturelands, Daberath with its pasturelands, ²⁹ Jarmuth with its pasturelands, and En-gannim with its pasturelands—four cities.

³⁰ From the tribe of Asher ⌊they gave⌋:

Mishal with its pasturelands, Abdon with its pasturelands, ³¹ Helkath with its pasturelands, and Rehob with its pasturelands—four cities.

³² From the tribe of Naphtali ⌊they gave⌋:

Kedesh in Galilee, the city of refuge for the one who commits manslaughter, with its pasturelands, Hammoth-dor with its pasturelands, and Kartan with its pasturelands—three cities.

³³ All 13 cities with their pasturelands were for the Gershonites by their clans.

Cities of Merari's Descendants

³⁴ From the tribe of Zebulun, ⌊they gave⌋ to the clans of the descendants of Merari, who were the remaining Levites:

Jokneam with its pasturelands, Kartah with its pasturelands, ³⁵ Dimnah with its pasturelands, and Nahalal with its pasturelands—four cities.

³⁶ From the tribe of Reuben, ⌊they gave⌋:

Bezer with its pasturelands, Jahzah^b with its pasturelands, ³⁷ Kedemoth with its pasturelands, and Mephaath with its pasturelands—four cities.^c

³⁸ From the tribe of Gad, ⌊they gave⌋:

Ramoth in Gilead, the city of refuge for the one who commits manslaughter, with its pasturelands, Mahanaim with its pasturelands, ³⁹ Heshbon with its pasturelands, and Jazer with its pasturelands—four cities in all. ⁴⁰ All 12 cities were allotted to the clans of Merari's descendants, the remaining Levite clans.

⁴¹ Within the Israelite possession there were 48 cities in all with their pasturelands for the Levites. ⁴² Each of these cities had its own surrounding pasturelands; this was true for all the cities.

The LORD's Promises Fulfilled

⁴³ So the LORD gave Israel all the land He had sworn to give their fathers, and they took possession of it and settled there. ⁴⁴ The LORD gave them rest on every side according to all He had sworn to their fathers. None of their enemies were able to stand against them, for the LORD handed over all their enemies to them. ⁴⁵ None of the good promises the LORD had made to the house of Israel failed. Everything was fulfilled.

Eastern Tribes Return Home

22 Joshua summoned the Reubenites, Gadites, and half the tribe of Manasseh, ² and told them, "You have done everything Moses the LORD's servant commanded you and have obeyed me in everything I commanded you. ³ You have not deserted your brothers even once this whole time but have carried out the requirement of the command of the LORD your God. ⁴ Now that He has given your brothers rest, just as He promised them, return to your homes in your own land that Moses the LORD's servant gave you across the Jordan. ⁵ Only carefully obey the command and instruction that Moses the LORD's servant gave you: to love the LORD your God, walk in all His ways, keep His commands, remain faithful^d to Him, and serve Him with all your heart and all your soul."

⁶ Joshua blessed them and sent them on their way, and they went to their homes. ⁷ Moses had given ⌊territory⌋ to half the tribe of Manasseh in Bashan, but Joshua had given ⌊territory⌋ to the other half,^e with their brothers, on the west side of the Jordan. When Joshua sent them to their homes and blessed them, ⁸ he said,

---

^a**21:25** Or *Ibleam* ^b**21:36** Or *Jahaz* ^c**21:36–37** Some Hb mss omit these vv. ^d**22:5** Lit *commands, hold on* ^e**22:7** Lit *to his half*

---

was a fortress with interior rooms that everyone entering and leaving the city had to pass through.

20:7-8 So they designated. Northern, central, and southern cities of refuge were designated on the eastern and western sides of the Jordan River. All citizens had easy ac-

cess to one of these cities.

21:1-45 The towns and pasturelands given to the Levites were distributed evenly throughout the other tribes. Their priestly service to the Lord was considered the inheritance of the Levites (13:33; 18:7).

21:11-12 Hebron. Caleb was free to shep-

herd the range of fields and outlying villages of Hebron, the resting place of Sarah and her family (Gen. 23:1-2). But the priests and Levites considered the city of Hebron their home.

21:43-45 promises the LORD had made. God reminded these battle-weary warriors

"Return to your homes with great wealth: a huge number of cattle, and silver, gold, bronze, iron, and a large quantity of clothing. Share the spoil of your enemies with your brothers."

Eastern Tribes Build an Altar

9 The Reubenites, Gadites, and half the tribe of Manasseh left the Israelites at Shiloh in the land of Canaan to go to their own land of Gilead, which they took possession of according to the LORD's command through Moses. 10 When they came to the region of[a] the Jordan in the land of Canaan, the Reubenites, Gadites, and half the tribe of Manasseh built a large, impressive altar there by the Jordan.

11 Then the Israelites heard ⌊it⌋ said, "Look, the Reubenites, Gadites, and half the tribe of Manasseh have built an altar on the frontier of the land of Canaan at the region of[b] the Jordan, on the Israelite side." 12 When the Israelites heard ⌊this⌋, the entire Israelite community assembled at Shiloh to go to war against them.

Explanation of the Altar

13 The Israelites sent Phinehas son of Eleazar the priest to the Reubenites, Gadites, and half the tribe of Manasseh, in the land of Gilead. 14 ⌊They sent⌋ 10 leaders with him—one family leader for each tribe of Israel. All of them were heads of their families among the clans of Israel. 15 They went to the Reubenites, Gadites, and half the tribe of Manasseh, in the land of Gilead, and told them, 16 "This is what the LORD's entire community says: 'What is this treachery you have committed today against the God of Israel by turning away from the LORD and building an altar for yourselves, so that you are in rebellion against the LORD today? 17 Wasn't the sin of Peor, which brought a plague on the LORD's community, enough for us, so that we have not cleansed ourselves from it even to this day, 18 and now, you would turn away from the LORD? If you rebel against the LORD today, tomorrow He will be angry with the entire community of Israel. 19 But if the land you possess is defiled, cross over to the land the LORD possesses where the LORD's tabernacle stands, and take possession ⌊of it⌋ among us. But don't rebel against the LORD or against us by building for yourselves an altar other than the altar of the LORD our God. 20 Wasn't Achan son of Zerah unfaithful regarding what was •set apart for destruction, bringing wrath on the entire community of Israel? He was not the only one who perished because of his sin.'"

21 The Reubenites, Gadites, and half the tribe of Manasseh answered the leaders of the Israelite clans,

22 "The LORD is the God of gods! The LORD is the God of gods![c] He knows, and may Israel also know. Do not spare us today, if ⌊it was⌋ in rebellion or treachery against the LORD 23 that we have built for ourselves an altar to turn away from Him. May the LORD Himself hold us accountable if ⌊we intended⌋ to offer •burnt offerings and •grain offerings on it, or to sacrifice •fellowship offerings on it. 24 We actually did this from a specific concern that in the future your descendants might say to our descendants, 'What relationship do you have with the LORD,[d] the God of Israel? 25 For the LORD has made the Jordan a border between us and you descendants of Reuben and Gad. You have no share in the LORD!' So your descendants may cause our descendants to stop fearing the LORD.

26 "Therefore we said: Let us take action and build an altar for ourselves, but not for burnt offering or sacrifice. 27 Instead, it is to be a witness between us and you, and between the generations after us, so that we may carry out the worship of the LORD in His presence with our burnt offerings, sacrifices, and fellowship offerings. Then in the future, your descendants will not be able to say to our descendants, 'You have no share in the LORD!' 28 We thought that if they said this to us or to our generations in the future, we would reply: Look at the replica of the LORD's altar that our fathers made, not for burnt offering or sacrifice, but as a witness between us and you. 29 We would never rebel against the LORD or turn away from Him today by building an altar for burnt offering, grain offering, or sacrifice, other than the altar of the LORD our God, which is in front of His tabernacle."

Conflict Resolved

30 When Phinehas the priest and the community leaders, the heads of Israel's clans who were with him, heard what the descendants of Reuben, Gad, and Manasseh had to say, they were pleased. 31 Phinehas son of Eleazar the priest said to the descendants of Reuben, Gad, and Manasseh, "Today we know that the LORD is among us, because you have not committed this treachery against Him. As a result, you have delivered the Israelites from the LORD's power."

32 Then Phinehas son of Eleazar the priest and the leaders returned from the Reubenites and Gadites in the land of Gilead to the Israelites in the land of Canaan and brought back a report to them. 33 The Israelites were pleased with the report, and they praised God. They spoke no more about going to war against them to ravage the land where the Reubenites and Gadites

---

a 22:10 Or to Geliloth by   b 22:11 Or at Geliloth by   c 22:22 Or The Mighty One, God, the LORD! The Mighty One, God, the LORD!, or God, the LORD God! God, the LORD God!   d 22:24 Lit What to you and to the LORD

---

that every victory, every conquest, and every blade of grass in this land was a gift from Him.

22:2 obeyed me in everything I commanded you. Joshua had asked a lot of these warriors. He had separated them from their families on the eastern side of the Jordan River for seven years to fight for their brothers' rights.

22:5 Only carefully obey. Joshua expressed his concern for the infant nation among such a pagan people.

22:11 the Israelites heard ... built an altar. The story of this altar got passed around from tribe to tribe until it was blown out of proportion. What was meant to be a symbol of a

common faith was now rumored to be rebellion against God.

22:12 to go to war against them. Some of the Israelite tribes were actually considering going to war against the tribes on the eastern side of the Jordan River.

22:13-14 They sent 10 leaders with him.

lived. ³⁴ So the Reubenites and Gadites named the altar: It[a] is a witness between us that the LORD is God.

Joshua's Farewell Address

23 A long time after the LORD had given Israel rest from all the enemies around them, Joshua was old, getting on in years. ² So Joshua summoned all Israel, including its elders, leaders, judges, and officers, and said to them, "I am old, getting on in years, ³ and you have seen for yourselves everything the LORD your God did to all these nations on your account, because it was the LORD your God who was fighting for you. ⁴ See, I have allotted these remaining nations to you as an inheritance for your tribes, including all the nations I have destroyed, from the Jordan westward to the Mediterranean Sea. ⁵ The LORD your God will force them back on your account and drive them out before you, so that you can take possession of their land, as the LORD your God promised you.

⁶ "Be very strong, and continue obeying all that is written in the book of the law of Moses, so that you do not turn from it to the right or left ⁷ and so that you do not associate with these nations remaining among you. Do not call on the names of their gods or make an oath to them; do not worship them or bow down to them. ⁸ Instead, remain faithful to the LORD your God, as you have done to this day.

⁹ "The LORD has driven out great and powerful nations before you, and no one has been able to stand against you to this day. ¹⁰ One of you routed a thousand, because the LORD your God was fighting for you, as He promised.[b] ¹¹ So be very diligent to love the LORD your God for your own well-being. ¹² For if you turn away and cling to the rest of these nations remaining among you, and if you intermarry or associate with them and they with you, ¹³ know for certain that the LORD your God will not continue to drive these nations out before you. They will become a snare and a trap for you, a scourge for your sides and thorns in your eyes, until you disappear from this good land the LORD your God has given you.

¹⁴ "I am now going the way of all the earth,[c] and you know with all your heart and all your soul that none of the good promises the LORD your God made to you has failed. Everything was fulfilled for you; not one promise has failed. ¹⁵ Since every good thing the LORD your God promised you has come about, so He will bring on you every bad thing until He has annihilated you from this good land the LORD your God has given you. ¹⁶ If you break the covenant of the LORD your God, which He

commanded you, and go and worship other gods, and bow down to them, the LORD's anger will burn against you, and you will quickly disappear from this good land He has given you."

Review of Israel's History

24 Joshua assembled all the tribes of Israel at Shechem and summoned Israel's elders, leaders, judges, and officers, and they presented themselves before God. ² Joshua said to all the people, "This is what the LORD, the God of Israel, says: 'Long ago your ancestors, including Terah, the father of Abraham and Nahor, lived beyond the Euphrates River and worshiped other gods. ³ But I took your father Abraham from the region beyond the Euphrates River, led him throughout the land of Canaan, and multiplied his descendants. I gave him Isaac, ⁴ and to Isaac I gave Jacob and Esau. I gave the hill country of Seir to Esau as a possession, but Jacob and his sons went down to Egypt.

⁵ "'Then I sent Moses and Aaron, I plagued Egypt by what I did there, and afterwards I brought you out. ⁶ When I brought your fathers out of Egypt and you reached the •Red Sea, the Egyptians pursued your fathers with chariots and horsemen as far as the sea. ⁷ Your fathers cried out to the LORD, so He put darkness between you and the Egyptians, and brought the sea over them, engulfing them. Your own eyes saw what I did to Egypt. After that, you lived in the wilderness a long time.

⁸ "'Later, I brought you to the land of the Amorites who lived beyond the Jordan. They fought against you, but I handed them over to you. You possessed their land, and I annihilated them before you. ⁹ Balak son of Zippor, king of Moab, set out to fight against Israel. He sent for Balaam son of Beor to curse you, ¹⁰ but I would not listen to Balaam. Instead, he repeatedly blessed you, and I delivered you from his hand.

¹¹ "'You then crossed the Jordan and came to Jericho. The people of Jericho—as well as the Amorites, Perizzites, Canaanites, Hittites, Girgashites, Hivites, and Jebusites—fought against you, but I handed them over to you. ¹² I sent the hornet[d] ahead of you, and it drove out the two Amorite kings before you. It was not by your sword or bow. ¹³ I gave you a land you did not labor for, and cities you did not build, though you live in them; you are eating from vineyards and olive groves you did not plant.'

The Covenant Renewal

¹⁴ "Therefore, •fear the LORD and worship Him in sincerity and truth. Get rid of the gods your ancestors

---

[a]**22:34** Some Hb mss, Syr, Tg read *altar Witness because it*   [b]**23:10** Lit *promised you*   [c]**23:14** = I am going to die   [d]**24:12** Or *sent terror*

One delegate from each tribe went with Phinehas to investigate the altar erected by the eastern tribes.

22:27 in His presence. The tabernacle at Shiloh housed the one true altar for worship. The law required all the Israelite men to gather there three times a year (Ex. 23:17).

The eastern tribes had not intended to worship at the altar they had built—it was just symbolic.

22:31 you have delivered the Israelites from the LORD's power. One tribe's sin would have meant disaster for the entire nation. Phinehas was not exaggerating when he

thanked the eastern tribes for sparing their lives as well.

23:1-2 Joshua summoned all Israel. Sensing the end of his life was near, Joshua summoned the leaders of Israel. He reviewed the past and exhorted the people to continue obeying the Lord.

worshiped beyond the Euphrates River and in Egypt, and worship the LORD. [15] But if it doesn't please you to worship the LORD, choose for yourselves today the one you will worship: the gods your fathers worshiped beyond the Euphrates River, or the gods of the Amorites in whose land you are living. As for me and my family, we will worship the LORD."

[16] The people replied, "We will certainly not abandon the LORD to worship other gods! [17] For the LORD our God brought us and our fathers out of the land of Egypt, the place of slavery and performed these great signs before our eyes. He also protected us all along the way we went and among all the peoples whose lands we traveled through. [18] The LORD drove out before us all the peoples, including the Amorites who lived in the land. We too will worship the LORD, because He is our God."

[19] But Joshua told the people, "You will not be able to worship the LORD, because He is a holy God. He is a jealous God; He will not remove your transgressions and sins. [20] If you abandon the LORD and worship foreign gods, He will turn against ⌊you⌋, harm you, and completely destroy you, after He has been good to you."

[21] "No!" the people answered Joshua. "We will worship the LORD."

[22] Joshua then told the people, "You are witnesses against yourselves that you yourselves have chosen to worship the LORD."

"We are witnesses," they said.

[23] "Then get rid of the foreign gods that are among you and offer your hearts to the LORD, the God of Israel."

[24] So the people said to Joshua, "We will worship the LORD our God and obey Him."

[25] On that day Joshua made a covenant for the people at Shechem and established a statute and ordinance for them. [26] Joshua recorded these things in the book of the law of God; he also took a large stone and set it up there under the oak next to the sanctuary of the LORD. [27] And Joshua said to all the people, "You see this stone—it will be a witness against us, for it has heard all the words the LORD said to us, and it will be a witness against you, so that you will not deny your God." [28] Then Joshua sent the people away, each to his own inheritance.

Burial of Three Leaders

[29] After these things, the LORD's servant, Joshua son of Nun, died at the age of 110. [30] They buried him in his allotted territory at Timnath-serah, in the hill country of Ephraim north of Mount Gaash. [31] Israel worshiped the LORD throughout Joshua's lifetime and during the lifetimes of the elders who outlived Joshua, and who had experienced all the works the LORD had done for Israel.

[32] Joseph's bones, which the Israelites had brought up from Egypt, were buried at Shechem in the parcel of land Jacob had purchased from the sons of Hamor, Shechem's father, for 100 qesitahs.[a] It was an inheritance for Joseph's descendants.

[33] And Eleazar son of Aaron died, and they buried him at Gibeah,[b] which had been given to his son Phinehas in the hill country of Ephraim.

---

[a] 24:32 The value of this currency is unknown.   [b] 24:33 = the Hill

---

23:6 Be very strong. Joshua's last words to his people were the first words God had spoken to him at the beginning of his command (1:6).

23:12 if you ... associate with them. The temptation to compromise by associating with the pagan people would be strong for the young nation. But Joshua warned the people of Israel to avoid them.

24:14 fear the LORD. To "fear" the Lord means worshipful submission, reverential awe, and obedient respect.

24:15 As for me ... we will worship. Joshua knew he could not speak for Israel. The commitment to serve God must be an individual, personal decision.

24:17-18 For the LORD our God. What choice could the people make other than to promise to serve the Lord? But their claims of loyalty would return to haunt them in the future when they fell away.

24:19 You will not be able to worship the LORD. Joshua did not trust Israel's promise of allegiance to God. He feared they would not keep their commitment when they returned home. **jealous God.** God is only called jealous when idolatry is mentioned. God burns with possessive, protective anger toward His people when they follow false gods.

24:22 You are witnesses. Witnesses could be called to testify in court if one party was charged with breaking an agreement. Joshua made Israel function as their own witnesses to their oath to serve the Lord. They would indict themselves if they were untrue to God.

24:25 Joshua made a covenant for the people. As a symbol of personal commitment, Joshua signed and dated the terms of their agreement in "the book of the law of God" (v. 26).

24:26 next to the sanctuary of the LORD. Putting the memorial stone next to the sanctuary indicated that God Himself was witnessing the promise Israel made to remain true to Him.

24:31 throughout Joshua's lifetime. Joshua was able to keep Israel on course throughout the time when he led the nation.

24:32 Joseph's bones ... buried at Shechem. In fulfillment of prophecy, Joseph's bones were brought from a land of slavery to a land of freedom (Gen. 50:24-25). His grave was near the border between the territories settled by the descendants of his two sons, Ephraim and Manasseh.

JUGES

PERSONAL READING PLAN

AUTHOR

The author of Judges is not designated in the book. Some view Samuel as the author, but this is uncertain.

DATE

The exact date of authorship is unknown, but Judges may have been written during the early period of the reign of David (circa 1000–980 B.C.). The action recorded here spans the period between the conquest and the monarchy of Israel.

THEME

God is merciful and long-suffering despite the sin of His people.

HISTORICAL BACKGROUND

The title of the book describes Israel's leaders from Joshua to the time when Israel had kings. Two to three hundred years lapse between the conquest of Canaan (after Joshua's death) and the rise of Saul (circa 1050 B.C.). During this time Israel was a loose confederation of tribes spread throughout the promised land. This area was heavily influenced by Canaanite culture and religion. Because of this, Israel desires to have a king like her neighbors (17:6; 18:1; 19:1; 21:25).

CHARACTERISTICS

Once in Canaan, all the Israelites needed to do was to obey God; instead, they followed the sinful example of the Canaanites. Their disobedience resulted in a cycle observed throughout the book (see 2:11-19): (1) there is apostasy or rebellion by God's people; (2) God raises up foreign oppressors to chasten His people; (3) a cry of distress goes up from the Israelites; (4) God raises up a "deliverer" or "judge" who takes up arms to defend the homeland and rescue the repentant people. The Lord's covenant faithfulness arises out of these repeated cycles. The Book of Judges shows that even in dark, chaotic times, God is in control.

PASSAGES FOR TOPICAL GROUP STUDY

Judah's Leadership against the Canaanites

1 After the death of Joshua, the Israelites inquired of the LORD, "Who will be the first to fight for us against the Canaanites?"

2 The LORD answered, "Judah is to go. I have handed the land over to him."

3 Judah said to his brother Simeon, "Come with me to my territory, and let us fight against the Canaanites. I will also go with you to your territory." So Simeon went with him.

4 When Judah attacked, the LORD handed the Canaanites and Perizzites over to them. They struck down 10,000 men in Bezek. 5 They found Adoni-bezek in Bezek, fought against him, and struck down the Canaanites and Perizzites.

6 When Adoni-bezek fled, they pursued him, seized him, and cut off his thumbs and big toes. 7 Adoni-bezek said, "Seventy kings with their thumbs and big toes cut off used to pick up ⌊scraps⌋ᵃ under my table. God has repaid me for what I have done." They brought him to Jerusalem, and he died there.

8 The men of Judah fought against Jerusalem and captured it. They put the city to the sword and set it on fire. 9 Afterwards, the men of Judah marched down to fight against the Canaanites who were living in the hill country, the •Negev, and the Judean foothills.ᵇ 10 Judah also marched against the Canaanites who were living in Hebron (Hebron was formerly named Kiriath-arba). They struck down Sheshai, Ahiman, and Talmai. 11 From there they marched against the residents of Debir (Debir was formerly named Kiriath-sepher).

12 Caleb said, "Whoever strikes down and captures Kiriath-sepher, I will give my daughter Achsah to him as a wife." 13 So Othniel son of Kenaz, Caleb's youngest brother, captured it, and Caleb gave him Achsah to him as his wife.

14 When she arrived, she persuaded Othnielᶜ to ask her father for a field. As she got off her donkey, Caleb asked her,ᵈ "What do you want?" 15 She answered him, "Give me a blessing. Since you have given me land in the Negev, give me springs of water also." So Caleb gave her both the upper and lower springs.ᵉ

16 The descendants of the Kenite, Moses' father-in-law, had gone up with the men of Judah from the City of Palmsᶠ to the Wilderness of Judah, which was in the Negev of Arad. They went to live among the people.

17 Judah went with his brother Simeon, struck the Canaanites who were living in Zephath, and •completely destroyed the town. So they named the town Hormah. 18 Judah captured Gaza and its territory, Ashkelon and its territory, and Ekron and its territory.ᵍ 19 The LORD was with Judah and enabled them to take possession of the hill country, but they could not drive out the people who were living in the valley because those people had iron chariots.ʰ

20 Judah gave Hebron to Caleb, just as Moses had promised. Then Caleb drove out the three sons of Anak who lived there.ⁱ

Benjamin's Failure

21 At the same time the Benjaminites did not drive out the Jebusites who were living in Jerusalem. The Jebusites have lived among the Benjaminites in Jerusalem to this day.

Success of the House of Joseph

22 The house of Joseph also attacked Bethel, and the LORD was with them. 23 They sent spies to Bethel (the town was formerly named Luz). 24 The spies saw a man coming out of the town and said to him, "Please show us how to get into town, and we will treat you well." 25 When he showed them the way into the town, they put the town to the sword but released the man and his entire family. 26 Then the man went to the land of the Hittites, built a town, and named it Luz. That is its name to this day.

Failure of the Other Tribes

27 At that time Manasseh failed to take possession of Beth-sheanʲ and its villages,ᵏ or Taanach and its villages, or the residents of Dor and its villages, or the residents of Ibleamˡ and its villages, or the residents of Megiddo and its villages. But the Canaanites refused to leaveᵐ this land. 28 When Israel became stronger, they made the Canaanites serve as forced labor but never drove them out completely.

29 At that time Ephraim failed to drive out the Canaanites who were living in Gezer, so the Canaanites have lived among them in Gezer.ⁿ

ᵃ1:7 Lit toes are gathering   ᵇ1:9 Or the Shephelah   ᶜ1:14 LXX reads arrived, he pressured her   ᵈ1:14 LXX reads She grumbled while on the donkey, and she cried out from the donkey, "Into the southland you sent me out," and Caleb said   ᵉ1:15 LXX reads me redemption of water, and Caleb gave her according to her heart the redemption of the upper and the redemption of the lower   ᶠ1:16 = Jericho; Jdg 3:13; Dt 34:3; 2 Ch 28:15   ᵍ1:18 LXX reads Judah did not inherit Gaza and its borders nor Ashkelon and its borders nor Ekron and its borders or Azotus and its surrounding lands   ʰ1:19 LXX reads hill country, for they were not able to drive out the residents of the valley because Rechab separated it   ⁱ1:20 LXX reads And he inherited from there the three cities of the sons of Anak   ʲ1:27 LXX reads Beth-shean, which is a Scythian city   ᵏ1:27 LXX reads its villages nor the fields around it   ˡ1:27 LXX reads Balaam   ᵐ1:27 LXX reads Canaanites began to live in   ⁿ1:29 LXX reads Gezer, and became forced labor

---

1:1–3:6 Putting up with idolatry proved easier than putting out the pagans (2:2). Israel repeatedly disobeyed God and experienced defeat. The Lord sent leader-heroes to deliver them.
1:1 After the death of Joshua. Without their leader, Israel hesitated. **fight for us.** Each tribe wanted the other's help to drive out its enemies.

1:8 set it on fire. Burning the city made Israel's victory permanent.
1:12 I will give my daughter Achsah to him as a wife. Caleb gained a city and a son-in-law with this deal.
1:17 struck the Canaanites. Judah and Simeon were carrying out God's judgment.

1:21 Benjaminites. The tribe of Benjamin dropped the ball. David had to finish the job years later (see 2 Sam. 5:6-9).
1:22 house of Joseph. Ephraim and Manasseh were Joseph's sons (see Gen. 48:13).
1:25 released the man Like Rahab in Jericho

30 Zebulun failed to drive out the residents of Kitron or the residents of Nahalol, so the Canaanites lived among them and served as forced labor.

31 Asher failed to drive out the residents of Acco[a] or of Sidon, or Ahlab, Achzib, Helbah, Aphik, or Rehob. 32 The Asherites lived among the Canaanites who were living in the land, because they failed to drive them out.

33 Naphtali did not drive out the residents of Beth-shemesh or the residents of Beth-anath. They lived among the Canaanites who were living in the land, but the residents of Beth-shemesh and Beth-anath served as their forced labor.

34 The Amorites forced the Danites into the hill country and did not allow them to go down into the valley. 35 The Amorites refused to leave Har-heres, Aijalon, and Shaalbim. When the house of Joseph got the upper hand, the Amorites[b] were made to serve as forced labor. 36 The territory of the Amorites extended from the ascent of Akrabbim, that is from Sela upward.

Pattern of Sin and Judgment

2 The Angel of the LORD went up from Gilgal to Bochim[c] and said, "I brought you out of Egypt and led you into the land I had promised to your fathers. I also said: I will never break My covenant with you. 2 You are not to make a covenant with the people who are living in this land, and you are to tear down their altars.[d] But you have not obeyed Me. What is this you have done? 3 Therefore, I now say: I will not drive out these people before you. They will be thorns[e][f] in your sides, and their gods will be a trap to you." 4 When the Angel of the LORD had spoken these words to all the Israelites, the people wept loudly. 5 So they named that place Bochim[g] and offered sacrifices there to the LORD.

Joshua's Death

6 Joshua sent the people away, and the Israelites went to take possession of the land, each to his own inheritance. 7 The people worshiped the LORD throughout Joshua's lifetime and during the lifetimes of the elders who outlived[h] Joshua. They had seen all the LORD's great works He had done for Israel.

8 Joshua son of Nun, the servant of the LORD, died at the age of 110. 9 They buried him in the territory of his inheritance, in Timnath-heres, in the hill country of Ephraim, north of Mount Gaash. 10 That whole generation was also gathered to their ancestors. After them

another generation rose up who did not know the LORD or the works He had done for Israel.

11 The Israelites did what was evil in the LORD's sight. They worshiped the •Baals 12 and abandoned the LORD, the God of their fathers, who had brought them out of Egypt. They went after other gods from the surrounding peoples and bowed down to them. They infuriated the LORD, 13 for they abandoned Him and worshiped Baal and the •Ashtoreths.

14 The LORD's anger burned against Israel, and He handed them over to marauders who raided them. He sold them to[i] the enemies around them, so that they could no longer resist their enemies. 15 Whenever the Israelites went out, the LORD[j] was against them and brought disaster ⌊on them⌋, just as He had promised and sworn to them. So they suffered greatly.

16 The LORD raised up judges, who saved them from the power of their marauders, 17 but they did not listen to their judges. Instead, they prostituted themselves with other gods, bowing down to them. They quickly turned from the way of their fathers, who had walked in obedience to the LORD's commands. They did not do as their fathers did. 18 Whenever the LORD raised up a judge for the Israelites, the LORD was with him and saved the people from the power of their enemies while the judge was still alive.[k] The LORD was moved to pity whenever they groaned because of those who were oppressing and afflicting them. 19 Whenever the judge died, the Israelites would act even more corruptly than their fathers, going after other gods to worship and bow down to them. They did not turn from their ⌊evil⌋ practices or their obstinate ways.

20 The LORD's anger burned against Israel, and He declared, "Because this nation has violated My covenant that I made with their fathers and disobeyed Me, 21 I will no longer drive out before them any of the nations Joshua left when he died. 22 ⌊I did this⌋ to test Israel and to see whether they would keep the LORD's way by walking in it, as their fathers had." 23 The LORD left these nations and did not drive them out immediately. He did not hand them over to Joshua.

The LORD Tests Israel

3 These are the nations the LORD left in order to test Israel, since none of these Israelites had fought in[l] any of the wars with Canaan. 2 This was to teach the future generations of the Israelites ⌊how to fight in⌋ battle, especially those who had not fought before.[m]

---

a1:31 LXX reads Acco, and they became for him forced labor and the residents of Dor   b1:35 LXX reads Joseph became strong on the Amorites, they   c2:1 LXX reads to the weeping place and to Bethel and to the house of Israel   d2:2 LXX reads with those lying in wait in this land; neither are you to fall down in worship to their gods, but their carved images you must break to pieces and their altars you must destroy   e2:3 LXX reads affliction   f2:3 Lit traps   g2:5 Or Weeping   h2:7 Lit extended their days after   i2:14 Lit into the hand of   j2:15 Lit the hand of the LORD   k2:18 Lit enemies all the days of the judge   l3:1 Lit had known   m3:2 Lit not known it

---

(see Josh. 2:1-21), the man who helped the Israelites at Bethel was spared.

1:33 served as their forced labor. Inhabitants who were not destroyed were enslaved by the Israelites.

2:1-5 The Angel of the Lord confronted Israel with their broken vows.

2:6_3:6 Israel's commitment to principle ends and the cycle of disobedience, defeat, and delivery begins.

2:10 another generation rose up. The new generation knew nothing about the Red Sea or Jordan River miracles.

2:11 Baals. God kept the Israelites from win-

ning wars whenever they worshiped the Canaanite idols.

2:16-19 they did not listen. The judges were the leader-heroes of the land. Whenever a judge led Israel, relative calm resulted. Whenever Israel was between heroes, however, it soon forgot its priorities.

3 ⌊These nations included:⌋ the five rulers of the Philistines and all of the Canaanites, the Sidonians, and the Hivites who lived in the Lebanese mountainsa from Mount Baal-hermon as far as the entrance to Hamath.b 4 The LORD left them to test Israel, to determine if they would keep the LORD's commands He had given their fathers throughc Moses. 5 But they settled among the Canaanites, Hittites, Amorites, Perizzites, Hivites, and Jebusites. 6 The Israelites took their daughters as wives for themselves, gave their own daughters to their sons, and worshiped their gods.

Othniel, the First Judge

7 The Israelites did what was evil in the LORD's sight; they forgot the LORD their God and worshiped the •Baals and the •Asherahs. 8 The LORD's anger burned against Israel, and He sold them tod Cushan-rishathaime king of Aram of the Two Rivers,f and the Israelites served him eight years.

9 The Israelites cried out to the LORD. So the LORD raised up Othniel son of Kenaz, Caleb's youngest brother as a deliverer to save the Israelites. 10 The Spirit of the LORD was on him, and he judged Israel. Othniel went out to battle, and the LORD handed over Cushan-rishathaim king of Aram to him, so that Othniel overpowered him. 11 Then the land was peaceful 40 years, and Othniel son of Kenaz died.

Ehud

12 The Israelites again did what was evil in the LORD's sight. He gave Eglon king of Moab power over Israel, because they had done what was evil in the LORD's sight. 13 After Eglon convinced the Ammonites and the Amalekites to join forces with him, he attacked and defeated Israel and took possession of the City of Palms.g 14 The Israelites served Eglon king of Moab 18 years.

15 Then the Israelites cried out to the LORD, and He raised up Ehud son of Gera, a left-handed Benjaminite,h as a deliverer for them. The Israelites sent him to Eglon king of Moab with tribute ⌊money⌋.

16 Ehud made himself a double-edged sword 18 inches long.i He strapped it to his right thigh under his clothes 17 and brought the tribute to Eglon king of Moab, who was an extremely fat man. 18 When Ehud had finished presenting the tribute, he dismissed the people who had carried it. 19 At the carved images near Gilgal he returned and said, "King ⌊Eglon⌋, I have a secret message for you." The king called for silence,

and all his attendants left him. 20 Then Ehud approached him while he was sitting alone in his room upstairs ⌊where it was⌋ cool. Ehud said, "I have a word from God for you," and the king stood up from his throne.j 21 Ehudk reached with his left hand, took the sword from his right thigh, and plunged it into Eglon's belly. 22 Even the handle went in after the blade, and Eglon's fat closed in over it, so that Ehud did not withdraw the sword from his belly. And Eglon's insides came out. 23 Ehud escaped by way of the porch, closing and locking the doors of the upstairs room behind him.

24 Ehud was gone when Eglon's servants came in. They looked and found the doors of the upstairs room locked and thought he was relieving himselfl in the cool room. 25 The servants waited until they became worried and saw that he had still not opened the doors of the upstairs room. So they took the key and opened the doors—and there was their lord lying dead on the floor!

26 Ehud escaped while the servants waited. He crossed over ⌊the Jordan⌋ near the carved images and reached Seirah. 27 After he arrived, he sounded the ram's horn throughout the hill country of Ephraim. The Israelites came down with him from the hill country, and he became their leader. 28 He told them, "Follow me, because the LORD has handed over your enemies, the Moabites, to you." So they followed him, captured the fords of the Jordan leading to Moab, and did not allow anyone to cross over. 29 At that time they struck down about 10,000 Moabites, all strong and able-bodied men. Not one of them escaped. 30 Moab became subject to Israel that day, and the land was peaceful 80 years.

Shamgar

31 After Ehud, Shamgar son of Anath ⌊became judge⌋. He delivered Israel by striking down 600 Philistines with an oxgoad.

Deborah and Barak

4 The Israelites again did what was evil in the sight of the LORD after Ehud had died. 2 So the LORD sold them into the hand of Jabin king of Canaan, who reigned in Hazor. The commander of his forces was Sisera who lived in Harosheth of the Nations.m 3 Then the Israelites cried out to the LORD, because Jabin had 900 iron chariots, and he harshly oppressed them 20 years.

4 Deborah, a woman who was a prophet and the wife of Lappidoth, was judging Israel at that time. 5 It was

---

a 3:3 LXX reads in Lebanon, without reference to mountains   b 3:3 Or as Lebo-hamath   c 3:4 Lit by the hand of   d 3:8 Lit into the hand of   e 3:8 Lit Doubly-Evil   f 3:8 Or Aram-naharaim; = Mesopotamia   g 3:13 = Jericho; Jdg 1:16; Dt 34:3; 2 Ch 28:15   h 3:15 = son of the right hand   i 3:16 Lit sword a gomed in length   j 3:20 LXX reads "A word of my God for you, O king," and Eglon rose up from the throne near him.   k 3:21 LXX reads It happened that when he rose up, Ehud immediately   l 3:24 Lit was covering his feet   m 4:2 Or Harosheth-ha-goiim

---

3:1-6 The Israelites failed God's test, accepting the lifestyle of their pagan neighbors, worshiping their gods, and even intermarrying with them.

3:7-11 Othniel is the first of many judges of Israel.

3:10 The Spirit of the LORD. The judge symbolizes God's presence among the people.

3:12-30 After murdering the king of Moab, Ehud escapes to Israel, and then leads them in destroying the Moabite nation.

3:28 the LORD has handed over your enemies. Ehud realizes he was merely the Lord's tool.

3:31 Shamgar. A rugged fighter, Shamgar is credited with "saving" Israel.

4:1-24 The Lord again demonstrates His power through a deliverer—this time a female judge, Deborah.

4:4 Deborah. As a judge, Deborah settled disputes among the Israelites. As a prophetess,

her custom to sit under the palm tree of Deborah between Ramah and Bethel in the hill country of Ephraim, and the Israelites went up to her for judgment.

6 She summoned Barak son of Abinoam from Kedesh in Naphtali and said to him, "Hasn't the LORD, the God of Israel, commanded ⌊you⌋: 'Go, deploy ⌊the troops⌋ on Mount Tabor, and take with you 10,000 men from the Naphtalites and Zebulunites? 7 Then I will lure Sisera commander of Jabin's forces, his chariots, and his army at the •Wadi Kishon ⌊to fight⌋ against you, and I will hand him over to you.'"

8 Barak said to her, "If you will go with me, I will go. But if you will not go with me, I will not go."

9 "I will go with you," she said, "but you will receive no honor on the road you are about to take, because the LORD will sell Sisera into a woman's hand." So Deborah got up and went with Barak to Kedesh. 10 Barak summoned Zebulun and Naphtali to Kedesh; 10,000 men followed him, and Deborah also went with him.

11 Now Heber the Kenite had moved away from the Kenites, the sons of Hobab, Moses' father-in-law, and pitched his tent beside the oak tree of Zaanannim, which was near Kedesh.

12 It was reported to Sisera that Barak son of Abinoam had gone up Mount Tabor. 13 Sisera summoned all his 900 iron chariots and all the people who were with him from Harosheth of the Nations[a] to the Wadi Kishon. 14 Then Deborah said to Barak, "Move on, for this is the day the LORD has handed Sisera over to you. Hasn't the LORD gone before you?" So Barak came down from Mount Tabor with 10,000 men following him.

15 The LORD threw Sisera, all his charioteers, and all his army into confusion with the sword before Barak. Sisera left his chariot and fled on foot. 16 Barak pursued the chariots and the army as far as Harosheth of the Nations,[a] and the whole army of Sisera fell by the sword; not a single man was left.

17 Meanwhile, Sisera had fled on foot to the tent of Jael, the wife of Heber the Kenite, because there was peace between Jabin king of Hazor and the family of Heber the Kenite. 18 Jael went out to greet Sisera and said to him, "Come in, my lord. Come in with me. Don't be afraid." So he went into her tent, and she covered him with a rug. 19 He said to her, "Please give me a little water to drink for I am thirsty." She opened a container of milk, gave him a drink, and covered him ⌊again⌋. 20 Then he said to her, "Stand at the entrance to the tent. If a man comes and asks you, 'Is there a man here?' say, 'No.'" 21 While he was sleeping from

exhaustion, Heber's wife Jael took a tent peg, grabbed a hammer, and went silently to Sisera. She hammered the peg into his temple and drove it into the ground, and he died.

22 When Barak arrived in pursuit of Sisera, Jael went out to greet him and said to him, "Come and I will show you the man you are looking for." So he went in with her, and there was Sisera lying dead with a tent peg through his temple!

23 That day God subdued Jabin king of Canaan before the Israelites. 24 The power of the Israelites continued to increase against Jabin king of Canaan until they destroyed him.

Deborah's Song

5 On that day Deborah and Barak son of Abinoam sang:

2 When the leaders lead[b] in Israel,
   when the people volunteer,
   praise the LORD.
3 Listen, kings! Pay attention, princes!
   I will sing to the LORD;
   I will sing praise to the LORD God of Israel.
4 LORD, when You came from Seir,
   when You marched from the fields of Edom,
   the earth trembled,
   the heavens poured ⌊rain⌋,
   the clouds poured water.
5 The mountains melted before the LORD,
   even Sinai[c] before the LORD, the God of Israel.

6 In the days of Shamgar son of Anath,
   in the days of Jael,
   the main ways were deserted,
   because travelers kept to the side roads.
7 Villages were deserted,[d]
   they were deserted in Israel,
   until I,[e] Deborah,
   I[e] arose, a mother in Israel.
8 Israel chose new gods,
   then war was in the gates.
   Not a shield or spear was seen
   among 40,000 in Israel.
9 My heart is with the leaders of Israel,
   with the volunteers of the people.
   Praise the LORD!
10 You who ride on white[d] donkeys,
   who sit on saddle blankets,
   and who travel on the road, give praise!
11 Let them tell the righteous acts of the LORD,
   the righteous deeds of His warriors in Israel,

---

[a]4:13,16 Or *Harosheth-ha-goiim*   [b]5:2 Lit *the locks of hair are loose*   [c]5:5 Or LORD, *this [One of] Sinai*   [d]5:7,10 Hb obscure   [e]5:7 Or *you*

---

[*] she predicted victory for Israel against the Canaanites.

4:6 Barak. Deborah picked him to command Israel's troops.

4:7 I will lure Sisera. According to God's plan, an ideal battleground for Sisera turned into a muddy disaster.

4:9 a woman's hand. When Barak hesitated to go forward, Deborah predicted a woman would help secure the victory (vv. 18-22).

4:11 Heber the Kenite. This Kenite nomad was related to Moses, but he had been sleeping with the enemy (v. 17).

4:14 gone before you. Deborah herself would

not go into battle, but the Lord advanced before Barak and his army.

4:18 he went into her tent. As a family friend, Sisera did not suspect Jael's warm behavior.

4:21 hammered the peg into his temple. Accustomed to pitching and tearing down tents, Jael used familiar tools to murder the com-

with the voices of the singers
at the watering places.[a]

Then the LORD's people went down to the gates.

12 "Awake! Awake, Deborah!
Awake! Awake, sing a song!
Arise Barak,
and take hold of your captives,
son of Abinoam!"

13 The survivors came down to the nobles;
the LORD's people came down to me[b]
with the warriors.

14 Those with their roots in Amalek[c] [came]
from Ephraim;
Benjamin [came with] your people after you.
The leaders came down from Machir,
and those who carry a marshal's staff [came]
from Zebulun.

15 The princes of Issachar were with Deborah;
Issachar was with Barak.
They set out at his heels in the valley.
There was great searching[d] of heart
among the clans of Reuben.

16 Why did you sit among the sheepfolds
listening to the playing of pipes for the flocks?
There was great searching of heart
among the clans of Reuben.

17 Gilead remained beyond the Jordan.
Dan, why did you linger at the ships?
Asher remained at the seashore
and stayed in his harbors.

18 Zebulun was a people risking their lives,
Naphtali also, on the heights of the battlefield.

19 Kings came and fought.
Then the kings of Canaan fought
at Taanach by the waters of Megiddo,
but they took no spoil of silver.

20 The stars fought from the heavens;
the stars fought with Sisera from their courses.

21 The river Kishon swept them away,
the ancient river, the river Kishon.
March on, my soul, in strength!

22 The horses' hooves then hammered—
the galloping, galloping of his[e] stallions.

23 "Curse Meroz," says the Angel of the LORD,
"Bitterly curse her inhabitants,
for they did not come to help the LORD,
to help the LORD against the mighty warriors."

24 Jael is most blessed of women,
the wife of Heber the Kenite;
she is most blessed among
tent-dwelling women.

25 He asked for water; she gave him milk.
She brought him curdled milk
in a majestic bowl.

26 She reached for a tent peg,
her right hand, for a workman's mallet.
Then she hammered Sisera—
she crushed his head;
she shattered and pierced his temple.

27 He collapsed, he fell, he lay down at[f] her feet;
he collapsed, he fell at her feet;
where he collapsed, there he fell—dead.

28 Sisera's mother looked through the window;
she [peered] through the lattice, crying out:
"Why is his chariot so long in coming?
Why don't I hear the hoofbeats of his horses?"[g]

29 Her wisest princesses answer her;
she even answers herself:[h]

30 "Are they not finding and dividing the spoil—
a girl or two for each warrior,
the spoil of colored garments for Sisera,
the spoil of an embroidered garment or two
for my neck?"[i]

31 LORD, may all your enemies perish
as Sisera did.[j]
But may those who love Him
be like the rising of the sun in its strength.

And the land was peaceful 40 years.

Midian Oppresses Israel

6 The Israelites did what was evil in the sight of
the LORD. So the LORD handed them over to Midian seven years, 2 and they oppressed Israel. Because
of Midian, the Israelites made hiding places for themselves in the mountains, caves, and strongholds.
3 Whenever the Israelites planted crops, the Midianites, Amalekites, and the eastern peoples came and
attacked them. 4 They encamped against them and
destroyed the produce of the land, even as far as Gaza.
They left nothing for Israel to eat, as well as no sheep,
ox or donkey. 5 For the Midianites came with their cattle and their tents like a great swarm of locusts. They
and their camels were without number, and they
entered the land to waste it. 6 So Israel became pov-

[a]5:11 Verse obscure [b]5:13 LXX reads *down for him* [c]5:14 LXX reads *in the valley* [d]5:15 Some Hb mss, Syr read *There were great resolves*
[e]5:22 = Sisera's [f]5:27 Lit *between* [g]5:28 Lit *Why have the hoofbeats of his chariot delayed* [h]5:29 Lit *answers her words* [i]5:30 Hb obscure
[j]5:31 Lit *perish thus*

mander as Deborah had predicted (v. 9).
5:1-31 Deborah's celebrates the great victory
over the Canaanites with one of the oldest poems in the Bible.
5:5 Sinai. Deborah reminds the people of their
ancestors' commitment to the covenant with
God at Mt. Sinai (see Ex. 19:17-20).

5:13-18 Deborah reviews those who contributed to Israel's campaign. Tribes who did not
join the united effort are criticized for their indifference.
5:31 peaceful. The period of peace completes
the cycle the Israelites experienced. Upon the
death of Deborah, however, the cycle begins

again with Israel's disobedience.
6:1-9:57 Despite a series of judges and their
heroic efforts, Israel continued to deteriorate.
The account of Gideon's victory shows that Israel had a real opportunity to change its course
and return to God. Even Gideon, however, ultimately disobeyed God (8:24-27). Abimelech's

erty-stricken because of Midian, and the Israelites cried out to the LORD.

[7] When the Israelites cried out to Him because of Midian, [8] the LORD sent a prophet to them. He said to them, "This is what the LORD God of Israel says: 'I brought you out of Egypt and out of the place of slavery. [9] I delivered you from the power of Egypt and the power of all who oppressed you. I drove them out before you and gave you their land. [10] I said to you: I am the LORD your God. Do not fear the gods of the Amorites whose land you live in. But you did not obey Me.'"

The LORD Calls Gideon

[11] The Angel[a] of the LORD came, and He[b] sat under the oak that was in Ophrah, which belonged to Joash, the Abiezrite. His son Gideon was threshing wheat in the wine vat in order to hide it from the Midianites. [12] Then the Angel of the LORD appeared to him and said: "The LORD is with you, mighty warrior."

[13] Gideon said to Him, "Please Sir,[c] if the LORD is with us, why has all this happened?[d] And where are all His wonders that our fathers told us about? They said, 'Hasn't the LORD brought us out of Egypt?' But now the LORD has abandoned us and handed us over to Midian."

[14] The LORD[e] turned to him and said, "Go in the strength you have and deliver Israel from the power of Midian. Am I not sending you?"

[15] He said to Him, "Please, Lord, how can I deliver Israel? Look, my family is the weakest in Manasseh, and I am the youngest in my father's house."

[16] "But I will be with you," the LORD said to him. "You will strike Midian down ⌊as if it were⌋ one man."

[17] Then he said to Him, "If I have found favor in Your sight, give me a sign that You are speaking with me. [18] Please do not leave this place until I return to You. Let me bring my gift and set it before You."

And He said, "I will stay until you return."

[19] So Gideon went and prepared a young goat and unleavened bread from a half bushel[f] of flour. He placed the meat in a basket and the broth in a pot. He brought them out and offered them to Him under the oak.

[20] The Angel of God said to him, "Take the meat with the unleavened bread, put it on this stone, and pour the broth ⌊on it⌋." And he did so.

[21] The Angel of the LORD extended the tip of the staff that was in His hand and touched the meat and the unleavened bread. Fire came up from the rock and consumed the meat and the unleavened bread. Then the Angel of the LORD vanished from his sight.

[22] When Gideon realized that He was the Angel of the LORD, he said, "Oh no, Lord GOD! I have seen the Angel of the LORD face to face!"

[23] But the LORD said to him, "Peace to you. Don't be afraid, for you will not die." [24] So Gideon built an altar to the LORD there and called it Yahweh Shalom.[g] It is in Ophrah of the Abiezrites until today.

Gideon Tears Down a Baal Altar

[25] On that very night the LORD said to him, "Take your father's young bull and a second bull seven years old. Then tear down the altar of •Baal that belongs to your father and cut down the •Asherah pole beside it. [26] Build a well-constructed altar to the LORD your God on the top of this rock. Take the second bull and offer it as a •burnt offering with the wood of the Asherah pole you cut down." [27] So Gideon took 10 of his male servants and did as the LORD had told him. But because he was too afraid of his father's household and the men of the city to do it in the daytime, he did it at night.

[28] When the men of the city got up in the morning, they found Baal's altar torn down, the Asherah pole beside it cut down, and the second bull offered up on the altar that had been built. [29] They said to each other, "Who did this?" After they made a thorough investigation, they said, "Gideon son of Joash did it."

[30] Then the men of the city said to Joash, "Bring out your son. He must die, because he tore down Baal's altar and cut down the Asherah pole beside it." [31] But Joash said to all who stood against him, "Would you plead Baal's case for him? Would you save him? Whoever pleads his case will be put to death by morning! If he is a god, let him plead his own case, because someone tore down his altar." [32] That day, Gideon's father called him Jerubbaal, saying, "Let Baal plead his case with him," because he tore down his altar.

The Sign of the Fleece

[33] All the Midianites, Amalekites, and Qedemites gathered together, crossed over ⌊the Jordan⌋, and camped in the Valley of Jezreel.

[34] The Spirit of the LORD enveloped Gideon, and he blew the ram's horn and the Abiezrites rallied behind him. [35] He sent messengers throughout all of Manasseh, who rallied behind him. He also sent messengers throughout Asher, Zebulun, and Naphtali, who ⌊also⌋ came to meet him.

[36] Then Gideon said to God, "If You will deliver Israel by my hand, as You said, [37] I will put a fleece of

---

[a]6:11 Or *angel*   [b]6:11 Or *he* (and so throughout this chap if this angel is a divine messenger and not a theophany)   [c]6:13 Lit *Please, my Lord,* or *Please, my lord*   [d]6:13 Lit *this found us out*   [e]6:14 LXX reads *The Angel of the LORD*   [f]6:19 Lit *an ephah*   [g]6:24 = *The LORD Is Peace*

---

self-proclaimed royalty (9:1-57) contributes to the decline.

6:7 because of Midian. The Israelites blamed the Midianites for their problems, but God had used Midian to punish the Israelites' unfaithfulness to Him.

6:11 threshing wheat in the wine vat. People

usually threshed wheat in the open air so the wind could take away the chaff. With the threat of Midianite attack, however, Gideon sought safety in the winepress.

6:12 mighty warrior. The Angel of the Lord saw the potential for a mighty warrior in this laborer.

6:14 Am I not sending you? Gideon did not know it then, but he was being selected as the next judge to deliver Israel.

6:15 how can I deliver Israel? Gideon's focus was not on his faith in God but on his small family. How could he be a hero?

6:17 give me a sign. Gideon's small faith

wool here on the threshing floor. If dew is only on the fleece, and all the ground is dry, I will know that You will deliver Israel by my strength, as You said." 38 And that is what happened. When he got up early in the morning, he squeezed the fleece and wrung dew out of it, filling a bowl with water.

39 Gideon then said to God, "Don't be angry with me; let me speak one more time. Please allow me to make one more test with the fleece. Let it remain dry, and the dew be all over the ground." 40 That night God did ⌊as Gideon requested⌋: only the fleece was dry, and dew was all over the ground.

God Selects Gideon's Army

7 Jerubbaal (that is, Gideon) and everyone who was with him, got up early and camped beside the spring of Harod. The camp of Midian was north of them, below the hill of Moreh, in the valley. 2 The LORD said to Gideon, "You have too many people for Me to hand the Midianites over to you,ᵃ or else Israel might brag:ᵇ 'I did it myself.' 3 Now announce in the presence of the people: 'Whoever is fearful and trembling may turn back and leave Mount Gilead.'" So 22,000 of the people turned back, but 10,000 remained.

4 Then the LORD said to Gideon, "There are still too many people. Take them down to the water, and I will test them for you there. If I say to you, 'This one can go with you,' he can go. But if I say about anyone, 'This one cannot go with you,' he cannot go." 5 So he brought the people down to the water, and the LORD said to Gideon, "Separate everyone who laps water with his tongue like a dog. Do the same with everyone who kneels to drink." 6 The number of those who lapped with their hands to their mouths was 300 men, and all the rest of the people knelt to drink water. 7 The LORD said to Gideon, "I will deliver you with the 300 men who lapped and hand the Midianites over to you. But everyone else is to go home." 8 So Gideon sent all the Israelites to their tents, but kept the 300 who tookᶜ the people's provisions and their trumpets. The camp of Midian was below him in the valley.

Gideon Spies on the Midianite Camp

9 That night the LORD said to him, "Get up and go into the camp, for I have given it into your hand. 10 But if you are afraid to go to the camp, go with Purah your servant. 11 Listen to what they say, and then you will be strengthened to go to the camp." So he went with Purah his servant to the outpost of the troopsᵈ who were in the camp.

12 Now the Midianites, Amalekites, and all the Qedemites had settled down in the valley like a swarm of locusts, and their camels were as innumerable as the sand on the seashore. 13 When Gideon arrived, there was a man telling his friend ⌊about⌋ a dream. He said, "Listen, I had a dream: a loaf of barley bread came tumbling into the Midianite camp, struck a tent, and it fell. The loaf turned the tent upside down so that it collapsed."

14 His friend answered: "This is nothing less than the sword of Gideon son of Joash, the Israelite. God has handed the entire Midianite camp over to him."

An Upset Victory

1. What is the biggest "upset victory" you have experienced? Were you a winner or loser?

Judges 7:1-25
2. Why did God ask Gideon to reduce the size of his army?
3. Why did He select the men who drank water while looking around? What does this suggest about how to be a good "soldier" for Christ?
4. How did God use the man's dream (v. 13) to bring about victory? How has God used circumstances in your own life to bring about His will?
5. Are you facing an overpowering "enemy" in competition? In your life? In your mental attitude? How do you need God's help in fighting the battle?

Gideon Attacks the Midianites

15 When Gideon heard the account of the dream and its interpretation, he bowed in worship. He returned to Israel's camp and said, "Get up, for the LORD has handed the Midianite camp over to you." 16 Then he divided the 300 men into three companies and gave each of the men a trumpet in one hand and an empty pitcher with a torch inside it ⌊in the other⌋.

17 "Watch me," he said,ᵉ "and do the same. When I come to the outpost of the camp, do as I do. 18 When I and everyone with me blow our trumpets, you are also to blow your trumpets all around the camp. Then you will say, 'The sword of the LORD and of Gideon!'"

ᵃ**7:2** Lit them   ᵇ**7:2** Lit brag against Me   ᶜ**7:8** Lit took in their hands   ᵈ**7:11** Lit of those who were arranged in companies of 50   ᵉ**7:17** Lit said to them

---

needed more assurance.
6:25 tear down the altar of Baal that belongs to your father. Sacrificing the symbol of his father's pagan faith would demonstrate God's superiority and Gideon's new start.
6:34 Spirit of the LORD. God's Spirit empowered Gideon to do His work. He now feels more

confident about God's instructions for his life.

7:1-8 Large numbers were not high on God's list of requirements for success. In fact, he shaved thousands of men off Gideon's battle plan and accomplished victory—with only 300 warriors.
7:3 may turn back. God wanted warriors who

were confident in His ability to make them strong.

7:4-8 lapped with their hands to their mouths. Another test weeded the army down from 10,000 to just 300, to go against the Midianites' army of 135,000. God wanted to leave no doubt that the victory was His doing.

19 Gideon and the 100 men who were with him went to the outpost of the camp at the beginning of the middle watch after the sentries had been stationed. They blew their trumpets and broke the pitchers that were in their hands. 20 The three companies blew their trumpets and shattered their pitchers. They held their torches in their left hands, their trumpets[a] in their right hands, and shouted, "The sword of the LORD and of Gideon!" 21 Each Israelite took his position around the camp, and the entire ⌊Midianite⌋ army fled, and cried out as they ran. 22 When Gideon's men blew their 300 trumpets, the LORD set the swords of each man in the army against each other. They fled to Beth-shittah in the direction of Zererah as far as the border of Abel-meholah near Tabbath. 23 Then the men of Israel were called from Naphtali, Asher, and Manasseh, and they pursued the Midianites.

The Men of Ephraim Join the Battle

24 Gideon sent messengers throughout the hill country of Ephraim with this message: "Come down to intercept the Midianites and take control of the watercourses ahead of them as far as Beth-barah and the Jordan." So all the men of Ephraim were called out, and they took control of the watercourses as far as Beth-barah and the Jordan. 25 They captured Oreb and Zeeb, the two princes of Midian; they killed Oreb at the rock of Oreb and Zeeb at the winepress of Zeeb, while they were pursuing the Midianites. They brought the heads of Oreb and Zeeb to Gideon across the Jordan.

8 The men of Ephraim said to him, "Why have you done this to us, not calling us when you went to fight against the Midianites?" And they argued with him violently.

2 So he said to them, "What have I done now compared to you? Is not the gleaning of Ephraim better than the vintage of Abiezer? 3 God handed over to you Oreb and Zeeb, the two princes of Midian. What was I able to do compared to you?" When he said this, their anger against him subsided.

Gideon Pursues the Kings of Midian

4 Gideon and the 300 men came to the Jordan and crossed it. They were exhausted, but still in pursuit. 5 He said to the men of Succoth, "Please give some loaves of bread to the people who are following me,[b] because they are exhausted, for I am pursuing Zebah and Zalmunna, the kings of Midian."

6 But the princes of Succoth asked, "Are[c] Zebah and Zalmunna now in your hands that we should give bread to your army?"

7 Gideon replied, "Very well, when the LORD has handed Zebah and Zalmunna over to me, I will trample[d] your flesh on thorns and briers from the wilderness!" 8 He went from there to Penuel and asked the same thing from them. The men of Penuel answered just as the men of Succoth had answered. 9 He also told the men of Penuel, "When I return in peace, I will tear down this tower!"

10 Now Zebah and Zalmunna were in Karkor, and with them was their army of about 15,000 men, who were all those left of the entire army of the Qedemites. Those who had been killed were 120,000 warriors.[e] 11 Gideon traveled on the caravan route,[f] east of Nobah and Jogbehah, and attacked their army while the army was unsuspecting. 12 Zebah and Zalmunna fled, and he pursued them. He captured these two kings of Midian and routed the entire army.

13 Gideon son of Joash returned from the battle by the ascent of Heres. 14 He captured a youth from the men of Succoth and interrogated him. The youth wrote down for him the ⌊names of the⌋ 77 princes and elders of Succoth. 15 Then he went to the men of Succoth and said, "Here are Zebah and Zalmunna. You taunted me about them, saying, 'Are[c] Zebah and Zalmunna now in your power that we should give bread to your exhausted men?'" 16 So he took the elders of the city, as well as some thorns and briers from the wilderness, and he disciplined the men of Succoth with them. 17 He also tore down the tower of Penuel and killed the men of the city.

18 He asked Zebah and Zalmunna, "What kind of men did you kill at Tabor?"

"They were like you," they said. "Each resembled the son of a king."

19 So he said, "They were my brothers, the sons of my mother! As the LORD lives, if you had let them live, I would not kill you." 20 Then he said to Jether, his first-born, "Get up and kill them." The youth did not draw his sword, because he was afraid, for he was still a youth.

21 Zebah and Zalmunna said, "Get up and kill us yourself, for a man is judged by his strength." So Gideon got up, killed Zebah and Zalmunna, and took the crescent ornaments that were on the necks of their camels.

---

a7:20 Lit trumpets to blow   b8:5 Lit are at my feet   c8:6,15 Lit Are the hands of   d8:7 Or tear   e8:10 Lit men who drew the sword   f8:11 Lit on the route of those who live in tents

---

7:8-14 Eavesdropping became an important morale booster and battle strategy for Gideon when an enemy's dream was interpreted to predict the Israelites' victory.

7:13-14 dream. A loaf of barley bread. A crushed tent. These images in a Midianite's dream spelled victory for the Israelites. While

Gideon's confidence increased at the news, a sleepless night awaited the worried Midianite warriors.

7:19 middle watch. About 10:00 p.m., according to the Jewish custom of dividing the night into three parts.

7:22 against each other. In the confusion, the

Midianites began fighting each other. Gideon's band got into the action only after the Midianite soldiers began to flee.

7:24 take control of the watercourses. Gideon knew that streams and oases would be critically important to the fleeing army.

8:1 men of Ephraim. Gideon handles their

Gideon's Legacy

22 Then the Israelites said to Gideon, "Rule over us, you as well as your sons and your grandsons, for you delivered us from the power of Midian."

23 But Gideon said to them, "I will not rule over you, and my son will not rule over you; the LORD will rule over you." 24 Then he said to them, "Let me make a request of you: Everyone give me an earring from his plunder." Now the enemy had gold earrings because they were Ishmaelites.

25 They said, "We agree to give them." So they spread out a mantle, and everyone threw an earring from his plunder on it. 26 The weight of the gold earrings he requested was about 43 pounds[a] of gold, in addition to the crescent ornaments and ear pendants, the purple garments on the kings of Midian, and the chains on the necks of their camels. 27 Gideon made an ephod from all this and put it in Ophrah, his hometown. Then all Israel prostituted themselves with it there, and it became a snare to Gideon and his household.

28 So Midian was subdued before the Israelites, and they were no longer a threat.[b] The land was peaceful 40 years during the days of Gideon. 29 Jerubbaal ⌊(that is, Gideon)⌋ son of Joash went back to live at his house.

30 Gideon had 70 sons, his own offspring, since he had many wives. 31 His concubine who was in Shechem also bore him a son, and he named him Abimelech. 32 Then Gideon son of Joash died at a ripe old age and was buried in the tomb of his father Joash in Ophrah of the Abiezrites.

33 When Gideon died, the Israelites turned and prostituted themselves with the •Baals and made Baal-berith[c] their god. 34 The Israelites did not remember the LORD their God who had delivered them from the power of the enemies around them. 35 They did not show kindness to the house of Jerubbaal (⌊that is,⌋ Gideon) for all the good he had done for Israel.

Abimelech Becomes King

9 Abimelech son of Jerubbaal went to his mother's brothers at Shechem and spoke to them and to all his maternal grandfather's clan, saying, 2 "Please speak in the presence of all the lords of Shechem, 'Is it better for you that 70 men, all the sons of Jerubbaal, rule over you or that one man rule over you?' Remember that I am your own flesh and blood."[d]

3 His mother's relatives spoke all these words about him in the presence of all the lords of Shechem, and they were favorable to Abimelech, for they said, "He is our brother." 4 So they gave him 70 pieces of silver from the temple of Baal-berith.[c] Abimelech hired worthless and reckless men with this money, and they followed him. 5 He went to his father's house in Ophrah and killed his 70 brothers, the sons of Jerubbaal, on top of a large stone. But Jotham, the youngest son of Jerubbaal, survived, because he hid himself. 6 Then all the lords of Shechem and of Beth-millo gathered together and proceeded to make Abimelech king at the oak of the pillar in Shechem.

Jotham's Parable

7 When they told Jotham, he climbed to the top of Mount Gerizim, raised his voice, and called to them:

Listen to me, lords of Shechem,
and may God listen to you:

8 The trees set out
to anoint a king over themselves.
They said to the olive tree, "Reign over us."

9 But the olive tree said to them,
"Should I stop giving my oil
that honors both God and man,
and rule[e] over the trees?"

10 Then the trees said to the fig tree,
"Come and reign over us."

11 But the fig tree said to them,
"Should I stop giving
my sweetness and my good fruit,
and rule[e] over trees?"

12 Later, the trees said to the grapevine,
"Come and reign over us."

13 But the grapevine said to them,
"Should I stop giving my wine
that cheers both God and man,
and rule[e] over trees?"

14 Finally, all the trees said to the bramble,
"Come and reign over us."

15 The bramble said to the trees,
"If you really are anointing me
as king over you,
come and find refuge in my shade.
But if not,
may fire come out from the bramble
and consume the cedars of Lebanon."

---

a 8:26 Lit 1,700 shekels b 8:28 Lit they no longer raised their head c 8:33; 9:4 Lit Baal of the Covenant, or Lord of the Covenant d 9:2 Lit your bone and your flesh e 9:9,11,13 Lit and go to sway

---

criticism with grace, averting trouble and even skirting a potential civil war.

8:2 gleaning of Ephraim. Gideon expresses his view in language familiar to many of his worker-warriors. Gleanings were the leftovers—we might call it a "mop-up operation."
8:3 their anger against him subsided. Gid-

eon points out that the mighty Ephraimites have no right to complain. After all, Ephraim took top honors, killing two of the top Midianite officers (7:25).

8:23 The LORD will rule. Although Gideon is theologically correct here, he will quickly fall into idolatry (v. 27).

8:27 ephod. This golden chest piece usually was worn by a priest (see Ex. 28:6-30). However, Gideon and the people worshiped the golden object as an idol.

8:31 bore him a son. Gideon had several wives who bore him at least 70 children. **Abimelech.** The mother of Abimelech was Gideon's

16 "Now if you have acted faithfully and honestly in making Abimelech king, if you have done well by Jerubbaal and his family, and if you have rewarded him appropriately for what he did— 17 for my father fought for you, risked his life, and delivered you from the hand of Midian, 18 and now you have attacked my father's house today, killed his 70 sons on top of a large stone, and made Abimelech, the son of his slave, king over the lords of Shechem 'because he is your brother'— 19 if then, you have acted faithfully and honestly with Jerubbaal and his house this day, rejoice in Abimelech and may he also rejoice in you. 20 But if not, may fire come from Abimelech and consume the lords of Shechem and Beth-millo, and may fire come from the lords of Shechem and Beth-millo and consume Abimelech." 21 Then Jotham fled, escaping to Beer, and lived there because of his brother Abimelech.

Abimelech's Punishment

22 When Abimelech had ruled over Israel three years, 23 God sent an evil spirit between Abimelech and the lords of Shechem. They treated Abimelech deceitfully, 24 so that the crime against the 70 sons of Jerubbaal might come to justice and their blood would be avenged on their brother Abimelech, who killed them, and on the lords of Shechem, who had helped him kill his brothers. 25 The lords of Shechem rebelled against him by putting people on the tops of the mountains to ambush and rob everyone who passed by them on the road. So this was reported to Abimelech.

26 Gaal son of Ebed came with his brothers and crossed into Shechem, and the lords of Shechem trusted him. 27 So they went out to the countryside and harvested grapes from their vineyards. They trod the grapes and held a celebration. Then they went to the house of their god, and as they ate and drank, they cursed Abimelech. 28 Gaal son of Ebed said, "Who is Abimelech and who is Shechem that we should serve him? Isn't he the son of Jerubbaal, and isn't Zebul his officer? You are to serve the men of Hamor, the father of Shechem. Why should we serve Abimelech? 29 If only these people were in my power, I would remove Abimelech." So he said[a] to Abimelech, "Gather your army and come out."

30 When Zebul, the ruler of the city, heard the words of Gaal son of Ebed, he was angry. 31 So he sent messengers secretly to Abimelech, saying, "Look, Gaal son of Ebed, with his brothers, have come to Shechem and are turning the city against you.[b] 32 Now tonight, you and the people with you are to come wait in ambush in

the countryside. 33 Then get up early and at sunrise, charge the city. When he and the people who are with him come out against you, do to him whatever you can."[c] 34 So Abimelech and all the people with him got up at night and waited in ambush for Shechem in four units.

35 Gaal son of Ebed went out and stood at the entrance of the city gate. Then Abimelech and the people who were with him got up from their ambush. 36 When Gaal saw the people, he said to Zebul, "Look, people are coming down from the mountaintops!" But Zebul said to him, "The shadows of the mountains look like men to you."

37 Then Gaal spoke again: "Look, people are coming down from the central part of the land, and one unit is coming from the direction of the Diviners' Oak." 38 Zebul replied,[d] "Where is your mouthing off now? You said, 'Who is Abimelech that we should serve him?' Aren't these the people you despised? Now go and fight them!"

39 So Gaal went out leading the lords of Shechem and fought against Abimelech, 40 but Abimelech pursued him, and Gaal fled before him. Many wounded died as far as the entrance of the gate. 41 Abimelech stayed in Arumah, and Zebul drove Gaal and his brothers from Shechem.

42 The next day when the people went into the countryside, this was reported to Abimelech. 43 He took the people, divided them into three companies, and waited in ambush in the countryside. He looked, and the people were coming out of the city, so he arose against them and struck them down. 44 Then Abimelech and the units that were with him rushed forward and took their stand at the entrance of the city gate. The other two units rushed against all who were in the countryside and struck them down. 45 So Abimelech fought against the city that entire day, captured it, and killed the people who were in it. Then he tore down the city and sowed it with salt.

46 When all the lords of the Tower of Shechem heard, they entered the inner chamber[e] of the temple of El-berith.[f] 47 Then it was reported to Abimelech that all the lords of the Tower of Shechem had gathered together. 48 So Abimelech and all the people who were with him went up to Mount Zalmon. Abimelech took his ax in his hand and cut a branch from the trees. He picked up the branch, put it on his shoulder, and said to the people who were with him, "Hurry and do what you have seen me do." 49 Each person also cut his own

---

a**9:29** DSS read They said; LXX reads I would say   b**9:31** Hb obscure   c**9:33** Lit him as your hand will find   d**9:38** Lit replied to him   e**9:46** Or the crypt, or the vault   f**9:46** = God of the Covenant

---

slave, but her son soon proclaimed himself king (9:2).

8:33 When Gideon died. With their leader gone, the cycle of disobedience starts over again for the Israelites.

9:1-57 Abimelech rises to power by murdering his own family members (v. 5). Renouncing his

father's faith, Abimelech looks toward Baal for assistance in his plot. Overcome with evil, Abimelech dies an ignominious death after just three years in power (vv. 52-54).

9:1 Jerubbaal. Another name for Gideon (7:1).

9:5 his 70 brothers. Abimelech murdered his father's sons in an attempt to secure his royal

position.

9:9-13 Jotham used familiar cultural images to make his point.

9:14 bramble. Thornbushes, sometimes called brambles, are only good for pricking bare heels and kindling fires.

9:15 cedars of Lebanon. The influential men

branch and followed Abimelech. They put the branches against the inner chamber and set it on fire around the people, and all the people in the Tower of Shechem died—about 1,000 men and women.

50 Abimelech went to Thebez, camped against it, and captured it. 51 There was a strong tower inside the city, and all the men, women, and lords of the city fled there. They locked themselves in and went up to the roof of the tower. 52 When Abimelech came to attack the tower, he approached its entrance to set it on fire. 53 But a woman threw the upper portion of a millstone on Abimelech's head and fractured his skull. 54 He quickly called his armor-bearer and said to him, "Draw your sword and kill me, or they'll say about me, 'A woman killed him.'" So his armor-bearer thrust him through, and he died. 55 When the Israelites saw that Abimelech was dead, they all went home.

56 In this way, the evil that Abimelech had done against his father, by killing his 70 brothers, God turned back on him. 57 And God also returned all the evil of the men of Shechem on their heads. So the curse of Jotham son of Jerubbaal came on them.

Tola and Jair

10 After Abimelech, Tola son of Puah, son of Dodo ⌊became judge⌋ and began to deliver Israel. He was from Issachar and lived in Shamir in the hill country of Ephraim. 2 Tola judged Israel 23 years, and when he died, was buried in Shamir.

3 After him came Jair the Gileadite, who judged Israel 22 years. 4 He had 30 sons who rode on 30 young donkeys. They had 30 townsa in Gilead, which are called Jair's Villagesb to this day. 5 When Jair died, he was buried in Kamon.

Israel's Rebellion and Repentance

6 Then the Israelites again did what was evil in the sight of the LORD. They worshiped the •Baals and the •Ashtoreths, the gods of Aram, Sidon, and Moab, and the gods of the Ammonites and the Philistines. They abandoned the LORD and did not worship Him. 7 So the LORD's anger burned against Israel, and He sold them toc the Philistines and the Ammonites. 8 They shattered and crushed the Israelites that year, and for 18 years ⌊they did the same to⌋ all the Israelites who were on the other side of the Jordan in the land of the Amorites in Gilead. 9 The Ammonites also crossed the Jordan to fight against Judah, Benjamin, and the house of Ephraim. Israel was greatly oppressed, 10 so they cried out to the LORD, saying, "We have sinned against You.

We have abandoned our God and worshiped the Baals."

11 The LORD said to the Israelites, "When the Egyptians, Amorites, Ammonites, Philistines, 12 Sidonians, Amalekites, and Maonitesd oppressed you, and you cried out to Me, did I not deliver you from their power? 13 But you have abandoned Me and worshiped other gods. Therefore, I will not deliver you again. 14 Go and cry out to the gods you have chosen. Let them deliver you in the time of your oppression."

15 But the Israelites said, "We have sinned. Deal with us as You see fit;e only deliver us today!" 16 So they got rid of the foreign gods among them and worshiped the LORD, but He became weary of Israel's misery.

17 The Ammonites were called together, and they camped in Gilead. So the Israelites assembled and camped at Mizpah. 18 The rulersf of Gilead said to one another, "Which man will lead the fight against the Ammonites? He will be the leader of all the inhabitants of Gilead."

Jephthah Becomes Israel's Leader

11 Jephthah the Gileadite was a great warrior, but he was the son of a prostitute, and Gilead was his father. 2 Gilead's wife bore him sons, and when they grew up, they drove Jephthah out and said to him, "You will have no inheritance in our father's house, because you are the son of another woman." 3 So Jephthah fled from his brothers and lived in the land of Tob. Then some lawless men joined Jephthah and traveled with him.

4 Some time later, the Ammonites fought against Israel. 5 When the Ammonites made war with Israel, the elders of Gilead went to get Jephthah from the land of Tob. 6 They said to him, "Come, be our commander, and let's fight against the Ammonites."

7 Jephthah replied to the elders of Gilead, "Didn't you hate me and drive me from my father's house? Why then have you come to me now when you're in trouble?"

8 They answered Jephthah, "Since that's true, we now turn to you. Come with us, fight the Ammonites, and you will become leader of all the inhabitants of Gilead."

9 So Jephthah said to them, "If you are bringing me back to fight the Ammonites and the LORD gives them to me, I will be your leader."

10 The elders of Gilead said to Jephthah, "The LORD is our witness if we don't do as you say." 11 So Jephthah went with the elders of Gilead. The people put him

---

a10:4 LXX; MT reads donkeys   b10:4 Or called Havvoth-jair   c10:7 Lit into the hand of   d10:12 LXX reads Midianites   e10:15 Lit Do to us what is good in Your eyes   f10:18 Lit The people, rulers

---

of Shechem saw themselves in this image. The worthless thornbush would summarily destroy the valuable cedars.

9:23 evil spirit. Unable to escape his deadly deeds, Abimelech has a falling out with his allies.

9:26 Gaal. With Abimelech fallen from grace,

Gaal appears on the scene to further deceive the willing people.

9:32 wait in ambush. In a favorite military tactic, the governor recommends an ambush to guarantee Abimelech's success.

9:34 got up at night. Although they took their places at night, the attack does not come until

the morning light.

10:1 Tola. Without foreign oppression, Tola could focus on Israel's spiritual woes.

10:3 Gileadite. Number seven in the line of judges, Jair was from Gilead, within the tribe of Manasseh.

10:6–12:7 Rejected by his own people as a

over themselves as leader and commander, and Jephthah repeated all his terms in the presence of the LORD at Mizpah.

Jephthah Rejects Ammonite Claims

12 Jephthah sent messengers to the king of the Ammonites, saying, "What do you have against me that you have come to fight against me in my land?"

13 The king of the Ammonites said to Jephthah's messengers, "When Israel came from Egypt, they seized my land from the Arnon to the Jabbok and the Jordan. Now restore it peaceably."

14 Jephthah again sent messengers to the king of the Ammonites 15 to tell him, "This is what Jephthah says: Israel did not take away the land of Moab or the land of the Ammonites. 16 But when they came from Egypt, Israel traveled through the wilderness to the •Red Sea and came to Kadesh. 17 Israel sent messengers to the king of Edom, saying, 'Please let us travel through your land,' but the king of Edom would not listen. They also sent ⌊messengers⌋ to the king of Moab, but he refused. So Israel stayed in Kadesh.

18 "Then they traveled through the wilderness and around the lands of Edom and Moab. They came to the east side of the land of Moab and camped on the other side of the Arnon but did not enter into the territory of Moab, for the Arnon was the boundary of Moab.

19 "Then Israel sent messengers to Sihon king of the Amorites, king of Heshbon. Israel said to him, 'Please let us travel through your land to our country,' 20 but Sihon did not trust Israel.ᵃ Instead, Sihon gathered all his people, camped at Jahaz, and fought with Israel. 21 Then the LORD God of Israel handed over Sihon and all his people to Israel, and they defeated them. So Israel took possession of the entire land of the Amorites who lived in that country. 22 They took possession of all the territory of the Amorites from the Arnon to the Jabbok and from the wilderness to the Jordan.

23 "The LORD God of Israel has now driven out the Amorites before His people Israel, but will you drive us out? 24 Isn't it true that you may possess whatever your god Chemosh drives out for you, and we may possess everything the LORD our God drives out before us? 25 Now are you any better than Balak son of Zippor, king of Moab? Did he ever contend with Israel or fight against them? 26 While Israel lived 300 years in Heshbon and its villages, in Aroer and its villages, and in all the cities that are on the banks of the Arnon, why didn't you take them back at that time? 27 I have not sinned against you, but you have wronged me by fighting against me. Let the LORD ⌊who is⌋ the Judge decide today between the Israelites and the Ammonites."

28 But the king of the Ammonites would not listen to Jephthah's message that he sent him.

Jephthah's Vow and Sacrifice

29 The Spirit of the LORD came on Jephthah, who traveled through Gilead and Manasseh, and then through Mizpah of Gilead. He crossed over to the Ammonites from Mizpah of Gilead. 30 Jephthah made this vow to the LORD: "If You will hand over the Ammonites to me, 31 whatever comes out of the doors of my house to greet me when I return in peace from the Ammonites will belong to the LORD, and I will offer it as a •burnt offering."

32 Jephthah crossed over to the Ammonites to fight against them, and the LORD handed them over to him. 33 He defeated 20 of their cities with a great slaughter from Aroer all the way to the entrance of Minnith and to Abel-keramim. So the Ammonites were subdued before the Israelites.

34 When Jephthah went to his home in Mizpah, there was his daughter, coming out to meet him with tambourines and dancing! She was his only child; he had no other son or daughter besides her. 35 When he saw her, he tore his clothes and said, "No! ⌊Not⌋ my daughter! You have devastated me! You have brought great misery on me.ᵇ I have given my word to the LORD and cannot take ⌊it⌋ back."

36 Then she said to him, "My father, you have given your word to the LORD. Do to me as you have said, for the LORD brought vengeance on your enemies, the Ammonites." 37 She also said to her father, "Let me do this one thing: Let me wander two months through the mountains with my friends and mourn my virginity."

38 "Go," he said. And he sent her away two months. So she left with her friends and mourned her virginity as she wandered through the mountains. 39 At the end of two months, she returned to her father, and he kept the vow he had made about her. And she had never been intimate with a man. Now it became a custom in Israel 40 ⌊that⌋ four days each year the young women of Israel would commemorate the daughter of Jephthah the Gileadite.

Conflict with Ephraim

12 The men of Ephraim were called together and crossed ⌊the Jordan⌋ to Zaphon. They said to Jephthah, "Why have you crossed over to fight against

---

ᵃ**11:20** Lit *Israel to travel through his territory*   ᵇ**11:35** Lit *have been among those who trouble me*

---

young man (11:3), Jephthah eventually became Israel's judge for six years.

10:12 did I not deliver you? A series of judges over many decades had represented God's faithfulness by delivering the people from oppression.

10:18 "Which man will lead the fight?" A desperate people looked for military leadership.

11:1 the son of a prostitute. Jephthah was the illegitimate son of Gilead and a prostitute, and likely half-Canaanite—a social outcast.

11:8 leader. The elders of Gilead were willing to promise Jephthah leadership of their region if he would lead them militarily.

11:13 seized my land. The king twisted history to make his case.

11:14-27 Jephthah's letter to the Ammonite king clarified Israel's claim to the land: They attained it from the Amorites, not the Ammonites; Israel's God had given them the land; and Is-

the Ammonites but didn't call us to go with you? We will burn your house down with you ⌊in it⌋!"

2 Then Jephthah said to them, "My people and I had a serious conflict with the Ammonites. So I called for you, but you didn't deliver me from their power. 3 When I saw that you weren't going to deliver me, I took my life in my own hands and crossed over to the Ammonites, and the LORD handed them over to me. Why then have you come[a] today to fight against me?"

4 Then Jephthah gathered all of the men of Gilead. They fought and defeated Ephraim, because Ephraim had said, "You Gileadites are Ephraimite fugitives in ⌊the territories of⌋ Ephraim and Manasseh." 5 The Gileadites captured the fords of the Jordan leading to Ephraim. Whenever a fugitive from Ephraim said, "Let me cross over," the Gileadites asked him, "Are you an Ephraimite?" If he answered, "No," 6 they told him, "Please say Shibboleth." If he said, "Sibboleth," because he could not pronounce it correctly, they seized him and killed him at the fords of the Jordan. At that time, 42,000 from Ephraim died.

7 Jephthah judged Israel six years, and when he died, he was buried in one of the cities of Gilead.[b]

Ibzan, Elon, and Abdon

8 Ibzan, who was from Bethlehem, judged Israel after Jephthah 9 and had 30 sons. He gave his 30 daughters in marriage ⌊to men⌋ outside the tribe and brought back 30 wives for his sons from outside ⌊the tribe⌋. Ibzan judged Israel seven years, 10 and when he died, he was buried in Bethlehem.

11 Elon, who was from Zebulun, judged Israel after Ibzan. He judged Israel 10 years, 12 and when he died, he was buried in Aijalon in the land of Zebulun.

13 After Elon, Abdon son of Hillel, who was from Pirathon, judged Israel. 14 He had 40 sons and 30 grandsons, who rode on 70 donkeys. Abdon judged Israel eight years, 15 and when he died, he was buried in Pirathon in the land of Ephraim, in the hill country of the Amalekites.

Birth of Samson, the Last Judge

13 The Israelites again did what was evil in the LORD's sight, so the LORD handed them over to the Philistines 40 years. 2 There was a certain man from Zorah, from the family of Dan, whose name was Manoah; his wife was barren and had no children. 3 The Angel of the LORD appeared to the woman and said to her, "It is true that you are barren and have no children, but you will conceive and give birth to a son.

4 Now please be careful not to drink wine or other alcoholic beverages, or to eat anything unclean; 5 for indeed, you will conceive and give birth to a son. You must never cut his hair,[c] because the boy will be a Nazirite to God from birth, and he will begin to save Israel from the power of the Philistines."

6 Then the woman went and told her husband, "A man of God came to me. He looked like the awe-inspiring Angel of God. I didn't ask Him where He came from, and He didn't tell me His name. 7 He said to me, 'You will conceive and give birth to a son. Therefore, do not drink wine or other alcoholic beverages, and do not eat anything unclean, because the boy will be a Nazirite to God from birth until the day of his death.'"

8 Manoah prayed to the LORD and said, "Please Lord, let the man of God you sent come again to us and teach us what we should do for the boy who will be born."

9 God listened to[d] Manoah, and the Angel of God came again to the woman. She was sitting in the field, and her husband Manoah was not with her. 10 The woman ran quickly to her husband and told him, "The man who came to me today has just come back!"

11 So Manoah got up and followed his wife. When he came to the man, he asked, "Are You the man who spoke to my wife?"

"I am," He said.

12 Then Manoah asked, "When Your words come true, what will the boy's responsibilities and mission[e] be?"

13 The Angel of the LORD answered Manoah, "Your wife needs to do everything I told her. 14 She must not eat anything that comes from the grapevine or drink wine or other alcoholic beverages. And she must not eat anything unclean. Your wife must do everything I have commanded her."

15 "Please stay here," Manoah told Him, "and we will prepare a young goat for You."

16 The Angel of the LORD said to him, "If I stay, I won't eat your food. But if you want to prepare a •burnt offering, offer it to the LORD." For Manoah did not know He was the Angel of the LORD.

17 Then Manoah said to Him, "What is Your name, so that we may honor You when Your words come true?"

18 "Why do you ask My name," the Angel of the LORD asked him, "since it is wonderful."

19 Manoah took a young goat and a •grain offering and offered them on a rock to the LORD, and He did a wonderful thing[f] while Manoah and his wife were

---

---

rael had occupied the land for many years.
11:30 made this vow. Vows were taken seriously in Israel. Their very existence as a people began with a vow between Abraham and God.
11:34 dancing. The entire community celebrated a military victory. Young girls often led the celebration (see Ex. 15:20, 1 Sam. 18:6).

11:35 tore his clothes. An act of extreme grief.
11:37 wander ... through the mountains. Jephthah's daughter did not defy her father or resist the terrible consequence of his vow. Her father may have offered her as a human sacrifice, or he may simply have kept her from ever marrying.

11:39-40 custom in Israel. This custom is mentioned nowhere else in the Old Testament.
12:2 Jephthah said to them. Jephthah's first response to the threat was diplomacy.
12:6 Shibboleth. Gileadites used a verbal test to identify Ephraimites.
13:1_16:31 Like Israel, Samson was blessed

watching. 20 When the flame went up from the altar to the sky, the Angel of the LORD went up in its flame. When Manoah and his wife saw ⌊this⌋, they fell face-down on the ground. 21 The Angel of the LORD did not appear again to Manoah and his wife. Then Manoah realized that it was the Angel of the LORD.

22 "We're going to die," he said to his wife, "because we have seen God!"

23 But his wife said to him, "If the LORD had intended to kill us, He wouldn't have accepted the burnt offering and the grain offering from us, and He would not have shown us all these things or spoken to us now like this."

24 So the woman gave birth to a son and named him Samson. The boy grew, and the LORD blessed him. 25 Then the Spirit of the LORD began to direct him in the Camp of Dan,a between Zorah and Eshtaol.

Faith under Fire

1. In choosing a date, what is more important: Body build? Looks? Brains? Personality? Spirituality?

Judges 14:1-20

2. God commanded the Israelites not to marry Gentiles, such as the Philistines. How did Samson demand that his parents help him sin?

3. How did Samson's bad choices cause harm to others? When have you seen your own sins hurt innocent people?

4. What did Samson put his faith in most: God? His strength? His clever wit? His parents? Other?

5. Do you sometimes do things your own way, even though you know it's not God's way? What happened the last time you did this?

Samson's Riddle

14 Samson went down to Timnah and saw a young Philistine woman there. 2 He went back and told his father and his mother: "I have seen a young Philistine woman in Timnah. Now get her for me as a wife."

3 But his father and mother said to him, "Can't you findb a young woman among your relatives or among

any of our people? Must you go to the uncircumcised Philistines for a wife?"

But Samson told his father, "Get her for me, because I want her."c 4 Now his father and mother did not know this was from the LORD, who was seeking an occasion against the Philistines. At that time, the Philistines were ruling over Israel.

5 Samson went down to Timnah with his father and mother and came to the vineyards of Timnah. Suddenly a young lion came roaring at him, 6 the Spirit of the LORD took control ofd him, and he tore the lion apart with his bare hands as he might have torn a young goat. But he did not tell his father or mother what he had done. 7 Then he went and spoke to the woman, because Samson wanted her.

8 After some time, when he returned to get her, he left ⌊the road⌋ to see the lion's carcass, and there was a swarm of bees with honey in the carcass. 9 He scooped ⌊some honey⌋ into his hands and ate ⌊it⌋ as he went along. When he returned to his father and mother, he gave ⌊some⌋ to them and they ate ⌊it⌋. But he did not tell them that he had scooped the honey from the lion's carcass.

10 His father went ⌊to visit⌋ the woman, and Samson prepared a feast there, as young men were accustomed to do. 11 When the Philistines saw him, they brought 30 men to accompany him.

12 "Let me tell you a riddle," Samson said to them. "If you can explain it to me during the seven days of the feast and figure it out, I will give you 30 linen garments and 30 changes of clothes. 13 But if you can't explain it to me, you must give me 30 linen garments and 30 changes of clothes."

"Tell us your riddle," they replied.e "Let's hear it."

14 So he said to them:

Out of the eater came something to eat,
    and out of the strong came something sweet.

After three days, they were unable to explain the riddle. 15 On the fourthf day they said to Samson's wife, "Persuade your husband to explain the riddle to us, or we will burn you and your father's household to death. Did you invite us here to rob us?"

16 So Samson's wife came to him, weeping, and said, "You hate me and don't love me! You told my people the riddle, but haven't explained it to me."

"Look," he said,g "I haven't even explained it to my father or mother, so ⌊why⌋ should I explain it to you?"

---

a13:25 Or in Mahaneh-dan b14:3 Lit Is there not c14:3 Lit because she is right in my eyes d14:6 Lit LORD rushed on e14:13 Lit replied to him
f14:15 LXX, Syr; MT reads seventh g14:16 Lit said to her

---

by God and consecrated to Him, but he also had an attraction for ungodly things.

13:2 had no children. A woman was not considered complete until she bore children. But compare Manoah's wife with Sarah (Gen. 11:30), Rebekah (Gen. 25:21), and Hannah (1 Sam. 1:2).

13:3 you will … give birth to a son. God sent an angel to announce Samson's coming birth; compare Ishmael (Gen. 16:11), John the Baptist (Luke 1:13), and Jesus Christ (Luke 1:31).

13:5 Nazirite to God from birth. Samson was "set apart" by God as a Nazirite for life, which involved not cutting one's hair, abstaining from

fermented beverages, and avoiding contact with dead bodies (see Num. 6:1-21).

13:6 A man of God came to me. Manoah's wife knew something significant had happened, but she was clear only about the Nazirite requirements.

13:8 teach us. Manoah believed his wife about

¹⁷ She wept the whole seven days of the feast, and at last, on the seventh day, he explained it to her, because she had nagged him so much. Then she explained it to her people. ¹⁸ On the seventh day before sunset, the men of the city said to him:

> What is sweeter than honey?
> What is stronger than a lion?

So he said to them:

> If you hadn't plowed with my young cow,
> you wouldn't know my riddle now!

¹⁹ The Spirit of the LORD took control of him, and he went down to Ashkelon and killed 30 of their men. He stripped them and gave their clothes to those who had explained the riddle. In a rage, Samson returned to his father's house, ²⁰ and his wife was given to one of the men who had accompanied him.

Samson's Revenge

15 Later on, during the wheat harvest, Samson ⌊took⌋ a young goat ⌊as a gift⌋ and visited his wife. "I want to go to my wife in her room," he said. But her father would not let him enter.

² "I was sure you hated her," her father said, "so I gave her to one of the men who accompanied you. Isn't her younger sister more beautiful than she is? Why not take her instead?"

³ Samson said to them, "This time I won't be responsible when I harm the Philistines." ⁴ So he went out and caught 300 foxes. He took torches, turned the foxes tail-to-tail, and put a torch between each pair of tails. ⁵ Then he ignited the torches and released the foxes into the standing grain of the Philistines. He burned up the piles of grain and the standing grain as well as the vineyards and olive groves.

⁶ Then the Philistines asked, "Who did this?"

They were told, "⌊It was⌋ Samson, the Timnite's son-in-law, because he has taken Samson's wife and given her to another man." So the Philistines went to her and her father and burned ⌊them⌋ to death.

⁷ Then Samson told them, "Because you did this, I swear that I won't rest until I have taken vengeance on you." ⁸ He tore them limb from limb[a] with a great slaughter, and he went down and stayed in the cave at the rock of Etam.

⁹ The Philistines went up, camped in Judah, and raided Lehi. ¹⁰ So the men of Judah said, "Why have you attacked us?"

They replied, "We have come to arrest Samson and pay him back for what he did to us."

¹¹ Then 3,000 men of Judah went to the cave at the rock of Etam, and they asked Samson, "Don't you realize that the Philistines rule over us? What have you done to us?"

"I have done to them what they did to me," he answered.[b]

¹² They said to him, "We've come to arrest you and hand you over to the Philistines."

Then Samson told them, "Swear to me that you yourselves won't kill me."

¹³ "No," they said,[c] "we won't kill you, but we will tie you up securely and hand you over to them." So they tied him up with two new ropes and led him away from the rock.

¹⁴ When he came to Lehi, the Philistines came to meet him shouting. The Spirit of the LORD took control of[d] him, and the ropes that were on his arms became like burnt flax and his bonds fell off his wrists. ¹⁵ He found a fresh jawbone of a donkey, reached out his hand, took it, and killed 1,000 men with it. ¹⁶ Then Samson said:

> With the jawbone of a donkey
> I have piled them in a heap.
> With the jawbone of a donkey
> I have killed 1,000 men.

¹⁷ When he finished speaking, he threw away the jawbone and named that place Ramath-lehi.[e] ¹⁸ He became very thirsty and called out to the LORD: "You have accomplished this great victory through[f] Your servant. Must I now die of thirst and fall into the hands of the uncircumcised?" ¹⁹ So God split a hollow place ⌊in the ground⌋ at Lehi, and water came out of it. After Samson drank, his strength returned, and he revived. That is why he named it En-hakkore,[g] which is in Lehi to this day. ²⁰ And he judged Israel 20 years in the days of the Philistines.

Samson and Delilah

16 Samson went to Gaza, where he saw a prostitute and went to bed with her. ² When the Gazites ⌊heard⌋ that Samson was there, they surrounded the place and waited in ambush for him all that night at the city gate. While they were waiting quietly,[h] they said, "Let us wait until dawn; then we will kill him." ³ But Samson stayed in bed until midnight when he got up, took hold of the doors of the city gate along with the two gateposts, and pulled

---

[a]**15:8** Lit *He struck them hip on thigh*   [b]**15:11** Lit *answered them*   [c]**15:13** Lit *said to him*   [d]**15:14** Lit *LORD rushed on*   [e]**15:17** = High Place of the Jawbone   [f]**15:18** Lit *through the hand of*   [g]**15:19** = Spring of the One Who Cried Out   [h]**16:2** Lit *quietly all night*

---

the birth of a child. His concern was that they be prepared to carry out the Lord's will for their child.

13:17 What is Your name? Manoah was sure that the promise would come true, so he wanted to know whom to honor.

14:3 uncircumcised. In Israel, calling some-

one "uncircumcised" implied ungodly behavior.

14:4 seeking an occasion. God used Samson's wrong desire for a Philistine woman to further his work against the enemies of God's people (see Gen. 50:20; Acts 2:23; Rom. 8:28).

14:12 riddle. Riddles were a form of entertain-

ment. Samson was showing off his cleverness.

14:16 You hate me and don't love me! This accusation was one to which Samson would prove extremely vulnerable.

14:19 took control of him. The Spirit of God empowered Samson to take revenge against the Philistines.

A Really Bad Hair Day

1. When was your hair the shortest? Longest? Craziest?

Judges 16:1-22

2. What caused Samson to go back to Delilah again and again, knowing she would betray him?

3. Samson was probably sleeping with Delilah, though they weren't married. How did Samson's own sinful choices bring about his destruction?

4. Why didn't Samson know that "the LORD had left him" (v. 20)? Is there evidence in your own life of God's Holy Spirit?

5. What one weakness of yours is in danger of taking away your spiritual strength?

them out, bar and all. He put them on his shoulders and took them to the top of the mountain overlooking Hebron.

⁴ Some time later, he fell in love with a woman named Delilah, who lived in the Sorek Valley. ⁵ The Philistine leaders went to her and said, "Persuade him to tell youᵃ where his great strength comes from, so we can overpower him, tie him up, and make him helpless. Each of us will then give you 1,100 pieces of silver."

⁶ So Delilah said to Samson, "Please tell me, where does your great strength ⌊come from⌋? How could ⌊someone⌋ tie you up and make you helpless?"

⁷ Samson told her, "If they tie me up with seven fresh bowstrings that have not been dried, I will become weak and be like any other man."

⁸ The Philistine leaders brought her seven fresh bowstrings that had not been dried, and she tied him up with them. ⁹ While the men in ambush were waiting in her room, she called out to him, "Samson, the Philistines are here!"ᵇ But he snapped the bowstrings as a strand of yarn snaps when it touches fire. ⌊The secret of⌋ his strength remained unknown.

¹⁰ Then Delilah said to Samson, "You have mocked me and told me lies! Won't you please tell me how you can be tied up?"

¹¹ He told her, "If they tie me up with new ropes that have never been used, I will become weak and be like any other man."

¹² Delilah took new ropes, tied him up with them, and shouted, "Samson, the Philistines are here!"ᵇ But while the men in ambush were waiting in her room, he snapped the ropes off his arms like a thread.

¹³ Then Delilah said to Samson, "You have mocked me all along and told me lies! Tell me how you can be tied up."

He told her, "If you weave the seven braids on my head with the web of a loom—"ᶜ

¹⁴ She fastened the braids with a pin and called to him, "Samson, the Philistines are here!"ᵇ He awoke from his sleep and pulled out the pin, with the loom and the web.

¹⁵ "How can you say, 'I love you,'" she told him, "when your heart is not with me? This is the third time you have mocked me and not told me what makes your strength so great!"

¹⁶ Because she nagged him day after day and pled with him until she wore him out,ᵈ ¹⁷ he told her the whole truth and said to her, "My hair has never been cut,ᵉ because I am a Nazirite to God from birth. If I am shaved, my strength will leave me, and I will become weak and be like any other man."

¹⁸ When Delilah realized that he had told her the whole truth, she sent this message to the Philistine leaders: "Come one more time, for he has told me the whole truth." The Philistine leaders came to her and brought the money with them.

¹⁹ Then she let him fall asleep on her lap and called a man to shave off the seven braids on his head. In this way, she rendered him helpless,ᶠ and his strength left him. ²⁰ Then she cried, "Samson, the Philistines are here!"ᵇ When he awoke from his sleep, he said, "I will escape as I did before and shake myself free." But he did not know that the LORD had left him.

Samson's Defeat and Death

²¹ The Philistines seized him and gouged out his eyes. They brought him down to Gaza and bound him with bronze shackles, and he was forced to grind grain in the prison. ²² But his hair began to grow back after it had been shaved.

ᵃ**16:5** Lit him and see ᵇ**16:9,12,14,20** Lit are on you ᶜ**16:13–14** LXX reads loom and fasten [them] with a pin into the wall and I will become weak and be like any other man." ¹⁴ And while he was sleeping, Delilah wove the seven braids on his head into the loom. ᵈ**16:16** Lit him and he became short to death ᵉ**16:17** Lit A razor has not gone up on my head ᶠ**16:19** LXX reads way he began to weaken

---

15:5 burned up. Samson struck back at the Philistines by burning their food.

15:7 vengeance. Usually revenge led to an escalation of violence as the conflict grew from man against man, to family against family, to tribe against tribe, to nation against nation.

15:11 What have you done to us? The tribe of

Judah preferred being under Philistine rule to being the enemy of the Philistines. Samson was upsetting the status quo (13:5).

15:15 killed 1,000 men. Compare this report with Shamgar's killing of 600 Philistines with an oxgoad (3:31).

15:19 water came out of it. As God provided

water for the wandering Israelites (Ex. 17:1-7), He provided it for Samson.

16:3 put them on his shoulders and took them. Samson's act was one of defiance and pride, telling the Philistines their gates couldn't hold him.

16:5 tie him up, and make him helpless. The

23 Now the Philistine leaders gathered together to offer a great sacrifice to their god Dagon. They rejoiced and said:

> Our god has handed over
> our enemy Samson to us.

24 When the people saw him, they praised their god and said:

> Our god has handed over to us
> our enemy who destroyed our land
> and who multiplied our dead.

The Secret of Strength

1. Who is the strongest (physically, intellectually, emotionally or spiritually) person you know? What makes that person so strong?

Judges 16:21-31

2. What was the real secret of Samson's strength (v. 28)?

3. What caused God to depart from Samson? How might he have avoided this tragic death?

4. How does God's Spirit bring strength to His people today? What is required of us if we are to have His strength in our lives?

5. In what area of your life do you most need the strength of God's Spirit today?

25 When they were drunk, they said, "Bring Samson here to entertain us." So they brought Samson from prison, and he entertained them. They had him stand between the pillars.

26 Samson said to the young man who was leading him by the hand, "Lead me where I can feel the pillars supporting the temple, so I can lean against them." 27 The temple was full of men and women; all the leaders of the Philistines were there, and about 3,000 men and women were on the roof watching Samson entertain [them]. 28 He called out to the LORD: "Lord GOD, please remember me. Strengthen me, God, just once more. With one act of vengeance, let me pay back the Philistines for my two eyes." 29 Samson took hold of the two middle pillars supporting the temple and leaned against them, one on his right hand and the other on his left. 30 Samson said, "Let me die with the Philistines." He pushed with all his might, and the temple fell on the leaders and all the people in it. And the dead he killed at his death were more than those he had killed in his life.

31 Then his brothers and his father's family came down, carried him back, and buried him between Zorah and Eshtaol in the tomb of his father Manoah. So he judged Israel 20 years.

Micah's Priest

17 There was a man from the hill country of Ephraim named Micah. 2 He said to his mother, "The 1,100 pieces of silver taken from you, and that I heard you utter a curse about—here, I have the silver with me. I took it. So now I return it to you."a

Then his mother said, "My son, you are blessed by the LORD!"

3 He returned the 1,100 pieces of silver to his mother, and his mother said, "I personally consecrate the silver to the LORD for my son's benefit to make a carved image overlaid with silver."b 4 So he returned the silver to his mother, and she took five pounds of silver and gave it to a silversmith. He made it into a carved image overlaid with silver,b and it was in Micah's house.

5 This man Micah had a shrine, and he made an •ephod and household idols, and installed one of his sons to be his priest. 6 In those days there was no king in Israel; everyone did whatever he wanted.c

7 There was a young man, a Levite, from Bethlehem in Judah, who resided within the clan of Judah. 8 The man left the town of Bethlehem in Judah to settle wherever he could find a place. On his way he came to Micah's home in the hill country of Ephraim.

9 "Where do you come from?" Micah asked him.

He answered him, "I am a Levite from Bethlehem in Judah, and I'm going to settle wherever I can find a place.

10 Micah replied,d "Stay with me and be my father and priest, and I will give you four ounces of silver a year, along with your clothing and provisions." So the Levite went in 11 and agreed to stay with the man, and the young man became like one of his sons. 12 Micah consecrated the Levite, and the young man became his priest and lived in Micah's house. 13 Then Micah said, "Now I know that the LORD will be good to me, because a Levite has become my priest."

---

a17:2 MT places this sentence at the end of v. 3. b17:3,4 Or *image and a cast image* c17:6 Lit *did what was right in his eyes* d17:10 Lit *replied to him*

Philistines were still out for revenge. They wanted to torture and humiliate Samson.

16:7 seven fresh bowstrings. Samson tried to deceive the Philistines by repeatedly using the number seven, which was believed to have magical powers.

16:11 new ropes. The Philistines had forgotten

that they had tried new ropes before with terrible results (15:13-14).

16:13 mocked me all along and told me lies. Delilah was correct; Samson had been playing games with her and her people.

16:19-20 his strength left him … the LORD had left him. Samson's strength was from the

Spirit of the Lord. When he betrayed his vow, he lost that special blessing.

16:21 gouged out his eyes. By blinding Samson the Philistines were able to both control and humiliate him.

16:27 all the leaders of the Philistines were there. The Philistines had planned a public hu-

Dan's Invasion and Idolatry

18 In those days, there was no king in Israel, and the Danite tribe was looking for territory to occupy. Up to that time no territory had been captured ⌊by them⌋ among the tribes of Israel. ² So the Danites sent out five brave men from all their clans, from Zorah and Eshtaol, to spy out the land and explore it. They told them, "Go and explore the land."

They came to the hill country of Ephraim as far as the home of Micah and spent the night there. ³ While they were near Micah's home, they recognized the speech of the young Levite. So they went over to him and asked, "Who brought you here? What are you doing in this place? What is keeping you here?" ⁴ He told them what Micah had done for him and that he had hired him as his priest.

⁵ Then they said to him, "Please inquire of God so we will know if we will have a successful journey."

⁶ The priest told them, "Go in peace. The LORD is watching over the journey you are going on."

⁷ The five men left and came to Laish. They saw that the people who were there were living securely, in the same way as the Sidonians, quiet and unsuspecting. There was nothing lacking in the land and no oppressive ruler. They were far from the Sidonians, having no alliance with anyone.ᵃ

⁸ When the men went back to their clans at Zorah and Eshtaol, their people asked them, "What did you find out?"

⁹ They answered, "Come on, let's go up against them, for we have seen the land, and it is very good. Why wait? Don't hesitate to go and invade and take possession of the land! ¹⁰ When you get there, you will come to an unsuspecting people and a wide-open land, for God has handed it over to you. It is a place where nothing on earth is lacking." ¹¹ Six hundred Danites departed from Zorah and Eshtaol armed with weapons of war. ¹² They went up and camped at Kiriath-jearim in Judah. This is why the place is called the Camp of Danᵇ to this day; it is west of Kiriath-jearim. ¹³ From there they traveled to the hill country of Ephraim and arrived at Micah's house.

¹⁴ The five men who had gone to spy out the land of Laish told their brothers, "Did you know that there are an •ephod, household gods, and a carved image overlaid with silverᶜ in these houses? Now think about what you should do." ¹⁵ So they detoured there and went to the house of the young Levite at the home of Micah and greeted him. ¹⁶ The 600 Danite men were standing by the entrance of the gate, armed with their weapons of war. ¹⁷ Then the five men who had gone to spy out the land went in and took the carved image overlaid with silver,ᶜ the ephod, and the household idols, while the priest was standing by the entrance of the gate with the 600 men armed with weapons of war.

¹⁸ When they entered Micah's house and took the carved image overlaid with silver,ᶜ the ephod, and the household idols, the priest said to them, "What are you doing?"

¹⁹ They told him, "Be quiet. Keep your mouth shut.ᵈ Come with us and be a father and a priest to us. Is it better for you to be a priest for the house of one person or for you to be a priest for a tribe and family in Israel?" ²⁰ So the priest was pleased and took his ephod, household idols, and carved image, and went with the people. ²¹ They prepared to leave, putting their small children, livestock, and possessions in front of them.

²² After they were some distance from Micah's house, the men who were in the houses near it mobilized and caught up with the Danites. ²³ They called to the Danites, who turned to face them, and said to Micah, "What's the matter with you that you mobilized ⌊the men⌋?"

²⁴ He said, "You took the gods I had made and the priest, and went away. What do I have left? How can you say to me, 'What's the matter with you?' "

²⁵ The Danites said to him, "Don't raise your voice against us, or angry men will attack you, and you and your family will lose your lives." ²⁶ The Danites went on their way, and Micah turned to go back home, because he saw that they were stronger than he was.

²⁷ After they had taken the gods Micah had made and the priest that belonged to him, they went to Laish, to a quiet and unsuspecting people. They killed them with their swords and burned down the city. ²⁸ There was no one to save them, because it was far from Sidon and they had no alliance with anyone. It was in a valley that belonged to Beth-rehob. They rebuilt the city and lived in it. ²⁹ They named the city Dan, after the name of their ancestor Dan, who was born to Israel. The city was formerly named Laish.

³⁰ The Danites set up the carved image for themselves. Jonathan son of Gershom, son of Moses,ᵉ and his sons were priests for the Danite tribe until the time of the exile from the land. ³¹ So they set up for themselves Micah's carved image that he had made, ⌊and it was there⌋ as long as the house of God was in Shiloh.

ᵃ**18:7** MT; some LXX mss, Sym, Lat, Syr read *Aram*   ᵇ**18:12** Or *called Mahaneh-dan*   ᶜ**18:14,17,18** Or *image, the cast image*   ᵈ**18:19** Lit *Put your hand on your mouth*   ᵉ**18:30** Some Hb mss, LXX, Vg; other Hb mss read *Manasseh*

---

miliation of Samson at their pagan temple, but God had other plans.

16:30 the dead he killed at his death. He took more than 3,000 Philistines with him.

17:1–18:31 This story tells of theft, curses, idols, the love of money, and abandonment of God's plan. It involved the tribes of Ephraim and Dan and a corrupt young Levite.

17:2 heard you utter a curse. Uttering a curse irresponsibly was an immoral act. Both Micah and his mother had lost any real faith and had descended into superstition.

17:3 consecrate the silver ... to make a carved image overlaid with silver. In one

breath she wanted to dedicate her wealth to God, and with the next she disobeyed His commands by making a graven image.

17:6 there was no king in Israel. Most scholars think that the book of Judges was written during Israel's monarchy, partly to show how the monarchy had brought order out of chaos.

Outrage in Benjamin

19 In those days, when there was no king in Israel, a Levite living in a remote part of the hill country of Ephraim acquired a woman from Bethlehem in Judah as his concubine. ² But she was unfaithful to[a] him and left him for her father's house in Bethlehem in Judah. She was there for a period of four months. ³ Then her husband got up and went after her to speak kindly to her[b] and bring her back. His servant and a couple of donkeys were with him. So she brought him to her father's house, and when the girl's father saw him, he gladly welcomed him. ⁴ His father-in-law, the girl's father, detained him, and he stayed with him for three days. They ate, drank, and spent the nights there.

⁵ On the fourth day, they got up early in the morning and prepared to go, but the girl's father said to his son-in-law, "Have something to eat to keep up your strength and then you can go." ⁶ So they sat down and the two of them ate and drank together. Then the girl's father said to the man, "Please agree to stay overnight and enjoy yourself." ⁷ The man got up to go, but his father-in-law persuaded him, so he stayed and spent the night there again. ⁸ He got up early in the morning of the fifth day to leave, but the girl's father said to him, "Please keep up your strength." So they waited until late afternoon and the two of them ate. ⁹ The man got up to go with his concubine and his servant, when his father-in-law, the girl's father, said to him, "Look, night is coming. Please spend the night. See, the day is almost over. Spend the night here, enjoy yourself, then you can get up early tomorrow for your journey and go home."

¹⁰ But the man was unwilling to spend the night. He got up, departed, and arrived opposite Jebus (that is, Jerusalem). The man had his two saddled donkeys and his concubine with him. ¹¹ When they were near Jebus and the day was almost gone, the servant said to his master, "Please, why not[c] let us stop at this Jebusite city and spend the night here?"

¹² But his master replied to him, "We will not stop at a foreign city where there are no Israelites. Let's move on to Gibeah." ¹³ "Come on," he said,[d] "let's try to reach one of these places and spend the night in Gibeah or Ramah." ¹⁴ So they continued on their journey, and the sun set as they neared Gibeah in Benjamin. ¹⁵ They stopped[e] to go in and spend the night in Gibeah. The Levite went in and sat down in the city square, but no one took them into their home to spend the night.

¹⁶ In the evening, an old man came in from his work in the field. He was from the hill country of Ephraim but was residing in Gibeah, and the men of that place were Benjaminites. ¹⁷ When he looked up and saw the traveler in the city square, the old man asked, "Where are you going, and where do you come from?"

¹⁸ He answered him, "We're traveling from Bethlehem in Judah to the remote hill country of Ephraim, where I am from. I went to Bethlehem in Judah, and now I'm going to the house of the LORD.[f] No one has taken me into his home, ¹⁹ although we have both straw and feed for our donkeys, and bread and wine for me, your female servant, and the young man with your servant.[g] There is nothing we lack."

²⁰ "Peace to you," said the old man. "I'll take care of everything you need. Only don't spend the night in the square." ²¹ So he brought him to his house and fed the donkeys. Then they washed their feet and ate and drank. ²² While they were enjoying themselves, all of a sudden, •perverted men of the city surrounded the house and beat on the door. They said to the old man who was the owner of the house, "Bring out the man who came to your house so we can have sex with him!"

²³ The owner of the house went out and said to them, "No, don't do ⌊this⌋ evil, my brothers. After all, this man has come into my house. Don't do this horrible thing. ²⁴ Here, let me bring out my virgin daughter and the man's concubine now. Use them and do whatever you want[h] to them. But don't do this horrible thing to this man."

²⁵ But the men would not listen to him, so the man seized his concubine and took her outside to them. They raped[i] her and abused her all night until morning. At daybreak they let her go. ²⁶ Early that morning, the woman made her way back, and as it was getting light, she collapsed at the doorway of the man's house where her master was.

²⁷ When her master got up in the morning, opened the doors of the house, and went out to leave on his journey, there was the woman, his concubine, collapsed near the doorway of the house with her hands on the threshold. ²⁸ "Get up," he told her. "Let's go." But there was no response. So the man put her on his donkey and set out for home.

²⁹ When he entered his house, he picked up a knife, took hold of his concubine, cut her into 12 pieces, limb

---

[a]**19:2** LXX, Vg read *was angry with* [b]**19:3** Lit *speak to her heart* [c]**19:11** Lit *Come, please* [d]**19:13** Lit *said to his servant* [e]**19:15** Lit *stopped there* [f]**19:18** LXX reads *to my house* [g]**19:19** Some Hb mss, Syr, Tg, Vg; other Hb mss read *servants* [h]**19:24** Lit *do what is good in your eyes* [i]**19:25** Lit *knew*

17:10 four ounces of silver. The young Levite's main concerns were exactly what Micah offered: money, clothes, and food.

17:12 became his priest. Micah wanted his own priest, idols, and all the trappings that imply piety.

18:1 territory to occupy. Dan had never been able to defeat the Canaanite residents and claim their homeland.

18:3 recognized the speech. At this time Israel was still a loose confederation of tribes, each with its distinct accent and dialect.

18:19 a tribe and family in Israel. The Danites appealed to the young Levite's greed and pride.

18:30 set up the carved image for themselves. The Danites based their new city around some stolen idols and a corrupt Levite priest.

19:1–21:25 The second story is one of moral

by limb, and sent her throughout the territory of Israel. ³⁰ Everyone who saw it said, "Nothing like this has ever happened or been seen since the day the Israelites came out of the land of Egypt to this day.ᵃ Think it over, discuss it, and speak up!"

War against Benjamin

20 All the Israelites from Dan to Beer-sheba and from the land of Gilead came out, and the community assembled as one body before the LORD at Mizpah. ² The leaders of all the people and of all the tribes of Israel presented themselves in the assembly of God's people: 400,000 armed foot soldiers. ³ The Benjaminites heard that the Israelites had gone up to Mizpah.

The Israelites asked, "Tell us, how did this outrage occur?"

⁴ The Levite, the husband of the murdered woman, answered: "I went to Gibeah in Benjamin with my concubine to spend the night. ⁵ Citizens of Gibeah ganged up on me and surrounded the house at night. They intended to kill me, but they raped my concubine, and she died. ⁶ Then I took my concubine and cut her in pieces, and sent her throughout Israel's territory, because they committed a horrible shame in Israel. ⁷ Look, all of you are Israelites. Give your judgment and verdict here ⌊and now⌋."

⁸ Then all the people stood united and said, "None of us will go to his tent or return to his house. ⁹ Now this is what we will do to Gibeah: we will go against it by lot. ¹⁰ We will take 10 men out of every 100 from all the tribes of Israel, and 100 out of every 1,000, and 1,000 out of every 10,000 to get provisions for the people when they go to Gibeah in Benjamin to punish them for all the horror they did in Israel."

¹¹ So all the men of Israel gathered united against the city. ¹² Then the tribes of Israel sent men throughout the tribe of Benjamin, saying, "What is this outrage that has occurred among you? ¹³ Hand over the •perverted men in Gibeah so we can put them to death and eradicate evil from Israel." But the Benjaminites would not obey their fellow Israelites. ¹⁴ Instead, the Benjaminites gathered together from their cities to Gibeah to go out and fight against the Israelites. ¹⁵ On that day the Benjaminites rallied 26,000 armed men from their cities, besides 700 choice men rallied by the inhabitants of Gibeah. ¹⁶ There were 700 choice men who were left-handed among all these people; all could sling a stone at a hair and not miss.

¹⁷ The Israelites, apart from Benjamin, rallied 400,000 armed men, every one an experienced warrior. ¹⁸ They set out, went to Bethel, and inquired of God. The Israelites asked, "Who is to go first to fight for us against the Benjaminites?"

And the LORD answered, "Judah will be first."

¹⁹ In the morning, the Israelites set out and camped near Gibeah. ²⁰ The men of Israel went out to fight against Benjamin and took their battle positions against Gibeah. ²¹ The Benjaminites came out of Gibeah and slaughtered 22,000 men of Israel on the field that day. ²² But the Israelite army rallied and again took their battle positions in the same place where they positioned themselves on the first day. ²³ They went up, wept before the LORD until evening, and inquired of Him: "Should we again fight against our brothers the Benjaminites?"

And the LORD answered: "Fight against them."

²⁴ On the second day the Israelites advanced against the Benjaminites. ²⁵ That same day the Benjaminites came out from Gibeah to meet them and slaughtered an additional 18,000 Israelites on the field; all were armed men.

²⁶ The whole Israelite army went to Bethel where they wept and sat before the LORD. They fasted that day until evening and offered •burnt offerings and •fellowship offerings to the LORD. ²⁷ Then the Israelites inquired of the LORD. In those days, the ark of the covenant of God was there, ²⁸ and Phinehas son of Eleazar, son of Aaron, was serving before it. The Israelites asked: "Should we again fight against our brothers the Benjaminites or should we stop?"

The LORD answered: "Fight, because I will hand them over to you tomorrow." ²⁹ So Israel set up an ambush around Gibeah. ³⁰ On the third day the Israelites fought against the Benjaminites and took their battle positions against Gibeah as before. ³¹ Then the Benjaminites came out against the people and were drawn away from the city. They began to attack the people as before, killing about 30 men of Israel on the highways, one of which goes up to Bethel and the other to Gibeah through the open country. ³² The Benjaminites said, "We are defeating them as before."

But the Israelites said, "Let's flee and draw them away from the city to the highways." ³³ So all the men of Israel got up from their places and took their battle positions at Baal-tamar, while the Israelites in ambush charged out of their places west ofᵇ Geba. ³⁴ Then 10,000 choice men from all Israel made a frontal

---

ᵃ **19:30** LXX reads *day." He commanded the men he sent out, saying, "You will say this to all the men of Israel: Has anything like this happened since the day the Israelites came out of Egypt until this day?* ᵇ **20:33** LXX, Syr, Vg; MT reads *places in the plain of,* or *places in the cave of*

---

decadence and tribal foolishness. The Gibeah incident is remarkably similar to Lot's experience in Sodom (see Gen. 19:1-13). There are no moral heroes in the story.

19:21 brought him to his house and fed the donkeys. The old man showed the Levite the proper hospitality for a fellow Israelite.

19:22 perverted men. The men of Gibeah exhibited perversions usually associated with the pagan Canaanites.

19:23 Don't do this horrible thing. Though the owner of the house called their homosexual demands "evil," he also called them "brothers."

19:24 my virgin daughter, and the man's

concubine. The old man was willing to sacrifice his daughter and his guest's concubine to the mob, but he refused to violate the code of hospitality covering his guest.

19:29 cut her into 12 pieces. The Levite's action of dismembering his concubine's body was meant to send a message to the tribes

assault against Gibeah, and the battle was fierce, but the Benjaminites did not know that disaster was about to strike them. ³⁵ The LORD defeated Benjamin in the presence of Israel, and on that day the Israelites slaughtered 25,100 men of Benjamin; all were armed men. ³⁶ Then the Benjaminites realized they had been defeated.

The men of Israel had retreated before Benjamin, because they were confident in the ambush they had set against Gibeah. ³⁷ The men in ambush had rushed quickly against Gibeah; they advanced and put the whole city to the sword. ³⁸ The men of Israel had a prearranged signal with the men in ambush: when they sent up a great cloud of smoke from the city, ³⁹ the men of Israel would return to the battle. When Benjamin had begun to strike them down, killing about 30 men of Israel, they said, "They're defeated before us, just as they were in the first battle." ⁴⁰ But when the column of smoke began to go up from the city, Benjamin looked behind them, and the whole city was going up in smoke.ᵃ ⁴¹ Then the men of Israel returned, and the men of Benjamin were terrified when they realized that disaster had struck them. ⁴² They retreated before the men of Israel toward the wilderness, but the battle overtook them, and those who came out of the citiesᵇ slaughtered those between them. ⁴³ They surrounded the Benjaminites, pursued them, and easily overtook them near Gibeah toward the east. ⁴⁴ There were 18,000 men who died from Benjamin; all were warriors. ⁴⁵ Then Benjamin turned and fled toward the wilderness to the rock of Rimmon, and Israel killed 5,000 men on the highways. They overtook them at Gidom and struck 2,000 more dead.

⁴⁶ All the Benjaminites who died that day were 25,000 armed men; all were warriors. ⁴⁷ But 600 men escaped into the wilderness to the rock of Rimmon and stayed there four months. ⁴⁸ The men of Israel turned back against the ₗotherₗ Benjaminites and killed them with their swords—the entire city, the animals, and everything that remained. They also burned down all the cities that remained.

Brides for Benjamin

21 The men of Israel had sworn an oath at Mizpah: "None of us will give his daughter to a Benjaminite in marriage." ² So the people went to Bethel and sat there before God until evening. They wept loudly and bitterly, ³ and cried out, "Why, LORD God of Israel, has it occurredᶜ that one tribe is ₗmissingₗ in Israel today?" ⁴ The next day the people got up

early, built an altar there, and offered •burnt offerings and •fellowship offerings. ⁵ The Israelites asked, "Who of all the tribes of Israel didn't come to the LORD with the assembly?" For a great oath had been taken that anyone who had not come to the LORD at Mizpah would certainly be put to death.

⁶ But the Israelites had compassion on their brothers, the Benjaminites, and said, "Today a tribe has been cut off from Israel. ⁷ What should we do about wives for the survivors? We've sworn to the LORD not to give them any of our daughters as wives." ⁸ They asked, "Which city among the tribes of Israel didn't come to the LORD at Mizpah?" It turned out that no one from Jabesh-gilead had come to the camp and the assembly. ⁹ For when the people were counted, no one was there from the inhabitants of Jabesh-gilead.

¹⁰ The congregation sent 12,000 brave warriorsᵈ there and commanded them: "Go and kill the inhabitants of Jabesh-gilead with the sword, including women and children. ¹¹ This is what you should do: •Completely destroy every male, as well as every female who has slept with a man." ¹² They found among the inhabitants of Jabesh-gilead 400 young virgins, who had not had sexual relations with a man, and they brought them to the camp at Shiloh in the land of Canaan.

¹³ The whole congregation sent a message of peace to the Benjaminites who were at the rock of Rimmon. ¹⁴ Benjamin returned at that time, and Israel gave them the women they had kept alive from Jabesh-gilead. But there were not enough for them.

¹⁵ The people had compassion on Benjamin, because the LORD had made this gap in the tribes of Israel. ¹⁶ The elders of the congregation said, "What should we do about wives for those who are left, since the women of Benjamin have been destroyed?" ¹⁷ They said, "There must be heirs for the survivors of Benjamin, so that a tribe of Israel will not be wiped out. ¹⁸ But we can't give them our daughters as wives." For the Israelites had sworn: "Anyone who gives a wife to a Benjaminite is cursed." ¹⁹ They also said, "Look, there's an annual festival to the LORD in Shiloh, which is north of Bethel, east of the highway that goes up from Bethel to Shechem, and south of Lebonah."

²⁰ Then they commanded the Benjaminites: "Go and hide in the vineyards. ²¹ Watch, and when you see the young women of Shiloh come out to perform the dances, each of you leave the vineyards and catch a wife for yourself from the young women of Shiloh, and go to the land of Benjamin. ²² When their fathers or brothers come to us and protest, we will tell them, 'Show favor

---

ᵃ20:40 Lit up to the sky ᵇ20:42 LXX, Vg read city ᶜ21:3 Lit has this occurred in Israel ᵈ21:10 Lit 12,000 of their sons of valor

---

about Benjamin's morally degenerate state. He did not recognize that by his inaction in protecting his concubine he virtually condoned her assault.

20:1-48 The dismembered concubine got Israel's attention and prompted immediate action.
20:1 Dan to Beer-sheba. This phrase indi-

cated that all of Israel was involved in this conflict.

20:10 10 men out of every 100. This method for provisioning an army seemed equitable and possible in the tribal confederation of the time.
20:13 Hand over the perverted men. Israel made a reasonable demand that the guilty men

be turned over for execution. This would have brought a peaceful end to the conflict, but the Benjaminites chose to fight.

20:21 22,000 men of Israel. Israel was in the right and had the Lord's guidance, but the Benjaminites scored a big victory in the first battle.
20:35 the LORD defeated Benjamin. After two

to them, since we did not get enough wives for each of them in the battle. You didn't actually give ⌊the women⌋ to them, so[a] you are not guilty ⌊of breaking your oath⌋.' "

23 The Benjaminites did this and took the number of women they needed from the dancers they caught. They went back to their own inheritance, rebuilt their cities, and lived in them. 24 At that time, each of the Israelites returned from there to his own tribe and family. Each returned from there to his own inheritance.

25 In those days there was no king in Israel; everyone did whatever he wanted.[b]

□ Ruth 3:1-18
□ Ruth 4:1-22

□ Ruth 1:1-22
□ Ruth 2:1-23

---

days of heavy losses, Israel prevailed the third day, slaughtering 25,100 Benjaminite warriors.

20:47 600 men escaped into the wilderness. If these 600 had not escaped, the tribe of Benjamin would have been wiped out.

21:1-25 The Israelites mourned the loss of their kinsmen and realized that some provision had to be made for the survival of the tribe of Benjamin.

21:1 sworn an oath. The oath not to allow a daughter to marry a Benjaminite also had a curse attached for anyone who violated it (v. 18).

21:2 wept loudly and bitterly. Israel had done the right thing, but the consequences of that action were still disastrous. The people wept because "one tribe is missing in Israel today."

21:5 didn't come to the Lord with the assembly. The Israelites also had vowed to kill any of their own people who failed to participate in the campaign against the Benjaminites. They discovered that no assistance had come from the city of Jabesh-gilead.

21:11 Completely destroy every male, as well as every female who has slept with a man. This punishment seems brutal, but it was what the strict covenant law required.

21:12 brought them to the camp. Israel decided that by providing the Benjaminites with virgins from Jabesh-gilead, they could skirt around the demands of both vows (vv. 1, 5).

21:21 catch a wife. The Benjaminites still needed another 200 wives, so the Israelites decided to just allow them to "kidnap" women. Since the women weren't actually given to them, the vow was not formally breached.

21:22 When their fathers or brothers come to us and protest. Israel prepared a standard response to the kidnapped girls' family members.

267

RUTH

AUTHOR

The author of Ruth is unknown.

DATE

The date of composition is difficult to fix, though it was probably written during the period of the Israelite monarchy (c. 1000-722 B.C.). An early date is likely, as suggested by the fact that the genealogy in 4:17-22 ends with David.

THEME

Divine providence and human loyalty in the life of one family. The legal procedure of kinsman-redeemer also serves to illustrate the larger biblical theme of redemption.

HISTORICAL BACKGROUND

The action of the Book of Ruth is set in the tumultuous period of the judges (circa 1100 B.C.). In a time of foreign oppression and spiritual decline, this encouraging story takes place at a temporary time of peace and presents a picture of genuine faith. It may be that the book's original intention was to provide a politically important genealogy for David (4:17-22). The story goes to great lengths to legitimize his Moabite connections. This was important since Moabite

women were considered immoral by many in Israel (see Gen. 19:30-38; Num. 25:1-3). Modern readers of Ruth, unfamiliar with the background of the "kinsman-redeemer" motif, will also want to read about the plight of bereft widows and disenfranchised poor people, and how the next of kin was obliged to extend the family name (see Deut. 25:5-10), and redeem their lost property (see Lev. 25:23-28).

CHARACTERISTICS

The Book of Ruth presents its themes in the form of a dramatic love story. The book is interesting for its contrast to the Book of Judges. Though set during the time of the judges, the story of Ruth does not present the dramatic acts of God; in fact, God is not often mentioned in the book. Nonetheless, implied throughout is the quiet and tangible presence of God superintending the action of the story.

Above all, this is a book about a loving and righteous woman. The author takes a foreigner (and one who is not Jewish), Ruth, and shows her to be a person about whom God is vitally concerned. Throughout the book, Ruth displays an unconditional loyalty to her desolate mother-in-law, Naomi. In her love, and in Boaz's kindness to these two widows, we see an illustration of God's self-giving love.

Naomi's Family in Moab

1 During the time[a] of the judges, there was a famine in the land. A man left Bethlehem[b] in Judah with his wife and two sons to live in the land of Moab for a while. 2 The man's name was Elimelech,[c] and his wife's name was Naomi.[d] The names of his two sons were Mahlon and Chilion. They were Ephrathites from Bethlehem in Judah. They entered the land of Moab and ⌊settled⌋ there. 3 Naomi's husband Elimelech died, and she was left with her two sons. 4 Her sons took Moabite women as their wives: one was named Orpah and the second was named Ruth. After they lived in Moab about 10 years, 5 both Mahlon and Chilion also died, and Naomi was left without her two children and without her husband.

Ruth's Loyalty to Naomi

6 She and her daughters-in-law prepared to leave the land of Moab, because she had heard in Moab that the LORD had paid attention to His people's ⌊need⌋ by providing them food. 7 She left the place where she had been living, accompanied by her two daughters-in-law, and traveled along the road leading back to the land of Judah.

8 She said to them, "Each of you go back to your mother's home. May the LORD show faithful love to you as you have shown to the dead and to me. 9 May the LORD enable each of you to find security in the house of your ⌊new⌋ husband." She kissed them, and they wept loudly.

10 "No," they said to her. "We will go with you to your people."

11 But Naomi replied, "Return home, my daughters. Why do you want to go with me? Am I able to have any more sons[e] who could become your husbands? 12 Return home, my daughters. Go on, for I am too old to have another husband. Even if I thought there was ⌊still⌋ hope for me to have a husband tonight and to bear sons, 13 would you be willing to wait for them to grow up? Would you restrain yourselves from remarrying?[f] No, my daughters, ⌊my life⌋ is much too bitter for you ⌊to share⌋,[g] because the LORD's hand has turned against me." 14 Again they wept loudly, and Orpah kissed her mother-in-law, but Ruth clung to her. 15 Naomi said, "Look, your sister-in-law has gone back to her people and to her god. Follow your sister-in-law."

16 But Ruth replied:

Do not persuade me to leave you
or go back and not follow you.

For wherever you go, I will go,
and wherever you live, I will live;
your people will be my people,
and your God will be my God.
17 Where you die, I will die,
and there I will be buried.
May the LORD do this to me,[h]
and even more,
if anything but death separates you and me.

18 When Naomi saw that Ruth was determined to go with her, she stopped trying to persuade her.

19 The two of them traveled until they came to Bethlehem. When they entered Bethlehem, the whole town was excited about their arrival[i] and ⌊the local women⌋ exclaimed, "Can this be Naomi?"

20 "Don't call me Naomi. Call me Mara,"[j] she answered,[k] "for the •Almighty has made me very bitter. 21 I left full, but the LORD has brought me back empty. Why do you call me Naomi, since the LORD has pronounced ⌊judgment⌋ on[l] me, and the Almighty has afflicted me?"

22 So Naomi came back from the land of Moab with her daughter-in-law Ruth the Moabitess. They arrived in Bethlehem at the beginning of the barley harvest.

Ruth and Boaz Meet

2 Now Naomi had a relative on her husband's side named Boaz.[m] He was a prominent man of noble character from Elimelech's family.

2 Ruth the Moabitess asked Naomi, "Will you let me go into the fields and gather fallen grain behind someone who allows me to?"

Naomi answered her, "Go ahead, my daughter." 3 So Ruth left and entered the field to gather ⌊grain⌋ behind the harvesters. She happened to be in the portion of land belonging to Boaz, who was from Elimelech's family.

4 Later, when Boaz arrived from Bethlehem, he said to the harvesters, "The LORD be with you."

"The LORD bless you," they replied.

5 Boaz asked his servant who was in charge of the harvesters, "Whose young woman is this?"

6 The servant answered, "She is the young Moabite woman who returned with Naomi from the land of Moab. 7 She asked, 'Will you let me gather fallen grain among the bundles behind the harvesters?' She came and has remained from early morning until now, except that she rested a little in the shelter."[n]

---

[a]1:1 Lit In the days of the judging [b]1:1 = House of Bread [c]1:2 = My God Is King [d]1:2 = Pleasant [e]1:11 Lit More to me sons in my womb [f]1:13 Lit marrying a man [g]1:13 Lit daughters, for more bitter to me than you [h]1:17 A solemn oath formula; 1 Sm 3:17; 1 Sm 3:9,35; 1 Kg 2:23; 2 Kg 6:31 [i]1:19 Lit excited because of them [j]1:20 = Bitter [k]1:20 Lit answered them [l] 1:21 LXX, Syr, Vg read has humiliated [m]2:1 = Quickness [n]2:7 LXX reads until evening she has not stopped in the field; Vg reads now and she did not return to the house; Hb uncertain

---

1:4 Moabite. The Moabites were descendants of Lot's son Moab (Gen. 19:30-36). Lot was Abraham's nephew. God had forbidden the Hebrews to marry the Canaanites, but not the Moabites.

1:16 I will go. Ruth gave up her national identity, her religion, and her home with no promise for any future or reward except to share in Naomi's sorrow.

1:20 Naomi. This name meant "sweetness" or "pleasantness." **Mara.** This name meant "bitterness." During the Exodus, the Hebrews arrived at a place named "Marah," which was known for its bitter water (Ex. 15:23).

2:1 relative. The Law brought hope for a widowed woman, if a brother or other relative stepped in to carry on some of the deceased husband's responsibilities (Deut. 25:5-6).

2:2 fallen grain. In Leviticus 19:9-10, the Hebrews were instructed to leave grain in

8 Then Boaz said to Ruth, "Listen, my daughter.ᵃ Don't go and gather ⌊grain⌋ in another field, and don't leave this one, but stay here close to my young women. 9 See which field they are harvesting, and follow ⌊them⌋. Haven't I ordered the young men not to touch you?ᵇ When you are thirsty, go and drink from the jars the young men have filled."

10 She bowed with her face to the ground and said to him, "Why are you so kind to notice me, although I am a foreigner?"

11 Boaz answered her, "Everything you have done for your mother-in-law since your husband's death has been fully reported to me: ⌊how⌋ you left your father and mother, and the land of your birth, and ⌊how⌋ you came to a people you didn't previously know. 12 May the LORD reward you for what you have done, and may you receive a full reward from the LORD God of Israel, under whose wings you have come for refuge."

13 "My lord," she said, "you have been so kind to me, for you have comforted and encouragedᶜ your slave, although I am not like one of your female servants."

14 At mealtime Boaz told her, "Come over here and have some bread and dip it in the vinegar sauce." So she sat beside the harvesters, and he offered her roasted grain. She ate and was satisfied and had ⌊some⌋ left over.

15 When she got up to gather ⌊grain⌋, Boaz ordered his young men, "Be sure to let her gather ⌊grain⌋ among the bundles, and don't humiliate her. 16 Pull out ⌊some⌋ stalks from the bundles for her and leave ⌊them⌋ for her to gather. Don't rebuke her." 17 So Ruth gathered ⌊grain⌋ in the field until evening. She beat out what she had gathered, and it was about 26 quartsᵈ of barley. 18 She picked up ⌊the grain⌋ and went into the city, where her mother-in-law saw what she had gleaned. Then she brought out what she had left over from her meal and gave ⌊it⌋ to her.

19 Then her mother-in-law said to her, "Where did you gather ⌊barley⌋ today, and where did you work? May ⌊the LORD⌋ bless the man who noticed you."

Ruth told her mother-in-law about the men she had worked ⌊with⌋ and said, "The name of the man I worked with today is Boaz."

20 Then Naomi said to her daughter-in-law, "May he be blessed by the LORD, who has not forsaken hisᵉ kindness to the living or the dead." Naomi continued,

"The man is a close relative. He is one of our •family redeemers."

21 Ruth the Moabitess said, "He also told me, 'Stay with my young men until they have finished all of my harvest.

22 So Naomi said to her daughter-in-law Ruth, "My daughter, it is good for you to workᶠ with his young women, so that nothing will happen to you in another field." 23 Ruth stayed close to Boaz's young women and gathered ⌊grain⌋ until the barley and the wheat harvests were finished. And she lived withᵍ her mother-in-law.

Ruth's Appeal to Boaz

3 Ruth's mother-in-law Naomi said to her, "My daughter, shouldn't I find security for you, so that you will be taken care of? 2 Now isn't Boaz our relative? Haven't you been working with his young women? This evening he will be winnowing barley on the threshing floor. 3 Wash, put on ⌊perfumed⌋ oil, and wear your ⌊best⌋ clothes. Go down to the threshing floor, but don't let the man know you are there until he has finished eating and drinking. 4 When he lies down, notice the place where he's lying, go in and uncover his feet, and lie down. Then he will explain to you what you should do."

5 So ⌊Ruth⌋ said to her, "I will do everything you say."ʰ 6 She went down ⌊to⌋ the threshing floor and did everything her mother-in-law had instructed her. 7 After Boaz ate, drank, and was in good spirits,ⁱ he went to lie down at the end of the pile of barley. Then she went in secretly, uncovered his feet, and lay down.

8 At midnight, Boaz was startled, turned over, and there lying at his feet was a woman! 9 So he asked, "Who are you?"

"I am Ruth, your slave," she replied. "Spreadʲ your cloak over me, for you are a •family redeemer."

10 Then he said, "May the LORD bless you, my daughter. You have shown more kindness now than before,ᵏ because you have not pursued younger men, whether rich or poor. 11 Now don't be afraid, my daughter. I will do for you whatever you say,ˡ since all the people in my townᵐ know that you are a woman of noble character. 12 Yes, it is true that I am a family redeemer, but there is a redeemer closer than I am. 13 Stay ⌊here⌋ tonight, and in the morning, if he wants to redeem you, ⌊that's⌋ good. Let him redeem ⌊you⌋. But if he doesn't want to redeem you, as the LORD lives, I will. Now, lie down until morning."

ᵃ2:8 Lit Haven't you heard, my daughter? ᵇ2:9 Either sexual or physical harassment ᶜ2:13 Lit and spoken to the heart of ᵈ2:17 Lit about an ephah ᵉ2:20 Or His ᶠ2:22 Lit go out ᵍ2:23 A few Hb mss, Vg read she returned to ʰ3:5 Alt Hb tradition reads say to me ⁱ3:7 Lit and his heart was glad ʲ3:9 Lit Spread the wing of; Ru 2:12 ᵏ3:10 Lit kindness at the last than at the first ˡ3:11 Some Hb mss, Origen, Syr, Tg, Vg read say to me ᵐ3:11 Lit all the gate of my people

---

their fields and grapes in their vineyards for the poor and widowed to glean from.

2:12 under whose wings. Boaz used a beautiful image of protection to describe his hopes for Ruth. This same image is used by the psalmist in Psalm 91:4, and by Jesus Himself in Matthew 23:37.

2:17 26 quarts. About half a bushel—a large amount for one day of gleaning.

3:4 uncover his feet. A request for marriage in that culture.

3:9 Spread your cloak over me. Some translations speak of "the corner of your gar-

ment," and the word used for "corner" also means "wings." Boaz's blessing to Ruth earlier had mentioned her being under God's wing. Now Ruth was asking to be under Boaz's wing as well.

3:12 closer than I. Here is an example of sophisticated ancient legal customs that in-

¹⁴ So she lay down at his feet until morning but got up while it was still dark.ᵃ Then Boaz said, "Don't let it be known that aᵇ woman came to the threshing floor." ¹⁵ And he told ⌊Ruth⌋, "Bring the shawl you're wearing and hold it out." When she held it out, he shoveled six ⌊measures⌋ of barley into her shawl, and sheᶜ went into the city.

¹⁶ She went to her mother-in-law, Naomi, who asked ⌊her⌋, "How did it go,ᵈ my daughter?"

Then Ruth told her everything the man had done for her. ¹⁷ She said, "He gave me these six ⌊measures⌋ of barley, because he said,ᵉ 'Don't go back to your mother-in-law empty-handed.' "

¹⁸ "Wait, my daughter," she said, "until you find out how things go, for he won't rest unless he resolves this today."

Ruth and Boaz Marry

4 Boaz went to the •gate ⌊of the town⌋ and sat down there. Soon, the family redeemer Boaz had spoken about came by. Boaz called him by name and said, "Comeᶠ over here and sit down." So he went over and sat down. ² Then Boaz took 10 men of the city's elders and said, "Sit here." And they sat down. ³ He said to the redeemer, "Naomi, who has returned from the land of Moab, is selling a piece of land that belonged to our brother Elimelech. ⁴ I thought I should inform you:ᵍ Buy ⌊it⌋ back in the presence of those seated here and in the presence of the elders of my people. If you want to redeem ⌊it⌋, do so. But if you doʰ not want to redeem ⌊it⌋, tell me, so that I will know, because there isn't anyone other than you to redeem ⌊it⌋, and I am next after you."

"I want to redeem ⌊it⌋," he answered.

⁵ Then Boaz said, "On the day you buy the land from Naomi, you will also acquireⁱ Ruth the Moabitess, the wife of the deceased man, to perpetuate the man's name on his property."

⁶ The redeemer replied, "I can't redeem ⌊it⌋ myself, or I will ruin my ⌊own⌋ inheritance. Take my right of redemption, because I can't redeem it."

⁷ At an earlier period in Israel, a man removed his sandal and gave ⌊it⌋ to the other party in order to make any matter ⌊legally⌋ binding concerning the right of redemption or the exchange of property. This was ⌊the method of⌋ legally binding a transaction in Israel.

⁸ So the redeemer removed his sandal and said to Boaz, "Buy back ⌊the property⌋ yourself."

⁹ Boaz said to the elders and all the people, "You are witnesses today that I am buying from Naomi everything that belonged to Elimelech, Chilion, and Mahlon. ¹⁰ I will also acquire Ruth the Moabitess, Mahlon's widow, as my wife, to perpetuate the deceased man's name on his property, so that his name will not disappear among his relatives or from the gate of his home. You are witnesses today."

¹¹ The elders and all the people who were at the gate said, "We are witnesses. May the LORD make the woman who is entering your house like Rachel and Leah, who together built the house of Israel. May you be powerful in Ephrathah and famous in Bethlehem. ¹² May your house become like the house of Perez, the son Tamar bore to Judah, because of the offspring the LORD will give you by this young woman."

¹³ Boaz took Ruth and she became his wife. When he was intimate with her, the LORD enabled her to conceive, and she gave birth to a son. ¹⁴ Then the women said to Naomi, "Praise the LORD, who has not left you without a family redeemer today. May his name be famous in Israel. ¹⁵ He will renew your life and sustain you in your old age. Indeed, your daughter-in-law, who loves you and is better to you than seven sons, has given birth to him." ¹⁶ Naomi took the child, placed him on her lap, and took care of him. ¹⁷ The neighbor women said, "A son has been born to Naomi," and they named him Obed.ʲ He was the father of Jesse, the father of David.

David's Genealogy from Judah's Son

¹⁸ Now this is the genealogy of Perez:

Perez fathered Hezron.
¹⁹ Hezron fathered Ram,ᵏ
who fathered Amminadab.
²⁰ Amminadab fathered Nahshon,
who fathered Salmon.
²¹ Salmon fathered Boaz,
who fathered Obed.
²² And Obed fathered Jesse,
who fathered David.

ᵃ3:14 Lit *up before a man could recognize his companion*   ᵇ3:14 LXX; MT reads *the*   ᶜ3:15 Some Hb mss, Aram, Syr, Vg; MT reads *he*   ᵈ3:16 Lit *Who are you*   ᵉ3:17 Alt Hb tradition, LXX, Syr, Tg read *said to me*   ᶠ4:1 Lit *Boaz said so-and-so come*   ᵍ4:4 Lit *should uncover your ear, saying*   ʰ4:4 Some Hb mss, LXX, Syr, Vg; other Hb mss read *if he does*   ⁱ4:5 Vg; MT reads *Naomi and from*   ʲ4:17 = Servant   ᵏ4:19 LXX reads *Aram*; Mt 1:3–4

---

volved inheritance and family structure. Boaz knew about a relative closer in bloodline to Ruth's husband than he was. Boaz had to deal with this legal matter before they could move ahead with any plan.

4:9 buying from Naomi. While Naomi was neither part of the proceedings nor the woman in question, ultimately her right to the land was being transferred.

4:13-17 gave birth to a son. At this point, Naomi had come full circle in her journey. She left Bethlehem with a family, then lost them all, and saved Ruth. But through God's provision, Naomi now held again the inheritance of her husband and family.

4:16 placed him on her lap. Joseph had done the same thing with his grandchildren as a symbol of ownership (Gen. 50:22-23), to

indicate that that they were as real to him as actual sons.

4:18-22 This genealogy stands as a reminder that God's plan reaches beyond generations. From Naomi's sorrow came a grandchild who established the family line of both King David and then Jesus, the Messiah.

INTRODUCTION TO
1 SAMUEL

AUTHOR

The author of 1 Samuel is not known with certainty. Perhaps a compiler drew from materials written by others such as Samuel, Gad, and Nathan (see 1 Chron. 29:29) in order to produce the final rendition. Note that 1 and 2 Samuel were originally composed as one unit.

DATE

The date of authorship is uncertain, though it is possible that this two-volume book was written around the time of Solomon's death (circa 930 B.C.).

THEME

The king-maker (Samuel) and the first king (Saul).

HISTORICAL BACKGROUND AND CHARACTERISTICS

The first Book of Samuel narrates a major transition in the life of Israel—the shift from government under judges to a monarchy. Samuel, the last judge, anoints Saul as Israel's first king (circa 1050 B.C.). He later anoints David as the king who will succeed Saul.

This historical book highlights the lives of three central figures: Samuel, Saul, and David. Sad elements abound: Eli's sons rebel; faithless Israel rejects her great King; Saul self-destructs in his vicious pursuit of David, reaching his lowest point when he consults a witch. But bright notes also punctuate this sordid story: Samuel stands firm and godly as the prophet of God who is ever faithful to his Lord; David (with soul mate Jonathan) appears youthful, courageous, popular, and abounding in faith in the mighty God of Israel. In the context of almost constant warfare, trust in God is either conspicuously present or conspicuously absent. God is seen as the rejected King, the revealer of the unknown, the judge of the rebellious, as well as the deliverer of His people.

PASSAGES FOR TOPICAL GROUP STUDY

3:1-14 . . . . SPEAKING OUT . . . . A Warning in the Night

8:1-22 . . . . . . MOTIVES AND DECISIONS . . Detrimental Desires

13:1-15 . . . . . . MAKING EXCUSES . . . "The Devil Made Me Do It"

16:1-13 . . . . . . LOOKING INSIDE AND OUT . . . . Seeing the Heart and Soul

17:20-50 . . . . DISCIPLINE and PREPARATION. . . . . Training for Action

18:1-16 . . . . . . FRIENDS and JEALOUS . . . . Friends and Foes

20:1-13,18-42 REBELLING FOR GOD . . . . Okay to Disobey

24:1-22 . . . . . AUTHORITIES and POWER. . . . . Respecting Authority

31:1-13 . . . . . . ASSISTED SUICIDE . . . . Saul's Suicide

Hannah's Vow

1 There was a man from Ramathaim-zophim in[a] the hill country of Ephraim. His name was Elkanah son of Jeroham, son of Elihu, son of Tohu, son of Zuph, an Ephraimite. ² He had two wives, the first named Hannah and the second Peninnah. Peninnah had children, but Hannah was childless. ³ This man would go up from his town every year to worship and to sacrifice to the LORD of •Hosts at Shiloh, where Eli's two sons, Hophni and Phinehas, were the LORD's priests.

⁴ Whenever Elkanah offered a sacrifice, he always gave portions of the meat to his wife Peninnah and to each of her sons and daughters. ⁵ But he gave a double[b] portion to Hannah, for he loved her even though the LORD had kept her from conceiving. ⁶ Her rival would taunt her severely just to provoke her, because the LORD had kept Hannah from conceiving. ⁷ Whenever she went up to the LORD's house, her rival taunted her in this way every year. Hannah wept and would not eat. ⁸ "Hannah, why are you crying?" her husband Elkanah asked. "Why won't you eat? Why are you troubled? Am I not better to you than 10 sons?"

⁹ Hannah got up after they ate and drank at Shiloh.[c] Eli the priest was sitting on a chair by the doorpost of the LORD's tabernacle. ¹⁰ Deeply hurt, Hannah prayed to the LORD and wept with many tears. ¹¹ Making a vow, she pleaded, "LORD of Hosts, if You will take notice of Your servant's affliction, remember and not forget me, and give Your servant a son,[d] I will give him to the LORD all the days of his life, and his hair will never be cut."[e]

¹² While she was praying in the LORD's presence, Eli watched her lips. ¹³ Hannah was speaking to herself,[f] and although her lips were moving, her voice could not be heard. Eli thought she was drunk ¹⁴ and scolded her, "How long are you going to be drunk? Get rid of your wine!"

¹⁵ "No, my lord," Hannah replied. "I am a woman with a broken heart. I haven't had any wine or beer; I've been pouring out my heart before the LORD. ¹⁶ Don't think of me as a wicked woman; I've been praying from the depth of my anguish and resentment."

¹⁷ Eli responded, "Go in peace, and may the God of Israel grant the petition you've requested from Him."

¹⁸ "May your servant find favor with you," she replied. Then Hannah went on her way; she ate and no longer appeared downcast.[g]

Samuel's Birth and Dedication

¹⁹ The next morning Elkanah and Hannah got up early to bow and to worship the LORD. Afterwards, they returned home to Ramah. Then Elkanah was intimate with his wife Hannah, and the LORD remembered her. ²⁰ After some time,[h] Hannah conceived and gave birth to a son. She named him Samuel,[i] because ⌊she said⌋, "I requested him from the LORD."

²¹ When Elkanah and all his household went up to make the annual sacrifice and his vow offering to the LORD, ²² Hannah did not go and explained to her husband, "After the child is weaned, I'll take him to appear in the LORD's presence and to stay there permanently."

²³ Her husband Elkanah replied, "Do what you think is best,[j] and stay here until you've weaned him. May the LORD confirm your[k] word." So Hannah stayed there and nursed her son until she weaned him. ²⁴ When she had weaned him, she took him with her to Shiloh, as well as a three-year-old bull,[l] two and one-half gallons[m] of flour, and a jar of wine. Though the boy was ⌊still⌋ young,[n] she took him to the LORD's house at Shiloh. ²⁵ Then they slaughtered the bull and brought the boy to Eli.

²⁶ "Please, my lord," she said, "as sure as you live, my lord, I am the woman who stood here beside you praying to the LORD. ²⁷ I prayed for this boy, and since the LORD gave me what I asked Him for, ²⁸ I now give the boy to the LORD. For as long as he lives, he is given to the LORD." Then he[o] bowed and worshiped the LORD there.[p]

Hannah's Triumphant Prayer

2 Hannah prayed:

My heart rejoices in the LORD;
my •horn is lifted up by the LORD.
My mouth boasts over my enemies,
because I rejoice in Your salvation.

² There is no one holy like the LORD.
There is no one besides You!
And there is no rock like our God.

³ Do not boast so proudly,
or let arrogant ⌊words⌋ come out of your mouth,
for the LORD is a God of knowledge,
and actions are weighed by Him.

⁴ The bows of the warriors are broken,
but the feeble are clothed with strength.

⁵ Those who are full hire themselves out for food,

ᵃ**1:1** Or *from Ramathaim, a Zuphite from*   ᵇ**1:5** Or *gave only one*; Hb obscure   ᶜ**1:9** LXX adds *and presented herself before the LORD*   ᵈ**1:11** Lit *a seed of men*   ᵉ**1:11** Lit *no razor will go up on his head*   ᶠ**1:13** Lit *to her heart*   ᵍ**1:18** Lit *and her face was not to her again*   ʰ**1:20** Lit *In the turning of the days*   ⁱ**1:20** Possibly a wordplay for *requested from God*   ʲ**1:23** Lit *what is good in your eyes*   ᵏ**1:23** DSS, LXX, Syr; MT reads *His*   ˡ**1:24** DSS, LXX, Syr; MT reads *Shiloh with three bulls*   ᵐ**1:24** Lit *bull and an ephah*   ⁿ**1:24** Lit *And the youth was a youth*   ᵒ**1:28** DSS read *she*; some Hb mss, Syr, Vg read *they*   ᵖ**1:28** LXX reads *Then she left him there before the LORD*

1:1 Ramathaim-sophim. This probably referred to Ramah, about 15 miles north of Jerusalem. Samuel was born and buried here. **Ephraimite.** Elkanah, Samuel's father, was Ephraimite by residence, but his ancestry was through the tribe of Levi. It was appropriate, then, for Samuel to become a priest even though his family was from Ephraim.

1:3 every year. Three times a year, Hebrews journeyed to a central location of worship, in this case at Shiloh in Ephraim, to celebrate a national feast. The temple had not yet been built. Joshua had settled the tabernacle there as a more permanent structure (Josh. 18:1). This remained the central place of worship until the ark of the covenant was stolen.

1:5 kept her from conceiving. During this time in history, infertility was always considered a curse from God. To be barren was the greatest shame any woman could bear.

2:10 His king. Through Samuel's leadership God would anoint the first and second kings, Saul and David.

but those who are starving ⌊hunger⌋ no more.
The barren woman gives birth to seven,
but the woman with many sons pines away.

6 The LORD brings death and gives life;
He sends ⌊some⌋ to •Sheol, and He raises
⌊others⌋ up.

7 The LORD brings poverty and gives wealth;
He humbles and He exalts.

8 He raises the poor from the dust
and lifts the needy from the garbage pile.
He seats them with noblemen
and gives them a throne of honor.a
For the foundations of the earth are the LORD's;
He has set the world on them.

9 He guards the stepsb of His faithful ones,
but the wicked are silenced in darkness,
for a man does not prevail by ⌊his own⌋ strength.

10 Those who oppose the LORD will be shattered;c
He will thunder in the heavens against them.
The LORD will judge the ends of the earth.
He will give power to His king;
He will lift up the horn of His anointed.

11 Elkanah went home to Ramah, but the boy served the LORD in the presence of Eli the priest.

Eli's Family Judged

12 Eli's sons were •wicked men; they had no regard for the LORD 13 or for the priests' share ⌊of the sacrifices⌋ from the people. When any man offered a sacrifice, the priest's servant would come with a three-pronged meat fork while the meat was boiling 14 and plunge it into the container or kettle or caldron or cooking pot. The priest would claim for himself whatever the meat fork brought up. This is the way they treated all the Israelites who came there to Shiloh. 15 Even before the fat was burned, the priest's servant would come and say to the man who was sacrificing, "Give the priest ⌊some⌋ meat to roast, because he won't accept boiled meat from you—only raw." 16 If that man said to him, "The fat must be burned first; then you can take whatever you want for yourself," the servant would reply, "No, I insist that you hand it over right now. If you don't, I'll take it by force!" 17 So the servants' sin was very severe in the presence of the LORD, because they treated the LORD's offering with contempt.

18 The boy Samuel served in the LORD's presence and wore a linen ephod. 19 Each year his mother made him a little robe and took it to him when she went with her husband to offer the annual sacrifice. 20 Eli would bless Elkanah and his wife: "May the LORD give you children by this woman in place of the one shed has given to the LORD." Then they would go home.

21 The LORD paid attention to Hannah's ⌊need⌋, and she conceived and gave birth to three sons and two daughters. Meanwhile, the boy Samuel grew up in the presence of the LORD.

22 Now Eli was very old. He heard about everything his sons were doing to all Israel and how they were sleeping with the women who served at the entrance to the tent of meeting. 23 He said to them, "Why are you doing these things? I have heard about your evil actions from all these people. 24 No, my sons, the report I hear from the LORD's people is not good. 25 If a man sins against another man, God can intercede for him, but if a man sins against the LORD, who can intercede for him?" But they would not listen to their father, since the LORD intended to kill them. 26 By contrast, the boy Samuel grew in stature and in favor with the LORD and with men.

27 A man of God came to Eli and said to him, "This is what the LORD says: 'Didn't I reveal Myself to your ancestral house when it was in Egypt and belonged to Pharaoh's palace? 28 I selected your housee from the tribes of Israel to be priests, to offer sacrifices on My altar, to burn incense, and to wear an •ephod in My presence. I also gave your house all the Israelite fire offerings. 29 Why, then, do all of you despise My sacrifices and offerings that I require at the place of worship? You have honored your sons more than Me, by making yourselves fat with the best part of all of the offerings of My people Israel.'

30 "Therefore, the LORD, the God of Israel, says:

'Although I said
your family and your ancestral house
would walk before Me forever,
the LORD now says, "No longer!"
I will honor those who honor Me,
but those who despise Me will be disgraced.

31 "'Look, the days are coming when I will cut off your strength and the strength of your ancestral family, so that none in your family will reach old age. 32 You will see distress ⌊in the⌋ place of worship, in spite of all that is good in Israel, and no one in your family will ever again reach old age. 33 Any man from your ⌊family⌋ I do not cut off from My altar will bring grieff and sadness to you. All your descendants will die violently.g h 34 This will be the sign that will come to you

---

a2:8 DSS, LXX add *He gives the vow of the one who makes a vow and He blesses the years of the just* b2:9 Lit *feet* c2:10 DSS, LXX read *The LORD shatters those who dispute with Him* d2:20 DSS; Hb reads *he* e2:28 Lit *selected him* f2:33 Lit *grief to your eyes* g2:33 DSS, LXX read *die by the sword of men* h2:33 Lit *die men*

2:13-16 The priests lived off *some* of the offerings. The three-pronged fork was a random method of giving the priests some food. Eli's sons chose a method that put the choice in their hands rather than God's.

2:15 Even before the fat was burned. For the priests to take meat before the fat had been boiled or burned off was to claim for themselves what belonged to God by His own decree. It was the ultimate disregard and disrespect.

2:16 I'll take it by force. Sacrifices were to be voluntary to have any meaning at all. This coercion turned an "offering" into a "do it or else."

2:18 ephod. The high priest wore a sacred, ornamental ephod, a sleeveless, tunic-like garment. Samuel's was linen.

2:22 women who served. These women are mentioned only one other time (Ex. 38:8) with-

concerning your two sons Hophni and Phinehas: both of them will die on the same day.

[35] "'Then I will raise up a faithful priest for Myself. He will do whatever is in My heart and mind. I will establish a lasting dynasty for him, and he will walk before My anointed one for all time. [36] Anyone who is left in your family will come and bow down to him for a piece of silver or a loaf of bread. He will say: Please appoint me to some priestly office so I can have a piece of bread to eat.'"

Samuel's Call

3 The boy Samuel served the LORD in Eli's presence. In those days the word of the LORD was rare and prophetic visions were not widespread.

[2] One day Eli, whose eyesight was failing, was lying in his room. [3] Before the lamp of God had gone out, Samuel was lying down in the tabernacle of the LORD where the ark of God was located.

A Warning in the Night

1. Are you a light or heavy sleeper? What does it take to wake you?

1 Samuel 3:1-14

2. Samuel lived in the Lord's temple, yet "the word of the LORD had not yet been revealed to him" (v. 7). What does that say about Eli, the high priest?

3. Why is God going to judge Eli's family forever?

4. What might Eli have done to stop his sons? In what way is he responsible for their sins?

5. How are you responsible for speaking out against those who are doing wrong?

[4] Then the LORD called Samuel,[a] and he answered, "Here I am." [5] He ran to Eli and said, "Here I am; you called me."

"I didn't call," Eli replied. "Go and lie down." So he went and lay down.

[6] Once again the LORD called, "Samuel!"

Samuel got up, went to Eli, and said, "Here I am; you called me."

"I didn't call, my son," he replied. "Go and lie down."

[7] Now Samuel had not yet experienced the LORD, because the word of the LORD had not yet been revealed to him. [8] Once again, for the third time, the LORD called Samuel. He got up, went to Eli, and said, "Here I am; you called me."

Then Eli understood that the LORD was calling the boy. [9] He told Samuel, "Go and lie down. If He calls you, say, 'Speak, LORD, for Your servant is listening.'" So Samuel went and lay down in his place.

[10] The LORD came, stood there, and called as before, "Samuel, Samuel!"

Samuel responded, "Speak, for Your servant is listening."

[11] The LORD said to Samuel, "I am about to do something in Israel that everyone who hears about it will shudder. [12] On that day I will carry out against Eli everything I said about his family, from beginning to end. [13] I told him that I am going to judge his family forever because of the iniquity he knows about: his sons are defiling the sanctuary,[b] and he has not stopped them. [14] Therefore, I have sworn to Eli's family: The iniquity of Eli's family will never be wiped out by either sacrifice or offering."

[15] Samuel lay down until the morning; then he opened the doors of the LORD's house. He was afraid to tell Eli the vision, [16] but Eli called him and said, "Samuel, my son."

"Here I am," answered Samuel.

[17] "What was the message He gave you?" Eli asked. "Don't hide it from me. May God punish you and do so severely if you hide anything from me that He told you." [18] So Samuel told him everything and did not hide anything from him. Eli responded, "He is the LORD. He will do what He thinks is good."[c]

[19] Samuel grew, and the LORD was with him and let nothing he said prove false.[d] [20] All Israel from Dan to Beer-sheba knew that Samuel was a confirmed prophet of the LORD. [21] The LORD continued to appear in Shiloh, be-

4 cause there He revealed Himself to Samuel by His word. [1] And Samuel's words came to all Israel.

The Ark Captured by the Philistines

Israel went out to meet the Philistines in battle and[e] camped at Ebenezer while the Philistines camped at Aphek. [2] The Philistines lined up in battle formation

---

[a]**3:4** DSS, LXX read *called, "Samuel! Samuel!"* [b]**3:13** Alt Hb tradition, LXX read *are cursing God* [c]**3:18** Lit *what is good in His eyes* [d]**3:19** Lit *let no words fall to the ground* [e]**4:1** LXX reads *In those days the Philistines gathered together to fight against Israel, and Israel went out to engage them in battle. They*

---

out much detail. Pagan women offered sexual favors at their temples as worship to fertility gods. Eli's sons were blatantly insulting God in mimicking that behavior.

2:35 My anointed one. Ultimately Jesus Christ, it was fulfilled as well in ancient Israel when the priesthood was taken away from the

Ithamar's descendants (Eli, etc.) and given to the Eleazar's descendants (another son of Aaron).

3:1 the word of the LORD was rare. Samuel was about to usher in a new day.

3:17 do so severely. Ruth used this expres-

sion when making her vow of loyalty to Naomi (Ruth 1:17). Jonathan used it in committing his loyalty and protection to David (20:12-13). David, Abner, Ben-Hadad, and even Jezebel also spoke these same words.

4:7 The gods. While the ark represented the presence of the One true God, the Philistines

against Israel, and as the battle intensified, Israel was defeated by the Philistines, who struck down about 4,000 men on the battlefield.

3 When the troops returned to the camp, the elders of Israel asked, "Why did the LORD let us be defeated today by the Philistines? Let's bring the ark of the LORD's covenant from Shiloh. Then it^a will go with us and save us from the hand of our enemies." 4 So the people sent ⌊men⌋ to Shiloh to bring back the ark of the covenant of the LORD of •Hosts, who dwells ⌊between⌋ the •cherubim. Eli's two sons, Hophni and Phinehas, were there with the ark of the covenant of God. 5 When the ark of the covenant of the LORD entered the camp, all the Israelites raised such a loud shout that the ground shook.

6 The Philistines heard the sound of the war cry and asked, "What's this loud shout in the Hebrews' camp?" When the Philistines discovered that the ark of the LORD had entered the camp, 7 they panicked. "The gods have entered their camp!" they said. "Woe to us, nothing like this has happened before.^b 8 Woe to us, who will rescue us from the hand of these magnificent gods? These are the gods that slaughtered the Egyptians with all kinds of plagues in the wilderness. 9 Show some courage and be men, Philistines! Otherwise, you'll serve the Hebrews just like they served you. Now be men and fight!"

10 So the Philistines fought, and Israel was defeated, and each man fled to his tent. The slaughter was severe—30,000 of the Israelite foot soldiers fell. 11 The ark of God was captured, and Eli's two sons, Hophni and Phinehas, died.

Eli's Death and Ichabod's Birth

12 That same day, a Benjaminite man ran from the battle and came to Shiloh. His clothes were torn, and there was dirt on his head. 13 When he arrived, there was Eli sitting on his chair beside the road watching, because he was anxious about the ark of God. When the man entered the city to give a report, the entire city cried out.

14 Eli heard the outcry and asked, "Why this commotion?" The man quickly came and reported to Eli. 15 At that time Eli was 98 years old, and his gaze was fixed^c because he couldn't see.

16 The man said to Eli, "I'm the one who came from the battle.^d I fled from there today."

"What happened, my son?" Eli asked.

17 The messenger answered, "Israel has fled from the Philistines, and also there was a great slaughter among the people. Your two sons, Hophni and Phinehas, are both dead, and the ark of God has been captured." 18 When he mentioned the ark of God, Eli fell backwards off the chair by the city gate, and since he was old and heavy, his neck broke and he died. Eli had judged Israel 40 years.

19 Eli's daughter-in-law, the wife of Phinehas, was pregnant and about to give birth. When she heard the news about the capture of God's ark and the deaths of her father-in-law and her husband, she collapsed and gave birth because her labor pains came on her. 20 As she was dying,^e the women taking care of her said, "Don't be afraid. You've given birth to a son!" But she did not respond, and did not pay attention. 21 She named the boy Ichabod,^f saying, "The glory has departed from Israel," referring to the capture of the ark of God and to ⌊the deaths of⌋ her father-in-law and her husband. 22 "The glory has departed from Israel," she said, "because the ark of God has been captured."

The Ark in Philistine Hands

5 After the Philistines had captured the ark of God, they took it from Ebenezer to Ashdod, 2 brought it into the temple of Dagon^g and placed it next to his statue.^h 3 When the people of Ashdod got up early the next morning, there was Dagon, fallen with his face to the ground before the ark of the LORD. So they took Dagon and returned him to his place. 4 But when they got up early the next morning, there was Dagon, fallen with his face to the ground before the ark of the LORD. ⌊This time⌋, both Dagon's head and the palms of his hands were broken off and lying on the threshold. Only Dagon's torso remained.ⁱ 5 That is why, to this day, the priests of Dagon and everyone who enters the temple of Dagon in Ashdod do not step on Dagon's threshold.

6 The LORD severely oppressed^j the people of Ashdod, terrorizing and afflicting the people of Ashdod and its territory with tumors.^{k l} 7 When the men of Ashdod saw what was happening, they said, "The ark of Israel's God must not stay here with us, because His hand is severe against us and our god Dagon." 8 So they called all the Philistine rulers together and asked, "What should we do with the ark of Israel's God?"

"The ark of Israel's God should be moved to Gath," they replied. So the men of Ashdod moved the ark.

---

^a4:3 Or He ^b4:7 Lit yesterday or the day before ^c4:15 Lit his eyes stood; 1 Kg 14:4 ^d4:16 LXX reads camp ^e4:20 LXX reads And in her time of delivery, she was about to die ^f4:21 = Where is Glory? ^g5:2 A Philistine god of the sea, grain, or storm ^h5:2 Lit to Dagon ⁱ5:4 LXX; Hb reads Only Dagon remained on it ^j5:6 Lit The hand of the LORD was heavy on ^k5:6 LXX adds He brought up mice against them, and they swarmed in their ships. Then mice went up into the land and there was a mortal panic in the city. ^l5:6 Perhaps bubonic plague

---

thought many gods had come.

4:11 The ark of God was captured. The ark had not saved them—it was not their lucky charm. **Hophni and Phinehas.** God had prophesied their death because they misused their position as priests (2:25).

4:18 40 years. Eli's leadership probably overlapped with several of Israel's judges, including Samson.

5:2 the temple of Dagon. This temple was located 50 miles from Shiloh, the central sanctuary of the Hebrews. Dagon was the mythical father of Baal.

5:8 Gath. A town 12 miles southeast of Israel. The same fate that settled on Ashdod fell on the people of Gath and Ekron.

6:2 diviners. A "yes or no" test was often involved, such as the one Gideon proposed when he laid his fleece before God. For instance, animal livers gave such signs.

9 After they had moved it, the LORD's hand was against the city of Gath, causing a great panic. He afflicted the men of the city, from the youngest to the oldest, with an outbreak of tumors.

10 The Gathites then sent the ark of God to Ekron, but when it got there, the Ekronites cried out, "They've moved the ark of Israel's God to us to kill us and our people!"a

11 The Ekronites called all the Philistine rulers together. They said, "Send the ark of Israel's God away. It must return to its place so it won't kill us and our people!"b For the fear of death pervaded the city; God's hand was very heavy there. 12 The men who did not die were afflicted with tumors, and the outcry of the city went up to heaven.

The Return of the Ark

6 When the ark of the LORD had been in the land of the Philistines for seven months, 2 the Philistines summoned the priests and the diviners and pleaded, "What should we do with the ark of the LORD? Tell us how we can send it back to its place."

3 They replied, "If you send the ark of Israel's God away, you must not send it without ⌊an offering⌋. You must return it with a guilt offering, and you will be healed. Then the reason His hand hasn't been removed from you will be revealed."c

4 They asked, "What guilt offering should we send back to Him?"

And they answered, "Five gold tumors and five gold mice ⌊corresponding to⌋ the number of Philistine rulers, since there was one plague for both youd and your rulers. 5 Make images of your tumors and of your mice that are destroying the land. Give glory to Israel's God, and perhaps He will stop oppressing you,e your gods, and your land. 6 Why harden your hearts as the Egyptians and Pharaoh hardened theirs? When He afflicted them, didn't they send Israel away, and Israel left?

7 "Now then, prepare one new cart and two milk cows that have never been yoked. Hitch the cows to the cart, but take their calves away and pen them up. 8 Take the ark of the LORD, place it on the cart, and put the gold objects in a box beside it, which you're sending Him as a guilt offering. Send it off and let it go its way. 9 Then watch: If it goes up the road to its homeland toward Beth-shemesh, it is the LORD who has made this terrible trouble for us. However, if it doesn't, we will know that it was not His hand that

punished us—it was just something that happened to us by chance."

10 The men did this: They took two milk cows, hitched them to the cart, and confined their calves in the pen. 11 Then they put the ark of the LORD on the cart, along with the box ⌊containing⌋ the gold mice and the images of the tumors. 12 The cows went straight up the road to Beth-shemesh. They stayed on that one highway, lowing as they went; they never strayed to the right or to the left. The Philistine rulers were walking behind them to the territory of Beth-shemesh.

13 The people of Beth-shemesh were harvesting wheat in the valley, and when they looked up and saw the ark, they were overjoyed to see it. 14 The cart came to the field of Joshua of Beth-shemesh and stopped there near a large rock. The people of the city chopped up the cart and offered the cows as a •burnt offering to the LORD. 15 The Levites removed the ark of the LORD, along with the box containing the gold objects, and placed them on the large rock. That day the men of Beth-shemesh offered burnt offerings and made sacrifices to the LORD. 16 When the five Philistine rulers observed ⌊this⌋, they returned to Ekron that same day.

17 As a guilt offering to the LORD, the Philistines had sent back one gold tumor for each city: Ashdod, Gaza, Ashkelon, Gath, and Ekron. 18 The number of gold mice also ⌊corresponded⌋ to the number of Philistine cities of the five rulers, the fortified cities and the outlying villages. The large rockf on which the ark of the LORD was placed is in the field of Joshua of Beth-shemesh to this day.

19 God struck down the men of Beth-shemesh because they looked inside the ark of the LORD.g He struck down 70 men ⌊out of⌋ 50,000 men.h The people wept because the LORD struck them with a great slaughter. 20 The men of Beth-shemesh asked, "Who is able to stand in the presence of this holy LORD God? Who should the ark go to from here?"

21 They sent messengers to the residents of Kiriath-jearim, saying, "The Philistines have returned the ark of the LORD. Come down and get it."i

7 So the men of Kiriath-jearim came for the ark of the LORD and took it to Abinadab's house on the hill. They consecrated his son Eleazar to take care of it.

Victory at Mizpah

2 Time went by until 20 years had passed since the ark had been taken to Kiriath-jearim. Then the whole house

---

a 5:10 DSS, LXX read Why have you moved . . . people? b 5:11 DSS, LXX read Why don't you return it to . . . people? c 6:3 DSS, LXX read healed, and an atonement shall be made for you. Shouldn't His hand be removed from you? d 6:4 Many Hb mss, LXX; MT reads them e 6:5 Lit will lighten the heaviness of His hand from you f 6:18 Some Hb mss, DSS, LXX, Tg; MT reads meadow g 6:19 LXX reads But the sons of Jeconiah did not rejoice with the men of Beth-shemesh when they saw the ark of the LORD. h 6:19 Some Hb mss, Josephus read 70 men i 6:21 Lit and bring it up to you

---

6:4 tumors ... mice. The gold was in the form of the plagues the Philistines had suffered: tumors and mice. The mice may have been carriers of the disease that caused the plague of tumors.

6:7 prepare one new cart. The Philistines made the "test" as difficult as possible. Cows

new to the yoke would not know how to pull together. Leaving calves behind would force cows to go against their natural instincts to return the ark to Israel.

6:9 Beth-shemesh. An Israelite border town about 15 miles west of Jerusalem.

6:19 looked inside the ark. While they were

glad to have it their national treasure back, the people still were required to treat the ark with reverence, unlike kids who have found a prize.

7:1 Abinadab's house. The ark stayed in his family for about 100 years. David finally brought the ark to Jerusalem (2 Sam. 6:2-3).

of Israel began to seek the LORD. ³ Samuel told them, "If you are returning to the LORD with all your heart, get rid of the foreign gods and the •Ashtoreths that are among you, dedicate yourselves toª the LORD, and worship only Him. Then He will rescue you from the hand of the Philistines." ⁴ So the Israelites removed the •Baals and the Ashtoreths and only worshiped the LORD.

⁵ Samuel said, "Gather all Israel at Mizpah, and I will pray to the LORD on your behalf." ⁶ When they gathered at Mizpah, they drew water and poured it out in the LORD's presence. They fasted that day, and there they confessed, "We have sinned against the LORD." And Samuel ⌊began to lead⌋ the Israelites at Mizpah as ⌊their⌋ judge.

⁷ When the Philistines heard that the Israelites had gathered at Mizpah, their rulers marched up toward Israel. When the Israelites heard ⌊about it⌋, they were afraid because of the Philistines. ⁸ The Israelites said to Samuel, "Don't stop crying out to the LORD our God for us, so that He will save us from the hand of the Philistines."

⁹ Then Samuel took a young lamb and offered it as a whole •burnt offering to the LORD. He cried out to the LORD on behalf of Israel, and the LORD answered him. ¹⁰ Samuel was offering the burnt offering as the Philistines drew near to fight against Israel. The LORD thundered loudly against the Philistines that day and threw them into such confusion that they fled before Israel. ¹¹ Then the men of Israel charged out of Mizpah and pursued the Philistines striking them down all the way to a place below Beth-car.

¹² Afterwards, Samuel took a stone and set it upright between Mizpah and Shen. He named it Ebenezer,ᵇ explaining, "The LORD has helped us to this point." ¹³ So the Philistines were subdued andᶜ did not invade Israel's territory again. The LORD's hand was against the Philistines all of Samuel's life. ¹⁴ The cities from Ekron to Gath, which they had taken from Israel, were restored; Israel even rescued their surrounding territories from Philistine control. There was also peace between Israel and the Amorites.

¹⁵ Samuel judged Israel throughout his life. ¹⁶ Every year he would go on a circuit to Bethel, Gilgal, and Mizpah and would judge Israel at all these locations. ¹⁷ Then he would return to Ramah because his home was there, he judged Israel there, and he had built an altar to the LORD there.

Israel's Demand for a King

8 When Samuel grew old, he appointed his sons as judges over Israel. ² His firstborn son's name was Joel and his second was Abijah. They were judges in Beer-sheba. ³ However, his sons did not walk in his ways—they turned toward dishonest gain, took bribes, and perverted justice.

 ## Detrimental Desires

1. When have you wanted something "just like" someone else had? What was it? Did you get it?

1 Samuel 8:1-22

2. Why did the Israelites want a king? Why did Samuel consider their demand sinful (v. 6)?
3. The people wanted a king to fight their battles (v. 20). What seems to be their basic motive in demanding this? Who should they have trusted to fight their battles?
4. Does wanting to be like other people sometimes influence your motives? In what way?
5. Does fear ever motivate your decisions? How can faith in God help?

⁴ So all the elders of Israel gathered together and went to Samuel at Ramah. ⁵ They said to him, "Look, you are old, and your sons do not follow your example. Therefore, appoint a king to judge us the same as all the other nations have."

⁶ When they said, "Give us a king to judge us," Samuel considered their demand sinful, so he prayed to the LORD. ⁷ But the LORD told him, "Listen to the people and everything they say to you. They have not rejected you; they have rejected Me as their king. ⁸ They are doing the same thing to you that they have done to Me,ᵈ since the day I brought them out of Egypt until this day, abandoning Me and worshiping other gods. ⁹ Listen to them, but you must solemnly warn them and tell them about the rights of the king who will rule over them."

¹⁰ Samuel told all the LORD's words to the people who were asking him for a king. ¹¹ He said, "These are the rights of the king who will rule over you: He can take your sons and put them to his use in his chariots, on his horses, or running in front of his chariots. ¹² He can appoint them for his use as commanders of thousands or commanders of fifties, to plow his ground or reap his harvest, or to make his weapons of war or the

---

ª**7:3** Lit *you and set your hearts on*   ᵇ**7:12** = Stone of Help   ᶜ**7:13** LXX reads *The LORD humbled the Philistines and they*   ᵈ**8:8** LXX; MT omits *to Me*

7:5 Mizpah. A common gathering spot for Israel, Mizpah was seven miles north of Jerusalem. It was there that Saul would later be presented as king (10:17-21).

7:10 the Philistines drew near. This battle marked a new phase in relations between the two peoples: the bully would become the

beaten because Israel was obeying God.

7:12 took a stone … named it Ebenezer. To commemorate what God had done (see Gen. 28: 16-19).

8:5 the same as all the other nations have. Israel's real motive for requesting a monarchy was now public: "Everyone else is doing it."

Apparently the people expressed concerns about the wickedness of Samuel's sons, which while valid, was a cover.

8:7 they have rejected Me. God directed Samuel to look at the deeper spiritual issue. Samuel's wounds were understandable. His leadership was being rejected. The more im-

equipment for his chariots. 13 He can take your daughters to become perfumers, cooks, and bakers. 14 He can take your best fields, vineyards, and olive orchards and give them to his servants. 15 He can take a tenth of your grain and your vineyards and give them to his officials and servants. 16 He can take your male servants, your female servants, your best young men,a and your donkeys and use them for his work. 17 He can take a tenth of your flocks, and you yourselves can become his servants. 18 When that day comes, you will cry out because of the king you've chosen for yourselves, but the LORD won't answer you on that day."

19 The people refused to listen to Samuel. "No!" they said. "We must have a king over us. 20 Then we'll be like all the other nations: our king will judge us, go out before us, and fight our battles."

21 Samuel listened to all the people's words and then repeated them to the LORD.b 22 "Listen to them," the LORD told Samuel. "Appoint a king for them."

Then Samuel told the men of Israel, "Each of you, go back to your city."

Saul Anointed King

9 There was an influential man of Benjamin named Kish son of Abiel, son of Zeror, son of Becorath, son of Aphiah, son of a Benjaminite. 2 He had a son named Saul, an impressive young man. There was no one more impressive among the Israelites than he. He stood a head taller than anyone else.c

3 One day the donkeys of Saul's father Kish wandered off. Kish said to his son Saul, "Take one of the attendants with you and go look for the donkeys." 4 Saul and his attendant went through the hill country of Ephraim and then through the region of Shalishah, but they didn't find them. They went through the region of Shaalim—nothing. Then they went through the Benjaminite region but still didn't find them.

5 When they came to the land of Zuph, Saul said to the attendant who was with him, "Come on, let's go back, or my father will stop ⌊worrying⌋ about the donkeys and start worrying about us."

6 "Look," the attendant said, "there's a man of God in this city who is highly respected; everything he says is sure to come true. Let's go there now. Maybe he'll tell us which way we should go."

7 "Suppose we do go," Saul said to his attendant, "what do we take the man? The food from our packs is gone, and there's no gift to take to the man of God. What do we have?"

8 The attendant answered Saul: "Here, I have a piece d of silver. I'll give it to the man of God, and he will tell us our way."

9 Formerly in Israel, a man who was going to inquire of God would say, "Come, let's go to the seer," for the prophet of today was formerly called the seer.

10 "Good," Saul replied to his attendant. "Come on, let's go." So they went to the city where the man of God was. 11 As they were climbing the hill to the city, they found some young women coming out to draw water and asked, "Is the seer here?"

12 The women answered, "Yes, he is ahead of you. Hurry, he just now came to the city, because there's a sacrifice for the people at the •high place today. 13 If you go quickly, you can catch up with him before he goes to the high place to eat. The people won't eat until he comes because he must bless the sacrifice; after that, the guests can eat. Go up immediately—you can find him now." 14 So they went up toward the city.

Saul and his attendant were entering the city when they saw Samuel coming toward them on his way to the high place. 15 Now the day before Saul's arrival, the LORD had informed Samuel,e 16 "At this time tomorrow I will send you a man from the land of Benjamin. Anoint him ruler over My people Israel. He will save them from the hand of the Philistines because I have seen ⌊the affliction of⌋ My people, for their cry has come to Me." 17 When Samuel saw Saul, the LORD told him, "Here is the man I told you about; he will rule over My people."

18 Saul approached Samuel in the gate area and asked, "Would you please tell me where the seer's house is?"

19 "I am the seer," Samuel answered.f "Go up ahead of me to the high place and eat with me today. When I send you off in the morning, I'll tell you everything that's in your heart. 20 As for the donkeys that wandered away from you three days ago, don't worry about them because they've been found. And who does all Israel desire but you and all your father's family?"

21 Saul responded, "Am I not a Benjaminite from the smallest of Israel's tribes and isn't my clan the least important of all the clans of the Benjaminite tribe? So why have you said something like this to me?"

22 Samuel took Saul and his attendant, brought them to the banquet hall, and gave them a place at the head of the 30g or so men who had been invited. 23 Then Samuel said to the cook, "Get the portion of meat that I gave you and told you to set aside."

---

a 8:16 LXX reads best cattle   b 8:21 Lit them in the LORD's ears   c 9:2 Lit From his shoulder and up higher than any of the people   d 9:8 Lit a quarter of a shekel   e 9:15 Lit had uncovered Samuel's ear, saying   f 9:19 Lit answered Saul   g 9:22 LXX reads 70

---

portant issue, however, was that God's leadership was rejected.

9:16 Anoint. Anointing someone was a sign of special power. The ceremony usually involved oil poured over someone's head or placed on the face. Often anointing was accompanied by laying hands on the person.

Even today some churches anoint in prayers for healing and lay hands on new leaders as the people pray for wisdom and success (Ex. 28:41; 2 Tim. 1:6; James 5:14).

9:21 Benjaminite. Benjamin was the youngest of Israel's sons. The smallness of Saul's clan and tribe was an issue because in these

times those would be his base of support. Gideon voiced similar concerns when asked to lead Israel against the Midianites (Judg. 6:15.)

9:24 thigh. Saul's receiving the thigh, part of the sacrifice usually kept for the priests (Ex. 29:27; Lev. 7:32), foreshadowed the

24 The cook picked up the thigh and what was attached to it and set it before Saul. Then Samuel said, "Notice that the reserved piece is set before you. Eat it because it was saved for you for this solemn event at the time I said, 'I've invited the people.' " So Saul ate with Samuel that day. 25 Afterwards, they went down from the high place to the city, and Samuel spoke with Saul on ⌊the⌋ roof.[a]

26 They got up early, and just before dawn, Samuel called to Saul on the roof, "Get up, and I'll send you on your way!" Saul got up, and both he and Samuel went outside. 27 As they were going down to the edge of the city, Samuel said to Saul, "Tell the attendant to go on ahead of us, but you stay for awhile, and I'll reveal the word of God to you." So the attendant went on.

10 Samuel took the flask of oil, poured it out on Saul's head, kissed him, and said, "Hasn't the LORD anointed you ruler over His inheritance?[b] 2 Today when you leave me, you'll find two men at Rachel's Grave at Zelzah in the land of Benjamin. They will say to you, 'The donkeys you went looking for have been found, and now your father has stopped being concerned about the donkeys and is worried about you, asking: What should I do about my son?'

3 "You will proceed from there until you come to the oak of Tabor. Three men going up to God at Bethel will meet you there, one bringing three goats, one bringing three loaves of bread, and one bringing a skin of wine. 4 They will ask how you are and give you two ⌊loaves[c] of⌋ bread, which you will accept from them.

5 "After that you will come to the Hill of God[d] where there are Philistine garrisons.[e] When you arrive at the city, you will meet a group of prophets coming down from the •high place prophesying. They will be preceded by harps, tambourines, flutes, and lyres. 6 The Spirit of the LORD will control you, you will prophesy with them, and you will be transformed into a different person. 7 When these signs have happened to you, do whatever your circumstances require[f] because God is with you. 8 Afterwards, go ahead of me to Gilgal. I will come to you to offer •burnt offerings and to sacrifice •fellowship offerings. Wait seven days until I come to you and show you what to do."

9 When Saul turned around[g] to leave Samuel, God changed his heart,[h] and all the signs came about that day. 10 When Saul and his attendant arrived at Gibeah,

a group of prophets met him. Then the Spirit of God took control of him, and he prophesied along with them.

11 Everyone who knew him previously and saw him prophesy with the prophets asked each other, "What has happened to the son of Kish? Is Saul also among the prophets?"

12 Then a man who was from there asked, "And who is their father?"

As a result, "Is Saul also among the prophets?" became a popular saying. 13 Then Saul finished prophesying and went to the high place.

14 Saul's uncle asked him and his attendant, "Where did you go?"

"To look for the donkeys," Saul answered. "When we saw they weren't there, we went to Samuel."

15 "Tell me," Saul's uncle asked, "what did Samuel say to you?"

16 Saul told him, "He assured us the donkeys had been found." However, Saul did not tell him what Samuel had said about the matter of kingship.

Saul Received as King

17 Samuel summoned the people to the LORD at Mizpah 18 and said to the Israelites, "This is what the LORD, the God of Israel, says: 'I brought Israel out of Egypt, and I rescued you from the power of the Egyptians and all the kingdoms that were oppressing you.' 19 But today you have rejected your God, who saves you from all your troubles and afflictions. You said to Him, 'You[i] must set a king over us.' Now therefore present yourselves before the LORD by your tribes and clans."

20 Samuel had all the tribes of Israel come forward, and the tribe of Benjamin was selected. 21 Then he had the tribe of Benjamin come forward by its clans, and the Matrite clan was selected.[j] Finally, Saul son of Kish was selected. But when they searched for him, they could not find him. 22 They again inquired of the LORD, "Has the man come here yet?"

The LORD replied, "There he is, hidden among the supplies."

23 They ran and got him from there. When he stood among the people, he stood a head taller than anyone else.[k] 24 Samuel said to all the people, "Do you see the one the LORD has chosen? There is no one like him among the entire population."

And all the people shouted,[l] "Long live the king!"

---

a 9:25 LXX reads *city. They prepared a bed for Saul on the roof, and he slept.* b 10:1 LXX adds *And you will reign over the LORD's people, and you will save them from the hand of their enemies all around. And this is the sign to you that the LORD has anointed you ruler over his inheritance.* c 10:4 DSS, LXX read *wave offerings* d 10:5 Or *to Gibeath-elohim* e 10:5 Or *governors* f 10:7 Lit *do for yourself whatever your hand finds* g 10:9 Lit *turned his shoulder* h 10:9 Lit *God turned to him another heart* i 10:19 Other Hb mss, LXX, Syr, Vg read *You said, 'No, you . . .* j 10:21 LXX adds *And he had the Matrite clan come forward, man by man.* k 10:23 Lit *people, and he was higher than any of the people from his shoulder and up* l 10:24 LXX reads *acknowledged and said*

---

honor in store for him.

10:1 flask of oil ... poured it out. Kings were doused with oil as a sign of God's blessing. Jesus later became God's "Anointed One." "Christos" and "Messiah" means "Anointed One."

10:8 Gilgal. The site of the first Israelite camp after they crossed the Jordan (Josh. 4:19).

10:11 What has happened. Saul's people were shocked at his presumptuous new role. The citizens of Nazareth asked similar questions about Jesus (Matt. 13:54-56).

10:20 selected. Urim and Thummim were stones used in making decisions like drawing straws or throwing dice (Ex. 28:30).

10:25 rights of kingship. Included Moses' instructions about the responsibilities of the king (Deut. 17:14-20).

²⁵ Samuel proclaimed to the people the rights of kingship. He wrote them on a scroll, which he placed in the presence of the LORD. Then, Samuel sent all the people away, each to his home.

²⁶ Saul also went to his home in Gibeah, and brave men whose hearts God had touched went with him. ²⁷ But some •wicked men said, "How can this guy save us?" They despised him and did not bring him a gift, but Saul said nothing.ᵃ ᵇ

Saul's Deliverance of Jabesh-gilead

11 Nahashᶜ the Ammonite came up and laid siege to Jabesh-gilead. All the men of Jabesh said to him, "Make a treaty with us, and we will serve you."

² Nahash the Ammonite replied, "I'll make one with you on this condition: that I gouge out everyone's right eye and humiliate all Israel."

³ "Don't do anything to us for seven days," the elders of Jabesh said to him, "and let us send messengers throughout the territory of Israel. If no one saves us, we will surrender to you."

⁴ When the messengers came to Gibeah, Saul's ⌊hometown⌋, and told the terms toᵈ the people, all wept aloud. ⁵ Just then Saul was coming in from the field behind his oxen. "What's the matter with the people? Why are they weeping?" Saul inquired, and they repeated to him the words of the men from Jabesh.

⁶ When Saul heard these words, the Spirit of God suddenly took control of him, and his anger burned furiously. ⁷ He took a team of oxen, cut them in pieces, and sent them throughout the land of Israel by messengers who said, "This is what will be done to the ox of anyone who doesn't march behind Saul and Samuel." As a result, the terror of the LORD fell on the people, and they went out united.

⁸ Saul counted them at Bezek. There were 300,000ᵉ Israelites and 30,000ᶠ men from Judah. ⁹ He told the messengers who had come, "Tell this to the men of Jabesh-gilead: 'Deliverance will be yours tomorrow by the time the sun is hot.'" So the messengers told the men of Jabesh, and they rejoiced.

¹⁰ Then the men of Jabesh said to ⌊Nahash⌋, "Tomorrow we will come out, and you can do whatever you wantᵍ to us."

¹¹ The next day Saul organized the troops into three divisions. During the morning watch, they invaded the Ammonite camp and slaughtered them until the heat of the day. There were survivors, but they were so scattered that no two of them were left together.

Saul's Confirmation as King

¹² Afterwards, the people said to Samuel, "Who said that Saul should notʰ reign over us? Give us those men so we can kill them!"

¹³ But Saul ordered, "No one will be executed this day, for today the LORD has provided deliverance in Israel."

¹⁴ Then Samuel said to the people, "Come, let's go to Gilgal, so we can renew the kingship there." ¹⁵ So all the people went to Gilgal, and there in the LORD's presence they made Saul king. There they sacrificed •fellowship offerings in the LORD's presence, and Saul and all the men of Israel greatly rejoiced.

Samuel's Final Public Speech

12 Then Samuel said to all Israel, "I have carefully listened to everything you said to me and placed a king over you. ² But now, you can see that the king is leading you. As for me, I'm old and gray, and my sons are here with you. I have led you from my youth until today. ³ Here I am. Bring charges against me before the LORD and His anointed: Whose ox or donkey have I taken? Whom have I wronged or mistreated? From whose hand have I taken a bribe to overlook something?ⁱ ʲ I will return it to you."

⁴ "You haven't wronged us, you haven't mistreated us, and you haven't taken anything from anyone's hand," they responded.

⁵ He said to them, "The LORD is a witness against you, and His anointed is a witness today that you haven't found anything in my hand."

"⌊He is⌋ a witness," they said.

⁶ Then Samuel said to the people, "The LORD, who appointed Moses and Aaron and who brought your ancestors up from the land of Egypt, is a witness.ᵏ ⁷ Now present yourselves, so I may judge you before the LORD about all the righteous acts He has done for you and your ancestors.

⁸ "When Jacob went to Egypt,ˡ your ancestors cried out to the LORD, and He sent them Moses and Aaron, who led your ancestors out of Egypt and settled them in this place. ⁹ But they forgot the LORD their God, so He handed them over to Sisera commander of the army of

ᵃ10:27 DSS add *Nahash king of the Ammonites had been severely oppressing the Gadites and Reubenites. He gouged out the right eye of each of them and brought fear and trembling on Israel. Of the Israelites beyond the Jordan none remained whose right eye Nahash, king of the Ammonites, had not gouged out. But there were 7,000 men who had escaped from the Ammonites and entered Jabesh-gilead.* ᵇ10:27 Lit *gift, and he was like a mute person* ᶜ11:1 DSS, LXX read *About a month later, Nahash* ᵈ11:4 Lit *in the ears of* ᵉ11:8 LXX reads *600,000* ᶠ11:8 DSS, LXX read *70,000* ᵍ11:10 Lit *do what is good in your eyes* ʰ11:12 Some Hb mss, LXX; other Hb mss omit *not* ⁱ12:3 LXX reads *bribe or a pair of shoes? Testify against me.* ʲ12:3 Lit *bribe and will hide my eyes with it?* ᵏ12:6 LXX; MT omits *is a witness* ˡ12:8 LXX reads *When Jacob and his sons went to Egypt and Egypt humbled them*

11:6 Spirit of God. Beginning well, Saul's first official act was prompted by God's power and spirit. Saul's later rule would be characterized by pettiness and indecision.

11:15 they made Saul king. At this confirmation the people formally honored Saul as their choice, as well as God's choice. Now in battle he had proved himself.

12:3 Here I am. When the people first came to Samuel to request a king, they cited the failure of his sons to lead them (8:4-7). Here he defends himself.

12:6 The LORD, who appointed Moses and Aaron. Samuel confronted the people on their lack of wisdom in requesting a king. He referred to the history of God's leadership. God had chosen Moses and Aaron (Ex. 4:14-17), but the people chose a king.

12:7 judge you before the LORD. Samuel switched from defending himself to accusing the people. He seems to be playing the role

Hazor, to the Philistines, and to the king of Moab. ⌊These enemies⌋ fought against them. [10] Then they cried out to the LORD and said, 'We have sinned, for we abandoned the LORD and worshiped the •Baals and the •Ashtoreths. Now deliver us from the power of our enemies, and we will serve You.' [11] So the LORD sent Jerubbaal, Barak,[a] Jephthah, and Samuel. He rescued you from the power of the enemies around you, and you lived securely. [12] But when you saw that Nahash king of the Ammonites was coming against you, you said to me, 'No, we must have a king rule over us'—even though the LORD your God is your king.

[13] "Now here is the king you've chosen, the one you requested. Look, this is the king the LORD has placed over you. [14] If you •fear the LORD, worship and obey Him, and if you don't rebel against the LORD's command, then both you and the king who rules over you will follow the LORD your God. [15] However, if you disobey the LORD and rebel against His command, the LORD's hand will be against you and against your ancestors.[b]

[16] "Now, therefore, present yourselves and see this great thing that the LORD will do before your eyes. [17] Isn't the wheat harvest today? I will call on the LORD and He will send thunder and rain, so that you will know and see what a great evil you committed in the LORD's sight by requesting a king for yourselves." [18] Samuel called on the LORD, and on that day the LORD sent thunder and rain. As a result, all the people greatly feared the LORD and Samuel.

[19] They pleaded with Samuel, "Pray to the LORD your God for your servants, so we won't die! For we have added to all our sins the evil of requesting a king for ourselves."

[20] Samuel replied, "Don't be afraid. Even though you have committed all this evil, don't turn away from following the LORD. Instead, worship the LORD with all your heart. [21] Don't turn away to follow worthless[c] things that can't profit or deliver you; they are worthless. [22] The LORD will not abandon His people, because of His great name and because He has determined to make you His own people.

[23] "As for me, I vow that I will not sin against the LORD by ceasing to pray for you. I will teach you the good and right way. [24] Above all, fear the LORD and worship Him faithfully with all your heart, considering the great things He has done for you. [25] However, if you continue to do what is evil, both you and your king will be swept away."

Saul's Failure

13 Saul was 30 years[d] old when he became king, and he reigned 42 years[e] over Israel.[f] [2] He chose 3,000 men from Israel for himself: 2,000 were with Saul at Michmash and in Bethel's hill country, and 1,000 were with Jonathan in Gibeah of Benjamin. He sent the rest of the troops away, each to his own tent.

"The Devil Made Me Do It"

1. How many "tardies" have you had this school year? Are you generally late or on time for your scheduled appointments? For practices?

1 Samuel 13:1-15

2. Only the priests were allowed to offer sacrifices, so Saul sinned when he did this. What motivated him to disregard this law?

3. How did Saul excuse himself for his sin? Whose fault was it, according to Saul?

4. Why did Saul say, "I forced myself to offer the burnt offering" (v. 12)? How do we sometimes make the same excuses to God that Saul made?

5. What commands of God, your teachers, or your coach do you sometimes ignore? How do you make excuses?

[3] Jonathan attacked the Philistine garrison[g] that was in Geba, and the Philistines heard about it. So Saul blew the ram's horn throughout the land saying, "Let the Hebrews hear!"[h] [4] And all Israel heard the news, "Saul has attacked the Philistine garrison,[g] and Israel is now repulsive to the Philistines." Then the troops were summoned to join Saul at Gilgal.

[5] The Philistines also gathered to fight against Israel: 3,000[i] chariots, 6,000 horsemen, and troops as numerous as the sand on the seashore. They went up and camped at Michmash, east of Beth-aven.[j]

[6] The men of Israel saw that they were in trouble because the troops were in a difficult situation. They hid in caves, thickets, among rocks, and in holes and cisterns. [7] Some Hebrews even crossed the Jordan to the land of Gad and Gilead.

Saul, however, was still at Gilgal, and all his troops were gripped with fear. [8] He waited seven days for the

---

^a**12:11** LXX, Syr; MT reads *Bedan*; Jdg 4:6; Heb 11:32 ^b**12:15** LXX reads *your king* ^c**12:21** LXX reads *away after empty* ^d**13:1** Some LXX mss; MT reads *was one year* ^e**13:1** Text emended to *42*; MT reads *two years* ^f**13:1** Some LXX mss omit v. 1 ^g**13:3,4** Or *governor* ^h**13:3** LXX reads *The slaves have revolted* ⁱ**13:5** One LXX ms, Syr; MT reads *30,000* ^j**13:5** LXX reads *Michmash, opposite Beth-horon to the south*

---

of God's defense attorney. His key point: "God keeps promises. Do the people keep theirs?"

12:11 He rescued you. During the time of the judges (between Joshua and Samuel), the people had developed a repetitive cycle of drawing close to God when they needed help, then falling away after the crisis cooled.

12:14 you and the king ... follow the LORD. Samuel reminded the people that establishing a king would not change the original covenant (Deut. 6:1-7) in which God claimed them as His own and established Himself as their provider.

12:17 wheat harvest ... thunder and rain. These acts of nature were most unusual during the months of the wheat harvest.

12:24 considering the great things He has done. Before Moses died, he reminded the people about the exodus and God's miraculous provisions (Deut. 4:10; 5:15; 7:18).

13:5 3,000 chariots. Without chariots, the Israelites were outnumbered and under-equipped.

appointed time that Samuel had set, but Samuel didn't come to Gilgal, and the troops were deserting him. 9 So Saul said, "Bring me the •burnt offering and the •fellowship offerings." Then he offered the burnt offering.

10 Just as he finished offering the burnt offering, Samuel arrived. So Saul went out to greet him, 11 and Samuel asked, "What have you done?"

Saul answered, "When I saw that the troops were deserting me and you didn't come within the appointed days and the Philistines were gathering at Michmash, 12 I thought: The Philistines will now descend on me at Gilgal, and I haven't sought the LORD's favor. So I forced myself to offer the burnt offering."

13 Samuel said to Saul, "You have been foolish. You have not kept the command which the LORD your God gave you. It was at this time that the LORD would have permanently established your reign over Israel, 14 but now your reign will not endure. The LORD has found a man loyal to Him,a and the LORD has appointed him as ruler over His people, because you have not done what the LORD commanded." 15 Then Samuel wentb from Gilgal to Gibeah in Benjamin. Saul registered the troops who were with him, about 600 men.

16 Saul, his son Jonathan, and the troops who were with them were staying in Geba of Benjamin, and the Philistines were camped at Michmash. 17 Raiding parties went out from the Philistine camp in three divisions. One division headed toward the Ophrah road leading to the land of Shual. 18 The next division headed toward the Beth-horon road, and the last division headed down the border road that looks out over the valley of Zeboim toward the wilderness.

19 No blacksmith could be found in all the land of Israel, because the Philistines had said, "Otherwise, the Hebrews will make swords or spears." 20 So all the Israelites went to the Philistines to sharpen their plowshares, mattocks, axes, and sickles.c 21 The price was two-thirds of a •shekeld for plowshares and mattocks, and one-third [of a shekel] for pitchforks and axes, and for putting a point on an oxgoad. 22 So on the day of battle not a sword or spear could be found in the hand of any of the troops who were with Saul and Jonathan; only Saul and his son Jonathan had [weapons].

Jonathan's Victory over the Philistines

14 23 Now a Philistine garrison took control of the pass at Michmash. 1 That same day Saul's son Jonathan said to the attendant who carried his weapons, "Come on, let's cross over to the Philistine garri-

son on the other side." However, he did not tell his father.

2 Saul was staying under the pomegranate tree in Migron on the outskirts of Gibeah.e The troops with him numbered about 600. 3 Ahijah, who was wearing an •ephod, [was also there]. He was the son of Ahitub, the brother of Ichabod son of Phinehas, son of Eli the LORD's priest at Shiloh. But the troops did not know that Jonathan had left.

4 There were sharp columnsf of rock on both sides of the pass that Jonathan intended to cross to reach the Philistine garrison. One was named Bozez and the other Seneh; 5 one stood to the north in front of Michmash and the other to the south in front of Geba. 6 Jonathan said to the attendant who carried his weapons, "Come on, let's cross over to the garrison of these uncircumcised men. Perhaps the LORD will help us. Nothing can keep the LORD from saving, whether by many or by few."

7 His armor-bearer responded, "Do what is in your heart. You choose. I'm right here with you whatever you decide."

8 "All right," Jonathan replied, "we'll cross over to the men and then let them see us. 9 If they say, 'Wait until we reach you,' then we will stay where we are and not go up to them. 10 But if they say, 'Come on up,' then we'll go up, because the LORD has handed them over to us—that will be our sign."

11 They let themselves be seen by the Philistine garrison, and the Philistines said, "Look, the Hebrews are coming out of the holes where they've been hiding!" 12 The men of the garrison called to Jonathan and his armor-bearer. "Come on up, and we'll teach you a lesson!" they said.

"Follow me," Jonathan told his armor-bearer, "for the LORD has handed them over to Israel." 13 Jonathan went up using his hands and feet, with his armor-bearer behind him. Jonathan cut them down, and his armor-bearer followed and finished them off. 14 In that first assault Jonathan and his armor-bearer struck down about 20 men in a half-acre field.

A Defeat for the Philistines

15 Terror spread through the [Philistine] camp and the open fields to all the troops. Even the garrison and the raiding parties were terrified. The earth shook, and terror from Godg spread. 16 When Saul's watchmen in Gibeah of Benjamin looked, they saw the panicking troops scattering in every direction. 17 So Saul said to the troops

---

a 13:14 Lit man according to His heart   b 13:15 LXX reads Samuel left Gilgal and went on his way, and the rest of the people followed Saul to join the people in his army. They went   c 13:20 LXX; MT reads plowshares   d 13:21 Lit was a pim; about ¼ ounce of silver   e 14:2 LXX reads on top of the hill   f 14:4 Lit There was a tooth   g 14:15 Or and a great terror

---

13:9 he offered the burnt offering. Saul was from the tribe of Benjamin, not Levi. Offering sacrifices was not his privilege. This choice was the watershed in Saul's reign. From this point, his decisions fail in wisdom and his influence plummets.

13:14 your reign will not endure. Though

Saul had three sons, his kingdom never passed through his family line. Because of David's kindness and loyalty, Mephibosheth, Jonathan's son and Saul's grandson, eventually ate at King David's table—the closest any of his descendants came to the monarchy (2 Sam. 9).

13:15 600 men. Saul had 3,000 soldiers at the start, but he lost 2,400 during the war at Gilgal.

13:22 sword or spear. The Philistines restricted the Israelites from working with metal. At a large disadvantage, they went to battle with weapons made only from natural

with him, "Call the roll and determine who has left us." They called the roll and saw that Jonathan and his armor-bearer were gone.

¹⁸ Saul told Ahijah, "Bring the ark of God," for it was with the Israelites[a] at that time. ¹⁹ While Saul spoke to the priest, the panic in the Philistine camp increased in intensity. So Saul said to the priest, "Stop what you're doing."[b]

²⁰ Saul and all the troops with him assembled and marched to the battle, and there, the Philistines were fighting against each other in great confusion! ²¹ There were Hebrews from the area who had gone earlier into the camp to join the Philistines, but even they joined the Israelites who were with Saul and Jonathan. ²² When all the Israelite men who had been hiding in the hill country of Ephraim heard that the Philistines were fleeing, they also joined Saul and Jonathan in the battle. ²³ So the LORD saved Israel that day.

Saul's Rash Oath

The battle extended beyond Beth-aven, ²⁴ and the men of Israel were worn out that day, for Saul had[c] placed the troops under an oath: "Cursed is the man who eats food before evening, before I have taken vengeance on my enemies." So none of the troops tasted ⌊any⌋ food.

²⁵ Everyone[d] went into the forest, and there was honey on the ground. ²⁶ When the troops entered the forest, they saw the flow of honey, but none of them ate any of it[e] because they feared the oath. ²⁷ However, Jonathan had not heard his father make the troops swear the oath. He reached out with the end of the staff he was carrying and dipped it into the honeycomb. When he ate the honey,[f] he had renewed energy. ²⁸ Then, one of the troops said, "Your father made the troops solemnly swear, 'Cursed is the man who eats food today,' and the troops are exhausted."

²⁹ Jonathan replied, "My father has brought trouble to the land. Just look at how I have renewed energy because I tasted a little honey. ³⁰ How much better if the troops had eaten freely today from the plunder they took from their enemies! Then the slaughter of the Philistines would have been much greater."

³¹ The Israelites struck down the Philistines that day from Michmash all the way to Aijalon. Since the Israelites were completely exhausted, ³² they rushed to the plunder, took sheep, cattle, and calves, slaughtered them on the ground, and ate ⌊meat⌋ with the blood ⌊still in it.⌋ ³³ Some reported to Saul: "Look, the troops are sinning against the LORD by eating ⌊meat⌋ with the blood ⌊still in it.⌋"

Saul said, "You have been unfaithful. Roll a large stone over here at once." ³⁴ He then said, "Go among the troops and say to them, 'Each man must bring me his ox or his sheep. Do the slaughtering here and then you can eat. Don't sin against the LORD by eating ⌊meat⌋ with the blood ⌊in it.⌋'" So every one of the troops brought his ox that night and slaughtered it there. ³⁵ Then Saul built an altar to the LORD; it was the first time he had built an altar to the LORD.

³⁶ Saul said, "Let's go down after the Philistines tonight and plunder them until morning. Don't let even one remain!"

"Do whatever you want,"[g] the troops replied.

But the priest said, "We must consult God here."

³⁷ So Saul inquired of God, "Should I go after the Philistines? Will You hand them over to Israel?" But God did not answer him that day.

³⁸ Saul said, "All you leaders of the troops, come here. Let us investigate how this sin has occurred today. ³⁹ As surely as the LORD lives who saves Israel, even if it is because of my son Jonathan, he must die!" Not one of the troops answered him.

⁴⁰ So he said to all Israel, "You will be on one side, and I and my son Jonathan will be on the other side."

And the troops replied, "Do whatever you want."[g]

⁴¹ So Saul said to the LORD, "God of Israel, give us the right ⌊decision⌋."[h] Jonathan and Saul were selected, and the troops were cleared ⌊of the charge⌋.

⁴² Then Saul said, "Cast ⌊the lot⌋ between me and my son Jonathan," and Jonathan was selected. ⁴³ Saul commanded him, "Tell me what you did."

Jonathan told him, "I tasted a little honey with the end of the staff I was carrying. I am ready to die!"

⁴⁴ Saul declared to him, "May God punish me severely if you do not die, Jonathan!"

⁴⁵ But the people said to Saul, "Must Jonathan die, who accomplished such a great deliverance for Israel? No, as the LORD lives, not a hair of his head will fall to the ground, for he worked with God's help today." So the people rescued Jonathan, and he did not die. ⁴⁶ Then Saul gave up the pursuit of the Philistines, and the Philistines returned to their own territory.

Summary of Saul's Kingship

⁴⁷ When Saul assumed the kingship over Israel, he fought against all his enemies in every direction:

ᵃ**14:18** LXX reads "Bring the ephod.î For he wore the ephod before Israel ᵇ**14:19** Lit Withdraw your hand ᶜ**14:24** LXX adds committed a great act of ignorance and ᵈ**14:25** Lit All the land ᵉ**14:26** Lit but there was none who raised his hand to his mouth ᶠ**14:27** Lit he returned his hand to his mouth ᵍ**14:36,40** Lit Do what is good in your eyes ʰ**14:41** LXX reads Israel, why have You not answered Your servant today? If the unrighteousness is in me or in my son Jonathan, LORD God of Israel, give Urim; but if the guilt is in Your people Israel, give Thummim.î

---

substances—bows, arrows, and slingshots.

14:15 terror from God. When the Philistines captured the ark, God sent a panic, but through plagues rather than earthquakes (5:9-10).

14:19 Stop what you're doing. The priests made decisions by reaching into the pocket of the ephod and pulling out stones. Saul was telling the priest to go ahead and check the stones.

14:24 I have taken vengeance. The conflict with the Philistines had become a personal agenda. Saul no longer representing God's interests.

14:33 [meat] with the blood [still in it]. The blood represented the life of the person or creature (Gen. 9:4; Lev. 17:11; Deut. 12:16). To this day, draining of blood is an important part of making meat kosher.

14:52 Philistines. The Philistines occupied the land between Israel and the Mediterra-

against Moab, the Ammonites, Edom, the kings of Zobah, and the Philistines. Wherever he turned, he caused havoc.ª ⁴⁸ He fought bravely, defeated the Amalekites, and delivered Israel from the hand of those who plundered them.

⁴⁹ Saul's sons were Jonathan, Ishvi, and Malchishua. The names of his two daughters were: Merab, his firstborn, and Michal, the younger. ⁵⁰ The name of Saul's wife was Ahinoam daughter of Ahimaaz. The name of the commander of his army was Abner son of Saul's uncle Ner. ⁵¹ Saul's father was Kish. Abner's father was Ner son of Abiel.

⁵² The conflict with the Philistines was fierce all of Saul's days, so whenever Saul noticed any strong or brave man, he enlisted him.

Saul Rejected as King

15 Samuel told Saul, "The LORD sent me to anoint you as king over His people Israel. Now, listen to the words of the LORD. ² This is what the LORD of •Hosts says: 'I witnessedᵇ what the Amalekites did to the Israelites when they opposed them along the way as they were coming out of Egypt. ³ Now go and attack the Amalekites and •completely destroy everything they have. Do not spare them. Kill men and women, children and infants, oxen and sheep, camels and donkeys.' "

⁴ Then Saul summoned the troops and counted them at Telaim: 200,000 foot soldiers and 10,000 men from Judah. ⁵ Saul came to the city of Amalek and set up an ambush in the •wadi. ⁶ He warned the Kenites, "Since you showed kindness to all the Israelites when they came out of Egypt, go on and leave! Get away from the Amalekites, or I'll sweep you away with them." So the Kenites withdrew from the Amalekites.

⁷ Then Saul struck down the Amalekites from Havilah all the way to Shur, which is next to Egypt. ⁸ He captured Agag king of Amalek alive, but he completely destroyed all the rest of the people with the sword. ⁹ Saul and the troops spared Agag, and the best of the sheep, cattle, and fatlings,ᶜ as well as the young rams and the best of everything else. They were not willing to destroy them, but they did destroy all the worthless and unwanted things.

¹⁰ Then the word of the LORD came to Samuel: ¹¹ "I regret that I made Saul king, for he has turned away from following Me and has not carried out My instructions." So Samuel became angry and cried out to the LORD ⌊all⌋ night.

¹² Early in the morning Samuel got up to confront Saul, but it was reported to Samuel, "Saul went to Car-

mel where he set up a monument for himself. Then he turned around and went down to Gilgal." ¹³ When Samuel came to him, Saul said, "May the LORD bless you. I have carried out the LORD's instructions."

¹⁴ Samuel replied, "Then what is this sound of sheepᵈ and cattle I hear?"

¹⁵ Saul answered, "The troops brought them from the Amalekites and spared the best sheep and cattle in order to offer a sacrifice to the LORD your God, but the rest we destroyed."

¹⁶ "Stop!" exclaimed Samuel. "Let me tell you what the LORD said to me last night."

"Tell me," he replied.

¹⁷ Samuel continued, "Although you once considered yourself unimportant, have you not become the leader of the tribes of Israel? The LORD anointed you king over Israel ¹⁸ and then sent you on a mission and said: 'Go and completely destroy the sinful Amalekites. Fight against them until you have annihilated them.' ¹⁹ So why didn't you obey the LORD? Why did you rush on the plunder and do what was evil in the LORD's sight?"

²⁰ "But I did obey the LORD!" Saul answered.ᵉ "I went on the mission the LORD gave me: I brought back Agag, king of Amalek, and I completely destroyed the Amalekites. ²¹ The troops took sheep and cattle from the plunder—the best of what was •set apart for destruction—to sacrifice to the LORD your God at Gilgal."

²² Then Samuel said:

Does the LORD take pleasure in •burnt offerings
    and sacrifices
as much as in obeying the LORD?

Look: to obey is better than sacrifice,
    to pay attention ⌊is better⌋ than the fat of rams.
23 For rebellion is like the sin of •divination,
    and defiance is like wickedness and idolatry.
    Because you have rejected the word of the LORD,
    He has rejected you as king.

²⁴ Saul answered Samuel, "I have sinned. I have transgressed the LORD's command and your words. Because I was afraid of the people, I obeyed them. ²⁵ Now therefore, please forgive my sin and return with me so I can worship the LORD."

²⁶ Samuel replied to Saul, "I will not return with you. Because you rejected the word of the LORD, the LORD has rejected you from being king over Israel." ²⁷ When Samuel turned to go, Saul grabbed the hem of his robe,

---

ª 14:47 LXX reads he was victorious ᵇ 15:2 LXX reads I will avenge ᶜ 15:9 LXX, Syr, Tg; Hb reads and the second ᵈ 15:14 Lit sheep in my ears ᵉ 15:20 Lit answered Samuel

---

nean Sea. With no natural boundaries the dividing line was always in dispute.

15:3 destroy everything. Everything—and everyone—that might witness to their values and culture could pollute the values and faith God was seeking to build in Israel, and therefore must be destroyed. **Kill ... children and**

infants. Most people today have a hard time reconciling such an order with the loving God revealed through Jesus Christ. Still, this was a different era, and we can't always understand from our limited perspective all that was necessary in order to establish Israel and their faith in the true God over against the other

cultures around them.

15:13 I have carried out the Lord's instructions. Saul was already making foolish decisions. Here he lied, intentionally stealing from God and deceiving God's representative.

15:15 The troops. Without much subtlety, Saul passed the blame. He blamed his sol-

and it tore. ²⁸ Samuel said to him, "The LORD has torn the kingship of Israel away from you today and has given it to your neighbor who is better than you. ²⁹ Furthermore, the Eternal One of Israel does not lie or change His mind, for He is not man who changes his mind."

³⁰ Saul said, "I have sinned. Please honor me now before the elders of my people and before Israel. Come back with me so I can bow and worship the LORD your God." ³¹ Then Samuel went back, following Saul, and Saul bowed down to the LORD.

³² Samuel said, "Bring me Agag king of Amalek."

Agag came to him trembling,ᵃ for he thought, "Certainly the bitterness of death has come."ᵇ

³³ Samuel declared:

As your sword has made women childless,
so your mother will be childless among women.

Then he hacked Agag to pieces before the LORD at Gilgal.

³⁴ Samuel went to Ramah, and Saul went up to his home in Gibeah of Saul. ³⁵ Even to the day of his death, Samuel never again visited Saul. Samuel mourned for Saul, and the LORD regretted He had made Saul king over Israel.

Samuel Anoints David

16 The LORD said to Samuel, "How long are you going to mourn for Saul, since I have rejected him as king over Israel? Fill your horn with oil and go. I am sending you to Jesse of Bethlehem because I have selected a king from his sons."

² Samuel asked, "How can I go? Saul will hear ⌊about it⌋ and kill me!"

The LORD answered, "Take a young cow with you and say, 'I have come to sacrifice to the LORD.' ³ Then invite Jesse to the sacrifice, and I will let you know what you are to do. You are to anoint for Me the one I indicate to you."

⁴ Samuel did what the LORD directed and went to Bethlehem. When the elders of the town met him, they trembledᶜ and asked, "Doᵈ you come in peace?"

⁵ "In peace," he replied. "I've come to sacrifice to the LORD. Consecrate yourselves and come with me to the sacrifice."ᵉ Then he consecrated Jesse and his sons and invited them to the sacrifice. ⁶ When they arrived, Samuel saw Eliab and said, "Certainly the LORD's anointed one is here before Him."

⁷ But the LORD said to Samuel, "Do not look at his appearance or his stature, because I have rejected him.

Man does not see what the LORD sees,ᶠ for man sees what is visible,ᵍ but the LORD sees the heart."

Seeing the Heart and Soul

1. When the elementary kids picked teams on the playground, how long did it usually take you to get chosen?

1 Samuel 16:1-13

2. What does "man sees what is visible but the LORD sees the heart" mean (v. 7)?
3. Why do you think God skipped over the older brothers and chose David?
4. How can outward appearances be misleading? How can you learn to see more the way God sees?
5. When the Lord looks at your heart, what does He see?

⁸ Jesse called Abinadab and presented him to Samuel. "The LORD hasn't chosen this one either," Samuel said. ⁹ Then Jesse presented Shammah, but Samuel said, "The LORD hasn't chosen this one either." ¹⁰ After Jesse presented seven of his sons to him, Samuel told Jesse, "The LORD hasn't chosen any of these." ¹¹ Samuel asked him, "Are these all the sons you have?"

"There is still the youngest," he answered, "but right now he's tending the sheep." Samuel told Jesse, "Send for him. We won't sit down to eat until he gets here." ¹² So Jesse sent for him. He had beautiful eyes and a healthy,ʰ handsome appearance.

Then the LORD said, "Anoint him, for he is the one." ¹³ So Samuel took the horn of oil, anointed him in the presence of his brothers, and the Spirit of the LORD took control of David from that day forward. Then Samuel set out and went to Ramah.

David in Saul's Court

¹⁴ Now the Spirit of the LORD had left Saul, and an evil spirit from the LORD began to torment him, ¹⁵ so Saul's servants said to him, "You see that an evil spirit from God is tormenting you. ¹⁶ Let our lord command your servants here in your presence to look for some-

---

ᵃ**15:32** Hb obscure ᵇ**15:32** LXX reads *Is death bitter in this way?* ᶜ**16:4** LXX reads *were astonished* ᵈ**16:4** DSS, LXX read *Seer, do* ᵉ**16:5** LXX reads *and rejoice with me today* ᶠ**16:7** LXX reads *God does not see as a man sees* ᵍ**16:7** Lit *what is of the eyes* ʰ**16:12** Or *reddish*

---

diers and took no responsibility himself. Saul was like Adam when he said, "The woman You gave" and Eve saying, "It was serpent" (Gen. 3:12-13).

15:15 the LORD your God. Saul's choice of pronouns, from "my God" to "your God," is an indication of his shift in loyalty.

15:35 the LORD regretted. Before Noah and the flood, God was grieved that He had even created humankind (Gen. 6:6-8).

16:2 Saul will ... kill me. In order to go where God had commanded, he had to pass through Saul's town. Samuel had already told Saul that his kingdom would be replaced

(15:28), so Saul could have been paranoid. Anointing a new king would be seen as an act of treason.

16:7 appearance ... stature. The choice of Saul had been based on distinctive physical attributes. He was an "impressive young man ... a head taller than anyone else." (9:2). Now

one who knows how to play the harp. Whenever the evil spirit from God ⌊troubles⌋ you, that person can play the harp, and you will feel better."

17 Then Saul commanded his servants, "Find me someone who plays well and bring him to me."

18 One of the young men answered, "I have seen a son of Jesse of Bethlehem who knows how to play ⌊the harp⌋. He is also a valiant man, a warrior, eloquent, handsome, and the LORD is with him."

19 Then Saul dispatched messengers to Jesse and said, "Send me your son David, who is with the sheep."

20 So Jesse took a donkey loaded with bread, a skin of wine, and one young goat and sent them by his son David to Saul. 21 When David came to Saul and entered his service, Saul admired him greatly, and David became his armor-bearer. 22 Then Saul sent word to Jesse: "Let David remain in my service, for I am pleased with him." 23 Whenever the spirit from God ⌊troubled⌋ Saul, David would pick up his harp and play, and Saul would then be relieved, feel better, and the evil spirit would leave him.

David versus Goliath

17 The Philistines gathered their forces for war at Socoh in Judah and camped between Socoh and Azekah in Ephes-dammim. 2 Saul and the men of Israel gathered and camped in the Valley of Elah; then they lined up in battle formation to face the Philistines.

3 The Philistines were standing on one hill, and the Israelites were standing on another hill with a ravine between them. 4 Then a champion named Goliath, from Gath, came out from the Philistine camp. He was nine feet, nine inches tall[a] [b] 5 and wore a bronze helmet[c] and bronze scale armor that weighed 125 pounds.[d] 6 There was bronze armor on his shins, and a bronze sword was slung between his shoulders. 7 His spear shaft was like a weaver's beam, and the iron point of his spear weighed 15 pounds.[e] In addition, a shield-bearer was walking in front of him.

8 He stood and shouted to the Israelite battle formations: "Why do you come out to line up in battle formation?" He asked them, "Am I not a Philistine and are you not servants of Saul? Choose one of your men and have him come down against me. 9 If he wins in a fight against me and kills me, we will be your servants. But if I win against him and kill him, then you will be our servants and serve us." 10 Then the Philistine said, "I defy the ranks of Israel today. Send me a man so we can fight each other!" 11 When Saul and all Israel heard these words from the Philistine, they lost their courage and were terrified.

12 Now David was the son of the Ephrathite from Bethlehem of Judah named Jesse. Jesse had eight sons, and during Saul's reign was ⌊already⌋ an old man. 13 Jesse's three oldest sons had followed Saul to the war, and their names were Eliab, the firstborn, Abinadab, the next, and Shammah, the third, 14 and David was the youngest. The three oldest had followed Saul, 15 but David kept going back and forth from Saul to tend his father's flock in Bethlehem.

16 Every morning and evening for 40 days the Philistine came forward and took his stand. 17 ⌊One day⌋, Jesse had told his son David, "Take this half-bushel[f] of roasted grain along with these loaves of bread for your brothers and hurry to their camp. 18 Also, take these 10 portions of cheese to the field commander.[g] Check on the welfare of your brothers and bring a confirmation from them. 19 They are with Saul and all the men of Israel are in the Valley of Elah fighting with the Philistines."

20 So David got up early in the morning, left the flock with someone to keep it, loaded up, and set out as Jesse had instructed him.

He arrived at the perimeter of the camp as the army was marching out to its battle formation shouting their battle cry. 21 Israel and the Philistines lined up in battle formation facing each other. 22 David left his supplies in the care of the quartermaster and ran to the battle line. When he arrived, he asked his brothers how they were. 23 While he was speaking with them, suddenly the champion named Goliath, the Philistine from Gath, came forward from the Philistine battle line and shouted his usual words, which David heard. 24 When all the Israelite men saw Goliath, they retreated from him terrified.

25 Previously, an Israelite man had declared, "Do you see this man who keeps coming out? He comes to defy Israel. The king will make the man who kills him very rich and will give him his daughter. The king will also make the household of that man's father exempt from paying taxes in Israel."

26 David spoke to the men who were standing with him: "What will be done for the man who kills that Philistine and removes this disgrace from Israel? Just who is this uncircumcised Philistine that he should defy the armies of the living God?"

27 The people told him about the offer, concluding, "That is what will be done for the man who kills him."

---

a 17:4 DSS, LXX read four cubits and a span   b 17:4 Lit was six cubits and a span   c 17:5 Lit helmet on his head   d 17:5 Lit 5,000 shekels
e 17:7 Lit 600 shekels   f 17:17 Lit this ephah   g 17:18 Lit the leader of 1,000

Samuel is instructed to ignore those criteria.

16:11 There is still the youngest. Generally priority went with being the eldest, not the youngest. However, David came to the throne as the youngest of a long line of brothers. This may have resulted in the humility that David often showed. Significantly, Jesus later taught, "whoever is greatest among you must become like the youngest" (Luke 22:26.)

16:14 evil spirit from the LORD. Evil spirits, like everything else in creation, are ultimately under God's control and cannot move where they are not allowed. **torment him.** Saul was tormented with depression and jealousy.

16:16 the person can play the harp. David, the future king, calmed Saul's spirit with music. God's Spirit had left Saul and rested on David. And the Spirit, expressed through the music, was the reason Saul felt relief.

16:18-19 David. David was a warrior-musician. Music brought him to the palace, and

Training for Action

1. Who bullied you when you were a child?

1 Samuel 17:20-50

2. Why does David consider Goliath to be "a disgrace" to Israel (v. 26)?

3. What is David's real motivation in fighting Goliath: Fame? The reward? God's honor? His own glory?

4. How had God prepared David for this battle? How might small events in your life be preparing you for a significant event or challenge in the future? Are you disciplined in practices or preparations for upcoming events?

5. Why did David choose to fight with a sling instead of conventional weapons? How might God be able to use your skills to accomplish great things?

28 David's oldest brother Eliab listened as he spoke to the men, and became angry with him. "Why did you come down here?" he asked. "Who did you leave those few sheep with in the wilderness? I know your arrogance and your evil heart—you came down to see the battle!"

29 "What have I done now?" protested David. "It was just a question." 30 Then he turned from those beside him to others in front of him and asked about the offer. The people gave him the same answer as before.

31 What David said was overheard and reported to Saul, so he had David brought to him. 32 David said to Saul, "Don't let anyone be discouraged by[a] him; your servant will go and fight this Philistine!"

33 But Saul replied, "You can't go fight this Philistine. You're just a youth, and he's been a warrior since he was young."

34 David answered Saul, "Your servant has been tending his father's sheep. Whenever a lion or a bear came and carried off a lamb from the flock, 35 I went after it, struck it down, and rescued ⌊the lamb⌋ from its mouth. If it reared up against me, I would grab it by its fur,[b] strike it down, and kill it. 36 Your servant has killed lions and bears; this uncircumcised Philistine will be like one of them, for he has defied the armies of the living God." 37 Then David said, "The LORD who res-

cued me from the paw of the lion and the paw of the bear will rescue me from the hand of this Philistine."

Saul said to David, "Go, and may the LORD be with you."

38 Then Saul had his own military clothes put on David. He put a bronze helmet on David's head and had him put on armor. 39 David strapped his sword on over the military clothes and tried to walk, but he was not used to them. "I can't walk in these," David said to Saul, "I'm not used to them." So David took them off. 40 Instead, he took his staff in his hand and chose five smooth stones from the •wadi and put them in the pouch, in his shepherd's bag. Then, with his sling in his hand, he approached the Philistine.

41 The Philistine came closer and closer to David, with the shield-bearer in front of him. 42 When the Philistine looked and saw David, he despised him because he was just a youth, healthy[c] and handsome. 43 He said to David, "Am I a dog that you come against me with sticks?"[d] Then he cursed David by his gods. 44 "Come here," the Philistine called to David, "and I'll give your flesh to the birds of the sky and the wild beasts!"

45 David said to the Philistine, "You come against me with a dagger, spear, and sword, but I come against you in the name of the LORD of •Hosts, the God of Israel's armies—you have defied Him. 46 Today, the LORD will hand you over to me. Today, I'll strike you down, cut your head off, and give the corpses[e] of the Philistine camp to the birds of the sky and the creatures of the earth. Then all the world will know that Israel has a God, 47 and this whole assembly will know that it is not by sword or by spear that the LORD saves, for the battle is the LORD's. He will hand you over to us."

48 When the Philistine started forward to attack him, David ran quickly to the battle line to meet the Philistine. 49 David put his hand in the bag, took out a stone, slung ⌊it⌋, and hit the Philistine on his forehead. The stone sank into his forehead, and he fell on his face to the ground. 50 David defeated the Philistine with a sling and a stone. Even though David had no sword, he struck down the Philistine and killed him. 51 David ran and stood over him. He grabbed the Philistine's sword, pulled it from its sheath, and used it to kill him. Then he cut off his head. When the Philistines saw that their hero was dead, they ran. 52 The men of Israel and Judah rallied, shouting their battle cry, and chased the Philistines to the entrance of the valley and to the gates of Ekron.[f] Philistine bodies were strewn all along the Shaaraim road to Gath and Ekron.

---

[a]**17:32** Lit *let a man's heart fall over*   [b]**17:35** LXX reads *throat*   [c]**17:42** Or *reddish*   [d]**17:43** Some LXX mss add *and stones?" And David said, "No! Worse than a dog!"*   [e]**17:46** LXX reads *give your limbs and the limbs*   [f]**17:52** LXX reads *Ashkelon*

---

his fighting skills won the victory against Goliath (17:46-58) and fame among the Israelites. But faith would make him God's choice as king (13:14).

17:28 your arrogance. The words of Eliab, David's oldest brother, give insight into David's character. While a brother may per-

ceive conceit, it was David's confidence in himself and God that saved Israel that day.

17:33 You're just a youth. By this point, Saul saw only the physical dimensions of the battle. His eyes were blind to the more crucial spiritual battle underway.

17:34 lion. David wasn't the only hero to face

lions. Samson fought a young lion (Judg. 14:5-6). Benaiah, one of David's mighty men, was known for killing a lion (2 Sam. 23:20). And Daniel faced lions as punishment for his crime of praying (Dan. 6:22).

17:46 all the world will know. David's motivation for victory is completely different than

53 When the Israelites returned from the pursuit of the Philistines, they plundered their camps. 54 David took Goliath's^a head and brought it to Jerusalem, but he put Goliath's weapons in his ⌊own⌋ tent.

55 When^b Saul had seen David going out to confront the Philistine, he asked Abner the commander of the army, "Whose son is this youth, Abner?"

"⌊My⌋ king, as surely as you live, I don't know," Abner replied.

56 The king said, "Find out whose son this young man is!"

57 When David returned from killing the Philistine, Abner took him and brought him before Saul with the Philistine's head still in his hand. 58 Saul said to him, "Whose son are you, young man?"

"The son of your servant Jesse of Bethlehem," David answered.

David's Success

18 When David had finished speaking with Saul, Jonathan committed himself to David, and loved him as much as he loved himself. 2 Saul kept David with him from that day on and did not let him return to his father's house.

3 Jonathan made a covenant with David because he loved him as much as himself. 4 Then Jonathan removed the robe he was wearing and gave it to David, along with his military tunic, his sword, his bow, and his belt.

5 David marched out ⌊with the army⌋, and was successful in everything Saul sent him to do. Saul put him in command of the soldiers, which pleased all the people and Saul's servants as well.

6 As David was returning from killing the Philistine, the women came out from all the cities of Israel to meet King Saul, singing and dancing with tambourines, with shouts of joy, and with three-stringed instruments. 7 As they celebrated, the women sang:

> Saul has killed his thousands,
> but David his tens of thousands.

8 Saul was furious and resented this song.^c "They credited tens of thousands to David," he complained, "but they only credited me with thousands. What more can he have but the kingdom?" 9 So Saul watched David jealously from that day forward.

Saul Attempts to Kill David

10 The next day an evil spirit from God took control of Saul, and he began to rave^d inside the palace. David

Friends and Foes

1. Who was your best friend in grade school? Did you ever swap or give each other stuff?

1 Samuel 18:1-16

2. Why did Saul try to kill David?
3. Why did Jonathan give these particular gifts to David (v. 4)? As a warrior, how might these gifts have been costly to Jonathan and meaningful to David?
4. Is there jealousy in your life? How is it affecting you? What can you do about it?
5. Are you a generous friend like Jonathan? Who in your group or team has been such a friend to you?

was playing ⌊the harp⌋ as usual, but Saul was holding a spear, 11 and he threw it, thinking, "I'll pin David to the wall." But David got away from him twice.

12 Saul was afraid of David, because the LORD was with David but had left from Saul. 13 Therefore, Saul reassigned David and made him commander over 1,000 men. David led the troops 14 and continued to be successful in all his activities because the LORD was with him. 15 When Saul observed that David was very successful, he dreaded him. 16 But all Israel and Judah loved David because he was leading their troops. 17 Saul told David, "Here is my oldest daughter Merab. I'll give her to you as a wife, if you will be a warrior for me and fight the LORD's battles." But Saul was thinking, "My hand doesn't need to be against him; let the hand of the Philistines be against him."

18 Then David responded, "Who am I, and what is my family or my father's clan in Israel that I should become the king's son-in-law?" 19 When it was time to give Saul's daughter Merab to David, she was given to Adriel the Meholathite as a wife.

David's Marriage to Michal

20 Now Saul's daughter Michal loved David, and when it was reported to Saul, it pleased him.^e 21 "I'll give her to him," Saul thought. "She'll be a trap for him, and the hand of the Philistines will be against him." So

---

^a**17:54** Lit *the Philistine's*   ^b**17:55** LXX omits 1 Sm 17:55—18:5   ^c**18:8** Lit *furious; this saying was evil in his eyes*   ^d**18:10** Or *prophesy*   ^e**18:20** Lit *Saul, the thing was right in his eyes*

Saul's. David's ambitions are directed toward glorifying God.

17:54 Goliath's weapons. Later, when hiding from Saul, David was given Goliath's sword for protection. At the time it was in the tabernacle, so David must have dedicated the sword, if not the rest of the weap-

ons, to the Lord.

18:1 Jonathan. David and Jonathan became best friends. Eventually David would be crowned in Jonathan's place as Saul's successor. Their friendship survived even this test. **loved him as much as he loved himself.** Jonathan's love for David was like the

Law (Lev. 19:18) and later Jesus (Matt. 22:39) said we all should love.

18:13 reassigned David. In other words, Saul sent David to war. Saul hoped David would be killed in battle and thus be out of the way. Years later, David would use this same tactic with Uriah, Bathsheba's husband (2

Saul said to David a second time, "You can now be my son-in-law."

22 Saul then ordered his servants, "Speak to David in private and tell him, 'Look, the king is pleased with you, and all his servants love you. Therefore, you should become the king's son-in-law.' "

23 Saul's servants reported these words directly to David,[a] but he replied, "Is it trivial in your sight to become the king's son-in-law? I am a poor man who is common."

24 The servants reported back to Saul, "These are the words David spoke."

25 Then Saul replied, "Say this to David: 'The king desires no other bride-price except 100 Philistine foreskins, to take revenge on his enemies.' " Actually, Saul intended to cause David's death at the hands of the Philistines.

26 When the servants reported these terms to David, he was pleased[b] to become the king's son-in-law. Before the wedding day arrived,[c] 27 David and his men went out and killed 200[d] Philistines. He brought their foreskins and presented them as full payment to the king to become his son-in-law. Then Saul gave his daughter Michal to David as his wife. 28 Saul realized that the LORD was with David and that his daughter Michal loved him, 29 and he became even more afraid of David. As a result, Saul was David's enemy from then on.

30 Every time the Philistine commanders came out to fight, David was more successful than all of Saul's officers. So his name became very famous.

David Delivered from Saul

19 Saul ordered his son Jonathan and all his servants to kill David. But Saul's son Jonathan liked David very much, 2 so he told him: "My father Saul intends to kill you. Be on your guard in the morning and hide in a secret place and stay there. 3 I'll go out and stand beside my father in the field where you are and talk to him about you. When I see what [he says], I'll tell you."

4 Jonathan spoke well of David to his father Saul. He said to him: "The king should not sin against his servant David. He hasn't sinned against you; in fact, his actions have been a great advantage to you. 5 He took his life in his hands when he struck down the Philistine, and the LORD brought about a great victory for all Israel. You saw it and rejoiced, so why would you sin against innocent blood by killing David for no reason?"

6 Saul listened to Jonathan's advice and swore an oath: "As surely as the LORD lives, David will not be killed." 7 So Jonathan summoned David and told him all these words. Then Jonathan brought David to Saul, and he served him as [he did] before.

8 When war broke out again, David went out and fought against the Philistines. He defeated them with such a great force that they fled from him.

9 Now an evil spirit from the LORD came on Saul as he was sitting in his palace holding a spear. David was playing [the harp], 10 and Saul tried to pin David to the wall with the spear. As the spear struck the wall, David eluded Saul and escaped. That night he ran away. 11 Saul sent agents to David's house to watch for him and kill him in the morning. But his wife Michal warned David: "If you don't escape tonight, you will be dead tomorrow!" 12 So she lowered David from the window, and he fled and escaped. 13 Then Michal took the household idol and put it on the bed, placed some goats' hair on its head, and covered it with a garment. 14 When Saul sent agents to seize David, Michal said, "He's sick."

15 Saul sent the agents [back] to see David and said, "Bring him on his bed so I can kill him." 16 When the messengers arrived, to their surprise, the household idol was on the bed with some goats' hair on its head.

17 Saul asked Michal, "Why did you deceive me like this? You sent my enemy away, and he has escaped!"

She answered him, "He said to me, 'Let me go! Why should I kill you?' "

18 So David fled and escaped and went to Samuel at Ramah and told him everything Saul had done to him. Then he and Samuel left and stayed at Naioth.

19 When it was reported to Saul that David was at Naioth in Ramah, 20 Saul sent agents to seize David. However, when they saw the group of prophets prophesying with Samuel leading them, the Spirit of God came on Saul's agents, and they also started prophesying. 21 When they reported to Saul, he sent other agents, and they also began prophesying. So Saul tried again and sent a third group of agents, and even they began prophesying. 22 Then Saul himself went to Ramah. He came to the large cistern at Secu, looked around, and asked, "Where are Samuel and David?"

"At Naioth in Ramah," someone said.

23 So he went to Naioth in Ramah. The Spirit of God also came on him, and as he walked along, he prophesied until he entered Naioth in Ramah. 24 Saul then removed his clothes and also prophesied before Samuel; he collapsed [and lay] naked all that day and all that night. That is why they say, "Is Saul also among the prophets?"

---

[a] **18:23** Lit words in David's ears   [b] **18:26** Lit David, it was right in David's eyes   [c] **18:26** Lit And the days were not full   [d] **18:27** LXX reads 100

Sam. 11:14-15).

18:25 bride-price. A future husband brought some wealth to the father of the bride. This practice is still followed in many parts of the world.

18:28 Michal loved him. No matter how Saul tried to get rid of David, God used that very

scheme to bring David closer. Rather than falling in battle, David became a national hero, best friend of the king's son, and then husband to the king's daughter. Could Saul be getting a message?

19:1 kill David. He was so unaware of the dynamics in his family and court that he shared

that news with his son, David's best friend.

19:13 Michal took the household idol. That the family had such idols is disturbing and evidence of the fact that at very least Saul's family had less than full allegiance to the God of Israel. This one was large enough to be mistaken for an adult human being.

Jonathan Protects David

20 David fled from Naioth in Ramah and came to Jonathan and asked, "What have I done? What did I do wrong? How have I sinned against your father so that he wants to take my life?"

Okay to Disobey

1. What secret ways of communicating have you tried with a friend: Secret handshake? Sign language? Passing notes?

1 Samuel 20:1-13,18-42

2. Why did Jonathan take such risks to help David?

3. Was Jonathan right in helping David, instead of helping his father? Why?

4. When are Christians justified in disobeying human authorities? When are we not justified?

5. Jonathan and David fled from Saul, but didn't fight him. What does that suggest about how to "disobey" ungodly orders?

² Jonathan said to him, "No, you won't die. Listen, my father doesn't do anything, great or small, without telling me.ᵃ So why would he hide this matter from me? This can't be ⌊true⌋."

³ But David said, "Your father certainly knows that you have come to look favorably on me. He has said, 'Jonathan must not know of this, or else he will be grieved.'" David also swore, "As surely as the LORD lives and as you yourself live, there is but a step between me and death."

⁴ Jonathan said to David, "Whatever you say, I will do for you."

⁵ So David told him, "Look, tomorrow is the New Moon, and I'm supposed to sit down and eat with the king. Instead, let me go, and I'll hide in the field until the third night. ⁶ If your father misses me at all, say, 'David urgently requested my permission to quickly go to his town Bethlehem for an annual sacrifice there involving the whole clan.' ⁷ If he says, 'Good,' then your servant is safe, but if he becomes angry, you will know he has evil intentions. ⁸ Deal faithfully with your servant, for you have brought me into a covenant before the LORD with you. If I have done anything wrong, then kill me yourself; why take me to your father?"

⁹ "No!" Jonathan responded. "If I ever find out my father has evil intentions against you, wouldn't I tell you about it?"

¹⁰ So David asked Jonathan, "Who will tell me if your father answers you harshly?"

¹¹ He answered David, "Come on, let's go out to the field." So both of them went out to the field. ¹² "By the LORD, the God of Israel, if I sound out my father by this time tomorrow or the next day and I find out that he is favorable toward you, and if I do not send for you and tell you,ᵇ ¹³ then may God punish Jonathan and do so severely. If my father intends to bring evil on you, then I will tell you,ᶜ and I will send you away, and you will go in peace. May the LORD be with you, just as He was with my father. ¹⁴ If I continue to live, treat me with the LORD's faithful love, but if I die, ¹⁵ don't ever withdraw your faithful love from my household—not even when the LORD cuts off every one of David's enemies from the face of the earth." ¹⁶ Then Jonathan made a covenant with the house of David, saying, "May the LORD hold David's enemies accountable."ᵈ ¹⁷ Jonathan once again swore to David in his love for him, because he loved him as he loved himself.

¹⁸ Then Jonathan said to him, "Tomorrow is the New Moon; you'll be missed because your seat will be empty. ¹⁹ The following day hurry down and go to the place where you hid on the day this incident began and stay beside the rock Ezel. ²⁰ I will shoot three arrows beside it as if I'm aiming at a target. ²¹ Then I will send the young man ⌊and say⌋, 'Go and find the arrows!' Now, if I expressly say to the young man, 'Look, the arrows are on this side of you—get them,' then come, because as the LORD lives, it is safe for you and there is no problem. ²² But if I say this to the youth: 'Look, the arrows are beyond you!' then go, for the LORD is sending you away. ²³ As for the matter you and I have spoken about, the LORD will be a witnessᵉ between you and me forever." ²⁴ So David hid in the field.

At the New Moon, the king sat down to eat the meal. ²⁵ He sat at his usual place on the seat by the wall. Jonathan sat facing himᶠ and Abner took his place beside Saul, but David's place was empty. ²⁶ Saul did not say anything that day because he thought, "Something unexpected has happened; he must be ceremonially unclean—yes, that's it, he is unclean."

ᵃ**20:2** Lit *without uncovering my ear*   ᵇ**20:12** Lit *and uncover your ear*   ᶜ**20:13** Lit *will uncover your ears*   ᵈ**20:16** Lit *LORD require it from the hand of David's enemies*   ᵉ**20:23** LXX; MT omits *a witness*   ᶠ**20:25** Text emended; MT reads *Jonathan got up*

20:11 Jonathan's words to David were the same as Cain's to Abel (Gen. 4:8). Yet, Jonathan's motivation was to save the life of his friend.

20:14 treat me with the LORD's faithful love. In Jonathan's mind, as long as descendants of Saul existed, David might fear a rebellion.

In fact, it was common for a new monarch to kill any heirs from the previous royal line. Here, Jonathan requested the survival of his family amid the change of kings.

20:15 my household. Many years later, David invited Jonathan's son, Mephibosheth, to eat at the royal table (2 Sam. 9:6-10).

20:31 you and your kingship. Saul saw the end of their legacy and tried to kill the culprit. Jonathan saw the end of their legacy and wanted to be a part of what God was doing.

20:41 kissed each other and wept with each other. This was a culture where men were not afraid to show feelings, even show-

27 However, the day after the New Moon, the second day, David's place was ⌞still⌟ empty, and Saul asked his son Jonathan, "Why didn't Jesse's son come to the meal either yesterday or today?"

28 Jonathan answered, "David asked for my permission to go to Bethlehem. 29 He said, 'Please let me go because our clan is holding a sacrifice in the town, and my brother has told me to be there. So now, if you are pleased with me, let me go so I can see my brothers.' That's why he didn't come to the king's table."

30 Then Saul became angry with Jonathan and shouted, "You son of a perverse and rebellious woman! Don't I know that you are siding with Jesse's son to your own shame and to the disgrace of your mother?a 31 Every day Jesse's son lives on earth you and your kingship are not secure. Now send for him and bring him to me—he deserves to die."

32 Jonathan answered his father back: "Why is he to be killed? What has he done?"

33 Then Saul threw his spear at Jonathan to kill him, so he knew that his father was determined to kill David. 34 He got up from the table in fierce anger and did not eat any food that second day of the New Moon, for he was grieved because of his father's shameful behavior toward David.

35 In the morning Jonathan went out to the field for the appointed meeting with David. A small young man was with him. 36 He said to the young man, "Run and find the arrows I'm shooting." As the young man ran, Jonathan shot an arrow beyond him. 37 He came to the location of the arrow that Jonathan had shot, but Jonathan called to him and said, "The arrow is beyond you, isn't it?" 38 Then Jonathan called to him, "Hurry up and don't stop!" Jonathan's young man picked up the arrow and returned to his master. 39 He did not know anything; only Jonathan and David knew the arrangement. 40 Then Jonathan gave his equipment to the young man who was with him and said, "Go, take it back to the city."

41 When the young man had gone, David got up from the south side of the stone Ezel, fell with his face to the ground, and bowed three times. Then he and Jonathan kissed each other and wept with each other, though David wept more.

42 Jonathan then said to David, "Go in the assurance the two of us pledged in the name of the LORD when we said: The LORD will be ⌞a witness⌟ between you and me and between my offspring and your offspring forever."b Then David left, and Jonathan went into the city.

David Flees to Nob

21 David went to Ahimelech the priest at Nob. Ahimelech was afraid to meet David, so he said to him, "Why are you alone and no one is with you?"

2 David answered Ahimelech the priest, "The king gave me a mission, but he told me, 'Don't let anyone know anything about the mission I'm sending you on or what I have ordered you ⌞to do⌟.' I have stationed ⌞my⌟ young men at a certain place. 3 Now what do you have on hand? Give me five loaves of bread or whatever can be found."

4 The priest told him, "There is no ordinary bread on hand. However, there is consecrated bread, but the young men may eat itc only if they have kept themselves from women."

5 David answered him, "I swear that women are being kept from us, as always when I go out ⌞to battle⌟. The young men's bodiesd are consecrated even on an ordinary mission, so of course their bodies are consecrated today." 6 So the priest gave him the consecrated ⌞bread⌟, for there was no bread there except the bread of the Presence that had been removed from before the LORD. When the bread was removed, it had been replaced with warm bread.

7 One of Saul's servants, detained before the LORD, was there that day. His name was Doeg the Edomite, chief of Saul's shepherds.

8 David said to Ahimelech, "Do you have a spear or sword on hand? I didn't even bring my sword or my weapons since the king's mission was urgent."

9 The priest replied, "The sword of Goliath the Philistine, whom you killed in the valley of Elah, is here, wrapped in a cloth behind the •ephod. If you want to take it for yourself, then take it, for there isn't another one here."

"There's none like it!" David said. "Give it to me."

David Flees to Gath

10 David fled that day from Saul's presence and went to King Achish of Gath. 11 But Achish's servants said to him, "Isn't this David, the king of the land? Don't they sing about him during their dances:

Saul has killed his thousands,
but David his tens of thousands?"

12 David took this to hearte and became very afraid of King Achish of Gath, 13 so he pretended to be insane in their presence. He acted like a madman around them,f scribblingg on the doors of the gate and letting saliva run down his beard.

---

a20:30 Lit your mother's genitals   b20:42 The last sentence of v. 42 is 1 Sm 21:1 in Hb.   c21:4 DSS; MT omits may eat it   d21:5 Lit vessels   e21:12 Lit David placed these words in his heart   f21:13 Lit madman in their hand   g21:13 LXX reads drumming

---

ing affection to each other. The kisses would have been on the cheek.

21:2 Don't let anyone know. David was less than forthcoming with Ahimelech the priest. David's "the-less-you-know-the-better" tactic unraveled when the priest was killed (22:16-18).

21:4 bread. Bread was always kept at the tabernacle. When a fresh supply was made, the old was given to the priests. David's request was contrary to what this bread was supposed to be used for. Jesus referred to this incident in Matthew 12:3-4, implying that some laws and traditions are secondary to

human need.

22:4 Moab. David's great-grandmother, Ruth, came from Moab, so he had extended family there.

22:5 Gad. The prophet became a regular among David's entourage. Gad confronted

14 "Look! You can see the man is crazy," Achish said to his servants. "Why did you bring him to me? 15 Do I have such a shortage of crazy people that you brought this one to act crazy around me? Is this one going to come into my house?"

Saul's Increasing Paranoia

22 So David left Gath and took refuge in the cave of Adullam. When David's brothers and his father's whole family heard, they went down and joined him there. 2 In addition, every man who was desperate, in debt, or discontented rallied around him, and he became their leader. About 400 men were with him.

3 From there David went to Mizpeh of Moab where he said to the king of Moab, "Please let my father and mother stay with you until I know what God will do for me." 4 So he left them in the care of the king of Moab, and they stayed with him the whole time David was in the stronghold.

5 Then the prophet Gad said to David, "Don't stay in the stronghold. Leave and return to the land of Judah." So David left and went to the forest of Hereth.

6 Saul heard that David and his men had been discovered. At that time Saul was in Gibeah, sitting under the tamarisk tree at the •high place. His spear was in his hand, and all his servants were standing around him. 7 Saul said to his servants, "Listen, men of Benjamin: Is Jesse's son going to give all of you fields and vineyards? ⌊Do you think⌋ he'll make all of you commanders of thousands and commanders of hundreds? 8 That's why all of you have conspired against me! Nobody tells me[a] when my own son makes a covenant with Jesse's son. None of you cares about me or tells me[b] that my son has stirred up my own servant to wait in ambush for me, as ⌊is the case⌋ today."

9 Then Doeg the Edomite, who was in charge of Saul's servants, answered: "I saw Jesse's son come to Ahimelech son of Ahitub at Nob. 10 Ahimelech inquired of the LORD for him and gave him provisions. He also gave him the sword of Goliath the Philistine."

Slaughter of the Priests

11 The king sent ⌊messengers⌋ to summon Ahimelech the priest, son of Ahitub, and his father's whole family, who were priests in Nob. All of them came to the king. 12 Then Saul said, "Listen, son of Ahitub!"

"I'm at your service, my lord," he said.

13 Saul asked him, "Why did you and Jesse's son conspire against me? You gave him bread and a sword and inquired of God for him, so he could rise up against me and wait in ambush, as ⌊is the case⌋ today."

14 Ahimelech replied to the king: "Who among all your servants is as faithful as David? He is the king's son-in-law, captain of your bodyguard, and honored in your house. 15 Was today the first time I inquired of God for him? Of course not! Please don't let the king make an accusation against your servant or any of my father's household, for your servant didn't have any idea[c] about all this."

16 But the king said, "You will die, Ahimelech—you and your father's whole family!"

17 Then the king ordered the guards standing by him, "Turn and kill the priests of the LORD because they sided with David. For they knew he was fleeing, but they didn't tell me."[d] But the king's servants would not lift a hand to execute the priests of the LORD.

18 So the king said to Doeg, "Go and execute the priests!" So Doeg the Edomite went and executed the priests himself. On that day, he killed 85 men who wore linen •ephods. 19 He also struck down Nob, the city of the priests, with the sword—both men and women, children and infants, oxen, donkeys, and sheep.

20 However, one of the sons of Ahimelech son of Ahitub escaped. His name was Abiathar, and he fled to David. 21 Abiathar told David that Saul had killed the priests of the LORD. 22 Then David said to Abiathar, "I knew that Doeg the Edomite was there that day and that he was sure to report to Saul. I myself am responsible for[e] the lives of everyone in your father's family. 23 Stay with me. Don't be afraid, for the one who wants to take my life wants to take your life. You will be safe with me."

Deliverance at Keilah

23 It was reported to David: "Look, the Philistines are fighting against Keilah and raiding the threshing floors."

2 So David inquired of the LORD: "Should I launch an attack against these Philistines?"

The LORD answered David, "Launch an attack against the Philistines and rescue Keilah."

3 But David's men said to him, "Look, we're afraid here in Judah; how much more if we go to Keilah against the Philistine forces!"

4 Once again, David inquired of the LORD, and the LORD answered him: "Go at once to Keilah, for I will hand the Philistines over to you." 5 Then David and his men went to Keilah, fought against the Philistines,

---

a 22:8 Lit No one uncovers my ear   b 22:8 Lit or uncovers my ear   c 22:15 Lit didn't know a thing, small or large   d 22:17 Lit didn't uncover my ear
e 22:22 LXX, Syr, Vg; MT reads I myself turn in

David's sin (2 Sam. 24:11-14) and served as biographer (1 Chron. 29:29) and music arranger for some of David's psalms (2 Chron. 29:25).

22:7 Benjamin. Saul's strongest political support was from his own tribe, Benjamin. David was from the tribe of Judah.

22:17 they knew. It is unlikely that the priests knew David's plans, since David was cautious and guarded by Ahimelech. Saul's paranoia was talking louder than his reason.

22:20 Abiathar. Once the priest, Abiathar, joined the group, David's board of advisors was complete, though he had yet to

receive the crown.

23:2 inquired of the LORD. When Abiathar joined David, he brought the ephod with the Urim and Thummim. This gave David access to God's wisdom and direction.

23:18 Jonathan. This was the last meeting of Jonathan and David. Jonathan had been

drove their livestock away, and inflicted heavy losses on them. So David rescued the inhabitants of Keilah. ⁶ Abiathar son of Ahimelech fled to David at Keilah, and he brought an •ephod with him.

⁷ When it was reported to Saul that David had gone to Keilah, he said, "God has handed him over to me, for he has trapped himself by entering a town with barred gates." ⁸ Then Saul summoned all the troops to go to war at Keilah and besiege David and his men.

⁹ When David learned that Saul was plotting evil against him, he said to Abiathar the priest, "Bring the ephod."

¹⁰ Then David said, "LORD God of Israel, Your servant has heard that Saul intends to come to Keilah and destroy the town because of me. ¹¹ Will the citizens of Keilah hand me over to him? Will Saul come down as Your servant has heard? LORD God of Israel, please tell Your servant."

The LORD answered, "He will come down."

¹² Then David asked, "Will the citizens of Keilah hand me and my men over to Saul?"

"They will," the LORD responded.

¹³ So David and his men, numbering about 600, left Keilah at once and moved from place to place. When it was reported to Saul that David had escaped from Keilah, he called off the expedition. ¹⁴ David then stayed in the wilderness strongholds and in the hill country of the Wilderness of Ziph. Saul searched for him every day, but God did not hand David over to him.

A Renewed Covenant

¹⁵ David was in the Wilderness of Ziph in Horesh when he saw that Saul had come out to take his life. ¹⁶ Then Saul's son Jonathan came to David in Horesh and encouraged him ⌊his faith in⌋ God, ¹⁷ saying, "Don't be afraid, for my father Saul will never lay a hand on you. You yourself will be king over Israel, and I'll be your second-in-command. Even my father Saul knows it is true." ¹⁸ Then the two of them made a covenant in the LORD's presence. Afterwards, David remained in Horesh, while Jonathan went home.

David's Narrow Escape

¹⁹ Some Ziphites came up to Saul at Gibeah and said, "David is[a] hiding among us in the strongholds in Horesh on the hill of Hachilah south of Jeshimon. ²⁰ Now, whenever the king wants to come down, let him come down. Our part will be to hand him over to the king."

²¹ "May you be blessed by the LORD," replied Saul, "for you have taken pity on me. ²² Go and check again. Investigate and watch carefully where he goes[b] and who has seen him there; they tell me he is extremely cunning. ²³ Look and find out all the places where he hides. Then come back to me with accurate information, and I'll go with you. If it turns out he really is in the region, I'll search for him among all the clans[c] of Judah." ²⁴ So they went to Ziph ahead of Saul.

Now David and his men were in the wilderness near Maon in the •Arabah south of Jeshimon, ²⁵ and Saul and his men went to look for ⌊him⌋. When David was told about it, he went down to the rock and stayed in the Wilderness of Maon. Saul heard of this and pursued David there.

²⁶ Saul went along one side of the mountain and David and his men went along the other side. Even though David was hurrying to get away from Saul, Saul and his men were closing in on David and his men to capture them. ²⁷ Then a messenger came to Saul saying, "Come quickly, because the Philistines have raided the land!" ²⁸ So Saul broke off his pursuit of David and went to engage the Philistines. Therefore, that place was named the Rock of Separation. ²⁹[d] From there David went up and stayed in the strongholds of En-gedi.

David Spares Saul

24 When Saul returned from pursuing the Philistines, he was told, "David is in the wilderness near En-gedi." ² So Saul took 3,000 of Israel's choice men and went to look for David and his men in front of the Rocks of the Wild Goats. ³ When Saul came to the sheep pens along the road, a cave was there, and he went in to relieve himself.[e] David and his men were staying in the back of the cave, ⁴ so they said to him, "Look, this is the day the LORD told you about: 'I will hand your enemy over to you so you can do to him whatever you desire.'" Then David got up and secretly cut off the corner of Saul's robe.

⁵ Afterwards, David's conscience bothered[f] him because he had cut off the corner of Saul's robe.[g] ⁶ He said to his men, "I swear before the LORD: I would never do such a thing to my lord, the LORD's anointed. ⌊I will never⌋ lift my hand against him, since he is the LORD's anointed." ⁷ With these words David persuaded[h] his men, and he did not let them rise up against Saul.

Then Saul left the cave and went on his way. ⁸ After that, David got up, went out of the cave, and called to Saul, "My lord the king!" When Saul looked behind

---

ᵃ23:19 Lit Is David not . . . Jeshimon? ᵇ23:22 Lit watch his place where his foot will be ᶜ23:23 Or thousands ᵈ23:29 1 Sm 24:1 in Hb ᵉ24:3 Lit to cover his feet ᶠ24:5 Lit David's heart struck ᵍ24:5 Some Hb mss, LXX, Syr, Vg; other Hb mss omit robe ʰ24:7 Or restrained

---

faithful to David as Saul's successor even though it meant forfeiting his own chance at the top. Jonathan died in battle before David came to the throne, so he never served in David's kingdom (31:2).

24:4 the LORD told you about. The Bible

contains no record of God giving this word to David or his men. It may have been a prophecy not recorded, or an inference on the part of his men based on other statements about David.

24:6 the LORD's anointed. David was consistently loyal to God. Building God's king-

dom was his priority. Saul had allowed his reign to degenerate into the normal political games of survival, intrigue, and greed. Even so, David would not sink to that level by killing God's anointed king.

24:11 my father. Since David had married Michal, Saul was his father-in-law as well as

Respecting Authority

1. Is there a "hideout" in your neighborhood? Did you go there when you were growing up?

1 Samuel 24:1-22

2. How would David have been justified in killing Saul? Why didn't he?

3. What did David mean that Saul was "the LORD's anointed" (v. 6)? What does this suggest about people who are in positions of authority?

4. What affect did David's action have on Saul?

5. Is there someone in authority over you who is abusing his or her power? How should you respond to that person?

him, David bowed to the ground in homage. [9] David said to Saul, "Why do you listen to the words of people who say, 'Look, David intends to harm you'? [10] You can see with your own eyes that the LORD handed you over to me today in the cave. ⌊Someone⌋ advised ⌊me⌋ to kill you, but I[a] took pity on you and said: I won't lift my hand against my lord, since he is the LORD's anointed. [11] See, my father! Look at the corner of your robe in my hand, for I cut it off, but I didn't kill you. Look and recognize that there is no evil or rebellion in me. I haven't sinned against you even though you are hunting me down to take my life.

[12] "May the LORD judge between you and me, and may the LORD take vengeance on you for me, but my hand will never be against you. [13] As the old proverb says, 'Wickedness comes from wicked people.' My hand will never be against you. [14] Who has the king of Israel come after? What are you chasing after? A dead dog? A flea? [15] May the LORD be judge and decide between you and me. May He take notice and plead my case and deliver[b] me from you."

[16] When David finished saying these things to him, Saul replied, "Is that your voice, David my son?" Then Saul wept aloud [17] and said to David, "You are more righteous than I, for you have done what is good to me though I have done what is evil to you. [18] You yourself

have told me today what good you did for me: when the LORD handed me over to you, you didn't kill me. [19] When a man finds his enemy, does he let him go unharmed?[c] May the LORD repay you with good for what you've done for me today.

[20] "Now I know for certain you will be king, and the kingdom of Israel will be established[d] in your hand. [21] Therefore swear to me by the LORD that you will not cut off my descendants or wipe out my name from my father's family." [22] So David swore to Saul. Then Saul went back home, and David and his men went up to the stronghold.

David, Nabal, and Abigail

25 Samuel died, and all Israel assembled to mourn for him, and they buried him by his home in Ramah. David then went down to the Wilderness of Paran.[e]

[2] A man in Maon had a business in Carmel; he was a very rich man with 3,000 sheep and 1,000 goats and was shearing his sheep in Carmel. [3] The man's name was Nabal, and his wife's name, Abigail. The woman was intelligent and beautiful, but the man, a Calebite, was harsh and evil in ⌊his⌋ dealings.

[4] While David was in the wilderness, he heard that Nabal was shearing sheep, [5] so David sent 10 young men instructing them, "Go up to Carmel, and when you come to Nabal, greet him in my name.[f] [6] Then say this: 'Long life to you,[g] and peace to you, to your family, and to all that is yours. [7] I hear that you are shearing.[h] When your shepherds were with us, we did not harass them, and nothing of theirs was missing the whole time they were in Carmel. [8] Ask your young men, and they will tell you. So let ⌊my⌋ young men find favor with you, for we have come on a feast[i] day. Please give whatever you can afford to your servants and to your son David.' "

[9] David's young men went and said all these things to Nabal on David's behalf,[j] and they waited.[k] [10] Nabal asked them, "Who is David? Who is Jesse's son? Many slaves these days are running away from their masters. [11] Am I supposed to take my bread, my water, and my meat that I butchered for my shearers and give them to men who are from I don't know where?"

[12] David's men retraced their steps. When they returned to him, they reported all these words. [13] He said to his men, "All of you, put on your swords!" So David and all his men put on their swords. About 400 men followed David while 200 stayed with the supplies.

---

[a]**24:10** Or *my eye* [b]**24:15** Lit *render a verdict for* [c]**24:19** Lit *go on a good way* [d]**24:20** Or *will flourish* [e]**25:1** LXX mss read *to Maon* [f]**25:5** Or *Nabal, and ask him for peace* [g]**25:6** Lit *To life* [h]**25:7** Lit *you have shearers* [i]**25:8** Lit *good* [j]**25:9** Lit *name* [k]**25:9** LXX reads *and he became arrogant*

---

his king.

24:16 wept aloud. Saul operated at both extremes. Before long, he quickly resumed his posse and forced David into flight again.

24:22 stronghold. Saul had just proclaimed David's righteousness, but David knew better than to trust Saul's goodwill. He scampered to

a cave or similar hideout.

25:1 Samuel died. Samuel bridged the era of the judges and the kings. His impact on Israel's spiritual life was great, though his sons failed to carry on his work.

25:2-44 Nabal. His name meant "fool.". He certainly dealt with David foolishly. This pas-

sage describes a husband who was as foolish as his wife was wise. Abigail saved the situation, but Nabal didn't survive it.

25:22 punish me, and even more. This is a severe Hebrew curse. David's oath of revenge reveals the other side of his leadership: quick, sure, confident, and violent.

14 One of Nabal's young men informed Abigail, Nabal's wife: "Look, David sent messengers from the wilderness to greet our master, but he yelled at them. 15 The men treated us well. When we were in the field, we weren't harassed and nothing of ours was missing the whole time we were living among them. 16 They were a wall around us, both day and night, the entire time we were herding the sheep. 17 Now consider carefully what you must do, because there is certain to be trouble for our master and his entire family. He is such a worthless fool nobody can talk to him!"

18 Abigail hurried, taking 200 loaves of bread, two skins of wine, five butchered sheep, a bushel[a] of roasted grain, 100 clusters of raisins, and 200 cakes of pressed figs, and loaded them on donkeys. 19 Then she said to her male servants, "Go ahead of me. I will be right behind you." But she did not tell her husband Nabal.

20 As she rode the donkey down a mountain pass hidden from view, she saw David and his men coming toward her and met them. 21 David had just said, "I guarded everything that belonged to this man in the wilderness for nothing. He was not missing anything, yet he paid me back evil for good. 22 May God punish me,[b] and even more if I let any of his men[c] ⌊survive⌋ until morning."

23 When Abigail saw David, she quickly got off the donkey and fell with her face to the ground in front of David. 24 She fell at his feet and said, "The guilt is mine, my lord, but please let your servant speak to you directly. Listen to the words of your servant. 25 My lord should pay no attention to this worthless man Nabal, for he lives up to his name:[d] His name is Nabal,[e] and stupidity is all he knows.[f] I, your servant, didn't see my lord's young men whom you sent. 26 Now my lord, as surely as the LORD lives and as you yourself live, it is the LORD who kept you from participating in bloodshed and avenging yourself by your own hand. May your enemies and those who want trouble for my lord be like Nabal. 27 Accept this gift your servant has brought to my lord, and let it be given to the young men who follow my lord. 28 Please forgive your servant's offense, for the LORD is certain to make a lasting dynasty for my lord because he fights the LORD's battles. Throughout your life, may evil[g] not be found in you.

29 "When someone pursues you and attempts to take your life, my lord's life will be tucked safely in the place[h] where the LORD your God protects the living. However, He will fling away your enemies' lives like ⌊stones⌋ from a sling. 30 When the LORD does for my lord all the good He promised and appoints you ruler over Israel, 31 there will not be remorse or a troubled conscience for my lord because of needless bloodshed or my lord's revenge. And when the LORD does good things for my lord, may you remember ⌊me⌋ your servant."

32 Then David said to Abigail, "Praise to the LORD God of Israel, who sent you to meet me today! 33 Blessed is your discernment, and blessed are you. Today you kept me from participating in bloodshed and avenging myself by my own hand. 34 Otherwise, as surely as the LORD God of Israel lives, who prevented me from harming you, if you had not come quickly to meet me, Nabal wouldn't have had any men[i] left by morning light." 35 Then David accepted what she had brought him and said, "Go home in peace. See, I have heard what you said and have granted your request."

36 Then Abigail went to Nabal, and there he was in his house, feasting like a king. Nabal was in a good mood[j] and very drunk, so she didn't say anything[k] to him until morning light.

37 In the morning when Nabal sobered up,[l] his wife told him about these events. Then he had a seizure[m] and became paralyzed.[n] 38 About 10 days later, the LORD struck Nabal dead.

39 When David heard that Nabal was dead, he said, "Praise the LORD who championed my cause against Nabal's insults and restrained His servant from doing evil. The LORD brought Nabal's evil deeds back on his own head."

Then David sent messengers to speak to Abigail about marrying him. 40 When David's servants came to Abigail at Carmel, they said to her, "David sent us to bring you to him as a wife."

41 She bowed her face to the ground and said, "Here I am, your servant, to wash the feet of my lord's servants." 42 Then Abigail got up quickly, and with her five female servants accompanying her, rode on the donkey following David's messengers. And so she became his wife.

43 David also married Ahinoam of Jezreel, and the two of them became his wives. 44 But Saul gave his daughter Michal, David's wife, to Palti son of Laish, who was from Gallim.

David Again Spares Saul

26 Then the Ziphites came to Saul at Gibeah saying, "David is hiding on the hill of Hachilah

---

[a] 25:18 Lit sheep, five seahs [b] 25:22 LXX; MT reads my enemies [c] 25:22 Lit of those of his who are urinating against the wall [d] 25:25 Lit for as is his name is, so he is [e] 25:25 = Fool [f] 25:25 Lit and foolishness is with him [g] 25:28 Or trouble [h] 25:29 Lit bundle [i] 25:34 Lit had anyone urinating against a wall [j] 25:36 Lit Nabal's heart was good on him [k] 25:36 Lit anything small or great [l] 25:37 Lit when the wine had gone out of Nabal [m] 25:37 Lit Then his heart died within him [n] 25:37 Lit became a stone

---

25:25 His name is Nabal. "Nabal" meant "fool." Names often reflect the character of a person, especially during this era. Even in the New Testament book of Philemon, Paul makes a request based on the meaning of a name. He asks that Onesimus (whose name means "useful" or "profitable") be made useful again (Philem. 1:10-11).

25:28 may evil not be found in you. Abigail was a clever diplomat, and became David's wife (v. 42).

26:2 3,000 of the choice men of Israel. The size of Saul's posse reveals his priorities: set-tling personal vendettas rather than fighting enemies or governing the country.

26:5 Abner. Abner and Saul were cousins. Abner was the commander of Saul's army who first brought David to Saul after Goliath was defeated (17:55-58).

opposite Jeshimon." ² So Saul, accompanied by 3,000 of the choice men of Israel, went to the Wilderness of Ziph to search for David there. ³ Saul camped beside the road at the hill of Hachilah opposite Jeshimon. David was living in the wilderness and discovered Saul had come there after him. ⁴ So David sent out spies and knew for certain that Saul had come. ⁵ Immediately, David went to the place where Saul had camped. He saw the place where Saul and Abner son of Ner, the general of his army, had lain down. Saul was lying inside the inner circle of the camp with the troops camped around him. ⁶ Then David asked Ahimelech the Hittite and Joab's brother Abishai son of Zeruiah, "Who will go with me into the camp to Saul?"

"I'll go with you," answered Abishai.

⁷ That night, David and Abishai came to the troops, and Saul was lying there asleep in the inner circle of the camp with his spear stuck in the ground by his head. Abner and the troops were lying around him. ⁸ Then Abishai said to David, "Today God has handed your enemy over to you. Let me thrust the spear through him into the ground just once. I won't ⌊have to strike⌋ him twice!"

⁹ But David said to Abishai, "Don't destroy him, for who can lift a hand against the LORD's anointed and be blameless?" ¹⁰ David added, "As the LORD lives, the LORD will certainly strike him down: either his day will come and he will die, or he will go into battle and perish. ¹¹ However, because of the LORD, I will never lift my hand against the LORD's anointed. Instead, take the spear and the water jug by his head, and let's go."

¹² So David took the spear and the water jug by Saul's head, and they went their way. No one saw them, no one knew, and no one woke up; they all remained asleep because a deep sleep from the LORD came over them. ¹³ David crossed to the other side and stood on top of the mountain at a distance; there was a considerable space between them. ¹⁴ Then David shouted to the troops and to Abner son of Ner: "Aren't you going to answer, Abner?"

"Who are you who calls to the king?" Abner asked.

¹⁵ David called to Abner, "You're a man, aren't you? Who in Israel is your equal? So why didn't you protect your lord the king when one of the people came to destroy him? ¹⁶ What you have done is not good. As the LORD lives, all of you deserve to die since you didn't protect your lord, the LORD's anointed. Now look around; where are the king's spear and water jug that were by his head?"

¹⁷ Saul recognized David's voice and asked, "Is that your voice, my son David?"

"It is my voice, my lord and king," David said. ¹⁸ Then he continued, "Why is my lord pursuing his servant? What have I done? What evil is in my hand? ¹⁹ Now, may my lord the king please hear the words of his servant: If it is the LORD who has incited you against me, then may He accept an offering. But if it is people, may they be cursed in the presence of the LORD, for today they have driven me away from sharing in the inheritance of the LORD saying, 'Go and worship other gods.' ²⁰ So don't let my blood fall to the ground far from the LORD's presence, for the king of Israel has come out to search for a flea, like one who pursues a partridge in the mountains."

²¹ Saul responded, "I have sinned. Come back, my son David, I will never harm you again because today you considered my life precious. I have been a fool! I've committed a grave error."

²² David answered, "Here is the king's spear; have one of the young men come over and get it. ²³ May the LORD repay every man for his righteousness and his loyalty. I wasn't willing to lift my hand against the LORD's anointed, even though the LORD handed you over to me today. ²⁴ Just as I considered your life valuable today, so may the LORD consider my life valuable and rescue me from all trouble."

²⁵ Saul said to him, "You are blessed, my son David. You will certainly do great things and will also prevail." Then David went on his way, and Saul returned home.

David Flees to Ziklag

27 David said to himself, "One of these days I'll be swept away by Saul. There is nothing better for me than to escape immediately to the land of the Philistines. Then Saul will stop searching for me everywhere in Israel, and I'll escape from him." ² So David set out with his 600 men and went to Achish son of Maoch, the king of Gath. ³ David and his men stayed with Achish in Gath. Each man had his family with him, and David had his two wives: Ahinoam of Jezreel and Abigail of Carmel, Nabal's widow. ⁴ When it was reported to Saul that David had fled to Gath, he no longer searched for him.

⁵ Now David said to Achish, "If I have found favor with you, let me be given a place in one of the outlying towns, so I can live there. Why should your servant live in the royal city with you?" ⁶ That day Achish gave Ziklag to him, and it still belongs to the kings of Judah

---

26:20 search for a flea. The allusion to a flea is saying that David is too harmless and insignificant for Saul to be pursuing him in this way.

27:1 to the land of the Philistines. David had fled to Philistia before (21:10-15). On that occasion he had feigned insanity to escape

from the home of King Achish, the very king with whom he was about to establish an alliance.

27:2 Achish. The first time David faced Achish, he was afraid he'd be seen as Goliath's killer. This time his position was much safer. If he were seen as Saul's enemy,

Achish would easily accept him. If David were living in an outlying town, perhaps Achish would call on him less often.

27:7 Philistine territory. David lived in Ziklag (in Philistia) until Saul's death. Ziklag was thereafter a Judean city.

27:8 Geshurites. Two tribes had this name.

today. 7 The time that David stayed in the Philistine territory amounted to a year and four months.

8 David and his men went up and raided the Geshurites, the Girzites,a and the Amalekites. From ancient times they had been the inhabitants of the region through Shur as far as the land of Egypt. 9 Whenever David attacked the land, he did not leave a single person alive, either man or woman, but he took flocks, herds, donkeys, camels, and clothing. Then he came back to Achish, 10 who inquired, "Where did you raid today?"b

David replied, "The south country of Judah," "The south country of the Jerahmeelites," or "Against the south country of the Kenites."

11 David did not let a man or woman live to be brought to Gath, for he said, "Or they will inform on us and say, 'This is what David did.'" This was David's custom during the whole time he stayed in the Philistine territory. 12 So Achish trusted David, thinking, "Since he has made himself detestable to his people Israel, he will be my servant forever."

Saul and the Medium

28 At that time, the Philistines brought their military units together into one army to fight against Israel. So Achish said to David, "You know, of course, that you and your men must march out in the armyc with me."

2 David replied to Achish, "Good, you will find out what your servant can do."

So Achish said to David, "Very well, I will appoint you as my permanent bodyguard."

3 By this time Samuel had died, and all Israel had mourned for him and buried him in Ramah, his city, and Saul had removed the mediums and spiritists from the land. 4 The Philistines came together and camped at Shunem. So Saul gathered all Israel, and they camped at Gilboa. 5 When Saul saw the Philistine camp, he was afraid and trembled violently. 6 He inquired of the LORD, but the LORD did not answer him in dreams or by the Urim or by the prophets. 7 Saul then said to his servants, "Find me a woman who is a medium, so I can go and consult her."

His servants replied, "There is a woman at Endor who is a medium."

8 Saul disguised himself by putting on different clothes and set out with two of his men. They came to the woman at night, and Saul said, "Consult a spirit for me. Bring up for me the one I tell you."

9 But the woman said to him, "You surely know what Saul has done, how he has killed the mediums and spir-

itists in the land. Why are you setting a trap for me to get me killed?"

10 Then Saul swore to her by the LORD: "As surely as the LORD lives, nothing bad will happen to you because of this."

11 "Who is it that you want me to bring up for you?" the woman asked.

"Bring up Samuel for me," he answered.

12 When the woman saw Samuel, she screamed, and then she asked Saul, "Why did you deceive me? You are Saul!"

13 But the king said to her, "Don't be afraid. What do you see?"

"I see a spirit formd coming up out of the earth," the woman answered.

14 Then Saul asked her, "What does he look like?"

"An old man is coming up," she replied. "He's wearing a robe." Then Saul knew that it was Samuel, and he bowed his face to the ground and paid homage.

15 "Why have you disturbed me by bringing me up?" Samuel asked Saul.

"I'm in serious trouble," replied Saul. "The Philistines are fighting against me and God has turned away from me. He doesn't answer me any more, either through the prophets or in dreams. So I've called on you to tell me what I should do."

16 Samuel answered, "Since the LORD has turned away from you and has become your enemy, why are you asking me? 17 The LORD has donee exactly what He said through me: The LORD has torn the kingship out of your hand and given it to your neighbor David. 18 You did not obey the LORD and did not carry out His wrath against Amalek; therefore the LORD has done this to you today. 19 The LORD will also hand Israel over to the Philistines along with you. Tomorrow you and your sons will be with me,f and the LORD will hand Israel's army over to the Philistines."

20 Immediately, Saul fell flat on the ground. He was terrified by Samuel's words and was also weak because he hadn't had any food all day and all night. 21 The woman came over to Saul, and she saw that he was terrified and said to him, "Look, your servant has obeyed you. I took my life in my hands and did what you told me [to do]. 22 Now please listen to your servant. Let me set some food in front of you. Eat and it will give you strength so you can go on your way."

23 He refused, saying, "I won't eat," but when his servants and the woman urged him, he listened to them. He got up off the ground and sat on the bed.

---

a**27:8** Alt Hb tradition reads *Gezerites* b**27:10** Some Hb mss, Syr, Tg; LXX, Vg, DSS read *Against whom did you raid today?* c**28:1** DSS, LXX read *battle* d**28:13** Or *a god*, or *a divine being* e**28:17** Some Hb, LXX mss, Vg read *done to you* f**28:19** LXX reads *sons will fall*

The tribe David attacked, south of Philistia on the way to Egypt, were among the settlers Joshua had failed to conquer (Josh. 13:2).

27:9 did not leave a single person alive. David's complete destruction fulfilled God's original direction to Joshua and it covered David's lie to Achish. David had led the king

to believe that his fight was against Judah.

28:6 the LORD did not answer. Saul's connections to God as the source of wisdom and strength were dwindling. Samuel was dead (v. 3). The prophet Abiathar had aligned himself with David and taken the official ephod (with its Urim and Thummim for decision mak-

ing). The prophet Gad had aligned himself with David as well.

29:4 only to become our adversary. The Hebrews had allied with the Philistines before (14:20-22), and their memories of it were not pleasant. In the heat of battle they left the Philistines to join with Saul and Jonathan.

24 The woman had a fattened calf at her house, and she quickly slaughtered it. She also took flour, kneaded it, and baked unleavened bread. 25 She served it to Saul and his servants, and they ate. Afterwards, they got up and left that night.

Philistines Reject David

29 The Philistines brought all their military units together at Aphek while Israel was camped by the spring in Jezreel. 2 As the Philistine leaders were passing ⌊in review with their units of⌋ hundreds and thousands, David and his men were passing ⌊in review⌋ behind them with Achish. 3 Then the Philistine commanders asked, "What are these Hebrews ⌊doing here⌋?"

Achish answered the Philistine commanders, "That is David, servant of King Saul of Israel. He has been with me a considerable period of time.ᵃ From the day he defected until today, I've found no fault with him."

4 The Philistine commanders, however, were enraged with Achish and told him, "Send that man back and let him return to the place you assigned him. He must not go down with us into battle only to become our adversary during the battle. What better way could he regain his master's favor than with the heads of our men? 5 Isn't this the David they sing about during their dances:

Saul has killed his thousands,
but David his tens of thousands?"

6 So Achish summoned David and told him, "As the LORD lives, you are an honorable man. I think it is goodᵇ to have you workingᶜ with me in the camp, because I have found no fault in you from the day you came to me until today. But the leaders don't think you are reliable. 7 Now go back quietly and you won't be doing ⌊anything⌋ the Philistine leaders think is wrong."

8 "But what have I done?" David replied to Achish. "From the first day I was with you until today, what have you found against your servant to keep me from going along to fight against the enemies of my lord the king?"

9 Achish answered David, "I'm convinced that you are as reliable as an angel of God. But the Philistine commanders have said, 'He must not go into battle with us.' 10 So get up early in the morning, you and your masters' servants who came with you.ᵈ When you've all gotten up early, go as soon as it's light." 11 So David and his men got up early in the morning to return to the land of the Philistines. And the Philistines went up to Jezreel.

David's Defeat of the Amalekites

30 David and his men arrived in Ziklag on the third day. The Amalekites had raided the •Negev and attacked and burned down Ziklag. 2 They also had kidnapped the women and everyoneᵉ in it from the youngest to the oldest. They had killed no one but had carried them off as they went on their way.

3 When David and his men arrived at the town, they found it burned down. Their wives, sons, and daughters had been kidnapped. 4 David and the troops with him wept loudly until they had no strength left to weep. 5 David's two wives, Ahinoam the Jezreelite and Abigail the widow of Nabal the Carmelite, had also been kidnapped. 6 David was in a difficult position because the troops talked about stoning him, for they were all very bitter over ⌊the loss of⌋ their sons and daughters. But David found strength in the LORD his God.

7 David said to Abiathar the priest, son of Ahimelech, "Bring me the •ephod." So Abiathar brought it to him, 8 and David asked the LORD: "Should I pursue these raiders? Will I overtake them?"

The LORD replied to him, "Pursue ⌊them⌋, for you will certainly overtake ⌊them⌋ and rescue ⌊the people⌋."

9 David and the 600 men with him went as far as the •Wadi Besor, where 200 men who were to remain behind would stop. 10 They stopped because they were too exhausted to cross the Wadi Besor. David and 400 of the men continued in pursuit.

11 They found an Egyptian in the open country and brought him to David. They gave him some bread to eat and water to drink. 12 Then they gave him some pressed figs and two clusters of raisins. After he ate he revived, for he hadn't eaten food or drunk water for three days and three nights.

13 Then David said to him, "Who do you belong to? Where are you from?"

"I'm an Egyptian, the slave of an Amalekite man," he said. "My master abandoned me when I got sick three days ago. 14 We raided the south country of the Cherethites, ⌊the territory⌋ of Judah, and the south country of Caleb, and we burned down Ziklag."

15 David then asked him, "Will you lead me to these raiders?"

He said, "Swear to me by God that you won't kill me or turn me over to my master, and I will lead you to them."

16 So he led him, and there were the Amalekites, spread out over the entire area, eating, drinking, and celebrating because of the great amount of plunder they had taken from the land of the Philistines and the land

ᵃ29:3 Hb obscure ᵇ29:6 Lit It was good in my eyes ᶜ29:6 Lit you going out and coming in ᵈ29:10 LXX adds and go to the place I appointed you to. Don't take this evil matter to heart, for you are good before me. ᵉ30:2 LXX; MT omits and everyone

29:6 As the LORD lives. Whether Achish believed in the Lord or not, he was speaking a language David understood.

29:8 what have I done? David played along, but this turn of events was fortunate. Saul was still king; David's time had not yet come. Had he fought in this battle, David would have put his sword against his own countrymen.

30:1 Amalekites. These were people south of Philistia that David had raided while he claimed to be fighting his own tribe of Judah (27:8).

30:26 sent some of the plunder. The Amalekites had plundered Judah, and David was recovering lost goods. Crediting God with the victory gave David reason to spread the spoils evenly and win the people's allegiance in future conflict.

of Judah. 17 David slaughtered them from twilight until the evening of the next day. None of them escaped, except 400 young men who got on camels and fled.

18 David recovered everything the Amalekites had taken; he also rescued his two wives. 19 Nothing ⌊of theirs⌋ was missing from the youngest to the oldest, including the sons and daughters, of all the plunder the Amalekites had taken. David got everything back. 20 He took all the sheep and cattle, which were driven ahead of the other livestock, and the people shouted, "This is David's plunder!"

Saul's Suicide

1. What is your first memory about death: A pet or other animal? A friend or relative? A famous person in the news?

1 Samuel 31:1-13

2. Why did Saul commit suicide? Why did his armor-bearer? Were they justified in doing this?
3. How did Saul's suicide affect the Israelites? How does suicide do great harm to innocent people?
4. What should Saul have done instead of killing himself? What should his armor-bearer have done? How might things have ended differently if they had?
5. What is the world's view on assisted suicide? What is God's view?

21 When David came to the 200 men who had been too exhausted to go with him and had been left at the Wadi Besor, they came out to meet him and to meet the troops with him. When David approached the men, he greeted them, 22 but all the •worthless men among those who had gone with David retorted, "Because they didn't go with us, we will not give any of the plunder we recovered to them except for each man's wife and children. They may take them and go."

23 But David said, "My brothers, you must not do this with what the LORD has given us. He protected us and handed over to us the raiders who came against us. 24 Who can agree to your proposal? The share of the one who goes into battle is to be the same as the share of the one who remains with the supplies. They will share equally." 25 And it has been so from that day for-

ward. David established ⌊this policy⌋ as a law and an ordinance for Israel ⌊and it continues⌋ to this very day.

26 When David came to Ziklag, he sent some of the plunder to his friends, the elders of Judah, saying, "Here is a gift for you from the plunder of the LORD's enemies." 27 ⌊He sent gifts⌋ to those in Bethel, in Ramoth of the Negev, and in Jattir; 28 to those in Aroer, in Siphmoth, and in Eshtemoa; 29 to those in Racal, in the towns of the Jerahmeelites, and in the towns of the Kenites; 30 to those in Hormah, in Bor-ashan, and in Athach; 31 to those in Hebron, and to ⌊those in⌋ all the places where David and his men had roamed.

The Death of Saul and His Sons

31 The Philistines fought against Israel, and Israel's men fled from them. Many were killed on Mount Gilboa. 2 The Philistines overtook Saul and his sons and killed his sons, Jonathan, Abinadab, and Malchishua. 3 When the battle intensified against Saul, the archers caught up with him and severely wounded him.a 4 Then Saul said to his armor-bearer, "Draw your sword and run me through with it, or these uncircumcised men will come and run me through and torture me." But his armor-bearer would not do it because he was terrified. Then Saul took his sword and fell on it. 5 When his armor-bearer saw that Saul was dead, he also fell on his own sword and died with him. 6 So on that day, Saul died together with his three sons, his armor-bearer, and all his men.

7 When the men of Israel on the other side of the valley and on the other side of the Jordan saw that Israel's men had run away and that Saul and his sons were dead, they abandoned the cities and fled. So the Philistines came and settled in them.

8 The next day when the Philistines came to strip the slain, they found Saul and his three sons dead on Mount Gilboa. 9 They cut off Saul's head, stripped off his armor, and sent messengers throughout the land of the Philistines to spread the good news in the temples of their idols and among the people. 10 Then they put his armor in the temple of the •Ashtoreths and hung his body on the wall of Beth-shan.

11 When the residents of Jabesh-gilead heard what the Philistines had done to Saul, 12 all their brave men set out, journeyed all night, and retrieved the body of Saul and the bodies of his sons from the wall of Beth-shan. When they arrived at Jabesh, they burned the bodies there. 13 Afterwards, they took their bones and buried them under the tamarisk tree in Jabesh and fasted seven days.

a 31:3 LXX reads and he was wounded under the ribs

31:2 killed his sons. Saul had a fourth son, Ish-Bosheth (2 Sam. 2:8), who was not killed in this battle.

31:9 cut off Saul's head. Goliath received the same treatment. Decapitation was proof that the adversary had perished. Al-

lies of headless adversaries best take cover.

31:10 Ashtoreths. Idols representing the Philistine and Canaanite goddess—counterpart to Baal. Placing Saul's armor in the temple credited his defeat to a false god.

31:11-12 Jabesh-gilead. Saul had defended these people in his first act as king. **burned the bodies.** Cremation was not the typical burial for an Israelite. Later David exhumed the bones and reburied them in the territory of Benjamin, Saul's tribe.

2 SAMUEL

AUTHOR

The author is not known with certainty. Perhaps a compiler drew from materials written by others such as Samuel, Gad, and Nathan (see 1 Chron. 29:29) in order to produce the final rendition. Note that 1 and 2 Samuel were originally composed as one unit.

DATE

The date of authorship is uncertain, though it is possible that this two-volume book was written around the time of Solomon's death (circa 930 B.C.).

THEME

The life and times of King David.

HISTORICAL BACKGROUND

David had been on the run from Saul. Now that Saul is dead, David is able to take his rightful place on the throne over all of Israel, but only after he emerges triumphant from a political power struggle. Surrounding nations, especially the Philistines, still pose the threat of war; however, Israel is militarily strong under David's victorious reign.

CHARACTERISTICS

Second Samuel continues the historical narrative of 1 Samuel, where David's youth and troublesome exile were the focus. Now in "volume two" David reigns as Saul's successor and he must heal and unify the war-torn country. Chapters 1-10 narrate the prosperous early reign of David. He is anointed king over Judah and then over all Israel. He also sustains victory after victory on the battlefield. David's adultery with Bathsheba (chapters 11-12), however, marks a turning point in the book. In the chapters that follow, the "sword will never leave" David's house (12:10). Throughout the book, God is seen as the One who establishes David upon the throne of Israel and gives him victory over his enemies.

PASSAGES FOR TOPICAL GROUP STUDY

11:1-27 ...... SIN and TURNING TO GOD............. Busted!

12:1-14 ...... ACCOUNTABILITY .... Nathan's Parable and David's Repentance

13:1-22...... SEX and DATE RAPE.... Amnon's Rape of Tamar

13:23-39 .... RIVALRY and REVENGE..... Absalom's Revenge

PASSAGES FOR GENERAL GROUP STUDY

12:15-25 .... Tragic Consequences (David loses his son)

Responses to Saul's Death

1 After the death of Saul, David returned from defeating the Amalekites and stayed at Ziklag two days. ² On the third day a man with torn clothes and dust on his head came from Saul's camp. When he came to David, he fell to the ground and paid homage. ³ David asked him, "Where have you come from?"

He replied to him, "I've escaped from the Israelite camp."

⁴ "What was the outcome? Tell me," David asked him.

"The troops fled from the battle," he answered. "Many of the troops have fallen and are dead. Also, Saul and his son Jonathan are dead."

⁵ David asked the young man who had brought him the report, "How do you know Saul and his son Jonathan are dead?"

⁶ "I happened to be on Mount Gilboa," he replied, "and there was Saul, leaning on his spear. At that very moment the chariots and the cavalry were closing in on him. ⁷ When he turned around and saw me, he called out to me, so I answered: I'm at your service. ⁸ He asked me, 'Who are you?' I told him: I'm an Amalekite. ⁹ Then he begged me, 'Stand over me and kill me, for I'm mortally wounded,ᵃ but my life still lingers.' ¹⁰ So I stood over him and killed him because I knew that after he had fallen he couldn't survive. I took the crown that was on his head and the armband that was on his arm, and I've brought them here to my lord."

¹¹ Then David took hold of his clothes and tore them, and all the men with him did the same. ¹² They mourned, wept, and fasted until the evening for those who died by the sword—for Saul, his son Jonathan, the LORD's people, and the house of Israel.

¹³ David inquired of the young man who had brought him the report, "Where are you from?"

"I'm the son of a foreigner" he said. "I'm an Amalekite."

¹⁴ David questioned him, "How is it that you were not afraid to lift your hand to destroy the LORD's anointed?" ¹⁵ Then David summoned one of his servants and said, "Come here and kill him!" The servant struck him, and he died. ¹⁶ For David had said to the Amalekite, "Your blood is on your own head because your own mouth testified against you by saying, 'I killed the LORD's anointed.'"

¹⁷ David sang the following lament for Saul and his son Jonathan, ¹⁸ and he ordered that the Judahites be taught ⌊The Song of⌋ the Bow. It is written in the Book of Jashar:ᵇ

¹⁹ The splendor of Israel lies slain on your heights.
How the mighty have fallen!
²⁰ Do not tell it in Gath,
don't announce it in the streets of Ashkelon,
or the daughters of the Philistines will rejoice,
and the daughters of the uncircumcised
will gloat.
²¹ Mountains of Gilboa,
let no dew or rain be on you,
or fields of offerings,ᶜ
for there the shield of the mighty was defiled—
the shield of Saul, no longer anointed with oil.
²² Jonathan's bow never retreated,
Saul's sword never returned unstained,ᵈ
from the blood of the slain,
from the bodies of the mighty.
²³ Saul and Jonathan,
loved and delightful,
they were not parted in life or in death.
They were swifter than eagles,
stronger than lions.
²⁴ Daughters of Israel, weep for Saul,
who clothed you in scarlet,
with luxurious things,
who decked your garments
with gold ornaments.
²⁵ How the mighty have fallen in the thick
of battle!
Jonathan ⌊lies⌋ slain on your heights.
²⁶ I grieve for you, Jonathan my brother.
You were such a friend to me.
Your love for me was more wonderful
than the love of a woman ⌊for me⌋.
²⁷ How the mighty have fallen
and the weapons of war have perished!

David, King of Judah

2 Some time later, David inquired of the LORD: "Should I go to one of the towns of Judah?"

The LORD answered him, "Go."

Then David asked, "Where should I go?"

"To Hebron," the LORD replied.

² So David went there with his two wives, Ahinoam the Jezreelite and Abigail, the widow of Nabal the Carmelite. ³ In addition, David brought the men who were with him, each one with his household, and they settled in the towns near Hebron. ⁴ Then the men of Judah came, and there they anointed David king over the house of Judah. They told David: "It was the men of Jabesh-gilead who buried Saul."

ᵃ**1:9** LXX reads *for terrible darkness has taken hold of me*   ᵇ**1:18** Or *of the Upright*   ᶜ**1:21** LXX reads *firstfruits*   ᵈ**1:22** Lit *empty*

1:8 Amalekite. Contrary to 1 Samuel 31:4-6, the Amalekite is providing additional information to the previous account, or he is altering the story because he expects the action he claims to have taken will earn a reward.

1:11 David … and all the men with him. King Saul had forced David and his men into hiding.

Yet here they wept for their nation's loss.

1:13 Amalekite. David had just rescued his wives from Amalekite kidnappers. He wouldn't welcome an Amalekite deserter into his camp.

1:14 the LORD's anointed. On two occasions, David could have killed Saul but did not (1 Sam. 24:3-7; 26:9-12). It was not David's (nor

anyone else's) right to kill God's selected leader.

1:15 kill him. Years before, Saul was told he had lost his kingdom for failing to destroy the Amalekites (1 Sam. 15:3-9) as God commanded. Here, an Amalekite lost his life because he claimed to have destroyed Saul.

5 David sent messengers to the men of Jabesh-gilead and said to them, "The LORD bless you, because you have shown this special kindness to Saul your lord when you buried him. 6 Now, may the LORD show special kindness and faithfulness to you, and I will also show the same goodness to you because you have done this deed. 7 Therefore, be strong and courageous, for though Saul your lord is dead, the house of Judah has anointed me king over them."

8 Abner son of Ner, commander of Saul's army, took Saul's son Ish-bosheth[a] [b] and moved him to Mahanaim. 9 He made him king over Gilead, Asher, Jezreel, Ephraim, Benjamin—over all Israel. 10 Saul's son Ishbosheth was 40 years old when he began his reign over Israel; he ruled for two years. The house of Judah, however, followed David. 11 The length of time that David was king in Hebron over the house of Judah was seven years and six months.

12 Abner son of Ner and soldiers of Ish-bosheth son of Saul marched out from Mahanaim to Gibeon. 13 So Joab son of Zeruiah and David's soldiers marched out and met them by the pool of Gibeon. The two groups took up positions on opposite sides of the pool.

14 Then Abner said to Joab, "Let's have the young men get up and compete in front of us."

"Let them get up," Joab replied.

15 So they got up and were counted off—12 for Benjamin and Ish-bosheth son of Saul, and 12 from David's soldiers. 16 Then each man grabbed his opponent by the head and ⌊thrust⌋ his sword into his opponent's side so that they all died together. So this place, which is in Gibeon, is named Field of Blades.[c]

17 The battle that day was extremely fierce, and Abner and the men of Israel were defeated by David's soldiers. 18 The three sons of Zeruiah were there: Joab, Abishai, and Asahel. Asahel was a fast runner, like one of the wild gazelles. 19 He chased Abner and did not turn to the right or the left in his pursuit of him. 20 Abner glanced back and said, "Is that you, Asahel?"

"Yes it is," Asahel replied.

21 Abner said to him, "Turn to your right or left, seize one of the young soldiers, and take whatever you can get from him." But Asahel would not stop chasing him. 22 Once again, Abner warned Asahel, "Stop chasing me. Why should I strike you to the ground? How could I ever look your brother Joab in the face?"

23 But Asahel refused to turn away, so Abner hit him in the stomach with the end of his spear. The spear went through his body, and he fell and died right there.

When all who came to the place where Asahel had fallen and died, they stopped, 24 but Joab and Abishai pursued Abner. By sunset, they had gone as far as the hill of Ammah, which is opposite Giah on the way to the wilderness of Gibeon.

25 The Benjaminites rallied to Abner; they formed a single unit and took their stand on top of a hill. 26 Then Abner called out to Joab: "Must the sword devour forever? Don't you realize this will only end in bitterness? How long before you tell the troops to stop pursuing their brothers?"

27 "As God lives," Joab replied, "if you had not spoken up, the troops wouldn't have stopped pursuing their brothers until morning." 28 Then Joab blew the ram's horn, and all the troops stopped; they no longer pursued Israel or continued to fight. 29 So Abner and his men marched through the •Arabah all that night. They crossed the Jordan, marched all morning,[d] and arrived at Mahanaim.

30 When Joab had turned back from pursuing Abner, he gathered all the troops. In addition to Asahel, 19 of David's soldiers were missing, 31 but they had killed 360 of the Benjaminites and Abner's men. 32 Afterwards, they carried Asahel to his father's tomb in Bethlehem and buried him. Then Joab and his men marched all night and reached Hebron at dawn.

Civil War

3 The war between the house of Saul and the house of David was long and drawn out, with David growing stronger and the house of Saul becoming weaker.

2 Sons were born to David in Hebron:

his firstborn was Amnon,
by Ahinoam the Jezreelite;
3 his second was Chileab,
by Abigail, the widow of Nabal the Carmelite;
the third was Absalom,
son of Maacah the daughter of King Talmai
of Geshur;
4 the fourth was Adonijah,
son of Haggith;
the fifth was Shephatiah,
son of Abital;
5 the sixth was Ithream,
by David's wife Eglah.

These were born to David in Hebron.

6 During the war between the house of Saul and the house of David, Abner kept acquiring more power in

---

a 2:8 Some LXX mss read *Ishbaal*; = Man of Baal; 1 Ch 8:33; 9:39 b 2:8 = Man of Shame c 2:16 Or *Helkath-hazzurim* d 2:29 Or *marched through the Bithron*

1:18 Book of Jashar. This lost manuscript is also mentioned in the Book of Joshua (Josh. 10:13).

2:1 inquired More than likely, David inquired with the Urim and Thummin (1 Sam. 10:20; 23:1-6; 28:6).

2:8 Abner. Abner (Saul's cousin and the commander of his army) knew his best play for power was through Saul's one surviving son, Ish-Bosheth.

2:12 Gibeon. David went first to Judah, his own tribe, to establish his sovereignty. Abner took Ish-Bosheth to Gibeon, a town in the region of Benjamin, the tribe of Saul's heritage.

2:13 Joab. Joab, a distant nephew of David, was commander of David's army and had a reputation for ruthlessness that even David eventually criticized (3:39).

2:28 all the troops stopped. Even though the truce failed, each army had time to retreat to its home base.

the house of Saul. ⁷ Now Saul had a concubine whose name was Rizpah daughter of Aiah, and Ish-bosheth questioned Abner, "Why did you sleep with my father's concubine?"

⁸ Abner was very angry about Ish-bosheth's accusation. "Am I a dog's headª who belongs to Judah?" he asked. "All this time I've been loyal to the house of your father Saul, to his brothers, and to his friends and haven't handed you over to David, but now you accuse me of wrongdoing with this woman! ⁹ May God punish Abner and do so severely if I don't do for David what the LORD swore to him: ¹⁰ to transfer the kingdom from the house of Saul and establish the throne of David over Israel and Judah from Dan to Beer-sheba." ¹¹ Ish-bosheth could not answer Abner because he was afraid of him.

¹² Abner sent messengers as his representatives to say to David, "Whose land is it? Make your covenant with me, and you can be certain I am on your side to hand all Israel over to you."

¹³ David replied, "Good, I will make a covenant with you. However, there's one thing I require of you: Do not appear before me unless you bring Saul's daughter Michal here when you come to see me."

¹⁴ Then David sent messengers to say to Ish-bosheth son of Saul, "Give me back my wife, Michal. I was •engaged to her for the price of 100 Philistine foreskins."

¹⁵ So Ish-bosheth sent someone to take her away from her husband, Paltiel son of Laish. ¹⁶ Her husband followed her, weeping all the way to Bahurim. Abner said to him, "Go back." So he went back.

The Assassination of Abner

¹⁷ Abner conferred with the elders of Israel: "In the past you wanted David to be king over you. ¹⁸ Now take action, because the LORD has spoken concerning David: 'Through My servant David I will save My people Israel from the power of the Philistines and the power of all Israel's enemies.'"

¹⁹ Abner also informed the Benjaminites and went to Hebron to inform David about all that was agreed on by Israel and the whole house of Benjamin. ²⁰ When Abner and 20 men came to David at Hebron, David held a banquet for him and his men.

²¹ Abner said to David, "Let me now go and I will gather all Israel to my lord the king. They will make a covenant with you, and you will rule over all you desire." So David dismissed Abner, and he went in peace.

²² Just then David's soldiers and Joab returned from a raid and brought a large amount of plundered goods with them. Abner was not with David in Hebron because David had dismissed him, and he had gone in peace. ²³ When Joab and all his army arrived, Joab was informed, "Abner son of Ner came to see the king, the king dismissed him, and he went in peace."

²⁴ Joab went to the king and said, "What have you done? Look here, Abner came to you. Why did you dismiss him? Now he's getting away. ²⁵ You know that Abner son of Ner came to deceive you and to find out about your activities and everything you're doing." ²⁶ Then Joab left David and sent messengers after Abner. They brought him back from the wellᵇ of Sirah, but David was unaware of it. ²⁷ When Abner returned to Hebron, Joab pulled him aside to the middle of the gateway, as if to speak to him privately, and there Joab stabbed him in the stomach. So Abner died in revenge for the death of Asahel,ᶜ Joab's brother.

²⁸ David heard ⌊about it⌋ later and said: "I and my kingdom are forever innocent before the LORD concerning the blood of Abner son of Ner. ²⁹ May it hang over Joab's head and his father's whole house, and may the house of Joab never be without someone who has an infection or leprosy or a man who can only work a spindleᵈ or someone who falls by the sword or starves." ³⁰ Joab and his brother Abishai killed Abner because he had put their brother Asahel to death in the battle at Gibeon.

³¹ David then ordered Joab and all the people who were with him, "Tear your clothes, put on •sackcloth, and mourn over Abner." And King David walked behind the funeral procession.ᵉ

³² When they buried Abner in Hebron, the king wept aloud at Abner's tomb. All the people wept, ³³ and the king sang a lament for Abner:

> Should Abner die as a fool dies?
> 34 Your hands were not bound,
>   your feet not placed in bronze ⌊shackles⌋.
>   You fell like one who falls victim to criminals.

And all the people wept over him even more.

³⁵ Then they came to urge David to eat bread while it was still day, but David took an oath: "May God punish me and do so severely if I taste bread or anything else before sunset!" ³⁶ All the people took note of this, and it pleased them. In fact, everything the king did pleased them. ³⁷ On that day all the troops and all Israel were convinced that the king had no part in the killing of Abner son of Ner.

ª**3:8** = a despised person   ᵇ**3:26** Or *cistern*   ᶜ**3:27** Lit *And he died for the blood of Asahel*   ᵈ**3:29** LXX reads *who uses a crutch*   ᵉ**3:31** Lit *the bed; or the bier*

3:7 Rizpah ... my father's concubine? In the ancient Middle East, taking a former king's concubine was often a political statement. Ish-Bosheth worried that it indicated a conspiracy to take over the throne (12:8; 16:21; 1 Kings 2:22).

3:13 Michal. Michal (1 Sam. 18:27) had been given to another man, Paltiel. (1 Sam. 25:44). If reunited, it would aid David's claim to the throne as Saul's son-in-law.

3:17 David to be king. Benjamin and Gilead in the Transjordan seemed to provide most of Ish-Bosheth's support (2:8, 15; 1 Sam. 11:9-11; 31:11-13).

3:27 Joab. The murder was unjustified. No state of war existed at this point, and blood revenge (Num. 35:12; Deut. 19:11-13) did not apply because Joab's brother Asahel had been killed in battle (v. 30; 2:1, 23). Furthermore, the act occurred in Hebron, a city of refuge (Josh. 20:7) where a blood avenger was

38 Then the king said to his soldiers, "You must know that a great leader has fallen in Israel today. **39** As for me, even though I am the anointed king, I have little power today. These men, the sons of Zeruiah, are too fierce for me. May the LORD repay the evildoer according to his evil!"

The Assassination of Ish-bosheth

4 When Saul's son ⌊Ish-bosheth⌋ heard that Abner had died in Hebron, his courage failed, and all Israel was dismayed. **2** Saul's son had two men who were leaders of raiding parties: one named Baanah and the other Rechab, sons of Rimmon the Beerothite of the Benjaminites. Beeroth is also considered part of Benjamin, **3** and the Beerothites fled to Gittaim and still live there as aliens to this very day.

4 Saul's son Jonathan had a son whose feet were crippled. He was five years old when the report about Saul and Jonathan came from Jezreel. His nurse picked him up and fled, but as she was hurrying to flee, he fell and became lame. His name was Mephibosheth.

5 Rechab and Baanah, the sons of Rimmon the Beerothite, set out and arrived at Ish-bosheth's house during the heat of the day while the king was taking his midday nap. **6** They entered the interior of the house as if to get wheat and stabbed him in the stomach. Then Rechab and his brother Baanah escaped. **7** They had entered the house while Ish-bosheth was lying on his bed in his bedroom and stabbed and killed him. Then they beheaded him, took his head, and traveled by way of the •Arabah all night. **8** They brought Ish-bosheth's head to David at Hebron and said to the king, "Here's the head of Ish-bosheth son of Saul, your enemy who intended to take your life. Today the LORD has granted vengeance to my lord the king against Saul and his offspring."

9 But David answered Rechab and his brother Baanah, sons of Rimmon the Beerothite, "As surely as the LORD lives, ⌊the One⌋ who has redeemed my life from every distress, **10** when the person told me, 'Look, Saul is dead,' he thought he was a bearer of good news, but I seized him and put him to death at Ziklag. That was my reward to him for his news! **11** How much more when wicked men kill a righteous man in his own house on his own bed! So now, should I not require his blood from your hands and wipe you off the earth?"

12 So David gave orders to the young men, and they killed Rechab and Baanah. They cut off their hands and feet and hung ⌊their bodies⌋ by the pool in Hebron, but they took Ish-bosheth's head and buried it in Abner's tomb in Hebron.

David, King of Israel

5 All the tribes of Israel came to David at Hebron and said, "Here we are, your own flesh and blood.ᵃ **2** Even while Saul was king over us, you were the one who led us out ⌊to battle⌋ and brought us back. The LORD also said to you, 'You will shepherd My people Israel and be ruler over Israel.'"

3 So all the elders of Israel came to the king at Hebron. King David made a covenant with them at Hebron in the LORD's presence, and they anointed David king over Israel.

4 David was 30 years old when he began his reign; he reigned 40 years. **5** In Hebron he reigned over Judah seven years and six months, and in Jerusalem he reigned 33 years over all Israel and Judah.

6 The king and his men marched to Jerusalem against the Jebusites who inhabited the land. The Jebusites had said to David: "You will never get in here. Even the blind and lame can repel you," thinking, "David can't get in here."

7 Yet David did capture the stronghold of Zion, the city of David. **8** He said that day, "Whoever attacks the Jebusites must go through the water shaft to reach the lame and the blind who are despised by David."ᵇ For this reason it is said, "The blind and the lame will never enter the house."ᶜ

9 David took up residence in the stronghold, which he named the city of David. He built it up all the way around from the supporting terraces inward. **10** David became more and more powerful, and the LORD God of •Hosts was with him. **11** King Hiram of Tyre sent envoys to David; ⌊he also sent⌋ cedar logs, carpenters, and stonemasons, and they built a palace for David. **12** Then David knew that the LORD had established him as king over Israel and had exalted his kingdom for the sake of His people Israel.

13 After he arrived from Hebron, David took more concubines and wives in Jerusalem, and more sons and daughters were born to him. **14** These are the names of those born to him in Jerusalem: Shammua, Shobab, Nathan, Solomon, **15** Ibhar, Elishua, Nepheg, Japhia, **16** Elishama, Eliada, and Eliphelet.

17 When the Philistines heard that David had been anointed king over Israel, they all went in search of David, but he heard about it and went down to the stronghold. **18** So the Philistines came and spread out in the Valley of Rephaim.

19 Then David inquired of the LORD: "Should I go to war against the Philistines? Will you hand them over to me?"

ᵃ**5:1** Lit *your bone and flesh*   ᵇ**5:8** Alt Hb tradition, LXX, Tg, Syr read *who despise David*   ᶜ**5:8** Or *temple*, or *palace*

---

not permitted to deal with a murderer without a trial (Num. 35:22-24).

5:3 they anointed David. David's third anointing as king. First Samuel privately anointed him with his family (1 Sam. 16:13), the tribe of Judah anointed him publicly (2:4), and, finally, the northern tribes anoint him at Hebron.

5:6 Jebusites. The Jebusites (Gen. 10:15, 16; Num. 13:29) could boast because Jerusalem was easy to defend, surrounded on three sides by deep valleys. Its location on the border between the two parts of David's kingdom was strategic, since it favored neither.

5:8 For this reason it is said. They were for-

bidden to offer sacrifices in the temple (Lev. 21:18).

5:13 concubines and wives. The result of treaties and alliances with other nations, concubines were basically wives who did not enjoy the full rights of marriage. God had warned Israel against this practice (Deut. 17:17).

The LORD replied to David, "Go, for I will certainly hand the Philistines over to you."

20 So David went to Baal-perazim and defeated them there and said, "Like a bursting flood, the LORD has burst out against my enemies before me." Therefore, he named that place the Lord Bursts Out.a 21 The Philistines abandoned their idols there, and David and his men carried them off.

22 The Philistines came up again and spread out in the Valley of Rephaim. 23 So David inquired of the LORD, and He answered, "Do not make a frontal assault. Circle around behind them and attack them opposite the balsam trees. 24 When you hear the sound of marching in the tops of the balsam trees, act decisively, for then the LORD will have marched out ahead of you to attack the camp of the Philistines." 25 So David did exactly as the LORD commanded him, and he struck down the Philistines all the way from Geba to Gezer.

David Moves the Ark

6 David again assembled all the choice men in Israel, 30,000. 2 He and all his troops set out to bring the ark of God from Baale-judah.b The ark is called by the Name, the name of the LORD of •Hosts who dwells ⌊between⌋ the •cherubim. 3 They set the ark of God on a new cart and transported it from Abinadab's house, which was on the hill. Uzzah and Ahio,c sons of Abinadab, were guiding the cart 4 and brought it with the ark of God from Abinadab's house on the hill. Ahio walked in front of the ark. 5 David and the whole house of Israel were celebrating before the LORD with all ⌊kinds of⌋ fir wood ⌊instruments⌋,d lyres, harps, tambourines, sistrums,e and cymbals.

6 When they came to Nacon's threshing floor, Uzzah reached out to the ark of God and took hold of it, because the oxen had stumbled. 7 Then the LORD's anger burned against Uzzah, and God struck him dead on the spot for his irreverence, and he died there next to the ark of God. 8 David was angry because of the LORD's outburst against Uzzah, so he named that place an Outburst Against Uzzah,f as it is today. 9 David feared the LORD that day and said, "How can the ark of the LORD ever come to me?" 10 So he was not willing to move the ark of the LORD to the city of David; instead, he took it to the house of Obed-edom the Gittite. 11 The ark of the LORD remained in his house three months, and the LORD blessed Obed-edom and his whole family.

12 It was reported to King David: "The LORD has blessed Obed-edom's family and all that belongs to him because of the ark of God." So David went and had the ark of God brought up from Obed-edom's house to the city of David with rejoicing. 13 When those carrying the ark of the LORD advanced six steps, he sacrificed an ox and a fattened calf. 14 David was dancingg with all his might before the LORD wearing a linen •ephod. 15 He and the whole house of Israel were bringing up the ark of the LORD with shouts and the sound of the ram's horn. 16 As the ark of the LORD was entering the city of David, Saul's daughter Michal looked down from the window and saw King David leaping and dancing before the LORD, and she despised him in her heart.

17 They brought the ark of the LORD and set it in its place inside the tent David had set up for it. Then David offered •burnt offerings and •fellowship offerings in the LORD's presence. 18 When David had finished offering the burnt offering and the fellowship offerings, he blessed the people in the name of the LORD of Hosts. 19 Then he distributed a loaf of bread, a date cake, and a raisin cake to each one of the whole multitude of the people of Israel, both men and women. Then all the people left, each to his own home.

20 When David returned ⌊home⌋ to bless his household, Saul's daughter Michal came out to meet him. "How the king of Israel honored himself today!" she said. "He exposed himself today in the sight of the slave girls of his subjects like a vulgar person would expose himself."

21 David replied to Michal, "I was dancingh before the LORD who chose me over your father and his whole family to appoint me ruler over the LORD's people Israel. I will celebrate before the LORD, 22 and I will humble myself even more and humiliate myself.i j I will be honored by the slave girls you spoke about." 23 And Saul's daughter Michal had no child to the day of her death.

The LORD's Covenant with David

7 When the king had settled into his palace and the LORD had given him rest on every side from all his enemies, 2 the king said to Nathan the prophet, "Look, I am living in a cedar house while the ark of God sits inside tent curtains."

3 So Nathan told the king, "Go and do all that is on your heart, for the LORD is with you."

4 But that night the word of the LORD came to Nathan: 5 "Go to My servant David and say, 'This is what the LORD says: Are you to build a house for Me to live in? 6 From the time I brought the Israelites out of

---

a **5:20** Or *Baal-perazim*; 2 Sm 6:8; 1 Ch 13:11 b **6:2** Alt name for Kiriath-jearim c **6:3** Or *and his brothers* d **6:5** DSS, LXX read *with tuned instruments with strength, with songs*; 1 Ch 13:8 e **6:5** = an Egyptian percussion instrument f **6:8** Or *Perez-uzzah*; 2 Sm 5:20 g **6:14** Or *whirling* h **6:21** LXX; MT omits *I was dancing* i **6:22** LXX reads *more and I will be humble in your eyes* j **6:22** Lit *more and I will be humble in my own eyes*

5:24 sound of marching. God's angelic soldiers rustled the leaves as they moved in front of David (2 Kings 6:17).

6:3 new cart. The ark should only be carried by Levites (Ex. 25:12-14; Num. 4:5-15), but David used a cart like the Philistines (1 Sam. 6:7).

6:7 Uzzah. Uzzah broke God's clear command (Ex. 25:12-14; Num. 4:5-15; 1 Chron. 15:13-15).

6:8-9 David was angry. Sometimes David got angry with God for things he didn't understand.

6:12 blessed Obed-Edom's family. God showed he would also bless the ark's correct transportation, while David researched his mistake.

6:20 king of Israel ... exposed himself. Discarding kingly robes, was performing priestly duties while returning the ark in a linen ephod normally worn by Levites (1 Sam. 2:18)

Egypt until today I have not lived in a house; instead, I have been moving around with the tabernacle tent. 7 In all My journeys with all the Israelites, have I ever asked anyone among the tribes of Israel, whom I commanded to shepherd My people Israel: Why haven't you built Me a house of cedar?'

8 "Now this is what you are to say to My servant David: 'This is what the LORD of •Hosts says: I took you from the pasture and from following the sheep to be ruler over My people Israel. 9 I have been with you wherever you have gone, and I have destroyed all your enemies before you. I will make a name for you like that of the greatest in the land. 10 I will establish a place for My people Israel and plant them, so that they may live there and not be disturbed again. Evildoers will not afflict them as they have done 11 ever since the day I ordered judges to be over My people Israel. I will give you rest from all your enemies.

"'The LORD declares to you: The LORD Himself will make a house for you. 12 When your time comes and you rest with your fathers, I will raise up after you your descendant, who will come from your body, and I will establish his kingdom. 13 He will build a house for My name, and I will establish the throne of his kingdom forever. 14 I will be a father to him, and he will be a son to Me. When he does wrong, I will discipline him with a human rod and with blows from others. 15 But My faithful love will never leave him as I removed it from Saul; I removed him from your way. 16 Your house and kingdom will endure before Me[a] forever, and your throne will be established forever.' "

17 Nathan spoke all these words and this entire vision to David.

David's Prayer of Thanksgiving

18 Then King David went in, sat in the LORD's presence, and said, "Who am I, Lord GOD, and what is my house that You have brought me this far? 19 What You have done so far[b] was a little thing to You, Lord GOD, for You have also spoken about Your servant's house in the distant future. And this is a revelation[c] for mankind, Lord GOD. 20 What more can David say to You? You know Your servant, Lord GOD. 21 Because of Your word and according to Your will, You have revealed all these great things to Your servant.

22 "This is why You are great, Lord GOD. There is no one like You, and there is no God besides You, as all we have heard confirms. 23 And who is like Your people Israel? God came to one nation on earth in order to

redeem a people for Himself, to make a name for Himself, and to perform for them[d] great and awesome acts, driving out nations and their gods before Your people You redeemed for Yourself from Egypt. 24 You established Your people Israel Your own people forever, and You, LORD, have become their God.

25 "Now, LORD God, fulfill the promise forever that You have made to Your servant and his house. Do as You have promised, 26 so that Your name will be exalted forever, when it is said, 'The LORD of Hosts is God over Israel.' The house of Your servant David will be established before You 27 since You, LORD of Hosts, God of Israel, have revealed this to Your servant when You said, 'I will build a house for you.' Therefore, Your servant has found the courage to pray this prayer to You. 28 Lord GOD, You are God; Your words are true, and You have promised this grace to Your servant. 29 Now, please bless Your servant's house so that it will continue before You forever. For You, Lord GOD, have spoken, and with Your blessing Your servant's house will be blessed forever."

David's Victories

8 After this, David defeated the Philistines, subdued them, and took Metheg-ammah[e] from Philistine control.[f] 2 He also defeated the Moabites, and after making them lie down on the ground, he measured them off with a cord. He measured every two cord lengths ⌊of those⌋ to be put to death and one length ⌊of those⌋ to be kept alive. So the Moabites became David's subjects and brought tribute.

3 David also defeated Hadadezer son of Rehob, king of Zobah, who went to restore his control at the Euphrates River. 4 David captured 1,700 horsemen[g] and 20,000 foot soldiers from him, and he hamstrung all the horses, and he kept 100 chariots.[h]

5 When the Arameans of Damascus came to assist King Hadadezer of Zobah, David struck down 22,000 Aramean men. 6 Then he placed garrisons in Aram of Damascus, and the Arameans became David's subjects and brought tribute. The LORD made David victorious wherever he went.

7 David took the gold shields of Hadadezer's officers and brought them to Jerusalem. 8 King David also took huge quantities of bronze from Betah[i] and Berothai, Hadadezer's cities.

9 When King Toi of Hamath heard that David had defeated the entire army of Hadadezer, 10 he sent his son Joram to King David to greet him and to congratulate

---

a7:16 Some Hb mss, LXX, Syr; other Hb mss read you   b7:19 Lit Yet this   c7:19 Or custom, or instruction   d7:23 Some Hb mss, Tg, Vg, Syr; other Hb mss read you   e8:1 Or took control of the mother city; Hb obscure   f8:1 LXX reads them, and David took tribute out of the hand of the Philistines   g8:4 LXX, DSS read 1,000 chariots and 7,000 horsemen   h8:4 Or chariot horses   i8:8 Some LXX mss, Syr read Tebah

---

7:2 tent. David felt that since he had a palace, which represented his reign, God deserved more than a tent (Ps. 132:2-5; Acts 7:46).

7:3 told the king. Nathan approved what he assumed made sense.

7:5-7 Are you to build a house for Me to live in? Living in a stationary house might give the

impression that God is limited. As he had allowed a king, God would eventually allow a temple building.

7:14 When he does wrong. God promises not to remove his merciful love—as he had done with Saul (1 Sam. 13:13-14; 15:22-23).

7:21 Because of Your word. A reference to

God's covenant with Abraham regarding the nation and the land (Gen. 12:2-3; Deut. 7:6-8; 33:26-29).

7:23 to make a name. God chose Israel to spread His glory (Deut. 9:4-5; Isa. 63:12; Jer. 32:20-21; Ezek. 36:22-38).

8:3 restore ... Euphrates River. Saul had

him because David had fought against Hadadezer and defeated him, for Toi and Hadadezer had fought many wars. Joram had items of silver, gold, and bronze with him. ¹¹ King David also dedicated these to the LORD, along with the silver and gold he had dedicated from all the nations he had subdued—¹² from Edom,ᵃ Moab, the Ammonites, the Philistines, the Amalekites, and the spoil of Hadadezer son of Rehob, king of Zobah.

¹³ David made a reputation for himself when he returned from striking down 18,000 Edomitesᵇ in the Valley of Salt.ᶜ ¹⁴ He placed garrisons throughout Edom, and all the Edomites were subject to David. The LORD made David victorious wherever he went.

¹⁵ So David reigned over all Israel, administering justice and righteousness for all his people.

¹⁶ Joab son of Zeruiah was over the army;
Jehoshaphat son of Ahilud was court historian;

¹⁷ Zadok son of Ahitub
and Ahimelech son of Abiathar were priests;
Seraiah was court secretary;

¹⁸ Benaiah son of Jehoiada ⌊was over⌋
the Cherethites and the Pelethites;
and David's sons were chief officials.ᵈ

David's Kindness to Mephibosheth

9 David asked, "Is there anyone remaining from Saul's family I can show kindness to because of Jonathan?" ² There was a servant of Saul's family named Ziba. They summoned him to David, and the king said to him, "Are you Ziba?"

"⌊I am⌋ your servant," he replied.

³ So the king asked, "Is there anyone left of Saul's family I can show the kindness of God to?"

Ziba said to the king, "There is still Jonathan's son who is lame in both feet."

⁴ The king asked him, "Where is he?"

Ziba answered the king, "You'll find him in Lo-debar at the house of Machir son of Ammiel." ⁵ So King David had him brought from the house of Machir son of Ammiel in Lo-debar.

⁶ Mephibosheth son of Jonathan son of Saul came to David, bowed down to the ground and paid homage. David said, "Mephibosheth!"

"I am your servant," he replied.

⁷ "Don't be afraid," David said to him, "since I intend to show you kindness because of your father Jonathan. I will restore to you all your grandfather Saul's fields, and you will always eat meals at my table."

⁸ Mephibosheth bowed down and said, "What is your servant that you take an interest in a dead dog like me?"

⁹ Then the king summoned Saul's attendant Ziba and said to him, "I have given to your master's grandson all that belonged to Saul and his family. ¹⁰ You, your sons, and your servants are to work the ground for him, and you are to bring in ⌊the crops⌋ so your master's grandson will have food to eat. But Mephibosheth, your master's grandson, is always to eat at my table." Now Ziba had 15 sons and 20 servants.

¹¹ Ziba said to the king, "Your servant will do all my lord the king commands."

So Mephibosheth ate at David'sᵉ table just like one of the king's sons. ¹² Mephibosheth had a young son whose name was Mica. All those living in Ziba's house were Mephibosheth's servants. ¹³ However, Mephibosheth lived in Jerusalem because he always ate at the king's table. He was lame in both feet.

War with the Ammonites

10 Some time later the king of the Ammonites died, and his son Hanun became king in his place. ² Then David said, "I'll show kindness to Hanun son of Nahash, just as his father showed kindness to me."

So David sent his emissaries to console Hanun concerning his father. However, when they arrived in the land of the Ammonites, ³ the Ammonite leaders said to Hanun their lord, "Just because David has sent men with condolences for you, do you really believe he's showing respect for your father? Instead, hasn't David sent his emissaries in order to scout out the city, spy on it, and overthrow it?" ⁴ So Hanun took David's emissaries, shaved off half their beards, cut their clothes in half at the hips, and sent them away.

⁵ When this was reported to David, he sent ⌊someone⌋ to meet them, since they were deeply humiliated. The king said, "Stay in Jericho until your beards grow back; then return."

⁶ When the Ammonites realized they had become repulsive to David, they hired 20,000 foot soldiers from the Arameans of Beth-rehob and Zobah, 1,000 men from the king of Maacah, and 12,000 men from Tob.

⁷ David heard about it and sent Joab and all the fighting men. ⁸ The Ammonites marched out and lined up in battle formation at the entrance to the city gate while the Arameans of Zobah and Rehob and the men of Tob and Maacah were in the field by themselves. ⁹ When Joab saw that there was a battle line in front of him and

---

ᵃ**8:12** Some Hb mss, LXX, Syr; MT reads *Aram*; 1 Ch 18:11   ᵇ**8:13** A few Hb mss, LXX, Syr; MT reads *Arameans*; 1 Ch 18:12   ᶜ**8:13** = the Dead Sea region   ᵈ**8:18** LXX; MT reads *were priests*; 1 Ch 18:17   ᵉ**9:11** LXX; Syr reads *the king's*; Vg reads *your*; MT reads *my*

---

previously defeated Zobah (1 Sam. 14:47), partially fulfilling God's promise of the land from Egypt to the Euphrates (Gen. 15:18).

8:15 all Israel. David now occupies the entire area God promised Abraham.

8:18 Cherethites and Pelethites. Soldiers in David's army (15:18) and elite royal

guard (23:22-23).

9:1 can show kindness. David remembered his promise to Jonathan (1 Sam. 20:15, 42).

9:2 Ziba. Ziba was chief steward of Saul's estate: the inheritance of Jonathan's son Mephibosheth, Saul's grandson and primary heir. Saul did have other descendants (21:8).

9:4 Machir. Machir, who later assisted David (17:27), cared for the crippled Mephibosheth.

9:7 Don't be afraid. In the ancient Middle East heirs of previous dynasties were executed to protect new kings.

9:8 a dead dog like me. Mephibosheth, even though he was royalty, would feel despised as

another behind him, he chose some men out of all the elite troops of Israel and lined up in battle formation to engage the Arameans. ¹⁰ He placed the rest of the forces under the command of his brother Abishai who lined up in battle formation to engage the Ammonites.

¹¹ "If the Arameans are too strong for me," Joab said, "then you will be my help. However, if the Ammonites are too strong for you, I'll come to help you. ¹² Be strong! We must prove ourselves strong for our people and for the cities of our God. May the LORD's will be done."ᵃ

¹³ Joab and his troops advanced to fight against the Arameans, and they fled before him. ¹⁴ When the Ammonites saw that the Arameans had fled, they too fled before Abishai and entered the city. So Joab withdrew from the attack against the Ammonites and went to Jerusalem.

¹⁵ When the Arameans saw that they had been defeated by Israel, they regrouped. ¹⁶ Hadadezer sent ⌊messengers⌋ to bring the Arameans who were across the Euphrates River, and they came to Helam with Shobach, commander of Hadadezer's army, leading them.

¹⁷ When this was reported to David, he gathered all Israel, crossed the Jordan, and went to Helam. Then the Arameans lined up in formation to engage David in battle and fought against him. ¹⁸ But the Arameans fled before Israel, and David killed 700 of their charioteers and 40,000 foot soldiers.ᵇ He also struck down Shobach commander of their army, who died there. ¹⁹ When all the kings who were Hadadezer's subjects saw that they had been defeated by Israel, they made peace with Israel and became their subjects. After this, the Arameans were afraid to ever help the Ammonites again.

David's Adultery with Bathsheba

11 In the spring when kings march out ⌊to war⌋, David sent Joab with his officers and all Israel. They destroyed the Ammonites and besieged Rabbah, but David remained in Jerusalem.

² One evening David got up from his bed and strolled around on the roof of the palace. From the roof he saw a woman bathing—a very beautiful woman. ³ So David sent someone to inquire about her, and he reported, "This is Bathsheba, daughter of Eliam and wife of Uriah the Hittite."ᶜ

⁴ David sent messengers to get her, and when she came to him, he slept with her. Now she had just been purifying herself from her uncleanness. Afterwards, she returned home. ⁵ The woman conceived and sent word to inform David: "I am pregnant."

Adultery and Murder

1. Who is the most beautiful woman you know personally? What makes her so beautiful?

2 Samuel 11:1-27

2. David was the leader of his army. Why was he not in battle? How did avoiding his proper duty lead him into deeper sin?
3. Why did Uriah refuse to go home to his wife? How did his actions add even more shame to what David had done?
4. How did David's sins keep leading to more and worse sins? How have you seen this occur in your own life?

⁶ David sent orders to Joab: "Send me Uriah the Hittite." So Joab sent Uriah to David. ⁷ When Uriah came to him, David asked how Joab and the troops were doing and how the war was going. ⁸ Then he said to Uriah, "Go down to your house and wash your feet." So Uriah left the palace, and a gift from the king followed him. ⁹ But Uriah slept at the door of the palace with all his master's servants; he did not go down to his house.

¹⁰ When it was reported to David, "Uriah didn't go home," David questioned Uriah, "Haven't you just come from a journey? Why didn't you go home?"

¹¹ Uriah answered David, "The ark, Israel, and Judah are dwelling in tents, and my master Joab and his soldiersᵈ are camping in the open field. How can I enter my house to eat and drink and sleep with my wife? As surely as you live and by your life, I will not do this!"

¹² "Stay here today also," David said to Uriah, "and tomorrow I will send you back." So Uriah stayed in Jerusalem that day and the next. ¹³ Then David invited Uriah to eat and drink with him, and David got him drunk. He went out in the evening to lie down on his cot with his master's servants, but he did not go home.

Uriah's Death Arranged

¹⁴ The next morning David wrote a letter to Joab and sent it with Uriah. ¹⁵ In the letter he wrote:

ᵃ**10:12** Lit *the LORD do what is good in His eyes*   ᵇ**10:18** Some LXX mss; MT reads *horsemen;* 1 Ch 19:18   ᶜ**11:3** DSS add *Joab's armor-bearer*
ᵈ**11:11** Lit *servants*

---

dogs were because he was disabled. Disabilities were seen as God's punishment.
9:10 Ziba had 15 sons and 20 servants. 35 men were required to oversee Saul's estate.
9:13 lame. Mephibosheth was injured when his nurse fell with him while they fled from Gibeah after hearing that Saul and Jonathan

had been killed (4:4).
11:4. just been purifying herself. Bathsheba had just become ceremonially clean (following menstruation; Lev. 15:19-30); she could not have been pregnant by her husband Uriah when David slept with her.
11:5 The woman conceived. David and Bath-

sheba's adultery could not be hidden. The penalty was death for them both (Lev. 20:10; Deut. 22:22).
11:11 ark. The ark was being kept in a field tent with Israel's army—for blessing and guidance. **my master Joab and his soldiers.** Mindful of his comrades' sacrifice, Uriah would

Put Uriah at the front of the fiercest fighting, then withdraw from him so that he is struck down and dies.

¹⁶ When Joab was besieging the city, he put Uriah in the place where he knew the best ⌊enemy⌋ soldiers were. ¹⁷ Then the men of the city came out and attacked Joab, and some of the men from David's soldiers fell ⌊in battle⌋; Uriah the Hittite also died.

¹⁸ Joab sent someone to report to David all the details of the battle. ¹⁹ He commanded the messenger, "When you've finished telling the king all the details of the battle— ²⁰ if the king's anger gets stirred up and he asks you, 'Why did you get so close to the city to fight? Didn't you realize they would shoot from the top of the wall? ²¹ At Thebez, who struck Abimelech son of Jerubbesheth?ᵃ ᵇ Didn't a woman drop an upper millstone on him from the top of the wall so that he died? Why did you get so close to the wall?'—then say, 'Your servant Uriah the Hittite is dead also.'" ²² Then the messenger left.

When he arrived, he reported to David all that Joab had sent him ⌊to tell⌋. ²³ The messenger reported to David, "The men gained the advantage over us and came out against us in the field, but we counterattacked right up to the entrance of the gate. ²⁴ However, the archers shot down on your soldiers from the top of the wall, and some of the king's soldiers died. Your servant Uriah the Hittite is also dead."

²⁵ David told the messenger, "Say this to Joab: 'Don't let this matter upset you because the sword devours all alike. Intensify your fight against the city and demolish it.' Encourage him."

²⁶ When Uriah's wife heard that her husband Uriah had died, she mourned for him.ᶜ ²⁷ When the time of mourning ended, David had her brought to his house. She became his wife and bore him a son. However, the LORD considered what David had done to be evil.

Nathan's Parable and David's Repentance

12 So the LORD sent Nathan to David. When he arrived, he said to him:

There were two men in a certain city, one rich and the other poor. ² The rich man had a large number of sheep and cattle, ³ but the poor man had nothing except one small ewe lamb that he had bought. It lived and grew up with him and his children. It shared his meager food and drank from his cup; it slept in his arms, and it was like a daughter to him. ⁴ Now a traveler came to the rich man, but the rich man could not bring himself to take one of his own sheep or cattle to prepare for the traveler who had come to him. Instead, he took the poor man's lamb and prepared it for his guest.ᵈ

⁵ David was infuriated with the man and said to Nathan: "As surely as the LORD lives, the man who did this deserves to die! ⁶ Because he has done this thing and shown no pity, he must pay four lambs for that lamb."

 Busted!

1. Have you ever been caught with your hand in the cookie jar? How did you react?

2 Samuel 12:1-14

2. How was David like the man in Nathan's story who stole the sheep?

3. Did the man in Nathan's story deserve to die? Did David?

4. What was David's response when confronted with his sin? How does this reflect what God meant when He said, "David is a man after God's own heart"?

5. How do you respond when someone confronts you with sin? How can you become a man or woman after God's own heart?

⁷ Nathan replied to David, "You are the man! This is what the LORD God of Israel says: 'I anointed you king over Israel, and I delivered you from the hand of Saul. ⁸ I gave your master's house to you and your master's wives into your arms,ᵉ and I gave you the house of Israel and Judah, and if that was not enough, I would have given you even more. ⁹ Why then have you despised the command of the LORD by doing what I considerᶠ evil? You struck down Uriah the Hittite with the sword and took his wife as your own wife—you murdered him with the Ammonite's sword. ¹⁰ Now therefore, the sword will never leave your house because you despised Me and took the wife of Uriah the Hittite to be your own wife.'

¹¹ "This is what the LORD says, 'I am going to bring disaster on you from your own family: I will take your

---

ᵃ**11:21** LXX reads *Jerubbaal* ᵇ**11:21** = Gideon ᶜ**11:26** Lit *her husband* ᵈ**12:4** Lit *for the man who had come to him* ᵉ**12:8** Lit *bosom* ᶠ**12:9** Alt Hb tradition reads *what He considers*

---

not even sleep with his own wife. While an Israelite king is unfaithful, a non-Israelite soldier is faithful.

11:13 to eat and drink. David hoped that if Uriah were drunk, he might sleep with Bathsheba.

11:23, 24 Uriah, the Hittite, is also dead. Joab pursued a different plan than David had

ordered—namely, to have Uriah abandoned. As a cover up, Joab had Uriah's platoon engaged near the city wall where archers' arrows resulted in several fatalities.

12:1 the LORD sent Nathan. God the true King commissions His ambassador to rebuke the chosen king, and declare judgment.

12:5 David was infuriated. David was furious

over the injustice and called for the man's death; though not normally a death penalty crime.

12:6 pay four lambs for that lamb. Ironically, David knew God's law (Exod. 22:1).

12:8 your master's wives into your arms. Simply meaning that God had given David Saul's throne and all it entailed (new kings usu-

wives and give them to another[a] before your very eyes, and he will sleep with them publicly.[b] 12 You acted in secret, but I will do this before all Israel and in broad daylight.'"[c]

13 David responded to Nathan, "I have sinned against the LORD."

Then Nathan replied to David, "The LORD has taken away your sin; you will not die. 14 However, because you treated[d] the LORD with such contempt in this matter, the son born to you will die." 15 Then Nathan went home.

Tragic Consequences

1. What do you do when you're really upset: Do you eat? Not eat? Not sleep?

2 Samuel 12:15-25

2. Why did David react this way when his son became ill? Why did the elders try to make him stop?
3. Why did David get up, wash, and eat after the baby died? What would most people have done?
4. What did David mean when he said, "I'll go to him, but he will never return to me" (v. 23)? What does this suggest about babies who have died?

The Death of Bathsheba's Son

The LORD struck the baby that Uriah's wife had borne to David, and he became ill. 16 David pleaded with God for the boy. He fasted, went ⌊home⌋, and spent the night lying on the ground. 17 The elders of his house stood beside him to get him up from the ground, but he was unwilling and would not eat anything with them.

18 On the seventh day the baby died. But David's servants were afraid to tell him the baby was dead. They said, "Look, while the baby was alive, we spoke to him, and he wouldn't listen to us. So how can we tell him the baby is dead? He may do something desperate."

19 When David saw that his servants were whispering to each other, he guessed that the baby was dead. So he asked his servants, "Is the baby dead?"

"He is dead," they replied.

20 Then David got up from the ground. He washed, anointed himself, changed his clothes, went to the LORD's house, and worshiped. Then he went home and requested ⌊something to eat⌋. So they served him food, and he ate.

21 His servants asked him, "What did you just do? While the baby was alive, you fasted and wept, but when he died, you got up and ate food."

22 He answered, "While the baby was alive, I fasted and wept because I thought, 'Who knows? The LORD may be gracious to me and let him live.' 23 But now that he is dead, why should I fast? Can I bring him back again? I'll go to him, but he will never return to me."

The Birth of Solomon

24 Then David comforted his wife Bathsheba; he went and slept with her. She gave birth to a son and named[e] him Solomon.[f] The LORD loved him, 25 and He sent ⌊a message⌋ through Nathan the prophet, who named[g] him Jedidiah,[h] because of the LORD.

Capture of the City of Rabbah

26 Joab fought against Rabbah of the Ammonites and captured the royal fortress. 27 Then Joab sent messengers to David to say, "I have fought against Rabbah and have also captured the water supply. 28 Now therefore, assemble the rest of the troops, lay siege to the city, and capture it. Otherwise I will be the one to capture the city, and it will be named after me. 29 So David assembled all the troops and went to Rabbah; he fought against it and captured it. 30 He took the crown from the head of their king,[i] and it was ⌊placed⌋ on David's head. The crown weighed 75 pounds[j] of gold, and it had a precious stone ⌊in it⌋. In addition, David took away a large quantity of plunder from the city. 31 He removed the people who were in the city and put ⌊them to work⌋ with saws, iron picks, and iron axes, and to labor at brickmaking. He did the same to all the Ammonite cities. Then he and all his troops returned to Jerusalem.

Amnon Rapes Tamar

13 Some time passed. David's son Absalom had a beautiful sister named Tamar, and David's son Amnon was infatuated with her. 2 Amnon was frustrated to the point of making himself sick over his sister Tamar because she was a virgin, but it seemed impossible to do anything to her. 3 Amnon had a friend named Jonadab, a son of David's brother Shimeah.

---

[a]**12:11** Or to your neighbor   [b]**12:11** Lit in the eyes of this sun   [c]**12:12** Lit and before the sun   [d]**12:14** Alt Hb tradition, one LXX ms; MT reads treated the enemies of; DSS read treated the word of   [e]**12:24** Alt Hb tradition reads he named   [f]**12:24** = His Restoration, or His Peace   [g]**12:25** Or prophet to name   [h]**12:25** = Beloved of the LORD   [i]**12:30** LXX reads of Milcom; some emend to Molech; 1 Kg 11:5,33   [j]**12:30** Lit a talent

---

ally kept the prior king's harem).

12:10 the sword will never leave. This is fulfilled in the violent deaths of three sons: Amnon (13:23-31); Absalom (18:1-18); and Adonijah (1 Kings 2:13-25).

12:11 I am going to bring disaster on you. Fulfilled when his son Absalom forced David to flee Jerusalem (15:1-24).

12:13 I have sinned. David joined a list of people of faith who committed heinous crimes and depended on God's grace. Abraham lied about Sarah being his wife, resulting in her almost being taken sexually by another man (Gen.20:1-5); Peter denied Christ; Paul persecuted Christians. **The LORD has taken away your sin.** David sincerely repented (Ps. 32:1, 5; 51:8, 12).

12:15 the baby. No name is given, so apparently the child did not live long enough to be circumcised on the eighth day—the time a son was normally named.

Jonadab was a very shrewd man, 4 and he asked Amnon, "Why are you, the king's son, so miserable every morning? Won't you tell me?"

Amnon's Rape of Tamar

1. Have you ever been lovesick over someone who didn't like you? How did it affect you?

2 Samuel 13:1-22

2. What should Amnon have done if he was in love with Tamar?

3. How did Amnon feel about Tamar after he'd raped her? What does this suggest about his love in the first place?

4. What effect did Amnon's sin have on Tamar? On the family? (See verses 28-29.)

5. How do sexual sins affect people beyond just those involved?

6. Is someone pressuring you to have sex? Are you pressuring someone? How can you avoid this temptation?

Amnon replied, "I'm in love with Tamar, my brother Absalom's sister."

5 Jonadab said to him, "Lie down on your bed and pretend you're sick. When your father comes to see you, say to him, 'Please let my sister Tamar come and give me ⌊something⌋ to eat. Let her prepare food in my presence so I can watch and eat from her hand.' "

6 So Amnon lay down and pretended to be sick. When the king came to see him, Amnon said to him, "Please let my sister Tamar come and make a couple of cakes in my presence so I can eat from her hand."

7 David sent word to Tamar at the palace: "Please go to your brother Amnon's house and prepare a meal for him."

8 Then Tamar went to his house while Amnon was lying down. She took dough, kneaded it, made cakes in his presence, and baked them. 9 She brought the pan and set it down in front of him, but he refused to eat. Amnon said, "Everyone leave me!" And everyone left him. 10 "Bring the meal to the bedroom," Amnon told Tamar, "so I can eat from your hand." Tamar took the cakes she had made and went to her brother Amnon's bedroom. 11 When she brought ⌊them⌋ to him to eat, he grabbed her and said,[a] "Come sleep with me, my sister!"

12 "Don't, my brother!" she cried. "Don't humiliate me, for such a thing should never be done in Israel. Don't do this horrible thing! 13 Where could I ever go with my disgrace? And you—you would be like one of the immoral men in Israel! Please, speak to the king, for he won't keep me from you." 14 But he refused to listen to her, and because he was stronger than she was, he raped her.

15 After this, Amnon hated Tamar with such intensity that the hatred he hated her with was greater than the love he had loved her with. "Get out of here!" he said.

16 "No," she cried,[b] "sending me away is much worse than the great wrong you've already done to me!" But he refused to listen to her. 17 Instead, he called to the servant who waited on him: "Throw this woman out and bolt the door behind her!" 18 Amnon's servant threw her out and bolted the door behind her. Now Tamar was wearing a long-sleeved[c] garment, because this is what the king's virgin daughters wore. 19 Tamar put ashes on her head and tore the long-sleeved garment she was wearing. She put her hand on her head and went away weeping.

20 Her brother Absalom said to her: "Has your brother Amnon been with you? Be quiet for now, my sister. He is your brother. Don't take this thing to heart." So Tamar lived as a desolate woman in the house of her brother Absalom.

Absalom Murders Amnon

21 When King David heard about all these things, he was furious.[d] 22 Absalom didn't say anything to Amnon, either good or bad, because he hated Amnon since he disgraced his sister Tamar.

23 Two years later, Absalom's sheepshearers were at Baal-hazor near Ephraim, and Absalom invited all the king's sons. 24 Then he went to the king and said, "Your servant has just hired sheepshearers. Will the king and his servants please come with your servant?"

25 The king replied to Absalom, "No, my son, we should not all go, or we would be a burden to you." Although Absalom urged him, he wasn't willing to go, though he did bless him.

26 "If not," Absalom said, "please let my brother Amnon go with us."

The king asked him, "Why should he go with you?" 27 But Absalom urged him, so he sent Amnon and all the king's sons.[e]

---

[a] **13:11** Lit *said to her* [b] **13:16** Lit *she said to him* [c] **13:18** Or *an ornamented*; Gn 37:3 [d] **13:21** LXX, DSS add *but he did not grieve the spirit of Amnon his son, for he loved him because he was his firstborn*; 1 Kg 1:6 [e] **13:27** LXX adds *And Absalom prepared a feast like a royal feast*.

12:25 Jedidiah. Solomon's nickname means "loved by the Lord."

13:1 Amnon. Amnon was David's oldest son (3:2). Tamar was Amnon's half-sister and Absalom's full sister.

13:13 Where could I ever go with my disgrace? Amnon's suggestion was wicked (Lev.

18:9; 20:17, Deut. 27:22). Rape would cause her to be unfit for marriage (Deut. 22:13-21) and jeopardize Amnon's right to the throne.

13:16 sending me away. The law demanded that Amnon marry Tamar (Deut. 22:29), but in sending her away, he rejected her as a bride. No longer a virgin, Tamar was disgraced.

13:21 he was furious. Though livid, David did not punish his son as the law prescribed (Lev. 20:17). Perhaps he felt he had lost all moral authority on account of Bathsheba. His failure to discipline his children would cause him much grief.

13:23 invited all the king's sons. It was cus-

28 Now Absalom commanded his young men, "Watch Amnon until he is in a good mood from the wine. When I order you to strike Amnon, then kill him. Don't be afraid. Am I not the one who has commanded you? Be strong and courageous!" 29 So Absalom's young men did to Amnon just as Absalom had commanded. Then all ⌊the rest of⌋ the king's sons got up, and each fled on his mule.

30 While they were on the way, a report reached David: "Absalom struck down all the king's sons; not even one of them survived!" 31 In response the king stood up, tore his clothes, and lay down on the ground, and all his servants stood by with their clothes torn.

Absalom's Revenge

1. Who is your school's biggest rival in sports? Has this competition ever gotten out of control?

2 Samuel 13:23-39

2. What motivated Absalom's hatred? Was his anger justified? Were his actions justified?

3. How should Absalom have dealt with the sin of Amnon? How should David have dealt with it?

4. How did Absalom's vengeance injure innocent people? How has your own vengeance injured innocent people?

5. Are you angry with someone who has wronged you? Are you looking for revenge on your rival? What would God have you do about it?

32 But Jonadab, son of David's brother Shimeah, spoke up: "My lord must not think they have killed all the young men, the king's sons, because only Amnon is dead. In fact, Absalom has planned thisᵃ ever since the day Amnon disgraced his sister Tamar. 33 So now, my lord the king, don't take seriously the report that says all the king's sons are dead. Only Amnon is dead."

34 Meanwhile, Absalom had fled. When the young man who was standing watch looked up, there were many people coming from the road west of him from the side of the mountain.ᵇ 35 Jonadab said to the king, "Look, the king's sons have come! It's exactly like your servant said." 36 Just as he finished speaking, the king's

sons entered and wept loudly. Then the king and all his servants also wept bitterly.

37 Now Absalom fled and went to Talmai son of Ammihud, king of Geshur. And David mourned for his sonᶜ every day. 38 Absalom had fled and gone to Geshur where he stayed three years. 39 Then King Davidᵈ longed to go to Absalom, for David had finished grieving over Amnon's death.

Absalom Restored to David

14 Joab son of Zeruiah observed that the king's mind was on Absalom. 2 So Joab sent someone to Tekoa to bring a clever woman from there. He told her, "Pretend to be in mourning: dress in mourning clothes and don't put on any oil. Act like a woman who has been mourning for the dead for a long time. 3 Go to the king and speak these words to him." Then Joab told her exactly what to say.

4 When the woman from Tekoa cameᵉ to the king, she fell with her face to the ground in homage and said, "Help me, my king!"

5 "What's the matter?" the king asked her.

"To tell the truth, I am a widow; my husband died," she said. 6 "Your servant had two sons. They were fighting in the field with no one to separate them, and one struck the other and killed him. 7 Now the whole clan has risen up against your servant and said, 'Hand over the one who killed his brother so we may put him to death for the life of the brother he murdered. We will destroy the heir!' They would extinguish my one remaining ember by not preserving my husband's name or posterity on earth."

8 The king told the woman, "Go home. I will issue a command on your behalf."

9 Then the woman of Tekoa said to the king, "My lord the king, may any blame be on me and my father's house, and may the king and his throne be innocent."

10 "Whoever speaks to you," the king said, "bring him to me. He will not trouble you again!"

11 She replied, "Please, may the king invoke the LORD your God, so that the avenger of blood will not increase the loss, and they will not eliminate my son!"

"As the LORD lives," he vowed, "not a hair of your son will fall to the ground."

12 Then the woman said, "Please, may your servant speak a word to my lord the king?"

"Speak," he replied.

13 The woman asked, "Why have you devised something similar against the people of God? When the king

ᵃ**13:32** Lit In fact, it was established on the mouth of Absalom   ᵇ**13:34** LXX adds And the watchman came and reported to the king saying, "I see men on the Horonaim road on the side of the mountain."   ᶜ**13:37** Probably Amnon   ᵈ**13:39** DSS, LXX, Tg read David's spirit   ᵉ**14:4** Some Hb mss, LXX, Syr, Tg, Vg; other Hb mss read spoke

tomary in Israel to host an annual sheep-shearing festival (1 Sam. 25:2, 8).

13:26 let my brother Amnon go with us. Absalom requested that he send his heir Amnon instead. **Why should he go?** David was suspicious; well aware of the brothers' feud (v. 22).

13:28 to strike Amnon. Absalom's strategy, murdering Amnon when he least expected it— two long years after his sin and during a party he had been invited to— would also secure Absalom's position as successor to the throne.

14:2 Joab sent. Joab knew David missed Absalom and was concerned about the political

ramifications of David's estrangement from the heir. So he sent a Tekoan woman to tell David a story designed to convince him to pardon Absalom. Here Joab is the most active in restoring Absalom, later he kills him (18:14-15).

14:7 They would extinguish my one remaining ember. The death of the woman's remain-

spoke as he did about this matter, he has pronounced his own guilt. The king has not brought back his own banished one. [14] For we will certainly die and be like water poured out on the ground, which can't be recovered. But God would not take away a life; He would devise plans so that the one banished from Him does not remain banished.

[15] "Now therefore, I've come to present this matter to my lord the king because the people have made me afraid. Your servant thought: I must speak to the king. Perhaps the king will grant his servant's request. [16] The king will surely listen in order to rescue his servant from the hand of this man who would eliminate both me and my son from God's inheritance. [17] Your servant thought: May the word of my lord the king bring relief, for my lord the king is able to discern the good and the bad like the Angel of God. May the LORD your God be with you."

[18] Then the king answered the woman, "I'm going to ask you something; don't conceal it from me!"

"Let my lord the king speak," the woman replied.

[19] The king asked, "Did Joab put you up to[a] all this?"

The woman answered. "As surely as you live, my lord the king, no one can turn to the right or left from all my lord the king says. Yes, your servant Joab is the one who gave orders to me; he told your servant exactly what to say. [20] Joab your servant has done this to address the issue indirectly,[b] but my lord has wisdom like the wisdom of the Angel of God, knowing everything on earth."

[21] Then the king said to Joab, "I hereby grant this request. Go, bring back the young man Absalom."

[22] Joab fell with his face to the ground in homage and praised the king. "Today," Joab said, "your servant knows I have found favor with you, my lord the king, because the king has granted the request of your servant."

[23] So Joab got up, went to Geshur, and brought Absalom to Jerusalem. [24] However, the king added, "He may return to his house, but he may not see my face." So Absalom returned to his house, but he did not see the king.[c]

[25] No man in all Israel was as handsome and highly praised as Absalom. From the sole of his foot to the top of his head, he did not have a single flaw. [26] When he shaved his head—he shaved ⌊it⌋ every year because ⌊his hair⌋ got so heavy for him that he had to shave it off—he would weigh the hair from his head and it would be five pounds[d] according to the royal standard.

[27] Three sons were born to Absalom, and a daughter named Tamar, who was a beautiful woman. [28] Absalom resided in Jerusalem two years but never saw the king. [29] Then Absalom sent for Joab in order to send him to the king, but Joab was unwilling to come. So he sent again, a second time, but he still wouldn't come. [30] Then Absalom said to his servants, "See, Joab has a field right next to mine, and he has barley there. Go and set fire to it!" So Absalom's servants set the field on fire.[e]

[31] Then Joab came to Absalom's house and demanded, "Why did your servants set my field on fire?"

[32] "Look," Absalom explained to Joab, "I sent for you and said, 'Come here. I want to send you to the king to ask: Why have I come back from Geshur? I'd be better off if I were still there.' So now, let me see the king. If I am guilty, let him kill me."

[33] Joab went to the king and told him. So David summoned Absalom, who came to the king and bowed down with his face to the ground before the king. Then the king kissed Absalom.

Absalom's Revolt

15 After this, Absalom got himself a chariot, horses, and 50 men to run before him. [2] He would get up early and stand beside the road leading to the city •gate. Whenever anyone had a grievance to bring before the king for settlement, Absalom called out to him and asked, "What city are you from?" If he replied, "Your servant is from one of the tribes of Israel," [3] Absalom said to him, "Look, your claims are good and right, but the king does not have anyone to listen to you." [4] He added, "If only someone would appoint me judge in the land. Then anyone who had a grievance or dispute could come to me, and I would make sure he received justice." [5] When a person approached to bow down to him, Absalom reached out his hand, took hold of him, and kissed him. [6] Absalom did this to all the Israelites who came to the king for a settlement. So Absalom stole the hearts of the men of Israel.

[7] When four[f] years had passed, Absalom said to the king, "Please let me go to Hebron to fulfill a vow I made to the LORD. [8] For your servant made a vow when I lived in Geshur of Aram, saying: If the LORD really brings me back to Jerusalem, I will worship the LORD in Hebron."[g]

[9] "Go in peace," the king said to him. So he went to Hebron.

---

[a] **14:19** Lit *Is the hand of Joab in*   [b] **14:20** Lit *to go around the face of the matter*   [c] **14:24** Lit *king's face*   [d] **14:26** Lit *200 shekels*   [e] **14:30** DSS, LXX add *So Joab's servants came to him with their clothes torn and said, "Absalom's servants have set the field on fire!"*   [f] **15:7** Some LXX mss, Syr, Vg; other LXX mss, MT read *40*   [g] **15:8** Some LXX mss; MT omits *in Hebron*

---

ing son would mean the elimination of her only source of financial support and her dead husband's family name.

14:24 He may return to his house, but he may not see my face. David refused to grant Absalom access to the palace. In the end, David's coldness toward Absalom drove a wedge between them.

14:26 When he shaved his head. The mention of Absalom's hair is particularly notable because it eventually played a role in his death (18:9).

14:32 let me see the king. Absalom demanded to either be granted full pardon or be punished by death. He was outraged at how he was treated but gave no sign of repentance for killing Amnon.

14:33 the king kissed Absalom. The kiss was a symbol of David's forgiveness and Absalom's restoration to the royal family. David did not ask for Absalom to repent, thereby further failing to

10 Then Absalom sent messengers throughout the tribes of Israel with this message: "When you hear the sound of the ram's horn, you are to say, 'Absalom has become king in Hebron!'"

11 Two hundred men from Jerusalem went with Absalom. They had been invited and were going innocently, for they knew nothing about the whole matter. 12 While he was offering the sacrifices, Absalom sent for David's adviser Ahithophel the Gilonite, from his city of Giloh. So the conspiracy grew strong, and the people supporting Absalom continued to increase.

13 Then an informer came to David and reported, "The hearts of the men of Israel are with Absalom."

14 David said to all the servants with him in Jerusalem, "Get up. We have to flee, or we will not escape from Absalom! Leave quickly, or he will overtake us, heap disaster on us, and strike the city with the edge of the sword."

15 The king's servants said to him, "Whatever my lord the king decides, we are your servants." 16 Then the king set out, and his entire household followed him. But he left behind 10 concubines to take care of the palace. 17 So the king set out, and all the people followed him. They stopped at the last house 18 while all his servants marched past him. Then all the Cherethites, the Pelethites, and the Gittites—600 men who came with him from Gath—marched past the king.

19 The king said to Ittai the Gittite, "Why are you also going with us? Go back and stay with the king since you're both a foreigner and an exile from your homeland. 20 Besides, you only arrived yesterday; should I make you wander around with us today while I go wherever I can? Go back and take your brothers with you. May the LORD show you kindness and faithfulness."

21 But in response, Ittai vowed to the king, "As surely as the LORD lives and as my lord the king lives, wherever my lord the king is, whether it means life or death, your servant will be there!"

22 "March on," David replied to Ittai. So Ittai the Gittite marched past with all his men and the children who were with him. 23 Everyone in the countryside was weeping loudly while all the people were marching past. As the king was crossing the Kidron Valley, all the people were marching past on the road that leads to the desert.

24 Zadok was also there, and all the Levites with him were carrying the ark of the covenant of God. They set the ark of God down, and Abiathar offered ⌊sacrifices⌋a until the people had finished marching past. 25 Then

the king instructed Zadok, "Return the ark of God to the city. If I find favor in the LORD's eyes, He will bring me back and allow me to see both it and its dwelling place. 26 However, if He should say, 'I do not delight in you,' then here I am—He can do with me whatever pleases Him."b

27 The king also said to Zadok the priest, "Look,c return to the city in peace and your two sons with you: your son Ahimaaz and Abiathar's son Jonathan. 28 Remember, I'll wait at the fords of the wilderness until word comes from you to inform me." 29 So Zadok and Abiathar returned the ark of God to Jerusalem and stayed there.

30 David was climbing the slope of the Mount of Olives, weeping as he ascended. His head was covered, and he was walking barefoot. Each of the people with him covered their heads and went up, weeping as they ascended.

31 Then someone reported to David: "Ahithophel is among the conspirators with Absalom."

"LORD," David pleaded, "please turn the counsel of Ahithophel into foolishness!"

32 When David came to the summit where he used to worship God, there to meet him was Hushai the Archite with his robe torn and dust on his head. 33 David said to him, "If you go away with me, you'll be a burden to me, 34 but if you return to the city and tell Absalom, 'I will be your servant, my king! Previously, I was your father's servant, but now I will be your servant,' then you can counteract Ahithophel's counsel for me. 35 Won't Zadok and Abiathar the priests be there with you? Report everything you hear from the king's palace to Zadok and Abiathar the priests. 36 Take note: their two sons, Zadok's son Ahimaaz and Abiathar's son Jonathan, are there with them. Send me everything you hear through them." 37 So Hushai, David's personal adviser, entered Jerusalem just as Absalom was entering the city.

Ziba Helps David

16 When David had gone a little beyond the summit,d Ziba, Mephibosheth's servant, was right there to meet him. He had a pair of saddled donkeys loaded with 200 loaves of bread, 100 clusters of raisins, 100 ⌊bunches⌋ of summer fruit,e and a skin of wine. 2 The king said to Ziba, "Why do you have these?"

Ziba answered, "The donkeys are for the king's household to ride, the bread and summer fruit are for

---

a15:24 Or *Abiathar went up*   b15:26 Lit *me what is good in His eyes*   c15:27 LXX; MT reads *Are you a seer?*   d16:1 = Mount of Olives
e16:1 Probably dates or figs

---

deal with the situation justly. Absalom remained bitter at David's delay in forgiving him.

15:1-2 chariot, horses. Absalom was the first Israelite leader known to have a chariot. **stand beside the road.** Absalom gained popularity by making himself available to hear the complaints of the masses. He even supported their

complaints without investigating them. Then he told them that the king would not help them, an ancient version of dirty politics.

15:7 go to Hebron. This important city was 20 miles south of Jerusalem.

15:18 Cherethites, the Pelethites. These were elite units of David's army (8:18).

15:25 Return the ark of God. David understood that the Ark of the Covenant was the symbol of God's presence and belonged in the capital city regardless of where the king was.

15:27 Look, return to the city in peace. David wanted the priests to remain in the tab-

the young men to eat, and the wine is for those who become exhausted to drink in the desert."

³ "Where is your master's son?" the king asked.

"Why, he's staying in Jerusalem," Ziba replied to the king, "for he said, 'Today, the house of Israel will restore my father's kingdom to me.' "

⁴ The king said to Ziba, "All that belongs to Mephibosheth is now yours!"

"I bow ⌊before you⌋," Ziba said. "May you look favorably on me, my lord the king!"

Shimei Curses David

⁵ When King David got to Bahurim, a man belonging to the family of the house of Saul was just coming out. His name was Shimei son of Gera, and he was yelling curses as he approached. ⁶ He threw stones at David and at all the royalᵃ servants, the people and the warriors on David's right and left. ⁷ Shimei said as he cursed: "Get out, get out, you worthless murderer! ⁸ The LORD has paid you back for all the blood of the house of Saul in whose place you rule, and the LORD has handed the kingdom over to your son Absalom. Look, you are in trouble because you're a murderer!"

⁹ Then Abishai son of Zeruiah said to the king, "Why should this dead dog curse my lord the king? Let me go over and cut his head off!"

¹⁰ The king replied, "Sons of Zeruiah, do we agree on anything? He curses ⌊me⌋ this way because the LORDᵇ told him, 'Curse David!' Therefore, who can say, 'Why did you do that?' " ¹¹ Then David said to Abishai and all his servants, "Look, my own son, my own flesh and blood,ᶜ intends to take my life—how much more now this Benjaminite! Leave him alone and let him curse ⌊me⌋; the LORD has told him to. ¹² Perhaps the LORD will see my afflictionᵈ and restore goodness to me instead of Shimei's curses today." ¹³ So David and his men proceeded along the road as Shimei was going along the ridge of the hill opposite him. As Shimei went, he cursed ⌊David⌋, and threw stones and dirt at him. ¹⁴ Finally, the king and all the people with him arrivedᵉ exhausted, so they rested there.

Absalom's Advisers

¹⁵ Now Absalom and all the Israelites came to Jerusalem. Ahithophel was also with him. ¹⁶ When David's friend Hushai the Archite came to Absalom, Hushai said to Absalom, "Long live the king! Long live the king!"

¹⁷ "Is this your loyalty to your friend?" Absalom asked Hushai. "Why didn't you go with your friend?"

¹⁸ "Not at all," Hushai answered Absalom. "I am on the side of the one that the LORD, the people, and all the men of Israel have chosen. I will stay with him. ¹⁹ Furthermore, whom will I serve if not his son? As I served in your father's presence, I will also serve in yours."

²⁰ Then Absalom said to Ahithophel, "Give ⌊me⌋ your advice. What should we do?"

²¹ Ahithophel replied to Absalom, "Sleep with your father's concubines he left to take care of the palace. When all Israel hears that you have become repulsive to your father, everyone with you will be encouraged." ²² So they pitched a tent for Absalom on the roof, and he slept with his father's concubines in the sight of all Israel.

²³ Now the advice Ahithophel gave in those days was like someone asking about a word from God—such was the regard that both David and Absalom had for Ahithophel's advice. ¹ Ahithophel said to Absalom, "Let me choose 12,000 men, and I will set out in pursuit of David tonight. ² I will attack him while he is weak and weary, throw him into a panic, and all the people with him will scatter. I will strike down only the king ³ and bring all the people back to you. When everyone returns ⌊except⌋ the man you're seeking, allᶠ the people will be at peace." ⁴ This proposal seemed good to Absalom and all the elders of Israel.

⁵ Then Absalom said, "Summon Hushai the Archite also. Let's hear what he has to say as well."

⁶ So Hushai came to Absalom, and Absalom told him: "Ahithophel offered this proposal. Should we carry out his proposal? If not, what do you say?"

⁷ Hushai replied to Absalom, "The advice Ahithophel has given this time is not good." ⁸ Hushai continued, "You know your father and his men. They are warriors and are desperate like a wild bear robbed of her cubs. Your father is an experienced soldier who won't spend the night with the people. ⁹ He's probably already hiding in one of the cavesᵍ or some other place. If some of our troops fallʰ first, someone is sure to hear and say, 'There's been a slaughter among the people who follow Absalom.' ¹⁰ Then, even a brave man with the heart of a lion will melt because all Israel knows that your father and the valiant men with him are warriors. ¹¹ Instead, I advise that all Israel from Dan to Beer-sheba—as numerous as the sand by the sea—be gathered to you and that you personally go into battle. ¹² Then we will attack David wherever we find him, and we will descend on him like dew on the ground. Not even one

---

ᵃ **16:6** Lit *all King David's*   ᵇ **16:10** Alt Hb tradition reads *If he curses, and if the LORD*   ᶜ **16:11** Lit *son who came from my belly*   ᵈ **16:12** Some Hb mss, LXX, Syr, Vg; other Hb mss read *iniquity*   ᵉ **16:14** LXX adds *at the Jordan*   ᶠ **17:3** LXX reads *to you as a bride returns to her husband. You seek the life of only one man, and all*   ᵍ **17:9** Or *pits, or ravines*   ʰ **17:9** Lit *And it will be when a falling on them at*

---

ernacle and be available to receive any messages the Lord might give them to tell David.

16:4 All that belongs to Mephibosheth. David believed Ziba's story, assuming the worst. Later he ran into Mephibosheth (19:24-30), who claimed that Ziba lied.

16:7 you worthless murderer! While it is pos-

sible he was accusing David in the death of Saul or members of Saul's family, David may have taken it as a reference to Uriah's death.

16:8 The LORD has paid you back. Shimei blamed David for the downfall of Saul's family. His accusations were untrue because David did not even strike Saul and made every effort

on behalf of his surviving family.

16:21 Sleep with your father's concubines he left. This act signified that Absalom was claiming royal power and made it impossible for reconciliation. It also fulfilled Nathan's prophecy (12:11-12).

17:1-3 set out in pursuit of David tonight.

will be left of all the men with him. 13 If he retreats to some city, all Israel will bring ropes to that city, and we will drag its ⌊stones⌋ into the valley until not even a pebble can be found there." 14 Since the LORD had decreed that Ahithophel's good advice be undermined in order to bring about Absalom's ruin, Absalom and all the men of Israel said, "The advice of Hushai the Archite is better than Ahithophel's advice."

David Informed of Absalom's Plans

15 Hushai then told the priests Zadok and Abiathar, "This is whata Ahithophel advised Absalom and the elders of Israel, and this is whatb I advised. 16 Now send someone quickly and tell David, 'Don't spend the night at the wilderness ford ⌊of the Jordan⌋, but be sure to cross over, or the king and all the people with him will be destroyed.' "

17 Jonathan and Ahimaaz were staying at En-rogel, where a servant girl would come and pass along information to them. They in turn would go and inform King David, because they dared not be seen entering the city. 18 However, a young man did see them and informed Absalom. So the two left quickly and came to the house of a man in Bahurim. He had a well in his courtyard, and they climbed down into it. 19 Then his wife took the cover, placed it over the mouth of the well, and scattered grain on it so nobody would know anything.

20 Absalom's servants came to the woman at the house and asked, "Where are Ahimaaz and Jonathan?"

"They passed by toward the water,"c the woman replied to them. The men searched but did not find ⌊them⌋, so they returned to Jerusalem.

21 After they had gone, Ahimaaz and Jonathan climbed out of the well and went and informed King David. They told him, "Get up and immediately ford the river, for Ahithophel has given this advice against you." 22 So David and all the people with him got up and crossed the Jordan. By daybreak, there was no one who had not crossed the Jordan. 23 When Ahithophel realized that his advice had not been followed, he saddled his donkey and set out for his house in his hometown. He set his affairs in orderd and hanged himself. So he died and was buried in his father's tomb.

24 David had arrived at Mahanaim by the time Absalom crossed the Jordan with all the men of Israel. 25 Now Absalom had appointed Amasa over the army in Joab's place. Amasa was the son of a man named Ithrae

the Israelite;f Ithra had married Abigail daughter of Nahash.g Abigail was a sister to Zeruiah, Joab's mother. 26 And Israel and Absalom camped in the land of Gilead. 27 When David came to Mahanaim, Shobi son of Nahash from Rabbah of the Ammonites, Machir son of Ammiel from Lo-debar, and Barzillai the Gileadite from Rogelim 28 brought beds, basins,h and pottery items. ⌊They also brought⌋ wheat, barley, flour, roasted grain, beans, lentils,i 29 honey, curds, sheep, and cheesej from the herd for David and the people with him to eat. They had reasoned, "The people must be hungry, exhausted, and thirsty in the desert."

Absalom's Defeat

18 David reviewed his troops and appointed commanders of hundreds and of thousands over them. 2 He then sent out the troops, one third under Joab, one third under Joab's brother Abishai son of Zeruiah, and one third under Ittai the Gittite. The king said to the troops, "I will also march out with you."

3 "You must not go!" the people pleaded. "If we have to flee, they will not pay any attention to us. Even if half of us die, they will not pay any attention to us because you are worthk 10,000 of us. Therefore, it is better if you support us from the city."

4 "I will do whatever you think is best," the king replied to them. So he stood beside the gate while all the troops marched out by hundreds and thousands. 5 The king commanded Joab, Abishai, and Ittai, "Treat the young man Absalom gently for my sake." All the people heard the king's orders to all the commanders about Absalom.

6 Then David's forces marched into the field to engage Israel in battle, which took place in the forest of Ephraim. 7 The people of Israel were defeated by David's soldiers, and the slaughter there was vast that day—20,000 ⌊casualties⌋. 8 The battle spread over the entire region, and that day the forest claimed more people than the sword.

Absalom's Death

9 Absalom was riding on his mule when he happened to meet David's soldiers. When the mule went under the tangled branches of a large oak tree, Absalom's head was caught fast in the tree. The mule under him kept going, so he was suspended in midair.l 10 One of the men saw ⌊him⌋ and informed Joab. He said, "I just saw Absalom hanging in an oak tree!"

---

a17:15 Lit Like this and like this   b17:15 Lit and like this and like this   c17:20 Or brook; Hb obscure   d17:23 Lit He commanded his house   e17:25 Or Jether   f17:25 Some LXX mss read Ishmaelite   g17:25 Some LXX mss read Jesse   h17:28 LXX reads brought 10 embroidered beds with double coverings, 10 vessels   i17:28 LXX, Syr; MT adds roasted grain   j 17:29 Hb obscure   k18:3 Some Hb mss, LXX, Vg; other Hb mss read because there would now be about   l18:9 Lit was between heaven and earth

---

Ahithophel underestimated the loyalty of David's soldiers, assuming that with David absent, his armies would scatter.

17:7-13 Hushai, secretly loyal to David, convinced Absalom to disregard Ahithophel's advice and amass a huge army before attacking, hoping to buy David some time.

17:16 be sure to cross over. Hushai warned David to cross the Jordan in case Absalom changed his mind and followed Ahithophel's advice.

17:23 set his affairs in order and hanged himself. Ahithophel's suicide comes in response to two realities: (1) he had lost his role

as the most respected advisor in the land (16:23), and his advice had been spurned (17:14); and (2) he had cast his unsuccessful lot with Absalom. He faced most certain execution.

18:8 that day the forest claimed more people than the sword. Guerilla tactics favored

11 "You just saw ⌊him⌋!" Joab exclaimed.ᵃ "Why didn't you strike him to the ground right there? I would have given you 10 silver piecesᵇ and a belt!"

12 The man replied to Joab, "Even if I had the weight of 1,000 pieces of silverᶜ in my hand, I would not raise my hand against the king's son. For we heard the king command you, Abishai, and Ittai, 'Protect the young man Absalom for me.'ᵈ 13 If I had jeopardized my ownᵉ life—and nothing is hidden from the king—you would have abandoned me."

14 Joab said, "I'm not going to waste time with you!" He then took three spears in his hand and thrust them into Absalom's heart while he was still alive in the oak tree, 15 and 10 young men who were Joab's armor-bearers surrounded Absalom, struck him, and killed him.

16 Afterwards, Joab blew the ram's horn, and the troops broke off their pursuit of Israel because Joab restrained them. 17 They took Absalom, threw him into a large pit in the forest, and piled a huge mound of stones over him. And all Israel fled, each to his tent.

18 When he was alive, Absalom had erected for himself a pillar in the King's Valley, for he had said, "I have no son to preserve the memory of my name." So he gave the pillar his name. It is still called Absalom's Monument today.

19 Ahimaaz son of Zadok said, "Please let me run and tell the king the good news that the LORD has delivered him from his enemies."

20 Joab replied to him, "You are not the man to take good news today. You may do it another day, but today you aren't taking good news, because the king's son is dead." 21 Joab then said to the •Cushite, "Go tell the king what you have seen." The Cushite bowed to Joab and took off running.

22 However, Ahimaaz son of Zadok persisted and said to Joab, "No matter what, please let me run too behind the Cushite!"

Joab replied, "My son, why do you want to run since you won't get a reward?"

23 "No matter what I want to run!"

"Then run!" Joab said to him. So Ahimaaz ran by way of the plain and outran the Cushite.

24 David was sitting between the two gates when the watchman went up to the roof of the gate and over to the wall. The watchman looked out and saw a man running alone. 25 He called out and told the king.

The king said, "If he's alone, he bears good news."

As the first runner came closer, 26 the watchman saw another man running. He called out to the gatekeeper, "Look! Another man is running alone!"

"This one is also bringing good news," said the king.

27 The watchman said, "The way the first man runs looks to me like the way Ahimaaz son of Zadok runs."

"This is a good man; he comes with good news," the king commented.

28 Ahimaaz called out to the king, "All is well," and then bowed down to the king with his face to the ground. He continued, "May the LORD your God be praised! He delivered up the men who rebelled against my lord the king."

29 The king asked, "Is the young man Absalom all right?"

Ahimaaz replied, "When Joab sent the king's servant and your servant, I saw a big disturbance, but I don't know what ⌊it was⌋."

30 The king said, "Move aside and stand here." So he stood to one side.

31 Just then the Cushite came and said, "May my lord the king hear the good news: today the LORD has delivered you from all those rising up against you!"

32 The king asked the Cushite, "Is the young man Absalom all right?"

The Cushite replied, "May what has become of the young man happen to the enemies of my lord the king and to all who rise up against you with evil intent."

33ᶠ The king was deeply moved and went up to the gate chamber and wept. As he walked, he cried, "My son Absalom! My son, my son Absalom! If only I had died instead of you, Absalom, my son, my son!"

David's Kingdom Restored

19 It was reported to Joab, "The king is weeping. He's mourning over Absalom." 2 That day's victory was turned into mourning for all the troops because on that day the troops heard, "The king is grieving over his son." 3 So they returned to the city quietly that day like people come in when they are humiliated after fleeing in battle. 4 But the king hid his face and cried out at the top of his voice, "My son Absalom! Absalom, my son, my son!"

5 Then Joab went into the house to the king and said, "Today you have shamed all your soldiers—those who rescued your life and the lives of your sons and daughters, your wives, and your concubines. 6 You love your enemies and hate those who love you! Today you have made it clear that the commanders and soldiers mean nothing to you. In fact, today I know that if Absalom were alive and all of us were dead, it would be fine with you!ᵍ

ᵃ18:11 Lit Joab said to the man who told him   ᵇ18:11 c. 4 ounces   ᶜ18:12 c. 25 pounds   ᵈ18:12 Some Hb mss, LXX, Tg, Vg; other Hb mss read Protect, whoever, the young man Absalom; Hb obscure   ᵉ18:13 Alt Hb tradition reads jeopardized his   ᶠ18:33 2 Sm 19:1 in Hb   ᵍ19:6 Lit be right in your eyes

---

by David's warrior utilized he rough terrain against superior numbers.

18:9 Absalom's head. Ironically, Absalom's beautiful hair (14:25) became his undoing.

18:13 you would have abandoned me. This man knew political reality: lower level people get sacrificed in order to protect the

involvement of higher-ups.

18:17 a huge mound of stones The pile of stones may have been a memorial ridiculing the memorial Absalom made for himself (v. 18).

18:27 a good man ... with good news. Messengers were chosen based on what type of news was being delivered.

19:9 the people among all the tribes of Israel were arguing. On the one hand, David was an effective leader who accomplished great things for them in the past. On the other hand, he fled from the land—not a very kingly thing to do.

19:11 restore the king. David appealed to his

7 "Now get up! Go out and encourage[a] your soldiers, for I swear by the LORD that if you don't go out, not a man will remain with you tonight. This will be worse for you than all the trouble that has come to you from your youth until now!"

8 So the king got up and sat in the •gate, and all the people were told: "Look, the king is sitting in the gate." Then they all came into the king's presence.

Meanwhile, each Israelite had fled to his tent. 9 All the people among all the tribes of Israel were arguing: "The king delivered us from the grasp of our enemies, and he rescued us from the grasp of the Philistines, but now he has fled from the land because of Absalom. 10 But Absalom, the man we anointed over us, has died in battle. So why do you say nothing about restoring the king?"

11 King David sent word to the priests, Zadok and Abiathar: "Say to the elders of Judah, 'Why should you be the last to restore the king to his palace? The talk of all Israel has reached the king at his house. 12 You are my brothers, my flesh and blood. So why should you be the last to restore the king?' 13 And tell Amasa, 'Aren't you my flesh and blood? May God punish me and do so severely if you don't become commander of the army from now on instead of Joab!'"

14 So he won over[b] all the men of Judah, and they sent word to the king: "Come back, you and all your servants." 15 Then the king returned. When he arrived at the Jordan, Judah came to Gilgal to meet the king and escort him across the Jordan.

16 Shimei son of Gera, a Benjaminite from Bahurim, hurried down with the men of Judah to meet King David. 17 There were 1,000 men from Benjamin with him. Ziba, an attendant from the house of Saul, with his 15 sons and 20 servants also rushed down to the Jordan ahead of the king. 18 They forded the Jordan to bring the king's household across and do whatever the king desired.[c]

When Shimei son of Gera crossed the Jordan, he fell down before the king 19 and said to him, "My lord, don't hold me guilty, and don't remember your servant's wrongdoing on the day my lord the king left Jerusalem. May the king not take it to heart. 20 For your servant knows that I have sinned. But look! Today I am the first one of the entire house of Joseph to come down to meet my lord the king."

21 Abishai son of Zeruiah asked, "Shouldn't Shimei be put to death for this, because he ridiculed the LORD's anointed?"

22 David answered, "Sons of Zeruiah, do we agree on anything? Have you become my adversary today? Should any man be killed in Israel today? Am I not aware that today I'm king over Israel?" 23 So the king said to Shimei, "You will not die." Then the king gave him his oath.

24 Mephibosheth, Saul's grandson, also went down to meet the king. He had not taken care of his feet, trimmed his moustache, or washed his clothes from the day the king left until the day he returned safely. 25 When he came from Jerusalem to meet the king, the king asked him, "Mephibosheth, why didn't you come with me?"

26 "My lord the king," he replied, "my servant ⌊Ziba⌋ betrayed me. Actually your servant said: 'I'll saddle the donkey for myself[d] so that I may ride it and go with the king'—for your servant is lame. 27 Ziba slandered your servant to my lord the king. But my lord the king is like the Angel of God, so do whatever you think best.[e] 28 For my grandfather's entire family deserves death from my lord the king, but you set your servant among those who eat at your table. So what further right do I have to keep on making appeals to the king?"

29 The king said to him, "Why keep on speaking about ⌊these⌋ matters of yours? I hereby declare: you and Ziba are to divide the land."

30 Mephibosheth said to the king, "Instead, since my lord the king has come to his palace safely, let Ziba take it all!"

31 Barzillai the Gileadite had come down from Rogelim and accompanied the king to the Jordan River to see him off at the Jordan. 32 Barzillai was a very old man—80 years old—and since he was a very wealthy man, he had provided for the needs of the king while he stayed in Mahanaim.

33 The king said to Barzillai, "Cross over with me, and I'll provide for you[f] at my side in Jerusalem."

34 Barzillai replied to the king, "How many years of my life are left that I should go up to Jerusalem with the king? 35 I'm now 80 years old. Can I discern what is pleasant and what is not? Can your servant taste what he eats or drinks? Can I still hear the voice of male and female singers? Why should your servant be an added burden to my lord the king? 36 Since your servant is only going with the king a little way across the Jordan, why should the king repay me with such a reward? 37 Please let your servant return so that I may die in my own city near the tomb of my father and mother. But here is your servant Chimham: let him cross over with

---

a**19:7** Lit *speak to the heart of*   b**19:14** Lit *he turned the heart of*   c**19:18** Lit *do what is good in his eyes*   d**19:26** LXX, Syr, Vg read *said to him, "Saddle the donkey for me*   e**19:27** Lit *do what is good in your eyes*   f**19:33** LXX reads *for your old age*; Ru 4:15

---

faithful priests to take the initiative in inviting him back to the throne.

19:13 Amasa. As a further means of gaining support, particularly from Judah, David appointed Amasa commander of his army in place of Joab. Amasa had been commander of Absalom's army, thus gaining the allegiance

of the rebels. Apparently Joab's disagreements with David's policies and killing Absalom made David distrust him.

19:17 from Benjamin. This large contingent probably feared that they would be associated with Shimei's cursing. They were a sign to David that Saul's family had

at last accepted him as king.

19:23 Shimei, "You will not die." David kept the pledge he made that day. However, Shimei eventually paid for his sin at the hand of Solomon, at David's request (1 Kings 2:8-9, 36-46).

19:25 why didn't you come with me? Re-

my lord the king. Do for him what seems good to you."[a]

38 The king replied, "Chimham will cross over with me, and I will do for him what seems good to you,[a] and whatever you desire from me I will do for you." 39 So all the people crossed the Jordan, and then the king crossed. The king kissed Barzillai and blessed him, and Barzillai returned to his home.

40 The king went on to Gilgal, and Chimham went with him. All the troops of Judah and half of Israel's escorted the king. 41 Suddenly, all the men of Israel came to the king. They asked him, "Why did our brothers, the men of Judah, take you away secretly and transport the king and his household across the Jordan, along with all of David's men?"

42 All the men of Judah responded to the men of Israel, "Because the king is our relative. Why does this make you angry? Have we ever eaten anything of the king's or been honored at all?"[b]

43 The men of Israel answered the men of Judah: "We have 10 shares in the king, so we have a greater [claim] to David than you. Why then do you despise us? Weren't we the first to speak of restoring our king?" But the words of the men of Judah were harsher than those of the men of Israel.

Sheba's Revolt

20 Now a wicked man, a Benjaminite named Sheba son of Bichri, happened to be there. He blew the ram's horn and shouted:

We have no portion in David,
no inheritance in Jesse's son.
Each man to his tent, Israel!

2 So all the men of Israel deserted David and followed Sheba son of Bichri, but the men of Judah from the Jordan all the way to Jerusalem remained loyal to their king.

3 When David came to his palace in Jerusalem, he took the 10 concubines he had left to take care of the palace and placed them under guard. He provided for them, but he was not intimate with them. They were confined until the day of their death, living as widows.

4 The king said to Amasa, "Summon the men of Judah to me within three days and be here yourself." 5 Amasa went to summon Judah, but he took longer than the time allotted him. 6 So David said to Abishai, "Sheba son of Bichri will do more harm to us than Absalom. Take your lord's soldiers and pursue him, or he will find fortified cities and elude us."[c]

7 So Joab's men, the Cherethites, the Pelethites, and all the warriors marched out under Abishai's command;[d] they left Jerusalem to pursue Sheba son of Bichri. 8 They were at the great stone in Gibeon when Amasa joined them. Joab was wearing his uniform and over it was a belt around his waist with a sword in its sheath. As he approached, [the sword] fell out. 9 Joab asked Amasa, "Are you well, my brother?" Then with his right hand Joab grabbed Amasa by the beard to kiss him. 10 Amasa was not on guard against the sword in Joab's hand, and Joab stabbed him in the stomach with it and spilled his intestines out on the ground. Joab did not stab him again for Amasa was dead. Joab and his brother Abishai pursued Sheba son of Bichri.

11 One of Joab's young men had stood over Amasa saying, "Whoever favors Joab and whoever is for David, follow Joab!" 12 Now Amasa was writhing in his blood in the middle of the highway, and the man had seen that all the people stopped. So he moved Amasa from the highway to the field and threw a garment over him because he realized that all those who encountered Amasa were stopping. 13 When he was removed from the highway, all the men passed by and followed Joab to pursue Sheba son of Bichri.

14 Sheba passed through all the tribes of Israel to Abel of Beth-maacah. All the Berites[e] came together and followed him. 15 Joab's troops came and besieged Sheba in Abel of Beth-maacah. They built an assault ramp against the outer wall of the city. While all the troops with Joab were battering the wall to make it collapse, 16 a wise woman called out from the city, "Listen! Listen! Please tell Joab to come here and let me speak with him."

17 When he had come near her, the woman asked, "Are you Joab?"

"I am," he replied.

"Listen to the words of your servant," she said to him.

He answered, "I'm listening."

18 She said, "In the past they used to say, 'Seek counsel in Abel,' and that's how they settled [disputes]. 19 I am a peaceful person, one of the faithful in Israel, but you're trying to destroy a city that is like a mother in Israel. Why would you devour the LORD's inheritance?"

20 Joab protested: "Never! I do not want to destroy! 21 That is not [my] intention. There is a man named Sheba son of Bichri, from the hill country of Ephraim, who has rebelled against King David. Deliver this one man, and I will withdraw from the city."

---

[a]19:37,38 Lit what is good in your eyes   [b]19:42 LXX reads king's or has he given us a gift or granted us a portion   [c]20:6 Lit and snatch away our eyes   [d]20:7 Lit out following him   [e]20:14 LXX, Vg read Bichrites

---

membering Ziba's accusations, David questioned Mephibosheth's allegiance (16:3).
19:29 you and Ziba are to divide the land. In this way, David did not have to determine whose story was true.
19:43 a greater [claim] to David. Forming 10 of 12 tribes, Israel claimed a greater share in

David's kingship despite having just supported Absalom.
20:1 Benjaminite. The royal house had once been Benjamin under Saul, but was forfeited by his actions. **We have no portion in David.** Sheba played on Israel's fear of being treated with contempt (19:43).

20:3 took the 10 concubines. The concubines reminded everyone of the tragic consequences of Absalom's sin (15:16; 16:22).
20:10 Joab stabbed him in the stomach. Joab had a track record for treachery (3:26-30; 18:12-14). David would not let Joab's actions be forgotten or go unpunished (1 Kings 2:5-6).

The woman replied to Joab, "All right. His head will be thrown over the wall to you." 22 The woman went to all the people with her wise counsel, and they cut off the head of Sheba son of Bichri and threw it to Joab. So he blew the ram's horn, and they dispersed from the city, each to his own tent. Joab returned to the king in Jerusalem.

23 Joab commanded the whole army of Israel; Benaiah son of Jehoiada was over the Cherethites and Pelethites; 24 Adorama was in charge of forced labor; Jehoshaphat son of Ahilud was court historian; 25 Sheva was court secretary; Zadok and Abiathar were priests; 26 and in addition, Ira the Jairite was David's priest.

Justice for the Gibeonites

21 During David's reign there was a famine for three successive years, so David inquired of the LORD. The LORD answered, "It is because of the blood shed by Saul and his family when he killed the Gibeonites."

2 The Gibeonites were not Israelites but rather a remnant of the Amorites. The Israelites had taken an oath concerning them, but Saul had tried to kill them in his zeal for the Israelites and Judah. So David summoned the Gibeonites and spoke to them. 3 He asked the Gibeonites, "What should I do for you? How can I wipe out this guilt so that you will bring a blessing onb the LORD's inheritance?"

4 The Gibeonites said to him, "We are not asking for money fromc Saul or his family, and we cannot put anyone to death in Israel."

"Whatever you say, I will do for you," he said.

5 They replied to the king, "As for the man who annihilated us and plotted to exterminate us so we would not exist within the whole territory of Israel, 6 let seven of his male descendants be handed over to us so we may hangd them in the presence of the LORD at Gibeah of Saul, the LORD's chosen."

The king answered, "I will hand them over."

7 David spared Mephibosheth, the son of Saul's son Jonathan, because of the oath of the LORD that was between David and Jonathan, Saul's son. 8 But the king took Armoni and Mephibosheth, who were the two sons whom Rizpah daughter of Aiah had borne to Saul, and the five sons whom Merabe daughter of Saul had borne to Adriel son of Barzillai the Meholathite 9 and handed them over to the Gibeonites. They hangedf them on the hill in the presence of the LORD; the seven of them died together. They were executed in the first days of the harvest at the beginning of the barley harvest.g

The Burial of Saul's Family

10 Rizpah, Aiah's daughter, took •sackcloth and spread it out for herself on the rock from the beginning of the harvest until the rain poured down from heaven on the bodies.h She kept the birds of the sky from them by day and the wild animals by night.

11 When it was reported to David what Saul's concubine Rizpah, daughter of Aiah, had done, 12 he went and got the bones of Saul and his son Jonathan from the leaders of Jabesh-gilead. They had stolen them from the public square of Beth-shan where the Philistines had hung them the day the Philistines killed Saul at Gilboa. 13 David had the bones brought from there. They also gathered up the bones of Saul's family who had been hung.f 14 They ⌊also⌋ buried the bones of Saul and his son Jonathan at Zela in the land of Benjamin in the tomb of Saul's father Kish. They did everything the king commanded. After this, God answered prayer for the land.

The Philistine Giants

15 The Philistines again waged war against Israel. David went down with his soldiers, and they fought the Philistines, but David became exhausted. 16 Then Ishbi-benob, one of the descendants of the giant,i whose bronze spear weighed about eight poundsj and who wore new armor, intended to kill David. 17 But Abishai son of Zeruiah came to his aid, struck the Philistine, and killed him. Then David's men swore to him: "You must never again go out with us to battle. You must not extinguish the lamp of Israel."

18 After this, there was another battle with the Philistines at Gob. At that time Sibbecai the Hushathite killed Saph, who was one of the descendants of the giant.i

19 Once again there was a battle with the Philistines at Gob, and Elhanan son of Jaare-oregim the Bethlehemite killedk Goliath the Gittite. The shaft of his spear was like a weaver's beam.

20 At Gath there was still another battle. A huge man was there with six fingers on each hand and six toes on each foot—24 in all. He, too, was descended from the giant.i 21 When he taunted Israel, Jonathan, son of David's brother Shimei, killed him.

22 These four were descended from the gianti in Gath and were killed by David and his soldiers.

---

a20:24 Some Hb mss, LXX, Syr read Adoniram; 1 Kg 4:6; 5:14   b21:3 Lit will bless   c21:4 Lit "Not for us silver and gold with   d21:6 Or impale, or expose   e21:8 Some Hb mss, LXX, Syr, Tg; other Hb mss read Michal   f21:9,13 Or impaled, or exposed   g21:9 = March–April   h21:10 = April to October   i21:16,18,20,22 Or Raphah   j21:16 Lit 300 (shekels)   k21:19 1 Ch 20:5 adds the brother of

---

21:1 because of the blood shed by Saul ... when he killed the Gibeonites. Saul's zeal for Israel justified ignoring the promises made by God (v. 2). Even though the Gibeonites tricked Joshua into this treaty (Josh. 9:14-15), to God a promise is a promise.

21:3 bring a blessing on the LORD's inheri-tance. The tables of blessing had been turned. Through Israel all the peoples (nations) would be blessed (Gen. 12:3). Here David asked another nation to bless Israel.

21:4 Whatever you say, I will do for you. Though Saul had given the Gibeonites no rights, David was willing to do all that was necessary to make amends.

21:12 bones of Saul. The people of Jabesh-gilead had rescued the bodies of Saul and his sons from the Philistines and had buried the bones under a tamarisk tree (1 Sam. 31:11-13).

21:16 the giant. The Raphaites were strong, numerous, perhaps up to 8-10 feet tall, and

David's Song of Thanksgiving

22 David spoke the words of this song to the LORD on the day the LORD rescued him from the hand of all his enemies and from the hand of Saul. ² He said:

The LORD is my rock, my fortress,
    and my deliverer,
³ my God, my mountainª where I seek refuge.
    My shield, the •horn of my salvation,
    my stronghold, my refuge,
    and my Savior, You save me from violence.
⁴ I called to the LORD, who is worthy of praise,
    and I was saved from my enemies.
⁵ For the waves of death engulfed me;
    the torrents of destruction terrified me.
⁶ The ropes of •Sheol entangled me;
    the snares of death confronted me.

⁷ I called to the LORD in my distress;
    I called to my God.
    From His temple He heard my voice,
    and my cry for help ⌊reached⌋ His ears.
⁸ Then the earth shook and quaked;
    the foundations of the heavensᵇ trembled;
    they shook because He burned with anger.
⁹ Smoke rose from His nostrils,
    and consuming fire ⌊came⌋ from His mouth;
    coals were set ablaze by it.ᶜ
¹⁰ He parted the heavens and came down,
    a dark cloud beneath His feet.
¹¹ He rode on a cherub and flew,
    soaring on the wings of the wind.
¹² He made darkness a canopy around Him,
    a gatheringᵈ of water and thick clouds.
¹³ From the radiance of His presence,
    flaming coals were ignited.
¹⁴ The LORD thundered from heaven;
    the •Most High projected His voice.
¹⁵ He shot arrows and scattered them;
    ⌊He hurled⌋ lightning bolts and routed them.
¹⁶ The depths of the sea became visible,
    the foundations of the world were exposed
    at the rebuke of the LORD,
    at the blast of the breath of His nostrils.

¹⁷ He reached down from on high
    and took hold of me;
    He pulled me out of deep waters.

¹⁸ He rescued me from my powerful enemy
    and from those who hated me,
    for they were too strong for me.
¹⁹ They confronted me in the day of my distress,
    but the LORD was my support.
²⁰ He brought me out to a wide-open place;
    He rescued me because He delighted in me.
²¹ The LORD rewarded me
    according to my righteousness;
    He repaid me
    according to the cleanness of my hands.
²² For I have kept the ways of the LORD
    and have not turned from my God
        to wickedness.
²³ Indeed, I have kept all His ordinances in mindᵉ
    and have not disregarded His statutes.
²⁴ I was blameless before Him
    and kept myself from sinning.
²⁵ So the LORD repaid me
    according to my righteousness,
    according to my cleannessᶠ in His sight.
²⁶ With the faithful
    You prove Yourself faithful;
    with the blameless man
    You prove Yourself blameless;
²⁷ with the pure
    You prove Yourself pure,
    but with the crooked
    You prove Yourself shrewd.
²⁸ You rescue an afflicted people,
    but Your eyes are set against the proud—
    You humble them.
²⁹ LORD, You are my lamp;
    the LORD illuminates my darkness.
³⁰ With You I can attack a barrier,ᵍ
    and with my God I can leap over a wall.
³¹ God—His way is perfect;
    the word of the LORD is pure.
    He is a shield to all who take refuge in Him.

³² For who is God besides the LORD?
    And who is a rock? Only our God.
³³ God is my strong refuge;ʰ
    He makes my way perfect.ⁱ
³⁴ He makes my feet like ⌊the feet of⌋ a deer
    and sets me securely on theʲ heights.ᵏ
³⁵ He trains my hands for war;

ª**22:3** LXX; MT reads *God of my mountain*; Ps 18:2   ᵇ**22:8** Some Hb mss, Syr, Vg read *mountains*; Ps 18:7   ᶜ**22:9** Or *ablaze from Him*   ᵈ**22:12** Or *sieve*, or *mass*; Hb obscure   ᵉ**22:23** Lit *Indeed, all His ordinances have been in front of me*   ᶠ**22:25** LXX, Syr, Vg read *to the cleanness of my hands*; Ps 18:24   ᵍ**22:30** Or *ridge*   ʰ**22:33** DSS, some LXX mss, Syr, Vg read *God clothes me with strength*; Ps 18:32   ⁱ**22:33** Some LXX mss, Syr; MT reads *He sets free the blameless His way*; Hb obscure   ʲ**22:34** LXX; some Hb mss read *my*; other Hb mss read *His*   ᵏ**22:34** Or *on my high places*

---

also called Zamzummites (Deut. 2:20-21).

21:19 killed Goliath the Gittite. A relative of the Goliath that David killed at Socoh in Judah (1 Sam. 17:1-3, 50-54; 1 Chron. 20:5).

22:1 the words of this song. David wrote this song (Ps. 18) soon after God delivered him from Saul's hand (1 Sam. 31:8) and be-

fore his humiliation with Bathsheba (12:9-10).

22:2 my rock. Like Moses, David described God as his rock (Deut. 32:4, 15, 18, 30). David often refers to God as his rock, for example, "my rock and my Redeemer" (Ps. 19:14). It is also a prophetic reference to his descendant Jesus Christ.

22:11 He rode on a cherub. Heavenly creatures who act as escorts and guards of the God's throne room (Gen. 3:24).

22:14 The LORD thundered from heaven. The voice of God, like thunder, strikes fear in people's hearts (Deut. 5:25-26). By His powerful voice, God created the world (Gen. 1)

my arms can bend a bow of bronze.
36 You have given me the shield of Your salvation;
Your help[a] exalts me.
37 You widen ⌊a place⌋ beneath me for my steps,
and my ankles do not give way.
38 I pursue my enemies and destroy them;
I do not turn back until they are wiped out.
39 I wipe them out and crush them,
and they do not rise;
they fall beneath my feet.
40 You have clothed me with strength for battle;
You subdue my adversaries beneath me.
41 You have made my enemies retreat before me;[b]
I annihilate those who hated me.
42 They look, but there is no one to save ⌊them⌋—
⌊they look⌋ to the LORD, but He does not answer them.
43 I pulverize them like dust of the earth;
I crush them and trample them like mud in the streets.
44 You have freed me from the feuds among my people;
You have appointed me the head of nations;
a people I had not known serve me.
45 Foreigners submit to me grudgingly;
as soon as they hear, they obey me.
46 Foreigners lose heart
and come trembling from their fortifications.
47 The LORD lives—may my rock be praised!
God, the rock of my salvation, is exalted.
48 God—He gives me vengeance
and casts down peoples under me.
49 He frees me from my enemies.
You exalt me above my adversaries;
You rescue me from violent men.
50 Therefore I will praise You, LORD,
among the nations;
I will sing about Your name.
51 He is a tower of salvation for[c] His king;
He shows loyalty to His anointed,
to David and his descendants forever.

David's Last Words

23 These are the last words of David:

The proclamation of David son of Jesse,
the proclamation of the man raised on high,[d]
the one anointed by the God of Jacob,

the favorite singer of Israel:
2 The Spirit of the LORD spoke through me,
His word was on my tongue.
3 The God of Israel spoke;
the Rock of Israel said to me,
"The one who rules the people with justice,
who rules in the •fear of God,
4 is like the morning light when the sun rises
on a cloudless morning,
the glisten of rain on sprouting grass."
5 Is it not true my house is with God?
For He has established an everlasting covenant with me,
ordered and secured in every ⌊detail⌋.
Will He not bring about
my whole salvation and ⌊my⌋ every desire?
6 But all the wicked are like thorns raked aside;
they can never be picked up by hand.
7 The man who touches them
must be armed with iron and the shaft of a spear.
They will be completely burned up on the spot.

Exploits of David's Warriors

8 These are the names of David's warriors:
Josheb-basshebeth the Tahchemonite was chief of the officers.[e] He wielded his spear[f] against 800 ⌊men⌋ he killed at one time.

9 After him, Eleazar son of Dodo son of Ahohi was among the three warriors with David when they defied the Philistines. The men of Israel retreated in the place they had gathered for battle, 10 but Eleazar stood ⌊his ground⌋ and attacked the Philistines until his hand was tired and stuck to his sword. The LORD brought about a great victory that day. Then the troops came back to him, but only to plunder the dead.

11 After him was Shammah son of Agee the Hararite. The Philistines had assembled ⌊in formation⌋ where there was a field full of lentils. The troops fled from the Philistines, 12 but Shammah took his stand in the middle of the field, defended it, and struck down the Philistines. So the LORD brought about a great victory.

13 Three of the 30 leading ⌊warriors⌋ went down at harvest time and came to David at the cave of Adullam, while a company of Philistines was camping in the Valley of Rephaim. 14 At that time David was in the stronghold, and a Philistine garrison was at Bethlehem. 15 David was extremely thirsty[g] and said, "If only someone would bring me water to drink from the well at the

---

a**22:36** LXX reads humility; Ps 18:35   b**22:41** Lit You gave me the neck of my enemies   c**22:51** DSS read He gives great victory to   d**23:1** Or raised up by the high [God]   e**23:8** Some Hb mss, LXX read Three   f**23:8** Some Hb mss; other Hb mss, LXX read He was Adino the Eznite   g**23:15** Lit And David craved

---

and by it He can shake the world (Ps. 29).
22:28 the proud—You humble them. God humbled Nebuchadnezzar and then blessed him with new insight (Dan. 4:33-34).
22:51 to His anointed. David's third-person reference to himself teaches two lessons: 1) he was saved and blessed because of his po-

sition as king, not because he was better than others; 2) all great victories (salvation) are administered by God through David's descendants. Believers declare that all the blessings of salvation come through David's son, Jesus Christ (Rom. 1:3; 2 Tim. 2:8; Rev. 22:16).
23:2 The Spirit of the LORD spoke. David's

claim means that God "breathed" His words into and through David, who is credited with 73 of the 150 psalms. Second Peter 1:21 confirms that God gave biblical writers the thoughts He wanted included in His Scripture.

23:13 Valley of Rephaim. The Philistines spread out in this valley on the route to Jerusa-

city gate of Bethlehem!" 16 So three of the warriors broke through the Philistine camp and drew water from the well at the gate of Bethlehem. They brought it back to David, but he refused to drink it. Instead, he poured it out to the LORD. 17 David said, "LORD, I would never do such a thing! Is this not the blood of men who risked their lives?" So he refused to drink it. Such were the exploits of the three warriors.

18 Abishai, Joab's brother and son of Zeruiah, was leader of the Three.ᵃ He raised his spear against 300 ⌊men⌋ and killed them, gaining a reputation among the Three. 19 Was he not the most honored of the Three? He became their commander even though he did not become one of the Three.

20 Benaiah son of Jehoiada was the son of a brave man from Kabzeel, a man of many exploits. Benaiah killed two sonsᵇ of Arielᶜ of Moab, and he went down into a pit on a snowy day and killed a lion. 21 He also killed an Egyptian, a huge man. Even though the Egyptian had a spear in his hand, Benaiah went down to him with a club, snatched the spear out of the Egyptian's hand, and then killed him with his own spear. 22 These were the exploits of Benaiah son of Jehoiada, who had a reputation among the three warriors. 23 He was the most honored of the Thirty, but he did not become one of the Three. David put him in charge of his bodyguard.

24 Among the Thirty were:

Joab's brother Asahel,
Elhanan son of Dodo of Bethlehem,
25 Shammah the Harodite,
Elika the Harodite,
26 Helez the Paltite,
Ira son of Ikkesh the Tekoite,
27 Abiezer the Anathothite,
Mebunnai the Hushathite,
28 Zalmon the Ahohite,
Maharai the Netophathite,
29 Heleb son of Baanah the Netophahite,
Ittai son of Ribai from Gibeah
of the Benjaminites,
30 Benaiah the Pirathonite,
Hiddai from the •Wadis of Gaash,ᵈ
31 Abi-albon the Arbathite,
Azmaveth the Barhumite,
32 Eliahba the Shaalbonite,
the sons of Jashen,
Jonathan son ofᵉ 33 Shammah the Hararite,
Ahiam son of Sharar the Hararite,
34 Eliphelet son of Ahasbai son of the Maacathite,

Eliam son of Ahithophel the Gilonite,
35 Hezro the Carmelite,
Paarai the Arbite,
36 Igal son of Nathan from Zobah,
Bani the Gadite,
37 Zelek the Ammonite,
Naharai the Beerothite, the armor-bearer
for Joab son of Zeruiah,
38 Ira the Ithrite,
Gareb the Ithrite,
39 and Uriah the Hittite.

There were 37 in all.

David's Military Census

24 The LORD's anger burned against Israel again, and it stirred up David against them to say: "Go, count ⌊the people of⌋ Israel and Judah."

2 So the king said to Joab, the commander of his army, "Go through all the tribes of Israel from Dan to Beer-sheba and register the troops so I can know their number."

3 Joab replied to the king, "May the LORD your God multiply the troops 100 times more than they are— while my lord the king looks on! But why does my lord the king want to do this?"

4 Yet the king's order prevailed over Joab and the commanders of the army. So Joab and the commanders of the army left the king's presence to register the troops of Israel.

5 They crossed the Jordan and camped in Aroer, south of the town in the middle of the valley, and then ⌊proceeded⌋ toward Gad and Jazer. 6 They went to Gilead and to the land of the Hittitesᶠ and continued on to Dan-jaan and around to Sidon. 7 They went to the fortress of Tyre and all the cities of the Hivites and Canaanites. Afterwards, they went to the •Negev of Judah at Beer-sheba.

8 When they had gone through the whole land, they returned to Jerusalem at the end of nine months and 20 days. 9 Joab gave the king the total of the registration of the troops. There were 800,000 fighting men from Israel and 500,000 men from Judah.

10 David's conscience troubled him after he had taken a census of the troops. He said to the LORD, "I have sinned greatly in what I've done. Now, LORD, because I've been very foolish, please take away Your servant's guilt."

David's Punishment

11 When David got up in the morning, a revelation from the LORD had come to the prophet Gad, David's

---

ᵃ**23:18** Some Hb mss, Syr read *the Thirty*   ᵇ**23:20** LXX; MT omits *sons*   ᶜ**23:20** Or *two warriors*   ᵈ**23:30** Or *from Nahale-gaash*   ᵉ**23:32** Some LXX mss; MT omits *son of*; 1 Ch 11:34   ᶠ**24:6** LXX; MT reads *of Tahtim-hodshi*; Hb obscure

---

lem to do battle with David's men. The Philistine garrison was at Bethlehem, David's hometown.

23:20 Benaiah ... many exploits. An army commander with a division of 24,000 men, he was also in charge of David's personal bodyguards.

23:34 Eliam. Bathsheba's father and the son of Ahithophel, David's counselor, who joined Absalom's plot.

23:39 Uriah. Not until Nathan confronted David did he admit his sin of killing Uriah and repent (12:11-13).

24:1 Go, count [the people of] Israel and Ju-

dah. Just as God allowed Satan to afflict Job, he also allowed him to tempt David to take a census with sinful motives. It was not the census that displeased God, but rather the condition of David's heart; relying on military muscle to defend Israel, rather than on God alone.

24:3 Joab. Joab knew that God was able to

seer: ¹² "Go and say to David, 'This is what the LORD says: I am offering you three ⌊choices⌋. Choose one of them, and I will do it to you.'"

¹³ So Gad went to David, told him ⌊the choices⌋, and asked him, "Do you want three[a] years of famine to come on your land, to flee from your foes three months while they pursue you, or to have a plague in your land three days? Now, think it over and decide what answer I should take back to the One who sent me."

¹⁴ David answered Gad, "I have great anxiety. Please, let us fall into the LORD's hands because His mercies are great, but don't let me fall into human hands."

¹⁵ So the LORD sent a plague on Israel from that morning until the appointed time, and from Dan to Beer-sheba 70,000 men died. ¹⁶ Then the angel extended his hand toward Jerusalem to destroy it, but the LORD relented concerning the destruction and said to the angel who was destroying the people, "Enough, withdraw your hand now!" The angel of the LORD was then at the threshing floor of Araunah[b] the Jebusite.

¹⁷ When David saw the angel striking the people, he said to the LORD, "Look, I am the one who has sinned; I am the one[c] who has done wrong. But these sheep, what have they done? Please, let Your hand be against me and my father's family."

David's Altar

¹⁸ Gad came to David that day and said to him, "Go up and set up an altar to the LORD on the threshing floor of Araunah the Jebusite." ¹⁹ David went up in obedience to Gad's command, just as the LORD had commanded. ²⁰ Araunah looked down and saw the king and his servants coming toward him, so he went out and bowed to the king with his face to the ground.

²¹ Araunah said, "Why has my lord the king come to his servant?"

David replied, "To buy the threshing floor from you in order to build an altar to the LORD, so the plague on the people may be halted."

²² Araunah said to David, "My lord the king may take whatever he wants[d] and offer it. Here are the oxen for a •burnt offering and the threshing sledges and ox yokes for the wood. ²³ ⌊My⌋ king, Araunah gives everything here to the king." Then he said to the king, "May the LORD your God accept you."

²⁴ The king answered Araunah, "No, I insist on buying it from you for a price, for I will not offer to the LORD my God burnt offerings that cost ⌊me⌋ nothing." David bought the threshing floor and the oxen for 20 ounces[e] of silver. ²⁵ He built an altar to the LORD there and offered burnt offerings and •fellowship offerings. Then the LORD answered prayer on behalf of the land, and the plague on Israel ended.

---

[a]**24:13** LXX; MT reads *seven*; 1 Ch 21:12   [b]**24:16** = *Ornan*; 1 Ch 21:15–28; 2 Ch 3:1   [c]**24:17** LXX reads *shepherd*   [d]**24:22** Lit *take what is good in his eyes*   [e]**24:24** Lit *50 shekels*

---

provide the necessary manpower, and he believed David should trust God.

24:9 fighting men. David counted only men of military age. The counters began east of the Jordan River, went counterclockwise until they reached Beersheba in the south, and reported to David in Jerusalem nearly 10 months later.

24:16 angel extended. Angels' duties range from delivering joyful messages ("He is not here! For He has been resurrected," Matt. 28:6), guarding God's people (Ps. 91:11), caring for Jesus in the desert ("angels came and began to serve Him," Matt. 4:11), and destroying people (2 Chron. 32:21).

24:21 To buy the threshing floor. A further example of David's acceptance of responsibility for his sin. The property owner offered to give David whatever he needed for the altar and the burnt offerings but David bought the threshing floor and the oxen. He also bought the land surrounding the threshing floor for 600 shekels or 15 pounds of gold. This spot, Mount Moriah, was where Abraham had offered Isaac and where Solomon later built his splendid temple.

INTRODUCTION TO
1 KINGS

AUTHOR

The author of 1 and 2 Kings is not known, but the three literary sources that are named suggest multiple authors and editors: "the Book of Solomon's Events" (1 Kings 11:41); "the Historical Record of Israel's Kings" (1 Kings 14:19; 2 Kings 15:31); and "the Historical Record of Judah's Kings " (1 Kings 14:29; 2 Kings 24:5).

DATE

The account of Jehoiachin's release from prison in 2 Kings 25:27-30 means that the final form of

Kings was written after 561 B.C. However, the source materials could have been written at the time of the events they describe. These events span almost 400 years.

THEME

Israel's golden age—its coronation and corrosion.

HISTORICAL BACKGROUND

Solomon reaps the reward of David's military success. He inherits peace and security and so launches Israel's "Golden Age." Following Solomon's death, the country divides into two separate nations: Israel and Judah, bringing an end to this era of strength. Both nations then enter a period of decline.

CHARACTERISTICS

The atmosphere in the early chapters of 1 Kings is one of grandeur–displaying Solomon's wealth, wisdom, and fame. But Solomon's end is most pitiful, as he turns to foreign wives and their false gods. Jeroboam follows suit, as do other kings of northern Israel and southern Judah. All told, 19 kings in the north and 20 rulers in the south are alternately profiled in 1 Kings. Tracking the rise and fall of both kingdoms can be confusing, but it helps to remember that none of Israel's kings were faithful to God during this time and only half of Judah's rulers showed any faithfulness.

PASSAGES FOR
TOPICAL GROUP STUDY

3:16-28 . . . . . STRUGGLES and WISDOM . . . . . . .Life and Death Crisis

10:23-11:13. . . TEMPTATIONS . . . . Overwhelmed by Temptation

12:1-24 . . . . . . ADVICE and DECISIONS . . . . Free Advice

18:16-40 . . . . FALSE PROPHETS and JUDGEMENT . . .Fire from Heaven

David's Last Days

1 Now King David was old and getting on in years. Although they covered him with bedclothes, he could not get warm. 2 So his servants said to him: "Let us[a] search for a young virgin for my lord the king. She is to attend the king and be his caregiver. She is to lie by your side so that my lord the king will get warm." 3 They searched for a beautiful girl throughout the territory of Israel; they found Abishag the Shunammite[b] and brought her to the king. 4 The girl was of unsurpassed beauty, and she became the king's caregiver. She served him, but he was not intimate with[c] her.

Adonijah's Bid for Power

5 Adonijah son of Haggith kept exalting himself, saying, "I will be king!" He also assembled chariots, cavalry, and 50 men to run ahead of him.[d] 6 But his father had never once reprimanded[e] him by saying, "Why do you act this way?" In addition, he was quite handsome and was born after Absalom. 7 He conspired[f] with Joab son of Zeruiah and with Abiathar the priest. They supported Adonijah, 8 but Zadok the priest, Benaiah son of Jehoiada, Nathan the prophet, Shimei, Rei, and David's warriors did not side with Adonijah.

9 Adonijah sacrificed sheep, oxen, and fattened cattle near the stone of Zoheleth, which is next to En-rogel. He invited all his royal brothers and all the men of Judah, the servants of the king, 10 but he did not invite Nathan the prophet, Benaiah, the warriors, or his brother Solomon.

Nathan's and Bathsheba's Appeals

11 Then Nathan said to Bathsheba, Solomon's mother, "Have you not heard that Adonijah son of Haggith has become king and our lord David does not know [it]? 12 Now please come and let me advise you. Save your life and the life of your son Solomon. 13 Go, approach King David and say to him, 'My lord king, did you not swear to your servant: Your son Solomon is to become king after me, and he is the one who is to sit on my throne? So why has Adonijah become king?' 14 At that moment, while you are still there speaking with the king, I'll come in after you and confirm your words."

15 So Bathsheba went to the king in his bedroom. Since the king was very old, Abishag the Shunammite was serving him. 16 Bathsheba bowed down and paid homage to the king, and he asked, "What do you want?" 17 She replied, "My lord, you swore to your servant by the LORD your God, 'Your son Solomon is to become king after me, and he is the one who is to sit on my throne.' 18 Now look, Adonijah has become king. And,[g] my lord king, you didn't know [it]. 19 He has lavishly sacrificed oxen, fattened cattle, and sheep. He invited all the king's sons, Abiathar the priest, and Joab the commander of the army, but he did not invite your servant Solomon. 20 Now, my lord king, the eyes of all Israel are on you to tell them who will sit on the throne of my lord the king after him. 21 Otherwise, when my lord the king rests with his fathers, I and my son Solomon will be regarded as criminals."

22 At that moment, while she was still speaking with the king, Nathan the prophet arrived, 23 and it was announced to the king, "Nathan the prophet is here." He came into the king's presence and bowed to him with his face to the ground.

24 "My lord king," Nathan said, "did you say, 'Adonijah is to become king after me, and he is the one who is to sit on my throne'? 25 For today he went down and lavishly sacrificed oxen, fattened cattle, and sheep. He invited all the sons of the king, the commanders of the army, and Abiathar the priest. And look! They're eating and drinking in his presence, and they're saying, 'Long live King Adonijah!' 26 But he did not invite me—me, your servant—or Zadok the priest or Benaiah son of Jehoiada or your servant Solomon. 27 I'm certain my lord the king would not have let this happen without letting your servant[h] know who will sit on my lord the king's throne after him."

Solomon Confirmed King

28 King David responded by saying, "Call in Bathsheba for me." So she came into the king's presence and stood before him. 29 The king swore an oath and said, "As the LORD lives, who has redeemed my life from every difficulty, 30 just as I swore to you by the LORD God of Israel: Your son Solomon is to become king after me, and he is the one who is to sit on my throne in my place, that is exactly what I will do this very day."

31 Bathsheba bowed with her face to the ground, paying homage to the king, and said, "May my lord King David live forever!"

32 King David then said, "Call in Zadok the priest, Nathan the prophet, and Benaiah son of Jehoiada for me." So they came into the king's presence. 33 The king said to them, "Take my servants with you, have my son Solomon ride on my own mule, and take him down to Gihon. 34 There, Zadok the priest and Nathan the prophet are to anoint him as king over Israel. You are

---

a1:2 Lit them   b1:3 Shunem was a town in the hill country of Issachar at the foot of Mt. Moreh; Jos 19:17–18.   c1:4 Lit he did not know   d1:5 Heralds announcing his procession   e1:6 Or grieved   f1:7 Lit His words were   g1:18 Many Hb mss, LXX, Vg, Syr; MT reads And now   h1:27 Many Hb mss, LXX; alt Hb tradition reads servants

---

1:1 David … getting on in years. David was about 70 when he died.

1:5 Adonijah. David's fourth son, he was the oldest surviving heir to David's throne. **50 men to run ahead.** Adonijah sought to impress the people. Compare Absalom in 2 Samuel 15:1.

1:6 never once reprimanded him. Although David was a godly, capable leader, he neglected to properly parent his children.

1:7 Joab. David's nephew, Joab had been a brave warrior but didn't always obey David's orders; for example, he executed David's son Absalom against David's orders.

1:11 Nathan. This prophet had been David's spiritual advisor for years (see 2 Sam. 7:4-17; 12:1-14).

1:12 Save your life. It is likely that Bathsheba and Solomon would be executed if Adonijah became king.

1:14 confirm your words. Nathan arranged for the two witnesses required under Mosaic law.

to blow the ram's horn and say, 'Long live King Solomon!' 35 You are to come up after him, and he is to come in and sit on my throne. He is the one who is to become king in my place; he is the one I have commanded to be ruler over Israel and Judah."

36 "•Amen," Benaiah son of Jehoiada replied to the king. "May the LORD, the God of my lord the king, so affirm it. 37 Just as the LORD was with my lord the king, so may He[a] be with Solomon and make his throne greater than the throne of my lord King David."

38 Then Zadok the priest, Nathan the prophet, Benaiah son of Jehoiada, the Cherethites, and the Pelethites went down, had Solomon ride on King David's mule, and took him to Gihon. 39 Zadok the priest took the horn of oil from the tabernacle and anointed Solomon. Then they blew the ram's horn, and all the people proclaimed, "Long live King Solomon!" 40 All the people followed him, playing flutes and rejoicing with such a great joy that the earth split open from the sound.[b]

Adonijah Hears of Solomon's Coronation

41 Adonijah and all the invited guests who were with him heard ⌊the noise⌋ as they finished eating. Joab heard the sound of the ram's horn and said, "Why is the town in such an uproar?" 42 He was still speaking when Jonathan son of Abiathar the priest, suddenly arrived. Adonijah said, "Come in, for you are an excellent man, and you must be bringing good news."

43 "Unfortunately not," Jonathan answered him. "Our lord King David has made Solomon king. 44 And with Solomon, the king has sent Zadok the priest, Nathan the prophet, Benaiah son of Jehoiada, the Cherethites, and the Pelethites, and they have had him ride on the king's mule. 45 Zadok the priest and Nathan the prophet have anointed him king in Gihon. They have gone from there rejoicing. The town has been in an uproar; that's the noise you heard. 46 Solomon has even taken his seat on the royal throne.

47 "The king's servants have also gone to congratulate our lord King David, saying, 'May your God make the name of Solomon more famous than your name, and may He make his throne greater than your throne.' Then the king bowed in worship on his bed. 48 And the king went on to say this: 'May the LORD God of Israel be praised! Today He has provided one to sit on my throne, and I am a witness.' "[c]

49 Then all of Adonijah's guests got up trembling and went their separate ways. 50 Adonijah was afraid of Solomon, so he got up and went to take hold of the horns of the altar.

51 It was reported to Solomon: "Look, Adonijah fears King Solomon, and he has taken hold of the horns of the altar, saying, 'Let King Solomon first[d] swear to me that he will not kill his servant with the sword.' "

52 Then Solomon said, "If he is a man of character, then not a single hair of his will fall to the ground, but if evil is found in him, then he dies." 53 So King Solomon sent for him, and they took him down from the altar. He came and paid homage to King Solomon, and Solomon said to him, "Go to your home."

David's Dying Instructions to Solomon

2 As the time approached for David to die, he instructed his son Solomon, 2 "As for me, I am going the way of all of the earth. Be strong and brave, 3 and keep your obligation to the LORD your God to walk in His ways and to keep His statutes, commandments, judgments, and testimonies. This is written in the law of Moses, so that you will have success in everything you do and wherever you turn, 4 and so that the LORD will carry out His promise that He made to me: 'If your sons are careful to walk faithfully before Me with their whole mind and heart, you will never fail to have a man on the throne of Israel.'

5 "You also know what Joab son of Zeruiah did to me and what he did to the two commanders of Israel's army, Abner son of Ner and Amasa son of Jether. He murdered them ⌊in a time⌋ of peace to avenge blood shed in war. He spilled that blood on his own waistband and on the sandals of his feet.[e] 6 Act according to your wisdom, and do not let his gray head descend to •Sheol in peace.

7 "Show loyalty to the sons of Barzillai the Gileadite and let them be among those who eat at your table because they supported me when I fled from your brother Absalom.

8 "Keep an eye on Shimei son of Gera, the Benjaminite from Bahurim who is with you. He uttered malicious curses against me the day I went to Mahanaim. But he came down to meet me at the Jordan River, and I swore to him by the LORD: 'I will never kill you with the sword.' 9 So don't let him go unpunished, for you are a wise man. You know how to deal with him to bring his gray head down to Sheol with blood."

10 Then David rested with his fathers and was buried in the city of David. 11 The ⌊length of⌋ time David reigned over Israel was 40 years: he reigned seven years in Hebron and 33 years in Jerusalem. 12 Solomon sat on the throne of his father David, and his kingship was firmly established.

---

[a]1:37 Alt Hb tradition reads *so He will*   [b]1:40 LXX reads *the land resounded with their noise*   [c]1:48 Lit *and my eyes are seeing*   [d]1:51 Two Hb mss, LXX, Syr, Vg read *today*   [e]2:5 LXX, Lat read *on my waistband and . . . my feet; v. 31*

1:34 anoint him as king. See 1 Sam. 16:13.

1:38 Cherethites ... Pelethites. Originally associated with the Philistines, they became David's bodyguards.

1:50 the horns of the altar. The altar was a safe haven for people who had committed unintentional crimes.

1:52 a man of character. Although Adonijah's sin was not unintentional, Solomon showed mercy and pardoned him.

2:1 David ... instructed his son. Giving last instructions to sons was customary (Gen. 49).

2:4 His promise that He made to me. God's promise to David was unconditional. He would have a royal dynasty forever, but evil kings would not receive the benefits of walking with God (see Deut. 11:26-28). **never fail to have a man on the throne of Israel.** While Israel was divided and exiled because of disobedience to God, ultimately, the promised Messiah, an heir of David, will reign.

Adonijah's Foolish Request

13 Now Adonijah son of Haggith came to Bathsheba, Solomon's mother. She asked, "Do you come peacefully?"

"Peacefully," he replied, 14 and then asked, "May I talk with you?"[a]

"Go ahead," she answered.

15 "You know the kingship was mine," he said. "All Israel expected me to be king, but then the kingship was turned over to my brother, for the LORD gave it to him. 16 So now I have just one request of you; don't turn me down."[b]

She said to him, "Go on."

17 He replied, "Please speak to King Solomon since he won't turn you down. Let him give me Abishag the Shunammite as a wife."

18 "Very well," Bathsheba replied. "I will speak to the king for you."

19 So Bathsheba went to King Solomon to speak to him about Adonijah. The king stood up to greet her, bowed to her, sat down on his throne, and had a throne placed for the king's mother. So she sat down at his right hand.

20 Then she said, "I have just one small request of you. Don't turn me down."

"⌊Go ahead and⌋ ask, mother," the king replied, "for I won't turn you down."

21 So she said, "Let Abishag the Shunammite be given to your brother Adonijah as a wife."

22 King Solomon answered his mother, "Why are you requesting Abishag the Shunammite for Adonijah? Since he is my elder brother, you might as well ask the kingship for him, for Abiathar the priest, and for Joab son of Zeruiah."[c] 23 Then Solomon took an oath by the LORD: "May God punish me and do so severely if Adonijah has not made this request at the cost of his life. 24 And now, as the LORD lives, the One who established me, seated me on the throne of my father David, and made me a dynasty as He promised—I swear Adonijah will be put to death today!" 25 Then King Solomon gave the order to Benaiah son of Jehoiada, who struck down Adonijah, and he died.

Abiathar's Banishment

26 The king said to Abiathar the priest, "Go to your fields in Anathoth. Even though you deserve to die, I will not put you to death today, since you carried the ark of the Lord GOD in the presence of my father David and you suffered through all that my father suffered."

27 So Solomon banished Abiathar from being the LORD's priest, and it fulfilled the LORD's prophecy He had spoken at Shiloh against Eli's family.

Joab's Execution

28 The news reached Joab. Since he had supported Adonijah but not Absalom, Joab fled to the LORD's tabernacle and took hold of the horns of the altar.

29 It was reported to King Solomon: "Joab has fled to the LORD's tabernacle and is now beside the altar." Then Solomon sent[d] Benaiah son of Jehoiada and told ⌊him⌋, "Go and strike him down!"

30 So Benaiah went to the tabernacle and said to Joab, "This is what the king says: 'Come out!'"

But Joab said, "No, for I will die here."

So Benaiah took a message back to the king, "This is what Joab said, and this is how he answered me."

31 The king said to him, "Do just as he says. Strike him down and bury him in order to remove from me and from my father's house the blood that Joab shed without just cause. 32 The LORD will bring back his own blood on his own head because he struck down two men more righteous and better than he, without my father David's knowledge. With his sword, Joab murdered Abner son of Ner, commander of Israel's army, and Amasa son of Jether, commander of Judah's army. 33 Their blood will come back on Joab's head and on the head of his descendants forever, but for David, his descendants, his dynasty, and his throne, there will be peace from the LORD forever."

34 Benaiah son of Jehoiada went up, struck down Joab, and put him to death. He was buried at his house in the wilderness. 35 Then the king appointed Benaiah son of Jehoiada in Joab's place over the army, and he appointed Zadok the priest in Abiathar's place.

Shimei's Banishment and Execution

36 Then the king summoned Shimei and said to him, "Build a house for yourself in Jerusalem and live there, but don't leave there ⌊and go⌋ anywhere else. 37 On the day you do leave and cross the Kidron Valley, know for sure that you will certainly die. Your blood will be on your own head."

38 Shimei said to the king, "The sentence is fair; your servant will do as my lord the king has spoken." And Shimei lived in Jerusalem for a long time.

39 But then, at the end of three years, two of Shimei's slaves ran away to Achish son of Maacah, king of Gath. Shimei was informed, "Look, your slaves are in Gath." 40 So Shimei saddled his donkey and set out to Achish

---

a**2:14** Lit then said, "I have a word for you."   b**2:16** Lit don't make me turn my face   c**2:22** LXX, Vg, Syr read kingship for him, and on his side are Abiathar the priest and Joab son of Zeruiah   d**2:29** LXX adds Joab a message: "What is the matter with you, that you have fled to the altar?" And Joab replied, "Because I feared you, I have fled to the Lord." And Solomon the king sent

---

2:5 He spilled that blood. Although Joab had served David well for many years, David instructed Solomon to deal with Joab because of his revengeful act of murdering Amasa and Abner.

2:8 Shimei. He had cursed David and thrown stones at him when David fled from Absalom

(2 Sam. 16:5-11).

2:15 kingship was mine. Adonijah believed he should have been king and wanted compensation.

2:17 give me Abishag. She was in the royal harem. Adonijah's request to marry her was effectively a claim to the throne.

2:22 ask the kingship. Solomon perceived the plot.

2:26 Abiathar. The high priest had served David faithfully during Saul's pursuit of David (see 1 Sam. 22:20-23).

2:27 fulfilled the LORD's prophecy. God had said Eli's line of priests would be cut off be-

at Gath to search for his slaves. He went and brought them back from Gath.

[41] It was reported to Solomon that Shimei had gone from Jerusalem to Gath and had returned. [42] So the king summoned Shimei and said to him, "Didn't I make you swear by the LORD and warn you, saying, 'On the day you leave and go anywhere else, know for sure that you will certainly die'? And you said to me, 'The sentence is fair; I will obey.' [43] So why have you not kept the LORD's oath and the command that I gave you?" [44] The king also said, "You yourself know all the evil that you did to my father David. Therefore, the LORD has brought back your evil on your head, [45] but King Solomon will be blessed, and David's throne will remain established before the LORD forever."

[46] Then the king commanded Benaiah son of Jehoiada, and he went out and struck Shimei down, and he died. So the kingdom was established in Solomon's hand.

The LORD Appears to Solomon

3 Solomon made an alliance[a] with Pharaoh king of Egypt by marrying Pharaoh's daughter. Solomon brought her to the city of David until he finished building his palace, the LORD's temple, and the wall surrounding Jerusalem. [2] However, the people were sacrificing on the •high places, because until that time a temple for the LORD's name had not been built. [3] Solomon loved the LORD by walking in the statutes of his father David, but he also sacrificed and burned incense on the high places.

[4] The king went to Gibeon to sacrifice there because it was the most famous high place. He offered 1,000 •burnt offerings on that altar. [5] At Gibeon the LORD appeared to Solomon in a dream at night. God said, "Ask. What should I give you?"

[6] And Solomon replied, "You have shown great and faithful love to Your servant, my father David, because he walked before You in faithfulness, righteousness, and[b] integrity. You have continued this great and faithful love for him by giving him a son to sit on his throne, as it is today.

[7] "LORD my God, You have now made Your servant king in my father David's place. Yet I am just a youth with no experience in leadership.[c] [8] Your servant is among Your people You have chosen, a[d] people too numerous to be numbered or counted. [9] So give Your servant an obedient heart to judge Your people and to discern between good and evil. For who is able to judge this great people of Yours?"

[10] Now it pleased the Lord that Solomon had requested this. [11] So God said to him, "Because you have requested this and did not ask for long life[e] or riches for yourself, or the death[f] of your enemies, but you asked discernment for yourself to understand justice, [12] I will therefore do what you have asked. I will give you a wise and understanding heart, so that there has never been anyone like you before and never will be again. [13] In addition, I will give you what you did not ask for: both riches and honor, so that no man in any kingdom will be your equal during your entire life. [14] If you walk in My ways and keep My statutes and commandments just as your father David did, I will give you a long life."

[15] Then Solomon woke up and realized it had been a dream. He went to Jerusalem, stood before the ark of the Lord's covenant, and offered burnt offerings and •fellowship offerings. Then he held a feast for all his servants.

Life and Death Crisis

1. How did your parents settle disputes between you and your brothers or sisters?

1 Kings 3:16-28

2. Why would the King of Israel bother to settle a dispute between prostitutes? Whose life was actually on the line in this dispute?

3. Why did Solomon suggest cutting the baby in two? What did that suggestion accomplish?

4. How did Solomon know which woman was the real mother of the living baby?

5. For what crisis do you need the wisdom of Solomon?

Solomon's Wisdom

[16] Then two women who were prostitutes came to the king and stood before him. [17] One woman said, "Please my lord, this woman and I live in the same house, and I had a baby while she was in the house. [18] On the third day after I gave birth, she also had a baby and we were alone. No one else[g] was with us in

---

[a]3:1 Lit Solomon made himself a son-in-law [b]3:6 Lit and with You [c]3:7 Lit am a little youth and do not know to go out or come in [d]3:8 Lit chosen many [e]3:11 Lit for many days [f]3:11 Lit life [g]3:18 Lit No stranger

---

cause of their wickedness (see 1 Sam. 2:30-35).

2:28 took hold of the horns. The refuge was only for those who had committed unintentional sins (see Ex. 21:14).

2:46 struck Shimei. Shimei had violated the

terms of his house arrest. He deserved death for his sins against David (see verses 8-9).

3:2 high places. The Law forbade sacrificing anywhere besides the tabernacle, yet Solomon and the Israelites sacrificed at these Canaanite shrines.

3:5 LORD appeared ... in a dream. God also

revealed His will in dreams to Jacob (Gen. 28:10-15; 31:11), Joseph (Gen. 37:5-8), and Nebuchadnezzar (Dan. 2:28-30).

3:7 just a youth with no experience in leadership. Solomon was about 20 when he became king.

3:15 stood before the ark of the LORD's cov-

the house; just the two of us were there. ¹⁹ During the night this woman's son died because she lay on him. ²⁰ She got up in the middle of the night and took my son from my side while your servant was asleep. She laid him at her breast, and she put her dead son in my arms. ²¹ When I got up in the morning to nurse my son, I discovered he was dead. That morning, when I looked closely at him I realized that he was not the son I gave birth to."

²² "No," the other woman said. "My son is the living one; your son is the dead one."

The first woman said, "No, your son is the dead one; my son is the living one." So they argued before the king.

²³ The king replied, "This woman says, 'This is my son who is alive, and your son is dead,' but that woman says, 'No, your son is dead, and my son is alive.' " ²⁴ The king continued, "Bring me a sword." So they brought the sword to the king. ²⁵ Solomon said, "Cut the living boy in two and give half to one and half to the other."

²⁶ The woman whose son was alive spoke to the king because she felt great compassion[a] for her son. "My lord, give her the living baby," she said, "but please don't have him killed!"

But the other one said, "He will not be mine or yours. Cut ⌊him in two⌋!"

²⁷ The king responded, "Give the living baby to the first woman, and don't kill him. She is his mother." ²⁸ All Israel heard about the judgment the king had given, and they stood in awe of the king because they saw that God's wisdom was in him to carry out justice.

Solomon's Officials

4 King Solomon ruled over Israel, ² and these were his officials:

Azariah son of Zadok, priest;
³ Elihoreph and Ahijah the sons of Shisha, secretaries;
Jehoshaphat son of Ahilud, historian;
⁴ Benaiah son of Jehoiada, in charge of the army;
Zadok and Abiathar, priests;
⁵ Azariah son of Nathan, in charge of the deputies;
Zabud son of Nathan, a priest and adviser to the king;
⁶ Ahishar, in charge of the palace;
and Adoniram son of Abda, in charge of forced labor.

⁷ Solomon had 12 deputies for all Israel. They provided food for the king and his household; each one made provision for one month out of the year. ⁸ These were their names:

Ben-hur, in the hill country of Ephraim;
⁹ Ben-deker, in Makaz, Shaalbim, Beth-shemesh, and Elon-beth-hanan;
¹⁰ Ben-hesed, in Arubboth (he had Socoh and the whole land of Hepher);
¹¹ Ben-abinadab, in all Naphath-dor (Taphath daughter of Solomon was his wife);
¹² Baana son of Ahilud, in Taanach, Megiddo, and all Beth-shean which is beside Zarethan below Jezreel, from Beth-shean to Abel-meholah, as far as the other side of Jokmeam;
¹³ Ben-geber, in Ramoth-gilead (he had the villages of Jair son of Manasseh, which are in Gilead, and he had the region of Argob, which is in Bashan, 60 great cities with walls and bronze bars);
¹⁴ Ahinadab son of Iddo, ⌊in⌋ Mahanaim;
¹⁵ Ahimaaz, in Naphtali (he also had married a daughter of Solomon—Basemath);
¹⁶ Baana son of Hushai, in Asher and Bealoth;
¹⁷ Jehoshaphat son of Paruah, in Issachar;
¹⁸ Shimei son of Ela, in Benjamin;
¹⁹ Geber son of Uri, in the land of Gilead, the country of Sihon king of the Amorites and of Og king of Bashan.

There was one deputy in the land of Judah.[b]

Solomon's Provisions

²⁰ Judah and Israel were as numerous as the sand by the sea; ⌊they were⌋ eating, drinking, and rejoicing. ²¹c Solomon ruled over all the kingdoms from the Euphrates River to the land of the Philistines and as far as the border of Egypt. They offered tribute and served Solomon all the days of his life.

²² Solomon's provisions for one day were 150 bushels[d] of fine flour and 300 bushels[e] of meal, ²³ 10 fattened oxen, 20 range oxen, and 100 sheep, besides deer, gazelles, roebucks, and pen-fed poultry,[f] ²⁴ for he had dominion over everything west of the Euphrates from Tiphsah to Gaza and over all the kings west of the Euphrates. He had peace on all his surrounding borders. ²⁵ Throughout Solomon's ⌊reign⌋, Judah and Israel lived in safety from Dan to Beer-sheba, each man under his own vine and his own fig tree. ²⁶ Solomon had 40,000[g] stalls of horses for his chariots, and 12,000

---

a**3:26** Lit *because her compassion grew hot*   b**4:19** LXX; Hb omits *of Judah*   c**4:21** 1 Kg 5:1 in Hb   d**4:22** Lit *30 cors*   e**4:22** Lit *60 cors*   f**4:23** Hb obscure   g**4:26** Some LXX mss read *4,000*, as does 1 Ch 9:25; 1 Kg 10:26, 2 Ch 1:14 reads *1,400*

---

enant and offered. Instead of making an offering to God at the high place, Solomon went to the tabernacle. Since only the high priest could approach the ark, the king stood outside facing the ark and made his offerings.

4:4 Benaiah. Commander in chief of the entire army, he did not participate in Adonijah's

plots. He had participated in Solomon's anointing at Gihon and had executed Adonijah.

4:5 Azariah. He was in charge of the 12 district officers in verses 8-19. This is not Azariah the priest (verse 2).

4:6 in charge of the palace. Ahishar super-

vised the servants and other palace workers.

4:7 had 12 deputies. Solomon needed revenue to support his military forces. He divided Israel into 12 districts with a governor for each who collected taxes for the royal household. Two of the governors were Solomon's sons-in-law.

horsemen. [27] Each of those deputies for a month in turn provided food for King Solomon and for everyone who came to King Solomon's table. They neglected nothing. [28] Each man brought the barley and the straw for the chariot teams and the other horses to the required place according to his assignment.[a]

Solomon's Wisdom and Literary Gifts

[29] God gave Solomon wisdom, very great insight, and understanding as ⌊vast⌋ as the sand on the seashore. [30] Solomon's wisdom was greater than the wisdom of all the people of the East, greater than all the wisdom of Egypt. [31] He was wiser than anyone—wiser than Ethan the Ezrahite, and Heman, Calcol, and Darda, sons of Mahol. His reputation extended to all the surrounding nations.

[32] Solomon composed 3,000 proverbs, and his songs numbered 1,005. [33] He described trees, from the cedar in Lebanon to the hyssop growing out of the wall. He also taught about animals, birds, reptiles, and fish. [34] People came from everywhere, ⌊sent⌋ by every king on earth who had heard of his wisdom, to listen to Solomon's wisdom.

Hiram's Building Materials

5 [b] Hiram king of Tyre sent his servants to Solomon when he heard that he had been anointed king in his father's place, for Hiram had always been friends with David.

[2] Solomon sent ⌊this message⌋ to Hiram: [3] "You know my father David was not able to build a temple for the name of the LORD his God. This was because of the warfare all around him until the LORD put his enemies under his feet. [4] The LORD my God has now given me rest all around; there is no enemy or crisis. [5] So I plan to build a temple for the name of the LORD my God, according to what the LORD promised my father David: 'I will put your son on your throne in your place, and he will build the temple for My name.'

[6] "Therefore, command that cedars from Lebanon be cut down for me. My servants will be with your servants, and I will pay your servants' wages according to whatever you say, for you know that not a man among us knows how to cut timber like the Sidonians."

[7] When Hiram heard Solomon's words, he greatly rejoiced and said, "May the LORD be praised today! He has given David a wise son to be over this great people!" [8] Then Hiram sent ⌊a reply⌋ to Solomon, saying, "I have heard your message; I will do everything you want regarding the cedar and cypress timber. [9] My servants will bring ⌊the logs⌋ down from Lebanon to the sea, and I will make them into rafts to go by sea to the place you indicate. I will break them apart there, and you can take them away. You then can meet my needs by providing my household with food."

[10] So Hiram provided Solomon with all the cedar and cypress timber he wanted, [11] and Solomon provided Hiram with 100,000 bushels[c] of wheat as food for his household and 110,000 gallons[d] of beaten oil. Solomon did this for Hiram year after year.

[12] The LORD gave Solomon wisdom, as He had promised him. There was peace between Hiram and Solomon, and the two of them made a treaty.

Solomon's Work Force

[13] Then King Solomon drafted forced laborers from all Israel; the labor force numbered 30,000 men. [14] He sent 10,000 to Lebanon each month in shifts; one month they were in Lebanon, two months they were at home. Adoniram was in charge of the forced labor. [15] Solomon had 70,000 porters and 80,000 stonecutters in the mountains, [16] not including his 3,300[e] deputies in charge of the work. They ruled over the people doing the work. [17] The king commanded them to quarry large, costly stones to lay the foundation of the temple with dressed stones. [18] So Solomon's builders and Hiram's builders, along with the Gebalites, quarried ⌊the stone⌋ and prepared the timber and stone for the temple's construction.

Building the Temple

6 Solomon ⌊began to⌋ build the temple for the LORD in the four hundred eightieth year after the Israelites came out from the land of Egypt, in the fourth year of his reign over Israel, in the second month, in the month of Ziv.[f] [2] The temple that King Solomon built for the LORD was 90 feet[g] long, 30 feet[h] wide, and 45 feet[i] high. [3] The portico in front of the temple sanctuary was 30 feet[h] long extending across the temple's width, and 15 feet deep[j] in front of the temple. [4] He also made windows with beveled frames[k] for the temple.

[5] He then built a chambered structure[l] along the temple wall, encircling the walls of the temple, that is, the sanctuary and the inner sanctuary. And he made side chambers[m] all around. [6] The lowest chamber was seven and a half feet[n] wide, the middle was nine feet[o] wide, and the third was 10 and a half feet[p] wide. He also provided offset ledges for the temple all around the outside so that nothing would be inserted into the temple walls.

---

[a]4:28 Lit judgment [b]5:1 1 Kg 5:15 in Hb [c]5:11 Lit 20,000 cors [d]5:11 LXX reads 20,000 baths; MT reads 20 cors [e]5:16 Some LXX mss read 3,600; 2 Ch 2:2,18 [f]6:1 April–May [g]6:2 Lit 60 cubits [h]6:2,3 Lit 20 cubits [i]6:2 Lit 30 cubits [j]6:3 Lit 10 cubits wide [k]6:4 Hb obscure [l]6:5 Lit built the house of chamber [m]6:5 Lit made ribs or sides [n]6:6 Lit five cubits [o]6:6 Lit six cubits [p]6:6 Lit seven cubits

---

4:13 60 great cities with walls. The Israelites had captured these from Og, king of Bashan (see Deut. 3:3-5).

4:21 from the Euphrates River to the land of the Philistines. Solomon's kingdom reached from the Euphrates River on the east, Egypt on the south, and the land of the Philistines on the west.

4:31 the East. Probably Mesopotamia.

4:32 proverbs … songs. Some are preserved for us in the books of Proverbs, Ecclesiastes, and the Song of Songs.

5:1 Hiram. An ally of David, he had ruled Tyre for 34 years and had provided workers and supplies, including cedars from Lebanon east of Tyre, to build David's palace.

5:5 he will build the temple. David made preparations for the temple after God promised him that his son would build it (see 2 Sam. 7:1-17).

7 The temple's construction used finished stones cut at the quarry so that no hammer, chisel, or any iron tool was heard in the temple while it was being built.

8 The door for the lowest[a] side chamber was on the right side of the temple. They went up a stairway[b] to the middle ⌊chamber⌋, and from the middle to the third. 9 When he finished building the temple, he paneled it with boards and planks of cedar. 10 He built the chambers along the entire temple, joined to the temple with cedar beams; ⌊each story was⌋ seven and a half feet[c] high.

11 The word of the LORD came to Solomon: 12 "As for this temple you are building—if you walk in My statutes, execute My ordinances, and keep all My commandments by walking in them, I will fulfill My promise to you, which I made to your father David. 13 I will live among the Israelites and not abandon My people Israel."

14 When Solomon finished building the temple,[d] 15 he paneled the interior temple walls with cedar boards; from the temple floor to the surface of the ceiling he overlaid the interior with wood. He also overlaid the floor with cypress boards. 16 Then he lined 30 feet[e] of the rear of the temple with cedar boards from the floor to the surface of the ceiling,[f] and he built the interior as an inner sanctuary, the most holy place. 17 The temple, that is, the sanctuary in front of the most holy place,[g] was 60 feet[h] long. 18 The cedar paneling inside the temple was carved with ⌊ornamental⌋ gourds and flower blossoms. Everything was cedar; not a stone could be seen.

19 He prepared the inner sanctuary inside the temple to put the ark of the LORD's covenant there. 20 The interior of the sanctuary was 30 feet[e] long, 30 feet wide, and 30 feet high; he overlaid it with pure gold. He also overlaid the cedar altar. 21 Next, Solomon overlaid the interior of the temple with pure gold, and he hung[i] gold chains across the front of the inner sanctuary and overlaid it with gold. 22 So he added the gold overlay to the entire temple until everything was completely finished, including the entire altar that belongs in the inner sanctuary.

23 In the inner sanctuary he made two •cherubim 15 feet[j] high out of olive wood. 24 One wing of the ⌊first⌋ cherub was seven and a half feet long,[c] and the other wing was seven and a half feet long. The wingspan was 15 feet[j] from tip to tip. 25 The second cherub also was 15 feet;[j] both cherubim had the same size and shape. 26 The first cherub's height was 15 feet[j] and so was the second cherub's. 27 Then he put the cherubim inside the inner temple. Since their wings were spread out, the first one's wing touched ⌊one⌋ wall while the second cherub's wing touched the other[k] wall, and in the middle of the temple their wings were touching wing to wing. 28 He also overlaid the cherubim with gold.

29 He carved all the surrounding temple walls with carved engravings—cherubim, palm trees and flower blossoms—in both the inner and outer sanctuaries. 30 He overlaid the temple floor with gold in both the inner and outer sanctuaries.

31 For the entrance of the inner sanctuary, he made olive wood doors. The pillars of the doorposts were five-sided.[b] 32 The two doors were made of olive wood. He carved cherubim, palm trees and flower blossoms on them and overlaid them with gold, hammering gold over the cherubim and palm trees. 33 In the same way, he made four-sided[b] olive wood doorposts for the sanctuary entrance. 34 The two doors were made of cypress wood; the first door had two folding sides, and the second door had two folding panels. 35 He carved cherubim, palm trees and flower blossoms on them and overlaid them with gold applied evenly over the carving. 36 He built the inner courtyard with three rows of dressed stone and a row of trimmed cedar beams.

37 The foundation of the LORD's temple was laid in ⌊Solomon's⌋ fourth year in the month of Ziv. 38 In ⌊his⌋ eleventh year in the eighth month, in the month of Bul,[l] the temple was completed in every detail and according to every specification. So he built it in seven years.

Solomon's Palace Complex

7 Solomon completed his entire palace-complex after 13 years of construction. 2 He built the House of the Forest of Lebanon. It was 150 feet[m] long, 75 feet[n] wide, and 45 feet[o] high on four rows of cedar pillars, with cedar beams on top of the pillars. 3 It was paneled above with cedar at the top of the chambers that ⌊rested⌋ on 45 pillars, fifteen per row. 4 There were three rows of window frames, facing each other[p] in three tiers.[q] 5 All the doors and doorposts had rectangular frames, the openings facing each other[r] in three tiers.[q] 6 He made the hall of pillars 75 feet[n] long and 45 feet[o] wide. A portico was in front of the pillars, and a canopy with pillars[b] was in front of them. 7 He made the Hall of the Throne where he would judge—the Hall of Judgment. It was paneled with cedar from the floor to the rafters.[s] 8 Solomon's own palace where he would live, in the other courtyard behind the hall,

---

a 6:8 LXX, Tg; Hb reads *middle* b 6:8,31,33; 7:6 Hb obscure c 6:10,24 Lit *five cubits* d 6:11–14 LXX omits these vv. e 6:16,20 Lit *20 cubits* f 6:16 LXX; Hb omits *of the ceiling*; 1 Kg 6:15 g 6:17 Hb obscure; lit *front of me* h 6:17 Lit *40 cubits* i 6:21 Lit *he caused to pass across* j 6:23,24,25,26 Lit *10 cubits* k 6:27 Lit *the second* l 6:38 October–November m 7:2 Lit *100 cubits* n 7:2,6 Lit *50 cubits* o 7:2,6 Lit *30 cubits* p 7:4 Lit *frames, window to window* q 7:4,5 Lit *three times, that is, at 3 different places* r 7:5 Lit *frames, opposing window to window* s 7:7 Syr, Vg; Hb reads *floor*

5:9 providing my household with food. Wheat and olive oil were not plentiful in or around Tyre.

5:17 large, costly stones. Stonecutters cut massive limestone blocks out of the quarry in the hills north of Jerusalem.

6:1 four hundred eightieth. This helps set the time of the exodus at 1446 B.C.

6:2 temple. The temple was twice the size of the tabernacle.

6:12 if you walk in My statutes. God reaffirms the promise He had made to David (2 Sam. 7:13). If Solomon would obey God, it would bring blessing on his nation. Israel lost out on some of this fellowship because of Solomon's later sin.

6:19 ark of the LORD's covenant. This symbolized God's presence among His people and contained the two stone tablets of the Ten Commandments (see Deut. 10:1-5).

6:23 two cherubim. Creatures with the lions'

was of similar construction. And he made a house like this hall for Pharaoh's daughter, his wife.[a]

9 All of these ⌊buildings⌋ were of costly stones, cut to size and sawed with saws on the inner and outer surfaces, from foundation to coping and from the outside to the great courtyard. 10 The foundation was made of large, costly stones 12 and 15 feet long.[b] 11 Above were also costly stones, cut to size, as well as cedar wood. 12 Around the great courtyard, as well as the inner courtyard of the LORD's temple and the portico of the temple, were three rows of dressed stone and a row of trimmed cedar beams.

13 King Solomon had Hiram[c] brought from Tyre. 14 He was a widow's son from the tribe of Naphtali, and his father was a man of Tyre, a bronze craftsman. Hiram had great skill, understanding, and knowledge to do every kind of bronze work. So he came to King Solomon and carried out all his work.

The Bronze Pillars

15 He cast two ⌊hollow⌋ bronze pillars: each 27 feet[d] high and 18 feet[e] in circumference.[f] 16 He also made two capitals of cast bronze to set on top of the pillars; seven and a half feet[g] was the height of the first capital, and seven and a half feet[g] was also the height of the second capital. 17 The capitals on top of the pillars had gratings of latticework, wreaths[h] made of chainwork—seven for the first capital and seven for the second. 18 He made the pillars with two encircling rows of pomegranates on the one grating to cover the capital on top; he did the same for the second capital. 19 And the capitals on top of the pillars in the portico were shaped like lilies, six feet[i] ⌊high⌋. 20 The capitals on the two pillars were also immediately above the rounded surface next to the grating, and 200 pomegranates were in rows encircling each[j] capital. 21 He set up the pillars at the portico of the sanctuary: he set up the right pillar and named it Jachin;[k] then he set up the left pillar and named it Boaz.[l] 22 The tops of the pillars were shaped like lilies. Then the work of the pillars was completed.

The Reservoir

23 He made the cast ⌊metal⌋ reservoir,[m] 15 feet[n] from brim to brim, perfectly round. It was seven and a half feet[g] high and 45 feet[o] in circumference. 24 ⌊Ornamental⌋ gourds encircled it below the brim, 10 every half yard,[p]

completely encircling the reservoir. The gourds were cast in two rows when the reservoir was cast. 25 It stood on 12 oxen, three facing north, three facing west, three facing south, and three facing east. The reservoir was on top of them and all their hindquarters were toward the center. 26 The reservoir was three inches[q] thick, and its rim was fashioned like the brim of a cup or of a lily blossom. It held 11,000 gallons.[r]

The Bronze Water Carts

27 Then he made 10 bronze water carts.[s] Each water cart was six feet[i] long, six feet[i] wide, and four and a half feet[t] high. 28 This was the design of the carts: They had frames; the frames were between the cross-pieces, 29 and on the frames between the cross-pieces were lions, oxen, and •cherubim. On the cross-pieces there was a pedestal above, and below the lions and oxen were wreaths of hanging[u] work. 30 Each cart had four bronze wheels with bronze axles. Underneath the four corners of the basin were cast supports, each next to a wreath. 31 And the water cart's opening inside the crown on top was 18 inches[v] wide. The opening was round, made as a pedestal 27 inches[w] wide. On it were carvings, but their frames were square, not round. 32 There were four wheels under the frames, and the wheel axles were part of the water cart; each wheel was 27 inches[x] tall. 33 The wheels' design was similar to that of chariot wheels: their axles, rims, spokes, and hubs were all of cast metal. 34 Four supports were at the four corners of each water cart; each support was one piece with the water cart. 35 At the top of the cart was a band nine inches[y] high encircling it; also, at the top of the cart, its braces and its frames were one piece with it. 36 He engraved cherubim, lions, and palm trees on the plates of its braces and on its frames, wherever each had space, with encircling wreaths. 37 In this way he made the 10 water carts using the same casting, dimensions, and shape for all of them.

Bronze Basins and Other Utensils

38 Then he made 10 bronze basins—each basin holding 220 gallons[z] and each was six feet[i] wide—one basin for each of the 10 water carts. 39 He set five water carts on the right side of the temple and five on the left side. He put the reservoir near the right side of the temple toward the southeast. 40 Then Hiram made the basins, the shovels, and the sprinkling basins.

a7:8 Lit daughter he had taken   b7:10 Lit ten cubits and eight cubits   c7:13 = Huram in 2 Ch 2:13; here not the king of Tyre (1 Kg 5:1)   d7:15 Lit 18 cubits   e7:15 Lit 12 cubits   f7:15 LXX adds and the thickness of the pillar was four fingers hollowed and similarly the second pillar   g7:16,23 Lit five cubits   h7:17 Lit tassels   i7:19,27,38 Lit four cubits   j7:20 Lit encircling the second   k7:21 = He will establish   l7:21 = In Him is strength   m7:23 Lit sea   n7:23 Lit 10 cubits   o7:23 Lit 30 cubits   p7:24 Lit 10 per cubit   q7:26 Lit a handbreadth   r7:26 Lit 2,000 baths   s7:27 Lit bronze stands   t7:27 Lit three cubits   u7:29 Or hammered-down   v7:31 Lit a cubit   w7:31 Lit one and a half cubits   x7:32 Lit was one and a half cubits   y7:35 Lit half a cubit   z7:38 Lit 40 baths

6:34 doors. The doors folded in half to open.

6:36 inner courtyard. Only the priests could use this courtyard.

7:2 House of the Forest of Lebanon. Lebanese cedar was used extensively throughout this palace. It was 11,250 square feet—four times the size of the temple.

7:8 palace where he would live. Solomon's residence and a residence for Pharaoh's daughter, his wife. They were all attached.

7:9 sawed. Limestone can be cut with a saw as it is quarried, but it hardens after exposure to the air.

7:15 bronze pillars. These pillars stood near the temple entrance.

7:23 cast [metal] reservoir. This was a large wash basin for the priests. It also served as a reservoir for the temple.

7:27 10 bronze water carts. The carts were used during the butchering of animal sacri-

Completion of the Bronze Works

So Hiram finished all the work that he was doing for King Solomon on the LORD's temple: [41] two pillars; bowls for the capitals that were on top of the two pillars; the two gratings for covering both bowls of the capitals that were on top of the pillars; [42] the 400 pomegranates for the two gratings (two rows of pomegranates for each grating covering both capitals' bowls on top of the pillars); [43] the 10 water carts; the 10 basins on the water carts; [44] the reservoir; the 12 oxen underneath the reservoir; [45] and the pots, shovels, and sprinkling basins. All the utensils that Hiram made for King Solomon at the LORD's temple ⌊were made⌋ of burnished bronze. [46] The king had them cast in clay molds in the Jordan Valley between Succoth and Zarethan. [47] Solomon left all the utensils unweighed because there were so many; the weight of the bronze was not determined.

Completion of the Gold Furnishings

[48] Solomon also made all the equipment in the LORD's temple: the gold altar; the gold table that the bread of the Presence was placed on; [49] the pure gold lampstands in front of the inner sanctuary, five on the right and five on the left; the gold flowers, lamps, and tongs; [50] the pure gold ceremonial bowls, wick trimmers, sprinkling basins, ladles,[a] and firepans; and the gold hinges for the doors of the inner temple (that is, the most holy place) and for the doors of the temple sanctuary.

[51] So all the work King Solomon did in the LORD's temple was completed. Then Solomon brought in the consecrated things of his father David—the silver, the gold, and the utensils—and put them in the treasuries of the LORD's temple.

Solomon's Dedication of the Temple

8 At that time Solomon assembled the elders of Israel, all the tribal heads and the ancestral leaders of the Israelites before him at Jerusalem in order to bring the ark of the LORD's covenant from Zion, the city of David. [2] So all the men of Israel were assembled in the presence of King Solomon in the seventh month, the month of Ethanim at the festival.[b] [3] All the elders of Israel came, and the priests picked up the ark. [4] The priests and the Levites brought the ark of the LORD, the tent of meeting, and the holy utensils that were in the tent. [5] King Solomon and the entire congregation of Israel, who had gathered around him and were with him in front of the ark, were sacrificing sheep and cattle that could not be counted or num-

bered, because there were so many. [6] The priests brought the ark of the LORD's covenant to its place, into the inner sanctuary of the temple, to the most holy place beneath the wings of the •cherubim. [7] For the cherubim were spreading their wings over[c] the place of the ark, so that the cherubim covered the ark and its poles from above. [8] The poles were so long that their ends were seen from the holy place in front of the inner sanctuary, but they were not seen from outside ⌊the sanctuary⌋; they are there to this day. [9] Nothing was in the ark except the two stone tablets that Moses had put there at Horeb,[d] where the LORD made a covenant with the Israelites when they came out of the land of Egypt.

[10] When the priests came out of the holy place, the cloud filled the LORD's temple, [11] and because of the cloud, the priests were not able to continue ministering, for the glory of the LORD filled the temple.

[12] Then Solomon said:

> The LORD said that He would dwell
> in thick darkness,
> [13] but I have indeed built an exalted temple
> for You,
> a place for Your dwelling forever.

[14] The king turned around and blessed the entire congregation of Israel while they were standing. [15] He said:

> May the LORD God of Israel be praised!
> He spoke directly to my father David,
> and He has fulfilled ⌊the promise⌋ by His power.
> He said,
> [16] "Since the day I brought My people Israel
> out of Egypt,
> I have not chosen a city to build a temple in
> among any of the tribes of Israel,
> so that My name would be there.
> But I have chosen David to rule
> My people Israel."
> [17] It was in the desire of my father David
> to build a temple for the name of the LORD God
> of Israel.
> [18] But the LORD said to my father David,
> "Since it was your desire to build a temple
> for My name,
> you have done well to have this desire.
> [19] Yet you are not the one to build it;
> instead, your son, your own offspring,
> will build it for My name."
> [20] The LORD has fulfilled what He promised.
> I have taken the place of my father David,

---

[a]**7:50** Or *dishes*, or *spoons*; lit *palms*   [b]**8:2** September–October   [c]**8:7** LXX; MT reads *toward*   [d]**8:9** = Sinai

---

fices (2 Chron. 4:6). A basin holding 220 gallons of water rested on each cart.

7:40 shovels. These were used to remove ashes from the altar.

7:46 Succoth and Zarethan. An area about 35 miles north of the Dead Sea, east of the Jordan River.

7:48 gold altar ... table. These replaced the altar of incense (Ex. 30:2-4) and the table of the bread of the Presence (Ex. 25:23-30) in the tabernacle.

7:51 consecrated things. David had already prepared and dedicated furnishings for the temple (2 Sam. 8:11).

8:1 bring the ark. The ark was brought from its temporary shelter in Jerusalem. From now on, the temple would be the permanent center of worship.

8:4 priests and Levites. God required that the ark be carried by the priests and Levites (Num. 4:15; Deut. 10:8).

and I sit on the throne of Israel,
   as the LORD promised.
I have built the temple for the name of the LORD
   God of Israel.
21 I have provided a place there for the ark,
   where the LORD's covenant is
   that He made with our ancestors
   when He brought them out of the land of Egypt.

Solomon's Prayer

22 Then Solomon stood before the altar of the LORD
in front of the entire congregation of Israel and spread
out his hands toward heaven. 23 He said:

LORD God of Israel,
   there is no God like You
   in heaven above or on earth below,
   keeping the gracious covenant
   with Your servants who walk before You
   with their whole heart.
24 You have kept what You promised
   to Your servant, my father David.
   You spoke directly ⌊to him⌋
   and You fulfilled ⌊Your promise⌋ by Your power
   as it is today.
25 Therefore, LORD God of Israel,
   keep what You promised
   to Your servant, my father David:
   You will never fail to have a man
   to sit before Me on the throne of Israel,
   if only your sons guard their walk before Me
   as you have walked before Me.
26 Now LORD[a] God of Israel,
   please confirm what You promised
   to Your servant, my father David.

27 But will God indeed live on earth?
   Even heaven, the highest heaven,
      cannot contain You,
   much less this temple I have built.
28 Listen[b] to Your servant's prayer and his petition,
   LORD my God,
   so that You may hear the cry and the prayer
   that Your servant prays before You today,
29 so that Your eyes may watch over this temple
      night and day,
   toward the place where You said:
   My name will be there,
   and so that You may hear the prayer
   that Your servant prays toward this place.
30 Hear the petition of Your servant

and Your people Israel,
   which they pray toward this place.
May You hear in Your dwelling place in heaven.
May You hear and forgive.

31 When a man sins against his neighbor
   and is forced to take an oath,[c]
   and he comes to take an oath
   before Your altar in this temple,
32 may You hear in heaven and act.
   May You judge Your servants,
   condemning the wicked by bringing
   what he has done on his own head
   and providing justice for the righteous
   by rewarding him according to
      his righteousness.

33 When Your people Israel are defeated
      before an enemy,
   because they have sinned against You,
   and they return to You and praise Your name,
   and they pray and plead with You
   for mercy in this temple,
34 may You hear in heaven
   and forgive the sin of Your people Israel.
   May You restore them to the land
   You gave their ancestors.

35 When the skies are shut and there is no rain,
   because they have sinned against You,
   and they pray toward this place
   and praise Your name,
   and they turn from their sins
   because You are afflicting them,
36 may You hear in heaven
   and forgive the sin of Your servants
   and Your people Israel,
   so that You may teach them the good way
   they should walk in.
   May You send rain on Your land
   that You gave Your people for an inheritance.

37 When there is famine on the earth,
   when there is pestilence,
   when there is blight, mildew, locust,
      or grasshopper,
   when their enemy besieges them
   in the region of their fortified cities,[d]
   ⌊when there is⌋ any plague or illness,
38 whatever prayer or petition
   anyone from Your people Israel might have—

---

a 8:26 Many Hb mss, LXX, Syr, Tg ms, Vg mss, 2 Ch 6:16; MT omits LORD   b 8:28 Lit Turn   c 8:31 Lit and he lifts a curse against him to curse him
d 8:37 Lit besieges him in the land of his gates

8:8 poles ... were seen. The poles by which
the priests carried the ark were left in their
rings (Ex. 25:15).

8:9 two stone tablets. The tablets containing
the Ten Commandments were kept in the ark.
The pot of manna (Ex. 16:33-34) and Aaron's
rod (Num. 17:10) may have been lost by Solo-

mon's time.

8:10 the cloud. Just as a cloud had covered
the tabernacle, a cloud, the symbol of God's
glory, filled the temple. This is sometimes
called "shekinah glory," a visible representation of God's presence with His people.

8:23 no God like You. This was an especially

good reminder in view of the pagan deities of
the surrounding Canaanites.

8:25 sons ... walk before Me. Solomon knew
the need for his royal descendants to be faithful to God.

8:27 this temple I have built. Since God is infinite, no building—not even a magnificent

each man knowing his own afflictions[a]
and spreading out his hands
toward this temple—

39 may You hear in heaven, Your dwelling place,
and may You forgive, act, and repay the man,
according to all his ways, since You know
his heart,
for You alone know every human heart,

40 so that they may •fear You
all the days they live on the land
You gave our ancestors.

41 Even for the foreigner who is not
of Your people Israel
but has come from a distant land
because of Your name—

42 for they will hear of Your great name,
mighty hand, and outstretched arm,
and will come and pray toward this temple—

43 may You hear in heaven, Your dwelling place,
and do according to all the foreigner
asks You for.
Then all the people on earth will know
Your name,
to fear You as Your people Israel do
and know that this temple I have built
is called by Your name.

44 When Your people go out to fight
against their enemies,[b]
wherever You send them,
and they pray to the LORD
in the direction of the city You have chosen
and the temple I have built for Your name,

45 may You hear their prayer and petition
in heaven
and uphold their cause.

46 When they sin against You—
for there is no one who does not sin—
and You are angry with them
and hand them over to the enemy,
and their captors deport them
to the enemy's country—
whether distant or nearby—

47 and when they come to their senses[c]
in the land where they were deported
and repent and petition You
in their captors' land:
"We have sinned and done wrong;
we have been wicked,"

48 and when they return to You
with their whole mind and heart
in the land of their enemies
who took them captive,
and when they pray to You in the direction
of their land
that You gave their ancestors,
the city You have chosen,
and the temple I have built for Your name,

49 may You hear in heaven, Your dwelling place,
their prayer and petition and uphold their cause.

50 May You forgive Your people
who sinned against You
and all their rebellions[d] against You,
and may You give them compassion
in the eyes of their captors,
so that they may be compassionate to them.

51 For they are Your people and Your inheritance;
You brought them out of Egypt,
out of the middle of an iron furnace.

52 May Your eyes be open
to Your servant's petition
and to the petition of Your people Israel,
listening to them whenever they call to You.

53 For You, Lord GOD, have set them apart
as Your inheritance
from all the people on earth,
as You spoke through Your servant Moses
when You brought their ancestors out of Egypt.

Solomon's Blessing

54 When Solomon finished praying this entire prayer and petition to the LORD, he got up from kneeling before the altar of the LORD, with his hands spread out toward heaven, 55 and he stood and blessed the whole congregation of Israel with a loud voice: 56 "May the LORD be praised! He has given rest to His people Israel according to all He has said. Not one of all the good promises He made through His servant Moses has failed. 57 May the LORD our God be with us as He was with our ancestors. May He not abandon us or leave us. 58 May He incline our hearts toward Him to walk in all His ways and to keep His commands, ordinances, and judgments, which He commanded our ancestors. 59 May my words I have made my petition with before the LORD be near the LORD our God day and night, so that He may uphold His servant's cause and the cause of His people Israel, as each day requires, 60 and so that all the peoples of the earth may know that the LORD is God. There is no other! 61 Let your heart be completely

---

a 8:38 Lit knowing in his heart of a plague   b 8:44 Some Hb mss, most ancient versions, 2 Ch 6:34; MT reads enemy   c 8:47 Lit they return to their heart   d 8:50 Lit rebellions that they have rebelled

---

one—can contain Him. And yet God chooses to dwell among His people.
8:33 defeated before an enemy. Sin against God could cause defeat in battle (see Lev. 26:36-39; Josh. 7:11-12).
8:34 Israel ... to the land. One of the consequences of sin against God was being scat-

tered in foreign lands (see Lev. 26:41-45).
8:37 plague or illness. God allows His people to suffer trouble in order to restore relationships and renew their commitment to Him. Good things result from that. Not all disasters or diseases are the result of sin (John 9:3), but this verse lists some of the troubles sin brings.

8:40 fear You. Experiencing God produces a sense of fear or reverence that helps us to obey God.
8:42 Your great name. Solomon knew that those who heard of God's power would be impressed and would believe (see Deut. 3:24). In this way, Solomon hoped that news of God's

devoted to the LORD our God to walk in His ordinances and to keep His commands, as it is today."

62 The king and all Israel with him were offering sacrifices in the LORD's presence. 63 Solomon offered a sacrifice of •fellowship offerings to the LORD: 22,000 cattle and 120,000 sheep. In this manner the king and all the Israelites dedicated the LORD's temple.

64 On the same day, the king consecrated the middle of the courtyard that was in front of the LORD's temple because that was where he offered the •burnt offering, the •grain offering, and the fat of the fellowship offerings since the bronze altar before the LORD was too small to accommodate the burnt offerings, the grain offerings, and the fat of the fellowship offerings.

65 Solomon and all Israel with him—a great assembly, from the entrance of Hamath[a] to the Brook of Egypt—observed the festival at that time in the presence of the LORD our God, seven days, and seven ⌊more⌋ days—14 days.[b] 66 On the fifteenth day[c] he sent the people away. So they blessed the king and went home to their tents rejoicing and with joyful hearts for all the goodness that the LORD had done for His servant David and for His people Israel.

The LORD's Response

9 When Solomon finished building the temple of the LORD, the royal palace, and all that Solomon desired to do, 2 the LORD appeared to Solomon a second time just as He had appeared to him at Gibeon. 3 The LORD said to him:

I have heard your prayer and petition you have made before Me. I have consecrated this temple you have built, to put My name there forever; My eyes and My heart will be there at all times.

4 As for you, if you walk before Me as your father David walked, with integrity of heart and uprightness, doing everything I have commanded you, and if you keep My statutes and ordinances, 5 I will establish your royal throne over Israel forever, as I promised your father David: You will never fail to have a man on the throne of Israel.

6 If you or your sons turn away from following Me and do not keep My commands—My statutes that I have set before you—and if you go and serve other gods and worship them, 7 I will cut off[d] Israel from the land I gave them, and I will reject the temple I have sanctified for My name. Israel

will become an object of scorn and ridicule among all the peoples. 8 Though this temple is ⌊now⌋ exalted,[e] every passerby will be appalled and will hiss. They will say: Why did the LORD do this to this land and this temple? 9 Then they will say: Because they abandoned the LORD their God who brought their ancestors out of the land of Egypt. They clung to other gods and worshiped and served them. Because of this, the LORD brought all this ruin on them.

King Hiram's 20 Towns

10 At the end of 20 years during which Solomon had built the two houses, the LORD's temple and the royal palace— 11 Hiram king of Tyre having supplied him with cedar and cypress logs and gold for his every wish—King Solomon gave Hiram 20 towns in the land of Galilee. 12 So Hiram went out from Tyre to look over the towns that Solomon had given him, but he was not pleased with them. 13 So he said, "What are these towns you've given me, my brother?" So he called them the Land of Cabul,[f] as they are ⌊still called⌋ today. 14 Now Hiram had sent the king 9,000 pounds[g] of gold.

Solomon's Forced Labor

15 This is the account of the forced labor that King Solomon had imposed to build the LORD's temple, his own palace, the supporting terraces, the wall of Jerusalem, and Hazor, Megiddo, and Gezer. 16 Pharaoh king of Egypt had attacked and captured Gezer. He then burned it down, killed the Canaanites who lived in the city, and gave it as a dowry to his daughter, Solomon's wife. 17 Then Solomon rebuilt Gezer, Lower Bethhoron, 18 Baalath, Tamar[h] in the Wilderness of Judah, 19 all the storage cities that belonged to Solomon, the chariot cities, the cavalry cities, and whatever Solomon desired to build in Jerusalem, Lebanon, or anywhere else in the land of his dominion.

20 As for all the peoples who remained of the Amorites, Hittites, Perizzites, Hivites, and Jebusites, who were not Israelites— 21 their descendants who remained in the land after them, those whom the Israelites were unable to annihilate—Solomon imposed forced labor on them; ⌊it is this way⌋ until today. 22 But Solomon did not consign the Israelites to slavery; they were soldiers, his servants, his commanders, his captains, and commanders of his chariots and his cavalry. 23 These were the deputies who were over Solomon's work: 550 who ruled over the people doing the work.

---

a 8:65 Or from Lebo-hamath   b 8:65 Seven days for the dedication of the temple, and then seven days for the Festival of Tabernacles.   c 8:66 Lit the eighth day (after the second seven days)   d 9:7 Lit send from My presence   e 9:8 Some ancient versions read temple will become a ruin   f 9:13 = Like Nothing   g 9:14 Lit 120 talents   h 9:18 Alt Hb traditions, LXX, Syr, Tg, Vg, 2 Ch 8:4 read Tadmor. Tamar was a city in southern Judah; Ezk 47:19; 48:28.

---

greatness would spread all over the earth.
8:52 whenever they call to You. Solomon summarized his prayer by asking God to always listen to His people, despite their sin.
8:53 as Your inheritance. This is another reference to God's special love for Israel. (See also Ex. 19:5-6; Ps. 135:4.)

8:58 May He incline our hearts. Solomon prays for God's sovereign grace (see Ps. 119:36; Jer. 31:33).

9:4-5 walk before Me …with integrity of heart. This involved attitudes, actions, and words that were submissive to God's instructions. God said He would provide rulers of Is-

rael through Solomon if he would obey Him.

9:9 Because they abandoned the LORD their God. People would know that Israel suffered because of its idolatry. God's warnings were clear. He knew how easy it would be for Solomon, his descendants, and the people of Israel to be seduced by other gods.

Solomon's Other Activities

24 Pharaoh's daughter moved from the city of David to the house that Solomon had built for her; he then built the terraces.

25 Three times a year Solomon offered •burnt offerings and •fellowship offerings on the altar he had built for the LORD, and he burned incense with them in the LORD's presence. So he completed the temple.

26 King Solomon put together a fleet of ships at Ezion-geber, which is near Eloth on the shore of the •Red Sea in the land of Edom. 27 With the fleet, Hiram sent his servants, experienced seamen, along with Solomon's servants. 28 They went to Ophir and acquired gold there—16 tonsa—and delivered it to Solomon.

The Queen of Sheba

10 The queen of Sheba heard about Solomon's fame connected with the name of the LORD and came to test him with difficult questions. 2 She came to Jerusalem with a very large retinue, with camels bearing spices, gold in great abundance, and precious stones. She came to Solomon and spoke to him about everything that was on her mind. 3 So Solomon answered all her questions; nothing was too difficult for the king to explain to her. 4 When the queen of Sheba observed all of Solomon's wisdom, the palace he had built, 5 the food at his table, his servants' residence, his attendants' service and their attire, his cupbearers, and the •burnt offerings he offered at the LORD's temple, it took her breath away.

6 She said to the king, "The report I heard in my own country about your words and about your wisdom is true. 7 But I didn't believe the reports until I came and saw with my own eyes. Indeed, I was not even told half. Your wisdom and prosperity far exceed the report I heard. 8 How happy are your men.b How happy are these servants of yours, who always stand in your presence hearing your wisdom. 9 May the LORD your God be praised! He delighted in you and put you on the throne of Israel, because of the LORD's eternal love for Israel. He has made you king to carry out justice and righteousness."

10 Then she gave the king four and a half tonsc of gold, a great quantity of spices, and precious stones. Never again did such a quantity of spices arrive as those the queen of Sheba gave to King Solomon.

11 In addition, Hiram's fleet that carried gold from Ophir brought from Ophir a large quantity of almugd wood and precious stones. 12 The king made the almug wood into steps for the LORD's temple and the king's palace and into harps and lyres for the singers. Never ⌊before⌋ had such almug wood come, and ⌊the like⌋ has not been seen ⌊again⌋ even to this very day.

13 King Solomon gave the queen of Sheba her every desire—whatever she asked—besides what he had given her out of his royal bounty. Then she, along with her servants, returned to her own country.

Solomon's Wealth

14 The weight of gold that came to Solomon annually was 25 tons,e 15 besides what came from merchants, traders' merchandise, and all the Arabian kings and governors of the land.

16 King Solomon made 200 large shields of hammered gold; 15 poundsf of gold went into each shield. 17 He made 300 small shields of hammered gold; about four poundsg of gold went into each shield. The king put them in the House of the Forest of Lebanon.

18 The king also made a large ivory throne and overlaid it with fine gold. 19 The throne had six steps; there was a rounded top at the back of the throne, armrests on either side of the seat, and two lions standing beside the armrests. 20 Twelve lions were standing there on the six steps, one at each end. Nothing like it had ever been made in any other kingdom.

21 All of King Solomon's drinking cups were gold, and all the utensils of the House of the Forest of Lebanon were pure gold. There was no silver, since it was considered as nothing in Solomon's time, 22 for the king had ships of Tarshish at sea with Hiram's fleet, and once every three years the ships of Tarshish would arrive bearing gold, silver, ivory, apes, and peacocks.h

23 King Solomon surpassed all the kings of the world in riches and in wisdom. 24 The whole world wanted an audience with Solomon to hear the wisdom that God had put in his heart. 25 Every man would bring his annual tribute: itemsi of silver and gold, clothing, weapons,j spices, and horses and mules.

26 Solomon accumulated 1,400 chariots and 12,000 horsemen and stationed them in the chariot cities and with the king in Jerusalem. 27 The king made silver as common in Jerusalem as stones, and he made cedar as abundant as sycamore in the Judean foothills. 28 Solomon's horses were imported from Egypt and Kue.k The king's traders bought them from Kue at the going price. 29 A chariot was imported from Egypt for 15 poundsl ⌊of silver⌋, and a horse for about four pounds.m In the same way, they exported them to all

---

a9:28 Lit *420 talents*; about 31,500 pounds   b10:8 LXX, Syr read *your wives*   c10:10 Lit *120 talents*   d10:11 Spelled *algum* in 2 Ch 2:8; 9:10–11
e10:14 Lit *666 talents*   f10:16 Lit *600* (shekels)   g10:17 Lit *three minas*   h10:22 Or *baboons*   i10:25 Or *vessels*, or *weapons*   j10:25 Or *fragrant balsam*   k10:28 = Cilicia (modern Turkey)   l10:29 Lit *600 shekels*   m10:29 Lit *150 shekels*

9:11 Solomon gave Hiram. Hiram had provided cedar and pine and the equivalent of 9,000 pounds of gold for the temple.

9:12 he was not pleased with them. The towns were near unproductive land and did not meet with Hiram's approval.

9:15 supporting terraces. Probably large

level areas between hills. He also built a wall around Jerusalem that doubled the size of the city.

9:20 Amorites ... Jebusites ... not Israelites. These were descendants of the conquered Canaanites.

9:25 Three times a year ... burnt offerings.

The occasions were the Festival of Unleavened Bread, the Festival of Harvest, and the Festival of Booths—the major feasts of Israel (see Ex. 23:14-16). Solomon led his people in worship.

10:1 queen of Sheba. This is modern Yemen in Arabia, about 1,200 miles from Jerusalem. It

Overwhelmed by Temptation

1. Finish the sentence: "The one with the most toys _____": (a) wins, (b) sins, (c) is lucky, (d) must be God's favorite.

1 Kings 10:23-11:13

2. What was Solomon's biggest problem: His wealth? His women? His will? His worship?

3. Where did Solomon's great wisdom come from (10:24)? In what ways was Solomon's success as a king completely dependent upon God?

4. In what ways does your success in life depend upon God? What does God require from you?

5. What things in life tempt you to ignore God's commands? Are you avoiding those temptations or flirting with them?

the kings of the Hittites and to the kings of Aram through their agents.

Solomon's Unfaithfulness to God

11 King Solomon loved many foreign women in addition to Pharaoh's daughter: Moabite, Ammonite, Edomite, Sidonian, and Hittite women ² from the nations that the LORD had told the Israelites about, "Do not intermarry with them, and they must not intermarry with you, because they will turn you away ⌊from Me⌋ to their gods." Solomon was deeply attached to these women and loved ⌊them⌋. ³ He had 700 wives who were princesses and 300 concubines, and they turned his heart away ⌊from the LORD⌋.

⁴ When Solomon was old, his wives seduced him ⌊to follow⌋ other gods. His heart was not completely with the LORD his God, as his father David's heart had been. ⁵ Solomon followed •Ashtoreth, the goddess of the Sidonians, and •Milcom, the detestable idol of the Ammonites. ⁶ Solomon did what was evil in the LORD's sight, and unlike his father David, he did not completely follow the LORD.

⁷ At that time, Solomon built a •high place for Chemosh, the detestable idol of Moab, and for Milcom,ᵃ the detestable idol of the Ammonites on the hill across from Jerusalem. ⁸ He did the same for all his foreign wives, who were burning incense and offering sacrifices to their gods.

⁹ The LORD was angry with Solomon, because his heart had turned away from the LORD God of Israel, who had appeared to him twice. ¹⁰ He had commanded him about this, so that he would not follow other gods, but Solomon did not do what the LORD had commanded.

¹¹ Then the LORD said to Solomon, "Since you have done thisᵇ and did not keep My covenant and My statutes, which I commanded you, I will tear the kingdom away from you and give it to your servant. ¹² However, I will not do it during your lifetime because of your father David; I will tear it out of your son's hand. ¹³ Yet, I will not tear the entire kingdom away from him. I will give one tribe to your son because of my servant David and because of Jerusalem that I chose."

Solomon's Enemies

¹⁴ So the LORD raised up Hadad the Edomite as an enemy against Solomon. He was of the royal family in Edom. ¹⁵ Earlier, when David was in Edom, Joab, the commander of the army, had gone to bury the dead and had struck down every male in Edom. ¹⁶ For Joab and all Israel had remained there six months, until he had killed every male in Edom. ¹⁷ Hadad fled to Egypt, along with some Edomites from his father's servants. At the time Hadad was a small boy. ¹⁸ Hadad and his men set out from Midian and went to Paran. They took men with them from Paran and went to Egypt, to Pharaoh king of Egypt, who gave Hadad a house, ordered that he ⌊be given⌋ food, and gave him land. ¹⁹ Pharaoh liked Hadad so much that he gave him a wife, the sister of his own wife, Queen Tahpenes. ²⁰ Tahpenes' sister gave birth to Hadad's son Genubath. Tahpenes ⌊herself⌋ weaned him in Pharaoh's palace, and Genubath ⌊lived⌋ there along with Pharaoh's sons.

²¹ When Hadad heard in Egypt that David rested with his fathers and that Joab, the commander of the army, was dead, Hadad said to Pharaoh, "Let me leave, so I can go to my own country."

²² But Pharaoh asked him, "What do you lack here with me for you to want to go back to your own country?"

"Nothing," he replied, "but please let me leave."

²³ God raised up Rezon son of Eliada as an enemy against Solomon. Rezon had fled from his master Hadadezer king of Zobah ²⁴ and gathered men to himself. He became captain of a raiding party when David killed the Zobaites. Heᶜ went to Damascus, lived there, and became king in Damascus. ²⁵ Rezon was Israel's enemy throughout Solomon's reign, adding to the trouble Hadad ⌊had caused⌋. He ruled over Aram,ᵈ but he loathed Israel.

ᵃ**11:7** Lit *Molech* ᵇ**11:11** Lit *Since this was with you* ᶜ**11:24** LXX; Hb reads *They* ᵈ**11:25** Two Hb mss, LXX, Syr read *Edom*

was a prosperous trading country. Solomon's traders were able to go east and south by water and probably brought him news of this country. **connected with the ... LORD.** Solomon's legendary wisdom attracted many people. Sages from many countries visited him and learned that his wisdom came from God.

10:9 be praised. The queen of Sheba acknowledged Solomon's God, as Hiram had done in 5:7. Whether she became a worshiper or merely admired Solomon's giftedness is unknown.

11:1 loved many foreign women. God forbade a king multiple wives (see Deut. 17:17).

He also forbade marrying foreign women. Solomon's pagan wives led him into idolatry.

11:5 Ashtoreth. Canaanite goddess of fertility and war whose worship involved sexual rites. **Milcom.** Worship included child sacrifices, which was strictly forbidden (see Lev. 18:21).

11:6 unlike ... David. David never worshiped

26 Now Solomon's servant, Jeroboam son of Nebat, was an Ephraimite from Zeredah. His widowed mother's name was Zeruah. Jeroboam rebelled against Solomon, 27 and this is the reason he rebelled against the king: Solomon had built the supporting terraces ⌊and⌋ repaired the opening in the wall of the city of his father David. 28 Now the man Jeroboam was capable, and Solomon noticed the young man because he was getting things done. So he appointed him over the entire labor force of the house of Joseph.

29 During that time, the prophet Ahijah the Shilonite met Jeroboam on the road as Jeroboam came out of Jerusalem. Now Ahijah had wrapped himself with a new cloak, and the two of them were alone in the open field. 30 Then Ahijah took hold of the new cloak he had on, tore it into 12 pieces, 31 and said to Jeroboam, "Take 10 pieces for yourself, for this is what the LORD God of Israel says: 'I am about to tear the kingdom out of Solomon's hand. I will give you 10 tribes, 32 but one tribe will remain his because of my servant David and because of Jerusalem, the city I chose out of all the tribes of Israel. 33 For they have abandoned Me; they have bowed the knee to Ashtoreth, the goddess of the Sidonians, to Chemosh, the god of Moab, and to Milcom, the god of the Ammonites. They have not walked in My ways to do right in My eyes and to carry out My statutes and My judgments as his father David did.

34 " 'However, I will not take the whole kingdom from his hand but will let him be ruler all the days of his life because of My servant David, whom I chose and who kept My commandments and My statutes. 35 I will take 10 tribes of the kingdom from his son's hand and give them to you. 36 I will give one tribe to his son, so that My servant David will always have a lamp before Me in Jerusalem, the city I chose for Myself to put My name there. 37 I will appoint you, and you will reign as king over all you want, and you will be king over Israel.

38 " 'After that, if you obey all I command you, walk in My ways, and do what is right in My sight in order to keep My statutes and My commandments as My servant David did, I will be with you. I will build you a lasting dynasty just as I built for David, and I will give you Israel. 39 I will humble David's descendants, because of ⌊their unfaithfulness⌋, but not forever.' "[a]

40 Therefore, Solomon tried to kill Jeroboam, but he fled to Egypt, to Shishak king of Egypt, where he remained until Solomon's death.

Solomon's Death

41 The rest of the events of Solomon's ⌊reign⌋, along with all his accomplishments and his wisdom, are written about in the Book of Solomon's Events. 42 The length of Solomon's reign in Jerusalem over all Israel totaled 40 years. 43 Solomon rested with his fathers and was buried in the city of his father David. His son Rehoboam became king in his place.

The Kingdom Divided

12 Then Rehoboam went to Shechem, for all Israel had gone to Shechem to make him king. 2 When Jeroboam son of Nebat heard ⌊about it⌋, for he was still in Egypt where he had fled from King Solomon's presence, Jeroboam stayed in Egypt.[b] 3 They summoned him, and Jeroboam and the whole assembly of Israel came and spoke to Rehoboam: 4 "Your father made our yoke harsh. You, therefore, lighten your father's harsh service and the heavy yoke he put on us, and we will serve you."

 Free Advice

1. What issue divides the students in your school or on your team? Where do you stand on this issue?

1 Kings 12:1-24

2. Why do you think Rehoboam chose his friends' advice: He didn't trust old people? He gave in to peer pressure? God made him?

3. Do you listen more to the advice of your parents, teachers, and coaches ... or to your friends? Why?

4. Where do you usually go for advice? What do you do if you don't like what you hear?

5. Since giving your life to God, what has changed in the way you see things? In the way you make decisions?

5 Rehoboam replied, "Go home for three days and then return to me." So the people left. 6 Then King Rehoboam consulted with the elders who had served his father Solomon when he was alive, asking, "How do you advise me to respond to these people?"

7 They replied, "Today if you will be a servant to these people and serve them, and if you respond to

---

a11:38–39 LXX omits and I will give . . . but not forever b12:2 LXX, Vg, 2 Ch 10:2 read Jeroboam returned from Egypt

---

false gods and always repented when he sinned.

11:26 Jeroboam rebelled against Solomon. Solomon trusted Jeroboam, who supervised the labor force of Ephraim and Manasseh, but Jeroboam knew of discontent among the laborers.

11:31-32 ten tribes. The twelfth tribe may be Simeon, which became part of Judah. Benjamin may have served as a buffer area between Israel and Judah, linked occasionally with the Northern Kingdom.

11:36 David ... have a lamp before Me in Jerusalem. As forerunners of Jesus the kings in

ancient Israel were to act as light in a dark pagan world. God remembered His promise to David despite the chastening Solomon had brought on himself.

11:38 I will build you a lasting dynasty. God gave a promise to Jeroboam that was similar to David's, but for Jeroboam it was conditional:

them by speaking kind words to them, they will be your servants forever."

8 But he rejected the advice of the elders who had advised him and consulted with the young men who had grown up with him and served him. 9 He asked them, "What message do you advise that we send back to these people who said to me, 'Lighten the yoke your father put on us'?"

10 Then the young men who had grown up with him told him, "This is what you should say to these people who said to you, 'Your father made our yoke heavy, but you, make it lighter on us!' This is what you should tell them: 'My little finger is thicker than my father's loins! 11 Although my father burdened you with a heavy yoke, I will add to your yoke; my father disciplined you with whips, but I will discipline you with barbed whips.' "a

12 So Jeroboam and all the people came to Rehoboam on the third day, as the king had ordered: "Return to me on the third day." 13 Then the king answered the people harshly. He rejected the advice the elders had given him 14 and spoke to them according to the young men's advice: "My father made your yoke heavy, but I will add to your yoke; my father disciplined you with whips, but I will discipline you with barbed whips."a

15 The king did not listen to the people, because the turn of events came from the LORD to carry out His word, which the LORD had spoken through Ahijah the Shilonite to Jeroboam son of Nebat. 16 When all Israel saw that the king had not listened to them, the people answered him:

> What portion do we have in David?
> We have no inheritance in the son of Jesse.
> Israel, return to your tents;
> David, now look after your own house!

So Israel went to their tents, 17 but Rehoboam reigned over the Israelites living in the cities of Judah.

18 Then King Rehoboam sent Adoram,b who was in charge of forced labor, but all Israel stoned him to death. King Rehoboam managed to get into the chariot and flee to Jerusalem. 19 Israel is in rebellion against the house of David until today.

Rehoboam in Jerusalem

20 When all Israel heard that Jeroboam had come back, they summoned him to the assembly and made him king over all Israel. No one followed the house of David except the tribe of Judah alone. 21 When Rehoboam arrived in Jerusalem, he mobilized 180,000 choice warriors from the entire house of Judah and the tribe of Benjamin to fight against the house of Israel to restore the kingdom to Rehoboam son of Solomon. 22 But a revelation from God came to Shemaiah, the man of God: 23 "Say to Rehoboam son of Solomon, king of Judah, to the whole house of Judah and Benjamin, and to the rest of the people, 24 'This is what the LORD says: You are not to march up and fight against your brothers, the Israelites. Each of you must return home, for I have done this.' "

So they listened to what the LORD said and went back as He had told them.

Jeroboam's Idolatry

25 Jeroboam built Shechem in the hill country of Ephraim and lived there. From there he went out and built Penuel. 26 Jeroboam said to himself, "⌊The way things are going⌋ now, the kingdom might return to the house of David. 27 If these people regularly go to offer sacrifices in the LORD's temple in Jerusalem, the heart of these people will return to their lord, Rehoboam king of Judah. They will murder me and go back to the king of Judah." 28 So the king sought advice.

Then he made two gold calves, and he said to the people, "Going to Jerusalem is too difficult for you. Israel, here is your Godc who brought you out of the land of Egypt." 29 He set up one in Bethel, and put the other in Dan. 30 This led to sin; the people walked ⌊in procession⌋ before one of the calves all the way to Dan.

31 Jeroboam also built shrines on the •high places and set up priests from every class of people who were not Levites. 32 Jeroboam made a festival in the eighth month on the fifteenth day of the month, like the festival in Judah. He offered sacrifices on the altar; he made this offering in Bethel to sacrifice to the calves he had set up. He also stationed in Bethel the priests for the high places he had set up. 33 He offered sacrifices ond the altar he had set up in Bethel on the fifteenth day of the eighth month, the month he had decided on his own. He made a festival for the Israelites, offered sacrifices on the altar, and burned incense.

Judgment on Jeroboam

13 A man of God came from Judah to Bethel by a revelation from the LORD while Jeroboam was standing beside the altar to burn incense. 2 The man of God cried out against the altar by a revelation from the LORD: "Altar, altar, this is what the LORD says, 'A son will be born to the house of David, named Josiah, and he will sacrifice on you the priests of the •high places who are burning incense on you. Human bones will be burned on you.' " 3 He gave a sign that day. He said,

---

a **12:11,14** Lit with scorpions   b **12:18** LXX reads Adoniram; 1 Kg 4:6; 5:14   c **12:28** Or here are your gods   d **12:33** Or He went up to

---

only if he obeyed God.
11:39 not forever. Always faithful to His promises, God would restore David's line to the throne in Jesus Christ (see Jer. 30:8-10).
12:1 All Israel had gone to Shechem. Shechem was a northern city. The northern tribes were willing to accept Jeroboam, but he had to

meet them halfway.
12:4 we will serve you. In later years, Solomon weighed the Israelites down with heavy taxes and pressed them into labor gangs (4:27-28; 5:13-16). The northern tribes were willing to accept Solomon's son as their king on the condition that there be less work.

12:26 Jeroboam said to himself. Jeroboam had been promised that God would build him a lasting dynasty (11:37-38), but he did not trust God. He thought that if his people continued making pilgrimages to the temple in Jerusalem, he would lose control over them.
12:31 priests ... not Levites. Jeroboam re-

"This is the sign that the LORD has spoken: 'The altar will now be ripped apart, and the ashes that are on it will be spilled out.'"

4 When the king heard the word that the man of God had cried out against the altar at Bethel, Jeroboam stretched out his hand from the altar and said, "Arrest him!" But the hand he stretched out against him withered, and he could not pull it back to himself. 5 The altar was ripped apart, and the ashes spilled off the altar, according to the sign that the man of God had given by the word of the LORD.

6 Then the king responded to the man of God, "Please plead for the favor of the LORD your God and pray for me so that my hand may be restored to me." So the man of God pleaded for the favor of the LORD, and the king's hand was restored to him and became as it had been at first.

7 Then the king declared to the man of God, "Come home with me, refresh yourself, and I'll give you a reward."

8 But the man of God replied, "If you were to give me half your house, I still wouldn't go with you, and I wouldn't eat bread or drink water in this place, 9 for this is what I was commanded by the word of the LORD: 'You must not eat bread or drink water or go back the way you came.'" 10 So he went another way; he did not go back by the way he had come to Bethel.

The Old Prophet and the Man of God

11 Now a certain old prophet was living in Bethel. His son[a] came and told him all the deeds that the man of God had done that day in Bethel. His sons also told their father the words that he had spoken to the king. 12 Then their father said to them, "Which way did he go?" His sons had seen[b] the way taken by the man of God who had come from Judah. 13 Then he said to his sons, "Saddle the donkey for me." So they saddled the donkey for him, and he got on it. 14 He followed the man of God and found him sitting under an oak tree. He asked him, "Are you the man of God who came from Judah?"

"I am," he said.

15 Then he said to him, "Come home with me and eat bread."

16 But he answered, "I cannot go back with you, eat bread, or drink water with you in this place, 17 for a message came to me by the word of the LORD: 'You must not eat bread or drink water there or go back by the way you came.'"

18 He said to him, "I am also a prophet like you. An angel spoke to me by the word of the LORD: 'Bring him back with you to your house so that he may eat bread and drink water.'" The old prophet deceived him, 19 and the man of God went back with him, ate bread in his house, and drank water.

20 While they were sitting at the table, the word of the LORD came to the prophet who had brought him back, 21 and the prophet cried out to the man of God who had come from Judah, "This is what the LORD says: 'Because you rebelled against the command of the LORD and did not keep the commandment that the LORD your God commanded you, 22 but you went back and ate bread and drank water in the place that He said to you: Do not eat bread and do not drink water, your corpse will never reach the grave of your fathers.'"

23 So after he had eaten bread and after he had drunk, the old prophet saddled the donkey for the prophet he had brought back. 24 When he left,[c] a lion met him along the way and killed him. His corpse was thrown on the road, and the donkey was standing beside it; the lion was standing beside the corpse too.

25 There were men passing by who saw the corpse thrown on the road and the lion standing beside it, and they went and spoke ⌊about it⌋ in the city where the old prophet lived. 26 When the prophet who had brought him back from his way heard ⌊about it⌋, he said, "He is the man of God who disobeyed the command of the LORD. The LORD has given him to the lion, and it has mauled him and killed him, according to the word of the LORD that He spoke to him."

27 Then the old prophet instructed his sons, "Saddle the donkey for me." They saddled it, 28 and he went and found the corpse of the man of God thrown on the road with the donkey and the lion standing beside the corpse. The lion had not eaten the corpse or mauled the donkey. 29 So the prophet lifted the corpse of the man of God and laid it on the donkey and brought it back. The old prophet came into the city to mourn and to bury him. 30 Then he laid the corpse in his own grave, and they mourned over him: "Oh, my brother!"

31 After he had buried him, he said to his sons, "When I die, you must bury me in the grave where the man of God is buried; lay my bones beside his bones, 32 for the word that he cried out by a revelation from the LORD against the altar in Bethel and against all the shrines of the high places in the cities of Samaria is certain to happen."

33 After all this Jeroboam did not repent of his evil way but again set up priests from every class of people for the high places. Whoever so desired it, he ordained,

---

[a] **13:11** Some Hb mss, LXX, Syr, Vg read *sons* [b] **13:12** LXX, Syr, Tg, Vg read *sons showed him* [c] **13:23–24** LXX reads *donkey, and he turned* 24 *and left, and*

---

jected and banished God's priests (2 Chron. 11:13-17; 13:9) and made his own.

12:32 made a festival. The Israelites were required to worship God at the temple in Jerusalem during three great feasts every year. Jeroboam created a substitute festival.

13:3 a sign. When this prophecy was fulfilled,

Jeroboam would know that the judgment would also happen.

13:7 a reward. Jeroboam was not repentant (v. 33), but he wanted to placate God. Had the prophet accepted a gift, Jeroboam's guilty conscience would have been eased, so the prophet refused (see 2 Kings 5:13-16).

13:8 I still wouldn't. God did not want His prophet to share a meal in the Northern Kingdom because that would have implied that God was at peace with them.

13:19 went back with him. The man of God was tired (v. 14), hungry, and thirsty. He probably wished God hadn't forbidden him to eat

and they became priests of the high places. 34 For the house of Jeroboam, this was the sin that caused it to be wiped out and annihilated from the face of the earth.

Disaster on the House of Jeroboam

14 At that time Abijah son of Jeroboam became sick. 2 Jeroboam said to his wife, "Go disguise yourself, so they won't know that you're Jeroboam's wife, and go to Shiloh. Ahijah the prophet is there; it was he who told about me becoming king over this people. 3 Take with you 10 loaves of bread, some cakes, and a jar of honey, and go to him. He will tell you what will happen to the boy."

4 Jeroboam's wife did that: she went to Shiloh and arrived at Ahijah's house. Ahijah could not see; his gaze was fixed[a] due to his age. 5 But the LORD had said to Ahijah, "Jeroboam's wife is coming soon to ask you about her son, for he is sick. You are to say such and such to her. When she arrives, she will be disguised."

6 When Ahijah heard the sound of her feet entering the door, he said, "Come in, wife of Jeroboam! Why are you disguised? I have bad news for you. 7 Go tell Jeroboam, 'This is what the LORD God of Israel says: I raised you up from among the people, appointed you ruler over My people Israel, 8 tore the kingdom away from the house of David, and gave it to you. But you were not like My servant David, who kept My commandments and followed Me with all of his heart, doing only what is right in My eyes. 9 You behaved more wickedly than all who were before you. In order to provoke Me, you have proceeded to make for yourself other gods and cast images, but you have flung Me behind your back. 10 Because of all this, I am about to bring disaster on the house of Jeroboam:

I will eliminate all of Jeroboam's males,[b]
both slave and free,[c] in Israel;
I will sweep away the house of Jeroboam
as one sweeps away dung until it is all gone!
11 Anyone who belongs to Jeroboam and dies
in the city,
the dogs will eat,
and anyone who dies in the field,
the birds of the sky will eat,
for the LORD has said it!'

12 "As for you, get up and go to your house. When your feet enter the city, the boy will die. 13 All Israel will mourn for him and bury him, for this one alone out of Jeroboam's ⌊sons⌋ will come to the grave, because in him ⌊alone⌋ out of the house of Jeroboam something was found pleasing to the LORD God of Israel. 14 The LORD will raise up for Himself a king over Israel, who will eliminate the house of Jeroboam. This is the day, yes,[c] even today! 15 For the LORD will strike Israel ⌊and the people will shake⌋ as a reed shakes in water. He will uproot Israel from this good soil that He gave to their forefathers. He will scatter them beyond the Euphrates because they made their •Asherah poles, provoking the LORD. 16 He will give up Israel, because of Jeroboam's sins that he committed and caused Israel to commit."

17 Then Jeroboam's wife got up and left and went to Tirzah. As she was crossing the threshold of the house, the boy died. 18 He was buried, and all Israel mourned for him, according to the word of the LORD He had spoken through His servant Ahijah the prophet.

19 As for the rest of the events of Jeroboam's ⌊reign⌋, how he waged war and how he reigned, note that they are written about in the Historical Record of Israel's Kings. 20 The length of Jeroboam's reign was 22 years. He rested with his fathers, and his son Nadab became king in his place.

Judah's King Rehoboam

21 Now Rehoboam, Solomon's son, reigned in Judah. Rehoboam was 41 years old when he became king; he reigned 17 years in Jerusalem, the city the LORD had chosen from all the tribes of Israel to put His name. Rehoboam's mother's name was Naamah the Ammonite.

22 Judah did what was evil in the LORD's eyes. They provoked Him to jealous anger more than all that their ancestors had done with the sins they committed. 23 They also built for themselves •high places, sacred pillars, and Asherah poles on every high hill and under every green tree; 24 there were even male shrine prostitutes in the land. They imitated all the abominations of the nations the LORD had dispossessed before the Israelites.

25 In the fifth year of King Rehoboam, Shishak king of Egypt went to war against Jerusalem. 26 He seized the treasuries of the LORD's temple and the treasuries of the royal palace. He took everything. He took all the gold shields that Solomon had made. 27 King Rehoboam made bronze shields in their place and committed them into the care of the captains of the royal escorts[d] who guarded the entrance to the king's palace. 28 Whenever the king entered the LORD's temple, the royal escorts would carry the shields, then they would take them back to the royal escorts' armory.

29 The rest of the events of Rehoboam's ⌊reign⌋, along with all his accomplishments, are written about in the

---

[a]**14:4** Lit *see, for his eyes stood;* 1 Sm 4:15   [b]**14:10** Lit *eliminate Jeroboam's one who urinates against the wall*   [c]**14:10,14** Hb obscure   [d]**14:27** Lit *the runners*

---

or drink. The old prophet said what he wanted to hear.

13:24 a lion … killed him. This may seem harsh, but the fate of an entire nation was at stake. The death of the prophet was an example to Israel. **standing beside it.** The donkey didn't flee, and the lion didn't eat the man or attack the donkey.

This proved that the young prophet's death was a divine judgment. This story was told in Bethel (v. 25), and served notice to Jeroboam that God would judge him as well.

14:9 flung Me behind your back. This implies Jeroboam's forceful decision to turn his back on God.

14:14 will eliminate the household of Jeroboam. Baasha killed all his descendants (15:27-30).

14:15 He will uproot Israel. God gave Jeroboam an opportunity to have a godly dynasty. When Jeroboam chose evil, the nation's destruction was inevitable.

Historical Record of Judah's Kings. ³⁰ There was war between Rehoboam and Jeroboam throughout their reigns. ³¹ Rehoboam rested with his fathers and was buried with his fathers in the city of David. His mother's name was Naamah the Ammonite. His son Abijamª became king in his place.

Judah's King Abijam

15 In the eighteenth year of ⌊Israel's⌋ King Jeroboam son of Nebat, Abijam became king over Judah; ² he reigned three years in Jerusalem. His mother's name was Maacah daughterᵇ of Abishalom.

³ Abijam walked in all the sins his father had done before him, and he was not completely devoted to the LORD his God as his ancestor David had been. ⁴ But because of David, the LORD his God gave him a lamp in Jerusalem to raise up his son after him and to establish Jerusalem ⁵ because David did what was right in the LORD's eyes, and he did not turn aside from anything He had commanded him all the days of his life, except in the matter of Uriah the Hittite.

⁶ There had been war between Rehoboam and Jeroboam all the days of Rehoboam's life. ⁷ The rest of the events of Abijam's ⌊reign⌋, along with all his accomplishments, are written about in the Historical Record of Judah's Kings. There was also war between Abijam and Jeroboam. ⁸ Abijam rested with his fathers and was buried in the city of David. His son Asa became king in his place.

Judah's King Asa

⁹ In the twentieth year of Israel's King Jeroboam, Asa became king of Judah; ¹⁰ he reigned 41 years in Jerusalem. His grandmother'sᶜ name was Maacah daughterᵇ of Abishalom.

¹¹ Asa did what was right in the LORD's eyes, as his ancestor David had done. ¹² He banished the male shrine prostitutes from the land and removed all of the idols that his fathers had made. ¹³ He also removed his grandmotherᵈ Maacah from being queen mother because she had made an obscene image of •Asherah. Asa chopped down her obscene image and burned it in the Kidron Valley. ¹⁴ The •high places were not taken away; but Asa's heart was completely with the LORD his entire life. ¹⁵ He brought his father's consecrated gifts and his own consecrated gifts into the LORD's temple: silver, gold, and utensils.

¹⁶ There was war between Asa and Baasha king of Israel throughout their reigns. ¹⁷ Israel's King Baasha went to war against Judah. He built Ramah in order to deny anyone access to Judah's King Asa. ¹⁸ So Asa with-

drew all the silver and gold that remained in the treasuries of the LORD's temple and the treasuries of the royal palace and put it into the hands of his servants. Then King Asa sent them to Ben-hadad son of Tabrimmon son of Hezion king of Aram who lived in Damascus, saying, ¹⁹ "There is a treaty between me and you, between my father and your father. Look, I have sent you a gift of silver and gold. Go and break your treaty with Baasha king of Israel so that he will withdraw from me."

²⁰ Ben-hadad listened to King Asa and sent the commanders of his armies against the cities of Israel. He attacked Ijon, Dan, Abel-beth-maacah, all Chinneroth, and the whole land of Naphtali. ²¹ When Baasha heard ⌊about it⌋, he quit building Ramah and stayed in Tirzah. ²² Then King Asa gave a command to everyone without exception in Judah, and they carried away the stones of Ramah and the timbers Baasha had built it with. Then King Asa built Geba of Benjamin and Mizpah with them.

²³ The rest of all the events of Asa's ⌊reign⌋, along with all his might, all his accomplishments, and the cities he built, are written about in the Historical Record of Judah's Kings. But in his old age he developed a disease in his feet. ²⁴ Then Asa rested with his fathers and was buried in the city of his forefather David. His son Jehoshaphat became king in his place.

Israel's King Nadab

²⁵ Nadab son of Jeroboam became king over Israel in the second year of Judah's King Asa; he reigned over Israel two years. ²⁶ Nadab did what was evil in the LORD's sight and followed the example of his father and the sin he had caused Israel to commit.

²⁷ Then Baasha son of Ahijah of the house of Issachar conspired against Nadab, and Baasha struck him down at Gibbethon of the Philistines while Nadab and all Israel were besieging Gibbethon. ²⁸ In the third year of Judah's King Asa, Baasha killed Nadab and reigned in his place.

²⁹ When Baasha became king, he struck down the entire house of Jeroboam. He did not leave Jeroboam anyone alive until he had destroyed his family according to the word of the LORD He had spoken through His servant Ahijah the Shilonite. ³⁰ This was because of Jeroboam's sins he had committed and had caused Israel to commit in the provocation he had provoked the LORD God of Israel with.

³¹ The rest of the events of Nadab's ⌊reign⌋, along with all his accomplishments, are written about in the

---

ª**14:31** = Abijah; 2 Ch 13   ᵇ**15:2,10** Possibly *granddaughter*; 2 Ch 13:2   ᶜ**15:10** Lit *mother's*   ᵈ**15:13** Lit *mother*

14:23 sacred pillars. Stone pillars symbolizing a god. **Asherah poles.** Carved wooden poles, images of the goddess Asherah, probably imitating growing trees, full of life.

14:24 male shrine prostitutes. Contrary to God's commands, the Israelites imitated the Canaanites whom their forefathers left in the

land (see Deut. 18:9-13; 23:17; Ps. 106:34-39).

15:3 not completely devoted. Abijam tolerated idols but publicly claimed godliness (2 Chron. 13:4, 10-12).

15:13 grandmother Maacah. Maacah (vv. 2,9) was the queen mother. Her son had followed God only half-heartedly, likely due to

her influence. Asa was free from her control.

15:17 deny anyone access. Many godly people of Israel moved south to Judah (see 2 Chron. 11:16-17; 15:8-9). Baasha tried to stop this population drain.

15:19 a treaty. Asa thought Baasha was preparing to invade, so he paid the Arameans to

---

345

Historical Record of Israel's Kings. 32 There was war between Asa and Baasha king of Israel throughout their reigns.

Israel's King Baasha

33 In the third year of Judah's King Asa, Baasha son of Ahijah became king over all Israel at Tirzah; ⌊he reigned⌋ 24 years. 34 He did what was evil in the LORD's sight and followed the example of Jeroboam and the sin he had caused Israel to commit.

16 Now the word of the LORD came to Jehu son of Hanani against Baasha: 2 "Because I raised you up from the dust and made you ruler over My people Israel, but you have walked in the way of Jeroboam and have caused My people Israel to sin, provoking Me with their sins, 3 take note: I will sweep away Baasha and his house, and I will make your house like the house of Jeroboam son of Nebat:

4 Anyone who belongs to Baasha and dies
     in the city,
   the dogs will eat,
   and anyone who is his and dies in the field,
   the birds of the sky will eat.

5 The rest of the events of Baasha's ⌊reign⌋, along with all his accomplishments and might, are written about in the Historical Record of Israel's Kings. 6 Baasha rested with his fathers and was buried in Tirzah. His son Elah became king in his place. 7 Through the prophet Jehu son of Hanani the word of the LORD also came against Baasha and against his house because of all the evil he had done in the LORD's sight, provoking Him with the work of his hands and being like the house of Jeroboam, and because Baasha had struck down the house of Jeroboam.

Israel's King Elah

8 In the twenty-sixth year of Judah's King Asa, Elah son of Baasha became king over Israel in Tirzah; ⌊he reigned⌋ two years.

9 His servant Zimri, commander of half his chariots, conspired against him while Elah was in Tirzah drinking himself drunk in the house of Arza, who was in charge of the household at Tirzah. 10 In the twenty-seventh year of Judah's King Asa, Zimri went in, struck Elah down, and killed him. Then Zimri became king in his place.

11 When he became king, as soon as he was seated on his throne, Zimri struck down the entire house of Baasha. He did not leave him a single male,[a] whether of his kinsmen or his friends. 12 So Zimri exterminated the entire house of Baasha, according to the word of the LORD He had spoken against Baasha through Jehu the prophet, 13 because of all the sins of Baasha and the sins of his son Elah, which they committed and caused Israel to commit, provoking the LORD God of Israel with their worthless idols.

14 The rest of the events of Elah's ⌊reign⌋, along with all his accomplishments, are written about in the Historical Record of Israel's Kings.

Israel's King Zimri

15 In the twenty-seventh year of Judah's King Asa, Zimri became king for seven days in Tirzah. Now the troops were encamped against Gibbethon of the Philistines. 16 When the encamped troops heard that Zimri had not only conspired but also struck down the king, then all Israel made Omri, the army commander, king over Israel that very day in the camp. 17 Omri along with all Israel marched up from Gibbethon and besieged Tirzah. 18 When Zimri saw that the city was captured, he entered the citadel of the royal palace and burned down the royal palace over himself. He died 19 because of his sin he committed by doing what was evil in the LORD's sight and by following the example of Jeroboam and the sin he caused Israel to commit.

20 The rest of the events of Zimri's ⌊reign⌋, along with the conspiracy that he instigated, are written about in the Historical Record of Israel's Kings. 21 At that time the people of Israel were split in half: half the people followed Tibni son of Ginath, to make him king, and half followed Omri. 22 However, the people who followed Omri proved stronger than those who followed Tibni son of Ginath. So Tibni died and Omri became king.

Israel's King Omri

23 In the thirty-first year of Judah's King Asa, Omri became king over Israel; ⌊he reigned⌋ 12 years. He reigned six years in Tirzah, 24 then he bought the hill of Samaria from Shemer for 150 pounds of silver,[b] and he built up the hill. He named the city he built Samaria[c] based on the name Shemer, the owner of the hill.

25 Omri did what was evil in the LORD's sight; he did more evil than all who were before him. 26 He followed the example of Jeroboam son of Nebat and the sins he caused Israel to commit, provoking the LORD God of Israel with their worthless idols. 27 The rest of the events of Omri's ⌊reign⌋, along with his accomplishments and the might he exercised, are written about in the Historical Record of Israel's Kings. 28 Omri rested with his fathers and was buried in Samaria. His son Ahab became king in his place.

---

[a]**16:11** Lit *him one who urinates against the wall*   [b]**16:24** Lit *for two talents*   [c]**16:24** = Belonging to Shemer's Clan

---

threaten Israel's northern border.
15:21 Baasha ... quit building Ramah. Asa's plan worked, but instead of trusting God to protect him, Asa had relied on a pagan nation (see 2 Chron. 16:7).
15:23 events of Asa's ⌊reign⌋. More details are preserved in 2 Chronicles 14–16.

15:25 in the second year of Judah's King Asa. The author now backtracks to describe the kings that had ruled in Israel during this same period.
15:29 according to the word of the LORD. Ahijah had prophesied the end of Jeroboam's family (13:34; 14:14). In Baasha's mind, he

was simply securing his throne.
16:7 Baasha had struck down. God knew Baasha was going to do this, but Baasha was responsible for his deeds (see Matt. 26:24).
16:12 the word of the LORD. Zimri unwittingly fulfilled the prophecy of Jehu (vv. 1-4).
16:19 example of Jeroboam. Not a single

Israel's King Ahab

29 Ahab son of Omri became king over Israel in the thirty-eighth year of Judah's King Asa; Ahab son of Omri reigned over Israel in Samaria 22 years. 30 But Ahab son of Omri did what was evil in the LORD's sight more than all who were before him. 31 Then, as if following the sin of Jeroboam son of Nebat were a trivial matter, he married Jezebel, the daughter of Ethbaal king of the Sidonians, and then proceeded to serve •Baal and worship him. 32 He set up an altar for Baal in the temple of Baal that he had built in Samaria. 33 Ahab also made an •Asherah pole. Ahab did more to provoke the LORD God of Israel than all the kings of Israel who were before him.

34 During his reign, Hiel the Bethelite built Jericho. At the cost of Abiram his firstborn, he laid its foundation, and at the cost of Segub his youngest, he set up its gates, according to the word of the LORD He had spoken through Joshua son of Nun.

Elijah Announces Famine

17 Now Elijah the Tishbite, from the Gilead settlers,a said to Ahab, "As the LORD God of Israel lives, I stand before Him, and there will be no dew or rain during these years except by my command!"

2 Then a revelation from the LORD came to him: 3 "Leave here, turn eastward, and hide yourself at the •Wadi Cherith where it enters the Jordan. 4 You are to drink from the wadi. I have commanded the ravens to provide for you there."

5 So he did what the LORD commanded. Elijah left and lived by the Wadi Cherith where it enters the Jordan. 6 The ravens kept bringing him bread and meat in the morning and in the evening, and he drank from the wadi. 7 After a while, the wadi dried up because there had been no rain in the land.

Elijah and the Widow

8 Then the word of the LORD came to him: 9 "Get up, go to Zarephath that belongs to Sidon, and stay there. Look, I have commanded a woman who is a widow to provide for you there." 10 So Elijah got up and went to Zarephath. When he arrived at the city gate, there was a widow woman gathering wood. Elijah called to her and said, "Please bring me a little water in a cup and let me drink." 11 As she went to get it, he called to her and said, "Please bring me a piece of bread in your hand."

12 But she said, "As the LORD your God lives, I don't have anything baked—only a handful of flour in the jar and a bit of oil in the jug. Just now, I am gathering a couple of sticks in order to go prepare it for myself and my son so we can eat it and die."

13 Then Elijah said to her, "Don't be afraid; go and do as you have said. Only make me a small loaf from it and bring it out to me. Afterwards, you may make some for yourself and your son, 14 for this is what the LORD God of Israel says: 'The flour jar will not become empty and the oil jug will not run dry until the day the LORD sends rain on the surface of the land.'"

15 So she proceeded to do according to the word of Elijah. She and he and her household ate for many days. 16 The flour jar did not become empty, and the oil jug did not run dry, according to the word of the LORD He had spoken throughb Elijah.

The Widow's Son Raised

17 After this, the son of the woman who owned the house became ill. His illness became very severe until no breath remained in him. 18 She said to Elijah, "Man of God, what do we have in common? Have you come to remind me of my guilt and to kill my son?"

19 But Elijah said to her, "Give me your son." So he took him from her arms, brought him up to the upper room where he was staying, and laid him on his own bed. 20 Then he cried out to the LORD and said, "My LORD God, have You also brought tragedy on the widow I am staying with by killing her son?" 21 Then he stretched himself out over the boy three times. He cried out to the LORD and said, "My LORD God, please let this boy's life return to him!"

22 So the LORD listened to Elijah's voice, and the boy's life returned to him, and he lived. 23 Then Elijah took the boy, brought him down from the upper room into the house, and gave him to his mother. Elijah said, "Look, your son is alive."

24 Then the woman said to Elijah, "Now I know you are a man of God and the LORD's word in your mouth is the truth."

Elijah's Message to Ahab

18 After a long time, the word of the LORD came to Elijah in the third year: "Go and present yourself to Ahab. I will send rain on the surface of the land." 2 So Elijah went to present himself to Ahab.

The famine was severe in Samaria. 3 Ahab called for Obadiah, who was in charge of the palace. Obadiah was a man who greatly •feared the LORD 4 and took 100 prophets and hid them, 50 men to a cave, and provided them with food and water when Jezebel slaughtered the LORD's prophets. 5 Ahab said to Obadiah, "Go throughout the land to every spring of water and to every •wadi. Perhaps we'll find grass so we can keep the horses and mules alive and not have to destroy any

---

a 17:1 LXX reads from Tishbe of Gilead   b 17:16 Lit by the hand of

---

king of Israel turned from calf worship.
16:24 hill of Samaria. Omri was threatened on three sides, so he needed an easily defended capital.
16:31 married Jezebel. Ahab wanted an alliance with the Phoenicians against Assyria, but Jezebel brought Baal worship.

16:34 built Jericho. Hiel fulfilled Joshua's prophecy (see Josh. 6:26).

17:1 Elijah. When the Northern Kingdom was in its greatest spiritual darkness, Elijah appeared. Merely human (see Jas. 5:17), his power came from his relationship with God. He immediately obeyed God's commands and

was uncompromising in his message.
17:10 Zarephath. Zarephath was only eight miles from Sidon, Jezebel's hometown.
17:15 the word of Elijah. The widow was not only obeying Elijah but God (v. 9). She shared her last meal because she believed that God cared for her.

cattle." ⁶ They divided the land between them in order to cover it. Ahab went one way by himself, and Obadiah went the other way by himself.

⁷ While Obadiah was ⌊walking⌋ along the road, Elijah suddenly met him. When Obadiah recognized him, he fell with his face ⌊to the ground⌋ and said, "Is it you, my lord Elijah?"

⁸ "It is I," he replied. "Go tell your lord, 'Elijah is here!'"

⁹ But Obadiah said, "What sin have I committed, that you are handing your servant over to Ahab to put me to death? ¹⁰ As the LORD your God lives, there is no nation or kingdom where my lord has not sent someone to search for you. When they said, 'He is not here,' he made that kingdom or nation swear they had not found you.

¹¹ "Now you say, 'Go tell your lord, "Elijah is here!"'

¹² But when I leave you, the Spirit of the LORD may carry you off to some place I don't know. Then when I go report to Ahab and he doesn't find you, he will kill me. But ⌊I⌋, your servant, have feared the LORD from my youth. ¹³ Wasn't it reported to my lord what I did when Jezebel slaughtered the LORD's prophets? I hid 100 of the prophets of the LORD, 50 men to a cave, and I provided them with food and water. ¹⁴ Now you say, 'Go tell your lord, "Elijah is here!"' He will kill me!"

¹⁵ Then Elijah said, "As the LORD of •Hosts lives, before whom I stand, today I will present myself to Ahab."

¹⁶ Obadiah went to meet Ahab and report to him. Then Ahab went to meet Elijah. ¹⁷ When Ahab saw Elijah, Ahab said to him, "Is that you, you destroyer of Israel?"

¹⁸ He replied, "I have not destroyed Israel, but you and your father's house have, because you have abandoned the LORD's commandments and followed the •Baals. ¹⁹ Now summon all Israel to meet me at Mount Carmel, along with the 450 prophets of Baal and the 400 prophets of •Asherah who eat at Jezebel's table."

Elijah at Mount Carmel

²⁰ So Ahab summoned all the Israelites and gathered the prophets at Mount Carmel. ²¹ Then Elijah approached all the people and said, "How long will you hesitate between two opinions? If •Yahweh is God, follow Him. But if Baal, follow him." But the people didn't answer him a word.

²² Then Elijah said to the people, "I am the only remaining prophet of the LORD, but Baal's prophets are 450 men. ²³ Let two bulls be given to us. They are to choose one bull for themselves, cut it in pieces, and

place it on the wood but not light the fire. I will prepare the other bull and place it on the wood but not light the fire. ²⁴ Then you call on the name of your god, and I will call on the name of Yahweh. The God who answers with fire, He is God."

All the people answered, "That ⌊sounds⌋ good."

²⁵ Then Elijah said to the prophets of Baal, "Since you are so numerous, choose for yourselves one bull and prepare it first. Then call on the name of your god but don't light the fire."

 ## Fire from Heaven

1. Have you ever had an accident involving fire? What happened?

1 Kings 18:16-40

2. When Elijah told the people to follow either Yahweh (God) or Baal, why didn't they answer him (v. 21)? Why did Elijah then suggest a contest between God and Baal?

3. Why did Elijah mock the false prophets (v. 27)? What do his taunts ("maybe he has wandered away"; "perhaps he's sleeping") suggest about the character of God?

4. What does this story suggest about the seriousness of leading people away from God?

5. What "false prophets" lead people away from God today?

²⁶ So they took the bull that he gave them, prepared it, and called on the name of Baal from morning until noon, saying, "Baal, answer us!" But there was no sound; no one answered. Then they did their lame dance around the altar they had made.

²⁷ At noon Elijah mocked them. He said, "Shout loudly, for he's a god! Maybe he's thinking it over; maybe he has wandered away;ª or maybe he's on the road. Perhaps he's sleeping and will wake up!" ²⁸ They shouted loudly, and cut themselves with knives and spears, according to their custom, until blood gushed out on them. ²⁹ All afternoon, they kept on raving until the offering of the evening sacrifice, but there was no sound, no one answered, no one paid attention.

³⁰ Then Elijah said to all the people, "Come near me." So all the people approached him. Then he repaired the LORD's altar that had been torn down: ³¹ Elijah took 12

ª **18:27** Or *has turned aside*, possibly to relieve himself

---

17:24 Now I know you are a man of God. This miracle increased the widow's faith. This was God's purpose. Jesus raising Lazarus from the dead achieved similar results (see John 11:1-4, 40-45).

18:1 I will send rain. During the drought, Israel had prayed in vain to Baal, the god of rain.

Love for Baal was at an all-time low. The drought had accomplished God's purpose. Now God would send rain.

18:4 slaughtered the LORD's prophets. Soon Elijah would command the Israelites to slay the prophets of Baal (v. 40). That seems harsh, but it must be remembered that they had con-

sented to the murder of God's prophets. They also sacrificed children.

18:20 all the Israelites. Elijah wanted an audience. Ahab, more than ready for a showdown, complied.

18:22 the only remaining prophet. The other prophets were in hiding (v. 4). Elijah was the

stones—according to the number of the tribes of the sons of Jacob, to whom the word of the LORD had come, saying, "Israel will be your name"— 32 and he built an altar with the stones in the name of Yahweh. Then he made a trench around the altar large enough to hold about four gallons.a b 33 Next, he arranged the wood, cut up the bull, and placed it on the wood. He said, "Fill four water pots with water and pour it on the offering to be burned and on the wood." 34 Then he said, "A second time!" and they did it a second time. And then he said, "A third time!" and they did it a third time. 35 So the water ran all around the altar; he even filled the trench with water.

36 At the time for offering the ⌊evening⌋ sacrifice, Elijah the prophet approached ⌊the altar⌋ and said, "LORD God of Abraham, Isaac, and Israel, today let it be known that You are God in Israel and I am Your servant, and that at Your word I have done all these things. 37 Answer me, LORD! Answer me so that this people will know that You, Yahweh, are God and that You have turned their hearts back."

38 Then Yahweh's fire fell and consumed the •burnt offering, the wood, the stones, and the dust, and it licked up the water that was in the trench. 39 When all the people saw it, they fell facedown and said, "Yahweh, He is God! Yahweh, He is God!"

40 Then Elijah ordered them, "Seize the prophets of Baal! Do not let even one of them escape." So they seized them, and Elijah brought them down to the •Wadi Kishon and slaughtered them there. 41 Elijah said to Ahab, "Go up, eat and drink, for there is the sound of a rainstorm."

42 So Ahab went to eat and drink, but Elijah went up to the summit of Carmel. He bowed down to the ground and put his face between his knees. 43 Then he said to his servant, "Go up and look toward the sea."

So he went up, looked, and said, "There's nothing." Seven times Elijah said, "Go back."

44 On the seventh time, he reported, "There's a cloud as small as a man's hand coming from the sea."

Then Elijah said, "Go and tell Ahab, 'Get ⌊your chariot⌋ ready and go down so the rain doesn't stop you.' "

45 In a little while, the sky grew dark with clouds and wind, and there was a downpour. So Ahab got in ⌊his chariot⌋ and went to Jezreel. 46 The power of the LORD was on Elijah, and he tucked his mantle under his belt and ran ahead of Ahab to the entrance of Jezreel.

Elijah's Journey to Horeb

19 Ahab told Jezebel everything that Elijah had done and how he had killed all the prophets with the sword. 2 So Jezebel sent a messenger to Elijah, saying, "May the gods punish me and do so severely if I don't make your life like the life of one of them by this time tomorrow!"

3 Then Elijah became afraidc and immediately ran for his life. When he came to Beer-sheba that belonged to Judah, he left his servant there, 4 but he went on a day's journey into the wilderness. He sat down under a broom tree and prayed that he might die. He said, "⌊I have had⌋ enough! LORD, take my life, for I'm no better than my fathers." 5 Then he lay down and slept under the broom tree.

Suddenly, an angel touched him. The angel told him, "Get up and eat." 6 Then he looked, and there at his head was a loaf of bread baked over hot stones and a jug of water. So he ate and drank and lay down again. 7 Then the angel of the LORD returned a second time and touched him. He said, "Get up and eat, or the journey will be too much for you." 8 So he got up, ate, and drank. Then on the strength from that food, he walked 40 days and 40 nights to Horeb, the mountain of God. 9 He entered a cave there and spent the night.

Elijah's Encounter with the LORD

Then the word of the LORD came to him, and He said to him, "What are you doing here, Elijah?"

10 He replied, "I have been very zealous for the LORD God of •Hosts, but the Israelites have abandoned Your covenant, torn down Your altars, and killed Your prophets with the sword. I alone am left, and they are looking for me to take my life."

11 Then He said, "Go out and stand on the mountain in the LORD's presence."

At that moment, the LORD passed by. A great and mighty wind was tearing at the mountains and was shattering cliffs before the LORD, but the LORD was not in the wind. After the wind there was an earthquake, but the LORD was not in the earthquake. 12 After the earthquake there was a fire, but the LORD was not in the fire. And after the fire there was a voice, a soft whisper. 13 When Elijah heard ⌊it⌋, he wrapped his face in his mantle and went out and stood at the entrance of the cave.

Suddenly, a voice came to him and said, "What are you doing here, Elijah?"

14 "I have been very zealous for the LORD God of Hosts," he replied, "but the Israelites have abandoned Your covenant, torn down Your altars, and killed Your prophets with the sword. I alone am left, and they're looking for me to take my life."

---

a 18:32 LXX reads *trench containing two measures of seed* b 18:32 Lit *altar corresponding to a house of two seahs of seed* c 19:3 Some Hb mss, LXX, Syr, Vg; MT reads *he saw*

---

only prophet left with the courage to do what a prophet should do.

18:30 the LORD's altar. The altar was one of many ancient places of worship built before Solomon finished the temple (3:2).

18:36 Elijah … said. Elijah's brief, simple prayer was in direct contrast to the prophets of

Baal, who had prayed, chanted, danced, and mutilated themselves for hours (see Matt. 6:7).

18:40 slaughtered. Idolatrous prophets were to be slain (Deut. 13:12-17).

19:3 Elijah became afraid. With God's victory, Elijah was popular, but when Jezebel threatened, the people deserted Elijah. He

had been critical of timid prophets (18:22), now he felt their fear.

19:4 prayed that he might die. Elijah's entire life's work had culminated in a great victory that seemed poised to cause a national revival. When the victory vaporized, Elijah felt that his work amounted to nothing and

15 Then the LORD said to him, "Go and return by the way you came to the Wilderness of Damascus. When you arrive, you are to anoint Hazael as king over Aram. 16 You are to anoint Jehu son of Nimshi as king over Israel and Elisha son of Shaphat from Abel-meholah as prophet in your place. 17 Then Jehu will put to death whoever escapes the sword of Hazael, and Elisha will put to death whoever escapes the sword of Jehu. 18 But I will leave 7,000 in Israel—every knee that has not bowed to •Baal and every mouth that has not kissed him."

Elisha's Appointment as Elijah's Successor

19 Elijah left there and found Elisha son of Shaphat as he was plowing. Twelve teams of oxen were in front of him, and he was with the twelfth team. Elijah walked by him and threw his mantle over him. 20 Elisha left the oxen, ran to follow Elijah, and said, "Please let me kiss my father and mother, and then I will follow you."

"Go on back," he replied, "for what have I done to you?"

21 So he turned back from following him, took the team of oxen, and slaughtered them. With the oxen's wooden yoke and plow, he cooked the meat and gave it to the people, and they ate. Then he left, followed Elijah, and served him.

Victory over Ben-hadad

20 Now Ben-hadad king of Aram assembled his entire army. Thirty-two kings, along with horses and chariotry, were with him. He marched up, besieged Samaria, and fought against it. 2 He sent messengers into the city to Ahab king of Israel and said to him, "This is what Ben-hadad says: 3 'Your silver and your gold are mine! And your best wives and children are mine as well!'"

4 Then the king of Israel answered, "Just as you say, my lord king: I am yours, along with all that I have."

5 The messengers then returned and said, "This is what Ben-hadad says: 'I have sent ⌊messengers⌋ to you, saying: Your silver, your gold, your wives, and your children you are to give to me. 6 But at this time tomorrow I will send my servants to you, and they will search your palace and your servants' houses. Whatever is precious to you, they will lay their hands on and take away.'"

7 Then the king of Israel called for all the elders of the land and said, "Think it over and you will see that this one is only looking for trouble, for he demanded my wives, my children, my silver, and my gold, and I didn't turn him down."

8 All the elders and all the people said to him, "Don't listen or agree."

9 So he said to Ben-hadad's messengers, "Say to my lord the king, 'Everything you demanded of your servant the first time, I will do, but this thing I cannot do.'" So the messengers left and took word back to him.

10 Then Ben-hadad sent ⌊messengers⌋ to him and said, "May the gods punish me and do so severely if Samaria's dust amounts to a handful for each of the people who follow me."

11 The king of Israel answered, "Say this: 'Let not him who puts on his armor boast like the one who takes it off.'"

12 When Ben-hadad heard this response, while he and the kings were drinking in the tents, he said to his servants, "Take ⌊your⌋ positions." So they took ⌊their⌋ positions against the city.

13 A prophet came to Ahab king of Israel and said, "This is what the LORD says: 'Do you see this entire immense horde? Watch, I am handing it over to you today so that you may know that I am the LORD.'"

14 Ahab asked, "By whom?"

And the prophet said, "This is what the LORD says: 'By the young men of the provincial leaders.'"

Then he asked, "Who is to start the battle?"

He said, "You."

15 So Ahab counted the young men of the provincial leaders, and there were 232. After them he counted all the Israelite troops: 7,000. 16 They marched out at noon while Ben-hadad and the 32 kings who were helping him were getting drunk in the tents. 17 The young men of the provincial leaders marched out first. Then Ben-hadad sent out scouts, and they reported to him, saying, "Men are marching out of Samaria."

18 So he said, "If they have marched out in peace, take them alive, and if they have marched out for battle, take them alive."

19 The young men of the provincial leaders and the army behind them marched out from the city, 20 and each one struck down his opponent. So the Arameans fled and Israel pursued them, but Ben-hadad king of Aram escaped on a horse with the cavalry. 21 Then the king of Israel marched out and attacked the cavalry and the chariotry. He inflicted a great slaughter on Aram.

22 The prophet approached the king of Israel and said to him, "Go and strengthen yourself, then consider what you should do, for in the spring the king of Aram will march up against you."

23 Now the king of Aram's servants said to him, "Their gods are gods of the hill country. That's why they were stronger than we. Instead, we should fight with them on the plain; then we will certainly be stronger than they. 24 Also do this: remove each king from

---

19:10 very zealous. Elijah had been driven by intense devotion for God to the point of burnout, but in his uncompromising stand against idolatry he had lost his patience and empathy. **abandoned Your covenant.** The people had sinned and Elijah wanted God to judge them—

now. Elijah knew there were other prophets (18:13), but he had little respect for people who would not take a stand for God.

19:12 a soft whisper. When God sent wind, earthquake, and fire, He showed He could speak in power and judge His people. But God wanted to touch people's hearts rather

than drive them to obey out of fear, and He taught Elijah compassion in the process. **19:15 anoint Hazael as king over Aram.** Hazael would be such a merciless enemy of Israel that Elisha literally wept as he anointed him (2 Kings 8:7-15).

19:16 prophet in your place. Elijah had not

his position and appoint captains in their place. ²⁵ Raise another army for yourself like the army you lost—horse for horse, chariot for chariot—and let's fight with them on the plain; and we will certainly be stronger than they." The king listened to them and did so.

²⁶ In the spring, Ben-hadad mobilized the Arameans and went up to Aphek to battle Israel. ²⁷ The Israelites mobilized, gathered supplies, and went to fight them. The Israelites camped in front of them like two little flocks of goats, while the Arameans filled the landscape.

²⁸ Then the man of God approached and said to the king of Israel, "This is what the LORD says: 'Because the Arameans have said: The LORD is a god of the mountains and not a god of the valleys, I will hand over this entire immense horde to you. Then you will know that I am the LORD.'"

²⁹ They camped opposite each other for seven days. On the seventh day, the battle took place, and the Israelites struck down the Arameans—100,000 foot soldiers in one day. ³⁰ The ones who remained fled into the city of Aphek, and the wall fell on those 27,000 remaining men.

Ben-hadad also fled and went into an inner room in the city. ³¹ His servants said to him, "Consider this: we have heard that the kings of the house of Israel are kings ⌊who show⌋ special kindness. So let's put •sackcloth around our waists and ropes around our heads, and let's go out to the king of Israel. Perhaps he will spare your life."

³² So they dressed with sackcloth around their waists and ropes around their heads, went to the king of Israel, and said, "Your servant Ben-hadad says, 'Please spare my life.'"

So he said, "Is he still alive? He is my brother."

³³ Now the men were looking for a sign of hope, so they quickly latched onto the hintᵃ and said, "Yes, your brother Ben-hadad."

Then he said, "Go and bring him."

So Ben-hadad came out to him, and Ahab had him come up into the chariot. ³⁴ Then Ben-hadad said to him, "The cities that my father took from your father I restore to you, and you may set up marketplaces for yourself in Damascus, like my father set up in Samaria."

⌊Ahab responded⌋, "On the basis of this treaty, I release you." So he made a treaty with him and released him.

Ahab Rebuked by the LORD

³⁵ One of the sons of the prophets said to his fellow prophet by the word of the LORD, "Strike me!" But the man refused to strike him.

³⁶ He told him, "Because you did not listen to the voice of the LORD, mark my words: When you leave me, a lion will kill you." When he left him, a lion found him and killed him.

³⁷ The prophet found another man and said to him, "Strike me!" So the man struck him, inflicting a wound. ³⁸ Then the prophet went and waited for the king on the road. He disguised himself with a bandage over his eyes. ³⁹ As the king was passing by, he cried out to the king and said, "Your servant marched out into the midst of the battle. Suddenly, a man turned aside and brought someone to me and said, 'Guard this man! If he is ever missing, it will be your life in place of his life, or you will weigh out 75 poundsᵇ of silver.' ⁴⁰ But while your servant was busy here and there, he disappeared."

The king of Israel said to him, "That will be your sentence; you yourself have decided it."

⁴¹ He quickly removed the bandage from his eyes. The king of Israel recognized that he was one of the prophets. ⁴² The prophet said to him, "This is what the LORD says: 'Because you released from your hand the man I had •devoted to destruction, it will be your life in place of his life and your people in place of his people.'" ⁴³ The king of Israel left for home resentful and angry, and he entered Samaria.

Ahab and Naboth's Vineyard

21 Some time passed after these events. Naboth the Jezreelite had a vineyard; it was in Jezreel next to the palace of Ahab king of Samaria. ² So Ahab spoke to Naboth, saying, "Give me your vineyard so I can have it for a vegetable garden, since it is right next to my palace. I will give you a better vineyard in its place, or if you prefer, I will give you its value in silver."

³ But Naboth said to Ahab, "I will never give my fathers' inheritance to you."

⁴ So Ahab went to his palace resentful and angry, because of what Naboth the Jezreelite had told him. He had said, "I will not give you my fathers' inheritance." He lay down on his bed, turned his face away, and didn't eat any food.

⁵ Then his wife Jezebel came to him and said to him, "Why are you so upset that you refuse to eat?"

⁶ "Because I spoke to Naboth the Jezreelite," he replied. "I told him: Give me your vineyard for silver, or if you wish, I will give you a vineyard in its place. But he said, 'I won't give you my vineyard!'"

⁷ Then his wife Jezebel said to him, "Now, exercise your royal power over Israel. Get up, eat some food, and

---

ᵃ **20:33** LXX, some Hb mss, alt Hb tradition; MT reads *they hastened and caught hold; "Is this it?"* ᵇ **20:39** Lit *a talent*

---

finished God's work, but he learned that it didn't depend just on him. God could raise up someone to take his place.

19:19 threw his mantle over him. This immediately told Elisha that he had been chosen to succeed Elijah in ministry.

20:11 This proverb means, "Save your brag-ging until after you win."

20:13 so that you may know that I am the LORD. God's purpose never changes. He wants people to know and honor Him.

20:15 7,000. This was not a large army compared to Ben-hadad's. The smaller the army, though, the more obvious it was that victory belonged to the Lord.

20:22 in the spring. This was the favorite time for kings to go to war (2 Sam. 11:1).

20:28 man of God. This same prophet talked with Ahab earlier (vv. 13, 22).

20:32 brother. This does not mean a literal

be happy. ⌊For⌋ I will give you the vineyard of Naboth the Jezreelite." ⁸ So she wrote letters in Ahab's name and sealed them with his seal. She sent the letters to the elders and nobles who lived with Naboth in his city. ⁹ In the letters, she wrote:

> Proclaim a fast and seat Naboth at the head of the people. ¹⁰ Then seat two •wicked men opposite him and have them testify against him, saying, "You have cursed God and king!" Then take him out and stone him to death.

¹¹ The men of his city, the elders and nobles who lived in his city, did as Jezebel had commanded them, as was written in the letters she had sent them. ¹² They proclaimed a fast and seated Naboth at the head of the people. ¹³ The two wicked men came in and sat opposite him. Then the wicked men testified against Naboth in the presence of the people, saying, "Naboth has cursed God and king!" So they took him outside the city and stoned him to death with stones. ¹⁴ Then they sent ⌊word⌋ to Jezebel, "Naboth has been stoned to death."

¹⁵ When Jezebel heard that Naboth had been stoned to death, she said to Ahab, "Get up and take possession of the vineyard of Naboth the Jezreelite who refused to give it to you for silver, since Naboth isn't alive, but dead." ¹⁶ When Ahab heard that Naboth was dead, he got up to go down to the vineyard of Naboth the Jezreelite to take possession of it.

The LORD's Judgment on Ahab

¹⁷ Then the word of the LORD came to Elijah the Tishbite: ¹⁸ "Get up and go to meet Ahab king of Israel, who is in Samaria. You'll find him in Naboth's vineyard, where he has gone to take possession of it. ¹⁹ Tell him, 'This is what the LORD says: Have you murdered and also taken possession?' Then tell him, 'This is what the LORD says: In the place where the dogs licked Naboth's blood, the dogs will also lick your blood!' "

²⁰ Ahab said to Elijah, "So, you have caught me, my enemy."

He replied, "I have caught you because you devoted yourself to do what is evil in the LORD's sight. ²¹ This is what the LORD says:ᵃ 'I am about to bring disaster on you and will sweep away your descendants:

> I will eliminate all of Ahab's males,ᵇ
> both slave and free, in Israel;

²² I will make your house like the house of Jeroboam son of Nebat and like the house of Baasha son of Ahi-

jah, because you have provoked ⌊My⌋ anger and caused Israel to sin. ²³ The LORD also speaks of Jezebel: The dogs will eat Jezebel in the plot of landᶜ at Jezreel:

> ²⁴ He who belongs to Ahab and dies in the city,
> the dogs will eat,
> and he who dies in the field, the birds of the sky will eat.' "

²⁵ Still, there was no one like Ahab, who devoted himself to do what was evil in the LORD's sight, because his wife Jezebel incited him. ²⁶ He committed the most detestable acts by going after idols as the Amorites had, whom the LORD had dispossessed before the Israelites.

²⁷ When Ahab heard these words, he tore his clothes, put •sackcloth over his body, and fasted. He lay down in sackcloth and walked around subdued. ²⁸ Then the word of the LORD came to Elijah the Tishbite: ²⁹ "Have you seen how Ahab has humbled himself before Me? I will not bring the disaster during his lifetime, because he has humbled himself before Me. I will bring the disaster on his house during his son's lifetime."

Jehoshaphat's Alliance with Ahab

22 There was a lull of three years without war between Aram and Israel. ² However, in the third year, Jehoshaphat king of Judah went to visit the king of Israel. ³ The king of Israel had said to his servants, "Don't you know that Ramoth-gilead is ours, but we have failed to take it from the hand of the king of Aram?" ⁴ So he asked Jehoshaphat, "Will you go with me to fight Ramoth-gilead?"

Jehoshaphat replied to the king of Israel, "I am as you are, my people as your people, my horses as your horses." ⁵ But Jehoshaphat said to the king of Israel, "First, please ask what the LORD's will is."

⁶ So the king of Israel gathered the prophets, about 400 men, and asked them, "Should I go against Ramoth-gilead for war or should I refrain?"

They replied, "March up, and the Lord will hand it over to the king."

⁷ But Jehoshaphat asked, "Isn't there a prophet of •Yahweh here any more? Let's ask him."

⁸ The king of Israel said to Jehoshaphat, "There is still one man who can ask the LORD, but I hate him because he never prophesies good about me, but only disaster. He is Micaiah son of Imlah."

"The king shouldn't say that!" Jehoshaphat replied.

⁹ So the king of Israel called an officer and said, "Hurry ⌊and get⌋ Micaiah son of Imlah!"

ᵃ**21:21** LXX; Hb omits *This is what the LORD says* ᵇ**21:21** Lit *eliminate Ahab's one who urinates against the wall* ᶜ**21:23** Some Hb mss, Syr, Tg, Vg, 2 Kg 9:36; MT, LXX read *the rampart*

---

brother but "not an enemy."
20:34 your father. This phrase probably did not refer to Ahab's father, Omri, but to his predecessor, Baasha, who once had a treaty with Ben-hadad.
20:35 One of the sons of the prophets. The prophets were organized into schools where

they trained and studied the law of Moses.
20:42 Compare the prophet Nathan, who allowed David to pass judgment on a fictitious man who stole a lamb, then applied the judgment to David who had stolen another man's wife (see 2 Sam. 12:1-7).
21:7 Jezebel. She treated Ahab the way a

mother treats a spoiled child, making evil plans to give him whatever he wanted.
21:10 two wicked men. The law required two witnesses. **cursed God and king.** Mosaic law did prescribe death for cursing God, but not for cursing the king.
22:2 Jehoshaphat. Jehoshaphat, unlike

10 Now the king of Israel and Jehoshaphat king of Judah, clothed in royal attire, were each sitting on his own throne. They were on the threshing floor at the entrance to Samaria's •gate, and all the prophets were prophesying in front of them. 11 Then Zedekiah son of Chenaanah made iron horns and said, "This is what the LORD says: 'You will gore the Arameans with these until they are finished off.'" 12 And all the prophets were prophesying the same: "March up to Ramoth-gilead and succeed, for the LORD will hand it over to the king."

Micaiah's Message of Defeat

13 The messenger who went to call Micaiah instructed him, "Look, the words of the prophets are unanimously favorable for the king. So let your words be like theirs, and speak favorably."

14 But Micaiah said, "As the LORD lives, I will say whatever the LORD says to me."

15 So he went to the king, and the king asked him, "Micaiah, should we go to Ramoth-gilead for war, or should we refrain?"

Micaiah told him, "March up and succeed. The LORD will hand it over to the king."

16 But the king said to him, "How many times must I make you swear not to tell me anything but the truth in the name of the LORD?"

17 So Micaiah said:

I saw all Israel scattered on the hills
like sheep without a shepherd.
And the LORD said,
'They have no master;
let everyone return home in peace.'

18 So the king of Israel said to Jehoshaphat, "Didn't I tell you he never prophesies good about me, but only disaster?"

19 Then Micaiah said, "Therefore, hear the word of the LORD: I saw the LORD sitting on His throne, and the whole heavenly •host was standing by Him at His right hand and at His left hand. 20 And the LORD said, 'Who will entice Ahab to march up and fall at Ramoth-gilead?' So one was saying this and another was saying that.

21 "Then a spirit came forward, stood before the LORD, and said, 'I will entice him.'

22 "The LORD asked him, 'How?'

"He said, 'I will go and become a lying spirit in the mouth of all his prophets.'

"Then He said, 'You will certainly entice him and prevail. Go and do that.'

23 "You see, the LORD has put a lying spirit into the mouth of all these prophets of yours, and the LORD has pronounced disaster against you."

24 Then Zedekiah son of Chenaanah came up, hit Micaiah in the face, and demanded, "Did[a] the Spirit of the LORD leave me to speak to you?"

25 Micaiah replied, "You will soon see when you go to hide yourself in an inner chamber on that day."

26 Then the king of Israel ordered, "Take Micaiah and return him to Amon, the governor of the city, and to Joash, the king's son, 27 and say, 'This is what the king says: Put this guy in prison and feed him only bread and water[b] until I come back safely.'"

28 But Micaiah said, "If you ever return safely, the LORD has not spoken through me." Then he said, "Listen, all you people!"[c]

Ahab's Death

29 Then the king of Israel and Judah's King Jehoshaphat went up to Ramoth-gilead. 30 But the king of Israel said to Jehoshaphat, "I will disguise myself and go into battle, but you wear your royal attire." So the king of Israel disguised himself and went into battle.

31 Now the king of Aram had ordered his 32 chariot commanders, "Do not fight with anyone at all except the king of Israel."

32 When the chariot commanders saw Jehoshaphat, they shouted, "He must be the king of Israel!" So they turned to fight against him, but Jehoshaphat cried out. 33 When the chariot commanders saw that he was not the king of Israel, they turned back from pursuing him.

34 But a man drew his bow without taking special aim and struck the king of Israel through the joints of his armor. So he said to his charioteer, "Turn around and take me out of the battle,[d] for I am badly wounded!" 35 The battle raged throughout that day, and the king was propped up in his chariot facing the Arameans. He died that evening, and blood from his wound flowed into the bottom of the chariot. 36 Then the cry rang out in the army as the sun set, declaring:

Each man to his own city,
and each man to his own land!

37 So the king died and was brought to Samaria. They buried the king in Samaria. 38 Then someone washed the chariot at the pool of Samaria. The dogs licked up his blood, and the prostitutes bathed ⌊in it⌋, according to the word of the LORD that He had spoken.

39 The rest of the events of Ahab's ⌊reign⌋, along with all his accomplishments, the ivory palace he built, and

---

a 22:24 Lit Which way did   b 22:27 Lit him on bread of oppression and water of oppression   c 22:28 LXX omits Then he said, "Listen, all you people!"   d 22:34 LXX; Hb reads camp

---

Ahab, was a godly king.

22:4 go with me. Ahab was prepared to create an alliance with Judah against Aram. This switch of loyalties happened generation after generation. Jehoshaphat's father had made an alliance with the king of Aram against Israel.

22:5 the LORD's will. Even though Jehoshaphat gave lip service to confirming his decisions with God, he made a poor choice in this case, as the prophet Jehu pointed out (see 2 Chron. 19:2).

22:8 never prophecies anything good. This was Ahab's rule of thumb for a prophet: Did

the prophet tell him good things or bad? Ahab was not interested in truth. He had hated Elijah for this very reason.

22:23 lying spirit. There are other times in the Old Testament when an evil or unrighteous spirit seems to be sent from God (for instance, when King Saul was tormented by an evil

all the cities he built, are written about in the Historical Record of Israel's Kings. [40] Ahab rested with his fathers, and his son Ahaziah became king in his place.

Judah's King Jehoshaphat

[41] Jehoshaphat son of Asa became king over Judah in the fourth year of Israel's King Ahab. [42] Jehoshaphat was 35 years old when he became king; he reigned 25 years in Jerusalem. His mother's name was Azubah daughter of Shilhi. [43] He walked in all the ways of his father Asa; he did not turn away from them but did what was right in the LORD's sight. However, the •high places were not taken away;[a] the people still sacrificed and burned incense on the high places. [44] Jehoshaphat also made peace with the king of Israel.

[45] The rest of the events of Jehoshaphat's ⌊reign⌋, along with the might he exercised and how he waged war, are written about in the Historical Record of Judah's Kings. [46] He removed from the land the rest of the male shrine prostitutes who were left from the days of his father Asa. [47] There was no king in Edom; a deputy served as king. [48] Jehoshaphat made ships of Tarshish to go to Ophir for gold, but they did not go because the ships were wrecked at Ezion-geber. [49] At that time, Ahaziah son of Ahab said to Jehoshaphat, "Let my servants go with your servants in the ships," but Jehoshaphat was not willing. [50] Jehoshaphat rested with his fathers and was buried with his fathers in the city of his forefather David. His son Jehoram became king in his place.

Israel's King Ahaziah

[51] Ahaziah son of Ahab became king over Israel in Samaria in the seventeenth year of Judah's King Jehoshaphat; he reigned over Israel two years. [52] He did what was evil in the LORD's sight. He walked in the way of his father, in the way of his mother, and in the way of Jeroboam son of Nebat, who had caused Israel to sin. [53] He served •Baal and worshiped him. He provoked the LORD God of Israel just as his father had done.

---

[a] **22:43** LXX, Syr, Vg read *he did not remove the high places*

---

spirit, 1 Sam. 16:14).

22:31 the king of Israel. It was (and is) an excellent war strategy to attack the leadership so that the soldiers are disoriented and cannot finish the battle well.

22:34 without taking special aim. Ahab's disguise didn't protect him when it counted. The consequences of his actions found him no matter who he was trying to fool. **he said to his charioteer.** In those days, one drove and the other fought; a third sometimes commanded the other chariots.

22:38 dogs licked. Elijah had pronounced this prophecy (21:19). Ahab would die a death of shame. The dogs would lick his blood; his body would not be carefully prepared for a ceremonial burial.

22:42 became king. Jehoshaphat actually became king while his father (King Asa) was still alive. Because of King Asa's failing health, he and his son shared rule for three years. King David and his son Solomon had shared leadership as well. This was called "co-regency."

22:44 king of Israel. Three kings ruled Israel during Jehoshaphat's reign in Judah: Ahab, Ahaziah, and Joram. This statement probably meant that Jehoshaphat's kingdom lived peaceably with Israel's kingdom, regardless of who was king at the time.

2 KINGS

AUTHOR

The author of 1 and 2 Kings is not known, but the three literary sources that are named suggest multiple authors and editors: "the Book of Solomon's Events" (1 Kings 11:41); "the Historical Record of Israel's Kings" (1 Kings 14:19; 2 Kings 15:31); and "the Historical Record of Judah's Kings " (1 Kings 14:29; 2 Kings 24:5).

DATE

The account of Jehoiachin's release from prison in 2 Kings 25:27-30 means that the final form of Kings was written after 561 B.C. However, the source materials could have been written at the time of the events they describe. These events span almost 400 years.

THEME

Israel's and Judah's spiral to destruction.

HISTORICAL BACKGROUND

The divided kingdoms of Israel and Judah continue their political and moral decline. They are oppressed by their enemies, particularly Aram (Syria). Second Kings gives witness to the rise of Assyrian power that crushes Israel's capital, Samaria, in 722 B.C. (2 Kings 17). The Babylonians succeeded the Assyrians as the dominant power in the region. It was at their hands, in 586 B.C., that Judah's capital, Jerusalem, suffered a fate similar to that of Samaria (2 Kings 25).

CHARACTERISTICS

Second Kings completes the historical narrative begun in 1 Kings. It chronicles the succession of kings in both the Northern Kingdom of Israel and the Southern Kingdom of Judah. The verdict upon most of these kings is sadly repetitive: They "did evil in the eyes of the Lord." But God keeps speaking through Elijah and, Elisha, who succeeds the great prophet, and is "doubly blessed" with God's Spirit.

PASSAGES FOR TOPICAL GROUP STUDY

4:1-7 .... USING YOUR GIFTS AND TALENTS ... Miracles with What You Have

5:1-16 .... HURTING AND HEALING ..... Healing Phenomenon

6:8-23 .. MIRACLES and POWER.............. Struck Blind

Ahaziah's Sickness and Death

1 After the death of Ahab, Moab rebelled against Israel. ² Ahaziah had fallen through the latticed window of his upper room in Samaria and was injured. So he sent messengers instructing them: "Go inquire of Baal-zebub,ª the god of Ekron, if I will recover from this injury."

³ But the angel of the LORD said to Elijah the Tishbite, "Go and meet the messengers of the king of Samaria and ask them, 'Is it because there is no God in Israel that you are going to inquire of Baal-zebub, the god of Ekron?' ⁴ Therefore, this is what the LORD says: 'You will not get up from your sickbed—you will certainly die.'" Then Elijah left.

⁵ The messengers returned to the king, who asked them, "Why have you come back?"

⁶ They replied, "A man came to meet us and said, 'Go back to the king who sent you and declare to him: This is what the LORD says: Is it because there is no God in Israel that you're sending ⌊these men⌋ to inquire of Baal-zebub, the god of Ekron? Therefore, you will not get up from your sickbed—you will certainly die.'"

⁷ The king asked them: "What sort of man came up to meet you and spoke those words to you?"

⁸ They replied, "A hairy man with a leather belt around his waist."

He said, "It's Elijah the Tishbite."

⁹ So King Ahaziah sent a captain of 50 with his 50 ⌊men⌋ to Elijah. When the captain went up to him, he was sitting on top of the hill. He announced, "Man of God, the king declares, 'Come down!'"

¹⁰ Elijah responded to the captain of the 50, "If I am a man of God, may fire come down from heaven and consume you and your 50 ⌊men⌋." Then fire came down from heaven and consumed him and his 50 ⌊men⌋.

¹¹ So the king sent another captain of 50 with his 50 ⌊men⌋ to Elijah. He took in the situationᵇ and announced, "Man of God, this is what the king says: 'Come down immediately!'"

¹² Elijah responded, "If I am a man of God, may fire come down from heaven and consume you and your 50 ⌊men⌋." So a divine fireᶜ came down from heaven and consumed him and his 50 ⌊men⌋.

¹³ Then the king sent a third captain of 50 with his 50 ⌊men⌋. The third captain of 50 went up and fell on his knees in front of Elijah and begged him, "Man of God, please let my life and the lives of these 50 servants of yours be precious in your sight. ¹⁴ Already fire has come down from heaven and consumed the first two captains of 50 with their fifties, but this time let my life be precious in your sight."

¹⁵ The angel of the LORD said to Elijah, "Go down with him. Don't be afraid of him." So he got up and went down with him to the king.

¹⁶ Then Elijah said to King Ahaziah, "This is what the LORD says: 'Because you have sent messengers to inquire of Baal-zebub, the god of Ekron—is it because there is no God in Israel for you to inquire of His will? You will not get up from your sickbed; you will certainly die.'"

¹⁷ Ahaziah died according to the word of the LORD that Elijah had spoken. Since he had no son, Joramᵈ became king in his place. ⌊This happened⌋ in the second year of Judah's King Jehoram son of Jehoshaphat.ᵉ ¹⁸ The rest of the events of Ahaziah's ⌊reign⌋, along with his accomplishments, are written about in the Historical Record of Israel's Kings.ᶠ

Elijah in the Whirlwind

2 The time had come for the LORD to take Elijah up to heaven in a whirlwind. Elijah and Elisha were traveling from Gilgal, ² and Elijah said to Elisha, "Stay here; the LORD is sending me on to Bethel."

But Elisha replied, "As the LORD lives and as you yourself live, I will not leave you." So they went down to Bethel.

³ Then the sons of the prophets who were at Bethel came out to Elisha and said, "Do you know that today the LORD will take your master away from you?"

He said, "Yes, I know. Be quiet."

⁴ Elijah said to him, "Elisha, stay here; the LORD is sending me to Jericho."

But Elisha said, "As the LORD lives and as you yourself live, I will not leave you." So they went to Jericho.

⁵ Then the sons of the prophets who were in Jericho came up to Elisha and said, "Do you know that today the LORD will take your master away from you?"

He said, "Yes, I know. Be quiet."

⁶ Elijah said to him, "Stay here; the LORD is sending me to the Jordan."

But Elisha said, "As the LORD lives and as you yourself live, I will not leave you." So the two of them went on.

⁷ Fifty men from the sons of the prophets came and stood facing them from a distance while the two of them stood by the Jordan. ⁸ Elijah took his mantle, rolled it up, and struck the waters, which parted to the right and left. Then the two of them crossed over on dry ground. ⁹ After they had crossed over, Elijah said to Eli-

---

ª**1:2** = Lord of the Flies ᵇ**1:11** Lit *He answered* ᶜ**1:12** Lit *a fire of God* ᵈ**1:17** Lit *Jehoram*; 2 Kg 8:16 ᵉ**1:17** LXX omits *in the second year . . . Jehoshaphat* ᶠ**1:18** LXX adds 4 more vv. here, which essentially duplicate the information in 2 Kg 3:1–3.

1:10 fire came down from heaven. Elijah called on God to execute a trial by fire as He had done on Mt. Carmel (1 Kings 18:36–39).

1:17 Ahaziah died. Ahaziah's death because of his sin confirmed God's word as the true revelation.

2:2 I will not leave you. Elisha knew that Eli-jah's work was almost finished, and wanted to be at his side until the end.

2:3 sons of the prophets. Groups or companies of prophets.

2:9 a double portion. A double portion was the rightful inheritance of a firstborn son.

2:12 chariots and horsemen. Elisha recognized the chariot of fire as a manifestation of God.

2:14 He struck the waters himself. Elisha's inheritance and right of succession were confirmed when he duplicated Elijah's miracle.

2:16 the Spirit of the LORD has carried him

sha, "Tell ⌊me⌋ what I can do for you before I am taken from you."

So Elisha answered, "Please, let there be a double portion of your spirit on me."

10 Elijah replied, "You have asked for something difficult. If you see me being taken from you, you will have it. If not, you won't."

11 As they continued walking and talking, a chariot of fire with horses of fire suddenly appeared and separated the two of them. Then Elijah went up into heaven in the whirlwind. 12 As Elisha watched, he kept crying out, "My father, my father, the chariots and horsemen of Israel!" Then he never saw Elijah again. He took hold of his own clothes and tore them into two pieces.

Elisha Succeeds Elijah

13 Elisha picked up the mantle that had fallen off Elijah and went back and stood on the bank of the Jordan. 14 Then he took the mantle Elijah had dropped and struck the waters. "Where is the LORD God of Elijah?" he asked. He struck the waters himself, and they parted to the right and the left, and Elisha crossed over.

15 When the sons of the prophets from Jericho, who were facing him, saw him, they said, "The spirit of Elijah rests on Elisha." They came to meet him and bowed down to the ground in front of him.

16 Then the sons of the prophets said to Elisha, "Since there are 50 strong men here with your servants, please let them go and search for your master. Maybe the Spirit of the LORD has carried him away and put him on one of the mountains or into one of the valleys."

He answered, "Don't send ⌊them⌋."

17 However, they urged him to the point of embarrassment, so he said, "Send ⌊them⌋." They sent 50 men, who looked for three days but did not find him. 18 When they returned to him in Jericho where he was staying, he said to them, "Didn't I tell you not to go?"

19 Then the men of the city said to Elisha, "Even though our lord can see that the city's location is good, the water is bad and the land unfruitful."

20 He replied, "Bring me a new bowl and put salt in it." After they had brought him one, 21 Elisha went out to the spring of water, threw salt in it, and said, "This is what the LORD says: 'I have healed this water. No longer will death or unfruitfulness result from it.'" 22 Therefore, the water remains healthy to this very day according to the word that Elisha spoke.

23 From there Elisha went up to Bethel. As he was walking up the path, some small boys came out of the city and harassed him, chanting, "Go up, baldy! Go up, baldy!"

24 He turned around, looked at them, and cursed them in the name of the LORD. Then two female bears came out of the woods and mauled 42 of the youths. 25 From there Elisha went to Mount Carmel, and then he returned to Samaria.

Israel's King Joram

3 Joram son of Ahab became king over Israel in Samaria during the eighteenth year of Judah's King Jehoshaphat; he reigned 12 years. 2 He did what was evil in the LORD's sight, but not like his father and mother, for he removed the sacred pillar of •Baal his father had made. 3 Nevertheless, Joram clung to the sins that Jeroboam son of Nebat had caused Israel to commit. He did not turn away from them.

Moab's Rebellion against Israel

4 King Mesha of Moab was a sheep breeder. He used to pay the king of Israel 100,000 lambs and the wool of 100,000 rams, 5 but when Ahab died, the king of Moab rebelled against the king of Israel. 6 So King Joram marched out from Samaria at that time and mobilized all Israel. 7 Then he sent ⌊a message⌋ to King Jehoshaphat of Judah: "The king of Moab has rebelled against me. Will you go with me to fight against Moab?"

Jehoshaphat said, "I will go. I am as you are, my people as your people, my horses as your horses." 8 Then he asked, "Which route should we take?"

Joram replied, "The route of the wilderness of Edom."

9 So the king of Israel, the king of Judah, and the king of Edom set out. After they had traveled their indirect route for seven days, they had no water for the army or their animals.

10 Then the king of Israel said, "Oh no, the LORD has summoned us three kings, only to hand us over to Moab."

11 But Jehoshaphat said, "Isn't there a prophet of the LORD here? Let's inquire of the LORD through him."

One of the servants of the king of Israel answered, "Elisha son of Shaphat, who used to pour water on Elijah's hands, is here."

12 Jehoshaphat affirmed, "The LORD's words are with him." So the king of Israel and Jehoshaphat and the king of Edom went to him.

13 However, Elisha said to King ⌊Joram⌋ of Israel, "We have nothing in common. Go to the prophets of your father and your mother!"

But the king of Israel replied, "No, because it is the LORD who has summoned us three kings to hand us over to Moab."

14 Elisha responded, "As the LORD of •Hosts lives, I stand before Him. If I did not have respect for King

---

away. The prophets could not believe that Elijah would be spared the most universal of human experiences—death.

3:2 He did what was evil. King Joram stood in a line of progressively evil kings that had begun with Omri (1 Kings 16:25).

3:3 sins that Jeroboam. King Jeroboam turned the people of Israel away from worship of God to idol worship.

3:7 [a message] to King Jehoshaphat. King Joram hoped the Northern and Southern kingdoms could form an alliance between them against a common threat, the Moabites.

3:11 Isn't there a prophet of the LORD here? The rulers had followed their own wisdom nearly to destruction. Now desperate, they wanted God's help.

3:14 If I did not have respect for ... Judah. The kings of Israel (Northern Kingdom) had broken God's covenant. Joram was not as bad as his father and grandfather (v. 2), but neither

Jehoshaphat of Judah, I would not look at you; I wouldn't take notice of you. 15 Now, bring me a musician."

While the musician played, the LORD's hand came on Elisha. 16 Then he said, "This is what the LORD says: 'Dig ditch after ditch in this •wadi.' 17 For the LORD says, 'You will not see wind or rain, but the wadi will be filled with water, and you will drink—you and your cattle and your animals.' 18 This is easy in the LORD's sight. He will also hand Moab over to you. 19 Then you must attack every fortified city and every choice city. You must cut down every good tree and stop up every spring of water. You must ruin every good piece of land with stones."

20 About the time for the •grain offering the ⌊next⌋ morning, water suddenly came from the direction of Edom and filled the land.

21 All Moab had heard that the kings had come up to fight against them. So all who could bear arms, from the youngest to the oldest, were summoned and took their stand at the border. 22 When they got up early in the morning, the sun was shining on the water, and the Moabites saw that the water across from them was red like blood. 23 "This is blood!" they exclaimed. "The kings have clashed swords and killed each other. So, to the spoil, Moab!"

24 However, when the Moabites came to Israel's camp, the Israelites attacked them, and they fled from them. So Israel went into the land and struck down the Moabites. 25 They destroyed the cities, and each of them threw stones to cover every good piece of land. They stopped up every spring of water and cut down every good tree. In the end, only the buildings of Kir-hareseth were left. Then men with slings surrounded ⌊the city⌋ and attacked it.

26 When the king of Moab saw that the battle was too fierce for him, he took 700 swordsmen with him to try to break through to the king of Edom, but they could not do it. 27 So he took his firstborn son, who was to become king in his place, and offered him as a •burnt offering on the city wall. Great wrath was on the Israelites, and they withdrew from him and returned to their land.

The Widow's Oil Multiplied

4 One of the wives of the sons of the prophets cried out to Elisha, "Your servant, my husband, has died. You know that your servant •feared the LORD. Now the creditor is coming to take my two children as his slaves."

2 Elisha asked her, "What can I do for you? Tell me, what do you have in the house?"

She said, "Your servant has nothing in the house except a jar of oil."

3 Then he said, "Go and borrow empty containers from everyone—from all your neighbors. Do not get just a few. 4 Then go in and shut the door behind you and your sons, and pour oil into all these containers. Set the full ones to one side." 5 So she left.

After she had shut the door behind her and her sons, they kept bringing her ⌊containers⌋, and she kept pouring. 6 When they were full, she said to her son, "Bring me another container."

But he replied, "There aren't any more." Then the oil stopped.

7 She went and told the man of God, and he said, "Go sell the oil and pay your debt; you and your sons can live on the rest."

Miracles with What You Have

1. Do you or have you received an allowance? How does it compare to what your friends get?

2 Kings 4:1-7

2. This woman didn't know what Elisha was planning when he told her to gather empty containers. Why did she gather so many? How did her faith in God make her rich?

3. Why did God choose to use what the widow already had in the house (a small jar of oil)?

4. How has God used your gifts and talents to bless others?

5. How can you use your gifts and talents even more in God's service?

The Shunammite Woman's Hospitality

8 One day Elisha went to Shunem. A prominent woman who ⌊lived⌋ there persuaded him to eat some food. So whenever he passed by, he stopped there to eat. 9 Then she said to her husband, "I know that the one who often passes by here is a holy man of God, 10 so let's make a small room upstairs and put a bed, a table, a chair, and a lamp there for him. Whenever he comes, he can stay there."

The Shunammite Woman's Son

11 One day he came there and stopped and went to the room upstairs to lie down. 12 He ordered his atten-

was he a king after God's heart.

3:19 cut down ... ruin. God demanded the devastation of rebellious Moab.

3:23 killed each other. The Moabites saw water that looked like blood. They thought the weak alliance opposing them had come to blows.

3:27 offered him as a burnt offering. The king of Moab sacrificed his own son as a burnt offering to the Moabite god Chemosh. The sight of the sacrifice may have encouraged the Moabites to fight furiously and drive Israel away.

4:14 no son, and her husband is old. Without

a son to help her after her husband was gone, this woman would soon be in a desperate situation.

4:16-17 In spite of her unbelief, the Shunammite woman delivered a child, and she did so exactly as Elisha had predicted.

4:20 The child ... died. The child was a gift

dant Gehazi, "Call this Shunammite woman." So he called her and she stood before him.

[13] Then he said to Gehazi, "Say to her, 'Look, you've gone to all this trouble for us. What can ⌊we⌋ do for you? Can ⌊we⌋ speak on your behalf to the king or to the commander of the army?' "

She answered, "I am living among my own people."

[14] So he asked, "Then what should be done for her?"

Gehazi answered, "Well, she has no son, and her husband is old."

[15] "Call her," Elisha said. So Gehazi called her, and she stood in the doorway. [16] Elisha said, "At this time next year you will have a son in your arms."

Then she said, "No, my lord. Man of God, do not deceive your servant."

[17] The woman conceived and gave birth to a son at the same time the following year, as Elisha had promised her.

The Shunammite's Son Raised

[18] The child grew and one day went out to his father and the harvesters. [19] ⌊Suddenly⌋, he complained to his father, "My head! My head!"

His father told his servant, "Carry him to his mother." [20] So he picked him up and took him to his mother. The child sat on her lap until noon and then died. [21] Then she went up and laid him on the bed of the man of God, shut him in, and left.

[22] She summoned her husband and said, "Please send me one of the servants and one of the donkeys, so I can hurry to the man of God and then come back."

[23] But he said, "Why go to him today? It's neither New Moon or Sabbath."

She replied, "Everything is all right."

[24] Then she saddled the donkey and said to her servant, "Hurry, don't slow the pace for me unless I tell you." [25] So she set out and went to the man of God at Mount Carmel.

When the man of God saw her at a distance, he said to his attendant Gehazi, "Look, there's the Shunammite woman. [26] Run out to meet her and ask, 'Are you all right? Is your husband all right? Is your son all right?' "

And she answered, "Everything's all right."

[27] When she came up to the man of God at the mountain, she clung to his feet. Gehazi came to push her away, but the man of God said, "Leave her alone—she is in severe anguish, and the LORD has hidden it from me. He hasn't told me."

[28] Then she said, "Did I ask my lord for a son? Didn't I say, 'Do not deceive me?' "

[29] So Elisha said to Gehazi, "Tuck your mantle under your belt, take my staff with you, and go. If you meet anyone, don't ⌊stop to⌋ greet him, and if a man greets you, don't answer him. Then place my staff on the boy's face."

[30] The boy's mother said ⌊to Elisha⌋, "As the LORD lives and as you yourself live, I will not leave you." So he got up and followed her.

[31] Gehazi went ahead of them and placed the staff on the boy's face, but there was no sound or sign of life, so he went back to meet Elisha and told him, "The boy didn't wake up."

[32] When Elisha got to the house, he discovered the boy lying dead on his bed. [33] So he went in, closed the door behind the two of them, and prayed to the LORD. [34] Then he went up and lay on the boy: he put mouth to mouth, eye to eye, hand to hand. While he bent down over him, the boy's flesh became warm. [35] Elisha got up, went into the house, and paced back and forth. Then he went up and bent down over him again. The boy sneezed seven times and opened his eyes.

[36] Elisha called Gehazi and said, "Call the Shunammite woman." He called her and she came. Then Elisha said, "Pick up your son." [37] She came, fell at his feet, and bowed to the ground; she picked up her son and left.

The Deadly Stew

[38] When Elisha returned to Gilgal, there was a famine in the land. The sons of the prophets were sitting at his feet.[a] He said to his attendant, "Put on the large pot and make stew for the sons of the prophets."

[39] One went out to the field to gather herbs and found a wild vine from which he gathered as many wild gourds as his garment would hold. Then he came back and cut them up into the pot of stew, but they were unaware ⌊of what they were⌋.

[40] They served some for the men to eat, but when they ate the stew they cried out, "There's death in the pot, man of God!" And they were unable to eat it.

[41] Then Elisha said, "Get some meal." He threw it into the pot and said, "Serve it for the people to eat." And there was nothing bad in the pot.

The Multiplied Bread

[42] A man from Baal-shalishah came to the man of God with his sack full of 20 loaves of barley bread from the first bread of the harvest. Elisha said, "Give it to the people to eat."

[43] But Elisha's attendant asked, "What? Am I to set 20 loaves before 100 men?"

---

[a] 4:38 Lit sitting before him

---

from God in response to the woman's faith. His death tested her faith.

4:21–26 The woman was determined to keep her son's death a private matter until she had spoken to Elisha.

4:29 place my staff. Elisha assumed that the special powers he had from God could be transferred through his staff.

4:33 closed the door … and prayed. Elisha sought God's will in this act of healing, then acted on it.

4:38 famine in the land. Just as God provided for His people, He sometimes showed His displeasure by sending famine and other trouble

(see Lev. 26:19–20; Deut. 28:18,23–24).

4:39 found a wild vine. Just like Baal worship, the wild vine was native to the land, but it was poisonous and deadly.

4:42 first bread of the harvest. People in the Northern Kingdom had lost confidence in a corrupt priesthood, so their offerings went to

"Give it to the people to eat," Elisha said, "for this is what the LORD says: 'They will eat, and they will have some left over.' " ⁴⁴ So he gave it to them, and as the LORD had promised, they ate and had some left over.

 Healing Phenomenon

1. Does your family have any "home remedies" to cure the hiccups, a cold, or something else?

2 Kings 5:1-16

2. Why did Elisha heal this great enemy leader (v. 8)?

3. Why did Naaman get angry with Elisha? How did he expect to be healed? What does this show about his character?

4. In what way did God require that Naaman humble himself in order to be healed? What does this show about God's character?

5. When you ask God for help, is your attitude humble or proud? How might God want you to humble yourself before Him?

Naaman's Disease Healed

5 Naaman, commander of the army for the king of Aram, was a great man in his master's sight[a] and highly regarded because through him, the LORD had given victory to Aram. The man was a brave warrior, but he had a skin disease.

² Aram had gone on raids and brought back from the land of Israel a young girl who served Naaman's wife. ³ She said to her mistress, "If only my master would go to[b] the prophet who is in Samaria, he would cure him of his skin disease."

⁴ So Naaman went and told his master what the girl from the land of Israel had said. ⁵ Therefore, the king of Aram said, "Go and I will send a letter ⌊with you⌋ to the king of Israel."

So he went and took with him 750 pounds[c] of silver, 150 pounds[d] of gold, and 10 changes of clothes. ⁶ He brought the letter to the king of Israel, and it read:

When this letter comes to you, note that I have sent you my servant Naaman for you to cure him of his skin disease.

⁷ When the king of Israel read the letter, he tore his clothes and asked, "Am I God, killing and giving life that this man expects me to cure a man of his skin disease? Think it over and you will see that he is only picking a fight with[e] me."

⁸ When Elisha the man of God heard that the king of Israel tore his clothes, he sent ⌊a message⌋ to the king, "Why have you torn your clothes? Have him come to me, and he will know there is a prophet in Israel." ⁹ So Naaman came with his horses and chariots and stood at the door of Elisha's house.

¹⁰ Then Elisha sent him a messenger, who said, "Go wash seven times in the Jordan and your flesh will be restored and you will be clean."

¹¹ But Naaman got angry and left, saying, "I was telling myself: He will surely come out, stand and call on the name of •Yahweh his God, and will wave his hand over the spot and cure the skin disease. ¹² Aren't Abana and Pharpar, the rivers of Damascus, better than all the waters of Israel? Could I not wash in them and be clean?" So he turned and left in a rage.

¹³ But his servants approached and said to him, "My father, if the prophet had told you to do some great thing, would you not have done it? How much more ⌊should you do it⌋ when he tells you, 'Wash and be clean'?" ¹⁴ So Naaman went down and dipped himself in the Jordan seven times, according to the command of the man of God. Then his skin was restored ⌊and became⌋ like the skin of a small boy, and he was clean.

¹⁵ Then Naaman and his whole company went back to the man of God, stood before him, and declared, "I know there's no God in the whole world except in Israel. Therefore, please accept a gift from your servant."

¹⁶ But Elisha said, "As the LORD lives, I stand before Him. I will not accept it." Naaman urged him to accept it, but he refused.

¹⁷ Naaman responded, "If not, please let two mule-loads of dirt be given to your servant, for your servant will no longer offer a •burnt offering or a sacrifice to any other god but Yahweh. ¹⁸ However, in a particular matter may the LORD pardon your servant: When my master, ⌊the king of Aram⌋, goes into the temple of Rimmon to worship and I, as his right-hand man,[f] bow in the temple of Rimmon—when I bow[g] in the temple of Rimmon, may the LORD pardon your servant in this matter."

¹⁹ So he said to him, "Go in peace."

Gehazi's Greed Punished

After Naaman had traveled a short distance from Elisha, ²⁰ Gehazi, the attendant of Elisha the man of God,

---

a**5:1** Lit *man before his master*   b**5:3** Lit *master was before*   c**5:5** Lit *10 talents*   d**5:5** Lit *6,000 [shekels]*   e**5:7** Lit *only seeking an occasion against*   f**5:18** Lit *worship, and he leans on my hand, and I*   g**5:18** LXX, Vg read *when he bows himself*

---

prophets who still spoke God's truth.

5:2 a young girl. This passage contrasts the corrupt rulers of the Northern Kingdom with a faithful slave girl who had a compassionate heart.

5:8 Why have you torn your clothes? Elisha scolded King Joram for his fear and faithlessness. This was an opportunity to demonstrate God's power to a pagan ruler.

5:10 wash ... in the Jordan. There was nothing magical about washing in the Jordan River. What Elisha demanded was Naaman's obedience.

5:11–14 When Naaman became a servant of God and acknowledged God's sovereignty, he was healed.

5:15 no God ... except in Israel. At a time when Israel's people were worshipping other gods, it was left to a pagan to declare the power of the only true God.

thought: My master has let this Aramean Naaman off lightly by not accepting from him what he brought. As the LORD lives, I will run after him and get something from him.

²¹ So Gehazi pursued Naaman. When Naaman saw someone running after him, he got down from the chariot to meet him and asked, "Is everything all right?"

²² Gehazi said, "It's all right. My master has sent me to say, 'I have just now discovered that two young men from the sons of the prophets have come to me from the hill country of Ephraim. Please give them 75 poundsª of silver and two changes of clothes.' "

²³ But Naaman insisted, "Please, accept 150 pounds."ᵇ He urged Gehazi and then packed 150 poundsᵇ of silver in two bags with two changes of clothes. Naaman gave them to two of his young men who carried them ahead of Gehazi. ²⁴ When Gehazi came to the hill,ᶜ he took the gifts from them and stored them in the house. Then he dismissed the men, and they left.

²⁵ Gehazi came and stood by his master. "Where did you go, Gehazi?" Elisha asked him.

"Your servant didn't go anywhere," he replied.

²⁶ But Elisha questioned him, "Wasn't my spirit thereᵈ when the man got down from his chariot to meet you? Is it a time to accept money and clothes, olive orchards and vineyards, sheep and oxen, and male and female slaves? ²⁷ Therefore, Naaman's skin disease will cling to you and your descendants forever." So Gehazi went out from his presence diseased—⌊white⌋ as snow.

The Floating Ax Head

6 The sons of the prophets said to Elisha, "Please notice that the place where we live under your supervisionᵉ is too small for us. ² Please let us go to the Jordan where we can each get a log and can build ourselves a place to live there."

"Go," he said.

³ Then one said, "Please come with your servants."

"I'll come," he answered.

⁴ So he went with them, and when they came to the Jordan, they cut down trees. ⁵ As one of them was cutting down a tree, the iron ⌊ax head⌋ fell into the water, and he cried out: "Oh, my master, it was borrowed!"

⁶ Then the man of God asked, "Where did it fall?"

When he showed him the place, the man of God cut a stick, threw it there, and made the iron float. ⁷ Then he said, "Pick it up." So he reached out and took it.

Struck Blind

1. Recall a time when you got lost. How did you find your way?

2 Kings 6:8-23

2. To whom was Elisha referring when he said, "those who are with us outnumber those who are with them" (v. 16)?

3. Why did Elisha show mercy to those who were trying to kill him? What was the result?

4. What was God's purpose in working this great miracle: To save Elisha? To show His power to a foreign nation? Other?

5. How can this passage encourage you when you feel outnumbered by the world's forces?

The Aramean War

⁸ When the king of Aram was waging war against Israel, he conferred with his servants, "My camp will be at such and such a place."

⁹ But the man of God sent ⌊word⌋ to the king of Israel: "Be careful passing by this place, for the Arameans are going down there." ¹⁰ Consequently, the king of Israel sent ⌊word⌋ to the place the man of God had told him about. The man of God repeatedlyᶠ warned the king, so the king would be on his guard.

¹¹ The king of Aram was enraged because of this matter, and he called his servants and demanded of them, "Tell me, which one of us is for the king of Israel?"

¹² One of his servants said, "No one, my lord the king. Elisha, the prophet in Israel, tells the king of Israel even the words you speak in your bedroom."

¹³ So the king said, "Go and see where he is, so I can send ⌊men⌋ to capture him."

When he was told, "Elisha is in Dothan," ¹⁴ he sent horses, chariots, and a massive army there. They went by night and surrounded the city.

¹⁵ When the servant of the man of God got up early and went out, he discovered an army with horses and chariots surrounding the city. So he asked Elisha, "Oh, my master, what are we to do?"

ª**5:22** Lit *a talent* ᵇ**5:23** Lit *two talents* ᶜ**5:24** Or *citadel* ᵈ**5:26** Lit *"Did not my heart go* ᵉ**6:1** Lit *we are living before you* ᶠ**6:10** Lit *not once and not twice*

5:16 I will not accept it. Elisha recognized Naaman's healing as an act of God. He could not accept a reward for something God had done.

5:22 give them 75 pounds of silver. Gehazi's love of money led to other sins—coveting and lying.

5:26 time to accept money. Gehazi had acted no better than the pagan soothsayers, who were prophets for profit (see Num. 22).

6:1 sons of the prophets. Several groups of prophets who acknowledged the leadership of Elijah and Elisha clustered around the cities of Bethel, Jericho, and Gilgal (2:1,3,5).

6:5 borrowed! A person who lost an ax head was liable for it, and its loss might mean servitude to repay the debt.

6:9 man of God sent [word] to the king. Elisha was a spiritual leader and advisor to the king of Israel. He advised Joram in this situation on military intelligence.

16 Elisha said, "Don't be afraid, for those who are with us outnumber those who are with them."

17 Then Elisha prayed, "LORD, please open his eyes and let him see." So the LORD opened the servant's eyes. He looked and saw that the mountain was covered with horses and chariots of fire all around Elisha.

18 When the Arameans came against him, Elisha prayed to the LORD, "Please strike this nation with blindness." So He struck them with blindness, according to Elisha's word. 19 Then Elisha said to them, "This is not the way, and this is not the city. Follow me, and I will take you to the man you're looking for." And he led them to Samaria. 20 When they entered Samaria, Elisha said, "LORD, open these men's eyes and let them see." So the LORD opened their eyes. They looked and discovered ⌊they were⌋ in Samaria.

21 When the king of Israel saw them, he said to Elisha, "My father, should I kill them? I will kill them."

22 Elisha replied, "Don't kill them. Do you kill those you have captured with your sword or your bow? Set food and water in front of them so they can eat and drink and go to their master."

23 So he prepared a great feast for them. When they had eaten and drunk, he sent them away, and they went to their master. The Aramean raiders did not come into Israel's land again.

24 Some time later, King Ben-hadad of Aram brought all his military units together and marched up to besiege Samaria. 25 So there was a great famine in Samaria, and they continued the siege against it until a donkey's head ⌊sold for⌋ 80 silver ⌊•shekels⌋,a and a cupb of dove's dungc ⌊sold for⌋ five silver ⌊shekels⌋.d

26 As the king of Israel was passing by on the wall, a woman cried out to him, "My lord the king, help!"

27 He answered, "If the LORD doesn't help you, where can I get help for you? From the threshing floor or the winepress?" 28 Then the king asked her, "What's the matter?"

She said, "This woman said to me, 'Give up your son, and we will eat him today. Then we will eat my son tomorrow.' 29 So we boiled my son and ate him, and I said to her the next day, 'Give up your son, and we will eat him,' but she has hidden her son."

30 When the king heard the woman's words, he tore his clothes. Then, as he was passing by on the wall, the people saw that there was •sackcloth under his clothes next to his skin. 31 He announced, "May God punish me and do so severely if the head of Elisha son of Shaphat remains on his shoulders today."

32 Elisha was sitting in his house, and the elders were sitting with him. The king sent a man ahead of him, but before the messenger got to him, Elisha said to the elders, "Do you see how this murderer has sent ⌊someone⌋ to cut off my head? Look, when the messenger comes, shut the door to keep him out. Isn't the sound of his master's feet behind him?"

33 While Elisha was still speaking with them, the messengere came down to him. Then he said, "This disaster is from the LORD. Why should I trust the LORD any longer?"

Aram Defeated

7 Elisha said, "Hear the word of the LORD! This is what the LORD says: 'About this time tomorrow at the gate of Samaria, six quartsf of fine meal ⌊will sell⌋ for a •shekelg and 12 quartsh of barley ⌊will sell⌋ for a shekel.'"g

2 Then the captain, the king's right-hand man, responded to the man of God, "Look, ⌊even if⌋ the LORD were to make windows in heaven, could this really happen?"

Elisha announced, "You will in fact see it with your own eyes, but you won't eat any of it."

3 Four men with skin diseases were at the entrance to the gate. They said to each other, "Why just sit here until we die? 4 If we say, 'Let's go into the city,' we will die there because the famine is in the city, but if we sit here, we will also die. So now, come on. Let's go to the Arameans' camp. If they let us live, we will live; if they kill us, we will die."

5 So the diseased men got up at twilight to go to the Arameans' camp. When they came to the camp's edge, they discovered that there was not a ⌊single⌋ man there, 6 for the Lordi had caused the Aramean camp to hear the sound of chariots, horses, and a great army. The Arameans had said to each other, "The king of Israel must have hired the kings of the Hittites and the kings of Egypt to attack us." 7 So they had gotten up and fled at twilight abandoning their tents, horses, and donkeys. The camp was intact, and they had fled for their lives.

8 When these men came to the edge of the camp, they went into a tent to eat and drink. Then they picked up the silver, gold, and clothing and went off and hid them. They came back and entered another tent, picked ⌊things⌋ up, and hid them. 9 Then they said to each other, "We're not doing what is right. Today is a day of good news. If we are silent and wait until morning light, we will be punished. Let's go tell the king's household."

---

a6:25 About 2 pounds   b6:25 Lit a fourth of a kab   c6:25 Or seedpods, or wild onions   d6:25 About 2 ounces   e6:33 Some emend to king
f7:1 Lit a seah   g7:1 About ½ ounce (of silver)   h7:1 Lit two seahs   i7:6 Many Hb mss read LORD

6:13 capture him. The king of Aram wanted to capture Elisha to keep him from offering assistance to King Joram of Israel.

6:24 King Ben-hadad. This Aramean king had besieged Samaria in the past.

6:30 tore his clothes. King Joram was expressing his anger toward Elisha, whom he blamed for the famine that had struck Israel.

6:33 disaster is from the LORD. Joram believed that Elisha had deceived him and that God was actually responsible for the famine.

7:12 what the Arameans have done. Instead of recognizing God's provision and the fulfillment of Elisha's prophecy, Joram saw only deception.

8:2 She and her household lived as foreigners. The Shunammite woman was obedient to Elisha's warning. Her Obedience had saved her from the famine.

8:3 went ... to the king to beg for her house and field. In this woman's absence, someone

10 The diseased men went and called to the city's gatekeepers and told them, "We went to the Aramean camp and no one was there—no human sounds. There was nothing but tethered horses and donkeys, and the tents were intact." 11 The gatekeepers called out, and ⌊the news⌋ was reported to the king's household.

12 So the king got up in the night and said to his servants, "Let me tell you what the Arameans have done to us. They know we are starving, so they have left the camp to hide in the open country, thinking, 'When they come out of the city, we will take them alive and go into the city.'"

13 But one of his servants responded, "Please, let ⌊messengers⌋ take five of the horses that are left in the city. ⌊The messengers⌋ are like the whole multitude of Israelites who will die,a so let's send them and see."

14 ⌊The messengers⌋ took two chariots with horses, and the king sent them after the Aramean army, saying, "Go and see." 15 So they followed them as far as the Jordan. They saw that the whole way was littered with clothes and equipment the Arameans had thrown off in their haste. The messengers returned and told the king. 16 Then the people went out and plundered the Aramean camp.

It was then that six quartsb of fine meal ⌊sold⌋ for a shekeld and 12 quartsd of barley ⌊sold⌋ for a shekel,d according to the word of the LORD. 17 The king had appointed the captain, his right-hand man, to be in charge of the gate, but the people trampled him in the gateway. He died, just as the man of God had predicted when the king came to him. 18 When the man of God had said to the king, "About this time tomorrow 12 quartsd of barley ⌊will sell⌋ for a shekelc and six quartsb of fine meal ⌊will sell⌋ for a shekelc at the gate of Samaria," 19 this captain had answered the man of God, "Look, ⌊even if⌋ the LORD were to make windows in heaven, could this really happen?" Elisha had said, "You will in fact see it with your own eyes, but you won't eat any of it." 20 This is what happened to him: the people trampled him in the gateway, and he died.

The Shunammite's Land Restored

8 Elisha said to the woman whose son he had restored to life, "Get ready, you and your household, and go and live as a foreigner wherever you can. For the LORD has announced a seven-year famine, and it has already come to the land."

2 So the woman got ready and did what the man of God said. She and her household lived as foreigners in the land of the Philistines for seven years. 3 When the woman returned from the land of the Philistines at the end of seven years, she went to appeal to the king for her house and field.

4 The king had been speaking to Gehazi, the servant of the man of God, saying, "Tell me all the great things Elisha has done."

5 While he was telling the king how Elisha restored the dead ⌊son⌋ to life, the woman whose son he had restored to life came to appeal to the king for her house and field. So Gehazi said, "My lord the king, this is the woman and this is the son Elisha restored to life."

6 When the king asked the woman, she told him the story. So the king appointed a court official for her, saying, "Restore all that was hers, along with all the income from the field from the day she left the country until now."

Aram's King Hazael

7 Elisha came to Damascus while Ben-hadad king of Aram was sick, and the king was told, "The man of God has come here." 8 So the king said to Hazael, "Take a gift with you and go meet the man of God. Inquire of the LORD through him, 'Will I recover from this sickness?'"

9 Hazael went to meet Elisha, taking with him a gift: 40 camel-loads of all kinds of goods from Damascus. When he came and stood before him, he said, "Your son, Ben-hadad king of Aram, has sent me to ask you, 'Will I recover from this sickness?'"

10 Elisha told him, "Go say to him, 'You are sure toe recover.' But the LORD has shown me that he is sure to die." 11 Then Elisha stared steadily at him until Hazael was ashamed.

The man of God wept, 12 and Hazael asked, "Why is my lord weeping?"

He replied, "Because I know the evil you will do to the people of Israel. You will set their fortresses on fire. You will kill their young men with the sword. You will dash their little ones to pieces. You will rip open their pregnant women."

13 Hazael said, "How could your servant, a mere dog, do this monstrous thing?"

Elisha answered, "The LORD has shown me that you will be king over Aram."

14 Hazael left Elisha and went to his master, who asked him, "What did Elisha say to you?"

He responded, "He told me you are sure to recover."
15 The next day Hazael took a heavy cloth, dipped it in water, and spread it over the king's face. Ben-hadad died, and Hazael reigned instead of him.

---

a7:13 LXX, Syr, Vg, many Hb mss; MT reads left in it. Indeed, they are like the whole multitude of Israel that are left in it; indeed, they are like the whole multitude of Israel who will die.   b7:16 Lit a seah   c7:16,18 About ½ ounce (of silver)   d7:16 Lit two seahs   e8:10 Alt Hb tradition reads You will not

---

had illegally taken her property.
8:6 Restore all that was hers. God's blessing was not limited to restoration of lost property but included all the income her property had generated.
8:7 Elisha came. Elisha journeyed to Damascus to anoint Hazael as the new king of Syria,

in obedience of the instructions he had received earlier from the Lord (1 Kings 19:15-18).
8:8 Inquire of the LORD. Ironically, as the pagan king Ben-hadad of Aram faced death, he wanted to know his fate from Israel's God. This was the opposite of Ahaziah's actions in 1:1-3.

8:12 I know the evil you will do to the people of Israel. Elisha realized that God would use Hazael, an aide of King Ben-hadad, as an instrument of judgment against Israel.

8:15 spread it over the king's face. This story illustrates that God is in control of the entire world, not just Israel. He used a brutal pagan

Judah's King Jehoram

16 In the fifth year of Israel's King Joram son of Ahab, Jehoram[a] son of Jehoshaphat became king of Judah, replacing his father.[b] 17 He was 32 years old when he became king; he reigned eight years in Jerusalem. 18 He walked in the way of the kings of Israel, as the house of Ahab had done, for Ahab's daughter was his wife. He did what was evil in the LORD's sight. 19 The LORD was unwilling to destroy Judah because of His servant David, since He had promised to give a lamp to David and to his sons forever.

20 During Jehoram's reign, Edom rebelled against Judah's control and appointed their own king. 21 So Jehoram crossed over to Zair with all his chariots. Then at night he set out to attack the Edomites who had surrounded him and the chariot commanders, but his troops fled to their tents. 22 So Edom is still in rebellion against Judah's control today. Libnah also rebelled at that time.

23 The rest of the events of Jehoram's ⌊reign⌋, along with all his accomplishments, are written about in the Historical Record of Israel's Kings. 24 Jehoram rested with his fathers and was buried with his fathers in the city of David, and his son Ahaziah became king in his place.

Judah's King Ahaziah

25 In the twelfth year of Israel's King Joram son of Ahab, Ahaziah son of Jehoram became king of Judah. 26 Ahaziah was 22 years old when he became king; he reigned one year in Jerusalem. His mother's name was Athaliah, granddaughter of Israel's King Omri. 27 He walked in the way of the house of Ahab and did what was evil in the LORD's sight like the house of Ahab, for he was a son-in-law to Ahab's family.

28 Ahaziah went with Joram son of Ahab to fight against Hazael king of Aram in Ramoth-gilead, and the Arameans wounded Joram. 29 So King Joram returned to Jezreel to recover from the wounds that the Arameans had inflicted on him in Ramoth-gilead[c] when he fought against Aram's King Hazael. Then Judah's King Ahaziah son of Jehoram went down to Jezreel to visit Joram son of Ahab since Joram was ill.

Jehu Anointed as Israel's King

9 The prophet Elisha called one of the sons of the prophets and said, "Tuck your mantle under your belt, take this flask of oil with you, and go to Ramoth-gilead. 2 When you get there, look for Jehu son of Jehoshaphat, son of Nimshi. Go in, get him away from his colleagues, and take him to an inner room. 3 Then, take the flask of oil, pour it on his head, and say, 'This is what the LORD says: "I anoint you king over Israel."' Open the door and escape. Don't wait." 4 So the young prophet went to Ramoth-gilead.

5 When he arrived, the army commanders were sitting there, so he said, "I have a message for you, commander."

Jehu asked, "For which one of us?"

He answered, "For you, commander."

6 So Jehu got up and went into the house. The young prophet poured the oil on his head and said, "This is what the LORD God of Israel says: 'I anoint you king over the LORD's people, Israel. 7 You are to strike down the house of your master Ahab so that I may avenge the blood shed by the hand of Jezebel—the blood of My servants the prophets and of all the servants of the LORD. 8 The whole house of Ahab will perish, and I will eliminate all of Ahab's males,[d] both slave and free, in Israel. 9 I will make the house of Ahab like the house of Jeroboam son of Nebat and like the house of Baasha son of Ahijah. 10 The dogs will eat Jezebel in the plot of land at Jezreel—no one will bury her.'" Then the young prophet opened the door and escaped.

11 When Jehu came out to his master's servants, they asked, "Is everything all right? Why did this crazy person come to you?"

Then he said to them, "You know the sort and their ranting."

12 But they replied, "⌊That's⌋ a lie! Tell us!"

So Jehu said, "He talked to me about this and that and said, 'This is what the LORD says: I anoint you king over Israel.'"

13 Each man quickly took his garment and put it under Jehu on the bare steps.[e] They blew the ram's horn and proclaimed, "Jehu is king!"

14 Then Jehu son of Jehoshaphat, son of Nimshi, conspired against Joram. Joram and all Israel had been at Ramoth-gilead on guard against Hazael king of Aram. 15 But King Joram had returned to Jezreel to recover from the wounds that the Arameans had inflicted on him when he fought against Aram's King Hazael. Jehu said, "If you ⌊commanders⌋ wish ⌊to make me king⌋, then don't let anyone escape from the city to go tell about it in Jezreel."

Jehu Kills Joram and Ahaziah

16 Jehu got into his chariot and went to Jezreel since Joram was laid up there and Ahaziah king of Judah had gone down to visit Joram. 17 Now the watchman was

---

---

man, Hazael, as His instrument of divine judgment against King Ben-hadad (Isa. 10:5–19; Amos 1:4).

8:19 because of His servant David. The Lord spared Judah's unfaithful royal house, but only because of the promise made to David that one of his descendants would always rule on the throne of Judah (2 Sam. 7:16).

8:20 Edom rebelled. Judah had ruled over Edom for many years through a governor appointed by Judah's king.

8:21 he set out to attack. The rebel Edomites defeated King Jehoram's army.

8:28 Ahaziah went ... to fight against Hazael. First Kings 22 tells about King Jehoshaphat of Judah uniting with King Ahab of Israel to fight the Arameans. In a similar situation, the kings of Israel and Judah united their forces to fight the Arameans under Hazael's leadership.

9:7 strike down the house of ... Ahab. Jehu

standing on the tower in Jezreel. He saw Jehu's troops approaching and shouted, "I see troops!"

Joram responded, "Choose a rider and send him to meet them and have him ask, '⌊Do you come in⌋ peace?' "

[18] So a horseman went to meet Jehu and said, "This is what the king asks: '⌊Do you come in⌋ peace?' "

Jehu replied, "What do you have to do with peace?[a] Fall in behind me."

The watchman reported, "The messenger reached them but hasn't started back."

[19] So he sent out a second horseman, who went to them and said, "This is what the king asks: '⌊Do you come in⌋ peace?' "

Jehu answered, "What do you have to do with peace?[a] Fall in behind me."

[20] Again the watchman reported, "He reached them but hasn't started back. Also, the driving is like that of Jehu son of Nimshi—he drives like a madman."

[21] "Harness!" Joram shouted, and they harnessed his chariot. Then Joram king of Israel and Ahaziah king of Judah set out, each in his own chariot, and met Jehu at the plot of land of Naboth the Jezreelite. [22] When Joram saw Jehu he asked, "⌊Do you come in⌋ peace, Jehu?"

He answered, "What peace can there be as long as there is so much prostitution and witchcraft from your mother Jezebel?"

[23] Joram turned around and fled, shouting to Ahaziah, "It's treachery, Ahaziah!"

[24] Then Jehu drew his bow and shot Joram between the shoulders. The arrow went through his heart, and he slumped down in his chariot. [25] Jehu said to Bidkar his aide, "Pick him up and throw him on the plot of ground belonging to Naboth the Jezreelite. For remember when you and I were riding side by side behind his father Ahab, and the LORD uttered this •oracle against him: [26] 'As surely as I saw the blood of Naboth and the blood of his sons yesterday,' this is the LORD's message, 'so will I repay you on this plot of land,' this is the LORD's message. So now, according to the word of the LORD, pick him up and throw him on the plot of land."

[27] When King Ahaziah of Judah saw ⌊what was happening⌋, he fled up the road toward Beth-haggan. Jehu pursued him, shouting, "Shoot him too!" So they shot him in his chariot[b] at Gur Pass near Ibleam, but he fled to Megiddo and died there. [28] Then his servants carried him to Jerusalem in a chariot and buried him in his fathers' tomb in the city of David. [29] It was in the eleventh year of Joram son of Ahab that Ahaziah had become king over Judah.

Jehu Kills Jezebel

[30] When Jehu came to Jezreel, Jezebel heard about it, so she painted her eyes, adorned her head, and looked down from the window. [31] As Jehu entered the gate, she said, "⌊Do you come in⌋ peace, Zimri,[c] killer of your master?"

[32] He looked up toward the window and said, "Who is on my side? Who?" Two or three eunuchs looked down at him, [33] and he said, "Throw her down!" So they threw her down, and some of her blood splattered on the wall and on the horses, and Jehu rode over her.

[34] Then he went in, ate and drank, and said, "Take care of this cursed woman and bury her, since she's a king's daughter." [35] But when they went out to bury her, they did not find anything but her skull, her feet, and the palms of her hands. [36] So they went back and told him, and he said, "This ⌊fulfills⌋ the LORD's word that He spoke through His servant Elijah the Tishbite: 'In the plot of land at Jezreel, the dogs will eat Jezebel's flesh. [37] Jezebel's corpse will be like manure on the surface of the field in the plot of land at Jezreel so that no one will ⌊be able⌋ to say: This is Jezebel.' "

Jehu Kills the House of Ahab

10 Since Ahab had 70 sons in Samaria, Jehu wrote letters and sent them to Samaria to the rulers of Jezreel, to the elders, and to the guardians of Ahab's sons,[d] saying:

[2] When this letter arrives, since your master's sons are with you and you have chariots, horses, a fortified city, and weaponry, [3] select the most qualified[e] of your master's sons, set him on his father's throne, and fight for your master's house.

[4] However, they were terrified and reasoned, "Look, two kings couldn't stand against him; how can we?" [5] So the overseer of the palace, the overseer of the city, the elders, and the guardians sent ⌊a message⌋ to Jehu: "We are your servants, and we will do whatever you tell us. We will not make anyone king. Do whatever you think is right."[f]

[6] Then Jehu wrote them a second letter, saying:

If you are on my side, and if you will obey me, bring me the heads of your master's sons at this time tomorrow at Jezreel.

All 70 of the king's sons were being cared for by the city's prominent men. [7] When the letter came to them, they took the king's sons and slaughtered all 70, put their heads in baskets, and sent them to Jehu at Jezreel.

---

[a] **9:18,19** Lit *What to you and to peace*   [b] **9:27** LXX, Syr, some mss of Vg; Hb omits *So they shot him*   [c] **9:31** Zimri was another usurper; 1 Kg 16:8–20   [d] **10:1** LXX; MT reads *of Ahab*   [e] **10:3** Lit *the good and the upright*   [f] **10:5** Lit *Do what is good in your eyes*

---

learned that he was appointed to be king and would be the instrument of God's judgment against King Ahab and his descendants.

9:15 don't let anyone escape from the city. To succeed, Jehu's coup had to be a surprise. The celebration of verse 13 was a means of generating support for Jehu's rebellion.

9:31 Zimri. Jezebel compared Jehu to Zimri, who had killed Elah to become king of Israel.

9:36 This ⌊fulfills⌋ the LORD's word. Elijah had prophesied the terrible way that Jezebel would die (1 Kings 21:23). Her death happened just as God had promised (1 Kings 16:31–33; 18:13; 21:7–14.)

10:1-7 Killing the king was just the first step in taking the throne of Israel. Jehu would have to capture Samaria and murder Ahab's 70 sons. He played on the worst traits of the leaders of Samaria—their desire to survive at all costs. They were willing to commit mass murder against all of these

8 When the messenger came and told him, "They have brought the heads of the king's sons," the king said, "Pile them in two heaps at the entrance of the gate until morning."

9 The next morning when he went out and stood ⌊at the gate⌋, he said to all the people, "You are innocent. It was I who conspired against my master and killed him. But who struck down all these? 10 Know, then, that not a word the LORD spoke against the house of Ahab will fail, for the LORD has done what He promised through His servant Elijah." 11 So Jehu killed all who remained of the house of Ahab in Jezreel—all his great men, close friends, and priests—leaving him no survivors.

12 Then he set out and went on his way to Samaria. On the way, while he was at Beth-eked of the Shepherds, 13 Jehu met the relatives of Ahaziah king of Judah and asked, "Who are you?"

They answered, "We're Ahaziah's relatives. We've come down to greet the king's sons and the queen mother's sons."

14 Then Jehu ordered, "Take them alive." So they took them alive and then slaughtered them at the pit of Beth-eked—42 men. He didn't spare any of them.

15 When he left there, he found Jehonadab son of Rechab ⌊coming⌋ to meet him. He greeted him and then asked, "Is your heart one with mine?"a

"It is," Jehonadab replied.

Jehu said, "If it is,b give me your hand."

So he gave him his hand, and Jehu pulled him up into the chariot with him. 16 Then he said, "Come with me and see my zeal for the LORD!" So he let him ride with him in his chariot. 17 When Jehu came to Samaria, he struck down all who remained from ⌊the house of⌋ Ahab in Samaria until he had annihilated his house, according to the word of the LORD spoken to Elijah.

Jehu Kills the Baal Worshipers

18 Then Jehu brought all the people together and said to them, "Ahab served •Baal a little, but Jehu will serve him a lot. 19 Now, therefore, summon to me all the prophets of Baal, all his servants, and all his priests. None must be missing, for I have a great sacrifice for Baal. Whoever is missing will not live." However, Jehu was acting deceptively in order to destroy the servants of Baal. 20 Jehu commanded, "Consecrate a solemn assembly for Baal." So they called one.

21 Then Jehu sent ⌊messengers⌋ throughout all Israel, and all the servants of Baalc came; there was not a man left who did not come. They entered the temple of Baal,

and it was filled from one end to the other. 22 Then he said to the custodian of the wardrobe, "Bring out the garments for all the servants of Baal." So he brought out their garments.

23 Then Jehu and Jehonadab son of Rechab entered the temple of Baal, and Jehu said to the servants of Baal, "Look carefully to see that there are no servants of the LORD here among you—only servants of Baal." 24 Then they went in to offer sacrifices and •burnt offerings.

Now Jehu had stationed 80 men outside, and he warned ⌊them⌋, "Whoever allows any of the men I am delivering into your hands to escape ⌊will forfeit⌋ his life for theirs." 25 When he finished offering the •burnt offering, Jehu said to the guards and officers, "Go in and kill them. Don't let anyone out." So they struck them down with the sword. Then the guards and officers threw ⌊the bodies⌋ out and went into the inner room of the temple of Baal. 26 They brought out the pillars of the temple of Baal and burned them 27 and tore down the pillar of Baal. Then they tore down the temple of Baal and made it a latrine—⌊which it is⌋ to this day.

Evaluation of Jehu's Reign

28 Jehu eliminated Baal ⌊worship⌋ from Israel, 29 but he did not turn away from the sins that Jeroboam son of Nebat had caused Israel to commit—⌊worshiping⌋ the golden calves that were in Bethel and Dan. 30 Nevertheless, the LORD said to Jehu, "Because you have done well in carrying out what is right in My sight and have done to the house of Ahab all that was in My heart, four generations of your sons will sit on the throne of Israel."

31 Yet, Jehu was not careful to follow with all his heart the law of the LORD God of Israel. He did not turn from the sins that Jeroboam had caused Israel to commit.

32 In those days the LORD began to reduce the size of Israel. Hazael defeated the Israelites throughout their territory: 33 from the Jordan eastward, all the land of Gilead—the Gadites, the Reubenites, and the Manassites—from Aroer which is by the Arnon Valley through Gilead to Bashan.d

34 Now the rest of the events of Jehu's ⌊reign⌋, along with all his accomplishments and all his might, are written about in the Historical Record of Israel's Kings. 35 Jehu rested with his fathers, and he was buried in Samaria. His son Jehoahaz became king in his place. 36 The length of Jehu's reign over Israel in Samaria was 28 years.

a10:15 Lit heart upright like my heart is with your heart   b10:15 LXX, Syr, Vg; Hb reads mine?" Jehonadab said, "It is and it is   c10:21 LXX adds—all his priests and all his prophets—   d10:33 Lit Arnon Valley and Gilead and Bashan

sons in order to save themselves.
10:30 Because you have done well. God had chosen Jehu to carry out His vengeance against the house of Ahab. God blessed Jehu with the longest dynasty (one hundred years) of any leader of the Northern Kingdom.
10:34 the rest of the events of Jehu's

[reign]. Jehu paid tribute to the Assyrians. Israel's decline affected the balance of power in the region.
11:1-2 Athaliah was determined to kill all heirs to the throne of Judah and seize power. But King Joash's young son, was hidden away by his supporters.

11:4 commanders of hundreds. The conspiracy to install Joash as king was organized by a priest, Jehoiada, who enlisted many people to support the coup against Athaliah.
11:12 put the crown on him. The coup was staged as an official coronation. Joash was given the symbol of earthly kingship, the

Athaliah Usurps the Throne

11 When Athaliah, Ahaziah's mother, saw that her son was dead, she proceeded to annihilate all the royal heirs. ² Jehosheba, ⌊who was⌋ King Jehoram's daughter and Ahaziah's sister, secretly rescued Joash son of Ahaziah from the king's sons who were being killed and ⌊put⌋ him and his nurse in a bedroom. So he was hidden from Athaliah and was not killed. ³ Joash was in hiding with Jehosheba in the LORD's temple six years while Athaliah ruled over the land.

Athaliah Overthrown

⁴ Then, in the seventh year, Jehoiada sent ⌊messengers⌋ and brought in the commanders of hundreds, the Carites, and the guards. He had them come to him in the LORD's temple, where he made a covenant with them and put them under oath. He showed them the king's son ⁵ and commanded them, "This is what you are to do: one third of you who come on duty on the Sabbath are to provide protection for the king's palace. ⁶ A third are to be at the Sur gate and a third at the gate behind the guards. You are to take turns providing protection for the palace.ᵃ

⁷ Your two divisions that go off duty on the Sabbath are to provide protection for the LORD's temple. ⁸ You must completely surround the king with weapons in hand. Anyone who approaches the ranks is to be put to death. You must be with the king in all his daily tasks."ᵇ

⁹ So the commanders of hundreds did everything Jehoiada the priest commanded. They each brought their men—those coming on duty on the Sabbath and those going off duty—and went to Jehoiada the priest. ¹⁰ The priest gave to the commanders of hundreds King David's spears and shields that were in the LORD's temple. ¹¹ Then the guards stood with their weapons in hand surrounding the king—from the right side of the temple to the left side, by the altar and by the temple.

¹² He brought out the king's son, put the crown on him, gave him the •testimony,ᶜ and made him king. They anointed him and clapped their hands and cried, "Long live the king!"

¹³ When Athaliah heard the noise from the guard ⌊and⌋ the crowd, she went out to the people at the LORD's temple. ¹⁴ As she looked, there was the king standing by the pillar according to the custom. The commanders and the trumpeters were by the king, and all the people of the land were rejoicing and blowing trumpets. Athaliah tore her clothes and screamed "Treason! Treason!"

¹⁵ Then Jehoiada the priest ordered the commanders of hundreds in charge of the army, "Take her out between the ranks, and put anyone who follows her to death by the sword," for the priest had said, "She is not to be put to death in the LORD's temple." ¹⁶ So they arrested her, and she went out by way of the Horses' Entrance to the king's palace, where she was put to death.

Jehoiada's Reforms

¹⁷ Then Jehoiada made a covenant between the LORD, the king, and the people that they would be the LORD's people and ⌊another one⌋ between the king and the people.ᵈ ¹⁸ So all the people of the land went to the temple of •Baal and tore it down. They broke its altars and images into pieces, and they killed Mattan, the priest of Baal, at the altars.

Then ⌊Jehoiada⌋ the priest appointed guards for the LORD's temple. ¹⁹ He took ⌊with him⌋ the commanders of hundreds, the Carites, the guards, and all the people of the land, and they brought the king from the LORD's temple. They entered the king's palace by way of the guards' gate. Then Joash sat on the throne of the kings. ²⁰ All the people of the land rejoiced, and the city was quiet, for they had put Athaliah to death by the sword in the king's palace.

Judah's King Joash

12 ²¹ᵉJoashᶠ was seven years old when he became king. ¹ In the seventh year of Jehu, Joash became king; he reigned 40 years in Jerusalem. His mother's name was Zibiah, who was from Beer-sheba. ² Throughout the time Jehoiada the priest instructed him, Joash did what was right in the LORD's sight. ³ Yet the •high places were not taken away; the people continued sacrificing and burning incense on the high places.

Repairing the Temple

⁴ Then Joash said to the priests, "All the dedicated money brought to the LORD's temple, census money, money from vows, and all money voluntarily given for the LORD's temple, ⁵ each priest is to take from his assessorᵃ and repair whatever damage to the temple is found.ᵍ

⁶ But by the twenty-third year ⌊of the reign⌋ of King Joash, the priests had not repaired the damageʰ to the temple. ⁷ So King Joash called Jehoiada the priest and

---

ᵃ**11:6; 12:5** Hb obscure   ᵇ**11:8** Lit *king when he goes out and when he comes in*   ᶜ**11:12** Or *him the copy of the covenant,* or *him a diadem,* or *him jewels*   ᵈ**11:17** Some Gk versions, 2 Ch 23:16 omit *and [another one] between the king and the people*   ᵉ**11:21** 2 Kg 12:1 in Hb   ᶠ**11:21** = The LORD Has Bestowed   ᵍ**12:5** Lit *repair the breach of the house wherever there is found a breach*   ʰ**12:6** Lit *breach* in 2 Kg 12:5–12

---

crown, then proclaimed king and anointed.

11:17 covenant between the LORD, the king, and the people. The old Mosaic covenant had to be renewed before Judah could move forward as a godly nation under Joash. Also important was a renewal of covenant between king and people.

11:21 seven years old. The new king, who would carry on the lineage of David in the royal house of Judah, was a child who had been hidden away until the time was right for his coronation.

12:2 Joash did what was right. Joash was a good ruler who followed the Lord for a while. But after the priest Jehoiada died, his laxity led to the renewal of Baal worship.

12:4–5 Joash had a new financial plan for the temple. Funds given by the people were handled by assessors who would allocate funds back to priests to keep the temple in good repair.

the other priests and said, "Why haven't you repaired the temple's damage? Since you haven't, don't take any money from your assessors; instead, hand it over for the repair of the temple." 8 So the priests agreed they would not take money from the people and they would not repair the temple's damage.

9 Then Jehoiada the priest took a chest, bored a hole in its lid, and set it beside the altar on the right side as one enters the LORD's temple; in it the priests who guarded the threshold put all the money brought into the LORD's temple. 10 Whenever they saw there was a large amount of money in the chest, the king's secretary and the high priest would go to the LORD's temple and count the money found there and tie it up in bags. 11 Then they would put the counted money into the hands of those doing the work—those who oversaw the LORD's temple. They ⌊in turn⌋ would pay it out to those working on the LORD's temple—the carpenters, the builders, 12 the masons, and the stonecutters—and ⌊would use it⌋ to buy timber and quarried stone to repair the damage to the LORD's temple and for all spending for temple repairs.

13 However, no silver bowls, wick trimmers, sprinkling basins, trumpets, or any articles of gold or silver were made for the LORD's temple from the money brought into the temple. 14 Instead, it was given to those doing the work, and they repaired the LORD's temple with it. 15 No accounting was required from the men who received the money to pay those doing the work, since they worked with integrity. 16 The money from the •restitution offering and the •sin offering was not brought to the LORD's temple since it belonged to the priests.

Aramean Invasion of Judah

17 At that time Hazael king of Aram marched up and fought against Gath and captured it. Then he planned to attack Jerusalem. 18 So King Joash of Judah took all the consecrated items that his ancestors—Judah's kings Jehoshaphat, Jehoram, and Ahaziah—had consecrated, along with his own consecrated items and all the gold found in the treasuries of the LORD's temple and in the king's palace, and he sent ⌊them⌋ to Hazael king of Aram. Then Hazael withdrew from Jerusalem.

Joash Assassinated

19 The rest of the events of Joash's ⌊reign⌋, along with all his accomplishments, are written about in the Historical Record of Judah's Kings. 20 Joash's servants conspired against him and killed him at Beth-millo ⌊on the road that⌋ goes down to Silla. 21 His servants Jozabad[a]

son of Shimeath and Jehozabad son of Shomer struck him down, and he died. Then they buried him with his fathers in the city of David, and his son Amaziah became king in his place.

Israel's King Jehoahaz

13 In the twenty-third year of Judah's King Joash son of Ahaziah, Jehoahaz son of Jehu became king over Israel in Samaria; ⌊he reigned⌋ 17 years. 2 He did what was evil in the LORD's sight and followed the sins that Jeroboam son of Nebat had caused Israel to commit; he did not turn away from them. 3 So the LORD's anger burned against Israel, and He surrendered them to the power of Hazael king of Aram and his son Ben-hadad during their reigns.

4 Then Jehoahaz sought the LORD's favor, and the LORD heard him, for He saw the oppression the king of Aram inflicted on Israel. 5 Therefore, the LORD gave Israel a deliverer, and they escaped from the power of the Arameans. Then the people of Israel dwelt in their tents as before, 6 but they didn't turn away from the sins that the house of Jeroboam had caused Israel to commit. Jehoahaz walked in them, and the •Asherah pole also remained standing in Samaria. 7 Jehoahaz did not have an army left, except for 50 horsemen, 10 chariots, and 10,000 foot soldiers, because the king of Aram had destroyed them, making them like dust at threshing.

8 The rest of the events of Jehoahaz's ⌊reign⌋, along with all his accomplishments and his might, are written about in the Historical Record of Israel's Kings. 9 Jehoahaz rested with his fathers, and he was buried in Samaria. His son Jehoash[b] became king in his place.

Israel's King Jehoash

10 In the thirty-seventh year of Judah's King Joash, Jehoash son of Jehoahaz became king over Israel in Samaria; ⌊he reigned⌋ 16 years. 11 He did what was evil in the LORD's sight. He did not turn away from all the sins that Jeroboam son of Nebat had caused Israel to commit, but he walked in them.

12 The rest of the events of Jehoash's ⌊reign⌋, along with all his accomplishments and the power he had to wage war against Judah's King Amaziah, are written about in the Historical Record of Israel's Kings. 13 Jehoash rested with his fathers, and Jeroboam sat on his throne. Jehoash was buried in Samaria with the kings of Israel.

Elisha's Death

14 When Elisha became sick with the illness that he died from, Jehoash king of Israel went down and wept

---

[a] 12:21 Many Hb mss, LXX read Jozacar; 2 Ch 24:26 reads Zabad   [b] 13:9 = Joash

---

12:9-13 Public confidence in the funding process for the temple grew. So did the offerings.

12:17 Hazael ... planned to attack Jerusalem. King Hazael of Damascus captured the Philistine city of Gath, then turned toward Jerusalem.

12:18-20 Joash used the temple treasuries to

pay off Hazael and forestall the attack. His outrageous acts led his own officials to assassinate him while he was asleep.

13:3 Ben-hadad. Like his father before him, this Ben-hadad was also used as an instrument of God's punishment against the Northern Kingdom.

13:5 the LORD gave Israel a deliverer. Israel was able to break the Aramean stranglehold during the reigns of Jehoash and Jeroboam II.

13:14 the chariots and horsemen of Israel! This exclamation by King Jehoash recognized that God was the real strength of Israel.

13:16 Elisha put his hands on the king's

over him and said, "My father, my father, the chariots and horsemen of Israel!"

15 Elisha responded, "Take a bow and arrows." So he got a bow and arrows. 16 Then Elisha said to the king of Israel, "Put your hand on the bow." So the king put his hand on it, and Elisha put his hands on the king's hands. 17 Elisha said, "Open the east window." So he opened it. Elisha said, "Shoot!" So he shot. Then Elisha said, "The LORD's arrow of victory, yes, the arrow of victory over Aram. You are to strike down the Arameans in Aphek until you have put an end to them."

18 Then Elisha said, "Take the arrows!" So he took them, and he said to the king of Israel, "Strike the ground!" So he struck the ground three times and stopped. 19 The man of God was angry with him and said, "You should have struck the ground five or six times. Then you would have struck down Aram until you had put an end to them, but now you will only strike down Aram three times." 20 Then Elisha died and was buried.

Now marauding bands of Moabites used to come into the land in the spring of the year. 21 Once, as the Israelites were burying a man, suddenly they saw a marauding band, so they threw the man into Elisha's tomb. When he touched Elisha's bones, the man revived and stood up!

God's Mercy on Israel

22 Hazael king of Aram oppressed Israel throughout the reign of Jehoahaz, 23 but the LORD was gracious to them and had compassion on them and turned toward them because of His covenant with Abraham, Isaac, and Jacob. He was not willing to destroy them. Even now He has not banished them from His presence.

24 King Hazael of Aram died, and his son Ben-hadad became king in his place. 25 Then Jehoash son of Jehoahaz took back from Ben-hadad son of Hazael the cities that Hazael had taken in war from Jehoash's father Jehoahaz. Jehoash defeated Ben-hadad three times and recovered the cities of Israel.

Judah's King Amaziah

14 In the second year of Israel's King Jehoash[a] son of Jehoahaz,[b] Amaziah son of Joash became king of Judah. 2 He was 25 years old when he became king; he reigned 29 years in Jerusalem. His mother's name was Jehoaddan[c] and was from Jerusalem. 3 He did what was right in the LORD's sight, but not like his ancestor David. He did everything his father Joash had done. 4 Yet, the •high places were not taken away, and the people continued sacrificing and burning incense on the high places.

5 As soon as the kingdom was firmly in his grasp, Amaziah killed his servants who had murdered his father the king. 6 However, he did not put the children of the murderers to death, as it is written in the book of the law of Moses where the LORD commanded, "Fathers must not be put to death because of children, and children must not be put to death because of fathers; instead, each one will be put to death for his own sin."

7 Amaziah killed 10,000 Edomites in the Valley of Salt. He took Sela in battle and called it Joktheel, ⌊which is its name⌋ to this very day. 8 Amaziah then sent messengers to Jehoash son of Jehoahaz, son of Jehu, king of Israel, saying, "Come, let us meet face to face."

9 King Jehoash of Israel sent ⌊word⌋ to Amaziah king of Judah, saying, "The thistle that was in Lebanon once sent ⌊a message⌋ to the cedar that was in Lebanon, saying, 'Give your daughter to my son as a wife.' Then a wild animal that was in Lebanon passed by and trampled the thistle. 10 You have indeed defeated Edom, and you have become overconfident. Enjoy your glory and stay at home. Why should you stir up such trouble that you fall—you and Judah with you?"

11 But Amaziah would not listen, so King Jehoash of Israel advanced. He and King Amaziah of Judah faced off at Beth-shemesh that belongs to Judah. 12 Judah was routed before Israel, and ⌊Judah's men⌋ fled, each to his own tent. 13 King Jehoash of Israel captured Judah's King Amaziah son of Joash,[d] son of Ahaziah, at Beth-shemesh. Then Jehoash went to Jerusalem and broke down 200 yards[e] of Jerusalem's wall from the Ephraim Gate to the Corner Gate. 14 He took all the gold and silver and all the utensils found in the LORD's temple and in the treasuries of the king's palace, and the hostages. Then he returned to Samaria.

Jehoash's Death

15 The rest of the events of Jehoash's ⌊reign⌋, along with his accomplishments, his might, and how he waged war against Amaziah king of Judah, are written about in the Historical Record of Israel's Kings. 16 Jehoash rested with his fathers, and he was buried in Samaria with the kings of Israel. His son Jeroboam became king in his place.

Amaziah's Death

17 Judah's King Amaziah son of Joash lived 15 years after the death of Israel's King Jehoash son of Jehoahaz.

---

[a]14:1 = Joash   [b]14:1 = Joahaz   [c]14:2 Alt Hb tradition, many Hb mss, Syr, Tg, Vg, 2 Ch 25:1; MT, LXX read *Jehoaddin*   [d]14:13 = Jehoash
[e]14:13 Lit *400 cubits*

---

hands. By holding the bow with King Jehoash, Elisha demonstrated that God would give him victory over the Arameans.

13:21 the man revived and stood up. Even in death, Elisha's bones were able to transmit God's power (4:32–35).

13:23 covenant. Israel deserved the full punishment prescribed in the law for disobedience to the covenant, but God was full of mercy and grace toward His people.

14:3 not like his ancestor David. King Jeroboam promoted idol worship. David was considered the ideal king who was faithful to God in all ways.

14:7 Amaziah killed 10,000 Edomites. Edom had rebelled successfully against Judah in King Jehoram's time. Amaziah defeated the Edomites.

14:8 Come, let us meet face to face. Feeling bold after his victory over the Edomites, Amaziah challenged the Northern Kingdom to bat-

18 The rest of the events of Amaziah's ⌊reign⌋ are written about in the Historical Record of Judah's Kings. 19 A conspiracy was formed against him in Jerusalem, and he fled to Lachish. However, ⌊men⌋ were sent after him to Lachish, and they put him to death there. 20 They carried him back on horses, and he was buried in Jerusalem with his fathers in the city of David.

21 Then all the people of Judah took Azariah,[a] who was 16 years old, and made him king in place of his father Amaziah. 22 He rebuilt Elath[b] and restored it to Judah after ⌊Amaziah⌋ the king rested with his fathers.

Israel's King Jeroboam

23 In the fifteenth year of Judah's King Amaziah son of Joash, Jeroboam son of Jehoash[c] became king of Israel in Samaria; he reigned 41 years. 24 He did what was evil in the LORD's sight. He did not turn away from all the sins Jeroboam son of Nebat had caused Israel to commit.

25 It was he who restored Israel's border from Lebo-hamath as far as the Sea of the •Arabah, according to the word the LORD, the God of Israel, had spoken through His servant, the prophet Jonah son of Amittai from Gath-hepher. 26 For the LORD saw that the affliction of Israel was very bitter. There was no one to help Israel, neither bond nor free. 27 However, the LORD had not said He would blot out the name of Israel from under heaven, so He delivered them by the hand of Jeroboam son of Jehoash.[c]

28 The rest of the events of Jeroboam's ⌊reign⌋—along with all his accomplishments and the power he had to wage war and how he recovered for Israel Damascus and Hamath, which had belonged to Judah—are written about in the Historical Record of Israel's Kings. 29 Jeroboam rested with his fathers, the kings of Israel. His son Zechariah became king in his place.

Judah's King Azariah

15 In the twenty-seventh year of Israel's King Jeroboam, Azariah[d] son of Amaziah became king of Judah. 2 He was 16 years old when he became king; he reigned 52 years in Jerusalem. His mother's name was Jecoliah; ⌊she was⌋ from Jerusalem. 3 Azariah did what was right in the LORD's sight just as his father Amaziah had done. 4 Yet, the •high places were not taken away; the people continued sacrificing and burning incense on the high places.

5 The LORD afflicted the king, and he had a serious skin disease until the day of his death. He lived in a sep-

arate house,[e] while Jotham, the king's son, was over the household governing the people of the land.

6 The rest of the events of Azariah's ⌊reign⌋, along with all his accomplishments, are written about in the Historical Record of Judah's Kings. 7 Azariah rested with his fathers, and he was buried with his fathers in the city of David. His son Jotham became king in his place.

Israel's King Zechariah

8 In the thirty-eighth year of Judah's King Azariah, Zechariah son of Jeroboam became king over Israel in Samaria for six months. 9 He did what was evil in the LORD's sight as his fathers had done. He did not turn away from the sins Jeroboam son of Nebat had caused Israel to commit.

10 Shallum son of Jabesh conspired against Zechariah. He struck him down publicly,[f] killed him, and became king in his place. 11 As for the rest of the events of Zechariah's ⌊reign⌋, they are written about in the Historical Record of Israel's Kings. 12 The word of the LORD that He spoke to Jehu was, "Four generations of your sons will sit on the throne of Israel." And it was so.

Israel's King Shallum

13 In the thirty-ninth year of Judah's King Uzziah, Shallum son of Jabesh became king; he reigned in Samaria a full month. 14 Then Menahem son of Gadi came up from Tirzah to Samaria and struck down Shallum son of Jabesh there. He killed him and became king in his place. 15 As for the rest of the events of Shallum's ⌊reign⌋, along with the conspiracy that he formed, they are written about in the Historical Record of Israel's Kings.

Israel's King Menahem

16 At that time, ⌊starting⌋ from Tirzah, Menahem attacked Tiphsah, all who were in it, and its territory. Because they wouldn't surrender, he attacked ⌊it and⌋ ripped open all the pregnant women.

17 In the thirty-ninth year of Judah's King Azariah, Menahem son of Gadi became king over Israel; ⌊he reigned⌋ 10 years in Samaria. 18 He did what was evil in the LORD's sight. Throughout his reign, he did not turn away from the sins Jeroboam son of Nebat had caused Israel to commit.

19 Pul[g] king of Assyria invaded the land, so Menahem gave Pul 75,000 pounds[h] of silver so that Pul would support him to strengthen his grip on the kingdom. 20 Then Menahem exacted 20 ounces[i] of silver from

---

[a]14:21 = Uzziah in 2 Ch 26:1   [b]14:22 = Eloth in 2 Ch 26:2   [c]14:23,27 = Joash   [d]15:1 = Uzziah in 2 Ch   [e]15:5 Lit *a house of freedom* or *of exemption*   [f]15:10 Hb uncertain; some emend to *at Ibleam*, as some LXX mss read; Hb could mean *at Kabal-am.*   [g]15:19 = Tiglath-pileser   [h]15:19 Lit *1,000 talents*   [i]15:20 Lit *50 shekels*

---

tle. Military mercenaries hired by Israel killed three thousand people of Judah and plundered property (2 Chron. 25:10–17).

14:28 recovered for Israel Damascus and Hamath. These cities had been under David's rule but were lost to Syria. King Jeroboam finally brought them back under Israel's control.

15:6 Azariah's [reign], along with all his accomplishments. Azariah increased Judah's military strength and improved the organization of its government.

15:12 And it was so. Jehu had destroyed the worshipers of Baal in Ahab's wicked kingdom. God had promised Jehu that his dynasty

would continue for four generations, and it did so.

15:20 from each of the wealthy men of Israel. Rather than fight the Assyrians, King Menahem of Israel paid them off with a bribe.

15:30 Hoshea. This king of Israel aligned himself with Assyria. In fact, the king of Assyria

each of the wealthy men of Israel to give to the king of Assyria. So the king of Assyria withdrew and did not stay there in the land.

21 The rest of the events of Menahem's ⌊reign⌋, along with all his accomplishments, are written about in the Historical Record of Israel's Kings. 22 Menahem rested with his fathers, and his son Pekahiah became king in his place.

Israel's King Pekahiah

23 In the fiftieth year of Judah's King Azariah, Pekahiah son of Menahem became king over Israel in Samaria; ⌊he reigned⌋ two years. 24 He did what was evil in the LORD's sight and did not turn away from the sins Jeroboam son of Nebat had caused Israel to commit.

25 Then his officer, Pekah son of Remaliah, conspired against him and struck him down, as well as Argob and Arieh,a in Samaria at the citadel of the king's palace. There were 50 Gileadite men with Pekah. He killed Pekahiah and became king in his place.

26 As for the rest of the events of Pekahiah's ⌊reign⌋, along with all his accomplishments, they are written about in the Historical Record of Israel's Kings.

Israel's King Pekah

27 In the fifty-second year of Judah's King Azariah, Pekah son of Remaliah became king over Israel in Samaria; ⌊he reigned⌋ 20 years. 28 He did what was evil in the LORD's sight. He did not turn away from the sins Jeroboam son of Nebat had caused Israel to commit.

29 In the days of Pekah king of Israel, Tiglath-pileser king of Assyria came and captured Ijon, Abel-beth-maacah, Janoah, Kedesh, Hazor, Gilead, and Galilee—all the land of Naphtali—and deported the people to Assyria.

30 Then Hoshea son of Elah organized a conspiracy against Pekah son of Remaliah. He attacked him, killed him, and became king in his place in the twentieth year of Jotham son of Uzziah.

31 As for the rest of the events of Pekah's ⌊reign⌋, along with all his accomplishments, they are written about in the Historical Record of Israel's Kings.

Judah's King Jotham

32 In the second year of Israel's King Pekah son of Remaliah, Jotham son of Uzziah became king of Judah. 33 He was 25 years old when he became king; he reigned 16 years in Jerusalem. His mother's name was Jerusha daughter of Zadok. 34 He did what was right in the LORD's sight just as his father Uzziah had done. 35 Yet, the high places were not taken away; the people

continued sacrificing and burning incense on the high places.

It was Jotham who built the Upper Gate of the LORD's temple. 36 The rest of the events of Jotham's ⌊reign⌋, along with all his accomplishments, are written about in the Historical Record of Judah's Kings. 37 In those days the LORD began sending Rezin king of Aram and Pekah son of Remaliah against Judah. 38 Jotham rested with his fathers, and he was buried with his fathers in the city of his ancestor David. His son Ahaz became king in his place.

Judah's King Ahaz

16 In the seventeenth year of Pekah son of Remaliah, Ahaz son of Jotham became king of Judah. 2 Ahaz was 20 years old when he became king; he reigned 16 years in Jerusalem. He did not do what was right in the sight of the LORD his God like his ancestor David 3 but walked in the way of the kings of Israel. He even made his son pass through the fire,b imitating the abominations of the nations the LORD had dispossessed before the Israelites. 4 He sacrificed and burned incense on the •high places, on the hills, and under every green tree.

5 Then Aram's King Rezin and Israel's King Pekah son of Remaliah came to wage war against Jerusalem. They besieged Ahaz but were not able to conquer him. 6 At that time Rezin king of Aram recovered Elath for Aram and expelled the Judahites from Elath. Then the Arameans came to Elath, and they live there until today.

7 So Ahaz sent messengers to Tiglath-pileser king of Assyria, saying, "I am your servant and your son. March up and save me from the power of the king of Aram and of the king of Israel, who are rising up against me." 8 Ahaz also took the silver and gold found in the LORD's temple and in the treasuries of the king's palace and sent ⌊them⌋ to the king of Assyria as a gift. 9 So the king of Assyria listened to him and marched up to Damascus and captured it. He deported its people to Kir but put Rezin to death.

Ahaz's Idolatry

10 King Ahaz went to Damascus to meet Tiglath-pileser king of Assyria. When he saw the altar that was in Damascus, King Ahaz sent a model of the altar and complete plans for its construction to Uriah the priest. 11 Uriah built the altar according to all ⌊the instructions⌋ King Ahaz sent from Damascus. Therefore, by the time King Ahaz came back from Damascus, Uriah the priest had made it. 12 When the king came back from Damascus, he saw the

---

a15:25 Hb obscure   b16:3 Either a Canaanite cult practice or child sacrifice

---

15:35 **Upper Gate.** The restoration of the temple's Upper Gate was one of Jotham's greatest accomplishments. But he failed to remove the high places—areas designated for the worship of false gods.

15:37 **Rezin ... Pekah.** The alliance of King

claimed to have established Hoshea's rule.

Pekah of Israel with Rezin, king of Aram, strengthened his position against Judah.

16:2 **like his ancestor David.** King David was the standard of excellence for Judah's kings. Ahaz did not measure up.

16:3 **made his son pass through the fire.** God had forbidden His people to participate in

child sacrifice, yet the king of Judah succumbed to this terrible sin.

16:7 **Ahaz sent messengers.** Since Aram and Israel were uniting against Assyria, Assyria was a likely candidate for an alignment with Judah.

16:8 **found in the LORD's temple.** Ahaz fol-

altar. Then he approached the altar and ascended it. ¹³ He offered his •burnt offering and his •grain offering, poured out his drink offering, and sprinkled the blood of his •fellowship offerings on the altar. ¹⁴ He took the bronze altar that was before the LORD in front of the temple between ⌊his⌋ altar and the LORD's temple, and put it on the north side of ⌊his⌋ altar.

¹⁵ Then King Ahaz commanded Uriah the priest, "Offer on the great altar the morning burnt offering, the evening grain offering, and the king's burnt offering and his grain offering. ⌊Also offer⌋ the burnt offering of all the people of the land, their grain offering, and their drink offerings. Sprinkle on the altar all the blood of the burnt offering and all the blood of sacrifice. The bronze altar will be for me to seek guidance."ᵃ ¹⁶ Uriah the priest did everything King Ahaz commanded.

¹⁷ Then King Ahaz cut off the frames of the water cartsᵇ and removed the bronze basin from ⌊each of⌋ them. He took the reservoirᶜ from the bronze oxen that were under it and put it on a stone pavement. ¹⁸ To satisfy the king of Assyria, he removed from the LORD's temple the Sabbath canopy they had built in the palace, and ⌊he closed⌋ the outer entrance for the king.

Ahaz's Death

¹⁹ The rest of the events of Ahaz's ⌊reign⌋, along with his accomplishments, are written about in the Historical Record of Judah's Kings. ²⁰ Ahaz rested with his fathers and was buried with his fathers in the city of David, and his son Hezekiah became king in his place.

Israel's King Hoshea

17 In the twelfth year of Judah's King Ahaz, Hoshea son of Elah became king over Israel in Samaria; ⌊he reigned⌋ nine years. ² He did what was evil in the LORD's sight, but not like the kings of Israel who preceded him.

³ Shalmaneser king of Assyria attacked him, and Hoshea became his vassal and paid him tribute money. ⁴ But the king of Assyria discovered a conspiracy by Hoshea—he had sent envoys to So king of Egypt and had not paid tribute money to the king of Assyria as in previous years.ᵈ Therefore, the king of Assyria arrested him and put him in prison. ⁵ Then the king of Assyria invaded the whole land, marched up to Samaria, and besieged it for three years.

The Fall of Samaria

⁶ In the ninth year of Hoshea, the king of Assyria captured Samaria. He deported the Israelites to Assyria and settled them in Halah and by the Habor, Gozan's river, and in the cities of the Medes.

Why Israel Fell

⁷ ⌊This disaster⌋ happened because the people of Israel had sinned against the LORD their God who had brought them out of the land of Egypt from the power of Pharaoh king of Egypt and because they had worshipedᵉ other gods. ⁸ They had lived according to the customs of the nations that the LORD had dispossessed before the Israelites and the customs the kings of Israel had introduced. ⁹ The Israelites secretly did what was not rightᶠ against the LORD their God. They built •high places in all their towns from watchtower to fortified city. ¹⁰ They set up for themselves sacred pillars and •Asherah poles on every high hill and under every green tree. ¹¹ They burned incense on all the high places just like those nations that the LORD had driven out before them. They did evil things, provoking the LORD. ¹² They served idols, although the LORD had told them, "You must not do this." ¹³ Still, the LORD warned Israel and Judah through every prophet and every seer, saying, "Turn from your evil ways and keep My commandments and statutes according to all the law I commanded your ancestors and sent to you through My servants the prophets."

¹⁴ But they would not listen. Instead, they became obstinate likeᵍ their ancestors who did not believe the LORD their God. ¹⁵ They rejected His statutes and His covenant He had made with their ancestors and the warnings He had given them. They pursued worthless idols and became worthless themselves, following the surrounding nations the LORD had commanded them not to imitate.

¹⁶ They abandoned all the commandments of the LORD their God. They made for themselves molded images—even two calves—and an Asherah pole. They worshiped the whole heavenly •host and served •Baal. ¹⁷ They made their sons and daughters pass through the fire and practiced •divination and interpreted omens. They devoted themselves to do what was evil in the LORD's sight and provoked Him.

¹⁸ Therefore, the LORD was very angry with Israel, and He removed them from His presence. Only the tribe of Judah remained. ¹⁹ Even Judah did not keep the commandments of the LORD their God but lived according to the customs Israel had introduced. ²⁰ So the LORD rejected all the descendants of Israel, afflicted them, and handed them over to plunderers until He had banished them from His presence.

ᵃ**16:15** Hb obscure ᵇ**16:17** Lit *the stands* ᶜ**16:17** Lit *sea* ᵈ**17:4** Lit *as year by year* ᵉ**17:7** Lit *feared* ᶠ**17:9** Or *Israelites spoke untrue words* ᵍ**17:14** Lit *they stiffened their neck like the neck of*

---

lowed the example of King Joash, who had used the temple wealth to pay tribute to Hazael of Damascus (12:17–18). The treasures that Ahaz paid to Assyria had probably been restored during Jotham's reign.

16:13–14 King Ahaz placed his new altar in the most prominent place in the temple. This reflected the priority he placed on his alliance with Assyria.

17:5 besieged it for three years. Samaria, capital of Israel, was fortified with a massive defensive wall.

17:6 deported. This deportation to a foreign nation had been prophesied to Jeroboam, the first ruler of the Northern Kingdom (1 Kings 14:5–11).

17:7 they had worshiped other gods. Israel's chief betrayal in their covenant with God was worship of pagan gods.

17:16–17 abandoned all the commandments. God consistently reminded the people

Summary of Israel's History

21 When the LORD tore Israel from the house of David, Israel made Jeroboam son of Nebat king. Then Jeroboam led Israel away from following the LORD and caused them to commit great sin. 22 The Israelites persisted in all the sins that Jeroboam committed and did not turn away from them. 23 Finally, the LORD removed Israel from His presence just as He had declared through all His servants the prophets. So Israel has been exiled to Assyria from their homeland until today.

Foreign Refugees in Israel

24 Then the king of Assyria brought ⌊people⌋ from Babylon, Cuthah, Avva, Hamath, and Sepharvaim and settled them in place of the Israelites in the cities of Samaria. The settlers took possession of Samaria and lived in its cities. 25 When they first lived there, they did not •fear the LORD. So the LORD sent lions among them, which killed some of them. 26 The settlers spoke to the king of Assyria, saying, "The nations that you have deported and placed in the cities of Samaria do not know the custom of the God of the land. Therefore, He has sent lions among them, which are killing them because the people don't know the custom of the God of the land."

27 Then the king of Assyria issued a command: "Send back one of the priests you deported. Have him go and live there so he can teach them the custom of the God of the land." 28 So one of the priests they had deported came and lived in Bethel, and he began to teach them how they should fear the LORD.

29 But ⌊the people of⌋ each nation, in the cities where they lived, were still making their own gods and putting them in the shrines of the high places that the Samaritans had made. 30 The men of Babylon made Succoth-benoth, the men of Cuth made Nergal, the men of Hamath made Ashima, 31 the Avvites made Nibhaz and Tartak, and the Sepharvites burned their children in the fire to Adrammelech and Anammelech, the gods of the Sepharvaim. 32 So they feared the LORD, but they also appointed from their number, priests to serve them in the shrines of the high places. 33 They feared the LORD, but they also worshiped their own gods according to the custom of the nations where they had been deported from.

34 They are ⌊still⌋ practicing the former customs to this day. None of them fear the LORD or observe their statutes and ordinances, the law and commandments the LORD commanded the descendants of Jacob; He renamed him Israel. 35 The LORD made a covenant with them and commanded them, "Do not fear other gods; do not bow down to them; do not serve them; do not sacrifice to them. 36 Instead, fear the LORD, who brought you from the land of Egypt with great power and an outstretched arm. You are to bow down to Him, and you are to sacrifice to Him. 37 You are to be careful always to observe the statutes, the ordinances, the laws, and the commandment He wrote for you; do not fear other gods. 38 Do not forget the covenant that I have made with you. Do not fear other gods, 39 but fear the LORD your God, and He will deliver you from the hand of all your enemies."

40 However, they would not listen but continued practicing their former custom. 41 These nations feared the LORD but also served their idols. Their children and grandchildren continue doing as their fathers did until today.

Judah's King Hezekiah

18 In the third year of Israel's King Hoshea son of Elah, Hezekiah son of Ahaz became king of Judah. 2 He was 25 years old when he became king; he reigned 29 years in Jerusalem. His mother's name was Abi[a] daughter of Zechariah. 3 He did what was right in the LORD's sight just as his ancestor David had done. 4 He removed the •high places and shattered the sacred pillars and cut down the •Asherah ⌊poles⌋. He broke into pieces the bronze snake that Moses made, for the Israelites burned incense to it up to that time. He called it Nehushtan.[b]

5 Hezekiah trusted in the LORD God of Israel; not one of the kings of Judah was like him, either before him or after him. 6 He held fast to the LORD and did not turn from following Him but kept the commandments the LORD had commanded Moses.

7 The LORD was with him, and wherever he went, he prospered. He rebelled against the king of Assyria and did not serve him. 8 He defeated the Philistines as far as Gaza and its borders, from watchtower to fortified city.

Review of Israel's Fall

9 In the fourth year of King Hezekiah, which was the seventh year of Israel's King Hoshea son of Elah, Shalmaneser king of Assyria marched against Samaria and besieged it. 10 The Assyrians captured it at the end of three years. In the sixth year of Hezekiah, which was the ninth year of Israel's King Hoshea, Samaria was captured. 11 The king of Assyria deported the Israelites to Assyria and put them in Halah and by the Habor, Gozan's river, and in the cities of the Medes, 12 because they did not listen to the voice of the LORD their God

---

a**18:2** = Abijah in 2 Ch 29:1   b**18:4** = A bronze thing

---

not to take on the worship practices of the Canaanites. But they refused to listen.

17:24 settled them in place of the Israelites. The Assyrians deported the most influential Israelites and replaced them with citizens who were loyal to Assyria.

17:25 lions. The lions, much like the frogs in Egypt (Ex. 8) and the rats in Philista (1 Sam. 5–6), represented a plague of God to the new inhabitants in Samaria.

17:29–33 Samaria became a melting-pot culture, combining the truth of God with popular religions of the day.

17:41 children and grandchildren. God commanded His people to teach their children about His deliverance (Deut. 6:4–9). But they continued to participate in idol worship.

18:1–2 Hezekiah. At age 11, Hezekiah began serving as king under his father, Ahaz.

18:4 bronze snake. Other righteous kings of Judah had destroyed the idols used in false

but violated His covenant—all He had commanded Moses the servant of the LORD. They did not listen, and they did not obey.

Sennacherib's Invasion

13 In the fourteenth year of King Hezekiah, Sennacherib king of Assyria attacked all the fortified cities of Judah and captured them. 14 So Hezekiah king of Judah sent word to the king of Assyria at Lachish, saying, "I have done wrong. Withdraw from me. Whatever you demand from me, I will pay." The king of Assyria demanded from King Hezekiah of Judah 11 tonsᵃ of silver and one tonᵇ of gold. 15 So Hezekiah gave ⌊him⌋ all the silver found in the LORD's temple and in the treasuries of the king's palace.

16 At that time Hezekiah stripped ⌊the gold from⌋ the doors of the LORD's sanctuary and from the doorposts he had overlaid and gave it to the king of Assyria.

17 Then the king of Assyria sent the Tartan, the Rabsaris, and the •Rabshakeh,ᶜ along with a massive army, from Lachish to King Hezekiah at Jerusalem. They advanced and came to Jerusalem, andᵈ they took their position by the aqueduct of the upper pool, which is by the highway to the Fuller's Field. 18 Then they called for the king, but Eliakim son of Hilkiah, who was in charge of the palace, Shebnah the court secretary, and Joah son of Asaph, the court historian, came out to them.

The Rabshakeh's Speech

19 Then the Rabshakeh said to them, "Tell Hezekiah this is what the great king, the king of Assyria, says: 'What are you relying on?ᵉ 20 You think mere words are strategy and strength for war. What are you now relying on so that you have rebelled against me? 21 Look, you now trust in Egypt, the stalk of this splintered reed, which if a man leans on it will go into his palm and pierce it. This is how Pharaoh king of Egypt is to all who trust in him. 22 Suppose you say to me: We trust in the LORD our God. Isn't He the One whose high places and altars Hezekiah has removed, saying to Judah and to Jerusalem: You must worship at this altar in Jerusalem?'

23 "So now make a bargain with my master the king of Assyria. I'll give you 2,000 horses if you're able to supply riders for them! 24 How then can you drive back a single officer among the least of my master's servants and trust in Egypt for chariots and for horsemen? 25 Have I attacked this place to destroy it without the LORD's ⌊approval⌋? The LORD said to me, 'Attack this land and destroy it.'"

26 Then Eliakim son of Hilkiah, Shebnah, and Joah said to the Rabshakeh, "Please speak to your servants in Aramaic, since we understand ⌊it⌋. Don't speak with us in Hebrewᶠ within earshot of the people on the wall."

27 But the Rabshakeh said to them, "Has my master sent me only to your master and to you to speak these words? Hasn't ⌊he⌋ also ⌊sent me⌋ to the men who sit on the wall, ⌊destined⌋ with you to eat their own excrement and drink their own urine?"

28 The Rabshakeh stood and called out loudly in Hebrew.ᶠ Then he spoke: "Hear the word of the great king, the king of Assyria. 29 This is what the king says: 'Don't let Hezekiah deceive you; he can't deliver you from my hand. 30 Don't let Hezekiah persuade you to trust in the LORD by saying: Certainly the LORD will deliver us! This city will not be handed over to the king of Assyria.'

31 "Don't listen to Hezekiah, for this is what the king of Assyria says: 'Make peaceᵍ with me and surrender to me. Then every one of you may eat from his own vine and his own fig tree, and every one may drink water from his own cistern 32 until I come and take you away to a land like your own land—a land of grain and new wine, a land of bread and vineyards, a land of olive trees and honey—so that you may live and not die. But don't listen to Hezekiah when he misleads you, saying: The LORD will deliver us. 33 Has any of the gods of the nations ever delivered his land from the power of the king of Assyria? 34 Where are the gods of Hamath and Arpad? Where are the gods of Sepharvaim, Hena, and Ivvah?ʰ Have they delivered Samaria from my hand? 35 Who among all the gods of the lands has delivered his land from my power? So how is the LORD to deliver Jerusalem?'"

36 But the people kept silent; they answered him not a word, for the king's command was, "Don't answer him." 37 Then Eliakim son of Hilkiah, who was in charge of the palace, Shebna the court secretary, and Joah son of Asaph, the court historian, came to Hezekiah with their clothes torn and reported to him the words of the Rabshakeh.

Hezekiah Seeks Isaiah's Counsel

19 When King Hezekiah heard ⌊their report⌋, he tore his clothes, covered himself with •sackcloth, and went into the LORD's temple. 2 Then he sent Eliakim, who was in charge of the palace, Shebna the court secretary, and the elders of the priests, covered with sackcloth, to the prophet Isaiah son of Amoz.

ᵃ18:14 Lit 300 talents ᵇ18:14 Lit 30 talents ᶜ18:17 Assyrian military titles ᵈ18:17 LXX, Syr, Vg; MT reads and came and ᵉ18:19 Lit What is this trust which you trust ᶠ18:26,28 Lit Judahite ᵍ18:31 Lit a blessing ʰ18:34 Some LXX, Vg mss read Sepharvaim? Where are the gods of the land of Samaria?

---

worship. Hezekiah destroyed even this artifact made by Moses. It had become an idol to the Israelites.

18:7 rebelled against ... Assyria. During Ahaz's reign, Judah had became a vassal of Assyria. But Hezekiah refused to pay tribute to Assyria and to recognize its pagan gods.

18:14–16 Hezekiah refused at first to pay tribute to Assyria. But he eventually gave in and raided his own holdings as well as the temple treasures to pacify his Assyrian overseers.

18:23 I'll give you 2,000 horses. This statement implies that Judah's army was inferior to the Assyrian army.

18:26 speak to your servants in Aramaic. Only the most educated people understood Aramaic. The leaders of Judah were hoping that if they switched to Aramaic, the townspeople listening from the wall wouldn't be able to understand the conversation. This might cause them to grow discouraged.

³ They said to him, "This is what Hezekiah says: 'Today is a day of distress, rebuke, and disgrace, for children have come to the point of birth, but there is no strength to deliver [them]. ⁴ Perhaps the LORD your God will hear all the words of the •Rabshakeh, whom his master the king of Assyria sent to mock the living God, and will rebuke [him for] the words that the LORD your God has heard. Therefore, offer a prayer for the surviving remnant.'"

⁵ So the servants of King Hezekiah went to Isaiah, ⁶ who said to them, "Tell your master this, 'The LORD says: Don't be afraid because of the words you have heard, that the king of Assyria's attendants have blasphemed Me with. ⁷ I am about to put a spirit in him, and he will hear a rumor and return to his own land where I will cause him to fall by the sword.'"

Sennacherib's Departing Threat

⁸ When the Rabshakeh heard that the king of Assyria had left Lachish, he returned and found him fighting against Libnah. ⁹ The king had heard this about Tirhakah king of •Cush:ᵃ "Look, he has set out to fight against you." So he again sent messengers to Hezekiah, saying, ¹⁰ "Say this to Hezekiah king of Judah: 'Don't let your God, whom you trust, deceive you by promising that Jerusalem will not be handed over to the king of Assyria. ¹¹ Look, you have heard what the kings of Assyria have done to all the countries: they destroyed them completely. Will you be rescued? ¹² Did the gods of the nations that my predecessors destroyed rescue them—[nations such as] Gozan, Haran, Rezeph, and the Edenites in Telassar? ¹³ Where is the king of Hamath, the king of Arpad, the king of the city of Sepharvaim, Hena, or Ivvah?'"

Hezekiah's Prayer

¹⁴ Hezekiah took the letter from the hand of the messengers, read it, then went up to the LORD's temple, and spread it out before the LORD. ¹⁵ Then Hezekiah prayed before the LORD: "LORD God of Israel who is enthroned [above] the •cherubim, You are God—You alone—of all the kingdoms of the earth. You made the heavens and the earth. ¹⁶ Listen closely, LORD, and hear; open Your eyes, LORD, and see; hear the words that Sennacherib has sent to mock the living God. ¹⁷ LORD, it is true that the kings of Assyria have devastated the nations and their lands. ¹⁸ They have thrown their gods into the fire, for they were not gods but made by human hands—wood and stone. So they have destroyed them. ¹⁹ Now, LORD our God, please save us

from his hand so that all the kingdoms of the earth may know that You are the LORD God—You alone."

God's Answer through Isaiah

²⁰ Then Isaiah son of Amoz sent [a message] to Hezekiah: "The LORD, the God of Israel says: 'I have heard your prayer to Me about Sennacherib king of Assyria.' ²¹ This is the word the LORD has spoken against him:

The young woman, Daughter Zion,
despises you and scorns you;
Daughter Jerusalem
shakes [her] head behind your back.ᵇ
22 Who is it you mocked and blasphemed?
Against whom have you raised [your] voice
and lifted your eyes in pride?
Against the Holy One of Israel!
23 You have mocked the Lordᶜ throughᵈ your
    messengers.
You have said:

With my many chariots
I have gone up to the heights of the mountains,
to the far recesses of Lebanon.
I cut down its tallest cedars,
its choice cypress trees.
I came to its farthest outpost,
its densest forest.
24 I dug [wells],
and I drank foreign waters.
I dried up all the streams of Egypt
with the soles of my feet.

25 Have you not heard?
I designed it long ago;
I planned it in days gone by.
I have now brought it to pass,
and you have crushed fortified cities
into piles of rubble.
26 Their inhabitants have become powerless,
dismayed, and ashamed.
They are plants of the field,
tender grass,
grass on the rooftops,
blasted by the east wind.ᵉ

27 But I know your sitting down,ᶠ
your going out and your coming in,
and your raging against Me.
28 Because your raging against Me
and your arrogance have reached My ears,
I will put My hook in your nose

ᵃ**19:9** Or *Nubia*   ᵇ**19:21** Lit *behind you*   ᶜ**19:23** Many mss read *LORD*   ᵈ**19:23** Lit *by the hand of*   ᵉ**19:26** DSS; MT reads *blasted before standing grain*; Is 37:27   ᶠ**19:27** LXX; DSS read *your rising up and your sitting down*; Is 37:28

18:27–30 can't deliver you from my hand. The Assyrian commander's words were intended for all the people of Judah. He wanted to break their confidence so that they would surrender in fear.

19:2 Isaiah. The writer of the book of Isaiah and a prophet during the reigns of Uzziah,

Jotham, and Ahaz.

19:3 to the point of birth. In other words, this was a "do or die" situation—a huge threat.

19:4 mock. King Hezekiah's hope seemed based more on God's protection of his reputation than on God's compassion for Judah.

19:7 I will cause him to fall. The report Isaiah described may have been that Tirhakah, king of Egypt, was marching against Assyria (v. 9).

19:18 for they were not gods. Hezekiah answered the accusations of the Assyrian commander (18:33–35) and affirmed that the Lord is the only true God.

and My bit in your mouth;
I will make you go back
the way you came.

29 This will be the sign for you: This year you will eat what grows on its own, and in the second year what grows from that. But in the third year sow and reap, plant vineyards and eat their fruit. 30 The surviving remnant of the house of Israel will again take root downward and bear fruit upward. 31 For a remnant will go out from Jerusalem, and survivors from Mount Zion. The zeal of the LORD of •Hosts will accomplish this.

32 Therefore, this is what the LORD says
        about the king of Assyria:
    He will not enter this city
    or shoot an arrow there
    or come before it with a shield
    or build up an assault ramp against it.
33 He will go back
        on the road that he came
    and he will not enter this city,
        declares the LORD.
34 I will defend this city and rescue it
        for My sake and for the sake
        of My servant David.

Defeat and Death of Sennacherib

35 That night the angel of the LORD went out and struck down 185,000 in the camp of the Assyrians. When the people got up the ⌊next⌋ morning—there were all the dead bodies! 36 So Sennacherib king of Assyria broke camp and left. He returned ⌊home⌋ and lived in Nineveh.

37 One day, while he was worshiping in the temple of his god Nisroch, his sons Adrammelech and Sharezer struck him down with the sword and escaped to the land of Ararat. Then his son Esar-haddon became king in his place.

Hezekiah's Illness and Recovery

20 In those days Hezekiah became terminally ill. The prophet Isaiah son of Amoz came and said to him, "This is what the LORD says: 'Put your affairs in order,ᵃ for you are about to die; you will not recover.'"

2 Then Hezekiah turned his face to the wall and prayed to the LORD, 3 "Please LORD, remember how I have walked before You faithfully and wholeheartedly and have done what is good in Your sight." And Hezekiah wept bitterly.

4 Isaiah had not yet gone out of the inner courtyard when the word of the LORD came to him: 5 "Go back and tell Hezekiah, the leader of My people, 'This is what the LORD God of your ancestor David says: I have heard your prayer; I have seen your tears. Look, I will heal you. On the third day ⌊from now⌋ you will go up to the LORD's temple. 6 I will add 15 years to your life. I will deliver you and this city from the hand of the king of Assyria. I will defend this city for My sake and for the sake of My servant David.'"

7 Then Isaiah said, "Bring a lump of pressed figs." So they brought it and applied it to his infected skin, and he recovered.

8 Hezekiah had asked Isaiah, "What is the sign that the LORD will heal me and that I will go up to the LORD's temple on the third day?"

9 Isaiah said, "This is the sign to you from the LORD that He will do what He has promised: Should the shadow go ahead 10 steps or go back 10 steps?"

10 Then Hezekiah answered, "It's easy for the shadow to lengthen 10 steps. No, let the shadow go back 10 steps." 11 So Isaiah the prophet called out to the LORD, and He brought the shadowᵇ back the 10 steps it had descended on Ahaz's stairway.ᶜ

Hezekiah's Folly

12 At that time Merodach-baladanᵈ son of Baladan, king of Babylon, sent letters and a gift to Hezekiah since he heard that Hezekiah had been sick. 13 Hezekiah gave them a hearing and showed them his whole treasure house—the silver, the gold, the spices, and the precious oil—and his armory, and everything that was found in his treasuries. There was nothing in his palace and in all his realm that Hezekiah did not show them.

14 Then the prophet Isaiah came to King Hezekiah and asked him, "What did these men say, and where did they come to you from?"

Hezekiah replied, "They came from a distant country, from Babylon."

15 Isaiah asked, "What have they seen in your palace?"

Hezekiah answered, "They have seen everything in my palace. There isn't anything in my treasuries that I didn't show them."

16 Then Isaiah said to Hezekiah, "Hear the word of the LORD: 17 'The time will certainly come when everything in your palace and all that your fathers have stored up until this day will be carried off to Babylon; nothing will be left,' says the LORD. 18 'Some of your descendants who come from you will be taken away,

---

ᵃ20:1 Lit *Command your house*   ᵇ20:11 Lit *shadow on the steps*   ᶜ20:11 Tg, Vg; Is 38:8 DSS read *on the steps of Ahaz's roof chamber*
ᵈ20:12 A few Hb mss, LXX, Syr, Tg, some Vg mss, Is 39:1; MT reads *Berodach-baladan*

19:22 Against the Holy One. Assyria's offense was not just against the city of Jerusalem or the nation of Judah. It was against God.

19:28 will put My hook in your nose. Some ancient monuments picture Assyria's enemies being led around with hooks in their noses. Isaiah's prophecy reversed the image.

19:30–31 remnant of the house of Israel. Attacks on Samaria and Judah had forced survivors to settle in this last piece of the original nation of Israel.

19:32 He will not enter. God sometimes delivered His people through mighty military victories. In this case, a shift in Sennacherib's

schedule showed God's provision.

20:6 for the sake of My servant David. King David established Jerusalem as his capital and the site for Solomon's temple. God had made a similar promise to Solomon (1 Kings 11:13).

20:12 Merodach-baladan ... sent letters ...

and they will become eunuchs[a] in the palace of the king of Babylon.' "

19 Then Hezekiah said to Isaiah, "The word of the LORD that you have spoken is good," for he thought: Why not, if there will be peace and security during my lifetime?

Hezekiah's Death

20 The rest of the events of Hezekiah's ⌊reign⌋, along with all his might and how he made the pool and the tunnel and brought water into the city, are written about in the Historical Record of Judah's Kings. 21 Hezekiah rested with his fathers, and his son Manasseh became king in his place.

Judah's King Manasseh

21 Manasseh was 12 years old when he became king; he reigned 55 years in Jerusalem. His mother's name was Hephzibah. 2 He did what was evil in the LORD's sight, imitating the abominations of the nations that the LORD had dispossessed before the Israelites. 3 He rebuilt the •high places that his father Hezekiah had destroyed and reestablished the altars for •Baal. He made an •Asherah, as King Ahab of Israel had done; he also worshiped the whole heavenly •host and served them. 4 He would build altars in the LORD's temple, where the LORD had said, "Jerusalem is where I will put My name." 5 He built altars to the whole heavenly host in both courtyards of the LORD's temple. 6 He made his son pass through the fire, practiced witchcraft and •divination, and consulted mediums and spiritists. He did a great amount of evil in the LORD's sight, provoking ⌊Him⌋.

7 Manasseh set up the carved image of Asherah he made in the temple that the LORD had spoken about to David and his son Solomon, "I will establish My name forever in this temple and in Jerusalem, which I have chosen out of all the tribes of Israel. 8 I will never again cause the feet of the Israelites to wander from the land I gave to their ancestors if only they will be careful to do all I have commanded them—the whole law that My servant Moses commanded them." 9 But they did not listen; Manasseh caused them to stray so that they did greater evil than the nations the LORD had destroyed before the Israelites.

10 The LORD spoke through His servants the prophets, saying, 11 "Since Manasseh king of Judah has committed all these abominations—greater evil than the Amorites who preceded him had done—and by means of his idols has also caused Judah to sin, 12 this is what the LORD God of Israel says: 'I am about to bring such disaster on Jerusalem and Judah that everyone who hears about it will shudder. 13 I will stretch over Jerusalem the measuring line ⌊used on⌋ Samaria and the mason's level ⌊used on⌋ the house of Ahab, and I will wipe Jerusalem clean as one wipes a bowl—wiping it and turning it upside down. 14 I will abandon the remnant of My inheritance and hand them over to their enemies. They will become plunder and spoil to all their enemies, 15 because they have done what is evil in My sight and have provoked Me from the day their ancestors came out of Egypt until today.' "

16 Manasseh also shed so much innocent blood that he filled Jerusalem with it from one end to another. This was in addition to his sin he caused Judah to commit so that they did what was evil in the LORD's sight.

Manasseh's Death

17 The rest of the events of Manasseh's ⌊reign⌋, along with all his accomplishments and the sin that he committed, are written about in the Historical Record of Judah's Kings. 18 Manasseh rested with his fathers and was buried in the garden of his own house, the garden of Uzza. His son Amon became king in his place.

Judah's King Amon

19 Amon was 22 years old when he became king; he reigned two years in Jerusalem. His mother's name was Meshullemeth daughter of Haruz; ⌊she was⌋ from Jotbah. 20 He did what was evil in the LORD's sight as his father Manasseh had done. 21 He walked in all the ways his father had walked; he served the idols his father had served, and he worshiped them. 22 He abandoned the LORD God of his ancestors and did not walk in the way of the LORD.

23 Amon's servants conspired against the king and killed him in his own house. 24 Then the common people[b] executed all those who had conspired against King Amon and made his son Josiah king in his place.

25 The rest of the events of Amon's ⌊reign⌋, along with his accomplishments, are written about in the Historical Record of Judah's Kings. 26 He was buried in his tomb in the garden of Uzza, and his son Josiah became king in his place.

Judah's King Josiah

22 Josiah was eight years old when he became king; he reigned 31 years in Jerusalem. His mother's name was Jedidah the daughter of Adaiah; ⌊she was⌋ from Bozkath. 2 He did what was right in the LORD's sight and walked in all the ways of his ancestor David; he did not turn to the right or the left.

---

[a]**20:18** Or *court officials*   [b]**21:24** Lit *the people of the land*

---

to Hezekiah. This was more than a get-well card. This Babylonian king invited Hezekiah to join a political alliance.

20:13 showed them. Hezekiah realized that a wealthy and powerful king would stand a better chance of allying with Babylonia against Assyria.

20:14–17 Hezekiah reported his actions to Isaiah the prophet, but he held back any mention of an alliance. Hezekiah's plan eventually backfired. Judah was exiled to Babylon 115 years later.

20:20 the tunnel. Hezekiah's tunnel through solid rock connected Jerusalem to an outside water source so they could hold on during a long siege.

21:1 reigned 55 years. Manasseh's reign was the longest of any king of Israel or Judah.

21:2 evil. Manasseh rebuilt the pagan worship sites that his father, Hezekiah, had torn down and reverted to worship of Canaanite idols.

Josiah Repairs the Temple

3 In the eighteenth year of King Josiah, the king sent the court secretary Shaphan son of Azaliah, son of Meshullam, to the LORD's temple, saying, 4 "Go up to Hilkiah the high priest so that he may total up the money brought into the LORD's temple—⌊the money⌋ the doorkeepers have collected from the people. 5 It is to be put into the hands of those doing the work—those who oversee the LORD's temple. They ⌊in turn⌋ are to give it to the workmen in the LORD's temple to repair the damage. 6 ⌊They are to give it⌋ to the carpenters, builders, and masons to buy timber and quarried stone to repair the temple. 7 But no accounting is to be required from them for the money put into their hands since they work with integrity."

The Book of the Law Found

8 Hilkiah the high priest told Shaphan the court secretary, "I have found the book of the law in the LORD's temple," and he gave the book to Shaphan, who read it. 9 Then Shaphan the court secretary went to the king and reported,[a] "Your servants have emptied out the money that was found in the temple and have put it into the hand of those doing the work—those who oversee the LORD's temple." 10 Then Shaphan the court secretary told the king, "Hilkiah the priest has given me a book," and Shaphan read it in the presence of the king.

11 When the king heard the words of the book of the law, he tore his clothes. 12 Then he commanded Hilkiah the priest, Ahikam son of Shaphan, Achbor son of Micaiah, Shaphan the court secretary, and the king's servant Asaiah: 13 "Go and inquire of the LORD for me, the people, and all Judah about the instruction in this book that has been found. For great is the LORD's wrath that is kindled against us because our ancestors have not obeyed the words of this book in order to do everything written about us."

Huldah's Prophecy of Judgment

14 So Hilkiah the priest, Ahikam, Achbor, Shaphan, and Asaiah went to the prophetess Huldah, wife of Shallum son of Tikvah, son of Harhas,[b] keeper of the wardrobe. She lived in Jerusalem in the Second District. They spoke with her.

15 She said to them, "This is what the LORD God of Israel says, 'Say to the man who sent you to Me: 16 This is what the LORD says: I am about to bring disaster on this place and on its inhabitants, ⌊fulfilling⌋ all the words of the book that the king of Judah has read, 17 because

they have abandoned Me and burned incense to other gods in order to provoke Me with all the work of their hands. My wrath will be kindled against this place, and it will not be quenched. 18 Say this to the king of Judah who sent you to inquire of the LORD: This is what the LORD God of Israel says: As for the words that you heard, 19 because your heart was tender and you humbled yourself before the LORD when you heard what I spoke against this place and against its inhabitants, that they would become a desolation and a curse, and because you have torn your clothes and wept before Me, I Myself have heard you—declares the LORD. 20 Therefore, I will indeed gather you to your fathers, and you will be gathered to your grave in peace. Your eyes will not see all the disaster that I am bringing on this place.'"

Then they reported[c] to the king.

Covenant Renewal

23 So the king sent ⌊messengers⌋, and they gathered to him all the elders of Jerusalem and Judah. 2 Then the king went to the LORD's temple with all the men of Judah and all the inhabitants of Jerusalem, as well as the priests and the prophets—all the people from the youngest to the oldest. As they listened, he read all the words of the book of the covenant that had been found in the LORD's temple. 3 Next, the king stood by the pillar[d] and made a covenant in the presence of the LORD to follow the LORD and to keep His commandments, His decrees, and His statutes with all his mind and with all his heart, and to carry out the words of this covenant that were written in this book; all the people agreed to[e] the covenant.

Josiah's Reforms

4 Then the king commanded Hilkiah the high priest and the priests of the second rank and the doorkeepers to bring out of the LORD's temple all the articles made for •Baal, •Asherah, and the whole heavenly •host. He burned them outside Jerusalem in the fields of the Kidron and carried their ashes to Bethel. 5 Then he did away with the idolatrous priests the kings of Judah had appointed to burn incense at the •high places in the cities of Judah and in the areas surrounding Jerusalem. They had burned incense to Baal, and to the sun, moon, constellations, and the whole heavenly host. 6 He brought out the Asherah pole from the LORD's temple to the Kidron Valley outside Jerusalem. He burned it at the Kidron Valley, beat it to dust, and threw its dust on the graves of the common people.[f] 7 He also tore down

---

[a] 22:9 Lit and returned a word to the king and said   [b] 22:14 2 Ch 34:22 reads Hasrah   [c] 22:20 Lit returned a word   [d] 23:3 2 Ch 34:31 reads platform   [e] 23:3 Lit people took a stand in   [f] 23:6 Lit the sons of the people

---

21:14 abandon. God let His people suffer the consequences of their own choices.

21:15 they have done what is evil. From the time of the exodus, the Hebrews had lived in cycles of obedience and disobedience. Their exile in Babylonia would be the harshest judgment of their history.

22:1 Josiah. The last righteous king from the line of David before Judah's exile.

22:4 the money. This money had been collected specifically for restoration of the temple.

22:8 book of the law. Either the complete writings of Moses (Genesis through Deuteron-

omy) or a portion of the book of Deuteronomy by itself.

22:14 Huldah. A woman with great influence in Judah. The men considered her word a message from God.

22:20 Your eyes will not see. King Josiah received the same comfort as Hezekiah. Judg-

---

the houses of the male shrine prostitutes that were in the LORD's temple, in which the women were weaving tapestries[a] for Asherah.

8 Then Josiah brought all the priests from the cities of Judah, and he defiled the high places from Geba to Beersheba, where the priests had burned incense. He tore down the high places of the gates at the entrance of the gate of Joshua the governor of the city (on the left at the city gate). 9 The priests of the high places, however, did not come up to the altar of the LORD in Jerusalem; instead, they ate unleavened bread with their fellow priests.

10 He defiled •Topheth, which is in the Valley of Hinnom, so that no one could make his son or his daughter pass through the fire to Molech. 11 He did away with the horses that the kings of Judah had dedicated to the sun. ⌊They had been⌋ at the entrance of the LORD's temple in the precincts by the chamber of Nathan-melech the court official, and he burned up the chariots of the sun.

12 The king tore down the altars that were on the roof—Ahaz's upper chamber that the kings of Judah had made—and the altars that Manasseh had made in the two courtyards of the LORD's temple. Then he smashed them[b] there and threw their dust into the Kidron Valley. 13 The king also defiled the high places that were across from Jerusalem, to the south of the Mount of Destruction, which Solomon king of Israel had built for •Ashtoreth, the detestable idol of the Sidonians; for Chemosh, the detestable idol of Moab; and for •Milcom, the abomination of the Ammonites. 14 He broke the sacred pillars into pieces, cut down the Asherah poles, then filled their places with human bones.

15 He even tore down the altar at Bethel and the high place that Jeroboam son of Nebat, who caused Israel to sin, had made. Then he burned the high place, crushed it to dust, and burned the Asherah. 16 As Josiah turned, he saw the tombs there on the mountain. He sent ⌊someone⌋ to take the bones out of the tombs, and he burned them on the altar. He defiled it according to the word of the LORD proclaimed by the man of God[c] who proclaimed these things. 17 Then he said, "What is this monument I see?"

The men of the city told him, "It is the tomb of the man of God who came from Judah and proclaimed these things that you have done to the altar at Bethel."

18 So he said, "Let him rest. Don't let anyone disturb his bones." So they left his bones undisturbed with the bones of the prophet who came from Samaria.

19 Josiah also removed all the shrines of the high places that were in the cities of Samaria, which the

kings of Israel had made to provoke ⌊the LORD⌋. Josiah did the same things to them that he had done at Bethel. 20 He slaughtered on the altars all the priests of the high places who were there, and he burned human bones on the altars. Then he returned to Jerusalem.

Passover Observed

21 The king commanded all the people, "Keep the •Passover of the LORD your God as written in the book of the covenant." 22 No such Passover had ever been kept from the time of the judges who judged Israel through the entire time of the kings of Israel and Judah. 23 But in the eighteenth year of King Josiah, this Passover was observed to the LORD in Jerusalem.

Further Zeal for the LORD

24 In addition, Josiah removed the mediums, the spiritists, household idols, images, and all the detestable things that were seen in the land of Judah and in Jerusalem. He did this in order to carry out the words of the law that were written in the book that Hilkiah the priest found in the LORD's temple. 25 Before him there was no king like him who turned to the LORD with all his mind and with all his heart and with all his strength according to all the law of Moses, and no one like him arose after him.

26 In spite of all that, the LORD did not turn from the fierceness of His great wrath and anger, which burned against Judah because of all the provocations Manasseh had provoked Him with. 27 For the LORD had said, "I will also remove Judah from My sight just as I have removed Israel. I will reject this city Jerusalem, that I have chosen, and the temple about which I said, 'My name will be there.'"

Josiah's Death

28 The rest of the events of Josiah's ⌊reign⌋, along with all his accomplishments, are written about in the Historical Record of Judah's Kings. 29 During his reign, Pharaoh Neco king of Egypt marched up to the king of Assyria at the Euphrates river. King Josiah went to confront him, and at Megiddo when Neco saw him he killed him. 30 From Megiddo his servants carried his dead body in a chariot, brought him into Jerusalem, and buried him in his own tomb. Then the common people[d] took Jehoahaz son of Josiah, anointed him, and made him king in place of his father.

Judah's King Jehoahaz

31 Jehoahaz was 23 years old when he became king; he reigned three months in Jerusalem. His mother's

a23:7 Or clothing b23:12 Text emended; MT reads he ran from c23:16 LXX adds when Jeroboam stood by the altar of the feast. And he turned and raised his eyes to the tomb of the man of God d23:30 Lit the people of the land

ment was coming, but he would not be around to watch the ax fall.
23:2 words of the book of the covenant. They probably read sections of Deuteronomy 27–28 where God set the terms of His covenant.
23:9 did not come up to the altar. Josiah

honored the priests of the high places (those who led in pagan worship) by allowing them to fraternize with priests who led in the worship of God.
23:15 high place that Jeroboam ...had made. When King Jeroboam built this altar, he received a prophecy about its destruction.

23:20 slaughtered ... all the priests. This refers to the pagan priests, not the levitical priests who were incorporated back into Jerusalem.
23:21 as written. Deuteronomy 16:1–8 outlined the Passover as a community celebration at the temple sanctuary instead of a

name was Hamutal daughter of Jeremiah; ⌊she was⌋ from Libnah. ³² He did what was evil in the LORD's sight just as his ancestors had done. ³³ Pharaoh Neco imprisoned him at Riblah in the land of Hamath to keep him from reigning in Jerusalem, and he imposed on the land a fine of 7,500 pounds[a] of silver and 75 pounds[b] of gold.

Judah's King Jehoiakim

³⁴ Then Pharaoh Neco made Eliakim son of Josiah king in place of his father Josiah and changed Eliakim's name to Jehoiakim. But Neco took Jehoahaz and went to Egypt, and he died there. ³⁵ So Jehoiakim gave the silver and the gold to Pharaoh, but at Pharaoh's command he taxed the land to give the money. He exacted the silver and the gold from the people of the land, each man according to his valuation, to give it to Pharaoh Neco.

³⁶ Jehoiakim was 25 years old when he became king; he reigned 11 years in Jerusalem. His mother's name was Zebidah daughter of Pedaiah; ⌊she was⌋ from Rumah. ³⁷ He did what was evil in the LORD's sight just as his ancestors had done.

Jehoiakim's Rebellion and Death

24 During his reign, Nebuchadnezzar king of Babylon attacked, and Jehoiakim became his vassal for three years. Then he turned and rebelled against him. ² The LORD sent Chaldean, Aramean, Moabite, and Ammonite raiders against Jehoiakim. He sent them against Judah to destroy it, according to the word of the LORD He had spoken through His servants the prophets. ³ This happened to Judah only at the LORD's command to remove them from His sight. It was because of the sins of Manasseh, according to all he had done, ⁴ and also because of all the innocent blood he had shed. He had filled Jerusalem with innocent blood, and the LORD would not forgive.

⁵ The rest of the events of Jehoiakim's ⌊reign⌋, along with all his accomplishments, are written about in the Historical Record of Judah's Kings. ⁶ Jehoiakim rested with his fathers, and his son Jehoiachin became king in his place.

⁷ Now the king of Egypt did not march out of his land again, for the king of Babylon took everything that belonged to the king of Egypt, from the Brook of Egypt to the Euphrates River.

Judah's King Jehoiachin

⁸ Jehoiachin was 18 years old when he became king; he reigned three months in Jerusalem. His mother's name was Nehushta daughter of Elnathan; ⌊she was⌋ from Jerusalem. ⁹ He did what was evil in the LORD's sight as his father had done.

Deportations to Babylon

¹⁰ At that time the servants of Nebuchadnezzar king of Babylon marched up to Jerusalem, and the city came under siege. ¹¹ Then King Nebuchadnezzar of Babylon came to the city while his servants were besieging it. ¹² Jehoiachin king of Judah, along with his mother, his servants, his commanders, and his officials, surrendered to the king of Babylon.

So the king of Babylon took him ⌊captive⌋ in the eighth year of his reign. ¹³ He also carried off from there all the treasures of the LORD's temple and the treasures of the king's palace, and he cut into pieces all the gold articles that Solomon king of Israel had made for the LORD's sanctuary, just as God had predicted. ¹⁴ Then he deported all Jerusalem and all the commanders and all the fighting men, 10,000 captives, and all the craftsmen and metalsmiths. Except for the poorest people of the land, nobody remained.

¹⁵ Nebuchadnezzar deported Jehoiachin to Babylon. Also, he took the king's mother, the king's wives, his officials, and the leading men of the land into exile from Jerusalem to Babylon. ¹⁶ The king of Babylon also brought captive into Babylon all 7,000 fighting men and 1,000 craftsmen and metalsmiths—all strong and fit for war. ¹⁷ Then the king of Babylon made Mattaniah, Jehoiachin's[c] uncle,[d] king in his place and changed his name to Zedekiah.

Judah's King Zedekiah

¹⁸ Zedekiah was 21 years old when he became king; he reigned 11 years in Jerusalem. His mother's name was Hamutal daughter of Jeremiah; ⌊she was⌋ from Libnah. ¹⁹ Zedekiah did what was evil in the LORD's sight just as Jehoiakim had done. ²⁰ Because of the LORD's anger, it came to the point in Jerusalem and Judah that He finally banished them from His presence. Then, Zedekiah rebelled against the king of Babylon.

Nebuchadnezzar's Siege of Jerusalem

25 In the ninth year of Zedekiah's reign, on the tenth day of the tenth month, King Nebuchadnezzar of Babylon advanced against Jerusalem with his entire army. They laid siege to the city and built a siege wall against it all around. ² The city was under siege until King Zedekiah's eleventh year.

³ By the ninth day of the ⌊fourth⌋ month the famine was so severe in the city that the people of the land had no food. ⁴ Then the city was broken into, and all the warriors ⌊fled⌋ by night by way of the gate between the

---

a **23:33** Lit *100 talents*   b **23:33** Lit *one talent*   c **24:17** Lit *his*   d **24:17** 2 Ch 36:10 reads *brother*; Jr 37:1

---

family event held in homes.
23:22 No such Passover. King Josiah's attention to detail made this Passover special. He made sure that only Levites slaughtered the sacrificial lambs, and he brought people from Israel and Judah together for the celebration.
23:29 King Josiah went to confront him. Be-

cause Judah was located between Assyria and Egypt, Josiah opposed any alliance between the two nations.
23:30 Jehoahaz. The third son of Josiah, he opposed any alliance with Egypt and won the people's support.
23:33 he imposed on the land. When Neco of

Egypt killed Josiah of Judah, he took control of Judah.
23:34 Jehoiakim. Jehoahaz was formerly named Shallum; Jehoiakim was formerly named Eliakim.
24:1 Nebuchadnezzar king of Babylon. When Babylon conquered Egypt, Judah came

two walls near the king's garden, even though the Chaldeans surrounded the city. As the king made his way along the route to the •Arabah, 5 the Chaldean army pursued him and overtook him in the plains of Jericho. Zedekiah's entire army was scattered from him. 6 The Chaldeans seized the king and brought him up to the king of Babylon at Riblah, and they passed sentence on him. 7 They slaughtered Zedekiah's sons before his eyes. Finally, the king of Babylon blinded Zedekiah, bound him in bronze ⌊chains⌋, and took him to Babylon.

Jerusalem Destroyed

8 On the seventh day of the fifth month, which was the nineteenth year of King Nebuchadnezzar, king of Babylon, Nebuzaradan, the commander of the guards, a servant of the king of Babylon, entered Jerusalem. 9 He burned the LORD's temple, the king's palace, and all the houses of Jerusalem; he burned down all the great houses. 10 The whole Chaldean army ⌊with⌋ the commander of the guards tore down the walls surrounding Jerusalem. 11 Nebuzaradan, the commander of the guards, deported the rest of the people who were left in the city, the deserters who had defected to the king of Babylon, and the rest of the population. 12 But the commander of the guards left some of the poorest of the land to be vinedressers and farmers.

13 Now the Chaldeans broke into pieces the bronze pillars of the LORD's temple, the water carts, and the bronze reservoir, which were in the LORD's temple, and carried the bronze to Babylon. 14 They also took the pots, the shovels, the wick trimmers, the dishes, and all the bronze articles used in ⌊temple⌋ service. 15 The commander of the guards took away the firepans and the sprinkling basins—whatever was gold or silver.

16 As for the two pillars, the one reservoir, and the water carts that Solomon had made for the LORD's temple, the weight of the bronze of all these articles was beyond measure. 17 One pillar was 27 feet[a] tall and had a bronze capital on top of it. The capital, encircled by a grating and pomegranates of bronze, stood five feet[b] high. The second pillar was the same, with its own grating.

18 The commander of the guards also took away Seraiah the chief priest, Zephaniah the priest of the second rank, and the three doorkeepers. 19 From the city he took a court official who had been appointed over the warriors; five trusted royal aides[c] found in the city; the secretary of the commander of the army, who enlisted the people of the land for military duty; and 60 men from the common people[d] who were found within the city. 20 Nebuzaradan, the commander of the guards, took them and brought them to the king of Babylon at Riblah. 21 The king of Babylon put them to death at Riblah in the land of Hamath. So Judah went into exile from its land.

Gedaliah Made Governor

22 Nebuchadnezzar king of Babylon appointed Gedaliah son of Ahikam, son of Shaphan, over the rest of the people he left in the land of Judah. 23 When all the commanders of the armies—they and their men—heard that the king of Babylon had appointed Gedaliah, they came to Gedaliah at Mizpah. ⌊The commanders included⌋ Ishmael son of Nethaniah, Johanan son of Kareah, Seraiah son of Tanhumeth the Netophathite, and Jaazaniah son of the Maacathite—they and their men. 24 Gedaliah swore an oath to them and their men, assuring them, "Don't be afraid of the servants of the Chaldeans. Live in the land and serve the king of Babylon, and it will go well for you."

25 In the seventh month, however, Ishmael son of Nethaniah, son of Elishama, of the royal family, came with 10 men and struck down Gedaliah, and he died. Also, ⌊they killed⌋ the Jews and the Chaldeans who were with him at Mizpah. 26 Then all the people, from the youngest to the oldest, and the commanders of the army, left and went to Egypt, for they were afraid of the Chaldeans.

Jehoiachin Pardoned

27 On the twenty-seventh day of the twelfth month of the thirty-seventh year of the exile of Judah's King Jehoiachin, Evil-merodach king of Babylon, in the year he became king, pardoned King Jehoiachin of Judah ⌊and released him⌋ from prison. 28 He spoke kindly to him and set his throne over the thrones of the kings who were with him in Babylon. 29 So Jehoiachin changed his prison clothes, and he dined regularly in the presence of the king of Babylon for the rest of his life. 30 As for his allowance, a regular allowance was given to him by the king, a portion for each day, for the rest of his life.

---

[a]25:17 Lit 18 cubits   [b]25:17 Lit three cubits   [c]25:19 Lit five men who look on the king's face   [d]25:19 Lit the people of the land

---

under Nebuchadnezzar's rule. Eventually Nebuchadnezzar took captives, including Daniel, from Judah to Babylon (see Dan. 1).

24:2 Chaldean … Ammonite. The Babylonians commanded such power that all these countries were at King Nebuchadnezzar's disposal to launch an attack against Judah.

24:6 rested with his fathers. Jeremiah prophesied that Jehoiakim would not be given a royal burial (see Jer. 22:19).

24:7 did not march out. The Babylonians had become so strong that even Egypt would not take a stand against them.

24:13–16 deported. Nebuchadnezzar seized the riches of Judah and the most skilled and educated people. He carried them to Babylon, leaving the peasants to till the land.

24:17–19 Mattaniah … Zedekiah. When Babylonia came to power, Nebuchadnezzar named Josiah's youngest son as king and changed his name to Zedekiah.

25:7 slaughtered Zedekiah's sons. The prophet Jeremiah had warned Zedekiah to surrender to Babylonia, but Zedekiah did not listen (see Jer. 38:1–28). He suffered greatly for his rebellion.

25:8–10 nineteenth year. In 586 B.C. the temple was burned, and the walls of the city of Jerusalem were torn down. In their exile in Babylon, the people of Judah were cut off from their temple and their sacred city. It was about 50 years before a remnant of the people was allowed to return to Jerusalem.

25:22–23 Gedaliah. A man who had served as King Josiah's secretary of state.

25:24 serve the king of Babylon. Gedaliah heeded Jeremiah's advice that his predecessor, Zedekiah, had ignored (v. 7).

INTRODUCTION TO
1 CHRONICLES

PERSONAL READING PLAN

- ☐ 1 Chronicles 2:1-55
- ☐ 1 Chronicles 3:1-24
- ☐ 1 Chronicles 4:1-43
- ☐ 1 Chronicles 5:1-26
- ☐ 1 Chronicles 6:1-30
- ☐ 1 Chronicles 6:31-80
- ☐ 1 Chronicles 7:1-40
- ☐ 1 Chronicles 9:1-44
- ☐ 1 Chronicles 10:1-11:9
- ☐ 1 Chronicles 11:10-47
- ☐ 1 Chronicles 12:1-40

- ☐ 1 Chronicles 13:1-14:17
- ☐ 1 Chronicles 15:1-16:6
- ☐ 1 Chronicles 16:7-43
- ☐ 1 Chronicles 18:1-19:19
- ☐ 1 Chronicles 20:1-22:1
- ☐ 1 Chronicles 22:2-23:32
- ☐ 1 Chronicles 24:1-25:31
- ☐ 1 Chronicles 26:1-27:34
- ☐ 1 Chronicles 28:1-21
- ☐ 1 Chronicles 29:1-30

AUTHOR

Jewish tradition suggests Ezra as author, but there is no firm evidence.

DATE

First Chronicles was probably written toward the end of the fifth century B.C. or a little later. The actions narrated in the book are centered primarily in the reign of David (circa 1011-971 B.C.).

THEME

A family record to remind exiled and returning Israelites of God's chosen king, and of their place in the restored Jerusalem.

HISTORICAL BACKGROUND

The reign of David was the golden age of Jewish history. The country was united and military victories allowed David to enlarge his territory. He introduced new administrative organization, which brought stability and prosperity. He brought the ark of the covenant to Jerusalem and restructured the tabernacle worship.

CHARACTERISTICS

In his recounting of history long past, the author relied on many written sources. About half of his work was taken from Samuel and Kings and the rest he drew from the Pentateuch, Judges, Ruth,

Psalms, Isaiah, Jeremiah, Lamentations, and Zechariah. Chapters 1-9 trace Israel's family record back to Adam. God is evident behind the scenes selecting a people for Himself. Chapters 10-29 record the history of David's reign from the viewpoint of the chronicler's priestly interests. His concern is not the ups and downs of one man, but the lasting achievements of David—the monarchy and the temple. David is seen as God's chosen king around whom the welfare of the nation revolves. The chronicler omits much of the personal and family detail recorded in 2 Samuel. Instead, he records the nature of David's reorganization of worship in Jerusalem—detailing his appointments of not only priests, but singers, musicians, and gatekeepers.

From Adam to Abraham

1 Adam, Seth, Enosh, ² Kenan, Mahalalel, Jared, ³ Enoch, Methuselah, Lamech, ⁴ Noah, Noah's sons:ᵃ Shem, Ham, and Japheth.

⁵ Japheth's sons: Gomer, Magog, Madai, Javan, Tubal, Meshech, and Tiras. ⁶ Gomer's sons: Ashkenaz, Riphath,ᵇ and Togarmah. ⁷ Javan's sons: Elishah, Tarshish, Kittim, and Rodanim.ᶜ

⁸ Ham's sons: Cush, Mizraim,ᵈ Put, and Canaan. ⁹ Cush's sons: Seba, Havilah, Sabta, Raama, and Sabteca. Raama's sons: Sheba and Dedan. ¹⁰ Cush fathered Nimrod, who was the first to become a great warrior on earth. ¹¹ Mizraim fathered Ludim, Anamim, Lehabim, Naphtuhim, ¹² Pathrusim, Casluhim (the Philistines came from them), and Caphtorim. ¹³ Canaan fathered Sidon, his firstborn, and Heth, ¹⁴ the Jebusites, Amorites, Girgashites, ¹⁵ Hivites, Arkites, Sinites, ¹⁶ Arvadites, Zemarites, and Hamathites.

¹⁷ Shem's sons: Elam, Asshur, Arpachshad, Lud, Aram, Uz, Hul, Gether, and Meshech. ¹⁸ Arpachshad fathered Shelah, and Shelah fathered Eber. ¹⁹ Two sons were born to Eber. One of them was named Peleg,ᵉ because the earth was divided during his lifetime, and the name of his brother was Joktan. ²⁰ Joktan fathered Almodad, Sheleph, Hazarmaveth, Jerah, ²¹ Hadoram, Uzal, Diklah, ²² Ebal, Abimael, Sheba, ²³ Ophir, Havilah, and Jobab. All of these were Joktan's sons.

24 Shem, Arpachshad, Shelah,
25 Eber, Peleg, Reu,
26 Serug, Nahor, Terah,
27 and Abram (that is, Abraham).

Abraham's Descendants

28 Abraham's sons: Isaac and Ishmael.

²⁹ These are their family records: Nebaioth, Ishmael's firstborn, Kedar, Adbeel, Mibsam, ³⁰ Mishma, Dumah, Massa, Hadad, Tema,
³¹ Jetur, Naphish, and Kedemah. These were Ishmael's sons.

³² The sons born to Keturah, Abraham's concubine: Zimran, Jokshan, Medan, Midian, Ishbak, and Shuah. Jokshan's sons: Sheba and Dedan. ³³ Midian's sons: Ephah, Epher, Hanoch, Abida, and Eldaah. All of these were Keturah's sons.

34 Abraham fathered Isaac. Isaac's sons: Esau and Israel.

³⁵ Esau's sons: Eliphaz, Reuel, Jeush, Jalam, and Korah. ³⁶ Eliphaz's sons: Teman, Omar, Zephi, Gatam, and Kenaz; and by Timna, Amalek.ᶠ ³⁷ Reuel's sons: Nahath, Zerah, Shammah, and Mizzah.

The Edomites

³⁸ Seir's sons: Lotan, Shobal, Zibeon, Anah, Dishon, Ezer, and Dishan. ³⁹ Lotan's sons: Hori and Homam. Timna was Lotan's sister. ⁴⁰ Shobal's sons: Alian, Manahath, Ebal, Shephi, and Onam. Zibeon's sons: Aiah and Anah. ⁴¹ Anah's son: Dishon. Dishon's sons: Hamran, Eshban, Ithran, and Cheran. ⁴² Ezer's sons: Bilhan, Zaavan, and Jaakan. Dishan's sons: Uz and Aran.

43 These were the kings who ruled in the land of Edom before any king ruled over the Israelites: Bela son of Beor. Bela's town was named Dinhabah. 44 When Bela died, Jobab son of Zerah from Bozrah ruled in his place. 45 When Jobab died, Husham from the land of the Temanites ruled in his place. 46 When Husham died, Hadad son of Bedad, who defeated Midian in the country of Moab, ruled in his place. Hadad's town was named Avith. 47 When Hadad died, Samlah from Masrekah ruled in his place. 48 When Samlah died, Shaul from Rehoboth on the Euphrates River ruled in his place. 49 When Shaul died, Baal-hanan son of Achbor ruled in his place. 50 When Baal-hanan died, Hadad ruled in his place. Hadad's city was named Pai, and his wife's name was Mehetabel daughter of Matred, daughter of Me-zahab. 51 Then Hadad died.

ᵃ**1:4** LXX; MT omits *Noah's sons* ᵇ**1:6** Some Hb mss, LXX, Vg, other Hb mss read *Diphath*; Gn 10:3 ᶜ**1:7** Some Hb mss, Syr read *Dodanim*; Gn 10:4 ᵈ**1:8** = Egypt ᵉ**1:19** = Division ᶠ**1:36** LXX; MT reads *and Timna and Amalek*; Gn 36:12

1:1–9:44 The chronicler uses genealogies to capture volumes of family history, tracing Israel's history from Saul (9:35-44) back to Adam (vv. 1-4). The genealogies show the continuum of God's faithfulness. As the chronicler's contemporaries returned from exile, review of the past helped secure their faith in God's presence. Emphasizing David and the Davidic line is a major theme of both Chronicles. **1:1–2:1** The lineage between Adam and Jacob is a brief stop on the road to the chronicler's ultimate destination—King David. The chronicler leaves out names that do not directly contribute to the royal route between Adam and David. **1:29-36** Abraham's descendants are grouped according to mothers: Hagar, Keturah, Sarah. **Timna.** Eliphaz's concubine; their son, Amalek, led the Amalekites (see 1 Sam. 15). **1:43-51 kings.** The chronicler reveals the

Edom's chiefs: Timna, Alvah,[a] Jetheth, [52] Oholibamah, Elah, Pinon, [53] Kenaz, Teman, Mibzar, [54] Magdiel, and Iram. These were Edom's chiefs.

Israel's Sons

2 These were Israel's sons: Reuben, Simeon, Levi, Judah, Issachar, Zebulun, [2] Dan, Joseph, Benjamin, Naphtali, Gad, and Asher.

Judah's Descendants

[3] Judah's sons: Er, Onan, and Shelah. ⌊These⌋ three were born to him by Bath-shua the Canaanite woman. Er, Judah's firstborn, was evil in the LORD's sight, so He put him to death. [4] Judah's daughter-in-law Tamar bore him Perez and Zerah. Judah had five sons in all.

[5] Perez's sons: Hezron and Hamul.

[6] Zerah's sons: Zimri, Ethan, Heman, Calcol, and Dara[b]—five in all.

[7] Carmi's son: Achar,[c] who brought trouble on Israel when he was unfaithful ⌊by taking⌋ what was •devoted to destruction.

[8] Ethan's son: Azariah.

[9] Hezron's sons, who were born to him: Jerahmeel, Ram, and Chelubai.[d]

[10] Ram fathered Amminadab, and Amminadab fathered Nahshon, a leader of Judah's descendants.

[11] Nahshon fathered Salma, and Salma fathered Boaz.

[12] Boaz fathered Obed, and Obed fathered Jesse.

[13] Jesse fathered Eliab, his firstborn; Abinadab was ⌊born⌋ second, Shimea third, [14] Nethanel fourth, Raddai fifth, [15] Ozem sixth, and David seventh.

[16] Their sisters were Zeruiah and Abigail. Zeruiah's three sons: Abishai, Joab, and Asahel.

[17] Amasa's mother was Abigail, and his father was Jether the Ishmaelite.

[18] Caleb son of Hezron had children by ⌊his⌋ wife Azubah and by Jerioth. These were Azubah's sons: Jesher, Shobab, and Ardon. [19] When Azubah died, Caleb married Ephrath, and she bore him Hur. [20] Hur fathered Uri,

and Uri fathered Bezalel. [21] After this, Hezron slept with the daughter of Machir the father of Gilead. Hezron had married her when he was 60 years old, and she bore him Segub. [22] Segub fathered Jair, who possessed 23 towns in the land of Gilead. [23] But Geshur and Aram captured[e] Jair's Villages[f] along with Kenath and its villages—60 towns. All these were the sons of Machir father of Gilead. [24] After Hezron's death in Caleb-ephrathah, his wife Abijah bore him Ashhur the father of Tekoa.

[25] The sons of Jerahmeel, Hezron's firstborn: Ram, his firstborn, Bunah, Oren, Ozem, and Ahijah. [26] Jerahmeel had another wife named Atarah, who was the mother of Onam.

[27] The sons of Ram, Jerahmeel's firstborn: Maaz, Jamin, and Eker.

[28] Onam's sons: Shammai and Jada. Shammai's sons: Nadab and Abishur.

[29] Abishur's wife was named Abihail, who bore him Ahban and Molid.

[30] Nadab's sons: Seled and Appaim. Seled died without children.

[31] Appaim's son: Ishi. Ishi's son: Sheshan. Sheshan's descendant: Ahlai.

[32] The sons of Jada brother of Shammai: Jether and Jonathan. Jether died without children.

[33] Jonathan's sons: Peleth and Zaza. These were the descendants of Jerahmeel.

[34] Sheshan had no sons, only daughters, but he did have an Egyptian servant whose name was Jarha. [35] Sheshan gave his daughter in marriage to his servant Jarha, and she bore him Attai.

[36] Attai fathered Nathan, and Nathan fathered Zabad.

[37] Zabad fathered Ephlal, and Ephlal fathered Obed.

[38] Obed fathered Jehu, and Jehu fathered Azariah.

[39] Azariah fathered Helez, and Helez fathered Eleasah.

[40] Eleasah fathered Sismai, and Sismai fathered Shallum.

[41] Shallum fathered Jekamiah, and Jekamiah fathered Elishama.

[42] The sons of Caleb brother of Jerahmeel: Mesha, his firstborn, fathered Ziph, and Mareshah, his second son,[g] fathered Hebron.

---

[a]**1:51** Alt Hb tradition reads *Aliah* [b]**2:6** Some Hb mss, LXX, Syr, Tg, Vg read *Darda;* 1 Kg 4:31 [c]**2:7** = Trouble; = Achan; Jos 7:1,16–26 [d]**2:9** = Caleb [e]**2:23** Lit *took from them* [f]**2:23** Or *captured Havvoth-jair* [g]**2:42** Lit *and the sons of Mareshah*

---

longstanding relationship between the Edomites and Israel with their appearance here. (See also Gen. 36:31-43.)

1:51-54 Edom's chiefs. These are the military leaders.

2:1-2 Israel's sons. These two verses provide an introductory framework for the next eight

chapters. It's interest to note that not all of the twelve sons of Jacob (Israel) are listed. Dan and Zebulun are missing. One reason that Dan may be missing is the fact that a center of pagan worship was set up at Dan after the United Kingdom divided in 931 B.C. **Joseph.** There is no tribe of Joseph. Tribes are named

for his sons, Ephraim and Manasseh

2:3-9 Perez, son of Tamar, emerges to carry on the royal line amid the sordid tales of Judah's other sons.

2:7 Achar. Achar bookmarks a lesson learned from the tragedy of disobedience (see Josh. 7).

⁴³ Hebron's sons: Korah, Tappuah, Rekem,
and Shema.
⁴⁴ Shema fathered Raham, who fathered
Jorkeam,
and Rekem fathered Shammai.
⁴⁵ Shammai's son was Maon,
and Maon fathered Beth-zur.
⁴⁶ Caleb's concubine Ephah was the mother of
Haran, Moza, and Gazez.
Haran fathered Gazez.
⁴⁷ Jahdai's sons: Regem, Jotham, Geshan, Pelet,
Ephah, and Shaaph.
⁴⁸ Caleb's concubine Maacah was the mother of
Sheber and Tirhanah. ⁴⁹ She was also the mother
of Shaaph, Madmannah's father, and of Sheva,
the father of Machbenah and Gibea. Caleb's
daughter was Achsah.
⁵⁰ These were Caleb's descendants.

The sons of Hur, Ephrathah's firstborn:
Shobal fathered Kiriath-jearim;
⁵¹ Salma fathered Bethlehem,
and Hareph fathered Beth-gader.

⁵² These were the descendants of Shobal the father
of Kiriath-jearim: Haroeh, half of the Manahathites,^a
⁵³ and the families of Kiriath-jearim—the Ithrites,
Puthites, Shumathites, and Mishraites. The Zorathites
and Eshtaolites descended from these.

⁵⁴ Salma's sons: Bethlehem, the Netophathites,
Atroth-beth-joab, and half of the Manahathites,
the Zorites, ⁵⁵ and the families of scribes who
lived in Jabez—the Tirathites, Shimeathites, and
Sucathites. These are the Kenites who came from
Hammath, the father of Rechab's family.

David's Descendants

3 These were David's sons who were born to
him in Hebron:
Amnon was the firstborn, by Ahinoam of Jezreel;
Daniel was ⌊born⌋ second, by Abigail of Carmel;
² Absalom son of Maacah, daughter of King
Talmai of Geshur, was third;
Adonijah son of Haggith was fourth;
³ Shephatiah, by Abital, was fifth;
and Ithream, by David's wife Eglah, was sixth.
⁴ Six sons were born to David in Hebron, where
he ruled seven years and six months, and he
ruled in Jerusalem 33 years.
⁵ These ⌊sons⌋ were born to him in Jerusalem:

Shimea, Shobab, Nathan, and Solomon. These
four were ⌊born to him⌋ by Bath-shua daughter of
Ammiel.
⁶ ⌊David's other sons⌋: Ibhar, Elishua,^b Eliphelet,
⁷ Nogah, Nepheg, Japhia, ⁸ Elishama, Eliada, and
Eliphelet—nine sons.
⁹ ⌊These⌋ were all David's sons, with their sister
Tamar, in addition to the sons by his concubines.

Judah's Kings

¹⁰ Solomon's son was Rehoboam;
his son was Abijah, his son Asa,
his son Jehoshaphat, ¹¹ his son Jehoram,^{c d}
his son Ahaziah, his son Joash,
¹² his son Amaziah, his son Azariah,
his son Jotham, ¹³ his son Ahaz,
his son Hezekiah, his son Manasseh,
¹⁴ his son Amon, and his son Josiah.
¹⁵ Josiah's sons:
Johanan was the firstborn, Jehoiakim second,
Zedekiah third, and Shallum fourth.
¹⁶ Jehoiakim's sons:
his sons Jeconiah and Zedekiah.

David's Line After the Exile

¹⁷ The sons of Jeconiah the captive:
his sons Shealtiel, ¹⁸ Malchiram, Pedaiah,
Shenazzar, Jekamiah, Hoshama, and Nedabiah.
¹⁹ Pedaiah's sons: Zerubbabel and Shimei.
Zerubbabel's sons: Meshullam and Hananiah,
with their sister Shelomith; ²⁰ and five others—
Hashubah, Ohel, Berechiah, Hasadiah,
and Jushab-hesed.
²¹ Hananiah's descendants: Pelatiah, Jeshaiah,
and the sons of Rephaiah, Arnan, Obadiah,
and Shecaniah.^e
²² The son^f of Shecaniah: Shemaiah.
Shemaiah's sons: Hattush, Igal, Bariah, Neariah,
and Shaphat—six.
²³ Neariah's sons: Elioenai, Hizkiah, and
Azrikam—three.
²⁴ Elioenai's sons: Hodaviah, Eliashib, Pelaiah,
Akkub, Johanan, Delaiah, and Anani—seven.

Judah's Descendants

4 Judah's sons: Perez, Hezron, Carmi, Hur,
and Shobal.
² Reaiah son of Shobal fathered Jahath,
and Jahath fathered Ahumai and Lahad.
These were the families of the Zorathites.
³ These were Etam's sons:^g Jezreel, Ishma, and

---

^a**2:52** Lit *Manuhoth* ^b**3:6** Lit *Elishama*; 1 Ch 14:5; 2 Sm 5:15 ^c**3:11** Lit *Joram* ^d**3:11** = The LORD is Exalted ^e**3:21** LXX reads *Jeshaiah, his son Rephaiah, his son Arnan, his son Obadiah, and his son Shecaniah* ^f**3:22** LXX; MT reads *sons* ^g**4:3** LXX; MT reads *father*

2:10–3:24 The chronicler zeroes in on the genealogy related to David. The lineage begins with David's immediate family and half sisters (2:13-17). It concludes with a focus on the sons of David himself (3:1-9).

2:34-41 Subtle reference to God's favor is implied in the names of those rendered childless

(vv. 30, 32). In contrast, Sheshan's initially jeopardized status continues through his daughter's son, Attai (v. 34).

3:1-9 David's complex family unit is recorded. (See also 2 Sam. 3:2-5; 5:13-16; 13:1). Solomon, as the bearer of the royal lineage, stands out among David's other children. Obviously

omitted is Bathsheba's son who died at birth (2 Sam. 12:18).

3:9 Tamar. Only one of David's daughters is listed. She is here because of the injustice done to her by brother Amnon (see 2 Sam. 13:14-16). This sin brought shame on the family and resulted in a murder (see 2 Sam. 13:18-29).

Idbash, and their sister was named Hazzelelponi.
⁴ Penuel fathered Gedor,
and Ezer fathered Hushah.
These were the sons of Hur, Ephrathah's firstborn and the father of Bethlehem:
⁵ Ashhur fathered Tekoa and had two wives, Helah and Naarah. ⁶ Naarah bore him Ahuzzam, Hepher, Temeni, and Haahashtari. These were Naarah's sons.
⁷ Helah's sons: Zereth, Zohar,ᵃ and Ethnan.
⁸ Koz fathered Anub, Zobebah,ᵇ and the families of Aharhel son of Harum.

⁹ Jabezᶜ was more honorable than his brothers. His mother named him Jabez and said, "I gave birth to him in pain."
¹⁰ Jabez called out to the God of Israel: "If only You would bless me, extend my border, let Your hand be with me, and keep me from harm, so that I will not cause any pain."ᵈ And God granted his request.

¹¹ Chelub brother of Shuhah fathered Mehir, who was the father of Eshton. ¹² Eshton fathered Beth-rapha, Paseah, and Tehinnah the father of Irnahash. These were the men of Recah.
¹³ Kenaz's sons: Othniel and Seraiah.
Othniel's sons: Hathath and Meonothai.ᵉ
¹⁴ Meonothai fathered Ophrah,
and Seraiah fathered Joab, the ancestor of ⌊those in⌋ the Valley of Craftsmen,ᶠ for they were craftsmen.
¹⁵ The sons of Caleb son of Jephunneh: Iru, Elah, and Naam.
Elah's son: Kenaz.
¹⁶ Jehallelel's sons: Ziph, Ziphah, Tiria, and Asarel.
¹⁷ Ezrah's sons: Jether, Mered, Epher, and Jalon. Mered's wife Bithiahᵍ gave birth to Miriam, Shammai, and Ishbah the father of Eshtemoa.
¹⁸ These were the sons of Pharaoh's daughter Bithiah; Mered had married her. His Judean wife gave birth to Jered the father of Gedor, Heber the father of Soco, and Jekuthiel the father of Zanoah. ¹⁹ The sons of Hodiah's wife, the sister of Naham: the father of Keilah the Garmite and ⌊the father of⌋ Eshtemoa the Maacathite.
²⁰ Shimon's sons: Amnon, Rinnah, Ben-hanan, and Tilon.
Ishi's sons: Zoheth and Ben-zoheth.

²¹ The sons of Shelah son of Judah: Er the father of Lecah, Laadah the father of Mareshah, the families of the guildʰ of linen workers at Beth-ashbea, ²² Jokim, the men of Cozeba; and Joash and Saraph, who married Moabitesⁱ and returned to Lehem. These ⌊names⌋ are from ancient records. ²³ They were the potters and residents of Netaim and Gederah. They lived there in the service of the king.

Simeon's Descendants

²⁴ Simeon's sons: Nemuel, Jamin, Jarib, Zerah, and Shaul;
²⁵ ⌊Shaul's sons:⌋ his son Shallum, his son Mibsam, and his son Mishma.
²⁶ Mishma's sons: his son Hammuel, his son Zaccur, and his son Shimei.

²⁷ Shimei had 16 sons and six daughters, but his brothers did not have many children, so their whole family did not become as numerous as the Judeans. ²⁸ They lived in Beer-sheba, Moladah, Hazar-shual, ²⁹ Bilhah, Ezem, Tolad, ³⁰ Bethuel, Hormah, Ziklag, ³¹ Beth-marcaboth, Hazar-susim, Beth-biri, and Shaaraim. These were their cities until David became king. ³² Their villages were Etam, Ain, Rimmon, Tochen, and Ashan—five cities, ³³ and all their surrounding villages as far as Baal. These were their settlements, and they kept a genealogical record for themselves.

³⁴ Meshobab, Jamlech, Joshah son of Amaziah, ³⁵ Joel, Jehu son of Joshibiah, son of Seraiah, son of Asiel,
³⁶ Elioenai, Jaakobah, Jeshohaiah, Asaiah, Adiel, Jesimiel, Benaiah,
³⁷ and Ziza son of Shiphi, son of Allon, son of Jedaiah, son of Shimri, son of Shemaiah—

³⁸ these mentioned by name were leaders in their families. Their ancestral houses increased greatly. ³⁹ They went to the entrance of Gedor, to the east side of the valley to seek pasture for their flocks. ⁴⁰ They found rich, good pasture, and the land was broad, peaceful, and quiet, for some Hamites had lived there previously.

⁴¹ These who were recorded by name came in the days of King Hezekiah of Judah, attacked the Hamites' tents and the Meunim who were found there, and •set them apart for destruction, as they are today. Then they settled in their place because there was pasture for their flocks. ⁴² Now 500 men from these sons of Simeon went with Pelatiah, Neariah, Rephaiah, and Uzziel,

---

ᵃ4:7 Alt Hb tradition reads Izhar   ᵇ4:8 Or Hazzobebah   ᶜ4:9 The name Jabez sounds like Hb jazeb meaning "he causes pain."   ᵈ4:10 LXX reads and act in knowledge which doesn't hurt me   ᵉ4:13 LXX, Vg; MT omits and Meonothai   ᶠ4:14 Or the Ge-harashim   ᵍ4:17 Lit She; 1 Ch 4:18   ʰ4:21 Lit house   ⁱ4:22 Or who ruled over Moab

---

3:17-20 Jeconiah. None of Jehoiachin's sons succeeded him as king. Babylon took Judah captive at that time.
4:9-10 Jabez. Jabez depended on God for his needs. Certainly there was some selfishness in his prayer ("extend my border"), as well as some lack of realistic expectation. Not only

does he want to avoid all harm, but many versions (NIV, RSV, KJV) translate the second half of verse 10 as saying that he wants to even avoid all pain. In a world where the "rain falls on the righteous and the unrighteous" (Matt. 5:45), that is hardly realistic. However, that he took these requests to God when so many

were seeking their answers in other gods was highly commendable.

4:21-23 guild … linen workers … potters. Families passed along trade and craft secrets to their descendants.
4:24-43 The chronicler mentions Simeon as

the sons of Ishi, as their leaders to Mount Seir. 43 They struck down the remnant of the Amalekites who had escaped and still live there today.

Reuben's Descendants

5 [These were] the sons of Reuben the firstborn of Israel. He was the firstborn, but his birthright was given to the sons of Joseph son of Israel, because Reuben defiled his father's bed. He is not listed in the genealogy according to birthright. 2 Although Judah became strong among his brothers and a ruler came from him, the birthright was given to Joseph.

3 The sons of Reuben, Israel's firstborn:
   Hanoch, Pallu, Hezron, and Carmi.
4 Joel's sons: his son Shemaiah,
   his son Gog, his son Shimei,
5 his son Micah, his son Reaiah,
   his son Baal, 6 and his son Beerah.

Beerah was a leader of the Reubenites, and Tiglath-pileser[a] king of Assyria took him into exile. 7 His relatives by their families as they are recorded in their genealogy: Jeiel the chief, Zechariah, 8 and Bela son of Azaz, son of Shema, son of Joel. They settled in Aroer as far as Nebo and Baal-meon. 9 They also settled in the east as far as the edge of the desert that extends to the Euphrates River, because their herds had increased in the land of Gilead. 10 During Saul's reign they waged war against the Hagrites, who were defeated by their power. And they lived in their tents throughout the region east of Gilead.

Gad's Descendants

11 The sons of Gad lived next to them in the land of Bashan as far as Salecah:
12 Joel the chief, Shapham the second [in command], Janai, and Shaphat in Bashan.
13 Their relatives according to their ancestral houses: Michael, Meshullam, Sheba, Jorai, Jacan, Zia, and Eber—seven.
14 These were the sons of Abihail son of Huri, son of Jaroah, son of Gilead, son of Michael, son of Jeshishai, son of Jahdo, son of Buz.
15 Ahi son of Abdiel, son of Guni, was head of their ancestral houses. 16 They lived in Gilead, in Bashan and its towns, and throughout the pasturelands of Sharon. 17 All of them were registered in the genealogies during the reigns of Judah's King Jotham and Israel's King Jeroboam.

18 The sons of Reuben and Gad and half the tribe of Manasseh had 44,760 warriors who could serve in the army—men who carried shield and sword, drew the bow, and were trained for war. 19 They waged war against the Hagrites, Jetur, Naphish, and Nodab. 20 They received help against these enemies,[b] and the Hagrites and all their allies were handed over to them, because they cried out to God in battle. He granted their request because they trusted in Him. 21 They captured the Hagrites' livestock—50,000 of their camels, 250,000 sheep, and 2,000 donkeys—as well as 100,000 people. 22 Many of the Hagrites were killed because it was God's battle. And they lived there in the Hagrites' place until the exile.

Half the Tribe of Manasseh

23 The sons of half the tribe of Manasseh settled in the land from Bashan to Baal-hermon (that is, Senir or Mount Hermon). They were numerous. 24 These were the heads of their ancestral houses: Epher, Ishi, Eliel, Azriel, Jeremiah, Hodaviah, and Jahdiel. They were brave warriors, famous men, and heads of their patriarchal families. 25 But they were unfaithful to the God of their ancestors. They prostituted themselves with the gods of the nations[c] God had destroyed before them. 26 So the God of Israel put it into the mind of Pul (that is, Tiglath-pileser[a]) king of Assyria to take the Reubenites, Gadites, and half the tribe of Manasseh into exile. He took them to Halah, Habor, Hara, and Gozan's river, [where they are] until today.

The Levites

6 [d] Levi's sons: Gershom, Kohath, and Merari.
2 Kohath's sons: Amram, Izhar, Hebron, and Uzziel.
3 Amram's children: Aaron, Moses, and Miriam.
   Aaron's sons: Nadab, Abihu, Eleazar, and Ithamar.
4 Eleazar fathered Phinehas;
   Phinehas fathered Abishua;
5 Abishua fathered Bukki;
   Bukki fathered Uzzi;
6 Uzzi fathered Zerahiah;
   Zerahiah fathered Meraioth;
7 Meraioth fathered Amariah;
   Amariah fathered Ahitub;
8 Ahitub fathered Zadok;
   Zadok fathered Ahimaaz;
9 Ahimaaz fathered Azariah;
   Azariah fathered Johanan;

---

a 5:6,26 LXX; MT reads Tilgath-pilneser   b 5:20 Lit against them   c 5:25 Lit the peoples of the land   d 6:1 1 Ch 5:27 in Hb

---

part of the nation of Judah. With no land of their own (Josh .19:1-9), these people were taken in by the larger tribe of Judah, having lost their own identity by David's time.

4:41 set them apart for destruction, as they are today. Hamites were essentially Canaanites. They were "set apart for destruction" be-

cause they were in the land designated for the people of Israel.

5:20 He granted their request. Again, the chronicler gives an example of God's faithfulness throughout the generations.

5:25-26. They prostituted themselves. Sexual imagery is often used to describe the way

that Israel ran after other gods (see for example, Hosea 1:2). **into exile.** Tilgath-pileser III of Assyria carried these northern tribes off into exile. This was God's punishment for their unfaithfulness.

6:1-3 Levi's sons. The office of high priest was a family business—a person had to be

10 Johanan fathered Azariah, who served as priest
in the temple that Solomon built in Jerusalem;
11 Azariah fathered Amariah;
Amariah fathered Ahitub;
12 Ahitub fathered Zadok;
Zadok fathered Shallum;
13 Shallum fathered Hilkiah;
Hilkiah fathered Azariah;
14 Azariah fathered Seraiah;
and Seraiah fathered Jehozadak.
15 Jehozadak went into exile when the LORD sent
Judah and Jerusalem into exile at the hands of
Nebuchadnezzar.

16a Levi's sons: Gershom, Kohath, and Merari.
17 These are the names of Gershom's sons: Libni
and Shimei.
18 Kohath's sons: Amram, Izhar, Hebron
and Uzziel.
19 Merari's sons: Mahli and Mushi.
These are the Levites' families according to their
fathers:
20 Of Gershom: his son Libni,
his son Jahath, his son Zimmah,
21 his son Joah, his son Iddo,
his son Zerah, and his son Jeatherai.
22 Kohath's sons: his son Amminadab,
his son Korah, his son Assir,
23 his son Elkanah, his son Ebiasaph,
his son Assir, 24 his son Tahath,
his son Uriel, his son Uzziah,
and his son Shaul.
25 Elkanah's sons: Amasai and Ahimoth,
26 his son Elkanah, his son Zophai,
his son Nahath, 27 his son Eliab,
his son Jeroham, and his son Elkanah.
28 Samuel's sons: his firstborn Joel,[b]
and his second son Abijah.
29 Merari's sons: Mahli, his son Libni,
his son Shimei, his son Uzzah,
30 his son Shimea, his son Haggiah,
and his son Asaiah.

The Musicians

31 These are the men David put in charge of the
music in the LORD's temple after the ark came to rest
there. 32 They ministered with song in front of the tabernacle, the tent of meeting, until Solomon built the
LORD's temple in Jerusalem, and they performed their
task according to the regulations ⌊given⌋ to them.
33 These are the men who served with their sons.

From the Kohathites: Heman the singer,
son of Joel, son of Samuel,
34 son of Elkanah, son of Jeroham,
son of Eliel, son of Toah,
35 son of Zuph, son of Elkanah,
son of Mahath, son of Amasai,
36 son of Elkanah, son of Joel,
son of Azariah, son of Zephaniah,
37 son of Tahath, son of Assir,
son of Ebiasaph, son of Korah,
38 son of Izhar, son of Kohath,
son of Levi, son of Israel.

39 Heman's relative was •Asaph, who stood
at his right hand:
Asaph son of Berechiah, son of Shimea,
40 son of Michael, son of Baaseiah,
son of Malchijah, 41 son of Ethni,
son of Zerah, son of Adaiah,
42 son of Ethan, son of Zimmah,
son of Shimei, 43 son of Jahath,
son of Gershom, son of Levi.

44 On the left, their relatives were Merari's sons:
Ethan son of Kishi, son of Abdi,
son of Malluch, 45 son of Hashabiah,
son of Amaziah, son of Hilkiah,
46 son of Amzi, son of Bani,
son of Shemer, 47 son of Mahli,
son of Mushi, son of Merari,
son of Levi.

Aaron's Descendants

48 Their relatives the Levites were assigned to all the
service of the tabernacle, God's temple. 49 But Aaron
and his sons did all the work of the most holy place.
They presented the offerings on the altar of •burnt offerings and on the altar of incense to make atonement for
Israel according to all that Moses the servant of God had
commanded.

50 These are Aaron's sons: his son Eleazar,
his son Phinehas, his son Abishua,
51 his son Bukki, his son Uzzi,
his son Zerahiah, 52 his son Meraioth,
his son Amariah, his son Ahitub,
53 his son Zadok, and his son Ahimaaz.

The Settlements of the Levites

54 These were the places assigned to Aaron's sons
from the Kohathite family for their settlements in their
territory, because the ⌊first⌋ lot was for them. 55 They

---

a6:16 1 Ch 6:1 in Hb b6:28 Some LXX mss, Syr, Arabic; other Hb mss omit *Joel*; 1 Sm 8:2

---

born into the role.
6:4-15 Jehozadak. Aaron was the patriarchal
priest (Ex. 28:1). His lineage languished when
Jehozadak was taken captive (v. 15).
6:11 Azariah. High priest who led 80 priests to
oppose King Uzziah of Judah (792–740) when
he tried to burn incense in the temple rather

than let the priests. God struck Uzziah with a
dreaded skin disease (2 Chron. 26:16-21).

6:13 Hilkiah. High priest who aided in Josiah's
reform movement (2 Kings 22:4). He supported Josiah by overseeing the repair of the
temple. While the temple was being repaired,
Josiah found the book of the law in the temple.

When Josiah heard the reading from the book
of the law, he tore his clothes and was deeply
troubled. Josiah commanded Hilkiah and others to remove the pagan articles of worship
that had been placed in the LORD's temple.

6:22 Korah. Leader of rebellion against
Moses and Aaron while Israel was camped

were given Hebron in the land of Judah and its surrounding pasturelands, ⁵⁶ but the fields and villages around the city were given to Caleb son of Jephunneh. ⁵⁷ Aaron's sons were given:

Hebron (a city of refuge), Libnah and its pasturelands, Jattir, Eshtemoa and its pasturelands, ⁵⁸ Hilenᵃ and its pasturelands, Debir and its pasturelands, ⁵⁹ Ashan and its pasturelands, and Beth-shemesh and its pasturelands. ⁶⁰ From the tribe of Benjamin ⌊they were given⌋ Geba and its pasturelands, Alemeth and its pasturelands, and Anathoth and its pasturelands. They had 13 towns in all among their families.

⁶¹ To the rest of the Kohathites, 10 towns from the half tribe of Manasseh ⌊were assigned⌋ by lot.

⁶² The Gershomites ⌊were assigned⌋ 13 towns from the tribes of Issachar, Asher, Naphtali, and Manasseh in Bashan according to their families.

⁶³ The Merarites ⌊were assigned⌋ by lot 12 towns from the tribes of Reuben, Gad, and Zebulun according to their families. ⁶⁴ So the Israelites gave these towns and their pasturelands to the Levites. ⁶⁵ They assigned by lot the towns named above from the tribes of the Judahites, Simeonites, and Benjaminites.

⁶⁶ Some of the families of the Kohathites were given towns from the tribe of Ephraim for their territory:

⁶⁷ Shechem (a city of refuge) with its pasturelands in the hill country of Ephraim, Gezer and its pasturelands, ⁶⁸ Jokmeam and its pasturelands, Beth-horon and its pasturelands, ⁶⁹ Aijalon and its pasturelands, and Gath-rimmon and its pasturelands. ⁷⁰ From half the tribe of Manasseh, Aner and its pasturelands, and Bileam and its pasturelands ⌊were given⌋ to the rest of the families of the Kohathites.

⁷¹ The Gershomites ⌊received⌋:

Golan in Bashan and its pasturelands, and Ashtaroth and its pasturelands from the families of half the tribe of Manasseh. ⁷² From the tribe of Issachar ⌊they received⌋ Kedesh and its pasturelands, Daberath and its pasturelands, ⁷³ Ramoth and its pasturelands, and Anem and its pasturelands. ⁷⁴ From the tribe of Asher ⌊they received⌋ Mashal and its pasturelands, Abdon and its pasturelands, ⁷⁵ Hukok and its pasturelands, and Rehob and its pasturelands. ⁷⁶ From the tribe of Naphtali ⌊they received⌋ Kedesh in Galilee and its pasturelands, Hammon and its pasturelands, and Kiriathaim and its pasturelands.

⁷⁷ The rest of the Merarites ⌊received⌋:

From the tribe of Zebulun, ⌊they received⌋ Rimmono and its pasturelands and Tabor and its pasturelands. ⁷⁸ From the tribe of Reuben across the Jordan at Jericho, to the east of the Jordan, ⌊they received⌋ Bezer in the desert and its pasturelands, Jahzah and its pasturelands, ⁷⁹ Kedemoth and its pasturelands, and Mephaath and its pasturelands. ⁸⁰ From the tribe of Gad ⌊they received⌋ Ramoth in Gilead and its pasturelands, Mahanaim and its pasturelands, ⁸¹ Heshbon and its pasturelands, and Jazer and its pasturelands.

Issachar's Descendants

7 Issachar's sons: Tola, Puah, Jashub, and Shimron—four.
² Tola's sons: Uzzi, Rephaiah, Jeriel, Jahmai, Ibsam, and Shemuel, the heads of their ancestral houses. During David's reign, 22,600 descendants of Tola were recorded as warriors in their genealogies.
³ Uzzi's son: Izrahiah.
Izrahiah's sons: Michael, Obadiah, Joel, Isshiah. All five of them were chiefs. ⁴ Along with them, they had 36,000 troops for battle according to the genealogical records of their ancestral houses, for they had many wives and children.
⁵ Their tribesmen who were warriors belonging to all the families of Issachar totalled 87,000 in their genealogies.

Benjamin's Descendants

⁶ Three of Benjamin's ⌊sons⌋: Bela, Becher, and Jediael.
⁷ Bela's sons: Ezbon, Uzzi, Uzziel, Jerimoth, and Iri—five. They were warriors and heads of their ancestral houses; 22,034 were listed in their genealogies.
⁸ Becher's sons: Zemirah, Joash, Eliezer, Elioenai, Omri, Jeremoth, Abijah, Anathoth, and Alemeth; all these were Becher's sons. ⁹ Their genealogies were recorded according to the heads of their ancestral houses—20,200 warriors.
¹⁰ Jediael's son: Bilhan.
Bilhan's sons: Jeush, Benjamin, Ehud,

ᵃ**6:58** Some Hb mss, LXX; other Hb mss read *Hilez*

---

in the wilderness of Paran (Num. 16). He led a confederacy of 250 princes of the people against Aaron's claim to the priesthood and Moses' claim to authority in general. The rebels contended that the entire congregation was sanctified and therefore qualified to perform priestly functions. As punishment for their insubordination, God caused the earth to open and swallow the leaders. **6:28 Samuel's sons.** Samuel faithfully served in the tabernacle as an influential priest and leader. Samuel's family was described as Ephraimites (1 Sam. 1:1). He was clearly a Levite and was dedicated to service in the tabernacle (see 1 Sam. 2:11).

7:1-5 Issachar. The chronicler details Issachar's strength in numbers during its most populated era.

7:6-12 Benjamin. Other lists give varying figures for the number of Benjamin's sons (see

Chenaanah, Zethan, Tarshish, and Ahishahar. 11 All these sons of Jediael listed by heads of families were warriors; there were 17,200 who could serve in the army. 12 Shuppim and Huppim were sons of Ir, and the Hushim were the sons of Aher.

Naphtali's Descendants

13 Naphtali's sons: Jahziel, Guni, Jezer, and Shallum—Bilhah's sons.

Manasseh's Descendants

14 Manasseh's sons through his Aramean concubine: Asriel and Machir the father of Gilead. 15 Machir took wives from Huppim and Shuppim. The name of his sister was Maacah. Another descendant was named Zelophehad, but he had only daughters. 16 Machir's wife Maacah gave birth to a son, and she named ⌊him⌋ Peresh. His brother was named Sheresh, and his sons were Ulam and Rekem. 17 Ulam's son: Bedan. These were the sons of Gilead son of Machir, son of Manasseh. 18 His sister Hammolecheth gave birth to Ishhod, Abiezer, and Mahlah. 19 Shemida's sons: Ahian, Shechem, Likhi, and Aniam.

Ephraim's Descendants

20 Ephraim's sons: Shuthelah, and his son Bered,
his son Tahath, his son Eleadah,
his son Tahath, 21 his son Zabad,
his son Shuthelah, Ezer, and Elead.
The men of Gath who were born in the land killed Ezer and Elead because they went down to raid their cattle. 22 Their father Ephraim mourned a long time, and his relatives came to comfort him. 23 He slept with his wife, and she conceived and gave birth to a son. So he named him Beriah, because there had been misfortune in his home.a 24 His daughter was Sheerah, who built Lower and Upper Beth-horon and Uzzen-sheerah,
25 his son Rephah, his son Resheph,
his son Telah, his son Tahan,
26 his son Ladan, his son Ammihud,
his son Elishama, 27 his son Nun,
and his son Joshua.

28 Their holdings and settlements were Bethel and its villages; Naaran to the east, Gezer and its villages to the west, and Shechem and its villages

as far as Ayyah and its villages, 29 and along the borders of the sons of Manasseh, Beth-shean and its villages, Taanach and its villages, Megiddo and its villages, and Dor and its villages. The sons of Joseph son of Israel lived in these towns.

Asher's Descendants

30 Asher's sons: Imnah, Ishvah, Ishvi, and Beriah, with their sister Serah. 31 Beriah's sons: Heber, and Malchiel, who fathered Birzaith. 32 Heber fathered Japhlet, Shomer, and Hotham, with their sister Shua. 33 Japhlet's sons: Pasach, Bimhal, and Ashvath. These were Japhlet's sons. 34 Shemer's sons: Ahi, Rohgah, Hubbah, and Aram. 35 His brother Helem's sons: Zophah, Imna, Shelesh, and Amal. 36 Zophah's sons: Suah, Harnepher, Shual, Beri, Imrah, 37 Bezer, Hod, Shamma, Shilshah, Ithran, and Beera. 38 Jether's sons: Jephunneh, Pispa, and Ara. 39 Ulla's sons: Arah, Hanniel, and Rizia. 40 All these were Asher's sons. They were the heads of their ancestral houses, chosen men, warriors, and chiefs among the leaders. The number of men listed in their genealogies for military service was 26,000.

Benjamin's Descendants

8 Benjamin fathered Bela, his firstborn;
Ashbel was ⌊born⌋ second, Aharah third,
2 Nohah fourth, and Rapha fifth.
3 Bela's sons: Addar, Gera, Abihud,
4 Abishua, Naaman, Ahoah,
5 Gera, Shephuphan, and Huram.
6 These were Ehud's sons, who were the heads of the families living in Geba and who were deported to Manahath: 7 Naaman, Ahijah, and Gera. Gera deported them and was the father of Uzza and Ahihud.
8 Shaharaim had sons in the country of Moab after he had divorced his wives Hushim and Baara. 9 His sons by his wife Hodesh: Jobab, Zibia, Mesha, Malcam, 10 Jeuz, Sachia, and Mirmah. These were his sons, heads of families. 11 He also had sons by Hushim: Abitub and Elpaal.
12 Elpaal's sons: Eber, Misham, and Shemed who built Ono and Lod and its villages, 13 Beriah and

---

a **7:23** *Beriah* sounds like the Hb for "in misfortune."

8:1-2; Gen. 46:21). Genealogies provided various functions for the people, which is why the chronicler likely slanted his count to include only those in the military.

7:14-19 In a document of this period, highlighting women was an unusual, though legitimate, function of a genealogy.

7:30-40 Asher. Asher stood out from the clan, a tribe of leaders and outstanding warriors (see Gen. 30:9-13). Asher was the son of Jacob. His mother was Leah's servant Zilpah.

8:1-40 Benjamin's tribe, the tribe of Saul, earns a second helping of highlights (7:6-12). Understanding Saul's historical context early on

allows the chronicler to pick up the story at Saul's death in chapter ten.

8:28 lived in Jerusalem. Families of Benjamin lived in Jerusalem. It is interesting to note that Jerusalem was not occupied until David's time. With this representation of Saul's tribe Benjamin in Jerusalem, it is evident that David

Shema, who were the heads of families of Aijalon's residents and who drove out the residents of Gath, ¹⁴ Ahio,ᵃ Shashak, and Jeremoth.

¹⁵ Zebadiah, Arad, Eder, ¹⁶ Michael, Ishpah, and Joha were Beriah's sons.

¹⁷ Zebadiah, Meshullam, Hizki, Heber, ¹⁸ Ishmerai, Izliah, and Jobab were Elpaal's sons.

¹⁹ Jakim, Zichri, Zabdi, ²⁰ Elienai, Zillethai, Eliel, ²¹ Adaiah, Beraiah, and Shimrath were Shimei's sons.

²² Ishpan, Eber, Eliel, ²³ Abdon, Zichri, Hanan, ²⁴ Hananiah, Elam, Anthothijah, ²⁵ Iphdeiah, and Penuel were Shashak's sons.

²⁶ Shamsherai, Shehariah, Athaliah, ²⁷ Jaareshiah, Elijah, and Zichri were Jeroham's sons.

²⁸ These were heads of families, chiefs according to their genealogies, and lived in Jerusalem.

²⁹ Jeiel,ᵇ fathered Gibeon and lived in Gibeon. His wife's name was Maacah. ³⁰ Abdon was his firstborn son, then Zur, Kish, Baal, Nadab, ³¹ Gedor, Ahio, Zecher, ³² and Mikloth who fathered Shimeah. These also lived opposite their relatives in Jerusalem, with their [other] relatives.

³³ Ner fathered Kish, Kish fathered Saul, and Saul fathered Jonathan, Malchishua, Abinadab, and Esh-baal.ᶜ

³⁴ Jonathan's son was Merib-baal,ᵈ and Merib-baal fathered Micah.

³⁵ Micah's sons: Pithon, Melech, Tarea, and Ahaz.

³⁶ Ahaz fathered Jehoaddah, Jehoaddah fathered Alemeth, Azmaveth, and Zimri, and Zimri fathered Moza.

³⁷ Moza fathered Binea. His son was Raphah, his son Eleasah, and his son Azel.

³⁸ Azel had six sons, and these were their names: Azrikam, Bocheru, Ishmael, Sheariah, Obadiah, and Hanan. All these were Azel's sons.

³⁹ His brother Eshek's sons: Ulam was his firstborn, Jeush second, and Eliphelet third.

⁴⁰ Ulam's sons were warriors and archers. They had many sons and grandsons—150 of them. All these were among Benjamin's sons.

After the Exile

9 All Israel was registered in the genealogies that are written about in the Book of the Kings of Israel. But Judah was exiled to Babylon because of their unfaithfulness. ² The first to live in their towns on their own property again were Israelites, priests, Levites, and temple servants.

³ These people from the descendants of Judah, Benjamin, Ephraim, and Manasseh settled in Jerusalem:
⁴ Uthai son of Ammihud, son of Omri, son of Imri, son of Bani,
a descendantᵉ of Perez son of Judah;
⁵ from the Shilonites:
Asaiah the firstborn and his sons;
⁶ and from the sons of Zerah:
Jeuel and 690 of their relatives.

⁷ The Benjaminites: Sallu son of Meshullam, son of Hodaviah, son of Hassenuah;
⁸ Ibneiah son of Jeroham;
Elah son of Uzzi, son of Michri;
Meshullam son of Shephatiah, son of Reuel, son of Ibnijah;
⁹ and 956 of their relatives according to their genealogical records. All these men were heads of their ancestral houses.

¹⁰ The priests: Jedaiah; Jehoiarib; Jachin;
¹¹ Azariah son of Hilkiah, son of Meshullam, son of Zadok, son of Meraioth, son of Ahitub, the chief official of God's temple;
¹² Adaiah son of Jeroham, son of Pashhur, son of Malchijah; Maasai son of Adiel, son of Jahzerah, son of Meshullam, son of Meshillemith, son of Immer;
¹³ and 1,760 of their relatives, the heads of households. They were capable men employed in the ministry of God's temple.

¹⁴ The Levites: Shemaiah son of Hasshub, son of Azrikam, son of Hashabiah of the Merarites;
¹⁵ Bakbakkar, Heresh, Galal, and Mattaniah, son of Mica, son of Zichri, son of Asaph;
¹⁶ Obadiah son of Shemaiah, son of Galal, son of Jeduthun; and Berechiah son of Asa, son of Elkanah who lived in the villages of the Netophathites.

¹⁷ The gatekeepers: Shallum, Akkub, Talmon, Ahiman, and their relatives. Shallum was their chief; ¹⁸ he was previously stationed at the King's Gate on the east side. These were the gatekeepers from the camp of the Levites.

ᵃ 8:13–14 LXX reads *Gath* ¹⁴ *and their brother* ᵇ 8:29 LXX; MT omits *Jeiel*; 1 Ch 9:35 ᶜ 8:33 = Man of Baal ᵈ 8:34 = Baal Contends ᵉ 9:4 Lit *Bani, from the sons*

---

did not exclude Saul's relations from favorable positions in Israel.

8:33 Esh-baal. Also known as Ish-Bosheth, Saul's youngest son who ruled over Israel (see 2 Sam. 2:8-10). Esh-baal was a pagan name and illustrates the influence of paganism in even the best families.

9:1 But Judah was exiled to Babylon because of their unfaithfulness. As with the northern tribes, Judah was exiled because of unfaithfulness to God (see 5:25-6). Judah, however, did return. The books of 1 and 2 Chronicles were written in an attempt to help them learn from past mistakes.

9:4-6 descendant. The chronicler's records served as an important "who's who" directory for the returnees. Genealogy played a crucial role in restoring individual identities, family roles, and social class to a lost people.

9:10-13 capable men employed in the ministry of God's temple. In Nehemiah 11:10-14

¹⁹ Shallum son of Kore, son of Ebiasaph, son of Korah and his relatives from his household, the Korahites, were assigned to guard the thresholds of the tent.ᵃ Their ancestors had been assigned to the LORD's camp as guardians of the entrance. ²⁰ In earlier times Phinehas son of Eleazar had been their leader, and the LORD was with him. ²¹ Zechariah son of Meshelemiah was the gatekeeper at the entrance to the tent of meeting.

²² The total number of those chosen to be gatekeepers at the thresholds was 212. They were registered by genealogy in their villages. David and Samuel the seer had appointed them to their trusted positions. ²³ So they and their sons were assigned to the gates of the LORD's house, the house of the tent. ²⁴ The gatekeepers were on the four sides: east, west, north, and south. ²⁵ Their relatives came from their villages at fixed times to be with them seven days, ²⁶ but the four chief gatekeepers, who were Levites, were entrusted with the rooms and the treasuries of God's temple. ²⁷ They spent the night in the vicinity of God's temple, because they had guard duty and were in charge of opening it every morning.

²⁸ Some of them were in charge of the utensils used in worship. They would count them when they brought them in and when they took them out. ²⁹ Others were put in charge of the furnishings and all the utensils of the sanctuary, as well as the fine flour, wine, oil, incense, and spices. ³⁰ But some of the priests' sons mixed the spices. ³¹ A Levite called Mattithiah, the firstborn of Shallum the Korahite, was entrusted with baking the bread.ᵇ ³² Some of the Kohathites' relatives were responsible for preparing the rows of the bread ⌊of the Presence⌋ every Sabbath.

³³ The singers, the heads of Levite families, stayed in the ⌊temple⌋ chambers and were exempt from other tasks because they were on duty day and night. ³⁴ These were the heads of Levite families, chiefs according to their genealogies, and lived in Jerusalem.

Saul's Family

³⁵ Jeiel fathered Gibeon and lived in Gibeon. His wife's name was Maacah. ³⁶ Abdon was his firstborn son, then Zur, Kish, Baal, Ner, Nadab, ³⁷ Gedor, Ahio, Zechariah, and Mikloth. ³⁸ Mikloth fathered Shimeam. These also lived opposite their relatives in Jerusalem with their ⌊other⌋ relatives.

³⁹ Ner fathered Kish, Kish fathered Saul, and Saul fathered Jonathan, Malchishua, Abinadab, and Esh-baal. ⁴⁰ Jonathan's son was Merib-baal, and Merib-baal fathered Micah. ⁴¹ Micah's sons: Pithon, Melech, Tahrea, and Ahaz.ᶜ ⁴² Ahaz fathered Jarah; Jarah fathered Alemeth, Azmaveth, and Zimri; Zimri fathered Moza. ⁴³ Moza fathered Binea. His son was Rephaiah, his son Eleasah, and his son Azel. ⁴⁴ Azel had six sons, and these were their names: Azrikam, Bocheru, Ishmael, Sheariah, Obadiah, and Hanan. These were Azel's sons.

The Deaths of Saul and His Sons

10 The Philistines fought against Israel, and Israel's men fled from them and were killed on Mount Gilboa. ² The Philistines pursued Saul and his sons and killed Saul's sons Jonathan, Abinadab, and Malchishua. ³ When the battle intensified against Saul, the archers found him and severely wounded him. ⁴ Then Saul said to his armor-bearer, "Draw your sword and run me through with it, or these uncircumcised men will come and torture me!" But his armor-bearer wouldn't do it because he was terrified. Then Saul took his sword and fell on it. ⁵ When his armor-bearer saw that Saul was dead, he also fell on his own sword and died. ⁶ So Saul and his three sons died—his whole house died together.

⁷ When all the men of Israel in the valley saw that the army had run away and that Saul and his sons were dead, they abandoned their cities and fled. So the Philistines came and settled in them.

⁸ The next day when the Philistines came to strip the slain, they found Saul and his sons dead on Mount Gilboa. ⁹ They stripped Saul, cut off his head, took his armor, and sent messengers throughout the land of the Philistines to spread the good news to their idols and their people. ¹⁰ Then they put his armor in the temple of their gods and hung his skull in the temple of Dagon.

¹¹ When all Jabesh-gilead heard of everything the Philistines had done to Saul, ¹² all their brave men set out and retrieved the body of Saul and the bodies of his sons and brought them to Jabesh. They buried their bones under the oakᵈ in Jabesh and fasted seven days.

ᵃ**9:19** = the temple ᵇ**9:31** Lit *with things prepared in pans* ᶜ**9:41** LXX, Syr, Tg, Vg, Arabic; MT omits *and Ahaz*; 1 Ch 8:35 ᵈ**10:12** Or *terebinth or large tree*

---

a match was made between historical record (6:12-13) and contemporary record. The people's ties with the past gave them a perspective on the present and hope for the future.

9:19 Korah. These were descendants of Kohath who were close relations to the priests.

9:22-27 gatekeepers. The gatekeepers served as the neighborhood watch. Refugees rebuilt their lives amid ruin.

9:28-34 This division of duties among the Levites consisted of civic duty specialties. Levites cared for the house of God.

10:3-6 Draw your sword and run me through. Saul was requesting assisted suicide. The armor-bearer refused to cooperate, most likely because he was trained to respect the king. His whole purpose in life was to assist and protect him. When Saul did himself in, the armor-bearer probably felt he had nothing to live for, and followed the king's example. Saul's suicide was a final act of despair by one

13 Saul died for his unfaithfulness to the LORD because he did not keep the LORD's word. He even consulted a medium for guidance, 14 but he did not inquire of the LORD. So the LORD put him to death and turned the kingdom over to David son of Jesse.

David's Anointing as King

11 All Israel came together to David at Hebron and said, "Here we are, your own flesh and blood.ᵃ 2 Even when Saul was king, you led us out ⌊to battle⌋ and brought us back. The LORD your God also said to you, 'You will shepherd My people Israel and be ruler over My people Israel.' "

3 So all the elders of Israel came to the king at Hebron. David made a covenant with them at Hebron in the LORD's presence, and they anointed David king over Israel, in keeping with the LORD's word through Samuel.

David's Capture of Jerusalem

4 David and all Israel marched to Jerusalem (that is, Jebus); the Jebusites who inhabited the land were there. 5 The inhabitants of Jebus said to David, "You will never get in here." Yet David did capture the stronghold of Zion (that is, the city of David).

6 David said, "Whoever is first to kill a Jebusite will become commander-in-chief." Joab son of Zeruiah went up first, so he became the chief.

7 Then David took up residence in the stronghold; therefore, it was called the city of David. 8 He built up the city all the way around, from the supporting terraces to the surrounding parts, and Joab restored the rest of the city. 9 David steadily grew more powerful, and the LORD of •Hosts was with him.

Exploits of David's Warriors

10 The following were the chiefs of David's warriors who, together with all Israel, strongly supported him in his reign to make him king according to the LORD's word about Israel. 11 This is the list of David's warriors:

Jashobeam son of Hachmoni was chief of the Thirty;ᵇ he wielded his spear against 300 and killed them at one time.

12 After him, Eleazar son of Dodo the Ahohite was one of the three warriors. 13 He was with David at Pasdammim when the Philistines had gathered there for battle. A plot of ground full of barley was there, where the troops had fled from the Philistines. 14 But Eleazar and Davidᶜ took their stand in the middle of the plot and defended it. They killed the Philistines, and the LORD gave them a great victory.

15 Three of the 30 chief men went down to David, to the rock at the cave of Adullam, while the Philistine army was encamped in the Valley of Rephaim. 16 At that time David was in the stronghold, and a Philistine garrison was at Bethlehem. 17 David was extremely thirstyᵈ and said, "If only someone would bring me water from the well at the city gate of Bethlehem!" 18 So the Three broke through the Philistine camp and drew water from the well at the gate of Bethlehem. They brought it back to David, but he refused to drink it. Instead, he poured it out to the LORD. 19 David said, "I would never do such a thing in the presence of God! How can I drink the blood of these men who risked their lives?" For they brought it at the risk of their lives. So he would not drink it. Such were the exploits of the three warriors.

20 Abishai, Joab's brother, was the leader of the Three.ᵉ He raised his spear against 300 ⌊men⌋ and killed them, gaining a reputation among the Three. 21 He was the most honored of the Three and became their commander even though he did not become one of the Three.

22 Benaiah son of Jehoiada was the son of a brave manᶠ from Kabzeel, a man of many exploits. Benaiah killed two ⌊sons of⌋ Ariel of Moab,ᵍ and he went down into a pit on a snowy day and killed a lion. 23 He also killed an Egyptian who was seven and a half feet tall.ʰ Even though the Egyptian had a spear in his hand like a weaver's beam, Benaiah went down to him with a club, snatched the spear out of the Egyptian's hand, and then killed him with his own spear. 24 These were the exploits of Benaiah son of Jehoiada, who had a reputation among the three warriors. 25 He was the most honored of the Thirty, but he did not become one of the Three. David put him in charge of his bodyguard.

26 The fighting men were:

Joab's brother Asahel,
Elhanan son of Dodo of Bethlehem,
27 Shammoth the Harorite,
Helez the Pelonite,
28 Ira son of Ikkesh the Tekoite,
Abiezer the Anathothite,
29 Sibbecai the Hushathite,
Ilai the Ahohite,
30 Maharai the Netophathite,
Heled son of Baanah the Netophathite,
31 Ithai son of Ribai from Gibeah
of the Benjaminites,
Benaiah the Pirathonite,

ᵃ11:1 Lit *your bone and flesh*   ᵇ11:11 Alt Hb tradition reads *Three*   ᶜ11:14 Lit *But they*   ᵈ11:17 Lit *And David craved*   ᵉ11:20 Syr reads *Thirty*
ᶠ11:22 Or *was a valiant man*   ᵍ11:22 Or *He killed two Moabite warriors*   ʰ11:23 Lit *who measured five cubits*

---

who had entirely alienated himself from God. **his whole house died together.** While three sons of Saul died in this same battle (including Jonathan, David's friend), two sons of Saul, Mephibosheth and Ishbosheth, survived Saul's death.

11:2 You will shepherd My people Israel.

David grew up as a shepherd of sheep, and now he would use his skills as a protector of people. This phrase would also apply to the Messiah who would come from David's lineage (see Isa. 40:11; Matt. 2:6).

11:7 it was called the city of David. Bethlehem was the city of David's birth, but Jerusa-

lem was the city of David's triumph. Located near the juncture of the northern tribes of Israel and the southern tribes that became Judah, Jerusalem was an ideal place for a capital city that would bring the nation together under one king.

11:15-19 David's warriors demonstrate their

32 Hurai from the •wadis of Gaash,
Abiel the Arbathite,
33 Azmaveth the Baharumite,
Eliahba the Shaalbonite,
34 the sons of[a] Hashem the Gizonite,
Jonathan son of Shagee the Hararite,
35 Ahiam son of Sachar the Hararite,
Eliphal son of Ur,
36 Hepher the Mecherathite,
Ahijah the Pelonite,
37 Hezro the Carmelite,
Naarai son of Ezbai,
38 Joel the brother of Nathan,
Mibhar son of Hagri,
39 Zelek the Ammonite,
Naharai the Beerothite, the armor-bearer
for Joab son of Zeruiah,
40 Ira the Ithrite,
Gareb the Ithrite,
41 Uriah the Hittite,
Zabad son of Ahlai,
42 Adina son of Shiza the Reubenite, chief
of the Reubenites, and 30 with him,
43 Hanan son of Maacah,
Joshaphat the Mithnite,
44 Uzzia the Ashterathite,
Shama and Jeiel the sons of Hotham
the Aroerite,
45 Jediael son of Shimri and his brother Joha
the Tizite,
46 Eliel the Mahavite,
Jeribai and Joshaviah, the sons of Elnaam,
Ithmah the Moabite,
47 Eliel, Obed, and Jaasiel the Mezobaite.

David's First Supporters

12 The following were the men who came to David at Ziklag while he was still banned from the presence of Saul son of Kish. They were among the warriors who helped him in battle. 2 They were archers who, using either their right or left hand, could ⌊throw⌋ stones ⌊with a sling⌋ or ⌊shoot⌋ arrows with a bow. They were Saul's relatives from Benjamin:

3 Their chief was Ahiezer son of Shemaah the Gibeathite.
Then there was his brother Joash;
Jeziel and Pelet sons of Azmaveth;
Beracah, Jehu the Anathothite;
4 Ishmaiah the Gibeonite, a warrior among the

Thirty and ⌊a leader⌋ over the Thirty;
[b] Jeremiah, Jahaziel, Johanan, Jozabad
the Gederathite;
5 Eluzai, Jerimoth, Bealiah, Shemariah,
Shephatiah the Haruphite;
6 Elkanah, Isshiah, Azarel, Joezer,
and Jashobeam, the Korahites;
7 and Joelah and Zebadiah, the sons of Jeroham
from Gedor.

8 Some Gadites defected to David at his stronghold in the desert. They were fighting men, trained for battle, expert with shield and spear. Their faces were like the faces of lions, and they were as swift as gazelles on the mountains.

9 Ezer was the chief, Obadiah second,
Eliab third,
10 Mishmannah fourth, Jeremiah fifth,
11 Attai sixth, Eliel seventh,
12 Johanan eighth, Elzabad ninth,
13 Jeremiah tenth, and Machbannai eleventh.

14 These Gadites were army commanders; the least of them was a match for a hundred, and the greatest of them for a thousand. 15 These are the men who crossed the Jordan in the first month[c] when it was overflowing all its banks, and put to flight all ⌊those in⌋ the valleys to the east and to the west.

16 Other Benjaminites and men from Judah also went to David at the stronghold. 17 David went out to meet them and said to them, "If you have come in peace to help me, my heart will be united with you, but if you have come to betray me to my enemies even though my hands have done no wrong, may the God of our ancestors look on it and judge."

18 Then the Spirit took control of[d] Amasai, chief of the Thirty, ⌊and he said⌋:

⌊We are⌋ yours, David,
⌊we are⌋ with you, son of Jesse!
Peace, peace to you,
and peace to him who helps you,
for your God helps you.

So David received them and made them leaders of his troops.

19 Some Manassites defected to David when he went with the Philistines to fight against Saul. However, they did not help the Philistines because the Philistine rulers, following consultation, sent David away. They said, "It will be our heads if he defects to his master Saul."

---

[a] 11:34 LXX omits the sons of; 2 Sm 23:32   [b] 12:4 1 Ch 12:5 in Hb starts here, v. 5 is 1 Ch 12:6 in Hb, and so on throughout chap 12
[c] 12:15 March–April   [d] 12:18 Lit Spirit clothed; Jdg 6:34; 2 Ch 24:20

---

unselfish devotion. Their efforts prompt David to demonstrate his ultimate devotion to God.
11:20 Abishai. He was listed as bravest of the brave.
11:39, 41, 46 At least three of David's thirty were of Gentile origin: Zelek the Ammonite, Uriah the Hittite, and Ithmah the Moabite. This

is all the more remarkable since the Ammonites and the Moabites carried a curse on them (Deut. 23:3). Uriah the Hittite was the husband of Bathsheba.
12:2 either their right or left hand. In the ancient world, left-handedness was usually associated with evil or demons, so many

southpaws became ambidextrous. This could be turned to a huge advantage in battle, because when an army attacked from the left, the defenders shields would be facing away in their left hands, thus exposing their right side to immediate danger. Conversely, an ambidextrous attacker could switch their

20 When David went to Ziklag, some men from Manasseh defected to him: Adnah, Jozabad, Jediael, Michael, Jozabad, Elihu, and Zillethai, chiefs of thousands in Manasseh. 21 They helped David against the marauders, for they were all brave warriors and commanders in the army. 22 At that time, men came day after day to help David until there was a great army, like an army of God.a

David's Soldiers in Hebron

23 The numbers of the armed troops who came to David at Hebron to turn Saul's kingdom over to him, according to the LORD's word, were as follows:

24 From the Judahites: 6,800 armed troops bearing shields and spears.

25 From the Simeonites: 7,100 brave warriors ready for war.

26 From the Levites: 4,600 27 in addition to Jehoiada, leader of the house of Aaron, with 3,700 men; 28 and Zadok, a young brave warrior, with 22 commanders from his own ancestral house.

29 From the Benjaminites, the relatives of Saul: 3,000 (up to that time the majority of the Benjaminites maintained their allegiance to the house of Saul).

30 From the Ephraimites: 20,800 brave warriors who were famous men in their ancestral houses.

31 From half the tribe of Manasseh: 18,000 designated by name to come and make David king.

32 From the Issacharites, who understood the times and knew what Israel should do: 200 chiefs with all their relatives under their command.

33 From Zebulun: 50,000 who could serve in the army, trained for battle with all kinds of weapons of war, with singleness of purpose to help David.b

34 From Naphtali: 1,000 commanders accompanied by 37,000 men with shield and spear.

35 From the Danites: 28,600 trained for battle.

36 From Asher: 40,000 who could serve in the army, trained for battle.

37 From across the Jordan—from the Reubenites, Gadites, and half the tribe of Manasseh: 120,000 men equipped with all the military weapons of war.

38 All these warriors, lined up in battle formation, came to Hebron with wholehearted determination to make David king over all Israel. All the rest of Israel was also of one mind to make David king. 39 They were there with David for three days, eating and drinking, for their relatives had provided for them. 40 In addition, their neighbors from as far away as Issachar, Zebulun, and Naphtali came bringing food on donkeys, camels, mules, and oxen—abundant provisions of flour, fig cakes, raisins, wine and oil, oxen, and sheep. Indeed, there was joy in Israel.

David and the Ark

13 David consulted with all his leaders, the commanders of hundreds and of thousands. 2 Then he said to the whole assembly of Israel, "If it seems good to you, and if this is from the LORD our God, let us spread out and send the message to the rest of our relatives in all the districts of Israel, including the priests and Levites in their cities with pasturelands, that they should gather together with us. 3 Then let us bring back the ark of our God, for we did not inquire of Him in Saul's days." 4 Since the proposal seemed right to all the people, the whole assembly agreed to do it.

5 So David assembled all Israel, from the Shihor of Egypt to the entrance of Hamath,c to bring the ark of God from Kiriath-jearim. 6 David and all Israel went to Baalah (that is, Kiriath-jearim), which belongs to Judah, to take from there the ark of God, which is called by the name of the LORD who dwells ⌊between⌋ the •cherubim. 7 At Abinadab's house, they set the ark of God on a new cart. Uzzah and Ahiod were guiding the cart.

8 David and all Israel were celebrating with all their might before God with songs and with lyres, harps, tambourines, cymbals, and trumpets. 9 When they came to Chidon's threshing floor, Uzzah reached out to hold the ark, because the oxen had stumbled. 10 Then the LORD's anger burned against Uzzah, and He struck him dead because he had reached out to the ark. So he died there in the presence of God.

11 David was angry because of the LORD's outburst against Uzzah, so he named that place Outburst Against Uzzah,e as it is ⌊still named⌋ today. 12 David feared God that day, and said, "How can I ever bring the ark of God to me?" 13 So David did not move the ark of God homef to the city of David; instead, he took it to the house of Obed-edom the Gittite. 14 The ark of God remained with Obed-edom's family in his house for three months, and the LORD blessed his family and all that he had.

God's Blessing on David

14 King Hiram of Tyre sent envoys to David, along with cedar logs, stonemasons, and carpenters

---

a12:22 Or like the ultimate army   b12:33 LXX; Hb omits David   c13:5 Or to Lebo-hamath   d13:7 Or and his brothers   e13:11 Or Perez-uzzah   f13:13 Lit to himself

---

shield to their right hand and attack with their natural left. In the close-up manner in which most battles were decided, this was a decided benefit.

12:23-37 David warmly received the help of Saul's defectors and made many volunteers leaders of his army (v. 18).

12:38 one mind. Throughout Israel's history, the people were never of one mind about anything. The ten northern ten tribes (Israel) were always opposed to the two southern tribes (Judah). David's era was a golden era in part because he was able to unite a divided nation.

13:1-4 bring back the ark. The Philistines had

captured and then returned the ark years earlier, but it remained forgotten in a warehouse.

13:7 new cart. The ark was irreverently transported on a cart. The Levites alone were allowed to carry the ark. Even then, it could only be transported on poles inserted in its corner rings (see Ex. 25:13-15).

to build a palace for him. ² Then David knew that the LORD had established him as king over Israel and that his kingdom had been exalted for the sake of His people Israel.

³ David took more wives in Jerusalem, and he became the father of more sons and daughters. ⁴ These are the names of the children born to him in Jerusalem: Shammua, Shobab, Nathan, Solomon, ⁵ Ibhar, Elishua, Elpelet, ⁶ Nogah, Nepheg, Japhia, ⁷ Elishama, Beeliada, and Eliphelet.

⁸ When the Philistines heard that David had been anointed king over all Israel, they all went in search of David; when David heard of this, he went out to face them. ⁹ Now the Philistines had come and made a raid in the Valley of Rephaim, ¹⁰ so David inquired of God, "Should I go to war against the Philistines? Will You hand them over to me?"

The LORD replied, "Go, and I will hand them over to you."

¹¹ So the Israelites went up to Baal-perazim, and David defeated the Philistines there. Then David said, "Like a bursting flood, God has used me to burst out against my enemies." Therefore, they named that place the Lord Bursts Out.ᵃ ¹² The Philistines abandoned their idols there, and David ordered that they be burned in the fire.

¹³ Once again the Philistines made a raid in the valley. ¹⁴ So David again inquired of God, and God answered him, "Do not pursue them directly. Circle down away from them and attack them opposite the balsam trees. ¹⁵ When you hear the sound of marching in the tops of the balsam trees, then march out to battle, for God will have marched out ahead of you to attack the camp of the Philistines." ¹⁶ So David did exactly as God commanded him, and they struck down the Philistine army from Gibeon to Gezer. ¹⁷ Then David's fame spread throughout the lands, and the LORD caused all the nations to be terrified of him.

The Ark Comes to Jerusalem

15 David built houses for himself in the city of David, and he prepared a place for the ark of God and pitched a tent for it. ² Then David said, "No one but the Levites may carry the ark of God, because the LORD has chosen them to carry the ark of the LORD and to minister before Him forever."

³ David assembled all Israel at Jerusalem to bring the ark of the LORD to the place he had prepared for it. ⁴ Then he gathered together the descendants of Aaron and the Levites:

⁵ From the Kohathites, Uriel the leader and 120 of his relatives; ⁶ from the Merarites, Asaiah the leader and 220 of his relatives; ⁷ from the Gershomites, Joel the leader and 130 of his relatives; ⁸ from the Elizaphanites, Shemaiah the leader and 200 of his relatives; ⁹ from the Hebronites, Eliel the leader and 80 of his relatives; ¹⁰ from the Uzzielites, Amminadab the leader and 112 of his relatives.

¹¹ David summoned the priests Zadok and Abiathar and the Levites Uriel, Asaiah, Joel, Shemaiah, Eliel, and Amminadab. ¹² He said to them, "You are the heads of the Levite families. You and your relatives must consecrate yourselves so that you may bring the ark of the LORD God of Israel to ⌊the place⌋ I have prepared for it. ¹³ For the LORD our God burst out ⌊in anger⌋ against us because you Levites were not ⌊with⌋ us the first time, for we didn't inquire of Him about the proper procedures." ¹⁴ So the priests and the Levites consecrated themselves to bring up the ark of the LORD God of Israel. ¹⁵ Then the Levites carried the ark of God the way Moses had commanded according to the word of the LORD: on their shoulders with the poles.

¹⁶ Then David told the leaders of the Levites to appoint their relatives as singers and to have them raise their voices with joy accompanied by musical instruments—harps, lyres, and cymbals. ¹⁷ So the Levites appointed Heman son of Joel; from his relatives, Asaph son of Berechiah; and from their relatives the Merarites, Ethan son of Kushaiah. ¹⁸ With them were their relatives second in rank: Zechariah, Jaaziel,ᵇ Shemiramoth, Jehiel, Unni, Eliab, Benaiah, Maaseiah, Mattithiah, Eliphelehu, Mikneiah, and the gatekeepers Obed-edom and Jeiel. ¹⁹ The singers Heman, Asaph, and Ethan were to sound the bronze cymbals; ²⁰ Zechariah, Aziel, Shemiramoth, Jehiel, Unni, Eliab, Maaseiah, and Benaiah were to play harps according to *Alamoth;*ᶜ ²¹ and Mattithiah, Eliphelehu, Mikneiah, Obed-edom, Jeiel, and Azaziah were to lead the music with lyres according to the •*Sheminith.* ²² Chenaniah, the leader of the Levites in music, was to direct the music because he was skillful. ²³ Berechiah and Elkanah were to be gatekeepers for the ark. ²⁴ The priests, Shebaniah, Joshaphat, Nethanel, Amasai, Zechariah, Benaiah, and Eliezer, were to blow trumpets before the ark of God. Obed-edom and Jehiah were also to be gatekeepers for the ark.

²⁵ David, the elders of Israel, and the commanders of the thousands went with rejoicing to bring the ark of the covenant of the LORD from the house of Obed-

---

ᵃ**14:11** Or *Baal-perazim*   ᵇ**15:18** Some Hb mss, LXX; other Hb mss read *Zechariah son and Jaaziel*   ᶜ**15:20** This notation may refer to a high pitch, perhaps a tune sung by soprano voices; the Hb word means "young women."

13:10 reached out to the ark. Uzzah's punishment seems harsh, but it impressed the LORD's holiness on the people.

14:10 David inquired. "Inquired" reflects the same Hebrew word used to describe Saul's inquiry of the Lord (1 Sam. 28:6). Unlike David, when Saul did not immediately get an answer

from God he "consulted" (a stronger Hebrew word for "inquire") the witch-medium from Endor. How the mighty had fallen! God then replied to Saul that he would be defeated by the Philistines and die the next day; a stark contrast to the thumbs-up given David here. David was, after all, a man after God's own heart.

14:11 Baal-perazim. "Perazim" in Hebrew, means "broken out." Previously, it described God's anger directed towards the Israelites, who were worshipping idols in the wilderness (Ps. 106:29), and Uzzah (13:11). Here, Yahweh once again strikes against those who violate His holiness.

edom. ²⁶ And because God helped the Levites who were carrying the ark of the covenant of the LORD, they sacrificed seven bulls and seven rams.

²⁷ Now David was dressed in a robe of fine linen, as were all the Levites who were carrying the ark, as well as the singers and Chenaniah, the music leader of the singers. David also wore a linen •ephod. ²⁸ So all Israel was bringing the ark of the covenant of the LORD up with shouts, the sound of the ram's horn, trumpets, and cymbals, and the playing of harps and lyres. ²⁹ As the ark of the covenant of the LORD was entering the city of David, Saul's daughter Michal looked down from the window and saw King David dancing[a] and celebrating, and she despised him in her heart.

16

They brought the ark of God and placed it inside the tent David had pitched for it. Then they offered •burnt offerings and •fellowship offerings in God's presence. ² When David had finished offering the burnt offerings and the fellowship offerings, he blessed the people in the name of the LORD. ³ Then he distributed to each and every Israelite, both men and women, a loaf of bread, a date cake, and a raisin cake.

⁴ David appointed some of the Levites to be ministers before the ark of the LORD, to celebrate the LORD God of Israel, and to give thanks and praise to Him. ⁵ •Asaph was the chief and Zechariah was second to him. Jeiel, Shemiramoth, Jehiel, Mattithiah, Eliab, Benaiah, Obed-edom, and Jeiel played the harps and lyres, while Asaph ⌊sounded⌋ the cymbals ⁶ and the priests Benaiah and Jahaziel ⌊blew⌋ the trumpets regularly before the ark of the covenant of God.

David's Psalm of Thanksgiving

⁷ On that day David decreed for the first time that thanks be given to the LORD by Asaph and his relatives:

⁸ Give thanks to the LORD; call on His name;
proclaim His deeds among the peoples.
⁹ Sing to Him; sing praise to Him;
tell about all His wonderful works!
¹⁰ Honor His holy name;
let the hearts of those who seek the LORD
rejoice.
¹¹ Search for the LORD and for His strength;
seek His face always.
¹² Remember the wonderful works He has done,
His wonders, and the judgments
He has pronounced,[b]
¹³ you offspring of Israel His servant,
Jacob's descendants—His chosen ones.

¹⁴ He is the LORD our God;
His judgments ⌊govern⌋ the whole earth.
¹⁵ Remember His covenant forever—
the promise He ordained for a thousand
generations,
¹⁶ ⌊the covenant⌋ He made with Abraham,
swore[c] to Isaac,
¹⁷ and confirmed to Jacob as a decree,
and to Israel as an everlasting covenant:
¹⁸ "I will give the land of Canaan to you
as your inherited portion."
¹⁹ When they[d] were few in number,
very few indeed, and temporary residents
in Canaan
²⁰ wandering from nation to nation
and from one kingdom to another,
²¹ He allowed no one to oppress them;
He rebuked kings on their behalf:
²² "Do not touch My anointed ones
or harm My prophets."

²³ Sing to the LORD, all the earth.
Proclaim His salvation from day to day.
²⁴ Declare His glory among the nations,
His wonderful works among all peoples.

²⁵ For the LORD is great and is highly praised;
He is feared above all gods.
²⁶ For all the gods of the peoples are idols,
but the LORD made the heavens.
²⁷ Splendor and majesty are before Him;
strength and joy are in His place.
²⁸ Ascribe to the LORD, families of the peoples,
ascribe to the LORD glory and strength.
²⁹ Ascribe to the LORD the glory of His name;
bring an offering and come before Him.
Worship the LORD
in the splendor of ⌊His⌋ holiness;
³⁰ tremble before Him, all the earth.

The world is firmly established;
it cannot be shaken.
³¹ Let the heavens be glad and the earth rejoice,
and let them say among the nations, "The LORD
is King!"
³² Let the sea and everything in it resound;
let the fields and all that is in them exult.
³³ Then the trees of the forest will shout for joy
before the LORD,
for He is coming to judge the earth.

---

^a**15:29** Or *whirling* ^b**16:12** Lit *judgments of His mouth* ^c**16:16** Lit *and His oath* ^d**16:19** One Hb ms, LXX, Vg; MT reads *you*

15:12 consecrate yourselves. Rather than repeat history, the Levites are to be spiritually prepared for their assignment (see Ex. 29:1-37).

15:27 linen ephod. The ephod was a chest covering reserved for the office of priest. As a sort of priest-king, David exercises a new form of spiritual leadership over Israel.

15:29 she despised him. It seems that Michal's feeling was due to the fact that David was dancing nearly naked, which was beneath David's dignity as king—especially since servant girls were watching (see 2 Sam. 6:16-23.) David, however, was showing an un-

bridled exuberance, which was appropriate to this moment of celebration. Michal's displeasure also gives example to her disregard for things sacred, as her father had before her (1 Sam. 13:8-14).

16:8-36 The chronicler embellishes the celebration in Jerusalem by the addition of a com-

34 Give thanks to the LORD, for He is good;
His faithful love endures forever.

35 And say: "Save us, God of our salvation;
gather us and rescue us from the nations
so that we may give thanks to Your holy name
and rejoice in Your praise.

36 May the LORD, the God of Israel, be praised
from everlasting to everlasting."

Then all the people said, "•Amen" and "Praise the LORD."

37 So David left Asaph and his relatives there before the ark of the LORD's covenant to minister regularly before the ark according to the daily requirements. 38 ⌞He also left⌟ Obed-edom and his[a] 68 relatives. Obed-edom son of Jeduthun and Hosah were to be gatekeepers. 39 ⌞David left⌟ Zadok the priest and his fellow priests before the tabernacle of the LORD at the •high place in Gibeon 40 to offer burnt offerings regularly, morning and evening, to the LORD on the altar of burnt offerings and to do everything that was written in the law of the LORD, which He had commanded Israel to keep. 41 With them were Heman, Jeduthun, and the rest who were chosen and designated by name to give thanks to the LORD—for His faithful love endures forever. 42 Heman and Jeduthun had with them trumpets and cymbals to play and musical instruments of God. Jeduthun's sons were at the gate.

43 Then all the people left for their homes, and David returned ⌞home⌟ to bless his household.

The LORD's Covenant with David

17 When David had settled into his palace, he said to Nathan the prophet, "Look! I am living in a cedar house while the ark of the LORD's covenant is under tent curtains."

2 So Nathan told David, "Do all that is on your heart, for God is with you."

3 But that night the word of God came to Nathan: 4 "Go to David My servant and say, 'This is what the LORD says: You are not the one to build Me a house to dwell in. 5 From the time I brought Israel out of ⌞Egypt⌟ until today I have not lived in a house; instead, I have moved from tent to tent and from tabernacle ⌞to tabernacle⌟. 6 In all My travels throughout Israel, have I ever spoken a word to even one of the judges of Israel, whom I commanded to shepherd My people, asking: Why haven't you built Me a house of cedar?'

7 "Now this is what you will say to My servant David: 'This is what the LORD of •Hosts says: I took you from the pasture and from following the sheep, to be ruler over My people Israel. 8 I have been with you wherever you have gone, and I have destroyed all your enemies before you. I will make a name for you like that of the greatest in the land. 9 I will establish a place for My people Israel and plant them, so that they may live there and not be disturbed again. Evildoers will not continue to oppress them as they formerly have 10 ever since the day I ordered judges to be over My people Israel. I will also subdue all your enemies.

" 'Furthermore, I declare to you that the LORD Himself will build a house for you. 11 When your time comes to be with your fathers, I will raise up after you your descendant,[b] who is one of your own sons, and I will establish his kingdom. 12 He will build a house for Me, and I will establish his throne forever. 13 I will be a father to him, and he will be a son to Me. I will not take away My faithful love from him as I took it from the one who was before you. 14 I will appoint him over My house and My kingdom forever, and his throne will be established forever.' "

15 Nathan recounted all these words and this entire vision to David.

David's Prayer of Thanksgiving

16 Then King David went in, sat in the LORD's presence, and said, "Who am I, LORD God, and what is my house that You have brought me this far? 17 This was a little thing to You,[c] God, for You have spoken about Your servant's house in the distant future. You regard me as a man of distinction,[d] LORD God. 18 What more can David say to You for honoring Your servant? You know Your servant. 19 LORD, You have done all this greatness, making known all these great ⌞promises⌟ because of Your servant and according to Your will. 20 LORD, there is no one like You, and there is no God besides You, as all we have heard confirms. 21 And who is like Your people Israel? God, You came to one nation on earth to redeem a people for Yourself, to make a name for Yourself through great and awesome deeds by driving out nations before Your people You redeemed from Egypt. 22 You made Your people Israel Your own people forever, and You, LORD, have become their God.

23 "Now, LORD, let the word that You have spoken concerning Your servant and his house be confirmed forever, and do as You have promised. 24 Let your name be confirmed and magnified forever in the saying, 'The LORD of Hosts, the God of Israel, is God over Israel.' May the house of Your servant David be established before You. 25 Since You, my God, have revealed to[e] Your servant that You will build him a house, Your ser-

---

[a] 16:38 LXX, Syr, Vg; Hb reads their [b] 17:11 Lit seed [c] 17:17 Lit thing in Your eyes [d] 17:17 Hb obscure [e] 17:25 Lit have uncovered the ear of

---

pilation of psalms not found in the book of Samuel (see Pss. 96:1-13; 105:1-15; 106:1, 47-48). David compiles events from the past into a merry celebration of the present.

17:1 a cedar house ... tent curtains. Cedars of Lebanon provided the most sought after building material of the time, later used in the temple's construction. In humility, David did not feel he should have a better dwelling than God.

17:5 I have moved from tent to tent. God resists the idea of being penned up in one building. In the book of Acts Paul declares, "The God who made the world and everything in it ... does not live in shrines made by hands" (Acts 17:24).

17:10 the LORD Himself will build a house for you. God counters David's offer to build a house for Him by saying He will build a house for David. God is not talking about a physical house, but a dynasty, the "house" of David.

vant has found ⌊courage⌋ to pray in Your presence. [26] LORD, You indeed are God, and You have promised this good thing to Your servant. [27] So now, You have been pleased to bless Your servant's house that it may continue before You forever. For You, LORD, have blessed it, and it is blessed forever."

David's Military Campaigns

18 After this, David defeated the Philistines, subdued them, and took Gath and its villages from Philistine control. [2] He also defeated the Moabites, and they became David's subjects and brought tribute.

[3] David also defeated King Hadadezer of Zobah at Hamath when he went to establish his control at the Euphrates River. [4] David captured 1,000 chariots, 7,000 horsemen, and 20,000 foot soldiers from him and hamstrung all the horses, and he kept 100 chariots.[a]

[5] When the Arameans of Damascus came to assist King Hadadezer of Zobah, David struck down 22,000 Aramean men. [6] Then he placed garrisons[b] in Aram of Damascus, and the Arameans became David's subjects and brought tribute. The LORD made David victorious wherever he went.

[7] David took the gold shields carried by Hadadezer's officers and brought them to Jerusalem. [8] From Tibhath and Cun, Hadadezer's cities, David also took huge quantities of bronze, from which Solomon made the bronze reservoir, the pillars, and the bronze articles.

[9] When King Tou of Hamath heard that David had defeated the entire army of King Hadadezer of Zobah, [10] he sent his son Hadoram to King David to greet him and to congratulate him because David had fought against Hadadezer and defeated him, for Tou and Hadadezer had fought many wars. ⌊Hadoram brought⌋ all kinds of items of gold, silver, and bronze. [11] King David also dedicated these to the LORD, along with the silver and gold he had carried off from all the nations—from Edom, Moab, the Ammonites, the Philistines, and the Amalekites.

[12] Abishai son of Zeruiah struck down 18,000 Edomites in the Valley of Salt. [13] He put garrisons in Edom, and all the Edomites were subject to David. The LORD made David victorious wherever he went.

[14] So David reigned over all Israel, administering justice and righteousness for all his people.

[15] Joab son of Zeruiah was over the army;
Jehoshaphat son of Ahilud was court historian;
[16] Zadok son of Ahitub

and Ahimelech[c] son of Abiathar were priests;
Shavsha was court secretary;
[17] Benaiah son of Jehoiada was over
the Cherethites and the Pelethites;
and David's sons were the chief officials
at the king's side.

War with the Ammonites

19 Some time later, King Nahash of the Ammonites died, and his son became king in his place. [2] Then David said, "I'll show kindness to Hanun son of Nahash, because his father showed kindness to me."

So David sent messengers to console him concerning his father. However, when David's emissaries arrived in the land of the Ammonites to console him, [3] the Ammonite leaders said to Hanun, "Just because David has sent men with condolences for you, do you really believe he's showing respect for your father? Instead, hasn't David sent his emissaries in order to scout out, overthrow, and spy on the land?" [4] So Hanun took David's emissaries, shaved them, cut their clothes in half at the hips, and sent them away.

[5] Someone came and reported to David about his men, so he sent ⌊someone⌋ to meet them, since the men were deeply humiliated. The king said, "Stay in Jericho until your beards grow back; then return."

[6] When the Ammonites realized they had made themselves repulsive to David, Hanun and the Ammonites sent 38 tons[d] of silver to hire chariots and horsemen from Aram-naharaim, Aram-maacah, and Zobah. [7] They hired 32,000 chariots and the king of Maacah with his army, who came and camped near Medeba. The Ammonites also gathered from their cities and came for the battle.

[8] David heard about this and sent Joab and the entire army of warriors. [9] The Ammonites marched out and lined up in battle formation at the entrance of the city while the kings who had come were in the field by themselves. [10] When Joab saw that there was a battle line in front of him and another behind him, he chose some men out of all the elite troops[e] of Israel and lined up in battle formation to engage the Arameans. [11] He placed the rest of the forces under the command of his brother Abishai, and they lined up in battle formation to engage the Ammonites.

[12] "If the Arameans are too strong for me," Joab said, "then you'll be my help. However, if the Ammonites are too strong for you, I'll help you. [13] Be strong! We must prove ourselves strong for our people and for the cities of our God. May the LORD's will be done."[f]

---

[a]**18:4** Or *chariot horses* [b]**18:6** Some Hb mss, LXX, Vg; other Hb mss omit *garrisons*; 2 Sm 8:6 [c]**18:16** Some Hb mss, LXX, Syr, Vg; other Hb mss read *Abimelech*; 2 Sm 8:17 [d]**19:6** Lit *1,000 talents* [e]**19:10** Lit *the choice ones*; 2 Sm 10:1 [f]**19:13** Lit *the LORD do what is good in His eyes*

17:12 He will build a house for Me. God says David's son will build a physical house for Him. Perhaps this was a concession to human weakness—we need a physical place to go in our search for God.

17:14 established forever. God implies a heavenly, eternal reign through His own son,

Jesus (see Isa. 9:6-7; Luke 1:32-33), a promise made to David (Ps. 89:35-37).

18:1–20:8 David's victories assure God's blessings on his reign. He defeated Israel's archenemies: the Philistines and the Moabites.

19:1–20:3 David's risky battle against the Ammonites and their reinforcements pays off in a

secured victory. David began by showing kindness at the death of Nahash, who ruled some 50 years.

19:4-5 shaved them. It was traditional for all adult men to wear beards as a sign of virility; this was a great humiliation.

19:9 Ammonites. The battlefield consisted of

14 Joab and the people with him approached the Arameans for battle, and they fled before him. 15 When the Ammonites saw that the Arameans had fled, they likewise fled before Joab's brother Abishai and entered the city. Then Joab went to Jerusalem.

16 When the Arameans realized that they had been defeated by Israel, they sent messengers to bring out the Arameans who were across the Euphrates with Shophach, commander of Hadadezer's army, leading them.

17 When this was reported to David, he gathered all Israel and crossed the Jordan. He came up to them and lined up in battle formation against them. When David lined up to engage the Arameans in battle, they fought against him. 18 But the Arameans fled before Israel, and David killed 7,000 of their charioteers and 40,000 foot soldiers. He also killed Shophach, commander of the army. 19 When Hadadezer's subjects saw that they had been defeated by Israel, they made peace with David and became his subjects. After this, the Arameans were never willing to help the Ammonites again.

Capture of the City of Rabbah

20 In the spring[a] when kings march out ⌊to war⌋, Joab led the army and destroyed the Ammonites' land. He came to Rabbah and besieged it, but David remained in Jerusalem. Joab attacked Rabbah and demolished it. 2 Then David took the crown from the head of their king,[b] and it was ⌊placed⌋ on David's head. He discovered the crown weighed 75 pounds[c] of gold, and there was a precious stone in it. In addition, David took away a large quantity of plunder from the city. 3 He brought out the people who were in it and put them to work with saws,[d] iron picks, and axes.[e] David did the same to all the Ammonite cities. Then he and all his troops returned to Jerusalem.

The Philistine Giants

4 After this, a war broke out with the Philistines at Gezer. At that time Sibbecai the Hushathite killed Sippai, a descendant of the giants,[f] and the Philistines were subdued.

5 Once again there was a battle with the Philistines, and Elhanan son of Jair killed Lahmi the brother of Goliath the Gittite. The shaft of his spear was like a weaver's beam.

6 There was still another battle at Gath where there was a man of extraordinary stature with six fingers ⌊on each hand⌋ and six toes ⌊on each foot⌋—24 in all. He, too, was descended from the giant.[g] 7 When he taunted

Israel, Jonathan, son of David's brother Shimei, killed him.

8 These were the descendants of the giant[g] in Gath killed by David and his soldiers.

David's Military Census

21 Satan[h] stood up against Israel and incited David to count ⌊the people of⌋ Israel. 2 So David said to Joab and the commanders of the troops, "Go and count Israel from Beer-sheba to Dan and bring ⌊a report⌋ to me so I can know their number."

3 Joab replied, "May the LORD multiply the number of His people a hundred times over! My lord the king, aren't they all my lord's servants? Why does my lord want to do this? Why should he bring guilt on Israel?"

4 Yet the king's order prevailed over Joab. So Joab left and traveled throughout Israel and then returned to Jerusalem. 5 Joab gave David the total of the registration of the troops. In all Israel there were 1,100,000 swordsmen and in Judah itself 470,000 swordsmen. 6 But he did not include Levi and Benjamin in the count because the king's command was detestable to him. 7 This command was also evil in God's sight, so He afflicted Israel.

8 David said to God, "I have sinned greatly because I have done this thing. Now, because I've been very foolish, please take away Your servant's guilt."

David's Punishment

9 Then the LORD instructed Gad, David's seer, 10 "Go and say to David, 'This is what the LORD says: I am offering you three ⌊choices⌋. Choose one of them for yourself, and I will do it to you.'"

11 So Gad went to David and said to him, "This is what the LORD says: 'Take your ⌊choice⌋—12 either three years of famine, three months of devastation by your foes with the sword of your enemy overtaking you, or three days of the sword of the LORD—a plague on the land, the angel of the LORD bringing destruction to the whole territory of Israel.' Now decide what answer I should take back to the One who sent me."

13 David answered Gad, "I have great anxiety. Please, let me fall into the LORD's hands because His mercies are very great, but don't let me fall into human hands."

14 So the LORD sent a plague on Israel, and 70,000 Israelite men died. 15 Then God sent an angel to Jerusalem to destroy it, but when the angel was about to destroy the city,[i] the LORD looked, relented concerning the destruction, and said to the angel who was destroy-

---

a 20:1 Lit At the time of the return of the year   b 20:2 LXX, Vg read of Milcom; = Molech; 1 Kg 11:5,7   c 20:2 Lit a talent   d 20:3 Text emended; MT reads and sawed them with the saw; 2 Sm 12:31   e 20:3 Text emended; MT reads saws; 2 Sm 12:31   f 20:4 Or the Rephaites   g 20:6,8 Or Raphah   h 21:1 Or An adversary; Jb 1:6; Zch 3:1–2   i 21:15 Lit but as he was destroying

---

a heavy Ammonite front at the entrance to the city, with Arameans' reinforcements waiting in the open fields.

20:2-3 [placed] on David's head. Crowning himself with an enemy's royalty was the ultimate sign of victory.

21:1–22:1 In the midst of military momentum,

David takes stock of his might through the use of a census. David's conceit and foolishness angers God (see 2 Sam. 24:1). The problem with this census is that David is putting his faith in numbers, rather than in the promises of God.

21:5 Joab. Joab, ever loyal to David, has the

complex job of tallying the totals for David's census.

21:24 offerings that cost [me] nothing Although Araunah was willing to provide a ready-made sacrifice free of charge, David insists on purchasing it. If one's offering doesn't cost him anything, giving it to God

ing ⌊the people⌋, "Enough, withdraw your hand now!" The angel of the LORD was then standing at the threshing floor of Ornan the Jebusite.

¹⁶ When David looked up and saw the angel of the LORD standing between earth and heaven, with his drawn sword in his hand stretched out over Jerusalem, David and the elders, clothed in •sackcloth, fell down with their faces ⌊to the ground⌋. ¹⁷ David said to God, "Wasn't I the one who gave the order to count the people? I am the one who has sinned and acted very wickedly. But these sheep, what have they done? My LORD God, please let Your hand be against me and against my father's family, but don't let the plague be against Your people."

David's Altar

¹⁸ So the angel of the LORD ordered Gad to tell David to go and set up an altar to the LORD on the threshing floor of Ornan the Jebusite. ¹⁹ David went up at Gad's command spoken in the name of the LORD.

²⁰ Ornan was threshing wheat when he turned and saw the angel. His four sons, who were with him, hid themselves. ²¹ David came to Ornan, and when Ornan looked and saw David, he left the threshing floor and bowed to David with his face to the ground.

²² Then David said to Ornan, "Give me this threshing-floor plot so that I may build an altar to the LORD on it. Give it to me for the full price, so the plague on the people may be halted."

²³ Ornan said to David, "Take it! My lord the king may do whatever he wants.ᵃ See, I give the oxen for the •burnt offerings, the threshing sledges for the wood, and the wheat for the •grain offering—I give it all."

²⁴ King David answered Ornan, "No, I insist on paying the full price, for I will not take for the LORD what belongs to you or offer burnt offerings that cost ⌊me⌋ nothing."

²⁵ So David gave Ornan 15 pounds of goldᵇ for the plot. ²⁶ He built an altar to the LORD there and offered burnt offerings and •fellowship offerings. He called on the LORD, and He answered him with fire from heaven on the altar of burnt offering.

²⁷ Then the LORD spoke to the angel, and he put his sword back into its sheath. ²⁸ At that time, when David saw that the LORD answered him at the threshing floor of Ornan the Jebusite, he offered sacrifices there. ²⁹ At that time the tabernacle of the LORD, which Moses made in the desert, and the altar of burnt offering were at the •high place in Gibeon, ³⁰ but David could not go before it to inquire of God, because he was terrified of

22 the sword of the LORD's angel. ¹ Then David said, "This is the house of the LORD God, and this is the altar of •burnt offering for Israel."

David's Preparations for the Temple

² So David gave orders to gather the foreigners that were in the land of Israel, and he appointed stonemasons to cut finished stones for building God's house. ³ David supplied a great deal of iron to make the nails for the doors of the gateways and for the fittings, together with an immeasurable quantity of bronze, ⁴ and innumerable cedar logs, because the Sidonians and Tyrians had brought a large quantity of cedar logs to David. ⁵ David said, "My son Solomon is young and inexperienced, and the house that is to be built for the LORD must be exceedingly great and famous and glorious in all the lands. Therefore, I must make provision for it." So David made lavish preparations for it before his death.

⁶ Then he summoned his son Solomon and instructed him to build a house for the LORD God of Israel. ⁷ "My son," David said to Solomon, "It was in my heart to build a house for the name of the LORD my God, ⁸ but the word of the LORD came to me: 'You have shed much blood and waged great wars. You are not to build a house for My name because you have shed so much blood on the ground before Me. ⁹ But a son will be born to you; he will be a man of rest. I will give him rest from all his surrounding enemies, for his name will be Solomon,ᶜ and I will give peace and quiet to Israel during his reign. ¹⁰ He is the one who will build a house for My name. He will be My son, and I will be his father. I will establish the throne of his kingdom over Israel forever.'

¹¹ "Now, my son, may the LORD be with you, and may you succeed in building the house of the LORD your God, as He said about you. ¹² Above all, may the LORD give you insight and understanding when He puts you in charge of Israel so that you may keep the law of the LORD your God. ¹³ Then you will succeed if you carefully follow the statutes and ordinances the LORD commanded Moses for Israel. Be strong and courageous. Don't be afraid or discouraged.

¹⁴ "Notice I have taken great pains to provide for the house of the LORD—3,775 tons of gold, 37,750 tons of silver,ᵈ and bronze and iron that can't be weighed because there is so much of it. I have also provided timber and stone, but you will need to add more to them. ¹⁵ You also have many workers: stonecutters, masons, carpenters, and people skilled in every kind of work

---

ᵃ**21:23** Lit *do what is good in his eyes* ᵇ**21:25** Lit *600 shekels of gold by weight* ᶜ**22:9** The name *Solomon* sounds like Hb "peace." ᵈ**22:14** Lit *100,000 talents of gold and 1,000,000 talents of silver*

---

cannot really be a sacrifice.
22:2-19 Resigned to the fact that he will not actually build the temple, David makes its spiritual and material preparations. His intimate connection with the temple is a major theme of both 1 and 2 Chronicles.
22:8-9 You have shed much blood. Here we

have a great paradox: while God was the one who called David to make war, the fact that David was a man of war disqualified him from building a temple to God. Even though God's directives are associated with much violence in the Old Testament, God was still working to lessen the amount of violence in the world. He

sent the flood to end humanity's trend to violence (see Gen. 6:11). Then later He sent visions of peace through prophets like Isaiah, visions of turning swords into plows, and spears into pruning knives (Isa. 2:4); and visions of the wolf living with the lamb and a time when "No one will harm or destroy" (Isa. 11:6,9).

16 in gold, silver, bronze, and iron—beyond number. Now begin the work, and may the LORD be with you."

17 Then David ordered all the leaders of Israel to help his son Solomon: 18 "The LORD your God is with you, isn't He? And hasn't He given you rest on every side? For He has handed the land's inhabitants over to me, and the land has been subdued before the LORD and His people. 19 Now determine in your mind and heart to seek the LORD your God. Get started building the LORD God's sanctuary so that you may bring the ark of the LORD's covenant and the holy articles of God to the temple that is to be built for the name of the LORD."

The Divisions of the Levites

23 When David was old and full of days, he installed his son Solomon as king over Israel. 2 Then he gathered all the leaders of Israel, the priests, and the Levites. 3 The Levites 30 years old and above were counted; the total number of men was 38,000 by headcount. 4 "Of these," [David said], "24,000 are to be in charge of the work on the LORD's temple, 6,000 are to be officers and judges, 5 4,000 are to be gatekeepers, and 4,000 are to praise the LORD with the instruments that I have made for worship."

6 Then David divided them into divisions according to Levi's sons: Gershom,a Kohath, and Merari.

7 The Gershomites: Ladan and Shimei.

8 Ladan's sons: Jehiel was the first, then Zetham, and Joel—three.

9 Shimei's sons: Shelomoth, Haziel, and Haran—three. Those were the heads of the families of Ladan.

10 Shimei's sons: Jahath, Zizah,b Jeush, and Beriah. Those were Shimei's sons—four.

11 Jahath was the first and Zizah was the second; however, Jeush and Beriah did not have many sons, so they became an ancestral house [and received] a single assignment.

12 Kohath's sons: Amram, Izhar, Hebron, and Uzziel—four.

13 Amram's sons: Aaron and Moses.

Aaron, along with his descendants, was set apart forever to consecrate the most holy things, to burn incense in the presence of the LORD, to minister to Him, and to pronounce blessings in His name forever. 14 As for Moses the man of God, his sons were named among the tribe of Levi.

15 Moses' sons: Gershom and Eliezer.

16 Gershom's sons: Shebuel [was] first.

17 Eliezer's sons were Rehabiah, first; Eliezer did not have any other sons, but Rehabiah's sons were very numerous.

18 Izhar's sons: Shelomith was first.

19 Hebron's sons: Jeriah was first, Amariah second, Jahaziel third, and Jekameam fourth.

20 Uzziel's sons: Micah was first, and Isshiah second.

21 Merari's sons: Mahli and Mushi. Mahli's sons: Eleazar and Kish.

22 Eleazar died having no sons, only daughters. Their cousins, the sons of Kish, married them.

23 Mushi's sons: Mahli, Eder, and Jeremoth—three.

24 These were the sons of Levi by their ancestral houses—the heads of families, according to their registration by name in the headcount—20 years old or more, who worked in the service of the LORD's temple. 25 For David said, "The LORD God of Israel has given rest to His people, and He has come to stay in Jerusalem forever. 26 Also, the Levites no longer need to carry the tabernacle or any of the equipment for its service"— 27 for according to the last words of David, the Levites 20 years old or more were to be counted— 28 "but their duty will be to assist the sons of Aaron with the service of the LORD's temple, being responsible for the courts and the chambers, the purification of all the holy things, and the work of the service of God's temple— 29 as well as the rows [of the bread of the Presence], the fine flour for the •grain offering, the wafers of unleavened bread, the baking,c the mixing, and all measurements of volume and length. 30 They are also to stand every morning to give thanks and praise to the LORD, and likewise in the evening. 31 Whenever •burnt offerings are offered to the LORD on the Sabbaths, New Moons, and appointed festivals, they are to do so regularly in the LORD's presence according to the number prescribed for them. 32 They are to carry out their responsibilities to the tent of meeting, to the holy place, and to their relatives, the sons of Aaron, in the service of the LORD's temple."

The Divisions of the Priests

24 The divisions of the descendants of Aaron were as follows: Aaron's sons were Nadab, Abihu, Eleazar, and Ithamar. 2 But Nadab and Abihu died before their father, and they had no sons, so Eleazar and Ithamar served as priests. 3 Together with Zadok from the sons of Eleazar and Ahimelech from

a23:6 Lit Gershon   b23:10 LXX, Vg; MT reads Zina   c23:29 Lit the griddle

---

23:1 full of days, he installed his son Solomon as king. The chronicler smoothes the tough transition between David and Solomon's reign by leaving out its political implications (1 Kings 1-2).

23:3 Levites. By assembling the Levites, David showed concern for his son's spiritual as well as royal readiness.

24:2 Nadab and Abihu died before their father. This is like mentioning that John Wilkes Booth died in 1865 without mentioning that he assassinated Abraham Lincoln! Like Uzzah's mishandling of the ark (13:10), Nadab and Abihu had been extinguished for

offering unholy fire before the Lord with incense that was not lit from the tabernacle's altar flame (Lev. 10:1-7; Num. 26:61). Since most people would be familiar with this infamous episode and Chronicles is primarily a priestly history of Israel, praise is instead given for the preservation of the Aaronic

the sons of Ithamar, David divided them according to the assigned duties of their service. 4 Since more leaders were found among Eleazar's descendants than Ithamar's, they were divided ⌊accordingly⌋: 16 heads of ancestral houses were from Eleazar's descendants, and eight ⌊heads⌋ of ancestral houses were from Ithamar's. 5 They were divided impartially by lot, for there were officers of the sanctuary and officers of God among both Eleazar's and Ithamar's descendants.

6 The secretary, Shemaiah son of Nethanel, a Levite, recorded them in the presence of the king and the officers, Zadok the priest, Ahimelech son of Abiathar, and the heads of families of the priests and the Levites. One ancestral house was taken for Eleazar, and then one for Ithamar.

7 The first lot fell to Jehoiarib, the second
    to Jedaiah,
8 the third to Harim, the fourth to Seorim,
9 the fifth to Malchijah, the sixth to Mijamin,
10 the seventh to Hakkoz, the eighth to Abijah,
11 the ninth to Jeshua, the tenth to Shecaniah,
12 the eleventh to Eliashib, the twelfth to Jakim,
13 the thirteenth to Huppah, the fourteenth
    to Jeshebeab,
14 the fifteenth to Bilgah, the sixteenth to Immer,
15 the seventeenth to Hezir, the eighteenth
    to Happizzez,
16 the nineteenth to Pethahiah, the twentieth
    to Jehezkel,
17 the twenty-first to Jachin, the twenty-second
    to Gamul,
18 the twenty-third to Delaiah,
    and the twenty-fourth to Maaziah.

19 These had their assigned duties for service when they entered the LORD's temple, according to their regulations, which they received from their ancestor Aaron, as the LORD God of Israel had commanded him.

The Rest of the Levites

20 As for the rest of Levi's sons:
from Amram's sons: Shubael;
from Shubael's sons: Jehdeiah.
21 From Rehabiah:
from Rehabiah's sons: Isshiah was the first.
22 From the Izharites: Shelomoth;
from Shelomoth's sons: Jahath.
23 Hebron'sa sons:
Jeriah ⌊the first⌋, Amariah the second,

Jahaziel the third, and Jekameam the fourth.
24 ⌊From⌋ Uzziel's sons: Micah;
from Micah's sons: Shamir.
25 Micah's brother: Isshiah;
from Isshiah's sons: Zechariah.
26 Merari's sons: Mahli and Mushi,
⌊and from⌋ his sons, Jaaziah his son.b
27 Merari's sons, by his son Jaaziah:c
Shoham, Zaccur, and Ibri.
28 From Mahli: Eleazar, who had no sons.
29 From Kish, ⌊from⌋ Kish's sons: Jerahmeel.
30 Mushi's sons: Mahli, Eder, and Jerimoth.

Those were the sons of the Levites according to their ancestral houses. 31 They also cast lots the same way as their relatives, the sons of Aaron did in the presence of King David, Zadok, Ahimelech, and the heads of the families of the priests and Levites—the family heads and their younger brothers alike.

The Levitical Musicians

25 David and the officers of the army also set apart some of the sons of •Asaph, Heman, and Jeduthun, who were to prophesy accompanied by lyres, harps, and cymbals. This is the list of the men who performed their service:

2 From Asaph's sons:
Zaccur, Joseph, Nethaniah, and Asarelah,
sons of Asaph, under Asaph's authority,
who prophesied under the authority of the king.
3 From Jeduthun: Jeduthun's sons:
Gedaliah, Zeri, Jeshaiah, Shimei,d Hashabiah,
and Mattithiah—six—under the authority of
their father Jeduthun, prophesying to the
accompaniment of lyres, giving thanks and
praise to the LORD.
4 From Heman: Heman's sons:
Bukkiah, Mattaniah, Uzziel, Shebuel, Jerimoth,
Hananiah, Hanani, Eliathah, Giddalti, Romamti-
ezer, Joshbekashah, Mallothi, Hothir, and
Mahazioth. 5 All these sons of Heman, the king's
seer, were ⌊given⌋ by the promises of God to
exalt him,e for God had given Heman fourteen
sons and three daughters.

6 All these men were under their own fathers' authority for the music in the LORD's temple, with cymbals, harps, and lyres for the service of God's temple. Asaph, Jeduthun, and Heman were under the king's authority. 7 Together with their relatives who were all

---

a **24:23** Some Hb mss, some LXX mss; MT omits *Hebron's*; 1 Ch 23:19 b **24:26** Or *Mushi; Jaaziah's sons: Beno.* c **24:27** Or *sons, Jaaziah: Beno,*
d **25:3** One Hb ms, LXX; MT omits *Shimei* e **25:5** Or *Him;* lit *by the words of God to lift a horn*

---

priesthood through Eleazar and Ithamar.

25:1 and the officers of the army. No autocrat, David pulls together a cabinet of decision makers. **who were to prophesy** During David's reign, musically gifted priests were encouraged to add their gifts to the people's wor-

ship experience. **lyres, harps, and cymbals** A popular instrument in the ancient Near East, lyres often accompanied singing (Gen. 31:27; Job 21:12; Ps. 137:2; Isa. 23:16) and worship (1 Sam. 10:5; 2 Sam. 6:5; Pss. 33:2; 43:4; 98:5). It was the instrument David used to calm Saul (1 Sam. 16:16). The harp was an Egyptian

favorite with 10-20 strings (Ps. 144:9) used mostly in worship (2 Chron. 29:25; Pss. 33:2; 81:2; 150:3), and was popular at banquets (1 Kings 10:12; 2 Chron. 9:11; Isa. 5:12; 14:11; Amos 5:23). They were also used in the New Testament church (1 Cor. 14:7), and even in heaven as well (Rev. 15:8; 14:2; 15:2).

trained and skillful in music for the LORD, they numbered 288. 8 They cast lots impartially for their duties, the young and old alike, the teacher along with the pupil.

9 The first lot for Asaph fell to Joseph,
⌊his sons, and his brothers—⌋ 12⌋
⌊to⌋ Gedaliah the second: him,
his brothers, and his sons— 12
10 the third ⌊to⌋ Zaccur, his sons,
and his brothers— 12
11 the fourth to Izri,ᵃ his sons,
and his brothers— 12
12 the fifth ⌊to⌋ Nethaniah, his sons,
and his brothers— 12
13 the sixth ⌊to⌋ Bukkiah, his sons,
and his brothers— 12
14 the seventh ⌊to⌋ Jesarelah, his sons,
and his brothers— 12
15 the eighth ⌊to⌋ Jeshaiah, his sons,
and his brothers— 12
16 the ninth ⌊to⌋ Mattaniah, his sons,
and his brothers— 12
17 the tenth ⌊to⌋ Shimei, his sons,
and his brothers— 12
18 the eleventh ⌊to⌋ Azarel,ᵇ his sons,
and his brothers— 12
19 the twelfth to Hashabiah, his sons,
and his brothers— 12
20 the thirteenth ⌊to⌋ Shubael, his sons,
and his brothers— 12
21 the fourteenth ⌊to⌋ Mattithiah, his sons,
and his brothers— 12
22 the fifteenth to Jeremoth, his sons,
and his brothers— 12
23 the sixteenth to Hananiah, his sons,
and his brothers— 12
24 the seventeenth to Joshbekashah, his sons,
and his brothers— 12
25 the eighteenth to Hanani, his sons,
and his brothers— 12
26 the nineteenth to Mallothi, his sons,
and his brothers— 12
27 the twentieth to Eliathah, his sons,
and his brothers— 12
28 the twenty-first to Hothir, his sons,
and his brothers— 12
29 the twenty-second to Giddalti, his sons,
and his brothers— 12

30 the twenty-third to Mahazioth, his sons,
and his brothers— 12
31 and the twenty-fourth to Romamti-ezer,
his sons, and his brothers— 12.

The Levitical Gatekeepers

26 ⌊The following were⌋ the divisions of the gatekeepers:

From the Korahites: Meshelemiah son of Kore, one of the sons of •Asaph. 2 Meshelemiah had sons:
Zechariah the firstborn, Jediael the second,
Zebadiah the third, Jathniel the fourth,
3 Elam the fifth, Jehohanan the sixth,
and Eliehoenai the seventh.
4 Obed-edom also had sons:
Shemaiah the firstborn, Jehozabad the second,
Joah the third, Sachar the fourth,
Nethanel the fifth, 5 Ammiel the sixth,
Issachar the seventh, and Peullethai the eighth,
for God blessed him.
6 Also, to his son Shemaiah were born sons who ruled over their ancestral houses because they were strong, capable men. 7 Shemaiah's sons: Othni, Rephael, Obed, and Elzabad; his brothers Elihu and Semachiah were also capable men. 8 All of these were among the sons of Obed-edom with their sons and brothers; they were capable men with strength for the work—62 from Obed-edom. 9 Meshelemiah also had sons and brothers who were capable men—18. 10 Hosah, from the Merarites, also had sons: Shimri the first (although he was not the firstborn, his father had appointed him as the first), 11 Hilkiah the second, Tebaliah the third, and Zechariah the fourth. The sons and brothers of Hosah were 13 in all.

12 These divisions of the gatekeepers, under their leading men, had duties for ministering in the LORD's temple, just as their brothers did. 13 They cast lots according to their ancestral houses, young and old alike, for each gate.

14 The lot for the east ⌊gate⌋ fell to Shelemiah.ᶜ They also cast lots for his son Zechariah, an insightful counselor, and his lot came out for the north ⌊gate⌋. 15 Obed-edom's was the south ⌊gate⌋, and his sons' ⌊lot⌋ was the storehouses; 16 for Shuppim and Hosah it was the west

---

ᵃ**25:11** A variant of Zeri   ᵇ**25:18** A variant of Uzziel   ᶜ**26:14** A variant of Meshelemiah

---

25:10-13 Zaccur … Bukkiah. Filling the temple with music of praise was a priority for the nation. Like the tribal leaders, the great warriors, and the priest, the musicians held a place of honor. For the nation to prosper, it needed to be obediently serving God. The future was determined by the devotion of the people to God. Worship was essential.

26:1-15 gatekeepers. The gatekeepers, formed from over 4,000 participants (23:5), served in a group of 22 at a time. The assignments were made through lots, similar to the way musicians were called to perform.

26:16-18 role of the gatekeepers. The gatekeepers served as the temple police force.

One of their jobs was to prevent the access of "unclean" persons to the inner temple area (2 Chron. 23:19). They also guarded the temple treasuries and storehouses 9:26; Neh. 12:25)

26:20 for what had been dedicated. Temple officers served to receive and administrate the

⌊gate⌋ and the gate of Shallecheth on the ascending highway.

There were guards stationed at every watch. 17 There were six Levites each day[a] on the east, four each day on the north, four each day on the south, and two pair at the storehouses. 18 As for the court on the west, there were four at the highway and two at the court. 19 Those were the divisions of the gatekeepers from the sons of the Korahites and Merarites.

The Levitical Treasurers and Other Officials

20 From the Levites, Ahijah was in charge of the treasuries of God's temple and the treasuries for what had been dedicated. 21 From the sons of Ladan, who were the sons of the Gershonites through Ladan and were the heads of families belonging to Ladan the Gershonite: Jehieli. 22 The sons of Jehieli, Zetham and his brother Joel, were in charge of the treasuries of the LORD's temple.

23 From the Amramites, the Izharites, the Hebronites, and the Uzzielites: 24 Shebuel, a descendant of Moses' son Gershom, was the officer in charge of the treasuries. 25 His relative through Eliezer: his son Rehabiah, his son Jeshaiah, his son Joram, his son Zichri, and his son Shelomith.[b] 26 This Shelomith[c] and his brothers were in charge of all the treasuries for what had been dedicated by King David, by the heads of families who were the commanders of the thousands and of the hundreds, and by the army commanders. 27 They dedicated part of the plunder from their battles for the repair of the LORD's temple. 28 All that Samuel the seer, Saul son of Kish, Abner son of Ner, and Joab son of Zeruiah had dedicated, along with everything else that had been dedicated, were in the care of Shelomith[d] and his brothers.

29 From the Izrahites: Chenaniah and his sons had the outside duties as officers and judges over Israel. 30 From the Hebronites: Hashabiah and his relatives, 1,700 capable men, had assigned duties in Israel west of the Jordan for all the work of the LORD and for the service of the king. 31 From the Hebronites: Jerijah was the head of the Hebronites, according to the genealogical records of his ancestors. In the fortieth year of David's reign a search was made, and strong, capable men were found among them at Jazer in Gilead. 32 There were among Jerijah's relatives, 2,700 capable men who were heads of families. King David appointed them over the Reubenites, the Gadites, and half the tribe of Manasseh as overseers in every matter relating to God and the king.

David's Secular Officials

27 This is the list of the Israelites, the heads of families, the commanders of thousands and the commanders of hundreds, and their officers who served the king in every matter to do with the divisions that were on rotated military duty each month throughout[e] the year. There were 24,000 in each division:

2 Jashobeam son of Zabdiel was in charge of the first division, for the first month; 24,000 were in his division. 3 He was a descendant of Perez and chief of all the army commanders for the first month.

4 Dodai the Ahohite was in charge of the division for the second month, and Mikloth was the leader; 24,000 were in his division.

5 The third army commander, as chief for the third month, was Benaiah son of Jehoiada the priest; 24,000 were in his division. 6 This Benaiah was a mighty man among the Thirty and over the Thirty, and his son Ammizabad was in charge[f] of his division.

7 The fourth ⌊commander⌋, for the fourth month, was Joab's brother Asahel, and his son Zebadiah ⌊was commander⌋ after him; 24,000 were in his division.

8 The fifth, for the fifth month, was the commander Shamhuth the Izrahite; 24,000 were in his division.

9 The sixth, for the sixth month, was Ira son of Ikkesh the Tekoite; 24,000 were in his division.

10 The seventh, for the seventh month, was Helez the Pelonite from the sons of Ephraim; 24,000 were in his division.

11 The eighth, for the eighth month, was Sibbecai the Hushathite, a Zerahite; 24,000 were in his division.

12 The ninth, for the ninth month, was Abiezer the Anathothite, a Benjaminite; 24,000 were in his division.

13 The tenth, for the tenth month, was Maharai the Netophathite, a Zerahite; 24,000 were in his division.

14 The eleventh, for the eleventh month, was Benaiah the Pirathonite from the sons of Ephraim; 24,000 were in his division.

15 The twelfth, for the twelfth month, was Heldai the Netophathite, of Othniel's family;[g] 24,000 were in his division.

---

[a]**26:17** LXX; MT omits *each day* [b]**26:25** One Hb tradition, some LXX mss, Syr, Tg, Vg; alt Hb tradition, some LXX mss read *Shelomoth* [c]**26:26** Many Hb mss; MT, LXX read *Shelomoth* [d]**26:28** LXX reads *Shelomoth* [e]**27:1** Lit *that came in and went out month by month for all months of* [f]**27:6** LXX; Hb omits *in charge* [g]**27:15** Lit *belonging to Othniel*

---

plunder from battles. The silver and gold from enemy cities would be dedicated to God's glory.

26:30-32 appointed. The complexity of the civic arrangements concludes with the role of those who work outside of Jerusalem. These traveling legal experts helped to keep the peace and administer justice throughout the land. That men are still being selected in the last year of David's reign (v. 31) demonstrates that he carefully considered the preparations for the temple-centered administration of his son, Solomon.

27:2-20 David rotated his soldiers in twelve units consisting of 24,000 men. Each went on active duty one month each year. They were commanded by twelve of David's heroic commanders (11:11-47; 2 Sam. 23:8-9). These men were not part of the permanent bodyguard that surrounded the king (2 Sam. 15:18; 23:23).

16 ⌊The following were⌋ in charge of the tribes of Israel:

For the Reubenites, Eliezer son of Zichri was the chief official;

for the Simeonites, Shephatiah son of Maacah;

17 for the Levites, Hashabiah son of Kemuel;

for Aaron, Zadok;

18 for Judah, Elihu, one of David's brothers;

for Issachar, Omri son of Michael;

19 for Zebulun, Ishmaiah son of Obadiah;

for Naphtali, Jerimoth son of Azriel;

20 for the Ephraimites, Hoshea son of Azaziah;

for half the tribe of Manasseh, Joel son of Pedaiah;

21 for half the tribe of Manasseh in Gilead, Iddo son of Zechariah;

for Benjamin, Jaasiel son of Abner;

22 for Dan, Azarel son of Jeroham.

Those were the leaders of the tribes of Israel.

23 David didn't count the men aged 20 or under, for the LORD had said He would make Israel as numerous as the stars of heaven. 24 Joab son of Zeruiah began to count them, but he didn't complete it. There was wrath against Israel because of this ⌊census⌋, and the number was not entered in the Historical Record[a] of King David.

25 Azmaveth son of Adiel was in charge of the king's storehouses.

Jonathan son of Uzziah was in charge of the storehouses in the country, in the cities, in the villages, and in the fortresses.

26 Ezri son of Chelub was in charge of those who worked in the fields tilling the soil.

27 Shimei the Ramathite was in charge of the vineyards.

Zabdi the Shiphmite was in charge of the produce of the vineyards for the wine cellars.

28 Baal-hanan the Gederite was in charge of the olive and sycamore trees in the Shephelah.[b]

Joash was in charge of the stores of olive oil.

29 Shitrai the Sharonite was in charge of the herds that grazed in Sharon, while

Shaphat son of Adlai was in charge of the herds in the valleys.

30 Obil the Ishmaelite was in charge of the camels.

Jehdeiah the Meronothite was in charge of the donkeys.

31 Jaziz the Hagrite was in charge of the flocks.

All these were officials in charge of King David's property.

32 David's uncle Jonathan was a counselor; he was a man of understanding and a scribe. Jehiel son of Hachmoni attended[c] the king's sons. 33 Ahithophel was the king's counselor. Hushai the Archite was the king's friend. 34 After Ahithophel came Jehoiada son of Benaiah, then Abiathar. Joab was the commander of the king's army.

David Commissions Solomon to Build the Temple

28 David assembled in Jerusalem all the leaders of Israel: the leaders of the tribes, the leaders of the divisions in the king's service, the commanders of thousands and the commanders of hundreds, and the officials in charge of all the property and cattle of the king and his sons, along with the court officials, the fighting men, and all the brave warriors. 2 Then King David rose to his feet and said, "Listen to me, my brothers and my people. It was in my heart to build a house as a resting place for the ark of the LORD's covenant and as a footstool for our God. I had made preparations to build, 3 but God said to me, 'You are not to build a house for My name because you are a man of war and have shed blood.'

4 "Yet the LORD God of Israel chose me out of all my father's household to be king over Israel forever. For He chose Judah as leader, and from the house of Judah, my father's household, and from my father's sons, He was pleased to make me king over all Israel. 5 And out of all my sons—for the LORD has given me many sons—He has chosen my son Solomon to sit on the throne of the LORD's kingdom over Israel. 6 He said to me, 'Your son Solomon is the one who is to build My house and My courts, for I have chosen him to be My son, and I will be his father. 7 I will establish his kingdom forever if he perseveres in keeping My commandments and My ordinances as ⌊he is⌋ today.'

8 "So now in the sight of all Israel, the assembly of the LORD, and in the hearing of our God, observe and seek after all the commandments of the LORD your God so that you may possess this good land and leave it as an inheritance to your descendants forever.

9 "As for you, Solomon my son, know the God of your father, and serve Him with a whole heart and a willing mind, for the LORD searches every heart and understands the intention of every thought. If you seek Him, He will be found by you, but if you forsake Him, He will reject you forever. 10 Realize now that the LORD

---

a **27:24** LXX; MT reads *Number*   b **27:28** A strip of land west of the Judean mountains   c **27:32** Lit *was with*

27:16-22 Each tribe of Israel symbolizes its loyalty to King David through the representation of its officer. The tribes are similarly listed in Numbers 1:1–19.

27:23 numerous as the stars. The chronicler's phrase is reminiscent of God's promise to Abraham (see Gen. 12:2). Inspired by

God's assurance, David does not need to include the younger warriors in order to boost his confidence.

27:24 the number was not entered. David's military strength needed no fixed number. David counted on God's assurance.

28:1 David assembled ... all the leaders.

David proclaimed the succession of his son Solomon and his plans for the temple and the future of Israel.

28:5 He has chosen. David emphasized God's selection of the next king. Like his father, Solomon enjoyed the assurance of being divinely appointed to his throne.

has chosen you to build a house for the sanctuary. Be strong, and do it."

11 Then David gave his son Solomon the plans for the vestibule ⌊of the temple⌋ and its buildings, treasuries, upper rooms, inner rooms, and the room for the place of •atonement. 12 The plans contained everything he had in mind[a] for the courts of the LORD's house, all the surrounding chambers, the treasuries of God's house, and the treasuries for what is dedicated. 13 ⌊Also included were plans⌋ for the divisions of the priests and the Levites; all the work of service in the LORD's house; all the articles of service of the LORD's house; 14 the weight of gold for all the articles for every kind of service; the weight of all the silver articles for every kind of service; 15 the weight of the gold lampstands and their gold lamps, including the weight of each lampstand and its lamps; the weight of each silver lampstand and its lamps, according to the service of each lampstand; 16 the weight of gold for each table for the rows ⌊of the bread of the Presence⌋ and the silver for the silver tables; 17 the pure gold for the forks, sprinkling basins, and pitchers; the weight of each gold dish; the weight of each silver bowl; 18 the weight of refined gold for the altar of incense; and the plans for the chariot of[b] the gold •cherubim that spread out ⌊their wings⌋ and cover the ark of the LORD's covenant.

19 ⌊David concluded,⌋ "By the LORD's hand on me, He enabled me to understand everything in writing, all the details of the plan."[c]

20 Then David said to his son Solomon, "Be strong and courageous, and do the work. Don't be afraid or discouraged, for the LORD God, my God, is with you. He won't leave you or forsake you until all the work for the service of the LORD's house is finished. 21 Here are the divisions of the priests and the Levites for all the service of God's house. Every willing man of any skill will be at your disposal for the work, and the leaders and all the people are at your every command."

Contributions for Building the Temple

29 Then King David said to all the assembly, "My son Solomon—God has chosen him alone—is young and inexperienced. The task is great, for the temple will not be for man, but for the LORD God. 2 So to the best of my ability I've made provision for the house of my God: gold for the gold ⌊articles⌋, silver for the silver, bronze for the bronze, iron for the iron, and wood for the wood, as well as onyx, ⌊stones for⌋ mount-

ing,[d] antimony,[e] stones of various colors, all kinds of precious stones, and a great quantity of marble. 3 Moreover, because of my delight in the house of my God, I now give my personal treasures of gold and silver for the house of my God over and above all that I've provided for the holy house: 4 100 tons[f] of gold (gold of Ophir) and 250 tons[g] of refined silver for overlaying the walls of the buildings, 5 the gold for the gold ⌊work⌋ and the silver for the silver, for all the work to be done by the craftsmen. Now, who will volunteer to consecrate himself to the LORD today?"

6 Then the leaders of the households, the leaders of the tribes of Israel, the commanders of thousands and of hundreds, and the officials in charge of the king's work gave willingly. 7 For the service of God's house they gave 185 tons[h] of gold and 10,000 gold drachmas,[i] 375 tons[j] of silver, 675 tons[k] of bronze, and 4,000 tons[l] of iron. 8 Whoever had ⌊precious⌋ stones gave them to the treasury of the LORD's house under the care of Jehiel the Gershonite. 9 Then the people rejoiced because of their leaders'[m] willingness to give, for they had given to the LORD with a whole heart. King David also rejoiced greatly.

David's Prayer

10 Then David praised the LORD in the sight of all the assembly. David said, "May You be praised, LORD God of our father Israel, from eternity to eternity. 11 Yours, LORD, is the greatness and the power and the glory and the splendor and the majesty, for everything in the heavens and on earth belongs to You. Yours, LORD, is the kingdom, and You are exalted as head over all. 12 Riches and honor come from You, and You are the ruler of everything. In Your hand are power and might, and it is in Your hand to make great and to give strength to all. 13 Now therefore, our God, we give You thanks and praise Your glorious name.

14 "But who am I, and who are my people, that we should be able to give as generously as this? For everything comes from You, and we have given You only what comes from Your own hand.[n] 15 For we are foreigners and sojourners in Your presence as were all our ancestors. Our days on earth are like a shadow, without hope. 16 LORD our God, all this wealth that we've provided for building You a house for Your holy name comes from Your hand; everything belongs to You. 17 I know, my God, that You test the heart and that You are pleased with uprightness. I have willingly given all

---

[a] **28:12** Or *he received from the Spirit*; v. 19   [b] **28:18** Or *chariot, that is*; Ps 18:10; Ezk 1:5,15   [c] **28:19** Hb obscure   [d] **29:2** Or *mosaic*
[e] **29:2** Ex 28:18 reads *turquoise*, which is spelled nearly the same in Hb.   [f] **29:4** Lit *3,000 talents*; about 113 tons   [g] **29:4** Lit *7,000 talents*; about 263 tons   [h] **29:7** Lit *5,000 talents*; about 188 tons   [i] **29:7** The *drachma*, or *daric*, was a Persian gold coin, first minted by Darius I about 515 B.C.; 10,000 darics weighed about 185 pounds.   [j] **29:7** Lit *10,000 talents*; about 378 tons   [k] **29:7** Lit *18,000 talents*; about 680 tons   [l] **29:7** Lit *100,000 talents*; about 3,750 tons   [m] **29:9** Lit *because they*   [n] **29:14** Lit *and from Your hand we have given to You*

28:19 By the LORD's hand on me, He enabled me to understand everything. The plan for the temple was ultimately from God, not David. Hebrews asserts that the original tabernacle was built according to a heavenly pattern (see Heb. 8:5).

29:2-9 The capstone of David's reign was the

initiation of the building of the temple. David dedicated his personal wealth to its construction. The people gladly responded to his leadership and voluntarily gave their gifts.

29:15 we are foreigners and sojourners. The Hebrew people had spent much of their history as foreigners and sojourners,

having spent so many years in Egypt and the wilderness. But here David voices the realization that this is still their status since the land they had occupied was God's. The author of Hebrews may have had David in mind when he wrote of the people of faith who "confessed that they were foreigners

these things with an upright heart, and now I have seen Your people who are present[a] here giving joyfully and[b] willingly to You. 18 LORD God of Abraham, Isaac, and Israel, our ancestors, keep this desire forever in the thoughts of the hearts of Your people, and confirm their hearts toward You. 19 Give my son Solomon a whole heart to keep and to carry out all Your commandments, Your decrees, and Your statutes, and to build the temple for which I have made provision."

20 Then David said to the whole assembly, "Praise the LORD your God." So the whole assembly praised the LORD God of their ancestors. They bowed down and paid homage to the LORD and the king.

21 The following day they offered sacrifices to the LORD and •burnt offerings to the LORD: 1,000 bulls, 1,000 rams, and 1,000 lambs, along with their drink offerings, and sacrifices in abundance for all Israel. 22 They ate and drank with great joy in the LORD's presence that day.

The Enthronement of Solomon

Then, for a second time, they made David's son Solomon king; they anointed him[c] as the LORD's ruler, and Zadok as the priest. 23 Solomon sat on the LORD's throne as king in place of his father David. He prospered, and all Israel obeyed him. 24 All the leaders and the mighty men, and all of King David's sons as well, pledged their allegiance to King Solomon. 25 The LORD highly exalted Solomon in the sight of all Israel and bestowed on him such royal majesty as had not been ⌊bestowed⌋ on any king over Israel before him.

A Summary of David's Life

26 David son of Jesse was king over all Israel. 27 The length of his reign over Israel was 40 years; he reigned in Hebron for seven years and in Jerusalem for 33. 28 He died at a good old age, full of days, riches, and honor, and his son Solomon became king in his place. 29 As for the events of King David's ⌊reign⌋, from beginning to end, note that they are written about in the Events of Samuel the Seer, the Events of Nathan the Prophet, and the Events of Gad the Seer, 30 along with all his reign, his might, and the incidents that affected him and Israel and all the kingdoms of the ⌊surrounding⌋ lands.

---

and temporary residents on the earth" (Heb 11:13).

29:22 a second time. Nearly two years prior, David had appointed Solomon to be king (23:1). However, the time had come for the official transition of power.

29:24 All the leaders and the mighty men David's officers continued the chronicler's theme of unity among Israel in support for the king.

29:29 Events of Samuel the Seer, the Events of Nathan the Prophet, and the **Events of Gad the Seer.** These annals are apparently lost to history.

2 CHRONICLES

AUTHOR

Jewish tradition suggests Ezra as author, but there is no firm evidence.

DATE

Second Chronicles was probably written toward the end of the fifth century B.C. or a little later. The events narrated span 970-538 B.C.

THEME

Kingship and worship in Judah from Solomon to the Exile.

HISTORICAL BACKGROUND

After the glory days of Israel under Solomon, warfare and unrest divide the nation, the people forsake temple worship for idols, and they lose their national identity when Jerusalem is totally destroyed in 586 B.C. Along the way, the southern kingdom of Judah is led into slow decline by evil kings and, alternately, into periods of spiritual reformation and restored national pride by Asa, Jehoshaphat, Uzziah, Hezekiah, and Josiah. Judah's slow decline (and the chronicler's account) ends with the Exile, but a "postscript" gives us a brief glimpse of future restoration.

CHARACTERISTICS

The major interests of 1 Chronicles—the Davidic dynasty and the temple worship—are continued in 2 Chronicles. Compared to the colorful stories in the books of Samuel and Kings, the chronicler has written a blander account. The stains of David's or Solomon's past are not addressed. Instead, the great wealth, worldwide acclaim, political stability, and magnificent temple get primary attention (chapters 1-9). Each king is evaluated on the basis of his response to God, especially regarding worship of God and obedience to the Law. Those who introduce reforms are given top billing and the nature of their reforms is described in some detail.

Some of the details included in 2 Chronicles that are not mentioned in Samuel and Kings are: (1) God giving the plans for both the tabernacle and temple; (2) the spoils of war being used as building materials for both tabernacle and temple; (3) the people generously contributing for both structures; and (4) the glory cloud appearing at the dedication of both structures.

Solomon's Request for Wisdom

1 Solomon son of David strengthened his hold on his kingdom. The LORD his God was with him and highly exalted him. ² Then Solomon spoke to all Israel, to the commanders of thousands and of hundreds, to the judges, and to every leader in all Israel—the heads of the families. ³ Solomon and the whole assembly with him went to the •high place that was in Gibeon because God's tent of meeting, which the LORD's servant Moses had made in the wilderness, was there. ⁴ Now, David had brought the ark of God from Kiriath-jearim to the place^a he had set up for it, because he had pitched a tent for it in Jerusalem, ⁵ but he put^b the bronze altar, which Bezalel son of Uri, son of Hur, had made, in front of the LORD's tabernacle. Solomon and the assembly inquired of Him^c ⌊there⌋. ⁶ Solomon offered sacrifices there in the LORD's presence on the bronze altar at the tent of meeting; he offered 1,000 •burnt offerings on it.

⁷ That night God appeared to Solomon and said to him: "Ask. What should I give you?"

⁸ And Solomon said to God: "You have shown great faithful love to my father David, and You have made me king in his place. ⁹ LORD God, let Your promise to my father David now come true. For You have made me king over a people as numerous as the dust of the earth. ¹⁰ Now, grant me wisdom and knowledge so that I may lead these people, for who can judge this great people of Yours?"

¹¹ God said to Solomon, "Because this was in your heart, and you have not requested riches, wealth, or glory, or for the life of those who hate you, and you have not even requested long life, but you have requested for yourself wisdom and knowledge that you may judge My people over whom I have made you king, ¹² wisdom and knowledge are given to you. I will also give you riches, wealth, and glory, such that it was not like this for the kings who were before you, nor will it be like this for those after you." ¹³ So Solomon went to Jerusalem from^d the high place that was in Gibeon in front of the tent of meeting, and he reigned over Israel.

Solomon's Horses and Wealth

¹⁴ Solomon accumulated 1,400 chariots and 12,000 horsemen, which he stationed in the chariot cities and with the king in Jerusalem. ¹⁵ The king made silver and gold as common in Jerusalem as stones, and he made cedar as abundant as sycamore in the Judean foothills.

¹⁶ Solomon's horses came from Egypt and Kue.^{e} The king's traders would get them from Kue at the going price. ¹⁷ A chariot could be imported from Egypt for 15 pounds^f ⌊of silver⌋ and a horse for about four pounds.^{g} In the same way, they exported them to all the kings of the Hittites and to the kings of Aram through their agents.

Solomon's Letter to Hiram

2^h Solomon decided to build a temple for the name of the LORD and a royal palace for himself, ²^i so he assigned 70,000 men as porters, 80,000 men as stonecutters in the mountains, and 3,600 as supervisors over them.

³ Then Solomon sent ⌊word⌋ to King Hiram^j of Tyre:

⌊Do for me⌋ what you did for my father David. You sent him cedars to build him a house to live in. ⁴ Now I myself am building a temple for the name of the LORD my God in order to dedicate it to Him for burning sweet incense before Him, for ⌊displaying⌋ the rows ⌊of the bread of the Presence⌋ continuously, and for ⌊sacrificing⌋ •burnt offerings for the evening and the morning, the Sabbaths and the New Moons, and the appointed festivals of the LORD our God. This is ⌊ordained⌋ for Israel forever. ⁵ The temple that I am building will be great, for our God is greater than any of the gods. ⁶ But who is able to build a temple for Him, since even heaven and the highest heaven cannot contain Him? Who am I then that I should build a house for Him except as a place to burn incense before Him? ⁷ Therefore, send me a craftsman who is skilled in engraving to work with gold, silver, bronze, and iron, and with purple, crimson, and blue yarn. ⌊He will work⌋ with the craftsmen who are with me in Judah and Jerusalem, appointed by my father David. ⁸ Also, send me cedar, cypress, and algum^k logs from Lebanon, for I know that your servants know how to cut the trees of Lebanon. Note that my servants will be with your servants ⁹ to prepare logs for me in abundance because the temple I am building will be great and wonderful. ¹⁰ I will give your servants, the woodcutters who cut the trees, 100,000 bushels^l of wheat flour, 100,000 bushels^l of barley, 110,000 gallons^m of wine, and 110,000 gallons of oil.^{n}

---

^{a}1:4 Vg; MT omits *the place* ^{b}1:5 MT, Tg, Syr; some Hb mss, LXX, Vg read *but there was* ^{c}1:5 Or *it* ^{d}1:13 LXX, Vg, MT reads *to* ^{e}1:16 = Cilicia (modern Turkey) ^{f}1:17 Lit *600 shekels* ^{g}1:17 Lit *150 shekels* ^{h}2:1 2 Ch 1:18 in Hb ^{i}2:2 2 Ch 2:1 in Hb ^{j}2:3 Some Hb mss, LXX, Syr, Vg; MT reads *Huram*; 2 Sm 5:11; 1 Kg 5:1–2 ^{k}2:8 Spelled *almug* in 1 Kg 10:11–12 ^{l}2:10 Lit *20,000 cors* ^{m}2:10 Lit *20,000 baths* ^{n}2:10 Lit *20,000 baths of oil*

1:1 highly exalted him. Solomon became known as one of the greatest leaders in Israel's history. The nation enjoyed widespread stability and prosperity during his reign. Solomon's wisdom enabled him to accomplish much.

1:7 What should I give you? As a sign of His blessing, God tells Solomon that anything he requests will be granted.

2:1 temple. According to God's promise, Solomon began the construction of the temple. It would be the greatest accomplishment of his reign.

2:3–10 Solomon sent Hiram, king of Tyre, a specific order concerning Hiram's contribution to the construction of the temple. Hiram's participation would have spiritual and material significance. Solomon and Hiram had a close relationship. Both were respected world leaders.

2:6 even heaven ... cannot contain Him? Solomon realizes that in one sense what he

Hiram's Reply

[11] Then King Hiram of Tyre wrote a letter[a] and sent [it] to Solomon:

Because the LORD loves His people, He set you over them as king.

[12] Hiram also said:

May the LORD God of Israel, who made the heavens and the earth, be praised! He gave King David a wise son with insight and understanding, who will build a temple for the LORD and a royal palace for himself. [13] I have now sent Huram-abi,[b] a skillful man who has understanding. [14] He is the son of a woman from the daughters of Dan. His father is a man of Tyre. He knows how to work with gold, silver, bronze, iron, stone, and wood, with purple, blue, crimson yarn, and fine linen. He knows how to do all kinds of engraving and to execute any design that may be given him. I have sent him to be with your craftsmen and the craftsmen of my lord, your father David. [15] Now, let my lord send the wheat, barley, oil, and wine to his servants as promised. [16] We will cut logs from Lebanon, as many as you need, and bring them to you as rafts by sea to Joppa. You can then take them up to Jerusalem.

Solomon's Work Force

[17] Solomon took a census of all the foreign men in the land of Israel, after the census that his father David had conducted, and the total was 153,600. [18] Solomon made 70,000 of them porters, 80,000 stonecutters in the mountains, and 3,600 supervisors to make the people work.

Building the Temple

3 Then Solomon began to build the LORD's temple in Jerusalem on Mount Moriah where the LORD[c] had appeared to his father David, at the site David had prepared on the threshing floor of Ornan the Jebusite. [2] He began to build on the second [day] of the second month in the fourth year of his reign. [3] These are Solomon's foundations[d] for building God's temple: the length[e] was 90 feet,[f] and the width 30 feet.[g] [4] The portico, which was across the front extending across the width of the temple, was 30 feet[g] wide; its height was 30 feet;[h] [g] he overlaid its inner surface with pure gold.

[5] The larger room[i] he paneled with cypress wood, overlaid with fine gold, and decorated with palm trees and chains. [6] He adorned the temple with precious stones for beauty, and the gold was the gold of Parvaim. [7] He overlaid the temple—the beams, the thresholds, its walls and doors—with gold, and he carved •cherubim on the walls.

The Most Holy Place

[8] Then he made the most holy place; its length corresponded to the width of the temple, 30 feet,[g] and its width was 30 feet.[g] He overlaid it with 45,000 pounds[j] of fine gold. [9] The weight of the nails was 20 ounces[k] of gold, and he overlaid the ceiling with gold.

[10] He made two cherubim of sculptured work, for the most holy place, and he overlaid them with gold. [11] The overall length of the wings of the cherubim was 30 feet:[g] the wing of one was seven and a half feet,[l] touching the wall of the room; its other wing was seven and a half feet,[l] touching the wing of the other cherub. [12] The wing of the other[m] cherub was seven and a half feet,[l] touching the wall of the room; its other wing was seven and a half feet,[l] reaching the wing of the other cherub. [13] The wingspan of these cherubim was 30 feet.[g] They stood on their feet and faced the larger room.[n]

[14] He made the veil of blue, purple, and crimson yarn and fine linen, and he wove cherubim into it.

The Bronze Pillars

[15] In front of the temple he made two pillars, [each] 27 feet[o] [p] high. The capital on top of each was seven and half feet[l] high. [16] He had made chainwork in the inner sanctuary and also put it on top of the pillars. He made 100 pomegranates and fastened them into the chainwork. [17] Then he set up the pillars in front of the sanctuary, one on the right and one on the left. He named the one on the right Jachin[q] and the one on the left Boaz.[r]

The Altar, Reservoir, and Basins

4 He made a bronze altar 30 feet[g] long, 30 feet[g] wide, and 15 feet[s] high.

[2] Then he made the cast [metal] reservoir, 15 feet[s] from brim to brim, perfectly round. It was seven and a half feet[l] high, and 45 feet[t] in circumference. [3] The likeness of oxen[u] was below it, completely encircling it, 10 every half yard,[v] completely surrounding the reservoir. The oxen were cast in two rows when the

has tried to do in building a temple to God is inappropriate. God is bigger than the universe itself. He can't be limited to one building, no matter how ornate it is.

2:17-18 all the foreign men in the land of Israel. One way of keeping foreign enemies in the land from rebelling is to occupy them with forced labor.

3:1 the LORD's temple. The temple would rise over the spot where Abraham and his son, Isaac, learned the importance of an obedient sacrifice (see Gen. 22).

3:8 most holy place. When imagining the most holy place, think of a perfect cube. This proportionately square room would house the presence of God.

4:1 made a bronze altar. The bronze altar is located in the courtyard. Steps stretch across it in front of the temple.

4:2 cast [metal] reservoir … perfectly round. A huge round basin is erected for cer-

reservoir was cast. ⁴ It stood on 12 oxen, three facing north, three facing west, three facing south, and three facing east. The reservoir was on top of them and all their hindquarters were toward the center. ⁵ The reservoir was three inchesᵃ thick, and its rim was fashioned like the brim of a cup or a lily blossom. It could hold 11,000 gallons.ᵇ

⁶ He made 10 basins for washing and he put five on the right and five on the left. The parts of the •burnt offering were rinsed in them, but the reservoir was used by the priests for washing.

The Lampstands, Tables, and Courts

⁷ He made the 10 gold lampstands according to their specifications and put them in the sanctuary, five on the right and five on the left. ⁸ He made 10 tables and placed them in the sanctuary, five on the right and five on the left. He also made 100 gold bowls.

⁹ He made the courtyard of the priests and the large court, and doors for the court. He overlaid the doors with bronze. ¹⁰ He put the reservoir on the right side, toward the southeast. ¹¹ Then Huramᶜ made the pots, the shovels, and the bowls.

Completion of the Bronze Furnishings

So Huram finished doing the work that he was doing for King Solomon in God's temple: ¹² two pillars; the bowls and the capitals on top of the two pillars; the two gratings for covering both bowls of the capitals that were on top of the pillars; ¹³ the 400 pomegranates for the two gratings (two rows of pomegranates for each grating covering both capitals' bowls on top of the pillars). ¹⁴ He also made the water cartsᵈ and the basins on the water carts. ¹⁵ The one reservoir and the 12 oxen underneath it, ¹⁶ the pots, the shovels, the forks, and all their utensils—Huram-abiᵉ made them for King Solomon for the LORD's temple. ⌊All these were made⌋ of polished bronze. ¹⁷ The king had them cast in clay molds in the Jordan Valley between Succoth and Zeredah. ¹⁸ Solomon made all these utensils in such great abundance that the weight of the bronze was not determined.

Completion of the Gold Furnishings

¹⁹ Solomon also made all the equipment in God's temple: the gold altar; the tables on which ⌊to put⌋ the bread of the Presence; ²⁰ the lampstands and their lamps of pure gold to burn in front of the inner sanctuary according to specifications; ²¹ the flowers, lamps, and gold tongs—of purest gold; ²² the wick trimmers, sprinkling basins, ladles,ᶠ and firepans—of purest gold; and the entryway to the temple, its inner doors to the most holy place, and the doors of the temple sanctuary—of gold.

5 So all the work Solomon did for the LORD's temple was completed. Then Solomon brought the consecrated things of his father David—the silver, the gold, and all the utensils—and put them in the treasuries of God's temple.

Preparations for the Temple Dedication

² At that time Solomon assembled at Jerusalem the elders of Israel—all the tribal heads, the ancestral chiefs of the Israelites—in order to bring the ark of the covenant of the LORD up from the city of David, that is, Zion. ³ So all the men of Israel were assembled in the king's presence at the festival; this was in the seventh month.ᵍ

⁴ All the elders of Israel came, and the Levites picked up the ark. ⁵ They brought up the ark, the tent of meeting, and the holy utensils that were in the tent. The priests and the Levites brought them up. ⁶ King Solomon and the entire congregation of Israel who had gathered around him were in front of the ark sacrificing sheep and cattle that could not be counted or numbered because there were so many. ⁷ The priests brought the ark of the LORD's covenant to its place, into the inner sanctuary of the temple, to the most holy place, beneath the wings of the •cherubim. ⁸ And the cherubim spread their wings over the place of the ark so that the cherubim formed a cover above the ark and its poles. ⁹ The poles were so long that their ends were seen from the holy placeʰ in front of the inner sanctuary, but they were not seen from outside; they are there to this very day. ¹⁰ Nothing was in the ark except the two tablets that Moses had put ⌊in it⌋ at Horeb,ⁱ where the LORD had made a covenant with the Israelites when they came out of Egypt.

¹¹ When the priests came out of the holy place—for all the priests who were present had consecrated themselves regardless of their tour of dutyʲ— ¹² the Levitical singers of •Asaph, of Heman, of Jeduthun, and of their sons and their relatives, dressed in fine linen, with cymbals, harps and lyres, were standing east of the altar, and with them were 120 priests blowing trumpets. ¹³ The trumpeters and singers joined together to praise and thank the LORD with one voice. They raised ⌊their⌋ voices, accompanied by trumpets, cymbals, and musical instruments, in praise to the LORD:

ᵃ**4:5** Lit *a handbreadth* ᵇ**4:5** Emended to *2,000 baths* (1 Kg 7:26); MT reads *3,000 baths* ᶜ**4:11** Or *Hiram*; 1 Kg 7:13,40,45 ᵈ**4:14** Lit *the stands*
ᵉ**4:16** Lit *Huram my father* ᶠ**4:22** Or *dishes,* or *spoons;* lit *palms* ᵍ**5:3** = September–October ʰ**5:9** Some Hb mss, LXX; other Hb mss read *the ark;*
1 Kg 8:8 ⁱ**5:10** = Sinai ʲ**5:11** Lit *themselves; there was no maintaining of divisions*

---

emonial washings. The reservoir contains about 11,000 gallons of water.
4:4 It stood on 12 oxen. The twelve tribes are symbolized in the detailed statues, which face all four directions. In this way, Israel could always see itself in worship.
4:5 the reservoir was used by the priests

for washing. Offering animal sacrifices was messy. This meant that the priests had to have a place to scrub themselves often.
5:2 Solomon assembled ... to bring the ark. For the first time, the ark is housed in a permanent, glorious dwelling. Its significance in the temple makes the seven years of labor

worth every moment—God's presence is among them.
5:10 Nothing was in the ark except the two tablets. The Israelites recognize the significance of God's commands on the stone tablets inside the ark (Ex. 32:15-16). Though the ark had changed hands with Israel's enemies,

For He is good;
His faithful love endures forever;

the temple, the LORD's temple, was filled with a cloud. 14 And because of the cloud, the priests were not able to continue ministering, for the glory of the LORD filled God's temple.

Solomon's Dedication of the Temple

6 Then Solomon said:

The LORD said He would dwell
in thick darkness,
2 but I have built an exalted temple for You,
a place for Your residence forever.

3 Then the king turned and blessed the entire congregation of Israel while they were standing. 4 He said:

May the LORD God of Israel be praised!
He spoke directly to my father David,
and He has fulfilled ⌊the promise⌋
by His power.
He said,
5 "Since the day I brought My people Israel
out of the land of Egypt,
I have not chosen a city to build a temple in
among any of the tribes of Israel,
so that My name would be there,
and I have not chosen a man
to be ruler over My people Israel.
6 But I have chosen Jerusalem
so that My name will be there,
and I have chosen David
to be over My people Israel."

7 Now it was in the heart of my father David
to build a temple for the name of the LORD God
of Israel.
8 However, the LORD said to my father David,
"Since it was your desire to build a temple
for My name,
you have done well to have this desire.
9 Yet, you are not the one to build the temple,
but your son, your own offspring,
will build the temple for My name."
10 So the LORD has fulfilled what He promised.
I have taken the place of my father David
and I sit on the throne of Israel,
as the LORD promised.
I have built the temple for the name
of the LORD God of Israel.
11 I have put the ark there,

where the LORD's covenant is
that He made with the Israelites.

Solomon's Prayer

12 Then Solomon stood before the altar of the LORD in front of the entire congregation of Israel and spread out his hands. 13 For Solomon had made a bronze platform seven and a half feet[a] long, seven and a half feet[a] wide, and four and a half feet[b] high and put it in the court. He stood on it, knelt down in front of the entire congregation of Israel, and spread out his hands toward heaven. 14 He said:

LORD God of Israel,
there is no God like You
in heaven or on earth,
keeping His gracious covenant
with Your servants who walk before You
with their whole heart.
15 You have kept what You promised
to Your servant, my father David.
You spoke directly ⌊to him⌋,
and You fulfilled ⌊Your promise⌋ by Your power,
as it is today.
16 Therefore, LORD God of Israel,
keep what You promised
to Your servant, my father David:
You will never fail to have a man
to sit before Me on the throne of Israel,
if only your sons guard their way to walk
in My Law
as you have walked before Me.
17 Now, LORD God of Israel, please confirm
what You promised to Your servant David.
18 But will God indeed live on earth with man?
Even heaven, the highest heaven,
cannot contain You,
much less this temple I have built.
19 Listen[c] to Your servant's prayer and his petition,
LORD my God,
so that You may hear the cry and the prayer
that Your servant prays before You,
20 so that Your eyes watch over this temple
day and night,
toward the place where You said
You would put Your name;
and so that You may hear the prayer
Your servant prays toward this place.
21 Hear the petitions of Your servant
and Your people Israel,
which they pray toward this place.

a **6:13** Lit *five cubits*   b **6:13** Lit *three cubits*   c **6:19** Lit *Turn*

God's commandments are miraculously undisturbed.

5:14 glory of the LORD. A supernatural cloud symbolizes the Lord's presence (Ex. 40:34-35) and God's pleasure with the new "home." This is reminiscent of the pillar of cloud that led the people of Israel in the wilderness.

6:1 dwell in thick darkness. There is a holiness and mystery about God that prevents people from fully comprehending or "seeing" Him.

6:9 you are not the one to build the temple. In 1 Chronicles 22:8 we are told that David was rejected for this honor because he had been

involved in so much violence and warfare.

6:13 in front of the entire congregation of Israel. Solomon models a spirit of humility and submission before the people. In a time and culture where some kings saw themselves as gods, and most thought it more important to encourage people to bow to them, Solomon

May You hear in Your dwelling place in heaven.
May You hear and forgive.

22 If a man sins against his neighbor
and is forced to take an oath[a]
and he comes to take an oath
before Your altar in this temple,
23 may You hear in heaven and act.
May You judge Your servants,
condemning the wicked by bringing
what he has done on his own head
and providing justice for the righteous
by rewarding him according to
his righteousness.

24 If Your people Israel are defeated
before an enemy,
because they have sinned against You,
and they return [to You] and praise Your name,
and they pray and plead for mercy
before You in this temple,
25 may You hear in heaven
and forgive the sin of Your people Israel.
May You restore them to the land
You gave them and their ancestors.

26 When the skies are shut and there is no rain
because they have sinned against You,
and they pray toward this place
and praise Your name,
and they turn from their sins
because You are afflicting[b] them,
27 may You hear in heaven
and forgive the sin of Your servants
and Your people Israel,
so that You may teach them the good way
they should walk in. May You send rain
on Your land
that You gave Your people for an inheritance.

28 When there is famine on the earth,
when there is pestilence,
when there is blight, mildew, locust,
or grasshopper,
when their enemies besiege them
in the region of their fortified cities,[c]
[when there is] any plague or illness,
29 whatever prayer or petition
anyone from your people Israel might have—
each man knowing his own affliction[d]
and suffering,

30 may You hear in heaven, Your dwelling place,
and may You forgive and repay the man
according to all his ways, since You know
his heart,
for You alone know the human heart,
31 so that they may •fear You
and walk in Your ways
all the days they live on the land
You gave our ancestors.

32 Even for the foreigner who is not
of Your people Israel
but has come from a distant land
because of Your great name
and Your mighty hand and outstretched arm:
when he comes and prays toward this temple,
33 may You hear in heaven in Your dwelling place,
and do all the foreigner asks You for.
Then all the peoples of the earth will know
Your name,
to fear You as Your people Israel do
and know that this temple I have built
is called by Your name.

34 When Your people go out to fight
against their enemies,
wherever You send them,
and they pray to You
in the direction of this city You have chosen
and the temple that I have built for Your name,
35 may You hear their prayer and petition
in heaven
and uphold their cause.

36 When they sin against You—
for there is no one who does not sin—
and You are angry with them
and hand them over to the enemy,
and their captors deport them
to a distant or nearby country,
37 and when they come to their senses
in the land where they were deported
and repent and petition You
in their captors' land,
saying: "We have sinned and done wrong;
we have been wicked,"
38 and when they return to You
with their whole mind and heart

---

[a] 6:22 Lit and he lifts a curse against him to curse him [b] 6:26 LXX, Vg; MT reads answering; 1 Kg 8:35 [c] 6:28 Lit if his (Israel's) enemies besiege
him in the land of his gates; Jos 2:7; Jdg 16:2–3 [d] 6:29 Lit plague

---

shows that submission to God is what's important.

6:26-31 As spiritually focused as Solomon's people are at present, a weaker moment for them is on the horizon. Solomon requested God's mercy in advance of their inevitable mistakes. He reminded God that the land is a gift. He called on God to show mercy so all will fear Him.

6:36 their captors deport them to a distant or nearby country. This was a military strategy the Assyrians invented some 300 years after Solomon spoke these words. The Assyrians used it against the northern tribes of Israel. Later, the Babylonians used it against the southern kingdom of Judah. The prayer is that God will still listen to Israel even in this worst of all scenarios.

6:40-42 Solomon asked God to come among the Israelites, reminding Him of His promise to David. Solomon had brought the

in the land of their captivity
where they were taken captive,
and when they pray in the direction
of their land
that You gave their ancestors,
and the city You have chosen,
and toward the temple I have built
for Your name,
39 may You hear in heaven, in Your dwelling place,
their prayer and petitions and uphold
their cause.a
May You forgive Your people
who sinned against You.

40 Now, my God,
please let Your eyes be open
and Your ears attentive
to the prayer of this place.
41 Now therefore:

Arise, LORD God, ⌊come⌋ to Your resting place,
You and the ark ⌊that shows⌋ Your strength.
May Your priests, LORD God, be clothed
with salvation,
and may Your godly people rejoice in goodness.
42 LORD God, do not reject Your anointed one;b
remember the loyalty of Your servant David.

The Dedication Ceremonies

7 When Solomon finished praying, fire descended from heaven and consumed the •burnt offering and the sacrifices, and the glory of the LORD filled the temple. 2 The priests were not able to enter the LORD's temple because the glory of the LORD filled the temple of the LORD. 3 All the Israelites were watching when the fire descended and the glory of the LORD came on the temple. They bowed down with their faces to the ground on the pavement. They worshiped and praised the LORD:

For He is good,
for His faithful love endures forever.

4 The king and all the people were offering sacrifices in the LORD's presence. 5 King Solomon offered a sacrifice of 22,000 cattle and 120,000 sheep. In this manner the king and all the people dedicated God's temple. 6 The priests were standing at their stations, as were the Levites with the musical instruments of the LORD, which King David had made to praise the LORD—"for His faithful love endures forever"—when David offered praise with them. Across from them, the priests were blowing trumpets, and all the people were standing.

7 Solomon consecrated the middle of the courtyard that was in front of the LORD's temple because that was where he offered the burnt offerings and the fat of the •fellowship offerings since the bronze altar that Solomon had made could not accommodate the burnt offering, the •grain offering, and the fat ⌊of the fellowship offerings⌋.

8 So Solomon and all Israel with him—a very great assembly, from the entrance to Hamathc to the Brook of Egypt—observed the festival at that time for seven days. 9 On the eighth day they held a sacred assembly, for the dedication of the altar lasted seven days and the festival seven days. 10 On the twenty-third day of the seventh month he sent the people away to their tents, rejoicing and with happy hearts for the goodness the LORD had done for David, for Solomon, and for His people Israel.

11 So Solomon finished the LORD's temple and the royal palace. Everything that had entered Solomon's heart to do for the LORD's temple and for his own palace succeeded.

The LORD's Response

12 Then the LORD appeared to Solomon at night and said to him:

I have heard your prayer and have chosen this place for Myself as a temple of sacrifice. 13 If I close the sky so there is no rain, or if I command the grasshopper to consume the land, or if I send pestilence on My people, 14 and My people who are called by My name humble themselves, pray and seek My face, and turn from their evil ways, then I will hear from heaven, forgive their sin, and heal their land. 15 My eyes will now be open and My ears attentive to prayer from this place. 16 And I have now chosen and consecrated this temple so that My name may be there forever; My eyes and My heart will be there at all times.

17 As for you, if you walk before Me as your father David walked, doing everything I have commanded you, and if you keep My statutes and ordinances, 18 I will establish your royal throne, as I promised your father David: You will never fail to have a man on the throne of Israel.

19 However, if you turn away and abandon My statutes and My commands that I have set before you and if you go and serve other gods and worship them, 20 then I will uproot Israel from the soil that I gave them, and this temple that I have

---

a6:39 Lit and do their judgment or justice b6:42 Some Hb mss, LXX; other Hb mss read ones; Ps 132:10 c7:8 Or from Lebo-hamath

ark to the temple (5:2-14).

7:1-3 God concludes the ceremonies in a firework display of heavenly power. God consumes the sacrifice on the altar, showing He accepts the praise and prayers from His people. God's sending fire as a visible sign of His presence is reminiscent of His sending fire on

Sinai (Deut. 4:11; 5:22). He likewise sent fire when Moses and Aaron dedicated the tabernacle (Num. 9:24) and when David set up the altar on the threshing floor of Araunah (1 Chron. 21:26).

7:6 musical instruments. Israel rises to its feet in celebration. The Levites render praise

to God for His goodness.

7:14 humble themselves … then I will hear from heaven. Earlier, Solomon modeled what God was now calling for, a humility in which the people would pray and seek God whenever they had fallen away. When people honestly acknowledge God, He is at-

sanctified for My name I will banish from My presence; I will make it an object of scorn and ridicule among all the peoples. 21 As for this temple, which was exalted, every passerby will be appalled and will say: Why did the LORD do this to this land and this temple? 22 Then they will say: Because they abandoned the LORD God of their ancestors who brought them out of the land of Egypt. They clung to other gods and worshiped and served them. Because of this, He brought all this ruin on them.

Solomon's Later Building Projects

8 At the end of 20 years during which Solomon had built the LORD's temple and his own palace— 2 Solomon having rebuilt the cities Hirama gave him and having settled the Israelites there— 3 Solomon went to Hamath-zobah and seized it. 4 He built Tadmor in the wilderness along with all the storage cities that he built in Hamath. 5 He built Upper Beth-horon and Lower Beth-horon—fortified cities with walls, gates, and bars— 6 Baalath, all the storage cities that belonged to Solomon, all the chariot cities, the cavalry cities, and everything Solomon desired to build in Jerusalem, Lebanon, or anywhere else in the land of his dominion.

7 As for all the peoples who remained of the Hittites, Amorites, Perizzites, Hivites, and Jebusites, who were not from Israel— 8 their descendants who remained in the land after them, those whom the Israelites had not completely destroyed—Solomon imposed forced labor on them; ⌊it is this way⌋ today. 9 But Solomon did not consign the Israelites to be slaves for his work; they were soldiers, commanders of his captains, and commanders of his chariots and his cavalry. 10 These were King Solomon's deputies: 250 who ruled over the people.

11 Solomon brought the daughter of Pharaoh from the city of David to the house he had built for her, for he said, "My wife must not live in the houseb of David king of Israel because the places to which the ark of the LORD has come are holy."

Public Worship Established at the Temple

12 At that time Solomon offered •burnt offerings to the LORD on the LORD's altar he had made in front of the vestibule 13 following the daily requirement for offerings according to the commandment of Moses for Sabbaths, New Moons, and the three annual appointed festivals: the Festival of Unleavened Bread, the Festival of Weeks, and the Festival of Booths. 14 According to the ordinances of his father David, he appointed the divisions of the priests over their service, of the Levites over their responsibilities to offer praise and to minister before the priests following the daily requirement, and of the gatekeepers by their divisions with respect to each gate, for this had been the command of David, the man of God. 15 They did not turn aside from the king's command regarding the priests and the Levites concerning any matter or concerning the treasuries. 16 All of Solomon's work was carried out from the day the foundation ⌊was laid⌋ for the LORD's temple until it was finished. So the LORD's temple was completed.

Solomon's Fleet

17 At that time Solomon went to Ezion-geber and to Eloth on the seashore in the land of Edom. 18 So through his servants, Hiramc sent him ships with crews of experienced seamen. They went with Solomon's servants to Ophir, took from there 17 tonsd of gold, and delivered it to King Solomon.

The Queen of Sheba

9 The queen of Sheba heard of Solomon's fame, so she came to test Solomon with difficult questions at Jerusalem with a very large retinue, with camels bearing spices, gold in abundance, and precious stones. She came to Solomon and spoke with him about everything that was on her mind. 2 So Solomon answered all her questions; nothing was too difficult for Solomon to explain to her. 3 When the queen of Sheba observed Solomon's wisdom, the palace he had built, 4 the food at his table, his servants' residence, his attendants' service and their attire, his cupbearers and their attire, and the •burnt offerings he offered at the LORD's temple, it took her breath away.

5 She said to the king, "The report I heard in my own country about your words and about your wisdom is true. 6 But I didn't believe their reports until I came and saw with my own eyes. Indeed, I was not even told half of your great wisdom! You far exceed the report I heard. 7 How happy are your men.e How happy are these servants of yours, who always stand in your presence hearing your wisdom. 8 May the LORD your God be praised! He delighted in you and put you on His throne as king for the LORD your God. Because Your God loved Israel enough to establish them forever, He has set you over them as king to carry out justice and righteousness."

9 Then she gave the king four and a half tonsf of gold, a great quantity of spices, and precious stones. There

---

a8:2 = the king of Tyre   b8:11 LXX reads city   c8:18 Hb Huram   d8:18 Lit 450 talents   e9:7 LXX, Old Lat read wives; 1 Kg 10:8   f9:9 Lit 120 talents

---

tentive to their prayers.

8:1-2 In contrast to his battle-weary father, Solomon enjoyed a peaceful reign. Solomon originally gave Hiram 20 cities as partial payment for his help. Hiram wasn't pleased and eventually returned them (see 1 Kings 9:10-14).

8:11 the places to which the ark ... has

come are holy. Solomon was all too aware of the spiritual conflict represented in his idol-worshiping Egyptian wife. His care to remove her from David's palace betrayed his better sense (1 Kings 11:1-4).

8:12-16 Solomon demonstrated the detail of his religious success in the form of numerous

sacrifices. He kept pace with his father's outward religious acts, though he ultimately failed to replicate David's devotion (1 Kings 11:4).

8:17-18 The chronicler completes Solomon's success profile by including his economic achievements. King Hiram once again proved to be a royal relationship worth keeping. Tyre's

never were such spices as those the queen of Sheba gave to King Solomon. 10 In addition, Hiram's servants and Solomon's servants who brought gold from Ophir also brought algum wood and precious stones. 11 The king made the algum wood into walkways for the LORD's temple and for the king's palace and into harps and lyres for the singers. Never before had anything like them been seen in the land of Judah.

12 King Solomon gave the queen of Sheba her every desire, whatever she asked—far more than she had brought the king. Then she, along with her servants, returned to her own country.

Solomon's Wealth

13 The weight of gold that came to Solomon annually was 25 tons,a 14 besides what was brought by the merchants and traders. All the Arabian kings and governors of the land also brought gold and silver to Solomon.

15 King Solomon made 200 large shields of hammered gold; 15 poundsb of hammered gold went into each shield. 16 He made 300 small shields of hammered gold; about eight poundsc of gold went into each shield. The king put them in the House of the Forest of Lebanon.

17 The king also made a large ivory throne and overlaid it with pure gold. 18 The throne had six steps; there was a footstool covered in gold for the throne, armrests on either side of the seat, and two lions standing beside the armrests. 19 Twelve lions were standing there on the six steps, one at each end. Nothing like it had ever been made in any other kingdom.

20 All of King Solomon's drinking cups were gold, and all the utensils of the House of the Forest of Lebanon were pure gold. There was no silver, since it was considered as nothing in Solomon's time, 21 for the king's ships kept going to Tarshish with Hiram's servants, and once every three years the ships of Tarshish would arrive bearing gold, silver, ivory, apes, and peacocks.d

22 King Solomon surpassed all the kings of the world in riches and wisdom. 23 All the kings of the world wanted an audience with Solomon to hear the wisdom God had put in his heart. 24 Each of them would bring his own gift—itemse of silver and gold, clothing, weapons,f spices, and horses and mules—as an annual tribute.

25 Solomon had 4,000 stalls for horses and chariots, and 12,000 horsemen. He stationed them in the chariot cities and with the king in Jerusalem. 26 He ruled over all the kings from the Euphrates River to the land

of the Philistines and as far as the border of Egypt. 27 The king made silver as common in Jerusalem as stones, and he made cedar as abundant as sycamore in the Judean foothills. 28 They were bringing horses for Solomon from Egypt and from all the countries.

Solomon's Death

29 The remaining events of Solomon's ⌊reign⌋, from beginning to end, are written about in the Events of Nathan the Prophet, the Prophecy of Ahijah the Shilonite, and the Visions of Iddo the Seer concerning Jeroboam son of Nebat. 30 Solomon reigned in Jerusalem over all Israel for 40 years. 31 Solomon rested with his fathers and was buried in the city of his father David. His son Rehoboam became king in his place.

The Kingdom Divided

10 Then Rehoboam went to Shechem, for all Israel had gone to Shechem to make him king. 2 When Jeroboam son of Nebat heard ⌊about it⌋—for he was in Egypt where he had fled from King Solomon's presence—Jeroboam returned from Egypt. 3 So they summoned him. Then Jeroboam and all Israel came and spoke to Rehoboam: 4 "Your father made our yoke harsh. Therefore, lighten your father's harsh service and the heavy yoke he put on us, and we will serve you."

5 Rehoboam replied, "Return to me in three days." So the people left.

6 Then King Rehoboam consulted with the elders who had served his father Solomon when he was alive, asking, "How do you advise me to respond to this people?"

7 They replied, "If you will be kind to these people and please them by speaking kind words to them, they will be your servants forever."

8 But he rejected the advice of the elders who had advised him and consulted with the young men who had grown up with him, the ones serving him. 9 He asked them, "What message do you advise we send back to this people who said to me, 'Lighten the yoke your father put on us'?"

10 Then the young men who had grown up with him told him, "This is what you should say to the people who said to you, 'Your father made our yoke heavy, but you, make it lighter on us!' This is what you should say to them: 'My little finger is thicker than my father's loins.g 11 Now therefore, my father burdened you with a heavy yoke, but I will add to your yoke; my father disciplined you with whips, but I, with barbed whips.' "h

---

a **9:13** Lit 666 talents b **9:15** Lit 600 (shekels) c **9:16** Lit 300 (shekels) d **9:21** Or baboons e **9:24** Or vessels, or weapons f **9:24** Or fragrant balsam; LXX reads resin (oil of myrrh) g **10:10** Or waist h **10:11** Lit with scorpions

---

navy became an important resource.

9:8 delighted ... put you on his throne. The chronicler frames the queen's speech to affirm Solomon's divinely appointed rule. God enabled and enlightened this obscure but resplendent queen to speak courteously of the competition.

9:28 bringing horses for Solomon. Solomon's picture-perfect conclusion conveys the chronicler's biographical bias. The happy ending serves to contrast with the heritage of rebellion that came from his many foreign wives (1 Kings 11:1-40).

10:4 Your father made our yoke harsh. At

some point in time, Solomon went from merely conscripting foreign laborers to forcing hard labor on Israelites as well. This uncharacteristically unwise move helped sow the seeds for the division of the kingdom.

10:7 if you will be kind to these people. Here the advice of the elders points to an important

¹² So Jeroboam and all the people came to Rehoboam on the third day, just as the king had ordered, saying, "Return to me on the third day." ¹³ Then the king answered them harshly. King Rehoboam rejected the elders' advice ¹⁴ and spoke to them according to the young men's advice, saying, "My father made your yoke heavy,ᵃ but I will add to it; my father disciplined you with whips, but I, with barbed whips."ᵇ

¹⁵ The king did not listen to the people because the turn of events came from God, in order that the LORD might carry out His word that He had spoken through Ahijah the Shilonite to Jeroboam son of Nebat.

¹⁶ When all Israel sawᶜ that the king had not listened to them, the people answered the king:

What portion do we have in David?
We have no inheritance in the son of Jesse.
Israel, each man to your tent;
David, look after your own house now!

So all Israel went to their tents. ¹⁷ But as for the Israelites living in the cities of Judah, Rehoboam reigned over them.

¹⁸ Then King Rehoboam sent Hadoram,ᵈ who was in charge of the forced labor, but the Israelites stoned him to death. However, King Rehoboam managed to get up into the chariot to flee to Jerusalem. ¹⁹ Israel is in rebellion against the house of David until today.

Rehoboam in Jerusalem

11 When Rehoboam arrived in Jerusalem, he mobilized the house of Judah and Benjamin—180,000 choice warriors—to fight against Israel to restore the reign to Rehoboam. ² But the word of the LORD came to Shemaiah, the man of God: ³ "Say to Rehoboam son of Solomon, king of Judah, to all Israel in Judah and Benjamin, and to the rest of the people: ⁴ 'This is what the LORD says: You are not to march up and fight against your brothers. Each of you must return home, for this incident has come from Me.'"

So they listened to what the LORD said and turned back from going against Jeroboam.

Judah's King Rehoboam

⁵ Rehoboam stayed in Jerusalem, and he fortified citiesᵉ in Judah. ⁶ He built up Bethlehem, Etam, Tekoa, ⁷ Beth-zur, Soco, Adullam, ⁸ Gath, Mareshah, Ziph, ⁹ Adoraim, Lachish, Azekah, ¹⁰ Zorah, Aijalon, and Hebron, which are fortified cities in Judah and in Benjamin. ¹¹ He strengthened their fortifications and put

leaders in them with supplies of food, oil, and wine. ¹² He also put large shields and spears in each and every city to make them very strong. So Judah and Benjamin were his.

¹³ The priests and Levites from all their regions throughout Israel took their stand with Rehoboam, ¹⁴ for the Levites left their pasturelands and their possessions and went to Judah and Jerusalem, because Jeroboam and his sons refused to let them serve as priests of the LORD. ¹⁵ Jeroboam appointed his own priests for the •high places, the goat-demons, and the ⌊gold⌋ calves he had made. ¹⁶ Those from every tribe of Israel who had determined in their hearts to seek the LORD their God followed the Levites to Jerusalem to sacrifice to the LORD God of their ancestors. ¹⁷ So they strengthened the kingdom of Judah and supported Rehoboam son of Solomon for three years, because they walked in the way of David and Solomon for three years.

¹⁸ Rehoboam married Mahalath, daughter of David's son Jerimoth and of Abihail daughter of Jesse's son Eliab. ¹⁹ She bore him sons: Jeush, Shemariah, and Zaham. ²⁰ After her, he married Maacah daughterᶠ of Absalom. She bore him Abijah, Attai, Ziza, and Shelomith. ²¹ Rehoboam loved Maacah daughterᶠ of Absalom more than all his wives and concubines. He acquired 18 wives and 60 concubines and was the father of 28 sons and 60 daughters.

²² Rehoboam appointed Abijah son of Maacah as chief, leader among his brothers, intending to make him king. ²³ Rehoboam also showed discernment by dispersing some of his sons to all the regions of Judah and Benjamin and to all the fortified cities. He gave them plenty of provisions and sought many wives for them.

Shishak's Invasion

12 When Rehoboam had established his sovereignty and royal power, he abandoned the law of the LORD—he and all Israel with him. ² Because they were unfaithful to the LORD, in the fifth year of King Rehoboam, Shishak king of Egypt went to war against Jerusalem ³ with 1,200 chariots, 60,000 cavalrymen, and countless people who came with him from Egypt—Libyans, Sukkiim, and Ethiopians.ᵍ ⁴ He captured the fortified cities of Judah and came as far as Jerusalem.

⁵ Then Shemaiah the prophet went to Rehoboam and the leaders of Judah who were gathered at Jerusalem because of Shishak. He said to them: "This is what the

---

ᵃ**10:14** Some Hb mss, LXX; other Hb mss read *I will make your yoke heavy*; 1 Kg 12:14   ᵇ**10:14** Lit *with scorpions*   ᶜ**10:16** Some Hb mss, LXX; other Hb mss omit *saw*; 1 Kg 12:16   ᵈ**10:18** = Adoram; 1 Kg 12:18   ᵉ**11:5** Lit *he built cities for a fortress*   ᶠ**11:20,21** Possibly *granddaughter*; 2 Ch 13:2   ᵍ**12:3** Lit *Cushites*

---

secret of successful rule: being good to your people is the best way to assure their loyalty.

10:13 rejected the elder's advice. Lack of respect for the wisdom of those who have lived a long time often leads to downfall.

10:15 the turn of events came from God.

The wisdom of God operates through the foolishness of men. Abijah had prophesied to Jeroboam that he would become king over the ten tribes. This was a consequence of Solomon's disobedience to God. (1 Kings 11:3). God used Rehoboam's imperceptiveness to bring about what He had ordained.

11:5-10 Rehoboam. Rehoboam faces great opposition but is armed with only two tribes: Benjamin and Judah. Despite great odds, Rehoboam prepares his forces for a fight. He fortified the cities and brought the priests into them. Many supported him and strengthened the kingdom (v. 17).

LORD says: 'You have abandoned Me; therefore, I have abandoned you into the hand of Shishak.' "

6 So the leaders of Israel and the king humbled themselves and said, "The LORD is righteous."

7 When the LORD saw that they had humbled themselves, the LORD's message came to Shemaiah: "They have humbled themselves; I will not destroy them but will grant them a little deliverance. My wrath will not be poured out on Jerusalem through Shishak. 8 However, they will become his servants so that they may recognize [the difference between] serving Me and serving the kingdoms of the land."

9 So King Shishak of Egypt went to war against Jerusalem. He seized the treasuries of the LORD's temple and the treasuries of the royal palace. He took everything. He took the gold shields that Solomon had made. 10 King Rehoboam made bronze shields in their place and committed them into the care of the captains of the royal escortsª who guarded the entrance to the king's palace. 11 Whenever the king entered the LORD's temple, the royal escorts would carry the shields and take them back to the royal escorts' armory. 12 When Rehoboam humbled himself, the LORD's anger turned away from him, and He did not destroy [him] completely. Besides that, conditions were good in Judah.

Rehoboam's Last Days

13 King Rehoboam established his royal power in Jerusalem. Rehoboam was 41 years old when he became king; he reigned 17 years in Jerusalem, the city the LORD had chosen from all the tribes of Israel to put His name. Rehoboam's mother's name was Naamah the Ammonite. 14 Rehoboam did what was evil, because he did not determine in his heart to seek the LORD.

15 The events of Rehoboam's [reign], from beginning to end, are written about in the Events of Shemaiah the Prophet and of Iddo the Seer concerning genealogies. There was war between Rehoboam and Jeroboam throughout their reigns. 16 Rehoboam rested with his fathers and was buried in the city of David. His son Abijahᵇ became king in his place.

Judah's King Abijah

13 In the eighteenth year of [Israel's] King Jeroboam, Abijahᵇ became king over Judah; 2 he reigned three years in Jerusalem. His mother's name was Micaiahᶜ daughter of Uriel; [she was] from Gibeah.

There was war between Abijah and Jeroboam. 3 Abijah set his army of warriors in order with 400,000

choice men. Jeroboam arranged his mighty army of 800,000 choice men in battle formation against him. 4 Then Abijah stood on Mount Zemaraim, which is in the hill country of Ephraim, and said, "Jeroboam and all Israel, hear me. 5 Don't you know that the LORD God of Israel gave the kingship over Israel to David and his descendants forever by a covenant of salt? 6 But Jeroboam son of Nebat, a servant of Solomon son of David, rose up and rebelled against his lord. 7 Then worthless and •wicked men gathered around him to resist Rehoboam son of Solomon when Rehoboam was young, inexperienced, and unable to assert himself against them.

8 "And now you are saying you can assert yourselves against the LORD's kingdom in the hand of [one of] David's sons. You are a vast multitude and have with you the golden calves that Jeroboam made for you as gods.ᵈ 9 Didn't you banish the priests of the LORD, the descendants of Aaron and the Levites, and make your own priests like the peoples of [other] lands do? Whoever comes to ordain himself with a young bull and seven rams may become a priest of what are not gods.

10 "But as for us, the LORD is our God. We have not abandoned Him; the priests ministering to the LORD are descendants of Aaron, and the Levites [serve] at their tasks. 11 They offer a •burnt offering and fragrant incense to the LORD every morning and every evening, and [they set] the rows of the bread [of the Presence] on the ceremonially clean table. They light the lamps of the gold lampstand every evening. We are carrying out the requirements of the LORD our God, while you have abandoned Him. 12 Look, God and His priests are with us at our head. The trumpets are ready to sound the charge against you. Israelites, don't fight against the LORD God of your ancestors, for you will not succeed."

13 Now Jeroboam had sent an ambush around to advance from behind them. So they were in front of Judah, and the ambush was behind them. 14 Judah turned and discovered that the battle was in front of them and behind them, so they cried out to the LORD. Then the priests blew the trumpets, 15 and the men of Judah raised the battle cry. When the men of Judah raised the battle cry, God routed Jeroboam and all Israel before Abijah and Judah. 16 So the Israelites fled before Judah, and God handed them over to them. 17 Then Abijah and his people struck them with a mighty blow, and 500,000 choice men of Israel were killed. 18 The Israelites were subdued at that time. The Judahites

---

ª**12:10** Lit *the runners*   ᵇ**12:16; 13:1** = Abijam; 1 Kg 14:31—15:8   ᶜ**13:2** LXX, Syr, Arabic read *Maacah*; 2 Ch 11:22; 1 Kg 15:2   ᵈ**13:8** Or *God*; 1 Kg 12:28

11:12 Judah and Benjamin were his. The northern kingdom of Israel was made up of ten tribes, while the southern kingdom of Judah was made up of two tribes: Judah and Benjamin.

11:23 Abijah. Rehoboam thinks ahead to the succession of his favored son, Abijah. His re-

maining sons are given political prestige.

12:1 abandoned the law ... all Israel with him. The divided kingdom is represented in terms of Judah (to the south) and Israel (to the north). The chronicler implies the reference is to Israelites living in Judah who abandon God's ways.

13:1–14:1 The story in 1 Kings 15:1-8 parallels the details of Abijah's reign in 2 Chronicles, only with a different twist. First Kings' more negative portrayal is balanced by the chronicler's illustration of Abijah's battlefield plea.

13:9 Whoever comes to ordain himself. God must call those ordained to a ministry. These

succeeded because they depended on the LORD, the God of their ancestors.

[19] Abijah pursued Jeroboam and captured ⌊some⌋ cities from him: Bethel and its villages, Jeshanah and its villages, and Ephron[a] and its villages. [20] Jeroboam no longer retained his power[b] during Abijah's reign; ultimately, the LORD struck him and he died.

[21] However, Abijah grew strong, acquired 14 wives, and fathered 22 sons and 16 daughters. [22] The rest of the events of Abijah's ⌊reign⌋, along with his ways and his sayings, are written about in the Writing of the Prophet Iddo. [1c] Abijah rested with his fathers and was buried in the city of David. His son Asa became king in his place. During his reign the land experienced peace for 10 years.

Judah's King Asa

[2d] Asa did what was good and right in the sight of the LORD his God. [3] He removed the pagan altars and the •high places. He shattered their sacred pillars and chopped down their •Asherah poles. [4] He told ⌊the people of⌋ Judah to seek the LORD God of their ancestors and to carry out the instruction and the command. [5] He also removed the high places and the incense altars from all the cities of Judah, and the kingdom experienced peace under him.

[6] Because the land experienced peace, Asa built fortified cities in Judah. No one made war with him in those days because the LORD gave him rest. [7] So he said to ⌊the people of⌋ Judah, "Let's build these cities and surround them with walls and towers, with doors and bars. The land is still ours because we sought the LORD our God. We sought Him and He gave us rest on every side." So they built and succeeded.

The Ethiopian Invasion

[8] Asa had an army of 300,000 from Judah bearing large shields and spears, and 280,000 from Benjamin bearing regular shields and drawing the bow. All these were brave warriors. [9] Then Zerah the •Cushite came against them with an army of one million men and 300[e] chariots. They came as far as Mareshah. [10] So Asa marched out against him and lined up in battle formation in the Valley of Zephathah at Mareshah.

[11] Then Asa cried out to the LORD his God: "LORD, there is no one besides You to help the mighty and those without strength. Help us, LORD our God, for we depend on You, and in Your name we have come against this multitude. LORD, You are our God. Do not let a mere mortal hinder You."

[12] So the LORD routed the Cushites before Asa and before Judah, and the Cushites fled. [13] Then Asa and the people who were with him pursued them as far as Gerar. The Cushites fell until they had no survivors, for they were crushed before the LORD and before His army. So the people of Judah carried off a great supply of loot. [14] Then they attacked all the cities around Gerar because the terror of the LORD was on them. They also plundered all the cities, since there was a great deal of plunder in them. [15] They also attacked the tents of the herdsmen and captured many sheep and camels. Then they returned to Jerusalem.

Revival Under Asa

The Spirit of God came on Azariah son of Oded. [2] So he went out to meet Asa and said to him, "Asa and all Judah and Benjamin, hear me. The LORD is with you when you are with Him. If you seek Him, He will be found by you, but if you abandon Him, He will abandon you. [3] For many years Israel has been without the true God, without a teaching priest, and without law, [4] but when they turned to the LORD God of Israel in their distress and sought Him, He was found by them. [5] In those times there was no peace for those who went about their daily activities because the residents of the lands had many conflicts. [6] Nation was crushed by nation and city by city, for God troubled them with every possible distress. [7] But as for you, be strong; don't be discouraged,[f] for your work has a reward."

[8] When Asa heard these words and the prophecy of ⌊Azariah son of⌋ Oded the prophet, he took courage and removed the detestable idols from the whole land of Judah and Benjamin and from the cities he had captured in the hill country of Ephraim. He renovated the altar of the LORD that was in front of the vestibule of the LORD's ⌊temple⌋. [9] Then he gathered all Judah and Benjamin, as well as those from ⌊the tribes of⌋ Ephraim, Manasseh, and Simeon who had settled among them, for they had defected to him from Israel in great numbers when they saw that the LORD his God was with him.

[10] They were gathered in Jerusalem in the third month of the fifteenth year of Asa's reign. [11] At that time they sacrificed to the LORD 700 cattle and 7,000 sheep from all the plunder they had brought. [12] Then they entered into a covenant to seek the LORD God of their ancestors with all their mind and all their heart. [13] Whoever would not seek the LORD God of Israel would be put to death, young or old,[g] man or woman.

---

[a]**13:19** Alt Hb tradition reads *Ephrain*　[b]**13:20** Lit *He did not restrain the power of Jeroboam*　[c]**14:1** 2 Ch 13:23 in Hb　[d]**14:2** 2 Ch 14:1 in Hb　[e]**14:9** Syr, Arabic read *30,000*　[f]**15:7** Lit *don't let your hands fail*　[g]**15:13** Or *insignificant or great*

---

false priests were taking it upon themselves to elevate themselves to priesthood.

14:5 removed the high places and the incense altars. Asa attempted to reform worshiping in Judah. His mission was short-lived in the wake of overwhelming odds (15:17), and he wasn't able to remove the high places (see

1 Kings 15:14).

15:1-19 A prophet's encouragement goes a long way with Asa. He resumed his search-and-destroy mission against idols with great zeal.

15:13 put to death. Religious expression has significant social and political implications.

Rebellion against God is taken as a serious offense against the state. In keeping with the law, all who would not seek the LORD were to be put to death (see Deut. 13:6-9).

15:15 They had sought Him with all their heart. Christ promises us that those who seek will find (Matt. 7:7-8). To seek with our whole

14 They took an oath to the LORD in a loud voice, with shouting, with trumpets, and with rams' horns. 15 All Judah rejoiced over the oath, for they had sworn it with all their mind. They had sought Him with all their heart, and He was found by them. So the LORD gave them rest on every side.

16 King Asa also removed Maacah, his grandmother,[a] from being queen mother because she had made an obscene image of •Asherah. Asa chopped down her obscene image, then crushed it and burned it in the Kidron Valley. 17 The •high places were not taken away from Israel; nevertheless, Asa was wholehearted his entire life.[b] 18 He brought his father's consecrated gifts and his own consecrated gifts into God's temple: silver, gold, and utensils.

19 There was no war until the thirty-fifth year of Asa's reign.

Asa's Treaty with Aram

16 In the thirty-sixth year of Asa, Israel's King Baasha went to war against Judah. He built Ramah in order to deny anyone's access—going or coming—to Judah's King Asa. 2 So Asa brought out the silver and gold from the treasuries of the LORD's temple and the royal palace and sent it to Aram's King Ben-hadad, who lived in Damascus, saying, 3 "There's a treaty between me and you, between my father and your father. Look, I have sent you silver and gold. Go break your treaty with Israel's King Baasha so that he will withdraw from me."

4 Ben-hadad listened to King Asa and sent the commanders of his armies to the cities of Israel. They attacked Ijon, Dan, Abel-maim,[c] and all the storage cities[d] of Naphtali. 5 When Baasha heard ⌊about it⌋, he quit building Ramah and stopped his work. 6 Then King Asa brought all Judah, and they carried away the stones of Ramah and the timbers Baasha had built it with. Then he built Geba and Mizpah with them.

Hanani's Rebuke of Asa

7 At that time, Hanani the seer came to King Asa of Judah and said to him, "Because you depended on the king of Aram and have not depended on the LORD your God, the army of the king of Aram has escaped from your hand. 8 Were not the •Cushites and Libyans a vast army with very many chariots and horsemen? When you depended on the LORD, He handed them over to you. 9 For the eyes of the LORD range throughout the earth to show Himself strong for those whose hearts are completely His. You have been foolish in this matter,

for from now on, you will have wars." 10 Asa was angry with the seer and put him in prison[e] because of his anger over this. And Asa mistreated some of the people at that time.

Asa's Death

11 Note that the events of Asa's ⌊reign⌋, from beginning to end, are written about in the Book of the Kings of Judah and Israel. 12 In the thirty-ninth year of his reign, Asa developed a disease in his feet, and his disease became increasingly severe. Yet even in his disease he didn't seek the LORD but the physicians. 13 Asa died in the forty-first year of his reign and rested with his fathers. 14 He was buried in his own tomb that he had hewn out for himself in the city of David. They laid him out in a coffin that was full of spices and various mixtures of prepared ointments; then they made a great fire in his honor.

Judah's King Jehoshaphat

17 His son Jehoshaphat became king in his place and strengthened himself against Israel. 2 He stationed troops in every fortified city of Judah and set garrisons in the land of Judah and in the cities of Ephraim that his father Asa had captured.

3 Now the LORD was with Jehoshaphat because he walked in the former ways of his father David.[f] He did not seek the •Baals 4 but sought the God of his father and walked by His commands, not according to the practices of Israel. 5 So the LORD established the kingdom in his hand. Then all Judah brought him tribute, and he had riches and honor in abundance. 6 His mind rejoiced in the LORD's ways, and he again removed the •high places and •Asherah poles from Judah.

Jehoshaphat's Educational Plan

7 In the third year of his reign, Jehoshaphat sent his officials—Ben-hail,[g] Obadiah, Zechariah, Nethanel, and Micaiah—to teach in the cities of Judah. 8 The Levites with them were Shemaiah, Nethaniah, Zebadiah,[h] Asahel, Shemiramoth, Jehonathan, Adonijah, Tobijah, and Tob-adonijah; the priests, Elishama and Jehoram, were with these Levites. 9 They taught throughout Judah, ⌊having⌋ the book of the LORD's instruction with them. They went throughout the towns of Judah and taught the people.

10 The terror of the LORD was on all the kingdoms of the lands that surrounded Judah, so they didn't fight against Jehoshaphat. 11 Some of the Philistines also brought gifts and silver as tribute to Jehoshaphat, and

---

a15:16 Lit mother; 2 Ch 11:22; 1 Kg 15:2   b15:17 Lit wholehearted all his days   c16:4 1 Kg 15:20 reads Abel-beth-maacah   d16:4 1 Kg 15:20 reads all [the] Chinneroth   e16:10 Lit the house of stocks   f17:3 Some Hb mss, LXX omits David   g17:7 = Son of Power   h17:8 Some Hb mss, Syr, Tg, Arabic read Zechariah

---

hearts is to seek in a way that isn't debilitated by ulterior motives and conflicting pursuits.

16:9 For the eyes of the LORD range throughout the earth ... completely His. Even at this time God did not simply look for faith and allegiance from those who were in Israel. He chose Israel as a light to the people of

other nations, but He always wanted to win the allegiance of others too.

17:1–21:3 Jehoshaphat. Jehoshaphat receives high marks from the chronicler for his general devotion to God and his denouncement of idolatrous worship (vv. 3-4,6). The king also instituted a noteworthy emphasis on reli-

gious education (vv. 7-9). This account is longer than the parallel in 1 Kings 22:1-46 to emphasize retribution during Jehoshaphat's reign.

17:6 His mind rejoiced. Jehoshaphat is lauded for his good intentions. However, like others before him, he fell short of even his own

the Arabs brought him flocks: 7,700 rams and 7,700 male goats.

Jehoshaphat's Military Might

12 Jehoshaphat grew stronger and stronger. He built fortresses and storage cities in Judah 13 and carried out great works in the towns of Judah. He had fighting men, brave warriors, in Jerusalem. 14 These are their numbers according to their ancestral families. For Judah, the commanders of thousands:

Adnah the commander and 300,000 brave warriors with him;

15 next to him, Jehohanan the commander and 280,000 with him;

16 next to him, Amasiah son of Zichri, the volunteer of the LORD, and 200,000 brave warriors with him;

17 from Benjamin, Eliada, a brave warrior, and 200,000 with him armed with bow and shield;

18 next to him, Jehozabad and 180,000 with him equipped for war.

19 These were the ones who served the king, besides those he stationed in the fortified cities throughout all Judah.

Jehoshaphat's Alliance with Ahab

18 Now Jehoshaphat had riches and honor in abundance, and he made an alliance with Ahab through marriage.ᵃ 2 Then after some years, he went down to visit Ahab in Samaria. Ahab sacrificed many sheep and cattle for him and for the people who were with him. Then he persuaded him to march up to Ramoth-gilead, 3 for Israel's King Ahab asked Judah's King Jehoshaphat, "Will you go with me to Ramoth-gilead?"

He replied to him, "I am as you are, my people as your people; ⌊we will be⌋ with you in the battle." 4 But Jehoshaphat said to the king of Israel, "First, please ask what the LORD's will is."

5 So the king of Israel gathered the prophets, 400 men, and asked them, "Should we go to Ramoth-gilead for war or should I refrain?"

They replied, "March up, and God will hand it over to the king."

6 But Jehoshaphat asked, "Isn't there a prophet of •Yahweh here any more? Let's ask him."

7 The king of Israel said to Jehoshaphat, "There is still one man who can ask the LORD, but I hate him because he never prophesies good about me, but only disaster. He is Micaiah son of Imlah."

"The king shouldn't say that," Jehoshaphat replied.

8 So the king of Israel called an officer and said, "Hurry ⌊and get⌋ Micaiah son of Imlah!"

9 Now the king of Israel and King Jehoshaphat of Judah, clothed in royal attire, were each sitting on his own throne. They were sitting on the threshing floor at the entrance to Samaria's •gate, and all the prophets were prophesying in front of them. 10 Then Zedekiah son of Chenaanah made iron horns and said, "This is what the LORD says: 'You will gore the Arameans with these until they are finished off.'" 11 And all the prophets were prophesying the same, saying, "March up to Ramoth-gilead and succeed, for the LORD will hand it over to the king."

Micaiah's Message of Defeat

12 The messenger who went to call Micaiah instructed him, "Look, the words of the prophets are unanimously favorable for the king. So let your words be like theirs, and speak favorably."

13 But Micaiah said, "As the LORD lives, I will say whatever my God says."ᵇ

14 So he went to the king, and the king asked him, "Micaiah, should we go to Ramoth-gilead for war, or should Iᶜ refrain?"

Micaiah said, "March up and succeed, for they will be handed over to you."

15 But the king said to him, "How many times must I make you swear not to tell me anything but the truth in the name of the LORD?"

16 So Micaiah said:

I saw all Israel scattered on the hills
like sheep without a shepherd.
And the LORD said,
'They have no master;
let each return home in peace.'

17 So the king of Israel said to Jehoshaphat, "Didn't I tell you he never prophesies good about me, but only disaster?"

18 Then Micaiah said, "Therefore, hear the word of the LORD. I saw the LORD sitting on His throne, and the whole heavenly •host was standing at His right hand and at His left hand. 19 And the LORD said, 'Who will entice Ahab king of Israel to march up and fall at Ramoth-gilead?' So one was saying this and another was saying that.

20 "Then a spirit came forward, stood before the LORD, and said, 'I will entice him.'

"The LORD asked him, 'How?'

ᵃ**18:1** Lit *made himself a son-in-law to Ahab*; 1 Kg 3:1; Ezr 9:14   ᵇ**18:13** LXX, Vg add *to me*; 1 Kg 22:14   ᶜ**18:14** LXX reads *we*; 1 Kg 22:15

---

goals. He allowed the idols to be restored during his reign (20:33).

18:1 made an alliance. This subtle reference to a family alliance would prove near disastrous for Judah on more than one occasion. First, Jehoshaphat nearly loses his life, but he learns his lesson and recovers quickly (19:1-

3). However, the Davidic line itself would be at stake (22:10–23:21).

18:5 the king of Israel gathered the prophets. These prophets Ahab gathered were prophets of Baal.

18:7 he never prophesies good about me. Micaiah, whose name means "Who is like

Yah?", was the only one of Yahweh's prophets left in the region. The 400 prophets of Baal were Ahab's yes-men. They prophesied whatever he wanted.

18:29 disguised himself. Ahab arranges for his rival to become an easy target, and Jehoshaphat falls for it.

[21] "So he said, 'I will go and become a lying spirit in the mouth of all his prophets.'

"Then He said, 'You will entice him and also prevail. Go and do that.'

[22] "Now, you see, the LORD has put a lying spirit in the mouth of[a] these prophets of yours, and the LORD has pronounced disaster against you."

[23] Then Zedekiah son of Chenaanah came up, hit Micaiah in the face, and demanded, "Did[b] the Spirit of the LORD leave me to speak to you?"

[24] Micaiah replied, "You will soon see when you go to hide yourself in an inner chamber on that day."

[25] Then the king of Israel ordered, "Take Micaiah and return him to Amon, the governor of the city, and to Joash, the king's son, [26] and say, 'This is what the king says: Put this guy in prison and feed him only bread and water[c] until I come back safely.'"

[27] But Micaiah said, "If you ever return safely, the LORD has not spoken through me." Then he said, "Listen, all you people!"

Ahab's Death

[28] Then the king of Israel and Judah's King Jehoshaphat went up to Ramoth-gilead. [29] But the king of Israel said to Jehoshaphat, "I will disguise myself and go into battle, but you wear your royal attire." So the king of Israel disguised himself, and they went into battle.

[30] Now the king of Aram had ordered his chariot commanders, "Do not fight with anyone, small or great, except the king of Israel."

[31] When the chariot commanders saw Jehoshaphat, they shouted, "He must be the king of Israel!" So they turned to attack him, but Jehoshaphat cried out and the LORD helped him. God drew them away from him. [32] When the chariot commanders saw that he was not the king of Israel, they turned back from pursuing him.

[33] But a man drew his bow without taking special aim and struck the king of Israel through the joints of his armor. So he said to the charioteer, "Turn around and take me out of the battle,[d] for I am badly wounded!" [34] The battle raged throughout that day, and the king of Israel propped himself up in his chariot facing the Arameans until evening. Then he died at sunset.

Jehu's Rebuke of Jehoshaphat

19 Jehoshaphat king of Judah returned to his home in Jerusalem in peace. [2] Then Jehu son of

Hanani the seer went out to confront him[e] and said to King Jehoshaphat, "Do you help the wicked and love those who hate the LORD? Because of this, the LORD's wrath is on you. [3] However, some good is found in you, for you have removed the •Asherah poles from the land and have decided to seek God."

Jehoshaphat's Reforms

[4] Jehoshaphat lived in Jerusalem, and once again he went out among the people from Beer-sheba to the hill country of Ephraim and brought them back to the LORD God of their ancestors. [5] He appointed judges in all the fortified cities of the land of Judah, city by city. [6] Then he said to the judges, "Consider what you are doing, for you do not judge for man, but for the LORD, who is with you in the matter of judgment. [7] And now, may the terror of the LORD be on you. Watch what you do, for there is no injustice or partiality or taking bribes with the LORD our God."

[8] Jehoshaphat also appointed in Jerusalem some of the Levites and priests and some of the heads of the Israelite families for ⌊rendering⌋ the LORD's judgments and for ⌊settling⌋ disputes of the residents of[f] Jerusalem. [9] He commanded them, saying, "In the •fear of the LORD, with integrity, and with a whole heart, you are to do the following: [10] for every dispute that comes to you from your brothers who dwell in their cities—whether it regards differences of bloodguilt, law, commandment, statutes, or judgments—you are to warn them, so they will not incur guilt before the LORD and wrath will not come on you and your brothers. Do this, and you will not incur guilt.

[11] "Note that Amariah, the chief priest, is over you in all matters related to the LORD, and Zebadiah son of Ishmael, the ruler of the house of Judah, in all matters related to the king, and the Levites are officers in your presence. Be strong; may the LORD be with those who do what is good."

War against Eastern Enemies

20 After this, the Moabites and Ammonites, together with some of the Meunites,[g] came ⌊to fight⌋ against Jehoshaphat. [2] People came and told Jehoshaphat, "A vast multitude from beyond the Dead Sea and from Edom[h] has come ⌊to fight⌋ against you; they are already in Hazazon-tamar" (that is, En-gedi). [3] Jehoshaphat was afraid, so he resolved to seek the LORD. So he proclaimed a fast for all Judah, [4] who gathered to seek the LORD. They even came from all the cities of Judah to seek Him.

---

[a]**18:22** Some Hb mss, LXX, Syr, Vg add *all*; 1 Kg 22:23   [b]**18:23** Lit *Which way did*   [c]**18:26** Lit *him on bread of oppression and water of oppression*   [d]**18:33** LXX, Vg; MT reads *camp*   [e]**19:2** Lit *to his face*   [f]**19:8** LXX, Vg; MT reads *disputes and they returned to*   [g]**20:1** LXX; MT reads *Ammonites*; 2 Ch 26:7   [h]**20:2** Some Hb mss, Old Lat; other Hb mss read *Aram*

18:31 God drew them away. God intervenes despite human foolishness. Jehoshaphat narrowly escapes death.

19:2 Jehu ... the seer. Jehu carries a precautionary message to Jehoshaphat. The next time he might not be so lucky!

19:5 appointed judges in all the fortified cit-ies. The postexilic refugees reading the chronicler's message would refer to Jehoshaphat's system as a model for rebuilding the civil and judicial systems necessary to function as a nation.

19:7 no injustice. God's perfect, personal example is the standard for justice.

19:8 appointed ... some of the Levites. The Levites would oversee the fairness of this supreme court. Thus, a balance between religion and state would be achieved.

20:1-30 The mere mention of Moab caused worry and fear. A record of Jehoshaphat's decisive victory over the Moabites and Ammon-

Jehoshaphat's Prayer

5 Then Jehoshaphat stood in the assembly of Judah and Jerusalem in the LORD's temple before the new courtyard. **6** He said:

LORD God of our ancestors, are You not the God who is in heaven, and do You not rule over all the kingdoms of the nations? Power and might are in Your hand, and no one can stand against You. **7** Are You not our God who drove out the inhabitants of this land before Your people Israel and who gave it forever to the descendants of Abraham Your friend? **8** They have lived in the land and have built You a sanctuary in it for Your name and have said, **9** "If disaster comes on us— sword or judgment, pestilence or famine—we will stand before this temple and before You, for Your name is in this temple. We will cry out to You because of our distress, and You will hear and deliver."

10 Now here are the Ammonites, Moabites, and ⌊the inhabitants of⌋ Mount Seir. You did not let Israel invade them when Israel came out of the land of Egypt, but Israel turned away from them and did not destroy them. **11** Look how they repay us by coming to drive us out of Your possession that You gave us as an inheritance. **12** Our God, will You not judge them? For we are powerless before this vast multitude that comes ⌊to fight⌋ against us. We do not know what to do, but we look to You.ᵃ

God's Answer

13 All Judah was standing before the LORD with their infants, their wives, and their children. **14** In the midst of the congregation, the Spirit of the LORD came on Jahaziel (son of Zechariah, son of Benaiah, son of Jeiel, son of Mattaniah, a Levite from •Asaph's descendants), **15** and he said, "Listen carefully, all Judah and you inhabitants of Jerusalem, and King Jehoshaphat. This is what the LORD says: 'Do not be afraid or discouraged because of this vast multitude, for the battle is not yours, but God's. **16** Tomorrow, go down against them. You will see them coming up the ascent of Ziz, and you will find them at the end of the valley facing the Wilderness of Jeruel. **17** You do not have to fight this ⌊battle⌋. Position yourselves, stand still, and see the salvation of the LORD. ⌊He is⌋ with you, Judah and Jerusalem. Do not be afraid or discouraged. Tomorrow, go out to face them, for the LORD is with you.'"

18 Then Jehoshaphat bowed with his face to the ground, and all Judah and the inhabitants of Jerusalem fell down before the LORD to worship Him. **19** Then the Levites from the sons of the Kohathites and the Korahites stood up to praise the LORD God of Israel shouting in a loud voice.

Victory and Plunder

20 In the morning they got up early and went out to the wilderness of Tekoa. As they were about to go out, Jehoshaphat stood and said, "Hear me, Judah and you inhabitants of Jerusalem. Believe in the LORD your God, and you will be established; believe in His prophets, and you will succeed." **21** Then he consulted with the people and appointed some to sing for the LORD and some to praise the splendor of ⌊His⌋ holiness. When they went out in front of the armed forces, they kept singing:ᵇ

Give thanks to the LORD,
for His faithful love endures forever.

22 The moment they began ⌊their⌋ shouts and praises, the LORD set an ambush against the Ammonites, Moabites, and ⌊the inhabitants of⌋ Mount Seir who came ⌊to fight⌋ against Judah, and they were defeated. **23** The Ammonites and Moabites turned against the inhabitants of Mount Seir and completely annihilated them. When they had finished with the inhabitants of Seir, they helped destroy each other.

24 When Judah came to a place overlooking the wilderness, they looked toward the multitude, and there were corpses lying on the ground; nobody had escaped. **25** Then Jehoshaphat and his people went to gather the plunder. They found among themᶜ an abundance of goods on the bodiesᵈ and valuable items. So they stripped them until nobody could carry any more. They were gathering the plunder for three days because there was so much. **26** They assembled in the Valley of Beracahᵉ on the fourth day, for there they praised the LORD. Therefore, that place is still called the Valley of Beracah today.

27 Then all the men of Judah and Jerusalem turned back with Jehoshaphat at their head, returning joyfully to Jerusalem, for the LORD enabled them to rejoice over their enemies. **28** So they came into Jerusalem to the LORD's temple with harps, lyres, and trumpets.

29 The terror of God was on all the kingdoms of the lands when they heard that the LORD had fought against the enemies of Israel. **30** Then Jehoshaphat's kingdom was quiet, for his God gave him rest on every side.

ᵃ **20:12** Lit *but on You our eyes*　ᵇ **20:21** Lit *saying*　ᶜ **20:25** LXX reads *found cattle*　ᵈ **20:25** Some Hb mss, Old Lat, Vg read *goods, garments*
ᵉ **20:26** = Blessing

---

ites would be cause for celebration.
20:5-12 Jehoshaphat wrestled in prayer before battling in the field. In answer to his prayer, God granted Judah victory.
20:20 Believe in the LORD your God. As a military leader, Jehoshaphat might have instructed his warriors to hit first and hit hardest.

But his military strategy was spiritual.
20:22 the LORD set an ambush. While Judah celebrated, the enemies grew more confused. They ambushed each other, securing the victory for the Israelites who had yet to draw their weapons.
20:30 was quiet. After a weaponless victory,

Judah's reputation for godly assistance kept the enemy at bay. God's peace signified His blessing on Judah during the king's reign.

20:35-37 Despite Jehoshaphat's battlefield success, he proved to be an inept entrepreneur. He failed to carry godly trust into his business efforts, choosing instead to seek a

Summary of Jehoshaphat's Reign

31 Jehoshaphat became king over Judah. He was 35 years old when he became king; he reigned 25 years in Jerusalem. His mother's name was Azubah daughter of Shilhi. 32 He walked in the way of Asa his father; he did not turn away from it but did what was right in the LORD's sight. 33 However, the •high places were not taken away; the people had not yet determined in their hearts ⌊to worship⌋ the God of their ancestors.

34 The rest of the events of Jehoshaphat's ⌊reign⌋ from beginning to end are written about in the Events of Jehu son of Hanani, which is recorded in the Book of Israel's Kings.

Jehoshaphat's Fleet of Ships

35 After this, Judah's King Jehoshaphat made an alliance with Israel's King Ahaziah, who was guilty of wrongdoing. 36 Jehoshaphat formed an alliance with him to make ships to go to Tarshish, and they made the ships in Ezion-geber. 37 Then Eliezer son of Dodavahu of Mareshah prophesied against Jehoshaphat, saying, "Because you formed an alliance with Ahaziah, the LORD has broken up what you have made." So the ships were wrecked and were not able to go to Tarshish.

Jehoram Becomes King Over Judah

21 Jehoshaphat rested with his fathers and was buried with his fathers in the city of David. His son Jehoram[a] became king in his place. 2 He had brothers, sons of Jehoshaphat: Azariah, Jehiel, Zechariah, Azariah, Michael, and Shephatiah; all these were the sons of Jehoshaphat, king of Judah.[b] 3 Their father had given them many gifts of silver, gold, and valuable things, along with fortified cities in Judah, but he gave the kingdom to Jehoram because he was the firstborn. 4 When Jehoram had established himself over his father's kingdom, he strengthened his position by killing with the sword all his brothers as well as some of the princes of Israel.

Judah's King Jehoram

5 Jehoram was 32 years old when he became king; he reigned eight years in Jerusalem. 6 He walked in the way of the kings of Israel, as the house of Ahab had done, for Ahab's daughter was his wife. He did what was evil in the LORD's sight, 7 but because of the covenant the LORD had made with David, He was unwilling to destroy the house of David since the LORD had promised to give a lamp to David and to his sons forever.

8 During Jehoram's reign, Edom rebelled against Judah's domination and appointed their own king. 9 So Jehoram crossed ⌊into Edom⌋ with his commanders and all his chariots. Then at night he set out to attack the Edomites who had surrounded him and the chariot commanders. 10 So Edom is still in rebellion against Judah's domination today. Libnah also rebelled at that time against his domination because he had abandoned the LORD God of his ancestors. 11 Jehoram also built •high places in the hills[c] of Judah, and he caused the inhabitants of Jerusalem to prostitute themselves, and he led Judah astray.

Elijah's Letter to Jehoram

12 Then a letter came to Jehoram from Elijah the prophet, saying:

This is what the LORD God of your ancestor David says: "Because you have not walked in the ways of your father Jehoshaphat or in the ways of Asa king of Judah 13 but have walked in the way of the kings of Israel, have caused Judah and the inhabitants of Jerusalem to prostitute themselves like the house of Ahab prostituted itself, and also have killed your brothers, your father's family, who were better than you, 14 the LORD is now about to strike your people, your sons, your wives, and all your possessions with a horrible affliction. 15 You yourself ⌊will be struck⌋ with many illnesses, including a disease of the intestines, until your intestines come out day after day because of the disease."

Jehoram's Last Days

16 The LORD put it into the mind of the Philistines and the Arabs who live near the •Cushites to attack Jehoram. 17 So they went to war against Judah and invaded it. They carried off all the possessions found in the king's palace and also his sons and wives; not a son was left to him except Jehoahaz,[d] his youngest son.

18 After all these things, the LORD afflicted him in his intestines with an incurable disease. 19 This continued day after day until two full years passed. Then his intestines came out because of his disease, and he died from severe[e] illnesses. But his people did not hold a fire in his honor like the fire in honor of his fathers.

20 Jehoram was 32 years old when he became king; he reigned eight years in Jerusalem. He died to no one's regret[f] and was buried in the city of David but not in the tombs of the kings.

a 21:1 = Joram   b 21:2 Some Hb mss, LXX, Syr, Vg, Arabic; other Hb mss read *Israel*   c 21:11 Some Hb mss, LXX, Vg read *cities*   d 21:17 LXX, Syr, Tg read *Ahaziah*; = Jehoahaz   e 21:19 Lit *evil*   f 21:20 Lit *He walked in no desirability*

failed alliance with a pagan partner.
21:4-20 Jehoram. Jehoram tested the limits of God's merciful protection of the line of David. Apart from God's commitment to David, the evil king's family would have been entirely obliterated (2 Kings 8:16-24).
21:4 Jehoram was likely inspired by his wife's

evil heritage. He brutally snuffed out all the competition in the false belief that this treachery will secure his empire.

21:10 God of his ancestors. Jehoram's lean toward evil was not consistent with his family tree. He was from David's line, and his propensity toward evil was his own personal choice.

21:12-15 Elijah's wake-up call could not have come at a better time, yet Jehoram ignored this word of warning and suffered the consequences.

21:20 died … not in the tombs of the kings. Death has the final word on Jehoram's life. No funeral. No procession. Nothing was done to

Judah's King Ahaziah

22 Then the inhabitants of Jerusalem made Ahaziah, his youngest son, king in his place, because the troops that had come with the Arabs to the camp had killed all the older sons.[a] So Ahaziah son of Jehoram became king of Judah. ² Ahaziah was 22[b] years old when he became king; he reigned one year in Jerusalem. His mother's name was Athaliah, granddaughter[c] of Omri.

³ He walked in the ways of the house of Ahab, for his mother gave him evil advice. ⁴ So he did what was evil in the LORD's sight like the house of Ahab, for they were his advisers after the death of his father, to his destruction. ⁵ He also followed their advice and went with Joram[d] son of Israel's King Ahab to fight against Hazael, king of Aram, in Ramoth-gilead. The Arameans[e] wounded Joram, ⁶ so he returned to Jezreel to recover from the wounds they inflicted on him in Ramoth-gilead[f] when he fought against Aram's King Hazael. Then Judah's King Ahaziah[g] son of Jehoram went down to Jezreel to visit Joram son of Ahab since Joram was ill.

⁷ With his going to Joram, Ahaziah's downfall was from God, for when Ahaziah went, he went out with Joram to meet Jehu son of Nimshi, whom the LORD had anointed to destroy the house of Ahab. ⁸ So it happened when Jehu executed judgment on the house of Ahab, he found the rulers of Judah and the sons of Ahaziah's brothers who were serving Ahaziah, and he killed them. ⁹ Then Jehu looked for Ahaziah, and Jehu's soldiers captured him (he was hiding in Samaria). Then they brought him to Jehu, and they killed him. They buried him, for they said, "He is the grandson of Jehoshaphat who sought the LORD with all his heart." So the house of Ahaziah had no one to exercise power over the kingdom.

Athaliah Usurps the Throne

¹⁰ When Athaliah, Ahaziah's mother, saw that her son was dead, she proceeded to annihilate all the royal heirs[h] of the house of Judah. ¹¹ Jehoshabeath,[i] the king's daughter, rescued Joash son of Ahaziah from the king's sons who were being killed and put him and his nurse in a bedroom. Now Jehoshabeath was the daughter of King Jehoram and the wife of Jehoiada the priest. Since she was Ahaziah's sister, she hid Joash from Athaliah so that she did not kill him. ¹² While Athaliah ruled over the land, he was hiding with them in God's temple six years.

Athaliah Overthrown

23 Then, in the seventh year, Jehoiada summoned his courage and took the commanders of hundreds into a covenant with him: Azariah son of Jeroham, Ishmael son of Jehohanan, Azariah son of Obed, Maaseiah son of Adaiah, and Elishaphat son of Zichri. ² They made a circuit throughout Judah. They gathered the Levites from all the cities of Judah and the heads of the families of Israel, and they came to Jerusalem.

³ Then the whole assembly made a covenant with the king in God's temple. Jehoiada said to them, "Here is the king's son! He must reign, just as the LORD promised concerning David's sons. ⁴ This is what you are to do: one third of you, priests and Levites who are coming on duty on the Sabbath, are to be gatekeepers. ⁵ A third are to be at the king's palace, and a third are to be at the Foundation Gate, and all the troops will be in the courtyards of the LORD's temple. ⁶ No one is to enter the LORD's temple but the priests and those Levites who serve; they may enter because they are holy, but all the people are to obey the requirement of the LORD. ⁷ You must completely surround the king with weapons in hand. Anyone who enters the temple is to be put to death. You must be with the king in all his daily tasks."[j]

⁸ So the commanders of hundreds did everything Jehoiada the priest commanded. They each brought their men—those coming on duty on the Sabbath and those going off duty on the Sabbath—for Jehoiada the priest did not release the divisions. ⁹ Jehoiada the priest gave to the commanders of hundreds King David's spears, shields, and quivers[k] that were in God's temple. ¹⁰ Then he stationed all the troops with their weapons in hand surrounding the king—from the right side of the temple to the left side, by the altar and by the temple.

¹¹ They brought out the king's son, put the crown on him, gave him the •testimony, and made him king. Jehoiada and his sons anointed him and cried, "Long live the king!"

¹² When Athaliah heard the noise from the troops, the guards, and those praising the king, she went to the troops in the LORD's temple. ¹³ As she looked, there was the king standing by his pillar[l] at the entrance. The commanders and the trumpeters were by the king, and all the people of the land were rejoicing and blowing trumpets while the singers with musical instruments

---

[a]**22:1** Lit *the former ones*   [b]**22:2** Some LXX mss, Syr, MT reads *42*; 2 Kg 8:26   [c]**22:2** Lit *daughter*   [d]**22:5** = Jehoram (also vv. 6–7)   [e]**22:5** Lit *Rammites*; = Arameans; 2 Kg 8:28   [f]**22:6** Lit *in Ramah*   [g]**22:6** Some Hb mss, LXX, Syr, Vg; other Hb mss read *Azariah*; 2 Kg 8:29   [h]**22:10** Lit *seed*   [i]**22:11** = Jehosheba; 2 Kg 11:2   [j]**23:7** Lit *king when he comes in and when he goes out*   [k]**23:9** Or *spears and large and small shields*   [l]**23:13** LXX reads *post*

---

honor this relentlessly evil king.

22:2 Ahaziah was 22. Ahaziah's youth and inexperience played into his quick demise.

22:3-4 Ahaziah allowed himself to become a puppet of the Northern Kingdom. Unfortunately, his own mother was pulling the strings.

22:7 Ahaziah's downfall. Jehu, Israel's next king, assassinated Ahaziah, yet all was according to God's plan.

22:9 Ahaziah's end leaves the story in suspense. An occupied tomb leaves an empty throne. The only successor in Judah is a mere infant.

22:10-12 Athaliah, like Jehoram, attempted to eradicate every inch of the Davidic line. However, her efforts were thwarted by the ingenuity of a quick-thinking girl.

23:1–24:27 Joash. Joash leaned on Jehoiada for inspiration. Under his influence, the king restored the temple and combatted idol wor-

were leading the praise. Athaliah tore her clothes and screamed, "Treason, treason!"

¹⁴ Then Jehoiada the priest sent out the commanders of hundreds, those in charge of the army, saying, "Take her out between the ranks, and put anyone who follows her to death by the sword," for the priest had said, "Don't put her to death in the LORD's temple." ¹⁵ So they arrested her, and she went by the entrance of the Horses' Gate to the king's palace, where they put her to death.

Jehoiada's Reforms

¹⁶ Then Jehoiada made a covenant between himself, the king, and the people that they would be the LORD's people. ¹⁷ So all the people went to the temple of •Baal and tore it down. They broke its altars and images into pieces and killed Mattan, the priest of Baal, at the altars.

¹⁸ Then Jehoiada put the oversight of the LORD's temple into the hands of the Levitical priests, whom David had appointed over the LORD's temple, to offer •burnt offerings to the LORD as it is written in the law of Moses, with rejoicing and song ordained byᵃ David. ¹⁹ He stationed gatekeepers at the gates of the LORD's temple so that nothing unclean could enter for any reason. ²⁰ Then he took ⌊with him⌋ the commanders of hundreds, the nobles, the governors of the people, and all the people of the land and brought the king down from the LORD's temple. They entered the king's palace through the upper ⌊gate⌋ and seated the king on the throne of the kingdom. ²¹ All the people of the land rejoiced, and the city was quiet, for they had put Athaliah to death by the sword.

Judah's King Joash

24 Joash was seven years old when he became king; he reigned 40 years in Jerusalem. His mother's name was Zibiah; ⌊she was⌋ from Beer-sheba. ² Throughout the time of Jehoiada the priest, Joash did what was right in the LORD's sight. ³ Jehoiada acquired two wives for him, and he was the father of sons and daughters.

Repairing the Temple

⁴ Afterwards, Joash took it to heart to renovate the LORD's temple. ⁵ So he gathered the priests and Levites and said, "Go out to the cities of Judah and collect money from all Israel to repair the temple of your God as needed year by year, and do it quickly."

However, the Levites did not hurry. ⁶ So the king called Jehoiada the high ⌊priest⌋ and said, "Why haven't you required the Levites to bring from Judah and Jeru-

salem the tax ⌊imposed by⌋ the LORD's servant Moses and the assembly of Israel for the tent of the testimony? ⁷ For the sons of that wicked Athaliah broke into the LORD's temple and even used the sacred things of the LORD's temple for the •Baals."

⁸ At the king's command a chest was made and placed outside the gate of the LORD's temple. ⁹ Then a proclamation was issued in Judah and Jerusalem that the tax God's servant Moses ⌊imposed⌋ on Israel in the wilderness be brought to the LORD. ¹⁰ All the leaders and all the people rejoiced, brought ⌊the tax⌋, and put it in the chest until it was full. ¹¹ Whenever the chest was brought by the Levites to the king's overseers, and when they saw that there was a large amount of money, the king's secretary and the high priest's deputy came and emptied the chest, picked it up, and returned it to its place. They did this daily and gathered the money in abundance. ¹² Then the king and Jehoiada gave it to those in charge of the labor on the LORD's temple, who were hiring masons and carpenters to renovate the LORD's temple, also blacksmiths and coppersmiths to repair the LORD's temple.

¹³ The workmen did their work, and through them the repairs progressed. They restored God's temple to its specifications and reinforced it. ¹⁴ When they finished, they presented the rest of the money to the king and Jehoiada, who made articles for the LORD's temple with it—articles for ministry and for making •burnt offerings, and ladlesᵇ and articles of gold and silver. They regularly offered burnt offerings in the LORD's temple throughout Jehoiada's life.

Joash's Apostasy

¹⁵ Jehoiada died when he was old and full of days; he was 130 years old at his death. ¹⁶ He was buried in the city of David with the kings because he had done ⌊what was⌋ good in Israel with respect to God and His temple.

¹⁷ However, after Jehoiada died, the rulers of Judah came and paid homage to the king. Then the king listened to them, ¹⁸ and they abandoned the temple of the LORD God of their ancestors and served the •Asherah poles and the idols. So there was wrath against Judah and Jerusalem for this guilt of theirs. ¹⁹ Nevertheless, He sent them prophets to bring them back to the LORD; they admonished them, but they would not listen.

²⁰ The Spirit of God took control ofᶜ Zechariah son of Jehoiada the priest. He stood above the people and said to them, "This is what God says: 'Why are you transgressing the LORD's commands and you do not prosper? Because you have abandoned the LORD, He has

---

ᵃ **23:18** Lit *song on the hands of* ᵇ **24:14** Or *dishes,* or *spoons*; lit *palms* ᶜ **24:20** Lit *God clothed*; Jdg 6:34; 1 Ch 12:18

---

ship. When Jehoiada died, Joash's success soon soured.

23:1 Jehoiada summoned his courage. Jehoiada went from zero to hero as he shared the weight of a king's mantle with a seven-year-old. Jehoiada's decisions became royal rule.

23:13 Treason, treason! Athaliah could not believe her ears. The sound of celebration suffocated her dream for royal power. Joash, the boy-king, would take her place. Her plan failed and God's plan came into play.

24:2 Throughout the time of Jehoiada. With Jehoiada in the picture, King Joash could not

go wrong. However, he forfeited his borrowed enthusiasm for God at Jehoiada's death.

24:4 Joash ... renovate the LORD's temple. Athaliah had left true worship in disarray. Restoring the temple was job number one.

24:5 Joash sent his Levitical priests in search of long overdue tax monies (Ex. 30:12-16).

abandoned you.'" ²¹ But they conspired against him and stoned him at the king's command in the courtyard of the LORD's temple. ²² King Joash didn't remember the kindness that Zechariah's father Jehoiada had extended to him, but killed his son. While he was dying, he said, "May the LORD see and demand an account."

Aramean Invasion of Judah

²³ At the turn of the year, an Aramean army went to war against Joash. They entered Judah and Jerusalem and destroyed all the leaders of the people among them and sent all the plunder to the king of Damascus. ²⁴ Although the Aramean army came with only a few men, the LORD handed over a vast army to them because the people of Judah had abandoned the LORD God of their ancestors. So they executed judgment on Joash.

Joash Assassinated

²⁵ When the Arameans saw that Joash had many wounds, they left him. His servants conspired against him, and killed him on his bed, because he had shed the blood of the sons of Jehoiada the priest. So he died, and they buried him in the city of David, but they did not bury him in the tombs of the kings.

²⁶ Those who conspired against him were Zabad, son of the Ammonite woman Shimeath, and Jehozabad, son of the Moabite woman Shimrith.^a ²⁷ Concerning his sons, the many •oracles about him, and the restoration of the LORD's temple, they are recorded in the Writing of the Book of the Kings. His son Amaziah became king in his place.

Judah's King Amaziah

²⁵ Amaziah became king ⌊when he was⌋ 25 years old; he reigned 29 years in Jerusalem. His mother's name was Jehoaddan; ⌊she was⌋ from Jerusalem. ² He did what was right in the LORD's sight but not completely.

³ As soon as the kingdom was firmly in his grasp,^b he executed his servants who had murdered his father the king. ⁴ However, he did not put their children to death, because—as it is written in the Law, in the book of Moses, where the LORD commanded—"Fathers must not die because of children, and children must not die because of fathers, but each one will die for his own sin."

Amaziah's Campaign against Edom

⁵ Then Amaziah gathered Judah and assembled them according to patriarchal family, according to command-ers of thousands, and according to commanders of hundreds. He numbered those 20 years old or more for all Judah and Benjamin. He found there to be 300,000 choice men who could serve in the army, bearing spear and shield. ⁶ Then for 7,500 pounds^c of silver he hired 100,000 brave warriors from Israel.

⁷ However, a man of God came to him and said, "King, do not let Israel's army go with you, for the LORD is not with Israel—all the Ephraimites. ⁸ But if you go ⌊with them⌋, do it! Be strong for battle! ⌊But⌋ God will make you stumble before the enemy, for God has the power to help or to make one stumble."

⁹ Then Amaziah said to the man of God, "What should I do about the 7,500 pounds^c of silver I gave to Israel's division?"

The man of God replied, "The LORD is able to give you much more than this."

¹⁰ So Amaziah released the division that came to him from Ephraim to go home. But they got very angry with Judah and returned home in a fierce rage.

¹¹ Amaziah strengthened his position and led his people to the Valley of Salt. He struck down 10,000 Seirites,^d ¹² and the Judahites captured 10,000 alive. They took them to the top of a cliff where they threw them off, and all of them were dashed to pieces.

¹³ As for the men of the division that Amaziah sent back so they would not go with him into battle, they raided the cities of Judah from Samaria to Beth-horon, struck down 3,000 of their people, and took a great deal of plunder.

¹⁴ After Amaziah came from the attack on the Edom-ites, he brought the gods of the Seirites^d and set them up as his gods. He worshiped before them and burned incense to them. ¹⁵ So the LORD's anger was against Amaziah, and He sent a prophet to him, who said, "Why have you sought a people's gods that could not deliver their own people from your hand?"

¹⁶ While he was still speaking to him, the king asked, "Have we made you the king's counselor? Stop, why should you lose your life?"

So the prophet stopped, but he said, "I know that God intends to destroy you, because you have done this and have not listened to my advice."

Amaziah's War With Israel's King Joash

¹⁷ King Amaziah of Judah took counsel and sent ⌊word⌋ to Jehoash^e son of Jehoahaz, son of Jehu, king of Israel, saying, "Come, let us meet face to face."

¹⁸ King Jehoash of Israel sent ⌊word⌋ to King Amaziah of Judah, saying, "The thistle that was in Lebanon sent

---

^a**24:26** = Shomer; 2 Kg 12:21   ^b**25:3** LXX, Syr; MT reads *was strong on him*; 1 Kg 14:4   ^c**25:6,9** Lit *100 talents*   ^d**25:11,14** = Edomites
^e**25:17** = Joash

24:19 He sent them prophets ... but they would not listen. This is a summary of most of Israel's history. Only when prophets were dead and long gone did the people respect their voice.

24:21 stoned him at the king's command. This was the fate of far too many of the proph-ets. Jesus told the parable of the vineyard owner (Matt. 22:33-46) to condemn the way Is-rael had so often rejected and killed the proph-ets. Stephen was stoned for reminding the religious leaders of Israel of this tendency (see Acts 7:51-60).

24:24 executed judgment on Joash. The king pays for the sins of the people. Joash suf-fered an inexplicable defeat at the hands of a smaller army.

24:25 Joash ... killed ... buried ... did not bury him in the tombs of the kings. Like Je-horam before him, Joash's undignified burial marks the dishonor of his evil life.

⌊a message⌋ to the cedar that was in Lebanon, saying, 'Give your daughter to my son as a wife.' Then a wild animal that was in Lebanon passed by and trampled the thistle. 19 You have said, 'Look, Iᵃ have defeated Edom,' and you have become overconfident that you will get glory. Now stay at home. Why stir up such trouble so that you fall and Judah with you?"

20 But Amaziah would not listen, for this ⌊turn of events⌋ was from God in order to hand them over to ⌊their enemies⌋ because they went after the gods of Edom. 21 So King Jehoash of Israel advanced. He and King Amaziah of Judah faced off at Beth-shemesh in Judah. 22 Judah was routed before Israel, and each fled to his own tent. 23 King Jehoash of Israel captured Judah's King Amaziah son of Joash, son of Jehoahaz,ᵇ at Beth-shemesh. Then Jehoash took him to Jerusalem and broke down 200 yardsᶜ of Jerusalem's wall from the Ephraim Gate to the Corner Gate.ᵈ 24 He took all the gold, silver, all the utensils that were found with Obed-edom in God's temple, the treasures of the king's palace, and the hostages. Then he returned to Samaria.

Amaziah's Death

25 Judah's King Amaziah son of Joash lived 15 years after the death of Israel's King Jehoash son of Jehoahaz. 26 The rest of the events of Amaziah's ⌊reign⌋, from beginning to end, are written about in the Book of the Kings of Judah and Israel.

27 From the time Amaziah turned from following the LORD, a conspiracy was formed against him in Jerusalem, and he fled to Lachish. However, ⌊men⌋ were sent after him to Lachish, and they put him to death there. 28 They carried him back on horses and buried him with his fathers in the city of Judah.ᵉ

Judah's King Uzziah

26 All the people of Judah took Uzziah,ᶠ who was 16 years old, and made him king in place of his father Amaziah. 2 He rebuilt Elothᵍ and restored it to Judah after ⌊Amaziah⌋ the king rested with his fathers.

3 Uzziah was 16 years old when he became king; he reigned 52 years in Jerusalem. His mother's name was Jecoliah; ⌊she was⌋ from Jerusalem. 4 He did what was right in the LORD's sight as his father Amaziah had done. 5 He sought God throughout the lifetime of Zechariah, the teacher of the •fearʰ of God. During the time that he sought the LORD, God gave him success.

Uzziah's Exploits

6 Uzziah went out to wage war against the Philistines, and he tore down the wall of Gath, the wall of Jabneh, and the wall of Ashdod. Then he built cities in ⌊the vicinity of⌋ Ashdod and among the Philistines. 7 God helped him against the Philistines, the Arabs that live in Gur-baal, and the Meunites. 8 The Ammonitesⁱ gave Uzziah tribute money, and his fame spread as far as the entrance of Egypt, for ⌊God⌋ made ⌊him⌋ very powerful. 9 Uzziah built towers in Jerusalem at the Corner Gate, the Valley Gate, and the corner buttress, and he fortified them. 10 Since he had many cattle both in the lowlands and the plain, he built towers in the desert and dug many wells. And since he was a lover of the soil, he had farmers and vinedressers in the hills and in the fertile lands.ʲ

11 Uzziah had an army equipped for combat that went out to war by division according to their assignments, as recorded by Jeiel the court secretary and Maaseiah the officer under the authority of Hananiah, one of the king's commanders. 12 The total number of heads of families was 2,600 brave warriors. 13 Under their authority was an army of 307,500 equipped for combat, a powerful force to help the king against the enemy. 14 Uzziah provided the entire army with shields, spears, helmets, armor, bows and slingstones. 15 He made skillfully designed devices in Jerusalem to shoot arrows and ⌊catapult⌋ large stones for use on the towers and on the corners. So his fame spread even to distant places, for he was marvelously helped until he became strong.

Uzziah's Disease

16 But when he became strong, he grew arrogant and it led to his own destruction. He acted unfaithfully against the LORD his God by going into the LORD's sanctuary to burn incense on the incense altar. 17 Azariah the priest, along with 80 brave priests of the LORD, went in after him. 18 They took their stand against King Uzziah and said, "Uzziah, you have no right to offer incense to the LORD—only the consecrated priests, the descendants of Aaron, have the right to offer incense. Leave the sanctuary, for you have acted unfaithfully! You will not receive honor from the LORD God."

19 Uzziah, with a censer in his hand to offer incense, was enraged. But when he became enraged with the priests, in the presence of the priests in the LORD's temple beside the altar of incense, a skin disease broke out on his forehead. 20 Then Azariah the chief priest and all

---

ᵃ**25:19** Some LXX mss, Old Lat, Tg, Vg; MT reads *you* ᵇ**25:23** = Ahaziah ᶜ**25:23** Lit *400 cubits* ᵈ**25:23** Some Hb mss; other Hb mss read *to Happoneh*; 2 Kg 14:13 ᵉ**25:28** Some Hb mss read *city of David*; 2 Kg 14:20 ᶠ**26:1** = Azariah ᵍ**26:2** LXX, Syr, Vg read *Elath*; 2 Kg 14:22 ʰ**26:5** Some Hb mss, LXX, Syr, Tg, Arabic; other Hb mss, Vg read *visions* ⁱ**26:8** LXX reads *Meunites* ʲ**26:10** Or *in Carmel*

25:1 Amaziah. His reign was basically good, but not wholeheartedly godly.

25:2 Amaziah battled idolatry with lesser zeal than he should. Even though he did "what was right in the LORD's sight", he did not do so "completely."

25:7 the LORD is not with Israel. Hosting Is-

rael's troops within his ranks would invite a curse. Amaziah wisely dismissed them.

25:14-25 Amaziah was so taken with the spoils of victory that he actually worshiped his plunder. In heavenly irony, God used a taunting northern king to punish Amaziah's foolishness.

26:1 Uzziah ... 16 years old. He started his

reign as an adolescent and ended as a convalescent, 52 years later.

26:5 During the time that he sought the LORD. Uzziah's secret to success is no surprise. Obedience is the consistent key in the Davidic line.

26:16 when he became strong, he grew ar-

the priests turned to him and saw that he was diseased on his forehead. They rushed him out of there. He himself also hurried to get out because the LORD had afflicted him. 21 So King Uzziah was diseased to the time of his death. He lived in quarantine[a] with a serious skin disease and was excluded from access to the LORD's temple, while his son Jotham was over the king's household governing the people of the land.

22 Now the prophet Isaiah son of Amoz wrote about the rest of the events of Uzziah's ⌊reign⌋, from beginning to end. 23 Uzziah rested with his fathers, and he was buried with his fathers in the burial ground of the kings' cemetery, for they said, "He has a skin disease." His son Jotham became king in his place.

Judah's King Jotham

27 Jotham was 25 years old when he became king; he reigned 16 years in Jerusalem. His mother's name was Jerushah daughter of Zadok. 2 He did what was right in the LORD's sight as his father Uzziah had done, except that he didn't enter the LORD's sanctuary. However, the people still behaved corruptly.

3 Jotham built the Upper Gate of the LORD's temple, and he built extensively on the wall of Ophel. 4 He also built cities in the hill country of Judah and fortresses and towers in the forests. 5 He waged war against the king of the Ammonites. He overpowered the Ammonites, and that year they gave him 7,500 pounds[b] of silver, 50,000 bushels[c] of wheat, and 50,000 bushels[c] of barley. They paid him the same in the second and third years. 6 So Jotham strengthened himself because he did not waver in obeying[d] the LORD his God.

7 As for the rest of the events of Jotham's ⌊reign⌋, along with all his wars and his ways, note that they are written about in the Book of the Kings of Israel and Judah. 8 He was 25 years old when he became king; he reigned 16 years in Jerusalem. 9 Jotham rested with his fathers and was buried in the city of David. His son Ahaz became king in his place.

Judah's King Ahaz

28 Ahaz was 20 years old when he became king; he reigned 16 years in Jerusalem. He did not do what was right in the LORD's sight like his forefather David, 2 for he walked in the ways of the kings of Israel and made cast images of the •Baals. 3 He burned incense in the Valley of Hinnom and burned his children in[e] the fire, imitating the detestable practices of the nations the LORD had dispossessed before the Isra-

elites. 4 He sacrificed and burned incense on the •high places, on the hills, and under every green tree.

5 So the LORD his God handed Ahaz over to the king of Aram. He attacked him and took many captives to Damascus.

Ahaz was also handed over to the king of Israel, who struck him with great force: 6 Pekah son of Remaliah killed 120,000 in Judah in one day—all brave men—because they had abandoned the LORD God of their ancestors. 7 An Ephraimite warrior named Zichri killed the king's son Maaseiah, Azrikam governor of the palace, and Elkanah who was second to the king. 8 Then the Israelites took 200,000 captives from their brothers—women, sons, and daughters. They also took a great deal of plunder from them and brought it to Samaria.

9 A prophet of the LORD named Oded was there. He went out to meet the army that came to Samaria and said to them, "Look, the LORD God of your ancestors handed them over to you because of His wrath against Judah, but you slaughtered them in a rage that has reached heaven. 10 Now you plan to reduce the people of Judah and Jerusalem, male and female, to slavery. Are you not also guilty before the LORD your God? 11 Listen to me and return the captives you took from your brothers, for the LORD's fierce wrath is on you."

12 So some men who were leaders of the Ephraimites—Azariah son of Johanan, Berechiah son of Meshillemoth, Jehizkiah son of Shallum, and Amasa son of Hadlai—stood in opposition to those coming from the war. 13 They said to them, "You must not bring the captives here, for you plan to bring guilt on us from the LORD to add to our sins and our guilt. For we have much guilt, and fierce wrath is on Israel."

14 The army left the captives and the plunder in the presence of the officers and the congregation. 15 Then the men who were designated by name took charge of the captives and provided clothes for their naked ones from the plunder. They clothed them, gave them sandals, food and drink, dressed their wounds, and provided donkeys for all the feeble. The Israelites brought them to Jericho, the City of Palms, among their brothers. Then they returned to Samaria.

16 At that time King Ahaz asked the king of Assyria for help. 17 The Edomites came again, attacked Judah, and took captives. 18 The Philistines also raided the cities of the Judean foothills and the •Negev of Judah and captured Beth-shemesh, Aijalon, Gederoth, Soco and its villages, Timnah and its villages, Gimzo and its villages,

---

[a] **26:21** Lit *a house of freedom* [b] **27:5** Lit *100 talents* [c] **27:5** Lit *10,000 cors* [d] **27:6** Lit *he established his ways before* [e] **28:3** LXX, Syr, Tg read *and passed his children through*; 2 Kg 16:3

---

rogant. How one handles power and success is an important test of character. David remained humble even after his great victories (2 Sam. 6:22), but Uzziah became full of himself.

26:22 Isaiah son of Amoz. Isaiah got his famous call as a prophet "In the year that King Uzziah died" (Isa. 6:1).

27:1 16 years. Jotham began his rule alongside his incapacitated father during the last years of his leprosy-ridden reign.

27:6 So Jotham strengthened himself. Because Jotham was a righteous king, God gave him some prosperous and relatively

uneventful years.

28:1-27 Ahaz's life was riddled with reprehensible behavior (see 2 Kings 16:1-20). He was more akin to the wretchedness of the Northern Kingdom.

28:17-18 Just when Ahaz thought things could not get worse, they did. His enemies declared

and they lived there. [19] For the LORD humbled Judah because of King Ahaz of Judah,[a] who threw off restraint in Judah and was unfaithful to the LORD. [20] Then Tiglath-pileser[b] king of Assyria came against Ahaz; he oppressed him and did not give him support. [21] Although Ahaz plundered the LORD's temple and the palace of the king and of the rulers and gave the plunder to the king of Assyria, it did not help him.

[22] At the time of his distress, King Ahaz himself became more unfaithful to the LORD. [23] He sacrificed to the gods of Damascus which had defeated him; he said, "Since the gods of the kings of Aram are helping them, I will sacrifice to them so that they will help me." But they were the downfall of him and of all Israel.

[24] Then Ahaz gathered up the utensils of God's temple, cut them into pieces, shut the doors of the LORD's temple, and made himself altars on every street corner in Jerusalem. [25] He made high places in every city of Judah to offer incense to other gods, and he provoked the God of his ancestors.

Ahaz's Death

[26] As for the rest of his deeds and all his ways, from beginning to end, they are written about in the Book of the Kings of Judah and Israel. [27] Ahaz rested with his fathers and was buried in the city, in Jerusalem, and his son Hezekiah became king in his place.

Judah's King Hezekiah

29 Hezekiah was 25 years old when he became king; he reigned 29 years in Jerusalem. His mother's name was Abijah[c] daughter of Zechariah. [2] He did what was right in the LORD's sight just as his ancestor David had done.

[3] In the first year of his reign, in the first month, he opened the doors of the LORD's temple and repaired them. [4] Then he brought in the priests and Levites and gathered them in the eastern public square. [5] He said to them, "Hear me, Levites. Consecrate yourselves now and consecrate the temple of the LORD God of your ancestors. Remove everything detestable from the holy place. [6] For our fathers were unfaithful and did what is evil in the sight of the LORD our God. They abandoned Him, turned their faces away from the LORD's tabernacle, and turned their backs on Him.[d] [7] They also closed the doors of the vestibule, extinguished the lamps, did not burn incense, and did not offer •burnt offerings in the holy place of the God of Israel. [8] Therefore, the wrath of the LORD was on Judah and Jerusalem, and He made them an object of terror, horror, and hissing, as

you see with your own eyes. [9] Our fathers fell by the sword, and our sons, our daughters, and our wives are in captivity because of this. [10] It is in my heart now to make a covenant with the LORD God of Israel so that His fierce wrath may turn away from us. [11] My sons, don't be negligent now, for the LORD has chosen you to stand in His presence, to serve Him, and to be His ministers and burners of incense."

Cleansing the Temple

[12] Then the Levites stood up:

Mahath son of Amasai and Joel son of Azariah from the Kohathites;
Kish son of Abdi and Azariah son of Jehallelel from the Merarites;
Joah son of Zimmah and Eden son of Joah from the Gershonites;
[13] Shimri and Jeuel from the Elizaphanites;
Zechariah and Mattaniah from the Asaphites;
[14] Jehiel[e] and Shimei from the Hemanites;
Shemaiah and Uzziel from the Jeduthunites.

[15] They gathered their brothers together, consecrated themselves, and went according to the king's command by the words of the LORD to cleanse the LORD's temple.

[16] The priests went to the entrance of the LORD's temple to cleanse it. They took all the detestable things they found in the LORD's sanctuary to the courtyard of the LORD's temple. Then the Levites received them and took them outside to the Kidron Valley. [17] They began the consecration on the first day of the first month, and on the eighth day of the month they came to the vestibule of the LORD's [temple]. They consecrated the LORD's temple for eight days, and on the sixteenth day of the first month they finished.

[18] Then they went inside to King Hezekiah and said, "We have cleansed the whole temple of the LORD, the altar of burnt offering and all its utensils, and the table for the rows [of the bread of the Presence] and all its utensils. [19] All the utensils that King Ahaz rejected during his reign when he became unfaithful we have set up and consecrated. They are in front of the altar of the LORD."

Renewal of Temple Worship

[20] King Hezekiah got up early, gathered the city officials, and went up to the LORD's temple. [21] They brought seven bulls, seven rams, seven lambs, and seven male goats as a •sin offering for the kingdom, for

---

[a]**28:19** Some Hb mss; other Hb mss read *Israel* [b]**28:20** MT reads *Tilgath-pilneser* [c]**29:1** = Abi; 2 Kg 18:2 [d]**29:6** Lit *and they gave the back of the neck* [e]**29:14** Alt Hb tradition reads *Jehuel*

---

open season on Judah.

28:20 Tiglath-pileser king of Assyria. Assyria answered Ahaz's cry for help, but brought more harm than good.

28:24-25 Not only did Ahaz bar the temple shut, but he went one step further. He prohibited worshiping God—the faith of his fathers

was now a crime.

28:27 Ahaz ... buried in the city. He was ousted from the royal cemetery—a sign that he could not eradicate religion completely.

29:1–32:33 Hezekiah's rule is refreshing. Finally, a king with stamina to stand up against the rule of evil. He is noted for his religious re-

forms and restoration of the temple worship.

29:1 Hezekiah ... reigned 29 years. Halfway into his reign Hezekiah became deathly ill (2 Kings 20:1). The Lord was gracious and allowed him to rule another 15 years (2 Kings 20:6).

29:5-11 Hezekiah knew how to read the signs,

the sanctuary, and for Judah. Then he told the descendants of Aaron, the priests, to offer them on the altar of the LORD. 22 So they slaughtered the bulls, and the priests received the blood and sprinkled it on the altar. They slaughtered the rams and sprinkled the blood on the altar. They slaughtered the lambs and sprinkled the blood on the altar. 23 Then they brought the sin offering goats right into the presence of the king and the congregation, who laid their hands on them. 24 The priests slaughtered the goats and put their blood on the altar for a sin offering, to make •atonement for all Israel, for the king said that the burnt offering and sin offering were for all Israel.

25 Hezekiah stationed the Levites in the LORD's temple with cymbals, harps, and lyres according to the command of David, Gad the king's seer, and Nathan the prophet. For the command was from the LORD through His prophets. 26 The Levites stood with the instruments of David, and the priests with the trumpets.

27 Then Hezekiah ordered that the burnt offering be offered on the altar. When the burnt offerings began, the song of the LORD and the trumpets began, accompanied by the instruments of David king of Israel. 28 The whole assembly was worshiping, singing the song, and blowing the trumpets—all of this ⌊continued⌋ until the burnt offering was completed. 29 When the burnt offerings were completed, the king and all those present with him bowed down and worshiped. 30 Then King Hezekiah and the officials told the Levites to sing praise to the LORD in the words of David and of •Asaph the seer. So they sang praises with rejoicing and bowed down and worshiped.

31 Hezekiah concluded, "Now you are consecrated[a] to the LORD. Come near and bring sacrifices and thank offerings to the LORD's temple." So the congregation brought sacrifices and thank offerings, and all those with willing hearts brought burnt offerings. 32 The number of burnt offerings the congregation brought was 70 bulls, 100 rams, and 200 lambs; all these were for a burnt offering to the LORD. 33 Six hundred bulls and 3,000 sheep were consecrated.

34 However, since there were not enough priests, they weren't able to skin all the burnt offerings, so their Levite brothers helped them until the work was finished and until the priests consecrated themselves. For the Levites were more conscientious[b] to consecrate themselves than the priests were. 35 Furthermore, the burnt offerings were abundant, along with the fat of the •fellowship offerings and with the drink offerings for the burnt offering.

So the service of the LORD's temple was established. 36 Then Hezekiah and all the people rejoiced over how God had prepared the people, for it had come about suddenly.

Celebration of the Passover

30 Then Hezekiah sent ⌊word⌋ throughout all Israel and Judah, and he also wrote letters to Ephraim and Manasseh to come to the LORD's temple in Jerusalem to observe the •Passover of the LORD God of Israel. 2 For the king and his officials and the entire congregation in Jerusalem decided to observe the Passover of the LORD in the second month 3 because they were not able to observe it at the appropriate time, since not enough of the priests had consecrated themselves and the people hadn't been gathered together in Jerusalem. 4 The proposal pleased the king and the congregation, 5 so they affirmed the proposal and spread the message throughout all Israel, from Beer-sheba to Dan, to come to observe the Passover of the LORD God of Israel in Jerusalem, for they hadn't observed it often,[c] as prescribed.[d]

6 So the couriers went throughout Israel and Judah with letters from the hand of the king and his officials, and according to the king's command, saying, "Israelites, return to the LORD God of Abraham, Isaac, and Israel so that He may return to those of you who remain, who have escaped from the grasp of the kings of Assyria. 7 Don't be like your fathers and your brothers who were unfaithful to the LORD God of their ancestors so that He made them an object of horror as you yourselves see. 8 Don't become obstinate[e] now like your fathers did. Give your allegiance[f] to the LORD, and come to His sanctuary that He has consecrated forever. Serve the LORD your God so that He may turn His fierce wrath away from you, 9 for when you return to the LORD, your brothers and your sons ⌊will receive⌋ mercy in the presence of their captors and will return to this land. For the LORD your God is gracious and merciful; He will not turn ⌊His⌋ face away from you if you return to Him."

10 The couriers traveled from city to city in the land of Ephraim and Manasseh as far as Zebulun, but the inhabitants[g] laughed at them and mocked them. 11 But some from Asher, Manasseh, and Zebulun humbled themselves and came to Jerusalem. 12 Also, the hand of God was in Judah to give them one heart to carry out

---

[a]29:31 Lit Now you have filled your hands   [b]29:34 Lit upright of heart; Ps 32:11; 64:10   [c]30:5 Or in great numbers   [d]30:5 Lit often, according to what is written   [e]30:8 Lit Don't stiffen your neck   [f]30:8 Lit hand   [g]30:10 Lit but they

---

explaining the simple history lesson in terms of cause and effect.

29:7 burn incense ... burnt offerings. Solomon's solemn religious orders seem almost like ancient history (2:4; 4:7), but they are just the remedy needed to rejuvenate Judah's languishing faith.

29:35 offerings. These personal offerings express the repentance of the individual, not just the corporate response of the nation.

30:1-27 Now Hezekiah is getting somewhere. He celebrates his monumental progress with a Passover feast. The people of Judah and remnants of Israel witness an unprecedented spiritual renewal.

30:2 the Passover. The people plan a nationwide unity celebration, inviting refugees of the Northern Kingdom and Ephraim and Manasseh.

30:9 captors. The Assyrians now dominate the Northern Kingdom, having captured most

the command of the king and his officials by the word of the LORD.

13 A very large assembly of people was gathered in Jerusalem to observe the Festival of Unleavened Bread in the second month. 14 They proceeded to take away the altars that were in Jerusalem, and they took away the incense altars and threw them into the Kidron Valley. 15 They slaughtered the Passover lamb on the fourteenth day of the second month. The priests and Levites were ashamed, and they consecrated themselves and brought •burnt offerings to the LORD's temple. 16 They stood at their prescribed posts, according to the law of Moses the man of God. The priests sprinkled the blood ⌊received⌋ from the hand of the Levites, 17 for there were many in the assembly who had not consecrated themselves, and so the Levites were in charge of slaughtering the Passover ⌊lambs⌋ for every unclean person to consecrate ⌊the lambs⌋ to the LORD. 18 For a large number of the people—many from Ephraim, Manasseh, Issachar, and Zebulun—were unclean, yet they had eaten the Passover contrary to what was written. But Hezekiah had interceded for them, saying, "May the good LORD provide •atonement on behalf of 19 whoever sets his whole heart on seeking God, the LORD God of his ancestors, even though not according to the purification ⌊rules⌋ of the sanctuary." 20 So the LORD heard Hezekiah and healed the people. 21 The Israelites who were present in Jerusalem observed the Festival of Unleavened Bread seven days with great joy, and the Levites and the priests praised the LORD day after day with loud instruments. 22 Then Hezekiah encouraged[a] all the Levites who performed skillfully before the LORD. They ate the appointed feast for seven days, sacrificing •fellowship offerings and giving thanks to the LORD God of their ancestors.

23 The whole congregation decided to observe seven more days, so they observed seven days with joy, 24 for Hezekiah king of Judah contributed 1,000 bulls and 7,000 sheep for the congregation. Also, the officials contributed 1,000 bulls and 10,000 sheep for the congregation, and many priests consecrated themselves. 25 Then the whole assembly of Judah with the priests and Levites, the whole assembly that came from Israel, the foreigners who came from the land of Israel, and those who were living in Judah, rejoiced. 26 Such rejoicing had not been seen in Jerusalem since the days of Solomon son of David, the king of Israel.

27 Then the priests and the Levites stood to bless the people, and God heard their voice, and their prayer came into His holy dwelling place in heaven.

Removal of Idolatry

31 When all this was completed, all Israel who had attended went out to the cities of Judah and broke up the sacred pillars, chopped down the •Asherah poles, and tore down the •high places and altars throughout Judah and Benjamin, as well as in Ephraim and Manasseh, to the last one.[b] Then all the Israelites returned to their cities, each to his own possession.

Offerings for Levites

2 Hezekiah reestablished the divisions of the priests and Levites for the •burnt offerings and •fellowship offerings, for ministry, for giving thanks, and for praise in the gates of the camp of the LORD, each division corresponding to his service among the priests and Levites. 3 The king contributed[c] from his own possessions for the regular morning and evening burnt offerings, the burnt offerings of the Sabbaths, of the New Moons, and of the appointed feasts, as written in the law of the LORD. 4 He told the people who lived in Jerusalem to give a contribution for the priests and Levites so that they could devote their energy to the law of the LORD. 5 When the word spread, the Israelites gave liberally of the best of the grain, wine, oil, honey, and of all the produce of the field, and they brought an abundant tenth of everything. 6 As for the Israelites and Judahites who lived in the cities of Judah, they also ⌊brought⌋ a tenth of the cattle and sheep, and a tenth of the dedicated things that were consecrated to the LORD their God. They gathered ⌊them⌋ into large piles. 7 In the third month they began building up the piles, and they finished in the seventh month. 8 When Hezekiah and his officials came and viewed the piles, they praised the LORD and His people Israel.

9 Hezekiah asked the priests and Levites about the piles. 10 Azariah, the chief priest of the household of Zadok, answered him, "Since they began bringing the offering to the LORD's temple, we eat and are satisfied and there is plenty left over because the LORD has blessed His people; this abundance is what is left over."

11 Hezekiah told them to prepare chambers in the LORD's temple, and they prepared ⌊them⌋. 12 The offering, the tenth, and the dedicated things were brought faithfully. Conaniah the Levite was the officer in charge of them, and his brother Shimei was second. 13 Jehiel, Azaziah, Nahath, Asahel, Jerimoth, Jozabad, Eliel, Ismachiah, Mahath, and Benaiah were deputies under the authority of Conaniah and his brother Shimei by appointment of King Hezekiah and of Azariah the ruler of God's temple.

---

a30:22 Lit *spoke to the heart of*   b31:1 Lit *Manasseh, until finishing*   c31:3 Lit *The king's portion*

---

of its inhabitants. Those who remain are challenged to demonstrate their allegiance to God by attending the feast.

30:15 priests and Levites. In order to maintain the spiritual momentum, Hezekiah turns to those commissioned to be holy examples among the people.

30:17 Passover [lambs]. The Levites eagerly serve the people who come to the Passover unprepared. Just like in old times, the Levites slay the lambs for the people's sacrifice.

30:18-19 Hezekiah, ever the diplomat, smoothes the transition from heathen to holiness for those who attend the Passover.

30:26 Such rejoicing ... since the days of Solomon. The chronicler cannot resist drawing the parallels between the overt religious emphasis of Hezekiah and that of Solomon.

31:2 Hezekiah single-handedly motivates the people to an inspired movement. Then he directs the details of the operation among his staff.

14 Kore son of Imnah the Levite, the keeper of the East Gate, was over the freewill offerings to God to distribute the contribution to the LORD and the consecrated things. 15 Eden, Miniamin, Jeshua, Shemaiah, Amariah, and Shecaniah in the cities of the priests were to faithfully distribute ⌊it⌋ under his authority to their brothers by divisions, whether large or small. 16 In addition, ⌊they distributed it⌋ to males registered by genealogy threea years old and above; to all who would enter the LORD's temple for their daily duty, for their service in their responsibilities according to their divisions. 17 ⌊They distributed also⌋ to those recorded by genealogy of the priests by their ancestral families and the Levites 20 years old and above, by their responsibilities in their divisions; 18 to those registered by genealogy—with all their infants, wives, sons, and daughters —of the whole assembly (for they had faithfully consecrated themselves as holy); 19 and to the descendants of Aaron, the priests, in the common fields of their cities, in each and every city. ⌊There were⌋ men who were registered by name to distribute a portion to every male among the priests and to every Levite recorded by genealogy.

20 Hezekiah did this throughout all Judah. He did what was good and upright and true before the LORD his God. 21 He was diligent in every deed that he began in the service of God's temple, in the law and in the commandment, in order to seek his God, and he prospered.

Sennacherib's Invasion

32 After these faithful deeds, Sennacherib king of Assyria came and entered Judah. He laid siege to the fortified cities and intendedb to break into them. 2 Hezekiah saw that Sennacherib had come and that he plannedc war on Jerusalem, 3 so he consulted with his officials and his warriors about stopping up the waters of the springs that were outside the city, and they helped him. 4 Many people gathered and stopped up all the springs and the stream that flowed through the land; they said, "Why should the kings of Assyria come and find plenty of water?" 5 Then Hezekiah strengthened his position by rebuilding the entire broken-down wall and heightening the towers and the other outside wall. He repaired the supporting terraces of the city of David, and made an abundance of weapons and shields.

6 He set military commanders over the people and gathered the people in the square of the city gate. Then he encouraged them,d saying, 7 "Be strong and courageous! Don't be afraid or discouraged before the king of Assyria or before all the multitude with him, for there are more with us than with him. 8 He has only human strength,e but we have the LORD our God to help us and to fight our battles." So the people relied on the words of King Hezekiah of Judah.

Sennacherib's Servant's Speech

9 After this, while Sennacherib king of Assyria with all his armed forces besiegedf Lachish, he sent his servants to Jerusalem against King Hezekiah of Judah and against all those of Judah who were in Jerusalem, saying, 10 "This is what King Sennacherib of Assyria says: 'What are you trusting in, you who remain under the siege of Jerusalem? 11 Isn't Hezekiah misleading you to give you over to death by famine and thirst when he says, "The LORD our God will deliver us from the power of the king of Assyria"? 12 Didn't Hezekiah himself remove His •high places and His altars and say to Judah and Jerusalem: "You must worship before one altar, and you must burn incense on it"?

13 "'Don't you know what I and my fathers have done to all the peoples of the lands? Have any of the national gods of the lands been able to deliver their land from my power? 14 Who among all the gods of these nations that my fathers utterly destroyed was able to deliver his people from my power, that your God should be able to do the same for you? 15 So now, don't let Hezekiah deceive you, and don't let him mislead you like this. Don't believe him, for no god of any nation or kingdom has been able to deliver his people from my power or the power of my fathers. How much less will your gods deliver you from my power!'"

16 His servants said more against the LORD God and against His servant Hezekiah. 17 He also wrote letters to mock the LORD God of Israel, saying against Him:

> Just like the national gods of the lands that did not deliver their people from my power, so Hezekiah's God will not deliver His people from my power.

18 Then they called out loudly in Hebrewg to the people of Jerusalem who were on the wall to frighten and discourage them in order that he might capture the city. 19 They spoke against the God of Jerusalem like they had spoken against the gods of the peoples of the land, which were made by human hands.

Deliverance from Sennacherib

20 King Hezekiah and the prophet Isaiah son of Amoz prayed about this and cried out to heaven, 21 and the

---

a31:16 Or 30; 1 Ch 23:3   b32:1 Lit said to himself   c32:2 Lit that his face was for   d32:6 Lit he spoke to their hearts   e32:8 Lit With him an arm of flesh   f32:9 Lit with his dominion was against   g32:18 Lit Judahite

---

31:3 king contributed from his own possessions. David showed the power of example (1 Chron. 29:3-9). Hezekiah discovers its motivational strength by giving generously toward his own project.

31:5 they brought an abundant tenth of everything. Tithing (giving a tenth of one's income) is a solid biblical guideline for stewardship.

32:1-23 Hezekiah encountered an Assyrian king with an attitude. It is one thing to challenge a godly king. Sennacherib, however, defied God Himself (vv. 10-15). The result was humiliating disaster for Assyria (vv. 20-21).

32:5-8 Then Hezekiah strengthened his position ... Then he encouraged them. Hezekiah showed himself to be a good military leader by taking both practical steps (rebuilding) and spiritual steps (encouraging his people and pointing them to faith) to be able to resist their enemy.

LORD sent an angel who annihilated every brave warrior, leader, and commander in the camp of the king of Assyria. So the king of Assyria returned with shame to his land. He went to the temple of his god, and there some of his own children cut him down with the sword. [22] So the LORD saved Hezekiah and the inhabitants of Jerusalem from the power of King Sennacherib of Assyria and from the power of all others. He gave them rest[a] on every side. [23] Many were bringing an offering to the LORD to Jerusalem and valuable gifts to King Hezekiah of Judah, and he was exalted in the eyes of all the nations after that.

Hezekiah's Illness and Pride

[24] In those days Hezekiah became sick to the point of death, so he prayed to the LORD, and He spoke to him and gave him a miraculous sign. [25] However, because his heart was proud, Hezekiah didn't respond according to the benefit that had come to him. So there was wrath upon him, upon Judah, and upon Jerusalem. [26] Then Hezekiah humbled himself for the pride of his heart—he and the inhabitants of Jerusalem—so the LORD's wrath didn't come on them during Hezekiah's lifetime.

Hezekiah's Wealth and Works

[27] Hezekiah had abundant riches and glory, and he made himself treasuries for silver, gold, precious stones, spices, shields, and every desirable item. [28] He made warehouses for the harvest of grain, wine, and oil, and stalls for all kinds of cattle, and pens for flocks. [29] He made cities for himself, and he acquired herds of sheep and cattle in abundance, for God gave him abundant possessions.

[30] This same Hezekiah blocked the outlet of the water of the Upper Gihon and channeled it smoothly downward and westward to the city of David. Hezekiah succeeded in everything he did. [31] When the ambassadors of Babylon's rulers were sent[b] to him to inquire about the miraculous sign that happened in the land, God left him to test him and discover what was in his heart.

Hezekiah's Death

[32] As for the rest of the events of Hezekiah's ⌊reign⌋ and his deeds of faithful love, note that they are written about in the Visions of the Prophet Isaiah son of Amoz, and in the Book of the Kings of Judah and Israel. [33] Hezekiah rested with his fathers and was buried on the ascent to the tombs of David's descendants. All

Judah and the inhabitants of Jerusalem paid him honor at his death. His son Manasseh became king in his place.

Judah's King Manasseh

33 Manasseh was 12 years old when he became king; he reigned 55 years in Jerusalem. [2] He did what was evil in the LORD's sight, imitating the detestable practices of the nations that the LORD had dispossessed before the Israelites. [3] He rebuilt the •high places that his father Hezekiah had torn down and reestablished the altars for the •Baals. He made •Asherah poles, and he worshiped the whole heavenly •host and served them. [4] He built altars in the LORD's temple, where the LORD had said: "Jerusalem is where My name will remain forever." [5] He built altars to the whole heavenly host in both courtyards of the LORD's temple. [6] He passed his sons through the fire in the Valley of Hinnom. He practiced witchcraft, •divination, and sorcery, and consulted mediums and spiritists. He did a great deal of evil in the LORD's sight, provoking Him.

[7] Manasseh set up a carved image of the idol he had made, in God's temple, about which God had said to David and his son Solomon: "I will establish My name forever[c] in this temple and in Jerusalem, which I have chosen out of all the tribes of Israel. [8] I will never again remove the feet of the Israelites from upon the land where I stationed your[d] ancestors, if only they will be careful to do all that I have commanded them through Moses—all the law, statutes, and judgments." [9] So Manasseh caused Judah and the inhabitants of Jerusalem to stray so that they did worse evil than the nations the LORD had destroyed before the Israelites.

Manasseh's Repentance

[10] The LORD spoke to Manasseh and his people, but they didn't listen. [11] So He brought against them the military commanders of the king of Assyria. They captured Manasseh with hooks, bound him with bronze ⌊shackles⌋, and took him to Babylon. [12] When he was in distress, he sought the favor of the LORD his God and earnestly humbled himself before the God of his ancestors. [13] He prayed to Him, so He heard his petition and granted his request, and brought him back to Jerusalem, to his kingdom. So Manasseh came to know that the LORD is God.

[14] After this, he built the outer wall of the city of David from west of Gihon in the valley to the entrance of the Fish Gate; he brought it around the Ophel, and

---

[a]**32:22** Lit *He led them*; Ps 23:2 [b]**32:31** LXX, Tg, Vg; MT reads *of Babylon sent* [c]**33:7** LXX, Syr, Tg, Vg; MT reads *name for Elom*; 2 Kg 21:7
[d]**33:8** LXX, Syr, Vg read *land I gave to their*; 2 Kg 21:8

32:9 Sennacherib. Sennacherib began his battle with a war of words. He insulted Judah's king and Judah's God. His aim was to demoralize his enemy, to intimidate them into submission. The chronicler leaves out Hezekiah's response (2 Kings 18:14-16).

32:14 Who among all the gods. Sennacherib

was calling the people of Israel to question whether their God was truly different than the gods of those around them. There was in fact an important difference. The gods of other nations were simply objects "made by human hands" (v.19).

33:1-20 According to the chronicler, Manas-

seh was no less evil for having repented. His is the longest evil reign in Judah's history.

33:6 He passed his sons through the fire in the Valley of Hinnom. Sacrificing children to the foreign god Molech was one of the evils that God condemned the most. The Valley of Hinnom was infamous for this practice. The

he heightened it considerably. He also placed military commanders in all the fortified cities of Judah.

15 He removed the foreign gods and the idol from the LORD's temple, along with all the altars that he had built on the mountain of the LORD's temple and in Jerusalem, and he threw them outside the city. 16 He built[a] the altar of the LORD and offered •fellowship and thank offerings on it. Then he told Judah to serve the LORD God of Israel. 17 However, the people still sacrificed at the high places, but only to the LORD their God.

Manasseh's Death

18 The rest of the events of Manasseh's ⌊reign⌋, along with his prayer to his God and the words of the seers who spoke to him in the name of the LORD God of Israel, are ⌊written about⌋ in the Events of Israel's Kings. 19 His prayer and how God granted his request, and all his sin and unfaithfulness and the sites where he built high places and set up Asherah poles and carved images before he humbled himself, they are written about in the Records of Hozai. 20 Manasseh rested with his fathers, and he was buried in his own house. His son Amon became king in his place.

Judah's King Amon

21 Amon was 22 years old when he became king; he reigned two years in Jerusalem. 22 He did what was evil in the LORD's sight just as his father Manasseh had done. Amon sacrificed to all the carved images that his father Manasseh had made, and he served them. 23 But he did not humble himself before the LORD like his father Manasseh humbled himself; instead, Amon increased ⌊his⌋ guilt.

24 So his servants conspired against him and put him to death in his own house. 25 Then the common people[b] executed all those who conspired against King Amon and made his son Josiah king in his place.

Judah's King Josiah

34 Josiah was eight years old when he became king; he reigned 31 years in Jerusalem. 2 He did what was right in the LORD's sight and walked in the ways of his ancestor David; he did not turn aside to the right or the left.

Josiah's Reform

3 In the eighth year of his reign, while he was still a youth, Josiah began to seek the God of his ancestor David, and in the twelfth year he began to cleanse Judah and Jerusalem of the •high places, the •Asherah poles, the carved images, and the cast images. 4 Then in

his presence the altars of the •Baals were torn down, and the incense altars that were above them he chopped down. The Asherah poles, the carved images, and the cast images he shattered, crushed to dust, and scattered over the graves of those who had sacrificed to them. 5 He burned the bones of the priests on their altars. So he cleansed Judah and Jerusalem. 6 ⌊He did the same⌋ in the cities of Manasseh, Ephraim, and Simeon, and as far as Naphtali ⌊and⌋ on their surrounding mountain shrines.[c] 7 He tore down the altars, and he smashed the Asherah poles and the carved images to powder. He chopped down all the incense altars throughout the land of Israel and returned to Jerusalem.

Josiah's Repair of the Temple

8 In the eighteenth year of his reign, in order to cleanse the land and the temple, Josiah sent Shaphan son of Azaliah, along with Maaseiah the governor of the city and the recorder Joah son of Joahaz, to repair the temple of the LORD his God.

9 So they went to Hilkiah the high priest, and gave him the money brought into God's temple. The Levites and the doorkeepers had collected ⌊money⌋ from Manasseh, Ephraim, and from the entire remnant of Israel, and from all Judah, Benjamin, and the inhabitants of Jerusalem. 10 They put it into the hands of those doing the work—those who oversaw the LORD's temple. They ⌊in turn⌋ gave it to the workmen who were working in the LORD's temple, to repair and restore the temple; 11 they gave it to the carpenters and builders and ⌊also used it⌋ to buy quarried stone and timbers—for joining and to make beams—for the buildings that Judah's Kings had destroyed.

12 The men were doing the work with integrity. Their overseers were Jahath and Obadiah the Levites from the Merarites, and Zechariah and Meshullam from the Kohathites as supervisors. The Levites were all skilled on musical instruments. 13 ⌊They were⌋ also over the porters and were supervising all those doing the work task by task. Some of the Levites were secretaries, officers, and gatekeepers.

The Recovery of the Book of the Law

14 When they brought out the money that had been deposited in the LORD's temple, Hilkiah the priest found the book of the law of the LORD ⌊written⌋ by the hand of Moses. 15 Consequently, Hilkiah told Shaphan the court secretary, "I have found the book of the law in the LORD's temple," and he gave the book to Shaphan.

---

a**33:16** Some Hb mss, Syr, Tg, Arabic; other Hb mss, LXX, Vg read *restored*   b**33:25** Lit *the people of the land*   c**34:6** One Hb tradition reads *Naphtali with their swords*; alt Hb tradition, Syr, Vg read *Naphtali, the ruins all around*; Hb obscure

---

name "Valley of Hinnom" was later translated into "Gehenna," the word for "hell."

33:11-17 It took a ring in his nose and bars in front of his face for Manasseh to call on God, who always responds to sincere repentance.

33:11 captured Manasseh with hooks ... took him to Babylon. Leading prisoners into

captivity with hooks was similar to how animals were led to slaughter.

33:20 Manasseh ... buried in his own house. Manasseh's burial plot is not among the kings. Even in death he remains outside of God's favor. Five kings (Ahaz, Jehoram, Joash, Uzziah, and Manasseh) had this kind of burial.

34:1–36:1 Josiah. Josiah initiates religious reform that sweeps across the nation of Judah and into Israel (vv. 3-7). When he discovers the book of Moses and its long forgotten laws, his reform becomes revival (vv. 14,29-32).

34:3-7 Josiah follows in great-grandfather Hezekiah's steps. All his national reforms flow

16 Shaphan took the book to the king, and also reported, "Your servants are doing all that was placed in their hands. 17 They have emptied out the money that was found in the LORD's temple and have put it into the hand of the overseers and the hand of those doing the work." 18 Then Shaphan the court secretary told the king, "Hilkiah the priest gave me a book," and Shaphan read it in the presence of the king.

19 When the king heard the words of the law, he tore his clothes. 20 Then he commanded Hilkiah, Ahikam son of Shaphan, Abdon son of Micah, Shaphan the court secretary, and the king's servant Asaiah, 21 "Go. Inquire of the LORD for me and for those remaining in Israel and Judah, concerning the words of the book that was found. For great is the LORD's wrath that is poured out on us because our fathers have not kept the word of the LORD in order to do everything written in this book."

Huldah's Prophecy of Judgment

22 So Hilkiah and those the king had designated[a] went to the prophetess Huldah, the wife of Shallum son of Tokhath, son of Hasrah, keeper of the wardrobe. She lived in Jerusalem in the Second District. They spoke with her about this.

23 She said to them, "This is what the LORD God of Israel says: Say to the man who sent you to Me, 24 'This is what the LORD says: I am about to bring disaster on this place and on its inhabitants, [fulfilling] all the curses written in the book that they read in the presence of the king of Judah, 25 because they have abandoned Me and burned incense to other gods in order to provoke Me with all the works of their hands. My wrath will be poured out on this place, and it will not be quenched.' 26 Say this to the king of Judah who sent you to inquire of the LORD: 'This is what the LORD God of Israel says: As for the words that you heard, 27 because your heart was tender and you humbled yourself before God when you heard His words against this place and against its inhabitants, and because you humbled yourself before Me, and you tore your clothes and wept before Me, I Myself have heard'—this is the LORD speaking. 28 'I will indeed gather you to your fathers, and you will be gathered to your grave in peace. Your eyes will not see all the disaster that I am bringing on this place and on its inhabitants.' "

Then they reported to the king.

Affirmation of the Covenant by Josiah and the People

29 So the king sent [messengers] and gathered all the elders of Judah and Jerusalem. 30 Then the king went up to the LORD's temple with all the men of Judah and the inhabitants of Jerusalem, as well as the priests and the Levites—all the people from great to small. He read in their hearing all the words of the book of the covenant that had been found in the LORD's temple. 31 Next the king stood at his post and made a covenant in the LORD's presence to follow the LORD and to keep His commandments, His decrees, and His statutes with all his heart and with all his soul in order to carry out the words of the covenant written in this book.

32 Then he had all those present in Jerusalem and Benjamin enter[b] [the covenant]. So all the inhabitants of Jerusalem carried out the covenant of God, the God of their ancestors.

33 So Josiah removed everything that was detestable from all the lands belonging to the Israelites, and he required all who were present in Israel to serve the LORD their God. Throughout his reign they did not turn aside from following the LORD God of their ancestors.

Josiah's Passover Observance

35 Josiah observed the LORD's •Passover and slaughtered the Passover [lambs] on the fourteenth day of the first month. 2 He appointed the priests to their responsibilities and encouraged them to serve in the LORD's temple. 3 He said to the Levites who taught all Israel the holy things of the LORD, "Put the holy ark in the temple built by Solomon son of David king of Israel. Since you do not have to carry it on your shoulders, now serve the LORD your God and His people Israel.

4 "Organize your ancestral houses by your divisions according to the written instruction of David king of Israel and that of his son Solomon. 5 Serve in the holy place by the divisions of the ancestral houses for your brothers, the lay people,[c] and the distribution of the tribal household of the Levites. 6 Slaughter the Passover [lambs], consecrate yourselves, and make preparations for your brothers to carry out the word of the LORD through Moses."

7 Then Josiah donated 30,000 sheep, lambs, and kid goats, plus 3,000 bulls from his own possessions, for the Passover sacrifices for all the lay people[c] who were present.

8 His officials also donated willingly for the people, the priests, and the Levites. Hilkiah, Zechariah, and Jehiel, leaders of God's temple, gave 2,600 Passover sacrifices and 300 bulls for the priests. 9 Conaniah and his brothers Shemaiah and Nethanel, and Hashabiah, Jeiel, and Jozabad, officers of the Levites, donated

---

a **34:22** LXX; MT omits *designated*   b **34:32** Lit *take a stand.*   c **35:5,7** Lit *the sons of the people*

---

from his intimate relationship with God.

34:6 as far as Naphtali. Josiah's zeal knows no bounds. His reforms sweep to the northern borders by sheer spiritual momentum.

34:14 found the book of the law of the LORD. This book was probably the Book of Deuteronomy. This finding helped spur Josiah's reforms.

34:19 tore his clothes. This was a sign of mourning. The people of Israel had strayed so far from what God had commanded in the book that Josiah found.

35:3 Put the holy ark in the temple built by Solomon. The ark symbolizes God's presence among His people. Placing it back in the

temple communicates security and stability.

35:4 according to the written instruction. Josiah is a traditionalist. He takes his orders for religious reform from David and Solomon. Two other passages support this thought (7:10; 11:17).

35:18 No Passover had been observed like

5,000 Passover sacrifices for the Levites, plus 500 bulls.

10 So the service was established; the priests stood at their posts and the Levites in their divisions according to the king's command. 11 Then they slaughtered the Passover lambs, and while the Levites were skinning the animals, the priests sprinkled the blood[a] they had been given.[b] 12 They removed the •burnt offerings so that they might be given to the divisions of the ancestral houses of the lay people[c] to offer to the LORD, according to what is written in the book of Moses; they did the same with the bulls. 13 They roasted the Passover lambs with fire according to regulation. They boiled the holy sacrifices in pots, in kettles, and in bowls; and they quickly brought them to the lay people.[c] 14 Afterwards, they made preparations for themselves and for the priests, since the priests, the descendants of Aaron, were busy offering up burnt offerings and fat until night. So the Levites made preparations for themselves and for the priests, the descendants of Aaron.

15 The singers, the descendants of •Asaph, were at their stations according to the command of David, Asaph, Heman, and Jeduthun the king's seer. Also, the gatekeepers were at each gate. Because their Levite brothers had made preparations for them, none of them left their tasks.

16 So all the service of the LORD was established that day for observing the Passover and for offering burnt offerings on the altar of the LORD, according to the command of King Josiah. 17 The Israelites who were present in Judah also observed the Passover at that time and the Festival of Unleavened Bread for seven days. 18 No Passover had been observed like it in Israel since the days of Samuel the prophet. None of the kings of Israel ever observed a Passover like the one that Josiah observed with the priests, the Levites, all Judah, the Israelites who were present in Judah, and the inhabitants of Jerusalem. 19 In the eighteenth year of Josiah's reign, this Passover was observed.

Josiah's Last Deeds and Death

20 After all this that Josiah had prepared for the temple, Neco king of Egypt marched up to fight at Carchemish by the Euphrates, and Josiah went out to confront him. 21 But Neco sent messengers to him, saying, "What is the issue between you and me, king of Judah? I have not come against you today[d] but to the dynasty[e] I am fighting. God told me to hurry. Stop

opposing God who is with me; don't make Him destroy you!"

22 But Josiah did not turn away from him; instead, in order to fight with him he disguised himself.[f] He did not listen to Neco's words from the mouth of God, but went to the Valley of Megiddo to fight. 23 The archers shot King Josiah, and he said to his servants, "Take me away, for I am severely wounded!" 24 So his servants took him out of the war chariot, carried him in his second chariot, and brought him to Jerusalem. Then he died, and they buried him in the tomb of his fathers. All Judah and Jerusalem mourned for Josiah. 25 Jeremiah chanted a dirge over Josiah, and all the singing men and singing women still speak of Josiah in their dirges to this very day. They established them as a statute for Israel, and indeed they are written in the Dirges.

26 The rest of the events of Josiah's reign, along with his deeds of faithful love according to what is written in the law of the LORD, 27 and his words, from beginning to end, are written about in the Book of the Kings of Israel and Judah.

Judah's King Jehoahaz

36 Then the common people[g] took Jehoahaz son of Josiah and made him king in Jerusalem in place of his father.

2 Jehoahaz[h] was 23 years old when he became king; he reigned three months in Jerusalem. 3 The king of Egypt deposed him in Jerusalem and fined the land 7,500 pounds[i] of silver and 75 pounds[j] of gold.

Judah's King Jehoiakim

4 Then Neco king of Egypt made Jehoahaz's brother Eliakim king over Judah and Jerusalem and changed Eliakim's name to Jehoiakim. But Neco took his brother Jehoahaz[h] and brought him to Egypt.

5 Jehoiakim was 25 years old when he became king; he reigned 11 years in Jerusalem. He did what was evil in the sight of the LORD his God. 6 Now Nebuchadnezzar king of Babylon attacked him and bound him in bronze shackles to take him to Babylon. 7 Also Nebuchadnezzar took some of the utensils of the LORD's temple to Babylon and put them in his temple in Babylon.

8 The rest of the deeds of Jehoiakim, the detestable things he did, and what was found against him, are written about in the Book of Israel's Kings. His son Jehoiachin became king in his place.

---

a35:11 LXX, Vg, Tg; MT omits *blood*   b35:11 Lit *sprinkled from their hand*   c35:12,13 Lit *the sons of the people*   d35:21 LXX, Syr, Tg, Vg; MT reads *Not against you, you today*   e35:21 Lit *house*   f35:22 LXX reads *he was determined*   g36:1 Lit *the people of the land*   h36:2,4 = Joahaz   i36:3 Lit *100 talents*   j36:3 Lit *one talent*

---

it in Israel since the days of Samuel. The people had probably observed a Passover of sorts, but not with the pageantry and precise attention to regulation that was done here.

35:21 Stop opposing God who is with me. Anyone could claim to be acting according to God's direction. However, Josiah's mistake

was that he didn't do anything to consult God to see whether or not this was true.

35:25 The shocking news of Josiah's death caused the prophet Jeremiah to express his emotions in written laments. These laments remained popular even in the chronicler's day.

36:2-14 Josiah's offspring were neither as righteous nor influential as their ancestor.

36:15 the LORD God of their ancestors sent word against them. This is an important summary statement of all that the chronicler had described. God kept sending the people warnings; they kept ignoring them.

Judah's King Jehoiachin

9 Jehoiachin was 18[a] years old when he became king; he reigned three months and 10 days in Jerusalem. He did what was evil in the LORD's sight. 10 In the spring[b] Nebuchadnezzar sent ⌊for him⌋ and brought him to Babylon along with the valuable utensils of the LORD's temple. Then he made Jehoiachin's brother Zedekiah king over Judah and Jerusalem.

Judah's King Zedekiah

11 Zedekiah was 21 years old when he became king; he reigned 11 years in Jerusalem. 12 He did what was evil in the sight of the LORD his God and did not humble himself before Jeremiah the prophet at the LORD's command. 13 He also rebelled against King Nebuchadnezzar who had made him swear allegiance by God. He became obstinate[c] and hardened his heart against returning to the LORD God of Israel. 14 All the leaders of the priests and the people multiplied their unfaithful deeds, imitating all the detestable practices of the nations, and they defiled the LORD's temple that He had consecrated in Jerusalem.

The Destruction of Jerusalem

15 But the LORD God of their ancestors sent word against them by the hand of his messengers, sending them time and time again, for He had compassion on His people and on His dwelling place. 16 But they kept ridiculing God's messengers, despising His words, and scoffing at His prophets, until the LORD's wrath was so stirred up against His people that there was no remedy.

17 So He brought up against them the king of the Chaldeans, who killed their choice young men with the sword in the house of their sanctuary. He had no pity on young man and virgin or elderly and aged; He handed them all over to him. 18 He took everything to Babylon—all the articles of God's temple, large and small, the treasures of the LORD's temple, and the treasures of the king and his officials. 19 Then the Chaldeans burned God's temple. They tore down Jerusalem's wall, burned down all its palaces, and destroyed all its valuable utensils.

20 Those who escaped from the sword he deported to Babylon, and they became servants to him and his sons until the rise of the Persian[d] kingdom. 21 This fulfilled the word of the LORD through Jeremiah and the land enjoyed its Sabbath rest all the days of the desolation until 70 years were fulfilled.

The Decree of Cyrus

22 In the first year of Cyrus king of Persia, the word of the LORD spoken through[e] Jeremiah was fulfilled. The LORD put it into the mind of King Cyrus of Persia to issue a proclamation throughout his entire kingdom and also ⌊to put it⌋ in writing:

23 This is what King Cyrus of Persia says: The LORD, the God of heaven, has given me all the kingdoms of the earth and has appointed me to build Him a temple at Jerusalem in Judah. Whoever among you of His people may go up, and may the LORD his God be with him.

---

a**36:9** Some Hb mss, LXX; other Hb mss read *eight*; 2 Kg 24:8   b**36:10** Lit *At the return of the year*   c**36:13** Lit *He stiffened his neck*
d**36:20** LXX reads *Median*   e**36:22** Lit *LORD by the mouth of*

36:19 Then the Chaldeans burned God's temple. They tore down Jerusalem's wall. This was the response of God's judgment on what had been described in verse 15. It was the greatest tragedy of Israel's history.

36:20-21 The chronicler concludes with Nebuchadnezzar. This foreigner terminated the royal kingdom, taking Judah's people captive.

The authors of 1 and 2 Samuel and 1 and 2 Kings shared these reasons for why Israel was taken into exile, while the chronicler looks at the exile as a new beginning. **the land enjoyed its Sabbath.** This was quite a positive spin on what had happened! It was like the land itself enjoyed a little time where it didn't have to bear with the evil that had been done in it. And just as giving land some fallow time

can make it more productive, so too did this rest for the land prepare it for the people's return.

36:22-23 The Davidic dynasty did not die. A broken and contrite people arose from the rubble of ruined dreams. The King of Israel would be their newfound hope.

INTRODUCTION TO
EZRA

PERSONAL READING PLAN

- ☐ Ezra 1:1-11
- ☐ Ezra 2:1-70
- ☐ Ezra 3:1-4:24
- ☐ Ezra 5:1-17
- ☐ Ezra 6:1-22

- ☐ Ezra 7:1-28
- ☐ Ezra 8:1-36
- ☐ Ezra 9:1-15
- ☐ Ezra 10:1-44

AUTHOR

The book is named for the principal character, Ezra, but the book does not state its author. This unknown author may have also helped to compile the Book of Nehemiah and perhaps 1 and 2 Chronicles, as these books share many common characteristics:

1. A fondness for lists, for the descriptions of religious festivals and for the phrases "heads of families" and "the house of God."

2. The prominence of Levites and temple personnel.

3. The almost exclusive use of the Hebrew words for "singer," "gatekeeper," and "temple servants."

DATE

With an unstated author, precise dating is difficult to determine. The events narrated cover the years circa 538-458 B.C.

THEME

Beginning again by building the second temple.

HISTORICAL BACKGROUND

Originally this work was one book, united with Nehemiah. In the Latin Bible, Ezra and

Nehemiah are entitled 1 and 2 Esdras. This book chronicles the restoration of Israel after 70 years of captivity in Babylon. This is accomplished through the help of three Persian kings (Cyrus, Darius, and Artaxerxes I). Cyrus was an enlightened king who reversed the oppressive policies of his Assyrian and Babylonian predecessors and encouraged the return of the exiles and the rebirth of their religion. The traditional view is that Ezra arrived in Jerusalem in the seventh year of the reign of Artaxerxes I (458 B.C.) and Nehemiah in the twentieth year of the reign (445 B.C.).

CHARACTERISTICS

This book weaves together various lists, the first-person and third-person memoirs of Ezra, and official documents. These include: (1) the decree of Cyrus (1:2-4); (2) the accusation against the Jews (4:11-16); (3) the response of Artaxerxes (4:17-22); (4) the letter of Tattenai to Darius (5:7-17); (5) a memo (6:2b-5); (6) Darius' reply to Tattenai (6:6-12); and (7) a letter from Artaxerxes I to Ezra (7:12-26). God is shown using Persian kings and Jewish leaders both to bless and to discipline His people. Ezra is often seen as the "father of Judaism" because he promotes a way of life renewed by and centered on unswerving allegiance to the Torah (God's Law). Ezra's policies saved Judaism from oblivion in this crucial period of transition.

The Decree of Cyrus

1 In the first year of Cyrus king of Persia,[a] the word of the LORD spoken through Jeremiah was fulfilled. The LORD put it into the mind of King Cyrus to issue a proclamation throughout his entire kingdom and ⌊to put it⌋ in writing:

2 This is what King Cyrus of Persia says: "The LORD, the God of heaven, has given me all the kingdoms of the earth and has appointed me to build Him a house at Jerusalem in Judah. 3 Whoever is among His people, may his God be with him, and may he go to Jerusalem in Judah and build the house of the LORD, the God of Israel, the God who is in Jerusalem. 4 Let every survivor, wherever he lives, be assisted by the men of that region with silver, gold, goods, and livestock, along with a freewill offering for the house of God in Jerusalem."

Return from Exile

5 So the family leaders of Judah and Benjamin, along with the priests and Levites—everyone God had motivated[b]—prepared to go up and rebuild the LORD's house in Jerusalem. 6 All their neighbors supported them[c] with silver articles, gold, goods, livestock, and valuables, in addition to all that was given as a freewill offering. 7 King Cyrus also brought out the articles of the LORD's house that Nebuchadnezzar had taken from Jerusalem and had placed in the house of his gods. 8 King Cyrus of Persia had them brought out under the supervision of Mithredath the treasurer, who counted them out to Sheshbazzar the prince of Judah. 9 This was the inventory:

> 30 gold basins, 1,000 silver basins,
> 29 silver knives, 10 30 gold bowls,
> 410 various[d] silver bowls,
> and 1,000 other articles.

11 The gold and silver articles totaled 5,400. Sheshbazzar brought all of them when the exiles went up from Babylon to Jerusalem.

The Exiles Who Returned

2 These now are the people of the province who came from those captive exiles King Nebuchadnezzar of Babylon[e] had deported to Babylon. Each of them returned to his hometown Jerusalem and Judah. 2 They came with Zerubbabel, Jeshua, Nehemiah, Seraiah, Reelaiah, Mordecai, Bilshan, Mispar, Bigvai, Rehum, and Baanah.

The number of the Israelite men ⌊included⌋:[f]

3 Parosh's descendants	2,172
4 Shephatiah's descendants	372
5 Arah's descendants	775
6 Pahath-moab's descendants:	
Jeshua's and Joab's descendants	2,812
7 Elam's descendants	1,254
8 Zattu's descendants	945
9 Zaccai's descendants	760
10 Bani's descendants	642
11 Bebai's descendants	623
12 Azgad's descendants	1,222
13 Adonikam's descendants	666
14 Bigvai's descendants	2,056
15 Adin's descendants	454
16 Ater's descendants: Hezekiah's	98
17 Bezai's descendants	323
18 Jorah's descendants	112
19 Hashum's descendants	223
20 Gibbar's descendants	95
21 Bethlehem's people	123
22 Netophah's men	56
23 Anathoth's men	128
24 Azmaveth's people	42
25 Kiriatharim's, Chephirah's,	
and Beeroth's people	743
26 Ramah's and Geba's people	621
27 Michmas's men	122
28 Bethel's and Ai's men	223
29 Nebo's people	52
30 Magbish's people	156
31 the other Elam's people	1,254
32 Harim's people	320
33 Lod's, Hadid's, and Ono's people	725
34 Jericho's people	345
35 Senaah's people	3,630

36 The priests ⌊included⌋:

Jedaiah's descendants of the house of Jeshua	973
37 Immer's descendants	1,052
38 Pashhur's descendants	1,247
39 and Harim's descendants	1,017

40 The Levites ⌊included⌋:

Jeshua's and Kadmiel's descendants from Hodaviah's descendants	74

41 The singers ⌊included⌋:

•Asaph's descendants	128

---

a **1:1** Cyrus reigned 538–530 B.C.   b **1:5** Lit *everyone whose spirit God had stirred*   c **1:6** Lit *supported their hands*   d **1:10** Or *similar*
e **2:1** Nebuchadnezzar reigned 605–562 B.C.   f **2:2** Lit *the men of the people of Israel*

1:1 Cyrus. Cyrus the Great, founder of the greater Persian Empire, conquered Babylon without a struggle in 539 B.C. **spoken through Jeremiah.** God used Cyrus to fulfill Jeremiah's prophecy that the Jewish captivity in Babylon would last seventy years (Jer. 25:11-12). By the time the people returned and built the altar in

536 B.C., seventy years were nearly fulfilled (2 Chron. 36:22-23; Isa. 44:28). **1:3 build the house of the LORD.** Isaiah had referred to Cyrus by name 150 years earlier as the one who would allow the rebuilding of Jerusalem's temple (Isa. 44:28).

2:2 Zerubbabel. Listed in the genealogy of David (1 Chron. 3:19). **Jeshua.** This was Joshua, the high priest (Hag. 1:1).

2:40 Levites. During David's reign, 24,000 Levites assisted the temple priests and taught the Law. At the time of the return to Jerusalem, the ratio of Levites to priests was much smaller.

42 The gatekeepers' descendants ⌊included⌋:

Shallum's descendants, Ater's descendants,
Talmon's descendants, Akkub's descendants,
Hatita's descendants,
    Shobai's descendants, in all   139

43 The temple servants ⌊included⌋:

Ziha's descendants, Hasupha's descendants,
Tabbaoth's descendants, 44 Keros's descendants,
Siaha's descendants, Padon's descendants,
45 Lebanah's descendants, Hagabah's descendants,
Akkub's descendants, 46 Hagab's descendants,
Shalmai'sa descendants, Hanan's descendants,
47 Giddel's descendants, Gahar's descendants,
Reaiah's descendants, 48 Rezin's descendants,
Nekoda's descendants, Gazzam's descendants,
49 Uzza's descendants, Paseah's descendants,
Besai's descendants, 50 Asnah's descendants,
Meunim'sb descendants,
    Nephusim'sc descendants,
51 Bakbuk's descendants, Hakupha's descendants,
Harhur's descendants, 52 Bazluth's descendants,
Mehida's descendants, Harsha's descendants,
53 Barkos's descendants, Sisera's descendants,
Temah's descendants, 54 Neziah's descendants,
and Hatipha's descendants.

55 The descendants of Solomon's servants ⌊included⌋:

Sotai's descendants,
    Hassophereth's descendants,
    Peruda's descendants, 56 Jaalah's descendants,
Darkon's descendants, Giddel's descendants,
57 Shephatiah's descendants, Hattil's descendants,
Pochereth-hazzebaim's descendants,
    and Ami's descendants.
58 All the temple servants
and the descendants
    of Solomon's servants   392

59 The following are those who came from Tel-
melah, Tel-harsha, Cherub, Addan, and Immer but
were unable to prove that their families and ancestry
were Israelite:

60 Delaiah's descendants,
    Tobiah's descendants,
Nekoda's descendants   652

61 and from the descendants of the priests: the descendants of Habaiah, the descendants of Hakkoz, the

descendants of Barzillai—who had taken a wife from
the daughters of Barzillai the Gileadite and was called
by their name. 62 These searched for their entries in
the genealogical records, but they could not be found,
so they were disqualified from the priesthood. 63 The
governor ordered them not to eat the most holy things
until there was a priest who could consult the Urim
and Thummim.d

64 The whole combined assembly
    numbered   42,360
65 not including their 7,337 male
    and female slaves,
    and their 200 male and female singers.
66 They had 736 horses, 245 mules,
67 435 camels, and 6,720 donkeys.

Gifts for the Work

68 After they arrived at the LORD's house in Jerusalem, some of the family leaders gave freewill offerings
for the house of God in order to have it rebuilt on its
⌊original⌋ site. 69 Based on what they could give, they
gave 61,000 gold coins,e 6,250 poundsf of silver, and
100 priestly garments to the treasury for the project.
70 The priests, Levites, singers, gatekeepers, temple
servants, and some of the people settled in their towns,
and ⌊the rest of⌋ Israel ⌊settled⌋ in their towns.

Sacrifice Restored

3 By the seventh month, the Israelites had settled
in their towns, and the people gathered together
in Jerusalem. 2 Jeshua son of Jozadak and his brothers
the priests along with Zerubbabel son of Shealtiel and
his brothers began to build the altar of Israel's God in
order to offer •burnt offerings on it, as it is written in
the law of Moses the man of God. 3 They set up the
altar on its foundation and offered burnt offerings for
the morning and evening on it to the LORD even
though they feared the surrounding peoples. 4 They
celebrated the Festival of Booths as prescribed, and
⌊offered⌋ burnt offerings each day, based on the number specified by ordinance for each festival day. 5 After
that, ⌊they offered⌋ the regular burnt offering and the
offerings for the beginning of each monthg and for all
the LORD's appointed holy occasions, as well as the
freewill offerings brought toh the LORD.

6 On the first day of the seventh month they began to
offer burnt offerings to the LORD, even though the foundation of the LORD's temple had not ⌊yet⌋ been laid.
7 They gave money to the stonecutters and artisans, and

---

a 2:46 Alt Hb tradition reads Shamlai's or Salmai's   b 2:50 Alt Hb tradition reads Meinim's   c 2:50 Alt Hb tradition reads Nephisim's   d 2:63 Two
objects used to determine God's will; Ex 28:30   e 2:69 Lit drachmas   f 2:69 Lit 5,000 minas   g 3:5 Lit for the new moons   h 3:5 Lit well as those of
everyone making a freewill offering to

2:42 gatekeepers. The returning group included 139 Levite gatekeepers who prevented
unauthorized people from entering the temple's restricted area. During Solomon's reign,
there were 4,000 gatekeepers (1 Chron. 23:5;
2 Chron. 8:14).

2:59 unable to prove that their families and

ancestry were Israelite. Those who could not
prove their Levitical genealogy were excluded
from the priesthood. They were, however, allowed to return to Jerusalem.

2:66 736 horses. The large number of horses
indicates affluence. Previously, horses were
only used for war and ceremonies.

3:2 altar. The first job was to rebuild the altar of
burnt offerings essential for reestablishing the
sacrificial system that set the Jews apart.

3:7 Sidon and Tyre. Solomon purchased materials for the first temple from Sidon and Tyre
in Lebanon: well known for cedar forests and
expert woodworkers (2 Chron. 2:10-16). For

⌊gave⌋ food, drink, and oil to the people of Sidon and Tyre, so they could bring cedar wood from Lebanon to Joppa by sea, according to the authorization ⌊given⌋ them by King Cyrus of Persia.

Rebuilding the Temple

8 In the second month of the second year after they arrived at God's house in Jerusalem, Zerubbabel son of Shealtiel, Jeshua son of Jozadak, and the rest of their brothers, including the priests, the Levites, and all who had returned to Jerusalem from the captivity, began ⌊to build⌋. They appointed the Levites who were 20 years old or more to supervise the work on the LORD's house. 9 Jeshua with his sons and brothers, Kadmiel with his sons, and the sons of Judah[a] and of Henadad, with their sons and brothers, the Levites, joined together to supervise those working on the house of God.

Temple Foundation Completed

10 When the builders had laid the foundation of the LORD's temple, the priests, dressed in their robes and holding trumpets, and the Levites descended from •Asaph, holding cymbals, took their positions to praise the LORD, as King David of Israel had instructed. 11 They sang with praise and thanksgiving to the LORD: "For He is good; His faithful love to Israel endures forever." Then all the people gave a great shout of praise to the LORD because the foundation of the LORD's house had been laid.

12 But many of the older priests, Levites, and family leaders, who had seen the first temple, wept loudly when they saw the foundation of this house, but many ⌊others⌋ shouted joyfully. 13 The people could not distinguish the sound of the joyful shouting from that of the[b] weeping, because the people were shouting so loudly. And the sound was heard far away.

Opposition to Rebuilding the Temple

4 When the enemies of Judah and Benjamin heard that the returned exiles[c] were building a temple for the LORD, the God of Israel, 2 they approached Zerubbabel and the leaders of the families and said to them, "Let us build with you, for we also worship your God and have been sacrificing to Him[d] since the time King Esar-haddon of Assyria[e] brought us here."

3 But Zerubbabel, Jeshua, and the other leaders of Israel's families answered them, "You may have no part with us in building a house for our God, since we alone must build ⌊it⌋ for the LORD, the God of Israel, as King

Cyrus, the king of Persia has commanded us." 4 Then the people who were already in the land[f] discouraged[g] the people of Judah and made them afraid to build. 5 They also bribed officials ⌊to act⌋ against them to frustrate their plans throughout the reign of King Cyrus of Persia and until the reign of King Darius of Persia.[h]

Opposition to Rebuilding the City

6 At the beginning of the reign of Ahasuerus,[i] the people who were already in the land[f] wrote an accusation against the residents of Judah and Jerusalem. 7 During the time of ⌊King⌋ Artaxerxes of Persia,[j] Bishlam, Mithredath, Tabeel and the rest of his colleagues wrote to King Artaxerxes. The letter was written in Aramaic and translated.[k, l]

8 Rehum the chief deputy and Shimshai the scribe wrote a letter to King Artaxerxes concerning Jerusalem as follows:

9 ⌊From⌋ Rehum[m] the chief deputy, Shimshai the scribe, and the rest of their colleagues—the judges and magistrates[n] from Tripolis, Persia, Erech, Babylon, Susa (that is, the people of Elam),[o] 10 and the rest of the peoples whom the great and illustrious Ashurbanipal[p] deported and settled in the cities of Samaria and the region west of the Euphrates River.

11 This is the text of the letter they sent to him:

To King Artaxerxes from your servants, the men from the region west of the Euphrates River:

12 Let it be known to the king that the Jews who came from you have returned to us at Jerusalem. They are rebuilding that rebellious and evil city, finishing its walls, and repairing its foundations. 13 Let it now be known to the king that if that city is rebuilt and its walls are finished, they will not pay tribute, duty, or land tax, and the royal revenue[q] will suffer. 14 Since we have taken an oath of loyalty to the king,[r] and it is not right for us to witness his dishonor, we have sent to inform the king 15 that a search should be made in your fathers' record books. In these record books you will discover and verify that the city is a rebellious city, harmful to kings and provinces. There have been revolts in it since ancient times. That is why this city was destroyed. 16 We advise the king that if this city is rebuilt and its walls are

---

[a]3:9 Or Hodaviah; Ezr 2:40; Neh 7:43; 1 Esdras 5:58   [b]3:13 Lit the people   [c]4:1 Lit the sons of the exile   [d]4:2 Alt Hb tradition reads have not been sacrificing   [e]4:2 Esar-haddon reigned 681–669 B.C.; 2 Kg 19:37; Is 37:38   [f]4:4,6 Lit people of the land   [g]4:4 Lit relaxed the hands of   [h]4:5 Darius reigned 521–486 B.C.   [i]4:6 = Xerxes; he reigned 486–465 B.C.   [j]4:7 Artaxerxes reigned 465–425 B.C.   [k]4:7 Lit translated. Aramaic: [l]4:7 Ezr 4:8—6:18 is written in Aram.   [m]4:9 Lit Then Rehum   [n]4:9 Or ambassadors   [o]4:9 Aram obscure in this v.   [p]4:10 Lit Osnappar   [q]4:13 Aram obscure   [r]4:14 Lit have eaten the salt of the palace

---

the rebuilt temple, Cyrus authorized the sale of cedar logs.

3:10 trumpets. When David brought the ark to Jerusalem, priests blew trumpets and Asaph sounded cymbals (1 Chron. 16:5-6). This was repeated when Solomon returned the ark to the temple. Here again descen-

dants of Asaph play cymbals.

3:13 weeping. The old men could remember the splendor of Solomon's temple, destroyed fifty years earlier (586 B.C.), and they wept.

4:3 You may have no part with us. The Samaritans, who opposed rebuilding, offered their help in order to subvert the effort. The

Jewish leaders refused since they blended worship of God with idols.

4:10 Ashurbanipal. This Assyrian king had deported people to Samaria (in Israel) during 669-626 B.C. (2 Kings 17:24). Descendants of the deported Babylonians opposed the Jews' return.

finished, you will not have any possession west of the Euphrates.

Artaxerxes' Reply

17 The king sent a reply to his chief deputy Rehum, Shimshai the scribe, and the rest of their colleagues living in Samaria and elsewhere in the region west of the Euphrates River:

Greetings.

18 The letter you sent us has been translated and read[a] in my presence. 19 I issued a decree and a search was conducted. It was discovered that this city has had uprisings against kings since ancient times, and there have been rebellions and revolts in it. 20 Powerful kings have also ruled over Jerusalem and exercised authority over the whole region, and tribute, duty, and land tax were paid to them. 21 Therefore, issue an order for these men to stop, so that this city will not be rebuilt until a ⌊further⌋ decree has been pronounced by me. 22 See that you not neglect this matter. Otherwise, the damage will increase and the royal interests[b] will suffer.

23 As soon as the text of King Artaxerxes' letter was read to Rehum, Shimshai the scribe, and their colleagues, they immediately went to the Jews in Jerusalem and forcibly stopped them.

Rebuilding of the Temple Resumed

24 Now the construction of God's house in Jerusalem had stopped and remained at a standstill until the second 5 year of the reign of King Darius of Persia. 1 But when the prophets Haggai and Zechariah son of Iddo prophesied to the Jews who were in Judah and Jerusalem, in the name of the God of Israel who was over them, 2 Zerubbabel son of Shealtiel and Jeshua son of Jozadak began to rebuild God's house in Jerusalem. The prophets of God were with them, helping them.

3 At that time Tattenai the governor of the region west of the Euphrates River, Shethar-bozenai, and their colleagues came to the Jews and asked, "Who gave you the order to rebuild this temple and finish this structure?"[c] 4 They also asked them, "What are the names of the workers[d] who are constructing this building?" 5 But God was watching[e] over the Jewish elders. These men wouldn't stop them until a report was sent to Darius, so that they could receive written instructions about this ⌊matter⌋.

The Letter to Darius

6 This is the text of the letter that Tattenai the governor of the region west of the Euphrates River, Shethar-bozenai, and their colleagues, the officials in the region, sent to King Darius. 7 They sent him a report, written as follows:

To King Darius:

All greetings.

8 Let it be known to the king that we went to the house of the great God in the province of Judah. It is being built with cut[f] stones, and its beams are being set in the walls. This work is being done diligently and succeeding through the people's efforts. 9 So we questioned the elders and asked, "Who gave you the order to rebuild this temple and finish this structure?"[c] 10 We also asked them for their names, so that we could write down the names of their leaders for your information.

11 This is the reply they gave us:

We are the servants of the God of heaven and earth and are rebuilding the temple that was built many years ago, which a great king of Israel built and finished. 12 But since our fathers angered the God of heaven, He handed them over to King Nebuchadnezzar of Babylon, the Chaldean, who destroyed this temple and deported the people to Babylon. 13 However, in the first year of Cyrus king of Babylon, he issued a decree to rebuild this house of God. 14 He also took from the temple in Babylon the gold and silver articles of God's house that Nebuchadnezzar had taken from the temple in Jerusalem and carried ⌊them⌋ to the temple in Babylon. He released them from the temple in Babylon to a man named Sheshbazzar, the governor by the appointment of King Cyrus. 15 He told him, 'Take these articles, put them in the temple in Jerusalem, and let the house of God be rebuilt on its ⌊original⌋ site.' 16 Then this same Sheshbazzar came and laid the foundation of God's house in Jerusalem. It has been under construction from that time until now, yet it has not been completed.

17 So if it pleases the king, let a search of the royal archives[g] in Babylon be conducted ⌊to see⌋ if it is true that a decree was issued by King Cyrus to rebuild this house of God in Jerusalem. Let the king's decision regarding ⌊this matter⌋ be sent to us.

---

a 4:18 Or been read clearly   b 4:22 Lit the kings   c 5:3,9 Or finish its furnishings   d 5:4 One Aram ms, LXX, Syr; MT reads Then we told them exactly what the names of the men were   e 5:5 Lit But the eye of their God was   f 5:8 Or huge   g 5:17 Lit treasure house

---

4:13 tribute. The letter-writer tried to persuade Artaxerxes (465-424 B.C.) that if Jerusalem's walls were rebuilt, the city would no longer pay taxes and capture part of his territory.

4:21 issue an order. The archival search revealed that the people of Jerusalem had revolted against the Babylonians. Artaxerxes temporarily ordered the rebuilding to stop, but left the way open for future completion. When they received his order, the officials stopped the work, probably destroying sections of the wall already repaired (Neh. 2:12-16).

5:1 Haggai and Zechariah. Two important prophets who favored resumption of work on the temple (Hag. 1:1-3; Zech. 1:1, 16).

5:6 King Darius. In order to verify the report of the Jewish leaders, the governor inquired whether Darius had authorized the work.

5:11 rebuilding the temple. The Jews told Tattenai about Solomon and his temple. They said it had been destroyed and that they had been

Darius' Search

6 King Darius gave the order, and they searched in the library of Babylon in the archives.[a] 2 But it was in the fortress of Ecbatana in the province of Media that a scroll was found with this record written on it:

3 In the first year of King Cyrus, he issued a decree concerning the house of God in Jerusalem:

Let the house be rebuilt as a place for offering sacrifices, and let its ⌊original⌋ foundations be retained.[b] Its height is to be 90 feet[c] and its width 90 feet,[c] 4 with three layers of cut[d] stones and one of timber. The cost is to be paid from the royal treasury. 5 The gold and silver articles of God's house that Nebuchadnezzar took from the temple in Jerusalem and carried to Babylon must also be returned. They are to be brought to the temple in Jerusalem, where they belong,[e] and put into the house of God.

Darius' Decree

6 Therefore, you must stay away from that place, Tattenai governor of the region west of the Euphrates River, Shethar-bozenai, and your[f] colleagues, the officials in the region. 7 Leave the construction of this house of God alone. Let the governor and elders of the Jews rebuild this house of God on its ⌊original⌋ site.

8 I hereby issue a decree concerning what you must do, so that the elders of the Jews can rebuild this house of God:

The cost is to be paid in full to these men out of the royal revenues from the taxes of the region west of the Euphrates River, so that the ⌊work⌋ will not stop. 9 Whatever is needed—young bulls, rams, and lambs for •burnt offerings to the God of heaven, or wheat, salt, wine, and oil, as requested by the priests in Jerusalem—let it be given to them every day without fail, 10 so that they can offer sacrifices of pleasing aroma to the God of heaven and pray for the life of the king and his sons.

11 I also issue a decree concerning any man who interferes with this directive:

Let a beam be torn from his house and raised up; he will be impaled on it, and his house will be made into a garbage dump because of this ⌊offense⌋. 12 May the God who caused His name to dwell there overthrow any king or people who dares[g] to harm or interfere with this house of God in Jerusalem. I, Darius, have issued the decree. Let it be carried out diligently.

13 Then Tattenai governor of the region west of the Euphrates River, Shethar-bozenai, and their colleagues diligently carried out what King Darius had decreed. 14 So the Jewish elders continued successfully with the building under the prophesying of Haggai the prophet and Zechariah son of Iddo. They finished the building according to the command of the God of Israel and the decrees of Cyrus, Darius, and King Artaxerxes of Persia. 15 This house was completed on the third day of the month of Adar[h] in the sixth year of the reign of King Darius.

Temple Dedication and the Passover

16 Then the Israelites, including the priests, the Levites, and the rest of the exiles, celebrated the dedication of this house of God with joy. 17 For the dedication of God's house they offered 100 bulls, 200 rams, and 400 lambs, as well as 12 male goats as a •sin offering for all Israel—one for each Israelite tribe. 18 They also appointed the priests by their divisions and the Levites by their groups to the service of God in Jerusalem, according to what is written in the book of Moses.

19 The exiles observed the •Passover on the fourteenth day of the first month. 20 All of the priests and Levites were ceremonially clean, because they had purified themselves. They killed the Passover lamb for themselves, their priestly brothers, and all the exiles. 21 The Israelites who had returned from exile ate ⌊it⌋, together with all who had separated themselves from the uncleanness of the Gentiles of the land[i] in order to worship the LORD, the God of Israel. 22 They observed the Festival of Unleavened Bread for seven days with joy, because the LORD had made them joyful, having changed the Assyrian king's attitude toward them, so that he supported them[j] in the work on the house of the God of Israel.

Ezra's Arrival

7 After these events, during the reign of King Artaxerxes of Persia, Ezra—

Seraiah's son, Azariah's son,
Hilkiah's son, 2 Shallum's son,
Zadok's son, Ahitub's son,
3   Amariah's son, Azariah's son,

---

a6:1 Lit Babylon where the treasures were stored   b6:3 Lit be brought forth   c6:3 Lit 60 cubits   d6:4 Or huge   e6:5 Lit Jerusalem, to its place,   f6:6 Lit their   g6:12 Lit who stretches out its hand   h6:15 = February–March   i6:21 Lit land to them   j6:22 Lit their hands

---

deported because of their sin. They wanted Darius' decree to be found so that the temple could be completed. They were allowed to continue working while waiting.

6:7 Leave … alone. After reading Cyrus's official decree, Darius gave instructions that temple reconstruction be funded by taxes, and all nec-

essaries for sacrifices supplied. Work resumed in the second year of his reign (520 B.C.).

6:15 This house was completed. The temple was completed 70.5 years after its destruction and 21 years after reconstruction began (515 B.C.).

6:21 separated. God's prohibition against

marrying foreigners was specifically meant for the Jewish people to keep their race set apart for God. The Jews were only permitted to marry foreigners who truly converted. It was never intended as a timeless prohibition of intermarriage. Later, in New Testament times, the law of grace superseded Old Testament commands,

Meraioth's son, [4] Zerahiah's son,
Uzzi's son, Bukki's son,
[5] Abishua's son, Phinehas's son,
Eleazar's son, Aaron the chief priest's son

[6] —came up from Babylon. He was a scribe skilled in the law of Moses, which the LORD, the God of Israel, had given. The king had granted him everything he requested because the hand of the LORD his God was on him. [7] Some of the Israelites, priests, Levites, singers, gatekeepers, and temple servants accompanied ⌊him⌋ to Jerusalem in the seventh year of King Artaxerxes.

[8] Ezra[a] came to Jerusalem in the fifth month, during the seventh year of the king. [9] He began the journey from Babylon on the first day of the first month and arrived in Jerusalem on the first day of the fifth month. The gracious hand of his God was on him, [10] because Ezra had determined in his heart to study the law of the LORD, obey ⌊it⌋, and teach ⌊its⌋ statutes and ordinances in Israel.

Letter from Artaxerxes

[11] This is the text of the letter King Artaxerxes gave to Ezra the priest and scribe, an expert in matters of the LORD's commandments and statutes for Israel:[b]

[12] Artaxerxes, king of kings, to Ezra the priest, an expert in the law of the God of heaven:

Greetings ⌊to you⌋.

[13] I issue a decree that any of the Israelites in my kingdom, including their priests and Levites, who want to go to Jerusalem, may go with you. [14] You are sent by the king and his seven counselors to evaluate Judah and Jerusalem according to the law of your God, which is in your possession. [15] ⌊You are⌋ also to bring the silver and gold the king and his counselors have willingly given to the God of Israel, whose dwelling is in Jerusalem, [16] and all the silver and gold you receive throughout the province of Babylon, together with the freewill offerings given by the people and the priests to the house of their God in Jerusalem. [17] Then, you are to buy with this money as many bulls, rams, and lambs as needed, along with their •grain and drink offerings, and offer them on the altar at the house of your God in Jerusalem. [18] You may do whatever seems best to you and your brothers with the rest of the silver and gold, according to the will of your God. [19] You must deliver to the God of Jerusalem all the articles given to you for the service of the house of your God. [20] You may use the royal treasury to pay for anything else you have to supply ⌊to meet⌋ the needs of the house of your God.

[21] I, King Artaxerxes, issue a decree to all the treasurers in the region west of the Euphrates River:

Whatever Ezra the priest and expert in the law of the God of heaven asks of you must be provided promptly, [22] up to 7,500 pounds[c] of silver, 500 bushels[d] of wheat, 550 gallons[e] of wine, 550 gallons[e] of oil, and salt without limit.[f] [23] Whatever is commanded by the God of heaven must be done diligently for the house of the God of heaven, so that wrath will not fall on the realm of the king and his sons. [24] Be advised that tribute, duty, and land tax must not be imposed on any priests, Levites, singers, doorkeepers, temple servants, or ⌊other⌋ servants of this house of God.

[25] And you, Ezra, according to[g] God's wisdom that you possess, appoint magistrates and judges to judge all the people in the region west of the Euphrates who know the laws of your God and to teach anyone who does not know ⌊them⌋. [26] Anyone who does not keep the law of your God and the law of the king, let a fair judgment be executed against him, whether death, banishment, confiscation of property, or imprisonment.

[27] Praise the LORD God of our fathers, who has put it into the king's mind to glorify the house of the LORD in Jerusalem, [28] and who has shown favor to me before the king, his counselors, and all his powerful officers. So I took courage because I was strengthened by the LORD my God,[h] and I gathered Israelite leaders to return with me.

Those Returning with Ezra

8 These are the family leaders and the genealogical records of those who returned with me from Babylon during the reign of King Artaxerxes:

[2] Gershom, from Phinehas's descendants;
Daniel, from Ithamar's descendants;
Hattush, from David's descendants,
[3] who was of Shecaniah's descendants;
Zechariah, from Parosh's descendants,
and 150 men with him who were registered
by genealogy;

---

[a]7:8 LXX, Syr, Vg read *They*   [b]7:11 Ezr 7:12–26 is written in Aram.   [c]7:22 Lit *100 talents*   [d]7:22 Lit *100 cors*   [e]7:22 Lit *100 baths*   [f]7:22 Lit *without instruction*   [g]7:25 Lit *to your*   [h]7:28 Lit *because the hand of the LORD my God was on me*

---

so that distinctions between Jews and other races became meaningless (see Eph. 2:11-22; Gal. 3:27-29).

7:1 during the reign of King Artaxerxes. The events in Esther occurred during this 57 year gap.

7:16 freewill offerings given by the people.

Voluntary gifts from the Jewish people who remained in Babylon. God accepts gifts from those who do not know Him (the king and his counselors in verse 15 and the people of Babylon in verse 16) and from His followers. But He rejects gifts from people who appear to know Him but whose hearts are far from Him (Isa. 1:10-15).

7:26 Anyone who does not keep the law ... death, banishment, confiscation of property, or imprisonment. The king gave Ezra authority to administer justice to the Jews in Jerusalem, Syria, Phoenicia, and Palestine. Ezra later used this authority to punish sin.

8:1 These are the family leaders. There were

4 Eliehoenai son of Zerahiah
from Pahath-moab's descendants,
and 200 men with him;

5 Shecaniah[a] son of Jahaziel
from Zattu's descendants,
and 300 men with him;

6 Ebed son of Jonathan
from Adin's descendants,
and 50 men with him;

7 Jeshaiah son of Athaliah
from Elam's descendants,
and 70 men with him;

8 Zebadiah son of Michael
from Shephatiah's descendants,
and 80 men with him;

9 Obadiah son of Jehiel
from Joab's descendants,
and 218 men with him;

10 Shelomith[b] son of Josiphiah
from Bani's descendants,
and 160 men with him;

11 Zechariah son of Bebai
from Bebai's descendants,
and 28 men with him;

12 Johanan son of Hakkatan
from Azgad's descendants,
and 110 men with him;

13 these are the last ones,
from Adonikam's descendants,
and their names are:
Eliphelet, Jeuel, and Shemaiah,
and 60 men with them;

14 Uthai and Zaccur[c]
from Bigvai's descendants,
and 70 men with him.

15 I gathered them at the river[d] that flows to Ahava, and we camped there for three days. I searched among the people and priests, but found no Levites there. 16 Then I summoned the leaders: Eliezer, Ariel, Shemaiah, Elnathan, Jarib, Elnathan, Nathan, Zechariah, and Meshullam, as well as the teachers Joiarib and Elnathan. 17 I sent them to Iddo, the leader at Casiphia, with a message for[e] him and his brothers, the temple servants at Casiphia, that they should bring us ministers for the house of our God. 18 Since the gracious hand of our God was on us, they brought us Sherebiah—a man of insight from the descendants of Mahli, a descendant of Levi son of Israel—along with his sons

and brothers, 18 men, 19 plus Hashabiah, along with Jeshaiah, from the descendants of Merari, and his brothers and their sons, 20 men. 20 There were also 220 of the temple servants, who had been appointed by David and the leaders for the work of the Levites. All were identified by name.

Preparing to Return

21 I proclaimed a fast by the Ahava River,[f] so that we might humble ourselves before our God and ask Him for a safe journey for us, our children, and all our possessions. 22 |I did this| because I was ashamed to ask the king for infantry and cavalry to protect us from enemies during the journey, since we had told him, "The hand of our God is gracious to all who seek Him, but His great anger is against all who abandon Him." 23 So we fasted and pleaded with our God about this, and He granted our request.

24 I selected 12 of the leading priests, along with Sherebiah, Hashabiah, and 10 of their brothers. 25 I weighed out to them the silver, the gold, and the articles—the contribution for the house of our God that the king, his counselors, his leaders, and all the Israelites who were present had offered. 26 I weighed out to them 24 tons[g] of silver, silver articles weighing 7,500 pounds,[h] 7,500 pounds[h] of gold, 27 20 gold bowls worth 1,000 gold coins,[i] and two articles of fine gleaming bronze, as valuable as gold. 28 Then I said to them, "You are holy to the LORD, and the articles are holy. The silver and gold are a freewill offering to the LORD God of your fathers. 29 Guard |them| carefully until you weigh |them| out in the chambers of the LORD's house before the leading priests, Levites, and heads of the Israelite families in Jerusalem." 30 So the priests and Levites took charge of the silver, the gold, and the articles that had been weighed out, to bring |them| to the house of our God in Jerusalem.

Arrival in Jerusalem

31 We set out from the Ahava River[f] on the twelfth |day| of the first month to go to Jerusalem. We were strengthened by our God,[j] and He protected us from the power of the enemy and from ambush along the way. 32 So we arrived at Jerusalem and rested there for three days. 33 On the fourth day the silver, the gold, and the articles were weighed out in the house of our God into the care of Meremoth the priest, son of Uriah. Eleazar son of Phinehas was with him. The Levites Jozabad son of Jeshua and Noadiah son of Binnui were also with

---

a 8:5 LXX, 1 Esdras 8:32; MT reads the descendants of Shecaniah b 8:10 Some LXX; 1 Esdras 8:36; MT reads the descendants of Shelomith c 8:14 Alt Hb tradition, some LXX read Zabud d 8:15 Or canal e 8:17 Lit Casiphia, and I put in their mouth the words to speak to f 8:21,31 Or Canal g 8:26 Lit 650 talents h 8:26 Lit 100 talents i 8:27 Or 1,000 drachmas j 8:31 Lit The hand of our God was on us

---

1,496 heads of families who returned to Jerusalem with Ezra. Including women and children, the group probably numbered 5,000 people—far fewer than the 50,000 on the first return.

8:15 found no Levites there. Ezra discovered that the group lacked Levites to conduct tem-

ple ministry and teach the Law. Levites were also responsible for taking the precious metals and utensils back to Jerusalem.

8:17 bring us ministers for the house of our God. Ezra sent a group of leaders to Casiphia, a place probably on the Tigris River near modern Baghdad, to recruit Levites and temple ser-

vants. There may have been a Jewish temple in Casiphia.

8:18 Sherebiah. They found 38 Levites from the families of Sherebiah and Jeshaiah and 220 temple servants willing to go to Jerusalem.

8:22 I was ashamed to ask the king. Ezra did not want to ask for soldiers and horsemen to

them. ³⁴ Everything was ⌊verified⌋ by number and weight, and the total weight was recorded at that time.

³⁵ The exiles who had returned from the captivity offered •burnt offerings to the God of Israel: 12 bulls for all Israel, 96 rams, and 77 lambs, along with 12 male goats as a •sin offering. All this was a burnt offering for the LORD. ³⁶ They also delivered the king's edicts to the royal satraps and governors of the region west of the Euphrates, so that they would support the people and the house of God.

Israel's Intermarriage with Pagans

9 After these things had been done, the leaders approached me and said: "The people of Israel, the priests, and the Levites have not separated themselves from the surrounding peoples whose detestable practices are like those of the Canaanites, Hittites, Perizzites, Jebusites, Ammonites, Moabites, Egyptians, and Amorites. ² Indeed, they have taken some of their daughters as wives for themselves and their sons, so that the holy people^a has become mixed with the surrounding peoples. The leaders^b and officials have taken the lead in this unfaithfulness!" ³ When I heard this report, I tore my tunic and robe, pulled out some of the hair from my head and beard, and sat down devastated.

Ezra's Confession

⁴ Everyone who trembled at the words of the God of Israel gathered around me, because of the unfaithfulness of the exiles, while I sat devastated until the evening offering. ⁵ At the evening offering, I got up from my humiliation, with my tunic and robe torn. Then I fell on my knees and spread out my hands to the LORD my God. ⁶ And I said:

My God, I am ashamed and embarrassed to lift my face toward You, my God, because our iniquities are higher than ⌊our⌋ heads and our guilt is as high as the heavens. ⁷ Our guilt has been terrible from the days of our fathers until the present. Because of our iniquities we have been handed over, along with our kings and priests, to the surrounding kings, and to the sword, captivity, plundering, and open shame, as it is today. ⁸ But now, for a brief moment, grace has come from the LORD our God to preserve a remnant for us and give us a stake in His holy place. Even in our slavery, God has given us new life and light to our eyes. ⁹ Though we are slaves, our God has not abandoned us in our slavery. He has extended grace to us in the presence of the Persian kings, giving us new life, so that we can rebuild the house of our God and repair its ruins, to give us a wall in Judah and Jerusalem.

¹⁰ Now, our God, what can we say in light of^c this? For we have abandoned the commandments ¹¹ You gave through Your servants the prophets, saying: "The land you are entering to possess is an impure land. The surrounding peoples have filled it from end to end with their uncleanness by their impurity and detestable practices. ¹² So do not give your daughters to their sons in marriage or take their daughters for your sons. Never seek their peace or prosperity, so that you will be strong, eat the good things of the land, and leave ⌊it⌋ as an inheritance to your sons forever." ¹³ After all that has happened to us because of our evil deeds and terrible guilt—though You, our God, have punished ⌊us⌋ less than our sins ⌊deserve⌋ and have allowed us to survive^d — ¹⁴ should we break Your commandments again and intermarry with the peoples who commit these detestable practices? Wouldn't You become ⌊so⌋ angry with us that You would destroy us, leaving no survivors? ¹⁵ LORD God of Israel, You are righteous, for we survive as a remnant today. Here we are before You with our guilt, though no one can stand in Your presence because of this.

Sending Away Foreign Wives

10 While Ezra prayed and confessed, weeping and falling facedown before the house of God, an extremely large assembly of Israelite men, women, and children gathered around him. The people also wept bitterly. ² Then Shecaniah son of Jehiel, an Elamite, responded to Ezra: "We have been unfaithful to our God by marrying foreign women from the surrounding peoples, but there is still hope for Israel in spite of this. ³ Let us therefore make a covenant before our God to send away all the ⌊foreign⌋ wives and their children, according to the counsel of my lord and of those who tremble at the commandment of our God. Let it be done according to the law. ⁴ Get up, for this matter is your responsibility, and we support you. Be strong and take action!"

⁵ Then Ezra got up and made the leading priests, Levites, and all Israel take an oath to do what had been said; so they took the oath. ⁶ Ezra then went from the house of God, walked to the chamber of Jehohanan son of Eliashib, where he spent the night.^e He did not eat food or drink water, because he was mourning over the unfaithfulness of the exiles.

---

^a**9:2** Lit seed   ^b**9:2** Lit hand of the leaders   ^c**9:10** Lit say after   ^d**9:13** Lit and gave us a remnant like this   ^e**10:6** 1 Esdras 9:2, Syr; MT, Vg read he went

---

protect the group because he had publicly said that God would take care of His people. Later Nehemiah accepted a military escort for his return to Jerusalem.

9:2 leaders ... have taken the lead. The Law expressly forbade marrying Israel's pagan neighbors (Ex. 34:16). This practice often led Jews to worship the gods of their spouses (Neh. 13:23-27). Leaders, if anyone, should have known better.

9:6 iniquities. Ezra feared that God would send the people into captivity again.

9:8 light to our eyes. God gave the light of His will to those in sin's darkness. Not only were they free from the Babylonian captivity, but also from sin's bondage. Ezra warned against choosing to become its slave again.

10:5 Ezra ... the leading priests ... take an oath. A covenant was the most binding form of agreement. While God clearly prohibits and even "hates" divorce (Mal. 2:16), intermarriage

7 They circulated a proclamation throughout Judah and Jerusalem that all the exiles should gather at Jerusalem. 8 Whoever did not come within three days would forfeit all his possessions, according to the decision of the leaders and elders, and would be excluded from the assembly of the exiles.

9 So all the men of Judah and Benjamin gathered in Jerusalem within the three days. On the twentieth ⌊day⌋ of the ninth month, all the people sat in the square at the house of God, trembling because of this matter and because of the heavy rain. 10 Then Ezra the priest stood up and said to them, "You have been unfaithful by marrying foreign women, adding to Israel's guilt. 11 Therefore, make a confession to the LORD God of your fathers and do His will. Separate yourselves from the surrounding peoples and ⌊your⌋ foreign wives."

12 Then all the assembly responded with a loud voice: "Yes, we will do as you say! 13 But there are many people, and it is the rainy season. We don't have the stamina to stay out in the open. This isn't something that can be done in a day or two, for we have rebelled terribly in this matter. 14 Let our leaders represent the entire assembly. Then let all those in our towns who have married foreign women come at appointed times, together with the elders and judges of each town, in order to avert the fierce anger of our God concerning[a] this matter." 15 Only Jonathan son of Asahel and Jahzeiah son of Tikvah opposed this, with Meshullam and Shabbethai the Levite supporting them.

16 The exiles did what had been proposed. Ezra the priest selected men[b] who were family leaders, all ⌊identified⌋ by name, to represent[c] their ancestral houses. They convened on the first day of the tenth month to investigate the matter, 17 and by the first day of the first month they had dealt with all the men who had married foreign women.

Those Married to Foreign Wives

18 ⌊The following⌋ were found to have married foreign women from the descendants of the priests:

from the descendants of Jeshua son of Jozadak and his brothers: Maaseiah, Eliezer, Jarib, and Gedaliah. 19 They pledged[d] to send their wives away, and being guilty, ⌊they offered⌋ a ram from the flock for their guilt;

20 Hanani and Zebadiah
from Immer's descendants;

21 Maaseiah, Elijah, Shemaiah, Jehiel, and Uzziah from Harim's descendants;

22 Elioenai, Maaseiah, Ishmael, Nethanel, Jozabad, and Elasah from Pashhur's descendants.

23 The Levites:

Jozabad, Shimei, Kelaiah (that is Kelita), Pethahiah, Judah, and Eliezer.

24 The singers:

Eliashib.

The gatekeepers:

Shallum, Telem, and Uri.

25 The Israelites:

Parosh's descendants: Ramiah, Izziah, Malchijah, Mijamin, Eleazar, Malchijah,[e] and Benaiah;

26 Elam's descendants: Mattaniah, Zechariah, Jehiel, Abdi, Jeremoth, and Elijah;

27 Zattu's descendants: Elioenai, Eliashib, Mattaniah, Jeremoth, Zabad, and Aziza;

28 Bebai's descendants: Jehohanan, Hananiah, Zabbai, and Athlai;

29 Bani's descendants: Meshullam, Malluch, Adaiah, Jashub, Sheal, and Jeremoth;

30 Pahath-moab's descendants: Adna, Chelal, Benaiah, Maaseiah, Mattaniah, Bezalel, Binnui, and Manasseh;

31 Harim's descendants: Eliezer, Isshijah, Malchijah, Shemaiah, Shimeon,

32 Benjamin, Malluch, and Shemariah;

33 Hashum's descendants: Mattenai, Mattattah, Zabad, Eliphelet, Jeremai, Manasseh, and Shimei;

34 Bani's descendants: Maadai, Amram, Uel,

35 Benaiah, Bedeiah, Cheluhi,

36 Vaniah, Meremoth, Eliashib,

37 Mattaniah, Mattenai, Jaasu,

38 Bani, Binnui, Shimei,

39 Shelemiah, Nathan, Adaiah,

40 Machnadebai, Shashai, Sharai,

41 Azarel, Shelemiah, Shemariah,

42 Shallum, Amariah, and Joseph;

43 Nebo's descendants: Jeiel, Mattithiah, Zabad, Zebina, Jaddai, Joel, and Benaiah.

44 All of these had married foreign women, and some of the wives had borne children.

---

a **10:14** Some Hb mss, LXX, Vg; other Hb mss read *until*   b **10:16** 1 Esdras 9:16, Syr; MT, Vg read *priest and men were selected*   c **10:16** Lit *name, for*   d **10:19** Lit *gave their hand*   e **10:25** Some LXX mss, 1 Esdras 9:26 read *Hashabiah*

---

led the Israelites into worship of false deities and seduced them away from God. The Law permitted marriage with outside women only if they converted.

10:7 proclamation. Whoever ignored the proclamation would be stripped of legal rights. **10:8 within three days.** Even though it was the rainy season, the people gathered in the square east of the temple. They feared both God's wrath and family breakups. **forfeit.** Confiscated property was sold; proceeds went into the temple treasury.

10:16 investigate the matter. The elders and judges of each town knew whether the women worshiped the Lord or idols. All the marriages were examined within three months.

INTRODUCTION TO
NEHEMIAH

PERSONAL READING PLAN

- ❏ Nehemiah 1:1–2:20
- ❏ Nehemiah 3:1-32
- ❏ Nehemiah 4:1-23
- ❏ Nehemiah 5:1–6:14
- ❏ Nehemiah 6:15–7:73a
- ❏ Nehemiah 7:73b–8:18

- ❏ Nehemiah 9:1-37
- ❏ Nehemiah 9:38–10:39
- ❏ Nehemiah 11:1-36
- ❏ Nehemiah 12:1-26
- ❏ Nehemiah 12:27-47
- ❏ Nehemiah 13:1-31

AUTHOR

The book is named for the principal character, Nehemiah, but the book does not state its author. This unknown author may have also helped to compile the Book of Ezra and perhaps 1 and 2 Chronicles, as these books share many common characteristics:

1. A fondness for lists, for the descriptions of religious festivals, and for the phrases "heads of families" and "the house of God."

2. The prominence of Levites and temple personnel.

3. The almost exclusive use of the Hebrew words for "singer," "gatekeeper," and "temple servants."

DATE

With an unstated author, precise dating is difficult to determine. The events narrated cover the years circa 445-432 B.C.

THEME

Restoration of the second temple and revival of the people, providing a legacy of God-given leadership principles.

HISTORICAL BACKGROUND

Originally this work was one book, united with Ezra. In the Latin Bible, Ezra and Nehemiah are entitled 1 and 2 Esdras. This book complements Ezra in reporting the restoration of Israel after 70 years of captivity in Babylon. Nehemiah's distress over the broken-down walls of Jerusalem (1:3) is probably caused by the episode in Ezra 4:7-23. Ezra's return had revived spiritual and nationalistic fervor in God's people so that they worked to rebuild the walls of Jerusalem (chapters 8-9). But the completion of that task apparently fell to governor Nehemiah, a man dedicated to God.

CHARACTERISTICS

This book weaves together various lists with first-person and third-person memoirs of Nehemiah, who is the lead actor in this drama. Some of the most moving prayers outside the Psalms are found here (1:5-11; 9:5b-37). Sounding like a modern dramatic story, Nehemiah describes the rebuilding of the Jerusalem walls. The physical condition of the walls (chapters 1-7) parallels the spiritual condition of the people. As the walls are restored, the people are rehabilitated (chapters 8-13). As Nehemiah follows God wholeheartedly, he models invaluable, God-given leadership principles for all types of situations.

1

The words of Nehemiah son of Hacaliah:

News from Jerusalem

During the month of Chislev in the twentieth year,[a] when I was in the fortress city of Susa, [2] Hanani, one of my brothers, arrived with men from Judah, and I questioned them about Jerusalem and the Jewish remnant that had returned from exile. [3] They said to me, "The survivors in the province, who returned from the exile, are in great trouble and disgrace. Jerusalem's wall has been broken down, and its gates have been burned down."

Nehemiah's Prayer

[4] When I heard these words, I sat down and wept. I mourned for a number of days, fasting and praying before the God of heaven. [5] I said,

LORD God of heaven, the great and awe-inspiring God who keeps His gracious covenant with those who love Him and keep His commands, [6] let Your eyes be open and Your ears be attentive to hear Your servant's prayer that I now pray to You day and night for Your servants, the Israelites. I confess the sins[b] we have committed against You. Both I and my father's house have sinned. [7] We have acted corruptly toward You and have not kept the commands, statutes, and ordinances You gave Your servant Moses. [8] Please remember what You commanded Your servant Moses: "⌊If⌋ you are unfaithful, I will scatter you among the peoples. [9] But if you return to Me and carefully observe My commands, even though your exiles were banished to the ends of the earth,[c] I will gather them from there and bring them to the place where I chose to have My name dwell." [10] They are Your servants and Your people. You redeemed ⌊them⌋ by Your great power and strong hand. [11] Please, Lord, let Your ear be attentive to the prayer of Your servant and to that of Your servants who delight to revere Your name. Give Your servant success today, and have compassion on him in the presence of this man.[d]

⌊At the time,⌋ I was the king's cupbearer.

Nehemiah Sent to Jerusalem

2

During the month of Nisan in the twentieth year[e] of King Artaxerxes, when wine was set before him, I took the wine and gave it to the king. I had never been sad in his presence, [2] so the king said to me, "Why are you[f] sad, when you aren't sick? This is nothing but sadness of heart."

I was overwhelmed with fear [3] and replied to the king, "May the king live forever! Why should I[g] not be sad when the city where my ancestors are buried lies in ruins and its gates have been destroyed by fire?"

[4] Then the king asked me, "What is your request?"

So I prayed to the God of heaven [5] and answered the king, "If it pleases the king, and if your servant has found favor with you, send me to Judah and to the city where my ancestors are buried,[h] so that I may rebuild it."

[6] The king, with the queen seated beside him, asked me, "How long will your journey take, and when will you return?" So I gave him a definite time, and it pleased the king to send me.

[7] I also said to the king: "If it pleases the king, let me have letters ⌊written⌋ to the governors of the region west of the Euphrates River, so that they will grant me ⌊safe⌋ passage until I reach Judah. [8] And ⌊let me have⌋ a letter ⌊written⌋ to Asaph, keeper of the king's forest, so that he will give me timber to rebuild the gates of the temple's fortress, the city wall, and the home where I will live."[i] The king granted my ⌊requests⌋, for I was graciously strengthened by my God.[j]

[9] I went to the governors of the region west of the Euphrates and gave them the king's letters. The king had also sent officers of the infantry and cavalry with me. [10] When Sanballat the Horonite and Tobiah the Ammonite official heard that someone had come to seek the well-being of the Israelites, they were greatly displeased.

Preparing to Rebuild the Walls

[11] After I arrived in Jerusalem and had been there three days, [12] I got up at night and ⌊took⌋ a few men with me. I didn't tell anyone what my God had laid on my heart to do for Jerusalem. The only animal I took[k] was the one I was riding. [13] I went out at night through the Valley Gate toward the Serpent's[l] Well and the Dung Gate, and I inspected the walls of Jerusalem that had been broken down and its gates that had been destroyed by fire. [14] I went on to the Fountain Gate and the King's Pool, but farther down it became too narrow for my animal to go through. [15] So I went up at night by way of the valley and inspected the wall. Then heading back, I entered through the Valley Gate and returned. [16] The officials did not know where I had gone or what I was doing, for I had not yet told the Jews, priests,

---

a1:1 The twentieth year of King Artaxerxes of Persia, November–December 446 (or 445) B.C. b1:6 Lit sins of the Israelites c1:9 Lit skies d1:11 = the king e2:1 March–April 445 (or 444) B.C. f2:2 Lit Why is your face g2:3 Lit my face h2:5 Lit city, the house of the graves of my fathers, i2:8 Lit enter j2:8 Lit for the gracious hand of my God was on me k2:12 Lit animal with me l2:13 Or Dragon's

---

1:1 Nehemiah. Nehemiah served as personal cupbearer to King Artaxerxes.

1:2 Hanani. Nehemiah's brother brought him a disturbing report that Jerusalem's wall was broken down and its gates were burned.

1:6 I now pray to You. Nehemiah wept, fasted, and prayed over the condition of Jerusalem.

1:10 by Your great power. Recalling God's work on behalf of His people in the past (Ex. 32:11), Nehemiah asked Him to help them again.

2:3–6 Nehemiah received permission from the king to go to Jerusalem to rebuild its walls.

2:11 had been there three days. When he arrived in the city, Nehemiah prepared himself with prayer and research before trusting a few men with his plans.

2:13 inspected the walls of Jerusalem. He surveyed the walls at night, perhaps to make plans before informing others about his intentions.

nobles, officials, or the rest of those who would be doing the work. [17] So I said to them, "You see the trouble we are in. Jerusalem lies in ruins and its gates have been burned down. Come, let's rebuild Jerusalem's wall, so that we will no longer be a disgrace." [18] I told them how the gracious hand of my God had been on me, and what the king had said to me.

They said, "Let's start rebuilding," and they were encouraged[a] to ⌊do⌋ this good work.

[19] When Sanballat the Horonite, Tobiah the Ammonite official, and Geshem the Arab heard ⌊about this⌋, they mocked and despised us, and said, "What is this you're doing? Are you rebelling against the king?"

[20] I gave them this reply, "The God of heaven is the One who will grant us success. We, His servants, will start building, but you have no share, right, or historic claim in Jerusalem."

Rebuilding the Walls

3 Eliashib the high priest and his fellow priests began rebuilding the Sheep Gate. They dedicated it and installed its doors. ⌊After building the wall⌋ to the Tower of the Hundred and the Tower of Hananel, they dedicated it. [2] The men of Jericho built next to Eliashib, and next to them Zaccur son of Imri built.

Fish Gate

[3] The sons of Hassenaah built the Fish Gate. They built it with beams and installed its doors, bolts, and bars. [4] Next to them Meremoth son of Uriah, son of Hakkoz, made repairs. Beside them Meshullam son of Berechiah, son of Meshezabel, made repairs. Next to them Zadok son of Baana made repairs. [5] Beside them the Tekoites made repairs, but their nobles did not lift a finger to help[b] their supervisors.

Old Gate, Broad Wall, and Tower of the Ovens

[6] Joiada son of Paseah and Meshullam son of Besodeiah repaired the Old[c] Gate. They built it with beams and installed its doors, bolts, and bars. [7] Next to them Melatiah the Gibeonite, Jadon the Meronothite, and the men of Gibeon and Mizpah, who were under the authority[d] of the governor of the region west of the Euphrates River. [8] After him Uzziel son of Harhaiah, the goldsmith, made repairs, and next to him Hananiah son of the perfumer made repairs. They restored Jerusalem as far as the Broad Wall.

[9] Next to them Rephaiah son of Hur, ruler over half the district of Jerusalem, made repairs. [10] After them Jedaiah son of Harumaph made repairs across from his house. Next to him Hattush the son of Hashabneiah made repairs. [11] Malchijah son of Harim and Hasshub son of Pahath-moab made repairs to another section, as well as to the Tower of the Ovens. [12] Beside him Shallum son of Hallohesh, ruler over half the district of Jerusalem, made repairs—he and his daughters.

Valley Gate, Dung Gate, and Fountain Gate

[13] Hanun and the inhabitants of Zanoah repaired the Valley Gate. They rebuilt it and installed its doors, bolts, and bars, and repaired 500 yards[e] of the wall to the Dung Gate. [14] Malchijah son of Rechab, ruler over the district of Beth-haccherem, repaired the Dung Gate. He rebuilt it and installed its doors, bolts, and bars.

[15] Shallun[f] son of Col-hozeh, ruler over the district of Mizpah, repaired the Fountain Gate. He rebuilt it and roofed it. Then he installed its doors, bolts, and bars. He also made repairs to the wall of the Pool of Shelah near the king's garden, as far as the stairs that descend from the city of David.

[16] After him Nehemiah son of Azbuk, ruler over half the district of Beth-zur, made repairs up to ⌊a point⌋ opposite the tombs of David, as far as the artificial pool and the House of the Warriors. [17] Next to him the Levites made repairs ⌊under⌋ Rehum son of Bani. Beside him Hashabiah, ruler over half the district of Keilah, made repairs for his district. [18] After him their fellow ⌊Levites⌋ made repairs ⌊under⌋ Binnui[g] son of Henadad, ruler over half the district of Keilah. [19] Next to him Ezer son of Jeshua, ruler over Mizpah, made repairs to another section opposite the ascent to the armory at the Angle.

The Angle, Water Gate, and Tower on the Ophel

[20] After him Baruch son of Zabbai[h] diligently repaired another section, from the Angle to the door of the house of Eliashib the high priest. [21] Beside him Meremoth son of Uriah, son of Hakkoz, made repairs to another section, from the door of Eliashib's house to the end of his house. [22] And next to him the priests from the surrounding area made repairs.

[23] After them Benjamin and Hasshub made repairs opposite their house. Beside them Azariah son of Maaseiah, son of Ananiah, made repairs beside his house. [24] After him Binnui son of Henadad made repairs to another section, from the house of Azariah to the Angle and the corner. [25] Palal son of Uzai ⌊made repairs⌋ opposite the Angle and tower that juts out from the upper palace[i] of the king, by the courtyard of the guard. Beside

---

[a]2:18 Lit they put their hands   [b]3:5 Lit not bring their neck to the work of   [c]3:6 Or Jeshanah   [d]3:7 Or Mizpah, the seat; 2 Kg 25:23; Jr 40:5–12   [e]3:13 Lit 1,000 cubits   [f]3:15 Some Hb mss, Syr read Shallum   [g]3:18 Some Hb mss, Syr, LXX; other Hb mss, Vg read Bavvai; v. 24   [h]3:20 Alt Hb tradition, Vg read Zaccai; Ezr 2:9   [i]3:25 Or and the upper tower that juts out from the palace

---

2:15 Valley Gate. This was Nehemiah's starting point in the southwest wall of Jerusalem.

2:17 Jerusalem lies in ruins. The walls and gates of the city had been destroyed by the Babylonian army in 586 B.C.

2:18 gracious hand of my God. Nehemiah urged the people to rebuild the wall, noting its disgraceful condition.

3:1 Eliashib ... and his fellow priests. Eliashib and the other priests started rebuilding the walls under Nehemiah's supervision.

3:10 Jedaiah ... made repairs across from his house. It was sensible to have the workers make repairs near their homes.

4:1–4 Sanballat accused the Jews of rebelling against the king of Persia. He may have objected to the rebuilding because he wanted to gain control of Judah.

4:9 prayed to our God and stationed a guard. The workers joined in Nehemiah's prayer and prepared to resist any attack.

him Pedaiah son of Parosh, 26 and the temple servants living on Ophel^a ⌊made repairs⌋ opposite the Water Gate toward the east and the tower that juts out. 27 Next to him the Tekoites made repairs to another section from ⌊a point⌋ opposite the great tower that juts out, as far as the wall of Ophel.

Horse Gate, Inspection Gate, and Sheep Gate

28 Each of the priests made repairs above the Horse Gate, each opposite his own house. 29 After them Zadok son of Immer made repairs opposite his house. And beside him Shemaiah son of Shecaniah, guard of the East Gate, made repairs. 30 Next to him Hananiah son of Shelemiah and Hanun the sixth son of Zalaph made repairs to another section.

After them Meshullam son of Berechiah made repairs opposite his room. 31 Next to him Malchijah, one of the goldsmiths, made repairs to the house of the temple servants and the merchants, opposite the Inspection^b Gate, and as far as the upper room of the corner. 32 The goldsmiths and merchants made repairs between the upper room of the corner and the Sheep Gate.

Progress in Spite of Opposition

4 ^c When Sanballat heard that we were rebuilding the wall, he became furious. He mocked the Jews 2 before his colleagues and the powerful men^d of Samaria, and said, "What are these pathetic Jews doing? Can they restore ⌊it⌋ by themselves? Will they offer sacrifices? Will they ever finish it? Can they bring these burnt stones back to life from the mounds of rubble?" 3 Then Tobiah the Ammonite, who was beside him, said, "Indeed, even if a fox climbed up what they are building, he would break down their stone wall!"

4 Listen, our God, for we are despised. Make their insults return on their own heads and let them be taken as plunder to a land of captivity. 5 Do not cover their guilt or let their sin be erased from Your sight, because they have provoked^e the builders.

6 So we rebuilt the wall until the entire wall was joined together up to half its ⌊height⌋, for the people had the will to keep working.

7^f When Sanballat, Tobiah, and the Arabs, Ammonites, and Ashdodites heard that the repair to the walls of Jerusalem was progressing and that the gaps were being closed, they became furious. 8 They all plotted together to come and fight against Jerusalem and throw it into confusion. 9 So we prayed to our God and stationed a guard because of them day and night.

10 In Judah, it was said:^g

The strength of the laborer fails,
since there is so much rubble.
We will never be able
to rebuild the wall.

11 And our enemies said, "They won't know or see anything until we're among them and can kill them and stop the work." 12 When the Jews who lived nearby arrived, they said to us time and again,^h "Everywhere you turn, ⌊they⌋ attackⁱ us." 13 So I stationed ⌊people⌋ behind the lowest sections of the wall, at the vulnerable areas. I stationed them by families with their swords, spears, and bows. 14 After I made an inspection, I stood up and said to the nobles, the officials, and the rest of the people, "Don't be afraid of them. Remember the great and awe-inspiring Lord, and fight for your countrymen, your sons and daughters, your wives and homes."

Sword and Trowel

15 When our enemies realized that we knew their scheme and that God had frustrated it, every one of us returned to his own work on the wall. 16 From that day on, half of my men did the work while the other half held spears, shields, bows, and armor. The officers supported all the people of Judah, 17 who were rebuilding the wall. The laborers who carried the loads worked with one hand and held a weapon with the other. 18 Each of the builders had his sword strapped around his waist while he was building, and the trumpeter was beside me. 19 Then I said to the nobles, the officials, and the rest of the people: "The work is enormous and spread out, and we are separated far from one another along the wall. 20 Wherever you hear the trumpet sound, rally to us there. Our God will fight for us!" 21 So we continued the work, while half of the men were holding spears from daybreak until the stars came out. 22 At that time, I also said to the people, "Let everyone and his servant spend the night inside Jerusalem, so that they can stand guard by night and work by day." 23 And I, my brothers, my men, and the guards with me never took off our clothes. Each carried his weapon, even when washing.^j

Social Injustice

5 There was a widespread outcry from the people and their wives against their Jewish countrymen. 2 Some were saying, "We, our sons, and our daughters are numerous. Let us get grain so that we can eat and

---

^a3:26 = a hill in Jerusalem   ^b3:31 Or *Muster*   ^c4:1 Neh 3:33 in Hb   ^d4:2 Or *the army*   ^e4:5 Or *provoked [You] in front of*   ^f4:7 Neh 4:1 in Hb   ^g4:10 Lit *Judah said*   ^h4:12 Lit *us 10 times*   ⁱ4:12 Or *again from every place, "You must return to*   ^j4:23 Lit *Each his weapon the water;* Hb obscure

---

4:10 strength of the laborer fails. Posting a guard did not end the problem. The workers were exhausted, and the job was only half done. Discouragement set in.

4:11 our enemies said. Nehemiah's enemies started rumors to produce fear and weaken the people's resolve to complete the task.

4:13 stationed them by families. Placing families together was dangerous, but Nehemiah knew that fathers would fight to protect their families.

4:14 Don't be afraid of them. Nehemiah encouraged the people to remember God's strength and power.

4:17 worked with one hand. Armed by Nehemiah, the laborers held their weapons in one hand and worked with the other.

4:20 Our God will fight for us! Nehemiah combined faith and effort, trusting God to protect them.

4:23 even when washing. The urgency of

live." [3] Others were saying, "We are mortgaging our fields, vineyards, and homes to get grain during the famine." [4] Still others were saying, "We have borrowed money to pay the king's tax on our fields and vineyards. [5] We and our children are ⌊just⌋ like our countrymen and their children, yet we are subjecting our sons and daughters to slavery. Some of our daughters are already enslaved, but we are powerless[a] because our fields and vineyards belong to others."

[6] I became extremely angry when I heard their outcry and these complaints. [7] After seriously considering the matter, I accused the nobles and officials, saying to them, "Each of you is charging his countrymen interest." So I called a large assembly against them [8] and said, "We have done our best to buy back our Jewish countrymen who were sold to foreigners, but now you sell your own countrymen, and we have to buy them back." They remained silent and could not say a word. [9] Then I said, "What you are doing isn't right. Shouldn't you walk in the •fear of our God ⌊and not invite⌋ the reproach of our foreign enemies? [10] Even I, as well as my brothers and my servants, have been lending them money and grain. Please, let us stop charging this interest.[b] [11] Return their fields, vineyards, olive groves, and houses to them immediately, along with the percentage[c] of the money, grain, new wine, and olive oil that you have been assessing them."

[12] They responded: "We will return ⌊these things⌋ and require nothing more from them. We will do as you say."

So I summoned the priests and made everyone take an oath to do this. [13] I also shook the folds of my robe and said, "May God likewise shake from his house and property everyone who doesn't keep this promise. May he be shaken out and have nothing!"

The whole assembly said, "•Amen," and they praised the LORD. Then the people did as they had promised.

Good and Bad Governors

[14] Furthermore, from the day King Artaxerxes appointed me to be their governor in the land of Judah—from the twentieth year until his thirty-second year, 12 years—I and my associates never ate from the food allotted to the governor. [15] The governors who preceded me had heavily burdened the people, taking food and wine from them, as well as a pound[d] of silver. Their subordinates also oppressed the people, but I didn't do this, because of the fear of God. [16] Instead, I devoted myself to the construction of the wall, and all my subordinates were gathered there for the work. We didn't buy any land.

[17] There were 150 Jews and officials, as well as guests from the surrounding nations at my table. [18] Each[e] day, one ox, six choice sheep, and some fowl were prepared for me. An abundance of all kinds of wine was ⌊provided⌋ every 10 days. But I didn't demand the food allotted to the governor, because the burden on the people was so heavy.

[19] Remember me favorably, my God, for all that I have done for this people.

Attempts to Discourage the Builders

6 When Sanballat, Tobiah, Geshem the Arab, and the rest of our enemies heard that I had rebuilt the wall and that no gap was left in it—though at that time I had not installed the doors in the gates— [2] Sanballat and Geshem sent me a message: "Come, let's meet together in the villages of[f] the Ono Valley." But they were planning to harm me.

[3] So I sent messengers to them, saying, "I am doing a great work and cannot come down. Why should the work cease while I leave it and go down to you?" [4] Four times they sent me the same proposal, and I gave them the same reply.

[5] Sanballat sent me this same message a fifth time by his aide, who had an open letter in his hand. [6] In it was written:

It is reported among the nations—and Geshem[g] agrees—that you and the Jews plan to rebel. This is the reason you are building the wall. According to these reports, you are to become their king [7] and have even set up the prophets in Jerusalem to proclaim on your behalf: "There is a king in Judah." These rumors will be heard by the king. So come, let's confer together.

[8] Then I replied to him, "There is nothing to these rumors you are spreading; you are inventing them in your own mind." [9] For they were all trying to intimidate us, saying, "They will become discouraged[h] in the work, and it will never be finished."

But now, ⌊my God,⌋ strengthen me.[i]

Attempts to Intimidate Nehemiah

[10] I went to the house of Shemaiah son of Delaiah, son of Mehetabel, who was restricted ⌊to his house⌋. He said:

Let us meet at the house of God
inside the temple.
Let us shut the temple doors
because they are coming to kill you.
They are coming to kill you tonight![j]

---

[a] **5:5** Lit but there is not the power in our hand   [b] **5:10** Or us forgive these debts   [c] **5:11** Lit hundredth   [d] **5:15** Lit 40 shekels   [e] **5:18** Lit And that which was prepared each   [f] **6:2** Or together at Chephirim in   [g] **6:6** Lit Gashmu   [h] **6:9** Lit saying, "Their hands will fail   [i] **6:9** Lit my hands   [j] **6:10** Or by night

---

the project required the workers to work night and day and remain armed at all times.

5:1 people and their wives. Stress caused the people to complain. These complaints were as hard to deal with as outside opposition.

5:3–9 Nehemiah got angry when he learned that some of the Jews were charging their

fellow Jews exorbitant interest rates ⌊and then foreclosing on their property. He put a stop to the practice.

5:14-16 During his years as governor of Jerusalem, Nehemiah could have lent money, then foreclosed when the people could not repay their debts. But he would not abuse

his position as governor.

6:2-3 Nehemiah's enemies tried to trap him by luring him away from Jerusalem for a meeting. But he refused to leave.

6:5-8 His enemies then accused Nehemiah of planning to overthrow King Artaxerxes. But he explained the lie to the Jewish work-

¹¹ But I said, "Should a man like me run away? How can I enter the temple and live? I will not go." ¹² I realized that God had not sent him, because of the prophecy he spoke against me. Tobiah and Sanballat had hired him. ¹³ He was hired, so that I would be intimidated, do as he suggested, sin, and get a bad reputation, in order that they could discredit me.

¹⁴ My God, remember Tobiah and Sanballat for what they have done, and also Noadiah the prophetess and the other prophets who wanted to intimidate me.

The Wall Completed

¹⁵ The wall was completed in 52 days, on the twenty-fifth day of the month Elul. ¹⁶ When all our enemies heard this, all the surrounding nations were intimidated and lost their confidence,ᵃ for they realized that this task had been accomplished by our God.

¹⁷ During those days, the nobles of Judah sent many letters to Tobiah, and Tobiah's ⌊letters⌋ came to them. ¹⁸ For many in Judah were bound by oath to him, since he was a son-in-law of Shecaniah son of Arah, and his son Jehohanan had married the daughter of Meshullam son of Berechiah. ¹⁹ These nobles kept mentioning Tobiah's good deeds to me, and they reported my words to him. And Tobiah sent letters to intimidate me.

The Exiles Return

7 When the wall had been rebuilt and I had the doors installed, the gatekeepers, singers, and Levites were appointed. ² Then I put my brother Hanani in charge of Jerusalem, along with Hananiah, commander of the fortress, because he was a faithful man who •feared God more than most. ³ I said to them, "Do not open the gates of Jerusalem until the sun is hot, and let the doors be shut and securely fastened while the guards are on duty. Station the citizens of Jerusalem as guards, some at their posts and some at their homes."

⁴ The city was large and spacious, but there were few people in it, and no houses had been built yet. ⁵ Then my God put it into my mind to assemble the nobles, the officials, and the people to be registered by genealogy. I found the genealogical record of those who came back first, and I found ⌊the following⌋ written in it:

⁶ These are the people of the province who went up from among the captive exiles deported by King Nebuchadnezzar of Babylon. Each of them returned to his own town in Jerusalem and Judah. ⁷ They came with Zerubbabel, Jeshua, Nehemiah, Azariah, Raamiah, Nahamani, Mordecai, Bilshan, Mispereth, Bigvai, Nehum, and Baanah.

The number of the Israelite men ⌊included⌋:

⁸ Parosh's descendants	2,172
⁹ Shephatiah's descendants	372
¹⁰ Arah's descendants	652
¹¹ Pahath-moab's descendants:	
Jeshua's and Joab's descendants	2,818
¹² Elam's descendants	1,254
¹³ Zattu's descendants	845
¹⁴ Zaccai's descendants	760
¹⁵ Binnui's descendants	648
¹⁶ Bebai's descendants	628
¹⁷ Azgad's descendants	2,322
¹⁸ Adonikam's descendants	667
¹⁹ Bigvai's descendants	2,067
²⁰ Adin's descendants	655
²¹ Ater's descendants: of Hezekiah	98
²² Hashum's descendants	328
²³ Bezai's descendants	324
²⁴ Hariph's descendants	112
²⁵ Gibeon'sᵇ descendants	95
²⁶ Bethlehem's and Netophah's men	188
²⁷ Anathoth's men	128
²⁸ Beth-azmaveth's men	42
²⁹ Kiriath-jearim's, Chephirah's,	
and Beeroth's men	743
³⁰ Ramah's and Geba's men	621
³¹ Michmas's men	122
³² Bethel's and Ai's men	123
³³ the other Nebo's men	52
³⁴ the other Elam's people	1,254
³⁵ Harim's people	320
³⁶ Jericho's people	345
³⁷ Lod's, Hadid's, and Ono's people	721
³⁸ Senaah's people	3,930

³⁹ The priests ⌊included⌋:

Jedaiah's descendants of the house of Jeshua	973
⁴⁰ Immer's descendants	1,052
⁴¹ Pashhur's descendants	1,247
⁴² Harim's descendants	1,017

⁴³ The Levites ⌊included⌋:

Jeshua's descendants: of Kadmiel Hodevah's descendants	74

⁴⁴ The singers ⌊included⌋:

•Asaph's descendants	148

⁴⁵ The gatekeepers ⌊included⌋:

Shallum's descendants, Ater's descendants,

ᵃ6:16 Lit and fell greatly in their eyes ᵇ7:25 Gibbar's in Ezr 2:20

---

ers and prayed for strength.

6:10-12 Nehemiah's enemies enlisted Shemaiah, a priest, in their plan to frighten Nehemiah into hiding from assassins in the holy place, which was forbidden by the Law (Num. 3:10; 18:7). But Nehemiah knew that a true priest or prophet would not advise someone

to desecrate the sanctuary by disobeying the Law.

6:15 wall was completed. After lying in ruins for almost 150 years, the walls of Jerusalem were rebuilt in less than two months.

6:17 Tobiah. Many Jews traded with Tobiah and tried to convince Nehemiah of his loyalty

to the project. But Tobiah actually opposed the work.

7:2 he was a faithful man. This is one of the major lessons in Nehemiah: God brings success to those who are faithful to carry out His work.

7:3 let the doors be shut. Nehemiah took

Talmon's descendants, Akkub's descendants, Hatita's descendants,
Shobai's descendants   138

46 The temple servants ⌊included⌋:

Ziha's descendants, Hasupha's descendants, Tabbaoth's descendants, 47 Keros's descendants, Sia's descendants, Padon's descendants, 48 Lebana's descendants, Hagaba's descendants, Shalmai's descendants, 49 Hanan's descendants, Giddel's descendants, Gahar's descendants, 50 Reaiah's descendants, Rezin's descendants, Nekoda's descendants, 51 Gazzam's descendants, Uzza's descendants, Paseah's descendants, 52 Besai's descendants, Meunim's descendants, Nephishesim's[a] descendants, 53 Bakbuk's descendants, Hakupha's descendants, Harhur's descendants, 54 Bazlith's descendants, Mehida's descendants, Harsha's descendants, 55 Barkos's descendants, Sisera's descendants, Temah's descendants, 56 Neziah's descendants, Hatipha's descendants.

57 The descendants of Solomon's servants ⌊included⌋:

Sotai's descendants, Sophereth's descendants, Perida's descendants, 58 Jaala's descendants, Darkon's descendants, Giddel's descendants, 59 Shephatiah's descendants, Hattil's descendants, Pochereth-hazzebaim's descendants, Amon's descendants.

60 All the temple servants
and the descendants of Solomon's
servants   392

61 The following are those who came from Tel-melah, Tel-harsha, Cherub, Addon, and Immer, but were unable to prove that their families and ancestry were Israelite:

62 Delaiah's descendants,
Tobiah's descendants,
and Nekoda's descendants   642

63 and from the priests: the descendants of Hobaiah, the descendants of Hakkoz, and the descendants of Barzillai—who had taken a wife from the daughters of Barzillai the Gileadite and was called by their name. 64 These searched for their entries in the genealogical records, but they could not be found, so they were disqualified from the priesthood. 65 The governor ordered them not to eat the most holy things until there was a priest who could consult the Urim and Thummim.[b]

66 The whole combined assembly
numbered   42,360
67 not including their 7,337 male
and female slaves,
as well as their 245 male and female singers.
68 They had 736 horses, 245 mules,[c]
69 435 camels, and 6,720 donkeys.

70 Some of the family leaders gave to the project. The governor gave 1,000 gold drachmas,[d] 50 bowls, and 530 priestly garments to the treasury. 71 Some of the family leaders gave 20,000 gold drachmas and 2,200 silver minas[e] to the treasury for the project. 72 The rest of the people gave 20,000 gold drachmas, 2,000 silver minas, and 67 priestly garments. 73 So the priests, Levites, gatekeepers, temple singers, some of the people, temple servants, and all Israel settled in their towns.

Public Reading of the Law

8 When the seventh month came and the Israelites had settled in their towns, 1 all the people gathered together at the square in front of the Water Gate. They asked Ezra the scribe to bring the book of the law of Moses that the LORD had given Israel. 2 On the first day of the seventh month, Ezra the priest brought the law before the assembly of men, women, and all who could listen with understanding. 3 While he was facing the square in front of the Water Gate, he read out of it from daybreak until noon before the men, the women, and those who could understand. All the people listened attentively[f] to the book of the law. 4 Ezra the scribe stood on a high wooden platform made for this purpose. Mattithiah, Shema, Anaiah, Uriah, Hilkiah, and Maaseiah stood beside him on his right; to his left were Pedaiah, Mishael, Malchijah, Hashum, Hash-baddanah, Zechariah, and Meshullam. 5 Ezra opened the book in full view of all the people, since he was elevated above everyone. As he opened it, all the people stood up. 6 Ezra blessed the LORD, the great God, and with their hands uplifted all the people said, "•Amen, Amen!" Then they bowed down and worshiped the LORD with their faces to the ground.

7 Jeshua, Bani, Sherebiah, Jamin, Akkub, Shabbethai, Hodiah, Maaseiah, Kelita, Azariah, Jozabad, Hanan, and Pelaiah, who were Levites,[g] explained the law to the people as they stood in their places. 8 They read the

---

a7:52 Alt Hb tradition reads *Nephushesim's*   b7:65 Two objects used to determine God's will; Ex 28:30   c7:68 Some Hb mss, LXX; other Hb mss omit v. 68; Ezr 2:66   d7:70 Or *darics*; the official Persian gold coin   e7:71 A Babylonian coin worth 50 shekels   f8:3 Lit *The ears of all the people listened*   g8:7 Vg, 1 Esdras 9:48; MT reads *Pelaiah and the Levites*

---

sensible precautions by closing the city gates. Depending on God's protection does not excuse irresponsible behavior.

7:5 Then my God put it into my mind. While taking action and using his common sense, Nehemiah relied on God's leadership. This combination of faithful work and prayerful

obedience made him a great leader.

8:1 all the people gathered together. The people from throughout Judah gathered to hear Ezra read and teach the Law from the five books of Moses (Deut. 31:11-12).

8:2 first day of the seventh month. Taking place in the September-October period, the

Feast of Trumpets was a time when work stopped and a sacred assembly was observed.

8:3 read out of it from daybreak until noon. Adults and children who were old enough to understand (vv. 2-3) listened attentively all morning as Ezra read from the Law.

book of the law of God, translating and giving the meaning so that the people could understand what was read. ⁹ Nehemiah the governor, Ezra the priest and scribe, and the Levites who were instructing the people said to all of them, "This day is holy to the LORD your God. Do not mourn or weep." For all the people were weeping as they heard the words of the law. ¹⁰ Then he said to them, "Go and eat what is rich, drink what is sweet, and send portions to those who have nothing prepared, since today is holy to our Lord. Do not grieve, because your strength ⌊comes from⌋ rejoicing in the LORD." ¹¹ And the Levites quieted all the people, saying, "Be still, since today is holy. Do not grieve." ¹² Then all the people began to eat and drink, send portions, and have a great celebration, because they had understood the words that were explained to them.

Festival of Booths Observed

¹³ On the second day, the family leaders of all the people, along with the priests and Levites, assembled before Ezra the scribe to study the words of the law. ¹⁴ They found written in the law how the LORD had commanded through Moses that the Israelites should dwell in booths during the festival of the seventh month. ¹⁵ So they proclaimed and spread this news throughout all their towns and in Jerusalem, saying, "Go out to the hill country and bring back branches of olive, wild olive, myrtle, palm, and ⌊other⌋ leafy trees to make booths, just as it is written." ¹⁶ The people went out, brought back ⌊branches⌋, and made booths for themselves on each of their rooftops, and courtyards, the court of the house of God, the square by the Water Gate, and the square by the Gate of Ephraim. ¹⁷ The whole community that had returned from exile made booths and lived in them. They had not celebrated like this from the days of Joshua son of Nun until that day. And there was tremendous joy. ¹⁸ Ezra[a] read out of the book of the law of God every day, from the first day to the last. The Israelites celebrated the feast for seven days, and on the eighth day there was an assembly, according to the ordinance.

National Confession of Sin

9 On the twenty-fourth day of this month the Israelites assembled; they were fasting, ⌊wearing⌋ •sackcloth, ⌊and had put⌋ dust on their heads. ² Those of Israelite descent separated themselves from all foreigners, and they stood and confessed their sins and the guilt[b] of their fathers. ³ While they stood in their places, they read from the book of the law of the LORD their God for a fourth of the day and ⌊spent⌋ another

fourth of the day in confession and worship of the LORD their God. ⁴ Jeshua, Bani, Kadmiel, Shebaniah, Bunni, Sherebiah, Bani, and Chenani stood on the raised platform ⌊built⌋ for the Levites and cried out loudly to the LORD their God. ⁵ Then the Levites—Jeshua, Kadmiel, Bani, Hashabneiah, Sherebiah, Hodiah, Shebaniah, and Pethahiah—said:

Stand up. Bless the LORD your God
from everlasting to everlasting.
Praise Your glorious name,
and may it be exalted above all blessing
  and praise.
⁶ You[c] alone are the LORD.
You created the heavens,
the highest heavens with all their host,
the earth and all that is on it,
the seas and all that is in them.
You give life to all of them,
and the heavenly host worships You.
⁷ You are the LORD God
who chose Abram
and brought him out of Ur of the Chaldeans,
and changed his name to Abraham.
⁸ You found his heart faithful in Your sight,
and made a covenant with him
to give the land of the Canaanites,
Hittites, Amorites, Perizzites,
Jebusites, and Girgashites—
to give it to his descendants.
You have kept Your promise,
for You are righteous.

⁹ You saw the oppression of our ancestors in Egypt
and heard their cry at the •Red Sea.
¹⁰ You performed signs and wonders
  against Pharaoh,
all his officials, and all the people of his land,
for You knew how arrogantly they treated
  our ancestors.
You made a name for Yourself
that endures to this day.
¹¹ You divided the sea before them,
and they crossed through it on dry ground.
You hurled their pursuers into the depths
like a stone into churning waters.
¹² You led them with a pillar of cloud by day,
and with a pillar of fire by night,
to illuminate the way they should go.
¹³ You came down on Mount Sinai,
and spoke to them from heaven.

---

[a] 8:18 Other Hb mss, Syr read *They* [b] 9:2 = liability for punishment [c] 9:6 LXX reads *And Ezra said: You*

8:10 Go and eat what is rich. When the people heard the Law read and explained, they wept and repented of their sins. Pleased by their response, Nehemiah reminded them that it was a time to celebrate with feasting.

8:16 courtyards ... square. The priests and Levites built their booths to celebrate this feast in the courts of the temple. Residents of the cities built booths (temporary shelters for the feast) on the roofs of their houses or in the courtyards. People from the countryside set up huts in the streets. Booths commemorated the time of wandering in the wilderness when the people had no permanent homes (Lev. 23:43).

8:17 the days of Joshua ... until that day. Such joy in this celebration had not been expressed since Joshua's day, because the people themselves had helped rebuild the walls.

9:1 fasting ... sackcloth ... dust. These actions symbolized remorse over sin. Sackcloth

You gave them impartial ordinances,
reliable instructions,
and good decrees and commandments.
14 You revealed Your holy Sabbath to them,
and gave them commandments, statutes,
and a law
through Your servant Moses.
15 You provided bread from heaven
for their hunger;
You brought them water from the rock
for their thirst.
You told them to go in and possess the land
You had sworn[a] to give them.

16 But our ancestors acted arrogantly;
they became stiff-necked and did not listen
to Your commands.
17 They refused to listen
and did not remember Your wonders
You performed among them.
They became stiff-necked and appointed a leader
to return to their slavery in Egypt.[b]
But You are a forgiving God,
gracious and compassionate,
slow to anger and rich in faithful love,
and You did not abandon them.
18 Even after they had cast an image of a calf
for themselves and said,
"This is your God who brought you
out of Egypt,"
and they had committed terrible blasphemies,
19 You did not abandon them in the wilderness
because of Your great compassion.
During the day the pillar of cloud
never turned away from them,
guiding them on their journey.
And during the night the pillar of fire
illuminated the way they should go.
20 You sent Your good Spirit to instruct them.
You did not withhold Your manna
from their mouths,
and You gave them water for their thirst.
21 You provided for them in the wilderness
40 years
and they lacked nothing.
Their clothes did not wear out,
and their feet did not swell.

22 You gave them kingdoms and peoples
and assigned them to be a boundary.

They took possession
of the land of Sihon[c] king of Heshbon
and of the land of Og king of Bashan.
23 You multiplied their descendants
like the stars of heaven
and brought them to the land
You told their ancestors to go in
and take possession [of it].
24 So their descendants went in and possessed
the land:
You subdued the Canaanites who inhabited
the land before them
and handed their kings and the surrounding
peoples over to them,
to do as they pleased with them.
25 They captured fortified cities and fertile land
and took possession of well-supplied houses,
rock-hewn cisterns, vineyards,
olive groves, and fruit trees in abundance.
They ate, were filled,
became prosperous, and delighted
in Your great goodness.

26 But they were disobedient and rebelled
against You.
They flung Your law behind their backs
and killed Your prophets
who warned them to turn them back to You.
They committed terrible blasphemies.
27 So You handed them over to their enemies,
who oppressed them.
In their time of distress, they cried out to You,
and You heard from heaven.
In Your abundant compassion
You gave them deliverers, who rescued them
from the power of their enemies.
28 But as soon as they had relief,
they again did what was evil in Your sight.
So You abandoned them to the power
of their enemies,
who dominated them.
When they cried out to You again,
You heard from heaven and rescued them
many times in Your compassion.
29 You warned them to turn back to Your law,
but they acted arrogantly
and would not obey Your commandments.
They sinned against Your ordinances,
by which a person will live if he does them.
They stubbornly resisted,[d]

---

[a] **9:15** Lit *lifted Your hand*   [b] **9:17** Some Hb mss, LXX; other Hb mss read *in their rebellion*   [c] **9:22** One Hb ms, LXX; MT, Vg read *Sihon, even the land of the*   [d] **9:29** Lit *They gave a stubborn shoulder*

---

was a dark, coarse cloth made from goat's hair (Pss. 30:11; 35:13). Dust refers to ashes (1 Sam. 4:12).

9:5 Your glorious name. The importance of God's name is spelled out in the Law. The Levites recalled times when God showed His goodness to the Jews. They called attention

to the covenant and its requirement of obedience.

9:13 You gave....impartial ordinances. God took the initiative in calling Israel and giving them laws and instructions that would raise the quality of life for them as individuals and a society and would reflect God's glory

through them to the other nations. Those who have lived in societies with the rule of law may not be able to appreciate how much more desirable life in such a society than in societies where might makes right.

9:14 You revealed Your holy Sabbath. God's day of rest is a gift born of grace and

stiffened their necks, and would not obey.
³⁰ You were patient with them for many years,
and Your Spirit warned them
through Your prophets,
but they would not listen.
Therefore, You handed them over
to the surrounding peoples.
³¹ However, in Your abundant compassion,
You did not destroy them or abandon them,
for You are a gracious and compassionate God.

³² So now, our God—the great, mighty,
and awe-inspiring God who keeps
His gracious covenant—
do not view lightly all the hardships
that have afflicted us,
our kings and leaders,
our priests and prophets,
our ancestors and all Your people,
from the days of the Assyrian kings until today.
³³ You are righteous concerning all that has come
on us,
because You have acted faithfully,
while we have acted wickedly.
³⁴ Our kings, leaders, priests, and ancestors
did not obey Your law
or listen to Your commandments
and warnings You gave them.
³⁵ When they were in their kingdom,
with Your abundant goodness You gave them,
and in the spacious and fertile land You set
before them,
they would not serve You or turn
from their wicked ways.
³⁶ Here we are today,
slaves in the land You gave our ancestors
so that they could enjoy its fruit
and its goodness.
Here we are—slaves in it!
³⁷ Its abundant harvest goes to the kings
You have set over us,
because of our sins.
They rule over our bodies
and our livestock as they please.
We are in great distress.

Israel's Vow of Faithfulness

^{38a} In view of all this, we are making a binding agreement in writing on a sealed document ⌊containing the names of⌋ our leaders, Levites, and priests.

^a**9:38** Neh 10:1 in Hb   ^b**10:29** Lit *and enter in a curse and in an oath*

10 Those whose seals were ⌊on the document⌋ were:

Nehemiah the governor, son of Hacaliah,
and Zedekiah,
² Seraiah, Azariah, Jeremiah,
³ Pashhur, Amariah, Malchijah,
⁴ Hattush, Shebaniah, Malluch,
⁵ Harim, Meremoth, Obadiah,
⁶ Daniel, Ginnethon, Baruch,
⁷ Meshullam, Abijah, Mijamin,
⁸ Maaziah, Bilgai, and Shemaiah.
These were the priests.

⁹ The Levites were:
Jeshua son of Azaniah,
Binnui of the sons of Henadad, Kadmiel,
¹⁰ and their brothers
Shebaniah, Hodiah, Kelita, Pelaiah, Hanan,
¹¹ Mica, Rehob, Hashabiah,
¹² Zaccur, Sherebiah, Shebaniah,
¹³ Hodiah, Bani, and Beninu.

¹⁴ The leaders of the people were:
Parosh, Pahath-moab, Elam, Zattu, Bani,
¹⁵ Bunni, Azgad, Bebai,
¹⁶ Adonijah, Bigvai, Adin,
¹⁷ Ater, Hezekiah, Azzur,
¹⁸ Hodiah, Hashum, Bezai,
¹⁹ Hariph, Anathoth, Nebai,
²⁰ Magpiash, Meshullam, Hezir,
²¹ Meshezabel, Zadok, Jaddua,
²² Pelatiah, Hanan, Anaiah,
²³ Hoshea, Hananiah, Hasshub,
²⁴ Hallohesh, Pilha, Shobek,
²⁵ Rehum, Hashabnah, Maaseiah,
²⁶ Ahiah, Hanan, Anan,
²⁷ Malluch, Harim, Baanah.

²⁸ The rest of the people—the priests, Levites, singers, gatekeepers, and temple servants, along with their wives, sons, and daughters, everyone who is able to understand and who has separated themselves from the surrounding peoples to ⌊obey⌋ the law of God— ²⁹ join with their noble brothers and commit themselves with a sworn oath^b to follow the law of God given through God's servant Moses and to carefully obey all the commands, ordinances, and statutes of the LORD our Lord.

Details of the Vow

³⁰ We will not give our daughters in marriage to
the surrounding peoples and will not take their
daughters as wives for our sons.

---

31 When the surrounding peoples bring merchandise or any kind of grain to sell on the Sabbath day, we will not buy from them on the Sabbath or a holy day. We will also leave ⌊the land⌋ uncultivated in the seventh year and will cancel every debt.

32 We will impose ⌊the following⌋ commandments on ourselves:

To give an eighth of an ounce of silver[a] yearly for the service of the house of our God: 33 the bread displayed before the LORD,[b] the daily •grain offering, the regular •burnt offering, the Sabbath and New Moon offerings, the appointed festivals, the holy things, the •sin offerings to •atone for Israel, and for all the work of the house of our God.

34 We have cast lots among the priests, Levites, and people for the donation of wood by our ancestral houses at the appointed times each year. They are to bring ⌊the wood⌋ to our God's house to burn on the altar of the LORD our God, as it is written in the law.

35 ⌊We will⌋ bring the •firstfruits of our land and of every fruit tree to the LORD's house year by year. 36 ⌊We will also bring⌋ the firstborn of our sons and our livestock, as prescribed by the law, and will bring the firstborn of our herds and flocks to the house of our God, to the priests who serve in our God's house. 37 We will bring ⌊a loaf⌋ from our first batch of dough to the priests at the storerooms of the house of our God. We will also bring the firstfruits of our ⌊grain⌋ offerings, of every fruit tree, and of the new wine and oil. A tenth of our land's ⌊produce⌋ from our lands belongs to the Levites, for the Levites are to collect the one-tenth offering in all our agricultural towns. 38 A priest of Aaronic descent must accompany the Levites when they collect the tenth, and the Levites must take a tenth of this offering to the storerooms of the treasury in the house of our God. 39 For the Israelites and the Levites are to bring the contributions of grain, new wine, and oil to the storerooms where the articles of the sanctuary are kept and where the priests, gatekeepers, and singers serve. We will not neglect the house of our God.

Resettling Jerusalem

11 Now the leaders of the people stayed in Jerusalem, and the rest of the people cast lots for one out of ten to come and live in Jerusalem, the holy city, while the other nine-tenths remained in their towns. 2 The people praised all the men who volunteered to live in Jerusalem.

3 These are the heads of the province who stayed in Jerusalem (but in the villages of Judah each lived on his own property in their towns—the Israelites, priests, Levites, temple servants, and descendants of Solomon's servants— 4 while some of the descendants of Judah and Benjamin settled in Jerusalem):

Judah's descendants:

Athaiah son of Uzziah, son of Zechariah, son of Amariah, son of Shephatiah, son of Mahalalel, of Perez's descendants; 5 and Maaseiah son of Baruch, son of Col-hozeh, son of Hazaiah, son of Adaiah, son of Joiarib, son of Zechariah, a descendant of the Shilonite. 6 The total number of Perez's descendants, who settled in Jerusalem, was 468 capable men.

7 These were Benjamin's descendants:

Sallu son of Meshullam, son of Joed, son of Pedaiah, son of Kolaiah, son of Maaseiah, son of Ithiel, son of Jeshaiah, 8 and after him Gabbai ⌊and⌋ Sallai: 928. 9 Joel son of Zichri was the officer over them, and Judah son of Hassenuah was second in command over the city.

10 The priests:

Jedaiah son of Joiarib, Jachin, and 11 Seraiah son of Hilkiah, son of Meshullam, son of Zadok, son of Meraioth, son of Ahitub, the chief official of God's house, 12 and their relatives who did the work at the temple: 822. Adaiah son of Jeroham, son of Pelaliah, son of Amzi, son of Zechariah, son of Pashhur, son of Malchijah 13 and his relatives, the leaders of families: 242. Amashsai son of Azarel, son of Ahzai, son of Meshillemoth, son of Immer, 14 and their relatives, capable men: 128. Zabdiel son of Haggedolim, was their chief.

15 The Levites:

Shemaiah son of Hasshub, son of Azrikam, son of Hashabiah, son of Bunni; 16 and Shabbethai and Jozabad, from the leaders of the Levites, who supervised the work outside the house of God; 17 Mattaniah son of Mica, son of Zabdi, son of •Asaph, the leader who began the thanksgiving in prayer; Bakbukiah, second among his relatives;

---

a 10:32 Lit give one-third of a shekel b 10:33 Lit rows of bread

---

and Abda son of Shammua, son of Galal, son of Jeduthun. [18] All the Levites in the holy city: 284.

[19] The gatekeepers:

Akkub, Talmon, and their relatives, who guarded the gates: 172.

[20] The rest of Israel, the priests, and the Levites were in all the villages of Judah, each on his own inherited property. [21] The temple servants lived on Ophel;[a] Ziha and Gishpa supervised the temple servants.

The Levites and Priests

[22] The leader of the Levites in Jerusalem was Uzzi son of Bani, son of Hashabiah, son of Mattaniah, son of Mica, of the descendants of Asaph, who were singers for the service of God's house. [23] For there was a command of the king regarding them, and an ordinance regulating[b] the singers' daily tasks. [24] Pethahiah son of Meshezabel, of the descendants of Zerah son of Judah, was the king's agent[c] in every matter concerning the people.

[25] As for the farming settlements with their fields:

Some of Judah's descendants lived
    in Kiriath-arba and its villages,
Dibon and its villages, and Jekabzeel
    and its villages,
[26] in Jeshua, Moladah, Beth-pelet,
[27] Hazar-shual, and Beer-sheba and its villages;
[28] in Ziklag and Meconah and its villages,
[29] in En-rimmon, Zorah, Jarmuth, and
[30] Zanoah and Adullam with their villages;
    in Lachish with its fields and Azekah
    and its villages.
So they settled from Beer-sheba to the Valley
    of Hinnom.

[31] Benjamin's descendants:
from Geba,[d] Michmash, Aija,
    and Bethel—and its villages,
[32] Anathoth, Nob, Ananiah,
[33] Hazor, Ramah, Gittaim,
[34] Hadid, Zeboim, Neballat,
[35] Lod, and Ono, the valley of the craftsmen.
[36] Some of the Judean divisions of Levites were
    in Benjamin.

12 These are the priests and Levites who went up with Zerubbabel son of Shealtiel and with Jeshua:

Seraiah, Jeremiah, Ezra,
[2] Amariah, Malluch, Hattush,

[3] Shecaniah, Rehum, Meremoth,
[4] Iddo, Ginnethoi, Abijah,
[5] Mijamin, Maadiah, Bilgah,
[6] Shemaiah, Joiarib, Jedaiah,
[7] Sallu, Amok, Hilkiah, Jedaiah.

These were the leaders of the priests and their relatives in the days of Jeshua.

[8] The Levites:

Jeshua, Binnui, Kadmiel,
Sherebiah, Judah, and Mattaniah—
he and his relatives were in charge
    of the praise songs.
[9] Bakbukiah, Unni,[e] and their relatives ⌊stood⌋
    opposite them in the services.
[10] Jeshua fathered Joiakim,
Joiakim fathered Eliashib,
Eliashib fathered Joiada,
[11] Joiada fathered Jonathan,
and Jonathan fathered Jaddua.[f]

[12] In the days of Joiakim, the leaders of the priestly families were:

	Meraiah	of Seraiah,
	Hananiah	of Jeremiah,
[13]	Meshullam	of Ezra,
	Jehohanan	of Amariah,
[14]	Jonathan	of Malluchi,
	Joseph	of Shebaniah,
[15]	Adna	of Harim,
	Helkai	of Meraioth,
[16]	Zechariah	of Iddo,
	Meshullam	of Ginnethon,
[17]	Zichri	of Abijah,
	Piltai	of Moadiah, of Miniamin,
[18]	Shammua	of Bilgah,
	Jehonathan	of Shemaiah,
[19]	Mattenai	of Joiarib,
	Uzzi	of Jedaiah,
[20]	Kallai	of Sallai,
	Eber	of Amok,
[21]	Hashabiah	of Hilkiah,
	and Nethanel	of Jedaiah.

[22] In the days of Eliashib, Joiada, Johanan, and Jaddua, the leaders of the families of the Levites and priests were recorded while Darius the Persian ruled. [23] Levi's descendants, the leaders of families, were recorded in the Book of the Historical Records during the days of Johanan son of Eliashib. [24] The leaders of the Levites—

---

[a]**11:21** A hill in Jerusalem   [b]**11:23** Lit *for*   [c]**11:24** Lit *was at the king's hand*   [d]**11:31** Or *descendants from Geba [lived in]:*   [e]**12:9** Alt Hb tradition reads *Unno*   [f]**12:10–11** These men were high priests.

---

and debts forgiven every seventh year (Lev. 25:1-7). The word *Sabbath* literally means cessation or rest. The various periods of rest were design to help God's people depend on Him to supply their needs even in these times of cessation. Also, it served to remind them that the earth is the Lord's and they are only temporary stewards of it.

10:35 firstfruits of our land. This means giving to the Lord from the first and best crops to acknowledge that God owns the land. Firstfruits of the trees meant giving over and above what the Law required to provide wood to keep the altar fire burning constantly (Lev.

6:12-13). The people cast lots to put together a schedule by which families would be responsible for providing the wood for the altar.

10:37 at the storerooms. The precious metals and temple articles were stored in rooms in the temple courts.

11:1 one out of ten. Along with the leaders,

Hashabiah, Sherebiah, and Jeshua son of Kadmiel, along with their relatives opposite them—gave praise and thanks, division by division, as David the man of God had prescribed. 25 ⌊This included⌋ Mattaniah, Bakbukiah, and Obadiah. Meshullam, Talmon, and Akkub were gatekeepers who guarded the storerooms at the gates. 26 These ⌊served⌋ in the days of Joiakim son of Jeshua, son of Jozadak, and in the days of Nehemiah the governor and Ezra the priest and scribe.

Dedication of the Wall

27 At the dedication of the wall of Jerusalem, they sent for the Levites wherever they lived and brought them to Jerusalem to celebrate the joyous dedication with thanksgiving and singing accompanied by cymbals, harps, and lyres. 28 The singers gathered from the region around Jerusalem, from the villages of the Netophathites, 29 from Beth-gilgal, and from the fields of Geba and Azmaveth, for they had built villages for themselves around Jerusalem. 30 After the priests and Levites had purified themselves, they purified the people, the gates, and the wall.

31 Then I brought the leaders of Judah up on top of the wall, and I appointed two large processions that gave thanks. One went to the right on the wall, toward the Dung Gate. 32 Hoshaiah and half the leaders of Judah followed:

33 Azariah, Ezra, Meshullam,
34 Judah, Benjamin, Shemaiah, and Jeremiah.

35 Some of the priests' sons had trumpets:

Zechariah son of Jonathan, son of Shemaiah, son of Mattaniah, son of Micaiah, son of Zaccur, son of •Asaph,
36 and his relatives:
Shemaiah, Azarel, Milalai, Gilalai, Maai, Nethanel, Judah, and Hanani, with the musical instruments of David, the man of God.
Ezra the scribe went in front of them.

37 At the Fountain Gate they climbed the steps of the city of David on the ascent of the wall ⌊and went⌋ above the house of David to the Water Gate on the east.

38 The second thanksgiving procession went to the left, and I followed it with half the people along the top of the wall, past the Tower of the Ovens to the Broad Wall, 39 above the Gate of Ephraim, and by the Old Gate, the Fish Gate, the Tower of Hananel, and the Tower of the Hundred, to the Sheep Gate. They stopped at the Gate of the Guard. 40 The two thanksgiving processions stood in the house of God. So ⌊did⌋ I and half of the officials accompanying me, as well as 41 the priests:

Eliakim, Maaseiah, Miniamin,
Micaiah, Elioenai, Zechariah,
and Hananiah, with trumpets;
42 and Maaseiah, Shemaiah, Eleazar,
Uzzi, Jehohanan, Malchijah, Elam, and Ezer.

Then the singers sang, with Jezrahiah as the leader. 43 On that day they offered great sacrifices and rejoiced because God had given them great joy. The women and children also celebrated, and Jerusalem's rejoicing was heard far away.

Support of the Levites' Ministry

44 On that same day men were placed in charge of the rooms ⌊that housed⌋ the supplies, contributions, •firstfruits, and tenths. The legally required portions for the priests and Levites were gathered from the village fields, because Judah was grateful to the priests and Levites who were serving. 45 They performed the service of their God and the service of purification, along with the singers and gatekeepers, as David and his son Solomon had prescribed. 46 For long ago, in the days of David and Asaph, there were leaders[a] of the singers and songs of praise and thanksgiving to God. 47 So in the days of Zerubbabel and Nehemiah, all Israel contributed the daily portions for the singers and gatekeepers. They also set aside daily portions for the Levites, and the Levites set aside daily portions for the descendants of Aaron.

Nehemiah's Further Reforms

13 At that time the book of Moses was read publicly to[b] the people. The command was found written in it that no Ammonite or Moabite should ever enter the assembly of God, 2 because they did not meet the Israelites with food and water. Instead, they hired Balaam against them to curse them, but our God turned the curse into a blessing. 3 When they heard the law, they separated all those of mixed descent from Israel.

4 Now before this, Eliashib the priest had been put in charge of the storerooms of the house of our God. He was a relative[c] of Tobiah 5 and had prepared a large room for him where they had previously stored the •grain offerings, the frankincense, the articles, and the

---

a 12:46 Alt Hb tradition reads there was a leader   b 13:1 Lit read in the ears of   c 13:4 Or an associate

---

one-tenth of the people were to settle in Jerusalem to make it a strong and vital city.

11:10-18 priests ... Levites. The priests, from six family heads, totaled 1,192 (vv. 10-14). The number given in 1 Chronicles 9:13 is 1,760. There were fewer Levites, only 284 (vv. 15-18). Many Levites did not return to

Judah from the exile.

12:44 Judah was grateful to the priests and Levites. The joy of the celebration overflowed into generous provision for the temple. The priests and Levites followed the pattern of worship that David had established (1 Chron. 22–26), including the prominent role of music.

12:47 all Israel contributed. Giving firstfruits and tithes was to be a continual practice rather than a one-time event. Everyone participated in this contribution.

13:5-8 When Nehemiah returned to Jerusalem after an absence of several months, he discovered that the high priest had allowed

tenths of grain, new wine, and oil prescribed for the Levites, singers, and gatekeepers, along with the contributions for the priests.

[6] While all this was happening, I was not in Jerusalem, because I had returned to King Artaxerxes of Babylon in the thirty-second year of his ⌊reign⌋. It was only later that I asked the king for a leave of absence [7] so I could return to Jerusalem. Then I discovered the evil that Eliashib had done on behalf of Tobiah by providing him a room in the courts of God's house. [8] I was greatly displeased and threw all of Tobiah's household possessions out of the room. [9] I ordered that the rooms be purified, and I had the articles of the house of God restored there, along with the grain offering and frankincense. [10] I also found out that because the portions for the Levites had not been given, each of the Levites and the singers performing the service had gone back to his own field. [11] Therefore, I rebuked the officials, saying, "Why has the house of God been neglected?" I gathered the Levites and singers together and stationed them at their posts. [12] Then all Judah brought a tenth of the grain, new wine, and oil into the storehouses. [13] I appointed as treasurers over the storehouses Shelemiah the priest, Zadok the scribe, and Pedaiah of the Levites, with Hanan son of Zaccur, son of Mattaniah to assist them, because they were considered trustworthy. They were responsible for the distribution to their colleagues.

[14] Remember me for this, my God, and don't erase the good deeds I have done for the house of my God and for its services.

[15] At that time I saw people in Judah treading wine presses on the Sabbath. They were also bringing in stores of grain and loading ⌊them⌋ on donkeys, along with wine, grapes, and figs. All kinds of goods were being brought to Jerusalem on the Sabbath day. So I warned ⌊them⌋ against selling food on that day. [16] The Tyrians living there were importing fish and all kinds of merchandise and selling them on the Sabbath to the people of Judah in Jerusalem.

[17] I rebuked the nobles of Judah and said to them: "What is this evil you are doing—profaning the Sabbath day? [18] Didn't your ancestors do the same, so that our God brought all this disaster on us and on this city? And now you are rekindling ⌊His⌋ anger against Israel by profaning the Sabbath!"

[19] When shadows began to fall on the gates of Jerusalem just before the Sabbath, I gave orders that the gates be closed and not opened until after the Sabbath. I posted some of my men at the gates, so that no goods could enter during the Sabbath day. [20] Once or twice the merchants and those who sell all kinds of goods camped outside Jerusalem, [21] but I warned them, "Why are you camping in front of the wall? If you do it again, I'll use force[a] against you." After that they did not come again on the Sabbath. [22] Then I instructed the Levites to purify themselves and guard the gates in order to keep the Sabbath day holy.

Remember me for this also, my God, and look on me with compassion in keeping with Your abundant, faithful love.

[23] In those days I also saw Jews who had married women from Ashdod, Ammon, and Moab. [24] Half of their children spoke the language of Ashdod or of one of the other peoples but could not speak Hebrew.[b] [25] I rebuked them, cursed them, beat some of their men, and pulled out their hair. I forced them to take an oath before God and said: "You must not give your daughters in marriage to their sons or take their daughters as wives for your sons or yourselves! [26] Didn't King Solomon of Israel sin in matters like this? There was not a king like him among many nations. He was loved by his God and God made him king over all Israel, yet foreign women drew him into sin. [27] Why then should we hear about you doing all this terrible evil and acting unfaithfully against our God by marrying foreign women?"

[28] Even one of the sons of Jehoiada, son of Eliashib the high priest, had become a son-in-law to Sanballat the Horonite. So I drove him away from me.

[29] Remember them, my God, for defiling the priesthood as well as the covenant of the priesthood and the Levites.

[30] So I purified them from everything foreign and assigned specific duties to each of the priests and Levites. [31] I also arranged for the donation of wood at the appointed times and for the •firstfruits.

Remember me, my God, with favor.

---

[a] **13:21** Lit *again, I will send a hand*   [b] **13:24** Or *Judahite*

Tobiah to occupy one of the temple storerooms. Tobiah had opposed the rebuilding of Jerusalem's walls, so Nehemiah threw him out his belongings and refilled the storeroom with grain.

13:10-13 Nehemiah discovered that the people had not brought their tithes and offerings to support the temple. He reprimanded them for their laxity, then appointed several people to oversee these tithes. He realized that neglect could undo the reforms already accomplished.

13:17–19 Nehemiah stopped commercial activity on the Sabbath by shutting the city gates on Friday evening and posting guards.

13:23 Jews who had married women from Ashdod, Ammon, and Moab. Ezra had dealt with the problem of intermarriage thirty years earlier (Ezra 9:1-4), and the people had made a vow not to marry foreign wives.

13:25 You must not give your daughters in marriage. Nehemiah did not dissolve the foreign marriages as Ezra had done, but he reacted passionately, realizing that inter-marriage had led to Israel's captivity by Babylon.

13:26 King Solomon. Nehemiah reminded the people of this king of Israel, who drifted away from God when he married foreign women (1 Kings 11:1-8). Solomon worshipped his foreign wives' idols, which drew his heart away from God. He even built high places to the false gods (1 Kings 11:7).

INTRODUCTION TO
ESTHER

PERSONAL READING PLAN

☐ Esther 1:1-22
☐ Esther 2:1-23
☐ Esther 3:1-4:17

☐ Esther 5:1-6:14
☐ Esther 7:1-8:17
☐ Esther 9:1-10:3

AUTHOR

The author is unknown, but was most likely a Jewish nationalist who was a resident of a Persian city. Some suggest that Mordecai was the author.

DATE

The writing of Esther was no earlier than the reign of Xerxes (circa 486-465 B.C.), and probably no later than 331 B.C., when the Persian Empire fell to Greece.

THEME

The providence of God in the free decisions of people, especially in delivering the Jews under Xerxes ... also a profile in human courage.

HISTORICAL BACKGROUND

More than a generation had passed since Cyrus defeated the Babylonians and allowed the Jews to return to Israel. Still, many Jews remained scattered throughout the known world, making their home among their captors. The Book of Esther features some of these expatriates. It is

noteworthy that Artaxerxes, the son of Xerxes, was king during Nehemiah's time. He may have been influenced by Queen Esther in his handling of the Jews (see Neh. 2:6).

CHARACTERISTICS

The Book of Esther recounts how the Feast of Purim came to be celebrated—a feast still observed today by Jews in memory of God's sovereign, providential care of His people. The story revolves around 10 banquets (1:3-4; 1:5-8; 1:9; 2:18; 3:15; 5:1-8; 7:1-10; 8:17; 9:17; 9:18-32). The banquets culminate in the double celebration of the Feast of Purim. Interestingly, the Book of Esther does not directly name God. This conspicuous lack of any reference to God focuses attention on what He is doing, behind the scenes, to effect deliverance for the Jews. Esther is a literary masterpiece that reads like a modern suspense novel, complete with plot twists, coincidence, irony, intrigue, revenge, and plenty of feasting.

PASSAGES FOR TOPICAL GROUP STUDY

2:1-18.... POPULARITY and RISK .... A Beauty Contest

Vashti Angers the King

1 These events took place during the days of Ahasuerus,[a] who ruled 127 provinces from India to •Cush. ² In those days King Ahasuerus reigned from his royal throne in the fortress at Susa. ³ He held a feast in the third year of his reign for all his officials and staff, the army of Persia and Media, the nobles, and the officials from the provinces. ⁴ He displayed the glorious wealth of his kingdom and the magnificent splendor of his greatness for a total of 180 days.

⁵ At the end of this time, the king held a week-long banquet in the garden courtyard of the royal palace for all the people, from the greatest to the least, who were present in the fortress of Susa. ⁶ White and violet linen hangings were fastened with fine white and purple linen cords to silver rods on marble[b] columns. Gold and silver couches ⌊were arranged⌋ on a mosaic pavement of red feldspar,[c] marble,[b] mother-of-pearl, and precious stones.

⁷ Beverages were served in an array of gold goblets, each with a different design. Royal wine flowed freely, according to the king's bounty ⁸ and no restraint was placed on the drinking. The king had ordered every wine steward in his household to serve as much as each person wanted. ⁹ Queen Vashti also gave a feast for the women of King Ahasuerus' palace.

¹⁰ On the seventh day, when the king was feeling good from the wine, Ahasuerus commanded Mehuman, Biztha, Harbona, Bigtha, Abagtha, Zethar, and Carkas, the seven eunuchs who personally served him, ¹¹ to bring Queen Vashti before him with her royal crown. ⌊He wanted⌋ to show off her beauty to the people and the officials, because she was very beautiful. ¹² But Queen Vashti refused to come at the king's command that was delivered by his eunuchs. The king became furious and his anger burned within him.

The King's Decree

¹³ The king consulted the wise men who understood the times,[d] for it was his normal procedure to confer with experts in law and justice. ¹⁴ The most trusted ones[e] were Carshena, Shethar, Admatha, Tarshish, Meres, Marsena, and Memucan. They were the seven officials of Persia and Media who had personal access to the king and occupied the highest positions in the kingdom. ¹⁵ ⌊The king asked,⌋ "According to the law, what should be done with Queen Vashti, since she refused to obey King Ahasuerus' command that was delivered by the eunuchs?"

¹⁶ Memucan said in the presence of the king and his officials, "Queen Vashti has defied not only the king, but all the officials and the peoples who are in every one of King Ahasuerus' provinces. ¹⁷ For the queen's action will become public knowledge to all the women and cause them to despise their husbands and say, 'King Ahasuerus ordered Queen Vashti brought before him, but she did not come.' ¹⁸ ⌊Before⌋ this day ⌊is over⌋, the noble women of Persia and Media who hear about the queen's act will say ⌊the same thing⌋ to all the king's officials, resulting in more contempt and fury.

¹⁹ "If it meets the king's approval, he should personally issue a royal decree. Let it be recorded in the laws of Persia and Media, so that it cannot be revoked: Vashti is not to enter King Ahasuerus' presence, and her royal position is to be given to another woman who is more worthy than she. ²⁰ The decree the king issues will be heard throughout his vast kingdom, so all women will honor their husbands, from the least to the greatest."

²¹ The king and his counselors approved the proposal, and he followed Memucan's advice. ²² He sent letters to all the royal provinces, to each province in its own script and to each ethnic group in its own language, that every man should be master of his own house and speak in the language of his own people.

Search for a New Queen

2 Some time later, when King Ahasuerus' rage had cooled down, he remembered Vashti, what she had done, and what was decided against her. ² The king's personal attendants[f] suggested, "Let a search be made for beautiful young virgins for the king. ³ Let the king appoint commissioners in each province of his kingdom, so that they may assemble all the beautiful young virgins to the harem at the fortress of Susa. ⌊Put them⌋ under the care of Hegai, the king's eunuch, who is in charge of the women, and give them the required beauty treatments. ⁴ Then the young woman who pleases the king will reign in place of Vashti." This suggestion pleased the king, and he did accordingly.

⁵ A Jewish man was in the fortress of Susa named Mordecai son of Jair, son of Shimei, son of Kish, a Benjaminite. ⁶ He had been taken into exile from Jerusalem with the other captives when King Nebuchadnezzar of Babylon took King Jeconiah[g] of Judah into exile. ⁷ Mordecai was the legal guardian of his cousin[h] Hadassah (that is, Esther), because she didn't have a father or mother. The young woman had a beautiful figure and was extremely good-looking. When her father and

---

[a]1:1 = Xerxes   [b]1:6 Or alabaster   [c]1:6 Or of porphyry   [d]1:13 Or understood propitious times   [e]1:14 Lit Those near him   [f]2:2 Lit The young men of the king who served him   [g]2:6 Or Jehoiachin; 2 Kg 24; 25:27; 1 Ch 3:16–17   [h]2:7 Lit uncle's daughter

---

1:1 Ahasuerus, who ruled. His name is also written as Xerxes. Ahasuerus succeeded his father, Darius, as king. Ahasuerus ruled the Persian Empire for 21 years from 486 to 465 B.C.

1:13 The king consulted the wise men who understood the times. Astrologers and magicians served in the court by giving advice and attempting to predict the future. God's prophets viewed them with scorn (Isa. 44:24-25).

1:19 Vashti is not to enter King Ahasuerus' presence. One of Ahasuerus' wise men suggested deposing the queen so that the women of the kingdom would not follow Vashti's example and disobey their husbands. The king issued a royal decree demoting Vashti from her position of queen and banishing her from his sight.

2:7 the legal guardian of his cousin Hadassah. Esther's Hebrew name means "myrtle."

A Beauty Contest

1. Who is the most beautiful or handsome person you know? How has that person's looks affected him or her?

Esther 2:1-18

2. Besides being beautiful, what else did Esther have going for her?

3. What makes a person beautiful to God (1 Sam. 16:7)? How is this different from the world's standard?

4. God used Esther's beauty to put her in a position of power. Why would he have chosen her for that role?

5. Later, Esther risked everything to save God's people from murder. Are you willing to risk all that you have to serve God?

mother died, Mordecai had adopted her as his own daughter.

8 When the king's command and edict became public knowledge, many young women gathered at the fortress of Susa under Hegai's care. Esther was also taken to the palace and placed under the care of Hegai, who was in charge of the women. 9 The young woman pleased him and gained his favora so that he accelerated the process of the beauty treatments and the special diet that she received. He assigned seven hand-picked female servants to her from the palace and transferred her and her servants to the harem's best quarters.

10 Esther did not reveal her ethnic background or her birthplace, because Mordecai had ordered her not to. 11 Every day Mordecai took a walk in front of the harem's courtyard to learn how Esther was doing and to see what was happening to her.

12 During the year before each young woman's turn to go to King Ahasuerus, the harem regulation required her to receive beauty treatments with oil of myrrh for six months and then with perfumes and cosmetics for ⌊another⌋ six months. 13 When the young woman would go to the king, she was given whatever she requested to take with her from the harem to the palace. 14 She would go in the evening, and in the morning she would return to a second harem under the supervision of Shaashgaz, the king's eunuch in charge of the

concubines. She never went to the king again, unless he desired her and summoned her by name.

Esther Becomes Queen

15 Esther was the daughter of Abihail, the uncle of Mordecai who had adopted ⌊her⌋ as his own daughter. When her turn came to go to the king, she did not ask for anything except what Hegai, the king's trusted official in charge of the harem, suggested. Esther won approval in the sight of everyone who saw her.

16 Esther was taken to King Ahasuerus in the royal palace in the tenth month, the month Tebeth, in the seventh year of his reign. 17 The king loved Esther more than all the other women. She won more favor and approval from him than did any of the other virgins. He placed the royal crown on her head and made her queen in place of Vashti. 18 The king held a great banquet for all his officials and staff. It was Esther's banquet. He freed his provinces from tax payments and gave gifts worthy of the king's bounty.

19 When the young womenb were assembled together for a second time, Mordecai was sitting at the King's Gate. 20 Esther still had not revealed her birthplace or her ethnic background, as Mordecai had directed. She obeyed Mordecai's orders, as she always had while he raised her.

Mordecai Saves the King

21 During those days while Mordecai was sitting at the King's Gate, Bigthan and Teresh, two eunuchs who guarded the ⌊king's⌋ entrance, became infuriated and tried to assassinatec King Ahasuerus. 22 When Mordecai learned of the plot, he reported it to Queen Esther, and she told the king on Mordecai's behalf. 23 When the report was investigated and verified, both men were hanged on the gallows. This event was recorded in the court records of daily events in the king's presence.

Haman's Plan to Kill the Jews

3 After all this took place, King Ahasuerus honored Haman, son of Hammedatha the Agagite. He promoted him in rank and gave him a higher position than all the other officials. 2 The entire royal staff at the King's Gate bowed down and paid homage to Haman, because the king had commanded this to be done for him. But Mordecai would not bow down or pay homage. 3 The members of the royal staff at the King's Gate asked Mordecai, "Why are you disobeying the king's command?" 4 When they had warned him day after day and he still would not listen to them, they

a **2:9** Lit and carried faithful love before him   b **2:19** Or the virgins   c **2:21** Lit and they sought to stretch out a hand against

Esther is a Persian name, meaning "star." Her parents died when she was young.

2:10 ethnic background or her birthplace. Mordecai had warned Esther not to reveal her nationality. Jews were forbidden to marry pagans (Deut. 7:1-4) or to have sexual relations outside of marriage (Ex. 20:14). Joining the

king's harem violated these rules, but God protected and used Esther and Mordecai to save their people.

2:19 sitting at the King's Gate. The gate was where commercial and legal transactions were made. Mordecai probably held an official position in the judicial system that

helped him uncover the assassination plot against the king.

3:1 After all this took place. Four years after Mordecai saved the king from assassination, Haman was promoted to the highest position in the land. **Haman ... the Agagite.** Haman was an Amalekite, a group of people de-

told Haman to see if Mordecai's actions would be tolerated, since he had told them he was a Jew.

5 When Haman saw that Mordecai was not bowing down or paying him homage, he was filled with rage. 6 And when he learned of Mordecai's ethnic identity, Haman decided not to do away with[a] Mordecai alone. He set out to destroy all of Mordecai's people, the Jews, throughout Ahasuerus' kingdom.

7 In the first month, the month of Nisan,[b] in King Ahasuerus' twelfth year,[c] Pur (that is, the lot) was cast before Haman for each day in each month, and it fell on the twelfth month, the month Adar.[d] 8 Then Haman informed King Ahasuerus, "There is one ethnic group, scattered throughout the peoples in every province of your kingdom, yet living in isolation. Their laws are different from everyone else's, so that they defy the king's laws. It is not in the king's best interest to tolerate them. 9 If the king approves, let an order be drawn up authorizing their destruction, and I will pay 375 tons of silver to[e] the accountants for deposit in the royal treasury."

10 The king removed his signet ring from his finger and gave it to Haman son of Hammedatha the Agagite, the enemy of the Jewish people. 11 Then the king told Haman, "The money and people are given to you to do with as you see fit."

12 The royal scribes were summoned on the thirteenth day of the first month, and the order was written exactly as Haman commanded. [It was intended for] the royal satraps, the governors of each of the provinces, and the officials of each ethnic group and written for each province in its own script and to each ethnic group in its own language. It was written in the name of King Ahasuerus and sealed with the royal signet ring. 13 Letters were sent by couriers to each of the royal provinces [telling the officials] to destroy, kill, and annihilate all the Jewish people—young and old, women and children—and plunder their possessions on a single day, the thirteenth day of Adar, the twelfth month.[f]

14 A copy of the text, issued as law throughout every province, was distributed to all the peoples so that they might get ready for that day. 15 The couriers left, spurred on by royal command, and the law was issued in the fortress of Susa. The king and Haman sat down to drink, while the city of Susa was in confusion.

Mordecai Appeals to Esther

4 When Mordecai learned all that had occurred, he tore his clothes, put on •sackcloth and ashes, went into the middle of the city, and cried loudly and bitterly. 2 He only went as far as the King's Gate, since [the law] prohibited anyone wearing sackcloth from entering the King's Gate. 3 There was great mourning among the Jewish people in every province where the king's command and edict came. They fasted, wept, and lamented, and many lay on sackcloth and ashes.

4 Esther's female servants and her eunuchs came and reported the news to her, and the queen was overcome with fear. She sent clothes for Mordecai to wear so he could take off his sackcloth, but he did not accept [them].

5 Esther summoned Hathach, one of the king's eunuchs assigned to her, and dispatched him to Mordecai to learn what he was doing and why.[g] 6 So Hathach went out to Mordecai in the city square in front of the King's Gate. 7 Mordecai told him everything that had happened as well as the exact amount of money Haman had promised to pay the royal treasury for the slaughter of the Jews.

8 Mordecai also gave him a copy of the written decree issued in Susa ordering their destruction, so that Hathach might show it to Esther, explain it to her, and instruct her to approach the king, implore his favor, and plead with him personally for her people. 9 Hathach came and repeated Mordecai's response to Esther.

10 Esther spoke to Hathach and commanded him to tell Mordecai, 11 "All the royal officials and the people of the royal provinces know that one law applies to every man or woman who approaches the king in the inner courtyard and who has not been summoned—[the] death [penalty]. Only if the king extends the golden scepter will that person live. I have not been summoned to appear before the king for the last[h] 30 days." 12 Esther's response was reported to Mordecai.

13 Mordecai told [the messenger] to reply to Esther, "Don't think that you will escape the fate of all the Jews because you are in the king's palace. 14 If you keep silent at this time, liberation and deliverance will come to the Jewish people from another place, but you and your father's house will be destroyed. Who knows, perhaps you have come to the kingdom for such a time as this."

15 Esther sent this reply to Mordecai: 16 "Go and assemble all the Jews who can be found in Susa and fast for me. Don't eat or drink for three days, night and day. I and my female servants will also fast in the same way. After that, I will go to the king even if it is against the law. If I perish, I perish." 17 So Mordecai went and did everything Esther had ordered him.

Esther Approaches the King

5 On the third day, Esther dressed up in her royal clothing and stood in the inner courtyard of the

---

a 3:6 Lit to stretch out a hand against   b 3:7 March–April   c 3:7 474 B.C.   d 3:7 February–March   e 3:9 Lit will weigh 10,000 silver talents on the hands of   f 3:13 LXX adds the text of Ahasuerus' letter here   g 4:5 Lit what is this and why is this   h 4:11 Lit king these

---

palace facing it. The king was sitting on his royal throne in the royal courtroom, facing its entrance. 2 As soon as the king saw Queen Esther standing in the courtyard, she won his approval.ᵃ The king extended the golden scepter in his hand toward Esther, and she approached and touched the tip of the scepter.

3 "What is it, Queen Esther?" the king asked her. "Whatever you want, even to half the kingdom, will be given to you."

4 "If it pleases the king," Esther replied, "may the king and Haman come today to the banquet I have prepared for them."

5 The king commanded, "Hurry, and get Haman so we can do as Esther has requested." So the king and Haman went to the banquet Esther had prepared.

6 While drinking theᵇ wine, the king asked Esther, "Whatever you ask will be given to you. Whatever you want, even to half the kingdom, will be done."

7 Esther answered, "⌊This is⌋ my petition and my request: 8 If the king approves of meᶜ and if it pleases the king to grant my petition and perform my request, may the king and Haman come to the banquet I will prepare for them. Tomorrow I will do what the king has asked."

9 That day Haman left full of joy and in good spirits.ᵈ But when Haman saw Mordecai at the King's Gate, and Mordecai didn't rise or tremble in fear at his presence, Haman was filled with rage toward Mordecai. 10 Yet Haman controlled himself and went home. He sent for his friends and his wife Zeresh to join him. 11 Then Haman described for them his glorious wealth and his many sons. He told them all how the king had promoted him in rank and given him a high position over the other officials and the royal staff. 12 "What's more," Haman added, "Queen Esther invited no one but me to join the king at the banquet she had prepared. I am invited again tomorrow to join her with the king. 13 Still, none of this satisfies me since I see Mordecai the Jew sitting at the King's Gate all the time."

14 His wife Zeresh and all his friends told him, "Have them build a gallows 75 feetᵉ high. Ask the king in the morning to hang Mordecai on it. Then go to the banquet with the king and enjoy yourself." The advice pleased Haman, so he had the gallows constructed.

Mordecai Honored by the King

6 That night sleep escaped the king, so he ordered the book recording daily events to be brought and read to the king. 2 They found the written report of how Mordecai had informed on Bigthana and Teresh, two eunuchs who guarded the ⌊king's⌋ entrance, when they planned to assassinate King Ahasuerus. 3 The king inquired, "What honor and special recognition have been given to Mordecai for this ⌊act⌋?"

The king's personal attendants replied, "Nothing has been done for him."

4 The king asked, "Who's in the court?" Now Haman was just entering the outer court of the palace to ask the king to hang Mordecai on the gallows he had prepared for him.

5 The king's attendants answered him, "See, Haman is standing in the court."

"Have him enter," the king ordered.

6 Haman entered, and the king asked him, "What should be done for the man the king wants to honor?"

Haman thought to himself, "Who is it the king would want to honor more than me?" 7 Haman told the king, "For the man the king wants to honor: 8 Have them bring a royal garment that the king himself has worn and a horse the king himself has ridden, which has a royal diadem on its head. 9 Put the garment and the horse under the charge of one of the king's most noble officials. Have them clothe the man the king wants to honor, parade him on the horse through the city square, and proclaim before him, 'This is what is done for the man the king wants to honor.' "

10 The king told Haman, "Hurry, and do just as you proposed. Take a garment and a horse for Mordecai the Jew, who is sitting at the King's Gate. Do not leave out anything you have suggested." 11 So Haman took the garment and the horse. He clothed Mordecai and paraded him through the city square, crying out before him, "This is what is done for the man the king wants to honor."

12 Then Mordecai returned to the King's Gate, but Haman, overwhelmed,ᶠ hurried off for home with his head covered. 13 Haman told his wife Zeresh and all his friends everything that had happened. His advisers and his wife Zeresh said to him, "If Mordecai, before whom you have begun to fall, is Jewish, you won't overcome him, because your downfall is certain." 14 While they were still speaking with him, the eunuchs of the king arrived and rushed Haman to the banquet Esther had prepared.

Haman Is Executed

7 The king and Haman came to feastᵍ with Esther the queen. 2 Once again, on the second day while drinking wine, the king asked Esther, "Queen Esther, whatever you ask will be given to you. Whatever you seek, even to half the kingdom, will be done."

ᵃ5:2 Lit she obtained favor in his eyes; Est 2:15,17   ᵇ5:6 Lit During the banquet of   ᶜ5:8 Lit If I have found favor in the eyes of the king   ᵈ5:9 Lit left rejoicing and good of heart   ᵉ5:14 Lit 50 cubits   ᶠ6:12 Lit mourning   ᵍ7:1 Lit drink

---

proached the king. She didn't mention praying, but fasting normally included earnestly seeking God in prayer.

5:2 she won his approval. Although Esther had not seen the king in a month, he held out the gold scepter toward her, granting permission to approach him.

5:10 Zeresh. Haman and his wife were well suited to each other. After Haman's whining about Mordecai and his boasting about his favor with the king, Haman's wife encouraged him to murder Mordecai as an example to everyone that Haman was in control.

6:3 honor and special recognition. God

used a sleepless night to accomplish His purpose. The king read the official records and discovered that Mordecai had never been honored for saving his life five years before.

7:8 Haman was ... where Esther was reclining. The reason the king went out into the palace garden is not known. But Haman

3 Queen Esther answered, "If I have obtained your approval,ᵃ my king, and if the king is pleased, spare my life—⌊this is⌋ my request; and ⌊spare⌋ my people—⌊this is⌋ my desire. 4 For my people and I have been sold out to destruction, death, and extermination. If we had merely been sold as male and female slaves, I would have kept silent. Indeed, the trouble wouldn't be worth burdening the king."

5 King Ahasuerus spoke up and asked Queen Esther, "Who is this, and where is the one who would devise such a scheme?"ᵇ

6 Esther answered, "The adversary and enemy is this evil Haman."

Haman stood terrified before the king and queen. 7 Angered by this, the king arose from where they were drinking wine and ⌊went to⌋ the palace garden. Haman remained to beg Queen Esther for his life because he realized the king was planning something terrible for him. 8 Just as the king returned from the palace garden to the house of wine drinking, Haman was falling on the couch where Esther was reclining. The king exclaimed, "Would he actually violate the queen while I am in the palace?" As soon as the statement left the king's mouth, Haman's face was covered.

9 Harbona, one of the royal eunuchs, said: "There is a gallows 75 feetᶜ tall at Haman's house that he made for Mordecai, who ⌊gave⌋ the report that savedᵈ the king."

The king commanded, "Hang him on it."

10 They hanged Haman on the gallows he had prepared for Mordecai. Then the king's anger subsided.

Esther Intervenes for the Jews

8 That same day King Ahasuerus awarded Queen Esther the estate of Haman, the enemy of the Jews. Mordecai entered the king's presence because Esther had revealed her relationship to Mordecai. 2 The king removed his signet ring he had recovered from Haman and gave it to Mordecai, and Esther put him in charge of Haman's estate.

3 Then Esther addressed the king again. She fell at his feet, wept, and begged him to revoke the evil of Haman the Agagite, and his plot he had devised against the Jews. 4 The king extended the golden scepter toward Esther, so she got up and stood before the king.

5 She said, "If it pleases the king, and I have found approval before him, if the matter seems right to the king and I am pleasing in his sight, let ⌊a royal edict⌋ be written. Let it revoke the documents the scheming Haman son of Hammedatha the Agagite, wrote to destroy the Jews who ⌊reside⌋ in all the king's prov-inces. 6 For how could I bear to see the evil that would come on my people? How could I bear to see the destruction of my relatives?"

7 King Ahasuerus said to Esther the Queen and to Mordecai the Jew, "Look, I have given Haman's estate to Esther, and he was hanged on the gallows because he attackedᵉ the Jews. 8 You may write in the king's name whatever pleases you concerning the Jews, and seal it with the royal signet ring. A document written in the king's name and sealed with the royal signet ring cannot be revoked."

9 On the twenty-third day of the third month (that is, the month Sivan),ᶠ the royal scribes were summoned. Everything was written exactly as Mordecai ordered for the Jews, to the satraps, the governors, and the officials of the 127 provinces from India to •Cush. ⌊The edict was written⌋ for each province in its own script, for each ethnic group in its own language, and to the Jews in their own script and language.

10 Mordecai wrote in King Ahasuerus' name and sealed ⌊the edicts⌋ with the royal signet ring. He sent the documents by mounted couriers, who rode fast horses bred from the royal racing mares.

11 The king's edict gave the Jews in each and every city the right to assemble and defend themselves, to destroy, kill, and annihilate every ethnic and provincial army hostile to them, including women and children, and to take their possessions as spoils of war. 12 ⌊This would take place⌋ on a single day throughout all the provinces of King Ahasuerus, on the thirteenth day of the twelfth month, the month Adar.ᵍ

13 A copy of the document was to be issued as law in every province. It was to be published for every ethnic group so the Jews could be ready to avenge themselves against their enemies on that day. 14 On their royal horses, the couriers rode out in haste, at the king's urgent command. The law was also issued in the fortress of Susa.

15 Mordecai went out from the king's presence clothed in royal purple and white, with a great golden crown and a purple robe of fine linen. The city of Susa shouted and rejoiced, 16 and the Jews celebratedʰ with gladness, joy and honor. 17 In every province and every city, wherever the king's command and his law reached, rejoicing and jubilation took place among the Jews. There was a celebration and a holiday.ⁱ And, many of the ethnic groups of the land professed themselves to be Jews because fear of the Jews had overcome them.

ᵃ7:3 Lit If I have found favor in your eyes   ᵇ7:5 Lit who would fill his heart to do this   ᶜ7:9 Lit 50 cubits   ᵈ7:9 Lit who spoke good for   ᵉ8:7 Lit stretched out his hand against   ᶠ8:9 May–June   ᵍ8:12 February–March   ʰ8:16 Lit had light   ⁱ8:17 Lit good day

---

begged her for his life after the king left. He was not assaulting her, but he may have been grasping at her in desperation.

7:9 gallows. The eunuch informed the king of Haman's plot and reminded the king of Mordecai's bravery. The tables were turned as Haman was executed on the gallows he had prepared for Mordecai.

8:1 awarded Queen Esther the estate. Ironically, all of Haman's property was given to the Jews whom Haman had planned to strip of their property.

8:3 the evil of Haman. Although Haman was dead, his decree was still in effect. When Es-ther again approached the king without permission, he held out his gold scepter to her.

8:8 write in the king's name whatever pleases you. While Haman's decree could not be revoked, a second one could override it. The new decree gave the Jews the right to protect themselves against anyone who

Victories of the Jews

9 The king's command and law went into effect on the thirteenth day of the twelfth month, the month Adar.[a] On the day when the Jews' enemies had hoped to overpower them, just the opposite happened. The Jews overpowered those who hated them. [2] In each of King Ahasuerus' provinces the Jews assembled in their cities to attack those who intended to harm them.[b] Not a single person could withstand them; terror of them fell on every nationality.

[3] All the officials of the provinces, the satraps, the governors, and the royal civil administrators[c] aided the Jews because they were afraid of Mordecai. [4] For Mordecai [exercised] great power in the palace, and his fame spread throughout the provinces as he became more and more powerful.

[5] The Jews put all their enemies to the sword, killing and destroying them. They did what they pleased to those who hated them. [6] In the fortress of Susa the Jews killed and destroyed 500 men, [7] including Parshandatha, Dalphon, Aspatha, [8] Poratha, Adalia, Aridatha, [9] Parmashta, Arisai, Aridai, and Vaizatha. [10] They killed these 10 sons of Haman son of Hammedatha, the enemy of the Jews. However, they did not seize[d] any plunder.

[11] On that day the number of people killed in the fortress of Susa was reported to the king. [12] The king said to Queen Esther, "In the fortress of Susa the Jews have killed and destroyed 500 men, including Haman's 10 sons. What have they done in the rest of the royal provinces? Whatever you ask will be given to you. Whatever you seek will also be done."

[13] Esther answered, "If it pleases the king, may the Jews who are in Susa also have tomorrow to carry out today's law, and may [the bodies of] Haman's 10 sons be hung on the gallows." [14] The king gave the orders for this to be done, so a law was announced in Susa, and they hung [the bodies of] Haman's 10 sons. [15] The Jews in Susa assembled again on the fourteenth day of the month of Adar and killed 300 men in Susa, but they did not seize[d] any plunder.

[16] The rest of the Jews in the royal provinces assembled, defended themselves, and got rid of[e] their enemies. They killed 75,000[f] of those who hated them, but they did not seize[d] any plunder. [17] [They fought] on the thirteenth day of the month of Adar and rested on the fourteenth, and it became a day of feasting and rejoicing.

[18] But the Jews in Susa had assembled on the thirteenth and the fourteenth days of the month. They rested on the fifteenth day of the month, and it became a day of feasting and rejoicing. [19] This explains why the rural Jews who live in villages observe the fourteenth day of the month of Adar as [a time of] rejoicing and feasting. It is a holiday when they send gifts to one another.

[20] Mordecai recorded these events and sent letters to all the Jews in all of King Ahasuerus' provinces, both near and far. [21] [He ordered] them to celebrate the fourteenth and fifteenth days of the month Adar every year [22] because during those days the Jews got rid of[g] their enemies. That was the month when their sorrow was turned into rejoicing and their mourning into a holiday. They were to be days of feasting, rejoicing, and of sending gifts to one another and the poor.

[23] So the Jews agreed to continue the practice they had begun, as Mordecai had written them to do. [24] For Haman son of Hammedatha the Agagite, the enemy of all the Jews, had plotted against the Jews to destroy them. He cast the Pur (that is, the lot) to crush and destroy them. [25] But when the matter was brought before the king, he commanded by letter that the evil plan Haman had devised against the Jews return on his own head and that he should be hanged with his sons on the gallows. [26] For this reason these days are called Purim, from the word Pur.

Because of all the instructions in this letter as well as what they had witnessed and what had happened to them, [27] the Jews bound themselves, their descendants, and all who joined with them [to a commitment] that they would not fail to celebrate these two days each and every year according to the written instructions and according to the time appointed. [28] These days are remembered and celebrated by every generation, family, province, and city, so that these days of Purim will not lose their significance in Jewish life[h] and their memory will not fade from their descendants.

[29] Queen Esther daughter of Abihail, along with Mordecai the Jew, wrote this second letter with full authority to confirm the letter about Purim. [30] He sent letters with messages of peace and faithfulness to all the Jews who were in the 127 provinces of the kingdom of Ahasuerus, [31] in order to confirm these days of Purim at their proper time just as Mordecai the Jew and Queen Esther had established them and just as they had committed themselves and their descendants to the practices of fasting and lamentation. [32] So Esther's command confirmed these customs of Purim, which were then written into the record.

---

[a]9:1 February–March [b]9:2 Lit cities to send out a hand against the seekers of their evil [c]9:3 Lit and those who do the king's work; Est 3:9
[d]9:10,15,16 Lit not put their hands on [e]9:16 Lit and gained relief from [f]9:16 Some LXX mss read 10,107; other LXX mss read 15,000 [g]9:22 Lit Jews gained relief from [h]9:28 LXX reads will be celebrated into all times

---

sought to attack them. God had used Esther to help her people.

9:5 put all their enemies to the sword. The Jews gathered in various cities to face their attackers, and government authorities helped them. On the day of battle they killed 500 men plus Haman's ten sons. The Jews took no plunder, although the king had given them permission to do so.

9:16 defended themselves, and got rid of their enemies. After defeating their enemies, the Jews experienced peace, and Mordecai became a powerful leader. In Deuteronomy 25:17-19, Moses linked rest from their enemies with the command to blot out the Amalekites, Haman's people.

9:19 [a time of] rejoicing and feasting. The Feast of Purim was commanded by Mordecai and Esther to commemorate God's goodness in protecting His people from destruction. It was to be an annual event celebrated with

Mordecai's Fame

10 King Ahasuerus imposed a tax throughout the land even to the farthest shores.[a] 2 All of his powerful and magnificent accomplishments and the detailed account of Mordecai's great rank to which the king had promoted him, have they not been written in the court record of daily events of the kings of Media and Persia? 3 Mordecai the Jew was second only to King Ahasuerus, famous among the Jews, and highly popular with many of his relatives. He continued to seek good for his people and to speak for the welfare of all his kindred.

[a] **10:1** Or imposed forced labor on the land and the coasts of the sea

eating, rejoicing, and sharing with the poor. It was called Purim because of Haman's use of the *pur* (the lot) to determine the time for the Jews' execution (3:7). The *pur* became a symbol of God's rescue from desperate and dangerous events.

INTRODUCTION TO
JOB

AUTHOR

The writer is not likely Job himself, but an Israelite who is otherwise unknown.

DATE

The events described may have taken place in the patriarchal age, but the book was probably not written in its present form until much later, possibly 600-400 B.C.

THEME

The justice of God in the light of human suffering.

HISTORICAL BACKGROUND

Since there is little significant detail given, the precise situation cannot be established with certainty.

CHARACTERISTICS

The opening verses set the stage for this well-crafted drama. Job is a wealthy, leading citizen, reputed to be very wise. When he loses herds, house, and family and is struck down with a painful illness, we see in Job's life the suffering that afflicts so many in our world. As a clue to Job's apparent alienation from God, the reader is shown that Satan, as accuser, is actively driving a wedge between God and His beloved. If Job proves to be righteous only because "it pays," then Satan wins his bet with God. Job's friends do not have the benefit of this insight and their counsel does not comfort Job. They focus on three arguments:

1. God is almighty.

2. God is just.

3. No human is entirely innocent in God's eyes.

Therefore, say his friends, Job's suffering must be punishment for some sin—a logical answer, but not at all consoling to Job in his despair. Finally, all are silenced, as God breaks in, but He gives no "solution" except to point to His greatness, glory, and power. For the most profound insight, we look ahead to Jesus' death on the cross. There God takes on Himself human suffering and thus defeats it forever—a solution only hinted at in the Book of Job.

PASSAGES FOR
TOPICAL GROUP STUDY

1:6-22 . . . TRAGEDY and DISASTER . . . . Losing Everything

Job and His Family

1 There was a man in the country of Uz named Job. He was a man of perfect integrity, who •feared God and turned away from evil. ² He had seven sons and three daughters. ³ His estate included 7,000 sheep, 3,000 camels, 500 yoke of oxen, 500 female donkeys, and a very large number of servants. Job was the greatest man among all the people of the east.

⁴ His sons used to have banquets, each at his house in turn. They would send an invitation to their three sisters to eat and drink with them. ⁵ Whenever a round of banqueting was over, Job would send ⌊for his children⌋ and purify them, rising early in the morning to offer burnt offerings for^a all of them. For Job thought: Perhaps my children have sinned, having cursed God in their hearts. This was Job's regular practice.

Losing Everything

1. Do you know anyone who has lost all he or she owned? How did that person react?

Job 1:6-22

2. Why did Satan urge God to make Job suffer? Why did God agree?

3. If you suddenly lost all your money, possessions, and family, what would be your first response: Anger at God? Anger at Satan? Loss of faith? Peaceful acceptance?

4. Read Job's response in verse 21. Why did he respond that way? Why did he worship God?

5. How do you respond when tragedy strikes? How can you be like Job and learn to trust God?

Satan's First Test of Job

⁶ One day the sons of God came to present themselves before the LORD, and Satan also came with them. ⁷ The LORD asked Satan, "Where have you come from?"

"From roaming through the earth," Satan answered Him, "and walking around on it."

⁸ Then the LORD said to Satan, "Have you considered My servant Job? No one else on earth is like him, a man of perfect integrity, who fears God and turns away from evil."

⁹ Satan answered the LORD, "Does Job •fear God for nothing? ¹⁰ Haven't You placed a hedge around him, his household, and everything he owns? You have blessed the work of his hands, and his possessions are spread out in the land. ¹¹ But stretch out Your hand and strike everything he owns, and he will surely curse You to Your face."

¹² "Very well," the LORD told Satan, "everything he owns is in your power. However, you must not lay a hand on Job ⌊himself⌋." So Satan went out from the LORD's presence.

¹³ One day when Job's sons and daughters were eating and drinking wine in their oldest brother's house, ¹⁴ a messenger came to Job and reported: "While the oxen were plowing and the donkeys grazing nearby, ¹⁵ the Sabeans swooped down and took them away. They struck down the servants with the sword, and I alone have escaped to tell you!"

¹⁶ He was still speaking when another ⌊messenger⌋ came and reported: "A lightning storm^b struck from heaven. It burned up the sheep and the servants, and devoured them, and I alone have escaped to tell you!"

¹⁷ That messenger was still speaking when ⌊yet⌋ another came and reported: "The Chaldeans formed three bands, made a raid on the camels, and took them away. They struck down the servants with the sword, and I alone have escaped to tell you!"

¹⁸ He was still speaking when another ⌊messenger⌋ came and reported: "Your sons and daughters were eating and drinking wine in their oldest brother's house. ¹⁹ Suddenly a powerful wind swept in from the desert and struck the four corners of the house. It collapsed on the young people so that they died, and I alone have escaped to tell you!"

²⁰ Then Job stood up, tore his robe and shaved his head.^c He fell to the ground and worshiped, ²¹ saying:

> Naked I came from my mother's womb,
> and naked I will leave this life.^d
> The LORD gives, and the LORD takes away.
> Praise the name of the LORD.

²² Throughout all this Job did not sin or blame God for anything.^e

Satan's Second Test of Job

2 One day the sons of God came again to present themselves before the LORD, and Satan also came with them to present himself before the LORD. ² The LORD asked Satan, "Where have you come from?"

"From roaming through the earth," Satan answered Him, "and walking around on it."

---

^a**1:5** Lit *for the number of*   ^b**1:16** Lit *The fire of God*   ^c**1:20** = in mourning; Gn 37:29,34; Jos 7:6   ^d**1:21** Lit *will return there*; Ps 139:13,15
^e**1:22** Lit *or ascribe blame to God*

1:1 country of Uz. Some scholars believe that Uz was in Bashan, south of Damascus; others say Uz was east of Edom in northern Arabia.

1:6-7 sons of God. Sometimes called the "hosts" of heaven, they act as God's messengers by patrolling the earth (Zech. 1:10ff

and 6:5ff) and are active in human affairs (though invisible).

1:7 Where have you come from? At this point in Old Testament history, Satan was merely known as the adversary who delights in the downfall of God's people. (See also 2:2)

1:10 placed a hedge. God is *aware* of ev-

ery detail in our lives.

1:11 he will surely curse You to Your face. Satan said man's only motive in loving God is selfish because human love is bought with good gifts.

1:20 tore his robe and shaved his head. Job grieved greatly over his overwhelming

473

3 Then the LORD said to Satan, "Have you considered My servant Job? No one else on earth is like him, a man of perfect integrity, who •fears God and turns away from evil. He still retains his integrity, even though you incited Me against him, to destroy him without just cause."

4 "Skin for skin!" Satan answered the LORD. "A man will give up everything he owns in exchange for his life. 5 But stretch out Your hand and strike his flesh and bones, and he will surely curse You to Your face."

6 "Very well," the LORD told Satan, "he is in your power; only spare his life." 7 So Satan left the LORD's presence and infected Job with incurable boils from the sole of his foot to the top of his head. 8 Then Job took a piece of broken pottery to scrape himself while he sat among the ashes.a

9 His wife said to him, "Do you still retain your integrity? Curse God and die!"

10 "You speak as a foolish woman speaks," he told her. "Should we accept only good from God and not adversity?" Throughout all this Job did not sin in what he said.b

Job's Three Friends

11 Now when Job's three friends—Eliphaz the Temanite, Bildad the Shuhite, and Zophar the Naamathite—heard about all this adversity that had happened to him, each of them came from his home. They met together to go and offer sympathy and comfort to him. 12 When they looked from a distance, they could ⌊barely⌋ recognize him. They wept aloud, and each man tore his robe and threw dust into the air and on his head. 13 Then they sat on the ground with him seven days and nights, but no one spoke a word to him because they saw that his suffering was very intense.

Job's Opening Speech

3 After this Job began to speak and cursed the day he was born. 2 He said:

3   May the day I was born perish,
    and the night when they said,
    "A boy is conceived."
4   If only that day had turned to darkness!
    May God above not care about it,
    or light shine on it.
5   May darkness and gloom reclaim it,
    and a cloud settle over it.
    May an eclipse of the sunc terrify it.
6   If only darkness had taken that night away!

May it not appeard among the days of the year
  or be listed in the calendar.e
7   Yes, may that night be barren;
    may no joyful shout be heard in it.
8   Let those who curse ⌊certain⌋ days
    cast a spell on it,
    those who are skilled in rousing •Leviathan.
9   May its morning stars grow dark.
    May it wait for daylight but have none;
    may it not see the breakingf of dawn.
10 For that night did not shut
    the doors of my ⌊mother's⌋ womb,
    and hide sorrow from my eyes.

11 Why was I not stillborn;
    ⌊why⌋ didn't I die as I came from the womb?
12 Why did the knees receive me,
    and why were there breasts for me to nurse?
13 For then I would have laid down in peace;
    I would be asleep.
    Then I would be at rest
14 with the kings and counselors of the earth,
    who rebuilt ruined cities for themselves,
15 or with princes who had gold,
    who filled their houses with silver.
16 Or ⌊why⌋ was I not hidden
    like a miscarried child,
    like infants who never see daylight?
17 There the wicked cease to make trouble,
    and there the weary find rest.
18 The captives are completely at ease;
    they do not hear the voice of ⌊their⌋ oppressor.
19 Both the small and the great are there,
    and the slave is set free from his master.

20 Why is light given to one burdened with grief,
    and life to those whose existence is bitter,
21 who wait for death, but it does not come,
    and search for it more than for hidden treasure,
22 who are filled with much joy
    and are glad when they reach the grave?
23 ⌊Why is life given⌋ to a man whose path
    is hidden,
    whom God has hedged in?
24 I sigh when food is ⌊put⌋ before me,g
    and my groans pour out like water.
25 For the thing I feared has overtaken me,
    and what I dreaded has happened to me.
26 I cannot relax or be still;
    I have no rest, for trouble comes.

a2:8 = in mourning; Jb 42:6; 2 Sm 13:19   b2:10 Lit sin with his lips   c3:5 Lit May a darkening of daylight   d3:6 LXX, Syr, Tg, Vg; MT reads rejoice
e3:6 Lit or enter the number of months   f3:9 Lit the eyelids   g3:24 Or My sighing serves as my food

losses, and yet bowed in worship to God.
2:4-5 Skin for skin! Satan reasoned that personal, physical suffering would break Job if losing his children and wealth didn't.
2:7 incurable boils. The two Hebrew words used for "incurable boils" were used to describe the plague of festering boils in Egypt

(Ex. 9:8-11). "Painful boils" is one of the curses for disobedience and refers to an incurable disease (Deut. 28:35).
2:12 could ⌊barely⌋ recognize him. His maladies included ulcerous sores, itching, degenerative changes in facial skin, loss of appetite, depression, worms in the boils,

weight loss, running sores, and difficulty breathing.
2:13 sat ... with him. This silence was the best response of Job's friends.
3:13 rest. Job merely longs for relief from what he saw as the judgment he was already living, not judgment after death.

First Series of Speeches

Eliphaz Speaks

4 Then Eliphaz the Temanite replied:

2 Should anyone try to speak with you
   when you are exhausted?
   Yet who can keep from speaking?
3 Look! You have instructed many
   and have strengthened weak hands.
4 Your words have steadied the one
      who was stumbling,
   and braced the knees that were buckling.
5 But now that this has happened to you,
   you have become exhausted.
   It strikes you, and you are dismayed.
6 Isn't your piety your confidence,
   and the integrity of your life^a your hope?
7 Consider: who has perished when he
      was innocent?
   Where have the honest been destroyed?
8 In my experience, those who plow injustice
   and those who sow trouble reap the same.
9 They perish at a ⌊single⌋ blast from God
   and come to an end by the breath of His nostrils.
10 The lion may roar and the fierce lion growl,
   but the fangs of young lions are broken.
11 The strong lion dies if ⌊it catches⌋ no prey,
   and the cubs of the lioness are scattered.

12 A word was brought to me in secret;
   my ears caught a whisper of it.
13 Among unsettling thoughts from visions
      in the night,
   when deep sleep descends on men,
14 fear and trembling came over me
   and made all my bones shake.
15 A wind^b passed by me,
   and I shuddered with fear.^c
16 ⌊A figure⌋ stood there,
   but I could not recognize its appearance;
   a form loomed before my eyes.
   I heard a quiet voice:
17 "Can a person be more righteous than God,
   or a man more pure than his Maker?"
18 If God puts no trust in His servants
   and He charges His angels with foolishness,^d
19 how much more those who dwell
      in clay houses,
   whose foundation is in the dust,

who are crushed like a moth!
20 They are smashed to pieces from dawn to dusk;
   they perish forever while no one notices.
21 Are their tent cords not pulled up?
   They die without wisdom.

5 Call out if you please. Will anyone answer you?
   Which of the holy ones will you turn to?
2 For anger kills a fool,
   and jealousy slays the gullible.
3 I have seen a fool taking root,
   but I immediately pronounced a curse
      on his home.
4 His children are far from safety.
   They are crushed at the ⌊city⌋ •gate,
   with no one to defend ⌊them⌋.
5 The hungry consume his harvest,
   even taking it out of the thorns.^e
   The thirsty^f pant for his children's wealth.
6 For distress does not grow out of the soil,
   and trouble does not sprout from the ground.
7 But mankind is born for trouble
   as surely as sparks fly upward.

8 However, if I were you, I would appeal to God
   and would present my case to Him.
9 He does great and unsearchable things,
   wonders without number.
10 He gives rain to the earth
   and sends water to the fields.
11 He sets the lowly on high,
   and mourners are lifted to safety.
12 He frustrates the schemes of the crafty
   so that they^g achieve no success.
13 He traps the wise in their craftiness
   so that the plans of the deceptive
   are quickly brought to an end.
14 They encounter darkness by day,
   and they grope at noon
      as if it were night.
15 He saves the needy from their sharp words^h
   and from the clutches of the powerful.
16 So the poor have hope,
   and injustice shuts its mouth.
17 See how happy the man is God corrects;
   so do not reject the discipline of the •Almighty.
18 For He crushes but also binds up;
   He strikes, but His hands also heal.
19 He will rescue you from six calamities;
   no harm will touch you in seven.

---

^a**4:6** Lit *ways*   ^b**4:15** Or *A spirit*   ^c**4:15** Or *and the hair on my body stood up*   ^d**4:18** Or *error*; Hb obscure   ^e**5:5** Hb obscure   ^f**5:5** Aq, Sym, Syr, Vg; MT reads *snares*   ^g**5:12** Lit *their hands*   ^h**5:15** Lit *from the sword of their mouth*; Ps 55:21; 59:7

3:23 hedged in. While earlier God's hedge produced bounty and all good things, now it kept Job trapped in pain.
4:1 Eliphaz. Eliphaz, probably the oldest of the three friends, begins their counsel (which some suggest is Satanic).
4:3-6 You have instructed many. Eliphaz

reminds Job how he advised others to be patient under trial and should do likewise.
4:8 those who sow trouble reap the same. "You reap what you sow" appears throughout the Bible (Ps. 7:14-16; Prov. 11:18). God sometimes disciplines people (Heb. 12:7), yet Scripture is also clear that not all suffer-

ing is the result of personal sin (John 9:1-3; 1 Peter 2:19-20). Eliphaz encouraged Job to submit to his punishment since God shows mercy to the humble (1 Sam. 2:7).

5:1 holy ones. Eliphaz warned Job that angels would not intervene. Job later desired a mediator between himself and God (9:33; 16:19-21).

20 In famine He will redeem you from death,
and in battle, from the power of the sword.
21 You will be safe from slander^a
and not fear destruction when it comes.
22 You will laugh at destruction and hunger
and not fear the animals of the earth.
23 For you will have a covenant with the stones
of the field,
and the wild animals will be at peace with you.
24 You will know that your tent is secure,
and nothing will be missing when you inspect
your home.
25 You will also know that your offspring
will be many
and your descendants like the grass of the earth.
26 You will approach the grave in full vigor,
as a stack of sheaves is gathered in its season.

27 We have investigated this, and it is true!
Hear it and understand ⌞it⌟ for yourself.

Job's Reply to Eliphaz

6 Then Job answered:

2 If only my grief could be weighed
and my devastation placed with it on a scale.
3 For then it would outweigh the sand of the seas!
That is why my words are rash.
4 Surely the arrows of the •Almighty
have pierced^b me;
my spirit drinks their poison.
God's terrors are arrayed against me.
5 Does a wild donkey bray over fresh grass
or an ox low over its fodder?
6 Is bland food eaten without salt?
Is there flavor in an egg white?^c
7 I refuse to touch ⌞them⌟;
they are like contaminated food.

8 If only my request would be granted
and God would provide what I hope for:
9 that He would decide to crush me,
to unleash His power and cut me off!
10 It would still bring me comfort,
and I would leap for joy in unrelenting pain
that I have not denied^d the words
of the Holy One.
11 What strength do I have that I should continue
to hope?
What is my future, that I should be patient?

12 Is my strength that of stone,
or my flesh made of bronze?
13 Since I cannot help myself,
⌞the hope for⌟ success has been banished
from me.

14 A despairing man should receive loyalty
from his friends,^e
even if he abandons the •fear of the Almighty.
15 My brothers are as treacherous as a •wadi,
as seasonal streams that overflow
16 and become darkened^f because of ice,
and the snow melts into them.
17 The wadis evaporate in warm weather;
they disappear from their channels
in hot weather.
18 Caravans turn away from their routes,
go up into the desert, and perish.
19 The caravans of Tema look ⌞for these streams⌟.
The traveling merchants of Sheba hope
for them.
20 They are ashamed because they
had been confident ⌞of finding water⌟.
When they arrive there, they are frustrated.
21 So ⌞this⌟ is what you have now become
⌞to me⌟.^g
When you see something dreadful,
you are afraid.
22 Have I ever said: Give me ⌞something⌟
or Pay a bribe for me from your wealth
23 or Deliver me from the enemy's power
or Redeem me from the grasp of the ruthless?

24 Teach me, and I will be silent.
Help me understand what I did wrong.
25 How painful honest words can be!
But what does your rebuke prove?
26 Do you think that you can disprove ⌞my⌟ words
or that a despairing man's words are
⌞mere⌟ wind?
27 No doubt you would cast ⌞lots⌟
for a fatherless child
and negotiate a price to ⌞sell⌟ your friend.

28 But now, please look at me;
would I lie to your face?
29 Reconsider; don't be unjust.
Reconsider; my righteousness is still the issue.
30 Am I lying,
or can I^h not recognize lies?

---

^a5:21 Lit be hidden from the whip of the tongue ^b6:4 Lit Almighty are in ^c6:6 Hb obscure ^d6:10 Lit hidden ^e6:14 Lit To the despairing his friend loyalty; Hb obscure ^f6:16 Or turbid ^g6:21 Alt Hb tradition reads So you have now become nothing ^h6:30 Lit Is there injustice on my tongue, or can my palate

---

5:17 Almighty. The divine title *Shaddai* is found 31 times in Job and only 17 times in the rest of the Old Testament.
5:27 Hear it and understand [it] for yourself. In other words, the final word!
6:1 If only my grief could be weighed. Job's lofty response makes it seem like a

speech contest.
6:5-6 wild donkey ... ox low ... bland food. Rhetorical questions are often used in Wisdom Literature to point out something absurd.
6:8-10 unleash His power and cut me off. Job longs for death to release him from the

struggle of proving to (God and) his friends that he is innocent of sin.
6:15 My brothers. Job's friends supported him in good times, but in adversity their support "evaporates" (v.17; see also vv. 20-21).
6:22-23 Job could not expect friends to remove his pain, but he needed them to "be

7 Isn't mankind consigned to forced labor on earth?
Are not his days like those of a hired hand?
2 Like a slave he longs for shade;
like a hired man he waits for his pay.
3 So I have been made to inherit months
of futility,
and troubled nights have been assigned to me.
4 When I lie down I think:
When will I get up?
But the evening drags on endlessly,
and I toss and turn until dawn.
5 My flesh is clothed with maggots and encrusted
with dirt.ᵃ
My skin forms scabsᵇ and then oozes.

6 My days pass more swiftly
than a weaver's shuttle;
they come to an end without hope.
7 Remember that my life is ⌊but⌋ a breath.
My eye will never again see anything good.
8 The eye of anyone who looks on me
will no longer see me.
Your eyes will look for me, but I will be gone.
9 As a cloud fades away and vanishes,
so the one who goes down to •Sheol will never
rise again.
10 He will never return to his house;
his hometown will no longer rememberᶜ him.

11 Therefore I will not restrain my mouth.
I will speak in the anguish of my spirit;
I will complain in the bitterness of my soul.
12 Am I the seaᵈ or a sea monster,
that You keep me under guard?
13 When I say: My bed will comfort me,
and my couch will ease my complaint,
14 then You frighten me with dreams,
and terrify me with visions,
15 so that I prefer strangling,ᵉ
death rather than life in this body.ᶠ
16 I give up! I will not live forever.
Leave me alone, for my days are a breath.ᵍ

17 What is man, that You think so highly of him
and pay so much attention to him?
18 You inspect him every morning,
and put him to the test every moment.
19 Will You ever look away from me,
or leave me alone until I swallow my saliva?
20 ⌊If⌋ I have sinned, what have I done to You,

Watcher of mankind?
Why have You made me Your target,
so that I have become a burden to You?ʰ
21 Why not forgive my sin
and pardon my transgression?
For soon I will lie down in the grave.
You will eagerly seek me, but I will be gone.

Bildad Speaks

8 Then Bildad the Shuhite replied:

2 How long will you go on saying these things?
Your words are a blast of wind.
3 Does God pervert justice?
Does the •Almighty pervert what is right?
4 Since your children sinned against Him,
He gave them over to their rebellion.
5 But if you earnestly seek God
and ask the Almighty for mercy,
6 if you are pure and upright,
then He will move even now on your behalf
and restore the home where your righteousness
dwells.
7 Then, even if your beginnings were modest,
your final days will be full of prosperity.

8 For ask the previous generation,
and pay attention to what
their fathers discovered,
9 since we were ⌊born only⌋ yesterday and know
nothing.
Our days on earth are but a shadow.
10 Will they not teach you and tell you
and speak from their understanding?
11 Does papyrus grow where there is no marsh?
Do reeds flourish without water?
12 While still uncut shoots,
they would dry up quicker than
any ⌊other⌋ plant.
13 Such is the destinyⁱ of all who forget God;
the hope of the godless will perish.
14 His source of confidence is fragile;ʲ
what he trusts in is a spider's web.
15 He leans on his web, but it doesn't stand firm.
He grabs it, but it does not hold up.
16 He is an amply watered plant in the sunshine;
his shoots spread out over his garden.
17 His roots are intertwined around a pile
of rocks.
He looks for a home among the stones.

ᵃ**7:5** Or *and dirty scabs* ᵇ**7:5** Lit *skin hardens* ᶜ**7:10** Lit *know* ᵈ**7:12** Or *the sea god;* Jb 26:12; Ps 74:13 ᵉ**7:15** Or *suffocation* ᶠ**7:15** Lit *than my bones* ᵍ**7:16** Or *are futile* ʰ**7:20** LXX, one ancient Jewish tradition; MT, Vg read *myself* ⁱ**8:13** Lit *Such are the ways* ʲ**8:14** Or *cut off;* Hb obscure

---

there" for him in his suffering (12:1-3; 21:1-6; 26:1-4).

6:27 negotiate … to [sell] your friend. Job exaggerates their cruelty to make his point.

7:13 My bed will comfort. Job can't even get a good night's sleep.

7:20-21 [If] I have sinned. Job, allowing for the possibility of sinning without realizing it, longs for release from his suffering through forgiveness or death.

8:3 Bildad the Shuhite. Job's second friend arrives to speak "truth." Bildad quickly points out that Job is only getting his due.

8:5-6 if you earnestly seek God. Bildad's focus is on God's power and unwavering justice. However, Bildad's God is inflexible and without mercy.

8:6 if you are pure and upright. A sliver of sarcasm: If Job were really innocent, his healing would not be delayed.

18 If he is uprooted[a] from his place,
   it will deny [knowing] him, saying,
   "I never saw you."
19 Surely this is the joy of his way of life;
   yet others will sprout from the dust.
20 Look, God does not reject a person
   of integrity,
   and He will not support evildoers.
21 He will yet fill your mouth with laughter
   and your lips with a shout of joy.
22 Your enemies will be clothed with shame;
   the tent of the wicked will exist no longer.

Job's Reply to Bildad

9 Then Job answered:

2 Yes, I know what you've said is true,
   but how can a person be justified before God?
3 If one wanted to take Him to court,
   he could not answer God[b] once
   in a thousand [times].
4 God is wise and all-powerful.
   Who has opposed Him
   and come out unharmed?
5 He removes mountains
   without their knowledge,
   overturning them in His anger.
6 He shakes the earth from its place
   so that its pillars tremble.
7 He commands the sun not to shine
   and seals off the stars.
8 He alone stretches out the heavens
   and treads on the waves of the sea.[c]
9 He makes [the stars]: the Bear,[d] Orion,
   the Pleiades, and the constellations[e]
   of the southern sky.
10 He performs great and unsearchable things,
   wonders without number.
11 If He passes by me, I wouldn't see Him;
   [if] He goes right by, I wouldn't recognize Him.
12 If He snatches [something], who can stop[f] Him?
   Who can ask Him, "What are You doing?"
13 God does not hold back His anger;
   •Rahab's assistants cringe in fear
   beneath Him!
14 How then can I answer Him
   or choose my arguments against Him?
15 Even if I were in the right, I could not answer.
   I could only beg my judge for mercy.

16 If I summoned [Him] and He answered me,
   I do not believe He would pay attention to
   what I said.
17 He batters me with a whirlwind
   and multiplies my wounds without cause.
18 He doesn't let me catch my breath
   but soaks me with bitter experiences.
19 If it is a matter of strength, look, He is
   the Mighty One!
   If it is a matter of justice, who can
   summon Him?[g]
20 Even if I were in the right, my own mouth
   would condemn me;
   if I were blameless, my mouth would
   declare me guilty.
21 Though I am blameless,
   I no longer care about myself;
   I renounce my life.
22 It is all the same. Therefore I say,
   "He destroys both the blameless
   and the wicked."
23 When disaster brings sudden death,
   He mocks the despair of the innocent.
24 The earth[h] is handed over to the wicked;
   He blindfolds[i] its judges.
   If it isn't He, then who is it?
25 My days fly by faster than a runner;[j]
   they flee without seeing any good.
26 They sweep by like boats made of papyrus,
   like an eagle swooping down on [its] prey.
27 If I said, "I will forget my complaint,
   change my expression, and smile,"
28 I would still live in terror of all my pains.
   I know You will not acquit me.
29 Since I will be found guilty,
   why should I labor in vain?
30 If I wash myself with snow,
   and cleanse my hands with lye,
31 then You dip me in a pit [of mud],
   and my own clothes despise me!
32 For He is not a man like me, that I can
   answer Him,
   that we can take each other to court.
33 There is no one to judge between us,
   to lay his hand on both of us.
34 Let Him take His rod away from me
   so His terror will no longer frighten me.

---

[a]**8:18** Lit *swallowed* [b]**9:3** Or *court, God would not answer him* [c]**9:8** Or *and walks on the back of the sea god* [d]**9:9** Or *Aldebaran* [e]**9:9** Or *chambers* [f]**9:12** Or *dissuade* [g]**9:19** LXX; MT reads *me* [h]**9:24** Or *land* [i]**9:24** Lit *covers the faces of* [j]**9:25** = a royal messenger; 2 Sm 18:19–33; 1 Kg 1:5; Est 3:13,15

8:8 previous generation. Where Eliphaz turned to mysticism for insight (4:12-21), Bildad found straightforward wisdom in the pages of history. Bildad truly believes he KNOWS the answer for Job. He uses illustrations from nature in verses 11-19 to point out the logic of his "truth."

8:20 not reject a person of integrity. Bildad invited Job to read between the lines and recognize himself as a hypocrite or a liar.

9:2-3 Job recognized that Bildad was right: the wicked do deserve punishment. If only he had sinned.

9:3 take Him to court. In an imaginary court-room, Job "lawyers up" in describing his plight in legal terms (vv. 3, 15-16, 20, 24, 32).

9:17 without cause. Job is unaware of the heavenly drama that preceded all his troubles (1:6-12).

9:22-24 If it isn't He, then who is it? Without realizing it, Job is on the right track.

35 Then I would speak and not fear Him.
But that is not the case; I am on my own.

10

I am disgusted with my life.
I will express my complaint
and speak in the bitterness of my soul.

2 I will say to God:
Do not declare me guilty!
Let me know why You prosecute me.

3 Is it good for You to oppress,
to reject the work of Your hands,
and favor[a] the plans of the wicked?

4 Do You have eyes of flesh,
or do You see as a human sees?

5 Are Your days like those of a human,
or Your years like those of a man,

6 that You look for my wrongdoing
and search for my sin,

7 even though You know that I am not wicked
and that there is no one who can deliver
from Your hand?

8 Your hands shaped me and formed me.
Will You now turn around and destroy me?

9 Please remember that You formed me like clay.
Will You now return me to dust?

10 Did You not pour me out like milk
and curdle me like cheese?

11 You clothed me with skin and flesh,
and wove me together with bones and tendons.

12 You gave me life and faithful love,
and Your care has guarded my life.

13 Yet You concealed these ⌊thoughts⌋ in Your heart;
I know that this was Your hidden plan:[b]

14 if I sin, You would notice,[c]
and would not acquit me of my wrongdoing.

15 If I am wicked, woe to me!
And even if I am righteous, I cannot lift up
my head.
I am filled with shame
and aware of my affliction.

16 If I am proud, You hunt me like a lion
and again display Your miraculous power
against me.

17 You produce new witnesses[d] against me
and multiply Your anger toward me.
Hardships assault me, wave after wave.[e]

18 Why did You bring me out of the womb?
I should have died and never been seen.

19 I wish[f] I had never existed
but had been carried from the womb
to the grave.

20 Are my days not few? Stop ⌊it⌋![g]
Leave me alone, so that I can smile a little

21 before I go to a land of darkness and gloom,
never to return.

22 ⌊It is⌋ a land of blackness
like the deepest darkness,
gloomy and chaotic,
where even the light is like[h] the darkness.

Zophar Speaks

11

Then Zophar the Naamathite replied:

2 Should this stream of words go unanswered
and such a talker[i] be acquitted?

3 Should your babbling put others to silence,
so that you can keep on ridiculing
with no one to humiliate you?

4 You have said, "My teaching is sound,
and I am pure in Your sight."

5 But if only God would speak
and declare His case[j] against you,

6 He would show you the secrets of wisdom,
for true wisdom has two sides.
Know then that God has chosen to overlook
some of your sin.

7 Can you fathom the depths of God
or discover the limits of the •Almighty?

8 ⌊They are⌋ higher than the heavens—what can
you do?
⌊They are⌋ deeper than •Sheol—what can
you know?

9 Their measure is longer than the earth
and wider than the sea.

10 If He passes by and throws
⌊someone⌋ in prison
or convenes a court, who can stop Him?

11 Surely He knows which people are worthless.
If He sees iniquity, will He not take note ⌊of it⌋?

12 But a stupid man will gain understanding
as soon as a wild donkey is born a man!

13 As for you, if you redirect your heart
and lift up your hands to Him ⌊in prayer⌋—

14 if there is iniquity in your hand, remove it,
and don't allow injustice to dwell
in your tents—

---

a **10:3** Lit shine on b **10:13** Lit was with You c **10:14** Lit notice me d **10:17** Or You bring fresh troops e **10:17** Lit Changes and a host are with me f **10:19** Lit As if g **10:20** Alt Hb tradition reads Will He not leave my few days alone? h **10:22** Lit chaotic, and shines as i **11:2** Lit a man of lips
j **11:5** Lit and open His lips

9:32-3 He is not a man like me. Job sought in vain for an impartial arbiter. Who better than God Himself? Job has arrived at the painful place of admitting that God appears to be his "enemy" and yet there is no one else to whom he can go.

10:3 reject the work of Your hands. Job

assigned cruel intentions to God. Depressed and utterly discouraged, Job began to believe his rantings, though his ideas denied everything that Job had always believed about God.

10:8-17 As if addressing the witness stand, Job questions God's character by attribut-

ing to God the evil done to him (see v. 8).
11:1-20 Eliphaz started it. Bildad elaborated on it. Now, Zophar reiterates their condemnation.

11:5 speak … against you. Zophar wanted to put words in God's mouth, presuming he knew God's mind. Instead, God eventually

15 then you will hold your head high,
    free from fault.
  You will be firmly established and unafraid.
16 For you will forget your suffering,
    recalling ⌊it only⌋ as waters that have flowed by.
17 ⌊Your⌋ life will be brighter than noonday;
    ⌊its⌋ darknessª will be like the morning.
18 You will be confident, because there is hope.
  You will look carefully about and lie down
    in safety.

19 You will lie down without fear,
    and many will seek your favor.
20 But the sight of the wicked will fail.
  Their way of escape will be cut off,
    and their ⌊only⌋ hope will be to die.

Job's Reply to Zophar

12 Then Job answered:

2 No doubt you are the people,
    and wisdom will die with you!
3 But I also have a mind;
    I am not inferior to you.
  Who doesn't know the things you are
    talking about?ᵇ

4 I am a laughingstock to myᶜ friends,
    by calling on God, who answers me.ᵈ
  The righteous and upright man is
    a laughingstock.
5 The one who is at ease holds calamity
    in contempt
  ⌊and thinks⌋ it is prepared for those whose feet
    are slipping.
6 The tents of robbers are safe,
    and those who provoke God are secure;
  God's power provides this.

7 But ask the animals, and they will instruct you;
    ⌊ask⌋ the birds of the sky, and they will tell you.
8 Or speak to the earth, and it will instruct you;
    let the fish of the sea inform you.
9 Which of all these does not know
    that the hand of the LORD has done this?
10 The life of every living thing is in His hand,
    as well as the breath of all mankind.
11 Doesn't the ear test words
    as the palate tastes food?
12 Wisdom is found with the elderly,
    and understanding comes with long life.

13 Wisdom and strength belong to God;
    counsel and understanding are His.
14 Whatever He tears down cannot be rebuilt;
    whoever He imprisons cannot be released.
15 When He withholds the waters, everything
    dries up,
  and when He releases them, they destroy
    the land.
16 True wisdom and power belong to Him.
  The deceived and the deceiver are His.
17 He leads counselors away barefoot
    and makes judges go mad.
18 He releases the bondsᵉ put on by kings
    and ties a cloth around their waists.
19 He leads priests away barefoot
    and overthrows established leaders.
20 He deprives trusted advisers of speech
    and takes away the elders' good judgment.
21 He pours out contempt on nobles
    and disarmsᶠ the strong.
22 He reveals mysteries from the darkness
    and brings the deepest darkness into the light.
23 He makes nations great, then destroys them;
    He enlarges nations, then leads them away.
24 He deprives the world's leaders of reason,
    and makes them wander
    in a trackless wasteland.
25 They grope around in darkness without light;
    He makes them stagger like drunken men.

13 Look, my eyes have seen all this;
    my ears have heard and understood it.
2 Everything you know, I also know;
    I am not inferior to you.
3 Yet I prefer to speak to the •Almighty
    and argue my case before God.
4 But you coat ⌊the truth⌋ with lies;
    you are all worthless doctors.
5 If only you would shut up
    and let that be your wisdom!

6 Hear now my argument,
    and listen to my defense.ᵍ
7 Would you testify unjustly on God's behalf
    or speak deceitfully for Him?
8 Would you show partiality to Him
    or argue the case in His defense?
9 Would it go well if He examined you?
  Could you deceive Him as you would deceive
    a man?

ª **11:17** Text emended; MT reads *noonday; you are dark, you*   ᵇ **12:3** Lit *With whom are not such things as these*   ᶜ **12:4** Lit *his*   ᵈ **12:4** Lit *him*
ᵉ **12:18** Text emended; MT reads *discipline*   ᶠ **12:21** Lit *and loosens the belt of*   ᵍ **13:6** Lit *to the claims of my lips*

---

spoke against Zophar himself (42:7).
11:8-9 higher than the heavens. Zophar's (partial) portrait of God resembles God's self-description (38:1–42:6). Knowing about God is not the same as knowing God.
11:11-12 a stupid man. Zophar mocks Job's feeble understanding.

11:13-20 Despite Zophar's formula for happiness (vv. 16-17), relationship with God is not a formula.
12:1–14:22 Job's longest speech thus far (12:1–13:19). Finally, his attention turns again to God (13:20–14:22).
12:2 wisdom will die with you. Job

sneered at his friends' supposed monopoly on wisdom.
12:6 robbers are safe. Job repeatedly ponders why those who have committed real evil are not suffering as he is.
12:9-10 hand of the LORD. Not only is God's hand skillful in what He has created (Isa.

10 Surely He would rebuke you
  if you secretly showed partiality.
11 Would God's majesty not terrify you?
  Would His dread not fall on you?
12 Your memorable sayings are proverbs of ash;
  your defenses are made of clay.

13 Be quiet,ᵃ and I will speak.
  Let whatever comes happen to me.
14 Why do I put myself at riskᵇ
  and take my life in my own hands?
15 Even if He kills me, I will hope in Him.ᶜ
  I will still defend my ways before Him.
16 Yes, this will result in my deliverance,
  for no godless person can appear before Him.
17 Pay close attention to my words;
  let my declaration ⌊ring⌋ in your ears.
18 Now then, I have prepared ⌊my⌋ case;
  I know that I am right.
19 Can anyone indict me?
  If so, I will be silent and die.

20 Only grant ⌊these⌋ two things to me, ⌊God⌋,
  so that I will not have to hide
    from Your presence:
21 remove Your hand from me,
  and do not let Your terror frighten me.
22 Then call, and I will answer,
  or I will speak, and You can respond to me.
23 How many iniquities and sins
    have I committed?ᵈ
  Reveal to me my transgression and sin.
24 Why do You hide Your face
  and consider me Your enemy?
25 Will You frighten a wind-driven leaf?
  Will You chase after dry straw?
26 For You record bitter accusations against me
  and make me inherit the iniquities of my youth.
27 You put my feet in the stocks
  and stand watch over all my paths,
  setting a limit for the solesᵉ of my feet.

28 Man wears out like something rotten,
  like a moth-eaten garment.

14 Man born of woman
  is short of days and full of trouble.
2 He blossoms like a flower, then withers;
  he flees like a shadow and does not last.
3 Do You really take notice of one like this?
  Will You bring me into judgment against You?ᶠ

4 Who can produce something pure from what
    is impure?
  No one!
5 Since man's days are determined
  and the number of his months depends on You,
  and ⌊since⌋ You have setᵍ limits he cannot pass,
6 look away from him and let him rest
  so that he can enjoy his day like a hired hand.

7 There is hope for a tree:
  If it is cut down, it will sprout again,
  and its shoots will not die.
8 If its roots grow old in the ground
  and its stump starts to die in the soil,
9 the smell of water makes it thrive
  and produce twigs like a sapling.
10 But a man dies and fades away;
  he breathes his last—where is he?
11 As water disappears from the sea
  and a •wadi becomes parched and dry,
12 so man lies down never to rise again.
  They will not wake up until the heavens are
    no more;
  they will not stir from their sleep.

13 If only You would hide me in •Sheol
  and conceal me until Your anger passes,
  that You would appoint a time for me
  and then remember me.
14 When a man dies, will he come back to life?
  ⌊If so,⌋ I would wait all the days of my struggle
  until my relief comes.
15 You would call, and I would answer You.
  You would long for the work of Your hands.
16 For then You would count my steps
  but would not take note of my sin.
17 My rebellion would be sealed up in a bag,
  and You would cover over my iniquity.

18 But as a mountain collapses and crumbles
  and a rock is dislodged from its place,
19 as water wears away stones
  and torrents wash away the soil from the land,
  so You destroy a man's hope.
20 You completely overpower him, and he
    passes on;
  You change his appearance and send him away.
21 If his sons receive honor, he does not know it;
  if they become insignificant, he is unaware of it.
22 He feels only the pain of his own body
  and mourns only for himself.

ᵃ**13:13** Lit *quiet before me* ᵇ**13:14** Lit *I take my flesh in my teeth* ᶜ**13:15** Other Hb mss read *I will be without hope* ᵈ**13:23** Lit *sins are to me* ᵉ**13:27** Lit *paths. You mark a line around the roots* ᶠ**14:3** LXX, Syr, Vg read *him* ᵍ**14:5** Lit *set his*

66:2; Jer. 14:22), but his hand sustains human life and provides its direction.

12:12, 20 Wisdom is found with the elderly. Job insinuates that wisdom has not accompanied age in the case of his friends.

13:3 I prefer to speak to the Almighty. Job still waits to hear his verdict from God's mouth, rather than his friends' (see also v. 15).

13:7 testify unjustly on God's behalf. That the friends could be wrong doesn't seem to have occurred to them.

13:15 I will hope in Him. The climax of the book, Job asserts ultimate faith in God's character, and will die proclaiming it.

13:20-22 grant [these] two things. Here Job asked for relief from his torment (v. 21), if not at least a fair trial. Then Job would know that he and God were still communicating.

13:26 record bitter accusations. Job supposed that God had meticulously recorded

Second Series of Speeches

Eliphaz Speaks

15 Then Eliphaz the Temanite replied:

2 Does a wise man answer with empty[a] counsel
or fill himself[b] with the hot east wind?

3 Should he argue with useless talk
or with words that serve no good purpose?

4 But you even undermine the •fear [of God]
and hinder meditation before Him.

5 Your iniquity teaches you what to say,
and you choose the language of the crafty.

6 Your own mouth condemns you, not I;
your own lips testify against you.

7 Were you the first person ever born,
or were you brought forth before the hills?

8 Do you listen in on the council of God,
or have a monopoly on wisdom?

9 What do you know that we don't?
[What] do you understand that is not [clear]
to us?

10 Both the gray-haired and the elderly are with us,
men older than your father.

11 Are God's consolations not enough for you,
even the words that [deal] gently with you?

12 Why has your heart misled you,
and why do your eyes flash

13 as you turn your anger[c] against God
and allow such words to leave your mouth?

14 What is man, that he should be pure,
or one born of woman, that he
should be righteous?

15 If God puts no trust in His holy ones
and the heavens are not pure in His sight,

16 how much less one who is revolting
and corrupt,
who drinks injustice like water?

17 Listen to me and I will inform you.
I will describe what I have seen,

18 what was declared by wise men
and was not suppressed by their ancestors,

19 the land was given to them alone
when no foreigner passed among them.

20 A wicked man writhes in pain all his days;
few[d] years are stored up for the ruthless.

21 Dreadful sounds fill his ears;
when he is at peace, a robber attacks him.

22 He doesn't believe he will return from darkness;
he is destined for the sword.

23 He wanders about for food, [saying,]
"Where is it?"
He knows the day of darkness is at hand.

24 Trouble and distress terrify him,
overwhelming him like a king prepared
for battle.

25 For he has stretched out his hand against God
and has arrogantly opposed the •Almighty.

26 He rushes headlong at Him
with his thick, studded shields.

27 Though his face is covered with fat[e]
and his waistline bulges with it,

28 he will dwell in ruined cities,
in abandoned houses destined to become piles
of rubble.

29 He will no longer be rich; his wealth
will not endure.
His possessions[f] will not spread over the land.

30 He will not escape from the darkness;
flames will wither his shoots,
and he will depart by the breath of God's mouth.

31 Let him not put trust in worthless things, being
led astray,
for what he gets in exchange will prove worthless.

32 It will be accomplished before his time,
and his branch will not flourish.

33 He will be like a vine that drops
its unripe grapes
and like an olive tree that sheds its blossoms.

34 For the company of the godless will be barren,
and fire will consume the tents of those
who offer bribes.

35 They conceive trouble and give birth to evil;
their womb prepares deception.

Job's Reply to Eliphaz

16 Then Job answered:

2 I have heard many things like these.
You are all miserable comforters.

3 Is there [no] end to your empty[g] words?
What provokes you that you continue testifying?

4 If you were in my place I could also talk like you.
I could string words together against you
and shake my head at you, [but I wouldn't].

5 I would encourage you with my mouth,
and the consolation from my lips
would bring relief.

---

[a] **15:2** Lit *windy;* Jb 16:3 [b] **15:2** Lit *his belly* [c] **15:13** Or *spirit* [d] **15:20** Lit *the number of* [e] **15:27** Lit *with his fat* [f] **15:29** Text emended; Hb
uncertain [g] **16:3** Lit *windy;* Jb 15:2

His vendetta against him (7:19-20; 10:14;
31:4).

14:2-6 Job tried a bit of poetic psychology,
suggesting that a mere mortal is not worth
the time or effort of a magnificent God. So
why doesn't God just leave him alone (v. 6)?
14:13-17 Death would be safe, hiding place

until God chose to revive him.
14:18-22 Hope may await Job at death, but
what about the here and now? Worn out, Job
searched for any sign of hope in life.
15:1-6 Eliphaz serves a second helping of
advice. He is less compassionate and more
impatient this time around.

15:7-10 When it came to wisdom, Job
claimed equality with his elders, not superiority (12:3; 13:2). However, Eliphaz was indignant. Who did Job think he was, anyway?
Did he know more than they did?

15:10 gray-haired. Eliphaz relied on senior-
ity for his right to speak. **15:12 heart misled**

6 Even if I speak, my suffering is not relieved,
and if I hold back, what have I lost?
7 Surely He has now exhausted me.
You have devastated my entire family.
8 You have shriveled me up[a]—it has become
a witness;
My frailty rises up against me and testifies
to my face.
9 His anger tears [at me], and He harasses me.
He gnashes His teeth at me.
My enemy pierces me with His eyes.
10 They open their mouths against me
and strike my cheeks with contempt;
they join themselves together against me.
11 God hands me over to unjust men;[b]
He throws me into the hands of the wicked.
12 I was at ease, but He shattered me;
He seized [me] by the scruff of the neck
and smashed me to pieces.
He set me up as His target;
13 His archers[c] surround me.
He pierces my kidneys without mercy
and pours my bile on the ground.
14 He breaks through my defenses again and again;[d]
He charges at me like a warrior.
15 I have sewn •sackcloth over my skin;
I have buried my strength[e] in the dust.
16 My face has grown red with weeping,
and the shadow of death covers my eyes,
17 although my hands are free from violence
and my prayer is pure.
18 Earth, do not cover my blood;
may my cry for help find no resting place.
19 Even now my witness is in heaven,
and my advocate is in the heights!
20 My friends scoff at me
as I weep before God.
21 I wish that someone might arbitrate
between a man and God
just as a •man [pleads] for his friend.
22 For [only] a few years will pass
before I go the way of no return.

17 My spirit is broken.
My days are extinguished.
A graveyard awaits me.
2 Surely mockers surround[f] me
and my eyes must gaze at their rebellion.

3 Make arrangements! Put up security for me.[g]
Who [else] will be my sponsor?[h]
4 You have closed their minds to understanding,
therefore You will not honor [them].
5 If a man informs on his friends for a price,
the eyes of his children will fail.
6 He has made me an object of scorn
to the people;
I have become a man people spit at.[i]
7 My eyes have grown dim from grief,
and my whole body has become but a shadow.
8 The upright are appalled at this,
and the innocent are roused against the godless.
9 Yet the righteous person will hold to his way,
and the one whose hands are clean
will grow stronger.
10 But come back [and try] again, all of you.[j]
I will not find a wise man among you.
11 My days have slipped by;
my plans have been ruined,
even the things dear to my heart.
12 They turned night into day
and [made] light [seem] near in the face
of darkness.
13 If I await •Sheol as my home,
spread out my bed in darkness,
14 and say to the •Pit: You are my father,
and to the worm: My mother or my sister,
15 where then is my hope?
Who can see [any] hope for me?
16 Will it go down to the gates of Sheol,
or will we descend together to the dust?

Bildad Speaks

18 Then Bildad the Shuhite replied:
2 How long until you stop talking?
Show some sense, and then we can talk.
3 Why are we regarded as cattle,
as stupid in your sight?
4 You who tear yourself in anger[k]—
should the earth be abandoned on your account,
or a rock be removed from its place?
5 Yes, the light of the wicked is extinguished;
the flame of his fire does not glow.
6 The light in his tent grows dark,
and the lamp beside him is put out.

a 16:8 Or have seized me; Hb obscure   b 16:11 LXX, Vg; MT reads to a boy   c 16:13 Or arrows   d 16:14 Lit through me, breach on breach
e 16:15 Lit horn   f 17:2 Lit are with   g 17:3 Lit me with You   h 17:3 Lit Who is there that will strike himself into my hand   i 17:6 Lit become a spitting to
the faces   j 17:10 Some Hb mss, LXX, Vg; other Hb mss read them   k 18:4 Lit He who tears himself in his anger

you. Apparently Job fails to realize the good fortune that his friends are God's consolations.
15:14-16 what is man. Once more, Eliphaz attempts to force Job to a confession (4:17). How can a man be pure compared to God, if even angels are not pure? How much more

sinful Job must be than the angels!
15:20-35 Eliphaz describes a clear-cut moral world of cause and effect. Calamity befalls only the wicked (vv. 20-24); Job must be blind or stubborn not to see it.
16:10-14 Despite Eliphaz's accusation, Job did not see himself on the offensive with God

(15:25). God was on the offensive against him.
16:18-21 cry for help. Is there anyone who will be a true friend and testify to his innocence (9:33)?
17:3 security. Job asks God to post bail for him as a sign of Job's innocence (Ps.

7 His powerful stride is shortened,
and his own schemes trip him up.
8 For his own feet lead him into a net,
and he strays into its mesh.
9 A trap catches ⌊him⌋ by the heel;
a noose seizes him.
10 A rope lies hidden for him on the ground,
and a snare ⌊waits⌋ for him along the path.
11 Terrors frighten him on every side
and harass him at every step.
12 His strength is depleted;
disaster lies ready for him to stumble.ᵃ
13 Parts of his skin are eaten away;
death's firstborn consumes his limbs.
14 He is ripped from the security of his tent
and marched away to the king of terrors.
15 Nothing he owned remains in his tent.
Burning sulfur is scattered over his home.
16 His roots below dry up,
and his branches above wither away.
17 ⌊All⌋ memory of him perishes from the earth;
he has no name abroad.ᵇ
18 He is driven from light to darkness
and chased from the inhabited world.
19 He has no children or descendants
among his people,
no survivor where he used to live.
20 Those in the west are appalled at his fate,
while those in the east tremble in horror.
21 Indeed, such is the dwelling of the wicked,
and this is the place of the one who does not
know God.

Job's Reply to Bildad

19

Then Job answered:

2 How long will you torment me
and crush me with words?
3 You have humiliated me ten times now,
and you mistreatᶜ me without shame.
4 Even if it is true that I have sinned,
my mistake concerns onlyᵈ me.
5 If you really want to appear superior to me
and would use my disgrace as evidence against me,
6 then understand that it is God who has wronged me
and caught me in His net.
7 I cry out: Violence! but get no response;
I call for help, but there is no justice.

8 He has blocked my way so that I cannot
pass through;
He has veiled my paths with darkness.
9 He has stripped me of my honor
and removed the crown from my head.
10 He tears me down on every side so that
I am ruined.ᵉ
He uproots my hope like a tree.
11 His anger burns against me,
and He regards me as ⌊one of⌋ His enemies.
12 His troops advance together;
they construct a rampᶠ against me
and camp around my tent.
13 He has removed my brothers from me;
my acquaintances have abandoned me.
14 My relatives stop coming by,
and my close friends have forgotten me.
15 My house guestsᵍ and female servants regard me
as a stranger;
I am a foreigner in their sight.
16 I call for my servant, but he does not answer,
even if I beg him with my own mouth.
17 My breath is offensive to my wife,
and my own familyʰ find me repulsive.
18 Even young boys scorn me.
When I stand up, they mock me.
19 All of my best friendsⁱ despise me,
and those I love have turned against me.
20 My skin and my flesh cling to my bones;
I have escaped by the skin of my teeth.
21 Have mercy on me, my friends, have mercy,
for God's hand has struck me.
22 Why do you persecute me as God ⌊does⌋?
Will you never get enough of my flesh?
23 I wish that my words were written down,
that they were recorded on a scroll
24 or were inscribed in stone forever
by an iron stylus and lead!
25 But I know my living Redeemer,ʲ
and He will stand on the dustᵏ at last.ˡ
26 Even after my skin has been destroyed,ᵐ
yet I will see God inⁿ my flesh.
27 I will see Him myself;
my eyes will look at ⌊Him⌋, and not
as a stranger.ᵒ
My heart longsᵖ within me.

ᵃ**18:12** Or *disaster hungers for him* ᵇ**18:17** Or *name in the streets* ᶜ**19:3** Hb obscure ᵈ**19:4** Lit *mistake lives with* ᵉ**19:10** Lit *gone* ᶠ**19:12** Lit *they raise up their way* ᵍ**19:15** Or *The resident aliens in my household* ʰ**19:17** Lit *and the sons of my belly* ⁱ**19:19** Lit *of the men of my council* ʲ**19:25** Or *know that my Redeemer is living* ᵏ**19:25** Or *earth* ˡ**19:25** Or *dust at the last,* or *dust as the Last One* ᵐ**19:26** Lit *skin which they destroyed,* or *skin they destroyed in this way* ⁿ**19:26** Or *apart from* ᵒ**19:27** Or *not a stranger* ᵖ**19:27** Lit *My kidneys grow faint*

119:121-122). He certainly cannot ask his friends.

17:5 informs on his friends. Job quotes an ancient proverb in predicting that his friends' children would become blind on account of their parents' sin.

17:15 Who can see [any] hope for me. Job

could not see any other ending to the story than the certain darkness of death (v. 13).

18:1-4 Bildad was incensed at Job's insults that said the animals were smarter than these friends (12:7-9).

18:5-21 In Bildad's universe all people receive their due: the wicked suffer, the

righteous prosper.

19:4 my mistake concerns only me. Job politely told his friends he didn't need their advice. Notice the use of the word "mistake," (inadvertent sin). Job still did not admit deliberate sin.

19:8-12 Job felt like God's enemy since God

28 If you say, "How will we pursue him,
since the root of the problem lies with him?"ᵃ
29 be afraid of the sword,
because wrath ⌊brings⌋ punishment
by the sword,
so that you may know there is a judgment.

Zophar Speaks

20 Then Zophar the Naamathite replied:

2 This is why my unsettling thoughts compel me
to answer,
because I am upset!ᵇ
3 I have heard a rebuke that insults me,
and my understandingᶜ makes me reply.
4 Don't you know that ever since antiquity,
from ⌊the time⌋ man was placed on earth,
5 the joy of the wicked has been brief
and the happiness of the godless has lasted only
a moment?
6 Though his arrogance reaches heaven,
and his head touches the clouds,
7 he will vanish forever like his own dung.
Those who knowᵈ him will ask, "Where is he?"
8 He will fly away like a dream and never be found;
he will be chased away like a vision in the night.
9 The eye that saw him will see ⌊him⌋ no more,
and his household will no longer see him.
10 His children will beg fromᵉ the poor,
for his own hands must give back his wealth.
11 His bones may be full of youthful vigor,
but it will lie down with him in the grave.
12 Though evil tastes sweet in his mouth
and he conceals it under his tongue,
13 though he cherishes it and will not let it go
but keeps it in his mouth,
14 yet the food in his stomach turns
into cobras' venom inside him.
15 He swallows wealth but must vomit it up;
God will force it from his stomach.
16 He will suck the poison of cobras;
a viper's fangsᶠ will kill him.
17 He will not enjoy the streams,
the rivers flowing with honey and cream.
18 He must return the fruit of his labor
without consuming ⌊it⌋;
he doesn't enjoy the profits from his trading.

19 For he oppressed and abandoned the poor;
he seized a house he did not build.
20 Because his appetite is never satisfied,ᵍ
he does not escape hisʰ desires.
21 Nothing is left for him to consume;
therefore, his prosperity will not last.
22 At the height of his successⁱ distress will come
to him;
the full weight of miseryʲ will crush him.
23 When he fills his stomach,
God will send His burning anger against him,
raining ⌊it⌋ down on him while he is eating.ᵏ
24 If he flees from an iron weapon,
⌊an arrow from⌋ a bronze bow will pierce him.
25 He pulls it out of his back,
the flashing tip out of his liver.ˡ
Terrors come over him.
26 Total darkness is reserved for his treasures.
A fire unfanned ⌊by human hands⌋
will consume him;
it will feed on what is left in his tent.
27 The heavens will expose his iniquity,
and the earth will rise up against him.
28 The possessions in his house will be removed,
flowing away on the day of God's anger.
29 This is the wicked man's lot from God,
the inheritance God ordained for him.

Job's Reply to Zophar

21 Then Job answered:

2 Pay close attention to my words;
let this be the consolation you offer.
3 Bear with me while I speak;
then after I have spoken, you may
continue mocking.
4 As for me, is my complaint against a man?
Then why shouldn't I be impatient?
5 Look at me and shudder;
put ⌊your⌋ hand over ⌊your⌋ mouth.
6 When I think about ⌊it⌋, I am terrified
and my body trembles in horror.
7 Why do the wicked continue to live,
growing old and becoming powerful?
8 Their children are established while they are
still alive,ᵐ
and their descendants, before their eyes.

ᵃ**19:28** Some Hb mss, LXX, Vg; other Hb mss read *me* ᵇ**20:2** Lit *because of my feeling within me* ᶜ**20:3** Lit *and a spirit from my understanding*
ᵈ**20:7** Lit *have seen* ᵉ**20:10** Or *children must compensate* ᶠ**20:16** Lit *tongue* ᵍ**20:20** Lit *Because he does not know ease in his stomach*
ʰ**20:20** Or *satisfied he will not save what he* ⁱ**20:22** Lit *In the fullness of his excess* ʲ**20:22** Some Hb mss, LXX, Vg; other Hb mss read *the hand of
everyone in misery* ᵏ**20:23** Text emended; MT reads *him, against his flesh* ˡ**20:25** Or *gallbladder* ᵐ**21:8** Lit *established before them with them*

---

no longer honored him (9) or his former faithfulness.
19:23-27 From the bottom, Job suddenly rallies to express confidence. His sorry situation had caused him to rely on God alone for deliverance (v. 26).
19:25 I know my living Redeemer. Though

Job was ready to die, he confidently proclaimed that God would vindicate his innocence in the end. Job was referring to the end of his physical life.

19:26 Even after my skin has been destroyed, yet I will see God. Job expects to see God after his flesh is destroyed. This

was an amazing insight for anyone of his time, not to mention someone in those circumstances.

20:4-11 According to Zophar, wickedness always gets punished immediately (v. 5). Job would soon perish if he did not repent (v. 8).
20:10, 19 the poor. At least they agreed on

9 Their homes are secure and free of fear;
no rod from God ⌊strikes⌋ them.

10 Their bulls breed without fail;
their cows calve and do not miscarry.

11 They let their little ones run
around like lambs;
their children skip about,

12 singing to the tambourine and lyre
and rejoicing at the sound of the flute.

13 They spend[a] their days in prosperity
and go down to •Sheol in peace.

14 Yet they say to God: "Leave us alone!
We don't want to know Your ways.

15 Who is the •Almighty, that we
should serve Him,
and what will we gain by pleading with Him?"

16 But their prosperity is not of their own doing.
The counsel of the wicked is far from me!

17 How often is the lamp of the wicked put out?
Does disaster[b] come on them?
Does He apportion destruction in His anger?

18 Are they like straw before the wind,
like chaff a storm sweeps away?

19 God reserves a person's punishment
for his children.
Let God repay the person himself, so that
he may know ⌊it⌋.

20 Let his own eyes see his demise;
let him drink from the Almighty's wrath!

21 For what does he care about his family once
he is dead,
when the number of his months has run out?

22 Can anyone teach God knowledge,
since He judges the exalted ones?[c]

23 One person dies in excellent health,[d]
completely secure[e] and at ease.

24 His body is[f] well-fed,[g]
and his bones are full of marrow.[h]

25 Yet another person dies with a bitter soul,
having never tasted prosperity.

26 But they both lie in the dust,
and worms cover them.

27 Look, I know your thoughts,
the schemes you would wrong me with.

28 For you say, "Where now is
the nobleman's house?"
and "Where are the tents the wicked lived in?"

29 Have you never consulted those who travel
the roads?
Don't you accept their reports?[i]

30 Indeed, the evil man is spared from the day
of disaster,
rescued from the day of wrath.

31 Who would denounce his behavior to his face?
Who would repay him for what he has done?

32 He is carried to the grave,
and someone keeps watch over ⌊his⌋ tomb.

33 The dirt on his grave is⌋ sweet to him.
Everyone follows behind him,
and those who go before him are
without number.

34 So how can you offer me such futile comfort?
Your answers are deceptive.

Third Series of Speeches
Eliphaz Speaks

22 Then Eliphaz the Temanite replied:

2 Can a man be of ⌊any⌋ use to God?
Can even a wise man be of use to Him?

3 Does it delight the •Almighty if you
are righteous?
Does He profit if you perfect your behavior?

4 Does He correct you and take you to court
because of your piety?

5 Isn't your wickedness abundant
and aren't your iniquities endless?

6 For you took collateral from your brothers
without cause,
stripping off their clothes and leaving them
naked.

7 You gave no water to the thirsty
and withheld food from the famished,

8 while the land belonged to a powerful man
and an influential man lived on it.

9 You sent widows away empty-handed,
and the strength of the fatherless was[k] crushed.

10 Therefore snares surround you,
and sudden dread terrifies you,

11 or darkness, so you cannot see,
and a flood of water covers you.

12 Isn't God as high as the heavens?
And look at the highest stars—how lofty
they are!

---

a **21:13** Alt Hb tradition reads *fully enjoy* b **21:17** Lit *their disaster* c **22:1** Probably angels d **21:23** Lit *in bone of his perfection* e **21:23** Text emended; MT reads *health, all at ease* f **21:24** Or *His sides are*; Hb obscure g **21:24** Lit *is full of milk* h **21:24** Lit *and the marrow of his bones is watered* i **21:29** Lit *signs* j **21:33** Lit *The clods of the wadi are* k **22:9** LXX, Syr, Vg, Tg read *you have*

---

this: Oppressing the poor is wicked (31:16-23). The Jews were commanded to take care of the poor.

20:20-25 Zophar implied that since Job has been wealthy, perhaps this was his sin—that he had not cared adequately for the poor.

20:29 inheritance God ordained for him.

Zophar sounded very pleased at how God would repay the oppressors of the poor (despite the fact that he has just included Job in that group).

21:7-15 Contrary to the theology of his companions, Job acknowledged that indeed the wicked do grow powerful (v. 7), not power-

less (20:11). They may be blessed with offspring (v. 8, 11), not barren (18:19). Outwardly, the righteous and wicked may share a common happiness (5:17-27).

21:20 demise. Job knew the fate of the wicked. This Hebrew word for "demise" means to strike, crush, or destroy. Job felt

13 Yet you say: "What does God know?
Can He judge through thick darkness?
14 Clouds veil Him so that He cannot see,
as He walks on the circle of the sky."
15 Will you continue on the ancient path
that wicked men have walked?
16 They were snatched away before their time,
and their foundations were washed away
by a river.
17 They were the ones who said to God,
"Leave us alone!"
and "What can the Almighty do to us?"a
18 But it was He who filled their houses
with good things.
The counsel of the wicked is far from me!
19 The righteous see ⌊this⌋ and rejoice;
the innocent mock them, ⌊saying⌋,
20 "Surely our opponents are destroyed,
and fire has consumed what they left behind."
21 Come to terms with God and be at peace;
in this wayb good will come to you.
22 Receive instruction from His mouth,
and place His sayings in your heart.
23 If you return to the Almighty, you will be renewed.
If you banish injustice from your tent
24 and consign your gold to the dust,
⌊the gold of⌋ Ophir to the stones in the •wadis,
25 the Almighty will be your gold
and your finest silver.
26 Then you will delight in the Almighty
and lift up your face to God.
27 You will pray to Him, and He will hear you,
and you will fulfill your vows.
28 When you make a decision, it will be
carried out,c
and light will shine on your ways.
29 When others are humiliated and you say,
"Lift ⌊them⌋ up,"
God will save the humble.d
30 He will ⌊even⌋ rescue the guilty one,
who will be rescued by the purity of your hands.

Job's Reply to Eliphaz

23 Then Job answered:

2 Today also my complaint is bitter.e
Hisf hand is heavy despite my groaning.
3 If only I knew how to find Him,
so that I could go to His throne.

4 I would plead my case before Him
and fill my mouth with arguments.
5 I would learn howg He would answer me;
and understand what He would say to me.
6 Would He prosecute me forcefully?
No, He will certainly pay attention to me.
7 There an upright man could reason with Him,
and I would escape from my Judge forever.
8 If I go east, He is not there,
and if I go west, I cannot perceive Him.
9 When He is at work to the north, I cannot
see Him;
when He turns south, I cannot find Him.
10 Yet He knows the way I have taken;h
when He has tested me, I will emerge
as pure gold.
11 My feet have followed in His tracks;
I have kept to His way and not turned aside.
12 I have not departed from the commands
of His lips;
I have treasuredi the words of His mouth
more than my daily food.
13 But He is unchangeable; who can oppose Him?
He does what He desires.
14 He will certainly accomplish
what He has decreed for me,
and He has many more things like these in mind.j
15 Therefore I am terrified in His presence;
when I consider ⌊this⌋, I am afraid of Him.
16 God has made my heart faint;
the •Almighty has terrified me.
17 Yet I am not destroyedk by the darkness,
by the thick darkness that covers my face.

24 Why does the •Almighty not reserve times
for judgment?
Why do those who know Him never see His days?
2 The wicked displace boundary markers.
They steal a flock and provide pasture for ⌊it⌋.
3 They drive away the donkeys ⌊owned⌋
by the fatherless
and take the widow's ox as collateral.
4 They push the needy off the road;
the poor of the land are forced into hiding.
5 Like wild donkeys in the desert,
the poor go out to their task of foraging for food;
the wilderness provides nourishment
for their children.

a**22:17** LXX, Syr; MT reads *him* b**22:21** Lit *peace; by them* c**22:28** Lit *out for you* d**22:29** Lit *bowed of eyes* e**23:2** Syr, Tg, Vg; MT reads *rebellion* f**23:2** LXX, Syr; MT reads *My* g**23:5** Lit *the words* h**23:10** Lit *way with me* i**23:12** LXX, Vg read *treasured in my bosom* j**23:14** Lit *these with Him* k**23:17** Or *silenced*

this was exactly what had happened to him—unjustly.

22:1–26:14 For the third and final round of speeches, Eliphaz gave it his best shot, Bildad came up short, and Zophar gave up entirely. Neither Job nor his friends were willing to concede. The friends resorted to spe-

cific accusations, which Job resolutely refuted.

22:2-4 profit. Eliphaz erroneously concluded that God is indifferent to personal purity. In fact, the purity of the worshiper was at the heart of the heavenly question behind Job's suffering (1:8-12; 2:3-6).

22:5-11 Agreeing with Zophar (20:10), Eliphaz concludes that Job is guilty of oppressing the poor. But Job's reputation refuted the accusation (1:1-5).

22:12-20 Concern turned to callousness. Eliphaz assigned Job a dishonorable place in the evil hall of fame (v. 15).

6 They gather their fodder in the field
and glean the vineyards of the wicked.
7 Without clothing, they spend the night naked,
having no covering against the cold.
8 Drenched by mountain rains,
they huddle against[a] the rocks, shelterless.
9 The fatherless infant is snatched
from the breast;
the nursing child of the poor is seized
as collateral.[b]
10 Without clothing, they wander about naked.
They carry sheaves but go hungry.
11 They crush olives in their presses;[c]
they tread the winepresses, but go thirsty.
12 From the city, men[d] groan;
the mortally wounded cry for help,
yet God pays no attention to this crime.

13 The wicked are those who rebel
against the light.
They do not recognize its ways
or stay on its paths.
14 The murderer rises at dawn
to kill the poor and needy,
and by night he becomes a thief.
15 The adulterer's eye watches for twilight,
thinking: No eye will see me,
he covers [his] face.
16 In the dark they break[e] into houses;
by day they lock themselves in,[f]
never experiencing the light.
17 For the morning is like death's shadow to them.
Surely they are familiar with the terrors
of death's shadow!

18 They float[g] on the surface of the water.
Their section of the land is cursed,
so that they never go to [their] vineyards.
19 As dry ground and heat snatch away
the melted snow,
so •Sheol [steals] those who have sinned.
20 The womb forgets them;
worms feed on them;
they are remembered no more.
So injustice is broken like a tree.
21 They prey on[h] the barren, childless woman
and do not deal kindly with the widow.
22 Yet God drags away[i] the mighty by His power;
when He rises up, they have no assurance
of life.

23 He gives them a sense of security, so they
can rely [on it],
but His eyes [watch] over their ways.
24 They are exalted for a moment, then they
are gone;
they are brought low and shrivel up
like everything else.[j]
They wither like heads of grain.
25 If this is not true, then who can prove me a liar
and show that my speech is worthless?

Bildad Speaks

25 Then Bildad the Shuhite replied:

2 Dominion and dread belong to Him,
the One who establishes harmony
in the heavens.[k]
3 Can His troops be numbered?
Does His light not shine on everyone?
4 How can a person be justified before God?
How can one born of woman be pure?
5 If even the moon does not shine
and the stars are not pure in His sight,
6 how much less man, who is a maggot,
and the son of man, who is a worm!

Job's Reply to Bildad

26 Then Job answered:

2 How you have helped the powerless
and delivered the arm that is weak!
3 How you have counseled the unwise
and thoroughly explained [the path to] success!
4 Who did you speak these words to?
Whose breath came out of your [mouth]?

5 The departed spirits tremble
beneath the waters and [all] that inhabit them.
6 •Sheol is naked before God,
and •Abaddon has no covering.
7 He stretches the northern [skies]
over empty space;
He hangs the earth on nothing.
8 He enfolds the waters in His clouds,
yet the clouds do not burst beneath their weight.
9 He obscures the view of [His] throne,
spreading His cloud over it.
10 He laid out the horizon on the surface
of the waters
at the boundary between light and darkness.

[a]**24:8** Lit they embrace   [b]**24:9** Text emended; MT reads breast; they seize collateral against the poor   [c]**24:11** Lit olives between their rows
[d]**24:12** One Hb ms, Syr read the dying   [e]**24:16** Lit dig   [f]**24:16** Lit they seal for themselves   [g]**24:18** Lit are insignificant   [h]**24:21** LXX, Tg read They
harm   [i]**24:22** Or God prolongs [the life of]   [j]**24:24** LXX reads like a mallow plant in the heat   [k]**25:2** Lit in His heights

23:3 If only I knew how to find Him. This verse may well summarize the main message of the book and the strongest cry of Job's heart. He bears bravely with physical suffering and material loss. But his loss of relationship with God cannot be assuaged.
23:10 Yet he knows the way I have taken.

God alone knows his heart. Job is beginning to hope that God will yet find him blameless.
23:13 what He desires. Job may not have understood God's mysterious ways but He still trusted his history with God.
23:17 darkness. Job discovered that it the darkness has not destroyed him and his

spiritual eyes are adjusting to it.

24:1-12 Job outlined several outlandish injustices. Orphans and widows were robbed of their minimal possessions, leaving them hungry and homeless. However, the gap between the actual crime and the punishment made a mockery of justice.

11 The pillars ⌊that hold up⌋ the sky tremble,
  astounded at His rebuke.
12 By His power He stirred the sea,
  and by His understanding He crushed •Rahab.
13 By His breath the heavens gained their beauty;
  His hand pierced the fleeing serpent.ᵃ
14 These are but the fringes of His ways;
  how faint is the word we hear of Him!
  Who can understand His mighty thunder?

27 Job continued his discourse, saying:

2 As God lives, who has deprived me of justice,
  and the •Almighty who has made me bitter,
3 as long as my breath is still in me
  and the breath from God remains in my nostrils,
4 my lips will not speak unjustly,
  and my tongue will not utter deceit.
5 I will never affirm that you are right.
  I will maintain my integrityᵇ until I die.
6 I will cling to my righteousness and never
    let it go.
  My conscience will not accuse ⌊me⌋ as long as
    I live!

7 May my enemy be like the wicked
  and my opponent like the unjust.
8 For what hope does the godless man have when
    he is cut off,
  when God takes away his life?
9 Will God hear his cry
  when distress comes on him?
10 Will he delight in the Almighty?
  Will he call on God at all times?
11 I will teach you about God's power.
  I will not conceal what the Almighty
    has planned.ᶜ
12 All of you have seen ⌊this⌋ for yourselves,
  why do you keep up this empty talk?

13 This is a wicked man's lot from God,
  the inheritance the ruthless receive
    from the Almighty.
14 Even if his children increase, they are destined
    for the sword;
  his descendants will never have enough food.
15 Those who survive him will be buried
    by the plague,
  yet their widows will not weep ⌊for them⌋.
16 Though he piles up silver like dust
  and heaps up a wardrobe like clay—

17 he may heap ⌊it⌋ up, but the righteous
    will wear ⌊it⌋,
  and the innocent will divide up his silver.
18 The house he built is like a moth's ⌊cocoon⌋
  or a booth set up by a watchman.
19 He lies down wealthy, but will do so
    no more;
  when he opens his eyes, it is gone.
20 Terrors overtake him like a flood;
  a storm wind sweeps him away at night.
21 An east wind picks him up, and he is gone;
  it carries him away from his place.
22 It blasts at him without mercy,
  while he flees desperately from its grasp.
23 It claps its hands at him
  and scorns him from its place.

Job's Hymn to Wisdom

28 Surely there is a mine for silver
  and a place where gold is refined.
2 Iron is taken from the ground,
  and copper is smelted from ore.
3 A miner puts an end to the darkness;
  he probesᵈ the deepest recesses
    for ore in the gloomy darkness.
4 He cuts a shaft far from human habitation,
  ⌊in places⌋ unknown to those who walk
    above ground.ᵉ
  Suspended far away from people,
    the miners swing back and forth.
5 Food may come from the earth,
  but below the surface the earth is transformed
    as by fire.
6 Its rocks are a source of sapphire,ᶠ
  containing flecks of gold.
7 No bird of prey knows that path;
  no falcon's eye has seen it.
8 Proud beasts have never walked on it;
  no lion has ever prowled over it.
9 The miner strikes the flint
  and transforms the mountains
    at ⌊their⌋ foundations.
10 He cuts out channels in the rocks,
  and his eyes spot every treasure.
11 He dams up the streams from flowingᵍ
  so that he may bring to light
    what is hidden.

12 But where can wisdom be found,
  and where is understanding located?

ᵃ**26:13** = Leviathan; Is 27:1   ᵇ**27:5** Lit *will not remove my integrity from me*   ᶜ**27:11** Lit *what is with the Almighty*   ᵈ**28:3** Lit *probes all*   ᵉ**28:4** Lit *far from with inhabitant, things forgotten by foot*   ᶠ**28:6** Or *lapis lazuli*   ᵍ**28:11** LXX, Vg read *He explores the sources of the streams*

24:17 morning is like death's shadow to them. Job listed criminal activities that are conducted in the dark. Therefore, morning's light makes them highly visible. The mistake of evildoers was thinking that the darkness could hide their crimes from God.

24:18-25 The only justice Job could see was

that death would finally triumph over evildoers (see also 21:23-26).

25:1-6 Bildad made one last speech to convince Job of his folly.

25:6 maggot. Bildad's meaning is clear: there is no way for a mere human to be pure when compared to God.

26:2-14 Job launched into the longest speech in the entire book. This chapter is united with chapters 27–28 in theme. Job can speak at length now that the three friends have completed their arguments.

26:6 Abaddon. This Hebrew word means perishing or destruction. *Abaddon* is another

13 No man can know its value,[a]
   since it cannot be found in the land
      of the living.
14 The ocean depths say, "It's not in me,"
   while the sea declares, "I don't have it."
15 Gold cannot be exchanged for it,
   and silver cannot be weighed out for its price.
16 Wisdom cannot be valued in the gold of Ophir,
   in precious onyx or sapphire.[b]
17 Gold and glass do not compare with it,
   and articles of fine gold cannot be exchanged
      for it.
18 Coral and quartz are not worth mentioning.
   The price of wisdom is beyond pearls.
19 Topaz from •Cush cannot compare with it,
   and it cannot be valued in pure gold.

20 Where then does wisdom come from,
   and where is understanding located?
21 It is hidden from the eyes of every living thing
   and concealed from the birds of the sky.
22 •Abaddon and Death say,
   "We have heard news of it with our ears."
23 But God understands the way to wisdom,
   and He knows its location.
24 For He looks to the ends of the earth
   and sees everything under the heavens.
25 When God fixed the weight of the wind
   and limited the water by measure,
26 when He established a limit[c] for the rain
   and a path for the lightning,
27 He considered wisdom and evaluated it;
   He established it and examined it.
28 He said to mankind,
   "Look! The •fear of the Lord—that is wisdom,
   and to turn from evil is understanding."

Job's Final Claim of Innocence

29 Job continued his discourse, saying:

2 If only I could be as in months gone by,
   in the days when God watched over me,
3 when His lamp shone above my head,
   and I walked through darkness by His light!
4 [I would be] as I was in the days of my youth
   when God's friendship rested on my tent,
5 when the •Almighty was still with me
   and my children were around me,
6 when my feet were bathed in cream
   and the rock poured out streams of oil for me!

7 When I went out to the city •gate
   and took my seat in the town square,
8 the young men saw me and withdrew,
   while older men stood to their feet.
9 City officials stopped talking
   and covered their mouths with [their] hands.
10 The noblemen's voices were hushed,
   and their tongues stuck to the roof
      of their mouths.
11 When they heard me, they blessed me,
   and when they saw me, they spoke well of me.[d]
12 For I rescued the poor man who cried out
      for help,
   and the fatherless child who had no one
      to support him.
13 The dying man blessed me,
   and I made the widow's heart rejoice.
14 I clothed myself in righteousness, and it
      enveloped me;
   my just decisions were like a robe and a turban.
15 I was eyes to the blind
   and feet to the lame.
16 I was a father to the needy,
   and I examined the case of the stranger.
17 I shattered the fangs of the unjust
   and snatched the prey from his teeth.

18 So I thought: I will die in my own nest
   and multiply [my] days as the sand.[e]
19 My roots will have access to water,
   and the dew will rest on my branches all night.
20 My strength will be refreshed within me,
   and my bow will be renewed in my hand.

21 Men listened to me with expectation,
   waiting silently for my advice.
22 After a word from me they did not speak again;
   my speech settled on them [like dew].
23 They waited for me as for the rain
   and opened their mouths as for spring showers.
24 If I smiled at them, they couldn't believe [it];
   they were thrilled at[f] the light
      of my countenance.
25 I directed their course and presided as chief.
   I lived as a king among his troops,
   like one who comforts those who mourn.

30 But now they mock me,
   men younger than I am,
   whose fathers I would have refused to put
   with my sheep dogs.

---

[a]28:13 LXX reads *way* [b]28:16 Or *lapis lazuli* [c]28:26 Or *decree* [d]29:11 Lit *When an ear heard, it called me blessed, and when an eye saw, it testified for me* [e]29:18 Or *as the phoenix* [f]29:24 Lit *they did not cast down*

---

word for *Sheol* or the place of the dead.
26:14 fringes of His ways. Job doesn't claim to understand God but he knows enough to know that if God revealed all his glory, the experience would be thunderous and overwhelming.
27:1-6 His companions may question his in-

nocence, but they could not doubt Job's convictions about his innocence (vv. 2-6).
27:2-4 As God lives ... my lips will not speak unjustly. Notice that Job still swore by God ; "As God lives" was the preface to his oath taking. He still claimed God was just even when he could not see justice being

applied to his own case before God.
27:13-23 Job's list of calamities that befall the wicked are a jumble of metaphors ranging from moths to floods to windstorms. They convey the retribution due evildoers.
28:1-28 Chapter 28 defines wisdom as a mystery at best. This abstract description of

2 What use to me was the strength of their hands?
  Their vigor had left them.
3 Emaciated from poverty and hunger,
  they gnawed the dry land,
  the desolate wasteland by night.
4 They plucked mallowa among the shrubs,
  and the roots of the broom tree were their food.
5 They were expelled from human society;
  people shouted at them as ⌊if they were⌋ thieves.
6 They are living on the slopes of the •wadis,
  among the rocks and in holes in the ground.
7 They bray among the shrubs;
  they huddle beneath the thistles.
8 Foolish men, without even a name!
  They were forced to leave the land.

9 Now I am mocked by their songs;
  I have become an object of scorn to them.
10 They despise me and keep their distance
   from me;
   they do not hesitate to spit in my face.
11 Because God has loosened myb bowstring
   and oppressed me,
   they have cast off restraint in my presence.
12 The rabblec rise up at my right;
   they trapd my feet
   and construct their siege rampe against me.
13 They tear up my path;
   they contribute to my destruction,
   without anyone to help them.
14 They advance as through a gaping breach;
   they keep rolling in through the ruins.
15 Terrors are turned loose against me;
   they chase my dignity away like the wind,
   and my prosperity has passed by like a cloud.

16 Now my life is poured out before my ⌊eyes⌋,
   and days of suffering have seized me.
17 Night pierces my bones,
   and my gnawing pains never abate.
18 My clothing is distorted with great force;
   He chokes me by the neck of my garment.c
19 He throws me into the mud,
   and I have become like dust and ashes.

20 I cry out to You for help, but You do not
   answer me;
   when I stand up, You ⌊merely⌋ look at me.
21 You have turned against me with cruelty;
   You harass me with Your strong hand.

22 You lift me up on the wind and make me
   ride ⌊it⌋;
   You scatter me in the storm.
23 Yes, I know that You will lead me to death—
   the place appointed for all who live.
24 Yet no one would stretch out ⌊his⌋ hand
   against a ruined manf
   when he cries out to him for help
   because of his distress.
25 Have I not wept for those who have fallen
   on hard times?
   Has my soul not grieved for the needy?
26 But when I hoped for good, evil came;
   when I looked for light, darkness came.
27 I am churning withing and cannot rest;
   days of suffering confront me.
28 I walk about blackened, but not by the sun.h
   I stood in the assembly and cried out for help.
29 I have become a brother to jackals
   and a companion of ostriches.
30 My skin blackens and flakes off,i
   and my bones burn with fever.
31 My lyre is ⌊used⌋ for mourning
   and my flute for the sound of weeping.

31 I have made a covenant with my eyes.
  How then could I look at a young woman?j
2 For what portion ⌊would I have⌋
   from God above,
   or ⌊what⌋ inheritance from the •Almighty
   on high?
3 Doesn't disaster come to the wicked
   and misfortune to evildoers?
4 Does He not see my ways
   and number all my steps?
5 If I have walked in falsehood
   or my foot has rushed to deceit,
6 let God weigh me with an accurate balance,
   and He will recognize my integrity.
7 If my step has turned from the way,
   my heart has followed my eyes,
   or impurity has stained my hands,
8 let someone else eat what I have sown,
   and let my crops be uprooted.
9 If my heart has been seduced by
   ⌊my neighbor's⌋ wife
   or I have lurked at his door,

---

a30:4 Or saltwort   b30:11 Alt Hb tradition, LXX, Vg read His   c30:12,18 Hb obscure   d30:12 Lit stretch out; Hb obscure   e30:12 Lit and raise up their destructive paths   f30:24 Lit a heap of ruins   g30:27 Lit My bowels boil   h30:28 Or walk in sunless gloom   i30:30 Lit blackens away from me   j31:1 Or a virgin

---

wisdom foreshadows God's own response (38:1–41:34).

28:28 fear of the Lord ... is wisdom. This profound verse is found in several other places in Scripture (Ps. 111:10, Prov. 1:7, 9:10, Eccles. 12:13).
29:1–31:40 This long speech of Job's are his

last words in this book. He first recalled his former happy state, then his calamities, and finally a checklist of potential sins he might have committed. Once again, he proclaimed himself innocent.

29:4 God's friendship. Job's relationship with God still existed. However, his circum-

stances had prevented his feeling God's presence as in the past.

29:12-13 poor ... fatherless. Job summarized his claims of innocence. Chief among his claims was that he never oppressed the poor.

29:21-25 Job recalled past respect given to

10 let my own wife grind ⌊grain⌋ for another man,
and let other men sleep with^a her.

11 For that would be a disgrace;
it would be a crime deserving punishment.^b

12 For it is a fire that consumes down to •Abaddon;
it would destroy my entire harvest.

13 If I have dismissed the case of my male
or female servants
when they made a complaint against me,

14 what could I do when God stands up ⌊to judge⌋?
How should I answer Him when He calls ⌊me⌋
to account?

15 Did not the One who made me in the womb
also make them?
Did not the same God form us both
in the womb?

16 If I have refused the wishes of the poor
or let the widow's eyes go blind,

17 if I have eaten my few crumbs alone
without letting the fatherless eat any of it—

18 for from my youth, I raised him as ⌊his⌋ father,
and since the day I was born^c I guided
the widow—

19 if I have seen anyone dying for lack of clothing
or a needy person without a cloak,

20 if he^d did not bless me
while warming himself with the fleece
from my sheep,

21 if I ever cast my vote^e against a fatherless child
when I saw that I had support in the ⌊city⌋ •gate,

22 then let my shoulder blade fall from my back,
and my arm be pulled from its socket.

23 For disaster from God terrifies me,
and because of His majesty I could not do
⌊these things⌋.

24 If I placed my confidence in gold
or called fine gold my trust,

25 if I have rejoiced because my wealth is great
or because my own hand has acquired
⌊so⌋ much,

26 if I have gazed at the sun when it was shining
or at the moon moving in splendor,

27 so that my heart was secretly enticed
and I threw them a kiss,^f

28 this would also be a crime
deserving punishment,
for I would have denied God above.

29 Have I rejoiced over my enemy's distress,
or become excited when trouble came his way?

30 I have not allowed my mouth to sin
by asking for his life with a curse.

31 Haven't the members of my household said,
"Who is there who has not had enough to eat
at Job's table?"

32 No stranger had to spend the night
on the street,
for I opened my door to the traveler.

33 Have I covered my transgressions as others do^g
by hiding my guilt in my heart,

34 because I greatly feared the crowds,
and the contempt of the clans terrified me,
so I grew silent and would not go outside?

35 If only I had someone to hear my ⌊case⌋!
Here is my signature; let the Almighty
answer me.
Let my Opponent compose ⌊His⌋ indictment.

36 I would surely carry it on my shoulder
and wear it like a crown.

37 I would give Him an account of all my steps;
I would approach Him like a prince.

38 If my land cries out against me
and its furrows join in weeping,

39 if I have consumed its produce
without payment
or shown contempt for its tenants,^h

40 then let thorns grow instead of wheat
and stinkweed instead of barley.

The words of Job are concluded.

Elihu's Angry Response

32 So these three men quit answering Job,
because he was righteous in his own eyes.
2 Then Elihu son of Barachel the Buzite from the family of Ram became angry. He was angry at Job because he had justified himself rather than God. 3 He was also angry at Job's three friends because they had failed to refute ⌊him⌋, and yet had condemned him.

4 Now Elihu had waited to speak to Job because they were ⌊all⌋ older than he. 5 But when he saw that the three men could not answer Job, he became angry.

6 So Elihu son of Barachel the Buzite replied:

I am young in years,
while you are old;
therefore I was timid and afraid
to tell you what I know.

---

^a**31:10** Lit *men kneel down over*   ^b**31:11** Lit *crime judges*   ^c**31:18** Lit *and from my mother's womb*   ^d**31:20** Lit *his loins*   ^e**31:21** Lit *I raise my hand*   ^f**31:27** Lit *and my hand kissed my mouth*   ^g**31:33** Or *as Adam*   ^h**31:39** Lit *or caused the breath of its tenants to breathe out*

---

him. People listened and were blessed (vv. 21-23).

30:1-31 The haunting contrast of past and present (vv. 1-19) made reliving the agony all the more painful for Job (vv. 20-31).

30:8 without even a name. Since a name

bespoke dignity in the sense that Job was known to have perfect integrity (1:1), the nameless (whose animal behaviors are listed in vv. 2-8) were especially infamous; lacking all character.

30:20-23 You do not answer. If only Job could have known the prologue (1:6-12).

God's power was responsible for restraining further suffering, not causing it (1:12; 2:6).

30:29 companion of ostriches. Better jackals and ostriches than the nameless (v. 8).

31:1-40 Job issued his strongest denial yet. If he were guilty of any listed sin, he would gladly accept the consequence but he can-

7 I thought that age should speak
and maturity should teach wisdom.
8 But it is a spirit in man[a]
and the breath of the •Almighty
that give him understanding.
9 It is not ⌊only⌋ the old who are wise
or the elderly who understand how to judge.
10 Therefore I say, "Listen to me.
I too will declare what I know."
11 Look, I waited for your conclusions;
I listened to your insights
as you sought for words.
12 I paid close attention to you.
Yet no one proved Job wrong;
not one of you refuted his arguments.
13 So do not claim, "We have found wisdom;
let God deal with him, not man."
14 But Job has not directed his argument to me,
and I will not respond to him
with your arguments.

15 Job's friends are dismayed and can
no longer answer;
words have left them.
16 Should I continue to wait now that
they are silent,
now that they stand ⌊there⌋ and no longer answer?
17 I too will answer;[b]
yes, I will tell what I know.
18 For I am full of words,
and my spirit[c] compels me ⌊to speak⌋.
19 My heart[d] is like unvented wine;
it is about to burst like new wineskins.
20 I must speak so that I can find relief;
I must open my lips and respond.
21 I will be partial to no one,
and I will not give anyone an ⌊undeserved⌋ title.
22 For I do not know how to give ⌊such⌋ titles;
otherwise, my Maker would remove me
in an instant.

Elihu Confronts Job

33 But now, Job, pay attention to my speech,
and listen to all my words.
2 I am going to open my mouth;
my tongue will form words on my palate.
3 My words ⌊come from⌋ my upright heart,
and my lips speak what they know
with sincerity.

4 The Spirit of God has made me,
and the breath of the •Almighty gives me life.
5 Refute me if you can.
Prepare your case against me; take your stand.
6 I am just like you before God;
I was also pinched off from ⌊a piece of⌋ clay.
7 Fear of me should not terrify you;
the pressure I exert[e] against you will be light.

8 Surely you have spoken in my hearing,
and I have heard these very[f] words:
9 "I am pure, without transgression;
I am clean and have no guilt.
10 But He finds reasons to oppose me;
He regards me as his enemy.
11 He puts my feet in the stocks;
He stands watch over all my paths."

12 But I tell you that you are wrong in this ⌊matter⌋,
since God is greater than man.
13 Why do you take Him to court
for not answering anything a person asks?[g]
14 For God speaks time and again,
but a person may not notice it.
15 In a dream, a vision in the night,
when deep sleep falls on people
as they slumber on ⌊their⌋ beds,
16 He uncovers their ears at that time
and terrifies them[h] with warnings,
17 in order to turn a person ⌊from his⌋ actions
and suppress his pride.[i]
18 God spares his soul from the •Pit,
his life from crossing the river ⌊of death⌋.[j]
19 A person may be disciplined on his bed
with pain
and constant distress in his bones,
20 so that he detests bread,
and his soul ⌊despises his⌋ favorite food.
21 His flesh wastes away to nothing,[k]
and his unseen bones stick out.
22 He draws near the Pit,
and his life to the executioners.
23 If there is an angel on his side,
one mediator out of a thousand,
to tell a person what is right for him[l]
24 and to be gracious to him and say,
"Spare him from going down to the Pit;
I have found a ransom,"
25 then his flesh will be healthier[m] than
in his youth,

---

[a]**32:8** Or *is the Spirit in a person* [b]**32:17** Lit *answer my part* [c]**32:18** Lit *and the spirit of my belly* [d]**32:19** Lit *belly* [e]**33:7** Lit *you; my pressure*
[f]**33:8** Lit *heard a sound of* [g]**33:13** Lit *court, for he does not answer all his words* [h]**33:16** LXX; MT reads *and seals* [i]**33:17** Lit *and cover pride within a man* [j]**33:18** Or *from perishing by the sword* [k]**33:21** Lit *away from sight* [l]**33:23** Or *to vouch for a person's uprightness* [m]**33:25** Hb obscure

---

not deny the truth of his own conscience. The list of sins includes: lust, dishonesty, adultery, oppression, stinginess, greed, idolatry, vindictiveness, hypocrisy, and exploitation.
31:1-12 Job denied sexual longing (vv. 1-4), as well as sexual immorality (vv. 9-12). He

professed upright business practices as well (vv. 5-8).
31:24-28 Job's friends had accused him of secret covetousness (22:24), though he had forthrightly denounced greed.
32:1–37:24 Elihu, to this point silent before his elders, now spoke. His tone was tactful,

compared to the exasperated trio who had rushed to judgment (or so he thought) without fully considering the facts of Job's case (32:12). Job, for his part, seemed prideful in his pronouncements against God (40:2). Elihu addressed the different sides through four levels of speeches (32:5–33:33; chap-

and he will return to the days of his youthful vigor.

26 He will pray to God, and God will delight in him.
That man will behold His face with a shout
of joy,
and God will restore his righteousness to him.

27 He will look at men and say,
"I have sinned and perverted what was right;
yet I did not get what I deserved.[a]

28 He redeemed my soul from going down
to the Pit,
and I will continue to see the light."

29 God certainly does all these things
two or three times to a man

30 in order to turn him back from the Pit,
so he may shine with the light of life.

31 Pay attention, Job, and listen to me.
Be quiet, and I will speak.

32 But if you have something to say,[b] answer me;
speak, for I would like to justify you.

33 If not, then listen to me;
be quiet, and I will teach you wisdom.

34

Then Elihu continued,[c] saying:

2 Hear my words, you wise men,
and listen to me, you knowledgeable ones.

3 Doesn't the ear test words
as the palate tastes food?

4 Let us judge for ourselves what is right;
let us decide together what is good.

5 For Job has declared, "I am righteous,
yet God has deprived me of justice.

6 Would I lie about my case?
My wound[d] is incurable,
though I am without transgression."

7 What man is like Job?
He drinks derision like water.

8 He keeps company with evildoers
and walks with wicked men.

9 For he has said, "A man gains nothing
when he becomes God's friend."

10 Therefore listen to me, you men
of understanding.
It is impossible for God [to do] wrong,
and [for] the •Almighty [to act] unjustly.

11 For He repays a person [according to] his deeds,
and He brings his ways on him.

12 Indeed, it is true that God does not act wickedly
and the Almighty does not pervert justice.

13 Who gave Him authority over the earth?
Who put Him in charge of the entire world?

14 If He put His mind to it
and withdrew the spirit and breath He [gave],

15 every living thing would perish together
and mankind would return to the dust.

16 If you [have] understanding, hear this;
listen to what I have to say.

17 Could one who hates justice govern [the world]?
Will you condemn the mighty Righteous One,

18 who says to a king, "Worthless man!"
and to nobles, "Wicked men!"?

19 God is not partial to princes
and does not favor the rich over the poor,
for they are all the work of His hands.

20 They die suddenly in the middle of the night;
people shudder, then pass away.
Even the mighty are removed without effort.

21 For His eyes [watch] over a man's ways,
and He observes all his steps.

22 There is no darkness, no deep darkness,
where evildoers can hide themselves.

23 God does not [need to] examine a person further,
that one should[e] approach Him in court.

24 He shatters the mighty without an investigation
and sets others in their place.

25 Therefore, He recognizes their deeds
and overthrows [them] by night, and they
are crushed.

26 In full view of the public,[f]
He strikes them for their wickedness,

27 because they turned aside from following Him
and did not understand any of His ways

28 but caused the poor to cry out to Him,
and He heard the outcry of the afflicted.

29 But when God is silent, who can declare
[Him] guilty?
When He hides [His] face, who can see Him?
Yet He [watches] over both individuals and nations,

30 so that godless men should not rule
or ensnare the people.

31 Suppose someone says to God,
"I have endured [my punishment];
I will no [longer] act wickedly.

32 Teach me what I cannot see;
if I have done wrong, I won't do it again."

33 Should God repay [you] on your terms
when you have rejected [His]?

---

a **33:27** Lit and the same was not to me   b **33:32** Lit If there are words   c **34:1** Lit answered   d **34:6** Lit arrow   e **34:23** Some emend to God has not appointed a time for man to   f **34:26** Lit In a place of spectators

---

ters 34–35; chapters 36–37).

32:6, 10, 17 what I know. As the youngest, it is interesting that he claimed three times to *know* what no one else has been able to explain. So he confidently added his perspective.

32:21-22 In a twist of irony, the Hebrew text

implies, "I am not partial to you with flattery, because if I flattered you, God would not be partial to me."

33:1-33 In his speeches, Elihu addressed all of Job's major points. He began by refuting Job's charge concerning God's apparent silence. In fact, God sometimes speaks

through dreams (v. 15) and personal pain (v. 19).

33:7 Fear of me. Elihu was clearly full of his own importance. He almost sounded as if he was speaking for God in his overemphasis of equality while implying superior power (terror).

33:23-28 Eliphaz thought Job was a lost

You must choose, not I!
So declare what you know.
34 Reasonable men will say to me,
along with the wise men who hear me,
35 "Job speaks without knowledge;
his words are without insight."
36 If only Job were tested to the limit,
because ⌊his⌋ answers are ⌊like⌋ those
of wicked men.
37 For he adds rebellion to his sin;
he ⌊scornfully⌋ claps in our presence,
while multiplying his words against God.

35

Then Elihu continued, saying:

2 Do you think it is just when you say,
"I am righteous before God"?
3 For you ask, "What does it profit You,a
and what benefit comes to me, if I do not sin?"
4 I will answer you
and your friends with you.
5 Look at the heavens and see;
gaze at the clouds high above you.
6 If you sin, how does it affect God?
If you multiply your transgressions, what does it
do to Him?
7 If you are righteous, what do you give Him,
or what does He receive from your hand?
8 Your wickedness ⌊affects⌋ a person like yourself,
and your righteousness ⌊another⌋ human being.
9 People cry out because of severe oppression;
they shout for help from the arm
of the mighty.
10 But no one asks, "Where is God my Maker,
who provides ⌊us⌋ with songs in the night,
11 who gives us more understanding
than the animals of the earth
and makes us wiser than the birds of the sky?"
12 There they cry out, but He does not answer,
because of the pride of evil men.
13 Indeed, God does not listen to empty ⌊cries⌋,
and the •Almighty does not take note of it—
14 how much less whenb you complainc
that you do not see Him,
⌊that your⌋ case is before Him
and you are waiting for Him.
15 But now, because God's anger does not punish
and He does not pay attention
to transgression,d

16 Job opens his mouth in vain
and multiplies words without knowledge.

36

Then Elihu continued, saying:

2 Be patient with me a little longer, and I will
inform you,
for there is still more to be said on God's behalf.
3 I will get my knowledge from afar
and ascribe righteousness to my Maker.
4 For my arguments are without flaw;e
one who has perfect knowledge is with you.
5 Yes, God is mighty, but He despises ⌊no one⌋;
He understands all things.f
6 He does not keep the wicked alive,
but He gives justice to the afflicted.
7 He does not remove His gaze from the righteous,
but He seats them forever with enthroned kings,
and they are exalted.
8 If people are bound with chains
and trapped by the cords of affliction,
9 God tells them what they have done
and how arrogantly they have transgressed.
10 He opens their ears to correction
and insists they repent from iniquity.
11 If they serve Him obediently,
they will end their days in prosperity
and their years in happiness.
12 But if they do not obey,
they will cross the river ⌊of death⌋g
and die without knowledge.
13 Those who have a godless heart harbor anger;
even when God binds them, they do not cry
for help.
14 They die in their youth;
their life ⌊ends⌋ among male cult prostitutes.
15 God rescues the afflicted by afflicting them;
He instructs them by means of their torment.
16 Indeed, He lured you from the jawsh of distress
to a spacious and unconfined place.
Your table was spread with choice food.
17 Yet ⌊now⌋ you are obsessed with the judgment
due the wicked;
judgment and justice have seized you.
18 Be careful that no one lures you with riches;i
do not let a large ransomj lead you astray.
19 Can your wealthk or all ⌊your⌋ physical exertion

---

a35:3 Some emend to me b35:14 Or How then can c35:14 Lit say d35:15 LXX, Vg; MT reads folly, or arrogance; Hb obscure e36:4 Lit my words are not false f36:5 Lit He is mighty in strength of heart g36:12 Or will perish by the sword h36:16 Lit from a mouth of narrowness i36:18 Or you into mockery j36:18 Or bribe k36:19 Or cry for help

---

cause (5:1). Elihu, however, envisioned an angel mediating on Job's behalf.

33:33 I will teach you wisdom. Satisfied that he has convinced Job of his opening argument, Elihu rambles on for the next four chapters. Only God ultimately answers (38:1).

34:1-37 Satisfied that he had defended

God's silence, Elihu next took on the issue of God's fairness, or lack thereof. He systematically addressed the so-called wise companions (vv. 2-15), then Job (vv. 16-33), and then himself (vv. 34-37).

34:14-15 If He put His mind to it. Elihu's arguments centered around God's right to use His

power at His discretion. What he did not consider was that choices are based on His goodness.

34:35 without insight. Each person has part of the puzzle, but God alone fits the pieces together (38:2; 42:3).

35:1-3, 12-15 Elihu has misunderstood Job to mean that he is seeking God's acquittal

keep ⌊you⌋ from distress?

20 Do not long for the night
when nations will disappear from their places.

21 Be careful that you do not turn to iniquity,
for that is why you have been tested
by[a] affliction.

22 Look, God shows Himself exalted by His power.
Who is a teacher like Him?

23 Who has appointed His way for Him,
and who has declared, "You have done wrong"?

24 Remember that you should praise His work,
which people have sung about.

25 All mankind has seen it;
people have looked at it from a distance.

26 Look, God is exalted beyond our knowledge;
the number of His years cannot be counted.

27 For He makes waterdrops evaporate;[b]
they distill the rain into its[c] mist,

28 which the clouds pour out
and shower abundantly on mankind.

29 Can anyone understand how the clouds
spread out
or how the thunder roars from God's pavilion?

30 Look, He spreads His lightning around Him
and covers the depths of the sea.

31 For He judges the nations with these;
He gives food in abundance.

32 He covers ⌊His⌋ hands with lightning
and commands it to hit its mark.

33 The[d] thunder declares His presence;[e]
the cattle also, the approaching ⌊storm⌋.

37 My heart pounds at this
and leaps from my chest.[f]

2 Just listen to His thunderous voice
and the rumbling that comes from His mouth.

3 He lets it loose beneath the entire sky;
His lightning to the ends of the earth.

4 Then there comes a roaring sound;
God thunders with His majestic voice.
He does not restrain the lightning
when His ⌊rumbling⌋ voice is heard.

5 God thunders marvelously with His voice;
He does great things that
we cannot comprehend.

6 For He says to the snow, "Fall to the earth,"
and the torrential rains,
His mighty torrential rains,

7 serve as His signature to all mankind,

so that all men may know His work.

8 The wild animals enter ⌊their⌋ lairs
and stay in their dens.

9 The windstorm comes from its chamber,
and the cold from the driving north winds.

10 Ice is formed by the breath of God,
and watery expanses are frozen.

11 He saturates clouds with moisture;
He scatters His lightning through them.

12 They swirl about,
turning round and round at His direction,
accomplishing everything He commands them
over the surface of the inhabited world.

13 He causes this to happen for punishment,
for His land, or for His faithful love.

14 Listen to this, Job.
Stop and consider God's wonders.

15 Do you know how God directs His clouds
or makes their lightning flash?

16 Do you understand how the clouds float,
those wonderful works of Him who has
perfect knowledge?

17 You whose clothes get hot
when the south wind brings calm to the land,

18 can you help God spread out the skies
as hard as a cast metal mirror?

19 Teach us what we should say to Him;
we cannot prepare ⌊our case⌋ because of
our darkness.

20 Should He be told that I want to speak?
Can a man speak when he is confused?

21 Now men cannot ⌊even⌋ look at the sun
when it is in the skies,
after a wind has swept through and cleared
them away.

22 Yet out of the north He comes, ⌊shrouded⌋
in a golden ⌊glow⌋;
awesome majesty surrounds Him.

23 The •Almighty—we cannot reach Him—
He is exalted in power!
In His justice and righteousness,
He will not oppress.

24 Therefore, men •fear Him.
He does not look favorably on any who are wise
in heart.

The LORD Speaks

38 Then the LORD answered Job from the whirl-wind. He said:

---

[a]36:21 Or for you have preferred this to [b]36:27 Lit He draws in waterdrops [c]36:27 Or His [d]36:33 Lit His, or Its [e]36:33 Lit thunder announces concerning Him or it (the storm) [f]37:1 Lit from its place

---

while at the same time claiming that God does not punish the wicked.

35:5 Look at the heavens. Like Bildad (18:4), Elihu encouraged Job to see the big picture. God is so above it all that Job's sins cause their own consequences.

35:13 empty. Elihu claimed God does not

listen to empty (of wisdom or purity) prayers. Job misunderstood God's silence: God was ignoring such worthless prayers.

36:10 correction. Elihu posed his only original idea in his speeches: God uses discipline to teach us about Himself. He implied that Job had not yet learned his lesson (see also v. 15).

36:16-21 Elihu encouraged Job not to miss God's purpose: opportunities for growth in his affliction.

36:26 beyond our knowledge. Elihu returned to his claim from 33:12. He moved the argument from God's justice to God's wisdom—for the rightness of an action could be

2 Who is this who obscures ⌊My⌋ counsel
   with ignorant words?
3 Get ready to answer Me like a man;
   when I question you, you will inform Me.
4 Where were you when I established the earth?
   Tell ⌊Me⌋, if you have[a] understanding.
5 Who fixed its dimensions? Certainly you know!
   Who stretched a measuring line across it?
6 What supports its foundations?
   Or who laid its cornerstone
7 while the morning stars sang together
   and all the sons of God shouted for joy?

8 Who enclosed the sea behind doors
   when it burst from the womb,
9 when I made the clouds its garment
   and thick darkness its blanket,[b]
10 when I determined its boundaries[c]
   and put ⌊its⌋ bars and doors in place,
11 when I declared: "You may come this far,
      but no farther;
   your proud waves stop here"?

12 Have you ever in your life commanded
      the morning
   or assigned the dawn its place,
13 so it may seize the edges of the earth
   and shake the wicked out of it?
14 The earth is changed as clay is by a seal;
   ⌊its hills⌋ stand out like ⌊the folds of⌋ a garment.
15 Light[d] is withheld from the wicked,
   and the arm raised ⌊in violence⌋ is broken.

16 Have you traveled to the sources of the sea
   or walked in the depths of the oceans?
17 Have the gates of death been revealed to you?
   Have you seen the gates of death's shadow?
18 Have you comprehended the extent
      of the earth?
   Tell ⌊Me⌋, if you know all this.

19 Where is the road to the home of light?
   ⌊Do you know⌋ where darkness lives,
20 so you can lead it back to its border?
   Are you familiar with the paths to its home?
21 Don't you know? You were already born;
   you have lived so long![e]
22 Have you entered the ⌊place⌋ where the snow
      is stored?
   Or have you seen the storehouses of hail,

23 which I hold in reserve for times of trouble,
   for the day of warfare and battle?
24 What road leads to ⌊the place⌋ where light
      is dispersed?[f]
   ⌊Where is the source of⌋ the east wind
      that spreads across the earth?

25 Who cuts a channel for the flooding rain
   or clears the way for lightning,
26 to bring rain on an uninhabited land,
   ⌊on⌋ a desert with no human life,[g]
27 to satisfy the parched wasteland
   and cause the grass to sprout?
28 Does the rain have a father?
   Who fathered the drops of dew?
29 Whose womb did the ice come from?
   Who gave birth to the frost of heaven
30 when water becomes as hard as stone,[h]
   and the surface of the watery depths is frozen?

31 Can you fasten the chains of the Pleiades
   or loosen the belt of Orion?
32 Can you bring out the constellations[i]
      in their season
   and lead the Bear[j] and her cubs?
33 Do you know the laws of heaven?
   Can you impose its[k] authority on earth?
34 Can you command[l] the clouds
   so that a flood of water covers you?
35 Can you send out lightning bolts, and they go?
   Do they report to you: "Here we are"?
36 Who put wisdom in the heart[m]
   or gave the mind understanding?
37 Who has the wisdom to number the clouds?
   Or who can tilt the water jars of heaven
38 when the dust hardens like cast metal
   and the clods ⌊of dirt⌋ stick together?
39 Can you hunt prey for a lioness
   or satisfy the appetite of young lions
40 when they crouch in their dens
   and lie in wait within their lairs?
41 Who provides the raven's food
   when its young cry out to God
   and wander about for lack of food?

39 Do you know when mountain goats give birth?
   Have you watched the deer in labor?
2 Can you count the months they are pregnant[n]
   so you can know the time they give birth?

---

a **38:4** Lit *know*   b **38:9** Lit *swaddling clothes*   c **38:10** Lit *I broke My statute on it*   d **38:15** Lit *Their light*   e **38:21** Lit *born; the number of your days is great*   f **38:24** Or *where lightning is distributed*   g **38:26** Lit *life in it*   h **38:30** Lit *water hides itself as the stone*   i **38:32** Or *Mazzaroth*; Hb obscure   j **38:32** Or *lead Aldebaran*   k **38:33** Or *God's*   l **38:34** Lit *lift up your voice to*   m **38:36** Or *the inner self*; Ps 51:6   n **39:2** Lit *months they fulfill*

---

proved by wisdom even if it did not satisfy the standards of justice.

37:1-13 Elihu affirms God's power and sovereignty over nature. This focus sets the reader up for God's own words about creation in chapters 38–41.

38:3 Get ready to answer Me. Through all Job's sufferings, his hope had been that God would one day answer him, proving His concern for Job. At last God spoke, and Job knew that their relationship was still intact.

38:1–40:2 In these three chapters God questioned Job on at least 20 creatures as well as the cosmos. Obviously, Job did not know any answers.

38:1 whirlwind. A windstorm took away Job's children (1:19) and now God speaks from a whirlwind.

38:7 morning stars. Morning stars here stands in parallel to "the sons of God." Rather than the stars which were created on

3 They crouch down to give birth to their young;
   they deliver their newborn.[a]
4 Their offspring are healthy and grow up
      in the open field.
   They leave and do not return.[b]

5 Who set the wild donkey free?
   Who released the swift donkey from its harness?
6 I made the wilderness its home,
   and the salty wasteland its dwelling.
7 It scoffs at the noise of the village
   and never hears the shouts of a driver.
8 It roams the mountains for its pastureland,
   searching for anything green.

9 Would the wild ox be willing to serve you?
   Would it spend the night
      by your feeding trough?
10 Can you hold the wild ox by its harness
      to the furrow?
   Will it plow the valleys behind you?
11 Can you depend on it because of its strength?
   Would you leave it to do your hard work?
12 Can you trust the wild ox to harvest your grain
   and bring ⌊it⌋ to your threshing floor?

13 The wings of the ostrich flap joyfully,
   but are her feathers and plumage like the stork's?[c]
14 She abandons her eggs on the ground
   and lets them be warmed in the sand.
15 She forgets that a foot may crush them
   or that some wild animal may trample them.
16 She treats her young harshly, as if
      ⌊they⌋ were not her own,
   with no fear that her labor may have been
      in vain.
17 For God has deprived her of wisdom;
   He has not endowed her with understanding.
18 When she proudly[c] spreads her wings,
   she laughs at the horse and its rider.

19 Do you give strength to the horse?
   Do you adorn his neck with a mane?[c]
20 Do you make him leap like a locust?
   His proud snorting ⌊fills one with⌋ terror.
21 He paws[d] in the valley and rejoices
      in his strength;
   He charges into battle.[e]
22 He laughs at fear, since he is afraid of nothing;
   he does not run from the sword.
23 A quiver rattles at his side,

along with a flashing spear and a lance.[f]
24 He charges ahead[g] with trembling rage;
   he cannot stand still at the trumpet's sound.
25 When the trumpet blasts, he snorts defiantly.[h]
   He smells the battle from a distance;
   he hears the officers' shouts and the battle cry.

26 Does the hawk take flight by your understanding
   and spread its wings to the south?
27 Does the eagle soar at your command
   and make its nest on high?
28 It lives on a cliff where it spends the night;
   its stronghold is on a rocky crag.
29 From there it searches for prey;
   its eyes penetrate the distance.
30 Its brood gulps down blood,
   and wherever corpses lie, it is there.

40

The LORD answered Job:

2 Will the one who contends with the •Almighty
      correct ⌊Him⌋?
   Let him who argues with God give an answer.[i]

3 Then Job answered the LORD:

4 I am so insignificant. How can I answer You?
   I place my hand over my mouth.
5 I have spoken once, and I will not reply;
   twice, but ⌊now⌋ I can add nothing.

6 Then the LORD answered Job from the whirlwind:

7 Get ready to answer Me like a man;
   When I question you, you will inform Me.
8 Would you really challenge My justice?
   Would you declare Me guilty to justify yourself?
9 Do you have an arm like God's?
   Can you thunder with a voice like His?

10 Adorn yourself with majesty and splendor,
   and clothe yourself with honor and glory.
11 Unleash your raging anger;
   look on every proud person and humiliate him.
12 Look on every proud person and humble him;
   trample the wicked where they stand.[j]
13 Hide them together in the dust;
   imprison them in the grave.[k]
14 Then I will confess to you
   that your own right hand can deliver you.

15 Look at Behemoth,
   which I made along with you.

---

[a]39:3 Or they send away their labor pains [b]39:4 Lit return to them [c]39:13,18,19 Hb obscure [d]39:21 LXX, Syr; MT reads digs [e]39:21 Lit He
goes out to meet the weapon [f]39:23 Or scimitar [g]39:24 Lit He swallows the ground [h]39:25 Lit he says, "Aha!" [i]40:2 Lit God respond to it
[j]40:12 Lit wicked in their place [k]40:13 Lit together; bind their faces in the hidden place

---

the fourth day, both terms refer to angels
who existed with God prior to creation.
38:8-11 sea. God points out to Job how impossible it would be for Job to control the seas.
38:19-21 light … darkness. Light and
darkness were personified and pictured as
having homes. How could Job know where

they "lived"?
38:36 Who put wisdom in the heart? God
clearly announced that only the One who
possessed such wisdom as One who created rain (28) and stars (31-32) could also
give that wisdom to human creatures.
39:1-4 mountain goats … deer. God men-

tioned the creatures that lived in hiding to
highlight the mysteries of nature that we
never see. God, the Creator, has thought up
multitudes of natural wonders we may never
discover.

39:9-12 wild ox. The wild ox referred to here
may have been the aurochs (extinct since

He eats grass like an ox.

16 Look at the strength of his loins
and the power in the muscles of his belly.

17 He stiffens his tail like a cedar tree;
the tendons of his thighs are woven
firmly together.

18 His bones are bronze tubes;
his limbs are like iron rods.

19 He is the foremost of God's works;
⌊only⌋ his Maker can draw the sword
against him.

20 The hills yield food for him,
while all ⌊sorts of⌋ wild animals play there.

21 He lies under the lotus plants,
hiding in the protection[a] of marshy reeds.

22 Lotus plants cover him with their shade;
the willows by the brook surround him.

23 Though the river rages, Behemoth is unafraid;
he remains confident, even if
the Jordan surges up to his mouth.

24 Can anyone capture him while he looks on,[b]
or pierce his nose with snares?

41 [c] Can you pull in •Leviathan with a hook
or tie his tongue down with a rope?

2 Can you put a cord[d] through his nose
or pierce his jaw with a hook?

3 Will he beg you for mercy
or speak softly to you?

4 Will he make a covenant with you
so that you can take him as a slave forever?

5 Can you play with him like a bird
or put him on a leash[e] for your girls?

6 Will traders bargain for him
or divide him among the merchants?

7 Can you fill his hide with harpoons
or his head with fishing spears?

8 Lay a[f] hand on him.
You will remember the battle
and never repeat it!

9[g] Any hope of ⌊capturing⌋ him proves false.
Does a person not collapse at the very sight of him?

10 No one is ferocious ⌊enough⌋ to rouse Leviathan;
who then can stand against Me?

11 Who confronted Me, that I should repay him?
Everything under heaven belongs to Me.

12 I cannot be silent about his limbs,
his power, and his graceful proportions.

13 Who can strip off his outer covering?
Who can penetrate his double layer
of armor?[h]

14 Who can open his jaws,[i]
surrounded by those terrifying teeth?

15 ⌊His⌋ pride is in ⌊his⌋ rows of scales,
closely sealed together.

16 One scale is so close to another[j]
that no air can pass between them.

17 They are joined to one another,
so closely connected[k] they cannot
be separated.

18 His snorting[l] flashes with light,
while his eyes are like the rays[m] of dawn.

19 Flaming torches shoot from his mouth;
fiery sparks fly out!

20 Smoke billows from his nostrils
as from a boiling pot or ⌊burning⌋ reeds.

21 His breath sets coals ablaze,
and flames pour out of his mouth.

22 Strength resides in his neck,
and dismay dances before him.

23 The folds of his flesh are joined together,
solid as metal[n] and immovable.

24 His heart is as hard as a rock,
as hard as a lower millstone!

25 When Leviathan rises, the mighty[o]
are terrified;
they withdraw because of ⌊his⌋ thrashing.

26 The sword that reaches him will have
no effect,
nor will a spear, dart, or arrow.

27 He regards iron as straw,
and bronze as rotten wood.

28 No arrow can make him flee;
slingstones become like stubble to him.

29 A club is regarded as stubble,
and he laughs at the whirring of a javelin.

30 His undersides are jagged potsherds,
spreading the mud like a threshing sledge.

31 He makes the depths seethe like a caldron;
he makes the sea like an ointment jar.

32 He leaves a shining wake behind him;[p]
one would think the deep had white hair!

33 He has no equal on earth—
a creature devoid of fear!

34 He surveys everything that is haughty;
he is king over all the proud beasts.[q]

---

[a]**40:21** Lit plants, in the hiding place [b]**40:24** Lit capture it in its eyes [c]**41:1** Jb 40:25 in Hb [d]**41:2** Lit reed [e]**41:5** Lit or bind him [f]**41:8** Lit your [g]**41:9** Jb 41:1 in Hb [h]**41:13** LXX; MT reads double bridle [i]**41:14** Lit open the doors of his face [j]**41:16** Lit One by one they approach [k]**41:17** Lit another; they cling together and [l]**41:18** Or sneezing [m]**41:18** Lit eyelids [n]**41:23** Lit together, hard on him [o]**41:25** Or the divine beings [p]**41:32** Lit a path [q]**41:34** Lit the children of pride

---

1627). It was larger than a hippo and terrifyingly dangerous.

39:18-25 horse ... strength. Highlighted by God, perhaps again to point out His own strength.

40:1-2 Let him ... give an answer. This is the end of the first speech by God. Job's request

returned to haunt him. He now received his longed-for opportunity to dialogue with God.

40:3-5 place my hand over my mouth. Job has learned there was was no suitable reply to the grandeur of God. It was enough that God spoke with him.

40:6-9 challenge My justice? God still didn't

rebuke Job; He simply asked what right Job had to assume he understood God's ways.

40:15, 23 Behemoth. What was the behemoth? Suggestions include hippopotamus, elephant, or dinosaur. The identity is unclear, but the word means "great beast."

41:1 Leviathan. Meaning "sea serpent" and

Job Replies to the LORD

42

Then Job replied to the LORD:

2 I[a] know that You can do anything
and no plan of Yours can be thwarted.
3 ⌊You asked,⌋ "Who is this who conceals
⌊My⌋ counsel with ignorance?"
Surely I spoke about things I did not understand,
things too wonderful for me to[b] know.
4 ⌊You said,⌋ "Listen now, and I will speak.
When I question you, you will inform Me."
5 I had heard rumors about You,
but now my eyes have seen You.
6 Therefore I take back ⌊my words⌋
and repent in dust and ashes.[c]

7 After the LORD had finished speaking[d] to Job, He said to Eliphaz the Temanite: "I am angry with you and your two friends, for you have not spoken the truth about Me, as My servant Job has. 8 Now take seven bulls and seven rams, go to My servant Job, and offer a burnt offering for yourselves. Then My servant Job will pray for you. I will surely accept his ⌊prayer⌋ and not deal with you as your folly deserves. For you have not spoken the truth about Me, as My servant

Job has." 9 Then Eliphaz the Temanite, Bildad the Shuhite, and Zophar the Naamathite went and did as the LORD had told them, and the LORD accepted Job's ⌊prayer⌋.

God Restores Job

10 After Job had prayed for his friends, the LORD restored his prosperity and doubled his ⌊previous⌋ possessions. 11 All his brothers, sisters, and former acquaintances came to his house and dined with him in his house. They offered him sympathy and comfort concerning all the adversity the LORD had brought on him. Each one gave him a *qesitah*,[e] and a gold earring.

12 So the LORD blessed the latter part of Job's life more than the earlier. He owned 14,000 sheep, 6,000 camels, 1,000 yoke of oxen, and 1,000 female donkeys. 13 He also had seven sons and three daughters. 14 He named his first ⌊daughter⌋ Jemimah, his second Keziah, and his third Keren-happuch. 15 No women as beautiful as Job's daughters could be found in all the land, and their father granted them an inheritance with their brothers.

16 Job lived 140 years after this and saw his children and their children to the fourth generation. 17 Then Job died, old and full of days.

---

a **42:2** Alt Hb tradition reads *You*   b **42:3** Lit *me, and I did not*   c **42:6** LXX reads *I despise myself and melt; I consider myself dust and ashes*
d **42:7** Lit *speaking these words*   e **42:11** The value of the currency is unknown; Gn 33:19; Jos 24:32

---

considered more ferocious than the behemoth in Job's time, this vicious marine animal commonly symbolized chaos and evil. Some suggest it could be a crocodile or whale. Both illustrate the human folly of attempting to wrestle (including trying to wrestle God) something immensely more powerful than man. That an entire chapter is devoted to describing it emphasizes its overwhelming power.

41:2-5 Perhaps the "Croc Hunter" would be briefly able to get the upper hand on a crocodile, but he couldn't take him home and make him his pet. In other words, Job is unqualified to take over God's job of dealing with evil, which makes man its pet.

41:34 king over all proud beasts. Even a lion or tiger would hesitate to go swimming near a crocodile.

41:27 Ancient weapons made of bronze or iron had little effect on a crocodile's hide.

42:5 I had heard rumors about You. Speaking of the God he thought he knew before his trials, Job realizes how little he understood.

42:3 Who is this? After a litany of more than 70 rhetorical questions, Job's ears still burned with God's initial inquiry (38:2).

42:7 I am angry with you and your two friends. God was angry at those who claimed He was angry at Job!

42:7-8 My servant Job. Unlike his friends, God lavished the well-deserved title on Job (1:8; 2:3).

42:12 So the LORD blessed. Satan's scheme had failed (1:6-12). Job continued to love and trust God throughout the sufferings. And God chose to multiply Job's blessings beyond what he had lost.

42:13 seven sons and three daughters. Children, particularly sons, were considered a blessing from God. Job would have someone to take care of him in his old age (see also verse 16).

INTRODUCTION TO

PSALMS

AUTHOR

King David (Pss. 3; 7 and many others), King Solomon (Pss. 72; 127), the sons of Korah (Pss. 42-49; 84-85; 87-88), Asaph (Pss. 50; 73-83), Heman (Ps. 88), Ethan (Ps. 89), and Moses (Ps. 90) all have psalms attributed to them. Many psalms are anonymous.

DATE

Although composed over centuries (circa 1400-400 B.C.), the Psalms may well have been collected and arranged in their present form as the "hymn book" of Israel sometime in the fourth or third century B.C.

THEME

The range of human response to God and His world.

HISTORICAL BACKGROUND

The Book of Psalms is a collection of various smaller groupings of psalms that were used in Israel's worship over the centuries. Some psalms were associated with certain feasts (Ps. 130 - Yom Kippur; Ps. 135 - Passover), others with the Sabbath (Pss. 92-100), and others for confession (Pss. 32; 51) or praise (Pss. 111-118; 146-150).

CHARACTERISTICS

The moods of the various psalms embrace the whole range of human experience from exuberant praise (Ps. 145) to despair (Ps. 42); from intense anger (Ps. 137) and doubt about God's care (Ps. 73); to hope for a future based precisely upon God's care (Ps. 23). The Psalms help us express and pray with *all* our emotions. The Psalms capture the reality of our up-and-down relationship with God, but they also move us steadily along the path of knowing God.

PASSAGES FOR TOPICAL GROUP STUDY

17:1-15 .... ENEMIES .... Enemy Outlook

23:1-6 .... GOD'S RESCUE AND CARE .... The Great Shepherd

46:1-11 .... FIGHTING and REFUGE .... God, Our Refuge

139:1-24 .. GOD'S PRESENCE and ABORTION ... God's Perpetual Presence

501

BOOK I

(Psalms 1–41)

Psalm 1

The Two Ways

1 How happy is the man
who does not follow[a] the advice of the wicked,
or take[b] the path of sinners,
or join a group[c] of mockers!

2 Instead, his delight is in the LORD's instruction,
and he meditates on it day and night.

3 He is like a tree planted beside streams
of water[d]
that bears its fruit in season[e]
and whose leaf does not wither.
Whatever he does prospers.

4 The wicked are not like this;
instead, they are like chaff that the wind
blows away.

5 Therefore the wicked will not survive[b]
the judgment,
and sinners will not be in the community
of the righteous.

6 For the LORD watches over the way
of the righteous,
but the way of the wicked leads to ruin.

Psalm 2

Coronation of the Son

1 Why do the nations rebel[f]
and the peoples plot in vain?

2 The kings of the earth take their stand
and the rulers conspire together
against the LORD and His Anointed One:[g]

3 "Let us tear off their chains
and free ourselves from their restraints."[h]

4 The One enthroned[i] in heaven laughs;
the Lord ridicules them.

5 Then He speaks to them in His anger
and terrifies them in His wrath:

6 "I have consecrated My King[j]
on Zion, My holy mountain."

7 I will declare the LORD's decree:
He said to Me, "You are My Son;[k]
today I have become Your[l] Father.

8 Ask of Me,
and I will make the nations
Your[l] inheritance
and the ends of the earth Your[l] possession.

9 You will break[m] them with a rod of iron;
You[n] will shatter them like pottery."[o]

10 So now, kings, be wise;
receive instruction, you judges of the earth.

11 Serve the LORD with reverential awe,
and rejoice with trembling.

12 Pay homage to[p] the Son, or He[q] will be angry,
and you will perish in your rebellion,[r]
for His[s] anger may ignite at any moment.
All those who take refuge in Him[t] are happy.

Psalm 3

Confidence in Troubled Times

A psalm of David
when he fled
from his son Absalom.

1 LORD, how my foes increase!
There are many who attack me.

2 Many say about me,
"There is no help for him in God." •Selah

3 But You, LORD, are a shield around me,
my glory, and the One who lifts up my head.

4 I cry aloud to the LORD,
and He answers me from His holy mountain.
Selah

5 I lie down and sleep;
I wake again because the LORD sustains me.

6 I am not afraid of the thousands of people
who have taken their stand against me
on every side.

7 Rise up, LORD!
Save me, my God!
You strike all my enemies on the cheek;
You break the teeth of the wicked.

8 Salvation belongs to the LORD;
may Your blessing be on Your people. *Selah*

---

[a]1:1 Lit *not walk in* [b]1:1,5 Lit *stand in* [c]1:1 Or *or sit in the seat* [d]1:3 Or *beside irrigation canals* [e]1:3 Lit *in its season* [f]2:1 Or *conspire, or rage* [g]2:2 Or *anointed one* [h]2:3 Lit *and throw their ropes from us* [i]2:4 Lit *who sits* [j]2:6 Or *king* [k]2:7 Or *me, "You are My son* [l]2:7,8 Or *your* [m]2:9 LXX, Syr, Tg read *shepherd* [n]2:9 Or *you* [o]2:9 Lit *a potter's vessel* [p]2:12 Lit *Kiss* [q]2:12 Or *son, otherwise he* [r]2:12 Lit *perish way* [s]2:12 Or *his* [t]2:12 Or *him*

1:2 meditates on it day and night. The blessed person relishes God's law. (Word). God's ways are a necessary part of daily living.

1:3 Whatever he does prospers. The psalmist describes the rewards of godly living: strength, security, and prosperity. The picture of a godly person's life is like a tree

blessing others with fruit and shade.

2:7 My Son ... become Your Father. The king recognized God as his higher authority. This verse also points to God's proclamation of Christ as both Son and servant at His baptism and transfiguration. (See Matt. 3:17; 17:5.)

Ps. 3 David penned this psalm while running from his son Absalom (2 Sam. 15:13-30). First he focuses on the urgency of his problem (vv. 1-2). Then he asserts his unfailing trust (vv. 3-6), all the while soliciting God's help (vv. 7-8). Fourteen Psalms recount specific events in David's life: 3,7,18,30,34,51,56,57,59,60,63, and 142.

Psalm 4

A Night Prayer

For the choir director:
with stringed instruments.
A Davidic psalm.

1 Answer me when I call,
God, who vindicates me.[a]
You freed me from affliction;
be gracious to me and hear my prayer.

2 How long, exalted men, will my honor
be insulted?
⌊How long⌋ will you love what is worthless
and pursue a lie? •Selah

3 Know that the LORD has set apart
the faithful for Himself;
the LORD will hear when I call to Him.

4 Be angry[b] and do not sin;
on your bed, reflect in your heart and be still.
Selah

5 Offer sacrifices in righteousness[c]
and trust in the LORD.

6 Many are saying, "Who can show us
anything good?"
Look on us with favor, LORD.

7 You have put more joy in my heart
than they have when their grain and new wine
abound.

8 I will both lie down and sleep in peace,
for You alone, LORD, make me live in safety.

Psalm 5

The Refuge of the Righteous

For the choir director:
with the flutes. A Davidic psalm.

1 Listen to my words, LORD;
consider my sighing.

2 Pay attention to the sound of my cry,
my King and my God,
for I pray to You.

3 At daybreak, LORD, You hear my voice;
at daybreak I plead my case to You and watch
expectantly.

4 For You are not a God who delights
in wickedness;

evil cannot lodge with You.

5 The boastful cannot stand in Your presence;
You hate all evildoers.

6 You destroy those who tell lies;
the LORD abhors a man of bloodshed
and treachery.

7 But I enter Your house
by the abundance of Your faithful love;
I bow down toward Your holy temple
in reverential awe of You.

8 LORD, lead me in Your righteousness,
because of my adversaries;[d]
make Your way straight before me.

9 For there is nothing reliable in what they say;[e]
destruction is within them;
their throat is an open grave;
they flatter with their tongues.

10 Punish them, God;
let them fall by their own schemes.
Drive them out because of their many crimes,
for they rebel against You.

11 But let all who take refuge in You rejoice;
let them shout for joy forever.
May You shelter them,
and may those who love Your name boast
about You.

12 For You, LORD, bless the righteous one;
You surround him with favor like a shield.

Psalm 6

A Prayer for Mercy

For the choir director:
with stringed instruments,
according to •Sheminith.
A Davidic psalm.

1 LORD, do not rebuke me in Your anger;
do not discipline me in Your wrath.

2 Be gracious to me, LORD, for I am weak;[f]
heal me, LORD, for my bones are shaking;

3 my whole being is shaken with terror.
And You, LORD—how long?

4 Turn, LORD! Rescue me;
save me because of Your faithful love.

5 For there is no remembrance of You
in death;
who can thank You in •Sheol?

a **4:1** Or *God of my righteousness.* b **4:4** Or *Tremble* c **4:5** Or *Offer right sacrifices*; lit *Sacrifice sacrifices of righteousness* d **5:8** Or *Of those who lie in wait for me* e **5:9** Lit *in his mouth* f **6:2** Or *sick*

3:2 Selah. This word occurs often in the Psalms and its meaning has been debated. It may indicate a pause for the singers and musicians when the Psalms were being sung.

4:2-3 the LORD will hear. David criticizes his enemies who are intent on ruining his reputation. He reminds them the Lord will re-

spond to his cries for help.

4:4 angry and do not sin ... reflect in your heart. Anger is inappropriate when it substitutes for trust in God (Eph. 4:26).

Ps. 5 I pray. When his enemies verbally assault him, David turns to prayer. David be-

gins his morning with a petition for the Lord's help. Notice David habitually prays morning and night.

6:1-10 This is the first of David's seven 'penitential' psalms. (See also 32, 38, 51,102,130 and 142.) They follow a pattern of spoken fears, weeping, and a burst of faith.

6 I am weary from my groaning;
   with my tears I dampen my pillow[a]
   and drench my bed every night.
7 My eyes are swollen from grief;
   they[b] grow old because of all my enemies.

8 Depart from me, all evildoers,
   for the LORD has heard the sound
      of my weeping.
9 The LORD has heard my plea for help;
   the LORD accepts my prayer.
10 All my enemies will be ashamed and shake
      with terror;
   they will turn back and suddenly be disgraced.

Psalm 7

Prayer for Justice

A *Shiggaion*[c] of David,
which he sang to the LORD
concerning the words of •Cush,[d]
a Benjaminite.

1 LORD my God, I seek refuge in You;
   save me from all my pursuers and rescue me,
2 or they[e] will tear me like a lion,
   ripping me apart, with no one to rescue me.[f]

3 LORD my God, if I have done this,
   if there is injustice on my hands,
4 if I have done harm to one at peace with me
   or have plundered[g] my adversary without cause,
5 may an enemy pursue and overtake me;
   may he trample me to the ground
   and leave my honor in the dust.   •Selah

6 Rise up, LORD, in Your anger;
   lift Yourself up against the fury
      of my adversaries;
   awake for me;[h]
   You have ordained[i] a judgment.
7 Let the assembly of peoples gather around You;
   take Your seat[j] on high over it.
8 The LORD judges the peoples;
   vindicate me, LORD,
   according to my righteousness
   and my integrity.[k]

9 Let the evil of the wicked come to an end,
   but establish the righteous.

The One who examines the thoughts
   and emotions[l]
is a righteous God.
10 My shield is with[m] God,
   who saves the upright in heart.
11 God is a righteous judge,
   and a God who executes justice every day.

12 If anyone does not repent,
   God[n] will sharpen His sword;
   He has strung[o] His bow and made it ready.
13 He has prepared His deadly weapons;
   He tips His arrows with fire.

14 See, he is pregnant with evil,
   conceives trouble, and gives birth to deceit.
15 He dug a pit and hollowed it out,
   but fell into the hole he had made.
16 His trouble comes back on his own head,
   and his violence falls on the top of his head.

17 I will thank the LORD for His righteousness;
   I will sing about the name of the LORD,
      the •Most High.

Psalm 8

God's Glory, Man's Dignity

For the choir director: on the •*Gittith*.
A Davidic psalm.

1 LORD, our Lord,
   how magnificent is Your name
      throughout the earth!

   You have covered the heavens
      with Your majesty.[p]
2 Because of Your adversaries,
   You have established a stronghold[q]
   from the mouths of children
      and nursing infants,
   to silence the enemy and the avenger.

3 When I observe Your heavens,
   the work of Your fingers,
   the moon and the stars,
   which You set in place,
4 what is man that You remember him,
   the son of man that You look after him?
5 You made him little less than God[r][s]
   and crowned him with glory and honor.

---

a**6:6** Lit *bed*   b**6:7** LXX, Aq, Sym, Jer read *I*   cPerhaps a passionate song with rapid changes of rhythm, or a dirge   dLXX, Aq, Sym, Theod, Jer read *of the Cushite*   e**7:2** Lit *he*   f**7:2** Lit *ripping, and without a rescuer*   g**7:4** Or *me and have spared*   h**7:6** LXX reads *awake, Lord my God*   i**7:6** Or *me; ordain*   j**7:7** MT reads *and return*   k**7:8** Lit *integrity on me*   l**7:9** Lit *examines hearts and kidneys*   m**7:10** Lit *on*   n**7:12** Lit *He*   o**7:12** Lit *bent; that is, bent the bow to string it*   p**8:1** Lit *earth, which has set Your splendor upon the heavens*   q**8:2** LXX reads *established praise*   r**8:5** LXX reads *angels*   s**8:5** Or *gods, or a god, or heavenly beings*; Hb *Elohim*

6:7 eyes grow old. David has wept until he can barely see. He strains to see God's deliverance, but foes fill his vision.

6:8-10 The LORD has heard ... my enemies will ... shake. Regaining his second wind, David defiantly addresses his enemies. His concluding confidence in God is a common theme

in many psalms (7:10-17; 10:16-18; 12:7).

7:11 judge. This image is of a judge bringing a swift sentence (See also 7:8, 11; 68:18).

7:16 His trouble comes back on his own head. Disobedience to God's ways always results in unpleasant consequences of our own making!

8:1-5 how magnificent is Your name. This psalm exemplifies how God should be praised: for who He is and for all He does.

8:3-4 what is man that You remember him. God has built a universe for us to live in. How we deserve His wondrous love and concern is beyond David's comprehension.

⁶ You made him lord over the works of Your hands;
You put everything under his feet:ᵃ
⁷ all the sheep and oxen,
as well as animals in the wild,
⁸ birds of the sky,
and fish of the sea
passing through the currents of the seas.

⁹ LORD, our Lord,
how magnificent is Your name
throughout the earth!

Psalm 9

Celebration of God's Justice

For the choir director:
according to *Muth-labben*.ᵇ
A Davidic psalm.

¹ I will thank the LORD with all my heart;
I will declare all Your wonderful works.
² I will rejoice and boast about You;
I will sing about Your name, •Most High.

³ When my enemies retreat,
they stumble and perish before You.
⁴ For You have upheld my just cause;ᶜ
You are seated on Your throne
as a righteous judge.
⁵ You have rebuked the nations:
You have destroyed the wicked;
You have erased their name forever and ever.
⁶ The enemy has come to eternal ruin;
You have uprooted the cities,
and the very memory of them has perished.

⁷ But the LORD sits enthroned forever;
He has established His throne for judgment.
⁸ He judges the world with righteousness;
He executes judgment on the peoples
with fairness.
⁹ The LORD is a refuge for the oppressed,
a refuge in times of trouble.
¹⁰ Those who know Your name trust in You
because You have not abandoned
those who seek You, LORD.

¹¹ Sing to the LORD, who dwells in Zion;
proclaim His deeds among the peoples.
¹² For the One who seeks an accounting
for bloodshed remembers them;
He does not forget the cry of the afflicted.

¹³ Be gracious to me, LORD;
consider my affliction at the hands of those
who hate me.
Lift me up from the gates of death,
¹⁴ so that I may declare all Your praises.
I will rejoice in Your salvation
within the gates of Daughter Zion.ᵈ

¹⁵ The nations have fallen into the pit they made;
their foot is caught in the net
they have concealed.
¹⁶ The LORD has revealed Himself;
He has executed justice,
striking downᵉ the wickedᶠ
by the work of their hands.   •*Higgaion.* •*Selah*

¹⁷ The wicked will return to •Sheol—
all the nations that forget God.
¹⁸ For the oppressed will not always be forgotten;
the hope of the afflictedᵍ will not perish
forever.

¹⁹ Rise up, LORD! Do not let man prevail;
let the nations be judged in Your presence.
²⁰ Put terror in them, LORD;
let the nations know they are only men.   *Selah*

Psalm 10

¹ LORD,ʰ why do You stand so far away?
Why do You hide in times of trouble?
² In arrogance the wicked relentlessly pursue
the afflicted;
let them be caught in the schemes
they have devised.

³ For the wicked one boasts about
his own cravings;
the one who is greedy cursesⁱ and despises
the LORD.
⁴ In all his scheming,
the wicked arrogantly thinks:ʲ
"There is no accountability,
⌊since⌋ God does not exist."
⁵ His ways are always secure;ᵏ
Your lofty judgments are beyond his sight;
he scoffs at all his adversaries.
⁶ He says to himself, "I will never be moved—
from generation to generation
without calamity."
⁷ Cursing, deceit, and violence fill his mouth;
trouble and malice are under his tongue.

ᵃ**8:6** Or *authority* ᵇPerhaps a musical term ᶜ**9:4** Lit *my justice and my cause* ᵈ**9:14** Jerusalem ᵉ**9:16** Or *justice, snaring* ᶠ**9:16** LXX, Aq, Syr, Tg read *justice, the wicked is trapped* ᵍ**9:18** Alt Hb tradition reads *humble* ʰ**10:1** A few Hb mss and LXX connect Pss 9–10. Together these 2 psalms form a partial •acrostic. ⁱ**10:3** Or *he blesses the greedy* ʲ**10:4** Lit *wicked according to the height of his nose* ᵏ**10:5** Or *prosperous*

8:6-8 lord. The psalmist applies the job description given in the Garden of Eden (Gen. 1:28; 2:15). Also quoted in Heb. 2:6-8.

9:1 declare ... Your wonderful works. "Wonderful works" is a single word in Hebrew that is used to praise God's redemptive miracles. (See also Ps. 106:7, 22.)

9:3-6 Each victory carried national as well as personal meaning. David praises God for rescues and for justice.

9:7-10 the LORD sits enthroned forever. Before the psalm concludes, David extols God's continuous, righteous judgment.

9:18 oppressed will not always be forgotten.

David speaks prophetically of the reign of God's justice in the future.

9:19-20 let the nations know. David prompts God to awaken his enemies to a harsh reality. The original word used here for "man" emphasizes human frailty.

10:11 God has forgotten. Wicked people

8 He waits in ambush near the villages;
    he kills the innocent in secret places;
    his eyes are on the lookout for the helpless.
9 He lurks in secret like a lion in a thicket.
    He lurks in order to seize the afflicted.
    He seizes the afflicted and drags him
        in his net.
10 He crouches and bends down;
    the helpless fall because of his strength.
11 He says to himself, "God has forgotten;
    He hides His face and will never see."

12 Rise up, LORD God! Lift up Your hand.
    Do not forget the afflicted.
13 Why has the wicked despised God?
    He says to himself, "You will not demand
        an account."
14 But You Yourself have seen trouble and grief,
    observing it in order to take the matter
        into Your hands.
    The helpless entrusts himself to You;
    You are a helper of the fatherless.
15 Break the arm of the wicked and evil person;
    call his wickedness into account
    until nothing remains of it.ᵃ

16 The LORD is King forever and ever;
    the nations will perish from His land.
17 LORD, You have heard the desire
        of the humble;ᵇ
    You will strengthen their hearts.
    You will listen carefully,
18 doing justice for the fatherless
        and the oppressed,
    so that men of the earth may terrify ⌊them⌋
        no more.

Psalm 11

Refuge in the LORD

For the choir director. Davidic.

1 I have taken refuge in the LORD.
    How can you say to me,
    "Escape to the mountain like a bird!ᶜ
2 For look, the wicked string the bow;
    they put theᵈ arrow on the bowstring
    to shoot from the shadows at the upright
        in heart.

3 When the foundations are destroyed,
    what can the righteous do?"
4 The LORD is in His holy temple;
    the LORD's throne is in heaven.
    His eyes watch; He examinesᵉ •everyone.
5 The LORD examines the righteous
        and the wicked.
    He hates the lover of violence.
6 He will rain burning coals and sulfurᶠ
        on the wicked;
    a scorching wind will be their portion.ᵍ
7 For the LORD is righteous; He loves
    righteous deeds.
    The upright will see His face.

Psalm 12

Oppression by the Wicked

For the choir director:
according to •Sheminith.
A Davidic psalm.

1 Help, LORD, for no faithful one remains;
    the loyal have disappeared
        from the •human race.
2 They lie to one another;
    they speak with flattering lips
        and deceptive hearts.
3 May the LORD cut off all flattering lips
    and the tongue that speaks boastfully.
4 They say, "Through our tongues
        we have power;ʰ
    our lips are our own—who can be our master?"

5 "Because of the oppression of the afflicted
    and the groaning of the poor,
    I will now rise up," says the LORD.
    "I will put in a safe place the one
        who longs for it."

6 The words of the LORD are pure words,
    like silver refined in an earthen furnace,
    purified seven times.

7 You, LORD, will guard us;ⁱ
    You will protect usʲ from this generation forever.
8 The wicked wanderᵏ everywhere,
    and what is worthless is exalted
        by the human race.

ᵃ**10:15** Lit *account You do not find*   ᵇ**10:17** Other Hb mss, LXX, Syr read *afflicted*   ᶜ**11:1** LXX, Syr, Jer, Tg, MT reads *to your mountain, bird*
ᵈ**11:2** Lit *their*   ᵉ**11:4** Lit *His eyelids examine*   ᶠ**11:6** Sym; MT reads *rain snares, fire*; the difference between the 2 Hb words is 1 letter   ᵍ**11:6** Lit *be
the portion of their cup*   ʰ**12:4** Lit *That say, "By our tongues we are strengthened*   ⁱ**12:7** Some Hb mss, LXX, Jer; other Hb mss read *them*
ʲ**12:7** Some Hb mss, LXX; other Hb mss read *him*   ᵏ**12:8** Lit *walk about*

---

wink at evil and erroneously believe God does the same. God may not act immediately, but He is not indifferent to injustice (v. 14).

10:16-18 Nations are destroyed and prideful people are humbled—as in the previous psalm (9:19-20). The two psalms link to-

gether, portraying the whole of God's awesome power.

Ps. 13 Similar to other psalms of lament, this one details David's distress (vv.12), asks for deliverance (vv. 3-4), and ends on a confident note (vv.5-6).

13:1-2 how long will You continually forget me? David feels as if his prayers are going nowhere. Four times he asks God: "How long" must I survive without Your presence—personally and militarily?

13:5 trusted in Your faithful love. These hon-

Psalm 13

A Plea for Deliverance

For the choir director.
A Davidic psalm.

1 LORD, how long will You continually forget me?
How long will You hide Your face from me?
2 How long will I store up anxious concerns[a]
within me,
agony in my mind every day?
How long will my enemy dominate me?

3 Consider me and answer, LORD, my God.
Restore brightness to my eyes;
otherwise, I will sleep in death,
4 my enemy will say, "I have triumphed
over him,"
and my foes will rejoice because I am shaken.

5 But I have trusted in Your faithful love;
my heart will rejoice in Your deliverance.
6 I will sing to the LORD
because He has treated me generously.

Psalm 14

A Portrait of Sinners

For the choir director. Davidic.

1 The fool says in his heart,
"God does not exist."
They are corrupt; their actions are revolting.
There is no one who does good.
2 The LORD looks down from heaven
on the •human race
to see if there is one who is wise,
one who seeks God.
3 All have turned away;
all alike have become corrupt.
There is no one who does good,
not even one.[b]

4 Will evildoers never understand?
They consume my people
as they consume bread;
they do not call on the LORD.
5 Then[c] they will be filled with terror,
for God is with those who are[d] righteous.
6 You ⌊sinners⌋ frustrate the plans of the afflicted,
but the LORD is his refuge.

7 Oh, that Israel's deliverance would come
from Zion!
When the LORD restores His captive people,
Jacob will rejoice; Israel will be glad.[e]

Psalm 15

A Description of the Godly

A Davidic psalm.

1 LORD, who can dwell in Your tent?
Who can live on Your holy mountain?

2 The one who lives honestly,
practices righteousness,
and acknowledges the truth in his heart—
3 who does not slander with his tongue,
who does not harm his friend
or discredit his neighbor,
4 who despises the one rejected by the LORD,[f]
but honors those who •fear the LORD,
who keeps his word whatever the cost,
5 who does not lend his money at interest
or take a bribe against the innocent—
the one who does these things will never
be moved.

Psalm 16

Confidence in the LORD

A Davidic •Miktam.

1 Protect me, God, for I take refuge in You.
2 I[g] said to the LORD, "You are my Lord;
I have no good besides You."[h]
3 As for the holy people who are in the land,
they are the noble ones in whom is
all my delight.
4 The sorrows of those who take another ⌊god⌋
for themselves multiply;
I will not pour out their drink offerings of blood,
and I will not speak their names with my lips.

5 LORD, You are my portion[i]
and my cup ⌊of blessing⌋;
You hold my future.
6 The boundary lines have fallen for me
in pleasant places;
indeed, I have a beautiful inheritance.

7 I will praise the LORD who counsels me—
even at night my conscience instructs me.

---

a **13:2** Or *up counsels* b **14:3** Two Hb mss, some LXX mss add the material found in Rm 3:13–18 c **14:5** Or *There* d **14:5** Lit *with the generation of the* e **14:7** Or *let Jacob rejoice; let Israel be glad.* f **15:4** Lit *in his eyes the rejected is despised* g **16:2** Some Hb mss, LXX, Syr, Jer; other Hb mss read *You* h **16:2** Or *"Lord, my good; there is none besides You."* i **16:5** Or *allotted portion*

---

est expressions of emotions before God make the Psalms a comfort to people in every age.

14:1 fool. The Hebrew word for fool, *nabal,* implies aggressiveness and perversity such as seen in Nabal's story in I Samuel 25:25. This kind of fool believes God is irrelevant to the practicality of life (10:4).

14:4 consume. David is amazed at the audacity of evil. Wicked people attack God's people, disregarding their value to God.

15:1 dwell in Your tent? The Psalms provide two images for "tent": one of formal worship and sacrifice and the other of simple hospitality. God desires His people to be at home when worshipping Him.

15:5 lend his money at interest. Using excessive interest as a means to get ahead was condemned (Lev. 25; 35-38).

16:1-8 keep the Lord in mind always. Almost every verse in this half of the psalm proclaims David's single-minded faithfulness to God.

8 I keep the LORD in mind[a] always.
Because He is at my right hand,
I will not be shaken.

9 Therefore my heart is glad,
and my spirit rejoices;
my body also rests securely.

10 For You will not abandon me to •Sheol;
You will not allow Your Faithful One to see the •Pit.[b]

11 You reveal the path of life to me;
in Your presence is abundant joy;
in Your right hand are eternal pleasures.

Enemy Outlook

1. Have you ever had an eye injury? What happened? How did you react?

Psalm 17

2. When David prayed, "Guard me as the apple of Your eye" (v. 8), what was he asking of God? How does this show David's value to God?

3. Why did David ask God to destroy his enemies? How might an ungodly man have responded to his enemies, rather than praying?

4. What did David mean when he prayed, "I will be satisfied with Your presence" (v. 15)?

5. What lesson can you learn from David's attitude toward his enemies?

Psalm 17

A Prayer for Protection

A Davidic prayer.

1 LORD, hear a just cause;
pay attention to my cry;
listen to my prayer—
from lips free of deceit.

2 Let my vindication come from You,
⌊for⌋ You see what is right.

3 You have tested my heart;
You have visited by night;

You have tried me and found nothing ⌊evil⌋;
I have determined that my mouth will not sin.[c]

4 Concerning what people do:
by the word of Your lips[d]
I have avoided the ways of the violent.

5 My steps are on Your paths;
my feet have not slipped.

6 I call on You, God,
because You will answer me;
listen closely to me; hear what I say.

7 Display the wonders of Your faithful love,
Savior of all who seek refuge
from those who rebel against Your right hand.[e]

8 Guard me as the apple of Your eye;[f]
hide me in the shadow of Your wings

9 from[g] the wicked who treat me violently,[h]
my deadly enemies who surround me.

10 They have become hardened;[i]
their mouths speak arrogantly.

11 They advance against me;[j] now they surround me.
They are determined[k]
to throw ⌊me⌋ to the ground.

12 They are[l] like a lion eager to tear,
like a young lion lurking in ambush.

13 Rise up, LORD!
Confront him; bring him down.
With Your sword, save me from the wicked.

14 With Your hand, LORD, ⌊save me⌋ from men,
from men of the world,
whose portion is in this life:
You fill their bellies with what You have in store,
their sons are satisfied,
and they leave their surplus to their children.

15 But I will see Your face in righteousness;
when I awake, I will be satisfied
with Your presence.[m]

Psalm 18

Praise for Deliverance

For the choir director. Of the servant of the LORD, David, who spoke the words of this song to the LORD on the day the LORD rescued him from the hand of all his enemies and from the hand of Saul. He said:

1 I love You, LORD, my strength.
2 The LORD is my rock,

---

[a]**16:8** Lit *front of me*   [b]**16:10** LXX reads *see decay*   [c]**17:3** Or *[evil]; my mouth will not sin*   [d]**17:4** God's law   [e]**17:7** Or *love, You who save with Your right hand those seeking refuge from adversaries*   [f]**17:8** Lit *as the pupil, the daughter of the eye*   [g]**17:9** Lit *from the presence of*   [h]**17:9** Or *who plunder me*   [i]**17:10** Lit *have closed up their fat*   [j]**17:11**Vg; one Hb ms, LXX read *They cast me out*; MT reads *Our steps*   [k]**17:11** Lit *They set their eyes*   [l]**17:12** Lit *He is*   [m]**17:15** Lit *form*

16:9-11 path of life ... presence. This "path of life" provides both physical security and eternity in God's presence.

17:1-6 hear a just cause. David's first concern is to plead his innocence as a prelude to asking for God's protection again in the second half of this prayer (7-15).

17:3-5 You have ... found nothing. David contrasts the purity of his life with the evil people around him (vv. 9-12). He asks God to vindicate his innocence, to "test his heart."

17:15 when I awake. Sleep was a euphemism for death. He will awake to the glorious presence of God at the resurrection. (Dan. 12:2; Isa. 26:19).

18:4-6 David penned this psalm when King Saul's army was closing in. Much of its content, with a few variations, is also quoted in 2 Sam. 22.

18:4-5 ropes of death. David describes his

my fortress, and my deliverer,
my God, my mountain where I seek refuge,
my shield and the •horn of my salvation,
my stronghold.

3 I called to the LORD, who is worthy of praise,
and I was saved from my enemies.

4 The ropes of death were wrapped around me;
the torrents of destruction terrified me.

5 The ropes of •Sheol entangled me;
the snares of death confronted me.

6 I called to the LORD in my distress,
and I cried to my God for help.
From His temple He heard my voice,
and my cry to Him reached His ears.

7 Then the earth shook and quaked;
the foundations of the mountains trembled;
they shook because He burned with anger.

8 Smoke rose from His nostrils,
and consuming fire ⌊came⌋ from His mouth;
coals were set ablaze by it.ª

9 He parted the heavens and came down,
a dark cloud beneath His feet.

10 He rode on a cherub and flew,
soaring on the wings of the wind.

11 He made darkness His hiding place,
dark storm clouds His canopy around Him.

12 From the radiance of His presence,
His clouds swept onward with hail
and blazing coals.

13 The LORD thundered fromᵇ heaven;
the •Most High projected His voice.ᶜ

14 He shot His arrows and scattered them;
He hurledᵈ lightning bolts and routed them.

15 The depths of the sea became visible,
the foundations of the world were exposed,
at Your rebuke, LORD,
at the blast of the breath of Your nostrils.

16 He reached down from on high
and took hold of me;
He pulled me out of deep waters.

17 He rescued me from my powerful enemy
and from those who hated me,
for they were too strong for me.

18 They confronted me in the day of my distress,
but the LORD was my support.

19 He brought me out to a wide-open place;
He rescued me because He delighted in me.

20 The LORD rewarded me
according to my righteousness;
He repaid me
according to the cleanness of my hands.

21 For I have kept the ways of the LORD
and have not turned from my God
to wickedness.

22 Indeed, I have kept all His ordinances in mindᵉ
and have not disregarded His statutes.

23 I was blameless toward Him
and kept myself from sinning.

24 So the LORD repaid me
according to my righteousness,
according to the cleanness of my hands
in His sight.

25 With the faithful
You prove Yourself faithful;
with the blameless man
You prove Yourself blameless;

26 with the pure
You prove Yourself pure,
but with the crooked
You prove Yourself shrewd.

27 For You rescue an afflicted people,
but You humble those with haughty eyes.

28 LORD, You light my lamp;
my God illuminates my darkness.

29 With You I can attack a barrier,ᶠ
and with my God I can leap over a wall.

30 God—His way is perfect;
the word of the LORD is pure.
He is a shield to all who take refuge in Him.

31 For who is God besides the LORD?
And who is a rock? Only our God.

32 God—He clothes me with strength
and makes my way perfect.

33 He makes my feet like the feet of a deer
and sets me securely on the heights.ᵍ

34 He trains my hands for war;
my arms can bend a bow of bronze.

35 You have given me the shield of Your salvation;
Your right hand upholds me,
and Your humility exalts me.

36 You widen ⌊a place⌋ beneath me for my steps,
and my ankles do not give way.

37 I pursue my enemies and overtake them;
I do not turn back until they are wiped out.

ª 18:8 Or *ablaze from Him*   ᵇ 18:13 Some Hb mss, LXX, Tg, Jer; other Hb mss read *in*   ᶜ 18:13 Other Hb mss read *voice, with hail and fiery coals*
ᵈ 18:14 Or *multiplied*   ᵉ 18:22 Lit *Indeed, all His ordinances have been in front of me*   ᶠ 18:29 Or *ridge*   ᵍ 18:33 Or *on my high places*

---

near death experience.

18:8 Smoke ... fire. Smoke in Isaiah 6:4 depicts the reaction of God's holiness to sin. "Consuming fire" is also used in Deuteronomy 4:24 when God is described as being jealously eager for the people to keep the covenant.

18:16-19 rescued ... delighted in me. After the powerful images of God's might in the previous verses, the contrast here highlights the love and tenderness with which God cares for each of us. God's holiness paradoxically and simultaneously contains both wrath at our sin and love for us.

18:25-35 You ... God. David offers a catalog of the attributes of God's character: faithful, blameless (25); pure, shrewd (26); rescuer, humbler (27); light-bringer (28); perfect, pure, a shield (30); a rock (31); strength (32); security (33); trainer (34); protector (35).

38 I crush them, and they cannot get up;
   they fall beneath my feet.
39 You have clothed me with strength for battle;
   You subdue my adversaries beneath me.
40 You have made my enemies retreat before me;[a]
   I annihilate those who hate me.
41 They cry for help, but there is no one
      to save ⌊them⌋—
   ⌊they cry⌋ to the LORD, but He does not
      answer them.
42 I pulverize them like dust before the wind;
   I trample them[b] like mud in the streets.

43 You have freed me from the feuds
      among the people;
   You have appointed me the head of nations;
   a people I had not known serve me.
44 Foreigners submit to me grudgingly;
   as soon as they hear,[c] they obey me.
45 Foreigners lose heart
   and come trembling from their fortifications.

46 The LORD lives—may my rock be praised!
   The God of my salvation is exalted.
47 God—He gives me vengeance
   and subdues peoples under me.
48 He frees me from my enemies.
   You exalt me above my adversaries;
   You rescue me from violent men.
49 Therefore I will praise You, LORD,
      among the nations;
   I will sing about Your name.
50 He gives great victories to His king;
   He shows loyalty to His anointed,
   to David and his descendants forever.

Psalm 19

The Witness of Creation and Scripture

> For the choir director.
> A Davidic psalm.

1 The heavens declare the glory of God,
   and the sky[d] proclaims the work of His hands.
2 Day after day they pour out speech;
   night after night
      they communicate knowledge.[e]
3 There is no speech; there are no words;
   their voice is not heard.
4 Their message[f] has gone out to all the earth,

and their words to the ends
   of the inhabited world.

In the heavens[g] He has pitched a tent
   for the sun.
5 It is like a groom coming from
      the[h] bridal chamber;
   it rejoices like an athlete running a course.
6 It rises from one end of the heavens
   and circles[i] to their other end;
   nothing is hidden from its heat.

7 The instruction of the LORD is perfect,
   reviving the soul;
   the •testimony of the LORD is trustworthy,
   making the inexperienced wise.
8 The precepts of the LORD are right,
   making the heart glad;
   the commandment of the LORD is radiant,
   making the eyes light up.
9 The •fear of the LORD is pure,
   enduring forever;
   the ordinances of the LORD are reliable
   and altogether righteous.
10 They are more desirable than gold—
   than an abundance of pure gold;
   and sweeter than honey—
   than honey dripping from the comb.
11 In addition, Your servant is warned by them;
   there is great reward in keeping them.

12 Who perceives his unintentional sins?
   Cleanse me from my hidden faults.
13 Moreover, keep Your servant from willful sins;
   do not let them rule over me.
   Then I will be innocent,
   and cleansed from blatant rebellion.
14 May the words of my mouth
   and the meditation of my heart
   be acceptable to You,
   LORD, my rock and my Redeemer.

Psalm 20

Deliverance in Battle

> For the choir director.
> A Davidic psalm.

1 May the LORD answer you in a day of trouble;
   may the name of Jacob's God protect you.
2 May He send you help from the sanctuary

---

[a]18:40 Or *You gave me the necks of my enemies*   [b]18:42 Some Hb mss, LXX, Syr, Tg; other Hb mss read *I poured them out*   [c]18:44 Lit *At the hearing of the ear*   [d]19:1 Or *expanse*   [e]19:2 Or *Day to day pours out speech, and night to night communicates knowledge*   [f]19:4 LXX, Sym, Syr, Vg; MT reads *line*   [g]19:4 Lit *In them*   [h]19:5 Lit *his*   [i]19:6 Lit *its circuit is*

19:1-4 declare … they pour out speech. Though the heavens seem to be silent, they speak of God's glory through sheer beauty.

19:4-6 a tent for the sun. Ancient people described the sky as a canopy over the earth which housed the sun. The sun was worshiped in pagan societies who didn't know Creator-God.

19:11-13 reward in keeping them. God gave us divine law as both warning and promise. It warns that certain actions require forgiveness. It promises that faithfulness to the Law brings reward. Willful disregard for the Law results in separation from God.

Ps. 20 This psalm was sung by the people to

encourage their king to face the enemy in battle. Verses 1-5 ask God's blessing and success for the king. The second part, verses 6-9, is a confession of faith in God's willingness and power to answer.

21:1-2 Your strength. "Your help" and "your victory" are the same word in Hebrew. To have

and sustain you from Zion.

3 May He remember all your offerings
and accept your •burnt offering. •Selah

4 May He give you what your heart desires
and fulfill your whole purpose.

5 Let us shout for joy at your victory
and lift the banner in the name of our God.
May the LORD fulfill all your requests.

6 Now I know that the LORD gives victory
to His anointed;
He will answer him from His holy heaven
with mighty victories from[a] His right hand.

7 Some take pride in a chariot, and others
in horses,
but we take pride in the name of the LORD
our God.

8 They collapse and fall,
but we rise and stand firm.

9 LORD, give victory to the king!
May He[b] answer us on the day that we call.

Psalm 21

The King's Victory

For the choir director.
A Davidic psalm.

1 LORD, the king finds joy in Your strength.
How greatly he rejoices in Your victory!

2 You have given him his heart's desire
and have not denied the request of his lips.
•Selah

3 For You meet him with rich blessings;
You place a crown of pure gold on his head.

4 He asked You for life, and You gave it to him—
length of days forever and ever.

5 His glory is great through Your victory;
You confer majesty and splendor on him.

6 You give him blessings forever;
You cheer him with joy in Your presence.

7 For the king relies on the LORD;
through the faithful love of the •Most High
he is not shaken.

8 Your hand will capture all your enemies;
your right hand will seize those who hate you.

9 You will make them [burn]
like a fiery furnace when you appear;
the LORD will engulf them in His wrath,

and fire will devour them.

10 You will wipe their descendants from the earth
and their offspring from the •human race.

11 Though they intend to harm[c] you
and devise a wicked plan, they will not prevail.

12 Instead, you will put them to flight
when you aim your bow[d] at their faces.

13 Be exalted, LORD, in Your strength;
we will sing and praise Your might.

Psalm 22

From Suffering to Praise

For the choir director: according to
"The Deer of the Dawn."[e]
A Davidic psalm.

1 My God, my God, why have You forsaken me?
[Why are You] so far from my deliverance
and from my words of groaning?[f]

2 My God, I cry by day, but You do not answer,
by night, yet I have no rest.

3 But You are holy,
enthroned on the praises of Israel.

4 Our fathers trusted in You;
they trusted, and You rescued them.

5 They cried to You and were set free;
they trusted in You and were not disgraced.

6 But I am a worm and not a man,
scorned by men and despised by people.

7 Everyone who sees me mocks me;
they sneer[g] and shake their heads:

8 "He relies on[h] the LORD;
let Him rescue him;
let the LORD[i] deliver him,
since He takes pleasure in him."

9 You took me from the womb,
making me secure while at my mother's breast.

10 I was given over to You at birth;[j]
You have been my God
from my mother's womb.

11 Do not be far from me, because distress is near
and there is no one to help.

12 Many bulls surround me;
strong ones of Bashan encircle me.

13 They open their mouths against me—
lions, mauling and roaring.

---

a **20:6** Other Hb mss, Aq, Sym, Jer, Syr read *with the victorious might of*   b **20:9** Or *LORD, save. May the king*   c **21:11** Lit *they stretch out evil against*   d **21:12** Lit *aim with your bowstrings*   e Perhaps a musical term   f **22:1** Or *My words of groaning are so far from delivering me* (as a statement)   g **22:7** Lit *separate with the lip*   h **22:8** Or *Rely on*   i **22:8** Lit *let Him*   j **22:10** Lit *was cast on You from the womb*

God's help is to have victory secured. Verse 6 repeats this thought.

Ps. 22 why have You forsaken me? David is under siege from God's enemies, feeling hopeless and deserted by God who has helped him in the past. This psalm is the cry of a righteous sufferer. Gospel writers find striking parallels

between David in this psalm and Christ at His crucifixion (Matt. 27:35, 39, 43; John 19:23-24).

22:1 Jesus quotes this verse (and perhaps the entire Psalm) during His crucifixion (Matt. 27:46; Mark 15:34).

22:3-5 You are holy. These verses show us that true prayer is all about God's faithfulness.

22:9-10 You took me from the womb. God chose David in the same manner that He chose Jeremiah and Paul—before their births.

22:12-18 bulls … dogs. The psalmist uses a series of powerful images to portray his enemies (bulls, lions, dogs, and evil men). Bashan bulls were the heaviest breed of their day.

14 I am poured out like water,
and all my bones are disjointed;
my heart is like wax,
melting within me.

15 My strength is dried up like baked clay;
my tongue sticks to the roof of my mouth.
You put me into the dust of death.

16 For dogs have surrounded me;
a gang of evildoers has closed in on me;
they pierced[a] my hands and my feet.

17 I can count all my bones;
people[b] look and stare at me.

18 They divided my garments among themselves,
and they cast lots for my clothing.

19 But You, LORD, don't be far away.
My strength, come quickly to help me.

20 Deliver my life from the sword,
my very life[c] from the power of the dog.

21 Save me from the mouth of the lion!
You have rescued[d] me
from the horns of the wild oxen.

22 I will proclaim Your name to my brothers;
I will praise You in the congregation.

23 You who •fear the LORD, praise Him!
All you descendants of Jacob, honor Him!
All you descendants of Israel, revere Him!

24 For He has not despised or detested
the torment of the afflicted.
He did not hide His face from him,
but listened when he cried to Him for help.

25 I will give praise[e] in the great congregation
because of You;
I will fulfill my vows
before those who fear You.[f]

26 The humble[g] will eat and be satisfied;
those who seek the LORD will praise Him.
May your hearts live forever!

27 All the ends of the earth will remember
and turn to the LORD.
All the families of the nations
will bow down before You,

28 for kingship belongs to the LORD;
He rules over the nations.

29 All who prosper on earth will eat and bow down;
all those who go down to the dust
will kneel before Him—
even the one who cannot preserve his life.

30 Descendants will serve Him;
the next generation will be told about the Lord.

31 They will come and tell a people yet to be born
about His righteousness—
what He has done.

 The Great Shepherd

1. Have you ever been around sheep? What are they like?

Psalm 23

2. What does it mean to "lie down in green pastures" and to be led "beside quiet waters" (v. 2)?

3. A shepherd used his rod and staff to guide, discipline, protect, and rescue sheep. How is this a picture of God's care for His people? How are we like sheep?

4. Why would God's "rod and staff" actually comfort David, instead of making him afraid?

5. How have you experienced God's "rod and staff" in your life?

Psalm 23

The Good Shepherd

A Davidic psalm.

1 The LORD is my shepherd;
there is nothing I lack.

2 He lets me lie down in green pastures;
He leads me beside quiet waters.

3 He renews my life;
He leads me along the right paths[h]
for His name's sake.

4 Even when I go through the darkest valley,[i]
I fear no danger,
for You are with me;
Your rod and Your staff[j]—they comfort me.

5 You prepare a table before me
in the presence of my enemies;
You anoint my head with oil;
my cup overflows.

[a]**22:16** Some Hb mss, LXX, Syr; other Hb mss read *me; like a lion*   [b]**22:17** Lit *they*   [c]**22:20** Lit *my only one*   [d]**22:21** Lit *answered*   [e]**22:25** Lit *my praise*   [f]**22:25** Lit *Him*   [g]**22:26** Or *poor*, or *afflicted*   [h]**23:3** Or *me in paths of righteousness*   [i]**23:4** Or *the valley of the shadow of death*   [j]**23:4** A shepherd's rod and crook

"Dog" was a term used for barbarians.

22:14-17 I am poured out like water. David is exhausted from fighting off powerful enemies. He likens his weakness to water that has been poured out (gone), melting wax, baked clay (too hard for use), and dust (What can be done with *dust*?). These are strong images illustrat-ing that he has come to the end of his human ability to fight back.

23:1 shepherd. In the Psalms, the shepherd was a widely used metaphor for the king (78:71-72; 2 Sam. 5:2).

23:6 goodness and faithful love. The Hebrew word *hesed* combines mercy and love with eternal qualities to capture the nature of God's love for us.

Ps. 24 This Psalm celebrates the Lord's entrance into Zion. Three thousand years old, this Psalm is recited by Jews on the first day of each week as an act of worship.

6 Only goodness and faithful love will pursue me
   all the days of my life,
   and I will dwell in[a] the house of the LORD
   as long as I live.[b]

Psalm 24

The King of Glory

A Davidic psalm.

1 The earth and everything in it,
   the world and its inhabitants,
   belong to the LORD;
2 for He laid its foundation on the seas
   and established it on the rivers.

3 Who may ascend the mountain of the LORD?
   Who may stand in His holy place?
4 The one who has clean hands and a pure heart,
   who has not set his mind[c] on what is false,
   and who has not sworn deceitfully.
5 He will receive blessing from the LORD,
   and righteousness from the God
       of his salvation.
6 Such is the generation of those who seek Him,
   who seek the face of the God of Jacob.[d] •Selah

7 Lift up your heads, you gates!
   Rise up, ancient doors!
   Then the King of glory will come in.
8 Who is this King of glory?
   The LORD, strong and mighty,
   the LORD, mighty in battle.
9 Lift up your heads, you gates!
   Rise up, ancient doors!
   Then the King of glory will come in.
10 Who is He, this King of glory?
   The LORD of •Hosts,
   He is the King of glory.   Selah

Psalm 25

Dependence on the LORD

Davidic.

1 LORD,[e] I turn my hope to You.[f]
2 My God, I trust in You.
   Do not let me be disgraced;
   do not let my enemies gloat over me.
3 Not one person who waits for You
   will be disgraced;

those who act treacherously without cause
will be disgraced.

4 Make Your ways known to me, LORD;
   teach me Your paths.
5 Guide me in Your truth and teach me,
   for You are the God of my salvation;
   I wait for You all day long.
6 Remember, LORD, Your compassion
   and Your faithful love,
   for they ⌊have existed⌋ from antiquity.[g]
7 Do not remember the sins of my youth
   or my acts of rebellion;
   in keeping with Your faithful love, remember me
   because of Your goodness, LORD.

8 The LORD is good and upright;
   therefore He shows sinners the way.
9 He leads the humble in what is right
   and teaches them His way.
10 All the LORD's ways ⌊show⌋ faithful love
       and truth
   to those who keep His covenant and decrees.
11 Because of Your name, LORD,
   forgive my sin, for it is great.

12 Who is the person who •fears the LORD?
   He will show him the way he should choose.
13 He will live a good life,
   and his descendants will inherit the land.[h]
14 The secret counsel of the LORD
   is for those who fear Him,
   and He reveals His covenant to them.
15 My eyes are always on the LORD,
   for He will pull my feet out of the net.

16 Turn to me and be gracious to me,
   for I am alone and afflicted.
17 The distresses of my heart increase;[i]
   bring me out of my sufferings.
18 Consider my affliction and trouble,
   and take away all my sins.
19 Consider my enemies; they are numerous,
   and they hate me violently.
20 Guard me and deliver me;
   do not let me be put to shame,
   for I take refuge in You.
21 May integrity and uprightness keep me,
   for I wait for You.

22 God, redeem Israel, from all its distresses.

---

[a]**23:6** LXX, Sym, Syr, Tg, Vg, Jer; MT reads *will return to*   [b]**23:6** Lit *LORD for length of days*; traditionally *LORD forever*   [c]**24:4** Or *not lifted up his soul*   [d]**24:6** Some Hb mss, LXX, Syr; other Hb mss read *seek Your face, Jacob*   [e]**25:1** The lines of this poem form an •acrostic.   [f]**25:1** Or *To You, LORD, I lift up my soul*   [g]**25:6** Or *everlasting*   [h]**25:13** Or *earth*   [i]**25:17** Or *Relieve the distresses of my heart*

24:4 pure heart. Having a pure heart does not imply moral perfection. "Heart," in Hebrew, encompassed thoughts, attitudes, affections, and will. (See also Matt. 5:8).

24:5 blessing from the LORD. The products of righteousness ("clean hands and a pure heart") are blessings from God. The righteous

person is the one who desires righteousness and cooperates with God, but only God can impart righteousness.

24:7-10 Lift up your heads ... gates ... doors! The pilgrims sing and praise God as they, with God, enter the gates of Jerusalem.

25:7 Do not remember ... He prays that his

past sins might be swallowed up in the *chesed* (loving-kindness) of God's great heart.

26:1 lived with integrity. Integrity does not mean moral perfection. Here "integrity" refers to the writer's passionate and lifelong devotion to God. Verse 6 illustrates his continual presence at God's altar.

Psalm 26

Prayer for Vindication

Davidic.

1 Vindicate me, LORD,
because I have lived with integrity
and have trusted in the LORD without wavering.

2 Test me, LORD, and try me;
examine my heart and mind.

3 For Your faithful love is before my eyes,
and I live by Your truth.

4 I do not sit with the worthless
or associate with hypocrites.

5 I hate a crowd of evildoers,
and I do not sit with the wicked.

6 I wash my hands[a] in innocence
and go around Your altar, LORD,

7 raising my voice in thanksgiving
and telling about Your wonderful works.

8 LORD, I love the house where You dwell,
the place where Your glory resides.

9 Do not destroy me along with sinners,
or my life along with men of bloodshed

10 in whose hands are evil schemes,
and whose right hands are filled with bribes.

11 But I live with integrity;
redeem me and be gracious to me.

12 My foot stands on level ground;
I will praise the LORD in the assemblies.

Psalm 27

My Stronghold

Davidic.

1 The LORD is my light and my salvation—
whom should I fear?
The LORD is the stronghold of my life—
of whom should I be afraid?

2 When evildoers came against me to devour
my flesh,
my foes and my enemies stumbled and fell.

3 Though an army deploy against me,
my heart is not afraid;
though war break out against me,
still I am confident.

4 I have asked one thing from the LORD;
it is what I desire:
to dwell in the house of the LORD

all the days of my life,
gazing on the beauty of the LORD
and seeking [Him] in His temple.

5 For He will conceal me in His shelter
in the day of adversity;
He will hide me under the cover of His tent;
He will set me high on a rock.

6 Then my head will be high
above my enemies around me;
I will offer sacrifices in His tent with shouts of joy.
I will sing and make music to the LORD.

7 LORD, hear my voice when I call;
be gracious to me and answer me.

8 In Your behalf my heart says, "Seek My face."
LORD, I will seek Your face.

9 Do not hide Your face from me;
do not turn Your servant away in anger.
You have been my help;
do not leave me or abandon me,
God of my salvation.

10 Even if my father and mother abandon me,
the LORD cares for me.

11 Because of my adversaries,
show me Your way, LORD,
and lead me on a level path.

12 Do not give me over to the will of my foes,
for false witnesses rise up against me,
breathing violence.

13 I am certain that I will see the LORD's goodness
in the land of the living.

14 Wait for the LORD;
be courageous and let your heart be strong.
Wait for the LORD.

Psalm 28

My Strength

Davidic.

1 LORD, I call to You;
my rock, do not be deaf to me.
If You remain silent to me,
I will be like those going down to the •Pit.

2 Listen to the sound of my pleading
when I cry to You for help,
when I lift up my hands
toward Your holy sanctuary.

3 Do not drag me away with the wicked,
with the evildoers,

a 26:6 A ritual or ceremonial washing to express innocence

26:8 Your glory resides. The tabernacle was originally built as a tangible sign of the presence of the Lord among the Israelites. God's glory dwelt in the tent (Ex. 40:35) and later in the temple (1 Kings 8:11). The glory of God dwelling in the tabernacle assures Israel that God's covenant with them is still in place.

27:4-6 dwell in the house of the LORD. "To dwell" was to literally sit. Four postures for prayer were practiced: sitting, kneeling, bowing flat on the ground, and standing.

27:7-12 hear my voice. He asks God to show him the right way to handle his problem. The Lord has already answered: **Seek My face.**

Seeking God's face (thoughts) is the way to approach any problem.

27:11 Show me Your way. Notice that the psalmist's prayers are dialogue, as if he is asking a human teacher for guidance. The writer is also aware that learning God's ways will take years, and he is willing to wait. (See also vv. 13-14.)

who speak in friendly ways
  with their neighbors,
while malice is in their hearts.
4 Repay them according to what
    they have done—
  according to the evil of their deeds.
  Repay them according to the work
    of their hands;
  give them back what they deserve.
5 Because they do not consider
  what the LORD has done
  or the work of His hands,
  He will tear them down and not
    rebuild them.

6 May the LORD be praised,
  for He has heard the sound of my pleading.
7 The LORD is my strength and my shield;
  my heart trusts in Him, and I am helped.
  Therefore my heart rejoices,
  and I praise Him with my song.

8 The LORD is the strength of His people;[a]
  He is a stronghold of salvation
    for His anointed.
9 Save Your people, bless Your possession,
  shepherd them, and carry them forever.

Psalm 29

The Voice of the LORD

A Davidic psalm.

1 Give the LORD—you heavenly beings[b]—
  give the LORD glory and strength.
2 Give the LORD the glory due His name;
  worship the LORD
  in the splendor of ⌊His⌋ holiness.[c]

3 The voice of the LORD is above the waters.
  The God of glory thunders—
  the LORD, above vast waters,
4 the voice of the LORD in power,
  the voice of the LORD in splendor.
5 The voice of the LORD breaks the cedars;
  the LORD shatters the cedars of Lebanon.
6 He makes Lebanon skip like a calf,
  and Sirion,[d] like a young wild ox.
7 The voice of the LORD flashes flames of fire.
8 The voice of the LORD shakes the wilderness;
  the LORD shakes the wilderness of Kadesh.

9 The voice of the LORD makes the deer give birth[e]
  and strips the woodlands bare.

In His temple all cry, "Glory!"

10 The LORD sat enthroned at the flood;
  the LORD sits enthroned, King forever.
11 The LORD gives His people strength;
  the LORD blesses His people with peace.

Psalm 30

Joy in the Morning

*A psalm; a dedication song
for the house. Davidic.*

1 I will exalt You, LORD,
  because You have lifted me up
  and have not allowed my enemies
  to triumph over me.
2 LORD my God,
  I cried to You for help, and You healed me.
3 LORD, You brought me up from •Sheol;
  You spared me from among those
  going down[f] to the •Pit.

4 Sing to the LORD, you His faithful ones,
  and praise His holy name.
5 For His anger lasts only a moment,
  but His favor, a lifetime.
  Weeping may spend the night,
  but there is joy in the morning.

6 When I was secure, I said,
  "I will never be shaken."
7 LORD, when You showed Your favor,
  You made me stand like a strong mountain;
  when You hid Your face, I was terrified.
8 LORD, I called to You;
  I sought favor from my Lord:
9 "What gain is there in my death,
  in my descending to the Pit?
  Will the dust praise You?
  Will it proclaim Your truth?
10 LORD, listen and be gracious to me;
  LORD, be my helper."

11 You turned my lament into dancing;
  You removed my •sackcloth
  and clothed me with gladness,
12 so that I can sing to You and not be silent.
  LORD my God, I will praise You forever.

---

[a] **28:8** Some Hb mss, LXX, Syr; other Hb mss read *strength for them*   [b] **29:1** Or *you angels*, or *you sons of the mighty*; lit *LORD sons of [the] gods*
[c] **29:2** Or *in holy attire*, or *in holy appearance*   [d] **29:6** Mount Hermon; Dt 3:9   [e] **29:9** Or *the oaks shake*   [f] **30:3** Some Hb mss, LXX, Theod, Orig, Syr; other Hb mss, Aq, Sym, Tg, Jer read *from going down*

29:9 temple. The temple can be understood on three levels: the faithful who worship at the temple (tabernacle) in Jerusalem, the heavenly temple of God (Isa. 6:1), or all of creation.

30:1-3 lifted me up. David has been healed by God (2) from some illness he thought would kill him.

30:11-12 You turned … removed … clothed. God answers David's cries. The Lord turns lament into dancing. Despair ("sackcloth") becomes gladness. David reminded that God is the source of all blessings, vows to praise God forever.

31:1 righteousness. In the feminine form of

this Hebrew word, righteousness takes on the connotation of the transformation that God creates in us, making us into loving, creative personalities.

31:5 Into Your hand I entrust my spirit. In Hebrew, "commit" literally means "to deposit." David gives up control of his life and places it

Psalm 31

A Plea for Protection

For the choir director.
A Davidic psalm.

1 LORD, I seek refuge in You;
let me never be disgraced.
Save me by Your righteousness.

2 Listen closely to me; rescue me quickly.
Be a rock of refuge for me,
a mountain fortress to save me.

3 For You are my rock and my fortress;
You lead and guide me
because of Your name.

4 You will free me from the net
that is secretly set for me,
for You are my refuge.

5 Into Your hand I entrust my spirit;
You redeem[a] me, LORD, God of truth.

6 I[b] hate those who are devoted
to worthless idols,
but I trust in the LORD.

7 I will rejoice and be glad in Your faithful love
because You have seen my affliction.
You have known the troubles of my life

8 and have not handed me over to the enemy.
You have set my feet in a spacious place.

9 Be gracious to me, LORD,
because I am in distress;
my eyes are worn out from angry sorrow—
my whole being[c] as well.

10 Indeed, my life is consumed with grief,
and my years with groaning;
my strength has failed
because of my sinfulness,[d]
and my bones waste away.

11 I am ridiculed by all my adversaries
and even by my neighbors.
I am an object of dread to my acquaintances;
those who see me in the street run from me.

12 I am forgotten: gone from memory
like a dead person—like broken pottery.

13 I have heard the gossip of many;
terror is on every side.
When they conspired against me,
they plotted to take my life.

14 But I trust in You, LORD;
I say, "You are my God."

15 The course of my life is in Your power;
deliver me from the power of my enemies
and from my persecutors.

16 Show Your favor to Your servant;
save me by Your faithful love.

17 LORD, do not let me be disgraced when I call
on You.
Let the wicked be disgraced;
let them be silent[e] [f] in •Sheol.

18 Let lying lips be quieted;
they speak arrogantly against the righteous
with pride and contempt.

19 How great is Your goodness
that You have stored up for those who •fear You,
and accomplished in the sight of •everyone
for those who take refuge in You.

20 You hide them in the protection
of Your presence;
You conceal them in a shelter[g]
from the schemes of men,
from quarrelsome tongues.

21 May the LORD be praised,
for He has wonderfully shown His faithful love
to me
in a city under siege.[h]

22 In my alarm I had said,
"I am cut off from Your sight."
But You heard the sound of my pleading
when I cried to You for help.

23 Love the LORD, all His faithful ones.
The LORD protects the loyal,
but fully repays the arrogant.

24 Be strong and courageous,
all you who put your hope in the LORD.

Psalm 32

The Joy of Forgiveness

Davidic. A •Maskil.

1 How happy is the one
whose transgression is forgiven,
whose sin is covered!

2 How happy is the man
the LORD does not charge with sin,
and in whose spirit is no deceit!

---

a31:5 Or *You have redeemed*, or *You will redeem*, or *spirit. Redeem*. b31:6 One Hb ms, LXX, Syr, Vg, Jer read *You* c31:9 Lit *my soul and my belly* d31:10 LXX, Syr, Sym read *affliction* e31:17 LXX reads *brought down* f31:17 Or *them perish* or *wail* g31:20 Lit *canopy* h31:21 Or *a fortified city*

---

in God's hands for safekeeping. This phrase is quoted by Jesus just before He dies (see Luke 23:46).

32:3-5 conceal … confess. The psalmist shares his personal experience with hidden sin. The sin itself is not specified, but the effects of it drain life away.

32:4 strength was drained. God's disapproval of the psalmist's sin is like a heavy hand that holds him down. Though he might fight against it, that heavy hand is a burden he must carry. Under that burden he wilts like a plant in the hot summer sun.

32:9 mule. Mules are symbols of stubbornness

and resistance to the master. We are exhorted to mature in spiritual understanding and be like mules.

33:1-3 lyre … harp. The instructions for the musicians and instruments in these verses require a more sophisticated orchestra and choir, like the one mentioned in Daniel 3:5.

3 When I kept silent,[a] my bones became brittle
from my groaning all day long.
4 For day and night Your hand was heavy on me;
my strength was drained[b]
as in the summer's heat.   •Selah
5 Then I acknowledged my sin to You
and did not conceal my iniquity.
I said,
"I will confess my transgressions to the LORD,"
and You took away the guilt of my sin.   Selah

6 Therefore let everyone who is faithful pray to You
at a time that You may be found.[c]
When great floodwaters come,
they will not reach him.
7 You are my hiding place;
You protect me from trouble.
You surround me with joyful shouts
of deliverance.   Selah

8 I will instruct you and show you the way to go;
with My eye on you, I will give counsel.
9 Do not be like a horse or mule,
without understanding,
that must be controlled with bit and bridle,
or else it will not come near you.

10 Many pains come to the wicked,
but the one who trusts in the LORD
will have faithful love surrounding him.
11 Be glad in the LORD and rejoice,
you righteous ones;
shout for joy,
all you upright in heart.

Psalm 33
Praise to the Creator

1 Rejoice in the LORD, you righteous ones;
praise from the upright is beautiful.
2 Praise the LORD with the lyre;
make music to Him with a ten-stringed harp.
3 Sing a new song to Him;
play skillfully on the strings, with a joyful shout.

4 For the word of the LORD is right,
and all His work is trustworthy.
5 He loves righteousness and justice;
the earth is full of the LORD's unfailing love.

6 The heavens were made by the word of the LORD,
and all the stars, by the breath of His mouth.

7 He gathers the waters of the sea into a heap;[d]
He puts the depths into storehouses.
8 Let the whole earth tremble before the LORD;
let all the inhabitants of the world stand in awe
of Him.
9 For He spoke, and it came into being;
He commanded, and it came into existence.

10 The LORD frustrates the counsel of the nations;
He thwarts the plans of the peoples.
11 The counsel of the LORD stands forever,
the plans of His heart from generation
to generation.
12 Happy is the nation whose God is the LORD—
the people He has chosen to be
His own possession!

13 The LORD looks down from heaven;
He observes everyone.
14 He gazes on all the inhabitants of the earth
from His dwelling place.
15 He alone crafts their hearts;
He considers all their works.
16 A king is not saved by a large army;
a warrior will not be delivered by great strength.
17 The horse is a false hope for safety;
it provides no escape by its great power.

18 Now the eye of the LORD is on those who •fear
Him—
those who depend on His faithful love
19 to deliver them from death
and to keep them alive in famine.

20 We wait for the LORD;
He is our help and shield.
21 For our hearts rejoice in Him,
because we trust in His holy name.
22 May Your faithful love rest on us, LORD,
for we put our hope in You.

Psalm 34
The LORD Delivers the Righteous

Concerning David, when he pretended to
be insane in the presence of Abimelech,[e]
who drove him out, and he departed.

1 I[f] will praise the LORD at all times;
His praise will always be on my lips.
2 I will boast in the LORD;
the humble will hear and be glad.

---

[a]**32:3** Probably a reference to a refusal to confess sin   [b]**32:4** Hb obscure   [c]**32:6** Lit *time of finding*   [d]**33:7** LXX, Tg, Syr, Vg, Jer read *sea as in a bottle*   [e]A reference to Achish, king of Gath   [f]**34:1** The lines of this poem form an •acrostic.

33:12-19 the nation. Israel is the blessed beneficiary of God's plan, chosen as a witness of His saving power. God's protection of Israel is assured, for He is the Lord of creation and He will not be frustrated (vv. 6-11).

33:16-17 army ... horse ... safety. These verses regarding military might have always been ignored by warring men who do not truly believe in God's sovereignty.

33:18, 22 faithful love. The love described here is God's continual passion for His covenant people.

34:8-14 I will teach you. The psalmist moves from praise to instruction, concentrating on human senses and emotions. By tasting (v. 8), fearing (v. 9), listening (v. 11), loving and desiring (v. 12), and speaking well (v. 13), a person learns to fear God and do His will.

34:15-18 eyes of the LORD are on the righ-

3 Proclaim with me the LORD's greatness;
let us exalt His name together.

4 I sought the LORD, and He answered me
and delivered me from all my fears.

5 Those who look to Him are[a] radiant with joy;
their faces will never be ashamed.

6 This poor man cried, and the LORD heard ⌊him⌋
and saved him from all his troubles.

7 The angel of the LORD encamps
around those who •fear Him, and rescues them.

8 Taste and see that the LORD is good.
How happy is the man who takes refuge
in Him!

9 Fear the LORD, you His saints,
for those who fear Him lack nothing.

10 Young lions[b] lack food and go hungry,
but those who seek the LORD
will not lack any good thing.

11 Come, children, listen to me;
I will teach you the fear of the LORD.

12 Who is the man who delights in life,
loving a long life to enjoy what is good?

13 Keep your tongue from evil
and your lips from deceitful speech.

14 Turn away from evil and do what is good;
seek peace and pursue it.

15 The eyes of the LORD are on the righteous,
and His ears are open to their cry for help.

16 The face of the LORD is set
against those who do what is evil,
to erase all memory of them from the earth.

17 The righteous[c] cry out, and the LORD hears,
and delivers them from all their troubles.

18 The LORD is near the brokenhearted;
He saves those crushed in spirit.

19 Many adversities come to the one
who is righteous,
but the LORD delivers him from them all.

20 He protects all his bones;
not one of them is broken.

21 Evil brings death to the sinner,
and those who hate the righteous
will be punished.

22 The LORD redeems the life of His servants,
and all who take refuge in Him will not
be punished.

Psalm 35

Prayer for Victory

Davidic.

1 Oppose my opponents, LORD;
fight those who fight me.

2 Take Your shields—large and small—
and come to my aid.

3 Draw the spear and javelin against my pursuers,
and assure me: "I am your deliverance."

4 Let those who seek to kill me
be disgraced and humiliated;
let those who plan to harm me
be turned back and ashamed.

5 Let them be like husks in the wind,
with the angel of the LORD driving them away.

6 Let their way be dark and slippery,
with the angel of the LORD pursuing them.

7 They hid their net for me without cause;
they dug a pit for me without cause.

8 Let ruin come on him unexpectedly,
and let the net that he hid ensnare him;
let him fall into it—to his ruin.

9 Then I will rejoice in the LORD;
I will delight in His deliverance.

10 My very bones will say,
"LORD, who is like You,
rescuing the poor from one too strong for him,
the poor or the needy from one who robs him?"

11 Malicious witnesses come forward;
they question me about things I do not know.

12 They repay me evil for good,
making me desolate.

13 Yet when they were sick,
my clothing was •sackcloth;
I humbled myself with fasting,
and my prayer was genuine.[d]

14 I went about ⌊grieving⌋ as if for my friend
or brother;
I was bowed down with grief,
like one mourning a mother.

15 But when I stumbled, they gathered in glee;
they gathered against me.
Assailants I did not know
tore at me and did not stop.

16 With godless mockery[e]
they gnashed their teeth at me.

---

[a] **34:5** Some Hb mss, LXX, Aq, Syr, Jer read *Look to Him and be*   [b] **34:10** LXX, Syr, Vg read *The rich*   [c] **34:17** Lit *They*   [d] **35:13** Lit *prayer returned to my chest*   [e] **35:16** Hb obscure

---

teous. The Lord sees the righteous (v. 15) and hears their cry (vv. 15, 17). To hear their cry implies rescue.

34:19-22 Evil brings death to the sinner. A righteous person can be delivered from troubles and saved from sin. The wicked must suffer the consequence of sin: death (Rom. 6:23).

35:1-3 shield ... spear ... javelin. David mentions military gear figuratively to emphasize his need of God's might to save him.

35:15 stumbled. David stumbled morally at times, causing himself grief and suffering.

35:27-28 shout for joy. David ends his prayer with shouts of joy to the faithful God

he trusts to rescue him—again.

36:1-4 the wicked. The wicked do not fear the Lord. They judge their own behavior (See "in his own eyes," v. 2) and so act as their own god.

36:4 on his bed. A wicked person even uses leisure time to plot wickedness. Why waste

17 Lord, how long will You look on?
Rescue my life from their ravages,
my very life[a] from the young lions.

18 I will praise You in the great congregation;
I will exalt You among many people.

19 Do not let my deceitful enemies rejoice over me;
do not let those who hate me without cause
look at me maliciously.

20 For they do not speak in friendly ways,
but contrive deceitful schemes[b]
against those who live peacefully in the land.

21 They open their mouths wide against me
and say,
"Aha, aha! We saw it!"[c]

22 You saw it, LORD; do not be silent.
Lord, do not be far from me.

23 Wake up and rise to my defense,
to my cause, my God and my LORD!

24 Vindicate me, LORD, my God,
in keeping with Your righteousness,
and do not let them rejoice over me.

25 Do not let them say in their hearts,
"Aha! Just what we wanted."
Do not let them say,
"We have swallowed him up!"

26 Let those who rejoice at my misfortune
be disgraced and humiliated;
let those who exalt themselves over me
be clothed with shame and reproach.

27 Let those who want my vindication
shout for joy and be glad;
let them continually say,
"The LORD be exalted,
who wants His servant's well-being."

28 And my tongue will proclaim
Your righteousness,
Your praise all day long.

Psalm 36

Human Wickedness and God's Love

For the choir director. ⌊A psalm⌋
of David, the LORD's servant.

1 An oracle within my heart
concerning the transgression of the wicked:
There is no dread of God before his eyes,

2 for in his own eyes he flatters himself ⌊too much⌋
to discover and hate his sin.

3 The words of his mouth are malicious
and deceptive;
he has stopped acting wisely and doing good.

4 Even on his bed he makes malicious plans.
He sets himself on a path that is not good
and does not reject evil.

5 LORD, Your faithful love ⌊reaches⌋ to heaven,
Your faithfulness to the skies.

6 Your righteousness is like the highest mountain;
Your judgments, like the deepest sea.
LORD, You preserve man and beast.

7 God, Your faithful love is so valuable
that •people take refuge in the shadow
of Your wings.

8 They are filled from the abundance
of Your house;
You let them drink from Your refreshing stream,

9 for with You is life's fountain.
In Your light we will see light.

10 Spread Your faithful love over those
who know You,
and Your righteousness over the upright
in heart.

11 Do not let the foot of the arrogant come near me
or the hand of the wicked drive me away.

12 There the evildoers fall;
they have been thrown down and cannot rise.

Psalm 37

Instruction in Wisdom

Davidic.

1 Do[d] not be agitated by evildoers;
do not envy those who do wrong.

2 For they wither quickly like grass
and wilt like tender green plants.

3 Trust in the LORD and do what is good;
dwell in the land and live securely.[e]

4 Take delight in the LORD,
and He will give you your heart's desires.

5 Commit your way to the LORD;
trust in Him, and He will act,

6 making your righteousness shine like the dawn,
your justice like the noonday.

7 Be silent before the LORD and wait expectantly
for Him;

---

[a]35:17 Lit my only one   [b]35:20 Lit but devise deceitful words   [c]35:21 Lit Our eyes saw!   [d]37:1 The lines of this poem form an •acrostic.
[e]37:3 Or and cultivate faithfulness

---

time meditating on God's law (1:2) or praying (42:8) when evil is your goal?

36:5-6 love ... faithfulness ... righteousness ... judgments. The psalmist sees these four virtues, which are central to God's character, evident in all of nature.

37:11 humble will inherit the land. This phrase is quoted by Jesus in the Beatitudes (Matt. 5:5). The meek are those who are humble before the Lord, acknowledging their dependence on God.

37:22 blessed ... cursed. Four times in this

psalm a choice of two ways is given: God's way or our own (wicked) way. (See also v. 9, 11; 29).

37:29 permanently. God's blessings to His people are eternal. In contrast, the prosperity of the wicked is temporary (vv. 10, 28).

do not be agitated by one who prospers
　　in his way,
by the man who carries out evil plans.

8　Refrain from anger and give up ⌊your⌋ rage;
　　do not be agitated—it can only bring harm.
9　For evildoers will be destroyed,
　　but those who put their hope in the LORD
　　will inherit the land.[a]

10　A little while, and the wicked will be no more;
　　though you look for him, he will not be there.
11　But the humble will inherit the land[a]
　　and will enjoy abundant prosperity.

12　The wicked schemes against the righteous
　　and gnashes his teeth at him.
13　The Lord laughs at him
　　because He sees that his day is coming.

14　The wicked have drawn the sword and strung
　　the[b] bow
　　to bring down the afflicted and needy
　　and to slaughter those whose way is upright.
15　Their swords will enter their own hearts,
　　and their bows will be broken.

16　Better the little that the righteous man has
　　than the abundance of many wicked people.
17　For the arms[c] of the wicked will be broken,
　　but the LORD supports the righteous.

18　The LORD watches over the blameless
　　all their days,
　　and their inheritance will last forever.
19　They will not be disgraced in times
　　of adversity;
　　they will be satisfied in days of hunger.

20　But the wicked will perish;
　　the LORD's enemies, like the glory
　　of the pastures,
　　will fade away—
　　they will fade away like smoke.

21　The wicked borrows and does not repay,
　　but the righteous is gracious and giving.
22　Those who are blessed by Him will inherit
　　the land,[a]
　　but those cursed by Him will be destroyed.

23　A man's steps are established by the LORD,
　　and He takes pleasure in his way.

24　Though he falls, he will not be overwhelmed,
　　because the LORD holds his hand.[d]
25　I have been young and now I am old,
　　yet I have not seen the righteous abandoned
　　or his children begging bread.
26　He is always generous, always lending,
　　and his children are a blessing.

27　Turn away from evil and do what is good,
　　and dwell there[e] forever.
28　For the LORD loves justice
　　and will not abandon His faithful ones.
　　They are kept safe forever,
　　but the children of the wicked
　　will be destroyed.
29　The righteous will inherit the land[a]
　　and dwell in it permanently.

30　The mouth of the righteous utters wisdom;
　　his tongue speaks what is just.
31　The instruction of his God is in his heart;
　　his steps do not falter.

32　The wicked lies in wait for the righteous
　　and seeks to kill him;
33　the LORD will not leave him in his hand[c]
　　or allow him to be condemned
　　when he is judged.

34　Wait for the LORD and keep His way,
　　and He will exalt you to inherit the land.
　　You will watch when the wicked
　　are destroyed.

35　I have seen a wicked, violent man
　　well-rooted[f] like a flourishing native tree.
36　Then I passed by and[g] noticed he was gone;
　　I searched for him, but he could not
　　be found.

37　Watch the blameless and observe the upright,
　　for the man of peace will have a future.[h]
38　But transgressors will all be eliminated;
　　the future[h] of the wicked will be destroyed.

39　The salvation of the righteous is from the LORD,
　　their refuge in a time of distress.
40　The LORD helps and delivers them;
　　He will deliver them from the wicked
　　and will save them
　　because they take refuge in Him.

---

a 37:9,11,22,29 Or earth　b 37:14 Lit their　c 37:17,33 Or power　d 37:24 Or LORD supports with His hand　e 37:27 Dwell in the land　f 37:35 Hb obscure　g 37:36 DSS, LXX, Syr, Vg, Jer; MT reads Then he passed away, and I　h 37:37,38 Or posterity

---

37:32 lies in wait … seeks to kill him. The wicked are predatory but cowardly. They prefer ambush tactics to steal the blessings of the righteous (10:8-9), even bringing false charges against them in court (v. 33).

37:39-40 He will deliver them. Despite all the efforts of the wicked, the righteous will prevail.

The Lord helps, delivers, and saves them.

Ps. 38 wounds … pain … affliction. David begs the Lord to heal him of a serious illness. David interprets the illness as a rebuke from God. He suffers pain and anguish (vv. 3-8), social alienation (v. 11), and political turmoil (v. 12).

38:11 loved ones … stand back. David often finds himself undeservedly abandoned by friends and under attack by enemies (31:11-12).

38:17-20 about to fall. David grows weaker because of his illness and guilt. His cries to God are reminiscent of Job's.

Psalm 38

Prayer of a Suffering Sinner

A Davidic psalm for remembrance.

1 LORD, do not punish me in Your anger
or discipline me in Your wrath.
2 For Your arrows have sunk into me,
and Your hand has pressed down on me.

3 There is no soundness in my body
because of Your indignation;
there is no health in my bones because of my sin.
4 For my sins have flooded over my head;
they are a burden too heavy for me to bear.
5 My wounds are foul and festering
because of my foolishness.
6 I am bent over and brought low;
all day long I go around in mourning.
7 For my loins are full of burning pain,
and there is no health in my body.
8 I am faint and severely crushed;
I groan because of the anguish of my heart.

9 Lord, my every desire is known to[a] You;
my sighing is not hidden from You.
10 My heart races, my strength leaves me,
and even the light of my eyes has faded.[b]
11 My loved ones and friends stand back
from my affliction,
and my relatives stand at a distance.
12 Those who seek my life set traps,
and those who want to harm me threaten
to destroy me;
they plot treachery all day long.

13 I am like a deaf person; I do not hear.
I am like a speechless person
who does not open his mouth.
14 I am like a man who does not hear
and has no arguments in his mouth.
15 I put my hope in You, LORD;
You will answer, Lord my God.
16 For I said, "Don't let them rejoice over me—
those who are arrogant toward me
when I stumble."
17 For I am about to fall,
and my pain is constantly with me.
18 So I confess my guilt;
I am anxious because of my sin.
19 But my enemies are vigorous and powerful;[c]
many hate me for no reason.

20 Those who repay evil for good
attack me for pursuing good.
21 LORD, do not abandon me;
my God, do not be far from me.
22 Hurry to help me,
Lord, my Savior.

Psalm 39

The Fleeting Nature of Life

For the choir director, for Jeduthun.
A Davidic psalm.

1 I said, "I will guard my ways
so that I may not sin with my tongue;
I will guard my mouth with a muzzle
as long as the wicked are in my presence."
2 I was speechless and quiet;
I kept silent, even from ⌊speaking⌋ good,
and my pain intensified.
3 My heart grew hot within me;
as I mused, a fire burned.
I spoke with my tongue:

4 "LORD, reveal to me the end of my life
and the number of my days.
Let me know how transitory I am.
5 You, indeed, have made my days short in length,
and my life span as nothing in Your sight.
Yes, every mortal man is only a vapor.   •Selah
6 Certainly, man walks about like a mere shadow.
Indeed, they frantically rush around in vain,
gathering possessions
without knowing who will get them.

7 "Now, Lord, what do I wait for?
My hope is in You.
8 Deliver me from all my transgressions;
do not make me the taunt of fools.
9 I am speechless; I do not open my mouth
because of what You have done.
10 Remove Your torment from me;
I fade away because of the force of Your hand.
11 You discipline a man with punishment for sin,
consuming like a moth what is precious to him;
every man is a mere vapor.   Selah

12 "Hear my prayer, LORD,
and listen to my cry for help;
do not be silent at my tears.
For I am a foreigner residing with You,
a sojourner like all my fathers.

---

[a]**38:9** Lit *is in front of* [b]**38:10** Or *and the light of my eyes—even that is not with me* [c]**38:19** Or *numerous*

39:1 sin with my tongue. As spiritual leader and king, David must control his anger and not speak evil words that would give the wicked even more ammunition against him while betraying the righteous (73:15).
39:4-6 Let me know. David prays for understanding. He recognizes the brevity of human life and wants to understand what is most important from God's point of view.
40:6 do not delight ... do not ask. Though the Law demands sacrifice and offerings, they are actually tools to teach us obedience (see 1 Sam. 15:22).
40:8 delight. David has learned true obedience, desiring and delighting in the things God desires and delights in.
40:12 troubles ... sins. David's troubles are products of sin. David claims his sins and trou-

13 Turn Your angry gaze from me
so that I may be cheered up
before I die and am gone."

Psalm 40
Thanksgiving and a Cry for Help

For the choir director.
A Davidic psalm.

1 I waited patiently for the LORD,
and He turned to me and heard my cry
for help.
2 He brought me up from a desolate[a] pit,
out of the muddy clay,
and set my feet on a rock,
making my steps secure.
3 He put a new song in my mouth,
a hymn of praise to our God.
Many will see and fear,
and put their trust in the LORD.

4 How happy is the man
who has put his trust in the LORD
and has not turned to the proud
or to those who run after lies!
5 LORD my God, You have done many things—
Your wonderful works and Your plans for us;
none can compare with You.
If I were to report and speak ⌊of them⌋,
they are more than can be told.

6 You do not delight in sacrifice and offering;
You open my ears to listen.[b]
You do not ask for a whole •burnt offering
or a •sin offering.
7 Then I said, "See, I have come;
it is written about me in the volume
of the scroll.
8 I delight to do Your will, my God;
Your instruction resides within me."[c]

9 I proclaim righteousness in the great assembly;
see, I do not keep my mouth closed[d]
—as You know, LORD.
10 I did not hide Your righteousness in my heart;
I spoke about Your faithfulness and salvation;
I did not conceal Your constant love and truth
from the great assembly.

11 LORD, do not withhold Your compassion
from me;

Your constant love and truth will always
guard me.
12 For troubles without number
have surrounded me;
my sins have overtaken me; I am unable to see.
They are more than the hairs of my head,
and my courage leaves me.
13 LORD, be pleased to deliver me;
hurry to help me, LORD.

14 Let those who seek to take my life
be disgraced and confounded.
Let those who wish me harm
be driven back and humiliated.
15 Let those who say to me, "Aha, aha!"
be horrified because of their shame.

16 Let all who seek You rejoice and be glad in You;
let those who love Your salvation continually say,
"The LORD is great!"
17 I am afflicted and needy;
the Lord thinks of me.
You are my help and my deliverer;
my God, do not delay.

Psalm 41
Victory in spite of Betrayal

For the choir director.
A Davidic psalm.

1 Happy is one who cares for the poor;
the LORD will save him in a day of adversity.
2 The LORD will keep him and preserve him;
he will be blessed in the land.
You will not give him over to the desire
of his enemies.
3 The LORD will sustain him on his sickbed;
You will heal him on the bed where he lies.

4 I said, "LORD, be gracious to me;
heal me, for I have sinned against You."
5 My enemies speak maliciously about me:
"When will he die and be forgotten?"
6 When one ⌊of them⌋ comes to visit,
he speaks deceitfully;
he stores up evil in his heart;
he goes out and talks.
7 All who hate me whisper together about me;
they plan to harm me.
8 "Lethal poison has been poured into him,
and he won't rise again from where he lies!"

---

[a]40:2 Or watery [b]40:6 Lit You hollow out ears for me [c]40:8 Lit instruction within my inner being [d]40:9 Lit not restrain my lips

---

bles are more numerous than the hairs on his head.
40:16-17 continually say. These two verses compose the chorus to be sung, praising God's deliverance.
41:1-3 he will be blessed. The Psalms are di-

vided into books. This Psalm ends Book I with "Blessed be the Lord." This book of Psalms began with "Blessed is the man." Worship always moves from human orientation God-ward.
41:9 friend ... ate my bread. Sharing meals together implies intimacy. One of David's inner circle has betrayed him. In

John 13:18, Jesus quotes this passage to predict His own betrayal by Judas.
41:13 LORD ... be praised. This psalm ends with a doxology of praise.
42:1 deer longs for water. Drought is implied here as David's long spiritual ordeal has exhausted him and spiritually dehydrated him.

9 Even my friend[a] in whom I trusted,
one who ate my bread,
has lifted up his heel against me.

10 But You, LORD, be gracious to me
and raise me up;
then I will repay them.

11 By this I know that You delight in me:
my enemy does not shout in triumph over me.

12 You supported me because of my integrity
and set me in Your presence forever.

13 May the LORD, the God of Israel, be praised
from everlasting to everlasting.
•Amen and amen.

BOOK II

(Psalms 42–72)
Psalm 42

Longing for God

For the choir director. A •Maskil
of the sons of Korah.

1 As a deer longs for streams of water,
so I long for You, God.

2 I thirst for God, the living God.
When can I come and appear before God?

3 My tears have been my food day and night,
while all day long people say to me,
"Where is your God?"

4 I remember this as I pour out my heart:
how I walked with many,
leading the festive procession to the house
of God,
with joyful and thankful shouts.

5 Why am I so depressed?
Why this turmoil within me?
Put your hope in God, for I will still praise Him,
my Savior and my God.

6 I[b] am deeply depressed;
therefore I remember You from the land
of Jordan
and the peaks of Hermon, from Mount Mizar.

7 Deep calls to deep in the roar
of Your waterfalls;
all Your breakers and Your billows have swept
over me.

8 The LORD will send His faithful love by day;
His song will be with me in the night—
a prayer to the God of my life.

9 I will say to God, my rock,
"Why have You forgotten me?
Why must I go about in sorrow
because of the enemy's oppression?"

10 My adversaries taunt me,
as if crushing my bones,
while all day long they say to me,
"Where is your God?"

11 Why am I so depressed?
Why this turmoil within me?
Put your hope in God, for I will still praise Him,
my Savior and my God.

Psalm 43[c]

1 Vindicate me, God, and defend my cause
against an ungodly nation;
rescue me from the deceitful and unjust man.

2 For You are the God of my refuge.
Why have You rejected me?
Why must I go about in sorrow
because of the enemy's oppression?

3 Send Your light and Your truth; let them lead me.
Let them bring me to Your holy mountain,
to Your dwelling place.

4 Then I will come to the altar of God,
to God, my greatest joy.
I will praise You with the lyre,
God, my God.

5 Why am I so depressed?
Why this turmoil within me?
Put your hope in God, for I will still praise Him,
my Savior and my God.

Psalm 44

Israel's Complaint

For the choir director. A •Maskil
of the sons of Korah.

1 God, we have heard with our ears—
our forefathers have told us—
the work You accomplished in their days,
in days long ago:

2 to plant them,
You drove out the nations with Your hand;
to settle them,

---

[a] 41:9 Lit Even a man of my peace [b] 42:5–6 Some Hb mss, LXX, Syr; other Hb mss read Him, the salvation of His presence. 6 My God, I
[c] Ps 43 Many Hb mss connect Pss 42–43

He longs for God's restoring power to stand against oppressors.

42:5 hope in God. This stanza, repeated in verse 11, serves as the refrain of the psalm. Its theme: To overcome difficulty, praise God.

43:1-4 The psalmist prays for deliverance from enemies who are "deceitful and unjust." He longs to return safely to the temple where God dwells, so he can properly commune with God and praise Him.

43:3 light … truth. God's light and truth are personified as messengers who will guide the

psalmist back to the temple where restoration will take place.

44:1-8 These words compose a communal lament upon Israel's defeat. Before crying out for help, the psalmist reviews how God has helped the Israelites in the past. Verses 1-3 recall how God aided the Israelites in capturing the prom-

You crushed the peoples.

3 For they did not take the land
   by their sword—
  their arm did not bring them victory—
  but by Your right hand, Your arm,
  and the light of Your face,
  for You were pleased with them.

4 You are my King, my God,
  who ordains[a] victories for Jacob.

5 Through You we drive back our foes;
  through Your name we trample our enemies.

6 For I do not trust in my bow,
  and my sword does not bring me victory.

7 But You give us victory over our foes
  and let those who hate us be disgraced.

8 We boast in God all day long;
  we will praise Your name forever.   •Selah

9 But You have rejected and humiliated us;
  You do not march out with our armies.

10 You make us retreat from the foe,
   and those who hate us
   have taken plunder for themselves.

11 You hand us over to be eaten like sheep
   and scatter us among the nations.

12 You sell Your people for nothing;
   You make no profit from selling them.

13 You make us an object of reproach
    to our neighbors,
   a source of mockery and ridicule to those
    around us.

14 You make us a joke among the nations,
   a laughingstock[b] among the peoples.

15 My disgrace is before me all day long,
   and shame has covered my face,

16 because of the voice of the scorner and reviler,
   because of the enemy and avenger.

17 All this has happened to us,
   but we have not forgotten You
   or betrayed Your covenant.

18 Our hearts have not turned back;
   our steps have not strayed from Your path.

19 But You have crushed us in a haunt of jackals
   and have covered us with deepest darkness.

20 If we had forgotten the name of our God
   and spread out our hands to a foreign god,

21 wouldn't God have found this out,
   since He knows the secrets of the heart?

22 Because of You we are slain all day long;
   we are counted as sheep to be slaughtered.

23 Wake up, LORD! Why are You sleeping?
   Get up! Don't reject us forever!

24 Why do You hide Yourself
   and forget our affliction and oppression?

25 For we have sunk down to the dust;
   our bodies cling to the ground.

26 Rise up! Help us!
   Redeem us because of Your faithful love.

Psalm 45

A Royal Wedding Song

For the choir director: according to
"The Lilies."[c] A •Maskil of the sons
of Korah. A love song.

1 My heart is moved by a noble theme
  as I recite my verses to the king;
  my tongue is the pen of a skillful writer.

2 You are the most handsome of •men;
  grace flows from your lips.
  Therefore God has blessed you forever.

3 Mighty warrior, strap your sword at your side.
  In your majesty and splendor—

4 in your splendor ride triumphantly
  in the cause of truth, humility, and justice.
  May your right hand show your awe-
    inspiring deeds.

5 Your arrows pierce the hearts
    of the king's enemies;
  the peoples fall under you.

6 Your throne, God, is[d] forever and ever;
  the scepter of Your[e] kingdom is a scepter
    of justice.

7 You love righteousness and hate wickedness;
  therefore God, your God, has anointed you,
  more than your companions, with the oil of joy.

8 Myrrh, aloes, and cassia ⌊perfume⌋
    all your garments;
  from ivory palaces harps bring you joy.

9 Kings' daughters are
    among your honored women;
  the queen, adorned with gold from Ophir,
  stands at your right hand.

10 Listen, daughter, pay attention and consider:
   forget your people and your father's house,

11 and the king will desire your beauty.
   Bow down to him, for he is your lord.

12 The daughter of Tyre, the wealthy people,
   will seek your favor with gifts.

---

[a]44:4 LXX, Syr, Aq; MT reads King, God; ordain   [b]44:14 Lit shaking of the head   [c]Apparently a hymn tune; compare Pss 60; 69; 80   [d]45:6 Or Your divine throne is, or Your throne is God's   [e]45:6 Or your

---

ised land. Verses 4-8 review how He has helped them keep the land given them.

45:1 noble theme. This psalm was recited at a royal wedding. Two other wedding poems in the Old Testament can be found in I Kings 16:31 and I Samuel 18:27. This is a love song sung to the tune: "The lilies." It sounds some-

what like Song of Solomon (v.2).

45:3-5 strap your sword. The psalmist encourages the king to be a warrior for good, to go out and fight on behalf of "truth, humility, and righteousness."

45:16 succeed your ancestors. The psalmist

pronounces a subtle blessing on the king by assuming his new bride will bear him sons.

46:1-3 We will not be afraid. The psalmist confesses his complete trust in God as his personal and national refuge. The powerful imagery here is reminiscent of the creation process itself. He claims that even if creation were to fall

13 In ⌊her chamber⌋, the royal daughter
    is all glorious,
    her clothing embroidered with gold.
14 In colorful garments she is led to the king;
    after her, the virgins, her companions,
    are brought to you.
15 They are led in with gladness and rejoicing;
    they enter the king's palace.
16 Your sons will succeed your ancestors;
    you will make them princes
    throughout the land.
17 I will cause your name to be remembered
    for all generations;
    therefore the peoples will praise you forever
    and ever.

God, Our Refuge

1. What is the worst disaster you've been in:
Earthquake? Tornado? Hurricane? Flood?
Your room?

Psalm 46
2. How is God "our refuge and strength" (v. 1)?
3. Why does God say that we must stop fighting
in order to know that He is God (v. 10)?
4. Is there someone you've been fighting with
lately? How can you stop fighting and spend
time with God?
5. In what way do you need to find refuge in
God? How can His strength rescue you from
trouble?

Psalm 46
God Our Refuge

For the choir director. A song
of the sons of Korah. According to
Alamoth.[a]

1 God is our refuge and strength,
   a helper who is always found
   in times of trouble.

2 Therefore we will not be afraid,
   though the earth trembles
   and the mountains topple
   into the depths of the seas,
3 though its waters roar and foam
   and the mountains quake with its turmoil. •*Selah*

4 ⌊There is⌋ a river—
   its streams delight the city of God,
   the holy dwelling place of the •Most High.
5 God is within her; she will not be toppled.
   God will help her when the morning dawns.
6 Nations rage, kingdoms topple;
   the earth melts when He lifts His voice.
7 The LORD of •Hosts is with us;
   the God of Jacob is our stronghold.   *Selah*

8 Come, see the works of the LORD,
   who brings devastation on the earth.
9 He makes wars cease throughout the earth.
   He shatters bows and cuts spears to pieces;
   He burns up the chariots.[b]
10 "Stop ⌊your fighting⌋—and know that I am God,
   exalted among the nations,
   exalted on the earth."
11 The LORD of Hosts is with us;
   the God of Jacob is our stronghold.   *Selah*

Psalm 47
God Our King

For the choir director. A psalm
of the sons of Korah.

1 Clap your hands, all you peoples;
   shout to God with a jubilant cry.
2 For the LORD •Most High is awe-inspiring,
   a great King over all the earth.
3 He subdues peoples under us
   and nations under our feet.
4 He chooses for us our inheritance—
   the pride of Jacob, whom He loves.   •*Selah*

5 God ascends amid shouts of joy,
   the LORD, amid the sound of trumpets.
6 Sing praise to God, sing praise;
   sing praise to our King, sing praise!
7 Sing a song of instruction,[c]
   for God is King of all the earth.

8 God reigns over the nations;
   God is seated on His holy throne.

[a] This notation may refer to a high pitch, perhaps a tune sung by soprano voices; the Hb word means "young women."   [b] **46:9** Lit *chariots with fire*
[c] **47:7** Hb *a Maskil*

apart, God would still stand.
46:4-6 river. The psalmist continues the water images of verses 1-3. Jerusalem has no actual river, but it sits on top of a natural spring just outside the city wall.
46:10 "Stop [your fighting]—and know that I am God." God interrupts the psalmist and

commands the people to quit fighting and be still long enough to perceive His presence. This is a frequent theme in Psalms (47:9; 65:8; 66:1-7).

47:1-4 all you peoples. These verses expand on the idea in 46:10 that God will be exalted among all nations.

47:9 the leaders of the earth belong to God. In fulfillment of the promise to Abraham (Gen. 12:2-3), all nations will be blessed through Israel.

48:1 His holy mountain. Jerusalem commands a wide view, which makes it difficult to attack.

9 The nobles of the peoples have assembled
⌊with⌋ the people of the God of Abraham.
For the leaders[a] of the earth belong to God;
He is greatly exalted.

Psalm 48

Zion Exalted

A song.
A psalm of the sons of Korah.

1 The LORD is great and is highly praised
in the city of our God.
His holy mountain, 2 rising splendidly,
is the joy of the whole earth.
Mount Zion on the slopes of the north
is the city of the great King.
3 God is known as a stronghold
in its citadels.

4 Look! The kings assembled;
they advanced together.
5 They looked, and froze with fear;
they fled in terror.
6 Trembling seized them there,
agony like that of a woman in labor,
7 as You wrecked the ships of Tarshish
with the east wind.

8 Just as we heard, so we have seen
in the city of the LORD of •Hosts,
in the city of our God;
God will establish it forever.   •Selah

9 God, within Your temple,
we contemplate Your faithful love.
10 Your name, God, like Your praise,
reaches to the ends of the earth;
Your right hand is filled with justice.
11 Mount Zion is glad.
The towns[b] of Judah rejoice
because of Your judgments.

12 Go around Zion, encircle it;
count its towers,
13 note its ramparts; tour its citadels
so that you can tell a future generation:
14 "This God, our God forever and ever—
He will lead us eternally."[c]

Psalm 49

Misplaced Trust in Wealth

For the choir director. A psalm
of the sons of Korah.

1 Hear this, all you peoples;
listen, all who inhabit the world,
2 both low and high,[d]
rich and poor together.
3 My mouth speaks wisdom;
my heart's meditation ⌊brings⌋ understanding.
4 I turn my ear to a proverb;
I explain my riddle with a lyre.

5 Why should I fear in times of trouble?
The iniquity of my foes surrounds me.
6 They trust in their wealth
and boast of their abundant riches.
7 Yet these cannot redeem a person[e]
or pay his ransom to God—
8 since the price of redeeming him is too costly,
one should forever stop trying[f]—
9 so that he may live forever
and not see the •Pit.

10 For one can see that wise men die;
the foolish and the senseless also pass away.
Then they leave their wealth to others.
11 Their graves are their eternal homes,[g]
their homes from generation to generation,
though they have named estates after themselves.
12 But despite ⌊his⌋ assets,[h] man will not last;
he is like the animals that perish.

13 This is the way of those who are arrogant,
and of their followers,
who approve of their words.[i]   •Selah
14 Like sheep they are headed for •Sheol;
Death will shepherd them.
The upright will rule over them in the morning,
and their form will waste away in Sheol,
far from their lofty abode.
15 But God will redeem my life
from the power of Sheol,
for He will take me.   Selah

16 Do not be afraid when a man gets rich,
when the wealth[j] of his house increases.

---

[a]**47:9** Lit shields [b]**48:11** Lit daughters [c]**48:14** Some Hb mss, LXX; other Hb mss read over death [d]**49:2** Lit both sons of Adam and sons of man [e]**49:7** Or Certainly he cannot redeem himself, or Yet he cannot redeem a brother [f]**49:8** Or costly, it will cease forever [g]**49:11** LXX, Syr, Tg; MT reads Their inner thought is that their houses are eternal [h]**49:12** Or honor [i]**49:13** Lit and after them with their mouth they were pleased [j]**49:16** Or glory

---

49:1 All peoples. Knowledge of God is for all nations, not just the Jews.

49:15 God will redeem my life. Is there hope anywhere? Can the cycle of life and death be broken and meaning to life restored? Only God holds the keys to Sheol.

49:16-19 his wealth will not follow him. We cannot take it with us, though some followers of pagan religions tried to.

50:1 God, the LORD. The many titles for God in this psalm serve to accent His ability and right to judge Israel.

50:7-15 sacrifices … honors Me. The people have come to believe that they can legalistically offer sacrifices while disobeying God in other ways, but they can't keep sinning and still keep the law.

50:14-15 thank offering. One way Israel acknowledged its total dependence on

17 For when he dies, he will take nothing at all;
his wealth[a] will not follow him down.
18 Though he praises himself during his lifetime—
and people praise you when you do well
for yourself—
19 he will go to the generation of his fathers;
they will never see the light.
20 A man with valuable possessions[b]
but without understanding
is like the animals that perish.

Psalm 50
God as Judge
A psalm of •Asaph.

1 God, the LORD God[c] speaks;
He summons the earth from east to west.[d]
2 From Zion, the perfection of beauty,
God appears in radiance.[e]
3 Our God is coming; He will not be silent!
Devouring fire precedes Him,
and a storm rages around Him.
4 On high, He summons heaven and earth
in order to judge His people.
5 "Gather My faithful ones to Me,
those who made a covenant with Me by sacrifice."
6 The heavens proclaim His righteousness,
for God is the judge.   •Selah

7 "Listen, My people, and I will speak;
I will testify against you, Israel.
I am God, your God.
8 I do not rebuke you for your sacrifices
or for your •burnt offerings,
which are continually before Me.
9 I will not accept a bull from your household
or male goats from your pens,
10 for every animal of the forest is Mine,
the cattle on a thousand hills.
11 I know every bird of the mountains,[f]
and the creatures of the field are Mine.
12 If I were hungry, I would not tell you,
for the world and everything in it is Mine.
13 Do I eat the flesh of bulls
or drink the blood of goats?
14 Sacrifice a thank offering to God,
and pay your vows to the •Most High.
15 Call on Me in a day of trouble;
I will rescue you, and you will honor Me."

16 But God says to the wicked:
"What right do you have to recite
My statutes
and to take My covenant on your lips?
17 You hate instruction
and turn your back on My words.[g]
18 When you see a thief,
you make friends with him,
and you associate with adulterers.
19 You unleash your mouth for evil
and harness your tongue for deceit.
20 You sit, maligning your brother,
slandering your mother's son.
21 You have done these things, and I kept silent;
you thought I was just like you.
But I will rebuke you
and lay out the case before you.[h]

22 "Understand this, you who forget God,
or I will tear you apart,
and there will be no rescuer.
23 Whoever sacrifices a thank offering
honors Me,
and whoever orders his conduct,
I will show him the salvation of God."

Psalm 51
A Prayer for Restoration
For the choir director.
A Davidic psalm, when Nathan the
prophet came to him after he had
gone to Bathsheba.

1 Be gracious to me, God,
according to Your faithful love;
according to Your abundant compassion,
blot out my rebellion.
2 Wash away my guilt,
and cleanse me from my sin.
3 For I am conscious of my rebellion,
and my sin is always before me.
4 Against You—You alone—I have sinned
and done this evil in Your sight.
So You are right when You pass sentence;
You are blameless when You judge.
5 Indeed, I was guilty ⌊when I⌋ was born;
I was sinful when my mother conceived me.
6 Surely You desire integrity in the inner self,
and You teach me wisdom deep within.

God—an acknowledgment God desires.
50:16-23 to the wicked. The Lord reproves the wicked for sinful behavior, especially their hypocrisy (vv. 16-17), thievery (v. 18), adultery (v. 18), and lying (vv. 19-20).
Ps. 51 A Prayer of Restoration. This psalm is David's prayer for forgiveness after Na-

than the prophet confronts him regarding his adultery with Bathsheba (see 2 Samuel 11:2-17).

51:5 guilty [when I] was born. David cannot claim that his sin is a onetime failure. His nature is to be sinful. He feels deeply that he has grieved the heart of God.

51:6 integrity in the inner self. David realizes that he cannot keep God's laws without God's help.

51:10 create a clean heart. Only God is described in the Old Testament as creating. The psalmist wants to be a new man, free of the burden and stain of sin.

7 Purify me with hyssop, and I will be clean;
wash me, and I will be whiter than snow.
8 Let me hear joy and gladness;
let the bones You have crushed rejoice.
9 Turn Your face away[a] from my sins
and blot out all my guilt.

10 God, create a clean heart for me
and renew a steadfast[b] spirit within me.
11 Do not banish me from Your presence
or take Your Holy Spirit from me.
12 Restore the joy of Your salvation to me,
and give me a willing spirit.[c]
13 Then I will teach the rebellious Your ways,
and sinners will return to You.

14 Save me from the guilt of bloodshed, God,
the God of my salvation,
and my tongue will sing of Your righteousness.
15 Lord, open my lips,
and my mouth will declare Your praise.
16 You do not want a sacrifice, or I would give it;
You are not pleased with a •burnt offering.
17 The sacrifice pleasing to God is[d] a broken spirit.
God, You will not despise a broken
and humbled heart.

18 In Your good pleasure, cause Zion to prosper;
build[e] the walls of Jerusalem.
19 Then You will delight in righteous sacrifices,
whole burnt offerings;
then bulls will be offered on Your altar.

Psalm 52

God Judges the Proud

For the choir director.
A Davidic •*Maskil.* When Doeg the
Edomite went and reported to Saul,
telling him, "David went to
Ahimelech's house."

1 Why brag about evil, you hero!
God's faithful love is constant.
2 Like a sharpened razor,
your tongue devises destruction,
working treachery.
3 You love evil instead of good,
lying instead of speaking truthfully.   •*Selah*
4 You love any words that destroy,
you treacherous tongue!

5 This is why God will bring you down forever.
He will take you, ripping you out of your tent;
He will uproot you from the land of the living.
Selah
6 The righteous will look on with awe
and will ridicule him:
7 "Here is the man
who would not make God his refuge,
but trusted in the abundance of his riches,
taking refuge in his destructive behavior."[f]

8 But I am like a flourishing olive tree
in the house of God;
I trust in God's faithful love forever and ever.
9 I will praise You forever for what You have done.
In the presence of Your faithful people,
I will put my hope in Your name, for it is good.

Psalm 53

A Portrait of Sinners

For the choir director: on *Mahalath.*[g]
A Davidic •*Maskil.*

1 The fool says in his heart, "God does not exist."
They are corrupt, and they do vile deeds.
There is no one who does good.
2 God looks down from heaven
on the •human race
to see if there is one who is wise
and who seeks God.
3 Everyone has turned aside;
they have all become corrupt.
There is no one who does good,
not even one.

4 Will evildoers never understand?
They consume My people
as they consume bread;
they do not call on God.
5 Then they will be filled with terror—
terror like no other—
because God will scatter
the bones of those who besiege you.
You will put them to shame,
for God has rejected them.

6 Oh, that Israel's deliverance would come
from Zion!
When God restores His captive people,
Jacob will rejoice; Israel will be glad.

---

[a]**51:9** Lit *Hide Your face* [b]**51:10** Or *right* [c]**51:12** Or *and sustain me with a noble spirit* [d]**51:17** Lit *The sacrifices of God are* [e]**51:18** Or *rebuild*
[f]**52:7** Or *riches, and grew strong in his evil desire;* lit *his destruction* [g]Perhaps a song tune, a musical instrument, or a dance; may be related to Hb
for "sickness"

Ps. 52 This passage relates one of David's bitterest experiences. While fleeing Saul, David asks help of a priest, Ahimelech. The priest is massacred along with his whole town for helping David (see 1 Sam. 21:7-22:23).
52:8 like a flourishing olive tree. Olive trees live for hundreds of years and can withstand

harsh conditions (v. 5). As an olive tree produces good fruit, the righteous person produces praise for God.

Ps. 53 Mahalath. The phrase "to Mahalath" probably means "set to a sad melody." Appropriately, the psalm tells the sad truth that many people think God is irrelevant.

53:4-6 evildoers never understand? Verses 4 and 6 are identical to 14:4, 7. Verse 5, however, is quite different. In 14:5 the psalmist portrays evildoers as afraid because of the presence of God. In verse 5 here, evildoers are afraid without reason. They lack security because they lack faith.

Psalm 54

Prayer for Deliverance

For the choir director:
with stringed instruments.
A Davidic •*Maskil.* When the
Ziphites went and said to Saul, "Is
David not hiding among us?"

1 God, save me by Your name,
and vindicate me by Your might!
2 God, hear my prayer;
listen to the words of my mouth.
3 For strangers rise up against me,
and violent men seek my life.
They have no regard for God.ᵃ   •*Selah*

4 God is my helper;
the Lord is the sustainer of my life.ᵇ
5 He will repay my adversaries for ⌊their⌋ evil.
Because of Your faithfulness, annihilate them.

6 I will sacrifice a freewill offering to You.
I will praise Your name, LORD,
because it is good.
7 For He has delivered me from every trouble,
and my eye has looked down on my enemies.

Psalm 55

Betrayal by a Friend

For the choir director:
with stringed instruments.
A Davidic •*Maskil.*

1 God, listen to my prayer
and do not ignoreᶜ my plea for help.
2 Pay attention to me and answer me.
I am restless and in turmoil with my complaint,
3 because of the enemy's voice,
because of the pressureᵈ of the wicked.
For they bring down disaster on meᵉ
and harass me in anger.

4 My heart shudders within me;
terrors of death sweep over me.
5 Fear and trembling grip me;
horror has overwhelmed me.
6 I said, "If only I hadᶠ wings like a dove!
I would fly away and find rest.
7 How far away I would flee;

I would stay in the wilderness.   •*Selah*
8 I would hurry to my shelter
from the raging wind and the storm."

9 Lord, confuseᵍ and confound their speech,ʰ
for I see violence and strife in the city;
10 day and night they make the rounds on its walls.
Crime and trouble are within it;
11 destruction is inside it;
oppression and deceit never leave its marketplace.

12 Now, it is not an enemy who insults me—
otherwise I could bear it;
it is not a foe who rises up against me—
otherwise I could hide from him.
13 But it is you, a man who is my peer,
my companion and good friend!
14 We used to have close fellowship;
we walked with the crowd into the house of God.

15 Let death take them by surprise;
let them go down to •Sheol alive,
because evil is in their homes and within them.
16 But I call to God,
and the LORD will save me.
17 I complain and groan morning, noon, and night,
and He hears my voice.
18 Though many are against me,
He will redeem me from my battle unharmed.
19 God, the One enthroned from long ago,
will hear, and will humiliate them   *Selah*
because they do not change
and do not •fear God.

20 Heⁱ acts violently
against those at peace with him;
he violates his covenant.
21 His buttery words are smooth,ʲ
but war is in his heart.
His words are softer than oil,
but they are drawn swords.

22 Cast your burden on the LORD,
and He will support you;
He will never allow the righteous to be shaken.

23 You, God, will bring them down
to the pit of destruction;
men of bloodshed and treachery
will not live out half their days.
But I will trust in You.

ᵃ54:3 Lit *They do not set God before them*   ᵇ54:4 Or *is with those who sustain my life*   ᶜ55:1 Lit *hide Yourself from*   ᵈ55:3 Or *threat,* or *oppression*   ᵉ55:3 LXX, Syr, Sym; MT reads *they cause me to totter*   ᶠ55:6 Lit *"Who will give to me . . . dove?* (as a question)   ᵍ55:9 Or *destroy*   ʰ55:9 Lit *and divide their tongue*   ⁱ55:20 The evil man   ʲ55:21 Other Hb mss, Sym, Syr, Tg, Jer read *His speech is smoother than butter*

55:1-3 Maskil. Psalm 55 is also a teaching psalm. Its title refers to a betrayal by a friend.

55:4-8 My heart shudders. His present enemy is a former friend. David feels betrayed and fears for his life (v. 4). And he fears that the present conflict will destroy all the work he has done as king (vv. 9-11). His first thought

is just to escape and have some peace.

55:9 confuse and confound their speech. At the center of any conspiracy, plans are discussed and plots are hatched. David prays that God will disrupt enemy communication and render conspiracy harmless, as happened at the Tower of Babel (Gen.11:5-9).

Ps. 56 Miktam. A Miktam is a teaching psalm of pithy, expressive sayings. This psalm could fit well into David's story in I Samuel 21:10-15.

57:2 God Most High ... who fulfills [His purpose] for me. God appointed David as king with a divine purpose. He will not allow

Psalm 56

A Call for God's Protection

For the choir director: according to
"A Silent Dove Far Away."[a]
A Davidic •Miktam. When the Philistines
seized him in Gath.

1 Be gracious to me, God, for man tramples me;
   he fights and oppresses me all day long.
2 My adversaries trample me all day,
   for many arrogantly fight against me.[b]

3 When I am afraid,
   I will trust in You.
4 In God, whose word I praise,
   in God I trust; I will not fear.
   What can man do to me?

5 They twist my words all day long;
   all their thoughts are against me for evil.
6 They stir up strife,[c] they lurk;
   they watch my steps
   while they wait to take my life.
7 Will they escape in spite of such sin?
   God, bring down the nations in wrath.

8 You Yourself have recorded my wanderings.[d]
   Put my tears in Your bottle.
   Are they not in Your records?
9 Then my enemies will retreat on the day
      when I call.
   This I know: God is for me.

10 In God, whose word I praise,
    in the LORD, whose word I praise,
11 in God I trust; I will not fear.
    What can man do to me?

12 I am obligated by vows[e] to You, God;
    I will make my thank offerings to You.
13 For You delivered me from death,
    even my feet from stumbling,
    to walk before God in the light of life.

Psalm 57

Praise for God's Protection

For the choir director: "Do Not Destroy."[f]
A Davidic •Miktam. When he fled
before Saul into the cave.

1 Be gracious to me, God, be gracious to me,

for I take refuge in You.
I will seek refuge in the shadow of Your wings
until danger passes.
2 I call to God •Most High,
   to God who fulfills [His purpose] for me.[g]
3 He reaches down from heaven and saves me,
   challenging the one who tramples me.   •Selah
   God sends His faithful love and truth.
4 I am in the midst of lions;
   I lie down with those who devour •men.
   Their teeth are spears and arrows,
   their tongues are sharp swords.
5 God, be exalted above the heavens;
   let Your glory be above the whole earth.

6 They prepared a net for my steps;
   I was downcast.
   They dug a pit ahead of me,
   but they fell into it!   Selah

7 My heart is confident, God, my heart is confident.
   I will sing; I will sing praises.
8 Wake up, my soul![h]
   Wake up, harp and lyre!
   I will wake up the dawn.
9 I will praise You, Lord, among the peoples;
   I will sing praises to You among the nations.
10 For Your faithful love is as high as the heavens;
    Your faithfulness reaches to the clouds.
11 God, be exalted above the heavens;
    let Your glory be over the whole earth.

Psalm 58

A Cry against Injustice

For the choir director:
"Do Not Destroy."[i]
A Davidic •Miktam.

1 Do you really speak righteously,
      you mighty ones?[i]
   Do you judge •people fairly?
2 No, you practice injustice in your hearts;
   with your hands you weigh out violence
      in the land.

3 The wicked go astray from the womb;
   liars err from birth.
4 They have venom like the venom of a snake,
   like the deaf cobra that stops up its ears,
5 that does not listen to the sound of the charmers
   who skillfully weave spells.

---

[a] Possibly a song tune   [b] 56:2 Or many fight against me, O exalted One, or many fight against me from the heights   [c] 56:6 Or They attack
[d] 56:8 Or misery   [e] 56:12 Lit Upon me the vows   [f] Possibly a song tune   [g] 57:2 Or who avenges me   [h] 57:8 Lit glory   [i] Possibly a song tune
[i] 58:1 Or Can you really speak righteousness in silence?

Saul to kill David (see I Samuel 22 and 24).

57:6 They dug a pit. The psalmist described his enemies as lions (v. 4). Here those enemies had set a net and dug a pit as if they were hunters and David the lion. But God changes the roles, and the enemies fall into the trap. The lions fall prey to David and to God.

58:6-8 God, knock … tear. David prays that Israel will be purged of such evil judges. The tone of the verses is much more like a curse than a prayer.

59:1 Deliver me. The Hebrew words for this phrase literally mean "raise me to a high, secure place." David prays for a safe deliverance

from Saul's soldiers who have surrounded David's house in an effort to kill him. (See also I Samuel 19:11-17.)

59:3-5 For no fault of mine. Though others lie (v. 12) and slander (v. 10), the psalmist proclaims innocence. He asks God to judge these enemies and to punish them for wickedness.

6 God, knock the teeth out of their mouths;
LORD, tear out the young lions' fangs.

7 They will vanish like water that flows by;
they will aim their useless arrows.ᵃ ᵇ

8 Like a slug that moves along in slime,
like a woman's miscarried ⌊child⌋,
they will not see the sun.

9 Before your pots can feel the heat of the thorns—
whether green or burning—
He will sweep them away.ᶜ

10 The righteous will rejoice
when he sees the retribution;
he will wash his feet in the blood of the wicked.

11 Then people will say,
"Yes, there is a reward for the righteous!
There is a God who judges on earth!"

Psalm 59
God Our Stronghold

For the choir director: "Do Not Destroy."ᵈ
A Davidic •Miktam. When Saul sent ⌊agents⌋
to watch the house and kill him.

1 Deliver me from my enemies, my God;
protect me from those who rise up against me.

2 Deliver me from those who practice sin,
and save me from men of bloodshed.

3 LORD, look! They set an ambush for me.
Powerful men attack me,
but not because of any sin or rebellion of mine.

4 For no fault of mine,
they run and take up a position.
Awake to help me, and take notice.

5 You, LORD God of •Hosts, God of Israel,
rise up to punish all the nations;
do not show grace to any wicked traitors. •Selah

6 They return at evening, snarling like dogs
and prowling around the city.

7 Look, they spew from their mouths—
sharp words fromᵉ their lips.
"For who," ⌊they say,⌋ "will hear?"

8 But You laugh at them, LORD;
You ridicule all the nations.

9 I will keep watch for You, myᶠ strength,
because God is my stronghold.

10 My faithful Godᵍ will come to meet me;
God will let me look down on my adversaries.

11 Do not kill them; otherwise, my people will forget.
By Your power, make them homeless wanderers
and bring them down,
Lord, our shield.

12 The sin of their mouths is the word of their lips,
so let them be caught in their pride.
They utter curses and lies.

13 Consume ⌊them⌋ in rage;
consume ⌊them⌋ until they are gone.
Then they will know to the ends of the earth
that God rules over Jacob. Selah

14 And they return at evening, snarling like dogs
and prowling around the city.

15 They scavenge for food;
they growl if they are not satisfied.

16 But I will sing of Your strength
and will joyfully proclaim
Your faithful love in the morning.
For You have been a stronghold for me,
a refuge in my day of trouble.

17 To You, my strength, I sing praises,
because God is my stronghold—
my faithful God.

Psalm 60
Prayer in Difficult Times

For the choir director: according to
"The Lily of Testimony."ʰ A Davidic •Miktam
for teaching. When he fought with Aram-naharaim
and Aram-zobah, and Joab returned and struck
Edom in the Valley of Salt, ⌊killing⌋ 12,000.

1 God, You have rejected us;
You have broken outⁱ against us;
You have been angry. Restore us!ʲ

2 You have shaken the land and split it open.
Heal its fissures, for it shudders.

3 You have made Your people suffer hardship;
You have given us a wine to drink
that made us stagger.

4 You have given a signal flag to those who •fear You,
so that they can flee before the archers.ᵏ •Selah

5 Save with Your right hand, and answer me,
so that those You love may be rescued.

6 God has spoken in His sanctuary:ˡ
"I will triumph! I will divide up Shechem.

ᵃ**58:7** Or *their arrows as if they were circumcised,* Hb obscure   ᵇ**58:7** Or *they wither like trampled grass*   ᶜ**58:9** Or *thorns, He will sweep it away, whether raw or cooking,* or *thorns, He will sweep him away alive in fury*   ᵈPossibly a song tune   ᵉ**59:7** Lit *swords are on*   ᶠ**59:9** Some Hb mss, LXX, Vg, Tg; other Hb mss read *his*   ᵍ**59:10** Alt Hb traditions read *God in His faithful love,* or *My God, His faithful love*   ʰPossibly a song tune   ⁱ**60:1** Lit *have burst through*   ʲ**60:1** Or *Turn back to us*   ᵏ**60:4** Or *can rally before the archers,* or *can rally because of the truth*   ˡ**60:6** Or *has promised by His holy nature*

60:1 Aram-naharaim. This is the Hebrew word for Mesopotamia, the area and people that have just defeated Israel. The Valley of Ghor was a flat area south of the Dead Sea where they lost 12,000 in battle.

60:4 flag. In the middle of battle, flags were used to establish a rallying point, a place

where an army could regroup and counterattack.

60:6-8 Shechem … Ephraim. Shechem was comprised of patriarchal settlements (Gen. 33:17-20). Although they were far from Jerusalem and the temple, God has not forgotten them. Ephraim became the

name for the northern tribes of Israel.

61:2 rock that is high. God is pictured as solid rock—an image first used by Moses (Deut. 32:4) and echoed elsewhere in the Psalms (62:2; 71:3; 91:1, 2; 144:1).

Ps. 62 If the writer was David, the events prompting this wisdom psalm could be the at-

I will apportion the Valley of Succoth.
7 Gilead is Mine, Manasseh is Mine,
and Ephraim is My helmet;
Judah is My scepter.
8 Moab is My washbasin;
on Edom I throw My sandal.
Over Philistia I shout in triumph."

9 Who will bring me to the fortified city?
Who will lead me to Edom?
10 Is it not You, God, who have rejected us?
God, You do not march out with our armies.
11 Give us aid against the foe,
for human help is worthless.
12 With God we will perform valiantly;
He will trample our foes.

Psalm 61
Security in God

For the choir director:
on stringed instruments. Davidic.

1 God, hear my cry;
pay attention to my prayer.
2 I call to You from the ends of the earth
when my heart is without strength.
Lead me to a rock that is high above me,
3 for You have been a refuge for me,
a strong tower in the face of the enemy.
4 I will live in Your tent forever
and take refuge under the shelter
of Your wings. •Selah

5 God, You have heard my vows;
You have given a heritage
to those who fear Your name.
6 Add days to the king's life;
may his years span many generations.
7 May he sit enthroned before God forever;
appoint faithful love and truth to guard him.
8 Then I will continually sing of Your name,
fulfilling my vows day by day.

Psalm 62
Trust in God Alone

For the choir director:
according to Jeduthun. A Davidic psalm.

1 I am at rest in God alone;
my salvation comes from Him.

2 He alone is my rock and my salvation,
my stronghold; I will never be shaken.
3 How long will you threaten a man?
Will all of you attack[a]
as if he were a leaning wall
or a tottering stone fence?
4 They only plan to bring him down
from his high position.
They take pleasure in lying;
they bless with their mouths,
but they curse inwardly. •Selah

5 Rest in God alone, my soul,
for my hope comes from Him.
6 He alone is my rock and my salvation,
my stronghold; I will not be shaken.
7 My salvation and glory depend on God;
my strong rock, my refuge, is in God.
8 Trust in Him at all times, you people;
pour out your hearts before Him.
God is our refuge. Selah

9 •Men are only a vapor;
exalted men, an illusion.
On a balance scale, they go up;
together they ⌊weigh⌋ less than a vapor.
10 Place no trust in oppression,
or false hope in robbery.
If wealth increases,
pay no attention to it.[b]

11 God has spoken once;
I have heard this twice:
strength belongs to God,
12 and faithful love belongs to You, LORD.
For You repay each according to his works.

Psalm 63
Praise God Who Satisfies

A Davidic psalm. When he was
in the Wilderness of Judah.

1 God, You are my God; I eagerly seek You.
I thirst for You;
my body faints for You
in a land that is dry, desolate, and without water.
2 So I gaze on You in the sanctuary
to see Your strength and Your glory.
3 My lips will glorify You
because Your faithful love is better than life.

---

a **62:3** Other Hb mss read *you be struck down*   b **62:10** Lit *increases, do not set heart*

---

tempt of Saul's family to remove David from the throne. The writer feels weak (v. 3), perhaps due to his age, and seeks God's strength. Structurally the psalm has three parts: reliance on God, trust and hope, and an explanation of why those are possible.

62:12 repay each. Ultimately God will judge each person according to his actions.

63:2 the sanctuary. David had sought God's presence at Nob (1 Sam. 21:1). Later the sanctuary was moved to Jerusalem.

63:6 on my bed. In the darkness the psalmist turns to God and anticipates the morning when God will rescue him. **night watches.**

The Jews divided the night into three watches.

63:8 Your right hand. The right hand of God refers to His power and authority—the same power that delivered Israel from Egypt (Ex. 15:6).

63:9-10 jackals' prey. Bodies left on battle-

4 So I will praise You as long as I live;
    at Your name, I will lift up my hands.
5 You satisfy me as with rich food;[a]
    my mouth will praise You with joyful lips.

6 When, on my bed, I think of You,
    I meditate on You during the night watches
7 because You are my help;
    I will rejoice in the shadow of Your wings.
8 I follow close to You;
    Your right hand holds on to me.

9 But those who seek to destroy my life
    will go into the depths of the earth.
10 They will be given over to the power
        of the sword;
    they will become the jackals' prey.
11 But the king will rejoice in God;
    all who swear by Him[b] will boast,
    for the mouths of liars will be shut.

Psalm 64

Protection from Evildoers

For the choir director.
A Davidic psalm.

1 God, hear my voice when I complain.
    Protect my life from the terror of the enemy.
2 Hide me from the scheming of the wicked,
    from the mob of evildoers,
3 who sharpen their tongues like swords
    and aim bitter words like arrows,
4 shooting from concealed places at the innocent.
    They shoot at him suddenly and are not afraid.
5 They encourage each other in an evil plan;[c] [d]
    they talk about hiding traps and say,
    "Who will see them?"[e]
6 They devise crimes ⌊and say,⌋
    "We have perfected a secret plan."
    The inner man and the heart are mysterious.

7 But God will shoot them with arrows;
    suddenly, they will be wounded.
8 They will be made to stumble;
    their own tongues work against them.
    All who see them will shake their heads.
9 Then everyone will fear
    and will tell about God's work,
    for they will understand what He has done.

10 The righteous rejoice in the LORD
    and take refuge in Him;
    all the upright in heart offer praise.

Psalm 65

God's Care for the Earth

For the choir director.
A Davidic psalm. A song.

1 Praise is rightfully Yours,[f]
    God, in Zion;[g]
    vows to You will be fulfilled.
2 All humanity will come to You,
    the One who hears prayer.
3 Iniquities overwhelm me;
    only You can •atone for[h] our rebellions.
4 How happy is the one You choose
    and bring near to live in Your courts!
    We will be satisfied with the goodness
        of Your house,
    the holiness of Your temple.[i]

5 You answer us in righteousness,
    with awe-inspiring works,
    God of our salvation,
    the hope of all the ends of the earth
    and of the distant seas;
6 You establish the mountains by Your[j] power,
    robed with strength;
7 You silence the roar of the seas,
    the roar of their waves,
    and the tumult of the nations.
8 Those who live far away are awed by Your signs;
    You make east and west shout for joy.

9 You visit the earth and water it abundantly,
    enriching it greatly.
    God's stream is filled with water,
    for You prepare the earth[k] in this way,
    providing ⌊people⌋ with grain.
10 You soften it with showers and bless its growth,
    soaking its furrows and leveling its ridges.
11 You crown the year with Your goodness;
    Your ways overflow with plenty.[l]
12 The wilderness pastures overflow,
    and the hills are robed with joy.
13 The pastures are clothed with flocks,
    and the valleys covered with grain.
    They shout in triumph; indeed, they sing.

---

[a]**63:5** Lit *with fat and fatness*   [b]**63:11** Or *him,* referring to the king; 1 Sm 17:55; 2 Sm 14:19   [c]**64:5** Lit *word,* or *thing*   [d]**64:5** Or *They hold fast to an evil purpose,* or *They establish for themselves an evil purpose*   [e]**64:5** Or *us,* or *it*   [f]**65:1** Or *Praise is silence to You,* or *Praise awaits You*   [g]**65:1** Jerusalem   [h]**65:3** Or *can forgive,* or *can wipe out*   [i]**65:4** Or *house, Your holy temple*   [j]**65:6** Some LXX mss, Vg; MT reads *His*   [k]**65:9** Lit *prepare it*   [l]**65:11** Lit *ways drip with fat*

---

fields were eaten by jackals.
64:3 tongues. Psalmists often complain about slanderous tongues, which are more painful than the sword (5:9). They are called swords and deadly arrows for the curses and lies they tell (59:7, 12).
64:7-8 But God will. The psalmist expresses

his certain trust in God's justice. God will surely act with righteousness, doing to them what they planned to do to him (63:9, 10).

Ps. 65 This psalm was sung at the harvest thanksgiving service (end of September) and at the celebration of a new year during an eight day festival.

65:3 atone for our rebellions. The people offered God the prescribed sacrifices for atonement. As a result, God forgave them (32:1,2; 78:38; 79:9).

66:10 tested … refined. Precious metals were refined by fire to remove any impurities and increase their value. The psalmist uses the met-

Psalm 66

Praise for God's Mighty Acts

For the choir director. A song.
A psalm.

1 Shout joyfully to God, all the earth!
2 Sing the glory of His name;
make His praise glorious.
3 Say to God, "How awe-inspiring are Your works!
Your enemies will cringe before You
because of Your great strength.
4 All the earth will worship You
and sing praise to You.
They will sing praise to Your name." •Selah

5 Come and see the works of God;
His acts toward •mankind are awe-inspiring.
6 He turned the sea into dry land,
and they crossed the river on foot.
There we rejoiced in Him.
7 He rules forever by His might;
He keeps His eye on the nations.
The rebellious should not exalt themselves. Selah

8 Praise our God, you peoples;
let the sound of His praise be heard.
9 He keeps us alive[a]
and does not allow our feet to slip.

10 For You, God, tested us;
You refined us as silver is refined.
11 You lured us into a trap;
You placed burdens on our backs.
12 You let men ride over our heads;
we went through fire and water,
but You brought us out to abundance.[b]

13 I will enter Your house with •burnt offerings;
I will pay You my vows
14 that my lips promised
and my mouth spoke during my distress.
15 I will offer You fattened sheep as burnt offerings,
with the fragrant smoke of rams;
I will sacrifice oxen with goats. Selah

16 Come and listen, all who •fear God,
and I will tell what He has done for me.
17 I cried out to Him with my mouth,
and praise was on my tongue.
18 If I had been aware of malice in my heart,
the Lord would not have listened.

19 However, God has listened;
He has paid attention to the sound of my prayer.
20 May God be praised!
He has not turned away my prayer
or turned His faithful love from me.

Psalm 67

All Will Praise God

For the choir director:
with stringed instruments. A psalm.
A song.

1 May God be gracious to us and bless us;
look on us with favor •Selah
2 so that Your way may be known on earth,
Your salvation among all nations.

3 Let the peoples praise You, God;
let all the peoples praise You.
4 Let the nations rejoice and shout for joy,
for You judge the peoples with fairness
and lead the nations on earth. Selah
5 Let the peoples praise You, God,
let all the peoples praise You.

6 The earth has produced its harvest;
God, our God, blesses us.
7 God will bless us,
and all the ends of the earth will •fear Him.

Psalm 68

God's Majestic Power

For the choir director.
A Davidic psalm. A song.

1 God arises. His enemies scatter,
and those who hate Him flee from His presence.
2 As smoke is blown away,
so You blow ⌊them⌋ away.
As wax melts before the fire,
so the wicked are destroyed before God.
3 But the righteous are glad;
they rejoice before God and celebrate with joy.

4 Sing to God! Sing praises to His name.
Exalt Him who rides on the clouds[c]—
His name is •Yahweh[d]—and rejoice before Him.
5 A father of the fatherless
and a champion of widows
is God in His holy dwelling.
6 God provides homes for those who are deserted.

---

[a] 66:9 Lit He sets our soul in life [b] 66:12 Or a place of satisfaction [c] 68:4 Or rides through the desert [d] 68:4 Lit Yah

---

aphor to describe spiritual maturing (12:6; 17:3).

66:17 praise. Old Testament believers praised God even in the face of the difficulties from which they were seeking deliverance (Phil. 4:6; 1 Tim. 2:1).

67:1 God be gracious to us. The psalmist uses Aaron's benediction (Num. 6:24-26).

68:4 rides on the clouds. This description, used often of the Canaanite god Baal, is applied to the true God who rules over all (v. 33; 104:3; Matt. 26:64).

68:11 brought the good news. God clearly re-

vealed beforehand that He would defeat the Canaanites in order to give His people the land (Ex. 23:22-31; Deut. 7:10-24).

68:14 the Almighty. The Hebrew name is Shaddai, referring to God's strength and majesty (91:1).

68:15-16 Mount Bashan. Bashan was a fertile

He leads out the prisoners to prosperity,[a]
but the rebellious live in a scorched land.

7 God, when You went out before Your people,
when You marched through the desert, •Selah
8 the earth trembled, and the skies
poured down ⌊rain⌋
before God, the God of Sinai,[b]
before God, the God of Israel.
9 You, God, showered abundant rain;
You revived Your inheritance
when it languished.
10 Your people settled in it;
by Your goodness You provided
for the poor, God.

11 The Lord gave the command;
a great company of women brought
the good news:
12 "The kings of the armies flee—they flee!"
She who stays at home divides the spoil.
13 While[c] you lie among the sheepfolds,[d]
the wings of a dove are covered with silver,
and its feathers with glistening gold.
14 When the •Almighty scattered kings
in the land,
it snowed on Zalmon.[e]

15 Mount Bashan is God's towering mountain;
Mount Bashan is a mountain of many peaks.
16 Why gaze with envy, you mountain peaks,
at the mountain[f] God desired for His dwelling?
The Lord will live ⌊there⌋ forever!
17 God's chariots are tens of thousands,
thousands and thousands;
the Lord is among them in the sanctuary[g]
as He was at Sinai.
18 You ascended to the heights,
taking away captives;
You received gifts from[h] people,
even from the rebellious,
so that the Lord God might live ⌊there⌋.[i]

19 May the Lord be praised!
Day after day He bears our burdens;
God is our salvation. Selah
20 Our God is a God of salvation,
and escape from death belongs to the Lord God.

21 Surely God crushes the heads of His enemies,
the hairy head of one who goes on
in his guilty acts.
22 The Lord said, "I will bring ⌊them⌋ back
from Bashan;
I will bring ⌊them⌋ back from the depths
of the sea
23 so that your foot may wade[j] in blood
and your dogs' tongues may have their share
from the enemies."
24 People have seen Your procession, God,
the procession of my God,
my King, in the sanctuary.[g]
25 Singers[k] lead the way,
with musicians following;
among them are young women
playing tambourines.
26 Praise God in the assemblies;
⌊praise⌋ the Lord from the fountain of Israel.
27 There is Benjamin, the youngest, leading them,
the rulers of Judah in their assembly,[l]
the rulers of Zebulun, the rulers of Naphtali.

28 Your God has decreed your strength.
Show Your strength, God,
You who have acted on our behalf.
29 Because of Your temple at Jerusalem,
kings will bring tribute to You.
30 Rebuke the beast[m] in the reeds,
the herd of bulls with the calves of the peoples.
Trample underfoot those with bars of silver.[n]
Scatter the peoples who take pleasure in war.
31 Ambassadors will come[o] from Egypt;
•Cush[p] will stretch out its hands[q] to God.

32 Sing to God, you kingdoms of the earth;
sing praise to the Lord, Selah
33 to Him who rides in the ancient,
highest heavens.
Look, He thunders with His powerful voice!
34 Ascribe power to God.
His majesty is over Israel,
His power among the clouds.
35 God, You are awe-inspiring in Your sanctuaries.
The God of Israel gives power and strength
to His people.
May God be praised!

[a]68:6 Or prisoners with joyous music; Hb uncertain [b]68:8 Lit God, this Sinai [c]68:13 Or If [d]68:13 Or campfires, or saddlebags; Hb obscure
[e]68:14 Or Black Mountain [f]68:16 Mount Zion [g]68:17,24 Or in holiness [h]68:18 Lit among [i]68:18 Or even those rebelling against the Lord God's
living there, or even rebels are living with the Lord God; Hb obscure [j]68:23 LXX, Syr read dip [k]68:25 Some Hb mss, LXX, Syr read Officials
[l]68:27 Hb obscure [m]68:30 Probably Egypt [n]68:30 Or peoples, trampling on those who take pleasure in silver, or peoples, trampling on the bars of
silver, or peoples, who trample each other for bars of silver [o]68:31 Or They bring red cloth, or They bring bronze [p]68:31 Modern Sudan
[q]68:31 Probably with tribute or in submission

---

area to the northeast of the Sea of Galilee. Mt. Bashan is pictured here as being envious over God's choice of Mt. Zion as His throne—thus making it the "highest" of all mountains (48:2).

68:17 God's chariots. A reference to the vast host of God's angelic beings, likened to a powerful force of charioteers (2 Kings 6:17; Hab. 3:8).

68:29 bring tribute. Gifts of homage were made to Solomon (1 Kings 10:1-10), but this also may look forward to the time when kings would bring gifts to the baby Jesus (Matt. 2:1-12).

Ps. 69 A Plea for Rescue. A lament psalm with messianic references similar to Psalm 22, fore-

shadowing Christ's agony.

69:1-2 deep waters … flood. This figurative language is used to describe deep pain and distress. The cause of the pain is enemy attacks (vv. 14, 15, 29), but also God's own "wounding" of the psalmist (v. 26).

69:13-15 Rescue. The psalmist refers to "res-

Psalm 69

A Plea for Rescue

For the choir director: according to
"The Lilies."[a] Davidic.

1 Save me, God,
for the water has risen to my neck.
2 I have sunk in deep mud, and there is
no footing;
I have come into deep waters,
and a flood sweeps over me.
3 I am weary from my crying;
my throat is parched.
My eyes fail, looking for my God.
4 Those who hate me without cause
are more numerous than the hairs of my head;
my deceitful enemies, who would destroy me,
are powerful.
Though I did not steal, I must repay.

5 God, You know my foolishness,
and my guilty acts are not hidden from You.
6 Do not let those who put their hope in You
be disgraced because of me,
Lord GOD of •Hosts;
do not let those who seek You
be humiliated because of me,
God of Israel.
7 For I have endured insults because of You,
and shame has covered my face.
8 I have become a stranger to my brothers
and a foreigner to my mother's sons
9 because zeal for Your house has consumed me,
and the insults of those who insult You
have fallen on me.
10 I mourned and fasted,
but it brought me insults.
11 I wore •sackcloth as my clothing,
and I was a joke to them.
12 Those who sit at the city •gate talk about me,
and drunkards make up songs about me.

13 But as for me, LORD,
my prayer to You is for a time of favor.
In Your abundant, faithful love, God,
answer me with Your sure salvation.
14 Rescue me from the miry mud;
don't let me sink.
Let me be rescued from those who hate me,
and from the deep waters.

15 Don't let the floodwaters sweep over me
or the deep swallow me up;
don't let the •Pit close its mouth over me.
16 Answer me, LORD,
for Your faithful love is good;
in keeping with Your great compassion,
turn to me.
17 Don't hide Your face from Your servant,
for I am in distress.
Answer me quickly!
18 Draw near to me and redeem me;
ransom me because of my enemies.

19 You know the insults I endure—
my shame and disgrace.
You are aware of all my adversaries.
20 Insults have broken my heart,
and I am in despair.
I waited for sympathy,
but there was none;
for comforters, but found no one.
21 Instead, they gave me gall[b] for my food,
and for my thirst
they gave me vinegar to drink.

22 Let their table set before them be a snare,
and let it be a trap for [their] allies.
23 Let their eyes grow too dim to see,
and let their loins continually shake.
24 Pour out Your rage on them,
and let Your burning anger overtake them.
25 Make their fortification desolate;
may no one live in their tents.
26 For they persecute the one You struck
and talk about the pain of those You wounded.
27 Add guilt to their guilt;
do not let them share in Your righteousness.
28 Let them be erased from the book of life
and not be recorded with the righteous.

29 But as for me—poor and in pain—
let Your salvation protect me, God.
30 I will praise God's name with song
and exalt Him with thanksgiving.
31 That will please the LORD more than an ox,
more than a bull with horns and hooves.
32 The humble will see it and rejoice.
You who seek God, take heart!
33 For the LORD listens to the needy
and does not despise
His own who are prisoners.

[a] Apparently a hymn tune; compare Pss 45; 60; 80   [b] **69:21** A bitter substance

cue" as answered prayer.
69:23 eyes … loins. The psalmist's enemies
made fun of him because of his pain. Now he
asks God to give them the same painful blind
eyes (v. 3) and bent backs (38:5-8).
69:24-28 anger overtake them. The writer
asks God to judge his enemies in a display of

anger. Verse 25 was fulfilled by Judas Iscariot
(Acts 1:20 combines these words with those of
109:8).
69:28 book of life. God's divine list of all the
righteous who enjoy His blessing of life (37:17,
29; 55:22; 75:10). The New Testament use of
the term includes those who have received

God's gift of eternal life (Phil. 4:3; Rev. 3:5).

Ps. 71 Psalm 71 may be a continuation of
Psalm 70 since there is no inscription and it
carries the same theme.

71:1-3 These verses are duplicates of Psalm
31:1-3. But they are developed in a different

34 Let heaven and earth praise Him,
the seas and everything that moves in them,
35 for God will save Zion
and build up[a] the cities of Judah.
They will live there and possess it.
36 The descendants of His servants will inherit it,
and those who love His name will live in it.

Psalm 70

A Call for Deliverance

For the choir director. Davidic.
To bring remembrance.

1 God, deliver me.
Hurry to help me, LORD!

2 Let those who seek my life
be disgraced and confounded;
let those who wish me harm
be driven back and humiliated.
3 Let those who say, "Aha, aha!"
retreat because of their shame.

4 Let all who seek You rejoice and be glad in You;
let those who love Your salvation
continually say, "God is great!"
5 I am afflicted and needy;
hurry to me, God.
You are my help and my deliverer;
LORD, do not delay.

Psalm 71

God's Help in Old Age

1 LORD, I seek refuge in You;
never let me be disgraced.
2 In Your justice, rescue and deliver me;
listen closely to me and save me.
3 Be a rock of refuge for me,
where I can always go.
Give the command to save me,
for You are my rock and fortress.
4 Deliver me, my God, from the hand
of the wicked,
from the grasp of the unjust and oppressive.
5 For You are my hope, Lord GOD,
my confidence from my youth.
6 I have leaned on You from birth;
You took me from my mother's womb.
My praise is always about You.
7 I have become an ominous sign to many,
but You are my strong refuge.

8 My mouth is full of praise
and honor to You all day long.
9 Don't discard me in my old age:
as my strength fails, do not abandon me.
10 For my enemies talk about me,
and those who spy on me plot together,
11 saying, "God has abandoned him;
chase him and catch him,
for there is no one to rescue ⌊him⌋."
12 God, do not be far from me;
my God, hurry to help me.
13 May my adversaries be disgraced and confounded;
may those who seek my harm
be covered with disgrace and humiliation.
14 But I will hope continually
and will praise You more and more.
15 My mouth will tell about Your righteousness
and Your salvation all day long,
though I cannot sum them up.
16 I come because of the mighty acts of the Lord GOD;
I will proclaim Your righteousness, Yours alone.
17 God, You have taught me from my youth,
and I still proclaim Your wonderful works.
18 Even when I am old and gray,
God, do not abandon me.
Then I will[b] proclaim Your power
to ⌊another⌋ generation,
Your strength to all who are to come.
19 Your righteousness reaches heaven, God,
You who have done great things;
God, who is like You?
20 You caused me to experience
many troubles and misfortunes,
but You will revive me again.
You will bring me up again,
even from the depths of the earth.
21 You will increase my honor
and comfort me once again.
22 Therefore, with a lute I will praise You
for Your faithfulness, my God;
I will sing to You with a harp,
Holy One of Israel.
23 My lips will shout for joy
when I sing praise to You,
because You have redeemed me.
24 Therefore, my tongue will proclaim
Your righteousness all day long,
for those who seek my harm
will be disgraced and confounded.

---

[a]**69:35** Or *and rebuild*   [b]**71:18** Lit *me until I*

---

way since now the psalmist is an old man with a memory of a long life of grace.

71:14 hope continually. This verse marks the turning point of the psalm. After his plea for help in verses 1-13, the psalmist here determines to hope in God as he has since his youth.

71:20 depths of the earth. This metaphor expresses the psalmist's desperation. He feels as though he were in the realm of the dead, cast down beyond the grave.

72:1 justice … righteousness. The entire prayer may be summed up in this verse.

Ps. 73 This is the first of eleven psalms (73–83)

attributed to Asaph. He and his descendants were the leaders of one of David's Levitical choirs.

Ps. 74 for Israel. This psalm is a communal lament such as was prayed when Israel was exiled, the promised land devastated, and the temple lay in ruins. (See also Zech. 7;1-6, 8:18-

Psalm 72

A Prayer for the King

Solomonic.

1 God, give Your justice to the king
    and Your righteousness to the king's son.
2 He will judge Your people with righteousness
    and Your afflicted ones with justice.
3 May the mountains bring prosperity[a]
        to the people,
    and the hills, righteousness.
4 May he vindicate the afflicted among the people,
    help the poor,
    and crush the oppressor.

5 May he continue[b] while the sun endures,
    and as long as the moon,
        throughout all generations.
6 May he be like rain that falls on the cut grass,
    like spring showers that water the earth.
7 May the righteous[c] flourish in his days,
    and prosperity[a] abound
    until the moon is no more.

8 And may he rule from sea to sea
    and from the Euphrates
    to the ends of the earth.
9 May desert tribes kneel before him
    and his enemies lick the dust.
10 May the kings of Tarshish
    and the coasts and islands bring tribute,
    the kings of Sheba and Seba offer gifts.
11 And let all kings bow down to him,
    all nations serve him.
12 For he will rescue the poor who cry out
    and the afflicted who have no helper.
13 He will have pity on the poor and helpless
    and save the lives of the poor.
14 He will redeem them from oppression
        and violence,
    for their lives are precious[d] in his sight.

15 May he live long!
    May gold from Sheba be given to him.
    May prayer be offered for him continually,
    and may he be blessed all day long.
16 May there be plenty of grain in the land;
    may it wave on the tops of the mountains.
    May its crops be like Lebanon.
    May people flourish in the cities

like the grass of the field.
17 May his name endure forever;
    as long as the sun shines,
    may his fame increase.
    May all nations be blessed by him
    and call him blessed.

18 May the LORD God, the God of Israel, be praised,
    who alone does wonders.
19 May His glorious name be praised forever;
    the whole earth is filled with His glory.
    •Amen and amen.

20 The prayers of David son of Jesse are concluded.

BOOK III

(Psalms 73–89)
Psalm 73

God's Ways Vindicated

A psalm of •Asaph.

1 God is indeed good to Israel,
    to the pure in heart.
2 But as for me, my feet almost slipped;
    my steps nearly went astray.
3 For I envied the arrogant;
    I saw the prosperity of the wicked.

4 They have an easy time until they die,[e]
    and their bodies are well-fed.[f]
5 They are not in trouble like others;
    they are not afflicted like most people.
6 Therefore, pride is their necklace,
    and violence covers them like a garment.
7 Their eyes bulge out from fatness;
    the imaginations of their hearts run wild.
8 They mock, and they speak maliciously;
    they arrogantly threaten oppression.
9 They set their mouths against heaven,
    and their tongues strut across the earth.
10 Therefore His people turn to them[g]
    and drink in their overflowing waters.[h]
11 They say, "How can God know?
    Does the •Most High know everything?"
12 Look at them—the wicked!
    They are always at ease,
    and they increase their wealth.
13 Did I purify my heart

---

[a]**72:3,7** Or *peace*   [b]**72:5** LXX; MT reads *May they fear you*   [c]**72:7** Some Hb mss, LXX, Syr, Jer read *May righteousness*   [d]**72:14** Or *valuable*
[e]**73:4** Lit *For there are no pangs to their death*   [f]**73:4** Lit *fat*   [g]**73:10** Lit *turn here*   [h]**73:10** Lit *and waters of fullness are drained by them*

19.)

74:1 Why. The first word of the psalm introduces a lament—a cry to God.

74:2 Remember. The psalm is punctuated with pleas for God to "remember." The wording of this verse and verses 12-17 recalls the victory song of Exodus 15.

74:3-8 destroyed. These verses detail the Babylonians' methods for destroying the temple.

74:9 no longer a prophet. Most troubling to Asaph was the absence of prophets to speak God's words to them and tell them when these troubles would end. During the exile, Jeremiah

was taken to Egypt (Jer. 43:6-7), and Ezekiel was deported to Babylon (Ezek. 1:1).

74:13-14 sea monster. Asaph recalls God's deliverance of His people from Egypt. The sea monster concept comes from Near Eastern creation myths, in which the creator battled a many-headed sea monster before establishing

and wash my hands in innocence for nothing?

14 For I am afflicted all day long,
and punished every morning.

15 If I had decided to say these things ⌊aloud⌋,
I would have betrayed Your people.ᵃ

16 When I tried to understand all this,
it seemed hopelessᵇ

17 until I entered God's sanctuary.
Then I understood their destiny.

18 Indeed You put them in slippery places;
You make them fall into ruin.

19 How suddenly they become a desolation!
They come to an end, swept away by terrors.

20 Like one waking from a dream,
Lord, when arising, You will despise their image.

21 When I became embittered
and my innermost beingᶜ was wounded,

22 I was a fool and didn't understand;
I was an unthinking animal toward You.

23 Yet I am always with You;
You hold my right hand.

24 You guide me with Your counsel,
and afterwards You will take me up in glory.ᵈ

25 Whom do I have in heaven but You?
And I desire nothing on earth but You.

26 My flesh and my heart may fail,
but God is the strengthᵉ of my heart,
my portion forever.

27 Those far from You will certainly perish;
You destroy all who are unfaithful to You.

28 But as for me, God's presence is my good.
I have made the Lord GOD my refuge,
so I can tell about all You do.

Psalm 74

Prayer for Israel

A •Maskil of •Asaph.

1 Why have You rejected ⌊us⌋ forever, God?
Why does Your anger burn
against the sheep of Your pasture?

2 Remember Your congregation,
which You purchased long ago
and redeemed as the tribe
for Your own possession.
⌊Remember⌋ Mount Zion where You dwell.

3 Make Your wayᶠ to the everlasting ruins,

to all that the enemy has destroyed
in the sanctuary.

4 Your adversaries roared in the meeting place
where You met with us.ᵍ
They set up their emblems as signs.

5 It was like men in a thicket of trees,
wielding axes,

6 then smashing all the carvings
with hatchets and picks.

7 They set Your sanctuary on fire;
they utterlyʰ desecrated
the dwelling place of Your name.

8 They said in their hearts,
"Let us oppress them relentlessly."
They burned down every place
throughout the land
where God met with us.ⁱ

9 We don't see any signs for us.
There is no longer a prophet.
And none of us knows how long this will last.

10 God, how long will the foe mock?
Will the enemy insult Your name forever?

11 Why do You hold back Your hand?
Stretch outʲ Your right hand and destroy ⌊them⌋!

12 God my king is from ancient times,
performing saving acts on the earth.

13 You divided the sea with Your strength;
You smashed the heads of the sea monsters
in the waters;

14 You crushed the heads of •Leviathan;
You fed him to the creatures of the desert.

15 You opened up springs and streams;
You dried up ever-flowing rivers.

16 The day is Yours, also the night;
You established the moon and the sun.

17 You set all the boundaries of the earth;
You made summer and winter.

18 Remember this: the enemy has mocked the LORD,
and a foolish people has insulted Your name.

19 Do not give the life of Your dove to beasts;ᵏ
do not forget the lives of Your poor people forever.

20 Consider the covenant,
for the dark places of the land
are full of violence.

21 Do not let the oppressed turn away in shame;
let the poor and needy praise Your name.

ᵃ73:15 Lit betrayed the generation of Your sons ᵇ73:16 Lit it was trouble in my eyes ᶜ73:21 Lit my kidneys ᵈ73:24 Or will receive me with honor ᵉ73:26 Lit rock ᶠ74:3 Lit Lift up Your steps ᵍ74:4 Lit in Your meeting place ʰ74:7 Lit they to the ground ⁱ74:8 Lit every meeting place of God in the land ʲ74:11 Lit From Your bosom ᵏ74:19 One Hb ms, LXX, Syr read Do not hand over to beasts a soul that praises You

---

order in creation. **Leviathan.** This may be a symbol for Satan; it may refer to the Egyptians—the monster of their captivity. God opened the Red Sea for the Hebrews but destroyed the Egyptians when they tried to follow.

74:15 springs and streams. God performed many water miracles. He gave the Israelites water in the wilderness (Ex. 17:5, 6; Num. 20:8-13), and enabled them to cross the Red Sea (Ex. 14) and the Jordan River (Josh. 3).

74:22-23 defend Your cause! Asaph thinks God should save His people for His own glory. Israel is His nation, so its suffering causes

God's name to be mocked. Israel's enemies are God's enemies.

75:2 When I choose a time. God will judge all people, but His judgment comes in His time, not ours. When He judges, no one on earth can help those under His wrath (v. 6).

22 Arise, God, defend Your cause!
Remember the insults
that fools bring against You all day long.
23 Do not forget the clamor of Your adversaries,
the tumult of Your opponents that goes up
constantly.

Psalm 75

God Judges the Wicked

For the choir director:
"Do Not Destroy."[a] A psalm
of •Asaph. A song.

1 We give thanks to You, God;
we give thanks to You, for Your name is near.
People tell about Your wonderful works.

2 "When I choose a time,
I will judge fairly.
3 When the earth and all its inhabitants shake,
I am the One who steadies its pillars.   •Selah
4 I say to the boastful, 'Do not boast,'
and to the wicked, 'Do not lift up your •horn.
5 Do not lift up your horn against heaven
or speak arrogantly.' "

6 Exaltation does not come
from the east, the west, or the desert,
7 for God is the judge:
He brings down one and exalts another.
8 For there is a cup in the LORD's hand,
full of wine blended with spices, and He pours
from it.
All the wicked of the earth will drink,
draining it to the dregs.

9 As for me, I will tell about Him forever;
I will sing praise to the God of Jacob.

10 "I will cut off all the horns of the wicked,
but the horns of the righteous will be lifted up."

Psalm 76

God, the Powerful Judge

For the choir director:
with stringed instruments. A psalm
of •Asaph. A song.

1 God is known in Judah;
His name is great in Israel.
2 His tent is in Salem,[b]
His dwelling place in Zion.

3 There He shatters the bow's flaming arrows,
the shield, the sword, and the weapons of war.
•Selah

4 You are resplendent and majestic
⌊coming down⌋ from the mountains of prey.
5 The brave-hearted have been plundered;
they have slipped into their ⌊final⌋ sleep.
None of the warriors was able to lift
a hand.
6 At Your rebuke, God of Jacob,
both chariot and horse lay still.

7 And You—You are to be •feared.[c]
When You are angry,
who can stand before You?
8 From heaven You pronounced judgment.
The earth feared and grew quiet
9 when God rose up to judge
and to save all the lowly of the earth.   Selah
10 Even human wrath will praise You;
You will clothe Yourself
with their remaining wrath.[d]

11 Make and keep your vows
to the LORD your God;
let all who are around Him bring tribute
to the awe-inspiring One.[e]
12 He humbles the spirit of leaders;
He is feared by the kings of the earth.

Psalm 77

Confidence in a Time of Crisis

For the choir director: according to
Jeduthun. Of •Asaph. A psalm.

1 I cry aloud to God,
aloud to God, and He will hear me.
2 In my day of trouble I sought the Lord.
My hands were lifted up all night long;
I refused to be comforted.
3 I think of God; I groan;
I meditate; my spirit becomes weak.   •Selah

4 You have kept me from closing my eyes;
I am troubled and cannot speak.
5 I consider days of old,
years long past.
6 At night I remember my music;
I meditate in my heart, and my spirit ponders.

7 "Will the Lord reject forever
and never again show favor?

---

[a] Apparently a tune for the psalm   [b] 76:2 Jerusalem   [c] 76:7 Or are awe-inspiring   [d] 76:10 Hb obscure   [e] 76:11 Or tribute with awe

---

75:4 boastful ... wicked. God warns those who misinterpret His delay. Make no mistake—judgment will come. The wicked are described in Psalm 73:4-12.

76:1 God is known. The good news of God's truth and power will be known particularly after the defeat of the enemies of Judah and Israel, His covenant people. Isaiah 36–37.

76:2 tent. This refers to the temple. Salem means Jerusalem.

Ps. 77 A picture of ordinary self-centered prayers—full of "I" references. I cry, I think, I groan. But at verse 11 Asaph changes his focus to God and is encouraged by remembering God's past deliverances.

77:16-19 trembled ... shook ... flashed. In vivid language, the poet describes God's display of power in delivering the Israelites from the Egyptians at the Red Sea (see Ex. 14).

8 Has His faithful love ceased forever?
  Is ⌊His⌋ promise at an end for all generations?
9 Has God forgotten to be gracious?
  Has He in anger withheld His compassion?"
                                    Selah

10 So I say, "It is my sorrow[a]
   that the right hand of the •Most High
      has changed."
11 I will remember the LORD's works;
   yes, I will remember Your ancient wonders.
12 I will reflect on all You have done
   and meditate on Your actions.

13 God, Your way is holy.
   What god is great like God?
14 You are the God who works wonders;
   You revealed Your strength among the peoples.
15 With power You redeemed Your people,
   the descendants of Jacob and Joseph.   *Selah*

16 The waters saw You, God.
   The waters saw You; they trembled.
   Even the depths shook.
17 The clouds poured down water.
   The storm clouds thundered;
   Your arrows flashed back and forth.
18 The sound of Your thunder was
      in the whirlwind;
   lightning lit up the world.
   The earth shook and quaked.
19 Your way went through the sea,
   and Your path through the great waters,
   but Your footprints were unseen.
20 You led Your people like a flock
   by the hand of Moses and Aaron.

Psalm 78

Lessons from Israel's Past

A •*Maskil* of •Asaph.

1 My people, hear my instruction;
  listen to what I say.
2 I will declare wise sayings;
  I will speak mysteries from the past—
3 things we have heard and known
  and that our fathers have passed down to us.
4 We must not hide them from their children,
  but must tell a future generation
  the praises of the LORD,
  His might, and the wonderful works
  He has performed.

5 He established a •testimony in Jacob
  and set up a law in Israel,
  which He commanded our fathers
  to teach to their children
6 so that a future generation—
  children yet to be born—might know.
  They were to rise and tell their children
7 so that they might put their confidence in God
  and not forget God's works,
  but keep His commandments.
8 Then they would not be like their fathers,
  a stubborn and rebellious generation,
  a generation whose heart was not loyal
  and whose spirit was not faithful to God.

9 The Ephraimite archers turned back
  on the day of battle.
10 They did not keep God's covenant
   and refused to live by His law.
11 They forgot what He had done,
   the wonderful works He had shown them.
12 He worked wonders in the sight of their fathers,
   in the land of Egypt, the region of Zoan.
13 He split the sea and brought them across;
   the water stood firm like a wall.
14 He led them with a cloud by day
   and with a fiery light throughout the night.
15 He split rocks in the wilderness
   and gave them drink as abundant as the depths.
16 He brought streams out of the stone
   and made water flow down like rivers.

17 But they continued to sin against Him,
   rebelling in the desert against the •Most High.
18 They deliberately[b] tested God,
   demanding the food they craved.
19 They spoke against God, saying,
   "Is God able to provide food in the wilderness?
20 Look! He struck the rock and water gushed out;
   torrents overflowed.
   But can He also provide bread
   or furnish meat for His people?"
21 Therefore, the LORD heard and became furious;
   then fire broke out against Jacob,
   and anger flared up against Israel
22 because they did not believe God
   or rely on His salvation.
23 He gave a command to the clouds above
   and opened the doors of heaven.
24 He rained manna for them to eat;
   He gave them grain from heaven.

[a]**77:10** Lit *"My piercing* [b]**78:18** Lit *in their heart*

78:2 wise sayings. The Hebrew word for wise sayings, *mashal*, also included the idea that the saying was concrete enough to be pictured in the mind's eye. Also used were dark sayings or secrets (*hidoth*). What he means here is that God's words make sense only to those whose eyes see the truth.

78:9-16 They forgot. The northern kingdom had forgotten God's miraculous acts and had broken God's covenantal law.

78:17-72 This passage is a long history lesson of God's gracious acts among His people. These lessons were repeated from one generation to the next to teach them the kind of God

they worshiped.

78:44-51 blood ... flies ... frogs. These verses recount the plagues God brought on Egypt (Ex. 7-12).

78:60 Shiloh. Located in Ephraim, Shiloh was the center of worship during the latter period of the judges until it was destroyed, most likely by

25 People[a] ate the bread of angels.[b]
   He sent them an abundant supply of food.
26 He made the east wind blow in the skies
   and drove the south wind by His might.
27 He rained meat on them like dust,
   and winged birds like the sand of the seas.
28 He made ⌊them⌋ fall in His camp,
   all around His tent.[c] [d]
29 They ate and were completely satisfied,
   for He gave them what they craved.
30 Before they had satisfied their desire,
   while the food was still in their mouths,
31 God's anger flared up against them,
   and He killed some of their best men.
   He struck down Israel's choice young men.
32 Despite all this, they kept sinning
   and did not believe His wonderful works.
33 He made their days end in futility,
   their years in sudden disaster.
34 When He killed ⌊some of⌋ them,
   ⌊the rest⌋ began to seek Him;
   they repented and searched for God.
35 They remembered that God was their rock,
   the Most High God, their Redeemer.
36 But they deceived Him with their mouths,
   they lied to Him with their tongues,
37 their hearts were insincere toward Him,
   and they were unfaithful to His covenant.
38 Yet He was compassionate;
   He •atoned for[e] ⌊their⌋ guilt
   and did not destroy ⌊them⌋.
   He often turned His anger aside
   and did not unleash[f] all His wrath.
39 He remembered that they were ⌊only⌋ flesh,
   a wind that passes and does not return.
40 How often they rebelled against Him
   in the wilderness
   and grieved Him in the desert.
41 They constantly tested God
   and provoked the Holy One of Israel.
42 They did not remember His power ⌊shown⌋
   on the day He redeemed them from the foe,
43 when He performed His miraculous signs
   in Egypt
   and His marvels in the region of Zoan.
44 He turned their rivers into blood,
   and they could not drink from their streams.

45 He sent among them swarms of flies,
   which fed on them,
   and frogs, which devastated them.
46 He gave their crops to the caterpillar
   and the fruit of their labor to the locust.
47 He killed their vines with hail
   and their sycamore-fig trees with a flood.
48 He handed over their livestock to hail
   and their cattle to lightning bolts.
49 He sent His burning anger against them:
   fury, indignation, and calamity—
   a band of deadly messengers.[g]
50 He cleared a path for His anger.
   He did not spare them from death,
   but delivered their lives to the plague.
51 He struck all the firstborn in Egypt,
   the first progeny of the tents of Ham.[h]
52 He led His people out like sheep
   and guided them like a flock in the wilderness.
53 He led them safely, and they were not afraid;
   but the sea covered their enemies.
54 He brought them to His holy land,
   to the mountain His right hand acquired.
55 He drove out nations before them.
   He apportioned their inheritance by lot
   and settled the tribes of Israel in their tents.

56 But they rebelliously tested
   the Most High God,
   for they did not keep His decrees.
57 They treacherously turned away
   like their fathers;
   they became warped like a faulty bow.
58 They enraged Him with their •high places
   and provoked His jealousy
   with their carved images.
59 God heard and became furious;
   He completely rejected Israel.
60 He abandoned the tabernacle at Shiloh,
   the tent where He resided among men.[i]
61 He gave up His strength[j] to captivity
   and His splendor to the hand of a foe.
62 He surrendered His people to the sword
   because He was enraged with His heritage.
63 Fire consumed His chosen young men,
   and His young women had no wedding songs.[k]
64 His priests fell by the sword,
   but the[l] widows could not lament.[m]

[a]78:25 Lit Man [b]78:25 Lit mighty ones [c]78:28 LXX, Syr read in their camp . . . their tents [d]78:28 Or in its camp, all around its tents [e]78:38 Or He wiped out, or He forgave [f]78:38 Or stir up [g]78:49 Or angels [h]78:51 Ham's descendants who settled in Egypt; Ps 105:23,27 [i]78:60 Hb adam [j]78:61 See Ps 132:8 where the ark of the covenant is the ark of His strength. [k]78:63 Lit virgins were not praised [l]78:64 Lit His [m]78:64 War probably prevented customary funerals.

the Philistines.

79:1-4 Jerusalem ... ruins. The psalm opens with a review of the nations' sin. Asaph laments the devastation of Jerusalem by foreign nations. God's temple had been defiled and destroyed. God's people lay slaughtered, their bodies eaten by animals because no one was

alive to bury the dead.

79:6 Pour out Your wrath. A prayer for curses on one's enemies is often part of psalms of lament. These prayers are based on God's covenant promise to Abraham to curse those who curse him (Gen. 12:2–3).

79:9-11 Deliver us. This is a prayer for God to help, to forgive His people, and to punish their enemies. The appeal claims God is not being true to Himself; He should present Himself as a God of vengeance to the nations.

80:1 Shepherd. God is portrayed as a shepherd of Israel, as in Psalm 23. Sheep have a

65 Then the Lord awoke as if from sleep,
   like a warrior from the effects of wine.
66 He beat back His foes;
   He gave them lasting shame.
67 He rejected the tent of Joseph
   and did not choose the tribe of Ephraim.
68 He chose instead the tribe of Judah,
   Mount Zion, which He loved.
69 He built His sanctuary like the heights,ᵃ
   like the earth that He established forever.
70 He chose David His servant
   and took him from the sheepfolds;
71 He brought him from tending ewes
   to be shepherd over His people Jacob—
   over Israel, His inheritance.
72 He shepherded them with a pure heart
   and guided them with his skillful hands.

Psalm 79

Faith amid Confusion

A psalm of •Asaph.

1 God, the nations have invaded Your inheritance,
   desecrated Your holy temple,
   and turned Jerusalem into ruins.
2 They gave the corpses of Your servants
   to the birds of the sky for food,
   the flesh of Your godly ones
   to the beasts of the earth.
3 They poured out their blood
   like water all around Jerusalem,
   and there was no one to bury ⌊them⌋.
4 We have become an object of reproach
   to our neighbors,
   a source of mockery and ridicule
   to those around us.

5 How long, LORD? Will You be angry forever?
   Will Your jealousy keep burning like fire?
6 Pour out Your wrath on the nations
   that don't acknowledge You,
   on the kingdoms that don't call on Your name,
7 for they have devoured Jacob
   and devastated his homeland.
8 Do not hold past sinsᵇ against us;
   let Your compassion come to us quickly,
   for we have become weak.

9 God of our salvation, help us—
   for the glory of Your name.

Deliver us and •atone forᶜ our sins,
   because of Your name.
10 Why should the nations ask,
   "Where is their God?"
   Before our eyes,
   let vengeance for the shed blood
      of Your servants
   be known among the nations.
11 Let the groans of the prisoners reach You;
   according to Your great power,
   preserve those condemned to die.

12 Pay back sevenfold to our neighbors
   the reproach they have hurled at You, Lord.
13 Then we, Your people, the sheep
      of Your pasture,
   will thank You forever;
   we will declare Your praise
   to generation after generation.

Psalm 80

A Prayer for Restoration

For the choir director:
according to "The Lilies."ᵈ
A testimony of •Asaph. A psalm.

1 Listen, Shepherd of Israel,
   who guides Joseph like a flock;
   You who sit enthroned ⌊on⌋ the •cherubim,
   rise up
2 at the head of Ephraim,
   Benjamin, and Manasseh.ᵉ
   Rally Your power and come to save us.
3 Restore us, God;
   look ⌊on us⌋ with favor,
   and we will be saved.

4 LORD God of •Hosts,
   how long will You be angry
   with Your people's prayers?
5 You fed them the bread of tears
   and gave them a full measureᶠ
   of tears to drink.
6 You set us at strife with our neighbors;
   our enemies make fun of us.
7 Restore us, God of Hosts;
   look ⌊on us⌋ with favor, and we will be saved.

8 You uprooted a vine from Egypt;
   You drove out the nations and planted it.

ᵃ**78:69** Either the heights of heaven or the mountain heights ᵇ**79:8** Or *hold the sins of past generations* ᶜ**79:9** Or *and wipe out,* or *and forgive*
ᵈPossibly a hymn tune; compare Pss 45; 60; 69 ᵉ**80:2** See Nm 2:17–24 for the order of these names in the marching order of the camp of Israel.
ᶠ**80:5** Lit *a one-third measure*

---

tendency to wander and get lost without a shepherd to lead them. See also, John 10.

80:3 look ⌊on us⌋ with favor. The phrasing of this verse echoes the priestly benediction "The LORD make His face shine on you" (Num. 6:25).

80:5 bread of tears. This is a reference to the manna and water that God provided for Israel

in the wilderness (Ex. 16:4; Num. 20:1-13).

80:8-16 vine … planted. This passage shows God as a gardener caring for Israel, the vine (Isa. 5:1-7; Hos. 10:1; John 15).

80:12 broken down its walls. The Lord removed His hand of protection from Israel.

Ps. 81 This festival psalm begins as a psalm of praise and becomes a call to obedience. It was probably used at the Feast of Tabernacles (v. 3) that commemorated God's care of His people during the desert journey.

81:6 I relieved his … burden. God delivered His people from forced labor in Egypt

⁹ You cleared ⌊a place⌋ for it;
it took root and filled the land.
¹⁰ The mountains were covered by its shade,
and the mighty cedars[a] with its branches.
¹¹ It sent out sprouts toward the Sea[b]
and shoots toward the River.[c]

¹² Why have You broken down its walls
so that all who pass by pick its fruit?
¹³ The boar from the forest gnaws at it,
and creatures of the field feed on it.
¹⁴ Return, God of Hosts.
Look down from heaven and see;
take care of this vine,
¹⁵ the root[d] Your right hand has planted,
the shoot[e] that You made strong for Yourself.
¹⁶ It was cut down and burned up;[f]
they[g] perish at the rebuke of Your countenance.
¹⁷ Let Your hand be with the man
at Your right hand,
with the son of man
You have made strong for Yourself.
¹⁸ Then we will not turn away from You;
revive us, and we will call on Your name.
¹⁹ Restore us, LORD God of Hosts;
look ⌊on us⌋ with favor, and we will be saved.

Psalm 81

A Call to Obedience

For the choir director: on the •Gittith.
Of •Asaph.

¹ Sing for joy to God our strength;
shout in triumph to the God of Jacob.
² Lift up a song—play the tambourine,
the melodious lyre, and the harp.
³ Blow the horn during the new moon
and during the full moon,
on the day of our feast.[h]
⁴ For this is a statute for Israel,
a judgment of the God of Jacob.
⁵ He set it up as an ordinance for Joseph
when He went throughout[i] the land of Egypt.

I heard an unfamiliar language:
⁶ "I relieved his shoulder from the burden;
his hands were freed from ⌊carrying⌋ the basket.
⁷ You called out in distress, and I rescued you;
I answered you from the thundercloud.
I tested you at the waters of Meribah.   •Selah

⁸ Listen, My people, and I will admonish you.
Israel, if you would only listen to Me!
⁹ There must not be a strange god
among you;
you must not bow down to a foreign god.
¹⁰ I am •Yahweh your God,
who brought you up from the land of Egypt.
Open your mouth wide, and I will fill it.

¹¹ "But My people did not listen to Me;
Israel did not obey Me.
¹² So I gave them over to their stubborn hearts
to follow their own plans.
¹³ If only My people would listen to Me
and Israel would follow My ways,
¹⁴ I would quickly subdue their enemies
and turn My hand against their foes."
¹⁵ Those who hate the LORD
would pretend submission to Him;
their doom would last forever.
¹⁶ But He would feed Israel[j]
with the best wheat.
"I would satisfy you with honey
from the rock."

Psalm 82

A Plea for Righteous Judgment

A psalm of •Asaph.

¹ God has taken His place in the divine assembly;
He judges among the gods:[k]
² "How long will you judge unjustly
and show partiality to the wicked?   •Selah
³ Provide justice for the needy
and the fatherless;
uphold the rights of the oppressed
and the destitute.
⁴ Rescue the poor and needy;
save them from the hand of the wicked."

⁵ They do not know or understand;
they wander in darkness.
All the foundations of the earth are shaken.

⁶ I said, "You are gods;
you are all sons of the •Most High.
⁷ However, you will die like men
and fall like any other ruler."

⁸ Rise up, God, judge the earth,
for all the nations belong to You.

---

[a]**80:10** Lit *the cedars of God*   [b]**80:11** The Mediterranean   [c]**80:11** The Euphrates   [d]**80:15** Hb obscure   [e]**80:15** Or *son*   [f]**80:16** Lit *burned with fire*   [g]**80:16** Or *may they*   [h]**81:3** Either Passover or Tabernacles   [i]**81:5** LXX, Syr, Jer read *out of*   [j]**81:16** Lit *him*   [k]**82:1** Either heavenly beings or earthly rulers

---

where they made and hauled bricks (Ex. 1).

81:16 best wheat ... honey from the rock. God promised prosperity for obedience. Wheat and honey (which often came from hives built among rocks) were symbols of prosperity.

82:1 divine assembly. This is the psalmist's vision of God presiding over the court of judgment in heaven. The rulers and judges of the earth are called before Him to give account of their judgments.

83:1-4 Asaph calls on God to judge the wicked and to protect Israel in the face of grave dan-

ger. The Jews took God for granted, believing He would automatically answer any time they prayed.

83:15 Your tempest ... Your storm. God, pictured here as a heavenly warrior, uses natural disasters as a weapon against enemies.

Psalm 83

Prayer against Enemies

A song. A psalm of •Asaph.

1 God, do not keep silent.
  Do not be deaf, God; do not be idle.
2 See how Your enemies make an uproar;
  those who hate You have
    acted arrogantly.ª
3 They devise clever schemes
    against Your people;
  they conspire against Your treasured ones.
4 They say, "Come, let us wipe them out
    as a nation
  so that Israel's name will no longer
    be remembered."
5 For they have conspired with one mind;
  they form an allianceᵇ against You—
6 the tents of Edom and the Ishmaelites,
  Moab and the Hagrites,
7 Gebal, Ammon, and Amalek,
  Philistia with the inhabitants of Tyre.
8 Even Assyria has joined them;
  they lend supportᶜ to the sons of Lot.ᵈ •Selah

9 Deal with them as ⌊You did⌋ with Midian,
  as ⌊You did⌋ with Sisera
  and Jabin at the Kishon River.
10 They were destroyed at En-dor;
  they became manure for the ground.
11 Make their nobles like Oreb and Zeeb,
  and all their tribal leaders like Zebah
    and Zalmunna,
12 who said, "Let us seize God's pastures
    for ourselves."

13 Make them like tumbleweed, my God,
  like straw before the wind.
14 As fire burns a forest,
  as a flame blazes through mountains,
15 so pursue them with Your tempest
  and terrify them with Your storm.
16 Cover their faces with shame
  so that they will seek Your name, LORD.
17 Let them be put to shame
    and terrified forever;
  let them perish in disgrace.
18 May they know that You alone—
  whose name is •Yahweh—
  are the •Most High over all the earth.

Psalm 84

Longing for God's House

For the choir director: on the •Gittith.
A psalm of the sons of Korah.

1 How lovely is Your dwelling place,
  LORD of •Hosts.
2 I long and yearn
  for the courts of the LORD;
  my heart and flesh cry out forᵉ the living God.

3 Even a sparrow finds a home,
  and a swallow, a nest for herself
  where she places her young—
  near Your altars, LORD of Hosts,
  my King and my God.
4 How happy are those who reside in Your house,
  who praise You continually. •Selah

5 Happy are the people whose strength is in You,
  whose hearts are set on pilgrimage.
6 As they pass through the Valley of Baca,ᶠ
  they make it a source of springwater;
  even the autumn rain will cover it with blessings.ᵍ
7 They go from strength to strength;
  each appears before God in Zion.

8 LORD God of Hosts, hear my prayer;
  listen, God of Jacob. Selah
9 Consider our shield,ʰ God;
  look on the face of Your anointed one.

10 Better a day in Your courts
  than a thousand ⌊anywhere else⌋.
  I would rather be at the door of the house
    of my God
  than to live in the tents of the wicked.
11 For the LORD God is a sun and shield.
  The LORD gives grace and glory;
  He does not withhold the good
  from those who live with integrity.
12 LORD of Hosts,
  happy is the person who trusts in You!

Psalm 85

Restoration of Favor

For the choir director. A psalm
of the sons of Korah.

1 LORD, You showed favor to Your land;
  You restored Jacob's prosperity.ⁱ

ª83:2 Lit have lifted their head ᵇ83:5 Lit they cut a covenant ᶜ83:8 Lit they are an arm ᵈ83:8 Moab and Edom ᵉ84:2 Or flesh shout for joy to
ᶠ84:6 Or Valley of Tears ᵍ84:6 Or pools ʰ84:9 The king ⁱ85:1 Or restored Jacob from captivity

---

83:18 May they know. Asaph's motive in asking God to wipe out Israel's enemies is that God's name will be glorified.

84:5 whose strength is in You. Happy are the people who love God and come to Zion, not so much from obligation as for joy at drawing near to God.

84:6 Valley of Baca. Also translated Valley of Weeping, this phrase refers to the difficulties pilgrims face on their journey through life.

85:9 glory. The manifestation of God's presence is called His glory. Recall that Moses could only see the back of God's glory lest it kill him (Ex. 33).

86:1 poor and needy. "Poor" here does not necessarily mean those who are economically destitute, but those who realize they are totally dependent on God (see 34:6; 35:10).

86:5-7 I call … You will answer. In the middle of trouble David trusts God. Clearly, David knows the meaning of praying without ceasing.

2 You took away Your people's guilt;
You covered all their sin.   •Selah

3 You withdrew all Your fury;
You turned from Your burning anger.

4 Return to us, God of our salvation,
and abandon Your displeasure with us.

5 Will You be angry with us forever?
Will You prolong Your anger for all generations?

6 Will You not revive us again
so that Your people may rejoice in You?

7 Show us Your faithful love, LORD,
and give us Your salvation.

8 I will listen to what God will say;
surely the LORD will declare peace
to His people, His godly ones,
and not let them go back to foolish ways.

9 His salvation is very near those who fear Him,
so that glory may dwell in our land.

10 Faithful love and truth will join together;
righteousness and peace will embrace.

11 Truth will spring up from the earth,
and righteousness will look down from heaven.

12 Also, the LORD will provide what is good,
and our land will yield its crops.

13 Righteousness will go before Him
to prepare the way for His steps.

Psalm 86

Lament and Petition

A Davidic prayer.

1 Listen, LORD, and answer me,
for I am poor and needy.

2 Protect my life, for I am faithful.
You are my God; save Your servant who trusts
in You.

3 Be gracious to me, Lord,
for I call to You all day long.

4 Bring joy to Your servant's life,
since I set my hope on You, Lord.

5 For You, Lord, are kind and ready to forgive,
abundant in faithful love to all who call on You.

6 LORD, hear my prayer;
listen to my plea for mercy.

7 I call on You in the day of my distress,
for You will answer me.

8 Lord, there is no one like You among the gods,
and there are no works like Yours.

a87:2 Places in Israel   b87:4 Modern Sudan

9 All the nations You have made
will come and bow down before You, Lord,
and will honor Your name.

10 For You are great and perform wonders;
You alone are God.

11 Teach me Your way, LORD,
and I will live by Your truth.
Give me an undivided mind to fear Your name.

12 I will praise You with all my heart, Lord my God,
and will honor Your name forever.

13 For Your faithful love for me is great,
and You deliver my life from the depths
of •Sheol.

14 God, arrogant people have attacked me;
a gang of ruthless men seeks my life.
They have no regard for You.

15 But You, Lord, are a compassionate
and gracious God,
slow to anger and abundant in faithful love
and truth.

16 Turn to me and be gracious to me.
Give Your strength to Your servant;
save the son of Your female servant.

17 Show me a sign of Your goodness;
my enemies will see and be put to shame
because You, LORD, have helped
and comforted me.

Psalm 87

Zion, the City of God

A psalm of the sons of Korah.
A song.

1 His foundation is on the holy mountains.

2 The LORD loves the gates of Zion
more than all the dwellings of Jacob.a

3 Glorious things are said about you,
city of God.   •Selah

4 "I will mention those who know Me:
•Rahab, Babylon, Philistia, Tyre, and •Cushb —
each one was born there."

5 And it will be said of Zion,
"This one and that one were born in her."
The •Most High Himself will establish her.

6 When He registers the peoples,
the LORD will record,
"This one was born there."   Selah

7 Singers and dancers alike [will say],
"All my springs are in you."

86:9 All the nations. God's work on behalf of Israel will cause the whole world to acknowledge Him—a prominent theme throughout Psalms (22:27; 47:9; 66:1-7; 86:9) and the Old Testament (Ex. 7:5; Lev. 26:45; 1 Sam. 17:46; 1 Kings 8:41-43; Ezek. 20:41).

86:14 ruthless. The Hebrew word includes the concept of ferocious violence that has no regard for God (Jer. 20:11). Throughout the Psalms, God is described as the enemy of the proud and the helper of the humble (138:6; 147:6).

87:1 His foundation. God Himself established the foundations of the city on a mountain, Mt.

Zion (48:2; 68:15-16; Isa. 14:32). The city included the temple Solomon built.

87:4 Rahab. This is a reference to Egypt (Isa. 30:7) rather than to the legendary sea monster.

87:5 This one and that one. Wherever God's people are scattered in the world, their "home"

Psalm 88

A Cry of Desperation

A song. A psalm of the sons
of Korah. For the choir director:
according to *Mahalath Leannoth*.
A •*Maskil* of Heman the Ezrahite.

1 LORD, God of my salvation,
I cry out before You day and night.
2 May my prayer reach Your presence;
listen to my cry.

3 For I have had enough troubles,
and my life is near •Sheol.
4 I am counted among those going down to the •Pit.
I am like a man without strength,
5 abandoned[a] among the dead.
I am like the slain lying in the grave,
whom You no longer remember,
and who are cut off from Your care.[b]

6 You have put me in the lowest part of the Pit,
in the darkest places, in the depths.
7 Your wrath weighs heavily on me;
You have overwhelmed me
with all Your waves. *Selah*

8 You have distanced my friends from me;
You have made me repulsive to them.
I am shut in and cannot go out.
9 My eyes are worn out from crying.
LORD, I cry out to You all day long;
I spread out my hands to You.

10 Do You work wonders for the dead?
Do departed spirits rise up to praise You? *Selah*
11 Will Your faithful love be declared in the grave,
Your faithfulness in •Abaddon?
12 Will Your wonders be known in the darkness,
or Your righteousness in the land of oblivion?

13 But I call to You for help, LORD;
in the morning my prayer meets You.
14 LORD, why do You reject me?
Why do You hide Your face from me?
15 From my youth,
I have been afflicted and near death.
I suffer Your horrors; I am desperate.
16 Your wrath sweeps over me;
Your terrors destroy me.
17 They surround me like water all day long;
they close in on me from every side.

18 You have distanced loved one and neighbor
from me;
darkness is my ⌊only⌋ friend.[c]

Psalm 89

Perplexity about God's Promises

A •*Maskil* of Ethan the Ezrahite.

1 I will sing about the LORD's faithful love forever;
with my mouth
I will proclaim Your faithfulness to all generations.
2 For I will declare,
"Faithful love is built up forever;
You establish Your faithfulness in the heavens."

3 ⌊The LORD said,⌋
"I have made a covenant with My chosen one;
I have sworn an oath to David My servant:
4 'I will establish your offspring forever
and build up your throne
for all generations.'" *Selah*

5 LORD, the heavens praise Your wonders—
Your faithfulness also—
in the assembly of the holy ones.
6 For who in the skies can compare
with the LORD?
Who among the heavenly beings[d] is like the LORD?
7 God is greatly feared in the council
of the holy ones,
more awe-inspiring than[e] all who surround Him.
8 LORD God of •Hosts,
who is strong like You, LORD?
Your faithfulness surrounds You.
9 You rule the raging sea;
when its waves surge, You still them.
10 You crushed •Rahab like one who is slain;
You scattered Your enemies
with Your powerful arm.
11 The heavens are Yours; the earth also is Yours.
The world and everything in it—
You founded them.
12 North and south—You created them.
Tabor and Hermon shout for joy at Your name.
13 You have a mighty arm;
Your hand is powerful;
Your right hand is lifted high.
14 Righteousness and justice are the foundation
of Your throne;
faithful love and truth go before You.

---

a **88:5** Or *set free*   b **88:5** Or *hand*   c **88:18** Or *from me, my friends. Oh darkness!*   d **89:6** Or *the angels, or the sons of the mighty*   e **89:7** Or *ones, revered by*

---

is in God's covenant and His holy city, Zion.
87:7 springs. Zion is a refreshing spring, the only source of God and salvation.
88:1-2 I cry out. The psalmist cries out to God for salvation. The verb indicates a loud scream or desperate weeping.

88:5 no longer remember. God's care appears to end at death, after which God no longer needs to rescue the suffering one (25:7; 106:4).
89:19-29 David My servant. The psalmist recounts God's eternal covenant with David as king and steward of God's peo-

ple.

89:27 firstborn. This verse prefigures Christ as God's firstborn.
89:52 Amen. This verse was probably added later to conclude Book III of the Psalms on a note of praise.

15 Happy are the people who know the joyful shout;
LORD, they walk in the light of Your presence.
16 They rejoice in Your name all day long,
and they are exalted by Your righteousness.
17 For You are their magnificent strength;
by Your favor our •horn is exalted.
18 Surely our shield[a] belongs to the LORD,
our king to the Holy One of Israel.

19 You once spoke in a vision to Your loyal ones
and said: "I have granted help to a warrior;
I have exalted one chosen[b] from the people.
20 I have found David My servant;
I have anointed him with My sacred oil.
21 My hand will always be with him,
and My arm will strengthen him.
22 The enemy will not afflict[c] him;
no wicked man will oppress him.
23 I will crush his foes before him
and strike those who hate him.
24 My faithfulness and love will be with him,
and through My name
his horn will be exalted.
25 I will extend his power to the sea
and his right hand to the rivers.
26 He will call to Me, 'You are my Father,
my God, the rock of my salvation.'
27 I will also make him My firstborn,
greatest of the kings of the earth.
28 I will always preserve My faithful love for him,
and My covenant with him will endure.
29 I will establish his line forever,
his throne as long as heaven lasts.[d]
30 If his sons forsake My instruction
and do not live by My ordinances,
31 if they dishonor My statutes
and do not keep My commandments,
32 then I will call their rebellion
to account with the rod,
their sin with blows.
33 But I will not withdraw
My faithful love from him
or betray My faithfulness.
34 I will not violate My covenant
or change what My lips have said.
35 Once and for all
I have sworn an oath by My holiness;
I will not lie to David.
36 His offspring will continue forever,
his throne like the sun before Me,

37 like the moon, established forever,
a faithful witness in the sky." *Selah*
38 But You have spurned and rejected him;
You have become enraged with Your anointed.
39 You have repudiated the covenant
with Your servant;
You have completely dishonored his crown.[e]
40 You have broken down all his walls;
You have reduced his fortified cities to ruins.
41 All who pass by plunder him;
he has become a joke to his neighbors.
42 You have lifted high the right hand of his foes;
You have made all his enemies rejoice.
43 You have also turned back his sharp sword
and have not let him stand in battle.
44 You have made his splendor[f] cease
and have overturned his throne.
45 You have shortened the days of his youth;
You have covered him with shame. *Selah*

46 How long, LORD? Will You hide Yourself forever?
Will Your anger keep burning like fire?
47 Remember how short my life is.
Have You created •everyone for nothing?
48 What man can live and never see death?
Who can save himself from the power of •Sheol?
Selah

49 Lord, where are the former acts
of Your faithful love
that You swore to David in Your faithfulness?
50 Remember, Lord, the ridicule
against Your servants—
in my heart I carry ⌊abuse⌋ from all the peoples—
51 how Your enemies have ridiculed, LORD,
how they have ridiculed every step
of Your anointed.

52 May the LORD be praised forever.
•Amen and amen.

BOOK IV
(Psalms 90–106)
Psalm 90
Eternal God and Mortal Man

A prayer of Moses the man of God.

1 Lord, You have been our refuge[g]
in every generation.

---

a **89:18** The king   b **89:19** Or *exalted a young man*   c **89:22** Or *not exact tribute from*   d **89:29** Lit *as days of heaven*   e **89:39** Lit *have dishonored his crown to the ground*   f **89:44** Hb obscure   g **90:1** A few Hb mss, LXX; MT reads *dwelling place*

Ps. 90 Several characteristics of God are highlighted in this psalm: a safe place (1); creative (2); eternal (4); present (8); angry at sin (7,11); compassionate (13); loving (14); splendid (16). Only this psalm is attributed to Moses, who wrote two other poems in the Pentateuch (Ex. 15; Deut. 32).

90:10 seventy ... eighty. Human life is brief and death is inevitable.

91:3 hunter's net. The net depicted danger from any enemy. "Refuge" and "fortress" (v. 2), present the opposite image for

God, making it clear that security resides only in a right relationship with Him.

91:12 against a stone. God constantly watches over His people, sending angels to guard and protect them even from common mishaps. This does not mean believers won't ever have difficulties; instead, it reminds us

2 Before the mountains were born,
before You gave birth to the earth
and the world,
from eternity to eternity, You are God.

3 You return mankind to the dust,
saying, "Return, descendants of Adam."
4 For in Your sight a thousand years
are like yesterday that passes by,
like a few hours of the night.
5 You end their life;[a] they sleep.
They are like grass that grows in the morning—
6 in the morning it sprouts and grows;
by evening it withers and dries up.

7 For we are consumed by Your anger;
we are terrified by Your wrath.
8 You have set our unjust ways before You,
our secret sins in the light of Your presence.
9 For all our days ebb away under Your wrath;
we end our years like a sigh.
10 Our lives last[b] seventy years
or, if we are strong, eighty years.
Even the best of them are[c] struggle and sorrow;
indeed, they pass quickly and we fly away.
11 Who understands the power of Your anger?
Your wrath matches the fear that is due You.
12 Teach us to number our days carefully
so that we may develop wisdom in our hearts.[d]

13 LORD—how long?
Turn and have compassion on Your servants.
14 Satisfy us in the morning with Your faithful love
so that we may shout with joy and be glad
all our days.
15 Make us rejoice for as many days
as You have humbled us,
for as many years as we have seen adversity.
16 Let Your work be seen by Your servants,
and Your splendor by their children.
17 Let the favor of the Lord our God be on us;
establish for us the work of our hands—
establish the work of our hands!

Psalm 91

The Protection of the Most High

1 The one who lives under the protection
of the •Most High
dwells in the shadow of the •Almighty.

2 I will say[e] to the LORD, "My refuge
and my fortress,
my God, in whom I trust."

3 He Himself will deliver you from the hunter's net,
from the destructive plague.
4 He will cover you with His feathers;
you will take refuge under His wings.
His faithfulness will be a protective shield.
5 You will not fear the terror of the night,
the arrow that flies by day,
6 the plague that stalks in darkness,
or the pestilence that ravages at noon.
7 Though a thousand fall at your side
and ten thousand at your right hand,
the pestilence will not reach you.
8 You will only see it with your eyes
and witness the punishment of the wicked.

9 Because you have made the LORD—my refuge,
the Most High—your dwelling place,
10 no harm will come to you;
no plague will come near your tent.
11 For He will give His angels orders
concerning you,
to protect you in all your ways.
12 They will support you with their hands
so that you will not strike your foot
against a stone.
13 You will tread on the lion and the cobra;
you will trample the young lion and the serpent.

14 Because he is lovingly devoted to Me,
I will deliver him;
I will exalt him because he knows My name.
15 When he calls out to Me, I will answer him;
I will be with him in trouble.
I will rescue him and give him honor.
16 I will satisfy him with a long life
and show him My salvation.

Psalm 92

God's Love and Faithfulness

A psalm. A song for
the Sabbath day.

1 It is good to praise the LORD,
to sing praise to Your name, •Most High,
2 to declare Your faithful love in the morning
and Your faithfulness at night,

---

a **90:5** Or *You overwhelm them*; Hb uncertain   b **90:10** Lit *The days of our years in them*   c **90:10** LXX, Tg, Syr, Vg read *Even their span is*; Hb obscure   d **90:12** Or *develop a heart of wisdom*   e **91:1–2** LXX, Syr, Jer read *Almighty, saying*, or *Almighty, he will say*

---

of God's constant awareness and concern for us.

91:13 lion ... cobra ... young lion ... serpent. Lions, cobras, and snakes are common in the Middle East and posed an unpredictable and deadly threat to people. God is not unaware of

attack and can protect us.

Ps. 92 For the Sabbath day. Psalm 92 is a song to be sung at morning worship on the Sabbath. Every day of the week had a psalm designated for morning worship.

92:4-5 I will shout for joy. God's works are worthy of being joyfully shouted to the whole

world. These verses are more exclamations or shouts than mere words to recite.

92:10-11 horn. The "horn" symbolized strength, and so the writer is grateful to God for exalting him with strength like that of an ox.

92:12-13 palm tree ... cedar. Palms were valued for their straightness and height. Cedars of

3 with a ten-stringed harp
   and the music of a lyre.

4 For You have made me rejoice, LORD,
   by what You have done;
   I will shout for joy
   because of the works of Your hands.

5 How magnificent are Your works, LORD,
   how profound Your thoughts!

6 A stupid person does not know,
   a fool does not understand this:

7 though the wicked sprout like grass
   and all evildoers flourish,
   they will be eternally destroyed.

8 But You, LORD, are exalted forever.

9 For indeed, LORD, Your enemies—
   indeed, Your enemies will perish;
   all evildoers will be scattered.

10 You have lifted up my •horn
   like that of a wild ox;
   I have been anointed[a] with oil.

11 My eyes look down on my enemies;
   my ears hear evildoers when they attack me.

12 The righteous thrive like a palm tree
   and grow like a cedar tree in Lebanon.

13 Planted in the house of the LORD,
   they thrive in the courtyards of our God.

14 They will still bear fruit in old age,
   healthy and green,

15 to declare: "The LORD is just;
   He is my rock,
   and there is no unrighteousness in Him."

Psalm 93
God's Eternal Reign

1 The LORD reigns! He is robed in majesty;
   The LORD is robed, enveloped in strength.
   The world is firmly established;
   it cannot be shaken.

2 Your throne has been established
   from the beginning;[b]
   You are from eternity.

3 The floods have lifted up, LORD,
   the floods have lifted up their voice;
   the floods lift up their pounding waves.

4 Greater than the roar of many waters—
   the mighty breakers of the sea—
   the LORD on high is majestic.

5 LORD, Your testimonies are completely reliable;
   holiness is the beauty of[c] Your house
   for all the days to come.

Psalm 94
The Just Judge

1 LORD, God of vengeance—
   God of vengeance, appear.

2 Rise up, Judge of the earth;
   repay the proud what they deserve.

3 LORD, how long will the wicked—
   how long will the wicked gloat?

4 They pour out arrogant words;
   all the evildoers boast.

5 LORD, they crush Your people;
   they afflict Your heritage.

6 They kill the widow and the foreigner
   and murder the fatherless.

7 They say, "The LORD doesn't see it.
   The God of Jacob doesn't pay attention."

8 Pay attention, you stupid people!
   Fools, when will you be wise?

9 Can the One who shaped the ear not hear,
   the One who formed the eye not see?

10 The One who instructs nations,
   the One who teaches man knowledge—
   does He not discipline?

11 The LORD knows man's thoughts;
   they are meaningless.[d]

12 LORD, happy is the man You discipline
   and teach from Your law

13 to give him relief from troubled times
   until a pit is dug for the wicked.

14 The LORD will not forsake His people
   or abandon His heritage,

15 for justice will again be righteous,
   and all the upright in heart will follow[e] it.

16 Who stands up for me against the wicked?
   Who takes a stand for me
   against evildoers?

17 If the LORD had not been my help,
   I would soon rest in the silence [of death].

18 If I say, "My foot is slipping,"
   Your faithful love will support me, LORD.

19 When I am filled with cares,
   Your comfort brings me joy.

---

[a] 92:10 Syr reads You have anointed me [b] 93:2 Lit from then [c] 93:5 Or holiness characterizes [d] 94:11 Or futile [e] 94:15 Or heart will support; lit heart after

---

Lebanon were magnificent trees that grew up to 120 feet tall and 40 feet in circumference. Supposedly there are cedars growing there today which are 2,000 years old.
93:1-2 The LORD ... is robed. To help the people connect to an invisible God, He is pictured as wearing a robe and crown (see 47 and 95-

99).
94:1 vengeance. Vengeance is God's privilege because only God is holy and wise enough to mete out true justice. (Deut. 32:35, 41; Rom. 12:19; Heb. 10:30).
94:12-15 discipline ... teach. Our entire lives are to be spent learning the ways of God.

95:3-5 in His hand. God holds all of creation in His hand. Many ancient religions had gods that ruled over various aspects of creation (the sea, fire, the skies).
95:6-11 worship. True worship of God involves obedience.
95:8 Meribah ... Massah. The psalmist re-

20 Can a corrupt throne—
one that creates trouble by law—
become Your ally?
21 They band together against the life
of the righteous
and condemn the innocent to death.
22 But the LORD is my refuge;
my God is the rock of my protection.
23 He will pay them back for their sins
and destroy them for their evil.
The LORD our God will destroy them.

Psalm 95
Worship and Warning

1 Come, let us shout joyfully to the LORD,
shout triumphantly to the rock of our salvation!
2 Let us enter His presence with thanksgiving;
let us shout triumphantly to Him in song.

3 For the LORD is a great God,
a great King above all gods.
4 The depths of the earth are in His hand,
and the mountain peaks are His.
5 The sea is His; He made it.
His hands formed the dry land.

6 Come, let us worship and bow down;
let us kneel before the LORD our Maker.
7 For He is our God,
and we are the people of His pasture,
the sheep under His care.[a]

Today, if you hear His voice:
8 "Do not harden your hearts as at Meribah,
as on that day at Massah in the wilderness
9 where your fathers tested Me;
they tried Me, though they had seen what I did.
10 For 40 years I was disgusted
with that generation;
I said, 'They are a people whose hearts
go astray;
they do not know My ways.'
11 So I swore in My anger,
'They will not enter My rest.'"

Psalm 96
King of the Earth

1 Sing a new song to the LORD;
sing to the LORD, all the earth.

2 Sing to the LORD, praise His name;
proclaim His salvation from day to day.
3 Declare His glory among the nations,
His wonderful works among all peoples.

4 For the LORD is great and is highly praised;
He is feared above all gods.
5 For all the gods of the peoples are idols,
but the LORD made the heavens.
6 Splendor and majesty are before Him;
strength and beauty are in His sanctuary.

7 Ascribe to the LORD, you families of the peoples,
ascribe to the LORD glory and strength.
8 Ascribe to the LORD the glory of His name;
bring an offering and enter His courts.
9 Worship the LORD in the splendor
of [His] holiness;
tremble before Him, all the earth.

10 Say among the nations: "The LORD reigns.
The world is firmly established; it cannot
be shaken.
He judges the peoples fairly."
11 Let the heavens be glad and the earth rejoice;
let the sea and all that fills it resound.
12 Let the fields and everything in them exult.
Then all the trees of the forest will shout for joy
13 before the LORD, for He is coming—
for He is coming to judge the earth.
He will judge the world with righteousness
and the peoples with His faithfulness.

Psalm 97
The Majestic King

1 The LORD reigns! Let the earth rejoice;
let the many coasts and islands be glad.

2 Clouds and thick darkness surround Him;
righteousness and justice are the foundation
of His throne.
3 Fire goes before Him
and burns up His foes on every side.
4 His lightning lights up the world;
the earth sees and trembles.
5 The mountains melt like wax
at the presence of the LORD—
at the presence of the Lord of all the earth.

6 The heavens proclaim His righteousness;
all the peoples see His glory.

---

a **95:7** Lit sheep of His hand

minds the readers of their ancestors' disobedience against God. After all the miracles in Egypt, the people complained. At Meribah and Massah, God told Moses to strike a rock with his staff and give water to the people (Ex. 17:1-7).

95:10 40 years. The people's lack of faith in God was evident throughout the travels to the promised land. They feared and rebelled (Num. 14:1-38) until God was so angry that He sent them to wander forty years in the desert.

97:1 coasts. The Lord reigns not just in the land of Israel.

97:3 fire. Fire may represent destruction of enemies, but it can also be a refining and cleansing agent.

97:8-12 Zion. This is another name for Jerusalem, the holy city. They will rejoice when God is exalted there.

7 All who serve carved images,
those who boast in idols, will be put to shame.
All the gods[a] must worship Him.

8 Zion hears and is glad,
and the towns[b] of Judah rejoice
because of Your judgments, LORD.
9 For You, LORD,
are the •Most High over all the earth;
You are exalted above all the gods.

10 You who love the LORD, hate evil!
He protects the lives of His godly ones;
He rescues them from the hand of the wicked.
11 Light dawns[c] [d] for the righteous,
gladness for the upright in heart.
12 Be glad in the LORD, you righteous ones,
and praise His holy name.[e]

Psalm 98

Praise the King

A psalm.

1 Sing a new song to the LORD,
for He has performed wonders;
His right hand and holy arm
have won Him victory.
2 The LORD has made His victory known;
He has revealed His righteousness
in the sight of the nations.
3 He has remembered His love
and faithfulness to the house of Israel;
all the ends of the earth
have seen our God's victory.

4 Shout to the LORD, all the earth;
be jubilant, shout for joy, and sing.
5 Sing to the LORD with the lyre,
with the lyre and melodious song.
6 With trumpets and the blast of the ram's horn
shout triumphantly
in the presence of the LORD, our King.

7 Let the sea and all that fills it,
the world and those who live in it, resound.
8 Let the rivers clap their hands;
let the mountains shout together for joy
9 before the LORD,
for He is coming to judge the earth.
He will judge the world righteously
and the peoples fairly.

Psalm 99

The King Is Holy

1 The LORD reigns! Let the peoples tremble.
He is enthroned above the •cherubim.
Let the earth quake.
2 The LORD is great in Zion;
He is exalted above all the peoples.
3 Let them praise Your great
and awe-inspiring name.
He is holy.

4 The mighty King loves justice.
You have established fairness;
You have administered justice
and righteousness in Jacob.
5 Exalt the LORD our God;
bow in worship at His footstool.
He is holy.

6 Moses and Aaron were among His priests;
Samuel also was among those calling on
His name.
They called to the LORD, and He answered them.
7 He spoke to them in a pillar of cloud;
they kept His decrees and the statutes
He gave them.
8 LORD our God, You answered them.
You were a God who forgave them,
but punished[f] their misdeeds.[g]

9 Exalt the LORD our God;
bow in worship at His holy mountain,
for the LORD our God is holy.

Psalm 100

Be Thankful

A psalm of thanksgiving.

1 Shout triumphantly to the LORD, all the earth.
2 Serve the LORD with gladness;
come before Him with joyful songs.
3 Acknowledge that the LORD is God.
He made us, and we are His[h]—
His people, the sheep of His pasture.
4 Enter His gates with thanksgiving
and His courts with praise.
Give thanks to Him and praise His name.
5 For the LORD is good, and His love is eternal;
His faithfulness endures through all generations.

[a]97:7 LXX, Syr read *All His angels*; Heb 1:6 [b]97:8 Lit *daughters* [c]97:11 One Hb ms, LXX, other versions read *rises to shine*; Ps 112:4 [d]97:11 Lit *Light is sown* [e]97:12 Lit *praise the mention*, or *memory, of His holiness* [f]99:8 Lit *avenged* [g]99:8 Or *but avenged misdeeds done against them* [h]100:3 Alt Hb tradition, other Hb mss, LXX, Syr, Vg read *and not we ourselves*

98:9 judge the earth. For God's people, the day when He judges will not bring sorrow. It will be a day of rejoicing because He will judge in righteousness and fairness.

99:6 Moses … Aaron … Samuel. These three men had served as priests to the nation of Israel. Moses served as the first priest, anointing Aaron to serve as Israel's high priest (Ex. 24:1-7; 28:1). Samuel was both a priest and a prophet who served Israel during a time when they had no strong leaders (1 Sam. 7:2-17).

99:7 pillar of cloud. This image recalls the desert when God led His people with a pillar of cloud by day and a pillar of fire by night. God's presence was in the cloud, and He spoke to Moses (Ex. 33:9) and Aaron (Num. 12:5-6).

100:1 all the earth. The psalmist sends out a call to pagan nations to acknowledge God as the supreme God.

101:2-5 integrity of heart. David understood that obedience is a matter of the heart, so he

Psalm 101

A Vow of Integrity

A Davidic psalm.

1 I will sing of faithful love and justice;
   I will sing praise to You, LORD.
2 I will pay attention to the way of integrity.
   When will You come to me?
   I will live with integrity of heart in my house.
3 I will not set anything godless before my eyes.
   I hate the doing of transgression;
   it will not cling to me.
4 A devious heart will be far from me;
   I will not be involved with^a evil.

5 I will destroy anyone
   who secretly slanders his neighbor;
   I cannot tolerate anyone
   with haughty eyes or an arrogant heart.
6 My eyes ⌊favor⌋ the faithful of the land
   so that they may sit down with me.
   The one who follows the way of integrity
   may serve me.
7 No one who acts deceitfully
   will live in my palace;
   no one who tells lies
   will remain in my presence.^b
8 Every morning I will destroy
   all the wicked of the land,
   eliminating all evildoers from the LORD's city.

Psalm 102

Affliction in Light of Eternity

A prayer of an afflicted person
who is weak and pours out
his lament before the LORD.

1 LORD, hear my prayer;
   let my cry for help come before You.
2 Do not hide Your face from me in my day
   of trouble.
   Listen closely to me;
   answer me quickly when I call.

3 For my days vanish like smoke,
   and my bones burn like a furnace.
4 My heart is afflicted, withered like grass;
   I even forget to eat my food.
5 Because of the sound of my groaning,
   my flesh sticks to my bones.

6 I am like a desert owl,^c
   like an owl among the ruins.
7 I stay awake;
   I am like a solitary bird on a roof.
8 My enemies taunt me all day long;
   they ridicule and curse me.
9 I eat ashes like bread
   and mingle my drinks with tears
10 because of Your indignation and wrath;
   for You have picked me up and thrown me aside.
11 My days are like a lengthening shadow,
   and I wither away like grass.

12 But You, LORD, are enthroned forever;
   Your fame ⌊endures⌋ to all generations.
13 You will arise and have compassion on Zion,
   for it is time to show favor to her—
   the appointed time has come.
14 For Your servants take delight in its stones
   and favor its dust.

15 Then the nations will fear the name of the LORD,
   and all the kings of the earth Your glory,
16 for the LORD will rebuild Zion;
   He will appear in His glory.
17 He will pay attention to the prayer of the destitute
   and will not despise their prayer.

18 This will be written for a later generation,
   and a newly created people will praise the LORD:
19 He looked down from His holy heights—
   the LORD gazed out from heaven to earth—
20 to hear a prisoner's groaning,
   to set free those condemned to die,^d
21 so that they might declare
   the name of the LORD in Zion
   and His praise in Jerusalem,
22 when peoples and kingdoms are assembled
   to serve the LORD.

23 He has broken my^e strength in midcourse;
   He has shortened my days.
24 I say: "My God, do not take me
   in the middle of my life!^f
   Your years continue through all generations.
25 Long ago You established the earth,
   and the heavens are the work of Your hands.
26 They will perish, but You will endure;
   all of them will wear out like clothing.
   You will change them like a garment,
   and they will pass away.

---

^a**101:4** Lit *not know* ^b**101:7** Lit *in front of my eyes* ^c**102:6** Or *a pelican of the desert* ^d**102:20** Lit *free sons of death* ^e**102:23** Other Hb mss, LXX read *His* ^f**102:24** Lit *my days*

---

carefully guarded his heart from sin. Old Testament believers understood sinful actions to result from following their hearts (inward compulsion) or eyes (external influences). (See Num. 15:39; Job 31:7; Prov. 21:4.)

101:5-8 David made seven pledges: to be loyal to God's way; to stop people from speaking evil

behind backs; to have peace reign in the court; to encourage stability in the community; to encourage godliness; to not tolerate deceit; and to convene court first thing every morning.

102:14 delight in its stones. Jerusalem (Zion) symbolized the nation's prosperity and relationship with God (2 Sam. 5:6-12; Ps. 48).

103:10-12 As far as the east is from the west. So great is God's grace that when He forgives, He also forgets our sins.

103:17 eternity to eternity. God's love is infinite; it extends beyond our finite lives, across all generations, and into eternity.

104:2 light. The reference to light pictures

27 But You are the same,
and Your years will never end.

28 Your servants' children will dwell [securely],
and their offspring will be established before You."

Psalm 103

The Forgiving God

Davidic.

1 My soul, praise the LORD,
and all that is within me, praise His holy name.

2 My soul, praise the LORD,
and do not forget all His benefits.

3 He forgives all your sin;
He heals all your diseases.

4 He redeems your life from the •Pit;
He crowns you with faithful love and compassion.

5 He satisfies you[a] with goodness;
your youth is renewed like the eagle.

6 The LORD executes acts of righteousness
and justice for all the oppressed.

7 He revealed His ways to Moses,
His deeds to the people of Israel.

8 The LORD is compassionate and gracious,
slow to anger and full of faithful love.

9 He will not always accuse [us]
or be angry forever.

10 He has not dealt with us as our sins deserve
or repaid us according to our offenses.

11 For as high as the heavens are above the earth,
so great is His faithful love
toward those who fear Him.

12 As far as the east is from the west,
so far has He removed
our transgressions from us.

13 As a father has compassion on his children,
so the LORD has compassion on those who fear Him.

14 For He knows what we are made of,
remembering that we are dust.

15 As for man, his days are like grass—
he blooms like a flower of the field;

16 when the wind passes over it, it vanishes,
and its place is no longer known.[b]

17 But from eternity to eternity
the LORD's faithful love is toward
those who fear Him,
and His righteousness toward the grandchildren

18 of those who keep His covenant,
who remember to observe His instructions.

19 The LORD has established His throne in heaven,
and His kingdom rules over all.

20 Praise the LORD,
[all] His angels of great strength,
who do His word,
obedient to His command.

21 Praise the LORD, all His armies,
His servants who do His will.

22 Praise the LORD, all His works
in all the places where He rules.
My soul, praise the LORD!

Psalm 104

God the Creator

1 My soul, praise the LORD!
LORD my God, You are very great;
You are clothed with majesty and splendor.

2 He wraps Himself in light as if it were a robe,
spreading out the sky like a canopy,

3 laying the beams of His palace
on the waters [above],
making the clouds His chariot,
walking on the wings of the wind,

4 and making the winds His messengers,[c]
flames of fire His servants.

5 He established the earth on its foundations;
it will never be shaken.

6 You covered it with the deep
as if it were a garment;
the waters stood above the mountains.

7 At Your rebuke the waters fled;
at the sound of Your thunder
they hurried away—

8 mountains rose and valleys sank[d] —
to the place You established for them.

9 You set a boundary they cannot cross;
they will never cover the earth again.

10 He causes the springs to gush into the valleys;
they flow between the mountains.

11 They supply water for every wild beast;
the wild donkeys quench their thirst.

12 The birds of the sky live beside [the springs];
they sing among the foliage.

13 He waters the mountains from His palace;
the earth is satisfied by the fruit of Your labor.

---

[a] 103:5 Lit satisfies your ornament; Hb obscure [b] 103:16 Lit place no longer knows it [c] 104:4 Or angels [d] 104:7–8 Or away. They flowed over the mountains and went down valleys

---

that first day of creation when God said, "Let there be light" (Gen. 1:3). The stretching out of the heavens pictures that second day of creation when God separated the sky from the water (Gen. 1:6-8).
104:9 set a boundary. God set in place boundaries for the waters so that they would

never again flood the earth (see Genesis 9:15). **104:15 food ... wine ... bread.** God's extravagant blessings are illustrated by grapes to make wine, olives to make the oil, and grain to make bread—all of which make His people glow with health.

104:31 glory of the LORD. Here glory refers to all of creation. God's glory is visible in His creation.

104:35 wicked ... no more. Creation, for all its beauty, has been marred by sin. The writer longs for the day when all sin will vanish from the earth.

14 He causes grass to grow for the livestock
and ⌊provides⌋ crops for man to cultivate,
producing food from the earth,
15 wine that makes man's heart glad—
making his face shine with oil—
and bread that sustains man's heart.

16 The trees of the LORD flourish,[a]
the cedars of Lebanon that He planted.
17 There the birds make their nests;
the stork makes its home in the pine trees.
18 The high mountains are for the wild goats;
the cliffs are a refuge for hyraxes.

19 He made the moon to mark the[b] seasons;
the sun knows when to set.
20 You bring darkness, and it becomes night,
when all the forest animals stir.
21 The young lions roar for their prey
and seek their food from God.
22 The sun rises; they go back
and lie down in their dens.
23 Man goes out to his work
and to his labor until evening.

24 How countless are Your works, LORD!
In wisdom You have made them all;
the earth is full of Your creatures.[c]
25 Here is the sea, vast and wide,
teeming with creatures beyond number—
living things both large and small.
26 There the ships move about,
and •Leviathan, which You formed
to play there.

27 All of them wait for You
to give them their food at the right time.
28 When You give it to them,
they gather it;
when You open Your hand,
they are satisfied with good things.
29 When You hide Your face,
they are terrified;
when You take away their breath,
they die and return to the dust.
30 When You send Your breath,[d]
they are created,
and You renew the face of the earth.

31 May the glory of the LORD
endure forever;
may the LORD rejoice in His works.

32 He looks at the earth, and it trembles;
He touches the mountains,
and they pour out smoke.
33 I will sing to the LORD all my life;
I will sing praise to my God while I live.
34 May my meditation be pleasing to Him;
I will rejoice in the LORD.
35 May sinners vanish from the earth
and the wicked be no more.
My soul, praise the LORD!
•Hallelujah!

Psalm 105
God's Faithfulness to His People

1 Give thanks to the LORD, call on His name;
proclaim His deeds among the peoples.
2 Sing to Him, sing praise to Him;
tell about all His wonderful works!
3 Honor His holy name;
let the hearts of those who seek
the LORD rejoice.
4 Search for the LORD and for His strength;
seek His face always.
5 Remember the wonderful works He has done,
His wonders,
and the judgments He has pronounced,[e]
6 you offspring of Abraham His servant,
Jacob's descendants—His chosen ones.

7 He is the LORD our God;
His judgments ⌊govern⌋ the whole earth.
8 He forever remembers His covenant,
the promise He ordained
for a thousand generations—
9 ⌊the covenant⌋ He made with Abraham,
swore[f] to Isaac,
10 and confirmed to Jacob as a decree
and to Israel as an everlasting covenant:
11 "I will give the land of Canaan to you
as your inherited portion."

12 When they were few in number,
very few indeed,
and temporary residents in Canaan,
13 wandering from nation to nation
and from one kingdom to another,
14 He allowed no one to oppress them;
He rebuked kings on their behalf:
15 "Do not touch My anointed ones,
or harm My prophets."

---

a 104:16 Lit are satisfied   b 104:19 Lit moon for   c 104:24 Lit possessions   d 104:30 Or Spirit   e 105:5 Lit judgments of His mouth   f 105:9 Lit and His oath

---

Ps. 105 Remember … works … wonders. This psalm was composed by David (1 Chron. 16:7) to sing at one of the festivals. The first 15 verses of the psalm are the same as the song recorded in 1 Chronicles 16:8-22. The entire psalm rehearses Israel's history, giving thanks to the Lord for all he has done on the nation's behalf. (See also 78; 106.)

105:8-11 covenant. God's covenant with Abraham is recorded in Genesis 15:9-21. This covenant promised that Abraham would receive the land of Canaan, which Israel possessed at the time this psalm was written.
105:12-41 My anointed ones. This section of the psalm describes God's fulfillment of

His covenant to Abraham—from the days of the patriarchs who were nomads in the land, to the days of God's protection of the people through the leadership of Moses. God never failed to keep His covenant promises.

105:25 whose hearts He turned to hate. This is probably a reference to Pharaoh, whose

16 He called down famine against the land
and destroyed the entire food supply.

17 He had sent a man ahead of them—
Joseph, who was sold as a slave.

18 They hurt his feet with shackles;
his neck was put in an iron collar.

19 Until the time his prediction came true,
the word of the LORD tested him.

20 The king sent ⌊for him⌋ and released him;
the ruler of peoples set him free.

21 He made him master of his household,
ruler over all his possessions—

22 binding[a] his officials at will
and instructing his elders.

23 Then Israel went to Egypt;
Jacob lived as a foreigner in the land of Ham.[b]

24 The LORD[c] made His people very fruitful;
He made them more numerous than their foes,

25 whose hearts He turned to hate His people
and to deal deceptively with His servants.

26 He sent Moses His servant,
and Aaron, whom He had chosen.

27 They performed His miraculous signs
among them,
and wonders in the land of Ham.[b]

28 He sent darkness, and it became dark—
for did they[d] not defy His commands?

29 He turned their waters into blood
and caused their fish to die.

30 Their land was overrun with frogs,
even in their kings' chambers.

31 He spoke, and insects came—
gnats throughout their country.

32 He gave them hail for rain,
and lightning throughout their land.

33 He struck their vines and fig trees
and shattered the trees of their territory.

34 He spoke and locusts came—
young locusts without number.

35 They devoured all the vegetation in their land
and consumed the produce of their soil.

36 He struck all the firstborn in their land,
all their first progeny.

37 Then He brought Israel out with silver and gold,
and no one among His tribes stumbled.

38 Egypt was glad when they left,
for dread of Israel[e] had fallen on them.

39 He spread a cloud as a covering
and ⌊gave⌋ a fire to light up the night.

40 They asked, and He brought quail
and satisfied them with bread from heaven.

41 He opened a rock, and water gushed out;
it flowed like a stream in the desert.

42 For He remembered His holy promise
to Abraham His servant.

43 He brought His people out with rejoicing,
His chosen ones with shouts of joy.

44 He gave them the lands of the nations,
and they inherited
what other peoples had worked for.

45 ⌊All this happened⌋
so that they might keep His statutes
and obey His laws.
•Hallelujah!

Psalm 106

Israel's Unfaithfulness to God

1 •Hallelujah!
Give thanks to the LORD, for He is good;
His faithful love endures forever.

2 Who can declare the LORD's mighty acts
or proclaim all the praise due Him?

3 How happy are those who uphold justice,
who practice righteousness at all times.

4 Remember me, LORD,
when You show favor to Your people.
Come to me with Your salvation

5 so that I may enjoy the prosperity
of Your chosen ones,
rejoice in the joy of Your nation,
and boast about Your heritage.

6 Both we and our fathers have sinned;
we have gone astray and have acted wickedly.

7 Our fathers in Egypt did not grasp
⌊the significance of⌋ Your wonderful works
or remember Your many acts of faithful love;
instead, they rebelled by the sea—the •Red Sea.

8 Yet He saved them because of His name,
to make His power known.

9 He rebuked the Red Sea, and it dried up;
He led them through the depths as through
a desert.

10 He saved them from the hand of the adversary;
He redeemed them from the hand
of the enemy.

11 Water covered their foes;
not one of them remained.

---

[a]**105:22** LXX, Syr, Vg read *teaching*   [b]**105:23,27** Egypt   [c]**105:24** Lit *He*   [d]**105:28** LXX, Syr read *for they did . . .* (as a statement)   [e]**105:38** Lit *them*

---

heart God hardened so that he would not let the people go (Ex. 4:21). This allowed God to show the Egyptians His powerful signs and wonders on behalf of His enslaved people.

105:45 statutes. This is from the same Hebrew word translated "decree" in verse 10. God's work of redeeming the Israelites through fulfill-ing His covenant promises was also to teach them to love Him and conform their lives to His will.

106:6-43 Israel's Unfaithfulness. The previous psalm focused on God's great works on behalf of Israel; this psalm chronicles Israel's history of rebellion that occurred despite God's care for the nation.

106:13 not wait for His counsel. Not long after Israel had experienced deliverance from Egypt at the Red Sea, the people began to complain against God. They did not wait for God's "counsel" (His divine plan and power), but gave in to fear and rebelled.

12 Then they believed His promises
and sang His praise.

13 They soon forgot His works
and would not wait for His counsel.

14 They were seized with craving
in the wilderness
and tested God in the desert.

15 He gave them what they asked for,
but sent a wasting disease among them.

16 In the camp they were envious of Moses
and of Aaron, the LORD's holy one.

17 The earth opened up and swallowed Dathan;
it covered the assembly of Abiram.

18 Fire blazed throughout their assembly;
flames consumed the wicked.

19 At Horeb they made a calf
and worshiped the cast metal image.

20 They exchanged their glorya
for the image of a grass-eating ox.

21 They forgot God their Savior,
who did great things in Egypt,

22 wonderful works in the land of Ham,b
awe-inspiring deeds at the Red Sea.

23 So He said He would have destroyed them—
if Moses His chosen one
had not stood before Him in the breach
to turn His wrath away from destroying ⌊them⌋.

24 They despised the pleasant land
and did not believe His promise.

25 They grumbled in their tents
and did not listen to the LORD's voice.

26 So He raised His hand against them
⌊with an oath⌋
that He would make them fall in the desert

27 and would disperse their descendantsc
among the nations,
scattering them throughout the lands.

28 They aligned themselves with •Baal of Peor
and ate sacrifices offered to lifeless gods.d

29 They provoked the LORD with their deeds,
and a plague broke out against them.

30 But Phinehas stood up and intervened,
and the plague was stopped.

31 It was credited to him as righteousness
throughout all generations to come.

32 They angered ⌊the LORD⌋ at the waters
of Meribah,
and Moses sufferede because of them;

33 for they embittered his spirit,f
and he spoke rashly with his lips.

34 They did not destroy the peoples
as the LORD had commanded them,

35 but mingled with the nations
and adopted their ways.

36 They served their idols,
which became a snare to them.

37 They sacrificed their sons and daughters
to demons.

38 They shed innocent blood—
the blood of their sons and daughters
whom they sacrificed to the idols of Canaan;
so the land became polluted with blood.

39 They defiled themselves by their actions
and prostituted themselves by their deeds.

40 Therefore the LORD's anger burned
against His people,
and He abhorred His own inheritance.

41 He handed them over to the nations;
those who hated them ruled them.

42 Their enemies oppressed them,
and they were subdued under their power.

43 He rescued them many times,
but they continued to rebel deliberately
and were beaten down by their sin.

44 When He heard their cry,
He took note of their distress,

45 remembered His covenant with them,
and relented according to the abundance
of His faithful love.

46 He caused them to be pitied
before all their captors.

47 Save us, LORD our God,
and gather us from the nations,
so that we may give thanks
to Your holy name
and rejoice in Your praise.

48 May the LORD, the God of Israel, be praised
from everlasting to everlasting.
Let all the people say, "•Amen!"
Hallelujah!

---

a106:20 = God b106:22 Egypt c106:27 Syr; MT reads *would make their descendants fall* d106:28 Lit *sacrifices for dead ones* e106:32 Lit *and it was evil for Moses* f106:33 Some Hb mss, LXX, Syr, Jer; other Hb mss read *they rebelled against His Spirit*

106:34-39 served their idols. Rebellion took the form of idol worship and even child-sacrifice to Canaanite gods. Ultimately, worshiping other gods (breaking the first commandment and God's heart) resulted in exile.

106:40-43 the LORD's anger burned. Because of their constant idol worship, God

caused the Babylonians to overpower them. Eventually they were exiled to Babylon, who destroyed their temple and cities and took the people into captivity.

107:3 gathered them. The writer rejoices in Israel's return from the Babylonian Exile. The people who had been dispersed were gath-

ered and returned to rebuild the land, the city of Jerusalem, and the temple (Ezra 2; Neh. 1:8-9; Isa. 11:12; 43:5-6).

107:24 His wonderful works in the deep. Probably the Mediterranean Sea.

107:33-42 thirsty ground … fruitful land. The

BOOK V

(Psalms 107–150)
Psalm 107

Thanksgiving for God's Deliverance

1 Give thanks to the LORD, for He is good;
His faithful love endures forever.

2 Let the redeemed of the LORD proclaim
that He has redeemed them from the hand
of the foe

3 and has gathered them from the lands—
from the east and the west,
from the north and the south.

4 Some[a] wandered in the desolate wilderness,
finding no way to a city where they could live.

5 They were hungry and thirsty;
their spirits failed[b] within them.

6 Then they cried out to the LORD
in their trouble;
He rescued them from their distress.

7 He led them by the right path
to go to a city where they could live.

8 Let them give thanks to the LORD
for His faithful love
and His wonderful works for the •human race.

9 For He has satisfied the thirsty
and filled the hungry with good things.

10 Others[c] sat in darkness and gloom[d]—
prisoners in cruel chains—

11 because they rebelled against God's commands
and despised the counsel of the •Most High.

12 He broke their spirits[e] with hard labor;
they stumbled, and there was no one to help.

13 Then they cried out to the LORD in their trouble;
He saved them from their distress.

14 He brought them out of darkness and gloom[d]
and broke their chains apart.

15 Let them give thanks to the LORD
for His faithful love
and His wonderful works for the human race.

16 For He has broken down the bronze gates
and cut through the iron bars.

17 Fools suffered affliction
because of their rebellious ways and their sins.

18 They loathed all food
and came near the gates of death.

19 Then they cried out to the LORD in their trouble;
He saved them from their distress.

20 He sent His word and healed them;
He rescued them from the •Pit.

21 Let them give thanks to the LORD
for His faithful love
and His wonderful works for the human race.

22 Let them offer sacrifices of thanksgiving
and announce His works with shouts of joy.

23 Others[c] went to sea in ships,
conducting trade on the vast waters.

24 They saw the LORD's works,
His wonderful works in the deep.

25 He spoke and raised a tempest
that stirred up the waves of the sea.[f]

26 Rising up to the sky, sinking down to the depths,
their courage[g] melting away in anguish,

27 they reeled and staggered like drunken men,
and all their skill was useless.

28 Then they cried out to the LORD in their trouble,
and He brought them out of their distress.

29 He stilled the storm to a murmur,
and the waves of the sea[h] were hushed.

30 They rejoiced when the waves[i] grew quiet.
Then He guided them to the harbor
they longed for.

31 Let them give thanks to the LORD
for His faithful love
and His wonderful works for the human race.

32 Let them exalt Him in the assembly
of the people
and praise Him in the council of the elders.

33 He turns rivers into desert,
springs of water into thirsty ground,

34 and fruitful land into salty wasteland,
because of the wickedness of its inhabitants.

35 He turns a desert into a pool of water,
dry land into springs of water.

36 He causes the hungry to settle there,
and they establish a city where they can live.

37 They sow fields and plant vineyards
that yield a fruitful harvest.

38 He blesses them, and they multiply greatly;
He does not let their livestock decrease.

39 When they are diminished and are humbled
by cruel oppression and sorrow,

40 He pours contempt on nobles
and makes them wander in trackless wastelands.

Lord sometimes disciplined His wayward people by causing drought (34). When the people repented, He restored the land and made it prosperous so that it would yield a crop (v. 37). Repeatedly, sin led to judgment, and God would discipline the people by oppression, calamity and sorrow (v. 39), through powerful enemy armies that destroyed the land and cities, and through deportation.

107:40 nobles. The corruption of Israel's leaders led to the downfall of both the northern and southern kingdoms (2 Kings 17:1-18; 24:18-20).

Ps. 108 The psalmist praises God for love and faithfulness, and then prays for God to deliver His people from their enemies. The psalm combines sections from other psalms (57:7-11; 60:5-12).

108:1-5 higher than the heavens. God's love toward His people is not just for earth but reaches the heavens—spanning life and eter-

41 But He lifts the needy out of their suffering
and makes their families [multiply]
like flocks.

42 The upright see it and rejoice,
and all injustice shuts its mouth.

43 Let whoever is wise pay attention
to these things,
and consider[a] the LORD's acts of faithful love.

Psalm 108

A Plea for Victory

A song. A Davidic psalm.

1 My heart is confident, God;[b]
I will sing; I will sing praises
with the whole of my being.[c]

2 Wake up, harp and lyre!
I will wake up the dawn.

3 I will praise You, LORD,
among the peoples;
I will sing praises to You
among the nations.

4 For Your faithful love is higher
than the heavens;
Your faithfulness reaches the clouds.

5 God, be exalted above the heavens;
let Your glory be over the whole earth.

6 Save with Your right hand and answer me
so that those You love may be rescued.

7 God has spoken in His sanctuary:[d]
"I will triumph!
I will divide up Shechem.
I will apportion the Valley of Succoth.

8 Gilead is Mine, Manasseh is Mine,
and Ephraim is My helmet;
Judah is My scepter.

9 Moab is My washbasin;
on Edom I throw My sandal.
Over Philistia I shout in triumph."

10 Who will bring me to the fortified city?
Who will lead me to Edom?

11 Have You not rejected us, God?
God, You do not march out
with our armies.

12 Give us aid against the foe,
for human help is worthless.

13 With God we will perform valiantly;
He will trample our foes.

Psalm 109

Prayer against an Enemy

For the choir director.
A Davidic psalm.

1 God of my praise, do not be silent.

2 For wicked and deceitful mouths open
against me;
they speak against me with lying tongues.

3 They surround me with hateful words
and attack me without cause.

4 In return for my love they accuse me,
but I continue to pray.[e]

5 They repay me evil for good,
and hatred for my love.

6 Set a wicked person over him;
let an accuser[f] stand at his right hand.

7 When he is judged, let him be found guilty,
and let his prayer be counted as sin.

8 Let his days be few;
let another take over his position.

9 Let his children be fatherless
and his wife a widow.

10 Let his children wander as beggars,
searching [for food] far[g]
from their demolished homes.

11 Let a creditor seize all he has;
let strangers plunder what he has worked for.

12 Let no one show him kindness,
and let no one be gracious
to his fatherless children.

13 Let the line of his descendants be cut off;
let their name be blotted out
in the next generation.

14 Let his forefathers' guilt
be remembered before the LORD,
and do not let his mother's sin be blotted out.

15 Let their sins[h] always remain before the LORD,
and let Him cut off [all] memory of them
from the earth.

16 For he did not think to show kindness,
but pursued the wretched poor
and the brokenhearted
in order to put them to death.

17 He loved cursing—let it fall on him;
he took no delight in blessing—let it be far
from him.

---

[a]107:43 Lit and let them consider   [b]108:1 Some Hb mss, LXX, Syr add my heart is confident; Ps 57:7   [c]108:1 Lit praises, even my glory   [d]108:7 Or has promised by His holy nature   [e]109:4 Lit but I, prayer   [f]109:6 Or adversary   [g]109:10 LXX reads beggars, driven far   [h]109:15 Lit Let them

---

nity (v. 4).

109:4 I continue to pray. David begins by praising God and cursing his "enemies." Scholars debate whether the enemies were real persons or enemies within himself. Imprecatory Psalms make for difficult reading as we have the benefit of Jesus' teaching to love our

enemies. But David's curses are generally offered on behalf of God's reputation.

109:14-15 forefathers' guilt. The Old Testament placed the guilt for sin not only on the sinner but also on all his or her family and possessions (Josh. 7:24). Punishment was often extended to the family (Ex. 20:5).

109:17-18 cursing. This referred not to swearing but to pronouncements of evil upon someone. David asks that his enemy's curses would return on his enemy's own head.

Ps. 110 This psalm, written by David, is a prophetic picture of the coming Messiah (King). Verses 1 and 4 are quoted in the New Testa-

18 He wore cursing like his coat—
let it enter his body like water
and go into his bones like oil.
19 Let it be like a robe he wraps around himself,
like a belt he always wears.
20 Let this be the LORD's payment to my accusers,
to those who speak evil against me.

21 But You, GOD my Lord,
deal ⌊kindly⌋ with me because of Your name;
deliver me because of the goodness
of Your faithful love.
22 For I am poor and needy;
my heart is wounded within me.
23 I fade away like a lengthening shadow;
I am shaken off like a locust.
24 My knees are weak from fasting,
and my body is emaciated.ᵃ
25 I have become an object of ridicule to my accusers;ᵇ
when they see me, they shake their heads
⌊in scorn⌋.

26 Help me, LORD my God;
save me according to Your faithful love
27 so they may know that this is Your hand
and that You, LORD, have done it.
28 Though they curse, You will bless.
When they rise up, they will be put to shame,
but Your servant will rejoice.
29 My accusers will be clothed with disgrace;
they will wear their shame like a cloak.
30 I will fervently thank the LORD with my mouth;
I will praise Him in the presence of many.
31 For He stands at the right hand of the needy,
to save him from those who would condemn him.

Psalm 110

The Priestly King

A Davidic psalm.

1 The LORD declared to my Lord:
"Sit at My right hand
until I make Your enemies Your footstool."
2 The LORD will extend Your mighty scepter
from Zion.
Ruleᶜ over Your surroundingᵈ enemies.
3 Your people will volunteer
on Your day of battle.ᵉ
In holy splendor, from the womb of the dawn,
the dew of Your youth belongs to You.ᶠ

4 The LORD has sworn an oath and will not
take it back:
"Forever, You are a priest
like Melchizedek."
5 The Lord is at Your right hand;
He will crush kings on the day of His anger.
6 He will judge the nations, heaping up corpses;
He will crush leaders over the entire world.
7 He will drink from the brook by the road;
therefore, He will lift up His head.

Psalm 111

Praise for the LORD's Works

1 •Hallelujah!ᵍ
I will praise the LORD with all my heart
in the assembly of the upright
and in the congregation.

2 The LORD's works are great,
studied by all who delight in them.
3 All that He does is splendid and majestic;
His righteousness endures forever.
4 He has caused His wonderful works
to be remembered.
The LORD is gracious and compassionate.
5 He has provided food for those who fear Him;
He remembers His covenant forever.
6 He has shown His people the power
of His works
by giving them the inheritance of the nations.
7 The works of His hands are truth and justice;
all His instructions are trustworthy.
8 They are established forever and ever,
enacted in truth and uprightness.
9 He has sent redemption to His people.
He has ordained His covenant forever.
His name is holy and awe-inspiring.
10 The •fear of the LORD is the beginning
of wisdom;
all who follow His instructionsʰ have
good insight.
His praise endures forever.

Psalm 112

The Traits of the Righteous

1 •Hallelujah!ᵍ
Happy is the man who •fears the LORD,
taking great delight in His commandments.

ᵃ**109:24** Lit denied from fat   ᵇ**109:25** Lit to them   ᶜ**110:2** One Hb ms, LXX, Tg read You will rule   ᵈ**110:2** Lit Rule in the midst of Your   ᵉ**110:3** Lit power   ᶠ**110:3** Hb obscure   ᵍ**111:1; 112:1** The lines of this poem form an •acrostic.   ʰ**111:10** Lit follow them

---

ment as referring to Jesus Christ (Matt. 22:41-46; Mark 12:35-37; Luke 20:41-44; Heb. 1:13; 5:6; 7:11-28).

111:2 Psalms 111–118 are a collection of "hallelujah" psalms expressing praise to the Lord.

112:7-8 heart is confident. No matter how

people's circumstances are affecting them, they can remain steadfast in faith.

Ps. 113 Praise. Psalm 113, being a Hallel Psalm and containing the word "Hallelujah," focuses on praising God. These Hallel Psalms are still sung in the synagogues on great festival days such as Passover.

113:4 exalted. God's name tells us what God is like. To say that God's name is exalted above the heavens is to assert His supremacy over everything we know.

113:9 childless woman. In ancient cultures, childlessness was the greatest of tragedies (Gen. 30:1; 1 Sam. 1:2-8). Some even thought

2 His descendants will be powerful in the land;
the generation of the upright will be blessed.
3 Wealth and riches are in his house,
and his righteousness endures forever.
4 Light shines in the darkness for the upright.
He is gracious, compassionate, and righteous.
5 Good will come to a man who lends generously
and conducts his business fairly.
6 He will never be shaken.
The righteous will be remembered forever.
7 He will not fear bad news;
his heart is confident, trusting in the LORD.
8 His heart is assured; he will not fear.
In the end he will look in triumph on his foes.
9 He distributes freely to the poor;
his righteousness endures forever.
His •horn will be exalted in honor.

10 The wicked man will see ⌊it⌋ and be angry;
he will gnash his teeth in despair.
The desire of the wicked will come to nothing.

Psalm 113

Praise to the Merciful God

1 •Hallelujah!
Give praise, servants of the LORD;
praise the name of the LORD.
2 Let the name of the LORD be praised
both now and forever.
3 From the rising of the sun to its setting,
let the name of the LORD be praised.

4 The LORD is exalted above all the nations,
His glory above the heavens.
5 Who is like the LORD our God—
the One enthroned on high,
6 who stoops down to look
on the heavens and the earth?
7 He raises the poor from the dust
and lifts the needy from the garbage pile
8 in order to seat them with nobles—
with the nobles of His people.
9 He gives the childless woman a household,
⌊making her⌋ the joyful mother of children.
Hallelujah!

Psalm 114

God's Deliverance of Israel

1 When Israel came out of Egypt—
the house of Jacob from a people

who spoke a foreign language—
2 Judah became His sanctuary,
Israel, His dominion.

3 The sea looked and fled;
the Jordan turned back.
4 The mountains skipped like rams,
the hills, like lambs.
5 Why was it, sea, that you fled?
Jordan, that you turned back?
6 Mountains, that you skipped like rams?
Hills, like lambs?

7 Tremble, earth, at the presence of the Lord,
at the presence of the God of Jacob,
8 who turned the rock into a pool of water,
the flint into a spring of water.

Psalm 115

Glory to God Alone

1 Not to us, LORD, not to us,
but to Your name give glory
because of Your faithful love, because of
Your truth.
2 Why should the nations say,
"Where is their God?"
3 Our God is in heaven
and does whatever He pleases.

4 Their idols are silver and gold,
made by human hands.
5 They have mouths, but cannot speak,
eyes, but cannot see.
6 They have ears, but cannot hear,
noses, but cannot smell.
7 They have hands, but cannot feel,
feet, but cannot walk.
They cannot make a sound with their throats.
8 Those who make them are[a] just like them,
as are all who trust in them.

9 Israel,[b] trust in the LORD!
He is their help and shield.
10 House of Aaron, trust in the LORD!
He is their help and shield.
11 You who •fear the LORD, trust in the LORD!
He is their help and shield.
12 The LORD remembers us and will bless ⌊us⌋.
He will bless the house of Israel;
He will bless the house of Aaron;
13 He will bless those who fear the LORD—
small and great alike.

a**115:8** Or *May those who make them become*   b**115:9** Other Hb mss, LXX, Syr read *House of Israel*

barrenness indicated God's displeasure with the woman or her family. God, who controls all of creation, can provide a barren woman with children, as with Sarah (Gen. 21:2), Rebekah (Gen. 25:21), Rachel (Gen. 30:23), Hannah (1 Sam. 1:19-20) and Elizabeth (Luke 1:7, 13).

Ps. 114 Delivered Israel. This psalm cele-

brates God's works in creating the nation of Israel (1-2); and delivering them as a nation from bondage in Egypt.

114:3 sea … Jordan. The parting of the Red Sea (Ex. 14:21-22) and the parting of the Jordan River to allow entrance to the promised land are recalled (Josh. 3:14-17).

116:3 ropes of death. This could refer to a severe sickness or to the fear of death experienced in times of war or bondage.

116:15 valuable in the LORD's sight. The word "valuable" suggests that God carefully watches over His people, caring for them as precious ones at the time of their death and re-

14 May the LORD add to ⌊your numbers⌋,
   both yours and your children's.
15 May you be blessed by the LORD,
   the Maker of heaven and earth.
16 The heavens are the LORD's,[a]
   but the earth He has given to the •human race.
17 It is not the dead who praise the LORD,
   nor any of those descending into the silence
   ⌊of death⌋.
18 But we will praise the LORD,
   both now and forever.
   •Hallelujah!

Psalm 116

Thanks to God for Deliverance

1 I love the LORD because He has heard
   my appeal for mercy.
2 Because He has turned His ear to me,
   I will call ⌊out to Him⌋ as long as I live.

3 The ropes of death were wrapped around me,
   and the torments of •Sheol overcame me;
   I encountered trouble and sorrow.
4 Then I called on the name of the LORD:
   "LORD, save me!"

5 The LORD is gracious and righteous;
   our God is compassionate.
6 The LORD guards the inexperienced;
   I was helpless, and He saved me.
7 Return to your rest, my soul,
   for the LORD has been good to you.
8 For You, ⌊LORD,⌋ rescued me from death,
   my eyes from tears,
   my feet from stumbling.
9 I will walk before the LORD
   in the land of the living.
10 I believed, even when I said,
   "I am severely afflicted."
11 In my alarm I said,
   "Everyone is a liar."

12 How can I repay the LORD
   all the good He has done for me?
13 I will take the cup of salvation
   and worship[b] the LORD.
14 I will fulfill my vows to the LORD
   in the presence of all His people.

15 The death of His faithful ones
   is valuable in the LORD's sight.

16 LORD, I am indeed Your servant;
   I am Your servant, the son of Your female servant.
   You have loosened my bonds.
17 I will offer You a sacrifice of thanksgiving
   and will worship[b] the LORD.
18 I will fulfill my vows to the LORD,
   in the very presence of all His people,
19 in the courts of the LORD's house—
   within you, Jerusalem.
   •Hallelujah!

Psalm 117

Universal Call to Praise

1 Praise the LORD, all nations!
   Glorify Him, all peoples!
2 For great is His faithful love to us;
   the LORD's faithfulness endures forever.
   •Hallelujah!

Psalm 118

Thanksgiving for Victory

1 Give thanks to the LORD, for He is good;
   His faithful love endures forever.
2 Let Israel say,
   "His faithful love endures forever."
3 Let the house of Aaron say,
   "His faithful love endures forever."
4 Let those who fear the LORD say,
   "His faithful love endures forever."

5 I called to the LORD in distress;
   the LORD answered me
   ⌊and put me⌋ in a spacious place.[c]
6 The LORD is for me; I will not be afraid.
   What can man do to me?
7 With the LORD for me as my helper,
   I will look in triumph on those who hate me.

8 It is better to take refuge in the LORD
   than to trust in man.
9 It is better to take refuge in the LORD
   than to trust in nobles.

10 All the nations surrounded me;
   in the name of the LORD I destroyed them.
11 They surrounded me, yes, they surrounded me;
   in the name of the LORD I destroyed them.
12 They surrounded me like bees;
   they were extinguished like a fire among thorns;
   in the name of the LORD I destroyed them.

---

[a]115:16 Lit LORD's heavens   [b]116:13,17 Or proclaim or invoke the name of; lit call on the name of   [c]118:5 Or answered me with freedom

---

ceiving them into His presence (72:14).

117:1-2 Call to praise. This is the shortest psalm and the shortest chapter in the Bible.

Ps. 118 Give thanks. This is the last of the Hallel psalms (Ps. 111–118). As the last song of that liturgy, this may have been the hymn sung

by Jesus and the disciples at the conclusion of the Last Supper (Matt. 26:30).

118:5 spacious place. The Hebrew word for "free" literally means a "spacious place," as opposed to being in bondage.

118:19-20 gates of righteousness. This

song, situated at the end of the hallelujah psalms, may have been the final song sung as pilgrims approached the city of Jerusalem on festival days (v. 27). The call to "open the gates of righteousness" could be a call to open the gates of the city and of the temple.

13 You[a] pushed me[b] hard to make me fall,
but the LORD helped me.

14 The LORD is my strength and my song;
He has become my salvation.

15 There are shouts of joy and victory
in the tents of the righteous:
"The LORD's right hand strikes with power!

16 The LORD's right hand is raised!
The LORD's right hand strikes with power!"

17 I will not die, but I will live
and proclaim what the LORD has done.

18 The LORD disciplined me severely
but did not give me over to death.

19 Open the gates of righteousness for me;
I will enter through them
and give thanks to the LORD.

20 This is the gate of the LORD;
the righteous will enter through it.

21 I will give thanks to You
because You have answered me
and have become my salvation.

22 The stone that the builders rejected
has become the cornerstone.

23 This came from the LORD;
it is wonderful in our eyes.

24 This is the day the LORD has made;
let us rejoice and be glad in it.

25 LORD, save us!
LORD, please grant us success!

26 Blessed is he who comes
in the name of the LORD.
From the house of the LORD we bless you.

27 The LORD is God and has given us light.
Bind the festival sacrifice with cords
to the horns of the altar.

28 You are my God, and I will give You thanks.
⌊You are⌋ my God; I will exalt You.

29 Give thanks to the LORD, for He is good;
His faithful love endures forever.

Psalm 119

Delight in God's Word

א *Alef*

1 How[c] happy are those whose way is blameless,
who live according to the law of the LORD!

2 Happy are those who keep His decrees
and seek Him with all their heart.

3 They do nothing wrong;
they follow His ways.

4 You have commanded that Your precepts
be diligently kept.

5 If only my ways were committed
to keeping Your statutes!

6 Then I would not be ashamed
when I think about all Your commands.

7 I will praise You with a sincere heart
when I learn Your righteous judgments.

8 I will keep Your statutes;
never abandon me.

ב *Bet*

9 How can a young man keep his way pure?
By keeping Your[d] word.

10 I have sought You with all my heart;
don't let me wander from Your commands.

11 I have treasured Your word in my heart
so that I may not sin against You.

12 LORD, may You be praised;
teach me Your statutes.

13 With my lips I proclaim
all the judgments from Your mouth.

14 I rejoice in the way ⌊revealed by⌋ Your decrees
as much as in all riches.

15 I will meditate on Your precepts
and think about Your ways.

16 I will delight in Your statutes;
I will not forget Your word.

ג *Gimel*

17 Deal generously with Your servant
so that I might live;
then I will keep Your word.

18 Open my eyes so that I may see
wonderful things in Your law.

19 I am a stranger on earth;
do not hide Your commands from me.

20 I am continually overcome
by longing for Your judgments.

21 You rebuke the proud, the accursed,
who wander from Your commands.

22 Take insult and contempt away from me,
for I have kept Your decrees.

23 Though princes sit together speaking against me,
Your servant will think about Your statutes;

24 Your decrees are my delight
and my counselors.

---

a **118:13** Perhaps the enemy b **118:13** LXX, Syr, Jer read *I was pushed* c **119:1** The stanzas of this poem form an •acrostic. d **119:9** Or *keeping it according to Your*

118:22 The stone that the builders rejected. This was the stone at the corner of a building's foundation which supports the greatest weight. (See also, Matt. 21:42-44; Acts 4:8-12; 1 Peter 2:7).

Ps. 119 This is the longest psalm and the longest chapter in the Bible as well as an outstanding example of an acrostic (alphabetical) poem. This carefully constructed psalm has 22 stanzas containing eight verses each. The repetitive structure of this psalm, with built-in memory aids, allowed for easy memorization.

119:13 proclaim. The Jews committed great portions of Scripture to memory.

119:29 way of deceit. In Hebrew, "the way of lying." The writer prays to not be like those who deceive themselves and depart from God's law.

119:32 broaden my understanding. Literally "enlarge my heart," or "cause my heart to swell

ד *Dalet*

25 My life is down in the dust;
    give me life through Your word.
26 I told You about my life,
    and You listened to me;
    teach me Your statutes.
27 Help me understand
    the meaning of Your precepts
    so that I can meditate on Your wonders.
28 I am weary[a] from grief;
    strengthen me through Your word.
29 Keep me from the way of deceit,
    and graciously give me Your instruction.
30 I have chosen the way of truth;
    I have set Your ordinances ⌊before me⌋.
31 I cling to Your decrees;
    LORD, do not put me to shame.
32 I pursue the way of Your commands,
    for You broaden my understanding.[b]

ה *He*

33 Teach me, LORD, the meaning of Your statutes,
    and I will always keep them.[c]
34 Help me understand Your instruction,
    and I will obey it
    and follow it with all my heart.
35 Help me stay on the path of Your commands,
    for I take pleasure in it.
36 Turn my heart to Your decrees
    and not to material gain.
37 Turn my eyes
    from looking at what is worthless;
    give me life in Your ways.[d]
38 Confirm what You said to Your servant,
    for it produces reverence for You.
39 Turn away the disgrace I dread;
    indeed, Your judgments are good.
40 How I long for Your precepts!
    Give me life through Your righteousness.

ו *Vav*

41 Let Your faithful love come to me, LORD,
    Your salvation, as You promised.
42 Then I can answer the one who taunts me,
    for I trust in Your word.
43 Never take the word of truth from my mouth,
    for I hope in Your judgments.
44 I will always keep Your law,
    forever and ever.

45 I will walk freely in an open place
    because I seek Your precepts.
46 I will speak of Your decrees before kings
    and not be ashamed.
47 I delight in Your commands,
    which I love.
48 I will lift up my hands to Your commands,
    which I love,
    and will meditate on Your statutes.

ז *Zayin*

49 Remember ⌊Your⌋ word to Your servant;
    You have given me hope through it.
50 This is my comfort in my affliction:
    Your promise has given me life.
51 The arrogant constantly ridicule me,
    but I do not turn away from Your instruction.
52 LORD, I remember Your judgments from long ago
    and find comfort.
53 Rage seizes me because of the wicked
    who reject Your instruction.
54 Your statutes are ⌊the theme of⌋ my song
    during my earthly life.[e]
55 I remember Your name in the night, LORD,
    and I keep Your law.
56 This is my ⌊practice⌋:
    I obey Your precepts.

ח *Khet*

57 The LORD is my portion;[f]
    I have promised to keep Your words.
58 I have sought Your favor with all my heart;
    be gracious to me according to Your promise.
59 I thought about my ways
    and turned my steps back to Your decrees.
60 I hurried, not hesitating
    to keep Your commands.
61 Though the ropes of the wicked
    were wrapped around me,
    I did not forget Your law.
62 I rise at midnight to thank You
    for Your righteous judgments.
63 I am a friend to all who •fear You,
    to those who keep Your precepts.
64 LORD, the earth is filled with Your faithful love;
    teach me Your statutes.

ט *Tet*

65 LORD, You have treated Your servant well,
    just as You promised.

---

[a] **119:28** Or *My soul weeps*   [b] **119:32** Lit *You enlarge my heart*   [c] **119:33** Or *will keep it as my reward*   [d] **119:37** Other Hb mss, Tg read *word*
[e] **119:54** Lit *song in the house of my sojourning*   [f] **119:57** Lit *You are my portion, LORD*

---

with joy." The writer had gone from being "weary from grief" (v. 28) to bursting with joy.

119:41 faithful love. The Law repeatedly stated God's unfailing love for His covenant people. It composed the foundation of life for Hebrew believers. Whatever else they might have to face, God's love would get them through.

119:42 Then I can answer. The writer did not seek prosperity and security. He merely wanted to be able to stand and say, "God has provided for me and protected me just as He promised He would if I trusted Him."

119:53 Rage seizes me. He did not burn with anger at the wicked for oppressing him, nor for

their proud boasts; he was indignant because they were mocking the Word of God.

119:54 earthly life. Literally, "in my temporary house." He may have been referring to his brief pilgrimage on this earth (v. 19).

119:67 I was afflicted. Literally, "lowered,

66 Teach me good judgment and discernment,
for I rely on Your commands.
67 Before I was afflicted I went astray,
but now I keep Your word.
68 You are good, and You do what is good;
teach me Your statutes.
69 The arrogant have smeared me with lies,
but I obey Your precepts with all my heart.
70 Their hearts are hard and insensitive,
but I delight in Your instruction.
71 It was good for me to be afflicted
so that I could learn Your statutes.
72 Instruction from Your lips is better for me
than thousands of gold and silver pieces.

י Yod

73 Your hands made me and formed me;
give me understanding
so that I can learn Your commands.
74 Those who fear You will see me and rejoice,
for I put my hope in Your word.
75 I know, LORD, that Your judgments are just
and that You have afflicted me fairly.
76 May Your faithful love comfort me,
as You promised Your servant.
77 May Your compassion come to me
so that I may live,
for Your instruction is my delight.
78 Let the arrogant be put to shame
for slandering me with lies;
I will meditate on Your precepts.
79 Let those who fear You,
those who know Your decrees, turn to me.
80 May my heart be blameless
regarding Your statutes
so that I will not be put to shame.

כ Kaf

81 I long for Your salvation;
I put my hope in Your word.
82 My eyes grow weary
⌊looking⌋ for what You have promised;
I ask, "When will You comfort me?"
83 Though I have become like a wineskin ⌊dried⌋
by smoke,
I do not forget Your statutes.
84 How many days ⌊must⌋ Your servant ⌊wait⌋?
When will You execute judgment
on my persecutors?
85 The arrogant have dug pits for me;
they violate Your instruction.

86 All Your commands are true;
people persecute me with lies—help me!
87 They almost ended my life on earth,
but I did not abandon Your precepts.
88 Give me life in accordance with
Your faithful love,
and I will obey the decree You have spoken.

ל Lamed

89 LORD, Your word is forever;
it is firmly fixed in heaven.
90 Your faithfulness is for all generations;
You established the earth, and it stands firm.
91 They stand today in accordance with
Your judgments,
for all things are Your servants.
92 If Your instruction had not been my delight,
I would have died in my affliction.
93 I will never forget Your precepts,
for You have given me life through them.
94 I am Yours; save me,
for I have sought Your precepts.
95 The wicked hope to destroy me,
but I contemplate Your decrees.
96 I have seen a limit to all perfection,
but Your command is without limit.

מ Mem

97 How I love Your teaching!
It is my meditation all day long.
98 Your command makes me wiser
than my enemies,
for it is always with me.
99 I have more insight than all my teachers
because Your decrees are my meditation.
100 I understand more than the elders
because I obey Your precepts.
101 I have kept my feet from every evil path
to follow Your word.
102 I have not turned from Your judgments,
for You Yourself have instructed me.
103 How sweet Your word is to my taste—
⌊sweeter⌋ than honey to my mouth.
104 I gain understanding from Your precepts;
therefore I hate every false way.

נ Nun

105 Your word is a lamp for my feet
and a light on my path.
106 I have solemnly sworn
to keep Your righteous judgments.

---

humbled." God's servant had been trodden underfoot, "laid low in the dust" (v. 25) with suffering and pain.

119:83 wineskin [dried] by smoke. The psalmist felt as if he had been dried out and shriveled through as would happen to an old wineskin left hanging by a fire.

119:99 teachers. His teachers had been able scholars, but the writer had given himself *completely* to the Word all day long (v. 97).

119:105 light on my path. This verse echoes Proverbs 6:23, which says that God's commands show clearly which moral choices lead to life and which do not.

119:113 double-minded. Describes a person of divided loyalties. Such a person lacks integrity, wholeness. He is fickle and so is undependable. He wants to serve God and the world and so violates the first commandment.

119:130 revelation of Your words. God's Word is simple and straightforward. Only those

107 I am severely afflicted;
LORD, give me life through Your word.
108 LORD, please accept my willing offerings
of praise,
and teach me Your judgments.
109 My life is constantly in danger,[a]
yet I do not forget Your instruction.
110 The wicked have set a trap for me,
but I have not wandered from Your precepts.
111 I have Your decrees as a heritage forever;
indeed, they are the joy of my heart.
112 I am resolved to obey Your statutes
to the very end.[b]

ס Samek

113 I hate the double-minded,
but I love Your instruction.
114 You are my shelter and my shield;
I put my hope in Your word.
115 Depart from me, you evil ones,
so that I may obey my God's commands.
116 Sustain me as You promised, and I will live;
do not let me be ashamed of my hope.
117 Sustain me so that I can be safe
and be concerned with Your statutes continually.
118 You reject all who stray from Your statutes,
for their deceit is a lie.
119 You remove all the wicked on earth
as if they were[c] dross;
therefore, I love Your decrees.
120 I tremble[d] in awe of You;
I fear Your judgments.

ע Ayin

121 I have done what is just and right;
do not leave me to my oppressors.
122 Guarantee Your servant's well-being;
do not let the arrogant oppress me.
123 My eyes grow weary ⌊looking for⌋ Your salvation
and for Your righteous promise.
124 Deal with Your servant based on
Your faithful love;
teach me Your statutes.
125 I am Your servant; give me understanding
so that I may know Your decrees.
126 It is time for the LORD to act,
⌊for⌋ they have broken Your law.
127 Since I love Your commandments
more than gold, even the purest gold,

128 I carefully follow[e] all Your precepts
and hate every false way.

פ Pe

129 Your decrees are wonderful;
therefore I obey them.
130 The revelation of Your words brings light
and gives understanding to the inexperienced.
131 I pant with open mouth
because I long for Your commands.
132 Turn to me and be gracious to me,
as is ⌊Your⌋ practice toward those who love
Your name.
133 Make my steps steady through Your promise;
don't let sin dominate me.
134 Redeem me from human oppression,
and I will keep Your precepts.
135 Show favor to Your servant,
and teach me Your statutes.
136 My eyes pour out streams of tears
because people do not follow Your instruction.

צ Tsade

137 You are righteous, LORD,
and Your judgments are just.
138 The decrees You issue are righteous
and altogether trustworthy.
139 My anger overwhelms me
because my foes forget Your words.
140 Your word is completely pure,
and Your servant loves it.
141 I am insignificant and despised,
but I do not forget Your precepts.
142 Your righteousness is an everlasting righteousness,
and Your instruction is true.
143 Trouble and distress have overtaken me,
but Your commands are my delight.
144 Your decrees are righteous forever.
Give me understanding, and I will live.

ק Qof

145 I call with all my heart; answer me, LORD.
I will obey Your statutes.
146 I call to You; save me,
and I will keep Your decrees.
147 I rise before dawn and cry out for help;
I put my hope in Your word.
148 I am awake through each watch of the night
to meditate on Your promise.

---

[a]**119:109** Lit in my hand [b]**119:112** Or statutes; the reward is eternal [c]**119:119** Other Hb mss, DSS, LXX, Aq, Sym, Jer read All the wicked of the earth You count as [d]**119:120** Lit My flesh shudders [e]**119:128** Lit I therefore follow carefully

---

who refuse to understand are confounded.
119:164 seven times a day. Seven is a number signifying completeness. The psalmist was in constant communion with God, praising Him throughout the activities of his day.
119:176 I wander like a lost sheep. He prayed, "Do not let me stray" (v. 10); but he had

longed for the wealth that others enjoyed. The proud had strayed from God's law in their scramble for things (v. 113), and the psalmist recognizes that he sinned in similar ways.

Ps. 120 A song of ascents. This psalm is the first of a group of psalms (120–134) which have this heading. Some take "ascents" to

mean the stairs leading up to the temple or that they were sung by pilgrims as they "ascended" to the temple in Jerusalem for the annual Jewish festivals (Ex. 23:14-17; Micah 4:2). Crowds of pilgrims traveling to Jerusalem often rejoiced, sang, and played musical instruments as they traveled (Isa. 30:29). This group of

149 In keeping with Your faithful love,
hear my voice.
LORD, give me life, in keeping with Your justice.

150 Those who pursue evil plans[a] come near;
they are far from Your instruction.

151 You are near, LORD,
and all Your commands are true.

152 Long ago I learned from Your decrees
that You have established them forever.

ר Resh

153 Consider my affliction and rescue me,
for I have not forgotten Your instruction.

154 Defend my cause, and redeem me;
give me life, as You promised.

155 Salvation is far from the wicked
because they do not seek Your statutes.

156 Your compassions are many, LORD;
give me life, according to Your judgments.

157 My persecutors and foes are many.
I have not turned from Your decrees.

158 I have seen the disloyal and feel disgust
because they do not keep Your word.

159 Consider how I love Your precepts;
LORD, give me life, according to
Your faithful love.

160 The entirety of Your word is truth,
and all Your righteous judgments
endure forever.

ש Sin/ ש Shin

161 Princes have persecuted me without cause,
but my heart fears |only| Your word.

162 I rejoice over Your promise
like one who finds vast treasure.

163 I hate and abhor falsehood,
|but| I love Your instruction.

164 I praise You seven times a day
for Your righteous judgments.

165 Abundant peace belongs to those
who love Your instruction;
nothing makes them stumble.

166 LORD, I hope for Your salvation
and carry out Your commands.

167 I obey Your decrees
and love them greatly.

168 I obey Your precepts and decrees,
for all my ways are before You.

ת Tav

169 Let my cry reach You, LORD;
give me understanding according to Your word.

170 Let my plea reach You;
rescue me according to Your promise.

171 My lips pour out praise,
for You teach me Your statutes.

172 My tongue sings about Your promise,
for all Your commandments are righteous.

173 May Your hand be ready to help me,
for I have chosen Your precepts.

174 I long for Your salvation, LORD,
and Your instruction is my delight.

175 Let me live, and I will praise You;
may Your judgments help me.

176 I wander like a lost sheep;
seek Your servant,
for I do not forget Your commands.

Psalm 120
A Cry for Truth and Peace
A •song of ascents.

1 In my distress I called to the LORD,
and He answered me:

2 "LORD, deliver me from lying lips
and a deceitful tongue."

3 What will He give you,
and what will He do to you,
you deceitful tongue?

4 A warrior's sharp arrows,
with burning charcoal![b]

5 What misery that I have stayed in Meshech,
that I have lived among the tents of Kedar![c]

6 I have lived too long
with those who hate peace.

7 I am for peace; but when I speak,
they are for war.

Psalm 121
The LORD Our Protector
A •song of ascents.

1 I raise my eyes toward the mountains.
Where will my help come from?

2 My help comes from the LORD,
the Maker of heaven and earth.

---

[a]**119:150** Some Hb mss, LXX, Sym, Jer read *who maliciously persecute me* [b]**120:4** Lit *with coals of the broom bush* [c]**120:5** *Meshech*: a people far to the north of Palestine; *Kedar*: a nomadic people of the desert to the southeast

---

psalms is known in Jewish liturgy as the Great Hallel (from *halal*, "to praise."

120:5 I have stayed in Meshech … Kedar. After the Exile, Jews lived throughout the Persian Empire (Est. 3:8). They lived from Meshech (central Asia Minor) in the north to Kedar in Arabia to the south.

121:1 mountains. Refers to the group of hills on which Jerusalem is situated. Because the temple was there, help was to come from the temple, from God.

121:3 not allow your foot to slip. This could refer to physical protection (91:9-12) as well as spiritual protection.

122:3-5 Jerusalem. To the scattered Jews, Jerusalem was a holy city, the center of their faith. God's presence resided in the temple.

122:6 love. In Hebrew a beautiful wordplay unites the words "pray," "peace," "Jerusalem," and "be secure." To *love* Jerusalem meant to love God and to love the nation—

3 He will not allow your foot to slip;
   your Protector will not slumber.
4 Indeed, the Protector of Israel
   does not slumber or sleep.

5 The LORD protects you;
   the LORD is a shelter right by your side.ᵃ
6 The sun will not strike you by day,
   or the moon by night.

7 The LORD will protect you from all harm;
   He will protect your life.
8 The LORD will protect your coming and going
   both now and forever.

Psalm 122

A Prayer for Jerusalem

A Davidic •song of ascents.

1 I rejoiced with those who said to me,
   "Let us go to the house of the LORD."
2 Our feet are standing
   within your gates, Jerusalem—

3 Jerusalem, built as a city ⌊should be⌋,
   solidly joined together,
4 where the tribes, the tribes of the LORD,
      go up
   to give thanks to the name of the LORD.
   (This is an ordinance for Israel.)
5 There, thrones for judgment are placed,
   thrones of the house of David.

6 Pray for the peace of Jerusalem:
   "May those who love you prosper;
7 may there be peace within your walls,
   prosperity within your fortresses."
8 Because of my brothers and friends,
   I will say, "Peace be with you."
9 Because of the house of the LORD our God,
   I will seek your good.

Psalm 123

Looking for God's Favor

A •song of ascents.

1 I lift my eyes to You,
   the One enthroned in heaven.
2 Like a servant's eyes on His master's hand,
   like a servant girl's eyes on her mistress's hand,
   so our eyes are on the LORD our God
   until He shows us favor.

3 Show us favor, LORD, show us favor,
   for we've had more than enough contempt.
4 We've had more than enough
   scorn from the arrogant
   ⌊and⌋ contempt from the proud.

Psalm 124

The LORD Is on Our Side

A Davidic •song of ascents.

1 If the LORD had not been on our side—
   let Israel say—
2 If the LORD had not been on our side
   when men attacked us,
3 then they would have swallowed us alive
   in their burning anger against us.
4 Then the waters would have engulfed us;
   the torrent would have swept over us;
5 the raging waters would have swept over us.

6 Praise the LORD,
   who has not let us be ripped apart
      by their teeth.
7 We have escaped like a bird
      from the hunter's net;
   the net is torn, and we have escaped.
8 Our help is in the name of the LORD,
   the Maker of heaven and earth.

Psalm 125

Israel's Stability

A •song of ascents.

1 Those who trust in the LORD are
      like Mount Zion.
   It cannot be shaken; it remains forever.
2 Jerusalem—the mountains surround her.
   And the LORD surrounds His people,
   both now and forever.

3 The scepter of the wicked will not remain
   over the land allotted to the righteous,
   so that the righteous will not apply their hands
      to injustice.
4 Do what is good, LORD, to the good,
   to those whose hearts are upright.
5 But as for those who turn aside
      to crooked ways,
   the LORD will banish them with the evildoers.

Peace be with Israel.

ᵃ**121:5** Lit *is your shelter at your right hand*

---

which were all one in the minds of the Jews.

123:2 servant. Humble, faithful men and women of God are utterly dependent upon Him. Just as slaves and maids look to their masters, God's people look to Him for mercy.

125:1–2 Those who trust in the LORD. For-

eign oppressors tried to push the Jews around, but trusting in God made Israel as unmovable as a mountain. The LORD surrounded His people by placing a ring of protection and blessing around them that the enemy could not penetrate (Job 1:10).

126:2 filled with laughter. As the returning ex-

iles caught sight of Mt. Zion, they were filled with joy to be back in their own land. The surrounding nations knew what had happened to the Jews. Now they looked on in awe as God fulfilled his Word and brought His people back.

127:1–2 Unless the LORD builds. If God's peo-

Psalm 126

Zion's Restoration

A •song of ascents.

1 When the LORD restored the fortunes of Zion,[a]
we were like those who dream.
2 Our mouths were filled with laughter then,
and our tongues with shouts of joy.
Then they said among the nations,
"The LORD has done great things for them."
3 The LORD had done great things for us;
we were joyful.

4 Restore our fortunes,[b] LORD,
like watercourses in the •Negev.[c]
5 Those who sow in tears
will reap with shouts of joy.
6 Though one goes along weeping,
carrying the bag of seed,
he will surely come back with shouts of joy,
carrying his sheaves.

Psalm 127

The Blessing of the LORD

A Solomonic •song of ascents.

1 Unless the LORD builds a house,
its builders labor over it in vain;
unless the LORD watches over a city,
the watchman stays alert in vain.
2 In vain you get up early and stay up late,
eating food earned by hard work;
certainly He gives sleep to the one He loves.[d]

3 Sons are indeed a heritage from the LORD,
children, a reward.
4 Like arrows in the hand of a warrior
are the sons born in one's youth.
5 Happy is the man who has filled his quiver
with them.
Such men will never be put to shame
when they speak with ⌊their⌋ enemies
at the city •gate.

Psalm 128

Blessings for Those Who Fear God

A •song of ascents.

1 How happy is everyone who •fears the LORD,
who walks in His ways!

2 You will surely eat
what your hands have worked for.
You will be happy,
and it will go well for you.
3 Your wife will be like a fruitful vine
within your house,
your sons, like young olive trees
around your table.
4 In this very way
the man who fears the LORD
will be blessed.

5 May the LORD bless you from Zion,
so that you will see the prosperity of Jerusalem
all the days of your life,
6 and will see your children's children!

Peace be with Israel.

Psalm 129

Protection of the Oppressed

A •song of ascents.

1 Since my youth they have often attacked me—
let Israel say—
2 Since my youth they have often attacked me,
but they have not prevailed against me.
3 Plowmen plowed over my back;
they made their furrows long.
4 The LORD is righteous;
He has cut the ropes of the wicked.

5 Let all who hate Zion
be driven back in disgrace.
6 Let them be like grass on the rooftops,
which withers before it grows up[e]
7 and can't even fill the hands of the reaper
or the arms of the one who binds sheaves.
8 Then none who pass by will say,
"May the LORD's blessing be on you."

We bless you in the name of the LORD.

Psalm 130

Awaiting Redemption

A •song of ascents.

1 Out of the depths I call to You, LORD!
2 Lord, listen to my voice;
let Your ears be attentive
to my cry for help.

---

[a]**126:1** Or *LORD returned those of Zion who had been captives* [b]**126:4** Or *Return our captives* [c]**126:4** *Seasonal streams in the arid south country* [d]**127:2** Or *work; He gives such things to His loved ones while [they] sleep* [e]**129:6** Or *it can be pulled out*

---

ple fail to trust Him as their ultimate source of shelter, security, and food, their efforts result in failure.

128:3 Your wife. Psalm 128 is called the marriage prayer as it was often sung at Jewish weddings. Culturally, a woman's role was to provide children.

129:6 withers before it grows up. Grass cannot take deep root on a hard, sun baked roof. It is scorched before it bears fruit.

132:2 he swore an oath. David had a special relationship with God. When God committed Himself to David and his descendants (v. 11), David responded by committing himself to the

work of God (v. 8). (See also 2 Sam. 6-7).

132:6 We heard. David was a youth in Ephrathah (Bethlehem) when he heard of the ark not having a "house." The ark spent twenty years in "the fields of Jaar" (Kiriath Jearim). David moved it from there to Jerusalem (1 Sam. 7:1-2; 2 Sam. 6:1-3).

³ LORD, if You considered sins,
Lord, who could stand?
⁴ But with You there is forgiveness,
so that You may be revered.

⁵ I wait for the LORD; I wait,
and put my hope in His word.
⁶ I ⌊wait⌋ for the Lord
more than watchmen for the morning—
more than watchmen for the morning.

⁷ Israel, put your hope in the LORD.
For there is faithful love with the LORD,
and with Him is redemption in abundance.
⁸ And He will redeem Israel
from all its sins.

Psalm 131

A Childlike Spirit

A Davidic •song of ascents.

¹ LORD, my heart is not proud;
my eyes are not haughty.
I do not get involved with things
too great or too difficult for me.
² Instead, I have calmed and quieted myself
like a little weaned child with its mother;
I am like a little child.

³ Israel, put your hope in the LORD,
both now and forever.

Psalm 132

David and Zion Chosen

A •song of ascents.

¹ LORD, remember David
and all the hardships he endured,
² and how he swore an oath to the LORD,
making a vow to the Mighty One of Jacob:
³ "I will not enter my houseᵃ
or get into my bed,ᵇ
⁴ I will not allow my eyes to sleep
or my eyelids to slumber
⁵ until I find a place for the LORD,
a dwelling for the Mighty One of Jacob."

⁶ We heard of ⌊the ark⌋ in Ephrathah;ᶜ
we found it in the fields of Jaar.ᵈ
⁷ Let us go to His dwelling place;
let us worship at His footstool.

⁸ Arise, LORD, come to Your resting place,
You and the ark ⌊that shows⌋ Your strength.
⁹ May Your priests be clothed with righteousness,
and may Your godly people shout for joy.
¹⁰ Because of Your servant David,
do not reject Your anointed one.ᵉ

¹¹ The LORD swore an oath to David,
a promise He will not abandon:
"I will set one of your descendantsᶠ
on your throne.
¹² If your sons keep My covenant
and My decrees that I will teach them,
their sons will also sit on your throne, forever."

¹³ For the LORD has chosen Zion;
He has desired it for His home:
¹⁴ "This is My resting place forever;
I will make My home here
because I have desired it.
¹⁵ I will abundantly bless its food;
I will satisfy its needy with bread.
¹⁶ I will clothe its priests with salvation,
and its godly people will shout for joy.
¹⁷ There I will make a •horn grow for David;
I have prepared a lamp for My anointed one.
¹⁸ I will clothe his enemies with shame,
but the crown he wearsᵍ will be glorious."

Psalm 133

Living in Harmony

A Davidic •song of ascents.

¹ How good and pleasant it is
when brothers can live together!
² It is like fine oil on the head,
running down on the beard,
running down Aaron's beard,
on his robes.
³ It is like the dew of Hermonʰ
falling on the mountains of Zion.
For there the LORD has appointed the blessing—
life forevermore.

Psalm 134

Call to Evening Worship

A •song of ascents.

¹ Now praise the LORD,
all you servants of the LORD

ᵃ**132:3** Lit *enter the tent of my house* ᵇ**132:3** Lit *into the couch of my bed* ᶜ**132:6** Bethlehem or the district around it; Gen 35:19 ᵈ**132:6** Kiriath-jearim; 1 Sm 7:1–2 ᵉ**132:10** The king ᶠ**132:11** Lit *set the fruit of your womb* ᵍ**132:18** Lit *but on him his crown* ʰ**133:3** The tallest mountain in the region, noted for its abundant precipitation

---

132:12 keep My covenant. This covenant was the law of Moses, given at Mt. Sinai. When the Israelites agreed to obey it, the terms of this "contract" were made binding upon them and blessing resulted (see I Kings 2:3-4).

133:1 good and pleasant. God desires that His people love one another and live in peace

with one another (1 Cor. 1:10). In Israel, this unity was most evident when the entire nation came together to celebrate the feasts.

133:3 dew of Hermon ... of Zion. Israel was a dry land, and the Jews depended on dew to water the ground and sustain life. Dew was therefore a symbol of the blessing of God on Is-

rael (Gen. 27:28; Hos. 14:5). Mt. Hermon was a tall, cold mountain, so heavy dew fell upon it. God compared that to the blessings which drenched Mt. Zion.

Ps. 136 In Jewish tradition, this psalm is known as the Great Hallel, repeating many of the themes of Psalm 135. It is intended for

who stand in the LORD's house at night!

2 Lift up your hands in the holy place,
and praise the LORD!

3 May the LORD,
Maker of heaven and earth,
bless you from Zion.

Psalm 135

The LORD Is Great

1 •Hallelujah!
Praise the name of the LORD.
Give praise, you servants of the LORD

2 who stand in the house of the LORD,
in the courts of the house of our God.

3 Praise the LORD, for the LORD is good;
sing praise to His name, for it is delightful.

4 For the LORD has chosen Jacob for Himself,
Israel as His treasured possession.

5 For I know that the LORD is great;
our Lord is greater than all gods.

6 The LORD does whatever He pleases
in heaven and on earth,
in the seas and all the depths.

7 He causes the clouds to rise from the ends
of the earth.
He makes lightning for the rain
and brings the wind from His storehouses.

8 He struck down the firstborn of Egypt,
both people and animals.

9 He sent signs and wonders against you, Egypt,
against Pharaoh and all his officials.

10 He struck down many nations
and slaughtered mighty kings:

11 Sihon king of the Amorites,
Og king of Bashan,
and all the kings of Canaan.

12 He gave their land as an inheritance,
an inheritance to His people Israel.

13 LORD, Your name [endures] forever,
Your reputation, LORD,
through all generations.

14 For the LORD will judge His people
and have compassion on His servants.

15 The idols of the nations are of silver and gold,
made by human hands.

16 They have mouths, but cannot speak,
eyes, but cannot see.

17 They have ears, but cannot hear;

indeed, there is no breath in their mouths.

18 Those who make them are just like them,
as are all who trust in them.

19 House of Israel, praise the LORD!
House of Aaron, praise the LORD!

20 House of Levi, praise the LORD!
You who revere the LORD, praise the LORD!

21 May the LORD be praised from Zion;
He dwells in Jerusalem.
Hallelujah!

Psalm 136

God's Love Is Eternal

1 Give thanks to the LORD, for He is good.
His love is eternal.

2 Give thanks to the God of gods.
His love is eternal.

3 Give thanks to the Lord of lords.
His love is eternal.

4 He alone does great wonders.
His love is eternal.

5 He made the heavens skillfully.
His love is eternal.

6 He spread the land on the waters.
His love is eternal.

7 He made the great lights:
His love is eternal.

8 the sun to rule by day,
His love is eternal.

9 the moon and stars to rule by night.
His love is eternal.

10 He struck the firstborn of the Egyptians
His love is eternal.

11 and brought Israel out from among them
His love is eternal.

12 with a strong hand and outstretched arm.
His love is eternal.

13 He divided the •Red Sea
His love is eternal.

14 and led Israel through,
His love is eternal.

15 but hurled Pharaoh and his army
into the Red Sea.
His love is eternal.

16 He led His people in the wilderness.
His love is eternal.

17 He struck down great kings
His love is eternal.

18 and slaughtered famous kings—
His love is eternal.

---

public worship. A Levite or song leader would sing one verse after another, and the choir or worshipers would respond with, "His love endures forever" (see 2 Chron. 5:12-14). God's love for His people is the reason He blesses and protects them.

137:1 rivers of Babylon. This refers to the Ti-

gris and Euphrates Rivers and the great network of canals between them.

137:2,3 hung up our lyres. Overcome with grief, the exiled Jews had no heart for music (Lam. 5:14-18). The songs of Zion were worship songs sung in the temple on Mount Zion. The Israelites could not bring themselves to

sing happy songs of victory and praise.

137:7 Edomites. Like the Israelites, the Edomites descended from Abraham and Isaac. God had told the Israelites to respect the Edomites as brothers (Deut. 23:7), so it was especially painful to know that the Edomites had urged the Babylonians to mercilessly attack the Isra-

19 Sihon king of the Amorites
His love is eternal.
20 and Og king of Bashan—
His love is eternal.
21 and gave their land as an inheritance,
His love is eternal.
22 an inheritance to Israel His servant.
His love is eternal.
23 He remembered us in our humiliation
His love is eternal.
24 and rescued us from our foes.
His love is eternal.
25 He gives food to every creature.
His love is eternal.
26 Give thanks to the God of heaven!
His love is eternal.

Psalm 137

Lament of the Exiles

1 By the rivers of Babylon—
there we sat down and wept
when we remembered Zion.
2 There we hung up our lyres
on the poplar trees,
3 for our captors there asked us for songs,
and our tormentors, for rejoicing:
"Sing us one of the songs of Zion."
4 How can we sing the LORD's song
on foreign soil?
5 If I forget you, Jerusalem,
may my right hand forget ⌊its skill⌋.
6 May my tongue stick to the roof
of my mouth
if I do not remember you,
if I do not exalt Jerusalem
as my greatest joy!
7 Remember, LORD, ⌊what⌋ the Edomites said
that day[a] at Jerusalem:
"Destroy it! Destroy it
down to its foundations!"
8 Daughter Babylon,
doomed to destruction,
happy is the one who pays you back
what you have done to us.
9 Happy is he who takes
your little ones
and dashes them against the rocks.

Psalm 138

A Thankful Heart

Davidic.

1 I will give You thanks with all my heart;
I will sing Your praise
before the heavenly beings.[b]
2 I will bow down toward Your holy temple
and give thanks to Your name
for Your constant love and faithfulness.
You have exalted Your name
and Your promise above everything else.
3 On the day I called, You answered me;
You increased strength within me.[c]
4 All the kings on earth
will give You thanks, LORD,
when they hear what You have promised.[d]
5 They will sing of the LORD's ways,
for the LORD's glory is great.
6 Though the LORD is exalted,
He takes note of the humble;
but He knows the haughty from afar.
7 If I walk in the thick of danger,
You will preserve my life
from the anger of my enemies.
You will extend Your hand;
Your right hand will save me.
8 The LORD will fulfill ⌊His purpose⌋ for me.
LORD, Your love is eternal;
do not abandon the work of Your hands.

Psalm 139

The All-Knowing, Ever-Present God

For the choir director.
A Davidic psalm.

1 LORD, You have searched me and known me.
2 You know when I sit down and when I stand up;
You understand my thoughts from far away.
3 You observe my travels and my rest;
You are aware of all my ways.
4 Before a word is on my tongue,
You know all about it, LORD.
5 You have encircled me;
You have placed Your hand on me.
6 ⌊This⌋ extraordinary knowledge is beyond me.
It is lofty; I am unable to ⌊reach⌋ it.

---

[a] **137:7** The day Jerusalem fell to the Babylonians in 586 B.C.   [b] **138:1** Or *the gods* (Jb 1:6; 2:1), or *before judges* or *kings* (Ps 82:1,6–7; Ex 21:6; 22:7–8); Hb *Elohim*   [c] **138:3** Hb obscure   [d] **138:4** Lit *hear the words of Your mouth*

---

elites (Obad. 8-15).

Ps. 138 This psalm begins a collection of eight Davidic Psalms, including six prayers and two songs in Psalms 138—145.

138:2 Your name. Out of the many so-called gods, Yahweh's name rises above all others—Yahweh, the God of Israel. The Law was God's

Word, His covenant with Israel. Within the Law are many promises of blessing. God's name and God's Word were the same in Jewish thinking.

Ps. 139 All Knowing, Ever Present. God is aware of and cares for the birth and life of each individual.

139:7-12 Where can I go to escape Your Spirit? No place in all creation is a hiding place from God. Even complete darkness hides nothing from Him.

139:13 You who created. God is the One who creates the unique mental and physical attributes of each individual. This implies loving

God's Perpetual Presence

1. Who knows you so well that they know what you are going to say before you even say it?

Psalm 139

2. How is it a comfort that you cannot "escape" God? How is it sobering?

3. What do verses 13-16 suggest about abortion? If God knits us together in the womb and plans all our days, what are we doing if we abort a baby?

4. Why does David say that he hates those who hate God (v. 21)?

5. Have you been walking more in an "offensive way" or an "everlasting way" (v. 24)? How do you need God's help to change?

7   Where can I go to escape Your Spirit?
    Where can I flee from Your presence?
8   If I go up to heaven, You are there;
    if I make my bed in •Sheol, You are there.
9   If I live at the eastern horizon
    ⌊or⌋ settle at the western limits,ᵃ
10 even there Your hand will lead me;
    Your right hand will hold on to me.
11 If I say, "Surely the darkness will hide me,
    and the light around me
        will become night"—
12 even the darkness is not dark to You.
    The night shines like the day;
    darkness and light are alike to You.

13 For it was You who created my inward parts;ᵇ
    You knit me together in my mother's womb.
14 I will praise You,
    because I have been remarkably
        and wonderfully made.ᶜ ᵈ
    Your works are wonderful,
    and I know ⌊this⌋ very well.
15 My bones were not hidden from You
    when I was made in secret,
    when I was formed in the depths of the earth.

16 Your eyes saw me when I was formless;
    all ⌊my⌋ days were written in Your book
        and planned
    before a single one of them began.

17 God, how difficultᵉ Your thoughts are
    for me ⌊to comprehend⌋;
    how vast their sum is!
18 If I counted them,
    they would outnumber the grains of sand;
    when I wake up,ᶠ I am still with You.

19 God, if only You would kill the wicked—
    you bloodthirsty men, stay away from me—
20 who invoke You deceitfully.
    Your enemies swear ⌊by You⌋ falsely.
21 LORD, don't I hate those who hate You,
    and detest those who rebel against You?
22 I hate them with extreme hatred;
    I consider them my enemies.

23 Search me, God, and know my heart;
    test me and know my concerns.
24 See if there is any offensiveᵍ way in me;
    lead me in the everlasting way.

Psalm 140

Prayer for Rescue

For the choir director.
A Davidic psalm.

1   Rescue me, LORD, from evil men.
    Keep me safe from violent men
2   who plan evil in their hearts.
    They stir up wars all day long.
3   They make their tongues
    as sharp as a snake's bite;
    viper's venom is under their lips.   •*Selah*

4   Protect me, LORD,
    from the clutches of the wicked.
    Keep me safe from violent men
    who plan to make me stumble.ʰ
5   The proud hide a trap with ropes for me;
    they spread a net along the path
    and set snares for me.   *Selah*

6   I say to the LORD, "You are my God."
    Listen, LORD, to my cry for help.
7   Lord GOD, my strong Savior,
    You shield my head on the day of battle.

ᵃ**139:9** Lit *I take up the wings of the dawn; I dwell at the end of the sea* ᵇ**139:13** Lit *my kidneys* ᶜ**139:14** DSS, some LXX mss, Syr, Jer read *because You are remarkable and wonderful* ᵈ**139:14** Hb obscure ᵉ**139:17** Or *precious* ᶠ**139:18** Other Hb mss read *I come to an end* ᵍ**139:24** Or *idolatrous* ʰ**140:4** Lit *to trip up my steps*

---

care for each detail of our own complexity.

139:16 Your eyes saw. God sees every human being as he or she is being formed in the womb. He has determined the length of each person's life.

140:10 fire ... abyss. This is similar to the fiery coals and burning sulfur (11:6) which God rains

on the wicked. It foreshadows the final place of punishment for the wicked (Rev. 19:20).

141:8 do not grant the desires. David asked God to judge the wicked, but knew that he was not altogether innocent himself (v. 4). He asked God to spare him, not because of his righteousness, but because of his steady trust in God.

142:3 spirit is weak. David was overwhelmed from being daily beset with "trouble" (v. 2), plots, and danger. David knew that enemies were all around and didn't know which way to turn. He needed God's wisdom to proceed.

143:2 no one alive is righteous. This is one of David's most beautiful prayers and begins with

⁸ LORD, do not grant the desires of the wicked;
do not let them achieve their goals.
⌊Otherwise,⌋ they will become proud.   *Selah*

⁹ As for the heads of those who surround me,
let the trouble their lips cause
overwhelm ⌊them⌋.

¹⁰ Let hot coals fall on them.
Let them be thrown into the fire,
into the abyss, never again to rise.

¹¹ Do not let a slanderer stay in the land.
Let evil relentlessly[a] hunt down a violent man.

¹² I[b] know that the LORD upholds
the just cause of the poor,
justice for the needy.

¹³ Surely the righteous will praise Your name;
the upright will live in Your presence.

Psalm 141

Protection from Sin and Sinners

A Davidic psalm.

¹ LORD, I call on You; hurry to ⌊help⌋ me.
Listen to my voice when I call on You.

² May my prayer be set before You as incense,
the raising of my hands as the evening offering.

³ LORD, set up a guard for my mouth;
keep watch at the door of my lips.

⁴ Do not let my heart turn to any evil thing
or wickedly perform reckless acts
with men who commit sin.
Do not let me feast on their delicacies.

⁵ Let the righteous one strike me—
it is ⌊an act of⌋ faithful love;
let him rebuke me—
it is oil for my head;
let me[c] not refuse it.
Even now my prayer is against
the evil acts of the wicked.[d]

⁶ When their rulers[e] will be thrown off
the sides of a cliff,
the people[f] will listen to my words,
for they are pleasing.

⁷ As when one plows and breaks up the soil,
⌊turning up rocks⌋,
so our[g] bones have been scattered
at the mouth of •Sheol.

⁸ But my eyes ⌊look⌋ to You, Lord GOD.
I seek refuge in You; do not let me die.[h]

⁹ Protect me from[i] the trap they have set for me,
and from the snares of evildoers.

¹⁰ Let the wicked fall into their own nets,
while I pass ⌊safely⌋ by.

Psalm 142

A Cry of Distress

A Davidic •*Maskil*. When he was
in the cave. A prayer.

¹ I cry aloud to the LORD;
I plead aloud to the LORD for mercy.

² I pour out my complaint before Him;
I reveal my trouble to Him.

³ Although my spirit is weak within me,
You know my way.

Along this path I travel
they have hidden a trap for me.

⁴ Look to the right and see:[j]
no one stands up for me;
there is no refuge for me;
no one cares about me.

⁵ I cry to You, LORD;
I say, "You are my shelter,
my portion in the land of the living."

⁶ Listen to my cry,
for I am very weak.
Rescue me from those who pursue me,
for they are too strong for me.

⁷ Free me from prison
so that I can praise Your name.
The righteous will gather around me
because You deal generously with me.

Psalm 143

A Cry for Help

A Davidic psalm.

¹ LORD, hear my prayer.
In Your faithfulness listen to my plea,
and in Your righteousness answer me.

² Do not bring Your servant into judgment,
for no one alive is righteous in Your sight.

³ For the enemy has pursued me,
crushing me to the ground,

---

[a]**140:11** Hb obscure   [b]**140:12** Alt Hb tradition reads *You*   [c]**141:5** Lit *my head*   [d]**141:5** Lit *of them*   [e]**141:6** Or *judges*   [f]**141:6** Lit *cliff, and they*
[g]**141:7** DSS reads *my*; some LXX mss, Syr read *their*   [h]**141:8** Or *not pour out my life*   [i]**141:9** Lit *from the hands of*   [j]**142:4** DSS, LXX, Syr, Vg, Tg
read *I look to the right and I see*

---

an honest admission of his own sinfulness.
David asks God to answer him, not because
David is righteous or for the fact that David deserves God's righteousness, but because God
is righteous.

143:12 for I am Your servant. David could ask
God to destroy his foes because he stood for

the principles of God. Those who fought him
made themselves enemies of the God he
served.

144:2 He is my faithful love. In the midst of
battle, David declared that the source of his
strength was God's unfailing love.

144:3-4 what is man. David marveled that a
God so powerful cared for insignificant humans, for creatures whose entire life is like a
fleeting shadow (see Psalm 8:4).

145:3-7 They will proclaim. Israel's history
was a long list of miracles that God had done
to protect them. Jewish parents were in-

making me live in darkness
like those long dead.
4 My spirit is weak within me;
my heart is overcome with dismay.

5 I remember the days of old;
I meditate on all You have done;
I reflect on the work of Your hands.
6 I spread out my hands to You;
I am like parched land before You. •Selah

7 Answer me quickly, LORD;
my spirit fails.
Don't hide Your face from me,
or I will be like those
going down to the •Pit.
8 Let me experience
Your faithful love in the morning,
for I trust in You.
Reveal to me the way I should go,
because I long for You.
9 Rescue me from my enemies, LORD;
I come to You for protection.ᵃ
10 Teach me to do Your will,
for You are my God.
May Your gracious Spirit
lead me on level ground.

11 Because of Your name, •Yahweh,
let me live.
In Your righteousness deliver me from trouble,
12 and in Your faithful love destroy my enemies.
Wipe out all those who attack me,
for I am Your servant.

Psalm 144

A King's Prayer
Davidic.

1 May the LORD my rock be praised,
who trains my hands for battle
and my fingers for warfare.
2 He is my faithful love and my fortress,
my stronghold and my deliverer.
He is my shield, and I take refuge in Him;
He subdues my peopleᵇ under me.

3 LORD, what is man, that You care for him,
the son of man, that You think of him?
4 Man is like a breath;
his days are like a passing shadow.

5 LORD, part Your heavens and come down.
Touch the mountains,
and they will smoke.
6 Flash ⌊Your⌋ lightning and scatter the foe;ᶜ
shoot Your arrows and rout them.
7 Reach downᵈ from on high;
rescue me from deep water,
and set me free
from the grasp of foreigners
8 whose mouths speak lies,
whose right hands are deceptive.

9 God, I will sing a new song to You;
I will play on a ten-stringed harp for You—
10 the One who gives victory to kings,
who frees His servant David
from the deadly sword.
11 Set me free and rescue me
from the grasp of foreigners
whose mouths speak lies,
whose right hands are deceptive.

12 Then our sons will be like plants
nurtured in their youth,
our daughters, like corner pillars
that are carved in the palace style.
13 Our storehouses will be full,
supplying all kinds of produce;
our flocks will increase by thousands
and tens of thousands in our open fields.
14 Our cattle will be well fed.ᵉ
There will be no breach ⌊in the walls⌋,
no going ⌊into captivity⌋,ᶠ
and no cry of lament in our public squares.
15 Happy are the people with such ⌊blessings⌋.
Happy are the people whose God is the LORD.

Psalm 145

Praising God's Greatness
A Davidic hymn.

1 Iᵍ exalt You, my God the King,
and praise Your name forever and ever.
2 I will praise You every day;
I will honor Your name forever and ever.

3 •Yahweh is great and is highly praised;
His greatness is unsearchable.
4 One generation will declare Your works to the next
and will proclaim Your mighty acts.

ᵃ143:9 One Hb ms, LXX; MT reads *I cover myself to You*   ᵇ144:2 Other Hb mss, DSS, Aq, Syr, Tg, Jer read *subdues peoples*; Ps 18:47; 2 Sm 22:48
ᶜ144:6 Lit *scatter them*   ᵈ144:7 Lit *down Your hands*   ᵉ144:14 Or *will bear heavy loads*, or *will be pregnant*   ᶠ144:14 Or *be no plague, no miscarriage*   ᵍ145:1 The lines of this poem form an •acrostic.

---

structed to tell God's mighty acts to their children, so they too would be in awe of God (Ex. 13:14-15).

146:5-9 God alone has power to truly help. God's infinite compassion motivates His use of power to stop oppressors and help the oppressed.

Ps. 147 This joyful psalm was likely composed and sung when Nehemiah and the Jews finished rebuilding the walls of Jerusalem (vv. 2, 13; Neh. 12:27-43).

147:4-6 stars … gives names. Untold numbers of galaxies comprise the universe, each one containing billions of stars. God created

and knows each one by name.

147:19-20 any nation. God chose Israel, gave them His law and made a covenant with them. God did not create this relationship with any other nation (Ezra 4:1-4). Through Israel, salvation would come to all (John 4:22).

148:8-10 cloud. All of nature praises God

5 I[a] will speak of Your glorious splendor
and[b] Your wonderful works.
6 They will proclaim the power of Your awe-
inspiring works,
and I will declare Your greatness.[c]
7 They will give a testimony of Your great goodness
and will joyfully sing of Your righteousness.
8 The LORD is gracious and compassionate,
slow to anger and great in faithful love.
9 The LORD is good to everyone;
His compassion ⌊rests⌋ on all He has made.
10 All You have made will praise You, LORD;
the[d] godly will bless You.
11 They will speak of the glory of Your kingdom
and will declare Your might,
12 informing ⌊all⌋ people[e] of Your mighty acts
and of the glorious splendor of Your[f] kingdom.
13 Your kingdom is an everlasting kingdom;
Your rule is for all generations.
The LORD is faithful in all His words
and gracious in all His actions.[g]
14 The LORD helps all who fall;
He raises up all who are oppressed.[h]
15 All eyes look to You,
and You give them their food in due time.
16 You open Your hand
and satisfy the desire of every living thing.
17 The LORD is righteous in all His ways
and gracious in all His acts.
18 The LORD is near all who call out to Him,
all who call out to Him with integrity.
19 He fulfills the desires of those who •fear Him;
He hears their cry for help and saves them.
20 The LORD guards all those who love Him,
but He destroys all the wicked.
21 My mouth will declare the LORD's praise;
let every living thing
praise His holy name forever and ever.

Psalm 146
The God of Compassion

1 •Hallelujah!
My soul, praise the LORD.
2 I will praise the LORD all my life;
I will sing to the LORD as long as I live.

3 Do not trust in nobles,
in man, who cannot save.

4 When his breath[i] leaves him,
he returns to the ground;
on that day his plans die.
5 Happy is the one whose help is
the God of Jacob,
whose hope is in the LORD his God,
6 the Maker of heaven and earth,
the sea and everything in them.
He remains faithful forever,
7 executing justice for the exploited
and giving food to the hungry.
The LORD frees prisoners.
8 The LORD opens ⌊the eyes of⌋ the blind.
The LORD raises up those
who are oppressed.[j]
The LORD loves the righteous.
9 The LORD protects foreigners
and helps the fatherless and the widow,
but He frustrates the ways of the wicked.

10 The LORD reigns forever;
Zion, your God ⌊reigns⌋
for all generations.
Hallelujah!

Psalm 147
God Restores Jerusalem

1 •Hallelujah!
How good it is to sing to our God,
for praise is pleasant and lovely.

2 The LORD rebuilds Jerusalem;
He gathers Israel's exiled people.
3 He heals the brokenhearted
and binds up their wounds.
4 He counts the number of the stars;
He gives names to all of them.
5 Our Lord is great, vast in power;
His understanding is infinite.[k]
6 The LORD helps the afflicted
but brings the wicked to the ground.

7 Sing to the LORD with thanksgiving;
play the lyre to our God,
8 who covers the sky with clouds,
prepares rain for the earth,
and causes grass to grow on the hills.
9 He provides the animals with their food,
and the young ravens, what they cry for.

[a]145:5 LXX, Syr read They   [b]145:5 LXX, Syr read and they will tell of   [c]145:6 Alt Hb tradition, Jer read great deeds   [d]145:10 Lit Your   [e]145:12 Lit informing the sons of man   [f]145:12 LXX, Syr, Jer; MT reads His   [g]145:13 One Hb ms, DSS, LXX, Syr; most Hb mss omit The LORD is faithful in all His words and gracious in all His actions.   [h]145:14 Lit bowed down   [i]146:4 Or spirit   [j]146:8 Lit bowed down   [k]147:5 Lit understanding has no number

by declaring His glory (19:1-4). Likewise, all living things, by their very existence, praise God. Their complex design declares the existence of an intelligent Creator.

149:4 adorns ... salvation. Here these words mean deliverance or victory, both physically and spiritually. They also have the deeper spiritual meaning of eternal life (Matt. 5:3; James 1:12).

149:5 on their beds. For the people, being able to lie down on their beds and sleep without fear resulted from God's protection.

149:6-9 When battling enemies, the Israelites knew that strength was not primarily in the swords they held but in the God they trusted and praised (Rev. 19:14-15).

150:1–2 Praise God. This triumphant, joyous psalm gives a rousing call to believers to praise God. It is a fitting finale to the book of Psalms. We should praise God for the miracles He has done, for His surpassing greatness, and because He is powerful, great, and glorious.

10 He is not impressed by the strength of a horse;
  He does not value the power[a] of a man.
11 The LORD values those who fear Him,
  those who put their hope in His faithful love.

12 Exalt the LORD, Jerusalem;
  praise your God, Zion!
13 For He strengthens the bars of your gates
  and blesses your children within you.
14 He endows your territory with prosperity;[b]
  He satisfies you with the finest wheat.

15 He sends His command throughout the earth;
  His word runs swiftly.
16 He spreads snow like wool;
  He scatters frost like ashes;
17 He throws His hailstones like crumbs.
  Who can withstand His cold?
18 He sends His word and melts them;
  He unleashes His winds,[c] and the waters flow.

19 He declares His word to Jacob,
  His statutes and judgments to Israel.
20 He has not done this for any nation;
  they do not know[d] ⌊His⌋ judgments.
  Hallelujah!

Psalm 148
Creation's Praise of the LORD

1 •Hallelujah!
  Praise the LORD from the heavens;
  praise Him in the heights.
2 Praise Him, all His angels;
  praise Him, all His •hosts.
3 Praise Him, sun and moon;
  praise Him, all you shining stars.
4 Praise Him, highest heavens,
  and you waters above the heavens.
5 Let them praise the name of the LORD,
  for He commanded, and they were created.
6 He set them in position forever and ever;
  He gave an order that will never pass away.

7 Praise the LORD from the earth,
  all sea monsters and ocean depths,
8 lightning[e] and hail, snow and cloud,
  powerful wind that executes His command,
9 mountains and all hills,
  fruit trees and all cedars,
10 wild animals and all cattle,
  creatures that crawl and flying birds,
11 kings of the earth and all peoples,
  princes and all judges of the earth,

12 young men as well as young women,
  old and young together.
13 Let them praise the name of the LORD,
  for His name alone is exalted.
  His majesty covers heaven and earth.
14 He has raised up a •horn for His people,
  praise from all His godly ones,
  from the Israelites, the people close to Him.
  Hallelujah!

Psalm 149
Praise for God's Triumph

1 •Hallelujah!
  Sing to the LORD a new song,
  His praise in the assembly of the godly.
2 Let Israel celebrate its Maker;
  let the children of Zion rejoice in their King.
3 Let them praise His name with dancing
  and make music to Him with tambourine and lyre.
4 For the LORD takes pleasure in His people;
  He adorns the humble with salvation.
5 Let the godly celebrate in triumphal glory;
  let them shout for joy on their beds.

6 Let the exaltation of God be in their mouths[f]
  and a two-edged sword in their hands,
7 inflicting vengeance on the nations
  and punishment on the peoples,
8 binding their kings with chains
  and their dignitaries with iron shackles,
9 carrying out the judgment decreed against them.
  This honor is for all His godly people.
  Hallelujah!

Psalm 150
Praise the LORD

1 •Hallelujah!
  Praise God in His sanctuary.
  Praise Him in His mighty heavens.
2 Praise Him for His powerful acts;
  praise Him for His abundant greatness.
3 Praise Him with trumpet blast;
  praise Him with harp and lyre.
4 Praise Him with tambourine and dance;
  praise Him with flute and strings.
5 Praise Him with resounding cymbals;
  praise Him with clashing cymbals.
6 Let everything that breathes praise the LORD.
  Hallelujah!

---

a 147:10 Lit *legs* b 147:14 Or *peace* c 147:18 Or *breath* d 147:20 DSS, LXX, Syr, Tg read *He has not made known to them* e 148:8 Or *fire*
f 149:6 Lit *throat*

150:3 Praise Him with. Worship here is de-   picted as a rousing, loud celebration accom-   panied by a full array of musical instruments.

INTRODUCTION TO
PROVERBS

PERSONAL READING PLAN

- ☐ Proverbs 1:1-2:22
- ☐ Proverbs 3:1-4:27
- ☐ Proverbs 5:1-6:35
- ☐ Proverbs 7:1-8:36
- ☐ Proverbs 9:1-10:32

- ☐ Proverbs 11:1-12:28
- ☐ Proverbs 13:1-14:35
- ☐ Proverbs 15:1-16:33
- ☐ Proverbs 17:1-18:24
- ☐ Proverbs 19:1-20:30

- ☐ Proverbs 21:1-22:29
- ☐ Proverbs 23:1-24:29
- ☐ Proverbs 25:1-26:28
- ☐ Proverbs 27:1-28:28
- ☐ Proverbs 29:1-31:31

AUTHOR

Proverbs has multiple authors and compilers who are named in the section subtitles. Solomon (1:1-22:16; 25:1-29:27) is the most prominent of these, plus the introduction to the work (1:1-7) is attributed to him. The group of authors entitled "the wise" (22:17-24:34) may have been royal scribes. The sayings of Agur (chapter 30) and Lemuel (chapter 31) conclude the book.

DATE

Solomon reigned in Israel circa 970-930 B.C. During that time he wrote thousands of proverbs and songs (1 Kings 4:32). The final compilation of this work occurred after Hezekiah's time (25:1), more than 200 years later, possibly as late as 500 B.C.

THEME

To impart moral wisdom and uncommon sense for right living.

HISTORICAL BACKGROUND

Following Solomon's ascension to the throne of Israel, the Lord appeared to him in a dream and offered him the desire of his heart (1 Kings 3:1-28; 4:29-34). Solomon chose wisdom. The Book of Proverbs collects this God-given wisdom in poetic figures of speech, along with the trusted sayings of wise men, accumulated over 200-plus years. Given the international nature of Solomon's court and Israel's mixing with its neighbors, it is not surprising that many parallels to the Proverbs have been found in extra-biblical texts.

CHARACTERISTICS

Following the Book of Psalms, which focuses on our devotional lives, we find the Book of Proverbs, which focuses on our practical lives. The English word "proverb" means a brief saying in place of many words. The Hebrew word for proverb, however, has a much broader meaning including longer sentences and discourses. The Book of Proverbs is a part of the Wisdom Literature of the Hebrews. Drawn from the everyday life of common people, these proverbs are couched in figurative, poetic speech laced with analogies and word pictures. Therefore, Book of Proverbs leaves a visual as well as verbal impact upon the reader.

As the introduction states, Proverbs was written to give "shrewdness to the inexperienced" (1:4). The repeated references to "my son" (1:8,10; 2:1; 3:1; 4:1; 5:1) focus on guiding the young to make righteous and moral choices. Because these proverbs were written particularly for instruction, they are frequently given in the form of commands.

PASSAGES FOR
TOPICAL GROUP STUDY

3:1-8 .... TRUSTING GOD .... Health for Body and Mind

The Purpose of Proverbs

1 The proverbs of Solomon son of David,
    king of Israel:

2 For gaining wisdom and being instructed;
    for understanding insightful sayings;

3 for receiving wise instruction
    ⌊in⌋ righteousness, justice, and integrity;

4 for teaching shrewdness to the inexperienced,[a]
    knowledge and discretion to a young man—

5 a wise man will listen and increase his learning,
    and a discerning man will obtain guidance—

6 for understanding a proverb or a parable,[b]
    the words of the wise, and their riddles.

7 The •fear of the LORD
    is the beginning of knowledge;
    fools despise wisdom and instruction.[c]

Avoid the Path of the Violent

8 Listen, my son, to your father's instruction,
    and don't reject your mother's teaching,

9 for they will be a garland of grace on your head
    and a ⌊gold⌋ chain around your neck.

10 My son, if sinners entice you,
    don't be persuaded.

11 If they say—"Come with us!
    Let's set an ambush and kill someone.[d]
    Let's attack some innocent person just for fun![e]

12 Let's swallow them alive, like •Sheol,
    still healthy as they go down to the •Pit.

13 We'll find all kinds of valuable property
    and fill our houses with plunder.

14 Throw in your lot with us,
    and we'll all share our money"[f]—

15 my son, don't travel that road with them
    or set foot on their path,

16 because their feet run toward trouble
    and they hurry to commit murder.[g]

17 It is foolish to spread a net
    where any bird can see it,

18 but they set an ambush to kill themselves;[h]
    they attack their own lives.

19 Such are the paths of all who pursue
    gain dishonestly;
    it takes the lives of those who profit from it.[i]

Wisdom's Plea

20 Wisdom calls out in the street;
    she raises her voice in the public squares.

21 She cries out above[j] the commotion;

she speaks at the entrance of the city •gates:

22 "How long, foolish ones, will you
    love ignorance?
    ⌊How long⌋ will ⌊you⌋ mockers enjoy mocking
    and ⌊you⌋ fools hate knowledge?

23 If you turn to my discipline,[k]
    then I will pour out my spirit on you
    and teach you my words.

24 Since I called out and you refused,
    extended my hand and no one paid attention,

25 since you neglected all my counsel
    and did not accept my correction,

26 I, in turn, will laugh at your calamity.
    I will mock when terror strikes you,

27 when terror strikes you like a storm
    and your calamity comes like a whirlwind,
    when trouble and stress overcome you.

28 Then they will call me, but I won't answer;
    they will search for me, but won't find me.

29 Because they hated knowledge,
    didn't choose to fear the LORD,

30 were not interested in my counsel,
    and rejected all my correction,

31 they will eat the fruit of their way
    and be glutted with their own schemes.

32 For the waywardness of the inexperienced
    will kill them,
    and the complacency of fools will destroy them.

33 But whoever listens to me will live securely
    and be free from the fear of danger."

Wisdom's Worth

2 My son, if you accept my words
    and store up my commands within you,

2 listening closely[l] to wisdom
    and directing your heart to understanding;

3 furthermore, if you call out to insight
    and lift your voice to understanding,

4 if you seek it like silver
    and search for it like hidden treasure,

5 then you will understand the •fear of the LORD
    and discover the knowledge of God.

6 For the LORD gives wisdom;
    from His mouth come knowledge
    and understanding.

7 He stores up success[m] for the upright;
    He is a shield for those who live with integrity

8 so that He may guard the paths of justice
    and protect the way of His loyal followers.

---

[a]1:4 Or *simple*, or *gullible*   [b]1:6 Or *an enigma*   [c]1:7 This verse states the theme of Pr.   [d]1:11 Lit *Let's ambush for blood*   [e]1:11 Lit *person for no reason*   [f]1:14 Lit *us; one bag will be for all of us*   [g]1:16 Lit *to shed blood*   [h]1:18 Lit *they ambush for their blood*   [i]1:19 Lit *takes the life of its masters*   [j]1:21 Lit *at the head of*   [k]1:23 Lit *back to my reprimands*   [l]2:2 Lit *you, stretching out your ear*   [m]2:7 Or *resourcefulness*

1:2 gaining wisdom. True wisdom begins with fearing the Lord (v. 7).

1:7 fear of the LORD. The fear of the Lord involves acknowledging God's power and sovereignty.

1:13 valuable property. Thieves disregard

what truly matters for stolen trinkets and wasted lives.

1:18 attack … own lives. Those who live apart from God are like people who set a trap, only to catch themselves in it.

1:26 laugh … mock. Wisdom derives joy from

the works of God and condemns those who reject His will.

1:32 kill … destroy. Living outside of God's wisdom brings destruction—a message repeated throughout the New Testament (Rom. 6:23).

1:33 live securely. Obedience may seem like a burden, but consider the difference between

9 Then you will understand righteousness, justice,
and integrity—every good path.
10 For wisdom will enter your mind,
and knowledge will delight your heart.
11 Discretion will watch over you,
and understanding will guard you,
12 rescuing you from the way of evil—
from the one who says perverse things,
13 ⌊from⌋ those who abandon the right paths
to walk in ways of darkness,
14 ⌊from⌋ those who enjoy doing evil
and celebrate perversity,
15 whose paths are crooked,
and whose ways are devious.
16 It will rescue you from a forbidden woman,
from a stranger[a] with her flattering talk,
17 who abandons the companion of her youth
and forgets the covenant of her God;
18 for her house sinks down to death
and her ways to the land of the departed spirits.
19 None return who go to her;
none reach the paths of life.
20 So follow the way of good people,
and keep to the paths of the righteous.
21 For the upright will inhabit the land,
and those of integrity will remain in it;
22 but the wicked will be cut off from the land,
and the treacherous uprooted from it.

Trust the LORD

3 My son, don't forget my teaching,
but let your heart keep my commands;
2 for they will bring you
many days, a full life,[b] and well-being.
3 Never let loyalty and faithfulness leave you.
Tie them around your neck;
write them on the tablet of your heart.
4 Then you will find favor and high regard
in the sight of God and man.

5 Trust in the LORD with all your heart,
and do not rely on your own understanding;
6 think about Him in all your ways,
and He will guide you on the right paths.
7 Don't consider yourself to be wise;
•fear the LORD and turn away from evil.
8 This will be healing for your body[c]
and strengthening for your bones.
9 Honor the LORD with your possessions
and with the first produce of your entire harvest;
10 then your barns will be completely filled,

Health for Body and Mind

1. What's your favorite "health food?" What's your least favorite?

Proverbs 3:1-8
2. What does it mean to tie loyalty and faithfulness "around your neck" and to "write them on the tablet of your heart" (v. 3)? How do we do accomplish this?
3. How does relying on our own understanding interfere with trusting God (v. 5)?
4. In what ways do you sometimes consider yourself wise? How has this gotten you in trouble?
5. Are you relying more on your own wisdom or on God's guidance?

and your vats will overflow with new wine.
11 Do not despise the LORD's instruction,
my son,
and do not loathe His discipline;
12 for the LORD disciplines the one He loves,
just as a father, the son he delights in.

Wisdom Brings Happiness

13 Happy is a man who finds wisdom
and who acquires understanding,
14 for she is more profitable than silver,
and her revenue is better than gold.
15 She is more precious than jewels;
nothing you desire compares with her.
16 Long life[d] is in her right hand;
in her left, riches and honor.
17 Her ways are pleasant,
and all her paths, peaceful.
18 She is a tree of life to those who embrace her,
and those who hold on to her are happy.

19 The LORD founded the earth by wisdom
and established the heavens by understanding.
20 By His knowledge the watery depths
broke open,
and the clouds dripped with dew.

21 Maintain ⌊your⌋ competence and discretion.
My son, don't lose sight of them.

---

a **2:16** Or *foreign woman*   b **3:2** Lit *days, years of life*   c **3:8** Lit *navel*   d **3:16** Lit *Length of days*

---

honesty and deception—living openly before others as opposed to having to keep track of lies and half-truths.
2:4 seek ... treasure. To find wisdom, a person must search and dig.
2:10-19 Wisdom is our protection against evil people who would lure us into self-destruction.

2:12 perverse. The original word translated as "perverse" means "to turn away from the upright." Throughout Proverbs this word describes a person who chooses wickedness over wisdom or self over God (see 8:13; 10:31).
2:21 upright will inhabit the land. The Jews' history involved a journey back to the land God

had promised their ancestor Abraham—their reward for following God.
3:2 well-being. This word is often translated "peace." It suggests wholeness, health, and harmony.
3:5 with all your heart. The Bible uses this phrase to express total commitment. The

22 They will be life for you[a]
  and adornment[b] for your neck.
23 Then you will go safely on your way;
  your foot will not stumble.
24 When you lie[c] down, you will not be afraid;
  you will lie down, and your sleep will be pleasant.
25 Don't fear sudden danger
  or the ruin of the wicked when it comes,
26 for the LORD will be your confidence[d]
  and will keep your foot from a snare.

Treat Others Fairly

27 When it is in your power,[e]
  don't withhold good from the one to whom
    it is due.
28 Don't say to your neighbor, "Go away!
    Come back later.
  I'll give it tomorrow"—when it is there with you.
29 Don't plan any harm against your neighbor,
  for he trusts you and lives near you.
30 Don't accuse anyone without cause,
  when he has done you no harm.
31 Don't envy a violent man
  or choose any of his ways;
32 for the devious are detestable to the LORD,
  but He is a friend[f] to the upright.
33 The LORD's curse is on the household
    of the wicked,
  but He blesses the home of the righteous;
34 He mocks those who mock,
  but gives grace to the humble.
35 The wise will inherit honor,
  but He holds up fools to dishonor.[g]

A Father's Example

4 Listen, ⌊my⌋ sons, to a father's discipline,
  and pay attention so that
    you may gain understanding,
2 for I am giving you good instruction.
  Don't abandon my teaching.
3 When I was a son with my father,
  tender and precious to my mother,
4 he taught me and said:
  "Your heart must hold on to my words.
  Keep my commands and live.
5 Get wisdom, get understanding;
  don't forget or turn away from the words
    of my mouth.
6 Don't abandon wisdom, and she will
    watch over you;

love her, and she will guard you.
7 Wisdom is supreme—so get wisdom.
  And whatever else you get, get understanding.
8 Cherish her, and she will exalt you;
  if you embrace her, she will honor you.
9 She will place a garland of grace on your head;
  she will give you a crown of beauty."

Two Ways of Life

10 Listen, my son. Accept my words,
  and you will live many years.
11 I am teaching you the way of wisdom;
  I am guiding you on straight paths.
12 When you walk, your steps will not be hindered;
  when you run, you will not stumble.
13 Hold on to instruction; don't let go.
  Guard it, for it is your life.
14 Don't set foot on the path of the wicked;
  don't proceed in the way of evil ones.
15 Avoid it; don't travel on it.
  Turn away from it, and pass it by.
16 For they can't sleep
  unless they have done what is evil;
  they are robbed of sleep unless they make
    someone stumble.
17 They eat the bread of wickedness
  and drink the wine of violence.
18 The path of the righteous is like the light of dawn,
  shining brighter and brighter until midday.
19 But the way of the wicked is
    like the darkest gloom;
  they don't know what makes them stumble.

The Straight Path

20 My son, pay attention to my words;
  listen closely to my sayings.
21 Don't lose sight of them;
  keep them within your heart.
22 For they are life to those who find them,
  and health to one's whole body.
23 Guard your heart above all else,[h]
  for it is the source of life.
24 Don't let your mouth speak dishonestly,
  and don't let your lips talk deviously.
25 Let your eyes look forward;
  fix your gaze[i] straight ahead.
26 Carefully consider the path[j] for your feet,
  and all your ways will be established.
27 Don't turn to the right or to the left;
  keep your feet away from evil.

---

[a]**3:22** Or *be your throat*; Hb *nephesh* can mean *throat, soul,* or *life.*   [b]**3:22** Or *grace*   [c]**3:24** LXX reads *sit*   [d]**3:26** Or *be at your side*   [e]**3:27** Lit *in the power of your hands*   [f]**3:32** Or *confidential counsel*   [g]**3:35** Or *but haughty fools dishonor,* or *but fools exalt dishonor*   [h]**4:23** Or *heart with all diligence*   [i]**4:25** Lit *eyelids*   [j]**4:26** Or *Clear a path*

Shema in Deuteronomy 6:5 calls us to love God with all our hearts, minds, and souls. Jesus described this as the first and greatest commandment.

3:6 guide … paths. This implies more than guidance. It means God removes obstacles from our path.

3:10 vats will overflow. Plenty of wine meant prosperity to Old Testament worshippers. Often the wealth of a land was described in terms of its vineyards, grapes, or wine.

3:11-12 discipline. The Lord corrects those whom He loves.

4:3 son with my father. Solomon's father was

King David. Because Solomon was "young and inexperienced" (1 Chron. 22:5), David envisioned a temple whose construction became Solomon's great achievement.

4:4 he taught me. Solomon transfers the wisdom of his father David to his own sons, as was the Hebrew custom.

Avoid Seduction

5 My son, pay attention to my wisdom;
listen closely[a] to my understanding

2 so that ⌊you⌋ may maintain discretion
and your lips safeguard knowledge.

3 Though the lips of the forbidden woman
drip honey
and her words are[b] smoother than oil,

4 in the end she's as bitter as •wormwood
and as sharp as a double-edged sword.

5 Her feet go down to death;
her steps head straight for •Sheol.

6 She doesn't consider the path of life;
she doesn't know that her ways are unstable.

7 So now, ⌊my⌋ sons, listen to me,
and don't turn away from the words
of my mouth.

8 Keep your way far from her.
Don't go near the door of her house.

9 Otherwise, you will give up your vitality
to others
and your years to someone cruel;

10 strangers will drain your resources,
and your earnings will end up
in a foreigner's house.

11 At the end of your life, you will lament
when your physical body has been consumed,

12 and you will say, "How I hated discipline,
and how my heart despised correction.

13 I didn't obey my teachers
or listen closely[c] to my mentors.

14 I was on the verge of complete ruin
before the entire community."

Enjoy Marriage

15 Drink water from your own cistern,
water flowing from your own well.

16 Should your springs flow in the streets,
streams of water in the public squares?

17 They should be for you alone
and not for you ⌊to share⌋ with strangers.

18 Let your fountain be blessed,
and take pleasure in the wife of your youth.

19 A loving doe, a graceful fawn—
let her breasts always satisfy you;
be lost in her love forever.

20 Why, my son, would you be infatuated
with a forbidden woman
or embrace the breast of a stranger?

21 For a man's ways are before the LORD's eyes,
and He considers all his paths.

22 A wicked man's iniquities entrap him;
he is entangled in the ropes of his own sin.

23 He will die because there is no instruction,
and be lost because of his great stupidity.

Financial Entanglements

6 My son, if you have put up security
for your neighbor[d]
or entered into an agreement with[e] a stranger,[f]

2 you have been trapped by the words
of your lips[g] —
ensnared by the words of your mouth.

3 Do this, then, my son, and free yourself,
for you have put yourself
in your neighbor's power:
Go, humble yourself, and plead
with your neighbor.

4 Don't give sleep to your eyes
or slumber to your eyelids.

5 Escape like a gazelle from a hunter,[h]
like a bird from a fowler's trap.[h]

Laziness

6 Go to the ant, you slacker!
Observe its ways and become wise.

7 Without leader, administrator, or ruler,

8 it prepares its provisions in summer;
it gathers its food during harvest.

9 How long will you stay in bed, you slacker?
When will you get up from your sleep?

10 A little sleep, a little slumber,
a little folding of the arms to rest,

11 and your poverty will come like a robber,
your need, like a bandit.

The Malicious Man

12 A worthless person, a wicked man,
who goes around speaking dishonestly,

13 who winks his eyes, signals with his feet,
and gestures with his fingers,

14 who plots evil with perversity in his heart—
he stirs up trouble constantly.

15 Therefore calamity will strike him suddenly;
he will be shattered instantly—
beyond recovery.

What the LORD Hates

16 Six things the LORD hates;
in fact, seven are detestable to Him:

---

a 5:1 Lit wisdom; stretch out your ear   b 5:3 Lit her palate is   c 5:13 Lit or turn my ear   d 6:1 Or friend   e 6:1 Lit or shaken hands for or with
f 6:1 The Hb word for stranger can refer to a foreigner, an Israelite outside one's family, or simply to another person.   g 6:2 Lit mouth   h 6:5 Lit hand

---

4:10 live many years. The Bible often equates obedience with long life, but a long life is measured by quality of life as well as number of years.

4:18-19 Throughout the Bible righteousness and wickedness are compared to light and darkness. God's presence and guidance are described in terms of light. Jesus called Himself "the Light of the World" (see John 8:12).

5:3 honey ... oil. Honey was the *sweetest* substance, and olive oil was the *smoothest* substance in Hebrew culture. Both are metaphors for folly.

5:7-14 Sexual infidelity carries a price. It costs a person dearly, including self-respect.

5:11 you will lament. "Lament" may refer to old age, but more likely it refers to the cumulative, debilitating effects of living immorally.

5:13 my teachers. This phrase could refer to parents or teachers of the law.

17 arrogant eyes, a lying tongue,
hands that shed innocent blood,

18 a heart that plots wicked schemes,
feet eager to run to evil,

19 a lying witness who gives false testimony,
and one who stirs up trouble among brothers.

Warning against Adultery

20 My son, keep your father's command,
and don't reject your mother's teaching.

21 Always bind them to your heart;
tie them around your neck.

22 When you walk here and there, they will
guide you;
when you lie down, they will watch over you;
when you wake up, they will talk to you.

23 For a commandment is a lamp, teaching is a light,
and corrective instructions are the way to life.

24 They will protect you from an evil woman,[a]
from the flattering[b] tongue of a stranger.

25 Don't lust in your heart for her beauty
or let her captivate you with her eyelashes.

26 For a prostitute's fee is only a loaf of bread,[c]
but an adulteress[d] goes after [your] very life.

27 Can a man embrace fire[e]
and his clothes not be burned?

28 Can a man walk on coals
without scorching his feet?

29 So it is with the one who sleeps with
another man's wife;
no one who touches her will go unpunished.

30 People don't despise the thief if he steals
to satisfy himself when he is hungry.

31 Still, if caught, he must pay seven times
as much;
he must give up all the wealth in his house.

32 The one who commits adultery[f] lacks sense;
whoever does so destroys himself.

33 He will get a beating[g] and dishonor,
and his disgrace will never be removed.

34 For jealousy enrages a husband,
and he will show no mercy
when he takes revenge.

35 He will not be appeased by anything
or be persuaded by lavish gifts.

7 My son, obey my words,
and treasure my commands.

2 Keep my commands and live;
protect my teachings
as you would the pupil of your eye.

3 Tie them to your fingers;
write them on the tablet of your heart.

4 Say to wisdom, "You are my sister,"
and call understanding [your] relative.

5 She will keep you from a forbidden woman,
a stranger with her flattering talk.

A Story of Seduction

6 At the window of my house
I looked through my lattice.

7 I saw among the inexperienced,[h]
I noticed among the youths,
a young man lacking sense.

8 Crossing the street near her corner,
he strolled down the road to her house

9 at twilight, in the evening,
in the dark of the night.

10 A woman came to meet him,
dressed like a prostitute,
having a hidden agenda.[i]

11 She is loud and defiant;
her feet do not stay at home.

12 Now in the street, now in the squares,
she lurks at every corner.

13 She grabs him and kisses him;
she brazenly says[j] to him,

14 "I've made •fellowship offerings;[k]
today I've fulfilled my vows.

15 So I came out to meet you,
to search for you, and I've found you.

16 I've spread coverings on my bed—
richly colored linen from Egypt.

17 I've perfumed my bed
with myrrh, aloes, and cinnamon.

18 Come, let's drink deeply of lovemaking
until morning.
Let's feast on each other's love!

19 My husband isn't home;
he went on a long journey.

20 He took a bag of money with him
and will come home at the time
of the full moon."

21 She seduces him with her persistent pleading;
she lures with her flattering[b] talk.

22 He follows her impulsively

---

a **6:24** LXX reads *from a married woman*   b **6:24; 7:21** Lit *smooth*   c **6:26** Or *On account of a prostitute, [one is left with] only a loaf of bread*   d **6:26** Lit *but a wife of a man*   e **6:27** Lit *man take fire to his bosom*   f **6:32** Lit *commits adultery with a woman*   g **6:33** Or *plague*   h **7:7** Or *simple, or gullible, or naive*   i **7:10** Or *prostitute, with a guarded heart*   j **7:13** Lit *she makes her face strong and says*   k **7:14** Meat from a fellowship offering had to be eaten on the day it was offered; therefore she is inviting him to a feast at her house.

6:1 security … agreement. The equivalent of cosigning a loan and being responsible for someone else's debt. Charging interest on loans to fellow countrymen was not considered honorable among the Hebrews.

6:6 slacker. A slacker was a lazy and shiftless person who chose a lifestyle of irresponsibility over actively doing the right things.

6:12 worthless person. A worthless and wicked person (Judg. 19:22; 1 Sam. 25:25) was also a troublemaker. Eventually this term became associated with Satan (2 Cor. 6:14-15).

6:17 arrogant eyes. A proud look. God does not reward pride or arrogance. Pride leads to destruction (16:18; 18:12).

6:23 lamp … light. This writer describes parents teaching truth to their children in the same way the psalmist describes the Word of God: "A lamp for my feet and a light on my path" (Ps. 119:105).

like an ox going to the slaughter,
like a deer bounding toward a trap[a]

23 until an arrow pierces its[b] liver,
like a bird darting into a snare—
he doesn't know it will cost him his life.

24 Now, ⌊my⌋ sons, listen to me,
and pay attention to the words of my mouth.

25 Don't let your heart turn aside to her ways;
don't stray onto her paths.

26 For she has brought many down to death;
her victims are countless.[c]

27 Her house is the road to •Sheol,
descending to the chambers of death.

Wisdom's Appeal

8 Doesn't Wisdom call out?
Doesn't Understanding make her voice heard?

2 At the heights overlooking the road,
at the crossroads, she takes her stand.

3 Beside the gates at the entry to[d] the city,
at the main entrance, she cries out:

4 "People, I call out to you;
my cry is to mankind.

5 Learn to be shrewd, you who are inexperienced;
develop common sense, you who are foolish.

6 Listen, for I speak of noble things,
and what my lips say is right.

7 For my mouth tells the truth,
and wickedness is detestable to my lips.

8 All the words of my mouth are righteous;
none of them are deceptive or perverse.

9 All of them are clear to the perceptive,
and right to those who discover knowledge.

10 Accept my instruction instead of silver,
and knowledge rather than pure gold.

11 For wisdom is better than precious stones,
and nothing desirable can compare with it.

12 I, Wisdom, share a home with shrewdness
and have knowledge and discretion.

13 To •fear the LORD is to hate evil.
I hate arrogant pride, evil conduct,
and perverse speech.

14 I possess good advice and competence;[e]
I have understanding and strength.

15 It is by me that kings reign
and rulers enact just law;

16 by me, princes lead,
as do nobles ⌊and⌋ all righteous judges.[f]

17 I love those who love me,

and those who search for me find me.

18 With me are riches and honor,
lasting wealth and righteousness.

19 My fruit is better than solid gold,
and my harvest than pure silver.

20 I walk in the way of righteousness,
along the paths of justice,

21 giving wealth as an inheritance to those
who love me,
and filling their treasuries.

22 The LORD made[g] me
at the beginning of His creation,[h]
before His works of long ago.

23 I was formed before ancient times,
from the beginning, before the earth began.

24 I was brought forth
when there were no watery depths
and no springs filled with water.

25 I was brought forth
before the mountains and hills were established,

26 before He made the land, the fields,
or the first soil on earth.

27 I was there when He established the heavens,
when He laid out the horizon on the surface
of the ocean,

28 when He placed the skies above,
when the fountains of the ocean gushed forth,

29 when He set a limit for the sea
so that the waters would not violate
His command,
when He laid out the foundations of the earth.

30 I was a skilled craftsman[i] beside Him.
I was His[j] delight every day,
always rejoicing before Him.

31 I was rejoicing in His inhabited world,
delighting in the •human race.

32 And now, ⌊my⌋ sons, listen to me;
those who keep my ways are happy.

33 Listen to instruction and be wise;
don't ignore it.

34 Anyone who listens to me is happy,
watching at my doors every day,
waiting by the posts of my doorway.

35 For the one who finds me finds life
and obtains favor from the LORD,

36 but the one who sins against me
harms himself;
all who hate me love death."

---

[a]7:22 Text emended; lit *like shackles for the discipline of a fool*; Hb obscure   [b]7:23 Or *his*   [c]7:26 Or *and powerful men are all her victims*   [d]8:3 Lit *the mouth of*   [e]8:14 Or *resourcefulness*   [f]8:16 Some Hb mss, LXX read *nobles who judge the earth*   [g]8:22 Or *possessed*, or *begot*   [h]8:22 Lit *way*   [i]8:30 Or *a confidante*, or *a child*   [j]8:30 LXX; Hb omits *His*

6:31 seven times. Seven is a number representing completion. Hebrew law did not require more than a fivefold restitution for stolen property. "Seven times" implies full restoration or "whatever it takes." No penalty could pardon adultery.

7:3 Tie them. Moses' last charge to the Israel-

ites was to bind God's Law to their foreheads and hands (Deut. 6:8). Solomon echoes Moses' command here.

7:21 persistent. An accurate picture of sin and temptation. The immoral woman sets out deliberately to cause a man to fall into sin.

8:14 Wisdom is highlighted here as a source of

strength. This chapter draws a stark contrast between the wise person and the helpless victim caught in the web of sin.

8:22-31 Wisdom is personified in this hymn-like passage. New Testament writers describe Jesus in similar terms. He was the Word that was with God during creation (John 1:1-3) as

Wisdom versus Foolishness

9 Wisdom has built her house;
she has carved out her seven pillars.
2 She has prepared her meat; she has mixed
her wine;
she has also set her table.
3 She has sent out her servants;
she calls out from the highest points of the city:
4 "Whoever is inexperienced, enter here!"
To the one who lacks sense, she says,
5 "Come, eat my bread,
and drink the wine I have mixed.
6 Leave inexperience behind, and you will live;
pursue the way of understanding.
7 The one who corrects a mocker
will bring dishonor on himself;
the one who rebukes a wicked man will get hurt.[a]
8 Don't rebuke a mocker, or he will hate you;
rebuke a wise man, and he will love you.
9 Instruct a wise man, and he will be wiser still;
teach a righteous man, and he will learn more.

10 The •fear of the LORD is the beginning
of wisdom,
and the knowledge of the Holy One
is understanding.
11 For by Wisdom your days will be many,
and years will be added to your life.
12 If you are wise, you are wise
for your own benefit;
if you mock, you alone will bear
⌊the consequences⌋."
13 The woman Folly is rowdy;
she is gullible and knows nothing.
14 She sits by the doorway of her house,
on a seat at the highest point of the city,
15 calling to those who pass by,
who go straight ahead on their paths:
16 "Whoever is inexperienced, enter here!"
To the one who lacks sense, she says,
17 "Stolen water is sweet,
and bread ⌊eaten⌋ secretly is tasty!"
18 But he doesn't know that the departed spirits
are there,
that her guests are in the depths of •Sheol.

A Collection of Solomon's Proverbs

10 Solomon's proverbs:

A wise son brings joy to his father,
but a foolish son, heartache to his mother.

2 Ill-gotten gains do not profit anyone,
but righteousness rescues from death.

3 The LORD will not let the righteous go hungry,
but He denies the wicked what they crave.

4 Idle hands make one poor,
but diligent hands bring riches.

5 The son who gathers during summer is prudent;
the son who sleeps during harvest is disgraceful.

6 Blessings are on the head of the righteous,
but the mouth of the wicked conceals violence.

7 The remembrance of the righteous is a blessing,
but the name of the wicked will rot.

8 A wise heart accepts commands,
but foolish lips will be destroyed.

9 The one who lives with integrity lives securely,
but whoever perverts his ways will be
found out.

10 A sly wink of the eye causes grief,
and foolish lips will be destroyed.

11 The mouth of the righteous is a fountain of life,
but the mouth of the wicked conceals violence.

12 Hatred stirs up conflicts,
but love covers all offenses.

13 Wisdom is found on the lips of the discerning,
but a rod is for the back of the one
who lacks sense.

14 The wise store up knowledge,
but the mouth of the fool hastens destruction.

15 A rich man's wealth is his fortified city;
the poverty of the poor is their destruction.

16 The labor of the righteous leads to life;
the activity of the wicked leads to sin.

17 The one who follows instruction is on the path
to life,
but the one who rejects correction goes astray.

18 The one who conceals hatred has lying lips,
and whoever spreads slander is a fool.

19 When there are many words, sin is unavoidable,
but the one who controls his lips is wise.

20 The tongue of the righteous is pure silver;
the heart of the wicked is of little value.

---

[a]**9:7** Lit *man his blemish*

---

well as the wisdom of God (1 Cor. 1:24,30).

8:32 those who keep my ways are happy. Blessings that follow wisdom are not so much mystical rewards as the natural consequences of good choices and a life well-lived.

8:36 harms himself. The Bible equates sin,

choosing our own way over God's, with self-destruction.

9:1 house ... seven pillars. "Seven pillars" could refer to the seven days of creation or to the seven constellations in the heavens.

9:5 eat ... drink. Wisdom is like wine and food.

9:7 mocker. A wicked person will lash out at correction and retaliate against discipline.

9:8 he will love you. Even a rebuke is a pleasant thing because a wise person will learn from it.

9:11 years will be added. Generally speaking,

21 The lips of the righteous feed many,
    but fools die for lack of sense.

22 The LORD's blessing enriches,
    and struggle adds nothing to it.[a]

23 As shameful conduct is pleasure for a fool,
    so wisdom is for a man of understanding.

24 What the wicked dreads will come to him,
    but what the righteous desires will be given
        to him.

25 When the whirlwind passes,
    the wicked are no more,
    but the righteous are secure forever.

26 Like vinegar to the teeth and smoke
        to the eyes,
    so the slacker is to the one who sends him
        [on an errand].

27 The •fear of the LORD prolongs life,[b]
    but the years of the wicked are cut short.

28 The hope of the righteous is joy,
    but the expectation of the wicked
        comes to nothing.

29 The way of the LORD is a stronghold
        for the honorable,
    but destruction awaits the malicious.

30 The righteous will never be shaken,
    but the wicked will not remain on the earth.

31 The mouth of the righteous produces wisdom,
    but a perverse tongue will be cut out.

32 The lips of the righteous know
        what is appropriate,
    but the mouth of the wicked,
        [only] what is perverse.

11 Dishonest scales are detestable to the LORD,
    but an accurate weight is His delight.

2 When pride comes, disgrace follows,
    but with humility comes wisdom.

3 The integrity of the upright guides them,
    but the perversity of the treacherous
        destroys them.

4 Wealth is not profitable on a day of wrath,
    but righteousness rescues from death.

5 The righteousness of the blameless
        clears his path,
    but the wicked person will fall because of
        his wickedness.

6 The righteousness of the upright rescues them,
    but the treacherous are trapped
        by their own desires.

7 When the wicked dies,
    his expectation comes to nothing,
    and hope placed in wealth[c] [d] vanishes.

8 The righteous is rescued from trouble;
    in his place, the wicked goes in.

9 With his mouth the ungodly
        destroys his neighbor,
    but through knowledge the righteous
        are rescued.

10 When the righteous thrive, a city rejoices,
    and when the wicked die, there is
        joyful shouting.

11 A city is built up by the blessing of the upright,
    but it is torn down by the mouth of the wicked.

12 Whoever shows contempt for his neighbor
        lacks sense,
    but a man with understanding keeps silent.

13 A gossip goes around revealing a secret,
    but the trustworthy keeps a confidence.

14 Without guidance, people fall,
    but with many counselors there is deliverance.

15 If someone puts up security for a stranger,
    he will suffer for it,
    but the one who hates such agreements
        is protected.

16 A gracious woman gains honor,
    but violent[e] men gain [only] riches.

17 A kind man benefits himself,
    but a cruel man brings disaster on himself.

18 The wicked man earns an empty wage,
    but the one who sows righteousness,
        a true reward.

19 Genuine righteousness [leads] to life,
    but pursuing evil [leads] to death.

---

[a]**10:22** Or *and He adds no trouble to it* [b]**10:27** Lit *LORD adds to days* [c]**11:7** LXX reads *hope of the ungodly* [d]**11:7** Or *strength* [e]**11:16** Or *ruthless*

---

wisdom adds to the quality and longevity of life.

9:12 The rewards of wisdom and folly work on the same principle that Paul described in Galatians 6:7. What a person sows will yield consequences.

10:1 Solomon's proverbs. Chapters 10–22

are collections of individual proverbs that do not have a common theme.

10:4 poor. In Proverbs poverty is associated with laziness or a lack of discipline.

10:5 harvest. Solomon often uses the image of harvest to illustrate a person who understands

the discipline of taking care of himself.

10:13 rod. Beatings were a form of punishment in Solomon's time. Even in Jesus' day, beatings accompanied capital punishment (Matt. 27:26).

10:25 Jesus may have had this proverb in mind

20 Those with twisted minds are detestable
    to the LORD,
but those with blameless conduct are
    His delight.

21 Be assured[a] that the wicked
will not go unpunished,
but the offspring of the righteous will escape.

22 A beautiful woman who rejects good sense
is like a gold ring in a pig's snout.

23 The desire of the righteous ⌊turns out⌋ well,
but the hope of the wicked ⌊leads to⌋ wrath.

24 One person gives freely,
yet gains more;
another withholds what is right,
only to become poor.

25 A generous person will be enriched,
and the one who gives a drink of water
will receive water.

26 People will curse anyone who hoards grain,
but a blessing will come to the one who sells it.

27 The one who searches for what is good finds favor,
but if someone looks for trouble, it will come
    to him.

28 Anyone trusting in his riches will fall,
but the righteous will flourish like foliage.

29 The one who brings ruin on his household
will inherit the wind,
and a fool will be a slave
to someone whose heart is wise.

30 The fruit of the righteous is a tree of life,
but violence[b] takes lives.

31 If the righteous will be repaid on earth,
how much more the wicked and sinful.

12 Whoever loves instruction loves knowledge,
    but one who hates correction is stupid.

2 The good obtain favor from the LORD,
but He condemns a man who schemes.

3 Man cannot be made secure by wickedness,
but the root of the righteous is immovable.

4 A capable wife[c] is her husband's crown,
but a wife who causes shame
is like rottenness in his bones.

5 The thoughts of the righteous ⌊are⌋ just,
but guidance from the wicked ⌊leads to⌋ deceit.

6 The words of the wicked are a deadly ambush,
but the speech of the upright rescues them.

7 The wicked are overthrown and perish,
but the house of the righteous will stand.

8 A man is praised for his insight,
but a twisted mind is despised.

9 Better to be dishonored, yet have a servant,
than to act important but have no food.

10 A righteous man cares about
    his animal's health,
but ⌊even⌋ the merciful acts of the wicked
    are cruel.

11 The one who works his land will have plenty
    of food,
but whoever chases fantasies lacks sense.

12 The wicked desire what evil men have,[d]
but the root of the righteous produces ⌊fruit⌋.

13 An evil man is trapped
    by ⌊his⌋ rebellious speech,
but the righteous escapes from trouble.

14 A man will be satisfied with good
by the words of his mouth,
and the work of a man's hands will reward him.

15 A fool's way is right in his own eyes,
but whoever listens to counsel is wise.

16 A fool's displeasure is known at once,
but whoever ignores an insult is sensible.

17 Whoever speaks the truth declares
    what is right,
but a false witness, deceit.

18 There is one who speaks rashly,
like a piercing sword;
but the tongue of the wise ⌊brings⌋ healing.

19 Truthful lips endure forever,
but a lying tongue, only a moment.

20 Deceit is in the hearts of those who plot evil,
but those who promote peace have joy.

21 No disaster ⌊overcomes⌋ the righteous,
but the wicked are full of misery.

---

[a]11:21 Lit Hand to hand   [b]11:30 LXX, Syr; MT reads but a wise one   [c]12:4 Or A wife of quality, or A wife of good character   [d]12:12 Or desire a stronghold of evil

---

when He told the parable of the wise man who built his house on a rock and thus withstood a fierce storm, while the foolish man built on the unstable sand (Matt. 7:24-29).

11:4 day of wrath. It is righteousness, not wealth, that will save us when we face God's judgment at the end of our lives.

11:7 hope ... vanishes. Beyond this life, wealth and power mean nothing. To trade righteousness or wisdom for either is a futile attempt at happiness. This passage is reminiscent of the teaching of Ecclesiastes on futility or meaninglessness. Only hope built on Christ and His teachings will last.

11:16 This proverb makes its point by comparing the value of respect to material wealth. The reader is not left to doubt which is the prize. Riches cannot buy good relationships, contentment, and respect from others.

11:24 gives freely, yet gains. Generosity

22 Lying lips are detestable to the LORD,
but faithful people are His delight.

23 A shrewd person conceals knowledge,
but a foolish heart publicizes stupidity.

24 The diligent hand will rule,
but laziness will lead to forced labor.

25 Anxiety in a man's heart weighs it down,
but a good word cheers it up.

26 A righteous man is careful in dealing
with his neighbor,[a]
but the ways of wicked men lead them astray.

27 A lazy man doesn't roast his game,
but to a diligent man, his wealth is precious.

28 There is life in the path of righteousness,
but another path leads to death.[b]

13 A wise son [hears his] father's instruction,
but a mocker doesn't listen to rebuke.

2 From the words of his mouth,
a man will enjoy good things,
but treacherous people have an appetite
for violence.

3 The one who guards his mouth protects his life;
the one who opens his lips invites his own ruin.

4 The slacker craves, yet has nothing,
but the diligent is fully satisfied.

5 The righteous hate lying,
but the wicked act disgustingly and disgracefully.

6 Righteousness guards people of integrity,[c]
but wickedness undermines the sinner.

7 One man pretends to be rich but has nothing;
another pretends to be poor but has
great wealth.

8 Riches are a ransom for a man's life,
but a poor man hears no threat.

9 The light of the righteous shines brightly,
but the lamp of the wicked is extinguished.

10 Arrogance leads to nothing but strife,
but wisdom is gained by those who take advice.

11 Wealth obtained by fraud will dwindle,
but whoever earns it through labor[d]
will multiply it.

12 Delayed hope makes the heart sick,
but fulfilled desire is a tree of life.

13 The one who has contempt for instruction
will pay the penalty,
but the one who respects a command
will be rewarded.

14 A wise man's instruction is a fountain of life,
turning people away from the snares of death.

15 Good sense wins favor,
but the way of the treacherous never changes.[e]

16 Every sensible person acts knowledgeably,
but a fool displays his stupidity.

17 A wicked messenger falls into trouble,
but a trustworthy courier [brings] healing.

18 Poverty and disgrace [come to] those
who ignore instruction,
but the one who accepts rebuke
will be honored.

19 Desire fulfilled is sweet to the taste,
but fools hate to turn from evil.

20 The one who walks with the wise
will become wise,
but a companion of fools will suffer harm.

21 Disaster pursues sinners,
but good rewards the righteous.

22 A good man leaves an inheritance
to his[f] grandchildren,
but the sinner's wealth is stored up
for the righteous.

23 The field of the poor yields abundant food,
but without justice, it is swept away.

24 The one who will not use the rod hates his son,
but the one who loves him disciplines
him diligently.

25 A righteous man eats until he is satisfied,
but the stomach of the wicked is empty.

14 Every wise woman builds her house,
but a foolish one tears it down
with her own hands.

2 Whoever lives with integrity •fears the LORD,
but the one who is devious in his ways
despises Him.

---

[a]12:26 Or man guides his neighbor [b]12:28 Or righteousness, and in its path there is no death [c]13:6 Lit guards integrity of way [d]13:11 Lit whoever gathers upon (his) hand [e]13:15 LXX, Syr, Tg read treacherous will perish [f]13:22 Or inheritance: his

---

toward others, not hoarding what we own, is the path to prosperity.

11:28 trusting. The problem is not having riches, but *trusting* in them. Jesus touched on this topic (Matt. 19:23-24). The second half of this verse refers to attitude more than material wealth.

11:31 repaid. This phrase can be interpreted both in terms of blessings and consequences. David suffered because of his sin with Bathsheba (2 Sam. 12:7-10). Moses suffered because of his lack of trust in the Lord (Num. 20:9-12).

12:11 whoever chases fantasies. Consistent,

constructive work, not daydreaming or fantasizing, yields the provisions we need for daily living.

12:14 words of his mouth. Literally, "the words he speaks" (25:11). The good things we do and say bring rewards.

12:16 ignores. Sometimes this word is trans-

3 The proud speech of a fool ⌊brings⌋ a rod
  ⌊of discipline⌋,[a]
  but the lips of the wise protect them.

4 Where there are no oxen, the feeding-trough
    is empty,[b]
  but an abundant harvest ⌊comes⌋
  through the strength of an ox.

5 An honest witness does not deceive,
  but a dishonest witness utters lies.

6 A mocker seeks wisdom and doesn't find it,
  but knowledge ⌊comes⌋ easily to the perceptive.

7 Stay away from a foolish man;
  you will gain no knowledge from his speech.

8 The sensible man's wisdom is to consider
    his way,
  but the stupidity of fools deceives ⌊them⌋.

9 Fools mock at making restitution,[c]
  but there is goodwill among the upright.

10 The heart knows its own bitterness,
   and no outsider shares in its joy.

11 The house of the wicked will be destroyed,
   but the tent of the upright will stand.[d]

12 There is a way that seems right to a man,
   but its end is the way[e] to death.

13 Even in laughter a heart may be sad,
   and joy may end in grief.

14 The disloyal will get
     what their conduct deserves,
   and a good man, what his ⌊deeds deserve⌋.

15 The inexperienced believe anything,
   but the sensible watch[f] their steps.

16 A wise man is cautious and turns from evil,
   but a fool is easily angered and is careless.[g]

17 A quick-tempered man acts foolishly,
   and a man who schemes is hated.

18 The gullible inherit foolishness,
   but the sensible are crowned with knowledge.

19 The evil bow before those who are good,
   the wicked, at the gates of the righteous.

20 A poor man is hated even by his neighbor,
   but there are many who love the rich.

21 The one who despises his neighbor sins,
   but whoever shows kindness to the poor
     will be happy.

22 Don't those who plan evil go astray?
   But those who plan good find loyalty
     and faithfulness.

23 There is profit in all hard work,
   but endless talk[h] leads only to poverty.

24 The crown of the wise is their wealth,
   but the foolishness of fools produces foolishness.

25 A truthful witness rescues lives,
   but one who utters lies is deceitful.

26 In the fear of the LORD one has
     strong confidence
   and his children have a refuge.

27 The fear of the LORD is a fountain of life,
   turning people from the snares of death.

28 A large population is a king's splendor,
   but a shortage of people is a ruler's devastation.

29 A patient person ⌊shows⌋ great understanding,
   but a quick-tempered one promotes foolishness.

30 A tranquil heart is life to the body,
   but jealousy is rottenness to the bones.

31 The one who oppresses the poor insults
     their Maker,
   but one who is kind to the needy honors Him.

32 The wicked are thrown down by their own sin,
   but the righteous have a refuge when they die.

33 Wisdom resides in the heart of the discerning;
   she is known[i] even among fools.

34 Righteousness exalts a nation,
   but sin is a disgrace to any people.

35 A king favors a wise servant,
   but his anger falls on a disgraceful one.

15

A gentle answer turns away anger,
but a harsh word stirs up wrath.

2 The tongue of the wise
    makes knowledge attractive,
  but the mouth of fools blurts out foolishness.

3 The eyes of the LORD are everywhere,
  observing the wicked and the good.

---

a14:3 Or In the mouth of a fool is a rod for his back, if text is emended   b14:4 Or clean   c14:9 Or at guilt offerings   d14:11 Lit flourish   e14:12 Lit ways   f14:15 Lit the prudent understand   g14:16 Or and falls   h14:23 Lit but word of lips   i14:33 LXX reads unknown

---

lated "covers." The concept here is diplomacy and tact rather than avoidance.
12:27 roast. This may refer to the preparation of food or to preparation for the hunt. A lazy person doesn't provide adequately for himself and his family.
13:3 guards his mouth. Words produce con-

sequences. James reinforced the wisdom of taming the tongue (James 3:5-9).
13:8 Which is the greater protection—to have the money to ransom yourself or to have so little property that no thief would try to steal from you?
13:11 fraud. This refers to money gained ille-

gally (10:2, Jer. 17:11), by extortion (Ps. 62:10) or deceit (Prov. 21:6).
13:22 inheritance. Throughout Proverbs the long-term legacy of the righteous is compared to the short life of the unrighteous (10:27).
13:24 the rod. The rod was used for spanking. Proverbs consistently reinforces the impor-

4 The tongue that heals is a tree of life,
but a devious tongue[a] breaks the spirit.

5 A fool despises his father's instruction,
but a person who heeds correction is sensible.

6 The house of the righteous has great wealth,
but trouble accompanies the income
of the wicked.

7 The lips of the wise broadcast knowledge,
but not so the heart of fools.

8 The sacrifice of the wicked is detestable
to the LORD,
but the prayer of the upright is His delight.

9 The LORD detests the way of the wicked,
but He loves the one
who pursues righteousness.

10 Discipline is harsh for the one who leaves
the path;
the one who hates correction will die.

11 •Sheol and •Abaddon lie open
before the LORD—
how much more, human hearts.

12 A mocker doesn't love one who corrects him;
he will not consult the wise.

13 A joyful heart makes a face cheerful,
but a sad heart ⌊produces⌋ a broken spirit.

14 A discerning mind seeks knowledge,
but the mouth of fools feeds on foolishness.

15 All the days of the oppressed are miserable,
but a cheerful heart has a continual feast.

16 Better a little with the •fear of the LORD
than great treasure with turmoil.

17 Better a meal of vegetables
where there is love
than a fattened calf with hatred.

18 A hot-tempered man stirs up conflict,
but a man slow to anger calms strife.

19 A slacker's way is like a thorny hedge,
but the path of the upright is a highway.

20 A wise son brings joy to his father,
but a foolish one despises his mother.

21 Foolishness brings joy to one without sense,

but a man with understanding walks
a straight path.

22 Plans fail when there is no counsel,
but with many advisers they succeed.

23 A man takes joy in giving an answer;[b]
and a timely word—how good that is!

24 For the discerning the path of life
leads upward,
so that he may avoid going down to Sheol.

25 The LORD destroys the house of the proud,
but He protects the widow's territory.

26 The LORD detests the plans of an evil man,
but pleasant words are pure.

27 The one who profits dishonestly troubles
his household,
but the one who hates bribes will live.

28 The mind of the righteous person thinks
before answering,
but the mouth of the wicked blurts out
evil things.

29 The LORD is far from the wicked,
but He hears the prayer of the righteous.

30 Bright eyes cheer the heart;
good news strengthens[c] the bones.

31 An ear that listens to life-giving rebukes
will be at home among the wise.

32 Anyone who ignores instruction
despises himself,
but whoever listens to correction acquires
good sense.[d]

33 The fear of the LORD is wisdom's instruction,
and humility comes before honor.

16 The reflections of the heart belong to man,
but the answer of the tongue is from the LORD.

2 All a man's ways seem right in his own eyes,
but the LORD weighs the motives.[e]

3 Commit your activities to the LORD
and your plans will be achieved.

4 The LORD has prepared everything
for His purpose—
even the wicked for the day of disaster.

---

a **15:4** Lit *but crookedness in it*   b **15:23** Lit *in an answer of his mouth*   c **15:30** Lit *makes fat*   d **15:32** Lit *acquires a heart*   e **16:2** Lit *weighs spirits*

---

tance of discipline, especially for children

14:4 abundant harvest. In order to realize a harvest, the farmer must invest money and work. **feeding-trough.** An empty manger implies laziness.

14:21 despises. Holds in contempt, belittles, ridicules. God made it clear that His people

should show concern for the poor.

14:22 loyalty and faithfulness. The New Testament equivalent would be grace and truth.

14:29 quick-tempered. Quick-tempered people often act before thinking. James encouraged his readers to be slow to speak and slow to anger (James 1:19).

14:31 God protects the poor (22:22-23). Our actions toward the poor reflect our attitude toward God.

15:1 The way we use speech says a lot about what kind of people we are (James 3:5-8). Whether we use gentle or harsh words, our conversation reflects our character.

5 Everyone with a proud heart is detestable
    to the LORD;
  be assured,[a] he will not go unpunished.

6 Wickedness is •atoned for by loyalty
    and faithfulness,
  and one turns from evil by the •fear of the LORD.

7 When a man's ways please the LORD,
  He[b] makes even his enemies to be at peace
    with him.

8 Better a little with righteousness
  than great income with injustice.

9 A man's heart plans his way,
  but the LORD determines his steps.

10 God's verdict is on the lips of a king;[c]
   his mouth should not err in judgment.

11 Honest balances and scales are the LORD's;
   all the weights in the bag[d] are His concern.

12 Wicked behavior[e] is detestable to kings,
   since a throne is established
     through righteousness.

13 Righteous lips are a king's delight,
   and he loves one who speaks honestly.

14 A king's fury is a messenger of death,
   but a wise man appeases it.

15 When a king's face lights up, there is life;
   his favor is like a cloud with spring rain.

16 Acquire wisdom—
   how much better it is than gold!
   And acquire understanding—
   it is preferable to silver.

17 The highway of the upright avoids evil;
   the one who guards his way protects his life.

18 Pride comes before destruction,
   and an arrogant spirit before a fall.

19 Better to be lowly of spirit with the humble[f]
   than to divide plunder with the proud.

20 The one who understands a matter
     finds success,
   and the one who trusts in the LORD
     will be happy.

21 Anyone with a wise heart is called discerning,
   and pleasant speech[g] increases learning.

22 Insight is a fountain of life for its possessor,
   but folly is the instruction of fools.

23 A wise heart instructs its mouth
   and increases learning with its speech.[h]

24 Pleasant words are a honeycomb:
   sweet to the taste[i] and health to the body.[j]

25 There is a way that seems right to a man,
   but in the end it is the way of death.

26 A worker's appetite works for him
   because his hunger[k] urges him on.

27 A worthless man digs up evil,
   and his speech is like a scorching fire.

28 A contrary man spreads conflict,
   and a gossip separates friends.

29 A violent man lures his neighbor,
   leading him in a way that is not good.

30 The one who narrows his eyes
     is planning deceptions;
   the one who compresses his lips
     brings about evil.

31 Gray hair is a glorious crown;
   it is found in the way of righteousness.

32 Patience is better than power,
   and controlling one's temper[l] than capturing
     a city.

33 The lot is cast into the lap,
   but its every decision is from the LORD.

17 Better a dry crust with peace
   than a house full of feasting with strife.

2 A wise servant will rule over a disgraceful son
   and share an inheritance among brothers.

3 A crucible is for silver and a smelter for gold,
   but the LORD is a tester of hearts.

4 A wicked person listens to malicious talk;[m]
   a liar pays attention to a destructive tongue.

5 The one who mocks the poor insults his Maker,
   and one who rejoices over disaster
   will not go unpunished.

---

[a] **16:5** Lit hand to hand [b] **16:7** Or he [c] **16:10** Or A divination is on the lips of a king [d] **16:11** Merchants kept the stones for their balance scales in a bag. [e] **16:12** Whether the wicked behavior is on the part of the king or someone else is ambiguous in Hb. [f] **16:19** Alt Hb tradition reads afflicted [g] **16:21** Lit and sweetness of lips [h] **16:23** Lit learning upon his lips [i] **16:24** Lit throat [j] **16:24** Lit bones [k] **16:26** Lit mouth [l] **16:32** Lit and ruling over one's spirit [m] **17:4** Lit to lips of iniquity

---

15:3 observing. That God sees everything we do evokes different responses from people: to the righteous this brings comfort; to the wicked, a threat.

15:4 devious. Our words have the power to influence people around us for good or evil.

15:8 sacrifice. God wants devoted hearts—not cold obedience.

15:11 Sheol and Abaddon. This is probably an allusion to the fact that God sees the dead in their graves or in their eternal homes. How much more is God able to see the hearts of living people?

15:15 the oppressed. People bowed down by affliction who cannot overcome their circumstances.

15:32 instruction. God's discipline or moral correction is a part of His love for us (Heb. 12:7-11).

16:4 disaster. God's justice includes punishment for wickedness as well as rewards for righteousness.

6 Grandchildren are the crown of the elderly,
and the pride of sons is their fathers.

7 Excessive speech is not appropriate
on a fool's lips;
how much worse are lies for a ruler.

8 A bribe seems like a magic stone to its owner;
wherever he turns, he succeeds.

9 Whoever conceals an offense promotes love,
but whoever gossips about it separates friends.

10 A rebuke cuts into a perceptive person
more than a hundred lashes into a fool.

11 An evil man seeks only rebellion;
a cruel messenger[a] will be sent against him.

12 Better for a man to meet a bear robbed
of her cubs
than a fool in his foolishness.

13 If anyone returns evil for good,
evil will never depart from his house.

14 To start a conflict is to release a flood;
stop the dispute before it breaks out.

15 Acquitting the guilty and condemning the just—
both are detestable to the LORD.

16 Why does a fool have money in his hand
with no intention of buying wisdom?

17 A friend loves at all times,
and a brother is born for a difficult time.

18 One without sense enters an agreement[b]
and puts up security for his friend.

19 One who loves to offend loves strife;
one who builds a high threshold invites injury.

20 One with a twisted mind will not succeed,
and one with deceitful speech will fall into ruin.

21 A man fathers a fool to his own sorrow;
the father of a fool has no joy.

22 A joyful heart is good medicine,
but a broken spirit dries up the bones.

23 A wicked man secretly takes a bribe
to subvert the course of justice.

24 Wisdom is the focus of the perceptive,
but a fool's eyes roam to the ends of the earth.

25 A foolish son is grief to his father
and bitterness to the one who bore him.

26 It is certainly not good to fine
an innocent person,
or to beat a noble for his honesty.[c]

27 The intelligent person restrains his words,
and one who keeps a cool head[d]
is a man of understanding.

28 Even a fool is considered wise
when he keeps silent,
discerning, when he seals his lips.

18 One who isolates himself pursues
⌊selfish⌋ desires;
he rebels against all sound judgment.

2 A fool does not delight in understanding,
but only wants to show off his opinions.[e]

3 When a wicked man comes,
shame does also,
and along with dishonor, disgrace.

4 The words of a man's mouth are deep waters,
a flowing river, a fountain of wisdom.

5 It is not good to show partiality to the guilty
by perverting the justice due the innocent.

6 A fool's lips lead to strife,
and his mouth provokes a beating.

7 A fool's mouth is his devastation,
and his lips are a trap for his life.

8 A gossip's words are like choice food
that goes down to one's innermost being.[f]

9 The one who is truly lazy in his work
is brother to a vandal.[g]

10 The name of the LORD is a strong tower;
the righteous run to it and are protected.[h]

11 A rich man's wealth is his fortified city;
in his imagination it is like a high wall.

12 Before his downfall a man's heart is proud,
but before honor comes humility.

13 The one who gives an answer
before he listens—
this is foolishness and disgrace for him.

---

[a] **17:11** Or *a merciless angel*, Ps 78:49   [b] **17:18** Lit *sense shakes hands*   [c] **17:26** Or *noble unfairly*   [d] **17:27** Lit *spirit*   [e] **18:2** Lit *to uncover his heart*   [f] **18:8** Lit *to the chambers of the belly*   [g] **18:9** Lit *master of destruction*   [h] **18:10** Lit *raised high*

16:6 loyalty and faithfulness. This is *God's loyalty* and *God's faithfulness*. We avoid evil through God's saving grace and our relationship with Him.

16:7 please the LORD. Habits that please God include pure thoughts (15:26) and honesty (20:23).

16:9 plans his way. God's sovereignty should not keep us from planning and setting goals. But we need God's wisdom to guide us as we make these plans.

16:10 king. Originally the nation of Israel was a theocracy governed by God. Later, Israel was ruled by judges, and finally by kings. The first two kings, Saul and David (Solomon's father), were chosen by God. Even though these early kings were political rulers, they were also God's representatives.

17:2 wise servant. The truth of this proverb is revealed in Solomon's own life. His son Rehoboam was rejected by the northern tribes,

14 A man's spirit can endure sickness,
but who can survive a broken spirit?

15 The mind of the discerning acquires knowledge,
and the ear of the wise seeks it.

16 A gift opens doors[a] for a man
and brings him before the great.

17 The first to state his case seems right
until another comes and cross-examines him.

18 ⌊Casting⌋ the lot ends quarrels
and separates powerful opponents.

19 An offended brother is ⌊harder to reach⌋[b]
than a fortified city,
and quarrels are like the bars of a fortress.

20 From the fruit of his mouth a man's stomach
is satisfied;
he is filled with the product of his lips.

21 Life and death are in the power of the tongue,
and those who love it will eat its fruit.

22 A man who finds a wife finds a good thing
and obtains favor from the LORD.

23 The poor man pleads,
but the rich one answers roughly.

24 A man with many friends may be harmed,[c]
but there is a friend who stays closer
than a brother.

19

Better a poor man who walks in integrity
than someone who has deceitful lips and is
a fool.

2 Even zeal is not good without knowledge,
and the one who acts hastily[d] sins.

3 A man's own foolishness leads him astray,
yet his heart rages against the LORD.

4 Wealth attracts many friends,
but a poor man is separated from his friend.

5 A false witness will not go unpunished,
and one who utters lies will not escape.

6 Many seek the favor of a ruler,
and everyone is a friend of one who gives gifts.

7 All the brothers of a poor man hate him;
how much more do his friends

keep their distance from him!
He may pursue ⌊them with⌋ words,
⌊but⌋ they are not ⌊there⌋.[e]

8 The one who acquires good sense[f]
loves himself;
one who safeguards understanding finds success.

9 A false witness will not go unpunished,
and one who utters lies perishes.

10 Luxury is not appropriate for a fool—
how much less for a slave to rule over princes!

11 A person's insight gives him patience,
and his virtue is to overlook an offense.

12 A king's rage is like a lion's roar,
but his favor is like dew on the grass.

13 A foolish son is his father's ruin,
and a wife's nagging is an endless dripping.

14 A house and wealth are inherited from fathers,
but a sensible wife is from the LORD.

15 Laziness induces deep sleep,
and a lazy person will go hungry.

16 The one who keeps commands
preserves himself;
one who disregards[g] his ways will die.

17 Kindness to the poor is a loan to the LORD,
and He will give a reward to the lender.[h]

18 Discipline your son while there is hope;
don't be intent on killing him.[i]

19 A person with great anger bears the penalty;
if you rescue him, you'll have to do it again.

20 Listen to counsel and receive instruction
so that you may be wise in later life.[j]

21 Many plans are in a man's heart,
but the LORD's decree will prevail.

22 A man's desire should be loyalty
to the covenant;
better to be a poor man than a perjurer.

23 The •fear of the LORD leads to life;
one will sleep at night[k] without danger.

24 The slacker buries his hand in the bowl;
he doesn't even bring it back to his mouth.

[a]18:16 Lit gift makes room   [b]18:19 LXX, Syr, Tg, Vg read is stronger   [c]18:24 Some LXX mss, Syr, Tg, Vg read friends must be friendly   [d]19:2 Lit who is hasty with feet   [e]19:7 Hb uncertain in this line   [f]19:8 Lit acquires a heart   [g]19:16 Or despises, or treats lightly   [h]19:17 Lit to him   [i]19:18 Lit don't lift up your soul to his death   [j]19:20 Lit in your end   [k]19:23 Lit will spend the night satisfied

which broke away into Israel, or the Northern Kingdom.

17:9 conceals. To conceal a sin is to overwhelm it with forgiveness and love.

17:17 friend ... brother. This verse does not focus on the difference between a friend and a brother, but on the commitment required in both relationships. Solomon likely heard stories about his father David's friendship with Jonathan (see 1 Sam. 18:1).

17:19 high threshold. Either a door that is tall to show off wealth or a symbol for boasting.

18:8 choice food. An apt description of a "juicy" piece of gossip. Just as a rich and delicious food is digested, gossip becomes a part of us and affects our attitudes.

18:11 like a high wall. Cities were surrounded with walls to provide protection; money is also viewed by many people as a form of security. Jesus addressed this security issue with the rich young ruler (Matt. 19:21-24).

25 Strike a mocker, and the inexperienced learn
    a lesson;
   rebuke the discerning, and he gains knowledge.

26 The one who assaults his father and evicts
    his mother
   is a disgraceful and shameful son.

27 If you stop listening to instruction, my son,
   you will stray from the words of knowledge.

28 A worthless witness mocks justice,
   and a wicked mouth swallows iniquity.

29 Judgments are prepared for mockers,
   and beatings for the backs of fools.

20 Wine is a mocker, beer is a brawler,
    and whoever staggers because of them
     is not wise.

2 A king's terrible wrath is like the roaring
   of a lion;
   anyone who provokes him endangers himself.

3 It is honorable for a man to resolve a dispute,
   but any fool can get himself into a quarrel.

4 The slacker does not plow
    during planting season;ᵃ
   at harvest time he looks,ᵇ and there is nothing.

5 Counsel in a man's heart is deep water;
   but a man of understanding draws it up.

6 Many a man proclaims his own loyalty,
   but who can find a trustworthy man?

7 The one who lives with integrity is righteous;
   his childrenᶜ who come after him
    will be happy.

8 A king sitting on a throne to judge
   sifts out all evil with his eyes.

9 Who can say, "I have kept my heart pure;
   I am cleansed from my sin"?

10 Differing weights and varying measuresᵈ—
   both are detestable to the LORD.

11 Even a young man is known by his actions—
   by whether his behavior is pure and upright.

12 The hearing ear and the seeing eye—
   the LORD made them both.

13 Don't love sleep, or you will become poor;
   open your eyes, and you'll have enough to eat.

14 "It's worthless, it's worthless!" the buyer says,
   but after he is on his way, he gloats.

15 There is gold and a multitude of jewels,
   but knowledgeable lips are a rare treasure.

16 Take his garment,ᵉ
   for he has put up security for a stranger;
   get collateral if it is for foreigners.

17 Food gained by fraud is sweet to a man,
   but afterwards his mouth is full of gravel.

18 Finalize plans through counsel,
   and wage war with sound guidance.

19 The one who reveals secrets is
    a constant gossip;
   avoid someone with a big mouth.

20 Whoever curses his father or mother—
   his lamp will go out in deep darkness.

21 An inheritance gained prematurely
   will not be blessed ultimately.

22 Don't say, "I will avenge this evil!"
   Wait on the LORD, and He will rescue you.

23 Differing weightsᶠ are detestable to the LORD,
   and dishonest scales are unfair.

24 A man's steps are determined by the LORD,
   so how can anyone understand his own way?

25 It is a trap for anyone to dedicate
    something rashly
   and later to reconsider his vows.

26 A wise king separates out the wicked
   and drives the threshing wheel over them.

27 A person's breath is the lamp of the LORD,
   searching the innermost parts.ᵍ

28 Loyalty and faithfulness deliver a king;
   through loyalty he maintains his throne.

29 The glory of young men is their strength,
   and the splendor of old men is gray hair.

30 Lashes and wounds purge away evil,
   and beatings cleanse the innermost parts.ʰ

ᵃ20:4 Lit plow in winter ᵇ20:4 Lit inquires ᶜ20:7 Lit sons ᵈ20:10 Lit Stone and stone, measure and measure ᵉ20:16 A debtor's outer garment held as collateral; Dt 24:12–13,17; Jb 22:6 ᶠ20:23 Lit A stone and a stone ᵍ20:27 Lit the chambers of the belly ʰ20:30 Lit beatings the chambers of the belly

---

18:17 Hearing both sides of the story before making a decision is wisdom that extends beyond the courtroom.

19:3 his heart rages. God did not accept Cain's sacrifice. He became angry with God and killed his brother (Heb. 11:4; 1 John 3:12).

19:13 nagging. Sometimes translated as "dis-sension" (10:12) or "strife" (23:29), this word is used more in Proverbs than in any other Old Testament book.

20:1 Wine … beer. Wine refers to fermented grape juice. Beer was made from barley, dates, or pomegranates. Priests were forbidden to drink beer.

20:3 avoid strife. The wise person avoids arguments.

20:9 cleansed from my sin. Before Christ's once-for-all sacrifice, cleansing from sin was gained through sacrificial offerings. These had to be repeated for each new sin or offense, so a person could not stay cleansed for long.

21 A king's heart is a water channel
in the LORD's hand:
He directs it wherever He chooses.

2 All the ways of a man seem right to him,
but the LORD evaluates the motives.

3 Doing what is righteous and just
is more acceptable to the LORD than sacrifice.

4 The lamp[a] that guides the wicked—
haughty eyes and an arrogant heart—is sin.

5 The plans of the diligent certainly lead to profit,
but anyone who is reckless only becomes poor.

6 Making a fortune through a lying tongue
is a vanishing mist,[b] a pursuit of death.[c] [d]

7 The violence of the wicked sweeps them away
because they refuse to act justly.

8 A guilty man's conduct is crooked,
but the behavior of the innocent is upright.

9 Better to live on the corner of a roof
than to share a house with a nagging wife.

10 A wicked person desires evil;
he has no consideration[e] for his neighbor.

11 When a mocker is punished,
the inexperienced become wiser;
when one teaches a wise man,
he acquires knowledge.

12 The Righteous One considers the house
of the wicked;
He brings the wicked to ruin.

13 The one who shuts his ears to the cry of the poor
will himself also call out and not be answered.

14 A secret gift soothes anger,
and a covert bribe,[f] fierce rage.

15 Justice executed is a joy to the righteous
but a terror to those who practice iniquity.

16 The man who strays from the way of wisdom
will come to rest
in the assembly of the departed spirits.

17 The one who loves pleasure will become
a poor man;
whoever loves wine and oil will not get rich.

18 The wicked are a ransom for the righteous,
and the treacherous, for[g] the upright.

19 Better to live in a wilderness
than with a nagging and hot-tempered wife.

20 Precious treasure and oil are in the dwelling
of the wise,
but a foolish man consumes them.[h]

21 The one who pursues righteousness
and faithful love
will find life, righteousness, and honor.

22 The wise conquer a city of warriors
and bring down its mighty fortress.

23 The one who guards his mouth and tongue
keeps himself out of trouble.

24 The proud and arrogant person,
named "Mocker,"
acts with excessive pride.

25 A slacker's craving will kill him
because his hands refuse to work.

26 He is filled with craving[i] all day long,
but the righteous give and don't hold back.

27 The sacrifice of a wicked person is detestable—
how much more so
when he brings it with ulterior motives!

28 A lying witness will perish,
but the one who listens will speak successfully.

29 A wicked man puts on a bold face,
but the upright man considers his way.

30 No wisdom, no understanding, and no counsel
⌊will prevail⌋ against the LORD.

31 A horse is prepared for the day of battle,
but victory comes from the LORD.

22 A good name is to be chosen
over great wealth;
favor is better than silver and gold.

2 The rich and the poor have this in common:[j]
the LORD made them both.[k]

3 A sensible person sees danger and takes cover,
but the inexperienced keep going
and are punished.

---

[a]**21:4** Some Hb mss, ancient versions read *tillage*   [b]**21:6** Or *a breath blown away*   [c]**21:6** Some Hb mss, LXX, Vg read *a snare of death*   [d]**21:6** Lit *is vanity, ones seeking death*   [e]**21:10** Or *favor*   [f]**21:14** Lit *a bribe in the bosom*   [g]**21:18** Or *in place of*   [h]**21:20** Lit *it*   [i]**21:26** Lit *He craves a craving*   [j]**22:2** Lit *poor meet*   [k]**22:2** Lit *all*

20:20 deep darkness. Cursing one's parents was punishable by death (see Lev. 20:9).
20:21 gained prematurely. The inheritance described here could be gained by deceit, or by request, as in the case of the prodigal son (Luke 15:12-13).
20:25 dedicate something rashly. Jephthah

promised God that he would sacrifice the first thing he saw at his house. Because of his rash vow, He was forced to take the life of his own daughter (see Judg. 11:34-35).
21:1 water channel. Just as a farmer controls the direction and amount of water that runs into irrigation canals, God also controls government.

21:3 sacrifice. While the sacrificial system was an important part of Hebrew life, God's greatest desire was for His people to honor Him through their righteousness and justice.
21:13 will himself also. We reap what we sow. People will receive the same treatment they give to the poor.

4 The result of humility is •fear of the LORD,
along with wealth, honor, and life.

5 There are thorns and snares on the path
    of the crooked;
the one who guards himself stays far from them.

6 Teach a youth about the way he should go;
even when he is old he will not depart from it.

7 The rich rule over the poor,
and the borrower is a slave to the lender.

8 The one who sows injustice will reap disaster,
and the rod of his fury will be destroyed.

9 A generous person[a] will be blessed,
for he shares his food with the poor.

10 Drive out a mocker, and conflict goes too;
then lawsuits and dishonor will cease.

11 The one who loves a pure heart
and gracious lips—the king is his friend.

12 The LORD's eyes keep watch over knowledge,
but He overthrows the words of the treacherous.

13 The slacker says, "There's a lion outside!
I'll be killed in the streets!"

14 The mouth of the forbidden woman is
    a deep pit;
a man cursed by the LORD will fall into it.

15 Foolishness is tangled up in the heart of a youth;
the rod of discipline will drive it away from him.

16 Oppressing the poor to enrich oneself,
and giving to the rich—both lead
    only to poverty.

Words of the Wise

17 Listen closely,[b] pay attention to the words
    of the wise,
and apply your mind to my knowledge.

18 For it is pleasing if you keep them within you
and if[c] they are constantly on your lips.

19 I have instructed you today—even you—
so that your confidence may be in the LORD.

20 Haven't I written for you thirty sayings[d]
about counsel and knowledge,

21 in order to teach you true and reliable words,
so that you may give a dependable report[e]
to those who sent you?

22 Don't rob a poor man because he is poor,
and don't crush the oppressed at the •gate,

23 for the LORD will take up their case
and will plunder those who plunder them.

24 Don't make friends with an angry man,[f]
and don't be a companion of a hot-tempered man,

25 or you will learn his ways
and entangle yourself in a snare.

26 Don't be one of those who enter agreements,[g]
who put up security for loans.

27 If you have no money to pay,
even your bed will be taken from under you.

28 Don't move an ancient property line
that your fathers set up.

29 Do you see a man skilled in his work?
He will stand in the presence of kings.
He will not stand in the presence
    of unknown men.

23 When you sit down to dine with a ruler,
consider carefully what[h] is before you,

2 and stick a knife in your throat
if you have a big[i] appetite;

3 don't desire his choice food,
for that food is deceptive.

4 Don't wear yourself out to get rich;
stop giving your attention to it.

5 As soon as your eyes fly to it, it disappears,
for it makes wings for itself
and flies like an eagle to the sky.

6 Don't eat a stingy person's bread,[j]
and don't desire his choice food,

7 for as he thinks within himself, so he is.
"Eat and drink," he says to you,
but his heart is not with you.

8 You will vomit the little you've eaten
and waste your pleasant words.

9 Don't speak to[k] a fool,
for he will despise the insight of your words.

10 Don't move an ancient property line,
and don't encroach on the fields
    of the fatherless,

11 for their Redeemer is strong,
and He will take up their case against you.

---

[a]**22:9** Lit *Good of eye* [b]**22:17** Lit *Stretch out your ear* [c]**22:18** Or *you; let them be, or you, so that* [d]**22:20** Text emended; one Hb tradition reads *you previously;* alt Hb tradition reads *you excellent things;* LXX, Syr, Vg read *you three times* [e]**22:21** Lit *give dependable words* [f]**22:24** Lit *with a master of anger* [g]**22:26** Lit *who shakes hands* [h]**23:1** Or *who* [i]**23:2** Lit *you are the master of an* [j]**23:6** Lit *eat bread of an evil eye* [k]**23:9** Lit *in the ears of*

21:14 secret gift. The purpose of this verse is not to condone bribery, but to emphasize a gift's ability to ease a tense situation (18:16; 19:6).

22:1 good name. An honorable reputation was highly esteemed. A "good name" comes through love and faithfulness (3:3-4).

22:7 slave. In Bible times people often had to sell themselves into slavery to pay off their debts.

22:9 shares his food with the poor. Stewardship is more than giving; it also involves a compassionate attitude that reaches out to people in need.

22:13 slacker. A lazy, irresponsible person. A slacker will go to any length to avoid work and justify his laziness.

22:14 mouth. Not just the immoral woman's kisses, but also her empty promises endanger anyone who believes her.

22:17 apply your mind. Believers should be

12 Apply yourself to instruction
   and listen to words of knowledge.
13 Don't withhold correction from a youth;
   if you beat him with a rod, he will not die.
14 Strike him with a rod,
   and you will rescue his life from •Sheol.

15 My son, if your heart is wise,
   my heart will indeed rejoice.
16 My innermost being will cheer
   when your lips say what is right.

17 Don't be jealous of sinners;
   instead, always •fear the LORD.
18 For then you will have a future,
   and your hope will never fade.

19 Listen, my son, and be wise;
   keep your mind on the right course.
20 Don't associate with those who drink
      too much wine,
   or with those who gorge themselves on meat.
21 For the drunkard and the glutton
      will become poor,
   and grogginess will clothe ⌊them⌋ in rags.

22 Listen to your father who gave you life,
   and don't despise your mother when[a] she is old.
23 Buy—and do not sell—truth,
   wisdom, instruction, and understanding.
24 The father of a righteous son will rejoice greatly,
   and one who fathers a wise son will delight
      in him.
25 Let your father and mother have joy,
   and let her who gave birth to you rejoice.

26 My son, give me your heart,
   and let your eyes observe my ways.
27 For a prostitute is a deep pit,
   and a forbidden woman is a narrow well;
28 indeed, she sets an ambush like a robber
   and increases those among men
      who are unfaithful.

29 Who has woe? Who has sorrow?
   Who has conflicts? Who has complaints?
   Who has wounds for no reason?
   Who has red eyes?
30 Those who linger over wine,
   those who go looking for mixed wine.
31 Don't gaze at wine when it is red,
   when it gleams in the cup

and goes down smoothly.
32 In the end it bites like a snake
   and stings like a viper.
33 Your eyes will see strange things,
   and you will say absurd things.[b]
34 You'll be like someone sleeping out at sea
   or lying down on the top of a ship's mast.
35 "They struck me, but[c] I feel no pain!
   They beat me, but I didn't know it!
   When will I wake up?
   I'll look for another ⌊drink⌋."

24 Don't envy evil men
   or desire to be with them,
2 for their hearts plan violence,
   and their words stir up trouble.

3 A house is built by wisdom,
   and it is established by understanding;
4 by knowledge the rooms are filled
   with every precious and beautiful treasure.

5 A wise warrior is better than a strong one,
   and a man of knowledge than one of strength;
6 for you should wage war with sound guidance—
   victory comes with many counselors.

7 Wisdom is inaccessible to[d] a fool;
   he does not open his mouth at the •gate.
8 The one who plots evil
   will be called a schemer.
9 A foolish scheme is sin,
   and a mocker is detestable to people.

10 If you do nothing in a difficult time,
   your strength is limited.
11 Rescue those being taken off to death,
   and save those stumbling toward slaughter.
12 If you say, "But we didn't know about this,"
   won't He who weighs hearts consider it?
   Won't He who protects your life know?
   Won't He repay a person according to his work?

13 Eat honey, my son, for it is good,
   and the honeycomb is sweet to your palate;
14 realize that wisdom is the same for you.
   If you find it, you will have a future,
   and your hope will never fade.

15 Don't set an ambush, wicked man,
   at the camp[e] of the righteous man;
   don't destroy his dwelling.
16 Though a righteous man falls seven times,

---

a **23:22** Or *because*   b **23:33** Or *will speak perversities* or *inverted things*   c **23:35** LXX, Syr, Tg, Vg read *me," you will say, "But*   d **24:7** Lit *is too high for*   e **24:15** A rural encampment or home not under the protection of a city

---

open to wisdom and truth from the Lord and His appointed leaders.
23:1-3 A guest should show restraint in order to honor his host.
23:5 makes wings for itself. Accumulating earthly wealth is foolish. It can take wings and fly away at any moment.

23:6 stingy. While a stingy host will offer food to appear generous, he is more concerned with counting the cost.
23:10 move … property line. Moving property lines was a form of stealing a neighbor's land. **encroach on the fields.** Not leaving grain in the fields for the poor after gathering the harvest

was also considered stealing (see Ruth 2:1-3).
23:11 Redeemer is strong. God is a defender of the fatherless and a redeemer of widows. This passage also alludes to a kinsman-redeemer, a person who cares for the family of a dead relative (see Ruth 2:20).
24:11 those being taken. This probably refers

he will get up,
but the wicked will stumble into ruin.

17 Don't gloat when your enemy falls,
and don't let your heart rejoice
when he stumbles,
18 or the LORD will see, be displeased,
and turn His wrath away from him.

19 Don't worry because of evildoers,
and don't envy the wicked.
20 For the evil have no future;
the lamp of the wicked will be put out.

21 My son, •fear the LORD, as well as the king,
and don't associate with rebels,[a]
22 for their destruction will come suddenly;
who knows what disaster these two can bring?

23 These [sayings] also belong to the wise:

It is not good to show partiality in judgment.
24 Whoever says to the guilty,
"You are innocent"—
people will curse him, and tribes
will denounce him;
25 but it will go well with those who convict
the guilty,
and a generous blessing will come to them.

26 He who gives an honest answer
gives a kiss on the lips.

27 Complete your outdoor work, and prepare
your field;
afterwards, build your house.

28 Don't testify against your neighbor
without cause.
Don't deceive with your lips.
29 Don't say, "I'll do to him what he did to me;
I'll repay the man for what he has done."

30 I went by the field of a slacker
and by the vineyard of a man lacking sense.
31 Thistles had come up everywhere,
weeds covered the ground,
and the stone wall was ruined.
32 I saw, and took it to heart;
I looked, and received instruction:
33 a little sleep, a little slumber,
a little folding of the arms to rest,
34 and your poverty will come like a robber,
your need, like a bandit.

Hezekiah's Collection

25 These too are proverbs of Solomon,
which the men of Hezekiah, king of Judah,
copied.

2 It is the glory of God to conceal a matter
and the glory of kings to investigate a matter.
3 As the heaven is high and the earth is deep,
so the hearts of kings cannot be investigated.

4 Remove impurities from silver,
and a vessel will be produced[b] for a silversmith.
5 Remove the wicked from the king's presence,
and his throne will be established
in righteousness.

6 Don't brag about yourself before the king,
and don't stand in the place of the great;
7 for it is better for him to say to you,
"Come up here!"
than to demote you in plain view of a noble.[c]

8 Don't take a matter to court hastily.
Otherwise, what will you do afterwards
if your opponent[d] humiliates you?
9 Make your case with your opponent[d]
without revealing another's secret;
10 otherwise, the one who hears will disgrace you,
and you'll never live it down.[e]

11 A word spoken at the right time
is like golden apples on a silver tray.[f]
12 A wise correction to a receptive ear
is like a gold ring or an ornament of gold.

13 To those who send him,
a trustworthy messenger
is like the coolness of snow on a harvest day;
he refreshes the life of his masters.

14 The man who boasts about a gift
that does not exist
is like clouds and wind without rain.
15 A ruler can be persuaded through patience,
and a gentle tongue can break a bone.
16 If you find honey, eat only what you need;
otherwise, you'll get sick from it and vomit.
17 Seldom set foot in your neighbor's house;
otherwise, he'll get sick of you and hate you.

18 A man giving false testimony
against his neighbor
is like a club, a sword, or a sharp arrow.

---

[a] **24:21** Or *those given to change* [b] **25:4** Lit *will come out;* Ex 32:24 [c] **25:7** Lit *you before a noble whom your eyes see* [d] **25:8,9** Or *neighbor*
[e] **25:10** Lit *and your evil report will not turn back* [f] **25:11** Or *like apples of gold in settings of silver*

---

to people who have been unjustly accused.

24:12 we didn't know. God judges those who are aware of injustice but do not oppose it.

24:17-18 gloat. God detests an attitude of superiority.

24:20 evil have no future. No matter how

prosperous the wicked may seem, their future without God is dismal and hopeless.

24:27 afterwards, build your house. The first priority in an agricultural society was preparing the land and planting the seed. After that the people could build houses and establish families.

25:4 impurities. Impurities must be removed from silver before it can be made into beautiful and useful things.

25:8 hastily. Before going to court, a person should ask if this is sensible. He should consider the possibility of losing and the consequences of an unfavorable decision.

19 Trusting an unreliable person in a time of trouble
is like a rotten tooth or a faltering foot.

20 Singing songs to a troubled heart
is like taking off clothing on a cold day,
or like [pouring] vinegar on soda.ᵃ

21 If your enemy is hungry, give him food to eat,
and if he is thirsty, give him water to drink;

22 for you will heap coals on his head,
and the LORD will reward you.

23 The north wind produces rain,
and a backbiting tongue, angry looks.

24 Better to live on the corner of a roof
than in a house shared with a nagging wife.

25 Good news from a distant land
is like cold water to a parched throat.ᵇ

26 A righteous person who yields to the wicked
is like a muddied spring or a polluted well.

27 It is not good to eat too much honey,
or to seek glory after glory.

28 A man who does not control his temper
is like a city whose wall is broken down.

26

Like snow in summer and rain at harvest,
honor is inappropriate for a fool.

2 Like a flitting sparrow or a fluttering swallow,
an undeserved curse goes nowhere.

3 A whip for the horse, a bridle for the donkey,
and a rod for the backs of fools.

4 Don't answer a fool according to his foolishness,
or you'll be like him yourself.

5 Answer a fool according to his foolishness,
or he'll become wise in his own eyes.

6 The one who sends a message by a fool's hand
cuts off his own feet and drinks violence.

7 A proverb in the mouth of a fool
is like lame legs that hang limp.

8 Giving honor to a fool
is like binding a stone in a sling.ᶜ

9 A proverb in the mouth of a fool
is like a stick with thorns,
brandished byᵈ the hand of a drunkard.

10 The one who hires a fool, or who hires
those passing by,
is like an archer who wounds everyone.

11 As a dog returns to its vomit,
so a fool repeats his foolishness.

12 Do you see a man who is wise in his own eyes?
There is more hope for a fool than for him.

13 The slacker says, "There's a lion in the road—
a lion in the public square!"

14 A door turns on its hinge,
and a slacker, on his bed.

15 The slacker buries his hand in the bowl;
he is too weary to bring it to his mouth.

16 In his own eyes, a slacker is wiser
than seven men who can answer sensibly.

17 A passerby who meddles in a quarrel
that's not his
is like one who grabs a dog by the ears.

18 Like a madman who throws flaming darts
and deadly arrows,

19 so is the man who deceives his neighbor
and says, "I was only joking!"

20 Without wood, fire goes out;
without a gossip, conflict dies down.

21 As charcoal for embers and wood for fire,
so is a quarrelsome man for kindling strife.

22 A gossip's words are like choice food
that goes down to one's innermost being.ᵉ

23 Smoothᶠ lips with an evil heart
are like glaze on an earthen vessel.

24 A hateful person disguises himself
with his speech
and harbors deceit within.

25 When he speaks graciously, don't believe him,
for there are seven abominations in his heart.

26 Though his hatred is concealed by deception,
his evil will be revealed in the assembly.

27 The one who digs a pit will fall into it,
and whoever rolls a stone—
it will come back on him.

28 A lying tongue hates those it crushes,
and a flattering mouth causes ruin.

27

Don't boast about tomorrow,
for you don't know what a day might bring.

2 Let another praise you, and not
your own mouth—
a stranger, and not your own lips.

3 A stone is heavy and sand, a burden,
but aggravation from a fool
outweighs them both.

4 Fury is cruel, and anger is a flood,
but who can withstand jealousy?

ᵃ **25:20** Lit *natron,* or *sodium carbonate*   ᵇ **25:25** Or *a weary person*   ᶜ **26:8** A stone bound in a sling would not release and could harm the person using the sling. A modern equivalent is jamming a cork in a gun barrel.   ᵈ **26:9** Lit *thorn that goes up into*   ᵉ **26:22** Lit *to the chambers of the belly*
ᶠ **26:23** LXX; MT reads *Burning*

25:9-10 Make your case. When you make your accusation public, the court of public opinion will make its judgment and you will be held accountable.

25:11 word spoken. This "word" can be an encouragement or a rebuke spoken in good timing and the right spirit. Used correctly,

words make us appear wise. Used incorrectly, they make us appear foolish.

26:14 door turns on its hinge. The point is not the way a slacker twists and turns, but the fact that a slacker never gets up.

26:18-19 only joking. Pranks and practical jokes can cause serious damage.

26:27 Haman prepared a gallows on which to execute Mordecai. But in a twist of fate, he died on it instead (Esth. 9:24-25).

26:28 A lying tongue hates. Lying and hating are connected. When we lie, we disrespect the people to whom we lie.

27:10. Family ties are important, but close

5 Better an open reprimand
  than concealed love.

6 The wounds of a friend are trustworthy,
  but the kisses of an enemy are excessive.

7 A person who is full tramples on a honeycomb,
  but to a hungry person, any bitter thing is sweet.

8 A man wandering from his home
  is like a bird wandering from its nest.

9 Oil and incense bring joy to the heart,
  and the sweetness of a friend is better
      than self-counsel.[a]

10 Don't abandon your friend or your father's friend,
   and don't go to your brother's house
   in your time of calamity;
   better a neighbor nearby than a brother
       far away.

11 Be wise, my son, and bring my heart joy,
   so that I can answer anyone who taunts me.

12 The sensible see danger and take cover;
   the foolish keep going and are punished.

13 Take his garment,[b]
   for he has put up security for a stranger;
   get collateral if it is for foreigners.[c]

14 If one blesses his neighbor
   with a loud voice early in the morning,
   it will be counted as a curse to him.

15 An endless dripping on a rainy day
   and a nagging wife are alike.

16 The one who controls her controls the wind
   and grasps oil with his right hand.

17 Iron sharpens iron,
   and one man sharpens another.[d]

18 Whoever tends a fig tree will eat its fruit,
   and whoever looks after his master
       will be honored.

19 As the water reflects the face,
   so the heart reflects the person.

20 •Sheol and •Abaddon are never satisfied,
   and people's eyes are never satisfied.

21 Silver is ⌊tested⌋ in a crucible, gold in a smelter,
   and a man, by the praise he receives.[e]

22 Though you grind a fool
   in a mortar with a pestle along with grain,
   you will not separate his foolishness from him.

23 Know well the condition of your flock,
   and pay attention to your herds,
24 for wealth is not forever;
   not even a crown lasts for all time.
25 When hay is removed and new growth appears
   and the grain from the hills is gathered in,
26 lambs will provide your clothing,
   and goats, the price of a field;
27 there will be enough goat's milk
       for your food—
   food for your household and nourishment
       for your servants.

28 The wicked flee when no one
      is pursuing ⌊them⌋,
   but the righteous are as bold as a lion.

2 When a land is in rebellion, it has many rulers,
  but with a discerning
      and knowledgeable person, it endures.

3 A destitute leader[f] who oppresses the poor
  is like a driving rain that leaves no food.

4 Those who reject the law praise the wicked,
  but those who keep the law battle
      against them.

5 Evil men do not understand justice,
  but those who seek the LORD
      understand everything.

6 Better a poor man who lives with integrity
  than a rich man who distorts right and wrong.[g]

7 A discerning son keeps the law,
  but a companion of gluttons humiliates
      his father.

8 Whoever increases his wealth
      through excessive interest
  collects it for one who is kind to the poor.

9 Anyone who turns his ear away from hearing
      the law—
  even his prayer is detestable.

10 The one who leads the upright into an evil way
   will fall into his own pit,
   but the blameless will inherit what is good.

---

[a] 27:9 LXX reads *heart, but the soul is torn up by affliction*   [b] 27:13 A debtor's outer garment held as collateral; Dt 24:12–13; Am 2:8   [c] 27:13 Lit a *foreign woman*   [d] 27:17 Lit *and a man sharpens his friend's face*   [e] 27:21 Lit *The crucible for silver and the smelter for gold, and a man for a mouth of praise.*   [f] 28:3 LXX reads *A wicked man*   [g] 28:6 Lit *who twists two ways*

---

friends are our family in times of need.
27:17 Iron sharpens iron. Good relationships are tools that God uses to develop our character.
27:23-27 This passage celebrates the security and the cycle of an agricultural society.
28:5 Wickedness perverts a person's sense

of justice and fairness. When Solomon became king, he prayed for wisdom and the ability to distinguish between right and wrong (1 Kings 3:9).
28:11 wise in his own eyes. To be unteachable or proud. Proverbs describes the fool (26:5) and the sluggard (26:16) as people who

refuse instruction and learning.
28:13 conceals his sins. David, after committing adultery with Bathsheba, tried to hide his sin by murdering her husband (2 Sam. 12:7-9).
28:15 A wicked ruler ... is like a roaring lion. A ruler like this does not realize that his security as king depends on the well being

11 A rich man is wise in his own eyes,
but a poor man who has discernment
sees through him.

12 When the righteous triumph,
there is great rejoicing,ᵃ
but when the wicked come to power,
people hide themselves.

13 The one who conceals his sins
will not prosper,
but whoever confesses and renounces them
will find mercy.

14 Happy is the one who is always reverent,
but one who hardens his heart falls into trouble.

15 A wicked ruler over a helpless people
is like a roaring lion or a charging bear.

16 A leader who lacks understanding
is very oppressive,
but one who hates unjust gain
prolongs his life.

17 A man burdened by bloodguiltᵇ
will be a fugitive until death.
Let no one help him.

18 The one who lives with integrity will be helped,
but one who distorts right and wrongᶜ
will suddenly fall.

19 The one who works his land
will have plenty of food,
but whoever chases fantasies
will have his fill of poverty.

20 A faithful man will have many blessings,
but one in a hurry to get rich
will not go unpunished.

21 It is not good to show partiality—
yet a man may sin for a piece of bread.

22 A greedy manᵈ is in a hurry for wealth;
he doesn't know that poverty will come to him.

23 One who rebukes a person will later find
more favor
than one who flattersᵉ with his tongue.

24 The one who robs his father or mother
and says, "That's no sin,"
is a companion to a man who destroys.

25 A greedy person provokes conflict,
but whoever trusts in the LORD will prosper.

26 The one who trusts in himselfᶠ is a fool,
but one who walks in wisdom will be safe.

27 The one who gives to the poor
will not be in need,
but one who turns his eyes awayᵍ
will receive many curses.

28 When the wicked come to power,
people hide,
but when they are destroyed,
the righteous flourish.

29 One who becomes stiff-necked,
after many reprimands
will be broken suddenly—
and without a remedy.

2 When the righteous flourish, the people rejoice,
but when the wicked rule, people groan.

3 A man who loves wisdom brings joy
to his father,
but one who consorts with prostitutes destroys
his wealth.

4 By justice a king brings stability to a land,
but a man ⌊who demands⌋ "contributions"ʰ
demolishes it.

5 A man who flattersⁱ his neighbor
spreads a net for his feet.

6 An evil man is caught by sin,
but the righteous one sings and rejoices.

7 The righteous person knows the rightsʲ
of the poor,
but the wicked one does not understand
these concerns.

8 Mockers inflame a city,
but the wise turn away anger.

9 If a wise man goes to court with a fool,
there will be ranting and raving
but no resolution.ᵏ

10 Bloodthirsty men hate an honest person,
but the upright care about him.ˡ

11 A fool gives full vent to his anger,ᵐ
but a wise man holds it in check.

ᵃ28:12 Lit glory ᵇ28:17 Lit the blood of a person ᶜ28:18 Lit who is twisted regarding two ways ᵈ28:22 Lit A man with an evil eye ᵉ28:23 Lit is smooth ᶠ28:26 Lit his heart ᵍ28:27 Lit who shuts his eyes ʰ29:4 The Hb word usually refers to offerings in worship. ⁱ29:5 Lit is smooth on ʲ29:7 Lit justice ᵏ29:9 Lit rest ˡ29:10 Or person, and seek the life of the upright ᵐ29:11 Lit spirit

of those over whom he rules.
28:20 get rich. Get-rich-quick schemes are contrasted with being faithful to God. Proverbs listed those who will not go unpunished, including the adulterer (6:29), the wicked (11:21), the proud (16:5), the person who mocks the poor (17:5), and the false witness (19:9).

28:23 Rebukes are welcomed by the wise. But flattery is never effective with those who are wise and discerning.

29:7 poor. Feeble or helpless. A righteous person demonstrates concern for others. A wicked person has no such compassion.

29:9 ranting and raving. Fools love turmoil

and strife more than resolving problems and living peaceably with others.

29:18 Without revelation. When people do not hear God's truth, they live lawless lives.

30:2-3 least intelligent. Agur comes up lacking when he compares his knowledge with God's (9:10).

12 If a ruler listens to lies,
all his servants will be wicked.

13 The poor and the oppressor have this in common:[a]
the LORD gives light to the eyes of both.

14 A king who judges the poor with fairness—
his throne will be established forever.

15 A rod of correction imparts wisdom,
but a youth left to himself[b]
is a disgrace to his mother.

16 When the wicked increase, rebellion increases,
but the righteous will see their downfall.

17 Discipline your son, and he will give you comfort;
he will also give you delight.

18 Without revelation[c] people run wild,
but one who keeps the law will be happy.

19 A servant cannot be disciplined by words;
though he understands, he doesn't respond.

20 Do you see a man who speaks too soon?
There is more hope for a fool than for him.

21 A slave pampered from his youth
will become arrogant[d] later on.

22 An angry man stirs up conflict,
and a hot-tempered man[e] increases rebellion.

23 A person's pride will humble him,
but a humble spirit will gain honor.

24 To be a thief's partner is to hate oneself;
he hears the curse but will not testify.[f]

25 The fear of man is a snare,
but the one who trusts in the LORD is protected.[g]

26 Many seek a ruler's favor,
but a man receives justice from the LORD.

27 An unjust man is detestable to the righteous,
and one whose way is upright
is detestable to the wicked.

The Words of Agur

30 The words of Agur son of Jakeh. The oracle.[h]

The man's oration to Ithiel, to Ithiel and Ucal:[i]

2 I am the least intelligent of men,[j]
and I lack man's ability to understand.

3 I have not gained wisdom,
and I have no knowledge of the Holy One.

4 Who has gone up to heaven and come down?
Who has gathered the wind in His hands?
Who has bound up the waters in a cloak?
Who has established all the ends of the earth?
What is His name,
and what is the name of His Son—
if you know?

5 Every word of God is pure;[k]
He is a shield to those who take refuge in Him.

6 Don't add to His words,
or He will rebuke you, and you will be proved
a liar.

7 Two things I ask of You;
don't deny them to me before I die:

8 Keep falsehood and deceitful words far from me.
Give me neither poverty nor wealth;
feed me with the food I need.

9 Otherwise, I might have too much
and deny You, saying, "Who is the LORD?"
or I might have nothing and steal,
profaning[l] the name of my God.

10 Don't slander a servant to his master,
or he will curse you, and you will become guilty.

11 There is a generation that curses its father
and does not bless its mother.

12 There is a generation that is pure
in its own eyes,
yet is not washed from its filth.

13 There is a generation—how haughty its eyes
and pretentious its looks.[m]

14 There is a generation whose teeth are swords,
whose fangs are knives,
devouring the oppressed from the land
and the needy from among mankind.

15 The leech has two daughters: Give, Give.
Three things are never satisfied;
four never say, "Enough!":

16 •Sheol; a barren womb;
earth, which is never satisfied with water;
and fire, which never says, "Enough!"

---

[a] **29:13** Lit *oppressor meet* [b] **29:15** Lit *youth sent away*; Jb 39:5; Is 16:2 [c] **29:18** Lit *vision* [d] **29:21** Hb obscure [e] **29:22** Lit *a master of rage*
[f] **29:24** When a call for witnesses was made public, anyone with information who did not submit his testimony was under a curse; Lv 5:1. [g] **29:25** Lit *raised high* [h] **30:1** Or *The burden,* or *Jakeh from Massa*; Pr 31:1 [i] **30:1** Hb uncertain. Sometimes read with different word division as *oration: I am weary, God, I am weary, God, and I am exhausted,* or *oration: I am not God, I am not God, that I should prevail.* LXX reads *My son, fear my words and when you have received them repent. The man says these things to the believers in God, and I pause.* [j] **30:2** Lit *I am more stupid than a man*
[k] **30:5** Lit *refined,* like metal [l] **30:9** Lit *grabbing* [m] **30:13** Lit *and its eyelids lifted up*

30:6 Don't add. Let God's Word stand on its own authority and serve as its own interpreter.
30:9 Who is the LORD? When Israel prospered, the people strayed from God, thinking they were self-sufficient.
30:12 pure in its own eyes. People who believe they are morally pure are blind to the danger of self-righteousness.
30:16 Sheol; a barren womb. In Solomon's day, being barren was compared to Sheol (the place of the dead) because it caused a feeling of emptiness.
30:20 I've done nothing wrong. The sexual appetite of the adulteress is no more sinful to her than eating a meal.
30:27 locusts. Locusts are capable of destroying crops with the precision of a military invasion.
30:28 lizard. Lizards had the run of the palace—illustrating that strength comes in many forms.

17 As for the eye that ridicules a father
and despises obedience to a mother,
may ravens of the valley pluck it out
and young vultures eat it.

18 Three things are beyond me;
four I can't understand:

19 the way of an eagle in the sky,
the way of a snake on a rock,
the way of a ship at sea,
and the way of a man with a young woman.

20 This is the way of an adulteress:
she eats and wipes her mouth
and says, "I've done nothing wrong."

21 The earth trembles under three things;
it cannot bear up under four:

22 a servant when he becomes king,
a fool when he is stuffed with food,

23 an unloved woman when she marries,
and a serving girl when she ousts her lady.

24 Four things on earth are small,
yet they are extremely wise:

25 the ants are not a strong people,
yet they store up their food in the summer;

26 hyraxes are not a mighty people,
yet they make their homes in the cliffs;

27 locusts have no king,
yet all of them march in ranks;

28 a lizard[a] can be caught in your hands,
yet it lives in kings' palaces.

29 Three things are stately in their stride,
even four are stately in their walk:

30 a lion, which is mightiest among beasts
and doesn't retreat before anything,

31 a strutting rooster,[b] a goat,
and a king at the head of his army.[c]

32 If you have been foolish by exalting yourself,
or if you've been scheming,
put your hand over your mouth.

33 For the churning of milk produces butter,
and twisting a nose draws blood,
and stirring up anger produces strife.

The Words of Lemuel

31 The words of King Lemuel,
an oracle[d] that his mother taught him:

2 What ⌊should I say⌋, my son?
What, son of my womb?
What, son of my vows?

3 Don't spend your energy on women
or your efforts on those who destroy kings.

4 It is not for kings, Lemuel,
it is not for kings to drink wine
or for rulers ⌊to desire⌋ beer.

5 Otherwise, they[e] will drink,
forget what is decreed,
and pervert justice for all the oppressed.[f]

6 Give beer to one who is dying,
and wine to one whose life is bitter.

7 Let him drink so that he can forget his poverty
and remember his trouble no more.

8 Speak up[g] for those who have no voice,[h]
for the justice of all who are dispossessed.[i]

9 Speak up,[g] judge righteously,
and defend the cause of[j] the oppressed
and needy.

In Praise of a Capable Wife

10 Who can find a capable wife?[k]
She is far more precious than jewels.[l]

11 The heart of her husband trusts in her,
and he will not lack anything good.

12 She rewards him with good, not evil,
all the days of her life.

13 She selects wool and flax[m]
and works with willing hands.

14 She is like the merchant ships,
bringing her food from far away.

15 She rises while it is still night
and provides food for her household
and portions[n] for her servants.

16 She evaluates a field and buys it;
she plants a vineyard with her earnings.[o]

17 She draws on her strength[p]
and reveals that her arms are strong.

18 She sees that her profits are good,
and her lamp never goes out at night.

19 She extends her hands to the spinning staff,
and her hands hold the spindle.

20 Her hands reach[q] out to the poor,
and she extends her hands to the needy.

21 She is not afraid for her household
when it snows,
for all in her household are doubly clothed.[r]

---

[a] 30:28 Or spider   [b] 30:31 Or a greyhound   [c] 30:31 LXX reads king haranguing his people   [d] 31:1 Or of Lemuel, king of Massa   [e] 31:5 Lit he
[f] 31:5 Lit sons of affliction   [g] 31:8,9 Lit Open your mouth   [h] 31:8 Lit who are mute   [i] 31:8 Lit all the sons of passing away   [j] 31:9 Lit and justice for
[k] 31:10 Or a wife of quality, or a wife of good character; Ru 2:1; 3:11   [l] 31:10 Vv. 10–31 form an •acrostic in Hb.   [m] 31:13 Plant from which linen is
made   [n] 31:15 Or tasks   [o] 31:16 Or vineyard by her own labors   [p] 31:17 Lit She wraps strength around her like a belt   [q] 31:20 Lit Her hand
reaches   [r] 31:21 LXX, Vg; MT reads are dressed in scarlet

31:2 vows. Perhaps his mother had committed Lemuel to God—much as Hannah did done with Samuel (1 Sam. 1:11).
31:3 Don't spend your energy. A king's strength would be foolishly spent if all he did was chase women.
31:4-7 An alcoholic king posed a double dan-

ger. His people and his politics depended on judgment and clear thinking.
31:8-9 defend the cause. Jewish law required that the king also represent those who had nothing to give in return.
31:14 merchant ships. The ideal wife in this verse is a wise consumer.

31:15 rises while it is still night. This woman is the opposite of the sluggard who loves to sleep (6:9; 20:13).
31:18 her lamp never goes out. The ideal wife manages her resources well so she does not run out of oil for her lamp.
31:22 fine linen and purple. The clothes worn

22 She makes her own bed coverings;
   her clothing is fine linen and purple.
23 Her husband is known at the city •gates,
   where he sits among the elders of the land.
24 She makes and sells linen garments;
   she delivers belts[a] to the merchants.
25 Strength and honor are her clothing,
   and she can laugh at the time to come.
26 She opens her mouth with wisdom,
   and loving instruction[b] is on her tongue.
27 She watches over the activities of her household

and is never idle.[c]
28 Her sons rise up and call her blessed.
   Her husband also praises her:
29 "Many women[d] are capable,
   but you surpass them all!"
30 Charm is deceptive and beauty is fleeting,
   but a woman who •fears the LORD
      will be praised.
31 Give her the reward of her labor,[e]
   and let her works praise her
      at the city gates.

---

[a]31:24 Or sashes [b]31:26 Or and the teaching of kindness [c]31:27 Lit and does not eat the bread of idleness [d]31:29 Lit daughters [e]31:31 Lit the fruit of her hands

---

by this woman reflect her family's high position. Purple was a color worn by royalty.

31:23 known at the city gate. The wise men of the town gathered here to share wisdom, settle disputes, and transact business. Their reputations were enhanced by the skills of their wives.

31:24 makes ... and sells. The ideal wife not

only supplies her home, but she is productive enough to supply merchants with her wares.

31:26 wisdom, and loving instruction. This woman's wisdom is shared with her children and servants.

31:28-29 capable. This wise wife enjoys a good reputation in the community and in her own household.

31:30 praised. Beauty and charm are temporary, but a life lived for the Lord is worthy of praise.

31:31 city gates. A place where only men received recognition. Good character and wisdom surpass gender and cultural bias.

ECCLESIASTES

PERSONAL READING PLAN

☐ Ecclesiastes 1:1–2:16
☐ Ecclesiastes 2:17–4:12
☐ Ecclesiastes 4:13–6:12

☐ Ecclesiastes 7:1–8:17
☐ Ecclesiastes 9:1–10:20
☐ Ecclesiastes 11:1–12:14

AUTHOR

The writing of Ecclesiastes is traditionally attributed to Solomon because of references to "son of David" and "king over Israel" (see 1:1,12). No writer is named in the book, and Ecclesiastes may have been the product of a writer from a later period who sought to emulate Solomon's wisdom.

DATE

The book may perhaps be dated after the return from exile, in the fifth century B.C. If Solomon were the author, the book would date from circa 950 B.C.

THEME

Life not focused on God is purposeless and meaningless. Without Him, nothing can satisfy (2:25). With Him, all of life is to be enjoyed to the full (2:26; 11:8).

HISTORICAL BACKGROUND

With so little information available about the author or date, it is difficult to place Ecclesiastes into a historical context. One possibility is that it was produced by a wisdom movement in Judaism that was responsible for collecting stories and sayings.

CHARACTERISTICS

Ecclesiastes has always raised questions concerning its appropriateness in the Old Testament canon (the authoritative list of books accepted as Holy Scripture). Its philosophical attitude of questioning beliefs central to Judaism and Christianity has led many to dismiss it. It may be, however, that the work is a foil against which we discern our tendency to overestimate or over-spiritualize our relationship with God. The book is unsparingly forthright in recording the author's desperate search for meaning. While he might be accused of overstating his case, hints of his true piety are evident (see 7:29), and the conclusion challenges the reader to obey God (12:13-14).

Near the end of the book, young people are specifically addressed (11:7-12:8). Youth are challenged to "let your heart be glad in the days of your youth" (11:9). The author exhorts to "remember your Creator in the days of your youth" (12:1)—because without focusing on God, "Everything is futile" (12:8). The book climaxes in 12:13-14 where the message is finally spelled out: Life without God and the fear of God is futility.

Everything is Futile

1 The words of the Teacher,[a] son of David, king in Jerusalem.

2 "Absolute futility," says the Teacher.
"Absolute futility. Everything is futile."
3 What does a man gain for all his efforts
he labors at under the sun?
4 A generation goes and a generation comes,
but the earth remains forever.
5 The sun rises and the sun sets;
panting, ⌊it returns⌋ to its place
where it rises.
6 Gusting to the south,
turning to the north,
turning, turning, goes the wind,
and the wind returns in its cycles.
7 All the streams flow to the sea,
yet the sea is never full.
The streams are flowing to the place,
and they flow there again.
8 All things[b] are wearisome;
man is unable to speak.
The eye is not satisfied by seeing
or the ear filled with hearing.
9 What has been is what will be,
and what has been done is what will be done;
there is nothing new under the sun.
10 Can one say about anything,
"Look, this is new"?
It has already existed in the ages before us.
11 There is no memory of those who[c] came before;
and of those who[c] will come after
there will also be no memory
among those who follow ⌊them⌋.

The Limitations of Wisdom

12 I, the Teacher, have been[d] king over Israel in Jerusalem. 13 I applied my mind to seek and explore through wisdom all that is done under heaven. God has given •people this miserable task to keep them occupied. 14 I have seen all the things that are done under the sun and have found everything to be futile, a pursuit of the wind.[e]

15 What is crooked cannot be straightened;
what is lacking cannot be counted.

16 I said to myself,[f] "Look, I have amassed wisdom far beyond all those who were over Jerusalem before me, and my mind has thoroughly grasped[g] wisdom and knowledge." 17 I applied my mind to know wisdom and knowledge, madness and folly; I learned that this too is a pursuit of the wind.[e]

18 For with much wisdom is much sorrow;
as knowledge increases, grief increases.

The Emptiness of Pleasure

2 I said to myself, "Go ahead, I will test you with pleasure and enjoy what is good." But it turned out to be futile. 2 I said about laughter, "It is madness," and about pleasure, "What does this accomplish?" 3 I explored with my mind how to let my body enjoy life[h] with wine and how to grasp folly—my mind still guiding me with wisdom—until I could see what is good for •people to do under heaven[i] during the few days of their lives.

The Emptiness of Possessions

4 I increased my achievements. I built houses and planted vineyards for myself. 5 I made gardens and parks for myself and planted every kind of fruit tree in them. 6 I constructed reservoirs of water for myself from which to irrigate a grove of flourishing trees. 7 I acquired male and female servants and had slaves who were born in my house. I also owned many herds of cattle and flocks, more than all who were before me in Jerusalem. 8 I also amassed silver and gold for myself, and the treasure of kings and provinces. I gathered male and female singers for myself, and many concubines, the delights of men.[j] 9 Thus, I became great and surpassed all who were before me in Jerusalem; my wisdom also remained with me. 10 All that my eyes desired, I did not deny them. I did not refuse myself any pleasure, for I took pleasure in all my struggles. This was my reward for all my struggles. 11 When I considered all that I had accomplished[k] and what I had labored to achieve, I found everything to be futile and a pursuit of the wind. There was nothing to be gained under the sun.

The Relative Value of Wisdom

12 Then I turned to consider wisdom, madness, and folly, for what will the man be like who comes after the king? He[l] will do what has already been done. 13 And I realized that there is an advantage to wisdom over folly, like the advantage of light over darkness.

14 The wise man has eyes in his head,
but the fool walks in darkness.

---

a1:1 Or of Qoheleth, or of the Leader of the Assembly b1:8 Or words c1:11 Or of the things that d1:12 Or Teacher, was e1:14,17 Or a feeding on wind, or an affliction of spirit f1:16 Lit said with my heart g1:16 Or discerned h2:3 Lit to pull my body i2:3 Two Hb mss, LXX, Syr read the sun j2:8 LXX, Theod, Syr read and male cupbearers and female cupbearers; Aq, Tg, Vg read a cup and cups; Hb obscure k2:11 Lit all my works that my hands had done l2:12 Other Hb mss read They

---

1:2 Futility. This concept is the main theme of Ecclesiastes. Occurring 38 times in the book, "absolute futility" emphasizes the uselessness of life apart from God. In Hebrew, futility (or vanity) means "breath" or "vapor." Thus, Ecclesiastes repeats the theme of wisdom literature—that all our concerns are

temporary as the morning mist.

1:3 under the sun. This key phrase is used 29 times in this book to refer to our limited view of life.

1:8 All things are wearisome. Many things God created are wonderful, but we are not to

find our meaning in creation itself. This search for meaning in the creation, rather than the Creator, becomes unbearably wearisome.

1:13 God. The name used for God throughout Ecclesiastes (Elohim, used 40 times) emphasizes divine sovereignty over all things.

Yet I also knew that one fate comes to them both. 15 So I said to myself, "What happens to the fool will also happen to me. Why then have I been overly wise?" And I said to myself that this is also futile. 16 For, just like the fool, there is no lasting remembrance of the wise man, since in the days to come both will be forgotten. How is it that the wise man dies just like the fool? 17 Therefore, I hated life because the work that was done under the sun was distressing to me. For everything is futile and a pursuit of the wind.

The Emptiness of Work

18 I hated all my work at which I labored under the sun because I must leave it to the man who comes after me. 19 And who knows whether he will be a wise man or a fool? Yet he will take over all my work that I labored at skillfully under the sun. This too is futile. 20 So I began to give myself over[a] to despair concerning all my work I had labored at under the sun. 21 For there is a man whose work was done with wisdom, knowledge, and skill, but he must give his portion to a man who has not worked for it. This too is futile and a great wrong. 22 For what does a man get with all his work and all his efforts that he labors with under the sun? 23 For all his days are filled with grief, and his occupation is sorrowful; even at night, his mind does not rest. This too is futile.

24 There is nothing better for man than to eat, drink, and to enjoy[b] [c] his work. I have seen that even this is from God's hand. 25 For who can eat and who can enjoy life[d] apart from Him?[e] 26 For to the man who is pleasing in His sight, He gives wisdom, knowledge, and joy, but to the sinner He gives the task of gathering and accumulating in order to give to the one who is pleasing in God's sight. This too is futile and a pursuit of the wind.

The Mystery of Time

3 There is an occasion for everything,
and a time for every activity under heaven:
2 a time to give birth and a time to die;
a time to plant and a time to uproot;[f]
3 a time to kill and a time to heal;
a time to tear down and a time to build;
4 a time to weep and a time to laugh;
a time to mourn and a time to dance;
5 a time to throw stones and a time
to gather stones;

6 a time to embrace and a time
to avoid embracing;
6 a time to search and a time to count as lost;
a time to keep and a time to throw away;
7 a time to tear and a time to sew;
a time to be silent and a time to speak;
8 a time to love and a time to hate;
a time for war and a time for peace.

9 What does the worker gain from his struggles? 10 I have seen the task that God has given •people to keep them occupied. 11 He has made everything appropriate[g] in its time. He has also put eternity in their hearts,[h] but man cannot discover the work God has done from beginning to end. 12 I know that there is nothing better for them than to rejoice and enjoy the[i] good life. 13 It is also the gift of God whenever anyone eats, drinks, and enjoys all his efforts. 14 I know that all God does will last forever; there is no adding to it or taking from it. God works so that people will be in awe of Him. 15 Whatever is, has already been, and whatever will be, already is. God repeats what has passed.[j]

The Mystery of Injustice and Death

16 I also observed under the sun: there is wickedness at the place of judgment and there is wickedness at the place of righteousness. 17 I said to myself, "God will judge the righteous and the wicked, since there is a time for every activity and every work." 18 I said to myself, "This happens concerning people, so that God may test them and they may see for themselves that they are like animals." 19 For the fate of people and the fate of animals is the same. As one dies, so dies the other; they all have the same breath. People have no advantage over animals, for everything is futile. 20 All are going to the same place; all come from dust, and all return to dust. 21 Who knows if the spirit of people rises upward and the spirit of animals goes downward to the earth? 22 I have seen that there is nothing better than for a person to enjoy his activities, because that is his reward. For who can enable him to see what will happen after he dies?[k]

4 Again, I observed all the acts of oppression being done under the sun. Look at the tears of those who are oppressed; they have no one to comfort them. Power is with those who oppress them; they have no one to comfort them. 2 So I admired the dead, who have already died, more than the living, who are still

---

[a]2:20 Lit *And I turned to cause my heart* [b]2:24 Syr, Tg; MT reads *There is no good in man who eats and drinks and enjoys* [c]2:24 Lit *and his soul sees good* [d]2:25 LXX, Theod, Syr read *can drink* [e]2:25 Other Hb mss, LXX, Syr read *me* [f]3:2 Lit *uproot what is planted* [g]3:11 Or *beautiful* [h]3:11 Or *has put a sense of past and future into their minds*, or *has placed ignorance in their hearts* [i]3:12 Lit *his* [j]3:15 Lit *God seeks [the] pursued*; or *God calls the past to account*, or *God seeks what is past*, or *God seeks the persecuted* [k]3:22 Lit *after him*

1:17 wisdom and knowledge. Even vast wisdom and knowledge are insufficient to provide meaning in life. In fact, wisdom and knowledge increase the seeker's sorrow rather than providing elusive happiness.

2:1 pleasure. In its simplest form, the Hebrew word for pleasure (*towb*), means "to be

good"—not in a moral sense but through blessing or prosperity. Related words are bounty, cheer, joy, gladness, prosperity, wealth, love, and mercy. The writer tried the best life had to offer and found it lacking meaning.

2:24 eat, drink and to enjoy his work. The

Teacher concludes that there is pleasure and joy in eating, drinking, and work. But we must be careful not to expect more from simple pleasures than they can give. (See also 5:18, 8:17.)

3:11 He has also put eternity in their hearts. Humans are made for eternity.

alive. [3] But better than either of them is the one who has not yet existed, who has not seen the evil activity that is done under the sun.

The Loneliness of Wealth

[4] I saw that all labor and all skillful work is due to a man's jealousy of his friend. This too is futile and a pursuit of the wind.

[5] The fool folds his arms
and consumes his own flesh.
[6] Better one handful with rest,
than two handfuls with effort and pursuit
of the wind.

[7] Again, I saw futility under the sun: [8] There is a person without a companion,[a] without even a son or brother, and though there is no end to all his struggles, his eyes are still not content with riches. "So who am I struggling for," ⌊he asks,⌋ "and depriving myself from good?" This too is futile and a miserable task.

[9] Two are better than one because they have a good reward for their efforts. [10] For if either falls, his companion can lift him up; but pity the one who falls without another to lift him up. [11] Also, if two lie down together, they can keep warm; but how can one person alone keep warm? [12] And if somebody overpowers one person, two can resist him. A cord of three strands is not easily broken.

[13] Better is a poor but wise youth than an old but foolish king who no longer pays attention to warnings. [14] For he came from prison to be king, even though he was born poor in his kingdom. [15] I saw all the living who move about under the sun follow[b] a second youth who succeeds him. [16] There is no limit to all the •people who were before them, yet those who come later will not rejoice in him. This too is futile and a pursuit of the wind.

Caution in God's Presence

5[c] Guard your step when you go to the house of God. Better to draw near in obedience than to offer the sacrifice as fools do, for they are ignorant and do wrong. [2][d] Do not be hasty to speak, and do not be impulsive to make a speech before God. God is in heaven and you are on earth, so let your words be few. [3] For dreams result from much work and a fool's voice from many words. [4] When you make a vow to God, don't delay fulfilling it, because He does not delight in fools. Fulfill what you vow. [5] Better that you do not vow than that you vow and not fulfill it. [6] Do not let

your mouth bring guilt on you, and do not say in the presence of the messenger that it was a mistake. Why should God be angry with your words and destroy the work of your hands? [7] For many dreams bring futility, also many words. So, •fear God.

The Realities of Wealth

[8] If you see oppression of the poor and perversion of justice and righteousness in the province, don't be astonished at the situation, because one official protects another official, and higher officials ⌊protect⌋ them. [9] The profit from the land is taken by all; the king is served by the field.[e]

[10] The one who loves money is never satisfied with money, and whoever loves wealth ⌊is⌋ never ⌊satisfied⌋ with income. This too is futile. [11] When good things increase, the ones who consume them multiply; what, then, is the profit to the owner, except to gaze at them with his eyes? [12] The sleep of the worker is sweet, whether he eats little or much; but the abundance of the rich permits him no sleep.

[13] There is a sickening tragedy I have seen under the sun: wealth kept by its owner to his harm. [14] That wealth was lost in a bad venture, so when he fathered a son, he was empty-handed. [15] As he came from his mother's womb, so he will go again, naked as he came; he will take nothing for his efforts that he can carry in his hands. [16] This too is a sickening tragedy: exactly as he comes, so he will go. What does he gain who struggles for the wind? [17] What is more, he eats in darkness all his days, with much sorrow, sickness, and anger.

[18] Here is what I have seen to be good: it is appropriate to eat, drink, and experience good in all the labor one does under the sun during the few days of his life God has given him, because that is his reward. [19] God has also given riches and wealth to every man, and He has allowed him to enjoy them, take his reward, and rejoice in his labor. This is a gift of God, [20] for he does not often consider the days of his life because God keeps him occupied with the joy of his heart.

6 Here is a tragedy I have observed under the sun, and it weighs heavily on humanity:[f] [2] God gives a man riches, wealth, and honor so that he lacks nothing of all he desires for himself, but God does not allow him to enjoy them. Instead, a stranger will enjoy them. This is futile and a sickening tragedy. [3] A man may father a hundred children and live many years. No matter how long he lives,[g] if he is not satisfied by good things and does not even have a proper burial, I say that a stillborn child is better off than he. [4] For he

---

[a] **4:8** Lit person, but there is not a second, [b] **4:15** Lit with [c] **5:1** Ec 4:17 in Hb [d] **5:2** Ec 5:1 in Hb [e] **5:9** Or An advantage for the land in every respect is a king for a cultivated field; Hb obscure [f] **6:1** Or it is common among men [g] **6:3** Lit how many years

---

3:16-18 see for themselves that they are like animals. This verse implies that we all need to recognize our own unjust acts. We are part of the problem.

4:5 fool folds his arms. The idle person (fool) is consistently portrayed in Scripture as coming to ruin (10:18; Prov. 6:6-11; 24:30-34).

4:9-12 Two are better than one. The human solution to life's misery is companionship. Life is better with a companion, but even with intimate friendship one still experiences the troubles life brings.

5:1-7 This more up-beat section of the book gives commands about how to worship God

properly. The writer encourages readers to worship God sincerely, not merely to talk of faith, but to humbly obey the Lord. He also warns that vows made to God must be promptly kept.

5:2 Do not be hasty to speak. We should not be hasty to make vows to the Lord. Jesus

comes in futility and he goes in darkness, and his name is shrouded in darkness. 5 Though a stillborn child does not see the sun and is not conscious, it has more rest than he. 6 And if he lives a thousand years twice, but does not experience happiness, do not both go to the same place?

7 All man's labor is for his stomach,[a]
yet the appetite is never satisfied.

8 What advantage then does the wise man have over the fool? What ⌊advantage⌋ is there for the poor person who knows how to conduct himself before others? 9 Better what the eyes see than wandering desire. This too is futile and a pursuit of the wind.

10 Whatever exists was given its name long ago,[b] and who man is, is known. But he is not able to contend with the One stronger than he. 11 For when there are many words, they increase futility. What is the advantage for man? 12 For who knows what is good for man in life, in the few days of his futile life that he spends like a shadow? Who can tell man what will happen after him under the sun?

Wise Sayings

7 A good name is better than fine perfume,
  and the day of one's death than the day
    of one's birth.
2 It is better to go to a house of mourning
  than to go to a house of feasting,
  since that is the end of all mankind,
  and the living should take it to heart.
3 Grief is better than laughter,
  for when a face is sad, a heart may be glad.
4 The heart of the wise is in a house of mourning,
  but the heart of fools is in a house of pleasure.
5 It is better to listen to rebuke
    from a wise person
  than to listen to the song of fools.
6 For like the crackling of ⌊burning⌋ thorns
    under the pot,
  so is the laughter of the fool.
  This too is futile.
7 Surely, the practice of extortion turns
    a wise person into a fool,
  and a bribe destroys the mind.
8 The end of a matter is better
    than its beginning;
  a patient spirit is better than a proud spirit.
9 Don't let your spirit rush to be angry,
  for anger abides in the heart of fools.

10 Don't say, "Why were the former days
    better than these?"
  For it is not wise of you to ask this.
11 Wisdom is as good as an inheritance,
  and an advantage to those who see the sun.
12 For wisdom is protection as money is protection,
  and the advantage of knowledge is that wisdom
    preserves the life of its owner.
13 Consider the work of God;
  for who can straighten out what He has made
    crooked?

14 In the day of prosperity be joyful, but in the day of adversity, consider: without question, God has made the one as well as the other, so that man cannot discover anything that will come after him.

Avoiding Extremes

15 In my futile life[c] I have seen everything: there is a righteous man who perishes in spite of his righteousness, and there is a wicked man who lives long in spite of his evil. 16 Don't be excessively righteous, and don't be overly wise. Why should you destroy yourself? 17 Don't be excessively wicked, and don't be foolish. Why should you die before your time? 18 It is good that you grasp the one and do not let the other slip from your hand. For the one who •fears God will end up with both of them.

19 Wisdom makes the wise man stronger
  than ten rulers of a city.
20 There is certainly no righteous man on the earth
  who does good and never sins.

21 Don't pay attention[d] to everything •people say, or you may hear your servant cursing you; 22 for you know that many times you yourself have cursed others.

What the Teacher Found

23 I have tested all this by wisdom. I resolved, "I will be wise," but it was beyond me. 24 What exists is beyond ⌊reach⌋ and very deep. Who can discover it? 25 I turned my thoughts to know, explore, and seek wisdom and an explanation ⌊for things⌋, and to know that wickedness is stupidity and folly is madness. 26 And I find more bitter than death the woman who is a trap, her heart a net, and her hands chains. The one who pleases God will escape her, but the sinner will be captured by her. 27 "Look," says the Teacher, "this I have discovered, by adding one thing to another to find out the explanation, 28 which my soul continually searches for but does not find: among a thousand ⌊people⌋ I have

---

[a]6:7 Lit mouth [b]6:10 Lit name already [c]7:15 Lit days [d]7:21 Lit Don't give your heart

---

gave this same advice in Matthew 5:33-37.

5:7 fear God. Fearing, or reverencing, God is the main theme of the Wisdom literature.

5:20 God keeps him occupied with the joy of his heart. The person whose heart is caught up in enjoying God and His good

gifts will find life fulfilling and enjoyable.

6:12 who knows what is good for man in life ...? We don't have the ability to change ourselves; without God we don't even know what we should aim to become.

7:9-10 anger ... the former days. Neither

anger nor nostalgia are proper responses to life's sorrows.

7:13-14 what He has made crooked? Crooked refers to the twists and turns of life. Rather than fighting against our circumstances, we are to trust that God is present in them and will take care of our needs.

found one ⌊true⌋ man, but among all these I have not found a true woman. 29 Only see this: I have discovered that God made people upright, but they pursued many schemes."

Wisdom, Authorities, and Inequities

8 Who is like the wise person, and who knows the interpretation of a matter? A man's wisdom brightens his face, and the sternness of his face is changed.

2 Keep[a] the king's command. Concerning an oath by God, 3 do not be in a hurry. Leave his presence, and don't persist in a bad cause, since he will do whatever he wants. 4 For the king's word is authoritative, and who can say to him, "What are you doing?" 5 The one who keeps a command will not experience anything harmful, and a wise heart knows the right time and procedure. 6 For every activity there is a right time and procedure, even though man's troubles are heavy on him. 7 Yet no one knows what will happen, because who can tell him what will happen? 8 No one has authority over the wind[b] to restrain it, and there is no authority over the day of death; there is no furlough in battle, and wickedness will not allow those who practice it to escape. 9 All this I have seen, applying my mind to all the work that is done under the sun, at a time when one man has authority over another to his harm.

10 In such circumstances, I saw the wicked buried. They came and went from the holy place, and they were praised[c] in the city where they did so. This too is futile. 11 Because the sentence against a criminal act is not carried out quickly, therefore the heart of •people is filled ⌊with the desire⌋ to commit crime. 12 Although a sinner commits crime a hundred times and prolongs his life, yet I also know that it will go well with God-fearing people, for they are reverent before Him. 13 However, it will not go well with the wicked, and they will not lengthen their days like a shadow, for they are not reverent before God.

14 There is a futility that is done on the earth: there are righteous people who get what the actions of the wicked deserve, and there are wicked people who get what the actions of the righteous deserve. I say that this too is futile. 15 So I commended enjoyment, because there is nothing better for man under the sun except to eat, drink, and enjoy himself, for this will accompany him in his labor during the years of his days that God gives him under the sun.

16 When I applied my mind to know wisdom and to observe the activity that is done on the earth (even though one's eyes do not close in sleep day or night), 17 I observed all the work of God ⌊and concluded⌋ that man is unable to discover the work that is done under the sun. Even though a man labors hard to explore it, he cannot find it; even if the wise man claims to know it, he is unable to discover it.

Enjoy Life Despite Death

9 Indeed, I took all this to heart and explained it all: the righteous, the wise, and their works are in God's hands. •People don't know whether ⌊to expect⌋ love or hate. Everything lies ahead of them. 2 Everything is the same for everyone: there is one fate for the righteous and the wicked, for the good and the bad,[d] for the clean and the unclean, for the one who sacrifices and the one who does not sacrifice. As it is for the good, so it is for the sinner, as for the one who takes an oath, so for the one who fears an oath. 3 This is an evil in all that is done under the sun: there is one fate for everyone. In addition, the hearts of people are full of evil, and madness is in their hearts while they live—after that they go to the dead. 4 But there is hope for whoever is joined[e] with all the living, since a live dog is better than a dead lion. 5 For the living know that they will die, but the dead don't know anything. There is no longer a reward for them because the memory of them is forgotten. 6 Their love, their hate, and their envy have already disappeared, and there is no longer a portion for them in all that is done under the sun.

7 Go, eat your bread with pleasure, and drink your wine with a cheerful heart, for God has already accepted your works. 8 Let your clothes be white all the time, and never let oil be lacking on your head. 9 Enjoy life with the wife you love all the days of your fleeting[f] life, which has been given to you under the sun, all your fleeting days. For that is your portion in life and in your struggle under the sun. 10 Whatever your hands find to do, do with ⌊all⌋ your strength, because there is no work, planning, knowledge, or wisdom in •Sheol where you are going.

The Limitations of Wisdom

11 Again I saw under the sun that the race is not to the swift, or the battle to the strong, or bread to the wise, or riches to the discerning, or favor to the skillful; rather, time and chance happen to all of them. 12 For man certainly does not know his time: like fish caught in a cruel net, or like birds caught in a trap, so people are trapped in an evil time, as it suddenly falls on them.

---

[a]8:2 Some Hb mss, LXX, Vg, Tg, Syr; other Hb mss read *I, keep* [b]8:8 Or *life-breath* [c]8:10 Some Hb mss, LXX, Aq, Theod, Sym; other Hb mss read *forgotten* [d]9:2 LXX, Aq, Syr, Vg; MT omits *and the bad* [e]9:4 Alt Hb tradition reads *chosen* [f]9:9 Or *futile*

7:26-28 man ... woman. The writer says of relationships that he has only found one man he could trust and no trustworthy women. Why? We all lack wisdom and understanding. (See also v. 20.)

7:29 God made people right ... but. God is not to blame for troubles on earth. He created humans perfectly, but we chose to disobey.

8:1 Who is like the wise person ...? The Hebrew word for "wise" involves intelligence, cunning, subtlety, and the skillful use of wisdom. It brings to mind a thinking person—one who doesn't simply *react* but reflects on a situation and considers the best response.

8:10-14 The writer poses a problem and then offers a solution. The problem (vv. 10-11) is that wicked people are often praised and punishment is often delayed. The solution (vv. 12-13) is that in the end, the right thing will be done in every case. God knows our hearts.

¹³ I have observed that this also is wisdom under the sun, and it is significant to me: ¹⁴ There was a small city with few men in it. A great king came against it, surrounded it, and built large siege works against it. ¹⁵ Now a poor wise man was found in the city, and he delivered the city by his wisdom. Yet no one remembered that poor man. ¹⁶ And I said, "Wisdom is better than strength, but the wisdom of the poor man is despised, and his words are not heeded."

¹⁷ The calm words of the wise are heeded
more than the shouts of a ruler over fools.
¹⁸ Wisdom is better than weapons of war,
but one sinner can destroy much good.

The Burden of Folly

10 Dead flies make a perfumer's oil ferment
and stink;
so a little folly outweighs wisdom and honor.
² A wise man's heart ⌊goes⌋ to theᵃ right,
but a fool's heart to theᵃ left.
³ Even when the fool walks along the road,
his heart lacks sense,
and he shows everyone he is a fool.
⁴ If the ruler's anger rises against you,
don't leave your place,
for calmness puts great offenses to rest.

⁵ There is an evil I have seen under the sun, an error proceeding from the presence of the ruler:

⁶ The fool is appointed to great heights,
but the rich remain in lowly positions.
⁷ I have seen slaves on horses,
but princes walking on the ground like slaves.
⁸ The one who digs a pit may fall into it,
and the one who breaks through a wall
may be bitten by a snake.
⁹ The one who quarries stones may be hurt
by them;
the one who splits trees may be endangered
by them.
¹⁰ If the ax is dull, and one does not sharpen
its edge,
then one must exert more strength;
however, the advantage of wisdom is that
it brings success.
¹¹ If the snake bites before it is charmed,
then there is no advantage for the charmer.ᵇ
¹² The words from the mouth of a wise man
are gracious,

but the lips of a fool consume him.
¹³ The beginning of the words of his mouth is folly,
but the end of his speaking is evil madness.
¹⁴ Yet the fool multiplies words.
No one knows what will happen,
and who can tell anyone what will happen
after him?
¹⁵ The struggles of fools weary them,
for they don't know how to go to the city.
¹⁶ Woe to you, land, when your king is
a household servant,
and your princes feast in the morning.
¹⁷ Blessed are you, land, when your king is
a son of nobles
and your princes feast at the proper time—
for strength and not for drunkenness.
¹⁸ Because of laziness the roof caves in,
and because of negligent hands the house leaks.
¹⁹ A feast is prepared for laughter,
and wine makes life happy,
and money is the answer for everything.
²⁰ Do not curse the king even in your thoughts,
and do not curse a rich person
even in your bedroom,
for a bird of the sky may carry the message,
and a winged creature may report the matter.

Invest in Life

11 Send your bread on the surface of the waters,
for after many days you may find it.
² Give a portion to seven or even to eight,
for you don't know what disaster may happen
on earth.
³ If the clouds are full, they will pour out rain
on the earth;
whether a tree falls to the south or the north,
the place where the tree falls, there it will lie.
⁴ One who watches the wind will not sow,
and the one who looks at the clouds
will not reap.
⁵ Just as you don't know the path of the wind,
or how bones ⌊develop⌋ inᶜ the womb
of a pregnant woman,
so you don't know the work of God who makes
everything.
⁶ In the morning sow your seed,
and at evening do not let your hand rest,
because you don't know which will succeed,
whether one or the other,
or if both of them will be equally good.

ᵃ**10:2** Lit his ᵇ**10:11** Lit master of the tongue ᶜ**11:5** Or know how the life-breath comes to the bones in

---

8:15 enjoyment. Here, again man is encouraged to "eat, drink, and enjoy himself." This is not a license for thoughtless Hedonism but is encouragement for humbly enjoying the life God has given us, whatever it holds. (See also 2:24 and 5:18.)

8:17 man is unable. God allows humans to

understand a little, but we are limited by our finite minds.

9:2 Everything is the same for everyone. Through a series of opposites, we see that all people—no matter how privileged or oppressed they were in life—share the common destiny of death.

9:10 Sheol. Life after death is a rare concept in the Old Testament. Sheol is the shadowy idea of the place of the dead.

10:2 goes to the right. The right may refer to the right hand, the place of protection, or may simply be a contrast between the way of good and the way of evil.

7 Light is sweet,
and it is pleasing for the eyes to see the sun.
8 For if a man should live many years,
let him rejoice in them all,
and let him remember the days of darkness,
since they will be many.
All that comes is futile.
9 Rejoice, young man, while you are young,
and let your heart be glad in the days
of your youth.
And walk in the ways of your heart
and in the sights of your eyes;
but know that for all of these things
God will bring you to judgment.
10 Remove sorrow from your heart,
and put away pain from your flesh,
because youth and the prime of life are fleeting.

The Twilight of Life

12 So remember your Creator in the days of your
youth:

Before the days of adversity come,
and the years approach when you will say,
"I have no delight in them";
2 before the sun and the light are darkened,
and the moon and the stars,
and the clouds return after[a] the rain;
3 on the day when the guardians of the house
tremble,
and the strong men stoop,
the women who grind cease because
they are few,
and the ones who watch through the windows
see dimly,
4 and the doors at the street are shut

while the sound of the mill fades;
when one rises at the sound of a bird,
and all the daughters of song grow faint.
5 Also, they are afraid of heights and dangers
on the road;
the almond tree blossoms,
the grasshopper loses its spring,[b]
and the caper berry has no effect;
for man is headed to his eternal home,
and mourners will walk around in the street;
6 before the silver cord is snapped,[c]
and the golden bowl is broken,
and the jar is shattered at the spring,
and the wheel is broken into the well;
7 and the dust returns to the earth as it once was,
and the spirit returns to God who gave it.

8 "Absolute futility," says the Teacher. "Everything is futile."

The Teacher's Objectives and Conclusion

9 In addition to the Teacher being a wise man, he constantly taught the •people knowledge; he weighed, explored, and arranged many proverbs. 10 The Teacher sought to find delightful sayings and to accurately write words of truth. 11 The sayings of the wise are like goads, and those from masters of collections are like firmly embedded nails. The sayings are given by one Shepherd.[d]

12 But beyond these, my son, be warned: there is no end to the making of many books, and much study wearies the body. 13 When all has been heard, the conclusion of the matter is: •fear God and keep His commands, because this ⌊is for⌋ all humanity. 14 For God will bring every act to judgment, including every hidden thing, whether good or evil.

---

[a]12:2 Or with   [b]12:5 Or grasshopper is weighed down, or grasshopper drags itself along   [c]12:6 Alt Hb tradition reads removed   [d]12:11 Or by a shepherd

---

10:12-14 words. Here the writer reminds us of the importance of being wise in our choice of words. The book of James gives us instructions in taming our tongues.

11:2 give a portion to seven. Since wealth is meaningless and uncertain, be generous with money. Since disaster is always possible, make investments in people instead of hoarding your resources for a "rainy day."

11:8 days of darkness. Darkness may involve misery, destruction, sorrow, or death. It is inevitable that all will know their share of dark days as well as "light" (v. 7).

11:9 Rejoice, young man. Young people are urged to enjoy whatever their hearts desire, but should temper their desires with an awareness of God's commands. Ignoring them results in judgment.

12:1-8 men stoop. The writer uses a variety of images to describe old age.

12:2 darkened … clouds. Darkness and clouds may be metaphors for weakening eyesight as well as the darkened ideals of youth (see v. 1).

12:3-4 Age is compared to a disintegrating house. The writer describes the trembling hands, stooping shoulders, lost teeth, poor eyesight, loss of hearing, sleeplessness, and confused speech of the elderly.

12:5 afraid. Old people fear going out, partly because their waning vigor and feebleness make movement dangerous. **almond tree blossoms.** This refers to the white hair of the aging. **grasshopper loses its spring.** People previously as agile as grasshoppers become stiff and frail in old age. **caper berry.** These berries were used to stimulate sexual desire when sex no longer appealed. All these images capture the fragility of human life.

12:6 cord … bowl … jar. Remember God before your life is broken and comes to an end, like the household objects described in this verse.

12:8 futility. The writer repeats the theme of the book. Life apart from God is futile.

12:9-10 explored. The writer diligently sought true wisdom; he weighed and explored, seeking out meaning and truth.

12:11-12 given by one Shepherd. The writer affirms that Scripture, unlike any other book, is full of wisdom. Earthly wisdom, which comes through the study of many books, is tiring. But the Bible is full of spiritual wisdom and does not lack.

12:13-14 fear God and keep His commands. All the Teacher's investigations have led to this truth: life's meaning is found in God alone. God's commands provide all the meaning and truth we desire.

INTRODUCTION TO
SONG OF SONGS

PERSONAL READING PLAN

❏ Song of Songs 1:1-2:13
❏ Song of Songs 2:14-3:11
❏ Song of Songs 4:1-16

❏ Song of Songs 5:1-16
❏ Song of Songs 6:1-7:9a
❏ Song of Songs 7:9b-8:14

AUTHOR

Traditionally, Song of Songs is attributed to King Solomon. However, its title, "Solomon's Finest Song" (1:1), can mean a song *by, for,* or *about* Solomon. Thus, the identity of the author remains an open question.

DATE

Song of Songs was perhaps written during Solomon's reign, circa 970–930 B.C., but the presence of non-Hebrew words or expressions suggests a later date for the final editing.

THEME

A celebration of love between a man and woman, which is akin to God's love for His people.

HISTORICAL BACKGROUND

Solomon's dynasty, his unsurpassed wisdom and wealth, and his many wives and concubines are thought-provoking contrasts to the simple, rustic purity of the Song of Songs.

CHARACTERISTICS

Interpretations of this "best of all songs" vary widely. Some view it literally, as a human love poem about King Solomon and his bride. Others see a third character in a triangle of relationships: a shepherd-figure who is the true lover and who wins the Shulammite girl's hand over against the advances of Solomon. Some understand the book to be an anthology of unrelated love poems, with no overall story to tell. Others interpret this lovers' song as an allegory, depicting either God's love for Israel or Christ's love for His bride, the church. Still others think it is natural to extol the wonders of human love. Readers are sometimes surprised to find an explicit love song in the Bible, hence the many attempts to spiritualize away its sensual lyrics. Another problem in understanding the Song of Songs has to do with the frequent change of voice and scene. The captions in the text are designed to help follow the lovers' dialogue.

PASSAGES FOR
TOPICAL GROUP STUDY

Love Song

1. Ladies: What celebrity fits your idea of a "Prince Charming"? Guys: What celebrity fits your idea of a "Dream Girl"?

Song of Songs 1:1–2:7

2. What does the woman find attractive in the man? The man in the woman?
3. What does this love song suggest about God's views on love and romance?
4. What do you think the beloved meant when she said, "do not stir up or awaken love until the appropriate time" (2:7)?
5. What or who can help you to wait until the "appropriate time" when you're in a romantic relationship?

1 Solomon's Finest Song[a]

W[b] 2 Oh, that he would kiss me with the kisses
 of his mouth!
 For your[c] love is[d] more delightful than wine.
 3 The fragrance of your perfume is intoxicating;
 your name is perfume poured out.
 No wonder young women[e] adore you.
 4 Take me with you—let us hurry.
 Oh, that the king would bring[f] me
 to his chambers.
Y We will rejoice and be glad for you;
 we will praise your love more than wine.
W It is only right that they adore you.

 5 Daughters of Jerusalem,
 I am dark like the tents of Kedar,
 yet lovely like the curtains of Solomon.
 6 Do not stare at me because I am dark,
 for the sun has gazed on me.
 My mother's sons were angry with me;
 they made me a keeper of the vineyards.
 I have not kept my own vineyard.[g]

 7 Tell me, you, the one I love:
 Where do you pasture your sheep?
 Where do you let them rest at noon?
 Why should I be like one who veils herself[h] [i]
 beside the flocks of your companions?

M[j] 8 If you do not know,
 most beautiful of women,
 follow[k] the tracks of the flock,
 and pasture your young goats
 near the shepherds' tents.

 9 I compare you, my darling,
 to a[l] mare among Pharaoh's chariots.[m]
 10 Your cheeks are beautiful with jewelry,
 your neck with its necklace.
 11 We will make gold jewelry for you,
 accented with silver.

W 12 While the king is on his couch,[n]
 my perfume[o] releases its fragrance.
 13 My love is a sachet of myrrh to me,
 spending the night between my breasts.
 14 My love is a cluster of henna blossoms to me,
 in the vineyards of En-gedi.[p]

M 15 How beautiful you are, my darling.
 How very beautiful!
 Your eyes are doves.

W 16 How handsome you are, my love.
 How delightful!
 Our bed is lush with foliage;
 17 the beams of our house are cedars,
 and our rafters are cypresses.[q]

2 I am a rose[r] of Sharon,
 a lily[s] of the valleys.

M 2 Like a lily among thorns,
 so is my darling among the young women.

W 3 Like an apricot[t] tree among the trees
 of the forest,
 so is my love among the young men.
 I delight to sit in his shade,
 and his fruit is sweet to my taste.
 4 He brought me to the banquet hall,[u]
 and he looked on me with love.[v]
 5 Sustain me with raisins;

[a]**1:1** Or *The Song of Songs, which is Solomon's* [b]**1:2** The **W, M, Y, N,** and **B** indicate the editors' opinions of the changes of speakers: **W** = Woman, **M** = Man, **Y** = Young women of Jerusalem, **N** = Narrator, **B** = Brothers. If a letter is in parenthesis **(W)**, there is a question about the identity of the speaker. [c]**1:2** Unexpected change of grammatical persons, here from *he* and *his* to *your*, is a Hb poetic device. [d]**1:2** Or *your caresses are*, or *your lovemaking is* [e]**1:3** Or *wonder virgins* [f]**1:4** Or *The king has brought* [g]**1:6** Lit *my vineyard, which is mine*; Sg 8:12 [h]**1:7** Or *who wanders* [i]**1:7** To express shame or grief, or to conceal identity as a prostitute would; Gn 38:14–15 [j]**1:8** Some understand the young women to be the speakers in this verse. [k]**1:8** Lit *go out for yourself into* [l]**1:9** Lit *my* [m]**1:9** Pharaoh's chariot horses were stallions. [n]**1:12** Or *is at his table* [o]**1:12** Lit *nard* [p]**1:14** = Wellspring of the Young Goat; Sg 1:8 [q]**1:17** Or *firs*, or *pines* [r]**2:1** Not the modern flower, but a common wildflower in northern Israel; perhaps a meadow saffron [s]**2:1** Or *lotus* [t]**2:3** Or *apple* [u]**2:4** Lit *the house of wine* [v]**2:4** Or *and his banner over me is love* [w]**2:5** Or *apples*

1:1 Solomon's Finest Song. Solomon (the assumed lover here) wrote more than 1,000 songs (1 Kings 4:32). This is a poetic description of joyful, marital sexual love.

1:2. kisses of his mouth. Illustrates greater desire. Nose kisses were common in the Ancient Near East.

1:5 I am dark. Deeply tanned skin was not considered attractive compared to the court's pale maidens.

1:7 one who veils herself. Prostitutes wore veils. She fears shepherds would mistake her for one if she pursued her lover among his flocks.

1:9 mare. Solomon purchased the best horses

from Pharaoh (1 Kings 10:28).

1:13 sachet of myrrh. Aromatic sap from balsam trees that grew in Arabia, Ethiopia, and India kept in a small pouch around a woman's neck for perfume (Esth. 2:12; Prov. 7:17). Royal wedding clothes were also perfumed with myrrh (3:6; Ps. 45:8). Myrrh was not found in Is-

refresh me with apricots,[w]
for I am lovesick.

6 His left hand is under my head,
and his right hand embraces me.[a]

7 Young women of Jerusalem, I charge you,
by the gazelles and the wild does of the field:
do not stir up or awaken love
until the appropriate time.[b]

8 Listen! My love ⌊is approaching⌋.
Look! Here he comes,
leaping over the mountains,
bounding over the hills.

9 My love is like a gazelle
or a young stag.
Look, he is standing behind our wall,
gazing through the windows,
peering through the lattice.

10 My love calls to me:

M   Arise, my darling.
Come away, my beautiful one.

11 For now the winter is past;
the rain has ended and gone away.

12 The blossoms appear in the countryside.
The time of singing[c] has come,
and the turtledove's cooing is heard in our land.

13 The fig tree ripens its figs;
the blossoming vines give off their fragrance.
Arise, my darling.
Come away, my beautiful one.

14 My dove, in the clefts of the rock,
in the crevices of the cliff,
let me see your face,[d]
let me hear your voice;
for your voice is sweet,
and your face is lovely.

(W)15 Catch the foxes for us—
the little foxes that ruin the vineyards—
for our vineyards are in bloom.

W   16 My love is mine and I am his;
he feeds among the lilies.

17 Before the day breaks[e]
and the shadows flee,
turn ⌊to me⌋, my love, and be like a gazelle
or a young stag on the divided mountains.

3 In my bed at night[f]
I sought the one I love;

I sought him, but did not find him.[g]

2 I will arise now and go about the city,
through the streets and the plazas.
I will seek the one I love.
I sought him, but did not find him.

3 The guards who go about the city found me.
"Have you seen the one I love?"
⌊I asked them⌋.

4 I had just passed them
when I found the one I love.
I held on to him and would not let him go
until I brought him to my mother's house—
to the chamber of the one who conceived me.

5 Young women of Jerusalem, I charge you,
by the gazelles and the wild does of the field:
do not stir up or awaken love
until the appropriate time.[b]

N   6 What is this coming up from the wilderness
like columns of smoke,
scented with myrrh and frankincense
from every fragrant powder of the merchant?

7 It is Solomon's royal litter[h]
surrounded by 60 warriors
from the mighty of Israel.

8 All of them are skilled with swords
and trained in warfare.
Each has his sword at his side
⌊to guard⌋ against the terror of the night.[i]

9 King Solomon made a sedan chair[j] for himself
with wood from Lebanon.

10 He made its posts of silver,
its back[k] of gold,
and its seat of purple.
Its interior is inlaid with love[l]
by the young women of Jerusalem.

11 Come out, young women of Zion,
and gaze at King Solomon,
wearing the crown his mother placed on him
the day of his wedding—
the day of his heart's rejoicing.

M

4   How beautiful you are, my darling.
How very beautiful!
Behind your veil,
your eyes are doves.
Your hair is like a flock of goats
streaming down Mount Gilead.

---

[a] 2:6 Or Let his left hand be under . . . , and his right hand embrace me   [b] 2:7; 3:5 Lit until it pleases   [c] 2:12 Or pruning   [d] 2:14 Or form   [e] 2:17 Lit breathes   [f] 3:1 Or bed night after night   [g] 3:1 LXX adds I called him, but he did not answer me   [h] 3:7 A conveyance carried on the shoulders of servants   [i] 3:8 Of the night is the same Hb word translated at night in Sg 3:1.   [j] 3:9 Perhaps a synonym for the Hb word translated litter in Sg 3:7; also called a palanquin   [k] 3:10 Or base, or canopy   [l] 3:10 Or leather

---

rael, increasing its value.

2:15 foxes … vineyards. Foxes were common pests in vineyards but here are probably symbols of threats to their relationship, perhaps other admirers.

3:5 Do not stir up or awaken love. This is a poetic warning against premarital relations,

against opening the fragrant garden of sexual love before a commitment to marriage is sealed (2:7).

3:7-10 royal litter. A specially built sedan chair on which bearers carried the beloved to the wedding.

4:1 a flock of goats. Goats in Canaan were

generally black; the lover sees his beloved's dark hair cascading down.

4:2 newly shorn [sheep]. The sheep would thus have been clean and white.

4:3 Your lips … scarlet. Egyptian women often painted their lips, and her beautiful lips incite the lover's desire to kiss her.

2 Your teeth are like a flock
   of newly shorn ⌊sheep⌋
coming up from washing,
each one having a twin,
and not one missing.ᵃ
3 Your lips are like a scarlet cord,
and your mouthᵇ is lovely.
Behind your veil,
your browᶜ is like a slice of pomegranate.
4 Your neck is like the tower of David,
constructed in layers.
A thousand bucklers are hung on it—
all of them shields of warriors.ᵈ
5 Your breasts are like two fawns,
twins of a gazelle, that feed among the lilies.
6 Before the day breaksᵉ
and the shadows flee,
I will make my way to the mountain of myrrh
and the hill of frankincense.
7 You are absolutely beautiful, my darling,
with no imperfection in you.

8 Come with me from Lebanon,ᶠ my bride—
with me from Lebanon!
Descend from the peak of Amana,
from the summit of Senir and Hermon,
from the dens of the lions,
from the mountains of the leopards.
9 You have captured my heart, my sister,ᵍ
   my bride.
You have captured my heart with one glance
   of your eyes,
with one jewel of your necklace.
10 How delightful your love is, my sister,
   my bride.
Your love is much better than wine,
and the fragrance of your perfume
   than any balsam.
11 Your lips drip ⌊sweetness like⌋ the honeycomb,
   my bride.
Honey and milk are under your tongue.
The fragrance of your garments is like
   the fragrance of Lebanon.
12 My sister, my bride, ⌊you are⌋
   a locked garden—
a locked gardenʰ and a sealed spring.
13 Your branches are a paradiseⁱ of pomegranates
with choicest fruits,

henna with nard—
14 nard and saffron, calamus and cinnamon,
with all the trees of frankincense,
myrrh and aloes,
with all the best spices.
15 ⌊You are⌋ a garden spring,
a well of flowing water
streaming from Lebanon.

W 16 Awaken, north wind—
come, south wind.
Blow on my garden,
and spread the fragrance of its spices.
Let my love come to his garden
and eat its choicest fruits.

M

5

I have come to my garden—my sister,
   my bride.
I gatherʲ my myrrh with my spices.
I eat my honeycomb with my honey.
I drink my wine with my milk.

N   Eat, friends!
Drink, be intoxicated with love!ᵏ

W 2 I sleep, but my heart is awake.
A sound! My love is knocking!

M   Open to me, my sister, my darling,
my dove, my perfect one.
For my head is drenched with dew,
my hair with droplets of the night.

W 3 I have taken off my clothing.
How can I put it back on?
I have washed my feet.
How can I get them dirty?
4 My love thrust his hand
   through the opening,
and my feelings were stirred for him.
5 I rose to open for my love.
My hands dripped with myrrh,
my fingers with flowing myrrh
on the handles of the bolt.
6 I opened to my love,
but my love had turned and gone away.
I was crushedˡ that he had left.ᵐ
I sought him, but did not find him.
I called him, but he did not answer.
7 The guards who go about the city found me.
They beat and wounded me;

ᵃ4:2 Lit and no one bereaved among them   ᵇ4:3 Or speech   ᶜ4:3 Or temple, or cheek, or lips   ᵈ4:4 The imagery in this v. may have been
suggested by the woman's necklace.   ᵉ4:6 Lit breathes   ᶠ4:8 The Hb word for Lebanon is similar to the word for frankincense; Sg 4:6,14,15.
ᵍ4:9 A term of endearment; Pr 7:4   ʰ4:12 Other Hb mss read locked fountain   ⁱ4:13 Or park, or orchard   ʲ5:1 Lit pluck   ᵏ5:1 Or Drink your fill,
lovers   ˡ5:6 Lit My soul went out   ᵐ5:6 Or spoken

4:4 Your neck is like the tower. Her neck,
adorned with beautiful necklaces, was, strong
and straight as David's military tower.
4:9 captured my heart, my sister. Lovers often call each other "brother" and "sister" (vv.
10, 12; 5:1) as terms of endearment.
4:12 locked garden. A garden is full of beauty,

refreshment, and sensual delight—a beautiful
description of love (v. 16; 5:1; 6:2). The locked
garden may refer to the beloved's virginity.

4:16 Let my love come to his garden. An invitation to enjoy sexual intimacy for the first
time. He expresses his complete satisfaction
as a result in 5:1.

5:5 My hands dripped with myrrh. The beloved's hands are oiled with perfume for her
lover's arrival. Other interpretations suggest
that myrrh may also symbolize her readiness
for sexual encounter. But he has left by the time
she opens the door (5:6).

5:8 I charge you. This refrain (used also in 2:7;

they took my cloak[a] from me—
the guardians of the walls.
8 Young women of Jerusalem, I charge you:
if you find my love,
tell him that I am lovesick.

Y 9 What makes the one you love better than
another,
most beautiful of women?
What makes him better than another,
that you would give us this charge?

W 10 My love is fit and strong,[b]
notable among ten thousand.
11 His head is purest gold.
His hair is wavy[c]
and black as a raven.
12 His eyes are like doves
beside streams of water,
washed in milk
and set like jewels.[d]
13 His cheeks are like beds of spice,
towers of[e] perfume.
His lips are lilies,
dripping with flowing myrrh.
14 His arms[f] are rods of gold
set[g] with topaz.[h]
His body[i] is an ivory panel
covered with sapphires.
15 His legs are alabaster pillars
set on pedestals of pure gold.
His presence[j] is like Lebanon,
as majestic as the cedars.
16 His mouth is sweetness.
He is absolutely desirable.
This is my love, and this is my friend,
young women of Jerusalem.

Y
6 Where has your love gone,
most beautiful of women?
Which way has he[k] turned?
We will seek him with you.

W 2 My love has gone down to his garden,
to beds of spice,
to feed in the gardens
and gather lilies.
3 I am my love's and my love is mine;
he feeds among the lilies.

M 4 You are as beautiful as Tirzah,[l] my darling,
lovely as Jerusalem,
awe-inspiring as an army with banners.
5 Turn your eyes away from me,
for they captivate me.
Your hair is like a flock of goats
streaming down from Gilead.
6 Your teeth are like a flock of ewes
coming up from washing,
each one having a twin,
and not one missing.[m]
7 Behind your veil,
your brow[n] is like a slice of pomegranate.
8 There are 60 queens
and 80 concubines
and young women[o] without number.
9 But my dove, my virtuous one, is unique;
she is the favorite of her mother,
perfect to the one who gave her birth.
Women see her and declare her fortunate;
queens and concubines also, and they sing
her praises:

Y[p] 10 Who is this[q] who shines like the dawn—
as beautiful as the moon,
bright as the sun,
awe-inspiring as an army with banners?

W 11 I came down to the walnut grove
to see the blossoms of the valley,
to see if the vines were budding
and the pomegranates blooming.
12 Before I knew it,
my desire put me
⌊among⌋ the chariots of my noble people.[r]

Y 13s Come back, come back, Shulammite![t]
Come back, come back, that we may look at you!

M Why are you looking at the Shulammite,
as you ⌊look⌋ at the dance of the two camps?[u]
7 How beautiful are your sandaled feet,
princess![v]
The curves of your thighs are like jewelry,
the handiwork of a master.
2 Your navel is a rounded bowl;
it never lacks mixed wine.
Your waist[w] is a mound of wheat
surrounded by lilies.

[a]5:7 Or veil, or shawl [b]5:10 Or is radiant and ruddy [c]5:11 Or is [like] palm leaves; Hb obscure [d]5:12 Lit milk sitting in fullness [e]5:13 LXX, Vg read spice, yielding [f]5:14 Lit hands [g]5:14 Lit filled; Sg 5:2,12 [h]5:14 Probably yellow topaz [i]5:14 Lit abdomen [j]5:15 The total effect of his appearance [k]6:1 Lit your love [l]6:4 = a mountain city in Manasseh [m]6:6 Lit and no one bereaved among them [n]6:7 Or temple, or cheek, or lips [o]6:8 Or and virgins; Sg 1:3 [p]6:10 Some see v. 10 as spoken by M [q]6:10 The pronoun this is feminine in Hb. [r]6:12 Or of Amminadib, or of my people of a prince; Hb obscure [s]6:13 Sg 7:1 in Hb [t]6:13 Perhaps an inhabitant of the town of Shunem, or "the peaceable one," or a feminine form of Solomon's name [u]6:13 Or dance of Mahanaim; Gn 32:2 [v]7:1 Lit daughter of a nobleman or prince [w]7:2 Or belly

3:5) comprises an oath to wait for a love such as this before entering into intimacy.
5:10 notable. Like Israel's princes (Lam. 4:7).
6:2-3 gather lilies. Imaginative language that portrays the lover as a gazelle (2:7) nibbling on the alluring lilies in the exotic garden, thus enjoying intimate moments with his beloved.

6:4 Tirzah. Tirzah was the capitol of Israel's northern kingdom, known for its grand architecture.
6:5 Turn your eyes. The lover is captivated by the deep love he sees through his beloved's eyes—it is almost too wonderful to bear (4:9).
6:8-9 queens ... concubines ... young women. Naming the notable women in the

kingdom or even compared to all the women in the kingdom, his lover is still "unique."
6:13 Shulammite. This name is ambiguous, either referring to her origin as a girl from Shunem ("Shunammite," 1 Kings 1:3), or as a feminine version of Solomon's name meaning, "Solomon's girl" Or even perhaps an oblique reference to a

3 Your breasts are like two fawns,
  twins of a gazelle.
4 Your neck is like a tower of ivory,
  your eyes like pools in Heshbon
  by the gate of Bath-rabbim.
  Your nose is like the tower of Lebanon
  looking toward Damascus.
5 Your head crowns you[a] like Mount Carmel,
  the hair of your head like purple cloth—
  a king could be held captive in your tresses.
6 How beautiful you are and how pleasant,
  ⌊my⌋ love, with such delights!
7 Your stature is like a palm tree;
  your breasts are clusters ⌊of fruit⌋.
8 I said, "I will climb the palm tree
  and take hold of its fruit."
  May your breasts be like clusters of grapes,
  and the fragrance of your breath like apricots.
9 Your mouth[b] is like fine wine—

W flowing smoothly for my love
  gliding past my lips and teeth![c]
10 I belong to my love,
  and his desire is for me.

11 Come, my love,
  let's go to the field;
  let's spend the night
    among the henna blossoms.[d]
12 Let's go early to the vineyards;
  let's see if the vine has budded,
  if the blossom has opened,
  if the pomegranates are in bloom.
  There I will give you my love.
13 The mandrakes give off a fragrance,
  and at our doors is every delicacy—
  new as well as old.
  I have treasured them up for you, my love.

8 If only I could treat you like my brother,[e]
  one who nursed at my mother's breasts,
  I would find you in public and kiss you,
  and no one would scorn me.
2 I would lead you, I would take you,
  to the house of my mother who taught me.[f]
  I would give you spiced wine to drink
  from my pomegranate juice.
3 His left hand is under my head,

and his right hand embraces me.
4 Young women of Jerusalem, I charge you:
  do not stir up or awaken love
  until the appropriate time.

Y 5 Who is this coming up from the wilderness,
  leaning on the one she loves?

W I awakened you under the apricot tree.
  There your mother conceived you;
  there she conceived and gave you birth.
6 Set me as a seal on your heart,
  as a seal on your arm.
  For love is as strong as death;
  ardent love is as unrelenting as •Sheol.
  Love's flames are fiery flames—
  the fiercest of all.[g]
7 Mighty waters cannot extinguish love;
  rivers cannot sweep it away.
  If a man were to give all his wealth[h] for love,
  it would be utterly scorned.

B 8 Our sister is young;
  she has no breasts.
  What will we do for our sister
  on the day she is spoken for?
9 If she is a wall,
  we will build a silver parapet on it.
  If she is a door,
  we will enclose it with cedar planks.[i]

W 10 I am[j] a wall
  and my breasts like towers.
  So in his eyes I have become
  like one who finds peace.[k]

11 Solomon owned a vineyard in Baal-hamon.
  He leased the vineyard to tenants.
  Each was to bring for his fruit
  1,000 pieces of silver.
12 I have my own vineyard.[l]
  The 1,000 are for you, Solomon,
  but 200 for those who guard its fruits.

M 13 You[m] who dwell in the gardens—
  companions are listening for your voice—
  let me hear you!

W 14 Hurry ⌊to me⌋, my love,
  and be like a gazelle
  or a young stag
  on the mountains of spices.

---

[a] 7:5 Lit head upon you is [b] 7:9 Lit palate [c] 7:9 LXX, Syr, Vg; MT reads past lips of sleepers [d] 7:11 Or the villages [e] 8:1 Lit Would that you were like a brother to me [f] 8:2 LXX adds and into the chamber of the one who bore me [g] 8:6 Or the blaze of the LORD [h] 8:7 Lit all the wealth of his house [i] 8:8–9 Vv. 8–9 may record what the girl's brothers (Sg 1:6) used to say; Gn 24:29; 34:6–18. [j] 8:10 Or was [k] 8:10 Shalom, the Hb word for peace, sounds similar to Solomon and Shulammite in Hb. [l] 8:12 Lit My vineyard, which is mine, is before me; Sg 1:6 [m] 8:13 You is feminine in Hb.

Mesopotamian goddess of love, Sulmanitu.

7:4 neck … tower of ivory. Ivory is used to describe the shape, color, and smoothness of the beloved's neck.

7:7 palm tree. This reference likely refers to her tall slim, appearance with breasts like clusters of fruit at the top of the tree.

7:13 mandrakes. These flowering herbs with a pungent fragrance were used for fertility (see Gen. 30:14-16).

8:1 like my brother. She longs to be as free and affectionate in public as she could be with a brother (though unacceptable between lovers in that culture).

8:12 I have my own vineyard. A poetic reference to her own body (1:6).

8:13 dwell in the gardens. The beloved had earlier invited her lover to her vineyards in the country (7:11-12).

8:14 like a gazelle or a young stag. The beloved desires her lover to be graceful, virile, strong and he return quickly to her (1:13; 4:6).

ISAIAH

PERSONAL READING PLAN

AUTHOR

In the opening verse of the book, the author is declared to be Isaiah son of Amoz (see also 2:1; 13:1). Chapters 1-39 ("The Book of Judgment") reflect the kingdom of Isaiah's day, but chapters 40-66 ("The Book of Comfort") envision the return from exile (536 B.C.) and the coming kingdom of God. There are some who believe that these visionary chapters may have been written later by other prophets.

DATE

Isaiah ministered in Judah circa 740-681 B.C.

THEME

The sovereign Lord, judging, and redeeming the whole earth.

HISTORICAL BACKGROUND

Assyria, the invincible superpower of the day, was threatening Jerusalem with conquest (2 Kings 15-20; 2 Chron. 26-32). Isaiah saw in this the culmination of God's judgment against the widespread apostasy of Judah under King Ahaz. He predicted the fall of Jerusalem (which occurred in 586 B.C.). The only hope for escape, Isaiah declared, was God's intervention, not political alliances, material wealth, or religious pretense. Chapters 40-66 focus on events 150-200 years after Isaiah's day, foretelling God's deliverance of His people from their Babylonian captors (in 538 B.C.), and pointing ahead to the greater deliverance from sin through Christ.

CHARACTERISTICS

As a prophet, poet, and politician, Isaiah was a giant in his day, respected in royal circles despite his unpopular message. Known for his beautiful images and profound insights into the nature of God (whom Isaiah calls "The Holy One of Israel"), the prophet Isaiah is quoted in the New Testament more than all other prophets combined. Isaiah's use of fire as a symbol of punishment (1:31), his references to the "holy mountain" of Jerusalem (2:2-4), and his mention of the highway to Jerusalem (11:16), are images that recur throughout the book.

PASSAGES FOR TOPICAL GROUP STUDY

40:25-31 . . . . . GOD'S HELP . . . . The Source of All Strength
52:13-53:12 . . PROPHECY OF JESUS . . The Suffering Servant

1 The vision concerning Judah and Jerusalem that Isaiah son of Amoz saw during the reigns[a][b] of Uzziah, Jotham, Ahaz, and Hezekiah, kings of Judah.

Judah on Trial

² Listen, heavens, and pay attention, earth,
for the LORD has spoken:
"I have raised children[c] and brought them up,
but they have rebelled against Me.
³ The ox knows its owner,
and the donkey its master's feeding-trough,
⌊but⌋ Israel does not know;
My people do not understand."

⁴ Oh—sinful nation,
people weighed down with iniquity,
brood of evildoers,
depraved children![c]
They have abandoned the LORD;
they have despised the Holy One of Israel;
they have turned their backs ⌊on Him⌋.

⁵ Why do you want more beatings?
Why do you keep on rebelling?
The whole head is hurt,
and the whole heart is sick.
⁶ From the sole of the foot even to the head,
no spot is uninjured—
wounds, welts, and festering sores
not cleansed, bandaged,
or soothed with oil.

⁷ Your land is desolate,
your cities burned with fire;
before your very eyes
foreigners devour your fields—
a desolation overthrown by foreigners.
⁸ Daughter Zion is abandoned
like a shelter in a vineyard,
like a shack in a cucumber field,
like a besieged city.
⁹ If the LORD of •Hosts
had not left us a few survivors,
we would be like Sodom,
we would resemble Gomorrah.

¹⁰ Hear the word of the LORD,
you rulers of Sodom!
Listen to the instruction of our God,
you people of Gomorrah!
¹¹ "What are all your sacrifices to Me?"
asks the LORD.

"I have had enough of •burnt offerings and rams
and the fat of well-fed cattle;
I have no desire for the blood of bulls,
lambs, or male goats.
¹² When you come to appear before Me,
who requires this from you—
⌊this⌋ trampling of My courts?
¹³ Stop bringing useless offerings.
I despise ⌊your⌋ incense.
New Moons and Sabbaths,
and the calling of solemn assemblies—
I cannot stand iniquity with a festival.
¹⁴ I hate your New Moons and prescribed festivals.
They have become a burden to Me;
I am tired of putting up with ⌊them⌋.
¹⁵ When you lift up your hands ⌊in prayer⌋,
I will refuse to look at you;
even if you offer countless prayers,
I will not listen.
Your hands are covered with blood.

Purification of Jerusalem

¹⁶ "Wash yourselves. Cleanse yourselves.
Remove your evil deeds from My sight.
Stop doing evil.
¹⁷ Learn to do what is good.
Seek justice.
Correct the oppressor.[d]
Defend the rights of the fatherless.
Plead the widow's cause.

¹⁸ "Come, let us discuss this,"
says the LORD.
"Though your sins are like scarlet,
they will be as white as snow;
though they are as red as crimson,
they will be like wool.
¹⁹ If you are willing and obedient,
you will eat the good things of the land.
²⁰ But if you refuse and rebel,
you will be devoured by the sword."
For the mouth of the LORD has spoken.

²¹ The faithful city—
what an adulteress she has become!
She was once full of justice.
Righteousness once dwelt in her—
but now, murderers!
²² Your silver has become dross,[e]
your beer[f] is diluted with water.
²³ Your rulers are rebels,

---

[a]1:1 Lit *saw in the days*   [b]1:1 c. 792–686 B.C.   [c]1:2,4 Or *sons*   [d]1:17 Or *Aid the oppressed*   [e]1:22 Or *burnished lead;* = lead oxide   [f]1:22 Or *wine*

1:1 kings of Judah. The nation of Israel had been divided into Judah in the south and Israel in the north. Isaiah focuses his message on Judah, listing the four kings who ruled from 792 to 686 B.C., during the time when he received God's prophetic visions and words.

1:9-10 Sodom ... Gomorrah. So far Judah has escaped total destruction, but the precedent has already been set by these sinful cities God utterly destroyed (see 3:9; Gen. 13:13; 18:20, 21; 19:5, 24, 25). God compares the Judeans to the depraved people of Sodom and Gomorrah.

1:17 Defend ... fatherless. Plead the

widow's cause. This guidance is echoed in Jeremiah 22:16 and James 1:27. These types of people are symbolic of all oppressed peoples in society. Their treatment by the nation as a whole was a barometer for the nation's spiritual and moral health; rulers were not to take advantage of them (see v. 23; 10:2; Jer. 22:3).

friends of thieves.
They all love graft
and chase after bribes.
They do not defend the rights of the fatherless,
and the widow's case never comes
before them."

24 Therefore the Lord GOD of Hosts,
the Mighty One of Israel, declares:
"Ah, I will gain satisfaction against My foes;
I will take revenge against My enemies.

25 I will turn My hand against you
and will burn away your dross[a] completely;[b]
I will remove all your impurities.

26 I will restore your judges to what
they once were,[c]
and your advisers to their former state.[d]
Afterwards you will be called the Righteous City,
a Faithful City."

27 Zion will be redeemed by justice,
her repentant ones by righteousness.

28 But both rebels and sinners will be destroyed,
and those who abandon the LORD will perish.

29 Indeed, they[e] will be ashamed
of the sacred trees
you desired,
and you will be embarrassed because of
the gardens
you have chosen.

30 For you will become like an oak
whose leaves are withered,
and like a garden without water.

31 The strong one will become tinder,
and his work a spark;
both will burn together,
with no one to quench ⌊the flames⌋.

The City of Peace

2 The vision that Isaiah son of Amoz saw concerning Judah and Jerusalem:

2 In the last days
the mountain of the LORD's house
will be established
at the top of the mountains
and will be raised above the hills.
All nations will stream to it,

3 and many peoples will come and say,
"Come, let us go up to the mountain
of the LORD,

to the house of the God of Jacob.
He will teach us about His ways
so that we may walk in His paths."
For instruction will go out of Zion
and the word of the LORD from Jerusalem.

4 He will settle disputes among the nations
and provide arbitration for many peoples.
They will turn their swords into plows
and their spears into pruning knives.
Nations will not take up the sword
against ⌊other⌋ nations,
and they will never again train for war.

The Day of the LORD

5 House of Jacob,
come and let us walk in the LORD's light.

6 For You have abandoned Your people,
the house of Jacob,
because they are full of ⌊•divination⌋
from the East
and of fortune-tellers like the Philistines.
They are in league[f] with foreigners.

7 Their[g] land is full of silver and gold,
and there is no limit to their treasures;
their land is full of horses,
and there is no limit to their chariots.

8 Their land is full of idols;
they bow down to the work of their hands,
to what their fingers have made.

9 So humanity is brought low,
and man is humbled.
Do not forgive them!

10 Go into the rocks
and hide in the dust
from the terror of the LORD
and from His majestic splendor.

11 Human pride[h] will be humbled,
and the loftiness of men will be brought low;
the LORD alone will be exalted on that day.

12 For a day belonging to the LORD of •Hosts
is ⌊coming⌋
against all that is proud and lofty,
against all that is lifted up—it will be humbled—

13 against all the cedars of Lebanon,
lofty and lifted up,
against all the oaks of Bashan,

14 against all the high mountains,
against all the lofty hills,

15 against every high tower,

---

[a]1:25 Or burnished lead; = lead oxide [b]1:25 Lit dross as with lye [c]1:26 Lit judges as at the first [d]1:26 Lit advisers as at the beginning
[e]1:29 Some Hb mss; other Hb mss, Tg read you [f]2:6 Or They teem, or They partner; Hb obscure [g]2:7 Lit Its; = the house of Jacob [h]2:11 Lit
Mankind's proud eyes

1:18 let us discuss this. This was not an invitation to compromise, but a call to come to a legal decision in alignment with God's perfect will regarding their sin. **scarlet.** God has caught His people "red handed." Blood covers their hands as it would a murderer's (vv. 15, 21). **as snow.** God's forgiveness provides complete cleansing (Ps. 51:7)—but the

offer depends on the people's receptiveness and true repentance (v. 19).

2:2-4 Isaiah often refers to the "mountain of the LORD," which is quite similar to Micah 4:1-3.

2:7 silver and gold ... horses ... chariots. Kings were specifically forbidden to accumulate these things (see Deut. 17:16-17) be-

cause they tended to cause the king, and the nation, to put their trust in money rather than in God (31:1).

3:1-3 God would remove the nation's leaders, either through death or exile (2 Kings 24:14; 25:18-21).

3:12 women rule. Ancient Near Eastern cul-

against every fortified wall,

16 against every ship of Tarshish,
and against every splendid sea vessel.

17 So human pride will be brought low,
and the loftiness of men will be humbled;
the LORD alone will be exalted on that day.

18 The idols will vanish completely.

19 People will go into caves in the rocks
and holes in the ground,
away from the terror of the LORD
and from His majestic splendor,
when He rises to terrify the earth.

20 On that day people will throw
their silver and gold idols,
which they made to worship,
to the moles and the bats.

21 They will go into the caves of the rocks
and the crevices in the cliffs,
away from the terror of the LORD
and from His majestic splendor,
when He rises to terrify the earth.

22 Put no more trust in man,
who has only the breath in his nostrils.
What is he really worth?

Judah's Leaders Judged

3 Observe this: The Lord GOD of •Hosts
is about to remove from Jerusalem
and from Judah
every kind of security:
the entire supply of bread and water,

2 the hero and warrior,
the judge and prophet,
the fortune-teller and elder,

3 the commander of 50 and the dignitary,
the counselor, cunning magician,[a]
and necromancer.[b]

4 "I will make youths their leaders,
and the unstable[c] will govern them."

5 The people will oppress one another,
man against man, neighbor against neighbor;
the youth will act arrogantly toward the elder,
and the worthless toward the honorable.

6 A man will even seize his brother
in his father's house, [saying:]
"You have a cloak—you be our leader!
This heap of rubble will be under your control."

7 On that day he will cry out, saying:
"I'm not a healer.
I don't even have food or clothing in my house.

Don't make me the leader of the people!"

8 For Jerusalem has stumbled
and Judah has fallen
because they have spoken and acted
against the LORD,
defying His glorious presence.

9 The look on their faces testifies against them,
and like Sodom, they flaunt their sin.
They do not conceal it.
Woe to them!
For they have brought evil on themselves.

10 Tell the righteous that it will go well [for them],
for they will eat the fruit of their deeds.

11 Woe to the wicked—[it will go] badly [for them],
for what they have done will be done to them.

12 Youths oppress My people,
and women rule over them.
My people, your leaders mislead you;
they confuse the direction of your paths.

13 The LORD rises to argue the case
and stands to judge the people.

14 The LORD brings [this] charge
against the elders and leaders of His people:
"You have devastated the vineyard.
The plunder from the poor is in your houses.

15 Why do you crush My people
and grind the faces of the poor?"
says the Lord GOD of Hosts.

Jerusalem's Women Judged

16 The LORD also says:

Because the daughters of Zion are haughty,
walking with heads held high
and seductive eyes,
going along with prancing steps,
jingling their ankle bracelets,

17 the Lord will put scabs on the heads
of the daughters of Zion,
and the LORD will shave their foreheads bare.

18 On that day the Lord will strip their finery: ankle bracelets, headbands, crescents, 19 pendants, bracelets, veils, 20 headdresses, ankle jewelry, sashes, perfume bottles, amulets, 21 signet rings, nose rings, 22 festive robes, capes, cloaks, purses, 23 garments, linen clothes, turbans, and veils.

24 Instead of perfume there will be a stench;
instead of a belt, a rope;
instead of beautifully styled hair, baldness;

---

a**3:3** Or *skilled craftsman* b**3:3** Or *medium* c**3:4** Or *mischief-makers*

---

ture looked down on the exercise of leadership by women or youth.
3:15 crush ... grind. Just as grain was crushed by millstones, the nation's poor have been ground down by their leaders.
3:21 signet rings, nose rings. Signet rings, worn by those in authority, featured an official

seal (see Gen. 41:42). Nose rings made of gold or other precious metals were worn by brides.
3:24 rope ... branding. Those taken captive would be herded and treated like cattle—a far cry from the opulent ease they were accustomed to.

4:2 branch of the LORD. This title is used of the Messiah because He will be the "branch" that will grow from "the stump" (11:1; 53:2; Jer. 23:5), a descendant of David. However, some scholars take this reference to be Judah rather than the Messiah.
4:5-6 cloud of smoke ... canopy. God's

instead of fine clothes, •sackcloth;
instead of beauty, branding.a

25 Your men will fall by the sword,
your warriors in battle.

26 Then her gates will lament and mourn;
deserted, she will sit on the ground.

4 On that day seven women
will seize one man, saying,
"We will eat our own bread
and provide our own clothing.
Just let us be called by your name.
Take away our disgrace."

Zion's Future Glory

2 On that day the branch of the LORD will be beautiful and glorious, and the fruit of the land will be the pride and glory of Israel's survivors. 3 Whoever remains in Zion and whoever is left in Jerusalem will be called holy—all in Jerusalem who are destined to live— 4 when the Lord has washed away the filth of the daughters of Zion and cleansed the bloodguilt from the heart of Jerusalem by a spirit of judgment and a spirit of burning. 5 Then the LORD will create a cloud of smoke by day and a glowing flame of fire by night over the entire site of Mount Zion and over its assemblies. For there will be a canopy over all the glory,b 6 and there will be a booth for shade from heat by day, and a refuge and shelter from storm and rain.

Song of the Vineyard

5 I will sing about the one I love,
a song about my loved one's vineyard:
The one I love had a vineyard
on a very fertile hill.

2 He broke up the soil, cleared it of stones,
and planted it with the finest vines.
He built a tower in the middle of it
and even hewed out a winepress there.
He expected it to yield good grapes,
but it yielded worthless grapes.

3 So now, residents of Jerusalem
and men of Judah,
please judge between Me
and My vineyard.

4 What more could I have done for My vineyard
than I did?
Why, when I expected a yield of good grapes,
did it yield worthless grapes?

5 Now I will tell you
what I am about to do to My vineyard:

I will remove its hedge,
and it will be consumed;
I will tear down its wall,
and it will be trampled.

6 I will make it a wasteland.
It will not be pruned or weeded;
thorns and briers will grow up.
I will also give orders to the clouds
that rain should not fall on it.

7 For the vineyard of the LORD of •Hosts
is the house of Israel,
and the menc of Judah,
the plant He delighted in.
He looked for justice
but saw injustice,
for righteousness,
but heard cries of wretchedness.

Judah's Sins Denounced

8 Woe to those who add house to house
and join field to field
until there is no more room
and you alone are left in the land.

9 In my hearing the LORD of Hosts ⌊has taken an oath⌋:

Indeed, many houses will become desolate,
grand and lovely ones without inhabitants.

10 For a ten-acred vineyard will yield
only six gallons,e
and 10 bushelsf of seed will yield
only ⌊one⌋ bushel.g

11 Woe to those who rise early in the morning
in pursuit of beer,
who linger into the evening,
inflamed by wine.

12 At their feasts they have lyre, harp,
tambourine, flute, and wine.
They do not perceive the LORD's actions,
and they do not see the work of His hands.

13 Therefore My people go into exile
because they lack knowledge;
theh dignitaries are starving,
and theh masses are parched with thirst.

14 Therefore •Sheol enlarges its throat
and opens wide its enormous jaws,
and down go Zion's dignitaries, her masses,
her crowds, and those who carouse in her!

15 Humanity is brought low, man is humbled,

---

a3:24 DSS read shame b4:5 Or For glory will be a canopy over all c5:7 Lit man d5:10 Lit ten-yoke e5:10 Lit one bath f5:10 Lit one homer g5:10 Lit [one] ephah h5:13 Lit its

---

glory in the wilderness was enshrouded in a cloud. In the Messianic kingdom of Christ, Israel will be restored and a canopy will cover Jerusalem. This is the same word used for a wedding canopy, a khuppah. The picture is of God reunited with his bride, Israel.

5:7 vineyard of the Lord. This verse pro-

vides the interpretation of verses 1-6, the "Song of the Vineyard."

5:8 house to house ... field to field until there is no more room. The land of Israel had been given permanently to specific families, so it could only be rented to others, not sold (see Num. 27:7-11; 1 Kings 21:1-3). God

declared the land "Mine" (Lev. 25:23), but greedy landowners sought to control the best plots of land in Israel for themselves.

6:1 King Uzziah died. Uzziah, a good king who ruled well, reigned from 792 until he died in 740 B.C. He contracted leprosy as a judgment upon his insistence on burning incense

and haughty eyes are humbled.

16 But the LORD of Hosts is exalted by His justice,
  and the holy God is distinguished
    by righteousness.

17 Lambs will graze
  as ⌊if in⌋a their own pastures,
  and strangersb will eat
  ⌊among⌋ the ruins of the rich.

18 Woe to those who drag wickedness
  with cords of deceit
  and ⌊pull⌋ sin along with cart ropes,

19 to those who say:
  "Let Him hurry up and do His work quickly
  so that we can see it!
  Let the plan of the Holy One of Israel take place
  so that we can know it!"

20 Woe to those who call evil good
  and good evil,
  who substitute darkness for light
  and light for darkness,
  who substitute bitter for sweet
  and sweet for bitter.

21 Woe to those who are wise in their own opinion
  and clever in their own sight.c

22 Woe to those who are heroes at drinking wine,
  who are fearless at mixing beer,

23 who acquit the guilty for a bribe
  and deprive the innocent of justice.

24 Therefore, as a tongue of fire consumes straw
  and as dry grass shrivels in the flame,
  so their roots will become like something rotten
  and their blossoms will blow away like dust,
  for they have rejected
  the instruction of the LORD of Hosts,
  and they have despised
  the word of the Holy One of Israel.

25 Therefore the LORD's anger burns
    against His people.
  He raised His hand against them
    and struck them;
  the mountains quaked,
  and their corpses were like garbage
    in the streets.
  In all this, His anger is not removed,
  and His hand is still raised ⌊to strike⌋.

26 He raises a signal flag for the distant nations
  and whistles for them from the ends
    of the earth.

Look—how quickly and swiftly they come!

27 None of them grows weary or stumbles;
  no one slumbers or sleeps.
  No belt is loose,
  and no sandal strap broken.

28 Their arrows are sharpened,
  and all their bows strung.
  Their horses' hooves are like flint;
  their ⌊chariot⌋ wheels are like a whirlwind.

29 Their roaring is like a lion's;
  they roar like young lions;
  they growl and seize their prey
  and carry ⌊it⌋ off,
  and no one can rescue ⌊it⌋.

30 On that day they will roar over it,
  like the roaring of the sea.
  When one looks at the land,
  there will be darkness and distress;
  light will be obscured by clouds.d

Isaiah's Call and Mission

6 In the year that King Uzziah died, I saw the Lord seated on a high and lofty throne, and His robee filled the temple. 2 Seraphimf were standing above Him; each one had six wings: with two he covered his face, with two he covered his feet, and with two he flew. 3 And one called to another:

Holy, holy, holy is the LORD of •Hosts;
His glory fills the whole earth.

4 The foundations of the doorways shook at the sound of their voices, and the temple was filled with smoke. 5 Then I said:

Woe is me, for I am ruined,
because I am a man of unclean lips
and live among a people of unclean lips,
⌊and⌋ because my eyes have seen the King,
the LORD of Hosts.

6 Then one of the seraphim flew to me, and in his hand was a glowing coal that he had taken from the altar with tongs. 7 He touched my mouth ⌊with it⌋ and said:

Now that this has touched your lips,
your wickedness is removed,
and your sin is atoned for.

8 Then I heard the voice of the Lord saying:

Who should I send?
Who will go for Us?

---

a **5:17** Syr reads *graze in* b **5:17** LXX reads *sheep* c **5:21** Lit *clever before their face* d **5:30** Lit *its clouds* e **6:1** Lit *seam* f **6:2** = heavenly beings

---

in God's temple and died with that condition (2 Chron. 26:16-21).

6:2 Seraphim. These angels are mentioned by name only here in the Bible. Their name comes from a Hebrew word meaning "burn," possibly speaking of God's purity (v. 6; Rev. 4:6-9). Note the contrast between their wor-

ship of God and the rebellious pride of humanity.

7:14 will give you a sign ... virgin. There are two possible interpretations for this verse. First, that this was a direct prophecy of the virgin birth of Jesus or second, that this was a sign given in the days of King Ahaz. For a sign

to help Ahaz's faith, it would seemingly have to happen in his days. Matthew 1:23 seems to say that Isaiah 7:14 is a prophecy of Jesus' virgin birth. Yet, Matthew 1:23 can be understood as comparing Jesus' birth to the announcement in Isaiah 7:14: a special messenger (prophet/angel) announces a

I said:

Here I am. Send me.

⁹ And He replied:

Go! Say to these people:
Keep listening, but do not understand;
keep looking, but do not perceive.

¹⁰ Dull the minds^a of these people;
deafen their ears and blind their eyes;
otherwise they might see with their eyes
and hear with their ears,
understand with their minds,
turn back, and be healed.

¹¹ Then I said, "Until when, Lord?" And He replied:

Until cities lie in ruins without inhabitants,
houses are without people,
the land is ruined and desolate,

¹² and the LORD drives the people far away,
leaving great emptiness in the land.

¹³ Though a tenth will remain in the land,
it will be burned again.
Like the terebinth or the oak,
which leaves a stump when felled,
the holy •seed is the stump.

The Message to Ahaz

7 This took place during the reign of Ahaz, son of Jotham, son of Uzziah king of Judah: Rezin king of Aram, along with Pekah, son of Remaliah, king of Israel, waged war against Jerusalem, but he could not succeed. ² When it became known to the house of David that Aram had occupied Ephraim, the heart of Ahaz^b and the hearts of his people trembled like trees of a forest shaking in a wind.

³ Then the LORD said to Isaiah, "Go out with your son Shear-jashub to meet Ahaz at the end of the conduit of the upper pool, by the road to the Fuller's Field. ⁴ Say to him: Calm down and be quiet. Don't be afraid or fainthearted because of these two smoldering stubs of firebrands, Rezin of Aram, and the son of Remaliah. ⁵ For Aram, along with Ephraim and the son of Remaliah, has plotted harm against you. They say: ⁶ Let us go up against Judah, terrorize it, and conquer it for ourselves. Then we can install Tabeel's son as king in it."

⁷ This is what the Lord GOD says:

It will not happen; it will not occur.

⁸ The^c head of Aram is Damascus,
the head of Damascus is Rezin

(within 65 years
Ephraim will be too shattered to be a people),

⁹ the head of Ephraim is Samaria,
and the head of Samaria is the son of Remaliah.
If you do not stand firm in your faith,
then you will not stand at all.

The Immanuel Prophecy

¹⁰ Then the LORD spoke again to Ahaz: ¹¹ "Ask for a sign from the LORD your God—from the depths of •Sheol to the heights of heaven." ¹² But Ahaz replied, "I will not ask. I will not test the LORD." ¹³ Isaiah said, "Listen, house of David! Is it not enough for you to try the patience of men? Will you also try the patience of my God? ¹⁴ Therefore, the Lord Himself will give you^d a sign: The virgin will conceive,^e have a son, and name him Immanuel.^f ¹⁵ By the time he learns to reject what is bad and choose what is good, he will be eating butter^g and honey. ¹⁶ For before the boy knows to reject what is bad and choose what is good, the land of the two kings you dread will be abandoned. ¹⁷ The LORD will bring on you, your people, and the house of your father, such a time as has never been since Ephraim separated from Judah—the king of Assyria ⌊is coming⌋.

¹⁸ On that day
the LORD will whistle to the fly
that is at the farthest streams of the Nile
and to the bee that is in the land of Assyria.

¹⁹ All of them will come and settle
in the steep ravines, in the clefts of the rocks,
in all the thornbushes, and in all the
water holes.

²⁰ On that day the Lord will use a razor hired from beyond the Euphrates River—the king of Assyria—to shave the head, the hair on the legs, and to remove the beard as well.

²¹ On that day
a man will raise a young cow and two sheep,

²² and from the abundant milk they give
he will eat butter,
for every survivor in the land will eat butter
and honey.

²³ And on that day
every place where there were 1,000 vines,
worth 1,000 pieces of silver,
will become thorns and briers.

---

^a**6:10** Lit *heart* ^b**7:2** Lit *Aram has rested upon Ephraim, his heart* ^c**7:8** Lit *For the* ^d**7:14** The pronoun *you* is pl ^e**7:14** Or *virgin is pregnant, will* ^f**7:14** = God With Us; Is 8:10 ^g**7:15** Or *sour milk*

---

special child whose birth will signify God's presence with us. It is possible that Isaiah's verse referred to a child in his day and also to Jesus (double fulfillment). **Immanuel.** The name means "God is with us," assuring King Ahaz that God would protect him from enemy nations (see Num. 14:9; 2 Chron. 13:12; Ps.

46:7). The same name appears in 8:8,10, perhaps in reference to Maher-Shalal-Hash-Baz, whose name means "quick to the plunder, swift to the spoil" (8:3). Of course, the final application of the name is to Jesus Christ who truly became "God with us" (9:6-7; Matt. 1:23).

8:11 the Lord said to me with great power. The prophets were clearly aware that their word was inspired and that God was using them for divine purposes (see Ezek. 1:3; 37:1; 40:1).

8:17 wait. Isaiah still hopes in God, confidently expecting that the people will ulti-

24 A man will go there with bow and arrows
because the whole land will be thorns
and briers.
25 You will not go to all the hills
that were once tilled with a hoe,
for fear of the thorns and briers.
⌊Those hills⌋ will be places for oxen to graze
and for sheep to trample.

The Coming Assyrian Invasion

8 Then the LORD said to me, "Take a large piece of parchment[a] and write on it with an ordinary pen:[b] Maher-shalal-hash-baz.[c] 2 I have appointed[d] trustworthy witnesses—Uriah the priest and Zechariah son of Jeberechiah."

3 I was then intimate with the prophetess, and she conceived and gave birth to a son. The LORD said to me, "Name him Maher-shalal-hash-baz, 4 for before the boy knows how to call out father or mother, the wealth of Damascus and the spoils of Samaria will be carried off to the king of Assyria."

5 The LORD spoke to me again:

6 Because these people rejected
the slowly flowing waters of Shiloah
and rejoiced with[e] Rezin
and the son of Remaliah,
7 the Lord will certainly bring against them
the mighty rushing waters
of the Euphrates River—
the king of Assyria and all his glory.
It will overflow its channels
and spill over all its banks.
8 It will pour into Judah,
flood over it, and sweep through,
reaching up to the neck;
and its spreading streams[f]
will fill your entire land, Immanuel!

9 Band together, peoples, and be broken;
pay attention, all you distant lands;
prepare for war, and be broken;
prepare for war, and be broken.
10 Devise a plan; it will fail.
Make a prediction; it will not happen.
For God is with us.[g]

The LORD of Hosts, the Only Refuge

11 For this is what the LORD said to me with great power, to keep[h] me from going the way of this people:

12 Do not call everything an alliance
these people say is an alliance.
Do not fear what they fear;
do not be terrified.
13 You are to regard only the LORD of •Hosts
as holy.
Only He should be •feared;
only He should be held in awe.
14 He will be a sanctuary;
but for the two houses of Israel,
He will be a stone to stumble over
and a rock to trip over,
and a trap and a snare to the inhabitants
of Jerusalem.
15 Many will stumble over these;
they will fall and be broken;
they will be snared and captured.

16 Bind up the •testimony.
Seal up the instruction among my disciples.
17 I will wait for the LORD,
who is hiding His face from the house of Jacob.
I will wait for Him.

18 Here I am with the children the LORD has given me to be signs and wonders in Israel from the LORD of Hosts who dwells on Mount Zion. 19 When they say to you, "Consult the spirits of the dead and the spiritists who chirp and mutter," shouldn't a people consult their God?[i] ⌊Should they consult⌋ the dead on behalf of the living? 20 To the law and to the testimony! If they do not speak according to this word, there will be no dawn for them.

21 They will wander through the land, dejected and hungry. When they are famished, they will become enraged, and, looking upward, will curse their king and their God. 22 They will look toward the earth and see only distress, darkness, and the gloom of affliction, and they will be driven into thick darkness.

Birth of the Prince of Peace

9[i] Nevertheless, the gloom of the distressed land will not be like that of the former times when He humbled the land of Zebulun and the land of Naphtali. But in the future He will bring honor to the Way of the Sea, to the land east of the Jordan, and to Galilee of the nations.

2[k] The people walking in darkness
have seen a great light;
on those living in the land of darkness,

---

a**8:1** Hb obscure b**8:1** Lit with the pen of a man c**8:1** Or Speeding to the Plunder, Hurrying to the Spoil d**8:2** Vg; MT, one DSS ms read I will appoint; one DSS ms, LXX, Syr, Tg read Appoint e**8:6** Or and rejoiced over f**8:8** Or wings g**8:10** Or For Immanuel; Is 7:14; 8:8 h**8:11** Or instruct i**8:19** Or gods j**9:1** Is 8:23 in Hb k**9:2** Is 9:1 in Hb

---

mately be delivered.

8:19 Consult the spirits of the dead and the spiritists. In crises the people sometimes sought help through the practice of necromancy (contact with the spirits of dead people in an effort to influence present reality). King Saul consulted the deceased Samuel to

ascertain what would happen to him (see 1 Sam. 28:8-11). God abhors this practice because it demonstrated a lack of trust in Him.

9:1-2 Galilee of the nations ... have seen a great light. At times in Israel's history, Galilee has had a mixed population of Jews and Gentiles. God would reveal His person and bless-

ing to the people of Galilee in the days of Jesus. Later Isaiah would refer to the Messiah as a "light for the nations" (42:6).

9:6 A child will be born to us. This is a prophecy about Messiah Jesus. **He will be named Wonderful Counselor.** Like other names in Isaiah, this one should be made into

a light has dawned.

3 You have enlarged the nation
and increased its joy.[a]
⌊The people⌋ have rejoiced before You
as they rejoice at harvest time
and as they rejoice when dividing spoils.

4 For You have shattered their burdensome yoke
and the rod on their shoulders,
the staff of their oppressor,
just as ⌊You did⌋ on the day of Midian.

5 For the trampling boot of battle
and the bloodied garments of war
will be burned as fuel for the fire.

6 For a child will be born for us,
a son will be given to us,
and the government will be on His shoulders.
He will be named
Wonderful Counselor, Mighty God,
Eternal Father, Prince of Peace.

7 The dominion will be vast,
and its prosperity will never end.
He will reign on the throne of David
and over his kingdom,
to establish and sustain it
with justice and righteousness from now on
and forever.
The zeal of the LORD of •Hosts
will accomplish this.

The Hand Raised against Israel

8 The Lord sent a message against Jacob;
it came against Israel.

9 All the people—
Ephraim and the inhabitants of Samaria—
will know it.
They will say with pride and arrogance:

10 "The bricks have fallen,
but we will rebuild with cut stones;
the sycamores have been cut down,
but we will replace them with cedars."

11 The LORD has raised up Rezin's adversaries
against him
and stirred up his enemies.

12 Aram from the east and Philistia from the west
have consumed Israel with open mouths.
In all this, His anger is not removed,
and His hand is still raised ⌊to strike⌋.

13 The people did not turn to Him
who struck them;
they did not seek the LORD of Hosts.

14 So the LORD cut off Israel's head and tail,
palm branch and reed in a single day.

15 The head is the elder, the honored one;
the tail is the prophet, the lying teacher.

16 The leaders of the people mislead ⌊them⌋,
and those they mislead are swallowed up.[b]

17 Therefore the Lord does not rejoice over[c]
Israel's[d] young men
and has no compassion
on its fatherless and widows,
for everyone is a godless evildoer,
and every mouth speaks folly.
In all this, His anger is not removed,
and His hand is still raised ⌊to strike⌋.

18 For wickedness burns like a fire
that consumes thorns and briers
and kindles the forest thickets
so that they go up in a column of smoke.

19 The land is scorched
by the wrath of the LORD of Hosts,
and the people are like fuel for the fire.
No one has compassion on his brother.

20 They carve ⌊meat⌋ on the right,
but they are ⌊still⌋ hungry;
they have eaten on the left,
but they are ⌊still⌋ not satisfied.
Each one eats the flesh of his own arm.

21 Manasseh is with Ephraim,
and Ephraim with Manasseh;
together, both are against Judah.
In all this, His anger is not removed,
and His hand is still raised ⌊to strike⌋.

10 Woe to those enacting crooked statutes
and writing oppressive laws

2 to keep the poor from getting a fair trial
and to deprive the afflicted among my people
of justice,
so that widows can be their spoil
and they can plunder the fatherless.

3 What will you do on the day of punishment
when devastation comes from far away?
Who will you run to for help?
Where will you leave your wealth?

4 ⌊There will be nothing to do⌋
except crouch among the prisoners
or fall among the slain.
In all this, His anger is not removed,
and His hand is still raised ⌊to strike⌋.

---

a **9:3** Alt Hb tradition reads *have not increased joy*   b **9:16** Or *are confused*   c **9:17** DSS read *not spare*   d **9:17** Lit *its*

---

a sentence: "A Wonderful Counselor is Almighty God, the Eternal Father is a Prince of Peace." God has a plan and nothing takes Him by surprise. He is all-powerful and eternal. Under His reign the people will experience "shalom," peace, well-being, and wholeness.

9:7 throne of David ... forever. Unlike the human kings of Israel—even the good ones like Ahaz—Messiah Jesus will eternally rule with perfect wisdom, justice, and righteousness (11:3-5; 2 Sam. 7:12, 13, 16; Jer. 33:15,20-22).

10:5 rod of My anger. God will ultimately de-

stroy the weapons of the oppressor, Assyria (9:4). Babylon also was used by God as a club of punishment against rebellious nations (see Jer. 50:23; 51:20; Hab. 1:6).

10:10 idols. Despite God's clear word concerning idols, Israelites routinely worshiped them (2:8). Just as God had chastened Sa-

Assyria, the Instrument of Wrath

5 Woe to Assyria, the rod of My anger—
the staff in their hands is My wrath.
6 I will send him against a godless nation;
I will command him ⌊to go⌋
against a people destined for My rage,
to take spoils, to plunder,
and to trample them down like clay
in the streets.
7 But this is not what he intends;
this is not what he plans.
It is his intent to destroy
and to cut off many nations.
8 For he says:
Aren't all my commanders kings?
9 Isn't Calno like Carchemish?
Isn't Hamath like Arpad?
Isn't Samaria like Damascus?ᵃ
10 As my hand seized the idolatrous kingdoms,
whose idols exceeded those of Jerusalem
and Samaria,
11 and as I did to Samaria and its idols
will I not also do to Jerusalem and its idols?

Judgment on Assyria

12 But when the Lord finishes all His work against
Mount Zion and Jerusalem, ⌊He will say,⌋ "Iᵇ will punish
the king of Assyria for his arrogant acts and the proud
look in his eyes." 13 For he said:

I have done ⌊this⌋ by my own strength
and wisdom, for I am clever.
I abolished the borders of nations
and plundered their treasures;
like a mighty warrior, I subjugated
the inhabitants.ᶜ
14 My hand has reached out, as if into a nest,
to seize the wealth of the nations.
Like one gathering abandoned eggs,
I gathered the whole earth.
No wing fluttered;
no beak opened or chirped.

15 Does an ax exalt itself
above the one who chops with it?
Does a saw magnify itself
above the one who saws with it?
As if a staff could wave those who liftᵈ it!
As if a rod could lift what isn't wood!ᵉ
16 Therefore the Lord GOD of •Hosts
will inflict an emaciating disease

on the well-fed of Assyria,
and He will kindle a burning fire
under its glory.
17 Israel's Light will become a fire,
and its Holy One, a flame.
In one day it will burn up Assyria's thorns
and thistles.
18 He will completely destroy
the glory of its forests and orchards
as a sickness consumes a person.
19 The remaining trees of its forest
will be so few in number
that a child could count them.

The Remnant Will Return

20 On that day the remnant of Israel and the survivors of the house of Jacob will no longer depend on the
one who struck them, but they will faithfully depend on
the LORD, the Holy One of Israel.

21 The remnant will return, the remnant of Jacob,
to the Mighty God.
22 Israel, even if your people were as numerous
as the sand of the sea,
⌊only⌋ a remnant of them will return.
Destruction has been decreed;
justice overflows.
23 For throughout the land
the Lord GOD of Hosts
is carrying out a destruction that was decreed.

24 Therefore, the Lord GOD of Hosts says this: "My
people who dwell in Zion, do not fear Assyria, though
he strikes you with a rod and raises his staff over you as
the Egyptians did. 25 In just a little while My wrath will
be spent and My anger will turn to their destruction."
26 And the LORD of Hosts will brandish a whip against
him as ⌊He did when He⌋ struck Midian at the rock of
Oreb; and He will raise His staff over the sea as ⌊He did⌋
in Egypt.

God Will Judge Assyria

27 On that day
his burden will fall from your shoulders,
and his yoke from your neck.
The yoke will be broken because of ⌊his⌋ fatness.ᶠ
28 Assyria has come to Aiath
and has gone through Migron,
storing his equipment at Michmash.
29 They crossed over at the ford, saying,
"We will spend the night at Geba."

ᵃ10:9 Cities conquered by Assyria ᵇ10:12 LXX reads *Jerusalem, He* ᶜ10:13 Or *I brought down their kings* ᵈ10:15 Some Hb mss, Syr, Vg read *wave he who lifts* ᵉ10:15 A human being ᶠ10:27 Hb obscure

---

maria because of idolatry (through defeat by
Shalmaneser V and Sargon II in 722–21 B.C.),
God would be forced to do the same to Israel.

10:16 will inflict an emaciating disease.
This probably refers to a plague, as happened to Sennacherib when 185,000 Assyrian soldiers were put to death by an angel of

God in 701 B.C..(See also 37:36; 2 Sam.
24:15,16; 1 Chron. 21:22,27.)

10:25 just a little while. From a human point
of view the present difficulty would be long
and hard; but in the context of eternity, the
time would be very brief.

11:1 stump of Jesse. The figurative stump of

David's father Jesse is all that remained of
David's dynasty after Judah was exiled to
Babylon in 586 B.C. Yet just as a shoot will
come up from a stump and make a new tree,
so too would a branch from David's line rise:
Jesus the Messiah. (See also Zech. 6:12;
Acts 13:23.)

The people of Ramah are trembling;
those at Gibeah of Saul have fled.
30 Cry aloud, daughter of Gallim!
Listen, Laishah!
Anathoth is miserable.
31 Madmenah has fled.
The inhabitants of Gebim have sought refuge.
32 Today he will stand at Nob,
shaking his fist at the mountain
of Daughter Zion,
the hill of Jerusalem.
33 Look, the Lord GOD of Hosts
will chop off the branches with terrifying power,
and the tall ⌊trees⌋ will be cut down,
the high ⌊trees⌋ felled.
34 He is clearing the thickets of the forest
with an ax,
and Lebanon with its majesty will fall.

Reign of the Davidic King

11 Then a shoot will grow from the stump of Jesse,
and a branch from his roots will bear fruit.
2 The Spirit of the LORD will rest on Him—
a Spirit of wisdom and understanding,
a Spirit of counsel and strength,
a Spirit of knowledge and of the •fear
of the LORD.
3 His delight will be in the fear of the LORD.
He will not judge
by what He sees with His eyes,
He will not execute justice
by what He hears with His ears,
4 but He will judge the poor righteously
and execute justice for the oppressed
of the land.
He will strike the land
with discipline[a] from His mouth,
and He will kill the wicked
with a command[b] from His lips.
5 Righteousness and faithfulness
will be a belt around His waist.
6 The wolf will live with the lamb,
and the leopard will lie down with the goat.
The calf, the young lion, and the fatling
will be together,
and a child will lead them.
7 The cow and the bear will graze,
their young ones will lie down together,
and the lion will eat straw like an ox.
8 An infant will play beside the cobra's pit,

and a toddler will put his hand
into a snake's den.
9 No one will harm or destroy
on My entire holy mountain,
for the land will be as full
of the knowledge of the LORD
as the sea is filled with water.

Israel Regathered

10 On that day the root of Jesse
will stand as a banner for the peoples.
The nations will seek Him,
and His resting place will be glorious.

11 On that day the Lord will ⌊extend⌋ His hand a second time to recover—from Assyria, Egypt, Pathros, •Cush, Elam, •Shinar, Hamath, and the coasts and islands of the west—the remnant of His people who survive.

12 He will lift up a banner for the nations
and gather the dispersed of Israel;
He will collect the scattered of Judah
from the four corners of the earth.
13 Ephraim's envy will cease;
Judah's harassment will end.
Ephraim will no longer be envious of Judah,
and Judah will not harass Ephraim.
14 But they will swoop down
on the Philistine flank to the west.
Together they will plunder the people
of the east.
They will extend their power over Edom
and Moab,
and the Ammonites will be their subjects.
15 The LORD will divide[c] the Gulf of Suez.[d]
He will wave His hand over the Euphrates
with His mighty wind
and will split it into seven streams,
letting people walk through on foot.
16 There will be a highway for the remnant
of His people
who will survive from Assyria,
as there was for Israel
when they came up from the land of Egypt.

A Song of Praise

12 On that day you will say:
"I will praise You, LORD,
although You were angry with me.
Your anger has turned away,
and You have had compassion on me.
2 Indeed, God is my salvation.

---

a**11:4** Lit *the rod*   b**11:4** Lit *with the breath*   c**11:15** Or *destroy,* or *dry up* (text emended)   d**11:15** Lit *the Sea of Egypt*

11:2 The Spirit of the LORD will rest on Him. Like David, the Messiah would be empowered by the Holy Spirit (see Luke 3:22; John 1:32-34) and characterized by wisdom, understanding, counsel, power, knowledge, and fear of the Lord, making Him the Wonderful Counselor of 9:6. With Judah's history of

bad kings, this promise of a Spirit-empowered king was significant. Isaiah refers to the Holy Spirit more than any other Old Testament prophet (16 times).

12:3 springs of salvation. Water is salvation in the desert and in the dry climate of the Middle East. God's salvation is like a spring in the

desert. Drawing water from this spring means living according to God's instructions and enjoying the blessings God provides.

13:1 oracle against Babylon. Sometimes translated "burden," as in a weighty message to deliver. Isaiah's oracle concerned Babylon, which had been a pagan city ever since Gen-

I will trust ⌊Him⌋ and not be afraid.
Because •Yah, the LORD,
is my strength and my song,
He has become my salvation."

3 You will joyfully draw water
from the springs of salvation,

4 and on that day you will say:
"Give thanks to the LORD; proclaim His name!
Celebrate His deeds among the peoples.
Declare that His name is exalted.

5 Sing to the LORD, for He has done
glorious things.
Let this be known throughout the earth.

6 Cry out and sing, citizen of Zion,
for the Holy One of Israel is among you
in ⌊His⌋ greatness."

An Oracle against Babylon

13 An •oracle against Babylon that Isaiah son of Amoz saw:

2 Lift up a banner on a barren mountain.
Call out to them.
Wave your hand, and they will go
through the gates of the nobles.

3 I have commanded My chosen ones;
I have also called My warriors,
who exult in My triumph,
to execute My wrath.

4 Listen, a tumult on the mountains,
like that of a mighty people!
Listen, an uproar among the kingdoms,
like nations being gathered together!
The LORD of •Hosts is mobilizing an army
for war.

5 They are coming from a far land,
from the distant horizon—
the LORD and the weapons of His wrath—
to destroy the whole country.[a]

6 Wail! For the day of the LORD is near.
It will come like destruction from the •Almighty.

7 Therefore everyone's hands will become weak,
and every man's heart will melt.

8 They will be horrified;
pain and agony will seize ⌊them⌋;
they will be in anguish like a woman in labor.
They will look at each other,
their faces flushed with fear.

9 Look, the day of the LORD is coming—
cruel, with rage and burning anger—

to make the earth a desolation
and to destroy the sinners on it.

10 Indeed, the stars of the sky
and its constellations[b]
will not give their light.
The sun will be dark when it rises,
and the moon will not shine.

11 I will bring disaster on the world,
and their ⌊own⌋ iniquity, on the wicked.
I will put an end to the pride of the arrogant
and humiliate the insolence of tyrants.

12 I will make man scarcer than gold,
and mankind more rare than the gold of Ophir.

13 Therefore I will make the heavens tremble,
and the earth will shake from its foundations
at the wrath of the LORD of Hosts,
on the day of His burning anger.

14 Like wandering gazelles
and like sheep without a shepherd,
each one will turn to his own people,
each one will flee to his own land.

15 Whoever is found will be stabbed,
and whoever is caught will die by the sword.

16 Their children will be smashed ⌊to death⌋
before their eyes;
their houses will be looted,
and their wives raped.

17 Look! I am stirring up the Medes against them,
who cannot be bought off with[c] silver
and who have no desire for gold.

18 ⌊Their⌋ bows will cut young men to pieces.
They will have no compassion on little ones;
they will not look with pity on children.

19 And Babylon, the jewel of the kingdoms,
the glory of the pride of the Chaldeans,
will be like Sodom and Gomorrah
when God overthrew them.

20 It will never be inhabited
or lived in from generation to generation;
a nomad will not pitch his tent there,
and shepherds will not let ⌊their flocks⌋ rest there.

21 But wild animals will lie down there,
and owls will fill the houses.
Ostriches will dwell there,
and wild goats will leap about.

22 Hyenas will howl in the fortresses,
and jackals, in the luxurious palaces.
Babylon's time is almost up;
her days are almost over.

---

a **13:5** Or *earth* b **13:10** Or *Orions* c **13:17** Lit *who have no regard for*

---

esis 11:1-9. This is significant because Isaiah made this prophecy before the fall of Babylon occurred. The Book of Isaiah takes a major turn at 13:1 and focuses on God's judgments against the nations.

13:3 I have commanded My chosen ones. God calls this army from many places. The

army's purpose is to serve as an instrument of His judgment upon sinful nations (see Joel 3:11).

13:6 the day of the LORD is near. This refers to the time of God's judgment on the wicked and deliverance of His people. The political upheaval resulting in the fall of Babylon to the

Assyrians in 689 B.C. parallels the turmoil coming upon the world just before God establishes a kingdom of peace.

14:12 Shining morning star. Many people see this as a description of Satan, who fell from heaven (see Luke 10:18). Others see this as the Babylonian king (v. 4) or perhaps

Israel's Return

14 For the LORD will have compassion on Jacob and will choose Israel again. He will settle them on their own land. The foreigner will join them and be united with the house of Jacob. ² The nations will escort Israel and bring it to its homeland. Then the house of Israel will possess them as male and female slaves in the LORD's land. They will make captives of their captors and will rule over their oppressors.

Downfall of the King of Babylon

³ When the LORD gives you rest from your pain, torment, and the hard labor you were forced to do, ⁴ you will sing this song ⌊of contempt⌋ about the king of Babylon and say:

How the oppressor has quieted down,
and how the raging^a has become quiet!

⁵ The LORD has broken the staff of the wicked,
the scepter of the rulers.

⁶ It struck the peoples in anger
with unceasing blows.
It subdued the nations in rage
with relentless persecution.

⁷ All the earth is calm and at rest;
people shout with a ringing cry.

⁸ Even the cypresses and the cedars of Lebanon
rejoice over you:
"Since you have been laid low,
no woodcutter has come against us."

⁹ •Sheol below is eager to greet your coming.
He stirs up the spirits of the departed for you—
all the rulers^b of the earth.
He makes all the kings of the nations
rise from their thrones.

¹⁰ They all respond to you, saying:
"You too have become as weak as we are;
you have become like us!

¹¹ Your splendor has been brought down to Sheol,
⌊along with⌋ the music of your harps.
Maggots are spread out under you,
and worms cover you."

¹² Shining morning star,^c
how you have fallen from the heavens!
You destroyer of nations,
you have been cut down to the ground.

¹³ You said to yourself:
"I will ascend to the heavens;
I will set up my throne
above the stars of God.

I will sit on the mount of the ⌊gods'⌋ assembly,
in the remotest parts of the North.^d

¹⁴ I will ascend above the highest clouds;
I will make myself like the •Most High."

¹⁵ But you will be brought down to Sheol
into the deepest regions of the •Pit.

¹⁶ Those who see you will stare at you;
they will look closely at you:
"Is this the man who caused the earth to tremble,
who shook the kingdoms,

¹⁷ who turned the world into a wilderness,
who trampled its cities
and would not release the prisoners
to return home?"

¹⁸ All the kings of the nations
lie in splendor, each in his own tomb.

¹⁹ But you are thrown out without a grave,
like a worthless branch,
covered by those slain with the sword
and dumped into a rocky pit
like a trampled corpse.

²⁰ You will not join them in burial,
because you destroyed your land
and slaughtered your own people.
The offspring of evildoers
will never be remembered.

²¹ Prepare a place of slaughter for his sons,
because of the iniquity of their fathers.
They never rise up to possess a land
or fill the surface of the earth with cities.

²² "I will rise up against them"—the declaration of the LORD of •Hosts—"and I will cut off from Babylon her reputation, remnant, offspring, and posterity"—the LORD's declaration. ²³ "I will make her a swampland and a region for wild animals,^e and I will sweep her away with a broom of destruction."

⌊This is⌋ the declaration
of the LORD of Hosts.

Assyria to Be Destroyed

²⁴ The LORD of Hosts has sworn:

As I have planned, so it will be;
as I have purposed it, so it will happen.

²⁵ I will break Assyria in My land;
I will tread him down on My mountain.
Then his yoke will be taken from them,
and his burden will be removed
from their shoulders.

²⁶ This is the plan prepared

the Babylonian king under Satan's influence. The language here does not need to be taken literally, but could refer to the Babylonian king's own mythological beliefs about himself and the gods.

14:17 would not release the prisoners. King Cyrus would send the exiles home, but

the king of Babylon kept them in captivity.

15:2 Every head is shaved. Shaving one's head and cutting off one's beard were signs of humiliation. Wearing sackcloth (coarse, dark cloth) symbolized mourning. The Moabites were lamenting the destruction of their cities.

15:9 waters of Dibon ... blood. So much death and destruction had occurred there that the water supply ran with blood.

16:1 Send lambs. The Moabites fled to strongholds 50 miles away, but they should have fled to Jerusalem, sending lambs on ahead as gifts. Isaiah had already prophe-

for the whole earth,
and this is the hand stretched out
against all the nations.
27 The LORD of Hosts Himself has planned it;
therefore, who can stand in its way?
It is His hand that is outstretched,
so who can turn it back?

An Oracle against Philistia

28 In the year that King Ahaz died, this •oracle came:

29 Don't rejoice, all of you ⌊in⌋ Philistia,
because the rod of the one who struck you
is broken.
For a viper will come out of the root[a] of a snake,
and from its egg comes a flying serpent.
30 Then the firstborn of the poor will be well fed,
and the impoverished will lie down in safety,
but I will kill your root with hunger,
and your remnant will be slain.[b]
31 Wail, you gates! Cry out, city!
Tremble with fear, all Philistia!
For a cloud of dust is coming from the north,
and there is no one missing from
⌊the invader's⌋ ranks.
32 What answer will be given to the messengers
from that nation?
The LORD has founded Zion,
and His afflicted people find refuge in her.

An Oracle against Moab

15 An •oracle against Moab:

Ar in Moab is devastated,
destroyed in a night.
Kir in Moab is devastated,
destroyed in a night.
2 Dibon went up to its temple
to weep at its •high places.
Moab wails on Nebo and at[c] Medeba.
Every head is shaved;
every beard is cut off.
3 In its streets they wear •sackcloth;
on its rooftops and in its public squares
everyone wails,
falling down and weeping.
4 Heshbon and Elealeh cry out;
their voices are heard as far away as Jahaz.
Therefore the soldiers of Moab cry out,
and they tremble.[d]
5 My heart cries out over Moab,

whose fugitives ⌊flee⌋ as far as Zoar,
to Eglath-shelishiyah;
they go up the slope of Luhith weeping;
they raise a cry of destruction
on the road to Horonaim.
6 The waters of Nimrim are desolate;
the grass is withered, the foliage is gone,
and the vegetation has vanished.
7 So they carry their wealth and belongings
over the •Wadi of the Willows.
8 For their cry echoes
throughout the territory of Moab.
Their wailing reaches Eglaim;
their wailing reaches Beer-elim.
9 The waters of Dibon[e] are full of blood,
but I will bring on Dibon[e] even more
⌊than this⌋—
a lion for those who escape from Moab,
and for the survivors in the land.

16 Send lambs to the ruler of the land,
from Sela in the desert
to the mountain of Daughter Zion.
2 Like a bird fleeing,
forced from the nest,
the daughters of Moab
will be at the fords of the Arnon.
3 Give us counsel and make a decision.
⌊Shelter us⌋ at noonday
with shade that is as dark as night.
Hide the refugee;
do not betray the one who flees.
4 Let my refugees stay with you;
be a refuge for Moab[f] from the aggressor.

When the oppressor has gone,
destruction has ended,
and marauders have vanished from the land.
5 Then in the tent of David
a throne will be established by faithful love.
A judge who seeks what is right
and is quick to execute justice
will sit on the throne forever.

6 We have heard of Moab's pride—
how very proud he is—
his haughtiness, his pride, his arrogance,
and his empty boasting.
7 Therefore let Moab wail;
let every one of them wail for Moab.

---

[a]**14:29** Or stock   [b]**14:30** DSS, Syr, Tg; MT reads and he will kill   [c]**15:2** Or wails over Nebo and over   [d]**15:4** Lit out, he trembles within himself
[e]**15:9** DSS, some LXX mss, Vg; MT reads Dimon   [f]**16:4** Or you; Moab—be a refuge for him

---

sied that Jerusalem would be saved from attacks by Assyria.
16:6 heard of Moab's pride. Moab was a small, boastful country whose people thought they could defeat the Assyrians without God's help (see Jer. 48:29).
16:9 weep for the vines. Due to the people's

pride, Moab's harvests would be lost. The combination of the invading army and drought would wipe out its crops and orchards. Isaiah had compassion for them as they experienced judgment.
17:3 Ephraim. This refers to northern Israel, which was allied with Damascus, Syria's cap-

ital. Isaiah predicted judgment against both nations. Assyria defeated Damascus in 732 B.C. and Israel in 722.
17:5 in the Valley of Rephaim. A fertile area west of Jerusalem where David had defeated the Philistines twice (see 2 Sam. 5:18-20,22-25). Rephaim is the Hebrew word for ghosts,

Mourn, you who are completely devastated,
for the raisin cakes of Kir-hareseth.
8 For Heshbon's terraced vineyards
and the grapevines of Sibmah have withered.
The rulers of the nations
have trampled its choice vines
that reached as far as Jazer
and spread to the desert.
Their shoots spread out
and reached the Dead Sea.
9 So I join with Jazer
to weep for the vines of Sibmah;
I drench Heshbon and Elealeh
with my tears.
Triumphant shouts have fallen silent[a]
over your summer ⌊fruit⌋ and your harvest.
10 Joy and rejoicing have been removed
from the orchard;
no one is singing or shouting for joy
in the vineyards.
No one tramples grapes[b] in the winepresses.
I have put an end to the shouting.
11 Therefore I moan like ⌊the sound of⌋ a lyre
for Moab,
⌊as does⌋ my innermost being for Kir-heres.
12 When Moab appears on the •high place,
when he tires[c] himself out
and comes to his sanctuary to pray,
it will do him no good.

13 This is the message that the LORD previously announced about Moab. 14 And now the LORD says, "In three years, as a hired worker counts years, Moab's splendor will become an object of contempt, in spite of a very large population. And those who are left will be few and weak."

An Oracle against Damascus

17

An •oracle against Damascus:

Look, Damascus is no longer a city.
It has become a ruined heap.
2 The cities of Aroer are forsaken;
they will be ⌊places⌋ for flocks.
They will lie down without fear.
3 The fortress disappears from Ephraim,
and a kingdom from Damascus.
The remnant of Aram will be
like the splendor of the Israelites.
⌊This is⌋ the declaration
of the LORD of •Hosts.

Judgment against Israel

4 On that day
the splendor of Jacob will fade,
and his healthy body[d] will become emaciated.
5 It will be as if a reaper had gathered
standing grain—
his arm harvesting the heads of grain—
and as if one had gleaned heads of grain
in the valley of Rephaim.
6 Only gleanings will be left in Israel,
as if an olive tree had been beaten—
two or three berries at the very top of the tree,
four or five on its fruitful branches.
⌊This is⌋ the declaration of the LORD,
the God of Israel.

7 On that day people will look to their Maker and will turn their eyes to the Holy One of Israel. 8 They will not look to the altars they made with their hands or to the •Asherahs and incense altars they made with their fingers.

9 On that day their strong cities will be
like the abandoned woods and mountaintops[e]
that were abandoned because of the Israelites;
there will be desolation.
10 For you have forgotten the God
of your salvation,
and you have failed to remember
the rock of your strength;
therefore you will plant beautiful plants
and set out cuttings from exotic vines.
11 On the day that you plant,
you will help them to grow,
and in the morning
you will help your seed to sprout,
⌊but⌋ the harvest will vanish
on the day of disease and incurable pain.

Judgment against the Nations

12 Ah! The roar of many peoples—
they roar like the roaring of the seas.
The raging of the nations—
they rage like the raging of mighty waters.
13 The nations rage like the raging of many waters.
He rebukes them, and they flee far away,
driven before the wind like chaff on the hills
and like dead thistles before a gale.
14 In the evening—sudden terror!
Before morning—it is gone!
This is the fate of those who plunder us
and the lot of those who ravage us.

---

[a]16:9 Or Battle cries have fallen [b]16:10 Lit wine [c]16:12 DSS read place, he will tire [d]17:4 Lit and the fat of his flesh [e]17:9 LXX reads like the Amorites and the Hivites; some Hb mss read like the Horesh and the Amir

---

so this is the Valley of Death.

17:8 Asherahs. Wooden symbols of the Canaanite fertility goddess in the Baal worship system. Many Asherah-worshipers lived in the Northern Kingdom of Israel. But under Assyrian attack, Israel would realize that wooden idols could not help them.

17:13 chaff on the hills. Chaff is the lightweight and useless part of grain that blows away during threshing, leaving the valuable wheat behind. The enemies of Israel would become insignificant and easily defeated.

19:3 seek idols. Some Israelites hoped that Egypt would help against Assyria, but God

announced His judgment on Egypt. Its idols and mediums would be unable to help this once cruel master of the Israelites. Now Egypt would have its own cruel master in the Assyrian Empire.

19:19 altar to the LORD. This promise must have been remarkable to Israelites who con-

The LORD's Message to Cush

18 Ah! The land of buzzing insect wings[a]
beyond the rivers of •Cush
2   sends envoys by sea,
     in reed vessels on the waters.

Go, swift messengers,
to a nation tall and smooth-skinned,
to a people feared near and far,
a powerful nation with a strange language,[b]
whose land is divided by rivers.
3   All you inhabitants of the world
     and you who live on the earth,
     when a banner is raised on the mountains, look!
     When a trumpet sounds, listen!

4   For, the LORD said to me:

I will quietly look out from My place,
     like shimmering heat in sunshine,
     like a rain cloud in harvest heat.
5   For before the harvest, when the blossoming
          is over
     and the blossom becomes a ripening grape,
He will cut off the shoots with a pruning knife,
and tear away and remove the branches.
6   They will all be left for the birds of prey
          on the hills
     and for the wild animals of the land.
The birds will spend the summer on them,
and all the animals, the winter on them.

7 At that time a gift will be brought to the LORD of
•Hosts from[c] a people tall and smooth-skinned, a people
feared near and far, a powerful nation with a strange
language, whose land is divided by rivers—to Mount
Zion, the place of the name of the LORD of Hosts.

An Oracle against Egypt

19 An •oracle against Egypt:

Look, the LORD rides on a swift cloud
and is coming to Egypt.
Egypt's idols will tremble before Him,
and Egypt's heart will melt within it.
2   I will provoke Egypt against Egypt;
     each will fight against his brother
     and each against his friend,
     city against city, kingdom against kingdom.
3   Egypt's spirit will be disturbed within it,
     and I will frustrate its plans.
     Then they will seek idols, ghosts,

spirits of the dead, and spiritists.
4   I will deliver Egypt into the hands
          of harsh masters,
     and a strong king will rule it.
          ⌊This is⌋ the declaration
               of the Lord GOD of •Hosts.

5   The waters of the sea will dry up,
     and the river will be parched and dry.
6   The channels will stink;
     they will dwindle, and Egypt's canals
          will be parched.
     Reed and rush will die.[d]
7   The reeds by the Nile, by the mouth
          of the river,
     and all the cultivated areas of the Nile
     will wither, blow away, and vanish.
8   Then the fishermen will mourn.
     All those who cast hooks into the Nile will lament,
     and those who spread nets on the water
          will shrivel up.
9   Those who work with flax will be dismayed;
     the combers and weavers will turn pale.[e]
10 ⌊Egypt's⌋ weavers[f] will be dejected;
     all her wage earners will be demoralized.

11 The princes of Zoan are complete fools;
     Pharaoh's wisest advisers give stupid advice!
     How can you say to Pharaoh,
     "I am one[g] of the wise,
     a student of eastern[h] kings."
12 Where then are your wise men?
     Let them tell you and reveal
     what the LORD of Hosts has planned against Egypt.
13 The princes of Zoan have been fools;
     the princes of Memphis are deceived.
     Her tribal chieftains have led Egypt astray.
14 The LORD has mixed within her a spirit
          of confusion.
     ⌊The leaders⌋ have made Egypt stagger
          in all she does,
     as a drunkard staggers in his vomit.
15 No head or tail, palm or reed,
     will be able to do anything for Egypt.

Egypt Will Know the LORD

16 On that day Egypt will be like women. She will
tremble with fear because of the threatening hand of
the LORD of Hosts when He raises it against her. 17 The
land of Judah will terrify Egypt; whenever Judah is men-

---

a **18:1** Or of sailing ships   b **18:2** Hb obscure   c **18:7** DSS, LXX, Vg; MT omits from   d **19:6** Or wilt, or become black   e **19:9** DSS, Tg; MT reads
weavers of white cloth   f **19:10** Or foundations   g **19:11** Lit a son   h **19:11** Lit a son of ancient

---

sidered Egypt a perpetual enemy.
19:20 oppressors ... savior. When the
Egyptians turn to God and ask for help, God
will give it. This will take place after the Messiah has returned and established His millennial kingdom (43:11).
19:23 highway from Egypt to Assyria.

Egypt and Assyria had been enemies for centuries. People from both nations and from Israel will worship together peacefully in the
millennial kingdom. This will fulfill part of
God's promise to Abraham that all peoples
would be blessed through him (Gen. 12:3).
19:25 My people ... My handiwork ... My in-

heritance. Here these titles for Israel are applied to nations typically considered enemies.
God will restore other nations besides Israel
in the Messianic kingdom.

20:1 Ashdod. The capture of this Philistine
city by Assyrian King Sargon II demonstrated to Israel that foreign alliances could

tioned, Egypt will tremble because of what the LORD of Hosts has planned against it.

18 On that day five cities in the land of Egypt will speak the language of Canaan and swear loyalty to the LORD of Hosts. One of the cities will be called the City of the Sun.a b

19 On that day there will be an altar to the LORD in the center of the land of Egypt and a pillar to the LORD near her border. 20 It will be a sign and witness to the LORD of Hosts in the land of Egypt. When they cry out to the LORD because of their oppressors, He will send them a savior and leader, and he will rescue them. 21 The LORD will make Himself known to Egypt, and Egypt will know the LORD on that day. They will offer sacrifices and offerings; they will make vows to the LORD and fulfill them. 22 The LORD will strike Egypt, striking and healing. Then they will return to the LORD and He will hear their prayers and heal them.

23 On that day there will be a highway from Egypt to Assyria. Assyria will go to Egypt, Egypt to Assyria, and Egypt will worship with Assyria.

24 On that day Israel will form a triple ⌊alliance⌋ with Egypt and Assyria—a blessing within the land. 25 The LORD of Hosts will bless them, saying, "Blessed be Egypt My people, Assyria My handiwork, and Israel My inheritance."

No Help from Cush or Egypt

20 In the year that the commander-in-chief, sent by Sargon king of Assyria, came to Ashdod and attacked and captured it— 2 during that time the LORD had spoken through Isaiah son of Amoz, saying, "Go, take off your •sacklothc and remove the sandals from your feet," and he did so, going naked and barefoot— 3 the LORD said, "As My servant Isaiah has gone naked and barefoot three years as a sign and omen against Egypt and •Cush, 4 so the king of Assyria will lead the captives of Egypt and the exiles of Cush, young and old alike, naked and barefoot, with bared buttocks, to Egypt's shame. 5 Those who made Cush their hope and Egypt their boast will be dismayed and ashamed. 6 And the inhabitants of this coastland will say on that day: Look, this is what has happened to those we relied on and fled to for help to rescue ⌊us⌋ from the king of Assyria! Now, how will we escape?"

A Judgment on Babylon

21 An •oracle against the desert by the sea:

Like storms that pass over the •Negev,
it comes from the desert, from the land of terror.

2 A troubling vision is declared to me:
"The treacherous one acts treacherously,
and the destroyer destroys.
Advance, Elam! Lay siege, you Medes!
I will put an end to all her groaning."

3 Therefore I amd filled with anguish.
Pain grips me, like the pain of a woman in labor.
I am too perplexed to hear,
too dismayed to see.

4 My heart staggers;
horror terrifies me.
He has turned my last glimmer of hopee
into sheer terror.

5 Prepare a table, and spread out a carpet!
Eat and drink!
Rise up, you princes, and oil the shields!

6 For the Lord has said to me,
"Go, post a lookout;
let him report what he sees.

7 When he sees riders—
pairs of horsemen,
riders on donkeys,
riders on camels—
pay close attention."

8 Then the lookoutf reported,
"Lord, I stand on the watchtower all day,
and I stay at my post all night.

9 Look, riders come—
horsemen in pairs."
And he answered, saying,
"Babylon has fallen, has fallen.
All the idols of her gods
have been shattered on the ground."

10 My downtrodden and threshed people,
I have declared to you
what I have heard from the LORD of •Hosts,
the God of Israel.

An Oracle against Dumah

11 An oracle against Dumah:g

One calls to me from Seir,
"Watchman, what is ⌊left⌋ of the night?
Watchman, what is ⌊left⌋ of the night?"

12 The watchman said,
"Morning has come, and also night.
If you want to ask, ask!
Come back again."

a 19:18 Some Hb mss, DSS, Sym, Tg, Vg, Arabic; other Hb mss read of Destruction; LXX reads of Righteousness   b 19:18 The ancient Egyptian city Heliopolis   c 20:2 Lit off the sackcloth from your loins   d 21:3 Lit Therefore my loins are   e 21:4 Lit my twilight   f 21:8 DSS, Syr; MT reads Then a lion   g 21:11 Some Hb mss, LXX read Edom

20:2 naked and barefoot. To represent exile and captivity, Isaiah probably did not wear clothing. This showed how Egypt and Cush would be treated by a victorious Assyria, a warning that Israel should not look to foreign allies for protection.

21:5 Eat and drink! The Babylonians were living in confident self-assurance, but Isaiah warned them of coming battle (Dan. 5:4-5). Rise up! He urged them to stop feasting and prepare for war.

21:9 Babylon has fallen. Israel hoped that Babylon would defeat the Assyrians, so this news was devastating (see Jer. 51:8).

22:9 city of David. The defense of the city depended upon available water. Hezekiah had repaired broken sections of the wall and also preserved the water supply (2 Chron. 32:1-5). lower pool. A reservoir in Jerusalem's southwestern valley. Hezekiah con-

An Oracle against Arabia

13 An oracle against Arabia:

You will camp for the night
in the scrublands of the desert,[a]
you caravans of Dedanites.
14 Bring water for the thirsty.
The inhabitants of the land of Tema
meet[b] the refugees with food.
15 For they have fled from swords,
from the drawn sword,
and from the bent bow,
from the stress of battle.

16 For the Lord said this to me: "Within one year, as a hired worker counts years, all the glory of Kedar will be gone. 17 The remaining Kedarite archers will be few in number." For the LORD, the God of Israel, has spoken.

An Oracle against Jerusalem

22 An •oracle against the Valley of Vision:

What's the matter with you?
Why have all of you gone up to the rooftops?
2 The noisy city, the jubilant town,
is filled with revelry.
Your dead did not die by the sword;
they were not killed in battle.
3 All your rulers have fled together,
captured without a bow.
All your fugitives were captured together;
they had fled far away.
4 Therefore I said,
"Look away from me! Let me weep bitterly!
Do not try to comfort me
about the destruction of my dear[c] people."
5 For the Lord GOD of •Hosts
had a day of tumult, trampling,
and bewilderment
in the Valley of Vision—
people shouting[d] and crying to the mountains;
6 Elam took up a quiver
with chariots and horsemen,[e]
and Kir uncovered the shield.
7 Your best valleys were full of chariots,
and horsemen were positioned at the gates.
8 He removed the defenses of Judah.

On that day you looked to the weapons in the House of the Forest. 9 You saw that there were many breaches in ⌊the walls of⌋ the city of David. You collected water from the lower pool. 10 You counted the houses of Jerusalem so that you could tear them down to fortify the wall. 11 You made a reservoir between the walls for the waters of the ancient pool, but you did not look to the One who made it, or consider the One who created it long ago.

12 On that day the Lord GOD of Hosts
called for weeping, for wailing,
for shaven heads,
and for the wearing of •sackcloth.
13 But look: joy and gladness,
butchering of cattle, slaughtering of sheep,
eating of meat, and drinking of wine—
"Let us eat and drink, for tomorrow we die!"
14 The LORD of Hosts has revealed ⌊this⌋
in my hearing:
"This sin of yours will never[f] be wiped out."
The Lord GOD of Hosts has spoken.

An Oracle against Shebna

15 The Lord GOD of Hosts said: "Go to Shebna, that steward who is in charge of the palace, ⌊and say to him:⌋ 16 What are you doing here? Who authorized you to carve out a tomb for yourself here, carving your tomb on the height and cutting a crypt for yourself out of rock? 17 Look, young man! The LORD is about to shake you violently. He will take hold of you, 18 wind you up into a ball, and sling you into a wide land.[g] There you will die, and there your glorious chariots will be—a disgrace to the house of your lord. 19 I will remove you from your office; you will be ousted from your position.

20 "On that day I will call for my servant, Eliakim son of Hilkiah. 21 I will clothe him with your robe and tie your sash around him. I will put your authority into his hand, and he will be like a father to the inhabitants of Jerusalem and to the House of Judah. 22 I will place the key of the House of David on his shoulder; what he opens, no one can close; what he closes, no one can open. 23 I will drive him, like a peg, into a firm place. He will be a throne of honor for his father's house. 24 They will hang on him the whole burden of his father's house: the descendants and the offshoots—all the small vessels, from bowls to every kind of jar. 25 On that day"—the declaration of the LORD of Hosts—"the peg that was driven into a firm place will give way, be cut off, and fall, and the load on it will be destroyed." Indeed, the LORD has spoken.

---

a 21:13 LXX, Syr, Tg, Vg read scrublands at evening   b 21:14 LXX, Syr, Tg, Vg read meet as a command   c 22:4 Lit of the daughter of my   d 22:5 Or Vision—a tearing down of a wall, or Vision—Kir raged; Hb obscure   e 22:6 Lit chariots of man   f 22:14 Lit will not until you die   g 22:17–18 Hb obscure

---

nected it, by a 1,777-foot tunnel carved out of rock under the city, to the Old Pool, the water source in the eastern valley.
22:11 the One who made it. Hezekiah's tunnel was insufficient to protect the people. They refused to turn to God, who alone could save them.

22:25 peg ... will give way. Eliakim was the palace administrator and a godly man. He would be a respected leader and a firm and stable foundation for the nation. But even he would come to an end, and the kingdom of Judah would be taken into captivity.

23:1 Tyre. This seaport city was captured several times over a period of 400 years before being destroyed by Alexander the Great in 332 B.C. King Hiram of Tyre supplied the cedars and craftsmen for Solomon's temple.

23:15 forgotten for 70 years. This represented a king's lifetime. The period referred to was probably from about 700 to 630 B.C.

An Oracle against Tyre

23 An •oracle against Tyre:

Wail, ships of Tarshish,
for your haven has been destroyed.
Word has reached them from the land
of Cyprus.ᵃ

2 Mourn, inhabitants of the coastland,
you merchants of Sidon;
your agentsᵇ have crossed the sea
3 on many waters.
Tyre's revenue was the grain from Shihor—
the harvest of the Nile.
She was the merchant among the nations.
4 Be ashamed Sidon, the stronghold of the sea,
for the sea has spoken:
"I have not been in labor or given birth.
I have not raised young men
⌊or⌋ brought up young women."
5 When the news reaches Egypt,
they will be in anguish over the news
about Tyre.
6 Cross over to Tarshish;
wail, inhabitants of the coastland!
7 Is this your jubilant ⌊city⌋,
whose origin was in ancient times,
whose feet have taken her
to settle far away?
8 Who planned this against Tyre,
the bestower of crowns,
whose traders are princes,
whose merchants are the honored ones
of the earth?
9 The LORD of •Hosts planned it,
to desecrate all ⌊its⌋ glorious beauty,
to disgrace all the honored ones of the earth.
10 Overflowᶜ your land like the Nile,
daughter of Tarshish;
there is no longer anything to restrain ⌊you⌋.ᵈ
11 He stretched out His hand over the sea;
He made kingdoms tremble.
The LORD has commanded
that the Canaanite fortresses be destroyed.
12 He said,
"You will not rejoice any more,
ravished young woman, daughter of Sidon.
Get up and cross over to Cyprus—
even there you will have no rest!"
13 Look at the land of Chaldeans—
a people who no longer exist.

Assyria destined it for wild beasts.
They set up their siege towers
and stripped its palaces.
They made it a ruin.
14 Wail, ships of Tarshish,
because your fortress is destroyed!

15 On that day Tyre will be forgotten for 70 years—the life span of one king. At the end of 70 years, what the song ⌊says⌋ about the prostitute will happen to Tyre:

16 Pick up ⌊your⌋ harp,
stroll through the city,
prostitute forgotten ⌊by men⌋.
Play skillfully,
sing many a song,
and you will be thought of again.

17 And at the end of the 70 years, the LORD will restore Tyre and she will go back into business, prostituting herself with all the kingdoms of the world on the face of the earth. 18 But her profits and wages will be dedicated to the LORD. They will not be stored or saved, for her profit will go to those who live in the LORD's presence, to provide them with ample food and sacred clothing.

The Earth Judged

24 Look, the LORD is stripping the earth bare
and making it desolate.
He will twist its surface and scatter
its inhabitants:
2 people and priest alike,
servant and master,
female servant and mistress,
buyer and seller,
lender and borrower,
creditor and debtor.
3 The earth will be stripped completely bare
and will be totally plundered,
for the LORD has spoken this message.

4 The earth mourns and withers;
the world wastes away and withers;
the exalted people of the earth waste away.
5 The earth is polluted by its inhabitants,
for they have transgressed teachings,
overstepped decrees,
and broken the everlasting covenant.
6 Therefore a curse has consumed the earth,
and its inhabitants have become guilty;
the earth's inhabitants have been burned,

ᵃ23:1 Hb *Kittim*   ᵇ23:2 DSS; MT reads *Sidon, whom the seafarers have filled*   ᶜ23:10 DSS, LXX read *Work*   ᵈ23:10 Or *longer any harbor*

---

when Phoenicia's trade was reduced by the Assyrians. After 630 B.C. Assyria declined, and Tyre rebuilt its successful trading operations.

23:17 prostituting. Tyre's reestablished (and profitable) trade activities, often conducted with unethical partners, is compared to a

prostitute who stops her trade in illicit sex but returns to it more successful than ever.

24:6 a curse has consumed the earth. God's judgment in consequence of sin. **only a few survive.** A remnant will be preserved (10:20).

25:4 stronghold for the poor ... humble

person. God's protection was described as a shelter and a shade (Ps. 91:1-3). He protects the needy from the storm and stills the storms created by the ruthless.

25:6 a feast ... a feast of aged wine. There will be a banquet on Mt. Zion for those who will be saved (Dan. 7:14). Perhaps this is sim-

and only a few survive.

7 The new wine mourns;
the vine withers.
All the carousers now groan.

8 The joyful tambourines have ceased.
The noise of the jubilant has stopped.
The joyful lyre has ceased.

9 They no longer sing and drink wine;
beer is bitter to those who drink it.

10 The city of chaos is shattered;
every house is closed to entry.

11 In the streets they cry[a] for wine.
All joy grows dark;
earth's rejoicing goes into exile.

12 Only desolation remains in the city;
its gate has collapsed in ruins.

13 For this is how it will be on earth
among the nations:
like a harvested olive tree,
like a gleaning after a grape harvest.

14 They raise their voices, they sing out;
they proclaim in the west
the majesty of the LORD.

15 Therefore in the east honor the LORD!
In the islands of the west [honor]
the name of the LORD, the God of Israel.

16 From the ends of the earth we hear songs:
The Splendor of the Righteous One.

But I said, "I waste away! I waste away![b]
Woe is me."
The treacherous act treacherously;
the treacherous deal very treacherously.

17 Terror, pit, and snare [await] you
who dwell on the earth.

18 Whoever flees at the sound of terror
will fall into a pit,
and whoever escapes from the pit
will be caught in a snare.
For the windows are opened from above,
and the foundations of the earth are shaken.

19 The earth is completely devastated;
the earth is split open;
the earth is violently shaken.

20 The earth staggers like a drunkard
and sways like a hut.
Earth's rebellion weighs it down,
and it falls, never to rise again.

21 On that day the LORD will punish
the host of heaven above
and kings of the earth below.

22 They will be gathered together
like prisoners in a pit.
They will be confined to a dungeon;
after many days they will be punished.

23 The moon will be put to shame
and the sun disgraced,
because the LORD of •Hosts will reign as king
on Mount Zion in Jerusalem,
and He will [display His] glory
in the presence of His elders.

Salvation and Judgment on That Day

25 LORD, You are my God;
I will exalt You. I will praise Your name,
for You have accomplished wonders,
plans [formed] long ago,
with perfect faithfulness.

2 For You have turned the city into a pile
of rubble,
a fortified city, into a ruin;
the fortress of barbarians is no longer a city;
it will never be rebuilt.

3 Therefore, a strong people will honor You.
A city of violent people[c] will •fear You.

4 For You have been a stronghold for the poor,
a stronghold for the humble person
in his distress,
a refuge from the rain, a shade from the heat.
When the breath of the violent
is like rain [against] a wall,

5 like heat in a dry land,
You subdue the uproar of barbarians.
As[d] the shade of a cloud [cools] the heat
of the day,
[so] He stills the song of the violent.

6 The LORD of •Hosts will prepare a feast
for all the peoples on this mountain[e] —
a feast of aged wine, choice meat,[f]
finely aged wine.

7 On this mountain
[He] will destroy the [burial] shroud,
the shroud over all the peoples,
the sheet covering all the nations;

8 He will destroy death forever.
The Lord GOD will wipe away the tears
from every face

---

[a] **24:11** Lit *streets she* (the city) *cries* [b] **24:16** Hb obscure [c] **25:3** Lit *nations* [d] **25:5** Lit *In* [e] **25:6** Mount Zion; Is 2:2–4; 24:23 [f] **25:6** Lit *wine, fat full of marrow*

---

ilar to the wedding supper of the Lamb (see Rev. 19:9).
26:1 a strong city. Refers to Jerusalem where the Messiah will reign. The humble will be exalted and oppressors vanquished, a reversal of the world's wicked system.
26:8 we wait for You … Your name and re-

nown. The righteous trust in God's care (Ps. 40:1). Problems will certainly come, but God will lead the faithful through life's trials and will reward them with goodness and joy at the end.
26:13 other lords than You. This included rulers of Egypt in the past; Assyria in the

present and Babylon in the future (2 Chron. 12:8).

26:19 dead will live … bodies will rise. God made a promise here for the first time: assuring the people that the believing dead will rise to life at Christ's second coming (Dan. 12:2).
morning dew. As dew refreshes grass, so

and remove His people's disgrace
from the whole earth,
for the LORD has spoken.

9 On that day it will be said,
"Look, this is our God;
we have waited for Him, and He has saved us.
This is the LORD; we have waited for Him.
Let us rejoice and be glad in His salvation."

10 For the LORD's power will rest
on this mountain.

But Moab will be trampled in his place[a]
as straw is trampled in a dung pile.

11 He will spread out his arms in the middle of it,
as a swimmer spreads out [his arms] to swim.
His pride will be brought low,
along with the trickery of his hands.

12 The high-walled fortress will be brought down,
thrown to the ground, to the dust.

The Song of Judah

26 On that day this song will be sung in the land of Judah:

We have a strong city.
Salvation is established as walls and ramparts.

2 Open the gates
so a righteous nation can come in—
one that remains faithful.

3 You will keep in perfect peace
the mind [that is] dependent [on You],
for it is trusting in You.

4 Trust in the LORD forever,
because in •Yah, the LORD, is
an everlasting rock!

5 For He has humbled those who live
in lofty places—
an inaccessible city.
He brings it down; He brings it down
to the ground;
He throws it to the dust.

6 Feet trample it,
the feet of the humble,
the steps of the poor.

God's People Vindicated

7 The path of the righteous is level;
You clear a straight path for the righteous.

8 Yes, LORD, we wait for You
in the path of Your judgments.
Our desire is for Your name and renown.

9 I long for You in the night;

---

yes, my spirit within me diligently seeks You,
for when Your judgments are [in] the land,
the inhabitants of the world
will learn righteousness.

10 [But if] the wicked is shown favor,
he does not learn righteousness.
In a righteous land he acts unjustly
and does not see the majesty of the LORD.

11 LORD, Your hand is lifted up [to take action],
but they do not see it.
They will see [Your] zeal for [Your] people,
and they will be put to shame.
The fire for Your adversaries will consume them!

12 LORD, You will establish peace for us,
for You have also done all our work for us.

13 LORD, our God, other lords than You have ruled
over us,
but we remember Your name alone.

14 The dead do not live;
departed spirits do not rise up.
Indeed, You have visited and destroyed them;
You have wiped out all memory of them.

15 You have added to the nation, LORD.
You have added to the nation; You are honored.
You have expanded all the borders of the land.

16 LORD, they went to You in their distress;
they poured out whispered [prayers
because] Your discipline [fell] on them.[b]

17 As a pregnant woman about to give birth
writhes and cries out in her pains,
so we were before You, LORD.

18 We became pregnant, we writhed in pain;
we gave birth to wind.
We have won no victories on earth,
and the earth's inhabitants have not fallen.

19 Your dead will live; their bodies[c] will rise.
Awake and sing, you who dwell in the dust!
For you will be covered with the morning dew,[d]
and the earth will bring forth
the departed spirits.

20 Go, my people, enter your rooms
and close your doors behind you.
Hide for a little while until the wrath has passed.

21 For look, the LORD is coming from His place
to punish the inhabitants of the earth
for their iniquity.
The earth will reveal the blood shed on it
and will no longer conceal her slain.

---

[a]25:10 Or trampled under Him   [b]26:16 Hb obscure   [c]26:19 Lit live; my body they   [d]26:19 Lit For your dew is a dew of lights

---

will believers experience new life along with God's blessing at the resurrection (Ps. 133:3).

26:20 Hide ... a little while ... wrath. Isaiah urged the future believing remnant to hide during the Tribulation when God pours out His anger. They should wait for God to deliver them.

26:21 to punish. God will judge people for both open and secret sins. **conceal her slain.** Since God knows all the bloodshed and evil on earth and will judge its perpetrators, this statement encourages believers to completely obey God.

27:1 sword ... Leviathan. God will triumph over all who oppose Him, including this large sea creature, which symbolizes the chaos and evil in the world (Ps. 74:13-14).

27:2 vineyard. Israel (see Isa. 5).

27:5 My strength ... peace. While God must judge sin, He prefers that believers repent and obey Him, living in the proper covenant

Leviathan Slain

27 On that day the LORD with His harsh, great, and strong sword, will bring judgment on •Leviathan, the fleeing serpent—Leviathan, the twisting serpent. He will slay the monster that is in the sea.

The LORD's Vineyard

2 On that day
sing about a desirable vineyard:

3 I, the LORD, watch over it;
I water it regularly.
I guard it night and day
so that no one disturbs it.

4 I am not angry,
but if it produces thorns and briers for Me,
I will fight against it, trample it,
and burn it to the ground.

5 Or let it take hold of My strength;
let it make peace with Me—
make peace with Me.

6 In days to come, Jacob will take root.
Israel will blossom and bloom
and fill the whole world with fruit.

7 Did the LORD strike Israel
as He struck the one who struck Israel?
Was he killed like those killed by Him?

8 You disputed with her
by banishing and driving her away.[a]
He removed ⌊her⌋ with His severe storm
on the day of the east wind.

9 Therefore Jacob's iniquity will be purged
in this way,
and the result of the removal of his sin will be this:
when he makes all the altar stones
like crushed bits of chalk,
no •Asherah poles or incense altars
will remain standing.

10 For the fortified city will be deserted,
pastures abandoned and forsaken
like a wilderness.
Calves will graze there,
and there they will spread out and strip
its branches.

11 When its branches dry out, they will be
broken off.
Women will come and make fires with them,
for they are not a people with understanding.
Therefore their Maker will not have compassion
on them,
and their Creator will not be gracious to them.

12 On that day
the LORD will thresh grain
from the Euphrates River
as far as the •Wadi of Egypt,
and you Israelites will be gathered one by one.

13 On that day
a great trumpet will be blown,
and those lost in the land of Assyria will come,
as well as those dispersed in the land of Egypt;
and they will worship the LORD
at Jerusalem on the holy mountain.

Woe to Samaria

28 Woe to the majestic crown
of Ephraim's drunkards,
and to the fading flower of its beautiful splendor,
which is on the summit above the rich valley.
⌊Woe⌋ to those overcome with wine.

2 Look, the Lord has a strong and mighty one—
like a devastating hail storm,
like a storm with strong flooding waters.
He will bring it across the land with ⌊His⌋ hand.

3 The majestic crown of Ephraim's drunkards
will be trampled underfoot.

4 The fading flower of his beautiful splendor,
which is on the summit above the rich valley,
will be like a ripe fig before the summer harvest.
Whoever sees it will swallow it
while it is still in his hand.

5 On that day
the LORD of •Hosts will become a crown
of beauty
and a diadem of splendor
to the remnant of His people,

6 a spirit of justice
to the one who sits in judgment,
and strength
to those who turn back the battle at the gate.

7 These also stagger because of wine
and stumble under the influence of beer:
priest and prophet stagger because of beer,
they are confused by wine.
They stumble because of beer,
they are muddled in ⌊their⌋ visions,
they stumble in ⌊their⌋ judgments.

8 Indeed, all their tables are covered with vomit;
there is no place without a stench.

9 Who is he[b] trying to teach?
Who is he[b] trying to instruct?
Infants[c] ⌊just⌋ weaned from milk?

---

[a] 27:8 Hb obscure   [b] 28:9 Or He   [c] 28:9 Lit Those

---

relationship and receiving His blessings (Job 22:21).

27:10 deserted ... abandoned ... forsaken. Because of Israel's sin, Jerusalem was destroyed in 586 B.C.

27:12 the LORD will thresh. Like the oxen that thresh wheat and gather it from the fields,

God will bring the Israelites from Assyria and Egypt to Jerusalem where the Messiah will reign.

28:12 let the weary rest. Although God had offered Israel peace and rest, they refused to listen.

28:15, 18 a deal with death. Isaiah's way of

describing Israel's covenant with Egypt. Jerusalem's leaders trusted in other gods, such as the god of the underworld, to save them.

28:20 bed ... cover. Looking for protection from false gods was as futile as trying to sleep in a small, uncomfortable bed with only a thin blanket to keep out the cold.

Babies[a] removed from the breast?

10 For ⌊he says⌋: "Law after law, law after law,
line after line, line after line,
a little here, a little there."[b]

11 So He will speak to this people
with stammering speech
and in a foreign language.

12 He had said to them:
"This is the place of rest,
let the weary rest;
this is the place of repose."
But they would not listen.

13 Then the word of the LORD came to them:
"Law after law, law after law,
line after line, line after line,
a little here, a little there,"[c]
so they go stumbling backwards,
to be broken, trapped, and captured.

A Deal with Death

14 Therefore hear the word of the LORD, you mockers
who rule this people in Jerusalem.

15 For you said, "We have cut a deal with Death,
and we have made an agreement with •Sheol;
when the overwhelming scourge
    passes through,
it will not touch us,
because we have made falsehood our refuge
and have hidden behind treachery."

16 Therefore the Lord GOD said:
"Look, I have laid a stone in Zion,
a tested stone,
a precious cornerstone, a sure foundation;
the one who believes will be unshakable.[d]

17 And I will make justice the measuring line
and righteousness the mason's level."
Hail will sweep away the false refuge,
and water will flood your hiding place.

18 Your deal with Death will be dissolved,
and your agreement with Sheol will not last.
When the overwhelming scourge passes through,
you will be trampled.

19 Every time it passes through,
it will carry you away;
it will pass through every morning—
every day and every night.
Only terror will cause you
to understand the message.[e]

20 Indeed, the bed is too short to stretch out on,
and its cover too small to wrap up in.

21 For the LORD will rise up as ⌊He did⌋
    at Mount Perazim.
He will rise in wrath, as at the valley of Gibeon,
to do His work, His strange work,
and to perform His task, His disturbing task.

22 So now, do not mock,
or your shackles will become stronger.
Indeed, I have heard from the Lord GOD of Hosts
a decree of destruction for the whole land.

God's Wonderful Advice

23 Listen and hear my voice.
Pay attention and hear what I say.

24 Does the plowman plow every day to plant seed?
Does he ⌊continuously⌋ break up and cultivate
    the soil?

25 When he has leveled its surface,
does he not then scatter cumin and sow
    black cumin?
He plants wheat in rows and barley in plots,
with spelt as their border.

26 His God teaches him order;
He instructs him.

27 Certainly black cumin is not threshed
with a threshing board,
and a cart wheel is not rolled over the cumin.
But black cumin is beaten out with a stick,
and cumin with a rod.

28 Bread grain is crushed,
but is not threshed endlessly.
Though the wheel of ⌊the farmer's⌋ cart rumbles,
his horses do not crush it.

29 This also comes from the LORD of Hosts.
He gives wonderful advice;
He gives great wisdom.

Woe to Jerusalem

29 Woe to Ariel,[f] Ariel,
the city where David camped!
Continue year after year;
let the festivals recur.

2 I will oppress Ariel,
and there will be mourning and crying,
and she will be to Me like an Ariel.[f]

3 I will camp in a circle around you;
I will besiege you with earth ramps,
and I will set up my siege towers against you.

---

[a]28:9 Lit *Those* [b]28:10 Hb obscure; perhaps the mockers of v. 9 are mimicking the prophet's words as baby talk. [c]28:13 Hb obscure; the LORD quotes the mockers' words in v. 10 to represent the unintelligible language of the Assyrian invaders. [d]28:16 Lit *will not hurry* [e]28:19 Or *The understanding of the message will cause sheer terror* [f]29:1,2 Hb obscure; perhaps = "altar hearth" or "lion of God"

28:24 the plowman. Isaiah compared God's judgment to the work of a farmer who must grind certain of his crops to get out the small seeds. Though God will judge sin, He will also save and restore.

29:1–2, 7 Ariel. Means "lion of God" and is a fitting name for Jerusalem, the capital of Judah who is a lion (Gen. 49:9). Yet the name also means altar hearth (Ezek. 43:15) and refers to Jerusalem, where so much bloodshed would make the city appear like an altar where sacrifices had been slain (see Ezek. 24:6,9).

29:4 voice will be like that of a spirit. Refers to the deceptive "voices" of the dead who supposedly spoke through mediums. A humbled Jerusalem will only be able to speak in a whisper.

29:6 you will be visited by the LORD of Hosts. As God intervened and spared Jerusalem from destruction by Assyrian soldiers,

4 You will be brought down;
  you will speak from the ground,
  and your words will come from low in the dust.
  Your voice will be like that of a spirit
    from the ground;
  your speech will whisper from the dust.

5 The multitude of your foes[a] will be
    like fine dust,
  and the multitude of the ruthless,
    like blowing chaff.
  Then suddenly, in an instant,

6 you will be visited by the LORD of •Hosts
  with thunder, earthquake, and loud noise,
  storm, tempest, and a flame of consuming fire.

7 The multitude of all the nations
  going out to battle against Ariel—
  all the attackers, the siege-works against her,
  and those who oppress her—
  will then be like a dream, a vision in the night.

8 It will be like a hungry one who dreams
    he is eating,
  then wakes and is still hungry;
  and like a thirsty one who dreams he is drinking,
  then wakes and is still thirsty, longing for water.
  So will be the multitude of all the nations
  who go to battle against Mount Zion.

9 Stop and be astonished;
  blind yourselves and be blind!
  They are drunk,[b] but not with wine;
  they stagger,[c] but not with beer.

10 For the LORD has poured out on you
  an overwhelming urge to[d] sleep;
  He has shut your eyes—the prophets,
  and covered your heads—the seers.

11 For you the entire vision will be like the words of a sealed document. If it is given to one who can read and he is asked to read it,[e] he will say, "I can't read it, because it is sealed." 12 And if the document is given to one who cannot read and he is asked to read it,[f] he will say, "I can't read."

13 The Lord said:

Because these people approach Me
    with their mouths
  to honor Me with lip-service[g]—
  yet their hearts are far from Me,
  and their worship ⌊consists of⌋ man-made rules
  learned ⌊by rote⌋—

14 therefore I will again confound these people
  with wonder after wonder.
  The wisdom of their wise men will vanish,
  and the understanding of the perceptive
    will be hidden.

15 Woe to those who go to great lengths
  to hide their plans from the LORD.
  ⌊They do⌋ their works in darkness,
  and say, "Who sees us? Who knows us?"

16 You have turned things around,
  as if the potter were the same as the clay.
  How can what is made say about its maker,
  "He didn't make me"?
  How can what is formed
  say about the one who formed it,
  "He doesn't understand ⌊what he's doing⌋"?

17 Isn't ⌊it true that⌋ in just a little while
  Lebanon will become an orchard,
  and the orchard will seem like a forest?

18 On that day the deaf will hear
  the words of a document,
  and out of a deep darkness
  the eyes of the blind will see.

19 The humble will have joy
  after joy in the LORD,
  and the poor people will rejoice
  in the Holy One of Israel.

20 For the ruthless one will vanish,
  the scorner will disappear,
  and all those who lie in wait with evil intent
  will be killed—

21 those who, with ⌊their⌋ speech,
  accuse a person of wrongdoing,
  who set a trap at the •gate for the mediator,
  and without cause deprive the righteous
    of justice.

22 Therefore, the LORD who redeemed Abraham says this about the house of Jacob:

Jacob will no longer be ashamed
  and his face will no longer be pale.

23 For when he sees his children,
  the work of My hands within his ⌊nation⌋,
  they will honor My name,
  they will honor the Holy One of Jacob
  and stand in awe of the God of Israel.

24 Those who are confused will gain understanding
  and those who grumble will accept instruction.

---

a 29:5 Lit foreigners   b 29:9 LXX, Tg, Vg read Be drunk   c 29:9 Tg, Vg read wine; stagger   d 29:10 Lit you a spirit of   e 29:11 Lit If one gives it to one who knows the document, saying, "Read this, please"   f 29:12 Lit who does not know the document, saying, "Read this, please"   g 29:13 Lit their mouth and honor Me with its lips

---

He will come and destroy the nations attacking His people (see Zech. 14:1-3).

29:13 their hearts are far from Me. Professing to know God or engaging in acts of worship do not necessarily mean that a person's heart is turned toward Him.

29:22 the LORD who redeemed. God re-newed His covenant with Abraham, promising to deliver and bless Israel (see Josh. 24:3; Acts 7:2-4). **no longer be ashamed.** God's deliverance from the Assyrian army was a preview of a future day when God's people will no longer be dominated by either foreign oppression or their own sin.

30:1 an alliance. King Hezekiah's advisors wanted to join Egypt to fight against the Assyrians, although Egypt was then a weak player on the Near East scene.

30:8 write it ... inscribe it. Even though the people would not obey God's instructions, Isaiah was to write them down so the people

Condemnation of the Egyptian Alliance

30 Woe to the rebellious children!

[This is]
the LORD's declaration.
They carry out a plan, but not Mine,
They make an alliance,
but against My will,
piling sin on top of sin.
2 They set out to go down to Egypt
without asking My advice,
in order to seek shelter
under Pharaoh's protection
and take refuge in Egypt's shadow.
3 But Pharaoh's protection will become
your shame,
and refuge in Egypt's shadow your disgrace.
4 For though his[a] princes are at Zoan
and his messengers reach as far as Hanes,
5 everyone will be ashamed
because of a people who can't help.
They are of no benefit, they are no help;
they are good for nothing but shame
and reproach.

6 An •oracle about the animals of the •Negev:[b]

Through a land of trouble and distress,
of lioness and lion,
of viper and flying serpent,
they carry their wealth on the backs of donkeys
and their treasures on the humps of camels,
to a people who will not help them.
7 Egypt's help is completely worthless;
therefore, I call her:
•Rahab Who Just Sits.

8 Go now, write it on a tablet in their presence
and inscribe it on a scroll;
it will be for the future,
forever and ever.
9 They are a rebellious people,
deceptive children,
children who do not obey the LORD's instruction.
10 They say to the seers, "Do not see,"
and to the prophets,
"Do not prophesy the truth to us.
Tell us flattering things.
Prophesy illusions.
11 Get out of the way!
Leave the pathway.
Rid us of the Holy One of Israel."

12 Therefore the Holy One of Israel says:
"Because you have rejected this message
and have trusted in oppression and deceit,
and have depended on them,
13 this iniquity of yours will be
like a spreading breach,
a bulge in a high wall
whose collapse will come very suddenly.
14 Its collapse will be like the shattering
of a potter's jar, crushed to pieces,
so that not even a fragment of pottery
will be found among its shattered remains—
no fragment large enough to take fire
from a hearth
or scoop water from a cistern."
15 For the Lord GOD, the Holy One of Israel,
has said:
"You will be delivered by returning and resting;
your strength will lie in quiet confidence.
But you are not willing."
16 You say, "No!
We will escape on horses"—
therefore you will escape!—
and, "We will ride on fast horses"—
but those who pursue you will be faster.
17 One thousand [will flee] at the threat of one,
at the threat of five you will flee,
until you alone remain
like a [solitary] pole on a mountaintop
or a banner on a hill.

The LORD's Mercy to Israel

18 Therefore the LORD is waiting
to show you mercy,
and is rising up to show you compassion,
for the LORD is a just God.
Happy are all who wait patiently for Him.

19 For you people will live on Zion in Jerusalem and
will never cry again. He will show favor to you at the
sound of your cry; when He hears, He will answer you.
20 The Lord will give you meager bread and water during
oppression, but your Teacher[c] will not hide Himself[d] any
longer. Your eyes will see your Teacher,[c] 21 and whenever you turn to the right or to the left, your ears will
hear this command behind you: "This is the way. Walk
in it." 22 Then you will defile your silver-plated idols and
your gold-plated images. You will throw them away like
menstrual cloths, and call them filth.

23 Then He will send rain for your seed that you have
sown in the ground, and the food, the produce of the

---

could not say they had never heard them.
30:13 iniquity … like … a high wall. The
simile meant that judgment would come suddenly and completely (see Jer. 19:11).
30:15 quiet confidence. The peace and confidence available to people who trust totally in
God's strength are part of the promise of the

new life of faith.
30:18 waiting to show you mercy. Although
God judges the unrepentant, His desire is for
all men to be saved. He is waiting to show
mercy if Israel will repent.
**30:26 bandages His people's injuries …
heals the wounds.** God will restore and

bless His people after purging and judging
their sin. God will heal the people from their
wickedness.
31:4 lion. God was not intimidated by the Assyrians, just as a lion is not afraid of shepherds (see Hos. 11:10).
31:5 birds … will protect Jerusalem. A pic-

ground, will be rich and plentiful. On that day your cattle will graze in open pastures. 24 The oxen and donkeys that work the ground will eat salted fodder scattered with winnowing shovel and fork. 25 Streams and watercourses will be on every high mountain and every raised hill on the day of great slaughter when the towers fall. 26 The moonlight will be as bright as the sunlight, and the sunlight will be seven times brighter—like the light of seven days—on the day that the LORD bandages His people's injuries and heals the wounds He inflicted.

Annihilation of the Assyrians

27 Look, •Yahweh[a] comes from far away,
His anger burning and heavy with smoke.[b]
His lips are full of fury,
and His tongue is like a consuming fire.
28 His breath is like an overflowing torrent
that rises to the neck.
⌊He comes⌋ to sift the nations in a sieve
of destruction
and to put a bridle on the jaws of the peoples
to lead ⌊them⌋ astray.
29 Your singing will be like that
on the night of a holy festival,
And ⌊your⌋ heart will rejoice
like one who walks ⌊to the music⌋ of a flute,
going up to the mountain of the LORD,
to the Rock of Israel.
30 And the LORD will make the splendor
of His voice heard
and reveal His arm striking
in angry wrath and a flame of consuming fire,
in driving rain, a torrent, and hailstones.
31 Assyria will be shattered by the voice
of the LORD.
He will strike with a rod.
32 And every stroke of the appointed[c] staff
that the LORD brings down on him
will be ⌊to the sound⌋ of tambourines
and lyres;
He will fight against him
with brandished weapons.
33 Indeed! •Topheth has been ready
for the king for a long time now.
His funeral pyre is deep and wide,
with plenty of fire and wood.
The breath of the LORD, like a torrent
of brimstone,
kindles it.

The LORD, the Only Help

31 Woe to those who go down to Egypt for help
and who depend on horses!
They trust in the number of chariots
and in the great strength of charioteers.
They do not look to the Holy One of Israel
and they do not seek the LORD's help.
2 But He also is wise and brings disaster.
He does not go back on what He says;
He will rise up against the house
of wicked men
and against the allies of evildoers.
3 Egyptians are men, not God;
their horses are flesh, not spirit.
When the LORD raises His hand ⌊to strike⌋,
the helper will stumble and the helped
will fall;
both will perish together.

4 For this is what the LORD said to me:

As a lion or young lion growls over its prey
when a band of shepherds is called out
against it,
and is not terrified by their shouting
or subdued by their noise,
so the LORD of •Hosts will come down
to fight on Mount Zion
and on its hill.

5 Like hovering birds,
so the LORD of Hosts will protect Jerusalem—
by protecting ⌊it⌋, He will rescue ⌊it⌋,
by sparing ⌊it⌋, He will deliver ⌊it⌋.

6 Return to the One the Israelites have greatly rebelled against. 7 For on that day, each one will reject the silver and gold idols that your own hands have sinfully made.

8 Then Assyria will fall,
but not by human sword;
a sword will devour him,
but not one made by man.
He will flee from the sword,
his young men will be put to forced labor.
9 His rock[d] will pass away because of fear,
and his officers will be afraid because of
the signal flag.

⌊This is⌋ the LORD's declaration—whose fire is in Zion and whose furnace is in Jerusalem.

---

[a] 30:27 Lit the name Yahweh   [b] 30:27 Hb obscure   [c] 30:32 Some Hb mss read punishing   [d] 31:9 Perhaps the Assyrian king

---

ture of God's protection of Jerusalem against the enemy.

31:9 signal flag. A banner serving as the rallying point for battle. The Assyrian commanders would be terrified when they saw Judah's banner and the slaughter of their soldiers by God's angel.

32:1 king will reign righteously. The Messiah will reign in righteousness when God's justice is finally won over all the earth (see Jer. 23:5).

32:5 fool. A senseless person who teaches falsehood and gives no thought to the needs of others. **scoundrel.** A person who plots to

take advantage of the poor and needy (see Prov. 24:7-9).

32:8 noble person...noble things...noble causes. The righteous king will be noble. Noble in Hebrew has the connotation of being generous. Isaiah didn't live to see this ideal king.

The Righteous Kingdom Announced

32 Indeed, a king will reign righteously,
and rulers will rule justly.

2 Each will be like a shelter from the wind,
a refuge from the rain,
like streams of water in a dry land
and the shade of a massive rock in an arid land.

3 Then the eyes of those who see will not
be closed,
and the ears of those who hear will listen.

4 The reckless mind will gain knowledge,
and the stammering tongue will speak clearly
and fluently.

5 A fool will no longer be called a noble,
nor a scoundrel said to be important.

6 For a fool speaks foolishness
and his mind plots iniquity.
He lives in a godless way
and speaks falsely about the LORD.
He leaves the hungry empty
and deprives the thirsty of drink.

7 The scoundrel's weapons are destructive;
he hatches plots to destroy the needy with lies,
and by charging the poor during a judgment.

8 But a noble person plans noble things;
he stands up for noble causes.

9 Stand up, you complacent women;
listen to me.
Pay attention to what I say,
you overconfident daughters.

10 In a little more than a year
you overconfident ones will shudder,
for the vintage will fail
and the harvest will not come.

11 Shudder, you complacent ones;
tremble, you overconfident ones!
Strip yourselves bare
and put ⌊•sackcloth⌋ about your waists.

12 Beat your breasts ⌊in mourning⌋
for the delightful fields and the fruitful vines,

13 for the ground of my people
growing thorns and briers,
indeed, for every joyous house in the joyful city.

14 For the palace will be forsaken,
the busy city abandoned.
The hill and the watchtower will become
barren places forever,
the joy of wild donkeys,
and a pasture for flocks,

15 until the Spirit from heaven is poured out on us.
Then the desert will become an orchard,
and the orchard will seem like a forest.

16 Then justice will inhabit the wilderness,
and righteousness will dwell in the orchard.

17 The result of righteousness will be peace;
the effect of righteousness
will be quiet confidence forever.

18 Then my people will dwell in a peaceful place,
and in safe and restful dwellings.

19 But hail will level the forest,[a]
and the city will sink into the depths.

20 Happy are you who sow seed
beside abundant waters,
who let ox and donkey range freely.

The LORD Rises Up

33 Woe, you destroyer never destroyed,
you traitor never betrayed!
When you have finished destroying,
you will be destroyed.
When you have finished betraying,
they will betray you.

2 LORD, be gracious to us! We wait for You.
Be our strength every morning,
and our salvation in time of trouble.

3 The peoples flee at the thunderous noise;
the nations scatter when You rise
in Your majesty.

4 Your spoil will be gathered as locusts
are gathered;
people will swarm over it like an infestation
of locusts.

5 The LORD is exalted, for He dwells on high;
He has filled Zion with justice
and righteousness.

6 There will be times of security for you—
a storehouse of salvation, wisdom,
and knowledge.
The •fear of the LORD is Zion's treasure.

7 Listen! Their warriors cry loudly in the streets;
the messengers of peace weep bitterly.

8 The highways are deserted;
travel has ceased.
An agreement has been broken,
cities[b] despised,
and human life disregarded.

9 The land mourns and withers;
Lebanon is ashamed and decayed.

---

a**32:19** Hb obscure   b**33:8** DSS read *witnesses*

32:9 women. A warning to the women of Judah who thought that judgment would not come (3:16-23). **complacent ... overconfident.** The wicked relied on Egypt for security, while the righteous trusted in the Lord.

32:15 until the Spirit. The outpouring of God's Spirit will bring fertility, justice, productivity, and security, as promised in the Deuteronomic covenant. But the people must obey God (see Deut. 5:2-3; 29:9; Joel 2:28).

33:2 our strength ... our salvation. Isaiah and the believing remnant longed for God's deliverance and defeat of their opponents. God has shown His power by defeating their opponents many times before.

33:16 heights ... rocky fortresses. God will make Jerusalem into a fortress, protected not by walls but by His power.

33:24 forgiven their iniquity. Both sickness and sin will be removed in the coming kingdom (see Jer. 31:34). The Messiah will be

Sharon is like a desert;
Bashan and Carmel shake off [their] leaves.

10 "Now I will rise up," says the LORD.
"Now I will lift Myself up.
Now I will be exalted.

11 You will conceive chaff;
you will give birth to stubble.
Your breath is fire that will consume you.

12 The peoples will be burned to ashes,
like thorns cut down and burned in a fire.

13 You who are far off, hear what I have done;
you who are near, know My strength."

14 The sinners in Zion are afraid;
trembling seizes the ungodly:
"Who among us can dwell
with a consuming fire?
Who among us can dwell
with ever-burning flames?"

15 The one who lives righteously
and speaks rightly,
who refuses gain from extortion,
whose hand never takes a bribe,
who stops his ears from listening
to murderous plots[a]
and shuts his eyes to avoid endorsing evil[b]—

16 he will dwell on the heights;
his refuge will be the rocky fortresses,
his food provided, his water assured.

17 Your eyes will see the king in his beauty;
you will see a vast land.

18 Your mind will meditate on the [past] terror:
"Where is the accountant?[c]
Where is the tribute collector?[d]
Where is the one who spied out our defenses?"[e]

19 You will no longer see the barbarians,
a people whose speech is difficult
to comprehend—
who stammer in a language that is
not understood.

20 Look at Zion, the city of our festival times.
Your eyes will see Jerusalem,
a peaceful pasture, a tent that does not wander;
its tent pegs will not be pulled up
nor will any of its cords be loosened.

21 For there the majestic One, the LORD, will be
for us,
a place of rivers and broad streams,
where ships that are rowed will not go,

and majestic vessels will not pass.

22 For the LORD is our Judge,
the LORD is our lawgiver,
the LORD is our King.
He will save us.

23 Your ropes are slack;
they cannot hold the base of the mast
or spread out the flag.
Then abundant spoil will be divided,
the lame will plunder it,

24 and none there will say, "I am sick."
The people who dwell there
will be forgiven [their] iniquity.

The Judgment of the Nations

34 You nations, come here and listen;
you peoples, pay attention!
Let the earth hear, and all that fills it,
the world and all that comes from it.

2 The LORD is angry with all the nations—
furious with all their armies.
He will set them apart for destruction,
giving them over to slaughter.

3 Their slain will be thrown out,
and the stench of their corpses will rise;
the mountains flow[f] with their blood.

4 All[g] the heavenly bodies will dissolve.
The skies will roll up like a scroll,
and their stars will all wither
as leaves wither on the vine,
and foliage on the fig tree.

The Judgment of Edom

5 When My sword has drunk its fill[h]
in the heavens
it will then come down on Edom
and on the people I have •set apart
for destruction.

6 The LORD's sword is covered with blood.
It drips with fat,
with the blood of lambs and goats,
with the fat of the kidneys of rams.
For the LORD has a sacrifice in Bozrah,
a great slaughter in the land of Edom.

7 The wild oxen will be struck[i] down with them,
and young bulls with the mighty bulls.
Their land will be soaked with[j] blood,
and their soil will be saturated with fat.

8 For the LORD has a day of vengeance,
a time of paying back [Edom].

[a]33:15 Lit to bloods   [b]33:15 Lit eyes from seeing evil   [c]33:18 Lit counter   [d]33:18 Lit weigher   [e]33:18 Lit who counts towers   [f]34:3 Or melt, or dissolve   [g]34:4 DSS read And the valleys will be split, and all   [h]34:5 DSS read sword will appear   [i]34:7 Or will go   [j]34:7 Or will drink its fill of

judge, lawgiver, and king.
34:2 angry ... furious. God responds to sin by destroying it (13:5). Even the stars will be dissolved in His final judgment.
34:7 wild oxen ... mighty bulls. May symbolize Edom's soldiers or leaders who will attack Israel. God will destroy them at Bozrah,

about 25 miles southeast of the Dead Sea.
34:9 pitch ... sulfur. Pitch is a tar like substance that seems to burn forever. Sulfur burns with great heat and intensity. This may refer to the destruction of Sodom and Gomorrah.
34:16 read the scroll. This scroll of the Lord

may refer to the prophecy in verses 1-15 where God will judge all nations hostile to Israel (Mal. 3:16).
35:3 Strengthen the weak hands. Isaiah encouraged the believing remnant to live by God's instructions and to encourage the fainthearted and weak (see Josh. 1:6; Heb. 12:12).

for its hostility against Zion.
9 ⌊Edom's⌋ streams will be turned into pitch,
   her soil into sulfur;
   her land will become burning pitch.
10 It will never go out—day or night.
   Its smoke will go up forever.
   It will be desolate, from generation
      to generation;
   no one will pass through it forever and ever.
11 The desert owl[a] and the hedgehog[b]
      will possess it,
   and the great owl and the raven
      will dwell there.
   ⌊The LORD⌋ will stretch out a measuring line
   and a plumb line over her
   for ⌊her⌋ destruction and chaos.
12 No nobles will be left to proclaim a king,
   and all her princes will come to nothing.
13 Her palaces will be overgrown with thorns;
   her fortified cities, with thistles and briers.
   She will become a dwelling for jackals,
   an abode[c] for ostriches.
14 The wild beasts will meet hyenas,
   and one wild goat will call to another.
   Indeed, the screech owl will stay there
   and will find a resting place for herself.
15 The sand partridge[d] will make her nest there;
   she will lay and hatch her eggs
   and will gather ⌊her brood⌋ under her shadow.
   Indeed, the birds of prey will gather there,
   each with its mate.
16 Search and read the scroll of the LORD:
   Not one of them will be missing,
   none will be lacking its mate,
   because He has ordered it by my[e] mouth,
   and He will gather them by His Spirit.
17 He has ordained a lot for them;
   His hand allotted their portion
      with a measuring line.
   They will possess it forever;
   they will dwell in it from generation
      to generation.

The Ransomed Return to Zion

35 The wilderness and the dry land will be glad;
   the desert will rejoice and blossom like a rose.[f]
2 It will blossom abundantly
   and will also rejoice with joy and singing.
   The glory of Lebanon will be given to it,
   the splendor of Carmel and Sharon.

They will see the glory of the LORD,
   the splendor of our God.
3 Strengthen the weak hands,
   steady the shaking knees!
4 Say to the faint-hearted:
   "Be strong; do not fear!
   Here is your God; vengeance is coming.
   God's retribution is coming; He will save you."
5 Then the eyes of the blind will be opened,
   and the ears of the deaf unstopped.
6 Then the lame will leap like a deer,
   and the tongue of the mute will sing for joy,
   for water will gush in the wilderness,
   and streams in the desert;
7 the parched ground will become a pool of water,
   and the thirsty land springs of water.
   In the haunt of jackals, in their lairs,
   there will be grass, reeds, and papyrus.
8 A road will be there and a way;
   it will be called the Holy Way.
   The unclean will not travel on it,
   but it will be for him who walks the path.
   Even the fool will not go astray.
9 There will be no lion there,
   and no vicious beast will go up on it;
   they will not be found there.
   But the redeemed will walk ⌊on it⌋,
10 and the ransomed of the LORD will return
   and come to Zion with singing,
   crowned with unending joy.
   Joy and gladness will overtake ⌊them⌋,
   and sorrow and sighing will flee.

Sennacherib Threatens Hezekiah

36 In the fourteenth year of King Hezekiah, Sennacherib king of Assyria advanced against all the fortified cities of Judah and captured them. 2 Then the king of Assyria sent the •Rabshakeh, along with a massive army, from Lachish to King Hezekiah at Jerusalem. The Assyrian stood near the conduit of the upper pool, by the road to the Fuller's Field. 3 Eliakim son of Hilkiah, who was in charge of the palace, Shebna the scribe, and Joah son of Asaph, the record keeper, came out to him.

4 The Rabshakeh said to them, "Tell Hezekiah:

The great king, the king of Assyria, says this: 'What are you basing your confidence on?[g] 5 I[h] say that your plans and military preparedness are mere words. Now who are you trusting in that

---

[a]**34:11** Or *The pelican*   [b]**34:11** Or *owl*   [c]**34:13** DSS, LXX, Syr, Tg; MT reads *jackals, grass*   [d]**34:15** Or *The arrow snake,* or *The owl*   [e]**34:16** Some Hb mss; other Hb mss, DSS, Syr, Tg read *His*   [f]**35:1** Or *meadow saffron*   [g]**36:4** Lit *What is this trust that you trust*   [h]**36:5** DSS read *You;* 2 Kg 18:20

35:5 eyes ... opened ... ears ... unstopped. The Messiah will heal the people and the land. Jesus accomplished both spiritual and physical healing during His life on earth. He alluded to this verse when answering John the Baptist (see Matt. 11:5).

35:8 road ... called the Holy Way. This highway will lead to God's city, Jerusalem, where His ways will be followed (Joel 3:17). Only the righteous will travel on this road.

36:4 king of Assyria. Sennacherib and his proud army believed themselves invincible. They believed they were gods. The field commander did not even acknowledge Hezekiah as king in this message.

36:7 high places and altars. High places (hilltops) were the locations of pagan worship. The Assyrian commander knew that Hezekiah had removed many pagan sites that his father Ahaz had built in Judah (2 Chron. 31:1-3). The commander may have

you have rebelled against me? ⁶ Look, you are trusting in Egypt, that splintered reed of a staff, which will enter and pierce the hand of anyone who leans on it. This is how Pharaoh king of Egypt is to all who trust in him. ⁷ Suppose you say to me: We trust in the LORD our God. Isn't He the One whose •high places and altars Hezekiah has removed, saying to Judah and Jerusalem: You are to worship at this altar?

⁸ Now make a deal with my master, the king of Assyria. I'll give you 2,000 horses if you can put riders on them! ⁹ How then can you repel ⌊the attackᵃ of even⌋ the weakest of my master's officers, and trust in Egypt for chariots and horsemen? ¹⁰ Have I attacked this land to destroy it without the LORD's ⌊approval⌋? The LORD said to me, 'Attack this land and destroy it.'"

¹¹ Then Eliakim, Shebna, and Joah said to the Rabshakeh, "Please speak to your servants in Aramaic, for we understand ⌊it⌋; don't speak to us in Hebrewᵇ within earshot of the people who are on the wall."

¹² But the Rabshakeh replied, "Has my master sent me to speak these words to your master and to you, and not to the men who sit on the wall, ⌊who are destined⌋ with you to eat their excrement and drink their urine?"

¹³ Then the Rabshakeh stood and called out loudly in Hebrew:ᵇ

Listen to the words of the great king, the king of Assyria! ¹⁴ The king says: "Don't let Hezekiah deceive you, for he cannot deliver you. ¹⁵ Don't let Hezekiah persuade you to trust the LORD, saying, 'The LORD will surely deliver us. This city will not be handed over to the king of Assyria.'"

¹⁶ Don't listen to Hezekiah. For the king of Assyria says: "Make peaceᶜ with me and surrender to me; then every one of you will eat from his own vine and his own fig tree and drink water from his own cistern ¹⁷ until I come and take you away to a land like your land, a land of grain and new wine, a land of bread and vineyards. ¹⁸ ⌊Beware⌋ that Hezekiah does not mislead you by saying, 'The LORD will deliver us.' Has any one of the gods of the nations delivered his land from the hand of the king of Assyria? ¹⁹ Where are the gods of Hamath and Arpad? Where are the gods of Sepharvaim? Have they delivered Samaria from my hand? ²⁰ Who of all the gods of these lands ⌊ever⌋ delivered his land from my hand, that the LORD should deliver Jerusalem?"

²¹ But they were silent and did not answer him at all, for the king's command was, "Don't answer him." ²² Then Eliakim son of Hilkiah, who was in charge of the palace, Shebna the scribe, and Joah son of Asaph, the record keeper, came to Hezekiah with their clothes torn, and they reported to him the words of the Rabshakeh.

Hezekiah Seeks Isaiah's Counsel

37 When King Hezekiah heard ⌊their report⌋, he tore his clothes, put on •sackcloth, and went to the house of the LORD. ² Then he sent Eliakim, who was in charge of the palace, Shebna the scribe, and the older priests, wearing sackcloth, to the prophet Isaiah son of Amoz. ³ They said to him, "Hezekiah says: 'Today is a day of distress, rebuke, and disgrace, ⌊as⌋ when children come to the point of birth, and there is no strength to deliver them. ⁴ Perhaps the LORD your God will hear the words of the •Rabshakeh, whom his master, the king of Assyria, sent to mock the living God, and will rebuke ⌊him for⌋ the words that the LORD your God has heard. Therefore offer a prayer for the surviving remnant.'"

⁵ When King Hezekiah's servants came to Isaiah, ⁶ Isaiah said to them, "Say this to your master, 'The LORD says: Don't be afraid because of the words you have heard, which the king of Assyria's attendants have blasphemed Me with. ⁷ Look! I am putting a spirit in him and he will hear a rumor and return to his own land, where I will cause him to fall by the sword.'"

Sennacherib's Letter

⁸ When the Rabshakeh heard that the king had left Lachish, he returned and discovered that the king of Assyria was fighting against Libnah. ⁹ The king had heard this about Tirhakah, king of •Cush:ᵈ "He has set out to fight against you." So when he heard this, he sent messengers to Hezekiah, saying, ¹⁰ "Say this to Hezekiah king of Judah: 'Don't let your God, whom you trust, deceive you by saying that Jerusalem won't be handed over to the king of Assyria. ¹¹ Look, you have heard what the kings of Assyria have done to all the countries; they destroyed them completely. Will you be rescued? ¹² Did the gods of the nations that my predecessorsᵉ destroyed rescue them—Gozan, Haran, Rezeph, and the Edenites in Telassar? ¹³ Where is the king of Hamath, the king of Arpad, the king of the city of Sepharvaim, Hena, or Ivvah?'"

ᵃ**36:9** Or *you refuse [a request]* ᵇ**36:11,13** Or *the Judean language* ᶜ**36:16** Lit *a blessing* ᵈ**37:9** Or *Nubia* ᵉ**37:12** Lit *fathers*

---

thought Hezekiah had stopped trusting in any god altogether.

36:10 The LORD said to me, "Attack this land." Ancient conquerors often claimed that the gods of their defeated enemies had joined their side (2 Chron. 35:21). The commander used this tactic to intimidate the Israelites.

36:11 Don't speak … in Hebrew. The negotiators thought panic might spread if the people heard the Assyrian demands in Hebrew. The confident commander went ahead and spoke in Hebrew anyway.

36:12 eat … excrement. The commander predicted that the Assyrian siege would cause famine in Judah. Famine would cause people to do horrific things.

36:18 Hezekiah … mislead you. The commander tried to undermine the king of Judah by tempting the people with prosperity if they surrendered to Assyria. He reasoned that since the gods of other nations had not been

Hezekiah's Prayer

[14] Hezekiah took the letter from[a] the messengers, read it, then went up to the LORD's house and spread it out before the LORD. [15] Hezekiah prayed to the LORD: [16] "LORD of •Hosts, God of Israel, who is enthroned above the •cherubim, You are God—You alone—of all the kingdoms of the earth. You made the heavens and the earth. [17] Listen closely, LORD, and hear; open Your eyes, LORD, and see; hear all the words that Sennacherib has sent to mock the living God. [18] LORD, it is true that the kings of Assyria have devastated all these countries and their lands [19] and have thrown their gods into the fire; for they were not gods but made by human hands—wood and stone. So they have destroyed them. [20] Now, LORD our God, save us from his hand so that all the kingdoms of the earth may know that You are the LORD—You alone."

God's Answer to Hezekiah

[21] Then Isaiah son of Amoz sent ⌊a message⌋ to Hezekiah: "The LORD, the God of Israel, says: 'Because you prayed to Me about Sennacherib king of Assyria, [22] this is the word the LORD has spoken against him:

The young woman, Daughter Zion,
despises you and scorns you:
Daughter Jerusalem shakes ⌊her⌋ head
behind your back.[b]
[23] Who is it you have mocked and blasphemed?
Who have you raised ⌊your⌋ voice against
and lifted your eyes in pride?
Against the Holy One of Israel!
[24] You have mocked the LORD
through[c] your servants.
You have said: With my many chariots
I have gone up to the heights of the mountains,
to the far recesses of Lebanon.
I cut down its tallest cedars,
its choice cypress trees.
I came to its remotest heights,
its densest forest.
[25] I dug ⌊wells⌋[d] and drank water.
I dried up all the streams of Egypt
with the soles of my feet.

[26] Have you not heard?
I designed it long ago;
I planned it in days gone by.
I have now brought it to pass,
and you have crushed fortified cities
into piles of rubble.
[27] Their inhabitants have become powerless,

dismayed, and ashamed.
They are plants of the field,
tender grass,
grass on the rooftops,
blasted by the east wind.[e]

[28] But I know[f] your sitting down,
your going out and your coming in,
and your raging against Me.
[29] Because your raging against Me
and your arrogance has reached My ears,
I will put My hook in your nose
and My bit in your mouth;
I will make you go back
the way you came.

[30] "'This will be the sign for you: This year you will eat what grows on its own, and in the second year what grows from that. But in the third year sow and reap, plant vineyards and eat their fruit. [31] The surviving remnant of the house of Judah will again take root downward and bear fruit upward. [32] For a remnant will go out from Jerusalem, and survivors from Mount Zion. The zeal of the LORD of Hosts will accomplish this.'

[33] "'Therefore, this is what the LORD says about the king of Assyria:

He will not enter this city
or shoot an arrow there
or come before it with a shield
or build up an assault ramp against it.
[34] He will go back
on the road that he came
and he will not enter this city.

⌊This is⌋
the LORD's declaration.

[35] I will defend this city and rescue it,
because of Me
and because of My servant David.'"

Sennacherib's Defeat and Death

[36] Then the angel of the LORD went out and struck down 185,000 in the camp of the Assyrians. When the people got up the ⌊next⌋ morning—there were all the dead bodies! [37] So Sennacherib king of Assyria broke camp and left. He returned ⌊home⌋ and lived in Nineveh. [38] One day, while he was worshiping in the temple of his god Nisroch, his sons Adrammelech and Sharezer struck him down with the sword and escaped to the land of Ararat. Then his son Esar-haddon became king in his place.

[a]**37:14** Lit from the hand of [b]**37:22** Lit behind you [c]**37:24** Lit by the hand of [d]**37:25** DSS add in foreign lands; 2 Kg 19:24 [e]**37:27** DSS, MT reads rooftops, field before standing grain [f]**37:28** DSS read know your rising up and

---

able to protect them from Assyria, God could not protect His people either.

37:23 lifted your eyes. In response to Hezekiah's prayer, God said that the Assyrians would be defeated because of their blasphemy and pride.

37:30 second … third year. Any part of a

year was counted as a year, so the third year could have been 13 to 15 months from that time. The third year is the normal time it takes for a vineyard to begin producing grapes.

37:38 worshiping in the temple. God slaughtered the Assyrians overnight, as Isaiah had predicted. Sennacherib was assassi-

nated twenty years later in 681 B.C. by two of his sons.

38:3 walked … wholeheartedly. He asked God to remember the good things he had done.

38:17 You have thrown all my sins. Apparently Hezekiah's illness was connected to his

Hezekiah's Illness and Recovery

38 In those days Hezekiah became terminally ill. The prophet Isaiah son of Amoz came and said to him, "This is what the LORD says: 'Put your affairs in order,[a] for you are about to die; you will not recover.' "[b]

2 Then Hezekiah turned his face to the wall and prayed to the LORD. 3 He said, "Please, LORD, remember how I have walked before You faithfully and wholeheartedly, and have done what is good in Your sight." And Hezekiah wept bitterly.

4 Then the word of the LORD came to Isaiah: 5 "Go and tell Hezekiah that this is what the LORD God of your ancestor David says: I have heard your prayer; I have seen your tears. Look, I am going to add 15 years to your life.[c] 6 And I will deliver you and this city from the hand of the king of Assyria; I will defend this city. 7 This is the sign to you from the LORD that the LORD will do what[d] He has promised:[e] 8 I am going to make the sun's shadow that goes down on Ahaz's stairway return by 10 steps." So the sun's shadow[f] went back the 10 steps it had descended.

9 A poem by Hezekiah king of Judah after he had been sick and had recovered from his illness:

10   I said: In the prime[g] of my life[c]
     I must go to the gates of •Sheol;
     I am deprived of the rest of my years.
11   I said: I will never see the LORD,
     the LORD in the land of the living;
     I will not look on humanity any longer
     with the inhabitants of what is passing away.[h]
12   My dwelling is plucked up and removed
       from me
     like a shepherd's tent.
     I have rolled up my life like a weaver;
     He cuts me off from the loom.[i]
     You make an end of me from day until night.
13   I thought until the morning:
     He will break all my bones like a lion;
     You make an end of me day and night.
14   I chirp like a swallow [or] a crane;
     I moan like a dove.
     My eyes grow weak looking upward.
     Lord, I am oppressed; support me.
15   What can I say?
     He has spoken to me,
     and He Himself has done it.
     I walk along slowly all my years

     because of the bitterness of my soul,
16   Lord, because of these [promises] people live,
     and in all of them is the life of my spirit as well;
     You have restored me to health
     and let me live.
17   Indeed, it was for [my own] welfare
     that I had such great bitterness;
     but Your love [has delivered] me
     from the •Pit of destruction,
     for You have thrown all my sins behind Your back.
18   For Sheol cannot thank You;
     Death cannot praise You.
     Those who go down to the Pit
     cannot hope for Your faithfulness.
19   The living, only the living can thank You,
     as I do today;
     a father will make Your faithfulness known
       to children
20   The LORD will[j] save me;
     we will play stringed instruments
     all the days of our lives
     at the house of the LORD.

21 Now Isaiah had said, "Let them take a lump of figs and apply it to his infected skin, so that he may recover." 22 And Hezekiah had asked, "What is the sign that I will go up to the LORD's temple?"

Hezekiah's Folly

39 At that time Merodach-baladan son of Baladan, king of Babylon, sent letters and a gift to Hezekiah since he heard that he had been sick and had recovered. 2 Hezekiah was pleased with them, and showed them his treasure house—the silver, the gold, the spices, and the precious oil—and all his armory, and everything that was found in his treasuries. There was nothing in his palace and in all his realm that Hezekiah did not show them.

3 Then Isaiah the prophet came to King Hezekiah and asked him, "What did these men say? The men who came to you—where were they from?"

Hezekiah replied, "They came to me from a distant country, from Babylon."

4 And he asked, "What have they seen in your palace?"

Hezekiah answered, "They have seen everything in my palace. There isn't anything in my storehouses that I didn't show them."

5 Then Isaiah said to Hezekiah, "Hear the word of the LORD of •Hosts: 6 'The time will certainly come

---

[a] **38:1** Lit *Command your house*   [b] **38:1** Lit *live*   [c] **38:5,10** Lit *days*   [d] **38:7** Lit *this thing*   [e] **38:7** Lit *said*   [f] **38:8** Lit *And the sun*   [g] **38:10** Lit *quiet*
[h] **38:11** Some Hb mss, Tg read *of the world*   [i] **38:12** Lit *thrum*   [j] **38:20** Lit *to*

---

sin. Not all sickness is the result of a personal sin (see John 9:2-3). **behind Your back.** When God forgives, He puts our sins far away forever (see Ps. 103:12; Jer. 31:34).

38:21 take a lump of figs. God used medical procedures of that day to heal Hezekiah.

39:2 treasure house. Hezekiah proudly

showed his riches, perhaps because he was trusting in his wealth and the foreign armies he could hire.

39:6 carried off to Babylon. Since the enemy at the time was Assyria, this prediction was surprising (Jer. 20:4). Babylon hardly seemed a threat.

40:1 Comfort, comfort My people. The last part of Isaiah (chapters 40–66) is even more Messianic and future-oriented than the first. Many of the promises were for those who would return from exile about 200 years after Isaiah's lifetime. Many of the prophecies are still to come, in the millennial reign of Christ.

when everything in your palace and all that your fathers have stored up until this day will be carried off to Babylon; nothing will be left,' says the LORD. 7 'Some of your descendants who come from you will be taken away, and they will be eunuchs in the palace of the king of Babylon.' "

8 Then Hezekiah said to Isaiah, "The word of the LORD that you have spoken is good." For he thought: There will be peace and security during my lifetime.

God's People Comforted

40 "Comfort, comfort My people," says your God.
2 Speak tenderly to[a] Jerusalem,
and announce to her
that her time of servitude is over,
her iniquity has been pardoned,
and she has received from the LORD's hand
double for all her sins.

3 A voice of one crying out:

Prepare the way of the LORD in the wilderness;
make a straight highway for our God
in the desert.
4 Every valley will be lifted up,
and every mountain and hill will be leveled;
the uneven ground will become smooth,
and the rough places a plain.
5 And the glory of the LORD will appear,
and all humanity[b] will see [it] together,
for the mouth of the LORD has spoken.

6 A voice was saying, "Cry out!"
Another[c] said, "What should I cry out?"
"All humanity is grass,
and all its goodness is like the flower of the field.
7 The grass withers, the flowers fade
when the breath[d] of the LORD blows on them;[e]
indeed, the people are grass.
8 The grass withers, the flowers fade,
but the word of our God remains forever."

9 Zion, herald of good news,
go up on a high mountain.
Jerusalem, herald of good news,
raise your voice loudly.
Raise it, do not be afraid!
Say to the cities of Judah,
"Here is your God!"
10 See, the Lord GOD comes with strength,
and His power establishes His rule.

His reward is with Him,
and His gifts accompany Him.
11 He protects His flock like a shepherd;
He gathers the lambs in His arms
and carries [them] in the fold of His [garment].
He gently leads those that are nursing.

12 Who has measured the waters in the hollow
of his hand
or marked off the heavens with the span
[of his hand]?
Who has gathered the dust of the earth
in a measure
or weighed the mountains in a balance
and the hills in scales?
13 Who has directed[f] the Spirit of the LORD,
or who gave Him His counsel?
14 Who did He consult with?
Who gave Him understanding
and taught Him the paths of justice?
Who taught Him knowledge
and showed Him the way of understanding?
15 Look, the nations are like a drop in a bucket;
they are considered as a speck of dust
on the scales;
He lifts up the islands like fine dust.
16 Lebanon is not enough for fuel,
or its animals enough for a •burnt offering.
17 All the nations are as nothing before Him;
they are considered by Him
as nothingness and emptiness.

18 Who will you compare God with?
What likeness will you compare Him to?
19 To an idol?—[something that] a smelter casts,
and a metalworker plates with gold
and makes silver welds [for it]?
20 To one who shapes a pedestal,
choosing wood that does not rot?[g]
He looks for a skilled craftsman
to set up an idol that will not fall over.

21 Do you not know?
Have you not heard?
Has it not been declared to you
from the beginning?
Have you not considered
the foundations of the earth?
22 God is enthroned above the circle of the earth;
its inhabitants are like grasshoppers.
He stretches out the heavens like thin cloth

---

a **40:2** Lit *Speak to the heart of* b **40:5** Lit *flesh* c **40:6** DSS, LXX, Vg read *I* d **40:7** Or *wind*, or *Spirit* e **40:7** Lit *it* f **40:13** Or *measured*, or *comprehended* g **40:20** Or *who is too poor for such an offering*, or *who chooses mulberry wood as a votive gift*; Hb obscure

---

40:2 Jerusalem. That is, the exiles who would return there. **double for all her sins.** God had punished Israel enough in the exile and was ready to restore her.

40:3 voice of one crying out. Each Gospel writer applied this verse to John the Baptist who prepared the way for Jesus Christ (see

Matt. 3:1-4; Mark 1:1-4; Luke 1:76-78; John 1:23). **a straight highway.** The image is of a highway through the desert, leading people straight back from Assyria and Babylon to Israel.

40:5 the glory of the LORD. When God restores Israel, the world will see His glory.

40:17 nothingness. This word is translated "formless" in Genesis 1:2.

40:27 Jacob ... Israel. That is, all 12 tribes. God's people should never think He does not see or remember them or fail to keep His promises.

40:31 trust in the LORD. Implies confident

and spreads them out like a tent to live in.
23 He reduces princes to nothing
and makes the judges of the earth
to be irrational.
24 They are barely planted, barely sown,
their stem hardly takes root in the ground
when He blows on them and they wither,
and a whirlwind carries them away like stubble.

The Source of All Strength

1. Who is the strongest person you know? The smartest?

Isaiah 40:25-31

2. What does it mean in verse 26 that God "brings out the starry host by number"? That "He calls all of them by name"? That "not one of them is missing"?
3. When have you wanted to say, "My way is hidden from the Lord, and my claim is ignored by my God" (v. 27)?
4. Are you feeling powerless right now? How can God strengthen you for an event or performance ahead?
5. Do you feel that God is ignoring you? How can He show you His great understanding?

25 "Who will you compare Me to,
or who is My equal?" asks the Holy One.
26 Look up[a] and see:
who created these?
He brings out the starry host by number;
He calls all of them by name.
Because of His great power and strength,
not one of them is missing.

27 Jacob, why do you say,
and Israel, why do you assert:
"My way is hidden from the LORD,
and my claim is ignored by my God"?
28 Do you not know?
Have you not heard?
•Yahweh is the everlasting God,
the Creator of the whole earth.
He never grows faint or weary;
there is no limit to His understanding.

29 He gives strength to the weary
and strengthens the powerless.
30 Youths may faint and grow weary,
and young men stumble and fall,
31 but those who trust in the LORD
will renew their strength;
they will soar on wings like eagles;
they will run and not grow weary;
they will walk and not faint.

The LORD versus the Nations' Gods

41 "Be silent before Me, islands!
And let peoples renew their strength.
Let them approach, then let them testify;
let us come together for the trial.
2 Who has stirred him up from the east?
He calls righteousness to his feet.[b]
The LORD[c] hands nations over to him,
and he subdues kings.
He makes ⌊them⌋ like dust ⌊with⌋ his sword,
like wind-driven stubble ⌊with⌋ his bow.
3 He pursues them, going on safely,
hardly touching the path with his feet.
4 Who has performed and done ⌊this⌋,
calling the generations from the beginning?
I, the LORD, am the first,
and with the last—I am He."

5 The islands see and are afraid,
the ends of the earth tremble.
They approach and arrive.
6 Each one helps the other,
and says to another, "Take courage!"
7 The craftsman encourages the metalworker;
the one who flattens with the hammer
⌊supports⌋ the one who strikes the anvil,
saying of the soldering, "It is good."
He fastens it with nails so that it will not fall over.

8 But you, Israel, My servant,
Jacob, whom I have chosen,
descendant of Abraham, My friend—
9 I brought[d] you from the ends of the earth
and called you from its farthest corners.
I said to you: You are My servant;
I have chosen you and not rejected you.
10 Do not fear, for I am with you;
do not be afraid, for I am your God.
I will strengthen you; I will help you;
I will hold on to you with My righteous
right hand.

---

[a] **40:26** Lit *Lift up your eyes on high*   [b] **41:2** Hb obscure   [c] **41:2** Lit *He*   [d] **41:9** Or *seized*

---

expectation rather than passive resignation (see Ps. 40:1). Faith brings spiritual transformation. Weary captives returning from the exile would be emotionally uplifted.

41:1 peoples renew their strength. This phrase contrasts the strength resulting from faith in God with mere human strength. The is-

lands and nations refer all the world's peoples whom God invites to come.

41:2 from the east. Cyrus, king of Persia from 559–530 B.C. **calls righteousness.** Because of God's promise to Abraham, He brought the exiles back. Cyrus was to carry out God's righteous plan, fulfilling God's will, even if he

was unaware of it.

41:14 Your Redeemer. Isaiah used this title for God 13 times. The redeemer was the family protector who helped distressed relatives, avenged murders, and reclaimed indentured slaves.

41:19 cedars in the desert. In the millennial

11 Be sure that all who are enraged against you
will be ashamed and disgraced;
those who contend with you
will become as nothing and will perish.
12 You will look for those who contend with you,
but you will not find them.
Those who war against you
will become absolutely nothing.
13 For I, the LORD your God,
hold your right hand
and say to you: Do not fear,
I will help you.
14 Do not fear, you worm Jacob,
you men[a] of Israel:
I will help you—
the LORD's declaration.
Your Redeemer is the Holy One of Israel.
15 See, I will make you
into a sharp threshing board,
new, with many teeth.
You will thresh mountains and pulverize ⌊them⌋,
and make hills like chaff.
16 You will winnow them
and a wind will carry them away,
and a gale will scatter them.
But you will rejoice in the LORD;
you will boast in the Holy One of Israel.

17 The poor and the needy seek water,
but there is none;
their tongues are parched with thirst.
I, the LORD, will answer them;
I, the God of Israel, do not forsake them.
18 I will open rivers on the barren heights,
and springs in the middle of the plains.
I will turn the desert into a pool of water
and dry land into springs of water.
19 I will plant cedars in the desert,
acacias, myrtles, and olive trees.
I will put cypress trees in the desert,
elms and box trees together,
20 so that all may see and know,
consider and understand,
that the hand of the LORD has done this,
the Holy One of Israel has created it.

21 "Submit your case," says the LORD.
"Present your arguments," says Jacob's King.
22 "Let them come and tell us
what will happen.

Tell us the past events,
so that we may reflect on it
and know the outcome.
Or tell us the future.
23 Tell us the coming events,
then we will know that you are gods.
Indeed, do ⌊something⌋ good or bad,
then we will be in awe[b] and perceive.
24 Look, you are nothing
and your work is worthless.
Anyone who chooses you is detestable.

25 "I have raised up one from the north,
and he has come,
one from the east who invokes My[c] name.
He will march over rulers as if they were mud,
like a potter who treads the clay.
26 Who told about this from the beginning,
so that we might know,
and from times past,
so that we might say: He is right?
No one announced it,
no one told it,
no one heard your words.
27 I was the first to say to Zion:[d]
Look! Here they are!
and I gave a herald of good news to Jerusalem.
28 When I look, there is no one;
there is no counselor among them;
when I ask them, they have nothing to say.
29 Look, all of them are a delusion;[e]
their works are nonexistent;
their images are wind and emptiness.

The Servant's Mission

42 "This is My Servant; I strengthen Him,
⌊this is⌋ My Chosen One; I delight in Him.
I have put My Spirit on Him;
He will bring justice[f] to the nations.
2 He will not cry out or shout
or make His voice heard in the streets.
3 He will not break a bruised reed,
and He will not put out a smoldering wick;
He will faithfully bring justice.
4 He will not grow weak or be discouraged
until He has established justice on earth.
The islands will wait for His instruction."

5 This is what God the LORD says—
who created the heavens and stretched
them out,

[a]**41:14** MT; LXX reads *small number*; DSS read *dead ones*   [b]**41:23** DSS read *we may hear*   [c]**41:25** DSS read *his*   [d]**41:27** Lit *First to Zion*
[e]**41:29** DSS, Syr read *are nothing*   [f]**42:1** DSS read *His justice*

kingdom, the climate will be changed so that even the desert is fertile.
41:20 Holy One of Israel has created it. Only God can truly create.
41:25 one from the north. This refers to King Cyrus of Persia whose territories were both to the north and east of Israel. **invokes My name.** Although Cyrus did not know God, he called on God's name (2 Chron. 36:23).
42:1 My Servant ... strengthen. Jesus Christ will bring universal justice and peace in the millennium. These verses are quoted in Matt. 12:15-21.
42:3 bruised reed. The promise points to Christ who will be gentle to those who are hurting, poor, and needy. **smoldering wick.** People who have nearly lost their faith in God. Jesus will restore their hope.
42:13 warrior. God will be a conquering warrior on behalf of His people, just as He was when He fought for them at the Red Sea (Ex. 15:3).

who spread out the earth and what comes
  from it,
who gives breath to the people on it
and life[a] to those who walk on it—

6 "I, the LORD, have called you
  for a righteous ⌊purpose⌋,[b]
  and I will hold you by your hand.
  I will keep you, and I make you
  a covenant for the people
  ⌊and⌋ a light to the nations,

7 in order to open blind eyes,
  to bring out prisoners from the dungeon,
  ⌊and⌋ those sitting in darkness
    from the prison house.

8 I am •Yahweh, that is My name;
  I will not give My glory to another,
  or My praise to idols.

9 The past events have indeed happened.
  Now I declare new events;
  I announce them to you before they occur."

A Song of Praise

10 Sing a new song to the LORD;
  ⌊sing⌋ His praise from the ends of the earth,
  you who go down to the sea with all that fills it,
  you islands with your[c] inhabitants.

11 Let the desert and its cities shout,
  the settlements where Kedar dwells ⌊cry aloud⌋.
  Let the inhabitants of Sela sing for joy;
  let them cry out from the mountaintops.

12 Let them give glory to the LORD,
  and declare His praise in the islands.

13 The LORD advances like a warrior;
  He stirs up His zeal like a soldier.
  He shouts, He roars aloud,
  He prevails over His enemies.

14 "I have kept silent from ages past;
  I have been quiet and restrained Myself.
  ⌊But now,⌋ I will groan like a woman in labor,
  gasping breathlessly.

15 I will lay waste mountains and hills,
  and dry up all their vegetation.
  I will turn rivers into islands,
  and dry up marshes.

16 I will lead the blind by a way they did not know;
  I will guide them on paths they have not known.
  I will turn darkness to light in front of them,
  and rough places into level ground.
  This is what I will do for them,

and I will not forsake them.

17 They will be turned back ⌊and⌋ utterly ashamed—
  those who trust in idols
  and say to metal-plated images:
  You are our gods!

Israel's Blindness and Deafness

18 "Listen, you deaf!
  Look, you blind, so that you may see.

19 Who is blind but My servant,
  or deaf like My messenger I am sending?
  Who is blind like ⌊My⌋ dedicated one,[d]
  or blind like the servant of the LORD?

20 Though seeing many things,[e] you do not obey.
  Though ⌊his⌋ ears are open, he does not listen."

21 The LORD was pleased, because of
    His righteousness,
  to magnify ⌊His⌋ instruction and make it glorious.

22 But this is a people plundered and looted,
  all of them trapped in holes
  or imprisoned in dungeons.
  They have become plunder,
  with no one to rescue them,
  and loot, with no one saying "Give ⌊it⌋ back!"

23 Who among you will pay attention to this?
  Let him listen and obey in the future.

24 Who gave Jacob to the robber,[f]
  and Israel to the plunderers?
  Was it not the LORD?
  Have we not sinned against Him?
  They were not willing to walk in His ways,
  and they would not listen to His instruction.

25 So He poured out on Jacob His furious anger
  and the power of war.
  It surrounded him with fire, but he did not
    know ⌊it⌋;
  it burned him, but he paid no attention.[g]

Restoration of Israel

43 Now this is what the LORD says—
  the One who created you, Jacob,
  and the One who formed you, Israel—
  "Do not fear, for I have redeemed you;
  I have called you by your name; you are Mine.

2 I will be with you
  when you pass through the waters,
  and ⌊when you pass⌋ through the rivers,
  they will not overwhelm you.
  You will not be scorched
  when you walk through the fire,

---

[a] 42:5 Lit spirit [b] 42:6 Or you by [My] righteousness; lit you in righteousness [c] 42:10 Lit their [d] 42:19 Hb obscure [e] 42:20 Alt Hb tradition reads
You see many things; [f] 42:24 Lit to loot [g] 42:25 Lit he did not put on heart

---

42:15 mountains and hills. Obstacles that could prevent Israel's return to Jerusalem. **dry up.** Recalled the passage through the Red Sea on dry land (Ex. 14:16-29). God can cause land to become barren.

42:24 Who gave Jacob to the robber. Since Israel was blind to her sin, God allowed her to

be plundered and taken into captivity. The Messiah will open the people's eyes to their sin and to God's salvation.

42:25 poured out ... furious anger. God's anger against sin would destroy Jerusalem with flames; God's people already had a taste of His wrath (2 Kings 25:9; Jer. 10:25).

43:3 your Savior. The name Jesus is derived from the Hebrew word for Savior. Israel is precious because of God's love and protection, because God chose to favor this people. **Egypt ... Cush ... Seba.** To reward Cyrus for releasing the Jewish captives, God allowed Persia to conquer these lands. Cush con-

and the flame will not burn you.
3 For I the LORD your God,
the Holy One of Israel, and your Savior,
give Egypt as a ransom for you,
•Cush and Seba in your place.
4 Because you are precious in My sight
and honored, and I love you,
I will give human beings in your place,
and peoples in place of your life.
5 Do not fear, for I am with you;
I will bring your descendants from the east,
and gather you from the west.
6 I will say to the north: Give ⌊them⌋ up!
and to the south: Do not hold ⌊them⌋ back!
Bring My sons from far away,
and My daughters from the ends of the earth—
7 everyone called by My name
and created for My glory.
I have formed him; indeed, I have made him."

8 Bring out a people who are blind, yet have eyes,
and are deaf, yet have ears.
9 All the nations are gathered together,
and the peoples are assembled.
Who among them can declare this,
and tell us the former things?
Let them present their witnesses
to vindicate ⌊themselves⌋,
so that people may hear and say, "It is true."
10 "You are My witnesses"—
the LORD's declaration—
"and My servant whom I have chosen,
so that you may know and believe Me
and understand that I am He.
No god was formed before Me,
and there will be none after Me.
11 I, I am the LORD,
and there is no other Savior but Me.
12 I alone declared, saved, and proclaimed—
and not some foreign god[a] among you.
So you are My witnesses"—
the LORD's declaration—
"and[b] I am God.
13 Also, from today on I am He ⌊alone⌋,
and no one can take ⌊anything⌋ from My hand.
I act, and who can reverse it?"

God's Deliverance of Rebellious Israel

14 This is what the LORD, your Redeemer, the Holy
One of Israel says:

Because of you, I will send to Babylon
and bring all of them as fugitives,[c]
even the Chaldeans in the ships in which
they rejoice.[d]
15 I am the LORD, your Holy One,
the Creator of Israel, your King.

16 This is what the LORD says—
who makes a way in the sea,
and a path through surging waters,
17 who brings out the chariot and horse,
the army and the mighty one together
(they lie down, they do not rise again;
they are extinguished, quenched like a wick)—
18 "Do not remember the past events,
pay no attention to things of old.
19 Look, I am about to do something new;
even now it is coming. Do you not see it?
Indeed, I will make a way in the wilderness,
rivers[e] in the desert.
20 The animals of the field will honor Me,
jackals and ostriches,
because I provide water in the wilderness,
and rivers in the desert,
to give drink to My chosen people.
21 The people I formed for Myself
will declare My praise.

22 "But Jacob, you have not called on Me,
because, Israel, you have become weary of Me.
23 You have not brought Me your sheep
for •burnt offerings
or honored Me with your sacrifices.
I have not burdened you with offerings
or wearied you with incense.[f]
24 You have not bought Me aromatic cane
with silver,
or satisfied Me with the fat of your sacrifices.
But you have burdened Me with your sins;
you have wearied Me with your iniquities.

25 "It is I who sweep away your transgressions
for My own sake
and remember your sins no more.
26 Take Me to court; let us argue our case together.
State your ⌊case⌋, so that you may be vindicated.
27 Your first father sinned,
and your mediators have rebelled against Me.
28 So I defiled the officers of the sanctuary,
and gave Jacob over to total destruction
and Israel to abuse.

a43:12 Lit not a foreigner b43:12 Or that c43:14 Or will break down all their bars d43:14 Hb obscure e43:19 DSS read paths f43:23 With demands for offerings and incense

sisted of modern-day Sudan, southern Egypt and northern Ethiopia. Seba may be Sheba in southern Arabia.

43:14 bring all of them as fugitives ... in the ships. God would turn the Babylonians into conquered people, rather than conquerors (see Jer. 51:1-44). The ships may have been

trading vessels.

43:20 jackals and ostriches. Although Israel would travel through desolate areas on the way back to Jerusalem, God would provide refreshment even in the desert.

43:22 not called ... become weary. The people had worshiped God only halfheart-

edly without troubling themselves with the sacrificial system God required.

43:25 for My own sake. Through grace God loves people even though we do not deserve it.

44:1 Jacob My servant. Many times in Isaiah, "servant" refers to Israel. Other times it re-

Spiritual Blessing

44 "And now listen, Jacob My servant,
Israel whom I have chosen.
2 This is the word of the LORD
your Maker who shaped you from birth;
He[a] will help you:
Do not fear; Jacob is My servant;
I have chosen Jeshurun.
3 For I will pour water on the thirsty land,
and streams on the dry ground;
I will pour out My Spirit on your descendants
and My blessing on your offspring.
4 They will sprout among[b] the grass
like poplars by the streambeds.
5 This one will say: I am the LORD's;
another will call ⌊himself⌋ by the name of Jacob;
still another will write on his hand: The LORD's,
and name ⌊himself⌋ by the name of Israel."

No God Other Than Yahweh

6 This is what the LORD, the King of Israel and its Redeemer, the LORD of •Hosts, says:

I am the first and I am the last.
There is no God but Me.
7 Who, like Me, can announce ⌊the future⌋?
Let him say so and make a case before Me,
since I have established an ancient people.
Let these gods declare[c] the coming things,
and what will take place.
8 Do not be startled or afraid.
Have I not told you and declared it long ago?
You are my witnesses!
Is there any God but Me?
There is no ⌊other⌋ Rock; I do not know any.

9 All who make idols are nothing,
and what they treasure does not profit.
Their witnesses do not see or know ⌊anything⌋,
so they will be put to shame.
10 Who makes a god or casts a metal image
for no profit?
11 Look, all its worshipers will be put to shame,
and the craftsmen are humans.
They all will assemble and stand;
they all will be startled and put to shame.

12 The ironworker labors over the coals,
shapes the idol with hammers,
and works it with his strong arm.

Also he grows hungry and his strength fails;
he doesn't drink water and is faint.
13 The woodworker stretches out a measuring line,
he outlines it with a stylus;
he shapes it with chisels
and outlines it with a compass.
He makes it according to a human likeness,
like a beautiful person,
to dwell in a temple.
14 He cuts down[d] cedars for his use,
or he takes a cypress[e] or an oak.
He lets it grow strong among the trees
of the forest.
He plants a laurel, and the rain makes it grow.
15 It serves as fuel for man.
He takes some of it and warms himself;
also he kindles a fire and bakes bread;
he even makes it into a god and worships it;
he makes it an idol and bows down to it.
16 He burns half of it in a fire,
and he roasts meat on that half.
He eats the roast and is satisfied.
He warms himself and says, "Ah!
I am warm, I see the blaze."
17 He makes a god or his idol with the rest of it.
He bows down to it and worships;
He prays to it, "Save me, for you are my god."
18 Such people[f] do not comprehend
and cannot understand,
for He has shut their eyes[g] so they cannot see,
and their minds so they cannot understand.
19 No one reflects,
no one has the perception or insight to say,
"I burned half of it in the fire,
I also baked bread on its coals,
I roasted meat and ate.
I will make something detestable with the rest
of it,
and I will bow down to a block of wood."
20 He feeds on[h] ashes.
⌊His⌋ deceived mind has led him astray,
and he cannot deliver himself,
or say, "Isn't there a lie in my right hand?"

21 Remember these things, Jacob,
and Israel, for you are My servant;
I formed you, you are My servant;
Israel, you will never be forgotten by Me.[i]

---

[a]44:2 Lit *from the womb, and He* [b]44:4 DSS, LXX, a few Hb mss read *as among* [c]44:7 Lit *declare them—* [d]44:14 Lit *To cut down for himself*
[e]44:14 Exact type of tree uncertain [f]44:18 Lit *They* [g]44:18 Or *for their eyes are shut* [h]44:20 Or *He shepherds* [i]44:21 DSS, LXX, Tg read *Israel, do not forget Me*

---

fers to the Messiah. There is a relationship: Jesus the Messiah fulfills Israel's calling, living as Israel was supposed to as God's servant.

44:4 sprout among the grass. A symbol of prosperity. When the Messiah comes, God will pour water on the land and pour His Holy Spirit on the people.

44:5 I am the LORD's. Israel will want to be known as the Lord's obedient people. **write on his hand.** Signified ownership.

44:6 first ... last. God is sovereign over time, and He is eternal.

44:9 nothing ... does not profit. This warn-

ing to future generations condemned idolatry and noted the foolishness of worshiping a stone or metal image.

44:17 you are my god. The idolater prayed to an inanimate object incapable of helping him. Anything that comes before God in a person's life is an idol.

22 I have swept away your transgressions
    like a cloud,
and your sins like a mist.
Return to Me,
for I have redeemed you.
23 Rejoice, heavens, for the LORD has acted;
shout, depths of the earth.
Break out into singing, mountains,
forest, and every tree in it.
For the LORD has redeemed Jacob,
and glorifies Himself through Israel.

Restoration of Israel through Cyrus

24 This is what the LORD, your Redeemer who
formed you from the womb, says:

I am the LORD, who made everything;
who stretched out the heavens by Myself;
who alone spread out the earth;
25 who destroys the omens
    of the false prophets
and makes fools of diviners;
who confounds the wise
and makes their knowledge foolishness;
26 who confirms the message of His servant
and fulfills the counsel of His messengers;
who says to Jerusalem: She will be inhabited,
and to the cities of Judah: They will be rebuilt,
and I will restore her ruins;
27 who says to the depths of the sea: Be dry,
and I will dry up your rivers;
28 who says to Cyrus: My shepherd,
he will fulfill all My pleasure
and say to Jerusalem: She will be rebuilt,
and of the temple: Its foundation will be laid.

45 The LORD says this to Cyrus, His anointed,
    whose right hand I have grasped
to subdue nations before him,
to unloose the loins[a] of kings,
to open the doors before him
and the gates will not be shut:
2 "I will go before you
and level the uneven places;[b]
I will shatter the bronze doors
and cut the iron bars in two.
3 I will give you the treasures of darkness
and riches from secret places,
so that you may know that I, the LORD,
the God of Israel call you by your name.

4 I call you by your name,
because of Jacob My servant
and Israel My chosen one.
I give a name to you,
though you do not know Me.
5 I am the LORD, and there is no other;
there is no God but Me.
I will strengthen[c] you,
though you do not know Me,
6 so that all may know from the rising of the sun
    to its setting
that there is no one but Me.
I am the LORD, and there is no other.
7 I form light and create darkness,
I make success and create disaster;
I, the LORD, do all these things.

8 "Heavens, sprinkle from above,
and let the skies shower righteousness.
Let the earth open up
that salvation sprout
and righteousness spring up with it.
I, the LORD, have created it.

9 "Woe to the one who argues
    with his Maker—
one clay pot among many.[d]
Does clay say to the one forming it:
What are you making?
Or does your work [say]:
He has no hands?[e]
10 How absurd is the one who says to [his] father:
What are you fathering?
or to [his] mother:
What are you giving birth to?"
11 This is what the LORD,
the Holy One of Israel and its Maker, says:
"Ask Me what is to happen to[f] My sons,
and instruct Me about the work of My hands.
12 I made the earth,
and created man on it.
It was My hands that stretched out the heavens,
and I commanded all their host.
13 I have raised him up in righteousness,
and will level all roads for him.
He will rebuild My city,
and set My exiles free,
not for a price or a bribe,"
says the LORD of •Hosts.

---

a**45:1** To gird *the loins* is to prepare for battle (2 Sm 20:8), so to *unloose* them is to surrender.   b**45:2** DSS, LXX read *the mountains*   c**45:5** Lit *gird*
d**45:9** Lit *a clay pot with clay pots of the ground*   e**45:9** Or . . . *making? Your work has no hands* (or *handles*).   f**45:11** Or *Me the coming things about*

44:22 swept away your transgressions like a cloud. God offers total forgiveness (40:2; 43:25). Israel's punishment made forgiveness and restoration possible. **redeemed.** God will buy back His people.

44:27 depths of the sea. The sea was deemed chaotic and fearful. In pagan myth,

the sea was a force of evil. Yet God has power over the sea while Babylon's gods are non-existent.

45:1 His anointed. Hebrew *messiah*. Anointing was a ceremony of pouring fragrant oil over a king or priest being appointed. Cyrus is not the Messiah, but a messiah, one

anointed by God for an important task. As the Persian king (who lived over 200 years after Isaiah), he would decree Israel's freedom to return from exile.

45:9 clay pot. The thing created by another has no right to question its creator (see Jer. 18:6).

God Alone is the Savior

14 This is what the LORD says:

The products of Egypt and the merchandise
  of •Cush
and the Sabeans, men of stature,
will come over to you
and will be yours;
they will follow you,
they will come over in chains;
and bow down to you.
They will confess[a] to you:
God is indeed with you, and there is no other;
there is no other God.

15 Yes, You are a God who hides Himself,
God of Israel, Savior.

16 All of them are put to shame, even humiliated;
the makers of idols go in humiliation together.

17 Israel will be saved by the LORD
with an everlasting salvation;
you will not be put to shame or humiliated
for all eternity.

18 For this is what the LORD says—
God is the Creator of the heavens.
He formed the earth and made it;
He established it;
He did not create it to be empty,
⌊but⌋ formed it to be inhabited—
"I am the LORD,
and there is no other.

19 I have not spoken in secret,
somewhere in a land of darkness.
I did not say to the descendants of Jacob:
Seek Me in a wasteland.
I, the LORD, speak truthfully;
I say what is right.

20 "Come, gather together,
and draw near, you fugitives of the nations.
Those who carry their wooden idols,
and pray to a god who cannot save,
have no knowledge.

21 Speak up and present ⌊your case⌋[b] —
yes, let them take counsel together.
Who predicted this long ago?
Who announced it from ancient times?
Was it not I, the LORD?
There is no other God but Me,
a righteous God and Savior;
there is no one except Me.

22 Turn to Me and be saved,
all the ends of the earth.
For I am God,
and there is no other.

23 By Myself I have sworn;[c]
Truth has gone from My mouth,
a word that will not be revoked:
Every knee will bow to Me,
every tongue will swear allegiance.

24 It will be said to Me: Only in the LORD
is righteousness and strength."
All who are incensed against Him
will come to Him and be put to shame.

25 All the descendants of Israel
will be justified and find glory through the LORD.

There is No One Like God

46 Bel crouches; Nebo cowers.
Their idols are consigned to beasts and cattle.
The ⌊images⌋ you carry are loaded,
as a burden for the weary ⌊animal⌋.

2 The gods cower; they crouch together;
they are not able to rescue the burden,
but they themselves go into captivity.

3 "Listen to Me, house of Jacob,
all the remnant of the house of Israel,
who have been sustained from the womb,
carried along since birth.

4 I will be the same until ⌊your⌋ old age,
and I will bear ⌊you⌋ up when you turn gray.
I have made ⌊you⌋, and I will carry ⌊you⌋;
I will bear and save ⌊you⌋.

5 "Who will you compare Me or make Me
  equal to?
Who will you measure Me with,
so that we should be like each other?

6 Those who pour out their bags of gold
and weigh out silver on scales—
they hire a goldsmith and he makes it
  into a god.
Then they kneel and bow down to it.

7 They lift it to their shoulder and bear it along;
they set it in its place, and there it stands;
it does not budge from its place.
They cry out to it but it doesn't answer;
it saves no one from his trouble.

8 "Remember this and be brave;[d]
take it to heart, you transgressors!

9 Remember what happened long ago,

---

[a] 45:14 Lit pray [b] 45:21 Lit and approach [c] 45:23 God takes an oath based on His own character. [d] 46:8 Hb obscure

---

45:14 come over to you … bow down. People from Egypt and Cush would acknowledge the God of Israel as Lord and would bow down to Israel. They would submit to God's truth and worship Him (1 Cor. 14:25).

45:15 a God who hides Himself. Although it seems as if God is hiding and unavailable as a result of human sin, God is in fact present as the Scriptures tell (Ps. 44:24). The hand of God is not always apparent.

45:24 All who are incensed against Him. Everyone is invited by God to repent of sin, yet many will continue to angrily oppose Him. These people will have no part in His eternal kingdom.

46:2 they themselves go into captivity. The idols were heavy burdens to carry around, and they could not help the Babylonians escape defeat. Instead, they were carried off into captivity along with the people.

46:12 Listen … hardhearted. God is calling

for I am God, and there is no other;
[I am] God, and no one is like Me.

10 I declare the end from the beginning,
and from long ago what is not yet done,
saying: My plan will take place,
and I will do all My will.

11 I call a bird of prey[a] from the east,
a man for My purpose from a far country.
Yes, I have spoken; so I will also bring it about.
I have planned it; I will also do it.

12 Listen to me, you hardhearted,
far removed from justice:

13 I am bringing My justice near;
it is not far away,
and My salvation will not delay.
I will put salvation in Zion,
My splendor in Israel.

The Fall of Babylon

47 "Go down and sit in the dust,
Virgin Daughter Babylon.
Sit on the ground without a throne,
Daughter Chaldea!
For you will no longer be called pampered
and spoiled.

2 Take millstones and grind meal;
remove your veil,
strip off [your] skirt, bare your thigh,
wade through the streams.

3 Your nakedness will be uncovered,
and your shame will be exposed.
I will take vengeance;
I will spare no one.[b]

4 The Holy One of Israel is our Redeemer;
the LORD of •Hosts is His name.

5 "Daughter Chaldea,
sit in silence and go into darkness.
For you will no longer be called mistress
of kingdoms.

6 I was angry with My people;
I profaned My possession,
and I placed them under your control.
You showed them no mercy;
you made your yoke very heavy on the elderly.

7 You said: I will be the mistress forever.
You did not take these things to heart
or think about their outcome.

8 "So now hear this, lover of luxury,
who sits securely,

who says to herself:
I, and no one else,
will never be a widow
or know the loss of children.

9 These two things will happen to you
suddenly, in one day:
loss of children and widowhood.
They will happen to you in their entirety,
in spite of your many sorceries
and the potency of your spells.

10 You were secure in your wickedness;
you said: No one sees me.
Your wisdom and knowledge
led you astray.
You said to yourself:
I, and no one else.

11 But disaster will happen to you;
you will not know how to avert it.
And it will fall on you,
but you will be unable to ward it off.[c]
Devastation will happen to you suddenly
and unexpectedly.

12 So take your stand with your spells
and your many sorceries,
which you have wearied yourself with
from your youth.
Perhaps you will be able to succeed;
perhaps you will inspire terror!

13 You are worn out
with your many consultations.
So let them stand and save you—
the astrologers,[d] who observe the stars,
who predict monthly
what will happen to you.

14 Look, they are like stubble;
fire burns them up.
They cannot deliver themselves
from the power[e] of the flame.
This is not a coal for warming themselves,
or a fire to sit beside!

15 This is what they are to you—
those who have wearied you
and have traded with you
from your youth—
each wanders on his own way;
no one can save you.

Israel Must Leave Babylon

48 "Listen to this, house of Jacob—
those who are called by the name Israel

---

[a]46:11 = Cyrus; Is 41:2-3; 44:28—45:1 [b]47:3 Hb obscure [c]47:11 Or to atone for it [d]47:13 Lit dividers of the heavens [e]47:14 Lit hand

---

Israel to repent of their sin by telling them the great things He will do for them in the future.
47:3 nakedness. Indicated disgrace, vulnerability, and impropriety (Gen. 9:22-23). Babylon will be humbled and shamed. She will be like a prostitute caught in the act.
47:9 loss of children and widowhood.

Boastful Babylon believed she would never be defeated. But God would judge her, causing desolation in a single day.
47:10 wickedness ... wisdom ... knowledge. The leaders of Babylon believed they would rule forever. Babylon's religions included sorcery and magic, practices forbid-

den by God (8:19; 44:24-25).
47:14 cannot deliver themselves. Astrologers could not save Babylon any more than idols could. Some idols were carved out of firewood.
47:15 traded with you from your youth. Referred to the merchants whose trade made

and have descended from[a] Judah,
who swear by the name of the LORD
and declare the God of Israel,
[but] not in truth or righteousness.
2 For they are named after the Holy City,
and lean on the God of Israel;
His name is •Yahweh of •Hosts.
3 I declared the past events long ago;
they came out of My mouth; I proclaimed them.
Suddenly I acted, and they occurred.
4 Because I know that you are stubborn,
and your neck is iron[b]
and your forehead bronze,
5 therefore I declared to you long ago;
I announced it to you before it occurred,
so you could not claim: My idol caused them;
my carved image and cast idol control them.
6 You have heard it. Observe it all.
Will you not acknowledge it?
From now on I will announce new things to you,
hidden things that you have not known.
7 They have been created now, and not long ago;
you have not heard of them before today,
so you could not claim, "I already knew them!"
8 You have never heard; you have never known;
For a long time your ears have not been open.
For I knew that you were very treacherous,
and were known as a rebel from birth.
9 I will delay My anger for the honor of My name,
and I will restrain Myself for your benefit
and [for] My praise,
so that you will not be destroyed.
10 Look, I have refined you, but not as silver;
I have tested[c] you in the furnace of affliction.
11 I will act for My own sake, indeed, My own,
for how can I[d] be defiled?
I will not give My glory to another.
12 "Listen to Me, Jacob,
and Israel, the one called by Me:
I am He; I am the first,
I am also the last.
13 My own hand founded the earth,
and My right hand spread out the heavens;
when I summoned them,
they stood up together.
14 All of you, assemble and listen!
Who among the idols[e] has declared
these things?

The LORD loves him;[f]
he will accomplish His will against Babylon,
and His arm [will be against] the Chaldeans.
15 I—I have spoken;
yes, I have called him;
I have brought him,
and he will succeed in his mission.
16 Approach Me and listen to this.
From the beginning I have not spoken in secret;
from the time anything existed, I was there."
And now the Lord GOD
has sent me and His Spirit.

17 This is what the LORD, your Redeemer, the Holy One of Israel says:

I am the LORD your God,
who teaches you for [your] benefit,
who leads you in the way you should go.
18 If only you had paid attention to My commands.
Then your peace would have been like a river,
and your righteousness like the waves
of the sea.
19 Your descendants would have been
as [countless] as the sand,
and the offspring of your body like its grains;
their name would not be cut off
or eliminated from My presence.

20 Leave Babylon,
flee from the Chaldeans!
Declare with a shout of joy,
proclaim this,
let it go out to the end of the earth;
announce,
"The LORD has redeemed His servant Jacob!"
21 They did not thirst
when He led them through the deserts;
He made water flow for them from the rock;
He split the rock, and water gushed out.
22 "There is no peace," says the LORD,
"for the wicked."

The Servant Brings Salvation

49 Coastlands,[g] listen to me;
distant peoples, pay attention.
The LORD called me before I was born.
He named me while I was
in my mother's womb.
2 He made my words like a sharp sword;
He hid me in the shadow of His hand.

[a]48:1 Lit have come from the waters of [b]48:4 Lit is an iron sinew [c]48:10 Or chosen [d]48:11 DSS, Syr; MT reads it [e]48:14 Lit among them
[f]48:14 Cyrus [g]49:1 Or Islands

Babylon wealthy.
48:6 announce new things. The new things included Cyrus' activities, the fall of Babylon, and Israel's restoration. The new era of God's kingdom that the Messiah would usher in is also in view here.
48:10 furnace of affliction. The captivity in

Babylon purified the people like gold and silver are refined in high heat.
48:16 Lord GOD has sent me and His Spirit. Just as God helped Cyrus accomplish his task, the Messiah, with the Holy Spirit on Him, will accomplish God's mission.
48:18 peace ... like a river. The Israelites

could have avoided captivity by obeying God's law (Ps. 81:11-16).
48:21 made water flow for them from the rock. After the Hebrews left Egypt, God provided water in the desert out of a rock (Ex. 17:1-7). God would provide for them as they left Babylon too.

He made me like a sharpened arrow;
He hid me in His quiver.
3 He said to me, "You are My servant, Israel;
I will be glorified in him."
4 But I myself said: I have labored in vain,
I have spent my strength for nothing and futility;
yet my vindication is with the LORD,
and my reward is with my God.
5 And now, says the LORD,
who formed me from the womb to be
His servant,
to bring Jacob back to Him
so that Israel might be gathered to Him;
for I am honored in the sight of the LORD,
and my God is my strength—
6 He says,
"It is not enough for you to be My servant
raising up the tribes of Jacob
and restoring the protected ones of Israel.
I will also make you a light for the nations,
to be My salvation to the ends of the earth."
7 This is what the LORD,
the Redeemer of Israel, his Holy One says
to one who is despised,
to one abhorred by people,ᵃ
to a servant of rulers:
"Kings will see and stand up,
and princesᵇ will bow down,
because of the LORD, who is faithful,
the Holy One of Israel—
and He has chosen you."

8 This is what the LORD says:

I will answer you in a time of favor,
and I will help you in the day of salvation.
I will keep you, and I will appoint you
to be a covenant for the people,
to restore the land,
to make them possess the desolate inheritances,
9 saying to the prisoners: Come out,
and to those who are in darkness:
Show yourselves.
They will feed along the pathways,
and their pastures will be on all
the barren heights.
10 They will not hunger or thirst,
the scorching heat or sun will not strike them;
for their compassionate One will guide them,
and lead them to springs of water.

11 I will make all My mountains into a road,
and My highways will be raised up.
12 See, these will come from far away,
from the north and from the west,ᶜ
and from the land of Sinim.ᵈ

13 Shout for joy, you heavens!
Earth, rejoice!
Mountains break into joyful shouts!
For the LORD has comforted His people,
and will have compassion on His afflicted ones.

Zion Remembered

14 Zion says, "The LORD has abandoned me;
The Lord has forgotten me!"
15 "Can a woman forget her nursing child,
or lack compassion for the child of her womb?
Even if these forget,
yet I will not forget you.
16 Look, I have inscribed you on the palms
of My hands;
your walls are continually before Me.
17 Your buildersᵉ hurry;
those who destroy and devastate you
will leave you.
18 Look up, and look around.
They all gather together; they come to you.
As I live"—

the LORD's declaration—

"you will wear all your childrenᶠ as jewelry,
and put them on as a bride does.
19 For your waste and desolate places
and your land marked by ruins—
will now be indeed too small for the inhabitants,
and those who swallowed you up will be far away.
20 The children that you have been deprived of
will yet say in your hearing:
This place is too small for me;
make room for me so that I may settle.
21 Then you will say within yourself:
Who fathered these for me?
I was deprived of my children and barren,
exiled and wandering—
but who brought them up?
See, I was left by myself—
but these, where did they come from?"ᵍ

22 This is what the Lord GOD says:

Look, I will lift up My hand to the nations,
and raise My banner to the peoples.

ᵃ49:7 Or by [the] nation ᵇ49:7 Lit princes and they ᶜ49:12 Lit sea ᵈ49:12 MT; DSS read of the Syenites; perhaps modern Aswan in southern Egypt ᵉ49:17 DSS, Aq, Theod, Vg; MT, Syr, Sym read sons ᶠ49:18 Lit all of them ᵍ49:21 Lit where are (or were) they

---

49:2 my words like a sharp sword. Jesus Christ will conquer the earth through the word of the gospel (Rev. 1:16; 2:12). God's Word is also depicted as a sword (Eph. 6:17; Heb. 4:12).

49:3 My servant, Israel. The Messiah is called Israel because He epitomizes the na-

tion, fulfilling what it failed to do (Zech. 3:8). **49:4 labored in vain.** This pointed to Christ's rejection by the nation of Israel and His suffering. **yet my vindication is with the LORD.** Jesus' vindication was His resurrection. **49:6 raising up the tribes of Jacob ... light for the nations.** Jesus' mission is twofold: He

will restore Israel and already has brought the light of God's truth to the Gentiles.

49:7 despised ... abhorred. Although rejected by Israel (John 1:10-11), the Servant would succeed in His ministry to the Gentiles.

49:8 time of favor ... day of salvation. God's offer of salvation is always current.

They will bring your sons in their arms,
and your daughters will be carried
on their shoulders.
23 Kings will be your foster fathers,
and their queens[a] your nursing mothers.
They will bow down to you
with their faces to the ground,
and lick the dust at your feet.
Then you will know that I am the LORD;
those who put their hope in Me
will not be put to shame.
24 Can the prey be taken from the mighty,
or the captives of the righteous[b] be delivered?
25 For this is what the LORD says:
"Even the captives of a mighty man
will be taken,
and the prey of a tyrant will be delivered;
I will contend with the one who contends
with you,
and I will save your children.
26 I will make your oppressors eat their own flesh,
and they will be drunk with their own blood
as with sweet wine.
Then all flesh will know
that I, the LORD, am your Savior,
and your Redeemer, the Mighty One of Jacob."

50

This is what the LORD says:

Where is your mother's divorce certificate
that I used to send her away?
Or who were My creditors that I sold you to?
Look, you were sold for your iniquities,
and your mother was put away
because of your transgressions.
2 Why was no one there when I came?
Why was there no one to answer when I called?
Is My hand too short to redeem?
Or do I have no power to deliver?
Look, I dry up the sea by My rebuke;
I turn the rivers into a wilderness;
their fish rot because of lack of water
and die of thirst.
3 I dress the heavens in black
and make •sackcloth their clothing.

The Obedient Servant

4 The Lord GOD has given Me
the tongue of those who are instructed
to know how to sustain the weary with a word.

He awakens [Me] each morning;
He awakens My ear to listen like those
being instructed.
5 The Lord GOD has opened My ear,
and I was not rebellious;
I did not turn back.
6 I gave My back to those who beat Me,
and My cheeks to those who tore out My beard.
I did not hide My face from scorn and spitting.
7 The Lord GOD will help Me;
therefore I have not been humiliated;
therefore I have set My face like flint,
and I know I will not be put to shame.
8 The One who justifies Me is near;
who will contend with Me?
Let us confront each other.[c]
Who has a case against Me?[d]
Let him come near Me!
9 In truth, the Lord GOD will help Me;
who is he who will condemn Me?
Indeed, all of them will wear out like a garment;
a moth will devour them.
10 Who among you •fears the LORD,
listening to the voice of His servant?
Who [among you] walks in darkness,
and has no light?
Let him trust in the name of the LORD;
let him lean on his God.
11 Look, all you who kindle a fire,
who encircle yourselves with[e] firebrands;
walk in the light of your fire
and in the firebrands you have lit!
This is what you'll get from My hand:
you will lie down in a place of torment.

Salvation for Zion

51

Listen to Me, you who pursue righteousness,
you who seek the LORD:
Look to the rock from which you were cut,
and to the quarry from which you were dug.
2 Look to Abraham your father,
and to Sarah who gave birth to you in pain.
When I called him, he was only one;
I blessed him and made him many.
3 For the LORD will comfort Zion;
He will comfort all her waste places,
and He will make her wilderness like Eden,
and her desert like the garden of the LORD.
Joy and gladness will be found in her,
thanksgiving and melodious song.

---

[a]**49:23** Lit *princesses* [b]**49:24** DSS, Syr, Vg read *fearsome one*, or *tyrant* [c]**50:8** Lit *us stand* [d]**50:8** Lit *Who is lord of My judgment* [e]**50:11** Syr reads *who set ablaze*

49:22 bring your sons in their arms. Gentiles will support Israel in the millennium and will bring Jews into the land at the beginning of Christ's rule.

50:1 your mother's divorce certificate...who were My creditors. God denies that He has given His people a divorce certif-

icate or that he has sold his children to pay His debts.

50:6 gave My back to those who beat Me. Yet another prophecy of Messiah. Isaiah is speaking as though he is the Servant (42:1); the Messiah who will be rejected before He takes His throne.

51:3 Zion ... Eden. Both referred to places of fellowship with God that were free from sin and guarded by angels (see Gen. 3:24). Zion will be fruitful and lush like the garden of Eden.

51:4 instruction ... My justice for a light to the nations. The word for instruction is Torah,

4 Pay attention to Me, My people,
and listen to Me, My nation;
for instruction will come from Me,
and My justice for a light to the nations.
I will bring it about quickly.

5 My righteousness is near,
My salvation appears,
and My arms will bring justice to the nations.
The coastlands[a] will put their hope in Me,
and they will look to My strength.[b]

6 Look up to the heavens,
and look at the earth beneath;
for the heavens will vanish like smoke,
the earth will wear out like a garment,
and its inhabitants will die in like manner.[c]
But My salvation will last forever,
and My righteousness will never be shattered.

7 Listen to Me, you who know righteousness,
the people in whose heart is My instruction:
do not fear disgrace by men,
and do not be shattered by their taunts.

8 For the moth will devour them like a garment,
and the worm will eat them like wool.
But My righteousness will last forever,
and My salvation for all generations.

9 Wake up, wake up!
Put on the strength of the LORD's power.
Wake up as in days past,
as in generations of long ago.
Wasn't it who hacked •Rahab to pieces,
who pierced the sea monster?

10 Wasn't it You who dried up the sea,
the waters of the great deep,
who made the sea-bed into a road
for the redeemed to pass over?

11 And the ransomed of the LORD will return
and come to Zion with singing,
crowned with unending joy.
Joy and gladness will overtake ⌊them⌋,
and sorrow and sighing will flee.

12 I—I am the One who comforts you.
Who are you that you should fear man who dies,
or a son of man who is given up like grass?

13 But you have forgotten the LORD, your Maker,
who stretched out the heavens
and laid the foundations of the earth.
You are in constant dread all day long
because of the fury of the oppressor,

who has set himself to destroy.
But where is the fury of the oppressor?

14 The prisoner[d] is soon to be set free;
he will not die ⌊and go⌋ to the •Pit,
and his food will not be lacking.

15 For I am the LORD your God
who stirs up the sea so that its waves roar—
His name is •Yahweh of •Hosts.

16 I have put My words in your mouth,
and covered you in the shadow of My hand,
in order to plant[e] the heavens,
to found the earth,
and to say to Zion, "You are My people."

17 Wake yourself, wake yourself up!
Stand up, Jerusalem,
you who have drunk the cup of His fury
from the hand of the LORD;
you who have drunk the goblet to the dregs—
the cup that ⌊causes people⌋ to stagger.

18 There is no one to guide her
among all the children she has raised;
there is no one to take hold of her hand
among all the offspring she has brought up.

19 These two things have happened to you:
devastation and destruction,
famine and sword.
Who will grieve for you?
How can I[f] comfort you?

20 Your children have fainted;
they lie at the head of every street
like an antelope in a net.
They are full of the LORD's fury,
the rebuke of your God.

21 So listen to this, afflicted
and drunken one—but not with wine.

22 This is what your Lord says—
Yahweh, even your God,
who defends His people—
"Look, I have removed
the cup of staggering from your hand;
that goblet, the cup of My fury.
You will never drink it again.

23 I will put it into the hands of your tormenters,
who said to you:
Lie down, so we can walk over you.
You made your back like the ground,
and like a street for those who walk on it.

52 "Wake up, wake up;
put on your strength, Zion!

---

a51:5 Or islands b51:5 Lit arm c51:6 Some DSS read die like gnats d51:14 Hb obscure e51:16 Syr reads to stretch out f51:19 MT, Tg, DSS,
LXX, Syr, Vg read you? Who can

the law of God. God's law will be known and
justice will prevail all over the world. God's
law will be light for the world in the millennial
reign of Christ.

51:9 Wake up! While it appeared to the Israelites that God was asleep, God is ever vigilant on behalf of His people (see Ps. 121:3-4).

51:14 prisoner is soon to be set free. These
were captives in exile in Babylon, yet meaning extends to everyone living in the darkness
of sin and alienated from God.

51:17 cup … dregs. The empty cup referred
to suffering God's judgment. While in exile,
the Israelites truly felt God's punishment (see

Jer. 25:15-29; Lam. 4:21).

51:18 no one to take hold of her hand.
Many young men of Jerusalem were killed
during the destruction of the city. This phrase
depicted Jerusalem as a sick woman with no
sons to care for her.

52:7 feet of the herald. Messengers ran with

Put on your beautiful garments,
Jerusalem, the Holy City!
For the uncircumcised and the unclean
will no longer enter you.
2 Stand up, shake the dust off yourself!
Take your seat, Jerusalem.
Remove the bonds[a] from your neck,
captive Daughter Zion."
3 For this is what the LORD says:
"You were sold for nothing,
and you will be redeemed without silver."
4 For this is what the Lord GOD says:
"At first My people went down to Egypt
to live there,
then Assyria oppressed them without cause.[b]
5 So now what have I here"—
the LORD's declaration—
"that My people are taken away for nothing?
Its rulers wail"—
the LORD's declaration—
"and My name is continually blasphemed
all day long.
6 Therefore My people will know My name;
therefore ⌊they will know⌋ on that day
that I am He who says:
Here I am."

7 How beautiful on the mountains
are the feet of the herald,
who proclaims peace,
who brings news of good things,
who proclaims salvation,
who says to Zion, "Your God reigns!"
8 The voices of your watchmen—
they lift up their voices,
shouting for joy together;
for every eye will see
when the LORD returns to Zion.
9 Be joyful, rejoice together,
you ruins of Jerusalem!
For the LORD has comforted His people;
He has redeemed Jerusalem.
10 The LORD has displayed His holy arm
in the sight of all the nations;
all the ends of the earth will see
the salvation of our God.

11 Leave, leave, go out from there!
Do not touch anything unclean;
go out from her, purify yourselves,

you who carry the vessels of the LORD.
12 For you will not leave in a hurry,
and you will not have to take flight;
because the LORD is going before you,
and the God of Israel is your rear guard.

The Suffering Servant

1. When have you suffered for someone else's misbehavior? When has someone else suffered because of your misbehavior?

Isaiah 52:13–53:12

2. Who is the "Servant" to whom this passage is referring? Why did He suffer? What did His suffering accomplish?
3. What does it mean that "We all went astray like sheep; we all have turned to our own way" (53:6)? Why did the Lord punish the Servant for us all?
4. What does it mean that God made the Servant a "restitution offering" (53:10)?
5. How does this passage teach that Jesus is the only way to finding peace with God?

The Servant's Suffering and Exaltation

13 See, My servant[c] will act wisely;[d]
He will be raised and lifted up
and greatly exalted.
14 Just as many were appalled at You[e] —
His appearance was so disfigured
that He did not look like a man,
and His form did not resemble
a human being—
15 so He will sprinkle[f] many nations.[g]
Kings will shut their mouths because of Him,
For they will see
what had not been told them,
and they will understand
what they had not heard.

53 Who has believed what we have heard?[h]
And who has the arm of the LORD
been revealed to?
2 He grew up before Him like a young plant
and like a root out of dry ground.

---

[a]**52:2** Alt Hb tradition reads *The bonds are removed* [b]**52:4** Or *them at last*, or *them for nothing* [c]**52:13** Tg adds *the Messiah* [d]**52:13** Or *will be successful* [e]**52:14** Some Hb mss, Syr, Tg read *Him* [f]**52:15** As the blood of a sacrifice is sprinkled on the altar on behalf of the people [g]**52:15** LXX reads *so many nations will marvel at Him* [h]**53:1** Or *believed our report*

---

news of battles (2 Sam. 18:26). **Your God reigns!** The gospel is the good news that God is king (see Mark 1:14-15).
52:10 His holy arm. God's power and strength.
52:13 lifted up and greatly exalted. From here to 53:12 the Servant's death for the sins

of His people is predicted. This phrase referred to His resurrection and glorification (Rom. 4:24-25).
52:14 appalled at You. Many were shocked at Israel's exile, so would many be surprised at Jesus' humiliation.
52:15 sprinkle. Sprinkling with blood for

cleansing from sin (Lev. 4:6). **shut their mouths.** Stunned respect. **they will see.** The nations will finally understand that the Messiah is Lord (Rom. 15:21).
53:2 young plant. He will seem frail before His exaltation.
53:4 bore our sicknesses. Sickness is used

He had no form or splendor that we should
    look at Him,
no appearance that we should desire Him.
3 He was despised and rejected by men,
    a man of suffering who knew what sickness was.
    He was like one people turned away from;[a]
    He was despised, and we didn't value Him.

4 Yet He Himself bore our sicknesses,
    and He carried our pains;
    but we in turn regarded Him stricken,
    struck down by God, and afflicted.
5 But He was pierced because of
        our transgressions,
    crushed because of our iniquities;
    punishment for our peace was on Him,
    and we are healed by His wounds.
6 We all went astray like sheep;
    we all have turned to our own way;
    and the LORD has punished Him
    for[b] the iniquity of us all.

7 He was oppressed and afflicted,
    yet He did not open His mouth.
    Like a lamb led to the slaughter
    and like a sheep silent before her shearers,
    He did not open His mouth.
8 He was taken away because of oppression
        and judgment;
    and who considered His fate?[c]
    For He was cut off from the land of the living;
    He was struck because of My people's rebellion.
9 They[d] made His grave with the wicked,
    and with a rich man at His death,
    although He had done no violence
    and had not spoken deceitfully.

10 Yet the LORD was pleased to crush Him,
    and He made Him sick.
    When[e] You make Him a •restitution offering,
    He will see ⌊His⌋ •seed, He will prolong His days,
    and the will of the LORD will succeed
        by His hand.
11 He will see ⌊it⌋[f] out of His anguish,
    and He will be satisfied with His knowledge.
    My righteous servant will justify many,
    and He will carry their iniquities.
12 Therefore I will give Him[g] the many
        as a portion,
    and He will receive[h] the mighty as spoil,

because He submitted Himself to death,
    and was counted among the rebels;
    yet He bore the sin of many
    and interceded for the rebels.

Future Glory for Israel

54 "Rejoice, barren one, who did not give birth;
        burst into song and shout,
    you who have not been in labor!
    For the children of the forsaken one
        will be more
    than the children of the married woman,"
    says the LORD.
2 "Enlarge the site of your tent,
    and let your tent curtains be stretched out;
    do not hold back;
    lengthen your ropes,
    and drive your pegs deep.
3 For you will spread out to the right
        and to the left,
    and your descendants will dispossess nations
    and inhabit the desolate cities.

4 "Do not be afraid, for you will not
        be put to shame;
    don't be humiliated, for you will not
        be disgraced.
    For you will forget the shame of your youth,
    and you will no longer remember
    the disgrace of your widowhood.
5 For your husband is your Maker—
    His name is •Yahweh of •Hosts—
    and the Holy One of Israel is your Redeemer;
    He is called the God of all the earth.
6 For the LORD has called you,
    like a wife deserted and wounded in spirit,
    a wife of one's youth when she is rejected,"
    says your God.
7 "I deserted you for a brief moment,
    but I will take you back with great compassion.
8 In a surge of anger
    I hid My face from you for a moment,
    but I will have compassion on you
    with everlasting love,"
    says the LORD your Redeemer.
9 "For this is like the days[i] of Noah to Me:
    when I swore that the waters of Noah
    would never flood the earth again,
    so I have sworn that I will not be angry with you
    or rebuke you.

---

[a] **53:3** Lit *And like a hiding of faces from Him*   [b] **53:6** Lit *with;* or *has placed on Him*   [c] **53:8** Or *and as for His generation, who considered [Him]?*
[d] **53:9** DSS; MT reads *He*   [e] **53:10** Or *If*   [f] **53:11** DSS, LXX read *see light*   [g] **53:12** Or *Him with*   [h] **53:12** Or *receive with*   [i] **54:9** DSS, Cairo Geniza;
MT, LXX read *waters*

---

as a metaphor for spiritual sickness: sin. Christ was punished for our sins.

53:5 crushed because of our iniquities. The Servant suffered in our place in order to reconcile us with God. **punishment for our peace.** The punishment Jesus received brought peace (wholeness) for us.

53:6 punished Him for the iniquity of us all. God punished Jesus for our sins so that we won't have to be punished for them.

53:9 wicked … rich man. Jesus was crucified as a criminal but was buried by a wealthy man, Joseph of Arimathea (see Matt. 27:57-60). This is a remarkable detail showing that

this prophecy from over 700 years before the time of Jesus is truly from God.

53:10 the LORD was pleased to crush Him. God gladly took on Himself the punishment we deserve. **He will see His seed.** This is a prophecy of the resurrection, since it means Jesus will be alive after His death.

10 Though the mountains move
and the hills shake,
My love will not be removed from you
and My covenant of peace will not be shaken,"
says your compassionate LORD.

11 "Poor ⌊Jerusalem⌋, storm-tossed,
and not comforted,
I will set your stones in black mortar,[a]
and lay your foundations in sapphires.[b]

12 I will make your battlements[c] of rubies,
your gates of sparkling stones,
and all your walls of precious stones.

13 Then all your children will be taught
by the LORD,
their prosperity will be great,

14 and you will be established
on ⌊a foundation of⌋ righteousness.
You will be far from oppression,
you will certainly not be afraid;
you will be far from terror,
it will certainly not come near you.

15 If anyone attacks you,
it is not from Me;
whoever attacks you
will fall before you.

16 Look, I have created the craftsman
who blows on the charcoal fire
and produces a weapon suitable for its task;
and I have created the destroyer to work havoc.

17 No weapon formed against you will succeed,
and you will refute any accusation[d]
raised against you in court.
This is the heritage of the LORD's servants,
and their righteousness is from Me."

⌊This is⌋
the LORD's declaration.

Come to the LORD

55 "Come, everyone who is thirsty,
come to the waters;
and you without money,
come, buy, and eat!
Come, buy wine and milk
without money and without cost!

2 Why do you spend money on what is not food,
and your wages on what does not satisfy?
Listen carefully to Me, and eat what is good,
and you will enjoy the choicest of foods.[e]

3 Pay attention and come to Me;
listen, so that you will live.

I will make an everlasting covenant with you,
the promises assured to David.

4 Since I have made him a witness to the peoples,
a leader and commander for the peoples,

5 so you will summon a nation you do not know,
and nations who do not know you will run
to you.
For the LORD your God,
even the Holy One of Israel,
has glorified you."

6 Seek the LORD while He may be found;
call to Him while He is near.

7 Let the wicked one abandon his way,
and the sinful one his thoughts;
let him return to the LORD,
so He may have compassion on him,
and to our God, for He will freely forgive.

8 "For My thoughts are not your thoughts,
and your ways are not My ways."

⌊This is⌋
the LORD's declaration.

9 "For as heaven is higher than earth,
so My ways are higher than your ways,
and My thoughts than your thoughts.

10 For just as rain and snow fall from heaven,
and do not return there
without saturating the earth,
and making it germinate and sprout,
and providing seed to sow
and food to eat,

11 so My word that comes from My mouth
will not return to Me empty,
but it will accomplish what I please,
and will prosper in what I send it ⌊to do⌋."

12 You will indeed go out with joy
and be peacefully guided;
the mountains and the hills will break
into singing before you,
and all the trees of the field will clap ⌊their⌋ hands.

13 Instead of the thornbush, a cypress will come up,
and instead of the brier, a myrtle will come up;
it will make a name for the LORD
as an everlasting sign that will not be destroyed.

A House of Prayer for All

56 This is what the LORD says:

Preserve justice and do what is right,
for My salvation is coming soon,

---

[a] 54:11 Lit in antimony [b] 54:11 Or lapis lazuli [c] 54:12 Lit suns; perhaps shields; Ps 84:11 [d] 54:17 Lit refute every tongue [e] 55:2 Lit enjoy fatness

---

55:1 thirsty, come to the waters. Thirst speaks of the desire for spiritual answers to life's mysteries. Waters represent the satisfaction of knowing God as Savior and Provider (John 4:10-14).

55:2 spend money ... wages on what does not satisfy? Throughout history, people have tried to find satisfaction through many things other than God. But the joy of salvation cannot be obtained except through God's free gift.

55:5 nations who do not know you. Many nations will recognize the splendor of the Lord and will go to Israel to worship Him. This is a reversal of the exile when Israel was taken to a foreign nation.

56:2 the man ... who keeps the Sabbath. Keeping the Sabbath was an important part of the law because it signified God's covenant with Israel. Refraining from work on that day showed trust in God's ability to provide.

and My righteousness will be revealed.

2 Happy is the man who does this,
anyone who maintains this,
who keeps the Sabbath without desecrating it,
and keeps his hand from doing any evil.

3 No foreigner who has converted to the LORD
should say,
"The LORD will exclude me from His people";
and the eunuch should not say,
"Look, I am a dried-up tree."

4 For the LORD says this:
"For the eunuchs who keep My Sabbaths,
and choose what pleases Me,
and hold firmly to My covenant,

5 I will give them, in My house and within
My walls,
a memorial and a name
better than sons and daughters.
I will give each ⌊of them⌋ an everlasting name
that will never be cut off.

6 And the foreigners who convert to the LORD,
minister to Him, love the LORD's name,
and are His servants,
all who keep the Sabbath without desecrating it,
and who hold firmly to My covenant—

7 I will bring them to My holy mountain
and let them rejoice in My house of prayer.
Their •burnt offerings and sacrifices
will be acceptable on My altar,
for My house will be called a house of prayer
for all nations."

8 ⌊This is⌋ the declaration
of the Lord GOD,
who gathers
the dispersed of Israel:
"I will gather to them still others
besides those already gathered."

Unrighteous Leaders Condemned

9 All you animals of the field and forest,
come and eat!

10 Israel'sa watchmen are blind, all of them,
they know nothing;
all of them are mute dogs,
they cannot bark;
they dream, lie down,
and love to sleep.

11 These dogs have fierce appetites;
they never have enough.

And they are shepherds
who have no discernment;
all of them turn to their own way,
every last one for his own gain.

12 "Come, let me get ⌊some⌋ wine,
let's guzzle ⌊some⌋ beer;
and tomorrow will be like today,
only far better!"

57 The righteous one perishes,
and no one takes it to heart;
faithful men are swept away,
with no one realizing
that the righteous one is swept away
from the presenceb of evil.

2 He will enter into peace—
they will rest on their bedsc—
everyone who lives uprightly.

Pagan Religion Denounced

3 But come here,
you sons of a sorceress,
offspring of an adulterer and a prostitute!d

4 Who is it you are mocking?
Who is it you are opening your mouth
and sticking out your tongue at?
Isn't it you, you rebellious children,
you race of liars,

5 who burn with lust among the oaks,
under every flourishing tree,
who slaughter children in the •wadis
below the clefts of the rocks?

6 Your portion is among the smooth ⌊stones⌋
of the wadi;
indeed, they are your lot.
You have even poured out a drink offering
to them;
you have offered a •grain offering;
should I be satisfied with these?

7 You have placed your bed
on a high and lofty mountain;
you also went up there to offer sacrifice.

8 You have set up your memorial
behind the door and doorpost.
For away from Me, you stripped,
went up, and made your bed wide,
and you have made a bargaine for yourself
with them.
You have loved their bed;
you have gazed on their genitals.f

---

a**56:10** Or *His*, or *Its* b**57:1** Or *away because* c**57:2** Either their deathbed or their grave d**57:3** Lit *and she acted as a harlot* e**57:8** Lit *you cut*
f**57:8** Lit *hand*; probably a euphemism for the male organ

---

56:3 No foreigner. Gentiles, who were not part of the covenant, would also find God's peace if they turned to God in faith. **eunuch.** Eunuchs were excluded from entry into the temple under the Mosaic law (Deut. 23:1), but they will be part of Christ's kingdom.

56:7 house of prayer. Being included in the

covenantal family of Israel will mean access to the temple, which will be rebuilt before Christ returns.

56:8 gather ... still others. God promised Abraham that through him all peoples of the world would be blessed (see Gen. 12:3). People everywhere who repent and come to God

are welcomed into His kingdom with joy.

57:3 an adulterer and a prostitute. This referred to the Canaanite fertility rites in which some Israelites participated. Supposedly, engaging in sexual relations with prostitutes in the temple helped guarantee fertility in crops, animals, and families.

9 You went to the king with oil
and multiplied your perfumes;
you sent your envoys far away
and sent ⌊them⌋ down even to •Sheol.

10 You became weary on your many journeys,
⌊but⌋ you did not say, "I give up!"
You found a renewal of your strength;ᵃ
therefore you did not grow weak.

11 Who was it you dreaded and feared,
so that you lied and didn't remember Me
or take it to heart?
Have I not kept silent for such a long timeᵇ
and you do not •fear Me?

12 I will expose your righteousness,
and your works—they will not profit you.

13 When you cry out,
let your collection ⌊of idols⌋ deliver you!
The wind will carry all of them off,
a breath will take them away.
But whoever takes refuge in Me
will inherit the land
and possess My holy mountain.

Healing and Peace

14 He said,
"Build it up, build it up, prepare the way,
remove ⌊every⌋ obstacle from My people's way."

15 For the High and Exalted One
who lives forever, whose name is Holy says this:
"I live in a high and holy place,
and with the oppressed and lowly of spirit,
to revive the spirit of the lowly
and revive the heart of the oppressed.

16 For I will not accuse ⌊you⌋ forever,
and I will not always be angry;
for then the spirit would grow weak before Me,
even the breath ⌊of man⌋, which I have made.

17 Because of his sinful greed I was angry,
so I struck him; I was angry and hid;ᶜ
but he went on turning back to the desires
of his heart.

18 I have seen his ways, but I will heal him;
I will lead him and comfort him
and his mourners,

19 creating words of praise."ᵈ
The LORD says,
"Peace, peace to the one who is far or near,
and I will heal him.

20 But the wicked are like the storm-tossed sea,

for it cannot be still,
and its waters churn up mire and muck.

21 There is no peace for the wicked,"
says my God.

True Fasting

58 "Cry out loudly,ᵉ don't hold back!
Raise your voice like a trumpet.
Tell My people their transgression,
and the house of Jacob their sins.

2 They seek Me day after day
and delight to know My ways,
like a nation that does what is right
and does not abandon the justice of their God.
They ask Me for righteous judgments;
they delight in the nearness of God."

3 "Why have we fasted, but You have not seen?
We have denied ourselves,
but You haven't noticed!"ᶠ
"Look, you do as you please on the day
of your fast,
and oppress all your workers.

4 You fast ⌊with⌋ contention and strife
to strike viciously with ⌊your⌋ fist.
You cannot fast as ⌊you do⌋ today,
⌊hoping⌋ to make your voice heard on high.

5 Will the fast I choose be like this:
A day for a person to deny himself,
to bow his head like a reed,
and to spread out •sackcloth and ashes?
Will you call this a fast
and a day acceptable to the LORD?

6 Isn't the fast I choose:
To break the chains of wickedness,
to untie the ropes of the yoke,
to set the oppressed free,
and to tear off every yoke?

7 Is it not to share your bread with the hungry,
to bring the poor and homeless
into your house,
to clothe the naked when you see him,
and to not ignoreᵍ your own flesh ⌊and blood⌋?

8 Then your light will appear like the dawn,
and your recovery will come quickly.
Your righteousness will go before you,
and the LORD's glory will be your rear guard.

9 At that time, when you call, the LORD
will answer;
when you cry out, He will say: Here I am.

ᵃ**57:10** Lit *found life of your hand*   ᵇ**57:11** MT, DSS; LXX reads *And I, when I see you, I pass by*   ᶜ**57:17** Lit *him; hiding and I am angry*   ᵈ**57:19** Lit *creating fruit of the lips*   ᵉ**58:1** Lit *with throat*   ᶠ**58:3** *"Why have we . . . but You haven't noticed!"* are Israel's words to God.   ᵍ**58:7** Lit *not hide yourself from*

57:10 [but] you did not say, "I give up!" The people continued in sin, refusing to give up their false religious practices (Jer. 2:25).
57:11 Have I not kept silent? Israel appeared to forget God because He seemed silent to them (Ps. 50:21).
57:15 high and holy place, and with the ...

lowly. Though God is transcendent (above everything), He is present with us. His presence is even stronger with the lowly, because God helps the needy and exalts the humble.

58:2 They seek Me day after day. God is speaking sarcastically. The people seem to be religious, but He knows their motives are

not right.

58:3 fasted ... denied ourselves. Refraining from food, repenting of sin, and praying signified a humble people before God in times of national calamity. Here the people continued in sin, going through the religious motions, without truly turning their hearts and minds to-

If you get rid of the yoke from those
   around you,[a]
the finger-pointing and malicious speaking,
10 and if you offer yourself[b] to the hungry,
and satisfy the afflicted one,
then your light will shine in the darkness,
and your night will be like noonday.
11 The LORD will always lead you,
satisfy you in a parched land,
and strengthen your bones.
You will be like a watered garden
and like a spring whose waters never run dry.
12 Some of you will rebuild the ancient ruins;
you will restore the foundations laid long ago;[c]
you will be called the repairer of broken walls,
the restorer of streets where people live.

13 "If you keep from desecrating[d] the Sabbath,
from doing whatever you want on My holy day;
if you call the Sabbath a delight,
and the holy ⌊day⌋ of the LORD honorable;
if you honor it, not going your own ways,
seeking your own pleasure, or talking
   too much;[e]
14 then you will delight yourself in the LORD,
and I will make you ride over the heights
   of the land,
and let you enjoy the heritage
   of your father Jacob."
For the mouth of the LORD has spoken.

Sin and Redemption

59 Indeed, the LORD's hand is not too short
   to save,
and His ear is not too deaf to hear.
2 But your iniquities have built barriers
between you and your God,
and your sins have made Him hide ⌊His⌋ face
   from you
so that He does not listen.
3 For your hands are defiled with blood,
and your fingers with iniquity;
your lips have spoken lies,
and you mutter injustice.
4 No one makes claims justly;
no one pleads honestly.
They trust in empty and worthless words;
they conceive trouble and give birth to iniquity.
5 They hatch viper's eggs
and weave spider's webs.

Whoever eats their eggs will die;
crack one open, and a viper is hatched.
6 Their webs cannot become clothing,
and they cannot cover themselves
   with their works.
Their works are sinful works,
and violent acts are in their hands.
7 Their feet run after evil,
and they rush to shed innocent blood.
Their thoughts are sinful thoughts;
ruin and wretchedness are in their paths.
8 They have not known the path of peace,
and there is no justice in their ways.
They have made their roads crooked;
no one who walks on them will know peace.

9 Therefore justice is far from us,
and righteousness does not reach us.
We hope for light, but there is darkness;
for brightness, but we live in the night.
10 We grope along a wall like the blind;
we grope like those without eyes.
We stumble at noon as though
   it were twilight;
⌊we are⌋ like the dead among those
   who are healthy.
11 We all growl like bears
and moan like doves.
We hope for justice, but there is none;
for salvation, ⌊but⌋ it is far from us.
12 For our transgressions have multiplied
   before You,
and our sins testify against us.
For our transgressions are with us,
and we know our iniquities:
13 transgression and deception against the LORD,
turning away from following our God,
speaking oppression and revolt,
conceiving and uttering lying words
   from the heart.
14 Justice is turned back,
and righteousness stands far off.
For truth has stumbled in the public square,
and honesty cannot enter.
15 Truth is missing,
and whoever turns from evil is plundered.

The LORD saw that there was no justice,
and He was offended.
16 He saw that there was no man—

---

[a] **58:9** Lit *from your midst* [b] **58:10** Some Hb mss, LXX, Syr read *offer your bread* [c] **58:12** Lit *foundations generation and generation* [d] **58:13** Lit *keep your foot from* [e] **58:13** Lit *or speak a word*

---

ward God.

58:5 a day acceptable to the LORD? God exposed their hypocrisy. Their self-righteous behavior did not hide their exploitation of employees. Religious activity without obedience is never acceptable to God.

58:7 share your bread. Inner righteousness

manifests itself in a concern for others and in acts of justice and mercy.

59:4 No one makes claims justly. The poor received no fairness in the courts. This was evidence of the nation's spiritual depravity.

59:7 Their feet run ... to shed innocent blood. Used in Romans 3:15-17 to demon-

strate the universality of sin. **sinful thoughts.** Sin begins in the mind (James 1:14-15).

59:10 like the blind. This was part of the covenant curse on the disobedient (Deut. 28:29). Without God's light in our lives, we live in spiritual darkness.

59:11 growl like bears. Expressed frustra-

He was amazed that there was
no one interceding;
so His own arm brought salvation,
and His own righteousness supported Him.
17 He put on righteousness like a breastplate,
and a helmet of salvation on His head;
He put on garments of vengeance for clothing,
and He wrapped Himself in zeal as in a cloak.
18 Thus He will repay according to [their] deeds:
fury to His enemies,
retribution to His foes,
and He will repay the coastlands.
19 They will •fear the name of the LORD
in the west,
and His glory in the east;
for He will come like a rushing stream
driven by the wind of the LORD.
20 The Redeemer will come to Zion,
and to those in Jacob who turn
from transgression.

[This is]
the LORD's declaration.

21 "As for Me, this is My covenant with them," says
the LORD: "My Spirit who is on you, and My words that
I have put in your mouth, will not depart from your
mouth, or from the mouth of your children, or from the
mouth of your children's children, from now on and
forever," says the LORD.

The LORD's Glory in Zion

60 Arise, shine, for your light has come,
and the glory of the LORD shines over you.[a]
2 For look, darkness covers the earth,
and total darkness the peoples;
but the LORD will shine over you,
and His glory will appear over you.
3 Nations will come to your light,
and kings to the brightness of your radiance.
4 Raise your eyes and look around:
they all gather and come to you;
your sons will come from far away,
and your daughters will be carried on the hip.
5 Then you will see and be radiant,
and your heart will tremble and rejoice,[b]
because the riches of the sea will become yours,
and the wealth of the nations will come to you.
6 Caravans of camels will cover your land[c]—
young camels of Midian and Ephah—
all of them will come from Sheba.
They will carry gold and frankincense

and proclaim the praises of the LORD.
7 All the flocks of Kedar will be gathered to you;
the rams of Nebaioth will serve you
and go up on My altar
as an acceptable [sacrifice].
I will glorify My beautiful house.
8 Who are these who fly like a cloud,
like doves to their shelters?
9 Yes, the islands will wait for Me
with the ships of Tarshish in the lead,
to bring your children from far away,
their silver and gold with them,
for the honor of the LORD your God,
the Holy One of Israel,
who has glorified you.
10 Foreigners will build up your walls,
and their kings will serve you.
Although I struck you in My wrath,
yet I will show mercy to you with My favor.
11 Your gates will always be open;
they will never be shut day or night
so that the wealth of the nations
may be brought into you,
with their kings being led [in procession].
12 For the nation and the kingdom
that will not serve you will perish;
those nations will be annihilated.
13 The glory of Lebanon will come to you—
[its] pine, fir, and cypress together—
to beautify the place of My sanctuary,
and I will glorify My dwelling place.[d]
14 The sons of your oppressors
will come and bow down to you;
all who reviled you
will fall down on their faces at your feet.
They will call you the City of the LORD,
Zion of the Holy One of Israel.
15 Instead of your being deserted and hated,
with no one passing through,
I will make you an object of eternal pride,
a joy from age to age.
16 You will nurse on the milk of nations,
and nurse at the breast of kings;
you will know that I, the LORD, am your Savior
and Redeemer, the Mighty One of Jacob.
17 I will bring gold instead of bronze;
I will bring silver instead of iron,
bronze instead of wood,
and iron instead of stones.

---

[a]60:1 *You* refers to Jerusalem. [b]60:5 Lit *expand* [c]60:6 Lit *cover you* [d]60:13 Lit *glorify the place of My feet*

---

tion and despair.
59:17 put on righteousness like a breastplate. God fights for His people like a warrior. Believers need to put on Christ's armor in the fight against Satan (see Eph. 6:14-17).
59:20 who turn from transgression. Jesus Christ will save all who turn from sin and put

their faith in Him (see Rom. 11:26).
59:21 My covenant. The Messiah will return in judgment and enter into a new covenant with believing Israel (Jer. 31:31), pouring His Spirit on them.
60:1 Arise, shine. Zion will both receive and reflect God's light and blessing. God is the

light—His light will endure forever.
60:5 wealth of the nations will come to you. At the beginning of the Millennium when Israel is restored to her land, redeemed people from other nations will bring great wealth to Israel.
60:11 gates will always be open. Zion will

I will appoint peace as your guard
and righteousness as your ruler.
18 Violence will never again be heard of
in your land;
devastation and destruction
⌊will be gone from⌋ your borders.
But you will name your walls salvation,
and your gates praise.
19 The sun will no longer be your light by day,
and the brightness of the moon will not shine
on you;
but the LORD will be your everlasting light,
and your God will be your splendor.
20 Your sun will no longer set,
and your moon will not fade;
for the LORD will be your everlasting light,
and the days of your sorrow will be over.
21 Then all your people will be righteous;
they will possess the land forever;
they are the branch I planted,
the work of My[a] hands,
so that I may be glorified.
22 The least will become a thousand,
the smallest a mighty nation.
I am the LORD;
I will accomplish it quickly in its time.

Messiah's Jubilee

61 The Spirit of the Lord GOD is on Me,
because the LORD has anointed Me
to bring good news to the poor.
He has sent Me to heal[b] the brokenhearted,
to proclaim liberty to the captives,
and freedom to the prisoners;
2 to proclaim the year of the LORD's favor,
and the day of our God's vengeance;
to comfort all who mourn,
3 to provide for those who mourn in Zion;
to give them a crown of beauty instead of ashes,
festive oil instead of mourning,
and splendid clothes instead of despair.[c]
And they will be called righteous trees,
planted by the LORD,
to glorify Him.

4 They will rebuild the ancient ruins;
they will restore the former devastations;
they will renew the ruined cities,
the devastations of many generations.
5 Strangers will stand and feed your flocks,

and foreigners will be your plowmen
and vinedressers.
6 But you will be called the LORD's priests;
they will speak of you as ministers of our God;
you will eat the wealth of the nations,
and you will boast in their riches.
7 Because your shame was double,
and they cried out, "Disgrace is their portion,"
therefore, they will possess double in their land,
and eternal joy will be theirs.

8 For I the LORD love justice;
I hate robbery and injustice;[d]
I will faithfully reward them
and make an everlasting covenant with them.
9 Their descendants will be known
among the nations,
and their posterity among the peoples.
All who see them will recognize
that they are a people the LORD has blessed.

10 I greatly rejoice in the LORD,
I exult in my God;
for He has clothed me with the garments
of salvation
and wrapped me in a robe of righteousness,
as a bridegroom wears a turban
and as a bride adorns herself with her jewels.
11 For as the earth brings forth its growth,
and as a garden enables what is sown
to spring up,
so the Lord GOD will cause righteousness
and praise
to spring up before all the nations.

Zion's Restoration

62 I will not keep silent because of Zion,
and I will not keep still because of Jerusalem
until her righteousness shines like a bright light,
and her salvation like a flaming torch.
2 Nations will see your righteousness,
and all kings your glory.
You will be called by a new name
that the LORD's mouth will announce.
3 You will be a glorious crown in the LORD's hand,
and a royal diadem in the palm of your God.
4 You will no longer be called Deserted,
and your land will not be called Desolate;
instead, you will be called My Delight is in Her,[e]
and your land Married;[f]
for the LORD delights in you,

---

[a]**60:21** LXX, DSS read *His* [b]**61:1** Lit *bind up* [c]**61:3** Lit *a dim spirit* [d]**61:8** Some Hb mss, DSS, LXX, Syr, Tg, Vg; other Hb mss read *robbery with a burnt offering* [e]**62:4** Hb *Hephzibah* [f]**62:4** Hb *Beulah*

---

be secure and won't need locked gates for protection.

61:1 to proclaim liberty. Jesus read these verses from a scroll in the synagogue (see Luke 4:16-21). All who heard knew these verses to be a prophecy of the Messiah. Jesus said that He was fulfilling them.

61:3 a crown of beauty. In place of the ashes that signify mourning, the Israelites will wear a crown symbolizing joy (Ps. 30:11). This is to be a time of celebration—the mourning period is over.

61:4 rebuild the ancient ruins. The cities of Israel, destroyed many years ago, will be re-

built after the exile.

61:6 priests. Israel will finally fulfill the calling given to them at Mt. Sinai. They will be God's priests to the world (see Ex. 19:6).

62:2 new name. Signified a new status and a new righteous character. Names often represented one's anticipated or present character.

and your land will be married.
5 For as a young man marries a virgin,
so your sons will marry you;
and as a bridegroom rejoices[a] over ⌊his⌋ bride,
so your God will rejoice over you.

6 Jerusalem,
I have appointed watchmen on your walls;
they will never be silent, day or night.
You, who remind the LORD,
no rest for you!
7 Do not give Him rest
until He establishes and makes her Jerusalem
the praise of the earth.

8 The LORD has sworn with His right hand
and His strong arm:
I will no longer give your grain
to your enemies for food,
and foreigners will not drink your new wine
you have labored for.
9 For those who gather grain will eat it
and praise the LORD,
and those who harvest the grapes will drink
⌊the wine⌋
in My holy courts.

10 Go out, go out through the gates;
prepare a way for the people!
Build it up, build up the highway;
clear away the stones!
Raise a banner for the peoples.
11 Look, the LORD has proclaimed
to the end of the earth,
"Say to Daughter Zion:
Look, your salvation is coming,
His reward is with Him,
and His recompense is before Him."
12 And they will be called[b] the Holy People,
the LORD's Redeemed;
and you will be called Cared For,
A City Not Deserted.

The LORD's Day of Vengeance

63 Who is this coming from Edom
in crimson-stained garments from Bozrah—
this One who is splendid in His apparel,
rising up proudly[c] in His great might?

It is I, proclaiming vindication,[d]
powerful to save.

2 Why is Your clothing red,
and Your garments like one who treads
a winepress?

3 I trampled the winepress alone,
and no one from the nations was with Me.
I trampled them in My anger
and ground them underfoot in My fury;
their blood spattered My garments,
and all My clothes were stained.
4 For I planned the day of vengeance,[e]
and the year of My redemption[f] came.
5 I looked, but there was no one to help,
and I was amazed that no one assisted;
so My arm accomplished victory for Me,
and My wrath assisted Me.
6 I crushed nations in My anger;
I made them drunk with My wrath
and poured out their blood on the ground.

Remembrance of Grace

7 I will make known the LORD's faithful love
⌊and⌋ the LORD's praiseworthy acts,
because of all the LORD has done for us—
even the many good things
⌊He has done⌋ for the house of Israel
and has done for them based on
His compassions
and the abundance of His faithful love.
8 He said, "They are indeed My people,
children who will not be disloyal,"
and He became their Savior.
9 In all their suffering, He suffered,[g]
and the Angel of His Presence saved them.
He redeemed them
because of His love and compassion;
He lifted them up and carried them
all the days of the past.
10 But they rebelled,
and grieved His Holy Spirit.
So He became their enemy
⌊and⌋ fought against them.
11 Then He[h] remembered the days of the past,
⌊the days⌋ of Moses ⌊and⌋ his people.
Where is He who brought them up
out of the sea
with the shepherds[i] of His flock?
Where is He who put His Holy Spirit
among the flock?

[a]**62:5** Lit *and the rejoicing of the bridegroom* [b]**62:12** Lit *will call them* [c]**63:1** Syr, Vg read *apparel, striding forward* [d]**63:1** Or *righteousness* [e]**63:4** Lit *For day of vengeance in My heart* [f]**63:4** Or *blood revenge* [g]**63:9** Alt Hb tradition reads *did not suffer* [h]**63:11** Or *he,* or *they* [i]**63:11** LXX, Tg, Syr read *shepherd*

62:6 watchmen on your walls. Guards stationed on city walls looked for any approaching enemy. Here it refers to prophets who call on the Lord. **no rest.** The prophets are like watchmen who keep waiting for God to do what He promised. God's promises give Him no rest until He fulfills them.

63:1 Bozrah. The main town of Edom, an enemy of Israel that God would judge.
63:5 wrath assisted me. In the final battle of Armageddon, God will defeat His enemies. Sin produces anger in God because it offends His holiness.
63:7 I will make known. As a representative

of the people, Isaiah publicly proclaimed God's mercy, love, and goodness. Recalling God's loving actions in the past helps believers to trust in His provision for the present and future.

63:17 make us stray from Your ways. As with Pharaoh, God allowed Israel's heart to

12 He sent His glorious arm
     at Moses' right hand,
   divided the waters before them
     to obtain eternal fame for Himself,
13 and led them through the depths
     like a horse in the wilderness,
   so that they did not stumble.
14 Like cattle that go down into the valley,
     the Spirit of the LORD gave them[a] rest.
   You led Your people this way
     to make a glorious name for Yourself.

Israel's Prayer

15 Look down from heaven and see
     from Your lofty home—holy and beautiful.
   Where is Your zeal and Your might?
   Your yearning[b] and Your compassion
     are withheld from me.
16 Yet You are our Father,
     even though Abraham does not know us
     and Israel doesn't recognize us.
   You, LORD, are our Father;
     from ancient times,
   Your name is our Redeemer.
17 Why, LORD, do You make us stray
     from Your ways?
   You harden our hearts so we do not •fear[c] You.
   Return, because of Your servants,
     the tribes of Your heritage.
18 Your holy people had a possession[d]
     for a little while,
   ⌊but⌋ our enemies have trampled down
     Your sanctuary.
19 We have become like those
     You never ruled over,
   like those not called by Your name.

64 [e] If only You would tear the heavens open
     ⌊and⌋ come down,
   so that mountains would quake
     at Your presence—
2[f] as fire kindles the brushwood,
     and fire causes water to boil—
   to make Your name known to Your enemies,
   so that nations will tremble at Your presence!
3 When You did awesome deeds
     that we did not expect,
   You came down,
   and the mountains quaked at Your presence.

4 From ancient times no one has heard,
     no one has listened,
   no eye has seen any God except You,
   who acts on behalf of the one who waits
     for Him.
5 You welcome the one who joyfully does
     what is right;
   they remember You in Your ways.
   But we have sinned, and You were angry;
   we will remain in Your ways[g] and be saved.
6 All of us have become like something unclean,
     and all our righteous acts are
     like a polluted[h] garment;
   all of us wither like a leaf,
   and our iniquities carry us away like the wind.
7 No one calls on Your name,
     striving to take hold of You.
   For You have hidden Your face from us
   and made us melt because of[i] [j] our iniquity.

8 Yet LORD, You are our Father;
     we are the clay, and You are our potter;
   we all are the work of Your hands.
9 LORD, do not be terribly angry
     or remember ⌊our⌋ iniquity forever.
   Please look—all of us are Your people!
10 Your holy cities have become a wilderness;
     Zion has become a wilderness,
   Jerusalem a desolation.
11 Our holy and beautiful[k] temple,
     where our fathers praised You,
   has been burned with fire,
   and all that was dear to us lies in ruins.
12 LORD, after all this, will You restrain Yourself?
   Will You keep silent and afflict severely?

The LORD's Response

65 "I was sought by those who did not ask;[l]
     I was found by those who did not seek Me.
   I said: Here I am, here I am,
     to a nation that was not called by[m] My name.
2 I spread out My hands all day long
     to a rebellious people
   who walk in the wrong path,
     following their own thoughts.
3 These people continually provoke Me
     to My face,
   sacrificing in gardens,
   burning incense on bricks,

---

[a]63:14 Lit him [b]63:15 Lit The agitation of Your inward parts [c]63:17 Lit our heart from fearing [d]63:18 Or Your people possessed Your holy place [e]64:1 Is 63:19b in Hb [f]64:2 Is 64:1 in Hb [g]64:5 Lit in them [h]64:6 Lit menstrual [i]64:7 LXX, Syr, Vg, Tg read and delivered us into the hand of [j]64:7 Lit melt by the hand [k]64:11 Or glorious; Is 60:7 [l]65:1 LXX, Syr, DSS, Tg read ask for Me [m]65:1 LXX, Syr, DSS, Tg, Vg read that did not call on

---

harden further once they started straying.
64:1 tear the heavens open [and] come down. The sky was depicted as a piece of cloth God would tear as He came to destroy Israel's enemies.
64:6 righteous acts are like a polluted garment. Sins were described as the color red—

a warning of loss, of hurt, of defeat—in 1:18. Compared to God's righteousness, even our good behavior is worthless.

65:1 did not ask … did not seek. God allowed Himself to be found as He continually reached out in love to Israel. He was ready to help them, but they did not respond to

His voice.
65:3 continually provoke Me. The people disobeyed God by worshiping idols and consulting mediums and spiritists. **to My face.** They did not hide their shameful activities, but they defiantly and boldly sacrificed to idols.
65:5 I am too holy for you! Idolaters are like

4 sitting among the graves,
spending nights in secret places,
eating swine's flesh,
and putting polluted broth in their bowls.[a]
5 They say: Keep to yourself,
don't come near me, for I am too holy for you!
These practices are smoke in My nostrils,
a fire that burns all day long.
6 It is written before Me:
I will not keep silent, but I will repay;
I will repay them fully[b]
7 [for] your iniquities and the iniquities
of your[c] fathers together,"
says the LORD.
"Because they burned incense
on the mountains
and reproached Me on the hills,
I will reward them fully[d]
for their former deeds."

8 The LORD says this:

As the new wine is found in a bunch of grapes,
and one says: Don't destroy it,
for there's some good[e] in it,
so I will act because of My servants
and not destroy them all.
9 I will produce descendants from Jacob,
and heirs to My mountains from Judah;
My chosen ones will possess it,
and My servants will dwell there.
10 Sharon will be a pasture for flocks,
and the Valley of Achor a place for cattle
to lie down,
for My people who have sought Me.
11 But you who abandon the LORD,
who forget My holy mountain,
who prepare a table for Fortune[f]
and fill bowls of mixed wine for Destiny,
12 I will destine you for the sword,
and all of you will kneel down to be slaughtered,
because I called and you did not answer,
I spoke and you did not hear;
you did what was evil in My sight
and chose what I did not delight in.

13 Therefore, this is what the Lord GOD says:

My servants will eat,
but you will be hungry;
My servants will drink,

but you will be thirsty;
My servants will rejoice,
but you will be put to shame.
14 My servants will shout for joy from a glad heart,
but you will cry out from an anguished heart,
and you will lament out of a broken spirit.
15 You will leave your name behind
as a curse for My chosen ones,
and the Lord GOD will kill you;
but He will give His servants another name.
16 Whoever is blessed in the land
will be blessed by the God of truth,
and whoever swears in the land
will swear by the God of truth.
For the former troubles will be forgotten
and hidden from My sight.

A New Creation

17 "For I will create a new heaven
and a new earth;
the past events will not be remembered or come
to mind.
18 Then be glad and rejoice forever
in what I am creating;
for I will create Jerusalem to be a joy,
and its people to be a delight.
19 I will rejoice in Jerusalem
and be glad in My people.
The sound of weeping and crying
will no longer be heard in her.
20 In her, a nursing infant will no longer live
only a few days,[g]
or an old man not live out his days.
Indeed, the youth will die at a hundred years,
and the one who misses a hundred years
will be cursed.
21 People will build houses and live [in them];
they will plant vineyards and eat their fruit.
22 They will not build and others live [in them];
they will not plant and others eat.
For My people's lives will be
like the lifetime of a tree.
My chosen ones will fully enjoy
the work of their hands.
23 They will not labor without success
or bear children [destined] for disaster,
for they will be a people blessed by the LORD
along with their descendants.
24 Even before they call, I will answer;
while they are still speaking, I will hear.

[a]65:3–4 These vv. catalog pagan worship. [b]65:6 Lit repay into their lap [c]65:7 LXX, Syr read [for] their iniquities and the iniquities of their
[d]65:7 Lit reward into their lap [e]65:8 Or there's a blessing [f]65:11 A pagan god [g]65:20 Lit her, no longer infant of days

the New Testament Pharisees whom Jesus called children of the Devil (see John 8:44). They thought of themselves as better than others.

65:13 my servants will eat...you will be hungry. The call for God to tear open the heavens and come down (64:1) is a call to

blessing and judgment. Verses 13-16 describe the very different results of God's coming.

65:15 as a curse for My chosen ones. Believers will refer to rebellious Israelites as an example of those receiving judgment. The name of evil King Ahab was used as a curse.

The restored remnant would receive both a new name and a new character as a blessing.

65:18 create Jerusalem to be a joy. As God created the earth and heavens, so will He create a new world for the enjoyment of His people when Christ returns (Rev. 21:1).

65:24 before they call, I will answer. Some

25 The wolf and the lamb will feed together,[a]
and the lion will eat straw like the ox,
but the serpent's food will be dust!
They will not do what is evil or destroy
on My entire holy mountain,"
says the LORD.

Final Judgment and Joyous Restoration

66 This is what the LORD says:

Heaven is My throne,
and earth is My footstool.
What house could you possibly build for Me?
And what place could be My home?
2 My hand made all these things,
and so they all came into being.

⌊This is⌋
the LORD's declaration.
I will look favorably on this kind of person:
one who is humble, submissive[b] in spirit,
and who trembles at My word.
3 One slaughters an ox, one kills a man;
one sacrifices a lamb, one breaks a dog's neck;
one offers a •grain offering, one offers
swine's blood;
one offers incense, one praises an idol—
all these have chosen their ways
and delight in their abominations.
4 So I will choose their punishment,
and I will bring on them what they dread,
because I called and no one answered;
I spoke and they didn't hear;
they did what is evil in My sight
and chose what I didn't delight in.

5 You who tremble at His word,
hear the word of the LORD:
"Your brothers who hate and exclude you
because of Me have said:
Let the LORD be glorified,
so that we can see your joy!
But they will be put to shame."

6 A sound of uproar from the city!
A voice from the temple—
the voice of the LORD,
paying back His enemies what they deserve!

7 Before Zion was in labor, she gave birth;
before she was in pain, she delivered a boy.
8 Who has heard of such a thing?

Who has seen such things?
Can a land be born in one day,
or a nation be delivered in an instant?
Yet as soon as Zion was in labor,
she gave birth to her sons.
9 "Will I bring a baby to the point of birth
and not deliver ⌊it⌋?"
says the LORD;
"or will I who deliver, close ⌊the womb⌋?"
says your God.
10 Be glad for Jerusalem and rejoice over her,
all who love her.
Rejoice greatly with her,
all who mourn over her—
11 so that you may nurse and be satisfied
from her comforting breast
and drink deeply and delight yourselves
from her glorious breasts.

12 For this is what the LORD says:

I will make peace flow to her like a river,
and the wealth[c] of nations like a flood;
you will nurse and be carried on ⌊her⌋ hip,
and bounced on ⌊her⌋ lap.
13 As a mother comforts her son,
so I will comfort you,
and you will be comforted in Jerusalem.

14 You will see, you will rejoice,
and you[d] will flourish like grass;
then the LORD's power will be revealed
to His servants,
but He will show His wrath against His enemies.
15 Look, the LORD will come with fire—
His chariots are like the whirlwind—
to execute His anger with fury,
and His rebuke with flames of fire.
16 For the LORD will execute judgment
on all flesh with His fiery sword,
and many will be slain by the LORD.

17 "Those who dedicate and purify themselves to
⌊enter⌋ the groves following their leader,[e] eating
meat from pigs, vermin, and rats, will perish together."

⌊This is⌋
the LORD's declaration.
18 "Knowing[f] their works and their thoughts, I have
come to gather all nations and languages; they will
come and see My glory. 19 I will establish a sign among

---

[a]65:25 Lit as one   [b]66:2 Lit broken   [c]66:12 Or glory   [d]66:14 Lit your bones   [e]66:17 Hb obscure   [f]66:18 LXX, Syr; MT omits Knowing

---

refuse to pray because God knows everything. But prayer is God's appointed means
for bringing His blessings.

66:1 What house? God cannot be contained in any building (1 Kings 8:27). Jesus
told the Samaritan woman "an hour is coming
when you will worship the Father neither on

this mountain nor in Jerusalem...God is spirit,
and those who worship Him must worship in
spirit and truth."

**66:7 Before ... labor ... before she was in
pain.** Israel's return to the land will happen so
quickly that it will occur without pain. Zion
here is pictured as the mother of Israel, which

is also the Messiah.

66:11 drink deeply and delight yourselves.
The people in Jerusalem will enjoy the city as
an infant enjoys food provided by its mother.
Everyone will rejoice.

66:20 They will bring. The Gentiles will bring
Jews into the land at the beginning of the mil-

them, and I will send survivors from them to the nations—to Tarshish, Put,[a] Lud (who are archers), Tubal, Javan, and the islands far away—who have not heard of My fame or seen My glory. And they will proclaim My glory among the nations. 20 They will bring all your brothers from all the nations as a gift to the LORD on horses and chariots, in litters, and on mules and camels, to My holy mountain Jerusalem, says the LORD, just as the Israelites bring an offering in a clean vessel to the house of the LORD. 21 I will also take some of them as priests and Levites," says the LORD.

22   "For just as the new heavens and the new earth,

which I will make,
will endure before Me"—
              the LORD's declaration—
"so will your offspring and your name endure.
23   All mankind will come to worship Me,
from one New Moon to another,
and from one Sabbath to another,"
says the LORD.

24 "As they leave, they will see the dead bodies of the men who have rebelled against Me; for their maggots will never die, their fire will never go out, and they will be a horror to all mankind."

---

[a] **66:19** LXX; MT reads *Put*; Jr 46:9

---

lennium. Gentiles too will worship God in the land in those days (56:6-7).

66:23 all mankind. Referred to believing Jews and Gentiles from all nations, in contrast to those who reject God (Zech. 14:16). **from**

one Sabbath to another. Many provisions of the law of Moses will be practiced in the millennium.

66:24 their fire will never go out. Jesus quoted this verse from the end of Isaiah as the

destiny of the lost who are confined to hell (Mark 9:48). Hell is eternal torment and separation from God.

INTRODUCTION TO
JEREMIAH

AUTHOR

These are the words of Jeremiah, who was both a prophet and a priest. They were written down by his secretary, Baruch (36:4-32), who may have finalized Jeremiah's prophecies in written form.

DATE

Events recorded here span the years 626-585 B.C. The book was compiled sometime later. Jeremiah's ministry was immediately preceded by that of Zephaniah. Habakkuk, Obadiah, and Ezekiel were all possibly contemporaries of Jeremiah.

THEME

God is just and must punish sin. But God in His grace promises Israel restoration and covenant renewal.

HISTORICAL BACKGROUND

The prophet Jeremiah ministered in the context of three major kings. Under King Josiah (640-609 B.C.), Jeremiah was free to preach and join in Josiah's reform movement. Under King Jehoiakim (609-598 B.C.), Jeremiah fell out of royal favor and experienced frequent imprisonments. Under King Zedekiah (597-586 B.C.), Jeremiah was treated more kindly but still feared for his life. The judgment that Jeremiah announced was brought about by King Nebuchadnezzar of Babylon. He besieged Jerusalem three times, culminating in the sacking of Jerusalem in 586 B.C. and a full-scale exile of Jews to Babylon. Jewish tradition asserts that while Jeremiah was living in exile in Egypt, he was stoned to death (see Heb. 11:37).

CHARACTERISTICS

The book is constructed thematically, not chronologically. In it, Jeremiah speaks God's words and he is obviously distressed. He complains to God about the job allotted to him more than any other prophet. Jeremiah denounces Judah's kings for their folly and weakness and the people for going their own way. Equally a part of his message, however, is a God of love who is determined to mold a people worthy of His name. Jeremiah is allowed to see that the divine wrath had a 70-year limit. After that—forgiveness and cleansing would come—bringing a new day in which all expectations would be fulfilled in a manner transcending all God's mercies of old.

1 The words of Jeremiah, the son of Hilkiah, one of the priests living in Anathoth in the territory of Benjamin. [2] The word of the LORD came to him in the thirteenth year of the reign of Josiah son of Amon, king of Judah. [3] It also came throughout the days of Jehoiakim son of Josiah, king of Judah, until the fifth month of the eleventh year of Zedekiah son of Josiah, king of Judah, when the people of Jerusalem went into exile.

The Call of Jeremiah

[4] The word of the LORD came to me:

[5] I chose you before I formed you in the womb;
I set you apart before you were born.
I appointed you a prophet to the nations.

[6] But I protested, "Oh no, Lord GOD! Look, I don't know how to speak since I am ⌊only⌋ a youth."

[7] Then the LORD said to me:

Do not say: I am ⌊only⌋ a youth,
for you will go to everyone I send you to
and speak whatever I tell you.
[8] Do not be afraid of anyone,
for I will be with you to deliver you.

⌊This is⌋
the LORD's declaration.

[9] Then the LORD reached out His hand, touched my mouth, and told me:

Look, I have filled your mouth with My words.
[10] See, today I have set you
over nations and kingdoms
to uproot and tear down,
to destroy and demolish,
to build and plant.

Two Visions

[11] Then the word of the LORD came to me, asking, "What do you see, Jeremiah?"

I replied, "I see a branch of an almond tree."

[12] The LORD said to me, "You have seen correctly, for I watch over My word to accomplish it." [13] Again the word of the LORD came to me inquiring, "What do you see?"

And I replied, "I see a boiling pot, its mouth tilted from the north ⌊to the south⌋."

[14] Then the LORD said to me, "Disaster will be poured out[a] from the north on all who live in the land. [15] Indeed, I am about to summon all the clans and kingdoms of the north."

⌊This is⌋ the LORD's declaration.

They will come, and each ⌊king⌋ will set up his throne
at the entrance to Jerusalem's gates.
They will attack all her surrounding walls
and all the other cities of Judah.

[16] "I will pronounce My judgments against them for all the evil they did when they abandoned Me to burn incense to other gods and to worship the works of their own hands.

[17] "Now, get ready. Stand up and tell them everything that I command you. Do not be intimidated by them or I will cause you to cower before them. [18] Today, I am the One who has made you a fortified city, an iron pillar, and bronze walls against the whole land—against the kings of Judah, its officials, its priests, and the population. [19] They will fight against you but never prevail over you, since I am with you to rescue you."

⌊This is⌋
the LORD's declaration.

Israel Accused of Apostasy

2 The word of the LORD came to me: [2] "Go and announce directly to Jerusalem that this is what the LORD says:

I remember the loyalty of your youth,
your love as a bride—
how you followed Me in the wilderness,
in a land not sown.
[3] Israel was holy to the LORD,
the •firstfruits of His harvest.
All who ate of it found themselves guilty;
disaster came on them."

⌊This is⌋
the LORD's declaration.

[4] Hear the word of the LORD, house of Jacob
and all families of the house of Israel.
[5] Here is what the LORD says:

What fault did your fathers find in Me
that they went so far from Me,
followed worthless idols,
and became worthless themselves?
[6] They stopped asking: Where is the LORD
who brought us from the land of Egypt,
who led us through the wilderness,
through a land of deserts and ravines,
through a land of drought and darkness,[b]
a land no one traveled through
and where no one lived?

---

[a]**1:14** LXX reads *will boil*   [b]**2:6** Or *shadow of death*

1:2 Josiah. Josiah, the last godly king of Judah, became king at age eight. When he matured, he realized Israel had drifted from obedience to the Law and initiated reforms (2 Kings 22:11). The subsequent spiritual deterioration of Judah gave rise to Jeremiah.

1:3 Jehoiakim. After Josiah was killed by Pharaoh Neco (2 Kings 23:29), pharaoh named his evil son Jehoiakim as king.

1:6 don't know how to speak. Jeremiah tried the same excuse as Moses (Ex. 4:10).

1:9 touched my mouth. When Moses bemoaned his lack of speaking skill, God appointed Aaron his spokesman (Ex. 4:10-16).

For Jeremiah, God simply reached down and placed His words in the prophet's mouth.

2:2 your love as a bride. Marriage often illustrated the relationship between God and His people (Isa. 54:5; Hos. 2:16). In the New Testament, Paul compared the husband/wife relationship to that of Jesus and His church (Eph. 5:23).

7 I brought you to a fertile land
to eat its fruit and bounty,
but after you entered, you defiled My land;
you made My inheritance detestable.

8 The priests quit asking: Where is the LORD?
The experts in the law no longer knew Me,
and the rulers rebelled against Me.
The prophets prophesied by •Baal
and followed useless idols.

9 Therefore, I will bring a case against you again.
⌊This is⌋
the LORD's declaration.
I will bring a case against your children's children.

10 Cross over to Cyprusª and take a look.
Send ⌊someone⌋ to Kedar and consider carefully;
see if there has ever been anything like this:

11 Has a nation ⌊ever⌋ exchanged its gods?
(but they were not gods!)
Yet My people have exchanged theirᵇ Glory
for useless idols.

12 Be horrified at this, heavens;
be shocked and utterly appalled.
⌊This is⌋
the LORD's declaration.

13 For My people have committed a double evil:
They have abandoned Me,
the fountain of living water,
and dug cisterns for themselves,
cracked cisterns that cannot hold water.

Consequences of Apostasy

14 Is Israel a slave?
Was he born into slavery?ᶜ
Why else has he become a prey?

15 The young lions have roared at him;
they have roared loudly.
They have laid waste his land.
His cities are in ruins, without inhabitants.

16 The men of Memphis and Tahpanhes
have also broken your skull.

17 Have you not brought this on yourself
by abandoning the LORD your God
while He was leading you along the way?

18 Now what will you gain
by traveling along the way to Egypt
to drink the waters of the Nile?ᵈ
What will you gain
by traveling along the way to Assyria
to drink the waters of the Euphrates?

19 Your own evil will discipline you;
your own apostasies will reprimand you.
Think it over and see how evil and bitter it is
for you to abandon the LORD your God
and to have no •fear of Me.
⌊This is⌋ the declaration
of the Lord GOD of •Hosts.

20 For long ago Iᵉ broke your yoke;
Iᵉ tore off your fetters.
You insisted: I will not serve!
On every high hill
and under every leafy tree
you lie down ⌊like⌋ a prostitute.

21 I planted you, a choice vine
from the very best seed.
How then could you turn into
a degenerate, foreign vine?

22 Even if you wash with lye
and use a great amount of soap,
the stain of your guilt is still in front of Me.
⌊This is⌋ the Lord GOD's declaration.

23 How can you protest: I am not defiled;
I have not followed the Baals?
Look at your behavior in the valley;
acknowledge what you have done.
⌊You are⌋ a swift young camel
twisting and turning on her way,

24 a wild donkey at homeᶠ in the wilderness.
She sniffs the wind in the heat of her desire.
Who can control her passion?
All who look for her will not become tired;
they will find her in her mating season.ᵍ

25 Keep your feet from going bare
and your throat from thirst.
But you say: It's hopeless;
I love strangers,
and I will continue to follow them.

26 Like the shame of a thief when he is caught,
so the house of Israel has been put to shame.
They, their kings, their officials,
their priests, and their prophets

27 say to a tree: You are my father,
and to a stone: You gave birth to me.
For they have turned their back to Me
and not their face;
but in their time of disaster they beg:
Rise up and save us!

ª**2:10** Lit *to the islands of Kittim*   ᵇ**2:11** Alt Hb tradition reads *My.*   ᶜ**2:14** Lit *born of a house*   ᵈ**2:18** Lit *of Shichor*   ᵉ**2:20** LXX reads *you*   ᶠ**2:24** Lit *donkey taught*   ᵍ**2:24** Lit *her month*

2:13 cracked cisterns. Note the contrast between God and the pagan deities represented by idols. God was the source of life-sustaining water while cisterns could not hold even a drop for the people to drink.

2:18 to drink the waters. Jeremiah returned to the illustration of verse 13. God had pro-

vided spiritual and physical food in the desert (v. 6), yet the people turned away and looked to enemies for political and spiritual guidance.

2:19 evil ... apostasies. The Hebrew word translated "apostasies" implied repeated descents into backsliding. Other passages fur-

ther demonstrate Jeremiah's understanding of apostasy (3:22; 5:6; 14:7).

2:20 broke your yoke. Jeremiah compared Judah to a stubborn draft animal that rebelled against its master. Judah was more than willing to degrade itself as a prostitute serves her customer.

28 But where are your gods you made for yourself?
Let them rise up and save you
in your time of disaster if they can,
for your gods are as numerous as your cities, Judah.

Judgment Deserved

29 Why do you bring a case against Me?
All of you have rebelled against Me.

[This is]
the LORD's declaration.

30 I have struck down your children in vain;
they would not accept discipline.
Your own sword has devoured your prophets
like a ravaging lion.

31 [Evil] generation,
pay attention to the word of the LORD!
Have I been a wilderness to Israel
or a land of dense darkness?
Why do My people claim:
We will go where we want;[a]
we will no longer come to You?

32 Can a young woman forget her jewelry
or a bride her wedding sash?
Yet My people have forgotten Me
for countless days.

33 How skillfully you pursue love;
you also teach evil women your ways.

34 Moreover, your skirts are stained
with the blood of the innocent poor.
You did not catch them breaking and entering.
But in spite of all these things

35 you claim: I am innocent.
His anger is sure to turn away from me.
But I will certainly judge you
because you have said: I have not sinned.

36 How unstable you are,
constantly changing your way!
You will be put to shame by Egypt
just as you were put to shame by Assyria.

37 Moreover, you will be led out from here
with your hands on your head
since the LORD has rejected those you trust;
you will not succeed even with their help.[b]

Wages of Apostasy

3 If[c] a man divorces his wife
and she leaves him to marry another,
can he ever return to her?
Wouldn't such a land[d] become totally defiled?
But you!

You have played the prostitute
with many partners—
can you return to Me?

[This is]
the LORD's declaration.

2 Look to the barren heights and see.
Where have you not been immoral?
You sat waiting for them beside the highways
like a nomad in the desert.
You have defiled the land
with your prostitution and wickedness.

3 This is why the showers haven't come—
why there has been no spring rain.
You have the brazen look of a prostitute[e]
and refuse to be ashamed.

4 Have you not lately called Me: My Father,
my youthful companion?

5 Will He bear a grudge forever?
Will He be endlessly infuriated?
This is what you have spoken and done,
the evil you are capable of.

Unfaithful Israel, Treacherous Judah

6 In the days of King Josiah the LORD asked me, "Have you seen what unfaithful Israel has done? She has ascended every high hill and gone under every green tree to prostitute herself there. 7 I thought: After she has done all these things, she will return to Me. But she didn't return, and her treacherous sister Judah saw it. 8 I[f] observed that it was because unfaithful Israel had committed adultery that I had sent her away and had given her a certificate of divorce. Nevertheless, her treacherous sister Judah was not afraid but also went and prostituted herself. 9 Indifferent to[g] her prostitution, she defiled the land and committed adultery with stone and tree. 10 Yet in spite of all this, her treacherous sister Judah didn't return to Me with all her heart—only in pretense."

[This is]
the LORD's declaration.

11 The LORD announced to me, "Unfaithful Israel has shown herself more righteous than treacherous Judah. 12 Go, proclaim these words to the north, and say:

Return, unfaithful Israel.

[This is]
the LORD's declaration.

I will not look on you with anger,[h]
for I am unfailing in My love.

[This is]
the LORD's declaration.

---

[a]2:31 Or We have taken control, or We can roam   [b]2:37 Lit with them   [c]3:1 One Hb ms, LXX, Syr; other Hb mss read Saying: If   [d]3:1 LXX reads woman   [e]3:3 Lit have a prostitute's forehead   [f]3:8 One Hb ms, Syr read She   [g]3:9 Lit From the lightness of   [h]3:12 Lit not cause My face to fall on you

---

2:22 wash … stain. The stain of sin is only removed by the grace and forgiveness of God.

3:1 return to Me. Jeremiah reminded the people that the covenant relationship was not only contractual, it was personal at its core. The faithlessness of Israel was bad enough (v. 8), but Judah's sin was worse. She had prostituted herself with other gods. Would Judah's men forgive and take back an unfaithful wife?

3:7 treacherous sister. Ezekiel expanded on this metaphor of Judah and Israel as unfaithful sisters (Ezek. 23).

3:8 was not afraid. Judah had watched the decline and fall of Israel (2 Kings 15:17–17:41). Yet the Southern Kingdom never seemed to worry that the same fate might befall them.

3:10 only in pretense. Judah had only pretended to embrace Josiah's reforms (2 Kings 23:1-25).

I will not be angry forever.
13 Only acknowledge your guilt—
you have rebelled against the LORD your God.
You have scattered your favors to strangers
under every green tree
and have not obeyed My voice.

⌊This is⌋
the LORD's declaration.

14 "Return, you faithless children"—⌊this is⌋ the LORD's declaration—"for I am your master, and I will take you, one from a city and two from a family, and I will bring you to Zion. 15 I will give you shepherds who are loyal to Me,[a] and they will shepherd you with knowledge and skill. 16 When you multiply and increase in the land, in those days"—the LORD's declaration—"no one will say any longer: The ark of the LORD's covenant. It will never come to mind, and no one will remember or miss it. It will never again be made. 17 At that time Jerusalem will be called, The LORD's Throne, and all the nations will be gathered to it, to the name of the LORD in Jerusalem. They will cease to follow the stubbornness of their evil hearts. 18 In those days the house of Judah will join with the house of Israel, and they will come together from the land of the north to the land I have given your ancestors to inherit."

True Repentance

19 I thought: How I long to make you ⌊My⌋ sons
and give you a desirable land,
the most beautiful inheritance of all
the nations.
I thought: You will call Me, my Father,
and never turn away from Me.
20 However, as a woman may betray her lover,[b]
so you have betrayed Me, house of Israel.

⌊This is⌋
the LORD's declaration.

21 A sound is heard on the barren heights,
the children of Israel weeping and begging
for mercy,
for they have perverted their way;
they have forgotten the LORD their God.
22 Return, you faithless children.
I will heal your unfaithfulness.
"Here we are, coming to You,
for You are the LORD our God.
23 Surely, falsehood comes from the hills,
commotion from the mountains,
but the salvation of Israel

is only in the LORD our God.
24 From the time of our youth
the shameful one[c] has consumed
what our fathers have worked for—
their flocks and their herds,
their sons and their daughters.
25 Let us lie down in our shame;
let our disgrace cover us.
We have sinned against the LORD our God,
both we and our fathers,
from the time of our youth even to this day.
We have not obeyed the voice of the LORD
our God."

Blessing or Curse

4 If you return,[d] Israel—

⌊this is⌋
the LORD's declaration—
⌊if⌋ you return to Me,
if you remove your detestable idols
from My presence
and do not waver,
2 if you swear, As the LORD lives,
in truth, in justice, and in righteousness,
then the nations will be blessed[e] by Him
and will pride themselves in Him.

3 For this is what the LORD says to the men of Judah and Jerusalem:

Break up the unplowed ground;
do not sow among the thorns.
4 Circumcise yourselves to the LORD;
remove the foreskin of your hearts,
men of Judah and residents of Jerusalem.
Otherwise, My wrath will break out like fire
and burn with no one to extinguish ⌊it⌋
because of your evil deeds.

Judgment from the North

5 Declare in Judah, proclaim in Jerusalem, and say:

Blow the ram's horn throughout the land.
Cry out loudly and say:
Assemble yourselves,
and let's flee to the fortified cities.
6 Lift up a signal flag toward Zion.
Run for cover! Don't stand still!
For I am bringing disaster from the north—
a great destruction.
7 A lion has gone up from his thicket;
a destroyer of nations has set out.
He has left his lair

---

a 3:15 Lit shepherds according to My heart   b 3:20 Lit friend   c 3:24 = a euphemism for Baal   d 4:1 Or Repent   e 4:2 Or will bless themselves

---

3:12 to the north. Many of Israel's citizens had been taken into exile by Assyria and removed to that empire's Northern provinces. Those who remained in Israel lived north of Judah.

3:16 In those days ... It will never come to mind. Even the ark of the covenant will be ir-

relevant and forgotten. Jeremiah did not imply that this coming Messianic age would be godless, but rather that the old covenant would be superseded by something better.

3:17 called The LORD's Throne. The ark of the covenant had contained the atonement cover. Golden cherubim sat on each end,

and God was enthroned between the cherubim (see 2 Chron. 5:8). In the Messianic age, however, Jesus' throne will be in Jerusalem instead of the ark.

3:18 house of Judah will join ... Israel. God's people had become a divided nation (1 Kings 11-12). In the Messianic age,

to make your land a waste.
Your cities will be reduced to uninhabited ruins.

8 Because of this, put on •sackcloth;
mourn and wail,
for the LORD's burning anger
has not turned away from us.

9 "On that day"—[this is] the LORD's declaration—
"the king and the officials will lose their courage. The
priests will tremble in fear, and the prophets will be
scared speechless."

10 I said, "Oh no, Lord GOD, You have certainly
deceived this people and Jerusalem, by announcing,
'You will have peace,' while a sword is at[a] our throats."

11 At that time it will be said to this people and to
Jerusalem, "A searing wind [blows] from the barren
heights in the wilderness on the way to My dear[b] people. [It comes] not to winnow or to sift; 12 a wind too
strong for this comes at My call.[c] Now I will also pronounce judgments against them."

13 Look, he advances like clouds;
his chariots are like a storm.
His horses are swifter than eagles.
Woe to us, for we are ruined!

14 Wash the evil from your heart, Jerusalem,
so that you will be delivered.
How long will you harbor
malicious thoughts within you?

15 For a voice announces from Dan,
proclaiming malice from Mount Ephraim.

16 Warn the nations: Look!
Proclaim to Jerusalem:
Those who besiege are coming
from a distant land;
they raise their voices
against the cities of Judah.

17 They have her surrounded
like those who guard a field,
because she has rebelled against Me.
[This is]
the LORD's declaration.

18 Your way of life and your actions
have brought this on you.
This is your punishment. It is very bitter,
because it has reached your heart!

Jeremiah's Lament

19 My anguish, my anguish![d] I writhe in agony!
Oh, the pain in[e] my heart!
My heart pounds;
I cannot be silent.

For you, my soul,
have heard the sound of the ram's horn—
the shout of battle.

20 Disaster after disaster is reported,
for the whole land is destroyed.
Suddenly my tents are destroyed,
my tent curtains, in a moment.

21 How long must I see the signal flag
and hear the sound of the ram's horn?

22 For My people are fools;
they do not know Me.
They are foolish children,
without understanding.
They are skilled in doing what is evil,
but they do not know how to do what is good.

23 I looked at the earth,
and it was formless and empty.
[I looked] to the heavens,
and their light was gone.

24 I looked at the mountains,
and they were quaking;
all the hills shook.

25 I looked, and no man was left;
all the birds of the sky had fled.

26 I looked, and the fertile field was a wilderness.
All its cities were torn down
because of the LORD
and His burning anger.

27 For this is what the LORD says:

The whole land will be a desolation,
but I will not finish it off.

28 Because of this, the earth will mourn;
the skies above will grow dark.
I have spoken; I have planned,
and I will not relent or turn back from it.

29 Every city flees
at the sound of the horseman and the archer.
They enter the thickets
and climb among the rocks.
Every city is abandoned;
no inhabitant is left.

30 And you devastated one, what are you doing
that you dress yourself in scarlet,
that you adorn yourself with gold jewelry,
that you enlarge your eyes with paint?
You beautify yourself for nothing.
Your lovers reject you;

ᵃ4:10 Lit sword touches   ᵇ4:11 Lit to the daughter of My   ᶜ4:12 Lit comes for Me   ᵈ4:19 Lit My inner parts, my inner parts   ᵉ4:19 Lit the walls of

---

God's people would be united again.
4:2 nations will be blessed. God promised
to make Abram's descendants into a great
nation and that other nations would be
blessed by his descendants (Gen. 12:2-3).
4:10 You have certainly deceived. God had
not directly deceived, but allowed false

prophets to promulgate untruths for various
reasons (see 1 Kings 22:20-23.)
4:11 searing wind … [blows]. The Babylonians were speedily approaching with the
goal of destroying Israel.
4:12 a wind too strong for this. A light
breeze separates good (wheat) and bad

(chaff) (Ps. 35:5.) The Lord will soon send a
wind that destroys.
4:23 earth … was formless and empty. Israel and Judah's destruction would return the
world to the state of pre-creation chaos. Genesis 1:2 is the only other use of this phrase in
the Bible.

they want to take your life.

31 I hear a cry like a woman in labor,
⌊a cry of⌋ anguish like one bearing her first child.
The cry of Daughter Zion gasping for breath,
stretching out her hands:
Woe is me, for my life is weary
because of the murderers!

The Depravity of Jerusalem

5 Roam through the streets of Jerusalem.
Look and take note;
search in her squares.
If you find a single person,
anyone who acts justly,
who seeks to be faithful,
then I will forgive her.

2 When they say, "As the LORD lives,"
they are swearing falsely.

3 LORD, don't Your eyes ⌊look for⌋ faithfulness?
You have struck them, but they felt no pain.
You finished them off,
but they refused to accept discipline.
They made their faces harder than rock,
and they refused to return.

4 Then I thought:

They are just the poor;
they have played the fool.
For they don't understand the way of the LORD,
the justice of their God.

5 I will go to the powerful
and speak to them.
Surely they know the way of the LORD,
the justice of their God.
However, these also had broken the yoke
and torn off the fetters.

6 Therefore, a lion from the forest
will strike them down.
A wolf from an arid plain will ravage them.
A leopard keeps watch over their cities.
Anyone who leaves them will be torn to pieces
because their rebellious acts are many,
their unfaithful deeds numerous.

7 Why should I forgive you?
Your children have abandoned Me
and sworn by those who are not gods.
I satisfied their needs, yet they
committed adultery;
they gashed themselves
at the prostitute's house.

8 They are well-fed,[a] eager[b] stallions,
each neighing after someone else's wife.

9 Should I not punish them for these things?
⌊This is⌋
the LORD's declaration.
Should I not avenge Myself
on such a nation as this?

10 Go up among her vineyard terraces
and destroy them,
but do not finish them off.
Prune away her shoots,
for they do not belong to the LORD.

11 They, the house of Israel and the house of Judah,
have dealt very treacherously with Me.
⌊This is⌋
the LORD's declaration.

12 They have contradicted the LORD
and insisted, "It won't happen.[c]
Harm won't come to us;
we won't see sword or famine."

13 The prophets become ⌊only⌋ wind,
for the ⌊LORD's⌋ word is not in them.
This will in fact happen to them.

Coming Judgment

14 Therefore, this is what the Lord GOD of •Hosts says:

Because you have spoken this word,
I am going to make My words
become fire in your mouth.
These people are the wood,
and the fire will consume them.

15 I am about to bring a nation
from far away against you,
house of Israel.

⌊This is⌋
the LORD's declaration.

It is an established nation,
an ancient nation,
a nation whose language you do not know
and whose speech you do not understand.

16 Their quiver is like an open grave;
they are all mighty warriors.

17 They will consume your harvest and your food.
They will consume your sons and your daughters.
They will consume your flocks and your herds.
They will consume your vines
and your fig trees.
They will destroy with the sword
your fortified cities in which you trust.

ª5:8 Lit well-equipped; Hb obscure   ᵇ5:8 Lit early-rising; Hb obscure   ᶜ5:12 Lit He does not exist

---

4:25-26 I looked, and no man was left. The world reduced to the state which existed before God had created life (Gen. 1:1-10).

4:27 I will not finish it off. The coming devastation would be terrible, but God's judgment would be tempered with mercy.

5:1 find a single person. Like His challenge to Abraham at Sodom (Gen. 18:26-33), God would spare Jerusalem for only one honest person.

5:6 lion … wolf …leopard. Not only has the ox broken from his yoke, he has wandered

beyond the farmer's protection (5:5). Some see lions, wolves, and leopards as literal animals of God's judgment (Lev 26:22; 2 Kings 2:24; 17:25; Ezek. 14:15). Yet, it is easier to see them as the nations referred to in chapters 4 and 6 (2:15; 4:7; 6:3; Hosea 13:7-8; Hab. 1:8; Zeph. 3:3). While the text says "will

18 "But even in those days"—⌊this is⌋ the LORD's declaration—"I will not finish you off. 19 When people ask: For what offense has the LORD our God done all these things to us? You will respond to them: Just as you abandoned Me and served foreign gods in your land, so will you serve strangers in a land that is not yours.

20 "Declare this in the house of Jacob; proclaim it in Judah, saying:

21 Hear this,
you foolish and senseless[a] people.
They have eyes, but they don't see.
They have ears, but they don't hear.
22 Do you not •fear Me?

⌊This is⌋
the LORD's declaration.

Do you not tremble before Me,
the One who set the sand as the boundary
of the sea,
an enduring barrier that it cannot cross?
The waves surge, but they cannot prevail.
They roar but cannot pass over it.
23 But these people have stubborn
and rebellious hearts.
They have turned aside and have gone away.
24 They have not said to themselves:
Let's fear the LORD our God,
who gives the rain, both early and late,
in its season,
who guarantees to us the fixed weeks
of the harvest.
25 Your guilty acts have diverted these things
⌊from you⌋.
Your sins have withheld ⌊My⌋ bounty from you,
26 for wicked men live among My people.
They watch like fowlers lying in wait.[b]
They set a trap;
they catch men.
27 Like a cage full of birds,
so their houses are full of deceit.
Therefore they have grown powerful and rich.
28 They have become fat and sleek.
They have also excelled in evil matters.
They have not taken up cases,
such as the case of orphans,
so they might prosper,
and they have not defended the rights of the needy.
29 Should I not punish them for these things?

⌊This is⌋
the LORD's declaration.

Should I not avenge Myself
on such a nation as this?

30 A horrible, terrible thing
has taken place in the land.
31 The prophets prophesy falsely,
and the priests rule by their own authority.
My people love it like this.
But what will you do at the end of it?

Threatened Siege of Jerusalem

6 Run for cover, Benjaminites,
out of Jerusalem!
Sound the ram's horn in Tekoa;
raise a smoke signal over Beth-haccherem,[c]
for disaster threatens from the north,
even great destruction.
2 ⌊Though she is⌋ beautiful and delicate,
I will destroy[d] Daughter Zion.
3 Shepherds and their flocks will come against her;
they will pitch ⌊their⌋ tents all around her.
Each will pasture his own portion.
4 Set ⌊them⌋ apart for war against her;
rise up, let's attack at noon.
Woe to us, for the day is passing;
the evening shadows grow long.
5 Rise up, let's attack by night.
Let us destroy her fortresses."

6 For this is what the LORD of •Hosts says:

Cut down the trees;
raise a siege ramp against Jerusalem.
This city must be punished.
There is nothing but oppression within her.
7 As a well gushes out its water,
so she pours forth her evil.[e]
Violence and destruction resound in her.
Sickness and wounds keep coming
to My attention.
8 Be warned, Jerusalem,
or I will be torn away from you;
I will make you a desolation,
a land devoid of inhabitant.

Wrath on Israel

9 This is what the LORD of Hosts says:

Glean as thoroughly as a vine
the remnant of Israel.
Pass your hand once more like a grape gatherer
over the branches.

---

a5:21 Lit without heart   b5:26 Hb obscure   c6:1 Or House of the Vineyard; Neh 3:14   d6:2 Or silence   e6:7 Or well keeps its water fresh, so she keeps her evil fresh

---

strike … ravage … be torn," the verbs used are in the perfect tense (in Hebrew). The prophetic writings regularly used this tense to underscore that prophecies were as good as done (Amos 5:2).

5:12 won't see sword or famine. Jeremiah mentions two of God's weapons. The third was plague. (14:12).

5:23 stubborn and rebellious hearts. Israel and Judah "refused to accept discipline" (v. 3) and kept on sinning (adultery and idolatry, v. 7).

5:28 excelled in evil matters. The sins of the people are doubly terrible because they not only committed sins but also neglected to do right for the poor and unfortunate.

6:1 out of Jerusalem. There was a certain safety implied in the "fortified cities" (4:5), but even that refuge would be swept away by the onslaught of Babylonians serving as the

10 Who can I speak to and give such a warning[a]
that they will listen?
Look, their ear is uncircumcised,[b]
so they cannot pay attention.
See, the word of the LORD
    has become contemptible to them—
they find no pleasure in it.

11 But I am full of the LORD's wrath;
I am tired of holding it back.
Pour ⌊it⌋ out on the children in the street,
on the gang of young men as well.
For both husband and wife will be captured,
the old with the very old.[c]

12 Their houses will be turned over to others,
⌊their⌋ fields and wives as well,
for I will stretch out My hand
against the residents of the land.

⌊This is⌋
the LORD's declaration.

13 For from the least to the greatest of them,
everyone is gaining profit unjustly.
From prophet to priest,
everyone deals falsely.

14 They have treated
    My people's brokenness superficially,
claiming: Peace, peace,
when there is no peace.

15 Were they ashamed when they acted
    so abhorrently?
They weren't at all ashamed.
They can no longer feel humiliation.
Therefore, they will fall among the fallen.
When I punish them, they will collapse,
says the LORD.

Disaster Because of Disobedience

16 This is what the LORD says:

Stand by the roadways and look.
Ask about the ancient paths:
Which is the way to what is good?
Then take it
and find rest for yourselves.
But they protested: We won't!

17 I appointed watchmen over you
⌊and said:⌋ Listen for the sound of the ram's horn.
But they protested: We won't listen!

18 Therefore listen, you nations
and you witnesses,
learn what ⌊the charge⌋ is against them.

19 Listen, earth!
I am about to bring disaster on these people,
the fruit of their own plotting,
for they have paid no attention to My word.
They have rejected My law.

20 What use to Me is frankincense from Sheba
or sweet cane from a distant land?
Your •burnt offerings are not acceptable;
your sacrifices do not please Me.

21 Therefore, this is what the LORD says:
I am going to place stumbling blocks
    before these people;
fathers and sons together will stumble
    over them;
friends and neighbors will ⌊also⌋ perish.

A Cruel Nation from the North

22 This is what the LORD says:

Look, an army is coming from a northern land;
a great nation will be awakened
from the remote regions of the earth.

23 They grasp bow and javelin.
They are cruel and show no mercy.
Their voice roars like the sea,
and they ride on horses,
lined up like men in battle formation
against you, Daughter Zion.

24 We have heard about it,
and we are discouraged.[d]
Distress has seized us—
pain like a woman in labor.

25 Don't go out to the fields;
don't walk on the road.
For the enemy has a sword;
terror is on every side.

26 My dear[e] people, dress yourselves in •sackcloth
and roll in the dust.
Mourn ⌊as you would for⌋ an only son,
a bitter lament,
for suddenly the destroyer will come on us.

Jeremiah Appointed as an Examiner

27 I have appointed you to be an assayer
    among My people—
a refiner[f]—
so you may know and assay their way of life.

28 All are stubborn rebels
spreading slander.

a**6:10** Or *and bear witness.*   b**6:10** = unresponsive to God   c**6:11** Lit *with fullness of days*   d**6:24** Lit *and our hands fail*   e**6:26** Lit *Daughter of My*
f**6:27** Text emended; MT reads *fortress*

Lord's instruments of judgment. The Babylonians served without knowing better, while the Israelites should have known.

6:4 Set [them] apart for war. The Babylonians speak in verses 4 and 5. In contrast to the panic felt by the people of Judah (v. 1), the invaders were calm and calculating. The

Babylonians prepared themselves for war, but the people of Judah looked only to escape.

6:10 ear is uncircumcised. The people were so caught up in their sin that they would not listen. Though the people were physically circumcised, they acted like pagans.

6:11 full of the LORD's wrath. He had been Jeremiah had "ingested" the Word of God through visions and is filled with the Lord's righteous anger.

6:14 Peace, peace, when there is no peace. Corrupt priests and prophets taught a "feel-good" message that aimed to treat the symp-

[They are] bronze and iron;
all of them are corrupt.
29 The bellows blow,
blasting the lead with fire.
The refining is completely in vain;
the evil ones are not separated out.
30 They are called rejected silver,
for the LORD has rejected them.

False Trust in the Temple

7 [This is] the word that came to Jeremiah from the LORD: 2 "Stand in the gate of the house of the LORD and there call out this word: Hear the word of the LORD, all [you people] of Judah who enter through these gates to worship the LORD.

3 "This is what the LORD of •Hosts, the God of Israel, says: Correct your ways and your deeds, and I will allow you to live in this place. 4 Do not trust deceitful words, chanting: This is the temple of the LORD, the temple of the LORD, the temple of the LORD. 5 Instead, if you really change your ways and your actions, if you act justly toward one another,a 6 if you no longer oppress the alien, the fatherless, and the widow and no longer shed innocent blood in this place or follow other gods, bringing harm on yourselves, 7 I will allow you to live in this place, the land I gave to your ancestors forever and ever. 8 [But] look, you keep trusting in deceitful words that cannot help.

9 "Do you steal, murder, commit adultery, swear falsely, burn incense to •Baal, and follow other gods that you have not known? 10 Then do you come and stand before Me in this house called by My name and insist: We are safe? As a result, you are free to continue doing all these detestable acts! 11 Has this house, which is called by My name, become a den of robbers in your view? Yes, I too have seen [it]."

[This is] the LORD's declaration.

Shiloh As a Warning

12 "But return to My place that was at Shiloh, where I made My name dwell at first. See what I did to it because of the evil of My people Israel. 13 Now, because you have done all these things"—[this is] the LORD's declaration—"and because I have spoken to you time and time againb but you wouldn't listen, and I have called to you, but you wouldn't answer, 14 what I did to Shiloh I will do to the house that is called by My name—the house in which you trust—the place that I gave you and your ancestors. 15 I will drive you from

My presence, just as I drove out all of your brothers, all the descendants of Ephraim.

Do Not Pray for Judah

16 "As for you, do not pray for these people. Do not offer a cry or a prayer on their behalf, and do not beg Me, for I will not listen to you. 17 Don't you see how they behave in the cities of Judah and in the streets of Jerusalem? 18 The sons gather wood, the fathers light the fire, and the women knead dough to make cakes for the queen of heaven,c and they pour out drink offerings to other gods so that they provoke Me to anger. 19 But are they really provoking Me?" [This is] the LORD's declaration. "Isn't it they themselves [being provoked] to disgrace?"

20 Therefore, this is what the Lord GOD says: "Look, My anger—My burning wrath—is about to be poured out on this place, on man and beast, on the tree of the field, and on the fruit of the ground. My wrath will burn and not be quenched."

Obedience Over Sacrifice

21 This is what the LORD of Hosts, the God of Israel, says: "Add your •burnt offerings to your other sacrifices, and eat the meat yourselves, 22 for when I brought your ancestors out of the land of Egypt, I did not speak with them or command them concerning burnt offering and sacrifice. 23 However, I did give them this command: Obey Me, and then I will be your God, and you will be My people. You must walk in every way I command you so that it may go well with you." 24 Yet they didn't listen or pay attention but walked according to their own advice and according to their own stubborn, evil heart. They went backward and not forward. 25 Since the day your ancestors came out of the land of Egypt until this day, I have sent all My servants the prophets to you time and time again.d 26 However, they wouldn't listen to Me or pay attention but became obstinate;e they did more evil than their ancestors.

A Lament for Disobedient Judah

27 "When you speak all these things to them, they will not listen to you. When you call to them, they will not answer you. 28 You must therefore declare to them: This is the nation that would not listen to the voice of the LORD their God and would not accept discipline. Truthf has perished—it has disappeared from their mouths. 29 Cut off the hair of your sacred vowg and throw it away. Raise up a dirge on the barren heights,

---

a 7:5 Lit justly between a man and his neighbor   b 7:13 Lit you rising early and speaking   c 7:18 = a pagan goddess   d 7:25 Lit you, each day rising early and sending   e 7:26 Lit but stiffened their neck   f 7:28 Or Faithfulness   g 7:29 Lit off your consecration

---

toms of the people's spiritual disease instead of treating the disease itself. Instead of calling for repentance, they tried to console the people with lies.

6:17 appointed watchmen. God appointed true prophets to serve His people so that His Word could be heard and His

warnings understood. (Ezek. 3:17.)

6:20 Your burnt offerings are not acceptable. God would rather see a spirit of repentance than hardened people doing rituals.

6:29-30 refining is completely in vain. To refine silver, the refiner would add lead which

would oxidize and remove other impurities. The result was pure silver. In this refining, however, the ore was so corrupt that its impurities couldn't be purged.

7:4 deceitful words ... the temple of the Lord. The corrupt priests and prophets proclaimed that Jerusalem would not be de-

for the LORD has rejected and abandoned the generation under His wrath.

30 "For the Judeans have done what is evil in My sight." ⌊This is⌋ the LORD's declaration. "They have set up their detestable things in the house that is called by My name and defiled it. 31 They have built the •high places of Topheth[a] in the Valley of Hinnom[b] in order to burn their sons and daughters in the fire, a thing I did not command; I never entertained the thought.[c]

32 "Therefore, take note! Days are coming"—the LORD's declaration—"when ⌊this place⌋ will no longer be called Topheth and the Valley of Hinnom, but the Valley of Slaughter. Topheth will become a cemetery,[d] because there will be no other burial place. 33 The corpses of these people will become food for the birds of the sky and for the wild animals of the land, with no one to scare them off. 34 I will remove from the cities of Judah and the streets of Jerusalem the sound of joy and gladness and the voices of the bridegroom and the bride, for the land will become a desolate waste.

Death over Life

8 "At that time"—⌊this is⌋ the LORD's declaration—"the bones of the kings of Judah, the bones of her officials, the bones of the priests, the bones of the prophets, and the bones of the residents of Jerusalem will be brought out of their graves. 2 They will be exposed to the sun, the moon, and the whole heavenly •host, which they have loved, served, followed, pursued, and worshiped. ⌊Their bones⌋ will not be collected and buried but will become like manure on the surface of the soil. 3 Death will be chosen over life by all the survivors of this evil family, those who remain wherever I have banished them." ⌊This is⌋ the declaration of the LORD of Hosts.

4 You are to say to them: This is what the LORD says:

Do ⌊people⌋ fall and not get up again?
If they turn away, do they not return?
5 Why have these people turned away?
Why is Jerusalem always turning away?
They take hold of deceit;
they refuse to return.
6 I have paid careful attention.
They do not speak what is right.
No one regrets his evil,
asking: What have I done?
Everyone has stayed his course
like a horse rushing into battle.
7 Even the stork in the sky

knows her seasons.
The turtledove, swallow, and crane[e]
are aware of their migration,
but My people do not know
the requirements of the LORD.

Punishment for Judah's Leaders

8 How can you claim: We are wise;
the law of the LORD is with us?
In fact, the lying pen of scribes
has produced falsehood.
9 The wise will be put to shame;
they will be dismayed and snared.
They have rejected the word of the LORD,
so what wisdom do they really have?
10 Therefore, I will give their wives to other men,
their fields to new occupants,
for from the least to the greatest,
everyone is gaining profit unjustly.
From prophet to priest,
everyone deals falsely.
11 They have treated superficially the brokenness
of My dear[f] people,
claiming: Peace, peace,
when there is no peace.
12 Were they ashamed when they acted
so abhorrently?
They weren't at all ashamed.
They can no longer feel humiliation.
Therefore, they will fall among the fallen.
When I punish them, they will collapse,
says the LORD.
13 I will gather them and bring them to an end.[g]
⌊This is⌋
the LORD's declaration.

There will be no grapes on the vine,
no figs on the fig tree,
and even the leaf will wither.
Whatever I have given them will be lost to them.

God's People Unrepentant

14 Why are we just sitting here?
Gather together; let us enter the fortified cities
and there suffer our fate,[h]
for the LORD our God has condemned[i] us.
He has given us poisoned water to drink,
because we have sinned against the LORD.
15 We hoped for peace, but there was
nothing good;
for a time of healing, but there was only terror.

---

a 7:31 Lit of the fireplace   b 7:31 A valley south of Jerusalem   c 7:31 Lit command, and it did not arise on My heart   d 7:32 Lit They will bury in Topheth   e 8:7 Hb obscure   f 8:11 Lit of the daughter of My   g 8:13 Lit Gathering I will end them   h 8:14 Or there be silenced   i 8:14 Or silenced

---

stroyed because of God's temple.

7:12 place that was at Shiloh. After the conquest of Canaan, the tabernacle was set up at Shiloh (Josh. 18:1) and remained there through the period of the judges (1 Sam. 1:9). Though 1 Samuel 1-4 does not actually record Shiloh's destruction by the Philistines,

Jeremiah implies this historical precedent. Later, the tabernacle is at Gibeon in David's reign (1 Chron. 21:29).

7:25 My servants the prophets. Jeremiah was part of a long roster specially chosen for this role (see Deut. 18:15-22).

7:30 set up their detestable things in the

house that is called by my Name. King Hezekiah tried to end paganism among the people (2 Kings 18:3-4). His son Manasseh, however, built altars in the temple to pagan gods (2 Kings 21:4). During Jeremiah's time, Josiah renewed the covenant (2 Kings 23) and tried to stop idolatry (2 Kings 23:24).

16 From Dan is heard
the snorting of horses.
At the sound of the neighing
of mighty steeds,
the whole land quakes.
They come to devour the land and everything
in it,
the city and all its residents.

17 Indeed, I am about to send snakes
among you,
poisonous vipers that cannot be charmed.
They will bite you.

⌊This is⌋
the LORD's declaration.

Lament over Judah

18 My joy has flown away;
grief has settled on me.
My heart is sick.

19 Listen—the cry of my dear[a] people
from a far away land:
Is the LORD no longer in Zion,
her King not in her midst?
Why have they provoked Me to anger
with their graven images,
with their worthless foreign idols?

20 Harvest has passed, summer has ended,
but we have not been saved.

21 I am broken by the brokenness
of my dear[a] people.
I mourn; horror has taken hold of me.

22 Is there no balm[b] in Gilead?
Is there no physician there?
So why has the healing
of my dear[a] people
not come about?

9 [c] If my head were water,
my eyes a fountain of tears,
I would weep day and night
over the slain of my dear[d] people.

2[e] If only I had a traveler's lodging place
in the wilderness,
I would abandon my people
and depart from them,
for they are all adulterers,
a solemn assembly of treacherous people.

3 They bent their tongues ⌊like⌋ their bows;
lies and not faithfulness prevail
in the land,

for they proceed from one evil to another,
and they do not take Me into account.

⌊This is⌋
the LORD's declaration.

Imminent Ruin and Exile

4 Everyone has to be on guard against his friend.
Don't trust any brother,
for every brother will certainly deceive,
and every friend spread slander.

5 Each one betrays his friend;
no one tells the truth.
They have taught their tongues to speak lies;
they wear themselves out doing wrong.

6 You live in ⌊a world⌋ of deception.[f]
In ⌊their⌋ deception they refuse to know Me.

⌊This is⌋
the LORD's declaration.

7 Therefore, this is what the LORD of •Hosts says:

I am about to refine them and test them,
for what else can I do
because of My dear[g] people?[h]

8 Their tongues are deadly arrows—
they speak deception.
With his mouth
a man speaks peaceably with his friend,
but inwardly he sets up an ambush.

9 Should I not punish them for these things?

⌊This is⌋
the LORD's declaration.

Should I not take My revenge[i]
against a nation such as this?

10 I will raise weeping and a lament
over the mountains,
a dirge over the wilderness grazing land,
for they have been so scorched
that no one passes through.
The sound of cattle is no longer heard.
From the birds of the sky to the animals,
⌊everything⌋ has fled—they have gone away.

11 I will make Jerusalem a heap of rubble,
a jackals' den.
I will make the cities of Judah a desolation,
an uninhabited place.

12 Who is the man wise enough to understand this?
Who has the LORD spoken to, that he may explain it?
Why is the land destroyed and scorched like a wilderness, so no one can pass through?

[a] 8:19,21,22 Lit of the daughter of my   [b] 8:22 = a medicine   [c] 9:1 Jr 8:23 in Hb   [d] 9:1 Lit slain among the daughter of my   [e] 9:2 Jr 9:1 in Hb   [f] 9:6 LXX reads Oppression on oppression, deceit on deceit   [g] 9:7 Lit of the daughter of My   [h] 9:7 LXX, Tg read because of their evils   [i] 9:9 Or not vindicate Myself

These reforms failed as well. Less than 20 years after Jeremiah's death, Ezekiel reported that idols again occupied the temple courts (see Ezek. 8:3, 5-6).

7:31 to burn their sons and daughters. Here trash was dumped and children were sacrificed to pagan gods. Though prohibited

by the Law (Lev. 18:21), child sacrifice was practiced by Ahaz (2 Kings 16:2-3) and Manasseh (2 Kings 21:1, 6). The Hebrew name for the Valley of Hinnom ("ge' hinnom") became "Gehenna," which was translated in the New Testament as "hell" (Matt. 18:9).

8:19 Is the LORD no longer in Zion? The

people wondered how their sovereign God-King could allow such a terrible fate to befall them. The correct answer: God had always been with them, but they had not been "with" God.

9:1 my eyes a fountain of tears. Jeremiah, the "weeping prophet," was a tenderhearted

13 The LORD said, "It is because they abandoned My law I set in front of them and did not obey My voice or walk according to it. 14 Instead, they followed the stubbornness of their hearts and the •Baals, as their fathers taught them." 15 Therefore, this is what the LORD of Hosts, the God of Israel, says: "I am about to feed this people •wormwood and give them poisonous waters to drink. 16 I will scatter them among nations that they and their fathers have not known. I will send a sword after them until I have finished them off."

Mourning over Judah

17 This is what the LORD of Hosts says:

Consider, and summon the women
who mourn;
send for the skillful women.
18 Let them come quickly to raise a lament
over us
so that our eyes may overflow with tears,
our eyelids soaked with weeping.
19 For a sound of lamentation is heard from Zion:
How devastated we are.
We are greatly ashamed,
for we have abandoned the land;
our dwellings have been torn down.

20 Now hear the word of the LORD,
you women.
Pay attention to[a] the word of His mouth.
Teach your daughters a lament
and one another a dirge,
21 for Death has climbed through our windows;
it has entered our fortresses,
cutting off children from the streets,
young men from the squares.

22 Speak as follows:
This is what the LORD says:

Human corpses will fall
like manure on the surface of the field,
like newly cut grain after the reaper
with no one to gather [it].

Boast in the LORD

23 This is what the LORD says:

The wise must not boast in his wisdom;
the mighty must not boast in his might;
the rich must not boast in his riches.
24 But the one who boasts should boast in this,
that he understands and knows Me—
that I am the LORD, showing faithful love,

justice, and righteousness on the earth,
for I delight in these things.

[This is]
the LORD's declaration.

25 "The days are coming"—the LORD's declaration—"when I will punish all the circumcised yet uncircumcised: 26 Egypt, Judah, Edom, the Ammonites, Moab, all those who clip the hair on their temples[b] and reside in the wilderness. All these nations are uncircumcised, and the whole house of Israel is uncircumcised in heart."

False Gods Contrasted with the Creator

10 Hear the word that the LORD has spoken to[c] you, house of Israel. 2 This is what the LORD says:

Do not learn the way of the nations
or be terrified by signs in the heavens,
although the nations are terrified by them,
3 for the customs of the peoples are worthless.
Someone cuts down a tree from the forest;
[it is] worked by the hands of a craftsman
with a chisel.
4 He decorates it with silver and gold.
It is fastened with hammer and nails,
so it won't totter.
5 Like scarecrows in a cucumber patch,
their idols cannot speak.
They must be carried because
they cannot walk.
Do not fear them for they can do no harm—
and they cannot do any good.

6 LORD, there is no one like You.
You are great;
Your name is great in power.
7 Who should not •fear You,
King of the nations?
It is what You deserve.
For among all the wise people of the nations
and among all their kingdoms,
there is no one like You.
8 They are both senseless and foolish,
instructed by worthless idols
[made of] wood!
9 Beaten silver is brought from Tarshish,
and gold from Uphaz[d]
from the hands of a goldsmith,
the work of a craftsman.
Their clothing is blue and purple,
all the work of skilled artisans.

---

a 9:20 Lit Your ears must receive   b 9:26 Or who live in distant places; Jr 25:23; 49:32; Lv 19:27   c 10:1 Or against   d 10:9 Or Ophir

---

man. (see 9:10; 13:17, and the book of Lamentations.)

9:2 abandon my people and depart from them. Jeremiah wanted to get away from his wicked countrymen. He despised their unfaithfulness, and even used the term "adulterers" to describe their sin of desiring other gods.

9:12 Who ... Who ... Why. The first two questions are rhetorical. God's answer could only be "You, Jeremiah." Jeremiah's task was to be wise about God's ways, to be instructed by Him, and to explain His Word to the people. Verses 13-16 are God's answer to the third question.

9:13 abandoned My law. Ongoing disobedience without repentance was a breach in the covenant between God and Israel—with terrible consequences for the nation (11:9-13).

9:17 summon the women who mourn. These were professionals who led funeral processions.

10 But the LORD is the true God;
He is the living God and eternal King.
The earth quakes at His wrath,
and the nations cannot endure His rage.

11 You are to say this to them: The gods that did not make the heavens and the earth will perish from the earth and from under these heavens.ᵃ

12 He made the earth by His power,
established the world by His wisdom,
and spread out the heavens
by His understanding.

13 When He thunders,ᵇ
the waters in the heavens are in turmoil,
and He causes the clouds to rise
from the ends of the earth.
He makes lightning for the rain
and brings the wind from His storehouses.

14 Everyone is stupid and ignorant.
Every goldsmith is put to shame
by ⌊his⌋ carved image,
for his cast images are a lie;
there is no breath in them.

15 They are worthless, a work to be mocked.
At the time of their punishment
they will be destroyed.

16 Jacob's Portionᶜ is not like these
because He is the One who formed all things.
Israel is the tribe of His inheritance;
the LORD of •Hosts is His name.

Exile After the Siege

17 Gather up your belongingsᵈ from the ground,
you who live under siege.

18 For this is what the LORD says:

Look, I am slinging out
the land's residents at this time
and bringing them such distress
that they will feel it.

Jeremiah Grieves

19 Woe to me because of my brokenness—
I am severely wounded!
I exclaimed, "This is my intense suffering,
but I must bear it."

20 My tent is destroyed;
all my tent cords are snapped.
My sons have departed from me and are
no more.

⌊I have⌋ no one to pitch my tent again
or to hang up my curtains.

21 For the shepherds are stupid:
they don't seek the LORD.
Therefore they have not prospered,
and their whole flock is scattered.

22 Listen! A noise—it is coming—
a great commotion from the land
to the north.
The cities of Judah will be made desolate,
a jackals' den.

23 I know, LORD,
that a man's way of life is not his own;
no one who walks determines his own steps.

24 Discipline me, LORD, but with justice—
not in Your anger,
or You will reduce me to nothing.

25 Pour out Your wrath on the nations
that don't recognize You
and on the families
that don't call on Your name,
for they have consumed Jacob;
they have consumed him and finished him off
and made his homeland desolate.

Reminder of the Covenant

11 ⌊This is⌋ the word that came to Jeremiah from the LORD: 2 "Listen to the words of this covenant, and tell them to the men of Judah and the residents of Jerusalem. 3 You must tell them: This is what the LORD, the God of Israel, says: Let a curse be on the man who does not obey the words of this covenant, 4 which I commanded your ancestors when I brought them out of the land of Egypt, out of the iron furnace. I declared: 'Obey Me, and do everything that I command you, and you will be My people, and I will be your God,' 5 in order to establish the oath I swore to your ancestors, to give ⌊them⌋ a land flowing with milk and honey, as it is today."

I answered, "•Amen, LORD."

6 The LORD said to me, "Proclaim all these words in the cities of Judah and in the streets of Jerusalem: Obey the words of this covenant and carry them out. 7 For I strongly warned your ancestors when I brought them out of the land of Egypt until today, warning them time and time again:ᵉ Obey My voice. 8 Yet they would not obey or pay attention; each one followed the stubbornness of his evil heart. So I brought on them all the curses of this covenant, because they had not done what I commanded ⌊them⌋ to do."

ᵃ10:11 This is the only Aram v. in Jr.   ᵇ10:13 Lit At His giving of the voice   ᶜ10:16 = the LORD   ᵈ10:17 Lit bundle   ᵉ11:7 Lit today, rising early and warning

---

9:24 boast ... that he understands and knows Me. Boasting is risky, but if one is going to boast, let it be in knowing and understanding the eternal God. (See also 1 Corinthians 1:31.)

10:1-25 In the last of these temple messages, Jeremiah contrasts the powerlessness of idols with the might of God. Idolatry creates a breach in the covenant (9:13) by forsaking trust in God alone (2:11)—a violation of the divine law and a personal betrayal (3:9).

10:4 decorates it with silver and gold. Wooden idols, often plated with silver or gold to preserve them and make them more beautiful, would still rot away—pretty packages with no permanence.

10:11 them. This verse was written in Aramaic (other examples include Ezra 4:8–6:18; 7:12–26; and Dan. 2:4b–7:28), the common language during that period, and may have been inserted (and spoken) for emphasis.

⁹ The LORD said to me, "A conspiracy has been discovered among the men of Judah and the residents of Jerusalem. ¹⁰ They have returned to the sins of their ancestors who refused to obey My words and have followed other gods to worship them. The house of Israel and the house of Judah broke My covenant I made with their ancestors.

¹¹ "Therefore, this is what the LORD says: I am about to bring on them disaster that they cannot escape. They will cry out to Me, but I will not hear them. ¹² Then the cities of Judah and the residents of Jerusalem will go and cry out to the gods they have been burning incense to, but they certainly will not save them in their time of disaster. ¹³ Your gods are indeed as numerous as your cities, Judah, and the altars you have set up to Shameᵃ—altars to burn incense to •Baal—as numerous as the streets of Jerusalem.

¹⁴ "As for you, do not pray for these people. Do not raise up a cry or a prayer on their behalf, for I will not be listening when they call out to Me at the time of their disaster.

¹⁵ What ⌊right⌋ does My beloved have
to be in My house,
having carried out so many evil schemes?
Can holy meatᵇ prevent your disasterᶜ
so you can rejoice?
¹⁶ The LORD named you
a flourishing olive tree,
beautiful with well-formed fruit.
He has set fire to it,
and its branches are consumedᵈ
with a great roaring sound.

¹⁷ "The LORD of •Hosts who planted you has decreed disaster against you, because of the harm the house of Israel and the house of Judah brought on themselves, provoking Me to anger by burning incense to Baal."

¹⁸ The LORD informed me, so I knew.
Then You helped me to see their deeds,
¹⁹ for I was like a docileᵉ lamb led to slaughter.
I didn't know that they had devised plots
against me:
"Let's destroy the tree with its fruit;ᶠ
let's cut him off from the land of the living
so that his name will no longer be remembered."
²⁰ But, LORD of Hosts, who judges righteously,
who tests heartᵍ and mind,
let me see Your vengeance on them,
for I have presented my case to You.

²¹ Therefore, here is what the LORD says concerning the people of Anathoth who want to take your life. They warn, "You must not prophesy in the name of the LORD, or you will certainly die at our hand." ²² Therefore, this is what the LORD of Hosts says: "I am about to punish them. The young men will die by the sword; their sons and daughters will die by famine. ²³ They will have no remnant, for I will bring disaster on the people of Anathoth ⌊in⌋ the year of their punishment."

Jeremiah's Complaint

12 You will be righteous, LORD,
even if I bring a case against You.
Yet, I wish to contend with You:
Why does the way of the wicked prosper?
⌊Why⌋ do the treacherous live at ease?
² You planted them, and they have taken root.
They have grown and produced fruit.
You are ever on their lips,ʰ
but far from their conscience.ⁱ
³ As for You, You know me, LORD; You see me.
You test whether my heart is with You.
Drag the wicked away like sheep to slaughter,
and set them apart for the day of killing.
⁴ How long will the land mourn
and the grass of every field wither?
Because of the evil of its residents,
animals and birds have been swept away,
for ⌊the people⌋ have said,
"He cannot see what our end will be."ʲ

The LORD's Response

⁵ If you have raced with runners
and they have worn you out,
how can you compete with horses?
If you stumble in a peaceful land,
what will you do in the thickets of the Jordan?
⁶ Even your brothers—
your own father's household—
even they were treacherous to you;
even they have cried out loudly after you.
Do not have confidence in them,
though they speak well of you.

⁷ I have abandoned My house;
I have deserted My inheritance.
I have given the love of My life
into the hand of her enemies.
⁸ My inheritance has acted toward Me
like a lion in the forest.
She has roared against Me.

ᵃ**11:13** = Baal ᵇ**11:15** = sacrifices ᶜ**11:15** LXX; MT reads *meat pass from you* ᵈ**11:16** Vg; MT reads *broken* ᵉ**11:19** Or *pet* ᶠ**11:19** Lit *bread*
ᵍ**11:20** Lit *kidneys* ʰ**12:2** Lit *are near in their mouth* ⁱ**12:2** Lit *kidneys* ʲ**12:4** LXX reads *see our ways*

The message was clear: since idols were worthless in God's eyes, so were idolmakers. Idols were valueless not only for God's people but also for the pagans who built and worshiped them.

10:19-20 Woe to me. Jeremiah evoked the image of the old, pastoral-nomadic lifestyle to illustrate the disappearance of the culture the Israelites had planted in the promised land. Towns would become empty with no one left to even pitch a tent (v. 25).

11:3 a curse be on the man who does not obey. Moses used this phrase 12 times in Deuteronomy 27:15-26. There, Moses instructed the people that obedience resulted in blessings (Deut. 28:1-14), and disobedience, in curses (Deut. 28:15-68).

11:21 Anathoth. A priestly city in Benjamin, which was Jeremiah's hometown (1:1).

11:23 no remnant. Only the conspirators of Anathoth were annihilated. After the Exile,

Therefore, I hate her.
9 Is My inheritance like a hyena[a] to Me?
Are birds of prey circling her?
Go, gather all the wild animals;
bring them to devour ⌊her⌋.
10 Many shepherds have destroyed My vineyard;
they have trampled My plot of land.
They have turned My desirable plot
into a desolate wasteland.
11 They have made it a desolation.
It mourns, desolate, before Me.
All the land is desolate,
but no one takes it to heart.
12 Over all the barren heights in the wilderness
the destroyers have come,
for the LORD has a sword that devours
from one end of the earth to the other.
No one has peace.
13 They have sown wheat but harvested thorns.
They have exhausted themselves
but have no profit.
Be put to shame by your harvests
because of the LORD's burning anger.

14 This is what the LORD says: "Concerning all My evil neighbors who attack the inheritance that I bequeathed to My people, Israel, I am about to uproot them from their land, and I will uproot the house of Judah from among them. 15 After I have uprooted them, I will once again have compassion on them and return each one to his inheritance and to his land. 16 If they will diligently learn the ways of My people—to swear by My name, 'As the LORD lives,' just as they taught My people to swear by •Baal—they will be built up among My people. 17 However, if they will not obey, then I will uproot and destroy that nation."

⌊This is⌋
the LORD's declaration.

Linen Underwear

13 This is what the LORD said to me: "Go and buy yourself linen underwear and put it on,[b] but don't get it wet." 2 So I bought underwear as the LORD instructed me and put it on.

3 Then the word of the LORD came to me a second time: 4 "Take the underwear that you bought and are wearing,[c] and go at once to the Euphrates River and hide it in a rocky crevice." 5 So I went and hid it by the Euphrates, as the LORD commanded me.

6 A long time later the LORD said to me, "Go at once to the Euphrates and get the underwear that I com-

manded you to hide there." 7 So I went to the Euphrates and dug up the underwear and got it from the place where I had hidden it, but it was ruined—of no use whatsoever.

8 Then the word of the LORD came to me: 9 "This is what the LORD says: Just like this I will ruin the great pride of both Judah and Jerusalem. 10 These evil people, who refuse to listen to Me, who walk in the stubbornness of their own hearts, and who have followed other gods to serve and worship—they will be like this underwear, of no use whatsoever. 11 Just as underwear clings to one's waist, so I fastened the whole house of Israel and of Judah to Me"—⌊this is the LORD's declaration⌋—"so that they might be My people for My fame, praise, and glory, but they would not obey.

The Wine Jars

12 "Say this to them: This is what the LORD, the God of Israel, says: Every jar should be filled with wine. Then they will respond to you: Don't we know that every jar should be filled with wine? 13 And you will say to them, This is what the LORD says: I am about to fill all who live in this land—the kings who reign for David on his throne, the priests, the prophets and all the residents of Jerusalem—with drunkenness. 14 I will smash them against each other, fathers and sons alike"—the LORD's declaration. "I will allow no mercy, pity, or compassion ⌊to keep Me⌋ from destroying them."

The LORD's Warning

15 Listen and pay attention. Do not be proud,
for the LORD has spoken.
16 Give glory to the LORD your God
before He brings darkness,
before your feet stumble
on the mountains at dusk.
You wait for light,
but He brings darkest gloom[d]
and makes thick darkness.
17 But if you will not listen,
my innermost being will weep in secret
because of your pride.
My eyes will overflow with tears,
for the LORD's flock has been taken captive.

18 Say to the king and the queen mother:
Take a humble seat,
for your glorious crowns
have fallen from your heads.
19 The cities of the •Negev are under siege;
no one can help ⌊them⌋.
All of Judah has been taken into exile,

---

[a]**12:9** Hb obscure   [b]**13:1** Lit around your waist   [c]**13:4** Lit wearing around your waist   [d]**13:16** Or brings a shadow of death

---

128 other men returned to the village (Ezra 2:23).

12:1 Why does the way of the wicked prosper? Jeremiah was not alone in asking this question (see Job 21:7-15, Mal. 3:15). God answered that the wicked *seem* to prosper but will perish (v. 7-13), and the invaders who

seem to benefit from his people's misery will surely be destroyed.

12:3 sheep to slaughter. Jeremiah requested that the same fate be given the wicked in Judah as his enemies planned for him (11:19).

12:6 Even your brothers. Members of Jere-

miah's own family were conspiring to kill him. (God said in v. 5 that things would get worse—they just did.) There is a direct connection to verse 7 in which Jeremiah disavows his family.

13:1 linen underwear. The priests' garments, made of linen, symbolized the nation

taken completely into exile.
20 Look up and see
those coming from the north.
Where is the flock entrusted to you,
the sheep ⌊that were⌋ your pride?

The Destiny of Jerusalem

21 What will you say when He appoints
close friends as leaders over you,
ones you yourself trained?
Won't labor pains seize you,
as ⌊they do⌋ a woman in labor?
22 And when you ask yourself:
Why have these things happened to me?—
it is because of your great guilt
that your skirts have been stripped off,
your body ravished.ᵃ
23 Can the •Cushite change his skin,
or a leopard his spots?
If so, you might be able to do what is good,
you who are instructed in evil.
24 I will scatter youᵇ like drifting chaff
before the desert wind.
25 This is your lot,
what I have decreed for you—

⌊this is⌋
the LORD's declaration—

because you have forgotten Me
and trusted in Falsehood.ᶜ
26 I will pull your skirts up over your face
so that your shame might be seen.
27 Your adulteries and your ⌊lustful⌋ neighings,
your heinous prostitution
on the hills, in the fields—
I have seen your detestable acts.
Woe to you, Jerusalem!
You are unclean—
for how long yet?

The Drought

14 The word of the LORD that came to Jeremiah
concerning the drought:

2 Judah mourns;
her gates languish.
⌊Her people⌋ are on the ground in mourning;
Jerusalem's cry rises up.
3 Their nobles send their servantsᵈ for water.
They go to the cisterns;
they find no water;
their containers return empty.
They are ashamed and humiliated;

they cover their heads.
4 The ground is cracked
since no rain ⌊has fallen⌋ on the land.
The farmers are ashamed;
they cover their heads.
5 Even the doe in the field
gives birth and abandons ⌊her fawn⌋
since there is no grass.
6 Wild donkeys stand on the barren heights
panting for air like jackals.
Their eyes fail
because there are no green plants.
7 Though our guilt testifies against us,
LORD, act for Your name's sake.
Indeed, our rebellions are many;
we have sinned against You.
8 Hope of Israel,
its Savior in time of distress,
why are You like an alien in the land,
like a traveler stopping only for the night?
9 Why are You like a helpless man,
like a warrior unable to save?
Yet You are among us, LORD,
and we are called by Your name.
Don't leave us!

10 This is what the LORD says concerning these people:

Truly they love to wander;
they never rest their feet.
So the LORD does not accept them.
Now He will remember their guilt
and punish their sins.

False Prophets to be Punished

11 Then the LORD said to me, "Do not pray for the well-being of these people. 12 If they fast, I will not hear their cry of despair. If they offer •burnt offering and •grain offering, I will not accept them. Rather, I will finish them off by sword, famine, and plague."

13 And I replied, "Oh no, Lord GOD! The prophets are telling them, 'You won't see sword or suffer famine. I will certainly give you true peace in this place.' "

14 But the LORD said to me, "These prophets are prophesying a lie in My name. I did not send them, nor did I command them or speak to them. They are prophesying to you a false vision, worthless •divination, the deceit of their own minds.

15 "Therefore, this is what the LORD says concerning the prophets who prophesy in My name, though I did not send them, and who say: There will never be sword

---

ᵃ **13:22** Lit *your heels have suffered violence* ᵇ **13:24** Lit *them* ᶜ **13:25** = Baal ᵈ **14:3** Lit *little ones*

---

as a "kingdom of priests" (Ex. 19:6). Putting on a priestly garment must have been hard for Jeremiah, since he was a descendant of the deposed priest Abiathar. Jeremiah's family was not allowed to officiate in the temple.

13:7 it was ruined—of no use whatsoever. The linen underwear was meant to be worn,

symbolizing the close connection between God and His people. When taken off and hidden (exiled), it became ruined by the elements.

13:13 fill ... with drunkenness. Instead of continuing to be prospered by God as his vessels, he would cause them to become de-

fenseless before their enemies as vessels of destruction.

13:18 king and the queen mother. If this refers to king and queen Jehoiachin and Nehushta (2 Kings 24:8), then it was just before Nebuchadnezzar laid siege to Jerusalem in 597 B.C.

or famine in this land: By sword and famine these prophets will meet their end. [16] The people they are prophesying to will be thrown into the streets of Jerusalem because of the famine and the sword. There will be no one to bury them—they, their wives, their sons, and their daughters. I will pour out their own evil on them."

Jeremiah's Request

[17] You are to speak this word to them:
Let my eyes overflow with tears;
day and night may [they] not stop,
for the virgin daughter of my people
has been destroyed by a great disaster,
an extremely severe wound.

[18] If I go out to the field,
look—those slain by the sword!
If I enter the city,
look—those ill from famine!
For both prophet and priest
travel to a land they do not know.

[19] Have You completely rejected Judah?
Do You detest Zion?
Why do You strike us
with no hope of healing for us?
We hoped for peace,
but there was nothing good;
for a time of healing,
but there was only terror.

[20] We acknowledge our wickedness, LORD,
the guilt of our fathers;
indeed, we have sinned against You.

[21] Because of Your name, don't despise [us].
Don't disdain Your glorious throne.
Remember Your covenant with us;
do not break it.

[22] Can any of the worthless idols of the nations
bring rain?
Or can the skies alone give showers?
Are You not the LORD our God?
We therefore put our hope in You,
for You have done all these things.

The LORD's Negative Response

15 Then the LORD said to me: "Even if Moses and Samuel should stand before Me, My compassions would not [reach out] to these people. Send them from My presence, and let them go. [2] If they ask you: Where will we go? you must tell them: This is what the LORD says:

Those [destined] for death, to death;
those [destined] for the sword, to the sword.
Those [destined] for famine, to famine;
those [destined] for captivity, to captivity.

[3] "I will ordain four kinds[a] [of judgment] for them"—[this is] the LORD's declaration—"the sword to kill, the dogs to drag away, and the birds of the sky and the wild animals of the land to devour and destroy. [4] I will make them a horror to all the kingdoms of the earth because of Manasseh son of Hezekiah, the king of Judah, for what he did in Jerusalem.

[5] Who will have pity on you, Jerusalem?
Who will show sympathy toward you?
Who will turn aside
to ask about your welfare?

[6] You have left Me.
[This is]
the LORD's declaration.
You have turned your back,
so I have stretched out My hand against you
and destroyed you.
I am tired of showing compassion.

[7] I scattered them with a winnowing fork
at the gates of the land.
I made [them] childless; I destroyed My people.
They would not turn from their ways.

[8] I made their widows more numerous
than the sand of the seas.
I brought against the mother of young men
a destroyer at noon.
I suddenly released on her
agitation and terrors.

[9] The mother of seven grew faint;
she breathed her [last] breath.
Her sun set while it was still day;
she was ashamed and humiliated.
The rest of them I will give over
to the sword
in the presence of their enemies."
[This is]
the LORD's declaration.

Jeremiah's Complaint

[10] Woe is me, my mother,
that you gave birth to me,
a man who incites dispute and conflict
in all the land.
I did not lend or borrow,
yet everyone curses me.

---

[a] **15:3** Lit *families*

13:22 skirts have been stripped off. Defeat by the Babylonians would mean total humiliation. Judah and Babylon had been allies in the past (v. 21), but now defeat would reduce Judah to a prostitute's status. This was a proper fate because Judah had acted like a prostitute in adultery with other gods.

14:1 drought. Drought was one of the curses of disobedience (Lev. 26:19-20). This drought was especially terrible because it came during the Babylonian invasion. No food, no water, no safety (v. 18).

14:4 no rain [has fallen] on the land. Judah and Israel occupy arid land. Normally enough

rain falls to sustain life, but Israel and Judah were dependent on rainfall to fill wells and cisterns to keep their water supply adequate.

14:10-11 these people ... wander. God rejected His people for a time. They might offer sacrifices, but God would not accept them.

14:16 no one to bury them. For an Israelite

The LORD's Response

11 The LORD said:

Assuredly, I will set you free and care for you.[a]
Assuredly, I will intercede for you
in a time of trouble,
in your time of distress, with the enemy.

12 Can anyone smash iron,
iron from the north, or bronze?

13 Your wealth and your treasures
I will give as plunder, without cost,
for all your sins,
and within all your borders.

14 Then I will make you serve your enemies[b]
in a land you do not know,
for My anger will kindle a fire
that will burn against you.

Jeremiah's Prayer for Vengeance

15 You know, LORD;
remember me and take note of me.
Avenge me against my persecutors.
In Your patience,[c] don't take me away.
Know that I suffer disgrace for Your honor.

16 Your words were found, and I ate them.
Your words became a delight to me
and the joy of my heart,
for I am called by Your name,
LORD God of •Hosts.

17 I never sat with the band of revelers,
and I did not celebrate [with them].
Because Your hand was [on me], I sat alone,
for You filled me with indignation.

18 Why has my pain become unending,
my wound incurable,
refusing to be healed?
You truly have become like a mirage to me—
water that is not reliable.

Jeremiah Told to Repent

19 Therefore, this is what the LORD says:

If you return, I will restore you;
you will stand in My presence.
And if you speak noble [words],
rather than worthless ones,
you will be My spokesman.
It is they who must return to you;
you must not return to them.

20 Then I will make you a fortified wall of bronze
to this people.

They will fight against you
but will not overcome you,
for I am with you
to save you and deliver you.

There you will worship other

[This is]
the LORD's declaration.

21 I will deliver you from the power of evil people
and redeem you from the control of the ruthless.

No Marriage for Jeremiah

16 The word of the LORD came to me: 2 "You must not marry or have sons or daughters in this place. 3 For this is what the LORD says concerning sons and daughters born in this place as well as concerning the mothers who bear them and the fathers who father them in this land: 4 They will die from deadly diseases. They will not be mourned or buried but will be like manure on the face of the earth. They will be finished off by sword and famine. Their corpses will become food for the birds of the sky and for the wild animals of the land.

5 "For this is what the LORD says: Don't enter a house where a mourning feast is taking place.[d] Don't go to lament or sympathize with them, for I have removed My peace from these people"—[this is] the LORD's declaration—"[as well as My] faithful love and compassion. 6 Both great and small will die in this land without burial. No lament will be made for them, nor will anyone cut himself or shave his head for them.[e] 7 Food won't be provided for the mourner to comfort him because of the dead. A cup of consolation won't be given him because of [the loss of] his father or mother. 8 You must not enter the house where feasting is taking place to sit with them to eat and drink. 9 For this is what the LORD of •Hosts, the God of Israel, says: I am about to eliminate from this place, before your very eyes and in your time, the sound of joy and gladness, the voice of the bridegroom and the bride.

Abandoning the LORD and His Law

10 "When you tell these people all these things, they will say to you: Why has the LORD declared all this great disaster against us? What is our guilt? What is our sin that we have committed against the LORD our God? 11 Then you will answer them: Because your fathers abandoned Me"—the LORD's declaration—"and followed other gods, served them, and worshiped them. Indeed, they abandoned Me and did not keep My law. 12 You did more evil than your fathers. Look, each one of you was following the stubbornness of his evil heart,

---

[a]**15:11** Lit *free for good*   [b]**15:14** Some Hb mss, LXX, Syr, Tg; other Hb mss read *you pass through*   [c]**15:15** Lit *In the slowness of Your anger*   [d]**16:5** Lit *house of mourning*   [e]**16:6** Cutting and shaving were pagan mourning rituals; Jr 41:5; 47:5; Dt 14:1.

---

to remain unburied was a terrible violation of dignity, a sign of awful calamity (Ezek. 6:5; 37:1; Amos 2:1). Even today, natural and other disasters are so overwhelming that it often takes days to deal with all the corpses. That is what is pictured here.

14:21 Remember Your covenant with us.

Jeremiah desperately pleaded with God to fulfill His part of the covenant. Judah had forsaken the Law, and God's punishment was intensely felt (9:13).

15:2 [destined] for death ... sword ... famine ... captivity. The people had failed to worship and serve God and now punish-

ment had arrived.

15:5-9 Much of this poem (vv. 8-9) about the destruction of Jerusalem (in 586 B.C.) focuses on widows and mothers. Even these miserable survivors, who would normally receive special consideration, would be treated without mercy.

not obeying Me. 13 So I will hurl you from this land into a land that you and your fathers are not familiar with. There you will worship other gods both day and night, for I will not grant you grace.ᵃ

14 "However, take note! The days are coming"—the LORD's declaration—"when it will no longer be said: As the LORD lives who brought the Israelites from the land of Egypt, 15 but rather: As the LORD lives who brought the Israelites from the land of the north and from all the other lands where He had banished them. For I will return them to their land that I gave to their ancestors.

Punishment of Exile

16 "I am about to send for many fishermen"—the LORD's declaration—"and they will fish for them. Then I will send for many hunters, and they will hunt them down on every mountain and hill and out of the clefts of the rocks, 17 for My gaze takes in all their ways. They are not concealed from Me, and their guilt is not hidden from My sight. 18 I will first repay them double for their guilt and sin because they have polluted My land. They have filled My inheritance with the lifelessness of their detestable and abhorrent idols."

> 19 LORD, my strength and my stronghold,
> my refuge in a time of distress,
> the nations will come to You
> from the ends of the earth, and they will say,
> "Our fathers inherited only lies,
> worthless idols of no benefit at all."
> 20 Can one make gods for himself?
> But they are not gods.
> 21 "Therefore, I am about to inform them,
> and this time I will make them know
> My power and My might;
> then they will know that My name is •Yahweh."

The Persistent Sin of Judah

17 The sin of Judah is written
with an iron stylus.
With a diamond point
it is engraved on the tablet of their hearts
and on the horns of theirᵇ altars,
2 while their children remember their altars
and their •Asherah poles, by the green trees
on the high hills—
3 My mountains in the countryside.
Your wealth and all your treasures
I will give up as plunder
because of the sin of your •high placesᶜ
within all your borders.

4 You will, of yourself, relinquish your inheritance
that I gave you.
I will make you serve your enemies
in a land you do not know,
for you have set My anger on fire;
it will burn forever.

Curse and Blessing

5 This is what the LORD says:

> Cursed is the man who trusts in mankind,
> who makes ⌊human⌋ flesh his strength
> and turns his heart from the LORD.
> 6 He will be like a juniper in the •Arabah;
> he cannot see when good comes
> but dwells in the parched places
> in the wilderness,
> in a salt land where no one lives.
> 7 Blessed is the man who trusts in the LORD,
> whose confidence indeed is the LORD.
> 8 He will be like a tree planted by water:
> it sends its roots out toward a stream,
> it doesn't fear when heat comes,
> and its foliage remains green.
> It will not worry in a year of drought
> or cease producing fruit.

The Deceitful Heart

> 9 The heart is more deceitful than anything else
> and desperately sick—who can understand it?
> 10 I, the LORD, examine the mind,
> I test the heartᵈ
> to give to each according to his way,
> according to what his actions deserve.
> 11 He who makes a fortune unjustly
> is ⌊like⌋ a partridge that hatches eggs
> it didn't lay.
> In the middle of his days
> ⌊his riches⌋ will abandon him,
> so in the end he will be a fool.
>
> 12 A throne of glory
> on high from the beginning
> is the place of our sanctuary,
> 13 LORD, the hope of Israel,
> all who abandon You
> will be put to shame.
> All who turn away from Me
> will be written in the dirt,
> for they have abandoned
> the fountain of living water, the LORD.

ᵃ**16:13** Or *compassion* ᵇ**17:1** Some Hb mss, Syr, Vg; other Hb mss read *your* ᶜ**17:3** Lit *plunder, your high places because of sin* ᵈ**17:10** Lit *kidneys*

15:15 You know ... remember me. Judah had lost its connection with God, but Jeremiah called on his own relationship with the Lord to support his request for vengeance against his enemies.

15:19-21 If you return, I will restore you. Jeremiah was neither exempt from the temptation to sin nor immune to sin's consequences. God called him to repent for doubting God. He understood Jeremiah (v.15) and encouraged him by promising protection from enemies and salvation from the wicked.

16:2 You must not marry. God prohibited Jeremiah from marrying and having children. The language here is the same as the absolute commands of the Ten Commandments (Ex. 20:3-4, 7, 13-17).

16:5 Don't enter a house where. The times would become so bad that Jeremiah was not to participate in either mourning or feasting.

Jeremiah's Plea

14 Heal me, LORD, and I will be healed;
save me, and I will be saved,
for You are my praise.

15 Hear how they keep challenging me,
"Where is the word of the LORD?
Let it come!"

16 But I have not run away from being
Your shepherd,
and I have not longed for the fatal day.
You know my words were spoken
in Your presence.

17 Don't become a terror to me.
You are my refuge in the day of disaster.

18 Let my persecutors be put to shame,
but don't let me be put to shame.
Let them be terrified, but don't let me
be terrified.
Bring on them the day of disaster;
shatter them with total[a] destruction.

Observing the Sabbath

19 This is what the LORD said to me, "Go and stand in the People's Gate, through which the kings of Judah enter and leave, and in all the gates of Jerusalem. 20 Announce to them: Hear the word of the LORD, kings of Judah, all Judah, and all the residents of Jerusalem who enter through these gates. 21 This is what the LORD says: Watch yourselves; do not pick up a load and bring it in through the gates of Jerusalem on the Sabbath day. 22 You must not carry a load out of your houses on the Sabbath day or do any work, but you must consecrate the Sabbath day, just as I commanded your ancestors. 23 They wouldn't listen or pay attention but became obstinate, not listening or accepting discipline.

24 "However, if you listen to Me, says the LORD, and do not bring loads through the gates of this city on the Sabbath day and consecrate the Sabbath day and do no work on it, 25 kings and princes will enter through the gates of this city. They will sit on the throne of David, riding in chariots and on horses with their officials, the men of Judah, and the residents of Jerusalem. This city will be inhabited forever. 26 Then ⌊people⌋ will come from the cities of Judah and from the area around Jerusalem, from the land of Benjamin and from the Judean foothills, from the hill country and from the •Negev bringing •burnt offerings and sacrifice, •grain offerings and frankincense, and thank offerings to the house of the LORD. 27 If you do not listen to Me to consecrate the Sabbath day by not carrying a load while entering the gates of Jerusalem on the Sabbath day, I will set fire to its gates, and it will consume the citadels of Jerusalem and not be extinguished."

Parable of the Potter

18 ⌊This is⌋ the word that came to Jeremiah from the LORD: 2 "Go down at once to the potter's house; there I will reveal My words to you." 3 So I went down to the potter's house, and there he was, working away at the wheel.[b] 4 But the jar that he was making from the clay became flawed in the potter's hand, so he made it into another jar, as it seemed right for him to do.

5 The word of the LORD came to me: 6 "House of Israel, can I not treat you as this potter ⌊treats his clay⌋?"—⌊this is⌋ the LORD's declaration. "Just like clay in the potter's hand, so are you in My hand, house of Israel. 7 At one moment I might announce concerning a nation or a kingdom that I will uproot, tear down, and destroy ⌊it⌋. 8 However, if that nation I have made an announcement about, turns from its evil, I will not bring the disaster on it I had planned. 9 At ⌊another⌋ time I announce that I will build and plant a nation or a kingdom. 10 However, if it does what is evil in My sight by not listening to My voice, I will not bring the good I had said I would do to it. 11 So now, say to the men of Judah and to the residents of Jerusalem: This is what the LORD says: I am about to bring harm to you and make plans against you. Turn now, each from your evil way, and correct your ways and your deeds. 12 But they will say: It's hopeless. We will continue to follow our plans, and each of us will continue to act according to the stubbornness of his evil heart."

Deluded Israel

13 Therefore, this is what the LORD says:

Ask among the nations,
Who has heard ⌊things⌋ like these?
Virgin Israel has done a most terrible thing.

14 Does the snow of Lebanon ever leave
the highland crags?
Or does cold water flowing from a distance
ever fail?

15 Yet My people have forgotten Me.
They burn incense to false ⌊idols⌋
that make them stumble in their ways—
in the ancient roads—
to walk on ⌊new⌋ paths, not the highway.

16 They have made their land a horror,
a perpetual object of scorn;[c]
everyone who passes by it will be horrified
and shake his head.

---

a17:18 Lit double   b18:3 Lit pair of stones   c18:16 Lit hissing

---

The present mourning was only a shadow of what was to come, and nothing warranted celebrating.

16:14 the days are coming. Mirroring Isaiah 40-55, the Lord announces that a new exodus will take place (23:7-8).

16:16 many fishermen ... many hunters. Like these, conquerors snare their victims in a net (Ezek. 12:13) or hook the jaws of enemies (Ezek. 29:4).

17:1 tablet of their hearts. When God writes his law on human hearts in the new covenant (31:31-34), obedience rather than rebellion becomes possible for those who confess Jesus as Lord (Luke 22:20; 1 Cor. 11:15; Heb. 8:8-9:28).

17:2 Asherah poles. During King Josiah's time, the worship of Asherah had gotten so bad that an Asherah pole was brought into the temple precinct. Josiah had it removed and burned in the Kidron Valley (2 Kings 23:6).

17 I will scatter them before the enemy
  like the east wind.
I will show them^a ⌊My⌋ back and not ⌊My⌋ face
  on the day of their calamity.

Plot against Jeremiah

18 Then certain ones said, "Come, let's make plans against Jeremiah, for the law will never be lost from the priest, or counsel from the wise, or an oracle from the prophet. Come, let's denounce him^b and pay no attention to all his words."

19 Pay attention to me, LORD.
  Hear what my opponents are saying!
20 Should good be repaid with evil?
  Yet they have dug a pit for me.
  Remember how I stood before You
  to speak good on their behalf,
  to turn Your anger from them.
21 Therefore, hand their children over to famine,
  and pour the sword's power on them.
  Let their wives become childless and widowed,
  their husbands slain by deadly disease,^c
  their young men struck down by the sword
    in battle.
22 Let a cry be heard from their houses
  when You suddenly bring raiders against them,
  for they have dug a pit to capture me
  and have hidden snares for my feet.
23 But You, LORD, know
  all their deadly plots against me.
  Do not wipe out their guilt;
  do not blot out their sin before You.
  Let them be forced to stumble before You;
  deal with them in the time of Your anger.

The Clay Jug

19 This is what the LORD says: "Go, buy a potter's clay jug. Take^d some of the elders of the people and some of the elders of the priests 2 and go out to the Valley of Hinnom near the entrance of the Potsherd Gate. Proclaim there the words I speak to you. 3 Say: Hear the word of the LORD, kings of Judah and residents of Jerusalem. This is what the LORD of •Hosts, the God of Israel, says: I am going to bring such disaster on this place that everyone who hears about it will shudder^e 4 because they have abandoned Me and made this a foreign place. They have burned incense in it to other gods that they, their fathers, and the kings of Judah have never known. They have filled this place with the blood of the innocent. 5 They have built

•high places to •Baal on which to burn their children in the fire as burnt offerings to Baal, something I have never commanded or mentioned; I never entertained the thought.^f

6 "Therefore, take note! The days are coming"—⌊this is⌋ the LORD's declaration—"when this place will no longer be called Topheth and the Valley of Hinnom, but the Valley of Slaughter. 7 I will spoil the plans of Judah and Jerusalem in this place. I will make them fall by the sword before their enemies, by the hand of those who want to take their life. I will provide their corpses as food for the birds of the sky and for the wild animals of the land. 8 I will make this city desolate, an object of scorn. Everyone who passes by it will be horrified and scoff because of all its wounds. 9 I will make them eat the flesh of their sons and their daughters, and they will eat each other's flesh in the siege and distress that their enemies, those who want to take their life, inflict on them.

10 "Then you are to shatter the jug in the presence of the people traveling with you, 11 and you are to proclaim to them: This is what the LORD of Hosts says: I will shatter these people and this city, like one shatters a potter's jar that can never again be mended. They will bury in Topheth until there is no place left to bury. 12 I will do so to this place"—⌊this is⌋ the declaration of the LORD—"and to its residents, making this city like Topheth. 13 The houses of Jerusalem and the houses of the kings of Judah will become impure like that place Topheth—all the houses on whose rooftops they have burned incense to the whole heavenly host and poured out drink offerings to other gods."

14 Jeremiah came back from Topheth, where the LORD had sent him to prophesy, stood in the courtyard of the LORD's temple, and proclaimed to all the people, 15 "This is what the LORD of Hosts, the God of Israel, says: 'I am about to bring on this city—and on all its ⌊dependent⌋ villages—all the disaster that I spoke against it, for they have become obstinate, not obeying My words.'"

Jeremiah Beaten by Pashhur

20 Pashhur the priest, the son of Immer and chief officer in the house of the LORD, heard Jeremiah prophesying these things. 2 So Pashhur had Jeremiah the prophet beaten and put him in the stocks at the Upper Benjamin Gate in the LORD's temple. 3 The next day, when Pashhur released Jeremiah from the stocks, Jeremiah said to him, "The LORD does not call you Pashhur, but Magor-missabib,^g 4 for this is what

---

^a18:17 LXX, Lat, Syr, Tg; MT reads *will look at them*   ^b18:18 Lit *let's strike him with the tongue*   ^c18:21 Lit *by death*   ^d19:1 Syr, Tg; MT omits *Take*
^e19:3 Lit *shudder their ears*; 1 Sm 3:11; 2 Kg 21:12   ^f19:5 Lit *mentioned, and it did not arise on My heart*   ^g20:3 = Terror Is on Every Side; Jr 6:25; 20:10; 46:5

18:14-15 Nature conformed to the laws of God. While nature behaved as prescribed, Judah wandered from the path God set for the people.

19:1-15 In chapter 18, a clay pot illustrated how God, the master potter, could reshape a repentant person. Here, however, the pot was

useless. God would smash Judah.

19:1 elders of the people ... priests. Since leaders of the nation disregarded God's warning to urge a covenant renewal, all levels of the culture would feel the heat of punishment.

19:7 spoil the plans. The Hebrew verb

means "to empty." Judah and Jerusalem had made plans without concern for God's will and commands. Jeremiah may have poured water out of the clay jar to illustrate the point that plans turn to nothing without God.

19:11 shatter these people ... like one shatters a potter's jar. The elders had seen

the LORD says, 'I am about to make you a terror to both yourself and those you love. They will fall by the sword of their enemies before your very eyes. I will hand Judah over to the king of Babylon, and he will deport them to Babylon and put them to the sword. 5 I will give away all the wealth of this city, all its products and valuables. Indeed, I will hand all the treasures of the kings of Judah over to their enemies. They will plunder them, seize them, and carry them off to Babylon. 6 As for you, Pashhur, and all who live in your house, you will go into captivity. You will go to Babylon. There you will die, and there you will be buried, you and all your friends that you prophesied falsely to.' "

Jeremiah Compelled to Preach

7 You deceived me, LORD, and I was deceived.
You seized me and prevailed.
I am a laughingstock all the time;
everyone ridicules me.
8 For whenever I speak, I cry out—
I proclaim: Violence and destruction!
because the word of the LORD has become
for me
constant disgrace and derision.
9 If I say: I won't mention Him
or speak any longer in His name,
His message becomes a fire burning in my heart,
shut up in my bones.
I become tired of holding it in,
and I cannot prevail.
10 For I have heard the gossip of the multitudes,
"Terror is on every side!a
Report [him]; let's report him!"
Everyone I trustedb watches for my fall.
"Perhaps he will be deceived
so that we might prevail against him
and take our vengeance on him."
11 But the LORD is with me like a violent warrior.
Therefore, my persecutors will stumble
and not prevail.
Since they have not succeeded, they will be
utterly shamed,
an everlasting humiliation that will
never be forgotten.
12 LORD of •Hosts, testing the righteous
and seeing the heartc and mind,
let me see Your vengeance on them,
for I have presented my case to You.
13 Sing to the LORD!
Praise the LORD,

for He rescues the life of the needy
from the hand of evil people.

Jeremiah's Lament

14 Cursed be the day
on which I was born.
The day my mother bore me—
let it never be blessed.
15 Cursed be the man
who brought the news to my father, saying,
"A male child is born to you,"
bringing him great joy.
16 Let that man be like the cities
the LORD overthrew without compassion.
Let him hear an outcry in the morning
and a war cry at noontime
17 because he didn't kill me in the womb
so that my mother might have been
my grave,
her womb eternally pregnant.
18 Why did I come out of the womb
to see [only] struggle and sorrow,
to end my life in shame?

Zedekiah's Request Denied

21 [This is] the word that came to Jeremiah from the LORD when King Zedekiah sent Pashhur son of Malchijah and the priest Zephaniah son of Maaseiah to Jeremiah, asking, 2 "Ask the LORD on our behalf, since Nebuchadnezzard king of Babylon is making war against us. Perhaps the LORD will perform for us something like all His [past] wonderful works so that [Nebuchadnezzar] will withdraw from us."

3 But Jeremiah answered, "This is what you are to say to Zedekiah: 4 'This is what the LORD, the God of Israel, says: I will repel the weapons of war in your hands, those you are using to fight the king of Babylon and the Chaldeanse who are besieging you outside the wall, and I will bring them into the center of this city. 5 I will fight against you with an outstretched hand and a mighty arm, with anger, rage, and great wrath. 6 I will strike the residents of this city, both man and beast. They will die in a great plague. 7 Afterwards' "—[this is] the LORD's declaration—" 'King Zedekiah of Judah, his officers, and the people—those in this city who survive the plague, the sword, and the famine—I will hand over to King Nebuchadnezzar of Babylon, to their enemies, yes, to those who want to take their lives. He will put them to the sword; he won't spare them or show pity or compassion.'

---

a 20:10 Hb Magor-missabib; Jr 20:3   b 20:10 Lit Every man of my peace; Ps 41:9   c 20:12 Lit kidneys   d 21:2 Lit Nebuchadrezzar
e 21:4 = Babylonians

---

many terrible things—drought, disease, and military defeat—but never irreparable devastation.

20:2 Jeremiah … beaten. Pashur probably had Jeremiah beaten in accordance with the Law covering disputes (Deut. 25:1-3).

20:6 you prophesied falsely to. Pashur was

a priest but not a true prophet. Perhaps he was among the false prophets who proclaimed peace (6:14). His prophecies failed the test; they did not come about; they were lies (Deut. 18:22).

20:8-9 Whenever I speak … I won't mention Him. Jeremiah was caught in a paradox.

Both options brought misery.

20:14 Cursed be the day. Jeremiah's calling as a prophet began before he was conceived (1:5). Therefore, he saw his conception day as misery. In that way, he was like Job who regarded birth as the beginning of sorrow (Job 3:3).

A Warning for the People

8 "But you must say to this people, 'This is what the LORD says: Look, I am presenting to you the way of life and the way of death. 9 Whoever stays in this city will die by the sword, famine, and plague, but whoever goes out and surrenders to the Chaldeans who are besieging you will live and will retain his life like the spoils ⌊of war⌋. 10 For I have turned[a] against this city to ⌊bring⌋ disaster and not good' "—⌊this is⌋ the LORD's declaration. "'It will be handed over to the king of Babylon, who will burn it down.'

11 "And to the house of the king of Judah ⌊say this⌋: 'Hear the word of the LORD! 12 House of David, this is what the LORD says:

> Administer justice every morning,
> and rescue the victim of robbery
> from the hand of his oppressor,
> or My anger will flare up like fire
> and burn unquenchably
> because of their evil deeds.
13 Beware! I am against you,
> you who sit above the valley,
> ⌊you atop⌋ the rocky plateau—
>> ⌊this is⌋
>> the LORD's declaration—
> you who say: Who can come down against us?
> Who can enter our hiding places?
14 I will punish you according to
> what you have done—
>> ⌊this is⌋
>> the LORD's declaration.
> I will kindle a fire in its forest
> that will consume everything around it.' "

Judgment against Sinful Kings

22 This is what the LORD says: "Go down to the palace of the king of Judah and announce this word there. 2 You are to say: Hear the word of the LORD, king of Judah, you who sit on the throne of David—you, your officers, and your people who enter these gates. 3 This is what the LORD says: Administer justice and righteousness. Rescue the victim of robbery from the hand of his oppressor. Don't exploit or brutalize the alien, the fatherless, or the widow. Don't shed innocent blood in this place. 4 For if you conscientiously carry out this word, then kings sitting on David's throne will enter through the gates of this palace riding on chariots and horses—they, their officers, and their people. 5 But if you do not obey these words, then I swear by Myself"—⌊this is⌋

the LORD's declaration—"that this house will become a ruin."

6 For this is what the LORD says concerning the house of the king of Judah:

> You are like Gilead to Me,
> ⌊or⌋ the summit of Lebanon,
> but I will certainly turn you into a wilderness,
> uninhabited cities.
7 I will appoint destroyers against you,
> each with his weapons.
> They will cut down the choicest of your cedars
> and throw them into the fire.

8 "Many nations will pass by this city and ask one another: Why did the LORD do such a thing to this great city? 9 They will answer: Because they abandoned the covenant of the LORD their God and worshiped and served other gods."

A Message concerning Shallum

10 Do not weep for the dead;
> do not mourn for him.[b]
> Weep bitterly for the one who has gone away,
> for he will never return again
> and see his native land.

11 For this is what the LORD says concerning Shallum son of Josiah, king of Judah, who succeeded Josiah his father as king: "He has left this place—he will never return here again, 12 but he will die in the place where they deported him, never seeing this land again."

A Message concerning Jehoiakim

13 Woe for the one who builds his palace
> through unrighteousness,
> his upper rooms through injustice,
> who makes his fellow man serve without pay
> and will not give him his wages,
14 who says: I will build myself a massive palace,
> with spacious upper rooms.
> He will cut windows[c] in it,
> and it will be paneled with cedar
> and painted with vermilion.
15 Are you a king because you excel in cedar?
> Your own father, did he not eat and drink?
> He administered justice and righteousness,
> then it went well with him.
16 He took up the case of the poor and needy,
> then it went well.
> Is this not what it means to know Me?
>> ⌊This is⌋
>> the LORD's declaration.

---

[a]**21:10** Lit *set My face*   [b]**22:10** The person referred to in this v. is the Shallum of v.11   [c]**22:14** Lit *My windows*

21:2 Ask the LORD on our behalf. Whether the king requested the Lord's help would depend on other factors, including the information he received. (Gen. 25:22, 2 Kings 22:13.) In many ways, this inquiry resembled seeking the advice of a fortuneteller, not the will of God.

21:8 the way of life and the way of death. God did not condemn the Israelites to death but offered them the opportunity to live, albeit in captivity. At least choosing life brought opportunity to love God and be loved by Him (Deut. 30:19-20).

21:9 goes out and surrenders. Jeremiah

was branded a traitor for advising surrender to the Babylonians (37:13). But he was not a traitor at all. He was simply explaining to the people their choice of living or dying. Jeremiah himself wanted to remain in Judah even after Jerusalem was destroyed (37:14; 40:6).

22:2 king of Judah ... on the throne of

17 But you have eyes and heart for nothing
except your own unjust gain,
shedding innocent blood
and committing extortion and oppression.

18 Therefore, this is what the LORD says concerning
Jehoiakim son of Josiah, king of Judah:

They will not mourn for him, ⌊saying,⌋
Woe, my brother! or Woe, ⌊my⌋ sister!
They will not mourn for him, saying,
Woe, lord! Woe, his majesty!

19 He will be buried ⌊like⌋ a donkey,
dragged off and thrown
outside the gates of Jerusalem.

20 Go up to Lebanon and cry out;
raise your voice in Bashan;
cry out from Abarim,
for all your lovers[a] have been crushed.

21 I spoke to you when you were secure.
You said: I will not listen.
This has been your way since youth;
indeed, you have never listened to Me.

22 The wind will take charge of[b] all
your shepherds,
and your lovers[a] will go into captivity.
Then you will be ashamed and humiliated
because of all your evil.

23 You residents of Lebanon,
nestled among the cedars,
how you will groan[c] when labor pains
come on you,
agony like a woman in labor.

A Message concerning Coniah

24 "As I live," says the LORD, "though you, Coniah[d]
son of Jehoiakim, the king of Judah, were a signet ring
on My right hand, I would tear you from it. 25 In fact, I
will hand you over to those you dread, who want to
take your life, to Nebuchadnezzar king of Babylon and
the Chaldeans. 26 I will hurl you and the mother who
gave birth to you into another land, where neither of
you were born, and there you will both die. 27 They will
never return to the land they long to return to."

28 Is this man Coniah a despised, shattered pot,
a jar no one wants?
Why are he and his descendants hurled out
and cast into a land they have not known?

29 Earth, earth, earth,
hear the word of the LORD!

30 This is what the LORD says:

Record this man as childless,
a man who will not be successful in his lifetime.
None of his descendants will succeed
in sitting on the throne of David
or ruling again in Judah.

The LORD and His Sheep

23 "Woe to the shepherds who destroy and scatter the sheep of My pasture!" ⌊This is⌋ the LORD's declaration. 2 "Therefore, this is what the LORD, the God of Israel, says about the shepherds who shepherd My people: You have scattered My flock, banished them, and have not attended to them. I will attend to you because of your evil acts"—the LORD's declaration. 3 "I will gather the remnant of My flock from all the lands where I have banished them, and I will return them to their grazing land. They will become fruitful and numerous. 4 I will raise up shepherds over them who will shepherd them. They will no longer be afraid or dismayed, nor will any be missing." ⌊This is⌋ the LORD's declaration.

The Righteous Branch of David

5 "The days are coming"—⌊this is⌋ the LORD's declaration—"when I will raise up a righteous Branch of David. He will reign wisely as king and administer justice and righteousness in the land. 6 In His days Judah will be saved, and Israel will dwell securely. This is what He will be named: The LORD Is Our Righteousness. 7 The days are coming"—the LORD's declaration—"when it will no longer be said: As the LORD lives who brought the Israelites from the land of Egypt, 8 but: As the LORD lives, who brought and led the descendants of the house of Israel from the land of the north and from all the other countries where I[e] had banished them. They will dwell once more in their own land."

False Prophets Condemned

9 Concerning the prophets:

My heart is broken within me,
and all my bones tremble.
I have become like a drunkard,
like a man overcome by wine,
because of the LORD,
because of His holy words.

10 For the land is full of adulterers;
the land mourns because of the curse,
and the grazing lands in the wilderness
have dried up.

---

[a] 22:20,22 Or friends, or allies   [b] 22:22 Lit will shepherd   [c] 22:23 LXX, Syr, Vg; MT reads will be pitied   [d] 22:24 = Jehoiachin   [e] 23:8 LXX reads He

---

David. The king was likely Zedekiah (21:3). The dynasty founded by David had endured, though the path was strewn with failures.
22:10 Do not weep for the dead. Though his reforms were quickly reversed, the beloved King Josiah was mourned (2 Chron. 35:25).
22:28 a despised, shattered pot. Jeremiah

returned to an image used in 18:1-10 and 19:1-15. Jehoiachin was "cast away" and taken into exile where he became utterly irrelevant.

22:30 as childless ... None of his descendants. Although Jehoiachin had at least seven children, none of them sat on the

throne of Judah. Thus, Jehoiachin was the last king of the Davidic line. Jehoiachin's line was restored, however, in the time of Zerubbabel. Christ came from his restored line (Matt. 1:12).

23:5 I will raise up a righteous Branch of David. One of Messiah's titles. The title signi-

Their way of life[a] has become evil,
and their power is not rightly used

11 because both prophet and priest are ungodly,
even in My house I have found their evil.
⌊This is⌋
the LORD's declaration.

12 Therefore, their way will be to them
like slippery paths in the gloom.
They will be driven away and fall down there,
for I will bring disaster on them,
the year of their punishment.
⌊This is⌋
the LORD's declaration.

13 Among the prophets of Samaria
I saw something disgusting:
They prophesied by •Baal
and led My people Israel astray.

14 Among the prophets of Jerusalem also
I saw a horrible thing:
They commit adultery and walk in lies.
They strengthen the hands of evildoers,
and none turns his back on evil.
They are all like Sodom to Me;
Jerusalem's residents are like Gomorrah.

15 Therefore, this is what the LORD of •Hosts says
concerning the prophets:

I am about to feed them •wormwood
and give them poisoned water to drink,
for from the prophets of Jerusalem
ungodliness[b] has spread throughout the land.

16 This is what the LORD of Hosts says: "Do not listen
to the words of the prophets who prophesy to you. They
are making you worthless. They speak visions from
their own minds, not from the LORD's mouth. 17 They
keep on saying to those who despise Me: The LORD has
said: You will have peace. To everyone who walks in
the stubbornness of his heart they have said, No harm
will come to you."

18 For who has stood in the council of the LORD
to see and hear His word?
Who has paid attention to His word and obeyed?

19 Look, a storm from the LORD!
Wrath has gone forth,
a whirling storm.
It will whirl about the head of the wicked.

20 The LORD's anger will not turn back
until He has completely fulfilled the purposes
of His heart.

In time to come you will
understand it clearly.

21 I did not send these prophets,
yet they ran ⌊with a message⌋.
I did not speak to them,
yet they prophesied.

22 If they had really stood in My council,
they would have enabled My people
to hear My words
and would have turned them back
from their evil ways
and their evil deeds.

23 "Am I a God who is only near"—⌊this is⌋ the
LORD's declaration—"and not a God who is far away?
24 Can a man hide himself in secret places where I cannot see him?"—the LORD's declaration. "Do I not fill
the heavens and the earth?"—the LORD's declaration.

25 "I have heard what the prophets who prophesy a lie
in My name have said: I had a dream! I had a dream!
26 How long will this continue in the minds of the prophets prophesying lies, prophets of the deceit of their own
minds? 27 Through their dreams that they tell one
another, they make plans to cause My people to forget
My name as their fathers forgot My name through Baal
worship. 28 The prophet who has ⌊only⌋ a dream should
recount the dream, but the one who has My word should
speak My word truthfully, for what is straw ⌊compared⌋
to grain?"—the LORD's declaration. 29 "Is not My word
like fire"—the LORD's declaration—"and like a sledge-
hammer that pulverizes rock? 30 Therefore, take note! I
am against the prophets"—the LORD's declaration—
"who steal My words from each other. 31 I am against
the prophets"—the LORD's declaration—"who use their
own tongues to deliver an oracle. 32 I am against those
who prophesy false dreams"—the LORD's declaration—
"telling them and leading My people astray with their
falsehoods and their boasting. It was not I who sent or
commanded them, and they are of no benefit at all to
these people"—⌊this is⌋ the LORD's declaration.

The Burden of the LORD

33 "Now when these people or a prophet or a priest
asks you: What is the burden of the LORD? you will
respond to them: What is the burden? I will throw you
away"—⌊this is⌋ the LORD's declaration. 34 "As for the
prophet, priest, or people who say: The burden of the
LORD, I will punish that man and his household. 35 This
is what each man is to say to his friend and to his
brother: What has the LORD answered? or What has the
LORD spoken? 36 But no longer refer to[c] the burden of

---

[a] 23:10 Lit Their manner of running [b] 23:15 Or pollution [c] 23:36 Or longer remember

---

fies that Messiah is a branch from David's line
(Isa. 11:1), which would be cut off for centu-
ries and restored in the person of Jesus
Christ.

**23:6 will be named: The LORD Is Our Righ-
teousness.** The Messiah will represent the
fact that our righteousness does not come

from ourselves, but from God.

23:14 Sodom … Gomorrah. The relationship
of false prophets (Sodom) to Jerusalem (Gomorrah) replicates the connection of the false
prophets of the northern kingdom to the fall of
Samaria in 722 B.C. (23:27). Though the people did not need a prophet to cause them to

sin, those who presume to speak for God will
incur stricter judgment (James 3:1).

23:16 speak visions from their own minds.
True prophets were God's messengers. False
prophets spoke their own mind, not God's
mind.

23:17 You will have peace … No harm.

the LORD, for each man's word becomes his burden and you pervert the words of the living God, the LORD of Hosts, our God. 37 You must say to the prophet: What has the LORD answered you? and What has the LORD spoken? 38 But if you say: The burden of the LORD, then this is what the LORD says: Because you have said, The burden of the LORD, and I specifically told you not to say, The burden of the LORD, 39 I will surely forget you[a] and throw away from My presence both you and the city that I gave you and your fathers. 40 I will bring on you everlasting shame and humiliation that will never be forgotten."

The Good and the Bad Figs

24 After Nebuchadnezzar king of Babylon had deported Jeconiah[b] son of Jehoiakim king of Judah, the officials of Judah, and the craftsmen and metalsmiths from Jerusalem and had brought them to Babylon, the LORD showed me two baskets of figs placed before the temple of the LORD. 2 One basket [contained] very good figs, like early figs, but the other basket contained very bad figs, so bad they were inedible. 3 The LORD said to me, "What do you see, Jeremiah?" I said, "Figs! The good figs are very good, but the bad figs are extremely bad, so bad they are inedible."

4 The word of the LORD came to me: 5 "This is what the LORD, the God of Israel, says: Like these good figs, so I regard as good the exiles from Judah I sent away from this place to the land of the Chaldeans. 6 I will keep My eyes on them for their good and will return them to this land. I will build them up and not demolish them; I will plant them and not uproot them. 7 I will give them a heart to know Me, that I am the LORD. They will be My people, and I will be their God because they will return to Me with all their heart.

8 "But as for the bad figs, so bad they are inedible, this is what the LORD says: in this way I will deal with Zedekiah king of Judah, his officials, and the remnant of Jerusalem—those remaining in this land and those living in the land of Egypt. 9 I will make them an object of horror and disaster to all the kingdoms of the earth, a disgrace, an object of scorn, ridicule, and cursing, wherever I have banished them. 10 I will send the sword, famine, and plague against them until they have perished from the land I gave to them and their ancestors."

The Seventy-Year Exile

25 [This is] the word that came to Jeremiah concerning all the people of Judah in the fourth year of Jehoiakim son of Josiah, king of Judah (which was the first year of Nebuchadnezzar king of Babylon). 2 The prophet Jeremiah spoke concerning all the people of Judah and all the residents of Jerusalem as follows: 3 "From the thirteenth year of Josiah son of Amon, king of Judah, until this very day—23 years— the word of the LORD has come to me, and I have spoken to you time and time again,[c] but you have not obeyed. 4 The LORD sent all His servants the prophets to you time and time again,[d] but you have not obeyed or even paid attention.[e] 5 He announced, 'Turn, each of you, from your[f] evil way of life and from your evil deeds. Live in the land the LORD gave to you and your ancestors forever and ever. 6 Do not follow other gods to serve them and to worship them, and do not provoke Me to anger by the work of your hands. Then I will do you no harm.

7 " 'But you would not obey Me'—[this is] the LORD's declaration—'in order that you might provoke Me to anger by the work of your hands and bring disaster on yourselves.'

8 "Therefore, this is what the LORD of •Hosts says: 'Because you have not obeyed My words, 9 I am going to send for all the families of the north'—[this is] the LORD's declaration—'and [send for] My servant Nebuchadnezzar king of Babylon, and I will bring them against this land, against its residents, and against all these surrounding nations, and I will •completely destroy them and make them a desolation, a derision, and ruins forever. 10 I will eliminate the sound of joy and gladness from them—the voice of the bridegroom and the bride, the sound of the millstones and the light of the lamp. 11 This whole land will become a desolate ruin, and these nations will serve the king of Babylon for 70 years. 12 When the 70 years are completed, I will punish the king of Babylon and that nation'—[this is] the LORD's declaration—'the land of the Chaldeans, for their guilt, and I will make it a ruin forever. 13 I will bring on that land all My words I have spoken against it, all that is written in this book that Jeremiah prophesied against all the nations. 14 For many nations and great kings will enslave them, and I will repay them according to their deeds and the work of their hands.' "

The Cup of God's Wrath

15 This is what the LORD, the God of Israel, said to me: "Take this cup of the wine of wrath from My hand and make all the nations I am sending you to drink from it. 16 They will drink, stagger,[g] and go out of their minds because of the sword I am sending among them."

False prophets lulled their listeners into a false assurance. God would punish them for their foolishness.

23:23 near ... far away. There was nowhere to hide. God heard every word of their deceit.

23:31 use their own tongues to deliver an oracle. The false prophets enjoyed a prophetic position without heeding principles. They declared lies as "feel good" truths.

24:1 deported. Babylon selectively captured the influential leaders of Judah. **showed me.** Jeremiah had a prophetic vision from God.

24:5-6 Figs were a favored, oft-preserved delicacy of this culture. God's people were a similar delight—well worth saving.

25:3 I have spoken ... you have not obeyed. Jeremiah's message had not changed for over two decades. Yet his warnings were unheeded.

25:9 Nebuchadnezzar. The king of Babylon was decidedly pagan. However, in God's

¹⁷ So I took the cup from the LORD's hand and made all the nations drink ⌊from it⌋, everyone the LORD sent me to. ¹⁸ ⌊These included:⌋

Jerusalem and the ⌊other⌋ cities of Judah, its kings and its officials, to make them a desolate ruin, an object of scorn and cursing—as it is today;
¹⁹ Pharaoh king of Egypt, his officers, his leaders, all his people,
²⁰ and all the mixed peoples;
all the kings of the land of Uz;
all the kings of the land of the Philistines—
Ashkelon, Gaza, Ekron, and the remnant of Ashdod;
²¹ Edom, Moab, and the Ammonites;
²² all the kings of Tyre,
all the kings of Sidon,
and the kings of the coastlands across the sea;
²³ Dedan, Tema, Buz, and all those who shave their temples;^a
²⁴ all the kings of Arabia,
and all the kings of the mixed peoples who have settled in the desert;
²⁵ all the kings of Zimri,
all the kings of Elam,
and all the kings of Media;
²⁶ all the kings of the north, both near and far from one another;
that is, all the kingdoms of the world which are on the face of the earth.
Finally, the king of Sheshach^b will drink after them.

²⁷ "Then you are to say to them: This is what the LORD of Hosts, the God of Israel, says: Drink, get drunk, and vomit. Fall down and never get up again, as a result of the sword I am sending among you. ²⁸ If^c they refuse to take the cup from you and drink, you are to say to them: This is what the LORD of Hosts says: You must drink! ²⁹ For I am already bringing disaster on the city that bears My name, so how could you possibly go unpunished? You will not go unpunished, for I am summoning a sword against all the inhabitants of the earth"—⌊this is⌋ the declaration of the LORD of Hosts.

Judgment on the Whole World

³⁰ "As for you, you are to prophesy all these things to them, and say to them:

The LORD roars from on high;
He raises His voice from His holy dwelling.
He roars loudly over His grazing land;

He calls out with a shout, like those
who tread ⌊grapes⌋,
against all the inhabitants of the earth.
³¹ The tumult reaches to the ends of the earth
because the LORD brings a case
against the nations.
He enters into judgment with all flesh.
As for the wicked, He hands them over
to the sword—

⌊This is⌋
the LORD's declaration.

³² "This is what the LORD of Hosts says:

Pay attention! Disaster goes forth
from nation to nation.
A great storm is stirred up
from the ends of the earth."

³³ Those slain by the LORD on that day will be ⌊spread⌋ from one end of the earth to the other. They will not be mourned, gathered, or buried. They will be like manure on the surface of the ground.

³⁴ Wail, you shepherds, and cry out.
Roll ⌊in the dust⌋,^d you leaders of the flock.
Because the days of your slaughter have come,
you will fall and become shattered
like a precious vase.
³⁵ Flight will be impossible for the shepherds,
and escape, for the leaders of the flock.
³⁶ ⌊Hear⌋ the sound of the shepherds' cry,
the wail of the leaders of the flock,
for the LORD is destroying their pasture.
³⁷ Peaceful grazing land will become lifeless
because of the LORD's burning anger.
³⁸ He has left His den like a lion,
for their land has become a desolation
because of the sword^e of the oppressor,
because of His burning anger.

Jeremiah's Speech in the Temple

26 At the beginning of the reign of Jehoiakim son of Josiah, king of Judah, this word came from the LORD: ² "This is what the LORD says: Stand in the courtyard of the LORD's temple and speak all the words I have commanded you to speak to all Judah's cities that are coming to worship there. Do not hold back a word. ³ Perhaps they will listen and return—each from his evil way of life—so that I might relent concerning the disaster that I plan to do to them because of the evil of their deeds. ⁴ You are to say to them: This is

^a**25:23** Or *who live in distant places*; Jr 9:26; 49:32; Lv 19:27 ^b**25:26** Probably a code name for Babylon ^c**25:28** Or *When* ^d**25:34** = a mourning custom ^e**25:38** Some Hb mss, LXX, Tg; other Hb mss read *burning*; Jr 46:16

grand scheme, even a pagan can be used as a tool to accomplish His will.
25:11-12 nations will serve ... 70 years. Jeremiah's warnings concerned an extensive exile. The Babylonians punished the exiled people for over half a century.
25:12 punish. God used the Babylonians; He

did not favor them. He would eventually punish them for brutalizing His people.
25:15 drink from it. God's wrath is unavoidable. His enemies will experience it.
25:17 the cup. The book of Numbers speaks of a drink of bitter water a husband would give his wife as a test for adultery (Num. 5:22-28).

Here, such a cup is applied to the many nations. Though it refers to Babylon in 51:7, it usually is directly related to God and His judgment (49:12; Pss. 60:3; 75:9; Isa. 51:17-23; Lam. 4:21; Ezek. 23:31-34; Hab. 2:16). As host, God offers this cup to Judah first, then those who have persecuted her. Jeremiah

what the LORD says: If you do not listen to Me by living according to My law that I set before you [5] and by listening to the words of My servants the prophets I have been sending you time and time again,[a] though you did not listen, [6] I will make this temple like Shiloh. I will make this city an object of cursing for all the nations of the earth."

Jeremiah Seized

[7] The priests, the prophets, and all the people heard Jeremiah speaking these words in the temple of the LORD. [8] He finished the address the LORD had commanded him to deliver to all the people. Then the priests, the prophets, and all the people took hold of him, yelling, "You must surely die! [9] How dare you prophesy in the name of the LORD, 'This temple will become like Shiloh and this city will become an uninhabited ruin'!" Then all the people assembled against Jeremiah at the LORD's temple.

[10] When the officials of Judah heard these things, they went up from the king's palace to the LORD's temple and sat at the entrance of the New Gate.[b] [11] Then the priests and prophets said to the officials and all the people, "This man deserves the death sentence because he has prophesied against this city, as you have heard with your own ears."

Jeremiah's Defense

[12] Then Jeremiah said to all the officials and the people, "The LORD sent me to prophesy all the words that you have heard against this temple and city. [13] So now, correct your ways and deeds and obey the voice of the LORD your God so that He might relent concerning the disaster that He warned about. [14] As for me, here I am in your hands; do to me what you think is good and right. [15] But know for certain that if you put me to death, you will bring innocent blood on yourselves, on this city, and on its residents, for it is certain the LORD has sent me to speak all these things directly to you."

Jeremiah Released

[16] Then the officials and all the people told the priests and prophets, "This man doesn't deserve the death sentence, for he has spoken to us in the name of the LORD our God!"

[17] Some of the elders of the land stood up and said to all the assembled people, [18] "Micah the Moreshite prophesied ins the days of Hezekiah king of Judah and said to all the people of Judah, 'This is what the LORD of •Hosts says:

Zion will be plowed like a field,
Jerusalem will become ruins,
and the temple mount a forested hill.'

[19] Did Hezekiah king of Judah and all ⌊the people of⌋ Judah put him to death? Did he not •fear the LORD and plead for the LORD's favor,[c] and did not the LORD relent concerning the disaster He had pronounced against them? We are about to bring great harm on ourselves!"

The Prophet Uriah

[20] Another man was also prophesying in the name of the LORD—Uriah son of Shemaiah from Kiriath-jearim. He prophesied against this city and against this land in words like all those of Jeremiah. [21] King Jehoiakim, all his warriors, and all the officials heard his words, and the king tried to put him to death. When Uriah heard, he fled in fear and went to Egypt. [22] But King Jehoiakim sent men to Egypt: Elnathan son of Achbor and ⌊certain other⌋ men with him ⌊went⌋ to Egypt. [23] They brought Uriah out of Egypt and took him to King Jehoiakim, who executed him with the sword and threw his corpse into the burial place of the common people.[d]

[24] But Ahikam son of Shaphan supported Jeremiah, so he was not handed over to the people to be put to death.

The Yoke of Babylon

27 At the beginning of the reign of Zedekiah[e] son of Josiah, king of Judah, this word came to Jeremiah from the LORD:[f] [2] "This is what the LORD said to me: Make fetters and yoke bars for yourself and put them on your neck. [3] Send ⌊word⌋ to the king of Edom, the king of Moab, the king of the Ammonites, the king of Tyre, and the king of Sidon through messengers who are coming to Zedekiah king of Judah in Jerusalem. [4] Command them ⌊to go⌋ to their masters, saying: This is what the LORD of •Hosts, the God of Israel, says: This is what you must say to your masters: [5] By My great strength and outstretched arm, I made the earth, and the people, and animals on the face of the earth. I give it to anyone I please.[g] [6] So now I have placed all these lands under the authority of My servant Nebuchadnezzar, king of Babylon. I have even given him the wild animals to serve him. [7] All nations will serve him, his son, and his grandson until the time for his own land comes, and then many nations and great kings will enslave him.

---

[a] **26:5** Lit *you, rising early and sending* [b] **26:10** Some Hb mss, Syr, Tg, Vg add *of the house* [c] **26:19** Or *and appease the LORD* [d] **26:23** Lit *the sons of the people* [e] **27:1** Some Hb mss, Syr, Arabic; other Hb mss, DSS read *Jehoiakim*; Jr 27:3,12 [f] **27:1** LXX omits this v. [g] **27:5** Lit *to whoever is upright in My eyes*

---

probably offered the actual cup (though symbolic) to each nation's representative in Jerusalem (27:3).

25:18 Judah. God's own people drink first (see Ezek. 9:6; 1 Pet. 4:17).

25:19-26 Though Babylon performs as God's "cup of wrath," it would drink too.

25:30 roars from on high. God is said to roar like a lion (Hosea 11:10; Amos 3:8).

25:16 he has spoken. The people and their elders were more obedient to God than the priests and so-called prophets of the land in acquitting Jeremiah. Obedience, not opposition, was the proper response to a prophet's message.

26:17-19 Some elders gave the priests and prophets a history lesson. Because of Hezekiah's repentance in 701 B.C., judgment on Jerusalem was averted (Micah 3:12; 4:12).

26:20-23 God's judgment was not news. King Jehoiakim's disrespect for the messenger could not silence the message.

8 "As for the nation or kingdom that does not serve Nebuchadnezzar king of Babylon and does not place its neck under the yoke of the king of Babylon, that nation I will punish by sword, famine, and plague"—⌊this is⌋ the LORD's declaration—"until through him I have destroyed it. 9 But as for you, do not listen to your prophets, your diviners, your dreamers, your fortune-tellers, or your sorcerers who say to you: Don't serve the king of Babylon! 10 for they prophesy a lie to you so that you will be removed from your land. I will banish you, and you will perish. 11 But as for the nation that will put its neck under the yoke of the king of Babylon and serve him, I will leave it in its own land, and that nation will till[a] it and reside in it." ⌊This is⌋ the LORD's declaration.

Warning to Zedekiah

12 I spoke to Zedekiah king of Judah in the same way: "Put your necks under the yoke of the king of Babylon, serve him and his people, and live! 13 Why should you and your people die by the sword, famine, or plague as the LORD has threatened against any nation that does not serve the king of Babylon? 14 Do not listen to the words of the prophets who are telling you, 'You must not serve the king of Babylon,' for they are prophesying a lie to you. 15 'I have not sent them'—⌊this is⌋ the LORD's declaration—'and they are prophesying falsely in My name; therefore, I will banish you, and you will perish—you and the prophets who are prophesying to you.' "

16 Then I spoke to the priests and all these people, saying, "This is what the LORD says, 'Do not listen to the words of your prophets. They are prophesying to you, claiming: Look, very soon now the articles of the LORD's temple will be brought back from Babylon. They are prophesying a lie to you. 17 Do not listen to them. Serve the king of Babylon and live! Why should this city become a ruin? 18 If they are indeed prophets and if the word of the LORD is with them, let them intercede with the LORD of Hosts not to let the articles that remain in the LORD's temple, in the palace of the king of Judah, and in Jerusalem go to Babylon.' 19 For this is what the LORD of Hosts says about the pillars, the sea, the water carts, and the rest of the articles that still remain in this city, 20 those Nebuchadnezzar king of Babylon did not take when he deported Jeconiah[b] son of Jehoiakim, king of Judah, from Jerusalem to Babylon along with all the nobles of Judah and Jerusalem. 21 Yes, this is what the LORD of Hosts, the God of Israel, says about the articles that remain in the temple of the LORD, in the palace

of the king of Judah, and in Jerusalem: 22 'They will be brought to Babylon and will remain there until I attend to them again.' ⌊This is⌋ the LORD's declaration. 'Then I will bring them up and restore them to this place.' "

Hananiah's False Prophecy

28 In that same year, at the beginning of the reign of Zedekiah king of Judah, in the fifth month of the fourth year, the prophet Hananiah son of Azzur from Gibeon said to me in the temple of the LORD in the presence of the priests and all the people, 2 "This is what the LORD of •Hosts, the God of Israel, says: 'I have broken the yoke of the king of Babylon. 3 Within two years I will restore to this place all the articles of the LORD's temple that Nebuchadnezzar king of Babylon took from here and transported to Babylon. 4 And I will restore to this place Jeconiah[b] son of Jehoiakim, king of Judah, and all the exiles from Judah who went to Babylon'—⌊this is⌋ the LORD's declaration—'for I will break the yoke of the king of Babylon.' "

Jeremiah's Response to Hananiah

5 The prophet Jeremiah replied to the prophet Hananiah in the presence of the priests and all the people who were standing in the temple of the LORD. 6 The prophet Jeremiah said, "•Amen! May the LORD do so. May the LORD make the words you have prophesied come true and may He restore the articles of the LORD's temple and all the exiles from Babylon to this place! 7 Only listen to this message I am speaking in your hearing and in the hearing of all the people. 8 The prophets who preceded you and me from ancient times prophesied war, disaster,[c] and plague against many lands and great kingdoms. 9 As for the prophet who prophesies peace—only when the word of the prophet comes true will the prophet be recognized as one whom the LORD has truly sent."

Hananiah Breaks Jeremiah's Yoke

10 The prophet Hananiah then took the yoke bar from the neck of Jeremiah the prophet and broke it. 11 In the presence of all the people Hananiah proclaimed, "This is what the LORD says: 'In this way, within two years I will break the yoke of Nebuchadnezzar, king of Babylon, from the neck of all the nations.'" Jeremiah the prophet then went on his way.

The LORD's Word against Hananiah

12 The word of the LORD came to Jeremiah after Hananiah the prophet had broken the yoke bar from the neck of Jeremiah the prophet: 13 "Go say to Hananiah: This is what the LORD says: You broke a wooden yoke

---

[a]27:11 Lit work   [b]27:20; 28:4 = Jehoiachin   [c]28:8 Some Hb mss, Vg read famine

---

26:20 Uriah ... prophesied. Uriah responded to the Lord and spoke boldly of God's prophecy with fear and reverence.

27:2 Make fetters and yoke bars. Fetters were restraints for prisoners, and yokes were used to keep oxen in line while plowing. God used Jeremiah as a human word-picture. Ju-

dah and other rebellious nations would not listen to his warnings; perhaps they would pay attention to his example.

27:12 Put your necks under the yoke. Jeremiah told the king that God had handed the people over to Babylon's domination and the king should submit like an ox under a yoke.

28:1 prophet Hananiah. This prophet's name means, "The Lord is gracious." However, Hananiah exhibited wishful thinking rather than a true revelation of God's plans. He may have been falsely encouraged by a revolt Nebuchadnezzar was dealing with at the time and recorded in the Babylonian

bar, but in its place you will make an iron yoke bar. [14] For this is what the LORD of Hosts, the God of Israel, says: I have put an iron yoke on the neck of all these nations that they might serve Nebuchadnezzar king of Babylon, and they will serve him. I have also put the wild animals under him."

[15] The prophet Jeremiah said to the prophet Hananiah, "Listen, Hananiah! The LORD did not send you, but you have led these people to trust in a lie. [16] Therefore, this is what the LORD says: 'I am about to send you off the face of the earth. You will die this year because you have spoken rebellion against the LORD.'" [17] And the prophet Hananiah died that year in the seventh month.

Jeremiah's Letter to the Exiles

29 This is the text of the letter that Jeremiah the prophet sent from Jerusalem to the rest of the elders of the exiles, the priests, the prophets, and all the people Nebuchadnezzar had deported from Jerusalem to Babylon. [2] ⌊This was⌋ after King Jeconiah,[a] the queen mother, the court officials, the officials of Judah and Jerusalem, the craftsmen, and the metalsmiths had left Jerusalem. [3] ⌊The letter was sent⌋ by Elasah son of Shaphan and Gemariah son of Hilkiah whom Zedekiah king of Judah had sent to Babylon to Nebuchadnezzar king of Babylon. ⌊The letter⌋ stated:

[4] This is what the LORD of •Hosts, the God of Israel, says to all the exiles I deported from Jerusalem to Babylon: [5] "Build houses and live ⌊in them⌋. Plant gardens and eat their produce. [6] Take wives and have sons and daughters. Take wives for your sons and give your daughters to men ⌊in marriage⌋ so that they may bear sons and daughters. Multiply there; do not decrease. [7] Seek the welfare of the city I have deported you to. Pray to the LORD on its behalf, for when it has prosperity, you will prosper."

[8] For this is what the LORD of Hosts, the God of Israel, says: "Don't let your prophets who are among you and your diviners deceive you, and don't listen to the dreams you elicit from them, [9] for they are prophesying falsely to you in My name. I have not sent them." ⌊This is⌋ the LORD's declaration.

[10] For this is what the LORD says: "When 70 years for Babylon are complete, I will attend to you and will confirm My promise concerning you to restore you to this place. [11] For I know the plans I have for you"—⌊this is⌋ the LORD's declaration—"plans for ⌊your⌋ welfare, not for disaster, to give you a future and a hope. [12] You will call to Me and come and pray to Me, and I will listen to you. [13] You will seek Me and find Me when you search for Me with all your heart. [14] I will be found by you"—the LORD's declaration—"and I will restore your fortunes[b] and gather you from all the nations and places where I banished you"—the LORD's declaration. "I will restore you to the place I deported you from."

[15] You have said, "The LORD has raised up prophets for us in Babylon!" [16] But this is what the LORD says concerning the king sitting on David's throne and concerning all the people living in this city—that is, concerning your brothers who did not go with you into exile. [17] This is what the LORD of Hosts says: "I am about to send against them sword, famine, and plague and will make them like rotten figs that are inedible because they are so bad. [18] I will pursue them with sword, famine, and plague. I will make them a horror to all the kingdoms of the earth—a curse and a desolation, an object of scorn and a disgrace among all the nations where I will have banished them. [19] ⌊I will do this⌋ because they have not listened to My words"—⌊this is⌋ the LORD's declaration—"that I sent to them with My servants the prophets time and time again.[c] And you too have not listened." ⌊This is⌋ the LORD's declaration.

[20] Hear the word of the LORD, all you exiles I have sent from Jerusalem to Babylon. [21] This is what the LORD of Hosts, the God of Israel, says to Ahab son of Kolaiah and to Zedekiah son of Maaseiah, the ones prophesying a lie to you in My name: "I am about to hand them over to Nebuchadnezzar king of Babylon, and he will kill them before your very eyes. [22] Based on ⌊what happens to⌋ them, all the exiles of Judah who are in Babylon will create a curse that says: May the LORD make you like Zedekiah and Ahab, whom the king of Babylon roasted in the fire! [23] because they have committed an outrage in Israel by committing adultery with their neighbors' wives and have spoken a lie in My name, which I did not command them. I am He who knows, and I am a witness." ⌊This is⌋ the LORD's declaration.

[24] To Shemaiah the Nehelamite you are to say, [25] "This is what the LORD of Hosts, the God of

---

[a]**29:2** = Jehoiachin [b]**29:14** Or *will end your captivity* [c]**29:19** Lit *prophets, rising up early and sending*

Israel, says: You[a] in your own name have sent out letters to all the people of Jerusalem, to the priest Zephaniah son of Maaseiah, and to all the priests, saying: 26 The LORD has appointed you priest in place of Jehoiada the priest to be the chief officer in the temple of the LORD, responsible for every madman who acts like a prophet. You must confine him in stocks and an iron collar. 27 So now, why have you not rebuked Jeremiah of Anathoth who has been acting like a prophet among you? 28 For he has sent ⌊word⌋ to us in Babylon, claiming: The exile will be long. Build houses and settle down. Plant gardens and eat their produce."

29 Zephaniah the priest read this letter in the hearing of Jeremiah the prophet.

A Message about Shemaiah

30 Then the word of the LORD came to Jeremiah: 31 "Send ⌊a message⌋ to all the exiles, saying: This is what the LORD says concerning Shemaiah the Nehelamite. Because Shemaiah prophesied to you, though I did not send him, and made you trust a lie, 32 this is what the LORD says: I am about to punish Shemaiah the Nehelamite and his descendants. There will not be even one of his ⌊descendants⌋ living among these people, nor will any ever see the good that I will bring to My people"—⌊this is⌋ the LORD's declaration—"for he has preached rebellion against the LORD."

Restoration from Captivity

30 ⌊This is⌋ the word that came to Jeremiah from the LORD. 2 This is what the LORD, the God of Israel, says: "Write down on a scroll all the words that I have spoken to you, 3 for the days are certainly coming"—⌊this is⌋ the LORD's declaration—"when I will restore the fortunes[b] of My people Israel and Judah"— the LORD's declaration. "I will restore them to the land I gave to their ancestors and they will possess it."

4 These are the words the LORD spoke to Israel and Judah. 5 Yes, this is what the LORD says:

We have heard a cry of terror,
of dread—there is no peace.
6 Ask and see
whether a male can give birth.
Why then do I see every man
with his hands on his stomach like a woman
in labor
and every face turned pale?
7 How awful that day will be!
There will be none like it!

It will be a time of trouble for Jacob,
but he will be delivered out of it.

8 "On that day"—⌊this is⌋ the declaration of the LORD of •Hosts—"I will break his yoke from your neck and snap your fetters so strangers will never again enslave him. 9 They will serve the LORD their God and I will raise up David their king for them."

10 As for you, My servant Jacob,
do not be afraid—

⌊this is⌋
the LORD's declaration—
and do not be dismayed, Israel,
for I will without fail save you from far away,
your descendants, from the land
of their captivity!
Jacob will return and have calm and quiet
with no one to frighten him.
11 For I will be with you—

⌊this is⌋
the LORD's declaration—
to save you!
I will bring destruction on all the nations
where I have scattered you;
however, I will not bring destruction on you.
I will discipline you justly,
but I will by no means leave you unpunished.

Healing Zion's Wounds

12 For this is what the LORD says:

Your injury is incurable;
your wound most severe.
13 No one takes up the case for your sores.
You have nothing that can heal you.
14 All your lovers have forgotten you;
they no longer look for you,
for I have struck you like an enemy would,
with the discipline of someone cruel,
because of your enormous guilt
and your innumerable sins.
15 Why do you cry out about your injury?
Your pain has no cure!
I have done these things to you
because of your enormous guilt
and your innumerable sins.
16 Nevertheless, all who devoured you
will be devoured,
and all your adversaries—all of them—
will go off into exile.
Your despoilers will become spoil,

---

[a] **29:25** Lit Because you   [b] **30:3** Or will end the captivity

---

God Himself. He delivered encouragement to their Babylonian doorstep.

29:8 deceive you. False prophets were eager to draw an audience with their message of false hope.

29:13 You will seek Me and find Me. God's promise is still for the Jewish people

scattered in every nation. Though they were scattered from the land, they would find God again if they sought Him (see Deut. 30:1-6, Rom. 11:26).

29:21 hand them over to Nebuchadnezzar. Once again, a pagan king was God's tool for assigning punishment. The false prophets

were finally silenced.

29:31-32 God made it easier for His people to understand His true intentions. He identified and silenced false prophets like Shemaiah.

30:1–33:26 Jeremiah balanced his message of doom with that of hope. He described a postexilic day of restoration that would serve

and all who plunder you will be plundered.
17 But I will bring you health
and will heal you of your wounds—

⌊this is⌋
the LORD's declaration—
for they call you The Outcast,
that Zion no one cares about.

Restoration of the Land

18 This is what the LORD says:

I will certainly restore the fortunes[a]
of Jacob's tents
and show compassion on his dwellings.
Every city will be rebuilt on its mound;
every citadel will stand on its proper site.
19 Thanksgiving will come out of them,
a sound of celebration.
I will multiply them, and they will not decrease;
I will honor them, and they will not
be insignificant.
20 His children will be as in past days;
his congregation will be established
in My presence.
I will punish all his oppressors.
21 Jacob's leader will be one of them;
his ruler will issue from him.
I will invite him to Me, and he will
approach Me,
for who would otherwise risk his life
to approach Me?

⌊This is⌋
the LORD's declaration.
22 You will be My people,
and I will be your God.

The Wrath of God

23 Look, a storm from the LORD!
Wrath has gone forth.
A churning storm,
it will whirl about the head of the wicked.
24 The LORD's burning anger will not turn back
until He has completely fulfilled the purposes
of His heart.
In time to come you will understand it.

God's Relationship with His People

31 "At that time"—⌊this is⌋ the LORD's declaration—"I will be God of all the families of Israel,
and they will be My people."
2 This is what the LORD says:

They found favor in the wilderness—
the people who survived the sword.
⌊When⌋ Israel went to find rest,
3 the LORD appeared to him[b] from far away.
I have loved you with an everlasting love;
therefore, I have continued to extend
faithful love to you.
4 Again I will build you so that you will be rebuilt,
Virgin Israel.
You will take up your tambourines again
and go forth in joyful dancing.
5 You will plant vineyards again
on the mountains of Samaria;
the planters will plant and will enjoy ⌊the fruit⌋.
6 For there will be a day when watchmen
will call out
in the hill country of Ephraim:
Get up, let's go up to Zion,
to the LORD our God!

God's People Brought Home

7 For this is what the LORD says:

Sing with joy for Jacob;
shout for the chief of the nations!
Proclaim, praise, and say:
LORD, save Your people,
the remnant of Israel!
8 Watch! I am going to bring them
from the northern land.
I will gather them from remote regions
of the earth—
the blind and the lame will be with them,
along with those who are pregnant and those
about to give birth.
They will return here as a great assembly!
9 They will come weeping,
but I will bring them back with consolation.[c]
I will lead them to •wadis ⌊filled⌋ with water
by a smooth way where they will not stumble,
for I am Israel's Father,
and Ephraim is My firstborn.
10 Nations, hear the word of the LORD,
and tell it among the far off coastlands!
Say: The One who scattered Israel
will gather him.
He will watch over him as a shepherd
⌊guards⌋ his flock,
11 for the LORD has ransomed Jacob
and redeemed him from the power of one
stronger than he.

_a**30:18** Or *certainly end the captivity*   ^b**31:3** LXX; MT reads *me*   ^c**31:9** LXX; MT reads *supplications*

---

as an encouraging reminder to the returning exiles.

30:1–31:40 Jeremiah used poetic language to describe the people's physical deliverance (30:1-11). Additionally, he described the ensuing spiritual healing (30:12-17) and joyful results (31:2-40).

30:3 days are certainly coming. The first exiles would not return to their homeland until many years later (537 B.C.). Yet even then, God's full promise was not fulfilled. In the days of Christ's kingdom, Israel will possess the land and be fully restored.

30:9 their king. David is the king whose line

leads to the Messiah. Jesus Christ is the Son of David who will rule physically in Israel during the Millennium.

30:20 as in past days. In the midst of such a chaotic state, thoughts of David's reign inspired a desire for a future restoration characterized by the peace and stability that David's

12 They will come and shout for joy on the heights
   of Zion;
   they will be radiant with joy
   because of the LORD's goodness,
   because of the grain, the new wine, the fresh oil,
   and because of the young of the flocks
   and herds.
   Their life will be like an irrigated garden,
   and they will no longer grow weak ⌊from hunger⌋.
13 Then the virgin will rejoice with dancing,
   while young and old men ⌊rejoice⌋ together.
   I will turn their mourning into joy,
   give them consolation,
   and ⌊bring⌋ happiness out of grief.
14 I will give the priests their fill with abundance,[a]
   and My people will be satisfied
   with My goodness.

⌊This is⌋
the LORD's declaration.

Lament Turned to Joy

15 This is what the LORD says:

A voice was heard in Ramah,
a lament with bitter weeping—
Rachel weeping for her children,
refusing to be comforted for her children
because they are no more.

16 This is what the LORD says:

Keep your voice from weeping
and your eyes from tears,
for the reward for your work will come—

⌊this is⌋
the LORD's declaration—
and your children will return
   from the enemy's land.
17 There is hope for your future—

⌊this is⌋
the LORD's declaration—
and your children will return
   to their own territory.
18 I have heard Ephraim moaning:
   You disciplined me, and I have been disciplined
   like an untrained calf.
   Restore me, and I will return,
   for you, LORD, are my God.
19 After I returned, I repented;
   After I was instructed, I struck my thigh
   ⌊in grief⌋.

I was ashamed and humiliated
because I bore the disgrace
   of my youth.
20 Isn't Ephraim a precious son to Me,
   a delightful child?
   Whenever I speak against him,
   I certainly still think about him.
   Therefore, My inner being yearns
      for him;
   I will truly have compassion on him.

⌊This is⌋
the LORD's declaration.

Repentance and Restoration

21 Set up road markers for yourself;
   establish signposts!
   Keep the highway in mind,
   the way you have traveled.
   Return, Virgin Israel!
   Return to these cities of yours.
22 How long will you turn here and there,
   faithless daughter?
   For the LORD creates something new
      in the land[b]—
   a female[c] will shelter[d] a man.

23 This is what the LORD of •Hosts, the God of Israel,
says: "When I restore their fortunes,[e] they will once
again speak this word in the land of Judah and in its cities: May the LORD bless you, righteous settlement, holy
mountain. 24 Judah and all its cities will live in it
together—also farmers and those who move[f] with the
flocks— 25 for I satisfy the thirsty person and feed all
those who are weak."
26 At this I awoke and looked around. My sleep had
been most pleasant to me.
27 "The days are coming"—⌊this is⌋ the LORD's declaration—"when I will sow the house of Israel and the
house of Judah with the seed of man and the seed of
beast. 28 Just as I watched over them to uproot and to
tear them down, to demolish and to destroy, and to
cause disaster, so will I be attentive to build and to plant
them," says the LORD. 29 "In those days, it will never
again be said:

The fathers have eaten sour grapes,
and the children's teeth are set on edge.

30 Rather, each will die for his own wrongdoing. Anyone who eats sour grapes—his own teeth will be set
on edge.

---

[a]31:14 Lit fatness   [b]31:22 Or new on earth   [c]31:22 Or woman   [d]31:22 Or female surrounds (Dt 32:10; Ps 32:7,10), or female courts; Hb obscure
[e]31:23 Or I end their captivity   [f]31:24 Tg, Vg, Aq, Sym; MT reads and they will move

---

rule brought to their nation.

30:22 You will be my people. This is the traditional covenant formula (7:23; 11:4; Gen.
17:7–8; Exod. 6:7; 19:6; Lev. 26:12; Deut.
7:26; Ezek. 36:28). Looking ahead, the basis
for this will not be the Mosaic covenant but a
new relationship (31:31–34).

31:6 Zion. This verse anticipates when the inhabitants of the northern kingdom will once
again worship in Jerusalem.

31:7 shout for the chief. Israel is the "chief of
the nations" by God's favor (Deut. 7:6-8). Israel was chosen to bring God's story to the
world.

31:11 stronger than he. God redeemed Israel from Babylon, a power far stronger than
Israel but not stronger than God.

31:15 Rachel weeping. Jeremiah described
the disappearance of the tribes of Manasseh
and Ephraim (Rachel's grandchildren, Gen.
46:19). Their defeat by Assyria symbolized

The New Covenant

31 "Look, the days are coming"—⌊this is⌋ the LORD's declaration—"when I will make a new covenant with the house of Israel and with the house of Judah. 32 ⌊This one will⌋ not be like the covenant I made with their ancestors when I took them by the hand to bring them out of the land of Egypt—a covenant they broke even though I had married them"—the LORD's declaration. 33 "Instead, this is the covenant I will make with the house of Israel after those days"—the LORD's declaration. "I will place My law[a] within them and write it on their hearts. I will be their God, and they will be My people. 34 No longer will one teach his neighbor or his brother, saying: Know the LORD, for they will all know Me, from the least to the greatest of them"—the LORD's declaration. "For I will forgive their wrongdoing and never again remember their sin."

35 This is what the LORD says:

The One who gives the sun for light by day,
the fixed order of moon and stars for light
   by night,
who stirs up the sea and makes its waves roar—
the LORD of Hosts is His name:
36   If this fixed order departs from My presence—
      ⌊this is⌋ the LORD's declaration—
   then also Israel's descendants will cease
   to be a nation before Me forever.

37 This is what the LORD says:

If the heavens above can be measured
and the foundations of the earth below explored,
I will reject all of Israel's descendants
because of all they have done—
      ⌊this is⌋
   the LORD's declaration.

38 "Look, the days are coming"—the LORD's declaration—"when the city[b] from the Tower of Hananel to the Corner Gate will be rebuilt for the LORD. 39 A measuring line will once again stretch out straight to the hill of Gareb and then turn toward Goah. 40 The whole valley—the corpses, the ashes, and all the fields as far as the Kidron Valley to the corner of the Horse Gate to the east—will be holy to the LORD. It will never be uprooted or demolished again."

Jeremiah's Land Purchase

32 ⌊This is⌋ the word that came to Jeremiah from the LORD in the tenth year of Zedekiah king of Judah, which was the eighteenth year of Nebuchadnezzar. 2 At that time, the army of the king of Babylon was besieging Jerusalem, and Jeremiah the prophet was imprisoned in the guard's courtyard in the palace of the king of Judah. 3 Zedekiah king of Judah had imprisoned him, saying: "Why are you prophesying, 'This is what the LORD says: Look, I am about to hand this city over to Babylon's king, and he will capture it. 4 Zedekiah king of Judah will not escape from the Chaldeans; indeed, he will certainly be handed over to Babylon's king. They will speak face to face[c] and meet eye to eye. 5 He will take Zedekiah to Babylon where he will stay until I attend to him'—⌊this is⌋ the LORD's declaration. 'You will fight the Chaldeans, but you will not succeed'?"

6 Jeremiah replied, "The word of the LORD came to me: 7 'Watch! Hanamel, the son of your uncle Shallum, is coming to you to say: Buy my field in Anathoth for yourself, for you own the right of redemption to buy it.'

8 "Then my cousin Hanamel ⌊came⌋ to the guard's courtyard as the LORD had said and urged me, 'Please buy my field in Anathoth in the land of Benjamin, for you own the right of inheritance and redemption. Buy it for yourself.' Then I knew that this was the word of the LORD. 9 So I bought the field in Anathoth from my cousin Hanamel, and I weighed out to him the money—17 •shekels[d] of silver. 10 I recorded it on a scroll, sealed it, called in witnesses, and weighed out the silver on a scale. 11 I took the purchase agreement—the sealed copy with its terms and conditions and the open copy— 12 and gave the purchase agreement to Baruch son of Neriah, son of Mahseiah. ⌊I did this⌋ in the sight of my cousin[e] Hanamel, the witnesses who were signing the purchase agreement, and all the Judeans sitting in the guard's courtyard. 13 "I instructed Baruch in their sight, 14 'This is what the LORD of •Hosts, the God of Israel, says: Take these scrolls—this purchase agreement with the sealed copy and this open copy—and put them in an earthen storage jar so they will last a long time. 15 For this is what the LORD of Hosts, the God of Israel, says: Houses, fields, and vineyards will again be bought in this land.'

16 "After I had given the purchase agreement to Baruch, son of Neriah, I prayed to the LORD: 17 Ah, Lord GOD! You Yourself made the heavens and earth by Your great power and with Your outstretched arm. Nothing is too difficult for You! 18 You show faithful love to thousands but lay the fathers' sins on their sons' laps after them, great and mighty God whose name is the LORD of

---

[a]31:33 Or instruction   [b]31:38 = Jerusalem   [c]32:4 Lit His mouth will speak with his mouth   [d]32:9 About 7 ounces   [e]32:12 Some Hb mss, LXX, Syr; other Hb mss read uncle

---

true heartache among the people. Yet God promised to restore Ephraim in the future (v.17-20).

31:29 never ... be said. A common complaint in Jeremiah's day, the people falsely accused God of unfairly assigning consequence of their ancestors' sins on them (Ezek. 18:2-4).

31:30 Rather. God justly assigned blame to individuals for their sins (Deut. 24:16). The exile was prompted by the sheer extent of apostasy and so the punishment appeared to be on the nation as a whole.

31:31 I will make a new covenant. God said He would make a new covenant with Israel

and Judah (Gentiles are included by faith in this covenant). This promise is very significant, for it shows that God's revelation through Moses was not the end, but the beginning. The New Covenant was inaugurated by Jesus' death (see 1 Cor. 11:25; 2 Cor. 3:6; Heb. 9:15).

Hosts, ¹⁹ the One great in counsel and mighty in deed, whose eyes are on all the ways of the sons of men in order to give to each person according to his ways and the result of his deeds. ²⁰ You performed signs and wonders in the land of Egypt and do so to this very day both in Israel and among mankind. You made a name for Yourself, as ⌊is the case⌋ today. ²¹ You brought Your people Israel out of Egypt with signs and wonders, with a strong hand and an outstretched arm, and with great terror. ²² You gave them this land You swore ⌊to give⌋ to their ancestors, a land flowing with milk and honey. ²³ They entered and possessed it, but they did not obey Your voice or live according to Your law. They failed to perform all You commanded them to do, and so You have brought all this disaster on them. ²⁴ Look! Siege ramps have come against the city to capture it, and the city, as a result of the sword, famine, and plague, has been handed over to the Chaldeans who are fighting against it. What You have spoken has happened. Look, You can see it! ²⁵ Yet You, Lord GOD, have said to me: Buy the field with silver and call in witnesses—even though the city has been handed over to the Chaldeans!"

²⁶ Then the word of the LORD came to Jeremiah: ²⁷ "Look, I am the LORD, the God of all flesh. Is anything too difficult for Me? ²⁸ Therefore, this is what the LORD says: I am about to hand this city over to the Chaldeans, to Babylon's king Nebuchadnezzar, and he will capture it. ²⁹ The Chaldeans who are going to fight against this city will come, set this city on fire, and burn it along with the houses where incense has been burned to •Baal on their rooftops and where drink offerings have been poured out to other gods to provoke Me to anger. ³⁰ From their youth, the Israelites and Judeans have done nothing but what is evil in My sight! They have done nothing but provoke Me to anger by the work of their hands"—⌊this is⌋ the LORD's declaration— ³¹ "for this city has been up against My wrath and fury from the day it was built until now. I will therefore remove it from My presence, ³² because of all the evil the Israelites and Judeans have done to provoke Me to anger— they, their kings, their officials, their priests, and their prophets, the men of Judah, and the residents of Jerusalem. ³³ They have turned their backs to Me and not their faces. Though I taught them time and time again,ᵃ they do not listen and receive discipline. ³⁴ They have placed their detestable things in the house that is called by My name and have defiled it. ³⁵ They have built the •high places of Baal in the Valley of Hinnom to make

their sons and daughters pass through ⌊the fire⌋ to •Molech—something I had not commanded them. I had never entertained the thoughtᵇ that they do this detestable act causing Judah to sin!

³⁶ "Now therefore, this is what the LORD, the God of Israel, says to this city about which you said: It has been handed over to Babylon's king through sword, famine, and plague: ³⁷ I am about to gather them from all the lands where I have banished them in My wrath, rage, and great fury, and I will return them to this place and make them live in safety. ³⁸ They will be My people, and I will be their God. ³⁹ I will give them one heart and one way so that for their good and for ⌊the good of⌋ their descendants after them, they will •fear Me always.

⁴⁰ "I will make with them an everlasting covenant: I will never turn away from doing good to them, and I will put fear of Me in their hearts so they will never again turn away from Me. ⁴¹ I will rejoice over them to do what is good to them, and I will plant them faithfully in this land with all My mind and heart.

⁴² "For this is what the LORD says: Just as I have brought all this great disaster on these people, so am I about to bring on them all the good I am promising them. ⁴³ Fields will be bought in this land about which you are saying: It's a desolation without man or beast; it has been handed over to the Chaldeans! ⁴⁴ Fields will be purchased with silver, the transaction written on a scroll and sealed, and witnesses will be called on in the land of Benjamin, in the areas surrounding Jerusalem, and in Judah's cities—the cities of the hill country, the cities of the Judean foothills, and the cities of the •Negev—because I will restore their fortunes."ᶜ

⌊This is⌋
the LORD's declaration.

Israel's Restoration

33 While he was still confined in the guard's courtyard, the word of the LORD came to Jeremiah a second time: ² "The LORD who made the earth,ᵈ the LORD who forms it to establish it, the LORD is His name, says this: ³ Call to Me and I will answer you and tell you great and wondrous things you do not know. ⁴ For this is what the LORD, the God of Israel, says concerning the houses of this city and the palaces of Judah's kings, the ones torn down ⌊for defense⌋ against the siege ramps and the sword: ⁵ The people coming to fight the Chaldeans will fill the houses with the corpses of ⌊their own⌋ men I strike down in My wrath and rage. I have hidden My face from this city

---

ᵃ**32:33** Lit *them, rising up early and teaching*   ᵇ**32:35** Lit *them, and it did not arise on My heart*   ᶜ**32:44** Or *will end their captivity*   ᵈ**33:2** LXX; MT reads *made it*

31:33 place My law within them. Far from being rendered obsolete, God's law is being internalized in those who have the indwelling Holy Spirit that enables one to obey it in spirit. Ezekiel speaks of God replacing hearts of stone with hearts of flesh—hearts that want to do God's will. This is parallel to

Jesus' statement in the Sermon on the Mount that He did not come to destroy the law but to fulfill it (Matt. 5:17-20).

32:1 tenth year. Jeremiah carefully noted the dates of his messages. The destruction of Judah was quickly approaching within a year.

32:7 right of... redemption. Jeremiah followed

an ancient law (Lev. 25:23-25). It required him to buy land from a financially struggling relative in order to keep it within the family.

32:25 buy the field. Despite the city's inevitable fate, Jeremiah purchased the land as another word-picture. He put a down payment on Judah's eventual return to their homeland.

because of all their evil. ⁶ Yet I will certainly bring health and healing to it and will indeed heal them. I will let them experience the abundance^a of peace and truth. ⁷ I will restore the fortunes^b of Judah and of Israel and will rebuild them as in former times. ⁸ I will purify them from all the wrongs they have committed against Me, and I will forgive all the wrongs they have committed against Me, rebelling against Me. ⁹ This city will bear on My behalf a name of joy, praise, and glory before all the nations of the earth, who will hear of all the good I will do for them. They will tremble with awe because of all the good and all the peace I will bring about for them.

¹⁰ "This is what the LORD says: In this place which you say is a ruin, without man or beast—that is, in Judah's cities and Jerusalem's streets that are a desolation without man, without inhabitant, and without beast—there will be heard again ¹¹ a sound of joy and gladness, the voice of the bridegroom and the bride, and the voice of those saying,

Praise the LORD of •Hosts,
for the LORD is good;
His faithful love endures forever

as they bring thank offerings to the temple of the LORD. For I will restore the fortunes^b of the land as in former times, says the LORD.

¹² "This is what the LORD of Hosts says: In this desolate place—without man or beast—and in all its cities there will once more be a grazing land where shepherds may rest flocks. ¹³ The flocks will again pass under the hands of the one who counts them in the cities of the hill country, the cities of the Judean foothills, the cities of the •Negev, the land of Benjamin—the cities surrounding Jerusalem and Judah's cities, says the LORD.

God's Covenant with David

¹⁴ "Look, the days are coming"—⌊this is⌋ the LORD's declaration—"when I will fulfill the good promises that I have spoken concerning the house of Israel and the house of Judah. ¹⁵ In those days and at that time I will cause a Branch of righteousness to sprout up for David, and He will administer justice and righteousness in the land. ¹⁶ In those days Judah will be saved, and Jerusalem will dwell securely, and this is what she will be named: The LORD Is Our Righteousness. ¹⁷ For this is what the LORD says: David will never fail to have a man sitting on the throne of the house of Israel. ¹⁸ The Levitical priests will never fail to have a man always before

Me to offer •burnt offerings, to burn •grain offerings, and to make sacrifices."

¹⁹ The word of the LORD came to Jeremiah: ²⁰ "This is what the LORD says: If you can break My covenant with the day and My covenant with the night so that day and night cease to come at their regular time, ²¹ then also My covenant with My servant David may be broken so that he will not have a son reigning on his throne, and the Levitical priests will not be My ministers. ²² The hosts of heaven cannot be counted; the sand of the sea cannot be measured. So, too, I will make the descendants of My servant David and the Levites who minister to Me innumerable."

²³ The word of the LORD came to Jeremiah: ²⁴ "Have you not noticed what these people have said? They say: The LORD has rejected the two families He had chosen. My people are treated with contempt and no longer regarded as a nation among them. ²⁵ This is what the LORD says: If I do not ⌊keep⌋ My covenant with the day and with the night and fail to establish the fixed order of heaven and earth, ²⁶ then I might also reject the •seed of Jacob and of My servant David—not taking from his descendants rulers over the descendants of Abraham, Isaac, and Jacob. Instead, I will restore their fortunes^c and have compassion on them."

Jeremiah's Word to King Zedekiah

34 ⌊This is⌋ the word that came to Jeremiah from the LORD when Nebuchadnezzar, king of Babylon, all his army, all the earthly kingdoms under his control, and all other nations were fighting against Jerusalem and all its surrounding cities: ² "This is what the LORD, the God of Israel, says: Go, speak to Zedekiah, king of Judah, and tell him: This is what the LORD says: I am about to hand this city over to the king of Babylon, and he will burn it down. ³ As for you, you will not escape from his hand but are certain to be captured and handed over to him. You will meet the king of Babylon eye to eye and speak face to face;^d you will go to Babylon.

⁴ "Yet hear the LORD's word, Zedekiah, king of Judah. This is what the LORD says concerning you: You will not die by the sword; ⁵ you will die peacefully. There will be a burning ceremony for you just like the burning ceremonies for your fathers, the former kings who preceded you. Alas, lord! will be the lament for you, for I have spoken ⌊this⌋ word." ⌊This is⌋ the LORD's declaration.

⁶ So Jeremiah the prophet related all these words to Zedekiah king of Judah in Jerusalem ⁷ while the king of

---

^a**33:6** Or *fragrance*; Hb obscure ^b**33:7,11** Or *will end the captivity* ^c**33:26** Or *instead end their captivity* ^d**34:3** Lit *and his mouth will speak to your mouth*

32:39 fear. The Lord complains of the lack of fear three times in Jeremiah (2:27; 5:22-24; 44:10). "Fear of the Lord" in the Old Testament can be variously defined as dread (Deut. 1:29), respect (Ps. 19:9), worship (2 Kings 17:7), love (Deut. 10:12, 20), wisdom (Prov. 1:29), service (Deut. 6:13), or obedi-

ence (Gen. 20:11; Job 1:8). Rather than isolate a single meaning, perhaps "fear of the Lord" should encapsulate all of these. The Israelites wish they knew, and "new covenanters" would come to learn, that total reverence of the Lord obliterates human fear (1 John 4:18).

33:4 torn down. Babylon's relentless siege required entire homes to be dismantled. The materials were then reassembled to fill gaps in the city walls.

33:8 purify. God promised what His people needed most: forgiveness. His grace would wash away their unrighteousness

Babylon's army was attacking Jerusalem and all of Judah's remaining cities—against Lachish and Azekah, for only they were left among Judah's fortified cities.

The People and Their Slaves

8 [This is] the word that came to Jeremiah from the LORD after King Zedekiah made a covenant with all the people who were in Jerusalem to proclaim freedom to them, 9 so each man would free his male and female Hebrew slaves and no one enslave his Judean brother. 10 All the officials and people who entered into covenant to free their male and female slaves—in order not to enslave them any longer—obeyed and freed them. 11 Afterwards, however, they changed their minds and took back their male and female slaves they had freed and forced them to become slaves [again].

12 Then the word of the LORD came to Jeremiah from the LORD: 13 "This is what the LORD, the God of Israel, says: I made a covenant with your ancestors when I brought them out of the land of Egypt, out of the place of slavery, saying: 14 At the end of seven years, each of you must free his Hebrew brother who sold himselfa to you. He may serve you six years, but then you must send him out free from you. But your ancestors did not obey Me or pay any attention. 15 Today you repented and did what pleased Me, each of you proclaiming freedom for his neighbor. You made a covenant before Me at the temple called by My name. 16 But you have changed your minds and profaned My name. Each has taken back his male and female slaves who had been freed [to go] wherever they wanted, and you have [again] subjugated them to be your slaves.

17 "Therefore, this is what the LORD says: You have not obeyed Me by proclaiming freedom, each man for his brother and for his neighbor. I hereby proclaim freedom for you"—[this is] the LORD's declaration—"to the sword, to plague, and to famine! I will make you a horror to all the earth's kingdoms. 18 As for those who disobeyed My covenant, not keeping the terms of the covenant they made before Me, I will treat them like the calf they cut in two in order to pass between its pieces. 19 The officials of Judah and Jerusalem, the court officials, the priests, and all the people of the land who passed between the pieces of the calf 20 will be handed over to their enemies, to those who want to take their life. Their corpses will become food for the birds of the sky and for the wild animals of the land. 21 I will hand Zedekiah king of Judah and his officials over to their enemies, to those who want to take their life, to the king of Babylon's army that is withdrawing. 22 I am about to give the command"—[this is] the LORD's

The Rechabites' Example

35 [This is] the word that came to Jeremiah from the LORD in the days of Jehoiakim son of Josiah, king of Judah: 2 "Go to the house of the Rechabites, speak to them, and bring them to one of the chambers of the temple of the LORD to offer them a drink of wine."

3 So I took Jaazaniah son of Jeremiah, son of Habazziniah, and his brothers and all his sons—the entire house of the Rechabites— 4 and I brought them into the temple of the LORD to a chamber [occupied by] the sons of Hanan son of Igdaliah, a man of God, who had a chamber near the officials' chamber, which was above the chamber of Maaseiah son of Shallum the doorkeeper. 5 I set jars filled with wine and some cups before the sons of the house of the Rechabites and said to them, "Drink wine!"

6 But they replied, "We do not drink wine, for Jonadab, son of our ancestor Rechab, commanded: 'You and your sons must never drink wine. 7 You must not build a house or sow seed or plant a vineyard. [Those things] are not for you. Rather, you must live in tents your whole life, so you may live a long time on the soil where you stay as a resident alien.' 8 We have obeyed the voice of Jonadab, son of our ancestor Rechab, in all he commanded us. So we haven't drunk wine our whole life—we, our wives, our sons, and our daughters. 9 We also have not built houses to live in and do not have vineyard, field, or seed. 10 But we have lived in tents and have obeyed and done as our ancestor Jonadab commanded us. 11 However, when Nebuchadnezzar king of Babylon marched into the land, we said: Come, let's go into Jerusalem to get away from the Chaldean and Aramean armies. So we have been living in Jerusalem."

12 Then the word of the LORD came to Jeremiah: 13 "This is what the LORD of •Hosts, the God of Israel, says: Go, say to the men of Judah and the residents of Jerusalem: Will you not accept discipline by listening to My words?"—[this is] the LORD's declaration. 14 "The words of Jonadab, son of Rechab, have been carried out. He commanded his sons not to drink wine, and they have not drunk to this very day because they have obeyed their ancestor's command. But I have spoken to you time and time again,b and you have not obeyed Me! 15 Time and time againc I have sent you all My servants

---

a 34:14 Or who was sold   b 35:14 Lit you, rising up early and speaking   c 35:15 Lit Rising up early and sending

---

and provide a new start.

33:18 When God restores Israel, the temple will be rebuilt and the priests will again function (Ezek. 40-48). This will continue throughout Christ's millennial reign.

33:22 cannot be counted. God used a phrase that was familiar throughout the generations of His people (see Gen. 22:17). God will not fail to keep His promises made to Abraham and the patriarchs.

33:24 The LORD has rejected. Other nations were not oblivious to the plight of Judah and Israel. However, they did not realize God's plan to use apparent rejec-

tion as a preface to Israel's restoration.

34:5 you will die peacefully. Zedekiah's rebellion against Nebuchadnezzar was worthy of execution. However, God graciously sustained his life as a sign of hope to Israel that His favor was not gone forever.

34:8 freedom. In accordance with the Law of

the prophets, proclaiming: Turn, each one from his evil way of life, and correct your actions. Stop following other gods to serve them. Live in the land that I gave you and your ancestors. But you would not pay attention or obey Me. [16] Yes, the sons of Jonadab son of Rechab carried out their ancestor's command he gave them, but these people have not obeyed Me. [17] Therefore, this is what the LORD, the God of Hosts, the God of Israel, says: I will certainly bring to Judah and to all the residents of Jerusalem all the disaster I have pronounced against them because I have spoken to them, but they have not obeyed, and I have called to them, but they would not answer."

[18] Jeremiah said to the house of the Rechabites: "This is what the LORD of Hosts, the God of Israel, says: 'Because you have obeyed the command of your ancestor Jonadab and have kept all his commands and have done all that he commanded you, [19] this is what the LORD of Hosts, the God of Israel, says: Jonadab son of Rechab will never fail to have a man to always stand before Me.' "

Jeremiah Dictates a Scroll

36 In the fourth year of Jehoiakim son of Josiah, king of Judah, this word came to Jeremiah from the LORD: [2] "Take a scroll, and write on it all the words I have spoken to you concerning Israel, Judah, and all the nations from the time I [first] spoke to you during Josiah's reign until today. [3] Perhaps, when the house of Judah hears about all the disaster I am planning to bring on them, each one of them will turn from his evil way. Then I will forgive their wrongdoing and sin."

[4] So Jeremiah summoned Baruch son of Neriah. At Jeremiah's dictation,[a] Baruch wrote on a scroll all the words the LORD had spoken to Jeremiah. [5] Then Jeremiah commanded Baruch, "I am restricted; I cannot enter the temple of the LORD, [6] so you must go and read from the scroll—which you wrote at my dictation[b] — the words of the LORD in the hearing of the people at the temple of the LORD on a day of fasting. You must also read them in the hearing of all the Judeans who are coming from their cities. [7] Perhaps their petition will come before the LORD, and each one will turn from his evil way, for the anger and fury that the LORD has pronounced against this people are great." [8] So Baruch son of Neriah did everything Jeremiah the prophet had commanded him. At the LORD's temple he read the LORD's words from the scroll.

Baruch Reads the Scroll

[9] In the fifth year of Jehoiakim son of Josiah, king of Judah, in the ninth month, all the people of Jerusalem

and all those coming in from Judah's cities into Jerusalem proclaimed a fast before the LORD. [10] Then at the LORD's temple, in the chamber of Gemariah son of Shaphan the scribe, in the upper courtyard at the opening of the New Gate of the LORD's temple, in the hearing of all the people, Baruch read Jeremiah's words from the scroll.

[11] When Micaiah son of Gemariah, son of Shaphan, heard all the words of the LORD from the scroll, [12] he went down to the scribe's chamber in the king's palace. All the officials were sitting there—Elishama the scribe, Delaiah son of Shemaiah, Elnathan son of Achbor, Gemariah son of Shaphan, Zedekiah son of Hananiah, and all the other officials. [13] Micaiah reported to them all the words he had heard when Baruch read from the scroll in the hearing of the people. [14] Then all the officials sent [word] to Baruch through Jehudi son of Nethaniah, son of Shelemiah, son of Cushi, saying, "Bring the scroll that you read in the hearing of the people, and come." So Baruch son of Neriah took the scroll and went to them. [15] They said to him, "Sit down and read [it] in our hearing." So Baruch read [it] in their hearing.

[16] When they had heard all the words, they turned to each other in fear and said to Baruch, "We must surely tell the king all these things." [17] Then they asked Baruch, "Tell us—how did you write all these words? At his dictation?"[c]

[18] Baruch said to them, "At his dictation.[c] He recited all these words to me while I was writing on the scroll in ink."

Jehoiakim Burns the Scroll

[19] The officials said to Baruch, "You and Jeremiah must hide yourselves and tell no one where you are." [20] Then they came to the king at the courtyard, having deposited the scroll in the chamber of Elishama the scribe, and reported everything in the hearing of the king. [21] The king sent Jehudi to get the scroll, and he took it from the chamber of Elishama the scribe. Jehudi then read it in the hearing of the king and all the officials who were standing by the king. [22] Since it was the ninth month, the king was sitting in his winter quarters with a fire burning in front of him. [23] As soon as Jehudi would read three or four columns, Jehoiakim would cut the scroll[d] with a scribe's knife and throw the columns into the blazing fire until the entire scroll was consumed by the fire in the brazier. [24] As they heard all these words, the king and all of his servants did not become terrified or tear their garments. [25] Even though Elnathan, Delaiah, and Gemariah had urged the king

---

[a]**36:4** Lit *From Jeremiah's mouth*   [b]**36:6** Lit *wrote from my mouth*   [c]**36:17,18** Lit *From his mouth*   [d]**36:23** Lit *columns, he would tear it*

---

the year of Jubilee (Lev. 25:10). Zedekiah proclaimed freedom for the Hebrews who were slaves of their own people.

34:14 did not obey. Unfortunately, Judah's attempts to reinstate the Law were half-hearted at best (see Deut. 15:12). They eventually recaptured their slaves (v. 16).

34:18 treat them like the calf. God had passed through the sacrifice in making the covenant (Gen. 15:8-11, 17). Judah's punishment was to be treated like the original sacrifice.

35:2 house of the Rechabites. Fiercely loyal to the Lord, the Rechabites were nomads who

joined Israel in the wilderness and took a special vow of holiness with God, including abstention from alcohol. They helped Jehu destroy the Baal worshippers in 2 Kings 10.

35:6 We do not drink wine. An object lesson of faithfulness to Judah, the Rechabites steadfastly refused the wine prohibited by their forefather.

not to burn the scroll, he would not listen to them. [26] Then the king commanded Jerahmeel the king's son, Seraiah son of Azriel, and Shelemiah son of Abdeel to seize Baruch the scribe and Jeremiah the prophet, but the LORD had hidden them.

Jeremiah Dictates Another Scroll

[27] After the king had burned the scroll with the words Baruch had written at Jeremiah's dictation,[a] the word of the LORD came to Jeremiah: [28] "Take another scroll, and once again write on it the very words that were on the original scroll that Jehoiakim king of Judah burned. [29] You are to proclaim concerning Jehoiakim king of Judah: This is what the LORD says: You have burned the scroll, saying: Why have you written on it: The king of Babylon will certainly come and destroy this land and cause it to be without man or beast? [30] Therefore, this is what the LORD says concerning Jehoiakim king of Judah: He will have no one to sit on David's throne, and his corpse will be thrown out ⌊to be exposed⌋ to the heat of day and the frost of night. [31] I will punish him, his descendants, and his officers for their wrongdoing. I will bring on them, on the residents of Jerusalem, and on the men of Judah all the disaster, which I warned them about but they did not listen."

[32] Then Jeremiah took another scroll and gave it to Baruch son of Neriah, the scribe, and he wrote on it at Jeremiah's dictation[b] all the words of the scroll that Jehoiakim, Judah's king, had burned in the fire. And many other words like them were added.

Jerusalem's Last Days

37 Zedekiah son of Josiah reigned as king in the land of Judah in place of Jehoiachin[c] son of Jehoiakim, for Nebuchadnezzar king of Babylon made him king. [2] He and his officers and the people of the land did not obey the words of the LORD that He spoke through Jeremiah the prophet.

[3] Nevertheless, King Zedekiah sent Jehucal son of Shelemiah and Zephaniah son of Maaseiah, the priest, to Jeremiah the prophet, requesting, "Please pray to the LORD our God for us!" [4] Jeremiah was going about his daily tasks[d] among the people, for they had not ⌊yet⌋ put him into the prison. [5] Pharaoh's army had left Egypt, and when the Chaldeans, who were besieging Jerusalem, heard the report, they withdrew from Jerusalem.

[6] The word of the LORD came to Jeremiah the prophet: [7] "This is what the LORD, the God of Israel, says: This is what you will say to Judah's king, who is sending you to inquire of Me: Watch: Pharaoh's army, which has come out to help you, is going to return to its own land of Egypt. [8] The Chaldeans will then return and fight against this city. They will capture it and burn it down. [9] This is what the LORD says: Don't deceive yourselves by saying: The Chaldeans will leave us for good, for they will not leave. [10] Indeed, if you were to strike down the entire Chaldean army that is fighting with you, and there remained among them only the badly wounded[e] men, each in his tent, they would get up and burn this city down."

Jeremiah's Imprisonment

[11] When the Chaldean army withdrew from Jerusalem because of Pharaoh's army, [12] Jeremiah ⌊started to⌋ leave Jerusalem to go to the land of Benjamin to claim his portion there among the people. [13] But when he was at the Benjamin Gate, an officer of the guard was there, whose name was Irijah son of Shelemiah, son of Hananiah, and he apprehended Jeremiah the prophet, saying, "You are deserting to the Chaldeans."

[14] "⌊That's⌋ a lie," Jeremiah replied. "I am not deserting to the Chaldeans!" Irijah would not listen to him but apprehended Jeremiah and took him to the officials. [15] The officials were angry at Jeremiah and beat him and placed him in jail in the house of Jonathan the scribe, for it had been made into a prison. [16] So Jeremiah went into a cell in the dungeon and stayed there many days.

Jeremiah Summoned by Zedekiah

[17] King Zedekiah later sent ⌊for him⌋ and received him, and in his house privately asked him, "Is there a word from the LORD?"

"There is," Jeremiah responded, and he continued, "You will be handed over to the king of Babylon." [18] Then Jeremiah said to King Zedekiah, "How have I sinned against you or your servants or these people that you have put me in prison? [19] Where are your prophets who prophesied to you, claiming, 'The king of Babylon will not come against you and this land'? [20] So now please listen, my lord the king. May my petition come before you. Don't send me back to the house of Jonathan the scribe, or I will die there."

[21] So King Zedekiah gave orders, and Jeremiah was placed in the guard's courtyard. He was given a loaf of bread each day from the baker's street until all the bread was gone from the city. So Jeremiah remained in the guard's courtyard.

---

[a]**36:27** Lit *written from Jeremiah's mouth*   [b]**36:32** Lit *it from Jeremiah's mouth*   [c]**37:1** = Coniah   [d]**37:4** Lit *was coming in and going out*   [e]**37:10** Lit *the pierced*

35:13 Will you not accept discipline. If this nomadic tribe could be obedient to family tradition, why did Judah resist God's laws?
36:1 The fourth year of Jehoiakim's reign marks the beginning of the Babylonian siege.
36:2 scroll. This was Jeremiah's first attempt to pen his prophecies. A written record could

be read aloud, hopefully warning more people.

36:5 I am restricted. Despite having been threatened (20:2), the unpopular Jeremiah found a way to propagate his message (26:7-11). His assistant, Baruch, took the message to the temple.

36:19 hide yourselves. The news was so disturbing, the officials instructed Baruch to run for safety. They feared the king would react to the messenger as well as the message.

36:23 throw the columns into the blazing fire. Jeremiah's message was all but wasted on Judah's King Jehoiakim, who demon-

Jeremiah Thrown into a Cistern

38 Now Shephatiah son of Mattan, Gedaliah son of Pashhur, Jucal[a] son of Shelemiah, and Pashhur son of Malchijah heard the words Jeremiah was speaking to all the people: [2] "This is what the LORD says: 'Whoever stays in this city will die by the sword, famine, and plague, but whoever surrenders to the Chaldeans will live. He will keep his life like the spoils ⌊of war⌋ and will live.' [3] This is what the LORD says: 'This city will most certainly be handed over to the king of Babylon's army, and he will capture it.' "

[4] The officials then said to the king, "This man ought to die, because he is weakening the morale of the warriors who remain in this city and of all the people by speaking to them in this way. This man is not seeking the well-being of this people, but disaster."

[5] King Zedekiah said, "Here he is; he's in your hands since the king can't do anything against you." [6] So they took Jeremiah and dropped him into the cistern of Malchiah the king's son, which was in the guard's courtyard, lowering Jeremiah with ropes. There was no water in the cistern, only mud, and Jeremiah sank in the mud.

[7] But Ebed-melech, a •Cushite court official employed in the king's palace, heard Jeremiah had been put into the cistern. While the king was sitting at the Benjamin Gate, [8] Ebed-melech went from the king's palace and spoke to the king: [9] "My lord king, these men have been evil in all they have done to Jeremiah the prophet. They have dropped him into the cistern where he will die from hunger, because there is no more bread in the city."

[10] So the king commanded Ebed-melech, the Cushite, "Take from here 30 men under your authority and pull Jeremiah the prophet up from the cistern before he dies."

[11] So Ebed-melech took the men under his authority and went to the king's palace to a place below the storehouse.[b] From there he took old rags and worn-out clothes and lowered them by ropes to Jeremiah in the cistern. [12] Ebed-melech the Cushite cried out to Jeremiah, "Place these old rags and clothes between your armpits and the ropes." Jeremiah did so, [13] and they pulled him up with the ropes and lifted him out of the cistern, but he continued to stay in the guard's courtyard.

Zedekiah's Final Meeting with Jeremiah

[14] King Zedekiah sent for Jeremiah the prophet and received him at the third entrance of the LORD's temple. The king said to Jeremiah, "I am going to ask you something; don't hide anything from me."

[15] Jeremiah replied to Zedekiah, "If I tell you, you will kill me, won't you? Besides, if I give you advice, you won't listen to me anyway."

[16] King Zedekiah swore to Jeremiah in private, "As the LORD lives, who has given us this life, I will not kill you or hand you over to these men who want to take your life."

[17] Jeremiah therefore said to Zedekiah, "This is what the LORD, the God of •Hosts, the God of Israel, says: 'If indeed you surrender to the officials of the king of Babylon, then you will live, this city will not be burned down, and you and your household will survive. [18] But if you do not surrender to the officials of the king of Babylon, then this city will be handed over to the Chaldeans. They will burn it down, and you yourself will not escape from them.' "

[19] But King Zedekiah said to Jeremiah, "I am worried about the Judeans who have deserted to the Chaldeans. They may hand me over to them to abuse me."

[20] "They will not hand you over," Jeremiah replied. "Obey the voice of the LORD in what I am telling you, so it may go well for you and you can live. [21] But if you refuse to surrender, this is the verdict[c] that the LORD has shown me: [22] 'All the women[d] who remain in the palace of Judah's king will be brought out to the officials of the king of Babylon and will say:

> Your trusted friends[e] misled[f] you
> and overcame you.
> Your feet sank into the mire,
> and they deserted you.

[23] All your wives and sons will be brought out to the Chaldeans. You yourself will not escape from them, for you will be seized by the king of Babylon and this city will burn down.' "

[24] Then Zedekiah warned Jeremiah, "Don't let anyone know about these things or you will die. [25] If the officials hear that I have spoken with you and come and demand of you, 'Tell us what you said to the king; don't hide anything from us and we won't kill you. Also, what did the king say to you?' [26] then you will tell them, 'I was bringing before the king my petition that he not return me to the house of Jonathan to die there.' "

[27] When all the officials came to Jeremiah and questioned him, he reported the exact words to them the king had commanded, and they quit speaking with him because nothing had been heard. [28] Jeremiah remained

a38:1 = Jehucal; Jr 37:3 b38:11 Or treasury c38:21 Or promise; lit word d38:22 Or wives e38:22 Lit The men of your peace f38:22 Or incited

strated his disdain by burning the message instead of heeding it.

36:30 no one to sit on David's throne. Although God eliminated Jehoiakim's line from the Davidic throne succession, his line was restored after the exile when Zerubbabel was placed as a signet ring on God's hand (see

Hag. 2:23). Jesus was descended from Zerubbabel, and thus from Jehoiakim (see Matt. 1:11-12).

37:1–38:28 With the threat of Babylon closing in on the inhabitants of Jerusalem, the unpopular prophet was imprisoned for treason (37:11-16). King Zedekiah tried protecting the

prisoner (37:17-21); however, Jeremiah ended up in a dark cistern (38:1-6). Jeremiah's rescue proved to be a timely turn of events (38:7-13).

37:3 Please pray. Zedekiah enjoyed a cafeteria-style relationship with Jeremiah—picking and choosing what he wanted to hear (v. 2).

in the guard's courtyard until the day Jerusalem was captured, and he was ⌊there⌋ when it happened.[a]

The Fall of Jerusalem to Babylon

39 In the ninth year of Zedekiah king of Judah, in the tenth month, King Nebuchadnezzar of Babylon advanced against Jerusalem with his entire army and laid siege to it. ² In the fourth month of Zedekiah's eleventh year, on the ninth day of the month, the city was broken into. ³ All the officials of the king of Babylon entered and sat at the Middle Gate: Nergal-sharezer, Samgar-nebo, Sarsechim the Rab-saris, Nergal-sharezer the Rab-mag, and all the rest of the officials of Babylon's king.

⁴ When he saw them, Zedekiah king of Judah and all the soldiers fled. They left the city at night by way of the king's garden through the gate between the two walls. They left along the route to the •Arabah. ⁵ However, the Chaldean army pursued them and overtook Zedekiah in the plains[b] of Jericho, arrested him, and brought him to Nebuchadnezzar, Babylon's king, at Riblah in the land of Hamath. The king passed sentence on him ⌊there⌋.

⁶ At Riblah the king of Babylon slaughtered Zedekiah's sons before his eyes, and he ⌊also⌋ slaughtered all Judah's nobles. ⁷ Then he blinded Zedekiah and put him in bronze chains to take him to Babylon. ⁸ The Chaldeans next burned down the king's palace and the people's houses and tore down the walls of Jerusalem. ⁹ Nebuzaradan, the commander of the guards, deported to Babylon the rest of the people—those who had remained in the city and those deserters who had defected to him along with the rest of the people who had remained. ¹⁰ ⌊However,⌋ Nebuzaradan, the commander of the guards, left in the land of Judah some of the poor people who owned nothing, and he gave them vineyards and fields at that time.

Jeremiah Freed by Nebuchadnezzar

¹¹ ⌊Speaking⌋ through Nebuzaradan, captain of the guard, King Nebuchadnezzar of Babylon gave orders concerning Jeremiah, saying: ¹² "Take him, look after him, and don't let any harm come to him; do for him whatever he says." ¹³ Nebuzaradan, captain of the guard, Nebushazban the Rab-saris, Nergal-sharezer the Rab-mag, and all the captains of the king of Babylon ¹⁴ had Jeremiah brought from the guard's courtyard and turned him over to Gedaliah son of Ahikam, son of Shaphan, to take him home. So he settled among ⌊his own⌋ people.

¹⁵ Now the word of the LORD had come to Jeremiah when he was confined in the guard's courtyard: ¹⁶ "Go tell Ebed-melech the •Cushite: This is what the LORD of •Hosts, the God of Israel, says: I am about to fulfill My words for harm and not for good against this city. They will take place before your eyes on that day. ¹⁷ But I will rescue you on that day"—⌊this is⌋ the LORD's declaration—"and you will not be handed over to the men you fear. ¹⁸ Indeed, I will certainly deliver you so that you do not fall by the sword. Because you have trusted in Me, you will keep your life like the spoils ⌊of war⌋." ⌊This is⌋ the LORD's declaration.

Jeremiah Stays in Judah

40 ⌊This is⌋ the word that came to Jeremiah from the LORD after Nebuzaradan, captain of the guard, released him at Ramah when he had been bound in chains with all the exiles of Jerusalem and Judah who were being exiled to Babylon. ² The captain of the guard took Jeremiah and said to him, "The LORD your God decreed this disaster on this place, ³ and the LORD has fulfilled ⌊it⌋. He has done just what He decreed. Because you ⌊people⌋ have sinned against the LORD and have not obeyed Him, this thing has happened. ⁴ Now pay attention ⌊to what I say⌋. Today I am setting you free from the chains that were on your hands. If it pleases you to come with me to Babylon, come, and I will take care of you. But if it seems wrong to you to come with me to Babylon, go no farther.[c] Look—the whole land is in front of you. Wherever it seems good and right for you to go, there." ⁵ When Jeremiah had not yet turned ⌊to go, Nebuzaradan said to him:⌋ "Return[d] to Gedaliah son of Ahikam, son of Shaphan, whom the king of Babylon has appointed over the cities of Judah, and stay with him among the people or go wherever you want to go." So the captain of the guard gave him a ration and a gift and released him. ⁶ Jeremiah therefore went to Gedaliah son of Ahikam at Mizpah, and he stayed with him among the people who remained in the land.

Gedaliah Advises Peace

⁷ When all the commanders of the armies in the field—they and their men—heard that the king of Babylon had appointed Gedaliah son of Ahikam over the land and that he had put him in charge of the men, women, and children, the poorest of the land who had not been deported to Babylon, ⁸ they came to Gedaliah at Mizpah. ⌊The commanders included⌋ Ishmael son of Nethaniah, Johanan and Jonathan the sons of Kareah,

---

[a]**38:28** Or *captured. This is what happened when Jerusalem was captured;*   [b]**39:5** Lit *Arabah*   [c]**40:4** Lit *Babylon, stop*   [d]**40:5** LXX reads *But if not, run, return;* Hb obscure

---

37:5 they withdrew from Jerusalem. The Babylonians were drawn away from smaller prey to pursue the powerful pharaoh. The Egyptians proved an insufficient ally against the Babylonians.

38:5 he's in your hands. Zedekiah eagerly released himself from responsibility in a po-

tentially volatile situation.

38:7 Ebed-melech, a Cushite. His name means "king's servant." He actually became a servant by helping Jeremiah, who was about 60 years old at the time. Jeremiah would have died at the hands of unjust men apart from the protests of this appalled offi-

cial. Ebed-melech was rewarded for acting justly and rescuing Jeremiah (39:15-18).

38:12 Ebed-melech exercised extra-mile effort. He managed the process with concern for Jeremiah's safety and comfort.

38:19 I am worried. Zedekiah was right to be afraid. Before his eyes were put out (2 Kings

Seraiah son of Tanhumeth, the sons of Ephai the Netophathite, and Jezaniah son of the Maacathite—they and their men.

9 Gedaliah son of Ahikam, son of Shaphan, swore an oath to them and their men, assuring them, "Don't be afraid to serve the Chaldeans. Live in the land and serve the king of Babylon, and it will go well for you. 10 As for me, I am going to live in Mizpah to represent[a] ⌊you⌋ before the Chaldeans who come to us. As for you, gather wine, summer fruit, and oil, place them in your ⌊storage⌋ jars, and live in the cities you have captured."

11 When all the Judeans in Moab and among the Ammonites and in Edom and in all the other lands also heard that the king of Babylon had left a remnant in Judah and had appointed Gedaliah son of Ahikam, son of Shaphan, over them, 12 they all returned from all the places where they had been banished and came to the land of Judah, to Gedaliah at Mizpah, and harvested a great amount of wine and summer fruit.

13 Meanwhile, Johanan son of Kareah and all the commanders of the armies in the field came to Gedaliah at Mizpah 14 and warned him, "Don't you realize that Baalis, king of the Ammonites, has sent Ishmael son of Nethaniah to strike you down?" But Gedaliah son of Ahikam would not believe them. 15 Then Johanan son of Kareah suggested to Gedaliah in private at Mizpah, "Let me go kill Ishmael son of Nethaniah. No one will know it. Why should he strike you down and scatter all of Judah that has gathered to you so that the remnant of Judah would perish?"

16 But Gedaliah son of Ahikam responded to Johanan son of Kareah, "Don't do that! What you're saying about Ishmael is a lie."

Gedaliah Assassinated by Ishmael

41 In the seventh month, Ishmael son of Nethaniah, son of Elishama, of the royal family and one of the king's chief officers, came with 10 men to Gedaliah son of Ahikam at Mizpah. They ate a meal together there in Mizpah, 2 but then Ishmael son of Nethaniah and the 10 men who were with him got up and struck down Gedaliah son of Ahikam, son of Shaphan, with the sword; he killed the one king of Babylon had appointed in the land. 3 Ishmael also struck down all the Judeans who were with Gedaliah at Mizpah, as well as the Chaldean soldiers who were there.

4 On the second day after he had killed Gedaliah, when no one knew ⌊yet⌋, 5 80 men came from Shechem, Shiloh, and Samaria who had shaved their beards, torn their garments, and gashed themselves,

and who were carrying •grain and incense offerings to bring to the temple of the LORD. 6 Ishmael son of Nethaniah came out of Mizpah to meet them, weeping as he came. When he encountered them, he said: "Come to Gedaliah son of Ahikam!" 7 But when they came into the city, Ishmael son of Nethaniah and the men with him slaughtered them and threw them into[b] a cistern.

8 However, there were 10 men among them who said to Ishmael, "Don't kill us, for we have hidden treasure in the field—wheat, barley, oil, and honey!" So he stopped and did not kill them along with their companions. 9 Now the cistern where Ishmael had thrown all the corpses of the men he had struck down was a large one[c] that King Asa had made in the encounter with Baasha king of Israel. Ishmael son of Nethaniah filled ⌊it⌋ with the slain.

10 Then Ishmael took captive all the remnant of the people of Mizpah including the daughters of the king—all those who remained in Mizpah over whom Nebuzaradan, captain of the guard, had appointed Gedaliah son of Ahikam. Ishmael son of Nethaniah took them captive and set off to cross over to the Ammonites.

The Captives Rescued by Johanan

11 When Johanan son of Kareah and all the commanders of the armies with him heard of all the evil that Ishmael son of Nethaniah had done, 12 they took all their men and went to fight with Ishmael son of Nethaniah and found him by the great pool in Gibeon. 13 When all the people with Ishmael saw Johanan son of Kareah and all the commanders of the army with him, they rejoiced, 14 and all the people whom Ishmael had taken captive from Mizpah turned around and rejoined Johanan son of Kareah. 15 But Ishmael son of Nethaniah escaped from Johanan with eight men and went to the Ammonites. 16 Johanan son of Kareah and all the commanders of the armies with him then took from Mizpah all the remnant of the people whom he had recovered from Ishmael son of Nethaniah after Ishmael had killed Gedaliah son of Ahikam—men, soldiers, women, children, and court officials whom he brought back from Gibeon. 17 They left, stopping in Geruth Chimham, which is near Bethlehem, in order to make their way into Egypt 18 away from the Chaldeans. For they feared them because Ishmael son of Nethaniah had struck down Gedaliah son of Ahikam, whom the king of Babylon had appointed in the land.

The People Seek Jeremiah's Counsel

42 Then all the commanders of the armies, along with Johanan son of Kareah, Jazaniah son of

---

[a]**40:10** Lit *to stand* [b]**41:7** Syr; MT reads *slaughtered them in* [c]**41:9** LXX; MT reads *down by the hand of Gedaliah*

25:7), his sons would be put to death before his eyes.

38:27 nothing had been heard. Zedekiah instructed Jeremiah not to disclose their private conversation. When asked about this by the officials, Jeremiah backtracked to his earlier pleas to Zedekiah regarding

his safekeeping (37:20).

39:2 A pile of rubble marked the beginning of the end for Jerusalem. After a two-month siege, the Babylonians captured the stalwart city.

39:14 among [his own] people. In the midst of deportation, Jeremiah was identified and

released from his political imprisonment.

39:18 trusted in Me. Ebed-melech's past heroism proved to be invaluable (38:7-13). He escaped certain death.

40:1 the word that came to Jeremiah. Jeremiah began another chapter of post-prison prophecies. His job was not yet over. He con-

Hoshaiah, and all the people from the least to the greatest, approached 2 Jeremiah the prophet and said, "May our petition come before you; pray to the LORD your God on our behalf, on behalf of this entire remnant (for few of us remain out of the many, as you can see with your own eyes), 3 that the LORD your God may tell us the way we should walk and the thing we should do."

4 So Jeremiah the prophet said to them, "I have heard. I will now pray to the LORD your God according to your words, and every word that the LORD answers you I will tell you; I won't withhold a word from you."

5 And they said to Jeremiah, "As for every word the LORD your God sends you to ⌊tell⌋ us, if we don't act accordingly, may the LORD be a true and faithful witness against us. 6 Whether it is pleasant or unpleasant, we will obey the voice of the LORD our God to whom we are sending you so that it may go well with us. We will certainly obey the voice of the LORD our God!"

Jeremiah's Advice to Stay

7 Now at the end of 10 days, the word of the LORD came to Jeremiah, 8 and he summoned Johanan son of Kareah, all the commanders of the armies who were with him, and all the people from the least to the greatest.

9 He said to them, "This is what the LORD says, the God of Israel to whom you sent me to bring your petition before Him: 10 'If you will indeed stay in this land, then I will rebuild and not demolish you, and I will plant and not uproot you, because I relent concerning the disaster that I have brought on you. 11 Don't be afraid of the king of Babylon whom you now fear; don't be afraid of him'—⌊this is⌋ the LORD's declaration—'because I am with you to save you and deliver you from him. 12 I will grant you compassion, and hea will have compassion on you and allow you to return to your own soil. 13 But if you say: We will not stay in this land, so as not to obey the voice of the LORD your God, 14 and if you say: No, instead we'll go to the land of Egypt where we will not see war or hear the sound of the ram's horn or hunger for food, and we'll live there, 15 then hear the word of the LORD, remnant of Judah! This is what the LORD of •Hosts, the God of Israel, says: If you are firmly resolved to go to Egypt and live there for a while, 16 then the sword you fear will overtake you there in the land of Egypt, and the famine you are worried about will follow on your heelsb there to Egypt, and you will die there. 17 All who resolve to go to Egypt to live there for a while will die by the sword, famine, and plague.

They will have no survivor or escapee from the disaster I will bring on them.'

18 "For this is what the LORD of Hosts, the God of Israel, says: 'Just as My anger and fury were poured out on Jerusalem's residents, so will My fury pour out on you if you go to Egypt. You will become an object of execration, scorn, cursing, and disgrace, and you will never see this place again.' 19 The LORD has spoken concerning you, remnant of Judah: 'Don't go to Egypt.' Know for certain that I have warned you today! 20 You have led your own selves astray because you are the ones who sent me to the LORD your God, saying, 'Pray to the LORD our God on our behalf, and as for all that the LORD our God says, tell it to us, and we'll act accordingly.' 21 For I have told you today, but you have not obeyed the voice of the LORD your God in everything He has sent me to ⌊tell⌋ you. 22 Now therefore, know for certain that by the sword, famine, and plague you will die in the place where you desired to go to live for a while."

Jeremiah's Counsel Rejected

43 When Jeremiah had finished speaking to all the people all the words of the LORD their God—all these words the LORD their God had sent him to give them— 2 then Azariah son of Hoshaiah, Johanan son of Kareah, and all the other arrogant men responded to Jeremiah, "You are speaking a lie! The LORD our God has not sent you to say, 'You must not go to Egypt to live there for a while!' 3 Rather, Baruch son of Neriah is inciting you against us to hand us over to the Chaldeans to put us to death or to deport us to Babylon!"

4 So Johanan son of Kareah and all the commanders of the armies did not obey the voice of the LORD to stay in the land of Judah. 5 Instead, Johanan son of Kareah and all the commanders of the armies took the whole remnant of Judah, those who had returned from all the nations where they had been banished to live in the land of Judah for a while— 6 the men, women, children, king's daughters, and everyone whom Nebuzaradan, captain of the guard, had allowed to remain with Gedaliah son of Ahikam son of Shaphan, along with Jeremiah the prophet and Baruch son of Neriah— 7 and they went to the land of Egypt because they did not obey the voice of the LORD. They went as far as Tahpanhes.

God's Sign to the People in Egypt

8 Then the word of the LORD came to Jeremiah at Tahpanhes: 9 "Pick up some large stones and set them in the mortar of the brick pavement that is at the open-

---

a 42:12 LXX reads I b 42:16 Lit will cling after you

---

tinued the task at hand, even though he had just been given freedom.

42:2-3 Jeremiah's insightful prophecies against Judah were not lost on the pagan officials of Babylon. The first exiles likely spread the word as his predictions came true.

40:5 Gedaliah. An impression from a royal

seal reading "Belonging to Gedaliah, Over the House," was found at Lachish. It is dated from the early sixth century B. C.

40:10 represent [you] before the Chaldeans. As governor, Gedaliah served as a national link between the remnants of Jews in Judah and the powerful Babylon.

40:16 Don't do that! The last thing Gedaliah wanted was to upset his peacekeeping position. Little did he know his advisers were right, and he would soon be killed by Ishmael (41:1-3). Gedaliah serves as a reminder that one should not assume that everyone sees things alike or aspires to the same lofty goals.

ing of Pharaoh's palace at Tahpanhes. ⌊Do this⌋ in the sight of the Judean men 10 and tell them: This is what the LORD of •Hosts, the God of Israel, says: I will send for My servant Nebuchadnezzar king of Babylon, and I will place his throne on these stones that I have embedded, and he will pitch his pavilion over them. 11 He will come and strike down the land of Egypt—those ⌊destined⌋ for death, to death; those ⌊destined⌋ for captivity, to captivity; and those ⌊destined⌋ for the sword, to the sword. 12 Iª will kindle a fire in the temples of Egypt's gods, and he will burn them and take them prisoner. He will clean the land of Egypt as a shepherd picks lice offᵇ his garment, and he will leave there unscathed. 13 He will smash the sacred pillars of the sun templeᶜ in the land of Egypt and burn down the temples of the Egyptian gods."

God's Judgment against His People in Egypt

44 ⌊This is⌋ the word that came to Jeremiah for all the Jews living in the land of Egypt—at Migdol, Tahpanhes, Memphis, and in the land of Pathros: 2 "This is what the LORD of •Hosts, the God of Israel, says: You have seen all the disaster I brought against Jerusalem and all Judah's cities; look, they are a ruin today without an inhabitant in them 3 because of their evil ways that provoked Me to anger, going and burning incense to serve other gods they, you, and your fathers did not know. 4 So I sent you all My servants the prophets time and time again,ᵈ saying, Don't do this detestable thing that I hate. 5 But they did not listen or pay attention; they did not turn from their evil or stop burning incense to other gods. 6 So My fierce wrath poured forth and burned in Judah's cities and Jerusalem's streets so that they became the desolate ruin they are today.

7 "So now, this is what the LORD, the God of Hosts, the God of Israel, says: Why are you doing such great harm to yourselves? You are cutting off man and woman, child and infant from Judah, leaving yourselves without a remnant. 8 You are provoking Me to anger by the work of your hands. You are burning incense to other gods in the land of Egypt where you have gone to live for a while. As a result, you will be cut off and become an object of cursing and insult among all the nations of earth. 9 Have you forgotten the evils of your fathers, the evils of Judah's kings, the evils of their wives, your own evils, and the evils of your wives that were committed in the land of Judah and in the streets of Jerusalem? 10 They have not become humble to this day, and they have not •feared or walked by My law or My statutes that I set before you and your ancestors.

11 "Therefore, this is what the LORD of Hosts, the God of Israel, says: I am about to turn against you to ⌊bring⌋ disaster, to cut off all Judah. 12 And I will take away the remnant of Judah, those who have resolved to go to the land of Egypt to live there for a while; they will meet their end. All of them in the land of Egypt will fall by the sword; they will meet their end by famine. From the least to the greatest, they will die by the sword and by famine. Then they will become an object of execration, of scorn, of cursing, and of disgrace. 13 I will punish those living in the land of Egypt just as I punished Jerusalem by sword, famine, and plague. 14 Then the remnant of Judah—those going to live for a while there in the land of Egypt—will have no fugitive or survivor to return to the land of Judah where they are longingᵉ to return to live, for they will not return except ⌊for a few⌋ fugitives."

The People's Stubborn Response

15 However, all the men who knew that their wives were burning incense to other gods, all the women standing by—a great assembly—and all the people who were living in the land of Egypt at Pathros answered Jeremiah, 16 "As for the word you spoke to us in the name of the LORD, we are not going to listen to you! 17 Instead, we will do everything we said we would: burn incense to the queen of heavenᶠ and offer drink offerings to her just as we, our fathers, our kings, and our officials did in Judah's cities and in Jerusalem's streets. Then we had enough food and good things and saw no disaster, 18 but from the time we ceased to burn incense to the queen of heaven and to offer her drink offerings, we have lacked everything, and through sword and famine we have met our end."

19 And the women said,ᵍ "When we burned incense to the queen of heaven and poured out drink offerings to her, was it apart from our husbands' knowledge that we made sacrificial cakes in her image and poured out drink offerings to her?"

20 But Jeremiah responded to all the people—the men, women, and all the people who were answering him—saying, 21 "As for the incense you burned in Judah's cities and in Jerusalem's streets—you, your fathers, your kings, your officials, and the people of the land—did the LORD not remember them? He brought this to mind. 22 The LORD can no longer bear your evil deeds and the detestable acts you have committed, so

---

ª**43:12** LXX, Syr, Vg read *He*   ᵇ**43:12** Or *will wrap himself in the land of Egypt as a shepherd wraps himself in*   ᶜ**43:13** = *of Heliopolis*; Hb *Beth-shemesh*   ᵈ**44:4** Lit *prophets, rising up early and sending*   ᵉ**44:14** Lit *lifting up their soul*   ᶠ**44:17** =Ashtoreth, or Astarte   ᵍ**44:19** LXX, Syr; MT omits *And the women said*

41:1 meal. Gedaliah's first feast would be his last official event. Ishmael's mealtime murder caught him off guard, although he had been warned that Ishmael was involved in a plot to assassinate him (40:13-16). Fearing Babylonian reprisal, the Jewish remnant fled to Egypt (vv. 16-18). The Holy Land would be bereft of Jews until there return from exile. Thereafter, they remembered the anniversary of Gedaliah's death (Zech. 7:5; 8:19).

42:6 we will obey. The army officers' good intentions prove to be short-lived. Like many in the prophet's presence, they heard only what they wanted (43:2).

42:7 at the end of 10 days. Jeremiah spent 10 days in prayer for the people. His message came as a result of his persistence.

43:1-3 Since the Jewish remnant did not like the message (even though Jeremiah's predictions had proven to be incredibly accurate), they once again blamed the mes-

your land has become a waste, a desolation, and an object of cursing, without inhabitant, as ⌊you see⌋ today. 23 Because you burned incense and sinned against the LORD and didn't obey the LORD's voice and didn't walk in His law, His statutes, and His testimonies, this disaster has come to you, as ⌊you see⌋ today."

24 Then Jeremiah said to all the people, including all the women, "Hear the word of the LORD, all Judah who are in the land of Egypt. 25 This is what the LORD of Hosts, the God of Israel, says: 'As for you and your wives, you women have spoken with your mouths, and you men fulfilled it by your deeds, saying: We will keep our vows we have made to burn incense to the queen of heaven and to pour out drink offerings for her. ⌊Go ahead,⌋ confirm your vows! Pay your vows!'

26 "Therefore, hear the word of the LORD, all you Judeans who live in the land of Egypt: 'I have sworn by My great name, says the LORD, that My name will never again be invoked by anyone of Judah in all the land of Egypt, saying, As the Lord GOD lives. 27 I am watching over them for disaster and not for good, and every man of Judah who is in the land of Egypt will meet his end by sword or famine until they are finished off. 28 Those who escape the sword will return from the land of Egypt to the land of Judah only few in number, and the whole remnant of Judah, the ones going to the land of Egypt to live there for a while, will know whose word stands, Mine or theirs! 29 This will be a sign to you'—⌊this is⌋ the LORD's declaration—'that I am about to punish you in this place, so you may know that My words of disaster concerning you will certainly come to pass. 30 This is what the LORD says: I am about to hand over Pharaoh Hophra, Egypt's king, to his enemies, to those who want to take his life, just as I handed over Judah's King Zedekiah to Babylon's King Nebuchadnezzar, who was his enemy, the one who wanted to take his life.' "

The LORD's Message to Baruch

45 ⌊This is⌋ the word that Jeremiah the prophet spoke to Baruch son of Neriah when he wrote these words on a scroll at Jeremiah's dictation[a] in the fourth year of Jehoiakim son of Josiah, king of Judah: 2 "This is what the LORD, the God of Israel, says to you, Baruch: 3 'You have said, Woe is me, because the LORD has added misery to my pain! I am worn out with[b] groaning and have found no rest.

4 " 'This is what you are to say to him: This is what the LORD says: What I have built I am about to demolish, and what I have planted I am about to uproot—the whole land! 5 But as for you, do you seek great things for yourself? Stop seeking! For I am about to bring disas-

Prophecies Against the Nations

46 The word of the LORD that came to Jeremiah the prophet about the nations:

Prophecies against Egypt

2 About Egypt and the army of Pharaoh Neco, Egypt's king, which was defeated at Carchemish on the Euphrates River by Nebuchadnezzar king of Babylon in the fourth year of Judah's King Jehoiakim son of Josiah:

3 Deploy small shields and large;
   draw near for battle!
4 Harness the horses;
   mount the steeds;[c]
   take your positions with helmets on!
   Polish the lances;
   put on armor!
5 Why have I seen ⌊this⌋?
   They are terrified,
   they are retreating,
   their warriors are crushed,
   they flee headlong,
   they never look back,
   terror is on every side!
                              ⌊This is⌋
                     the LORD's declaration.
6 The swift cannot flee,
   and the warrior cannot escape!
   In the north by the bank of the Euphrates River,
   they stumble and fall.
7 Who is this, rising like the Nile,
   like rivers whose waters churn?
8 Egypt rises like the Nile,
   and its waters churn like rivers.
   He boasts: I will go up, I will cover the earth;
   I will destroy cities with their residents.
9 Rise up, you cavalry!
   Race furiously, you chariots!
   Let the warriors go forth—
   •Cush and Put,
   who are able to handle shields,
   and the Ludim,
   who are able to handle and string the bow.
10 That day belongs to the Lord, the GOD of •Hosts,
   a day of vengeance to avenge Himself
   against His adversaries.
   The sword will devour and be satisfied;

<hr>

a45:1 Lit scroll from Jeremiah's mouth   b45:3 Lit I labored in my   c46:4 Or mount up, riders

<hr>

senger. Jeremiah's message was exactly opposite of what they had planned; even if their plan contradicted the Lord's promise to bless and protect them (42:9-12), and disregarded His warning that they would be severely punished by choosing to go to Egypt (42:13-18).

43:8 Tahpanhes. Tahpanhes was a frontier town in the eastern Nile delta. Having once reached the Egyptian border in 601 B.C., Nebuchadnezzar's army returned there in 567 (46:14; Ezek. 29:17-20).
43:13 sun temple. Just as Nebuchadnezzar had demolished the temple in Jerusalem, he

would destroy the temple of the sun god Re in the Egyptian worship center at Heliopolis.
44:1 Migdol. Previously mentioned as near the exodus route (Ex. 14:2) and a place where some Jewish refugees fled, Egypt's doom was proclaimed there (46:13-14).
44:18 queen of heaven. The people refused

it will drink its fill of their blood,
because it will be a sacrifice to the Lord,
  the GOD of Hosts,
in the northern land by the Euphrates River.

11 Go up to Gilead and get balm,
  Virgin Daughter Egypt!
  You have multiplied remedies in vain;
  there is no healing for you.
12 The nations have heard of your dishonor,
  and your outcry fills the earth,
  because warrior stumbles against warrior
  and together both of them have fallen.

13 ⌊This is⌋ the word the LORD spoke to Jeremiah the prophet about the coming of Nebuchadnezzar king of Babylon to defeat the land of Egypt:

14 Announce it in Egypt, and proclaim it in Migdol!
  Proclaim it in Memphis and in Tahpanhes!
  Say: Take positions! Prepare yourself,
  for the sword devours all around you.
15 Why have your strong ones been swept away?
  Each has not stood,
  for the LORD has thrust him down.
16 He continues to stumble.
  Indeed, each falls over the other.
  They say: Get up! Let's return to our people
  and to the land of our birth,
  away from the sword that oppresses.
17 There they will cry out:
  Pharaoh king of Egypt was all noise;
  he let the opportune moment pass.

18 As I live—
              ⌊this is⌋ the King's declaration;
              the LORD of Hosts is His name.
  He will come like Tabor among the mountains
  and like Carmel by the sea.
19 Pack your bags for exile,
  inhabitant of Daughter Egypt!
  For Memphis will become a desolation,
  uninhabited ruins.

20 Egypt is a beautiful young cow,
  but a horsefly from the north is coming
    against her.[a]
21 Even her mercenaries among her
  are like stall-fed calves.
  They too will turn back;
  together they will flee;
  they will not take their stand,

for the day of their calamity is coming on them,
  the time of their punishment.
22 Egypt will hiss like a slithering snake,[b]
  for ⌊the enemy⌋ will come with an army;
  with axes they will come against her
  like those who cut trees.
23 They cut down her forest—
              ⌊this is⌋
              the LORD's declaration—
  though it is dense,
  for they are more numerous than locusts;
  they cannot be counted.
24 Daughter Egypt will be put to shame,
  handed over to a northern people.

25 The LORD of Hosts, the God of Israel, says: "I am about to punish Amon, ⌊god⌋ of Thebes, along with Pharaoh, Egypt, her gods, and her kings—Pharaoh and those trusting in him. 26 I will hand them over to those who want to take their lives—to Nebuchadnezzar king of Babylon and his officers. But after this, it will be inhabited again as in ancient times."
              ⌊This is⌋
              the LORD's declaration.

Reassurance for Israel

27 But you, My servant Jacob, do not be afraid,
  and do not be discouraged, Israel,
  for without fail I will save you from far away
  and your descendants, from the land
    of their captivity!
  Jacob will return and have calm and quiet
  with no one to frighten him.
28 And you, My servant Jacob, do not be afraid—
              ⌊this is⌋
              the LORD's declaration—
  for I will be with you.
  I will bring destruction on all the nations
  where I have banished you,
  but I will not bring destruction on you.
  I will discipline you with justice,
  but I will by no means leave you unpunished.

Prophecies against the Philistines

47 ⌊This is⌋ the word of the LORD that came to Jeremiah the prophet about the Philistines before Pharaoh defeated Gaza. 2 This is what the LORD says:

Look, waters are rising from the north
  and becoming an overflowing •wadi.
  They will overflow the land and everything in it,

---

[a] **46:20** Some Hb mss, LXX, Syr; other Hb mss read *is coming, coming* [b] **46:22** Lit *Her sound, she will go like a snake*

---

the cities and their inhabitants.
The people will cry out,
and every inhabitant of the land will wail.
3 At the sound of the stomping hooves
    of his stallions,
the rumbling of his chariots,
and the clatter of their wheels,
fathers will not turn back for their sons,
because they will be utterly helpless[a]
4 on account of the day that is coming
to destroy all the Philistines,
to cut off from Tyre and Sidon
every remaining ally.
Indeed, the LORD is about to destroy
    the Philistines,
the remnant of the islands of Caphtor.[b]
5 Baldness is coming to Gaza.
Ashkelon will become silent,
a remnant of their valley.
How long will you gash yourself?

6 Ah, sword of the LORD!
How long will you be restless?
Go back to your scabbard;
be still; be silent!
7 How can it[c] rest
when the LORD has given it a command?
He has assigned it
against Ashkelon and the shore of the sea.

Prophecies against Moab

48 About Moab, this is what the LORD of •Hosts,
the God of Israel, says:

Woe to Nebo, because it is about to be destroyed;
Kiriathaim will be put to shame; it will be
    taken captive.
The fortress will be put to shame and dismayed!
2 There is no longer praise for Moab;
they plan harm against her in Heshbon:
Come, let's cut her off from nationhood.
You madmen will also be silenced;
the sword will pursue you.
3 A voice cries out from Horonaim:
devastation and great disaster!
4 Moab will be shattered;
her little ones will cry out.
5 For on the ascent to Luhith
they will be weeping continually,[d]

and on the descent to Horonaim
will be heard cries of distress over the destruction:
6 Flee! Save your lives!
Be like a juniper bush[e] in the wilderness.
7 Because you trust in your works[f] and treasures,
you will be captured also.
Chemosh will go into exile
with his priests and officials.
8 The destroyer will move against every town;
not one town will escape.
The valley will perish,
and the plain will be annihilated,
as the LORD has said.
9 Make Moab a salt marsh,[g] [h]
for she will run away;[i]
her towns will become a desolation,
without inhabitant.

10 Cursed is the one
who does the LORD's business deceitfully,[j]
and cursed is the one
who withholds his sword from bloodshed.

11 Moab has been left quiet since his youth,
settled ⌊like wine⌋ on its dregs.
He hasn't been poured from one container
    to another
or gone into exile.
So his taste has remained the same,
and his aroma hasn't changed.
12 Therefore look, the days are coming—
                                        ⌊this is⌋
                        the LORD's declaration—
when I will send those to him,
    who will pour him out.
They will empty his containers
and smash his jars.
13 Moab will be put to shame because of Chemosh,
just as the house of Israel was put to shame
because of Bethel that they trusted in.

14 How can you say, We are warriors—
mighty men ⌊ready⌋ for battle?
15 The destroyer of Moab and its towns
has come up,[k]
and the best of its young men
have gone down to slaughter.
                ⌊This is⌋ the King's declaration;
                the LORD of Hosts is His name.

---

[a]47:3 Lit because of laziness of hands   [b]47:4 Probably Crete; Gn 10:14; Dt 2:23; Am 9:7   [c]47:7 LXX, Vg; MT reads you   [d]48:5 Lit Luhith, weeping goes up with weeping   [e]48:6 Or like Aroer; Jr 48:19; Is 17:2   [f]48:7 LXX reads strongholds   [g]48:9 LXX reads a sign; Vg reads a flower; Syr, Tg read a crown; others read Moab fly away   [h]48:9 = to make a conquered city uninhabitable; Jdg 9:45   [i]48:9 Hb obscure   [j]48:10 Or negligently   [k]48:15 Or Moab is destroyed; he has come up against its city

---

tor (43:1-3). Baruch was feeling sorry for himself. God's response (v. 4) was to remind him of the message of judgment he had been given. In Egypt, God was not yet through. Thus, Baruch's original message uttered in chapter 36 is placed here as a reminder.
45:5 Stop seeking! Rather than seeking reward for faithfulness, Baruch should be grateful that his life was spared. A similar promise had been made to Ebed-melech (39:15-18). Thorough judgment would precede complete restoration (1:10; 31:28; 42:10).

46:1-51:64 Just as chapters 36-45 are largely concerned with the judgment against Judah commencing in 605 B.C. and running to Babylon's catching up with the Jewish exiles in Egypt (567 B.C.), chapter 46 begins with the original judgment of Egypt through its defeat by Nebuchadnezzar at the battle of Carchemish in 605 B.C. and ending with the Babylonian onslaught within Egypt itself (567 B.C.).

16 Moab's calamity is near at hand;
    his disaster is rushing swiftly.
17 Mourn for him, all you surrounding ⌊nations⌋,
    everyone who knows his name.
    Say: How the mighty scepter is shattered,
    the glorious staff!
18 Come down from glory; sit on parched ground,
    resident of the daughter of Dibon,
    for the destroyer of Moab has come against you;
    he has destroyed your fortresses.
19 Stand by the highway and look,
    resident of Aroer!
    Ask him who is fleeing or her who is escaping,
    What happened?
20 Moab is put to shame, indeed dismayed.
    Wail and cry out!
    Declare by the Arnon
    that Moab is destroyed.

21 "Judgment has come to the land of the plateau—
to Holon, Jahzah, Mephaath, 22 Dibon, Nebo, Beth-
diblathaim, 23 Kiriathaim, Beth-gamul, Beth-meon,
24 Kerioth, Bozrah, and all the towns of the land of
Moab, those far and near. 25 Moab's •horn is chopped
off; his arm is shattered."

                                        ⌊This is⌋
                            the LORD's declaration.

26 "Make him drunk, because he has exalted himself
against the LORD. Moab will wallow in his own vomit,
and he will also become a laughingstock. 27 Wasn't
Israel a laughingstock to you? Was he ever found among
thieves? For whenever you speak of him you shake
⌊your head⌋."

28 Abandon the towns! Live in the cliffs,
    residents of Moab!
    Be like a dove
    that nests inside the mouth of a cave.

29 We have heard of Moab's pride,
    great pride, indeed—
    his insolence, arrogance, pride,
    and haughty heart.
30 I know his outburst.

                                        ⌊This is⌋
                            the LORD's declaration.

    It is empty.
    His boast is empty.
31 Therefore, I will wail over Moab.
    I will cry out for Moab, all of it;
    he will moan for the men of Kir-heres.

32 I will weep for you, vine of Sibmah,
    with more than the weeping for Jazer.
    Your tendrils have extended to the sea;
    they have reached to the sea ⌊and to⌋ Jazer.[a]
    The destroyer has fallen on your summer fruit
        and grape harvest.
33 Joy and celebration are taken
        from the fertile field
    and from the land of Moab.
    I have stopped the flow of wine
        from the winepresses;
    no one will tread with shouts of joy.
    The shouting is not a shout of joy.

34 "There is a cry from Heshbon to Elealeh; they raise
their voices as far as Jahaz—from Zoar to Horonaim ⌊and⌋
Eglath-shelishiyah—because even the waters of Nimrim
have become desolate. 35 In Moab, I will stop"—⌊this is⌋
the LORD's declaration—"the one who offers sacrifices
on the •high place and burns incense to his gods.
36 Therefore, My heart moans like flutes for Moab, and
My heart moans like flutes for the people of Kir-heres.
And therefore, the wealth he has gained has perished.
37 Indeed, every head is bald and every beard clipped; on
every hand is a gash and •sackcloth around the waist.
38 On all the rooftops of Moab and in her public squares,
everyone is mourning because I have shattered Moab
like a jar no one wants." ⌊This is⌋ the LORD's declaration.
39 "How broken it is! They wail! How Moab has turned
his back! He is ashamed. Moab will become a laughingstock and a shock to all those around him."

40 For this is what the LORD says:

    He will swoop down like an eagle
        and spread his wings against Moab.
41 The towns have[b] been captured,
    and the strongholds seized.
    In that day the heart of Moab's warriors
    will be like the heart of a woman
        with contractions.
42 Moab will be destroyed as a people
    because he has exalted himself
        against the LORD.
43 Panic, pit, and trap
    await you, resident of Moab.

                                        ⌊This is⌋
                            the LORD's declaration.

44 He who flees from the panic
        will fall in the pit,
    and he who climbs from the pit
    will be captured in the trap,

---

a48:32 Some Hb mss read reached as far as Jazer; Is 16:8   b48:41 Or Kerioth has

---

Proceeding from the southwest to the distant
east, the oracles continue. They concern the
other nations that surround and had oppressed Israel (chs. 47-49), and conclude
with the 539 B.C. fall of the Lord's instrument
in these judgments; Babylon (chs. 50-51).
This final judgment ultimately resulted in Is-

rael's return from exile.
46:16 to our people. Warriors from smaller,
nearby nations would turn their backs on the
losing Egyptian army. They would rather return home alive with what they had, than end
up with nothing.
48:1 About Moab. Tracing its ancestry to Lot

(Gen. 19:37) and assigned to Reuben's tribe
(Num. 32; Josh. 13:15–23) Moab was located
east of the Dead Sea. David subjected the Moabites (2 Sam 8:2, 12), and Solomon continued control. After Ahab's death, Moab
rebelled against Israel and regained independence (2 Kgs 1:1; 3:4–27). Afterwards its influ-

for I will bring against Moab
the year of their punishment.

⌊This is⌋
the LORD's declaration.

45 Those who flee will stand exhausted
in Heshbon's shadow
because fire has come out from Heshbon
and a flame from within Sihon.
It will devour Moab's forehead
and the skull of the noisemakers.
46 Woe to you, Moab!
The people of Chemosh have perished
because your sons have been taken captive
and your daughters have gone into captivity.
47 Yet, I will restore the fortunes[a] of Moab
in the last days.

⌊This is⌋
the LORD's declaration.

The judgment on Moab ends here.

Prophecies against Ammon

49 About the Ammonites, this is what the LORD
says:

Does Israel have no sons?
Is he without an heir?
Why then has •Milcom[b][c] dispossessed Gad
and his people settled in their cities?
2 Therefore look, the days are coming—
⌊this is⌋
the LORD's declaration—
when I will make the shout
of battle heard
against Rabbah of the Ammonites.
It will become a desolate mound,
and its villages will be burned down.
Israel will dispossess their dispossessors,
says the LORD.
3 Wail, Heshbon, for Ai is devastated;
cry out, daughters of Rabbah!
Clothe yourselves with •sackcloth,
and lament;
run back and forth within your walls,[d]
because Milcom will go into exile
together with his priests and officials.
4 Why do you brag about your valleys,
your flowing valley,[e]
you faithless daughter?
You who trust in your treasures
⌊and boast⌋: Who can attack me?

5 Look, I am about to bring terror on you—
⌊this is⌋ the declaration of the Lord,
the GOD of •Hosts—
from all those around you.
You will be banished, each man headlong,
with no one to gather up the fugitives.
6 But after that, I will restore the fortunes[a]
of the Ammonites.

⌊This is⌋
the LORD's declaration.

Prophecies against Edom

7 About Edom, this is what the LORD of Hosts says:

Is there no longer wisdom in Teman?[f]
Has counsel perished from the prudent?
Has their wisdom rotted away?
8 Run! Turn back! Lie low,
residents of Dedan,
for I will bring Esau's calamity on him
at the time I punish him.
9 If grape harvesters came to you,
wouldn't they leave some gleanings?
Were thieves to come in the night,
they would destroy only what they wanted.
10 But I will strip Esau bare;
I will uncover his secret places.
He will try to hide himself,
but he will be unable.
His descendants will be destroyed
along with his relatives and neighbors.
He will exist no longer.
11 Abandon your orphans; I will preserve them;
let your widows trust in Me.

12 "For this is what the LORD says: If those who do not
deserve to drink the cup must drink it, can you possibly
remain unpunished? You will not remain unpunished, for
you must drink ⌊it⌋ too. 13 For by Myself I have sworn"—
the LORD's declaration—"Bozrah[g] will become a desolation, a disgrace, a ruin, and a curse, and all her cities will
become ruins forever."

14 I have heard a message from the LORD;
an envoy has been sent among the nations:
Assemble yourselves to come against her.
Rise up for war!

15 Look, I will certainly make you insignificant
among the nations,
despised among humanity.

---

[a] 48:47; 49:6 Or will end the captivity [b] 49:1 LXX, Syr, Vg; MT reads Malkam [c] 49:1 = Molech; 1 Kg 11:5 [d] 49:3 Or sheep pens [e] 49:4 Or about your strength, your ebbing strength [f] 49:7 = southern Edom, or Edom; Ezk 25:13; Ob 9 [g] 49:13 = Edom's capital; Am 1:12

---

ence waned and it became Assyria's vassal
(734 B.C.). In 605 it came under Babylonian
control and aided Nebuchadnezzar against
Judah's rebellion under Jehoiakim (2 Kings
24:2). Along with Ammon, Moab lost its freedom to Nebuchadnezzar in 582. Soon after an
Arab invasion from the east eliminated Moab

as a nation.᠎ Except for Babylon, Moab received more attention from Jeremiah than any
other nation, including Egypt (Jer. 9:26;
25:21). It was a favorite target of other prophets as well (Isa. 15–16; Ezek. 25:8–11; Amos
2:1–3; Zeph. 2:8–11).

48:26 Make him drunk. The mighty Moab

once brought fear to Judah's inhabitants.
Now, God would numb the nation with His
wrath (49:12; Pss. 60:3; 75:9; Isa. 51:17-23;
Lam. 4:21; Ezek. 23:31-34; Hab. 2:16).

48:27 laughingstock. Apparently Moab
joined Edom in jeering the captives of Jerusalem as they were taken to Babylon in ex-

16 As to the terror you cause,[a]
   your presumptuous heart has deceived you.
   You who live in the clefts of the rock,[b]
   you who occupy the mountain summit,
   though you elevate your nest like the eagle,
   even from there I will bring you down.

⌊This is⌋
the LORD's declaration.

17 "Edom will become a desolation. Everyone who passes by her will be horrified and scoff because of all her wounds. 18 As when Sodom and Gomorrah were overthrown along with their neighbors," says the LORD, "no one will live there; no human being will even stay in it as a resident alien.

19 "Look, it will be like a lion coming up from the thickets[c] of the Jordan to the perennially watered grazing land. Indeed, I will chase Edom away from her ⌊land⌋ in a flash. I will appoint whoever is chosen for her. For who is like Me? Who will summon Me? Who is the shepherd who can stand against Me?"

20 Therefore, hear the plans that the LORD has drawn up against Edom and the strategies He has devised against the people of Teman: The flock's little lambs will certainly be dragged away, and their grazing land will be made desolate because of them. 21 At the sound of their fall the earth will quake; the sound of her cry will be heard at the •Red Sea. 22 Look! It will be like an eagle soaring upward, then swooping down and spreading its wings over Bozrah. In that day the hearts of Edom's warriors will be like the heart of a woman with contractions.

Prophecies against Damascus

23 About Damascus:

Hamath and Arpad are put to shame,
   for they have heard a bad report
   and are agitated;
in the sea there is anxiety that cannot
   be calmed.
24 Damascus has become weak;
   she has turned to run;
   panic has gripped her.
Distress and labor pains
   have seized her
   like a woman in labor.
25 How can the city of praise
   not be abandoned,
   the town that brings Me joy?

26 Therefore, her young men will fall
   in her public squares;
all the warriors will be silenced in that day.

⌊This is⌋ the declaration of
the LORD of Hosts.

27 I will set fire to the wall of Damascus;
   it will devour Ben-hadad's citadels.

Prophecies against Kedar and Hazor

28 About Kedar and the kingdoms of Hazor, which Nebuchadnezzar, Babylon's king, defeated, this is what the LORD says:

Rise up, go against Kedar,
   and destroy the people of the east!
29 They will take their tents and their flocks
   along with their tent curtains
   and all their equipment.
They will take their camels
   for themselves.
They will call out to them:
   Terror is on every side!
30 Run! Escape quickly! Lie low,
   residents of Hazor—

⌊this is⌋
the LORD's declaration—

for Nebuchadnezzar king of Babylon
   has drawn up a plan against you;
he has devised a strategy against you.

31 Rise up, go up against a nation at ease,
   one living in security.

⌊This is⌋
the LORD's declaration.

They have no doors, not even a gate bar;
   they live alone.
32 Their camels will become plunder,
   and their massive herds of cattle will
   become spoil.
I will scatter them to the wind
   in every direction,
   those who shave their temples;
I will bring calamity on them
   across all their borders.

⌊This is⌋
the LORD's declaration.

33 Hazor will become a jackals' den,
   a desolation forever.
No one will live there;

---

[a] 49:16 Lit Your horror   [b] 49:16 = Petra; Jdg 1:36; 2 Kg 14:7; Is 16:1   [c] 49:19 Lit pride; Jr 12:5; 50:44; Zch 11:3

---

ile (Lam. 2:15-16).

48:29 We have heard. Moab's pride brought God to bitter tears (see Isa.16:7, 11). Ultimately, the nation's arrogance incurred God's wrath as well. Like-sounding Hebrew verbs emphasize God's condemnation: pride (ga'on), great pride (ge'eh) insolence (ga-

boah) and arrogance (ga'awa). These words rightly hiss in succession.
48:43 Panic, pit, and trap. God's wrath would sweep throughout Moab and trap His enemy like a hunter.
48:44 He who flees. There was no place to hide from God's wrath—all escape attempts

would be thwarted (see Amos 5:18-20). There would be no turning back.

49:1 About the Ammonites. Like Moab, Ammon was descended from Lot (Gen. 19:30-38). Solomon married an Ammonite princess and built a pagan temple on the temple mount (1 Kings 11:7). Their king Baalis was

no human being will even stay in it
    as a resident alien.

Prophecies against Elam

34 ⌊This is⌋ the word of the LORD that came to Jeremiah the prophet about Elam[a] at the beginning of the reign of Zedekiah king of Judah. 35 This is what the LORD of Hosts says:

I am about to shatter Elam's bow,
    the source[b] of their might.
36 I will bring the four winds against Elam
    from the four corners of the heavens,
and I will scatter them to all these winds.
There will not be a nation
    to which Elam's banished ones will not go.
37 I will devastate Elam before their enemies,
    before those who want to take their lives.
I will bring disaster on them,
    My burning anger.

            ⌊This is⌋
      the LORD's declaration.
I will send the sword after them
    until I finish them off.
38 I will set My throne in Elam,
    and I will destroy the king and officials
      from there.

            ⌊This is⌋
      the LORD's declaration.

39 In the last days,
    I will restore the fortunes[c] of Elam.

            ⌊This is⌋
      the LORD's declaration.

Prophecies against Babylon

50 The word the LORD spoke about Babylon, the land of the Chaldeans, through Jeremiah the prophet:

2 Announce to the nations;
    proclaim and raise up a signal flag;
    proclaim, and hide nothing.
Say: Babylon is captured;
Bel is put to shame;
Marduk is devastated;
    her idols are put to shame;
    her false gods, devastated.
3 For a nation from the north will come
    against her;
    it will make her land desolate.
No one will be living in it—

both man and beast will escape.[d]
4 In those days and at that time—

            ⌊this is⌋
      the LORD's declaration—
the Israelites and Judeans
    will come together,
weeping as they come,
and will seek the LORD their God.
5 They will ask about Zion,
    ⌊turning⌋ their faces to this road.
They will come and join themselves[e]
    to the LORD
in an everlasting covenant that will never
    be forgotten.

6 My people are lost sheep;
    their shepherds have led them astray,
    guiding them the wrong way in the mountains.
They have wandered from mountain to hill;
    they have forgotten their resting place.
7 All who found them devoured them.
Their adversaries said: We're not guilty;
    instead, they have sinned against the LORD,
    their righteous grazing land,
the hope of their ancestors, the LORD.

8 Escape from Babylon;
    depart from the Chaldeans' land.
Be like the rams that lead the flock.
9 For I will soon stir up and bring against Babylon
    an assembly of great nations
      from the north country.
They will line up in battle formation
    against her;
    from there she will be captured.
Their arrows will be like those
    of a skilled[f] warrior
who does not return empty-handed.
10 The Chaldeans will become plunder;
    all her plunderers will be fully satisfied.

            ⌊This is⌋
      the LORD's declaration.

11 Because you rejoice,
    because you sing in triumph—
you who plundered My inheritance—
because you frolic like a young cow
    treading grain
    and neigh like stallions,
12 your mother will be utterly humiliated;
    she who bore you will be put to shame.

---

[a] **49:34** = modern Iran; Ezr 4:9; Dn 8:2; Ac 2:9   [b] **49:35** Lit *first*   [c] **49:39** Or *will end the captivity*   [d] **50:3** Lit *escape; they will walk*   [e] **50:5** LXX; MT reads *Come and join yourselves*   [f] **50:9** Some Hb mss, LXX, Syr; other Hb mss read *bereaving*

---

instrumental in the Gedaliah's murder (chs. 40-41). Ammon had taken territory from the tribe of Gad after the deportation of northern Israel in 733 B.C. The Lord intended to reclaim it. The Babylonians initially accomplished this in 582 B.C. Eventually the Jewish Maccabeans reclaimed it for Israel from 149-

63 B.C. until the Romans took over. A large portion of Ammon is presently occupied by Israel on the West Bank.

49:7 About Edom. The Edomites, related to Israel through Esau (Gen. 36), were eventually destroyed by Arabs (Mal. 1:2-5). Many moved to Idumea in southern Judah, and

may have been Herod the Great's ancestors **no ... wisdom.** Edomites were known for their wisdom (Job 2:11).

49:12 unpunished. Some see Edom's punishment as relating to her alliance with Philistia against Judah's King Jehoram (2 Chron. 21:15-16; Amos 1:9, 11; Obad. 10). Esau

Look! She will lag behind all[a] the nations—
a dry land, a wilderness, an •Arabah.

13 Because of the LORD's wrath,
she will not be inhabited;
she will become a desolation, every bit of her.
Everyone who passes through Babylon
will be horrified
and scoff because of all her wounds.

14 Line up in battle formation around Babylon,
all you archers!
Shoot at her! Do not spare an arrow,
for she has sinned against the LORD.

15 Raise a war cry against her on every side!
She has thrown up her hands ⌊in surrender⌋;
her defense towers have fallen;
her walls are demolished.
Since this is the LORD's vengeance,
take out your vengeance on her;
as she has done, do the same to her.

16 Cut off the sower from Babylon
as well as him who wields the sickle
at harvest time.
Because of the oppressor's sword,
each will turn to his own people,
each will flee to his own land.

The Return of God's People

17 Israel is a stray lamb, chased by lions.
The first who devoured him was the king
of Assyria;
this last who has crunched his bones
was Nebuchadnezzar king of Babylon.

18 Therefore, this is what the LORD of •Hosts, the
God of Israel, says: "I am about to punish the king of
Babylon and his land just as I punished the king of
Assyria.

19 I will return Israel to his grazing land,
and he will feed on Carmel and Bashan;
he will be satisfied
in the hill country of Ephraim and of Gilead.

20 In those days and at that time—

⌊this is⌋
the LORD's declaration—

one will search for Israel's guilt,
but there will be none,
and for Judah's sins,
but they will not be found,
for I will forgive those I leave as a remnant.

The Invasion of Babylon

21 Go against the land of Merathaim,
and against those living in Pekod.
Put them to the sword;
•completely destroy them—

⌊this is⌋
the LORD's declaration—

do everything I have commanded you.

22 The sound of war is in the land—
a great destruction.

23 How the hammer of the whole earth
is cut down and smashed!
What a horror Babylon has become
among the nations!

24 Babylon, I laid a trap for you, and you
were caught,
but you did not even know it.
You were found and captured
because you fought against the LORD.

25 The LORD opened His armory
and brought out His weapons of wrath,
because it is a task of the Lord GOD of Hosts
in the land of the Chaldeans.

26 Come against her from the most distant places.[b]
Open her granaries;
pile her up like mounds of grain
and completely destroy her.
Leave her no survivors.

27 Put all her young bulls to the sword;
let them go down to the slaughter.
Woe to them, because their day has come,
the time of their punishment.

The Humiliation of Babylon

28 ⌊There is⌋ a voice of fugitives and escapees
from the land of Babylon
announcing in Zion the vengeance of the LORD
our God,
the vengeance for His temple.

29 Summon the archers to Babylon,
all who string the bow;
camp all around her; let none escape.
Repay her according to her deeds;
just as she has done, do the same to her,
for she has acted arrogantly
against the LORD,
against the Holy One of Israel.

30 Therefore, her young men will fall
in her public squares;

---

[a]**50:12** Lit *Look! The last of*   [b]**50:26** Lit *from the end*

(Edom) was supposed to be Jacob's brother.
49:13 Bozrah. Edom's capital was located 25
miles southeast of the Dead Sea. The terms
used to describe its destruction usually refer
to Judah (15:4; 21:7; 25:9; 29:18; 34:17; Deut.
28:37; Ps. 44:14-15).
49:16 deceived you. Edom was a powerful

and respected nation. However, these
well-intentioned accolades proved to be a
disastrous disservice. Pride was one
downfall that led to her defeat.

49:17 scoff. The Edomites jeered Jerusalem's
defeated residents in 586 B.C. (Ps. 137:7; Lam.
2:15-16), and would be repaid in kind.

49:22 eagle. God used a bird of prey to illustrate His watchful gaze over his enemy. God
seemed remote and removed, yet soon He
would swoop down upon Edom like an eagle.

49:34 about Elam. Jeremiah's predicted
Elam's defeat in 597 B.C. The capital of Elam,
Susa, became the center of the Persian Em-

all the warriors will be silenced
  in that day.
      ⌊This is⌋
      the LORD's declaration.

31 Look, I am against you, you arrogant one—
      ⌊this is⌋ the declaration of
      the Lord GOD of Hosts—
  because your day has come,
  the time when I will punish you.
32 The arrogant will stumble and fall
  with no one to pick him up.
  I will set fire to his cities,
  and it will consume everything around him."

The Desolation of Babylon

33 This is what the LORD of Hosts says:

  Israelites and Judeans alike
    have been oppressed.
  All their captors hold them fast;
  they refuse to release them.
34 Their Redeemer is strong;
  the LORD of Hosts is His name.
  He will fervently plead their case
  so that He might bring rest to the earth
  but turmoil to those who live in Babylon.
35 A sword is over the Chaldeans—
      ⌊this is⌋
      the LORD's declaration—
  against those who live in Babylon,
  against her officials, and against her sages.
36 A sword is against the diviners,
  and they will act foolishly.
  A sword is against her heroic warriors,
  and they will be terrified.
37 A sword is against his horses and chariots
  and against all the foreigners among them,
  and they will be like women.
  A sword is against her treasuries,
  and they will be plundered.
38 A drought will come on her waters,
  and they will be dried up.
  For it is a land of carved images,
  and they go mad because of terrifying things.[a]

39 Therefore, desert creatures[b] will live
    with jackals,
  and ostriches will also live in her.
  It will never again be inhabited
  or lived in through all generations.

40 Just as when God overthrew Sodom
    and Gomorrah
  and their neighboring towns—
      ⌊this is⌋
      the LORD's declaration—
  so no one will live there;
  no human being will even stay in it
  as a resident alien.

The Conquest of Babylon

41 Look! A people comes from the north.
  A great nation and many kings
    will be stirred up
  from the remote regions of the earth.
42 They grasp bow and javelin.
  They are cruel and show no mercy.
  Their voice roars like the sea,
  and they ride on horses,
  lined up like men in battle formation
  against you, Daughter of Babylon.
43 The king of Babylon has heard reports
    about them,
  and his hands fall helpless.
  Distress has seized him—
  pain, like a woman in labor.

44 "Look, it will be like a lion coming up from the thickets[c] of the Jordan to the perennially watered grazing land. Indeed, I will chase Babylon[d] away from her ⌊land⌋ in a flash. I will appoint whoever is chosen for her. For who is like Me? Who will summon Me? Who is the shepherd who can stand against Me?"

45 Therefore, hear the plans that the LORD has drawn up against Babylon and the strategies He has devised against the land of the Chaldeans: Certainly the flock's little lambs will be dragged away; certainly the grazing land will be made desolate because of them. 46 At the sound of Babylon's conquest the earth will quake; a cry will be heard among the nations.

God's Judgment on Babylon

51 This is what the LORD says:

  I am about to stir up a destructive wind[e]
    against Babylon
  and against the population of Leb-qamai.[f]
2 I will send strangers to Babylon
  who will scatter her and strip her land bare,
  for they will come against her
  from every side in the day of disaster.

---

[a]50:38 Or of dreaded gods   [b]50:39 Or desert demons; Rv 18:2   [c]50:44 Lit pride; Jr 12:5; 50:44; Zch 11:3   [d]50:44 Lit them   [e]51:1 Or stir up the spirit of a destroyer   [f]51:1 = a name for Chaldeans

---

pire after 539 B.C. (Neh. 1:1; Dan. 8:2).
49:35 bow. Modern Iran —a nation of notable archers— continues Elam's legacy.
49:38 set My throne. In 567 B.C., the Lord set up Nebuchadnezzar's throne at Tahpanhes (Egypt). He may have done likewise to Elam just one year after Jeremiah's prophecy

(596 B.C.).
49:39 restore the fortunes of Elam. Like other nations, Elam is promised restoration in the last days (Isa. 19:21, 25).
50:2 Babylon. Finally, the conqueror gets conquered. The nation that enjoyed seemingly endless conquests was temporarily

halted by many northern nations. All of Babylon was doomed to eventual defeat.

50:11 plundered My inheritance. God resented Babylon's indifference to His chosen people Judah's plight. The people's inheritance was promised by God Himself. Babylon would suffer for its harshness.

3 Don't let the archer string his bow;
  don't let him put on[a] his armor.
  Don't spare her young men;
  •completely destroy her entire army!

4 Those who were slain will fall in the land
    of the Chaldeans,
  those who were pierced through, in her streets.

5 For Israel and Judah are not left widowed
  by their God, the LORD of •Hosts,
  though their land is full of guilt
  against the Holy One of Israel.

6 Leave Babylon;
  save your lives, each of you!
  Don't be silenced by her guilt.
  For this is the time of the LORD's vengeance—
  He will pay her what she deserves.

7 Babylon was a golden cup in the LORD's hand
  making the whole earth drunk.
  The nations drank her wine;
  therefore, the nations go mad.

8 Suddenly Babylon fell and was shattered.
  Wail for her;
  get balm for her wound—
  perhaps she can be healed.

9 We tried to heal Babylon,
  but she could not be healed.
  Abandon her!
  Let each of us go to his own land,
  for her judgment extends to the sky
  and reaches as far as the clouds.

10 The LORD has brought about our vindication;
   come, let's tell in Zion
   what the LORD our God has accomplished.

11 Sharpen the arrows!
   Fill the quivers!
   The LORD has put it into the mind
   of the kings of the Medes
   because His plan is aimed at Babylon
   to destroy her,
   for it is the LORD's vengeance,
   vengeance for His temple.

12 Raise up a signal flag
   against the walls of Babylon;
   fortify the watch post;
   set the watchmen in place;
   prepare the ambush.
   For the LORD has both planned
     and accomplished

what He has threatened
against those who live in Babylon.

13 You who reside by many waters,
   rich in treasures,
   your end has come,
   your life thread is cut.

14 The LORD of Hosts has sworn by Himself:
   I will fill you up with men as with locusts,
   and they will sing the victory song over you.

15 He made the earth by His power,
   established the world by His wisdom,
   and spread out the heavens
     by His understanding.

16 When He thunders,[b]
   the waters in the heavens are in turmoil,
   and He causes the clouds
   to rise from the ends of the earth.
   He makes lightning for the rain
   and brings the wind from His storehouses.

17 Everyone is stupid and ignorant.
   Every goldsmith is put to shame
     by ⌊his⌋ carved image,
   for his cast images are a lie;
   there is no breath in them.

18 They are worthless, a work to be mocked.
   At the time of their punishment they will
     be destroyed.

19 Jacob's Portion[c] is not like these
   because He is the One who formed all things.
   ⌊Israel is⌋ the tribe of His inheritance;
   the LORD of Hosts is His name.

20 You are My battle club,
   My weapons of war.
   With you I will smash nations;
   with you I will bring kingdoms to ruin.

21 With you I will smash the horse and its rider;
   with you I will smash the chariot and its rider.

22 With you I will smash man and woman;
   with you I will smash the old man
     and the youth;
   with you I will smash the young man
     and the virgin.

23 With you I will smash the shepherd
     and his flock;
   with you I will smash the farmer
     and his ox-team.[d]
   With you I will smash governors and officials.

---

[a]51:3 Hb obscure   [b]51:16 Lit At His giving of the voice   [c]51:19 = the LORD   [d]51:23 Lit yoke

---

50:17-18 Assyria had conquered the northern kingdom in 722 B.C. Babylon had conquered the southern kingdom in 586 B.C. As Assyria had passed into the horizon, to be replaced by Babylon, so too would Babylon come to pass, to be replaced by another (Persia) who would allow the Israelites to return to their homeland.

50:19 Carmel ... Bashan ... Gilead. Originally granted to Moses (Num. 21:33; Josh. 13:29-31) but lost to Assyria during Micah's time (2 Kings 14:25), Jeremiah prophecies that Israel will be returned to its initial prosperity (Ezek. 34:13-14; Micah 7:14). The ultimate realization of this prophecy is yet future.

50:20 Judah' sins ... not be found. God has forgiven (31:31-34) the remnant (39:10; 52:16).

50:25 His weapons of wrath. A great coalition of neighboring northern nations would bring God's punishment on Babylon. Those who Babylon had once fought would now be

731

24 "I will repay Babylon and all the residents of Chaldea for all their evil they have done in Zion before your very eyes."

⌊This is⌋
the LORD's declaration.

25 Look, I am against you, devastating mountain—
⌊this is⌋
the LORD's declaration—
you devastate the whole earth.
I will stretch out My hand against you,
roll you down from the cliffs,
and turn you into a burned-out mountain.
26 No one will be able to retrieve a cornerstone
or a foundation stone from you,
because you will become
desolate forever.

⌊This is⌋
the LORD's declaration.

27 Raise a signal flag in the land;
blow a ram's horn among the nations;
set apart the nations against her.
Summon kingdoms against her—
Ararat, Minni, and Ashkenaz.
Appoint a marshal against her;
bring up horses like a swarm[a] of locusts.
28 Set apart the nations for battle against her—
the kings of Media,
her governors and all her officials,
and all the lands they rule.
29 The earth quakes and trembles,
because the LORD's purposes against Babylon
stand:
to make the land of Babylon
an uninhabited desolation.
30 Babylon's warriors have
stopped fighting;
they sit in their strongholds.
Their might is exhausted;
they have become like women.
Babylon's homes have been set ablaze,
her gate bars are shattered.
31 Messenger races to meet messenger,
and herald to meet herald,
to announce to the king of Babylon
that his city has been captured
from end ⌊to end⌋.
32 The fords have been seized,
the marshes set on fire,
and the soldiers are terrified.

33 For this is what the LORD of Hosts, the God of Israel, says:

The daughter of Babylon is like a threshing floor
at the time it is trampled.
In just a little while her harvest time will come.

34 "Nebuchadnezzar of Babylon has devoured me;
he has crushed me.
He has set me aside like an empty dish;
he has swallowed me like a sea monster;
he filled his belly with my delicacies;
he has vomited me out,"[b]
35 says the inhabitant of Zion;
"Let the violence ⌊done⌋ to me and my family
⌊be done⌋ to Babylon.
Let my blood be on the inhabitants of Chaldea,"
says Jerusalem.

36 Therefore, this is what the LORD says:

I am about to plead your case
and take vengeance on your behalf;
I will dry up her sea
and make her fountain run dry.
37 Babylon will become a heap of rubble,
a jackals' den,
a desolation and an object of scorn,
without inhabitant.
38 They will roar together like young lions;
they will growl like lion cubs.
39 While they are flushed with heat,
I will serve them a feast,
and I will make them drunk so that they revel.[c]
Then they will fall asleep forever
and never wake up.

⌊This is⌋
the LORD's declaration.

40 I will bring them down like lambs
to the slaughter,
like rams together with male goats.

41 How Sheshach has been captured,
the praise of the whole earth seized.
What a horror Babylon has become
among the nations!
42 The sea has risen over Babylon;
she is covered with its turbulent waves.
43 Her cities have become a desolation,
a dry and arid land,
a land where no one lives,
where no human being passes through.

---

[a]**51:27** Hb obscure [b]**51:34** Lit *has rinsed me off* [c]**51:39** LXX reads *pass out*

---

turning to conquer her.
50:32 consume. God's anger burns hot (15:14; Lam. 4:11; Amos 1:4-14; 2:2-5).
50:43 a woman in labor. The prophets commonly pictured Daughter Zion crying out in such agony (4:31; 6:24; 13:21; 22:23; 30:6; Isa. 26:17; Micah 4:9-10). In the oracles

against the nations (chs. 46-51), Israel's oppressors are pictured in the same way (48:41; 49:22; 50:43; Ps. 48:6; Isa. 13:8; 21:3) In contrast to Daughter Zion's pangs, Daughter of Babylon (v. 42) suffers here. Similar language is often used to describe the terrifying aspects of the Day of the Lord (Dan. 12:1; Zeph. 1:14-

15), whose fury will be unsurpassed and gives a picture of the kind of torments the nations who oppose God will experience in Jeremiah. Birth pangs can also be the occasion for joy when seen as introductory to the crowning of Messiah and the renewal of Israel (Isa. 66:6-9; Micah 5:3; John 16:21; Rev. 12:2).

44 I will punish Bel in Babylon.
I will make him vomit what he swallowed.
The nations will no longer stream to him;
even Babylon's wall will fall.

45 Come out from among her, My people!
Save your lives, each of you,
from the LORD's burning anger.

46 May you not become faint-hearted
and fearful
when the report is proclaimed in the land,
for the report will come one year,
and then another the next year.
There will be violence in the land
with ruler against ruler.

47 Therefore, look, the days are coming
when I will punish Babylon's carved images.
Her entire land will suffer shame,
and all her slain will lie fallen within her.

48 Heaven and earth and everything in them
will shout for joy over Babylon
because the destroyers from the north
will come against her.

⌊This is⌋
the LORD's declaration.

49 Babylon must fall ⌊because of⌋ the slain
of Israel,
even as the slain of all the earth fell
because of Babylon.

50 You who have escaped the sword,
go and do not stand still!
Remember the LORD from far away,
and let Jerusalem come to your mind.

51 We are ashamed
because we have heard insults.
Humiliation covers our faces
because foreigners have entered
the holy places of the LORD's temple.

52 Therefore, look, the days are coming—

⌊this is⌋
the LORD's declaration—
when I will punish her carved images,
and the wounded will groan
throughout her land.

53 Even if Babylon should ascend
to the heavens
and fortify her tall fortresses,
destroyers will come against her from Me.

⌊This is⌋
the LORD's declaration.

54 The sound of a cry from Babylon!
The sound of great destruction
from the land of the Chaldeans!

55 For the LORD is going to devastate Babylon;
He will silence her mighty voice.
Their waves roar like abundant waters;
the tumult of their voice resounds,

56 for a destroyer is coming against her,
against Babylon.
Her warriors will be captured,
their bows shattered,
for the LORD is a God of retribution;
He will certainly repay.

57 I will make her princes and sages drunk,
along with her governors, officials,
and warriors.
Then they will fall asleep forever
and never wake up.

⌊This is⌋ the King's declaration;
the LORD of Hosts is His name.

58 This is what the LORD of Hosts says:

Babylon's thick walls will be
totally demolished,
and her high gates consumed by fire.
The peoples will have labored
for nothing;
the nations will exhaust themselves
⌊only to feed⌋ the fire.

59 ⌊This is⌋ what Jeremiah the prophet commanded Seraiah son of Neriah son of Mahseiah, the quartermaster, when he went to Babylon with Zedekiah king of Judah in the fourth year of Zedekiah's reign. 60 Jeremiah wrote on one scroll about all the disaster that would come to Babylon; all these words were written against Babylon.

61 Jeremiah told Seraiah, "When you get to Babylon, see that you read all these words aloud. 62 You must say, 'LORD, You have threatened to cut off this place so that no one will live in it—man or beast. Indeed, it will remain desolate forever.' 63 When you have finished reading this scroll, tie a stone to it and throw it into the middle of the Euphrates River. 64 Then say, 'In the same way, Babylon will sink and never rise again because of the disaster I am bringing on her. They will grow weary.'"

The words of Jeremiah end here.

The Fall of Jerusalem

52 Zedekiah was 21 years old when he became king; he reigned 11 years in Jerusalem. His

---

51:6 Leave Babylon. Earlier, Jeremiah instructed the people of Judah to surrender to Babylon. Even though God was going to discipline His people, He had a plan for restoration after the exile.

51:11–12 God's avengers are to prepare for battle. Babylon will be vanquished for its destruction of the Lord's temple (50:28; Ps 74:3–8). The avengers are identified as the "kings of the Medes." This is the first mention of Media as the agent of Babylon's destruction. Media, an ancient kingdom northwest of India, was conquered by Cyrus in 550 B.C (Isa. 44:28; 45:1). His mother was a Mede. The

"kings" referred to here could be those who served under Cyrus as vassals (v. 27; Ararat, Minni, and Ashkenaz). Cyrus' decree (2 Chron. 36:22-23; Ezra 1:1-4) allowed the Jews to return to Israel. Thus, Cyrus was not only God's avenger, but His redeemer as well.

mother's name was Hamutal daughter of Jeremiah; ⌊she was⌋ from Libnah. ² Zedekiah did what was evil in the LORD's sight just as Jehoiakim had done. ³ Because of the LORD's anger, it came to the point in Jerusalem and Judah that He finally banished them from His presence. Nevertheless, Zedekiah rebelled against the king of Babylon.

⁴ In the ninth year of Zedekiah's reign, on the tenth day of the tenth month, King Nebuchadnezzar of Babylon advanced against Jerusalem with his entire army. They laid siege to the city and built a siege wall all around it. ⁵ The city was under siege until King Zedekiah's eleventh year.

⁶ By the ninth day of the fourth month the famine was so severe in the city that the people of the land had no food. ⁷ Then the city was broken into, and all the warriors fled. They left the city by night by way of the gate between the two walls near the king's garden, though the Chaldeans surrounded the city. They made their way along the route to the •Arabah. ⁸ The Chaldean army pursued the king and overtook Zedekiah in the plains of Jericho. Zedekiah's entire army was scattered from him. ⁹ The Chaldeans seized the king and brought him to the king of Babylon at Riblah in the land of Hamath, and he passed sentence on him.

¹⁰ At Riblah the king of Babylon slaughtered Zedekiah's sons before his eyes and also slaughtered the Judean commanders. ¹¹ Then he blinded Zedekiah and bound him with bronze chains. The king of Babylon brought Zedekiah to Babylon, where he kept him in custody[a] until his dying day.

¹² On the tenth day of the fifth month—which was the nineteenth year of King Nebuchadnezzar, king of Babylon—Nebuzaradan, the commander of the guards, entered Jerusalem as the representative of[b] the king of Babylon. ¹³ He burned the LORD's temple, the king's palace, all the houses of Jerusalem, and all the houses of the nobles. ¹⁴ The whole Chaldean army with the commander of the guards tore down all the walls surrounding Jerusalem. ¹⁵ Nebuzaradan, the commander of the guards, deported some of the poorest of the people, as well as the rest of the people who were left in the city, the deserters who had defected to the king of Babylon, and the rest of the craftsmen. ¹⁶ But some of the poor people of the land Nebuzaradan, the commander of the guards, left to be vinedressers and farmers.

¹⁷ Now the Chaldeans broke into pieces the bronze pillars for the LORD's temple and the water carts and the bronze reservoir that were in the LORD's temple, and carried all the bronze to Babylon. ¹⁸ They took the pots, the shovels, the wick trimmers, the sprinkling basins, the dishes, and all the bronze articles used in ⌊temple⌋ service. ¹⁹ The commander of the guards took away the bowls, the firepans, the sprinkling basins, the pots, the lampstands, the pans, and the drink offering bowls—whatever was gold or silver.

²⁰ As for the two pillars, the one reservoir, and the 12 bronze bulls under the water carts that King Solomon had made for the LORD's temple, the weight of the bronze of all these articles was beyond measure. ²¹ One pillar was 27 feet[c] tall, had a circumference of 18 feet,[d] was hollow—four fingers thick— ²² and had a bronze capital on top of it. One capital, encircled by bronze latticework and pomegranates, stood seven and a half feet[e] high. The second pillar was the same, with pomegranates. ²³ ⌊Each capital had⌋ 96 pomegranates all around it. All the pomegranates around the latticework numbered 100.

²⁴ The commander of the guards also took away Seraiah the chief priest, Zephaniah the priest of the second rank, and the three doorkeepers. ²⁵ From the city he took a court official who had been appointed over the warriors; seven trusted royal aides[f] found in the city; the secretary of the commander of the army, who enlisted the people of the land for military duty; and 60 men from the common people who were found within the city. ²⁶ Nebuzaradan, the commander of the guards, took them and brought them to the king of Babylon at Riblah. ²⁷ The king of Babylon put them to death at Riblah in the land of Hamath. Thus Judah went into exile from its land.

²⁸ These are the people Nebuchadnezzar deported: in the seventh year, 3,023 Jews; ²⁹ in his eighteenth year,[g] 832 people from Jerusalem; ³⁰ in Nebuchadnezzar's twenty-third year, Nebuzaradan, the commander of the guards, deported 745 Jews. All together 4,600 people ⌊were deported⌋.

---

a**52:11** Lit *in a house of guards*   b**52:12** Lit *Jerusalem; he stood before*   c**52:21** Lit *18 cubits*   d**52:21** Lit *12 cubits*   e**52:22** Lit *five cubits*
f**52:25** Lit *seven men who look on the king's face*   g**52:29** Some Hb mss, Syr add *he deported*

50:34-44 As in Lamentations, Jerusalem itself speaks of the terror inflicted upon her by Babylon. Babylon's gods are also judged, specifically Bel (v. 44; Isa. 46:1-2).

51:36 case. The Lord presented Jerusalem's case against Babylon. "Case" is often used in the context of God's judgments. Jeremiah pleads his case (12:1; 20:12), then the Lord pleads His case (25:31).

51:39. I will make them drunk. It might seem strange for God to throw a party for a defendant. But, sure enough, the ancient historians Herodotus and Xenophon reported that one of Cyrus' commanders, Gobryus, took advantage of a drunken party held in the palace by Belshazzar in 539 B.C. Gobryus and his soldiers had been able to slip under Babylon's impressive walls because a dam they built suitably lowered the Euphrates' water-level. As God said, the celebrants in the palace did not awake (Dan. 5:30-31).

Jehoiachin Pardoned

31 On the twenty-fifth day of the twelfth month of the thirty-seventh year of the exile of Judah's King Jehoiachin, Evil-merodach king of Babylon, in the ⌊first⌋ year of his reign, pardoned King Jehoiachin of Judah and released him from the prison. 32 He spoke kindly to him and set his throne above the thrones of the kings who were with him in Babylon. 33 So Jehoiachin changed his prison clothes, and he dined regularly in the presence of the king of Babylon for the rest of his life. 34 As for his allowance, a regular allowance was given to him by the king of Babylon, a portion for each day until the day of his death, for the rest of his life.

51:46 when the report is proclaimed. God warned His people not to be discouraged by false information (see Matt. 24:6). Babylon's end was certain. They only needed to take Him at His word.

51:51 foreigners have entered … the LORD's temple. The physical conquest of Jerusalem was not as shameful as the spiritual toll on the people. Seeing their temple defiled by pagan warriors was heartbreaking.

52:1-27, 31-34 Baruch probably penned the addendum to Jeremiah's prophecies (see the parallel in 2 Kings 24:18–25:21, 27-30). Hindsight validated Jeremiah's prophecies against Jerusalem. The eventual fulfillment of his prophecies regarding the exiles' return was an encouragement to them. The plan of God was a help to the people as they endured in a foreign land.

52:1 Zedekiah. Baruch framed Zedekiah's ambition in the bigger picture of God's plan. Zedekiah's attempted heroism resulted in rebellion against God's design for His people.

692-693 (179 words-short last page)

52:1-34 Chapter 52 parallels the account given at the end of 2 Kings (2 Kings 24:20-25:30). Israel, who had badly wanted a king back in the day of Saul (a man known for his stature), ended with a king whose stature did not exceed the walls of Jerusalem within which he was enclosed (586 B.C.). Saul faced a giant (Goliath) and won (through David). Zedekiah faced a giant without God's blessing, and ended up imprisoned, blinded, and dead in a foreign land (52:11). One day the true King would restore them.

52:28 These are the people. The staged deportation represented the Babylonian's systematic conquest. Piece by piece, the nation of Judah was disassembled and taken away.

52:30 twenty-third year. This second deportation was probably a result of the governor Gedaliah's assassination (41:1-3). The numbers likely represent only males. The few Jews left fled to Egypt (ch. 44).

52:31 Jehoiachin. Jehoiachin represented the hope of the people. His release and restoration kindled the exiles' belief in Jeremiah's prophecies of future prosperity. Jehoiachin was treated well until his death.

INTRODUCTION TO
LAMENTATIONS

AUTHOR

Early Jewish and Christian tradition ascribes this anonymous book to Jeremiah. Although this is likely, the evidence for this view is not certain. It is clear, however, that the author was an eyewitness to the fall of Jerusalem and Judah's forced exile to Babylon.

DATE

Lamentations was probably written between 586 B.C. (the fall of Jerusalem) and 516 B.C. (the dedication of the rebuilt temple).

THEME

Grief over Judah's fall and Jerusalem's destruction.

HISTORICAL BACKGROUND

Jerusalem lay under siege by Babylon for 18 months. Outside the city, the Babylonians captured and killed many of the people of Judah. While inside the city, disease and famine claimed many more. Reflecting on these stark days, and then the fall of Jerusalem, Lamentations depicts the incredible grief and loss accompanying the invasion and destruction of Jerusalem—including the temple—and the exile of Judah's residents.

CHARACTERISTICS

Lamentations is a good example of ancient Near Eastern "dirge" poetry that was read aloud at funerals. It is used by Jews praying at the western (wailing) wall, even to this day. The author of this book crafted his theological lessons and channeled his emotions to fit his lament into an "acrostic" poem. (An acrostic poem is one in which the verses each begin with the successive 22 letters of the Hebrew alphabet.) An interesting thematic parallel to Lamentations is the Book of Job (see the introduction page for Job). Job grieves over the calamity that has struck him on a personal level, while the author of Lamentations pours out his grief over the destruction of the city of Jerusalem. Whereas Job has done nothing to deserve his disaster and thus wonders how God can be just, the poet of Lamentations readily confesses that Judah is guilty and that God is just. Lamentations provides a sad "post-mortem" on the prophetic warnings that Judah had repeatedly ignored. Although appalled at the severity of the national destruction, the poet still trusts God. Having confessed the people's sin, the poet desperately hopes that the God who brings grief will also renew mercy (see 3:21-33; 5:21-22). Because of its profound reflection on the problem of suffering, Lamentations, like Job, (which finds no easy answers, but is content to trust God's mercy), has inspired Christian devotion and hymn-writing.

Lament over Jerusalem

א Alef

1 How[a] she sits alone,
the city ⌊once⌋ crowded with people!
She who was great among the nations
has become like a widow.
The princess among the provinces
has become a slave.

ב Bet

2 She weeps aloud during the night,
with tears on her cheeks.
There is no one to offer her comfort,
⌊not one⌋ from all her lovers.[b]
All her friends have betrayed her;
they have become her enemies.

ג Gimel

3 Judah has gone into exile
following[c] affliction and harsh slavery;
she lives among the nations
but finds no place to rest.
All her pursuers have overtaken her
in narrow places.

ד Dalet

4 The roads to Zion mourn,
for no one comes to the appointed festivals.
All her gates are deserted;
her priests groan,
her young women grieve,
and she herself is bitter.

ה He

5 Her adversaries have become ⌊her⌋ masters;
her enemies are at ease,
for the LORD has made her suffer
because of her many transgressions.
Her children have gone away
as captives before the adversary.

ו Vav

6 All her splendor has vanished
from Daughter Zion.
Her leaders are like stags
that find no pasture;
they walk away exhausted
before the hunter.

ז Zayin

7 During the days of her affliction
and homelessness
Jerusalem remembers all
her precious belongings
that were ⌊hers⌋ in days of old.
When her people fell
into the adversary's hand,
she had no one to help.
The adversaries looked at her,
laughing over her downfall.

ח Khet

8 Jerusalem has sinned grievously;
therefore, she has become an object of scorn.[d]
All who honored her ⌊now⌋ despise her,
for they have seen her nakedness.
She herself groans and turns away.

ט Tet

9 Her uncleanness ⌊stains⌋ her skirts.
She never considered her end.
Her downfall was astonishing;
there was no one to comfort her.
LORD, look on my affliction,
for the enemy triumphs!

י Yod

10 The adversary has seized
all her precious belongings.
She has even seen the nations
enter her sanctuary—
those You had forbidden
to enter Your assembly.

כ Kaf

11 All her people groan
while they search for bread.
They have traded their precious belongings
for food
in order to stay alive.
LORD, look and see
how I have become despised.

ל Lamed

12 Is this nothing to you, all you who pass by?
Look and see!
Is there any pain like mine,
which was dealt out to me,

---

[a] **1:1** The stanzas in Lm 1–4 form an •acrostic. [b] **1:2** = Jerusalem's political allies; Jr 22:20–22; Ezk 23 [c] **1:3** Or *because of* [d] **1:8** Or *become impure*

1:1 How she sits alone. Jerusalem has been devastated by Babylon, and this poetic lament beautifully and woefully portrays the tragedy of God's Holy City as deserted and desolate. The first four chapters follow an acrostic pattern; each verse begins with the Hebrew letter that corresponds to A-Z. Chapter 5 is a scrambled alphabet, perhaps symbolizing despair.

1:2 princess. The Hebrew word used here (Sara) is also the name given Abraham's wife and the mother of the nation. As such, it illustrates Jerusalem's preeminence. **from all her lovers.** Such destruction befell Judah as a consequence of the nation's passionate idolatry. Now, in Judah's time of need, her gods proved useless.

1:9 uncleanness. The image is gruesome. Jerusalem is compared to a woman in her time of uncleanness who does not seclude herself or even stem the flow of blood (see Lev. 15:19). Jerusalem was obvious about its idolatry.

which the LORD made ⌊me⌋ suffer
on the day of His burning anger?

מ Mem

13 He sent fire from on high into my bones;
He made it descend.ᵃ
He spread a net for my feet
and turned me back.
He made me desolate,
sick all day long.

נ Nun

14 My transgressions have been formed
   into a yoke,ᵇ ᶜ
fastened together by His hand;
they have been placed on my neck,
and the Lord has broken my strength.
He has handed me over
to those I cannot withstand.

ס Samek

15 The Lord has rejected
all the mighty men within me.
He has summoned an armyᵈ against me
to crush my young warriors.
The Lord has trampled Virgin Daughter Judah
⌊like grapes⌋ in a winepress.

ע Ayin

16 I weep because of these things;
my eyes flowᵉ with tears.
For there is no one nearby to comfort ⌊me⌋,
no one to keep me alive.
My children are desolate
because the enemy has prevailed.

פ Pe

17 Zion stretches out her hands;
there is no one to comfort her.
The LORD has issued a decree against Jacob
that his neighbors should be his adversaries.
Jerusalem has become
something impure among them.

צ Tsade

18 The LORD is in the right,
for I have rebelled against His command.
Listen, all you people;

look at my pain.
My young men and women
have gone into captivity.

ק Qof

19 I called to my lovers,
but they betrayed me.
My priests and elders
perished in the city
while searching for food
to keep themselves alive.

ר Resh

20 LORD, see how I am in distress.
I am churning within;
my heart is broken,ᶠ
for I have been very rebellious.
Outside, the sword takes the children;
inside, there is death.

ש Shin

21 People have heard me groaning,
but there is no one to comfort me.
All my enemies have heard of my misfortune;
they are glad that You have caused ⌊it⌋.
Bring on the day You have announced,
so that they may become like me.

ת Tav

22 Let all their wickedness come before You,
and deal with them
as You have dealt with me
because of all my transgressions.
For my groans are many,
and I am sick at heart.

Judgment on Jerusalem

א Alef

2 How the Lord has overshadowed
Daughter Zion with His anger!
He has thrown down Israel's glory
from heaven to earth.
He has abandoned His footstoolᵍ
in the day of His anger.

ב Bet

2 Without compassion the Lord has swallowed up
all the dwellings of Jacob.

ᵃ**1:13** DSS, LXX; MT reads *bones, and it prevailed against them*   ᵇ**1:14** Some Hb mss, LXX read *He kept watch over my transgressions*   ᶜ**1:14** Or *The yoke of my transgressions is bound*; Hb obscure   ᵈ**1:15** Or *has announced an appointed time*   ᵉ**1:16** Lit *my eye, my eye flows*   ᶠ**1:20** Lit *is turned within me*   ᵍ**2:1** Either the ark of the covenant or the temple

---

1:16-17 No one ... to comfort. A frequent refrain (see also vv. 2, 9, 21) in chapter one, hope actually exists (Isa. 40:1-2). Yet in the near-context, it would appear that the possibility of such consolation is beyond possibility (2:13, Jer. 19:10-11). This is also true of tragedy in our own lives, when God's purposes initially appear inscrutable. Even when God harshly disciplines us, there is yet hope. God meant to purify his people, and exile accomplished it well.

1:20 Outside ... inside, there is death. Judah was in a no-win situation. For 18 months, the city was under Nebuchadnezzar's attack. Certain death awaited any escapees, while starvation stifled those within the city walls.

1:21 day You have announced. The author selfishly wished their Babylonian captor would share Judah's same fate—that God's judgment would be severe (Jer. 25:15-38). He understood the impartiality of

In His wrath He has demolished
the fortified cities of Daughter Judah.
He brought ⌊them⌋ to the ground
and defiled the kingdom and its leaders.

ג Gimel

3 He has cut off every •horn of Israel
in His burning anger
and withdrawn His right hand
in the presence of the enemy.
He has blazed against Jacob like a flaming fire
that consumes everything ⌊in its path⌋.

ד Dalet

4 Like an enemy He has bent His bow;
His right hand is positioned like an adversary.
He has killed everyone who was loved,[a]
pouring out His wrath like fire
on the tent of Daughter Zion.

ה He

5 The Lord is like an enemy;
He has swallowed up Israel.
He swallowed up all its palaces
and destroyed its fortified cities.
He has multiplied mourning and lamentation
within Daughter Judah.

ו Vav

6 He has done violence to His temple[b]
as if ⌊it were⌋ a garden ⌊booth⌋,
destroying His place of meeting.
The LORD has abolished
appointed festivals and Sabbaths in Zion.
He has despised king and priest
in His fierce anger.

ז Zayin

7 The Lord has rejected His altar,
repudiated His sanctuary;
He has handed the walls of her palaces
over to the enemy.
They have raised a shout in the house
of the LORD
as on the day of an appointed festival.

ח Khet

8 The LORD determined to destroy
the wall of Daughter Zion.

He stretched out a measuring line
and did not restrain Himself from destroying.
He made the ramparts and walls grieve;
together they waste away.

ט Tet

9 Zion's gates have fallen to the ground;
He has destroyed and shattered the bars
on her ⌊gates⌋.
Her king and her leaders ⌊live⌋ among the nations,
instruction[c] is no more,
and even her prophets receive
no vision from the LORD.

י Yod

10 The elders of Daughter Zion
sit on the ground in silence.
They have thrown dust on their heads
and put on •sackcloth.
The young women of Jerusalem
have bowed their heads to the ground.

כ Kaf

11 My eyes are worn out from weeping;
I am churning within.
My heart is poured out in grief[d]
because of the destruction of my dear people,
because children and infants faint
in the streets of the city.

ל Lamed

12 They cry out to their mothers:
Where is the grain and wine?
as they faint like the wounded
in the streets of the city,
as their lives fade away
in the arms of their mothers.

מ Mem

13 What can I say on your behalf?
To what can I compare you, Daughter Jerusalem?
What can I liken you to,
so that I may console you, Virgin Daughter Zion?
For your ruin is as vast as the sea.
Who can heal you?

נ Nun

14 Your prophets saw visions for you
that were empty and deceptive;

---

[a] **2:4** Lit killed all the delights of the eye; Ezk 24:16   [b] **2:6** Lit booth   [c] **2:9** Or the law   [d] **2:11** Lit My liver is poured out on the ground

divine retribution for disobedience.
2:6 violence to His temple. Judah recognized the temple as a sign of God's presence among them. Their spiritual indifference resulted in its destruction. **LORD has abolished appointed festivals.** The festivals of Leviticus 23 were signs of great joy that God had removed.

2:7 raised a shout. The pilfering pagans struck the author with sadness. Their irreverent and mocking shouts of victory in the temple added insult to injury.

2:9 prophets receive no vision from the LORD. God stopped sending the people warning or hope through the prophets. The only

message left for Judah was that of mass destruction. However, during the Exile, God would continue to encourage his people through the prophet Daniel.

2:14 empty and misleading. A true prophet, like Jeremiah, spoke only God's message. False prophets encouraged the kind of cove-

they did not reveal your guilt
and so restore your fortunes.
They saw •oracles for you
that were empty and misleading.

ס Samek

15 All who pass by
⌊scornfully⌋ clap their hands at you.
They hiss and shake their heads
at Daughter Jerusalem:
Is this the city that was called
the perfection of beauty,
the joy of the whole earth?

פ Pe

16 All your enemies
open their mouths against you.
They hiss and gnash ⌊their⌋ teeth,
saying, "We have swallowed ⌊her⌋ up.
This is the day we have waited for!
We have lived to see ⌊it⌋."

ע Ayin

17 The LORD has done what He planned;
He has accomplished His decree,
which He ordained in days of old.
He has demolished without compassion,
letting the enemy gloat over you
and exalting the horn of your adversaries.

צ Tsade

18 The hearts of the people cry out
to the Lord.
Wall of Daughter Zion,
let ⌊your⌋ tears run down like a river
day and night.
Give yourself no relief
and your[a] eyes no rest.

ק Qof

19 Arise, cry out in the night,
from the first watch of the night.
Pour out your heart like water
before the Lord's presence.
Lift up your hands to Him
for the lives of your children
who are fainting from hunger
on the corner of every street.

ר Resh

20 LORD, look and consider
who You have done this to.
Should women eat their own children,
the infants they have nurtured?[b]
Should priests and prophets
be killed in the Lord's sanctuary?

ש Shin

21 ⌊Both⌋ young and old
are lying on the ground in the streets.
My young men and women
have fallen by the sword.
You have killed ⌊them⌋ in the day of Your anger,
slaughtering without compassion.

ת Tav

22 You summoned my attackers[c] on every side,
as if ⌊for⌋ an appointed festival day;
on the day of the LORD's anger
no one escaped or survived.
My enemy has destroyed
those I nurtured[d] and reared.

Hope through God's Mercy

א Alef

3 I am the man who has seen affliction
under the rod of God's wrath.
2 He has driven me away and forced ⌊me⌋ to walk
in darkness instead of light.
3 Yes, He repeatedly turns His hand
against me all day long.

ב Bet

4 He has worn away my flesh and skin;
He has shattered my bones.
5 He has laid siege against me,
encircling me with bitterness and hardship.
6 He has made me dwell in darkness
like those who have been dead for ages.

ג Gimel

7 He has walled me in so I cannot escape;
He has weighed me down with chains.
8 Even when I cry out and plead for help,
He rejects my prayer.
9 He has walled in my ways with cut stones;
He has made my paths crooked.

---

a **2:18** Lit *and the daughter of your*   b **2:20** Or *infants in a healthy condition*; Hb obscure   c **2:22** Or *terrors*   d **2:22** Or *I bore healthy*; Hb obscure

---

nantal disobedience that Scripture calls spiritual adultery (Jer. 2-6; Ezek. 16, 20, 23; Hosea 1-3).
2:15 clap ... hiss ... shake. "The perfection of beauty" (Ps. 50:2; Ezek. 27:3; 28:12) and "the joy of the whole earth" (Ps. 48:2) that was Jerusalem was now laid waste. They "clap their hands" utilizes the same words used to describe the hostile scorn that God places on the wicked (Job 27:23). Similarly "hiss" (1 Kings 9:8; Job 27:23; Jer. 19:8), and "shake their heads" also implies scornful derision (Job 16:4; Pss. 22:7; 109:25; Isa. 37:22). Such may have been the case with Edom, Israel's archival since the days of Exodus. Edom is said to have aided Babylon against Jerusalem in 586 B.C., and even exploited Judah to its own benefit (4:21; Ps. 137:7; Jer. 49:7-22; Ezek. 25:12-14; Obad.).There's nothing worse than being laughed at while in misery (Jer. 18:18-23).

ד Dalet

10 He is[a] a bear waiting in ambush,
a lion in hiding;

11 He forced me off my way and tore me to pieces;
He left me desolate.

12 He bent His bow
and set me as the target for His arrow.

ה He

13 He pierced my kidneys
with His arrows.

14 I am a laughingstock to all my people,[b]
mocked by their songs all day long.

15 He filled me with bitterness,
sated me with •wormwood.

ו Vav

16 He ground my teeth on gravel
and made me cower[c] in the dust.

17 My soul has been deprived[d] of peace;
I have forgotten what happiness is.

18 Then I thought: My future[e] is lost,
as well as my hope from the LORD.

ז Zayin

19 Remember[f] my affliction and my homelessness,
the wormwood and the poison.

20 I continually remember ⌊them⌋
and have become depressed.[g]

21 Yet I call this to mind,
and therefore I have hope:

ח Khet

22 ⌊Because of⌋ the LORD's faithful love
we do not perish,[h]
for His mercies never end.

23 They are new every morning;
great is Your faithfulness!

24 I say: The LORD is my portion,
therefore I will put my hope in Him.

ט Tet

25 The LORD is good to those who wait for Him,
to the person who seeks Him.

26 It is good to wait quietly
for deliverance from the LORD.

27 It is good for a man to bear the yoke
while he is ⌊still⌋ young.

י Yod

28 Let him sit alone and be silent,
for God has disciplined him.

29 Let him put his mouth in the dust—
perhaps there is ⌊still⌋ hope.

30 Let him offer ⌊his⌋ cheek
to the one who would strike him;
let him be filled with shame.

כ Kaf

31 For the Lord
will not reject ⌊us⌋ forever.

32 Even if He causes suffering,
He will show compassion
according to His abundant, faithful love.

33 For He does not enjoy bringing affliction
or suffering on •mankind.

ל Lamed

34 Crushing all the prisoners of the land[i]
beneath one's feet,

35 denying justice to a man
in the presence of the •Most High,

36 or suppressing a person's lawsuit—
the Lord does not approve ⌊of these things⌋.

מ Mem

37 Who is there who speaks and it happens,
unless the Lord has ordained ⌊it⌋?

38 Do not both adversity and good
come from the mouth of the Most High?

39 Why should ⌊any⌋ living person complain,
⌊any⌋ man, because of the punishment
for his sins?

נ Nun

40 Let us search out and examine our ways,
and turn back to the LORD.

41 Let us lift up our hearts and ⌊our⌋ hands
to God in heaven:

42 We have sinned and rebelled;
You have not forgiven.

ס Samek

43 You have covered Yourself in anger
and pursued us;
You have killed without compassion.

44 You have covered Yourself with a cloud

---

[a]3:10 Lit is to me [b]3:14 Some Hb mss, LXX, Vg; other Hb mss, Syr read all peoples [c]3:16 Or and trampled me [d]3:17 Syr, Vg; MT reads You deprived my soul [e]3:18 Or splendor [f]3:19 Or I remember [g]3:20 Alt Hb tradition reads and You cause me to collapse [h]3:22 One Hb mss, Syr, Tg read The LORD's faithful love, indeed, does not perish [i]3:34 Or earth

---

2:19 Pour out your heart like water. The image pictures a full confession here (Ps. 62:8).

3:15 bitterness … wormwood. The pungent taste of punishment plagued the nation of Judah (Jer. 9:15). Even food, their source for life, was bitterly unsatisfying. At Passover, bitter herbs such as these remind of hardship.

3:23 new every morning; great is Your faithfulness. The basis of a popular hymn, this verse beautifully describes the kindness of God even in judgment.

3:24 portion. With nothing but rubble to call their own, Judah's only valuable belonging was God (Num. 18:20). **I will put my hope in Him.** No hope for a second wind. No will for fighting back. There was nothing else Judah could do but wait on God.

3:27 bear the yoke The author realized this overbearing trial (v. 1) might turn out for their good.

3:36 suppressing a person's lawsuit. The

so that no prayer can pass through.
45 You have made us disgusting filth
among the peoples.

פ Pe

46 All our enemies
open their mouths against us.
47 We have experienced panic and pitfall,
devastation and destruction.
48 My eyes flow with streams of tears
because of the destruction of my dear people.

ע Ayin

49 My eyes overflow unceasingly,
without end,
50 until the LORD looks down
from heaven and sees.
51 My eyes bring me grief
because of [the fate of] all the women in my city.

צ Tsade

52 For no [apparent] reason, my enemies[a]
hunted me like a bird.
53 They dropped me alive into[b] a pit
and threw stones at me.
54 Water flooded over my head,
and I thought: I'm going to die!

ק Qof

55 I called on Your name, •Yahweh,
from the depths of the •Pit.
56 You hear my plea:
Do not ignore my cry for relief.
57 You come near when I call on You;
You say: "Do not be afraid."

ר Resh

58 You defend my cause, Lord;
You redeem my life.
59 LORD, You see the wrong done to me;
judge my case.
60 You see all their malice,
all their plots against me.

ש Sin/ ש Shin

61 LORD, You hear their insults,
all their plots against me.
62 The slander[c] and murmuring of my opponents
attack me all day long.

63 When they sit and when they rise, look,
I am mocked by their songs.

ת Tav

64 You will pay them back
what they deserve, LORD,
according to the work of their hands.
65 You will give them a heart filled with anguish.[d]
May Your curse be on them!
66 You will pursue [them] in anger and destroy them
under Your heavens.[e] [f]

Terrors of the Besieged City

א Alef

4 How the gold has become tarnished,
the fine gold become dull!
The stones of the temple[g] lie scattered
at the corner of every street.

ב Bet

2 Zion's precious people—
[once] worth their weight in pure gold—
how they are regarded as clay jars,
the work of a potter's hands!

ג Gimel

3 Even jackals offer [their] breasts
to nurse their young,
but my dear people have become cruel
like ostriches in the wilderness.

ד Dalet

4 The nursing infant's tongue
clings to the roof of his mouth from thirst.
Little children beg for bread,
but no one gives them [any].

ה He

5 Those who used to eat delicacies
are destitute in the streets;
those who were reared in purple [garments]
huddle in garbage heaps.

ו Vav

6 The punishment of my dear people
is greater than that of Sodom,
which was overthrown in an instant
without a hand laid on it.

---

[a]3:52 Or Those who were my enemies for no reason   [b]3:53 Or They ended my life in; Hb obscure   [c]3:62 Lit lips   [d]3:65 Or them an obstinate heart; Hb obscure   [e]3:66 LXX, Syr, Vg read heavens, LORD   [f]3:66 Lit under the LORD's heavens   [g]4:1 Or The sacred gems

---

author built a case for God's compassion through rhetorical questions. Judah could hardly call her situation unjust.

3:46-47 Verse 46 repeats the thought of 2:16. Verse 47 summarizes the destruction that had devastated Jerusalem (Isa 24:17-18; Jer 48:43-44).

3:57 when I call on You. Jeremiah looks back to his personal experience and gives testimony to God's faithfulness. Crisis is met with compassion. God is real to those He loves (Ps. 145:18).

3:63 I am mocked. In dire straits, Judah was the joke of many nations (vv. 46-47).

Where was Judah's God now?

4:1 fine gold become dull! Jerusalem was a tragic before-and-after comparison. Before their calamity, the people were priceless. Now, sin devalued them (v. 2). The Temple valuables are gone and even the people, the greater treasure, are now almost worthless (v. 2).

ז Zayin

7 Her dignitaries were brighter than snow,
whiter than milk;
⌊their⌋ bodiesª were more ruddy than coral,
their appearance ⌊like⌋ sapphire.ᵇ

ח Khet

8 ⌊Now⌋ they appear darker than soot;
they are not recognized in the streets.
Their skin has shriveled on their bones;
it has become dry like wood.

ט Tet

9 Those slain by the sword are better off
than those slain by hunger,
who waste away, pierced ⌊with pain⌋
because the fields lack produce.

י Yod

10 The hands of compassionate women
have cooked their own children;
they became their food
during the destruction of my dear people.

כ Kaf

11 The LORD has exhausted His wrath,
poured out His burning anger;
He has ignited a fire in Zion,
and it has consumed her foundations.

ל Lamed

12 The kings of the earth
and all the world's inhabitants
    did not believe
that an enemy or adversary
could enter Jerusalem's gates.

מ Mem

13 ⌊Yet it happened⌋ because of the sins
    of her prophets
and the guilt of her priests,
who shed the blood of the righteous
within her.

נ Nun

14 Blind, they stumbled in the streets,
defiled by this blood,
so that no one dared
to touch their garments.

ס Samek

15 "Stay away! Unclean!" people shouted at them.
"Away, away! Don't touch ⌊us⌋!"
So they wandered aimlessly.
It was said among the nations,
"They can stay here no longer."

פ Pe

16 The LORD Himself has scattered them;
He regards them no more.
The priests are not respected;
the elders find no favor.

ע Ayin

17 All the while our eyes were failing
⌊as we looked⌋ in vain for assistance;
we watched from our towers
for a nationᶜ that refused to help.

צ Tsade

18 Our steps were closely followed,
so that we could not walk in our streets.
Our end drew near; our time ran out.
Our end had come!

ק Qof

19 Those who chased us were swifter
than eagles in the sky;
they relentlessly pursued us over the mountains
and ambushed us in the wilderness.

ר Resh

20 The LORD's anointed,ᵈ the breath of our life,ᵉ
was captured in their traps;
we had said about him:
We will live under his protection
    among the nations.

ש Sin

21 So rejoice and be glad, Daughter Edom,
you resident of the land of Uz!
Yet the cup will pass to you as well;
you will get drunk and expose yourself.

ת Tav

22 Daughter Zion, your punishment is complete;
He will not lengthen your exile.ᶠ
But He will punish your iniquity, Daughter Edom,
and will expose your sins.

ª **4:7** Lit bones ᵇ **4:7** Or lapis lazuli ᶜ **4:17** Probably Egypt ᵈ **4:20** = King Zedekiah; 2 Kg 25:7 ᵉ **4:20** Lit nostrils ᶠ **4:22** Or not deport you again

---

4:6 Sodom … overthrown in an instant. God's punishment on Sodom, although equally thorough, was mercifully quick (Gen. 19:24-29). By contrast, Jerusalem's painful siege went on month after month.

4:10 cooked their own children. The Israel-ites fulfill the curse of eating their own children

as a result of disobedience to the Lord and breaking His covenant (Lev. 26:29; Deut. 28:53-57). It is also reminiscent of cannibalism during the siege of Samaria in Elisha's time (2 Kings 6:28-29).

4:17 a nation that refused to help. Egypt proved to be an impotent ally against God's

plan to use Babylon against Jerusalem.

4:21 Daughter Edom. The poet mocks Edom in return (see note on 2:15), telling them to en-joy it while it lasts, because it won't last long. She will endure the same kind of humiliation that Jerusalem endured.

4:22 Daughter Zion, your punishment is

Prayer for Restoration

5 •Yahweh, remember what has happened to us.
Look, and see our disgrace!

2 Our inheritance has been turned over
to strangers,
our houses to foreigners.

3 We have become orphans, fatherless;
our mothers are widows.

4 We must pay for the water we drink;
our wood comes at a price.

5 We are closely pursued;
we are tired, and no one offers us rest.

6 We made a treaty with[a] Egypt
and with Assyria, to get enough food.

7 Our fathers sinned; they no longer exist,
but we bear their punishment.

8 Slaves rule over us;
no one rescues ⌊us⌋ from their hands.

9 We secure our food at the risk of our lives
because of the sword in the wilderness.

10 Our skin is as hot[b] as an oven
from the ravages of hunger.

11 Women are raped in Zion,
virgins in the cities of Judah.

12 Princes are hung up by their hands;
elders are shown no respect.

13 Young men labor at millstones;
boys stumble under ⌊loads of⌋ wood.

14 The elders have left the city •gate,
the young men, their music.

15 Joy has left our hearts;
our dancing has turned to mourning.

16 The crown has fallen from our head.
Woe to us, for we have sinned.

17 Because of this, our heart is sick;
because of these, our eyes grow dim:

18 because of Mount Zion, which lies desolate
⌊and has⌋ jackals prowling in it.

19 You, LORD, are enthroned forever;
Your throne endures from generation
to generation.

20 Why have You forgotten us forever,
abandoned us for ⌊our⌋ entire lives?

21 LORD, restore us to Yourself, so we may return;
renew our days as in former times,

22 unless You have completely rejected us
and are intensely angry with us.

---

a5:6 Lit We gave the hand to b5:10 Or black; Hb obscure

---

complete. In the end, Judah's sole hope was in God's covenant with His people (Gen. 12:2-3; Deut. 28-30) and His assurance of a new covenant (Jer. 31:31). Because of God's promises, the nation would be restored.

5:1 Yahweh remember. The people failed to remember their obligations as covenant people, and God failed to remember them (1:9; 2:1). In 3:19, the poet asked Yahweh to remember him. Here he emphatically begs Yahweh to remember His people.

5:7 punishment. The people of Judah realized their present condition was the result of years of sin. Their heritage was one of pain and disobedience.

5:16 crown has fallen. Jerusalem's royal destiny was displaced by rebellion. Thus, the golden city was ruined.

5:19 enthroned forever. Despite the destruc-tion of God's throne room in the temple, the Lord still reigned as everlasting king.

5:20 forgotten. For the last time, the poet asks God why He has abandoned them.

5:22 completely rejected. The author feared the one thing God would never do (Jer. 31:37; Rom. 11:2). Despite Judah's rebellious streak, God would never abandon them completely. He was always near (Ps. 145:18).

INTRODUCTION TO
EZEKIEL

PERSONAL READING PLAN

- ❏ Ezekiel 1:1-3:15
- ❏ Ezekiel 3:16-5:17
- ❏ Ezekiel 6:1-8:18
- ❏ Ezekiel 9:1-11:25
- ❏ Ezekiel 12:1-13:23
- ❏ Ezekiel 14:1-15:8
- ❏ Ezekiel 16:1-63
- ❏ Ezekiel 17:1-18:32
- ❏ Ezekiel 19:1-20:49
- ❏ Ezekiel 21:1-22:31
- ❏ Ezekiel 23:1-49
- ❏ Ezekiel 24:1-25:17

- ❏ Ezekiel 26:1-27:36
- ❏ Ezekiel 28:1-29:21
- ❏ Ezekiel 30:1-31:18
- ❏ Ezekiel 32:1-33:33
- ❏ Ezekiel 34:1-35:15
- ❏ Ezekiel 36:1-37:14
- ❏ Ezekiel 37:15-39:29
- ❏ Ezekiel 40:1-47
- ❏ Ezekiel 40:48-42:20
- ❏ Ezekiel 43:1-44:31
- ❏ Ezekiel 45:1-46:24
- ❏ Ezekiel 47:1-48:35

AUTHOR

The writer was Ezekiel, a Jewish priest and prophet, exiled in Babylon. He was a man of broad knowledge, not only of his own traditions but also of international affairs and history.

DATE

Ezekiel's prophecies can be dated with precision, more easily than any other prophet. His first dates from 593 B.C., seven years before the fall of Jerusalem and his last dates from 571 B.C. The Book of Ezekiel contains more dates than any other Old Testament prophetic book. In addition, archaeologists (from Babylonian records) and astronomers (from accurate dating of eclipses referred to in ancient archives), provide precise modern calendar equivalents.

THEME

God acts in the events of human history so that everyone may come to know Him and find new life.

HISTORICAL BACKGROUND

Like his contemporary, Jeremiah, Ezekiel prophesied in politically volatile times. After Israel was destroyed by the Assyrians in 722 B.C., only the southern kingdom of Judah was left. Assyria

lost its domination in 612 B.C. and was replaced as a world power by Babylon. Judah was a subservient state of Babylon, but rebelled, hoping for Egypt's support. Egypt proved unreliable, and Judah was subdued by King Nebuchadnezzar of Babylon in 605 and again in 598-597 B.C. He took thousands of Jews captive each time; Ezekiel was among those in the second wave of exiles.

CHARACTERISTICS

Ezekiel is a book of heavenly visions, poems, parables, and dramatically acted-out prophetic symbolism. However, to get the people's attention, God uses more than Ezekiel's vivid images and symbolic actions. He allows the people to suffer. Fortunately, Ezekiel's message of imminent doom turns to ultimate hope in the end. There is symmetry in the book with (1) the vision of the desecrated temple balanced by that of the restored temple, (2) the message of God's anger balanced by the truth of God's mercy, and (3) the appointment of Ezekiel as a watchman of judgment balanced by his role as a watchman of consolation. In writing to the Jews in exile, Ezekiel communicated that the God of Israel was God *even* in idolatrous Babylon. Ezekiel warned the people that their own idolatry would be judged, and offered them the encouragement that the Lord would return them to their homeland.

1 In the thirtieth year, in the fourth ⌊month⌋, on the fifth ⌊day⌋ of the month, while I was among the exiles by the Chebar Canal, the heavens opened and I saw visions of God. 2 On the fifth ⌊day⌋ of the month— it was the fifth year of King Jehoiachin's exile— 3 the word of the LORD came directly to Ezekiel the priest, the son of Buzi, in the land of the Chaldeans by the Chebar Canal. And the LORD's hand was on him there.

Vision of the LORD's Glory

4 I looked and there was a whirlwind coming from the north, a great cloud with fire flashing back and forth and brilliant light all around it. In the center of the fire, there was a gleam like amber. 5 The form of four living creatures came from it. And this was their appearance: They had human form, 6 but each of them had four faces and four wings. 7 Their legs were straight, and the soles of their feet were like the hooves of a calf, sparkling like the gleam of polished bronze. 8 ⌊They had⌋ human hands under their wings on their four sides. All four of them had faces and wings. 9 Their wings were touching. The creatures did not turn as they moved; each one went straight ahead. 10 The form of ⌊each of⌋ their faces was that of a man, and each of the four had the face of a lion on the right, the face of an ox on the left, and the face of an eagle. 11 ⌊That is what⌋ their faces ⌊were like⌋. Their wings were spread upward; each had two ⌊wings⌋ touching that of another and two wings covering its body. 12 Each creature went straight ahead. Wherever the Spirit[a] wanted to go, they went without turning as they moved.

13 The form of the living creatures was like the appearance of burning coals of fire and torches. Fire was moving back and forth between the living creatures; it was bright, with lightning coming out of it. 14 The creatures were darting back and forth like flashes of lightning.

15 When I looked at the living creatures, there was one wheel on the ground beside each creature that had four faces. 16 The appearance of the wheels and their craftsmanship was like the gleam of beryl, and all four had the same form. Their appearance and craftsmanship was like a wheel within a wheel. 17 When they moved, they went in any of the four directions, without pivoting as they moved. 18 Their rims were large and frightening. Each of their four rims were full of eyes all around. 19 So when the living creatures moved, the wheels moved beside them, and when the creatures rose from the earth, the wheels also rose. 20 Wherever the Spirit[a] wanted to go, the creatures went in the

direction the Spirit was moving. The wheels rose alongside them, for the spirit of the living creatures was in the wheels. 21 When the creatures moved, the wheels moved; when the creatures stood still, the wheels stood still; and when the creatures rose from the earth, the wheels rose alongside them, for the spirit of the living creatures was in the wheels.

22 The shape of an expanse, with a gleam like awe-inspiring crystal, was spread out over the heads of the living creatures. 23 And under the expanse their wings extended one toward another. Each of them also had two wings covering their bodies. 24 When they moved, I heard the sound of their wings like the roar of mighty waters, like the voice of the •Almighty, and a sound of commotion like the noise of an army. When they stood still, they lowered their wings.

25 A voice came from above the expanse over their heads; when they stood still, they lowered their wings. 26 The shape of a throne with the appearance of sapphire[b] stone was above the expanse.[c] There was a form with the appearance of a human on the throne high above. 27 From what seemed to be His waist up, I saw a gleam like amber, with what looked like fire enclosing it all around. From what seemed to be His waist down, I also saw what looked like fire. There was a brilliant light all around Him. 28 The appearance of the brilliant light all around was like that of a rainbow in a cloud on a rainy day. This was the appearance of the form of the LORD's glory. When I saw ⌊it⌋, I fell facedown and heard a voice speaking.

Mission to Rebellious Israel

2 He said to me, "Son of man, stand up on your feet and I will speak with you." 2 As He spoke to me, the Spirit entered me and set me on my feet, and I listened to the One who was speaking to me. 3 He said to me: "Son of man, I am sending you to the Israelites ⌊and⌋ to the rebellious nations[d] who have rebelled against Me. The Israelites and their ancestors have transgressed against Me to this day. 4 The children are obstinate[e] and hardhearted. I am sending you to them, and you must say to them: This is what the Lord GOD says. 5 Whether they listen or refuse ⌊to listen⌋—for they are a rebellious house—they will know that a prophet has been among them.

6 "But you, son of man, do not be afraid of them or their words, though briers and thorns are beside you and you live among scorpions. Don't be afraid of their words or be discouraged by ⌊the look on⌋ their faces, for they are a rebellious house. 7 But speak My words to

---

[a] 1:12,20 Or spirit   [b] 1:26 Or lapis lazuli   [c] 1:26 Lit expanse that was over their head   [d] 2:3 LXX omits to the rebellious nations   [e] 2:4 Lit hard of face

---

1:1 thirtieth year. Ezekiel celebrated his thirtieth birthday, which ordinarily would have marked the beginning of his priesthood (see Num. 4:3), in Babylonian exile.

1:2 fifth year of King Jehoiachin's exile. In 597 B.C., the Babylonians captured Jehoiachin, Ezekiel, and many other Jews. Ezekiel's pro-

phetic role began in the fifth year of their exile.

1:5-6 four living creatures ... and four wings. They are identified as cherubim—special angelic beings (ch. 10).

1:12 the Spirit. The chariot-throne (God's Spirit) moves wherever God wants. Ezekiel is communicating to the exiles that God is

not limited to Israel.

2:1 Son of man. Expression used in these ways: (1) as a poetic synonym for "man" or "human," as in Pss. 8:4 and 80:17; (2) in Ezekiel as the title by which God regularly addresses the prophet (2:1,3; 3:1,3); and (3) in Dan. 7 as the identity of the glorious person whom the

them whether they listen or refuse ⌊to listen⌋, for they are rebellious.

8 "And you, son of man, listen to what I tell you: Do not be rebellious like that rebellious house. Open your mouth and eat what I am giving you." 9 So I looked and saw a hand reaching out to me, and there was a written scroll in it. 10 When He unrolled it before me, it was written on the front and back; ⌊words of⌋ lamentation, mourning, and woe were written on it.

3 He said to me: "Son of man, eat what you find ⌊here⌋. Eat this scroll, then go and speak to the house of Israel." 2 So I opened my mouth, and He fed me the scroll. 3 "Son of man," he said to me, "eat[a] and fill your stomach with this scroll I am giving you." So I ate ⌊it⌋, and it was as sweet as honey in my mouth.

4 Then He said to me: "Son of man, go to the house of Israel and speak My words to them. 5 For you are not being sent to a people of unintelligible speech or difficult language but to the house of Israel. 6 ⌊You are⌋ not ⌊being sent⌋ to many peoples of unintelligible speech or difficult language, whose words you cannot understand. No doubt, if I sent you to them, they would listen to you. 7 But the house of Israel will not want to listen to you because they do not want to listen to Me. For the whole house of Israel is hardheaded and hardhearted. 8 Look, I have made your face as hard as their faces and your forehead as hard as their foreheads. 9 I have made your forehead like a diamond, harder than flint. Don't be afraid of them or discouraged by ⌊the look on⌋ their faces, even though they are a rebellious house."

10 Next He said to me: "Son of man, listen carefully to all My words that I speak to you and take ⌊them⌋ to heart. 11 Go to your people, the exiles, and speak to them. Tell them: This is what the Lord GOD says, whether they listen or refuse ⌊to listen⌋."

12 The Spirit then lifted me up, and I heard a great rumbling sound behind me—praise the glory of the LORD in His place!— 13 with the[b] sound of the living creatures' wings brushing against each other and the sound of the wheels beside them, a great rumbling sound. 14 So the Spirit lifted me up and took me away. I left in bitterness and in an angry spirit, and the LORD's hand was on me powerfully. 15 I came to the exiles at Tel-abib, who were living by the Chebar Canal, and I sat there stunned for seven days.

Ezekiel as a Watchman

16 Now at the end of seven days the word of the LORD came to me: 17 "Son of man, I have made you a watchman over the house of Israel. When you hear a word

from My mouth, give them a warning from Me. 18 If I say to the wicked person: You will surely die, but you do not warn him—you don't speak out to warn him about his wicked way in order to save his life—that wicked person will die for his iniquity. Yet I will hold you responsible for his blood. 19 But if you warn a wicked person and he does not turn from his wickedness or his wicked way, he will die for his iniquity, but you will have saved your life. 20 Now if a righteous person turns from his righteousness and practices iniquity, and I put a stumbling block in front of him, he will die. If you did not warn him, he will die because of his sin and the righteous acts he did will not be remembered. Yet I will hold you responsible for his blood. 21 But if you warn the righteous person that he should not sin, and he does not sin, he will indeed live because he listened to ⌊your⌋ warning, and you will have saved your life."

22 Then the hand of the LORD was on me there, and He said to me, "Get up, go out to the plain, and I will speak with you there." 23 So I got up and went out to the plain. The LORD's glory was present there, like the glory I had seen by the Chebar Canal, and I fell facedown. 24 The Spirit entered me and set me on my feet. He spoke with me and said: "Go, shut yourself inside your house. 25 And you, son of man, they will put ropes on you and bind you with them so you cannot go out among them. 26 I will make your tongue stick to the roof of your mouth, and you will be mute and unable to rebuke them, for they are a rebellious house. 27 But when I speak with you, I will open your mouth, and you will say to them: This is what the Lord GOD says. Let the one who listens, listen, and let the one who refuses, refuse—for they are a rebellious house.

Jerusalem's Siege Dramatized

4 "Now you, son of man, take a brick, set it in front of you, and draw the city of Jerusalem on it. 2 Then lay siege against it: construct a siege wall, build a ramp, pitch military camps, and place battering rams against it on all sides. 3 Take an iron plate and set it up as an iron wall between yourself and the city. Turn your face toward it so that it is under siege, and besiege it. This will be a sign for the house of Israel.

4 "Then lie down on your left side and place the iniquity[c] of the house of Israel on it. You will bear their iniquity for the number of days you lie on your side. 5 For I have assigned you the years of their iniquity according to the number of days ⌊you lie down⌋, 390 days; so you will bear the iniquity of the house of Israel. 6 When you

---

a3:3 Lit feed your belly b3:12–13 Some emend to behind me as the glory of the LORD rose from His place: 13 the c4:4 Or punishment

---

prophet sees coming with the clouds of heaven to approach the Ancient of Days. "The Son of Man" is a designation of Christ found frequently in the NT.

3:9 forehead … diamond. The forehead represented a person's determination or stubbornness (see Isa. 48:4). Ezekiel needed to

toughen up in order to deliver bad news to an unreceptive people.

3:11 whether they listen or refuse [to listen]. A prophet's success was not in a receptive hearing, but a faithful delivery of God's message.

3:17 a watchman. Ezekiel was like one positioned on the city walls to warn of impending physical danger.

4:5 you will bear the iniquity. Ezekiel was commanded to lie down for 430 days as a word-picture of Judah and Israel's guilt, which corresponded to the 430 years of Israel's bondage in Egypt (see Ex. 12:41).

have completed these days, lie down again, but on your right side, and bear the iniquity of the house of Judah. I have assigned you 40 days, a day for each year. 7 You must turn your face toward the siege of Jerusalem with your arm bared, and prophesy against it. 8 Be aware that I will put cords on you so you cannot turn from side to side until you have finished the days of your siege.

9 "Also take wheat, barley, beans, lentils, millet, and spelt. Put them in a single container and make them into bread for yourself. You are to eat it during the number of days you lie on your side, 390 days. 10 The food you eat each day will be eight ounces[a] by weight; you will eat it from time to time.[b] 11 You are also to drink water by measure, one-sixth of a gallon,[c] ⌊which⌋ you will drink from time to time. 12 You will eat it as ⌊you would⌋ a barley cake and bake it over dried human excrement in their sight." 13 The LORD said, "This is how the Israelites will eat their bread—ceremonially unclean—among the nations where I will banish them."

14 But I said, "Ah, Lord GOD, I have never been defiled. From my youth until now I have not eaten anything that died naturally or was mauled by wild beasts. And impure meat has never entered my mouth."

15 He replied to me, "Look, I will let you ⌊use⌋ cow dung instead of human excrement, and you can make your bread over that." 16 Then He said to me, "Son of man, I am going to cut off the supply of bread in Jerusalem. They will anxiously eat bread ⌊rationed⌋ by weight and in dread drink water by measure. 17 So they will lack bread and water; everyone will be devastated and waste away because of their iniquity.

Ezekiel Dramatizes Jerusalem's Fall

5 "Now you, son of man, take a sharp sword, use it as you would a barber's razor, and shave your head and beard. Then take a pair of scales and divide the hair. 2 You are to burn up one third ⌊of it⌋ in the city when the days of the siege have ended; you are to take one third and slash ⌊it⌋ with the sword all around the city; and you are to scatter one third to the wind, for I will draw a sword ⌊to chase⌋ after them. 3 But you are to take a few strands from the hair and secure them in the folds of your ⌊robe⌋. 4 Take some more of them, throw them into the fire, and burn them in it. A fire will spread from it to the whole house of Israel.

5 "This is what the Lord GOD says: I have set this Jerusalem in the center of the nations, with countries all around her. 6 But she has rebelled against My ordinances with more wickedness than the nations, and

against My statutes more than the countries that surround her. For her people have rejected My ordinances and have not walked in My statutes.

7 "Therefore, this is what the Lord GOD says: Because you have been more insubordinate than the nations around you—you have not walked in My statutes or kept My ordinances; you have not even kept the ordinances of the nations around you—8 therefore, this is what the Lord GOD says: See, I am against you, ⌊Jerusalem⌋, and I will execute judgments within you in the sight of the nations. 9 Because of all your abominations, I will do to you what I have never done before and what I will never do again. 10 As a result, fathers will eat ⌊their⌋ sons within Jerusalem,[d] and sons will eat their fathers. I will execute judgments against you and scatter all your survivors to every direction of the wind.

11 "Therefore, as I live"—⌊this is⌋ the declaration of the Lord GOD—"I am going to cut ⌊you⌋ off and show ⌊you⌋ no pity, because you have defiled My sanctuary with all your detestable practices and abominations. Yes, I will not spare ⌊you⌋. 12 One third of your people will die by plague and be consumed by famine within you; one third will fall by the sword all around you; and I will scatter one third to every direction of the wind, and I will draw a sword ⌊to chase⌋ after them. 13 When My anger is spent and I have vented My wrath on them, I will be appeased. Then, after I have spent My wrath on them, they will know that I, the LORD, have spoken in My jealousy.

14 "I will make you a ruin and a disgrace among the nations around you, in the sight of everyone who passes by. 15 So you[e] will be a disgrace and a taunt, a warning and a horror, to the nations around you when I execute judgments against you in anger, wrath, and furious rebukes. I, the LORD, have spoken. 16 When I shoot deadly arrows of famine at them, arrows for destruction that I will send to destroy you, ⌊inhabitants of Jerusalem⌋, I will intensify the famine against you and cut off your supply of bread. 17 I will send famine and dangerous animals against you. They will leave you childless, ⌊Jerusalem⌋. Plague and bloodshed will sweep through you, and I will bring a sword against you. I, the LORD, have spoken."

Prophecy against Israel's Idolatry

6 The word of the LORD came to me: 2 "Son of man, turn your face toward the mountains of Israel and prophesy against them. 3 You are to say: Mountains of Israel, hear the word of the Lord GOD! This is what the Lord GOD says to the mountains and

---

[a]4:10 Lit 20 shekels [b]4:10 Or it at set times [c]4:11 Lit hin [d]5:10 Lit you [e]5:15 DSS, LXX, Syr, Tg, Vg; MT reads she

---

4:9 Some call it Ezekiel bread. Because wheat was sparse in times of famine, bread had to be supplemented with inferior grains and legumes.

4:15 cow dung. Manure could be used as a fuel for cooking. Ezekiel requested cow dung rather than human waste that is regarded as rit-

ually impure. Ezekiel's concern for purity especially reflects his priestly role.

5:1 sharp ... sword. Conquering armies sometimes humiliated enemies by forcibly shaving them.

5:10 fathers will eat [their] sons. During sieges, starvation kills children and the elderly

first. Sometimes survivors eat the deceased to stay alive (see 2 Kings 6:29). God had warned Israel that rejecting His law would bring this very punishment (see Deut. 28:53).

6:3 destroy your high places. Israel and Judah disobeyed God by building shrines, some to God and some to foreign gods, on the same

the hills, to the ravines and the valleys: I am about to bring a sword against you, and I will destroy your •high places. 4 Your altars will be desolated and your incense altars smashed. I will throw down your slain in front of your idols. 5 I will lay the corpses of the Israelites in front of their idols and scatter your bones around your altars. 6 Wherever you live the cities will be in ruins and the high places will be desolate, so that your altars will lie in ruins and be desecrated,ᵃ your idols smashed and obliterated, your incense altars cut down, and your works wiped out. 7 The slain will fall among you, and you will know that I am the LORD.

8 "Yet I will leave a remnant when you are scattered among the nations, for throughout the countries there will be some of you who will escape the sword. 9 Then your survivors will remember Me among the nations where they are taken captive, how I was crushed by their promiscuous hearts that turned away from Me and by their eyes that lusted after their idols. They will loathe themselves because of the evil things they did, their abominations of every kind. 10 And they will know that I am the LORD; I did not threaten to bring this disaster on them without a reason.

Lament over the Fall of Jerusalem

11 "This is what the Lord GOD says: Clap your hands, stamp your feet, and cry out over all the evil abominations of the house of Israel, who will fall by the sword, famine, and plague. 12 The one who is far off will die by plague; the one who is near will fall by the sword; and the one who remains and is sparedᵇ will die of famine. In this way I will exhaust My wrath on them. 13 You will ⌊all⌋ know that I am the LORD when their slain lie among their idols around their altars, on every high hill, on all the mountaintops, and under every green tree and every leafy oak—the places where they offered pleasing aromas to all their idols. 14 I will stretch out My hand against them, and wherever they live I will make the land a desolate waste, from the wilderness to Diblah.ᶜ Then they will know that I am •Yahweh."

Announcement of the End

7 And the word of the LORD came to me: 2 "Son of man, this is what the Lord GOD says to the land of Israel:

An end! The end has come
on the four corners of the land.
3 The end is now on you;
I will send My anger against you
and judge you according to your ways.

I will punish you for all your abominations.
4 I will not look on you with pity or spare ⌊you⌋,
but I will punish you for your ways
and for your abominations within you.
Then you will know that I am the LORD."

5 This is what the Lord GOD says:

Look, one disaster after another is coming!
6 An end has come; the end has come!
It has awakened against you.
Look, it is coming!
7 Doomᵃ has come on you,
inhabitants of the land.
The time has come; the day is near.
There will be panic on the mountains
and not celebration.

8 I will pour out My wrath on you very soon;
I will exhaust My anger against you
and judge you according to your ways.
I will punish you for all your abominations.
9 I will not look on ⌊you⌋ with pity or spare ⌊you⌋.
I will punish you for your ways
and for your abominations within you.
Then you will know
that it is I, the LORD, who strikes.

10 Look, the day is coming!
Doom has gone out.
The rod has blossomed;
arrogance has bloomed.
11 Violence has grown into a rod of wickedness;
none of them ⌊will remain⌋:
none of their multitude,
none of their wealth,
and none of the eminentᵈ among them.

12 The time has come; the day has arrived.
Let the buyer not rejoice
and the seller not mourn,
for wrath is on all her multitude.
13 The seller will certainly not return
to what was sold
as long as he and the buyer remain alive.ᵉ
For the vision concerning all its people
will not be revoked,
and none of them will preserve
his life because of his iniquity.

14 They have blown the trumpet
and prepared everything,

ᵃ6:6; 7:7 Hb obscure   ᵇ6:12 Or besieged   ᶜ6:14 Some Hb mss, some LXX mss read Riblah; 2 Kg 23:33; Jr 39:5   ᵈ7:11 Some Hb mss, Syr, Vg read and no rest   ᵉ7:13 Lit sold, while still in life is their life

---

hilltops pagan Canaanites used as shrines.

6:11 Clap your hands. This kind of clapping usually resembles the hostile, taunting jeers of opponents and rival crowds at athletic contests. It describes how spectators treated captives being marched away in disgrace (25:6; Job 27:23; Lam. 2:15; Nahum 3:19). Here,

however, it is not a smug gesture. Ezekiel is instructed to act as God's agent in expressing His extreme anger over their abominations (21:14, 17; 22:13).

7:2 end … four corners of the land. Enough was enough! No one would escape God's punishment. "Four" is used throughout Ezekiel to

represent the four directions. God's power moves freely about in all directions and is not limited by boundaries or obstacles.

7:14 They have blown the trumpet. The devastation will be so complete they will not be able to defend themselves. No one will be able to respond to the trumpet call to war.

but no one goes to war,
for My wrath is on all her multitude.

15 The sword is on the outside;
plague and famine are on the inside.
Whoever is in the field will die by the sword,
and famine and plague will devour
whoever is in the city.

16 The survivors among them will escape
and live on the mountains
like doves of the valley,
all of them moaning,
each over his own iniquity.

17 All their hands will become weak,
and all ⌊their⌋ knees will turn to water.

18 They will put on •sackcloth,
and horror will overwhelm them.
Shame will cover all ⌊their⌋ faces,
and all their heads will be bald.

19 They will throw their silver into the streets,
and their gold will seem like something filthy.
Their silver and gold will be unable to save them
in the day of the LORD's wrath.
They will not satisfy their appetites
or fill their stomachs,
for these were the stumbling blocks
that brought about their iniquity.

20 He appointed His beautiful ornaments
for majesty,
but[a] they made their abhorrent images
from them,
their detestable things.
Therefore, I have made these
into something filthy for them.

21 I will hand these things over
to foreigners as plunder
and to the wicked of the earth as spoil,
and they will profane them.

22 I will turn My face from the wicked
as they profane My treasured place.
Violent men will enter it and profane it.

23 Forge the chain,
for the land is filled with crimes of bloodshed,
and the city is filled with violence.

24 So I will bring the most evil of nations
to take possession of their houses.
I will put an end to the pride of the strong,
and their sacred places will be profaned.

25 Anguish is coming!

They will seek peace, but there will be none.

26 Disaster after disaster will come,
and there will be rumor after rumor.
Then they will seek a vision from a prophet,
but instruction will perish from the priests
and counsel from the elders.

27 The king will mourn;
the prince will be clothed in grief;
and the hands of the people of the land
will tremble.
I will deal with them according to
their own conduct,
and I will judge them by their own standards.
Then they will know that I am the LORD.

Visionary Journey to Jerusalem

8 In the sixth year, in the sixth ⌊month⌋, on the fifth ⌊day⌋ of the month, I was sitting in my house and the elders of Judah were sitting in front of me, and there the hand of the Lord GOD came down on me. [2] I looked, and there was a form that had the appearance of a man.[b] From what seemed to be His waist down was fire, and from His waist up was something that looked bright, like the gleam of amber. [3] He stretched out what appeared to be a hand and took me by the hair of my head. Then the Spirit lifted me up between earth and heaven and carried me in visions of God to Jerusalem, to the entrance of the inner gate that faces north, where the offensive statue that provokes jealousy was located. [4] I saw the glory of the God of Israel there, like the vision I had seen in the plain.

Pagan Practices in the Temple

[5] The LORD said to me, "Son of man, look toward the north." I looked to the north, and there was this offensive statue north of the altar gate, at the entrance. [6] He said to me, "Son of man, do you see what they are doing, the great abominations that the house of Israel is committing here, so that I must depart from My sanctuary? You will see even greater abominations."

[7] Then He brought me to the entrance of the court, and when I looked there was a hole in the wall. [8] He said to me, "Son of man, dig through the wall." So I dug through the wall, and there was a doorway. [9] He said to me, "Go in and see the terrible abominations they are committing here." [10] I went in and looked, and there engraved all around the wall was every form of detestable thing, crawling creatures and beasts, as well as all the idols of the house of Israel.

[11] Seventy elders from the house of Israel were standing before them, with Jaazaniah son of Shaphan

---

[a]7:20 Or They turned their beautiful ornaments into objects of pride, and [b]8:2 LXX; MT, Vg read of fire

---

8:3 carried me ... Jerusalem. In a dream-vision, God showed Ezekiel the idolatry practiced in the temple by those still living in Jerusalem.

8:11 Seventy elders. Ezekiel was disgusted to find 70 Jewish elders worshiping the animal gods of Egypt while seeking release from

Babylonian domination. Ironically, seventy leaders had confirmed the Mosaic Covenant that delivered the Hebrews from bondage to Egyptian gods (Exod 24:1, 9). Facing slavery once again, they appealed to Egypt's gods for help. Such an incredible flip-flop goes to show just how far downhill the people had gone (cf.

Deut 4:16–19; Lev 11:40–42). Having lost faith in God, they concluded that, because Babylon had conquered Judah, God had forsaken them (9:9). Furthermore, this passage shows that what people do in secret shows their real character. The elders claimed to be believers but acted exactly like unbelievers in Yahweh.

standing among them. Each had an incense burner in his hand, and a fragrant cloud of incense was rising up. [12] Then He said to me, "Son of man, do you see what the elders of the house of Israel are doing in the darkness, each at the shrine of his idol? For they are saying: The LORD does not see us. The LORD has abandoned the land." [13] Again He said to me, "You will see even greater abominations, which they are committing."

[14] So He brought me to the entrance of the north gate of the LORD's house, and I saw women sitting there weeping for Tammuz. [15] And He said to me, "Do you see ⌊this⌋, son of man? You will see even greater abominations than these."

[16] So He brought me to the inner court of the LORD's house, and there were about 25 men at the entrance of the LORD's temple, between the portico and the altar, with their backs to the LORD's temple and their faces ⌊turned⌋ to the east. They were bowing to the east in worship of the sun. [17] And He said to me, "Do you see ⌊this⌋, son of man? Is it not enough for the house of Judah to commit the abominations they are practicing here, that they must also fill the land with violence and repeatedly provoke Me to anger, even putting the branch to their nose?ᵃ [18] Therefore I will respond with wrath. I will not show pity or spare ⌊them⌋. Though they cry out in My ears with a loud voice, I will not listen to them."

Vision of Slaughter in Jerusalem

9 Then He called to me directly with a loud voice, "Come near, executioners of the city, each ⌊of you⌋ with a destructive weapon in his hand." [2] And I saw six men coming from the direction of the Upper Gate, which faces north, each with a war club in his hand. There was another man among them, clothed in linen, with writing equipment at his side. They came and stood beside the bronze altar.

[3] Then the glory of the God of Israel rose from above the •cherubim where it had been, to the threshold of the temple. He called to the man clothed in linen with the writing equipment at his side. [4] "Pass throughout the city of Jerusalem," the LORD said to him, "and put a mark on the foreheads of the men who sigh and groan over all the abominations committed in it."

[5] To the others He said in my hearing, "Pass through the city after him and start killing; do not show pity or spare ⌊them⌋! [6] Slaughter the old men, the young men and women, as well as the ⌊older⌋ women and little children, but do not come near anyone who has the mark. Now begin at My sanctuary." So they began with the

elders who were in front of the temple. [7] Then He said to them, "Defile the temple and fill the courts with the slain. Go!" So they went out killing ⌊people⌋ in the city.

[8] While they were killing, I was left alone. And I fell facedown and cried out, "Ah, Lord GOD! Are You going to destroy the entire remnant of Israel when You pour out Your wrath on Jerusalem?"

[9] He answered me: "The iniquity of the house of Israel and Judah is extremely great; the land is full of bloodshed, and the city full of perversity. For they say: The LORD has abandoned the land; He does not see. [10] But as for Me, I will not show pity or spare ⌊them⌋. I will bring their actions down on their own heads." [11] Then the man clothed in linen with the writing equipment at his side reported back, "I have done as You commanded me."

God's Glory Leaves the Temple

10 Then I looked, and there above the expanse over the heads of the •cherubim was something like sapphireᵇ stone resembling the shape of a throne that appeared above them. [2] The LORD spoke to the man clothed in linen and said, "Go inside the wheelwork beneath the cherubim. Fill your hands with hot coals from among the cherubim and scatter ⌊them⌋ over the city." So he went in as I watched.

[3] Now the cherubim were standing to the south of the temple when the man went in, and the cloud filled the inner court. [4] Then the glory of the LORD rose from above the cherubim to the threshold of the temple. The temple was filled with the cloud, and the court was filled with the brightness of the LORD's glory. [5] The sound of the cherubim's wings could be heard as far as the outer court; it was like the voice of •God Almighty when He speaks.

[6] After the LORD commanded the man clothed in linen, saying, "Take fire from inside the wheelwork, from among the cherubim," the man went in and stood beside a wheel. [7] Then one of the cherubim reached out his hand to the fire that was among them. He took ⌊some⌋, and put ⌊it⌋ into the hands of the man clothed in linen, who took it and went out. [8] The cherubim appeared to have the form of human hands under their wings.

[9] I looked, and there were four wheels beside the cherubim, one wheel beside each cherub. The luster of the wheels was like the gleam of beryl. [10] In appearance, all four had the same form, like a wheel within a wheel. [11] When they moved, they would go in any of the four directions, without pivoting as they moved.

ᵃ **8:17** Possibly a pagan ritual or a euphemism for offensive behavior   ᵇ **10:1** Or *lapis lazuli*

8:14 Tammuz. According to Mesopotamian religion, Tammuz was a god who died every winter and was reborn every spring. The pagan ceremony of weeping for Tammuz was believed to aid the arrival of a fertile spring.

9:8 pour out Your wrath. Ezekiel, like Moses, interceded with God to ease the se-

verity of His punishment (Ezek. 4:14; 11:13.).

10:2 Fill your hands with hot coals. In the temple, hot coals from the altar were used with incense to form a cloud that separated the people from God's glory. Angels—much like priests—perform the same ceremony in heaven to create a cloud of smoke around

God's throne (v. 1). Here, God is about to remove His glory from the temple because of Israel's sins. The spreading of these coals anticipates Jerusalem's burning (2 Kings 25:9); a visible sign of God's departure.

10:19 glory of the God of Israel was above them. Israel and Judah failed to keep the land

But wherever the head faced, they would go in that direction,[a] without pivoting as they went. 12 Their entire bodies, including their backs, hands, wings, and the wheels that the four of them had, were full of eyes all around. 13 As I listened the wheels were called "the wheelwork." 14 Each one had four faces: the first face was that of a cherub, the second that of a man, the third that of a lion, and the fourth that of an eagle.

15 The cherubim ascended; these were the living creatures I had seen by the Chebar Canal. 16 When the cherubim moved, the wheels moved beside them, and when they lifted their wings to rise from the earth, even then the wheels did not veer away from them. 17 When the cherubim stood still, the wheels stood still, and when they ascended, the wheels ascended with them, for the spirit of the living creatures was in them.

18 Then the glory of the LORD moved away from the threshold of the temple and stood above the cherubim. 19 The cherubim lifted their wings and ascended from the earth right before my eyes; the wheels were beside them as they went. The glory of the God of Israel was above them, and it stood at the entrance to the eastern gate of the LORD's house.

20 These were the living creatures I had seen beneath the God of Israel by the Chebar Canal, and I recognized that they were cherubim. 21 Each had four faces and each had four wings, with the form of human hands under their wings. 22 Their faces looked like the same faces I had seen by the Chebar Canal. Each creature went straight ahead.

Vision of Israel's Corrupt Leaders

11 The Spirit then lifted me up and brought me to the eastern gate of the LORD's house, which faces east, and at the gate's entrance were 25 men. Among them I saw Jaazaniah son of Azzur, and Pelatiah son of Benaiah, leaders of the people. 2 The LORD said to me, "Son of man, these are the men who plan evil and give wicked advice in this city. 3 They are saying: Isn't the time near to build houses?[b] The city is the pot, and we are the meat. 4 Therefore, prophesy against them. Prophesy, son of man!"

5 Then the Spirit of the LORD came on me, and He told me, "You are to say: This is what the LORD says: That is what you are thinking, house of Israel; and I know the thoughts that arise in your mind. 6 You have multiplied your slain in this city, filling its streets with the dead.

7 "Therefore, this is what the Lord GOD says: The slain you have put within it are the meat, and the city is the pot, but I[c] will remove you from it. 8 You fear the sword, so I will bring the sword against you." ⌊This is⌋ the declaration of the Lord GOD. 9 "I will bring you out of the city and hand you over to foreigners; I will execute judgments against you. 10 You will fall by the sword, and I will judge you at the border of Israel. Then you will know that I am the LORD. 11 The city will not be a pot for you, and you will not be the meat within it. I will judge you at the border of Israel, 12 so you will know that I am the LORD, whose statutes you have not followed and whose ordinances you have not practiced. Instead, you have acted according to the ordinances of the nations around you."

13 Now while I was prophesying, Pelatiah son of Benaiah died. Then I fell facedown and cried out with a loud voice: "Ah, Lord GOD! Will You bring to an end the remnant of Israel?"

Promise of Israel's Restoration

14 The word of the LORD came to me again: 15 "Son of man, your own relatives, those who have the right to redeem you,[d] [e] and the entire house of Israel, all of them, are those the residents of Jerusalem have said this to: Stay away from the LORD; this land has been given to us as a possession.

16 "Therefore say: This is what the Lord GOD says: Though I sent them far away among the nations and scattered them among the countries, yet for a little while I have been a sanctuary for them in the countries where they have gone.

17 "Therefore say: This is what the Lord GOD says: I will gather you from the peoples and assemble you from the countries where you have been scattered, and I will give you the land of Israel.

18 "When they arrive there, they will remove all its detestable things and all its abominations from it. 19 And I will give them one heart and put a new spirit within them; I will remove their heart of stone from their bodies[f] and give them a heart of flesh, 20 so they may follow My statutes, keep My ordinances, and practice them. Then they will be My people, and I will be their God. 21 But as for those whose hearts pursue their desire for detestable things and abominations, I will bring their actions down on their own heads." ⌊This is⌋ the declaration of the Lord GOD.

God's Glory Leaves Jerusalem

22 Then the •cherubim, with the wheels beside them, lifted their wings, and the glory of the God of Israel was above them. 23 The glory of the LORD rose

---

[a]10:11 Lit go after it [b]11:3 Or The time is not near to build houses. [c]11:7 Some Hb mss, LXX, Syr, Tg, Vg; other Hb mss read He [d]11:15 LXX, Syr read your relatives, your fellow exiles [e]11:15 Or own brothers, your relatives [f]11:19 Lit flesh

---

holy, so God's glory left the temple and moved above the chariot-throne.

11:3 city is the pot. Wishful thinkers believed that Jerusalem's walls were all the protection they needed. Not so (v. 11).

11:16 sanctuary. The people's prior conception of God's presence was tied to a place—the temple. Now, God made it clear that His presence went outside the temple's physical limitations.

11:19 give them one heart and put a new spirit within them. God will bring the exiles back and will one day revive them to a spiritual depth the nation had never held. God will give new spirits, making them new creations (see 2 Cor. 5:17).

11:20 follow My statutes. When God restores Israel and Judah, the people will obey the Law of Moses.

up from within the city and stood on the mountain east of the city.[a] 24 The Spirit lifted me up and brought me to Chaldea and to the exiles in a vision from the Spirit of God. After the vision I had seen left me, 25 I spoke to the exiles about all the things the LORD had shown me.

Ezekiel Dramatizes the Exile

12 The word of the LORD came to me: 2 "Son of man, you are living among a rebellious house. They have eyes to see but do not see, and ears to hear but do not hear, for they are a rebellious house.

3 "Son of man, pack your bags for exile and go into exile in their sight during the day. You will go into exile from your place to another place while they watch; perhaps they will understand, though they are a rebellious house. 4 During the day, bring out your bags like an exile's bags while they look on. Then in the evening go out in their sight like those going into exile. 5 As they watch, dig through the wall and take the ⌊bags⌋ out through it. 6 And while they look on, lift ⌊the bags⌋ to ⌊your⌋ shoulder and take ⌊them⌋ out in the dark; cover your face so that you cannot see the land. For I have made you a sign to the house of Israel."

7 So I did just as I was commanded. I brought out my bags like an exile's bags in the daytime. In the evening I dug through the wall by hand; I took ⌊them⌋ out in the dark, carrying ⌊them⌋ on my shoulder in their sight.

8 Then the word of the LORD came to me in the morning: 9 "Son of man, hasn't the house of Israel, that rebellious house, asked you: What are you doing? 10 Say to them: This is what the Lord GOD says: This •oracle is about the prince[b] in Jerusalem and all the house of Israel who are living there.[c] 11 You are to say: I am a sign for you. Just as I have done, so it will be done to them; they will go into exile, into captivity. 12 The prince who is among them will lift ⌊his bags⌋ to his shoulder in the dark and go out. They[d] will dig through the wall to bring ⌊him⌋ out through it. He will cover his face so he cannot see the land with his eyes. 13 But I will spread My net over him, and he will be caught in My snare. I will bring him to Babylon, the land of the Chaldeans, yet he will not see it, and he will die there. 14 I will also scatter all the attendants who surround him and all his troops to every direction of the wind, and I will draw a sword ⌊to chase⌋ after them. 15 They will know that I am the LORD when I disperse them among the nations and scatter them among the countries. 16 But I will spare a few of them from the sword, famine, and plague so they can tell about all their abominations among the nations where they go. Then they will know that I am the LORD."

Ezekiel Dramatizes Israel's Anxiety

17 The word of the LORD came to me: 18 "Son of man, eat your bread with trembling and drink your water with shaking and anxiety. 19 Then say to the people of the land: This is what the Lord GOD says about the residents of Jerusalem in the land of Israel: They will eat their bread with anxiety and drink their water in dread, for their[e] land will be stripped of everything in it because of the violence of all who live there. 20 The inhabited cities will be destroyed, and the land will become a desolation. Then you will know that I am the LORD."

A Deceptive Proverb Stopped

21 Again the word of the LORD came to me: 22 "Son of man, what is this proverb you ⌊people⌋ have about the land of Israel, which goes:

> The days keep passing by,
> and every vision fails?

23 Therefore say to them: This is what the Lord GOD says: I will put a stop to this proverb, and they will not use it again in Israel. But say to them: The days draw near, as well as the fulfillment of every vision. 24 For there will no longer be any false vision or flattering •divination within the house of Israel. 25 But I, the LORD, will speak whatever message I will speak, and it will be done. It will no longer be delayed. For in your days, rebellious house, I will speak a message and bring it to pass." ⌊This is⌋ the declaration of the Lord GOD.

26 The word of the LORD came to me: 27 "Son of man, notice that the house of Israel is saying: The vision that he sees concerns many years ⌊from now⌋; he prophesies about distant times. 28 Therefore say to them: This is what the Lord GOD says: None of My words will be delayed any longer. The message I speak will be fulfilled." ⌊This is⌋ the declaration of the Lord GOD.

Israel's False Prophets Condemned

13 The word of the LORD came to me: 2 "Son of man, prophesy against the prophets of Israel who are prophesying. Say to those who prophesy out of their own imagination: Hear the word of the LORD! 3 This is what the Lord GOD says: Woe to the foolish prophets who follow their own spirit and have seen nothing. 4 Your prophets, Israel, are like jackals among ruins. 5 You did not go up to the gaps or restore the

---

[a]11:23 = the Mount of Olives   [b]12:10 = King Zedekiah   [c]12:10 Lit are among them   [d]12:12 LXX, Syr read He   [e]12:19 Lit its; = Jerusalem's

---

12:2 eyes to see but do not see. The central theme of chapters 8 and 9 is the Israelites' claim that "The Lord does not see us. The Lord has abandoned the land" (8:12; 9:9). In chapters 10 and 11, Ezekiel not only sees what the Lord sees, but forwards the message. Still, they dogmatically stick to their defenses even though they have been told that these are no defenses at all. It is important to remember that the Lord not only sees us now, but he sees how we will respond in the future to what He graciously allows.

12:8 word … came to me in the morning. The very next day God evaluated the success of Ezekiel's unusual demonstration of obedience. Ezekiel had followed God's instruction (v. 7).

12:27 years [from now]. The people thought the prophecy's fulfillment was far off; it wasn't.

13:6 the fulfillment of [their] message. Accuracy was the mark of true prophets. False

wall around the house of Israel so that it might stand in battle on the day of the LORD. 6 They see false visions and speak lying •divinations. They claim: ⌊This is⌋ the LORD's declaration, when the LORD did not send them, yet they wait for the fulfillment of ⌊their⌋ message. 7 Didn't you see a false vision and speak a lying divination when you proclaimed: ⌊This is⌋ the LORD's declaration, even though I had not spoken?

8 "Therefore, this is what the Lord GOD says: I am against you because you have spoken falsely and had lying visions." ⌊This is⌋ the declaration of the Lord GOD. 9 "My hand will be against the prophets who see false visions and speak lying divinations. They will not be present in the fellowship of My people or be recorded in the register of the house of Israel, and they will not enter the land of Israel. Then you will know that I am the Lord GOD.

10 "Since they have led My people astray saying: Peace, when there is no peace, for when someone builds a wall they plaster it with whitewash, 11 therefore, tell those who plaster ⌊it⌋ that it will fall. Torrential rain will come, and I will send hailstones plunginga down, and a windstorm will be released. 12 Now when the wall has fallen, will you not be asked: Where is the coat of whitewash that you put on ⌊it⌋?

13 "So this is what the Lord GOD says: I will release a windstorm in My wrath. Torrential rain will come in My anger, and hailstones ⌊will fall⌋ in destructive fury. 14 I will tear down the wall you plastered with whitewash and knock it to the ground so that its foundation is exposed. The city will fall, and you will be destroyed within it. Then you will know that I am the LORD. 15 After I exhaust My wrath against the wall and against those who plaster it with whitewash, I will say to you: The wall is no more and neither are those who plastered it— 16 those prophets of Israel who prophesied to Jerusalem and saw a vision of peace for her when there was no peace." ⌊This is⌋ the declaration of the Lord GOD.

17 "Now, son of man, turnb toward the women of your people who prophesy out of their own imagination. Prophesy against them 18 and say: This is what the Lord GOD says: Woe to the women who sew ⌊magic⌋ bands on the wrist of every hand and who make veils for the heads of people of every height in order to ensnare lives. Will you ensnare the lives of My people but preserve your own? 19 You profane Me in front of My people for handfuls of barley and scraps of bread; you kill those who should not die and spare those who should not live, when you lie to My people, who listen to lies.

20 "Therefore, this is what the Lord GOD says: I am against your ⌊magic⌋ bands that you ensnare people with like birds, and I will tear them from your arms. I will free the people you have ensnared like birds. 21 I will also tear off your veils and deliver My people from your hands, so that they will no longer be prey in your hands. Then you will know that I am the LORD. 22 Because you have disheartened the righteous person with lies, even though I have not caused him grief, and because you have encouraged the wicked person not to turn from his evil way to save his life, 23 therefore you will no longer see false visions or practice divination. I will deliver My people from your hands. Then you will know that I am the LORD."

Idolatrous Elders Punished

14 Some of the elders of Israel came to me and sat down in front of me. 2 Then the word of the LORD came to me: 3 "Son of man, these men have set up idols in their hearts and have put sinful stumbling blocks before their faces. Should I be consulted by them at all?

4 "Therefore, speak to them and tell them: This is what the Lord GOD says: When anyone from the house of Israel sets up idols in his heart, puts a sinful stumbling block before his face, and then comes to the prophet, I, the LORD, will answer him appropriately.c ⌊I will answer him⌋ according to his many idols, 5 so that I may take hold of the house of Israel by their hearts, because they are all estranged from Me by their idols.

6 "Therefore, say to the house of Israel: This is what the Lord GOD says: Repent and turn away from your idols; turn your faces away from all your abominations. 7 For when anyone from the house of Israel or from the foreigners who reside in Israel separates himself from Me, setting up idols in his heart and putting a sinful stumbling block before his face, and then comes to the prophet to inquire of Me,d I, the LORD, will answer him Myself. 8 I will turn against that one and make him a sign and a proverb; I will cut him off from among My people. Then you will know that I am the LORD.

9 "But if the prophet is deceived and speaks a message, it was I, the LORD, who deceived that prophet. I will stretch out My hand against him and destroy him from among My people Israel. 10 They will bear their punishment—the punishment of the one who inquires will be the same as that of the prophet— 11 in order that the house of Israel may no longer stray from following Me and no longer defile themselves with all their

---

a 13:11 One Hb ms, LXX, Vg; MT reads and you, hailstones, will plunge   b 13:17 Lit set your face   c 14:4 Alt Hb tradition reads him who comes   d 14:7 Lit Me for himself

---

prophets spoke lies.

13:10 plaster it with whitewash. A laborer used white paste to cover inconsistencies in a rock-hewn wall. Likewise, God's people focused on appearances rather than the condition of their hearts. God is concerned about the heart (see 1 Sam. 16:7).

13:11 Torrential rain will come ... hailstones. Reverting back to the storm imagery, Ezekiel described how their sin would be exposed (1:4).

14:3 Should I be consulted. Pagans seeking advice from Ezekiel seemed hypocritical. Why consult two opposing sources?

14:4 stumbling block. The idolatrous people tripped on their own sins—a costly mistake that resulted in death.

14:6 Repent and turn. Ezekiel urged repentance while there was still time. Repentance is turning from sin to God. Without repentance, there is no real faith in God or Jesus.

transgressions. Then they will be My people and I will be their God." ⌊This is⌋ the declaration of the Lord GOD.

Four Devastating Judgments

12 The word of the LORD came to me: 13 "Son of man, if a land sins against Me by acting faithlessly, and I stretch out My hand against it to cut off its supply of bread, to send famine through it, and to wipe out ⌊both⌋ man and animal from it, 14 even ⌊if⌋ these three men— Noah, Daniel, and Job—were in it, they would deliver ⌊only⌋ themselves by their righteousness." ⌊This is⌋ the declaration of the Lord GOD.

15 "If I allow dangerous animals to pass through the land and depopulate it so that it becomes desolate, with no one passing through ⌊it⌋ for ⌊fear of⌋ the animals, 16 even ⌊if⌋ these three men were in it, as I live"—the declaration of the Lord GOD—"they could not deliver ⌊their⌋ sons or daughters. They alone would be delivered, but the land would be desolate.

17 "Or if I bring a sword against that land and say: Let a sword pass through it, so that I wipe out ⌊both⌋ man and animal from it, 18 even ⌊if⌋ these three men were in it, as I live"—the declaration of the Lord GOD—"they could not deliver ⌊their⌋ sons or daughters, but they alone would be delivered.

19 "Or if I send a plague into that land and pour out My wrath on it with bloodshed to wipe out ⌊both⌋ man and animal from it, 20 even ⌊if⌋ Noah, Daniel, and Job were in it, as I live"—the declaration of the Lord GOD—"they could not deliver ⌊their⌋ son or daughter. They would deliver ⌊only⌋ themselves by their righteousness.

21 "For this is what the Lord GOD says: How much worse will it be when I send My four devastating judgments against Jerusalem—sword, famine, dangerous animals, and plague—in order to wipe out ⌊both⌋ man and animal from it! 22 Even so, there will be survivors left in it, sons and daughters who will be brought out. Indeed, they will come out to you, and you will observe their conduct and actions. Then you will be consoled about the devastation I have brought on Jerusalem, about all I have brought on it. 23 They will bring you consolation when you see their conduct and actions, and you will know that it was not without cause that I have done what I did to it." ⌊This is⌋ the declaration of the Lord GOD.

Parable of the Useless Vine

15 Then the word of the LORD came to me: 2 "Son of man, how does the wood of the vine, that branch among the trees of the forest, compare to any other wood? 3 Can wood be taken from it to make something useful? Or can anyone make a peg from it to hang things on? 4 In fact, it is put into the fire as fuel. The fire devours both of its ends, and the middle is charred. Can it be useful for anything? 5 Even when it was whole it could not be made into a useful object. How much less can it ever be made into anything useful when the fire has devoured it and it is charred!

6 "Therefore, this is what the Lord GOD says: Like the wood of the vine among the trees of the forest, which I have given to the fire as fuel, so I will give up the residents of Jerusalem. 7 I will turn against them. They may have escaped from the fire, but it will ⌊still⌋ consume them. And you will know that I am the LORD when I turn against them. 8 I will make the land desolate because they have acted unfaithfully." ⌊This is⌋ the declaration of the Lord GOD.

Parable of God's Adulterous Wife

16 The word of the LORD came to me again: 2 "Son of man, explain Jerusalem's abominations to her. 3 You are to say: This is what the Lord GOD says to Jerusalem: Your origin and your birth were in the land of the Canaanites. Your father was an Amorite and your mother a Hittite. 4 As for your birth, your umbilical cord wasn't cut on the day you were born, and you weren't washed cleanᵃ with water. You were not rubbed with salt or wrapped in cloths. 5 No one cared ⌊enough⌋ about you to do even one of these things out of compassion for you. But you were thrown out into the open field because you were despised on the day you were born.

6 "I passed by you and saw you lying in your blood, and I said to you ⌊as you lay⌋ in your blood: Live! Yes, I said to you ⌊as you lay⌋ in your blood: Live!ᵇ 7 I made you thriveᶜ like plants of the field. You grew up and matured and became very beautiful.ᵈ Your breasts were formed and your hair grew, but you were stark naked.

8 "Then I passed by you and saw you, and you were indeed at the age for love. So I spread the edge of My garment over you and covered your nakedness. I pledged Myself to you, entered into a covenant with you, and you became Mine." ⌊This is⌋ the declaration of the Lord GOD. 9 "I washed you with water, rinsed off your blood, and anointed you with oil. 10 I clothed you in embroidered cloth and provided you with leather sandals. I also wrapped you in fine linen and covered you with silk. 11 I adorned you with jewelry, putting bracelets on your wrists and a chain around your neck. 12 I put a ring in your nose, earrings on your ears, and

---

ᵃ16:4 Hb obscure   ᵇ16:6 Some Hb mss, LXX, Syr omit Yes, I said to you [as you lay] in your blood: Live!   ᶜ16:7 LXX reads Thrive; I made you
ᵈ16:7 Or matured and developed the loveliest of ornaments

14:14, 20 Noah, Daniel, and Job. Even biblical characters who sought after God's heart would have no saving influence over such a wicked society. They could save only themselves.

15:2 wood of the vine. Isaiah called Israel God's vineyard (see also John 15), but Ezekiel

sarcastically pointed out that God would burn the branches.

15:7 it will [still] consume them. Jerusalem's remaining inhabitants considered escaping the initial wave of capture in 597 B.C. a close call. Yet, total destruction was only a few years away.

16:3 Jerusalem. This city was also called the fortress of Zion and remained a Canaanite hotspot until David completely conquered it (1 Chron. 11:4-9).

16:8 spread the edge of My garment over you. God's relationship with Israel, as with the church, is analogous to marriage (see Eph.

a beautiful tiara on your head. 13 So you were adorned with gold and silver, and your clothing was ⌊made⌋ of fine linen, silk, and embroidered cloth. You ate fine flour, honey, and oil. You became extremely beautiful and attained royalty. 14 Your fame spread among the nations because of your beauty, for it was perfect through My splendor, which I had bestowed on you." ⌊This is⌋ the declaration of the Lord GOD.

15 "But you were confident in your beauty and acted like a prostitute because of your fame. You lavished your sexual favors on everyone who passed by. Your beauty became his.a 16 You took some of your garments and made colorful •high places for yourself, and you engaged in prostitution on them. These places should not have been built, and this should never have happened!a 17 You also took your beautiful jewelry made from the gold and silver I had given you, and you made male images so that you could engage in prostitution with them. 18 Then you took your embroidered garments to cover them, and set My oil and incense before them. 19 You also set before them as a pleasing aroma the food I gave you—the fine flour, oil, and honey that I fed you. That is what happened." ⌊This is⌋ the declaration of the Lord GOD.

20 "You even took your sons and daughters you bore to Me and sacrificed them to these images as food. Wasn't your prostitution enough? 21 You slaughtered My children and gave them up when you passed them through ⌊the fire⌋ to the images. 22 In all your abominations and acts of prostitution, you did not remember the days of your youth when you were stark naked and lying in your blood.

23 "Then after all your evil—Woe, woe to you!"—the declaration of the Lord GOD— 24 "you built yourself a mound and made yourself an elevated place in every square. 25 You built your elevated place at the head of every street and turned your beauty into an abomination. You spread your legs to everyone who passed by and increased your prostitution. 26 You engaged in promiscuous acts with Egyptian men, your well-endowed neighbors, and increased your prostitution to provoke Me to anger.

27 "Therefore, I stretched out My hand against you and reduced your provisions. I gave you over to the desire of those who hate you, the Philistine women, who were embarrassed by your indecent behavior. 28 Then you engaged in prostitution with the Assyrian men because you were not satisfied. Even though you did this with them, you were still not satisfied. 29 So you extended your prostitution to Chaldea, the land of merchants, but you were not even satisfied with this!

30 "How your heart was inflamed ⌊with lust⌋"—the declaration of the Lord GOD—"when you did all these things, the acts of a brazen prostitute, 31 building your mound at the head of every street and making your elevated place in every square. But you were unlike a prostitute because you scorned payment. 32 You adulterous wife, who receives strangers instead of her husband! 33 Men give gifts to all prostitutes, but you gave gifts to all your lovers. You bribed them to come to you from all around for your sexual favors. 34 So you were the opposite of other women in your acts of prostitution; no one solicited you. When you paid a fee instead of one being paid to you, you were the opposite.

35 "Therefore, you prostitute, hear the word of the LORD! 36 This is what the Lord GOD says: Because your lust was poured out and your nakedness exposed by your acts of prostitution with your lovers, and because of all your detestable idols and the blood of your children that you gave to them, 37 I am therefore going to gather all the lovers you pleased—all those you loved as well as all those you hated. I will gather them against you from all around and expose your nakedness to them so they see you completely naked. 38 I will judge you the way adulteresses and those who shed blood are judged. Then I will bring about your bloodshed in wrath and jealousy. 39 I will hand you over to them, and they will level your mounds and tear down your elevated places. They will strip off your clothes, take your beautiful jewelry, and leave you stark naked. 40 They will bring a mob against you to stone you and cut you to pieces with their swords. 41 Then they will burn down your houses and execute judgments against you in the sight of many women. I will stop you from being a prostitute, and you will never again pay fees for lovers. 42 So I will satisfy My wrath against you, and My jealousy will turn away from you. Then I will be silent and no longer angry. 43 Because you did not remember the days of your youth but enraged Me with all these things, I will also bring your actions down on your own head." ⌊This is⌋ the declaration of the Lord GOD. "Haven't you committed immoral acts in addition to all your abominations?

44 "Look, everyone who uses proverbs will say this proverb about you:

Like mother, like daughter.

45 You are the daughter of your mother, who despised her husband and children. You are the sister of your sisters, who despised their husbands and children. Your mother was a Hittite and your father an Amorite.

a 16:15,16 Hb obscure

5:22-32). He found an orphan girl, Jerusalem, and loved her as His wife.

16:15 confident in your beauty. God's gift to Jerusalem became a pitfall as the city asserted its independence.

16:16-19 You took. Israel, the Lord's precious wife, took everything that the He had provided; the best clothing, food, and even precious jewelry, and pawned it in service to her idols. The imagery of melting precious metal into idols recalls episodes in Israel's past when it similarly prostituted itself (Exod. 32:2-4; Judg. 8:24-27).

16:37 gather them against you. God's sovereignty over the scenario allowed Him to turn Jerusalem's so-called lovers into enemies.

16:44 proverb. The Lord is fond of turning Israel's proverbs on their heads (12:21-25; 14:8; 18:2). Jerusalem shared a common bond and a common fate with the rebellious Canaanite

46 Your older sister was Samaria, who lived with her daughters to the north of you, and your younger sister was Sodom, who lived with her daughters to the south of you. 47 Didn't you walk in their ways and practice their abominations? It was only a short time before you behaved more corruptly than they did.[a]

48 "As I live"—the declaration of the Lord GOD—"your sister Sodom and her daughters have not behaved as you and your daughters have. 49 Now this was the iniquity of your sister Sodom: she and her daughters had pride, plenty of food, and comfortable security, but didn't support the poor and needy. 50 They were haughty and did detestable things before Me, so I removed them when I saw ⌊this⌋.[b] 51 But Samaria did not commit ⌊even⌋ half your sins. You have multiplied your abominations beyond theirs and made your sisters appear righteous by all the abominations you have committed. 52 You must also bear your disgrace, since you have been an advocate for your sisters. For they appear more righteous than you because of your sins, which you committed more abhorrently than they ⌊did⌋. So you also, be ashamed and bear your disgrace, since you have made your sisters appear righteous.

53 "I will restore their fortunes, the fortunes of Sodom and her daughters and those of Samaria and her daughters. I will also restore[c] your fortunes among them, 54 so you will bear your disgrace and be ashamed of all you did when you comforted them. 55 As for your sisters, Sodom and her daughters and Samaria and her daughters will return to their former state. You and your daughters will also return to your former state. 56 Didn't you treat your sister Sodom as an object of scorn when you were proud, 57 before your wickedness was exposed? It was like the time you were scorned by the daughters of Aram[d] and all those around her, and by the daughters of the Philistines—those who treated you with contempt from every side. 58 You yourself must bear the consequences of your indecency and abominations"—the LORD's declaration.

59 "For this is what the Lord GOD says: I will deal with you according to what you have done, since you have despised the oath by breaking the covenant. 60 But I will remember the covenant I made with you in the days of your youth, and I will establish an everlasting covenant with you. 61 Then you will remember your ways and be ashamed when you[e] receive your older and younger sisters. I will give them to you as daughters, but not because of your covenant. 62 I will establish My covenant with you, and you will know that I am the LORD, 63 so that when I make •atonement for all you have done, you will remember and be ashamed, and never open your mouth again because of your disgrace." ⌊This is⌋ the declaration of the Lord GOD.

Parable of the Eagles

17 The word of the LORD came to me: 2 "Son of man, pose a riddle and speak a parable to the house of Israel. 3 You are to say: This is what the Lord GOD says:

A great eagle with great wings, long pinions,
and full plumage of many colors
came to Lebanon and took the top of the cedar.
4 He plucked off its topmost shoot,
brought it to the land of merchants,
and set it in a city of traders.
5 Then he took some of the land's seed
and put it in a fertile field;
he set it ⌊like⌋ a willow,
a plant[f] by abundant waters.
6 It sprouted and became a spreading vine,
low in height with its branches turned
        toward him,
yet its roots stayed under it.
So it became a vine,
produced branches, and sent forth shoots.

7 But there was another great eagle
with great wings and thick plumage.
And this vine bent its roots toward him!
It stretched out its branches to him
from its planting bed,
so that he might water it.
8 It had been planted
in a good field by abundant waters
in order to produce branches,
bear fruit, and become a splendid vine.

9 You are to say: This is what the Lord GOD says:

Will it flourish?
Will he not tear out its roots
and strip off its fruit
so that it shrivels?
All its fresh leaves will wither!
Great strength and many people
will not be needed to pull it from its roots.
10 Even though it is planted, will it flourish?
Won't it completely wither
when the east wind strikes it?
It will wither on the bed where it sprouted."

---

a 16:47 Lit *they in all your ways*   b 16:50 Or *them as you have seen*   c 16:53 LXX, Vg; MT reads *Samaria and her daughters and the fortunes of*
d 16:57 Other Hb mss, Syr read *Edom*   e 16:61 Some LXX, Syr read *I*   f 17:5 Hb obscure

---

people who first inhabited the land (v. 45) and were banished by Joshua (Gen. 15:16; Josh. 3:10). Yet, the Lord will remember His covenant with them (v. 60).

16:47 more corruptly than they. Comparing a city to Sodom was the ultimate insult (Jer. 23:14).

16:49 but didn't support the poor and needy. Sodom focused completely on her own needs and didn't care for those who needed help.

16:56 treat your sister Sodom. Ezekiel reminisced about Jerusalem's sense of superiority over Sodom. The people never even mentioned the name Sodom for fear of lowering themselves to Sodom's standards.

17:2-10 The prophet contrasted the imagery of a vine (Judah) with that of two powerful eagles: (Babylon (v. 3) and Egypt (v. 7). He demonstrated how Judah's varying allegiances played a role in Judah's downfall. King Zede-

¹¹ The word of the LORD came to me: ¹² "Now say to that rebellious house: Don't you know what these things mean? Tell ⌊them⌋: The king of Babylon came to Jerusalem, took its king and officials, and brought them back with him to Babylon. ¹³ He took one of the royal family and made a covenant with him, putting him under oath. Then he took away the leading men of the land, ¹⁴ so the kingdom might be humble and not exalt itself but might keep his covenant in order to endure. ¹⁵ However, this king revolted against him by sending his ambassadors to Egypt so they might give him horses and a large army. Will he flourish? Will the one who does such things escape? Can he break a covenant and ⌊still⌋ escape?

¹⁶ "As I live"—⌊this is⌋ the declaration of the Lord GOD—"he will die in Babylon, in the land of the king who put him on the throne, whose oath he despised and whose covenant he broke. ¹⁷ Pharaoh will not help him with ⌊his⌋ great army and vast horde in battle, when ramps are built and siege walls constructed to destroy many lives. ¹⁸ He despised the oath by breaking the covenant. He did all these things even though he gave his hand ⌊in pledge⌋. He will not escape!"

¹⁹ Therefore, this is what the Lord GOD says: "As I live, I will bring down on his head My oath that he despised and My covenant that he broke. ²⁰ I will spread My net over him, and he will be captured in My snare. I will bring him to Babylon and execute judgment on him there for the treachery he committed against Me. ²¹ All the fugitives[a] among his troops will fall by the sword, and those who survive will be scattered to every direction of the wind. Then you will know that I, •Yahweh, have spoken."

²² This is what the Lord GOD says:

I will take ⌊a sprig⌋
from the lofty top of the cedar and plant ⌊it⌋.
I will pluck a tender sprig
from its topmost shoots,
and I will plant ⌊it⌋
on a high towering mountain.
²³ I will plant it on Israel's high mountain
so that it may bear branches, produce fruit,
and become a majestic cedar.
Birds of every kind will nest under it,
taking shelter in the shade of its branches.
²⁴ Then all the trees of the field will know
that I am the LORD.
I bring down the tall tree,
and make the low tree tall.

I cause the green tree to wither
and make the withered tree thrive.
I, Yahweh, have spoken
and I will do ⌊it⌋.

Personal Responsibility for Sin

18 The word of the LORD came to me: ² "What do you mean by using this proverb concerning the land of Israel:

The fathers eat sour grapes,
and the children's teeth are set on edge?

³ As I live"—⌊this is⌋ the declaration of the Lord GOD—"you will no longer use this proverb in Israel. ⁴ Look, every life belongs to Me. The life of the father is like the life of the son—both belong to Me. The person who sins is the one who will die.

⁵ "Now suppose a man is righteous and does what is just and right: ⁶ He does not eat at the mountain ⌊shrines⌋ or raise his eyes to the idols of the house of Israel. He does not defile his neighbor's wife or come near a woman during her menstrual impurity. ⁷ He doesn't oppress anyone but returns his collateral to the debtor. He does not commit robbery, but gives his bread to the hungry and covers the naked with clothing. ⁸ He doesn't lend at interest or for profit but keeps his hand from wrongdoing and carries out true justice between men. ⁹ He follows My statutes and keeps My ordinances, acting faithfully. Such a person is righteous; he will certainly live." ⌊This is⌋ the declaration of the Lord GOD.

¹⁰ "Now suppose the man has a violent son, who sheds blood and does any of these ⌊things⌋, ¹¹ though the father has done none of them. Indeed, when the son eats at the mountain ⌊shrines⌋ and defiles his neighbor's wife, ¹² and ⌊when⌋ he oppresses the poor and needy, commits robbery, and does not return collateral, and ⌊when⌋ he raises his eyes to the idols, commits abominations, ¹³ and lends at interest or for profit, will he live? He will not live! Since he has committed all these abominations, he will certainly die. His blood will be on him.

¹⁴ "Now suppose he has a son who sees all the sins his father has committed, and though he sees them, he does not do likewise. ¹⁵ He does not eat at the mountain ⌊shrines⌋ or raise his eyes to the idols of the house of Israel. He does not defile his neighbor's wife. ¹⁶ He doesn't oppress anyone, hold collateral, or commit robbery. He gives his bread to the hungry and covers the naked with clothing. ¹⁷ He keeps his hand from ⌊harm-

---

^a**17:21** Some Hb mss, LXX, Syr, Tg read *choice men*

---

kiah (v. 15) recruited Egypt to help rebel against Babylon (2 Kings 24:20), that proved to be a total failure. Ezekiel predicted the king's revolt and the resulting Babylonian retribution nearly three years in advance (vv. 19-21).

17:23 I will plant it on Israel's high mountain. In the last days, God will restore Jerusa-

lem as chief of the world's cities. The high mountain is Zion, the mount on which Jerusalem rests. The cedar tree in the image represents the beauty and majesty of the city when God restores it.

18:2 sour grapes. This was a popular saying that implied that it was inevitable that a child

would suffer blame for a parent's sins. Once again, God turns this proverb upside down (12:21; 14:8; 16:44).

18:4 every life belongs to Me. God contrasted a common saying with His sovereign command. Individuals would be accountable for their own sins.

ing the poor, not taking interest or profit on a loan. He practices My ordinances and follows My statutes. Such a person will not die for his father's iniquity. He will certainly live.

18 "As for his father, he will die for his own iniquity because he practiced fraud, robbed his brother, and did what was wrong among his people. 19 But you may ask: Why doesn't the son suffer punishment for the father's iniquity? Since the son has done what is just and right, carefully observing all My statutes, he will certainly live. 20 The person who sins is the one who will die. A son won't suffer punishment for the father's iniquity, and a father won't suffer punishment for the son's iniquity. The righteousness of the righteous person will be on him, and the wickedness of the wicked person will be on him.

21 "Now if the wicked person turns from all the sins he has committed, keeps all My statutes, and does what is just and right, he will certainly live; he will not die. 22 None of the transgressions he has committed will be held against him. He will live because of the righteousness he has practiced. 23 Do I take any pleasure in the death of the wicked?" This is the declaration of the Lord GOD. "Instead, don't I take pleasure when he turns from his ways and lives? 24 But when a righteous person turns from his righteousness and practices iniquity, committing the same abominations that the wicked do, will he live? None of the righteous acts he did will be remembered. He will die because of the treachery he has engaged in and the sin he has committed.

25 "But you say: The Lord's way isn't fair. Now listen, house of Israel: Is it My way that is unfair? Instead, isn't it your ways that are unfair? 26 When a righteous person turns from his righteousness and practices iniquity, he will die for this. He will die because of the iniquity he has practiced. 27 But if a wicked person turns from the wickedness he has committed and does what is just and right, he will preserve his life. 28 He will certainly live because he thought it over and turned from all the transgressions he had committed; he will not die. 29 But the house of Israel says: The Lord's way isn't fair. Is it My ways that are unfair, house of Israel? Instead, isn't it your ways that are unfair?

30 "Therefore, house of Israel, I will judge each one of you according to his ways." This is the declaration of the Lord GOD. "Repent and turn from all your transgressions, so they will not be a stumbling block that causes your punishment. 31 Throw off all the transgressions you have committed, and make yourselves a new

heart and a new spirit. Why should you die, house of Israel? 32 For I take no pleasure in anyone's death." This is the declaration of the Lord GOD. "So repent and live!

A Lament for Israel's Princes

19 "Now, lament for the princes of Israel 2 and say:

What was your mother? A lioness!
She lay down among the lions;
she reared her cubs among the young lions.
3 She brought up one of her cubs,
and he became a young lion.
After he learned to tear prey,
he devoured people.
4 When the nations heard about him,
he was caught in their pit.
Then they led him away with hooks
to the land of Egypt.

5 When she saw that she waited in vain,
that her hope was lost,
she took another of her cubs
and made him a young lion.
6 He prowled among the lions,
and he became a young lion.
After he learned to tear prey,
he devoured people.
7 He devastated[a] their strongholds
and destroyed their cities.
The land and everything in it shuddered
at the sound of his roaring.
8 Then the nations from
the surrounding provinces
set out against him.
They spread their net over him;
he was caught in their pit.
9 They put a wooden yoke on him[b] with hooks
and led him away to the king of Babylon.
They brought him into the fortresses
so his roar could no longer be heard
on the mountains of Israel.

10 Your mother was like a vine in your vineyard,[c]
planted by the water;
it was fruitful and full of branches
because of plentiful waters.
11 It had strong branches, fit for the scepters
of rulers;
its height towered among the clouds.[d]

---

[a]**19:7** Tg, Aq; LXX reads *fed on*; MT reads *knew*   [b]**19:9** Or *put him in a cage*   [c]**19:10** Some Hb mss; other Hb mss read *blood*   [d]**19:11** Or *thick foliage*

18:9 he will certainly live. Ezekiel gave God's decree about the physical, not eternal, context of life and death (Deut. 30:15-20). He further illustrated how righteousness is rewarded on its own merit, despite family history.

18:21 he will not die. Through repentance, a wicked person changes course.

18:32 I take no pleasure in anyone's death. In this summary statement, Ezekiel revealed an important aspect of God's character. God is consistent, not capricious, in His judgment. He is not willing for any to perish (see 2 Peter 3:9).

19:1 princes of Israel. Ezekiel, lamenting the fate of all the wicked people in Jerusa-

lem, rehearsed a mournful poem.

19:3-14 Ezekiel used a pair of analogies to illustrate Jerusalem's demise. The cubs symbolized Kings Jehoahaz (v. 3) and Zedekiah (v. 5). They were full brothers (2 Kings 23:31; 24:18; Jer. 52:1). Their reigns were separated by Jehoiakim and Jehoiachin's reigns. Both died in

So it was conspicuous for its height
as well as its many branches.
12 But it was uprooted in fury,
thrown to the ground,
and the east wind dried up its fruit.
Its strong branches were torn off and dried up;
fire consumed them.
13 Now it is planted in the wilderness,
in a dry and thirsty land.
14 Fire has gone out from its main branch[a]
and has devoured its fruit,
so that it no longer has a strong branch,
a scepter for ruling.

This is a lament and should be used as a lament."

Israel's Rebellion

20 In the seventh year, in the fifth ⌊month⌋, on the tenth ⌊day⌋ of the month, some of Israel's elders came to consult the LORD, and they sat down in front of me. 2 Then the word of the LORD came to me: 3 "Son of man, speak with the elders of Israel and tell them: This is what the Lord GOD says: Are you coming to consult Me? As I live, I will not be consulted by you." ⌊This is⌋ the declaration of the Lord GOD.

4 "Will you pass judgment against them, will you pass judgment, son of man? Explain to them the abominations of their fathers. 5 Say to them: This is what the Lord GOD says: On the day I chose Israel, I swore an oath[b] to the descendants of Jacob's house and made Myself known to them in the land of Egypt. I swore to them, saying: I am the LORD your God. 6 On that day I swore[c] to them that I would bring them out of the land of Egypt into a land I had searched out for them, ⌊a land⌋ flowing with milk and honey, the most beautiful of all lands. 7 I also said to them: Each of you must throw away the detestable things that are before your eyes and not defile yourselves with the idols of Egypt. I am the LORD your God.

8 "But they rebelled against Me and were unwilling to listen to Me. None of them threw away the detestable things that were before their eyes, and they did not forsake the idols of Egypt. So I considered pouring out My wrath on them, exhausting My anger against them within the land of Egypt. 9 But I acted for the sake of My name, so that it would not be profaned in the eyes of the nations they were living among, in whose sight I had made Myself known to Israel by bringing them out of Egypt.

10 "So I brought them out of the land of Egypt and led them into the wilderness. 11 Then I gave them My stat-

utes and explained My ordinances to them—the person who does them will live by them. 12 I also gave them My Sabbaths to serve as a sign between Me and them, so they will know that I am the LORD who sets them apart as holy.

13 "But the house of Israel rebelled against Me in the wilderness. They did not follow My statutes and they rejected My ordinances—the person who does them will live by them. They also completely profaned My Sabbaths. So I considered pouring out My wrath on them in the wilderness to put an end to them. 14 But I acted because of My name, so that it would not be profaned in the eyes of the nations in whose sight I had brought them out. 15 However, I swore[c] to them in the wilderness that I would not bring them into the land I had given ⌊them⌋—the most beautiful of all lands, flowing with milk and honey— 16 because they rejected My ordinances, profaned My Sabbaths, and did not follow My statutes. For their hearts went after their idols. 17 But I spared them from destruction and did not bring them to an end in the wilderness.

18 "Then I said to their children in the wilderness: Don't follow the statutes of your fathers, defile yourselves with their idols, or keep their ordinances. 19 I am the LORD your God. Follow My statutes, keep My ordinances, and practice them. 20 Keep My Sabbaths holy, and they will be a sign between Me and you, so you may know that I am the LORD your God.

21 "But the children rebelled against Me. They did not follow My statutes or carefully keep My ordinances—the person who does them will live by them. They also profaned My Sabbaths. So I considered pouring out My wrath on them and exhausting My anger against them in the wilderness. 22 But I withheld My hand and acted because of My name, so that it would not be profaned in the eyes of the nations in whose sight I brought them out. 23 However, I swore[c] to them in the wilderness that I would disperse them among the nations and scatter them among the countries. 24 For they did not practice My ordinances but rejected My statutes and profaned My Sabbaths, and their eyes were fixed on their fathers' idols. 25 I also gave them statutes that were not good and ordinances that did not bring them life. 26 When they made every firstborn pass through ⌊the fire⌋, I defiled them through their gifts in order to devastate them so they would know that I am the LORD.

27 "Therefore, son of man, speak to the house of Israel, and tell them: This is what the Lord GOD says: In this way also your fathers blasphemed Me by commit-

---

a**19:14** Lit *from the branch of its parts*   b**20:5** Lit *I lifted My hand*   c**20:6,15,23** Lit *lifted My hand*

---

captivity—Jehoahaz in Egypt (2 Kings 23:34), and Zedekiah in Babylon (2 Kings 25:7). The story of the vine (vv. 10-14) parallels Judah's rebellion that led to its uprooting.
20:1 seventh year ... fifth month. The summer of 591 B.C., five years away from Jerusalem's fall. It had been almost eleven

months since the last date given by Ezekiel (8:1). God will not dignify the elders request with an answer (cf. 14:3) other than an extended history lesson (vv. 5-45). To understand the present, the elders need to be reminded of God's gracious choice of Israel in spite of their rebellion during their years in

Egypt and throughout their history to the present.

20:25 I also gave them statutes that were not good ... not bring them life. This does not refer to God's law, which is good (Rom. 7:12), but to the Canaanite statutes that Israel followed.

ting treachery against Me: 28 When I brought them into the land that I swore[a] to give them and they saw any high hill or leafy tree, they offered their sacrifices and presented their offensive offerings there. They also sent up their pleasing aromas and poured out their drink offerings there. 29 So I asked them: What is this •high place you are going to? And it is called High Place to this day.

30 "Therefore say to the house of Israel: This is what the Lord GOD says: Are you defiling yourselves the way your fathers did, and prostituting yourselves with their detestable things? 31 When you offer your gifts, making your children pass through the fire, you continue to defile yourselves with all your idols to this day. So should I be consulted by you, house of Israel? As I live"—[this is] the declaration of the Lord GOD—"I will not be consulted by you!

Israel's Restoration

32 "When you say: Let us be like the nations, like the peoples of [other] countries, worshiping wood and stone, what you have in mind will never happen. 33 As I live"—the declaration of the Lord GOD—"I will rule over you with a strong hand, an outstretched arm, and outpoured wrath. 34 I will bring you from the peoples and gather you from the countries where you were scattered, with a strong hand, an outstretched arm, and outpoured wrath. 35 I will lead you into the wilderness of the peoples and enter into judgment with you there face to face. 36 Just as I entered into judgment with your fathers in the wilderness of the land of Egypt, so I will enter into judgment with you." [This is] the declaration of the Lord GOD. 37 "I will make you pass under the rod and will bring you into the bond of the covenant. 38 And I will also purge you of those who rebel and transgress against Me. I will bring them out of the land where they live as foreign residents, but they will not enter the land of Israel. Then you will know that I am the LORD.

39 "As for you, house of Israel, this is what the Lord GOD says: Go and serve your idols, each of you. But afterwards you will surely listen to Me, and you will no longer defile My holy name with your gifts and idols. 40 For on My holy mountain, Israel's high mountain"— the declaration of the Lord GOD—"there the entire house of Israel, all of them, will serve Me in the land. There I will accept them and will require your contributions and choicest gifts, all your holy offerings. 41 When I bring you from the peoples and gather you from the countries where you have been scattered, I will accept you as a pleasing aroma. And I will demonstrate My holiness through you in the sight of the nations. 42 When I lead you into the land of Israel, the land I swore[a] to give your fathers, you will know that I am the LORD. 43 There you will remember your ways and all your deeds you have defiled yourselves with, and you will loathe yourselves for all the evil things you have done. 44 You will know that I am the LORD, house of Israel, when I have dealt with you because of My name rather than according to your evil ways and corrupt acts." [This is] the declaration of the Lord GOD.

Fire in the South

45b The word of the LORD came to me: 46 "Son of man, face the south and preach against it. Prophesy against the forest land in the •Negev, 47 and say to the forest there: Hear the word of the LORD! This is what the Lord GOD says: I am about to ignite a fire in you, and it will devour every green tree and every dry tree in you. The blazing flame will not be extinguished, and every face from the south to the north will be scorched by it. 48 Then all people will see that I, •Yahweh, have kindled it. It will not be extinguished."

49 Then I said, "Ah, Lord GOD, they are saying of me: Isn't he [just] posing riddles?"

God's Sword of Judgment

21[c] The word of the LORD came to me again: 2 "Son of man, turn your face toward Jerusalem and preach against the sanctuaries. Prophesy against the land of Israel, 3 and say to it: This is what the LORD says: I am against you. I will draw My sword from its sheath and cut off both the righteous and the wicked from you. 4 Since I will cut off[d] [both] the righteous and the wicked, My sword will therefore come out of its sheath against everyone from the south to the north. 5 So all the people will know that I, the LORD, have taken My sword from its sheath—it will not be sheathed again.

6 "But you, son of man, groan! Groan bitterly with a broken heart[e] right before their eyes. 7 And when they ask you: Why are you groaning? then say: Because of the news that is coming. Every heart will melt, and every hand will become weak. Every spirit will be discouraged, and every knee will turn to water. Yes, it is coming and it will happen." [This is] the declaration of the Lord GOD.

8 The word of the LORD came to me: 9 "Son of man, prophesy: This is what the Lord says! You are to proclaim:

---

a 20:28,42 Lit lifted My hand   b 20:45 Ezk 21:1 in Hb   c 21:1 Ezk 21:6 in Hb   d 21:4 Lit off from you   e 21:6 Lit with broken loins

---

20:26 pass through [the fire]. Child sacrifice is the ultimate example of a Canaanite statute that was not good.

20:32 will never happen. Forget it! God would not release His people from His loving grip.

20:33 strong hand, an outstretched arm. Reminiscent of the delivery language used to describe God's rescue of Israel through the Exodus (Exod. 6:6; 32:11; Deut. 4:34; 5:15; 7:19; 11:2; Ps. 132:12), God's hand and arm will now purify Israel of rebels once again.

20:39 But afterwards. At the end of this age, God will end Israel's rebellious streak and all Israel will be saved (see Rom. 11:26). At that time, Israel will acknowledge Yahweh as a faithful God who forgives His people (vv. 42-44).

21:3 My sword ... cut off ... the wicked. God would soon use Babylon to carry out His discipline on His people—both righteous and wicked.

A sword! A sword is sharpened
and also polished.
10 It is sharpened for slaughter,
polished to flash like lightning!
Should we rejoice?
The scepter of My son,
the sword despises every tree.[a]
11 The sword is given to be polished,
to be grasped in the hand.
It is sharpened, and it is polished,
to be put in the hand of the slayer.
12 Cry out and wail, son of man,
for it is against My people.
It is against all the princes of Israel!
They are given over to the sword
with My people.
Therefore strike [your] thigh [in grief].
13 Surely it will be a trial!
And what if the sword despises
even the scepter?
The scepter will not continue.[a]
[This is] the declaration
of the Lord GOD.

14 Therefore, son of man, prophesy
and clap [your] hands together.
Let the sword strike two times, even three.
It is a sword for massacre,
a sword for great massacre—
it surrounds[b] them!
15 I have appointed a sword for slaughter[a]
at all their gates,
so that their hearts may melt
and many may stumble.
Alas! It is ready to flash like lightning;
it is drawn[a] for slaughter.
16 Slash to the right;
turn to the left—
wherever your blade is directed.
17 I also will clap My hands together,
and I will satisfy My wrath.
I, the LORD, have spoken."

18 Then the word of the LORD came to me: 19 "Now you, son of man, mark out two roads that the sword of Babylon's king can take. Both of them should originate from the same land. And make a signpost at the fork in the road to [each] city. 20 Mark out a road that the sword can take to Rabbah of the Ammonites and to Judah into fortified Jerusalem. 21 For the king of Bab-

ylon stands at the split in the road, at the fork of the two roads, to practice •divination: he shakes the arrows, consults the idols, and observes the liver. 22 The answer marked[c] Jerusalem appears in his right hand, [indicating] that he should set up battering rams, give the order to[d] slaughter, raise a battle cry, set battering rams against the gates, build a ramp, and construct a siege wall. 23 It will seem like false divination in the eyes of those who have sworn an oath to the Babylonians, but it will draw attention to [their] guilt so that they will be captured.

24 "Therefore, this is what the Lord GOD says: Because you have drawn attention to your guilt, exposing your transgressions, so that your sins are revealed in all your actions, since you have done this, you will be captured by them.

25 And you, profane and wicked prince of Israel,[e]
the day has come
for your punishment."[f]

26 This is what the Lord GOD says:

Remove the turban, and take off the crown.
Things will not remain as they are;[g]
exalt the lowly and bring down the exalted.
27 A ruin, a ruin,
I will make it a ruin!
Yet this will not happen
until He comes;
I have given the judgment to Him.[h]

28 "Now prophesy, son of man, and say: This is what the Lord GOD says concerning the Ammonites and their contempt. You are to proclaim:

Sword, sword!
[You are] drawn for slaughter,
polished to consume, to flash like lightning.
29 While they offer false visions
and lying divinations about you,
[the time] has come to put you
to the necks of the profane wicked ones;
the day has come
for your punishment.[f]

30 Return [it] to its sheath!

I will judge you[i]
in the place where you were created,
in the land of your origin.
31 I will pour out My indignation on you;

---

[a]21:10,13,15 Hb obscure [b]21:14 Or penetrates [c]21:22 Lit The divination for [d]22:22 Lit rams, open the mouth in [e]21:25 = King Zedekiah
[f]21:25,29 Lit come in the time of the punishment of the end [g]21:26 Lit This not this [h]21:27 Or comes to whom it rightfully belongs, and I will give it to Him; Gn 49:10 [i]21:30 = the Ammonites

---

21:9 sword. Ezekiel referenced battle imagery to indicate Jerusalem's pending siege and destruction. This was actually written as a song.

21:10 the scepter of my son. The people of Judah should not place false hope in their king (scepter), for God's judgment (with fire and sword) would destroy both the righteous

and wicked trees (20:47; 21:3-4).

21:21 observes the liver. At Damascus, Nebuchadnezzar is undecided on which road to take: towards Rabbah in Ammon or towards Jerusalem. For this he consulted two marked arrows shaken up (one picked). Then he turned to his household idols. Finally, sheep

were slaughtered so as to observe spots or irregularities on their livers. Apparently, the livers said Jerusalem, and the arrow and idols agreed.

21:25 day has come. Zedekiah would be king at the time of Jerusalem's fall.

21:27 A ruin! … until He comes. God will re-

I will blow the fire of My fury on you.
I will hand you over to brutal men,
skilled at destruction.

³² You will be fuel for the fire.
Your blood will be ⌊spilled⌋ in the land.
You will not be remembered,
for I, the LORD, have spoken."

Indictment of Sinful Jerusalem

22 The word of the LORD came to me: ² "Now, son of man, will you pass judgment? Will you pass judgment against the city of blood? Then explain all her abominations to her. ³ You are to say: This is what the Lord GOD says: A city that sheds blood within her ⌊walls⌋ so that her time of judgment has come and who makes idols for herself so that she is defiled! ⁴ You are guilty of the blood you have shed, and you are defiled from the idols you have made. You have brought your ⌊judgment⌋ days near and have come to your years ⌊of punishment⌋. Therefore, I have made you a disgrace to the nations and a mockery to all the lands. ⁵ Those who are near and those far away from you will mock you, you infamous one full of turmoil.

⁶ "Look, every prince of Israel within you has used his strength to shed blood. ⁷ Father and mother are treated with contempt, and the foreign resident is exploited within you. The fatherless and widow are oppressed in you. ⁸ You despise My holy things and profane My Sabbaths. ⁹ There are men within you who slander in order to shed blood. People who ⌊live⌋ in you eat at the mountain ⌊shrines⌋; they commit immoral acts within you. ¹⁰ Men within you have sexual intercourse with ⌊their⌋ father's wife, and violate women during their menstrual impurity. ¹¹ One man within you commits an abomination with his neighbor's wife; another wickedly defiles his daughter-in-law; and ⌊yet⌋ another violates his sister, his father's daughter. ¹² People who ⌊live⌋ in you accept bribes in order to shed blood. You take interest and profit ⌊on a loan⌋ and brutally extort your neighbors. You have forgotten Me." ⌊This is⌋ the declaration of the Lord GOD.

¹³ "Now look, I clap My hands together against the unjust gain you have made and against the blood shed among you. ¹⁴ Will your courage endure or your hands be strong in the days when I deal with you? I, the LORD, have spoken, and I will act. ¹⁵ I will disperse you among the nations and scatter you among the countries; I will purge your uncleanness. ¹⁶ You^a will be profaned in the sight of the nations. Then you will know that I am the LORD."

Jerusalem as God's Furnace

¹⁷ The word of the LORD came to me: ¹⁸ "Son of man, the house of Israel has become dross to Me. All of them are copper, tin, iron, and lead inside the furnace; they are the dross of silver. ¹⁹ Therefore, this is what the Lord GOD says: Because all of you have become dross, I am about to gather you into Jerusalem. ²⁰ Just as one gathers silver, copper, iron, lead, and tin into the furnace to blow fire on them and melt them, so I will gather ⌊you⌋ in My anger and wrath, put you ⌊inside⌋, and melt you. ²¹ Yes, I will gather you together and blow on you with the fire of My fury, and you will be melted within the city. ²² As silver is melted inside a furnace, so you will be melted inside the city. Then you will know that I, the LORD, have poured out My wrath on you."

Indictment of a Sinful Land

²³ The word of the LORD came to me: ²⁴ "Son of man, say to her: You are a land that has not been cleansed, that has not received rain in the day of indignation. ²⁵ The conspiracy of her prophets within her is^b like a roaring lion tearing ⌊its⌋ prey: they devour people, seize wealth and valuables, and multiply the widows within her. ²⁶ Her priests do violence to My law and profane My holy things. They make no distinction between the holy and the common, and they do not explain the difference between the clean and the unclean. They disregard^c My Sabbaths, and I am profaned among them.

²⁷ "Her officials within her are like wolves tearing ⌊their⌋ prey, shedding blood, and destroying lives in order to get unjust gain. ²⁸ Her prophets plaster with whitewash for them by seeing false visions and lying •divinations, and they say: This is what the Lord GOD says, when the LORD has not spoken. ²⁹ The people of the land have practiced extortion and committed robbery. They have oppressed the poor and needy and unlawfully exploited the foreign resident. ³⁰ I searched for a man among them who would repair the wall and stand in the gap before Me on behalf of the land so that I might not destroy it, but I found no one. ³¹ So I have poured out My indignation on them and consumed them with the fire of My fury. I have brought their actions down on their own heads." ⌊This is⌋ the declaration of the Lord GOD.

The Two Immoral Sisters

23 The word of the LORD came to me again: ² "Son of man, there were two women, daughters of the same mother, ³ who acted like prostitutes in Egypt, behaving promiscuously in their youth. Their

---

^a**22:16** One Hb ms, LXX, Syr, Vg read *I* / ^b**22:24–25** LXX reads *indignation,* ²⁵ *whose princes within her are* / ^c**22:26** Lit *close their eyes from*

---

store Jerusalem at the second coming of Jesus.

21:28 Ammonites. Evil nations were standing in line for judgment. The Ammonites were next.

22:13 clap My hands. Returning to the judgment motif of clapped hands (6:11; 21:14),

the sentence on Judah is formally pronounced because of their disregard for Moses' warning (Lev. 26:27-39; Deut. 28:64-68) that disobedience would result in exile (12:15; 20:23; 36:19). God cared less that His reputation would be tarnished by Israel's failure than He cares that Israel acts like His

people. Earlier, he had condemned false prophets for whitewashing their messages (13:10-15), and does so again (22:28). Similarly, Jesus condemns phony Pharisees for being more concerned with outward appearance than inner holiness (Matt. 23:27). God would much rather have us publicly fail as

breasts were fondled there, and their virgin nipples caressed. [4] The older one was named Oholah,[a] and her sister was Oholibah.[b] They became Mine and gave birth to sons and daughters. As for their names, Oholah represents Samaria and Oholibah represents Jerusalem.

[5] "Oholah acted like a prostitute even though she was Mine. She lusted after her lovers, the Assyrians: warriors [6] dressed in blue, governors and prefects, all of them desirable young men, horsemen riding on steeds. [7] She offered her sexual favors to them; all of them were the elite of Assyria. She defiled herself with all those she lusted after and with all their idols. [8] She didn't give up her promiscuity that began in Egypt, when men slept with her in her youth, caressed her virgin nipples, and poured out their lust on her. [9] Therefore, I handed her over to her lovers, the Assyrians she lusted for. [10] They exposed her nakedness, seized her sons and daughters, and killed her with the sword. Since they executed judgment against her, she became notorious among women.

[11] "Now her sister Oholibah saw ⌊this⌋, but she was ⌊even⌋ more depraved in her lust than Oholah, and made her promiscuous acts worse than those of her sister. [12] She lusted after the Assyrians: governors and prefects, warriors splendidly dressed, horsemen riding on steeds, all of them desirable young men. [13] And I saw that she had defiled herself; both of them ⌊had taken⌋ the same path. [14] But she increased her promiscuity when she saw male figures carved on the wall, images of the Chaldeans, engraved in vermilion, [15] wearing belts on their waists and flowing turbans on their heads; all of them looked like officers, a depiction of the Babylonians in Chaldea, the land of their birth. [16] At the sight of them[c] she lusted after them and sent messengers to them in Chaldea. [17] Then the Babylonians came to her, to the bed of love, and defiled her with their lust. But after she was defiled by them, she turned away from them in disgust. [18] When she flaunted her promiscuity and exposed her nakedness, I turned away from her in disgust just as I turned away from her sister. [19] Yet she multiplied her acts of promiscuity, remembering the days of her youth when she acted like a prostitute in the land of Egypt [20] and lusted after their lovers, whose sexual members were like those of donkeys and whose emission was like that of stallions. [21] So you revisited the indecency of your youth, when the Egyptians caressed your nipples to enjoy your youthful breasts.

[22] "Therefore Oholibah, this is what the Lord GOD says: I am going to incite your lovers against you, those you turned away from in disgust. I will bring them against you from every side: [23] the Babylonians and all the Chaldeans; Pekod, Shoa, and Koa; and all the Assyrians with them—desirable young men, all of them governors and prefects, officers and administrators, all of them riding on horses. [24] They will come against you with an alliance of nations and with weapons, chariots, and[d] wagons. They will set themselves against you on every side with shields, bucklers, and helmets. I will delegate judgment to them, and they will judge you by their own standards. [25] When I vent My jealous rage on you, they will deal with you in wrath. They will cut off your nose and ears, and your descendants will fall by the sword. They will seize your sons and daughters, and your descendants will be consumed by fire. [26] They will strip off your clothes and take your beautiful jewelry. [27] So I will put an end to your indecency and sexual immorality, which began in the land of Egypt, and you will not look longingly at them or remember Egypt any more.

[28] "For this is what the Lord GOD says: I am going to hand you over to those you hate, to those you turned away from in disgust. [29] They will treat you with hatred, take all you have worked for, and leave you stark naked, so that the shame of your debauchery will be exposed, both your indecency and promiscuity. [30] These things will be done to you because you acted like a prostitute with the nations, defiling yourself with their idols. [31] You have followed the path of your sister, so I will put her cup in your hand."

[32] This is what the Lord GOD says:

> You will drink your sister's cup,
>   which is deep and wide.
> You will be an object of[e] ridicule and scorn,
>   for it holds ⌊so⌋ much.
[33]
> You will be filled with drunkenness and grief,
>   with a cup of devastation and desolation,
>   the cup of your sister Samaria.
[34]
> You will drink it and drain ⌊it⌋;
>   then you will gnaw its broken pieces,
>   and tear your breasts.
> For I have spoken.

> > ⌊This is⌋ the declaration
> > of the Lord GOD.

[35] Therefore, this is what the Lord GOD says: "Because you have forgotten Me and cast Me behind

---

[a]**23:4** = Her Tent   [b]**23:4** = My Tent Is in Her   [c]**23:16** Lit of her eyes   [d]**23:24** LXX reads nations, from the north, chariots and; Hb obscure
[e]**23:32** Or It will bring

Christians than to be privately hypocritical in our activities.

22:30 stand in the gap. The great divide between a holy God and His rebellious people was often bridged by a prophet's pleas (see Jer. 37:3; 42:2).
23:5 lusted. Judah relied on foreign alliances

instead of her true love, God.

23:8 give up her promiscuity ... in Egypt. God's people pursued a political relationship with Egypt, though she proved to be an ineffective ally (see Ex. 17:3; Num. 11:5, 18, 20).
23:19 land of Egypt. From 600-586 B.C., Judah twice attempted to enlist Egypt's aid

against Babylon. In the first instance, King Jehoiakim rebelled in 600 B.C. after Egypt defeated Babylon in battle (2 Kings 24:1). In the second instance, Zedekiah relied on Egypt's promises of help in 588 B.C. (29:6-7; 2 Kings 25:1; Jer. 37:5-8).

23:31 her cup. The cup of intoxicating strong

your back, you must bear the consequences of your indecency and promiscuity."

36 Then the LORD said to me: "Son of man, will you pass judgment against Oholah and Oholibah? Then declare their abominations to them. 37 For they have committed adultery, and blood is on their hands; they have committed adultery with their idols. They have even made the children they bore to Me pass through ⌊the fire⌋ as food for the idols. 38 They also did this to Me: they defiled My sanctuary on that same day and profaned My Sabbaths. 39 On the same day they slaughtered their children for their idols, they entered My sanctuary to profane it. Yes, that is what they did inside My house.

40 "In addition, they sent for men who came from far away when a messenger was dispatched to them. And look how they came! You bathed, painted your eyes, and adorned yourself with jewelry for them. 41 You sat on a luxurious couch with a table spread before it, on which you had set My incense and oil. 42 The sound of a carefree crowd was there. Drunkards[a] from the desert were brought in, along with common men. They put bracelets on the women's hands and beautiful crowns on their heads. 43 Then I said concerning this woman worn out by adultery: Will they now have illicit sex with her, even her? 44 Yet they had sex with her as one does with a prostitute. This is how they had sex with Oholah and Oholibah, those obscene women. 45 But righteous men will judge them the way adulteresses and those who shed blood are judged, for they are adulteresses and blood is on their hands.

46 "This is what the Lord GOD says: Summon[b] an assembly against them and consign them to terror and plunder. 47 The assembly will stone them and cut them down with their swords. They will kill their sons and daughters and burn their houses with fire. 48 So I will put an end to indecency in the land, and all the women will be admonished not to imitate your indecent behavior. 49 They will repay you for your indecency, and you will bear the consequences for your sins of idolatry. Then you will know that I am the Lord GOD."

Parable of the Boiling Pot

24 The word of the LORD came to me in the ninth year, in the tenth month, on the tenth ⌊day⌋ of the month: 2 "Son of man, write down today's date, this very day. The king of Babylon has laid siege to Jerusalem this very day. 3 Now speak a parable to the rebellious house. Tell them: This is what the Lord GOD says:

Put the pot on ⌊the fire⌋—
put ⌊it⌋ on,
and then pour water into it!
4 Place the pieces of meat in it,
every good piece—
thigh and shoulder.
Fill it with choice bones.
5 Take the choicest of the flock
and also pile up the fuel[c] under it.
Bring it to a boil
and cook the bones in it."

6 Therefore, this is what the Lord GOD says:

Woe to the city of bloodshed,
the pot that has rust inside it,
and whose rust will not come off!
Empty it piece by piece;
lots should not be cast for its contents.
7 For the blood she shed[d] is in her midst.
She put it out on the bare rock;
she didn't pour it on the ground
to cover it with dust.
8 In order to stir up wrath and take vengeance,
I have put her blood on the bare rock,
so that it would not be covered.

9 Therefore, this is what the Lord GOD says:

Woe to the city of bloodshed!
I Myself will make the pile of kindling large.
10 Pile on the logs and kindle the fire!
Cook the meat well
and mix in the spices![e] [f]
Let the bones be burned!
11 Set the empty pot on its coals
so that it becomes hot and its copper glows.
Then its impurity will melt inside it;
its rust will be consumed.
12 It has frustrated every effort;[g]
its thick rust will not come off.
Into the fire with its rust!
13 Because of the indecency of your uncleanness—
since I tried to purify you,
but you would not be purified
from your uncleanness—
you will not be pure again
until I have satisfied My wrath on you.
14 I, the LORD, have spoken.
It is coming, and I will do it!
I will not refrain, I will not show pity,

---

a 23:42 Or Sabeans b 23:46 Or I will summon c 24:5 Lit bones d 24:7 Lit For her blood e 24:10 Some Hb mss read well; remove the broth; LXX reads fire so that the meat may be cooked and the broth may be reduced f 24:10 Or and stir the broth g 24:12 Hb obscure

---

drink that a guilty party drank left them reeling because God's judgment was contained in the cup (see Jer. 25:15-29; Hab. 2:15). This cup of wrath is also a theme found in the New Testament (Mark 14:36).

23:37-38 children ... pass through [the fire]. The people would not give up their pagan

practices of idolatry and child sacrifice, even committing these sins in God's temple.

24:2 laid siege. While hundreds of miles away in Babylon, Ezekiel received the news of Jerusalem's siege through a vision.

24:3 rebellious house. The house would soon receive its dues. It would be cooked

like meat in a pot.

24:4 Place the pieces of meat in it. Those arrogant leaders who remained from the first exile thought they had opted out of judgment. However, God revealed they were indeed special—special enough to be included on the menu (11:3).

and I will not relent.
I[a] will judge you
according to your ways and deeds.

⌊This is⌋ the declaration
of the Lord GOD.

The Death of Ezekiel's Wife: A Sign

15 Then the word of the LORD came to me: 16 "Son of man, I am about to take the delight of your eyes away from you with a fatal blow. But you must not lament or weep or let your tears flow. 17 Groan quietly; do not observe mourning rites for the dead. Put on your turban and strap your sandals on your feet; do not cover ⌊your⌋ mustache or eat the bread of mourners."[b]

18 I spoke to the people in the morning, and my wife died in the evening. The next morning I did just as I was commanded. 19 Then the people asked me, "Won't you tell us what these things you are doing mean for us?"

20 So I answered them: "The word of the LORD came to me: 21 'Say to the house of Israel: This is what the Lord GOD says: I am about to desecrate My sanctuary, the pride of your power, the delight of your eyes, and the desire of your heart. Also, the sons and daughters you left behind will fall by the sword. 22 Then you will do just as I have done: You will not cover ⌊your⌋ mustache or eat the bread of mourners.[b] 23 Your turbans will remain on your heads and your sandals on your feet. You will not lament or weep but will waste away because of your sins and will groan to one another. 24 Now Ezekiel will be a sign for you. You will do everything that he has done. When this happens, you will know that I am the Lord GOD.

25 " 'Son of man, know that on the day I take their stronghold from them, their pride and joy, the delight of their eyes and the longing of their hearts, ⌊as well as⌋ their sons and daughters, 26 on that day a fugitive will come to you and report the news. 27 On that day your mouth will be opened ⌊to talk⌋ with him; you will speak and no longer be mute. So you will be a sign for them, and they will know that I am the LORD.' "

Prophecies Against the Nations

Judgment against Ammon

25 Then the word of the LORD came to me: 2 "Son of man, turn your face toward the Ammonites and prophesy against them. 3 Say to the Ammonites: Hear the word of the Lord GOD: This is what the Lord GOD says: Because you said: Good! about My sanctuary when it was desecrated, about the land of Israel when

it was laid waste, and about the house of Judah when they went into exile, 4 therefore I am about to give you to the people of the east as a possession. They will set up their encampments and pitch their tents among you. They will eat your fruit and drink your milk. 5 I will make Rabbah a pasture for camels and Ammon a sheepfold. Then you will know that I am the LORD."

6 For this is what the Lord GOD says: "Because you clapped ⌊your⌋ hands, stamped ⌊your⌋ feet, and rejoiced over the land of Israel with wholehearted contempt, 7 therefore I am about to stretch out My hand against you and give you as plunder to the nations. I will cut you off from the peoples and eliminate you from the countries. I will destroy you, and you will know that I am the LORD."

Judgment against Moab

8 This is what the Lord GOD says: "Because Moab and Seir said: Look, the house of Judah is like all the ⌊other⌋ nations, 9 therefore I am about to expose Moab's flank beginning with its[c] frontier cities, the pride of the land: Beth-jeshimoth, Baal-meon, and Kiriathaim. 10 I will give it along with Ammon to the people of the east as a possession, so that Ammon will not be remembered among the nations. 11 So I will execute judgments against Moab, and they will know that I am the LORD."

Judgment against Edom

12 This is what the Lord GOD says: "Because Edom acted vengefully against the house of Judah and incurred grievous guilt by taking revenge on them, 13 therefore this is what the Lord GOD says: I will stretch out My hand against Edom and cut off both man and animal from it. I will make it a wasteland; they will fall by the sword from Teman to Dedan. 14 I will take My vengeance on Edom through My people Israel, and they will deal with Edom according to My anger and wrath. So they will know My vengeance." ⌊This is⌋ the declaration of the Lord GOD.

Judgment against Philistia

15 This is what the Lord GOD says: "Because the Philistines acted in vengeance and took revenge with deep contempt, destroying ⌊because of their⌋ ancient hatred, 16 therefore this is what the Lord GOD says: I am about to stretch out My hand against the Philistines, cutting off the Cherethites and wiping out what remains of the coastal peoples.[d] 17 I will execute great vengeance against them with furious rebukes. They will know that I am the LORD when I take My vengeance on them."

---

[a]24:14 Some Hb mss, LXX, Syr, Tg, Vg; other Hb mss read They   [b]24:17,22 Lit men   [c]25:9 Lit with the cities, with its   [d]25:16 Lit the seacoast

---

24:6 Empty ... lots should not be cast In the previous deportation, the Babylonians had cast lots to determine who would go. Now, nobody would wait for unlucky names to be called. This time, *everyone* would be deported.

24:27 you will be a sign for them. Ezekiel, the widower (his wife was taken in an instant by

God—24:15-19), offered a living picture of the agony and grief that awaited Judah. Just as Ezekiel was told not to mourn for his wife (v. 17), the exiles would be so stunned by news of Jerusalem's fall that they would be unable to mourn (vv. 22-27).

25:1-32:18. Just as Jeremiah devoted much of

his prophecy to a section of oracles concerning God's judgment of the nations surrounding Israel (Jer. 46-51), so Ezekiel prophesies against surrounding nations. The first five nations in Ezekiel's oracles match Jeremiah, while Tyre and Sidon to the northwest of Israel are added in Ezekiel. Syria, Elam, and Babylon,

The Downfall of Tyre

26 In the eleventh year, on the first ⌞day⌟ of the month, the word of the LORD came to me: 2 "Son of man, because Tyre said about Jerusalem: Good! The gateway to the peoples is shattered. She has been turned over to me. I will be filled ⌞now that⌟ she lies in ruins, 3 therefore this is what the Lord GOD says: See, I am against you, Tyre! I will raise up many nations against you, just as the sea raises its waves. 4 They will destroy the walls of Tyre and demolish her towers. I will scrape the soil from her and turn her into a bare rock. 5 She will become a place in the sea to spread nets, for I have spoken." ⌞This is⌟ the declaration of the Lord GOD. "She will become plunder for the nations, 6 and her villages on the mainland will be slaughtered by the sword. Then they will know that I am the LORD."

7 For this is what the Lord GOD says: "See, I am about to bring King Nebuchadnezzar of Babylon, king of kings, against Tyre from the north with horses, chariots, cavalry, and a vast company of troops. 8 He will slaughter your villages on the mainland with the sword. He will set up siege works against you, and will build a ramp[a] and raise a wall of shields against you. 9 He will direct the blows of his battering rams against your walls and tear down your towers with his iron tools. 10 His horses will be so numerous that their dust will cover you. When he enters your gates as ⌞an army⌟ entering a breached city, your walls will shake from the noise of cavalry, wagons, and chariots. 11 He will trample all your streets with the hooves of his horses. He will slaughter your people with the sword, and your mighty pillars will fall to the ground. 12 They will take your wealth as spoil and plunder your merchandise. They will also demolish your walls and tear down your beautiful homes. Then they will throw your stones, timber, and soil into the water. 13 I will put an end to the noise of your songs, and the sound of your lyres will no longer be heard. 14 I will turn you into a bare rock, and you will be a place to spread nets. You will never be rebuilt, for I, the LORD, have spoken." ⌞This is⌟ the declaration of the Lord GOD.

15 This is what the Lord GOD says to Tyre: "Won't the coasts and islands quake at the sound of your downfall, when the wounded groan and slaughter occurs within you? 16 All the princes of the sea will descend from their thrones, remove their robes, and strip off their embroidered garments. They will clothe themselves with trembling; they will sit on the ground, trem-

ble continually, and be appalled at you. 17 Then they will lament for you and say of you:

> How you have perished, city of renown,
> you who were populated from the seas![b]
> She who was powerful on the sea,
> she and all of her inhabitants
> inflicted their terror.[c]

18 Now the coastlands tremble
on the day of your downfall;
the islands in the sea
are alarmed by your demise."

19 For this is what the Lord GOD says: "When I make you a ruined city like ⌞other⌟ deserted cities, when I raise up the deep against you so that the mighty waters cover you, 20 then I will bring you down ⌞to be⌟ with those who descend to the •Pit, to the people of antiquity. I will make you dwell in the underworld[d] like[e] the ancient ruins, with those who descend to the Pit, so that you will no longer be inhabited or display ⌞your⌟ splendor[f] in the land of the living. 21 I will make you an object of horror, and you will no longer exist. You will be sought but will never be found again." ⌞This is⌟ the declaration of the Lord GOD.

The Sinking of Tyre

27 The word of the LORD came to me: 2 "Now, son of man, lament for Tyre. 3 Say to Tyre, who is located at the entrance of the sea, merchant of the peoples to many coasts and islands: This is what the Lord GOD says:

> Tyre, you declared:
> I am perfect in beauty.
> 4 Your realm was in the heart of the sea;
> your builders perfected your beauty.
> 5 They constructed all your planking
> with pine trees from Senir.[g]
> They took a cedar from Lebanon
> to make a mast for you.
> 6 They made your oars of oaks from Bashan.
> They made your deck of cypress wood
> from the coasts of Cyprus,
> ⌞inlaid⌟ with ivory.
> 7 Your sail was ⌞made of⌟
> fine embroidered linen from Egypt,
> and served as your banner.
> Your awning was of blue and purple fabric
> from the coasts of Elishah.
> 8 The inhabitants of Sidon and Arvad

---

[a] **26:8** Lit *ramp against you*   [b] **26:17** Some LXX mss read *How you were destroyed from the seas, city of renown!*   [c] **26:17** Lit *and all her inhabitants who put their terror on all her inhabitants*; Hb obscure   [d] **26:20** Lit *the lower parts of the earth*   [e] **26:20** Some Hb mss, LXX; other Hb mss, Syr read *in*   [f] **26:20** LXX reads *or appear*   [g] **27:5** = Mount Hermon

---

lands to the north and east, are addressed in Jeremiah. Tyre was overthrown by Nebuchadnezzar in 572 B.C. Babylon itself was defeated by Persia in 539 B.C.

26:2 Good! Tyre wasted no time laying claim to the monopoly of trade opportunities that became available after Jerusalem's demise.

26:5 she will become a place in the sea to spread nets. Much later than Ezekiel, Alexander the Great completed Tyre's doom, destroying the city completely. Today, only a land bridge exists where Tyre once was—a land bridge used by fishermen.

26:8 set up siege works. Babylon besieged

the nation of Tyre for 15 years. Tyre was able to hold out because of its navy.

27:3 Tyre ... I am perfect in beauty. Tyre was a city located on the coast and was known for its great navy, variety of goods, and trading port. The city of Tyre believed it was invincible—even against a formidable foe such as

were your rowers.
Your wise men were within you, Tyre;
they were your helmsmen.
9 The elders of Gebal and its wise men
were within you, repairing your leaks.

All the ships of the sea and their sailors
came to[a] you to barter for your goods.
10 ⌊Men of⌋ Persia, Lud, and Put
were in your army, ⌊serving⌋ as your warriors.
They hung shields and helmets in you;
they gave you splendor.
11 Men of Arvad and Helech
were ⌊stationed⌋ on your walls all around,
and Gamadites were in your towers.
They hung their shields[b] all around your walls;
they perfected your beauty.

12 "Tarshish was your trading partner because of
⌊your⌋ great wealth of every kind. They exchanged silver, iron, tin, and lead for your merchandise. 13 Javan, Tubal, and Meshech were your merchants. They exchanged slaves[c] and bronze utensils for your goods. 14 Those from Beth-togarmah exchanged horses, war horses, and mules for your merchandise. 15 Men of Dedan[d] were also your merchants; many coasts and islands were your regular markets. They brought back ivory tusks and ebony as your payment. 16 Aram[e] [f] was your trading partner because of your numerous products. They exchanged turquoise,[g] purple and embroidered cloth, fine linen, coral,[h] and rubies[i] for your merchandise. 17 Judah and the land of Israel were your merchants. They exchanged wheat from Minnith, meal,[j] honey, oil, and balm for your goods. 18 Damascus was also your trading partner because of your numerous products and your great wealth of every kind, ⌊trading⌋ in wine from Helbon and white wool.[k] 19 Vedan[l] and Javan from Uzal[m] dealt in your merchandise; wrought iron, cassia, and aromatic cane were ⌊exchanged⌋ for your goods. 20 Dedan was your merchant in saddlecloths for riding. 21 Arabia and all the princes of Kedar were your business[n] partners, trading with you in lambs, rams, and goats. 22 The merchants of Sheba and Raamah traded with you. They exchanged gold, the best of all spices, and all kinds of precious stones for your merchandise. 23 Haran, Canneh, Eden, the merchants of Sheba, Asshur, and Chilmad traded with you. 24 They were your merchants in choice garments, cloaks of blue and embroidered materials, and multicolored carpets,[m] which were bound and secured with cords in your marketplace. 25 Ships of Tarshish were the carriers for your goods.

So you became full and heavily loaded[o]
in the heart of the sea.
26 Your rowers have brought you
onto the high seas,
but the east wind has shattered you
in the heart of the sea.
27 Your wealth, merchandise, and goods,
your sailors and helmsmen,
those who repair your leaks,
those who barter for your goods,
and all the warriors within you,
with all the other people on board,[p]
sink into the heart of the sea
on the day of your downfall.

28 The countryside shakes
at the sound of your sailors' cries.
29 All those who handle an oar
disembark from their ships.
The sailors and all the helmsmen of the sea
stand on the shore.
30 They raise their voices over you
and cry out bitterly.
They throw dust on their heads;
they roll in ashes.
31 They shave their heads because of you
and wrap themselves in •sackcloth.
They weep over you
with deep anguish and bitter mourning.

32 In their wailing they lament for you,
mourning over you:
Who was like Tyre,
silenced[m] in the middle of the sea?
33 When your merchandise was unloaded
from the seas,
you satisfied many peoples.
You enriched the kings of the earth
with your abundant wealth and goods.
34 Now you are shattered by the sea
in the depths of the waters;
your goods and the people within you
have gone down.
35 All the inhabitants of the coasts and islands
are appalled at you.

---

a27:9 Lit sailors were with   b27:11 Or quivers; Hb obscure   c27:13 Lit souls of men   d27:15 LXX reads Rhodes   e27:16 Some Hb mss, Aq, Syr read Edom   f27:16 = Syria   g27:16 Hb obscure; Ezk 28:13; Ex 28:18; 39:11   h27:16 Hb obscure; Jb 28:18   i27:16 Hb obscure; Is 54:12   j27:17 Or resin; Hb obscure   k27:18 Or and wool from Zahar   l27:19 Or Dan   m27:19,24,32 Hb obscure   n27:21 Lit trading   o27:25 Or and very glorious   p27:27 Lit with all your assembly among you

---

Babylon. Chapter 28 refers to Tyre as a city of beauty and pride.

27:10–24 Mercenaries "hung their shields" and "helmets" on the walls to signal that they were on the job and ready to go. For Tyre, mercenaries would have been easy to come by in the normal order of trade. The scope of Tyre's commerce was extensive. Ammon sold wheat to Judah and Israel to use in trade with Tyre (v. 17). Helbon, a wine center northwest of Damascus, and Zahar, a desert area also northwest of Damascus, traded wine and wool with Damascus for use in trade with Tyre (v. 18). Many nations that traded with Tyre still exist today by the same name. Others have changed their names or no longer exist. Examples of these are the regions of Togarmah (Armenia); Aram (Syria); Kedar in Arabia; Dedan, northwest of Edom; and Haran, Cannah, and Eden in Mesopotamia.

Their kings shudder with fear;
⌊their⌋ faces are contorted.
36 Those who trade among the peoples
hiss at you;
you have become an object of horror
and will never exist again.”

The Fall of Tyre's Ruler

28 The word of the LORD came to me: 2 “Son of man, say to the ruler of Tyre: This is what the Lord GOD says:

Your[a] heart is proud,
and you have said: I am a god;
I sit in the seat of gods
in the heart of the sea.
Yet you are a man and not a god,
though you have regarded your heart
as that of a god.
3 Yes, you are wiser than Daniel;
no secret is hidden from you!
4 By your wisdom and understanding
you have acquired wealth for yourself.
You have acquired gold and silver
for your treasuries.
5 By your great skill in trading
you have increased your wealth,
but your heart has become proud
because of your wealth.”

6 Therefore this is what the Lord GOD says:

Because you regard your heart as that of a god,
7 I am about to bring strangers against you,
ruthless men from the nations.
They will draw their swords
against your magnificent wisdom
and will defile your splendor.
8 They will bring you down to the •Pit,
and you will die a violent death
in the heart of the sea.
9 Will you still say: I am a god,
in the presence of those who kill[b] you?
Yet you will be ⌊shown to be⌋ a man, not a god,
in the hands of those who kill you.
10 You will die the death of the uncircumcised
at the hands of strangers.
For I have spoken.

⌊This is⌋ the declaration
of the Lord GOD.

A Lament for Tyre's King

11 The word of the LORD came to me: 12 “Son of man, lament for the king of Tyre and say to him: This is what the Lord GOD says:

You were the seal[c] of perfection,[d]
full of wisdom and perfect in beauty.
13 You were in Eden, the garden of God.
Every kind of precious stone covered you:
carnelian, topaz, and diamond,[d]
beryl, onyx, and jasper,
sapphire,[e] turquoise[f] and emerald.[g]
Your mountings and settings were crafted in gold;
they were prepared on the day
you were created.
14 You were an anointed guardian cherub,
for[h] I had appointed you.
You were on the holy mountain of God;
you walked among the fiery stones.
15 From the day you were created
you were blameless in your ways
until wickedness was found in you.
16 Through the abundance of your trade,
you were filled with violence, and you sinned.
So I expelled you in disgrace
from the mountain of God,
and banished you, guardian cherub,[i]
from among the fiery stones.
17 Your heart became proud because of your beauty;
For the sake of your splendor
you corrupted your wisdom.
So I threw you down to the earth;
I made a spectacle of you before kings.
18 You profaned your sanctuaries
by the magnitude of your iniquities
in your dishonest trade.
So I sent out fire from within you,
and it consumed you.
I reduced you to ashes on the ground
in the sight of everyone watching you.
19 All those who know you among the nations
are appalled at you.
You have become an object of horror
and will never exist again.”

A Prophecy against Sidon

20 The word of the LORD came to me: 21 “Son of man, turn your face toward Sidon and prophesy against it. 22 You are to say: This is what the Lord GOD says:

---

[a]**28:2** Lit *Because your* [b]**28:9** Some Hb mss, LXX, Syr, Vg; other Hb mss read *of the one who kills* [c]**28:12** Or *sealer* [d]**28:12,13** Hb obscure [e]**28:13** Or *lapis lazuli* [f]**28:13** Or *malachite, or garnet* [g]**28:13** Or *beryl* [h]**28:14** Or *With an anointed guardian cherub* [i]**28:16** Or *and the guardian cherub banished you*

27:17 Judah and Israel also traded with Tyre.
28:7 ruthless men from the nations. Babylon, the unchallenged superpower among all nations, would besiege Tyre. Centuries later, Alexander the Great would besiege the city too.
28:13 Eden, the garden of God. Many see this

lament as a song about Satan, who likewise empowered wicked kings like the one in Tyre as he empowered the serpent in the garden of Eden. Others see here poetic language drawn from the very mythology the pagan kings believed—stories which had many parallels to the Genesis account of Eden.

28:14 guardian cherub. Cherubim were angelic beings with flaming swords that guarded the entrance to Eden (Gen. 3:24).
28:17 threw you down to the earth. God cannot tolerate pride in His presence, and drove the king of Tyre out.
28:21 Sidon. A sister city to Tyre. Sidon was

Look! I am against you, Sidon,
and I will display My glory within you.
They will know that I am the LORD
when I execute judgments against her
and demonstrate My holiness through her.
23 I will send a plague against her
and bloodshed in her streets;
the slain will fall within her,
while the sword is against her[a] on every side.
Then they will know that I am the LORD.

24 "The house of Israel will no longer be hurt by[b] prickling briers or painful thorns from all their neighbors who treat them with contempt. Then they will know that I am the Lord GOD.

25 "This is what the Lord GOD says: When I gather the house of Israel from the peoples where they are scattered and demonstrate My holiness through them in the sight of the nations, then they will live in their own land, which I gave to My servant Jacob. 26 They will live there securely, build houses, and plant vineyards. They will live securely when I execute judgments against all their neighbors who treat them with contempt. Then they will know that I am the LORD their God."

A Prophecy of Egypt's Ruin

29 In the tenth year, in the tenth ⌊month⌋ on the twelfth ⌊day⌋ of the month, the word of the LORD came to me: 2 "Son of man, turn your face toward Pharaoh king of Egypt and prophesy against him and against all of Egypt. 3 Speak ⌊to him⌋ and say: This is what the Lord GOD says:

Look, I am against you, Pharaoh king of Egypt,
the great monster[c] lying in the middle
of his Nile,
who says: My Nile is my own;
I made ⌊it⌋ for myself.
4 I will put hooks in your jaws
and make the fish of your streams
cling to your scales.
I will haul you up
from the middle of your Nile,
and all the fish of your streams
will cling to your scales.
5 I will leave you in the desert,
you and all the fish of your streams.
You will fall on the open ground
and will not be taken away
or gathered ⌊for burial⌋.

I have given you
to the beasts of the earth
and the birds of the sky as food.
6 Then all the inhabitants of Egypt
will know that I am the LORD,
for they[d] have been a staff ⌊made⌋ of reed
to the house of Israel.
7 When Israel grasped you by the hand,
you splintered, tearing all their shoulders;
when they leaned on you,
you shattered and made all their hips unsteady.[e]

8 "Therefore this is what the Lord GOD says: I am going to bring a sword against you and wipe out man and animal from you. 9 The land of Egypt will be a desolate ruin. Then they will know that I am the LORD. Because you[f] said: The Nile is my own; I made ⌊it⌋, 10 therefore, I am against you and your Nile. I will turn the land of Egypt into ruins, a desolate waste from Migdol to Syene, as far as the border of •Cush. 11 No human foot will pass through it, and no animal foot will pass through it. It will be uninhabited for 40 years. 12 I will make the land of Egypt a desolation among[g] desolate lands, and its cities will be a desolation among[h] ruined cities for 40 years. I will disperse the Egyptians among the nations and scatter them across the countries.

13 "For this is what the Lord GOD says: At the end of 40 years I will gather the Egyptians from the nations where they were dispersed. 14 I will restore the fortunes of Egypt and bring them back to the land of Pathros, the land of their origin. There they will be a lowly kingdom. 15 Egypt will be the lowliest of kingdoms and will never again exalt itself over the nations. I will make them so small they cannot rule over the nations. 16 It will never again be an object of trust for the house of Israel, drawing attention to their sin of turning to the Egyptians. Then they will know that I am the Lord GOD."

Babylon Receives Egypt as Compensation

17 In the twenty-seventh year in the first ⌊month⌋, on the first ⌊day⌋ of the month, the word of the LORD came to me: 18 "Son of man, Nebuchadnezzar king of Babylon made his army labor strenuously against Tyre. Every head was made bald and every shoulder chafed, but he and his army received no compensation from Tyre for the labor he expended against it. 19 Therefore this is what the Lord GOD says: I am going to give the land of Egypt to Nebuchadnezzar king of Babylon, who will carry off its wealth, seizing its spoil and taking its plun-

a 28:23 Or within her by the sword   b 28:24 Lit longer have   c 29:3 Or crocodile   d 29:6 LXX, Syr, Vg read you   e 29:7 LXX, Syr, Vg; MT reads and you caused their hips to stand   f 29:9 LXX, Syr, Vg; MT reads he   g 29:12 Or Egypt the most desolate of   h 29:12 Or be the most desolate of

both a center of commercial vitality and a place of sin.
28:24 prickling briers and painful thorns. Pagan nations would no longer be allowed to torment Israel.
28:25 demonstrate My holiness. God would redeem His reputation before the nations by re-

deeming His people.
29:3 Pharaoh ... great monster. Ezekiel portrayed Egypt as a menacing force lying in wait in the peaceful Nile.
29:1–32:32 As Jeremiah had focused on the judgment against Babylon, Ezekiel occupies himself here with the judgment of Egypt in

these four chapters. Six of seven oracles concerning Egypt date from 587-585 B.C., while 29:17-21 dates to 571 B.C. This oracle, which predicted Babylon's destruction of Egypt in 567 B.C., was placed here as a logical extension of the first oracle (vv. 1-16).
29:1 In the tenth year. This prophecy is dated

der. This will be his army's compensation. **20** I have given him the land of Egypt as the pay he labored for, since they worked for Me." ⌊This is⌋ the declaration of the Lord GOD. **21** "In that day I will cause a •horn to sprout for the house of Israel, and I will enable you to speak out among them. Then they will know that I am the LORD."

Egypt's Doom

30 The word of the LORD came to me: **2** "Son of man, prophesy and say: This is what the Lord GOD says:

Wail: Alas for the day!
3 For a day is near;
a day belonging to the LORD is near.
It will be a day of clouds,
a time ⌊of doom⌋ for the nations.
4 A sword will come against Egypt,
and there will be anguish in •Cush
when the slain fall in Egypt,
and its wealth is taken away,
and its foundations are torn down.
5 Cush, Put, and Lud,
and all the various foreign troops,ᵃ
plus Libyaᵇ and the men of the covenant landᶜ
will fall by the sword along with them.
6 This is what the LORD says:
Those who support Egypt will fall,
and its proud strength will collapse.
From Migdol to Syene
they will fall within it by the sword.
⌊This is⌋ the declaration
of the Lord GOD.
7 They will be desolate
amongᵈ desolate lands,
and their cities will lie
among ruinedᵉ cities.
8 They will know that I am the LORD
when I set fire to Egypt
and all its allies are shattered.

9 On that day, messengers will go out from Me in ships to terrify confident Cush. Anguish will come over them on the day of Egypt's ⌊doom⌋. For indeed it is coming."

10 This is what the Lord GOD says:

I will put an end to the hordesᶠ of Egypt
by the hand of Nebuchadnezzar king of Babylon.
11 He along with his people,

ruthless men from the nations,
will be brought in to destroy the land.
They will draw their swords against Egypt
and fill the land with the slain.
12 I will make the streams dry
and sell the land into the hands of evil men.
I will bring desolation
on the land and everything in it
by the hands of foreigners.
I, the LORD, have spoken.

13 This is what the Lord GOD says:

I will destroy the idols and put an end
to the false gods in Memphis.
There will no longer be
a prince from the land of Egypt.
So I will instill fear in that land.
14 I will make Pathros desolate,
set fire to Zoan,
and execute judgments on Thebes.
15 I will pour out My wrath on Pelusium,
the stronghold of Egypt,
and will wipe out the crowdsᶠ of Thebes.
16 I will set fire to Egypt;
Pelusium will writhe in anguish,
Thebes will be breached,
and Memphis will face foes in broad daylight.ᵍ
17 The young men of Onʰ and Pi-beseth
will fall by the sword,
and those citiesⁱ will go into captivity.
18 The day will be darkʲ in Tehaphnehes,
when I break the yoke of Egypt there
and its proud strength
comes to an end in the city.
A cloud will cover Tehaphnehes,ᵏ
and its villages will go into captivity.
19 So I will execute judgments against Egypt,
and they will know that I am the LORD.

Pharaoh's Power Broken

20 In the eleventh year, in the first ⌊month⌋, on the seventh ⌊day⌋ of the month, the word of the LORD came to me: **21** "Son of man, I have broken the arm of Pharaoh king of Egypt. Look, it has not been bandaged— ⌊no⌋ medicine has been applied and no splint put on to bandage it so that it can grow strong ⌊enough⌋ to handle a sword. **22** Therefore this is what the Lord GOD says: Look! I am against Pharaoh king of Egypt. I will break his arms, both the strong one and the one ⌊already⌋

ᵃ**30:5** Or all Arabia ᵇ**30:5** Lit Cub; Hb obscure ᶜ**30:5** Probably = Israel ᵈ**30:7** Or be the most desolate of ᵉ**30:7** Or will be the most ruined of ᶠ**30:10,15** Or pomp, or wealth ᵍ**30:16** Or foes daily ʰ**30:17** LXX, Vg; MT reads iniquity ⁱ**30:17** Or and the women; lit and they ʲ**30:18** Some Hb mss, LXX, Syr, Tg, Vg; MT reads will withhold ᵏ**30:18** Or Egypt; lit it

to January 587 B.C.; about a year after the siege of Jerusalem began and about a year and a half before she fell.

30:3 a day is near. The "day of the Lord" is sometimes used generally to mean a day of judgment. Sometimes it is used to refer to God's judgment on the nations at the end of human history. Sometimes it refers to a day of blessing and deliverance for Israel (v. 3). Ezekiel's prior prophecies (7:19; 13:15) that refer to the "day of the Lord" are in the context of the imminent destruction of Judah. Here it refers to the imminent destruction of Egypt. Other prophets, like Joel, refer to "day of the

Lord" as close at hand (Joel 1:15–2:11), and a future context (2:28:32; 3:1-21) when all nations are judged and the covenant with Israel is restored.

30:21 not been bandaged. A prior defeat by Nebuchadnezzar was only the beginning of Egypt's pain and suffering. Soon, Babylon

broken, and will make the sword fall from his hand. 23 I will disperse the Egyptians among the nations and scatter them among the countries. 24 I will strengthen the arms of Babylon's king and place My sword in his hand. But I will break the arms of Pharaoh, and he will groan before him as a mortally wounded man. 25 I will strengthen the arms of Babylon's king, but Pharaoh's arms will fall. They will know that I am the LORD when I place My sword in the hand of Babylon's king and he wields it against the land of Egypt. 26 When I disperse the Egyptians among the nations and scatter them among the countries, they will know that I am the LORD."

Downfall of Egypt and Assyria

31 In the eleventh year, in the third ⌊month⌋, on the first ⌊day⌋ of the month, the word of the LORD came to me: 2 "Son of man, say to Pharaoh king of Egypt and to his hordes:

Who are you like in your greatness?
3 Think of Assyria, a cedar in Lebanon,
with beautiful branches and shady foliage,
and of lofty height.
Its top was among the clouds.ᵃ
4 The waters caused it to grow;
the underground springs made it tall,
directing their rivers all around
the place where the tree was planted
and sending their channels
to all the trees of the field.
5 Therefore the cedar became greater in height
than all the trees of the field.
Its branches multiplied,
and its boughs grew long
as it spread ⌊them⌋ out
because of the plentiful water.
6 All the birds of the sky
nested in its branches,
and all the animals of the field
gave birth beneath its boughs;
all the great nations lived in its shade.
7 It was beautiful in its greatness,
in the length of its limbs,
for its roots extended to abundant water.
8 The cedars in God's garden could not rival it;
the pine trees couldn't compare
  with its branches,
nor could the plane trees match its boughs.
No tree in the garden of God

could compare with it in beauty.
9 I made it beautiful with its many limbs,
and all the trees of Eden,
which were in God's garden, envied it.

10 "Therefore this is what the Lord GOD says: Since itᵇ became great in height and set its top among the clouds,ᵃ and itᶜ grew proud on account of its height, 11 I determined to hand it over to a ruler of nations; he would surely deal with it. I banished it because of its wickedness. 12 Foreigners, ruthless men from the nations, cut it down and left it lying. Its limbs fell on the mountains and in every valley; its boughs lay broken in all the earth's ravines. All the peoples of the earth left its shade and abandoned it. 13 All the birds of the sky nested on its fallen trunk, and all the animals of the field were among its boughs. 14 ⌊This happened⌋ so that no trees ⌊planted⌋ beside water would become great in height and set their tops among the clouds,ᵃ and so that no ⌊other⌋ well-watered trees would reach them in height. For they have all been consigned to death, to the underworld, among the •people who descend to the •Pit.

15 "This is what the Lord GOD says: I caused grieving on the day the cedar went down to •Sheol. I closed off the underground deep because of it:ᵈ I held back the rivers of the deep, and ⌊its⌋ abundant waters were restrained. I made Lebanon mourn on account of it, and all the trees of the field fainted because of it. 16 I made the nations quake at the sound of its downfall, when I threw it down to Sheol ⌊to be⌋ with those who descend to the Pit. Then all the trees of Eden, all the well-watered trees, the choice and best of Lebanon, were comforted in the underworld. 17 They too descended with it to Sheol, to those slain by the sword. As its alliesᵉ ᶠ they had lived in its shade among the nations.

18 "Who then are you like in glory and greatness among Eden's trees? You also will be brought down to the underworld ⌊to be⌋ with the trees of Eden. You will lie among the uncircumcised with those slain by the sword. This is Pharaoh and all his hordes"—the declaration of the Lord GOD.

A Lament for Pharaoh

32 In the twelfth year, in the twelfth month, on the first ⌊day⌋ of the month, the word of the LORD came to me: 2 "Son of man, lament for Pharaoh king of Egypt and say to him:

You compare yourself to a lion of the nations,
butᵍ you are like a monster in the seas.

ᵃ31:3,10,14 Or thick foliage   ᵇ31:10 Syr, Vg; MT, LXX read you   ᶜ31:10 Lit its heart   ᵈ31:15 Or I covered it with the underground deep
ᵉ31:17 LXX, Syr read offspring   ᶠ31:17 Lit arm   ᵍ32:2 Or Lion of the nations, you are destroyed;

---

would crush every bone.
30:23, 26 disperse the Egyptians. Egypt followed Judah into exile (29:12), and was likewise allowed to return by Cyrus.

31:3 Assyria. In case Egypt needed more proof of its pending punishment, God encouraged them to consider once-powerful Assyria.

It came to ruin by the hand of Babylon.
31:12 Babylon felled the mighty cedar of Assyria.

31:16 the trees of Eden … were comforted. Trees are used in this passage to represent nations. "Trees of Eden" represent the beautiful nations that were consoled by the fact that

even the mightiest nation could not withstand Babylon.

31:17 slain by the sword. Smaller nations preceded Assyria in defeat. They shared the same murderous fate.

31:18 God made sure the pharaoh got the message. His end was near.

You thrash about in your rivers,
churn up the waters with your feet,
and muddy the[a] rivers.”

3 This is what the Lord GOD says:

I will spread My net over you
with an assembly of many peoples,
and they[b] will haul you up in My net.
4 I will abandon you on the land
and hurl you on the open field.
I will cause all the birds of the sky
to settle on you
and let the beasts of the entire earth
eat their fill of you.
5 I will put your flesh on the mountains
and fill the valleys with your carcass.
6 I will drench the land
with the flow of your blood,
[even] to the mountains;
the ravines will be filled with your [gore].

7 When I snuff you out,
I will cover the heavens
and darken their stars.
I will cover the sun with a cloud,
and the moon will not give its light.
8 I will darken all the shining lights
in the heavens over you,
and will bring darkness on your land.
                    [This is] the declaration
                        of the Lord GOD.

9 I will trouble the hearts of many peoples,
when I bring about your destruction
among the nations,
in countries you do not know.
10 I will cause many nations to be appalled at you,
and their kings will shudder with fear
    because of you
when I brandish My sword in front of them.
On the day of your downfall
each of them will tremble
every moment for his life.

11 For this is what the Lord GOD says:

The sword of Babylon's king
will come against you!
12 I will make your hordes fall
by the swords of warriors,
all of them ruthless men from the nations.

They will ravage Egypt's pride,
and all its hordes will be destroyed.
13 I will slaughter all its cattle
that are beside many waters.
No human foot will churn them again,
and no cattle hooves will disturb them.
14 Then I will let their waters settle
and will make their rivers flow like oil.
                    [This is] the declaration
                        of the Lord GOD.
15 When I make the land of Egypt a desolation,
so that it is emptied of everything in it,
when I strike down all who live there,
then they will know that I am the LORD.

16 “This is a lament that will be chanted; the women of the nations will chant it. They will chant it over Egypt and all its hordes.” [This is] the declaration of the Lord GOD.

Egypt in Sheol

17 In the twelfth year,[c] on the fifteenth [day] of the month, the word of the LORD came to me: 18 “Son of man, wail over the hordes of Egypt and bring Egypt and the daughters of mighty nations down to the underworld,[d] [to be] with those who descend to the •Pit:

19 Whom do you surpass in loveliness?
Go down and be laid to rest
with the uncircumcised!
20 They will fall among those slain by the sword.
A sword is appointed!
They drag her and all her hordes away.
21 Warrior leaders will speak
from the middle of •Sheol
about him[e] and his allies:
They have come down;
the uncircumcised lie
slain by the sword.

22 Assyria is there with all her company;
her graves are all around her.
All of them are slain, fallen by the sword.
23 Her graves are set in the deepest regions
of the Pit,
and her company is all around her burial place.
All of them are slain, fallen by the sword—
they who [once] spread terror
in the land of the living.

24 Elam is there
with all her hordes around her grave.

---

a 32:2 Lit their   b 32:3 LXX, Vg read I   c 32:17 LXX reads year, in the first month,   d 32:18 Lit the lower parts of the earth   e 32:21 Either Pharaoh or Egypt

---

32:2 lion. Lions were symbols of strength and dominance (cf. Judah's kings, 19:23-9). Such was the apparent power of the pharaoh.

32:17–25 In Ezekiel's final message against Egypt (April 585 B.C.), he recounts all the powers fallen under the Lord's hand and reminds Egypt that she is next. Egypt will join the “uncir-cumcised” nations already in the “pit” (v. 18) who suffer God's judgment for their oppression of Israel. Egypt would join Assyria in the pit.

32:24 Elam. Elam, located east of Babylon, was devastated by the Assyrians in the late seventh century B.C. Jeremiah also prophe-sied against Elam in 597 B.C. (Jer. 49:34-39), probably because she had joined As-syria in the conquest of Israel's northern kingdom (Isa. 22:6). Elam was invaded by Nebuchadnezzar in 596. Later she joined Babylon in the destruction and exile of Jeru-salem (Ezra 2:7, 31; 8:7). Elam was taken over by the Medo-Persians (sixth century

All of them are slain, fallen by the sword—
they who went down
   to the underworld[a] uncircumcised,
who ⌊once⌋ spread their terror
in the land of the living.
They bear their disgrace
with those who descend to the Pit.

25 Among the slain
they prepare a resting place for Elam
with all her hordes.
Her graves are all around her.
All of them are uncircumcised,
slain by the sword,
although their terror was ⌊once⌋ spread
in the land of the living.
They bear their disgrace
with those who descend to the Pit.
They are placed among the slain.

26 Meshech and Tubal[b] are there,
with all their hordes.
Their graves are all around them.
All of them are uncircumcised,
   slain by the sword,
although their terror was ⌊once⌋ spread
in the land of the living.

27 They do[c] not lie down
with the fallen warriors of the uncircumcised,[d]
who went down to Sheol
with their weapons of war,
whose swords were placed under their heads.
The punishment for their sins
rested on their bones,
although the terror of ⌊these⌋ warriors
was ⌊once⌋ in the land of the living.

28 But you will be shattered
and will lie down among the uncircumcised,
with those slain by the sword.

29 Edom is there, her kings and all her princes,
who, despite their strength, have been placed
among those slain by the sword.
They lie down with the uncircumcised,
with those who descend to the Pit.

30 All the leaders of the north
and all the Sidonians are there.
They went down in shame with the slain,
despite the terror their strength inspired.
They lie down uncircumcised
with those slain by the sword.

They bear their disgrace
with those who descend to the Pit.

31 Pharaoh will see them
and be comforted over all his hordes—
Pharaoh and all his army,
slain by the sword.

⌊This is⌋ the declaration
of the Lord GOD.

32 For I will spread My[e] terror
in the land of the living,
so Pharaoh and all his hordes
will be laid to rest among the uncircumcised,
with those slain by the sword."

⌊This is⌋ the declaration
of the Lord GOD.

Ezekiel as Israel's Watchman

33 The word of the LORD came to me: 2 "Son of man, speak to your people and tell them: Suppose I bring the sword against a land, and the people of that land select a man from among them, appointing him as their watchman, 3 and he sees the sword coming against the land and blows his trumpet to warn the people. 4 Then, if anyone hears the sound of the trumpet but ignores the warning, and the sword comes and takes him away, his blood will be on his own head. 5 ⌊Since⌋ he heard the sound of the trumpet but ignored the warning, his blood is on his own hands.[f] If he had taken warning, he would have saved his life. 6 However, if the watchman sees the sword coming but doesn't blow the trumpet, so that the people aren't warned, and the sword comes and takes away their lives, then they have been taken away because of their iniquity, but I will hold the watchman accountable for their blood.

7 "As for you, son of man, I have made you a watchman for the house of Israel. When you hear a word from My mouth, give them a warning from Me. 8 If I say to the wicked: Wicked one, you will surely die, but you do not speak out to warn him about his way, that wicked person will die for his iniquity, yet I will hold you responsible for his blood. 9 But if you warn a wicked person to turn from his way and he doesn't turn from it, he will die for his iniquity, but you will have saved your life.

10 "Now as for you, son of man, say to the house of Israel: You have said this: Our transgressions and our sins are ⌊heavy⌋ on us, and we are wasting away because of them! How then can we survive? 11 Tell them: As I live"—the declaration of the Lord GOD—"I take no

---

[a]**32:24** Lit *the lower parts of the earth* [b]**32:26** Lit *Meshech-tubal* [c]**32:27** Or *Do they . . . ?* [d]**32:27** LXX reads *of antiquity* [e]**32:32** Alt Hb tradition, LXX, Syr read *his* [f]**33:5** Lit *on him*

B.C.), but full judgment was still to come.

33:1–48:35 The last section of Ezekiel's prophecy is concerned with the fulfillment of God's covenant ideal for Israel. He would renew his commitment with them (ch. 33), raise a new David to shepherd them (ch. 34), defeat their enemies and return them to prosperity (chs.

35-36) resurrect the covenant community (ch. 37) defeat the last-ditch efforts of nations hostile to Israel (chs. 38-39), and dwell with His people in a renewed Jerusalem (chs. 40-48).

33:6 accountable for their blood. The watchman was held responsible for the safety of all the inhabitants inside the city walls. The spiri-

tual condition of Jerusalem was of vital importance.

33:10 sins are [heavy] on us. The exiles finally made a significant spiritual breakthrough. They recognized their weighty sinfulness.

33:11 that the wicked person should turn from his ways. God's remedy is sincere re-

---

pleasure in the death of the wicked, but rather that the wicked person should turn from his way and live. Repent, repent of your evil ways! Why will you die, house of Israel?

12 "Now, son of man, say to your people: The righteousness of the righteous person will not save him on the day of his transgression; neither will the wickedness of the wicked person cause him to stumble on the day he turns from his wickedness. The righteous person won't be able to survive by his righteousness on the day he sins. 13 When I tell the righteous person that he will surely live, but he trusts in his righteousness and commits iniquity, then none of his righteousness will be remembered, and he will die because of the iniquity he has committed.

14 "So when I tell the wicked person: You will surely die, but he repents of his sin and does what is just and right— 15 he returns collateral, makes restitution for what he has stolen, and walks in the statutes of life without practicing iniquity—he will certainly live; he will not die. 16 None of the sins he committed will be held against him. He has done what is just and right; he will certainly live.

17 "But your people say: The Lord's way isn't fair, even though it is their own way that isn't fair. 18 When a righteous person turns from his righteousness and commits iniquity, he will die on account of this. 19 But when a wicked person turns from his wickedness and does what is just and right, he will live because of this. 20 Yet you say: The Lord's way isn't fair. I will judge each of you according to his ways, house of Israel."

The News of Jerusalem's Fall

21 In the twelfth year of our exile, in the tenth ⌊month⌋, on the fifth ⌊day⌋ of the month, a fugitive from Jerusalem came to me and reported, "The city has been taken!" 22 Now the hand of the LORD had been on me the evening before the fugitive arrived, and He opened my mouth before the man came to me in the morning. So my mouth was opened and I was no longer mute.

Israel's Continued Rebellion

23 Then the word of the LORD came to me: 24 "Son of man, those who live in the[a] ruins in the land of Israel are saying: Abraham was only one person, yet he received possession of the land. But we are many; the land has been given to us as a possession. 25 Therefore say to them: This is what the Lord GOD says: You eat ⌊meat⌋ with blood ⌊in it⌋, raise your eyes to your idols, and shed blood. Should you then receive possession of the land? 26 You have relied on your swords, you have

committed abominations, and each of you has defiled his neighbor's wife. Should you then receive possession of the land?

27 "Tell them this: This is what the Lord GOD says: As surely as I live, those who are in the ruins will fall by the sword, those in the open field I have given to wild animals to be devoured, and those in the strongholds and caves will die by plague. 28 I will make the land a desolate waste, and its proud strength will come to an end. The mountains of Israel will become desolate, with no one passing through. 29 They will know that I am the LORD when I make the land a desolate waste because of all the abominations they have committed.

30 "Now, son of man, your people are talking about you near the ⌊city⌋ walls and in the doorways of their houses. One person speaks to another, each saying to his brother: Come and hear what the message is that comes from the LORD! 31 So My people come to you in crowds,[b] sit in front of you, and hear your words, but they don't obey them. Although they express love with their mouths, their hearts pursue unjust gain. 32 Yes, to them you are like a singer of love songs who has a beautiful voice and plays skillfully on an instrument. They hear your words, but they don't obey them. 33 Yet when it comes—and it will definitely come—then they will know that a prophet has been among them."

The Shepherds and God's Flock

34 The word of the LORD came to me: 2 "Son of man, prophesy against the shepherds of Israel. Prophesy, and say to them: This is what the Lord GOD says to the shepherds: Woe to the shepherds of Israel, who have been feeding themselves! Shouldn't the shepherds feed their flock? 3 You eat the fat, wear the wool, and butcher the fatlings, but you do not tend the flock. 4 You have not strengthened the weak, healed the sick, bandaged the injured, brought back the strays, or sought the lost. Instead, you have ruled them with violence and cruelty. 5 They were scattered for lack of a shepherd; they became food for all the wild animals when they were scattered. 6 My flock went astray on all the mountains and every high hill. They were scattered over the whole face of the earth, and there was no one searching or seeking ⌊for them⌋.

7 "Therefore, you shepherds, hear the word of the LORD. 8 As I live"—the declaration of the Lord GOD— "because My flock has become ⌊prey and⌋ food for every wild animal since ⌊they⌋ lack a shepherd, for My shepherds do not search for My flock, and ⌊because⌋ the

---

pentance, without which there is not true faith.

33:12-20 In God's justice system, every person is held accountable for personal choices (18:21-29). Judgment is meted out on a fair and equitable scale (vv. 17-20).

33:22 I was no longer mute. When Babylon finally took over Jerusalem, God's restric-

tions on Ezekiel were lifted (see 3:26).

33:24 only one person … But we are many. The remaining Jews appealed to strength in numbers, hoping to change God's plans. Like homesick children, they wanted to stay in their homeland.

34:2 shepherds of Israel. Leaders were often regarded as shepherds (Num 27:17; Isa. 44:28; Jer. 23:2). These misfit shepherds disregarded the physical well-being and spiritual condition of the people under their care.

34:5 scattered for lack of a shepherd. As a result of their leaders' selfishness, the entire

shepherds feed themselves rather than My flock, [9] therefore, you shepherds, hear the word of the LORD!

[10] "This is what the Lord GOD says: Look, I am against the shepherds. I will demand My flock from them[a] and prevent them from shepherding the flock. The shepherds will no longer feed themselves, for I will rescue My flock from their mouths so that they will not be food for them.

[11] "For this is what the Lord GOD says: See, I Myself will search for My flock and look for them. [12] As a shepherd looks for his sheep on the day he is among his scattered flock, so I will look for My flock. I will rescue them from all the places where they have been scattered on a cloudy and dark day. [13] I will bring them out from the peoples, gather them from the countries, and bring them into their own land. I will shepherd them on the mountains of Israel, in the ravines, and in all the inhabited places of the land. [14] I will tend them with good pasture, and their grazing place will be on Israel's lofty mountains. There they will lie down in a good grazing place; they will feed in rich pasture on the mountains of Israel. [15] I will tend My flock and let them lie down." ⌊This is⌋ the declaration of the Lord GOD. [16] "I will seek the lost, bring back the strays, bandage the injured, and strengthen the weak, but I will destroy[b] the fat and the strong. I will shepherd them with justice.

[17] "The Lord GOD says to you, My flock: I am going to judge between one sheep and another, between the rams and male goats. [18] Isn't it enough for you to feed on the good pasture? Must you also trample the rest of the pasture with your feet? Or ⌊isn't it enough⌋ that you drink the clear water? Must you also muddy the rest with your feet? [19] Yet My flock has to feed on what your feet have trampled, and drink what your feet have muddied.

[20] "Therefore, this is what the Lord GOD says to them: See, I Myself will judge between the fat sheep and the lean sheep. [21] Since you have pushed with flank and shoulder and butted all the weak ones with your horns until you scattered them all over, [22] I will save My flock, and they will no longer be prey for you. I will judge between one sheep and another. [23] I will appoint over them a single shepherd, My servant David, and he will shepherd them. He will tend them himself and will be their shepherd. [24] I, the LORD, will be their God, and My servant David will be a prince among them. I, the LORD, have spoken.

[25] "I will make a covenant of peace with them and eliminate dangerous animals in the land, so that they may live securely in the wilderness and sleep in the forest. [26] I will make them and the area around My hill a blessing: I will send down showers in their season—showers[c] of blessing. [27] The trees of the field will give their fruit, and the land will yield its produce; My flock will be secure in their land. They will know that I am the LORD when I break the bars of their yoke and rescue them from the hands of those who enslave them. [28] They will no longer be prey for the nations, and the wild animals of the land will not consume them. They will live securely, and no one will frighten ⌊them⌋. [29] I will establish for them a place renowned for ⌊its⌋ agriculture,[d] and they will no longer be victims of famine in the land. They will no longer endure the insults of the nations. [30] Then they will know that I, the LORD their God, am with them, and that they, the house of Israel, are My people." ⌊This is⌋ the declaration of the Lord GOD. [31] "You are My flock, the human flock of My pasture, and I am your God." ⌊This is⌋ the declaration of the Lord GOD.

A Prophecy against Edom

35 The word of the LORD came to me: [2] "Son of man, turn your face toward Mount Seir and prophesy against it. [3] Say to it: This is what the Lord GOD says:

Look! I am against you, Mount Seir.
I will stretch out My hand against you
and make you a desolate waste.
[4] I will turn your cities into ruins,
and you will become a desolation.
Then you will know that I am the LORD.

[5] "Because you maintained an ancient hatred and handed over the Israelites to the power of the sword in the time of their disaster, the time of final punishment, [6] therefore, as I live"—⌊this is⌋ the declaration of the Lord GOD—"I will destine you for bloodshed, and it will pursue you. Since you did not hate bloodshed, it will pursue you. [7] I will make Mount Seir a desolate waste and will cut off from it those who come and go. [8] I will fill its mountains with the slain; those slain by the sword will fall on your hills, in your valleys, and in all your ravines. [9] I will make you a perpetual desolation; your cities will not be inhabited. Then you will know that I am the LORD.

---

[a] **34:10** Lit *their hand* [b] **34:16** Some Hb mss, LXX, Syr, Vg read *watch over* [c] **34:26** Lit *season; they will be showers* [d] **34:29** LXX, Syr read *a plant of peace*

---

flock would suffer. Ezekiel referred to the divide-and-conquer strategy of the Exile as a flock without a shepherd (see Mark 6:34).

34:16 the fat and the strong. The tables were turned. The selfish leaders would now be destroyed. Then God would respond and tend to the discarded sheep Himself.

34:17 I am going to judge. God turned His attention to the individuals represented in the flock. Judgment would be handed out to each.

34:23-24 My servant David. Ezekiel described a future united kingdom with a king who would truly care for the sheep. Some see this as a reference to Jesus' rule of the king-

dom, while others believe David will rule under Jesus.

35:2 Mount Seir. While on the subject of peace, God encouraged His people by judging one of their worst enemies, Edom (see Gen. 32-33).

35:5 time of final punishment. The Edomites

10 "Because you said: These two nations and two lands will be mine, and we will possess them—though the LORD was there— 11 therefore, as I live"—the declaration of the Lord GOD—"I will treat ⌊you⌋ according to the anger and jealousy you showed in your hatred of them. I will make Myself known among them[a] when I judge you. 12 Then you will know that I, the LORD, have heard all the blasphemies you uttered against the mountains of Israel, saying: They are desolate. They have been given to us to devour! 13 You boasted against Me with your mouth, and spoke many words against Me. I heard ⌊it⌋ Myself!

14 "This is what the Lord GOD says: While the whole world rejoices, I will make you a desolation. 15 Just as you rejoiced over the inheritance of the house of Israel because it became a desolation, so I will deal with you: you will become a desolation, Mount Seir, and ⌊so will⌋ all Edom in its entirety. Then they will know that I am the LORD.

Restoration of Israel's Mountains

36 "Son of man, prophesy to the mountains of Israel and say: Mountains of Israel, hear the word of the LORD. 2 This is what the Lord GOD says: Because the enemy has said about you, 'Good! The ancient heights have become our possession,' 3 therefore, prophesy and say: This is what the Lord GOD says: Because they have made you desolate and have trampled you from every side, so that you became a possession for the rest of the nations and an object of people's gossip and slander, 4 therefore, mountains of Israel, hear the word of the Lord GOD. This is what the Lord GOD says to the mountains and hills, to the ravines and valleys, to the desolate ruins and abandoned cities, which have become plunder and a mockery to the rest of the nations all around.

5 "This is what the Lord GOD says: Certainly in My burning zeal I speak against the rest of the nations and all of Edom, who took[b] My land as their own possession with wholehearted rejoicing and utter contempt, so that its pastureland became[c] plunder. 6 Therefore, prophesy concerning the land of Israel and say to the mountains and hills, to the ravines and valleys: This is what the Lord GOD says: Look, I speak in My burning zeal because you have endured the insults of the nations. 7 Therefore this is what the Lord GOD says: I swear[d] that the nations all around you will endure their own insults.

8 "You, mountains of Israel, will put forth your branches and bear your fruit for My people Israel, since their arrival is near. 9 Look! I am on your side; I will turn toward you, and you will be tilled and sown. 10 I will fill you with people, with the whole house of Israel in its entirety. The cities will be inhabited and the ruins rebuilt. 11 I will fill you with people and animals, and they will increase and be fruitful. I will make you inhabited as you once were and make ⌊you⌋ better off than you were before. Then you will know that I am the LORD. 12 I will cause people, My people Israel, to walk on you; they will possess you, and you will be their inheritance. You will no longer deprive them of ⌊their⌋ children.

13 "This is what the Lord GOD says: Because people are saying to you: You devour men and deprive your nation of children, 14 therefore, you will no longer devour men and deprive your nation of children."[e] ⌊This is⌋ the declaration of the Lord GOD. 15 "I will no longer allow the insults of the nations to be heard against you, and you will not have to endure the reproach of the peoples anymore; you will no longer cause your nation to stumble."[f] ⌊This is⌋ the declaration of the Lord GOD.

Restoration of Israel's People

16 The word of the LORD came to me: 17 "Son of man, while the house of Israel lived in their land, they defiled it with their conduct and actions. Their behavior before Me was like menstrual impurity. 18 So I poured out My wrath on them because of the blood they had shed on the land, and because they had defiled it with their idols. 19 I dispersed them among the nations, and they were scattered among the countries. I judged them according to their conduct and actions. 20 When they came to the nations where they went, they profaned My holy name, because it was said about them: These are the people of the LORD, yet they had to leave His land ⌊in exile⌋. 21 Then I had concern for My holy name, which the house of Israel profaned among the nations where they went.

22 "Therefore, say to the house of Israel: This is what the Lord GOD says: It is not for your sake that I will act, house of Israel, but for My holy name, which you profaned among the nations where you went. 23 I will honor the holiness of My great name, which has been profaned among the nations—the name you have profaned among them. The nations will know that I am •Yahweh"—the declaration of the Lord GOD—"when I demonstrate My holiness through you in their sight.

24 "For I will take you from the nations and gather you from all the countries, and will bring you into your

---

a35:11 LXX reads you b36:5 Lit gave c36:5 Or contempt, to empty it of; Hb obscure d36:7 Lit lift up My hand e36:14 Alt Hb tradition reads and cause your nation to stumble f36:15 Some Hb mss, Tg read no longer bereave your nation of children

---

showed their true colors when they raided the weakened Jerusalem (Obad. 12-14). They cheered when Nebuchadnezzar destroyed the city (_Ps. 137_; _Joel 3:19_).

36:1, 4 mountains. Earlier, the prophet has pronounced judgment on the mountains of Israel because of Israel's worship of idols in the "high places" (6:1-14). After this judgment had been fulfilled, Ezekiel then pronounced a double judgment on Edom's Mount Seir (35:1-3, 14) for Edom's role in reducing Israel's Holy Mount (Jerusalem). Now the prophet again speaks to the mountains of Israel, but this time to announce judgment on the "rest of the nations" the Lord employed to chastise His daughter Israel. Israel's mountains would flourish once more as she is brought back from exile and enjoys prosperity and security (vv. 8-15).

36:22 It is not for your sake. God's restoration of his people was not a personal favor to the

own land. 25 I will also sprinkle clean water on you, and you will be clean. I will cleanse you from all your impurities and all your idols. 26 I will give you a new heart and put a new spirit within you; I will remove your heart of stone[a] and give you a heart of flesh. 27 I will place My Spirit within you and cause you to follow My statutes and carefully observe My ordinances. 28 Then you will live in the land that I gave your fathers; you will be My people, and I will be your God. 29 I will save you from all your uncleanness. I will summon the grain and make it plentiful, and will not bring famine on you. 30 I will also make the fruit of the trees and the produce of the field plentiful, so that you will no longer experience reproach among the nations on account of famine.

31 "Then you will remember your evil ways and your deeds that were not good, and you will loathe yourselves for your iniquities and abominations. 32 It is not for your sake that I will act"—the declaration of the Lord GOD—"let this be known to you. Be ashamed and humiliated because of your ways, house of Israel!

33 "This is what the Lord GOD says: On the day I cleanse you from all your iniquities, I will cause the cities to be inhabited, and the ruins will be rebuilt. 34 The desolate land will be cultivated instead of lying desolate in the sight of everyone who passes by. 35 Then they will say: This land that was desolate has become like the garden of Eden. The cities that were once ruined, desolate, and destroyed are ⌊now⌋ fortified and inhabited. 36 Then the nations that remain around you will know that I, the LORD, have rebuilt what was destroyed and have replanted what was desolate. I, the LORD, have spoken and I will do ⌊it⌋.

37 "This is what the Lord GOD says: I will respond to the house of Israel and do this for them: I will multiply them in number like a flock.[b] 38 So the ruined cities will be filled with a flock of people, just as the flock of sheep for sacrifice is filled[c] in Jerusalem during its appointed festivals. Then they will know that I am the LORD."

The Valley of Dry Bones

37 The hand of the LORD was on me, and He brought me out by His Spirit and set me down in the middle of the valley; it was full of bones. 2 He led me all around them. There were a great many of them on the surface of the valley, and they were very dry. 3 Then He said to me, "Son of man, can these bones live?"

I replied, "Lord GOD, ⌊only⌋ You know."

4 He said to me, "Prophesy concerning these bones and say to them: Dry bones, hear the word of the LORD!

5 This is what the Lord GOD says to these bones: I will cause breath to enter you, and you will live. 6 I will put tendons on you, make flesh grow on you, and cover you with skin. I will put breath in you so that you come to life. Then you will know that I am the LORD."

7 So I prophesied as I had been commanded. While I was prophesying, there was a noise, a rattling sound, and the bones came together, bone to bone. 8 As I looked, tendons appeared on them, flesh grew, and skin covered them, but there was no breath in them. 9 He said to me, "Prophesy to the breath,[d] prophesy, son of man. Say to it: This is what the Lord GOD says: Breath, come from the four winds and breathe into these slain so that they may live!" 10 So I prophesied as He commanded me; the breath[d] entered them, and they came to life and stood on their feet, a vast army.

11 Then He said to me, "Son of man, these bones are the whole house of Israel. Look how they say: Our bones are dried up, and our hope has perished; we are cut off. 12 Therefore, prophesy and say to them: This is what the Lord GOD says: I am going to open your graves and bring you up from them, My people, and lead you into the land of Israel. 13 You will know that I am the LORD, My people, when I open your graves and bring you up from them. 14 I will put My Spirit in you, and you will live, and I will settle you in your own land. Then you will know that I am the LORD. I have spoken, and I will do ⌊it⌋." ⌊This is⌋ the declaration of the LORD.

The Reunification of Israel

15 The word of the LORD came to me: 16 "Son of man, take a single stick and write on it: Belonging to Judah and the Israelites associated with him. Then take another stick and write on it: Belonging to Joseph—the stick of Ephraim—and all the house of Israel associated with him. 17 Then join them together into a single stick so that they become one in your hand. 18 When your people ask you: Won't you explain to us what you mean by these things?— 19 tell them: This is what the Lord GOD says: I am going to take the stick of Joseph—which is in the hand of Ephraim—and the tribes of Israel associated with him, and put them together with the stick of Judah. I will make them into a single stick so that they become one in My hand.

20 "When the sticks you have written on are in your hand and in full view of the people, 21 tell them: This is what the Lord GOD says: I am going to take the Israelites out of the nations where they have gone. I will gather them from all around and bring them into their own land. 22 I will make them one nation in the land,

---

[a]36:26 Lit stone from your flesh   [b]36:37 Lit flock of people   [c]36:38 Lit the flock of consecrated things, as the flock   [d]37:9,10 Or wind, or spirit

---

people. He recovered His nation for His own sake, to demonstrate His glory. This is the reason He gave for withholding wrath (20:9).

36:26-27 new heart ... new spirit ... My Spirit ... follow My statutes. In the New Covenant promise, all Israel will be saved (Rom. 11:26) and God's law will be written on their hearts

(Jer. 31:33). In that day, Israel will finally obey the Law and have faith in God.

37:8 but there was no breath. Similar to an airless balloon, the lifeless shape lacked the mysterious and divine quality needed to bring it to life (see also Gen. 2:7). Ezekiel saw Israel's restoration in stages; first in belief and later

when God's Spirit was poured into them.

37:17 together. Although Israel had been divided into two kingdoms for centuries, Ezekiel illustrated a united future.

37:24 David. David was Israel's ultimate king because he obeyed God's law and had great faith. In the millennial kingdom Jesus will rule,

on the mountains of Israel, and one king will rule over all of them. They will no longer be two nations and will no longer be divided into two kingdoms. 23 They will not defile themselves any more with their idols, their detestable things, and all their transgressions. I will save them from all their apostasies by which[a] they sinned, and I will cleanse them. Then they will be My people, and I will be their God. 24 My servant David will be king over them, and there will be one shepherd for all of them. They will follow My ordinances, and keep My statutes and obey them.

25 "They will live in the land that I gave to My servant Jacob, where your fathers lived. They will live in it forever with their children and grandchildren, and My servant David will be their prince forever. 26 I will make a covenant of peace with them; it will be an everlasting covenant with them. I will establish and multiply them, and will set My sanctuary among them forever. 27 My dwelling place will be with them; I will be their God, and they will be My people. 28 When My sanctuary is among them forever, the nations will know that I, the LORD, sanctify Israel."

The Defeat of Gog

38 The word of the LORD came to me: 2 "Son of man, turn your face toward Gog, of the land of Magog, the chief prince of[b] Meshech and Tubal. Prophesy against him 3 and say: This is what the Lord GOD says: Look, I am against you, Gog, chief prince of Meshech and Tubal. 4 I will turn you around, put hooks in your jaws, and bring you out with all your army, including horses and riders, who are all splendidly dressed, a huge company armed with shields and bucklers, all of them brandishing swords. 5 Persia, •Cush, and Put are with them, all of them with shields and helmets; 6 Gomer with all its troops; and Beth-togarmah from the remotest parts of the north along with all its troops—many peoples are with you.

7 "Be prepared and get yourself ready, you and all your company who have been mobilized around you; you will be their guard. 8 After a long time you will be summoned. In the last years you will enter a land that has been restored from war[c] and regathered from many peoples to the mountains of Israel, which had long been a ruin. They were brought out from the peoples, and all of them [now] live securely. 9 You, all of your troops, and many peoples with you will advance, coming like a thunderstorm; you will be like a cloud covering the land.

10 "This is what the Lord GOD says: On that day, thoughts will arise in your mind, and you will devise an evil plan. 11 You will say: I will go up against a land of open villages; I will come against a tranquil people who are living securely, all of them living without walls and without bars or gates— 12 in order to seize spoil and carry off plunder, to turn your hand against ruins now inhabited and against a people gathered from the nations, who have been acquiring cattle and possessions and who live at the center of the world. 13 Sheba and Dedan and the merchants of Tarshish with all its rulers[d] will ask you: Have you come to seize spoil? Have you assembled your hordes to carry off plunder, to make off with silver and gold, to take cattle and possessions, to seize great spoil?

14 "Therefore prophesy, son of man, and say to Gog: This is what the Lord GOD says: On that day when My people Israel are dwelling securely, will you not know [this] 15 and come from your place in the remotest parts of the north—you and many peoples with you, who are all riding horses—a mighty horde, a huge army? 16 You will advance against My people Israel like a cloud covering the land. It will happen in the last days, Gog, that I will bring you against My land so that the nations may know Me, when I show Myself holy through you in their sight.

17 "This is what the Lord GOD says: Are you the one I spoke about in former times through My servants, the prophets of Israel, who for years prophesied in those times that I would bring you against them? 18 Now on that day, the day when Gog comes against the land of Israel"—[this is] the declaration of the Lord GOD—"My wrath will flare up.[e] 19 I swear in My zeal and fiery rage: On that day there will be a great earthquake in the land of Israel. 20 The fish of the sea, the birds of the sky, the animals of the field, every creature that crawls on the ground, and every human being on the face of the earth will tremble before Me. The mountains will be thrown down, the cliffs will collapse, and every wall will fall to the ground. 21 I will call for a sword against him on all My mountains"—the declaration of the Lord GOD—"and every man's sword will be against his brother. 22 I will execute judgment on him with plague and bloodshed. I will pour out torrential rain, hailstones, fire, and brimstone on him, as well as his troops and the many peoples who are with him. 23 I will display My greatness and holiness, and will reveal Myself in the sight of many nations. Then they will know that I am the LORD.

---

[a] 37:23 Some Hb mss, LXX, Sym; other Hb mss read *their settlements where*; Ezk 6:6,13–14   [b] 38:2 Or *the prince of Rosh*,   [c] 38:8 Lit *from the sword*   [d] 38:13 Lit *young lions*, or *villages*   [e] 38:18 Lit *up in My anger*

---

and perhaps David will rule under Him.

38:8 summoned. Gog would be summoned to battle against Israel once God's people were finally resettled. Some see this as coming after Israel's physical regathering, but before the spiritual restoration. Others picture Gog and Magog as participants in the final battle at the end of the millennial kingdom (Rev. 20:8).

38:11 open villages. A peaceful and restored Israel would have no use for protective barriers. In this surreal future battle, Gog would take advantage of its vulnerability.

38:17 Are you the one. Gog is identified as the subject of similar prophecies of days gone by (Joel 3:9-14).

38:19 great earthquake. God would intervene, announcing His presence in the form of a thunderous earthquake. He would shatter Gog's plans for victory.

38:22 The enemy's internal confusion (v. 21) would be compounded by God's use of super-

The Disposal of Gog

39 "As for you, son of man, prophesy against Gog and say: This is what the Lord GOD says: Look, I am against you, Gog, chief prince of[a] Meshech and Tubal. 2 I will turn you around, drive you on, and lead you up from the remotest parts of the north. I will bring you against the mountains of Israel. 3 Then I will knock your bow from your left hand and make your arrows drop from your right hand. 4 You, all your troops, and the peoples who are with you will fall on the mountains of Israel. I will give you as food to every kind of predatory bird and to the wild animals. 5 You will fall on the open field, for I have spoken." ⌊This is⌋ the declaration of the Lord GOD.

6 "I will send fire against Magog and those who live securely on the coasts and islands. Then they will know that I am the LORD. 7 So I will make My holy name known among My people Israel and will no longer allow it to be profaned. Then the nations will know that I am the LORD, the Holy One in Israel. 8 Yes, it is coming, and it will happen." ⌊This is⌋ the declaration of the Lord GOD. "This is the day I have spoken about.

9 "Then the inhabitants of Israel's cities will go out, kindle fires, and burn the weapons—the bucklers and shields, the bows and arrows, the clubs and spears. For seven years they will use them to make fires. 10 They will not gather wood from the countryside or cut ⌊it⌋ down from the forests, for they will use the weapons to make fires. They will take the loot from those who looted them and plunder those who plundered them." ⌊This is⌋ the declaration of the Lord GOD.

11 "Now on that day I will give Gog a burial place there in Israel—the Valley of the Travelers[b] east of the Sea. It will block those who travel through, for Gog and all his hordes will be buried there. So ⌊it⌋ will be called the Valley of Hamon-gog.[c] 12 The house of Israel will spend seven months burying them in order to cleanse the land. 13 All the people of the land will bury ⌊them⌋ and their fame will spread on the day I display My glory." ⌊This is⌋ the declaration of the Lord GOD.

14 "They will appoint men on a full-time basis to pass through the land and bury the invaders[d] who remain on the surface of the ground, in order to cleanse it. They will make ⌊their⌋ search at the end of the seven months. 15 When they pass through the land and one of them sees a human bone, he will erect a marker next to it until the buriers have buried it in the Valley of Hamon-

gog. 16 There will even be a city named Hamonah[e] ⌊there⌋. So they will cleanse the land.

17 "Son of man, this is what the Lord GOD says: Tell every kind of bird and all the wild animals: Assemble and come! Gather from all around to My sacrificial feast that I am slaughtering for you, a great feast on the mountains of Israel; you will eat flesh and drink blood. 18 You will eat the flesh of mighty men and drink the blood of the earth's princes: rams, lambs, male goats, and bulls, all of them fatlings of Bashan. 19 You will eat fat until you are satisfied and drink blood until you are drunk, at My sacrificial feast that I have prepared for you. 20 At My table you will eat your fill of horses and riders, of mighty men and all the warriors." ⌊This is⌋ the declaration of the Lord GOD.

Israel's Restoration to God

21 "I will display My glory among the nations, and all the nations will see the judgment I have executed and the hand I have laid on them. 22 From that day forward the house of Israel will know that I am the LORD their God. 23 And the nations will know that the house of Israel went into exile on account of their iniquity, because they dealt unfaithfully with Me. Therefore, I hid My face from them and handed them over to their enemies, so that they all fell by the sword. 24 I dealt with them according to their uncleanness and transgressions, and I hid My face from them.

25 "So this is what the Lord GOD says: Now I will restore the fortunes of Jacob and have compassion on the whole house of Israel, and I will be jealous for My holy name. 26 They will feel remorse for[f] [g] their disgrace and all the unfaithfulness they committed against Me, when they live securely in their land with no one to frighten ⌊them⌋. 27 When I bring them back from the peoples and gather them from the countries of their enemies, I will demonstrate My holiness through them in the sight of many nations. 28 They will know that I am the LORD their God when I regather them to their own land after having exiled them among the nations. I will leave none of them behind.[h] 29 I will no longer hide My face from them, for I will pour out My Spirit on the house of Israel." ⌊This is⌋ the declaration of the Lord GOD.

The New Temple

40 In the twenty-fifth year of our exile, at the beginning of the year, on the tenth day of the month in the fourteenth year after Jerusalem had been captured, on that very day the LORD's hand was on me, and He brought me there. 2 In visions of God He took

---

[a]**39:1** Or *Gog, prince of Rosh*, [b]**39:11** Hb obscure [c]**39:11** = Hordes of Gog [d]**39:14** Or *basis, some to pass through the land, and with them some to bury those* [e]**39:16** *Hamonah* is related to the Hb word for "horde." [f]**39:26** Some emend to *will forget* [g]**39:26** Lit *will bear* [h]**39:28** Lit *behind*

---

natural plagues and storms. Israel did not even need an army.

39:4 food to every kind. The worst curse imaginable was not to receive proper burial and so be vulnerable to weather and animals. To a Hebrew, there was no clear distinction between body and soul. Those not buried were

thought to be aware of such an awful fate and were restless until they were properly interred.

39:112 seven months. In Israel, it required seven days to be cleansed from touching a dead body (Num. 19:11-22). That the contamination here will take a week of months, rather than a regular week, not only implies the sheer

number of dead bodies, but the time it would take to purify the land.

39:22-23 God's reputation is one of justice and mercy (v. 25) when it comes to His own people. He showed compassion and safeguarded His name.

me to the land of Israel and set me down on a very high mountain. On its southern ⌊slope⌋ was a structure resembling a city. 3 He brought me there, and I saw a man whose appearance was like bronze, with a linen cord and a measuring rod in his hand. He was standing by the gate. 4 He spoke to me: "Son of man, look with your eyes, listen with your ears, and pay attention to everything I am going to show you, for you have been brought here so that I might show ⌊it⌋ to you. Report everything you see to the house of Israel."

The Wall and Outer Gates

5 Now there was a wall surrounding the outside of the temple. The measuring rod in the man's hand was six units of 21 inches;[a] each unit was the standard length plus three inches.[b] He measured the thickness of the ⌊wall⌋ structure; it was about 10 feet,[c] and its height was the same.[c] 6 Then he came to the gate that faced east and climbed its steps. He measured the threshold of the gate; it was 10 feet deep—the first threshold was 10 feet deep. 7 Each recess was about 10 feet[c] long and 10 feet[d] deep, and there was ⌊a space of⌋ eight and three-quarter feet[e] between the recesses. The ⌊inner⌋ threshold of the gate on the temple side next to the gate's portico was about 10 feet.[c] 8 Next he measured the portico of the gate; 9 it[f] was 14 feet,[g] and its pilasters were three and a half feet.[h] The portico of the gate was on the temple side.

10 There were three recesses on each side of the east gate, each with the same measurements, and the pilasters on either side also had the same measurements. 11 Then he measured the width of the gate's entrance; it was 17 and a half feet,[i] while the width[j] of the gateway was 22 and three-quarter feet.[k] 12 There was a barrier of 21 inches[l] in front of the recesses on both sides, and the recesses on each side were 10 and a half feet[m] square. 13 Then he measured the gateway from the roof of one recess to the roof of the ⌊opposite⌋ one; the distance was 43 and three-quarter feet.[n] The openings of the recesses faced each other. 14 Next, he measured the pilasters—105 feet.[o] The gate extended around to the pilaster of the court.[p] 15 ⌊The distance⌋ from the front of the gate at the entrance to the front of the gate's portico on the inside was 87 and a half feet.[q] 16 The recesses and their pilasters had beveled windows all around the inside of the gateway. The porticos also had windows all around on the inside. Each pilaster was decorated with palm trees.

17 Then he brought me into the outer court, and there were chambers and a paved surface laid out all around the court. Thirty chambers faced the pavement, 18 which flanked the gates and corresponded to the length of the gates; ⌊this⌋ was the lower pavement. 19 Then he measured the distance from the front of the lower gate to the exterior front of the inner court; it was 175 feet.[r] ⌊This⌋ was the east; next the north ⌊is described⌋.

20 He measured the gate of the outer court facing north, ⌊both⌋ its length and width. 21 Its three recesses on each side, its pilasters, and its portico had the same measurements as the first gate: 87 and a half feet[q] long and 43 and three-quarter feet[n] wide. 22 Its windows, portico, and palm trees had the same measurements as those of the gate that faced east. Seven steps led up to the gate, and its portico was ahead of them. 23 The inner court had a gate facing the north gate, like the one on the east. He measured the distance from gate to gate; it was 175 feet.[r]

24 He brought me to the south side, and there was also a gate on the south. He measured its pilasters and portico; they had the same measurements as the others. 25 Both the gate and its portico had windows all around, like the other windows. It was 87 and a half feet[q] long and 43 and three-quarter feet[n] wide. 26 Its stairway had seven steps, and its portico was ahead of them. It had palm trees on its pilasters, one on each side. 27 The inner court had a gate on the south. He measured from gate to gate on the south; it was 175 feet.[r]

The Inner Gates

28 Then he brought me to the inner court through the south gate. When he measured the south gate, it had the same measurements as the others. 29 Its recesses, pilasters, and portico had the same measurements as the others. Both it and its portico had windows all around. It was 87 and a half feet[q] long and 43 and three-quarter feet[n] wide. 30 (There were porticoes all around, 43 and three-quarter feet long and eight and three-quarter feet[e] wide.[s]) 31 Its portico faced the outer court, and its pilasters were decorated with palm trees. Its stairway had eight steps.

32 Then he brought me to the inner court on the east side. When he measured the gate, it had the same measurements as the others. 33 Its recesses, pilasters, and portico had the same measurements as the others. Both it and its portico had windows all around. It was 87 and

[a] **40:5** This unit of measure approximately = a long cubit (perhaps 20½ inches) [b] **40:5** Lit *six cubits by the cubit and a handbreadth* [c] **40:5,7** Lit *was one rod* [d] **40:7** Lit *and one rod* [e] **40:7,30** Lit *five cubits* [f] **40:8–9** Some Hb mss, Syr, Vg; other Hb mss read *gate facing the temple side; it was one rod. 9 Then he measured the portico of the gate; it* [g] **40:9** Lit *eight cubits* [h] **40:9** Lit *two cubits* [i] **40:11** Lit *10 cubits* [j] **40:11** Lit *length* [k] **40:11** Lit *13 cubits* [l] **40:12** Lit *one cubit* [m] **40:12** Lit *six cubits* [n] **40:13,21,25,29** Lit *25 cubits* [o] **40:14** Lit *60 cubits* [p] **40:14** Hb obscure [q] **40:15,21,25,29** Lit *50 cubits* [r] **40:19,23,27** Lit *100 cubits* [s] **40:30** Some Hb mss, LXX omit v. 30

40:2 a very high mountain. A reference to Mt. Zion in a restored Jerusalem of the future.

40:4 pay attention to everything I ... show you. Some interpreters feel the temple God showed Ezekiel is symbolic and not a literal temple. Others point out that the description is very specific and must refer to a temple not yet built: the temple of the millennial kingdom of Christ.

40:6_. the gate that faced east. God's glory left the temple through the east gate (_10:19_), and would likewise return through it (_43:1–5_). The restoration of the temple would be the capstone of Israel's reemergence (37:26–27). It's magnificence would exceed Solomon's and then Herod's temple. The temple of the last days would be a beacon and sign to the world that God once again dwelt in the midst of Israel (48:35; Rev. 21:3–4; 22:1–4).

40:15 was 87 and a half feet. The gate excavated at Lachish is nearly eighty-two feet deep.

a half feet[a] long and 43 and three-quarter feet[b] wide. [34] Its portico faced the outer court, and its pilasters were decorated with palm trees on each side. Its stairway had eight steps.

[35] Then he brought me to the north gate. When he measured ⌊it⌋, it had the same measurements as the others, [36] ⌊as did⌋ its recesses, pilasters, and portico. It also had windows all around. It was 87 and a half feet[a] long and 43 and three-quarter feet[b] wide. [37] Its portico[c] faced the outer court, and its pilasters were decorated with palm trees on each side. Its stairway had eight steps.

Rooms for Preparing Sacrifices

[38] There was a chamber whose door ⌊opened⌋ into the portico of the gate.[d] The •burnt offering was to be washed there. [39] Inside the portico of the gate there were two tables on each side, on which to slaughter the burnt offering, •sin offering, and •restitution offering. [40] Outside, as one approaches the entrance of the north gate, there were two tables on one side and two ⌊more⌋ tables on the other side of the gate's portico. [41] So there were four tables inside the gate and four outside, eight tables ⌊in all⌋ on which the slaughtering was to be done. [42] There were also four tables of cut stone for the burnt offering, ⌊each⌋ 31 and a half inches[e] long, 31 and a half inches wide, and 21 inches[f] high. The utensils used to slaughter the burnt offerings and ⌊other⌋ sacrifices were placed on them. [43] There were three-inch[g] hooks[h] fastened all around the inside of the room, and the flesh of the offering was to be laid on the tables.

Rooms for Singers and Priests

[44] Outside the inner gate, within the inner court, there were chambers for the singers:[i] one[j] beside the north gate, facing south, and another beside the south[k] gate, facing north. [45] Then the man said to me: "This chamber that faces south is for the priests who keep charge of the temple. [46] The chamber that faces north is for the priests who keep charge of the altar. These are the sons of Zadok, the ones from the sons of Levi who may approach the LORD to serve Him." [47] Next he measured the court. It was square, 175 feet[l] long and 175 feet wide. The altar was in front of the temple.

[48] Then he brought me to the portico of the temple and measured the pilasters of the portico; they were eight and three-quarter feet[m] ⌊thick⌋ on each side. The width of the gateway was 24 and a half feet,[n] and the sidewalls of the gate were[o] five and a quarter feet[p] ⌊wide⌋ on each side. [49] The portico was 35 feet[q] across and 21[r] feet[s] deep, and 10 steps led[t] up to it. There were pillars by the pilasters, one on each side.

Inside the Temple

41

Next he brought me into the great hall and measured the pilasters; on each side the width of the pilaster was 10 and a half feet.[u] [v] [2] The width of the entrance was 17 and a half feet,[w] and the sidewalls of the entrance were eight and three-quarter feet[m] ⌊wide⌋ on each side. He also measured the length of the great hall, 70 feet,[x] and the width, 35 feet.[q] [3] He went inside ⌊the next room⌋ and measured the pilasters at the entrance; they were three and a half feet[y] ⌊wide⌋. The entrance was 10 and a half feet[v] ⌊wide⌋, and the width of the entrance's sidewalls on each side[z] was 12 and a quarter feet.[aa] [4] He then measured the length of the room adjacent to the great hall, 35 feet,[q] and the width, 35 feet. And he said to me, "This is the most holy place."

Outside the Temple

[5] Then he measured the wall of the temple; it was 10 and a half feet[v] ⌊thick⌋. The width of the side rooms all around the temple was seven feet.[ab] [6] The side rooms were arranged one above another in three stories of 30 rooms each.[ac] There were ledges on the wall of the temple all around to serve as supports for the side rooms, so that the supports would not be in the temple wall ⌊itself⌋. [7] The side rooms surrounding ⌊the temple⌋ widened at each successive story, for the structure surrounding the temple ⌊went up⌋ by stages. This was the reason for the temple's broadness as it rose. And so, one would go up from the lowest story to the highest by means of the middle one.[ad]

[8] I saw that the temple had a raised platform surrounding ⌊it⌋; this foundation for the side rooms was 10 and a half feet high.[ae] [9] The thickness of the outer wall of the side rooms was eight and three-quarter feet.[m] The free space between the side rooms of the temple [10] and the ⌊outer⌋ chambers was 35 feet[q] wide all around the temple. [11] The side rooms opened into the free space, one entrance toward the north and another

[a]40:33,36 Lit 50 cubits [b]40:33,36 Lit 25 cubits [c]40:37 LXX; MT reads pilasters [d]40:38 Text emended; MT reads door was by the pilasters, at the gates [e]40:42 Lit one and a half cubits [f]40:42 Lit one cubit [g]40:43 Lit one-handbreadth [h]40:43 Or ledges [i]40:44 LXX reads were two chambers [j]40:44 LXX; MT reads singers, which was [k]40:44 LXX; MT reads east [l]40:47 Lit 100 cubits [m]40:48; 41:2,9 Lit five cubits [n]40:48 Lit 14 cubits [o]40:48 MT omits 24 and a half feet, and the sidewalls of the gate were [p]40:48 Lit three cubits [q]40:48; 41:2,4,10 Lit 20 cubits [r]40:49 LXX; MT reads 19 and a quarter [s]40:49 Lit 12 cubits [t]40:49 MT reads and it was on steps that they would go [u]41:1 LXX; MT reads pilasters; they were 10 and a half feet wide on each side—the width of the tabernacle [v]41:1,3,5 Lit six cubits [w]41:2 Lit 10 cubits [x]41:2 Lit 40 cubits [y]41:3 Lit two cubits [z]41:3 LXX; MT reads width of the entrance [aa]41:3 Lit seven cubits [ab]41:5 Lit four cubits [ac]41:6 Lit another three and 30 times [ad]41:7 Hb obscure [ae]41:8 Lit a full rod of six cubits of a joint; Hb obscure

41:1-12 The guide speaks little in these chapters, letting God's awesomeness speak for itself (40:4, 45; 41:22; 42:13; 43:18; 46:20, 24; 47:8). His description of the temple is reminiscent of the Solomonic temple (1 Kings 6:5–8). The temple sanctuary had three divisions: (1) a porch, (2) an outer "holy place", (3) and an inner sanctuary known as the "holy of holies". This inner sanctuary was inaccessible to ordinary mortals (not even Ezekiel in his vision), and symbolized God's divine presence in Israel's heart. In the real temple, only the High Priest could enter the innermost sanctuary, and that only once a year on the Day of Atonement. God, who is transcendent (above it all), cannot really be limited to a single place. Ezekiel's vision strikes a balance. God is indeed present in the world as a holy presence, and should be treated with appropriate awe.

41:22 altar. This wooden altar, the only furniture listed, may be where the bread of Pres-

to the south. The area of free space was eight and three-quarter feet[a] wide all around.

[12] Now the building that faced the temple yard toward the west was 122 and a half feet[b] wide. The wall of the building was eight and three-quarter feet[a] thick on all sides, and the building's length was 157 and a half feet.[c]

[13] Then the man measured the temple; it was 175 feet[d] long. In addition, the temple yard and the building, including its walls, were 175 feet long. [14] The width of the front of the temple along with the temple yard to the east was 175 feet. [15] Next he measured the length of the building facing the temple yard to the west, with its galleries[e] on each side; it was 175 feet.

Interior Wooden Structures

The interior of the great hall and the porticoes of the court— [16] the thresholds, the beveled windows, and the balconies all around with their three levels opposite the threshold—were overlaid with wood on all sides. ⌊They were paneled⌋ from the ground to the windows (but the windows were covered), [17] reaching to the top of the entrance, and as far as the inner temple and on the outside. On every wall all around, on the inside and outside, was a pattern [18] carved with •cherubim and palm trees. There was a palm tree between each pair of cherubim. Each cherub had two faces: [19] a human face turned toward the palm tree on one side, and a lion's face turned toward it on the other. They were carved throughout the temple on all sides. [20] Cherubim and palm trees were carved from the ground to the top of the entrance and on the wall of the great hall.

[21] The doorposts of the great hall were square, and the front of the sanctuary had the same appearance. [22] The altar was[f] made of wood, five and a quarter feet[g] high and three and a half feet[h] long.[i] It had corners, and its length[j] and sides were of wood. The man told me, "This is the table that stands before the LORD."

[23] The great hall and the sanctuary each had a double door, [24] and each of the doors had two swinging panels. There were two panels for one door and two for the other. [25] Cherubim and palm trees were carved on the doors of the great hall like those carved on the walls. There was a wooden canopy[k] outside, in front of the portico. [26] There were beveled windows and palm trees on both sides, on the sidewalls of the portico, the side rooms of the temple, and the canopies.[k]

The Priests' Chambers

42 Then the man led me out by way of the north gate into the outer court. He brought me to the group of chambers opposite the temple yard and opposite the building to the north. [2] Along the length ⌊of the chambers⌋, which was 175 feet,[d] there was an entrance on the north; the width was 87 and a half feet.[l] [3] Opposite the 35 ⌊foot space⌋[m] belonging to the inner court and opposite the paved surface belonging to the outer court, ⌊the structure rose⌋ gallery by gallery in three tiers. [4] In front of the chambers was a walkway toward the inside, 17 and a half feet[n] wide and 175 feet[d] long,[o] and their entrances were on the north. [5] The upper chambers were narrower because the galleries took away more space from them than from the lower and middle stories of the building. [6] For they were arranged in three stories and had no pillars like the pillars of the courts; therefore the upper chambers were set back from the ground more than the lower and middle stories. [7] A wall on the outside ran in front of the chambers, parallel to them, toward the outer court; it was 87 and a half feet[l] long. [8] For the chambers on the outer court were 87 and a half feet long, while those facing the great hall were 175 feet[d] ⌊long⌋. [9] At the base of these chambers there was an entryway on the east side as one enters them from the outer court.

[10] In the thickness of the wall of the court toward the south,[p] there were chambers facing the temple yard and the ⌊western⌋ building, [11] with a passageway in front of them, just like the chambers that faced north. Their length and width, as well as all their exits, measurements, and entrances, were identical. [12] The entrance at the beginning of the passageway, the way in front of the corresponding[q] wall as one enters on the east side, was similar to the entrances of the chambers that were on the south side.

[13] Then the man said to me, "The northern and southern chambers that face the temple yard are the holy chambers where the priests who approach the LORD will eat the most holy offerings. There they will deposit the most holy offerings—the •grain offerings, •sin offerings, and •restitution offerings—for the place is holy. [14] Once the priests have entered, they must not go out from the holy area to the outer court until they have removed the clothes they minister in, for these are holy. They are to put on other clothes before they approach the public area."

a 41:11,12 Lit *five cubits* b 41:12 Lit *70 cubits* c 41:12 Lit *90 cubits* d 41:13; 42:2,4,8 Lit *100 cubits* e 41:15 Or *ledges* f 41:21–22 Or *and in front of the sanctuary was something that looked like* 22 *an altar* g 41:22 Lit *three cubits* h 41:22 Lit *two cubits* i 41:22 LXX reads *long and three and a half feet wide* j 41:22 LXX reads *base* k 41:25,26 Hb obscure l 42:2,7 Lit *50 cubits* m 42:3 Lit *20 [cubits]* n 42:4 Lit *10 cubits* o 42:4 LXX, Syr; MT reads *wide, a way of one cubit* p 42:10 LXX; MT reads *east* q 42:12 Or *protective;* Hb obscure

ence was placed (see Ex. 25:30).
42:1 chambers. These two buildings served three purposes: (a) the priests ate offering portions there, (b) offerings were stored there, and (c) the priests changed from their official vestments back to street clothes there. According to the Law, the priests received a portion of

some offerings. From the whole burnt offering they received only the animal's skin (Lev. 7:8). A memorial portion of grain offerings was burned on the altar and the remainder given to the priests (Lev. 2:3, 10; 6:16–18; 7:14–15). The priests received the brisket and right thigh from the peace offering (Lev. 7:30–34). Finally,

the fat of the sin and trespass offerings were burned on the altar and the remainder eaten by the priests (Lev. 6:26; 7:6–7).

43:2 God, who previously abandoned the defiled temple in Jerusalem (11:22-23), will return in triumphant procession to reclaim His place among His people. God's glory

Outside Dimensions of the Temple Complex

15 When he finished measuring inside the temple complex, he led me out by way of the gate that faced east and measured all around the complex.

16 He measured the east side with a measuring rod; it was 875 feet[a] by the measuring rod.[b]
17 He[c] measured the north side;
it was 875 feet by the measuring rod.[b]
18 He[d] measured the south side;
it was 875 feet by the measuring rod.
19 Then he turned to the west side
and measured 875 feet by the measuring rod.

20 He measured the temple complex on all four sides. It had a wall all around ⌊it⌋, 875 ⌊feet⌋ long and 875 ⌊feet⌋ wide, to separate the holy from the common.

Return of the LORD's Glory

43 He led me to the gate, the one that faces east, 2 and I saw the glory of the God of Israel coming from the east. His voice sounded like the roar of mighty waters, and the earth shone with His glory. 3 The vision I saw was like the one I had seen when He[e] came to destroy the city, and like the ones I had seen by the Chebar Canal. I fell facedown. 4 The glory of the LORD entered the temple by way of the gate that faced east. 5 Then the Spirit lifted me up and brought me to the inner court, and the glory of the LORD filled the temple.

6 While the man was standing beside me, I heard someone speaking to me from the temple. 7 He said to me: "Son of man, this is the place of My throne and the place for the soles of My feet, where I will dwell among the Israelites forever. ⌊The house of⌋ Israel and their kings will no longer defile My holy name by their ⌊religious⌋ prostitution and by the corpses[f] of their kings at their •high places.[g] 8 Whenever they placed their threshold next to My threshold and their doorposts beside My doorposts, with ⌊only⌋ a wall between Me and them, they were defiling My holy name by the abominations they committed. So I destroyed them in My anger. 9 Now let them remove their prostitution and the corpses[f] of their kings far from Me, and I will dwell among them forever.

10 "As for you, son of man, describe the temple to the house of Israel, so that they may be ashamed of their iniquities. Let them measure ⌊its⌋ pattern, 11 and they will be ashamed of all that they have done. Reveal[h] the design of the temple to them—its layout with its exits and entrances—its complete design along with all its statutes, design specifications, and laws. Write it down in their sight so that they may observe its complete design and all its statutes and may carry them out. 12 This is the law of the temple: all its surrounding territory on top of the mountain will be especially holy. Yes, this is the law of the temple.

The Altar

13 "These are the measurements of the altar in units of length (each unit being the standard length plus three inches):[i] the gutter is 21 inches ⌊deep⌋ and 21 inches wide, with a rim of nine inches[k] around its edge. This is the base[l] of the altar. 14 ⌊The distance⌋ from the gutter on the ground to the lower ledge is three and a half feet,[m] and the width ⌊of the ledge⌋ is 21 inches.[j] There are seven feet[n] from the small ledge to the large ledge, ⌊whose⌋ width is also 21 inches. 15 The altar hearth[o] is seven feet[n] ⌊high⌋, and four horns project upward from the hearth. 16 The hearth is square, 21 feet[p] long by 21 feet wide. 17 The ledge is 24 and a half feet[q] long by 24 and a half feet wide, with four equal sides. The rim all around it is 10 and a half inches,[r] and its gutter is 21 inches[j] all around it. The altar's steps face east."

18 Then He said to me: "Son of man, this is what the Lord GOD says: These are the statutes for the altar on the day it is constructed, so that •burnt offerings may be sacrificed on it and blood may be sprinkled on it: 19 You are to give a bull from the herd as a •sin offering to the Levitical priests who are from the offspring of Zadok, who approach Me in order to serve Me." ⌊This is⌋ the declaration of the Lord GOD. 20 "You must take some of its blood and apply ⌊it⌋ to the four horns of the altar, the four corners of the ledge, and all around the rim. In this way you will purify the altar and make •atonement for it. 21 Then you must take away the bull for the sin offering, and it must be burned outside the sanctuary in the place appointed for the temple.

22 "On the second day you are to present an unblemished male goat as a sin offering. They will purify the altar just as they did with the bull. 23 When you have finished the purification, you are to present a young, unblemished bull and an unblemished ram from the

---

[a] 42:16 Lit 500 in rods; also in vv. 17–20   [b] 42:16,17 Lit rod all around   [c] 42:17 LXX reads Then he turned to the north and   [d] 42:18 LXX reads Then he turned to the south and   [e] 43:3 Some Hb mss, Theod, Vg; other Hb mss, LXX, Syr read I.   [f] 43:7,9 Or monuments   [g] 43:7 Some Hb mss, Theod, Tg read their death   [h] 43:10–11 LXX, Vg; MT reads pattern. 11 And if they are ashamed . . . done, reveal   [i] 43:13 Lit in cubits (a cubit being a cubit plus a handbreadth)   [j] 43:13,14,17 Lit one cubit   [k] 43:13 Lit one span   [l] 43:13 LXX reads height   [m] 43:14 Lit two cubits   [n] 43:14,15 Lit four cubits   [o] 43:15 Hb obscure   [p] 43:16 Lit 12 cubits   [q] 43:17 Lit 14 cubits   [r] 43:17 Lit one-half cubit

---

was not in the second temple built by Herod, but will be in the third.

43:5 glory. The long-awaited day finally came. God's presence, symbolized by splendor and glory, filled the temple (v. 4).

43:8 Solomon built his palace close to the temple, blurring the distinction between what was holy and what was his (1 Kings 7:1-12). God resented the confusion.

43:13-15 Ezekiel describes the future temple whose altar will be considerably larger than Solomon's.

43:19 sin offering to the Levitical priests. After it is built, the temple must be cleansed and purified with blood.

43:21 The blood of the sacrifice is necessary to accomplish the offering. The animal carcasses are burned outside of the temple (see Lev. 4:12, 21).

flock. 24 You must present them before the LORD; the priests will throw salt on them and sacrifice them as a burnt offering to the LORD. 25 You will offer a goat for a sin offering each day for seven days. A young bull and a ram from the flock, both unblemished, must also be offered. 26 For seven days the priests are to make atonement for the altar and cleanse it. In this way they will consecrate it[a] 27 and complete the days ⌊of purification⌋. Then on the eighth day and afterwards, the priests will offer your burnt offerings and •fellowship offerings on the altar, and I will accept you." ⌊This is⌋ the declaration of the Lord GOD.

The Prince's Privilege

44 The man then brought me back toward the sanctuary's outer gate that faced east, and it was closed. 2 The LORD said to me: "This gate will remain closed. It will not be opened, and no one will enter through it, because the LORD, the God of Israel, has entered through it. Therefore it will remain closed. 3 The prince himself will sit in the gateway to eat a meal before the LORD. He must enter by way of the portico of the gate and go out the same way."

4 Then the man brought me by way of the north gate to the front of the temple. I looked, and the glory of the LORD filled His temple. And I fell facedown. 5 The LORD said to me: "Son of man, pay attention; look with your eyes and listen with your ears to everything I tell you about all the statutes and laws of the LORD's temple. Take careful note of the entrance of the temple along with all the exits of the sanctuary.

The Levites' Duties and Privileges

6 "Say to the rebellious people, the house of Israel: This is what the Lord GOD says: ⌊I have had⌋ enough of all your abominations, house of Israel. 7 When you brought in foreigners, uncircumcised in both heart and flesh, to occupy My sanctuary, you defiled My temple while you offered My food—the fat and the blood. You[b] broke My covenant with all your abominations. 8 You have not kept charge of My holy things but have appointed ⌊others⌋ to keep charge of My sanctuary for you.

9 "This is what the Lord GOD says: No foreigner, uncircumcised in heart and flesh, may enter My sanctuary, not even a foreigner who is among the Israelites. 10 Surely the Levites who wandered away from Me when Israel went astray, and who strayed from Me after their idols, will bear the consequences of their sin. 11 Yet they will occupy My sanctuary, serving as guards at the temple gates and ministering at the temple. They will slaughter the •burnt offerings and ⌊other⌋ sacrifices for the people and will stand before them to serve them. 12 Because they ministered to the house of Israel before their idols and became a sinful stumbling block to them, therefore I swore an oath[c] against them"— ⌊this is⌋ the declaration of the Lord GOD—"that they would bear the consequences of their sin. 13 They must not approach Me to serve Me as priests or come near any of My holy things or the most holy things. They will bear their disgrace and the consequences of the abominations they committed. 14 Yet I will make them responsible for the duties of the temple—for all its work and everything done in it.

The Priests' Duties and Privileges

15 "But the Levitical priests descended from Zadok, who kept charge of My sanctuary when the Israelites went astray from Me, will approach Me to serve Me. They will stand before Me to offer Me fat and blood." ⌊This is⌋ the declaration of the Lord GOD. 16 "They are the ones who may enter My sanctuary and draw near to My table to serve Me. They will keep My mandate. 17 When they enter the gates of the inner court they must wear linen garments; they must not have on them anything made of wool when they minister at the gates of the inner court and within ⌊it⌋. 18 They must wear linen turbans on their heads and linen undergarments around their waists. They are not to put on ⌊anything that makes them⌋ sweat. 19 Before they go out to the outer court,[d] to the people, they must take off the clothes they have been ministering in, leave them in the holy chambers, and dress in other clothes so that they do not transmit holiness to the people through their clothes.

20 "They may not shave their heads or let their hair grow long, but must carefully trim their hair. 21 No priest may drink wine before he enters the inner court. 22 He is not to marry a widow or a divorced woman, but must marry a virgin from the offspring of the house of Israel, or a widow who is the widow of a priest. 23 They must teach My people the difference between the holy and the common, and explain to them the difference between the clean and the unclean.

24 "In a dispute, they will officiate as judges and decide the case according to My ordinances. They must observe My laws and statutes regarding all My appointed festivals, and keep My Sabbaths holy. 25 A priest may not come ⌊near⌋ a dead person so that he becomes defiled. However, he may defile himself for a

---

a 43:26 Lit will fill its hands   b 44:7 LXX, Syr, Vg; MT reads They   c 44:12 Lit I lifted My hand   d 44:19 Some Hb mss, LXX, Syr, Vg; other Hb mss read court, to the outer court

---

44:2 gate. No one else could enter the sealed gate (symbolic of God's holiness), as God had when He first entered the temple (43:4).

44:7 defiled My temple. God would forbid history repeating itself by allowing faithless foreigners to enter the sanctuary.

44:10 bear the consequences. The Levites were supposed to be the spiritual leader-priests (Deut. 33:8-11). As a result of their sins, they (except those related to Zadok) would be limited in their future role (vv. 13-15).

44:15 But the Levitical priests. Zadok's descendants will be allowed full access to the temple as a reward for their devotion and purity (see 1 Sam. 2:27-36).

44:17 linen garments. Linen, representing holiness and distinction (9:2), produced less sweat and odor than wool.

44:23 difference between the holy and the common. With the temple system having been defunct for centuries, the Israelites

785

father, a mother, a son, a daughter, a brother, or an unmarried sister. 26 After he is cleansed, he is to count off seven days for himself. 27 On the day he goes into the sanctuary, into the inner court to minister in the sanctuary, he must present his •sin offering." ⌊This is⌋ the declaration of the Lord GOD.

28 "This will be their inheritance: I am their inheritance. You are to give them no possession in Israel: I am their possession. 29 They will eat the •grain offering, the sin offering, and the •restitution offering. Everything in Israel that is permanently dedicated ⌊to the LORD⌋ will belong to them. 30 The best of all the •firstfruits of every kind and contribution of every kind from all your gifts will belong to the priests. You are to give your first batch of dough to the priest so that a blessing may rest on your homes. 31 The priests may not eat any bird or animal that died naturally or was mauled by wild beasts.

The Sacred Portion of the Land

45 "When you divide the land by lot as an inheritance, you must set aside a donation to the LORD, a holy portion of the land, eight and one-third ⌊miles⌋[a] long and six and two-thirds ⌊miles⌋[b] wide. This entire tract of land will be holy. 2 In this area there will be a square ⌊section⌋[c] for the sanctuary, 875 by 875 ⌊feet⌋,[d] with 87 and a half feet[e] of open space all around it. 3 From this holy portion,[f] you will measure off an area eight and one-third ⌊miles⌋[a] long and three and one-third ⌊miles⌋[g] wide, in which the sanctuary, the most holy place, will stand.[h] 4 It will be a holy area of the land to be used by the priests who minister in the sanctuary, who draw near to serve the LORD. It will be a place for their houses, as well as a holy area for the sanctuary. 5 There will be ⌊another area⌋ eight and one-third ⌊miles⌋[a] long and three and one-third ⌊miles⌋[g] wide for the Levites who minister in the temple; it will be their possession for towns to live in.[i]

6 "As the property of the city, you must set aside an area one and two-thirds ⌊of a mile⌋[j] wide and eight and one-third ⌊miles⌋[a] long, adjacent to the holy donation ⌊of land⌋. It will be for the whole house of Israel. 7 And the prince will have the area on each side of the holy donation ⌊of land⌋ and the city's property, adjacent to the holy donation and the city's property, stretching to the west on the west side and to the east on the east side. ⌊Its⌋ length will correspond to one of the ⌊tribal⌋ portions

from the western boundary to the eastern boundary. 8 This will be his land as a possession in Israel. My princes will no longer oppress My people but give the ⌊rest of the⌋ land to the house of Israel according to their tribes.

9 "This is what the Lord GOD says: You have gone too far,[k] princes of Israel! Put away violence and oppression and do what is just and right. Put an end to your evictions of My people." ⌊This is⌋ the declaration of the Lord GOD. 10 "You must have honest balances, an honest dry measure,[l] and an honest liquid measure.[m] 11 The dry measure[n] and the liquid measure[o] will be uniform, with the liquid measure containing five and a half gallons[p] and the dry measure ⌊holding⌋ half a bushel.[p] Their measurement will be one-tenth of the standard larger capacity measure.[q] 12 The •shekel will weigh 20 gerahs. Your mina will equal 60 shekels.

The People's Contribution to the Sacrifices

13 "This is the contribution you are to offer: Three quarts[r] from five bushels[s] of wheat and[t] three quarts from five bushels of barley. 14 The quota of oil in liquid measures[u] will be one percent of every[v] cor. ⌊The cor equals⌋ 10 liquid measures ⌊or⌋ one standard larger capacity measure,[w] since 10 liquid measures equal one standard larger capacity measure. 15 And ⌊the quota⌋ from the flock is one animal out of every 200 from the well-watered pastures of Israel. ⌊These are⌋ for the •grain offerings, •burnt offerings, and •fellowship offerings, to make •atonement for the people." ⌊This is⌋ the declaration of the Lord GOD. 16 "All the people of the land must take part in this contribution for the prince in Israel. 17 Then the burnt offerings, grain offerings, and drink offerings for the festivals, New Moons, and Sabbaths—for all the appointed times of the house of Israel—will be the prince's responsibility. He will provide the •sin offerings, grain offerings, burnt offerings, and fellowship offerings to make atonement on behalf of the house of Israel.

18 "This is what the Lord GOD says: In the first ⌊month⌋, on the first ⌊day⌋ of the month, you are to take a young, unblemished bull and purify the sanctuary. 19 The priest must take some of the blood from the sin offering and apply ⌊it⌋ to the temple doorposts, the four corners of the altar's ledge, and the doorposts of the gate to the inner court. 20 You must do the same thing on the seventh ⌊day⌋ of the month for everyone who

a 45:1,3,5,6 Lit 25,000 [cubits]   b 45:1 LXX = 20,000 [cubits]; MT reads 10,000 [cubits], or four and one-third [miles]   c 45:2 Lit square all around   d 45:2 Lit 500 by 500 [cubits]   e 45:2 Lit 50 cubits   f 45:3 Lit this measured [portion]   g 45:3,5 Lit 10,000 [cubits]   h 45:3 Lit be   i 45:5 LXX; MT, Syr, Tg, Vg read possession—20 chambers   j 45:6 Lit 5,000 [cubits]   k 45:9 Lit Enough of you   l 45:10 Lit an honest ephah   m 45:10 Lit and an honest bath   n 45:11 Lit the ephah   o 45:11 Lit the bath   p 45:11 Lit one-tenth of a homer   q 45:11 Lit be [based] on the homer   r 45:13 Lit One-sixth of an ephah   s 45:13 Lit a homer   t 45:13 LXX, Vg; MT reads and you are to give   u 45:14 Lit oil, the bath, the oil   v 45:14 Lit be one-tenth of the bath from the   w 45:14 Lit 10 baths, a homer

would need to relearn the laws.

45:2 open space. No building permits would be given out for the area around the sanctuary this time! God's holiness would be set apart.

45:4 holy area of the land to be used by the priests. In Israel's history, the priests were scattered throughout the land as references of

religious service and justice (Josh. 21:1-42). In the new temple era, they would be centralized around the sanctuary.

45:5 In the Old Testament, priests lived in special "holy" areas they did not own. In the new temple era, however, the Levites would be allowed to own property.

45:7 prince will have the area. Unlike that of Solomon's time, the new palace would be separate from the new temple.

45:10 have honest balances. God established common ground rules to guard against fraud. Following these guidelines, the people would not find themselves re-

sins unintentionally or through ignorance. In this way you will make atonement for the temple.

21 "In the first ⌊month⌋, on the fourteenth day of the month, you are to celebrate the •Passover, a festival of seven days ⌊during which⌋ unleavened bread will be eaten. 22 On that day the prince will provide a bull as a sin offering on behalf of himself and all the people of the land. 23 During the seven days of the festival, he will provide seven bulls and seven rams without blemish as a burnt offering to the LORD on each of the seven days, along with a male goat each day for a sin offering. 24 He will also provide a grain offering of half a bushel[a] per bull and half a bushel per ram, along with a gallon[b] of oil for every half bushel. 25 At the festival ⌊that begins⌋ on the fifteenth day of the seventh month,[c] he will provide the same things for seven days—the same sin offerings, burnt offerings, grain offerings, and oil.

Sacrifices at Appointed Times

46 "This is what the Lord GOD says: The gate of the inner court that faces east must be closed during the six days of work, but it will be opened on the Sabbath day and opened on the day of the New Moon. 2 The prince should enter from the outside by way of the gate's portico and stand at the doorpost of the gate while the priests sacrifice his •burnt offerings and •fellowship offerings. He will bow in worship at the threshold of the gate and then depart, but the gate must not be closed until evening. 3 The people of the land will also bow in worship before the LORD at the entrance of that gate on the Sabbaths and New Moons.

4 "The burnt offering that the prince presents to the LORD on the Sabbath day is to be six unblemished lambs and an unblemished ram. 5 The •grain offering will be half a bushel[a] with the ram, and the grain offering with the lambs will be whatever he wants to give, as well as a gallon[b] of oil for every half bushel. 6 On the day of the New Moon, ⌊the burnt offering⌋ is to be a young, unblemished bull, as well as six lambs and a ram without blemish. 7 He will provide a grain offering of half a bushel[a] with the bull, half a bushel with the ram, and whatever he can afford with the lambs, together with a gallon[b] of oil for every half bushel. 8 When the prince enters, he must go in by way of the gate's portico and go out the same way.

9 "When the people of the land come before the LORD at the appointed times,[d] whoever enters by way of the north gate to worship must go out by way of the south gate, and whoever enters by way of the south gate must go out by way of the north gate. No one must return through the gate by which he entered, but must go out by the opposite gate. 10 When the people enter, the prince will enter with them, and when they leave, he will leave. 11 At the festivals and appointed times, the grain offering will be half a bushel[a] with the bull, half a bushel with the ram, and whatever he wants to give with the lambs, along with a gallon[b] of oil for every half bushel.

12 "When the prince makes a freewill offering, whether a burnt offering or a fellowship offering as a freewill offering to the LORD, the gate that faces east must be opened for him. He is to offer his burnt offering or fellowship offering just as he does on the Sabbath day. Then he will go out, and the gate must be closed after he leaves.

13 "You must offer an unblemished year-old male lamb as a daily burnt offering to the LORD; you will offer it every morning. 14 You must also prepare a grain offering every morning along with it: three quarts,[e] with one-third of a gallon[f] of oil to moisten the fine flour—a grain offering to the LORD. ⌊This is⌋ a permanent statute ⌊to be observed⌋ regularly. 15 They will offer the lamb, the grain offering, and the oil every morning as a regular burnt offering.

Transfer of Royal Lands

16 "This is what the Lord GOD says: If the prince gives a gift to each of his sons as their inheritance, it will belong to his sons. It will become their property by inheritance. 17 But if he gives a gift from his inheritance to one of his servants, it will belong to that servant until the year of freedom, when it will revert to the prince. His inheritance belongs only to his sons; it is theirs. 18 The prince must not take any of the people's inheritance, evicting them from their property. He is to provide an inheritance for his sons from his own property, so that none of My people will be displaced from his own property."

The Temple Kitchens

19 Then he brought me through the entrance that was at the side of the gate, into the priests' holy chambers, which faced north. I saw a place there at the far western end. 20 He said to me, "This is the place where the priests will boil the •restitution offering and the •sin offering, and where they will bake the grain offering, so that they do not bring ⌊them⌋ into the outer court and transmit holiness to the people." 21 Next he brought me into the outer court and led me past its four corners. There was a ⌊separate⌋ court in each of its corners. 22 In

---

a 45:24; 46:5,7,11 Lit an ephah   b 45:24; 46:5,7,11 Lit a hin   c 45:25 = the Festival of Booths; Lv 23:33–43; Dt 16:13–15   d 46:9 Or the festivals
e 46:14 Lit one-sixth of an ephah   f 46:14 Lit one-third of a hin

---

learning old lessons against greed.
45:25 festival. The Feast of Tabernacles was a seven-day celebration at the end of the year (see Num. 29:12; Deut. 16:16). Sacrifices were made on each of these seven days.
46:3 worship … Sabbaths. One of the few references to Old Testament worship on the Sab-

bath. Usually referred to in terms of proscribed limitations, this Sabbath had its limits too. The people usually worshipped in the outer court; they could look through the eastern gate to the altar in the inner court where the sacrifices were offered, but were not permitted to enter it. The prince could pass through the eastern

gate, but was only allowed to stand by the inner gatepost and watch.

46:16 property by inheritance. Since the Law required land to be kept within clans and tribes (Lev. 25:1-13), servants of a different clan had to return land at the Jubilee.

the four corners of the ⌊outer⌋ court there were enclosed[a] courts, 70 ⌊feet⌋[b] long by 52 and a half ⌊feet⌋[c] wide. All four corner areas had the same dimensions. 23 There was a ⌊stone⌋ wall[d] around the inside of them, around the four of them, with ovens built at the base of the walls on all sides. 24 He said to me: "These are the kitchens where those who minister at the temple will cook the people's sacrifices."

The Life-Giving River

47 Then he brought me back to the entrance of the temple and there was water flowing from under the threshold of the temple toward the east, for the temple faced east. The water was coming down from under the south side ⌊of the threshold⌋ of the temple, south of the altar. 2 Next he brought me out by way of the north gate and led me around the outside to the outer gate that faced east; there the water was trickling from the south side. 3 As the man went out east with a measuring line in his hand, he measured off a third of a mile[e] and led me through the water. It came up to ⌊my⌋ ankles. 4 Then he measured off a third ⌊of a mile⌋ and led me through the water. It came up to ⌊my⌋ knees. He measured off another third ⌊of a mile⌋ and led me through ⌊the water⌋. It came up to ⌊my⌋ waist. 5 Again he measured off a third of a ⌊mile⌋, and it was a river that I could not cross ⌊on foot⌋. For the water had risen; it was deep enough to swim in, a river that could not be crossed ⌊on foot⌋.

6 He asked me, "Do you see ⌊this⌋, son of man?" Then he led me back to the bank of the river. 7 When I had returned, I saw a very large number of trees along both sides of the riverbank. 8 He said to me, "This water flows out to the eastern region and goes down to the •Arabah. When it enters the sea, the sea of foul water,[f] g the water ⌊of the sea⌋ becomes fresh. 9 Every ⌊kind of⌋ living creature that swarms will live wherever the river flows,[h] and there will be a huge number of fish because this water goes there. Since the water will become fresh, there will be life everywhere the river goes. 10 Fishermen will stand beside it from En-gedi to En-eglaim.[i] These will become places where nets are spread out to dry. Their fish will consist of many different kinds, like the fish of the Mediterranean Sea. 11 Yet its swamps and marshes will not be healed; they will be left for salt. 12 All ⌊kinds of⌋ trees providing food will grow along both

banks of the river. Their leaves will not wither, and their fruit will not fail. Each month they will bear fresh fruit because the water ⌊comes⌋ from the sanctuary. Their fruit will be used for food and their leaves for medicine."

The Borders of the Land

13 This is what the Lord GOD says: "This is[j] the border you will ⌊use to⌋ divide the land as an inheritance for the 12 tribes of Israel. Joseph will receive two shares. 14 You will inherit it in equal portions, since I swore[k] to give it to your ancestors. So this land will fall to you as an inheritance.

15 "This is to be the border of the land:

On the north side it will extend from the Mediterranean Sea by way of Hethlon and Lebo-hamath to Zedad,[l] 16 Berothah, and Sibraim (which is between the border of Damascus and the border of Hamath), ⌊as far as⌋ Hazer-hatticon, which is on the border of Hauran. 17 So the border will run from the sea to Hazar-enon at the border of Damascus, with the territory of Hamath to the north. This will be the northern side.

18 On the east side it will run between Hauran and Damascus, along the Jordan between Gilead and the land of Israel; you will measure from the ⌊northern⌋ border to the eastern sea.g This will be the eastern side.

19 On the south side it will run from Tamar to the waters of Meribath-kadesh,[m] and on to the Brook ⌊of Egypt⌋ as far as the Mediterranean Sea. This will be the southern side.

20 On the west side the Mediterranean Sea will be the border, from the ⌊southern⌋ border up to a point opposite Lebo-hamath. This will be the western side.

21 "You are to divide this land among yourselves according to the tribes of Israel. 22 You will allot it as an inheritance for yourselves and for the foreigners living among you, who have fathered children among you. You will treat them[n] like native-born Israelites; along with you, they will be allotted an inheritance among the tribes of Israel. 23 In whatever tribe the foreigner lives, you will assign his inheritance there." ⌊This is⌋ the declaration of the Lord GOD.

---

a46:22 Hb obscure   b46:22 Lit 40 [cubits]   c46:22 Lit 30 [cubits]   d46:23 Or a row   e47:3 Lit 1,000 cubits; also in vv. 4–5   f47:8 Or enters the sea, being brought out to the sea; Hb obscure   g47:8,18 = the Dead Sea   h47:9 LXX, Vg; MT reads the two rivers flow   i47:10 Two springs near the Dead Sea   j47:13 Tg, Vg; Syr reads The valley of   k47:14 Lit lifted My hand   l47:15 LXX; MT reads [and] Lebo to Zedad, Hamath; Ezk 48:1   m47:19 = Kadesh-barnea   n47:22 Lit They will be to you

---

47:1 water. A river will flow from Messiah's temple to the Dead Sea that will become alive (see Rev. 22:1). Freshwater marine life will thrive inside it. Vegetation and trees will grow beside it.

47:10 where nets are spread. For the first time, fishermen will find their livelihood on

the banks of the former Dead Sea.

47:14 equal portions. God has pre-apportioned the land to be divided amongst the Israelites in the millennial kingdom.

47:15 This is to be the border of the land. The boundaries of the future allotment will be greater than even the borders in David and Sol-

omon's days. Future Israel will include Lebanon and part of Syria. Also, the land will undergo geographical changes, probably making it larger in other ways.

47:22 foreigners living among you. Some non-Jews will live in the land peacefully in the days of Messiah's kingdom.

The Tribal Allotments

48 "Now these are the names of the tribes:

From the northern end, along the road of Hethlon, to Lebo-hamath as far as Hazar-enon, at the northern border of Damascus, alongside Hamath and extending from the eastern side to the sea, will be Dan—one portion. ² Next to the territory of Dan, from the east side to the west, will be Asher—one ⌊portion⌋. ³ Next to the territory of Asher, from the east side to the west, will be Naphtali—one ⌊portion⌋. ⁴ Next to the territory of Naphtali, from the east side to the west, will be Manasseh—one ⌊portion⌋. ⁵ Next to the territory of Manasseh, from the east side to the west, will be Ephraim—one ⌊portion⌋. ⁶ Next to the territory of Ephraim, from the east side to the west, will be Reuben—one ⌊portion⌋. ⁷ Next to the territory of Reuben, from the east side to the west, will be Judah—one ⌊portion⌋.

⁸ "Next to the territory of Judah, from the east side to the west, will be the portion you donate ⌊to the LORD⌋, eight and one-third ⌊miles⌋ᵃ wide, and as long as one of the ⌊tribal⌋ portions from the east side to the west. The sanctuary will be in the middle of it. ⁹ "The ⌊special⌋ portion you donate to the LORD will be eight and one-third ⌊miles⌋ᵃ long and three and one-third ⌊miles⌋ᵇ wide. ¹⁰ This holy donation will be set apart for the priests ⌊alone⌋. It will be eight and one-third ⌊miles long⌋ᵃ on the northern side, three and one-third ⌊miles⌋ᵇ wide on the western side, three and one-third ⌊miles⌋ wide on the eastern side, and eight and one-third ⌊miles⌋ᵃ long on the southern side. The LORD's sanctuary will be in the middle of it. ¹¹ It is for the consecrated priests, the sons of Zadok, who kept My charge and did not go astray as the Levites did when the Israelites went astray. ¹² It will be a special donation for them out of the ⌊holy⌋ donation of the land, a most holy place adjacent to the territory of the Levites.

¹³ "Next to the territory of the priests, the Levites ⌊will have an area⌋ eight and one-third ⌊miles⌋ᵃ long and three and one-third ⌊miles⌋ᵇ wide. The total length will be eight and one-third ⌊miles⌋ᵃ and the width three and one-third ⌊miles⌋.ᵇ ¹⁴ They must not sell or exchange any of it, and they must not transfer this choice ⌊part⌋ of the land, for it is holy to the LORD.

¹⁵ "The remaining ⌊area⌋, one and two-thirds ⌊of a mile⌋ᶜ wide and eight and one-third ⌊miles long⌋,ᵃ will be for common use by the city, for ⌊both⌋ residential and open space. The city will be in the middle of it. ¹⁶ These are the city's measurements:

one and a half ⌊miles⌋ᵈ on the north side;
one and a half ⌊miles⌋ on the south side;
one and a half ⌊miles⌋ on the east side;
and one and a half ⌊miles⌋ on the west side.

¹⁷ The city's open space will extend:

425 ⌊feet⌋ᵉ to the north,
425 ⌊feet⌋ to the south,
425 ⌊feet⌋ to the east,
and 425 ⌊feet⌋ to the west.

¹⁸ "The remainder of the length alongside the holy donation will be three and one-third ⌊miles⌋ᵇ to the east and three and one-third ⌊miles⌋ to the west. It will run alongside the holy donation. Its produce will be food for the workers of the city. ¹⁹ The city's workers from all the tribes of Israel will cultivate it. ²⁰ The entire donation will be eight and one-third ⌊miles⌋ᵃ by eight and one-third ⌊miles⌋; you are to set apart the holy donation along with the city property as a square ⌊area⌋.

²¹ "The remaining ⌊area⌋ on both sides of the holy donation and the city property will belong to the prince. He will own ⌊the land⌋ adjacent to the ⌊tribal⌋ portions, next to the eight and one-third ⌊miles⌋ᵃ of the donation as far as the eastern border andᶠ next to the eight and one-third ⌊miles of the donation⌋ᵃ as far as the western border. The holy donation and the sanctuary of the temple will be in the middle of it. ²² Except for the Levitical property and the city property in the middle of the area belonging to the prince, the area between the territory of Judah and that of Benjamin will belong to the prince.

²³ "As for the rest of the tribes:

From the east side to the west, will be Benjamin—one ⌊portion⌋.
²⁴ Next to the territory of Benjamin, from the east side to the west, will be Simeon—one ⌊portion⌋.
²⁵ Next to the territory of Simeon, from the east side to the west, will be Issachar—one ⌊portion⌋.
²⁶ Next to the territory of Issachar, from the east side to the west, will be Zebulun—one ⌊portion⌋.
²⁷ Next to the territory of Zebulun, from the east side to the west, will be Gad—one ⌊portion⌋.

ᵃ**48:8,9,10,13,15,20,21** Lit *25,000 [cubits]* ᵇ**48:9,10,13,18** Lit *10,000 [cubits]* ᶜ**48:15** Lit *5,000 [cubits]* ᵈ**48:16** Lit *4,500 [cubits]* ᵉ**48:17** Lit *250 [cubits]* ᶠ**48:21** Lit *border, and to the west,*

48:1 The land will be divided according to the names of the tribes of Israel—Jacob's descendants. All of the tribes are listed, proving that there are no lost tribes.

48:2 Asher—one [portion]. Asher will receive the most northern section of land—away from the sanctuary. Six other tribes

will live in the north.

48:7 Judah—one [portion]. As the tribe of the Messianic royal line, this tribe would take a privileged position next to God's own portion. Four other tribes will live in the south.

48:14 choice [part] of the land. The sacred district at the geographical center of the land

will be reserved d**m all the tribes of Israel.** The remaining portion of land will function as a "national park" for all the holy city's residents, who represent every tribe.

48:31 gates. Ezekiel's description is similar to John's vision in Revelation 21 (Rev. 21:12–14). Twelve gates will surround the millennial Jeru-

28 Next to the territory of Gad toward the south side, the border will run from Tamar to the waters of Meribath-kadesh, to the Brook ⌊of Egypt⌋, and out to the Mediterranean Sea. 29 This is the land you are to allot as an inheritance to Israel's tribes, and these will be their portions." ⌊This is⌋ the declaration of the Lord God.

The New City

30 "These are the exits of the city:

On the north side, which measures one and a half ⌊miles⌋,a 31 there will be three gates facing north, the gates of the city being named for the tribes of Israel: one, the gate of Reuben; one, the gate of Judah; and one, the gate of Levi.

32 On the east side, which is one and a half ⌊miles⌋,b there will be three gates: one, the gate of Joseph; one, the gate of Benjamin; and one, the gate of Dan.

33 On the south side, which measures one and a half ⌊miles⌋, there will be three gates: one, the gate of Simeon; one, the gate of Issachar; and one, the gate of Zebulun.

34 On the west side, which is one and a half ⌊miles⌋, there will be three gates: one, the gate of Gad; one, the gate of Asher; and one, the gate of Naphtali.

35 The perimeter ⌊of the city⌋ will be six ⌊miles⌋,c and the name of the city from that day on will be: •Yahweh Is There."

---

a 48:30 Lit 4,500 ⌊cubits⌋   b 48:32 Lit 4,500 ⌊cubits⌋; also in vv. 33–34   c 48:35 Lit 18,000 ⌊cubits⌋

---

salem. Israel's future restoration will be complete. In cities of the ancient world such as Babylon the gates were often named after the gods. The more common practice in Israel, however, was for gates to be named for where they led. In the end, Ezekiel demonstrates what

has been true all along. The gateway to God is through His twelve tribes; first in his covenant with them, then through the New Covenant in which the twelve tribes are representative of all the people of God (11:19; 16:60; 36:26-27; Jer. 31:31; Luke 22:20; Rom. 11:27; 2 Cor. 3:6;

Heb. 7:22; 9:15). God keeps His covenant promises, even beyond the end.

INTRODUCTION TO
DANIEL

AUTHOR

Daniel (whose name means "God is my judge") was an exiled Israelite statesman in the dominating empires of his time.

DATE

The date for the writing of this book has been vigorously debated. Scholars who regard the book as genuine predictive prophecy date it circa 530 B.C., near the end of Daniel's life. The events depicted in the life of Daniel and his friends (chapters 1-6) are set in the time of the Babylonian captivity (605-538 B.C.) and the onset of the Persian Empire. The visions (chapters 7-12) look ahead to succeeding history, at least to 160 B.C., and perhaps to events still in the future even today.

THEME

God is sovereign over the kingdoms of men (2:21; 5:21).

HISTORICAL BACKGROUND

In 605 B.C. Nebuchadnezzar took Daniel and other captives to Babylon. Daniel rose quickly to prominence under Nebuchadnezzar. After the king's death, Daniel seems to have fallen from favor only to regain it by interpreting the handwriting on the wall at Belshazzar's feast (5:13-29). With the capture of Babylon by Darius, Daniel maintained his official position, serving under both Darius and Cyrus, the king of Persia.

CHARACTERISTICS

Daniel was written in the context of the Exile. It called for a commitment to God's law amongst the people of God who were suffering persecution (even unto death). Daniel appeals to them to awaken and be prepared for the unexpected intervention of God into world affairs. Jesus referred to Daniel in His teachings (Matt. 24:15) and quoted from 9:27, 11:31, and 12:11. The Book of Revelation draws heavily from Daniel's apocalyptic imagery (in chapters 7-12).

PASSAGES FOR
TOPICAL GROUP STUDY

1:1-21 . . . . . . PEER PRESSURE and DISCIPLINE . . Pure Discipline

3:1-12,19-27. . . . PERSECUTION and FAITH. . . . . A Fiery Test

6:1-24 . . . . COURAGE and PRAYER. . . . . . . The Den of Lions

Daniel's Captivity in Babylon

1 In the third year of the reign of Jehoiakim king of Judah, Nebuchadnezzar[a] king of Babylon came to Jerusalem and laid siege to it. [2] The Lord handed Jehoiakim king of Judah over to him, along with some of the vessels from the house of God. Nebuchadnezzar carried them to the land of Babylon,[b] to the house of his god,[c] and put the vessels in the treasury of his god.

[3] The king ordered Ashpenaz, the chief of his court officials,[d] to bring some of the Israelites from the royal family and from the nobility— [4] young men without any physical defect, good-looking, suitable for instruction in all wisdom, knowledgeable, perceptive, and capable of serving in the king's palace—and to teach them the Chaldean language and literature. [5] The king assigned them daily provisions from the royal food and from the wine that he drank. They were to be trained for three years, and at the end of that time they were to serve in the king's court.[e] [6] Among them, from the descendants of Judah, were Daniel, Hananiah, Mishael, and Azariah. [7] The chief official gave them ⌊different⌋ names: to Daniel, he gave the name Belteshazzar; to Hananiah, Shadrach; to Mishael, Meshach; and to Azariah, Abednego.

Faithfulness in Babylon

[8] Daniel determined that he would not defile himself with the king's food or with the wine he drank. So he asked permission from the chief official not to defile himself. [9] God had granted Daniel favor and compassion from the chief official, [10] yet he said to Daniel, "My lord the king assigned your food and drink. I'm afraid ⌊of what would happen⌋ if he saw your faces looking thinner than those of the other young men your age. You would endanger my life[f] with the king."

[11] So Daniel said to the guard whom the chief official had assigned to Daniel, Hananiah, Mishael, and Azariah, [12] "Please test your servants for 10 days. Let us be given vegetables to eat and water to drink. [13] Then examine our appearance and the appearance of the young men who are eating the king's food, and deal with your servants based on what you see." [14] He agreed with them in this matter and tested them for 10 days. [15] At the end of 10 days they looked better and healthier[g] than all the young men who were eating the king's food. [16] So the guard continued to remove their food and the wine they were to drink and gave them vegetables.

Pure Discipline

1. What is your favorite food? Your favorite drink?

Daniel 1:1-21

2. Why did Daniel refuse to eat some of the food he was given? How might food have "defiled" him?

3. How did Daniel handle this difficult situation? How can you be like Daniel when you're asked to do something that violates your conscience?

4. What are some things in the world that might "defile" you? How do your peers pressure you to defile yourself?

5. What were the results of Daniel's obedience (vv. 17-20)? How might obedient discipline make you a better student? Athlete?

Faithfulness Rewarded

[17] God gave these four young men knowledge and understanding in every kind of literature and wisdom. Daniel also understood visions and dreams of every kind. [18] At the end of the time that the king had said to present them, the chief official presented them to Nebuchadnezzar. [19] The king interviewed them, and among all of them, no one was found equal to Daniel, Hananiah, Mishael, and Azariah. So they began to serve in the king's court. [20] In every matter of wisdom and understanding that the king consulted them about, he found them 10 times[h] better than all the diviner-priests and mediums in his entire kingdom. [21] Daniel remained there until the first year of King Cyrus.

Nebuchadnezzar's Dream

2 In the second year of his reign, Nebuchadnezzar had dreams that troubled him, and sleep deserted him. [2] So the king gave orders to summon the diviner-priests, mediums, sorcerers, and Chaldeans[i] to tell the king his dreams. When they came and stood before the king, [3] he said to them, "I have had a dream and am anxious to understand it."

[4] The Chaldeans spoke to the king (Aramaic[j] begins here): "May the king live forever. Tell your servants the dream, and we will give the interpretation."

---

[a]**1:1** Or *Nebuchadrezzar* [b]**1:2** Lit *Shinar*; Gn 10:10; 11:2; 14:1,9 [c]**1:2** Or *gods* [d]**1:3** Or *his eunuchs* [e]**1:5** Lit *to stand before the king* [f]**1:10** Lit *would make my head guilty* [g]**1:15** Lit *fatter of flesh* [h]**1:20** Lit *hands* [i]**2:2** In this chap *Chaldeans* = influential Babylonian wise men [j]**2:4** The text from here through chap 7 is written in *Aramaic.*

1:1 Jehoiakim. Jehoiakim reigned from 609-598 B.C. Babylonian texts claim that Nebuchadnezzar attacked Israel in 605 B.C. when Daniel and his three friends were captured. Jehoikim was Nebuchadnezzar's vassal for three years, then rebelled. Jerusalem was finally overrun by the Babylonians in 586 B.C.

1:8 determined that he would not defile himself. The food served at the king's table was unclean according to Mosaic law. It had been prepared by Gentiles, probably included things that the Jews were forbidden to eat, and had been sacrificed to idols. Daniel decided not to eat these things that would displease God—even though to refuse royal food would endanger his position and perhaps his life.

1:9-10 I'm afraid. The official liked Daniel, but he feared that granting Daniel's request would put his own career at risk. He was responsible for keeping his captives in good

5 The king replied to the Chaldeans, "My word is final: If you don't tell me the dream and its interpretation, you will be torn limb from limb,[a] and your houses will be made a garbage dump. 6 But if you make the dream and its interpretation known to me, you'll receive gifts, a reward, and great honor from me. So make the dream and its interpretation known to me."

7 They answered a second time, "May the king tell the dream to his servants, and we will give the interpretation."

8 The king replied, "I know for certain you are trying to gain some time, because you see that my word is final. 9 If you don't tell me the dream, there is one decree for you. You have conspired to tell me something false or fraudulent until the situation changes. So tell me the dream and I will know you can give me its interpretation."

10 The Chaldeans answered the king, "No one on earth can make known what the king requests. Consequently, no king, however great and powerful, has ever asked anything like this of any diviner-priest, medium, or Chaldean. 11 What the king is asking is so difficult that no one can make it known to him except the gods, whose dwelling is not with mortals." 12 Because of this, the king became violently angry and gave orders to destroy all the wise men of Babylon. 13 The decree was issued that the wise men were to be executed, and they searched for Daniel and his friends, to execute them.

14 Then Daniel responded with tact and discretion to Arioch, the commander of the king's guard,[b] who had gone out to execute the wise men of Babylon. 15 He asked Arioch, the king's officer, "Why is the decree from the king so harsh?"[c] Then Arioch explained the situation to Daniel. 16 So Daniel went and asked the king to give him some time, so that he could give the king the interpretation.

17 Then Daniel went to his house and told his friends Hananiah, Mishael, and Azariah about the matter, 18 ⌊urging⌋ them to ask the God of heaven for mercy concerning this mystery, so Daniel and his friends would not be killed with the rest of Babylon's wise men. 19 The mystery was then revealed to Daniel in a vision at night, and Daniel praised the God of heaven 20 and declared:

> May the name of God
> be praised forever and ever,
> for wisdom and power belong to Him.
> 21 He changes the times and seasons;
> He removes kings and establishes kings.
> He gives wisdom to the wise

and knowledge to those
who have understanding.
22 He reveals the deep and hidden things;
He knows what is in the darkness,
and light dwells with Him.
23 I offer thanks and praise to You,
God of my fathers,
because You have given me
wisdom and power.
And now You have let me know
what we asked of You,
for You have let us know
the king's mystery.[d]

24 Therefore Daniel went to Arioch, whom the king had assigned to destroy the wise men of Babylon. He came and said to him, "Don't kill the wise men of Babylon! Bring me before the king, and I will give him the interpretation."

25 Then Arioch quickly brought Daniel before the king and said to him, "I have found a man among the Judean exiles who can let the king know the interpretation."

26 The king said in reply to Daniel, whose name was Belteshazzar, "Are you able to tell me the dream I had and its interpretation?"

27 Daniel answered the king: "No wise man, medium, diviner-priest, or astrologer is able to make known to the king the mystery he asked about. 28 But there is a God in heaven who reveals mysteries, and He has let King Nebuchadnezzar know what will happen in the last days. Your dream and the visions ⌊that came into⌋ your mind ⌊as you lay⌋ in bed were these: 29 Your Majesty, while you were in your bed, thoughts came ⌊to your mind⌋ about what will happen in the future.[e] The revealer of mysteries has let you know what will happen. 30 As for me, this mystery has been revealed to me, not because I have more wisdom than anyone living, but in order that the interpretation might be made known to the king, and that you may understand the thoughts of your mind.

The Dream's Interpretation

31 "My king, as you were watching, a colossal statue appeared. That statue, tall and dazzling, was standing in front of you, and its appearance was terrifying. 32 The head of the statue was pure gold, its chest and arms were silver, its stomach and thighs were bronze, 33 its legs were iron, and its feet were partly iron and partly fired clay. 34 As you were watching, a stone broke off without a hand touching it,[f] struck the statue on its feet

---

a 2:5 Lit be made into limbs   b 2:14 Or executioners   c 2:15 Or urgent   d 2:23 Lit matter   e 2:29 Lit happen after this   f 2:34 Lit off not by hands

---

physical shape to prepare them for whatever tasks the king would assign them.

1:12 vegetables to eat and water to drink. The four Hebrews didn't eat the meat or drink the wine because they had most likely been offered to idols.

1:17 Daniel also understood visions and

dreams. God gave these four young men knowledge and understanding. But the most important gift was Daniel's ability to understand visions and dreams—a talent that no earthly knowledge or training could give.

2:18 ask the God of heaven for mercy concerning this mystery. Even though

Daniel was well educated and had great abilities, he asked his friends to join him in prayer concerning this mystery. A vision was the answer to the mystery.

2:31-43 a colossal statue. Nebuchadnezzar's dream had four empires that can be interpreted as Babylon (gold head), Medo-

of iron and fired clay, and crushed them. ³⁵ Then the iron, the fired clay, the bronze, the silver, and the gold were shattered and became like chaff from the summer threshing floors. The wind carried them away, and not a trace of them could be found. But the stone that struck the statue became a great mountain and filled the whole earth.

³⁶ "This was the dream; now we will tell the king its interpretation. ³⁷ Your Majesty, you are king of kings. The God of heaven has given you sovereignty, power, strength, and glory. ³⁸ Wherever people live—or wild animals, or birds of the air—He has handed them over to you and made you ruler over them all. You are the head of gold.

³⁹ "After you, there will arise another kingdom, inferior to yours, and then another, a third kingdom, of bronze, which will rule the whole earth. ⁴⁰ A fourth kingdom will be as strong as iron; for iron crushes and shatters everything, and like iron that smashes, it will crush and smash all the others.ᵃ ⁴¹ You saw the feet and toes, partly of a potter's fired clay and partly of iron—it will be a divided kingdom, though some of the strength of iron will be in it. You saw the iron mixed with clay, ⁴² and that the toes of the feet were part iron and part fired clay—part of the kingdom will be strong, and part will be brittle. ⁴³ You saw the iron mixed with clay— the peoples will mix with one anotherᵇ but will not hold together, just as iron does not mix with fired clay.

⁴⁴ "In the days of those kings, the God of heaven will set up a kingdom that will never be destroyed, and this kingdom will not be left to another people. It will crush all these kingdoms and bring them to an end, but will itself endure forever. ⁴⁵ You saw a stone break off from the mountain without a hand touching it,ᶜ and it crushed the iron, bronze, fired clay, silver, and gold. The great God has told the king what will happen in the future.ᵈ The dream is true, and its interpretation certain."

Nebuchadnezzar's Response

⁴⁶ Then King Nebuchadnezzar fell down, paid homage to Daniel, and gave orders to present an offering and incense to him. ⁴⁷ The king said to Daniel, "Your God is indeed God of gods, Lord of kings, and a revealer of mysteries, since you were able to reveal this mystery." ⁴⁸ Then the king promoted Daniel and gave him many generous gifts. He made him ruler over the entire province of Babylon and chief governor over all the wise men of Babylon. ⁴⁹ At Daniel's request, the king

appointed Shadrach, Meshach, and Abednego to manage the province of Babylon. But Daniel remained at the king's court.

A Fiery Test

1. What's the worst experience you've had with fire?
2. What idols do you face in your school? How do fellow students treat people at your school who do not "bow down" to them?

Daniel 3:1-12,19-27

3. Why did these three young men refuse to bow down to the idol? What did they risk by refusing?
4. Who was the "fourth man" who appeared in the furnace (v. 25)? What does this teach us about God's intervention for those who are faithful to Him?
5. When you are persecuted for your faith, how do you respond?

Nebuchadnezzar's Gold Statue

3 King Nebuchadnezzar made a gold statue, 90 feet high and nine feet wide.ᵉ He set it up on the plain of Dura in the province of Babylon. ² King Nebuchadnezzar sent word to assemble the satraps, prefects, governors, advisers, treasurers, judges, magistrates, and all the rulers of the provinces to attend the dedication of the statue King Nebuchadnezzar had set up. ³ So the satraps, prefects, governors, advisers, treasurers, judges, magistrates, and all the rulers of the provinces assembled for the dedication of the statue the king had set up. Then they stood before the statue Nebuchadnezzar had set up.

⁴ A herald loudly proclaimed, "People of every nation and language, you are commanded: ⁵ When you hear the sound of the horn, flute, zither,ᶠ lyre,ᵍ harp, drum,ʰ and every kind of music, you are to fall down and worship the gold statue that King Nebuchadnezzar has set up. ⁶ But whoever does not fall down and worship will immediately be thrown into a furnace of blazing fire."

⁷ Therefore, when all the people heard the sound of the horn, flute, zither, lyre, harp, and every kind of

---

ᵃ2:40 Lit *all these* ᵇ2:43 Lit *another in the seed of men* ᶜ2:45 Lit *mountain, not by hands* ᵈ2:45 Lit *happen after this* ᵉ3:1 Lit *statue, its height 60 cubits, its width six cubits* ᶠ3:5 Or *lyre* ᵍ3:5 Or *sambuke; a type of triangular harp with 4 or more strings* ʰ3:5 Or *pipe; the identity of these instruments is uncertain.*

Persia (silver chest and arms), Greece (bronze belly and thighs) and Rome (iron legs and feet).

2:44-45 kingdom that will never be destroyed. This kingdom is the kingdom of God. Jesus is the rock not made by human hands that will conquer all other political

powers and have authority over all things. Amillennialists believe that this kingdom is a spiritual kingdom that was introduced by Jesus at His first coming. Premillennialists believe that this is a literal kingdom that will be established at the second coming.

3:1 A gold statue. After hearing that he

would play a significant role in Gentile history, Nebuchadnezzar built a 90-foot gold statue to symbolize the greatness of Babylon under his rule. He hoped that this impressive structure would unify the nation.

3:2 dedication. Nebuchadnezzar called together officials of every rank in the kingdom.

music, people of every nation and language fell down and worshiped the gold statue that King Nebuchadnezzar had set up.

The Furnace of Blazing Fire

8 Some Chaldeans took this occasion to come forward and maliciously accuse[a] the Jews. 9 They said to King Nebuchadnezzar, "May the king live forever. 10 You as king have issued a decree that everyone who hears the sound of the horn, flute, zither, lyre, harp, drum, and every kind of music must fall down and worship the gold statue. 11 Whoever does not fall down and worship will be thrown into a furnace of blazing fire. 12 There are some Jews you have appointed to manage the province of Babylon: Shadrach, Meshach, and Abednego. These men have ignored you, the king; they do not serve your gods or worship the gold statue you have set up."

13 Then in a furious rage Nebuchadnezzar gave orders to bring in Shadrach, Meshach, and Abednego. So these men were brought before the king. 14 Nebuchadnezzar asked them, "Shadrach, Meshach, and Abednego, is it true that you don't serve my gods or worship the gold statue I have set up? 15 Now if you're ready, when you hear the sound of the horn, flute, zither, lyre, harp, drum, and every kind of music, fall down and worship the statue I made. But if you don't worship it, you will immediately be thrown into a furnace of blazing fire—and who is the god who can rescue you from my power?"

16 Shadrach, Meshach, and Abednego replied to the king, "Nebuchadnezzar, we don't need to give you an answer to this question. 17 If the God we serve exists, then He can rescue us from the furnace of blazing fire, and He can rescue us from the power of you, the king. 18 But even if He does not rescue us,[b] we want you as king to know that we will not serve your gods or worship the gold statue you set up."

19 Then Nebuchadnezzar was filled with rage, and the expression on his face changed toward Shadrach, Meshach, and Abednego. He gave orders to heat the furnace seven times more than was customary, 20 and he commanded some of the strongest soldiers in his army to tie up Shadrach, Meshach, and Abednego and throw them into the furnace of blazing fire. 21 So these men, in their trousers, robes, head coverings,[c] and other clothes, were tied up and thrown into the furnace of blazing fire. 22 Since the king's command was so urgent[d] and the furnace extremely hot, the raging flames[e] killed those men who carried Shadrach, Meshach, and Abednego up. 23 And these three men,

Shadrach, Meshach, and Abednego fell, bound, into the furnace of blazing fire.

Delivered from the Fire

24 Then King Nebuchadnezzar jumped up in alarm. He said to his advisers, "Didn't we throw three men, bound, into the fire?"

"Yes, of course, Your Majesty," they replied to the king.

25 He exclaimed, "Look! I see four men, not tied, walking around in the fire unharmed; and the fourth looks like a son of the gods."[f]

26 Nebuchadnezzar then approached the door of the furnace of blazing fire and called: "Shadrach, Meshach, and Abednego, you servants of the •Most High God—come out!" So Shadrach, Meshach, and Abednego came out of the fire. 27 When the satraps, prefects, governors, and the king's advisers gathered around, they saw that the fire had no effect on[g] the bodies of these men: not a hair of their heads was singed, their robes were unaffected, and there was no smell of fire on them. 28 Nebuchadnezzar exclaimed, "Praise to the God of Shadrach, Meshach, and Abednego! He sent His angel[h] and rescued His servants who trusted in Him. They violated the king's command and risked their lives rather than serve or worship any god except their own God. 29 Therefore I issue a decree that anyone of any people, nation, or language who says anything offensive against the God of Shadrach, Meshach, and Abednego will be torn limb from limb and his house made a garbage dump. For there is no other god who is able to deliver like this." 30 Then the king rewarded Shadrach, Meshach, and Abednego in the province of Babylon.

Nebuchadnezzar's Proclamation

4[i] King Nebuchadnezzar,

To those of every people, nation, and language, who live in all the earth:

May your prosperity increase. 2 I am pleased to tell you about the miracles and wonders the •Most High God has done for me.

3 How great are His miracles,
and how mighty His wonders!
His kingdom is an eternal kingdom,
and His dominion is from generation
to generation.

The Dream

4[j] I, Nebuchadnezzar, was at ease in my house and flourishing in my palace. 5 I had a dream, and it frightened

a3:8 Lit and eat the pieces of   b3:18 Lit But if not   c3:21 The identity of these articles of clothing is uncertain.   d3:22 Or harsh   e3:22 Lit the flame of the fire   f3:25 Or of a divine being   g3:27 Lit fire had not overcome   h3:28 Or messenger   i4:1 Dn 3:31 in Hb   j4:4 Dn 4:1 in Hb

He wanted the officials to swear allegiance to him and publicly recognize his absolute authority in the kingdom.

3:12 These men have ignored you, the king. Shadrach, Meshach, and Abednego chose to obey God rather than the king. The officials who pointed this out to Nebuchad-

nezzar were probably trying to gain favor with the king by contrasting their worship of the golden image with the disobedience of the three Jews.

3:18 even if He does not rescue us. As they faced the fiery furnace, Nebuchadnezzar gave the three Jews another chance to

bow down to the golden image. But the Jews were obedient to God—even in the face of death. They were confident that God could rescue them, but were willing to obey even if rescue did not come. This was a test of their faith.

4:1-3 To those ... to generation. Nebu-

me; while in my bed, the images and visions in my mind alarmed me. 6 So I issued a decree to bring all the wise men of Babylon to me in order that they might make the dream's interpretation known to me. 7 When the diviner-priests, mediums, Chaldeans, and astrologers came in, I told them the dream, but they could not make its interpretation known to me.

8 Finally Daniel, named Belteshazzar after the name of my god—and the spirit of the holy gods is in him—came before me. I told him the dream: 9 Belteshazzar, head of the diviners, because I know that you have a spirit of the holy gods and that no mystery puzzles you, explain to me the visions of my dream that I saw, and its interpretation. 10 In the visions of my mind as I was lying in bed, I saw this:

There was a tree in the middle of the earth,
and its height was great.
11 The tree grew large and strong;
its top reached to the sky,
and it was visible to the ends of thea earth.
12 Its leaves were beautiful, its fruit was abundant,
and on it was food for all.
Wild animals found shelter under it,
the birds of the air lived in its branches,
and every creature was fed from it.

13 As I was lying in my bed, I also saw in the visions of my mind an observer, a holy one,b coming down from heaven. 14 He called out loudly:

Cut down the tree and chop off its branches;
strip off its leaves and scatter its fruit.
Let the animals flee from under it,
and the birds from its branches.
15 But leave the stump with its roots in the ground,
and with a band of iron and bronze around it,
in the tender grass of the field.
Let him be drenched with dew from the sky
and share the plants of the earth
with the animals.
16 Let his mind be changed from that of a man,
and let him be given the mind of an animal
for seven periods of time.c d
17 This word is by decree of the observers;
the matter is a command from the holy ones.
This is so the living will know
that the Most High is ruler
over the kingdom of men.
He gives it to anyone He wants
and sets over it the lowliest of men.

18 This is the dream that I, King Nebuchadnezzar, had. Now, Belteshazzar, tell me the interpretation, because none of the wise men of my kingdom can make the interpretation known to me. But you can, because you have the spirit of the holy gods.

The Dream Interpreted

19 Then Daniel, whose name is Belteshazzar, was stunned for a moment, and his thoughts alarmed him. The king said, "Belteshazzar, don't let the dream or its interpretation alarm you."

Belteshazzar answered, "My lord, may the dream apply to those who hate you, and its interpretation to your enemies! 20 The tree you saw, which grew large and strong, whose top reached to the sky and was visible to all the earth, 21 whose leaves were beautiful and its fruit abundant—and on it was food for all, under it the wild animals lived, and in its branches the birds of the air lived— 22 that tree is you, the king. For you have become great and strong: your greatness has grown and even reaches the sky, and your dominion ⌊extends⌋ to the ends of the earth.

23 "The king saw an observer, a holy one, coming down from heaven and saying, 'Cut down the tree and destroy it, but leave the stump with its roots in the ground and with a band of iron and bronze around it, in the tender grass of the field. Let him be drenched with dew from the sky, and share ⌊food⌋ with the wild animals for seven periods of time.' 24 This is the interpretation, Your Majesty, and this is the sentence of the Most High that has been passed against my lord the king: 25 You will be driven away from people to live with the wild animals. You will feed on grass like cattle and be drenched with dew from the sky for seven periods of time, until you acknowledge that the Most High is ruler over the kingdom of men, and He gives it to anyone He wants. 26 As for the command to leave the tree's stump with its roots, your kingdom will be restorede to you as soon as you acknowledge that Heavenf rules. 27 Therefore, may my advice seem good to you my king. Separate yourself from your sins by doing what is right, and from your injustices by showing mercy to the needy. Perhaps there will be an extension of your prosperity."

The Sentence Executed

28 All this happened to King Nebuchadnezzar. 29 At the end of 12 months, as he was walking on the roof of the royal palace in Babylon, 30 the king exclaimed, "Is this not Babylon the Great that I have built by my vast power to be a royal residence and to display my majestic glory?"

---

a4:11 Lit of all the b4:13 = an angel c4:16 Lit animal as seven times pass over him d4:16 Perhaps = 7 years e4:26 Lit enduring f4:26 = God

---

chadnezzar issued this official proclamation of God's greatness in response to the events described in verses 4-37.
4:5 I had a dream. This was 30 years after the dream in chapter 2.
4:11-12 tree. The tree in Nebuchadnezzar's dream represents Nebuchadnezzar himself,

whose kingdom spread farther than any kingdom before it.
4:13 an observer, a holy one. Nebuchadnezzar didn't recognize the messenger, but Jews knew that this was an angel from heaven.
4:15 leave the stump with its roots in the

ground. The fact that the stump and roots remained in the ground suggested that the tree would be revived later. There would eventually be new growth.

4:17 the Most High is ruler over the kingdom of men. The lesson that Nebuchadnezzar was supposed to learn from his

31 While the words were still in the king's mouth, a voice came from heaven: "King Nebuchadnezzar, to you it is declared that the kingdom has departed from you. 32 You will be driven away from people to live with the wild animals, and you will feed on grass like cattle for seven periods of time, until you acknowledge that the Most High is ruler over the kingdom of men, and He gives it to anyone He wants."

33 At that moment the sentence against Nebuchadnezzar was executed. He was driven away from people. He ate grass like cattle, and his body was drenched with dew from the sky, until his hair grew like eagles' ⌊feathers⌋ and his nails like birds' ⌊claws⌋.

Nebuchadnezzar's Praise

34 But at the end of those days, I, Nebuchadnezzar, looked up to heaven, and my sanity returned to me. Then I praised the Most High and honored and glorified Him who lives forever:

> For His dominion is an everlasting dominion,
> and His kingdom is from generation
>   to generation.
35 All the inhabitants of the earth are counted
>   as nothing,
> and He does what He wants with the army
>   of heaven
> and the inhabitants of the earth.
> There is no one who can hold back His hand
> or say to Him, "What have You done?"

36 At that time my sanity returned to me, and my majesty and splendor returned to me for the glory of my kingdom. My advisers and my nobles sought me out, I was reestablished over my kingdom, and even more greatness came to me. 37 Now I, Nebuchadnezzar, praise, exalt, and glorify the King of heaven, because all His works are true and His ways are just. And He is able to humble those who walk in pride.

Belshazzar's Feast

5 King Belshazzar held a great feast for 1,000 of his nobles and drank wine in their presence. 2 Under the influence of[a] the wine, Belshazzar gave orders to bring in the gold and silver vessels that his predecessor[b] Nebuchadnezzar had taken from the temple in Jerusalem, so that the king and his nobles, wives, and concubines could drink from them. 3 So they brought in the gold[c] vessels that had been taken from the temple, the house of God in Jerusalem, and the king and his nobles, wives, and concubines drank from them.

4 They drank the wine and praised their gods made of gold and silver, bronze, iron, wood, and stone.

The Handwriting on the Wall

5 At that moment the fingers of a man's hand appeared and began writing on the plaster of the king's palace wall next to the lampstand. As the king watched the hand[d] that was writing, 6 his face turned pale,[e] and his thoughts so terrified him that his hip joints shook and his knees knocked together. 7 The king called out to bring in the mediums, Chaldeans, and astrologers. He said to these wise men of Babylon, "Whoever reads this inscription and gives me its interpretation will be clothed in purple, have a gold chain around his neck, and have the third highest position in the kingdom." 8 So all the king's wise men came in, but none could read the inscription or make known its interpretation to him. 9 Then King Belshazzar became even more terrified, his face turned pale,[f] and his nobles were bewildered.

10 Because of the outcry of the king and his nobles, the queen[g] came to the banquet hall. "May the king live forever," she said. "Don't let your thoughts terrify you or your face be pale.[h] 11 There is a man in your kingdom who has the spirit of the holy gods in him. In the days of your predecessor he was found to have insight, intelligence, and wisdom like the wisdom of the gods. Your predecessor, King Nebuchadnezzar, appointed him chief of the diviners, mediums, Chaldeans, and astrologers. Your own predecessor, the king, 12 ⌊did this⌋ because Daniel, the one the king named Belteshazzar, was found to have an extraordinary spirit, knowledge and perception, and the ability to interpret dreams, explain riddles, and solve problems. Therefore, summon Daniel, and he will give the interpretation."

Daniel before the King

13 Then Daniel was brought before the king. The king said to him, "Are you Daniel, one of the Judean exiles that my predecessor the king brought from Judah? 14 I've heard that you have the spirit of the gods in you, and that you have insight, intelligence, and extraordinary wisdom. 15 Now the wise men and mediums were brought before me to read this inscription and make its interpretation known to me, but they could not give its interpretation. 16 However, I have heard about you that you can give interpretations and solve problems. Therefore, if you can read this inscription and give me its interpretation, you will be clothed in purple, have a gold chain around your neck, and have the third highest position in the kingdom."

---

a**5:2** Or *When he tasted* b**5:2** Or *father,* or *grandfather* c**5:3** Theod, Vg add *and silver* d**5:5** Lit *part of the hand* e**5:5–6** Lit *writing,* 6 *the king's brightness changed* f**5:9** Lit *his brightness changed on him* g**5:10** Perhaps the queen mother h**5:10** Lit *your brightness change*

---

experience was that God is sovereign over all rulers of the earth. It is God who chooses to set rulers over the people, and God has the power to take away their authority.
4:26 Heaven rules. This is similar to "kingdom of heaven" used by Jesus in Matthew.
4:28 All this happened to … Nebuchad-

nezzar. Daniel's prophecy came true because Nebuchadnezzar refused to heed his warning and acknowledge God's sovereignty. God had given Nebuchadnezzar the opportunity to turn from his ways.

5:1 Belshazzar. Here Belshazzar is said to be Nebuchadnezzar's son. This could also mean

grandson or heir. Other documents tell us that Belshazzar, a descendant of Nebuchadnezzar, was the oldest son of Nabonidus, the reigning king. Nabonidus appointed Belshazzar co-regent, so he was called a king and thus exercised the authority of a king.

5:5 king's palace. Remarkably, this palace

¹⁷ Then Daniel answered the king, "You may keep your gifts, and give your rewards to someone else; however, I will read the inscription for the king and make the interpretation known to him. ¹⁸ Your Majesty, the •Most High God gave sovereignty, greatness, glory, and majesty to your predecessor Nebuchadnezzar. ¹⁹ Because of the greatness He gave him, all peoples, nations, and languages were terrified and fearful of him. He killed anyone he wanted and kept alive anyone he wanted; he exalted anyone he wanted and humbled anyone he wanted. ²⁰ But when his heart was exalted and his spirit became arrogant, he was deposed from his royal throne and his glory was taken from him. ²¹ He was driven away from people, his mind was like an animal's, he lived with the wild donkeys, he was fed grass like cattle, and his body was drenched with dew from the sky until he acknowledged that the Most High God is ruler over the kingdom of men and sets anyone He wants over it.

²² "But you his successor, Belshazzar, have not humbled your heart, even though you knew all this. ²³ Instead, you have exalted yourself against the Lord of heaven. The vessels from His houseᵃ were brought to you, and as you and your nobles, wives, and concubines drank wine from them, you praised the gods made of silver and gold, bronze, iron, wood, and stone, which do not see or hear or understand. But you have not glorified the God who holds your life-breath in His hand and who controls the whole course of your life.ᵇ ²⁴ Therefore, He sent the hand, and this writing was inscribed.

The Inscription's Interpretation

²⁵ "This is the writing that was inscribed:

MENE, MENE, TEKEL, PARSIN

²⁶ This is the interpretation of the message:

MENEᶜ ⌊means that⌋ God has numbered ⌊the days of⌋ your kingdom and brought it to an end.

²⁷ TEKELᵈ ⌊means that⌋ you have been weighed in the balance and found deficient.

²⁸ PERESᵉ ⌊means that⌋ your kingdom has been divided and given to the Medes and Persians."

²⁹ Then Belshazzar gave an order, and they clothed Daniel in purple, ⌊placed⌋ a gold chain around his neck, and issued a proclamation concerning him that he should be the third ruler in the kingdom.

³⁰ That very night Belshazzar the king of the Chaldeans was killed, ³¹ᶠ and Darius the Mede received the kingdom at the age of 62.

The Den of Lions

1. Have you ever been close to a real lion? Where? What was it like?

Daniel 6:1-24

2. Why were the king's officials out to get Daniel (v. 3)?

3. Why were they unable to find any charge to bring against Daniel (v. 4)? Why did they decide to "find something against him concerning the law of his God" (v. 5)? What does this say about Daniel's character?

4. What saved Daniel: His faith? His innocence? His prayers? The king's prayers? God's faithfulness? Lazy lions?

5. What can you learn from Daniel's prayer habits? From his courage in obeying God?

The Plot against Daniel

6 Darius decidedᵍ to appoint 120 satraps over the kingdom, stationed throughout the realm, ² and over them three administrators, including Daniel. These satraps would be accountable to them so that the king would not be defrauded. ³ Danielʰ distinguished himself above the administrators and satraps because he had an extraordinary spirit, so the king planned to set him over the whole realm. ⁴ The administrators and satraps, therefore, kept trying to find a charge against Daniel regarding the kingdom. But they could find no charge or corruption, for he was trustworthy, and no negligence or corruption was found in him. ⁵ Then these men said, "We will never find any charge against this Daniel unless we find something against him concerning the law of his God."

⁶ So the administrators and satraps went together to the king and said to him, "May King Darius live forever. ⁷ All the administrators of the kingdom, the prefects, satraps, advisers, and governors have agreed that the

---

ᵃ**5:23** = God's temple   ᵇ**5:23** Lit and all your ways belong to Him   ᶜ**5:26** Or numbered, or a mina; = a weight of 500 to 600 grams   ᵈ**5:27** Or weighed, or a shekel; = a weight of 10 grams   ᵉ**5:28** Or divided, or half a shekel; sg form of PARSIN in v. 25   ᶠ**5:31** Dn 6:1 in Hb   ᵍ**6:1** Lit It was pleasing before Darius   ʰ**6:3** Lit Now this Daniel

---

in the southern citadel was discovered by German archaeologist R. Koldewey in the early twentieth century. Indeed, most scholars agree with his identification of the very same throne room, with walls covered in script-friendly white gypsum.

5:13 Judean exiles. It is now over 60 years

from the opening of the book. Daniel is possibly over 80 years old.

5:22-23 you ... Belshazzar, have not humbled your heart. Belshazzar knew all that had happened to Nebuchadnezzar, but he failed to learn from his predecessor's experience. He openly defied God by drinking

from the temple goblets and worshiping idols.

5:25-28 The inscription on the wall is a play on words. Mene is from a verb meaning "to number, to reckon" and refers to a weight of fifty shekels (a mina). Tekel is from the verb "to weigh" and refers to a shekel. Parsin is

king should establish an ordinance and enforce an edict that for 30 days, anyone who petitions any god or man except you, the king, will be thrown into the lions' den. [8] Therefore, Your Majesty, establish the edict and sign the document so that, as a law of the Medes and Persians, it is irrevocable and cannot be changed." [9] So King Darius signed the document.

Daniel in the Lions' Den

[10] When Daniel learned that the document had been signed, he went into his house. The windows in its upper room opened toward Jerusalem, and three times a day he got down on his knees, prayed, and gave thanks to his God, just as he had done before. [11] Then these men went as a group and found Daniel petitioning and imploring his God. [12] So they approached the king and asked about his edict: "Didn't you sign an edict that for 30 days any man who petitions any god or man except you, the king, will be thrown into the lions' den?"

The king answered, "As a law of the Medes and Persians, the order stands and is irrevocable."

[13] Then they replied to the king, "Daniel, one of the Judean exiles, has ignored you, the king, and the edict you signed, for he prays three times a day." [14] As soon as the king heard this, he was very displeased; he set his mind on rescuing Daniel and made every effort until sundown to deliver him.

[15] Then these men went to the king and said to him, "You as king know it is a law of the Medes and Persians that no edict or ordinance the king establishes can be changed."

[16] So the king gave the order, and they brought Daniel and threw him into the lions' den. The king said to Daniel, "May your God, whom you serve continually, rescue you!" [17] A stone was brought and placed over the mouth of the den. The king sealed it with his own signet ring and with the signet rings of his nobles, so that nothing in regard to Daniel could be changed. [18] Then the king went to his palace and spent the night fasting. No diversions[a] were brought to him, and he could not sleep.

Daniel Released

[19] At the first light of dawn the king got up and hurried to the lions' den. [20] When he reached the den, he cried out in anguish to Daniel. "Daniel, servant of the living God," the king said,[b] "has your God whom you serve continually been able to rescue you from the lions?"

[21] Then Daniel spoke with the king: "May the king live forever. [22] My God sent His angel and shut the lions' mouths. They haven't hurt me, for I was found innocent before Him. Also, I have not committed a crime against you my king."

[23] The king was overjoyed and gave orders to take Daniel out of the den. So Daniel was taken out of the den, uninjured, for he trusted in his God. [24] The king then gave the command, and those men who had maliciously accused Daniel[c] were brought and thrown into the lions' den—they, their children, and their wives. They had not reached the bottom of the den before the lions overpowered them and crushed all their bones.

Darius Honors God

[25] Then King Darius wrote to those of every people, nation, and language who live in all the earth: "May your prosperity abound. [26] I issue a decree that in all my royal dominion, people must tremble in fear before the God of Daniel:

> For He is the living God,
> and He endures forever;
> His kingdom will never be destroyed,
> and His dominion has no end.
> [27] He rescues and delivers;
> He performs signs and wonders
> in the heavens and on the earth,
> for He has rescued Daniel
> from the power of the lions."

[28] So Daniel prospered during the reign of Darius and[d] the reign of Cyrus the Persian.

Daniel's Vision of the Four Beasts

7 In the first year of Belshazzar king of Babylon, Daniel had a dream with visions in his mind as he was lying in his bed. He wrote down the dream, and here is the summary[e] of his account. [2] Daniel said, "In my vision at night I was watching, and suddenly the four winds of heaven stirred up the great sea. [3] Four huge beasts came up from the sea, each different from the other.

[4] "The first was like a lion but had eagle's wings. I continued watching until its wings were torn off. It was lifted up from the ground, set on its feet like a man, and given a human mind.

[5] "Suddenly, another beast appeared, a second one, that looked like a bear. It was raised up on one side, with three ribs in its mouth between its teeth. It was told, 'Get up! Gorge yourself on flesh.'

[6] "While I was watching, another beast appeared. It was like a leopard with four wings of a bird on its back. It had four heads and was given authority to rule.

---

[a]**6:18** Hb obscure   [b]**6:20** Lit *said to Daniel*   [c]**6:24** Lit *had eaten his pieces*   [d]**6:28** Or *Darius, even*   [e]**7:1** Lit *beginning*

---

from the verb "to break in two, to divide" and refers to a half-mina.

5:27 Tekel. Belshazzar's moral and spiritual life did not measure up to the standard of God's righteousness, so he was rejected as unacceptable. As a result, his reign would come to an end and his kingdom would be di-

vided between the Medes and the Persians.

6:7 Certainly not all the royal administrators agreed to this edict, since Daniel was not even aware of it and would not support it. The conspirators lied in order to get the king to agree to their scheme. The tables would be turned on them shortly (v. 24).

6:20 he cried out in anguish That Darius was in anguish indicates his distress at having been hoodwinked by his administrators and the unlikelihood that Daniel had survived.

6:23 uninjured, for he trusted in his God. The king was fully expecting to find Daniel

7 "While I was watching in the night visions, a fourth beast appeared, frightening and dreadful, and incredibly strong, with large iron teeth. It devoured and crushed, and it trampled with its feet whatever was left. It was different from all the beasts before it, and it had 10 horns.

8 "While I was considering the horns, suddenly another horn, a little one, came up among them, and three of the first horns were uprooted before it. There were eyes in this horn like a man's, and it had a mouth that spoke arrogantly.

The Ancient of Days and the Son of Man

9 "As I kept watching,

> thrones were set in place,
> and the Ancient of Days took His seat.
> His clothing was white like snow,
> and the hair of His head like whitest wool.
> His throne was flaming fire;
> its wheels were blazing fire.
> 10 A river of fire was flowing,
> coming out from His presence.
> Thousands upon thousands served Him;
> ten thousand times ten thousand
> stood before Him.
> The court was convened,
> and the books were opened.

11 "I watched, then, because of the sound of the arrogant words the horn was speaking. As I continued watching, the beast was killed and its body destroyed and given over to the burning fire. 12 As for the rest of the beasts, their authority to rule was removed, but an extension of life was granted to them for a certain period of time. 13 I continued watching in the night visions,

> and I saw One like a son of man
> coming with the clouds of heaven.
> He approached the Ancient of Days
> and was escorted before Him.
> 14 He was given authority to rule,
> and glory, and a kingdom;
> so that those of every people,
> nation, and language
> should serve Him.
> His dominion is an everlasting dominion
> that will not pass away,
> and His kingdom is one
> that will not be destroyed.

Interpretation of the Vision

15 "As for me, Daniel, my spirit was deeply distressed within me,[a] and the visions in my mind terrified me. 16 I approached one of those who were standing by and asked him the true meaning of all this. So he let me know the interpretation of these things: 17 'These huge beasts, four in number, are four kings who will rise from the earth. 18 But the holy ones of the •Most High will receive the kingdom and possess it forever, yes, forever and ever.'

19 "Then I wanted to know the true meaning of the fourth beast, the one different from all the others, extremely terrifying, with iron teeth and bronze claws, devouring, crushing, and trampling with its feet whatever was left. 20 ⌊I also wanted to know⌋ about the 10 horns on its head and about the other horn that came up, before which three fell—the horn that had eyes, and a mouth that spoke arrogantly, and that was more visible than the others. 21 As I was watching, this horn made war with the holy ones and was prevailing over them 22 until the Ancient of Days arrived and a judgment was given in favor of the holy ones of the Most High, for the time had come, and the holy ones took possession of the kingdom.

23 "This is what he said: 'The fourth beast will be a fourth kingdom on the earth, different from all the other kingdoms. It will devour the whole earth, trample it down, and crush it. 24 The 10 horns are 10 kings who will rise from this kingdom. Another, different from the previous ones, will rise after them and subdue three kings. 25 He will speak words against the Most High and oppress[b] the holy ones of the Most High. He will intend to change religious festivals[c] and laws, and the holy ones will be handed over to him for a time, times, and half a time.[d] 26 But the court will convene, and his dominion will be taken away, to be completely destroyed forever. 27 The kingdom, dominion, and greatness of the kingdoms under all of heaven will be given to the people, the holy ones of the Most High. His kingdom will be an everlasting kingdom, and all rulers will serve and obey Him.'

28 "This is the end of the interpretation. As for me, Daniel, my thoughts terrified me greatly, and my face turned pale,[e] but I kept the matter to myself."

The Vision of a Ram and a Goat

8 In the third year of King Belshazzar's reign, a vision appeared to me, Daniel, after the one that had appeared to me earlier. 2 I saw the vision, and as I watched, I was in the fortress city of Susa, in the prov-

---

[a] 7:15 Lit was distressed in the middle of its sheath   [b] 7:25 Lit wear out   [c] 7:25 Lit change times   [d] 7:25 Or for three and a half years   [e] 7:28 Lit my brightness changed on me; Dn 5:6,9–10

---

devoured. Not only was Daniel's life miraculously preserved, but he did not even have a single scratch from his night with the ravenous lions. God proved His power to save believers.

7:1-8 Daniel is given a vision of four beasts. They have been seen by some to

represent Babylon, Medo-Persia, Greece, and Rome. Chapter 2:36-43 refers to another dream with four statues.

7:13-14 son of man. This is the first time this title is used for the Messiah. Here Christ approaches the Ancient of Days and is given all the authority, glory, and sovereign power

that had previously been given to earthly rulers.

7:18 holy ones of the Most High. Those who believe in Christ will inherit the kingdom. (Matt. 19:28-29; Rev. 20:4-6.)

7:24-26 Another ... will rise after them. After the ten divided kings, one king will take

ince of Elam. I saw in the vision that I was beside the Ulai Canal. [3] I looked up,[a] and there was a ram standing beside the canal. He had two horns. The two horns were long, but one was longer than the other, and the longer one came up last. [4] I saw the ram charging to the west, the north, and the south. No animal could stand against him, and there was no rescue from his power. He did whatever he wanted and became great.

[5] As I was observing, a male goat appeared, coming from the west across the surface of the entire earth without touching the ground. The goat had a conspicuous horn[b] between his eyes. [6] He came toward the two-horned ram I had seen standing beside the canal and rushed at him with savage fury. [7] I saw him approaching the ram, and infuriated with him, he struck the ram, shattering his two horns, and the ram was not strong enough to stand against him. The goat threw him to the ground and trampled him, and there was no one to rescue the ram from his power. [8] Then the male goat became very great, but when he became powerful, the large horn was shattered. Four conspicuous horns came up in its place, ⌊pointing⌋ toward the four winds of heaven.

The Little Horn

[9] From one of them a little horn emerged and grew extensively toward the south and the east and toward the beautiful land.[c] [10] It grew as high as the heavenly •host, made some of the stars and some of the host fall to the earth, and trampled them. [11] It made itself great, even up to the Prince of the host; it removed His daily sacrifice and overthrew the place of His sanctuary. [12] Because of rebellion, a host, together with the daily sacrifice, will be given over. The horn will throw truth to the ground and will be successful in whatever it does.

[13] Then I heard a holy one speaking, and another holy one said to the speaker, "How long will ⌊the events of⌋ this vision last—the daily sacrifice, the rebellion that makes desolate, and the giving over of the sanctuary and of the host to be trampled?"

[14] He said to me,[d] "For 2,300 evenings and mornings; then the sanctuary will be restored."

Interpretation of the Vision

[15] While I, Daniel, was watching the vision and trying to understand it, there stood before me someone who appeared to be a man. [16] I heard a human voice calling from the middle of the Ulai: "Gabriel, explain the vision to this man."

[17] So he approached where I was standing; when he came near, I was terrified and fell facedown. "Son of man," he said to me, "understand that the vision refers to the time of the end." [18] While he was speaking to me, I fell into a deep sleep, with my face ⌊to the ground⌋. Then he touched me, made me stand up, [19] and said, "I am here to tell you what will happen at the conclusion of the time of wrath, because it refers to the appointed time of the end. [20] The two-horned ram that you saw represents the kings of Media and Persia. [21] The shaggy goat represents the king of Greece, and the large horn between his eyes represents the first king.[e] [22] The four horns that took the place of the shattered horn represent four kingdoms. They will rise from that nation, but without its power.

[23] Near the end of their kingdoms,
when the rebels have reached
the full measure of their sin,[f]
an insolent king, skilled in intrigue,[g]
will come to the throne.
[24] His power will be great,
but it will not be his own.
He will cause terrible destruction
and succeed in whatever he does.
He will destroy the powerful
along with the holy people.
[25] He will cause deceit to prosper
through his cunning and by his influence,
and in his own mind he will make himself great.
In ⌊a time of⌋ peace, he will destroy many;
he will even stand against the Prince of princes.
But he will be shattered, not by human hands.
[26] The vision of the evenings and the mornings
that has been told is true.
Now you must seal up the vision
because it refers to many days ⌊in the future⌋."

[27] I, Daniel, was overcome and lay sick for days. Then I got up and went about the king's business. I was greatly disturbed by the vision and could not understand it.

Daniel's Prayer

9 In the first year of Darius, who was the son of Ahasuerus, was a Mede by birth, and was ruler over the kingdom of the Chaldeans— [2] in the first year of his reign, I, Daniel, understood from the books according to the word of the LORD to Jeremiah the prophet that the number of years for the desolation of Jerusalem would be 70. [3] So I turned my attention to

---

[a]**8:3** Lit *I lifted my eyes and looked*   [b]**8:5** Lit *a horn of a vision*   [c]**8:9** = Israel   [d]**8:14** LXX, Theod, Syr, Vg read *him*   [e]**8:21** = Alexander the Great
[f]**8:23** Lit *have become complete*   [g]**8:23** Lit *king, and understanding riddles*

---

over three of the ten. But he will oppose God's authority, oppress the saints, and abandon old laws to institute his own governmental system. This king will persecute Israel for three and a half years (a time that may be figurative or could refer to the three and one-half years of the Great Tribulation,

Rev. 12:14). After that Jesus will sit as judge, remove him from power, and set up His eternal kingdom.

8:3 He had two horns. The ram represents the Medo-Persian Empire, with the longer horn signifying the superior position of Persia. The Medo-Persian Empire would charge

in all directions until it dominated the entire area.

8:5-7 conspicuous horn. The goat represents Greece, with the prominent horn as a symbol for Alexander the Great. Greece would crush the Medo-Persian Empire.

8:8 large horn was shattered. Alexander

the Lord God to seek Him by prayer and petitions, with fasting, •sackcloth, and ashes.

[4] I prayed to the LORD my God and confessed:

Ah, Lord—the great and awe-inspiring God who keeps His gracious covenant with those who love Him and keep His commandments— [5] we have sinned, done wrong, acted wickedly, rebelled, and turned away from Your commandments and ordinances. [6] We have not listened to Your servants the prophets, who spoke in Your name to our kings, leaders, fathers, and all the people of the land.

[7] Lord, righteousness belongs to You, but this day public shame belongs to us: the men of Judah, the residents of Jerusalem, and all Israel—those who are near and those who are far, in all the countries where You have dispersed them because of the disloyalty they have shown toward You. [8] LORD, public shame belongs to us, our kings, our leaders, and our fathers, because we have sinned against You. [9] Compassion and forgiveness belong to the Lord our God, though we have rebelled against Him [10] and have not obeyed the voice of the LORD our God by following His instructions that He set before us through His servants the prophets.

[11] All Israel has broken Your law and turned away, refusing to obey You. The promised curse[a] written in the law of Moses, the servant of God, has been poured out on us because we have sinned against Him. [12] He has carried out His words that He spoke against us and against our rulers[b] by bringing on us so great a disaster that nothing like what has been done to Jerusalem has ever been done under all of heaven. [13] Just as it is written in the law of Moses, all this disaster has come on us, yet we have not appeased the LORD our God by turning from our injustice and paying attention to Your truth. [14] So the LORD kept the disaster in mind and brought it on us, for the LORD our God is righteous in all He has done. But we have not obeyed Him.

[15] Now, Lord our God, who brought Your people out of the land of Egypt with a mighty hand and made Your name ⌊renowned⌋ as it is this day, we have sinned, we have acted wickedly. [16] Lord, in keeping with all Your righteous acts, may Your anger and wrath turn away from Your city Jerusalem, Your holy mountain; for because of our sins and the injustices of our fathers, Jerusalem and Your people have become an object of ridicule to all those around us.

[17] Therefore, our God, hear the prayer and the petitions of Your servant. Show Your favor to Your desolate sanctuary for the Lord's sake. [18] Listen,[c] my God, and hear. Open Your eyes and see our desolations and the city called by Your name. For we are not presenting our petitions before You based on our righteous acts, but based on Your abundant compassion. [19] Lord, hear! Lord, forgive! Lord, listen and act! My God, for Your own sake, do not delay, because Your city and Your people are called by Your name.

The 70 Weeks of Years

[20] While I was speaking, praying, confessing my sin and the sin of my people Israel, and presenting my petition before •Yahweh my God concerning the holy mountain of my God— [21] while I was praying, Gabriel, the man I had seen in the first vision, came to me in my extreme weariness, about the time of the evening offering. [22] He gave me this explanation: "Daniel, I've come now to give you understanding. [23] At the beginning of your petitions an answer went out, and I have come to give it, for you are treasured ⌊by God⌋. So consider the message and understand the vision:

[24] Seventy weeks[d] are decreed
about your people and your holy city—
to bring the rebellion to an end,
to put a stop to sin,
to wipe away injustice,
to bring in everlasting righteousness,
to seal up vision and prophecy,
and to anoint the most holy place.

[25] Know and understand this:
From the issuing of the decree
to restore and rebuild Jerusalem
until •Messiah the Prince[e]
will be seven weeks and 62 weeks.[f]
It will be rebuilt with a plaza and a moat,
but in difficult times.

[26] After those 62 weeks[g]
the Messiah will be cut off
and will have nothing.
The people of the coming prince
will destroy the city and the sanctuary.

---

[a]9:11 Lit The curse and the oath   [b]9:12 Lit against rulers who ruled us   [c]9:18 Lit Stretch out Your ear   [d]9:24 = 490 years; 2 Ch 36:21; Jr 25:11–12; 29:10   [e]9:25 Or until an anointed one, a prince   [f]9:25 = 49 years and 434 years   [g]9:26 = 434 years

---

died at the height of power. The four prominent horns are his four generals who carved up the Macedonian Empire.

8:9-12 The horn that started small but grew in power was Antiochus IV Epiphanes. Antiochus took control of Israel, refused to allow the Jews to make sacrifices, and killed many for their faith. Then he declared himself to be God's equal and was eventually defeated by Judas Maccabeus, who rededicated the temple to the Lord and began the Feast of Hanukkah.

9:18 Your abundant compassion. Daniel based his requests on God's character, not on Israel's worthiness. Daniel was asking God for His mercy. God answers prayer because He is gracious, not because we deserve it.

9:25 issuing of the decree. There are several possibilities as to the identity of this decree: by Cyrus (Ezra 1:2-4), the decree by

The^a end will come with a flood,
and until the end there will be^b war;
desolations are decreed.

27 He will make a firm covenant^c
with many for one week,^d
but in the middle of the week
he will put a stop to sacrifice and offering.
And the abomination of desolation
will be on a wing of the temple^{e f}
until the decreed destruction
is poured out on the desolator."

Vision of a Glorious One

10 In the third year of Cyrus king of Persia, a message was revealed to Daniel, who was named Belteshazzar. The message was true and was about a great conflict. He understood the message and had understanding of the vision.

2 In those days I, Daniel, was mourning for three full weeks. 3 I didn't eat any rich food, no meat or wine entered my mouth, and I didn't put any oil ⌊on my body⌋ until the three weeks were over. 4 On the twenty-fourth day of the first month,^g as I was standing on the bank of the great river, the Tigris, 5 I looked up, and there was a man dressed in linen, with a belt of gold from Uphaz^h around his waist. 6 His body was like topaz,ⁱ his face like the brilliance of lightning, his eyes like flaming torches, his arms and feet like the gleam of polished bronze, and the sound of his words like the sound of a multitude.

7 Only I, Daniel, saw the vision. The men who were with me did not see it, but a great terror fell on them, and they ran and hid. 8 I was left alone, looking at this great vision. No strength was left in me; my face grew deathly pale,^j and I was powerless. 9 I heard the words he said, and when I heard them I fell into a deep sleep,^k with my face to the ground.

Angelic Conflict

10 Suddenly, a hand touched me and raised me to my hands and knees. 11 He said to me, "Daniel, you are a man treasured ⌊by God⌋. Understand the words that I'm saying to you. Stand on your feet, for I have now been sent to you." After he said this to me, I stood trembling.

12 "Don't be afraid, Daniel," he said to me, "for from the first day that you purposed to understand and to humble yourself before your God, your prayers were heard. I have come because of your prayers. 13 But the prince of the kingdom of Persia opposed me for 21 days. Then Michael, one of the chief princes, came to help me after I had been left there with the kings of Persia. 14 Now I have come to help you understand what will happen to your people in the last days, for the vision refers to those days."

15 While he was saying these words to me, I turned my face toward the ground and was speechless. 16 Suddenly one with human likeness touched my lips. I opened my mouth and said to the one standing in front of me, "My lord, because of the vision, I am overwhelmed and powerless. 17 How can someone like me, your servant,^l speak with someone like you, my lord? Now I have no strength, and there is no breath in me."

18 Then the one with human likeness touched me again and strengthened me. 19 He said, "Don't be afraid, you who are^m treasured ⌊by God⌋. Peace to you; be very strong!"

As he spoke to me, I was strengthened and said, "Let my lord speak, for you have strengthened me."

20 He said, "Do you know why I've come to you? I must return at once to fight against the prince of Persia, and when I leave, the prince of Greece will come. 21 No one has the courage to support me against them except Michael, your prince. However, I will tell you what is recorded in the book of truth. 1 In the first year of Darius the Mede, I stood up to strengthen and protect him. 2 Now I will tell you the truth.

11

Prophecies about Persia and Greece

"Three more kings will arise in Persia, and the fourth will be far richer than the others. By the power he gains through his riches, he will stir up everyone against the kingdom of Greece. 3 Then a warrior king will arise; he will rule a vast realm and do whatever he wants. 4 But as soon as he is established, his kingdom will be broken up and divided to the four winds of heaven, but not to his descendants; it will not be the same kingdom that he ruled, because his kingdom will be uprooted and will go to others besides them.

Kings of the South and the North

5 "The king of the South will grow powerful, but one of his commanders will grow more powerful and will rule a kingdom greater than his. 6 After some years they will form an alliance, and the daughter of the king of the South will go to the king of the North to seal the agreement. She will not retain power, and his strength will not endure. She will be given up, together with her

---

a**9:26** Lit *Its*, or *His* b**9:26** Or *end of a* c**9:27** Or *will enforce a covenant* d**9:27** = 7 years e**9:27** LXX; MT reads *of abominations* f**9:27** Or *And the desolator will be on the wing of abominations*, or *And the desolator will come on the wings of monsters* (or *of horror*); Hb obscure g**10:4** Nisan (March–April) h**10:5** Some Hb mss read *Ophir* i**10:6** The identity of this stone is uncertain. j**10:8** Lit *my splendor was turned on me to ruin* k**10:9** Lit *a sleep on my face* l**10:17** Lit *Can I, a servant of my lord* m**10:19** Lit *afraid, man*

Darius (Ezra 6:3-12), the decree by Artaxerxes (Ezra 7:13-26) or the decree by Artaxerxes (Neh. 2:7-9). This most likely refers to the decree by Artaxerxes Longimanus in 444 B.C. that allowed the Jews permission to rebuild Jerusalem's city walls. Sixty-nine "sevens" (7 plus 62), the equivalent of 483 years, elapsed between this decree and the crucifixion of the Messiah.

9:26 Messiah will be cut off. This is a reference to the crucifixion of Christ.

9:27 make a firm covenant. A ruler will come who will guarantee Israel's safety, but he will break the covenant after only three and a half years. Many believe that this is a reference to the Antichrist, who will set up an abomination against God until the end. Others see this as a reference to the Messiah's instituting a new covenant and putting an end to the Old Testament sacrificial system.

entourage, her father,[a] and the one who supported her during those times. 7 In the place of the king of the South, one from her family[b] will rise up, come against the army, and enter the fortress of the king of the North. He will take action against them and triumph. 8 He will take even their gods captive to Egypt, with their metal images and their precious articles of silver and gold. For some years he will stay away from the king of the North, 9 who will enter the kingdom of the king of the South and then return to his own land.

10 "His sons will mobilize for war and assemble a large number of armed forces. They will advance, sweeping through like a flood,[c] and will again wage war as far as his fortress. 11 Infuriated, the king of the South will march out to fight with the king of the North, who will raise a great multitude, but the multitude will be handed over to his enemy. 12 When the multitude is carried off, he will become arrogant and cause tens of thousands to fall, but he will not triumph. 13 The king of the North will again raise a multitude larger than the first. After some years[d] he will advance with a great army and many supplies.

14 "In those times many will rise up against the king of the South. Violent ones among your own people will assert themselves to fulfill a vision, but they will fail. 15 Then the king of the North will come, build up an assault ramp, and capture a well-fortified city. The forces of the South will not stand; even their select troops will not be able to resist. 16 The king of the North who comes against him will do whatever he wants, and no one can oppose him. He will establish himself in the beautiful land[e] with total destruction in his hand. 17 He will resolve to come with the force of his whole kingdom and will reach an agreement with him.[f] He will give him a daughter in marriage[g] to destroy it,[h] but she will not stand with him or support him. 18 Then he will turn his attention to the coasts and islands[i] and capture many. But a commander will put an end to his taunting; instead, he will turn his taunts against him. 19 He will turn his attention back to the fortresses of his own land, but he will stumble, fall, and be no more.

20 "In his place one will arise who will send out a tax collector for the glory of the kingdom; but within a few days he will be shattered, though not in anger[j] or in battle.

21 "In his place a despised person will arise; royal honors will not be given to him, but he will come during a time of peace[k] and seize the kingdom by intrigue.

22 A flood of forces will be swept away before him; they will be shattered, as well as the covenant prince. 23 After an alliance is made with him, he will act deceitfully. He will rise to power with a small nation.[l] 24 During a time of peace,[m] he will come into the richest parts of the province and do what his fathers and predecessors never did. He will lavish plunder, loot, and wealth on his followers, and he will make plans against fortified cities, but only for a time.

25 "With a large army he will stir up his power and his courage against the king of the South. The king of the South will prepare for battle with an extremely large and powerful army, but he will not succeed, because plots will be made against him. 26 Those who eat his provisions will destroy him; his army will be swept away, and many will fall slain. 27 The two kings, whose hearts are bent on evil, will speak lies at the same table but to no avail, for still the end will come at the appointed time. 28 The king of the North will return to his land with great wealth, but his heart will be set against the holy covenant;[n] he will take action, then return to his own land.

29 "At the appointed time he will come again to the South, but this time[o] will not be like the first. 30 Ships of Kittim[p] will come against him, and being intimidated, he will withdraw. Then he will rage against the holy covenant and take action. On his return, he will favor those who abandon the holy covenant. 31 His forces will rise up and desecrate the temple fortress. They will abolish the daily sacrifice and set up the abomination of desolation. 32 With flattery he will corrupt those who act wickedly toward the covenant, but the people who know their God will be strong and take action. 33 Those who are wise among the people will give understanding to many, yet they will die by sword and flame, and be captured and plundered for a time. 34 When defeated, they will be helped by some, but many others will join them insincerely. 35 Some of the wise will fall so that they may be refined, purified, and cleansed until the time of the end, for it will still come at the appointed time.

36 "Then the king will do whatever he wants. He will exalt and magnify himself above every god, and he will say outrageous things against the God of gods. He will be successful until the time of wrath is completed, because what has been decreed will be accomplished. 37 He will not show regard for the gods[q] of his fathers, the god longed for by women, or for any other god, because he

---

a 11:6 One Hb ms, Theod read child; Vg, Syr read children   b 11:7 Lit from the shoot of her roots   c 11:10 Lit advance and overflow and pass through   d 11:13 Lit At the end of the times   e 11:16 = Israel   f 11:17 = the king of the South   g 11:17 Lit him the daughter of women   h 11:17 Perhaps the kingdom   i 11:18 = of the Mediterranean   j 11:20 Or not openly   k 11:21 Or come without warning   l 11:23 Or a few people   m 11:24 Or Without warning   n 11:28 Or the Jewish people and religion   o 11:29 Lit but the last   p 11:30 = the Romans   q 11:37 Or God

---

10:5 a man dressed in linen. This is either an angel or, as some think, a pre-incarnate appearance of Christ.

10:13 prince of the kingdom of Persia. Possibly a reference to a demonic figure because of the lengthy battle with the angel, Michael.

10:21 book of truth. This is a reference to God's absolute authority over all of mankind's history—past, present, and future.

11:1 first year of Darius. This is still the same year since chapter nine. This is the year 539 B.C. when Cyrus was appointed as administrator of Babylon.

11:16 king of the North. After the Egyptian defeat at the battle of Sidon, Antiochus III was welcomed by Jerusalem's inhabitants in 198 B.C. This change in government set up the brutal reign of his son, Antiochus Epiphanes IV, 23 years later.

11:21-35 Gabriel, the master angel (8:16;

will magnify himself above all. 38 Instead, he will honor a god of fortresses—a god his fathers did not know—with gold, silver, precious stones, and riches. 39 He will deal with the strongest fortresses with ⌊the help of⌋ a foreign god. He will greatly honor those who acknowledge him,[a] making them rulers over many and distributing land as a reward.

40 "At the time of the end, the king of the South will engage him in battle, but the king of the North will storm against him with chariots, horsemen, and many ships. He will invade countries and sweep through them like a flood. 41 He will also invade the beautiful land, and many will fall. But these will escape from his power: Edom, Moab, and the prominent people[b] of the Ammonites. 42 He will extend his power against the countries, and not even the land of Egypt will escape. 43 He will get control over the hidden treasures of gold and silver and over all the riches of Egypt. The Libyans and •Cushites will also be in submission.[c] 44 But reports from the east and the north will terrify him, and he will go out with great fury to destroy and annihilate many. 45 He will pitch his royal tents between the sea and[d] the beautiful holy mountain, but he will meet his end with no one to help him.

12 At that time
Michael the great prince
who stands watch over your people will rise up.
There will be a time of distress
such as never has occurred
since nations came into being until that time.
But at that time all your people
who are found written in the book will escape.
2 Many of those who sleep in the dust
of the earth will awake,

some to eternal life,
and some to shame and eternal contempt.
3 Those who are wise will shine
like the bright expanse ⌊of the heavens⌋,
and those who lead many to righteousness,
like the stars forever and ever.

4 "But you, Daniel, keep these words secret and seal the book until the time of the end. Many will roam about, and knowledge will increase."[e]

5 Then I, Daniel, looked, and two others were standing there, one on this bank of the river and one on the other. 6 One said to the man dressed in linen, who was above the waters of the river, "How long until the end of these extraordinary things?" 7 Then I heard the man dressed in linen, who was above the waters of the river. He raised both his hands[f] toward heaven and swore by Him who lives eternally that it would be for a time, times, and half ⌊a time⌋. When the power of the holy people is shattered, all these things will be completed.

8 I heard but did not understand. So I asked, "My lord, what will be the outcome of these things?"

9 He said, "Go on your way, Daniel, for the words are secret and sealed until the time of the end. 10 Many will be purified, cleansed, and refined, but the wicked will act wickedly; none of the wicked will understand, but the wise will understand. 11 From the time the daily sacrifice is abolished and the abomination of desolation is set up, there will be 1,290 days. 12 Blessed is the one who waits for and reaches 1,335 days. 13 But as for you, go on your way to the end;[g] you will rest, then rise to your destiny at the end of the days."

---

a11:39 Or those he acknowledges b11:41 Lit the first c11:43 Lit Cushites at his steps d11:45 Or the seas at e12:4 LXX reads and the earth will be filled with unrighteousness f12:7 Lit raised his right and his left g12:13 LXX omits to the end

---

9:21) who will eventually announce the birth of Jesus 530 years later (Lk. 1:19, 26), has set the stage (vv. 2-20) for the appearance of the "little horn" (8:9-12, 23-25); Antiochus Epiphanes (175-163 B.C.) The profound effect he would have on Israel makes this section especially climactic.

11:31 desecrate the temple. Antiochus polluted the temple with a pagan altar in 168 B.C.

11:36 the king will do whatever he wants. From here to the end of chapter 11, the king

referred to is the Antichrist. He will set himself up completely independent of any power, even exalting himself above God.

11:40-45 Just before Christ's return, the Antichrist will battle his political enemies. At the battle of Armageddon he will be killed on the "beautiful holy mountain," Jerusalem's temple mount (Rev. 19:11-21).

12:1 Michael. Michael (10:13, 21) reappears in a big way in the New Testament (Jude 9; Rev. 12:7, 14), where once again he will be arrayed against the forces of evil.

12:2 those who sleep in the dust. This is the first clear scriptural reference to a resurrection. The godly will rise to everlasting life, while the wicked will be resurrected to eternal shame and contempt.

12:13 rise to your destiny. Daniel would die before many of the events he prophesied took place. But he would be raised from the dead, according to the promise, to receive his reward and inheritance for his service to God.

INTRODUCTION TO
HOSEA

PERSONAL READING PLAN

☐ Hosea 1:1–2:23
☐ Hosea 3:1–5:15
☐ Hosea 6:1–8:14

☐ Hosea 9:1–10:15
☐ Hosea 11:1–12:14
☐ Hosea 13:1–14:9

AUTHOR

The author is identified as Hosea, son of Beeri—a prophet to the northern kingdom (Israel). He was the only one of the writing prophets to come from Israel, and his prophecy is mainly directed to them

DATE

Hosea's prophetic career spanned four decades, from the prosperous latter years of Jeroboam II (793-753 B.C.) to the 720s shortly before the fall of Samaria and the exile of Israel.

THEME

God's undying love for His people.

HISTORICAL BACKGROUND

The dominant faith of Israel during Hosea's time was not Mosaic Judaism but a mixture of the worship of Yahweh and the local polytheistic Baal religions. Israel was prosperous and complacent under Jeroboam II, but after his death, and a succession of six kings in 30 years, life became increasingly insecure and the nation's resources weakened. Israel stubbornly sought help from other nations instead of from the Lord.

CHARACTERISTICS

Hosea's language relies heavily upon the covenant stipulations of blessings and curses (see Lev. 26; Deut. 28-32). While reciting the case against Israel and the consequential curses she will face, Hosea interjects God's promise to restore her to the land and to Himself in covenant faithfulness.

The beginning of the book (chapters 1-3) tells the story of Hosea's intriguing family situation, which demonstrates his message from God to Israel. First, Hosea obeys the Lord's command to marry an adulterous woman, Gomer. They have three children—each given a name symbolic of Hosea's message. Then, even though Hosea and Gomer are separated by her unfaithfulness, the Lord says to Hosea, "Go again; show love to a woman who is loved by another man and is an adulteress" (3:1). This unusual story raises questions. Is the story allegorical or is it meant to be taken literally? The precise nature of Gomer's relationship to Hosea cannot be established with certainty. God's purpose in this "enacted" prophecy is clear, however. Bound to the Lord by covenant, Israel still "prostitutes" herself and bears "illegitimate children." In word and deed, the Book of Hosea communicates that despite Israel's faithlessness, God remains faithful and longs to take them back, just as Hosea forgives Gomer. This reunion is described with imagery recalling the exodus from Egypt and settlement in Canaan (see 1:11; 3:5; 14:4-7).

1

The word of the LORD that came to Hosea son of Beeri during the reigns of Uzziah, Jotham, Ahaz, and Hezekiah, kings of Judah, and of Jeroboam son of Joash, king of Israel.

Hosea's Marriage and Children

2 When the LORD first spoke to Hosea, He said this to him:

Go and marry a promiscuous wife
and ⌊have⌋ children of promiscuity,
for the whole land has been promiscuous
by abandoning the LORD.

3 So he went and married Gomer daughter of Diblaim, and she conceived and bore him a son. 4 Then the LORD said to him:

Name him Jezreel, for in a little while
I will avenge the bloodshed of Jezreel
on the house of Jehu
and put an end to the kingdom of the house
of Israel.
5 On that day I will break the bow of Israel
in the valley of Jezreel.ᵃ

6 She conceived again and gave birth to a daughter, and the LORD said to him:

Name her No Compassion,ᵇ
for I will no longer have compassion
on the house of Israel.
I will certainly take them away.
7 But I will have compassion on the house
of Judah,
and I will deliver them by the LORD their God.
I will not deliver them by bow, sword, or war,
or by horses and cavalry.

8 After Gomer had weaned No Compassion, she conceived and gave birth to a son. 9 Then the LORD said:

Name him Not My People,ᶜ
for you are not My people,
and I will not be your God.ᵈ
10ᵉ Yet the number of the Israelites
will be like the sand of the sea,
which cannot be measured or counted.
And in the place where they were told:
You are not My people,
they will be called: Sons of the living God.
11 And the Judeans and the Israelites
will be gathered together.

They will appoint for themselves a single ruler,
and go up fromᶠ the land.
For the day of Jezreel will be great.

2

ᵍ Callʰ your brothers: My People
and your sisters: Compassion.

Israel's Adultery Rebuked

2 Rebuke your mother; rebuke ⌊her⌋.
For she is not My wife and I am not
her husband.
Let her remove the promiscuous look
from her face
and her adultery from between her breasts.
3 Otherwise, I will strip her naked
and expose her as she was on the day
of her birth.
I will make her like a desert
and like a parched land,
and I will let her die of thirst.
4 I will have no compassion on her children
because they are the children of promiscuity.
5 For their mother is promiscuous;
she conceived them and acted shamefully.
For she thought: I will go after my lovers,
the men who give me my food and water,
my wool and flax, my oil and drink.
6 Therefore, this is what I will do:
I will block herⁱ way with thorns;
I will enclose her with a wall,
so that she cannot find her paths.
7 She will pursue her lovers but not catch them;
she will seek them but not find ⌊them⌋.
Then she will think:
I will go back to my former husband,
for then it was better for me than now.
8 She does not recognize
that it is I who gave her the grain,
the new wine, and the oil.
I lavished silver and gold on her,
which they used for •Baal.
9 Therefore, I will take back My grain in its time
and My new wine in its season;
I will take away My wool and linen,
which were to cover her nakedness.
10 Now I will expose her shame
in the sight of her lovers,
and no one will rescue her from My hands.
11 I will put an end to all her celebrations:
her feasts, New Moons, and Sabbaths—
all her festivals.

ᵃ1:5 = God sows ᵇ1:6 Hb Lo-ruhamah ᶜ1:9 Hb Lo-ammi ᵈ1:9 Lit not be yours ᵉ1:10 Hs 2:1 in Hb ᶠ1:11 Or and flourish in; Hb obscure
ᵍ2:1 Hs 2:3 in Hb ʰ2:1 Lit Say to ⁱ2:6 LXX, Syr; MT reads your

---

1:1 Hosea. Hosea's message was good news for Israel; his name means "salvation."
1:3 Gomer daughter of Diblaim. It is debatable whether Hosea's wife was unfaithful at the time he married her or that the child she bore is not Hosea's.
1:6 Name her No Compassion. God empha-

sized the seriousness of the breach in the love relationship with His people by naming one of the children "No Compassion."
1:9 Name him Not My People. Their third child's name carried the ultimate insult. God dared to disown His people.
1:11 the Judeans ... gathered together. The

Lord foresaw a future time when the two kingdoms would be ruled under His own leadership.
2:2 not My wife ... not her husband. Hosea spoke about Gomer as God felt about Israel.
2:10 no one will rescue her from My hands. None of Israel's false gods could save the na-

12 I will devastate her vines and fig trees.
   She thinks that these are her wages
   that her lovers have given her.
   I will turn them into a thicket,
   and the wild animals will eat them.

13 And I will punish her for the days of the Baals
   when she burned incense to them,
   put on her rings and jewelry,
   and went after her lovers,
   but forgot Me.

⌊This is⌋
the LORD's declaration.

Israel's Adultery Forgiven

14 Therefore, I am going to persuade her,
   lead her to the wilderness,
   and speak tenderly to her.ᵃ

15 There I will give her vineyards back to her
   and make the Valley of Achorᵇ
   into a gateway of hope.
   There she will respond as ⌊she did⌋
   in the days of her youth,
   as in the day she came out of the land of Egypt.

16 In that day—

the LORD's declaration—
   you will call ⌊Me⌋: My husband,
   and no longer call Me: My Baal.ᶜ

17 For I will remove the names of the Baals
   from her mouth;
   they will no longer be remembered
     by their names.

18 On that day I will make a covenant for them
   with the wild animals, the birds of the sky,
   and the creatures that crawl on the ground.
   I will shatter bow, sword,
   and weapons of war in the landᵈ
   and will enable the people to rest securely.

19 I will take you to be My wife forever.
   I will take you to be My wife in righteousness,
   justice, love, and compassion.

20 I will take you to be My wife in faithfulness,
   and you will know the LORD.

21 On that day I will respond—
the LORD's declaration.
   I will respond to the sky,
   and it will respond to the earth.

22 The earth will respond to the grain,
   the new wine, and the oil,
   and they will respond to Jezreel.

23 I will sow herᵉ in the land for Myself,
   and I will have compassion
   on No Compassion;
   I will say to Not My People:
   You are My people,
   and he will say: ⌊You are⌋ My God.

Waiting for Restoration

3 Then the LORD said to me, "Go again; show love to a woman who is loved by another man and is an adulteress, just as the LORD loves the Israelites though they turn to other gods and love raisin cakes." 2 So I bought her for 15 •shekels of silver and five bushels of barley.ᶠ ᵍ 3 I said to her, "You must live with me many days. Don't be promiscuous or belong to any man, and I will act the same way toward you."

4 For the Israelites must live many days without king or prince, without sacrifice or sacred pillar, and without •ephod or household idols. 5 Afterwards, the people of Israel will return and seek the LORD their God and David their king. They will come with awe to the LORD and to His goodness in the last days.

God's Case against Israel

4 Hear the word of the LORD, people of Israel,
   for the LORD has a case
   against the inhabitants of the land:
   There is no truth, no faithful love,
   and no knowledge of God in the land!

2 Cursing, lying, murder, stealing,
   and adultery are rampant;
   one act of bloodshed follows another.

3 For this reason the land mourns,
   and everyone who lives in it languishes,
   along with the wild animals and the birds
     of the sky;
   even the fish of the sea disappear.

4 But let no one dispute; let no one argue,
   for My case is against you priests.ʰ ⁱ

5 You will stumble by day;
   the prophet will also stumble with you by night.
   And I will destroy your mother.

6 My people are destroyed for lack of knowledge.
   Because you have rejected knowledge,
   I will reject you from serving as My priest.
   Since you have forgotten the law of your God,
   I will also forget your sons.

7 The more they multiplied,
   the more they sinned against Me.

ᵃ2:14 Lit speak to her heart   ᵇ2:15 = Trouble; Jos 7:26   ᶜ2:16 Or My master   ᵈ2:18 Or war on the earth   ᵉ2:23 = Israel   ᶠ3:2 LXX reads barley and a measure of wine   ᵍ3:2 Lit silver, a homer of barley, and a lethek of barley   ʰ4:4 Text emended; MT reads argue, and your people are like those contending with a priest   ⁱ4:4 Hb obscure

---

tion from punishment.
2:12 devastate her vines ... her wages that her lovers have given her. Although the Lord had abundantly blessed Israel, Israel credited its harvests to other gods.
2:16-17 My Husband ... My Baal. Ironically, the Hebrew word for Baal is "master." The Lord

predicted that Israel would disassociate from its current "master" as a sign of repentance.
2:20 take you to be My wife in faithfulness. The context of Hosea's story illustrates the unfaithfulness of a nation portrayed as a wayward wife. In contrast, God was consistently characterized as stubbornly faithful.

3:3 You must live with me. Hosea risked heartbreak by inviting an adulterous woman into his household.
4:2 rampant. Israel broke every law in the Ten Commandments with reckless enthusiasm (Ex. 20:13-16).
4:4-9 let no one dispute. The priests, respon-

I[a] will change their honor into disgrace.

8 They feed on the sin[b] of My people;
they have an appetite for their transgressions.

9 ⌊The same judgment⌋ will happen
to both people and priests.
I will punish them for their ways
and repay them for their deeds.

10 They will eat but not be satisfied;
they will be promiscuous but not multiply;
for they have abandoned their devotion
to the LORD.

11 Promiscuity, wine, and new wine
take away ⌊one's⌋ understanding.

12 My people consult their wooden ⌊idols⌋,
and their divining rods inform them.
For a spirit of promiscuity leads them astray;
they act promiscuously
in disobedience to[c] their God.

13 They sacrifice on the mountaintops,
and they burn offerings on the hills,
and under oaks, poplars, and terebinths,
because their shade is pleasant.
And so your daughters act promiscuously
and your daughters-in-law commit adultery.

14 I will not punish your daughters
when they act promiscuously
or your daughters-in-law
when they commit adultery,
for the men themselves go off with prostitutes
and make sacrifices with cult prostitutes.
People without discernment are doomed.

Warnings for Israel and Judah

15 Israel, if you act promiscuously,
don't let Judah become guilty!
Do not go to Gilgal
or make a pilgrimage to Beth-aven,[d]
and do not swear an oath: As the LORD lives!

16 For Israel is as obstinate as a stubborn cow.
Can the LORD now shepherd them
like a lamb in an open meadow?

17 Ephraim is attached to idols;
leave him alone!

18 When their drinking is over,
they turn to promiscuity.
Israel's leaders[e] fervently love disgrace.[f]

19 A wind with its wings will carry them off,[g]
and they will be ashamed of their sacrifices.

5 Hear this, priests!
Pay attention, house of Israel!
Listen, royal house!
For the judgment applies to you
because you have been a snare at Mizpah
and a net spread out on Tabor.

2 Rebels are deeply involved in slaughter;
I will be a punishment for all of them.[f]

3 I know Ephraim,
and Israel is not hidden from Me.
For now, Ephraim,
you have acted promiscuously;
Israel is defiled.

4 Their actions do not allow ⌊them⌋
to return to their God,
for a spirit of promiscuity is among them,
and they do not know the LORD.

5 Israel's arrogance testifies against them.[h]
Both Israel and Ephraim stumble
because of their wickedness;
even Judah will stumble with them.

6 They go with their flocks and herds
to seek the LORD
but do not find ⌊Him⌋;
He has withdrawn from them.

7 They betrayed the LORD;
indeed, they gave birth to illegitimate children.
Now the New Moon will devour them
along with their fields.

8 Blow the horn in Gibeah,
the trumpet in Ramah;
raise the war cry in Beth-aven:
After you, Benjamin!

9 Ephraim will become a desolation
on the day of punishment;
I announce what is certain
among the tribes of Israel.

10 The princes of Judah are like those
who move boundary markers;
I will pour out My fury on them like water.

11 Ephraim is oppressed, crushed in judgment,
for he is determined to follow
what is worthless.[i]

12 So I am like rot to Ephraim
and like decay to the house of Judah.

13 When Ephraim saw his sickness
and Judah his wound,
Ephraim went to Assyria

---

a4:7 Alt Hb tradition, Syr, Tg read They   b4:8 Or sin offerings   c4:12 Lit promiscuously from under   d4:15 = House of Wickedness   e4:18 Lit Her shields; Ps 47:9; 89:18   f4:18; 5:2 Hb obscure   g4:19 Lit wind will bind it in its wings   h5:5 Lit against his face   i5:11 Or follow a command; Hb obscure

---

sible for the nation's religious life, could not blame the people for Israel's dilemma. They too were sinners.

4:8 an appetite for their transgressions. The priests cheerfully led the people in idol worship and received part of their offerings as a bonus.
4:17 Ephraim ... leave him alone. Here Israel

is referred to as Ephraim because it is the largest of the northern kingdom's 10 tribes. God, increasingly frustrated with Ephraim, would eventually abandon that influential tribe.

4:19 wind. Although Israel felt invincible at the time, God would soon ordain Assyria to destroy Israel's sense of security (9:3).

5:5 Judah. The southern kingdom fell prey to spiritual adultery as well, worshiping Canaanite gods.

5:7 gave birth to illegitimate children. Concerns the legitimacy of Hosea fathering Gomer's children (4:13-15).

5:10 those who move boundary markers.

and sent ⌊a delegation⌋ to the great king.[a]
But he cannot cure you or heal your wound.

14 For I am like a lion to Ephraim
and like a young lion to the house of Judah.
Yes, I will tear ⌊them⌋ to pieces and depart.
I will carry ⌊them⌋ off,
and no one can rescue ⌊them⌋.

15 I will depart and return to My place
until they recognize their guilt and seek
My face;
they will search for Me in their distress.

A Call to Repentance

6 Come, let us return to the LORD.
For He has torn ⌊us⌋,
and He will heal us;
He has wounded ⌊us⌋,
and He will bind up our wounds.

2 He will revive us after two days,
and on the third day He will raise us up
so we can live in His presence.

3 Let us strive to know the LORD.
His appearance is as sure as the dawn.
He will come to us like the rain,
like the spring showers that water the land.

The LORD's First Lament

4 What am I going to do with you, Ephraim?
What am I going to do with you, Judah?
Your loyalty is like the morning mist
and like the early dew that vanishes.

5 This is why I have used the prophets
to cut them down;[b]
I have killed them with the words of My mouth.
My judgment strikes like lightning.[c]

6 For I desire loyalty and not sacrifice,
the knowledge of God rather than
•burnt offerings.

7 But they, like Adam,[d] have violated
the covenant;
there they have betrayed Me.

8 Gilead is a city of evildoers,
tracked with bloody footprints.

9 Like robbers who wait in ambush for someone,
a band of priests murders on the road
to Shechem.
They commit atrocities.

10 I have seen something horrible in the house
of Israel:

Ephraim's promiscuity is there; Israel is defiled.

11 A harvest is also appointed for you, Judah.

When I[e] return My people from captivity,
7 1 when I heal Israel,
the sins of Ephraim and the crimes of Samaria
will be exposed.
For they practice fraud;
a thief breaks in;
a gang pillages outside.

2 But they never consider that I remember
all their evil.
Now their sins are all around them;
they are right in front of My face.

Israel's Corruption

3 They please the king with their evil,
the princes with their lies.

4 All of them commit adultery;
⌊they are⌋ like an oven heated by a baker
who stops stirring ⌊the fire⌋
from the kneading of the dough
until it is leavened.

5 On the day of our king,
the princes are sick with the heat of wine—
there is a conspiracy with traitors.[f]

6 For they—their hearts like an oven—
draw him into their oven.
Their anger smolders all night;
in the morning it blazes like a flaming fire.

7 All of them are as hot as an oven,
and they consume their rulers.
All their kings fall;
not one of them calls on Me.[g]

8 Ephraim has allowed himself to get mixed up
with the nations.
Ephraim is unturned bread, baked on a griddle.

9 Foreigners consume his strength,
but he does not notice.
Even his hair is streaked with gray,
but he does not notice.

10 Israel's arrogance testifies against them,[h]
yet they do not return to the LORD their God,
and for all this, they do not seek Him.

11 So Ephraim has become like a silly,
senseless dove;
they call to Egypt, and they go to Assyria.

12 As they are going, I will spread My net
over them;

---

a **5:13** Or to King Yareb b **6:5** Or have cut down the prophets c **6:5** LXX, Syr, Tg; MT reads Your judgments go out as light d **6:7** Or they, as at
Adam, or they, like men; e **6:11** Or you. Judah, when I f **7:5** Lit wine—he stretches out his hand to scorners; Hb obscure g **7:3–7** These vv. may
refer to a king's assassination; Hb obscure. h **7:10** Lit against his face

---

Judah took over some of Israel's territory with complete disregard for God's law (Deut. 19:14).

5:13 Ephraim went to Assyria. Instead of turning to God for help, Israel sought aid from a pagan nation.

6:2 two days. Perhaps an example of wishful

thinking—Israel predicted that its punishment would not last long.

6:6 knowledge. God was looking for more than lip service. Israel must demonstrate its love for Him by adhering to covenant promises of obedience (Josh. 24:16-27).

7:2 I remember all their evil. Like Gomer, Is-

rael thought it sinned in secret. However, God saw and remembered every misdeed.

7:5 day of our king. Most likely an innocent celebration that had turned into a disgrace.

7:8 unturned bread. Using baker's imagery, Hosea showed that Israel's foolish political intentions were half-baked at best.

I will bring them down like birds of the sky.
I will discipline them in accordance
    with the news that reaches[a] their assembly.

The LORD's Second Lament

13 Woe to them, for they fled from Me;
    destruction to them, for they rebelled
        against Me!
    Though I want to redeem ⌊them⌋,
    they speak lies against Me.
14 They do not cry to Me from their hearts;
    rather, they wail on their beds.
    They slash themselves[b] for grain and wine;
    they turn away from Me.
15 I trained and strengthened their arms,
    but they plot evil against Me.
16 They turn, but not to what is above;[c]
    they are like a faulty bow.
    Their leaders will fall by the sword
    because of the cursing of their tongue.
    They will be ridiculed for this in the land
        of Egypt.

Israel's False Hopes

8 ⌊Put⌋ the horn to your mouth!
    One like an eagle comes
    against the house of the LORD,
    because they transgress My covenant
    and rebel against My law.
2 Israel cries out to Me:
    My God, we know You!
3 Israel has rejected what is good;
    an enemy will pursue him.

4 They have installed kings,
    but not through Me.
    They have appointed leaders,
    but without My approval.
    They make their silver and gold
    into idols for themselves
    for their own destruction.[d]
5 Your calf-idol[e] is rejected, Samaria.
    My anger burns against them.
    How long will they be incapable of innocence?
6 For this thing is from Israel—
    a craftsman made it, and it is not God.
    The calf of Samaria will be smashed to bits!

7 Indeed, they sow the wind
    and reap the whirlwind.
    There is no standing grain;

what sprouts fails to yield flour.
    Even if they did,
    foreigners would swallow it up.
8 Israel is swallowed up!
    Now they are among the nations
    like discarded pottery.
9 For they have gone up to Assyria
    ⌊like⌋ a wild donkey going off on its own.
    Ephraim has paid for love.
10 Even though they hire ⌊lovers⌋
        among the nations,
    I will now round them up,
    and they will begin to decrease in number
    under the burden of the king and leaders.

11 When Ephraim multiplied his altars for sin,
    they became his altars for sinning.
12 Though I were to write out for him
    ten thousand points of My law,
    they would be[f] regarded as something alien.
13 Though they ⌊offer⌋ sacrificial gifts[g]
    and eat the flesh,
    the LORD does not accept them.
    Now He will remember their guilt
    and punish their sins;
    they will return to Egypt.
14 Israel has forgotten his Maker and built palaces;
    Judah has also multiplied fortified cities.
    I will send fire on their cities,
    and it will consume their citadels.

The Coming Exile

9 Israel, do not rejoice jubilantly as the nations do,
    for you have acted promiscuously,
        leaving your God.
    You have loved the wages of a prostitute
    on every grain-threshing floor.
2 Threshing floor and wine vat will not
        sustain them,
    and the new wine will fail them.
3 They will not stay in the land of the LORD.
    Instead, Ephraim will return to Egypt,
    and they will eat unclean food in Assyria.

4 They will not pour out
    their wine offerings to the LORD,
    and their sacrifices will not please Him.
    Their ⌊food⌋ will be like the bread of mourners;
    all who eat it become defiled.
    For their bread will be for their appetites ⌊alone⌋;
    it will not enter the house of the LORD.

---

a7:12 Lit *news to*   b7:14 Some Hb mss, LXX; other Hb mss read *They stay*; 1 Kg 18:28   c7:16 Others emend to *turn to what is useless*   d8:4 Lit *themselves that it might be cut off*   e8:5 Lit *calf*   f8:12 Or *Though I wrote out . . . law, they are*   g8:13 Hb obscure

---

7:9 consume his strength. Israel bought protection with lavish tributes to foreign kings. (See Tiglath-Pileser as an example in 2 Kings 15:19-20, 29.)

7:11 silly, senseless dove. Hosea showed the ignorance involved in Israel's fickle political policies. Israel relied on whatever country seemed

strong at the moment.

7:15 I trained and strengthened their arms. Israel had taken the credit for its military endeavors.

7:16 faulty bow. A faulty bow would consistently miss its target, just as Israel consistently failed to understand God's purposes.

8:1 eagle. The eagle represented the eagerness of Israel's enemy, Assyria.

8:5 calf-idol. Jeroboam had fashioned a golden image for the people of Israel to worship (1 Kings 12:26-30).

8:8 discarded pottery. Israel's people were not the successful nation God once envisioned

5 What will you do on a festival day,
on the day of the LORD's feast?
6 For even if they flee from devastation,
Egypt will gather them, and Memphis
will bury them.
Thistles will take possession
of their precious silver;
thorns will invade their tents.

7 The days of punishment have come;
the days of retribution have come.
Let Israel recognize it!
The prophet is a fool,
and the inspired man is insane,
because of the magnitude
of your guilt and hostility.
8 Ephraim's watchman is with my God.
The prophet ⌊encounters⌋ a fowler's snare
on all his ways.
Hostility is in the house of his God!
9 They have deeply corrupted themselves
as in the days of Gibeah.
He will remember their guilt;
He will punish their sins.

Ephraim Bereaved of Offspring
10 I discovered Israel
like grapes in the wilderness.
I saw your fathers
like the first fruit of the fig tree
in its first season.
But they went to Baal-peor,
consecrated themselves to Shame,[a]
and became detestable,
like the thing they loved.
11 Ephraim's glory will fly away like a bird:
no birth, no gestation, no conception.
12 Even if they raise children,
I will bereave them of each one.
Yes, woe to them when I depart from them!
13 I have seen Ephraim like Tyre,
planted in a meadow,
so Ephraim will bring out his children
to the executioner.
14 Give them, LORD—
What should You give?
Give them a womb that miscarries
and breasts that are dry!

15 All their evil appears at Gilgal,
for there I came to hate them.

I will drive them from My house
because of their evil, wicked actions.
I will no longer love them;
all their leaders are rebellious.
16 Ephraim is blighted;
their roots are withered;
they cannot bear fruit.
Even if they bear children,
I will kill the precious offspring of their wombs.
17 My God will reject them
because they have not listened to Him;
they will become wanderers among the nations.

The Vine and the Calf
10 Israel is a lush[b] vine;
it yields fruit for itself.
The more his fruit increased,
the more he increased the altars.
The better his land produced,
the better they made the sacred pillars.
2 Their hearts are devious;[c]
now they must bear their guilt.
The LORD will break down their altars
and demolish their sacred pillars.
3 In fact, they are now saying:
"We have no king!
For we do not •fear the LORD.
What can a king do for us?"
4 They speak ⌊mere⌋ words,
taking false oaths while making covenants.
So lawsuits break out
like poisonous weeds in the furrows of a field.

5 The residents of Samaria will have anxiety
over the calf of Beth-aven.
Indeed, its idolatrous priests rejoiced over it;
the people will mourn over it,
over its glory.
It will certainly depart from them.
6 The calf itself will be taken to Assyria
as an offering to the great king.[d]
Ephraim will experience shame;
Israel will be ashamed of its counsel.
7 Samaria's king will disappear[e]
like foam[f] on the surface of the water.
8 The •high places of Aven, the sin of Israel,
will be destroyed;
thorns and thistles will grow over their altars.
They will say to the mountains, "Cover us!"
and to the hills, "Fall on us!"

---

[a] 9:10 = a Hb term of derision for *Baal* [b] 10:1 Or *ravaged* [c] 10:2 Or *divided* [d] 10:6 Or *to King Yareb* [e] 10:7 Or *will be cut off* [f] 10:7 Or *a stick*

---

and commanded them to be (Ex. 19:5). They had become as useless as broken pottery.
8:13 Egypt. Egypt could only mean one thing: captivity. Assyria would be the actual site of Israel's torture (11:5).
9:3 will not stay in the land of the Lord. Like tenants kicked out by the landlord, Israel would

be removed from the promised land. The land promised to the Israelites belonged to the Lord (Josh. 22:19).
9:5 festival day. The point being, Israel will be too far removed from Jerusalem to have any opportunity to celebrate its festivals (i.e., Passover, Unleavened Bread, Weeks, and Booths).

So, technically, they would be unable to observe the law (which they were rampantly breaking away). Eventually, in 70 A.D., this change of circumstance became permanent.
9:9 days of Gibeah. Compared to a brutal rape and murder in its past, Israel's present sins were worse (Judg. 19-20).

Israel's Defeat because of Sin

9 Israel, you have sinned
since the days of Gibeah;
they have taken their stand there.
Will not war against the unjust
overtake them in Gibeah?

10 I will discipline them at my discretion;
nations will be gathered against them
to put them in bondage[a]
for their two crimes.

11 Ephraim is a well-trained young cow
that loves to thresh,
but I will place a yoke on[b] her fine neck.
I will harness Ephraim;
Judah will plow;
Jacob will do the final plowing.

12 Sow righteousness for yourselves
and reap faithful love;
break up your untilled ground.
It is time to seek the LORD
until He comes and sends righteousness
on you like the rain.

13 You have plowed wickedness
and reaped injustice;
you have eaten the fruit of lies.
Because you have trusted in your own way[c]
and in your large number of soldiers,

14 the roar of battle will rise against your people,
and all your fortifications will be demolished
in a day of war,
like Shalman's destruction of Beth-arbel.
Mothers will be dashed to pieces
along with ⌊their⌋ children.

15 So it will be done to you, Bethel,
because of your extreme evil.
At dawn the king of Israel will be
totally destroyed.

The LORD's Love for Israel

11 When Israel was a child, I loved him,
and out of Egypt I called My son.

2 ⌊The more⌋ they[d] called them,[e]
⌊the more⌋ they[e] departed from Me.[f]
They kept sacrificing to the •Baals
and burning offerings to idols.

3 It was I who taught Ephraim to walk,
taking them[g] in My arms,

but they never knew that I healed them.

4 I led them with human cords,
with ropes of kindness.
To them I was like one
who eases the yoke from their jaws;
I bent down to give them food.

5 Israel will not return to the land of Egypt
and Assyria will be his king,
because they refused to repent.

6 A sword will whirl through his cities;
it will destroy and devour the bars
of his gates,[h]
because of their schemes.

7 My people are bent on turning from Me.
Though they call to Him on high,
He will not exalt them at all.

8 How can I give you up, Ephraim?
How can I surrender you, Israel?
How can I make you like Admah?
How can I treat you like Zeboiim?
I have had a change of heart;
My compassion is stirred!

9 I will not vent the full fury of My anger;
I will not turn back to destroy Ephraim.
For I am God and not man,
the Holy One among you;
I will not come in rage.[i]

10 They will follow the LORD;
He will roar like a lion.
When He roars,
His children will come trembling from the west.

11 They will be roused like birds from Egypt
and like doves from the land of Assyria.
Then I will settle them in their homes.

⌊This is⌋
the LORD's declaration.

12[j] Ephraim surrounds me with lies,
the house of Israel, with deceit.
Judah still wanders with El[k]
and is faithful to holy ones.[l] [m]

God's Case against Jacob's Heirs

12 Ephraim chases[n] the wind
and pursues the east wind.
He continually multiplies lies and violence.
He makes a covenant with Assyria,
and olive oil is carried to Egypt.

---

[a]**10:10** LXX, Syr, Vg read *against them when they are disciplined*   [b]**10:11** Lit *will pass over*   [c]**10:13** LXX reads *your chariots*   [d]**11:2** Perhaps the prophets   [e]**11:2** = Israel   [f]**11:2** LXX; MT reads *them*   [g]**11:3** LXX, Syr, Vg; MT reads *him*   [h]**11:6** Or *devour his empty talkers*, or *devour his limbs*; Hb obscure   [i]**11:9** Or *come into any city*; Hb obscure   [j]**11:12** Hs 12:1 in Hb   [k]**11:12** Or *God*   [l]**11:12** Or *Judah walks with God and is faithful to the Holy One*; Hb obscure   [m]**11:12** Possibly angels, or less likely, pagan gods or idols   [n]**12:1** Or *feeds on*, or *tends*

9:10 grapes in the wilderness. Sweet grapes amid desolation would be a rare find indeed! In the same way, God had once prized Israel for her purity among the nations.

10:1 a lush vine. Before its idolatry, Israel was full of promise and hope like a vine full of fruit.

10:4 making covenants. Israel knew when it

was in political trouble. However, its kings turned to the wrong power for help.

10:9 Gibeah. Like Gibeah (9:9), Israel would endure war and hardship as a consequence of sin (Judg. 19:12-30).

11:1 called My son. God went back to Israel's past, when He and Israel were like Father and

son (Ex. 4:22-23).

11:4 ropes of kindness. A compassionate farmer repositioned the yoke on a work animal so that it can enjoy its food.

11:5 return to the land of Egypt. Returning to Egypt was a major step backward: from freedom to slavery, blessing to punishment, suc-

2 The LORD also has a dispute with Judah.
He is about to punish Jacob
  according to his ways;
He will repay him based on his actions.

3 In the womb he grasped his brother's heel,
and as an adult he wrestled with God.

4 Jacob struggled with the Angel and prevailed;
he wept and sought His favor.
He found him[a] at Bethel,
and there He spoke with him.[b]

5 •Yahweh is the God of •Hosts;
Yahweh is His name.

6 But you must return to your God.
Maintain love and justice,
and always put your hope in God.

7 A merchant loves to extort
with dishonest scales in his hands.

8 But Ephraim says:
"How rich I have become;
I made it all myself.
In all my earnings,
no one can find any crime in me
that I can be punished for!"[c]

Judgment on Apostate Israel

9 I have been the LORD your God
ever since[d] the land of Egypt.
I will make you live in tents again,
as in the festival days.

10 I spoke through the prophets
and granted many visions;
I gave parables through the prophets.

11 Since Gilead is full of evil,
they will certainly come to nothing.
They sacrifice bulls in Gilgal;
even their altars will be like heaps of rocks
on the furrows of a field.

Further Indictment of Jacob's Heirs

12 Jacob fled to the land of Aram.
Israel worked to earn a wife;
he tended flocks for a wife.

13 The LORD brought Israel from Egypt
  by a prophet,
and Israel was tended by a prophet.

14 Ephraim has provoked bitter anger,
so his Lord will leave his bloodguilt on him
and repay him for his contempt.

13 When Ephraim spoke, there was trembling;
he was exalted in Israel.
But he incurred guilt through •Baal and died.

2 Now they continue to sin
and make themselves a cast image,
idols skillfully made from their silver,
all of them the work of craftsmen.
People say about them,
"Let the men who sacrifice[e] kiss the calves."

3 Therefore, they will be like the morning mist,
like the early dew that vanishes,
like chaff blown from a threshing floor,
or like smoke from a window.

Death and Resurrection

4 I have been the LORD your God
ever since[f] the land of Egypt;
you know no God but Me,
and no Savior exists besides Me.

5 I knew[g] you in the wilderness,
in the land of drought.

6 When they had pasture,
they became satisfied;
they were satisfied,
and their hearts became proud.
Therefore they forgot Me.

7 So I will be like a lion to them;
I will lurk like a leopard on the path.

8 I will attack them
like a bear robbed of her cubs
and tear open the rib cage over their hearts.
I will devour them there like a lioness,
like a wild beast that would rip them open.

9 I will destroy you, Israel;
you have no help but Me.[h]

10 Where now is your king,[i]
that he may save you in all your cities,
and the[j] rulers[k] you demanded, saying:
Give me a king and leaders?

11 I give you a king in My anger
and take away ⌊a king⌋ in My wrath.

12 Ephraim's guilt is preserved;
his sin is stored up.

13 Labor pains come on him.
He is not a wise son;
when the time comes,
he will not be born.[l]

---

[a]**12:4** Or *Him* [b]**12:4** LXX, Syr; MT reads *us* [c]**12:8** Lit *crime which is sin* [d]**12:9** LXX reads *God who brought you out of* [e]**13:2** Or *Those who make human sacrifices*; 2 Kg 17:16–17 [f]**13:4** DSS, LXX read *God who brought you out of* [g]**13:5** LXX, Syr read *fed* [h]**13:9** LXX reads *At your destruction, Israel, who will help you?* [i]**13:10** LXX, Syr, Vg; MT reads *I will be your king* [j]**13:10** Lit *your* [k]**13:10** Or *judges* [l]**13:13** Lit *he will not present himself at the opening of the womb for sons*

---

cess to inferiority.

11:8 God compared Ephraim's fate to that of cities overthrown by the destruction of Sodom (Deut. 29:23).

11:9 For I am God and not man. A father may punish a child and then regret it. However, God was grieved by the punishment before it began.

12:1 olive oil is carried to Egypt. Israel gave olive oil in hopes of endearing themselves to the Egyptians.

12:6 return. Jacob turned his life around after encountering God (Gen. 32:24-30), and Israel could choose the same.

12:8 Ephraim. Hosea interchanged "Ephraim"

(the most influential northern tribe) and "Israel" for the same northern kingdom.

12:12 Jacob fled. God reminded Israel of its humble beginnings through the story of Jacob. Jacob tended sheep and worked faithfully for his prosperity (Gen. 29:20-28).

13:3 vanishes. Although Ephraim thrived for a

14 I will[a] ransom them from the power of •Sheol.
I will[a] redeem them from death.
Death, where are your barbs?
Sheol, where is your sting?
Compassion is hidden from My eyes.

The Coming Judgment

15 Although he flourishes among ⌊his⌋ brothers,[b]
an east wind will come,
a wind from the Lᴏʀᴅ rising up from the desert.
His water source will fail,
and his spring will run dry.
The wind[c] will plunder the treasury
of every precious item.

16d Samaria will bear her guilt
because she has rebelled against her God.
They will fall by the sword;
their little ones will be dashed to pieces,
and their pregnant women ripped open.

A Plea to Repent

14 Israel, return to the Lᴏʀᴅ your God,
for you have stumbled in your sin.
2 Take words ⌊of repentance⌋ with you
and return to the Lᴏʀᴅ.
Say to Him: "Forgive all ⌊our⌋ sin
and accept what is good,
so that we may repay You
with praise[e] from our[f] lips.
3 Assyria will not save us,
we will not ride on horses,

and we will no longer proclaim: Our gods!
to the work of our hands.
For the fatherless receives compassion
in You."

A Promise of Restoration

4 I will heal their apostasy;
I will freely love them,
for My anger will have turned from him.
5 I will be like the dew to Israel;
he will blossom like the lily
and take root like ⌊the cedars of⌋ Lebanon.
6 His new branches will spread,
and his splendor will be like the olive tree,
his fragrance, like ⌊the forest of⌋ Lebanon.
7 The people will return and live
beneath his shade.
They will grow grain
and blossom like the vine.
His renown will be like the wine of Lebanon.

8 Ephraim, why should I[g] have anything more
to do with idols?
It is I who answer and watch over him.
I am like a flourishing pine tree;
your fruit comes from Me.

9 Let whoever is wise understand these things,
and whoever is insightful recognize them.
For the ways of the Lᴏʀᴅ are right,
and the righteous walk in them,
but the rebellious stumble in them.

---

[a]**13:14** Or *Should I . . . ?*   [b]**13:15** Or *among reeds*   [c]**13:15** Probably = the Assyrian king   [d]**13:16** Hs 14:1 in Hb   [e]**14:2** LXX reads *with the fruit*   [f]**14:2** Lit *repay the bulls of our*   [g]**14:8** LXX reads *he*

---

brief moment, its self-destructive practices would bring the nation down forever.

13:7-8 wild beast. From shepherd to predator, the imagery shifts to express God's frustration with His people. If Israel did not acknowledge His tender mercy, His justice would have to get their attention.

13:10 Where now is your king. Hosea wrote at a time when kings were assassinated as quickly as they were inaugurated. This also implies that the nation needed to seek their help from God, not human rulers.

13:15 east wind. According to God's plan, As-syria blew onto the scene at the right time, de-stroyed Israel, and took her people captive.

13:16 Samaria. The description of the fall of the capital city of the northern kingdom is similar to language used by other prophets (Isa. 13:6; Amos 1:13; Nahum 3:10). This prediction is ful-filled in 2 Kings 17:5.

14:1 Israel, return. God's command has a greater context at the conclusion of His mes-sage than earlier references (10:12; 12:6). Lip service will not suffice. Genuine repentance is the only acceptable means for returning to God.

14:8 your fruit comes from Me. God revealed the secret of success to a farming community whose existence was tied to the fruit of a har-vest. God alone blesses the bounty.

14:9 ways of the Lᴏʀᴅ are right. Hosea con-cludes with a cause and effect lesson. Rebel-lion leads to stumbling: righteousness provides a clear path to God.

INTRODUCTION TO
JOEL

PERSONAL READING PLAN

☐ Joel 1:1-20
☐ Joel 2:1-17

☐ Joel 2:18-32
☐ Joel 3:1-21

AUTHOR

The author is identified as the prophet Joel, son of Pethuel (1:1). While there are 12 other Old Testament characters with this name, none of them can be identified with this prophet.

DATE

The date is uncertain. Joel could have been written as early as the ninth and as late as the fourth century B.C. Since Joel uses quotes or paraphrases from several other prophets and does not refer to either the Babylonian or Assyrian Empire, a later date seems probable—sometime during the Persian period (539-331 B.C.).

THEME

A plague of locusts is a sign of the coming Day of the Lord.

HISTORICAL BACKGROUND

The occasion for Joel's prophetic ministry was a plague of locusts that was consuming Judah. The fact that no historical record of such a plague has endured does not mean this event was simply an allegorical device of the writer. Rather, this underscores the truth that even the worst natural or national disasters fade from memory when attention is turned to something that endures forever– an eternal God and His future kingdom (see 2:28-3:21).

CHARACTERISTICS

The literary genius of Joel shines throughout the book's structure; each section flows into the next. Hence, it helps to read the whole book in one sitting before studying its parts. The focus of the book is twofold:

(1) The ever-present, practical problem of what to do about the locust plague (1:1-2:27); and

(2) The future Day of the Lord, of which the current plague is a sign (2:28-3:21).

In combining the two—event plus interpretation—Joel is performing the classic function of an Old Testament prophet, that of conveying God's revelation. Likewise, the borrowing of phrases from other prophets to speak a "new word" from the Lord in a new setting shows that Joel was probably an educated person. Joel had perhaps heard the prophecies of Micah, Jeremiah, and Isaiah. In 2:28-3:21 Joel expands the apocalyptic dimensions of these prophets. In Acts 2, the Apostle Peter expounds the meaning of Joel's prophecy. Specifically, Joel's prediction about the outpouring of the Holy Spirit was fulfilled on the Day of Pentecost.

1

The word of the LORD that came to Joel son of Pethuel:

A Plague of Locusts

2 Hear this, you elders;
listen, all you inhabitants of the land.
Has anything like this ever happened
in your days
or in the days of your ancestors?
3 Tell your children about it,
and let your children tell their children,
and their children the next generation.
4 What the devouring locust has left,
the swarming locust has eaten;
what the swarming locust has left,
the young locust has eaten;
and what the young locust has left,
the destroying locust has eaten.

5 Wake up, you drunkards, and weep;
wail, all you wine drinkers,
because of the sweet wine,
for it has been taken from your mouth.
6 For a nation has invaded My land,
powerful and without number;
its teeth are the teeth of a lion,
and it has the fangs of a lioness.
7 It has devastated My grapevine
and splintered My fig tree.
It has stripped off its bark and thrown it away;
its branches have turned white.
8 Grieve like a young woman dressed
in •sackcloth,
⌊mourning⌋ for the husband of her youth.
9 •Grain and drink offerings have been cut off
from the house of the LORD;
the priests, who are ministers
of the LORD, mourn.
10 The fields are destroyed;
the land grieves;
indeed, the grain is destroyed;
the new wine is dried up;
and the olive oil fails.
11 Be ashamed, you farmers,
wail, you vinedressers,[a]
over the wheat and the barley,
because the harvest of the field has perished.
12 The grapevine is dried up,
and the fig tree is withered;
the pomegranate, the date palm,
and the apple—

all the trees of the orchard—have withered.
Indeed, human joy has dried up.

13 Dress ⌊in sackcloth⌋ and lament, you priests;
wail, you ministers of the altar.
Come and spend the night in sackcloth,
you ministers of my God,
because grain and drink offerings
are withheld from the house of your God.
14 Announce a sacred fast;
proclaim an assembly!
Gather the elders
and all the residents of the land
at the house of the LORD your God,
and cry out to the LORD.

The Day of the LORD

15 Woe because of that day!
For the Day of the LORD is near
and will come as devastation
from the •Almighty.
16 Hasn't the food been cut off
before our eyes,
joy and gladness
from the house of our God?
17 The seeds lie shriveled in their casings.[b]
The storehouses are in ruin,
and the granaries are broken down,
because the grain has withered away.
18 How the animals groan!
The herds of cattle wander in confusion
since they have no pasture.
Even the flocks of sheep suffer punishment.
19 I call to You, LORD,
for fire has consumed
the pastures of the wilderness,
and flames have devoured
all the trees of the countryside.
20 Even the wild animals cry out to[c] You,
for the river beds are dried up,
and fire has consumed
the pastures of the wilderness.

2

Blow the horn in Zion;
sound the alarm on My holy mountain!
Let all the residents of the land tremble,
for the Day of the LORD is coming;
in fact, it is near—
2 a day of darkness and gloom,
a day of clouds and dense overcast,
like the dawn spreading over the mountains;

---

[a]1:11 Or *The farmers are dismayed, the vinedressers wail*   [b]1:17 Or *clods*; Hb obscure   [c]1:20 Or *animals pant for*; Hb obscure

---

1:1 Joel. Joel's prophetic message focuses on God's supreme power and might. As if to emphasize his point, Joel's name means, "The Lord is God."

1:6 invaded. Locusts had invaded the land. Joel uses locusts as a metaphor for God's judgment of their sin. In great numbers lo-

custs can create large-scale devastation (see Ex 10:13-15).

1:14 cry out to the Lord. Joel encouraged the people to cry out to the Lord in repentance, humility, and desperation (see also Judg. 20:26).

1:15 Day of the Lord is near. The Day of the Lord signifies both a present event and

foreshadowing of a final future event.

2:2 darkness and gloom. Darkness symbolizes a day of destruction, wrath, and judgment on sin. During the time Jesus hung on the cross, darkness descended on the earth even though it was the middle of the day (see Matt. 27:44-46).

a great and strong people [appears],
such as never existed in ages past
and never will again
in all the generations to come.

3 A fire destroys[a] in front of them,
and behind them a flame devours.
The land in front of them
is like the Garden of Eden,
but behind them,
it is like a desert wasteland;
there is no escape from them.

4 Their appearance is like that of horses,
and they gallop like war horses.

5 They bound on the tops of the mountains.
Their sound is like the sound of chariots,
like the sound of fiery flames
    consuming stubble,
like a mighty army deployed for war.

6 Nations writhe in horror before them;
all faces turn pale.

7 They attack as warriors [attack];
they scale walls as men of war [do].
Each goes on his own path,
and they do not change their course.

8 They do not push each other;
each man proceeds on his own path.
They dodge the missiles, never stopping.

9 They storm the city;
they run on the wall;
they climb into the houses;
they enter through the windows like thieves.

10 The earth quakes before them;
the sky shakes.
The sun and moon grow dark,
and the stars cease their shining.

11 The LORD raises His voice
in the presence of His army.
His camp is very large;
Those who carry out His command are powerful.
Indeed, the Day of the LORD is terrible
    and dreadful—
who can endure it?

God's Call for Repentance

12 Even now—

                        [this is]
            the LORD's declaration—
turn to Me with all your heart,
    with fasting, weeping, and mourning.

13 Tear your hearts,
not just your clothes,
and return to the LORD your God.
For He is gracious and compassionate,
slow to anger, rich in faithful love,
and He relents from sending disaster.

14 Who knows? He may turn and relent
and leave a blessing behind Him,
[so you can] offer grain and wine
to the LORD your God.

15 Blow the horn in Zion!
Announce a sacred fast;
proclaim an assembly.

16 Gather the people;
sanctify the congregation;
assemble the aged;[b]
gather the children,
even those nursing at the breast.
Let the bridegroom leave his bedroom,
and the bride her honeymoon chamber.

17 Let the priests, the LORD's ministers,
weep between the portico[c] and the altar.
Let them say:
"Have pity on Your people, LORD,
and do not make Your inheritance a disgrace,
an object of scorn among the nations.
Why should it be said among the peoples,
'Where is their God?'"

God's Response to His People

18 Then the LORD became jealous for His land and spared His people. 19 The LORD answered His people:

Look, I am about to send you
grain, new wine, and olive oil.
You will be satiated with them,
and I will no longer make you
a disgrace among the nations.

20 I will drive the northerner far from you
and banish him to a dry and desolate land,
his front ranks into the Dead Sea,
and his rear guard into the Mediterranean Sea.
His stench will rise;
yes, his rotten smell will rise,
for he has done catastrophic things.

21 Don't be afraid, land;
rejoice and be glad,
for the LORD has done great things.

22 Don't be afraid, wild animals,

---

[a]2:3 Lit consumes   [b]2:16 Or elders   [c]2:17 = the temple porch; 1 Kg 6:3; 7:6–21

2:10 sun and moon ... stars. Joel extended God's judgment to the cosmos. Even the sun, moon, and stars were dimmed by the massive destruction (see Isa. 13:10).

2:13 compassionate. God's wrath and might are tempered by grace, compassion, slowness to anger, and faithful love. Those who love and obey God will experience His compassion, while those who defy God will experience wrath.

2:21-23 Everything came to life again as a symbol of God's restorative power. Animals (v. 22) and people (v. 23) enjoy the rebirth of the land (v. 21).

2:27 I am the Lord ... there is no other. The blessings (vv. 25-26) were a sign of God's presence among His people.

2:30-31 wonders. These cosmic wonders, formerly a scene of destruction (v. 10), now proclaimed God's provision through His Spirit. Joel described it as both a day of

for the wilderness pastures have turned green,
the trees bear their fruit,
and the fig tree and grapevine yield
their riches.

23 Children of Zion, rejoice and be glad
in the LORD your God,
because He gives you the autumn rain
for your vindication.[a]
He sends showers for you,
both autumn and spring rain as before.

24 The threshing floors will be full of grain,
and the vats will overflow
with new wine and olive oil.

25 I will repay you for the years
that the swarming locust ate,
the young locust, the destroying locust,
and the devouring locust—
My great army that I sent against you.

26 You will have plenty to eat and be satisfied.
You will praise the name of •Yahweh your God,
who has dealt wondrously with you.
My people will never again be put to shame.

27 You will know that I am present in Israel
and that I am the LORD your God,
and there is no other.
My people will never again be put to shame.

God's Promise of His Spirit

28b After this
I will pour out My Spirit on all humanity;
then your sons and your daughters
will prophesy,
your old men will have dreams,
and your young men will see visions.

29 I will even pour out My Spirit
on the male and female slaves in those days.

30 I will display wonders
in the heavens and on the earth:
blood, fire, and columns of smoke.

31 The sun will be turned to darkness
and the moon to blood
before the great and awe-inspiring Day
of the LORD comes.

32 Then everyone who calls
on the name of Yahweh will be saved,
for there will be an escape
for those on Mount Zion and in Jerusalem,
as the LORD promised,
among the survivors the LORD calls.

Judgment of the Nations

3[c] Yes, in those days and at that time,
when I restore the fortunes of Judah
and Jerusalem,

2 I will gather all the nations
and take them to the Valley of Jehoshaphat.[d]
I will enter into judgment with them there
because of My people, My inheritance Israel.
The nations have scattered the Israelites
in foreign countries
and divided up My land.

3 They cast lots for My people;
they bartered a boy for a prostitute
and sold a girl for wine to drink.

4 And also: Tyre, Sidon, and all the territories of Philistia—what are you to Me? Are you paying Me back or trying to get even with Me? I will quickly bring retribution on your heads. 5 For you took My silver and gold and carried My finest treasures to your temples. 6 You sold the people of Judah and Jerusalem to the Greeks to remove them far from their own territory. 7 Look, I am about to rouse them up from the place where you sold them; I will bring retribution on your heads. 8 I will sell your sons and daughters into the hands of the people of Judah, and they will sell them to the Sabeans,[e] to a distant nation, for the LORD has spoken.

9 Proclaim this among the nations:
Prepare for holy war;
rouse the warriors;
let all the men of war advance and attack!

10 Hammer your plowshares into swords
and your pruning knives into spears.
Let even the weakling say: I am a warrior.

11 Come quickly,[f] all you surrounding nations;
gather yourselves.
Bring down Your warriors there, LORD.

12 Let the nations be roused
and come to the Valley of Jehoshaphat,
for there I will sit down
to judge all the surrounding nations.

13 Swing the sickle
because the harvest is ripe.
Come and trample ⌊the grapes⌋
because the winepress is full;
the wine vats overflow
because the wickedness of the nations is great.

14 Multitudes, multitudes
in the valley of decision!

---

[a]2:23 Or righteousness [b]2:28 Jl 3:1 in Hb [c]3:1 Jl 4:1 in Hb [d]3:2 = The LORD Will Judge [e]3:8 Probably = the south Arabian kingdom of Sheba (modern Yemen) [f]3:11 LXX, Syr, Tg read Gather yourselves and come; Hb obscure

---

judgment for sin and a time of deliverance for God's people.
3:1 at that time. God offers a plan of hope to the Israelites. Their enemies will be judged and Israel's fortunes will be restored.
3:2 enter into judgment. In this supernatural event, evil will ultimately be judged and the

righteous delivered (see also Rev. 20:8-10).
3:4-8 Specific nations were summoned before the Lord for their destructive attitudes toward God.
3:9-11 holy war. The mighty assembly of the Lord's army gears up for battle (see also Rev. 19:14). Joel exhorted the Lord to reveal

His protection and provision (v. 11).
3:10 plowshares into swords. Instead of enjoying peace, the nations prepared for war by turning tools for plowing into battle weapons, foreshadowing their inevitable defeat (Isa. 2:4, Mic. 4:3).
3:14 in the valley of decision. All of human-

For the Day of the LORD is near
in the valley of decision.

15 The sun and moon will grow dark,
and the stars will cease their shining.

16 The LORD will roar from Zion
and raise His voice from Jerusalem;
heaven and earth will shake.
But the LORD will be a refuge for His people,
a stronghold for the Israelites.

Israel Blessed

17 Then you will know
that I am the LORD your God,
who dwells in Zion, My holy mountain.
Jerusalem will be holy,
and foreigners will never overrun it again.

18 In that day
the mountains will drip with sweet wine,
and the hills will flow with milk.
All the streams of Judah will flow with water,
and a spring will issue from the LORD's house,
watering the Valley of Acacias.[a]

19 Egypt will become desolate,
and Edom a desert wasteland,
because of the violence ⌊done⌋ to the people
of Judah
in whose land they shed innocent blood.

20 But Judah will be inhabited forever,
and Jerusalem from generation to generation.

21 I will pardon their bloodguilt,[b]
⌊which⌋ I have not pardoned,
for the LORD dwells in Zion.

---

a3:18 Or *Shittim*   b3:21 LXX, Syr read *I will avenge their blood*

---

kind was represented in this decision that all must make: repent or continue to rebel and sin against God.

3:16 refuge … stronghold. The Day of the Lord will be a place of safety for the righ-teous and bring delight to those who are saved by faith in God.

3:18 In that day. Joel looked forward to a day when God's people would fully experience the fullness of God's creation forever (2:28–3:1).

3:21 the Lord dwells. At the close of the prophecy, Joel emphasized God's presence among His people; God's covenant will finally be the rule of the day. This, as many of Joel's prophecies, foreshadows future events at the end of the age.

INTRODUCTION TO
AMOS

AUTHOR

Amos, who came from the small town of Tekoa (six miles south of Bethlehem and 11 miles from Jerusalem), was a citizen of the southern state of Judah, but ministered in the northern state of Israel, alongside the prophet Hosea. Amos was a shepherd (1:1) and fruit farmer (7:14), not a professional prophet. However, his skill with words and the strikingly broad range of his general knowledge of history and the world indicate that he was not an ignorant peasant.

DATE

Amos ministered during the reigns of Uzziah, king of Judah (783-742 B.C.), and Jeroboam II, king of Israel (786-746 B.C.), possibly circa 760-750 B.C.

THEME

God's judgment on injustice.

HISTORICAL BACKGROUND

By 800 B.C. both the northern kingdom (Israel) and the southern kingdom (Judah) had reached new political and military heights. Peace reigned and business was booming. Even religion was on the rise. However, the exterior calm belied Israel's inner disease. Idolatry, extravagant indulgence, and a corrupt judicial system ran beneath the surface. In this context, Amos calls for justice—particularly social justice as the foundation for true piety (5:24).

CHARACTERISTICS

Whereas his contemporary, Hosea, focuses on the love of God and spiritual adultery, Amos focuses on the righteousness of God and social injustice. He often makes his points by use of a simple rhetorical question (e.g., 5:25). Amos speaks as a simple Judean farmer burdened for the materialistic nation of Israel. His prayer averts the total destruction of Israel (7:1-6), and yet his message was most unpopular. However, social acceptance didn't matter to one whose job was not on the line (7:12-15). In Amos, God roars like a lion (1:2) and brings hope only at the end (9:11-15). The Book of Amos is constantly shadowed by clouds of judgment as the Lord reacts to the cruel social behaviors in the land. Amos passionately declares both God's concern for the poor and His wrath on those who would exploit them. His message is an uncomfortable one in any age as he challenges followers of God to examine themselves and their society, confronting injustice wherever it exists.

1 The words of Amos, who was one of the sheep breeders[a] from Tekoa—what he saw regarding Israel in the days of Uzziah, king of Judah, and Jeroboam son of Joash, king of Israel, two years before the earthquake.

2 He said:

The LORD roars from Zion
and raises His voice from Jerusalem;
the pastures of the shepherds mourn,[b]
and the summit of Carmel withers.

Judgment on Israel's Neighbors

3 The LORD says:

I will not relent from punishing Damascus
for three crimes, even four,
because they threshed Gilead with iron sledges.
4 Therefore, I will send fire against Hazael's palace,
and it will consume Ben-hadad's citadels.
5 I will break down the gates[c] of Damascus.
I will cut off the ruler from the Valley of Aven,
and the one who wields the scepter
from Beth-eden.
The people of Aram will be exiled to Kir.
The LORD has spoken.

6 The LORD says:

I will not relent from punishing Gaza
for three crimes, even four,
because they exiled a whole community,
handing them over to Edom.
7 Therefore, I will send fire against the walls
of Gaza,
and it will consume its citadels.
8 I will cut off the ruler from Ashdod,
and the one who wields the scepter
from Ashkelon.
I will also turn My hand against Ekron,
and the remainder of the Philistines will perish.
The Lord GOD has spoken.

9 The LORD says:

I will not relent from punishing Tyre
for three crimes, even four,
because they handed over
a whole community of exiles to Edom
and broke[d] a treaty of brotherhood.
10 Therefore, I will send fire against the walls
of Tyre,
and it will consume its citadels.

11 The LORD says:

I will not relent from punishing Edom
for three crimes, even four,
because he pursued his brother with the sword.
He stifled his compassion,
his anger tore [at them] continually,
and he harbored his rage incessantly.
12 Therefore, I will send fire against Teman,
and it will consume the citadels of Bozrah.

13 The LORD says:

I will not relent from punishing
the Ammonites
for three crimes, even four,
because they ripped open
the pregnant women of Gilead
in order to enlarge their territory.
14 Therefore, I will set fire to the walls of Rabbah,
and it will consume its citadels.
There will be shouting on the day of battle
and a violent wind on the day of the storm.
15 Their king and his princes
will go into exile together.
The LORD has spoken.

2 The LORD says:

I will not relent from punishing Moab
for three crimes, even four,
because he burned to lime
the bones of the king of Edom.
2 Therefore, I will send fire against Moab,
and it will consume the citadels of Kerioth.
Moab will die with a tumult,
with shouting and the sound of the ram's horn.
3 I will cut off the judge from the land
and kill all its officials with him.
The LORD has spoken.

Judgment on Judah

4 The LORD says:

I will not relent from punishing Judah
for three crimes, even four,
because they have rejected the law
of the LORD
and have not kept His statutes.
The lies that their ancestors followed
have led them astray.
5 Therefore, I will send fire against Judah,
and it will consume the citadels of Jerusalem.

---

a 1:1 Or the shepherds   b 1:2 Or dry up   c 1:5 Lit gate bars   d 1:9 Lit and did not remember

---

1:1 Tekoa. Tekoa was in a desolate area 12 miles south of Jerusalem. There Amos was a shepherd and a keeper of fig trees around 750 B.C.

1:2 roars. God's words were as fearful as a lion's roar. As a shepherd, Amos knew the power of God's words of judgment (see 3:4).

1:3 for three crimes. Amos pictured God losing patience over repeated disobedience (vv. 6,9,11,13; 2:1,4,6).

2:6 sell a righteous person. Amos admonished the Israelites for devaluing human life. God's policy of working off a debt (Deut. 15:12) was stretched into extortion.

2:8 stretch out beside every altar. Sinful Israel slept soundly on its own guilty conscience near places of pagan idol worship.

2:9 I destroyed the Amorite. God reminded Israel that they did not arrive at success by their own efforts. God had uprooted and destroyed Israel's enemies in Canaan, repre-

Judgment on Israel

6 The LORD says:

I will not relent from punishing Israel
for three crimes, even four,
because they sell a righteous person for silver
and a needy person for a pair of sandals.
7 They trample the heads of the poor
on the dust of the ground
and block the path of the needy.
A man and his father have sexual relations
with the same girl,
profaning My holy name.
8 They stretch out beside every altar
on garments taken as collateral,
and they drink in the house of their God
wine obtained through fines.

9 Yet I destroyed the Amorite as Israel advanced;
his height was like the cedars,
and he was as sturdy as the oaks;
I destroyed his fruit above and his roots beneath.
10 And I brought you from the land of Egypt
and led you 40 years in the wilderness
in order to possess the land of the Amorite.
11 I raised up some of your sons as prophets
and some of your young men as Nazirites.
Is this not the case, Israelites?

[This is]
the LORD's declaration.

12 But you made the Nazirites drink wine
and commanded the prophets:
Do not prophesy.
13 Look, I am about to crush[a] [you] in your place
as a wagon full of sheaves crushes [grain].
14 Escape will fail the swift,
the strong one will not prevail by his strength,
and the brave will not save his life.
15 The archer will not stand [his ground],
the [one who is] swift of foot
will not save himself,
and the one riding a horse will not save his life.
16 Even the most courageous of the warriors
will flee naked on that day—
the LORD's declaration.

God's Reasons for Punishing Israel

3 Listen to this message that the LORD has spoken
against you, Israelites, against the entire clan that
I brought from the land of Egypt:

2 I have known only you
out of all the clans of the earth;
therefore, I will punish you for all
your iniquities.
3 Can two walk together
without agreeing to meet?[b]
4 Does a lion roar in the forest
when it has no prey?
Does a young lion growl from its lair
unless it has captured [something]?
5 Does a bird land in a trap on the ground
if there is no bait for it?
Does a trap spring from the ground
when it has caught nothing?
6 If a ram's horn is blown in a city,
aren't people afraid?
If a disaster occurs in a city,
hasn't the LORD done it?
7 Indeed, the Lord GOD does nothing
without revealing His counsel
to His servants the prophets.
8 A lion has roared;
who will not fear?
The Lord GOD has spoken;
who will not prophesy?

9 Proclaim on the citadels in Ashdod
and on the citadels in the land of Egypt:
Assemble on the mountains of Samaria
and see the great turmoil in the city
and the acts of oppression within it.
10 The people are incapable of doing right—
the LORD's declaration—
those who store up violence and destruction
in their citadels.

11 Therefore, the Lord GOD says:

An enemy will surround the land;
he will destroy your strongholds
and plunder your citadels.

12 The LORD says:

As the shepherd snatches two legs
or a piece of an ear
from the lion's mouth,
so the Israelites who live in Samaria
will be rescued
with [only] the corner of a bed
or the[c] cushion[d] of a couch.[e]

a 2:13 Or hinder; Hb obscure b 3:3 LXX reads without meeting c 3:12 Or Israelites will be rescued, those who sit in Samaria on a corner of a bed or a d 3:12 Hb obscure e 3:12 LXX, Aq, Sym, Theod, Syr, Tg, Vg read or in Damascus

---

sented here by the formidable Amorites.

2:10 I brought you … led you. God reminded the people of their roots. They are a chosen people with high hopes and a high calling.

2:11 raised up … prophets. Amos was a living example of God's guidance. Rebelliously, Israel ignored God's messengers

and would now suffer the consequences.

2:16 on that day. Little did Israel know that Assyria would soon conquer Israel and take the nation captive.

3:2 of all the clans of the earth. God specifically and lovingly chose Israel as His own people to be a witness to the nations. How

then could Israel be so blind to its privileges and responsibilities?

3:8 lion. The lion reappears as an image of the Lord's vengeance on Israel (see also 1:2).

3:12 cushion of a couch. Amos' warnings of a lion attack fell on the lazy ears of those lounging in luxury.

13 Listen and testify against the house of Jacob—
⌊this is⌋ the declaration
of the Lord GOD,
the God of •Hosts.
14 I will punish the altars of Bethel
on the day I punish Israel for its crimes;
the horns of the altar will be cut off
and fall to the ground.
15 I will demolish the winter house
and the summer house;
the houses ⌊inlaid with⌋ ivory will be destroyed,
and the great houses will come to an end—
the LORD's declaration.

Social and Spiritual Corruption

4 Listen to this message, you cows of Bashan
who are on the hill of Samaria,
women who oppress the poor
and crush the needy,
who say to their husbands,
"Bring us something to drink."

2 The Lord GOD has sworn by His holiness:

Look, the days are coming[a]
when you will be taken away with hooks,
every last ⌊one⌋ of you with fishhooks,
3 You will go through breaches in the wall,
each woman straight ahead,
and you will be driven along toward Harmon.
⌊This is⌋
the LORD's declaration.

4 Come to Bethel and rebel;
rebel even more at Gilgal!
Bring your sacrifices every morning,
your tenths every three days.
5 Offer leavened bread as a thank offering,
and loudly proclaim your freewill offerings,
for that is what you Israelites love ⌊to do⌋!
⌊This is⌋
the LORD's declaration.

God's Discipline and Israel's Apostasy

6 I gave you absolutely nothing to eat[b]
in all your cities,
a shortage of food in all your communities,
yet you did not return to Me—
the LORD's declaration.

7 I also withheld the rain from you
while there were still three months
until harvest.

I sent rain on one city
but no rain on another.
One field received rain
while a field with no rain withered.
8 Two or three cities staggered
to another city to drink water
but were not satisfied,
yet you did not return to Me—
the LORD's declaration.

9 I struck you with blight and mildew;
the locust devoured
your many gardens and vineyards,
your fig trees and olive trees,
yet you did not return to Me—
the LORD's declaration.

10 I sent plagues like those of Egypt;
I killed your young men with the sword,
along with your captured horses.
I caused the stench of your camp
to fill your nostrils,
yet you did not return to Me—
the LORD's declaration.

11 I overthrew some of you
as I[c] overthrew Sodom and Gomorrah,
and you were like a burning stick
snatched from a fire,
yet you did not return to Me—
the LORD's declaration.

12 Therefore, Israel, that is what I will do to you,
and since I will do that to you,
Israel, prepare to meet your God!
13 He is here:
the One who forms the mountains,
creates the wind,
and reveals His[d] thoughts to man,
the One who makes the dawn out of darkness
and strides on the heights of the earth.
•Yahweh, the God of •Hosts, is His name.

Lamentation for Israel

5 Listen to this message that I am singing for you, a
lament, house of Israel:

2 She has fallen;
Virgin Israel will never rise again.
She lies abandoned on her land,
with no one to raise her up.

[a] **4:2** Lit coming on you   [b] **4:6** Lit you cleanness of teeth   [c] **4:11** Lit God   [d] **4:13** Or his

---

4:1 cows of Bashan. Bashan, a lush pastureland, catered to its cattle (Ps. 22:12). Likewise, the men of Israel pampered the needs of these luxury-loving women.

4:4 Come to Bethel ... Gilgal. Amos pinpointed holy places for worshipping Yahweh (God's self-proclaimed name). However, Is-

rael shamelessly used them as sites for engaging in sinful idol worship.
4:5 that is what you Israelites love [to do]. Israel wanted a pick-and-choose religion, rather than obeying the whole law of God.
4:6-11 Amos described five disasters in Israel's past: shortage of food (6); drought (vv.

7-8); blight and mildew (v. 9); locusts (v. 9); plagues (v. 10); God's direct judgments (v. 11). But Israel stubbornly refused to repent even after these disasters.

4:13 Amos listed God's credentials in order to remind Israel that God was fully able and prepared to carry out all He had decreed.

3 For the Lord GOD says:

The city that marches out a thousand ⌊strong⌋
will have ⌊only⌋ a hundred left,
and the one that marches out a hundred ⌊strong⌋
will have ⌊only⌋ ten left in the house of Israel.

Seek God and Live

4 For the LORD says to the house of Israel:

Seek Me and live!
5 Do not seek Bethel
or go to Gilgal
or journey to Beer-sheba,
for Gilgal will certainly go into exile,
and Bethel will come to nothing.
6 Seek •Yahweh and live,
or He will spread like fire
⌊throughout⌋ the house of Joseph;
it will consume ⌊everything,⌋
with no one at Bethel to extinguish it.
7 Those who turn justice into •wormwood
throw righteousness to the ground.

8 The One who made the Pleiades and Orion,
who turns darknessᵃ into dawn
and darkens day into night,
who summons the waters of the sea
and pours them out over the face of the earth—
Yahweh is His name.
9 He brings destructionᵇ on the strong,ᶜ
and it falls on the stronghold.

10 They hate the one who convicts ⌊the guilty⌋
at the city •gate
and despise the one who speaks with integrity.
11 Therefore, because you trample on the poor
and exact a grain tax from him,
you will never live in the houses of cut stone
you have built;
you will never drink the wine
from the lush vineyards
you have planted.
12 For I know your crimes are many
and your sins innumerable.
They oppress the righteous, take a bribe,
and deprive the poor of justice at the gates.
13 Therefore, the wise person will keep silent
at such a time,
for the days are evil.

14 Seek good and not evil
so that you may live,
and the LORD, the God of •Hosts,
will be with you,
as you have claimed.
15 Hate evil and love good;
establish justice in the gate.
Perhaps the LORD, the God of Hosts,
will be gracious
to the remnant of Joseph.

16 Therefore Yahweh, the God of Hosts, the Lord,
says:

There will be wailing in all the public squares;
they will cry out in anguishᵈ in all the streets.
The farmer will be called on to mourn,
and professional mournersᵉ to wail.
17 There will be wailing in all the vineyards,
for I will pass among you.
The LORD has spoken.

The Day of the LORD

18 Woe to you who long for the Day of the LORD!
What will the Day of the LORD be for you?
It will be darkness and not light.
19 It will be like a man who flees from a lion
only to have a bear confront him.
He goes home and rests his hand against the wall
only to have a snake bite him.
20 Won't the Day of the LORD
be darkness rather than light,
even gloom without any brightness in it?
21 I hate, I despise your feasts!
I can't stand the stench
of your solemn assemblies.
22 Even if you offer Me
your •burnt offerings and •grain offerings,
I will not accept ⌊them⌋;
I will have no regard
for your •fellowship offerings of fattened cattle.
23 Take away from Me the noise of your songs!
I will not listen to the music of your harps.
24 But let justice flow like water,
and righteousness, like an unfailing stream.

25 "House of Israel, was it sacrifices and grain offerings that you presented to Me during the 40 years in the wilderness? 26 But you have taken upᶠ Sakkuthᵍ ʰ your kingⁱ and Kaiwanʲ ᵏ your star god, images you have

---

ᵃ**5:8** Or *turns the shadow of death*   ᵇ**5:9** Hb obscure   ᶜ**5:9** Or *stronghold*   ᵈ**5:16** Lit *it will say, "Alas! Alas!"*   ᵉ**5:16** Lit *and those skilled in lamentation*   ᶠ**5:26** Or *you will lift up*   ᵍ**5:26** LXX, Sym, Syr, Vg read *the tent*; Ac 7:43   ʰ**5:26** Lit *Sikkuth*; probably a Mesopotamian war god also called Adar or Ninurta   ⁱ**5:26** LXX, Vg read *up the tent of Molech*; Ac 7:43   ʲ**5:26** LXX reads *Rephan*; Ac 7:43   ᵏ**5:26** Lit *Kiyyun*; probably a Mesopotamian god identified with Saturn

---

5:7 justice into wormwood. Wormwood is a metaphor for bitterness.

5:8-9 The One. Amos beautifully reminds the people of God's incredible power—the omnipotence with which they were dealing.

5:11 trample on the poor. Amos exposed the social injustice against the poor (2:7).

5:16-17 wailing ... anguish. Vineyards, which typically represented bounty and gladness, would now be sites of sorrow (Isa. 16:10). God's presence among them would bring sadness over their plight, and not comfort.

5:18 Day of the Lord. Amos describes a future day of God's ultimate victory over evil (Isa. 5:19) **darkness.** A day that Israel thought would bring reward to God's people would instead bring unexpected doom (Joel 2:1-2).

5:21-23 stench ... noise. Even Israel's intentions were not pure. Hypocrisy tainted every religious effort.

made for yourselves. ²⁷ So I will send you into exile beyond Damascus." Yahweh, the God of Hosts, is His name. He has spoken.

Woe to the Complacent

6 Woe to those who are at ease in Zion
and to those who feel secure on the hill
of Samaria—
the notable people in this first of the nations,
those the house of Israel comes to.

2 Cross over to Calneh and see;
go from there to great Hamath;
then go down to Gath of the Philistines.
Are you better than these kingdoms?
Is their territory larger than yours?

3 You dismiss any thought of the evil day
and bring in a reign of violence.

4 They lie on beds [inlaid with] ivory,
sprawled out on their couches,
and dine on lambs from the flock
and calves from the stall.

5 They improvise songs^a to the sound
of the harp
and invent^b their own musical instruments
like David.

6 They drink wine by the bowlful
and anoint themselves with the finest oils
but do not grieve over the ruin of Joseph.

7 Therefore, they will now go into exile
as the first of the captives,
and the feasting of those who sprawl out
will come to an end.

Israel's Pride Judged

8 The Lord GOD has sworn by Himself—the declaration of •Yahweh, the God of •Hosts:

I loathe Jacob's pride
and hate his citadels,
so I will hand over the city and everything
in it.

9 And if there are 10 men left in one house, they will die. 10 A close relative^c and a burner,^d will remove his corpse^e from the house. He will call to someone in the inner recesses of the house, "Any more with you?"

That person will reply, "None."

Then he will say, "Silence, because Yahweh's name must not be invoked."

11 For the LORD commands:

The large house will be smashed to pieces,
and the small house to rubble.

12 Do horses run on rock,
or does someone plow [it] with oxen?^f
Yet you have turned justice into poison
and the fruit of righteousness
into •wormwood—

13 you who rejoice over Lo-debar
and say, "Didn't we capture Karnaim
for ourselves by our own strength?"

14 But look, I am raising up a nation
against you, house of Israel—
[this is] the declaration
of the Lord,
the GOD of Hosts—
and they will oppress you
from the entrance of Hamath^g
to the Brook of the •Arabah.^h

First Vision: Locusts

7 The Lord GOD showed me this: He was forming a swarm of locusts at the time the spring crop first began to sprout—after the cutting of the king's hay. 2 When the locusts finished eating the vegetation of the land, I said, "Lord GOD, please forgive! How will Jacob survive since he is so small?"

3 The LORD relented concerning this. "It will not happen," He said.

Second Vision: Fire

4 The Lord GOD showed me this: The Lord GOD was calling for a judgment by fire. It consumed the great deep and devoured the land. 5 Then I said, "Lord GOD, please stop! How will Jacob survive since he is so small?"

6 The LORD relented concerning this. "This will not happen either," said the Lord GOD.

Third Vision: A Plumb Line

7 He showed me this: The Lord was standing there by a vertical wall with a plumb line in His hand. 8 The LORD asked me, "What do you see, Amos?"

I replied, "A plumb line."

Then the Lord said, "I am setting a plumb line among My people Israel; I will no longer spare them:

9 Isaac's •high places will be deserted,
and Israel's sanctuaries will be in ruins;
I will rise up against the house of Jeroboam
with a sword."

^a**6:5** Hb obscure   ^b**6:5** Or *compose on*   ^c**6:10** Lit *His uncle*   ^d**6:10** Or *burner of incense, or burner of a memorial fire, or burner of a body;* Hb obscure   ^e**6:10** Lit *remove bones*   ^f**6:12** Others emend to *plow the sea*   ^g**6:14** Or *from Lebo-hamath;* 2 Kg 14:25,28   ^h**6:14** Probably the Valley of Zared at the southeast end of the Dead Sea

5:24 like an unfailing stream. Israel's dried-up enthusiasm for its religious traditions should have been replaced by a recommitment to justice to the poor which could have brought peaceful living.

6:10-11 corpse … smashed to pieces … rubble. Amos described devastating vengeance

on the citizens of the Northern Kingdom.

6:10 must not be invoked. The Lord's destruction would be so severe even a survivor would not be allowed to mention the Lord's name. Doing so might incur God's wrath.

6:13 by our own strength. Israel may have won the battles in nearby cities, but it would

soon lose the war to conquering Assyria.

7:1 the Lord God showed me. God spoke to Amos in a dramatic vision, which Amos communicated to the people: doom for their next crops. Remember that they lived in dependency on each year's crop.

7:8 plumb line. A plumb line is an essential

Amaziah's Opposition

[10] Amaziah the priest of Bethel sent ⌊word⌋ to Jeroboam king of Israel, saying, "Amos has conspired against you ⌊right here⌋ in the house of Israel. The land cannot endure all his words, [11] for Amos has said this: 'Jeroboam will die by the sword, and Israel will certainly go into exile from its homeland.' "

[12] Then Amaziah said to Amos, "Go away, you seer! Flee to the land of Judah. Earn your living[a] and give ⌊your⌋ prophecies there, [13] but don't ever prophesy at Bethel again, for it is the king's sanctuary and a royal temple."

[14] So Amos answered Amaziah, "I was[b] not a prophet or the son of a prophet;[c] rather, I was[d] a herdsman, and I took care of sycamore figs. [15] But the LORD took me from following the flock and said to me, 'Go, prophesy to My people Israel.' "

[16] Now hear the word of the LORD. You say:

Do not prophesy against Israel;
do not preach against the house of Isaac.

[17] Therefore, this is what the LORD says:

Your wife will be a prostitute in the city,
your sons and daughters will fall by the sword,
and your land will be divided up
with a measuring line.
You yourself will die on pagan[e] soil,
and Israel will certainly go into exile
from its homeland.

Fourth Vision: A Basket of Summer Fruit

8 The Lord GOD showed me this: A basket of summer fruit. [2] He asked me, "What do you see, Amos?"

I replied, "A basket of summer fruit."

The LORD said to me, "The end has come for My people Israel; I will no longer spare them. [3] In that day the temple[f] songs will become wailing"—the Lord GOD's declaration. "Many dead bodies, thrown everywhere! Silence!"

[4] Hear this, you who trample on the needy
and do away with the poor of the land,
[5] asking, "When will the New Moon be over
so we may sell grain,
and the Sabbath,
so we may market wheat?
We can reduce the measure
while increasing the price[g]

and cheat with dishonest scales.
[6] We can buy the poor with silver
and the needy for a pair of sandals
and even sell the wheat husks!"

[7] The LORD has sworn by the Pride of Jacob:[h]

I will never forget all their deeds.
[8] Because of this, won't the land quake
and all who dwell in it mourn?
All of it will rise like the Nile;
it will surge and then subside
like the Nile in Egypt.

[9] And in that day—

⌊this is⌋ the declaration
of the Lord GOD—

I will make the sun go down at noon;
I will darken the land in the daytime.
[10] I will turn your feasts into mourning
and all your songs into lamentation;
I will cause everyone[i] to wear •sackcloth
and every head to be shaved.
I will make that grief
like mourning for an only son
and its outcome like a bitter day.

[11] Hear this! The days are coming—

⌊this is⌋ the declaration
of the Lord GOD—

when I will send a famine through the land:
not a famine of bread or a thirst for water,
but of hearing the words of the LORD.
[12] People will stagger from sea to sea
and roam from north to east,
seeking the word of the LORD,
but they will not find it.
[13] In that day the beautiful young women,
the young men also, will faint from thirst.
[14] Those who swear by the guilt of Samaria
and say, "As your god lives, Dan,"
or "As the way[j] [k] of Beer-sheba lives"—
they will fall, never to rise again.

Fifth Vision: The LORD beside the Altar

9 I saw the LORD standing beside the altar, and He said:

Strike the capitals of the pillars
so that the thresholds shake;
knock them down on the heads of all the people.
Then I will kill the rest of them with the sword.

---

[a]**7:12** Lit *Eat bread* [b]**7:14** Or *am* [c]**7:14** = a prophet's disciple or a member of a prophetic guild; 2 Kg 2:3–15; 4:38; 9:1 [d]**7:14** Or *am* [e]**7:17** Lit *unclean* [f]**8:3** Or *palace* [g]**8:5** Lit *reduce the ephah and make the shekel great* [h]**8:7** = the LORD or the promised land; Am 6:8; Ps 47:4; Nah 2:2 [i]**8:10** Lit *every loin* [j]**8:14** LXX reads *god* [k]**8:14** Or *power*

---

carpenter's tool, composed of a weighted string used to accurately create a straight wall. This symbol highlights Israel's crookedness versus God's holiness (straightness).

7:11 Jeroboam will die. Amaziah mistook Amos' spiritual exhortation as a political threat against the king.

7:17 prostitute in the city. In the end, Amaziah's intolerance for Amos' warnings would result in his total loss. Amaziah's abandoned wife would resort to prostitution in order to support herself. His children would die violently, and his land would be scattered. Amaziah had repeated these same words in verse 11.

8:2 basket of summer fruit. What seemed an innocent image of ready-to-eat fruit was actually a picture of impending punishment.

8:6 buy the poor with silver. God reiterated the oppressive situation Israel's extortion

None of those who flee will get away;
none of their fugitives will escape.
2 If they dig down to •Sheol,
from there My hand will take them;
if they climb up to heaven,
from there I will bring them down.
3 If they hide themselves
on the top of Carmel,
from there I will track them down
and seize them;
if they conceal themselves
from My sight on the sea floor,
from there I will command
the ⌊sea⌋ serpent to bite them.
4 And if they are driven
by their enemies into captivity,
from there I will command
the sword to kill them.
I will fix My eyes on them
for harm and not for good.
5 The Lord, the GOD of •Hosts—
He touches the earth;
it melts, and all who dwell on it mourn;
all of it rises like the Nile
and subsides like the Nile of Egypt.
6 He builds His upper chambers
in the heavens
and lays the foundation of His vault
on the earth.
He summons the waters of the sea
and pours them out on the face of the earth.
•Yahweh is His name.

Announcement of Judgment

7 Israelites, are you not like the •Cushites to Me?
⌊This is⌋
the LORD's declaration.
Didn't I bring Israel from the land of Egypt,
the Philistines from Caphtor,[a]
and the Arameans from Kir?
8 Look, the eyes of the Lord GOD
are on the sinful kingdom,
and I will destroy it

from the face of the earth.
However, I will not totally destroy
the house of Jacob—
the LORD's declaration—
9 for I am about to give the command,
and I will shake the house of Israel
among all the nations,
as one shakes a sieve,
but not a pebble will fall to the ground.
10 All the sinners among My people,
who say: Disaster will never overtake[b]
or confront us,
will die by the sword.

Announcement of Restoration

11 In that day
I will restore the fallen booth of David:
I will repair its gaps,
restore its ruins,
and rebuild it as in the days of old,
12 so that they may possess
the remnant of Edom
and all the nations
that are called by My name[c]—
⌊this is⌋
the LORD's declaration—
He will do this.

13 Hear this! The days are coming—
the LORD's declaration—
when the plowman will overtake the reaper
and the one who treads grapes,
the sower of seed.
The mountains will drip with sweet wine,
and all the hills will flow ⌊with it⌋.
14 I will restore the fortunes of My people Israel.[d]
They will rebuild and occupy ruined cities,
plant vineyards and drink their wine,
make gardens and eat their produce.
15 I will plant them on their land,
and they will never again be uprooted
from the land I have given them.
Yahweh your God has spoken.

---

[a]9:7 = Crete; Dt 2:23; Jr 47:4 [b]9:10 Or You will not let disaster come near [c]9:12 LXX reads so that the remnant of man and all the nations . . . may seek [Me]; Ac 15:17 [d]9:14 Or restore My people Israel from captivity

---

among the poor had caused. Crimes against a seemingly insignificant sector of society resulted in large-scale devastation (2:6). God's concern for the poor and justice are strong themes seen throughout the entire Bible.

9:1 I saw the Lord. Amos' final vision is one of destruction (vv. 1-10) and hope for what is yet to come (vv. 11-15).

9:2-4 if they hide themselves. The fugitives in this vision instinctively hide. However, there is no refuge from God's wrath (See also Ps. 139:7-8).

9:8 not totally destroy. What was only hinted at earlier (5:15) was now confirmed. A remnant of people would remain as a symbol of hope.

9:11 I will repair. Amos' words are pure refreshment to those who would repent and turn back to God's ways.

9:12 Edom. Edom was Israel's greatest enemy at the time, as far as Israel was concerned. Conquering Edom represented complete victory for Israel.

9:13-15 plowman will overtake the reaper. Contrasting an earlier description of agricultural disaster (4:6-11), Amos now portrays a farmer's fantasy. God restores the land so that the people could hardly keep up with its bounty.

9:14 restore. A once devastated people, God would rebuild their lives from the ground up as a symbol of their restoration.

INTRODUCTION TO
OBADIAH

PERSONAL READING PLAN

❑ Obadiah 1-21

AUTHOR

This short book is referred to as the "vision of Obadiah" (v. 1). This prophet's name means "the servant of the LORD." While there are 11 other Old Testament characters with this name, none of them can be identified with this prophet.

DATE

The date of composition is uncertain, depending upon which of these two events in Israel's history correlates with verses 11-14:

(1) The Philistine invasion of Jerusalem during the reign of Jehoram (853-841 B.C.; see 2 Chron. 21:8-20). If this event is referred to, Obadiah would be a ninth-century contemporary of Elisha.

(2) The Babylonian campaign against Jerusalem (605-585 B.C.), in which case Obadiah would be a sixth-century contemporary of Jeremiah. The latter seems more likely.

THEME

God's judgment of proud Edom and the restoration of Israel.

HISTORICAL BACKGROUND

The Edomites apparently took advantage of the fall of Jerusalem to Babylon in 586 B.C. They plundered the land and looted the homes of survivors. Obadiah speaks God's judgment on Edom for the way they took advantage of "brother Jacob" in his moment of weakness. The term

"Edom" is used in the Old Testament for the name of Esau (the brother of Jacob) and for the race made up of his descendants. The area this tribe occupied was originally the land of Seir. It was a rugged, mountainous region that extended from the Dead Sea south to the Gulf of Aqabah. The hatred and hostility between Edom and Israel was long-standing. The history of the blood feud between the two peoples can be traced by a study of the relevant Old Testament passages (see Gen. 27:41-45; 32:1-21; 33; Num. 20:14-21; Deut. 2:1-6; 2 Sam. 8:13-14; 2 Kings 8:20-22; Ezek. 35).

Edom was known for sitting smugly in her fortified cities atop rocky clefts, and Obadiah prophesies against her for relying on this for her sense of security. In the fifth century the Edomites were driven out of their own land by the Nabateans. After this, many Edomites moved into southern Palestine.

CHARACTERISTICS

Obadiah is the shortest book in all of the Old Testament. While other prophets often announced oracles directed at other nations (along with their words for Israel), nearly the whole Book of Obadiah consists of the words of a Jewish prophet to another country. In this respect Obadiah is like Nahum, who preached against Nineveh. With respect to language, Obadiah is like Jeremiah (compare vv. 1-9 with Jer. 49:7-22), which suggests interdependence on an unknown third source. The language of this book is characterized by vivid and striking metaphors (see vv. 4,5,16,18).

The vision of Obadiah.

Edom's Certain Judgment

This is what the Lord GOD has said about Edom:

We have heard a message from the LORD;
an envoy has been sent among the nations:
Rise up, and let us go to war against her.[a]

2 Look, I will make you insignificant
among the nations;
you will be deeply despised.

3 Your presumptuous heart has deceived you,
you who live in clefts of the rock[b]
in your home on the heights,
who say to yourself:
Who can bring me down to the ground?

4 Though you seem to soar[c] like an eagle
and make your nest among the stars,
even from there I will bring you down.
[This is] the LORD's declaration.

5 If thieves came to you,
if marauders by night—
how ravaged you will be!—
wouldn't they steal only what they wanted?
If grape pickers came to you,
wouldn't they leave some grapes?

6 How Esau will be pillaged,
his hidden treasures searched out!

7 Everyone who has a treaty with you
will drive you to the border;
everyone at peace with you
will deceive and conquer you.
Those who eat your bread
will set[d] a trap for you.
He will be unaware of it.

8 In that day—
the LORD's declaration—
will I not eliminate the wise ones of Edom
and those who understand
from the hill country of Esau?

9 Teman,[e] your warriors will be terrified
so that everyone from the hill country of Esau
will be destroyed by slaughter.

Edom's Sins against Judah

10 You will be covered with shame
and destroyed forever
because of violence done to your brother Jacob.

11 On the day you stood aloof,
on the day strangers captured his wealth,[f]
while foreigners entered his •gate
and cast lots for Jerusalem,
you were just like one of them.

12 Do not gloat[g] over your brother
in the day of his calamity;
do not rejoice over the people of Judah
in the day of their destruction;
do not boastfully mock[h]
in the day of distress.

13 Do not enter the gate of My people
in the day of their disaster.
Yes, you—do not gloat over their misery
in the day of their disaster
and do not appropriate their possessions
in the day of their disaster.

14 Do not stand at the crossroads[i]
to cut off their fugitives,
and do not hand over their survivors
in the day of distress.

Judgment of the Nations

15 For the Day of the LORD is near,
against all the nations.
As you have done, so it will be done to you;
what you deserve will return on your own head.

16 For as you have drunk on My holy mountain,
so all the nations will drink[j] continually.
They will drink and gulp down
and be as though they had never been.

17 But there will be a deliverance on Mount Zion,
and it will be holy;
the house of Jacob will dispossess
those who dispossessed them.[k]

18 Then the house of Jacob will be a [blazing] fire,
and the house of Joseph a [burning] flame,
but the house of Esau will be stubble;
they[l] will set them on fire and consume them.[a]
Therefore no survivor will remain
of the house of Esau,
for the LORD has spoken.

Future Blessing for Israel

19 [People from] the •Negev will possess
the hill country of Esau;
[those from] the Judean foothills will possess
[the land of] the Philistines.
They[l] will possess
the territories of Ephraim and Samaria,

---

[a]**1,18** = Edom [b]**3** Or *in Sela*; probably = Petra; Jdg 1:36; 2 Kg 14:7; Is 16:1 [c]**4** Or *to build high* [d]**7** Some LXX mss, Sym, Tg, Vg; MT reads *They will set your bread as* [e]**9** = a region or city in Edom [f]**11** Or *forces* [g]**12–14** Or *You should not have gloated . . .* (using the same form *You should not have . . .* in each of the following 8 commands) [h]**12** Lit *not make your mouth big* [i]**14** Hb obscure [j]**16** = drink a cup of judgment [k]**17** DSS, LXX, Syr, Vg, Tg; MT reads *Jacob will possess its inheritance* [l]**18,19** = the house of Jacob

---

1 let us go to war. An envoy had been sent to the nations, urging them to rise up against the nation of Edom. The prophet, Obadiah, announces that God is stirring up other nations to judge Edom for its arrogance and hostility toward Israel.

4 like an eagle. Eagles symbolized strength and pride. Edom was considered a powerful, and even invincible nation.

5-6 Esau. Another name used for Edom because the nation descended from Esau, Jacob's older brother (Gen. 25ff). Edom would be completely desolated because of their attacks against Israel. Although Israelites were commanded to leave a little bit behind for the poor, all of Edom's hidden treasures would be carried away.

15 Day of the Lord. The Day of the Lord will bring judgment for all nations, not just Edom. Edom's imminent humiliation foreshadows God's judgment on all nations.

while Benjamin will possess Gilead.
20 The exiles of the Israelites who are in Halah[a]
who are among the Canaanites
as far as Zarephath
and the exiles of Jerusalem who are in Sepharad

will possess the cities of the Negev.
21 Saviors[b] will ascend Mount Zion
to rule over the hill country
of Esau,
but the kingdom will be the LORD's.

---

[a]20 Or of this host of the Israelites; Hb obscure   [b]21 Or Those who have been delivered

---

16 drunk on My holy mountain. The Lord was angry with the Edomites for holding a drunken celebration in Jerusalem, God's holy habitation. But, all the other nations who have opposed Israel will also feel God's wrath.

19 possess the hill country. Other peoples will occupy Edom's land, probably the remnant of Israel described in verse 20.

21 Saviors. Also could be translated as "forces." The Hebrews who have been taken away as captives will return as victors and rule over Edom. **the kingdom will be the LORD's.** Edom will not be beyond the reach of God, despite their arrogance. Once Israel returns to overcome Edom, God will rule.

INTRODUCTION TO
JONAH

PERSONAL READING PLAN

- ☐ Jonah 1:1-17
- ☐ Jonah 2:1-10

- ☐ Jonah 3:1-10
- ☐ Jonah 4:1-11

AUTHOR

The prophet Jonah originally told the story of this book, though others may have written it down. The author is not identified in the text.

DATE

The book was written sometime after Jonah's ministry circa 800-770 B.C., before Nineveh's destruction (612 B.C.) and Samaria's fall (722-721 B.C.).

THEME

God's love for the Gentiles, even Nineveh.

HISTORICAL BACKGROUND

Israel had just restored her northern borders under King Jeroboam II (793-753 B.C.), as Jonah had prophesied (2 Kings 14:25). At this time, Israel was politically secure, spiritually smug, and morally corrupt. Nineveh, the city to which Jonah was sent by God, was the capital of Assyria. Assyria was a ruthless empire that threatened tiny Israel, and eventually conquered it in 722 B.C. Nineveh was 500 miles east of Joppa, but Jonah boarded a ship heading 2,000 miles west, revealing how desperately Jonah wanted to get away from a people he despised. The Israelites had many reasons to hate the proud Ninevites, as Nahum points out in a

prophecy dedicated exclusively to the Ninevites (see the Introduction to Nahum). Nineveh's repentance and revival under Jonah was short-lived. The second time around for proud, cruel Nineveh resulted in her fall in 612 B.C and they were never heard from again.

CHARACTERISTICS

Unlike most other Old Testament prophetic books, Jonah gives an account of a single incident in the life of the prophet. The story is briefly told in some 40 verses. His prayer consumes the remaining eight verses. Some regard this book as an imaginative tale, akin to a modern "fish story." Others view Jonah as an allegory or parable, teaching God's universal love. However, the Jews accepted this book as reflecting the experience of the actual prophet Jonah. And Jesus' refers to Jonah (Matt. 12:38-41) substantiating that the book recounts actual events. Jonah's missionary message finds later parallels in the message of Peter (see Acts 10:1-11:18) and Paul (see Rom. 9-11). The theological emphases in Jonah (on God's universal love, sovereignty, and redemption) are equally applicable today.

PASSAGES FOR
TOPICAL GROUP STUDY

Jonah's Flight

1 The word of the LORD came to Jonah son of Amittai: ² "Get up! Go to the great city of Nineveh and preach against it, because their wickedness has confronted Me." ³ However, Jonah got up to flee to Tarshish from the LORD's presence. He went down to Joppa and found a ship going to Tarshish. He paid the fare and went down into it to go with them to Tarshish, from the LORD's presence.

Running Away

1. Did you ever try to run away from home? How far did you get?

Jonah 1:1-17

2. Why did Jonah try to run away from God?
3. How did Jonah's disobedience endanger innocent people? In what way did the sailors, who didn't know God, act in a more godly way than Jonah?
4. When have you tried to run away from God? With what results?
5. When have you acted less godly than people who aren't even Christians? How did that damage God's reputation in your school or community?
6. How did God show grace toward Jonah? How has He shown grace toward you?

⁴ Then the LORD hurled a violent wind on the sea, and such a violent storm arose on the sea that the ship threatened to break apart. ⁵ The sailors were afraid, and each cried out to his god. They threw the ship's cargo into the sea to lighten the load. Meanwhile, Jonah had gone down to the lowest part of the vessel and had stretched out and fallen into a deep sleep.

⁶ The captain approached him and said, "What are you doing sound asleep? Get up! Call to your god.ᵃ Maybe this god will consider us, and we won't perish."

⁷ "Come on!" the sailors said to each other. "Let's cast lots. Then we will know who is to blame for this trouble we're in." So they cast lots, and the lot singled out Jonah. ⁸ Then they said to him, "Tell us who is to blame for this trouble we're in. What is your business and where are you from? What is your country and what people are you from?"

⁹ He answered them, "I am a Hebrew. I worshipᵇ •Yahweh, the God of the heavens, who made the sea and the dry land."

¹⁰ Then the men were even more afraid and said to him, "What is this you've done?" For the men knew he was fleeing from the LORD's presence, because he had told them. ¹¹ So they said to him, "What should we do to you to calm this sea that's against us?" For the sea was getting worse and worse.

¹² He answered them, "Pick me up and throw me into the seaᶜ so it may quiet down for you, for I know that I'm to blame for this violent storm that is against you." ¹³ Nevertheless, the men rowed hard to get back to dry land, but they could not because the sea was raging against them more and more.

¹⁴ So they called out to the LORD: "Please, Yahweh, don't let us perish because of this man's life, and don't charge us with innocent blood! For You, Yahweh, have done just as You pleased." ¹⁵ Then they picked up Jonah and threw him into the sea, and the sea stopped its raging. ¹⁶ The men •feared the LORD even more, and they offered a sacrifice to the LORD and made vows. ¹⁷ᵈ Then the LORD appointed a great fish to swallow Jonah, and Jonah was inᵉ the fish three days and three nights.

Jonah's Prayer

2 Jonah prayed to the LORD his God from insideᶠ the fish:

²   I called to the LORD in my distress,
     and He answered me.
     I cried out for help in the belly of •Sheol;
     You heard my voice.
³   You threw me into the depths,
     into the heart of the seas,
     and the currentᵍ overcame me.
     All Your breakers and Your billows
       swept over me.
⁴   But I said: I have been banished
     from Your sight,
     yet I will look once moreʰ
     toward Your holy temple.
⁵   The waters engulfed me up to the neck;ⁱ
     the watery depths overcame me;
     seaweed was wrapped around my head.
⁶   I sank to the foundations of the mountains;
     the earth with its prison bars closed
       behind me forever!
     But You raised my life from the •Pit,
     LORD my God!

ᵃ**1:6** Or *God*   ᵇ**1:9** Or *fear*   ᶜ**1:12** Lit *sea that's against you*   ᵈ**1:17** Jnh 2:1 in Hb   ᵉ**1:17** Lit *in the belly of*   ᶠ**2:1** Lit *from the belly of*   ᵍ**2:3** Lit *river*   ʰ**2:4** LXX reads *said: Indeed, will I look . . . ?*   ⁱ**2:5** Or *me, threatening my life*

1:2 wickedness. Nineveh's wickedness is described in generic terms, but elsewhere we learn that they were "self-assured " (Zeph. 2:15), arrogantly declaring themselves to be invincible. Nahum later wrote that the city was brutal to war captives, and full of prostitution, witchcraft, and idolatry (Nah. 3:1-4).

1:3 going to Tarshish. Many scholars locate this city in the south of Spain. It was the most distant place known to the Israelites, in the opposite direction from Nineveh. Jonah was trying to get as far away from God's call as he could.

1:4 the LORD hurled a violent wind on the

sea. Jonah attempted unsuccessfully to runs away from God's presence.

1:16 The men feared the LORD. The pagan sailors who worshiped many gods could see that the God of Israel was more powerful. Note the contrast between Jonah's disobedience and the pagan sailors' respect for God.

A Big Fish Story

1. What is the biggest fish you have ever caught?

Jonah 2:1–3:10

2. How did Jonah react when he found himself inside the belly of a fish? How does this demonstrate that God allowed this for Jonah's own good?

3. How did Nineveh respond when they heard God's commands? How did this compare with Jonah's response?

4. Why did God "relent" from the disaster He was going to send to Nineveh? What did He want from those people in the first place (3:10)?

5. Is God asking you for obedience in some area of your life? How are you responding?

7   As my life was fading away,
    I remembered the LORD.
    My prayer came to You,
    to Your holy temple.
8   Those who cling to worthless idols
    forsake faithful love,
9   but as for me, I will sacrifice to You
    with a voice of thanksgiving.
    I will fulfill what I have vowed.
    Salvation[a] is from the LORD!

10 Then the LORD commanded the fish, and it vomited Jonah onto dry land.

Jonah's Preaching

3 Then the word of the LORD came to Jonah a second time: 2 "Get up! Go to the great city of Nineveh and preach the message that I tell you." 3 So Jonah got up and went to Nineveh according to the LORD's command.

Now Nineveh was an extremely large city,[b] a three-day walk.[c] 4 Jonah set out on the first day of his walk in the city and proclaimed, "In 40 days Nineveh will be overthrown!" 5 The men of Nineveh believed in God.[d] They proclaimed a fast and dressed in •sackcloth—from the greatest of them to the least.

6 When word reached the king of Nineveh, he got up from his throne, took off his royal robe, put on sack-cloth, and sat in ashes. 7 Then he issued a decree in Nineveh:

By order of the king and his nobles: No man or beast, herd or flock, is to taste anything at all. They must not eat or drink water. 8 Furthermore, both man and beast must be covered with sack-cloth, and everyone must call out earnestly to God. Each must turn from his evil ways and from the violence[e] he is doing.[f] 9 Who knows? God may turn and relent; He may turn from His burning anger so that we will not perish.

10 Then God saw their actions—that they had turned from their evil ways—so God relented from the disaster He had threatened to do to them. And He did not do it.

To Pout or Not to Pout?

1. Who is your biggest rival in school sports? Would you be happy if God started to do a great work among the players on that team?

Jonah 4:1–11

2. Why was Jonah angry that God spared Nineveh? Why did he react by pouting?

3. Why did God create a plant to give Jonah shade and then kill the plant?

4. Summarize in your own words what God said to Jonah in verses 10 and 11.

5. In what situations do you sometimes care more about your own comfort and blessings than about other people—friends or rivals?

Jonah's Anger

4 But Jonah was greatly displeased and became furious. 2 He prayed to the LORD: "Please, LORD, isn't this what I said while I was still in my own country? That's why I fled toward Tarshish in the first place. I knew that You are a merciful and compassionate God, slow to become angry, rich in faithful love, and One who relents from ⌊sending⌋ disaster. 3 And now, LORD, please take my life from me, for it is better for me to die than to live."

4 The LORD asked, "Is it right for you to be angry?"

---

[a] **2:9** Or *Deliverance*   [b] **3:3** Or *was a great city to God*   [c] **3:3** Probably = the time required to cover the city on foot   [d] **3:5** Or *believed God*   [e] **3:8** Or *injustice*   [f] **3:8** Lit *violence in their hands*

2:9 what I have vowed. In response to God's salvation, Jonah made a vow to praise and obey God.

3:5 The men of Nineveh believed. Much to Jonah's astonishment, the Ninevites repented. People from all classes of society put on sackcloth as a symbol of repentance.

Their repentance was short-lived, however, since they soon violently destroyed Israel.

3:9 God may turn and relent. The king knew that Nineveh's future lay in God's hands. Repentance did not guarantee survival however, because the final decision was up to God.

4:1 Jonah was greatly displeased. God's compassion on Nineveh angered Jonah. God should punish this evil city, Jonah surmised. He preached reluctantly, hoping that the obstinate Ninevites would get the punishment they deserved … with no mercy.

4:3 better for me to die. Jonah was so dis-

5 Jonah left the city and sat down east of it. He made himself a shelter there and sat in its shade to see what would happen to the city. 6 Then the LORD God appointed a plant,a and it grew up to provide shade over Jonah's head to ease his discomfort.b Jonah was greatly pleased with the plant. 7 When dawn came the next day, God appointed a worm that attacked the plant, and it withered.

8 As the sun was rising, God appointed a scorching east wind. The sun beat down on Jonah's head so that he almost fainted, and he wanted to die. He said, "It's better for me to die than to live."

9 Then God asked Jonah, "Is it right for you to be angry about the plant?"

"⌊Yes,⌋" he replied. "It is right. I'm angry enough to die!"

10 So the LORD said, "You cared about the plant, which you did not labor over and did not grow. It appeared in a night and perished in a night. 11 Should I not care about the great city of Nineveh, which has more than 120,000 peoplec who cannot distinguish between their right and their left, as well as many animals?"

---

a 4:6 = either a castor-oil plant or a climbing gourd   b 4:6 Lit to deliver him from his evil   c 4:11 Or men

---

appointed in God's mercy to the Ninevites that he wanted to die. Perhaps he thought that Israel had lost its favored standing with God, since Nineveh was such an enemy to Israel. Or he may have been embarrassed that his threats were not carried out.

4:10-11 You cared about the plant, which you did not labor over. God uses the vine to show Jonah how misplaced his affections were. Jonah did not truly care for the plant; only for the physical comfort it gave him. A gardener who cared for a plant would have

reason to regret its loss. Likewise God, whose love extends to all people, had even more reason to show compassion on Nineveh. Jonah had to acknowledge God's missionary heart: repentance and salvation are for all people.

MICAH

PERSONAL READING PLAN

☐ Micah 1:1-16
☐ Micah 2:1-13
☐ Micah 3:1-4:5

☐ Micah 4:6-5:15
☐ Micah 6:1-16
☐ Micah 7:1-20

AUTHOR

The author is identified as Micah, a contemporary of Isaiah and Hosea, who was probably from Moresheth-gath (1:14).

DATE

These prophecies were given during the reigns of Jotham, Ahaz, and Hezekiah (1:1)–kings of Judah who reigned circa 750-686 B.C. Since Micah predicted the fall of Israel's capital, Samaria (1:6-7), which occurred in circa 722 B.C., these prophecies would date from before that time.

THEME

A just and merciful God delivers His people from darkness. The lives of God's covenant people should reflect God's standards.

HISTORICAL BACKGROUND

It is helpful to understand the life and times during which Micah prophesied (1:1; see 2 Kings 15:32-20:21). During this dark time when the sins of the northern kingdom of Israel were being punished by Assyrian invaders, Micah could see that these same activities (idolatry, Baal worship, child sacrifice, sorcery) were creeping south to Judah and Jerusalem. As in the northern kingdom, this led to an increasing gap between the rich and the poor. The poor were oppressed with no recourse in the courts, because of corrupt judges, so Micah championed their cause. Religious life flourished but had little depth or reality. Micah draws a sharp contrast between this "pop religion" and true faith, which involves justice, faithfulness, and walking with God (6:8).

CHARACTERISTICS

Against this background, judgment is inevitable, says Micah. He stresses that God hates idolatry, injustice, rebellion, and empty ritualism. However, judgment will be followed by restoration, which will prepare the way for a new future. Micah emphasizes God's undeserved grace toward His people and His unstoppable initiative. Micah holds a long view of history, looking ahead several thousand years and intersperses this futuristic view in his prophecies. One moment he is talking about the promised Messiah; in the next fragment of verses he may focus on the imminent invasion of Assyria. Reading these short speeches with their rapid shifts of focus can be confusing. Furthermore, the Book of Micah shifts voices frequently–from God to Micah to the rebellious people and back again. Micah and Isaiah have similar literary styles. Both prophets use very descriptive language and many figures of speech. Micah also has a passion for punning, as seen in 1:10-15.

1 The word of the LORD that came to Micah the Moreshite—what he saw regarding Samaria and Jerusalem in the days of Jotham, Ahaz, and Hezekiah, kings of Judah.

Coming Judgment on Israel

2 Listen, all you peoples;
pay attention, earth[a] and everyone in it!
The Lord GOD will be a witness against you,
the Lord, from His holy temple.

3 Look, the LORD is leaving His place
and coming down to trample
the heights[b] of the earth.

4 The mountains will melt beneath Him,
and the valleys will split apart,
like wax near a fire,
like water cascading down a mountainside.

5 All this will happen because of Jacob's rebellion
and the sins of the house of Israel.
What is the rebellion of Jacob?
Isn't it Samaria?
And what is the •high place of Judah?
Isn't it Jerusalem?

6 Therefore, I will make Samaria
a heap of ruins in the countryside,
a planting area for a vineyard.
I will roll her stones into the valley
and expose her foundations.

7 All her carved images will be smashed to pieces,
all her wages will be burned in the fire,
and I will destroy all her idols.
Since she collected the wages of a prostitute,
they will be used again for a prostitute.

Micah's Lament

8 Because of this I will lament and wail;
I will walk barefoot and naked.
I will howl like the jackals
and mourn like ostriches.[c]

9 For her wound is incurable
and has reached even Judah;
it has approached the gate of my people,
as far as Jerusalem.

10 Don't announce it in Gath,
don't weep at all.
In Beth-leaphrah roll in the dust.

11 Depart in shameful nakedness,
you residents of Shaphir;
the residents of Zaanan will not come out.
Beth-ezel is lamenting;

its support[d] is taken from you.

12 Though the residents of Maroth
anxiously wait for something good,
calamity has come from the LORD
to the gate of Jerusalem.

13 Harness the horses to the chariot,
you residents of Lachish.
This was the beginning of sin for Daughter Zion,
because Israel's acts of rebellion can be traced
to you.

14 Therefore, send farewell gifts to Moresheth-gath;
the houses of Achzib are a deception
to the kings of Israel.

15 I will again bring a conqueror
against you who live in Mareshah.
The nobility[e] of Israel will come to Adullam.

16 Shave yourselves bald and cut off your hair
in sorrow for your precious children;
make yourselves as bald as an eagle,
for they have been taken from you into exile.

Oppressors Judged

2 Woe to those who dream up wickedness
and prepare evil ⌊plans⌋ on their beds!
At morning light they accomplish it
because the power is in their hands.

2 They covet fields and seize them;
they also take houses.
They deprive a man of his home,
a person of his inheritance.

3 Therefore, the LORD says:

I am now planning a disaster
against this nation;
you cannot free your necks from it.
Then you will not walk so proudly
because it will be an evil time.

4 In that day one will take up a taunt against you,
and lament mournfully, saying:
We are totally ruined!
He measures out the allotted land of my people.
How He removes ⌊it⌋ from me!
He allots our fields to traitors.

5 Therefore, there will be no one
in the assembly of the LORD
to divide the land by casting lots.[f]

God's Word Rejected

6 "Stop your preaching," they[g] preach.
"They should not preach these things;

---

[a]1:2 Or land [b]1:3 Or high places [c]1:8 Or eagle owls; lit daughters of the desert [d]1:11 Lit its standing place; Hb obscure [e]1:15 Lit glory
[f]2:5 Lit LORD stretching the measuring line by lot [g]2:6 = the prophets

---

1:1 Samaria and Jerusalem. The capitals of the northern kingdom (Israel) and the southern kingdom (Judah) represent all 12 tribes of Israel.

1:2-7 The prophet's synopsis urges all nations to hear God's judgment against them (v. 2), God's punishment (vv. 3-4), the reason (v. 5), and its results (vv. 6-7).

1:3 the heights of the earth. A common phrase for idol worship sites, this refers to Jerusalem and Samaria's mountain locations. I

1:6-7 Micah saw this prophecy fulfilled in 722 B.C. when the Assyrians captured Samaria (2 Kings 17:6).

1:11 Shaphir. The name Shaphir meant "beautiful or pleasant," but the town would soon be naked and ashamed, not beautiful. Nakedness here suggests captives with nowhere to hide.

2:2-3 covet. The people would certainly perish because of their violation of the 10th commandment.

shame will not overtake us."a

7 House of Jacob, should it be asked:
"Is the Spirit of the LORD impatient?
Are these the things He does?"
Don't My words bring good
to the one who walks uprightly?

8 But recently My people have risen up
like an enemy:
You strip off the splendid robe
from those who are passing through confidently,
like those returning from war.

9 You force the women of My people
out of their comfortable homes,
and you take My blessingb
from their children forever.

10 Get up and leave,
for this is not your place of rest,
because defilement brings destruction—
a grievous destruction!

11 If a man of spiritc comes
and invents lies:
"I will preach to you about wine and beer,"
he would be just the preacher for this people!

The Remnant Regathered

12 I will indeed gather all of you, Jacob;
I will collect the remnant of Israel.
I will bring them together like sheep in a pen,
like a flock in the middle of its fold.
It will be noisy with people.

13 One who breaks open ⌊the way⌋
will advance before them;
they will break out, pass through the gate,
and leave by it.
Their King will pass through before them,
the LORD as their leader.

Unjust Leaders Judged

3 Then I said: "Now listen, leaders of Jacob,
you rulers of the house of Israel.
Aren't you supposed to know what is just?

2 You hate good and love evil.
You tear off the skin of people
and ⌊strip⌋ their flesh from their bones.

3 You eat the flesh of my people
after you strip their skin from them
and break their bones.
You chop them up
like flesh for the cooking pot,
like meat in a caldron."

4 Then they will cry out to the LORD,

but He will not answer them.
He will hide His face from them at that time
because of the crimes they have committed.

False Prophets Judged

5 This is what the LORD says
concerning the prophets
who lead my people astray,
who proclaim peace
when they have ⌊food⌋ to sink their teeth into
but declare war against the one
who puts nothing in their mouths.

6 Therefore, it will be night for you—
without visions;
it will grow dark for you—
without •divination.
The sun will set on these prophets,
and the daylight will turn black over them.

7 Then the seers will be ashamed
and the diviners disappointed.
They will all cover their mouthsd
because there will be no answer from God.

8 But as for me, I am filled with power
by the Spirit of the LORD,
with justice and courage,
to proclaim to Jacob his rebellion
and to Israel his sin.

Zion's Destruction

9 Listen to this, leaders of the house of Jacob,
you rulers of the house of Israel,
who abhor justice
and pervert everything that is right,

10 who build Zion with bloodshed
and Jerusalem with injustice.

11 Her leaders issue rulings for a bribe,
her priests teach for payment,
and her prophets practice divination
for money.
Yet they lean on the LORD, saying,
"Isn't the LORD among us?
No calamity will overtake us."

12 Therefore, because of you,
Zion will be plowed like a field,
Jerusalem will become ruins,
and the hill of the temple mount
will be a thicket.

The LORD's Rule from Restored Zion

4 In the last days
the mountain of the LORD's house

---

a2:6 Text emended; MT reads things. Shame will not depart.   b2:9 Perhaps = land   c2:11 Lit wind   d3:7 Lit mustache

---

2:6-7 False prophets, believing God incapable of anger against His people, urged Micah not to prophesy judgment.

2:11 wine and beer. Like his contemporaries, Isaiah (5:11-12, 22; 28:7-8; 56:12) and Amos (4:1; 6:4-6), Micah inveighs against excess as demonstrated by the affluent's overindulgence of wine and beer. He mocks them for even applauding prophets who praise the virtues of their favorite vices. Such prophets become drunk themselves (Isa. 28:7; Amos 2:12). Other sages go further in denouncing the disadvantages of such vices (Prov. 20:1; 21:17; 23:20-21, 29-35; 31:4-7). Such is the folly of rejecting God's Word.

2:12-13 remnant. God will keep His covenant promises to Abraham and will gather and bless a remnant of Israel (Isa. 1:9; 4:3).

3:1-3 leaders of Jacob. In Micah's words,

will be established
at the top of the mountains
and will be raised above the hills.
Peoples will stream to it,
2 and many nations will come and say,
"Come, let us go up to the mountain of the LORD,
to the house of the God of Jacob.
He will teach us about His ways
so we may walk in His paths."
For instruction will go out of Zion
and the word of the LORD from Jerusalem.
3 He will settle disputes among many peoples
and provide arbitration for strong nations
that are far away.
They will beat their swords into plows,
and their spears into pruning knives.
Nation will not take up the sword against nation,
and they will never again train for war.
4 But each man will sit under his grapevine
and under his fig tree
with no one to frighten ⌊him⌋.
For the mouth of the LORD of •Hosts
has promised ⌊this⌋.
5 Though all the peoples each walk
in the name of their gods,
we will walk in the name of •Yahweh our God
forever and ever.
6 On that day—

⌊this is⌋
the LORD's declaration—
I will assemble the lame
and gather the scattered,
those I have injured.
7 I will make the lame into a remnant,
those far removed into a strong nation.
Then the LORD will rule over them
in Mount Zion
from this time on and forever.
8 And you, watchtower for the flock,
fortified hill[a] of Daughter Zion,
the former rule will come to you,
sovereignty will come to Daughter Jerusalem.

From Exile to Victory
9 Now, why are you shouting loudly?
Is there no king with you?
Has your counselor perished,
so that anguish grips you like a woman in labor?
10 Writhe and cry out,[b] Daughter Zion,

like a woman in labor.
For now you will leave the city
and camp in the open fields.
You will go to Babylon;
there you will be rescued;
there the LORD will redeem you
from the power of your enemies!
11 Many nations have now assembled against you;
they say, "Let her be defiled,
and let us feast our eyes on Zion."
12 But they do not know the LORD's intentions
or understand His plan,
that He has gathered them
like sheaves to the threshing floor.
13 Rise and thresh, Daughter Zion,
for I will make your horns iron
and your hooves bronze,
so you can crush many peoples.
Then you[c] will devote
what they plundered to the LORD,
their wealth to the Lord of all the earth.

From Defeated Ruler to Conquering King
5 [d] Now daughter ⌊who is⌋ under attack,
you slash yourself ⌊in grief⌋;
a siege is set against us!
They are striking the judge of Israel
on the cheek with a rod.
2[e] Bethlehem Ephrathah,
you are small among the clans of Judah;
One will come from you
to be ruler over Israel for Me.
His origin[f] is from antiquity,
from eternity.[g]
3 Therefore, He will abandon them
until the time
when she who is in labor has given birth;
then the rest of His brothers will return
to the people of Israel.
4 He will stand and shepherd ⌊them⌋
in the strength of •Yahweh,
in the majestic name of Yahweh His God.
They will live securely,
for then His greatness will extend
to the ends of the earth.
5 There[h] will be peace.
When Assyria invades our land,
when it marches against our fortresses,
we will raise against it seven shepherds,
even eight leaders of men.

their leaders were like hunters devouring their own people.
4:1-8 Micah prophesies that in the last days God will exalt Jerusalem as the center of Christ's rule. God will keep His promise to bless the world through Israel.
4:4 under his grapevine. Grapevines sym-

bolize harvests in times of peace and security.
4:7 lame. Micah contrasts those who walk after foreign gods (v. 5) with the Israelites who know their weakness (lameness) and dependency on Yahweh. Though Israel is spiritually lame and faces exile, God will save a remnant

to rebuild a strong nation under His rule.
4:9–13 Verses 9 and 10 may reflect Isaiah's rebuke of Hezekiah for showing the Babylonian king his treasure in 705 B.C. (2 Kings 20; Isa. 39); which eventually resulted in the Babylonian exile in 586 B.C. The Lord's lifting of the Assyrian siege of Jerusalem in 701 B.C.

⁶ They will shepherd the land of Assyria
with the sword,
the land of Nimrod with a drawn blade.^a
So He will rescue us from Assyria
when it invades our land,
when it marches against our territory.

The Glorious and Purified Remnant

⁷ Then the remnant of Jacob
will be among many peoples
like dew from the LORD,
like showers on the grass,
which do not wait for anyone
or linger for •mankind.
⁸ Then the remnant of Jacob
will be among the nations,
among many peoples,
like a lion among animals of the forest,
like a young lion among flocks of sheep,
which tramples and tears as it passes through,
and there is no one to rescue ⌊them⌋.
⁹ Your hand will be lifted up
against your adversaries,
and all your enemies will be destroyed.

¹⁰ In that day—
the LORD's declaration—
I will remove your horses from you
and wreck your chariots.
¹¹ I will remove the cities of your land
and tear down all your fortresses.
¹² I will remove sorceries from your hands,
and you will not have any more fortune-tellers.
¹³ I will remove your carved images
and sacred pillars from you,
so that you will not bow down again
to the work of your hands.
¹⁴ I will pull up the •Asherah poles
from among you
and demolish your cities.^b
¹⁵ I will take vengeance in anger and wrath
against the nations that have not obeyed ⌊Me⌋.

God's Lawsuit against Judah

6 Now listen to what the LORD is saying:

Rise, plead ⌊your⌋ case before the mountains,
and let the hills hear your voice.
² Listen to the LORD's lawsuit,
you mountains and enduring foundations
of the earth,

because the LORD has a case against His people,
and He will argue it against Israel.
³ My people, what have I done to you,
or how have I wearied you?
Testify against Me!
⁴ Indeed, I brought you up from the land of Egypt
and redeemed you from that place of slavery.
I sent Moses, Aaron, and Miriam ahead of you.
⁵ My people,
remember what Balak king of Moab proposed,
what Balaam son of Beor answered him,
and ⌊what happened⌋ from Acacia Grove^c
to Gilgal,
so that you may acknowledge
the LORD's righteous acts.

⁶ What should I bring before the LORD
when I come to bow before God on high?
Should I come before Him with •burnt offerings,
with year-old calves?
⁷ Would the LORD be pleased with thousands
of rams,
or with ten thousand streams of oil?
Should I give my firstborn for my transgression,
the child of my body for my own sin?
⁸ He has told you men what is good
and what it is the LORD requires of you:
Only to act justly,
to love faithfulness,
and to walk humbly with your God.

Verdict of Judgment

⁹ The voice of the LORD calls out to the city^d
(and it is wise to •fear Your name):
"Pay attention to the rod
and the One who ordained it.^e
¹⁰ Are there still^f the treasures of wickedness
and the accursed short measure
in the house of the wicked?
¹¹ Can I excuse wicked scales
or bags of deceptive weights?
¹² For the wealthy of the city are full of violence,
and its residents speak lies;
the tongues in their mouths are deceitful.
¹³ "As a result, I have begun to strike
you severely,^g
bringing desolation because of your sins.
¹⁴ You will eat but not be satisfied,
for there will be hunger within you.

a **5:6** Aq, Vg; MT, Sym read *Nimrod at its gateways* b **5:14** Or *shrines* c **6:5** Or *Shittim* d **6:9** = Jerusalem e **6:9** Or *attention, you tribe. Who has ordained it?*; Hb obscure f **6:10** Hb obscure g **6:13** LXX, Aq, Theod, Syr, Vg; MT reads *I have made [you] sick by striking you down*

(vv. 11-13) was a postponement of Jerusalem's destruction due to Hezekiah's prior repentance (2 Kings 19; Jer. 26:17-19). **5:2 Bethlehem.** This prophecy of Christ's coming was used by the wise men as a guide to find Jesus (see also Matthew 2:1-6). **5:7 the remnant of Jacob.** Micah goes into

elaborate detail describing the restoration and refreshment of believing Israelites who will take their rightful place over the enemies of God. Israel will then be all that God intended. **5:8-9** Like a lion who fears no other animal, the remnant of Israel will dominate other na-

tions. Jesus is also called the Lion of Judah. **5:10-11 remove your horses.** God will remove Israel's self-reliance. He will take away their military hardware and any other idols that keep them from depending upon Him. **6:4 out of Egypt.** The prophets frequently reminded Israel of this deliverance (7:15;

What you acquire, you cannot save,
and what you do save,
I will give to the sword.[a]

15 You will sow but not reap;
you will press olives
but not anoint yourself with oil;
and ⌊you will tread⌋ grapes
but not drink the wine.

16 The statutes of Omri
and all the practices of Ahab's house
have been observed;
you have followed their policies.
Therefore, I will make you a desolate place
and the city's[b] residents an object of contempt;[c]
you will bear the scorn of My people."[d]

Israel's Moral Decline

7 How sad for me!
For I am like one who—
when the summer fruit has been gathered
after the gleaning of the grape harvest—
⌊finds⌋ no grape cluster to eat,
no early fig, which I crave.

2 Godly people have vanished from the land;
there is no one upright among the people.
All of them wait in ambush to shed blood;
they hunt each other with a net.

3 Both hands are good at accomplishing evil:
the official and the judge demand a bribe;
when the powerful man communicates
his evil desire,
they plot it together.

4 The best of them is like a brier;
the most upright is worse than a hedge of thorns.
The day of your watchmen,
⌊the day of⌋ your punishment, is coming;
at this time their panic is here.

5 Do not rely on a friend;
don't trust in a close companion.
Seal your mouth
from the woman who lies in your arms.

6 For a son considers his father a fool,
a daughter opposes her mother,
and a daughter-in-law is
against her mother-in-law;
a person's enemies are the people
in his own home.

7 But as for me, I will look to the LORD;
I will wait for the God of my salvation.
My God will hear me.

Zion's Vindication

8 Do not rejoice over me, my enemy!
Though I have fallen, I will stand up;
though I sit in darkness,
the LORD will be my light.

9 Because I have sinned against Him,
I must endure the LORD's rage
until He argues my case
and establishes justice for me.
He will bring me into the light;
I will see His salvation.[e]

10 Then my enemy will see,
and she will be covered with shame,
the one who said to me,
"Where is the LORD your God?"
My eyes will look at her in triumph;
at that time she will be trampled
like mud in the streets.

11 A day will come for rebuilding your walls;
on that day ⌊your⌋ boundary will be extended.

12 On that day people will come to you
from Assyria and the cities of Egypt,
even from Egypt to the Euphrates River
and from sea to sea
and from mountain to mountain.

13 Then the earth will become a wasteland
because of its inhabitants,
and as a result of their actions.

Micah's Prayer Answered

14 Shepherd Your people with Your staff,
the flock that is Your possession.
They live alone in a scrubland,
surrounded by pastures.
Let them graze in Bashan and Gilead
as in ancient times.

15 I will show them[f] wondrous deeds
as in the days of your exodus
from the land of Egypt.

16 Nations will see and be ashamed
of[g] all their power.
They will put ⌊their⌋ hands
over ⌊their⌋ mouths,
and their ears will become deaf.

17 They will lick the dust like a snake;
they will come trembling out of
their hiding places
like reptiles slithering on the ground.

---

a 6:14 Hb obscure b 6:16 Lit *and its* c 6:16 Lit *residents a hissing* d 6:16 LXX reads *of the peoples* e 7:9 Or *righteousness* f 7:15 = Israel
g 7:16 Or *ashamed in spite of*

Hosea 2:15; 13:4; Amos 2:10; 3:1).

6:6-8 Micah asks what the people can do to regain God's favor. Then he answers his own question: God desires obedience that offers justice and mercy toward others and to humbly fellowship with Him. (See also 1 Sam. 15:22; Isa. 1:11-15).

6:16 statutes of Omri ... practices of Ahab's house. These were the worst kings of the northern kingdom; they ruled by idolatry and cruel violence.

7:2 Godly people have vanished. While Israelites thought they were obeying God, they held their own definitions of obedience, not those in Scripture. Godly people were as rare as summer fruit after the harvest.

7:7 But as for me. In contrast to the prophets who watched for judgment on a corrupt nation overseen by corrupt officials (vv. 1-6), Micah and the remnant "watch" for their future deliverance and salvation (vv. 8-16). God

They will tremble before the LORD our God;
they will stand in awe of You.

18 Who is a God like You,
removing iniquity and passing over rebellion
for the remnant of His inheritance?
He does not hold on to His anger forever,
because He delights in faithful love.

19 He will again have compassion on us;
He will vanquish our iniquities.
You will cast all our[a] sins
into the depths of the sea.

20 You will show loyalty to Jacob
and faithful love to Abraham,
as You swore to our fathers
from days long ago.

---

keeps both promises: the nation is judged but its faithful are saved.

7:15-17 Micah's hope for the salvation of Israel rests on the promise of a Messiah. When Christ comes, He will return Israel to her land. Nations will see this deliverance and be overwhelmed by fear of the Lord.

7:20 loyalty. God's deliverance is certain because of the covenant with Jacob and Abraham (Gen. 22:17). God will bless their descendants and fulfill His promise of blessing (Gen. 17:5).

INTRODUCTION TO
NAHUM

PERSONAL READING PLAN

☐ Nahum 1:1-15
☐ Nahum 2:1-13

☐ Nahum 3:1-19

AUTHOR

Nahum, "the Elkoshite," was probably from Judah. Nahum means "comfort" and is related to the name Nehemiah, meaning "The LORD comforts."

DATE

Nahum's oracle is dated between the overthrow of Thebes (in 663 B.C.; see 3:8-10) and the fall of Nineveh (in 612 B.C.). It is perhaps near the end of this period since he prophesies the fall of Nineveh as imminent (2:1; 3:14,19). This would place Nahum during the reign of Josiah and make him a contemporary of Zephaniah and a young Jeremiah.

THEME

The Lord's judgment of Nineveh.

HISTORICAL BACKGROUND

The northern kingdom of Israel had fallen to the Assyrians circa 722 B.C. The Assyrians were brutally cruel, their kings often pictured as gloating over the gruesome punishments inflicted on conquered peoples. No wonder the fear and dread of Assyria fell on all her neighbors! About 700 B.C., the Assyrian king Sennacherib made Nineveh, which was the greatest city of its day, the capital of the empire. Jonah had announced Nineveh's doom, but the people repented and were given a "stay of execution" (see the Intro-

duction to Jonah). However, they quickly returned to their evil ways. Poetic justice and Nineveh's destruction is the focus of Nahum's prophecy. Within a few years, Nahum's prophecies came true. Proud Nineveh fell so hard that it never rose again. The site of the city was obliterated; it was only rediscovered some 2,500 years later!

CHARACTERISTICS

Like Obadiah, but unlike the other minor prophets, Nahum does not address his homeland at all, but a foreign city—Nineveh. Still, the book was intended for Jewish readers. While the style of Nahum is that of traditional judgment oracles, the language is poetic, with many metaphors and similes, as well as other vivid images. Each of the three chapters in Nahum is a complete unit in itself. Chapter 1 is in the form of a poem in which Nahum declares the judgment that is to come. Chapter 2 describes the siege and subsequent sack of Nineveh. In chapter 3, Nineveh is described and compared to Thebes. Thebes, the capital of Upper Egypt, was a city like Nineveh that was strong and proud and yet its destruction had come. Thus Nahum shows that the God of Israel is, in fact, the God who controls the fate of all the nations. Nahum's purpose is to lift up the great God of Israel, and thus bring comfort to his people. This book is a powerful indictment of a nation that seeks glory by aggression and oppression. The God of Israel hates violence and pride and "will never leave the guilty unpunished" (1:3).

843

1 The •oracle concerning Nineveh. The book of the vision of Nahum the Elkoshite.

God's Vengeance

2 The LORD is a jealous and avenging God;
the LORD takes vengeance
and is fierce in[a] wrath.
The LORD takes vengeance against His foes;
He is furious with His enemies.
3 The LORD is slow to anger but great in power;
the LORD will never leave
⌊the guilty⌋ unpunished.
His path is in the whirlwind and storm,
and clouds are the dust beneath His feet.
4 He rebukes the sea so that it dries up,
and He makes all the rivers run dry.
Bashan and Carmel wither;
even the flower of Lebanon withers.
5 The mountains quake before Him,
and the hills melt;
the earth trembles[b][c] at His presence—
the world and all who live in it.
6 Who can withstand His indignation?
Who can endure His burning anger?
His wrath is poured out like fire,
even rocks are shattered before Him.

Destruction of Nineveh

7 The LORD is good,
a stronghold in a day of distress;
He cares for those who take refuge in Him.
8 But He will completely destroy Nineveh[d]
with an overwhelming flood,
and He will chase His enemies into darkness.

9 Whatever you[e] plot against the LORD,
He will bring ⌊it⌋ to complete destruction;
oppression will not rise up a second time.
10 For they will be consumed
like entangled thorns,
like a drunkard's drink,
and like straw that is fully dry.[f]
11 One has gone out from Nineveh,[g]
who plots evil against the LORD,
and is a wicked counselor.

Promise of Judah's Deliverance

12 This is what the LORD says:

Though they are strong[h] and numerous,
they will still be mowed down,

and he[i] will pass away.
Though I have afflicted you,[j]
I will afflict you no longer.
13 For I will now break off his[k] yoke from you
and tear off your shackles.

The Assyrian King's Demise

14 The LORD has issued an order concerning you:[k]

There will be no offspring
to carry on your name.[l]
I will eliminate the carved idol and cast image
from the house of your gods;
I will prepare your grave,
for you are contemptible.

15[m]Look to the mountains—
the feet of one bringing good news
and proclaiming peace!
Celebrate your festivals, Judah;
fulfill your vows.
For the wicked one will never again
march through you;
he will be entirely wiped out.

Attack against Nineveh

2 One who scatters is coming up against you.
Man the fortifications!
Watch the road!
Brace[n] yourself!
Summon all your strength!

2 For the LORD will restore the majesty of Jacob,
yes,[o] the majesty of Israel,
though ravagers have ravaged them
and ruined their vine branches.

3 The shields of his[p] warriors are dyed red;
the valiant men are dressed in scarlet.
The fittings of the chariot flash like fire
on the day of its ⌊battle⌋ preparations,
and the spears are brandished.
4 The chariots dash madly through the streets;
they rush around in the plazas.
They look like torches;
they dart back and forth like lightning.
5 He gives orders to his officers;
they stumble as they advance.
They race to its wall;
the protective shield is set in place.
6 The river gates are opened,
and the palace erodes away.

---

[a]**1:2** Lit *is a master of* [b]**1:5** Some emend to *is laid waste* [c]**1:5** Lit *lifts* [d]**1:8** Lit *her place* [e]**1:9** = Nineveh [f]**1:10** Hb obscure [g]**1:11** Lit *from you* [h]**1:12** Lit *intact* [i]**1:12** = either the king of Assyria or his army [j]**1:12** = Judah [k]**1:13,14** Probably = the king of Assyria [l]**1:14** Lit *It will not be sown from your name any longer* [m]**1:15** Nah 2:1 in Hb [n]**2:1** Lit *Strengthen* [o]**2:2** Or *like* [p]**2:3** = the army commander attacking Nineveh

---

1:3 The LORD is slow to anger. The vengeance described in verse 2 is slow in coming. God withholds judgment to give the people a chance to repent. Similarly, the Lord had previously sent Jonah to Nineveh to urge its people to repent.

1:15 one bringing good news. Nahum speaks of one who brings news of deliverance from Assyria. In Isaiah 52:7, this phrase is used of one who brings news of deliverance from exile in Babylon. Paul uses this phrase in Romans 10:15 to refer to those who tell about Christ and the good news of salvation.

2:3-4 shields ... fittings ... chariots. The equipment and speed of Assyria's attackers are described. Red may have been the color of the attackers' shields and armor, or a reference to blood on them from battle. Their chariots and swords move like lightning as they approach the city for battle.

7 Beauty[a] is stripped,[b]
  she is carried away;
  her ladies-in-waiting moan
  like the sound of doves,
  and beat their breasts.
8 Nineveh has been like a pool of water
  from her ⌊first⌋ days,[b]
  but they are fleeing.
  "Stop! Stop!" ⌊they cry,⌋
  but no one turns back.
9 "Plunder the silver! Plunder the gold!"
  There is no end to the treasure,
  an abundance of every precious thing.
10 Desolation, decimation, devastation!
  Hearts melt,
  knees tremble,
  loins shake,
  every face grows pale!

11 Where is the lions' lair,
  or the feeding ground of the young lions,
  where the lion and lioness prowled,
  and the lion's cub,
  with nothing to frighten them away?
12 The lion mauled whatever its cubs needed
  and strangled ⌊prey⌋ for its lionesses.
  It filled up its dens with the kill,
  and its lairs with mauled prey.
13 Beware, I am against you—
                    the declaration
                of the Lord of •Hosts.
  I will make your chariots go up in smoke[c]
  and the sword will devour your young lions.
  I will cut off your prey from the earth,
  and the sound of your messengers
  will never be heard again.

Nineveh's Downfall

3 Woe to the city of blood,
  totally deceitful,
  full of plunder,
  never without prey.
2 The crack of the whip
  and rumble of the wheel,
  galloping horse
  and jolting chariot!
3 Charging horseman,
  flashing sword,
  shining spear;
  heaps of slain,

mounds of corpses,
  dead bodies without end—
  they stumble over their dead.
4 Because of the continual prostitution
    of the prostitute,
  the attractive mistress of sorcery,
  who betrays nations by her prostitution
  and clans by her witchcraft,
5 I am against you—
                    the declaration
                of the Lord of •Hosts.
  I will lift your skirts over your face
  and display your nakedness to nations,
  your shame to kingdoms.
6 I will throw filth on you
  and treat you with contempt;
  I will make a spectacle of you.
7 Then all who see you will recoil
    from you, saying:
  Nineveh is devastated;
  who will show sympathy to her?
  Where can I find anyone to comfort you?

8 Are you better than Thebes[d]
  that sat along the Nile
  with water surrounding her,
  whose rampart was the sea,
  the river[e] [f] her wall?
9 •Cush and Egypt were her endless source
    of strength;
  Put and Libya were among her[g] allies.
10 Yet she became an exile;
  she went into captivity.
  Her children were also dashed to pieces
  at the head of every street.
  They cast lots for her dignitaries,
  and all her nobles were bound in chains.
11 You[h] also will become drunk;
  you will hide yourself.[i]
  You also will seek refuge from the enemy.

12 All your fortresses are fig trees
  with figs that ripened first;
  when shaken, they fall—
  right into the mouth of the eater!

13 Look, your troops are women among you;
  the gates of your land
  are wide open to your enemies.
  Fire will devour the bars ⌊of your gates⌋.

---

[a]**2:7** Text emended; MT reads *Huzzab* [b]**2:7,8** Hb obscure [c]**2:13** Lit *will burn her chariots in smoke* [d]**3:8** Lit *No-amon* [e]**3:8** LXX, Syr, Vg read *water* [f]**3:8** Lit *sea from sea* [g]**3:9** Lit *your*; = Thebes [h]**3:11** = Nineveh [i]**3:11** Or *will be overcome*

2:8 like a pool of water. With their city flooded by attackers, Ninevites would flee, leaving their possessions behind to be plundered. They would flee in panic as rapidly as water flowed out of a tank.

2:11-12 lions' lair. Using the metaphor of a lion's pride, Nahum taunts Assyria. They had fought as brutally as a lion hunting for his lioness and cubs. Yet now their capital, or lions' lair, was wasted by war.

3:4 prostitution of the prostitute. Nineveh had lusted for power it didn't deserve, just as a harlot lusts for men. They sold their military services to gain control over other nations.

This may also be a reference to Nineveh's goddess of sex and war.

3:7 Nineveh is devastated. On Nineveh's judgment day, she would lie in ruins with no one to comfort her. The atrocities committed by the people of Nineveh would catch up with them.

14 Draw water for the siege;
strengthen your fortresses.
Step into the clay and tread the mortar;
take hold of the brick-mold!

15 The fire will devour you there;
the sword will cut you down.
It will devour you like the young locust.
Multiply yourselves like the young locust,
multiply like the swarming locust!

16 You have made your merchants
more numerous than the stars of the sky.
The young locust strips[a] ⌊the land⌋
and flies away.

17 Your court officials are like the swarming locust,
and your scribes like clouds of locusts,

which settle on the walls on a cold day;
when the sun rises, they take off,
and no one knows where they are.

18 King of Assyria, your shepherds slumber;
your officers sleep.[b]
Your people are scattered
across the mountains
with no one to gather ⌊them⌋ together.

19 There is no remedy for your injury;
your wound is severe.
All who hear the news about you
will clap their hands because of you,
for who has not experienced
your constant cruelty?

---

a 3:16 Or sheds [its skin]   b 3:18 Probably = sleep in death

3:15 Multiply yourselves like the young locust. This is a command to the Ninevites to increase their numbers so they can defend themselves against inevitable attack.

3:16 locust strips [the land]. The merchants (locusts), who were once numerous in Nineveh, would strip the land until it had no more wealth.

3:17 locusts. The leaders in the city exploited Nineveh like locusts devouring a crop. But during Nineveh's destruction, they would panic and flee overnight.

INTRODUCTION TO
HABAKKUK

PERSONAL READING PLAN

☐ Habakkuk 1:1-11
☐ Habakkuk 1:12-2:1

☐ Habakkuk 2:2-20
☐ Habakkuk 3:1-19

AUTHOR

The book was written by the prophet Habakkuk, a contemporary of Jeremiah. He was a man of deep faith and rooted in the religious traditions of Israel.

DATE

Habakkuk was written in the latter part of the seventh century B.C., probably c. 610-605 B.C. Habakkuk, like Jeremiah, probably lived to see the beginning of the fulfillment of his prophecy when Jerusalem was attacked by the Babylonians in 597 B.C.

THEME

Faith triumphs over doubt. Habakkuk wrestles with a problem that faces every age: Why does God seem inactive in the face of evil and injustice?

HISTORICAL BACKGROUND

The northern kingdom (Israel) had fallen to Assyria circa 722 B.C. and now the rising Chaldean Empire (i.e., the second Babylonian Empire) was threatening on the horizon. In Habakkuk's day, the rulers of the southern kingdom (Judah) were known to "do what was evil in the LORD's sight" (see 2 Kings 23:31-24:7). As an agent of judgment in God's hand, the Chaldeans invaded Judah in 605 B.C. The king of Babylon, Nebuchadnezzar, made the Judean king, Jehoia-

kim, his vassal or puppet ruler. Chapters one and two of Habakkuk are historically rooted in the events preceding and following the 605 B.C. invasion under Nebuchadnezzar's leadership. While 3:1 contains Habakkuk's name, it is less certain whether this chapter should be dated at the time of the invasion, or later in the prophet's life.

CHARACTERISTICS

Habakkuk is unusual in that it contains no prophecy directed to Israel. Instead, it is a dialogue between the prophet and God. The book shares some of the structural and thematic traits of the psalms of lament (e.g. Pss. 13; 44; 74; 80). Complaint and petition are followed by the divine perspective on the problem. Like the psalmist, Habakkuk uses stark poetic images to color and convey his message. Like the psalmist, and unlike all other prophets (who mostly speak on God's behalf to the people), Habakkuk speaks for himself and on behalf of his people directly and only to God. Like Job, he receives no answer except that God is God. God is holy, does care, and will act as He sees fit, but only in His time.

Habakkuk 2:4—"the righteous one will live by his faith"—is quoted by several New Testament authors who use it in speaking of faith (see Rom. 1:17; Gal. 3:11; Heb. 10:38). The Book of Habakkuk was popular during the time between the Old and New Testaments. A complete commentary on its first two chapters has been found among the Dead Sea Scrolls.

1

The •oracle that Habakkuk the prophet saw.

Habakkuk's First Prayer

2 How long, LORD, must I call for help
and You do not listen,
or cry out to You about violence
and You do not save?

3 Why do You force me to look at injustice?
Why do You tolerate[a] wrongdoing?
Oppression and violence are right in front of me.
Strife is ongoing, and conflict escalates.

4 This is why the law is ineffective
and justice never emerges.
For the wicked restrict the righteous;
therefore, justice comes out perverted.

God's First Answer

5 Look at the nations[b] and observe—
be utterly astounded!
For something is taking place in your days
that you will not believe
when you hear about it.

6 Look! I am raising up the Chaldeans,[c]
that bitter, impetuous nation
that marches across the earth's open spaces
to seize territories not its own.

7 They are fierce and terrifying;
their views of justice and sovereignty
stem from themselves.

8 Their horses are swifter than leopards
and more fierce[d] than wolves of the night.
Their horsemen charge ahead;
their horsemen come from distant ⌊lands⌋.
They fly like an eagle, swooping to devour.

9 All of them come to do violence;
their faces are set in determination.[e]
They gather prisoners like sand.

10 They mock kings,
and rulers are a joke to them.
They laugh at every fortress
and build siege ramps to capture it.

11 Then they sweep by like the wind
and pass through.
They are guilty;[f] their strength is their god.

Habakkuk's Second Prayer

12 Are You not from eternity, •Yahweh my God?
My Holy One, You[g] will not die.

LORD, You appointed them to execute judgment;
⌊my⌋ Rock, You destined them to punish ⌊us⌋.

13 ⌊Your⌋ eyes are too pure to look on evil,
and You cannot tolerate wrongdoing.
So why do You tolerate those
who are treacherous?
Why are You silent
while one[h] who is wicked swallows up
one[i] who is more righteous than himself?

14 You have made mankind
like the fish of the sea,
like marine creatures that have no ruler.

15 The Chaldeans pull them all up with a hook,
catch them in their dragnet,
and gather them in their fishing net;
that is why they are glad and rejoice.

16 That is why they sacrifice to their dragnet
and burn incense to their fishing net,
for by these things their portion is rich
and their food plentiful.

17 Will they therefore empty their net[j]
and continually slaughter nations
without mercy?

Habakkuk Waits for God's Response

2

I will stand at my guard post
and station myself on the lookout tower.
I will watch to see what He will say to me
and what I should[k] reply about my complaint.

God's Second Answer

2 The LORD answered me:

Write down this vision;
clearly inscribe it on tablets
so one may easily read it.[l]

3 For the vision is yet for the appointed time;
it testifies about the end and will not lie.
Though it delays, wait for it,
since it will certainly come and not be late.

4 Look, his ego is inflated;[e]
he is without integrity.
But the righteous one will live by his faith.[m]

5 Moreover, wine[n] betrays;
an arrogant man is never at rest.[o]
He enlarges his appetite like •Sheol,
and like Death he is never satisfied.
He gathers all the nations to himself;
he collects all the peoples for himself.

---

a**1:3** Lit observe   b**1:5** DSS, LXX, Syr read Look, you treacherous people; Ac 13:41   c**1:6** = the Babylonians   d**1:8** Or and quicker   e**1:9; 2:4** Hb obscure   f**1:11** Or wind, and transgress and incur guilt   g**1:12** Alt Hb tradition reads we   h**1:13** = Babylon; perhaps personified in its king   i**1:13** = Judah   j**1:17** DSS read sword   k**2:1** Syr reads what He will   l**2:2** Lit one who reads in it may run   m**2:4** Or faithfulness   n**2:5** DSS read wealth   o**2:5** Or man does not endure; Hb obscure

---

1:1-17 How long ... Habakkuk asks God why evil goes unpunished, and God's response is that he is going to punish Judah by allowing Babylon (the Chaldeans) to conquer it. Habakkuk questions how God can use Babylon, which is even more wicked than Judah.

1:3 tolerate wrongdoing. Habakkuk saw the injustice around him and was appalled. Even worse, the righteous God seems to tolerate this evil.

1:12 from eternity. Habakkuk finds comfort and confidence in God's faithfulness.

1:13 why do You tolerate? Although he accepts that Judah must be punished, Habakkuk wonders why God would use such an evil nation to administer the discipline.

2:4 righteous one will live by his faith. In contrast to the arrogant **Chaldean**, the righteous follower of God will live by faith, pa-

The 5 Woe Oracles

6 Won't all of these take up a taunt against him,
with mockery and riddles about him?
They will say:

Woe to him who amasses what is not his—
how much longer?—
and loads himself with goods taken in pledge.
7 Won't your creditors suddenly arise,
and those who disturb you wake up?
Then you will become spoil for them.
8 Since you have plundered many nations,
all the peoples who remain will plunder you—
because of human bloodshed
and violence against lands, cities,
and all who live in them.

9 Woe to him who unjustly gains
wealth for his house^a
to place his nest on high,
to escape from the reach of disaster!
10 You have planned shame for your house
by wiping out many peoples
and sinning against your own self.
11 For the stones will cry out from the wall,
and the rafters will answer them
from the woodwork.

12 Woe to him who builds a city with bloodshed
and founds a town with injustice!
13 Is it not from the LORD of •Hosts,
that the peoples labor ⌊only⌋ to fuel the fire
and countries exhaust themselves for nothing?
14 For the earth will be filled
with the knowledge of the LORD's glory,
as the waters cover the sea.

15 Woe to him who gives his neighbors drink,
pouring out your wrath^b
and even making them drunk,
in order to look at their nakedness!
16 You will be filled with disgrace
instead of glory.
You also—drink,
and expose your uncircumcision!^c
The cup in the LORD's right hand
will come around to you,
and utter disgrace will cover your glory.
17 For ⌊your⌋ violence against Lebanon
will overwhelm you;
the destruction of animals will terrify you,^d

because of ⌊your⌋ human bloodshed and violence
against lands, cities, and all who live in them.

18 What use is a carved idol
after its craftsman carves it?
It is ⌊only⌋ a cast image, a teacher of lies.
For the one who crafts its shape trusts in it
and makes idols that cannot speak.
19 Woe to him who says to wood: Wake up!
or to mute stone: Come alive!
Can it teach?
Look! It may be plated with gold and silver,
yet there is no breath in it at all.

20 But the LORD is in His holy temple;
let everyone on earth
be silent in His presence.

Habakkuk's Third Prayer

3 A prayer of Habakkuk the prophet. According to
Shigionoth.^e

2 LORD, I have heard the report about You;
LORD, I stand in awe of Your deeds.
Revive ⌊Your work⌋ in these years;
make ⌊it⌋ known in these years.
In ⌊Your⌋ wrath remember mercy!

3 God comes from Teman,
the Holy One from Mount Paran.   •Selah
His splendor covers the heavens,
and the earth is full of His praise.
4 ⌊His⌋ brilliance is like light;
rays are flashing from His hand.
This is where His power is hidden.
5 Plague goes before Him,
and pestilence follows in His steps.
6 He stands and shakes^f the earth;
He looks and startles the nations.
The age-old mountains break apart;
the ancient hills sink down.
His pathways are ancient.
7 I see the tents of Cushan^g in distress;
the tent curtains of the land of Midian tremble.
8 Are You angry at the rivers, LORD?
Is Your wrath against the rivers?
Or is Your rage against the sea
when You ride on Your horses,
Your victorious chariot?
9 You took the sheath from Your bow;
the arrows are ready^h to be used with an oath.^i
Selah

---

^a **2:9** Or *dynasty*   ^b **2:15** Or *venom*   ^c **2:16** DSS, LXX, Aq, Syr, Vg read *and stagger*   ^d **2:17** DSS, LXX, Aq, Syr, Tg, Vg; MT reads *them*
^e **3:1** Perhaps a passionate song with rapid changes of rhythm, or a dirge   ^f **3:6** Or *surveys*   ^g **3:7** = Midian   ^h **3:9** Or *set*   ^i **3:9** Hb obscure

---

tiently experiencing God's blessing, and trusting God's promises. (See also Rom. 1:17; Gal. 3:11; Heb. 10:38).

2:6-8 Woe to him. This is the first of five woes that foretell Babylon's destruction.

2:9-11 unjustly gains wealth. The Chalde-ans are compared to eagles building nests on mountainsides for protection from preda-tors. The Babylonians used their stolen goods to build a seemingly invincible em-pire.

2:11 stones will cry out from the wall. The materials used to build the Babylonian

Empire were purchased with plundered wealth.

2:12-14 founds a town with injustice. To Babylon's greed and pride, add its love of sin. The Lord declares that this empire's la-bor is in vain because the people follow evil, not God.

You split the earth with rivers.
10 The mountains see You and shudder;
a downpour of water sweeps by.
The deep roars with its voice
and lifts its waves[a] high.
11 Sun and moon stand still
in [their] lofty residence,
at the flash of Your flying arrows,
at the brightness of Your shining spear.
12 You march across the earth with indignation;
You trample down the nations in wrath.
13 You come out to save Your people,
to save Your anointed.[b]
You crush the leader of the house of the wicked
and strip [him] from foot[c] to neck. **Selah**
14 You pierce his head
with his own spears;
his warriors storm out to scatter us,
gloating as if ready to secretly devour the weak.
15 You tread the sea with Your horses,
stirring up the great waters.

Habakkuk's Confidence in God Expressed

16 I heard, and I trembled within;
my lips quivered at the sound.
Rottenness entered my bones;
I trembled where I stood.
Now I must quietly wait for the day
of distress
to come against the people invading us.
17 Though the fig tree does not bud
and there is no fruit on the vines,
though the olive crop fails
and the fields produce no food,
though there are no sheep in the pen
and no cattle in the stalls,
18 yet I will triumph in the LORD;
I will rejoice in the God of my salvation!
19 •Yahweh my Lord is my strength;
He makes my feet like those of a deer
and enables me to walk on mountain heights!

For the choir director: on[d] stringed instruments.

---

a 3:10 Lit hands   b 3:13 = the Davidic king or the nation of Israel   c 3:13 Lit foundation   d 3:19 Lit on my

---

2:14 earth will be filled. God's judgment of evil will illustrate how much greater God's glory is than anything greed can assemble.

2:15-17 gives his neighbors drink. Babylon's inhumanity and violence is condemned. The nation is compared to someone who gives a neighbor alcohol to indulge in lustful behavior.

3:16 Now I must quietly wait. After seeing God's might in Israel's past, Habakkuk is left physically weak from his encounter with God. But he has greater confidence and peace as he waits for Judah's invasion and

Babylon's subsequent fall.

3:18-19 yet I will triumph. Even if the suffering is hard and relief many years away, Habakkuk will rejoice in the Lord. God gives strength to face any circumstance that will come along the way.

INTRODUCTION TO
ZEPHANIAH

PERSONAL READING PLAN

☐ Zephaniah 1:1-2:3
☐ Zephaniah 2:4-15

☐ Zephaniah 3:1-20

AUTHOR

Zephaniah was an aristocrat and a great-great grandson of Hezekiah, the king of Judah from 715 to 686 B.C. (see 1:1).

DATE

Zephaniah prophesied during the reign of Josiah (640-609 B.C.). His preaching as recorded here may have contributed to Josiah's reforms, which took place in 621 B.C. This makes Zephaniah an older contemporary and kindred spirit of Jeremiah.

THEME

The coming Day of the Lord.

HISTORICAL BACKGROUND

Zephaniah's twofold message—"gloom and doom" for Judah and its neighbors (1:1-3:8), then the Lord's purging and purifying of a faithful remnant (3:9-20)—is best appreciated within the context of what necessitated their judgment. The historical situation that he addressed is the same pervasive decadence that triggered King Josiah's reform movement (see 2 Chron. 34-35). Josiah was spurred on by the evils of King Manasseh and King Amon, by the rediscovery of Moses' Law, by hearing Jeremiah's early preach-

ing, and quite possibly by Zephaniah's preaching. Thus it was that Josiah removed the pagan centers of idol worship. The immediate occasion for Zephaniah's prophecy may have been a century-long invasion of Canaan by the Scythians (a fierce nomadic people). Fulfillment of Zephaniah's prophecy (destruction of Judah) came at the hands of King Nebuchadnezzar of Babylon who defeated the Assyrians in 612 B.C., thus establishing Babylonian supremacy in the Near East.

CHARACTERISTICS

Zephaniah consists of several brief oracles or utterances, heavy with an emphasis on judgment. The prophet foresaw a worldwide catastrophe, but he also saw beyond it. In the prophetic tradition, Zephaniah delivers his message with lament, exhortation, and hope. Zephaniah presents a beautiful picture of a God who delights in His people (3:14-20). The prophecies of Zephaniah against the nations are listed below:

Judah:	1:4-2:3
Philistia:	2:4-7
Ammon:	2:8-11
Moab:	2:8-11
Cush:	2:12
Assyria:	2:13-15

1 The word of the LORD that came to Zephaniah son of Cushi, son of Gedaliah, son of Amariah, son of Hezekiah, in the days of Josiah son of Amon, king of Judah.

The Great Day of the LORD

2 I will completely sweep away everything
from the face of the earth—
⌊this is⌋
the LORD's declaration.
3 I will sweep away man and animal;
I will sweep away the birds of the sky
and the fish of the sea,
and the ruins[a] along with the wicked.
I will cut off mankind
from the face of the earth—
the LORD's declaration.

4 I will stretch out My hand against Judah
and against all the residents of Jerusalem.
I will cut off from this place
every vestige of •Baal,
the names of the pagan priests
along with the priests;
5 those who bow in worship on the rooftops
to the heavenly host;
those who bow and pledge loyalty to the LORD
but also pledge loyalty to •Milcom;[b]
6 and those who turn back from following
the LORD,
who do not seek the LORD or inquire of Him.
7 Be silent in the presence of the Lord GOD,
for the Day of the LORD is near.
Indeed, the LORD has prepared a sacrifice;
He has consecrated His guests.

8 On the day of the LORD's sacrifice
I will punish the officials, the king's sons,
and all who are dressed in foreign clothing.
9 On that day I will punish
all who skip over the threshold,[c]
who fill their master's house
with violence and deceit.

10 On that day—
the LORD's declaration—
there will be an outcry from the Fish Gate,
a wailing from the Second District,
and a loud crashing from the hills.
11 Wail, you residents of the Hollow,[d]
for all the merchants[e] will be silenced;

all those loaded with silver
will be cut off.
12 And at that time I will search Jerusalem
with lamps
and punish the men
who settle down comfortably,[f]
who say to themselves:
The LORD will not do good or evil.
13 Their wealth will become plunder
and their houses a ruin.
They will build houses but never live ⌊in them⌋,
plant vineyards but never drink their wine.

14 The great Day of the LORD is near,
near and rapidly approaching.
Listen, the Day of the LORD—
there the warrior's cry is bitter.
15 That day is a day of wrath,
a day of trouble and distress,
a day of destruction and desolation,
a day of darkness and gloom,
a day of clouds and blackness,
16 a day of trumpet ⌊blast⌋ and battle cry
against the fortified cities,
and against the high corner towers.
17 I will bring distress on mankind,
and they will walk like the blind
because they have sinned against the LORD.
Their blood will be poured out like dust
and their flesh like dung.
18 Their silver and their gold
will not be able to rescue them
on the day of the LORD's wrath.
The whole earth will be consumed
by the fire of His jealousy.
For He will make a complete,
yes, a horrifying end
of all the inhabitants of the earth.

A Call to Repentance

2 Gather yourselves together;
gather together, undesirable[g] nation,
2 before the decree takes effect
and the day passes like chaff,
before the burning of the LORD's anger
overtakes you,
before the day of the LORD's anger
overtakes you.
3 Seek the LORD, all you humble of the earth,
who carry out what He commands.

---

[a]**1:3** Perhaps objects connected with idolatry   [b]**1:5** Some LXX mss, Syr, Vg; MT, other LXX mss read *their king*   [c]**1:9** Hb obscure   [d]**1:11** Or *the market district*   [e]**1:11** Or *Canaanites*   [f]**1:12** Lit *who thicken on their dregs*   [g]**2:1** Or *shameless*

1:4-7 Judah is condemned for its idolatry, particularly the worship of Baal, a Canaanite fertility god. Some scholars argue that these threats place Zephaniah's prophecy before the reign of Josiah since his reforms destroyed the altars of Baal (2 Kings 23:4-16). Another alternative is that Josiah's reforms did not last and the people of Judah were again worshiping Baal.

1:5-6 Zephaniah chastises three groups of idolaters: those who worshiped the sun, moon, and stars; those who combined worship of God with Molech, the Ammonite deity to which children were sacrificed; and those who didn't worship any god, including the true God.

1:18 not be able to rescue them. Riches can

save people from many of life's issues, but are totally worthless when God's wrath comes.

2:1-3 before the day of the LORD's anger overtakes you. Zephaniah's point in all these dire warnings: repentance is the only hope for Judah.

2:9-10 Moab … Ammonites. Because of

Seek righteousness, seek humility;
perhaps you will be concealed
on the day of the LORD's anger.

Judgment against the Nations

4 For Gaza will be abandoned,
and Ashkelon will become a ruin.
Ashdod will be driven out at noon,
and Ekron will be uprooted.

5 Woe, inhabitants of the seacoast,
nation of the Cherethites!a
The word of the LORD is against you,
Canaan, land of the Philistines:
I will destroy you until there is no one left.

6 The seacoast will become pasturelands
with caves for shepherds and folds for sheep.

7 The coastland will belong
to the remnant of the house of Judah;
they will find pasture there.
They will lie down in the evening
among the houses of Ashkelon,
for the LORD their God will return to them
and restore their fortunes.

8 I have heard the taunting of Moab
and the insults of the Ammonites,
who have taunted My people
and threatened their territory.

9 Therefore, as I live—
the declaration of the LORD of •Hosts,
the God of Israel—
Moab will be like Sodom
and the Ammonites like Gomorrah—
a place overgrown with weeds,
a salt pit, and a perpetual wasteland.
The remnant of My people will plunder them;
the remainder of My nation
will dispossess them.

10 This is what they get for their pride,
because they have taunted and acted arrogantly
against the people of the LORD of Hosts.

11 The LORD will be terrifying to them
when He starves all the gods of the earth.
Then all the distant coastlands of the nations
will bow in worship to Him,
each in its own place.

12 You •Cushites will also be slain
by My sword.

13 He will also stretch out His hand
against the north

and destroy Assyria;
He will make Nineveh a desolate ruin,
dry as the desert.

14 Herds will lie down in the middle of it,
every kind of wild animal.b
Both the desert owlc and the screech owld
will roost in the capitals of its pillars.
⌊Their⌋ calls will sounde from the window,
but devastationf will be on the threshold,
for He will expose the cedar work.g

15 This is the self-assured city
that lives in security,
that thinks to herself:
I am, and there is no one besides me.
What a desolation she has become,
a place for wild animals to lie down!
Everyone who passes by her
jeersh and shakes his fist.

Woe to Oppressive Jerusalem

3 Woe to the city that is rebelliousi and defiled,
the oppressive city!

2 She has not obeyed;
she has not accepted discipline.
She has not trusted in the LORD;
she has not drawn near to her God.

3 Thej princes within her are roaring lions;
her judges are wolves of the night,
which leave nothing fork the morning.

4 Her prophets are reckless—
treacherous men.
Her priests profane the sanctuary;
they do violence to instruction.

5 The righteous LORD is in her;
He does no wrong.
He applies His justice morning by morning;
He does not fail at dawn,
yet the one who does wrong knows no shame.

6 I have cut off nations;
their corner towers are destroyed.
I have laid waste their streets,
with no one to pass through.
Their cities lie devastated,
without a person, without an inhabitant.

7 I thought: You will certainly •fear Me
and accept correction.
Then her dwelling placel
would not be cut off
⌊based on⌋ all that I had allocated to her.

---

a2:5 = Sea Peoples; Ezk 25:16 b2:14 Lit every wild animal of a nation; Pr 30:25 c2:14 Or the pelican; Hb obscure d2:14 Or the hedgehog; Hb obscure e2:14 Lit sing f2:14 LXX, Vg read ravens g2:14 Hb obscure h2:15 Or hisses i3:1 Or filthy j3:3 Lit Her k3:3 Or that had nothing to gnaw in l3:7 LXX, Syr read her eyes

---

Moab's and Ammon's taunting, Judah's remnant (faithful few who survive) will conquer them and inhabit their lands.

2:12 Cushites will also be slain by My sword. The Cushites lived in what is today Egypt, Sudan, and northern Ethiopia; the southernmost point known to the people of Ju-

dah. Zephaniah may have intended that God would judge the whole earth.

2:15 self-assured city. For about 200 years Nineveh was the world's strongest city, so the claim "there is no one besides me" was partially accurate. But eventually the city lay in ruins; its haughtiness silenced.

3:3-4 princes ... judges ... prophets ... priests. The rulers and judges were so greedy that by dawn they had devoured prey caught the previous evening. Arrogant prophets twisted God's law for their own gain. Idolatrous priests profaned the places of worship, when they should have been teaching the law.

However, they became more corrupt
in all their actions.

8 Therefore, wait for Me—
 the LORD's declaration—
until the day I rise up for plunder.ᵃ
For My decision is to gather nations,
to assemble kingdoms,
in order to pour out My indignation on them,
all My burning anger;
for the whole earth will be consumed
by the fire of My jealousy.

Final Restoration Promised

9 For I will then restore
pure speech to the peoples
so that all of them may call
on the name of •Yahweh
and serve Him with a single purpose.ᵇ
10 From beyond the rivers of •Cush
My supplicants, My dispersed people,
will bring an offering to Me.
11 On that day youᶜ will not be put to shame
because of everything you have done
in rebelling against Me.
For then I will remove
your boastful braggarts from among you,
and you will never again be haughty
on My holy mountain.
12 I will leave
a meek and humble people among you,
and they will trust in the name of Yahweh.
13 The remnant of Israel will no longer
do wrong or tell lies;
a deceitful tongue will not be found
in their mouths.

But they will pasture and lie down,
with nothing to make [them] afraid.

14 Sing for joy, Daughter Zion;
shout loudly, Israel!
Be glad and rejoice with all [your] heart,
Daughter Jerusalem!
15 The LORD has removed your punishment;
He has turned back your enemy.
The King of Israel, the LORD, is among you;
you need no longer fear harm.
16 On that day it will be said to Jerusalem:
"Do not fear;
Zion, do not let your hands grow weak.
17 The LORD your God is among you,
a warrior who saves.
He will rejoice over you with gladness.
He will bring [you] quietnessᵈ with His love.
He will delight in you with shouts of joy."
18 I will gather those who have been driven
from the appointed festivals;
[They will be] a tribute from you,ᵉ
and reproach [on her].ᶠ
19 Yes, at that time
I will deal with all who afflict you.
I will save the lame and gather the scattered;
I will make those who were disgraced
throughout the earth
receive praise and fame.
20 At that time I will bring youᵍ back,
yes, at the time I will gather you.
I will make you famous and praiseworthy
among all the peoples of the earth,
when I restore your fortunes before your eyes.
Yahweh has spoken.

ᵃ**3:8** LXX, Syr read *for a witness;* Vg reads *up forever*   ᵇ**3:9** Lit *with one shoulder*   ᶜ**3:11** = Israel   ᵈ**3:17** LXX, Syr read *He will renew you*
ᵉ**3:18** = Jerusalem   ᶠ**3:18** Hb obscure   ᵍ**3:20** = people of Israel

---

3:8 the whole earth will be consumed by the fire of My jealousy. This section ends with a declaration of God's universal judgment on all nations, fueled by His jealous love.

3:9 I will then restore. After God punishes, God promises restoration and peace. God's judgment aims to purify the nations so they call on His name and serve Him.

3:15 The King of Israel, the Lord. Israel's redeemer and Messiah King will dwell among them (Isa. 9:7; Zech 14:9). No longer must Israel face God's wrath or her enemies (vv. 8, 19).

3:17-20 Zephaniah concludes his prophetic message with encouragement and hope. He reminds the Israelites that they are God's chosen people, and God still loves them. Then Zephaniah offers a series of promises of restoration from God. These would give hope to those that trusted in Yahweh, the almighty yet loving God who keeps His promises.

INTRODUCTION TO
HAGGAI

PERSONAL READING PLAN

☐ Haggai 1:1-15

☐ Haggai 2:1-23

AUTHOR

The author is not identified, although the book tells of Haggai's ministry and records his oracles. Haggai means "festal," which may suggest that the prophet was born during one of the three Jewish feasts (Unleavened Bread, Pentecost (or Weeks), or Tabernacles; see Deut. 16:16).

DATE

Haggai is quite specific as to the year, month, and day of his messages: August 29 (1:1); September 15 (1:15); October 17 (2:1); December 18 (2:10 and 2:20), 520 B.C.

THEME

Rebuilding the nation—the blessing is in the doing.

HISTORICAL BACKGROUND

This book is set in the context of the return of the Jews from the Babylonian exile and the subsequent rebuilding of Jerusalem and the temple (see the Introductions to Ezra and Nehemiah). It was through the ministry of Haggai (along with Zechariah) that the rebuilding of the temple began (see Ezra 5:1-2). The problem with getting the building started, it seems, was not just with the neighboring Samaritans who opposed the rebuilding projects (fearing that this would lead to a renewed and politically powerful Jewish state). The real problem had to do with the lethargy of the people. Hag-

gai's aim was to get the people enthusiastic about the project. The temple was completed and dedicated four years later in 516 B.C. No other prophet had results as direct, immediate, and identifiable as Haggai!

CHARACTERISTICS

There is only one book in the Old Testament that is shorter than Haggai (Obadiah). Yet in just 38 verses Haggai is able to show the contrasting consequences of disobedience vs. obedience, as well as point to the coming of the Messiah. Haggai was an older contemporary of Zechariah. Both dealt with the same themes, although in quite different ways (see the Introduction to Zechariah). Haggai was a practical doer, while Zechariah was an apocalyptic visionary. Haggai did not mince words while Zechariah mixed metaphors in a memorable way. Haggai exhorted the people to get to work on the project at hand (the rebuilding of the temple), while Zechariah encouraged them to put their hope in what lay ahead for them in the distant future (which also served to motivate the people to rebuild the temple, though in a different way). Haggai records not only his oracles, but also his ministry and the response of the people to it, while Zechariah emphasizes the prophecies.

Several times Haggai seems to echo other Scriptures (compare 1:6 with Deut. 28:38-39 and 2:17 with Deut. 28:22). The use of "be strong" three times in 2:4 corresponds with the encouragement given in Joshua 1:6-7,9,18.

Command to Rebuild the Temple

1 In the second year of King Darius,[a] on the first day of the sixth month, the word of the LORD came through Haggai the prophet to Zerubbabel son of Shealtiel, the governor of Judah, and to Joshua son of Jehozadak, the high priest:

2 "The LORD of •Hosts says this: These people say: The time has not come for the house of the LORD to be rebuilt."

3 The word of the LORD came through Haggai the prophet: 4 "Is it a time for you yourselves to live in your paneled houses, while this house[b] lies in ruins?" 5 Now, the LORD of Hosts says this: "Think carefully about[c] your ways:

6   You have planted much
but harvested little.
You eat
but never have enough to be satisfied.
You drink
but never have enough to become drunk.
You put on clothes
but never have enough to get warm.
The wage earner ⌊puts his⌋ wages
into a bag with a hole in it."

7 The LORD of Hosts says this: "Think carefully about[c] your ways. 8 Go up into the hills, bring down lumber, and build the house. Then I will be pleased with it and be glorified," says the LORD. 9 "You expected much, but then it amounted to little. When you brought ⌊the harvest⌋ to your house, I ruined[d] it. Why?" ⌊This is⌋ the declaration of the LORD of Hosts. "Because My house still lies in ruins, while each of you is busy with his own house.

10   So on your account,[e]
the skies have withheld the dew
and the land its crops.
11   I have summoned a drought
on the fields and the hills,
on the grain, new wine, olive oil,
and whatever the ground yields,
on the people and animals,
and on all that your hands produce."

The People's Response

12 Then Zerubbabel son of Shealtiel, the high priest Joshua son of Jehozadak, and the entire remnant of the people obeyed the voice of the LORD their God and the words of the prophet Haggai, because the LORD their God had sent him. So the people •feared the LORD.

13 Haggai, the LORD's messenger, delivered the LORD's message to the people, "I am with you"—the LORD's declaration.

14 The LORD stirred up the spirit of Zerubbabel son of Shealtiel, governor of Judah, the spirit of the high priest Joshua son of Jehozadak, and the spirit of all the remnant of the people. They began work on the house of •Yahweh of Hosts, their God, 15 on the twenty-fourth day of the sixth month, in the second year of King Darius.

Encouragement and Promise

2 On the twenty-first day of the seventh month, the word of the LORD came through Haggai the prophet: 2 "Speak to Zerubbabel son of Shealtiel, governor of Judah, to the high priest Joshua son of Jehozadak, and to the remnant of the people: 3 Who is left among you who saw this house in its former glory? How does it look to you now? Doesn't it seem like nothing to you?[f] 4 Even so, be strong, Zerubbabel"—the LORD's declaration. "Be strong, Joshua son of Jehozadak, high priest. Be strong, all you people of the land"—the LORD's declaration. "Work! For I am with you"—the declaration of the LORD of •Hosts. 5 "⌊This is⌋ the promise I made to you when you came out of Egypt, and My Spirit is present among you; don't be afraid."

6 For the LORD of Hosts says this: "Once more, in a little while, I am going to shake the heavens and the earth, the sea and the dry land. 7 I will shake all the nations so that the treasures of all the nations will come, and I will fill this house with glory," says the LORD of Hosts. 8 "The silver and gold belong to Me"—the declaration of the LORD of Hosts. 9 "The final glory of this house[g] will be greater than the first," says the LORD of Hosts. "I will provide peace in this place"—the declaration of the LORD of Hosts.

From Deprivation to Blessing

10 On the twenty-fourth day of the ninth ⌊month⌋, in the second year of Darius, the word of the LORD came to Haggai the prophet: 11 "This is what the LORD of Hosts says: Ask the priests for a ruling. 12 If a man is carrying consecrated meat in the fold of his garment, and with his fold touches bread, stew, wine, oil, or any other food, does it become holy?"

The priests answered, "No."

13 Then Haggai asked, "If someone defiled by ⌊contact with⌋ a corpse touches any of these, does it become defiled?"

The priests answered, "It becomes defiled."

---

[a]1:1 King of Persia 522–486 B.C.   [b]1:4 = the temple   [c]1:5,7 Lit *Place your heart on*   [d]1:9 Lit *blew on*   [e]1:10 Or *So above you*   [f]2:3 Lit *Is it not in your eyes?*   [g]2:9 Or *The glory of this latter house*

1:2 These people. The Israelites are called "these people," rather than the usual "my people," to emphasize that sin had separated them from God. They were making excuses for not building the temple as God had commanded.

1:3-4 live in your paneled houses. Haggai

rebukes the people for their selfishness and misplaced priorities. They were building comfortable houses for themselves but neglecting to build the house of God.

1:5-6,9-10 Think carefully about your ways. The people's apathy about building the temple has caused God to withhold

blessings, so that they will "think carefully" about their ways.

1:14 The LORD stirred up the spirit. God moved the hearts of his people, giving them a desire to return home and work on the temple.

2:1 On the twenty-first day of the seventh

14 Then Haggai replied, "So is this people, and so is this nation before Me"—the LORD's declaration. "And so is every work of their hands; even what they offer there is defiled.

15 "Now, reflect back from this day: Before one stone was placed on another in the LORD's temple, 16 what state were you in?a When someone came to a ⌊grain⌋ heap of 20 measures, it ⌊only⌋ amounted to 10; when one came to the winepress to dip 50 measures from the vat, it ⌊only⌋ amounted to 20. 17 I struck you—all the work of your hands—with blight, mildew, and hail, but you didn't turn to Me"—the LORD's declaration. 18 "Consider carefully from this day forward; from the twenty-fourth day of the ninth month, from the day the foundation of the LORD's temple was laid; consider it carefully. 19 Is there still seed left in the granary? The vine, the fig, the pomegranate, and the olive tree have not yet produced. But from this day on I will bless you."

Promise to Zerubbabel

20 The word of the LORD came to Haggai a second time on the twenty-fourth day of the month: 21 "Speak to Zerubbabel, governor of Judah: I am going to shake the heavens and the earth. 22 I will overturn royal thrones and destroy the power of the Gentile kingdoms. I will overturn chariots and their riders. Horses and their riders will fall, each by his brother's sword. 23 On that day"—the declaration of the LORD of Hosts—"I will take you, Zerubbabel son of Shealtiel, My servant"—the LORD's declaration—"and make you like My signet ring, for I have chosen you." ⌊This is⌋ the declaration of the LORD of Hosts.

---

a 2:16 Hb obscure

month. This was the final day of the week-long Feast of Tabernacles, a time of celebration for the summer harvest.

2:3 former glory. The people were discouraged as they compared the inferior rebuilt temple to Solomon's glorious temple.

2:7 I will fill this house with glory. To encourage the people, God promises that glory will fill the house of the Lord. This Messianic prophecy foretells Christ's coming (He is the radiance of God's glory, Heb. 1:3), and points toward the glory of God's kingdom fully realized at the end of time.

2:13-14 It becomes defiled. Just as ceremonial uncleanness is transferred from an "unclean" person to anything he touches, so the disobedience of a worshiper is transferred onto sacrifices, which renders them unacceptable to God.

2:15-19 reflect back. To convince the people to obey God, Haggai reminds them of the economic hardships God used to punish their sin. He then affirms that God has promised blessing for faithful obedience.

INTRODUCTION TO

ZECHARIAH

PERSONAL READING PLAN

- ☐ Zechariah 1:1-2:13
- ☐ Zechariah 3:1-5:11
- ☐ Zechariah 6:1-7:14
- ☐ Zechariah 8:1-9:17

- ☐ Zechariah 10:1-11:17
- ☐ Zechariah 12:1-13:6
- ☐ Zechariah 13:7-14:21

AUTHOR

The writer is Zechariah, the prophet and priest who was born in exile and returned from Babylon to Judah in 538 B.C. (1:1; see Ezra 5:1; 6:14).

DATE

Zechariah is specific as to the year, month, and day of the messages recorded in chapters 1-8. They span the years from 520 to 518 B.C. The date of his final prophecy (chapters 9-14) is uncertain, though it was probably not given until some 40 years later (e.g., after 480 B.C.).

THEME

Rebuilding the temple and the nation of Judah; the Lord's return.

HISTORICAL BACKGROUND

Zechariah tells of the return of the Jews from the Babylonian exile and the subsequent rebuilding of Jerusalem and the temple (see the Introductions to Ezra and Nehemiah). It was through the ministry of Zechariah (along with Haggai) that the rebuilding of the temple began (see Ezra 5:1-2). The temple was completed and dedicated four years later in 516 B.C.

CHARACTERISTICS

Zechariah was a younger contemporary of Haggai, with a ministry extending well beyond Haggai's, possibly into the reign of Artaxerxes I (465-424 B.C.). Both prophets dealt with the same theme (rebuilding the temple) but in contrasting ways (see the Introduction to Haggai). Zechariah was an apocalyptic visionary, while Haggai was a practical doer. The Book of Zechariah poses a study in contrast between Part I (chapters 1-8) and Part II (chapters 9-14), written some 40 years later. In Part I, Zechariah tries to instill enthusiasm for the rebuilding of the temple as the people begin to see how things ultimately result in their deliverance and God's greater glory. In Part II, he proclaims that rebuilding the temple will create the future transformation of God's people into a holy nation. The visions of Zechariah are listed below:

Horseman -	1:7-11
Four Horns and Craftsmen -	1:18-21
Surveyor -	2:1-13
High Priest and Branch -	3:1-10
Gold Lampstand -	4:1-14
Flying Scroll -	5:1-4
Woman in the Basket -	5:5-11
Four Chariots -	6:1-8

A Plea for Repentance

1 In the eighth month, in the second year of Darius, the word of the LORD came to the prophet Zechariah son of Berechiah, son of Iddo: 2 "The LORD was extremely angry with your ancestors. 3 So tell the people: This is what the LORD of •Hosts says: Return to Me"—[this is] the declaration of the LORD of Hosts— "and I will return to you, says the LORD of Hosts. 4 Do not be like your ancestors; the earlier prophets proclaimed to them: This is what the LORD of Hosts says: Turn from your evil ways and your evil deeds. But they did not listen or pay attention to Me"—the LORD's declaration. 5 "Where are your ancestors now? And do the prophets live forever? 6 But didn't My words and My statutes that I commanded My servants the prophets overtake your ancestors? They repented and said: As the LORD of Hosts purposed to deal with us for our ways and deeds, so He has dealt with us."

The Night Visions

7 On the twenty-fourth day of the eleventh month, which is the month of Shebat, in the second year of Darius, the word of the LORD came to the prophet Zechariah son of Berechiah, son of Iddo:

First Vision: Horsemen

8 I looked out in the night and saw a man riding on a red horse. He was standing among the myrtle trees in the valley. Behind him were red, sorrel, and white horses. 9 I asked, "What are these, my lord?"

The angel who was talking to me replied, "I will show you what they are."

10 Then the man standing among the myrtle trees explained, "They are the ones the LORD has sent to patrol the earth."

11 They reported to the Angel of the LORD standing among the myrtle trees, "We have patrolled the earth, and right now the whole earth is calm and quiet."

12 Then the Angel of the LORD responded, "How long, LORD of Hosts, will You withhold mercy from Jerusalem and the cities of Judah that You have been angry with these 70 years?" 13 The LORD replied with kind and comforting words to the angel who was speaking with me.

14 So the angel who was speaking with me said, "Proclaim: The LORD of Hosts says: I am extremely jealous for Jerusalem and Zion. 15 I am fiercely angry with the nations that are at ease, for I was a little angry, but they made it worse. 16 Therefore, this is what the LORD says: I have graciously returned to Jerusalem; My house will

be rebuilt within it"—the declaration of the LORD of Hosts—"and a measuring line will be stretched out over Jerusalem.

17 "Proclaim further: This is what the LORD of Hosts says: My cities will again overflow with prosperity; the LORD will once more comfort Zion and again choose Jerusalem."

Second Vision: Four Horns and Craftsmen

18a Then I looked up and saw four •horns. 19 So I asked the angel who was speaking with me, "What are these?"

And he said to me, "These are the horns that scattered Judah, Israel, and Jerusalem."

20 Then the LORD showed me four craftsmen. 21 I asked, "What are they coming to do?"

He replied, "These are the horns that scattered Judah so no one could raise his head. These [craftsmen] have come to terrify them, to cut off the horns of the nations that raised [their] horns against the land of Judah to scatter it."

Third Vision: Surveyor

2 b I looked up and saw a man with a measuring line in his hand. 2 I asked, "Where are you going?"

He answered me, "To measure Jerusalem to determine its width and length."

3 Then the angel who was speaking with me went out, and another angel went out to meet him. 4 He said to him, "Run and tell this young man: Jerusalem will be inhabited without walls because of the number of people and livestock in it." 5 The declaration of the LORD: "I will be a wall of fire around it, and I will be the glory within it."

6 "Get up! Leave the land of the north"—the LORD's declaration—"for I have scattered you like the four winds of heaven"—the LORD's declaration. 7 "Go, Zion! Escape, you who are living with Daughter Babylon." 8 For the LORD of •Hosts says this: "He has sent Me[c] for [His] glory against the nations who are plundering you, for anyone who touches you touches the pupil[d] of His[e] eye. 9 I will move against them with My[f] power, and they will become plunder for their own servants. Then you will know that the LORD of Hosts has sent Me.[c]

10 "Daughter Zion, shout for joy and be glad, for I am coming to dwell among you"—the LORD's declaration. 11 "Many nations will join themselves to the LORD on that day and become My[g] people. I will dwell among you, and you will know that the LORD of Hosts has sent Me[c] to you. 12 The LORD will take possession of Judah as His portion in the Holy Land, and He will

---

a**1:18** Zch 2:1 in Hb   b**2:1** Zch 2:5 in Hb   c**2:8,9,11** Or me   d**2:8** Or apple   e**2:8** Alt Hb tradition reads My   f**2:9** Or my   g**2:11** LXX, Syr read His

---

1:7-17 Zechariah's first vision of a rider among myrtle trees was a reassuring message. It soothed Israel's fears and inspired hope. The accompanying angel explained that their enemies would be punished (vv. 14-5), and Israel's prosperity would be restored (v. 17).

1:8 in the night ... saw. Zechariah experienced eight visions concerning the restoration of Israel, all in a single night.

2:1-13 The renovation projected in the third vision concerned the expansion of the restored city of Jerusalem (vv. 1-2). A city "without walls" was a symbol of the peace and

prosperity that awaited the Jews in their future dwelling (v. 4).

2:5 will be a wall of fire. This new nation would celebrate their stake in the glory of God.

2:12 in the Holy Land. Ordinary dirt became holy ground due to the presence of God as

once again choose Jerusalem. [13] Let all people be silent before the LORD, for He is coming from His holy dwelling."

Fourth Vision: High Priest and Branch

3 Then he showed me Joshua the high priest standing before the Angel of the LORD, with Satan[a] standing at his right side to accuse him. [2] The LORD[b] said to Satan: "The LORD rebuke you, Satan! May the LORD who has chosen Jerusalem rebuke you! Isn't this man a burning stick snatched from the fire?"

[3] Now Joshua was dressed with filthy[c] clothes as he stood before the Angel. [4] So He[d] spoke to those[e] standing before Him, "Take off his filthy clothes!" Then He said to him, "See, I have removed your guilt from you, and I will clothe you with splendid robes."

[5] Then I said, "Let them put a clean turban on his head." So a clean turban was placed on his head, and they clothed him in garments while the Angel of the LORD was standing nearby.

[6] Then the Angel of the LORD charged Joshua: [7] "This is what the LORD of •Hosts says: If you walk in My ways and keep My instructions, you will both rule My house and take care of My courts; I will also grant you access among these who are standing here.

[8] "Listen, Joshua the high priest, you and your colleagues sitting before you; indeed, these men are a sign that I am about to bring My servant, the Branch. [9] Notice the stone I have set before Joshua; on ⌊that⌋ one stone are seven eyes. I will engrave an inscription on it"—the declaration of the LORD of Hosts—"and I will take away the guilt of this land in a single day. [10] On that day, each of you will invite his neighbor to ⌊sit⌋ under ⌊his⌋ vine and fig tree." ⌊This is⌋ the declaration of the LORD of Hosts.

Fifth Vision: Gold Lampstand

4 The angel who was speaking with me then returned and roused me as one awakened out of sleep. [2] He asked me, "What do you see?"

I replied, "I see a solid gold lampstand there with a bowl on its top. It has seven lamps on it and seven channels for each of[f] the lamps on its top. [3] There are also two olive trees beside it, one on the right of the bowl and the other on its left."

[4] Then I asked the angel who was speaking with me, "What are these, my lord?"

[5] "Don't you know what they are?" replied the angel who was speaking with me.

I said, "No, my lord."

[6] So he answered me, "This is the word of the LORD to Zerubbabel: 'Not by strength or by might, but by My Spirit,' says the LORD of •Hosts. [7] 'What are you, great mountain? Before Zerubbabel you will become a plain. And he will bring out the capstone accompanied by shouts of: Grace, grace to it!'"

[8] Then the word of the LORD came to me: [9] "Zerubbabel's hands have laid the foundation of this house, and his hands will complete it. Then you will know that the LORD of Hosts has sent me to you. [10] For who scorns the day of small things? These seven eyes of the LORD, which scan throughout the whole earth, will rejoice when they see the plumb line[g] in Zerubbabel's hand."

[11] I asked him, "What are the two olive trees on the right and left of the lampstand?" [12] And I questioned him further, "What are the two olive branches beside the two gold conduits, from which golden ⌊oil⌋ pours out?"

[13] Then he inquired of me, "Don't you know what these are?"

"No, my lord," I replied.

[14] "These are the two anointed ones,"[h] he said, "who stand by the Lord of the whole earth."

Sixth Vision: Flying Scroll

5 I looked up again and saw a flying scroll. [2] "What do you see?" he asked me.

"I see a flying scroll," I replied, "30 feet[i] long and 15 feet[j] wide."

[3] Then he said to me, "This is the curse that is going out over the whole land, for every thief will be removed according to what is written on one side, and everyone who swears ⌊falsely⌋ will be removed according to what is written on the other side. [4] I will send it out,"—the declaration of the LORD of •Hosts—"and it will enter the house of the thief and the house of the one who swears falsely by My name. It will stay inside his house and destroy it along with its timbers and stones."

Seventh Vision: Woman in the Basket

[5] Then the angel who was speaking with me came forward and told me, "Look up and see what this is that is approaching."

[6] So I asked, "What is it?"

He responded, "It's a measuring basket[k] that is approaching." And he continued, "This is their iniquity[l] in all the land." [7] Then a lead cover was lifted, and there was a woman sitting inside the basket. [8] "This is

---

God again chooses Jerusalem for His residence.

3:8-9 Branch ... stone. Christ is represented here in two forms: as is a servant of God, a Branch from the King David's line, and the stone associated with the removal of sin.

4:1-14 Zechariah's fifth vision was the motiva-

tional force behind the Jews' temple restoration. The people would soon resume the groundbreaking from years earlier (vv. 7-8). God's Spirit would serve as the construction manager (v. 6).

4:2 gold lampstand. The gold lampstand, with a bowl of oil and channels supplying the

lights, was significant due to its continual flow. God's presence, symbolized in familiar items from the temple, would never be snuffed out.

4:3 two olive trees beside it. The key players in the temple reconstruction were symbolized in the stately trees. Judah's governor, Zerubbabel, and the high priest, Joshua,

Wickedness," he said. He shoved her down into the basket and pushed the lead weight over its opening. [9] Then I looked up and saw two women approaching with the wind in their wings. Their wings were like those of a stork, and they lifted up the basket between earth and sky.

[10] So I asked the angel who was speaking with me, "Where are they taking the basket?"

[11] "To build a shrine for it in the land of •Shinar,"[a] he told me. "When that is ready, ⌊the basket⌋ will be placed there on its pedestal."

Eighth Vision: Four Chariots

6 Then I looked up again and saw four chariots coming from between two mountains. And the mountains were made of bronze. [2] The first chariot had red horses, the second chariot black horses, [3] the third chariot white horses, and the fourth chariot dappled horses—⌊all⌋ strong horses. [4] So I inquired of the angel who was speaking with me, "What are these, my lord?"

[5] The angel told me, "These are the four spirits[b] of heaven going out after presenting themselves to the Lord of the whole earth. [6] The one with the black horses is going to the land of the north, the white horses are going after them, but the dappled horses are going to the land of the south." [7] As the strong horses went out, they wanted to go patrol the earth, and the LORD said, "Go, patrol the earth." So they patrolled the earth. [8] Then He summoned me saying, "See, those going to the land of the north have pacified My Spirit in the northern land."

Crowning of the Branch

[9] The word of the LORD came to me: [10] "Take ⌊an offering⌋ from the exiles, from Heldai, Tobijah, and Jedaiah, who have arrived from Babylon, and go that same day to the house of Josiah son of Zephaniah. [11] Take silver and gold, make crowns and place them on the head of Joshua son of Jehozadak, the high priest. [12] You are to tell him: This is what the LORD of •Hosts says: Here is a man whose name is Branch; He will branch out from His place and build the LORD's temple. [13] Yes, He will build the LORD's temple; He will be clothed in splendor and will sit on His throne and rule. There will also be a priest on His throne, and there will be peaceful counsel between the two of them. [14] The crown will reside in the LORD's temple as a memorial to Heldai, Tobijah, Jedaiah, and Hen[c] son of Zephaniah. [15] People who are far off will come and build the LORD's temple, and you will know that the LORD of Hosts has

sent Me to you. This will happen when you fully obey the LORD your God."

Disobedience and Fasting

7 In the fourth year of King Darius, the word of the LORD came to Zechariah on the fourth day of the ninth month, which is Chislev. [2] Now ⌊the people of⌋ Bethel had sent Sharezer, Regem-melech, and their men to plead for the LORD's favor [3] by asking the priests who were at the house of the LORD of •Hosts as well as the prophets, "Should we mourn and fast in the fifth month as we have done these many years?"

[4] Then the word of the LORD of Hosts came to me: [5] "Ask all the people of the land and the priests: When you fasted and lamented in the fifth and in the seventh ⌊months⌋ for these 70 years, did you really fast for Me? [6] When you eat and drink, don't you eat and drink ⌊simply⌋ for yourselves? [7] Aren't ⌊these⌋ the words that the LORD proclaimed through the earlier prophets when Jerusalem was inhabited and secure,[d] along with its surrounding cities, and when the southern region and the Judean foothills were inhabited?"

[8] The word of the LORD came to Zechariah: [9] "The LORD of Hosts says this: Render true justice. Show faithful love and compassion to one another. [10] Do not oppress the widow or the fatherless, the stranger or the poor, and do not plot evil in your hearts against one another. [11] But they refused to pay attention and turned a stubborn shoulder; they closed their ears so they could not hear. [12] They made their hearts like a rock so as not to obey the law or the words that the LORD of Hosts had sent by His Spirit through the earlier prophets. Therefore great anger came from the LORD of Hosts. [13] Just as He had called, and they would not listen, so when they called, I would not listen," says the LORD of Hosts. [14] "I scattered them with a windstorm over all the nations that had not known them, and the land was left desolate behind them, with no one coming or going. They turned a pleasant land into a desolation."

Obedience and Feasting

8 The word of the LORD of •Hosts came: [2] "The LORD of Hosts says this: I am extremely jealous for Zion; I am jealous for her with great wrath." [3] The LORD says this: "I will return to Zion and live in Jerusalem. Then Jerusalem will be called the Faithful City, the mountain of the LORD of Hosts, and the Holy Mountain." [4] The LORD of Hosts says this: "Old men and women will again sit along the streets of Jerusalem, each with a staff in hand because of advanced age. [5] The streets of the city will be filled with boys and

---

a5:11 = Babylon; Gn 10:10 b6:5 Or winds c6:14 Probably = Josiah; Zch 6:10; in Hb Hen = favor d7:7 Or prosperous

---

would lead the people in their efforts.

5:1-4 Zechariah's fifth vision held no tolerance for sin. The flying scroll portrayed swift judgment on all those who rejected God's commands.

5:2 flying scroll. The scroll served as God's giant billboard, announcing His judgment

against sin—large enough that nobody could miss the message.

5:6 basket. A super-sized basket (big enough to hold a person) carried a weighty mission. The corporate sins of all the people would be carried away in it.

5:7 a woman sitting inside the basket. Her

presence had less to do with her gender than it did the animated image of wickedness as alive and well. The wickedness must be destroyed.

6:1-8 The eighth vision fulfilled the punishment ordained in the first vision (1:7-17).

8:1-23 Zechariah itemized the blessings

girls playing in them." 6 The LORD of Hosts says this: "Though it may seem incredible to the remnant of this people in those days, should it also seem incredible to Me?"—the declaration of the LORD of Hosts. 7 The LORD of Hosts says this: "I will save My people from the land of the east and the land of the west. 8 I will bring them ⌊back⌋ to live in Jerusalem. They will be My people, and I will be their faithful and righteous God."

9 The LORD of Hosts says this: "Let your hands be strong, you who now hear these words that the prophets spoke when the foundations were laid for the rebuilding of the temple, the house of the LORD of Hosts. 10 For prior to those days neither man nor beast had wages. There was no safety from the enemy for anyone who came or went, for I turned everyone against his neighbor. 11 But now, I will not treat the remnant of this people as in the former days"—the declaration of the LORD of Hosts. 12 "For they will sow in peace: the vine will yield its fruit, the land will yield its produce, and the skies will yield their dew. I will give the remnant of this people all these things as an inheritance. 13 As you have been a curse among the nations, house of Judah and house of Israel, so I will save you, and you will be a blessing. Don't be afraid; let your hands be strong." 14 For the LORD of Hosts says this: "As I resolved to treat you badly when your fathers provoked Me to anger, and would not relent," says the LORD of Hosts, 15 "so I have resolved again in these days to do what is good to Jerusalem and the house of Judah. Don't be afraid. 16 These are the things you must do: Speak truth to one another; render honest and peaceful judgments in your •gates. 17 Do not plot evil in your hearts against your neighbor, and do not love perjury, for I hate all this"— the LORD's declaration.

18 Then the word of the LORD of Hosts came to me: 19 "The LORD of Hosts says this: The fast of the fourth ⌊month⌋, the fast of the fifth, the fast of the seventh, and the fast of the tenth will become times of joy, gladness, and cheerful festivals for the house of Judah. Therefore, love truth and peace." 20 The LORD of Hosts says this: "Peoples will yet come, the residents of many cities; 21 the residents of one city will go to another, saying: Let's go at once to plead for the LORD's favor and to seek the LORD of Hosts. I am also going. 22 Many peoples and strong nations will come to seek the LORD of Hosts in Jerusalem and to plead for the LORD's favor." 23 The LORD of Hosts says this: "In those days, 10 men from nations of every language will grab the robe of a Jewish man tightly, urging: Let us go with you, for we have heard that God is with you."

Judgment of Zion's Enemies

9 An •Oracle

The word of the LORD
is against the land of Hadrach,
and Damascus is its resting place—
for the eyes of men
and all the tribes of Israel
are on the LORDa—
2 and also against Hamath, which borders it,
as well as Tyre and Sidon,
though they are very shrewd.
3 Tyre has built herself a fortress;
she has heaped up silver like dust
and gold like the dirt of the streets.
4 Listen! The Lord will impoverish her
and cast her wealth into the sea;
she herself will be consumed by fire.
5 Ashkelon will see it and be afraid;
Gaza too, and will writhe in great pain,
as will Ekron, for her hope will fail.
There will cease to be a king in Gaza,
and Ashkelon will become uninhabited.
6 A mongrel people will live in Ashdod,
and I will destroy the pride
of the Philistines.
7 I will remove the blood from their mouths
and the detestable things
from between their teeth.
Then they too will become a remnant
for our God;
they will become like a clan in Judah
and Ekron like the Jebusites.
8 I will set up camp at My house
against an army,b
against those who march back and forth,
and no oppressor will march against them again,
for now I have seen with My own eyes.

The Coming of Zion's King

9 Rejoice greatly, Daughter Zion!
Shout in triumph, Daughter Jerusalem!
See, your King is coming to you;
He is righteous and victorious,c
humble and riding on a donkey,
on a colt, the foal of a donkey.
10 I will cut off the chariot from Ephraim
and the horse from Jerusalem.
The bow of war will be removed,
and He will proclaim peace to the nations.
His dominion will extend from sea to sea,

---

a9:1 Or eyes of the LORD are on mankind—   b9:8 Or house as a guard   c9:9 Or and has salvation

---

promised in his earlier visions (1:7–6:8). If the Lord Almighty said it, they could count on God delivering what He had promised.
8:9, 13 "Let your hands be strong." This exhortation of the Lord both opens and closes His word recorded in 8:9-13. Because God had promised His favor and protection to the

inhabitants of Judah, they were encouraged to look to the future with confidence and a commitment to complete the construction of the temple. This description contrasts strikingly with the description of their forebears, who refused to pay attention, turned a stubborn shoulder, stop their ears from hearing

and made their hearts like flint (7:11-12). Now Judah would be blessed and be a blessing to others.
8:11 But now. Zechariah emphasized the contrast between their present state of disobedience and God's coming restoration (see 8:12).

from the Euphrates River
to the ends of the earth.

11 As for you,
because of the blood of your covenant,
I will release your prisoners
from the waterless cistern.

12 Return to a stronghold,
you prisoners who have hope;
today I declare that I will restore double to you.

13 For I will bend Judah ⌊as My bow⌋;
I will fill that bow with Ephraim.
I will rouse your sons, Zion,
against your sons, Greece.ª
I will make you like a warrior's sword.

14 Then the LORD will appear over them,
and His arrow will fly like lightning.
The Lord GOD will sound the trumpet
and advance with the southern storms.

15 The LORD of •Hosts will defend them.
They will consume and conquer
    with slingstones;
they will drink and be rowdy as if with wine.
They will be as full as the sprinkling basin,
like ⌊those⌋ at the corners of the altar.

16 The LORD their God will save them on that day
as the flock of His people;
for they are like jewels in a crown,
sparkling over His land.

17 How lovely and beautiful they will be!
Grain will make the young men flourish,
and new wine, the young women.

The LORD Restores His People

10 Ask the LORD for rain
in the season of spring rain.
The LORD makes the rain clouds,
and He will give them showers of rain
and crops in the field for everyone.

2 For the idols speak falsehood,
and the diviners see illusions;
they relate empty dreams
and offer empty comfort.
Therefore ⌊the people⌋ wander like sheep;
they suffer affliction because there is
    no shepherd.

3 My anger burns against the shepherds,
so I will punish the leaders.ᵇ
For the LORD of •Hosts has tended His flock,
the house of Judah;

He will make them like His majestic steed
    in battle.

4 From themᶜ will come the cornerstone,
from them the tent peg,
from them the battle bow,
from them every ruler.
Together 5 they will be like warriors in battle
trampling down the mud of the streets.
They will fight because the LORD is with them,
and they will put horsemen to shame.

6 I will strengthen the house of Judah
and deliver the house of Joseph.ᵈ
I will restoreᵉ them
because I have compassion on them,
and they will be
as though I had never rejected them.
For I am the LORD their God,
and I will answer them.

7 Ephraim will be like a warrior,
and their hearts will be glad as if with wine.
Their children will see it and be glad;
their hearts will rejoice in the LORD.

8 I will whistle and gather them
because I have redeemed them;
they will be as numerous as they once were.

9 Though I sow them among the nations,
they will remember Me in the distant lands;
they and their children will live and return.

10 I will bring them back from the land of Egypt
and gather them from Assyria.
I will bring them to the land of Gilead
and to Lebanon,
but it will not be enough for them.

11 Heᶠ will pass through the sea of distress
and strike the waves of the sea;
all the depths of the Nile will dry up.
The pride of Assyria will be brought down,
and the scepter of Egypt will come to an end.

12 I will strengthen them in the LORD,
and they will march in His name—
⌊this is⌋
•Yahweh's declaration.

Israel's Shepherds: Good and Bad

11 Open your gates, Lebanon,
and fire will consume your cedars.

2 Wail, cypress, for the cedar has fallen;
the glorious ⌊trees⌋ are destroyed!
Wail, oaks of Bashan,

ª**9:13** Lit *Javan*; Gn 10:2; Dn 8:21   ᵇ**10:3** Lit *he-goats*   ᶜ**10:4** = Judah   ᵈ**10:6** = the northern kingdom   ᵉ**10:6** Other Hb mss, LXX read *settle*
ᶠ**10:11** = the LORD

8:19 fast. God would turn the deprivations of the past into future feasts. What were once annual seasons of mourning would turn into celebrations.

8:20-23 Yahweh's reputation would inspire many nations. As a result, previously pagan nations would gravitate toward Jeru-

salem to worship God (Isa. 2:3).

9:9 Chapter 9 marks the second half of Zechariah's prophecies. The concluding five chapters focus on the coming King: Jesus Christ. **Rejoice ... Daughter Zion!** Jerusalem's citizens are to prepare to receive their King who will come riding on a donkey. **riding**

on a donkey. Here, Zechariah prophesies Christ's peaceful entry into the city of Jerusalem (Matt. 21:5), which sets the stage for His eventual return.

11:5 those who buy them....those who sell them. God's people had been and would yet be oppressed by other nations who got rich at their

for the stately forest has fallen!
3 Listen to the wail of the shepherds,
  for their glory is destroyed.
  Listen to the roar of young lions,
  for the thickets of the Jordan
  are[a] destroyed.

4 The LORD my God says this: "Shepherd the flock intended for slaughter. 5 Those who buy them slaughter them but are not punished. Those who sell them say: Praise the LORD because I have become rich! Even their own shepherds have no compassion for them. 6 Indeed, I will no longer have compassion on the inhabitants of the land"—the LORD's declaration. "Instead, I will turn everyone over to his neighbor and his king. They will devastate the land, and I will not deliver ⌊it⌋ from them."

7 So I shepherded the flock intended for slaughter, the afflicted of the flock.[b] I took two staffs, calling one Favor and the other Union, and I shepherded the flock. 8 In one month I got rid of three shepherds. I became impatient with them, and they also detested me. 9 Then I said, "I will no longer shepherd you. Let what is dying die, and let what is going astray go astray; let the rest devour each other's flesh." 10 Next I took my staff called Favor and cut it in two, annulling the covenant I had made with all the peoples. 11 It was annulled on that day, and so the afflicted of the flock[c] who were watching me knew that it was the word of the LORD. 12 Then I said to them, "If it seems right to you, give me my wages; but if not, keep ⌊them⌋." So they weighed my wages, 30 pieces of silver.

13 "Throw it to the potter,"[d] the LORD said to me— this magnificent price I was valued by them. So I took the 30 pieces of silver and threw it into the house of the LORD, to the potter.[e] 14 Then I cut in two my second staff, Union, annulling the brotherhood between Judah and Israel.

15 The LORD also said to me: "Take the equipment of a foolish shepherd. 16 I am about to raise up a shepherd in the land who will not care for those who are going astray, and he will not seek the lost[f] or heal the broken. He will not sustain the healthy,[g] but he will devour the flesh of the fat ⌊sheep⌋ and tear off their hooves.

17 Woe to the worthless shepherd
  who deserts the flock!
  May a sword strike[h] his arm
  and his right eye!

May his arm wither away
and his right eye go completely blind!"

Judah's Security

12

An •Oracle

The word of the LORD concerning Israel. A declaration of the LORD, who stretched out the heavens, laid the foundation of the earth, and formed the spirit of man within him.

2 "Look, I will make Jerusalem a cup that causes staggering for the peoples who surround the city. The siege against Jerusalem will also involve Judah. 3 On that day I will make Jerusalem a heavy stone for all the peoples; all who try to lift it will injure themselves severely when all the nations of the earth gather against her. 4 On that day"—the LORD's declaration—"I will strike every horse with panic and its rider with madness. I will keep a watchful eye on the house of Judah but strike all the horses of the nations with blindness. 5 Then ⌊each of⌋ the leaders of Judah will think to himself: The residents of Jerusalem are my strength through the LORD of •Hosts, their God. 6 On that day I will make the leaders of Judah like a firepot in a woodpile, like a flaming torch among sheaves; they will consume all the peoples around them on the right and the left, while Jerusalem continues to be inhabited on its site, in Jerusalem. 7 The LORD will save the tents of Judah first, so that the glory of David's house and the glory of Jerusalem's residents may not be greater than that of Judah. 8 On that day the LORD will defend the inhabitants of Jerusalem, so that the one who is weakest among them will be like David on that day, and the house of David will be like God, like the Angel of the LORD, before them. 9 On that day I will set out to destroy all the nations that come against Jerusalem.

Mourning for the Pierced One

10 "Then I will pour out a spirit[i] of grace and prayer on the house of David and the residents of Jerusalem, and they will look at[j] Me whom they pierced. They will mourn for Him as one mourns for an only child and weep bitterly for Him as one weeps for a firstborn. 11 On that day the mourning in Jerusalem will be as great as the mourning of Hadad-rimmon in the plain of Megiddo. 12 The land will mourn, every family by itself: the family of David's house by itself and their women

---

a 11:3 Lit for the majesty of the Jordan is   b 11:7 LXX reads slaughter that belonged to the sheep merchants   c 11:11 LXX reads and the sheep merchants   d 11:13 Syr reads treasury; Mt 27:5   e 11:13 One Hb ms, Syr read treasury   f 11:16 Lit young   g 11:16 Or exhausted   h 11:17 Lit be against   i 12:10 Or out the Spirit   j 12:10 Or to

---

expense. **even their own shepherds.** Their own leaders, those who had been called to exercise compassion, cared only for themselves.
11:7 So I shepherded the flock. In the midst of this nation with abusive and self-serving shepherds, Zechariah is sent as good shepherd, one who foreshadows the

Good Shepherd. Like the Messiah, he was rejected. **two staffs.** Middle Eastern shepherds often carried two staffs. One to use against predatory animals and one designed to enable the shepherd to retrieve a lost sheep from a hard to reach place. **Favor...and Union** were the symbolic names

of the two staffs. Favor spoke of God's grace toward His oppressed people and Union symbolized the reuniting of the divided kingdom.
11:12 30 pieces of silver. The price of a slave gored by an ox. The amount for which Jesus was betrayed.
11:14 annulling the brotherhood. The Jews'

by themselves; the family of Nathan's[a] house by itself and their women by themselves; 13 the family of Levi's house by itself and their women by themselves; the family of Shimei[b] by itself and their women by themselves; 14 all the remaining families, every family by itself, and their women by themselves.

God's People Cleansed

13 "On that day a fountain will be opened for the house of David and for the residents of Jerusalem, ⌊to wash away⌋ sin and impurity. 2 On that day"—the declaration of the LORD of •Hosts—"I will erase the names of the idols from the land, and they will no longer be remembered. I will remove the prophets[c] and the unclean spirit from the land. 3 If a man still prophesies, his father and his mother who bore him will say to him: You cannot remain alive because you have spoken falsely in the name of the LORD. When he prophesies, his father and his mother who bore him will pierce him through. 4 On that day every prophet will be ashamed of his vision when he prophesies; they will not put on a hairy cloak in order to deceive. 5 He will say: I am not a prophet; I am a tiller of the soil, for a man purchased[d] me as a servant since my youth. 6 If someone asks him: What are these wounds on your chest?[e] —then he will answer: The wounds I received in the house of my friends.

7 Sword, awake against My shepherd,
against the man who is My associate—
the declaration of the LORD of Hosts.
Strike the shepherd, and the sheep
will be scattered;
I will also turn My hand against the little ones.
8 In the whole land—
the LORD's declaration—
two-thirds[f] will be cut off and die,
but a third will be left in it.
9 I will put this third through the fire;
I will refine them as silver is refined
and test them as gold is tested.
They will call on My name,
and I will answer them.
I will say: They are My people,
and they will say: The LORD is our God."

The LORD's Triumph and Reign

14 A day of the LORD is coming when your plunder will be divided in your presence. 2 I will gather all the nations against Jerusalem for battle. The city will be captured, the houses looted, and the women raped. Half the city will go into exile, but the rest of the people will not be removed from the city.

3 Then the LORD will go out to fight against those nations as He fights on a day of battle. 4 On that day His feet will stand on the •Mount of Olives, which faces Jerusalem on the east. The Mount of Olives will be split in half from east to west, forming a huge valley, so that half the mountain will move to the north and half to the south. 5 You will flee by My mountain valley,[g] for the valley of the mountains will extend to Azal. You will flee as you fled[h] from the earthquake in the days of Uzziah king of Judah. Then the LORD my God will come and all the holy ones with Him.[i]

6 On that day there will be no light; the sunlight and moonlight[j] will diminish.[k] 7 It will be a day known ⌊only⌋ to •Yahweh, without day or night, but there will be light at evening.

8 On that day living water will flow out from Jerusalem, half of it toward the eastern sea[l] and the other half toward the western sea,[m] in summer and winter alike. 9 On that day Yahweh will become king over all the earth—Yahweh alone, and His name alone. 10 All the land from Geba to Rimmon south of Jerusalem will be changed into a plain. But ⌊Jerusalem⌋ will be raised up and will remain[n] on its site from the Benjamin Gate to the place of the First Gate,[o] to the Corner Gate, and from the Tower of Hananel to the royal winepresses. 11 People will live there, and never again will there be a curse of destruction. So Jerusalem will dwell in security.

12 This will be the plague the LORD strikes all the peoples with, who have warred against Jerusalem: their flesh will rot while they stand on their feet, their eyes will rot in their sockets, and their tongues will rot in their mouths. 13 On that day a great panic from the LORD will be among them, so that each will seize the hand of another, and the hand of one will rise against the other. 14 Judah will also fight at Jerusalem, and the wealth of all the surrounding nations will be collected: gold, silver, and clothing in great abundance. 15 The same plague as the previous one will strike[p] the horses, mules, camels, donkeys, and all the animals that are in those camps.

16 Then all the survivors from the nations that came against Jerusalem will go up year after year to worship

---

[a] 12:12 = a son of David; 2 Sm 5:14; Lk 3:31   [b] 12:13 = a descendant of Levi; Ex 6:16–17; Nm 3:18; 1 Ch 6:17   [c] 13:2 = false prophets   [d] 13:5 Or sold   [e] 13:6 Lit wounds between my hands   [f] 13:8 Lit two-thirds in it   [g] 14:5 Some Hb mss, LXX, Sym, Tg read You will be blocked—the valley of My mountains—   [h] 14:5 LXX reads It will be blocked as it was blocked   [i] 14:5 Some Hb mss, LXX, Vg, Tg, Syr; other Hb mss read you   [j] 14:6 Lit light; the precious things   [k] 14:6 LXX, Sym, Syr, Tg, Vg read no light or cold or ice   [l] 14:8 = the Dead Sea   [m] 14:8 = the Mediterranean Sea   [n] 14:10 Or will be inhabited   [o] 14:10 Or the former gate   [p] 14:15 Lit be on

---

history was one of family hostility, not harmony. The role of the future Messiah-Shepherd would be to reunite the splintered flock (Ezek. 37:16-28).

11:15 foolish shepherd. In the absence of God's Shepherd, a deceiver would arrive on the scene. He would wound many (v. 17).

12:1 word of the LORD. Zechariah put God's message in the context of His powerful works. God's deeds were powerful, but His declaration was more so.

13:7 Sword. This sword, representing death, would be employed to bring God's vengeance—first on the Shepherd, then on even

the little ones... Without the Shepherd, God's people would be vulnerable and defenseless, as history attests (see Matt. 26:31,56).

14:3 The LORD will go out to fight. The LORD will fight on behalf of Jerusalem.

14:18 rain will not fall. Only those who worshiped God would enjoy His blessings.

the King, the LORD of •Hosts, and to celebrate the Festival of Booths. [17] Should any of the families of the earth not go up to Jerusalem to worship the King, the LORD of Hosts, rain will not fall on them. [18] And if the people[a] of Egypt will not go up and enter, then rain will not fall on them; this[b] will be the plague the LORD inflicts on the nations who do not go up to celebrate the Festival of Booths. [19] This will be the punishment of Egypt and all the nations that do not go up to celebrate the Festival of Booths. [20] On that day, ⌊the words⌋

HOLY TO THE LORD

will be on the bells of the horses. The pots in the house of the LORD will be like the sprinkling basins before the altar. [21] Every pot in Jerusalem and in Judah will be holy to the LORD of Hosts. Everyone who sacrifices will come and take some of the pots to cook in. And on that day there will no longer be a Canaanite[c] in the house of the LORD of Hosts.

---

[a]**14:18** Lit *family*   [b]**14:18** Lit *it*   [c]**14:21** Or *merchant*

14:20 Holy to the Lord. This phrase summarizes God's desire: that all may know God as holy, and recognize that there is no other god.

MALACHI

AUTHOR

This book is ascribed to Malachi, a contemporary of Ezra and Nehemiah. Since the word "Malachi" means "my messenger," some think that this is a title rather than the name of a person. The Greek translation of the Old Testament (the Septuagint) renders "Malachi" in 1:1 as "my messenger." However, the evidence is not conclusive, and there may well have been a specific prophet by this name.

DATE

The sins denounced by Nehemiah (see Neh. 13:6-31) correspond closely to the denunciation of Malachi (see 1:6-14; 2:14-16; 3:8-11). Hence, a date may be inferred any time after Nehemiah returned to Jerusalem the second time, that is, some time later than 433 B.C.

THEME

Repentance as a prescription to cure spiritual skepticism and indifference.

HISTORICAL BACKGROUND

In the face of stern opposition, the exiles finished the temple in 516 B.C. under the leadership of Zerubbabel and the prophecy of Haggai. The community was strengthened through the restoration of temple worship by Ezra in 458 B.C. In 445 B.C., Nehemiah returned to Jerusalem, rebuilt the walls, and brought many religious reforms.

Twelve years later, Nehemiah returned to serve the Persian king. With success behind them, the people lapsed into religious indifference. Malachi claims the people are "just going through the motions" of their faith, doubting the love and justice of God. Malachi was most likely the last prophet until the time of Christ, some 400 years later.

CHARACTERISTICS

Malachi uses a question-and-answer form of dialogue to develop his themes. Seven questions or complaints raised by the people are recorded. However, the book is dominated by God's voice—the voice of a loving father (1:6) having to discipline His children with "tough love". Malachi is written in forceful, lofty prose. He uses repetition (the name "LORD of Hosts" occurs 20 times) and vivid images to help the people he is addressing to sense the attitudes of God. When He judges, God will be "like a refiner's fire and like cleansing lye" (3:2), but for the righteous "the sun of righteousness will rise with healing in its wings, and you will go out and playfully jump like calves from the stall" (4:2).

The LORD's Love for Israel

1 An •oracle: The word of the LORD to Israel through Malachi.[a]

² "I have loved you," says the LORD.

But you ask: "How have You loved us?"

"Wasn't Esau Jacob's brother?" ⌊This is⌋ the LORD's declaration. "Even so, I loved Jacob, ³ but I hated Esau. I turned his mountains into a wasteland, and ⌊gave⌋ his inheritance to the desert jackals."

⁴ Though Edom says: "We have been devastated, but we will rebuild[b] the ruins," the LORD of •Hosts says this: "They may build, but I will demolish. They will be called a wicked country and the people the LORD has cursed[c] forever. ⁵ Your own eyes will see this, and you yourselves will say: The LORD is great, ⌊even⌋ beyond[d] the borders of Israel.

Disobedience of the Priests

⁶ "A son honors ⌊his⌋ father, and a servant his master. But if I am a father, where is My honor? And if I am a master, where is ⌊your⌋ •fear of Me? says the LORD of Hosts to you priests, who despise My name."

Yet you ask: "How have we despised Your name?"

⁷ "By presenting defiled food on My altar."

You ask: "How have we defiled You?"

When you say: "The LORD's table is contemptible."

⁸ "When you present a blind ⌊animal⌋ for sacrifice, is it not wrong? And when you present a lame or sick ⌊animal⌋, is it not wrong? Bring it to your governor! Would he be pleased with you or show you favor?" asks the LORD of Hosts. ⁹ "And now ask for God's favor. Will He be gracious to us? ⌊Since⌋ this has come from your hands, will He show any of you favor?" asks the LORD of Hosts. ¹⁰ "I wish one of you would shut the ⌊temple⌋ doors, so you would no longer kindle a useless ⌊fire on⌋ My altar! I am not pleased with you," says the LORD of Hosts, "and I will accept no offering from your hands.

¹¹ "For My name will be great among the nations, from the rising of the sun to its setting. Incense[e] and pure offerings will be presented in My name in every place because My name will be great among the nations,"[f] says the LORD of Hosts.

¹² But you are profaning it[g] when you say: "The Lord's table is defiled, and its product, its food, is contemptible." ¹³ You also say: "Look, what a nuisance!" "And you scorn[h] it," says the LORD of Hosts. "You bring stolen,[i] lame, or sick animals. You bring this as an offering! Am I to accept that from your hands?" asks the LORD.

¹⁴ "The deceiver is cursed who has an ⌊acceptable⌋ male in his flock and makes a vow but sacrifices a defective ⌊animal⌋ to the Lord. For I am a great King," says the LORD of Hosts, "and My name[j] will be feared among the nations.

Warning to the Priests

2 "Therefore, this decree is for you priests: ² If you don't listen, and if you don't take it to heart to honor My name," says the LORD of •Hosts, "I will send a curse among you, and I will curse your blessings. In fact, I have already begun to curse them because you are not taking it to heart.

³ "Look, I am going to rebuke your descendants, and I will spread animal waste[k] over your faces, the waste from your festival sacrifices, and you will be taken away with it. ⁴ Then you will know that I sent you this decree so My covenant with Levi may continue," says the LORD of Hosts. ⁵ "My covenant with him was one of life and peace, and I gave these to him; it called for reverence, and he revered Me and stood in awe of My name. ⁶ True instruction was in his mouth, and nothing wrong was found on his lips. He walked with Me in peace and fairness and turned many from sin. ⁷ For the lips of a priest should guard knowledge, and people should seek instruction from his mouth, because he is the messenger of the LORD of Hosts.

⁸ "You, on the other hand, have turned from the way. You have caused many to stumble by your instruction. You have violated[l] the covenant of Levi," says the LORD of Hosts. ⁹ "So I in turn have made you despised and humiliated before all the people because you are not keeping My ways but are showing partiality in ⌊your⌋ instruction."

Judah's Marital Unfaithfulness

¹⁰ Don't all of us have one Father? Didn't one God create us? Why then do we act treacherously against one another, profaning the covenant of our fathers? ¹¹ Judah has acted treacherously, and a detestable thing has been done in Israel and in Jerusalem. For Judah has profaned the LORD's sanctuary,[m] which He loves, and has married the daughter of a foreign god.[n] ¹² To the man who does this, may the LORD cut off any descendants[o] [p] from the tents of Jacob, even if they present an offering to the LORD of Hosts.

---

[a]**1:1** = My Messenger   [b]**1:4** Or *will return and build*   [c]**1:4** Or *LORD is angry with*   [d]**1:5** Or *great over*   [e]**1:11** Or *Burnt offerings*   [f]**1:11** Many translations supply present tense verbs in this v. rather than future tense.   [g]**1:12** = the LORD's name   [h]**1:13** Lit *blow at*   [i]**1:13** Or *injured*   [j]**1:14** Or *Because I am . . . LORD of Hosts, My name*   [k]**2:3** = dung or entrails   [l]**2:8** Lit *corrupted*   [m]**2:11** Or *profaned what is holy to the LORD*   [n]**2:11** = a woman who worshiped a foreign god; Nm 21:29   [o]**2:12** One Hb ms, LXX, DSS read *off one witnessing or answering*   [p]**2:12** Lit *off one waking or answering*; Hb obscure

---

1:7 defiled food. God gave the priests specific instructions in Leviticus 22:17-30 on how to make acceptable sacrifices. To offer sacrifices wrongly was to profane God's name (Lev. 22:2,32).

2:2 I will curse your blessings. Words spoken as a blessing or curse in biblical times were understood as bringing into reality whatever was spoken. So to revoke a blessing was unheard of.)

2:10 profaning the covenant. Malachi condemns the people for breaking the great covenant, which dictated true worship of God and kind, fair treatment of others.

2:15 the wife of your youth. God clearly views being treacherous to one's wife (or husband), as well as divorce as unjust and in violation of His plan for marriage. Marriage is used here as an illustration of the covenant God made with His "bride," the nation of Israel. God is faithful to His covenants and de-

13 And this is another thing you do: you cover the LORD's altar with tears, with weeping and groaning, because He no longer respects your offerings or receives ⌊them⌋ gladly from your hands.

14 Yet you ask, "For what reason?" Because the LORD has been a witness between you and the wife of your youth. You have acted treacherously against her, though she was your marriage partner and your wife by covenant. 15 Didn't the one ⌊God⌋ make ⌊us⌋ with a remnant of His life-breath? And what does the One seek?a A godly •offspring. So watch yourselves carefully,b and do not act treacherously against the wife of your youth.

16 "If he hates and divorces ⌊his wife⌋," says the LORD God of Israel, "hec covers his garment with injustice," says the LORD of Hosts. Therefore, watch yourselves carefully,d and do not act treacherously.

Judgment at the LORD's Coming

17 You have wearied the LORD with your words.

Yet you ask, "How have we wearied ⌊Him⌋?"

When you say, "Everyone who does evil is good in the LORD's sight, and He is pleased with them," or "Where is the God of justice?"

3 "See, I am going to send My messenger, and he will clear the way before Me. Then the Lord you seek will suddenly come to His temple, the Messenger of the covenant you desire—see, He is coming," says the LORD of •Hosts. 2 But who can endure the day of His coming? And who will be able to stand when He appears? For He will be like a refiner's fire and like cleansing lye. 3 He will be like a refiner and purifier of silver; He will purify the sons of Levi and refine them like gold and silver. Then they will present offerings to the LORD in righteousness. 4 And the offerings of Judah and Jerusalem will please the LORD as in days of old and years gone by.

5 "I will come to you in judgment, and I will be ready to witness against sorcerers and adulterers; against those who swear falsely; against those who oppress the widow and the fatherless, and cheat the wage earner; and against those who deny ⌊justice to⌋ the foreigner. They do not •fear Me," says the LORD of Hosts. 6 "Because I, •Yahweh, have not changed, you descendants of Jacob have not been destroyed.

Robbing God

7 "Since the days of your fathers, you have turned from My statutes; you have not kept ⌊them⌋. Return to Me, and I will return to you," says the LORD of Hosts.

But you ask: "How can we return?"

8 "Will a man rob God? Yet you are robbing Me!" You ask: "How do we rob You?"

"⌊By not making the payments⌋ of 10 percent and the contributions. 9 You are suffering under a curse, yet you—the whole nation—are ⌊still⌋ robbing Me. 10 Bring the full 10 percent into the storehouse so that there may be food in My house. Test Me in this way," says the LORD of Hosts. "See if I will not open the floodgates of heaven and pour out a blessing for you without measure. 11 I will rebuke the devourere for you, so that it will not ruin the produce of your ground, and your vine in your field will not be barren," says the LORD of Hosts. 12 "Then all the nations will consider you fortunate, for you will be a delightful land," says the LORD of Hosts.

The Righteous and the Wicked

13 "Your words against Me are harsh," says the LORD.

Yet you ask: "What have we spoken against You?"

14 You have said: "It is useless to serve God. What have we gained by keeping His requirements and walking mournfully before the LORD of Hosts? 15 So now we consider the arrogant to be fortunate. Not only do those who commit wickedness prosper, they even test God and escape."

16 At that time those who feared the LORD spoke to one another. The LORD took notice and listened. So a book of remembrance was written before Him for those who feared Yahweh and had high regard for His name. 17 "They will be Mine," says the LORD of Hosts, "a special possession on the day I am preparing. I will have compassion on them as a man has compassion on his son who serves him. 18 So you will again see the difference between the righteous and the wicked, between one who serves God and one who does not serve Him.

The Day of the LORD

4f "For indeed, the day is coming, burning like a furnace, when all the arrogant and everyone who commits wickedness will become stubble. The coming day will consume them," says the LORD of •Hosts, "not leaving them root or branches. 2 But for you who •fear My name, the sun of righteousness will rise with healing in its wings, and you will go out and playfully jump like calves from the stall.g 3 You will trample the wicked, for they will be ashes under the soles of your feet on the day I am preparing," says the LORD of Hosts.

a2:15 Or Did the One not make them? So their flesh and spirit belong to Him, or No one who does this even has a remnant of the Spirit in him; Hb obscure b2:15 Lit So guard yourselves in your spirit c2:16 Or The LORD God of Israel says that He hates divorce and the one who d2:16 Lit Therefore, guard yourselves in your spirit e3:11 Perhaps = locusts; Jl 1:4; 2:25 f4:1 Mal 3:19 in Hb g4:2 Or like stall-fed calves

sires that we be people of fidelity as well.

3:1 My messenger ... he will clear the way. The word for "messenger" in Hebrew means "prophet" or "priest." But scholars interpret this as a prophecy of John the Baptist. In fact, Jesus later identified the messenger as John the Baptist (Matt. 11:7-10), whose min-

istry signaled the coming of the Lord.

3:10-12 Bring the full 10 percent into the storehouse. Malachi reaffirms the Mosaic covenant of Deuteronomy 28. God had promised Israel that if Israel obeyed, they would be blessed; if they disobeyed, they would be cursed. They were currently expe-

riencing curses. However, if they would obey the Lord and bring offerings to the temple, God promised to pour blessing "without measure" on them.

4:2 sun of righteousness will rise with healing. This refers to the Day of the Lord, when righteousness and healing will fill the

A Final Warning

4 "Remember the instruction of Moses My servant, the statutes and ordinances I commanded him at Horeb for all Israel. 5 Look, I am going to send you Elijah the prophet before the great and awesome Day of the LORD comes. 6a And he will turn the hearts of fathers to ⌊their⌋ children and the hearts of children to their fathers. Otherwise, I will come and strike the landb with a curse."

new heavens and new earth like the bright morning sun.

4:4 Remember the instruction of Moses. This command, used many times throughout the Old Testament, can mean (1) pay attention to something mentally, (2) meditate as well as obey or (3) recite the Law. Here the emphasis is on recalling the people to obey.

4:5 I am going to send you Elijah the prophet. John the Baptist fulfilled this prophecy in part when he prepared the way for the Messiah. After Elijah appeared in the transfiguration, Christ told His disciples that another Elijah would come. Israel did not accept John the Baptist, so another forerunner will come before the Day of the Lord (Matt. 11:7-14; 17:10-13). Some scholars believe that Elijah is one of the two witnesses in Revelation 11:1-13.

THE NEW
TESTAMENT

MATTHEW

AUTHOR

Nowhere is the author named within the first Gospel. There is however, a long tradition that has assigned it to Matthew. Little is known about Matthew except that he was a tax collector. As such, he would have been bitterly hated by the general populace in Israel—with good reason. For one thing, tax collectors worked for Rome, the oppressor, and therefore were seen as traitors to Israel. For another, tax collectors made their living—and many were quite wealthy—by charging above and beyond what Rome required (only the tax collector knew what was owed). Matthew, the tax collector, stands in contrast to the poor and middle-class fishermen who composed the main body of the disciples.

DATE

When Matthew was written is uncertain, but it was probably between A.D. 50-70.

THEME

Jesus is the long-promised Messiah and authoritative teacher.

THE SYNOPTIC GOSPELS

The word "synoptic" means, literally, "able to be seen together." It refers to the first three Gospels—Matthew, Mark, and Luke—which cover the same events in Jesus' life, often in the same way. A parallel reading of the first three Gospels makes it clear that there is some sort of literary connection between them. The nature of this connection is not absolutely certain, but generally it is assumed that Mark was the first Gospel, that Matthew and Luke had Mark's text before them when they wrote, and that they included some of Mark's material in their own compositions. One reason scholars conclude this is that of the 105 sections of Mark, all but four occur in Matthew or Luke. In fact, Matthew uses 93 of these 105 sections (nearly 90%), including not just the general story, but also Mark's very words in 51% of the cases. However, Matthew and Luke also share some 200 verses not found in Mark, most of which consist of the teachings of Jesus. This material may have come from an early (but now lost) collection of Jesus' teachings.

In whatever order they were written, it is clear that when each of the Gospel writers put together their accounts, they did so with a definite purpose in mind. Each selected some stories

and left out others to produce an account of Jesus' life that would answer the questions and concerns of a particular audience. Mark probably wrote for Christians in Rome who were suffering under Nero's persecution, and so he told about Jesus who was the Suffering Servant. Luke wrote about the Son of Man who came to seek and to save the needy, the lost, and the outcasts. Matthew wrote to a Jewish audience and told the story of King Jesus, the Son of David, who came as the long-promised Messiah to claim His throne.

CHARACTERISTICS

Matthew is the most Jewish of all the Gospels. It was written by a Jew to other Jews to convince them that Jesus was, indeed, the Messiah foretold by Old Testament Scripture. Thus, the author cites numerous Old Testament prophecies that were fulfilled by Jesus. He uses phrases similar to, "all this has happened so that the prophetic Scriptures might be fulfilled" 16 times.

The Jewishness of the Gospel is also seen in the fact that Matthew mentions Jewish customs without explanation (e.g., "phylacteries" in 23:5), that he has a very high view of the law (5:17-20), and that even when recording Jesus' public rebukes, he shows more respect for the teachers of the law and the Pharisees than any other Gospel writer (23:2).

Yet one of the most interesting features of Matthew is that, although he is so Jewish in his concerns, his book clearly portrays the universal nature of the Gospel—that it is for all the peoples of the world. This emphasis emerges right at the beginning when the Gentile wise men bring gifts to the baby Jesus, and it runs through to the end when Jesus sends His followers out to "make disciples of all nations."

Other features of Matthew include his interests in the church (this is the only Gospel to use the word "church") and his concern about the end times—the second coming of Jesus, the end of the world, and the final judgment (his is the fullest account).

STRUCTURE

Matthew is the most orderly in structure of the four Gospel accounts. After an introductory section, the material is organized into five blocks of narrative alternated with five blocks of discourse or teaching. We can see that this is not an accidental arrangement, because Matthew ends each teaching section with a similar statement (compare 7:28; 11:1; 13:53; 19:1 and 26:1).

PASSAGES FOR TOPICAL GROUP STUDY

PASSAGES FOR GENERAL GROUP STUDY

The Genealogy of Jesus Christ

1 The historical record[a] of Jesus Christ, the Son of David, the Son of Abraham:

From Abraham to David

2 Abraham fathered[b] Isaac,
   Isaac fathered Jacob,
   Jacob fathered Judah and his brothers,
3 Judah fathered Perez and Zerah by Tamar,
   Perez fathered Hezron,
   Hezron fathered Aram,
4 Aram fathered Aminadab,
   Aminadab fathered Nahshon,
   Nahshon fathered Salmon,
5 Salmon fathered Boaz by Rahab,
   Boaz fathered Obed by Ruth,
   Obed fathered Jesse,
6 and Jesse fathered King David.

From David to the Babylonian Exile

   Then[c] David fathered Solomon by Uriah's wife,
7 Solomon fathered Rehoboam,
   Rehoboam fathered Abijah,
   Abijah fathered Asa,[d]
8 Asa[d] fathered Jehoshaphat,
   Jehoshaphat fathered Joram,
   Joram fathered Uzziah,
9 Uzziah fathered Jotham,
   Jotham fathered Ahaz,
   Ahaz fathered Hezekiah,
10 Hezekiah fathered Manasseh,
   Manasseh fathered Amon,[e]
   Amon[e] fathered Josiah,
11 and Josiah fathered Jechoniah and his brothers at the time of the exile to Babylon.

From the Exile to the Messiah

12 Then after the exile to Babylon
   Jechoniah fathered Salathiel,
   Salathiel fathered Zerubbabel,
13 Zerubbabel fathered Abiud,
   Abiud fathered Eliakim,
   Eliakim fathered Azor,
14 Azor fathered Zadok,
   Zadok fathered Achim,
   Achim fathered Eliud,
15 Eliud fathered Eleazar,
   Eleazar fathered Matthan,
   Matthan fathered Jacob,
16 and Jacob fathered Joseph the husband of Mary, who gave birth to[f] Jesus who is called the •Messiah.

17 So all the generations from Abraham to David were 14 generations; and from David until the exile to Babylon, 14 generations; and from the exile to Babylon until the Messiah, 14 generations.

God with Us

1. Do you know how your parents picked your name? What does your name mean?
2. What age do you think is a good age to get married? How long should you be engaged before getting married?

Matthew 1:18-25

3. Why did Joseph decide not to "divorce" Mary? What does this teach us of his character?
4. Why was Jesus born from a virgin? Why is that miracle important to our Christian faith?
5. What does "God with us" mean? In what ways have you experienced God with you?
6. When did Jesus really become your "Immanuel"—God with you? How are you experiencing Jesus "with you" in *your* life now?

The Nativity of the Messiah

18 The birth of Jesus Christ came about this way: After His mother Mary had been •engaged to Joseph, it

---

[a]**1:1** Or *The book of the genealogy*   [b]**1:2** In vv. 2–16 either a son, as here, or a later descendant, as in v. 8   [c]**1:6** Other mss add *King*   [d]**1:7,8** Other mss read *Asaph*   [e]**1:10** Other mss read *Amos*   [f]**1:16** Lit *Mary, from whom was born*

1:1 The historical record. It seems curious to the modern reader that Matthew would begin his Gospel with a long list of names. However, this makes perfect sense given that he was writing to a Jewish audience. By tracing the line of Jesus back to Abraham, Matthew was indicating that Jesus was a true Jew.

1:3-6 by Tamar ... Rahab ... Ruth ... Uriah's wife. Only four women are mentioned in these verses. It is surprising that women are mentioned at all in the genealogy since a man's line was never traced through his mother. All four were non-Jews and in each case, there was something suspect about their marriages. Although an unlikely to be named as part of the Messiah's line, they draw attention to the fact that God works in unusual ways. **Tamar.** Tamar was a Canaanite who tricked Judah, her father-in-

law, into sleeping with her. From this union came the twins, Perez and Zerah (Gen. 38). **Rahab.** She was a prostitute who assisted Joshua's spies when they were in Jericho (Josh. 2:1-21). **Ruth.** A Moabitess who married a Jew named Boaz. She is included in the royal line although Deuteronomy 23:3 forbids any Moabite from entering "the LORD's assembly." **Uriah's wife.** David seduced Bathsheba, the eventual mother of Solomon, and got her pregnant. He then arranged for her husband Uriah to be killed in battle (2 Sam. 11 - 12). Bathsheba may have been an Israelite, but she was married to a Hittite.

1:18-25 birth of Jesus. Matthew and Luke record different aspects of the birth of Jesus.

1:18 engaged. A first-century Jewish marriage had three parts to it: the engagement

(which often took place when the two people were children, and was usually arranged by a marriage broker); the betrothal (a one-year period in which the couple was considered virtually "married," although they did not have sexual relations); and the marriage. Mary and Joseph were at the second stage in their relationship. **she was pregnant.** The penalty in the Old Testament for sleeping with a woman betrothed to another was death by stoning for both parties (Deut. 22:23-24). By this time, however, the breaking of the engagement was the course that was followed. **by the Holy Spirit.** The agent in Jesus' birth was the Holy Spirit (Luke 1:35).

1:20 a dream. Dreams were often the means by which God revealed Himself to people. Matthew records four other occasions when dreams were crucial during the birth and

was discovered before they came together that she was pregnant by the Holy Spirit. ¹⁹ So her husband Joseph, being a righteous man, and not wanting to disgrace her publicly, decided to divorce her secretly.

²⁰ But after he had considered these things, an angel of the Lord suddenly appeared to him in a dream, saying, "Joseph, son of David, don't be afraid to take Mary as your wife, because what has been conceived in her is by the Holy Spirit. ²¹ She will give birth to a son, and you are to name Him Jesus,ᵃ because He will save His people from their sins."

²² Now all this took place to fulfill what was spoken by the Lord through the prophet:

²³   **See, the virgin will become pregnant**
     and give birth to a son,
     and they will name Him Immanuel,ᵇ

which is translated "God is with us."

²⁴ When Joseph got up from sleeping, he did as the Lord's angel had commanded him. He married her ²⁵ but did not know her intimately until she gave birth to a son.ᶜ And he named Him Jesus.

Wise Men Seek the King

2 After Jesus was born in Bethlehem of Judea in the days of King •Herod, •wise men from the east arrived unexpectedly in Jerusalem, ² saying, "Where is He who has been born King of the Jews? For we saw His star in the eastᵈ and have come to worship Him."ᵉ

³ When King Herod heard this, he was deeply disturbed, and all Jerusalem with him. ⁴ So he assembled all the •chief priests and •scribes of the people and asked them where the •Messiah would be born.

⁵ "In Bethlehem of Judea," they told him, "because this is what was written by the prophet:

⁶   **And you, Bethlehem,** in the land of Judah,
     are by no means **least among the leaders**
       of Judah:
     because out of you will come a leader
     who will shepherd My people Israel."ᶠ

⁷ Then Herod secretly summoned the wise men and asked them the exact time the star appeared. ⁸ He sent them to Bethlehem and said, "Go and search carefully for the child. When you find Him, report back to me so that I too can go and worship Him."ᵍ

⁹ After hearing the king, they went on their way. And there it was—the star they had seen in the east!ʰ It led them until it came and stopped above the place where the child was. ¹⁰ When they saw the star, they were overjoyed beyond measure. ¹¹ Entering the house, they saw the child with Mary His mother, and falling to their knees, they worshiped Him.ⁱ Then they opened their treasures and presented Him with gifts: gold, frankincense, and myrrh. ¹² And being warned in a dream not to go back to Herod, they returned to their own country by another route.

The Flight into Egypt

¹³ After they were gone, an angel of the Lord suddenly appeared to Joseph in a dream, saying, "Get up! Take the child and His mother, flee to Egypt, and stay there until I tell you. For Herod is about to search for the child to destroy Him." ¹⁴ So he got up, took the child and His mother during the night, and escaped to Egypt. ¹⁵ He stayed there until Herod's death, so that what was spoken by the Lord through the prophet might be fulfilled: **Out of Egypt I called My Son.**ʲ

The Massacre of the Innocents

¹⁶ Then Herod, when he saw that he had been outwitted by the wise men, flew into a rage. He gave orders to massacre all the male children in and around Bethlehem who were two yearsᵏ old and under, in keeping with the time he had learned from the wise men. ¹⁷ Then what was spoken through Jeremiah the prophet was fulfilled:

¹⁸   **A voice was heard in Ramah,**
     weeping,ˡ and great mourning,
     Rachel weeping for her children;

ᵃ**1:21** *Jesus* is the Gk form of the Hb name "Joshua," which = "The Lord saves" or "Yahweh saves." ᵇ**1:23** Is 7:14 ᶜ**1:25** Other mss read *to her firstborn son* ᵈ**2:2** Or *star at its rising* ᵉ**2:2** Or *to pay Him homage* ᶠ**2:6** Mc 5:2 ᵍ**2:8** Or *and pay Him homage* ʰ**2:9** Or *star . . . at its rising* ⁱ**2:11** Or *they paid Him homage* ʲ**2:15** Hs 11:1 ᵏ**2:16** Lit *were from two years* ˡ**2:18** Other mss read *Ramah, lamentation, and weeping,*

---

childhood of Jesus (2:12,13,19,22). **son of David.** The crucial link between Joseph and David is made quite clear by the angel. **take Mary as your wife.** The marriage was completed when the husband took his betrothed from her parents' home (where she lived during the betrothal) to his own home.

1:21 name Him. It was necessary for Joseph to name Jesus and thus formally accept Him as his son. **Jesus.** A common name and the Greek form of the Hebrew name Joshua which meant, "God is salvation."

2:1 King Herod. Herod the Great was a shrewd but cruel monarch who was appointed by Rome to rule over Palestine. His reign lasted from 40 B.C. to 4 B.C. **wise men.** These were astrologers who probably came from Babylon, and may have been in-

fluenced by Daniel's prophecies.

2:8 worship Him. This was either a cynical or deceptive statement from Herod, which contrasts with the genuine worship of the wise men (v. 11). By allowing the wise men to search for the child he had a better chance of finding Him than if he were to send troops.

2:11 presented Him with gifts. The giving of gifts signified allegiance. **gold.** A metal of great value; the currency of kings. **frankincense.** A sweet-smelling gum that was burned during worship. **myrrh.** Another gum, used as a perfume and as medicine. It was also used to embalm bodies. Taken together, the gifts represent the deity of Jesus as the royal Son of God Who gave His life for His people.

2:16 two years old. This indicates that some time had elapsed since Jesus' actual birth. That Herod was capable of killing children is testified to by another deed he did before his death. He arrested a number of leading people that were executed at the time of his death to assure that genuine mourning would occur when he died!

2:23 He will be called a Nazarene. There is no such quote in the Old Testament. Matthew may have been alluding in general terms to the prophets foretelling the contempt that men would have for Jesus (e.g. Isa. 52:13-53:12). The designation "Jesus of Nazareth" was at first a term of scorn and derision as illustrated in John 1:45-46.

3:1 John the Baptist. There is a gap of 25 to 30 years between the events in chapters 1–2 and the start of Jesus' ministry. John the

and she refused to be consoled,
because they were no more.[a]

The Holy Family in Nazareth

[19] After Herod died, an angel of the Lord suddenly appeared in a dream to Joseph in Egypt, [20] saying, "Get up! Take the child and His mother and go to the land of Israel, because those who sought the child's life are dead." [21] So he got up, took the child and His mother, and entered the land of Israel. [22] But when he heard that Archelaus[b] was ruling over Judea in place of his father Herod, he was afraid to go there. And being warned in a dream, he withdrew to the region of Galilee. [23] Then he went and settled in a town called Nazareth to fulfill what was spoken through the prophets, that He will be called a •Nazarene.

The Messiah's Herald

3 In those days John the Baptist came, preaching in the Wilderness of Judea [2] and saying, "Repent, because the kingdom of heaven has come near!" [3] For he is the one spoken of through the prophet Isaiah, who said:

A voice of one crying out in the wilderness:
"Prepare the way for the Lord;
make His paths straight!"[c]

[4] John himself had a camel-hair garment with a leather belt around his waist, and his food was locusts and wild honey. [5] Then ₎people from₍ Jerusalem, all Judea, and all the vicinity of the Jordan were flocking to him, [6] and they were baptized by him in the Jordan River as they confessed their sins.

[7] When he saw many of the •Pharisees and •Sadducees coming to the place of his baptism,[d] he said to them, "Brood of vipers! Who warned you to flee from the coming wrath? [8] Therefore produce fruit consistent with[e] repentance. [9] And don't presume to say to yourselves, 'We have Abraham as our father.' For I tell you that God is able to raise up children for Abraham from these stones! [10] Even now the ax is ready to strike the root of the trees! Therefore every tree that doesn't produce good fruit will be cut down and thrown into the fire.

Baptized with Spirit and Fire

1. Who is the craziest looking man of God you have ever met? Who is the wildest preacher you have heard?

Matthew 3:1-17
2. What does John mean, "produce fruit consistent with repentance?" What would that look like in your life?
3. How does Jesus "baptize you with the Holy Spirit?" How does He baptize you with "fire?"
4. Have you been baptized with the Holy Spirit? How does that affect your life?
5. Are you being "baptized with fire" lately? How can your group help?

[11] "I baptize you with[f] water for repentance,[g] but the One who is coming after me is more powerful than I. I am not worthy to take off[h] His sandals. He Himself will baptize you with[f] the Holy Spirit and fire. [12] His winnowing shovel[i] is in His hand, and He will clear His threshing floor and gather His wheat into the barn. But the chaff He will burn up with fire that never goes out."

The Baptism of Jesus

[13] Then Jesus came from Galilee to John at the Jordan, to be baptized by him. [14] But John tried to stop Him, saying, "I need to be baptized by You, and yet You come to me?"

---

[a]2:18 Jr 31:15 [b]2:22 A son of Herod the Great who ruled a portion of his father's kingdom 4 B.C.–A.D. 6 [c]3:3 Is 40:3 [d]3:7 Lit *to his baptism*
[e]3:8 Lit *fruit worthy of* [f]3:11 Or *in* [g]3:11 Baptism was the means by which repentance was expressed publicly. [h]3:11 Or *to carry* [i]3:12 A wooden farm implement used to toss threshed grain into the wind so the lighter chaff would blow away and separate from the heavier grain

---

Baptist was an extremely popular figure whose influence spread from Alexandria in Egypt to Asia Minor.

3:2 kingdom of heaven. Pious Jews did not mention God's name. To speak of God they referred to His abode—heaven. Most believe this phrase has the same meaning as the phrase "kingdom of God" in Mark (Mark 1:15). It refers to the messianic age that is yet to come in which God will reign.

3:3 Prepare the way. This is a quotation from Isaiah 40:3. The Jews expected that an Elijah-like figure would precede the Messiah and announce His coming (Mal. 3:1; 4:5; see also Matt. 17:3). This "voice" who would pave the way for the Lord was John the Baptist. Ancient roads were notoriously bad, and the only time they tended to be smoothed out was in preparation for a royal visit.

3:4 locusts and wild honey. This description is similar to that of Old Testament prophets, in particular Elijah (2 Kings 1:8; Zech. 13:4). The locusts John ate could have been either an insect (Lev. 11:22-23) or a kind of bean from the locust tree. Honey could refer either to what bees produce or to the sap of a certain tree. In either case, this was the food eaten by the poorest of people.

3:11 I am not worthy to take off His sandals. This would be the task of a slave. **fire.** Fire is a symbol of judgment that Matthew refers to a number of times (5:22; 7:19; 13:40,42; 18:8; 25:41).

3:12 gather His wheat. In the harvesting of wheat, after the grain is separated from the straw, the mixture is tossed up in the air. The heavier kernels fall to the ground, while the straw and chaff blow away and are later burned. This is an image of the judgment that will take place at the future return of Jesus.

3:13 baptized. By allowing Himself to be baptized, Jesus identifies with the people of Israel and with their sin, modeling an act of genuine repentance (although He Himself was without sin as 1 Peter 2:22 indicates).

3:16 like a dove. Matthew uses a dove as a symbol of the coming of the Holy Spirit

4:1 led up by the Spirit into the wilderness to be tempted. Jesus' victory over temptation would demonstrate three things: His sinless character; an example of endurance through times of testing; and how to use Scripture as a means of defense against the

¹⁵ Jesus answered him, "Allow it for now, because this is the way for us to fulfill all righteousness." Then he allowed Him ₍to be baptized₎.

¹⁶ After Jesus was baptized, He went up immediately from the water. The heavens suddenly opened for Him,ᵃ and He saw the Spirit of God descending like a dove and coming down on Him. ¹⁷ And there came a voice from heaven:

This is My beloved Son.
I take delight in Him!

The Temptation of Jesus

4 Then Jesus was led up by the Spirit into the wilderness to be tempted by the Devil. ² After He had fasted 40 days and 40 nights, He was hungry. ³ Then the tempter approached Him and said, "If You are the Son of God, tell these stones to become bread."

⁴ But He answered, "It is written:

Man must not live on bread alone
but on every word that comes
from the mouth of God."ᵇ

⁵ Then the Devil took Him to the holy city,ᶜ had Him stand on the pinnacle of the temple, ⁶ and said to Him, "If You are the Son of God, throw Yourself down. For it is written:

He will give His angels orders
concerning you, and
they will support you with their hands
so that you will not strike
your foot against a stone."ᵈ

⁷ Jesus told him, "It is also written: **Do not test the Lord your God.**"ᵉ

⁸ Again, the Devil took Him to a very high mountain and showed Him all the kingdoms of the world and their splendor. ⁹ And he said to Him, "I will give You all these things if You will fall down and worship me."ᶠ

¹⁰ Then Jesus told him, "Go away,ᵍ Satan! For it is written:

Worship the Lord your God,
and serve only Him."ʰ

¹¹ Then the Devil left Him, and immediately angels came and began to serve Him.

Ministry in Galilee

¹² When He heard that John had been arrested, He withdrew into Galilee. ¹³ He left Nazareth behind and went to live in Capernaum by the sea, in the region of Zebulun and Naphtali. ¹⁴ This was to fulfill what was spoken through the prophet Isaiah:

¹⁵ **Land of Zebulun and land of Naphtali,**
   along the sea road, beyond the Jordan,
   Galilee of the Gentiles!
¹⁶ **The people who live in darkness**
   have seen a great light,
   and for those living in the shadowland
   of death,
   light has dawned.ⁱ ʲ

¹⁷ From then on Jesus began to preach, "Repent, because the kingdom of heaven has come near!"

The First Disciples

¹⁸ As He was walking along the Sea of Galilee, He saw two brothers, Simon, who was called Peter, and his brother Andrew. They were casting a net into the sea, since they were fishermen. ¹⁹ "Follow Me," He told them, "and I will make you fish forᵏ people!" ²⁰ Immediately they left their nets and followed Him.

²¹ Going on from there, He saw two other brothers, James the son of Zebedee, and his brother John. They were in a boat with Zebedee their father, mending their nets, and He called them. ²² Immediately they left the boat and their father and followed Him.

Teaching, Preaching, and Healing

²³ Jesus was going all over Galilee, teaching in their •synagogues, preaching the good news of the kingdom, and healing everyˡ disease and sickness among the people. ²⁴ Then the news about Him spread throughout

---

ᵃ**3:16** Other mss omit *for Him* ᵇ**4:4** Dt 8:3 ᶜ**4:5** Jerusalem ᵈ**4:6** Ps 91:11–12 ᵉ**4:7** Dt 6:16 ᶠ**4:9** Or *and pay me homage* ᵍ**4:10** Other mss read *Get behind Me* ʰ**4:10** Dt 6:13 ⁱ**4:16** Lit *dawned on them* ʲ**4:15–16** Is 9:1–2 ᵏ**4:19** Lit *you fishers of* ˡ**4:23** Or *every kind of*

---

devil and a support in the face of evil.

4:2 40 days. Moses fasted 40 days on Mount Sinai while receiving the commandments (Ex. 34:28), and Israel was in the wilderness 40 years (Deut. 8:2).

4:3 the tempter approached. The Spirit led Jesus into the wilderness, but it was Satan who tested Him. His challenges to Jesus came only after Jesus had entered a condition of physical weakness because of His fast. **If You are the Son of God.** This was a temptation to verify the truth of what God had declared (3:17).

4:4 It is written. Jesus' response is drawn from Deuteronomy 8:3. Originally this was a reflection on the meaning of the manna in the desert. True life involves not just the physical, but also the spiritual (which the Word of

God feeds). Jesus will not heed Satan, but listens only to His Father, God.

4:5 temple. The Devil's challenge for Jesus is to prove this love and power of God by creating a peril from which God alone can rescue Him.

4:7 It is also written. Jesus responds that people are not to test God, as Deuteronomy 6:16 clearly states, but to trust Him.

4:8-9 I will give You. The final temptation has to do with gaining the kingdoms of the world without suffering the coming agonies of the cross.

4:12 John had been arrested. John's arrest and imprisonment are described in more detail in 14:1-12. **Galilee.** This was the northern province of Palestine. It was small, about 25

by 35 miles in size, but quite densely populated. In the time of Jesus, approximately 350,000 people lived there—100,000 of whom were Jews. It was a rich farming and fishing region.

4:13 Nazareth. This was a village located in the hill country of Galilee, 20 miles southwest of Capernaum.

4:20 Immediately they left. According to 4:12-17, Jesus had been living and preaching in Capernaum. These fishermen probably had the chance to hear His message prior to their call. Still, what they did was an act of great faith and courage.

5:1 on the mountain. To the original Jewish readers, this would have been an inescapable allusion to when Moses delivered the Law to Israel from Mount Sinai (Deut. 18:15).

Syria. So they brought to Him all those who were afflicted, those suffering from various diseases and intense pains, the demon-possessed, the epileptics, and the paralytics. And He healed them. 25 Large crowds followed Him from Galilee, •Decapolis, Jerusalem, Judea, and beyond the Jordan.

The Sermon on the Mount

5 When He saw the crowds, He went up on the mountain, and after He sat down, His disciples came to Him. 2 Then[a] He began to teach them, saying:

The Beatitudes

3 "Blessed are the poor in spirit,
because the kingdom of heaven is theirs.
4 Blessed are those who mourn,
because they will be comforted.
5 Blessed are the gentle,
because they will inherit the earth.
6 Blessed are those who hunger
and thirst for righteousness,
because they will be filled.
7 Blessed are the merciful,
because they will be shown mercy.
8 Blessed are the pure in heart,
because they will see God.
9 Blessed are the peacemakers,
because they will be called sons of God.
10 Blessed are those who are persecuted
for righteousness,
because the kingdom of heaven is theirs.

11 "Blessed are you when they insult you and persecute you and falsely say every kind of evil against you because of Me. 12 Be glad and rejoice, because your reward is great in heaven. For that is how they persecuted the prophets who were before you.

Believers Are Salt and Light

13 "You are the salt of the earth. But if the salt should lose its taste, how can it be made salty? It's no longer good for anything but to be thrown out and trampled on by men.

14 "You are the light of the world. A city situated on a hill cannot be hidden. 15 No one lights a lamp and puts it under a basket,[b] but rather on a lampstand, and it gives light for all who are in the house. 16 In the same way, let your light shine[c] before men, so that they may see your good works and give glory to your Father in heaven.

Attitude Adjustment

1. Do you pray or "say a blessing" before you eat meals? Why or why not?

Matthew 5:1-12

2. What does it mean to be "gentle?" How can a gentle person still be a good competitor?
3. What does it mean to be "pure in heart?" What things in school, sports, or the rest of life make it hard for you to be pure in heart?
4. On a scale of 1 (not at all) to 10 (totally), how much do you hunger and thirst for righteousness?
5. If God gave you an attitude adjustment, which of the eight "attitudes" in these verses would need the most work?

Christ Fulfills the Law

17 "Don't assume that I came to destroy the Law or the Prophets. I did not come to destroy but to fulfill. 18 For •I assure you: Until heaven and earth pass away, not the smallest letter[d] or one stroke of a letter will pass from the law until all things are accomplished. 19 Therefore, whoever breaks one of the least of these commandments and teaches people to do so will be called least in the kingdom of heaven. But whoever practices and teaches ⌊these commandments⌋ will be

---

a5:2 Lit *Then opening His mouth*   b5:15 A large basket used to measure grain   c5:16 Or *way, your light must shine*   d5:18 Or *not one iota; iota* is the *smallest letter* of the Gk alphabet.

---

sat down. When rabbis taught, they would sit rather than stand. This accents Jesus' authoritative position.

5:3 Blessed are. The Greek word *makarios* refers to people who are to be congratulated. It does not necessarily mean they are happy or prospering. Instead, whether they feel it or not, they are fortunate because their condition reflects that they are in a right relationship to God. **poor in spirit.** This phrase does not refer to those who are poor in the material sense, but to those who acknowledge their need of God.

5:5 the gentle. This involves a lifestyle marked by thoughtfulness, humility, and courteousness. **inherit the earth.** The irony of God's reign is that, despite the efforts of those who grasp for the world, it will one day be given not to those who have been covet-

ous, but to those who have been generous.

5:8 pure in heart. The call is for single-minded pursuit of God's way with every facet of our being. **see God.** In the Old Testament, this term described what it meant to experience God's favor.

5:13 salt. Salt was a very valuable commodity in ancient times. It was not only used to flavor foods, but it was indispensable in preserving them. The disciples are to flavor the world around them with God's love and direction; and they are to preserve that which is valuable in life from the spoilage of sin and hate.

5:17 the Law or the Prophets. The Law referred to the first five books of the Old Testament, while the Prophets referred to the Major and Minor Prophets, as well as the Historical Books.

5:18 I assure you. Literally, this is "for truly I say to you," a phrase characteristic of Jesus. No other teacher of His era was known to say this. **the smallest letter or one stroke of a letter.** Some Hebrew and Aramaic letters are distinguishable only by a small line or dot. Jesus accents the validity of the Law as the ethical norm for all God's people.

5:22 angry. The Greek word used here describes deep-seated, smoldering, inner anger rather than a flash of anger. **Fool!** An Aramaic term of contempt: "You good-for-nothing" or "I spit on you." **Sanhedrin.** The Sanhedrin (a group of 70 Jewish men) was the official ruling body of the Jews. This body was responsible for administering justice in matters related to Jewish law. **hellfire.** Literally, *Gehenna*, a ravine outside Jerusalem where children were once sacrificed to the god Molech (1 Kings 11:7).

called great in the kingdom of heaven. 20 For I tell you, unless your righteousness surpasses that of the •scribes and •Pharisees, you will never enter the kingdom of heaven.

Gouge Out Your Eyes

1. Who told you about the "birds and the bees"? Was the situation awkward? Boring? Interesting? Funny?

Matthew 5:27-30

2. What is "lust?" What is adultery? Why does Jesus speak so strongly against these two sins?

3. How can a person commit adultery in his heart, just by lusting after someone else? What is Jesus saying here?

4. Does Jesus really want you to gouge out your eyes if you look lustfully at another person (or picture)?

5. What is one thing that you would like your group to hold you accountable to in the next week?

Murder Begins in the Heart

21 "You have heard that it was said to our ancestors,[a] **Do not murder,**[b] and whoever murders will be subject to judgment. 22 But I tell you, everyone who is angry with his brother[c] will be subject to judgment. And whoever says to his brother, 'Fool!'[d] will be subject to the •Sanhedrin. But whoever says, 'You moron!' will be subject to •hellfire.[e] 23 So if you are offering your gift on the altar, and there you remember that your brother has something against you, 24 leave your gift there in front of the altar. First go and be reconciled with your brother, and then come and offer your gift. 25 Reach a

settlement quickly with your adversary while you're on the way with him, or your adversary will hand you over to the judge, the judge to[f] the officer, and you will be thrown into prison. 26 I assure you: You will never get out of there until you have paid the last penny![g]

Adultery in the Heart

27 "You have heard that it was said, **Do not commit adultery.**[h] 28 But I tell you, everyone who looks at a woman to lust for her has already committed adultery with her in his heart. 29 If your right eye •causes you to sin, gouge it out and throw it away. For it is better that you lose one of the parts of your body than for your whole body to be thrown into hell. 30 And if your right hand causes you to sin, cut it off and throw it away. For it is better that you lose one of the parts of your body than for your whole body to go into hell!

Divorce Practices Censured

31 "It was also said, **Whoever divorces his wife must give her a written notice of divorce.**[i] 32 But I tell you, everyone who divorces his wife, except in a case of sexual immorality,[j] causes her to commit adultery. And whoever marries a divorced woman commits adultery.

Tell the Truth

33 "Again, you have heard that it was said to our ancestors,[a] **You must not break your oath, but you must keep your oaths to the Lord.**[k] 34 But I tell you, don't take an oath at all: either by heaven, because it is God's throne; 35 or by the earth, because it is His footstool; or by Jerusalem, because it is the city of the great King. 36 Neither should you swear by your head, because you cannot make a single hair white or black. 37 But let your word 'yes' be 'yes,' and your 'no' be 'no.'[l] Anything more than this is from the evil one.

Go the Second Mile

38 "You have heard that it was said, **An eye for an eye and a tooth for a tooth.**[m] 39 But I tell you, don't

---

[a] **5:21,33** Lit to the ancients   [b] **5:21** Ex 20:13; Dt 5:17   [c] **5:22** Other mss add without a cause   [d] **5:22** Lit Raca, an Aram term of abuse similar to "airhead"   [e] **5:22** Lit the gehenna of fire   [f] **5:25** Other mss read judge will hand you over to   [g] **5:26** Lit quadrans, the smallest and least valuable Roman coin, worth 1/64 of a daily wage   [h] **5:27** Ex 20:14; Dt 5:18   [i] **5:31** Dt 24:1   [j] **5:32** Gk porneia = fornication, or possibly a violation of Jewish marriage laws   [k] **5:33** Lv 19:12; Nm 30:2; Dt 23:21   [l] **5:37** Say what you mean and mean what you say   [m] **5:38** Ex 21:24; Lv 24:20; Dt 19:21

Jews considered it a defiled place, good only as a garbage dump, which was continually burning. Gehenna became a symbol for the place of punishment and spiritual death.

5:23 altar. The primary responsibility for initiating reconciliation lies with the one who, whether on purpose or by accident, has offended another member of the community.

5:25 thrown into prison. The Romans threw debtors into jail where it was impossible for them to earn money to pay off their debt. Jesus uses this image to describe the situation before God of the person who refuses to seek reconciliation.

5:28 to lust. Just as anger is at the root of murder, so too lust is at the root of adultery.

This does not condemn sexual attraction as such, but rather the deliberate harboring of desire for an illicit relationship.

5:31-32 divorces his wife. As seen from Matthew 19 and Mark 10, divorce and remarriage is a departure from God's intention for marriage.

5:38 An eye an for eye. This is said to be the oldest law in the world. It is found in the codes of Hammurabi, a king who lived in the 18th century B.C., as well as three times in the Old Testament (Ex. 21:23-24; Lev. 24:20; Deut. 19:21). The Law's original intent was not to require an "eye for an eye," but to limit punishment to the extent of the crime.

5:40 coat. The Law (Ex. 22:25-26; Deut. 24:10-13) prohibited a person from seizing a person's cloak as the payment of a debt,

since this woolen outer robe was used as a blanket at night. Jesus' call here is for His followers to give beyond even what the Law would require.

5:41 forces you to go one mile. Roman soldiers had the right to press civilians into service to carry their gear for a distance up to one mile. The word used here is a technical term for such compulsory conscription.

5:43 Love your neighbor. Jesus quotes Leviticus 19:18. **hate your enemy.** This command is found neither in the Old Testament nor in the Talmud but must have been a current saying.

5:44 love your enemies. The word used here is agape. This is love that shows itself not by what a person feels, but by what the per-

resist[a] an evildoer. On the contrary, if anyone slaps you on your right cheek, turn the other to him also. ⁴⁰ As for the one who wants to sue you and take away your shirt,[b] let him have your coat[c] as well. ⁴¹ And if anyone forces[d] you to go one mile, go with him two. ⁴² Give to the one who asks you, and don't turn away from the one who wants to borrow from you.

Turn the Other Cheek

1. What causes you to reach the boiling point: A slow driver in the fast lane? "Technical problems" during your favorite TV show?
2. If someone attacks you, verbally, physically, or some other way, how do you usually respond?

Matthew 5:38-48

3. What does it mean, in practical terms, to "turn the other cheek?" To "go the extra mile?"
4. How can you both love your enemies and still be a good competitor?
5. Who do you need to forgive today? In what situation is God asking you to go an extra mile?

Love Your Enemies

⁴³ "You have heard that it was said, **Love your neighbor**[e] and hate your enemy. ⁴⁴ But I tell you, love your enemies[f] and pray for those who[g] persecute you, ⁴⁵ so that you may be[h] sons of your Father in heaven. For He causes His sun to rise on the evil and the good, and sends rain on the righteous and the unrighteous. ⁴⁶ For if you love those who love you, what reward will you have? Don't even the tax collectors do the same? ⁴⁷ And if you greet only your brothers, what are you doing out of the ordinary?[i] Don't even the Gentiles[j] do the same? ⁴⁸ Be perfect, therefore, as your heavenly Father is perfect.

How to Give

6 "Be careful not to practice your righteousness[k] in front of people, to be seen by them. Otherwise, you will have no reward from your Father in heaven. ² So whenever you give to the poor, don't sound a trumpet before you, as the hypocrites do in the •synagogues and on the streets, to be applauded by people. •I assure you: They've got their reward! ³ But when you give to the poor, don't let your left hand know what your right hand is doing, ⁴ so that your giving may be in secret. And your Father who sees in secret will reward you.[l]

How to Pray

⁵ "Whenever you pray, you must not be like the hypocrites, because they love to pray standing in the synagogues and on the street corners to be seen by people. I assure you: They've got their reward! ⁶ But when you pray, go into your private room, shut your door, and pray to your Father who is in secret. And your Father who sees in secret will reward you.[m] ⁷ When you pray, don't babble like the idolaters,[n] since they imagine they'll be heard for their many words. ⁸ Don't be like them, because your Father knows the things you need before you ask Him.

The Model Prayer

⁹ "Therefore, you should pray like this:

> Our Father in heaven,
> Your name be honored as holy.
> 10 Your kingdom come.
> Your will be done

---

[a]**5:39** Or *don't set yourself against*, or *don't retaliate against* [b]**5:40** Lit *tunic* = inner garment [c]**5:40** Lit *robe*, or *garment* = outer garment
[d]**5:41** Roman soldiers could require people to carry loads for them. [e]**5:43** Lv 19:18 [f]**5:44** Other mss add *bless those who curse you, do good to those who hate you*, [g]**5:44** Other mss add *mistreat you and* [h]**5:45** Or *may become*, or *may show yourselves to be* [i]**5:47** Lit *doing more*, or *doing that is superior* [j]**5:47** Other mss read *tax collectors* [k]**6:1** Other mss read *charitable giving* [l]**6:4** Other mss read *will Himself reward you openly*
[m]**6:6** Other mss add *openly* [n]**6:7** Or *Gentiles*, or *nations*, or *heathen*, or *pagans*

---

son chooses to do. It is love done on the behalf of another without the expectation of reward. **pray.** One way this love is demonstrated is by prayer for those who harass you.

5:46 tax collectors. Tax collectors grew rich by charging people more than what was required, keeping the excess for themselves. That they were doing this as agents of Rome made the offense even more grievous.

5:48 Be perfect. This means, "having attained the end or purpose" or "being complete." People can be "perfect" if they realize that for which they were made, which is to reflect God's image, and hence to love.

6:1 in front of people. In general terms, Jesus makes it clear that His followers are not to seek to make themselves look good by making a public display of religious devotion.

6:2 the hypocrites. It was not their lack of inner conviction that Jesus is faulting (they undoubtedly believed they ought to give to the poor), but their desire to make sure their observance of the traditions was seen by others.

6:7 babble like the idolaters. A common practice of pagan prayer was to recite a long list of divine names in hopes of invoking a god to action.

6:9 Our Father in heaven. This does not locate God somewhere beyond space, but stresses His majesty and dignity. **Your name be honored as holy.** The first petition is that God's character and nature be held in great esteem by all.

6:10 Your kingdom come. God's kingdom

is in evidence whenever His will is being followed. John the Baptist has already preached that "the kingdom of heaven has come near." But it will come in its fullness when all submit to the will of God. **on earth as it is in heaven.** God does not want to rule over just one part of His creation (heaven), but all of it.

6:11 our daily bread. This is a reminder that God is not just concerned about our "spiritual side" but our everyday physical needs as well.

6:13 temptation. The request is not a plea to be exempt from the common moral struggles of life, but that God would empower the disciple to have the moral strength to resist giving in to evil during such struggles.

on earth as it is in heaven.

11 Give us today our daily bread.ᵃ

12 And forgive us our debts,
as we also have forgiven our debtors.

13 And do not bring us intoᵇ temptation,
but deliver us from the evil one.ᶜ
[For Yours is the kingdom and the power
and the glory forever. •Amen.]ᵈ

Prayer Uplink

1. When do you pray: Before meals? In a crisis? Daily in devotions? Before a test? Other?

Matthew 6:5-18

2. What does "Your name be honored as holy" mean? Why does Jesus open His prayer this way?

3. How is God's will done in heaven? If His will were done that way in your life, how would your life be different?

4. According to verses 12-15, just how much is God going to forgive you your debts? How well do you forgive the debts (or injuries) of others?

5. What is the purpose of fasting? Is there a situation in your life right now that would be helped by fasting?

14 "For if you forgive people their wrongdoing,ᵉ your heavenly Father will forgive you as well. 15 But if you don't forgive people,ᶠ your Father will not forgive your wrongdoing.ᵉ

How to Fast

16 "Whenever you fast, don't be sad-faced like the hypocrites. For they make their faces unattractiveᵍ so their fasting is obvious to people. I assure you: They've got their reward! 17 But when you fast, put oil on your head, and wash your face, 18 so that you don't show your fasting to people but to your Father who is in secret. And your Father who sees in secret will reward you.ʰ

God and Possessions

19 "Don't collect for yourselves treasuresⁱ on earth, where moth and rust destroy and where thieves break in and steal. 20 But collect for yourselves treasures in heaven, where neither moth nor rust destroys, and where thieves don't break in and steal. 21 For where your treasure is, there your heart will be also.

22 "The eye is the lamp of the body. If your eye is good, your whole body will be full of light. 23 But if your eye is bad, your whole body will be full of darkness. So if the light within you is darkness—how deep is that darkness!

24 "No one can be a slave of two masters, since either he will hate one and love the other, or be devoted to one and despise the other. You cannot be slaves of God and of money.

The Cure for Anxiety

25 "This is why I tell you: Don't worry about your life, what you will eat or what you will drink; or about your body, what you will wear. Isn't life more than food and the body more than clothing? 26 Look at the birds of the sky: they don't sow or reap or gather into barns, yet your heavenly Father feeds them. Aren't you worth more than they? 27 Can any of you add a single •cubit to his heightʲ by worrying? 28 And why do you worry about clothes? Learn how the wildflowers of the field grow: they don't labor or spin thread. 29 Yet I tell you that not even Solomon in all his splendor was adorned like one of these! 30 If that's how God clothes the grass of the field, which is here today and thrown into the furnace tomorrow, won't He do much more for you—you of little faith? 31 So don't worry, saying, 'What will we eat?' or 'What will we drink?' or 'What will we wear?' 32 For the idolatersᵏ eagerly seek all

ᵃ**6:11** Or *our necessary bread,* or *our bread for tomorrow* ᵇ**6:13** Or *do not cause us to come into* ᶜ**6:13** Or *from evil* ᵈ**6:13** Other mss omit bracketed text ᵉ**6:14,15** Or *trespasses* ᶠ**6:15** Other mss add *their wrongdoing* ᵍ**6:16** Or *unrecognizable,* or *disfigured* ʰ**6:18** Other mss add *openly* ⁱ**6:19** Or *valuables* ʲ**6:27** Or *add one moment to his life-span* ᵏ**6:32** Or *Gentiles,* or *nations,* or *heathen,* or *pagans*

6:16 They've got their reward. Once again, as with giving and with prayer (6:2,5), those who play to the crowds and are admired by them for being "righteous" have received all the reward they will get.

6:19 moth and rust. The irony of building one's life around one's possessions was that even the most valuable treasures on earth were vulnerable to destruction by insignificant creatures and elements.

6:20 treasures in heaven. These would include relationships made eternal (1 Thess. 4:13-18) and a spiritual wholeness that comes from God's approval of us.

6:22 The eye is the lamp of the body. Both eye and heart are sometimes used in the Bible as metaphors to describe the motivating principle that guides the way a person lives

(Ps. 119:36-37). To have a good eye is to have a pure heart.

6:24 hate. This is using dramatic overstatement to express the fact that loyalty to one master makes loyalty to another master impossible. **money.** Dividing our loyalty between God and money turns money into a god.

6:25 Don't worry. When we are focused on that which cannot be taken away from us (treasures in heaven) we don't have to worry about what is essential.

6:27 a single cubit. If all the worry in the world cannot add height to a person, what is the purpose of worrying? (Modern medicine might add that worry actually will probably *reduce* one's stature and life span through stress-related diseases!)

6:33 But seek first the kingdom of God. The supreme ambition of the Christian is that all he or she thinks, says, and does be for the glory of God.

6:34 tomorrow. Worry generally has to do with the future, about what lies ahead. The disciple is to live one day at a time.

7:1-2 Do not judge. This is not to say that disciples are never to make moral judgments about the actions of others (7:15-20 requires them to do so in certain instances); rather, it condemns a harsh and censorious attitude toward others.

7:12 whatever you want others to do for, do also the same for them. This is the so-called Golden Rule. The negative form of this rule was widely known in the ancient world: "Do not do to others what you do not wish them to do to

these things, and your heavenly Father knows that you need them. 33 But seek first the kingdom of God[a] and His righteousness, and all these things will be provided for you. 34 Therefore don't worry about tomorrow, because tomorrow will worry about itself. Each day has enough trouble of its own.

Don't Sweat It!

1. What clothes are you most comfortable in? Are you a "fashion guru?" "Casual dresser?" "Neat freak?" "Slob?"
2. What things do you worry about most? Winning? Grades? Your love life? Other?

Matthew 6:25-34

3. Why does Jesus only address worrying about food and clothing? What about winning in sports, doing well in school, getting married? How does Jesus' teaching here apply to those things?
4. Does not worrying about tomorrow mean not planning ahead? How do you balance responsibility with faith?
5. What does it mean to "seek first the kingdom of God?" How can you do that this coming week?

Do Not Judge

7 "Do not judge, so that you won't be judged. 2 For with the judgment you use,[b] you will be judged, and with the measure you use,[c] it will be measured to you. 3 Why do you look at the speck in your brother's eye but don't notice the log in your own eye? 4 Or how can you say to your brother, 'Let me take the speck out of your eye,' and look, there's a log in your eye? 5 Hypocrite! First take the log out of your eye, and then you will see clearly to take the speck out of your brother's eye. 6 Don't give what is holy to dogs or toss your pearls before pigs, or they will trample them with their feet, turn, and tear you to pieces.

Keep Asking, Searching, Knocking

7 "Keep asking,[d] and it will be given to you. Keep searching,[e] and you will find. Keep knocking,[f] and the door[g] will be opened to you. 8 For everyone who asks receives, and the one who searches finds, and to the one who knocks, the door[h] will be opened. 9 What man among you, if his son asks him for bread, will give him a stone? 10 Or if he asks for a fish, will give him a snake? 11 If you then, who are evil, know how to give good gifts to your children, how much more will your Father in heaven give good things to those who ask Him! 12 Therefore, whatever you want others to do for you, do also the same for them—this is the Law and the Prophets.[i]

Entering the Kingdom

13 "Enter through the narrow gate. For the gate is wide and the road is broad that leads to destruction, and there are many who go through it. 14 How narrow is the gate and difficult the road that leads to life, and few find it.

15 "Beware of false prophets who come to you in sheep's clothing but inwardly are ravaging wolves. 16 You'll recognize them by their fruit. Are grapes gathered from thornbushes or figs from thistles? 17 In the same way, every good tree produces good fruit, but a bad tree produces bad fruit. 18 A good tree can't produce bad fruit; neither can a bad tree produce good fruit. 19 Every tree that doesn't produce good fruit is cut down and thrown into the fire. 20 So you'll recognize them by their fruit.

21 "Not everyone who says to Me, 'Lord, Lord!' will enter the kingdom of heaven, but ⌊only⌋ the one who does the will of My Father in heaven. 22 On that day many will say to Me, 'Lord, Lord, didn't we prophesy in Your name, drive out demons in Your name, and do many miracles in Your name?' 23 Then I will announce to them, 'I never knew you! **Depart from Me, you lawbreakers!**'[j] [k]

---

[a]**6:33** Other mss omit *of God*   [b]**7:2** Lit *you judge*   [c]**7:2** Lit *you measure*   [d]**7:7** Or *Ask*   [e]**7:7** Or *Search*   [f]**7:7** Or *Knock*   [g]**7:7** Lit *and it*   [h]**7:8** Lit *knocks, it*   [i]**7:12** When capitalized, *the Law and the Prophets* = the OT   [j]**7:23** Lit *you who work lawlessness*   [k]**7:23** Ps 6:8

---

you." Jesus alters this statement in a slight but highly significant way. He shifts the statement from the negative to the positive. Whereas the negative rule was fulfilled by inaction (not bothering others), the positive rule requires active benevolence. **this is the Law and the Prophets.** That love is the summary of the Law is one of Jesus' central themes (Mark 12:30-31). Paul had a similar focus (Rom. 13:8-10).

7:13 gate is wide ... road is broad. This is the way of the secular world that stands in contrast to the values taught in the Sermon on the Mount. **destruction.** This is where the "natural" way of the secular world leads. While ultimately such a lifestyle leads to the judgment of God against sin (Rom. 1:18), it also leads to destruction here and now in the sense of estranged relationships and inner chaos.

7:14 narrow is the gate and difficult the road. The narrower way is the way of life advocated by the Sermon. This way leads to an inner wholeness marked by the presence of God and fulfilling human relationships.

7:15 sheep's clothing. Prophets often wore animal skins (3:4; 2 Kings 1:8). People might dress in this fashion and claim to be prophets. Or, metaphorically, they might act as innocent as sheep while their true nature is that of vicious wolves who feed off others.

7:20 by their fruit. One important way to discern if a person is a genuine spokesperson for God is by considering what he or she does. Does the person reflect the values of the Sermon on the Mount in what he or she does?

7:21 Not everyone who says to me, 'Lord,

Lord'. The earliest Christian confession was "Jesus is Lord." However, Jesus emphasizes actions over words (25:31-46; James 1:19-27; 2:14-26).

7:22 On that day. This is the final day of judgment. Throughout the Bible, there is a clear expectation of a final accounting of humanity by God.

7:24-27 foundation was on a rock. In the autumn, rains produced flash floods that swept down ravines. While the two houses in the flood's path look alike, only the one built on a solid foundation will stand. Only those who build their lives on the foundation of the words of Jesus will stand.

8:2 serious skin disease. Often translated leprosy, no disease was more dreaded since it brought not only physical disfigure-

The Two Foundations

24 "Therefore, everyone who hears these words of Mine and acts on them will be like a sensible man who built his house on the rock. 25 The rain fell, the rivers rose, and the winds blew and pounded that house. Yet it didn't collapse, because its foundation was on the rock. 26 But everyone who hears these words of Mine and doesn't act on them will be like a foolish man who built his house on the sand. 27 The rain fell, the rivers rose, the winds blew and pounded that house, and it collapsed. And its collapse was great!"

Practicing the Right Stuff

1. What is the first thing you ever built? Did it last?
2. What happens when you ignore what your coach tells you to do? What happens when you practice what he teaches?

Matthew 7:24-29

3. What does it mean to hear Jesus' words and put them into practice? To hear, but not practice?
4. How will obedience to Jesus' words affect a person's life? How about disobedience?
5. What words of Jesus are you putting into action? What words do you need to get going on?

28 When Jesus had finished this sermon,ᵃ the crowds were astonished at His teaching, 29 because He was teaching them like one who had authority, and not like their •scribes.

Cleansing a Leper

8 When He came down from the mountain, large crowds followed Him. 2 Right away a man with a serious skin disease came up and knelt before Him, saying, "Lord, if You are willing, You can make me clean."ᵇ

3 Reaching out His hand He touched him, saying, "I am willing; be made clean." Immediately his disease was healed.ᶜ 4 Then Jesus told him, "See that you don't tell anyone; but go, show yourself to the priest, and offer the gift that Moses prescribed, as a testimony to them."

A Centurion's Faith

5 When He entered Capernaum, a •centurion came to Him, pleading with Him, 6 "Lord, my servant is lying at home paralyzed, in terrible agony!"

7 "I will come and heal him," He told him.

8 "Lord," the centurion replied, "I am not worthy to have You come under my roof. But only say the word, and my servant will be cured. 9 For I too am a man under authority, having soldiers under my command.ᵈ I say to this one, 'Go!' and he goes; and to another, 'Come!' and he comes; and to my slave, 'Do this!' and he does it."

10 Hearing this, Jesus was amazed and said to those following Him, "•I assure you: I have not found anyone in Israel with so great a faith! 11 I tell you that many will come from east and west, and recline at the table with Abraham, Isaac, and Jacob in the kingdom of heaven. 12 But the sons of the kingdom will be thrown into the outer darkness. In that place there will be weeping and gnashing of teeth." 13 Then Jesus told the centurion, "Go. As you have believed, let it be done for you." And his servant was cured that very moment.ᵉ

Healings at Capernaum

14 When Jesus went into Peter's house, He saw his mother-in-law lying in bed with a fever. 15 So He touched her hand, and the fever left her. Then she got up and began to serve Him. 16 When evening came,

---

ᵃ**7:28** Lit *had ended these words*   ᵇ**8:2** In these vv. 2–3, *clean* includes healing, ceremonial purification, return to fellowship with people, and worship in the temple; see Lv 14:1–32.   ᶜ**8:3** Lit *cleansed*   ᵈ**8:9** Lit *under me*   ᵉ**8:13** Or *that hour*; lit *very hour*

---

ment but also social banishment.

8:3 He touched him. Actually touching a leper was unimaginable to most first century Jews. Not only did one risk contracting the disease, but such contact also made the person ritually impure and thus unable to participate in the religious life of the community (Lev. 5:3-6).

8:4 don't tell anyone. Jesus had to prevent the crowds from proclaiming Him Messiah before they knew what kind of Messiah He was (one who would suffer and die, not the conquering hero they hoped for).

8:5 centurion. A Roman military officer, the commander of 100 men. To most Jews, such a soldier would be a hated symbol of Rome.

8:7 I will come. According to rabbinical law, if Jesus were to enter a Gentile's home he

would be made unclean. This does not create concern for Jesus, however.

8:13 As you have believed, let it be done for you. The testimony of New Testament Scripture is that belief is a powerful force when centered on God. The power of God is released into the world when people believe that "with God all things are possible" (19:26; Mark 10:27; 14:36; Luke 18:27).

8:15 He touched her hand. This is the only healing recorded by Matthew that is initiated by Jesus.

8:16 drove out the spirits with a word. First-century exorcists used elaborate incantations, spells, and magic apparatus to cast out demons—in contrast to Jesus whose word alone carried incredible power.

8:19 a scribe. Typically these teachers of the Law were opposed to Jesus because of His disregard for the oral law or tradition that was so important to them. However, individual scribes became followers of Jesus.

8:20 Son of Man. This is the title Jesus prefers for Himself. In the first century it was a rather colorless, indeterminate title with only some messianic overtones (based on Scriptures such as Dan. 7:13-14). This phrase could be translated as "man" or simply "I." This title is used 29 times in Matthew, always by Jesus, and never by others.

8:21 bury my father. The obligation of a son to bury his father was so important that it normally took precedence over other religious obligations.

8:22 let the dead bury their own. Jesus told

they brought to Him many who were demon-possessed. He drove out the spirits with a word and healed all who were sick, ¹⁷ so that what was spoken through the prophet Isaiah might be fulfilled:

> He Himself took our weaknesses
> and carried our diseases.ᵃ

Following Jesus

¹⁸ When Jesus saw large crowdsᵇ around Him, He gave the order to go to the other side ₁of the sea₁.ᶜ ¹⁹ A •scribe approached Him and said, "Teacher, I will follow You wherever You go!"

²⁰ Jesus told him, "Foxes have dens and birds of the sky have nests, but the Son of Man has no place to lay His head."

²¹ "Lord," another of His disciples said, "first let me go bury my father."ᵈ

²² But Jesus told him, "Follow Me, and let the dead bury their own dead."

Wind and Wave Obey the Master

²³ As He got into theᵉ boat, His disciples followed Him. ²⁴ Suddenly, a violent storm arose on the sea, so that the boat was being swamped by the waves. But He was sleeping. ²⁵ So the disciples came and woke Him up, saying, "Lord, save ₁us₁! We're going to die!"

²⁶ But He said to them, "Why are you fearful, you of little faith?" Then He got up and rebuked the winds and the sea. And there was a great calm.

²⁷ The men were amazed and asked, "What kind of man is this?—even the winds and the sea obey Him!"

Demons Driven Out by the Master

²⁸ When He had come to the other side, to the region of the Gadarenes,ᶠ two demon-possessed men met Him as they came out of the tombs. They were so violent that no one could pass that way. ²⁹ Suddenly they shouted, "What do You have to do with us,ᵍ ʰ Son of God? Have You come here to torment us before the time?"

³⁰ Now a long way off from them, a large herd of pigs was feeding. ³¹ "If You drive us out," the demons begged Him, "send us into the herd of pigs."

³² "Go!" He told them. So when they had come out, they entered the pigs. And suddenly the whole herd rushed down the steep bank into the sea and perished in the water. ³³ Then the men who tended them fled. They went into the city and reported everything—especially what had happened to those who were demon-possessed. ³⁴ At that, the whole town went out to meet Jesus. When they saw Him, they begged Him to leave their region.

The Son of Man Forgives and Heals

9 So He got into a boat, crossed over, and came to His own town. ² Just then some menⁱ brought to Him a paralytic lying on a stretcher. Seeing their faith, Jesus told the paralytic, "Have courage, son, your sins are forgiven."

³ At this, some of the •scribes said among themselves, "He's blaspheming!"

⁴ But perceiving their thoughts, Jesus said, "Why are you thinking evil things in your hearts?ʲ ⁵ For which is easier: to say, 'Your sins are forgiven,' or to say, 'Get up and walk'? ⁶ But so you may know that the •Son of Man has authority on earth to forgive sins"—then He told the paralytic, "Get up, pick up your stretcher, and go home." ⁷ And he got up and went home. ⁸ When the crowds saw this, they were awestruckᵏ ˡ and gave glory to God who had given such authority to men.

The Call of Matthew

⁹ As Jesus went on from there, He saw a man named Matthew sitting at the tax office, and He said to him, "Follow Me!" So he got up and followed Him.

¹⁰ While He was reclining at the table in the house, many tax collectors and sinners came as guests to eatᵐ with Jesus and His disciples. ¹¹ When the •Pharisees saw this, they asked His disciples, "Why does your Teacher eat with tax collectors and sinners?"

ᵃ8:17 Is 53:4   ᵇ8:18 Other mss read *saw a crowd*   ᶜ8:18 Sea of Galilee   ᵈ8:21 Not necessarily meaning his father was already dead   ᵉ8:23 Other mss read *to a*   ᶠ8:28 Other mss read *Gergesenes*   ᵍ8:29 Other mss add *Jesus*   ʰ8:29 Lit *What to us and to You*   ⁱ9:2 Lit *then they*   ʲ9:4 Or *minds*   ᵏ9:8 Other mss read *amazed*   ˡ9:8 Lit *afraid*   ᵐ9:10 Lit *came, they were reclining* (at the table); at important meals the custom was to recline on a mat at a low table and lean on the left elbow.

---

people that to be His followers, they had to put following Him above all other obligations.

8:24 a violent storm. The Sea of Galilee was a deep, freshwater lake, 13 miles long and 8 miles across at its widest point. It was pear-shaped and ringed by mountains, though open at its north and south ends. Fierce winds blew into this bowl-shaped lake, creating savage and unpredictable storms.

8:28 the region of the Gadarenes. Matthew, Mark, and Luke use different terms to describe the place where Jesus landed.

8:34 they begged Him to leave. This may have been in part out of fear of His power, but also because He had destroyed part of their livelihood (the pigs). To these towns-people, their pigs were worth more than the lives of the two madmen.

9:2 your sins are forgiven. Jesus repudiates the teaching that all illness and misfortune is an indication that a person had committed a worse sin than others (John 9:1-3).

9:3 blaspheming. Blasphemy is "contempt for God," and under Jewish law its penalty was death (Lev. 24:16). Jesus' was equating Himself with God and in the scribes' view this was blasphemy.

9:5 which is easier? It is far easier to say, "Your sins are for given" than it is to heal a person. There is no way to verify whether sins have been forgiven, but it is obvious whether a lame person walks or not.

9:8 authority. The issue here, as in each of the three stories in 8:23–9:8, is Jesus' authority. He has authority over the elements, demons, and even sin.

9:9 Matthew. Presumably the author of this Gospel. Matthew would have been hated by both the religious establishment and the common people because he was working for the Romans.

9:11 Why does your Teacher eat with tax collectors and sinners? The Pharisees could not understand how a truly religious person could eat with people whose moral life was disreputable and who violated the practices regarding ritual cleanliness.

9:12 Those who are well don't need a doctor, but the sick do. Jesus was not necessarily saying that the Pharisees *were* spiritually healthy, only that they perceived themselves to be so.

9:15 the groom. In the Old Testament, God is often referred to as the groom of Israel. **the**

12 But when He heard this, He said, "Those who are well don't need a doctor, but the sick do. 13 Go and learn what this means: **I desire mercy and not sacrifice.**[a] For I didn't come to call the righteous, but sinners."[b]

A Question about Fasting

14 Then John's disciples came to Him, saying, "Why do we and the Pharisees fast often, but Your disciples do not fast?"

15 Jesus said to them, "Can the wedding guests[c] be sad while the groom is with them? The days will come when the groom will be taken away from them, and then they will fast. 16 No one patches an old garment with unshrunk cloth, because the patch pulls away from the garment and makes the tear worse. 17 And no one puts[d] new wine into old wineskins. Otherwise, the skins burst, the wine spills out, and the skins are ruined. But they put new wine into fresh wineskins, and both are preserved."

A Girl Restored and a Woman Healed

18 As He was telling them these things, suddenly one of the leaders[e] came and knelt down before Him, saying, "My daughter is near death,[f] but come and lay Your hand on her, and she will live." 19 So Jesus and His disciples got up and followed him.

20 Just then, a woman who had suffered from bleeding for 12 years approached from behind and touched the •tassel on His robe, 21 for she said to herself, "If I can just touch His robe, I'll be made well!"[g]

22 But Jesus turned and saw her. "Have courage, daughter," He said. "Your faith has made you well."[h] And the woman was made well from that moment.[i]

23 When Jesus came to the leader's house, He saw the flute players and a crowd lamenting loudly. 24 "Leave," He said, "because the girl isn't dead, but sleeping." And they started laughing at Him. 25 But when the crowd had been put outside, He went in and took her by the hand, and the girl got up. 26 And this news spread throughout that whole area.

Healing the Blind

27 As Jesus went on from there, two blind men followed Him, shouting, "Have mercy on us, Son of David!"

28 When He entered the house, the blind men approached Him, and Jesus said to them, "Do you believe that I can do this?"

"Yes, Lord," they answered Him.

29 Then He touched their eyes, saying, "Let it be done for you according to your faith!" 30 And their eyes were opened. Then Jesus warned them sternly, "Be sure that no one finds out!"[j] 31 But they went out and spread the news about Him throughout that whole area.

Driving Out a Demon

32 Just as they were going out, a demon-possessed man who was unable to speak was brought to Him. 33 When the demon had been driven out, the man[k] spoke. And the crowds were amazed, saying, "Nothing like this has ever been seen in Israel!"

34 But the Pharisees said, "He drives out demons by the ruler of the demons!"

The Lord of the Harvest

35 Then Jesus went to all the towns and villages, teaching in their •synagogues, preaching the good news of the kingdom, and healing every[l] disease and every sickness.[m] 36 When He saw the crowds, He felt compassion for them, because they were weary and worn out, like sheep without a shepherd. 37 Then He said to His disciples, "The harvest is abundant, but the workers are few. 38 Therefore, pray to the Lord of the harvest to send out workers into His harvest."

Commissioning the Twelve

10 Summoning His 12 disciples, He gave them authority over unclean[n] spirits, to drive them out and to heal every[l] disease and sickness. 2 These are the names of the 12 apostles:

---

a9:13 Hs 6:6   b9:13 Other mss add to repentance   c9:15 Lit the sons of the bridal chamber   d9:17 Lit And they do not put   e9:18 A leader of a synagogue; Mk 5:22   f9:18 Lit daughter has now come to the end   g9:21 Or be delivered   h9:22 Or has saved you   i9:22 Lit hour   j9:30 Lit no one knows   k9:33 Lit the man who was unable to speak   l9:35; 10:1 Or every kind of   m9:35 Other mss add among the people   n10:1 Morally or ceremonially impure

---

groom will be taken away from them. This is a foreshadowing of Jesus' death. It will be as if the groom is suddenly, violently abducted just prior to his wedding.

9:20 a woman who had suffered from bleeding. She was probably undergoing a period of menstruation, which rendered her ritually impure (Lev. 15:25-33). As a result, she should not have been there in the crowd. She was considered "unclean," and if anyone touched her, that person too would become "unclean."

9:23 flute players and a crowd lamenting loudly. These were in all likelihood professional mourners. Even the poorest person was required to hire no less than two flutes and one wailing woman to mourn a death.

9:24 the girl isn't dead, but sleeping.

Jesus uses the same expression in reference to Lazarus who also died (John 11:11-15). What He means is that she is not permanently dead.

9:27 two blind men. Blindness was common in the ancient world, often due to infection. **Son of David.** There was a strong expectation that the Messiah would be a king in the line of David.

9:34 by the ruler of demons. The Pharisees dismiss Jesus' healings by attributing them to Satan.

10:1 12 disciples. This is the first time in Matthew that the 12 disciples are mentioned. The number 12 is significant. There were 12 sons of Jacob and they became the patriarchs of the 12 tribes of the old Israel.

10:5 Do not go among the Gentiles. The first mission of the Twelve was to the people of Israel. After the death and resurrection of Jesus, their mission expanded to include all nations (28:19).

10:7 The kingdom of heaven has come near. This is the same message that John the Baptist gave (3:2).

10:11 stay there until you leave. They are not to dishonor their hosts by accepting better accommodations.

10:14 shake the dust off your feet. When pious Jews left a Gentile region and returned to Israel, they shook off the dust of the land through which they had traveled to disassociate themselves from the coming judgment against the Gentiles.

886

First, Simon, who is called Peter,
and Andrew his brother;
James the son of Zebedee,
and John his brother;
3 Philip and Bartholomew;[a]
Thomas and Matthew the tax collector;
James the son of Alphaeus, and Thaddaeus;[b]
4 Simon the Zealot,[c] and Judas Iscariot,[d]
who also betrayed Him.

5 Jesus sent out these 12 after giving them instructions: "Don't take the road leading to other nations, and don't enter any •Samaritan town. 6 Instead, go to the lost sheep of the house of Israel. 7 As you go, announce this: 'The kingdom of heaven has come near.' 8 Heal the sick, raise the dead, cleanse those with skin diseases, drive out demons. You have received free of charge; give free of charge. 9 Don't take along gold, silver, or copper for your money-belts. 10 Don't take a traveling bag for the road, or an extra shirt, sandals, or a walking stick, for the worker is worthy of his food.

11 "When you enter any town or village, find out who is worthy, and stay there until you leave. 12 Greet a household when you enter it, 13 and if the household is worthy, let your peace be on it. But if it is unworthy, let your peace return to you. 14 If anyone will not welcome you or listen to your words, shake the dust off your feet when you leave that house or town. 15 •I assure you: It will be more tolerable on the day of judgment for the land of Sodom and Gomorrah than for that town.

Persecutions Predicted

16 "Look, I'm sending you out like sheep among wolves. Therefore be as shrewd as serpents and as harmless as doves. 17 Because people will hand you over to sanhedrins[e] and flog you in their •synagogues, beware of them. 18 You will even be brought before governors and kings because of Me, to bear witness to them and to the nations. 19 But when they hand you over, don't worry about how or what you should speak. For you will be given what to say at that hour,

20 because you are not speaking, but the Spirit of your Father is speaking through you.

21 "Brother will betray brother to death, and a father his child. Children will even rise up against their parents and have them put to death. 22 You will be hated by everyone because of My name. But the one who endures to the end will be delivered.[f] 23 When they persecute you in one town, escape to another. For I assure you: You will not have covered the towns of Israel before the •Son of Man comes. 24 A disciple[g] is not above his teacher, or a slave above his master. 25 It is enough for a disciple to become like his teacher and a slave like his master. If they called the head of the house '•Beelzebul,' how much more the members of his household!

Fear God

26 "Therefore, don't be afraid of them, since there is nothing covered that won't be uncovered, and nothing hidden that won't be made known. 27 What I tell you in the dark, speak in the light. What you hear in a whisper,[h] proclaim on the housetops. 28 Don't fear those who kill the body but are not able to kill the soul; rather, fear Him who is able to destroy both soul and body in •hell. 29 Aren't two sparrows sold for a penny?[i] Yet not one of them falls to the ground without your Father's consent.[j] 30 But even the hairs of your head have all been counted. 31 Don't be afraid therefore; you are worth more than many sparrows.

Acknowledging Christ

32 "Therefore, everyone who will acknowledge Me before men, I will also acknowledge him before My Father in heaven. 33 But whoever denies Me before men, I will also deny him before My Father in heaven. 34 Don't assume that I came to bring peace on the earth. I did not come to bring peace, but a sword. 35 For I came to turn

a man against his father,
a daughter against her mother,

---

[a]10:3 Probably the Nathanael of Jn 1:45–51 [b]10:3 Other mss read and Lebbaeus, whose surname was Thaddaeus [c]10:4 Lit the Cananaean [d]10:4 Iscariot probably = "a man of Kerioth," a town in Judea. [e]10:17 Local Jewish courts or local councils [f]10:22 Or saved [g]10:24 Or student [h]10:27 Lit in the ear [i]10:29 Gk assarion, a small copper coin [j]10:29 Lit ground apart from your Father

---

10:16 shrewd as serpents ... harmless as doves. While Jesus' disciples are to use cleverness—not force—to survive, they are to be honest and holy.

10:17-23 when they hand you over. This passage seems to have more applicability to the time after Jesus' resurrection and ascension. At that time, the early church certainly faced all the perils mentioned here.

10:17 sanhedrins ... synagogues. The sanhedrins were Jewish courts where religious troublemakers were tried and then beaten publicly in the synagogues.

10:18 governors and kings. Some of Jesus' disciples will stand before Roman provincial governors and kings.

10:22 the one who endures to the end will

be delivered. His disciples will not be spared persecution, but they are guaranteed entrance into the kingdom of God.

10:23 before the Son of Man comes. The early church expected an early return of Christ.

10:25 Beelzebul. This is probably a slang expression for a demon-prince, meaning something like "The Lord of Dung."

10:27 on the housetops. Important announcements would often be made from the roof of a building. What Jesus taught the disciples in private was to be broadcast to all.

10:28 don't fear. They are not to fear death, since those who have the power to kill them have no power over their souls. **rather, fear**

Him. This is not meant to imply that the motive for following Jesus is only fear of God's wrath, but that believers' lives are to be marked by a greater regard for God than for human opinion.

10:29 sparrows. Sparrows are worth next to nothing (two for a penny) and yet not one of them dies without God knowing it. **penny.** A penny was worth one sixteenth of a denarius. A denarius was the average day's wage of a manual laborer.

10:34 Don't assume that I came to bring peace on the earth. This should not be taken to mean that Jesus was in favor of war. Jesus turned away from the militaristic expectations of the Messiah. He also proclaimed that "all who take up a sword will perish by a sword" (26:52). He was saying that the demands He would make would

a daughter-in-law against her mother-in-law;
36 **and a man's enemies will be**
the members of his household.[a]

37 The person who loves father or mother more than Me is not worthy of Me; the person who loves son or daughter more than Me is not worthy of Me. 38 And whoever doesn't take up his cross and follow[b] Me is not worthy of Me. 39 Anyone finding[c] his life will lose it, and anyone losing[d] his life because of Me will find it.

A Cup of Cold Water

40 "The one who welcomes you welcomes Me, and the one who welcomes Me welcomes Him who sent Me. 41 Anyone who[e] welcomes a prophet because he is a prophet[f] will receive a prophet's reward. And anyone who[g] welcomes a righteous person because he's righteous[h] will receive a righteous person's reward. 42 And whoever gives just a cup of cold water to one of these little ones because he is a disciple[i]—I assure you: He will never lose his reward!"

In Praise of John the Baptist

11 When Jesus had finished giving orders to His 12 disciples, He moved on from there to teach and preach in their towns. 2 When John heard in prison what the •Messiah was doing, he sent ⌊a message⌋ by his disciples 3 and asked Him, "Are You the One who is to come, or should we expect someone else?"

4 Jesus replied to them, "Go and report to John what you hear and see: 5 the blind see, the lame walk, those with skin diseases are healed,[j] the deaf hear, the dead are raised, and the poor are told the good news. 6 And if anyone is not offended because of Me, he is blessed."

7 As these men went away, Jesus began to speak to the crowds about John: "What did you go out into the wilderness to see? A reed swaying in the wind? 8 What then did you go out to see? A man dressed in soft clothes? Look, those who wear soft clothes are in kings' palaces. 9 But what did you go out to see? A prophet? Yes, I tell you, and far more than a prophet. 10 This is the one it is written about:

Look, I am sending My messenger
ahead of You;[k]
he will prepare Your way before You.[l]

11 "•I assure you: Among those born of women no one greater than John the Baptist has appeared,[m] but the least in the kingdom of heaven is greater than he. 12 From the days of John the Baptist until now, the kingdom of heaven has been suffering violence,[n] and the violent have been seizing it by force. 13 For all the prophets and the law prophesied until John; 14 if you're willing to accept it, he is the Elijah who is to come. 15 Anyone who has ears[o] should listen!

An Unresponsive Generation

16 "To what should I compare this generation? It's like children sitting in the marketplaces who call out to each other:

17 We played the flute for you,
but you didn't dance;
we sang a lament,
but you didn't mourn![p]

18 For John did not come eating or drinking, and they say, 'He has a demon!' 19 The •Son of Man came eating and drinking, and they say, 'Look, a glutton and a drunkard, a friend of tax collectors and sinners!' Yet wisdom is vindicated[q] by her deeds."[r]

20 Then He proceeded to denounce the towns where most of His miracles were done, because they did not repent: 21 "Woe to you, Chorazin! Woe to you, Bethsaida! For if the miracles that were done in you had been done in Tyre and Sidon, they would have repented in sackcloth and ashes long ago! 22 But I tell you, it will be more tolerable for Tyre and Sidon on the day of judgment than for you. 23 And you, Capernaum, will you be exalted to heaven? You will go down to •Hades. For if the miracles that were done in you had

[a]**10:35–36** Mc 7:6 [b]**10:38** Lit *follow after* [c]**10:39** Or *The one who finds* [d]**10:39** Or *and the one who loses* [e]**10:41** Or *The one who* [f]**10:41** Lit *prophet in the name of a prophet* [g]**10:41** Or *And the one who* [h]**10:41** Lit *person in the name of a righteous person* [i]**10:42** Lit *little ones in the name of a disciple* [j]**11:5** Lit *cleansed* [k]**11:10** Lit *messenger before Your face* [l]**11:10** Mal 3:1 [m]**11:11** Lit *arisen* [n]**11:12** Or *has been forcefully advancing* [o]**11:15** Other mss add *to hear* [p]**11:17** Or *beat your breasts* [q]**11:19** Or *declared right* [r]**11:19** Other mss read *children*

---

create conflicts between people, even people in the same family. Jesus did not seek to avoid conflict when conflict was necessary.

10:37 loves father or mother. Jesus was not being anti-family here. He was saying that family ties can work against faithful discipleship, and that God's claim must be our clear and first loyalty.

10:38 cross. It would evoke for His hearers the image of a Roman execution.

10:39 finding his life. This is putting one's own natural inclinations ahead of loyalty to Christ.

10:40 welcomes. To receive someone is to offer hospitality (vv. 11-14). In a time of persecution this could be dangerous. Welcoming the disciple probably means that the host accepts the teaching of the disciple.

10:42 a cup of cold water. In the hot Middle-Eastern climate, cold water was a gift of life-sustaining importance.

11:2 in prison. Herod arrested John at the instigation of his wife Herodias, who was angry with John for denouncing their marriage (14:1-12).

11:4-6 Go and report. Jesus responds by inviting John's disciples to report what they have seen with their own eyes and heard with their own ears. His actions and His teaching are all the "proof" that is necessary to identify Him from Old Testament prophecies.

11:7-8 a reed swaying in the wind. John was not a weak and vacillating reed who was affected by every wind of opinion, nor was he a finely dressed courtier in the halls of King Herod.

11:9-10 far more than a prophet. John was a very special prophet. He had been foretold by Old Testament prophecy. His role, as the quotation from Malachi 3:1 shows, was to prepare for the coming of the Messiah.

11:19 Yet wisdom is vindicated by her deeds. Despite the leaders' rejection of Jesus and John, God's wisdom in sending them is demonstrated in that both will ultimately bear evidence to the kingdom of God at work.

11:20 repent. To repent is to change your mind about the direction in which you are going.

been done in Sodom, it would have remained until today. [24] But I tell you, it will be more tolerable for the land of Sodom on the day of judgment than for you."

The Son Gives Knowledge and Rest

[25] At that time Jesus said, "I praise[a] You, Father, Lord of heaven and earth, because You have hidden these things from the wise and learned and revealed them to infants. [26] Yes, Father, because this was Your good pleasure.[b] [27] All things have been entrusted to Me by My Father. No one knows[c] the Son except the Father, and no one knows the Father except the Son and anyone to whom the Son desires[d] to reveal Him.

[28] "Come to Me, all of you who are weary and burdened, and I will give you rest. [29] All of you, take up My yoke and learn from Me, because I am gentle and humble in heart, and you will find rest for yourselves. [30] For My yoke is easy and My burden is light."

Lord of the Sabbath

12 At that time Jesus passed through the grainfields on the Sabbath. His disciples were hungry and began to pick and eat some heads of grain. [2] But when the •Pharisees saw it, they said to Him, "Look, Your disciples are doing what is not lawful to do on the Sabbath!"

[3] He said to them, "Haven't you read what David did when he and those who were with him were hungry— [4] how he entered the house of God, and they ate[e] the •sacred bread, which is not lawful for him or for those with him to eat, but only for the priests? [5] Or haven't you read in the Law[f] that on Sabbath days the priests in the temple violate the Sabbath and are innocent? [6] But I tell you that something greater than the temple is here! [7] If you had known what this means: **I desire mercy and not sacrifice**,[g] you would not have condemned the innocent. [8] For the •Son of Man is Lord of the Sabbath."

The Man with the Paralyzed Hand

[9] Moving on from there, He entered their •synagogue. [10] There He saw a man who had a paralyzed hand. And in order to accuse Him they asked Him, "Is it lawful to heal on the Sabbath?"

[11] But He said to them, "What man among you, if he had a sheep[h] that fell into a pit on the Sabbath, wouldn't take hold of it and lift it out? [12] A man is worth far more than a sheep, so it is lawful to do good on the Sabbath."

[13] Then He told the man, "Stretch out your hand." So he stretched it out, and it was restored, as good as the other. [14] But the Pharisees went out and plotted against Him, how they might destroy Him.

The Servant of the Lord

[15] When Jesus became aware of this, He withdrew from there. Huge crowds[i] followed Him, and He healed them all. [16] He warned them not to make Him known, [17] so that what was spoken through the prophet Isaiah might be fulfilled:

> [18] Here is My Servant whom I have chosen,
>   My beloved in whom My soul delights;
>   I will put My Spirit on Him,
>   and He will proclaim justice to the nations.
> [19] He will not argue or shout,
>   and no one will hear His voice in the streets.
> [20] He will not break a bruised reed,
>   and He will not put out a smoldering wick,
>   until He has led justice to victory.[j]
> [21] The nations will put their hope in His name.[k]

A House Divided

[22] Then a demon-possessed man who was blind and unable to speak was brought to Him. He healed him, so that the man[l] could both speak and see. [23] And all the crowds were astounded and said, "Perhaps this is the Son of David!"

[24] When the Pharisees heard this, they said, "The man drives out demons only by •Beelzebul, the ruler of the demons."

[25] Knowing their thoughts, He told them: "Every kingdom divided against itself is headed for destruction, and no city or house divided against itself will stand.

---

a**11:25** Or *thank*   b**11:26** Lit *was well-pleasing in Your sight*   c**11:27** Or *knows exactly*   d**11:27** Or *wills*, or *chooses*   e**12:4** Other mss read *he ate*
f**12:5** The Torah (the Pentateuch)   g**12:7** Hs 6:6   h**12:11** Or *had one sheep*   i**12:15** Other mss read *Many*   j**12:20** Or *until He has successfully put forth justice*   k**12:18–21** Is 42:1–4   l**12:22** Lit *mute*

11:21 Chorazin. Apart from this reference (and the parallel in Luke 10:13) and one reference in rabbinic writing, there is no other mention of Chorazin. **Bethsaida.** The home of Peter, Andrew, and Philip (John 1:44; 12:21). **Tyre and Sidon.** These were two Phoenician port cities inhabited by Gentiles. **sackcloth and ashes.** As a sign of mourning and repentance from sin, people would wear rough clothing and cover themselves with ashes.

11:23 Capernaum. The village where Jesus performed many of His first miracles (8:5-17). **Sodom.** This city, destroyed by God because of its evil, was legendary for its wickedness (Gen. 18:20–19:29).

11:25 the wise and learned. The scribes and Pharisees, though educated and supposedly wise, are blind to God's plan (1 Cor. 1:19-20).

11:27 My Father. Jesus here defines His relationship with the One He calls "Father" in verse 25. This is one of the most explicit statements in the Gospels about who Jesus is. Three points are made: (1) All things are shared between the Father and the Son; (2) There is an intimate relationship between the two; (3) It is Jesus who reveals the Father to people (John 3:34-35; 10:15).

11:30 burden. The demands of discipleship, while costly in one way (5-7; 8:18-22) are "light" in comparison with the demands of ceremonial law.

12:1 Sabbath. The seventh day of the week (Saturday), begins Friday at sunset and ends Saturday at sunset. The Fourth Commandment is to rest from all labor on the Sabbath (Ex. 20:8-11). By the first century, scores of laws had evolved which defined what could not be done on the Sabbath.

pick and eat some heads of grain. It was permissible for hungry travelers to pluck and eat grain from a field (Deut. 23:25).

12:4 ate the sacred bread. Each Sabbath, 12 fresh loaves of bread were put in the Holy Place (Ex. 25:30; Num. 4:7). Only the priests were to eat the old bread. David did what was unlawful, providing a precedent that human need supersedes ceremonial law.

12:10 paralyzed hand. Rabbinic law allowed healing on the Sabbath only if there was danger to life. Clearly a paralyzed hand (which had probably been that way for some time) did not constitute an emergency.

12:13 Stretch out your hand. Just as He deliberately declared the paralytic's sins forgiven, knowing that this would be considered blasphemy by the teachers of the Law (9:1-8). Here He deliberately heals on the Sabbath,

²⁶ If Satan drives out Satan, he is divided against himself. How then will his kingdom stand? ²⁷ And if I drive out demons by Beelzebul, who is it your sons drive them out by? For this reason they will be your judges. ²⁸ If I drive out demons by the Spirit of God, then the kingdom of God has come to you. ²⁹ How can someone enter a strong man's house and steal his possessions unless he first ties up the strong man? Then he can rob his house. ³⁰ Anyone who is not with Me is against Me, and anyone who does not gather with Me scatters. ³¹ Because of this, I tell you, people will be forgiven every sin and blasphemy, but the blasphemy against[a] the Spirit will not be forgiven.[b] ³² Whoever speaks a word against the Son of Man, it will be forgiven him. But whoever speaks against the Holy Spirit, it will not be forgiven him, either in this age or in the one to come.

A Tree and Its Fruit

³³ "Either make the tree good and its fruit good, or make the tree bad[c] and its fruit bad; for a tree is known by its fruit. ³⁴ Brood of vipers! How can you speak good things when you are evil? For the mouth speaks from the overflow of the heart. ³⁵ A good man produces good things from his storeroom of good,[d] and an evil man produces evil things from his storeroom of evil. ³⁶ I tell you that on the day of judgment people will have to account for every careless word they speak.[e] ³⁷ For by your words you will be acquitted, and by your words you will be condemned."

The Sign of Jonah

³⁸ Then some of the •scribes and Pharisees said to Him, "Teacher, we want to see a sign from You."

³⁹ But He answered them, "An evil and adulterous generation demands a sign, but no sign will be given to it except the sign of the prophet Jonah. ⁴⁰ For as Jonah was in the belly of the great fish three days and three nights, so the Son of Man will be in the heart of the earth three days and three nights. ⁴¹ The men of Nineveh will stand up at the judgment with this generation and condemn it, because they repented at Jonah's proc-

lamation; and look—something greater than Jonah is here! ⁴² The queen of the south will rise up at the judgment with this generation and condemn it, because she came from the ends of the earth to hear the wisdom of Solomon; and look—something greater than Solomon is here!

An Unclean Spirit's Return

⁴³ "When an unclean[f] spirit comes out of a man, it roams through waterless places looking for rest but doesn't find any. ⁴⁴ Then it says, 'I'll go back to my house that I came from.' And when it arrives, it finds ⌊the house⌋ vacant, swept, and put in order. ⁴⁵ Then off it goes and brings with it seven other spirits more evil than itself, and they enter and settle down there. As a result, that man's last condition is worse than the first. That's how it will also be with this evil generation."

True Relationships

⁴⁶ He was still speaking to the crowds when suddenly His mother and brothers were standing outside wanting to speak to Him. ⁴⁷ Someone told Him, "Look, Your mother and Your brothers are standing outside, wanting to speak to You."[g]

⁴⁸ But He replied to the one who told Him, "Who is My mother and who are My brothers?" ⁴⁹ And stretching out His hand toward His disciples, He said, "Here are My mother and My brothers! ⁵⁰ For whoever does the will of My Father in heaven, that person is My brother and sister and mother."

The Parable of the Sower

13 On that day Jesus went out of the house and was sitting by the sea. ² Such large crowds gathered around Him that He got into a boat and sat down, while the whole crowd stood on the shore.

³ Then He told them many things in parables, saying: "Consider the sower who went out to sow. ⁴ As he was sowing, some seeds fell along the path, and the birds came and ate them up. ⁵ Others fell on rocky ground, where there wasn't much soil, and they sprang up quickly since the soil wasn't deep. ⁶ But when the sun

---

[a]**12:31** Or *of* [b]**12:31** Other mss add *people* [c]**12:33** Lit *rotten*, or *decayed* [d]**12:35** Other mss read *from the storehouse of his heart* [e]**12:36** Lit *will speak* [f]**12:43** Morally or ceremonially impure [g]**12:47** Other mss omit this v.

---

knowing that this too is anathema to His critics.

12:24 only by Beelzebul. Beelzebul was the Canaanite name for the chief god Baal. In Jewish terminology, this became identified as the chief among the demons. To be possessed by this demon meant to be controlled and empowered by him, which is how the teachers of the Law explained Jesus' miracles

12:31 blasphemy against the Spirit. This is to resist the Spirit's convicting work, and so not to see one's sin. Therefore rendering the person unable to experience forgiveness of sin and, ultimately, eternal life.

12:32 it will not be forgiven. It might be excusable to utter a word against the Son of Man, since who He is, at this point, is somewhat hidden. Even John the Baptist is not sure about Jesus' identity (11:3). To resist the insights brought by the Holy Spirit, who is the revealer of truth, is to put one's self deliberately

outside the orbit of God's revelation.

12:40 three days and three nights. Jesus' death and resurrection took place over a three-day period (Friday, Saturday, and Sunday).

12:41 men of Nineveh. The people of Nineveh repented when Jonah preached to them.

12:42 the queen of the south. This queen came all the way from Arabia to listen to the wisdom of Solomon (1 Kings 10:1-13). In both examples, Gentiles heeded the words of a Jew, but the Jews of this generation will not heed One greater than both Jonah and Solomon.

12:43-45 this evil generation. Jesus tells a parable about the spiritual state of His generation. By His message of healing, Jesus had swept out the demon that possessed the people. But the new Spirit, the Holy Spirit, is not in-

vited to take up residence in their hearts. So, evil returns in much greater power.

12:46 standing outside. According to Mark, Jesus' family thinks that He is "out of His mind" and so they go to "restrain Him" (Mark 3:21). When the family arrives, they find Him surrounded by the crowd. Not wanting to confront Him in that setting, they wait outside.

13:3 parables. Parables are comparisons that draw upon common experience in order to teach about kingdom realities. **sow.** Farmers would throw seed into the soil using a broadcast method.

13:4 the path. There were long, hard pathways between the various plots of land. The soil was so packed down that seed could not penetrate the soil and germinate.

13:5 rocky ground. Some of the soil covered a limestone base a few inches beneath the

came up they were scorched, and since they had no root, they withered. 7 Others fell among thorns, and the thorns came up and choked them. 8 Still others fell on good ground, and produced a crop: some 100, some 60, and some 30 times ⌊what was sown⌋. 9 Anyone who has ears[a] should listen!"

Why Jesus Used Parables

10 Then the disciples came up and asked Him, "Why do You speak to them in parables?"

Four Soils

1. Have you ever planted a garden? What kind? How did it do?

Matthew 13:1-23

2. Who first planted the "seed" of the kingdom of heaven in your life? What happened to this seed?

3. What are the "the worries of this age and the seduction of wealth" (v. 22)? How do these things "choke" the word of God?

4. Which of the four soils best describes the condition of your heart right now?

5. What "fertilizer" would help your spiritual "soil" right now? What "weeds" need to be pulled?

---

11 He answered them, "Because the secrets[b] of the kingdom of heaven have been given for you to know, but it has not been given to them. 12 For whoever has, ⌊more⌋ will be given to him, and he will have more than enough. But whoever does not have, even what he has will be taken away from him. 13 For this reason I speak to them in parables, because looking they do not see,

and hearing they do not listen or understand. 14 Isaiah's prophecy is fulfilled in them, which says:

> You will listen and listen,
> yet never understand;
> and you will look and look,
> yet never perceive.
> 15 For this people's heart has grown callous;
> their ears are hard of hearing,
> and they have shut their eyes;
> otherwise they might see with their eyes
> and hear with their ears,
> understand with their hearts
> and turn back—
> and I would cure them.[c]

16 "But your eyes are blessed because they do see, and your ears because they do hear! 17 For •I assure you: Many prophets and righteous people longed to see the things you see yet didn't see them; to hear the things you hear yet didn't hear them.

The Parable of the Sower Explained

18 "You, then, listen to the parable of the sower: 19 When anyone hears the word[d] about the kingdom and doesn't understand it, the evil one comes and snatches away what was sown in his heart. This is the one sown along the path. 20 And the one sown on rocky ground—this is one who hears the word and immediately receives it with joy. 21 Yet he has no root in himself, but is short-lived. When pressure or persecution comes because of the word, immediately he stumbles. 22 Now the one sown among the thorns—this is one who hears the word, but the worries of this age and the seduction[e] of wealth choke the word, and it becomes unfruitful. 23 But the one sown on the good ground—this is one who hears and understands the word, who does bear fruit and yields: some 100, some 60, some 30 times ⌊what was sown⌋."

The Parable of the Wheat and the Weeds

24 He presented another parable to them: "The kingdom of heaven may be compared to a man who sowed

---

[a]13:9 Other mss add *to hear*   [b]13:11 The Gk word *mysteria* does not mean "mysteries" in the Eng sense; it means what we can know only by divine revelation.   [c]13:14–15 Is 6:9–10   [d]13:19 Gk *logos* = *word*, or *message*, or *saying*, or *thing*   [e]13:22 Or *pleasure*, or *deceitfulness*

---

surface. Seed that fell here would germinate, but it would not last since a proper root system could not develop, because of the rock.

13:7 thorns. In other parts of the plot there were the roots of weeds. When the seed grew up, so did the weeds, which invariably stunted the growth of the good seed. Although it lived, such seed would not bear fruit.

13:8 good ground. However, some of the seed did fall where it was intended. **some 100, some 60, some 30 times.** The good soil yielded a spectacular crop. The normal yield for a Palestinian field is seven and a half times what is sown, while 10 times is an especially good harvest. This is where the emphasis in the parable lies: Not with the unproductive soil, but with the miracle crop.

13:9 Anyone who has ears should listen! Jesus urges His hearers to ponder His parable. Part of the power of a parable lies in the fact that people must reflect on it in order to understand it.

13:10 Why … parables? The disciples ask why Jesus uses parables. Behind this question lies the fact that parables do not always act as simple illustrations that illuminate spiritual truth. They can be hard to understand (13:36).

13:11 secrets. A secret in the New Testament is not something that is hidden as much as it is a mystery that is unclear to the outsider, but clear to the truth-seeking insider to whom its meaning has been revealed.

13:13-15 hearing they do not listen. The problem the Pharisees had with parables was not that they could not understand the

parables—they understood them all too well, but resisted their truth (21:43-46).

13:19 snatches away. The seed is the message about the kingdom. Some are so hardened (like the soil on the paths between farm plots) that the seed of the Word never even penetrates. It is, instead, snatched away by Satan. **hears … doesn't understand.** This person merely hears the message; there is no understanding of what is heard. To understand is to grasp the meaning of the message and then make it your own.

13:22 among the thorns. Still others allow the wrong concerns (specifically worries and wealth) to squeeze out their interest in Jesus and His way. **it becomes unfruitful.** The weeds do not kill the plant (in contrast to the seeds sown on hard ground or on rocky soil, which do not survive). But they do not allow it to bring forth fruit.

good seed in his field. 25 But while people were sleeping, his enemy came, sowed weeds[a] among the wheat, and left. 26 When the plants sprouted and produced grain, then the weeds also appeared. 27 The landowner's slaves came to him and said, 'Master, didn't you sow good seed in your field? Then where did the weeds come from?'

28 " 'An enemy did this!' he told them.

" 'So, do you want us to go and gather them up?' the slaves asked him.

29 " 'No,' he said. 'When you gather up the weeds, you might also uproot the wheat with them. 30 Let both grow together until the harvest. At harvest time I'll tell the reapers: Gather the weeds first and tie them in bundles to burn them, but store the wheat in my barn.' "

The Parables of the Mustard Seed and of the Yeast

31 He presented another parable to them: "The kingdom of heaven is like a mustard seed that a man took and sowed in his field. 32 It's the smallest of all the seeds, but when grown, it's taller than the vegetables and becomes a tree, so that the birds of the sky come and nest in its branches."

33 He told them another parable: "The kingdom of heaven is like yeast that a woman took and mixed into 50 pounds[b] of flour until it spread through all of it."[c]

Using Parables Fulfills Prophecy

34 Jesus told the crowds all these things in parables, and He would not speak anything to them without a parable, 35 so that what was spoken through the prophet might be fulfilled:

I will open My mouth in parables;
I will declare things kept secret
from the foundation of the world.[d]

Jesus Interprets the Wheat and the Weeds

36 Then He dismissed the crowds and went into the house. His disciples approached Him and said, "Explain the parable of the weeds in the field to us."

37 He replied: "The One who sows the good seed is the •Son of Man; 38 the field is the world; and the good seed—these are the sons of the kingdom. The weeds are the sons of the evil one, and 39 the enemy who sowed them is the Devil. The harvest is the end of the age, and the harvesters are angels. 40 Therefore just as the weeds are gathered and burned in the fire, so it will be at the end of the age. 41 The Son of Man will send out His angels, and they will gather from His kingdom everything that causes sin[e] and those guilty of lawlessness.[f] 42 They will throw them into the blazing furnace where there will be weeping and gnashing of teeth. 43 Then the righteous will shine like the sun in their Father's kingdom. Anyone who has ears[g] should listen!

The Parables of the Hidden Treasure and of the Priceless Pearl

44 "The kingdom of heaven is like treasure, buried in a field, that a man found and reburied. Then in his joy he goes and sells everything he has and buys that field.

45 "Again, the kingdom of heaven is like a merchant in search of fine pearls. 46 When he found one priceless[h] pearl, he went and sold everything he had, and bought it.

The Parable of the Net

47 "Again, the kingdom of heaven is like a large net thrown into the sea. It collected every kind [of fish], 48 and when it was full, they dragged it ashore, sat down, and gathered the good [fish] into containers, but threw out the worthless ones. 49 So it will be at the end of the age. The angels will go out, separate the evil people from the righteous, 50 and throw them into the blazing furnace. In that place there will be weeping and gnashing of teeth.

The Storehouse of Truth

51 "Have you understood all these things?"[i]

"Yes," they told Him.

52 "Therefore," He said to them, "every student of Scripture[j] instructed in the kingdom of heaven is like a

---

[a]13:25 Or darnel, a weed similar in appearance to wheat in the early stages   [b]13:33 Lit 3 sata; about 40 quarts   [c]13:33 Or until all of it was leavened   [d]13:35 Ps 78:2   [e]13:41 Or stumbling   [f]13:41 Or those who do lawlessness   [g]13:43 Other mss add to hear   [h]13:46 Or very precious   [i]13:51 Other mss add Jesus asked them   [j]13:52 Or every scribe

---

13:31 mustard seed. The mustard plant, which grows to about 10 feet, has the smallest seed. Its shade and tasty brown seeds attract flocks of birds.

13:33 yeast. A small piece of dough would be saved from the previous baking and allowed to ferment. It would then be added to the new bread mixture, causing it to rise. **50 pounds of flour.** Literally, "three measures." This would be almost 160 cups of flour, enough to make bread for about 100 people!

13:38 sons of the kingdom. To be a "son" of something or someone meant to be a person who reflected the characteristics of that particular thing or person. The "sons of the kingdom" are people whose lives are in conformity to the values of that kingdom. The "sons of the evil one" are those whose character reflects that of Satan.

13:40 burned in the fire. God's judgment was often described in terms of a consuming fire that would purify the world of all evil (2 Thess. 1:7; Heb. 12:28-29; 2 Peter 3:10; Rev. 19:20).

13:42 weeping and gnashing of teeth. This was a common phrase used to indicate extreme horror and suffering (8:12; 13:50; 22:13; 24:51; 25:30).

13:43 Anyone who has ears should listen! This is one common phrase used to call people to think about what they have heard: What does it mean? What are its implications? How are we to respond to this story (v. 9)?

13:44 treasure, buried in a field. People would often hide their valuables in jars, which they buried in the ground. **that a man found.** Probably a day laborer hired to till the field.

sells everything he has. It was not a sacrifice on the part of the man to do this. He knew what he was getting was worth all he had.

13:52 what is new and what is old. Jesus challenges people to draw not only from the Law and the Prophets, but also from His teachings. The coming of Jesus breathes fresh air into those writings.

13:54 His hometown. This was Nazareth, located in the hill country of Galilee.

13:57 except in his hometown. Familiarity often prevents people from acknowledging the accomplishments or wisdom of one they assume they know.

14:1 Herod. Herod Antipas was the ruler of the Roman provinces of Galilee and Perea from 4 B.C. to A.D. 39. He was the son of Herod the

landowner who brings out of his storeroom what is new and what is old." ⁵³ When Jesus had finished these parables, He left there.

Rejection at Nazareth

⁵⁴ He went to His hometown and began to teach them in their •synagogue, so that they were astonished and said, "How did this wisdom and these miracles come to Him? ⁵⁵ Isn't this the carpenter's son? Isn't His mother called Mary, and His brothers James, Joseph,ᵃ Simon, and Judas? ⁵⁶ And His sisters, aren't they all with us? So where does He get all these things?" ⁵⁷ And they were offended by Him.

But Jesus said to them, "A prophet is not without honor except in his hometown and in his household." ⁵⁸ And He did not do many miracles there because of their unbelief.

John the Baptist Beheaded

14 At that time •Herod the tetrarch heard the report about Jesus. ² "This is John the Baptist!" he told his servants. "He has been raised from the dead, and that's why supernatural powers are at work in him."

³ For Herod had arrested John, chainedᵇ him, and put him in prison on account of Herodias, his brother Philip's wife, ⁴ since John had been telling him, "It's not lawful for you to have her!" ⁵ Though he wanted to kill him, he feared the crowd, since they regarded him as a prophet.

⁶ But when Herod's birthday celebration came, Herodias' daughter danced before themᶜ and pleased Herod. ⁷ So he promised with an oath to give her whatever she might ask. ⁸ And prompted by her mother, she answered, "Give me John the Baptist's head here on a platter!" ⁹ Although the king regretted it, he commanded that it be granted because of his oaths and his guests. ¹⁰ So he sent orders and had John beheaded in the prison. ¹¹ His head was brought on a platter and given to the girl, who carried it to her mother. ¹² Then

his disciples came, removed the corpse,ᵈ buried it, and went and reported to Jesus.

Feeding 5,000

¹³ When Jesus heard about it, He withdrew from there by boat to a remote place to be alone. When the crowds heard this, they followed Him on foot from the towns. ¹⁴ As He stepped ashore,ᵉ He saw a huge crowd, felt compassion for them, and healed their sick.

¹⁵ When evening came, the disciples approached Him and said, "This place is a wilderness, and it is already late.ᶠ Send the crowds away so they can go into the villages and buy food for themselves."

¹⁶ "They don't need to go away," Jesus told them. "You give them something to eat."

¹⁷ "But we only have five loaves and two fish here," they said to Him.

¹⁸ "Bring them here to Me," He said. ¹⁹ Then He commanded the crowds to sit downᵍ on the grass. He took the five loaves and the two fish, and looking up to heaven, He blessed them. He broke the loaves and gave them to the disciples, and the disciples ₁gave them₁ to the crowds. ²⁰ Everyone ate and was filled. Then they picked up 12 baskets full of leftover pieces! ²¹ Now those who ate were about 5,000 men, besides women and children.

Walking on the Water

²² Immediately Heʰ made the disciples get into the boat and go ahead of Him to the other side, while He dismissed the crowds. ²³ After dismissing the crowds, He went up on the mountain by Himself to pray. When evening came, He was there alone. ²⁴ But the boat was already over a mileⁱ from land,ʲ battered by the waves, because the wind was against them. ²⁵ Around three in the morning,ᵏ He came toward them walking on the sea. ²⁶ When the disciples saw Him walking on the sea, they were terrified. "It's a ghost!" they said, and cried out in fear.

²⁷ Immediately Jesus spoke to them. "Have courage! It is I. Don't be afraid."

ᵃ**13:55** Other mss read *Joses*; Mk 6:3 ᵇ**14:3** Or *bound* ᶜ**14:6** Lit *danced in the middle* ᵈ**14:12** Other mss read *body* ᵉ**14:14** Lit *Coming out* (of the boat) ᶠ**14:15** Lit *and the time* (for the evening meal) *has already passed* ᵍ**14:19** Lit *to recline* ʰ**14:22** Other mss read *Jesus* ⁱ**14:24** Lit *already many stadia*; 1 *stadion* = 600 feet ʲ**14:24** Other mss read *already in the middle of the sea* ᵏ**14:25** Lit *fourth watch of the night* = 3 to 6 a.m.

Great, who had ordered the slaughter of the babies at the time of Jesus' birth.

14:2 This is John the Baptist. Herod was suffering from a guilty conscience. He was afraid that the holy man he had executed had come back with supernatural powers.

14:16 You give them something to eat. Jesus' statement, and the entire scene, is similar to when Elisha miraculously provided food for 100 people from 20 loaves of bread (2 Kings 4:42-44). Since that act authenticated Elisha's commission from God, how much more should this miracle demonstrate Jesus' innate divine power?

14:17 five loaves. These would have been small round cakes made of wheat or barley. **two fish.** These could have been smoked or pickled fish.

14:20 filled. As it will be at the messianic feast, the needs of God's people are abundantly met. **12.** This is the number of tribes of Israel. The number 12 connotes completeness, reinforcing the idea that this scene is meant to demonstrate how Jesus the Messiah provides nourishment for all God's people. **baskets.** Small wicker containers carried by the Jews.

14:21 besides women and children. Women and children in this culture were generally not counted.

14:22 He dismissed the crowds. According to John 6:14-15, the crowd, which saw the feeding as a sign that Jesus was the messianic King, tried in its enthusiasm to get Jesus to lead a revolt against Rome.

14:25 three in the morning. Referred to as

the fourth watch, this period ran from 3 a.m. to 6 a.m. **walking on the sea.** In no other situation did the pre-resurrection Jesus take a supernatural shortcut to expedite His travel plans. This event was intended to provide the disciples with further insight into His divine identity and compassionate motivation.

14:26 It's a ghost. The sea, especially at night, was thought at that time to be a dwelling place for demons.

14:27 Have courage! It is I. Don't be afraid. This is the language of God (Isa. 41:10; 43:5; Jer. 1:8). **It is I.** Literally, "I am." In the Old Testament this is a phrase used by God to describe Himself (Ex. 3:1-14). In the context of Jesus' ongoing revelation of Himself to the disciples, this is another indication of His divine identity.

28 "Lord, if it's You," Peter answered Him, "command me to come to You on the water."

29 "Come!" He said.

And climbing out of the boat, Peter started walking on the water and came toward Jesus. 30 But when he saw the strength of the wind,a he was afraid. And beginning to sink he cried out, "Lord, save me!"

Walking on Water

1. What is the most daring thing you have ever done?

Matthew 14:22-33

2. Why were the disciples afraid when they saw someone walking on the water? How would you have felt?

3. Why did Peter ask to walk on the water? Why did he sink? Would you have stepped out? Would you have sunk?

4. When have you asked God for a miracle? What happened? Did you begin to doubt afterward?

5. What are you facing in your life where you need Jesus to remind you, "Don't be afraid"?

31 Immediately Jesus reached out His hand, caught hold of him, and said to him, "You of little faith, why did you doubt?" 32 When they got into the boat, the wind ceased. 33 Then those in the boat worshiped Him and said, "Truly You are the Son of God!"

Miraculous Healings

34 Once they crossed over, they came to land at Gennesaret. 35 When the men of that place recognized Him, they alertedb the whole vicinity and brought to Him all who were sick. 36 They were begging Him that they might only touch the •tassel on His robe. And as many as touched it were made perfectly well.

The Tradition of the Elders

15 Then •Pharisees and •scribes came from Jerusalem to Jesus and asked, 2 "Why do Your disciples break the tradition of the elders? For they don't wash their hands when they eat!"c

3 He answered them, "And why do you break God's commandment because of your tradition? 4 For God said:d

> Honor your father and your mother;e and,
> The one who speaks evil of father or mother
> must be put to death.f

5 But you say, 'Whoever tells his father or mother, "Whatever benefit you might have received from me is a gift ⌊committed to the temple⌋,"'— 6 he does not have to honor his father.'g In this way, you have revoked God's wordh because of your tradition. 7 Hypocrites! Isaiah prophesied correctly about you when he said:

> 8 These peoplei honor Me with their lips,
>   but their heart is far from Me.
> 9 They worship Me in vain,
>   teaching as doctrines the commands
>   of men."j

Defilement Is from Within

10 Summoning the crowd, He told them, "Listen and understand: 11 It's not what goes into the mouth that defiles a man, but what comes out of the mouth, this defiles a man."

12 Then the disciples came up and told Him, "Do You know that the Pharisees took offense when they heard this statement?"

13 He replied, "Every plant that My heavenly Father didn't plant will be uprooted. 14 Leave them alone! They are blind guides.k And if the blind guide the blind, both will fall into a pit."

---

a**14:30** Other mss read *saw the wind*   b**14:35** Lit *sent into*   c**15:2** Lit *eat bread* = eat a meal   d**15:4** Other mss read *commanded, saying*
e**15:4** Ex 20:12; Dt 5:16   f**15:4** Ex 21:17; Lv 20:9   g**15:6** Other mss read *then he does not have to honor his father or mother*   h**15:6** Other mss read *commandment*   i**15:8** Other mss add *draws near to Me with their mouths, and*   j**15:8–9** Is 29:13 LXX   k**15:14** Other mss add *for the blind*

14:33 Truly You are the Son of God. In the other Gospels, this identification by the disciples does not happen until the incident at Caesarea Philippi (16:13-20). **the Son of God.** In the Old Testament, this term described God's appointed king who reigned over Israel in God's stead (Ps. 2:7). In the New Testament, this title is often connected with the title "Messiah."

14:34 Gennesaret. This was a thickly populated, fertile plain four miles southwest of Capernaum.

14:36 tassel on His robe. This recalls the healing of the bleeding woman (9:20-22).

15:2 the tradition. There were literally thousands of unwritten rules that developed over time in an attempt to define how the Old Testament Law applied in everyday life. **elders.**

These were respected Jewish rabbis whose decisions concerning points of religious law were considered binding. **they don't wash their hands.** The issue here is ceremonial holiness, not personal hygiene.

15:4 For God said. Jesus cites two commands in the Law regarding how parents are to be treated with respect (Ex. 20:12; 21:17). **put to death.** Jesus was not advocating putting people to death for such an action, but rather underlining the issue of respect taught by the Law.

15:5 But you say. The Law was clear. Before pension plans and Social Security, one aspect of that principle was providing for one's parents when they were too old or too sick to work. However, the traditions taught that if people dedicated some money to God, it was thereafter not considered their property.

Thus, a child could declare property or money as given over to God and therefore unavailable for his or her parents' support.

15:8 but their heart. This is the essence of what Jesus had against the Pharisees. They obeyed the laws, but their hearts were not in tune with the love of God. They were not yet part of that New Covenant spoken of by Jeremiah where God's law of love was written "on their hearts" (Jer. 31:33).

15:11 defiles. Those who came into contact with something considered taboo were thought to be unfit to worship or to have physical contact with others. For the Jew, unclean or defiled things included certain animals, dead bodies, lepers, Gentiles, and, as demonstrated here, certain food.

15:13 Every plant. God's people were com-

15 Then Peter replied to Him, "Explain this parable to us."

16 "Are even you still lacking in understanding?" He[a] asked. 17 "Don't you realize[b] that whatever goes into the mouth passes into the stomach and is eliminated?[c] 18 But what comes out of the mouth comes from the heart, and this defiles a man. 19 For from the heart come evil thoughts, murders, adulteries, sexual immoralities, thefts, false testimonies, blasphemies. 20 These are the things that defile a man, but eating with unwashed hands does not defile a man."

A Gentile Mother's Faith

21 When Jesus left there, He withdrew to the area of Tyre and Sidon. 22 Just then a Canaanite woman from that region came and kept crying out,[d] "Have mercy on me, Lord, Son of David! My daughter is cruelly tormented by a demon."

23 Yet He did not say a word to her. So His disciples approached Him and urged Him, "Send her away because she cries out after us."[e]

24 He replied, "I was sent only to the lost sheep of the house of Israel."

25 But she came, knelt before Him, and said, "Lord, help me!"

26 He answered, "It isn't right to take the children's bread and throw it to their dogs."

27 "Yes, Lord," she said, "yet even the dogs eat the crumbs that fall from their masters' table!"

28 Then Jesus replied to her, "Woman, your faith is great. Let it be done for you as you want." And from that moment[f] her daughter was cured.

Healing Many People

29 Moving on from there, Jesus passed along the Sea of Galilee. He went up on a mountain and sat there, 30 and large crowds came to Him, having with them the lame, the blind, the deformed, those unable to speak, and many others. They put them at His feet, and He healed them. 31 So the crowd was amazed when they saw those unable to speak talking, the deformed restored, the lame walking, and the blind seeing. And they gave glory to the God of Israel.

Feeding 4,000

32 Now Jesus summoned His disciples and said, "I have compassion on the crowd, because they've already stayed with Me three days and have nothing to eat. I don't want to send them away hungry; otherwise they might collapse on the way."

33 The disciples said to Him, "Where could we get enough bread in this desolate place to fill such a crowd?"

34 "How many loaves do you have?" Jesus asked them.

"Seven," they said, "and a few small fish."

35 After commanding the crowd to sit down on the ground, 36 He took the seven loaves and the fish, and He gave thanks, broke them, and kept on giving them to the disciples, and the disciples ¡gave them¡ to the crowds. 37 They all ate and were filled. Then they collected the leftover pieces—seven large baskets full. 38 Now those who ate were 4,000 men, besides women and children. 39 After dismissing the crowds, He got into the boat and went to the region of Magadan.[g]

The Yeast of the Pharisees and the Sadducees

16 The •Pharisees and •Sadducees approached, and as a test, asked Him to show them a sign from heaven.

2 He answered them: "When evening comes you say, 'It will be good weather because the sky is red.' 3 And in the morning, 'Today will be stormy because the sky is red and threatening.' You[h] know how to read the appearance of the sky, but you can't read the signs of the times.[i] 4 An evil and adulterous generation wants a sign, but no sign will be given to it except the sign of[j] Jonah." Then He left them and went away.

5 The disciples reached the other shore,[k] and they had forgotten to take bread.

---

[a]15:16 Other mss read Jesus [b]15:17 Other mss add yet [c]15:17 Lit and goes out into the toilet [d]15:22 Other mss read and cried out to Him [e]15:23 Lit she is yelling behind us or after us [f]15:28 Lit hour [g]15:39 Other mss read Magdala [h]16:3 Other mss read Hypocrites! You [i]16:2–3 Other mss omit When (v. 2) through end of v. 3 [j]16:4 Other mss add the prophet [k]16:5 Lit disciples went to the other side

---

monly described as a "planted by the LORD" (Isa. 60:21; 61:3). Jesus is declaring that the Pharisees, in spite of their pretense to holiness, had not been divinely planted. They were more like weeds that will be uprooted and cast away.

15:17 is eliminated. Literally, "goes into the toilet."

15:22 a Canaanite. The woman was a Syrophoenician (Mark 7:26). The Canaanites were ancient archetypal enemies of the Jews. By specifically referring to her as a Canaanite, Matthew accents how far removed she was from those normally considered God's people.

15:24 I was sent only. This seemingly callous statement by Jesus has caused much debate. Could Jesus really have been this ethnocentric? Likely, His actions here, however, is that He was voicing the predominant view of His time precisely with the idea in mind that it could be shown as shallow in light of this faithful foreigner.

15:26 dogs. There is a play on words here. While Jews commonly used a word that referred to wild street dogs when they discussed Gentiles, the word used here refers to a household pet dog.

15:28 your faith is great. Once again Jesus points out the faith of a foreigner (8:5-13), in contrast to the lack of faith of the people of His hometown (13:58) and even the disciples (14:31; 16:8).

15:32-39 4,000. The main difference between the feeding of the 4,000 and the feeding of the 5,000 (14:15-21) is the difference in audience. Just as the feeding of the 5,000 anticipated the coming salvation for Israel, so the feeding of the 4,000 promises this same salvation to Gentiles.

15:32 three days. The crowd had been with Him for a few days in contrast to the 5,000 who were fed on the day they gathered.

15:39 Magadan. It is not certain where this town is located. The point, however, is that Jesus left the Gentile region for Jewish soil at this time.

16:1 Sadducees. While prominent in the early chapters of Acts, the Sadducees, (whose main area of concern was with the worship at the temple in Jerusalem,) are rarely mentioned in the Gospels. It seems that they were a small, but highly influential, party of Jews composed mainly of wealthy, aristocratic priests.

⁶ Then Jesus told them, "Watch out and beware of the yeast[a] of the Pharisees and Sadducees."

⁷ And they discussed among themselves, "We didn't bring any bread."

⁸ Aware of this, Jesus said, "You of little faith! Why are you discussing among yourselves that you do not have bread? ⁹ Don't you understand yet? Don't you remember the five loaves for the 5,000 and how many baskets you collected? ¹⁰ Or the seven loaves for the 4,000 and how many large baskets you collected? ¹¹ Why is it you don't understand that when I told you, 'Beware of the yeast of the Pharisees and Sadducees,' it wasn't about bread?" ¹² Then they understood that He did not tell them to beware of the yeast in bread, but of the teaching of the Pharisees and Sadducees.

Peter's Confession of the Messiah

¹³ When Jesus came to the region of Caesarea Philippi,[b] He asked His disciples, "Who do people say that the •Son of Man is?"[c]

¹⁴ And they said, "Some say John the Baptist; others, Elijah; still others, Jeremiah or one of the prophets."

¹⁵ "But you," He asked them, "who do you say that I am?"

¹⁶ Simon Peter answered, "You are the •Messiah, the Son of the living God!"

¹⁷ And Jesus responded, "Simon son of Jonah,[d] you are blessed because flesh and blood did not reveal this to you, but My Father in heaven. ¹⁸ And I also say to you that you are Peter,[e] and on this rock[f] I will build My church, and the forces[g] of •Hades will not overpower it. ¹⁹ I will give you the keys of the kingdom of heaven, and whatever you bind on earth is already bound[h] in heaven, and whatever you loose on earth is already loosed[i] in heaven."

²⁰ And He gave the disciples orders to tell no one that He was[j] the Messiah.

His Death and Resurrection Predicted

²¹ From then on Jesus began to point out to His disciples that He must go to Jerusalem and suffer many things from the elders, •chief priests, and •scribes, be killed, and be raised the third day. ²² Then Peter took Him aside and began to rebuke Him, "Oh no,[k] Lord! This will never happen to You!"

²³ But He turned and told Peter, "Get behind Me, Satan! You are an offense to Me because you're not thinking about God's concerns,[l] but man's."

Deny Yourself

1. If your best friends were asked what one word best describes you, what would they say? What would you say?

Matthew 16:13-28
2. Who do you say Jesus is? Who does Jesus Himself say that He is (see v. 20)?
3. What does it mean to "deny yourself"? To "take up your cross"?
4. What does it mean to "lose your life" for Jesus? Give practical examples of times when you or someone you know "lost his life" to obey God.
5. How much is your soul worth? Are there things in your life that are endangering your soul?

Take Up Your Cross

²⁴ Then Jesus said to His disciples, "If anyone wants to come with Me, he must deny himself, take up his cross, and follow Me. ²⁵ For whoever wants to save his •life will lose it, but whoever loses his life because of Me will find it. ²⁶ What will it benefit a man if he gains the whole world yet loses his life? Or what will a man give in exchange for his life? ²⁷ For the Son of Man is

---

[a]**16:6** Or *leaven* [b]**16:13** A town north of Galilee at the base of Mount Hermon [c]**16:13** Other mss read *that I, the Son of Man, am* [d]**16:17** Or *son of John* [e]**16:18** *Peter* (Gk *Petros*) = a specific stone or rock [f]**16:18** *Rock* (Gk *petra*) = a rocky crag or bedrock [g]**16:18** Lit *gates* [h]**16:19** Or *earth will be bound* [i]**16:19** Or *earth will be loosed* [j]**16:20** Other mss add *Jesus* [k]**16:22** Lit *Mercy to You = May God have mercy on You* [l]**16:23** Lit *about the things of God*

16:4 An evil and adulterous generation. The Old Testament prophets often used adultery as a metaphor for the way Israel strayed from fidelity to God (Ezek. 16; Hos. 2:2).

16:6 yeast. Jews connected yeast with the process of fermentation, which they saw as a form of rotting. Hence, yeast became a metaphor for the profound effects of even a little bit of evil.

16:13 Caesarea Philippi. A beautiful city on the slopes of Mount Hermon, 25 miles north of Bethsaida. It had once been called Balinas when it was a center for Baal worship. It was later called Paneas because it was said that the god Pan had his birth in a nearby cave. At the time of Jesus, it was the location of a temple dedicated to the godhead of Caesar.

16:17 flesh and blood did not reveal this to you. Jesus told the disciples that it was not by reason that people came to faith, but rather it was by revelation. The Father granted knowledge or revelation to the seeker (John 6:65). Peter responded in belief in Jesus as the Messiah (John 6:68-69).

16:18 Peter. Peter (a nickname meaning "rock"), by way of his confession, articulates the central truth, forming the foundation upon which the new people of God will be built.

16:19 keys of the kingdom of heaven. This is an allusion to Isaiah 22:15-24 in which God declared that he would give the "key to the house of David" to a new steward who would replace the old one who had been irresponsible.

16:23 Get behind Me, Satan! By urging

Jesus to back away from His teaching about suffering, Peter, like Satan, is tempting Jesus with the promise that He can have the whole world without pain (4:8-10).

16:24 deny himself. This means to regard one's ambitions as irrelevant in light of the kingdom of God. **take up his cross.** This symbolized the grisly method of Roman execution, as the only people who bore crosses were prisoners on their way to their death. This would have startled the original hearers, as they thought the Messiah would overthrow Rome. **follow Me.** This is a call for the disciples to imitate the lifestyle and embrace the values of their Teacher.

16:28 see the Son of Man coming. Jesus had already said that the kingdom of God was near (4:17; 10:23; 12:28). While some see this as a prediction of His imminent Sec-

going to come with His angels in the glory of His Father, and then He will reward each according to what he has done. 28 •I assure you: There are some standing here who will not taste death until they see the Son of Man coming in His kingdom."

The Transfiguration

17 After six days Jesus took Peter, James, and his brother John, and led them up on a high mountain by themselves. 2 He was transformed[a] in front of them, and His face shone like the sun. Even His clothes became as white as the light. 3 Suddenly, Moses and Elijah appeared to them, talking with Him.

4 Then Peter said to Jesus, "Lord, it's good for us to be here! If You want, I will make[b] three •tabernacles here: one for You, one for Moses, and one for Elijah."

5 While he was still speaking, suddenly a bright cloud covered[c] them, and a voice from the cloud said:

> This is My beloved Son.
> I take delight in Him.
> Listen to Him!

6 When the disciples heard it, they fell facedown and were terrified.

7 Then Jesus came up, touched them, and said, "Get up; don't be afraid." 8 When they looked up they saw no one except Him[d] —Jesus alone. 9 As they were coming down from the mountain, Jesus commanded them, "Don't tell anyone about the vision until the •Son of Man is raised[e] from the dead."

10 So the disciples questioned Him, "Why then do the •scribes say that Elijah must come first?"

11 "Elijah is coming[f] and will restore everything," He replied.[g] 12 "But I tell you: Elijah has already come, and they didn't recognize him. On the contrary, they did whatever they pleased to him. In the same way the Son of Man is going to suffer at their hands."[h] 13 Then the disciples understood that He spoke to them about John the Baptist.

The Power of Faith over a Demon

14 When they reached the crowd, a man approached and knelt down before Him. 15 "Lord," he said, "have mercy on my son, because he has seizures[i] and suffers severely. He often falls into the fire and often into the water. 16 I brought him to Your disciples, but they couldn't heal him."

17 Jesus replied, "You unbelieving and rebellious[j] generation! How long will I be with you? How long must I put up with you? Bring him here to Me." 18 Then Jesus rebuked the demon,[k] and it[l] came out of him, and from that moment[m] the boy was healed.

19 Then the disciples approached Jesus privately and said, "Why couldn't we drive it out?"

20 "Because of your little faith," He[n] told them. "For •I assure you: If you have faith the size of[o] a mustard seed, you will tell this mountain, 'Move from here to there,' and it will move. Nothing will be impossible for you. [21 However, this kind does not come out except by prayer and fasting.]"[p]

The Second Prediction of His Death

22 As they were meeting[q] in Galilee, Jesus told them, "The Son of Man is about to be betrayed into the hands of men. 23 They will kill Him, and on the third day He will be raised up." And they were deeply distressed.

Paying the Temple Tax

24 When they came to Capernaum, those who collected the double-drachma tax[r] approached Peter and said, "Doesn't your Teacher pay the double-drachma tax?"

25 "Yes," he said.

When he went into the house, Jesus spoke to him first,[s] "What do you think, Simon? Who do earthly kings

---

a**17:2** Or *transfigured*   b**17:4** Other mss read *wish, let's make*   c**17:5** Or *enveloped*; Ex 40:34–35   d**17:8** Other mss omit *Him*   e**17:9** Other mss read *Man has risen*   f**17:11** Other mss add *first*   g**17:11** Other mss read *Jesus said to them*   h**17:12** Lit *suffer by them*   i**17:15** Lit *he is moonstruck*; thought to be a form of epilepsy   j**17:17** Or *corrupt*, or *perverted*, or *twisted*; Dt 32:5   k**17:18** Lit *rebuked him* or *it*   l**17:18** Lit *the demon*   m**17:18** Lit *hour*   n**17:20** Other mss read *your unbelief," Jesus*   o**17:20** Lit *faith like*   p**17:21** Other mss omit bracketed text; Mk 9:29   q**17:22** Other mss read *were staying*   r**17:24** Jewish men paid this tax to support the temple; Ex 30:11–16. A double-drachma could purchase 2 sheep.   s**17:25** Lit *Jesus anticipated him by saying*

---

ond Coming, it can also be seen as referring to either to the transfiguration (17:1-13) or to Christ's death and resurrection.

17:1 After six days. This phrase connects the transfiguration with Jesus' prediction that there are "some standing here who will not taste death until they see the Son of Man coming in His kingdom" (16:28). **Peter, James, and his brother John.** These three emerge as the inner circle around Jesus. **a high mountain.** This may well be Mount Hermon, a 9,000-foot mountain located 12 miles from Caesarea Philippi (though early tradition says it is Mount Tabor located southwest of the Sea of Galilee).

17:2 transformed. The description of Jesus here is similar to that used to picture the appearance of God when He appeared in a vision to Daniel (Dan. 7:9). In Revelation 1:9-

18 the resurrected, glorified Jesus is described in these same terms.

17:3 Moses. Moses was the greatest figure in the Old Testament. It was to him God gave the Law, which became the very heart of the nation. **Elijah.** The Jews expected that Elijah, one of the most esteemed prophets, would return just prior to the coming of the salvation they had been promised. These two figures together represent the Law and the Prophets, the whole of scriptural tradition.

17:4 tabernacles. Peter might have had in mind the huts of intertwined branches that were put up at the Festival of Tabernacles to commemorate Israel's time in the wilderness.

17:9 Don't tell. Jesus commands silence because the meaning of this event cannot be understood until Jesus dies and rises

again. Only then it will be clear what kind of Messiah He is.

17:16 they couldn't heal him. Based on the response of Jesus, it appears that the faith of the disciples is shown once again to be incomplete.

17:20 this mountain. "Removing mountains" is the overcoming of difficulties. **Nothing will be impossible for you.** This power is subject to acting with God's direction.

17:24 those who collected. These were not the "tax collectors" vilified by the Jewish community as traitors because they worked for Rome. Rather, they collected the temple tax. **Doesn't your Teacher pay the double-drachma tax?** If Jesus did not, it could be misconstrued as a scandalous rejection of a common duty. If He did, it could be miscon-

collect tariffs or taxes from? From their sons or from strangers?"[a]

²⁶ "From strangers," he said.[b]

"Then the sons are free," Jesus told him. ²⁷ "But, so we won't offend them, go to the sea, cast in a fishhook, and catch the first fish that comes up. When you open its mouth you'll find a coin.[c] Take it and give it to them for Me and you."

Who Is the Greatest?

18 At that time[d] the disciples came to Jesus and said, "Who is greatest in the kingdom of heaven?"

² Then He called a child to Him and had him stand among them. ³ "•I assure you," He said, "unless you are converted[e] and become like children, you will never enter the kingdom of heaven. ⁴ Therefore, whoever humbles himself like this child—this one is the greatest in the kingdom of heaven. ⁵ And whoever welcomes[f] one child like this in My name welcomes Me.

⁶ "But whoever •causes the downfall of one of these little ones who believe in Me—it would be better for him if a heavy millstone[g] were hung around his neck and he were drowned in the depths of the sea! ⁷ Woe to the world because of offenses.[h] For offenses must come, but woe to that man by whom the offense comes. ⁸ If your hand or your foot causes your downfall, cut it off and throw it away. It is better for you to enter life maimed or lame, than to have two hands or two feet and be thrown into the eternal fire. ⁹ And if your eye causes your downfall, gouge it out and throw it away. It is better for you to enter life with one eye, rather than to have two eyes and be thrown into •hellfire![i]

The Parable of the Lost Sheep

¹⁰ "See that you don't look down on one of these little ones, because I tell you that in heaven their angels continually view the face of My Father in heaven. [¹¹ For the •Son of Man has come to save the lost.][j] ¹² What do you think? If a man has 100 sheep, and one of them goes astray, won't he leave the 99 on the hillside and go and search for the stray? ¹³ And if he finds it, I assure you: He rejoices over that sheep[k] more than over the 99 that did not go astray. ¹⁴ In the same way, it is not the will of your Father in heaven that one of these little ones perish.

Forgive Him or Choke Him?

1. What's the most money you've ever owed? Been owed?
2. Are you quick or slow to forgive when you're hurt?

Matthew 18:21-35

3. Why did the master treat the unforgiving slave so harshly? What does this tell us about how God will treat us when we are unforgiving?
4. Why should the slave have forgiven the other man's debt? Why should we forgive others who hurt us?
5. Are you more like the forgiving master (v. 27) or the slave (v. 30)?
6. Who do you need to forgive? What's keeping you from forgiving them?

Restoring a Brother

¹⁵ "If your brother sins against you,[l] go and rebuke him in private.[m] If he listens to you, you have won your brother. ¹⁶ But if he won't listen, take one or two more with you, so that **by the testimony[n] of two or three witnesses every fact may be established.**[o] ¹⁷ If he pays no attention to them, tell the church.[p] But if he doesn't pay attention even to the church, let him be like an unbeliever[q] and a tax collector to you. ¹⁸ I assure you:

---

[a]**17:25** Or *foreigners* [b]**17:26** Other mss read *Peter said to Him* [c]**17:27** Gk *stater*, worth 2 double-drachmas [d]**18:1** Lit *hour* [e]**18:3** Or *are turned around* [f]**18:5** Or *receives* [g]**18:6** A millstone turned by a donkey [h]**18:7** Or *causes of stumbling* [i]**18:9** Lit *gehenna of fire* [j]**18:11** Other mss omit bracketed text [k]**18:13** Lit *over it* [l]**18:15** Other mss omit *against you* [m]**18:15** Lit *him between you and him alone* [n]**18:16** Lit *mouth* [o]**18:16** Dt 19:15 [p]**18:17** Or *congregation* [q]**18:17** Or *like a Gentile*

---

strued as an endorsement of the temple system that He generally seemed to reject (21:12-13).

17:27 But, so we won't offend them. Since such freedom would be interpreted by others as disrespect for God and the temple, it is appropriate to pay the tax.

18:2 a child. Children held little value among adult males in this society. To hold up a child as a model for an adult to emulate was unheard of.

18:3 unless you are converted. Literally, "turn around."

18:4 humbles himself. In the Bible, humility is not a denial of one's strengths, nor an attitude of passivity or timidity, but an attitude that values the interests of others above one's own.

18:6 causes the downfall. The influence of false teachers is probably in view (2 John 7-15), but it could also refer to disciples who abuse their freedom by refusing to be sensitive to the tender consciences of others (Rom. 14:1–15:2). **a heavy millstone.** The millstone in view here is the huge upper stone of a community grist mill, so big it had to be drawn around by a donkey.

18:7 Woe. A strong warning to false teachers and those who are not careful about how their lives affect others.

18:10 in heaven their angels. The picture is one of angels reporting to God on the condition of those in their charge. Disdain for others has no place in the Christian community since even those people who appear insignificant are divinely watched-over and cared for.

18:13 He rejoices over that sheep more than over the 99. This is not to minimize the shepherd's gladness over those sheep that remained in the fold, but to accent his joy over the recovery of the one who had strayed away.

18:21 how many times ... and I forgive him? The rabbis taught that a person ought to be forgiven for a particular offense up to three times. After that, the offended person was under no obligation to grant forgiveness.

18:22 70 times seven. Some translate this as "seventy-seven times." Whichever reading is correct, Jesus underscores the idea that learning to bestow the kind of forgiveness He has for us on others is a lifetime pursuit of choosing the health of the relationship over adherence to regulation.

Whatever you bind on earth is already bound[a] in heaven, and whatever you loose on earth is already loosed[b] in heaven. ¹⁹ Again, I assure you: If two of you on earth agree about any matter that you[c] pray for, it will be done for you[d] by My Father in heaven. ²⁰ For where two or three are gathered together in My name, I am there among them."

The Parable of the Unforgiving Slave

²¹ Then Peter came to Him and said, "Lord, how many times could my brother sin against me and I forgive him? As many as seven times?"

²² "I tell you, not as many as seven," Jesus said to him, "but 70 times seven.[e] ²³ For this reason, the kingdom of heaven can be compared to a king who wanted to settle accounts with his •slaves. ²⁴ When he began to settle accounts, one who owed 10,000 talents[f] was brought before him. ²⁵ Since he had no way to pay it back, his master commanded that he, his wife, his children, and everything he had be sold to pay the debt.

²⁶ "At this, the •slave fell facedown before him and said, 'Be patient with me, and I will pay you everything!' ²⁷ Then the master of that slave had compassion, released him, and forgave him the loan.

²⁸ "But that •slave went out and found one of his fellow slaves who owed him 100 •denarii.[g] He grabbed him, started choking him, and said, 'Pay what you owe!' ²⁹ "At this, his fellow •slave fell down[h] and began begging him, 'Be patient with me, and I will pay you back.' ³⁰ But he wasn't willing. On the contrary, he went and threw him into prison until he could pay what was owed. ³¹ When the other slaves saw what had taken place, they were deeply distressed and went and reported to their master everything that had happened.

³² "Then, after he had summoned him, his master said to him, 'You wicked •slave! I forgave you all that debt because you begged me. ³³ Shouldn't you also have had mercy on your fellow slave, as I had mercy on you?' ³⁴ And his master got angry and handed him over to the jailers[i] until he could pay everything that was owed.

³⁵ So My heavenly Father will also do to you if each of you does not forgive his brother[j] from his[k] heart."

The Question of Divorce

19 When Jesus had finished this instruction, He departed from Galilee and went to the region of Judea across the Jordan. ² Large crowds followed Him, and He healed them there. ³ Some •Pharisees approached Him to test Him. They asked, "Is it lawful for a man to divorce his wife on any grounds?"

Divorce ... Life Shredder

1. Describe your ideal husband or wife. What things are most important to you in finding the right person?

Matthew 19:1-12

2. What does it mean that a married couple "become one flesh?" If the two have become one, then what is divorce like?
3. When does Jesus allow for divorce?
4. How does Jesus' teaching differ from our culture's views on marriage and divorce? Who is right: Jesus? Modern culture? Somewhere in between?
5. How has your life been affected by divorce? How might Jesus' teaching help you to prepare for a "divorce-free" marriage?

⁴ "Haven't you read," He replied, "that He who created[l] them in the beginning **made them male and female,**[m] ⁵ and He also said:

> **For this reason a man will leave**
> **his father and mother**
> **and be joined to his wife,**
> **and the two will become one flesh?**[n]

---

[a]**18:18** Or *earth will be bound* [b]**18:18** Or *earth will be loosed* [c]**18:19** Lit *they* [d]**18:19** Lit *for them* [e]**18:22** Or *but 77 times* [f]**18:24** A huge sum of money that could never be repaid by a slave; a talent = 6,000 denarii [g]**18:28** A small sum compared to 10,000 talents [h]**18:29** Other mss add *at his feet* [i]**18:34** Or *torturers* [j]**18:35** Other mss add *his trespasses* [k]**18:35** Lit *your* [l]**19:4** Other mss read *made* [m]**19:4** Gn 1:27; 5:2 [n]**19:5** Gn 2:24

18:24 10,000 talents. Herod the Great, who ruled over Palestine at the time of Jesus' birth, had an annual revenue of only about 900 talents. The crowd listening to Jesus would have gasped at the thought of having to pay someone such a fantastically large amount of money.

18:25 he, his wife, his children. An Oriental king had total power. Thus, he decided to sell the man and the servant's family into slavery to recoup at least a fraction of his losses.

18:26 I will pay you everything. This was an impossible promise, given the amount. While it may reflect the slave's sincere desire to save himself and his family, he was so far in debt that he could never hope to repay the king.

18:27 released him. The man was free. The

impossible burden that must have crushed him with fear (while he wondered what would happen to him when his mismanagement was discovered) was suddenly gone. There was no judgment, no debt-restructuring to keep him in perpetual bondage, no more fear. Likewise, the disciple of Jesus is free from the punishment of sin (Rom. 8:1-2).

18:28 100 denarii. Since a denarius was a day's wage for a laborer, this was a reasonably large amount. However, at the rate of one denarius a day, it would have taken the first servant 15 years to pay back the king a single talent!

18:30 But he wasn't willing. Under the circumstances, this man would have been expected to forego the debt. Instead, he insists on carrying out the full weight of the law against the slave indebted to him. The mercy

he received from the king does not produce any moral change in this man.

18:33 Shouldn't you also have had mercy ... as I had mercy on you? This is the point of the parable.

18:34 to the jailers. Prisoners were often tortured to make them reveal hidden sources of money. The man will now be pressed for every cent he has. **until he could pay everything that was owed.** Given the amount owed, the man would be in prison until death.

18:35 from his heart. The depth and breadth of forgiveness is drawn from the limitless heavenly supply in the heart of the forgiven follower. To do this, we must be in touch with how much God in Christ has forgiven us, and invite that same Spirit of Christ into our heart, so it will flow to others.

6 So they are no longer two, but one flesh. Therefore what God has joined together, man must not separate."

7 "Why then," they asked Him, "did Moses command [us] to give divorce papers and to send her away?"

8 He told them, "Moses permitted you to divorce your wives because of the hardness of your hearts. But it was not like that from the beginning. 9 And I tell you, whoever divorces his wife, except for sexual immorality, and marries another, commits adultery."a

10 His disciples said to Him, "If the relationship of a man with his wife is like this, it's better not to marry!"

11 But He told them, "Not everyone can accept this saying, but only those it has been given to. 12 For there are eunuchs who were born that way from their mother's womb, there are eunuchs who were made by men, and there are eunuchs who have made themselves that way because of the kingdom of heaven. Let anyone accept this who can."

Blessing the Children

13 Then children were brought to Him so He might put His hands on them and pray. But the disciples rebuked them. 14 Then Jesus said, "Leave the children alone, and don't try to keep them from coming to Me, because the kingdom of heaven is made up of people like this."b 15 After putting His hands on them, He went on from there.

The Rich Young Ruler

16 Just then someone came up and asked Him, "Teacher, what good must I do to have eternal life?"

17 "Why do you ask Me about what is good?"c He said to him. "There is only One who is good.d If you want to enter into life, keep the commandments."

18 "Which ones?" he asked Him.

Jesus answered,

Do not murder;
do not commit adultery;
do not steal;

do not bear false witness;
19 honor your father and your mother;
and love your neighbor as yourself.e

20 "I have kept all these,"f the young man told Him. "What do I still lack?"

21 "If you want to be perfect,"g Jesus said to him, "go, sell your belongings and give to the poor, and you will have treasure in heaven. Then come, follow Me."

22 When the young man heard that command, he went away grieving, because he had many possessions.

Possessions and the Kingdom

23 Then Jesus said to His disciples, "•I assure you: It will be hard for a rich person to enter the kingdom of heaven! 24 Again I tell you, it is easier for a camel to go through the eye of a needle than for a rich person to enter the kingdom of God."

25 When the disciples heard this, they were utterly astonished and asked, "Then who can be saved?"

26 But Jesus looked at them and said, "With men this is impossible, but with God all things are possible."

27 Then Peter responded to Him, "Look, we have left everything and followed You. So what will there be for us?"

28 Jesus said to them, "I assure you: In the Messianic Age,h when the •Son of Man sits on His glorious throne, you who have followed Me will also sit on 12 thrones, judging the 12 tribes of Israel. 29 And everyone who has left houses, brothers or sisters, father or mother,i children, or fields because of My name will receive 100 times more and will inherit eternal life. 30 But many who are first will be last, and the last first.

The Parable of the Vineyard Workers

20 "For the kingdom of heaven is like a landowner who went out early in the morning to hire workers for his vineyard. 2 After agreeing with the workers on one •denarius for the day, he sent them into his vineyard. 3 When he went out about nine in the morning,j he saw others standing in the market-

---

a19:9 Other mss add *Also whoever marries a divorced woman commits adultery*; Mt 5:32   b19:14 Lit *heaven is of such ones*   c19:17 Other mss read *Why do you call Me good?*   d19:17 Other mss read *No one is good but One—God*   e19:18–19 Ex 20:12–16; Dt 5:16–20; Lv 19:18   f19:20 Other mss add *from my youth*   g19:21 Or *complete*   h19:28 Lit *the regeneration*   i19:29 Other mss add *or wife*   j20:3 Lit *about the third hour*

19:8 Moses permitted. Moses' concession was an accommodation to human sinfulness, not part of God's intention.

19:9 marries another. Commentators differ as to whether remarriage was prohibited regardless of whether or not the divorce was for reasons of marital unfaithfulness.

19:20 What do I still lack? He seems to know that he *is* lacking something. When we seek a status based on our own works, we always feel like we are short of what we need.

19:21 sell your belongings. By telling the young man to sell all his goods, Jesus exposed that the man's heart was gripped by his possessions rather than by God.

19:24 eye of a needle. Jesus uses an exag-

gerated form of speech (hyperbole) to make His point. The camel was the largest animal in Palestine and certainly could not get through the tiny opening of a needle.

19:25 Then who can be saved? The radical nature of Jesus' statement causes them to think about their own destiny. If the rich (who they believed were especially favored of God) will find it difficult to enter the kingdom, then what chance do they have?

19:26 with God all things are possible. This is asserted many times in the New Testament (Mark 9:23; 10:27; 14:36; Luke 1:37). Only the power of atonement and the persuasive pull of the Holy Spirit can overcome man's largest obstacles.

19:30 many who are first will be last. Jesus often makes the point that those who

expect to be part of the kingdom will not necessarily be part of it, and those who expect to be excluded will not necessarily be excluded. Jesus said the tax collectors and the prostitutes were entering the kingdom of heaven ahead of many who considered themselves to be pious (21:31).

20:2 one denarius. This was a subsistence wage that would meet one's daily needs, but not allow for any excess to be saved for the following day. It was considered a fair wage for a day's work.

20:3 about nine in the morning. Probably the first workers were hired at daybreak, about 6 a.m.

20:6 Then about five So near the end of the workday, it is unusual that they are there at all. They certainly were not expecting work to

place doing nothing. 4 To those men he said, 'You also go to my vineyard, and I'll give you whatever is right.' So off they went. 5 About noon and at three,ᵃ he went out again and did the same thing. 6 Then about fiveᵇ he went and found others standing around,ᶜ and said to them, 'Why have you been standing here all day doing nothing?'

Hey—That's Not Fair!

1. When you were a child, what chores were you expected to do? Were you paid?

Matthew 20:1-16

2. If you were hired in this story at 5 p.m., how would you have felt at pay time (vv. 8-9)? If you were hired at 6 a.m., how would you have felt (vv. 10-12)?

3. Why did the employer pay everyone the same, regardless of how much work they'd done? Is this fair? What might this teach us about God's attitude toward those who serve Him?

4. Do you find yourself resenting it when God blesses people that you think don't deserve it? What does this passage teach you about that attitude?

7 " 'Because no one hired us,' they said to him.

" 'You also go to my vineyard,' he told them.ᵈ 8 When evening came, the owner of the vineyard told his foreman, 'Call the workers and give them their pay, starting with the last and ending with the first.'ᵉ

9 "When those who were hired about fiveᵇ came, they each received one denarius. 10 So when the first ones came, they assumed they would get more, but they also received a denarius each. 11 When they received it, they began to complain to the landowner: 12 'These last men put in one hour, and you made them equal to us who bore the burden of the day and the burning heat!'

13 "He replied to one of them, 'Friend, I'm doing you no wrong. Didn't you agree with me on a denarius? 14 Take what's yours and go. I want to give this last man the same as I gave you. 15 Don't I have the right to do what I want with my business?ᶠ Are you jealousᵍ because I'm generous?'ʰ

16 "So the last will be first, and the first last."ⁱ

The Third Prediction of His Death

17 While going up to Jerusalem, Jesus took the 12 disciples aside privately and said to them on the way: 18 "Listen! We are going up to Jerusalem. The •Son of Man will be handed over to the •chief priests and •scribes, and they will condemn Him to death. 19 Then they will hand Him over to the Gentiles to be mocked, flogged,ʲ and crucified, and He will be resurrectedᵏ on the third day."

Suffering and Service

20 Then the mother of Zebedee's sons approached Him with her sons. She knelt down to ask Him for something. 21 "What do you want?" He asked her.

"Promise,"ˡ she said to Him, "that these two sons of mine may sit, one on Your right and the other on Your left, in Your kingdom."

22 But Jesus answered, "You don't know what you're asking. Are you able to drink the cupᵐ that I am about to drink?"ⁿ

"We are able," they said to Him.

23 He told them, "You will indeed drink My cup.ᵒ But to sit at My right and left is not Mine to give; instead, it belongs to those for whom it has been prepared by My Father." 24 When the 10 ₗdisciplesₗ heard this, they became indignant with the two brothers. 25 But Jesus called them over and said, "You know that the rulers of

---

ᵃ**20:5** Lit *about the sixth hour and the ninth hour* ᵇ**20:6,9** Lit *about the eleventh hour* ᶜ**20:6** Other mss add *doing nothing* ᵈ**20:7** Other mss add *'and you'll get whatever is right.'* ᵉ**20:8** Lit *starting from the last until the first* ᶠ**20:15** Lit *with what is mine* ᵍ**20:15** Lit *Is your eye evil*; an idiom for jealousy or stinginess ʰ**20:15** Lit *good* ⁱ**20:16** Other mss add *For many are called, but few are chosen.* ʲ**20:19** Or *scourged* ᵏ**20:19** Other mss read *will rise again* ˡ**20:21** Lit *Say* ᵐ**20:22** Figurative language referring to His coming suffering; Mt 26:39; Jn 18:11 ⁿ**20:22** Other mss add *and (or) to be baptized with the baptism that I am baptized with* ᵒ**20:23** Other mss add *and be baptized with the baptism that I am baptized with*

---

be offered. This also is a parallel of God's grace, given not when it is expected but when it is least expected.

20:8 When evening came. The laborer's day went from sunrise to sunset. According to the Old Testament Law, workers were to be paid their wages at the end of the day so that they would not have to go hungry (Deut. 24:14-15).

20:9-12 they assumed they would get more. As those hired last receive a denarius for an hour's work, they would have been joyfully surprised. Quite naturally, the spirits of the others in line suddenly rise—if those who worked only one hour received a denarius, what might those who worked all day receive? As the foreman continues to pay each one a denarius, the earlier workers grow angry. What at first seemed like a fair wage (v.

2), now appeared to be unjust and insulting.

20:13 Friend. In the other places where this form of address is used (22:12; 26:50), it has an ironic twist. The laborers are not relating to the landowner as a friend, but as an unjust man. **I'm doing you no wrong.** His actions were not unjust, since he was paying them what they had agreed to in the beginning.

20:15 Don't I have the right? In light of the ongoing conflict with the Pharisees regarding Jesus' interest in the religious outcasts of His time, Jesus, by means of this parable, declares that God's grace is not unjust.

20:20 the mother of Zebedee's sons. In Mark's account, James and John approach Jesus directly. Regardless of the role their mother played in this incident, it is clear that they are held responsible for it (v. 24).

20:22 drink the cup. This phrase means to share the same fate. In the Old Testament, drinking the cup is a metaphor for experiencing God's wrath (Ps. 75:8; Isa. 51:17-22). Here, the cup refers to Jesus' suffering and death for the sins of the world. **We are able.** Despite their bold assertion, they do not grasp what Jesus means by the question. They probably assumed He was referring to being willing to share in His future, which they imagine to be one of power and prestige.

20:24 they became indignant. All 12 share the view that the kingdom will be earthly and political, with Jesus as the reigning king and them as His chief lieutenants.

20:28 ransom. "Ransom" was a word used generally to describe the act of freeing people from bondage, whether through the lit-

Serve Others

1. What do your parents want you to be "when you grow up"?

Matthew 20:20-28

2. What exactly are the guys requesting of Jesus in this passage?
3. How does a person become great in God's kingdom? How is this different from becoming great in sports or business or school?
4. How did Jesus Himself set the example for serving others?
5. How can you serve the people on your team or in your group? How might that attitude help you all in the long run?

the Gentiles dominate them, and the men of high position exercise power over them. ²⁶ It must not be like that among you. On the contrary, whoever wants to become great among you must be your servant, ²⁷ and whoever wants to be first among you must be your slave; ²⁸ just as the Son of Man did not come to be served, but to serve, and to give His life—a ransom for many."

Two Blind Men Healed

²⁹ As they were leaving Jericho, a large crowd followed Him. ³⁰ There were two blind men sitting by the road. When they heard that Jesus was passing by, they cried out, "Lord, have mercy on us, Son of David!" ³¹ The crowd told them to keep quiet, but they cried out all the more, "Lord, have mercy on us, Son of David!"

³² Jesus stopped, called them, and said, "What do you want Me to do for you?"

³³ "Lord," they said to Him, "open our eyes!" ³⁴ Moved with compassion, Jesus touched their eyes. Immediately they could see, and they followed Him.

The Triumphal Entry

21 When they approached Jerusalem and came to Bethphage at the •Mount of Olives, Jesus then sent two disciples, ² telling them, "Go into the village ahead of you. At once you will find a donkey tied there, and a colt with her. Untie them and bring them to Me. ³ If anyone says anything to you, you should say that the Lord needs them, and immediately he will send them."

⁴ This took place so that what was spoken through the prophet might be fulfilled:

⁵ **Tell Daughter Zion,**
  "See, your King is coming to you,
  gentle, and mounted on a donkey,
  even on a colt,
  the foal of a beast of burden."ᵃ

⁶ The disciples went and did just as Jesus directed them. ⁷ They brought the donkey and the colt; then they laid their robes on them, and He sat on them. ⁸ A very large crowd spread their robes on the road; others were cutting branches from the trees and spreading them on the road. ⁹ Then the crowds who went ahead of Him and those who followed kept shouting:

  •*Hosanna* **to the Son of David!**
  Blessed is He who comes
  in the name of the Lord!ᵇ
  Hosanna **in the highest heaven!**

¹⁰ When He entered Jerusalem, the whole city was shaken, saying, "Who is this?" ¹¹ And the crowds kept saying, "This is the prophet Jesus from Nazareth in Galilee!"

Cleansing the Temple Complex

¹² Jesus went into the •temple complexᶜ and drove out all those buying and selling in the temple. He overturned the money changers' tables and the chairs of

ᵃ**21:5** Is 62:11; Zch 9:9 ᵇ**21:9** Ps 118:25-26 ᶜ**21:12** Other mss add *of God*

---

eral payment of a purchase price or through some act of deliverance.

20:29 Jericho. The journey begun in 19:1 is almost complete. Jericho, about 18 miles east of Jerusalem, was the place where travelers recrossed the Jordan back into Israel. **a large crowd.** These were pilgrims on their way to Jerusalem for the Passover Feast. Every male over 12 years of age was expected to attend.

20:30 two blind men. Mark and Luke only mention one. **Lord ... Son of David.** This is clearly a messianic title by which the men hail Jesus. The blind truly see who He is, while the Twelve still had not fully grasped this.

21:3 the Lord. Thus far in Matthew's Gospel, Jesus has not referred to Himself by this title.

While it can simply be a formal term for a master, the context of this occasion indicates He was implying divine authority as well.

21:8 spread their robes. This was a gesture of respect, given to kings (2 Kings 9:12-13), prophets, and other holy men.

21:9 Hosanna. Literally, "Save now!" This was commonly used as an expression of praise to God or as a greeting.

21:12 temple. Built by Herod the Great in 20 B.C., this magnificent structure covered about 30 acres. **buying and selling.** Temple worship required the sacrifice of an unblemished lamb or (for the poor) a dove. However, inspectors approved only those animals bought from certified vendors employed by the high priest's family. There was great profiteering, as such animals were

sold at a huge markup. **money changers.** At Passover each Jew was required to pay a temple tax of nearly two days' wages. Since only a relatively rare currency was acceptable, money changers set up business in the temple to provide people with the correct currency. They charged exorbitant fees for this service.

21:15 children ... cheering. In contrast to the bitterness created in the worshipers by the exploitation allowed in the temple, Jesus transforms it into a place where children celebrate His presence (18:2-4; 19:14).

21:17 Bethany, and spent the night. Jesus left the city of Jerusalem at night possibly because such opposition to Him was building among the authorities.

21:18-22 a lone fig tree. Fig trees were a

those selling doves. ¹³ And He said to them, "It is written, **My house will be called a house of prayer.**ᵃ But you are making it **a den of thieves!**"ᵇ

Children Cheer Jesus

¹⁴ The blind and the lame came to Him in the temple complex, and He healed them. ¹⁵ When the •chief priests and the •scribes saw the wonders that He did and the children in the temple complex cheering, "Hosanna to the Son of David!" they were indignant ¹⁶ and said to Him, "Do You hear what these ⌈children⌉ are saying?"

"Yes," Jesus told them. "Have you never read:

> **You have prepared**ᶜ **praise**
> **from the mouths of children**
> **and nursing infants?**"ᵈ

¹⁷ Then He left them, went out of the city to Bethany, and spent the night there.

The Barren Fig Tree

¹⁸ Early in the morning, as He was returning to the city, He was hungry. ¹⁹ Seeing a lone fig tree by the road, He went up to it and found nothing on it except leaves. And He said to it, "May no fruit ever come from you again!" At once the fig tree withered.

²⁰ When the disciples saw it, they were amazed and said, "How did the fig tree wither so quickly?"

²¹ Jesus answered them, "•I assure you: If you have faith and do not doubt, you will not only do what was done to the fig tree, but even if you tell this mountain, 'Be lifted up and thrown into the sea,' it will be done. ²² And if you believe, you will receive whatever you ask for in prayer."

Messiah's Authority Challenged

²³ When He entered the temple complex, the chief priests and the elders of the people came up to Him as He was teaching and said, "By what authority are You doing these things? Who gave You this authority?"

²⁴ Jesus answered them, "I will also ask you one question, and if you answer it for Me, then I will tell you by

what authority I do these things. ²⁵ Where did John's baptism come from? From heaven or from men?"

They began to argue among themselves, "If we say, 'From heaven,' He will say to us, 'Then why didn't you believe him?' ²⁶ But if we say, 'From men,' we're afraid of the crowd, because everyone thought John was a prophet." ²⁷ So they answered Jesus, "We don't know."

And He said to them, "Neither will I tell you by what authority I do these things.

The Parable of the Two Sons

²⁸ "But what do you think? A man had two sons. He went to the first and said, 'My son, go, work in the vineyard today.'

²⁹ "He answered, 'I don't want to!' Yet later he changed his mind and went. ³⁰ Then the man went to the other and said the same thing.

" 'I will, sir,' he answered. But he didn't go.

³¹ "Which of the two did his father's will?"

"The first," they said.

Jesus said to them, "I assure you: Tax collectors and prostitutes are entering the kingdom of God before you! ³² For John came to you in the way of righteousness,ᵉ and you didn't believe him. Tax collectors and prostitutes did believe him, but you, when you saw it, didn't even change your minds then and believe him.

The Parable of the Vineyard Owner

³³ "Listen to another parable: There was a man, a landowner, who planted a vineyard, put a fence around it, dug a winepress in it, and built a watchtower. He leased it to tenant farmers and went away. ³⁴ When the grape harvestᶠ drew near, he sent his slaves to the farmers to collect his fruit. ³⁵ But the farmers took his slaves, beat one, killed another, and stoned a third. ³⁶ Again, he sent other slaves, more than the first group, and they did the same to them. ³⁷ Finally, he sent his son to them. 'They will respect my son,' he said.

³⁸ "But when the tenant farmers saw the son, they said among themselves, 'This is the heir. Come, let's kill him and take his inheritance!' ³⁹ So they seized him and threw him out of the vineyard, and killed him.

ᵃ**21:13** Is 56:7 ᵇ**21:13** Jr 7:11 ᶜ**21:16** Or *restored* ᵈ**21:16** Ps 8:3 LXX ᵉ**21:32** John came preaching and practicing righteousness ᶠ**21:34** Lit *the season of fruits*

---

common prophetic symbol associated with Israel and with judgment (Jer. 8:13; Hos. 9:10; Mic. 7:1; Nah. 3:12). Just as the tree was judged for its failure to have fruit, so Israel, and the temple as a symbol of Israel's faith, was judged for its failure to have "fruit"—works that honored God.

21:19 nothing on it except leaves. The tree symbolized Israel. It had the outward appearance of life (bustling activity at the temple), but no fruit (the qualities of justice, love, and godliness that were to mark God's people). **At once the fig tree withered.** The immediacy of the event points out the divine power of Jesus and also the authority of Jesus as judge.

21:23 the chief priests and the elders. The chief priests were the key officers of the temple, just below the high priest in rank. The el-

ders were powerful and (reputedly) wise leaders of Israel. They were generally not priests, but administrators. These were representatives from the Sanhedrin, the Jewish ruling council.

21:31 Tax collectors and prostitutes. In this society, these two groups of people represented the lowest depths to which men and women respectively could sink. The tax collectors were Jewish men viewed as exploiting their own people for their own gain as they worked for Rome. Yet Jesus says that these along with prostitutes would be entering the kingdom ahead of the religious authorities!

21:32 the way of righteousness. John declared that the way to enter God's kingdom was through repentance—a change of heart and life.

21:33 vineyard. This vineyard was built with a wall around it to keep out animals, a pit in which to crush grapes to make wine, and a tower where the farmer kept a lookout for robbers and also where he slept during harvest.

21:37 he sent his son. The landowner assumed the tenants would acknowledge the authority of his own son, the heir of the vineyard.

21:38 take his inheritance. The arrival of the son was mistakenly understood by the servants as a sign that the landowner must have died. By law, a piece of ownerless property could be kept by those who first occupied and cultivated it. Since the tenants assumed the land would be ownerless if the son was dead, they killed him in order to lay claim to the land for themselves.

⁴⁰ Therefore, when the owner of the vineyard comes, what will he do to those farmers?"

⁴¹ "He will completely destroy those terrible men," they told Him, "and lease his vineyard to other farmers who will give him his produce at the harvest."ᵃ

⁴² Jesus said to them, "Have you never read in the Scriptures:

> The stone that the builders rejected
> has become the cornerstone.ᵇ
> This came from the Lord
> and is wonderful in our eyes?ᶜ

⁴³ Therefore I tell you, the kingdom of God will be taken away from you and given to a nation producing itsᵈ fruit. [⁴⁴ Whoever falls on this stone will be broken to pieces; but on whomever it falls, it will grind him to powder!"]ᵉ

⁴⁵ When the chief priests and the •Pharisees heard His parables, they knew He was speaking about them. ⁴⁶ Although they were looking for a way to arrest Him, they feared the crowds, because theyᶠ regarded Him as a prophet.

The Parable of the Wedding Banquet

22 Once more Jesus spoke to them in parables: ² "The kingdom of heaven may be compared to a king who gave a wedding banquet for his son. ³ He sent out his •slaves to summon those invited to the banquet, but they didn't want to come. ⁴ Again, he sent out other slaves, and said, 'Tell those who are invited: Look, I've prepared my dinner; my oxen and fattened cattle have been slaughtered, and everything is ready. Come to the wedding banquet.'

⁵ "But they paid no attention and went away, one to his own farm, another to his business. ⁶ And the others seized his •slaves, treated them outrageously and killed them. ⁷ The kingᵍ was enraged, so he sent out his troops, destroyed those murderers, and burned down their city.

⁸ "Then he told his •slaves, 'The banquet is ready, but those who were invited were not worthy. ⁹ Therefore, go to where the roads exit the city and invite everyone you find to the banquet.' ¹⁰ So those slaves went out on the roads and gathered everyone they found, both evil and good. The wedding banquet was filled with guests.ʰ ¹¹ But when the king came in to view the guests, he saw a man there who was not dressed for a wedding. ¹² So he said to him, 'Friend, how did you get in here without wedding clothes?' The man was speechless.

¹³ "Then the king told the attendants, 'Tie him up hand and foot,ⁱ and throw him into the outer darkness, where there will be weeping and gnashing of teeth.'

¹⁴ "For many are invited, but few are chosen."

God and Caesar

¹⁵ Then the •Pharisees went and plotted how to trap Him by what He said.ʲ ¹⁶ They sent their disciples to Him, with the •Herodians. "Teacher," they said, "we know that You are truthful and teach truthfully the way of God. You defer to no one, for You don't show partiality.ᵏ ¹⁷ Tell us, therefore, what You think. Is it lawful to pay taxes to Caesar or not?"

¹⁸ But perceiving their malice, Jesus said, "Why are you testing Me, hypocrites? ¹⁹ Show Me the coin used for the tax." So they brought Him a •denarius. ²⁰ "Whose image and inscription is this?" He asked them.

²¹ "Caesar's," they said to Him.

Then He said to them, "Therefore, give back to Caesar the things that are Caesar's, and to God the things that are God's." ²² When they heard this, they were amazed. So they left Him and went away.

The Sadducees and the Resurrection

²³ The same day some •Sadducees, who say there is no resurrection, came up to Him and questioned Him: ²⁴ "Teacher, Moses said, **if a man dies, having no children, his brother is to marry his wife and raise up offspring for his brother.**ˡ ²⁵ Now there were seven

---

ᵃ**21:41** Lit *him the fruits in their seasons*   ᵇ**21:42** Lit *the head of the corner*   ᶜ**21:42** Ps 118:22–23   ᵈ**21:43** The word *its* refers back to *kingdom.*
ᵉ**21:44** Other mss omit this v.   ᶠ**21:46** The crowds   ᵍ**22:7** Other mss read *But when the (that) king heard about it he*   ʰ**22:10** Lit *those reclining* (to eat)   ⁱ**22:13** Other mss add *take him away*   ʲ**22:15** Lit *trap Him in [a] word*   ᵏ**22:16** Lit *don't look on the face of men;* that is, on the outward appearance   ˡ**22:24** Dt 25:5

21:41 lease his vineyard to other farmers. Landowners would rent the vineyard to people who would meet the terms of their contracts. The implication of the parable is that God will raise up new leaders to care for His people.

21:42 The stone that the builders rejected has become the cornerstone. Here the stone is Jesus (the Messiah) whom the builders (the leaders) fail to recognize. The identification here of the Messiah (the stone) with the Son of God (v. 37) was unique to Jesus.

22:3 sent out his slaves to summon those invited. In well-to-do circles, invitations to banquets were issued well in advance, but the specific time to arrive was communicated on the day of the event when everything was ready (Est. 5:8; 6:14).

22:9 to where the roads exit the city. These are the public squares where beggars gathered hoping for handouts.

22:11-12 wedding clothes. In this allegorical parable, the wedding clothes represent the robes of righteousness God provides for His people (Zech. 3:3-5; Rev. 3:4, 5,18). Without God-given righteousness, one has no part in the kingdom. The false disciple, like the religious leaders (v. 34), is silenced before the king. He has no excuse.

22:13 weeping and gnashing of teeth. This is a common phrase used to indicate the extreme horror and suffering of God's judgment (8:12; 13:42,50).

22:16 Herodians. A political group made up of influential Jewish sympathizers of King Herod. Normally despised by the Pharisees as traitors who worked with Rome and associated with Gentiles, the Pharisees needed this group's assistance to secure the civil authority's opposition to Jesus.

22:17 taxes. An annual poll tax had to be paid to the Romans by all adult Jews. Many Jews felt that paying taxes to Caesar denied the belief that God was the rightful ruler of Israel.

22:18 Why are you testing Me? If the authorities can get Jesus to say that the people should *not* pay taxes to Caesar, then the Roman guard would have grounds to arrest Him. On the other hand, if Jesus says they *should* pay taxes, then He would lose the support of the crowds who resented being taxed by an occupying force.

22:19 the coin. Only the denarius, a small silver coin, could be used to pay the poll tax. Since it bore the picture of Tiberius Caesar and a description of him as "Son of the Divine Augustine," these coins were offensive

brothers among us. The first got married and died. Having no offspring, he left his wife to his brother. 26 The same happened to the second also, and the third, and so to all seven.ᵃ 27 Then last of all the woman died. 28 Therefore, in the resurrection, whose wife will she be of the seven? For they all had married her."ᵇ

29 Jesus answered them, "You are deceived, because you don't know the Scriptures or the power of God. 30 For in the resurrection they neither marry nor are given in marriage but are likeᶜ angels in heaven. 31 Now concerning the resurrection of the dead, haven't you read what was spoken to you by God: 32 **I am the God of Abraham and the God of Isaac and the God of Jacob?**ᵈ Heᵉ is not the God of the dead, but of the living."

33 And when the crowds heard this, they were astonished at His teaching.

The Primary Commandments

34 When the Pharisees heard that He had silenced the Sadducees, they came together in the same place. 35 And one of them, an expert in the law, asked a question to test Him: 36 "Teacher, which commandment in the law is the greatest?"ᶠ

37 He said to him, **"Love the Lord your God with all your heart, with all your soul, and with all your mind.**ᵍ 38 This is the greatest and most importantʰ commandment. 39 The second is like it: **Love your neighbor as yourself.**ⁱ 40 All the Law and the Prophets dependʲ on these two commandments."

The Question about the Messiah

41 While the Pharisees were together, Jesus questioned them, 42 "What do you think about the •Messiah? Whose Son is He?"

"David's," they told Him.

43 He asked them, "How is it then that David, inspired by the Spirit,ᵏ calls Him 'Lord':

44   **The Lord declared to my Lord,**
     'Sit at My right hand
     until I put Your enemies under Your feet'?ˡ ᵐ

45 "If David calls Him 'Lord,' how then can the Messiah be his Son?" 46 No one was able to answer Him at all,ⁿ and from that day no one dared to question Him any more.

Religious Hypocrites Denounced

23 Then Jesus spoke to the crowds and to His disciples: 2 "The •scribes and the •Pharisees are seated in the chair of Moses.ᵒ 3 Therefore do whatever they tell you and observe ⌊it⌋. But don't do what they do,ᵖ because they don't practice what they teach. 4 They tie up heavy loads that are hard to carry�qand put them on people's shoulders, but they themselves aren't willing to lift a fingerʳ to move them. 5 They do everythingˢ to be observed by others: They enlarge their phylacteriesᵗ and lengthen their •tassels.ᵘ 6 They love the place of honor at banquets, the front seats in the •synagogues, 7 greetings in the marketplaces, and to be called '•Rabbi' by people.

8 "But as for you, do not be called 'Rabbi,' because you have one Teacher,ᵛ and you are all brothers. 9 Do not call anyone on earth your father, because you have one Father, who is in heaven. 10 And do not be called masters either, because you have one Master,ʷ the •Messiah. 11 The greatest among you will be your servant. 12 Whoever exalts himself will be humbled, and whoever humbles himself will be exalted.

13 "But woe to you, scribes and Pharisees, hypocrites! You lock up the kingdom of heaven from people. For you don't go in, and you don't allow those entering to go in.

[14 "Woe to you, scribes and Pharisees, hypocrites! You devour widows' houses and make long prayers just for show.ˣ This is why you will receive a harsher punishment.]ʸ

ᵃ22:26 Lit so until the seven   ᵇ22:28 Lit all had her   ᶜ22:30 Other mss add God's   ᵈ22:32 Ex 3:6,15–16   ᵉ22:32 Other mss read God   ᶠ22:36 Lit is great   ᵍ22:37 Dt 6:5   ʰ22:38 Lit and first   ⁱ22:39 Lv 19:18   ʲ22:40 Or hang   ᵏ22:43 Lit David in Spirit   ˡ22:44 Other mss read until I make Your enemies Your footstool   ᵐ22:44 Ps 110:1   ⁿ22:46 Lit answer Him a word   ᵒ23:2 Perhaps a special chair for teaching in synagogues, or a metaphorical phrase for teaching with Moses' authority   ᵖ23:3 Lit do according to their works   q23:4 Other mss omit that are hard to carry   ʳ23:4 Lit lift with their finger   ˢ23:5 Lit do all their works   ᵗ23:5 Small leather boxes containing OT texts, worn by Jews on their arms and foreheads   ᵘ23:5 Other mss add on their robes   ᵛ23:8 Other mss add the Messiah   ʷ23:10 Or Teacher   ˣ23:14 Or prayers with false motivation   ʸ23:14 Other mss omit bracketed text

---

to strict Jews, who would not even handle them.

22:23 Sadducees. A small, but highly influential party of Jews composed mainly of wealthy, aristocratic priests. Up to this point Jesus has been no threat to the Sadducees since His ministry had been largely in Galilee, far from the temple they controlled. **resurrection.** Most Jews believed that at the end of history God would bring the dead to life for judgment. The Sadducees did not believe in the resurrection.

22:34-40 to test Him. In Mark's version, the scribe appears to ask Jesus a sincere question (Mark 12:28-34).

22:36 which commandment in the law is the greatest? The Pharisees, who generally regarded all the laws of God as equally important, probably hoped Jesus would isolate

one law and thus provide them with the opportunity to discredit Him for ignoring other laws.

22:37 Love the Lord. This is part of the *Shema* (Deut. 6:4-5). This passage, recited by pious Jews each morning and evening, captures what was essential about the people's relationship to God.

22:42 the Messiah. This title identifies Jesus as the expected deliverer of Israel.

23:2 chair of Moses. This refers to the seat in the front of each synagogue in which a rabbi sat while teaching.

23:5 phylacteries. These were small cases containing passages of the Law. They were tied to the forehead and left arm (Ex. 13:9,16; Deut. 6:8; 11:18). **tassels.** Jews were to tie tassels on the corners of their

robes to remind them of God's commands (Num. 15:37-39). The Pharisees wore these things in an ornamental way to draw attention to themselves.

23:6 the front seats in the synagogues. The choice seat was up front, with its back to the box containing the sacred Scriptures, and its front facing the congregation, ... so that all would see who sat there.

23:7 greetings. Out of respect for the authority of the teachers of the Law, people rose and called out titles of respect when they passed by. **Rabbi.** This official title for the scribes literally meant "my master."

23:13 You lock up the kingdom of heaven from people. Instead of unlocking the Scriptures, the traditions and rules of the scribes have the effect of securely locking away such knowledge from the people.

¹⁵ "Woe to you, scribes and Pharisees, hypocrites! You travel over land and sea to make one •proselyte, and when he becomes one, you make him twice as fit for •hell[a] as you are!

¹⁶ "Woe to you, blind guides, who say, 'Whoever takes an oath by the sanctuary, it means nothing. But whoever takes an oath by the gold of the sanctuary is bound by his oath.'[b] ¹⁷ Blind fools![c] For which is greater, the gold or the sanctuary that sanctified the gold? ¹⁸ Also, 'Whoever takes an oath by the altar, it means nothing. But whoever takes an oath by the gift that is on it is bound by his oath.'[b] ¹⁹ Blind people![d] For which is greater, the gift or the altar that sanctifies the gift? ²⁰ Therefore the one who takes an oath by the altar takes an oath by it and by everything on it. ²¹ The one who takes an oath by the sanctuary takes an oath by it and by Him who dwells in it. ²² And the one who takes an oath by heaven takes an oath by God's throne and by Him who sits on it.

²³ "Woe to you, scribes and Pharisees, hypocrites! You pay a tenth of[e] mint, dill, and cumin,[f] yet you have neglected the more important matters of the law—justice, mercy, and faith. These things should have been done without neglecting the others. ²⁴ Blind guides! You strain out a gnat, yet gulp down a camel!

²⁵ "Woe to you, scribes and Pharisees, hypocrites! You clean the outside of the cup and dish, but inside they are full of greed[g] and self-indulgence! ²⁶ Blind Pharisee! First clean the inside of the cup,[h] so the outside of it[i] may also become clean.

²⁷ "Woe to you, scribes and Pharisees, hypocrites! You are like whitewashed tombs, which appear beautiful on the outside, but inside are full of dead men's bones and every impurity. ²⁸ In the same way, on the outside you seem righteous to people, but inside you are full of hypocrisy and lawlessness.

²⁹ "Woe to you, scribes and Pharisees, hypocrites! You build the tombs of the prophets and decorate the monuments of the righteous, ³⁰ and you say, 'If we had lived in the days of our fathers, we wouldn't have taken part with them in shedding the prophets' blood.'[j] ³¹ You therefore testify against yourselves that you are sons of those who murdered the prophets. ³² Fill up, then, the measure of your fathers' sins![k]

³³ "Snakes! Brood of vipers! How can you escape being condemned to hell?[l] ³⁴ This is why I am sending you prophets, sages, and scribes. Some of them you will kill and crucify, and some of them you will flog in your synagogues and hound from town to town. ³⁵ So all the righteous blood shed on the earth will be charged to you,[m] from the blood of righteous Abel to the blood of Zechariah, son of Berechiah, whom you murdered between the sanctuary and the altar. ³⁶ •I assure you: All these things will come on this generation!

Jesus' Lamentation over Jerusalem

³⁷ "Jerusalem, Jerusalem! The city who kills the prophets and stones those who are sent to her. How often I wanted to gather your children together, as a hen gathers her chicks[n] under her wings, yet you were not willing! ³⁸ See, your house is left to you desolate. ³⁹ For I tell you, you will never see Me again until you say, **Blessed is He who comes in the name of the Lord!**"[o]

Destruction of the Temple Predicted

24 As Jesus left and was going out of the •temple complex, His disciples came up and called His attention to the temple buildings. ² Then He replied to them, "Don't you see all these things? •I assure you: Not one stone will be left here on another that will not be thrown down!"

Signs of the End of the Age

³ While He was sitting on the •Mount of Olives, the disciples approached Him privately and said, "Tell us, when will these things happen? And what is the sign of Your coming and of the end of the age?"

⁴ Then Jesus replied to them: "Watch out that no one deceives you. ⁵ For many will come in My name, saying,

---

[a]**23:15** Lit *twice the son of gehenna* [b]**23:16,18** Lit *is obligated* [c]**23:17** Lit *Fools and blind* [d]**23:19** Other mss read *Fools and blind* [e]**23:23** Or *You tithe* [f]**23:23** A plant whose seeds are used as a seasoning [g]**23:25** Or *full of violence* [h]**23:26** Other mss add *and dish* [i]**23:26** Other mss read *of them* [j]**23:30** Lit *have been partakers with them in the blood of the prophets* [k]**23:32** Lit *the measure of your fathers* [l]**23:33** Lit *escape from the judgment of gehenna* [m]**23:35** Lit *will come on you* [n]**23:37** Or *as a mother bird gathers her young* [o]**23:39** Ps 118:26

23:16 blind guides. The Pharisees prided themselves on being "guides for the blind." Instead, Jesus asserts they are blind themselves.

23:24 You strain out a gnat, yet gulp down a camel! This is an example of Jesus' use of humorous irony to make His point.

23:25 greed and self-indulgence. Jesus says it is as if they think using ritually "clean" utensils makes the consumption of food and drink gained by greed and violence acceptable. While concerned for the external demands of their tradition, they fail to consider what is going on inside of themselves.

23:26 clean the inside. Following the metaphor of the cup and dish, this is a call to self-examination and repentance. True holiness before God comes from the inside out, not from the outside in. A clean heart, not a clean dish, is required.

23:27 whitewashed tombs. Tombs would often be whitewashed. While this gave them an attractive appearance, it could do nothing about the decay inside the tomb.

23:28 lawlessness. Literally, "wickedness."

23:33 Brood of vipers! The image painted by these words is of snakes slithering through the undergrowth trying to escape the oncoming fire.

23:34 crucify. The Jews did not practice crucifixion. This may be a reference to how the Jewish authorities eventually led the Romans to carry out the execution of Jesus Himself.

23:35 Abel. Abel, the first person to be killed, was murdered by his brother, who, like these leaders, refused to listen to God

(Gen. 4:3-8). **Zechariah, son of Berechiah.** There were two known Zechariahs who were sons of men named Berechiah. One was the author of the Old Testament book by his name, but there is no record of how he died. The other was a man murdered by Jewish zealots in the temple in A.D. 67. This was contemporary with Matthew's writing, but after Jesus' earthly ministry.

23:38 your house. This is the temple from which the presence of God will depart because of the people's rejection of the Messiah (Jer. 12:7; Ezek. 10:18-19).

24:2 Not one stone will be left here. The temple was destroyed by Rome in 70 A.D.

24:6-8 You are going hear. Some feel that apocalyptic language uses graphic imagery to describe historical events. Others see this as a description of future events.

'I am the •Messiah,' and they will deceive many. ⁶ You are going to hear of wars and rumors of wars. See that you are not alarmed, because these things must take place, but the end is not yet. ⁷ For nation will rise up against nation, and kingdom against kingdom. There will be faminesᵃ and earthquakes in various places. ⁸ All these events are the beginning of birth pains.

Persecutions Predicted

⁹ "Then they will hand you over for persecution,ᵇ and they will kill you. You will be hated by all nations because of My name. ¹⁰ Then many will take offense, betray one another and hate one another. ¹¹ Many false prophets will rise up and deceive many. ¹² Because lawlessness will multiply, the love of many will grow cold. ¹³ But the one who endures to the end will be delivered.ᶜ ¹⁴ This good news of the kingdom will be proclaimed in all the worldᵈ as a testimony to all nations. And then the end will come.

The Great Tribulation

¹⁵ "So when you see **the abomination that causes desolation,**ᵉ ᶠ spoken of by the prophet Daniel, standing in the holy place" (let the reader understandᵍ), ¹⁶ "then those in Judea must flee to the mountains! ¹⁷ A man on the housetopʰ must not come down to get things out of his house. ¹⁸ And a man in the field must not go back to get his clothes. ¹⁹ Woe to pregnant women and nursing mothers in those days! ²⁰ Pray that your escape may not be in winter or on a Sabbath. ²¹ For at that time there will be great tribulation, the kind that hasn't taken place from the beginning of the world until now and never will again! ²² Unless those days were limited, no one wouldⁱ survive.ʲ But those days will be limited because of the elect.

²³ "If anyone tells you then, 'Look, here is the Messiah!' or, 'Over here!' do not believe it! ²⁴ False messiahsᵏ and false prophets will arise and perform great signs and wonders to lead astray, if possible, even the elect. ²⁵ Take

note: I have told you in advance. ²⁶ So if they tell you, 'Look, he's in the wilderness!' don't go out; 'Look, he's in the inner rooms!' do not believe it. ²⁷ For as the lightning comes from the east and flashes as far as the west, so will be the coming of the •Son of Man. ²⁸ Wherever the carcass is, there the vulturesˡ will gather.

The Coming of the Son of Man

²⁹ "Immediately after the tribulation of those days:

The sun will be darkened,
and the moon will not shed its light;
the stars will fall from the sky,
and the celestial powers will be shaken.

³⁰ "Then the sign of the Son of Man will appear in the sky, and then all the peoples of the earthᵐ will mourn;ⁿ and they will see the Son of Man coming on the clouds of heaven with power and great glory. ³¹ He will send out His angels with a loud trumpet, and they will gather His elect from the four winds, from one end of the sky to the other.

The Parable of the Fig Tree

³² "Now learn this parable from the fig tree: As soon as its branch becomes tender and sprouts leaves, you know that summer is near. ³³ In the same way, when you see all these things, recognizeᵒ that Heᵖ is near—at the door! ³⁴ I assure you: This generation will certainly not pass away until all these things take place. ³⁵ Heaven and earth will pass away, but My words will never pass away.

No One Knows the Day or Hour

³⁶ "Now concerning that day and hour no one knows—neither the angels in heaven, nor the Sonᑫ — except the Father only. ³⁷ As the days of Noah were, so the coming of the Son of Man will be. ³⁸ For in those days before the flood they were eating and drinking, marrying and giving in marriage, until the day Noah boarded the ark. ³⁹ They didn't knowʳ until the flood

---

ᵃ**24:7** Other mss add *epidemics* ᵇ**24:9** Or *tribulation,* or *distress* ᶜ**24:13** Or *be saved* ᵈ**24:14** Or *in all the inhabited earth* ᵉ**24:15** Or *abomination of desolation,* or *desolating sacrilege* ᶠ**24:15** Dn 9:27 ᵍ**24:15** These are, most likely, Matthew's words to his readers. ʰ**24:17** Or *roof* ⁱ**24:22** Lit *short, all flesh would not* ʲ**24:22** Or *be saved* or *delivered* ᵏ**24:24** Or *False christs* ˡ**24:28** Or *eagles* ᵐ**24:30** Or *all the tribes of the land* ⁿ**24:30** Lit *will beat;* = beat their breasts ᵒ**24:33** Or *things, you know* ᵖ**24:33** Or *it;* = summer ᑫ**24:36** Other mss omit *nor the Son* ʳ**24:39** They didn't know the day and hour of the coming judgment

---

24:9-13 hand you over. The focus shifts from the woes experienced by people in general to those Christians will face. Many will fall away, but Jesus calls for faithfulness (v. 13).

24:14 This good news. Despite the persecution, the mission of Jesus' disciples is to preach the Gospel and make disciples of all nations (28:18-20).

24:15 the abomination that causes desolation. This phrase (from Dan. 9:27; 11:31; 12:11) refers to an event so awful that Jews will flee from the temple in horror. Such an event occurred in 168 B.C. when Antiochus Epiphanes, a Syrian king, set up an altar to Zeus in the temple. Jesus warns that when that type of desecration occurs again, the fall of Jerusalem would be imminent (2 Thess. 2:1-4). Luke's version includes armies surrounding

Jerusalem as a further sign (Luke 21:20).

24:21 great tribulation. The destruction of Jerusalem in 70 A.D. was an unparalleled disaster for Israel. Some consider this the fulfillment of Jesus' words. Others are still looking for the completion of this prophecy.

24:22 the elect. These are the people God has called into His kingdom. They are akin to the survivors of God's wrath spoken of in Isaiah 1:9 and 4:2-4.

24:24 great signs and wonders. Miracles in themselves are no proof of a person's divine authority. Pharaoh's magicians in Egypt were able to imitate many of the miracles performed by Moses (Ex. 7:20-22).

24:30 the sign of the Son of Man. Jesus uses common military imagery to describe His coming. A "sign" was a banner, flag, or

standard under which an army would march. Isaiah 11:10 compares the Messiah to a banner that will be raised as a rallying point for all God's people.

24:31 a loud trumpet. Trumpets were used to communicate orders to the army. Isaiah 27:13 uses the image of a trumpet blast to describe how God's people will be gathered together when God comes to bring judgment upon their enemies.

24:32 parable from the fig tree. They knew that the fig tree only got its leaves in late spring. When the leaves came it was a sure sign that summer was near.

24:33 these things. Jesus evidently refers to those things that will occur prior to the fall of Jerusalem, and as a possible foreshadowing of things to come prior to the final judgment (vv. 4-15).

came and swept them all away. So this is the way the coming of the Son of Man will be: ⁴⁰ Then two men will be in the field: one will be taken and one left. ⁴¹ Two women will be grinding at the mill: one will be taken and one left. ⁴² Therefore be alert, since you don't know what day[a] your Lord is coming. ⁴³ But know this: If the homeowner had known what time[b] the thief was coming, he would have stayed alert and not let his house be broken into. ⁴⁴ This is why you also must be ready, because the Son of Man is coming at an hour you do not expect.

Faithful Service to the Messiah

⁴⁵ "Who then is a faithful and sensible slave, whom his master has put in charge of his household, to give them food at the proper time? ⁴⁶ That slave whose master finds him working when he comes will be rewarded. ⁴⁷ I assure you: He will put him in charge of all his possessions. ⁴⁸ But if that wicked slave says in his heart, 'My master is delayed,' ⁴⁹ and starts to beat his fellow slaves, and eats and drinks with drunkards, ⁵⁰ that slave's master will come on a day he does not expect and at an hour he does not know. ⁵¹ He will cut him to pieces[c] and assign him a place with the hypocrites. In that place there will be weeping and gnashing of teeth.

The Parable of the 10 Virgins

25 "Then the kingdom of heaven will be like 10 virgins[d] who took their lamps and went out to meet the groom. ² Five of them were foolish and five were sensible. ³ When the foolish took their lamps, they didn't take oil with them. ⁴ But the sensible ones took oil in their flasks with their lamps. ⁵ Since the groom was delayed, they all became drowsy and fell asleep.

⁶ "In the middle of the night there was a shout: 'Here's the groom! Come out to meet him.'

⁷ "Then all those virgins got up and trimmed their lamps. ⁸ But the foolish ones said to the sensible ones, 'Give us some of your oil, because our lamps are going out.'

⁹ "The sensible ones answered, 'No, there won't be enough for us and for you. Go instead to those who sell, and buy oil for yourselves.'

¹⁰ "When they had gone to buy some, the groom arrived. Then those who were ready went in with him to the wedding banquet, and the door was shut.

¹¹ "Later the rest of the virgins also came and said, 'Master, master, open up for us!'

¹² "But he replied, '•I assure you: I do not know you!'

¹³ "Therefore be alert, because you don't know either the day or the hour.[e]

Be Prepared

1. What happened the last time your electricity went off? How prepared were you?

Matthew 25:1-13

2. Why does Jesus describe five of these girls as foolish? What did they do that was foolish?

3. What would you call the refusal of the five girls in this parable to share their oil: Wise? Selfish? Fair? Unfair?

4. What is the meaning of this parable? What will happen to those people who are not prepared when Jesus returns?

5. If you knew Jesus would return next week, how would you live your life differently?

The Parable of the Talents

¹⁴ "For it is just like a man going on a journey. He called his own •slaves and turned over his possessions to them. ¹⁵ To one he gave five talents;[f] to another, two; and to another, one—to each according to his own ability. Then he went on a journey. Immediately ¹⁶ the man

---

[a]**24:42** Other mss read *hour*; = *time*   [b]**24:43** Lit *watch*; a division of the night in ancient times   [c]**24:51** Lit *him in two*   [d]**25:1** Or *bridesmaids*
[e]**25:13** Other mss add *in which the Son of Man is coming.*   [f]**25:15** Worth a very large sum of money; a talent = 6,000 •denarii

---

24:45-51 faithful and sensible slave. When the master was away, one slave would be appointed as the head of the household. If he abused this position for his own indulgence, the sudden appearance of his master would bring judgment.

25:1 10 virgins. There is no special meaning here to the numbers ten or five. They simply reflect two categories of people. **took their lamps.** Weddings typically occurred at night. The lamps, probably small earthen jars with a wick inserted to draw the oil used as fuel, would be held up on poles to brighten the way for the procession. **to meet the groom.** Prior to a wedding, the groom would go to the bride's home and lead her in a procession to his house where the wedding took place. These 10 women were probably either at the bride's house or somewhere along the

processional route waiting for the groom to come.

25:6 In the middle of the night. This emphasizes the unexpected delay of the groom, since this would have been long after most people would have expected him to come. **Come out to meet him.** People would gather around the groom to escort him to the bride's home and then back to the actual site of the wedding. The unexpected arrival of the groom, the shout of proclamation, and the people coming out to meet him all echo themes of the return of Christ as described in 1 Thessalonians 4:16-17.

25:8 our lamps are going out. Once the time for the procession arrived, the foolish women realized they were short on oil.

25:9 No. The refusal to share was not selfish,

but simply prudent. They carried only enough for themselves. This aspect of the story is thought to show that each person needs his or her own relationship with the Lord; such a relationship cannot be obtained by simply being around those who demonstrate faith. **Go instead to those who sell.** Since it is so late, it would be difficult to find a shopkeeper willing to open shop and sell them oil. Likewise, at the time of the Lord's return, it is too late to try to make up for one's lack of preparation.

25:15 talents. Originally this was a unit of weight. However, it was also used as the highest denomination of coinage. It would take a laborer almost 20 years to earn the equivalent of one talent.

25:16 earned five more. High interest rates in that time could make a thousand percent

who had received five talents went, put them to work, and earned five more. ¹⁷ In the same way the man with two earned two more. ¹⁸ But the man who had received one talent went off, dug a hole in the ground, and hid his master's money.

Making a Profit

1. When you were little, did you receive an allowance? How much? How did you usually spend it?

Matthew 25:14-30

2. In this parable, a "talent" is money. Why does the master praise those who earned him money, and condemn the guy who buried his?

3. Why was the master so hard on the slave with one talent? After all, he didn't steal or lose it. What principle is Jesus teaching about how we use what we are given for His service?

4. The master was looking for a profit on his investments. How are you making a "profit" for the kingdom of heaven?

5. What areas in your life are you "burying," rather than using for God?

¹⁹ "After a long time the master of those •slaves came and settled accounts with them. ²⁰ The man who had received five talents approached, presented five more talents, and said, 'Master, you gave me five talents. Look, I've earned five more talents.'

²¹ "His master said to him, 'Well done, good and faithful •slave! You were faithful over a few things; I will put you in charge of many things. Share your master's joy!'

²² "Then the man with two talents also approached. He said, 'Master, you gave me two talents. Look, I've earned two more talents.'

²³ "His master said to him, 'Well done, good and faithful •slave! You were faithful over a few things; I will put you in charge of many things. Share your master's joy!'

²⁴ "Then the man who had received one talent also approached and said, 'Master, I know you. You're a difficult man, reaping where you haven't sown and gathering where you haven't scattered seed. ²⁵ So I was afraid and went off and hid your talent in the ground. Look, you have what is yours.'

²⁶ "But his master replied to him, 'You evil, lazy •slave! If you knew that I reap where I haven't sown and gather where I haven't scattered, ²⁷ then^a you should have deposited my money with the bankers. And when I returned I would have received my money^b back with interest.

²⁸ " 'So take the talent from him and give it to the one who has 10 talents. ²⁹ For to everyone who has, more will be given, and he will have more than enough. But from the one who does not have, even what he has will be taken away from him. ³⁰ And throw this good-for-nothing slave into the outer darkness. In that place there will be weeping and gnashing of teeth.'

The Sheep and the Goats

³¹ "When the •Son of Man comes in His glory, and all the angels^c with Him, then He will sit on the throne of His glory. ³² All the nations^d will be gathered before Him, and He will separate them one from another, just as a shepherd separates the sheep from the goats. ³³ He will put the sheep on His right, and the goats on the left. ³⁴ Then the King will say to those on His right, 'Come, you who are blessed by My Father, inherit the kingdom prepared for you from the foundation of the world.

³⁵ For I was hungry
and you gave Me something to eat;
I was thirsty
and you gave Me something to drink;
I was a stranger and you took Me in;
³⁶ I was naked and you clothed Me;

---

^a**25:26–27** Or *So you knew . . . scattered? Then* (as a question) ^b**25:27** Lit *received what is mine* ^c**25:31** Other mss read *holy angels* ^d**25:32** Or *the Gentiles*

---

return possible (though undoubtedly difficult).

25:19 After a long time. The indefinite time reference hints that Christ's own return may be far off. After Jesus ascended to heaven, much of the church was expecting His early return (Heb. 10:37; 1 Peter 4:7; Rev. 1:3). When this did not happen, they had to be taught how to wait. Parables such as this helped, as did teachings (1 Thess. 4:13-18; 2 Peter 3:3-10).

25:21 Share your master's joy! The servants are not only given more responsibility; they are invited into a new relationship with the master. No longer simply servants, they now enjoy his friendship and respect. Jesus spoke of this same change in relationship in John 15:15 when He told the disciples, "I do not call you slaves anymore … I have called

you friends."

25:24 a difficult man. Literally, this is "exacting." He was generous in his original entrustment of his property to his servants. He was generous to the first and second servants upon his return. It would raise the question in the listeners' minds whether the problem was with the third servant's perceptions.

25:25 So I was afraid. The servant implies that his lack of having anything to show for having been entrusted with the talent is really the fault of the master: he expects too much, and he is too frightening.

25:32 All the nations. This is a universal, worldwide judgment. All people will be present at this judgment scene. **separates the sheep from the goats.** These animals

grazed in common herds during the day. At night, however, they were separated because the goats needed to be in shelters to be protected from the elements.

25:34 prepared for you from the foundation of the world. Contrast this with the punishment of the wicked in the eternal fire "prepared for the Devil and his angels" (v. 41).

25:36 in prison. Probably in view are those (like John the Baptist) who were in prison because they resisted the government out of fidelity to God. Visiting such a prisoner would put the visitor at risk since he or she might be identified as a sympathizer.

25:41 the eternal fire. The idea of hell, a place of eternal punishment by fire, reflects Israel's experience with the valley of Gehenna, a ra-

I was sick and you took care of Me;
I was in prison and you visited Me.'

37 "Then the righteous will answer Him, 'Lord, when did we see You hungry and feed You, or thirsty and give You something to drink? 38 When did we see You a stranger and take You in, or without clothes and clothe You? 39 When did we see You sick, or in prison, and visit You?'

40 "And the King will answer them, 'I assure you: Whatever you did for one of the least of these brothers of Mine, you did for Me.' 41 Then He will also say to those on the left, 'Depart from Me, you who are cursed, into the eternal fire prepared for the Devil and his angels!

Sheep and Goats

1. Have you ever been stopped by someone begging in the street? What did you do?

Matthew 25:31-46

2. Who will stand before God to be judged? What will happen after the judgment? Who will go to heaven, and who will go to hell?

3. What principle is Jesus teaching in this passage?

4. Who are "the least of these" that Jesus refers to?

5. When was the last time you did something for someone hungry, alone, poor, sick, or imprisoned?

6. What can your group can do to help someone in need?

42 For I was hungry
    and you gave Me nothing to eat;
    I was thirsty

and you gave Me nothing to drink;
43 I was a stranger
    and you didn't take Me in;
    I was naked
    and you didn't clothe Me,
    sick and in prison
    and you didn't take care of Me.'

44 "Then they too will answer, 'Lord, when did we see You hungry, or thirsty, or a stranger, or without clothes, or sick, or in prison, and not help You?'

45 "Then He will answer them, 'I assure you: Whatever you did not do for one of the least of these, you did not do for Me either.'

46 "And they will go away into eternal punishment, but the righteous into eternal life."

The Plot to Kill Jesus

26 When Jesus had finished saying all this, He told His disciples, 2 "You know[a] that the •Passover takes place after two days, and the •Son of Man will be handed over to be crucified."

3 Then the •chief priests[b] and the elders of the people assembled in the palace of the high priest, who was called Caiaphas, 4 and they conspired to arrest Jesus in a treacherous way and kill Him. 5 "Not during the festival," they said, "so there won't be rioting among the people."

The Anointing at Bethany

6 While Jesus was in Bethany at the house of Simon, a man who had a serious skin disease, 7 a woman approached Him with an alabaster jar of very expensive fragrant oil. She poured it on His head as He was reclining at the table. 8 When the disciples saw it, they were indignant. "Why this waste?" they asked. 9 "This might have been sold for a great deal and given to the poor."

10 But Jesus, aware of this, said to them, "Why are you bothering this woman? She has done a noble thing for Me. 11 You always have the poor with you, but you do not always have Me. 12 By pouring this fragrant oil on My body, she has prepared Me for burial. 13 •I assure you: Wherever this gospel is proclaimed in the whole

---

a 26:2 Or *Know* (as a command)   b 26:3 Other mss add *and the scribes*

---

vine outside Jerusalem where children were once sacrificed to the god Molech (1 Kings 11:7). Gehenna became a symbol for the place of punishment and spiritual death. **prepared for the Devil and his angels!** Satan, the Devil, led a rebellion of angels against God, and they have all been condemned for it (2 Peter 2:4; Rev. 19:20; 20:10).

25:44 Lord, when did we see You? With this teaching Jesus condemned those who look past the suffering of the world as they seek a detached religiosity. The New Testament is consistent in saying that love of God and love of people, especially people who are in need, must go together.

25:45 Whatever you did not do. It is not enough simply to avoid doing bad things— people will be judged also for the good things they neglect to do.

26:2 the Passover. This feast was a celebration of God's deliverance of Israel from Egypt (Ex. 12).

26:3 the high priest. This was the religious and civic head of the Jews.

26:5 Not during the festival. During Passover, Jerusalem's population rose from 50,000 to 250,000. Jesus' popularity with the crowds meant He could not be arrested publicly for fear that this might spark a riot that would lead to harsh Roman repression.

26:7 a woman approached Him. A woman would not be present at a meal like this except to serve. Her entrance would have been thought scandalous. **Poured it on His head.** Typically, this perfume was used very sparingly and only for special occasions. This was a lavish gesture indicating the high regard this woman had for Jesus. **reclining.**

People feasted while lying on low couches arranged around a table.

26:15 30 pieces of silver. This was not a very large amount, but aligns with the prophecy in Zechariah 11:12.

26:17 On the first day of Unleavened Bread. This feast did not officially start until the day after Passover. However, in the first century the day on which the lambs were sacrificed was sometimes referred to as the first day of the Feast of Unleavened Bread.

26:20 When evening came. The Passover could be eaten only after sunset.

26:23 dipped his hand with Me in the bowl. To share a meal was a sign of friendship, making the betrayal even more scandalous.

world, what this woman has done will also be told in memory of her."

[14] Then one of the Twelve—the man called Judas Iscariot—went to the chief priests [15] and said, "What are you willing to give me if I hand Him over to you?" So they weighed out 30 pieces of silver for him. [16] And from that time he started looking for a good opportunity to betray Him.

Betrayal at the Passover

[17] On the first day of •Unleavened Bread the disciples came to Jesus and asked, "Where do You want us to prepare the Passover so You may eat it?"

[18] "Go into the city to a certain man," He said, "and tell him, 'The Teacher says: My time is near; I am celebrating the Passover at your place[a] with My disciples. ' " [19] So the disciples did as Jesus had directed them and prepared the Passover. [20] When evening came, He was reclining at the table with the Twelve. [21] While they were eating, He said, "I assure you: One of you will betray Me."

[22] Deeply distressed, each one began to say to Him, "Surely not I, Lord?"

[23] He replied, "The one who dipped his hand with Me in the bowl—he will betray Me. [24] The Son of Man will go just as it is written about Him, but woe to that man by whom the Son of Man is betrayed! It would have been better for that man if he had not been born." [25] Then Judas, His betrayer, replied, "Surely not I, •Rabbi?"

"You have said it," He told him.

The First Lord's Supper

[26] As they were eating, Jesus took bread, blessed and broke it, gave it to the disciples, and said, "Take and eat it; this is My body." [27] Then He took a cup, and after giving thanks, He gave it to them and said, "Drink from it, all of you. [28] For this is My blood ⌊that establishes⌋ the covenant;[b] it is shed for many for the forgiveness of

sins. [29] But I tell you, from this moment I will not drink of this fruit of the vine until that day when I drink it in a new way[c] in My Father's kingdom with you." [30] After singing psalms,[d] they went out to the •Mount of Olives.

Peter's Denial Predicted

[31] Then Jesus said to them, "Tonight all of you will run away[e] because of Me, for it is written:

> I will strike the shepherd,
> and the sheep of the flock will be scattered.[f]

[32] But after I have been resurrected, I will go ahead of you to Galilee."

[33] Peter told Him, "Even if everyone runs away because of You, I will never run away!"

[34] "I assure you," Jesus said to him, "tonight—before the rooster crows, you will deny Me three times!"

[35] "Even if I have to die with You," Peter told Him, "I will never deny You!" And all the disciples said the same thing.

The Prayer in the Garden

[36] Then Jesus came with them to a place called Gethsemane,[g] and He told the disciples, "Sit here while I go over there and pray." [37] Taking along Peter and the two sons of Zebedee, He began to be sorrowful and deeply distressed. [38] Then He said to them, "My soul is swallowed up in sorrow[h]—to the point of death.[i] Remain here and stay awake with Me." [39] Going a little farther,[j] He fell facedown and prayed, "My Father! If it is possible, let this cup pass from Me. Yet not as I will, but as You will."

[40] Then He came to the disciples and found them sleeping. He asked Peter, "So, couldn't you[k] stay awake with Me one hour? [41] Stay awake and pray, so that you won't enter into temptation. The spirit is willing, but the flesh is weak."

[42] Again, a second time, He went away and prayed, "My Father, if this[l] cannot pass[m] unless I drink it, Your

---

[a]26:18 Lit *Passover with you*   [b]26:28 Other mss read *new covenant*   [c]26:29 Or *drink new wine*; lit *drink it new*   [d]26:30 Pss 113–118 were sung during and after the Passover meal.   [e]26:31 Or *stumble*   [f]26:31 Zch 13:7   [g]26:36 A garden east of Jerusalem at the base of the Mount of Olives; *Gethsemane* = olive oil press   [h]26:38 Or *I am deeply grieved*, or *I am overwhelmed by sorrow*; Ps 42:6,11; 43:5   [i]26:38 Lit *unto death*   [j]26:39 Other mss read *Drawing nearer*   [k]26:40 *You* = all 3 disciples because the verb in Gk is pl   [l]26:42 Other mss add *cup*   [m]26:42 Other mss add *from Me*

26:24 as it is written about Him. Passages such as Isaiah 53:1-6 point to the suffering of God's chosen servant.

26:26 this is My body. Jesus introduces a new meaning for the Passover bread. While it used to represent God's provision of food for His people while they wandered in the desert after the Exodus, now it is to represent Jesus' body that was brutally treated and nailed to the cross, later to be remembered in the bread at Communion.

26:27 cup. Jesus relates the Passover cup of red wine to the renewal of the covenant of God with His people by His sacrificial death.

26:28 covenant. This New Covenant is based on the promise of Jeremiah 31:31-34 that one day God would initiate a covenant which would result in a deep, inner

change in people's character and in the forgiveness of sin. This covenant is dependent upon Jesus' sacrificial death, rather than on human effort.

26:29 I will not drink. This may mean that Jesus chose to abstain from the fourth Passover cup, which was passed around at the close of the meal, indicating that the meal will only be consummated when the kingdom comes in its fullness.

26:34 before the rooster crows. The Romans called the watch from midnight to 3 a.m. "cock crow."

26:36 Gethsemane. This was an olive orchard in an estate at the foot of the Mount of Olives just outside the eastern wall of Jerusalem. The name literally means "an oil press" (for making olive oil).

26:39 prayed. He would have prayed aloud, as was customary for people at the time, so the disciples could hear His prayer as long as they were awake. **My Father.** This was not a title for God that was used in prayer in the first century. It expressed an intimacy that would have been considered inappropriate. **this cup.** In the Old Testament, drinking a cup of bitter wine was often used as a symbol for experiencing God's judgment (Ps. 75:8; Isa. 51:17-22).

26:41 The spirit ... the flesh. Probably as in Psalm 51:12, the spirit is the human spirit energized by God. The problem is that the disciples allowed their physical condition to dictate their response to an impending spiritual crisis.

26:50 arrested Him. No charge is given. Perhaps it was blasphemy (9:3), violation of the Sabbath (12:2,10,14), or the practice of

will be done." ⁴³ And He came again and found them sleeping, because they could not keep their eyes open.^a

⁴⁴ After leaving them, He went away again and prayed a third time, saying the same thing once more. ⁴⁵ Then He came to the disciples and said to them, "Are you still sleeping and resting?^b Look, the time is near. The Son of Man is being betrayed into the hands of sinners. ⁴⁶ Get up; let's go! See—My betrayer is near."

The Judas Kiss

⁴⁷ While He was still speaking, Judas, one of the Twelve, suddenly arrived. A large mob, with swords and clubs, was with him from the chief priests and elders of the people. ⁴⁸ His betrayer had given them a sign: "The One I kiss, He's the One; arrest Him!" ⁴⁹ So he went right up to Jesus and said, "Greetings, Rabbi!"—and kissed Him.

Betrayed by a Kiss

1. What is the closest you have come to getting arrested? What happened? Were you guilty?

Matthew 26:47-56

2. Why is Jesus being arrested here? What has He done to deserve it?

3. Why does Judas betray Jesus by kissing him? How does Jesus respond to that betrayal?

4. Why does Jesus insist that His disciples not fight back? What had to be "fulfilled" in Jesus' death?

5. How should we respond when we are betrayed by someone close to us? Why?

6. Why did Jesus' disciples run away? With that in mind, who should we turn to in times of trials?

⁵⁰ "Friend," Jesus asked him, "why have you come?"^c

Then they came up, took hold of Jesus, and arrested Him. ⁵¹ At that moment one of those with Jesus reached out his hand and drew his sword. He struck the high priest's slave and cut off his ear.

⁵² Then Jesus told him, "Put your sword back in place because all who take up a sword will perish by a sword. ⁵³ Or do you think that I cannot call on My Father, and He will provide Me at once with more than 12 legions^d of angels? ⁵⁴ How, then, would the Scriptures be fulfilled that say it must happen this way?"

⁵⁵ At that time Jesus said to the crowds, "Have you come out with swords and clubs, as if I were a criminal,^e to capture Me? Every day I used to sit, teaching in the •temple complex, and you didn't arrest Me. ⁵⁶ But all this has happened so that the prophetic Scriptures^f would be fulfilled." Then all the disciples deserted Him and ran away.

Jesus Faces the Sanhedrin

⁵⁷ Those who had arrested Jesus led Him away to Caiaphas the high priest, where the •scribes and the elders had convened. ⁵⁸ Meanwhile, Peter was following Him at a distance right to the high priest's courtyard.^g He went in and was sitting with the temple police^h to see the outcome.ⁱ

⁵⁹ The chief priests and the whole •Sanhedrin were looking for false testimony against Jesus so they could put Him to death. ⁶⁰ But they could not find any, even though many false witnesses came forward.^j Finally, two^k who came forward ⁶¹ stated, "This man said, 'I can demolish God's sanctuary and rebuild it in three days.'"

⁶² The high priest then stood up and said to Him, "Don't You have an answer to what these men are testifying against You?" ⁶³ But Jesus kept silent. Then the high priest said to Him, "By the living God I place You under oath: tell us if You are the •Messiah, the Son of God!"

---

^a**26:43** Lit *because their eyes were weighed down* ^b**26:45** Or *Sleep on now and take your rest.* ^c**26:50** Or *Jesus told him, "do what you have come for."* (as a statement) ^d**26:53** A Roman legion contained up to 6,000 soldiers. ^e**26:55** Lit *as against a criminal* ^f**26:56** Or *the Scriptures of the prophets* ^g**26:58** Or *high priest's palace* ^h**26:58** Or *the officers,* or *the servants* ⁱ**26:58** Lit *end* ^j**26:60** Other mss add *they found none* ^k**26:60** Other mss add *false witnesses*

---

sorcery (9:34).

26:51 one of those with Jesus. According to John's Gospel (John 18:10), this was Peter. **his sword.** That Peter should have a sword is not unusual. Travelers carried them as protection against robbers. **cut off his ear.** Why he was not seized for this act of aggression is unknown. Luke adds the detail that Jesus immediately healed the man (Luke 22:51).

26:53 12 legions of angels. If force were to be used to establish God's kingdom, Jesus would not be relying on the talents of 12 untrained men to do the job! Instead, more than 12 legions of angels could be at His disposal.

26:54 the Scriptures. Jesus is probably referring to Zechariah 13:7: "Strike the shep-

herd, and the sheep will be scattered" (Mark 14:27).

26:57 the high priest. The high priest oversaw the Sanhedrin, which was the highest Jewish court, made up of 71 leaders, both priests and laymen.

26:59 false testimony. To convict someone of a capital crime required the unanimous testimony of at least two witnesses (Deut. 19:15).

26:61 I can demolish God's sanctuary and rebuild it in three days. Although Matthew does not record it, John's Gospel puts a statement much like this on the lips of Jesus (John 2:19). However, Jesus did not say He would destroy the temple; simply that it would one day be destroyed. In addition, He was referring to the temple of His *body* being

destroyed (John 2:21) and being restored after three days, which was very different from how it was understood here.

26:63-64 the Messiah ... the Son of God ... the Son of Man. These are the three main titles that reveal who Jesus is. The time for secrecy is past. He is the Messiah, God's royal King. Jesus' statement (v. 64) is a combination of Psalm 110:1 and Daniel 7:13-14, passages with strong messianic implications.

26:64 You have said it. Jesus uses an ambiguous statement that places the responsibility of affirming it on the questioner. **seated at the right hand.** To sit at the right hand of a sovereign was to be in a place of honor and power.

26:65 tore his robes. By tearing his clothes,

64 "You have said it,"a Jesus told him. "But I tell you, in the futureb you will see **the Son of Man seated at the right hand** of the Power and **coming on the clouds of heaven.**"c

65 Then the high priest tore his robes and said, "He has blasphemed! Why do we still need witnesses? Look, now you've heard the blasphemy! 66 What is your decision?"d

They answered, "He deserves death!" 67 Then they spit in His face and beat Him; others slapped Him 68 and said, "Prophesy to us, Messiah! Who hit You?"

Peter Denies His Lord

69 Now Peter was sitting outside in the courtyard. A servant approached him and she said, "You were with Jesus the Galilean too."

70 But he denied it in front of everyone: "I don't know what you're talking about!"

71 When he had gone out to the gateway, another woman saw him and told those who were there, "This man was with Jesus the •Nazarene!"

72 And again he denied it with an oath, "I don't know the man!"

73 After a little while those standing there approached and said to Peter, "You certainly are one of them, since even your accente gives you away."

74 Then he started to cursef and to swear with an oath, "I do not know the man!" Immediately a rooster crowed, 75 and Peter remembered the words Jesus had spoken, "Before the rooster crows, you will deny Me three times." And he went outside and wept bitterly.

Jesus Handed Over to Pilate

27 When daybreak came, all the •chief priests and the elders of the people plotted against Jesus to put Him to death. 2 After tying Him up, they led Him away and handed Him over to •Pilate,g the governor.

Judas Hangs Himself

3 Then Judas, His betrayer, seeing that He had been condemned, was full of remorse and returned the 30 pieces of silver to the chief priests and elders. 4 "I have sinned by betraying innocent blood," he said.

"What's that to us?" they said. "See to it yourself!"

5 So he threw the silver into the sanctuary and departed. Then he went and hanged himself.

6 The chief priests took the silver and said, "It's not lawful to put it into the temple treasury,h since it is blood money."i 7 So they conferred together and bought the potter's field with it as a burial place for foreigners. 8 Therefore that field has been called "Blood Field" to this day. 9 Then what was spoken through the prophet Jeremiah was fulfilled:

> They took the 30 pieces of silver, the price of Him whose price was set by the sons of Israel, 10 and they gave them for the potter's field, as the Lord directed me.j

Jesus Faces the Governor

11 Now Jesus stood before the governor. "Are You the King of the Jews?" the governor asked Him.

Jesus answered, "You have said it."k 12 And while He was being accused by the chief priests and elders, He didn't answer.

13 Then Pilate said to Him, "Don't You hear how much they are testifying against You?" 14 But He didn't answer him on even one charge, so that the governor was greatly amazed.

Jesus or Barabbas

15 At the festival the governor's custom was to release to the crowd a prisoner they wanted. 16 At that time they had a notorious prisoner called Barabbas.l 17 So when they had gathered together, Pilate said to them, "Who is it you want me to release for you—Barabbas,l or Jesus who is called •Messiah?" 18 For he knew they had handed Him over because of envy.

19 While he was sitting on the judge's bench, his wife sent word to him, "Have nothing to do with that righteous man, for today I've suffered terribly in a dream because of Him!"

---

a**26:64** Or *That is true,* an affirmative oath; Mt 27:11; Mk 15:2   b**26:64** Lit *you, from now*   c**26:64** Ps 110:1; Dn 7:13   d**26:66** Lit *What does it seem to you?*   e**26:73** Or *speech*   f**26:74** To call down curses on himself if what he said weren't true   g**27:2** Other mss read *Pontius Pilate*   h**27:6** See Mk 7:11 where the same Gk word used here (*Corban*) means a gift (pledged to the temple).   i**27:6** Lit *the price of blood*   j**27:9–10** Jr 32:6–9; Zch 11:12–13   k**27:11** Or *That is true,* an affirmative oath; Mt 26:64; Mk 15:2   l**27:16,17** Other mss read *Jesus Barabbas*

---

the high priest signaled that he was profoundly disturbed by Jesus' statement. **blasphemy.** This is the act of dishonoring or slandering God. Under the Law, its penalty was death by stoning (Lev. 24:10-16).

26:67 spit ... beat ... slapped. These were traditional ways of expressing abhorrence and repudiation for someone (Num. 12:14; Deut. 25:9; Job 30:10; Isa. 50:6). These actions reflected the council's fierce opposition to what Jesus said.

26:68 Prophesy. Mark 14:65 says Jesus was first blindfolded. They are mocking His claim to be the Messiah by taunting Him to name who it was that had struck Him while He was unable to see.

27:1 When daybreak came. The Roman court began at daybreak, which made it necessary for the Sanhedrin to meet in an all-night session. They were anxious to get a quick conviction before the people found out what they had done. **plotted.** Legally, the Sanhedrin had no authority to order the death of Jesus (John 18:31). However, under Roman law, blasphemy was not a capital offense. Consequently, they needed to work out how to present the case to Pilate to ensure Jesus' conviction. Their decision was to charge Him with high treason.

27:2 Pilate. Pontius Pilate was the fifth procurator of Judea. He served from A.D. 26–36. While the Gospels present him as a fair-minded man, pressured by the Sanhedrin to do its bidding, historians of the time called him an "inflexible, merciless, and obstinate" man who was continually ignoring Jewish customs in his harsh leadership.

27:6 It's not lawful. The irony is intense. The priests will not put the money back into the temple treasury since it was defiled by having been used as bounty on a person's life. However, they make no reflection upon the fact that they are the ones who used the money for this purpose.

27:16 Barabbas. Barabbas was a genuine resistance leader who had led an armed insurrection against Rome. It was probably in relationship to this rebellion that he also had committed murder (Luke 23:19).

27:18 For he knew. While Pilate could have simply thrown the charges out of court, John's Gospel hints that the Sanhedrin made a not-too-subtle threat to Pilate that, if he should do so, they would bring charges to Caesar against him for releasing a man who claimed to be a rival king (John 19:12).

20 The chief priests and the elders, however, persuaded the crowds to ask for Barabbas and to execute Jesus. 21 The governor asked them, "Which of the two do you want me to release for you?"

"Barabbas!" they answered.

22 Pilate asked them, "What should I do then with Jesus, who is called Messiah?"

They all answered, "Crucify Him!"[a]

23 Then he said, "Why? What has He done wrong?"

But they kept shouting, "Crucify Him!" all the more.

24 When Pilate saw that he was getting nowhere,[b] but that a riot was starting instead, he took some water, washed his hands in front of the crowd, and said, "I am innocent of this man's blood.[c] See to it yourselves!"

25 All the people answered, "His blood be on us and on our children!" 26 Then he released Barabbas to them. But after having Jesus flogged,[d] he handed Him over to be crucified.

Mocked by the Military

27 Then the governor's soldiers took Jesus into •headquarters and gathered the whole •company around Him. 28 They stripped Him and dressed Him in a scarlet robe. 29 They twisted together a crown of thorns, put it on His head, and placed a reed in His right hand. And they knelt down before Him and mocked Him: "Hail, King of the Jews!" 30 Then they spit at Him, took the reed, and kept hitting Him on the head. 31 When they had mocked Him, they stripped Him of the robe, put His clothes on Him, and led Him away to crucify Him.

Crucified Between Two Criminals

32 As they were going out, they found a Cyrenian man named Simon. They forced this man to carry His cross. 33 When they came to a place called Golgotha (which means Skull Place), 34 they gave Him wine[e] mixed with gall to drink. But when He tasted it, He would not drink it. 35 After crucifying Him they divided His clothes by casting lots.[f] 36 Then they sat down and

A Crown of Thorns

1. Growing up, who were the "bullies" in your life? How did they pick on you? Did you stand up for yourself or someone else who was being bullied?

Matthew 27:26-31

2. Why did the soldiers mock Jesus?
3. What's the truth about Jesus' kingship? Why is it so fitting that His crown be made of thorns?
4. Why did Jesus put up with these things?
5. What was Jesus' response to His torturers (see Luke 23:34)? Is there anybody you need to forgive?
6. How do your sufferings compare to what Jesus went through? How does your response compare with His?

were guarding Him there. 37 Above His head they put up the charge against Him in writing:

> **THIS IS JESUS
> THE KING OF THE JEWS**

38 Then two criminals[g] were crucified with Him, one on the right and one on the left. 39 Those who passed by were yelling insults at[h] Him, shaking their heads 40 and saying, "The One who would demolish the sanctuary and rebuild it in three days, save Yourself! If You are the Son of God, come down from the cross!" 41 In the same way the chief priests, with the •scribes and elders,[i] mocked Him and said, 42 "He saved others, but He cannot save Himself! He is the King of Israel! Let Him[j]

---

a27:22 Lit "Him—be crucified!" b27:24 Lit that it availed nothing c27:24 Other mss read this righteous man's blood d27:26 Roman flogging was done with a whip made of leather strips embedded with pieces of bone or metal that brutally tore the flesh. e27:34 Other mss read sour wine f27:35 Other mss add that what was spoken by the prophet might be fulfilled: "They divided My clothes among them, and for My clothing they cast lots." g27:38 Or revolutionaries h27:39 Lit passed by blasphemed or were blaspheming i27:41 Other mss add and Pharisees j27:42 Other mss read If He . . . Israel, let Him

---

27:24 washed his hands. This was a Jewish custom used as a way to disassociate oneself from a criminal act (Deut. 21:1-9). Since it was not a practice of the Romans, Matthew took special note of this as a way of focusing the responsibility upon the Sanhedrin.

27:26 released Barabbas. The death of Jesus (who is innocent) in the place of Barabbas (who is guilty) is a visual statement on the meaning of substitutionary atonement. **flogged.** This was a terrible punishment. Soldiers would lash a naked and bound prisoner with a leather thong with pieces of bone and lead woven into it. The flesh would be cut to shreds. In itself, this punishment sometimes led to death due to shock and loss of blood.

27:32 Simon. This man was probably a Jew

who had come on a pilgrimage to Jerusalem for the Passover feast. Cyrene was a Greek city on the north shore of Africa.

27:33 Golgotha. This is the Aramaic word for a "skull."

27:34 wine mixed with gall. It was a custom to offer a pain-deadening narcotic to prisoners about to be killed.

27:35 crucifying. Crucifixion was the most feared of all punishments in the first-century world. It was cruel in the extreme and totally degrading. **divided His clothes.** This fulfills the prophecy of the suffering of God's righteous servant in Psalm 22:18.

27:40 If You are the Son of God, come down from the cross! This taunt is reminiscent of the temptations in 4:1-11.

27:46 Eli, Eli. This cry has the exact words of Psalm 22:1. While Jesus was bearing the sins of all people throughout all the ages, God the Father withdrew from Him. He ultimately experiences God's deliverance and is resurrected to life giving all believers new life (Ps. 22:19-31).

27:50 a loud voice. Generally a victim of crucifixion would be exhausted and unconscious at the point of death. While Jesus' cry reveals His agony, it is likely from the description of the strange incidents in verses 51-53 that it is a cry of victory.

27:51 curtain of the sanctuary was split in two. This was likely the curtain in the temple that stood between the people and God in the holy of holies. Only the high priest could go behind the curtain into God's presence. Jesus' death and God's tearing o the curtain

come down now from the cross, and we will believe in Him. [43] He has put His trust in God; let God rescue Him now—if He wants Him![a] For He said, 'I am God's Son.' " [44] In the same way even the criminals who were crucified with Him kept taunting Him.

The Death of Jesus

[45] From noon until three in the afternoon[b] darkness came over the whole land.[c] [46] At about three in the afternoon Jesus cried out with a loud voice, *"Eli, Eli, lemá sabachtháni?"* that is, *"My God, My God, why have You forsaken[d] Me?"*[e]

[47] When some of those standing there heard this, they said, "He's calling for Elijah!"

[48] Immediately one of them ran and got a sponge, filled it with sour wine, fixed it on a reed, and offered Him a drink. [49] But the rest said, "Let's see if Elijah comes to save Him!"

[50] Jesus shouted again with a loud voice and gave up His spirit. [51] Suddenly, the curtain of the sanctuary[f] was split in two from top to bottom; the earth quaked and the rocks were split. [52] The tombs also were opened and many bodies of the saints who had gone to their rest[g] were raised. [53] And they came out of the tombs after His resurrection, entered the holy city, and appeared to many.

[54] When the •centurion and those with him, who were guarding Jesus, saw the earthquake and the things that had happened, they were terrified and said, "This man really was God's Son!"[h]

[55] Many women who had followed Jesus from Galilee and ministered to Him were there, looking on from a distance. [56] Among them were •Mary Magdalene, Mary the mother of James and Joseph, and the mother of Zebedee's sons.

The Burial of Jesus

[57] When it was evening, a rich man from Arimathea named Joseph came, who himself had also become a disciple of Jesus. [58] He approached Pilate and asked for Jesus' body. Then Pilate ordered that it[i] be released. [59] So Joseph took the body, wrapped it in clean, fine linen, [60] and placed it in his new tomb, which he had cut into the rock. He left after rolling a great stone against the entrance of the tomb. [61] Mary Magdalene and the other Mary were seated there, facing the tomb.

The Closely Guarded Tomb

[62] The next day, which followed the preparation day, the chief priests and the •Pharisees gathered before Pilate [63] and said, "Sir, we remember that while this deceiver was still alive, He said, 'After three days I will rise again.' [64] Therefore give orders that the tomb be made secure until the third day. Otherwise, His disciples may come, steal Him, and tell the people, 'He has been raised from the dead.' Then the last deception will be worse than the first."

[65] "You have[j] a guard [of soldiers],"[k] Pilate told them. "Go and make it as secure as you know how." [66] Then they went and made the tomb secure by sealing the stone and setting the guard.[l]

Resurrection Morning

28 After the Sabbath, as the first day of the week was dawning, •Mary Magdalene and the other Mary went to view the tomb. [2] Suddenly there was a violent earthquake, because an angel of the Lord descended from heaven and approached [the tomb]. He rolled back the stone and was sitting on it. [3] His appearance was like lightning, and his robe was as white as snow. [4] The guards were so shaken from fear of him that they became like dead men.

[5] But the angel told the women, "Don't be afraid, because I know you are looking for Jesus who was crucified. [6] He is not here! For He has been resurrected, just as He said. Come and see the place where He lay. [7] Then go quickly and tell His disciples, 'He has been raised from the dead. In fact, He is going ahead of you

[a] **27:43** Or *if He takes pleasure in Him*; Ps 22:8 [b] **27:45** Lit *From the sixth hour to the ninth hour* [c] **27:45** Or *whole earth* [d] **27:46** Or *abandoned* [e] **27:46** Ps 22:1 [f] **27:51** A heavy curtain separated the inner room of the temple from the outer. [g] **27:52** Lit *saints having fallen asleep*; that is, they had died [h] **27:54** Or *the Son of God* [i] **27:58** Other mss read *that the body* [j] **27:65** Or *"Take* [k] **27:65** It is uncertain whether this guard consisted of temple police or Roman soldiers. [l] **27:66** Lit *stone with the guard*

from the top has opened the way for people to freely enter the presence of God (Heb. 10:19-20). **the earth quaked and the rocks were split.** Jewish thought held that at the end of the age the Mount of Olives would split in two and the righteous dead would emerge to live forever. Earthquakes were also seen as signs of God's judgment. They are referred to often in the Old Testament as a metaphor for political or social events that have a major effect upon God's people (Hab. 3:9-10).

27:55 Many women. Mary Magdalene was from the fishing village of Magdala on the west coast of Galilee (Luke 8:2). The other Mary had well-known sons in the early church. Zebedee's wife was probably Salome, the mother of James and John. In contrast to these women, all the male disciples had fled.

27:60 tomb. Isaiah 53:9 said God's servant would be laid to rest in the tomb of a rich man.

27:62 The next day. Jesus died on Friday about 3 p.m. The Sabbath began at 6 p.m., after which no work could be done. Yet it was on this day that the Sanhedrin met with Pilate in violation of its own tradition.

27:66 sealing the stone. This was the insignia of Pilate. It would be a capital offense to remove the stone without Pilate's approval. The seal and the guard represent the most powerful human forces available to keep Jesus' body in the tomb.

28:1 as the day of the first week was dawning. The Sabbath was considered over at 6 p.m. on Saturday. This scene takes place early on Sunday morning. This is why

Christians developed the tradition of worshiping on Sunday instead of on the Sabbath (Saturday).

28:2 earthquake. Earthquakes were often associated with manifestations of God's power (Hab. 3:6).

28:5 Don't be afraid. This is a standard reply of an angel to the people to whom the angel is sent (Dan. 10:12; Luke 1:12,30; 2:10).

28:7 go ... tell. Under Jewish law, women were not considered reliable witnesses. That they were the first to know of Jesus' resurrection was somewhat of an embarrassment to the early followers of Christ (Luke 24:11,22-24). Inclusion of this detail reinforces that this is historically accurate. (They certainly would not have invented the story this way!)

He is Risen!

1. What was the biggest or best surprise you've ever had?

Matthew 28:1-20

2. How would you react if told a dead friend was suddenly alive again?

3. What did Jesus prove beyond any doubt by rising from the dead? What or who has He gained final victory over?

4. How does the resurrection set Jesus apart from all other religious figures, such as Buddha or Confucius or Mohammed?

5. What story did the Romans invent to explain Jesus' resurrection? What stories have people invented in our own lifetime?

6. What does Jesus' resurrection mean to you? Have you received His gift of eternal life?

---

to Galilee; you will see Him there.' Listen, I have told you."

[8] So, departing quickly from the tomb with fear and great joy, they ran to tell His disciples the news. [9] Just then[a] Jesus met them and said, "Good morning!" They came up, took hold of His feet, and worshiped Him. [10] Then Jesus told them, "Do not be afraid. Go and tell My brothers to leave for Galilee, and they will see Me there."

The Soldiers Are Bribed to Lie

[11] As they were on their way, some of the guard came into the city and reported to the •chief priests everything that had happened. [12] After the priests[b] had assembled with the elders and agreed on a plan, they gave the soldiers a large sum of money [13] and told them, "Say this, 'His disciples came during the night and stole Him while we were sleeping.' [14] If this reaches the governor's ears,[c] we will deal with[d] him and keep you out of trouble." [15] So they took the money and did as they were instructed. And this story has been spread among Jewish people to this day.

The Great Commission

[16] The 11 disciples traveled to Galilee, to the mountain where Jesus had directed them. [17] When they saw Him, they worshiped,[e] but some doubted. [18] Then Jesus came near and said to them, "All authority has been given to Me in heaven and on earth. [19] Go, therefore, and make disciples of[f] all nations, baptizing them in the name of the Father and of the Son and of the Holy Spirit, [20] teaching them to observe everything I have commanded you. And remember,[g] I am with you always,[h] to the end of the age."

---

[a]**28:9** Other mss add *as they were on their way to tell the news to His disciples* [b]**28:12** Lit *After they* [c]**28:14** Lit *this is heard by the governor*
[d]**28:14** Lit *will persuade* [e]**28:17** Other mss add *Him* [f]**28:19** Lit *and instruct*, or *and disciple* (as a verb) [g]**28:20** Lit *look* [h]**28:20** Lit *all the days*

28:12 gave the soldiers a large sum of money. The Sanhedrin bought off the guards so that they would not tell what really happened.

28:13 His disciples ... stole Him while we were sleeping. This attempt at "damage control" was weak. The very reason the guards were posted was to keep the disciples from stealing the body and concocting a story about resurrection. It would be hard to believe that the disciples who had stolen Jesus' body—and hence knew that the resurrection was a hoax—would then go on to die for their faith, often in painful ways.

28:14 If this reaches the governor's ears. For a Roman guard to fall asleep on duty was an offense meriting execution.

28:16 to the mountain. Mountains were the places in times past where God revealed Himself in special ways to the leaders of Israel, such as when He revealed Himself to Moses in Exodus 24 and to Elijah in 1 Kings 19.

28:17 some doubted. So stupendous is the resurrection of Jesus that right from the beginning His disciples had difficulty accepting it. When the women reported what had happened at the tomb, the Eleven said that it sounded like nonsense (Luke 24:9-11). After 10 of the disciples (all but Thomas) met the resurrected Jesus and believed (Luke 24:36-48), Thomas still doubted (John 20:24-29).

28:18-20 Jesus came near and said to them. Because all authority in heaven and earth now belongs to Jesus, He sends His disciples to spread His message everywhere with the promise that He Himself is with them to the end of time.

28:18 All authority has been given to Me in heaven and on earth. This is the meaning of the statement "Jesus is Lord." Since there is no power greater than His (Rom. 8:38-39; Phil. 2:9-11; Col. 1:15-20), there is no other loyalty to which His disciples can give their absolute allegiance.

28:20 I am with you always. This is the climactic promise of the New Covenant. The presence of God with His people was always the goal toward which Israel looked under the Old Covenant. In Jesus, that presence is assured through the indwelling of Christ's Spirit (John 14:16-17). **to the end of the age.** This covers all time until the return of Christ when the new heaven and the new earth will be revealed.

MARK

PERSONAL READING PLAN

AUTHOR

In Mark's Gospel, we discover that Mark's full name was John Mark, that his mother's name was Mary, and that their home was used as a meeting place by the disciples. Peter went there directly after his miraculous release from prison (Acts 12:1-17). Consequently, as a young man, Mark was immersed in the life of the newly forming church.

We also learn that Mark was close to Peter as Peter referred to him as "my son Mark" (1 Peter 5:13). Many believe that Mark was Peter's secretary and that his Gospel reflects Peter's view of the events. Writing in A.D. 140, Bishop Papias says: "Mark, having become the interpreter of Peter, wrote down accurately all that he remembered of the things said and done by our Lord, but not, however, in order."

Mark was also closely connected with Paul. Along with his cousin, Barnabas, Mark accompanied the great apostle on the first missionary journey. Mark, for unknown reasons, left the party at Perga when they turned inland to Asia. Because of this, Paul refused to allow Mark to go on the second missionary journey. Thus, Barnabas went with Mark to Cyprus while Paul teamed up with Silas. For years Mark dropped out of sight. Tradition says he founded the church at Alexandria, Egypt. Eventually, Paul and Mark were reconciled and Mark became Paul's companion during Paul's imprisonment in a Roman jail.

DATE

Mark was written sometime between A.D. 50-70, probably in the mid-60s.

THEME

Jesus the Messiah, the Son of God.

HISTORICAL BACKGROUND

The 10 years between A.D. 60 and A.D. 70 when Mark wrote his Gospel were years of persecution for Christians living in Rome. Previously, they were regarded as an exotic religious sect. But after Nero burned Rome in A.D. 64, he blamed the Christians, and an era of persecution began. Nero fed them to the lions in the coliseum and burned them as human torches at his garden parties. Mark directed his Gospel to these Christians, who were dying for Jesus' name,

This was the first written account of Jesus' life. Thus it was, according to William Barclay, "the most important book in the world." Mark's collection of previously unrecorded stories was widely circulated and was used by Matthew and Luke when they wrote their Gospels. In fact, all but 24 verses of Mark's Gospel are found in their accounts.

CHARACTERISTICS

In the shortest of the Gospels, Mark races breathlessly through Jesus' life by linking a

series of short stories. Despite the way Mark hurries through the material, his account is the richest and most vivid in eyewitness detail. For example, when speaking of Jesus blessing the children, Mark alone tells us that Jesus first took them in his arms (Mark 10:13-16).

Mark's Gospel carefully orders the stories, resulting in a skillfully crafted outline. In fact, he tells the story of Jesus in a remarkably sophisticated way considering that Mark could not alter well-known stories, witnessed by many people. He was merely the chronicler of the tradition, not the creator of it. The church would not have used his Gospel if it had been inaccurate. Mark's creativity, under the guidance of the Holy Spirit, came in his sequencing of the stories. As you read through the Gospel, be alert to the significance of the sequencing.

Mark does not place his stories in chronological order as we might expect; instead, he groups his stories thematically. Mark uses several themes, simultaneously. However, it is clear that he has structured his story *geographically*. Jesus' ministry begins to the north in Galilee and then moves down to Jerusalem, where he is finally killed. Mark structures the story in terms of *Jesus' unfolding ministry*: preparation, proclamation, and completion. There is also an unfolding vision of *who Jesus is. Generally*, the first half of the book focuses on the discovery of Jesus as the Messiah, and the second half on the discovery of Jesus as the Son of God. Regarding the *disciples' growing awareness*, they move from experiencing Jesus as an excep-

tional rabbi, to seeing him as a man of power, and then as the healer of hardened hearts. After Caesarea Philippi and their realization that he is the Messiah, they know him as a teacher. In Jerusalem during the final week of his life, they come to realize that he is the Son of God.

PASSAGES FOR TOPICAL GROUP STUDY

PASSAGES FOR GENERAL GROUP STUDY

The Messiah's Herald

1 The beginning of the gospel of Jesus Christ, the Son of God. ² As it is written in Isaiah the prophet:[a]

Look, I am sending My messenger ahead
    of You,
who will prepare Your way.[b]
³ A voice of one crying out in the wilderness:
    "Prepare the way for the Lord;
    make His paths straight!"[c]

⁴ John came baptizing[d] in the wilderness and preaching a baptism of repentance[e] for the forgiveness of sins. ⁵ The whole Judean countryside and all the people of Jerusalem were flocking to him, and they were baptized by him in the Jordan River as they confessed their sins. ⁶ John wore a camel-hair garment with a leather belt around his waist and ate locusts and wild honey. ⁷ He was preaching: "Someone more powerful than I will come after me. I am not worthy to stoop down and untie the strap of His sandals. ⁸ I have baptized you with[f] water, but He will baptize you with[f] the Holy Spirit."

The Baptism of Jesus

⁹ In those days Jesus came from Nazareth in Galilee and was baptized in the Jordan by John. ¹⁰ As soon as He came up out of the water, He saw the heavens being torn open and the Spirit descending to Him like a dove. ¹¹ And a voice came from heaven:

You are My beloved Son;
    I take delight in You![g]

The Temptation of Jesus

¹² Immediately the Spirit drove Him into the wilderness. ¹³ He was in the wilderness 40 days, being tempted by Satan. He was with the wild animals, and the angels began to serve Him.

Ministry in Galilee

¹⁴ After John was arrested, Jesus went to Galilee, preaching the good news[h] [i] of God:[j] ¹⁵ "The time is fulfilled, and the kingdom of God has come near. Repent and believe in the good news!"

The First Disciples

¹⁶ As He was passing along by the Sea of Galilee, He saw Simon and Andrew, Simon's brother. They were casting a net into the sea, since they were fishermen. ¹⁷ "Follow Me," Jesus told them, "and I will make you fish for[k] people!" ¹⁸ Immediately they left their nets and followed Him. ¹⁹ Going on a little farther, He saw James the son of Zebedee and his brother John. They were in their boat mending their nets. ²⁰ Immediately He called them, and they left their father Zebedee in the boat with the hired men and followed Him.

Driving Out an Unclean Spirit

²¹ Then they went into Capernaum, and right away He entered the •synagogue on the Sabbath and began to teach. ²² They were astonished at His teaching because, unlike the •scribes, He was teaching them as one having authority.

²³ Just then a man with an unclean spirit was in their synagogue. He cried out,[l] ²⁴ "What do You have to do with us,[m] Jesus—Nazarene? Have You come to destroy us? I know who You are—the Holy One of God!"

²⁵ But Jesus rebuked him and said, "Be quiet,[n] and come out of him!" ²⁶ And the unclean spirit convulsed him, shouted with a loud voice, and came out of him.

²⁷ Then they were all amazed, so they began to argue with one another, saying, "What is this? A new teaching with authority![o] He commands even the unclean

ᵃ1:2 Other mss read *in the prophets* ᵇ1:2 Other mss add *before You* ᶜ1:2–3 Mal 3:1; Is 40:3 ᵈ1:4 Or *John the Baptist came*, or *John the Baptizer came* ᵉ1:4 Or *a baptism based on repentance* ᶠ1:8 Or *in* ᵍ1:11 Or *In You I am well pleased* ʰ1:14 Other mss add *of the kingdom* ⁱ1:14 Or *gospel* ʲ1:14 Either *from God* or *about God* ᵏ1:17 Lit *you to become fishers of* ˡ1:23 Other mss add to the beginning of v. 24: *"Leave us alone.* ᵐ1:24 Lit *What to us and to You* ⁿ1:25 Or *Be muzzled* ᵒ1:27 Other mss read *What is this? What is this new teaching? For with authority*

1:3 make His paths straight. When a king was planning to visit or pass through a town, a messenger was sent ahead of the royal entourage so that the towns along the way could get things ready for his coming, literally straightening and smoothing the roads. In this context, making straight paths for the Lord implies repentance from sin (v. 15).

1:5 The whole Judean countryside. Mark uses hyperbole to show John's popularity. **all the people of Jerusalem.** It was a difficult 20-mile trip from Jerusalem to where John was baptizing, and yet the crowds came. **the Jordan River.** John's ministry of baptism had a special meaning in this particular river which had an important place in Israel's history. After the exodus from Egypt, it was the miraculous crossing of this river

that brought the people of Israel into the land God promised them (Josh. 3).

1:13 40 days. It is possible that this is a symbolic reference to the 40 years Israel spent in the wilderness. The reason for their experience was unbelief; Jesus voluntarily entered His trial. **wild animals.** For the Christians to whom this letter was written (who were facing wild beasts in the Roman Coliseum), it must have been comforting to know that Jesus had also faced such beasts and was sustained by angels.

1:14 After John was arrested. There is a gap of perhaps a year between the incidents recorded in verses 9-13 and those recorded here. The story of John's imprisonment is told in 6:17-29. **Galilee.** The northern province of Palestine, considered by people from

Jerusalem as a cultural backwater populated by unsophisticated, uneducated country folk who spoke with an accent.

1:23 an unclean spirit. Malignant, supernatural beings that were able to harm and even possess people: these were Satan's legions.

1:25 Be quiet. At the beginning of his ministry, Jesus did not want His identity or power spoken about, probably because people would have misunderstood the meaning of His ministry. **rebuked.** The same word is used in Mark 4:39 when Jesus orders the tumult of the sea and wind to be still. **come out of him!** In Jesus' day there were exorcists who used a combination of religious and magical practices to try to release people. In contrast, Jesus issues a simple word of command which is immediately obeyed.

spirits, and they obey Him." ²⁸ His fame then spread throughout the entire vicinity of Galilee.

Perfect Priorities

1. Are you a morning person or an evening person?

Mark 1:29-39

2. Why did Simon's mother-in-law begin to serve Jesus and His disciples as soon as she was healed (v. 31)?

3. Why did Jesus spend so much time healing people? What response did people have to this (v. 33)?

4. Why did Jesus go off to "a deserted place" by Himself (v. 35)? What does this show of His priorities?

5. How often do you spend time alone with God? How can you make this more of a priority?

Healings at Capernaum

²⁹ As soon as they left the synagogue, they went into Simon and Andrew's house with James and John. ³⁰ Simon's mother-in-law was lying in bed with a fever, and they told Him about her at once. ³¹ So He went to her, took her by the hand, and raised her up. The fever left her,ᵃ and she began to serve them.

³² When evening came, after the sun had set, they began bringing to Him all those who were sick and those who were demon-possessed. ³³ The whole town was assembled at the door, ³⁴ and He healed many who were sick with various diseases and drove out many demons. But He would not permit the demons to speak, because they knew Him.

Preaching in Galilee

³⁵ Very early in the morning, while it was still dark, He got up, went out, and made His way to a deserted place. And He was praying there. ³⁶ Simon and his companions went searching for Him. ³⁷ They found Him and said, "Everyone's looking for You!"

³⁸ And He said to them, "Let's go on to the neighboring villages so that I may preach there too. This is why I have come." ³⁹ So He went into all of Galilee, preaching in their synagogues and driving out demons.

Cleansing a Leper

⁴⁰ Then a man with a serious skin disease came to Him and, on his knees,ᵇ begged Him: "If You are willing, You can make me clean."ᶜ

⁴¹ Moved with compassion, Jesus reached out His hand and touched him. "I am willing," He told him. "Be made clean." ⁴² Immediately the disease left him, and he was healed.ᵈ ⁴³ Then He sternly warned him and sent him away at once, ⁴⁴ telling him, "See that you say nothing to anyone; but go and show yourself to the priest, and offer what Moses prescribed for your cleansing, as a testimony to them." ⁴⁵ Yet he went out and began to proclaim it widely and to spread the news, with the result that Jesus could no longer enter a town openly. But He was out in deserted places, and they would come to Him from everywhere.

The Son of Man Forgives and Heals

2 When He entered Capernaum again after some days, it was reported that He was at home. ² So many people gathered together that there was no more room, not even in the doorway, and He was speaking the message to them. ³ Then they came to Him bringing a paralytic, carried by four men. ⁴ Since they were not able to bring him toᵉ Jesus because of the crowd, they removed the roof above where He was. And when they had broken through, they lowered the stretcher on which the paralytic was lying.

⁵ Seeing their faith, Jesus told the paralytic, "Son, your sins are forgiven."

ᵃ**1:31** Other mss add *at once* ᵇ**1:40** Other mss omit *on his knees* ᶜ**1:40** In these vv., *clean* includes healing, ceremonial purification, return to fellowship with people, and worship in the temple; Lv 14:1–32. ᵈ**1:42** Lit *made clean* ᵉ**2:4** Other mss read *able to get near*

1:40 serious skin disease. No disease was dreaded more than leprosy, since it brought not only physical disfigurement but social banishment. **came to Him.** What the leper did was forbidden by law. The leper should have sought to avoid drawing near Jesus. The rabbis taught that if a leper passed by a clean man, the clean man would not become unclean. However, if the leper stopped, then the clean man would become unclean. **If You are willing.** The leper had no doubt about Jesus' ability. However, since leprosy was considered a sign of God's judgment against a person because of sin, the man was uncertain of Jesus' willingness.

1:41 Moved with compassion. Human suffering evoked a deep, affective response from Jesus. He was not afraid of strong emotions. **touched.** Actually touching a leper was unimaginable to most first-century peo-

ple. From the leper's perspective, the effect of Jesus' touch must have been overwhelming. He had come to think of himself as untouchable and unlovable. This touch affirmed him as a fellow human in spite of his disease.

1:44 offer what Moses prescribed. In Leviticus 14:1-32 the ritual is outlined whereby a leper is declared "clean." Such certification was vital to a leper: it was that person's way back into normal contact with human society.

2:4 removed the roof. The roof of a typical Palestinian house was flat (it was often used for sleeping) and was reached by an outside ladder or stairway. It was constructed of earth and brushwood that was packed between wooden beams set about three feet apart. The roof was easily breached (and

easily repaired). A rather large opening would have been required to lower a man on a mat. While this was going on, with the noise and falling dirt, all attention inside would have been diverted from Jesus' sermon to the ever-growing hole.

2:5 faith. This is the first time in Mark that this word is used. It increasingly becomes the quality Jesus looks for in those to whom He ministers. **your sins are forgiven.** The friends, the man, and the crowd expected a healing; sin was a whole new issue that had not yet been raised by Jesus.

2:6 scribes. Literally, teachers and religious lawyers who interpreted Jewish law.

2:7 blaspheming. Blasphemy is "contempt for God," and under Jewish law its penalty is death (Lev. 24:16). The teachers of the law

6 But some of the •scribes were sitting there, thinking to themselves:[a] 7 "Why does He speak like this? He's blaspheming! Who can forgive sins but God alone?"

Healing Forgiveness

1. When was the last time you had to go to the emergency room? Who took you?
2. Do you have a friend with a disability? How do you help this person?

Mark 2:1-12

3. Why did Jesus forgive the paralyzed man before healing him?
4. What does it show us about Jesus that He could forgive the man's sins?
5. Who are the friends in your life that cared enough to bring you to Jesus? Who do you need to help "carry" to Jesus?

8 Right away Jesus understood in His spirit that they were reasoning like this within themselves and said to them, "Why are you reasoning these things in your hearts?[b] 9 Which is easier: to say to the paralytic, 'Your sins are forgiven,' or to say, 'Get up, pick up your stretcher, and walk'? 10 But so you may know that the •Son of Man has authority on earth to forgive sins," He told the paralytic, 11 "I tell you: get up, pick up your stretcher, and go home."

12 Immediately he got up, picked up the stretcher, and went out in front of everyone. As a result, they were all astounded and gave glory to God, saying, "We have never seen anything like this!"

The Call of Matthew

13 Then Jesus went out again beside the sea. The whole crowd was coming to Him, and He taught them. 14 Then, moving on, He saw Levi the son of Alphaeus sitting at the tax office, and He said to him, "Follow Me!" So he got up and followed Him.

Dining with Sinners

15 While He was reclining at the table in Levi's house, many tax collectors and sinners were also guests[c] with Jesus and His disciples, because there were many who were following Him. 16 When the scribes of the •Pharisees[d] saw that He was eating with sinners and tax collectors, they asked His disciples, "Why does He eat[e] with tax collectors and sinners?"

17 When Jesus heard this, He told them, "Those who are well don't need a doctor, but the sick ⌊do need one⌋. I didn't come to call the righteous, but sinners."

A Question about Fasting

18 Now John's disciples and the Pharisees[f] were fasting. People came and asked Him, "Why do John's disciples and the Pharisees' disciples fast, but Your disciples do not fast?"

19 Jesus said to them, "The wedding guests[g] cannot fast while the groom is with them, can they? As long as they have the groom with them, they cannot fast. 20 But the time[h] will come when the groom is taken away from them, and then they will fast in that day. 21 No one sews a patch of unshrunk cloth on an old garment. Otherwise, the new patch pulls away from the old cloth, and a worse tear is made. 22 And no one puts new wine into old wineskins. Otherwise, the wine will burst the skins, and the wine is lost as well as the skins.[i] But new wine is for fresh wineskins."

Lord of the Sabbath

23 On the Sabbath He was going through the grainfields, and His disciples began to make their way picking some heads of grain. 24 The Pharisees said to Him,

---

[a]**2:6** Or *there, reasoning in their hearts* [b]**2:8** Or *minds* [c]**2:15** Lit *reclining* (at the table) at important meals the custom was to recline on a mat at a low table and lean on the left elbow. [d]**2:16** Other mss read *scribes and Pharisees* [e]**2:16** Other mss add *and drink* [f]**2:18** Other mss read *the disciples of John and of the Pharisees* [g]**2:19** Lit *The sons of the bridal chamber* [h]**2:20** Lit *the days* [i]**2:22** Other mss read *the wine spills out and the skins will be ruined*

---

believed that illness was the direct result of sin (John 9:2), so the sick could not recover until their sin had been forgiven by God.

2:9 Which is easier. Jesus responds to their question (v. 7) in rabbinic fashion: He asks them a question. The answer to His question is obvious. It is far easier to say, "Your sins are for given," than it is to heal the man right then and there. There is no way to verify whether sins have been forgiven, but it is obvious whether a lame man walks or not.

2:10 But so you may know. If Jesus is able to heal the paralytic in terms of their own theology, which linked forgiveness and healing, the scribes would have to admit that the man's sins had been forgiven.

2:14 Levi. Elsewhere he is identified as Matthew (Matt. 9:9), the disciple who wrote one of the Gospels. In his role as a tax collector, Matthew would have been hated by both the religious establishment and the common people.

2:15 reclining at the table. Here speaks of sharing a meal with another, which was a significant event implying acceptance of that person. In this way, Jesus extends His forgiveness (v. 10) to those who were outside orthodox religious life. **tax collectors.** They were hated by the Jews for collecting taxes on behalf of pagan Rome and for growing rich by collecting more than was actually required.

2:20 taken away. An ominous note predicting Jesus' death.

2:22 new wine. New wine continues to ferment. Hence, no one would have poured it into a leather container which was old, dry, and crusty. New wine required new skins which were supple and flexible, able to expand as the wine fermented.

2:23 Sabbath. The seventh day of the week (Saturday) which begins Friday at sunset and ends Saturday at sunset. The fourth Commandment is to rest from all labor on the Sabbath (Ex. 20:8-11). By the first century scores of regulations had evolved which defined what could and could not be done on the Sabbath. **picking some heads of grain.** It was permissible for hungry travelers to pluck and eat grain from a field (Deut. 23:25). The issue is not stealing. What the Pharisees objected to was the "work" this involved.

3:2 they were watching Him closely. Here

"Look, why are they doing what is not lawful on the Sabbath?"

25 He said to them, "Have you never read what David and those who were with him did when he was in need and hungry— 26 how he entered the house of God in the time of Abiathar the high priest and ate the •sacred bread—which is not lawful for anyone to eat except the priests—and also gave some to his companions?" 27 Then He told them, "The Sabbath was made for[a] man and not man for[a] the Sabbath. 28 Therefore the Son of Man is Lord even of the Sabbath."

Remember the What?

1. When you were a kid, what were you not allowed to do on Sunday because it was the "Sabbath"?

Mark 2:23-3:6

2. Why did the Pharisees get angry with the disciples for eating grain from a field? (It was not considered stealing in Jesus' time.)

3. Read Exodus 20:8-11. Is Jesus disobeying Scripture by healing the man? If not, how have the Pharisees misused Scripture to accuse Jesus?

4. How should we "remember to dedicate the Sabbath" today? Are you doing that in your life at present?

The Man with the Paralyzed Hand

3 Now He entered the •synagogue again, and a man was there who had a paralyzed hand. 2 In order to accuse Him, they were watching Him closely to see whether He would heal him on the Sabbath. 3 He told the man with the paralyzed hand, "Stand before us."[b]

4 Then He said to them, "Is it lawful on the Sabbath to do good or to do evil, to save life or to kill?" But they were silent. 5 After looking around at them with anger and sorrow at the hardness of their hearts, He told the man, "Stretch out your hand." So he stretched it out, and his hand was restored. 6 Immediately the •Pharisees went out and started plotting with the •Herodians against Him, how they might destroy Him.

Ministering to the Multitude

7 Jesus departed with His disciples to the sea, and a great multitude followed from Galilee, Judea, 8 Jerusalem, Idumea, beyond the Jordan, and around Tyre and Sidon. The great multitude came to Him because they heard about everything He was doing. 9 Then He told His disciples to have a small boat ready for Him, so the crowd would not crush Him. 10 Since He had healed many, all who had diseases were pressing toward Him to touch Him. 11 Whenever the unclean spirits saw Him, those possessed fell down before Him and cried out, "You are the Son of God!" 12 And He would strongly warn them not to make Him known.

The 12 Apostles

13 Then He went up the mountain and summoned those He wanted, and they came to Him. 14 He also appointed 12—He also named them apostles[c]—to be with Him, to send them out to preach, 15 and to have authority to[d] drive out demons.

16 He appointed the Twelve:[e]

> To Simon, He gave the name Peter;
> 17 and to James the son of Zebedee,
> and to his brother John,
> He gave the name "Boanerges"
> (that is, "Sons of Thunder");
> 18 Andrew;
> Philip and Bartholomew;
> Matthew and Thomas;
> James the son of Alphaeus,
> and Thaddaeus;
> Simon the Zealot,[f]

---

[a]**2:27** Or *because of* [b]**3:3** Lit *Rise up in the middle* [c]**3:14** Other mss omit *He also named them apostles* [d]**3:15** Other mss add *heal diseases, and to* [e]**3:16** Other mss omit *He appointed the Twelve* [f]**3:18** Lit *the Cananaean*

---

the religious leaders were refraining from questioning Jesus. Now they simply watched to see if His actions betrayed a disregard for the law so they might accuse Him. **see whether He would heal him on the Sabbath.** The issue is not healing, but whether Jesus would do so on the Sabbath.

3:5 anger and sorrow. Jesus felt strongly about the injustice of a system that sacrificed the genuine needs of people for religious traditions that had nothing to do with God. **hardness of their hearts.** The Greek word, sometimes translated "stubborn" is also used to describe a gallstone or a tooth. **Stretch out your hand.** Just as He deliberately declared the paralytic's sins forgiven (knowing that this was blasphemy to the teachers of the law), here He deliberately heals on the Sabbath (knowing that this too was anathema to His critics).

3:6 Herodians. A political group made up of influential Jewish sympatizers of King Herod. They were normally despised by the Pharisees, who considered them traitors (for working with Rome) and irreligious (unclean as a result of their association with Gentiles). However, the Pharisees had no power to kill Jesus. Only the civil authority could do this, and hence the collaboration. **how they might destroy Him.** The Pharisees believed Jesus violated the Sabbath by healing on that day, but failed to see that they were violating the Sabbath law by plotting how to kill Him on that day!

3:8 The great multitude came to Him. They came from near (Galilee) and far, from the north (Tyre and Sidon), south (Idumea), and east (the region across the Jordan was called Perea). They came from Jewish and from Gentile regions. They

came from the country regions (Galilee) and from the heart of the nation (Jerusalem).

3:21 they set out. They undertook the 30-mile journey from Nazareth to Capernaum. **to restrain Him.** Their intent was to forcibly take Him home (6:17, the same word is translated "arrested"). **out of His mind.** Literally, "he is beside himself." His family concluded that He was suffering from some sort of ecstatic, religiously- induced mental illness.

3:22 He has Beelzebub in Him! Beelzebub was the Canaanite name for the chief god Baal. The religious leaders equated Beelzebub with Satan. To be possessed by this demon meant to be controlled by him, which is how the teachers of the law explained Jesus' power over demons.

3:29 whoever blasphemes against the

[19] and Judas Iscariot,[a] who also betrayed Him.

Eternal Family Ties

1. What's something you've done that made your family or friends wonder if you were crazy?

Mark 3:20-35

2. Why do you think Jesus' family thought he was "out of His mind" (v. 21)?

3. What did Jesus mean that we need to "tie up the strong man" (v. 27)? Who is that strong man? How do we tie him up?

4. Who did Jesus say are His true brothers and sisters? Are you a true brother or sister of Jesus? How do you know?

A House Divided

[20] Then He went home, and the crowd gathered again so that they were not even able to eat.[b] [21] When His family heard this, they set out to restrain Him, because they said, "He's out of His mind."

[22] The •scribes who had come down from Jerusalem said, "He has •Beelzebul in Him!" and, "He drives out demons by the ruler of the demons!"

[23] So He summoned them and spoke to them in parables: "How can Satan drive out Satan? [24] If a kingdom is divided against itself, that kingdom cannot stand. [25] If a house is divided against itself, that house cannot stand. [26] And if Satan rebels against himself and is divided, he cannot stand but is finished![c]

[27] "On the other hand, no one can enter a strong man's house and rob his possessions unless he first ties up the strong man. Then he will rob his house. [28] •I assure you: People will be forgiven for all sins[d] and whatever blasphemies they may blaspheme. [29] But whoever blasphemes against the Holy Spirit never has forgiveness, but is guilty of an eternal sin"[e] — [30] because they were saying, "He has an unclean spirit."

True Relationships

[31] Then His mother and His brothers came, and standing outside, they sent ⌊word⌋ to Him and called Him. [32] A crowd was sitting around Him and told Him, "Look, Your mother, Your brothers, and Your sisters[f] are outside asking for You."

[33] He replied to them, "Who are My mother and My brothers?" [34] And looking about at those who were sitting in a circle around Him, He said, "Here are My mother and My brothers! [35] Whoever does the will of God is My brother and sister and mother."

The Parable of the Sower

4 Again He began to teach by the sea, and a very large crowd gathered around Him. So He got into a boat on the sea and sat down, while the whole crowd was on the shore facing the sea. [2] He taught them many things in parables, and in His teaching He said to them: [3] "Listen! Consider the sower who went out to sow. [4] As he sowed, this occurred: Some seed fell along the path, and the birds came and ate it up. [5] Other seed fell on rocky ground where it didn't have much soil, and it sprang up right away, since it didn't have deep soil. [6] When the sun came up, it was scorched, and since it didn't have a root, it withered. [7] Other seed fell among thorns, and the thorns came up and choked it, and it didn't produce a crop. [8] Still others fell on good ground and produced a crop that increased 30, 60, and 100 times ⌊what was sown⌋." [9] Then He said, "Anyone who has ears to hear should listen!"

---

[a]3:19 *Iscariot* probably = "a man of Kerioth," a town in Judea.   [b]3:20 Lit *eat bread*, or *eat a meal*   [c]3:26 Lit *but he has an end*   [d]3:28 Lit *All things will be forgiven the sons of men*   [e]3:29 Other mss read *is subject to eternal judgment*   [f]3:32 Other mss omit *and Your sisters*

Holy Spirit never has forgiveness. The first three Gospels (Matt. 12:31-32; Luke 12:10) refer to this concept. In light of the context, the unpardonable sin can be defined as rejecting the power and authority of the Holy Spirit working in Jesus and crediting that authority to Satan. Such a person calls absolute good—the work of the Holy Spirit— absolute evil. No one wanting to repent of sin has committed this sin. No born again person can commit this sin.

3:34-35 My mother and My brothers. Jesus gives a new definition of family. Kinship is not a matter of heredity; it is a matter of spirit—doing God's will. Eventually His family will move from doubt to faith (John 19:25-27; Acts 1:14; 1 Cor. 15:7).

4:1 large crowd. The scene is similar to that described in 3:7-9. This crowd was probably also drawn to Jesus in hopes of seeking healing and exorcism. However, this time Jesus speaks from a boat in order that all of the people might hear Him.

4:2 parables. Parables are comparisons that draw upon common experience in order to teach the realities of God's kingdom. These metaphors or analogies are often presented in story form; they draw upon the known to explain the unknown.

4:3 Listen! Pay attention! There is more to this story than appears at first. **sow.** Farmers would throw seed into the soil by a broad cast method.

4:4 the path. The soil of the pathways was so hard packed that seed could not penetrate the soil to germinate.

4:5 rocky ground. Some soil covered a limestone base which was a few inches beneath the surface. Seed that fell here would germinate but not last, since a proper root system could not develop.

4:7 thorns. In other places, there were the roots of weeds. When the seed grew up, so did the weeds, which invariably stunted the growth of the good seed.

4:8 good ground. Some of the seed did fall where it could germinate, grow, and produce a crop. **30, 60, and 100 times.** The good soil yielded a spectacular crop. While 10 times is an especially good harvest, this is a miracle crop.

4:11 The secret. A secret in the New Testament is something which was previously unknown but has now been revealed to all who will hear. The secret given the disciples is that the kingdom of God is with them. **the kingdom of God.** How God establishes His reign in human affairs is what Jesus' para-

Why Jesus Used Parables

¹⁰ When He was alone with the Twelve, those who were around Him asked Him about the parables. ¹¹ He answered them, "The secret[a] of the kingdom of God has been granted to you, but to those outside, everything comes in parables ¹² so that

> they may look and look,
> yet not perceive;
> they may listen and listen,
> yet not understand;
> otherwise, they might turn back—
> and be forgiven."[b c]

The Parable of the Sower Explained

¹³ Then He said to them: "Do you not understand this parable? How then will you understand any of the parables? ¹⁴ The sower sows the word. ¹⁵ These[d] are the ones along the path where the word is sown: when they hear, immediately Satan comes and takes away the word sown in them.[e] ¹⁶ And these are[f] the ones sown on rocky ground: when they hear the word, immediately they receive it with joy. ¹⁷ But they have no root in themselves; they are short-lived. When affliction or persecution comes because of the word, they immediately stumble. ¹⁸ Others are sown among thorns; these are the ones who hear the word, ¹⁹ but the worries of this age, the seduction[g] of wealth, and the desires for other things enter in and choke the word, and it becomes unfruitful. ²⁰ But the ones sown on good ground are those who hear the word, welcome it, and produce a crop: 30, 60, and 100 times ₁what was sown₁."

Using Your Light

²¹ He also said to them, "Is a lamp brought in to be put under a basket or under a bed? Isn't it to be put on a lampstand? ²² For nothing is concealed except to be revealed, and nothing hidden except to come to light. ²³ If anyone has ears to hear, he should listen!" ²⁴ Then He said to them, "Pay attention to what you hear. By the measure you use,[h] it will be measured and added to you. ²⁵ For to the one who has, it will be given, and from the one who does not have, even what he has will be taken away."

The Parable of the Growing Seed

²⁶ "The kingdom of God is like this," He said. "A man scatters seed on the ground; ²⁷ he sleeps and rises—night and day, and the seed sprouts and grows—he doesn't know how. ²⁸ The soil produces a crop by itself—first the blade, then the head, and then the ripe grain on the head. ²⁹ But as soon as the crop is ready, he sends for the sickle, because harvest has come."

The Parable of the Mustard Seed

³⁰ And He said: "How can we illustrate the kingdom of God, or what parable can we use to describe it? ³¹ It's like a mustard seed that, when sown in the soil, is smaller than all the seeds on the ground. ³² And when sown, it comes up and grows taller than all the vegetables, and produces large branches, so that the birds of the sky can nest in its shade."

Using Parables

³³ He would speak the word to them with many parables like these, as they were able to understand. ³⁴ And He did not speak to them without a parable. Privately, however, He would explain everything to His own disciples.

Wind and Wave Obey the Master

³⁵ On that day, when evening had come, He told them, "Let's cross over to the other side ₁of the lake₁." ³⁶ So they left the crowd and took Him along since He was ₁already₁ in the boat. And other boats were with Him. ³⁷ A fierce windstorm arose, and the waves were breaking over the boat, so that the boat was already being swamped. ³⁸ But He was in the stern, sleeping on the cushion. So they woke Him up and said to Him, "Teacher! Don't you care that we're going to die?"

³⁹ He got up, rebuked the wind, and said to the sea, "Silence! Be still!" The wind ceased, and there was a

---

a⁴:11 The Gk word *mysterion* does not mean "mystery" in the Eng sense; it means what we can know only by divine revelation.   b⁴:12 Other mss read *and their sins be forgiven them*   c⁴:12 Is 6:9–10   d⁴:15 Some people   e⁴:15 Other mss read *in their hearts*   f⁴:16 Other mss read *are like*   g⁴:19 Or *pleasure, or deceitfulness*   h⁴:24 Lit *you measure*

---

bles in this section are all about. **has been granted to you.** Not even the disciples who have been given "the secret" perceive fully what is going on (v. 13). It is as the disciples follow Jesus that they will come to understand more fully what He means

4:12 look and look ... listen and listen. This quote is from Isaiah 6:9-10 in which God called the prophet to speak His word even though Israel would not listen. Although they saw God's messenger and heard his word, they refused to heed his message. **might turn back—and be forgiven.** In order to be forgiven, people must repent (turn). In order to repent, they must understand their true situation.

4:37 A fierce windstorm. The Sea of Galilee was pear-shaped and ringed by mountains, though open at its northern and southern ends. Fierce winds blew into this bowl-shaped sea, creating savage and unpredictable storms.

4:39 Instead of bailing, Jesus commands the wind and the waves to be still, and so they are. He has power over the very elements—in the same way God does (Ps. 65:7; 106:9). This was something no ordinary rabbi could do. **Be still!** This is literally, "Be muzzled!" as if the storm were some wild beast needing to be subdued. Pictured in this account is Jesus' divine power to calm the storms of life.

4:40 fearful. Once Jesus displays His power, their fear of the storm turns into fear of Him. This is the fear of the unknown and the unexplainable. This miracle would force the disciples to reconsider all they had heard and seen from Jesus.

4:41 terrified. Terror replaced fear. Terror is felt in the presence of an unknown force or power. **Who then is this?** This is the key question in Mark's Gospel. The congregation in the synagogue wondered about this (1:27). The religious leaders asked this question (2:7; 3:22). Now his disciples discover that they do not understand who He is. The rest of Mark describes how the disciples discover His true nature.

5:1 the region of the Gerasenes. The location of their landing is not clear. However, it is on the other side of the lake from Capernaum, in Gentile territory, probably near the lower end of the Sea of Galilee.

5:2 He got out of the boat. No mention is made of the disciples in this story. **a man with an unclean spirit.** There was widespread belief that demons could enter and

great calm. ⁴⁰ Then He said to them, "Why are you fearful? Do you still have no faith?"

⁴¹ And they were terrified and asked one another, "Who then is this? Even the wind and the sea obey Him!"

Calming the Storm

1. When you were little, what did you do when there was a big storm?

Mark 4:35-41

2. Why was Jesus sleeping while a dangerous storm was raging?

3. Why were the disciples so afraid during the storm? How did their fear show they lacked faith?

4. If "even the wind and the sea obey Him" (v. 41), what does that teach you about Jesus' power in your life?

5. What "storms" are raging in your life right now? How can Jesus calm them?

Demons Driven Out by the Master

5 Then they came to the other side of the sea, to the region of the Gerasenes.ᵃ ² As soon as He got out of the boat, a man with an unclean spirit came out of the tombs and met Him. ³ He lived in the tombs. No one was able to restrain him any more—even with chains— ⁴ because he often had been bound with shackles and chains, but had snapped off the chains and smashed the shackles. No one was strong enough to subdue him. ⁵ And always, night and day, he was crying out among the tombs and in the mountains and cutting himself with stones.

⁶ When he saw Jesus from a distance, he ran and knelt down before Him. ⁷ And he cried out with a loud voice, "What do You have to do with me,ᵇ Jesus, Son of the Most High God? I begᶜ You before God, don't torment me!" ⁸ For He had told him, "Come out of the man, you unclean spirit!"

⁹ "What is your name?" He asked him.

"My name is Legion,"ᵈ he answered Him, "because we are many." ¹⁰ And he kept begging Him not to send them out of the region.

¹¹ Now a large herd of pigs was there, feeding on the hillside. ¹² The demonsᵉ begged Him, "Send us to the pigs, so we may enter them." ¹³ And He gave them permission. Then the unclean spirits came out and entered the pigs, and the herd of about 2,000 rushed down the steep bank into the sea and drowned there. ¹⁴ The men who tended themᶠ ran off and reported it in the town and the countryside, and people went to see what had happened. ¹⁵ They came to Jesus and saw the man who had been demon-possessed by the legion, sitting there, dressed and in his right mind; and they were afraid. ¹⁶ The eyewitnesses described to them what had happened to the demon-possessed man and ₗtoldₗ about the pigs. ¹⁷ Then they began to beg Him to leave their region.

¹⁸ As He was getting into the boat, the man who had been demon-possessed kept begging Him to be with Him. ¹⁹ But He would not let him; instead, He told him, "Go back home to your own people, and report to them how much the Lord has done for you and how He has had mercy on you." ²⁰ So he went out and began to proclaim in the •Decapolis how much Jesus had done for him, and they were all amazed.

A Girl Restored and a Woman Healed

²¹ When Jesus had crossed over again by boat to the other side, a large crowd gathered around Him while He was by the sea. ²² One of the •synagogue leaders, named Jairus, came, and when he saw Jesus, he fell at His feet ²³ and kept begging Him, "My little daughter is at death's door.ᵍ Come and lay Your hands on her so she can get well and live."

ᵃ**5:1** Other mss read *Gadarenes*; other mss read *Gergesenes* ᵇ**5:7** Lit *What to me and to You* ᶜ**5:7** Or *adjure* ᵈ**5:9** A Roman legion contained up to 6,000 soldiers; here *legion* indicates a large number. ᵉ**5:12** Other mss read *All the demons* ᶠ**5:14** Other mss read *tended the pigs* ᵍ**5:23** Lit *My little daughter has it finally*; = to be at the end of life

---

take control of a person's body, speaking and acting through that person. The demons were understood to be Satan's legions. In overcoming them, Jesus was demonstrating His power over Satan and his work. **tombs.** The ragged limestone cliffs with their caves and depressions provided a natural burial site. The demoniac occupied the place of the dead, indicating the nature of the evil that was at work in him.

5:6 knelt down. Thus, the demons acknowledge Jesus' power over them. Likewise, in verse 7 they request that He not torture them, again acknowledging His superior power.

5:7 Son of the Most High God. The demons ask who Jesus is (4:41). The demon-filled man, with supernatural insight, points out Jesus' deity (1:11). Interestingly, this is how

God was often referred to by the Gentiles (Gen. 14:17-24; Dan. 4:17). **I beg You before God, don't torment me!** It is not clear what they feared.

5:9 Legion. The name for a company of 6,000 Roman soldiers. The man was occupied not by one, but by a huge number of demons.

5:15 they were afraid. It might be expected that they would rejoice that this man who had terrorized them (and whom they could no longer restrain) was now healed. But instead they are fearful of Jesus, who had the power to overcome the demons and destroy their herd.

5:20 Decapolis. This was a league of 10 Gentile cities patterned after the Greek way of life. This is the first of several ventures by

Jesus into Gentile areas, demonstrating what Mark later points out (13:10; 14:9). The gospel is to be preached to all nations.

5:22 synagogue leaders. In first-century Israel, synagogues were found in each city and town. People met there weekly on the Sabbath for worship and instruction. Synagogues were run by a committee of lay people (the rulers).

5:25 a woman. This woman should not have been in the crowd. Because of the nature of her illness she was considered "unclean" (Lev. 15:25-30). **suffering from bleeding.** Probably hemorrhaging from the womb. Since many people assumed that chronic problems like this were God's judgment upon a person for their sin, she undoubtedly experienced some measure of condemnation from others.

Miraculous Faith

1. How do you feel about a trip to the doctor's office? Would you rather suffer with pain than go see a doctor?

Mark 5:24-34

2. Why did the woman touch Jesus' robe? Why didn't she just ask Him for healing?

3. Why did Jesus ask who had touched Him? What did this force the woman to do?

4. What "faith" did the woman have? How did it make her well?

5. What needs healing in your own life—physically, spiritually, emotionally, or otherwise?

²⁴ So Jesus went with him, and a large crowd was following and pressing against Him. ²⁵ A woman suffering from bleeding for 12 years ²⁶ had endured much under many doctors. She had spent everything she had and was not helped at all. On the contrary, she became worse. ²⁷ Having heard about Jesus, she came behind Him in the crowd and touched His robe. ²⁸ For she said, "If I can just touch His robes, I'll be made well!" ²⁹ Instantly her flow of blood ceased, and she sensed in her body that she was cured of her affliction.

³⁰ At once Jesus realized in Himself that power had gone out from Him. He turned around in the crowd and said, "Who touched My robes?"

³¹ His disciples said to Him, "You see the crowd pressing against You, and You say, 'Who touched Me?'"

³² So He was looking around to see who had done this. ³³ Then the woman, knowing what had happened to her, came with fear and trembling, fell down before Him, and told Him the whole truth. ³⁴ "Daughter," He said to her, "your faith has made you well.ᵃ Go in peace and be freeᵇ from your affliction."

³⁵ While He was still speaking, people came from the synagogue leader's house and said, "Your daughter is dead. Why bother the Teacher any more?"

³⁶ But when Jesus overheard what was said, He told the synagogue leader, "Don't be afraid. Only believe." ³⁷ He did not let anyone accompany Him except Peter, James, and John, James' brother. ³⁸ They came to the leader's house, and He saw a commotion—people weeping and wailing loudly. ³⁹ He went in and said to them, "Why are you making a commotion and weeping? The child is not dead but •asleep." ⁴⁰ They started laughing at Him, but He put them all outside. He took the child's father, mother, and those who were with Him, and entered the place where the child was. ⁴¹ Then He took the child by the hand and said to her, *"Talitha koum!"*ᶜ (which is translated, "Little girl, I say to you, get up!"). ⁴² Immediately the girl got up and began to walk. (She was 12 years old.) At this they were utterly astounded. ⁴³ Then He gave them strict orders that no one should know about this and said that she should be given something to eat.

Rejection at Nazareth

6 He went away from there and came to His hometown, and His disciples followed Him. ² When the Sabbath came, He began to teach in the •synagogue, and many who heard Him were astonished. "Where did this man get these things?" they said. "What is this wisdom given to Him, and how are these miracles performed by His hands? ³ Isn't this the carpenter, the son of Mary, and the brother of James, Joses, Judas, and Simon? And aren't His sisters here with us?" So they were offended by Him.

⁴ Then Jesus said to them, "A prophet is not without honor except in his hometown, among his relatives, and in his household." ⁵ So He was not able to do any miraclesᵈ there, except that He laid His hands on a few

ᵃ**5:34** Or *has saved you*   ᵇ**5:34** Lit *healthy*   ᶜ**5:41** An Aram expression   ᵈ**6:5** Lit *miracle*

5:28 If I can just touch His robes, I'll be made well! There is no attempt on her part to establish genuine contact with Jesus: she simply wants to brush up against Him so that she can be brought in contact with His power. Nonetheless, by this action the woman showed that she had "ears to hear" (4:9) and had faith that Jesus could indeed heal her.

5:30 Who touched My robes? Jesus desired a relationship with those He helped; He was not an impersonal power source.

5:34 your faith has made you well. It was her faith that compelled her to reach out to Jesus—the source of healing power. **Go ... be free.** This phrase means "be complete, be whole."

5:38 people weeping and wailing loudly. These were in all likelihood professional mourners. Even the poorest person was required to hire not less than two flutes and one wailing woman to mourn a death.

6:1-2 His hometown. Nazareth, which was located in the hill country of Galilee some 20 miles southwest of Capernaum (Luke 4:14-30).

6:2 Where did this man get these things? The townspeople do not deny Jesus' wisdom or power to do miracles. But they are puzzled as to the origin of such abilities.

6:3 carpenter. The Greek word refers to a general craftsman who worked not only with wood but also with stone and metal. **son of Mary.** A man was never described as the son of his mother except as an insult. The townsfolk may have heard rumors of Jesus' unusual birth and may have taken Him to be

illegitimate. **brother ... sisters.** Mark names four brothers and indicates Jesus had sisters too. **they were offended by Him.** They could not get past His humble and familiar origins—therefore, they couldn't give credence to who He really was.

6:7 began to send them out. To go out on a ministry tour is not the idea or plan of the Twelve. Jesus does the sending. **in pairs.** He does not send them alone—perhaps as a protection against robbers; perhaps because two witnesses have more credibility than one (Deut. 17:6); perhaps so that they will support one another as they learn to minister. The parallel accounts in Matthew and Luke indicate their mission was to announce and demonstrate the fact that God's kingdom was now at hand (1:15). **gave them authority.** He empowers them to do battle with evil. It is in His name and power that they minister.

sick people and healed them. 6 And He was amazed at their unbelief.

Commissioning the Twelve

Now He was going around the villages in a circuit, teaching. 7 He summoned the Twelve and began to send them out in pairs and gave them authority over unclean spirits. 8 He instructed them to take nothing for the road except a walking stick: no bread, no traveling bag, no money in their belts. 9 They were to wear sandals, but not put on an extra shirt. 10 Then He said to them, "Whenever you enter a house, stay there until you leave that place. 11 If any place does not welcome you and people refuse to listen to you, when you leave there, shake the dust off your feet as a testimony against them."[a]

12 So they went out and preached that people should repent. 13 And they were driving out many demons, anointing many sick people with oil, and healing.

John the Baptist Beheaded

14 King •Herod heard of this, because Jesus' name had become well known. Some[b] said, "John the Baptist has been raised from the dead, and that's why supernatural powers are at work in him." 15 But others said, "He's Elijah." Still others said, "He's a prophet[c]—like one of the prophets."

16 When Herod heard of it, he said, "John, the one I beheaded, has been raised!" 17 For Herod himself had given orders to arrest John and to chain him in prison on account of Herodias, his brother Philip's wife, whom he had married. 18 John had been telling Herod, "It is not lawful for you to have your brother's wife!" 19 So Herodias held a grudge against him and wanted to kill him. But she could not, 20 because Herod was in awe of[d] John and was protecting him, knowing he was a righteous and holy man. When Herod heard him he would be very disturbed,[e] yet would hear him gladly.

21 Now an opportune time came on his birthday, when Herod gave a banquet for his nobles, military commanders, and the leading men of Galilee. 22 When

Herodias' own daughter[f] came in and danced, she pleased Herod and his guests. The king said to the girl, "Ask me whatever you want, and I'll give it to you." 23 So he swore oaths to her: "Whatever you ask me I will give you, up to half my kingdom."

Losing Your Head

1. When have you recently "lost your head?" What made you upset? What did you do?

Mark 6:14-29

2. Why did Herodias, Herod's wife, want to kill John the Baptist? Why did Herod not want to kill him?

3. What caused Herod to change his mind and kill John? How did his environment get him into trouble?

4. What sorts of "environments" can get you into trouble? Specifically, where do you draw the line when it comes to movies, music, etc. with sexual or violent content?

24 Then she went out and said to her mother, "What should I ask for?"

"John the Baptist's head!" she said.

25 Immediately she hurried to the king and said, "I want you to give me John the Baptist's head on a platter—right now!"

26 Though the king was deeply distressed, because of his oaths and the guests[g] he did not want to refuse her. 27 The king immediately sent for an executioner and commanded him to bring John's head. So he went and beheaded him in prison, 28 brought his head on a platter, and gave it to the girl. Then the girl gave it to

---

6:8 instructed. These instructions cause the Twelve to pare down to the bare minimum. They take only the clothes on their backs and a staff, the tool of a shepherd. By faith they must trust that God will provide the rest of their needs as they go about His work.

6:10 They are not to dishonor their host by accepting better accommodations.

6:14 King Herod. Herod Antipas was the ruler of the Roman provinces of Galilee and Perea from 4 B.C. to A.D. 39. He was the son of Herod the Great, the Jewish ruler who ordered the slaughter of the babies after Jesus' birth. Herod Antipas was not, in fact, the "king." When he went to Rome some years later to request this title, his power was taken away and he was banished.

6:18 It is not lawful. According to Leviticus 18:16 and 20:21, it was not lawful for a man to marry his brother's wife while that brother was still alive. Herod, a Jew himself, scandalized his people by divorcing the Nabatean Princess Aretas to marry Herodias who was his niece (the daughter of his half-brother) and his sister-in-law (the wife of a different brother).

6:21 an opportune time. Herodias was plotting a way to kill John (v. 19) because of his criticism of her marriage. **a banquet.** The sparseness of the lifestyle of the Twelve (vv. 8-11) would have contrasted greatly with the opulence of Herod's birthday party. The men in attendance would have been wealthy landowners, those in high government positions, and military officials.

6:22 Herodias' own daughter. This is Herodias' teenage daughter (from her first marriage), whose name is Salome.

6:25 John the Baptist's head on a platter. This was a gruesome act: serving John's head on a platter as if it were another course in the banquet.

6:33 ran there by land. The crowds are now wise to the disciples' tactic of sailing off across the lake and leaving them standing on the shore (4:35-36). So they follow on foot. The distances would not have been great since the lake was only eight miles at its widest. They could probably see where they were sailing to.

6:41 five loaves. These were small round cakes made of wheat or barley. **two fish.** These were probably smoked or pickled fish that were used as a sauce for the bread.

her mother. [29] When his disciples[a] heard about it, they came and removed his corpse and placed it in a tomb.

Rest and Refreshment

1. How do you unwind after a busy day?

Mark 6:30-44

2. Why did the disciples need a rest? How were they intending to spend their rest time?

3. How did Jesus actually provide rest and refreshment for everyone around Him?

4. The disciples thought they were getting a break (v. 31), but they ended up serving. What does this passage say to you about the use of your free time?

5. How can you use your free time this week in a God-pleasing way?

Feeding 5,000

[30] The apostles gathered around Jesus and reported to Him all that they had done and taught. [31] He said to them, "Come away by yourselves to a remote place and rest a while." For many people were coming and going, and they did not even have time to eat. [32] So they went away in the boat by themselves to a remote place, [33] but many saw them leaving and recognized them. People ran there by land from all the towns and arrived ahead of them.[b] [34] So as He stepped ashore, He saw a huge crowd and had compassion on them, because they were like sheep without a shepherd. Then He began to teach them many things.

[35] When it was already late, His disciples approached Him and said, "This place is a wilderness, and it is already late! [36] Send them away, so they can go into the surrounding countryside and villages to buy themselves something to eat."

[37] "You give them something to eat," He responded.

They said to Him, "Should we go and buy 200 •denarii worth of bread and give them something to eat?"

[38] And He asked them, "How many loaves do you have? Go look."

When they found out they said, "Five, and two fish."

[39] Then He instructed them to have all the people sit down[c] in groups on the green grass. [40] So they sat down in ranks of hundreds and fifties. [41] Then He took the five loaves and the two fish, and looking up to heaven, He blessed and broke the loaves. He kept giving them to His disciples to set before the people. He also divided the two fish among them all. [42] Everyone ate and was filled. [43] Then they picked up 12 baskets full of pieces of bread and fish. [44] Now those who ate the loaves were 5,000 men.

Walking on the Water

[45] Immediately He made His disciples get into the boat and go ahead of Him to the other side, to Bethsaida, while He dismissed the crowd. [46] After He said good-bye to them, He went away to the mountain to pray. [47] When evening came, the boat was in the middle of the sea, and He was alone on the land. [48] He saw them being battered as they rowed,[d] because the wind was against them. Around three in the morning[e] He came toward them walking on the sea and wanted to pass by them. [49] When they saw Him walking on the sea, they thought it was a ghost and cried out; [50] for they all saw Him and were terrified. Immediately He spoke with them and said, "Have courage! It is I. Don't be afraid." [51] Then He got into the boat with them, and the wind ceased. They were completely astounded,[f] [52] because they had not understood about the loaves. Instead, their hearts were hardened.

---

[a]**6:29** John's disciples [b]**6:33** Other mss add *and gathered around Him* [c]**6:39** Lit *people recline* [d]**6:48** Or *them struggling as they rowed*
[e]**6:48** Lit *Around the fourth watch of the night* = 3 to 6 a.m. [f]**6:51** Lit *were astounded in themselves*

6:42 filled. Miraculously, five loaves and two fish fed everyone, not meagerly but abundantly, so that they were filled.

6:43 12. The number of the tribes of Israel, reinforcing the idea that what Jesus is doing here has prophetic significance as a demonstration that Jesus provides nourishment for all God's people. **Baskets full.** Small wicker containers carried by all Jews. Each disciple returned with his full. The word used for basket describes a distinctly Jewish type of basket. **pieces.** The law required that the scraps of a meal be collected. **bread.** Bread and eating are recurring themes in these two cycles of stories (6:30-8:26).

6:44 men. Literally, "males" (Matt. 14:21). When all the women and children are taken into account, this was a huge crowd.

6:45 The reason for Jesus' abrupt dismissal of the disciples and the crowd is explained in the Gospel of John (John 6:14-15). Apparently the crowd wanted to make Jesus the king by force. **Bethsaida.** Literally, "house of the fisher." This is a village on the northern shore of the Sea of Galilee, several miles east of Capernaum. This was the birthplace of Philip, Andrew, and Peter.

6:46 He went ... to pray. In the midst of great success and popular acclaim, once again Jesus goes off to pray.

6:48 the wind was against them. Once again (4:37), the elements work against the disciples. This time the problem is not a storm, but a strong headwind that would make rowing difficult. **three in the morning.** This was the way Roman soldiers told time. The fourth watch ran from 3:00 to 6:00 a.m.

Assuming the disciples set out to sea in the late afternoon, they had been struggling at the oars for probably seven or more hours. **walking on the sea.** It has already been established that Jesus is Lord over the wind and the water (4:39,41). **wanted to pass by them.** This could be translated: "for He intended to pass their way," presumably to reveal His presence and remind them of His power in the midst of their distress.

6:49 a ghost. The sea, especially at night, was thought to be a dwelling place for demons. Hence the response of the disciples.

6:50 terrified. Once before on this lake they were terrified by an event they did not expect and did not understand (4:41). This is the terror of experiencing something that defies all categories of understanding. **It is I.** Literally, "I Am." This phrase is used by

Miraculous Healings

53 When they had crossed over, they came to land at Gennesaret and beached the boat. 54 As they got out of the boat, people immediately recognized Him. 55 They hurried throughout that vicinity and began to carry the sick on stretchers to wherever they heard He was. 56 Wherever He would go, into villages, towns, or the country, they laid the sick in the marketplaces and begged Him that they might touch just the •tassel of His robe. And everyone who touched it was made well.

The Traditions of the Elders

7 The •Pharisees and some of the •scribes who had come from Jerusalem gathered around Him. 2 They observed that some of His disciples were eating their bread with unclean—that is, unwashed—hands. 3 (For the Pharisees, in fact all the Jews, will not eat unless they wash their hands ritually, keeping the tradition of the elders. 4 When they come from the marketplace, they do not eat unless they have washed. And there are many other customs they have received and keep, like the washing of cups, jugs, copper utensils, and dining couches.a) 5 Then the Pharisees and the scribes asked Him, "Why don't Your disciples live according to the tradition of the elders, instead of eating bread with ritually uncleanb hands?"

6 He answered them, "Isaiah prophesied correctly about you hypocrites, as it is written:

These people honor Me with their lips,
but their heart is far from Me.
7 They worship Me in vain,
teaching as doctrines the commands of men.c

8 Disregarding the command of God, you keep the tradition of men."d 9 He also said to them, "You completely invalidate God's command in order to maintaine your tradition! 10 For Moses said:

Honor your father and your mother;f and,
Whoever speaks evil of father or mother
must be put to death.g

11 But you say, 'If a man tells his father or mother: Whatever benefit you might have received from me is Corban'" (that is, a gift ⌐committed to the temple⌐), 12 "you no longer let him do anything for his father or mother. 13 You revoke God's word by your tradition that you have handed down. And you do many other similar things." 14 Summoning the crowd again, He told them, "Listen to Me, all of you, and understand: 15 Nothing that goes into a person from outside can defile him, but the things that come out of a person are what defile him. 16 If anyone has ears to hear, he should listen!"h

17 When He went into the house away from the crowd, the disciples asked Him about the parable. 18 And He said to them, "Are you also as lacking in understanding? Don't you realize that nothing going into a man from the outside can defile him? 19 For it doesn't go into his heart but into the stomach and is eliminated."i (As a result, He made all foods clean.j) 20 Then He said, "What comes out of a person—that defiles him. 21 For from within, out of people's hearts, come evil thoughts, sexual immoralities, thefts, murders, 22 adulteries, greed, evil actions, deceit, lewdness, stinginess,k blasphemy, pride, and foolishness. 23 All these evil things come from within and defile a person."

A Gentile Mother's Faith

24 He got up and departed from there to the region of Tyre and Sidon.l He entered a house and did not want anyone to know it, but He could not escape notice. 25 Instead, immediately after hearing about Him, a woman whose little daughter had an unclean spirit came and fell at His feet. 26 Now the woman was Greek, a Syrophoenician by birth, and she kept asking Him to drive the demon out of her daughter. 27 He said to her,

---

a7:4 Other mss omit and dining couches b7:5 Other mss read with unwashed c7:6–7 Is 29:13 d7:8 Other mss add The washing of jugs, and cups, and many other similar things you practice. e7:9 Other mss read to establish f7:10 Ex 20:12; Dt 5:16 g7:10 Ex 21:17; Lv 20:9 h7:16 Other mss omit this verse i7:19 Lit goes out into the toilet j7:19 Other mss read is eliminated, making all foods clean." k7:22 Lit evil eye l7:24 Other mss omit and Sidon

---

God to describe Himself (Ex. 3:1-14).

6:52 their hearts were hardened. This is the problem. Like the Pharisees in the synagogue (3:5), the disciples' hearts are like calcified stone (the same Greek word is used here and in 3:5).

6:53 Gennesaret. Since the wind frustrated their plan to go north, they instead cross the lake to a thickly populated, fertile plain some four miles southwest of Capernaum. There, crowds again flock to Him as a healer.

7:3 wash their hands ritually. The issue was holiness, not hygiene (germs were unknown in the first century). Before each meal the hands were washed with special water in a particular way.

7:11 Corban. An oath, which when invoked, dedicated an item to God, rendering it thereafter unavailable for normal use. A son might declare his property "Corban" with the result that his parents would have no further claim on his support, even though the oath neither required him to transfer his property to the temple nor to cease using it himself.

7:15 defile him. This means "to render someone impure in a ritual sense."

7:20 What comes out of a person. Jesus calls the people to focus on what comes out of a person's heart and mind. Thoughts and actions reveal true uncleanness.

7:26 Greek, a Syrophoenician by birth. This woman is described first by her religion, language, and culture. She is a Greek-speaking Gentile. Then she is de-

scribed by her nationality. She came from Phoenicia (modern-day Lebanon).

7:27 first. Jesus' primary mission was to the children of Israel. By the use of the word "first," He implies that a mission to the Gentiles was intended from the beginning.

7:28 Instead of being insulted by His metaphor, she catches on to His wordplay and replies, in essence, "Carry on with the meal You are serving Israel, but allow us a few scraps."

7:29 Because of this reply. Jesus is impressed with the depth of her understanding as well as her clever and witty reply. In fact, this Gentile woman seems to understand more about Jesus than either the Twelve (6:45-56) or the Pharisees (vv. 1-13).

7:33 spitting. This was regarded by Jews

"Allow the children to be satisfied first, because it isn't right to take the children's bread and throw it to the dogs."

28 But she replied to Him, "Lord, even the dogs under the table eat the children's crumbs."

29 Then He told her, "Because of this reply, you may go. The demon has gone out of your daughter." 30 When she went back to her home, she found her child lying on the bed, and the demon was gone.

Jesus Does Everything Well

31 Again, leaving the region of Tyre, He went by way of Sidon to the Sea of Galilee, through a the region of the •Decapolis. 32 They brought to Him a deaf man who also had a speech difficulty, and begged Jesus to lay His hand on him. 33 So He took him away from the crowd privately. After putting His fingers in the man's ears and spitting, He touched his tongue. 34 Then, looking up to heaven, He sighed deeply and said to him, "Eph-phatha!" b (that is, "Be opened!"). 35 Immediately his ears were opened, his speech difficulty was removed, c and he began to speak clearly. 36 Then He ordered them to tell no one, but the more He would order them, the more they would proclaim it.

37 They were extremely astonished and said, "He has done everything well! He even makes deaf people hear, and people unable to speak, talk!"

Feeding 4,000

8 In those days there was again a large crowd, and they had nothing to eat. He summoned the disciples and said to them, 2 "I have compassion on the crowd, because they've already stayed with Me three days and have nothing to eat. 3 If I send them home famished, d they will collapse on the way, and some of them have come a long distance."

4 His disciples answered Him, "Where can anyone get enough bread here in this desolate place to fill these people?"

5 "How many loaves do you have?" He asked them.

"Seven," they said. 6 Then He commanded the crowd to sit down on the ground. Taking the seven loaves, He

gave thanks, broke the ⌊loaves⌋, and kept on giving ⌊them⌋ to His disciples to set before ⌊the people⌋. So they served the ⌊loaves⌋ to the crowd. 7 They also had a few small fish, and when He had blessed them, He said these were to be served as well. 8 They ate and were filled. Then they collected seven large baskets of left-over pieces. 9 About 4,000 ⌊men⌋ were there. He dismissed them 10 and immediately got into the boat with His disciples and went to the district of Dalmanutha. e

The Yeast of the Pharisees and Herod

11 The •Pharisees came out and began to argue with Him, demanding of Him a sign from heaven to test Him. 12 But sighing deeply in His spirit, He said, "Why does this generation demand a sign? •I assure you: No sign will be given to this generation!" 13 Then He left them, got on board ⌊the boat⌋ again, and went to the other side.

14 They had forgotten to take bread and had only one loaf with them in the boat. 15 Then He commanded them: "Watch out! Beware of the yeast of the Pharisees and the yeast of •Herod."

16 They were discussing among themselves that they did not have any bread. 17 Aware of this, He said to them, "Why are you discussing that you do not have any bread? Do you not yet understand or comprehend? Is your heart hardened? 18 Do you have eyes, and not see, and do you have ears, and not hear? f And do you not remember? 19 When I broke the five loaves for the 5,000, how many baskets full of pieces of bread did you collect?"

"Twelve," they told Him.

20 "When I broke the seven loaves for the 4,000, how many large baskets full of pieces of bread did you collect?"

"Seven," they said.

21 And He said to them, "Don't you understand yet?"

Healing a Blind Man

22 Then they came to Bethsaida. They brought a blind man to Him and begged Him to touch him. 23 He took the blind man by the hand and brought him out of the

---

a 7:31 Or into b 7:34 An Aram expression c 7:35 Lit opened, the bond of his tongue was untied d 8:3 Or fasting e 8:10 Probably on the western shore of the Sea of Galilee f 8:18 Jr 5:21; Ezk 12:2

---

and Greeks as a healing agent.

7:36 tell no one. This command stands in sharp contrast to what Jesus said on His previous visit to the region of the Decapolis. On that occasion, He told the ex-demoniac to "go and tell" the story of what the Lord had done for him (5:18-20). On this trip, Jesus sees the results of that man's witness. Instead of urgently requesting Jesus to leave as they had done on his previous visit (5:17), now not only do the townspeople bring a man to be healed, but they have developed expectations about who Jesus is and what He can do. This is why Jesus now commanded silence.

8:1-10 a large crowd. The major difference between the feeding of the four thousand and the feeding of the five thousand is the difference in audience. This feeding in-

cluded Gentiles (as well as Jews), whereas the earlier feeding involved Jews only.

8:10 Dalmanutha. It is not certain where this town is located. Possibly it is Magdala, a town near Tiberias on the west side of the lake. The point is clear. At this time Jesus left the Gentile region where He was ministering and returned to Jewish soil.

8:15 yeast. To the Jew, yeast was connected with fermentation, which they saw as a form of rotting. So yeast became a metaphor for evil and its expansion.

8:17 Do you not yet understand? Jesus asks this question twice in these verses (vv. 14-21). This is the issue: Although exposed to ample evidence of who Jesus is, they still fail to put it all together. **heart hardened?** This is the problem (3:5; 6:52). Their hearts

are stone-like. The seed of the Word can't penetrate (4:15).

8:22 Bethsaida. This was a town at the mouth of the Jordan River on the shore of the Sea of Galilee.

8:25 Again. This is the only healing that requires a second action on the part of Jesus. Mark's placement of this story right after the disciples' incomprehension of the meaning of the feedings, and just prior to their confession of faith in Him as the Messiah, indicates he is using this story to illustrate how difficult it was for the disciples to grasp Jesus' identity.

8:27 Caesarea Philippi. When Jesus and His disciples visited this city, there was a gleaming white marble temple dedicated to the godhead of Caesar. It is fitting that in this

village. Spitting on his eyes and laying His hands on him, He asked him, "Do you see anything?"

²⁴ He looked up and said, "I see people—they look to me like trees walking."

²⁵ Again Jesus placed His hands on the man's eyes, and he saw distinctly. He was cured and could see everything clearly. ²⁶ Then He sent him home, saying, "Don't even go into the village."ᵃ

Peter's Confession of the Messiah

²⁷ Jesus went out with His disciples to the villages of Caesarea Philippi. And on the road He asked His disciples, "Who do people say that I am?"

²⁸ They answered Him, "John the Baptist; others, Elijah; still others, one of the prophets."

²⁹ "But you," He asked them again, "who do you say that I am?"

Peter answered Him, "You are the •Messiah!"

³⁰ And He strictly warned them to tell no one about Him.

His Death and Resurrection Predicted

³¹ Then He began to teach them that the •Son of Man must suffer many things, and be rejected by the elders, the •chief priests, and the •scribes, be killed, and rise after three days. ³² He was openly talking about this. So Peter took Him aside and began to rebuke Him.

³³ But turning around and looking at His disciples, He rebuked Peter and said, "Get behind Me, Satan, because you're not thinking about God's concerns,ᵇ but man's!"

Take Up Your Cross

³⁴ Summoning the crowd along with His disciples, He said to them, "If anyone wants to be My follower, he must deny himself, take up his cross, and follow Me. ³⁵ For whoever wants to save his •life will lose it, but whoever loses his life because of Me and the gospel will save it. ³⁶ For what does it benefit a man to gain the whole world yet lose his life? ³⁷ What can a man give in exchange for his life? ³⁸ For whoever is ashamed of Me and of My words in this adulterous and sinful generation, the Son of Man will also be ashamed of him when

He comes in the glory of His Father with the holy angels."

9 Then He said to them, "•I assure you: There are some standing here who will not taste death until they see the kingdom of God come in power."

Precious Time

1. What's the highest place you've ever climbed?

Mark 9:2-13
2. Why did Jesus wait until He was alone with His disciples to be "transfigured" before them?
3. How did Peter react to this awesome event (vv. 5-6)? How would you have reacted?
4. When did you last spend an hour alone with Jesus?
5. Why is it so important that Christians spend time alone with Jesus?
6. How can you make time alone with Jesus a higher priority in your life?

The Transfiguration

² After six days Jesus took Peter, James, and John and led them up on a high mountain by themselves to be alone. He was transformedᶜ in front of them, ³ and His clothes became dazzling—extremely white as no launderer on earth could whiten them. ⁴ Elijah appeared to them with Moses, and they were talking with Jesus.

⁵ Then Peter said to Jesus, "•Rabbi, it is good for us to be here! Let us make three •tabernacles: one for You, one for Moses, and one for Elijah"— ⁶ because he did not know what he should say, since they were terrified.

⁷ A cloud appeared, overshadowing them, and a voice came from the cloud:

ᵃ**8:26** Other mss add *or tell anyone in the village*　ᵇ**8:33** Lit *about the things of God*　ᶜ**9:2** Or *transfigured*

---

place with rich associations to the religions of the world, Jesus, the Galilean, asks His disciples if they understand that He is the Anointed One sent by God.

8:29 who do you say that I am? This is the crucial question in Mark's Gospel. By it the author challenges his readers to consider how they will answer the question as well.

8:33 Get behind Me, Satan! By urging Jesus to back away from His teaching about suffering and death, Peter is doing what Satan did: tempting Jesus with the promise that He can have the whole world without pain (Matt. 4:8-10).

8:34 deny himself, take up his cross, and follow Me. These words would certainly have special meaning to those in the situation faced by the original recipients of the

gospel.

8:38 ashamed of Me. This would be indicated by failing to persist in one's Christian testimony in times of persecution.

9:2 After six days. By this phrase Mark connects the Transfiguration with Jesus' prediction that "some who are standing here will not taste death before they see the kingdom of God come with power" (9:1).

9:4 The presence of both Moses and Elijah on the mountain is meant to indicate that the Old Testament law and the prophets endorse Jesus as God's appointed Messiah.

9:5 tabernacles. Peter might have had in mind the huts of intertwined branches which were put up at the Festival of Tabernacles to commemorate Israel's time in the wilder-

ness. Or he might be thinking of the "Tent of Meeting" where God met with Moses.

9:6 terrified. Throughout the Bible, whenever God is manifested before people the human response is one of fear (Ex. 3:5-6; Judg. 6:20-23; Isa. 6:5; Dan. 10:7-8; Rev. 1:17).

9:11 Elijah must come first? The Jews believed God would send Elijah back before the Messiah appeared to again call Israel to faithfulness (Mal. 4:5).

9:18 The symptoms closely resemble those of a certain form of epilepsy.

9:19 unbelieving generation! This is the cry of anguish and loneliness of one who knows so clearly the way things really are, and yet is constantly confronted with disbelief in var-

This is My beloved Son;
listen to Him!

⁸ Then suddenly, looking around, they no longer saw anyone with them except Jesus alone.

⁹ As they were coming down from the mountain, He ordered them to tell no one what they had seen until the •Son of Man had risen from the dead. ¹⁰ They kept this word to themselves, discussing what "rising from the dead" meant.

¹¹ Then they began to question Him, "Why do the •scribes say that Elijah must come first?"

¹² "Elijah does come first and restores everything," He replied. "How then is it written about the Son of Man that He must suffer many things and be treated with contempt? ¹³ But I tell you that Elijah really has come, and they did to him whatever they wanted, just as it is written about him."

The Power of Faith over a Demon

¹⁴ When they came to the disciples, they saw a large crowd around them and scribes disputing with them. ¹⁵ All of a sudden, when the whole crowd saw Him, they were amazedᵃ and ran to greet Him. ¹⁶ Then He asked them, "What are you arguing with them about?"

¹⁷ Out of the crowd, one man answered Him, "Teacher, I brought my son to You. He has a spirit that makes him unable to speak. ¹⁸ Wherever it seizes him, it throws him down, and he foams at the mouth, grinds his teeth, and becomes rigid. So I asked Your disciples to drive it out, but they couldn't."

¹⁹ He replied to them, "You unbelieving generation! How long will I be with you? How long must I put up with you? Bring him to Me." ²⁰ So they brought him to Him. When the spirit saw Him, it immediately convulsed the boy. He fell to the ground and rolled around, foaming at the mouth. ²¹ "How long has this been happening to him?" Jesus asked his father.

"From childhood," he said. ²² "And many times it has thrown him into fire or water to destroy him. But if You can do anything, have compassion on us and help us."

²³ Then Jesus said to him, " 'If You can?'ᵇ ᶜ Everything is possible to the one who believes."

²⁴ Immediately the father of the boy cried out, "I do believe! Help my unbelief."

²⁵ When Jesus saw that a crowd was rapidly coming together, He rebuked the unclean spirit, saying to it, "You mute and deaf spirit,ᵈ I command you: come out of him and never enter him again!"

²⁶ Then it came out, shrieking and convulsing himᵉ violently. The boy became like a corpse, so that many said, "He's dead." ²⁷ But Jesus, taking him by the hand, raised him, and he stood up.

²⁸ After He went into a house, His disciples asked Him privately, "Why couldn't we drive it out?"

²⁹ And He told them, "This kind can come out by nothing but prayer [and fasting]."ᶠ

 Help My Unbelief

1. What was something you did as a child that drove your parents crazy?

Mark 9:14-29

2. Why did Jesus say "bring him to me" (v. 19) when His disciples had failed to heal the boy?

3. Why did Jesus challenge the father who had said, "But if You can do anything" (vv. 22-23)? What did the father's wording show about his lack of faith?

4. How did the father overcome his lack of faith? How can Jesus help you overcome your own lack of faith?

ᵃ**9:15** Or *surprised*   ᵇ**9:23** Other mss add *believe*   ᶜ**9:23** Jesus appears to quote the father's words in v. 22 and then comment on them.
ᵈ**9:25** A spirit that caused the boy to be deaf and unable to speak   ᵉ**9:26** Other mss omit *him*   ᶠ**9:29** Other mss omit bracketed text

---

ious forms.

9:23 If You can? The question is not whether Jesus has the ability to heal (which has been amply demonstrated); the issue is the man's faith.

9:24 unbelief. The problem here is one of *doubt* (being of two minds about an issue) not one of *disbelief* (certainty that something is not true). The father did not disbelieve. After all, he had brought his son to Jesus to be healed (v. 17). His faith has been shaken by the failure of the disciples to heal his son (v. 18) so that now, even though he desperately wants his child to be free of this demon, he wonders if it is possible (v. 22).

9:29 prayer. The disciples have been given the authority to cast out demons (6:7) and have, in fact, done so (6:13). However, as

this incident makes clear, this power was not their own. It required continuing dependence upon God.

9:30 made their way through Galilee. They leave Herod Philip's territory, but they do not return to Galilee as they have done in the past. Instead, they pass through enroute to Jerusalem and Jesus' death.

9:31 betrayed. This is a new note in His teaching. It is not just that He will be rejected by the leaders of Israel. There will be an element of treachery involved.

9:34 greatest. Once again the disciples have missed the point. In the face of Jesus' teaching about suffering and death, they are concerned about their position and personal power.

9:42 causes the downfall. Literally, something which snares a person or animal, causing them to trip up or enticing them to stray. **these little ones who believe in Me.** The reference is to Jesus' followers (v. 37). **a heavy millstone.** There are two words for millstone. One refers to a small hand mill used in a home; the other (which Jesus uses here) refers to the huge upper stone of a community mill, so big that it had to be drawn around by a donkey. **the sea.** Jews were terrified of the sea.

9:43 life. Spiritual life; life in the kingdom of God (v. 47). **hell.** Literally, Gehenna—a ravine outside Jerusalem where children were once sacrificed and garbage was burned during the time of Jesus.

9:50 Salt. Salt does not normally lose its taste, but salt from the Dead Sea was mixed

The Second Prediction of His Death

30 Then they left that place and made their way through Galilee, but He did not want anyone to know it. 31 For He was teaching His disciples and telling them, "The Son of Man is being betrayed[a] into the hands of men. They will kill Him, and after He is killed, He will rise three days later." 32 But they did not understand this statement, and they were afraid to ask Him.

Who is the Greatest?

33 Then they came to Capernaum. When He was in the house, He asked them, "What were you arguing about on the way?" 34 But they were silent, because on the way they had been arguing with one another about who was the greatest. 35 Sitting down, He called the Twelve and said to them, "If anyone wants to be first, he must be last of all and servant of all." 36 Then He took a child, had him stand among them, and taking him in His arms, He said to them, 37 "Whoever welcomes[b] one little child such as this in My name welcomes Me. And whoever welcomes Me does not welcome Me, but Him who sent Me."

In His Name

38 John said to Him, "Teacher, we saw someone[c] driving out demons in Your name, and we tried to stop him because he wasn't following us."

39 "Don't stop him," said Jesus, "because there is no one who will perform a miracle in My name who can soon afterwards speak evil of Me. 40 For whoever is not against us is for us. 41 And whoever gives you a cup of water to drink because of My name,[d] since you belong to the •Messiah—I assure you: He will never lose his reward.

Warnings from Jesus

42 "But whoever •causes the downfall of one of these little ones who believe in Me—it would be better for him if a heavy millstone[e] were hung around his neck and he were thrown into the sea. 43 And if your hand

causes your downfall, cut it off. It is better for you to enter life maimed than to have two hands and go to •hell—the unquenchable fire, [44 where

**Their worm does not die,
and the fire is not quenched.]**[f g]

45 And if your foot causes your downfall, cut it off. It is better for you to enter life lame than to have two feet and be thrown into hell—[the unquenchable fire, 46 where

**Their worm does not die,
and the fire is not quenched.]**[f g]

47 And if your eye causes your downfall, gouge it out. It is better for you to enter the kingdom of God with one eye than to have two eyes and be thrown into hell, 48 where

**Their worm does not die,
and the fire is not quenched.**[g]

49 For everyone will be salted with fire.[h i] 50 Salt is good, but if the salt should lose its flavor, how can you make it salty? Have salt among yourselves and be at peace with one another."

The Question of Divorce

10 He set out from there and went to the region of Judea and across the Jordan. Then crowds converged on Him again and, as He usually did, He began teaching them once more. 2 Some •Pharisees approached Him to test Him. They asked, "Is it lawful for a man to divorce ⌊his⌋ wife?"

3 He replied to them, "What did Moses command you?"

4 They said, "Moses permitted us to write divorce papers and send her away."

5 But Jesus told them, "He wrote this commandment for you because of the hardness of your hearts. 6 But from the beginning of creation God[j] **made them male and female.**[k]

a9:31 Or handed over b9:37 Or Whoever receives c9:38 Other mss add who didn't go along with us d9:41 Lit drink in the name; = Messiah e9:42 A millstone turned by a donkey f9:44,46 Other mss omit bracketed text g9:44,46,48 Is 66:24 h9:49 Other mss add and every sacrifice will be salted with salt i9:49 Lv 2:16; Ezk 43:24 j10:6 Other mss omit God k10:6 Gn 1:27; 5:2

with impurities and over time could acquire a stale taste. **be at peace with one another.** When His followers have a sense of service, peace is the outcome. Had the disciples grasped this concept of servant power instead of opting for power and greatness, they would not have been arguing on the road (v. 33).

10:1 from there. He begins His journey to Jerusalem in Capernaum (9:33), the place where His ministry began in the Gospel of Mark (1:16-45). **Judea.** A Roman province in the south of Palestine, similar in size and location to the land of Judah in the Old Testament. **across the Jordan.** This is a reference to a specific region called Perea, which was a narrow corridor on the east side of the Jordan. Pious Jews would cross over the Jordan into Perea to avoid traveling through Samaria. This is the territory of

Herod Antipas, the ruler who beheaded John the Baptist.

10:2 test Him. It is not by chance that the Pharisees question Jesus about divorce. It was this issue that led to John the Baptist's death (6:17-28). If Jesus responded that divorce was lawful, then the leaders could criticize Him as being in opposition to John the Baptist whom the people greatly respected for his courage in opposing Herod's sin. If Jesus said it was not lawful, then the leaders might be able to get Herod to arrest Him as well. **divorce.** All the Jewish parties agreed (on the basis of Deut. 24:1) that divorce was allowed. The issue in this debate concerned the grounds on which such divorce was permissible. It was only the husband who had the right of divorce. The most that a wife could do was to ask her husband to divorce her.

10:4 divorce papers. These were issued to the woman as a form of protection, verifying her release from marriage and giving her the right to remarry.

10:11 commits adultery against her. In the Jewish law of that era, adultery was considered to be an offense against the man. Jesus asserts the responsibility of the husband to be faithful to his wife under God's command.

10:13 little children. The age is uncertain. The term was used to describe infants and children up to 12 years old. **His disciples rebuked them.** The demands on Jesus were ceaseless. The disciples wanted to protect Him, and so in an era when children were expected to be kept in the background, it was not unreasonable that they would attempt to curb this particular demand.

7 **For this reason a man will leave**
  his father and mother
  [and be joined to his wife,]ª
8 **and the two will become one flesh.**ᵇ

So they are no longer two, but one flesh. 9 Therefore what God has joined together, man must not separate."

10 Now in the house the disciples questioned Him again about this matter. 11 And He said to them, "Whoever divorces his wife and marries another commits adultery against her. 12 Also, if she divorces her husband and marries another, she commits adultery."

Blessing the Children

13 Some people were bringing little children to Him so He might touch them, but His disciples rebuked them. 14 When Jesus saw it, He was indignant and said to them, "Let the little children come to Me. Don't stop them, for the kingdom of God belongs to such as these. 15 •I assure you: Whoever does not welcomeᶜ the kingdom of God like a little child will never enter it." 16 After taking them in His arms, He laid His hands on them and blessed them.

The Rich Young Ruler

17 As He was setting out on a journey, a man ran up, knelt down before Him, and asked Him, "Good Teacher, what must I do to inherit eternal life?"

18 "Why do you call Me good?" Jesus asked him. "No one is good but One—God. 19 You know the commandments:

Do not murder;
do not commit adultery;
do not steal;
do not bear false witness;
do not defraud;
honor your father and mother."ᵈ

20 He said to Him, "Teacher, I have kept all these from my youth."

21 Then, looking at him, Jesus loved him and said to him, "You lack one thing: Go, sell all you have and give to the poor, and you will have treasure in heaven. Then come,ᵉ follow Me." 22 But he was stunnedᶠ at this demand, and he went away grieving, because he had many possessions.

Perilous Possessions

1. What is the most valuable thing you own?

Mark 10:17-31

2. If God asked you to give up all your possessions and be a missionary in a distant land, what would you say?
3. Why is it so hard (v. 23) for a rich man to enter the kingdom of heaven?
4. What things in life can make it hard for people to serve God? What things in your life hinder you?
5. If Jesus said to you, "You lack one thing" (v. 21), what would be that one thing?

Possessions and the Kingdom

23 Jesus looked around and said to His disciples, "How hard it is for those who have wealth to enter the kingdom of God!" 24 But the disciples were astonished at His words. Again Jesus said to them, "Children, how hard it isᵍ to enter the kingdom of God! 25 It is easier for a camel to go through the eye of a needle than for a rich person to enter the kingdom of God."

26 So they were even more astonished, saying to one another, "Then who can be saved?"

ª**10:7** Other mss omit bracketed text ᵇ**10:7–8** Gn 2:24 ᶜ**10:15** Or *not receive* ᵈ**10:19** Ex 20:12–16; Dt 5:16–20 ᵉ**10:21** Other mss add *taking up the cross, and* ᶠ**10:22** Or *he became gloomy* ᵍ**10:24** Other mss add *for those trusting in wealth*

10:14 the kingdom of God belongs to such as these. Jesus says this humble inner disposition of soul must be evident in members of his kingdom.

10:20 kept all these from my youth. The man believes he has kept the commandments, and yet he is unsure whether he has gained eternal life. This was the fallacy of a system based on works/righteousness. People were struggling to be counted among the righteous until the judgment (and then it was too late). There was no hope for all failed.

10:21 loved him. Mark is the only Gospel to note Jesus' affection for this earnest and sincere young man. **Go, sell all you have.** It was felt in the Old Testament that riches by themselves were no hindrance to spiritual pursuit. But Jesus points out that accumulation of wealth can hinder participation in

God's kingdom. **follow Me.** The weight of emphasis is not on selling all, but on following Jesus. The man's possessions are in the way of his discipleship to Jesus.

10:24 astonished. The disciples are astonished because traditional Jewish wisdom saw wealth as a sign of God's favor; it was thought to be a verification that one had led a godly life (Job 1:10; 42:10; Ps. 128:1-2).

10:26 Then who can be saved? They realize the radical nature of Jesus' statement and wonder about their own fate. If it is difficult for anyone to enter the kingdom, even the rich who they had always assumed were favored by God, then what chance do they have?

10:32 Jerusalem. Jesus' destination is now revealed, as is the site of His betrayal, death, and resurrection (v. 33). **astonished ...**

afraid. Given the increasingly hostile response toward Jesus by the leaders, it was frightening that Jesus headed directly into a confrontation with them.

10:37 They interpret Jesus' heading toward Jerusalem as a sign that He will initiate His new kingdom in Jerusalem, over which He will rule as the new king of Israel.

10:38 drink the cup. This is a phrase which means "share the same fate." In the Old Testament, the cup is a metaphor for wrath (Ps. 75:8; Isa. 51: 17-22). **baptism.** In the Old Testament, the image of a deluge or flood overwhelming one is used as a metaphor for disaster (Ps. 42:7; Isa. 43:2). Both the cup and the baptism refer to Jesus' suffering and death for the sins of the world.

10:39 We are able. The disciples answer

[27] Looking at them, Jesus said, "With men it is impossible, but not with God, because all things are possible with God."

[28] Peter began to tell Him, "Look, we have left everything and followed You."

[29] "I assure you," Jesus said, "there is no one who has left house, brothers or sisters, mother or father,[a] children, or fields because of Me and the gospel, [30] who will not receive 100 times more, now at this time—houses, brothers and sisters, mothers and children, and fields, with persecutions—and eternal life in the age to come. [31] But many who are first will be last, and the last first."

The Third Prediction of His Death

[32] They were on the road, going up to Jerusalem, and Jesus was walking ahead of them. They were astonished, but those who followed Him were afraid. Taking the Twelve aside again, He began to tell them the things that would happen to Him.

[33] "Listen! We are going up to Jerusalem. The •Son of Man will be handed over to the •chief priests and the •scribes, and they will condemn Him to death. Then they will hand Him over to the Gentiles, [34] and they will mock Him, spit on Him, flog[b] Him, and kill Him, and He will rise after three days."

Suffering and Service

[35] Then James and John, the sons of Zebedee, approached Him and said, "Teacher, we want You to do something for us if we ask You."

[36] "What do you want Me to do for you?" He asked them.

[37] They answered Him, "Allow us to sit at Your right and at Your left in Your glory."

[38] But Jesus said to them, "You don't know what you're asking. Are you able to drink the cup I drink or to be baptized with the baptism I am baptized with?"

[39] "We are able," they told Him.

Jesus said to them, "You will drink the cup I drink, and you will be baptized with the baptism I am baptized with. [40] But to sit at My right or left is not Mine to give; instead, it is for those it has been prepared for."

Fierce Competition

1. Who is the most competitive person in your family? Do you see competitiveness as a positive or negative quality?

Mark 10:35-45

2. What were James and John asking of Jesus? How were their priorities wrong?

3. How is Christ's teaching about how to be great (v. 43) different from what the world teaches?

4. What does it mean to be a servant to others? Do you tend most often to be a servant or the one served?

5. How can you work this week to serve others?

[41] When the ⌊other⌋ 10 ⌊disciples⌋ heard this, they began to be indignant with James and John.

[42] Jesus called them over and said to them, "You know that those who are regarded as rulers of the Gentiles dominate them, and their men of high positions exercise power over them. [43] But it must not be like that among you. On the contrary, whoever wants to become great among you must be your servant, [44] and whoever wants to be first among you must be a •slave to all. [45] For even the Son of Man did not come to be served, but to serve, and to give His life—a ransom for many."[c]

A Blind Man Healed

[46] They came to Jericho. And as He was leaving Jericho with His disciples and a large crowd, Bartimaeus (the son of Timaeus), a blind beggar, was sitting by the road. [47] When he heard that it was Jesus the •Nazarene,

---

[a]**10:29** Other mss add *or wife*   [b]**10:34** Or *scourge*   [c]**10:45** Or *in the place of many*; Is 53:10–12

---

too readily Jesus' question as to whether they can share His cup and His baptism. They do not grasp what He means by this question, thinking perhaps that it is referring to being in fellowship with Him. Their leadership will not be expressed through positions of authority but through suffering and death.

10:43 servant. Rather than become masters (and exercise authority), they are to become servants (and meet the needs of others).

10:45 ransom. In the first century, a slave or a prisoner could gain freedom if a purchase price (ransom) was paid. Jesus would pay the ransom price "for many" by His death (Titus 2:14; 1 Peter 1:18-19).

10:46 Jericho. They've almost completed their journey from Galilee. Jericho is a city

some 18 miles east of Jerusalem and is the place where travelers recrossed the Jordan back into Israel. **a large crowd.** These were pilgrims on their way to Jerusalem for the Passover Feast. Every male over 12 years of age was expected to attend.

10:47, Son of David, Jesus. A debate was going on as to who the Messiah would be. Would he come from the tribe of Levi, or was he a king in the line of David? Clearly this is a messianic title by which Bartimaeus hails Jesus. Interestingly, Jesus does not silence him as He has done so often in the past when His identity is revealed. The time for secrecy is past. He accepts the title. This is the only use in Mark of this title, on the eve of Jesus' entry into Jerusalem as messianic King.

10:52 Your faith has healed you. Barti-

maeus demonstrated his faith in several ways: by his title for Jesus (showing he grasped who Jesus was), by his persistence (he will not let this opportunity go by), and by his request for healing (showing that he believed Jesus could do so).

11:2 a young donkey. According to Zechariah 9:9, the King would come riding on a colt. Jesus will not simply enter Jerusalem. He will come as the messianic King. He will not come as a warrior-king (as the people expected) riding a war horse. Matthew 21:2 states this was a donkey, specifically fulfilling Zechariah's prophecy and emphasizing the peaceful, gentle nature of the Messiah.

11:8 spread their robes. This was a gesture of respect, given to kings (2 Kin. 9:12-13).

he began to cry out, "Son of David, Jesus, have mercy on me!" [48] Many people told him to keep quiet, but he was crying out all the more, "Have mercy on me, Son of David!"

[49] Jesus stopped and said, "Call him."

So they called the blind man and said to him, "Have courage! Get up; He's calling for you." [50] He threw off his coat, jumped up, and came to Jesus.

[51] Then Jesus answered him, "What do you want Me to do for you?"

"*Rabbouni,*"[a] the blind man told Him, "I want to see!"

[52] "Go your way," Jesus told him. "Your faith has healed you." Immediately he could see and began to follow Him on the road.

The Triumphal Entry

11 When they approached Jerusalem, at Bethphage and Bethany near the •Mount of Olives, He sent two of His disciples [2] and told them, "Go into the village ahead of you. As soon as you enter it, you will find a young donkey tied there, on which no one has ever sat. Untie it and bring it here. [3] If anyone says to you, 'Why are you doing this?' say, 'The Lord needs it and will send it back here right away.'"

[4] So they went and found a young donkey outside in the street, tied by a door. They untied it, [5] and some of those standing there said to them, "What are you doing, untying the donkey?" [6] They answered them just as Jesus had said, so they let them go. [7] Then they brought the donkey to Jesus and threw their robes on it, and He sat on it.

[8] Many people spread their robes on the road, and others spread leafy branches cut from the fields.[b] [9] Then those who went ahead and those who followed kept shouting:

> •Hosanna!
> Blessed is He who comes
> in the name of the Lord![c]
> [10] Blessed is the coming kingdom
> of our father David!
> Hosanna in the highest heaven!

[11] And He went into Jerusalem and into the •temple complex. After looking around at everything, since it was already late, He went out to Bethany with the Twelve.

Taking a Stand

1. What does it take to get you to clean your room? How clean is it right now?

Mark 11:12-19

2. In what way had the temple area been made into "a den of thieves" (v. 17)?
3. Why did Jesus get so angry about it? Why did He, called the "Prince of Peace," react so violently?
4. If Jesus came to your town today, what might make Him react in anger?
5. Where do you need to take a righteous stand? How can you go about this?

The Barren Fig Tree Is Cursed

[12] The next day when they came out from Bethany, He was hungry. [13] After seeing in the distance a fig tree with leaves, He went to find out if there was anything on it. When He came to it, He found nothing but leaves, because it was not the season for figs. [14] He said to it, "May no one ever eat fruit from you again!" And His disciples heard it.

Cleansing the Temple Complex

[15] They came to Jerusalem, and He went into the temple complex and began to throw out those buying

---

[a] **10:51** Hb for *my teacher;* Jn 20:16   [b] **11:8** Other mss read *others were cutting leafy branches from the trees and spreading them on the road*
[c] **11:9** Ps 118:26

11:9 *Hosanna!* Literally, "Save now." **Blessed is He.** While the psalm from which this cry is taken (Ps. 118:26), originally served as a tribute to the king of Israel, it was applied to any pilgrim who traveled to Jerusalem for the feasts. It was later understood by the rabbis to be a messianic psalm, referring to the final redemption that would be ushered in by the Messiah.

11:11 temple. This was the third temple to be built on Mount Zion. It was built by Herod the Great in 20 B.C. and was a magnificent structure covering some 30 acres. The temple consisted of four concentric courts ringed by enormous walls.

11:13 fig tree. On the Mount of Olives, fig trees are in leaf by early April, but they would not have ripe fruit until June, long after the Passover. Fig trees were a common pro-

phetic symbol. They were associated with Israel and with judgment (Jer. 8:13; Hos. 9:10-11; Mic. 7:1).

11:15 buying and selling. Worship in the temple centered on sacrifice. Those wishing to participate were required to offer an unblemished animal, and apparently temple inspectors approved only those animals bought from certified vendors (who sold animals at a huge markup). **money changers.** At Passover, each Jew was required to pay a temple tax of one-half shekel (nearly two days' wages). No other currency was acceptable, necessitating money changers to exchange the money of pilgrims coming from outside. The money changers charged exorbitant amounts for the simple act of exchanging currency; up to one-half day's wages of working people. **those selling doves.** A dove was the lowliest of all sacri-

fices. While a lamb was normally required, the law had a provision that those too poor to afford a lamb could offer two doves instead (Lev. 5:7). While this provision was still observed, temple vendors charged 20 times what it cost to buy a dove outside the temple.

11:17 a house of prayer for all nations? The outermost area of the temple where all these activities were taking place was called the Court of the Gentiles. It was intended to be a place where pious Gentiles could pray.

11:23 this mountain. This is probably the Mount of Olives overlooking Jerusalem. **the sea.** The Dead Sea is visible from the Mount of Olives.

11:27 the chief priests, the scribes and the elders. The chief priests were the key officers of the temple, just below the high

and selling in the temple. He overturned the money changers' tables and the chairs of those selling doves, [16] and would not permit anyone to carry goods through the temple complex.

[17] Then He began to teach them: "Is it not written, **My house will be called a house of prayer for all nations?**[a] But you have made it **a den of thieves!**"[b] [18] Then the •chief priests and the •scribes heard it and started looking for a way to destroy Him. For they were afraid of Him, because the whole crowd was astonished by His teaching.

[19] And whenever evening came, they would go out of the city.

The Barren Fig Tree Is Withered

[20] Early in the morning, as they were passing by, they saw the fig tree withered from the roots up. [21] Then Peter remembered and said to Him, "•Rabbi, look! The fig tree that You cursed is withered."

[22] Jesus replied to them, "Have faith in God. [23] •I assure you: If anyone says to this mountain, 'Be lifted up and thrown into the sea,' and does not doubt in his heart, but believes that what he says will happen, it will be done for him. [24] Therefore, I tell you, all the things you pray and ask for—believe that you have received[c] them, and you will have them. [25] And whenever you stand praying, if you have anything against anyone, forgive him, so that your Father in heaven will also forgive you your wrongdoing.[d] [[26] But if you don't forgive, neither will your Father in heaven forgive your wrongdoing."][e]

Messiah's Authority Challenged

[27] They came again to Jerusalem. As He was walking in the temple complex, the chief priests, the scribes, and the elders came and asked Him, [28] "By what authority are You doing these things? Who gave You this authority to do these things?"

[29] Jesus said to them, "I will ask you one question; then answer Me, and I will tell you by what authority I am doing these things. [30] Was John's baptism from heaven or from men? Answer Me."

[31] They began to argue among themselves: "If we say, 'From heaven,' He will say, 'Then why didn't you believe him?' [32] But if we say, 'From men'"—they were afraid of the crowd, because everyone thought that John was a genuine prophet. [33] So they answered Jesus, "We don't know."

And Jesus said to them, "Neither will I tell you by what authority I do these things."

The Parable of the Vineyard Owner

12 Then He began to speak to them in parables: "A man planted a vineyard, put a fence around it, dug out a pit for a winepress, and built a watchtower. Then he leased it to tenant farmers and went away. [2] At harvest time he sent a •slave to the farmers to collect some of the fruit of the vineyard from the farmers. [3] But they took him, beat him, and sent him away empty-handed. [4] Again he sent another slave to them, and they[f] hit him on the head and treated him shamefully.[g] [5] Then he sent another, and they killed that one. ⌊He⌋ also ⌊sent⌋ many others; they beat some and they killed some.

[6] "He still had one to send, a beloved son. Finally he sent him to them, saying, 'They will respect my son.'

[7] "But those tenant farmers said among themselves, 'This is the heir. Come, let's kill him, and the inheritance will be ours!' [8] So they seized him, killed him, and threw him out of the vineyard.

[9] "Therefore, what will the owner[h] of the vineyard do? He will come and destroy the farmers and give the vineyard to others. [10] Haven't you read this Scripture:

> **The stone that the builders rejected**
> **has become the cornerstone.**[i]
> [11] **This came from the Lord**
> **and is wonderful in our eyes?**[j]

[12] Because they knew He had said this parable against them, they were looking for a way to arrest Him, but

---

[a]**11:17** Is 56:7 [b]**11:17** Jr 7:11 [c]**11:24** Other mss read *you receive*; other mss read *you will receive* [d]**11:25** These are the only uses of this word in Mk. It means "the violation of the Law" or "stepping over a boundary" or "departing from the path" or "trespass." [e]**11:26** Other mss omit bracketed text [f]**12:4** Other mss add *threw stones and* [g]**12:4** Other mss add *and sent him off* [h]**12:9** Or *lord* [i]**12:10** Lit *the head of the corner* [j]**12:10–11** Ps 118:22–23

---

priest in rank. The elders were powerful and (reputedly) wise leaders of Israel. They were generally not priests, but instead were administrators, judges, and military leaders of Israel. The teachers of the law were religious lawyers. Taken together, these three groups comprised the Sanhedrin—the ruling Jewish council—who opposed Him as Jesus prophesied they would (8:31).

12:1 A man planted a vineyard ... dug out a pit ... built a watchtower. For the religious leaders, Jesus' use of these phrases would surely call to mind the well-known imagery found in a poem originally delivered by the prophet Isaiah centuries before (Isa. 5:1-7). In Isaiah's song, the symbol of the vineyard was used to describe Israel. Although planted and cultivated by God, Israel was compared to a vineyard that produced only bad fruit. In this parable God is the landlord

who leaves his vineyard in the care of others who are responsible to Him. It produces fruit, but the tenants refuse to give Him His share of the produce.

12:6 a beloved son. The crowd didn't know the identity of the Son, yet Mark's readers know that it is Jesus. A central theme in chapters 11–16 is the discovery that Jesus is the Son of God.

12:10 cornerstone. The reference is to a stone that was rejected in the building of Solomon's temple, which was later found to be the keystone to the porch (a keystone held an arch in place).

12:13-17 to trap Him. Beaten badly in their first two confrontations with Jesus, the leaders regroup and consider their strategy. They decide to send representatives from

two groups with a trick question they hope will trap Jesus. The question deals with the explosive issue of taxes.

12:13 Pharisees and the Herodians. The origin of this unusual alliance is described in 3:1-6. The plan to destroy Jesus had now matured and was gaining momentum in Jerusalem.

12:14 You are truthful. By these and other flattering words they hoped to catch Jesus off guard. **taxes.** A poll tax had to be paid to the Romans each year by all adult Jews. This tax was deeply resented.

12:15 Bring Me a denarius. A denarius was a small, silver coin (worth about 25 cents today) bearing the picture of Tiberius Caesar. The denarius was the only coin that could be used to pay the poll tax.

they were afraid of the crowd. So they left Him and went away.

Money Matters

1. Whose picture appears on a five-dollar bill? Ten? Twenty? Fifty? Hundred?

Mark 12:13-17

2. How were the Pharisees trying to trap Jesus with their questions about paying taxes?

3. What did Jesus mean when he said, "Give back to Caesar the things that are Caesar's, and to God the things that are God's" (v. 17)?

4. Who is Caesar today? What things belong to "Caesar"? What things belong to God?

5. What do you need to give to God? Are you doing this?

God and Caesar

13 Then they sent some of the •Pharisees and the •Herodians to Him to trap Him by what He said.ᵃ 14 When they came, they said to Him, "Teacher, we know You are truthful and defer to no one, for You don't show partialityᵇ but teach truthfully the way of God. Is it lawful to pay taxes to Caesar or not? 15 Should we pay, or should we not pay?"

But knowing their hypocrisy, He said to them, "Why are you testing Me? Bring Me a •denarius to look at." 16 So they brought one. "Whose image and inscription is this?" He asked them.

"Caesar's," they said.

17 Then Jesus told them, "Give back to Caesar the things that are Caesar's, and to God the things that are God's." And they were amazed at Him.

The Sadducees and the Resurrection

18 Some •Sadducees, who say there is no resurrection, came to Him and questioned Him: 19 "Teacher, Moses wrote for us that **if a man's brother dies,** leaves his wife behind, and **leaves no child, his brother should take the wife and produce •offspring for his brother.**ᶜ 20 There were seven brothers. The first took a wife, and dying, left no offspring. 21 The second also took her, and he died, leaving no offspring. And the third likewise. 22 The seven alsoᵈ left no offspring. Last of all, the woman died too. 23 In the resurrection, when they rise,ᵉ whose wife will she be, since the seven had married her?"ᶠ

24 Jesus told them, "Are you not deceived because you don't know the Scriptures or the power of God? 25 For when they rise from the dead, they neither marry nor are given in marriage but are like angels in heaven. 26 Now concerning the dead being raised—haven't you read in the book of Moses, in the passage about the burning bush, how God spoke to him: **I am the God of Abraham and the God of Isaac and the God of Jacob?**ᵍ 27 He is not God of the dead but of the living. You are badly deceived."

The Primary Commandments

28 One of the •scribes approached. When he heard them debating and saw that Jesus answered them well, he asked Him, "Which commandment is the most important of all?"ʰ

29 "This is the most important,"ⁱ Jesus answered:

Listen, Israel! The Lord our God, the Lord is One.ʲ 30 **Love the Lord your God with all your heart, with all your soul, with all your mind, and with all your strength.**ᵏˡ

31 "The second is: **Love your neighbor as yourself.**ᵐ There is no other commandment greater than these."

ᵃ**12:13** Lit *trap Him in (a) word*   ᵇ**12:14** Lit *don't look on the face of men;* that is, on the outward appearance   ᶜ**12:19** Gn 38:8; Dt 25:5
ᵈ**12:22** Other mss add *had taken her and*   ᵉ**12:23** Other mss omit *when they rise*   ᶠ**12:23** Lit *the seven had her as a wife*   ᵍ**12:26** Ex 3:6,15–16
ʰ**12:28** Lit *Which commandment is first of all?*   ⁱ**12:29** Other mss add *of all the commandments*   ʲ**12:29** Or *The Lord our God is one Lord.*
ᵏ**12:30** Dt 6:4–5; Jos 22:5   ˡ**12:30** Other mss add *This is the first commandment.*   ᵐ**12:31** Lv 19:18

12:18 Sadducees. There is relatively little information available about this group. It seems they were a small but highly influential party of wealthy, aristocratic priests. Jesus had been no threat to the Sadducees. However, when He cleared the temple, He invaded their sphere of influence and so became their enemy. **resurrection.** The belief that at the end of the age God would bring the dead back to life for judgment. The Sadducees did not accept this belief.

12:24-27 Jesus told them. Jesus takes their question seriously (although it is not a sincere question, since they did not believe in the resurrection) and answers them directly. In so doing, He affirms that life after death is real.

12:28 scribes. Jesus has answered suc-

cessfully the Herodians, the Pharisees, and the Sadducees. It is now a scribe's turn to ask a question. His attitude toward Jesus is different from the others. He asks a genuine question. **saw that Jesus answered them well.** This teacher of the law is very impressed with the way Jesus answered the questions, so he asks an important question for Him personally. **Which commandment is the most important?** This phrase is, literally, "which is the chief (or first) commandment"; i.e., what commandment summarizes all the commandments?

12:29 Listen, Israel! The Shema (a statement of faith taken from Deut. 6:4), is recited by pious Jews each morning and evening. This affirmation captures what was clearly distinctive about Israel's God.

12:30 Love. In Greek, this is *agape.* It means

an active, benevolent giving to others without expectation of reward. **heart.** The inner life; the center of personality; where God reveals Himself to a person. **soul.** The seat of life itself; the personality or ego. **mind.** The organ of knowledge; the intellect. **strength.** The power of a living being; the total effort behind heart, soul, and mind.

12:38 long robes. Long, white linen garments fringed with tassels that touched the ground. In such a stately garment, a person could not run or work and would be reckoned to be one of leisure and importance. **greetings.** People considered the teachers of the law to be men of great insight and authority, and so they rose when they passed by and called out titles of respect.

12:39 the front seats in the synagogues.

32 Then the scribe said to Him, "You are right, Teacher! You have correctly said that He is One, and there is no one else except Him. 33 And to love Him with all your heart, with all your understanding,a and with all your strength, and to love your neighbor as yourself, is far more ⌊important⌋ than all the burnt offerings and sacrifices."

34 When Jesus saw that he answered intelligently, He said to him, "You are not far from the kingdom of God." And no one dared to question Him any longer.

The Question about the Messiah

35 So Jesus asked this question as He taught in the •temple complex, "How can the scribes say that the •Messiah is the Son of David? 36 David himself says by the Holy Spirit:

**The Lord declared to my Lord,
'Sit at My right hand
until I put Your enemies under Your feet.'b**

37 David himself calls Him 'Lord'; how then can the Messiah be his Son?" And the large crowd was listening to Him with delight.

Warning against the Scribes

38 He also said in His teaching, "Beware of the scribes, who want to go around in long robes, and who want greetings in the marketplaces, 39 the front seats in the •synagogues, and the places of honor at banquets. 40 They devour widows' houses and say long prayers just for show. These will receive harsher punishment."

The Widow's Gift

41 Sitting across from the temple treasury, He watched how the crowd dropped money into the treasury. Many rich people were putting in large sums. 42 And a poor widow came and dropped in two tiny coins worth very little.c 43 Summoning His disciples, He said to them, "•I assure you: This poor widow has put in more than all those giving to the temple treasury. 44 For they all gave out of their surplus, but she out of her poverty has put in everything she possessed—all she had to live on."

Meaningful Giving

1. What is your most priceless possession? What makes it so special?

Mark 12:41-44

2. What did Jesus mean that this poor widow had given more than all the others (v. 43)?

3. What did Jesus mean that other people had given "out of their surplus" (v. 44)?

4. Do you give to God out of your surplus or out of your poverty?

5. If you really get serious about God, what will have to change in the way you spend your money? Your time?

Destruction of the Temple Predicted

13 As He was going out of the •temple complex, one of His disciples said to Him, "Teacher, look! What massive stones! What impressive buildings!"

2 Jesus said to him, "Do you see these great buildings? Not one stone will be left here on another that will not be thrown down!"

Signs of the End of the Age

3 While He was sitting on the •Mount of Olives across from the temple complex, Peter, James, John, and Andrew asked Him privately, 4 "Tell us, when will these things happen? And what will be the sign when all these things are about to take place?"

5 Then Jesus began by telling them: "Watch out that no one deceives you. 6 Many will come in My name,

a 12:33 Other mss add with all your soul b 12:36 Ps 110:1 c 12:42 Lit dropped in two lepta, which is a quadrans; the lepton was the smallest and least valuable Gk coin in use. The quadrans, 1/64 of a daily wage, was the smallest Roman coin.

The choice seat was up front, with its back to the box which contained the sacred Scriptures, and its front facing the congregation so that all would see who sat there.

12:40 They devour widows' houses. Since the teachers of the law were forbidden to receive pay for their teaching, they lived off others, including, it seems, poor widows who were little able to support them.

12:41 temple treasury. This was located in the court of women (which was the first of the inner courts of the temple). It consisted of 13 trumpet-shaped receptacles used to collect donations for the temple.

12:42 tiny coins. The smallest coins in circulation, worth 1/400 shekel, or about 1/8 of a cent.

13:1 What impressive buildings! The temple was, indeed, a wonder to behold. It was built with huge white stones, some measuring 37 feet long by 12 feet high by 18 feet wide. At a distance the temple appeared to strangers, like a mountain covered with snow.

13:3-4 The disciples once again come to Jesus, privately asking Him to explain His teaching. To them, an event as cataclysmic as the temple's destruction must be one of the events that would usher in the new age (Matt. 24:3).

13:5 Watch out. This is a key theme in this section (vv. 21-23, 33-37). Vigilance, against being deceived by those who claim that the end times have begun, or claim that they are prophets, is essential.

13:14 the abomination that causes desolation. This phrase appears in the book of Daniel (Dan. 9:27; 11:31; 12:11). It refers to an event so awful that Jews will flee from the temple in horror. A similar event happened in 168 B.C. when Antiochus Epiphanes, a Syrian king, captured Jerusalem. He set up an altar to Zeus in the temple and sacrificed a pig there. He also put public brothels in the temple courts. Jesus warns that when such an event occurs again, the fall of Jerusalem is imminent (2 Thess. 2:1-4). **those in Judea must flee.** When the armies march against the city, Jesus' disciples are to recognize that this is the sign that God's judgment against Israel has come to a head. Instead of flocking to the city in anticipation of a dramatic messianic victory, they must run for their lives.

13:23 I have told you everything in ad-

saying, 'I am He,' and they will deceive many. [7] When you hear of wars and rumors of wars, don't be alarmed; these things must take place, but the end is not yet. [8] For nation will rise up against nation, and kingdom against kingdom. There will be earthquakes in various places, and famines.[a] These are the beginning of birth pains.

Persecutions Predicted

[9] "But you, be on your guard! They will hand you over to sanhedrins,[b] and you will be flogged in the •synagogues. You will stand before governors and kings because of Me, as a witness to them. [10] And the good news[c] must first be proclaimed to all nations. [11] So when they arrest you and hand you over, don't worry beforehand what you will say. On the contrary, whatever is given to you in that hour—say it. For it isn't you speaking, but the Holy Spirit. [12] Then brother will betray brother to death, and a father his child. Children will rise up against parents and put them to death. [13] And you will be hated by everyone because of My name. But the one who endures to the end will be delivered.[d]

The Great Tribulation

[14] "When you see the **abomination that causes desolation**[e] standing where it should not" (let the reader understand),[f] "then those in Judea must flee to the mountains! [15] A man on the housetop must not come down or go in to get anything out of his house. [16] And a man in the field must not go back to get his clothes. [17] Woe to pregnant women and nursing mothers in those days! [18] Pray it[g] won't happen in winter. [19] For those will be days of tribulation, the kind that hasn't been from the beginning of the world,[h] which God created, until now and never will be again! [20] Unless the Lord limited those days, no one would survive.[i] But He limited those days because of the elect, whom He chose.

[21] "Then if anyone tells you, 'Look, here is the •Messiah! Look—there!' do not believe it! [22] For false messiahs[j] and false prophets will rise up and will perform signs and wonders to lead astray, if possible, the elect. [23] And you must watch! I have told you everything in advance.

The Coming of the Son of Man

[24] "But in those days, after that tribulation:

The sun will be darkened,
and the moon will not shed its light;
[25] the stars will be falling from the sky,
and the celestial powers will be shaken.

[26] Then they will see the •Son of Man coming in clouds with great power and glory. [27] He will send out the angels and gather His elect from the four winds, from the end of the earth to the end of the sky.

The Parable of the Fig Tree

[28] "Learn this parable from the fig tree: As soon as its branch becomes tender and sprouts leaves, you know that summer is near. [29] In the same way, when you see these things happening, know[k] that He[l] is near—at the door! [30] •I assure you: This generation will certainly not pass away until all these things take place. [31] Heaven and earth will pass away, but My words will never pass away.

No One Knows the Day or Hour

[32] "Now concerning that day or hour no one knows—neither the angels in heaven nor the Son—except the Father. [33] Watch! Be alert![m] For you don't know when the time is ⌊coming⌋. [34] It is like a man on a journey, who left his house, gave authority to his •slaves, gave each one his work, and commanded the doorkeeper to be alert. [35] Therefore be alert, since you don't know when the master of the house is coming—whether in the evening or at midnight or at the crowing of the rooster or early in the morning. [36] Otherwise, he might come suddenly and find you sleeping. [37] And what I say to you, I say to everyone: Be alert!"

The Plot to Kill Jesus

14 After two days it was the •Passover and the Festival of •Unleavened Bread. The •chief

---

[a]**13:8** Other mss add *and disturbances*   [b]**13:9** Local Jewish courts or local councils   [c]**13:10** Or *the gospel*   [d]**13:13** Or *saved*   [e]**13:14** Dn 9:27   [f]**13:14** These are, most likely, Mark's words to his readers.   [g]**13:18** Other mss read *pray that your escape*   [h]**13:19** Lit *creation*   [i]**13:20** Lit *days, all flesh would not survive*   [j]**13:22** Or *false christs*   [k]**13:29** Or *you know*   [l]**13:29** Or *it; = summer*   [m]**13:33** Other mss add *and pray*

---

vance. Some see the fulfillment of Jesus' words in the fall of Jerusalem in AD 70. Others are still looking for the "Great Tribulation" yet to come (Rev. 7:14).

13:24-27 Jesus now describes the second coming of the Son of Man in power and glory. The destruction of Jerusalem is the result of human failure and evil. It will bring suffering and hardship. The second coming will bring salvation and blessing to the people of God.

13:27 gather His elect. It is God who will do this (Deut. 30:3-4; Ps. 50:4-5; Isa. 43:5-6). Jesus makes it quite clear who He is: the Son of God (vv. 26-27).

13:28 parable from the fig tree. They knew that the fig tree only got its leaves in late spring. When the leaves came, it was a sure

sign that summer was near. This is a reference to the rather mysterious cursing of the fig tree by Jesus in 11:12-14,20-21, and has to do with the judgment on Jerusalem, as Jesus' teaching here shows.

13:28-37 With all this as background (vv. 5-27), Jesus can now respond to the disciples' original question (v. 4). His response is that one event (the fall of Jerusalem) will occur within their lifetime, but are not to be deceived. This will not usher in the end time. The final event (the second coming) will be at a future, unspecified date known only to God the Father (v. 32). Jesus encourages the disciples to be vigilant, but not to worry about when all this will take place.

14:1 the Passover. A feast in which the people of Israel celebrated God's deliverance of

their nation from Egypt where they had been held as slaves (Ex. 12). **the Festival of Unleavened Bread.** By the time of the first century, this feast was coupled with the Passover so that there was a week of feasting.

14:3 a woman came. A woman would not be present at a meal like this except to serve. Her entrance would have been scandalous.

14:12 sacrifice the Passover lamb. Each pilgrim sacrificed his own lamb in the temple. A priest caught the blood in a bowl and this was thrown on the altar. After removing certain parts of the lamb for sacrifice, the carcass was returned to the pilgrim and was roasted and eaten for Passover.

14:13-16 Follow him. Instructions for Jesus' arrest had already been issued (John 11:57). He knew that the officials were look-

priests and the •scribes were looking for a treacherous way to arrest and kill Him. ² "Not during the festival," they said, "or there may be rioting among the people."

The Anointing at Bethany

³ While He was in Bethany at the house of Simon who had a serious skin disease, as He was reclining at the table, a woman came with an alabaster jar of pure and expensive fragrant oil of nard. She broke the jar and poured it on His head. ⁴ But some were expressing indignation to one another: "Why has this fragrant oil been wasted? ⁵ For this oil might have been sold for more than 300 •denarii and given to the poor." And they began to scold her.

⁶ Then Jesus said, "Leave her alone. Why are you bothering her? She has done a noble thing for Me. ⁷ You always have the poor with you, and you can do good for them whenever you want, but you do not always have Me. ⁸ She has done what she could; she has anointed My body in advance for burial. ⁹ •I assure you: Wherever the gospel is proclaimed in the whole world, what this woman has done will also be told in memory of her."

¹⁰ Then Judas Iscariot, one of the Twelve, went to the chief priests to hand Him over to them. ¹¹ And when they heard this, they were glad and promised to give him silver.ᵃ So he started looking for a good opportunity to betray Him.

Preparation for Passover

¹² On the first day of Unleavened Bread, when they sacrifice the Passover lamb, His disciples asked Him, "Where do You want us to go and prepare the Passover so You may eat it?"

¹³ So He sent two of His disciples and told them, "Go into the city, and a man carrying a water jug will meet you. Follow him. ¹⁴ Wherever he enters, tell the owner of the house, 'The Teacher says, "Where is the guest room for Me to eat the Passover with My disciples?" ' ¹⁵ He will show you a large room upstairs, furnished and ready. Make the preparations for us

there." ¹⁶ So the disciples went out, entered the city, and found it just as He had told them, and they prepared the Passover.

Betrayal at the Passover

¹⁷ When evening came, He arrived with the Twelve. ¹⁸ While they were reclining and eating, Jesus said, "I assure you: One of you will betray Me—one who is eating with Me!"

¹⁹ They began to be distressed and to say to Him one by one, "Surely not I?"

²⁰ He said to them, "[It is] one of the Twelve—the one who is dipping [bread] with Me in the bowl. ²¹ For the •Son of Man will go just as it is written about Him, but woe to that man by whom the Son of Man is betrayed! It would have been better for that man if he had not been born."

The First Lord's Supper

²² As they were eating, He took bread, blessed and broke it, gave it to them, and said, "Take [it];ᵇ this is My body."

²³ Then He took a cup, and after giving thanks, He gave it to them, and so they all drank from it. ²⁴ He said to them, "This is My blood [that establishes] the covenant;ᶜ it is shed for many. ²⁵ I assure you: I will no longer drink of the fruit of the vine until that day when I drink it in a new wayᵈ in the kingdom of God." ²⁶ After singing psalms,ᵉ they went out to the •Mount of Olives.

Peter's Denial Predicted

²⁷ Then Jesus said to them, "All of you will run away,ᶠ ᵍ because it is written:

I will strike the shepherd,
and the sheep will be scattered.ʰ

²⁸ But after I have been resurrected, I will go ahead of you to Galilee."

²⁹ Peter told Him, "Even if everyone runs away, I will certainly not!"

ᵃ14:11 Or *money*; in Mt 26:15 it is specified as 30 pieces of silver; see Zch 11:12–13 ᵇ14:22 Other mss add *eat*; ᶜ14:24 Other mss read *the new covenant* ᵈ14:25 Or *drink new wine*; lit *drink it new* ᵉ14:26 Pss 113–118 were sung during and after the Passover meal. ᶠ14:27 Other mss add *because of Me this night* ᵍ14:27 Or •*stumble* ʰ14:27 Zch 13:7

---

ing for Him in places away from the crowd. To guard against being arrested before His time, He would generally sleep in Bethany, which was outside the jurisdiction of the priests. But the law required that He eat the Passover meal in Jerusalem itself, hence the need for secret arrangements.

14:18 reclining and eating. People would eat festive meals by lying on couches or cushions arranged around a low table. **one who is eating with Me.** These words recall the prophecy in Psalm 41:9.

14:20 dipping bread with Me in the bowl. To share in a meal was a sign of friendship, accenting the act of betrayal.

14:22-26 bread ... cup. Jesus provides the model for how the church now celebrates communion (1 Cor. 11:23-26).

14:24 covenant. A treaty between two parties. Such an agreement was often sealed by the sacrifice of an animal. It refers to the arrangement that God made with Israel (Ex. 24:1-8) which was dependent on Israel's obedience. Now (as anticipated in Jer. 31:31-34) a new covenant is established, which is made dependent on Jesus' obedience (His sacrificial death). A covenant of law becomes a covenant of love. **shed.** Blood which was poured out symbolized a violent death (Gen. 4:10-11; Deut. 19:10; Matt. 23:35). This phrase points to the type of death Jesus would experience.

14:32 Gethsemane. An olive orchard in an estate at the foot of the Mount of Olives, just outside the eastern wall of Jerusalem. The name means literally "an oil press" (for making olive oil).

14:33 Peter, James, and John. Once again, these three men accompany Jesus during a time of great significance. Interestingly, neither the rebuke by Peter (8:32) nor the self-centered request of James and John (10:35-40) has damaged their relationship with Jesus. Also note each of these men has vowed to stay with Jesus through thick and thin (10:38-39; 14:29, 31). What Jesus asks them to share with Him here is not glory (which they wanted), but sorrow (which they kept denying would come). **deeply distressed.** Literally, filled with "shuddering awe." Jesus is filled with deep sorrow as the impact of submitting to His father's will hits Him.

14:35 fell to the ground. This accents the emotional distress He was feeling. **the hour.** This word is often used to refer to an event that represents a crucial turning point in

30 "I assure you," Jesus said to him, "today, this very night, before the rooster crows twice, you will deny Me three times!"

31 But he kept insisting, "If I have to die with You, I will never deny You!" And they all said the same thing.

Stay Awake

1. When have you fallen asleep at an embarrassing moment: In church? In class? On a date?

Mark 14:32-42

2. Why was Jesus so upset? What did He choose to do at this moment of personal crisis?

3. What does this teach us about how we should handle times of crisis?

4. Jesus told Peter, "Stay awake and pray" because "the spirit is willing, but the flesh is weak" (v. 38). How do these words apply to you?

5. Is someone in your group or team facing a time of crisis? How can you "stay awake" to help that person?

The Prayer in the Garden

32 Then they came to a place named Gethsemane, and He told His disciples, "Sit here while I pray." 33 He took Peter, James, and John with Him, and He began to be deeply distressed and horrified. 34 Then He said to them, "My soul is swallowed up in sorrow[a]—to the point of death. Remain here and stay awake." 35 Then He went a little farther, fell to the ground, and began to pray that if it were possible, the hour might pass from Him. 36 And He said, "•Abba, Father! All things are possible for You. Take this cup away from Me. Nevertheless, not what I will, but what You will."

37 Then He came and found them sleeping. "Simon, are you sleeping?" He asked Peter. "Couldn't you stay awake one hour? 38 Stay awake and pray so that you won't enter into temptation. The spirit is willing, but the flesh is weak."

39 Once again He went away and prayed, saying the same thing. 40 And He came again and found them sleeping, because they could not keep their eyes open.[b] They did not know what to say to Him. 41 Then He came a third time and said to them, "Are you still sleeping and resting? Enough! The time has come. Look, the Son of Man is being betrayed into the hands of sinners. 42 Get up; let's go! See—My betrayer is near."

The Judas Kiss

43 While He was still speaking, Judas, one of the Twelve, suddenly arrived. With him was a mob, with swords and clubs, from the chief priests, the scribes, and the elders. 44 His betrayer had given them a signal. "The One I kiss," he said, "He's the One; arrest Him and take Him away under guard." 45 So when he came, he went right up to Him and said, "•Rabbi!"—and kissed Him. 46 Then they took hold of Him and arrested Him. 47 And one of those who stood by drew his sword, struck the high priest's •slave, and cut off his ear.

48 But Jesus said to them, "Have you come out with swords and clubs, as though I were a criminal,[c] to capture Me? 49 Every day I was among you, teaching in the •temple complex, and you didn't arrest Me. But the Scriptures must be fulfilled." 50 Then they all deserted Him and ran away.

51 Now a certain young man,[d] having a linen cloth wrapped around his naked body, was following Him. They caught hold of him, 52 but he left the linen cloth behind and ran away naked.

Jesus Faces the Sanhedrin

53 They led Jesus away to the high priest, and all the chief priests, the elders, and the scribes convened. 54 Peter followed Him at a distance, right into the high priest's courtyard. He was sitting with the temple police,[e] warming himself by the fire.[f]

a 14:34 Or I am deeply grieved   b 14:40 Lit because their eyes were weighed down   c 14:48 Lit as against a criminal   d 14:51 Perhaps John Mark who later wrote this Gospel   e 14:54 Or the officers; lit the servants   f 14:54 Lit light

---

God's plan for a person or for the world. In reference to Jesus, it specifically refers to His crucifixion (John 12:23).

14:36 Abba. This is how a child would address his father: "Daddy." This was not a title that was used in prayer in the first century. **this cup.** Like the word "hour," "cup" was also used as a image referring to the destiny God had in store for a person.

14:43 a mob. The Sanhedrin commanded the services of the temple police (who were Levites) and of an auxiliary police force (servants of the court) who maintained order outside the temple area.

14:44 kiss. The intensive form of verb used here indicates that Judas' actual kiss was a warm and affectionate greeting and not merely perfunctory.

14:45 Rabbi! This title was a form of respect. It meant literally, "My Great One." By his greeting, by his kiss, and by sharing the same bowl (v. 20—to eat together was a sign of friendship), Judas conveys the sense of a warm relationship with Jesus.

14:47 one of those who stood by. According to John's Gospel (John 18:10), this was Peter. **drew his sword.** That Peter should have a sword is not unusual. Travelers carried them as protection against robbers and the disciples had just completed a journey from Jerusalem to Galilee (Luke 22:36-38).

14:51 young man. It has been suggested that this is Mark himself. He lived in Jerusalem (Acts 12:12), and there is a tradition that

the Last Supper was held in the upper room of his mother's house. **linen cloth.** Probably a bed sheet. The fact that it was linen means that he came from a wealthy family.

14:55 the whole Sanhedrin. A council consisting of 71 leaders, both priests and laymen, who made up the highest Jewish court. They were given authority by Rome to rule in matters of religious law. **testimony.** To convict someone of a capital crime required the unanimous testimony of at least two witnesses. Each witness gave his testimony individually to the judge in the presence of the accused. If two witnesses differed in their accounts, their testimony was thrown out of court (Deut. 19:15-18).

14:62 This is the first time in Mark that Jesus openly and unequivocally declares His Mes-

55 The chief priests and the whole •Sanhedrin were looking for testimony against Jesus to put Him to death, but they could find none. 56 For many were giving false testimony against Him, but the testimonies did not agree. 57 Some stood up and were giving false testimony against Him, stating, 58 "We heard Him say, 'I will demolish this sanctuary made by ⸢human⸣ hands, and in three days I will build another not made by hands.'" 59 Yet their testimony did not agree even on this.

60 Then the high priest stood up before them all and questioned Jesus, "Don't You have an answer to what these men are testifying against You?" 61 But He kept silent and did not answer anything. Again the high priest questioned Him, "Are You the •Messiah, the Son of the Blessed One?"

62 "I am," said Jesus, "and all of you[a] will see **the Son of Man seated at the right hand** of the Power and **coming with the clouds of heaven.**"[b]

63 Then the high priest tore his robes and said, "Why do we still need witnesses? 64 You have heard the blasphemy! What is your decision?"[c]

And they all condemned Him to be deserving of death. 65 Then some began to spit on Him, to blindfold Him, and to beat Him, saying, "Prophesy!" Even the temple police took Him and slapped Him.

Peter Denies His Lord

66 While Peter was in the courtyard below, one of the high priest's servants came. 67 When she saw Peter warming himself, she looked at him and said, "You also were with that •Nazarene, Jesus."

68 But he denied it: "I don't know or understand what you're talking about!" Then he went out to the entryway, and a rooster crowed.[d]

69 When the servant saw him again she began to tell those standing nearby, "This man is one of them!"

70 But again he denied it. After a little while those standing there said to Peter again, "You certainly are one of them, since you're also a Galilean!"[e]

71 Then he started to curse[f] and to swear with an oath, "I don't know this man you're talking about!"

72 Immediately a rooster crowed a second time, and Peter remembered when Jesus had spoken the word to him, "Before the rooster crows twice, you will deny Me three times." When he thought about it, he began to weep.[g]

Jesus Faces Pilate

15 As soon as it was morning, the •chief priests had a meeting with the elders, •scribes, and the whole •Sanhedrin. After tying Jesus up, they led Him away and handed Him over to •Pilate.

2 So Pilate asked Him, "Are You the King of the Jews?"

He answered him, "You have said it."[h]

3 And the chief priests began to accuse Him of many things. 4 Then Pilate questioned Him again, "Are You not answering anything? Look how many things they are accusing You of!" 5 But Jesus still did not answer anything, so Pilate was amazed.

Jesus or Barabbas

6 At the festival it was Pilate's custom to release for the people a prisoner they requested. 7 There was one named Barabbas, who was in prison with rebels who had committed murder during the rebellion. 8 The crowd came up and began to ask ⸢Pilate⸣ to do for them as was his custom. 9 So Pilate answered them, "Do you want me to release the King of the Jews for you?" 10 For he knew it was because of envy that the chief priests had handed Him over. 11 But the chief priests stirred up the crowd so that he would release Barabbas to them instead.

12 Pilate asked them again, "Then what do you want me to do with the One you call the King of the Jews?"

13 Again they shouted, "Crucify Him!"

14 Then Pilate said to them, "Why? What has He done wrong?"

But they shouted, "Crucify Him!" all the more.

---

[a]**14:62** Lit and you (pl in Gk)   [b]**14:62** Ps 110:1; Dn 7:13   [c]**14:64** Lit How does it appear to you?   [d]**14:68** Other mss omit and a rooster crowed   [e]**14:70** Other mss add and your speech shows it   [f]**14:71** To call down curses on himself if what he said weren't true   [g]**14:72** Or he burst into tears, or he broke down   [h]**15:2** Or That is true, an affirmative oath; Mt 26:64; 27:11

14:64 blasphemy. Dishonoring or slandering another. The penalty for blaspheming God was death by stoning (Lev. 24:10-16). **deserving of death.** At that point in history, the Sanhedrin did not have power to carry out a death sentence. Only the Roman procurator could do that.

14:71 started to curse. Peter goes so far as to call down on himself the wrath of God if he is not telling the truth (which he knows he is not)! **I don't know this man.** This, like his previous denial (v. 68), is an outright lie. **you're talking about.** Peter does not use Jesus' name (8:38).

14:72 a rooster crowed a second time. Roosters in Palestine crowed first at about 12:30 a.m., then again at about 1:30 a.m.,

and for a third time at about 2:30 a.m. As a result of this peculiar habit, the watch kept by soldiers in Palestine from midnight until 3 a.m. was called "cock-crow." Peter's denials were therefore spread over the early hours.

15:1 Pilate. Pontius Pilate was the fifth procurator of Judea. He served from A.D. 26-36. Historians of the time called him an "inflexible, merciless and obstinate" man who disliked the Jews and their customs.

15:8 The crowd. At the beginning of the week the crowd hailed Jesus as "He who comes in the name of the Lord" (11:9).

15:15 released Barabbas. The death of Jesus (who is innocent) in the place of Barabbas (who is guilty) is a visual statement of the meaning of substitutionary atonement. It explains what Jesus meant in

10:45 when He said that He came to "give His life as a ransom for many."

15:21 Simon. Possibly a Jew, from a Greek city on the north shore of Africa, who had come to Jerusalem for the Passover feast. **Rufus.** Romans 16:13 mentions a Rufus. Mark wrote this Gospel for the church at Rome, and if this is the same Rufus, he would be able to verify this detail about his father. **carry Jesus' cross.** The prisoner carried the heavy cross-beam through the winding streets as an example to others. Jesus, however, had already been without sleep for at least 24 hours and been beaten, flogged, and beaten again. He was physically unable to bear the weight of the cross-beam.

15:22 Golgotha. In Aramaic, "a skull." This was probably a round, bare hill outside Jerusalem.

Sacrificing For Us!

1. When someone accuses you of something you didn't do, how do you react?

Mark 15:1-15

2. Why do you think Jesus didn't answer the charges against him (v. 5)?

3. Why did the people ask for Barabbas instead of Jesus? What does this show about the human race?

4. How does the story of Barabbas illustrate what Christ did for you?

5. Have you come to the point in your life where you've asked Jesus to forgive your sins, realizing that He died for you? If not, why are you waiting?

---

¹⁵ Then, willing to gratify the crowd, Pilate released Barabbas to them. And after having Jesus flogged,^a he handed Him over to be crucified.

Mocked by the Military

¹⁶ Then the soldiers led Him away into the courtyard (that is, •headquarters) and called the whole •company together. ¹⁷ They dressed Him in a purple robe, twisted together a crown of thorns, and put it on Him. ¹⁸ And they began to salute Him, "Hail, King of the Jews!" ¹⁹ They kept hitting Him on the head with a reed and spitting on Him. Getting down on their knees, they were paying Him homage. ²⁰ When they had mocked Him, they stripped Him of the purple robe, put His clothes on Him, and led Him out to crucify Him.

Crucified between Two Criminals

²¹ They forced a man coming in from the country, who was passing by, to carry Jesus' cross. He was Simon, a Cyrenian, the father of Alexander and Rufus. ²² And they brought Jesus to the place called *Golgotha* (which means Skull Place). ²³ They tried to give Him wine mixed with myrrh, but He did not take it. ²⁴ Then they crucified Him and divided His clothes, casting lots for them to decide what each would get. ²⁵ Now it was nine in the morning^b when they crucified Him. ²⁶ The inscription of the charge written against Him was

> THE KING OF THE JEWS

²⁷ They crucified two criminals^c with Him, one on His right and one on His left. [²⁸ So the Scripture was fulfilled that says: **And He was counted among outlaws.**]^{d e 29} Those who passed by were yelling insults at^f Him, shaking their heads, and saying, "Ha! The One who would demolish the sanctuary and build it in three days, ³⁰ save Yourself by coming down from the cross!" ³¹ In the same way, the chief priests with the scribes were mocking Him to one another and saying, "He saved others; He cannot save Himself! ³² Let the •Messiah, the King of Israel, come down now from the cross, so that we may see and believe." Even those who were crucified with Him were taunting Him.

The Death of Jesus

³³ When it was noon,^g darkness came over the whole land^h until three in the afternoon.ⁱ ³⁴ And at threeⁱ Jesus cried out with a loud voice, "*Eloi, Eloi, lemá*^j *sabach-tháni?*" which is translated, "**My God, My God, why have You forsaken Me?**"^k

³⁵ When some of those standing there heard this, they said, "Look, He's calling for Elijah!" ³⁶ Someone ran and filled a sponge with sour wine, fixed it on a reed, offered Him a drink, and said, "Let's see if Elijah comes to take Him down!"

---

^a**15:15** Roman flogging was done with a whip made of leather strips embedded with pieces of bone or metal that brutally tore the flesh. ^b**15:25** Lit *was the third hour* ^c**15:27** Or *revolutionaries* ^d**15:28** Other mss omit bracketed text ^e**15:28** Is 53:12 ^f**15:29** Lit *passed by blasphemed* ^g**15:33** Lit *the sixth hour* ^h**15:33** Or *whole earth* ⁱ**15:33,34** Lit *the ninth hour* ^j**15:34** Other mss read *lama*; other mss read *lima* ^k**15:34** Ps 22:1

15:23 wine mixed with myrrh. A pain-deadening narcotic offered to prisoners about to be crucified (Ps. 69:21).

15:24 divided His clothes. The clothes of the condemned person belonged to the four soldiers who carried out the crucifixion (Ps. 22:18; John 19:23-24).

15:26 THE KING OF THE JEWS. By posting this sign on the cross, Pilate was simply attempting to further humiliate the Jews. The intent was to communicate that Jesus' fate would be shared by anyone else who tried to assert their authority against Rome.

15:27 one on His right and one on His left. Earlier on, James and John had asked for the honor to sit at Jesus' right and left-hand when He came into his kingdom (10:37), a request Jesus denied. Now these two criminals are given the positions on either side of Jesus as He completes His earthly mission.

15:31 He saved others ... He cannot save Himself! This is just the point! Because He is saving others, His own life is forfeited.

15:33 darkness. A supernatural event showing the significance of this death (Amos 8:9). There is darkness for three hours.

15:36 sour wine. Wine vinegar was considered a refreshing drink (Ruth 2:14).

15:38 curtain of the sanctuary. There were two curtains in the temple sanctuary. An outer curtain separated the sanctuary from the courtyard. The inner curtain covered the Holy of Holies where only the high priest was admitted. It is most likely it was the latter curtain that was torn by God to allow all access to the Father through Jesus Christ.

15:39 centurion. The supervising officer, a pagan soldier who may not have been aware of the significance of what he observed.

15:42 preparation day. Jesus died on Friday at 3 p.m. The Sabbath began at 6 p.m., after which no work could be done. Great haste was required.

15:43 Joseph of Arimathea. Little is known of him, except that he was from a wealthy and prominent family and was a member of the Sanhedrin.

15:44 Pilate was surprised. It often took two or three days for a person to die from crucifixion.

15:46 The body was washed, quickly wrapped, and then placed in a tomb. The tomb was then sealed against robbers or animals by means of a large stone. These stones were set in grooves which would guide the stone to the tomb's entrance. Ele-

37 But Jesus let out a loud cry and breathed His last. 38 Then the curtain of the sanctuary[a] was split in two from top to bottom. 39 When the •centurion, who was standing opposite Him, saw the way He[b] breathed His last, he said, "This man really was God's Son!"[c]

40 There were also women looking on from a distance. Among them were •Mary Magdalene, Mary the mother of James the younger and of Joses, and Salome. 41 When He was in Galilee, they would follow Him and help Him. Many other women had come up with Him to Jerusalem.

The Burial of Jesus

42 When it was already evening, because it was preparation day (that is, the day before the Sabbath), 43 Joseph of Arimathea, a prominent member of the Sanhedrin who was himself looking forward to the kingdom of God, came and boldly went in to Pilate and asked for Jesus' body. 44 Pilate was surprised that He was already dead. Summoning the centurion, he asked him whether He had already died. 45 When he found out from the centurion, he gave the corpse to Joseph. 46 After he bought some fine linen, he took Him down and wrapped Him in the linen. Then he placed Him in a tomb cut out of the rock, and rolled a stone against the entrance to the tomb. 47 Now Mary Magdalene and Mary the mother of Joses were watching where He was placed.

Resurrection Morning

16 When the Sabbath was over, •Mary Magdalene, Mary the mother of James, and Salome bought spices, so they could go and anoint Him. 2 Very early in the morning, on the first day of the week, they went to the tomb at sunrise. 3 They were saying to one another, "Who will roll away the stone from the entrance to the tomb for us?" 4 Looking up, they observed that the stone—which was very large—had been rolled away. 5 When they entered the tomb, they saw a young man[d] dressed in a long white robe sitting on the right side; they were amazed and alarmed.[e]

6 "Don't be alarmed," he told them. "You are looking for Jesus the •Nazarene, who was crucified. He has been resurrected! He is not here! See the place where they put Him. 7 But go, tell His disciples and Peter, 'He is going ahead of you to Galilee; you will see Him there just as He told you.'"

8 So they went out and started running from the tomb, because trembling and astonishment overwhelmed them. And they said nothing to anyone, since they were afraid.

Appearances of the Risen Lord

[9 Early on the first day of the week, after He had risen, He appeared first to Mary Magdalene, out of whom He had driven seven demons. 10 She went and reported to those who had been with Him, as they were mourning and weeping. 11 Yet, when they heard that He was alive and had been seen by her, they did not believe it. 12 Then after this, He appeared in a different form to two of them walking on their way into the country. 13 And they went and reported it to the rest, who did not believe them either.

The Great Commission

14 Later, He appeared to the Eleven themselves as they were reclining at the table. He rebuked their unbelief and hardness of heart, because they did not believe those who saw Him after He had been resurrected. 15 Then He said to them, "Go into all the world and preach the gospel to the whole creation. 16 Whoever believes and is baptized will be saved, but whoever does not believe will be condemned. 17 And these signs will accompany those who believe: In My name they will drive out demons; they will speak in new languages; 18 they will pick up snakes;[f] if they should drink anything deadly, it will never harm them; they will lay hands on the sick, and they will get well."

The Ascension

19 Then after speaking to them, the Lord Jesus was taken up into heaven and sat down at the right hand of God. 20 And they went out and preached everywhere, the Lord working with them and confirming the word by the accompanying signs.][g]

---

a **15:38** A heavy curtain separated the inner room of the temple from the outer.   b **15:39** Other mss read *saw that He cried out like this and*   c **15:39** Or *the Son of God*, Mk 1:1   d **16:5** In Mt 28:2, the young man = an angel   e **16:5** *Amazed and alarmed* translate the idea of one Gk word   f **16:18** Other mss add *with their hands*   g **16:9–20** Other mss omit bracketed text

---

vated above the tomb's entrance, it would not be too difficult to set the stone in motion to roll against the entrance. It would be extremely difficult to remove the stone from the entrance since it would have to be pushed uphill.

15:47 watching. Two of the three women at the crucifixion saw clearly where Jesus was entombed.

16:5 alarmed. A rare Greek word used in the New Testament only by Mark (9:15; 14:33),

indicating great astonishment in the face of the supernatural.

16:6 He has been resurrected! In the same way that Mark reports the crucifixion of Jesus in simple, stark terms (15:24), so too he describes his resurrection in a plain, unadorned way. The phrase is, literally, "he has been raised," showing that God is the One who accomplished this great act.

16:8 they said nothing. Eventually, of course, the women did report what hap-

pened (Matt. 28:8; Luke 24:10). **they were afraid.** This was the same sort of fear that the disciples felt on the Sea of Galilee when they discovered that Jesus had power over the elements themselves (4:41). This is how human beings respond in the face of the supernatural. Thus the Gospel of Mark ends on this note of astonishment and fear which was so characteristic of how he described people's reaction.

INTRODUCTION TO

LUKE

PERSONAL READING PLAN

- ☐ Luke 1:1-38
- ☐ Luke 1:39-80
- ☐ Luke 2:1-52
- ☐ Luke 3:1-4:13
- ☐ Luke 4:14-5:16
- ☐ Luke 5:17-6:11
- ☐ Luke 6:12-7:10
- ☐ Luke 7:11-50

- ☐ Luke 8:1-39
- ☐ Luke 8:40-9:36
- ☐ Luke 9:37-10:24
- ☐ Luke 10:25-11:28
- ☐ Luke 11:29-12:21
- ☐ Luke 12:22-59
- ☐ Luke 13:1-14:14
- ☐ Luke 14:15-15:32

- ☐ Luke 16:1-17:19
- ☐ Luke 17:20-18:43
- ☐ Luke 19:1-48
- ☐ Luke 20:1-47
- ☐ Luke 21:1-38
- ☐ Luke 22:1-53
- ☐ Luke 22:54-23:56
- ☐ Luke 24:1-53

AUTHOR

Although no author is named in the third Gospel, a second century tradition attributes it to Luke. Since Luke was *not* an apostle and he *was* a Gentile, it is unlikely that he would have received credit for it if he had not written it.

Internal evidence supports Luke's authorship. It is clear that the same person wrote both the third Gospel and the Book of Acts; both books are dedicated to Theophilus. Both books are similar in style, language, and interests. The author of Acts begins by saying, "I wrote the first narrative," which is surely the Gospel of Luke. Since Acts was traditionally credited to Luke, we assume Luke did indeed write this Gospel.

Additionally, the author of the third Gospel uses the language we would expect from a doctor (Luke was a physician). He describes illnesses with more precision than is found in Matthew and Mark (4:38; 5:12). He also omits the comment in Mark 5:26 that the woman who was subject to bleeding "had endured much under many doctors. She spent everything she had and was not helped at all."

Little is known about Luke from the New Testament except that he was a doctor beloved by Paul (Col. 4:14) and a coworker with Paul (2 Tim. 4:11; Philem. 24). In the book of Acts, Luke describes experiences while traveling with Paul. One early non-canonical document (writings not included in Holy Scripture), the *Prologue to*

Luke, states that Luke was a physician, that he was unmarried and childless, and that he died at the age of 84. Beyond this, we know Luke only through his two eloquent documents.

DATE

There is no strong evidence as to when Luke's Gospel was written. Many scholars date it between A.D. 75 and 85, although this is by no means conclusive. In fact, since Acts ends with Paul awaiting trial in Rome (probably before A.D. 67), if Luke wrote his Gospel before he wrote Acts, then a date in the early A.D. 60s is likely.

The place of writing was most likely Rome, though Achaia, Ephesus and Caesarea are also possibilities. The place to which it was sent depends on where Theophilus lived. By its details about Palestine, the Gospel seems to be written for readers who were unfamiliar with that land. The Christians in Antioch, Achaia, and Ephesus are possible recipients of this Gospel.

THEME

Jesus is the Savior of the whole world.

HISTORICAL BACKGROUND

Luke was a Gentile who wrote the story of Jesus for other Gentiles. Luke dedicates the book to Theophilus, probably a high-ranking Roman government official (the title "most honorable" was normally reserved for such officials). Theophilus was a common name among both Greeks and

Jews in New Testament times. It means "friend of God."

Luke then dates the conception and birth of John the Baptist and Jesus with reference to the Roman rulers governing at the time (1:5; 2:1-2). Luke makes a habit of translating Hebrew words into their Greek equivalents so that his Gentile readers will understand. For example, Luke never refers to Jesus as "Rabbi," the Hebrew title for a teacher, but always by the Greek equivalent, "Master." Luke identifies the place where Jesus was crucified not as *Golgotha, (Hebrew)*, but as *Kranion,* the Greek equivalent for "the place of the skull."

The Gentile character of the third Gospel is also seen in its identification of Jesus' lineage. Luke traces Him back to Adam, the founder of the human race, and not, as Matthew does, back to Abraham, the founder of the Jewish race. Also, Luke seldom quotes the Old Testament or demonstrates how Jesus fulfills Old Testament prophecy. This is a Gentile book about the Jewish Messiah who died for all people.

CHARACTERISTICS

Luke's account of Jesus' life is the longest book in the New Testament and it is extraordinarily joyful. It begins and ends with rejoicing (1:46-47 and 24:52-53). . Luke uses the words "joy" (6:23), "laugh" (6:21), and "celebrate" (15:23,32). Luke is the only writer to record the four great canticles of joy and worship: *Magnificat* (1:46-55), *Benedictus* (1:68-79), *Gloria in Exclesis* (2:14), and *Nunc Dimittis* (2:29-32).

STYLE

Despite Luke's meticulous documentation, his Gospel is no dry, academic document. It sparkles with life and vitality. Luke's portraits of people are particularly vivid and compassionate. People like Zacchaeus, Mary and Martha, Elizabeth and the mother of Jesus all spring to life through his talented pen.

PASSAGES FOR TOPICAL GROUP STUDY

PASSAGES FOR GENERAL GROUP STUDY

The Dedication to Theophilus

1 Many have undertaken to compile a narrative about the events that have been fulfilled[a] among us, [2] just as the original eyewitnesses and servants of the word handed them down to us. [3] It also seemed good to me, since I have carefully investigated everything from the very first, to write to you in orderly sequence, most honorable Theophilus, [4] so that you may know the certainty of the things about which you have been instructed.[b]

Gabriel Predicts John's Birth

[5] In the days of King •Herod of Judea, there was a priest of Abijah's division[c] named Zechariah. His wife was from the daughters of Aaron, and her name was Elizabeth. [6] Both were righteous in God's sight, living without blame according to all the commandments and requirements of the Lord. [7] But they had no children[d] because Elizabeth could not conceive,[e] and both of them were well along in years.[f]

[8] When his division was on duty and he was serving as priest before God, [9] it happened that he was chosen by lot, according to the custom of the priesthood, to enter the sanctuary of the Lord and burn incense. [10] At the hour of incense the whole assembly of the people was praying outside. [11] An angel of the Lord appeared to him, standing to the right of the altar of incense. [12] When Zechariah saw him, he was startled and overcome with fear.[g] [13] But the angel said to him:

Do not be afraid, Zechariah,
because your prayer has been heard.
Your wife Elizabeth will bear you a son,
and you will name him John.
[14] There will be joy and delight for you,
and many will rejoice at his birth.
[15] For he will be great in the sight of the Lord
and will never drink wine or beer.
He will be filled with the Holy Spirit
while still in his mother's womb.
[16] He will turn many of the sons of Israel

to the Lord their God.
[17] And he will go before Him
in the spirit and power of Elijah,
to turn the hearts of fathers
to their children,
and the disobedient
to the understanding of the righteous,
to make ready for the Lord a prepared people.

[18] "How can I know this?" Zechariah asked the angel. "For I am an old man, and my wife is well along in years."[h]

[19] The angel answered him, "I am Gabriel, who stands in the presence of God, and I was sent to speak to you and tell you this good news. [20] Now listen! You will become silent and unable to speak until the day these things take place, because you did not believe my words, which will be fulfilled in their proper time."

[21] Meanwhile, the people were waiting for Zechariah, amazed that he stayed so long in the sanctuary. [22] When he did come out, he could not speak to them. Then they realized that he had seen a vision in the sanctuary. He kept making signs to them and remained speechless. [23] When the days of his ministry were completed, he went back home.

[24] After these days his wife Elizabeth conceived and kept herself in seclusion for five months. She said, [25] "The Lord has done this for me. He has looked with favor in these days to take away my disgrace among the people."

Gabriel Predicts Jesus' Birth

[26] In the sixth month, the angel Gabriel was sent by God to a town in Galilee called Nazareth, [27] to a virgin •engaged to a man named Joseph, of the house of David. The virgin's name was Mary. [28] And [the angel] came to her and said, "Rejoice, favored woman! The Lord is with you."[i] [29] But she was deeply troubled by this statement, wondering what kind of greeting this could be. [30] Then the angel told her:

---

[a]**1:1** Or *events that have been accomplished*, or *events most surely believed*   [b]**1:4** Or *informed*   [c]**1:5** One of the 24 divisions of priests appointed by David for temple service; 1 Ch 24:10   [d]**1:7** Lit *child*   [e]**1:7** Lit *Elizabeth was sterile* or *barren*   [f]**1:7** Lit *in their days*   [g]**1:12** Lit *and fear fell on him*   [h]**1:18** Lit *in her days*   [i]**1:28** Other mss add *blessed are you among women*

1:1 Many. Mark and Luke contain similar material. Most of Mark is included in Luke. Unknown writers also recorded some of the teachings and stories about Jesus that Luke incorporated into his Gospel as well.

1:2 eyewitnesses and servants of the word. "The word" is a shorthand way of referring to the whole of Jesus' life and teaching (Acts 1:21-22; 2 Peter 1:16; 1 John 1:1). The stories that form the Gospels were passed on by those who were personally acquainted with and dedicated to Jesus.

1:3 carefully investigated. While Luke was not an eyewitness, his association with Paul and Mark (Col. 4:10-14; 2 Tim. 4:11), his travels to Judea (Acts 21), and his familiarity with other eyewitnesses afforded him ample opportunity to collect information from reliable witnesses. **Theophilus.** An unknown

figure. He may have been Luke's patron who underwrote the cost of writing the Gospel, or a Roman official (Acts 1:1).

1:7 Elizabeth could not conceive. Barrenness was seen as a tragedy and a valid reason for divorce.

1:12 overcome with fear. The fear of the angel he experienced is similar to that experienced other places in Scripture when an angel comes to an individual (vv. 29-30; Ex. 3:2-6; Dan. 10:7).

1:15 he ...will never drink wine ... He will be filled with the Holy Spirit. The first statement connects John to the Old Testament order of Nazirites (Num. 6); the second statement shows him to be the forerunner of the new era of the Messiah when God's Spirit would indwell His people.

1:17 in the spirit and power of Elijah. Elijah was one of the first great Old Testament prophets. Malachi, the last prophet to speak to the Jews, foresaw a time when Elijah would come again to prepare people for the Lord (Mal. 4:5). While Jewish tradition anticipated the literal return of Elijah, the angel's message is that John would be inspired by the same divine energy that led Elijah.

1:19 Gabriel. Literally, "man of God." In Jewish tradition, he was one of the select few angels who represent God as His special servants (Dan. 8:16; 9:21).

1:20 unable to speak. Old Testament saints questioned God without rebuke or punishment (Gen. 15:8; Judg. 6:13). Here, Zechariah's inability to speak is tied to his lack of trust. It may have also been a confirmation of Gabriel's words.

Do not be afraid, Mary,
for you have found favor with God.

³¹ Now listen:
You will conceive and give birth to a son,
and you will call His name JESUS.

³² He will be great
and will be called the Son of the Most High,
and the Lord God will give Him
the throne of His father David.

³³ He will reign over the house of Jacob forever,
and His kingdom will have no end.

Miracle Birth

1. How old were your parents when you were born?

Luke 1:26-38

2. Mary was young, perhaps only 14, when the angel appeared to her. How would you have reacted in her position?

3. What does Mary mean, "I am the Lord's slave" (v. 38)? What does her response show about her character?

4. Why was Jesus born from a woman who'd never had sex? Why was that important?

5. Mary was completely willing to follow God's plan for her life. How can you be more like her?

³⁴ Mary asked the angel, "How can this be, since I have not been intimate with a man?"ᵃ ³⁵ The angel replied to her:

"The Holy Spirit will come upon you,
and the power of the Most High
will overshadow you.

Therefore the holy One to be born
will be called the Son of God.

³⁶ And consider your relative Elizabeth—even she has conceived a son in her old age, and this is the sixth month for her who was called barren. ³⁷ For nothing will be impossible with God."

³⁸ "I am the Lord's •slave,"ᵇ said Mary. "May it be done to me according to your word." Then the angel left her.

Mary's Visit to Elizabeth

³⁹ In those days Mary set out and hurried to a town in the hill country of Judah ⁴⁰ where she entered Zechariah's house and greeted Elizabeth. ⁴¹ When Elizabeth heard Mary's greeting, the baby leaped inside her,ᶜ and Elizabeth was filled with the Holy Spirit. ⁴² Then she exclaimed with a loud cry:

You are the most blessed of women,
and your child will be blessed!ᵈ

⁴³ How could this happen to me, that the mother of my Lord should come to me? ⁴⁴ For you see, when the sound of your greeting reached my ears, the baby leaped for joy inside me!ᵉ ⁴⁵ She who has believed is blessed because what was spoken to her by the Lord will be fulfilled!"

Mary's Praise

⁴⁶ And Mary said:

My soul proclaims the greatness ofᶠ the Lord,
⁴⁷ and my spirit has rejoiced in God my Savior,
⁴⁸ because He has looked with favor
on the humble condition of His •slave.
Surely, from now on all generations
will call me blessed,
⁴⁹ because the Mighty One
has done great things for me,
and His name is holy.
⁵⁰ His mercy is from generation to generation
on those who fear Him.
⁵¹ He has done a mighty deed with His arm;

ᵃ**1:34** Lit *since I do not know a man* ᵇ**1:38** Lit *Look, the Lord's slave* ᶜ**1:41** Lit *leaped in her abdomen* or *womb* ᵈ**1:42** Lit *and the fruit of your abdomen* (or *womb*) *is blessed* ᵉ**1:44** Lit *in my abdomen* or *womb* ᶠ**1:46** Or *soul magnifies*

1:26 In the sixth month. This is the sixth month of Elizabeth's pregnancy. **a town in Galilee called Nazareth.** Nazareth was an insignificant little village (John 1:46) in the province of Galilee. God often uses what others see as small or insignificant, as with the "little town of Bethlehem."

1:27 a virgin engaged to a man. Betrothal, usually lasting for about a year, could occur as young as 12 years old. This was a far more binding arrangement than engagements today. Although sexual relations were not permitted, the woman had the legal status of a wife and the relationship could only be broken by divorce. The virgin birth of Jesus, although only mentioned in Matthew and Luke in the entire New Testament, traces its roots to the prophecy of the child spoken of in Isaiah 7:14. **Joseph, of the house of David.** The Messiah was to come through the line of

David, the most famous king of Israel's history (2 Sam. 7:16; Ps. 132:11).

1:28 favored woman! The angel is not commending her virtue, but recognizing the reality of God's grace to her. **The Lord is with you.** This phrase is often used as a statement of God's special intention to equip a person for His service (Josh. 1:5; Judg. 6:12; Matt. 28:20).

1:34 How can this be ...? Zechariah asked a similar question of the angel when informed that he and his wife Elizabeth would have a child (v. 18). He asked out of doubt that such a thing could come to pass. Mary, however, is not registering doubt as much as wonder.

1:43 my Lord. Elizabeth recognizes the sovereignty and power of Mary's child even prior to His birth.

1:45 She who has believed is blessed. In general, the Bible has many more male role models than female, but it is Mary's belief that has made her a model of faith for women through the centuries. Her faith contrasts with the doubt of Zechariah in verse 18.

1:46-55 And Mary said. Mary's song (known as the *Magnificat* after its first words in the Latin Vulgate translation) may have been used as a hymn by the early church as a means of describing the mission of Mary's Son. It celebrates God's action on behalf of Israel as the fulfillment of the enduring hopes of the nation.

2:1 Caesar Augustus. Luke roots Jesus' birth firmly in history. Augustus ruled the Roman Empire from 30 B.C. to 14 A.D. Originally known as Gaius Octavius (or Octavian), he was awarded the title Augustus (which means "majestic" or "highly revered") by the

He has scattered the proud
because of the thoughts of their hearts;

52 He has toppled the mighty from their thrones
and exalted the lowly.

53 He has satisfied the hungry with good things
and sent the rich away empty.

54 He has helped His servant Israel,
mindful of His mercy,[a]

55 just as He spoke to our ancestors,
to Abraham and his descendants[b] forever.

56 And Mary stayed with her about three months; then she returned to her home.

The Birth and Naming of John

57 Now the time had come for Elizabeth to give birth, and she had a son. 58 Then her neighbors and relatives heard that the Lord had shown her His great mercy,[c] and they rejoiced with her.

59 When they came to circumcise the child on the eighth day, they were going to name him Zechariah, after his father. 60 But his mother responded, "No! He will be called John."

61 Then they said to her, "None of your relatives has that name." 62 So they motioned to his father to find out what he wanted him to be called. 63 He asked for a writing tablet and wrote:

HIS NAME IS JOHN

And they were all amazed. 64 Immediately his mouth was opened and his tongue ⌊set free⌋, and he began to speak, praising God. 65 Fear came on all those who lived around them, and all these things were being talked about throughout the hill country of Judea. 66 All who heard about ⌊him⌋ took ⌊it⌋ to heart, saying, "What then will this child become?" For, indeed, the Lord's hand was with him.

Zechariah's Prophecy

67 Then his father Zechariah was filled with the Holy Spirit and prophesied:

68 Praise the Lord, the God of Israel,
because He has visited
and provided redemption for His people.

69 He has raised up a •horn of salvation[d] for us
in the house of His servant David,

70 just as He spoke by the mouth
of His holy prophets in ancient times;

71 salvation from our enemies
and from the clutches[e] of those who hate us.

72 He has dealt mercifully with our fathers
and remembered His holy covenant—

73 the oath that He swore to our father Abraham.
He has given us the privilege,

74 since we have been rescued
from our enemies' clutches,[f]
to serve Him without fear

75 in holiness and righteousness
in His presence all our days.

76 And child, you will be called
a prophet of the Most High,
for you will go before the Lord
to prepare His ways,

77 to give His people knowledge of salvation
through the forgiveness of their sins.

78 Because of our God's merciful compassion,
the Dawn from on high will visit us

79 to shine on those who live in darkness
and the shadow of death,
to guide our feet into the way of peace.

80 The child grew up and became spiritually strong, and he was in the wilderness until the day of his public appearance to Israel.

The Birth of Jesus

2 In those days a decree went out from Caesar Augustus[g] that the whole empire[h] should be regis-

---

[a]1:54 Because He remembered His mercy; see Ps 98:3 [b]1:55 Or offspring; lit seed [c]1:58 Lit the Lord magnified His mercy with her [d]1:69 A strong Savior [e]1:71 Lit the hand [f]1:74 Lit from the hand of enemies [g]2:1 Emperor who ruled the Roman Empire 27 B.C.–A.D. 14; also known as Octavian, he established the peaceful era known as the Pax Romana; Caesar was a title of Roman emperors. [h]2:1 Or the whole inhabited world

---

Roman senate and became known thereafter as Caesar Augustus. Augustus was a wise ruler who encouraged the arts and built many fine projects. He also brought an unprecedented period of peace to the world. **registered.** From about 30 B.C. onward, the Caesars ordered people in the various Roman provinces to be registered every 14 years for a census for purposes of taxation. Resistance from the population and from local rulers sometimes meant census-taking required several years to complete. While there is firm evidence of a census after King Herod's death in 6 A.D., there is no external source that allows us to know whether the census mentioned here was a separate, earlier one or the beginning stages of the census completed at that date.

2:3 everyone went to be registered, each to his own town. Since Joseph and Mary

lived in Galilee, they must have owned some property in Bethlehem. Roman custom required people who owned property in another location from where they lived to register there as well. Bethlehem, a three to four-day journey from Galilee, was the village where King David, through whose line the Messiah was to come, had lived.

2:5 to be registered along with Mary. In some provinces, the Romans charged a poll tax on women 12 years of age or older. **engaged to him and was pregnant.** Their betrothal had not yet been consummated by intercourse (Matt. 1:24-25).

2:7 firstborn. The firstborn of every Jewish family was dedicated to God in a special way (Ex. 13:12). **She wrapped Him snugly in cloth.** The tradition of the time was to wrap a baby in strips of cloth. Such cloths

would give the child the feeling of being securely held. **feeding trough.** A feeding trough for animals. **the inn.** This is either a building used for the accommodation of travelers or a spare room in a private home. Either way, there was no space for the couple, who stayed with the animals. A tradition dating back to the second century maintains this was in a cave on the site of which today is the Church of the Nativity.

2:8 shepherds. Since temple authorities kept flocks of sheep for sacrificial purposes pastured near Bethlehem, it might be that the shepherds of these flocks were the ones visited by the angels. This happened at a time of year when sheep could still be kept in the field, which was sometime between April and November. The date of December 25 as the birth of Christ was selected in the fourth century.

tered. ² This first registration took place while^a Quirinius was governing Syria. ³ So everyone went to be registered, each to his own town.

Heavenly Purpose

1. What's your favorite thing about Christmas?

Luke 2:1-20

2. Why were the shepherds terrified (v. 9)? How would you have reacted in their situation?

3. Why was Jesus sleeping "in the feeding trough" (v. 16)? Why would the Son of God be born into such poverty?

4. Why was Jesus born in the first place? What was His purpose on earth? What did He accomplish?

5. Have you personally been "born again" into the family of Jesus? If so, what does it mean to you to be part of that family?

⁴ And Joseph also went up from the town of Nazareth in Galilee, to Judea, to the city of David, which is called Bethlehem, because he was of the house and family line of David, ⁵ to be registered along with Mary, who was •engaged to him^b and was pregnant. ⁶ While they were there, the time came for her to give birth. ⁷ Then she gave birth to her firstborn Son, and she wrapped Him snugly in cloth and laid Him in a feeding trough— because there was no room for them at the inn.

The Shepherds and the Angels

⁸ In the same region, shepherds were staying out in the fields and keeping watch at night over their flock.

⁹ Then an angel of the Lord stood before^c them, and the glory of the Lord shone around them, and they were terrified.^d ¹⁰ But the angel said to them, "Don't be afraid, for look, I proclaim to you good news of great joy that will be for all the people: ¹¹ today a Savior, who is •Messiah the Lord, was born for you in the city of David. ¹² This will be the sign for you: you will find a baby wrapped snugly in cloth and lying in a feeding trough."

¹³ Suddenly there was a multitude of the heavenly host with the angel, praising God and saying:

¹⁴   Glory to God in the highest heaven,
      and peace on earth to people He favors!^{e f}

¹⁵ When the angels had left them and returned to heaven, the shepherds said to one another, "Let's go straight to Bethlehem and see what has happened, which the Lord has made known to us."

¹⁶ They hurried off and found both Mary and Joseph, and the baby who was lying in the feeding trough. ¹⁷ After seeing ⌊them⌋, they reported the message they were told about this child, ¹⁸ and all who heard it were amazed at what the shepherds said to them. ¹⁹ But Mary was treasuring up all these things^g in her heart and meditating on them. ²⁰ The shepherds returned, glorifying and praising God for all they had seen and heard, just as they had been told.

The Circumcision and Presentation of Jesus

²¹ When the eight days were completed for His circumcision, He was named JESUS—the name given by the angel before He was conceived.^h ²² And when the days of their purification according to the law of Moses were finished, they brought Him up to Jerusalem to present Him to the Lord ²³ (just as it is written in the law of the Lord: **Every firstborn maleⁱ will be dedicated^j to the Lord^k**) ²⁴ and to offer a sacrifice (according to what is stated in the law of the Lord: **a pair of turtledoves or two young pigeons^l**).

^a**2:2** Or *This registration was the first while,* or *This registration was before*   ^b**2:5** Other mss read *was his engaged wife*   ^c**2:9** Or *Lord appeared to*   ^d**2:9** Lit *they feared a great fear*   ^e**2:14** Other mss read *earth good will to people*   ^f**2:14** Or *earth to men of good will*   ^g**2:19** Lit *these words*   ^h**2:21** Or *conceived in the womb*   ⁱ**2:23** Lit *"Every male that opens a womb*   ^j**2:23** Lit *be called holy*   ^k**2:23** Ex 13:2,12   ^l**2:24** Lv 5:11; 12:8

2:9 an angel of the Lord. In some Old Testament passages, the angel of the Lord is identified as God himself (Gen. 16:7; Ex. 3:2; Judg. 6:11), indicating His divine authority and splendor. Throughout the Bible, angels serve as God's agents of instruction, judgment, and deliverance. **the glory of the Lord.** The overwhelmingly powerful light that accompanies the presence of God (Ps. 104:1-2; Ezek. 1:4). **they were terrified.** Often in the Bible when an angel appears to a person, the response is one of terror. It is the fear of being in the presence of something supernatural, powerful, and totally foreign to one's experience (1:29-30; Dan. 10:7).

2:10 for all the people. Another emphasis on the universality of the gospel, especially as presented by Luke.

2:11 a Savior ... Messiah the Lord. "Sav-

ior," a term in the Old Testament which only applies to God, is one who delivers his people from evil and harm. "Messiah" means one anointed by God. "Lord" implies both His authority and Deity.

2:12 the sign. In the Old Testament, God sometimes granted signs that pointed out to people the reliability of His message. The "sign" of the Lord is, ironically, that of a baby wrapped in cloths and lying in an animal's feeding trough.

2:13 heavenly host. At a birth, neighbors and friends would gather to celebrate. At this birth, the angels fulfill this function.

2:14 peace on earth to people He favors! While older versions divide this phrase into two clauses (peace on earth / good will toward men), the Holman translation, with its

single clause accenting God's promise of peace to His people, is to be preferred.

2:21 eight days were completed for His circumcision. The Old Testament Law required that male infants be circumcised on the eighth day (Lev. 12:3). **JESUS** Jesus was a common Jewish name meaning "God saves."

2:29 dismiss Your slave in peace. The thought is that of a slave requesting leave after fulfilling a task his master had given him. Simeon can approach death easily now, not only because God had kept His promise (v. 26), but because he could be assured that this child would "destroy death." (2 Tim. 1:10).

2:33 His father and mother were amazed. The references to Joseph as Jesus' father should be read simply as a shorthand way of

Simeon's Prophetic Praise

25 There was a man in Jerusalem whose name was Simeon. This man was righteous and devout, looking forward to Israel's consolation,a and the Holy Spirit was on him. 26 It had been revealed to him by the Holy Spirit that he would not see death before he saw the Lord's Messiah. 27 Guided by the Spirit, he enteredb the •temple complex. When the parents brought in the child Jesus to perform for Him what was customary under the law, 28 Simeon took Him up in his arms, praised God, and said:

29 Now, Master,
You can dismiss Your •slave in peace,
according to Your word.
30 For my eyes have seen Your salvation.
31 You have prepared ⌊it⌋
in the presence of all peoples—
32 a light for revelation to the Gentilesc
and glory to Your people Israel.

33 His father and motherd were amazed at what was being said about Him. 34 Then Simeon blessed them and told His mother Mary: "Indeed, this child is destined to cause the fall and rise of many in Israel and to be a sign that will be opposede — 35 and a sword will pierce your own soul—that the thoughtsf of many hearts may be revealed."

Anna's Testimony

36 There was also a prophetess, Anna, a daughter of Phanuel, of the tribe of Asher. She was well along in years,g having lived with her husband seven years after her marriage,h 37 and was a widow for 84 years.i She did not leave the temple complex, serving God night and day with fastings and prayers. 38 At that very moment,j she came up and began to thank God and to speak about Him to all who were looking forward to the redemption of Jerusalem.k

The Family's Return to Nazareth

39 When they had completed everything according to the law of the Lord, they returned to Galilee, to their own town of Nazareth. 40 The boy grew up and became strong, filled with wisdom, and God's grace was on Him.

 In Dad's House

1. Describe a time when you got lost, ran away, or were separated from your parents.

Luke 2:41-52
2. Why did Jesus "stay behind" in Jerusalem after His parents had left?
3. Why would Jesus, the Son of God, sit and ask questions about the Bible?
4. How did Joseph and Mary react? What would your parents have said?
5. What did Jesus mean when He said, "I had to be in my Father's house" (v. 49)?
6. Jesus grew "in favor with God" (v. 52). What can you do to grow in your relationship with God?

In His Father's House

41 Every year His parents traveled to Jerusalem for the •Passover Festival. 42 When He was 12 years old, they went up according to the custom of the festival. 43 After those days were over, as they were returning, the boy Jesus stayed behind in Jerusalem, but His parentsl did not know it. 44 Assuming He was in the traveling party, they went a day's journey. Then they began looking for Him among their relatives and

---

a2:25 The coming of the Messiah with His salvation for the nation; Lk 2:26,30; Is 40:1; 61:2 b2:27 Lit And in the Spirit, he came into the c2:32 Or the nations d2:33 Other mss read But Joseph and His mother e2:34 Or spoken against f2:35 Or schemes g2:36 Lit in many days h2:36 Lit years from her virginity i2:37 Or she was a widow until the age of 84 j2:38 Lit very hour k2:38 Other mss read in Jerusalem l2:43 Other mss read but Joseph and His mother

---

referring to Joseph, not as an implied denial of the virgin birth. While Joseph and Mary had already heard many strange things about their Son, they would certainly not be immune to such a startling declaration as Simeon's.

2:34-35 told His mother. Simeon foreshadows the rest of the Gospel by warning Mary that in the process of fulfilling Jesus' mission there will be great pain for her.

2:36 Asher. One of the 10 tribes "lost" in the Assyrian invasion of Israel in 722 B.C.

2:37 She did not leave the temple. Since it is unlikely that she could have lived at the temple, the stress is on her great devotion to God as she, like Simeon, prayed and waited for God to fulfill His promises to Israel.

2:39 returned to Galilee. In contrast, Matthew reports the family stayed much longer in Bethlehem, and then left for Egypt when threatened by Herod. Only after Herod's death did they return to Nazareth in Galilee (Matt. 2:13-23).

2:42 When He was 12 years old. At age 13, a Jewish boy was expected to take his place in the religious community of Israel. Age 12 would be a time of preparation for assuming responsibilities of adulthood.

2:43-44 Jesus stayed behind ... but His parents did not know it. Jewish pilgrims from outside Jerusalem traveled to and from the feast in large caravans. Typically, the women and children would be up front while the men and older boys traveled along behind. In the evenings, when the caravan stopped for the night, families would regroup.

It would have been easy during the day for Mary and Joseph to each assume that Jesus was with the other parent or with friends.

2:46 After three days. This does not mean they spent three days in Jerusalem looking for Jesus. Day one was the trip out of the city with the caravan—probably a walk of about 25 miles. Day two was their trip back to the city. Day three was when they found Him in the temple. **sitting among the teachers.** It was common for the rabbis to discuss theology in the temple courts. Interested listeners would sit with them and converse about questions that arose from their discussions. **asking them questions.** Even Jesus had to develop as a boy. We learn from this account that He was much different than any other child.

2:47 all those who heard Him were as-

friends. ⁴⁵ When they did not find Him, they returned to Jerusalem to search for Him. ⁴⁶ After three days, they found Him in the temple complex sitting among the teachers, listening to them and asking them questions. ⁴⁷ And all those who heard Him were astounded at His understanding and His answers. ⁴⁸ When His parents saw Him, they were astonished, and His mother said to Him, "Son, why have You treated us like this? Your father and I have been anxiously searching for You."

⁴⁹ "Why were you searching for Me?" He asked them. "Didn't you know that I had to be in My Father's house?"ᵃ ⁵⁰ But they did not understand what He said to them.

In Favor with God and with People

⁵¹ Then He went down with them and came to Nazareth and was obedient to them. His mother kept all these things in her heart. ⁵² And Jesus increased in wisdom and stature, and in favor with God and with people.

The Messiah's Herald

3 In the fifteenth year of the reign of Tiberius Caesar,ᵇ while Pontius •Pilate was governor of Judea, •Herod was tetrarchᶜ of Galilee, his brother Philip tetrarch of the region of Itureaᵈ and Trachonitis,ᵈ and Lysanias tetrarch of Abilene,ᵉ ² during the high priesthood of Annas and Caiaphas, God's word came to John the son of Zechariah in the wilderness. ³ He went into all the vicinity of the Jordan, preaching a baptism of repentanceᶠ for the forgiveness of sins, ⁴ as it is written in the book of the words of the prophet Isaiah:

A voice of one crying out in the wilderness:
"Prepare the way for the Lord;
make His paths straight!
⁵ Every valley will be filled,
and every mountain and hill will be
made low;ᵍ
the crooked will become straight,

the rough ways smooth,
⁶ and everyoneʰ will see the salvation of God."ⁱ

⁷ He then said to the crowds who came out to be baptized by him, "Brood of vipers! Who warned you to flee from the coming wrath? ⁸ Therefore produce fruit consistent with repentance. And don't start saying to yourselves, 'We have Abraham as our father,' for I tell you that God is able to raise up children for Abraham from these stones! ⁹ Even now the ax is ready to strikeʲ the root of the trees! Therefore every tree that doesn't produce good fruit will be cut down and thrown into the fire."

¹⁰ "What then should we do?" the crowds were asking him.

¹¹ He replied to them, "The one who has two shirtsᵏ must share with someone who has none, and the one who has food must do the same."

¹² Tax collectors also came to be baptized, and they asked him, "Teacher, what should we do?"

¹³ He told them, "Don't collect any more than what you have been authorized."

¹⁴ Some soldiers also questioned him: "What should we do?"

He said to them, "Don't take money from anyone by force or false accusation; be satisfied with your wages."

¹⁵ Now the people were waiting expectantly, and all of them were debating in their mindsˡ whether John might be the •Messiah. ¹⁶ John answered them all, "I baptize you withᵐ water, but One is coming who is more powerful than I. I am not worthy to untie the strap of His sandals. He will baptize you withᵐ the Holy Spirit and fire. ¹⁷ His winnowing shovelⁿ is in His hand to clear His threshing floor and gather the wheat into His barn, but the chaff He will burn up with a fire that never goes out." ¹⁸ Then, along with many other exhortations, he proclaimed good news to the people. ¹⁹ But Herod the tetrarch, being rebuked by him about Herodias, his brother's wife, and about all the evil things Herod had done, ²⁰ added this to everything else—he locked John up in prison.

ᵃ**2:49** Or *be involved in My Father's interests* (or *things*), or *be among My Father's people* ᵇ**3:1** Emperor who ruled the Roman Empire A.D. 14–37 ᶜ**3:1** Or *ruler* ᵈ**3:1** A small province northeast of Galilee ᵉ**3:1** A small Syrian province ᶠ**3:3** Or *baptism based on repentance* ᵍ**3:5** Lit *be humbled* ʰ**3:6** Lit *all flesh* ⁱ**3:4–6** Is 40:3–5 ʲ**3:9** Lit *the ax lies at* ᵏ**3:11** Lit *tunics* ˡ**3:15** Or *hearts* ᵐ**3:16** Or *in* ⁿ**3:17** A wooden farm implement used to toss threshed grain into the wind so the lighter chaff would blow away and separate from the heavier grain

---

tounded. This seems to be the first reason why Luke included this story. Jesus' insight into the Law drew the respect and wonder of His elders.

2:48 Mary's response is not amazement at Jesus' insight into the Law, but a motherly one of frustration and concern because of the worry Jesus' absence caused. **Your father and I.** Even though the infant narratives describe Jesus' birth as a virgin birth, Joseph took Jesus as his own child and acted as father to Him.

2:49 I had to be. Luke records several statements which reflect Jesus' sense of the necessity of His mission and the steps required to fulfill it (4:43; 9:22; 24:7). Mary and Joseph's inability to comprehend what He meant is paralleled later on by his family's misunderstanding of Him (8:19-21).

2:51 was obedient to them. Jesus may have had an awareness that He was God's unique Son, but that didn't keep Him from being obedient to His human parents.

2:52 increased. Jesus' growth was not one-dimensional. Jesus grew along several dimensions. He grew physically (in stature). He grew intellectually (in wisdom). He grew socially (in favor with men). But most of all He grew spiritually (in favor with God).

3:7 Brood of vipers! The image painted by these words is of snakes slithering through the undergrowth, trying to escape the on-coming fire.

3:8 Abraham as our father. John warns that they cannot retreat into an easy assumption that they will be spared judgment just because they are members of God's chosen race.

3:16 not worthy to untie the strap of His sandals. The task of removing the master's sandals was that of the lowest ranking slave in the household. The Messiah is so great that John feels unworthy to perform even that lowly function for Him.

3:21-22 Jesus also was baptized. This scene really belongs with verses 1-20 as it briefly records the baptism of Jesus by John. Unlike Matthew's longer account which includes His conversation with John, Luke's stress is that the importance of this event lay in Jesus' reception of the Spirit and the divine declaration of His status as Son.

3:32 Matthew's genealogy agrees with Luke's from David to Abraham (1 Chron. 2:1-15).

4:1 full of the Holy Spirit ... led by the Spirit. The work of the Holy Spirit is a major

The Baptism of Jesus

21 When all the people were baptized, Jesus also was baptized. As He was praying, heaven opened, 22 and the Holy Spirit descended on Him in a physical appearance like a dove. And a voice came from heaven:

> You are My beloved Son.
> I take delight in You!

The Genealogy of Jesus Christ

23 As He began ⌐His ministry⌐, Jesus was about 30 years old and was thought to be[a] the

son of Joseph, ⌐son⌐[b] of Heli,
24 ⌐son⌐ of Matthat, ⌐son⌐ of Levi,
⌐son⌐ of Melchi, ⌐son⌐ of Jannai,
⌐son⌐ of Joseph, 25 ⌐son⌐ of Mattathias,
⌐son⌐ of Amos, ⌐son⌐ of Nahum,
⌐son⌐ of Esli, ⌐son⌐ of Naggai,
26 ⌐son⌐ of Maath, ⌐son⌐ of Mattathias,
⌐son⌐ of Semein, ⌐son⌐ of Josech,
⌐son⌐ of Joda, 27 ⌐son⌐ of Joanan,
⌐son⌐ of Rhesa, ⌐son⌐ of Zerubbabel,
⌐son⌐ of Shealtiel, ⌐son⌐ of Neri,
28 ⌐son⌐ of Melchi, ⌐son⌐ of Addi,
⌐son⌐ of Cosam, ⌐son⌐ of Elmadam,
⌐son⌐ of Er, 29 ⌐son⌐ of Joshua,
⌐son⌐ of Eliezer, ⌐son⌐ of Jorim,
⌐son⌐ of Matthat, ⌐son⌐ of Levi,
30 ⌐son⌐ of Simeon, ⌐son⌐ of Judah,
⌐son⌐ of Joseph, ⌐son⌐ of Jonam,
⌐son⌐ of Eliakim, 31 ⌐son⌐ of Melea,
⌐son⌐ of Menna, ⌐son⌐ of Mattatha,
⌐son⌐ of Nathan, ⌐son⌐ of David,
32 ⌐son⌐ of Jesse, ⌐son⌐ of Obed,
⌐son⌐ of Boaz, ⌐son⌐ of Salmon,[c]
⌐son⌐ of Nahshon, 33 ⌐son⌐ of Amminadab,
⌐son⌐ of Ram,[d] ⌐son⌐ of Hezron,
⌐son⌐ of Perez, ⌐son⌐ of Judah,
34 ⌐son⌐ of Jacob, ⌐son⌐ of Isaac,
⌐son⌐ of Abraham, ⌐son⌐ of Terah,

⌐son⌐ of Nahor, 35 ⌐son⌐ of Serug,
⌐son⌐ of Reu, ⌐son⌐ of Peleg,
⌐son⌐ of Eber, ⌐son⌐ of Shelah,
36 ⌐son⌐ of Cainan, ⌐son⌐ of Arphaxad,
⌐son⌐ of Shem, ⌐son⌐ of Noah,
⌐son⌐ of Lamech, 37 ⌐son⌐ of Methuselah,
⌐son⌐ of Enoch, ⌐son⌐ of Jared,
⌐son⌐ of Mahalaleel, ⌐son⌐ of Cainan,
38 ⌐son⌐ of Enos, ⌐son⌐ of Seth,
⌐son⌐ of Adam, ⌐son⌐ of God.

That's Tempting!

1. What is the longest you have gone without food? What food did you miss most?

Luke 4:1-13

2. What ways did Satan use to tempt Jesus? How did Jesus resist those temptations?

3. Why would Jesus have even been tempted to throw Himself off the top of the temple? To what was Satan trying to appeal?

4. What areas of temptation are you facing lately? How would giving in to those temptations affect your life and the lives of those around you?

5. How can you follow Jesus' example in resisting those temptations?

The Temptation of Jesus

4 Then Jesus returned from the Jordan, full of the Holy Spirit, and was led by the Spirit in the wilderness 2 for 40 days to be tempted by the Devil. He ate nothing during those days, and when they were over,[e] He was hungry. 3 The Devil said to Him, "If

---

a3:23 People did not know about His virgin birth; Lk 1:26–38; Mt 1:18–25 b3:23 The relationship in some cases may be more distant than a son.
c3:32 Other mss read *Sala* d3:33 Other mss read *Amminadab, son of Aram, son of Joram;* other mss read *Amminadab, son of Admin, son of Arni*
e4:2 Lit *were completed*

---

concern for Luke both in his Gospel and in Acts. Satan's confrontation of Jesus was not a result of being apart from the Spirit, but an integral part of the Spirit's preparing Him for His mission.

4:2 40 days ... tempted. Moses fasted 40 days on Mount Sinai while receiving the commandments (Ex. 34:28). **He ate nothing.** Fasting was a means of communion with God. It was this communion that Satan sought to destroy as he tempted Jesus.

4:3 If You are the Son of God. Satan challenges Jesus at the point of His identity and authority. Surely it must have seemed ironic that the Son of God should be tired, hungry, and apparently alone in such a desolate area. **bread.** While there is nothing inherently wrong with turning stones to bread, the appeal of the temptation was for Jesus to use

His power to meet His own needs instead of trusting His Father to do so.

4:5-7 kingdoms of the world. The second temptation is an appeal to ambition and glory. Probably through some form of vision Satan enabled Jesus to see the splendor, wealth, and power that is represented by the world's political authorities. For the price tag of rejecting God, Satan offers Jesus a painless, immediate way to power and fame. It was only by His obedience to the Father Jesus would become the King of kings, possessing all authority and power (Ps. 2:8-9; Dan. 7:14).

4:8 Jesus answered. Jesus quotes Deuteronomy 6:13, again affirming His loyalty to God and God's ways.

4:9 If You are the Son of God. Once again

Jesus' identity as the Messiah is being attacked (v. 3). **the pinnacle of the temple.** Barclay says this would have been a point 450 feet above the Kidron Valley.

4:12 It is said. Jesus quotes Deuteronomy 6:16 and again asserts His complete trust in His Father. His Word does not need to be tested in foolish ways in order to find out it is true.

4:13 he departed. Having been resisted in his appeals to self-interest, power, and pride, Satan left Jesus. His opposition to Jesus surfaces again in Jesus' conflicts with demons later on and ultimately in his influence upon Judas, in the events leading to the betrayal of Jesus (22:3).

4:14 Galilee. From chapters 4:14–9:50, Luke records Jesus' ministry in Galilee, a province about 50 miles long and 25 miles

You are the Son of God, tell this stone to become bread."

[4] But Jesus answered him, "It is written: **Man must not live on bread alone.**"[a b]

[5] So he took Him up[c] and showed Him all the kingdoms of the world in a moment of time. [6] The Devil said to Him, "I will give You their splendor and all this authority, because it has been given over to me, and I can give it to anyone I want. [7] If You, then, will worship me,[d] all will be Yours."

[8] And Jesus answered him,[e] "It is written:

**Worship the Lord your God,
and serve Him only.**"[f]

[9] So he took Him to Jerusalem, had Him stand on the pinnacle of the temple, and said to Him, "If You are the Son of God, throw Yourself down from here. [10] For it is written:

**He will give His angels orders
concerning you,
to protect you,**[g] [11] and
**they will support you with their hands,
so that you will not strike
your foot against a stone.**"[h]

[12] And Jesus answered him, "It is said: **Do not test the Lord your God.**"[i]

[13] After the Devil had finished every temptation, he departed from Him for a time.

Ministry in Galilee

[14] Then Jesus returned to Galilee in the power of the Spirit, and news about Him spread throughout the entire vicinity. [15] He was teaching in their •synagogues, being acclaimed[j] by everyone.

Rejection at Nazareth

[16] He came to Nazareth, where He had been brought up. As usual, He entered the synagogue on the Sabbath day and stood up to read. [17] The scroll of the prophet Isaiah was given to Him, and unrolling the scroll, He found the place where it was written:

[18] **The Spirit of the Lord is on Me,
because He has anointed Me
to preach good news to the poor.
He has sent Me**[k]
to proclaim freedom[l] **to the captives
and recovery of sight to the blind,
to set free the oppressed,**
[19] **to proclaim the year of the Lord's favor.**[m n]

Get Out of Town

1. Where did you grow up? What did you like best/least about your hometown?

Luke 4:14-30

2. Why did Jesus choose this particular passage from Isaiah to read (vv. 18-19)?

3. What did Jesus mean by suggesting that He had come "to proclaim freedom to the captives" (v. 18)?

4. Why did the people get so angry that they "drove Him out of town" and tried to murder Him (v. 29)?

5. Jesus' words about Elijah meant that God would not heal those who rejected Him. Have you accepted Jesus or rejected Him?

---

[20] He then rolled up the scroll, gave it back to the attendant, and sat down. And the eyes of everyone in the synagogue were fixed on Him. [21] He began by saying to them, "Today as you listen, this Scripture has been fulfilled."

---

[a]4:4 Other mss add *but on every word of God*   [b]4:4 Dt 8:3   [c]4:5 Other mss read *So the Devil took Him up on a high mountain*   [d]4:7 Lit *will fall down before me*   [e]4:8 Other mss add *"Get behind Me, Satan!*   [f]4:8 Dt 6:13   [g]4:10 Ps 91:11   [h]4:11 Ps 91:12   [i]4:12 Dt 6:16   [j]4:15 Or *glorified*   [k]4:18 Other mss add *to heal the brokenhearted,*   [l]4:18 Or *release*, or *forgiveness*   [m]4:19 The time of messianic grace   [n]4:18–19 Is 61:1–2

---

wide in the north of Palestine. **in the power of the Spirit.** Just as the Spirit led Jesus into His time of testing (4:1; Matt. 4:1), so the Spirit now empowers Jesus' ministry.

4:15 synagogues. While the temple in Jerusalem was the religious center for all Jews, the community synagogue was the focal point of weekly worship and teaching. Jesus' initial ministry was as a well-received itinerant preacher.

4:16 stood up to read. As a sign of reverence for God, men would stand as they read the Scripture then sit down to teach.

4:17 the scroll. Since Nazareth was a small village, it is unlikely that the synagogue would have been able to afford to have scrolls of the entire sacred writings. The Isaiah scroll was undoubtedly a prized posses-

sion of the synagogue.

4:18 The passage Jesus read was from Isaiah 61:1-2 (with the addition of a phrase from 58:6). Using the metaphors of people in prison, blindness, and slavery, the prophet speaks of his God-given mission to proclaim freedom and pardon to people who are oppressed and burdened.

4:19 the year of the Lord's favor. This refers to the Jubilee Year of Leviticus 25. Every 50 years, the Jews were to release their slaves, cancel all debts, and return land to the families of its original owners. In this context it became a symbol of the deliverance and new order of justice that God intended to bring about.

4:21 Today ... this Scripture has been fulfilled. The phrase is reminiscent of Mark

1:15, with its announcement that the "kingdom of God has come near." In both cases, Jesus asserts that the new era foretold by Isaiah has begun because He has come to bring it about.

4:22 Joseph's son. This may be a slur, alluding to rumors of Jesus' illegitimacy (Mark 6:3). In stark contrast to God's declaration in 3:22 (Matt. 3:17) that Jesus is God's Son, the hometown people could only see Jesus as Joseph's boy.

4:24 No prophet is accepted in his hometown. This proverb also has Greek parallels.

4:32 His message had authority. Most rabbis taught the Law through quoting what other rabbis had said about it. In contrast, Jesus' teaching impressed His hearers with its relevancy, power, and directness.

22 They were all speaking well of Him[a] and were amazed by the gracious words that came from His mouth, yet they said, "Isn't this Joseph's son?"

23 Then He said to them, "No doubt you will quote this proverb[b] to Me: 'Doctor, heal yourself.' 'All we've heard that took place in Capernaum, do here in Your hometown also.' "

24 He also said, "•I assure you: No prophet is accepted in his hometown. 25 But I say to you, there were certainly many widows in Israel in Elijah's days, when the sky was shut up for three years and six months while a great famine came over all the land. 26 Yet Elijah was not sent to any of them—but to a widow at Zarephath in Sidon. 27 And in the prophet Elisha's time, there were many in Israel who had serious skin diseases, yet not one of them was healed[c]—only Naaman the Syrian."

28 When they heard this, everyone in the synagogue was enraged. 29 They got up, drove Him out of town, and brought Him to the edge[d] of the hill their town was built on, intending to hurl Him over the cliff. 30 But He passed right through the crowd and went on His way.

Driving Out an Unclean Spirit

31 Then He went down to Capernaum, a town in Galilee, and was teaching them on the Sabbath. 32 They were astonished at His teaching because His message had authority. 33 In the synagogue there was a man with an unclean demonic spirit who cried out with a loud voice, 34 "Leave us alone![e] What do You have to do with us,[f] Jesus—•Nazarene? Have You come to destroy us? I know who You are—the Holy One of God!"

35 But Jesus rebuked him and said, "Be quiet and come out of him!"

And throwing him down before them, the demon came out of him without hurting him at all. 36 They were all struck with amazement and kept saying to one another, "What is this message? For He commands the unclean spirits with authority and power, and they

come out!" 37 And news about Him began to go out to every place in the vicinity.

Healings at Capernaum

38 After He left the synagogue, He entered Simon's house. Simon's mother-in-law was suffering from a high fever, and they asked Him about her. 39 So He stood over her and rebuked the fever, and it left her. She got up immediately and began to serve them.

40 When the sun was setting, all those who had anyone sick with various diseases brought them to Him. As He laid His hands on each one of them, He would heal them. 41 Also, demons were coming out of many, shouting and saying, "You are the Son of God!" But He rebuked them and would not allow them to speak, because they knew He was the •Messiah.

Preaching in Galilee

42 When it was day, He went out and made His way to a deserted place. But the crowds were searching for Him. They came to Him and tried to keep Him from leaving them. 43 But He said to them, "I must proclaim the good news about the kingdom of God to the other towns also, because I was sent for this purpose." 44 And He was preaching in the synagogues of Galilee.[g]

The First Disciples

5 As the crowd was pressing in on Jesus to hear God's word, He was standing by Lake Gennesaret.[h] 2 He saw two boats at the edge of the lake;[i] the fishermen had left them and were washing their nets. 3 He got into one of the boats, which belonged to Simon, and asked him to put out a little from the land. Then He sat down and was teaching the crowds from the boat.

4 When He had finished speaking, He said to Simon, "Put out into deep water and let down[j] your nets for a catch."

5 "Master," Simon replied, "we've worked hard all night long and caught nothing! But at Your word, I'll let down the nets."[k]

---

[a]4:22 Or They were testifying against Him   [b]4:23 Or parable   [c]4:27 Lit cleansed   [d]4:29 Lit brow   [e]4:34 Or Ha!, or Ah!   [f]4:34 Lit What to us and to You   [g]4:44 Other mss read Judea   [h]5:1 = Sea of Galilee   [i]5:2 Lit boats standing by the lake   [j]5:4 Lit and you (Gk pl) let down   [k]5:5 Other mss read net (Gk sg)

4:33 an unclean demonic spirit. These were seen as malignant, supernatural agents of Satan, able to harm and possess people. In overcoming the demon, Jesus demonstrated His power over the Devil.

4:34 I know who You are. The demon clearly identified Jesus. He knew the person Jesus, the man from Nazareth and he knew the nature of God, the "Holy One," recognizing that Jesus had the power to destroy him.

4:41 You are the Son of God! While Satan attacked Jesus at the point of His divine nature (vv. 3,9), the defeated demons acknowledged His Deity. **would not allow them to speak.** Jesus silenced the demons. He did not want their witness and it was not yet time for this general announcement.

5:2 washing their nets. In the morning, fish-

ermen would clean and repair their nets..

5:3 the boats. While one belonged to Simon Peter, the other boat may have been owned by James and John (Mark 1:19), Simon's partners in the fishing business (v. 10) A fishing boat was an open craft about 20 to 30 feet long.

5:4-5 let down your nets. Jesus' command seemed foolish since mid-morning was not the time fish would be feeding. Picture tired and hungry men who have worked unsuccessfully all night. Why in the world should they listen to a religious teacher when it comes to their fishing business? Yet, Simon Peter decides to go along with Him and was rewarded for it.

5:6-7 nets began to tear. In contrast to Simon's doubt, Luke underscores the magni-

tude of the catch, so large that it tore the nets and threatened to sink Simon's boat as well as that of his partners!

5:8 he fell at Jesus' knees. Just what Simon Peter recognized about Jesus' identity at this point is unclear since "Lord" can be a title for God or a title of respect for an esteemed person. In any case, it is apparent that Peter was thoroughly convinced that Jesus was at least a rabbi.

5:12 a serious skin disease. Often identified as leprosy, the term was used to cover a wide range of skin diseases besides the true leprosy of Hanson's Disease; no diagnosis was dreaded more than leprosy since it led not only to physical disfigurement and a slow death, but social banishment as well.

5:13 He touched him. Since touching a

⁶ When they did this, they caught a great number of fish, and their nets[a] began to tear. ⁷ So they signaled to their partners in the other boat to come and help them; they came and filled both boats so full that they began to sink.

Giving It All Up

1. Where is the best fishing spot in your area? What is the biggest fish you've ever caught?

Luke 5:1-11

2. Jesus was not a professional fisherman, while Simon and the others were. How might you have reacted to Jesus telling you how to do your job?

3. Consider verse 8. Why did Simon Peter tell Jesus to "go away from me"? Why did he suddenly realize that he was a "sinful man"?

4. Peter, James, and John "left everything, and followed Him" (v. 11). Where is Jesus asking you to follow Him? What must you give up to follow Him?

⁸ When Simon Peter saw this, he fell at Jesus' knees and said, "Go away from me, because I'm a sinful man, Lord!" ⁹ For he and all those with him were amazed[b] at the catch of fish they took, ¹⁰ and so were James and John, Zebedee's sons, who were Simon's partners.

"Don't be afraid," Jesus told Simon. "From now on you will be catching people!" ¹¹ Then they brought the boats to land, left everything, and followed Him.

Cleansing a Leper

¹² While He was in one of the towns, a man was there who had a serious skin disease all over him. He saw Jesus, fell facedown, and begged Him: "Lord, if You are willing, You can make me clean."[c]

¹³ Reaching out His hand, He touched him, saying, "I am willing; be made clean," and immediately the disease left him. ¹⁴ Then He ordered him to tell no one: "But go and show yourself to the priest, and offer what Moses prescribed for your cleansing as a testimony to them."

¹⁵ But the news[d] about Him spread even more, and large crowds would come together to hear Him and to be healed of their sicknesses. ¹⁶ Yet He often withdrew to deserted places and prayed.

The Son of Man Forgives and Heals

¹⁷ On one of those days while He was teaching, •Pharisees and teachers of the law were sitting there who had come from every village of Galilee and Judea, and also from Jerusalem. And the Lord's power to heal was in Him. ¹⁸ Just then some men came, carrying on a stretcher a man who was paralyzed. They tried to bring him in and set him down before Him. ¹⁹ Since they could not find a way to bring him in because of the crowd, they went up on the roof and lowered him on the stretcher through the roof tiles into the middle of the crowd before Jesus.

²⁰ Seeing their faith He said, "Friend,[e] your sins are forgiven you."

²¹ Then the •scribes and the Pharisees began to reason: "Who is this man who speaks blasphemies? Who can forgive sins but God alone?"

²² But perceiving their thoughts, Jesus replied to them, "Why are you reasoning this in your hearts?[f] ²³ Which is easier: to say, 'Your sins are forgiven you,' or to say, 'Get up and walk'? ²⁴ But so you may know that the •Son of Man has authority on earth to forgive sins"—He told the paralyzed man, "I tell you: get up, pick up your stretcher, and go home."

²⁵ Immediately he got up before them, picked up what he had been lying on, and went home glorifying God. ²⁶ Then everyone was astounded, and they were

---

a 5:6 Other mss read *net* (Gk sg)   b 5:9 Or *For amazement had seized him and all those with him*   c 5:12 In these verses, *clean* includes healing, ceremonial purification, return to fellowship with people, and worship in the temple; Lv 14:1–32.   d 5:15 Lit *the word*   e 5:20 Lit *Man*   f 5:22 Or *minds*

---

leper was unimaginable due to the risk of contracting the disease and the violation of the Law that prohibited such contact, Jesus' touch of this leper communicated the tremendous extent of Jesus' compassion as well as His power.

5:14 ordered him to tell no one. There has been much speculation as to why Jesus in many instances discouraged people from telling others what He has done or who He is (Matt. 16:20; Mark 3:12; 5:43; 7:36). The most prevalent view of why He urged this "messianic secret" was that Jesus had to prevent the crowds from proclaiming Him Messiah before they knew what kind of Messiah He was (one who would suffer and die, not the conquering hero of popular imagination).

5:17 Pharisees. A small, powerful religious sect whose prime concern was keeping the law. Since their standards were too high for most Jews to keep in daily life, they were respected as especially devout, godly people. **teachers of the law.** Literally, "scribes." Originally, it was their job to make copies of the Old Testament. Because of their familiarity with Scripture, their role evolved into that of teachers of the law.

5:21 blasphemies. Blasphemy is "contempt for God" punishable by death (Lev. 24:16). Since the teachers of the law believed that illness was the direct result of sin (John 9:2), they assumed that the sick could not recover until their sin had been forgiven by God, who alone could offer forgiveness. Hence they are distressed that Jesus pronounced forgiveness, since this was tantamount to a claim of Deity.

5:23 Which is easier? There are certainly instances where paralysis has been related to unresolved guilt. That is not to say, however, that in *every* instance paralysis or disease is the result of sin. See Luke 13:1-5 and John 9:1-5.

5:27 Levi. Generally thought to be Matthew, referred to in Matthew 9:9.

5:33 fast. Fasting, almsgiving, and prayer were three traditional practices followed by all Jewish sects.

6:1 Sabbath. By Jesus' time the scribes had developed scores of laws that obscured the point that the Sabbath was meant to be a welcome day of rest. **picking heads of grain.** Not considered stealing since it was permissible for hungry travelers to pluck and eat grain from a field (Deut. 23:25).

giving glory to God. And they were filled with awe and said, "We have seen incredible things today!"

The Call of Levi

27 After this, Jesus went out and saw a tax collector named Levi sitting at the tax office, and He said to him, "Follow Me!" 28 So, leaving everything behind, he got up and began to follow Him.

Dining with Sinners

29 Then Levi hosted a grand banquet for Him at his house. Now there was a large crowd of tax collectors and others who were guests[a] with them. 30 But the Pharisees and their scribes were complaining to His disciples, "Why do you eat and drink with tax collectors and sinners?"

31 Jesus replied to them, "The healthy don't need a doctor, but the sick do. 32 I have not come to call the righteous, but sinners to repentance."

A Question about Fasting

33 Then they said to Him, "John's disciples fast often and say prayers, and those of the Pharisees do the same, but Yours eat and drink."[b]

34 Jesus said to them, "You can't make the wedding guests[c] fast while the groom is with them, can you? 35 But the days will come when the groom will be taken away from them—then they will fast in those days."

36 He also told them a parable: "No one tears a patch from a new garment and puts it on an old garment. Otherwise, not only will he tear the new, but also the piece from the new garment will not match the old. 37 And no one puts new wine into old wineskins. Otherwise, the new wine will burst the skins, it will spill, and the skins will be ruined. 38 But new wine should be put into fresh wineskins.[d] 39 And no one, after drinking old wine, wants new, because he says, 'The old is better.' "[e]

Lord of the Sabbath

6 On a Sabbath,[f] He passed through the grainfields. His disciples were picking heads of grain, rubbing them in their hands, and eating them. 2 But some of the •Pharisees said, "Why are you doing what is not lawful on the Sabbath?"

3 Jesus answered them, "Haven't you read what David and those who were with him did when he was hungry— 4 how he entered the house of God, and took and ate the •sacred bread, which is not lawful for any but the priests to eat? He even gave some to those who were with him." 5 Then He told them, "The •Son of Man is Lord of the Sabbath."

The Man with the Paralyzed Hand

6 On another Sabbath He entered the •synagogue and was teaching. A man was there whose right hand was paralyzed. 7 The •scribes and Pharisees were watching Him closely, to see if He would heal on the Sabbath, so that they could find a charge against Him. 8 But He knew their thoughts and told the man with the paralyzed hand, "Get up and stand here."[g] So he got up and stood there. 9 Then Jesus said to them, "I ask you: is it lawful on the Sabbath to do good or to do evil, to save life or to destroy it?" 10 After looking around at them all, He told him, "Stretch out your hand." He did so, and his hand was restored.[h] 11 They, however, were filled with rage and started discussing with one another what they might do to Jesus.

The 12 Apostles

12 During those days He went out to the mountain to pray and spent all night in prayer to God. 13 When daylight came, He summoned His disciples, and He chose 12 of them—He also named them apostles:

14 Simon, whom He also named Peter,
and Andrew his brother;
James and John;
Philip and Bartholomew;
15 Matthew and Thomas;
James the son of Alphaeus,
and Simon called the Zealot;
16 Judas the son of James,
and Judas Iscariot, who became a traitor.

---

[a]5:29 Lit were reclining (at the table); at important meals the custom was to recline on a mat at a low table and lean on the left elbow. [b]5:33 Other mss read "Why do John's . . . drink?" (as a question) [c]5:34 Or the friends of the groom; lit sons of the bridal chamber [d]5:38 Other mss add And so both are preserved. [e]5:39 Other mss read is good [f]6:1 Other mss read a second-first Sabbath; perhaps a special Sabbath [g]6:8 Lit stand in the middle [h]6:10 Other mss add as sound as the other

---

6:3 Haven't you read … ? David. By comparing His actions with those of David's, Jesus gave the first of several hints that He is the long-expected Son of David, the Messiah (Mark 10:46-48; 11:6-10; 12:35-37).

6:4 entered the house of God, and took and ate the sacred bread. This was technically unlawful since only the priests were allowed to eat this bread (Lev. 24:5-9).

6:7 if He would heal on the Sabbath. The issue is not healing, but whether Jesus would do so on the Sabbath in defiance of the oral tradition, which allowed healing on that day only if there was danger to life.

6:9 is it lawful …? Jesus points out that the Pharisees' concern for their traditions wrongfully overshadowed God's clear call for love and mercy.

6:17 a level place. As a matter of contrast, Matthew has Jesus saying many of the same things recorded here (such as the Beatitudes and the Lord's Prayer) on a mountaintop (Matt. 5:1). **from all Judea.** Luke emphasizes the breadth of Jesus' ministry. Judea and Jerusalem, known for Jewish orthodoxy, were to the south while Tyre and Sidon, Gentile areas, were to the north.

6:20 Blessed. Refers to people who are to be congratulated, not necessarily meaning they are happy or prospering. Instead, whether they feel it or not, they are fortunate because their condition reflects that they are in a right relationship to God. **poor.** The Beatitudes in Luke differ slightly from those reported in Matthew 5. Those who are materially poor are generally seen in the New Testament to be more receptive to God (18:18-25; James 2:5-7). **the kingdom of God.** Those who maintain loyalty to God, even if it means poverty rather than the wealth they might gain if they compromised their integrity, are assured an inheritance in His kingdom.

6:21 are hungry. In the Old Testament hunger and thirst are used as a way of describing the desire for spiritual fullness experienced by those who truly seek God (Ps. 42:1-2; Isa. 55:1; Amos 8:11). **will be filled.** The story of the rich man and Lazarus in chapter 16:19 illustrates future rewards for those who follow Christ.

6:23 their ancestors used to treat the prophets. Elijah, Jeremiah, Ezekiel, and other Old Testament prophets faced consistent rejection, ridicule, and abuse from the people of their day.

Teaching and Healing

[17] After coming down with them, He stood on a level place with a large crowd of His disciples and a great multitude of people from all Judea and Jerusalem and from the seacoast of Tyre and Sidon. [18] They came to hear Him and to be healed of their diseases; and those tormented by unclean spirits were made well. [19] The whole crowd was trying to touch Him, because power was coming out from Him and healing them all.

The Beatitudes

[20] Then looking up at[a] His disciples, He said:

Blessed are you who are poor,
because the kingdom of God is yours.
[21] Blessed are you who are hungry now,
because you will be filled.
Blessed are you who weep now,
because you will laugh.
[22] Blessed are you when people hate you,
when they exclude you, insult you,
and slander your name as evil,
because of the Son of Man.

[23] "Rejoice in that day and leap for joy! Take note—your reward is great in heaven, because this is the way their ancestors used to treat the prophets.

Woe to the Self-Satisfied

[24] But woe to you who are rich,
because you have received your comfort.
[25] Woe to you who are full now,
because you will be hungry.
Woe to you[b] who are laughing now,
because you will mourn and weep.
[26] Woe to you[b]
when all people speak well of you,
because this is the way their ancestors
used to treat the false prophets.

Love Your Enemies

[27] "But I say to you who listen: Love your enemies, do good to those who hate you, [28] bless those who curse you, pray for those who mistreat you. [29] If anyone hits you on the cheek, offer the other also. And if anyone takes away your coat, don't hold back your shirt either. [30] Give to everyone who asks from you, and from one who takes away your things, don't ask for them back. [31] Just as you want others to do for you, do the same for them. [32] If you love those who love you, what credit is that to you? Even sinners love those who love them. [33] If you do what is good to those who are good to you, what credit is that to you? Even sinners do that. [34] And if you lend to those from whom you expect to receive, what credit is that to you? Even sinners lend to sinners to be repaid in full. [35] But love your enemies, do what is good, and lend, expecting nothing in return. Then your reward will be great, and you will be sons of the Most High. For He is gracious to the ungrateful and evil. [36] Be merciful, just as your Father also is merciful.

Do Not Judge

[37] "Do not judge, and you will not be judged. Do not condemn, and you will not be condemned. Forgive, and you will be forgiven. [38] Give, and it will be given to you; a good measure—pressed down, shaken together, and running over—will be poured into your lap. For with the measure you use,[c] it will be measured back to you."

[39] He also told them a parable: "Can the blind guide the blind? Won't they both fall into a pit? [40] A disciple is not above his teacher, but everyone who is fully trained will be like his teacher.

[41] "Why do you look at the speck in your brother's eye, but don't notice the log in your own eye? [42] Or how can you say to your brother, 'Brother, let me take out the speck that is in your eye,' when you yourself don't see the log in your eye? Hypocrite! First take the log out of your eye, and then you will see clearly to take out the speck in your brother's eye.

A Tree and Its Fruit

[43] "A good tree doesn't produce bad fruit; on the other hand, a bad tree doesn't produce good fruit. [44] For each tree is known by its own fruit. Figs aren't gathered from thornbushes, or grapes picked from a bramble bush. [45] A good man produces good out of the good

---

[a]**6:20** Lit Then lifting up His eyes to   [b]**6:25,26** Other mss omit to you   [c]**6:38** Lit you measure

---

6:24 woe. Like "blessed," this is God's pronouncement on the peoples' real state of affairs regardless of what external circumstances feel like. Unless they repent, God's judgment is the only future they have.

6:25 are laughing. Sometimes in the Old Testament, joy and laughter are the spontaneous responses of people blessed by God (Isa. 51:11; 66:10; Jer. 31:13; 33:11). This is the meaning intended in verse 21.

6:27 Love. The orthodox Jew of the time only regarded fellow Jews as his neighbor, but Jesus makes it clear that there is no one to whom love is not owed. The word used for love is agape, benevolent action done for another without the expectation of reward.

6:29 coat. An outer robe made of wool, used as a blanket at night. **shirt.** The close-fitting under-robe. Jesus used the humorous picture of a robber being encouraged to take even more than he intended to steal in order to emphasize the spirit of giving that ought to characterize His followers (v. 30).

6:31 as you want others to do for you. This is the so-called Golden Rule. The negative form of this rule was widely known in the ancient world: "Do not do to others what you do not wish them to do to you." Jesus alters this statement in a slight but highly significant way.

6:36 Be merciful. The same principle found in the Lord's Prayer where we are told that if we expect God to forgive us of the offenses we have committed, we need to forgive others for their offenses against us (Matt. 6:14-15).

6:37 Do not judge. Moral discernment is not forbidden, but only God is righteous enough to pass final judgment without partiality or error. **you will not be judged.** Not that such people will escape judgment, but that they will be treated mercifully when judgment comes.

6:47–49 the flood came. Palestine was dry most of the year. In the autumn, heavy rains would turn what appeared to be dry land into a raging river as flash floods swept down the ravines. Only lives built on a solid foundation will withstand the trials of life.

7:1 Capernaum. This was a town on the north end of the Sea of Galilee, three miles west of the Jordan River. This was where Jesus often stayed during His ministry in Galilee.

storeroom of his heart. An evil man produces evil out of the evil storeroom, for his mouth speaks from the overflow of the heart.

The Two Foundations

46 "Why do you call Me 'Lord, Lord,' and don't do the things I say? 47 I will show you what someone is like who comes to Me, hears My words, and acts on them: 48 He is like a man building a house, who dug deepa and laid the foundation on the rock. When the flood came, the river crashed against that house and couldn't shake it, because it was well built. 49 But the one who hears and does not act is like a man who built a house on the ground without a foundation. The river crashed against it, and immediately it collapsed. And the destruction of that house was great!"

A Centurion's Faith

7 When He had concluded all His sayings in the hearing of the people, He entered Capernaum. 2 A •centurion's •slave, who was highly valued by him, was sick and about to die. 3 When the centurion heard about Jesus, he sent some Jewish elders to Him, requesting Him to come and save the life of his slave. 4 When they reached Jesus, they pleaded with Him earnestly, saying, "He is worthy for You to grant this, 5 because he loves our nation and has built us a •synagogue." 6 Jesus went with them, and when He was not far fromb the house, the centurion sent friends to tell Him, "Lord, don't trouble Yourself, since I am not worthy to have You come under my roof. 7 That is why I didn't even consider myself worthy to come to You. But say the word, and my servant will be cured.c 8 For I too am a man placed under authority, having soldiers under my command.d I say to this one, 'Go!' and he goes; and to another, 'Come!' and he comes; and to my slave, 'Do this!' and he does it."

9 Jesus heard this and was amazed at him, and turning to the crowd following Him, He said, "I tell you, I have not found so great a faith even in Israel!" 10 When those who had been sent returned to the house, they found the •slave in good health.

A Widow's Son Raised to Life

11 Soon afterwards He was on His way to a town called Nain. His disciples and a large crowd were traveling with Him. 12 Just as He neared the gate of the town, a dead man was being carried out. He was his mother's only son, and she was a widow. A large crowd from the city was also with her. 13 When the Lord saw her, He had compassion on her and said, "Don't cry." 14 Then He came up and touched the open coffin,e and the pallbearers stopped. And He said, "Young man, I tell you, get up!"

15 The dead man sat up and began to speak, and Jesus gave him to his mother. 16 Then fearf came over everyone, and they glorified God, saying, "A great prophet has risen among us," and "God has visitedg His people." 17 This report about Him went throughout Judea and all the vicinity.

In Praise of John the Baptist

18 Then John's disciples told him about all these things. So John summoned two of his disciples 19 and sent them to the Lord, asking, "Are You the One who is to come, or should we look for someone else?"

20 When the men reached Him, they said, "John the Baptist sent us to ask You, 'Are You the One who is to come, or should we look for someone else?' "

21 At that time Jesus healed many people of diseases, plagues, and evil spirits, and He granted sight to many blind people. 22 He replied to them, "Go and report to John the things you have seen and heard: The blind receive their sight, the lame walk, those with skin diseases are healed,h the deaf hear, the dead are raised, and the poor have the good news preached to them. 23 And anyone who is not offended because of Me is blessed." 24 After John's messengers left, He began to speak to the crowds about John: "What did you go out into the wilderness to see? A reed swaying in the wind? 25 What then did you go out to see? A man dressed in soft robes? Look, those who are splendidly dressedi and live in luxury are in royal palaces. 26 What then did you go out to see? A prophet? Yes, I tell you,

---

a6:48 Lit dug and went deep   b7:6 Lit and He already was not far from   c7:7 Other mss read and let my servant be cured   d7:8 Lit under me   e7:14 Or the bier   f7:16 Or awe   g7:16 Or come to help   h7:22 Lit cleansed   i7:25 Or who have glorious robes

---

7:2 centurion's. A commander of over 100 soldiers.

7:11 Nain. The modern-day town of Nen, six miles southeast of Nazareth and within a mile of where Elisha raised another woman's son centuries before (2 Kings 4:18-37).

7:12 his mother's only son, and she was a widow. This woman's situation was serious: children provided the only "Social Security" available for parents in their old age and this woman had no more children and no husband. Thus, she faced both loneliness and poverty. **A large crowd.** Mourners accompanied the woman to the burial site.

7:16 fear came over everyone. The response of both fear and praise is characteristic of people throughout the Bible when God's power is manifest.

7:18-20 Are You the One ...? The parallel passage in Matthew 11:1-19 indicates that at this point John was in Herod's prison. John's question as to whether Jesus was "the one" comes from confusion over the role of the Messiah. John preached of a Messiah who would come to execute God's wrath and judgment upon the unrighteous in Israel (3:17). Jesus' actions, while empowered by God, did not match John's expectation.

7:21-23 He replied to them. Jesus did not answer their question directly, but invited them to watch and reflect upon what He did as He healed and taught. The recovery of sight, the healing of the lame, the restoration of hearing to the deaf, the raising of the dead, and the preaching of the good news of God's mercy to the poor and oppressed are all marks of the Messiah's mission according to Isaiah (Isa. 26:19; 29:18-19; 35:5-6; 61:1).

7:24 A reed swaying in the wind? John, who stood firmly for God, was not a man to be swayed by the currents of popular opinion or pressure.

7:25 A man dressed in soft robes? Jesus accented how John's ascetic demeanor was in marked contrast to the indulgence and wastefulness that characterized those who served King Herod. One can imagine the crowd's smiles as they caught Jesus' irony in these two comparisons.

7:28 I tell you ... greater than he. This sentence was not in the least meant to disparage John or to diminish his place in the kingdom of God, but to emphasize the new order that Jesus was beginning. To play the least part in the kingdom of God is greater than to have the lead role in the old order represented by John and the Old Testament

and far more than a prophet. ²⁷ This is the one it is written about:

> Look, I am sending My messenger
> ahead of You;^a
> he will prepare Your way before You.^b

²⁸ I tell you, among those born of women no one is greater than John,^c but the least in the kingdom of God is greater than he."

²⁹ (And when all the people, including the tax collectors, heard this, they acknowledged God's way of righteousness,^d because they had been baptized with John's baptism. ³⁰ But since the •Pharisees and experts in the law had not been baptized by him, they rejected the plan of God for themselves.)

An Unresponsive Generation

³¹ "To what then should I compare the people of this generation, and what are they like? ³² They are like children sitting in the marketplace and calling to each other:

> We played the flute for you,
> but you didn't dance;
> we sang a lament,
> but you didn't weep!

³³ For John the Baptist did not come eating bread or drinking wine, and you say, 'He has a demon!' ³⁴ The •Son of Man has come eating and drinking, and you say, 'Look, a glutton and a drunkard, a friend of tax collectors and sinners!' ³⁵ Yet wisdom is vindicated^e by all her children."

Much Forgiveness, Much Love

³⁶ Then one of the Pharisees invited Him to eat with him. He entered the Pharisee's house and reclined at the table. ³⁷ And a woman in the town who was a sinner found out that Jesus was reclining at the table in the Pharisee's house. She brought an alabaster flask of fragrant oil ³⁸ and stood behind Him at His feet, weeping, and began to wash His feet with her tears. She wiped His feet with the hair of her head, kissing them and anointing them with the fragrant oil.

³⁹ When the Pharisee who had invited Him saw this, he said to himself, "This man, if He were a prophet, would know who and what kind of woman this is who is touching Him—she's a sinner!"

Guilty as Charged

1. What's something you are guilty of: Speeding? Breaking curfew? Borrowing clothes without asking? Other?

Luke 7:36-50

2. Why did the woman pour perfume on Jesus' feet, wipe His feet with her hair, and kiss His feet?
3. Why did the Pharisee react the way he did?
4. Who had more sin forgiven: The Pharisee? The woman? Both the same?
5. The point of Jesus' parable is not how much sin He forgives for each person, but how each person responds to Jesus' forgiveness. How have you responded to His forgiveness?

⁴⁰ Jesus replied to him, "Simon, I have something to say to you."

"Teacher," he said, "say it."

⁴¹ "A creditor had two debtors. One owed 500 •denarii, and the other 50. ⁴² Since they could not pay it back, he graciously forgave them both. So, which of them will love him more?"

⁴³ Simon answered, "I suppose the one he forgave more."

"You have judged correctly," He told him. ⁴⁴ Turning to the woman, He said to Simon, "Do you see this woman? I entered your house; you gave Me no water for My feet, but she, with her tears, has washed My feet and wiped them with her hair. ⁴⁵ You

---

^a**7:27** Lit *messenger before Your face*   ^b**7:27** Mal 3:1   ^c**7:28** Other mss read *women is not a greater prophet than John the Baptist*   ^d**7:29** Lit *they justified God*   ^e**7:35** Or *wisdom is declared right*

---

prophets—those who could only look forward to the Messiah.

7:36 reclined at the table. People ate by reclining on their left side on low couches arranged around a table, such that their feet would be stretched out behind them.

7:38 began to wash His feet with her tears. The woman's tears show her extreme conviction of her sin as she stood by the feet of Jesus. For a woman to loose her hair in public was scandalous; using it to dry her tears from Jesus' feet marked her great humility before Him. Normally, a person's head would be anointed as a sign of honor. (The Hebrew word *Messiah* means "anointed one.") Like John the Baptist, who felt unworthy to undo the thongs of the Messiah's sandals (3:16), perhaps this woman felt she was so unworthy that she dare only anoint Jesus'

feet. That Jesus accepted these acts shows much about His character. He did not let what people might think dictate how He related to people. He saw her love and penitence and responded to that instead of public opinion.

7:41-43 500 denarii ... 50. The difference here is between owing what one could earn in 18 months versus owing what could be earned in less than two months. Then, as now, it would be the rare moneylender who would cancel either debt! Part of what Jesus was saying was that God cancels debts (in the form of sins) that are far greater than most humans would cancel. A similar point is made in the parable of the unmerciful servant, where the amount the master forgave was greater still (Matt. 18:23-35). Simon rightly gets the point that the man with the greatest debt would be

most grateful.

7:47 Jesus is not saying that the woman is forgiven *because* she has shown such extravagant love, but her love expresses her gratitude for the forgiveness she has received.

7:50 Go in peace. Jesus utters this common saying not simply as a wish but as an expression of fact.

8:2-3 some women. Jesus' band was supported by these women who helped in gratitude for the healing they had received from Jesus. Mary and Joanna are mentioned at the resurrection (24:10). The presence of Joanna, who was married to the man charged with the responsibility for managing Herod's affairs, shows that Jesus' influence had reached to the higher social and eco-

gave Me no kiss, but she hasn't stopped kissing My feet since I came in. ⁴⁶ You didn't anoint My head with oil, but she has anointed My feet with fragrant oil. ⁴⁷ Therefore I tell you, her many sins have been forgiven; that's why ᵃ she loved much. But the one who is forgiven little, loves little." ⁴⁸ Then He said to her, "Your sins are forgiven."

⁴⁹ Those who were at the table with Him began to say among themselves, "Who is this man who even forgives sins?"

⁵⁰ And He said to the woman, "Your faith has saved you. Go in peace."

Many Women Support Christ's Work

8 Soon afterwards He was traveling from one town and village to another, preaching and telling the good news of the kingdom of God. The Twelve were with Him, ² and also some women who had been healed of evil spirits and sicknesses: Mary, called •Magdalene (seven demons had come out of her); ³ Joanna the wife of Chuza, •Herod's steward; Susanna; and many others who were supporting them from their possessions.

The Parable of the Sower

⁴ As a large crowd was gathering, and people were flocking to Him from every town, He said in a parable: ⁵ "A sower went out to sow his seed. As he was sowing, some fell along the path; it was trampled on, and the birds of the sky ate it up. ⁶ Other seed fell on the rock; when it sprang up, it withered, since it lacked moisture. ⁷ Other seed fell among thorns; the thorns sprang up with it and choked it. ⁸ Still other seed fell on good ground; when it sprang up, it produced a crop: 100 times what was sown." As He said this, He called out, "Anyone who has ears to hear should listen!"

Why Jesus Used Parables

⁹ Then His disciples asked Him, "What does this parable mean?" ¹⁰ So He said, "The secrets ᵇ of the kingdom of God have been given for you to know, but to the rest it is in parables, so that

Looking they may not see,
and hearing they may not understand. ᶜ

The Parable of the Sower Explained

¹¹ "This is the meaning of the parable: ᵈ The seed is the word of God. ¹² The seeds along the path are those who have heard. Then the Devil comes and takes away the word from their hearts, so that they may not believe and be saved. ¹³ And the seeds on the rock are those who, when they hear, welcome the word with joy. Having no root, these believe for a while and depart in a time of testing. ¹⁴ As for the seed that fell among thorns, these are the ones who, when they have heard, go on their way and are choked with worries, riches, and pleasures of life, and produce no mature fruit. ¹⁵ But the seed in the good ground—these are the ones who, ᵉ having heard the word with an honest and good heart, hold on to it and by enduring, bear fruit.

Using Your Light

¹⁶ "No one, after lighting a lamp, covers it with a basket or puts it under a bed, but puts it on a lampstand so that those who come in may see the light. ¹⁷ For nothing is concealed that won't be revealed, and nothing hidden that won't be made known and come to light. ¹⁸ Therefore, take care how you listen. For whoever has, more will be given to him; and whoever does not have, even what he thinks he has will be taken away from him."

True Relationships

¹⁹ Then His mother and brothers came to Him, but they could not meet with Him because of the crowd. ²⁰ He was told, "Your mother and Your brothers are standing outside, wanting to see You."

²¹ But He replied to them, "My mother and My brothers are those who hear and do the word of God."

Wind and Wave Obey the Master

²² One day He and His disciples got into a boat, and He told them, "Let's cross over to the other side of the lake." So they set out, ²³ and as they were sailing He fell asleep. Then a fierce windstorm came down on the lake; they

---

ᵃ**7:47** Her love shows that she has been forgiven ᵇ**8:10** The Gk word *mysteria* does not mean "mysteries" in the Eng sense; it means what we can know only by divine revelation. ᶜ**8:10** Is 6:9 ᵈ**8:11** Lit *But this is the parable:* ᵉ**8:15** Or *these are the kind who*

---

nomic classes. That women traveled with Jesus shows the difference between Him and other rabbis who often held women in low esteem.

8:5 sow his seed. Farmers sowed their fields by scattering seed with broad sweeping motions of the hand as they walked along the paths in their fields. Afterward, they would go through the field to plow the seed under. **the path.** There were hard pathways between the various plots of land. These were packed so hard that seed could not even penetrate the soil, thus making it easy for the birds to simply eat it.

8:6 on the rock. Some of the soil covered a limestone base a few inches beneath the surface. Seed that fell here would germinate, but it would not last since the roots could not

penetrate deeply enough into the ground to draw moisture during hot, dry times.

8:7 thorns. In other parts of the plot there were the roots of weeds that grew faster than the seedlings, stunting their growth. Although it lived, such seed would not bear fruit.

8:8 good ground. This was the soil in which the seed could grow and flourish. **100 times [what was sown].** A spectacular crop! A tenfold crop was considered an especially good harvest.

8:10 secrets of the kingdom. In the New Testament a secret is something hidden until God chooses to reveal it. The quote from Isaiah 6:9 does not mean Jesus spoke in parables to keep people from understanding, but that their lack of spiritual openness pre-

vented them from understanding.

8:16 lamp. A pottery vessel filled with olive oil.

8:23 a fierce windstorm. The Sea of Galilee was a deep, freshwater lake, 13 miles long and 8 miles wide. It was pear-shaped and ringed by mountains, though open at its north and south ends. Fierce winds often blew into this bowl-shaped lake, creating savage and unpredictable storms.

8:24 Master. A common term of address for a rabbi.

8:25 Where is your faith? This may not be so much a rebuke as an invitation for them to take a fresh look at who they think He is. Have they been listening (vv. 4-21)? **fearful and amazed.** The disciples' fear of the storm

were being swamped and were in danger. ²⁴ They came and woke Him up, saying, "Master, Master, we're going to die!" Then He got up and rebuked the wind and the raging waves. So they ceased, and there was a calm. ²⁵ He said to them, "Where is your faith?"

They were fearful and amazed, asking one another, "Who can this be?ᵃ He commands even the winds and the waves, and they obey Him!"

Dealing with Demons

1. What is the scariest place or situation you've ever been in?

Luke 8:26-39

2. What was wrong with the man who met Jesus? How had he gotten that way?

3. Why did Jesus send the demons into the herd of pigs? Why didn't He just send them to "the abyss" (v. 31)?

4. Why would Jesus tell this grateful man that he couldn't stay with Him, but had to go back home? What was the result of his return home?

5. How do you proclaim Jesus' healing power to the people you know?

Demons Driven Out by the Master

²⁶ Then they sailed to the region of the Gerasenes,ᵇ which is opposite Galilee. ²⁷ When He got out on land, a demon-possessed man from the town met Him. For a long time he had worn no clothes and did not stay in a house but in the tombs. ²⁸ When he saw Jesus, he cried out, fell down before Him, and said in a loud voice, "What do You have to do with me,ᶜ Jesus, You Son of the Most High God? I beg You, don't torment me!"

²⁹ For He had commanded the unclean spirit to come out of the man. Many times it had seized him, and although he was guarded, bound by chains and shackles, he would snap the restraints and be driven by the demon into deserted places.

³⁰ "What is your name?" Jesus asked him.

"Legion," he said—because many demons had entered him. ³¹ And they begged Him not to banish them to the •abyss.

³² A large herd of pigs was there, feeding on the hillside. The demons begged Him to permit them to enter the pigs, and He gave them permission. ³³ The demons came out of the man and entered the pigs, and the herd rushed down the steep bank into the lake and drowned. ³⁴ When the men who tended them saw what had happened, they ran off and reported it in the town and in the countryside. ³⁵ Then people went out to see what had happened. They came to Jesus and found the man the demons had departed from, sitting at Jesus' feet, dressed and in his right mind. And they were afraid. ³⁶ Meanwhile the eyewitnesses reported to them how the demon-possessed man was delivered. ³⁷ Then all the people of the Gerasene regionᵇ asked Him to leave them, because they were gripped by great fear. So getting into the boat, He returned.

³⁸ The man from whom the demons had departed kept begging Him to be with Him. But He sent him away and said, ³⁹ "Go back to your home, and tell all that God has done for you." And off he went, proclaiming throughout the town all that Jesus had done for him.

A Girl Restored and a Woman Healed

⁴⁰ When Jesus returned, the crowd welcomed Him, for they were all expecting Him. ⁴¹ Just then, a man named Jairus came. He was a leader of the •synagogue. He fell down at Jesus' feet and pleaded with Him to come to his house, ⁴² because he had an only daughter about 12 years old, and she was at death's door.ᵈ

While He was going, the crowds were nearly crushing Him. ⁴³ A woman suffering from bleeding for 12 years, who had spent all she had on doctorsᵉ yet could

---

ᵃ**8:25** Lit *Who then is this?*   ᵇ**8:26,37** Other mss read *the Gadarenes*   ᶜ**8:28** Lit *What to me and to You*   ᵈ**8:42** Lit *she was dying*   ᵉ**8:43** Other mss omit *who had spent all she had on doctors*

---

gives way to fear of the One who has power over that storm! It is the fear of an unknown force or power. **Who can this be?** This is the key question that emerges in these stories of Jesus' divine power. No rabbi could do what they have just seen Jesus do!

8:26 the region of the Gerasenes. The precise location of their landing is not clear. However, it is on the other side of the lake from Capernaum, in a burial ground in Gentile territory, probably near the lower end of the Sea of Galilee.

8:27 He got out on land. tombs. The ragged limestone cliffs with caves and depressions provided natural tombs.

8:28 don't torment me! The plea not to be tortured comes from the demons. Their plea

is ironic in light of their effect on the man whom they possessed.

8:30 Legion. The term for a company of Roman soldiers consisting of 6,000 men. The man was occupied by a huge number of demons.

8:31 the abyss. Despite popular belief that the underworld is the place where Satan and his demons have free reign, the Bible declares it to be the place of punishment for these evil beings (2 Peter 2:4).

8:32 pigs. This herd belonged to Gentiles since Jews considered pigs unclean animals. To associate with them would defile them before God (Lev. 11:1-8).

8:35 they were afraid. It might be expected that the people would rejoice that this man

who had terrorized them was now healed. Instead they are fearful of Jesus who had the power to overcome the demons.

8:43 A woman suffering. The woman should not have been there because her illness made her ceremonially "unclean" (Lev. 15:25-30), thus cutting her off from contact with other people, including her husband.

8:48 your faith has made you well. Spiritual as well as physical healing is in view here.

8:51 Peter, John, and James. These three disciples become a sort of inner circle around Jesus.

8:52 Everyone was crying. These were in all likelihood professional mourners. Even the poorest person was expected to hire not

not be healed by any, [44] approached from behind and touched the •tassel of His robe. Instantly her bleeding stopped.

[45] "Who touched Me?" Jesus asked.

When they all denied it, Peter[a] said, "Master, the crowds are hemming You in and pressing against You."[b]

[46] "Somebody did touch Me," said Jesus. "I know that power has gone out from Me." [47] When the woman saw that she was discovered,[c] she came trembling and fell down before Him. In the presence of all the people, she declared the reason she had touched Him and how she was instantly cured. [48] "Daughter," He said to her, "your faith has made you well.[d] Go in peace."

[49] While He was still speaking, someone came from the synagogue leader's ⌊house⌋, saying, "Your daughter is dead. Don't bother the Teacher anymore."

[50] When Jesus heard it, He answered him, "Don't be afraid. Only believe, and she will be made well." [51] After He came to the house, He let no one enter with Him except Peter, John, James, and the child's father and mother. [52] Everyone was crying and mourning for her. But He said, "Stop crying, for she is not dead but asleep."

[53] They started laughing at Him, because they knew she was dead. [54] So He[e] took her by the hand and called out, "Child, get up!" [55] Her spirit returned, and she got up at once. Then He gave orders that she be given something to eat. [56] Her parents were astounded, but He instructed them to tell no one what had happened.

Commissioning the Twelve

9 Summoning the Twelve, He gave them power and authority over all the demons, and ⌊power⌋ to heal[f] diseases. [2] Then He sent them to proclaim the kingdom of God and to heal the sick.

[3] "Take nothing for the road," He told them, "no walking stick, no traveling bag, no bread, no money; and don't take an extra shirt. [4] Whatever house you enter, stay there and leave from there. [5] If they do not welcome you, when you leave that town, shake off the dust from your feet as a testimony against them." [6] So they went out and traveled from village to village, proclaiming the good news and healing everywhere.

Herod's Desire to See Jesus

[7] •Herod the tetrarch heard about everything that was going on. He was perplexed, because some said that John had been raised from the dead, [8] some that Elijah had appeared, and others that one of the ancient prophets had risen. [9] "I beheaded John," Herod said, "but who is this I hear such things about?" And he wanted to see Him.

Feeding 5,000

[10] When the apostles returned, they reported to Jesus all that they had done. He took them along and withdrew privately to a[g] town called Bethsaida. [11] When the crowds found out, they followed Him. He welcomed them, spoke to them about the kingdom of God, and cured[h] those who needed healing.

[12] Late in the day,[i] the Twelve approached and said to Him, "Send the crowd away, so they can go into the surrounding villages and countryside to find food and lodging, because we are in a deserted place here."

[13] "You give them something to eat," He told them.

"We have no more than five loaves and two fish," they said, "unless we go and buy food for all these people." [14] (For about 5,000 men were there.)

Then He told His disciples, "Have them sit down[j] in groups of about 50 each." [15] They did so, and had them all sit down. [16] Then He took the five loaves and the two fish, and looking up to heaven, He blessed and broke them. He kept giving them to the disciples to set before the crowd. [17] Everyone ate and was filled. Then they picked up[k] 12 baskets of leftover pieces.

---

[a]**8:45** Other mss add *and those with him*   [b]**8:45** Other mss add *and You say, 'Who touched Me?'*   [c]**8:47** Lit *she had not escaped notice*   [d]**8:48** Or *has saved you*   [e]**8:54** Other mss add *having put them all outside*   [f]**9:1** In this passage, different Gk words are translated as *heal*. In Eng, "to heal" or "to cure" are synonyms with little distinction in meaning. Technically, we do not heal or cure diseases. People are healed or cured from diseases.   [g]**9:10** Other mss add *deserted place near a*   [h]**9:11** Or *healed*; in this passage, different Gk words are translated as *heal*. In Eng, "to heal" or "to cure" are synonyms with little distinction in meaning. Technically, we do not heal or cure diseases. People are healed or cured from diseases.   [i]**9:12** Lit *When the day began to decline*   [j]**9:14** Lit *them recline*   [k]**9:17** Lit *Then were picked up by them*

---

less than two flutes and one wailing woman to mourn a death. They were a sign that all knew the child was dead.

9:5 shake off the dust from your feet. When leaving Gentile areas, Jews would wipe off their feet as a symbolic action of cleansing themselves from the judgment of God that was to come. For the disciples to do this to Jewish villages would indicate that the village was not part of the true Israel.

9:7 Herod. Before his death in 4 B.C., Herod the Great divided his territory between three of his sons: Herod (Antipas) and Philip ruled over their areas until A.D. 39 and 33 respectively. The third son, Archelaus, was given Judea, Samaria, and Edom but was soon removed because of a petition by the Jews he ruled. **John had been raised.** Mark 6:14-29 tells the gruesome story of John's death.

9:8 Elijah. It was commonly believed that just prior to the coming of the Messiah, God would raise up Israel's famous prophet to prepare the way (Mal. 4:5).

9:10 Bethsaida. A town north of the Sea of Galilee.

9:12 a deserted place here. The disciples pointed out to Jesus that it would soon be too late for the crowd to find hospitality. It may be that they were in the predominately Gentile area on the east side of the Sea of Galilee where Jews could not be assured of being welcomed.

9:13 five loaves and two fish. If three loaves of bread was considered a generous meal for a guest (11:5-8), then the disciples' provision here was barely adequate for their own needs.

9:14 5000 men. Literally, "males" (Matt. 14:21). When all the women and children are added in, this was truly a huge crowd.

9:20 who do you say that I am? This is *the* critical question. Have the disciples heeded what they have seen and heard of Jesus (8:18)? **God's Messiah!** This is a Hebrew word meaning "the Anointed One"; that is, the prophesied future king of Israel.

9:21 tell this to no one. Jesus commanded them be silent about what they know. The problem was that, although they knew He was the Messiah, they did not yet know what *kind* of Messiah He was.

9:22 must suffer. The people did not understand that Messiah was to be a suffering servant. They thought His role meant only glory and victory. They didn't realize salvation

Peter's Confession of the Messiah

[18] While He was praying in private and His disciples were with Him, He asked them, "Who do the crowds say that I am?"

[19] They answered, "John the Baptist; others, Elijah; still others, that one of the ancient prophets has come back."[a]

[20] "But you," He asked them, "who do you say that I am?"

Peter answered, "God's •Messiah!"

His Death and Resurrection Predicted

[21] But He strictly warned and instructed them to tell this to no one, [22] saying, "The •Son of Man must suffer many things and be rejected by the elders, •chief priests, and •scribes, be killed, and be raised the third day."

Take Up Your Cross

[23] Then He said to ⌊them⌋ all, "If anyone wants to come with[b] Me, he must deny himself, take up his cross daily,[c] and follow Me. [24] For whoever wants to save his •life will lose it, but whoever loses his life because of Me will save it. [25] What is a man benefited if he gains the whole world, yet loses or forfeits himself? [26] For whoever is ashamed of Me and My words, the Son of Man will be ashamed of him when He comes in His glory and that of the Father and the holy angels. [27] I tell you the truth: there are some standing here who will not taste death until they see the kingdom of God."

The Transfiguration

[28] About eight days after these words, He took along Peter, John, and James, and went up on the mountain to pray. [29] As He was praying, the appearance of His face changed, and His clothes became dazzling white. [30] Suddenly, two men were talking with Him—Moses and Elijah. [31] They appeared in glory and were speaking of His death,[d] which He was about to accomplish in Jerusalem.

[32] Peter and those with him were in a deep sleep,[e] and when they became fully awake, they saw His glory and the two men who were standing with Him. [33] As the two men were departing from Him, Peter said to Jesus, "Master, it's good for us to be here! Let us make three •tabernacles: one for You, one for Moses, and one for Elijah"—not knowing what he said.

[34] While he was saying this, a cloud appeared and overshadowed them. They became afraid as they entered the cloud. [35] Then a voice came from the cloud, saying:

This is My Son, the Chosen One;[f]
listen to Him!

[36] After the voice had spoken, only Jesus was found. They kept silent, and in those days told no one what they had seen.

The Power of Faith over a Demon

[37] The next day, when they came down from the mountain, a large crowd met Him. [38] Just then a man from the crowd cried out, "Teacher, I beg You to look at my son, because he's my only ⌊child⌋. [39] Often a spirit seizes him; suddenly he shrieks, and it throws him into convulsions until he foams at the mouth;[g] wounding[h] him, it hardly ever leaves him. [40] I begged Your disciples to drive it out, but they couldn't."

[41] Jesus replied, "You unbelieving and rebellious[i] generation! How long will I be with you and put up with you? Bring your son here."

[42] As the boy was still approaching, the demon knocked him down and threw him into severe convulsions. But Jesus rebuked the unclean spirit, cured the boy, and gave him back to his father. [43] And they were all astonished at the greatness of God.

The Second Prediction of His Death

While everyone was amazed at all the things He was doing, He told His disciples, [44] "Let these words sink in:[j] the Son of Man is about to be betrayed into the hands of men."

[a]**9:19** Lit *has risen*   [b]**9:23** Lit *come after*   [c]**9:23** Other mss omit *daily*   [d]**9:31** Or *departure;* Gk *exodus*   [e]**9:32** Lit *were weighed down with sleep*   [f]**9:35** Other mss read *the Beloved*   [g]**9:39** Lit *convulsions with foam*   [h]**9:39** Or *bruising,* or *mauling*   [i]**9:41** Or *corrupt,* or *perverted,* or *twisted;* Dt 32:5   [j]**9:44** Lit *Put these words in your ears*

would be provided through the suffering and death of the Messiah. **rejected by the elders, chief priests, and scribes.** These three groups made up the Sanhedrin, the ruling Jewish body. For the first time, Jesus predicted His rejection by the officials of Israel.

9:23 come with Me. This is to take on the role of a disciple, one committed to the teachings of a master. **deny himself.** This is to no longer live with self-satisfaction as the primary aim of life. Self must be denied in favor of doing the will of God. **take up his cross.** It is a metaphor emphasizing the call for all Jesus' disciples to put aside one's own desires and interests out of loyalty to Jesus. **daily.** Luke alone included this. Following Jesus is a day-by-day commitment.

9:26 Comes in His glory! While His present suffering is real, the future glory of the Son of Man is pictured here (Dan. 7:13-14).

9:28 the mountain. This may be Mt. Hermon, a 9,000-foot mountain located 12 miles from Caesarea Philippi (though early tradition says the transfiguration occurred on Mt. Tabor, located southwest of the Sea of Galilee). In the past, God had revealed Himself on other mountains, such as when He appeared to Moses (Exod. 24) and Elijah (1 Kings 19) on Mt. Sinai (also called Mt. Horeb)..

9:30 Moses. It was to Moses God gave the law. **Elijah.** The Jews expected Elijah to return just prior to the coming of the day of the Lord (Mal. 4:5-6).

9:35 a voice. Once again, as He did at the baptism of Jesus (3:22), God proclaimed that Jesus is His Son.

9:41 You unbelieving and rebellious generation! This parallels God's cry when faced with Israel's stubborn refusal to listen to Him in the wilderness (Deut. 32:5,20).

9:42 rebuked ... cured ... gave. Jesus displayed the glory, power, and compassion of God by this decisive defeat of the demon.

9:47 took a little child. Children, like women and slaves, had few rights and little social significance in the eyes of men. By having this child stand beside Him, Jesus placed him in the position of honor that each of the Twelve coveted.

9:49 someone driving out demons. The disciples' lack of humility is matched by their lack of acceptance that God is at work outside of their circle. (See Num. 11:24-30 for a similar incident in the life of Moses.) Since a

45 But they did not understand this statement; it was concealed from them so that they could not grasp it, and they were afraid to ask Him about it.[a]

Who Is the Greatest?

46 Then an argument started among them about who would be the greatest of them. 47 But Jesus, knowing the thoughts of their hearts, took a little child and had him stand next to Him. 48 He told them, "Whoever welcomes[b] this little child in My name welcomes Me. And whoever welcomes Me welcomes Him who sent Me. For whoever is least among you—this one is great."

In His Name

49 John responded, "Master, we saw someone driving out demons in Your name, and we tried to stop him because he does not follow us."

50 "Don't stop him," Jesus told him, "because whoever is not against you is for you."[c]

The Journey to Jerusalem

51 When the days were coming to a close for Him to be taken up,[d] He determined[e] to journey to Jerusalem. 52 He sent messengers ahead of Him, and on the way they entered a village of the •Samaritans to make preparations for Him. 53 But they did not welcome Him, because He determined to journey to Jerusalem. 54 When the disciples James and John saw this, they said, "Lord, do You want us to call down fire from heaven to consume them?"[f] 55 But He turned and rebuked them,[g] 56 and they went to another village.

Following Jesus

57 As they were traveling on the road someone said to Him, "I will follow You wherever You go!"

58 Jesus told him, "Foxes have dens, and birds of the sky[h] have nests, but the Son of Man has no place to lay His head." 59 Then He said to another, "Follow Me."

"Lord," he said, "first let me go bury my father."[i]

60 But He told him, "Let the dead bury their own dead, but you go and spread the news of the kingdom of God."

61 Another also said, "I will follow You, Lord, but first let me go and say good-bye to those at my house."

62 But Jesus said to him, "No one who puts his hand to the plow and looks back is fit for the kingdom of God."

Sending Out the Seventy

10 After this, the Lord appointed 70[j] others, and He sent them ahead of Him in pairs to every town and place where He Himself was about to go. 2 He told them: "The harvest is abundant, but the workers are few. Therefore, pray to the Lord of the harvest to send out workers into His harvest. 3 Now go; I'm sending you out like lambs among wolves. 4 Don't carry a money-bag, traveling bag, or sandals; don't greet anyone along the road. 5 Whatever house you enter, first say, 'Peace to this household.' 6 If a son of peace[k] is there, your peace will rest on him; but if not, it will return to you. 7 Remain in the same house, eating and drinking what they offer, for the worker is worthy of his wages. Don't be moving from house to house. 8 When you enter any town, and they welcome you, eat the things set before you. 9 Heal the sick who are there, and tell them, 'The kingdom of God has come near you.' 10 When you enter any town, and they don't welcome you, go out into its streets and say, 11 'We are wiping off ¡as a witness¡ against you even the dust of your town that clings to our feet. Know this for certain: the kingdom of God has come near.' 12 I tell you, on that day it will be more tolerable for Sodom than for that town.

Unrepentant Towns

13 "Woe to you, Chorazin! Woe to you, Bethsaida! For if the miracles that were done in you had been done in Tyre and Sidon, they would have repented long ago, sitting in sackcloth and ashes! 14 But it will

---

[a]**9:45** Lit *about this statement*   [b]**9:48** Or *receives* throughout the verse   [c]**9:50** Other mss read *against us is for us*   [d]**9:51** His ascension   [e]**9:51** Lit *He stiffened His face to go*; Is 50:7   [f]**9:54** Other mss add *as Elijah also did*   [g]**9:55–56** Other mss add *and said, "You don't know what kind of spirit you belong to.* 56 *For the Son of Man did not come to destroy people's lives but to save them."*   [h]**9:58** Wild birds, as opposed to domestic birds   [i]**9:59** Not necessarily meaning his father was already dead   [j]**10:1** Other mss read *72*   [k]**10:6** A peaceful person; one open to the message of the kingdom

---

person's name represented his character and power, this exorcist recognized Jesus' authority over demons and called upon that authority in his work.

9:50 whoever is not against you is for you. The concern should be whether a person is seeking to glorify Jesus, not whether he or she is part of the "right" organization.

9:52 Samaritans. Samaritans and Jews were bitter enemies. The Samaritans did not want anything to do with someone traveling to Jerusalem, since they believed the true place of worship was on a mountain in *their* province.

9:54 do You want us to call down fire from heaven? Elijah once did this (2 Kings 1:9-12), so the disciples may have thought it was an appropriate fate for those who treated Jesus shabbily.

9:58 no place to lay His head. Once Jesus began His public ministry He had no settled home, but traveled throughout Palestine. To follow Jesus is to be a sojourner in this world (Heb. 11:13).

9:59 let me go bury my father. This does not mean that the man's father had just died, but that the son was putting off following Jesus until he was free from obligations to his father—the last of which would have been the duty of providing for his burial, a duty that took precedence over all other religious obligations. The kingdom outweighs responsibility even to family.

10:2 harvest. The harvest image was used in the Old Testament as a metaphor for the coming judgment when God would gather together all His people.

10:4 Don't carry ... don't greet. This lack of provisions and the command not to stop to greet anyone highlights the urgency of their task (2 Kings 4:29).

10:8 eat the things set before you. The concern here is not for proper etiquette in a host's home. If this trip involved going to the east side of the Jordan River, it would include visiting Gentile towns where the food would not meet Jewish dietary laws. Jesus' point is that the preaching of the kingdom is not to be deterred by religious traditions.

10:12 Sodom. An ancient city whose place in history was preserved because of the severity of God's judgment upon its evil (Gen. 19:1-29).

10:13 Woe to you. In spite of all the evidence concerning Jesus that they had seen

be more tolerable for Tyre and Sidon at the judgment than for you. ¹⁵ And you, Capernaum, will you be exalted to heaven? No, you will go down to •Hades! ¹⁶ Whoever listens to you listens to Me. Whoever rejects you rejects Me. And whoever rejects Me rejects the One who sent Me."

The Return of the Seventy

¹⁷ The Seventyᵃ returned with joy, saying, "Lord, even the demons submit to us in Your name."

¹⁸ He said to them, "I watched Satan fall from heaven like a lightning flash. ¹⁹ Look, I have given you the authority to trample on snakes and scorpions and over all the power of the enemy; nothing will ever harm you. ²⁰ However, don't rejoice thatᵇ the spirits submit to you, but rejoice that your names are written in heaven."

The Son Reveals the Father

²¹ In that same hour Heᶜ rejoiced in the Holyᵈ Spirit and said, "I praiseᵉ You, Father, Lord of heaven and earth, because You have hidden these things from the wise and the learned and have revealed them to infants. Yes, Father, because this was Your good pleasure.ᶠ ²² All things haveᵍ been entrusted to Me by My Father. No one knows who the Son is except the Father, and who the Father is except the Son, and anyone to whom the Son desiresʰ to reveal Him."

²³ Then turning to His disciples He said privately, "The eyes that see the things you see are blessed! ²⁴ For I tell you that many prophets and kings wanted to see the things you see yet didn't see them; to hear the things you hear yet didn't hear them."

The Parable of the Good Samaritan

²⁵ Just then an expert in the law stood up to test Him, saying, "Teacher, what must I do to inherit eternal life?"

²⁶ "What is written in the law?" He asked him. "How do you read it?"

²⁷ He answered:

Love the Lord your God with all your heart, with all your soul, with all your strength, and with all your mind; and your neighbor as yourself.ⁱ

²⁸ "You've answered correctly," He told him. "Do this and you will live."

²⁹ But wanting to justify himself, he asked Jesus, "And who is my neighbor?"

The Good Samaritan

1. Have you ever helped a stranger or been helped by a stranger? What happened?

Luke 10:25-37

2. "And who is my neighbor?" What was Jesus' answer to that question, according to this passage?

3. How would you answer the question the "expert in the law" asked in verse 25?

4. Samaritans were like social outcasts in Jesus' day. How did the Samaritan prove to be more like Jesus than the "religious" people in the parable?

5. Who has been a "neighbor" to you? To whom have you been a "neighbor" recently?

³⁰ Jesus took up ₗthe questionₗ and said: "A man was going down from Jerusalem to Jericho and fell into the hands of robbers. They stripped him, beat him up, and fled, leaving him half dead. ³¹ A priest happened to be going down that road. When he saw him, he passed by on the other side. ³² In the same way, a Levite, when he arrived at the place and saw him, passed by on the other side. ³³ But a •Samaritan on his journey came up

ᵃ **10:17** Other mss read *The Seventy-two*   ᵇ **10:20** Lit *don't rejoice in this, that*   ᶜ **10:21** Other mss read *Jesus*   ᵈ **10:21** Other mss omit *Holy*
ᵉ **10:21** Or *thank*, or *confess*   ᶠ **10:21** Lit *was well-pleasing in Your sight*   ᵍ **10:22** Other mss read *And turning to the disciples, He said, "Everything has*   ʰ **10:22** Or *wills*, or *chooses*   ⁱ **10:27** Dt 6:5; Lv 19:18

---

and heard, they still had not received Him as Messiah. **Chorazin.** Apart from this reference and Matthew 11:21, there is no other mention of Chorazin in the Bible. **Bethsaida!** The home of Peter, Andrew, and Philip (John 1:44; 12:21).

10:19 authority to trample on snakes. Snakes and scorpions are symbolic of Satan's forces unleashed in nature. These forces, which plague humanity, are rendered powerless at the reign of the Messiah (Ps. 91:13; Isa. 11:8). Nevertheless, the joy of the disciples should not be rooted in acts of supernatural authority, but in the assurance that they have a place in heaven (v. 20).

10:25 an expert in the law. This would have been a scribe, a man charged with the responsibility of interpreting the law and teaching people what was involved in its observance.

10:26-27 What is written in the law? Jesus' question points the lawyer back to the *Shema* (Deut. 6:5), which is recited in verse 27. The scribe also adds Leviticus 19:18 with its stress on the love of neighbor.

10:29 And who is my neighbor? In an attempt to regain the initiative, he asks Jesus another question. Given the understanding of "neighbor" at the time, his follow-up question was perfectly natural. The Jewish religious leaders of the time taught that only other Jews were neighbors.

10:31 A priest. This priest may have been returning home after his period of temple service. He may have passed by to avoid the ritual defilement of touching a dead man.

10:32 a Levite. These were men assigned to

aid the priests in various temple duties. Perhaps he was fearful of being attacked himself by the same robbers.

10:33 a Samaritan. These people were despised by most Jews, and hence making him the hero who acted like a neighbor would have caught the Jewish audience off guard.

10:34 pouring on oil and wine. While olive oil and wine were thought to have medicinal benefits, they were also used in acts of worship at the temple.

10:35 two denarii. Silver coins that would have been enough to care for the man for three weeks.

10:38 village. Bethany, just on the outskirts of Jerusalem, was the home of Martha and

to him, and when he saw ⌊the man⌋, he had compassion. [34] He went over to him and bandaged his wounds, pouring on oil and wine. Then he put him on his own animal, brought him to an inn, and took care of him. [35] The next day[a] he took out two •denarii, gave them to the innkeeper, and said, 'Take care of him. When I come back I'll reimburse you for whatever extra you spend.'

[36] "Which of these three do you think proved to be a neighbor to the man who fell into the hands of the robbers?"

[37] "The one who showed mercy to him," he said. Then Jesus told him, "Go and do the same."

One Necessary Thing

1. In your family, who does most of the preparation when company comes? What do you do?

Luke 10:38-42

2. Why did Mary sit "at the Lord's feet" (v. 39)? Why didn't Martha do that?

3. When is it good to be busy serving others? When is it not the best thing to do?

4. What "many tasks" tend to distract you from spending time with Jesus? How could you balance your schedule to allow more time to listen to Him?

5. In verse 42 Jesus says, "but one thing is necessary." What is that thing?

Martha and Mary

[38] While they were traveling, He entered a village, and a woman named Martha welcomed Him into her home.[b] [39] She had a sister named Mary, who also sat at the Lord's[c] feet and was listening to what He said.[d] [40] But Martha was distracted by her many tasks, and she came up and asked, "Lord, don't You care that my sister has left me to serve alone? So tell her to give me a hand."[e]

[41] The Lord[f] answered her, "Martha, Martha, you are worried and upset about many things, [42] but one thing is necessary. Mary has made the right choice,[g] and it will not be taken away from her."

The Model Prayer

11 He was praying in a certain place, and when He finished, one of His disciples said to Him, "Lord, teach us to pray, just as John also taught his disciples." [2] He said to them, "Whenever you pray, say:

> Father,[h]
> Your name be honored as holy.
> Your kingdom come.[i]
> [3] Give us each day our daily bread.[j]
> [4] And forgive us our sins,
> for we ourselves also forgive everyone
> in debt[k] to us.
> And do not bring us into temptation."[l]

Keep Asking, Searching, Knocking

[5] He also said to them: "Suppose one of you[m] has a friend and goes to him at midnight and says to him, 'Friend, lend me three loaves of bread, [6] because a friend of mine on a journey has come to me, and I don't have anything to offer him.'[n] [7] Then he will answer from inside and say, 'Don't bother me! The door is already locked, and my children and I have gone to bed. I can't get up to give you anything.' [8] I tell you, even though he won't get up and give him anything because he is his friend, yet because of his persistence,[o] he will get up and give him as much as he needs.

[9] "So I say to you, keep asking,[p] and it will be given to you. Keep searching,[q] and you will find. Keep knock-

---

[a]**10:35** Other mss add *as he was leaving* [b]**10:38** Other mss omit *into her home* [c]**10:39** Other mss read *at Jesus'* [d]**10:39** Lit *to His word* or *message* [e]**10:40** Or *tell her to help me* [f]**10:41** Other mss read *Jesus* [g]**10:42** Lit *has chosen the good part* [h]**11:2** Other mss read *Our Father in heaven* [i]**11:2** Other mss add *Your will be done on earth as it is in heaven* [j]**11:3** Or *our bread for tomorrow* [k]**11:4** Or *everyone who wrongs us* [l]**11:4** Other mss add *But deliver us from the evil one* [m]**11:5** Lit *Who of you* [n]**11:6** Lit *I have nothing to set before him* [o]**11:8** Or *annoying persistence,* or *shamelessness* [p]**11:9** Or *you, ask* [q]**11:9** Or *Search*

Mary and their brother Lazarus. **a woman named Martha.** Martha and Mary also appear in John 11:1-44, where their brother Lazarus dies and is raised from the dead by Jesus.

10:42 one thing is necessary. Jesus is not saying that a simple meal is all that is needed, but that listening and responding to Him is the single most critical thing in life.

11:1 teach us to pray. Various Jewish groups (including John's disciples) had their own distinctive prayers.

11:2 Father. While even the orthodox Jews of the day called God "our Father," this simple, personal form of address was new. Jesus at times used the term "Abba," a term more akin to "Dad" than "Father," which was being much more familiar with God than

other rabbis thought appropriate. He taught the disciples to approach God personally. **Your name be honored as holy.** The first petition is that the name of God (i.e., His character and nature) be honored by all. **Your kingdom come.** The prayer is that God will quickly establish the reign of His kingdom throughout the world. While the kingdom is in some sense already present (10:9), it will only come in its *fullness* when Christ returns.

11:4 for we ourselves also forgive. This is not an appeal for forgiveness as a reward for our forgiving others, but rather a reminder that God's forgiveness produces a willingness to extend that to others. Jesus told the parable of the unmerciful servant (Matt. 18:21-35) to make this point. **do not bring us into temptation.** The request is that the person will not have to face a trial so difficult

that he or she will fall into sin.

11:5-6 I don't have anything to offer him. Hospitality was held in high regard in the ancient Middle East. Hebrews urged Christians to continue to be hospitable to traveling strangers (Heb. 13:2). Since hospitality was such an important duty, it would be imperative that the host in this story provide some food for his surprise visitor.

11:7 The door is already locked. A wooden door secured by a wooden or iron bolt thrust through rings. It could not be opened without making a noise. **my children and I have gone to bed.** The whole family would sleep together on a mat on the floor of the simple one-room cottage envisioned here. If the man got up, he would disturb the whole household.

ing,[a] and the door will be opened to you. [10] For everyone who asks receives, and the one who searches finds, and to the one who knocks, the door will be opened. [11] What father among you, if his son[b] asks for a fish, will give him a snake instead of a fish? [12] Or if he asks for an egg, will give him a scorpion? [13] If you then, who are evil, know how to give good gifts to your children, how much more will the heavenly Father give[c] the Holy Spirit to those who ask Him?"

A House Divided

[14] Now He was driving out a demon that was mute.[d] When the demon came out, the man who had been mute, spoke, and the crowds were amazed. [15] But some of them said, "He drives out demons by •Beelzebul, the ruler of the demons!" [16] And others, as a test, were demanding of Him a sign from heaven.

[17] Knowing their thoughts, He told them: "Every kingdom divided against itself is headed for destruction, and a house divided against itself falls. [18] If Satan also is divided against himself, how will his kingdom stand? For you say I drive out demons by Beelzebul. [19] And if I drive out demons by Beelzebul, who is it your sons[e] drive them out by? For this reason they will be your judges. [20] If I drive out demons by the finger of God, then the kingdom of God has come to you. [21] When a strong man, fully armed, guards his estate, his possessions are secure.[f] [22] But when one stronger than he attacks and overpowers him, he takes from him all his weapons[g] he trusted in, and divides up his plunder. [23] Anyone who is not with Me is against Me, and anyone who does not gather with Me scatters.

An Unclean Spirit's Return

[24] "When an unclean spirit comes out of a man, it roams through waterless places looking for rest, and not finding rest, it then[h] says, 'I'll go back to my house where I came from.' [25] And returning, it finds ⌊the house⌋ swept and put in order. [26] Then it goes and brings seven other spirits more evil than itself, and they enter and settle down there. As a result, that man's last condition is worse than the first."

True Blessedness

[27] As He was saying these things, a woman from the crowd raised her voice and said to Him, "The womb that bore You and the one who nursed You are blessed!"

[28] He said, "Even more, those who hear the word of God and keep it are blessed!"

The Sign of Jonah

[29] As the crowds were increasing, He began saying: "This generation is an evil generation. It demands a sign, but no sign will be given to it except the sign of Jonah.[i] [30] For just as Jonah became a sign to the people of Nineveh, so also the •Son of Man will be to this generation. [31] The queen of the south will rise up at the judgment with the men of this generation and condemn them, because she came from the ends of the earth to hear the wisdom of Solomon, and look—something greater than Solomon is here! [32] The men of Nineveh will rise up at the judgment with this generation and condemn it, because they repented at Jonah's proclamation, and look—something greater than Jonah is here!

The Lamp of the Body

[33] "No one lights a lamp and puts it in the cellar or under a basket,[j] but on a lampstand, so that those who come in may see its light. [34] Your eye is the lamp of the body. When your eye is good, your whole body is also full of light. But when it is bad, your body is also full of darkness. [35] Take care then, that the light in you is not darkness. [36] If therefore your whole body is full of light, with no part of it in darkness, the whole body will be full of light, as when a lamp shines its light on you."[k]

Religious Hypocrisy Denounced

[37] As He was speaking, a •Pharisee asked Him to dine with him. So He went in and reclined at the table.

---

[a]**11:9** Or *Knock* [b]**11:11** Other mss read *son asks for bread, would give him a stone? Or if he* [c]**11:13** Lit *the Father from heaven will give* [d]**11:14** A demon that caused the man to be mute [e]**11:19** Your exorcists [f]**11:21** Lit *his possessions are in peace* [g]**11:22** Gk *panoplia*, the armor and weapons of a foot soldier; Eph 6:11,13 [h]**11:24** Other mss omit *then* [i]**11:29** Other mss add *the prophet* [j]**11:33** Other mss omit *or under a basket* [k]**11:36** Or *shines on you with its rays*

11:8 because of his persistence. Literally, "shamelessness."

11:9 keep asking ... Keep searching ... Keep knocking. Jesus is emphasizing that prayer is a continuous, ongoing process. Prayer is rooted in the assurance that the householder (God) will hear the prayers and meet the needs of his friend.

11:11-13 snake ... scorpion. These were creatures that Jews were forbidden to eat (Lev. 11:12,42). The snake may be an eel-like fish that likewise was forbidden to the Jews. The scorpion, at least, could be poisonous.

11:13 who are evil. A strong statement since "evil" is used elsewhere to characterize Satan (Matt. 6:13). Since not even a sinful human father would give such a repulsive, dangerous food to his own son, how much

less will the perfect heavenly Father fail to give what His children most need?

11:15 Beelzebul. Probably a slang expression for a demon-prince, meaning something like "The Lord of Dung." It is used here apparently as a synonym for Satan.

11:29 the sign of Jonah. This is a reference to Jesus' resurrection. After Jonah spent three days and three nights in the belly of the "great fish," he experienced a miraculous deliverance—which authenticated his call to preach in Nineveh (Jonah 1:17; 2:10).

11:31 The queen of the south. She came all the way from Arabia to listen to the wisdom of Solomon (1 Kings 10:1-13). **something greater.** Jesus claims to be greater than Solomon, under whose reign Israel achieved its apex of power and dominion.

He also claims to be greater than Jonah (v. 32), under whose preaching an entire Gentile city was brought to its knees before God.

11:34 Your eye is the lamp of the body. The comparison is between a lamp that provides light for one's path and a good eye (literally, an eye that is "single") that enables people to find their way toward a purposeful life of obedience to God.

11:38 he was amazed. Like Simon in 7:39, Jesus' unorthodox actions raised silent questions in the mind of His host. **He did not first perform the ritual washing.** This had nothing to do with hygiene, but everything to do with religious tradition.

11:41 give ... then. They should repent of their greed and give to the poor instead.

38 When the Pharisee saw this, he was amazed that He did not first perform the ritual washing[a] before dinner. 39 But the Lord said to him: "Now you Pharisees clean the outside of the cup and dish, but inside you are full of greed and evil. 40 Fools! Didn't He who made the outside make the inside too? 41 But give to charity what is within,[b] and then everything is clean for you.

42 "But woe to you Pharisees! You give a tenth[c] of mint, rue, and every kind of herb, and you bypass[d] justice and love for God.[e] These things you should have done without neglecting the others.

43 "Woe to you Pharisees! You love the front seat in the •synagogues and greetings in the marketplaces.

44 "Woe to you![f] You are like unmarked graves; the people who walk over them don't know it."

45 One of the experts in the law answered Him, "Teacher, when You say these things You insult us too."

46 Then He said: "Woe also to you experts in the law! You load people with burdens that are hard to carry, yet you yourselves don't touch these burdens with one of your fingers.

47 "Woe to you! You build monuments[g] to the prophets, and your fathers killed them. 48 Therefore you are witnesses that you approve[h] the deeds of your fathers, for they killed them, and you build their monuments.[i] 49 Because of this, the wisdom of God said, 'I will send them prophets and apostles, and some of them they will kill and persecute,' 50 so that this generation may be held responsible for the blood of all the prophets shed since the foundation of the world[j] — 51 from the blood of Abel to the blood of Zechariah, who perished between the altar and the sanctuary.

"Yes, I tell you, this generation will be held responsible.[k]

52 "Woe to you experts in the law! You have taken away the key of knowledge! You didn't go in yourselves, and you hindered those who were going in."

53 When He left there,[l] the •scribes and the Pharisees began to oppose Him fiercely and to cross-examine Him about many things; 54 they were lying in wait for Him to trap Him in something He said.[m]

Beware of Religious Hypocrisy

12 In these circumstances,[n] a crowd of many thousands came together, so that they were trampling on one another. He began to say to His disciples first: "Be on your guard against the yeast[o] of the •Pharisees, which is hypocrisy. 2 There is nothing covered that won't be uncovered, nothing hidden that won't be made known. 3 Therefore whatever you have said in the dark will be heard in the light, and what you have whispered in an ear in private rooms will be proclaimed on the housetops.

Fear God

4 "And I say to you, My friends, don't fear those who kill the body, and after that can do nothing more. 5 But I will show you the One to fear: Fear Him who has authority to throw ⌊people⌋ into •hell after death. Yes, I say to you, this is the One to fear! 6 Aren't five sparrows sold for two pennies?[p] Yet not one of them is forgotten in God's sight. 7 Indeed, the hairs of your head are all counted. Don't be afraid; you are worth more than many sparrows!

Acknowledging Christ

8 "And I say to you, anyone who acknowledges Me before men, the •Son of Man will also acknowledge him before the angels of God, 9 but whoever denies Me before men will be denied before the angels of God. 10 Anyone who speaks a word against the Son of Man will be forgiven, but the one who blasphemes against the Holy Spirit will not be forgiven. 11 Whenever they bring you before •synagogues and rulers and authorities, don't worry about how you should defend yourselves or what you should say. 12 For the Holy Spirit will teach you at that very hour what must be said."

---

a 11:38 Lit He did not first wash   b 11:41 Or But donate from the heart as charity   c 11:42 Or a tithe   d 11:42 Or neglect   e 11:42 Lit the justice and the love of God   f 11:44 Other mss read you scribes and Pharisees, hypocrites!   g 11:47 Or graves   h 11:48 Lit witnesses and approve   i 11:48 Other mss omit their monuments   j 11:50 Lit so that the blood of all . . . world may be required of this generation,   k 11:51 Lit you, it will be required of this generation   l 11:53 Other mss read And as He was saying these things to them   m 11:54 Other mss add so that they might bring charges against Him   n 12:1 Or Meanwhile, or At this time, or During this period   o 12:1 Or leaven   p 12:6 Lit two assaria; the assarion (sg) was a small copper coin

---

Such action would reflect a change of heart that would show inner cleanliness.

11:42 You give a tenth. The Old Testament required a tithe of garden and farm produce (Lev. 27:30-33; Deut. 14:22-29). Jesus attacked the Pharisees for holding fast to this (relatively) insignificant detail while they had totally neglected concerns like justice and love that dominate the Old Testament Law and prophets.

11:43 the front seat. The seats facing the congregation were the most important seats in the synagogue. To be seated there had become a sign of one's status in the congregation.

11:44 graves. Unmarked graves defile those who unknowingly come in contact with them (Num. 19:16).

11:46 load people with burdens. The scribes interpreted the law with a complex system of restrictions. Thus most felt condemned for their continual breaking of God's law. Jesus is incensed that the scribes assumed their duty stopped with interpreting the law. They made no attempt to help the people who struggled under the burden they created.

11:51 Abel. The first person to be murdered. It happened because his brother, like these leaders, refused to listen to God (Gen. 4:3-8). **Zechariah.** The context implies this was Zechariah (son of Jehoiada) who was murdered in the temple by people who refused to hear his word (2 Chron. 24:19-22).

11:52 taken away the key of knowledge! Instead of unlocking the Scriptures, the traditions of the scribes have securely locked away such knowledge from the people.

12:1 yeast. Yeast was often used as a metaphor for evil. Here it represents the hypocrisy of the Pharisees.

12:2-3 nothing covered...nothing hidden. In the context of Jesus' warning about the hypocrisy of the Pharisees, He reminds His disciples that everything is open before God's all-seeing gaze. We may pretend to be better than what we are, but God knows. Authentic worship and discipleship live constantly in this realization.

12:4 don't fear those who kill the body. Whatever we fear has control of us. Most people's greatest fear is physical death—and by extension—anyone or anything that can bring about our physical death. Jesus

Building True Wealth

1. If you could have fame, fortune, or good looks, which would you choose?

Luke 12:13-21

2. What is Jesus warning against in verse 15? How does greed lead to spiritual disaster?

3. "Take it easy; eat, drink, and enjoy yourself" (v. 19). What is your attitude toward this philosophy? The attitude of those in your school?

4. Why did God call the rich man a fool (v. 20): Because he was rich? Because of his attitude? Other?

5. How can you be "rich toward God" (v. 21)? How can you help others who put their trust "in the abundance of [their] possessions" (v. 15)?

The Parable of the Rich Fool

¹³ Someone from the crowd said to Him, "Teacher, tell my brother to divide the inheritance with me."

¹⁴ "Friend,"ᵃ He said to him, "who appointed Me a judge or arbitrator over you?" ¹⁵ He then told them, "Watch out and be on guard against all greed because one's life is not in the abundance of his possessions."

¹⁶ Then He told them a parable: "A rich man's land was very productive. ¹⁷ He thought to himself, 'What should I do, since I don't have anywhere to store my crops? ¹⁸ I will do this,' he said. 'I'll tear down my barns and build bigger ones and store all my grain and my goods there. ¹⁹ Then I'll say to myself, "Youᵇ have many goods stored up for many years. Take it easy; eat, drink, and enjoy yourself." '

²⁰ "But God said to him, 'You fool! This very night your •life is demanded of you. And the things you have prepared—whose will they be?'

²¹ "That's how it is with the one who stores up treasure for himself and is not rich toward God."

The Cure for Anxiety

²² Then He said to His disciples: "Therefore I tell you, don't worry about your life, what you will eat; or about the body, what you will wear. ²³ For life is more than food and the body more than clothing. ²⁴ Consider the ravens: they don't sow or reap; they don't have a storeroom or a barn; yet God feeds them. Aren't you worth much more than the birds? ²⁵ Can any of you add a •cubit to his heightᶜ by worrying? ²⁶ If then you're not able to do even a little thing, why worry about the rest?

Where's Your Treasure?

1. What "treasure" did you collect as a kid? Do those things still seem valuable to you now?

Luke 12:22-34

2. Jesus taught this lesson because of the rich man's request for help in verse 13. How might worry have been the motivating factor behind his request?

3. What does it mean to "seek His kingdom" (v. 31)?

4. How do we make "money-bags for [ourselves] that won't grow old" (v. 33)?

5. Jesus tells us in verse 34, "For where your treasure is, there your heart will be also." Where is your heart today—with treasures on earth or with Jesus in heaven?

²⁷ "Consider how the wildflowers grow: they don't labor or spin thread. Yet I tell you, not even Solomon in all his splendor was adorned like one of these! ²⁸ If that's how God clothes the grass, which is in the field today and is thrown into the furnace tomorrow, how

---

ᵃ**12:14** Lit Man   ᵇ**12:19** Lit say to my soul, "Soul, you   ᶜ**12:25** Or add one moment to his life-span

---

says this is a misplaced fear. He died to free us from this slavery (Heb. 2:15). Our only fear should be of Him who has the authority to send those who have died to hell. It was said of the Scottish reformer John Knox that he feared God so much, he feared no man.

12:6 sparrows. These small, common birds were eaten by poor people. **pennies.** A penny was worth one sixteenth of a denarius, which was the average day's wage.

12:13 Teacher. Literally, "Rabbi." As men schooled in the law of God, rabbis were often asked to settle legal disputes. **divide the inheritance.** If sons could not peaceably keep the father's estate together, one could sue for the property to be legally divided.

12:14 who appointed Me a judge or arbitrator over you? Jesus refused to be used as a

pawn for this man's material gain. Jesus effectively became the judge over both of them, exposing the motivation of their hearts.

12:15 be on guard against all greed. Jesus pinpointed the real motivating factor behind this appeal for justice. **life.** Then, as now, a person's happiness and well-being was often thought to be determined by what he or she owned. Jesus flatly rejected this as a standard for measuring the worth of one's life.

12:18 store all my grain and my goods there. Up to this point in the parable, the listeners would view the man as blessed by God. Even the plan to store the crop for future use could be commended, since the people of the Middle East would periodically suffer from famine. But God redirected the thought. He reminded the rich man that only God directs the future. The man was to live

respecting God, not confident in his own resources.

12:19 eat, drink, and enjoy yourself. The man was not following God's ways, but living as a pagan, concerned only with his own desires.

12:20 You fool! In the Bible, a fool is someone who lives without regard to God. **your life is demanded of you.** The word for "demanded" is a word used in banking circles when a loan was being called in for payment.

12:28 you of little faith? Faith is the opposite of anxiety.

12:29 Don't keep striving. Literally, "do not seek."

12:31 seek His kingdom. Having warned the

971

much more will He do for you—you of little faith? ²⁹ Don't keep striving for what you should eat and what you should drink, and don't be anxious. ³⁰ For the Gentile world eagerly seeks all these things, and your Father knows that you need them.

³¹ "But seek His kingdom, and these things will be provided for you. ³² Don't be afraid, little flock, because your Father delights to give you the kingdom. ³³ Sell your possessions and give to the poor. Make moneybags for yourselves that won't grow old, an inexhaustible treasure in heaven, where no thief comes near and no moth destroys. ³⁴ For where your treasure is, there your heart will be also.

Ready for the Master's Return

³⁵ "Be ready for service[a] and have your lamps lit. ³⁶ You must be like people waiting for their master to return[b] from the wedding banquet so that when he comes and knocks, they can open ⟨the door⟩ for him at once. ³⁷ Those •slaves the master will find alert when he comes will be blessed. •I assure you: He will get ready,[c] have them recline at the table, then come and serve them. ³⁸ If he comes in the middle of the night, or even near dawn,[d] and finds them alert, those slaves are blessed. ³⁹ But know this: if the homeowner had known at what hour the thief was coming, he would not have let his house be broken into. ⁴⁰ You also be ready, because the Son of Man is coming at an hour that you do not expect."

Rewards and Punishment

⁴¹ "Lord," Peter asked, "are You telling this parable to us or to everyone?"

⁴² The Lord said: "Who then is the faithful and sensible manager his master will put in charge of his household servants to give them their allotted food at the proper time? ⁴³ That •slave whose master finds him working when he comes will be rewarded. ⁴⁴ I tell you the truth: he will put him in charge of all his possessions. ⁴⁵ But if that slave says in his heart, 'My master is delaying his coming,' and starts to beat the male and

female slaves, and to eat and drink and get drunk, ⁴⁶ that slave's master will come on a day he does not expect him and at an hour he does not know. He will cut him to pieces[e] and assign him a place with the unbelievers.[f] ⁴⁷ And that slave who knew his master's will and didn't prepare himself or do it[g] will be severely beaten. ⁴⁸ But the one who did not know and did things deserving of blows will be beaten lightly. Much will be required of everyone who has been given much. And even more will be expected of the one who has been entrusted with more.[h]

Not Peace but Division

⁴⁹ "I came to bring fire on the earth, and how I wish it were already set ablaze! ⁵⁰ But I have a baptism to be baptized with, and how it consumes Me until it is finished! ⁵¹ Do you think that I came here to give peace to the earth? No, I tell you, but rather division! ⁵² From now on, five in one household will be divided: three against two, and two against three.

⁵³   **They will be divided, father against son,**
      son against father,
      mother against daughter,
      daughter against mother,
      mother-in-law against her daughter-in-law,
      and daughter-in-law against mother-in-law."[i]

Interpreting the Time

⁵⁴ He also said to the crowds: "When you see a cloud rising in the west, right away you say, 'A storm is coming,' and so it does. ⁵⁵ And when the south wind is blowing, you say, 'It's going to be a scorcher!' and it is. ⁵⁶ Hypocrites! You know how to interpret the appearance of the earth and the sky, but why don't you know how to interpret this time?

Settling Accounts

⁵⁷ "Why don't you judge for yourselves what is right? ⁵⁸ As you are going with your adversary to the ruler, make an effort to settle with him on the way. Then he won't drag you before the judge, the judge hand you

---

^a**12:35** Lit *Let your loins be girded*, an idiom for tying up loose outer clothing in preparation for action; Ex 12:11   ^b**12:36** Lit *master, when he should return*   ^c**12:37** Lit *will gird himself*   ^d**12:38** Lit *even in the second or third watch*   ^e**12:46** Lit *him in two*   ^f**12:46** Or *unfaithful,* or *untrustworthy*   ^g**12:47** Lit *or do toward his will*   ^h**12:48** Or *much*   ⁱ**12:53** Mc 7:6

---

disciples not to focus their attention on the material benefits of this life, Jesus encouraged them to seek the spiritual blessings of God's kingdom. **these things will be provided for you.** The promise is that if the disciples concentrate on doing the will of God, then their basic needs will be met by Him.

12:33 moth. The most expensive clothing is susceptible to insignificant creatures like moths (James 5:1-3; 1 Peter 1:4).

12:35 Be ready for service. To work or travel a man would gather up the garment with a belt to free his legs for uninhibited movement. This implies the disciples were to be ever ready to serve their Lord.

12:42 manager. When a wealthy homeowner was away, he would appoint one of

his servants to be in charge of his affairs during his absence. One of his responsibilities was the management of food rations.

12:46 He will cut him to pieces and assign him a place with the unbelievers. While the method of executing a person by cutting him into pieces is grotesque, the addition of the second phrase may imply that we are to understand it as a metaphor picturing the cutting off of this person from his former household.

12:49 fire. Fire is used both as a symbol of judgment (3:16; Acts 2:19) and of the Holy Spirit (3:16; Acts 2:4).

12:50 baptism. This word was used in a figurative way to describe being overwhelmed by a catastrophe. Before the Spirit's purify-

ing work can begin, the fire of God's judgment must first be experienced by Jesus on the cross. **finished!** The death of Jesus was the essential reason for His incarnation, His coming in the flesh (see John 19:30).

13:1 the Galileans whose blood Pilate had mixed with their sacrifices. While nothing is known of this specific act, similar acts of violence against worshipping Jews had been done in Jerusalem

13:4 the tower in Siloam. Siloam was a reservoir located near the southeast corner of Jerusalem. The tower Jesus refers to may have been one built for fortification or in conjunction with an aqueduct that was part of the city's water supply. As with the slain Galileans (vv. 2-3), those killed when the tower collapsed were not more sinful than the other residents of the city; indeed, all of them

over to the bailiff, and the bailiff throw you into prison. ⁵⁹ I tell you, you will never get out of there until you have paid the last cent."[a]

Repent or Perish

13 At that time, some people came and reported to Him about the Galileans whose blood •Pilate had mixed with their sacrifices. ² And He[b] responded to them, "Do you think that these Galileans were more sinful than all Galileans because they suffered these things? ³ No, I tell you; but unless you repent, you will all perish as well! ⁴ Or those 18 that the tower in Siloam fell on and killed—do you think they were more sinful than all the people who live in Jerusalem? ⁵ No, I tell you; but unless you repent, you will all perish as well!"

The Parable of the Barren Fig Tree

⁶ And He told this parable: "A man had a fig tree that was planted in his vineyard. He came looking for fruit on it and found none. ⁷ He told the vineyard worker, 'Listen, for three years I have come looking for fruit on this fig tree and haven't found any. Cut it down! Why should it even waste the soil?'

⁸ "But he replied to him, 'Sir,[c] leave it this year also, until I dig around it and fertilize it. ⁹ Perhaps it will bear fruit next year, but if not, you can cut it down.' "

Healing a Daughter of Abraham

¹⁰ As He was teaching in one of the •synagogues on the Sabbath, ¹¹ a woman was there who had been disabled by a spirit[d] for over 18 years. She was bent over and could not straighten up at all.[e] ¹² When Jesus saw her, He called out to her,[f] "Woman, you are free of your disability." ¹³ Then He laid His hands on her, and instantly she was restored and began to glorify God.

¹⁴ But the leader of the synagogue, indignant because Jesus had healed on the Sabbath, responded by telling the crowd, "There are six days when work should be done; therefore come on those days and be healed and not on the Sabbath day."

¹⁵ But the Lord answered him and said, "Hypocrites! Doesn't each one of you untie his ox or donkey from the feeding trough on the Sabbath and lead it to water? ¹⁶ Satan has bound this woman, a daughter of Abraham, for 18 years—shouldn't she be untied from this bondage on the Sabbath day?"

¹⁷ When He had said these things, all His adversaries were humiliated, but the whole crowd was rejoicing over all the glorious things He was doing.

The Parables of the Mustard Seed and of the Yeast

¹⁸ He said therefore, "What is the kingdom of God like, and what can I compare it to? ¹⁹ It's like a mustard seed that a man took and sowed in his garden. It grew and became a tree, and the birds of the sky nested in its branches."

²⁰ Again He said, "What can I compare the kingdom of God to? ²¹ It's like yeast that a woman took and mixed into 50 pounds[g] of flour until it spread through the entire mixture."[h]

The Narrow Way

²² He went through one town and village after another, teaching and making His way to Jerusalem. ²³ "Lord," someone asked Him, "are there few being saved?"[i]

He said to them, ²⁴ "Make every effort to enter through the narrow door, because I tell you, many will try to enter and won't be able ²⁵ once the homeowner gets up and shuts the door. Then you will stand[j] outside and knock on the door, saying, 'Lord, open up for us!' He will answer you, 'I don't know you or where you're from.' ²⁶ Then you will say,[k] 'We ate and drank in Your presence, and You taught in our streets!' ²⁷ But He will say, 'I tell you, I don't know you or where you're from. Get away from Me, all you workers of unrighteousness!' ²⁸ There will be weeping and gnashing of teeth in that place, when you see Abraham, Isaac, Jacob, and all the prophets in the kingdom of God but yourselves

[a]**12:59** Gk *lepton*, the smallest and least valuable copper coin in use   [b]**13:2** Other mss read *Jesus*   [c]**13:8** Or *Lord*   [d]**13:11** Lit *had a spirit of disability*   [e]**13:11** Or *straighten up completely*   [f]**13:12** Or *He summoned her*   [g]**13:21** Lit *3 sata*; about 40 quarts   [h]**13:21** Or *until all of it was leavened*   [i]**13:23** Or *are the saved few?* (in number); lit *are those being saved few?*   [j]**13:25** Lit *you will begin to stand*   [k]**13:26** Lit *you will begin to say*

needed to repent.

13:6 fig tree … vineyard. Since vineyards were really more like fruit gardens, the presence of such a tree was not unusual.

13:7-9 Perhaps it will bear fruit next year. While the owner wants to cut down the tree, the caretaker of the garden desires to cultivate. Jesus points out God's patience toward His people and the reality that a day of accounting is coming.

13:11 bent over. This woman's disease appears to have been a fusion of the spinal column, causing great pain and making it impossible for her to stand erect.

13:16 a daughter of Abraham. The severity of her infirmity may have led many to assume she was being punished for an espe-

cially bad sin and thus was not considered by God as one of His people. Jesus affirms her as a true Israelite (Gal. 3:7). **untied from this bondage on the Sabbath.** One of the purposes of the Sabbath was to be a weekly reminder of the freedom for which God had delivered His people from Egypt (Deut. 5:15). By overcoming Satan's grip on this woman on the Sabbath, Jesus, far from defiling the day, demonstrated its true significance.

13:19 mustard seed. The mustard plant is the smallest seed, yet its shrubs grew to about 10 feet high.

13:20-21 yeast. While yeast was generally a symbol of something evil (Mark 8:15), here it is positive, symbolizing growth and transformation.

13:21 50 pounds of flour. Literally, "three measures"—which would be almost 160 cups of flour! This would make enough bread for over 100 people.

13:23 saved? This word serves as a shorthand way of expressing deliverance from God's judgment and entrance into a relationship of peace with Him (Acts 2:47; 16:29-31; 1 Cor. 1:18; 2 Cor. 2:15). It is synonymous with entering the kingdom of God (12:32) and inheriting eternal life (18:18).

13:25-27 I don't know you. The picture is of people wishing at the last moment to respond to the invitation of a distinguished man holding a dinner party (14:15-24). While they protest that familiarity with the host should be grounds for their admission, the reason for their rejection is found in a paraphrase of Psalm 6:8 ("Depart from me, all

thrown out. 29 They will come from east and west, from north and south, and recline at the table in the kingdom of God. 30 Note this: some are last who will be first, and some are first who will be last."

Jesus and Herod Antipas

31 At that time some •Pharisees came and told Him, "Go, get out of here! •Herod wants to kill You!"

32 He said to them, "Go tell that fox, 'Look! I'm driving out demons and performing healings today and tomorrow, and on the third daya I will complete My work.'b 33 Yet I must travel today, tomorrow, and the next day, because it is not possible for a prophet to perish outside of Jerusalem!

Jesus' Lamentation over Jerusalem

34 "Jerusalem, Jerusalem! The city who kills the prophets and stones those who are sent to her. How often I wanted to gather your children together, as a hen gathers her chicks under her wings, but you were not willing! 35 See, your housec is abandoned to you. And I tell you, you will not see Me until the time comes when you say, **Blessed is He who comes in the name of the Lord!"**d

A Sabbath Controversy

14 One Sabbath, when He went to eate at the house of one of the leading •Pharisees, they were watching Him closely. 2 There in front of Him was a man whose body was swollen with fluid.f 3 In response, Jesus asked the law experts and the Pharisees, "Is it lawful to heal on the Sabbath or not?" 4 But they kept silent. He took the man, healed him, and sent him away. 5 And to them, He said, "Which of you whose son or ox falls into a well, will not immediately pull him out on the Sabbath day?" 6 To this they could find no answer.

Teachings on Humility

7 He told a parable to those who were invited, when He noticed how they would choose the best places for themselves: 8 "When you are invited by someone to a wedding banquet, don't recline at the best place, because a more distinguished person than you may have been invited by your host.g 9 The one who invited both of you may come and say to you, 'Give your place to this man,' and then in humiliation, you will proceed to take the lowest place.

10 "But when you are invited, go and recline in the lowest place, so that when the one who invited you comes, he will say to you, 'Friend, move up higher.' You will then be honored in the presence of all the other guests. 11 For everyone who exalts himself will be humbled, and the one who humbles himself will be exalted."

12 He also said to the one who had invited Him, "When you give a lunch or a dinner, don't invite your friends, your brothers, your relatives, or your rich neighbors, because they might invite you back, and you would be repaid. 13 On the contrary, when you host a banquet, invite those who are poor, maimed, lame, or blind. 14 And you will be blessed, because they cannot repay you; for you will be repaid at the resurrection of the righteous."

The Parable of the Large Banquet

15 When one of those who reclined at the table with Him heard these things, he said to Him, "The one who will eat bread in the kingdom of God is blessed!"

16 Then He told him: "A man was giving a large banquet and invited many. 17 At the time of the banquet, he sent his slave to tell those who were invited, 'Come, because everything is now ready.'

18 "But without exceptionh they all began to make excuses. The first one said to him, 'I have bought a field, and I must go out and see it. I ask you to excuse me.'

19 "Another said, 'I have bought five yoke of oxen, and I'm going to try them out. I ask you to excuse me.'

20 "And another said, 'I just got married,i and therefore I'm unable to come.'

21 "So the slave came back and reported these things to his master. Then in anger, the master of the house

---

a13:32 Very shortly   b13:32 Lit *I will be finished*   c13:35 Probably the temple; Jr 12:7; 22:5   d13:35 Ps 118:26   e14:1 Lit *eat bread*; = eat a meal
f14:2 Afflicted with dropsy or edema   g14:8 Lit *by him*   h14:18 Lit *And from one* (voice)   i14:20 Lit *I have married a woman*

---

evildoers ..."). They are evildoers shut out from God's presence.

13:30 last ... first. This saying of Jesus implies that Gentiles, the last to hear of God's grace, may actually respond to His invitation, while many in Israel will find it much more difficult to respond.

13:31 Herod. Herod's dominion included Galilee and Perea, the probable location of Jesus at this point.

13:32 tell that fox. Sometimes the fox was used as a symbol of a cunning person. Note that the image with strength like the lion isn't used here. The reference to the "third day" would bring Jesus' resurrection to mind for Luke's readers.

13:33 perish outside of Jerusalem! Prophets, like Jeremiah, did die outside Jerusalem. The force of the saying is that just as the authorities associated with the temple in Jerusalem consistently opposed the prophets and executed some of them, so Jesus will experience the same fate.

13:34-35 Jerusalem., Jerusalem!... see your house is abandoned to you. George Santayana observed that those who don't know history are doomed to repeat it. Sometimes even those who know history, repeat it. Nearly 600 year before Jesus spoke these words, the Babylonians leveled Jerusalem and its temple. Now, within forty years Jesus prophecy will be fulfilled as the Romans utterly destroy the city. "How she sits alone, the city [once] crowded with people" (Lamentations 1:1).

14:2 swollen with fluid. This fluid retention was not in actuality a disease, but a sign of disease of the heart, kidneys, or liver.

14:5 ox falls into a well. The first lesson of this dinner party lay in Jesus' exposure of their callous attitude toward people's needs in contrast to their sensitivity to the plight of animals (13:15; Matt. 12:11).

14:8 the best place. The scene envisioned here is that of the embarrassment that would be experienced by someone who assumed he or she should be in a place of honor and took that position apart from the host's invitation. When the guest for whom the host had reserved that spot arrived, the presumptuous guest would be humiliated by having to give up the seat.

14:15 The one ... is blessed! The bliss of life with God was often pictured in terms of a feast (Isa. 25:6; 55:2; 65:13).

14:16-17 invited ... sent his slave to tell. In well-to-do circles, invitations to honored

told his slave, 'Go out quickly into the streets and alleys of the city, and bring in here the poor, maimed, blind, and lame!'

²² " 'Master,' the slave said, 'what you ordered has been done, and there's still room.'

²³ "Then the master told the slave, 'Go out into the highways and lanes and make them come in, so that my house may be filled. ²⁴ For I tell you, not one of those men who were invited will enjoy my banquet!' "

The Best Invitation Ever

1. What's your favorite excuse to get out of going somewhere you don't want to go?

Luke 14:15-24

2. Why would people make excuses not to attend a big banquet with free food?
3. What happened to those people who rejected the invitation?
4. What lesson is Jesus teaching in this parable?
5. What excuses do people use to reject Jesus' offer of free salvation?
6. Have you accepted or rejected His invitation? Why or why not?

The Cost of Following Jesus

²⁵ Now great crowds were traveling with Him. So He turned and said to them: ²⁶ "If anyone comes to Me and does not hate his own father and mother, wife and children, brothers and sisters—yes, and even his own life—he cannot be My disciple. ²⁷ Whoever does not bear his own cross and come after Me cannot be My disciple.

ᵃ**14:33** Or *does not renounce* or *leave*

²⁸ "For which of you, wanting to build a tower, doesn't first sit down and calculate the cost to see if he has enough to complete it? ²⁹ Otherwise, after he has laid the foundation and cannot finish it, all the onlookers will begin to make fun of him, ³⁰ saying, 'This man started to build and wasn't able to finish.'

Salt of the Earth

1. Do you like salty food? Bland food?

Luke 14:25-35

2. What did Jesus mean by teaching that His followers should "hate" their families (v. 26)?
3. Why did Jesus use an illustration of going to war to describe the proper attitude toward possessions (vv. 31-33)?
4. What is so important about salt, especially to Jesus' audience? How are Christians like salt to this world?
5. Are you like good salt in your school, or are you more like salt that has lost its taste? How can you become "saltier" salt?

³¹ "Or what king, going to war against another king, will not first sit down and decide if he is able with 10,000 to oppose the one who comes against him with 20,000? ³² If not, while the other is still far off, he sends a delegation and asks for terms of peace. ³³ In the same way, therefore, every one of you who does not say goodbye toᵃ all his possessions cannot be My disciple.

³⁴ "Now, salt is good, but if salt should lose its taste, how will it be made salty? ³⁵ It isn't fit for the soil or for the manure pile; they throw it out. Anyone who has ears to hear should listen!"

---

guests for a formal dinner were issued well in advance, but the specific time to arrive was communicated on the day of the event when everything was ready (Esther 5:8; 6:14).

14:18-20 excuses. Jesus' listeners would immediately see these excuses as an obvious attempt to insult the host.

14:18 I must go out and see it. Then, as now, people would not buy property first and then look at it later!

14:20 married. Marriage plans were made far in advance; the man certainly would have known of his plans for marriage when he received the original invitation to the banquet. The net effect of all these excuses is that the guests didn't value the relationship enough to come, and so made excuses.

14:21 streets. These are probably the pub-

lic squares where beggars gathered, hoping for handouts. **the poor, maimed, blind, and lame!** These people were all social outcasts reduced to begging for survival. Those normally considered unworthy are indeed the ones who are included (1:52-53; 4:18-19; 6:20-22; 7:22).

14:23 make them come in. The persuasion in view here is meant to convince these incredulous outcasts that they really are welcomed to the banquet. Middle East etiquette requires people of a low social rank to refuse invitations from those of a higher social status.

14:27 bear his own cross. This does not mean followers of Christ should seek out ways to suffer. It means that a follower of Jesus needs to be willing to go where he is sent and do what God asks of him.

14:28-30 calculate the cost. This is the first of three parables communicating the need for serious consideration of what it means to be Jesus' disciple. Just as it would be foolish to begin building a tower before contemplating the costs involved, so Jesus is discouraging people from following Him based upon wrong assumptions and ideas of what His kingdom involves.

14:31-32 decide if he is able. The second parable reinforces the first. Only a foolish king would attempt to wage a war before considering if there is realistic hope for success. A would-be disciple had better consider what is involved in the course he or she is undertaking.

14:33 every one of you who does not say good-bye to all his possessions. Just as one should count the costs before begin-

The Parable of the Lost Sheep

15 All the tax collectors and sinners were approaching to listen to Him. ² And the •Pharisees and •scribes were complaining, "This man welcomes sinners and eats with them!"

³ So He told them this parable: ⁴ "What man among you, who has 100 sheep and loses one of them, does not leave the 99 in the open field[a] and go after the lost one until he finds it? ⁵ When he has found it, he joyfully puts it on his shoulders, ⁶ and coming home, he calls his friends and neighbors together, saying to them, 'Rejoice with me, because I have found my lost sheep!' ⁷ I tell you, in the same way, there will be more joy in heaven over one sinner who repents than over 99 righteous people who don't need repentance.

The Parable of the Lost Coin

⁸ "Or what woman who has 10 silver coins,[b] if she loses one coin, does not light a lamp, sweep the house, and search carefully until she finds it? ⁹ When she finds it, she calls her women friends and neighbors together, saying, 'Rejoice with me, because I have found the silver coin I lost!' ¹⁰ I tell you, in the same way, there is joy in the presence of God's angels over one sinner who repents."

The Parable of the Lost Son

¹¹ He also said: "A man had two sons. ¹² The younger of them said to his father, 'Father, give me the share of the estate I have coming to me.' So he distributed the assets[c] to them. ¹³ Not many days later, the younger son gathered together all he had and traveled to a distant country, where he squandered his estate in foolish living. ¹⁴ After he had spent everything, a severe famine struck that country, and he had nothing.[d] ¹⁵ Then he went to work for[e] one of the citizens of that country, who sent him into his fields to feed pigs. ¹⁶ He longed to eat his fill from[f] the carob pods[g] the pigs were eating, but no one would give him any. ¹⁷ When he came to his senses,[h] he said, 'How many of my father's hired hands have more than enough food, and here I am dying[i] of hunger![j] ¹⁸ I'll get up, go to my father, and say to him, Father, I have sinned against heaven and in your sight. ¹⁹ I'm no longer worthy to be called your son. Make me like one of your hired hands.' ²⁰ So he got up and went to his father. But while the son was still a long way off, his father saw him and was filled with compassion. He ran, threw his arms around his neck,[k] and kissed him. ²¹ The son said to him, 'Father, I have sinned against heaven and in your sight. I'm no longer worthy to be called your son.'

The Wasteful Son

1. Where would you like to be after you graduate?

Luke 15:11-32

2. Who does the younger son represent in this parable? The father? The older son?
3. Why did the father throw a party for the lost son when he returned? What does that teach us about God?
4. Why was the older son pouting? Why did his father go out to him and plead with him?
5. Who are you most like right now: The younger son living with pigs? The younger son returning home? The older son feeling cheated? How do you need God the Father's love and forgiveness?

²² "But the father told his •slaves, 'Quick! Bring out the best robe and put it on him; put a ring on his finger[l] and sandals on his feet. ²³ Then bring the fattened calf and slaughter it, and let's celebrate with a feast,

---

a15:4 Or *the wilderness* **b15:8** Gk *10 drachmas*; a *drachma* was a silver coin = a •denarius. **c15:12** Lit *livelihood,* or *living* **d15:14** Lit *and he began to be in need* **e15:15** Lit *went and joined with* **f15:16** Other mss read *to fill his stomach with* **g15:16** Seed casings of a tree used as food for cattle, pigs, and sometimes the poor **h15:17** Lit *to himself* **i15:17** The word *dying* is translated *lost* in vv. 4–9 and vv. 24,32. **j15:17** Or *dying in the famine*; v. 14 **k15:20** Lit *He ran, fell on his neck* **l15:22** Lit *hand*

---

ning, so the disciple must be ready to give up all to follow Jesus.

15:4 the open field. This was a desolate area with many cliffs. A lone sheep in such an environment was in great danger from wild animals or from falling over the cliffs.

15:8 10 silver coins. This might represent her dowry. One of these coins was equal to about a day's wage for a laborer and represented a substantial loss for a person who lived a hand-to-mouth existence. **light a lamp.** Peasant homes were poorly illuminated because of a lack of windows. **sweep the house.** A coin could easily be obscured since floors were just dirt covered with straw.

15:12 give me the share. Under Jewish law,

the younger of two sons would receive one-third of the estate upon his father's death. While a father might divide up his property before he died if he wished, this son's request would be considered unbelievably callous. In essence, he implies that the fact that his father still lives is getting in the way of his plans.

15:15 pigs. Ceremonially unclean animals (Lev. 11:7) that Jews would not eat, raise, or touch.

15:16 the carob pods. While eating the food of pigs sounds terrible even to modern readers, for the Pharisees it would have been utterly horrifying.

15:20 his father saw him. The implication is the father had been waiting and hoping to see his son return one day. **He ran.** It was degrading for an elderly man to run to any-

one, especially to someone who had so disgraced him. This presents staggering insight into the response of the Almighty Holy God to a repentant sinner.

15:22 the best robe. A sign that people should honor him as they honor the father. **a ring.** The signet ring gives the son the authority to represent the father. **sandals...** To wear shoes indicated a man was free to go where he pleased.

15:28 didn't want to go in. This son's refusal to enter the house would have been seen as a sign of grave disrespect, since the eldest son was expected to play the part of a gracious host at a family feast. As he did with the younger son, the father went out to plead with the older son. This too was an overwhelming display of grace.

24 because this son of mine was dead and is alive again; he was lost and is found!' So they began to celebrate.

25 "Now his older son was in the field; as he came near the house, he heard music and dancing. 26 So he summoned one of the servants and asked what these things meant. 27 'Your brother is here,' he told him, 'and your father has slaughtered the fattened calf because he has him back safe and sound.'ᵃ

28 "Then he became angry and didn't want to go in. So his father came out and pleaded with him. 29 But he replied to his father, 'Look, I have been slaving many years for you, and I have never disobeyed your orders, yet you never gave me a young goat so I could celebrate with my friends. 30 But when this son of yours came, who has devoured your assetsᵇ with prostitutes, you slaughtered the fattened calf for him.'

31 " 'Son,'ᶜ he said to him, 'you are always with me, and everything I have is yours. 32 But we had to celebrate and rejoice, because this brother of yours was dead and is alive again; he was lost and is found.' "

The Parable of the Dishonest Manager

16 He also said to the disciples: "There was a rich man who received an accusation that his manager was squandering his possessions. 2 So he called the manager in and asked, 'What is this I hear about you? Give an account of your management, because you can no longer be ⌊my⌋ manager.'

3 "Then the manager said to himself, 'What should I do, since my master is taking the management away from me? I'm not strong enough to dig; I'm ashamed to beg. 4 I know what I'll do so that when I'm removed from management, people will welcome me into their homes.'

5 "So he summoned each one of his master's debtors. 'How much do you owe my master?' he asked the first one.

6 " 'A hundred measures of oil,' he said.

" 'Take your invoice,' he told him, 'sit down quickly, and write 50.'

7 "Next he asked another, 'How much do you owe?'

" 'A hundred measures of wheat,' he said.

" 'Take your invoice,' he told him, 'and write 80.'

8 "The master praised the unrighteous manager because he had acted astutely. For the sons of this age are more astute than the sons of light ⌊in dealing⌋ with their own people.ᵈ 9 And I tell you, make friends for yourselves by means of the unrighteous money so that when it fails,ᵉ they may welcome you into eternal dwellings. 10 Whoever is faithful in very little is also faithful in much, and whoever is unrighteous in very little is also unrighteous in much. 11 So if you have not been faithful with the unrighteous money, who will trust you with what is genuine? 12 And if you have not been faithful with what belongs to someone else, who will give you what is your own? 13 No household slave can be the •slave of two masters, since either he will hate one and love the other, or he will be devoted to one and despise the other. You can't be slaves to both God and money."

Kingdom Values

14 The •Pharisees, who were lovers of money, were listening to all these things and scoffing at Him. 15 And He told them: "You are the ones who justify yourselves in the sight of others, but God knows your hearts. For what is highly admired by people is revolting in God's sight.

16 "The Law and the Prophets wereᶠ until John; since then, the good news of the kingdom of God has been proclaimed, and everyone is strongly urged to enter it.ᵍ 17 But it is easier for heaven and earth to pass away than for one stroke of a letter in the law to drop out.

18 "Everyone who divorces his wife and marries another woman commits adultery, and everyone who marries a woman divorced from her husband commits adultery.

The Rich Man and Lazarus

19 "There was a rich man who would dress in purple and fine linen, feasting lavishly every day. 20 But a poor man named Lazarus, covered with sores, was left at his gate. 21 He longed to be filled with what fell from the rich man's table, but instead the dogs would come and

---

ᵃ**15:27** Lit *him back healthy* ᵇ**15:30** Lit *livelihood*, or *living* ᶜ**15:31** Or *Child* ᵈ**16:8** Lit *own generation* ᵉ**16:9** Other mss read *when you fail* or *pass away* ᶠ**16:16** Perhaps *were proclaimed*, or *were in effect* ᵍ**16:16** Or *everyone is forcing his way into it*

15:29 Look. This would have been considered an extremely rude way for a son to address his father, since there is no hint of respect or affection. **I have been slaving ... for you.** Ironically, this son views his ongoing relationship with his father in the way the younger son hoped he might be privileged to have.

15:30 this son of yours. Instead of "my brother."

15:31-32 everything I have is yours. This would assure the older son that he is in no danger of losing his inheritance because of the presence of his younger brother. He, too, should celebrate his brother's homecoming. We are not told what the older son does. Jesus purposely leaves the story open-ended.

16:2. Give an account. This is better understood as "turn in your books." Since it would be assumed that a dishonest manager had probably doctored the books, they would not be looked at in order to find evidence to fire him; he is simply to "clean out his desk."

16:5-7 A hundred ... write 50. This reduction of debts was done quickly to avoid discovery by the master (v. 6). Since it would be assumed the manager was still in the employ of the landowner, the renters would be grateful to the manager for his concern for them. The tenants would quickly spread the news throughout the village that the master had been gracious, making it socially impossible for the master to deny that he had authorized such reductions.

16:6-7 The assumption is that the master has let out his land to tenants, who have agreed

to pay him a fixed return in grain and oil. The amounts owed indicate that this master was quite wealthy. The reduction of 400 gallons of olive oil and 200 bushels of wheat both amount to the same in cash value, about 500 denarii.

16:8 unrighteous. The man's moral sense is not being commended; his taking appropriate action to protect himself is. The disciple is likewise called to take action in the face of the coming judgment. **astute.** Hebrew and Aramaic translations of this word translate it as "wisdom." If an unjust man shows such wisdom in making provision for his future, how much more ought the children of light show wisdom in preparing for their future in the face of the certain judgment of God?

16:20 Lazarus. His name means "he whom

lick his sores. ²² One day the poor man died and was carried away by the angels to Abraham's side.ᵃ The rich man also died and was buried. ²³ And being in torment in •Hades, he looked up and saw Abraham a long way off, with Lazarus at his side. ²⁴ 'Father Abraham!' he called out, 'Have mercy on me and send Lazarus to dip the tip of his finger in water and cool my tongue, because I am in agony in this flame!'

Heaven and Hell

1. When can you remember being unbearably thirsty? How did you finally quench it?

Luke 16:19-31

2. What was Lazarus' life like? What was the rich man's life like?
3. What happened when Lazarus died? What happened when the rich man died? (Note the wording in verse 22.)
4. How are the five brothers going to learn the truth about heaven and hell (v. 28)? How will people today learn that truth?
5. Will you go to heaven when you die? How can you be sure?

²⁵ " 'Son,'ᵇ Abraham said, 'remember that during your life you received your good things, just as Lazarus received bad things, but now he is comforted here, while you are in agony. ²⁶ Besides all this, a great chasm has been fixed between us and you, so that those who want to pass over from here to you cannot; neither can those from there cross over to us.'

²⁷ " 'Father,' he said, 'then I beg you to send him to my father's house— ²⁸ because I have five brothers—to warn them, so they won't also come to this place of torment.'

²⁹ "But Abraham said, 'They have Moses and the prophets; they should listen to them.'

³⁰ " 'No, father Abraham,' he said. 'But if someone from the dead goes to them, they will repent.'

³¹ "But he told him, 'If they don't listen to Moses and the prophets, they will not be persuaded if someone rises from the dead.' "

Warnings from Jesus

17 He said to His disciples, "Offensesᶜ will certainly come,ᵈ but woe to the one they come through! ² It would be better for him if a millstoneᵉ were hung around his neck and he were thrown into the sea than for him to cause one of these little ones to •stumble. ³ Be on your guard. If your brother sins,ᶠ rebuke him, and if he repents, forgive him. ⁴ And if he sins against you seven times in a day, and comes back to you seven times, saying, 'I repent,' you must forgive him."

Faith and Duty

⁵ The apostles said to the Lord, "Increase our faith."

⁶ "If you have faith the size ofᵍ a mustard seed," the Lord said, "you can say to this mulberry tree, 'Be uprooted and planted in the sea,' and it will obey you.

⁷ "Which one of you having a slave plowing or tending sheep, will say to him when he comes in from the field, 'Come at once and sit down to eat'? ⁸ Instead, will he not tell him, 'Prepare something for me to eat, get ready,ʰ and serve me while I eat and drink; later you can eat and drink'? ⁹ Does he thank that slave because he did what was commanded?ⁱ ¹⁰ In the same way, when you have done all that you were commanded, you should say, 'We are good-for-nothing slaves; we've only done our duty.' "

The 10 Lepers

¹¹ While traveling to Jerusalem, He passed betweenʲ Samaria and Galilee. ¹² As He entered a village, 10 men

ᵃ**16:22** Lit *to the fold of Abraham's robe,* or *to Abraham's bosom;* see Jn 13:23   ᵇ**16:25** Lit *Child*   ᶜ**17:1** Or *Traps,* or *Bait-sticks,* or *Causes of stumbling,* or *Causes of sin*   ᵈ**17:1** Lit *It is impossible for offenses not to come*   ᵉ**17:2** Large stone used for grinding grains into flour   ᶠ**17:3** Other mss add *against you*   ᵍ**17:6** Lit *faith like*   ʰ**17:8** Lit *eat, tuck in your robe,* or *eat, gird yourself*   ⁱ**17:9** Other mss add *I don't think so*   ʲ**17:11** Or *through the middle of*

God helps," indicating the poor man's piety before God.

16:26 a great chasm has been fixed. The impassable gap between them indicated the finality of God's judgment on the matter. It is said earlier that the rich man could see Lazarus and Abraham (v. 23). However, since Lazarus never says anything on his own behalf, it is uncertain how much he is aware of the plight of the rich man.

16:27-28 send him ... to warn them. This introduces the second lesson of the passage. In light of his fate, the man urges Abraham to send Lazarus as a warning to his brothers who are following in his path. The rich man cared for his family; he just was unable to see poor Lazarus as worthy of the same sort of concern.

16:29 Moses and the prophets. Those who fail to hear Scripture will not be persuaded by resurrection.

17:2 millstone. This would be a large, round grinding stone with a hole in the middle. Such a horrible death is preferable to the judgment that will come upon one who leads another into sin. **cause ... to stumble.** Literally "to scandalize" (v. 1) in the sense of corrupting the life of another by offering an opportunity to sin or making sin appear legitimate.

17:6 mustard seed. This was the tiniest of all seeds. **Be uprooted.** This is not an invitation for believers to exercise capricious power in prayer, but to illustrate the point that astounding things can result for the person who exercises his or her faith through prayer (Matt. 21:21-22).

17:8-9 The point is not that the master is demanding or ungrateful, but simply that the servant's job involves these tasks. The performance of them is a normal, expected part of the role.

17:10 we've only done our duty. Obedience to Jesus' commands about purity, radical forgiveness, and faith do not merit special reward from God. They are simply qualities expected of those who follow Him.

17:12 serious skin diseases. Most typically, leprosy. Although "leprosy" was used to cover a wide range of skin diseases besides the true leprosy of Hanson's Disease, no diagnosis was dreaded more than leprosy since it brought not only a slow death and physical disfigurement but also social

with serious skin diseases met Him. They stood at a distance [13] and raised their voices, saying, "Jesus, Master, have mercy on us!"

An Attitude of Gratitude

1. How are you at writing thank-you notes: Always write them? Sometimes write them? What's a thank-you note?

Luke 17:11-19

2. How did the faith of the lepers make them well (v. 19)? How did they show faith?

3. The Jewish people considered Samaritans to be outcasts. Why does verse 16 mention that the one leper who was grateful was a Samaritan?

4. Why do you think the other nine healed lepers didn't return to thank Jesus?

5. When it comes to showing gratitude to God, are you more like the one who returned or the nine who didn't?

[14] When He saw them, He told them, "Go and show yourselves to the priests." And while they were going, they were healed.[a]

[15] But one of them, seeing that he was healed, returned and, with a loud voice, gave glory to God. [16] He fell facedown at His feet, thanking Him. And he was a •Samaritan.

[17] Then Jesus said, "Were not 10 cleansed? Where are the nine? [18] Didn't any return[b] to give glory to God except this foreigner?" [19] And He told him, "Get up and go on your way. Your faith has made you well."[c]

The Coming of the Kingdom

[20] Being asked by the •Pharisees when the kingdom of God will come, He answered them, "The kingdom of God is not coming with something observable; [21] no one will say,[d] 'Look here!' or 'There!' For you see, the kingdom of God is among you."

[22] Then He told the disciples: "The days are coming when you will long to see one of the days of the •Son of Man, but you won't see it. [23] They will say to you, 'Look there!' or 'Look here!' Don't follow or run after them. [24] For as the lightning flashes from horizon to horizon and lights up the sky, so the Son of Man will be in His day. [25] But first He must suffer many things and be rejected by this generation.

[26] "Just as it was in the days of Noah, so it will be in the days of the Son of Man: [27] people went on eating, drinking, marrying and giving in marriage until the day Noah boarded the ark, and the flood came and destroyed them all. [28] It will be the same as it was in the days of Lot: people went on eating, drinking, buying, selling, planting, building. [29] But on the day Lot left Sodom, fire and sulfur rained from heaven and destroyed them all. [30] It will be like that on the day the Son of Man is revealed. [31] On that day, a man on the housetop, whose belongings are in the house, must not come down to get them. Likewise the man who is in the field must not turn back. [32] Remember Lot's wife! [33] Whoever tries to make his •life secure[e] [f] will lose it, and whoever loses his life will preserve it. [34] I tell you, on that night two will be in one bed: one will be taken and the other will be left. [35] Two women will be grinding grain together: one will be taken and the other left. [[36] Two will be in a field: one will be taken, and the other will be left."][g]

[37] "Where, Lord?" they asked Him.

He said to them, "Where the corpse is, there also the vultures will be gathered."

The Parable of the Persistent Widow

18 He then told them a parable on the need for them to pray always and not become discouraged: [2] "There was a judge in one town who didn't fear God or respect man. [3] And a widow in that town kept coming to him, saying, 'Give me justice against my adversary.'

---

[a] **17:14** Lit *cleansed* [b] **17:18** Lit *Were they not found returning* [c] **17:19** Or *faith has saved you* [d] **17:21** Lit *they will not say* [e] **17:33** Other mss read to save his life [f] **17:33** Or *tries to retain his life* [g] **17:36** Other mss omit bracketed text

---

banishment. **stood at a distance.** Lepers were forbidden to approach uninfected people (Lev. 13:45-46).

17:14 show yourselves. Old Testament law required people with skin diseases feared to be leprous to be examined by a priest who would determine if the infection was clearing up or progressing (Lev. 14:1-7). Only upon the priest's declaration of healing could the leper reenter society.

17:15-16 Samaritan. The one man who came back to give thanks to Jesus was the one Jews would least expect to do so—a Samaritan.

17:17-19 Where are the nine? Only the foreigner caught the significance of his healing and glorified God because of it. The other nine people typify the response of Israel,

which saw sign after sign of Jesus' authority but failed to respond to Him with gratitude.

17:21 the kingdom of God is among you. This phrase has many different translations, all with some relevant meaning here. The Holman Christian Standard translation has "among you" emphasizing that the kingdom of God begins with the community of faith acting in obedience to Christ. The NIV translates the word "within you," which reminds us that it starts with letting God have the throne of our hearts. The ESV translates it "in the midst of you" which emphasizes its present reality. All essentially say that the kingdom of God is not just some future hope. It starts now with our response of obedience.

17:22 one of the days of the Son of Man. The implication is that before He returns

there will be a substantial delay during which his followers will have to wait patiently for Him—even when there is no external evidence of His coming (12:35-48).

17:26-30 eating, drinking, marrying ... The time of the second coming of Christ is compared to that of Noah (Gen. 6:9-9:17) and Lot (Gen. 18:16-19:29). The activities mentioned here (eating, drinking, marrying, buying, selling, planting.) are not evil; instead, the emphasis of the comparison is the unexpected nature of the sudden judgment that came upon the people in the course of their daily lives—as will be the case when Christ returns (1 Thess. 5:1-3).

17:37 Where the corpse is, there also the vultures will be gathered. Jesus quotes a common proverb used to illustrate the connection between any two closely related

4 "For a while he was unwilling, but later he said to himself, 'Even though I don't fear God or respect man, 5 yet because this widow keeps pestering me,ᵃ I will give her justice, so she doesn't wear me outᵇ by her persistent coming.' "

6 Then the Lord said, "Listen to what the unjust judge says. 7 Will not God grant justice to His elect who cry out to Him day and night? Will He delay ⌊to help⌋ them?ᶜ 8 I tell you that He will swiftly grant them justice. Nevertheless, when the •Son of Man comes, will He find that faithᵈ on earth?"

The Parable of the Pharisee and the Tax Collector

9 He also told this parable to some who trusted in themselves that they were righteous and looked down on everyone else: 10 "Two men went up to the •temple complex to pray, one a •Pharisee and the other a tax collector. 11 The Pharisee took his standᵉ and was praying like this: 'God, I thank You that I'm not like other peopleᶠ—greedy, unrighteous, adulterers, or even like this tax collector. 12 I fast twice a week; I give a tenthᵍ of everything I get.'

13 "But the tax collector, standing far off, would not even raise his eyes to heaven but kept striking his chestʰ and saying, 'God, turn Your wrath from meⁱ—a sinner!' 14 I tell you, this one went down to his house justified rather than the other; because everyone who exalts himself will be humbled, but the one who humbles himself will be exalted."

Blessing the Children

15 Some people were even bringing infants to Him so He might touch them, but when the disciples saw it, they rebuked them. 16 Jesus, however, invited them: "Let the little children come to Me, and don't stop them, because the kingdom of God belongs to such as these. 17 •I assure you: Whoever does not welcome the kingdom of God like a little child will never enter it."

The Rich Young Ruler

18 A ruler asked Him, "Good Teacher, what must I do to inherit eternal life?"

Going Down to Go Up

1. How are you at public speaking? At singing a solo? At praying aloud in a group?

Luke 18:9-14

2. Compare the physical postures of the Pharisee and tax collector as they prayed. What does each man's posture and prayer style show about his true character?

3. Why did the tax collector in this story go home "justified" (v. 14), rather than the Pharisee?

4. What does it mean to exalt yourself? To humble yourself?

5. Is your character more like the tax collector's or the Pharisee's? In what areas of your life do you need to pray for more humility?

19 "Why do you call Me good?" Jesus asked him. "No one is good but One—God. 20 You know the commandments:

> Do not commit adultery;
> do not murder;
> do not steal;
> do not bear false witness;
> honor your father and mother."ʲ

21 "I have kept all these from my youth," he said.

22 When Jesus heard this, He told him, "You still lack one thing: sell all that you have and distribute it to the

---

ᵃ**18:5** Lit *widow causes me trouble*   ᵇ**18:5** Or *doesn't give me a black eye*, or *doesn't ruin my reputation*   ᶜ**18:7** Or *Will He put up with them?*
ᵈ**18:8** Or *faith*, or *that kind of faith*, or *any faith*, or *the faith*, or *faithfulness*; the faith that persists in prayer for God's vindication   ᵉ**18:11** Or *Pharisee stood by himself*   ᶠ**18:11** Or *like the rest of men*   ᵍ**18:12** Or *give tithes*   ʰ**18:13** Mourning   ⁱ**18:13** Lit *God, be propitious*; = May Your wrath be turned aside by the sacrifice   ʲ**18:20** Ex 20:12–16; Dt 5:16–20

---

events. Here it means that God's judgment will occur wherever necessary. Such an enigmatic reply forces the disciples to consider their own preparedness for the sudden coming of the Lord in judgment.

18:1-8 The last line of this parable (v. 8) relates what appears to be a general admonition about prayer (11:5–8), specifically to the theme of being prepared for the return of Christ. The disciples are called to pray faithfully and steadfastly for the kingdom of God, never giving up hope for God's justice to be accomplished (v. 1).

18:8 He will swiftly grant them justice. If an unjust judge can be persuaded to act by a persistent widow, how much more will God respond to the prayers of His people.

18:9 trusted in themselves that they were

righteous. This typifies the attitude of a person who assumes that he or she has met God's standards for life. This attitude is marked by a concentration on external performance rather than on humble dependence on God's grace (Gal. 3:10-14; Phil. 3:3-9). **looked down on everyone else.** Literally, "to treat with contempt." This was a major flaw of the Pharisees, who would not even associate with those they considered to be "sinners."

18:10 Pharisee ... tax collector. The Pharisee and tax collector represent opposites in Jewish society. Tax collectors were looked down upon not only because they frequently cheated people, but because they raised money for the hated Roman government. Pharisees, on the other hand, were given a place of prestige in Jewish society.

18:12 a tenth of everything. While Jews were only required to fast on the Day of Atonement, Pharisees fasted every Monday and Thursday in an attempt to gain merit with God. Although all Jews were expected to tithe of one's produce, Pharisees carefully tithed even things that were not required (11:42). This man's external performance of religious obligations was exemplary.

18:13 standing far off. The tax collector may not even have dared to enter the court of the Jews, remaining in the outermost court of the temple where Gentiles met. **striking his chest.** This action, combined with his fear of even following the common custom of looking upwards in prayer, showed his shame and contrition.

18:14 went down to his house justified. The Pharisee left in his self-delusion while the tax collector was forgiven by God.

poor, and you will have treasure in heaven. Then come, follow Me."

²³ After he heard this, he became extremely sad, because he was very rich.

Possessions and the Kingdom

²⁴ Seeing that he became sad,ᵃ Jesus said, "How hard it is for those who have wealth to enter the kingdom of God! ²⁵ For it is easier for a camel to go through the eye of a needle than for a rich person to enter the kingdom of God."

²⁶ Those who heard this asked, "Then who can be saved?"

²⁷ He replied, "What is impossible with men is possible with God."

²⁸ Then Peter said, "Look, we have left what we had and followed You."

²⁹ So He said to them, "I assure you: There is no one who has left a house, wife or brothers, parents or children because of the kingdom of God, ³⁰ who will not receive many times more at this time, and eternal life in the age to come."

The Third Prediction of His Death

³¹ Then He took the Twelve aside and told them, "Listen! We are going up to Jerusalem. Everything that is written through the prophets about the Son of Man will be accomplished. ³² For He will be handed over to the Gentiles, and He will be mocked, insulted, spit on; ³³ and after they flog Him, they will kill Him, and He will rise on the third day."

³⁴ They understood none of these things. This sayingᵇ was hidden from them, and they did not grasp what was said.

A Blind Man Receives His Sight

³⁵ As He drew near Jericho, a blind man was sitting by the road begging. ³⁶ Hearing a crowd passing by, he inquired what this meant. ³⁷ "Jesus the •Nazarene is passing by," they told him.

³⁸ So he called out, "Jesus, Son of David, have mercy on me!" ³⁹ Then those in front told him to keep quiet,ᶜ but he kept crying out all the more, "Son of David, have mercy on me!"

⁴⁰ Jesus stopped and commanded that he be brought to Him. When he drew near, He asked him, ⁴¹ "What do you want Me to do for you?"

"Lord," he said, "I want to see!"

⁴² "Receive your sight!" Jesus told him. "Your faith has healed you."ᵈ ⁴³ Instantly he could see, and he began to follow Him, glorifying God. All the people, when they saw it, gave praise to God.

Out on a Limb

1. Did you like to climb trees when you were little? Do you still like to climb?

Luke 19:1-10
2. Why were people upset that Jesus was going to stay with Zacchaeus?
3. Tax collectors were notorious for cheating people. Why did Zacchaeus offer to pay back the people he'd cheated?
4. In verse 9 Jesus says, "Today salvation has come to this house." How did salvation come to Zacchaeus?
5. Zacchaeus realized that he needed to make restitution for cheating people. What wrongs do you need to make right?

Jesus Visits Zacchaeus

19 He entered Jericho and was passing through. ² There was a man named Zacchaeus who was a chief tax collector, and he was rich. ³ He was trying to see who Jesus was, but he was not able because of the crowd, since he was a short man. ⁴ So running ahead, he climbed up a sycamore tree to see Jesus, since He was about to pass that way. ⁵ When Jesus came to the place, He looked up and said to him,

---

ᵃ**18:24** Other mss omit *he became sad* ᵇ**18:34** The meaning of the saying ᶜ**18:39** Or *those in front rebuked him* ᵈ**18:42** Or *has saved you*

18:18 ruler. Perhaps this person was a leader of a synagogue (like Jairus—8:41) or even a member of the Sanhedrin, the official Jewish ruling council. **what must I do.** The emphasis on gaining the kingdom by virtue of one's religious activities stands in sharp contrast to Jesus' teaching about receiving the kingdom by faith (vv. 16-17).

18:20 the commandments. Jesus cited five of the Ten Commandments that deal with a person's relationship toward others (Ex. 20:12-16). Significantly, He omits both the first ("You shall have no other gods besides me") and the tenth ("You shall not covet"). Those are the commandments that later prove to be the stumbling blocks for this ruler.

18:22 You still lack one thing. Jesus did not refute the man's claim to be obedient to the demands of the commandments, but He

pointed out that this has not touched his inner attitude of love for God or his neighbor. **sell all that you have.** Jesus used this command to show the ruler that wealth is his true god and his self-centered use of his money his true love. Jesus was not saying with this teaching that *everyone* who seeks eternal life must sell all their possessions. He was saying to give full allegiance to God. **follow Me.** The ultimate demand of the kingdom is for absolute allegiance to Jesus over one's self and possessions (16:13). This the ruler does not accept.

18:24 How hard it is. Jesus contradicted the common assumption that wealth is the verification of love for God or a godly life (Job 1:10; Ps. 128:1-2). Instead, wealth is actually a barrier that can prevent people from seeing their need for God.

18:31 up to Jerusalem. Jews used the

phrase "going up to Jerusalem" as an idiomatic expression of planning to offer a sacrifice of worship at the temple.

18:35 Jericho. Jericho is 18 miles east of Jerusalem and the place where travelers from Galilee recrossed the Jordan back into Israel.

18:42 Your faith. The blind man demonstrated his faith: (1) by the title he used for Jesus (he grasped who Jesus was); (2) by his persistent pleas for Jesus' help (he would not let this opportunity go by); and (3) by his request for healing (he believed Jesus had the power to heal him).

19:2 rich. The wealth was undoubtedly the result of "legal" but callous exploitation of his own people through inflated tax rates.

19:4 a sycamore tree. This tree's short trunk and spreading branches make it easy to climb.

"Zacchaeus, hurry and come down, because today I must stay at your house."

⁶ So he quickly came down and welcomed Him joyfully. ⁷ All who saw it began to complain, "He's gone to lodge with a sinful man!"

⁸ But Zacchaeus stood there and said to the Lord, "Look, I'll give[a] half of my possessions to the poor, Lord! And if I have extorted anything from anyone, I'll pay[b] back four times as much!"

⁹ "Today salvation has come to this house," Jesus told him, "because he too is a son of Abraham. ¹⁰ For the •Son of Man has come to seek and to save the lost."[c]

The Parable of the 10 Minas

¹¹ As they were listening to this, He went on to tell a parable because He was near Jerusalem, and they thought the kingdom of God was going to appear right away.

¹² Therefore He said: "A nobleman traveled to a far country to receive for himself authority to be king[d] and then return. ¹³ He called 10 of his •slaves, gave them 10 minas,[e] and told them, 'Engage in business until I come back.'

¹⁴ "But his subjects hated him and sent a delegation after him, saying, 'We don't want this man to rule over us!'

¹⁵ "At his return, having received the authority to be king,[d] he summoned those •slaves he had given the money to so he could find out how much they had made in business. ¹⁶ The first came forward and said, 'Master, your mina has earned 10 more minas.'

¹⁷ " 'Well done, good[f] •slave!' he told him. 'Because you have been faithful in a very small matter, have authority over 10 towns.'

¹⁸ "The second came and said, 'Master, your mina has made five minas.'

¹⁹ "So he said to him, 'You will be over five towns.'

²⁰ "And another came and said, 'Master, here is your mina. I have kept it hidden away in a cloth ²¹ because I was afraid of you, for you're a tough man: you collect what you didn't deposit and reap what you didn't sow.'

²² "He told him, 'I will judge you by what you have said,[g] you evil •slave! ₍If₎ you knew I was a tough man, collecting what I didn't deposit and reaping what I didn't sow, ²³ why didn't you put my money in the bank? And when I returned, I would have collected it with interest!' ²⁴ So he said to those standing there, 'Take the mina away from him and give it to the one who has 10 minas.'

²⁵ "But they said to him, 'Master, he has 10 minas.'

²⁶ " 'I tell you, that to everyone who has, more will be given; and from the one who does not have, even what he does have will be taken away. ²⁷ But bring here these enemies of mine, who did not want me to rule over them, and slaughter[h] them in my presence.' "

The Triumphal Entry

²⁸ When He had said these things, He went on ahead, going up to Jerusalem. ²⁹ As He approached Bethphage and Bethany, at the place called the •Mount of Olives, He sent two of the disciples ³⁰ and said, "Go into the village ahead of you. As you enter it, you will find a young donkey tied there, on which no one has ever sat. Untie it and bring it here. ³¹ If anyone asks you, 'Why are you untying it?' say this: 'The Lord needs it.' "

³² So those who were sent left and found it just as He had told them. ³³ As they were untying the young donkey, its owners said to them, "Why are you untying the donkey?"

³⁴ "The Lord needs it," they said. ³⁵ Then they brought it to Jesus, and after throwing their robes on the donkey, they helped Jesus get on it. ³⁶ As He was going along, they were spreading their robes on the road. ³⁷ Now He came near the path down the Mount of Olives, and the whole crowd of the disciples began to praise God joyfully with a loud voice for all the miracles they had seen:

³⁸ **Blessed is the King**
who comes in the name of the Lord.[i]
Peace in heaven
and glory in the highest heaven!

ᵃ**19:8** Or *I give* ᵇ**19:8** Or *I pay* ᶜ**19:10** Or *save what was lost* ᵈ**19:12,15** Lit *to receive for himself a kingdom* or *sovereignty* ᵉ**19:13** = Gk coin worth 100 drachma or about 100 days' wages ᶠ**19:17** Or *capable* ᵍ**19:22** Lit *you out of your mouth* ʰ**19:27** Or *execute* ⁱ**19:38** The words *the King* are substituted for *He* in Ps 118:26. ʲ**19:38** Ps 118:26

19:5-7 I must stay at your house. Jesus invited Himself to Zacchaeus' house, shocking everyone! Not only would the self-righteous Pharisees disapprove, but Zacchaeus' ill-gotten wealth made this association difficult to accept even by the average person.

19:8 half of my possessions to the poor. Zacchaeus immediately did precisely what the ruler refused to do (18:22). **I'll pay back four times as much!** Giving half of his wealth to the poor did not mean he would keep the other half for himself. Instead, the remaining wealth would be used to recompense those he had defrauded. Zacchaeus was so eager to be restored to God and his community that he pledged to go far beyond what the law required (Lev. 6:1-5).

19:13 slaves. Wealthy people who had to travel on business would entrust their resources to servants who would act as managers of the estate. **10 minas.** A mina was worth about 100 denarii, about the equivalent of three months' wages for a laborer.

19:20-21 hidden away. In contrast to the other two, this servant had simply hidden the money away. In the parable found in Matthew 25, the man buries the money in the ground, an action that would have been considered a safe way to protect what he had been given.

19:21 a tough man. Literally, this is "an exacting man." This is a person who demanded that those who work for him give an unusually good return on investment.

19:29 Bethphage. A village near Jerusalem, probably across a ravine from Bethany. **Bethany.** A small village about two miles east

of Jerusalem. **Mount of Olives.** According to Zechariah 14:3-5, it is from the Mt. of Olives that God will commence the final judgment of Israel's enemies. It is not by accident that Jesus chose this place to prepare His entry into Jerusalem.

19:43-44 your enemies …will not leave one stone. In A.D. 70 the Romans literally tore Jerusalem apart stone by stone so that absolutely nothing—including the temple—was left standing. The final act of humiliation for the conquered Jews was to watch as the Romans ran a plow through what had been the center of the city as a sign that the Jews were now "plowed under."

19:45 those who were selling. Worshippers had to offer an unblemished animal, but inspectors approved only those animals bought from certified vendors who worked

Weeping for Others

1. Have you ever been in a parade? What was it like? What's the last parade you saw?

Luke 19:28-44

2. Why did Jesus enter Jerusalem on a donkey? Why not a white horse? Why not walking?

3. What caused Jesus to weep over Jerusalem (v. 41)? How can we show more concern for the souls of those around us?

4. What does Jesus mean that Jerusalem "did not recognize the time of your visitation" (v. 44)?

5. Have you recognized Jesus' "visitation" in your own life? Have you brought Him to visit others?

³⁹ Some of the •Pharisees from the crowd told Him, "Teacher, rebuke Your disciples."

⁴⁰ He answered, "I tell you, if they were to keep silent, the stones would cry out!"

Jesus' Love for Jerusalem

⁴¹ As He approached and saw the city, He wept over it, ⁴² saying, "If you knew this day what ⌊would bring⌋ peace—but now it is hidden from your eyes. ⁴³ For the days will come on you when your enemies will build an embankment against you, surround you, and hem you in on every side. ⁴⁴ They will crush you and your children within you to the ground, and they will not leave one stone on another in you, because you did not recognize the time of your visitation."

Cleansing the Temple Complex

⁴⁵ He went into the •temple complex and began to throw out those who were selling,ᵃ ⁴⁶ and He said, "It is

written, **My house will be a house of prayer,** but you have made it **a den of thieves!"**ᵇ

⁴⁷ Every day He was teaching in the temple complex. The •chief priests, the •scribes, and the leaders of the people were looking for a way to destroy Him, ⁴⁸ but they could not find a way to do it, because all the people were captivated by what they heard.ᶜ

The Authority of Jesus Challenged

20 One dayᵈ as He was teaching the people in the •temple complex and proclaiming the good news, the •chief priests and the •scribes, with the elders, came up ² and said to Him: "Tell us, by what authority are You doing these things? Who is it who gave You this authority?"

³ He answered them, "I will also ask you a question. Tell Me, ⁴ was the baptism of John from heaven or from men?"

⁵ They discussed it among themselves: "If we say, 'From heaven,' He will say, 'Why didn't you believe him?' ⁶ But if we say, 'From men,' all the people will stone us, because they are convinced that John was a prophet."

⁷ So they answered that they did not know its origin.ᵉ

⁸ And Jesus said to them, "Neither will I tell you by what authority I do these things."

The Parable of the Vineyard Owner

⁹ Then He began to tell the people this parable: "A man planted a vineyard, leased it to tenant farmers, and went away for a long time. ¹⁰ At harvest time he sent a •slave to the farmers so that they might give him some fruit from the vineyard. But the farmers beat him and sent him away empty-handed. ¹¹ He sent yet another slave, but they beat that one too, treated him shamefully, and sent him away empty-handed. ¹² And he sent yet a third, but they wounded this one too and threw him out.

¹³ "Then the owner of the vineyard said, 'What should I do? I will send my beloved son. Perhapsᶠ they will respect him.'

ᵃ**19:45** Other mss add *and buying in it* ᵇ**19:46** Is 56:7; Jr 7:11 ᶜ**19:48** Lit *people hung on what they heard* ᵈ**20:1** Lit *It happened on one of the days* ᵉ**20:7** Or *know where it was from* ᶠ**20:13** Other mss add *when they see him*

---

for members of the high priest's family. Thus, there was great profiteering as the priests and others took advantage of the religious obligations of the Jews by selling the animals at a huge markup.

19:46 a house of prayer. The outermost area of the temple was intended to be a place where pious Gentiles could pray (Isa. 56:7).

20:1 Luke records several conflicts (vv. 1-47) in which various groups of religious leaders confront Jesus one by one. Thus, the opposition begun in Galilee at the start of Jesus' ministry (5:17-6:11) is continued and completed in Jerusalem. **the chief priests.** These were the key officers of the temple, just below the high priest in rank. **the scribes.** Originally, it was the scribes' job to make copies of the Old Testament. Because

of their familiarity with Scripture, this evolved into their function as teachers of the law. **the elders.** These men served as administrators, judges, military leaders. This group was probably an official committee of the Sanhedrin chosen to confront Jesus for driving the merchants out of the temple (19:45-46).

20:2 Tell us. They asked: Where does He get His authority? While not as subtle as some of their later questions (vv. 20-22,27-33), it is still a trap. If Jesus says He acted on His own authority, they could detain Him as a hopeless megalomaniac. If He said that His authority came from God, they could accuse Him of blasphemy (for which the penalty was death).

20:3-6 Tell Me. Answering a question with a question was a common tactic in rabbinic debate.

20:7-8 they answered that they did not know. To accept that John's authority came from God was to admit that John was a true prophet. They would also have to accept that Jesus came from God, as John said. They would also have to explain why they had not supported John's ministry. On the other hand, to say that John just pretended to be a prophet was to risk an uprising of the crowd.

20:9 went away. Absentee landlords would commonly get tenant-farmers to work their large estates, requiring the tenant farmers to give them a portion of their harvest in payment for use of the land.

20:10 slave. In terms of this parable, the slaves represent the Old Testament prophets.

[14] "But when the tenant farmers saw him, they discussed it among themselves and said, 'This is the heir. Let's kill him, so the inheritance will be ours!' [15] So they threw him out of the vineyard and killed him.

"Therefore, what will the owner of the vineyard do to them? [16] He will come and destroy those farmers and give the vineyard to others."

But when they heard this they said, "No—never!"

[17] But He looked at them and said, "Then what is the meaning of this Scripture:[a]

> The stone that the builders rejected—
> this has become the cornerstone?[b] [c]

[18] Everyone who falls on that stone will be broken to pieces, and if it falls on anyone, it will grind him to powder!"

[19] Then the scribes and the chief priests looked for a way to get their hands on Him that very hour, because they knew He had told this parable against them, but they feared the people.

God and Caesar

[20] They[d] watched closely and sent spies who pretended to be righteous,[e] so they could catch Him in what He said,[f] to hand Him over to the governor's rule and authority. [21] They questioned Him, "Teacher, we know that You speak and teach correctly, and You don't show partiality,[g] but teach truthfully the way of God. [22] Is it lawful for us to pay taxes to Caesar or not?"

[23] But detecting their craftiness, He said to them,[h] [24] "Show Me a •denarius. Whose image and inscription does it have?"

"Caesar's," they said.

[25] "Well then," He told them, "give back to Caesar the things that are Caesar's and to God the things that are God's."

[26] They were not able to catch Him in what He said[f] in public,[i] and being amazed at His answer, they became silent.

The Sadducees and the Resurrection

[27] Some of the •Sadducees, who say there is no resurrection, came up and questioned Him: [28] "Teacher, Moses wrote for us that **if a man's brother** has a wife, and **dies childless, his brother should take the wife and produce •offspring for his brother.**[j] [29] Now there were seven brothers. The first took a wife and died without children. [30] Also the second[k] [31] and the third took her. In the same way, all seven died and left no children. [32] Finally, the woman died too. [33] Therefore, in the resurrection, whose wife will the woman be? For all seven had married her."[l]

[34] Jesus told them, "The sons of this age marry and are given in marriage. [35] But those who are counted worthy to take part in that age and in the resurrection from the dead neither marry nor are given in marriage. [36] For they cannot die anymore, because they are like angels and are sons of God, since they are sons of the resurrection. [37] Moses even indicated ₁in the passage₁ about the burning bush that the dead are raised, where he calls the Lord **the God of Abraham and the God of Isaac and the God of Jacob.**[m] [38] He is not God of the dead but of the living, because all are living to[n] Him."

[39] Some of the scribes answered, "Teacher, You have spoken well." [40] And they no longer dared to ask Him anything.

The Question about the Messiah

[41] Then He said to them, "How can they say that the •Messiah is the Son of David? [42] For David himself says in the Book of Psalms:

> The Lord declared to my Lord,
> 'Sit at My right hand
> [43] until I make Your enemies
> Your footstool.'[o]

[44] David calls Him 'Lord'; how then can the Messiah be his Son?"

---

[a]**20:17** Lit *What then is this that is written* [b]**20:17** Lit *the head of the corner* [c]**20:17** Ps 118:22 [d]**20:20** The scribes and chief priests of v. 19 [e]**20:20** Or *upright;* that is, loyal to God's law [f]**20:20,26** Lit *catch Him in [a] word* [g]**20:21** Lit *You don't receive a face* [h]**20:23** Other mss add *"Why are you testing Me?* [i]**20:26** Lit *in front of the people* [j]**20:28** Dt 25:5 [k]**20:30** Other mss add *took her as wife, and he died without children* [l]**20:33** Lit *had her as wife* [m]**20:37** Ex 3:6,15 [n]**20:38** Or *with* [o]**20:42–43** Ps 110:1

20:14 inheritance. The tenants apparently mistook the arrival of the son as a sign that the owner had died. By law, a piece of ownerless property (which it would be if they killed the son) could be kept by those who first seized it.

20:16 Having refused to pay rent three times over, and having killed the owner's son, the farmers suffered severe and immediate action. The owner could muster all the legal power available against these evil tenants. Their judgment would mean their death. The land they had so jealously guarded would be given over to others.

20:17 cornerstone. Stone laid at the corner to bind two walls together and to strengthen them. Used symbolically as a symbol of strength and prominence. The figure is often applied to rulers or leaders (Pss. 118:22;

144:12; Isa. 19:13 NIV, REB, NASB; Zech. 10:4).Here the reference is to Psalm 118 where the Messiah is identified as a cornerstone (Ps. 118:22). Jesus is both the cornerstone and a free-standing stone on which those who reject Him are destroyed.

20:24 Whose image and inscription? Jesus did what he did many times—answered a question by asking a question. Those trying to trick Jesus produce a silver denarius minted by the Roman government. On one side was the image of the emperor, Tiberius Caesar. Under Caesar's image was the inscription: "Tiberius, son of the divine Augustus." On the flip side of the coin was an image of Tiberius' mother, Livia.

20:25 give back to Caesar. While clearly implying that one's final loyalty must be to God and not the state, Jesus implied that there are

things owed to the state and that it was not his mission to detract from the state. In his letter to the Romans Paul clearly articulated God's design for the state: "Everyone must submit to the governing authorities, for there is no authority except from God, and those that exist are instituted by God" (Rom. 13:1).

20:27 Sadducees. There is relatively little information available about this group. However, it seems that they were a small but highly influential party of Jews composed mainly of wealthy, aristocratic priests. The Sadducees accepted only the first five books of the Old Testament as authoritative and denied the resurrection.

20:28-33 in the resurrection …? The question they pose has to do with levirate marriage (Deut. 25:5-10) which was designed to ensure the continuation of the family name

Warning against the Scribes

[45] While all the people were listening, He said to His disciples, [46] "Beware of the scribes, who want to go around in long robes and who love greetings in the marketplaces, the front seats in the •synagogues, and the places of honor at banquets. [47] They devour widows' houses and say long prayers just for show. These will receive greater punishment."[a]

The Widow's Gift

21 He looked up and saw the rich dropping their offerings into the temple treasury. [2] He also saw a poor widow dropping in two tiny coins.[b] [3] "I tell you the truth," He said. "This poor widow has put in more than all of them. [4] For all these people have put in gifts out of their surplus, but she out of her poverty has put in all she had to live on."

Destruction of the Temple Predicted

[5] As some were talking about the •temple complex, how it was adorned with beautiful stones and gifts dedicated to God,[c] He said, [6] "These things that you see— the days will come when not one stone will be left on another that will not be thrown down!"

Signs of the End of the Age

[7] "Teacher," they asked Him, "so when will these things be? And what will be the sign when these things are about to take place?"

[8] Then He said, "Watch out that you are not deceived. For many will come in My name, saying, 'I am He,' and, 'The time is near.' Don't follow them. [9] When you hear of wars and rebellions,[d] don't be alarmed. Indeed, these things must take place first, but the end won't come right away."

[10] Then He told them: "Nation will be raised up against nation, and kingdom against kingdom. [11] There will be violent earthquakes, and famines and plagues in various places, and there will be terrifying sights and great signs from heaven. [12] But before all these things, they will lay their hands on you and persecute you. They will hand you over to the •synagogues and prisons, and you will be brought before kings and governors because of My name. [13] It will lead to an opportunity for you to witness.[e] [14] Therefore make up your minds[f] not to prepare your defense ahead of time, [15] for I will give you such words[g] and a wisdom that none of your adversaries will be able to resist or contradict. [16] You will even be betrayed by parents, brothers, relatives, and friends. They will kill some of you. [17] You will be hated by everyone because of My name, [18] but not a hair of your head will be lost. [19] By your endurance gain[h] your •lives.

The Destruction of Jerusalem

[20] "When you see Jerusalem surrounded by armies, then recognize that its desolation has come near. [21] Then those in Judea must flee to the mountains! Those inside the city[i] must leave it, and those who are in the country must not enter it, [22] because these are days of vengeance to fulfill all the things that are written. [23] Woe to pregnant women and nursing mothers in those days, for there will be great distress in the land[j] and wrath against this people. [24] They will fall by the edge of the sword, and be led captive into all the nations, and Jerusalem will be trampled by the Gentiles[k] until the times of the Gentiles are fulfilled.

The Coming of the Son of Man

[25] "Then there will be signs in the sun, moon, and stars; and there will be anguish on the earth among nations bewildered by the roaring sea and waves. [26] People will faint from fear and expectation of the things that are coming on the world, because the celestial powers will be shaken. [27] Then they will see the •Son of Man coming in a cloud with power and great glory. [28] But when these things begin to take place, stand up and lift up your heads, because your redemption is near!"

The Parable of the Fig Tree

[29] Then He told them a parable: "Look at the fig tree, and all the trees. [30] As soon as they put out ⌜leaves⌝ you

---

[a] **20:47** Or *judgment* [b] **21:2** Lit *two lepta*; the *lepton* was the smallest and least valuable Gk coin in use. [c] **21:5** Gifts given to the temple in fulfillment of vows to God [d] **21:9** Or *insurrections*, or *revolutions* [e] **21:13** Lit *lead to a testimony for you* [f] **21:14** Lit *Therefore place* (determine) *in your hearts* [g] **21:15** Lit *you a mouth* [h] **21:19** Other mss read *endurance you will gain* [i] **21:21** Lit *inside her* [j] **21:23** Or *the earth* [k] **21:24** Or *nations*

---

as well as to keep property within a family. Their case study attempted to show the absurdity of resurrection.

20:34-36 they are like angels. Jesus affirmed that resurrection life will be more akin to the experience of angels (in which the Sadducees likewise did not believe) than to the social and physical laws that now govern life.

20:39 You have spoken well. The scribes (who were Pharisees) believed in the resurrection and in angels and would be glad to see the cynicism of the Sadducees refuted.

20:46 long robes. These were long, white linen garments fringed with tassels touching the ground. In such a stately garment, a person could not run or work and so would be reckoned to be a person of leisure and importance. **greetings.** People considered the

teachers of the law to be men of great insight and authority, so they rose when the teachers passed by and called out titles of respect.

20:47 They devour widows' houses. Since the teachers of the law were forbidden to receive pay for their teaching, they lived off others, including poor widows (21:1-4).

21:1 temple treasury. This was located in the court of women (which was the first of the inner courts of the temple). It consisted of 13 trumpet-shaped receptacles used to collect donations.

21:2 two tiny coins. The smallest coins in circulation, worth about 1/8 of a cent. Her donation, while small in amount, represented the depth of her dedication to God (12:22-34).

21:5 temple. The temple was constructed of huge white stones, some measuring 37 feet long by 12 feet high by 18 feet wide.

21:11 terrifying sights and great signs from heaven. This is apocalyptic language—graphic, calamitous, cosmic imagery. Such language was used often in the Old Testament (Isa. 2:6-21; 13:6-22).

21:21 those in Judea must flee. Those who follow Christ are to recognize that this is the sign that God's judgment against Israel is coming to a head. Instead of flocking to the city in anticipation of a Messianic appearance, they must run for their lives.

21:24 the times of the Gentiles. Some believe this may refer to the period of the Gentile ingathering to Christ and others to the completion of a time during the tribulation (Rom. 11:25).

can see for yourselves and recognize that summer is already near. [31] In the same way, when you see these things happening, recognize[a] that the kingdom of God is near. [32] •I assure you: This generation will certainly not pass away until all things take place. [33] Heaven and earth will pass away, but My words will never pass away.

The Need for Watchfulness

[34] "Be on your guard, so that your minds are not dulled[b] from carousing,[c] drunkenness, and worries of life, or that day will come on you unexpectedly [35] like a trap. For it will come on all who live on the face of the whole earth. [36] But be alert at all times, praying that you may have strength[d] to escape all these things that are going to take place and to stand before the Son of Man."

[37] During the day, He was teaching in the temple complex, but in the evening He would go out and spend the night on what is called the •Mount of Olives. [38] Then all the people would come early in the morning to hear Him in the temple complex.

The Plot to Kill Jesus

22 The Festival of •Unleavened Bread, which is called •Passover, was drawing near. [2] The •chief priests and the •scribes were looking for a way to put Him to death, because they were afraid of the people.

[3] Then Satan entered Judas, called Iscariot, who was numbered among the Twelve. [4] He went away and discussed with the chief priests and temple police how he could hand Him over to them. [5] They were glad and agreed to give him silver.[e] [6] So he accepted ⌐the offer⌐ and started looking for a good opportunity to betray Him to them when the crowd was not present.

Preparation for Passover

[7] Then the Day of Unleavened Bread came when the Passover lamb had to be sacrificed. [8] Jesus sent Peter and John, saying, "Go and prepare the Passover meal for us, so we can eat it."

[9] "Where do You want us to prepare it?" they asked Him.

Celebrating the Lord's Supper

1. What special meals does your family celebrate together: Thanksgiving? Sunday dinner? Birthday suppers?

Luke 22:7-23

2. What is the purpose of the Lord's Supper, according to Jesus?

3. What was the disciples' response during this first Lord's Supper (v. 23)? What is your focus at church: Worshiping God? Arguing with others?

4. Why should Christians today celebrate the Lord's Supper?

5. How often do you celebrate the Lord's Supper? What do you do in preparing to receive it?

---

[10] "Listen," He said to them, "when you've entered the city, a man carrying a water jug will meet you. Follow him into the house he enters. [11] Tell the owner of the house, 'The Teacher asks you, "Where is the guest room where I can eat the Passover with My disciples?" ' [12] Then he will show you a large, furnished room upstairs. Make the preparations there."

[13] So they went and found it just as He had told them, and they prepared the Passover.

The First Lord's Supper

[14] When the hour came, He reclined at the table, and the apostles with Him. [15] Then He said to them, "I have fervently desired to eat this Passover with you before I suffer. [16] For I tell you, I will not eat it again[f] until it is fulfilled in the kingdom of God." [17] Then He took a cup, and after giving thanks, He said, "Take this and share it among yourselves. [18] For I tell you, from now on I will

---

22:1 The Festival of Unleavened Bread. This feast was a seven-day period so closely related to Passover (Deut. 16:1-8) that the whole period was often called Passover. Passover, celebrated on the fourteenth day of the Jewish month of Nisan (March–April), was the celebration of God's deliverance of Israel from slavery in Egypt (Ex. 12).

22:2 looking for a way to put Him to death. The religious leadership had long ago decided that Jesus must be silenced (6:11; 20:19). It was only their fear of an uproar by the masses that had prevented them from doing so.

22:4 chief priests and temple police. The management of the temple was under the control of the high priest and those who aligned themselves with him. They controlled the temple guard and held them re-

sponsible for maintaining order in the temple area.

22:7–8 the Day of Unleavened Bread came when the Passover lamb had to be sacrificed. While the Feast of Unleavened Bread did not officially start until the day after Passover, the day on which the lambs were sacrificed was sometimes referred to as the first day of the Feast of Unleavened Bread. **the Passover meal.** Each pilgrim sacrificed his own lamb in the temple. A priest caught the blood in a bowl and threw it on the altar. The pilgrim then ate the sacrificial lamb for Passover.

22:10 a man carrying a water jug. Such a person would have been easy to spot since it was highly unusual for a man to carry a jar. Women carried jars, men carried wineskins.

22:14 When the hour came. The meal could be eaten only after sunset.

22:16-18 The Passover had a twofold significance: it looked back upon Israel's deliverance from Egypt and it looked forward to the final redemption that would be ushered in by the Messiah. The comments in verses 16 and 18 refer to that final consummation of the kingdom of God. In a sense, the meal will not be finished until the final messianic banquet. No longer is the Old Testament Passover the supreme act of God's deliverance of His people: From now on spiritual deliverance from the power and penalty of sin is secured by the death and resurrection of Jesus.

22:19 He simply says, "Do this in remembrance of Me." Jesus' use of the bread and the cup in a symbolic way was consistent

not drink of the fruit of the vine until the kingdom of God comes."

19 And He took bread, gave thanks, broke it, gave it to them, and said, "This is My body, which is given for you. Do this in remembrance of Me."

20 In the same way He also took the cup after supper and said, "This cup is the new covenant ⌊established by⌋ My blood; it is shed for you.a 21 But look, the hand of the one betraying Me is at the table with Me! 22 For the •Son of Man will go away as it has been determined, but woe to that man by whom He is betrayed!"

23 So they began to argue among themselves which of them it could be who was going to do this thing.

The Dispute over Greatness

24 Then a dispute also arose among them about who should be considered the greatest. 25 But He said to them, "The kings of the Gentiles dominate them, and those who have authority over them are calledb 'Bene-factors.'c 26 But it must not be like that among you. On the contrary, whoever is greatest among you must become like the youngest, and whoever leads, like the one serving. 27 For who is greater, the one at the table or the one serving? Isn't it the one at the table? But I am among you as the One who serves. 28 You are the ones who stood by Me in My trials. 29 I bestow on you a kingdom, just as My Father bestowed one on Me, 30 so that you may eat and drink at My table in My kingdom. And you will sit on thrones judging the 12 tribes of Israel.

Peter's Denial Predicted

31 "Simon, Simon,d look out! Satan has asked to sift youe like wheat. 32 But I have prayed for youf that your faith may not fail. And you, when you have turned back, strengthen your brothers."

33 "Lord," he told Him, "I'm ready to go with You both to prison and to death!"

34 "I tell you, Peter," He said, "the rooster will not crow today untilg you deny three times that you know Me!"

Money-Bag, Backpack, and Sword

35 He also said to them, "When I sent you out without money-bag, traveling bag, or sandals, did you lack any-thing?"

"Not a thing," they said.

36 Then He said to them, "But now, whoever has a money-bag should take it, and also a traveling bag. And whoever doesn't have a sword should sell his robe and buy one. 37 For I tell you, what is written must be ful-filled in Me: **And He was counted among the out-laws.**h Yes, what is written about Me is coming to its fulfillment."

38 "Lord," they said, "look, here are two swords." "Enough of that!"i He told them.

The Prayer in the Garden

39 He went out and made His way as usual to the •Mount of Olives, and the disciples followed Him. 40 When He reached the place, He told them, "Pray that you may not enter into temptation." 41 Then He with-drew from them about a stone's throw, knelt down, and began to pray, 42 "Father, if You are willing, take this cup away from Me—nevertheless, not My will, but Yours, be done."

[43 Then an angel from heaven appeared to Him, strengthening Him. 44 Being in anguish, He prayed more fervently, and His sweat became like drops of blood falling to the ground.]j 45 When He got up from prayer and came to the disciples, He found them sleep-ing, exhausted from their grief.k 46 "Why are you sleep-ing?" He asked them. "Get up and pray, so that you won't enter into temptation."

The Judas Kiss

47 While He was still speaking, suddenly a mob was there, and one of the Twelve named Judas was leading them. He came near Jesus to kiss Him, 48 but Jesus said to him, "Judas, are you betraying the Son of Man with a kiss?"

49 When those around Him saw what was going to happen, they asked, "Lord, should we strike with the

---

a22:19–20 Other mss omit which is given for you (v. 19) through the end of v. 20   b22:25 Or them call themselves   c22:25 Title of honor given to those who benefited the public good   d22:31 Other mss read Then the Lord said, "Simon, Simon   e22:31 you (pl in Gk)   f22:32 you (sg in Gk)   g22:34 Other mss read before   h22:37 Is 53:12   i22:38 Or It is enough!   j22:43–44 Other mss omit bracketed text   k22:45 Lit sleeping from grief

---

with the way in which the various elements of the Passover meal were used. The sym-bols in the Passover meal pointed back to the first covenant God made with Israel while Jesus' words here at the Last Supper pointed forward to His death and the new covenant.

22:20 covenant. This is a treaty between two parties, often sealed by the sacrifice of an animal. It refers to the agreement that God made with Israel which was dependent on Israel's obedience (Ex. 24:1-8). Now a new covenant (Jer. 31:31-33; Heb. 8:8,13) is established which is dependent on Jesus' obedience and sacrificial death. A covenant of law gives way to a covenant of love.

22:26 like the youngest. Prestige in this culture went with age and experience. The youngest people had little prestige or

honor. Jesus' followers should not think that true greatness requires any more prestige than the youngest person received in that culture.

22:32 I have prayed for you. This "you" is singular. While Peter will deny Jesus, he is also the one who will encourage the others to reaffirm their faith in Him. This pictures the conflict between Satan and Jesus in the on-going life of the church. While Satan has an influence, it is continually checked and countered by the intercession of Jesus as the High Priest of God's people (Heb. 4:14-16). **strengthen your brothers.** In Acts 1:15 and 2:14 Peter was the leading character among the original disciples. His faith and courage exemplified to all the others what it meant to follow Jesus (John 21:15-17).

22:37 counted among the outlaws. Jesus

will be crucified as a criminal with two crimi-nals (23:32). This is to fulfill the prophecy of Isaiah (Isa. 53:12).

22:42 Father. This distinguishes the nature of the relationship Jesus enjoyed with God. **this cup.** The Old Testament often pictured a person's destiny as related to the nature of the "cup" from which God gave the person to drink. For those who trust Him, it was seen as a cup of blessing (Ps. 16:5; 23:5), but His opponents would be forced to drink a cup full of wrath (Isa. 51:17; Lam. 4:21; Hab. 2:16). **nevertheless, not My will, but Yours, be done.** The wrestling in prayer re-solves itself in Jesus' entrustment of Himself to the Father.

22:54 the high priest's house. On the Day of Atonement the high priest alone could en-ter the most holy place and, with sprinkled

sword?" ⁵⁰ Then one of them struck the high priest's slave and cut off his right ear.

⁵¹ But Jesus responded, "No more of this!"^a And touching his ear, He healed him. ⁵² Then Jesus said to the chief priests, temple police, and the elders who had come for Him, "Have you come out with swords and clubs as if I were a criminal?^b ⁵³ Every day while I was with you in the •temple complex, you never laid a hand on Me. But this is your hour—and the dominion of darkness."

Confronting Sin

1. How do you usually react to failure: Kick yourself for days? Pray about it? Talk to someone about it? Try to learn from it?

Luke 22:54-62

2. Peter had just told Jesus that he would follow Him to death (v. 33). Why did he suddenly deny Jesus?

3. Have you ever denied Jesus? How? Why?

4. Peter "went outside and wept bitterly" (v. 62). How do you react when you find that you've somehow failed God?

5. Jesus "turned and looked at Peter" (v. 61). How does God turn and look at you to convict you of sin?

Peter Denies His Lord

⁵⁴ They seized Him, led Him away, and brought Him into the high priest's house. Meanwhile Peter was following at a distance. ⁵⁵ They lit a fire in the middle of the courtyard and sat down together, and Peter sat among them. ⁵⁶ When a servant saw him sitting in the firelight, and looked closely at him, she said, "This man was with Him too."

⁵⁷ But he denied it: "Woman, I don't know Him!"

⁵⁸ After a little while, someone else saw him and said, "You're one of them too!"

"Man, I am not!" Peter said.

⁵⁹ About an hour later, another kept insisting, "This man was certainly with Him, since he's also a Galilean."

⁶⁰ But Peter said, "Man, I don't know what you're talking about!" Immediately, while he was still speaking, a rooster crowed. ⁶¹ Then the Lord turned and looked at Peter. So Peter remembered the word of the Lord, how He had said to him, "Before the rooster crows today, you will deny Me three times." ⁶² And he went outside and wept bitterly.

Jesus Mocked and Beaten

⁶³ The men who were holding Jesus started mocking and beating Him. ⁶⁴ After blindfolding Him, they kept^c asking, "Prophesy! Who hit You?" ⁶⁵ And they were saying many other blasphemous things against Him.

Jesus Faces the Sanhedrin

⁶⁶ When daylight came, the elders^d of the people, both the chief priests and the •scribes, convened and brought Him before their •Sanhedrin. ⁶⁷ They said, "If You are the •Messiah, tell us."

But He said to them, "If I do tell you, you will not believe. ⁶⁸ And if I ask you, you will not answer. ⁶⁹ But from now on, the Son of Man will be seated at the right hand of the Power of God."

⁷⁰ They all asked, "Are You, then, the Son of God?"

And He said to them, "You say that I am."

⁷¹ "Why do we need any more testimony," they said, "since we've heard it ourselves from His mouth?"

Jesus Faces Pilate

23 Then their whole assembly rose up and brought Him before •Pilate. ² They began to accuse Him, saying, "We found this man subverting our nation, opposing payment of taxes to Caesar, and saying that He Himself is the •Messiah, a King."

³ So Pilate asked Him, "Are You the King of the Jews?"

He answered him, "You have said it."^e

---

^a**22:51** Lit *Permit as far as this* ^b**22:52** Lit *as against a criminal* ^c**22:64** Other mss add *striking Him on the face and* ^d**22:66** Or *council of elders* ^e**23:3** Or *That is true;* an affirmative oath

---

blood, make atonement for the sins of the people. Caiaphas was the high priest before whom Jesus came (Matt. 26:57).

22:60 a rooster crowed. Roosters in Palestine might crow anytime between midnight and 3 a.m. (which was the reason that particular watch was called "cock-crow"). Peter's denials therefore occurred in the very early morning hours.

22:61 the Lord turned. The other Gospels make it clear that Jesus was interrogated during the night by the high priest and at least some members of the Sanhedrin (Matt. 26:68). It may be at this point that Jesus was being transferred from the high priest's house to the meeting place of the full Sanhedrin for His early morning trial.

22:66 Sanhedrin. This was a council con-

sisting of 71 leaders (both priests and laymen) who made up the highest Jewish court. They were given authority by Rome to rule in matters of religious law.

22:67-68 If You are the Messiah, tell us. While the other Gospels record the failure of the Sanhedrin to produce any charges against Jesus (Mark 14:56), Luke zeroes in on the point of contention that most angered the council: They felt Jesus was making false claims to be Messiah. .

22:69 the Son of Man. Jesus openly and unequivocally declared His Messiahship. The three titles for Jesus, Christ, Son of Man, Son of God, are combined here for the first time in the Gospel. It becomes clear the Son of Man is the Messiah, who is the Son of God. **seated at the right hand of the Power of God.** This was the place of honor. Jesus, the

Son of Man like in Daniel 7:13-14, will be vindicated at the second coming when His accusers see that His claim was true.

22:71 we've heard it ourselves. The Sanhedrin heard all they needed. The Old Testament penalty for blaspheming God was death by stoning (Lev. 24:10-16), but at this point in history the Sanhedrin did not have the power to carry out a death sentence. They would need to get the Roman procurator to do that for them somehow.

23:1 brought Him before Pilate. Pilate served as procurator of Judea from A.D. 26 to 36. Historians of the time called him an "inflexible, merciless, and obstinate" man who disliked the Jews and their customs.

23:5-7 sent Him to Herod. Pilate decided to pass off the case to Herod who had authority

[4] Pilate then told the •chief priests and the crowds, "I find no grounds for charging this man."

[5] But they kept insisting, "He stirs up the people, teaching throughout all Judea, from Galilee where He started even to here."

Jesus Faces Herod Antipas

[6] When Pilate heard this,[a] he asked if the man was a Galilean. [7] Finding that He was under •Herod's jurisdiction, he sent Him to Herod, who was also in Jerusalem during those days. [8] Herod was very glad to see Jesus; for a long time he had wanted to see Him, because he had heard about Him and was hoping to see some miracle[b] performed by Him. [9] So he kept asking Him questions, but Jesus did not answer him. [10] The chief priests and the •scribes stood by, vehemently accusing Him. [11] Then Herod, with his soldiers, treated Him with contempt, mocked Him, dressed Him in a brilliant robe, and sent Him back to Pilate. [12] That very day Herod and Pilate became friends.[c] Previously, they had been hostile toward each other.

Jesus or Barabbas

[13] Pilate called together the chief priests, the leaders, and the people, [14] and said to them, "You have brought me this man as one who subverts the people. But in fact, after examining Him in your presence, I have found no grounds to charge this man with those things you accuse Him of. [15] Neither has Herod, because he sent Him back to us. Clearly, He has done nothing to deserve death. [16] Therefore I will have Him whipped[d] and ˌthenˌ release Him." [[17] For according to the festival he had to release someone to them.][e]

[18] Then they all cried out together, "Take this man away! Release Barabbas to us!" [19] (He had been thrown into prison for a rebellion that had taken place in the city, and for murder.)

[20] Pilate, wanting to release Jesus, addressed them again, [21] but they kept shouting, "Crucify! Crucify Him!"

[22] A third time he said to them, "Why? What has this man done wrong? I have found in Him no grounds for the death penalty. Therefore I will have Him whipped and ˌthenˌ release Him."

[23] But they kept up the pressure, demanding with loud voices that He be crucified. And their voices[f] won out. [24] So Pilate decided to grant their demand [25] and released the one they were asking for, who had been thrown into prison for rebellion and murder. But he handed Jesus over to their will.

The Way to the Cross

[26] As they led Him away, they seized Simon, a Cyrenian, who was coming in from the country, and laid the cross on him to carry behind Jesus. [27] A great multitude of the people followed Him, including women who were mourning and lamenting Him. [28] But turning to them, Jesus said, "Daughters of Jerusalem, do not weep for Me, but weep for yourselves and your children. [29] Look, the days are coming when they will say, 'Blessed are the barren, the wombs that never bore, and the breasts that never nursed!' [30] Then they will begin **to say to the mountains, 'Fall on us!' and to the hills, 'Cover us!'**[g] [31] For if they do these things when the wood is green, what will happen when it is dry?"

Crucified between Two Criminals

[32] Two others—criminals—were also led away to be executed with Him. [33] When they arrived at the place called The Skull, they crucified Him there, along with the criminals, one on the right and one on the left. [[34] Then Jesus said, "Father, forgive them, because they do not know what they are doing."][e] And they divided His clothes and cast lots.

[35] The people stood watching, and even the leaders kept scoffing: "He saved others; let Him save Himself if this is God's Messiah, the Chosen One!" [36] The soldiers also mocked Him. They came offering Him sour wine [37] and said, "If You are the King of the Jews, save Yourself!"

---

[a]**23:6** Other mss read *heard "Galilee"* [b]**23:8** Or *sign* [c]**23:12** Lit *friends with one another* [d]**23:16** Gk *paideuo;* to discipline or "teach a lesson"; 1 Kg 12:11,14 LXX; 2 Ch 10:11,14; perhaps a way of referring to the Roman scourging; Lat *flagellatio* [e]**23:17,34** Other mss omit bracketed text [f]**23:23** Other mss add *and those of the chief priests* [g]**23:30** Hs 10:8

---

over Galilee. This might have been done since Herod Antipas was Jewish, or simply to get a Jewish opinion of the case or to rid himself of the responsibility.

23:9 Jesus did not answer him. See Isaiah 53:7.

23:18 Barabbas. A genuine resistance leader who was also guilty of murder.

23:20-22 Pilate, wanting to release Jesus. Pilate argues again for Jesus' release, but the leaders will hear nothing of this. He then seeks to appease the crowd by punishing Jesus and then releasing Him.

23:25 released the one ... thrown into prison for ... murder. The death of the innocent in the place of the guilty is an individual application of the meaning of Jesus' death

as a substitutionary atonement for sinners. It explains what Jesus meant in Mark 10:45 when He said that He came to "give His life as a ransom for many."

23:26 Simon. Possibly a Jew, from a Greek city on the north shore of Africa who was in Jerusalem for the Passover feast. **laid the cross on him.** The fact that Jesus could not carry His crossbeam reveals the extent to which He had been beaten. Because of Jesus' weakened condition, Simon was grabbed out of the crowds and forced into service by the Roman soldiers.

23:31 For if they do these things when the wood is green, what will happen when it is dry? A proverbial saying that means, "If things are this bad now, what will happen later?"

23:33 The Skull. In Aramaic, this was

Golgotha. The name was given because it was a round, bare hillock outside Jerusalem. **they crucified Him.** Crucifixion was the most feared of all punishments in the first-century world.

23:34 Father, forgive them. Jesus' call for mercy reflected His radical call to His disciples to forgive their enemies (6:27-28; Acts 7:60). **divided His clothes.** The clothes of the condemned person belonged to the four soldiers who carried out the crucifixion (Ps. 22:18; John 19:23-24).

23:35 if this is God's Messiah. To the leaders, the disgraceful death Jesus was experiencing proved that He could not possibly be the Messiah.

23:44 darkness. This was some sort of supernatural event (Ex. 10:21-23) showing the

[38] An inscription was above Him:[a]

THIS IS THE KING OF THE JEWS

[39] Then one of the criminals hanging there began to yell insults at[b] Him: "Aren't You the Messiah? Save Yourself and us!"

[40] But the other answered, rebuking him: "Don't you even fear God, since you are undergoing the same punishment? [41] We are punished justly, because we're getting back what we deserve for the things we did, but this man has done nothing wrong." [42] Then he said, "Jesus, remember me[c] when You come into Your kingdom!"

[43] And He said to him, "•I assure you: Today you will be with Me in paradise."

On the Cross

1. When have you been punished for something you didn't do? How did it feel? Have you ever taken someone else's punishment? Why?

Luke 23:26-49

2. Why did Jesus die on the cross? What did His death accomplish?

3. Why did Jesus promise one thief, "Today you will be with Me in paradise" (v. 43)? Why didn't He promise that to the other thief?

4. When Jesus said, "Father, forgive them" (v. 34), who was he asking God to forgive?

5. When you die, will you be with Jesus in paradise? How do you know?

The Death of Jesus

[44] It was now about noon,[d] and darkness came over the whole land[e] until three,[f] [45] because the sun's light failed.[g] The curtain of the sanctuary was split down the middle. [46] And Jesus called out with a loud voice, "Father, **into Your hands I entrust My spirit.**"[h] Saying this, He breathed His last.

[47] When the •centurion saw what happened, he began to glorify God, saying, "This man really was righteous!" [48] All the crowds that had gathered for this spectacle, when they saw what had taken place, went home, striking their chests.[i] [49] But all who knew Him, including the women who had followed Him from Galilee, stood at a distance, watching these things.

The Burial of Jesus

[50] There was a good and righteous man named Joseph, a member of the •Sanhedrin, [51] who had not agreed with their plan and action. He was from Arimathea, a Judean town, and was looking forward to the kingdom of God. [52] He approached Pilate and asked for Jesus' body. [53] Taking it down, he wrapped it in fine linen and placed it in a tomb cut into the rock, where no one had ever been placed.[j] [54] It was preparation day, and the Sabbath was about to begin.[k] [55] The women who had come with Him from Galilee followed along and observed the tomb and how His body was placed. [56] Then they returned and prepared spices and perfumes. And they rested on the Sabbath according to the commandment.

Resurrection Morning

24 On the first day of the week, very early in the morning, they[l] came to the tomb, bringing the spices they had prepared. [2] They found the stone rolled away from the tomb. [3] They went in but did not find the body of the Lord Jesus. [4] While they were perplexed about this, suddenly two men stood by them in dazzling clothes. [5] So the women were terrified and bowed down to the ground.[m]

---

[a]**23:38** Other mss add *written in Greek, Latin, and Hebrew letters* [b]**23:39** Or *began to blaspheme* [c]**23:42** Other mss add *Lord* [d]**23:44** Lit *about the sixth hour* [e]**23:44** Or *whole earth* [f]**23:44** Lit *the ninth hour* [g]**23:45** Other mss read *three, and the sun was darkened* [h]**23:46** Ps 31:5 [i]**23:48** *Mourning* [j]**23:53** Or *interred, or laid* [k]**23:54** Lit *was dawning; not in the morning but at sundown Friday* [l]**24:1** Other mss add *and other women with them* [m]**24:5** Lit *and inclined their faces to the ground*

---

significance of the crucifixion (22:53; Amos 8:9).

23:45 curtain of the sanctuary. The curtain in the temple was probably the one that separated the holy place (where the priests performed their daily service) and the most holy place. The curtain stood as a visible sign of the barrier between people and God since only the high priest could pass through that curtain once a year on the Day of Atonement. Its rending was another supernatural sign of the significance of Jesus' death: He has opened the way for believers to have immediate and direct access to God (Heb. 10:19-20).

23:50-52 asked for Jesus' body. To ask for the body was to admit allegiance to the now discredited Jesus and was, therefore, potentially dangerous.

23:55 The women who had come ... from Galilee. See chapter 8:2-3. These women saw where Jesus was laid. Thus, Luke undermines any criticism that the women merely went to the wrong tomb later on.

24:1 On the first day of the week. This was early Sunday morning. **spices.** Aromatic oils to anoint the body, not so much to preserve it as to honor it. Clearly they did not expect Jesus to have risen from the dead.

24:2 The stone was rolled away not so that the resurrected Jesus could leave the tomb but so that His disciples could see that it was empty (John 20:8). **the stone.** It would have been fairly easy to roll the huge, disc-shaped stone down the groove cut for it so that it covered the opening, but once in place it would have been very difficult to push it back up the incline. **tomb.** Typically

such tombs had a large antechamber, with a small two-foot-high doorway at the back which led into the six- or seven-foot burial chamber.

24:4 two men. Matthew 28:2-3 says that an angel came down from heaven. The description of their clothing here confirms this is Luke's meaning, too.

24:9 the Eleven. Judas had committed suicide for his treachery (Matt. 27:5).

24:10 Mary Magdalene, Joanna. All the Gospel writers include Mary as one of the witnesses of Jesus' empty tomb. Under Jewish law, women were not considered reliable witnesses. **Mary the mother of James.** Literally, "Mary of James." Typically one would understand it to mean James' wife, but Mark 15:40 refers specifically to Mary as the

"Why are you looking for the living among the dead?" asked the men. [6] "He is not here, but He has been resurrected! Remember how He spoke to you when He was still in Galilee, [7] saying, 'The •Son of Man must be betrayed into the hands of sinful men, be crucified, and rise on the third day' ?" [8] And they remembered His words.

[9] Returning from the tomb, they reported all these things to the Eleven and to all the rest. [10] •Mary Magdalene, Joanna, Mary the mother of James, and the other women with them were telling the apostles these things. [11] But these words seemed like nonsense to them, and they did not believe the women. [12] Peter, however, got up and ran to the tomb. When he stooped to look in, he saw only the linen cloths.[a] So he went home, amazed at what had happened.

The Emmaus Disciples

[13] Now that same day two of them were on their way to a village called[b] Emmaus, which was about seven miles[c] from Jerusalem. [14] Together they were discussing everything that had taken place. [15] And while they were discussing and arguing, Jesus Himself came near and began to walk along with them. [16] But they[d] were prevented from recognizing Him. [17] Then He asked them, "What is this dispute that you're having[e] with each other as you are walking?" And they stopped ⌊walking and looked⌋ discouraged.

[18] The one named Cleopas answered Him, "Are You the only visitor in Jerusalem who doesn't know the things that happened there in these days?"

[19] "What things?" He asked them.

So they said to Him, "The things concerning Jesus the •Nazarene, who was a Prophet powerful in action and speech before God and all the people, [20] and how our •chief priests and leaders handed Him over to be sentenced to death, and they crucified Him. [21] But we were hoping that He was the One who was about to redeem Israel. Besides all this, it's the third day since these things happened. [22] Moreover, some women from our group astounded us. They arrived early at the tomb,

[23] and when they didn't find His body, they came and reported that they had seen a vision of angels who said He was alive. [24] Some of those who were with us went to the tomb and found it just as the women had said, but they didn't see Him."

An Eye-Opening Experience

1. What's the longest walk you've ever taken?

Luke 24:13-35

2. Why did Jesus ask the men to tell Him all about His own death and resurrection?

3. Why did "the Messiah have to suffer these things" (v. 25)—that is, dying on the cross and rising again from the dead?

4. Why were the men's "eyes opened" to who Jesus was when "He took the bread, blessed and broke it, and gave it to them" (vv. 30-31)? What does this teach us about the Lord's Supper?

5. Has Jesus "opened your eyes"? If not, will you ask Him to right now?

[25] He said to them, "How unwise and slow you are to believe in your hearts all that the prophets have spoken! [26] Didn't the •Messiah have to suffer these things and enter into His glory?" [27] Then beginning with Moses and all the Prophets, He interpreted for them the things concerning Himself in all the Scriptures.

[28] They came near the village where they were going, and He gave the impression that He was going farther. [29] But they urged Him: "Stay with us, because it's almost evening, and now the day is almost over." So He went in to stay with them.

---

[a]**24:12** Other mss add *lying there*   [b]**24:13** Lit *village, which name is*   [c]**24:13** Lit *about 60 stadia;* 1 *stadion* = 600 feet   [d]**24:16** Lit *their eyes*
[e]**24:17** Lit *What are these words that you are exchanging*

---

mother of James.

24:12 he saw only the linen cloths. John reports this curious fact in even greater detail (John 20:1–9). It was the custom to bind a dead body with strips of linen cloth. The head was bound with a separate cloth. Thus, when Jesus rose from the dead He would have passed through the cloth (as He later did through doors) and the whole mass would have collapsed. Had the body been stolen, grave clothes would have been taken or, at least, unwound and tossed aside.

24:13 two of them. These may not have been two of the remaining eleven apostles, but two followers of Jesus who lived in nearby Jerusalem. They were likely returning home after the Passover feast. **Emmaus.** The site of this village is uncertain.

24:14-16 As Jesus came up to the two, they were prevented from recognizing Him. Later on, they recognized Him as He broke bread (vv. 30-31).

24:18 Cleopas. While this man was probably a figure Luke's readers would know, his identity remains uncertain today.

24:21 to redeem Israel. To free the Jewish nation from bondage to Rome and establish the kingdom of God (1:68; 2:38; 21:28,31; Titus 2:14; 1 Peter 1:18). **the third day.** This could refer to the Jewish belief that after the third day the soul left the body or to Jesus' statement that He would be raised to life on the third day (9:22).

24:25-27 How unwise and slow you are. Jesus rebuked them for their lack of understanding of the Old Testament prophecies regarding the Messiah and explained

how these Scriptures foretold all that had taken place.

24:26 Didn't the Messiah have to suffer. The need for the Messiah to suffer was proclaimed in Isaiah 53. **and enter into His glory.** The messianic glory was a common expectation of the Jews, but His suffering was not.

24:27 Moses and all the Prophets. This was a way of referring to all the Old Testament Scriptures (16:31). Jesus claims that all the Old Testament teachings about the Servant of the Lord, the Son of Man, the Son of David, and the Messiah apply to Him. It is these teachings taken collectively that explain who He is and what He came to do.

24:30 He took the bread, blessed and broke it, and gave it to them. While this is a simple enough description of how a meal

30 It was as He reclined at the table with them that He took the bread, blessed and broke it, and gave it to them. 31 Then their eyes were opened, and they recognized Him, but He disappeared from their sight. 32 So they said to each other, "Weren't our hearts ablaze within us while He was talking with us on the road and explaining the Scriptures to us?" 33 That very hour they got up and returned to Jerusalem. They found the Eleven and those with them gathered together, 34 who said,ᵃ "The Lord has certainly been raised, and has appeared to Simon!" 35 Then they began to describe what had happened on the road and how He was made known to them in the breaking of the bread.

The Reality of the Risen Jesus

36 And as they were saying these things, He Himself stood among them. He said to them, "Peace to you!" 37 But they were startled and terrified and thought they were seeing a ghost. 38 "Why are you troubled?" He asked them. "And why do doubts arise in your hearts? 39 Look at My hands and My feet, that it is I Myself! Touch Me and see, because a ghost does not have flesh and bones as you can see I have." 40 Having said this, He showed them His hands and feet. 41 But while they still could not believeᵇ because of ₁their₁ joy and were amazed, He asked them, "Do you have anything here to eat?" 42 So they gave Him a piece of a broiled fish,ᶜ 43 and He took it and ate in their presence.

44 Then He told them, "These are My words that I spoke to you while I was still with you—that everything written about Me in the Law of Moses, the Prophets, and the Psalms must be fulfilled." 45 Then He opened their minds to understand the Scriptures. 46 He also said to them, "This is what is written:ᵈ the Messiah would suffer and rise from the dead the third day, 47 and repentance forᵉ forgiveness of sins would be proclaimed in His name to all the nations, beginning at Jerusalem. 48 You are witnesses of these things. 49 And look, I am sending youᶠ what My Father promised. As for you, stay in the cityᵍ until you are empoweredʰ from on high."

The Ascension of Jesus

50 Then He led them out as far as Bethany, and lifting up His hands He blessed them. 51 And while He was blessing them, He left them and was carried up into heaven. 52 After worshiping Him, they returned to Jerusalem with great joy. 53 And they were continually in the •temple complex blessing God.ⁱ

ᵃ**24:34** Gk is specific that this refers to the Eleven and those with them. ᵇ**24:41** Or *they still disbelieved* ᶜ**24:42** Other mss add *and some honeycomb* ᵈ**24:46** Other mss add *and thus it was necessary that* ᵉ**24:47** Other mss read *repentance and* ᶠ**24:49** Lit *upon you* ᵍ**24:49** Other mss add *of Jerusalem* ʰ**24:49** Lit *clothed with power* ⁱ**24:53** Other mss read *praising and blessing God. Amen.*

---

would begin, it is probably meant to carry overtones of the Lord's Supper (22:19).

24:31 He disappeared. The Gospels' accounts of the appearances of the resurrected Jesus indicate that while He was in His earthly form (vv. 39, 42-43; Matt. 28:9), He was not restricted by that body (John 20:19).

24:37-43 ghost. Luke described at some length the way in which Jesus proved to the disciples that He was not a ghost, an angel, nor a product of any hallucinations. The wound marks were still visible even in His resurrected body. When even that evidence seemed insufficient due to the disciples' amazement and shock, He ate before them to again show He was no ghost. Jesus truly, physically, rose from the dead (1 Cor. 15:35-49).

24:49 What My Father promised. The baptism of the Holy Spirit at Pentecost is what the Father had promised (Joel 2:28; Acts 2:14-18). It is this theme that is picked up and developed throughout the book of Acts in which Luke recorded how the Spirit empowered the early Christians (particularly Peter and Paul) to bear witness for Christ.

24:51 carried up into heaven. This is the first of two descriptions of Jesus' ascension (Acts 1:9-11).

24:53 The book ends with a note of expectancy that provides the setting for the opening of the book of Acts.

JOHN

PERSONAL READING PLAN

AUTHOR

Like the other three Gospels, the fourth Gospel is anonymous. The inscription "The Gospel According to John" or "According to John" (as found in some ancient manuscripts) was added to the text by early Christians. Yet the writer identifies himself by calling himself "the disciple who Jesus loved" (21:20-24; see also 13:23-25; 19:26-27; 20:2-8; 21:7). Who was he?

He must have been one of the 12 original disciples because he was present at the Last Supper (13:23-25; 21:20). In fact, the beloved disciple was "reclining close beside" Jesus (13:23). This gives us a valuable clue as to his identity. We know that the person reclining next to Jesus was not Peter, because Peter asked this disciple a question (13:24). The person was probably not Andrew, since Andrew is explicitly named several times in the text (1:40,44; 6:8; 12:22 Most of the other disciples are also named in this Gospel.

Some have suggested Lazarus as author of the fourth Gospel because in 11:5 Jesus is said to have loved him, but Lazarus is named in chapters 11-12. Of all the possible candidates, James and John are not named in the fourth Gospel. The beloved disciple could not have been James, since he died at the hands of Herod Agrippa I (Acts 12:2) early in the development of the church, and the fourth Gospel is written years after his death. Therefore, the author is most likely John. Indeed, early church tradition is unanimous that John the apostle wrote the fourth Gospel.

DATE

Most scholars agree that John was the last of the four Gospels to be written. It was probably composed in A.D. 80 or 90, though estimates range from the A.D. 50s to 90s.

THEME

Jesus is the giver of life.

PURPOSE

Why did John write as he did about Jesus? Two of his own statements provide the answer to this question. First, John claims: "we testify and declare to you the eternal life that was with the Father and was revealed to us ... what we have seen and heard we also declare to you, so that you may have fellowship along with us" (1 John 1:1-3). Second, John states at the end of his Gospel: "these are written so that you may believe Jesus is the Messiah, the Son of God, and by believing you may have life in His name" (John 20:31). John's Gospel also is a witness document. He tells us Jesus' story so that we will understand who Jesus is, put our faith in him as the unique Son of God, and so experience life in Christ and fellowship with other believers.

HISTORICAL BACKGROUND

What, then, do we know about John the apostle? We know that he and his brother James, along with Peter and his brother Andrew, were the first four disciples called by Jesus (Mark 1:16-20). Furthermore, James and John seem inseparable. On only one occasion is John recorded as acting alone (Luke 9:49-50). Together the two brothers want to call down fire on a village (Luke 9:54). Together they earn the title from Jesus of "Sons of Thunder" (Mark 3:17). The two of them request to be seated on Jesus' right and left in the coming kingdom (Mark 10:35-37). They are both with Jesus on the Mount of Transfiguration (Mark 9:2), in Gethsemane (Mark 14:33), and when Jairus' daughter is raised from the dead (Mark 5:37). John is right at the heart of Jesus' life and ministry.

CHARACTERISTICS

For those familiar with the Synoptic Gospels (Matthew, Mark, Luke), what strikes one so forcibly about John's Gospel is how *different* it is. John's account does not contradict the synoptics. Rather, John makes explicit what Matthew, Mark and Luke only hint at. He does not repeat material covered in the synoptics, but adds aspects of Jesus' ministry not included elsewhere. And he records for us some of Jesus' longer discourses (sermons) on great themes such as light, love, life, truth, and abiding. Here in the great *I Am* sections we listen to Jesus reveal who he is.

THE OMISSIONS

In John's Gospel, we find no information about Jesus' birth or His temptation. In this Gospel, Jesus casts out no demons, cures no lepers, almost never speaks in parables, and does not emphasize the "kingdom of God." John does not mention the institution of the Lord's Supper or Jesus' agony in the Garden of Gethsemane.

THE CONCLUSION

Instead, John tells us about portions of Jesus' ministry not discussed in the synoptics. We hear about Jesus' ministry before John the Baptist's imprisonment and Jesus' visits to Jerusalem. Perhaps most importantly, we read details of Jesus' ministry in Judea (the Synoptic Gospels focus on His Galilean ministry). John's Gospel is particularly rich when it comes to the teachings of Jesus.

John records for us some of the most beloved stories about Jesus: the wedding feast at Cana of Galilee (2:1-11); the night visit of Nicodemus (3:1-15); the conversation with the woman at the well (4:1-42); the raising of Lazarus from the dead (11:1-44); and the washing of the disciples' feet (13:1-17). In John's Gospel, we find the bulk of our Lord's teaching about the Holy Spirit, and here the "I" in the Sermon on the Mount in Matthew 5:21ff ("You have heard it said ... but I tell you) becomes the majestic "I am" who is God's own Son.

STYLE

John writes in very simple Greek with a relatively small vocabulary. He often repeats words and phrases. Yet the end is a compelling document whose very simplicity makes it impressive. In fact, some scholars suggest that this Greek sounds acquired, not native. Furthermore, the writing has a strong Jewish flavoring. This is exactly what one would expect of John, the son of Zebedee—a Jew who had lived for a long time in Galilee, an area whose population included more Gentiles than Jews.

STRUCTURE

Most scholars agree that John's Gospel begins with a distinct prologue (1:1-18) and then divides into two major parts. The first part of the Gospel concentrates on Jesus' *public ministry*. It is organized around His miracles, "signs" that reveal who He really is. This part covers most of the three years of Jesus' ministry.

In the second part, the focus shifts from the crowds to the disciples and Jesus' *private ministry* among them. The theme in this section is the *glory* that is revealed in Jesus' crucifixion and resurrection. The time period of this segment is short: from the Thursday night of the Last Supper through Jesus' post-resurrection appearances.

Additional themes run through the book. For example, the material is grouped around the major Jewish feasts. Also, the idea of the passion of Jesus is present throughout.

John recounted events from specially selected days in Jesus' life. These events present a Savior who knows "where I came from and where I am going" (8:14). Jesus' repeated references to the One "who sent me" emphasize he is truly God's Son.

John describes Jesus as the "Word" (1:1-14), the sum of all that God wanted to say to us. God communicated in the only way we could truly understand: by becoming one of us.

PASSAGES FOR TOPICAL GROUP STUDY

Prologue

1 In the beginning was the Word,[a]
and the Word was with God,
and the Word was God.

2 He was with God in the beginning.

3 All things were created through Him,
and apart from Him not one thing
was created
that has been created.

4 Life was in Him,[b]
and that life was the light of men.

5 That light shines in the darkness,
yet the darkness did not overcome[c] it.

6 There was a man named John
who was sent from God.

7 He came as a witness
to testify about the light,
so that all might believe through him.[d]

8 He was not the light,
but he came to testify about the light.

9 The true light, who gives light to everyone,
was coming into the world.[e]

10 He was in the world,
and the world was created through Him,
yet the world did not recognize Him.

11 He came to His own,[f]
and His own people[f] did not receive Him.

12 But to all who did receive Him,
He gave them the right to be[g] children of God,
to those who believe in His name,

13 who were born,
not of blood,[h]
or of the will of the flesh,
or of the will of man,[i]
but of God.

14 The Word became flesh[j]
and took up residence[k] among us.
We observed His glory,
the glory as the •One and Only Son[l]
from the Father,
full of grace and truth.

15 (John testified concerning Him and exclaimed,
"This was the One of whom I said,
'The One coming after me has surpassed me,
because He existed before me.' ")

16 Indeed, we have all received grace after grace
from His fullness,

17 for although the law was given
through Moses,
grace and truth came through Jesus Christ.

18 No one has ever seen God.[m]
The One and Only Son[n]—
the One who is at the Father's side[o]—
He has revealed Him.

John the Baptist's Testimony

19 This is John's testimony when the •Jews from Jerusalem sent priests and Levites to ask him, "Who are you?"

20 He did not refuse to answer, but he declared: "I am not the •Messiah."

21 "What then?" they asked him. "Are you Elijah?"
"I am not," he said.
"Are you the Prophet?"[p]
"No," he answered.

22 "Who are you, then?" they asked. "We need to give an answer to those who sent us. What can you tell us about yourself?"

---

[a]**1:1** The *Word* (Gk *Logos*) is a title for Jesus as the communication and the revealer of God the Father; Jn 1:14,18; Rv 19:13. [b]**1:3–4** Other punctuation is possible: . . . *not one thing was created. What was created in Him was life* [c]**1:5** Or *grasp,* or *comprehend,* or *overtake*; Jn 12:35 [d]**1:7** Or *through it* (the light) [e]**1:9** Or *The true light who comes into the world gives light to everyone,* or *The true light enlightens everyone coming into the world.* [f]**1:11** The same Gk adjective is used twice in this verse: the first refers to all that Jesus owned as Creator (*to His own*); the second refers to the Jews (*His own people*). [g]**1:12** Or *become* [h]**1:13** Lit *bloods*; the pl form of *blood* occurs only here in the NT. It may refer either to lineal descent (that is, blood from one's father and mother) or to the OT sacrificial system (that is, the various blood sacrifices). Neither is the basis for birth into the family of God. [i]**1:13** Or *not of human lineage, or of human capacity, or of human volition* [j]**1:14** The eternally existent Word (vv. 1–2) took on full humanity, but without sin; Heb 4:15. [k]**1:14** Lit *and tabernacled,* or *and dwelt in a tent*; this word occurs only here in John. A related word, referring to the Festival of Tabernacles, occurs only in 7:2; Ex 40:34–38. [l]**1:14** *Son* is implied from the reference to the Father and from Gk usage. [m]**1:18** Since God is an infinite being, no one can see Him in His absolute essential nature; Ex 33:18–23. [n]**1:18** Other mss read *God* [o]**1:18** Lit *is in the bosom of the Father* [p]**1:21** Probably = the Prophet in Dt 18:15

1:1 In the beginning. The coming of Jesus inaugurates a new creation (Gen. 1:1). **the Word.** This is the translation of the Greek word *Logos.* The Greeks taught that the *Logos* was a principle that gave order and meaning to the universe. The Old Testament spoke of the *Logos* as the divine wisdom active in creation and human affairs (Prov. 8:12-36).

1:4 life. This has a double meaning, referring to physical life and the supernatural illumination (*"the light"*) that brings spiritual life.

1:5 light ... darkness. This is another theme borrowed from Greek philosophy that is central to John's portrait of Jesus (8:12; 12:35). The light of God shines in spite of the efforts of the powers of darkness to extinguish it.

1:6 John. John the Baptist's influence was felt from Egypt to Asia Minor (Acts 18:24-26; 19:1-4).

1:10 He was in the world. This is the radically new dimension the gospel adds to Greek and Jewish ideas about the *Logos:* It is *not* an "it," but a person.

1:11 He came to His own. Israel, God's own people (Gen. 17:7), especially failed to see who Jesus was (12:37-41).

1:12 children of God. Entrance into God's family does not depend on birthright or race (v. 13), but on following God's will based on belief in Jesus.

1:14 became flesh. The Greeks believed the flesh was so worthless that the divine would have no relationship with it. They thought of spirituality as a matter of escaping the limits of the body. **took up residence among us.** Literally, "set His tent in us." This is an allusion to God's dwelling with Israel in the tabernacle

(Ex. 33:7-11). Temporarily, God lived among people in human form. **Only Son.** While Israel's kings were sometimes called "Sons of God" (Ps. 2), Jesus is God's Son in a unique sense (v. 18; 3:16,18).

1:17 Moses ... Jesus. The grace of Jesus brings life, whereas the Law of Moses could only point out the failure of people before God. **Jesus Christ.** "Christ" is the Greek term for the Hebrew title "Messiah," which means "the anointed one."

1:21 Elijah. Malachi 4:5-6 anticipated that someone like Elijah would return before the "Day of the LORD" came in final judgment. **the Prophet.** Deuteronomy 18:18 raised the expectation that one day a leader like Moses would come (4:25; 6:14).

1:23 Make straight the way of the Lord.

23 He said, "I am a **voice of one crying out in the wilderness: Make straight the way of the Lord**a—just as Isaiah the prophet said."

24 Now they had been sent from the •Pharisees. 25 So they asked him, "Why then do you baptize if you aren't the Messiah, or Elijah, or the Prophet?"

26 "I baptize withb water," John answered them. "Someone stands among you, but you don't know ⌊Him⌋. 27 He is the One coming after me,c whose sandal strap I'm not worthy to untie."

28 All this happened in Bethanyd across the Jordan,e where John was baptizing.

The Lamb of God

29 The next day John saw Jesus coming toward him and said, "Here is the Lamb of God, who takes away the sin of the world! 30 This is the One I told you about: 'After me comes a man who has surpassed me, because He existed before me.' 31 I didn't know Him, but I came baptizing withb water so He might be revealed to Israel."

32 And John testified, "I watched the Spirit descending from heaven like a dove, and He rested on Him. 33 I didn't know Him, but Hef who sent me to baptize withb water told me, 'The One you see the Spirit descending and resting on—He is the One who baptizes withb the Holy Spirit.' 34 I have seen and testified that He is the Son of God!"g

35 Again the next day, John was standing with two of his disciples. 36 When he saw Jesus passing by, he said, "Look! The Lamb of God!"

37 The two disciples heard him say this and followed Jesus. 38 When Jesus turned and noticed them following Him, He asked them, "What are you looking for?"

They said to Him, "•Rabbi" (which means "Teacher"), "where are You staying?"

39 "Come and you'll see," He replied. So they went and saw where He was staying, and they stayed with Him that day. It was about 10 in the morning.h

40 Andrew, Simon Peter's brother, was one of the two who heard John and followed Him. 41 He first found his own brother Simon and told him, "We have found the Messiah!"i (which means "Anointed One"), 42 and he brought ⌊Simon⌋ to Jesus.

When Jesus saw him, He said, "You are Simon, son of John.j You will be called •Cephas" (which means "Rock").

Philip and Nathanael

43 The next day Hek decided to leave for Galilee. Jesus found Philip and told him, "Follow Me!"

44 Now Philip was from Bethsaida, the hometown of Andrew and Peter. 45 Philip found Nathanaell and told him, "We have found the One Moses wrote about in the Law (and so did the prophets): Jesus the son of Joseph, from Nazareth!"

46 "Can anything good come out of Nazareth?" Nathanael asked him.

"Come and see," Philip answered.

47 Then Jesus saw Nathanael coming toward Him and said about him, "Here is a true Israelite; no deceit is in him."

48 "How do you know me?" Nathanael asked.

"Before Philip called you, when you were under the fig tree, I saw you," Jesus answered.

49 "Rabbi," Nathanael replied, "You are the Son of God! You are the King of Israel!"

50 Jesus responded to him, "Do you believe ⌊only⌋ because I told you I saw you under the fig tree? Youm will see greater things than this." 51 Then He said, "•I assure you: Youn will see heaven opened and the angels of God ascending and descending on the •Son of Man."

---

a**1:23** Is 40:3 b**1:26,31,33** Or *in* c**1:27** Other mss add *who came before me* d**1:28** Other mss read *in Bethabara* e**1:28** Another Bethany, near Jerusalem, was the home of Lazarus, Martha, and Mary; Jn 11:1. f**1:33** *He* refers to God the Father, who gave John a sign to help him identify the Messiah. Vv. 32–34 indicate that John did not know that Jesus was the Messiah until the Spirit descended upon Him at His baptism. g**1:34** Other mss read *is the Chosen One of God* h**1:39** Lit *about the tenth hour.* Various methods of reckoning time were used in the ancient world. John probably used a different method from the other 3 Gospels. If John used the same method of time reckoning as the other 3 Gospels, the translation would be: *It was about four in the afternoon.* i**1:41** In the NT, the word Messiah translates the Gk word *Christos* ("Anointed One"), except here and in Jn 4:25 where it translates *Messias.* j**1:42** Other mss read *Simon, son of Jonah* k**1:43** Or *he,* referring either to Peter (v. 42) or Andrew (vv. 40–41) l**1:45** Probably the Bartholomew of the other Gospels and Acts m**1:50** *You* (sg in Gk) refers to Nathanael. n**1:51** *You* is pl in Gk and refers to Nathanael and the other disciples.

When a royal figure traveled, a herald was sent ahead announcing the person's arrival so people could be prepared.

1:25 baptize. Prior to John, only Gentiles who converted to Judaism were baptized, as a sign of their cleansing from the pollutions of their Gentile past. **the Messiah.** The popular expectation was that the Messiah would be a military leader who would deliver Israel from the rule of the Romans.

1:29 the Lamb of God. Although Jesus is referred to as a lamb elsewhere in the Bible (1 Pet. 1:19; Rev. 5:6; 13:8), this exact title for Jesus occurs only here and in verse 36.

1:30 He existed before me. John speaks of the pre-existence of Jesus (vv. 1-3). This is a divine quality that Jesus claimed when He declared that He predates not only John but

Abraham (8:58).

1:32 the Spirit … and He rested upon Him. (See Isa. 11:2; 42:1.) God's Spirit would permanently abide with the Messiah, unlike the occasional movement of the Spirit on Old Testament kings and prophets.

1:38 Rabbi. Rabbis were teachers who gathered disciples around them. **staying.** This word hints that the concern in this question ("Where are you staying?") is on Jesus' true dwelling place. In this Gospel, recognition of Jesus' identity is tied up with recognizing where He is from and where He is going (8:21; 9:30; 14:2-6).

1:39 Come and you'll see. Jesus invites these followers to enter into the journey of discipleship with Him. Only as they commit themselves to follow Him will they learn His true

identity.

1:42 Cephas. The Aramaic name Cephas and the Greek name Peter both mean "rock." Although Peter seemed unstable at times (18:15-17,25-27), he eventually became the chief spokesman for the apostles and a leader in the early church (Acts 2:14).

1:43 Galilee. This province where Jesus was raised was 60 miles north of Jerusalem. The Pharisees couldn't believe that the Messiah would come from Galilee (7:41,52).

1:45 the One Moses wrote about in the Law. This refers to the Prophet to come (Deut. 18:18), the fulfillment of the Old Testament hope (v. 21).

1:46 Nazareth. This was a small, insignificant village in Galilee. It seemed impossible to Na-

The First Sign: Turning Water into Wine

2 On the third day a wedding took place in Cana of Galilee. Jesus' mother was there, and ²Jesus and His disciples were invited to the wedding as well. ³When the wine ran out, Jesus' mother told Him, "They don't have any wine."

 Wedding Woes

1. Have you ever been at a wedding where things didn't go right? What happened?

John 2:1-11

2. Why does Jesus initially tell His mother that her concerns and His are not the same?

3. Why does Jesus, after saying that, turn around and provide more wine?

4. Why would the Son of God concern Himself about whether there's enough wine at a wedding? What does this miracle show about Jesus?

5. How did this miracle display Jesus' glory (v. 11)?

6. How can you help meet a need of someone you know this week?

⁴"What has this concern of yours to do with Me,ᵃ •woman?" Jesus asked. "My hourᵇ has not yet come."

⁵"Do whatever He tells you," His mother told the servants.

⁶Now six stone water jars had been set there for Jewish purification. Each contained 20 or 30 gallons.ᶜ ⁷"Fill the jars with water," Jesus told them. So they filled them to the brim. ⁸Then He said to them, "Now draw some out and take it to the chief servant."ᵈ And they did.

⁹When the chief servant tasted the water (after it had become wine), he did not know where it came from—though the servants who had drawn the water knew. He called the groom ¹⁰and told him, "Everybody sets out the fine wine first, then, after people have drunk freely, the inferior. But you have kept the fine wine until now."

¹¹Jesus performed this first signᵉ in Cana of Galilee. He displayed His glory, and His disciples believed in Him.

¹²After this, He went down to Capernaum, together with His mother, His brothers, and His disciples, and they stayed there only a few days.

Cleansing the Temple Complex

¹³The Jewish •Passover was near, so Jesus went up to Jerusalem. ¹⁴In the •temple complex He found people selling oxen, sheep, and doves, and ⌊He also found⌋ the money changers sitting there. ¹⁵After making a whip out of cords, He drove everyone out of the temple complex with their sheep and oxen. He also poured out the money changers' coins and overturned the tables. ¹⁶He told those who were selling doves, "Get these things out of here! Stop turning My Father's house into a marketplace!"ᶠ

¹⁷And His disciples remembered that it is written: **Zeal for Your house will consume Me.**ᵍ

¹⁸So the Jews replied to Him, "What sign ⌊of authority⌋ will You show us for doing these things?"

¹⁹Jesus answered, "Destroy this sanctuary, and I will raise it up in three days."

²⁰Therefore the Jews said, "This sanctuary took 46 years to build, and will You raise it up in three days?"

²¹But He was speaking about the sanctuary of His body. ²²So when He was raised from the dead, His disciples remembered that He had said this. And they believed the Scripture and the statement Jesus had made.

²³While He was in Jerusalem at the Passover Festival, many trusted in His name when they saw the signs

---

ᵃ**2:4** Or *You and I see things differently*; lit *What to Me and to you*; Mt 8:29; Mk 1:24; 5:7; Lk 8:28 ᵇ**2:4** The time of His sacrificial death and exaltation; Jn 7:30; 8:20; 12:23,27; 13:1; 17:1 ᶜ**2:6** Lit *2 or 3 measures* ᵈ**2:8** Lit *ruler of the table*; perhaps *master of the feast*, or *headwaiter* ᵉ**2:11** Lit *this beginning of the signs*; Jn 4:54; 20:30. Seven miraculous signs occur in John's Gospel and are so noted in the headings. ᶠ**2:16** Lit *a house of business* ᵍ**2:17** Ps 69:9

---

thanael that the impressive person whom Philip described could come from such a place. **in Cana.** This village is believed to have been near Nazareth.

1:47 a true Israelite. Nathanael came to Jesus with sincerity. Israel was supposed to be a people prepared to respond to God, but it failed to reflect that purpose.

1:50 greater things. This is probably an allusion to the miracles Jesus will perform as signs of His divine identity.

1:51 the Son of Man. Of all the titles for Jesus in this chapter, this is the one He uses for Himself. Daniel 7:13 provides its background as the one invested with divine authority to rule the earth.

2:1 a wedding took place. Jesus' presence at this joyful occasion reminds us that He was not a sour ascetic who avoided the celebrations of life. **in Cana.** This village is believed to have been near Nazareth.

2:3 When the wine ran out. This situation was an embarrassment to the host because it suggested that he was too stingy to provide adequate refreshments for his guests. **Jesus' mother.** Mary appears only here and in 19:25. Her concern for this problem as well as her relationship to the servants (v. 5) indicates she may have been active in the planning of the wedding.

2:8 chief servant. This appears to be an honored guest at the wedding, serving in a role like that of a modern-day toastmaster.

2:10 Everybody sets out the fine wine first. Typically, the best wine was served when the guests were most able to appreciate it.

2:11 sign. John uses this term frequently to describe Jesus' miracles as more than acts of power. They pointed to God's presence in Jesus.

2:14 people selling oxen, sheep, and doves. This commercial activity began as a way to allow travelers to purchase animals for sacrifice at the temple rather than bringing them from long distances. But it had deteriorated into a money making scheme, with the sellers charging inflated prices.

2:18 the Jews. This word in the Gospel of John usually refers to the religious leaders in Jerusalem and Judea who were hostile to Jesus. It has more of a political sense (i.e., "the establishment") than an ethnic one.

2:19 Destroy this sanctuary, and I will raise it up in three days. The leaders misunder-

He was doing. 24 Jesus, however, would not entrust Himself to them, since He knew them all 25 and because He did not need anyone to testify about man; for He Himself knew what was in man.

Jesus and Nicodemus

3 There was a man from the •Pharisees named Nicodemus, a ruler of the Jews. 2 This man came to Him at night and said, "•Rabbi, we know that You have come from God as a teacher, for no one could perform these signs You do unless God were with him."

A Spiritual Birth

1. What is the favorite story your parents tell about the day you were born?

John 3:1-21

2. What does it mean to be "born again" (v. 3)?

3. What is the difference between being "born of the flesh" and "born of the Spirit" (v. 6)?

4. What does it really mean to believe in Jesus? How would you explain it to Nicodemus?

5. How can a person have eternal life? Is there any other way to eternal life (v. 18)?

6. Are you born again? If so, how do you know? If not, would you like to be?

3 Jesus replied, "•I assure you: Unless someone is born again,[a] he cannot see the kingdom of God."

4 "But how can anyone be born when he is old?" Nicodemus asked Him. "Can he enter his mother's womb a second time and be born?"

5 Jesus answered, "I assure you: Unless someone is born of water and the Spirit,[b] he cannot enter the kingdom of God. 6 Whatever is born of the flesh is flesh, and whatever is born of the Spirit is spirit. 7 Do not be amazed that I told you that you[c] must be born again. 8 The wind[d] blows where it pleases, and you hear its sound, but you don't know where it comes from or where it is going. So it is with everyone born of the Spirit."

9 "How can these things be?" asked Nicodemus.

10 "Are you a teacher[e] of Israel and don't know these things?" Jesus replied. 11 "I assure you: We speak what We know and We testify to what We have seen, but you[f] do not accept Our testimony.[g] 12 If I have told you about things that happen on earth and you don't believe, how will you believe if I tell you about things of heaven? 13 No one has ascended into heaven except the One who descended from heaven—the •Son of Man.[h] 14 Just as Moses lifted up the snake in the wilderness, so the Son of Man must be lifted up, 15 so that everyone who believes in Him will[i] have eternal life.

16 "For God loved the world in this way: He gave His •One and Only Son, so that everyone who believes in Him will not perish but have eternal life. 17 For God did not send His Son into the world that He might condemn the world, but that the world might be saved through Him. 18 Anyone who believes in Him is not condemned, but anyone who does not believe is already condemned, because he has not believed in the name of the One and Only Son of God.

19 "This, then, is the judgment: the light has come into the world, and people loved darkness rather than the light because their deeds were evil. 20 For everyone who practices wicked things hates the light and avoids it,[j] so that his deeds may not be exposed. 21 But anyone who lives by[k] the truth comes to the light, so that his works may be shown to be accomplished by God."[l]

a3:3 The same Gk word can mean *again* or *from above* (also in v. 7). b3:5 Or *spirit*, or *wind*; the Gk word *pneuma* can mean *wind*, *spirit*, or *Spirit*, each of which occurs in this context. c3:7 The pronoun is pl in Gk. d3:8 The Gk word *pneuma* can mean *wind*, *spirit*, or *Spirit*, each of which occurs in this context. e3:10 Or *the teacher* f3:11 The word *you* in Gk is pl here and throughout v. 12. g3:11 The pl forms (*We*, *Our*) refer to Jesus and His authority to speak for the Father. h3:13 Other mss add *who is in heaven* i3:15 Other mss add *not perish, but* j3:20 Lit *and does not come to the light* k3:21 Lit *who does* l3:21 It is possible that Jesus' words end at v. 15. Ancient Gk did not have quotation marks.

stood what Jesus means by this statement. After the resurrection, the disciples realized that Jesus was referring to Himself as the true place in which God dwells (1:14,51).

2:25 He Himself knew what was in man. The Scriptures (1 Kings 8:39) and the rabbis taught that only God could know this.

3:1 Pharisees. The Pharisees believed that religious and ethical purity was the way to secure God's favor. They were concerned for the fine points of the law, which tended to overshadow its purpose. **Nicodemus.** A respected religious authority (v. 10), Nicodemus also appears in 7:50 and 19:39 but in no other Gospel. **ruler of the Jews.** Nicodemus was a member of the Sanhedrin—the religious and political governing body of Judea.

3:3 born again. This phrase can be translated in two ways—"born again" or "born from

above." "Born again" emphasizes the radical reorientation of life that results from trusting Jesus. "Born from above" declares that spiritual life is a gift from God, not something we can earn (1:12-13).

3:13 ascended into heaven except. This Gospel's witness to Jesus is from the perspective of the whole story already told; hence the author can refer to the ascension of Jesus even at this point.

3:14 snake. Because of the Israelites' rebellion in the wilderness, God sent deadly serpents among them. Then in His mercy He instructed Moses to put a statue of a serpent on a pole. Whoever looked upon that serpent would not die (Num. 21:4-9). In a similar way, when people look with faith upon Jesus who is "lifted up" (on the cross), they are rescued from God's judgment (6:40).

3:15 eternal life. This type of life is more than never-ending existence. It also means the quality of fullness, goodness, and perfection of life with God.

3:16 God loved the world in this way. The great motivation behind God's plan of salvation (1 John 4:9-10). **He gave.** This is demonstrated especially in Jesus' incarnation and crucifixion.

3:17 that the world might be saved through Him. The purpose of Jesus' mission was to provide access to God for all who believe.

3:18 already condemned. It is our own behavior that condemns us. Through Jesus, God saves us from the condemnation that results from our own actions. **Only Son of God.** Jesus is the unique Son of God because He alone fully reflects the Father.

Jesus and John the Baptist

22 After this, Jesus and His disciples went to the Judean countryside, where He spent time with them and baptized. 23 John also was baptizing in Aenon near Salim, because there was plenty of water there. People were coming and being baptized, 24 since John had not yet been thrown into prison.

25 Then a dispute arose between John's disciples and a •Jew[a] about purification. 26 So they came to John and told him, "Rabbi, the One you testified about, and who was with you across the Jordan, is baptizing—and everyone is flocking to Him."

27 John responded, "No one can receive a single thing unless it's given to him from heaven. 28 You yourselves can testify that I said, 'I am not the •Messiah, but I've been sent ahead of Him.' 29 He who has the bride is the groom. But the groom's friend, who stands by and listens for him, rejoices greatly[b] at the groom's voice. So this joy of mine is complete. 30 He must increase, but I must decrease."

The One from Heaven

31 The One who comes from above is above all. The one who is from the earth is earthly and speaks in earthly terms.[c] The One who comes from heaven is above all. 32 He testifies to what He has seen and heard, yet no one accepts His testimony. 33 The one who has accepted His testimony has affirmed that God is true. 34 For God sent Him, and He speaks God's words, since He[d] gives the Spirit without measure. 35 The Father loves the Son and has given all things into His hands. 36 The one who believes in the Son has eternal life, but the one who refuses to believe in the Son will not see life; instead, the wrath of God remains on him.

Jesus and the Samaritan Woman

4 When Jesus[e] knew that the •Pharisees heard He was making and baptizing more disciples than John 2 (though Jesus Himself was not baptizing, but His disciples were), 3 He left Judea and went again to Galilee. 4 He had to travel through Samaria, 5 so He came to a town of Samaria called Sychar near the property[f] that Jacob had given his son Joseph. 6 Jacob's well was there, and Jesus, worn out from His journey, sat down at the well. It was about six in the evening.[g]

It's Alive!

1. When you're really thirsty, what quenches your thirst the best?

John 4:1-26

2. What is the "living water" that Jesus was talking about? What did the woman think He meant?

3. Why did Jesus tell the woman to go get her husband and bring him back? How did that question force the woman to understand what Jesus was saying?

4. What did Jesus mean when He said that "true worshipers will worship the Father in spirit and truth" (v. 23)?

5. What helps you to worship God in spirit and truth?

7 A woman of Samaria came to draw water.

"Give Me a drink," Jesus said to her, 8 for His disciples had gone into town to buy food.

9 "How is it that You, a Jew, ask for a drink from me, a Samaritan woman?" she asked Him. For Jews do not associate with[h] Samaritans.[i]

10 Jesus answered, "If you knew the gift of God, and who is saying to you, 'Give Me a drink,' you would ask Him, and He would give you living water."

11 "Sir," said the woman, "You don't even have a bucket, and the well is deep. So where do you get this 'living water'? 12 You aren't greater than our father

---

a**3:25** Other mss read *and the Jews*   b**3:29** Lit *with joy rejoices*   c**3:31** Or *of earthly things*   d**3:34** Other mss read *since God*   e**4:1** Other mss read *the Lord*   f**4:5** Lit *piece of land*   g**4:6** Lit *the sixth hour*; see note at Jn 1:39; an alternate time reckoning would be *noon*   h**4:9** Or *do not share vessels with*   i**4:9** Other mss omit *For Jews do not associate with Samaritans.*

3:19-20 light … darkness. Just as 3:16-18 sums up the good news of the gospel, so these verses sum up the human situation that makes the gospel necessary. The problem is not a lack of understanding of the "light," but a preference for the "darkness."

3:21 anyone who lives by the truth. This stands in parallel with "everyone who believes in Him" (v. 16) and in contrast with "everyone who practices wicked things" (v. 20). Together, these phrases show that belief in Jesus and a lifestyle marked by obedience to God's ways go hand-in-hand (1 John 3:10).

3:22 to the Judean countryside … baptized. The other Gospel writers do not mention this stage of Jesus' ministry. John 4:2 says it was not Jesus who baptized, but His disciples.

3:26 everyone is flocking to Him. Some of John's disciples were upset that Jesus was

becoming more popular than their master.

3:29 the groom's friend. This refers to John the Baptist, whose purpose was to prepare people for the coming of the Messiah (1:31).

4:1-3 the Pharisees heard. The Pharisees had already investigated John (1:24-27) because of his challenge to their beliefs and authority (Matt. 3:7-10; Mark 11:27-33). Jesus' popularity fueled their suspicions as well.

4:4 Samaria. This was a territory between the provinces of Judea and Galilee. When the northern kingdom of Israel was conquered in 722 B.C. by the Assyrians, many of its people were deported. Exiles from other areas of the vast Assyrian Empire were brought in (2 Kings 17:24-41). Many of these people intermarried with the remaining Israelites and adopted some of the Jewish religious practices. In Jesus' day, strict Jews avoided Samaria as an

unclean area, and the term "Samaritan" was used as an insult (8:48).

4:5 the property that Jacob had given his son Joseph. Genesis 48:22 tells of Jacob giving some land to Joseph.

4:7 came to draw water. Translations differ in the time of day of this encounter. The Samaritan woman probably came at this time to avoid other women, perhaps because of their criticism of the life she lived.

4:9 Jews do not associate with Samaritans. Since some sects of Judaism regarded Samaritans as unclean from birth, Jesus' request shocks the woman.

4:10 living water. This was a common phrase referring to water that flowed from a brook or spring. Water like this was better than the stagnant water of a well or a pond.

Jacob, are you? He gave us the well and drank from it himself, as did his sons and livestock."

¹³ Jesus said, "Everyone who drinks from this water will get thirsty again. ¹⁴ But whoever drinks from the water that I will give him will never get thirsty again— ever! In fact, the water I will give him will become a wellᵃ of water springing up within him for eternal life."

¹⁵ "Sir," the woman said to Him, "give me this water so I won't get thirsty and come here to draw water."

¹⁶ "Go call your husband," He told her, "and come back here."

¹⁷ "I don't have a husband," she answered.

"You have correctly said, 'I don't have a husband,'" Jesus said. ¹⁸ "For you've had five husbands, and the man you now have is not your husband. What you have said is true."

¹⁹ "Sir," the woman replied, "I see that You are a prophet. ²⁰ Our fathers worshiped on this mountain,ᵇ yet you ⌊Jews⌋ say that the place to worship is in Jerusalem."

²¹ Jesus told her, "Believe Me, •woman, an hour is coming when you will worship the Father neither on this mountain nor in Jerusalem. ²² You Samaritansᶜ worship what you do not know. We worship what we do know, because salvation is from the Jews. ²³ But an hour is coming, and is now here, when the true worshipers will worship the Father in spirit and truth. Yes, the Father wants such people to worship Him. ²⁴ God is spirit, and those who worship Him must worship in spirit and truth."

²⁵ The woman said to Him, "I know that •Messiahᵈ is coming" (who is called Christ). "When He comes, He will explain everything to us."

²⁶ "I am ⌊He⌋," Jesus told her, "the One speaking to you."

The Ripened Harvest

²⁷ Just then His disciples arrived, and they were amazed that He was talking with a woman. Yet no one said, "What do You want?" or "Why are You talking with her?"

²⁸ Then the woman left her water jar, went into town, and told the men, ²⁹ "Come, see a man who told me everything I ever did! Could this be the Messiah?" ³⁰ They left the town and made their way to Him.

³¹ In the meantime the disciples kept urging Him, "•Rabbi, eat something."

³² But He said, "I have food to eat that you don't know about."

³³ The disciples said to one another, "Could someone have brought Him something to eat?"

³⁴ "My food is to do the will of Him who sent Me and to finish His work," Jesus told them. ³⁵ "Don't you say, 'There are still four more months, then comes the harvest'? Listen ⌊to what⌋ I'm telling you: Openᵉ your eyes and look at the fields, for they are readyᶠ for harvest. ³⁶ The reaper is already receiving pay and gathering fruit for eternal life, so the sower and reaper can rejoice together. ³⁷ For in this case the saying is true: 'One sows and another reaps.' ³⁸ I sent you to reap what you didn't labor for; others have labored, and you have benefited fromᵍ their labor."

The Savior of the World

³⁹ Now many Samaritans from that town believed in Him because of what the woman saidʰ when she testified, "He told me everything I ever did." ⁴⁰ Therefore, when the Samaritans came to Him, they asked Him to stay with them, and He stayed there two days. ⁴¹ Many more believed because of what He said.ⁱ ⁴² And they told the woman, "We no longer believe because of what you said, for we have heard for ourselves and know that this really is the Savior of the world."ʲ

A Galilean Welcome

⁴³ After two days He left there for Galilee. ⁴⁴ Jesus Himself testified that a prophet has no honor in his own country. ⁴⁵ When they entered Galilee, the Galileans welcomed Him because they had seen everything He

---

ᵃ**4:14** Or *spring* ᵇ**4:20** Mount Gerizim, where there had been a Samaritan temple that rivaled Jerusalem's ᶜ**4:22** *Samaritans* is implied since the Gk verb and pronoun are pl. ᵈ**4:25** In the NT, the word Messiah translates the Gk word *Christos* ("Anointed One"), except here and in Jn 1:41 where it translates *Messias*. ᵉ**4:35** Lit *Raise* ᶠ**4:35** Lit *white* ᵍ**4:38** Lit *you have entered into* ʰ**4:39** Lit *because of the woman's word* ⁱ**4:41** Lit *because of His word* ʲ**4:42** Other mss add *the Messiah*

4:17-18 You have correctly said. Women in Bible times could be divorced by their husbands for trivial reasons, but they had no right to divorce their husbands. This Samaritan woman may have been abandoned by one or more of her husbands and was a mistress to the man she was living with at this time.

4:19 prophet. Jesus' knowledge of this woman's life led her to see Him as a prophet who must be taken seriously.

4:21-24 worship in spirit and in truth. In 2:18-22 Jesus had shown that He is the new temple that is superior to the physical building in Jerusalem. Here He shows that He is superior to the religious claims of the Samaritans. The point is not where a person worships, but whom.

4:23 an hour is coming, and is now here. This captures the tension of the gospel's announcement about the kingdom of God. It is both present and future.

4:29 Come, see. This is the same invitation to discipleship extended to Andrew and Nathanael (1:39-40,46). **Could this be the Messiah?** The phrase in Greek appears to require a negative answer, but it hopes for a positive response.

4:34 Him who sent Me. Jesus often uses this phrase as a title for the Father. It emphasizes His awareness of His mission and His sense of operating within His Father's will. This purpose filled Him with satisfaction ("My food").

4:35 four more months, then comes the harvest. This common saying may have in-

dicated that there was no great rush to finish a task (i.e., no matter what you do, it still takes four months for the harvest to grow). Jesus contradicted that proverb by insisting that, although He has only just "sown the seed" of the gospel with the woman, already a harvest is about to be gathered. The disciples are to see the urgency of the work of the kingdom.

4:37 One sows and another reaps. By talking with this woman, Jesus reaps the work of His Father, the sower. But in verse 38 it will be the disciples who reap what others (such as Jesus, John the Baptist, and the prophets) have sown.

4:42 Savior. This is the only place in the Gospels where this title is applied to Jesus. In the Old Testament, it refers to God as the one who rescues (Isa. 43:3,11; 49:6; Jer.

did in Jerusalem during the festival. For they also had gone to the festival.

The Second Sign: Healing an Official's Son

⁴⁶ Then He went again to Cana of Galilee, where He had turned the water into wine. There was a certain royal official whose son was ill at Capernaum. ⁴⁷ When this man heard that Jesus had come from Judea into Galilee, he went to Him and pleaded with Him to come down and heal his son, for he was about to die.

⁴⁸ Jesus told him, "Unless you ˌpeopleˌ see signs and wonders, you will not believe."

⁴⁹ "Sir," the official said to Him, "come down before my boy dies!"

⁵⁰ "Go," Jesus told him, "your son will live." The man believed whatᵃ Jesus said to him and departed.

⁵¹ While he was still going down, his •slaves met him saying that his boy was alive. ⁵² He asked them at what time he got better. "Yesterday at seven in the morningᵇ the fever left him," they answered. ⁵³ The father realized this was the very hour at which Jesus had told him, "Your son will live." Then he himself believed, along with his whole household.

⁵⁴ This therefore was the second sign Jesus performed after He came from Judea to Galilee.

The Third Sign: Healing the Sick

5 After this, a Jewish festival took place, and Jesus went up to Jerusalem. ² By the Sheep Gate in Jerusalem there is a pool, called Bethesdaᶜ in Hebrew, which has five colonnades.ᵈ ³ Within these lay a multitude of the sick—blind, lame, and paralyzed ˌ—waiting for the moving of the water, ⁴ because an angel would go down into the pool from time to time and stir up the water. Then the first one who got in after the water was stirred up recovered from whatever ailment he hadˌ.ᵉ

⁵ One man was there who had been sick for 38 years. ⁶ When Jesus saw him lying there and knew he had already been there a long time, He said to him, "Do you want to get well?"

⁷ "Sir," the sick man answered, "I don't have a man to put me into the pool when the water is stirred up, but while I'm coming, someone goes down ahead of me."

Exercising Faith Muscles

1. How important is it to you to stay physically fit? What are you doing to keep in shape?

John 5:1-15

2. Why did Jesus ask the man if he wanted to get well (vv. 5-6)?
3. Why did Jesus command him to pick up his bedroll and walk? How did that demonstrate the man's faith?
4. In what area of life might Jesus be asking you to exercise some faith?
5. Is there some healing that you need: Physical? Spiritual? Emotional? Other?

⁸ "Get up," Jesus told him, "pick up your bedroll and walk!" ⁹ Instantly the man got well, picked up his bedroll, and started to walk.

Now that day was the Sabbath, ¹⁰ so the •Jews said to the man who had been healed, "This is the Sabbath! It's illegal for you to pick up your bedroll."

¹¹ He replied, "The man who made me well told me, 'Pick up your bedroll and walk.' "

¹² "Who is this man who told you, 'Pick up ˌyour bedrollˌ and walk?'" they asked. ¹³ But the man who was cured did not know who it was, because Jesus had slipped away into the crowd that was there.ᶠ

¹⁴ After this, Jesus found him in the •temple complex and said to him, "See, you are well. Do not sin any

---

ᵃ**4:50** Lit *the word* ᵇ**4:52** Or *seven in the evening*; lit *at the seventh hour*; see note at Jn 1:39; an alternate time reckoning would be *at one in the afternoon* ᶜ**5:2** Other mss read *Bethzatha*; other mss read *Bethsaida* ᵈ**5:2** Rows of columns supporting a roof ᵉ**5:3–4** Other mss omit bracketed text ᶠ**5:13** Lit *slipped away, there being a crowd in that place*

14:8). It is another reference to the deity of Christ. **of the world.** The Gospel of John emphasizes that Jesus' mission involves all types of people (3:16; 8:12; 10:16; 17:20). The religious leaders rejected Jesus, but these "unclean Samaritans"—recognizing that God's plan included them—embraced it with joy!

4:44 a prophet has no honor in his own country. In the other Gospels this phrase is linked to Jesus' rejection in Nazareth (Matt. 13:57; Mark 6:4; Luke 4:24). Why it is mentioned here is uncertain. It may be in anticipation of the fact that while Jesus' initial reception in Galilee would be positive (v. 45), the people would ultimately reject Him.

4:48 you. Unless you people see ... you will not believe. The reliance on miracles as

an evidence to produce faith did not meet with Jesus' approval. Such faith lacked the depth of conviction found in people who believed because of the truth of what He said.

4:50 The man believed. The man stands in contrast to the crowds in verse 48 by becoming an example of what faith in Jesus is all about—to trust His promises upon His authority.

4:54 the second sign. John's Gospel numbers only the first sign of Jesus at Cana (2:11) and this one—in spite of the fact that many other signs are alluded to and five more are spelled out.

5:2 Bethesda. This pool in Jerusalem has been excavated. Fed by intermittent springs, it was seen as a healing shrine even by second-century Roman cults.

5:7 I don't have a man to put me into the pool. The man did not expect to be healed by Jesus. He only hoped that Jesus might help him get into the water at the next healing opportunity.

5:10 It's illegal for you to pick up your bedroll. This is one example of the many traditions the rabbis had developed to help people obey the law.

5:13 had slipped away. Apparently Jesus had not identified Himself to this man or others in the crowd. He didn't stay around to make sure He got the credit for this healing.

5:14 Do not sin any more, so that something worse doesn't happen to you. Jesus did not accept the common idea that suffering and disease were the result of personal sin (9:1-3).

more, so that something worse doesn't happen to you." [15] The man went and reported to the Jews that it was Jesus who had made him well.

Honoring the Father and the Son

[16] Therefore, the Jews began persecuting Jesus[a] because He was doing these things on the Sabbath. [17] But Jesus responded to them, "My Father is still working, and I am working also." [18] This is why the Jews began trying all the more to kill Him: not only was He breaking the Sabbath, but He was even calling God His own Father, making Himself equal with God.

[19] Then Jesus replied, "•I assure you: The Son is not able to do anything on His own, but only what He sees the Father doing. For whatever the Father[b] does, the Son also does these things in the same way. [20] For the Father loves the Son and shows Him everything He is doing, and He will show Him greater works than these so that you will be amazed. [21] And just as the Father raises the dead and gives them life, so the Son also gives life to anyone He wants to. [22] The Father, in fact, judges no one but has given all judgment to the Son, [23] so that all people will honor the Son just as they honor the Father. Anyone who does not honor the Son does not honor the Father who sent Him.

Life and Judgment

[24] "I assure you: Anyone who hears My word and believes Him who sent Me has eternal life and will not come under judgment but has passed from death to life. [25] "I assure you: An hour is coming, and is now here, when the dead will hear the voice of the Son of God, and those who hear will live. [26] For just as the Father has life in Himself, so also He has granted to the Son to have life in Himself. [27] And He has granted Him the right to pass judgment, because He is the •Son of Man. [28] Do not be amazed at this, because a time is coming when all who are in the graves will hear His voice [29] and come out—those who have done good things, to the resurrection of life, but those who have done wicked things, to the resurrection of judgment.

[30] "I can do nothing on My own. I judge only as I hear, and My judgment is righteous, because I do not seek My own will, but the will of Him who sent Me.

Four Witnesses to Jesus

[31] "If I testify about Myself, My testimony is not valid.[c] [32] There is Another who testifies about Me, and I know that the testimony He gives about Me is valid.[d] [33] You have sent messengers to John, and he has testified to the truth. [34] I don't receive man's testimony, but I say these things so that you may be saved. [35] John[e] was a burning and shining lamp, and for a time you were willing to enjoy his light.

[36] "But I have a greater testimony than John's because of the works that the Father has given Me to accomplish. These very works I am doing testify about Me that the Father has sent Me. [37] The Father who sent Me has Himself testified about Me. You have not heard His voice at any time, and you haven't seen His form. [38] You don't have His word living in you, because you don't believe the One He sent. [39] You pore over[f] the Scriptures because you think you have eternal life in them, yet they testify about Me. [40] And you are not willing to come to Me that you may have life.

[41] "I do not accept glory from men, [42] but I know you—that you have no love for God within you. [43] I have come in My Father's name, yet you don't accept Me. If someone else comes in his own name, you will accept him. [44] How can you believe? While accepting glory from one another, you don't seek the glory that comes from the only God. [45] Do not think that I will accuse you to the Father. Your accuser is Moses, on whom you have set your hope. [46] For if you believed Moses, you would believe Me, because he wrote about Me. [47] But if you don't believe his writings, how will you believe My words?"

The Fourth Sign: Feeding 5,000

6 After this, Jesus crossed the Sea of Galilee (or Tiberias). [2] And a huge crowd was following Him because they saw the signs that He was performing on

---

[a]5:16 Other mss add and trying to kill Him [b]5:19 Lit whatever that One [c]5:31 Or not true [d]5:32 Or true [e]5:35 Lit That man [f]5:39 In Gk this could be a command: Pore over . . .

5:25 An hour is coming, and is now here. Jesus says new life occurs as those who are spiritually dead respond to the Son who will give them true life (1:12).

5:32 Another. This means the Father.

5:35 John was a burning and shining lamp. A reference to the lamp of Psalm 132:17 which God would set up to light the way for His "Anointed One."

5:45 Your accuser is Moses. The Jewish religious leaders believed Jesus had rejected the law, but it was they who had abandoned it. Therefore, it was the law, in which they prided themselves, that would condemn them.

6:1 Sea of Galilee (or Tiberias). Tiberias was a city founded on the shore of the Sea of

Galilee in A.D. 20 by Herod, Roman ruler of the area. By the time this Gospel was written, this new name for the Sea of Galilee had become well known.

6:4 the Passover. Passover celebrated Israel's deliverance from Egypt (Ex. 12:1-13). At that time, each family of Israel was to sacrifice a lamb, eat it, and put its blood on the doorframes of their homes so God's avenging angel would "pass over" their houses as Egypt was punished. Hence the lamb's blood was accepted in place of their firstborn, and its flesh nourished them for their escape from Egypt. The Passover theme makes sense of the transition from "bread" to "flesh" later in verse 51, since Jesus is the true Lamb whose blood assures deliverance from God's wrath and whose flesh nurtures believers into life. This assurance is a gift each person must choose on his own.

6:9 five barley loaves and two fish. Barley bread was used by the poor because it was less expensive than wheat. From Luke 11:5 we may assume that three loaves were normally a meal. At most the boy had provisions for two people. **but what are they for so many?** The question asked by Andrew and Philip is similar to the response of Moses when the people asked for meat in the wilderness (Num. 11:23).

6:10 numbered about 5,000. According to Matthew 14:21, this number did not include women and children.

6:14-15 This really is the Prophet. The people see by this action that Jesus is far more than a healer. He has done far greater things than the prophets of old.

6:16-21 The inadequacy of the crowd's as-

the sick. ³ So Jesus went up a mountain and sat down there with His disciples.

⁴ Now the •Passover, a Jewish festival, was near. ⁵ Therefore, when Jesus looked up and noticed a huge crowd coming toward Him, He asked Philip, "Where will we buy bread so these people can eat?" ⁶ He asked this to test him, for He Himself knew what He was going to do.

⁷ Philip answered, "Two hundred •denarii worth of bread wouldn't be enough for each of them to have a little."

⁸ One of His disciples, Andrew, Simon Peter's brother, said to Him, ⁹ "There's a boy here who has five barley loaves and two fish—but what are they for so many?"

¹⁰ Then Jesus said, "Have the people sit down."

There was plenty of grass in that place, so they sat down. The men numbered about 5,000. ¹¹ Then Jesus took the loaves, and after giving thanks He distributed them to those who were seated—so also with the fish, as much as they wanted.

¹² When they were full, He told His disciples, "Collect the leftovers so that nothing is wasted." ¹³ So they collected them and filled 12 baskets with the pieces from the five barley loaves that were left over by those who had eaten.

¹⁴ When the people saw the signᵃ He had done, they said, "This really is the Prophet who was to come into the world!" ¹⁵ Therefore, when Jesus knew that they were about to come and take Him by force to make Him king, He withdrew againᵇ to the mountain by Himself.

The Fifth Sign: Walking on Water

¹⁶ When evening came, His disciples went down to the sea, ¹⁷ got into a boat, and started across the sea to Capernaum. Darkness had already set in, but Jesus had not yet come to them. ¹⁸ Then a high wind arose, and the sea began to churn. ¹⁹ After they had rowed about three or four miles,ᶜ they saw Jesus walking on the sea. He was coming near the boat, and they were afraid.

²⁰ But He said to them, "It is I.ᵈ Don't be afraid!" ²¹ Then they were willing to take Him on board, and at once the boat was at the shore where they were heading.

The Bread of Life

²² The next day, the crowd that had stayed on the other side of the sea knew there had been only one boat.ᵉ ⸤They also knew⸥ that Jesus had not boarded the boat with His disciples, but that His disciples had gone off alone. ²³ Some boats from Tiberias came near the place where they ate the bread after the Lord gave thanks. ²⁴ When the crowd saw that neither Jesus nor His disciples were there, they got into the boats and went to Capernaum looking for Jesus.

²⁵ When they found Him on the other side of the sea, they said to Him, "•Rabbi, when did You get here?"

²⁶ Jesus answered, "•I assure you: You are looking for Me, not because you saw the signs, but because you ate the loaves and were filled. ²⁷ Don't work for the food that perishes but for the food that lasts for eternal life, which the •Son of Man will give you, because God the Father has set His seal of approval on Him."

²⁸ "What can we do to perform the works of God?" they asked.

²⁹ Jesus replied, "This is the work of God: that you believe in the One He has sent."

³⁰ "What sign then are You going to do so we may see and believe You?" they asked. "What are You going to perform? ³¹ Our fathers ate the manna in the wilderness, just as it is written: **He gave them bread from heaven to eat.**"ᶠ ᵍ

³² Jesus said to them, "I assure you: Moses didn't give you the bread from heaven, but My Father gives you the real bread from heaven. ³³ For the bread of God is the One who comes down from heaven and gives life to the world."

³⁴ Then they said, "Sir, give us this bread always!"

³⁵ "I am the bread of life," Jesus told them. "No one who comes to Me will ever be hungry, and no one who

---

ᵃ**6:14** Other mss read *signs*   ᵇ**6:15** A previous withdrawal is mentioned in Mk 6:31–32, an event that occurred just before the feeding of the 5,000.
ᶜ**6:19** Lit *25 or 30 stadia; 1 stadion = 600 feet*   ᵈ**6:20** Lit *I am*   ᵉ**6:22** Other mss add *into which His disciples had entered*   ᶠ**6:31** Bread miraculously provided by God for the Israelites   ᵍ**6:31** Ex 16:4; Ps 78:24

---

sessment of Jesus as simply a political leader is shown in this scene of Old Testament allusions that reveal Jesus' divine glory to the Twelve.

6:19 three or four miles. This would be about halfway across the lake. The lake, surrounded by high hills, was often buffeted by strong winds and rainstorms.

6:20 It is I. While the disciples may have originally taken it only as a statement of identification, Jesus is calming them by the assurance of His presence. He is the Son of God who controls the wind and sea, so they shouldn't be afraid (Pss. 29:3; 77:19). **Don't be afraid!** The call not to fear echoes God's assurance to Israel of His presence and protection.

6:25 Rabbi, when did You get here? Their

real question of course is not "when," but "how"?

6:26 not because you saw the signs. The crowd saw Jesus only as a way of getting their physical needs met.

6:27 food that lasts for eternal life. Jesus challenges the crowd to examine their priorities and to realize that He has come to provide the "food" that will save them from spiritual hunger and death.

6:29 This is the work of God. The crowd was looking for the laws Jesus wanted them to obey so they might have God's favor (v. 28). Jesus lets them see that only one thing is required (note the singular "work" in contrast to the plural "works"—v. 28)—belief in Him.

6:30 What sign then are You going to do?

Some messianic expectations included the idea that the Messiah would display miracles greater than those that had been performed by Moses in the wilderness. Since Jesus had only fed the people once, they referred to this specific scene in hopes that He might provide for their needs continually as Moses had done. **so we may see and believe You?** As in 5:44, the problem was not a lack of evidence but a concern for people's praise more than God's. The people were unable to see what was going on because of their preoccupation with the things of this life.

6:34 give us this bread always! Just as the disciples thought in physical terms when they found Jesus talking with the Samaritan woman, so do these people (4:32-33).

6:37 I will never cast out. Those who come to

---

believes in Me will ever be thirsty again. ³⁶ But as I told you, you've seen Me,ᵃ and yet you do not believe. ³⁷ Everyone the Father gives Me will come to Me, and the one who comes to Me I will never cast out. ³⁸ For I have come down from heaven, not to do My will, but the will of Him who sent Me. ³⁹ This is the will of Him who sent Me: that I should lose none of those He has given Me but should raise them up on the last day. ⁴⁰ For this is the will of My Father: that everyone who sees the Son and believes in Him may have eternal life, and I will raise him up on the last day."

⁴¹ Therefore the Jews started complaining about Him, because He said, "I am the bread that came down from heaven." ⁴² They were saying, "Isn't this Jesus the son of Joseph, whose father and mother we know? How can He now say, 'I have come down from heaven'?"

⁴³ Jesus answered them, "Stop complaining among yourselves. ⁴⁴ No one can come to Me unless the Father who sent Me drawsᵇ him, and I will raise him up on the last day. ⁴⁵ It is written in the Prophets: **And they will all be taught by God.**ᶜ Everyone who has listened to and learned from the Father comes to Me— ⁴⁶ not that anyone has seen the Father except the One who is from God. He has seen the Father.

⁴⁷ "I assure you: Anyone who believesᵈ has eternal life. ⁴⁸ I am the bread of life. ⁴⁹ Your fathers ate the manna in the wilderness, and they died. ⁵⁰ This is the bread that comes down from heaven so that anyone may eat of it and not die. ⁵¹ I am the living bread that came down from heaven. If anyone eats of this bread he will live forever. The bread that I will give for the life of the world is My flesh."

⁵² At that, the Jews argued among themselves, "How can this man give us His flesh to eat?"

⁵³ So Jesus said to them, "I assure you: Unless you eat the flesh of the Son of Man and drink His blood, you do not have life in yourselves. ⁵⁴ Anyone who eats My flesh and drinks My blood has eternal life, and I will raise him up on the last day, ⁵⁵ because My flesh is real food and

My blood is real drink. ⁵⁶ The one who eats My flesh and drinks My blood lives in Me, and I in him. ⁵⁷ Just as the living Father sent Me and I live because of the Father, so the one who feeds on Me will live because of Me. ⁵⁸ This is the bread that came down from heaven; it is not like the mannaᵉ your fathers ate—and they died. The one who eats this bread will live forever."

⁵⁹ He said these things while teaching in the •synagogue in Capernaum.

Many Disciples Desert Jesus

⁶⁰ Therefore, when many of His disciples heard this, they said, "This teaching is hard! Who can acceptᶠ it?"

⁶¹ Jesus, knowing in Himself that His disciples were complaining about this, asked them, "Does this offend you? ⁶² Then what if you were to observe the Son of Man ascending to where He was before? ⁶³ The Spirit is the One who gives life. The flesh doesn't help at all. The words that I have spoken to you are spirit and are life. ⁶⁴ But there are some among you who don't believe." (For Jesus knew from the beginning those who would notᵍ believe and the one who would betray Him.) ⁶⁵ He said, "This is why I told you that no one can come to Me unless it is granted to him by the Father."

⁶⁶ From that moment many of His disciples turned back and no longer accompanied Him. ⁶⁷ Therefore Jesus said to the Twelve, "You don't want to go away too, do you?"

⁶⁸ Simon Peter answered, "Lord, who will we go to? You have the words of eternal life. ⁶⁹ We have come to believe and know that You are the Holy One of God!"ʰ

⁷⁰ Jesus replied to them, "Didn't I choose you, the Twelve? Yet one of you is the Devil!" ⁷¹ He was referring to Judas, Simon Iscariot's son,ⁱ ʲ one of the Twelve, because he was going to betray Him.

The Unbelief of Jesus' Brothers

7 After this, Jesus traveled in Galilee, since He did not want to travel in Judea because the •Jews were trying to kill Him. ² The Jewish Festival of Tabernaclesᵏ ˡ was near, ³ so His brothers said to Him, "Leave here and

---

^a**6:36** Other mss omit *Me* ^b**6:44** Or *brings*, or *leads*; see the use of this Gk verb in Jn 12:32; 21:6; Ac 16:19; Jms 2:6. ^c**6:45** Is 54:13 ^d**6:47** Other mss add *in Me* ^e**6:58** Other mss omit *the manna* ^f**6:60** Lit *hear* ^g**6:64** Other mss omit *not* ^h**6:69** Other mss read *You are the Messiah, the Son of the Living God* ⁱ**6:71** Other mss read *Judas Iscariot, Simon's son* ^j**6:71** Lit *Judas, of Simon Iscariot* ^k**7:2** Or *Booths* ^l**7:2** One of 3 great Jewish religious festivals, along with Passover and Pentecost; Ex 23:14; Dt 16:16

Jesus are a gift from the Father. As such, they enjoy a sense of ultimate security that no human can offer.

6:39 I should lose none of those. Jesus' purpose was to do the Father's will. God's desire is that none of those who come to His Son would be lost but will be raised from death on the last day.

6:40 the will of My Father. Two crucial themes, each emphasizing God's grace, are summed up here: (1) Salvation is open to all who will believe Jesus, and (2) Salvation is a gift to be received. It is God's desire that all people accept His gift (2 Pet. 3:9).

6:42 Isn't this Jesus the son of Joseph? Jesus' description of Himself as "the bread that came down from heaven" evoked complaints from the religious leaders. A common

saying in English is "familiarity breeds contempt." These religious leaders knew the small village Jesus came from and knew his father, Joseph. The very ordinariness of Jesus' background was a stumbling block to their seeing Jesus for Who He was (is). Their expectation was that Messiah would come as a warrior or as a heavenly Son of man coming on clouds of glory.

6:44 No one can come to me unless. Jesus answers the religious leaders' complaints by reminding them that God draws people to Jesus. Human perception and understanding are insufficient to see what God is doing. The religious leaders and Jesus read the same Scriptures but they weren't seeing or understanding the same thing. Rabbis quoted interpretations of the Scriptures at great length. Jesus' teaching was different. He taught in a direct, authoritative style and not like the reli-

gious teachers.

6:45 And they will all be taught by God. Jesus alludes to a marvelous promise in Isaiah: "Then all your children will be taught by the LORD, their prosperity will be great" (54:13). **Everyone who has listened to and learned from the Father.** The implication is that those who are listening to God will recognize and receive Jesus. The religious leaders are offended by Jesus because they are out of touch with God. Because Jesus, the Word, is the only one who has seen the Father, those who receive Him will learn much more of God than is possible apart from Jesus.

6:51 for the life of the world. Like the Passover lamb, Christ's death means life to those who feed spiritually on Him.

go to Judea so Your disciples can see Your works that You are doing. ⁴ For no one does anything in secret while he's seeking public recognition. If You do these things, show Yourself to the world." ⁵ (For not even His brothers believed in Him.)

⁶ Jesus told them, "My time has not yet arrived, but your time is always at hand. ⁷ The world cannot hate you, but it does hate Me because I testify about it—that its deeds are evil. ⁸ Go up to the festival yourselves. I'm not going up to the festival yet,ᵃ because My time has not yet fully come." ⁹ After He had said these things, He stayed in Galilee.

Jesus at the Festival of Tabernacles

¹⁰ After His brothers had gone up to the festival, then He also went up, not openly but secretly. ¹¹ The Jews were looking for Him at the festival and saying, "Where is He?" ¹² And there was a lot of discussion about Him among the crowds. Some were saying, "He's a good man." Others were saying, "No, on the contrary, He's deceiving the people." ¹³ Still, nobody was talking publicly about Him because they feared the Jews.

¹⁴ When the festival was already half over, Jesus went up into the •temple complex and began to teach. ¹⁵ Then the Jews were amazed and said, "How does He know the Scriptures, since He hasn't been trained?"

¹⁶ Jesus answered them, "My teaching isn't Mine but is from the One who sent Me. ¹⁷ If anyone wants to do His will, he will understand whether the teaching is from God or if I am speaking on My own. ¹⁸ The one who speaks for himself seeks his own glory. But He who seeks the glory of the One who sent Him is true, and there is no unrighteousness in Him. ¹⁹ Didn't Moses give you the law? Yet none of you keeps the law! Why do you want to kill Me?"

²⁰ "You have a demon!" the crowd responded. "Who wants to kill You?"

²¹ "I did one work, and you are all amazed," Jesus answered. ²² "Consider this: Moses has given you circumcision—not that it comes from Moses but from the fathers—and you circumcise a man on the Sabbath. ²³ If a man receives circumcision on the Sabbath so that the law of Moses won't be broken, are you angry at Me because I made a man entirely well on the Sabbath? ²⁴ Stop judging according to outward appearances; rather judge according to righteous judgment."

The Identity of the Messiah

²⁵ Some of the people of Jerusalem were saying, "Isn't this the man they want to kill? ²⁶ Yet, look! He's speaking publicly and they're saying nothing to Him. Can it be true that the authorities know He is the •Messiah? ²⁷ But we know where this man is from. When the Messiah comes, nobody will know where He is from."

²⁸ As He was teaching in the temple complex, Jesus cried out, "You know Me and you know where I am from. Yet I have not come on My own, but the One who sent Me is true. You don't know Him; ²⁹ I know Him because I am from Him, and He sent Me."

³⁰ Then they tried to seize Him. Yet no one laid a hand on Him because His hourᵇ had not yet come. ³¹ However, many from the crowd believed in Him and said, "When the Messiah comes, He won't perform more signs than this man has done, will He?"

³² The •Pharisees heard the crowd muttering these things about Him, so the •chief priests and the Pharisees sent temple police to arrest Him.

³³ Then Jesus said, "I am only with you for a short time. Then I'm going to the One who sent Me. ³⁴ You will look for Me, but you will not find Me; and where I am, you cannot come."

³⁵ Then the Jews said to one another, "Where does He intend to go so we won't find Him? He doesn't intend to go to the Dispersionᶜ among the Greeks and teach the Greeks, does He? ³⁶ What is this remark He made: 'You will look for Me, and you will not find Me; and where I am, you cannot come'?"

The Promise of the Spirit

³⁷ On the last and most important day of the festival, Jesus stood up and cried out, "If anyone is thirsty, he should come to Meᵈ and drink! ³⁸ The one who believes

---

ᵃ7:8 Other mss omit *yet*   ᵇ7:30 The time of His sacrificial death and exaltation; Jn 2:4; 8:20; 12:23,27; 13:1; 17:1   ᶜ7:35 Jewish people scattered throughout Gentile lands who spoke Gk and were influenced by Gk culture   ᵈ7:37 Other mss omit *to Me*

6:54 eternal life. Jesus makes it clear that He is not talking about the Passover. The subject is eternal life.

6:67 the Twelve. This is the first mention of the apostolic band in this Gospel (See also Mark 3:13-19). **You don't want to go away too, do you?** In Greek, this question anticipates a negative answer.

6:68 You have the words of eternal life. When this verse is compared with verse 63, it is clear that Peter has grasped Jesus' meaning.

7:2 Festival of Tabernacles. This, along with Passover and Pentecost, was a major feast when Jews from all over the Roman empire gathered in Jerusalem. This feast celebrated God's provision for Israel during their years of wandering in the wilderness (Lev. 23:39). By this time, it had also become a Thanksgiving celebration for the harvest (v. 37).

7:3-5 so His brothers said. The urging of Jesus' brothers bears similarities to that of His mother in John 2:3-5. Members of His family members are trying to advise Him about how He should carry out His mission. Verse 5 shows that His brothers, like the crowds in 6:66, misunderstood the nature of Jesus as Messiah and His mission on earth.

7:22-23 circumcision. Circumcision, a sign of God's covenant with His people, was initiated long before Moses by Abraham (Gen. 17). Yet circumcision was reinforced by Moses' Law which required that a male child be circumcised eight days after birth. Pharisaic tradition held that since the law of circumcision was more important than the laws prohibiting work on the Sabbath, it was lawful to circumcise a child on the Sabbath. Jesus uses their logic against them (v. 23). If it is lawful to perform an act that led to a person's ceremonial perfection on the Sabbath, how could it be wrong for Him to restore a person to wholeness on that day?

7:37 If anyone is thirsty, he should come to Me and drink! The vision in Ezekiel 47:1-12 of water flowing from the temple giving life to all the surrounding area is in view as Jesus, the new temple of God (2:19), who provides the water of life to all who believe.

8:3 the scribes and the Pharisees. The teachers of the law, or scribes, are not mentioned in the Gospel of John, but they play a prominent part in the other Gospels. They were ordained teachers, serving as the repre-

in Me, as the Scripture has said,[a] will have streams of living water flow from deep within him." [39] He said this about the Spirit, whom those who believed in Him were going to receive, for the Spirit[b] had not yet been received,[c] [d] because Jesus had not yet been glorified.

The People Are Divided over Jesus

[40] When some from the crowd heard these words, they said, "This really is the Prophet!"[e] [41] Others said, "This is the Messiah!" But some said, "Surely the Messiah doesn't come from Galilee, does He? [42] Doesn't the Scripture say that the Messiah comes from David's offspring[f] and from the town of Bethlehem, where David once lived?" [43] So a division occurred among the crowd because of Him. [44] Some of them wanted to seize Him, but no one laid hands on Him.

Debate over Jesus' Claims

[45] Then the temple police came to the chief priests and Pharisees, who asked them, "Why haven't you brought Him?"

[46] The police answered, "No man ever spoke like this!"[g]

[47] Then the Pharisees responded to them: "Are you fooled too? [48] Have any of the rulers believed in Him? Or any of the Pharisees? [49] But this crowd, which doesn't know the law, is accursed!"

[50] Nicodemus—the one who came to Him previously, being one of them—said to them, [51] "Our law doesn't judge a man before it hears from him and knows what he's doing, does it?"

[52] "You aren't from Galilee too, are you?" they replied. "Investigate and you will see that no prophet arises from Galilee."[h]

8 [53 So each one went to his house. [1] But Jesus went to the •Mount of Olives.

An Adulteress Forgiven

[2] At dawn He went to the •temple complex again, and all the people were coming to Him. He sat down and began to teach them.

[3] Then the •scribes and the •Pharisees brought a woman caught in adultery, making her stand in the center. [4] "Teacher," they said to Him, "this woman was caught in the act of committing adultery. [5] In the law Moses commanded us to stone such women. So what do You say?" [6] They asked this to trap Him, in order that they might have evidence to accuse Him.

Anyone Without Sin?

1. Have you ever written with chalk on the sidewalk? What things have you drawn or written?

John 8:1-11
2. How was the Pharisees' question intended to trap Jesus? How did He turn the trap back on them instead?
3. Who in the group was "without sin" (vv. 7-9)? Who in the group had the right to condemn or forgive sins?
4. What lesson was Jesus teaching here: Adultery is okay? Forgive others? Repent and stop sinning? Examine your own life instead of others?
5. How can you help others who are living in sin?

Jesus stooped down and started writing on the ground with His finger. [7] When they persisted in questioning Him, He stood up and said to them, "The one without sin among you should be the first to throw a stone at her." [8] Then He stooped down again and continued writing on the ground. [9] When they heard this, they left one by one, starting with the older men. Only He was left, with the woman in the center. [10] When Jesus stood up, He said to her, "•Woman, where are they? Has no one condemned you?"

---

[a]**7:38** Jesus may have had several OT passages in mind; Is 58:11; Ezk 47:1–12; Zch 14:8   [b]**7:39** Other mss read *Holy Spirit*   [c]**7:39** Other mss read *had not yet been given*   [d]**7:39** Lit *the Spirit was not yet*; the word *received* is implied from the previous clause.   [e]**7:40** Probably = the Prophet in Dt 18:15   [f]**7:42** Lit *seed*   [g]**7:46** Other mss read *like this man*   [h]**7:52** Jonah and probably other prophets did come from Galilee; 2 Kgs 14:25

---

sentatives of Moses in interpreting the law. They were taught as rabbis and acted as lawyers in legal cases. **a woman caught in adultery.** Since this sin cannot be committed alone, why was only one offender brought before the temple courts? The teachers of the law and the Pharisees likely staged this to trap Jesus (v. 6).

8:5 Moses commanded us to stone such women. This was only partially true. Leviticus 20:10 and Deuteronomy 22:22 prescribe that both parties should be put to death. Since it was said that the woman was caught in the act, the man was also there and should have been brought in as well. The Jews, under Roman law, had no authority to carry out such sentences. In Israel's past, this penalty was rarely carried out because capital offenses required two or three witnesses. The normal result of adultery (on the part of a woman) was

divorce. Women could not divorce their husbands for any reason.

8:6 They asked this to trap Him. See also Matthew 19:3 and 22:15 for other situations where Jesus' enemies attempted to find some reason for making a charge against Him. In this case, if He allowed stoning He would be in violation of Roman law and would be considered stricter than even the Pharisees in His application of the law. If Jesus tried to release her, He could be faulted for ignoring the Law of Moses. **started writing on the ground with His finger.** It is uncertain what Jesus wrote. But speculation centers on the possibility that He may have been writing the other commandments, which would remind the onlookers of commandments *they* may have broken.

8:7 The one without sin among you. Jesus affirms the validity of the law, but forces the ini-

tiative back on the accusers. Perhaps some of them were reminded of times when they "sowed some wild oats." This statement does not imply that judicial cases can only be tried by sinless people. But it is a rebuke to the motives of these leaders who ignored their own sins while using this woman to implicate Jesus.

8:9 starting with the older men. The older men may have had the wisdom of experience to recognize their own fallibilities more readily.

8:11 Neither do I condemn you. This story illustrates the truth of 3:17. The woman had come face-to-face with condemnation, shame, and death, but she was pardoned by the One to whom all judgment has been given (5:22). **Go, and from now on do not sin any more.** The compassion and mercy of Jesus is related to His call to people to live in obedience to the

11 "No one, Lord,"a she answered.

"Neither do I condemn you," said Jesus. "Go, and from now on do not sin any more."]b

Walking in the Light

1. When have you witnessed an accident or crime? Were you called to testify as a witness?
2. What do you have in common with your dad? What's something important he taught you?

John 8:12-20

3. How is Jesus "the light of the world" (v. 12a)? How does it feel to know that by following Him you "will never walk in the darkness but will have the light of life" (v. 12b)?
4. What did Jesus mean that the Pharisees judge "by human standards" (v. 15)? How can we learn to judge by God's standards?
5. Are you walking in Jesus' light or in darkness?

The Light of the World

12 Then Jesus spoke to them again: "I am the light of the world. Anyone who follows Me will never walk in the darkness but will have the light of life."

13 So the Pharisees said to Him, "You are testifying about Yourself. Your testimony is not valid."c

14 "Even if I testify about Myself," Jesus replied, "My testimony is valid,d because I know where I came from and where I'm going. But you don't know where I come from or where I'm going. 15 You judge by human standards.e I judge no one. 16 And if I do judge, My judgment

is true, because I am not alone, but I and the Father who sent Me ⌊judge together⌋. 17 Even in your law it is written that the witness of two men is valid. 18 I am the One who testifies about Myself, and the Father who sent Me testifies about Me."

19 Then they asked Him, "Where is Your Father?"

"You know neither Me nor My Father," Jesus answered. "If you knew Me, you would also know My Father." 20 He spoke these words by the treasury,f while teaching in the temple complex. But no one seized Him, because His hourg had not come.

Jesus Predicts His Departure

21 Then He said to them again, "I'm going away; you will look for Me, and you will die in your sin. Where I'm going, you cannot come."

22 So the Jews said again, "He won't kill Himself, will He, since He says, 'Where I'm going, you cannot come'?"

23 "You are from below," He told them, "I am from above. You are of this world; I am not of this world. 24 Therefore I told you that you will die in your sins. For if you do not believe that I am ⌊He⌋,h you will die in your sins."

25 "Who are You?" they questioned.

"Precisely what I've been telling you from the very beginning," Jesus told them. 26 "I have many things to say and to judge about you, but the One who sent Me is true, and what I have heard from Him—these things I tell the world."

27 They did not know He was speaking to them about the Father. 28 So Jesus said to them, "When you lift up the •Son of Man, then you will know that I am ⌊He⌋, and that I do nothing on My own. But just as the Father taught Me, I say these things. 29 The One who sent Me is with Me. He has not left Me alone, because I always do what pleases Him."

Truth and Freedom

30 As He was saying these things, many believed in Him. 31 So Jesus said to the Jews who had believed Him,

---

a8:11 Or *Sir*; Jn 4:15,49; 5:7; 6:34; 9:36   b8:11 Other mss omit bracketed text   c8:13 The law of Moses required at least 2 witnesses to make a claim legally valid (v. 17).   d8:14 Or *true*   e8:15 Lit *You judge according to the flesh*   f8:20 A place for offerings to be given, perhaps in the court of women   g8:20 The time of His sacrificial death and exaltation; Jn 2:4; 7:30; 12:23,27; 13:1; 17:1   h8:24 Jesus claimed to be deity, but the Pharisees didn't understand His meaning.

---

will of His Father. Paul, likewise, rejects the idea that people can claim God's mercy while pursuing a lifestyle in opposition to His will (Rom. 6:1-2,15).

8:12 Then Jesus spoke to them again. The place for this exchange between Jesus and the religious leaders is probably the Feast of Tabernacles (7:2). **I am the light of the world.** Jesus makes another bold assertion coupled with the promise that those who follow Him will not walk in darkness. Because the religious leaders were out of touch with God, they were walking in darkness and leading those who followed them away from the light. There is tragic irony here that the One who had created them and longed to dispel their darkness was viewed as an enemy.

8:13 Your testimony is not valid. The reli-

gious leaders viewed Jesus assertion to be the light of the world as lacking support. They were challenging Him to bring forth evidence to support His claim.

8:14 Even if I testify about Myself. Jesus answers their challenge by saying that His claim about Himself is based on His knowing where he came from and where he is going.

8:17 Even in your law...the witness of two men is valid. Jesus reminds the religious leaders of the rules of evidence in their law. No one could be put to death on the testimony of just one witness (Num. 35:30). At least two witnesses had to testify to the guilt of the accused. Jesus argues that His claim to be the light of the world has two witnesses: He and the Father, two impeccable witnesses. But from the perspective of the religious leaders,

this amounted to no witnesses at all.

8:28 lift up the Son of Man. This is to say, "crucify" Him.

8:31 if you continue in My word. Witnessing Jesus' miracles and hearing His teachings and conversations with the religious leaders, many Jews had come to believe His claims. To these who had come to an intellectual belief, Jesus sets forth the condition of being His followers. The condition is as true today as it was when Jesus first uttered these words: stay in My word. Again, this is more than an intellectual knowledge of His word. The religious leaders of Jesus' time had God's Word. They memorized it and could quote it readily. The problem was that for most of them the Word didn't move from their heads to their hearts. There was nothing wrong with the Word. It had

"If you continue in My word,[a] you really are My disciples. [32] You will know the truth, and the truth will set you free."

[33] "We are descendants[b] of Abraham," they answered Him, "and we have never been enslaved to anyone. How can You say, 'You will become free'?"

[34] Jesus responded, "•I assure you: Everyone who commits sin is a slave of sin. [35] A slave does not remain in the household forever, but a son does remain forever. [36] Therefore if the Son sets you free, you really will be free. [37] I know you are descendants[b] of Abraham, but you are trying to kill Me because My word[a] is not welcome among you. [38] I speak what I have seen in the presence of the Father,[c] and therefore you do what you have heard from your father."

[39] "Our father is Abraham!" they replied.

"If you were Abraham's children," Jesus told them, "you would do what Abraham did. [40] But now you are trying to kill Me, a man who has told you the truth that I heard from God. Abraham did not do this! [41] You're doing what your father does."

"We weren't born of sexual immorality," they said. "We have one Father—God."

[42] Jesus said to them, "If God were your Father, you would love Me, because I came from God and I am here. For I didn't come on My own, but He sent Me. [43] Why don't you understand what I say? Because you cannot listen to[d] My word. [44] You are of your father the Devil, and you want to carry out your father's desires. He was a murderer from the beginning and has not stood in the truth, because there is no truth in him. When he tells a lie, he speaks from his own nature,[e] because he is a liar and the father of liars.[f] [45] Yet because I tell the truth, you do not believe Me. [46] Who among you can convict Me of sin? If I tell the truth, why don't you believe Me? [47] The one who is from God listens to God's words. This is why you don't listen, because you are not from God."

Jesus and Abraham

[48] The Jews responded to Him, "Aren't we right in saying that You're a •Samaritan and have a demon?"

[49] "I do not have a demon," Jesus answered. "On the contrary, I honor My Father and you dishonor Me. [50] I do not seek My glory; the One who seeks it also judges. [51] I assure you: If anyone keeps My word, he will never see death—ever!"

[52] Then the Jews said, "Now we know You have a demon. Abraham died and so did the prophets. You say, 'If anyone keeps My word, he will never taste death—ever!' [53] Are You greater than our father Abraham who died? Even the prophets died. Who do You pretend to be?"[g]

[54] "If I glorify Myself," Jesus answered, "My glory is nothing. My Father—you say about Him, 'He is our God'—He is the One who glorifies Me. [55] You've never known Him, but I know Him. If I were to say I don't know Him, I would be a liar like you. But I do know Him, and I keep His word. [56] Your father Abraham was overjoyed that he would see My day; he saw it and rejoiced."

[57] The Jews replied, "You aren't 50 years old yet, and You've seen Abraham?"[h]

[58] Jesus said to them, "I assure you: Before Abraham was, I am."[i]

[59] At that, they picked up stones to throw at Him. But Jesus was hidden[j] and went out of the temple complex.[k]

The Sixth Sign: Healing a Man Born Blind

9 As He was passing by, He saw a man blind from birth. [2] His disciples questioned Him: "•Rabbi, who sinned, this man or his parents, that he was born blind?"

[3] "Neither this man nor his parents sinned," Jesus answered. "[This came about] so that God's works might be displayed in him. [4] We[l] must do the works of Him who sent Me[m] while it is day. Night is coming when no one can work. [5] As long as I am in the world, I am the light of the world."

---

[a]**8:31,37** Or *My teaching,* or *My message* [b]**8:33,37** Or *offspring;* lit *seed;* Jn 7:42 [c]**8:38** Other mss read *of My Father* [d]**8:43** Or *cannot hear* [e]**8:44** Lit *from his own things* [f]**8:44** Lit *of it* [g]**8:53** Lit *Who do you make Yourself?* [h]**8:57** Other mss read *and Abraham has seen You?* [i]**8:58** *I AM* is the name God gave Himself at the burning bush; Ex 3:13–14; see note at Jn 8:24. [j]**8:59** Or *Jesus hid Himself* [k]**8:59** Other mss add *and having gone through their midst, He passed by* [l]**9:4** Other mss read *I* [m]**9:4** Other mss read *sent us*

---

fallen onto hard ground, rocky ground, or among thorns (Mk. 4:1-20). The condition of the hearer will be a limiting or an enriching factor when God's Word is spoken. To stay in Jesus' word is to be transformed.

8:32 the truth will set you free. Jesus brings together two short but powerful words: *truth and freedom.* This saying is often quoted out of context in academic settings to support the claim that there is a strong link between intellectual pursuits and human freedom. The truth Jesus is talking about is not just intellectual. Being set free is not being able to do as we wish.

8:33 we are descendents of Abraham. The religious leaders responded by saying that they didn't need to be set free. They are children of Abraham.

8:34 Everyone who commits sin is a slave of sin. In this verse, the freedom Jesus spoke of in 8:32 and 8:36 becomes clearer. The freedom that every human being needs is freedom from sin. Sin is a cruel taskmaster. Truth is a gift of God that enables humans to see both the problem and its solution.

8:36 if the Son sets you free. The source of spiritual freedom is found in Jesus. Here He offers the solution to the problem He posed in verse 34.

8:41 your father. Having denied that they are Abraham's children in verse 40, Jesus' statement here raises the question of whose children they really are. **We weren't born of sexual immorality.** The crowd was probably referring to the irregular circumstances behind Jesus' birth.

8:59 they picked up stones. Stoning was the punishment for blasphemy against "the name of the LORD" (Lev. 24:16). The incredulity and scorn of verses 52 and 57 turn to fury at Jesus' bold assertion in verse 58.

9:1 As He was passing by. An indefinite time reference. **blind from birth.** The story of the healing of the blind man, which extends through 10:21, illustrates Jesus' ability to give new life to people in hopeless situations and the implications of discipleship in the face of opposition.

9:2 His disciples. These disciples may be the Twelve or a broader group of Judean followers. **who sinned?** Despite the book of Job's teaching, the rabbis taught that a person's misfortune was the result of his sin or a punishment inherited because of one's parents' sins. Some people taught that such handicaps

⁶ After He said these things He spit on the ground, made some mud from the saliva, and spread the mud on his eyes. ⁷ "Go," He told him, "wash in the pool of Siloam" (which means "Sent"). So he left, washed, and came back seeing.

⁸ His neighbors and those who formerly had seen him as a beggar said, "Isn't this the man who sat begging?" ⁹ Some said, "He's the one." "No," others were saying, "but he looks like him."

Power in Weakness

1. When you were a kid, what was your favorite "mud game?"

John 9:1-15,24-34

2. Why was this man born blind? What does this teach us about one reason for suffering in life?

3. When did the man actually start seeing (v. 11)? What does this teach us about God's healing and our own obedience?

4. How can a weakness in your life turn into an opportunity for God to show His power?

5. The Pharisees asked the blind man who Jesus was. How would you answer that question?

He kept saying, "I'm the one!"

¹⁰ Therefore they asked him, "Then how were your eyes opened?"

¹¹ He answered, "The man called Jesus made mud, spread it on my eyes, and told me, 'Go to Siloam and wash.' So when I went and washed I received my sight."

¹² "Where is He?" they asked.

"I don't know," he said.

The Healed Man's Testimony

¹³ They brought the man who used to be blind to the •Pharisees. ¹⁴ The day that Jesus made the mud and opened his eyes was a Sabbath. ¹⁵ So again the Pharisees asked him how he received his sight.

"He put mud on my eyes," he told them. "I washed and I can see."

¹⁶ Therefore some of the Pharisees said, "This man is not from God, for He doesn't keep the Sabbath!" But others were saying, "How can a sinful man perform such signs?" And there was a division among them.

¹⁷ Again they asked the blind man,ᵃ "What do you say about Him, since He opened your eyes?"

"He's a prophet," he said.

¹⁸ The Jews did not believe this about him—that he was blind and received sight—until they summoned the parents of the one who had received his sight.

¹⁹ They asked them, "Is this your son, ⌊the one⌋ you say was born blind? How then does he now see?"

²⁰ "We know this is our son and that he was born blind," his parents answered. ²¹ "But we don't know how he now sees, and we don't know who opened his eyes. Ask him; he's of age. He will speak for himself." ²² His parents said these things because they were afraid of the Jews, since the Jews had already agreed that if anyone confessed Him as •Messiah, he would be banned from the •synagogue. ²³ This is why his parents said, "He's of age; ask him."

²⁴ So a second time they summoned the man who had been blind and told him, "Give glory to God.ᵇ We know that this man is a sinner!"

²⁵ He answered, "Whether or not He's a sinner, I don't know. One thing I do know: I was blind, and now I can see!"

²⁶ Then they asked him, "What did He do to you? How did He open your eyes?"

²⁷ "I already told you," he said, "and you didn't listen. Why do you want to hear it again? You don't want to become His disciples too, do you?"

²⁸ They ridiculed him: "You're that man's disciple, but we're Moses' disciples. ²⁹ We know that God has

---

ᵃ**9:17** = the man who had been blind   ᵇ**9:24** *Give glory to God* was a solemn charge to tell the truth; Jos 7:19.

---

were a punishment for the sin that the child in the womb had committed (Luke 13:1-5). Ezekiel taught that people would not be punished by God for the sins of their parents, but the belief in such retribution lingered (Ezek. 18). **born blind.** The emphasis is on the fact that this man was born with this disability (vv. 1,19-20,32). This not only points out the longevity of his problem, but underscores the theological emphasis that people who are not "born again" will not "see the kingdom of God" (3:3). They walk in darkness (8:12).

9:3 Neither this man nor his parents sinned Jesus is not pronouncing the family sinless, but is dismissing the disciples' interest in the *cause* of the man's blindness. He focuses their attention on its *purpose*.

9:21 he's of age. The legal age was 13. The parents affirm he is old enough to speak for himself.

9:22 the Jews. From the account in 12:42, it is clear that the Pharisaic leaders are referred to here. They found Jesus offensive because He broke the traditional interpretations of the Mosaic Law which they attempted to keep in such detail.

9:24 Give glory to God. Although this saying is equivalent to the modern-day oath to "tell the truth, the whole truth, and nothing but the truth," the man did indeed give glory to God by affirming his conviction about Jesus, even though this was the exact opposite of what the Pharisees intended.

9:29 we don't know where He's from.! This implies that Jesus, unlike Moses, had no connection with God.

9:35 thrown the man out. Jesus said that He would never drive away those who came to Him (6:37). In contrast, the Pharisees reject those who are drawn by the Father.

10:1 sheep pen. At night sheep were herded into enclosures made of stone as a protection against predators and thieves.

10:3 The doorkeeper. Although both the shepherd and the gate clearly represent Jesus (vv. 7, 11), the figure of the watchman is not explained. In a parable, unlike an allegory, not all the details have a meaning. **calls his own sheep by name.** Shepherds had names and distinctive calls for their sheep. These calls helped them separate their flocks from other herds mixed in with their sheep in a sheep pen.

10:7 I am the door. This symbol is stated

spoken to Moses. But this man—we don't know where He's from!"

30 "This is an amazing thing," the man told them. "You don't know where He is from, yet He opened my eyes! 31 We know that God doesn't listen to sinners, but if anyone is God-fearing and does His will, He listens to him. 32 Throughout history[a] no one has ever heard of someone opening the eyes of a person born blind. 33 If this man were not from God, He wouldn't be able to do anything."

34 "You were born entirely in sin," they replied, "and are you trying to teach us?" Then they threw him out.[b]

The Blind Man's Sight and the Pharisees' Blindness

35 When Jesus heard that they had thrown the man out, He found him and asked, "Do you believe in the •Son of Man?"[c]

36 "Who is He, Sir, that I may believe in Him?" he asked.

37 Jesus answered, "You have seen Him; in fact, He is the One speaking with you."

38 "I believe, Lord!" he said, and he worshiped Him.

39 Jesus said, "I came into this world for judgment, in order that those who do not see will see and those who do see will become blind."

40 Some of the Pharisees who were with Him heard these things and asked Him, "We aren't blind too, are we?"

41 "If you were blind," Jesus told them, "you wouldn't have sin.[d] But now that you say, 'We see'—your sin remains.

The Ideal Shepherd

10 "•I assure you: Anyone who doesn't enter the sheep pen by the door but climbs in some other way, is a thief and a robber. 2 The one who enters by the door is the shepherd of the sheep. 3 The doorkeeper opens it for him, and the sheep hear his voice. He calls his own sheep by name and leads them out. 4 When he has brought all his own outside, he goes ahead of them. The sheep follow him because they recognize his voice.

5 They will never follow a stranger; instead they will run away from him, because they don't recognize the voice of strangers."

6 Jesus gave them this illustration, but they did not understand what He was telling them.

The Good Shepherd

7 So Jesus said again, "I assure you: I am the door of the sheep. 8 All who came before Me[e] are thieves and robbers, but the sheep didn't listen to them. 9 I am the door. If anyone enters by Me, he will be saved and will come in and go out and find pasture. 10 A thief comes only to steal and to kill and to destroy. I have come that they may have life and have it in abundance.

11 "I am the good shepherd. The good shepherd lays down his life for the sheep. 12 The hired man, since he is not the shepherd and doesn't own the sheep, leaves them[f] and runs away when he sees a wolf coming. The wolf then snatches and scatters them. 13 This happens because he is a hired man and doesn't care about the sheep.

14 "I am the good shepherd. I know My own sheep, and they know Me, 15 as the Father knows Me, and I know the Father. I lay down My life for the sheep. 16 But I have other sheep that are not of this fold; I must bring them also, and they will listen to My voice. Then there will be one flock, one shepherd. 17 This is why the Father loves Me, because I am laying down My life so I may take it up again. 18 No one takes it from Me, but I lay it down on My own. I have the right to lay it down, and I have the right to take it up again. I have received this command from My Father."

19 Again a division took place among the Jews because of these words. 20 Many of them were saying, "He has a demon and He's crazy! Why do you listen to Him?" 21 Others were saying, "These aren't the words of someone demon-possessed. Can a demon open the eyes of the blind?"

Jesus at the Festival of Dedication

22 Then the Festival of Dedication[g] took place in Jerusalem, and it was winter. 23 Jesus was walking in

---

a9:32 Lit *From the age* b9:34 = they banned him from the synagogue; v. 22 c9:35 Other mss read *the Son of God* d9:41 To *have sin* is an idiom that refers to guilt caused by sin. e10:8 Other mss omit *before Me* f10:12 Lit *leaves the sheep* g10:22 Or *Hanukkah*, also called *the Feast of Lights*; this festival commemorated the rededication of the temple in 164 B.C.

---

forthrightly in 14:6 where Jesus says He is the way to God.

10:8 thieves and robbers. Jesus is referring to the religious leaders who exploit the people for their own advantage (2:14-15; Ezek. 34:1-6).

10:10 have it in abundance. The eternal life a person has in Christ means more than length of life. It includes quality of life as well.

10:11 I am the good shepherd. In contrast to the hired hands who run away at danger, the true shepherd cares for the flock at risk of his life (1 Sam. 17:34-35). The image of the ruler as a shepherd was common in Israel (Ps. 23; Ezek. 34).

10:14 I know My own sheep. "To know" means "to love" (v. 17).

10:15 I lay down My life. This phrase accents the voluntary nature of Jesus' death (v. 18).

10:16 I have other sheep that are not of this fold. Since the Gospel of John has consistently emphasized that Jesus' mission was not just for Jews but for the entire world, it is likely that this is the meaning here. **one flock, one shepherd.** The Christian community is not to be marred by divisions, but it should model unity across racial and ethnic lines as all people respond to the voice of the Great Shepherd (11:52; Eph. 2:11-22).

10:22 Festival of Dedication. This feast (Hanukkah) commemorated Judas Maccabeus' deliverance of Jerusalem—and the temple—from the tyranny of the Syrian (Seleucid) king, Antiochus Epiphanes, who had profaned the temple by placing a statue of the Greek god Zeus in the Most Holy Place. The Pharisees try

to get Jesus to proclaim Himself as the Messiah so he will attract the attention and the displeasure of Rome.

10:23 Solomon's Colonnade. This was a large covered porch on the east side of the temple. The porch was constructed on a foundation that was believed to have been part of the original temple built by King Solomon.

11:2 Mary. Apparently the author of the Gospel of John, aware that the story of Jesus' anointing was a familiar one to his readers, used this incident to identify Mary even though it doesn't occur in this Gospel until chapter 12 (Mark 14:1-11).

11:4 the Son of God may be glorified. All the signs in this Gospel were meant as a demonstration of the reality of Jesus' unity with the Father (10:25-30).

the •temple complex in Solomon's Colonnade.ᵃ ²⁴ Then the Jews surrounded Him and asked, "How long are You going to keep us in suspense?ᵇ If You are the •Messiah, tell us plainly."ᶜ

²⁵ "I did tell you and you don't believe," Jesus answered them. "The works that I do in My Father's name testify about Me. ²⁶ But you don't believe because you are not My sheep.ᵈ ²⁷ My sheep hear My voice, I know them, and they follow Me. ²⁸ I give them eternal life, and they will never perish—ever! No one will snatch them out of My hand. ²⁹ My Father, who has given them to Me, is greater than all. No one is able to snatch them out of the Father's hand. ³⁰ The Father and I are one."ᵉ

Renewed Efforts to Stone Jesus

³¹ Again the Jews picked up rocks to stone Him. ³² Jesus replied, "I have shown you many good works from the Father. Which of these works are you stoning Me for?"

³³ "We aren't stoning You for a good work," the Jews answered, "but for blasphemy, because You—being a man—make Yourself God."

³⁴ Jesus answered them, "Isn't it written in your law,ᶠ I said, you are gods?ᵍ ³⁵ If He called those whom the word of God came to 'gods'—and the Scripture cannot be broken— ³⁶ do you say, 'You are blaspheming' to the One the Father set apart and sent into the world, because I said: I am the Son of God? ³⁷ If I am not doing My Father's works, don't believe Me. ³⁸ But if I am doing them and you don't believe Me, believe the works. This way you will know and understandʰ that the Father is in Me and I in the Father." ³⁹ Then they were trying again to seize Him, yet He eluded their grasp.

Many beyond the Jordan Believe in Jesus

⁴⁰ So He departed again across the Jordan to the place where John had been baptizing earlier, and He remained there. ⁴¹ Many came to Him and said, "John never did a sign, but everything John said about this man was true." ⁴² And many believed in Him there.

Lazarus Dies at Bethany

11 Now a man was sick, Lazarus, from Bethany, the village of Mary and her sister Martha. ² Mary was the one who anointed the Lord with fragrant oil and wiped His feet with her hair, and it was her brother Lazarus who was sick. ³ So the sisters sent a message to Him: "Lord, the one You love is sick."

⁴ When Jesus heard it, He said, "This sickness will not end in death but is for the glory of God, so that the Son of God may be glorified through it." ⁵ (Jesus loved Martha, her sister, and Lazarus.) ⁶ So when He heard that he was sick, He stayed two more days in the place where He was. ⁷ Then after that, He said to the disciples, "Let's go to Judea again."

⁸ "•Rabbi," the disciples told Him, "just now the Jews tried to stone You, and You're going there again?"

⁹ "Aren't there 12 hours in a day?" Jesus answered. "If anyone walks during the day, he doesn't stumble, because he sees the light of this world. ¹⁰ If anyone walks during the night, he does stumble, because the light is not in him." ¹¹ He said this, and then He told them, "Our friend Lazarus has fallen •asleep, but I'm on My way to wake him up."

¹² Then the disciples said to Him, "Lord, if he has fallen asleep, he will get well."

¹³ Jesus, however, was speaking about his death, but they thought He was speaking about natural sleep. ¹⁴ So Jesus then told them plainly, "Lazarus has died. ¹⁵ I'm glad for you that I wasn't there so that you may believe. But let's go to him."

¹⁶ Then Thomas (called "Twin") said to his fellow disciples, "Let's go so that we may die with Him."

The Resurrection and the Life

¹⁷ When Jesus arrived, He found that Lazarus had already been in the tomb four days. ¹⁸ Bethany was near Jerusalem (about two milesⁱ away). ¹⁹ Many of the Jews had come to Martha and Mary to comfort them about their brother. ²⁰ As soon as Martha heard that Jesus was

---

ᵃ**10:23** Rows of columns supporting a roof ᵇ**10:24** Lit *How long are you taking away our life?* ᶜ**10:24** Or *openly*, or *publicly* ᵈ**10:26** Other mss add *just as I told you* ᵉ**10:30** Lit *I and the Father—We are one.* ᶠ**10:34** Other mss read *in the law* ᵍ**10:34** Ps 82:6 ʰ**10:38** Other mss read *know and believe* ⁱ**11:18** Lit *15 stadia*; 1 *stadion* = 600 feet

---

11:6 He stayed two more days. At least two views are possible on why Jesus did this: (1) As in 2:3-4, Jesus seemingly ignores an urgent request to act in a needy situation. Jesus' delay communicates that His agenda is set neither by Himself (6:38) nor by the desires of those He loves, but by the Father; (2) He waited in order that through this trial His glory would be revealed in a new and dramatic way.

11:7 Let's go to Judea again. Jesus was in Perea on the other side of the Jordan River (10:40-42).

11:9 Aren't there 12 hours in a day? Jesus responds with a two-sentence parable which indicates there is no need to fear the Jewish leaders, since He is living in His Father's will and by His timetable. Until His "hour" comes, He is safe from harm and will do the Father's work. There is the implication, though, that the

"night" will soon come when He—the light of the world—is taken away. The parable also calls His disciples to consider whether they will take their cues from the "light of the world" or from those (like the Pharisees) who operate in the darkness.

11:11 fallen asleep. This was a common euphemism for death.

11:13 they thought. Like the Pharisees, the disciples failed to grasp the spiritual implications of Jesus' words (4:33).

11:16 Thomas (called "Twin"). Although Thomas has become famous for his doubt (20:25), here he demonstrates his deep faith and loyalty.

11:21 if You had been here, my brother wouldn't have died. This is not a rebuke but

an expression of regret. Martha apparently had faith that if Jesus had been there before his death, Lazarus could have survived.

11:23 will rise again. Martha would have understood Jesus' comment as an appropriate expression of comfort at a funeral.

11:25 I am the resurrection and the life. Jesus focuses Martha's attention not on the doctrine of the general resurrection, but on Him as the source of resurrection (5:24-29). **even if he dies, will live.** In this verse and in verse 26, Jesus is asserting His power over death and His ability to give life "to anyone He wants to" (5:21).

11:26 Do you believe this? Jesus confronts Martha with this claim. Does she see Him only as a healer or as the Lord of life?

coming, she went to meet Him. But Mary remained seated in the house.

²¹ Then Martha said to Jesus, "Lord, if You had been here, my brother wouldn't have died. ²² Yet even now I know that whatever You ask from God, God will give You."

Raising the Dead

1. What was the last funeral you attended? What was it like?

John 11:17-44

2. Why was Jesus "angry in His spirit and deeply moved" (v. 33) when He saw everyone weeping? What does this teach us about God's view of death? Sin?
3. Why did Jesus Himself weep (v. 35)? What does this show us about God's compassion and love?
4. What does the resurrection of Lazarus prove about Jesus? Why is it important to know that He has power over death?
5. Is there a "resurrection" that you need in your life right now?

²³ "Your brother will rise again," Jesus told her.

²⁴ Martha said, "I know that he will rise again in the resurrection at the last day."

²⁵ Jesus said to her, "I am the resurrection and the life. The one who believes in Me, even if he dies, will live. ²⁶ Everyone who lives and believes in Me will never die—ever. Do you believe this?"

²⁷ "Yes, Lord," she told Him, "I believe You are the •Messiah, the Son of God, who was to come into the world."

Jesus Shares the Sorrow of Death

²⁸ Having said this, she went back and called her sister Mary, saying in private, "The Teacher is here and is calling for you."

²⁹ As soon as she heard this, she got up quickly and went to Him. ³⁰ Jesus had not yet come into the village but was still in the place where Martha had met Him. ³¹ The Jews who were with her in the house consoling her saw that Mary got up quickly and went out. So they followed her, supposing that she was going to the tomb to cry there.

³² When Mary came to where Jesus was and saw Him, she fell at His feet and told Him, "Lord, if You had been here, my brother would not have died!"

³³ When Jesus saw her crying, and the Jews who had come with her crying, He was angryᵃ in His spirit and deeply moved. ³⁴ "Where have you put him?" He asked.

"Lord," they told Him, "come and see."

³⁵ Jesus wept.

³⁶ So the Jews said, "See how He loved him!" ³⁷ But some of them said, "Couldn't He who opened the blind man's eyes also have kept this man from dying?"

The Seventh Sign: Raising Lazarus from the Dead

³⁸ Then Jesus, angry in Himself again, came to the tomb. It was a cave, and a stone was lying against it. ³⁹ "Remove the stone," Jesus said.

Martha, the dead man's sister, told Him, "Lord, he already stinks. It's been four days."

⁴⁰ Jesus said to her, "Didn't I tell you that if you believed you would see the glory of God?"

⁴¹ So they removed the stone. Then Jesus raised His eyes and said, "Father, I thank You that You heard Me. ⁴² I know that You always hear Me, but because of the crowd standing here I said this, so they may believe You sent Me." ⁴³ After He said this, He shouted with a loud voice, "Lazarus, come out!" ⁴⁴ The dead man came out bound hand and foot with linen strips and with his face wrapped in a cloth. Jesus said to them, "Loose him and let him go."

ᵃ**11:33** The Gk word is very strong and probably indicates Jesus' anger against sin's tyranny and death.

11:27 In this verse, Martha declares by using several terms exactly who Jesus is. **the Messiah, the Son of God.** In calling Him the Christ, Martha acknowledges Jesus as the One who delivers and saves His people from sin and death. Her recognition of Him as the Son of God shows her insight into His divine identity. The meaning behind this title is that He is God, sharing the Father's nature just as a child shares the characteristics of his parents.

11:32 Mary. That Mary stayed in the house when Jesus arrived (v. 20) seems to indicate her despair. Mary does not add a statement of faith like Martha expressed—that Jesus could still do something powerful (v. 22). When Mary says, "Lord, if You had been here, my brother would not have died," it may have been an expression of disappointment rather than faith.

11:33 crying. Funerals were times for loud, public expressions of grief in Bible times. The word "crying" here indicates a type of wailing.

11:38 the tomb. Tombs for people of importance were either vertical shafts covered by a stone, or horizontal crevices carved out of a hill. Since this tomb was carved out of a cave, it was the latter type.

11:39 he already stinks. Even if Martha knew of the other people whom Jesus had raised (Matt. 11:5; Mark 5:22-43; Luke 7:11-15), they had been dead for only a short time. By the fourth day the decomposition of the body had begun, so resuscitation was not possible.

11:40 Didn't I tell you? This may be a reference to the message in verse 4, or the implication of what Jesus meant by His declaration to Martha in verse 25. The signs in the Gospel of

John have consistently been regarded as demonstrations of Jesus' identity. This final sign will reveal what has been alluded to all along—Jesus is God.

11:44 bound hand and foot with linen strips. Burial customs included wrapping the body with cloth and spices (19:40). This practice was not intended to preserve the body, like the ancient Egyptian process of mummification. It was a sign of honor for the deceased person.

11:48 everybody will believe in Him! What bothered these leaders was that people might interpret Jesus' miracles as a sign of His messiahship. Since they have already decided that He could not possibly be the Messiah (7:52), this was something they could not allow to happen.

The Plot to Kill Jesus

45 Therefore many of the Jews who came to Mary and saw what He did believed in Him. 46 But some of them went to the •Pharisees and told them what Jesus had done.

47 So the •chief priests and the Pharisees convened the •Sanhedrin and said, "What are we going to do since this man does many signs? 48 If we let Him continue in this way, everybody will believe in Him! Then the Romans will come and remove both our place[a] and our nation."

49 One of them, Caiaphas, who was high priest that year, said to them, "You know nothing at all! 50 You're not considering that it is to your[b] advantage that one man should die for the people rather than the whole nation perish." 51 He did not say this on his own, but being high priest that year he prophesied that Jesus was going to die for the nation, 52 and not for the nation only, but also to unite the scattered children of God. 53 So from that day on they plotted to kill Him. 54 Therefore Jesus no longer walked openly among the Jews but departed from there to the countryside near the wilderness, to a town called Ephraim. And He stayed there with the disciples.

55 The Jewish •Passover was near, and many went up to Jerusalem from the country to purify[c] themselves before the Passover. 56 They were looking for Jesus and asking one another as they stood in the •temple complex: "What do you think? He won't come to the festival, will He?" 57 The chief priests and the Pharisees had given orders that if anyone knew where He was, he should report it so they could arrest Him.

The Anointing at Bethany

12 Six days before the •Passover, Jesus came to Bethany where Lazarus[d] was, the one Jesus had raised from the dead. 2 So they gave a dinner for Him there; Martha was serving them, and Lazarus was one of those reclining at the table with Him. 3 Then Mary took a pound of fragrant oil—pure and expensive nard—anointed Jesus' feet, and wiped His feet with her hair. So the house was filled with the fragrance of the oil.

4 Then one of His disciples, Judas Iscariot (who was about to betray Him), said, 5 "Why wasn't this fragrant oil sold for 300 •denarii[e] and given to the poor?" 6 He didn't say this because he cared about the poor but because he was a thief. He was in charge of the money-bag and would steal part of what was put in it.

7 Jesus answered, "Leave her alone; she has kept it for the day of My burial. 8 For you always have the poor with you, but you do not always have Me."

The Decision to Kill Lazarus

9 Then a large crowd of the Jews learned He was there. They came not only because of Jesus, but also to see Lazarus the one He had raised from the dead. 10 Therefore the •chief priests decided to also kill Lazarus, 11 because he was the reason many of the Jews were deserting them[f] and believing in Jesus.

The Triumphal Entry

12 The next day, when the large crowd that had come to the festival heard that Jesus was coming to Jerusalem, 13 they took palm branches and went out to meet Him. They kept shouting: "•*Hosanna!* **Blessed is He who comes in the name of the Lord**[g] —the King of Israel!"

14 Jesus found a young donkey and sat on it, just as it is written: 15 **Fear no more, Daughter Zion; look! your King is coming, sitting on a donkey's colt.**[h]

16 His disciples did not understand these things at first. However, when Jesus was glorified, then they remembered that these things had been written about Him and that they had done these things to Him. 17 Meanwhile the crowd, which had been with Him when He called Lazarus out of the tomb and raised him from the dead, continued to testify.[i] 18 This is also why the crowd met Him, because they heard He had done this sign.

---

[a]**11:48** The temple or possibly all of Jerusalem   [b]**11:50** Other mss read *to our*   [c]**11:55** The law of Moses required God's people to purify or cleanse themselves so they could celebrate the Passover. Jews often came to Jerusalem a week early to do this; Nm 9:4–11.   [d]**12:1** Other mss read *Lazarus who died*   [e]**12:5** This amount was about a year's wages for a common worker.   [f]**12:11** Lit *going away*   [g]**12:13** Ps 118:25–26   [h]**12:15** Zch 9:9   [i]**12:17** Other mss read *Meanwhile the crowd, which had been with Him, continued to testify that He had called Lazarus out of the tomb and raised him from the dead.*

12:6 he was a thief. This is the only place in the Gospels that we are given any background about Judas. The author's point is not to dismiss legitimate caring for the poor, but to point out that in spite of his words, Judas' motives were self-serving.

12:7 for the day of My burial. Jesus uses this incident as a foreshadowing of His death. Bodies were often wrapped with spices for burial (19:39-40). Mary's expression was an act of thanksgiving to Jesus for what He had done for her brother.

12:8 you always have the poor with you. This is not meant to disparage acts of mercy, but to shift the focus to the upcoming death of Jesus.

12:10 the chief priests decided to also kill Lazarus. There is no record that this ironic plot

to kill a man who had just been raised from the dead ever got beyond the planning stage.

12:12 the large crowd. This was a large crowd of Jews in town for the Passover celebration.

12:13 Hosanna! Originally a one-word prayer for God to save (Ps. 118:25), this had become an expression of praise. **Blessed is He who comes in the name of the Lord.** Psalm 118:26 was used in the liturgy for Passover and celebrated God's deliverance of Israel from her enemies.

12:20 some Greeks. These were Gentile converts to Judaism such as the men described in Acts 10:2.

12:23 The hour has come. Throughout John's Gospel, the author has anticipated this time

(2:4; 7:6; 8:20). From here on, he speaks of how Jesus' "hour had come" (13:1). This is the time of His glorification initiated by His death (v. 28).

12:24 a grain of wheat. Just as a seed must be buried before it can become fruitful, so Christ's death is necessary so many people may be brought to life.

12:25 loves … hates. The only way to gain life is to be willing to lose it for the sake of Christ (Matt. 10:39; Luke 9:24).

12:27 My soul is troubled. The Gospel of John does not show us Jesus praying in the garden of Gethsemane as the other gospels do, but the same anguish that was expressed at that time is seen here.

12:31 the judgment of this world. Jesus has

¹⁹ Then the •Pharisees said to one another, "You see? You've accomplished nothing. Look—the world has gone after Him!"

Jesus Predicts His Crucifixion

²⁰ Now some Greeks were among those who went up to worship at the festival. ²¹ So they came to Philip, who was from Bethsaida in Galilee, and requested of him, "Sir, we want to see Jesus."

²² Philip went and told Andrew; then Andrew and Philip went and told Jesus. ²³ Jesus replied to them, "The hour has come for the •Son of Man to be glorified. ²⁴ "•I assure you: Unless a grain of wheat falls into the ground and dies, it remains by itself. But if it dies, it produces a large crop.ᵃ ²⁵ The one who loves his life will lose it, and the one who hates his life in this world will keep it for eternal life. ²⁶ If anyone serves Me, he must follow Me. Where I am, there My servant also will be. If anyone serves Me, the Father will honor him.

²⁷ "Now My soul is troubled. What should I say— Father, save Me from this hour? But that is why I came to this hour. ²⁸ Father, glorify Your name!"ᵇ

Then a voice came from heaven: "I have glorified it, and I will glorify it again!"

²⁹ The crowd standing there heard it and said it was thunder. Others said, "An angel has spoken to Him!" ³⁰ Jesus responded, "This voice came, not for Me, but for you. ³¹ Now is the judgment of this world. Now the ruler of this world will be cast out. ³² As for Me, if I am lifted upᶜ from the earth I will draw all ⌊people⌋ to Myself." ³³ He said this to signify what kind of death He was about to die.

³⁴ Then the crowd replied to Him, "We have heard from the law that the •Messiah will remain forever. So how can You say, 'The Son of Man must be lifted up'?ᶜ Who is this Son of Man?"

³⁵ Jesus answered, "The light will be with you only a little longer. Walk while you have the light so that darkness doesn't overtake you. The one who walks in darkness doesn't know where he's going. ³⁶ While you have the light, believe in the light so that you may become

sons of light." Jesus said this, then went away and hid from them.

Isaiah's Prophecies Fulfilled

³⁷ Even though He had performed so many signs in their presence, they did not believe in Him. ³⁸ But this was to fulfill the word of Isaiah the prophet, who said:ᵈ

> Lord, who has believed our message?
> And who has the arm of the Lord been
> revealed to?ᵉ

³⁹ This is why they were unable to believe, because Isaiah also said:

> ⁴⁰ He has blinded their eyes
> and hardened their hearts,
> so that they would not see with their eyes
> or understand with their hearts,
> and be converted,
> and I would heal them.ᶠ

⁴¹ Isaiah said these things becauseᵍ he saw His glory and spoke about Him.

⁴² Nevertheless, many did believe in Him even among the rulers, but because of the Pharisees they did not confess Him, so they would not be banned from the •synagogue. ⁴³ For they loved praise from men more than praise from God.ʰ

A Summary of Jesus' Mission

⁴⁴ Then Jesus cried out, "The one who believes in Me believes not in Me, but in Him who sent Me. ⁴⁵ And the one who sees Me sees Him who sent Me. ⁴⁶ I have come as a light into the world, so that everyone who believes in Me would not remain in darkness. ⁴⁷ If anyone hears My words and doesn't keep them, I do not judge him; for I did not come to judge the world but to save the world. ⁴⁸ The one who rejects Me and doesn't accept My sayings has this as his judge:ⁱ the word I have spoken will judge him on the last day. ⁴⁹ For I have not spoken on My own, but the Father Himself who sent Me has given Me a command as to what I should say

---

ᵃ**12:24** Lit *produces much fruit*   ᵇ**12:28** Other mss read *Your Son*   ᶜ**12:32,34** Or *exalted*   ᵈ**12:38** Lit *which he said*   ᵉ**12:38** Is 53:1   ᶠ**12:40** Is 6:10   ᵍ**12:41** Other mss read *when*   ʰ**12:43** Lit *loved glory of men more than glory of God*; v. 41; Jn 5:41   ⁱ**12:48** Lit *has the one judging him*

---

said repeatedly that His purpose was not to judge but to save. But His coming *does* bring judgment. His presence brings all people to a crisis point. If they receive Him, they will have life. If they refuse Him, they will experience death. **the ruler of this world.** Satan is often presented as having the world under his domination (Matt. 4:8; Eph. 2:2-3; Heb. 2:14-15).

12:32 if I am lifted up from the earth I will draw all people to Myself. There is a double meaning here. To be "lifted up" was understood by the crowds to mean crucifixion (v. 34), but it is also reminiscent of the "lifting up" of a military flag or standard as a rallying point for an army (6:40).

12:35-36 the light. Jesus does not answer the question of the crowds, but He describes Himself as "the light of the world" (8:12) to issue them one last call to trust in Him.

12:47 I did not come to judge the world but to save the world. Just as to believe in Jesus is to believe in the Father (vv. 44-46), so to refuse Him is to refuse the Father.

13:1 Jesus knew. Here and in verses 3 and 11, John points out what Jesus knew. This emphasizes that Jesus was in charge of the events leading to His death (10:18).

13:3 Jesus' self-knowledge was at the heart of His willingness and ability to serve. This verse says that He knew who He was in terms of where He had come from (the Father), where He was going (back to the Father), and what His role was while He was on earth.

13:4-5 to wash His disciples' feet. People's dusty, sandaled feet were usually washed by the lowest-ranking servant of the household before a meal was served. Jesus' action was

deliberate. Removing His outer clothing was a sign He was going to do some work, and it identified Him with a lowly servant who was dressed in the same way.

13:6 Lord, are You going to wash my feet? Peter is surprised at this departure from normal procedure.

13:7 afterwards you will know. This may refer to verse 17, but more likely it refers to the full understanding of Jesus' servanthood that will be made clear after His resurrection.

13:8 If I don't wash you, you have no part with me. This lifts the meaning of the footwashing to a higher plane than an object lesson about humility. Jesus' action was a symbol of the spiritual cleansing He would accomplish for His followers through the cross.

and what I should speak. ⁵⁰ I know that His command is eternal life. So the things that I speak, I speak just as the Father has told Me."

Jesus Washes His Disciples' Feet

13 Before the •Passover Festival, Jesus knew that His hour had come to depart from this world to the Father. Having loved His own who were in the world, He loved them to the end.ᵃ

Washing Stinking Feet

1. Who cleans the toilet where you live? When it comes to housework, what's the last job you would do?

John 13:1-17

2. Why did Jesus wash the disciples' feet? What does He mean by "wash one another's feet" (v. 14)?

3. How would you have reacted to Jesus washing your feet? Would you have been more like Peter in verse 8 or in verse 9?

4. What does Jesus mean, "If I don't wash you, you have no part with Me" (v. 8)?

5. In practical terms, how can you be "washing someone's feet" this week?

² Now by the time of supper, the Devil had already put it into the heart of Judas, Simon Iscariot's son, to betray Him. ³ Jesus knew that the Father had given everything into His hands, that He had come from God, and that He was going back to God. ⁴ So He got up from supper, laid aside His robe, took a towel, and tied it around Himself. ⁵ Next, He poured water into a basin and began to wash His disciples' feet and to dry them with the towel tied around Him.

⁶ He came to Simon Peter, who asked Him, "Lord, are You going to wash my feet?"

⁷ Jesus answered him, "What I'm doing you don't understand now, but afterwards you will know."

⁸ "You will never wash my feet—ever!" Peter said.

Jesus replied, "If I don't wash you, you have no part with Me."

⁹ Simon Peter said to Him, "Lord, not only my feet, but also my hands and my head."

¹⁰ "One who has bathed," Jesus told him, "doesn't need to wash anything except his feet, but he is completely clean. You are clean, but not all of you." ¹¹ For He knew who would betray Him. This is why He said, "You are not all clean."

The Meaning of Footwashing

¹² When Jesus had washed their feet and put on His robe, He reclinedᵇ again and said to them, "Do you know what I have done for you? ¹³ You call Me Teacher and Lord. This is well said, for I am. ¹⁴ So if I, your Lord and Teacher, have washed your feet, you also ought to wash one another's feet. ¹⁵ For I have given you an example that you also should do just as I have done for you.

¹⁶ "•I assure you: A slave is not greater than his master,ᶜ and a messenger is not greater than the one who sent him. ¹⁷ If you know these things, you are blessed if you do them. ¹⁸ I'm not speaking about all of you; I know those I have chosen. But the Scripture must be fulfilled: **The one who eats My bread**ᵈ **has raised his heel against Me.**ᵉ

¹⁹ "I am telling you now before it happens, so that when it does happen you will believe that I am [He]. ²⁰ I assure you: The one who receives whomever I send receives Me, and the one who receives Me receives Him who sent Me."

Judas' Betrayal Predicted

²¹ When Jesus had said this, He was troubled in His spirit and testified, "I assure you: One of you will betray Me!"

²² The disciples started looking at one another—uncertain which one He was speaking about. ²³ One of

---

ᵃ**13:1** to the end = completely or always   ᵇ**13:12** At important meals the custom was to recline on a mat at a low table and lean on the left elbow.   ᶜ**13:16** Or lord   ᵈ**13:18** Other mss read eats bread with Me   ᵉ**13:18** Ps 41:9

13:16 A slave is not greater than his master. If the master serves, how much more should the servants? **a messenger.** This is the same word as "apostle," which occurs only here in the Gospel of John. An apostle was a person sent with authority to represent another. Jesus' followers are to represent His servanthood to others.

13:18 the Scripture must be fulfilled. Psalm 41:9 is quoted as an example of a person being betrayed by close friends. Like David, Jesus must face being betrayed by His friends. **The one who eats My bread has raised his heel against Me.** Eating together was a sign of friendship. To lift up one's heel was a gesture of contempt, implying a desire to trample someone underfoot.

13:23 the one Jesus loved. This is the first mention of a disciple who will appear several

times in these final chapters (19:26-27; 20:2; 21:7,20). This is probably a reference to John, author of this Gospel. This title does not mean that Jesus loved this disciple more than the others, but that his identity was defined by Jesus' love for him.

13:26 He gave it to Judas. Although this was a signal that Judas was the person who would betray Jesus, it may also have been His final attempt to call Judas to repentance, since the sharing of food was a sign of friendship and peace.

13:27 Satan entered him. The relationship between Satan's activity and that of Judas is never explained. It is Judas's free choice to betray Jesus no matter his motives, but in so doing he was following the desires of the Devil. **What you're doing, do quickly.** Jesus' control of the timing of His death is evident even in

Judas's betrayal. His life was not taken from Him by others; He gave it willingly as a sacrifice on our behalf.

13:33 Where I am going you cannot come. Jesus used this same phrase with the Jewish religious leaders as a warning that they would not see the Father because they were heading in the wrong direction (8:21).

13:34-35 a new commandment. This is the first of several indications that at this meal Jesus is instituting a New Covenant between God and His people.

14:2 many dwelling places. The emphasis is not on having separate compartments in heaven, but on the abundance of room for all who will receive Jesus.

14:3 I will come back. This probably refers to

His disciples, the one Jesus loved, was reclining close beside Jesus.[a] 24 Simon Peter motioned to him to find out who it was He was talking about. 25 So he leaned back against Jesus and asked Him, "Lord, who is it?"

26 Jesus replied, "He's the one I give the piece of bread to after I have dipped it." When He had dipped the bread, He gave it to Judas, Simon Iscariot's son.[b] 27 After Judas ate₁ the piece of bread, Satan entered him. Therefore Jesus told him, "What you're doing, do quickly."

28 None of those reclining at the table knew why He told him this. 29 Since Judas kept the money-bag, some thought that Jesus was telling him, "Buy what we need for the festival," or that he should give something to the poor. 30 After receiving the piece of bread, he went out immediately. And it was night.

The New Commandment

31 When he had gone out, Jesus said, "Now the •Son of Man is glorified, and God is glorified in Him. 32 If God is glorified in Him,[c] God will also glorify Him in Himself and will glorify Him at once.

33 "Children, I am with you a little while longer. You will look for Me, and just as I told the Jews, 'Where I am going you cannot come,' so now I tell you.

34 "I give you a new commandment: love one another. Just as I have loved you, you must also love one another. 35 By this all people will know that you are My disciples, if you have love for one another."

Peter's Denials Predicted

36 "Lord," Simon Peter said to Him, "where are You going?"

Jesus answered, "Where I am going you cannot follow Me now, but you will follow later."

37 "Lord," Peter asked, "why can't I follow You now? I will lay down my life for You!"

38 Jesus replied, "Will you lay down your life for Me? I assure you: A rooster will not crow until you have denied Me three times.

The Way to the Father

14 "Your heart must not be troubled. Believe[d] in God; believe also in Me. 2 In My Father's house are many dwelling places;[e] if not, I would have told you. I am going away to prepare a place for you. 3 If I go away and prepare a place for you, I will come back and receive you to Myself, so that where I am you may be also. 4 You know the way where I am going."[f]

5 "Lord," Thomas said, "we don't know where You're going. How can we know the way?"

6 Jesus told him, "I am the way, the truth, and the life. No one comes to the Father except through Me.

Jesus Reveals the Father

7 "If you know Me, you will also know[g] My Father. From now on you do know Him and have seen Him."

8 "Lord," said Philip, "show us the Father, and that's enough for us."

9 Jesus said to him, "Have I been among you all this time without your knowing Me, Philip? The one who has seen Me has seen the Father. How can you say, 'Show us the Father'? 10 Don't you believe that I am in the Father and the Father is in Me? The words I speak to you I do not speak on My own. The Father who lives in Me does His works. 11 Believe Me that I am in the Father and the Father is in Me. Otherwise, believe[h] because of the works themselves.

Praying in Jesus' Name

12 "•I assure you: The one who believes in Me will also do the works that I do. And he will do even greater works than these, because I am going to the Father. 13 Whatever you ask in My name, I will do it so that the Father may be glorified in the Son. 14 If you ask Me[i] anything in My name, I will do it.[j]

---

a 13:23 Lit reclining at Jesus' breast; that is, on His right; Jn 1:18 b 13:26 Other mss read Judas Iscariot, Simon's son c 13:32 Other mss omit If God is glorified in Him d 14:1 Or You believe e 14:2 The Vg used the Lat term mansio, a traveler's resting place. The Gk word is related to the verb meno, meaning remain or stay, which occurs 40 times in John. f 14:4 Other mss read this verse: And you know where I am going, and you know the way g 14:7 Other mss read If you had known Me, you would have known h 14:11 Other mss read believe Me i 14:14 Other mss omit Me j 14:14 Other mss omit all of v. 14

---

the coming of Christ through His Spirit (vv. 15-21) rather than to the second coming, which receives very little attention in this Gospel. Through the Spirit, Jesus returns to the disciples (v. 18), and they are then "in" or "with" Him and the Father (vv. 20, 23). Seen in this way, this promise is not for the distant future, but it will be true for the disciples in a short time (20:22).

14:6 I am the way. The destination to which Jesus is going is not so much a place, but a person—the Father (7:33; 8:21). The way for the disciples to come to the Father is through the Son, who opens the way for them through His death (Heb. 10:19-22).

14:12 he will do even greater works. The work Jesus has done is revealing the truth about God. It is this mission that His disciples

will inherit after His death. The "greater" things that they will do should be understood in terms of their scope (i.e., they will bring the gospel to the Gentile world) rather than their power.

14:16 another Counselor. The Greek term paraclete has no adequate English translation. Words such as "Counselor" or "Helper" or "Comforter" emphasize only one of the many aspects of this term. Since this discourse presents the ministry of the Spirit in the same terms as that of Jesus, the Spirit can be referred to as another "Paraclete" like Jesus was (1 John 2:1).

14:17 He remains with you and will be in you. This indwelling of the Spirit with God's people ultimately makes the temple and the issue of where to worship irrelevant (4:21).

14:18 I am coming to you. The coming of Jesus spoken of here should be understood in terms of the coming of the Spirit. It is in that way that the believers will "see" Him, whereas the world will not (v. 19).

14:26 the Father will send Him. Here and in verse 16, it is the Father who sends the Spirit to the believer. In 15:26 and 16:7, Jesus says He will send the Spirit. **will teach you ... remind you.** These parallel verbs are two ways of saying the same thing. The purpose of the teaching of the Spirit is not to impart new information, but to remind believers of the truth that Jesus taught and to help them apply it to new situations.

15:1 I am the true vine. The image of the vine was used to describe Israel in the Old Testament (Ps. 80:14-18; Isa. 5:1-7). But Israel did

Another Counselor Promised

15 "If you love Me, you will keep[a] My commandments. 16 And I will ask the Father, and He will give you another •Counselor to be with you forever. 17 He is the Spirit of truth. The world is unable to receive Him because it doesn't see Him or know Him. But you do know Him, because He remains with you and will be[b] in you. 18 I will not leave you as orphans; I am coming to you.

Do You Really Love Me?

1. What was your most memorable Christmas or birthday gift?

John 14:15-27

2. If we love Jesus, what will we do (vv. 15,21,23)? What does this imply when we deliberately choose to sin?
3. What do you learn about the Holy Spirit in verses 16-17 and 25-27?
4. What sort of "peace" does the world give? What sort does Jesus give?
5. Do you love Jesus? How can you more fully obey Him?
6. Do you know the peace of Jesus, or are you seeking peace with the world?

The Father, the Son, and the Holy Spirit

19 "In a little while the world will see Me no longer, but you will see Me. Because I live, you will live too. 20 In that day you will know that I am in My Father, you are in Me, and I am in you. 21 The one who has My commands and keeps them is the one who loves

Me. And the one who loves Me will be loved by My Father. I also will love him and will reveal Myself to him."

22 Judas (not Iscariot) said to Him, "Lord, how is it You're going to reveal Yourself to us and not to the world?"

23 Jesus answered, "If anyone loves Me, he will keep My word. My Father will love him, and We will come to him and make Our home with him. 24 The one who doesn't love Me will not keep My words. The word that you hear is not Mine but is from the Father who sent Me.

25 "I have spoken these things to you while I remain with you. 26 But the Counselor, the Holy Spirit—the Father will send Him in My name—will teach you all things and remind you of everything I have told you.

Jesus' Gift of Peace

27 "Peace I leave with you. My peace I give to you. I do not give to you as the world gives. Your heart must not be troubled or fearful. 28 You have heard Me tell you, 'I am going away and I am coming to you.' If you loved Me, you would have rejoiced that I am going to the Father, because the Father is greater than I. 29 I have told you now before it happens so that when it does happen you may believe. 30 I will not talk with you much longer, because the ruler of the world is coming. He has no power over Me.[c] 31 On the contrary, ⌊I am going away⌋[d] so that the world may know that I love the Father. Just as the Father commanded Me, so I do.

"Get up; let's leave this place."

The Vine and the Branches

15 "I am the true vine, and My Father is the vineyard keeper. 2 Every branch in Me that does not produce fruit He removes, and He prunes every branch that produces fruit so that it will produce more fruit. 3 You are already clean because of the word I have spoken to you. 4 Remain in Me, and I in you. Just as a branch is unable to produce fruit by itself unless it remains on the vine, so neither can you unless you remain in Me.

---

a**14:15** Other mss read *If you love Me, keep* (as a command)   b**14:17** Other mss read *and is*   c**14:30** Lit *He has nothing in Me*   d**14:31** Probably refers to the cross

---

not produce the fruits God expected (Isa. 5:1-7; Matt. 21:43). Jesus transfers this image to Himself. He is the "true vine" who produces fruit because He always obeys the Father and does what pleases Him (8:29).

15:2 removes … prunes. A gardener cuts off dead branches that do not contribute to the plant and trims small branches to make them stronger when they grow back.

15:4 produce fruit. Although Paul uses the image of fruit to describe Christian character (Gal. 5:22-23), the fruit here probably relates to 4:35 and 12:24 where a similar agricultural image refers to the many people who would come to Christ. Just as Jesus' fruitfulness was dependent on His doing the Father's will, so the believer's fruitfulness results from following Jesus' teaching.

15:5 you can do nothing without Me. The disciples' relationship with Jesus is changing. He will no longer be visibly present to them. But His physical absence makes possible a relationship in which His disciples abide in Him and He in them. This mutual indwelling is not just a nice possibility but a vital necessity. Each of the disciples who heard these words understood clearly the relationship of the grape vine to its branches. They knew what happened when branches were severed from the vine.

15:6 If anyone does not remain in Me. Jesus elaborates on the metaphor of the vine and branches calling to mind a scene that His disciple has probably witnessed numerous times. Severed branches are worthless. Rather than letting them clutter up the vineyard, they are gathered and thrown in the fire.

15:7 ask whatever you want and it will be done for you. Here the promise is in the context of spiritual fruitfulness. In this verse, Jesus gives a further definition to what it means for his disciples to abide in Him and He in them: His words remain in His disciples. Words are the fuel of our lives. Observe yourself and other human beings. The attitudes and actions of every life are fueled by some kind of words. Our destinies are determined by the words that shape us. Jesus cleanses us by His words (15:3).By taking in Jesus' words that we grow into His likeness. Within this context His desires have become our desires and so whatever we ask, He will do.

15:8 My father is glorified by this. When God is glorified His weighty importance, divine power, and shining majesty are evident to both believers and nonbelievers. The same concept is seen in Jesus command to disciples to

5 "I am the vine; you are the branches. The one who remains in Me and I in him produces much fruit, because you can do nothing without Me. 6 If anyone does not remain in Me, he is thrown aside like a branch and he withers. They gather them, throw them into the fire, and they are burned. 7 If you remain in Me and My words remain in you, ask whatever you want and it will be done for you. 8 My Father is glorified by this: that you produce much fruit and prove to bea My disciples.

Christlike Love

9 "As the Father has loved Me, I have also loved you. Remain in My love. 10 If you keep My commands you will remain in My love, just as I have kept My Father's commands and remain in His love.

11 "I have spoken these things to you so that My joy may be in you and your joy may be complete. 12 This is My command: love one another as I have loved you. 13 No one has greater love than this, that someone would lay down his life for his friends. 14 You are My friends if you do what I command you. 15 I do not call you slaves anymore, because a slave doesn't know what his masterb is doing. I have called you friends, because I have made known to you everything I have heard from My Father. 16 You did not choose Me, but I chose you. I appointed you that you should go out and produce fruit and that your fruit should remain, so that whatever you ask the Father in My name, He will give you. 17 This is what I command you: love one another.

Persecutions Predicted

18 "If the world hates you, understand that it hated Me before it hated you. 19 If you were of the world, the world would love ¡you as¡ its own. However, because you are not of the world, but I have chosen you out of it, the world hates you. 20 Remember the word I spoke to you: 'A slave is not greater than his master.' If they persecuted Me, they will also persecute you. If they kept My word, they will also keep yours. 21 But they will do all these things to you on account of My name, because they don't know the One who sent Me. 22 If I had not come and spoken to them, they would not have sin.c Now they have no

excuse for their sin. 23 The one who hates Me also hates My Father. 24 If I had not done the works among them that no one else has done, they would not have sin. Now they have seen and hated both Me and My Father. 25 But ¡this happened¡ so that the statement written in their law might be fulfilled: **They hated Me for no reason.**d

Coming Testimony and Rejection

26 "When the •Counselor comes, the One I will send to you from the Father—the Spirit of truth who proceeds from the Father—He will testify about Me. 27 You also will testify, because you have been with Me from the beginning.

16 "I have told you these things to keep you from stumbling. 2 They will ban you from the •synagogues. In fact, a time is coming when anyone who kills you will think he is offering service to God. 3 They will do these things because they haven't known the Father or Me. 4 But I have told you these things so that when their timee comes you may remember I told them to you. I didn't tell you these things from the beginning, because I was with you.

The Counselor's Ministry

5 "But now I am going away to Him who sent Me, and not one of you asks Me, 'Where are You going?' 6 Yet, because I have spoken these things to you, sorrow has filled your heart. 7 Nevertheless, I am telling you the truth. It is for your benefit that I go away, because if I don't go away the •Counselor will not come to you. If I go, I will send Him to you. 8 When He comes, He will convict the world about sin, righteousness, and judgment: 9 about sin, because they do not believe in Me; 10 about righteousness, because I am going to the Father and you will no longer see Me; 11 and about judgment, because the ruler of this world has been judged.

12 "I still have many things to tell you, but you can't bear them now. 13 When the Spirit of truth comes, He will guide you into all the truth. For He will not speak on His own, but He will speak whatever He hears. He will also declare to you what is to come. 14 He will glorify Me, because He will take from what is Mine and

---

a15:8 Or *and become*   b15:15 Or *lord*   c15:22 To *have sin* is an idiom that refers to guilt caused by sin.   d15:25 Ps 69:4   e16:4 Other mss read *when the time*

---

let their lights shine through their good works. When others see this they recognize that God at work and they praise Him (Matt. 5:16).

15:15 friends. The disciples' relationship with Jesus is modeled upon that of Jesus with His Father. In 5:19-20 Jesus said the Father showed Him all that He does. In the same way, Jesus has now revealed to the disciples all that He has learned from the Father.

15:18 the world. This means that system of thinking and acting that sets humanity against the ways of God. **it hated Me before it hated you.** The reason for this hatred was "people loved darkness rather than the light because their deeds were evil" (3:19). It hates Jesus because He was from above while those who opposed Him were of this world and belonged to the Devil (8:23,44).

15:26 the Counselor ... will testify about Me. In times of persecution the Spirit will enable the disciples to speak the truth of the Father.

16:1 Throughout this discourse (13:1–17:26) Jesus prepares the disciples for what will be happening when He departs (v. 4; 13:19; 14:29). **stumbling.** Literally, "scandalize." The severity of persecution might dissuade the disciples from holding on to Jesus and His teaching. His warning is a corrective to any notions they may have that His kingdom will come about easily.

16:7 It is for your benefit that I go away. Jesus' departure means the coming of the Counselor (14:16), which really means His return to them in a deep, inner, spiritual way (7:39; 14:15-21).

16:8 He will convict the world about sin, righteousness, and judgment. The "world" held that Jesus was an unrighteous sinner under the judgment of God (9:25). The Spirit will prove that the world is wrong.

16:17-18 don't know what He's talking about! The riddle (v. 16) left the disciples confused. Their frustration here sums up the misunderstanding so common in this Gospel (2:21-22; 3:4; 4:15,32; 6:5,41,52; 7:35; 8:22,27,33,43; 10:19; 11:12). His closest followers do not know what He means. It will be resolved as He speaks without using any figurative language (v. 29).

16:20-22 weep and wail ... rejoice. This parable explains what the disciples will soon experience. While they are weeping over their loss of Jesus, the world (as personified by the

declare it to you. ¹⁵ Everything the Father has is Mine. This is why I told you that He takes from what is Mine and will declare it to you.

Sorrow Turned to Joy

¹⁶ "A little while and you will no longer see Me; again a little while and you will see Me."ᵃ

¹⁷ Therefore some of His disciples said to one another, "What is this He tells us: 'A little while and you will not see Me; again a little while and you will see Me'; and, 'because I am going to the Father'?" ¹⁸ They said, "What is this He is saying,ᵇ 'A little while'? We don't know what He's talking about!"

¹⁹ Jesus knew they wanted to question Him, so He said to them, "Are you asking one another about what I said, 'A little while and you will not see Me; again a little while and you will see Me'?

²⁰ "•I assure you: You will weep and wail, but the world will rejoice. You will become sorrowful, but your sorrow will turn to joy. ²¹ When a woman is in labor she has pain because her time has come. But when she has given birth to a child, she no longer remembers the suffering because of the joy that a person has been born into the world. ²² So you also have sorrowᶜ now. But I will see you again. Your hearts will rejoice, and no one will rob you of your joy. ²³ In that day you will not ask Me anything.

"I assure you: Anything you ask the Father in My name, He will give you. ²⁴ Until now you have asked for nothing in My name. Ask and you will receive, that your joy may be complete.

Jesus the Victor

²⁵ "I have spoken these things to you in figures of speech. A time is coming when I will no longer speak to you in figures, but I will tell you plainly about the Father. ²⁶ In that day you will ask in My name. I am not telling you that I will make requests to the Father on your behalf. ²⁷ For the Father Himself loves you, because you have loved Me and have believed that I came from God.ᵈ ²⁸ I came from the Father and have come into the world. Again, I am leaving the world and going to the Father."

²⁹ "Ah!" His disciples said. "Now You're speaking plainly and not using any figurative language. ³⁰ Now we know that You know everything and don't need anyone to question You. By this we believe that You came from God."

³¹ Jesus responded to them, "Do you now believe? ³² Look: An hour is coming, and has come, when each of you will be scattered to his own home, and you will leave Me alone. Yet I am not alone, because the Father is with Me. ³³ I have told you these things so that in Me you may have peace. You will have suffering in this world. Be courageous! I have conquered the world."

Jesus Prays for Himself

17 Jesus spoke these things, looked up to heaven, and said:

> Father,
> the hour has come.
> Glorify Your Son
> so that the Son may glorify You,
> ² for You gave Him authority
> over all flesh;ᵉ
> so He may give eternal life
> to all You have given Him.
> ³ This is eternal life:
> that they may know You, the only true God,
> and the One You have sent—Jesus Christ.
> ⁴ I have glorified You on the earth
> by completing the work You gave Me to do.
> ⁵ Now, Father, glorify Me in Your presence
> with that glory I had with You
> before the world existed.

Jesus Prays for His Disciples

> ⁶ I have revealed Your name
> to the men You gave Me from the world.
> They were Yours, You gave them to Me,
> and they have kept Your word.

ᵃ**16:16** Other mss add *because I am going to the Father*　ᵇ**16:18** Other mss omit *He is saying*　ᶜ**16:22** Other mss read *will have sorrow*　ᵈ**16:27** Other mss read *from the Father*　ᵉ**17:2** Or *people*

---

religious authorities) will rejoice that He is gone.

16:22 But I will see you again. Characteristically, this might mean either physically after Jesus' resurrection, or spiritually when He comes to them in the Spirit.

16:23 In that day. Again, this might mean the literal day of Jesus' resurrection, or the figurative Old Testament "day" of the Lord when salvation and judgment would be fulfilled. In the latter case, the "day" really extends from the first coming of Christ until His return in glory.

16:33 conquered. The powers of evil are overcome by Jesus' death and resurrection (Heb. 2:14; Rev. 5:5; 17:14).

17:6-8 They have received them. The disciples' insight that Jesus had indeed come from God (16:30) was a clue that Jesus' mission had been successful.

17:9 You have given Me. Jesus' disciples are not His, but the Father's—since it is because of the Father that they have come to Him (6:65).

17:12 I was protecting them. One part of God's work is protecting us—as He did His disciples—through His great power.

17:17 Sanctify them by the truth. Jesus prayed that the Father would keep His disciples from worldly concerns and empower them for service in His kingdom.

17:25 Righteous Father! God's righteousness means that He always does what is right. No matter what happens to us, we can trust Him, because He has our best interests at heart.

18:1 Kidron Valley. This valley was one of the borders of Jerusalem. During the rainy season it was a torrent. **a garden.** Luke 22:39 locates this on the Mt. of Olives, while Matthew 26:36 and Mark 14:32 refer to it as Gethsemane. It was a place of refuge that Jesus and the disciples often retreated to during visits to Jerusalem (v. 2; Luke 22:39).

18:2 Judas, who betrayed Him. The author of the Gospel of John gives no details about Judas' betrayal (Luke 22:1-6,47-48).

18:3 a company of soldiers. The word for "detachment" is a technical term meaning a force of 600 soldiers. Only Pilate would have the authority to dispatch these troops. This strong show of force would make sense if Pilate had been told by the Jewish authorities

7 Now they know that all things
You have given to Me are from You,

8 because the words that You gave Me,
I have given them.
They have received them
and have known for certain
that I came from You.
They have believed that You sent Me.

9 I pray[a] for them.
I am not praying for the world
but for those You have given Me,
because they are Yours.

10 All My things are Yours,
and Yours are Mine,
and I have been glorified in them.

11 I am no longer in the world,
but they are in the world,
and I am coming to You.
Holy Father,
protect[b] them by Your name
that You have given Me,
so that they may be one as We are one.

12 While I was with them,
I was protecting them by Your name
that You have given Me.
I guarded them and not one of them is lost,
except the son of destruction,[c]
so that the Scripture may be fulfilled.

13 Now I am coming to You,
and I speak these things in the world
so that they may have My joy completed
in them.

14 I have given them Your word.
The world hated them
because they are not of the world,
as I am not of the world.

15 I am not praying
that You take them out of the world
but that You protect them from the evil one.

16 They are not of the world,
as I am not of the world.

17 Sanctify[d] them by the truth;
Your word is truth.

18 As You sent Me into the world,
I also have sent them into the world.

19 I sanctify Myself for them,
so they also may be sanctified by the truth.

Jesus Prays for All Believers

20 I pray not only for these,
but also for those who believe in Me
through their message.

21 May they all be one,
as You, Father, are in Me and I am in You.
May they also be one[e] in Us,
so the world may believe You sent Me.

22 I have given them the glory You have given Me.
May they be one as We are one.

23 I am in them and You are in Me.
May they be made completely one,
so the world may know You have sent Me
and have loved them as You have loved Me.

24 Father,
I desire those You have given Me
to be with Me where I am.
Then they will see My glory,
which You have given Me
because You loved Me
before the world's foundation.

25 Righteous Father!
The world has not known You.
However, I have known You,
and these have known that You sent Me.

26 I made Your name known to them
and will make it known,
so the love You have loved Me with
may be in them and I may be in them.

Jesus Betrayed

18 After Jesus had said these things, He went out with His disciples across the Kidron Valley, where there was a garden, and He and His disciples went into it. 2 Judas, who betrayed Him, also knew the

---

a**17:9** Lit *ask* (throughout this passage)   b**17:11** Lit *keep* (throughout this passage)   c**17:12** The one destined for destruction, loss, or perdition
d**17:17** Set apart for special use   e**17:21** Other mss omit *one*

---

that Jesus and the disciples were planning an insurrection, which, according to 11:48, is what the authorities feared.

18:9 to fulfill the words He had said. This refers to 6:39; 17:12. This phrase is similar to the one used in 13:18; 15:25 when referring to Old Testament passages.

18:10 Peter, who had a sword. According to Luke 22:36-38, two of the disciples armed themselves with swords. These were daggers that could have been easy to hide. In John 13:37 Peter had pledged to die for Jesus. In light of the odds here, his attack could easily have caused that to happen. **Malchus.** The name of the servant is mentioned only here in the New Testament. Perhaps he was known to the community to which this Gospel was originally written.

18:11 Sheathe your sword! In verse 36 this refusal to meet force with force is used by Jesus as a sign of the true nature of His kingdom. **the cup.** In the Old Testament, drinking "the cup" is sometimes a symbol of experiencing God's judgment and wrath against sin (Ezek. 23:32-34; Hab. 2:16). This use of the metaphor reminds us that Jesus Himself will bear God's judgment against the sins of the people.

18:13 Annas. Annas was the high priest from A.D. 6 until A.D. 15, when he was deposed by the Roman authorities. But he held on to power by controlling the office through the appointment of family members, such as Caiaphas. In Acts 4:6 Annas is called the high priest even though that was no longer his title.

18:15 another disciple. The identity of this disciple is unknown. Although some interpret-

ers believe this is John, the author of this Gospel, it is unlikely that he is "the beloved disciple" mentioned elsewhere in the Gospel since he is not identified here as such.

18:20 I have spoken openly to the world. Jesus' teaching has been public all along. If the religious leaders wanted to know what He taught, they had ample opportunity to find out for themselves (8:43; 10:25). According to Jewish law, people were not required to testify against themselves, but witnesses were required. Jesus' answer and His suggestion that they call on others who had heard what He said (v. 21) may be His way of pointing out that this was an illegal hearing, since no witnesses were present.

18:28 headquarters. The Roman seat of power over Judea was located at Caesarea (Acts 23:33-35). This word refers to Pilate's

place, because Jesus often met there with His disciples. ³ So Judas took a •company of soldiers and some temple police from the •chief priests and the •Pharisees and came there with lanterns, torches, and weapons.

⁴ Then Jesus, knowing everything that was about to happen to Him, went out and said to them, "Who is it you're looking for?"

⁵ "Jesus the •Nazarene," they answered.

"I am He,"ᵃ Jesus told them.

Judas, who betrayed Him, was also standing with them. ⁶ When He told them, "I am He," they stepped back and fell to the ground.

⁷ Then He asked them again, "Who is it you're looking for?"

"Jesus the Nazarene," they said.

⁸ "I told you I am ⌊He⌋," Jesus replied. "So if you're looking for Me, let these men go." ⁹ This was to fulfill the words He had said: "I have not lost one of those You have given Me."

¹⁰ Then Simon Peter, who had a sword, drew it, struck the high priest's slave, and cut off his right ear. (The slave's name was Malchus.)

¹¹ At that, Jesus said to Peter, "Sheathe your sword! Am I not to drink the cup the Father has given Me?"

Jesus Arrested and Taken to Annas

¹² Then the company of soldiers, the commander, and the Jewish temple police arrested Jesus and tied Him up. ¹³ First they led Him to Annas, for he was the father-in-law of Caiaphas, who was high priest that year. ¹⁴ Caiaphas was the one who had advised the Jews that it was advantageous that one man should die for the people.

Peter Denies Jesus

¹⁵ Meanwhile Simon Peter was following Jesus, as was another disciple. That disciple was an acquaintance of the high priest; so he went with Jesus into the high priest's courtyard. ¹⁶ But Peter remained standing outside by the door. So the other disciple, the one known to the high priest, went out and spoke to the girl who was the doorkeeper and brought Peter in.

¹⁷ Then the slave girl who was the doorkeeper said to Peter, "You aren't one of this man's disciples too, are you?"

"I am not!" he said. ¹⁸ Now the slaves and the temple police had made a charcoal fire, because it was cold. They were standing there warming themselves, and Peter was standing with them, warming himself.

Jesus before Annas

¹⁹ The high priest questioned Jesus about His disciples and about His teaching.

²⁰ "I have spoken openly to the world," Jesus answered him. "I have always taught in the •synagogue and in the •temple complex, where all the Jews congregate, and I haven't spoken anything in secret. ²¹ Why do you question Me? Question those who heard what I told them. Look, they know what I said."

²² When He had said these things, one of the temple police standing by slapped Jesus, saying, "Is this the way you answer the high priest?"

²³ "If I have spoken wrongly," Jesus answered him, "give evidenceᵇ about the wrong; but if rightly, why do you hit Me?"

²⁴ Then Annas sent Him bound to Caiaphas the high priest.

Peter Denies Jesus Twice More

²⁵ Now Simon Peter was standing and warming himself. They said to him, "You aren't one of His disciples too, are you?"

He denied it and said, "I am not!"

²⁶ One of the high priest's slaves, a relative of the man whose ear Peter had cut off, said, "Didn't I see you with Him in the garden?"

²⁷ Peter then denied it again. Immediately a rooster crowed.

Jesus before Pilate

²⁸ Then they took Jesus from Caiaphas to the governor's •headquarters. It was early morning. They did not enter the headquarters themselves; otherwise they would be defiled and unable to eat the •Passover.

ᵃ**18:5** Lit *I am*; see note at Jn 8:58   ᵇ**18:23** Or *him, testify*

18:5 temporary residence in Jerusalem, a building that Herod the Great erected as a home for himself years before. **early morning.** Jesus' trial before the high priest was either late at night or very early in the morning. The trial before Pilate probably began around 6:00 to 7:00 a.m. since the Roman courts began early. **otherwise they would be defiled.** Rabbinic tradition taught that Gentile homes were unclean, defiling any Jew who entered. **the Passover.** According to the chronology of this Gospel, the Passover would be observed that evening. Any Jew ritually defiled would have to wait a month to observe this feast.

18:31 judge Him according to your law. Pilate's contempt for the Jews is seen throughout this account. He knew they had already tried Jesus or they would not have brought Him before his tribunal.

18:33 Are You the King of the Jews? This was probably asked in sarcasm or surprise. The Jewish religious leaders must have told Pilate that Jesus was claiming to be their king. They tried to portray Him as a threat to Roman rule (vv. 34-35).

19:1 flogged. This Roman punishment involved 39 lashes with a whip imbedded with metal and rock. It sometimes led to death from bleeding and shock.

19:2 a crown of thorns ... a purple robe. These were mock symbols of royalty.

19:7 He made Himself the Son of God. This was the charge that the leaders originally made against Jesus (5:18; 8:53; 10:33).

19:14 the preparation day. This was Friday. The Sabbath (which was also Passover ac-

cording to this Gospel) would begin that evening.

19:15 We have no king but Caesar! Even during the period of the Jewish kings, God was considered the only true King of Israel. In 8:33,41 the religious leaders protested against Jesus' implication that they served anyone but God. But they would rather affirm loyalty to a leader they despised than follow Jesus.

19:17 Carrying His own cross. Condemned prisoners had to carry at least the crossbar of the cross to the site of their execution, where the vertical posts were probably permanently installed.

19:19 Pilate also had a sign lettered and put on the cross. Some prisoners were required to wear signs around their necks that declared their crimes. This sign listed the name and ori-

²⁹ Then •Pilate came out to them and said, "What charge do you bring against this man?"

³⁰ They answered him, "If this man weren't a criminal,ᵃ we wouldn't have handed Him over to you."

³¹ So Pilate told them, "Take Him yourselves and judge Him according to your law."

"It's not legalᵇ for us to put anyone to death," the Jews declared. ³² They said this so that Jesus' words might be fulfilled signifying what sort of death He was going to die.

³³ Then Pilate went back into the headquarters, summoned Jesus, and said to Him, "Are You the King of the Jews?"

³⁴ Jesus answered, "Are you asking this on your own, or have others told you about Me?"

³⁵ "I'm not a Jew, am I?" Pilate replied. "Your own nation and the chief priests handed You over to me. What have You done?"

³⁶ "My kingdom is not of this world," said Jesus. "If My kingdom were of this world, My servantsᶜ would fight, so that I wouldn't be handed over to the Jews. As it is, My kingdom does not have its origin here."ᵈ

³⁷ "You are a king then?" Pilate asked.

"You say that I'm a king," Jesus replied. "I was born for this, and I have come into the world for this: to testify to the truth. Everyone who is of the truth listens to My voice."

³⁸ "What is truth?" said Pilate.

Jesus or Barabbas

After he had said this, he went out to the Jews again and told them, "I find no grounds for charging Him. ³⁹ You have a custom that I release one ⌊prisoner⌋ to you at the Passover. So, do you want me to release to you the King of the Jews?"

⁴⁰ They shouted back, "Not this man, but Barabbas!" Now Barabbas was a revolutionary.ᵉ

Jesus Flogged and Mocked

19 Then •Pilate took Jesus and had Him flogged. ² The soldiers also twisted together a crown of thorns, put it on His head, and threw a purple robe around Him. ³ And they repeatedly came up to Him and said, "Hail, King of the Jews!" and were slapping His face.

⁴ Pilate went outside again and said to them, "Look, I'm bringing Him outside to you to let you know I find no grounds for charging Him."

Pilate Sentences Jesus to Death

⁵ Then Jesus came out wearing the crown of thorns and the purple robe. Pilate said to them, "Here is the man!"

⁶ When the •chief priests and the temple police saw Him, they shouted, "Crucify! Crucify!"

Pilate responded, "Take Him and crucify Him yourselves, for I find no grounds for charging Him."

⁷ "We have a law," the Jews replied to him, "and according to that law He must die, because He made Himselfᶠ the Son of God."

⁸ When Pilate heard this statement, he was more afraid than ever. ⁹ He went back into the •headquarters and asked Jesus, "Where are You from?" But Jesus did not give him an answer. ¹⁰ So Pilate said to Him, "You're not talking to me? Don't You know that I have the authority to release You and the authority to crucify You?"

¹¹ "You would have no authority over Me at all," Jesus answered him, "if it hadn't been given you from above. This is why the one who handed Me over to you has the greater sin."ᵍ

¹² From that moment Pilate made every effortʰ to release Him. But the Jews shouted, "If you release this man, you are not Caesar's friend. Anyone who makes himself a king opposes Caesar!"

¹³ When Pilate heard these words, he brought Jesus outside. He sat down on the judge's bench in a place called the Stone Pavement (but in Hebrew *Gabbatha*). ¹⁴ It was the preparation day for the •Passover, and it was about six in the morning.ⁱ Then he told the Jews, "Here is your king!"

ᵃ**18:30** Lit *an evil doer*   ᵇ**18:31** According to Roman law   ᶜ**18:36** Or *attendants*, or *helpers*   ᵈ**18:36** Lit *My kingdom is not from here*   ᵉ**18:40** Or *robber*; see Jn 10:1,8 for the same Gk word used here   ᶠ**19:7** He claimed to be   ᵍ**19:11** To *have sin* is an idiom that refers to guilt caused by sin.
ʰ**19:12** Lit *Pilate was trying*   ⁱ**19:14** Lit *the sixth hour*; see note at Jn 1:39; an alternate time reckoning would be *about noon*

---

gin of Jesus as well as the "crime" for which He was convicted.

19:20 Hebrew, Latin, and Greek. These were the three common languages of the area. Jews from outside of Palestine would not necessarily have been able to read Aramaic (the local language of that area), nor Latin (the official language of the empire), but everyone would have known Greek since that was the common language of commerce.

19:25 His mother. Particularly touching is the presence of Jesus' mother at the cross. She watches her own son die a horrible death normally reserved for criminals. She had been told that her status as mother of the Son of God would make her blessed (Luke 1:42), but she did not feel "blessed" at this point.

19:26 the disciple He loved. It appears that

by this time Joseph, Mary's husband, was dead. As the oldest son, Jesus would have assumed the responsibility of caring for His mother (13:23).

19:29 sour wine. This was cheap wine. It may have been on the scene for the entertainment of the soldiers as they waited for the process of crucifixion to run its course. It would have done little for Jesus' thirst, and its bitterness symbolized the agony of the experience.

19:30 It is finished! Jesus is saying that His work had been accomplished. **gave up His spirit.** Jesus' death was voluntary. His life was not taken away by others; He sacrificed it freely (10:18).

19:31 the Jews did not want the bodies to remain on the cross. Although Roman custom left bodies on crosses as a warning for

criminals, Jewish law forbade bodies hung on a tree to remain there overnight (Deut. 21:22-23). **the men's legs broken.** By pressing their weight on their legs, victims could ease some of the pressure on their arms and chests, making breathing easier. But once their legs were broken, this relief was no longer possible; death by suffocation and shock would come quickly.

19:36 Not one of His bones will be broken. From the beginning of this Gospel, the ministry of Jesus has been pictured in terms of the Passover lamb (1:29; 6:4). One of the requirements about these lambs was that their bones should not be broken (Ex. 12:46).

19:38 Joseph. Although this Joseph is mentioned in all the Gospels, little is known about him. Luke says he was a member of the Sanhedrin who had opposed the plan of the major-

¹⁵ But they shouted, "Take Him away! Take Him away! Crucify Him!"

Pilate said to them, "Should I crucify your king?"

"We have no king but Caesar!" the chief priests answered.

¹⁶ So then, because of them, he handed Him over to be crucified.

The Crucifixion

Therefore they took Jesus away.ᵃ ¹⁷ Carrying His own cross, He went out to what is called Skull Place, which in Hebrew is called *Golgotha.* ¹⁸ There they crucified Him and two others with Him, one on either side, with Jesus in the middle. ¹⁹ Pilate also had a sign lettered and put on the cross. The inscription was:

> **JESUS THE NAZARENE**
> **THE KING OF THE JEWS**

²⁰ Many of the Jews read this sign, because the place where Jesus was crucified was near the city, and it was written in Hebrew,ᵇ Latin, and Greek. ²¹ So the chief priests of the Jews said to Pilate, "Don't write, 'The King of the Jews,' but that He said, 'I am the King of the Jews.'"

²² Pilate replied, "What I have written, I have written."

²³ When the soldiers crucified Jesus, they took His clothes and divided them into four parts, a part for each soldier. They also took the tunic, which was seamless, woven in one piece from the top. ²⁴ So they said to one another, "Let's not tear it, but toss for it, to see who gets it." ₁They did this₁ to fulfill the Scripture that says: **They divided My clothes among themselves, and they cast lots for My clothing.**ᶜ And this is what the soldiers did.

Jesus' Provision for His Mother

²⁵ Standing by the cross of Jesus were His mother, His mother's sister, Mary the wife of Clopas, and •Mary Magdalene. ²⁶ When Jesus saw His mother and the disciple He loved standing there, He said to His mother, "•Woman, here is your son." ²⁷ Then He said to the dis-

ciple, "Here is your mother." And from that hour the disciple took her into his home.

The Finished Work of Jesus

²⁸ After this, when Jesus knew that everything was now accomplished that the Scripture might be fulfilled, He said, "I'm thirsty!" ²⁹ A jar full of sour wine was sitting there; so they fixed a sponge full of sour wine on hyssopᵈ and held it up to His mouth.

³⁰ When Jesus had received the sour wine, He said, "It is finished!" Then bowing His head, He gave up His spirit.

Jesus' Side Pierced

³¹ Since it was the preparation day, the Jews did not want the bodies to remain on the cross on the Sabbath (for that Sabbath was a specialᵉ day). They requested that Pilate have the men's legs broken and that ₁their bodies₁ be taken away. ³² So the soldiers came and broke the legs of the first man and of the other one who had been crucified with Him. ³³ When they came to Jesus, they did not break His legs since they saw that He was already dead. ³⁴ But one of the soldiers pierced His side with a spear, and at once blood and water came out. ³⁵ He who saw this has testified so that you also may believe. His testimony is true, and he knows he is telling the truth. ³⁶ For these things happened so that the Scripture would be fulfilled: **Not one of His bones will be broken.**ᶠ ³⁷ Also, another Scripture says: **They will look at the One they pierced.**ᵍ

Jesus' Burial

³⁸ After this, Joseph of Arimathea, who was a disciple of Jesus—but secretly because of his fear of the Jews—asked Pilate that he might remove Jesus' body. Pilate gave him permission, so he came and took His body away. ³⁹ Nicodemus (who had previously come to Him at night) also came, bringing a mixture of about 75 poundsʰ of myrrh and aloes. ⁴⁰ Then they took Jesus' body and wrapped it in linen cloths with the aromatic spices, according to the burial custom of the Jews. ⁴¹ There was a garden in the place where He was crucified. A new

ᵃ**19:16** Other mss add *and led Him out* ᵇ**19:20** Or *Aramaic* ᶜ**19:24** Ps 22:18 ᵈ**19:29** Or *with hyssop* ᵉ**19:31** Lit *great* ᶠ**19:36** Ex 12:46; Nm 9:12; Ps 34:20 ᵍ**19:37** Zch 12:10 ʰ**19:39** Lit *100 litrai;* a Roman *litrai* = 12 ounces

ity to kill Jesus (Luke 23:50-51). The author's comment here that he was a secret disciple because of his fear of the Jews accords with what he said in 12:42-43.

19:39 a mixture of about 75 pounds of myrrh and aloes. This was a large amount of spices to use in the burial process. Normally, only royal figures were accorded such honor at death.

19:41 A new tomb. Tombs for the wealthy were carved in rock and closed by a stone rolled across the entrance. Matthew 27:59-60 says this was Joseph's own tomb.

20:1 the first day of the week. This was Sunday. **Mary Magdalene.** Mary is mentioned in the accounts of the resurrection of Jesus in all four Gospels. Luke 8:2 says that she was one of several women who traveled with the disci-

ples.

20:5-7 linen cloths. Grave robbers, in search of treasures entombed with the corpse, would either have taken the wrapped body of Jesus or scattered the strips as they tore them off. The fact that the clothes were neatly laid to one side was one of the evidences that led the "other disciple" to faith (v. 8).

20:14 she did not know it was Jesus. Mary may have been blinded by her grief. Or perhaps there was a difference in Jesus' appearance that caused her not to recognize Him.

20:15 gardener. The tomb was located in a garden owned by Joseph of Arimathea. As an aristocratic member of the Sanhedrin, he probably would have employed a gardener to care for his property.

20:16 Mary. When Jesus speaks Mary's name, she immediately recognizes who is speaking to her, thus proving her discipleship. **Rabbouni.** Literally, "my teacher." This is a title of respect for Jesus, as well as one that shows Mary's submission and love for Him.

20:17 Don't cling to Me. We need not think that Jesus refused to allow Mary to touch Him. After Mary expressed her joy and relief at seeing Him, He told her that all was not finished yet.

20:19 fear of the Jews. The disciples were afraid that the authorities, who had been successful in having Jesus killed, might now turn on them. **Jesus came.** Nothing is said about how Jesus came to be among the disciples, but the implication of the locked doors appears to be that Jesus simply appeared with them (v. 26; Luke 24:31). **Peace to you!** The

tomb was in the garden; no one had yet been placed in it. ⁴² They placed Jesus there because of the Jewish preparation and since the tomb was nearby.

The Empty Tomb

20 On the first day of the week •Mary Magdalene came to the tomb early, while it was still dark. She saw that the stone had been removedᵃ from the tomb. ² So she ran to Simon Peter and to the other disciple, the one Jesus loved, and said to them, "They have taken the Lord out of the tomb, and we don't know where they have put Him!"

Tomb Raiders

1. Have you ever seen someone you knew from your past, and you didn't recognize him or her? What happened? How did you feel when you suddenly realized who it was?

John 20:1-18

2. Why did Jesus ask Mary who she was looking for, when He undoubtedly knew? Why did she suddenly recognize Him when He said her name?

3. John, the "other disciple," "entered the tomb, saw, and believed" (v. 8). What did he believe? Why did the empty tomb convince him?

4. Do you believe in Jesus' death and resurrection? How does this belief affect your life?

³ At that, Peter and the other disciple went out, heading for the tomb. ⁴ The two were running together, but the other disciple outran Peter and got to the tomb first. ⁵ Stooping down, he saw the linen cloths lying there, yet he did not go in. ⁶ Then, following him, Simon Peter came also. He entered the tomb and saw the linen cloths lying there. ⁷ The wrapping that had been on His head was not lying with the linen cloths but was folded up in a separate place by itself. ⁸ The other disciple, who had reached the tomb first, then entered the tomb, saw, and believed. ⁹ For they still did not understand the Scripture that He must rise from the dead. ¹⁰ Then the disciples went home again.

Mary Magdalene Sees the Risen Lord

¹¹ But Mary stood outside facing the tomb, crying. As she was crying, she stooped to look into the tomb. ¹² She saw two angels in white sitting there, one at the head and one at the feet, where Jesus' body had been lying. ¹³ They said to her, "•Woman, why are you crying?"

"Because they've taken away my Lord," she told them, "and I don't know where they've put Him." ¹⁴ Having said this, she turned around and saw Jesus standing there, though she did not know it was Jesus.

¹⁵ "Woman," Jesus said to her, "why are you crying? Who is it you are looking for?"

Supposing He was the gardener, she replied, "Sir, if you've removed Him, tell me where you've put Him, and I will take Him away."

¹⁶ Jesus said, "Mary."

Turning around, she said to Him in Hebrew, "*Rabbouni!*"ᵇ—which means "Teacher."

¹⁷ "Don't cling to Me," Jesus told her, "for I have not yet ascended to the Father. But go to My brothers and tell them that I am ascending to My Father and your Father—to My God and your God."

¹⁸ Mary Magdalene went and announced to the disciples, "I have seen the Lord!" And she told them whatᶜ He had said to her.

The Disciples Commissioned

¹⁹ In the evening of that first day of the week, the disciples were ₗgathered togetherₗ with the doors locked because of their fear of the Jews. Then Jesus came, stood among them, and said to them, "Peace to you!"

²⁰ Having said this, He showed them His hands and His side. So the disciples rejoiced when they saw the Lord.

ᵃ**20:1** Lit *She saw the stone removed*   ᵇ**20:16** *Rabbouni* is also used in Mk 10:51   ᶜ**20:18** Lit *these things*

promise of peace was given in 14:27 and 16:33. It sums up the blessings and fullness of the New Covenant that Jesus has established between the Father and His people (14:27).

20:22 He breathed on them. As God originally breathed life into Adam at the first creation (Gen. 2:7), so now Jesus breathes spiritual life into His people at the re-creation of the people of God (1:12-13): **Receive the Holy Spirit.** The other Gospels do not mention the coming of the Spirit to the disciples, but Acts 2 indicates that Luke saw this promise being fulfilled on the day of Pentecost, seven weeks after Jesus' resurrection.

20:23 If you forgive … if you retain. The disciples are to pronounce forgiveness upon those who receive the gospel. Likewise, to those who refuse the gospel, they are to pronounce the words of warning just as Jesus did

(8:24).

20:26 Even though the doors were locked. This indicates that Jesus' resurrected body was not limited in the way a normal physical body is. He was able to enter a locked room and simply appear. Nevertheless His body could be felt (v. 27), and He ate (Luke 24:41-43). **Peace to you!** The word *peace* reflects the salvation that Christ's redemptive work achieves—total well being and inner rest of spirit, in fellowship with God.

20:28 My Lord and my God! Thomas clearly affirms the deity of Jesus. This is the last of a series of confessions of faith that sum up what the author of John's Gospel wants the reader to recognize about Jesus (11:27).

20:29 Those who believe without seeing are blessed. The author applies the words of Tho-

mas to the situation of his readers. They are not deprived because of never having seen Jesus. Indeed, He is with them through the Spirit (14:15-20).

21:1 After this. This is actually the same indefinite time reference that John used to begin chapters 5, 6, and 7. When this appearance of Jesus occurred is unclear. Since one of the themes in this section is Jesus' restoration of Peter, and since, like Mary in 20:15, they did not recognize Him at first, it may be that this event actually occurred before Jesus' climactic appearance to the disciples in 20:19. **Sea of Tiberias.** Tiberias, a city founded in A.D. 20 by Herod, was located on the shore of the Sea of Galilee. By the time the Gospel of John was written, this new name for the Sea of Galilee was well known.

21:7 the one Jesus loved. This is thought to

21 Jesus said to them again, "Peace to you! As the Father has sent Me, I also send you." 22 After saying this, He breathed on them and said,ᵃ "Receive the Holy Spirit. 23 If you forgive the sins of any, they are forgiven them; if you retain ⌊the sins of⌋ any, they are retained."

Thomas Sees and Believes

24 But one of the Twelve, Thomas (called "Twin"), was not with them when Jesus came. 25 So the other disciples kept telling him, "We have seen the Lord!"

You Gotta Believe

1. Are you more likely to believe what someone tells you, or do you have to see to believe?

John 20:24-31

2. Why do you suppose Thomas doubted? If you'd been in his place, what would your response have been?
3. How does Jesus deal with Thomas' doubt (v. 27)?
4. Why does John say that he wrote about Jesus' life, resurrection, and miracles (v. 31)? Why is "believing" such an important thing?
5. Are you an unbeliever or a believer? If you're an unbeliever, what would it take for you to believe?

But he said to them, "If I don't see the mark of the nails in His hands, put my finger into the mark of the nails, and put my hand into His side, I will never believe!"

26 After eight days His disciples were indoors again, and Thomas was with them. Even though the doors were locked, Jesus came and stood among them. He said, "Peace to you!"

27 Then He said to Thomas, "Put your finger here and observe My hands. Reach out your hand and put it into My side. Don't be an unbeliever, but a believer."

28 Thomas responded to Him, "My Lord and my God!"

29 Jesus said, "Because you have seen Me, you have believed.ᵇ Those who believe without seeing are blessed."

The Purpose of This Gospel

30 Jesus performed many other signs in the presence of His disciples that are not written in this book. 31 But these are written so that you may believe Jesus is the •Messiah, the Son of God,ᶜ and by believing you may have life in His name.

Jesus' Third Appearance to the Disciples

21 After this, Jesus revealed Himself again to His disciples by the Sea of Tiberias.ᵈ He revealed Himself in this way:

2 Simon Peter, Thomas (called "Twin"), Nathanael from Cana of Galilee, Zebedee's sons, and two others of His disciples were together.

3 "I'm going fishing," Simon Peter said to them.

"We're coming with you," they told him. They went out and got into the boat, but that night they caught nothing.

4 When daybreak came, Jesus stood on the shore. However, the disciples did not know it was Jesus.

5 "Men,"ᵉ Jesus called to them, "you don't have any fish, do you?"

"No," they answered.

6 "Cast the net on the right side of the boat," He told them, "and you'll find some." So they did,ᶠ and they were unable to haul it in because of the large number of fish.

7 Therefore the disciple, the one Jesus loved, said to Peter, "It is the Lord!"

When Simon Peter heard that it was the Lord, he tied his outer garment around himᵍ (for he was stripped) and plunged into the sea. 8 But since they were not far from land (about 100 yardsʰ away), the other disciples came in the boat, dragging the net full of fish. 9 When they got out on land, they saw a charcoal fire there, with fish lying on it, and bread.

ᵃ20:22 Lit He breathed and said to them ᵇ20:29 Or have you believed? (as a question) ᶜ20:31 Or that the Messiah, the Son of God, is Jesus ᵈ21:1 The Sea of Galilee; Sea of Tiberias is used only in John; Jn 6:1,23 ᵉ21:5 Lit Children ᶠ21:6 Lit they cast ᵍ21:7 Lit he girded his garment ʰ21:8 Lit about 200 cubits

be John, the author of the Gospel of John. **It is the Lord!** Just as Jesus' voice caused Mary to recognize Him (20:16), so here the enormous catch of fish revealed to the beloved disciple that the person with whom they were talking was the Lord.

21:12 breakfast. The Jesus whom the disciples met was no disembodied spirit. They could see Him, hear Him, and eat with Him. Jesus had been resurrected bodily. He had conquered death.

21:14 the third time. This is the third resurrection account in John's Gospel (20:19-23,24-29). The post-resurrection appearances are part of the proof of Jesus' resurrection. They also show that Jesus had conquered death and describe how the disciples learned of their mission. Their encounter with the living Jesus changed them from frightened men to bold witnesses for their Lord.

21:15 do you love Me more than these? Jesus gives Peter three opportunities to pledge his love for Him. **Feed My lambs.** After each query about his love, Jesus calls Peter to demonstrate that love by being a "good shepherd" to Jesus' sheep.

21:18 you will stretch out your hands. The stretching out of a person's hands was an early Christian idiom for crucifixion. This explains the author's comment on this quote in verse 19.

21:19 by what kind of death he would glorify God. Peter would indeed lay down his life for Jesus in the future. Since Peter is believed to have been killed during Nero's persecution of Christians in the early 60s, the manner and reality of his death would have been known by

this Gospel's first readers. **Follow Me!** The important thing for the disciple, whether Peter or any reader of the Gospel of John, is to keep on following Jesus, no matter where this might lead (12:26).

21:21 what about him? This question may be a clue about the purpose of this entire chapter. By the time of this writing, the beloved disciple (likely John) was probably old. So something had to be said about a rumor that had begun at the earliest stages of the Christian era which implied that John would live until Jesus' return (v. 23).

21:22 what is that to you? Jesus' response emphasized that Peter should mind his own business. The path of discipleship is different for each follower. We should follow the path He has laid out for us.

Cast Your Nets

1. What has been your best or worst fishing, camping, or hiking experience?

John 21:1-14

2. Why did Jesus cook breakfast for the disciples? How is this act similar to His washing their feet (13:1-7)?

3. What made John, "the one Jesus loved," recognize that it was Jesus on the beach (v. 7)?

4. Why did Peter jump into the lake (v. 7)?

5. Why did Jesus tell the disciples to cast their nets for fish? Why not just miraculously have them swim ashore?

6. Is Jesus calling you to "cast your nets" in faith? How? Where?

10 "Bring some of the fish you've just caught," Jesus told them. 11 So Simon Peter got up and hauled the net ashore, full of large fish—153 of them. Even though there were so many, the net was not torn.

12 "Come and have breakfast," Jesus told them. None of the disciples dared ask Him, "Who are You?" because they knew it was the Lord. 13 Jesus came, took the bread, and gave it to them. He did the same with the fish.

14 This was now the third time[a] Jesus appeared[b] to the disciples after He was raised from the dead.

Jesus' Threefold Restoration of Peter

15 When they had eaten breakfast, Jesus asked Simon Peter, "Simon, son of John,[c] do you love[d] Me more than these?"

"Yes, Lord," he said to Him, "You know that I love You."

"Feed My lambs," He told him. 16 A second time He asked him, "Simon, son of John, do you love Me?"

"Yes, Lord," he said to Him, "You know that I love You."

"Shepherd My sheep," He told him. 17 He asked him the third time, "Simon, son of John, do you love Me?"

Peter was grieved that He asked him the third time, "Do you love Me?" He said, "Lord, You know everything! You know that I love You."

"Feed My sheep," Jesus said. 18 "•I assure you: When you were young, you would tie your belt and walk wherever you wanted. But when you grow old, you will stretch out your hands and someone else will tie you and carry you where you don't want to go." 19 He said this to signify by what kind of death he would glorify God.[e] After saying this, He told him, "Follow Me!"

Correcting a False Report

20 So Peter turned around and saw the disciple Jesus loved following them. ⌊That disciple⌋ was the one who had leaned back against Jesus at the supper and asked, "Lord, who is the one that's going to betray You?" 21 When Peter saw him, he said to Jesus, "Lord—what about him?"

22 "If I want him to remain until I come," Jesus answered, "what is that to you? As for you, follow Me."

23 So this report[f] spread to the brothers[g] that this disciple would not die. Yet Jesus did not tell him that he would not die, but, "If I want him to remain until I come, what is that to you?"

Epilogue

24 This is the disciple who testifies to these things and who wrote them down. We know that his testimony is true.

25 And there are also many other things that Jesus did, which, if they were written one by one, I suppose not even the world itself could contain the books[h] that would be written.

a**21:14** The other two are in Jn 20:19–29.   b**21:14** Lit was revealed (see v. 1)   c**21:15–17** Other mss read Simon, son of Jonah; Jn 1:42; Mt 16:17   d**21:15–17** Two synonyms are translated love in this conversation: agapao, the first 2 times by Jesus (vv. 15–16); and phileo, the last time by Jesus (v. 17) and all 3 times by Peter (vv. 15–17). Peter's threefold confession of love for Jesus corresponds to his earlier threefold denial of Jesus; Jn 18:15–18,25–27.   e**21:19** Jesus predicts that Peter would be martyred. Church tradition says that Peter was crucified upside down.   f**21:23** Lit this word   g**21:23** The word brothers refers to the whole Christian community.   h**21:25** Lit scroll

21:23 Yet Jesus did not tell him that he would not die. The narrator thus sets the record straight on Jesus' comment about the beloved disciple. It was not a promise that He would return within this disciple's lifetime.

ACTS

AUTHOR

Although unnamed, there is an ancient tradition that Luke wrote Acts as a companion to the third Gospel. Little is known of Luke. He is mentioned only three times in the New Testament (Col. 4:14; Philem. 24; 2 Tim. 4:11). These references tell us that Luke was a physician, a valued companion of Paul, and a Gentile.

Luke's medical background is demonstrated by his use of medical terms, especially in his Gospel. For example, in recounting the story of the camel and the needle's eye (Luke 18:25), Luke's role as Paul's traveling companion is evident in *we* sections, the author suddenly switches from saying, "They did this" to "We did that" (Acts 16:10-17; 20:5-21:18; 27:1-28:16). At these points in Paul's journeys, Luke joined him as a colleague in ministry. And we learn that Luke was a Gentile from the list of greetings with which Paul concludes Colossians Col. 4:10-11.

DATE

The final events recorded here took place in early A.D. 60, so Acts must have been compiled after that time.

THEME

The spread of the Gospel to all the known world (1:8).

HISTORICAL BACKGROUND

Why did Luke write the book of Acts? Possibly he desired to commend Christianity to the Gentile world in general and to the Roman government in particular. We find in Acts not only Jews turning to Jesus (3,000 on the Day of Pentecost, see Acts 2:41) but also Gentiles. We see Peter (the apostle to the Jews) welcoming Cornelius, the Roman centurion, into the church. We see Philip preaching to the Samaritans and Jewish believers and evangelizing Gentiles in Antioch. We find Paul called by Christ to be the apostle to the Gentiles, setting up churches across the Roman Empire. Finally in Acts 15, there is formal affirmation that Gentiles are accepted in the church of Jesus Christ on equal terms with Jews.

Luke's response to the Roman government is fascinating. He seemed to go out of his way to show that Christians were loyal citizens and not lawbreakers and criminals (18:14-16; 19:37; 23:29; 25:25). He also took pains to point out that Roman officials had always treated Christians fairly and courteously (13:12; 18:12-17; 19:31). This was important to state lest Christianity be perceived as a political movement and therefore a threat to the Roman Empire.

However, commending Christianity to Gentiles was not Luke's central aim. His main purpose is implied in 1:8, "But you will receive power when the Holy Spirit has come upon you, and you will be My witnesses in Jerusalem, in all Judea and Samaria, and to the ends of the earth." Luke aims to show how Christianity had spread from Jerusalem to Rome in 30 years.

CHARACTERISTICS

The book of Acts is the bridge between the Gospel and the Epistles. On the one hand, Acts completes the story of Jesus--how his life, death, and resurrection created a whole new community: the church. On the other hand, Acts sets the stage for the correspondence to this church; the letters make up the rest of the New Testament. It would be

difficult to fully understand the Epistles without the data found in Acts.

Luke tells the story of the development of the church by opening a series of windows that allows us to glimpse important (and representative) developments in its growth.

1. Key Figure–The Holy Spirit

One thing that characterizes the entire story is the work of the Holy Spirit. There is little question in Luke's mind how the church spread: the Holy Spirit did it. So we see the church resulting from the baptism of the Holy Spirit (2:38-41). We then see the Holy Spirit gently but directly guide the early church (13:2 and 16:7). In fact, the presence of the Holy Spirit signals that a church is authentic and not false (19:1-6). Some have suggested that this book ought to have been labeled "The Acts of the Holy Spirit" and not "The Acts of the Apostles".

2. Leading Roles–Peter and Paul

The title "The Acts of the Apostles" is inaccurate for yet another reason. The book of Acts is the story of only two apostles–Peter and Paul. Peter's story is told first. In the initial 12 chapters, he is the central figure. But in chapter 13, the spotlight shifts to Paul, and he holds center stage until Acts concludes.

The stories of these two men are not dissimilar. Both heal cripples (3:1-10; 14:8-12); both have the experience of seeing cures brought about in unusual ways (5:15-16; 19:11-12); both bring people back to life (9:36-42; 20:9-12); both meet a sorcerer (8:9-25; 13:6-12); and both are released from prison as the result of a miracle (12:7; 16:26-28). The author of Acts focuses on Peter and on Paul in their roles as key leaders of the early church. Peter was the chief apostle to the Jews, while Paul was the chief apostle to the Gentiles.

3. Key Sources

Where did Luke get his information about the church's growth? The source of the second half of the book (chapters 13-28) is clear. Luke got this information directly from his friend and companion, Paul. We know Luke was traveling with Paul (the *we* sections), and he may well have kept a journal. We can also guess that during Paul's confinement in prison, the great apostle probably recounted his many adventures to Luke.

But how about the first 12 chapters that center around Peter? Luke tells us in Luke 1:3 that he "carefully investigated everything from the very first." How? Probably by talking to believers he met through Paul. For example, Luke knew Mark. Both men were with Paul when he wrote Colossians (Col. 4:10,14). From Mark he would have received valuable information about the growth of the church in Jerusalem and about Peter's role there. And Luke would have heard stories about Peter in the churches he visited. Finally, Luke may have had access to the official records (written and oral) of the key churches mentioned in the first 12 chapters–the churches in Jerusalem, Caesarea and Antioch.

4. Keen Historian

Luke's accuracy as a historian was validated by the archaeological research of Sir William Ramsay. Luke had the mind of a researcher: He was careful and paid attention to details. Thus, when reading his story of the early church, we have confidence that what Luke tells us is just what happened.

PASSAGES FOR TOPICAL GROUP STUDY

Prologue

1 I wrote the first narrative, Theophilus, about all that Jesus began to do and teach [2] until the day He was taken up, after He had given orders through the Holy Spirit to the apostles whom He had chosen. [3] After He had suffered, He also presented Himself alive to them by many convincing proofs, appearing to them during 40 days and speaking about the kingdom of God.

The Holy Spirit Promised

[4] While He was together with them,[a] He commanded them not to leave Jerusalem, but to wait for the Father's promise. "This," ⌊He said, "is what⌋ you heard from Me; [5] for John baptized with water, but you will be baptized with the Holy Spirit not many days from now."

[6] So when they had come together, they asked Him, "Lord, at this time are You restoring the kingdom to Israel?"

[7] He said to them, "It is not for you to know times or periods that the Father has set by His own authority. [8] But you will receive power when the Holy Spirit has come upon you, and you will be My witnesses in Jerusalem, in all Judea and Samaria, and to the ends[b] of the earth."

The Ascension

[9] After He had said this, He was taken up as they were watching, and a cloud received Him out of their sight. [10] While He was going, they were gazing into heaven, and suddenly two men in white clothes stood by them. [11] They said, "Men of Galilee, why do you stand looking up into heaven? This Jesus, who has been taken from you into heaven, will come in the same way that you have seen Him going into heaven."

United in Prayer

[12] Then they returned to Jerusalem from the mount called Olive Grove, which is near Jerusalem—a Sabbath day's journey away. [13] When they arrived, they went to the room upstairs where they were staying:

Peter, John,
James, Andrew,
Philip, Thomas,
Bartholomew, Matthew,
James the son of Alphaeus,
Simon the Zealot, and Judas the son of James.

[14] All these were continually united in prayer,[c] along with the women, including Mary[d] the mother of Jesus, and His brothers.

Baptism of the Holy Spirit

1. What long-awaited prize was worth the wait (concert tickets, driver's license, etc.)?

Acts 1:1-11

2. What does it mean to be "baptized with the Holy Spirit" (v. 5)? What does that image suggest about the Holy Spirit's work in our lives?

3. Why did Jesus tell the disciples, "It is not for you to know times or periods that the Father has set by His own authority" (v. 7)? What "times and periods" do you sometimes wonder about?

4. What "power" does the Holy Spirit bring to Christians? How do you specifically need the Holy Spirit's help in being a witness to others?

Matthias Chosen

[15] During these days Peter stood up among the brothers[e] — the number of people who were together was about 120—and said: [16] "Brothers, the Scripture had to be fulfilled that the Holy Spirit through the mouth of David spoke in advance about Judas, who became a guide to those who arrested Jesus. [17] For he was one of our number and was allotted a share in this

---

[a]**1:4** Or *He was eating with them,* or *He was lodging with them*   [b]**1:8** Lit *the end*   [c]**1:14** Other mss add *and petition*   [d]**1:14** Or *prayer, with their wives and Mary*   [e]**1:15** Other mss read *disciples*

1:1 the first narrative. That is, the Gospel of Luke. Luke authored both works. **all that Jesus began to do and teach.** Acts is the continuing story of the work of Jesus in the life of the church.

1:2 until the day He was taken up. See Luke 24:50–53. The ascension marks the beginning of a new phase in the work of Jesus. He now exercises His divine reign from heaven. **apostles.** Apostles were ambassadors especially commissioned to represent the one in whose name they were sent. In the Gospels, this term refers only to the Twelve. In Acts, others (like Paul and Barnabas in 14:3–4) are called apostles.

1:4–5 the Father's promise. From the very beginning the expectation was that through Jesus the Spirit of God would be poured out on all His people. **baptized with the Holy**

Spirit. Baptism was associated with cleansing. The metaphor would communicate being flooded with God's Spirit. Thus Jesus raised the expectations of the disciples about what the next step in His agenda for them might be.

1:6–8 are You restoring the kingdom to Israel. Jesus and the disciples had different ideas about the kingdom of God (Luke 9:46–55; 22:24ff). The question of verse 6 reflects three such misunderstandings: (1) it would not be Jesus who would be doing the work from now on, but the disciples empowered by His Spirit; (2) the time of the kingdom's establishment should not concern them; and (3) the kingdom is not a matter of the political destiny of Israel, but a spiritual realm involving the whole world.

1:8 the Holy Spirit has come upon you.

The mission of Jesus is continued through the work of His Spirit empowering the disciples to bear witness to Him (Luke 12:11–12; Matt. 28:20–21). The result of this empowering will be the spread of the gospel throughout the world.

1:9 a cloud received Him out of their sight. A declaration of Jesus' deity. The Bible often uses the cloud as a symbol of divine glory (Ex. 16:10; Ps. 104:3).

1:14 Mary ... and ... His brothers. Before the resurrection, Jesus' brothers had not believed in Him (Mark 3:21; John 7:5). One of His brothers, James, eventually became a leader of the Jerusalem church and the author of the epistle of James.

1:18–19 falling headfirst, he burst open. This statement about Judas' death differs

ministry." ¹⁸ Now this man acquired a field with his unrighteous wages; and falling headfirst, he burst open in the middle, and all his insides spilled out. ¹⁹ This became known to all the residents of Jerusalem, so that in their own language that field is called *Hakeldama,* that is, Field of Blood. ²⁰ "For it is written in the Book of Psalms:

Replacing a Starting Player

1. If you could add any one person to your athletic team now, who would you invite? To your group?

Acts 1:12-26

2. Why did the disciples decide to find another disciple to replace Judas?

3. Why did Judas commit suicide? Where does going it your own way instead of siding with Jesus lead?

4. Matthias was chosen, but he is never mentioned again; God chose Paul later. What does this suggest about man's views of qualified spiritual leaders?

5. Judas rejected Jesus, while Paul obeyed Him. How can you be a disciple more like Paul?

Let his dwelling become desolate;
let no one live in it;ᵃ and
Let someone else take his position.ᵇ

²¹ "Therefore, from among the men who have accompanied us during the whole time the Lord Jesus went in and out among us— ²² beginning from the baptism of John until the day He was taken up from us—from among these, it is necessary that one become a witness with us of His resurrection."

²³ So they proposed two: Joseph, called Barsabbas, who was also known as Justus, and Matthias. ²⁴ Then they prayed, "You, Lord, know the hearts of all; show which of these two You have chosen ²⁵ to take the placeᶜ in this apostolic service that Judas left to go to his own place." ²⁶ Then they cast lots for them, and the lot fell to Matthias. So he was numbered with the 11 apostles.

Pentecost

2 When the day of Pentecost had arrived, they were all together in one place. ² Suddenly a sound like that of a violent rushing wind came from heaven, and it filled the whole house where they were staying. ³ And tongues, like flames of fire that were divided, appeared to them and rested on each one of them. ⁴ Then they were all filled with the Holy Spirit and began to speak in different languages, as the Spirit gave them ability for speech.

⁵ There were Jews living in Jerusalem, devout men from every nation under heaven. ⁶ When this sound occurred, the multitude came together and was confused because each one heard them speaking in his own language. ⁷ And they were astounded and amazed, saying,ᵈ "Look, aren't all these who are speaking Galileans? ⁸ How is it that we hear, each of us, in our own native language? ⁹ Parthians, Medes, Elamites; those who live in Mesopotamia, in Judea and Cappadocia, Pontus and Asia, ¹⁰ Phrygia and Pamphylia, Egypt and the parts of Libya near Cyrene; visitors from Rome, both Jews and •proselytes, ¹¹ Cretans and Arabs—we hear them speaking in our own languages the magnificent acts of God." ¹² And they were all astounded and perplexed, saying to one another, "What could this be?" ¹³ But some sneered and said, "They're full of new wine!"

Peter's Sermon

¹⁴ But Peter stood up with the Eleven, raised his voice, and proclaimed to them: "Jewish men and all you residents of Jerusalem, let this be known to you and pay attention to my words. ¹⁵ For these people are not

---

ᵃ**1:20** Ps 69:25 ᵇ**1:20** Ps 109:8 ᶜ**1:25** Other mss read *to share* ᵈ**2:7** Other mss add *to one another*

---

considerably from the account in Matthew 27:3–10. It may be that he hanged himself, and then the rope broke, allowing his body to fall to the ground. The field, bought with Judas's betrayal money, may have come to be known as belonging to him.

1:22 from the baptism of John until the day He was taken up from us. Since the apostles were to bear witness to all Jesus said and did, it was important that they be eyewitnesses who were involved in His ministry from the very beginning.

1:23 Joseph, called Barsabbas ... Matthias. Nothing is known of these men. Of all the original 12 apostles, only Peter, James, and John are mentioned outside of the Gospels and Acts 1:13.

1:24 You, Lord, know the hearts of all.

Such knowledge is a divine attribute (1 Sam. 16:7; Jer. 17:10) which Jesus shares.

1:26 they cast lots. Making decisions by casting lots was common in biblical times (see Josh. 18:3–8; 1 Chron. 25:6–8; Neh. 10:34.) This was done by shaking stones on which names were written from a container. The person whose name came out of the container first would be selected.

2:1 the day of Pentecost. This was the Feast of Weeks (Ex. 23:16; Lev. 23:15–21; Deut. 16:9–12) held 50 days after Passover. Originally, a kind of Thanksgiving Day for gathered crops, it came to be associated with the commemoration of the giving of the Law at Sinai (Ex. 20:1–17). Pentecost was a celebration attended by thousands of Jews who had settled all over the Roman empire.

2:2–4 a violent rushing wind. In both Hebrew (the language in which the Old Testament was originally written) and Greek (the language in which the New Testament was originally written), the word translated as "Spirit" and "wind" and "breath" is all the same word. In Hebrew the word is *rhuah;* in Greek the word is *pneuma.* While this can lead to confusion, it also adds meaning. Is this "wind" from heaven truly a wind or is it the Spirit of God? Actually, it's both! Note also that it was a violent wind that came at Pentecost. This reminds us that while the Holy Spirit can bring peace to a person's soul, the Spirit is also a powerful force that we cannot control. **like flames of fire.** Fire is often associated with divine appearances (Ex. 3:2; 19:18). John the Baptist said Jesus would baptize his followers with the Holy Spirit and fire (Luke 3:16), symbolizing the purifying effect of the Spirit. Tongues were a

drunk, as you suppose, since it's only nine in the morning.[a] 16 On the contrary, this is what was spoken through the prophet Joel:

Real Fire Power

1. What are you usually doing at 9 a.m. on a Sunday? A weekday? A Saturday?

Acts 2:1-24,36-41

2. What do the images of wind and fire suggest about the Holy Spirit (vv. 2-3)?

3. Why did God "pour out" His Spirit (vv. 17-21)? What is one of the important works of the Holy Spirit (vv. 21,36)?

4. How does a person receive the Holy Spirit (v. 38)? Have you obeyed this step?

5. How have you seen the Holy Spirit at work in your own life? How can you increase His influence in your life?

17 And it will be in the last days, says God,
    that I will pour out My Spirit on all humanity;
    then your sons and your daughters
        will prophesy,
    your young men will see visions,
    and your old men will dream dreams.
18 I will even pour out My Spirit
    on My male and female slaves in those days,
    and they will prophesy.
19 I will display wonders in the heaven above
    and signs on the earth below:
    blood and fire and a cloud of smoke.
20 The sun will be turned to darkness,

and the moon to blood,
    before the great and remarkable
        day of the Lord comes;
21   then whoever calls on the name of the Lord
    will be saved.[b]

22 "Men of Israel, listen to these words: This Jesus the •Nazarene was a man pointed out to you by God with miracles, wonders, and signs that God did among you through Him, just as you yourselves know. 23 Though He was delivered up according to God's determined plan and foreknowledge, you used[c] lawless people[d] to nail Him to a cross and kill Him. 24 God raised Him up, ending the pains of death, because it was not possible for Him to be held by it. 25 For David says of Him:

    I saw the Lord ever before me;
    because He is at my right hand,
    I will not be shaken.
26   Therefore my heart was glad,
    and my tongue rejoiced.
    Moreover my flesh will rest in hope,
27   because You will not leave my soul in •Hades,
    or allow Your Holy One to see decay.
28   You have revealed the paths of life to me;
    You will fill me with gladness
        in Your presence.[e]

29 "Brothers, I can confidently speak to you about the patriarch David: he is both dead and buried, and his tomb is with us to this day. 30 Since he was a prophet, he knew that God had sworn an oath to him to seat one of his descendants[f] [g] on his throne. 31 Seeing this in advance, he spoke concerning the resurrection of the •Messiah:

    He[h] was not left in Hades,
    and His flesh did not experience decay.[i]

32 "God has resurrected this Jesus. We are all witnesses of this. 33 Therefore, since He has been exalted

---

[a]2:15 Lit it's the third hour of the day   [b]2:17–21 Jl 2:28–32   [c]2:23 Other mss read you have taken   [d]2:23 Or used the hand of lawless ones   [e]2:25–28 Ps 16:8–11   [f]2:30 Other mss add according to the flesh to raise up the Messiah   [g]2:30 Lit one from the fruit of his loin   [h]2:31 Other mss read His soul   [i]2:31 Ps 16:10

---

sign to the crowds of a supernatural event, the point of which was Jesus Christ.

2:9–11 Parthians, Medes, Elamites ... Mesopotamia. Present day Iran and Iraq, to the east of Jerusalem. These Jews traced their roots back to the Assyrian overthrow of Israel and the Babylonian overthrow of Judea several centuries before. **Judea.** Either the immediate environs around Jerusalem are in view, or Luke is referring to the days under David and Solomon when the land of Israel stretched from Egypt on the west to the Euphrates River on the east. **Cappadocia, Pontus and Asia, Phrygia and Pamphylia.** Present day Turkey to the north of Jerusalem. Much of Acts takes place in this region. **Egypt ... Libya near Cyrene.** To the west of Jerusalem on the northern coast of Africa. **proselytes.** Judaism's high morality and developed spiritual-

ity attracted many Gentiles from other religions. **Cretans.** An island south of Greece in the Mediterranean Sea. **Arabs.** The Nabetean kingdom was south of Jerusalem with borders on Egypt and the Euphrates.

2:22 miracles, wonders, and signs that God did ... through Him. The fact of Jesus' miracles is not debated. The stories of His work in Galilee had been widely reported (Mark 3:8; Luke 12:1; Acts 26:26). What was debated was the source of His power: early on some leaders accused Him of being possessed by Satan (Mark 3:22).

2:24–28 Death could not hold Jesus (v. 24) because the Messiah would not be subject to death (v. 27). This is supported by a quote from Psalm 16:8–11 which, in its original setting, was the prayer of a righteous person re-

joicing in the fact that because God supported him, he could be assured that he would not be left in Sheol or the Pit but enjoy God's presence forever. Some rabbis viewed this as a Messianic Psalm providing a precedent for Peter to read it as one that foretold the death and resurrection of the Messiah Jesus.

2:36 Lord. The full impact of the deity of Jesus gradually dawned upon the apostles. As the gospel spread beyond Palestine, He is referred to primarily as "the Lord," the title used for God in the Old Testament.

2:38 Repent. Repentance is the act of turning away from all other loyalties to affirm one's allegiance to Jesus (see Mark 1:15). **be baptized.** Baptism is the outward sign of the inward change of heart and mind, which shows the desire to be cleansed from sin. **in**

to the right hand of God and has received from the Father the promised Holy Spirit, He has poured out what you both see and hear. 34 For it was not David who ascended into the heavens, but he himself says:

> The Lord said to my Lord,
> 'Sit at My right hand
> 35 until I make Your enemies Your footstool.'ᵃ

A Loving Church

1. When have you visited a church that was very different from your own? What was it like? What was so different?

Acts 2:42-47

2. What does it mean that the church "devoted themselves to the apostles' teaching, to fellowship, to the breaking of bread, and to prayers" (v. 42)?
3. How is your church similar to the fellowship described here? How is it different?
4. Why did the early Christians sell "their possessions and property and distribute the proceeds to all, as anyone had a need" (v. 45)? How might you help your church to do this today?

36 "Therefore let all the house of Israel know with certainty that God has made this Jesus, whom you crucified, both Lord and Messiah!"

Forgiveness through the Messiah

37 When they heard this, they were pierced to the heart and said to Peter and the rest of the apostles: "Brothers, what must we do?"

38 "Repent," Peter said to them, "and be baptized, each of you, in the name of Jesus the Messiah for the forgiveness of your sins, and you will receive the gift of the Holy Spirit. 39 For the promise is for you and for your children, and for all who are far off,ᵇ as many as the Lord our God will call." 40 And with many other words he testified and strongly urged them, saying, "Be saved from this corruptᶜ generation!"

A Generous and Growing Church

41 So those who accepted his message were baptized, and that day about 3,000 people were added to them. 42 And they devoted themselves to the apostles' teaching, to fellowship, to the breaking of bread, and to prayers.

43 Then fear came over everyone, and many wonders and signs were being performed through the apostles. 44 Now all the believers were together and had everything in common. 45 So they sold their possessions and property and distributed the proceeds to all, as anyone had a need.ᵈ 46 And every day they devoted themselves [to meeting] together in the •temple complex, and broke bread from house to house. They ate their food with gladness and simplicity of heart, 47 praising God and having favor with all the people. And every day the Lord added to themᵉ those who were being saved.

Healing of a Lame Man

3 Now Peter and John were going up together to the •temple complex at the hour of prayer at three in the afternoon.ᶠ 2 And a man who was lame from his mother's womb was carried there and placed every day at the temple gate called Beautiful, so he could beg from those entering the temple complex. 3 When he saw Peter and John about to enter the temple complex, he asked for help. 4 Peter, along with John, looked at him intently and said, "Look at us." 5 So he turned to them,ᵍ expecting to get something from them. 6 But Peter said, "I have neither silver nor gold, but what I have, I give to you: In the name of Jesus Christ the •Nazarene, get up and walk!" 7 Then, taking him by the right hand he raised him up, and at once his feet and ankles became strong. 8 So he jumped up, stood, and started to walk, and he entered the tem-

---

ᵃ**2:34-35** Ps 110:1   ᵇ**2:39** Remote in time or space   ᶜ**2:40** Or crooked, or twisted   ᵈ**2:45** Or to all, according to one's needs   ᵉ**2:47** Other mss read to the church   ᶠ**3:1** Lit at the ninth hour   ᵍ**3:5** Or he paid attention to them

---

the name of Jesus the Messiah. The early Christians declared, "Jesus is Lord" as they were baptized (Rom. 10:9; 1 Cor. 12:3) affirming their allegiance and dependence on Him to save them. Recognition of Jesus' Messiahship was critical for a person's inclusion in the church. **receive the gift of the Holy Spirit.** The coming of the Holy Spirit is the distinctive reality that Jesus bestows on those who trust Him.

2:42 teaching. The foundation for the church's life was the instruction of the apostles as the representatives of Jesus. **fellowship.** While this may include the aspect of sharing to meet material needs (v. 45), it most likely refers to their common participation in the Spirit as they worshipped together (1 Cor. 12). **the breaking of bread.** The Lord's Supper in which they remembered Jesus' death (Luke 22:19) and recognized

His presence among them (Luke 24:30–31). **prayers.** This may refer to set times and forms of prayer—the typical practice of the Jews.

2:43–47 The picture of the church is one of continual growth (v. 47) marked by generous sharing (vv. 44–45) and joyful worship and fellowship (vv. 46–47). The worship at the temple continued as before since the line dividing Christianity from Judaism had not yet been drawn. Christians saw their faith as the natural climax of what the Jewish faith had always declared.

2:44–45 everything in common. The shared life that these early Christians practiced was an outgrowth of the intense love they had for one another through Jesus Christ. They believed that in Christ each person's need should become everyone's

need. This attitude is a key component of authentic Christian community.

3:1 the hour of prayer. The two daily times of sacrifice and prayer at the temple were in the early morning and around 3:00 p.m.

3:2 the temple gate called Beautiful. This gate was apparently near Solomon's Colonnade (v. 11) on the eastern side of the temple. Beggars would gather about the temple in hopes of receiving alms from passersby.

3:3–5 he asked for help. The man probably called out for alms without paying attention to whom he was talking. But Peter and John broke through his routine by insisting that he pay attention to them.

3:6–8 I have neither silver nor gold. To experience life fully is surely more valuable

ple complex with them—walking, leaping, and praising God. 9 All the people saw him walking and praising God, 10 and they recognized that he was the one who used to sit and beg at the Beautiful Gate of the temple complex. So they were filled with awe and astonishment at what had happened to him.

What I Have Is Yours!

1. What do you do when a beggar asks you for money?

Acts 3:1-16

2. Why do you think Peter and John "looked at [the lame man] intently" (v. 4)? Why didn't they just drop a coin and keep going?

3. What was the result of their act of faith? How did it affect the lame man (v. 8)? Others (vv. 9-10)?

4. Why did Peter and John heal the man: Out of compassion? They had no money? To glorify God? Other?

5. What was it that healed the man (v. 16)? How can your faith help others in need?

Preaching in Solomon's Colonnade

11 While he[a] was holding on to Peter and John, all the people, greatly amazed, ran toward them in what is called Solomon's Colonnade. 12 When Peter saw this, he addressed the people: "Men of Israel, why are you amazed at this? Or why do you stare at us, as though by our own power or godliness we had made him walk? 13 The God of Abraham, Isaac, and Jacob, the God of our fathers, has glorified His Servant Jesus, whom you handed over and denied in the presence of •Pilate, when he had decided to release Him. 14 But you denied the Holy and

Righteous One, and asked to have a murderer given to you. 15 And you killed the source[b] of life, whom God raised from the dead; we are witnesses of this. 16 By faith in His name, His name has made this man strong, whom you see and know. So the faith that comes through Him has given him this perfect health in front of all of you.

17 "And now, brothers, I know that you did it in ignorance, just as your leaders also did. 18 But what God predicted through the mouth of all the prophets—that His •Messiah would suffer—He has fulfilled in this way. 19 Therefore repent and turn back, that your sins may be wiped out so that seasons of refreshing may come from the presence of the Lord, 20 and He may send Jesus, who has been appointed Messiah for you. 21 Heaven must welcome[c] Him until the times of the restoration of all things, which God spoke about by the mouth of His holy prophets from the beginning. 22 Moses said:[d]

> The Lord your God will raise up for you a Prophet like me from among your brothers. You must listen to Him in everything He will say to you. 23 And it will be that everyone who will not listen to that Prophet will be completely cut off from the people.[e]

24 "In addition, all the prophets who have spoken, from Samuel and those after him, have also announced these days. 25 You are the sons of the prophets and of the covenant that God made with your forefathers, saying to Abraham, **And in your seed all the families of the earth will be blessed.**[f] 26 God raised up His Servant[g] and sent Him first to you to bless you by turning each of you from your evil ways."

Peter and John Arrested

4 Now as they were speaking to the people, the priests, the commander of the temple guard, and the •Sadducees confronted them, 2 because they were provoked that they were teaching the people and proclaiming in the person of Jesus[h] the resurrection from the dead. 3 So they seized them and put them in custody until the next day, since it was already evening.

---

[a]3:11 Other mss read *the lame man who was healed*   [b]3:15 Or *the Prince*, or *the Ruler*   [c]3:21 Or *receive*, or *retain*   [d]3:22 Other mss add *to the fathers*   [e]3:22–23 Dt 18:15–19   [f]3:25 Gn 12:3; 18:18; 22:18; 26:4   [g]3:26 Other mss add *Jesus*   [h]4:2 Lit *proclaiming in Jesus*

---

than money, and the healing which Peter was about to do would help this man live more fully. **In the name of Jesus Christ.** This man was healed by the authority of Jesus. Even those who were not Jesus' followers sought to heal by using His name. **jumped up ... praising God.** This man made no attempt to hide his excitement. That he jumped to his feet is also a sign of how complete the healing was (see Isa. 35:6.)

3:11 Solomon's Colonnade. A long porch extending along the eastern wall of the outer court of the temple. It was the typical gathering place for the early Christians (5:12).

3:17 you did it in ignorance. The Law of Moses allowed for forgiveness of sins committed unwittingly (Num. 15:27–31). While Peter acknowledges that the people did not

really know what they were doing when they had Jesus crucified (see also 13:27, Luke 23:34; 1 Cor. 2:8), he makes the point that if they resist him now, they are guilty of a conscious, willful rejection of the Messiah.

3:22 a Prophet like me. That God would send a new Moses who would restore God's people to Himself was a common expectation among the Jews (John 1:21; 4:25; 6:14).

4:1 the commander of the temple guard. A high-ranking official who had the responsibility of maintaining order in the temple. **the Sadducees.** The Sadducees were a wealthy group who believed only in the first five books of the Old Testament and denied the resurrection (see 23:6–8).

4:2 proclaiming ... the resurrection. The Sadducees considered the teaching to be a

priestly right alone. To further upset things, the disciples were preaching the resurrection, a doctrine that the Sadducees denied.

4:10 let it be known to all of you. The Sanhedrin represented the highest level of authority among the Jews. But Peter is not intimidated by them as he declares that the miracle was not a product of sorcery but of faith in the power of Jesus—the one they had condemned to death a few weeks before.

4:12 salvation. Peter declared that his audience could either repent and believe in order to experience God's salvation, or they could persist in their rejection of Jesus and forfeit the hope for which Israel had waited so long.

4:13 realized ... they had been with Jesus. The Sanhedrin identified the boldness with

1033

4 But many of those who heard the message believed, and the number of the men came to about 5,000.

Peter and John Face the Jewish Leadership

5 The next day, their rulers, elders, and •scribes assembled in Jerusalem 6 with Annas the high priest, Caiaphas, John and Alexander, and all the members of the high-priestly family.[a] 7 After they had Peter and John stand[b] before them, they asked the question: "By what power or in what name have you done this?"

8 Then Peter was filled with the Holy Spirit and said to them, "Rulers of the people and elders:[c] 9 If we are being examined today about a good deed done to a disabled man—by what means he was healed— 10 let it be known to all of you and to all the people of Israel, that by the name of Jesus Christ the •Nazarene—whom you crucified and whom God raised from the dead—by Him this man is standing here before you healthy. 11 This [Jesus] is

> The stone despised by you builders,
> who has become the cornerstone.[d]

12 There is salvation in no one else, for there is no other name under heaven given to people by which we must be saved."

The Name Forbidden

13 When they observed the boldness of Peter and John and realized that they were uneducated and untrained men, they were amazed and knew that they had been with Jesus. 14 And since they saw the man who had been healed standing with them, they had nothing to say in response. 15 After they had ordered them to leave the •Sanhedrin, they conferred among themselves, 16 saying, "What should we do with these men? For an obvious sign, evident to all who live in Jerusalem, has been done through them, and we cannot deny it! 17 But so this does not spread any further among the people, let's threaten them against speaking to anyone in this name again." 18 So they called for them and

ordered them not to preach or teach at all in the name of Jesus.

19 But Peter and John answered them, "Whether it's right in the sight of God [for us] to listen to you rather than to God, you decide; 20 for we are unable to stop speaking about what we have seen and heard."

21 After threatening them further, they released them. They found no way to punish them, because the people were all giving glory to God over what had been done; 22 for the man was over 40 years old on whom this sign of healing had been performed.

Prayer for Boldness

23 After they were released, they went to their own fellowship[e] and reported all that the •chief priests and the elders had said to them. 24 When they heard this, they raised their voices to God unanimously and said, "Master, You are the One who made the heaven, the earth, and the sea, and everything in them. 25 You said through the Holy Spirit, by the mouth of our father David Your servant:[f]

> Why did the Gentiles rage,
> and the peoples plot futile things?
> 26 The kings of the earth took their stand,
> and the rulers assembled together
> against the Lord and against His •Messiah.[g]

27 "For, in fact, in this city both •Herod and Pontius •Pilate, with the Gentiles and the peoples of Israel, assembled together against Your holy Servant Jesus, whom You anointed, 28 to do whatever Your hand and Your plan had predestined to take place. 29 And now, Lord, consider their threats, and grant that Your slaves may speak Your message with complete boldness, 30 while You stretch out Your hand for healing, signs, and wonders to be performed through the name of Your holy Servant Jesus." 31 When they had prayed, the place where they were assembled was shaken, and they were all filled with the Holy Spirit and began to speak God's message with boldness.

a 4:6 Or high-priestly class, or high-priestly clan   b 4:7 Lit had placed them   c 4:8 Other mss add of Israel   d 4:11 Ps 118:22   e 4:23 Or friends, or companions   f 4:25 Other mss read through the mouth of David Your servant   g 4:25–26 Ps 2:1–2

which Peter spoke as reminiscent of the way Jesus had spoken. **untrained men.** As fishermen by trade, Peter and John had not received formal rabbinical training.

4:16–17 we cannot deny it. Recognizing the undeniable fact that the man was healed and the widespread popular support for the disciples (v. 21), the Sanhedrin realized there was little they could do but try to intimidate the disciples into silence.

4:19–20 unable to stop speaking about what we have seen. Since the Sanhedrin had set itself against God and His Messiah, the disciples had no choice but to ignore its commands and remain faithful to God.

4:31 the place ... was shaken. Earthquakes were a common sign in the Old Testament of God's presence (Ex. 19:18; Ps. 114:7; Isa.

6:4; Ezek. 38:19). Through this sign, the disciples were assured that their prayer was heard.

4:32 those who believed were of one heart and soul. Compare with 2:44–45. This sharing was done freely by the early believers as an expression of love for one another; it may be intended as another sign of the Spirit at work (v. 31).

4:34 not a needy person among them. While this was the ideal for Old Testament Israel (Deut. 15:4), the generosity of the Christians allowed it to actually be experienced (see Luke 12:32–34; 18:18–30; 19:1–10).

4:35 laid them at the apostles' feet. The apostles were given the responsibility of distributing the resources so the needs of the people were met.

5:2 he kept back. The rare Greek word translated here is used in the Septuagint version of Joshua 7:1 to describe Achan's action of "keeping back" part of the booty from Jericho that was to be devoted to God. Luke may have used this word to make a connection between Achan's sin and that of Ananias.

5:4–10 Many find the death of Ananias and Sapphira disturbing. Capital punishment for an act of deceit seems harsh. But trust was vital to this early Christian community. Those who were not true to their word threatened the community's survival. Whether from heart failure at the exposure of their sin, or from some direct act of God, both Ananias and Sapphira died when their lie was revealed.

5:11 great fear came. The result of this inci-

Believers Sharing

³² Now the multitude of those who believed were of one heart and soul, and no one said that any of his possessions was his own, but instead they held everything in common. ³³ And with great power the apostles were giving testimony to the resurrection of the Lord Jesus, and great grace was on all of them. ³⁴ For there was not a needy person among them, because all those who owned lands or houses sold them, brought the proceeds of the things that were sold, ³⁵ and laid them at the apostles' feet. This was then distributed to each person as anyone had a need.

³⁶ Joseph, a Levite and a Cypriot by birth, whom the apostles named Barnabas, which is translated Son of Encouragement, ³⁷ sold a field he owned, brought the money, and laid it at the apostles' feet.

Lying to the Holy Spirit

5 But a man named Ananias, with Sapphira his wife, sold a piece of property. ² However, he kept back part of the proceeds with his wife's knowledge, and brought a portion of it and laid it at the apostles' feet.

³ Then Peter said, "Ananias, why has Satan filled your heart to lie to the Holy Spirit and keep back part of the proceeds from the field? ⁴ Wasn't it yours while you possessed it? And after it was sold, wasn't it at your disposal? Why is it that you planned this thing in your heart? You have not lied to men but to God!" ⁵ When he heard these words, Ananias dropped dead, and a great fear came on all who heard. ⁶ The young men got up, wrapped his body, carried him out, and buried him.

⁷ There was an interval of about three hours; then his wife came in, not knowing what had happened. ⁸ "Tell me," Peter asked her, "did you sell the field for this price?"

"Yes," she said, "for that price."

⁹ Then Peter said to her, "Why did you agree to test the Spirit of the Lord? Look! The feet of those who have buried your husband are at the door, and they will carry you out!"

Lying to Get in the Spotlight

1. When has someone caught you in a lie? How did you feel? What did you learn?

Acts 5:1-11

2. What were Ananias and Sapphira guilty of? Why did God punish them so severely?
3. What were they hoping to gain by lying about the price? Were they under some obligation to give any or all of the money to God?
4. Why did Peter ask Sapphira what price they had earned? What might she have done differently?
5. In your life, where are you most tempted to be dishonest or lack integrity in some way?

¹⁰ Instantly she dropped dead at his feet. When the young men came in, they found her dead, carried her out, and buried her beside her husband. ¹¹ Then great fear came on the whole church and on all who heard these things.

Apostolic Signs and Wonders

¹² Many signs and wonders were being done among the people through the hands of the apostles. By common consent they would all meet in Solomon's Colonnade. ¹³ None of the rest dared to join them, but the people praised them highly. ¹⁴ Believers were added to the Lord in increasing numbers—crowds of both men and women. ¹⁵ As a result, they would carry the sick out into the streets and lay them on beds and pallets so that when Peter came by, at least his shadow might fall on some of them. ¹⁶ In addition, a multitude came together from the towns surrounding Jerusalem, bringing sick

---

dent was that the entire community recognized the seriousness of the presence of God in their midst (Heb. 10:31; 12:28–29).

church. This is the first use of the word *ekklesia* in Acts. This word, along with *synagoge,* was commonly used in the Septuagint to translate the Hebrew word *qahal,* referring to the assembly of God's people. Since *synagoge* became tied in with the name for the Jewish places of worship (the synagogue), the Christians used *ekklesia* to refer to themselves. They claimed a common Old Testament term to identify themselves as the true "Israel" of God.

5:12 signs and wonders. Miracles that point to the reality of God's presence and power.

5:13–14 None of the rest. The lack of clarity of this passage leads to some questions.

There seems to be a contradiction here between verse 13, "None of the rest dared to join them," and verse 14, "Believers were added to the Lord's church in increasing numbers—crowds of both men and women." Verse 13 seems to say that people were still afraid to join with the followers of Christ, because of the persecution against them. But it is possible that the word translated here "join them" may be better translated "interfere with them," which makes more sense within the context.

5:15 Peter ... his shadow. This action reveals the esteem that the common people held for the church (and especially for Peter). The woman in Mark 5:28 had a similar superstitious idea about Jesus' garment which He corrected by telling her it was her faith in Him—not any magical properties about His clothes—that brought her healing

(see also 19:11–12 and Mark 6:56).

5:19–20 This is the first of three miraculous escapes from jail reported in Acts (12:6–19 and 16:26.)

5:21–26 The Sanhedrin was bewildered when they discovered the men they had imprisoned were back at the temple preaching!

5:28 you ... are determined to bring this man's blood on us! The Sanhedrin was concerned that the apostles' teaching would undermine their authority in the public eye. To them, Jesus was a blasphemer who deserved death.

5:29 "We must obey God rather than men." Peter and John had already made this statement in 4:19–20. We are called to

people and those who were tormented by unclean spirits, and they were all healed.

In and Out of Prison

17 Then the high priest took action. He and all his colleagues, those who belonged to the party of the •Sadducees, were filled with jealousy. 18 So they arresteda the apostles and put them in the city jail. 19 But an angel of the Lord opened the doors of the jail during the night, brought them out, and said, 20 "Go and stand in the •temple complex, and tell the people all about this life." 21 In obedience to this, they entered the temple complex at daybreak and began to teach.

The Apostles on Trial Again

When the high priest and those who were with him arrived, they convened the •Sanhedrin—the full Senate of the sons of Israel—and sent ⌊orders⌋ to the jail to have them brought. 22 But when the temple police got there, they did not find them in the jail, so they returned and reported, 23 "We found the jail securely locked, with the guards standing in front of the doors; but when we opened them, we found no one inside!" 24 Asb the captain of the temple police and the •chief priests heard these things, they were baffled about them, as to what could come of this.

25 Someone came and reported to them, "Look! The men you put in jail are standing in the temple complex and teaching the people." 26 Then the captain went with the temple police and brought them in without force, because they were afraid the people might stone them. 27 When they had brought them in, they had them stand before the Sanhedrin, and the high priest asked, 28 "Didn't we strictly order you not to teach in this name? And look, you have filled Jerusalem with your teaching and are determined to bring this man's blood on us!"

29 But Peter and the apostles replied, "We must obey God rather than men. 30 The God of our fathers raised up Jesus, whom you had murdered by hanging Him on a tree. 31 God exalted this man to His right hand as ruler and Savior, to grant repentance to Israel, and forgiveness of sins. 32 We are witnesses of these things, and so is the Holy Spirit whom God has given to those who obey Him."

Gamaliel's Advice

33 When they heard this, they were enraged and wanted to kill them. 34 A •Pharisee named Gamaliel, a teacher of the law who was respected by all the people, stood up in the Sanhedrin and ordered the menc to be taken outside for a little while. 35 He said to them, "Men of Israel, be careful about what you're going to do to these men. 36 Not long ago Theudas rose up, claiming to be somebody, and a group of about 400 men rallied to him. He was killed, and all his partisans were dispersed and came to nothing. 37 After this man, Judas the Galilean rose up in the days of the census and attracted a following.d That man also perished, and all his partisans were scattered. 38 And now, I tell you, stay away from these men and leave them alone. For if this plan or this work is of men, it will be overthrown; 39 but if it is of God, you will not be able to overthrow them. You may even be found fighting against God." So they were persuaded by him. 40 After they called in the apostles and had them flogged, they ordered them not to speak in the name of Jesus and released them. 41 Then they went out from the presence of the Sanhedrin, rejoicing that they were counted worthy to be dishonored on behalf of the name.e 42 Every day in the temple complex, and in various homes, they continued teaching and proclaiming the good news that the •Messiah is Jesus.f

Seven Chosen to Serve

6 In those days, as the number of the disciples was multiplying, there arose a complaint by the Hellenistic Jewsg against the Hebraic Jewsh that their widows were being overlooked in the daily distribution. 2 Then the Twelve summoned the whole company of the disciples and said, "It would not be right for us to give up preaching about God to wait on tables. 3 Therefore, brothers, select from among you seven

---

a5:18 Lit laid hands on   b5:24 Other mss add the high priest and   c5:34 Other mss read apostles   d5:37 Lit and drew people after him   e5:41 Other mss add of Jesus, or of Christ   f5:42 Or that Jesus is the Messiah   g6:1 Jews of Gk language and culture   h6:1 Jews of Aram or Hb language and culture

---

be good citizens of the state (Rom. 13:1–7), but we as believers have a higher citizenship. Our loyalty to the kingdom of God extends beyond national borders, and it is not governed by human authority.

5:30 hanging Him on a tree. Probably a deliberate reference to Deuteronomy 21:22–23, which taught that a curse rested upon a person whose body was hung on a tree. This is a reference to a cross that was sometimes called a "tree." Peter is highlighting the fact that these leaders are guilty of a serious crime (v. 28) because they condemned the Messiah to a shameful death.

5:34 A Pharisee. In the Gospels the Pharisees are the prime opponents of Jesus because of their conviction that he was a lawbreaker. But in Acts they are more supportive of the church than the Sadducees,

who felt that the apostles were encroaching on their power in temple affairs. **Gamaliel.** Other sources confirm Luke's comment that this man was greatly honored and loved by the people.

5:36 Theudas. To prove his point, Gamaliel mentions two former insurrectionists whose crusades fell apart shortly after their leaders died. The Theudas referred to here is unknown.

5:37 Judas the Galilean. This man led a revolt against Roman oppression in A.D. 6 when Judea came under Roman control.

5:40 flogged. "Flogging" referred to being whipped 13 times by a lash with three strands (thus amounting to 39 lashes). Deuteronomy 25:3 allowed a maximum of 40 lashes, but 39 became the norm so the law

would not be broken.

6:1 Hellenistic Jews. Jews who came from outside Palestine and for whom Aramaic and Hebrew were relatively unknown languages. Their synagogue worship was also conducted in their native languages. **Hebraic Jews.** Native Palestinians who spoke Aramaic as their daily language. Since all the apostles were Hebraic Jews, it is possible that they were more aware of the needs of those with whom they could easily communicate.

6:2 wait on tables. This does not refer to being a waiter. Since banking at that time was done by people sitting at a table, to "wait on tables" was a figure of speech for handling financial transactions.

6:5 They chose. The names of the men cho-

men of good reputation, full of the Spirit and wisdom, whom we can appoint to this duty. ⁴ But we will devote ourselves to prayer and to the preaching ministry." ⁵ The proposal pleased the whole company. So they chose Stephen, a man full of faith and the Holy Spirit, and Philip, Prochorus, Nicanor, Timon, Parmenas, and Nicolaus, a •proselyte from Antioch. ⁶ They had them stand before the apostles, who prayed and laid their hands on them.ᵃ

Glamour Ministry

1. If you worked in a restaurant, what job would you like to have? What would you not like to do?

Acts 6:1–7

2. Why did the disciples say, "It would not be right for us to give up preaching about God to wait on tables" (v. 2)?

3. Those who waited on tables needed to be "of good reputation, full of the Spirit and wisdom" (v. 3). What does that suggest about the importance of less glamorous ministries?

4. What ministry do you perform for your church? For your teammates? For your group?

⁷ So the preaching about God flourished, the number of the disciples in Jerusalem multiplied greatly, and a large group of priests became obedient to the faith.

Stephen Accused of Blasphemy

⁸ Stephen, full of grace and power, was performing great wonders and signs among the people. ⁹ Then some from what is called the Freedmen's •Synagogue, composed of both Cyrenians and Alexandrians, and some from Cilicia and Asia, came forward and disputed with Stephen. ¹⁰ But they were unable to stand up against the wisdom and the Spirit by whom he spoke. ¹¹ Then they induced men to say, "We heard him speaking blasphemous words against Moses and God!" ¹² They stirred up the people, the elders, and the •scribes; so they came up, dragged him off, and took him to the •Sanhedrin. ¹³ They also presented false witnesses who said, "This man does not stop speaking blasphemous words against this holy place and the law. ¹⁴ For we heard him say that Jesus, this •Nazarene, will destroy this place and change the customs that Moses handed down to us." ¹⁵ And all who were sitting in the Sanhedrin looked intently at him and saw that his face was like the face of an angel.

Stephen's Address

7 "Is this true?"ᵇ the high priest asked.
² "Brothers and fathers," he said, "listen: The God of glory appeared to our father Abraham when he was in Mesopotamia, before he settled in Haran, ³ and said to him:

> Get out of your country and away from
> your relatives,
> and come to the land that I will show you.ᶜ

⁴ "Then he came out of the land of the Chaldeans and settled in Haran. And from there, after his father died, God had him move to this land in which you now live. ⁵ He didn't give him an inheritance in it, not even a foot of ground, but He promised to give it to him as a possession, and to his descendants after him, even though he was childless. ⁶ God spoke in this way:

> His descendants would be strangers
> in a foreign country,
> and they would enslave and oppress them
> for 400 years.
> ⁷ I will judge the nation that they will serve
> as slaves, God said.
> After this, they will come out and worship Me
> in this place.ᵈ

ᵃ**6:6** The laying on of hands signified the prayer of blessing for the beginning of a new ministry. ᵇ**7:1** Lit *"Are these things so?"* ᶜ**7:3** Gn 12:1
ᵈ**7:6–7** Gn 15:13–14

---

sen indicate that all seven were Greek-speaking Jews. They perhaps also served as a bridge between the Palestinian apostles and the Greek-speaking Jews to help avoid further tensions between the two groups. **Stephen.** This man moves to center stage in chapter 7. **Philip.** Like Stephen, Philip demonstrated gifts of evangelism not unlike those of the apostles (see v. 8; 8:4–8; 21:8).

6:9 the Freedmen's Synagogue. The Freedmen were former Roman slaves (or their descendants) released by their masters and granted Roman citizenship. The Greek-speaking Jews who left home and family to settle in Jerusalem were especially devoted to the temple and its religious system.

6:14 Jesus … will destroy this place. The root of the complaint against Stephen was the charge that the followers of Jesus threat-

ened to destroy the temple and replace the laws of Moses with their own ways. Jesus spoke of destroying the temple in a way that was misunderstood (Mark 14:58; John 2:19–22). Jesus spoke of the destruction of the temple that was to come (Luke 21:5–6). Stephen, in repeating this warning of judgment that would result if the Jews rejected Jesus as their Messiah, may have been misunderstood as inferring that the Christians were plotting an attack on the temple.

6:15 like the face of an angel. The only other biblical character who shared this experience was Moses, the man of God whom Stephen was charged with defying (Ex. 34:29–31; 2 Cor. 3:12–13)!

7:6–7 God spoke in this way. This is a combination of quotes issued by God to Abraham and Moses in Genesis 15:13 and

Exodus 3:12. God would be with His people in Egypt and, after He delivered them from there, they would worship Him in the desert at Sinai.

7:9-10 Because the patriarchs were jealous of Joseph. Stephen does not quote directly from Genesis but summarizes the account of Joseph's brothers selling him into slavery. Stephen doesn't refer to them as brothers but as "the patriarchs." His choice of words may be intentional since they weren't acting like brothers. **God was with him.** Joseph suffered greatly in being separated from his father, Jacob, his younger brother, Benjamin. Stephen doesn't go into detail about Joseph's sufferings but chooses to focus on the fact that God was with him. **gave him wisdom and favor.** Joseph's painful losses were offset by great blessings from God. Through Joseph God

8 Then He gave him the covenant of circumcision. This being so, he fathered Isaac and circumcised him on the eighth day; Isaac did the same with Jacob, and Jacob with the 12 patriarchs.

The Patriarchs in Egypt

9 "The patriarchs became jealous of Joseph and sold him into Egypt, but God was with him 10 and rescued him out of all his troubles. He gave him favor and wisdom in the sight of Pharaoh, king of Egypt, who appointed him governor over Egypt and over his whole household. 11 Then a famine came over all of Egypt and Canaan, with great suffering, and our forefathers could find no food. 12 When Jacob heard there was grain in Egypt, he sent our forefathers the first time. 13 The second time, Joseph was revealed to his brothers, and Joseph's family became known to Pharaoh. 14 Joseph then invited his father Jacob and all his relatives, 75 people in all, 15 and Jacob went down to Egypt. He and our forefathers died there, 16 were carried back to Shechem, and were placed in the tomb that Abraham had bought for a sum of silver from the sons of Hamor in Shechem.

Moses, a Rejected Savior

17 "As the time was drawing near to fulfill the promise that God had made to Abraham, the people flourished and multiplied in Egypt 18 until a different king ruled over Egypt[a] who did not know Joseph. 19 He dealt deceitfully with our race and oppressed our forefathers by making them leave their infants outside so they wouldn't survive.[b] 20 At this time Moses was born, and he was beautiful before God. He was nursed in his father's home three months, 21 and when he was left outside, Pharaoh's daughter adopted and raised him as her own son. 22 So Moses was educated in all the wisdom of the Egyptians, and was powerful in his speech and actions.

23 "As he was approaching the age of 40, he decided[c] to visit his brothers, the sons of Israel. 24 When he saw one of them being mistreated, he came to his rescue and avenged the oppressed man by striking down the Egyptian. 25 He assumed his brothers would understand that God would give them deliverance through him, but they did not understand. 26 The next day he showed up while they were fighting and tried to reconcile them peacefully, saying, 'Men, you are brothers. Why are you mistreating each other?'

27 "But the one who was mistreating his neighbor pushed him[d] away, saying:

Who appointed you a ruler and a judge over us?
28 Do you want to kill me, the same way you killed the Egyptian yesterday?[e]

29 "At this disclosure, Moses fled and became an exile in the land of Midian, where he fathered two sons. 30 After 40 years had passed, an angel[f] appeared to him in the desert of Mount Sinai, in the flame of a burning bush. 31 When Moses saw it, he was amazed at the sight. As he was approaching to look at it, the voice of the Lord came: 32 I am the God of your forefathers— the God of Abraham, of Isaac, and of Jacob.[g] So Moses began to tremble and did not dare to look.

33 "Then the Lord said to him:

Take the sandals off your feet, because the place where you are standing is holy ground. 34 I have certainly seen the oppression of My people in Egypt; I have heard their groaning and have come down to rescue them. And now, come, I will send you to Egypt.[h]

35 "This Moses, whom they rejected when they said, Who appointed you a ruler and a judge?[e] — this one God sent as a ruler and a redeemer by means of the angel who appeared to him in the bush. 36 This man led them out and performed wonders and signs in the land of Egypt, at the Red Sea, and in the desert for 40 years.

Israel's Rebellion against God

37 "This is the Moses who said to the sons of Israel, God[i] will raise up for you a Prophet like me from among your brothers.[j] 38 He is the one who was in the

a7:18 Other mss omit *over Egypt*   b7:19 A common pagan practice of population control by leaving infants outside to die   c7:23 Lit *40, it came into his heart*   d7:27 Moses   e7:27–28,35 Ex 2:14   f7:30 Other mss add *of the Lord*   g7:32 Ex 3:6,15   h7:33–34 Ex 3:5,7–8,10   i7:37 Other mss read *The Lord your God*   j7:37 Dt 18:15

provided for Egypt and its neighbors, including Joseph's family from Canaan.

7:14 all his relatives, 75 people in all. The Hebrew text of Genesis 46:27 says 70, but the Septuagint text reads 75.

7:16 carried back to Shechem. Jacob was buried in Hebron (Gen. 50:13) at the cave that Abraham bought from Ephron. Joseph's bones were eventually laid to rest at Shechem in a field that Jacob bought from the sons of Hamor (Josh. 24:32). The Old Testament does not mention where the bones of the other sons of Jacob were buried, but a Samaritan tradition says it was at Shechem. Stephen appears to have telescoped events in order to get on with his main points.

7:17–34 A major portion of Stephen's sermon is given to what God accomplished through Moses. Stephen divides Moses' life into three segments: (1) his birth and education in Egypt, (2) the years in Midian where he fled as a fugitive after he killed an Egyptian who was dealing harshly with a Hebrew, and (3) the years of the Exodus and journey from Egypt to the Promised Land.

7::22 Moses was educated in all the wisdom of the Egyptians. The Old Testament accounts of Moses don't mention his education. The Jewish biblical interpreter, Philo of Alexandria (20 BC – AD 50, makes this point in his life of Moses. Philo says that the best teachers of both Egypt and Greece had a part in Moses' education and that Moses excelled them.

7:23 approaching the age of 40. The Exodus account does not mention Moses' age at the time of this event, but rabbinic tradi-

tion taught that he was 40.

7:51 stiff-necked people. The image is that of a people refusing to bow their head before God (Ex. 33:5; Deut. 10:16). **uncircumcised hearts and ears!** Physical circumcision was a symbol of a heart set apart for God and ears open to do His will.

7:52 Which of the prophets did your fathers not persecute? Jewish tradition held that Isaiah was sawn in two by the evil king Manasseh and that Jeremiah was stoned by Jews in Egypt. Jesus also warned the leaders that in rejecting Him they were following in the footsteps of their fathers (Luke 11:47–51).

7:53 have not kept it. The final accusation Stephen makes is that these leaders are the ones who violate Moses' law. **under the di-**

congregation in the desert together with the angel who spoke to him on Mount Sinai, and with our forefathers. He received living oracles to give to us. [39] Our forefathers were unwilling to obey him, but pushed him away, and in their hearts turned back to Egypt. [40] They told Aaron:

Make us gods who will go before us. As for this Moses who brought us out of the land of Egypt, we don't know what's become of him.[a]

[41] They even made a calf in those days, offered sacrifice to the idol, and were celebrating what their hands had made. [42] Then God turned away and gave them up to worship the host of heaven, as it is written in the book of the prophets:

Did you bring Me offerings and sacrifices
for 40 years in the desert,
O house of Israel?
[43] No, you took up the tent of Moloch[b]
and the star of your god Rephan,[c]
the images that you made to worship.
So I will deport you beyond Babylon![d]

God's Real Tabernacle

[44] "Our forefathers had the tabernacle of the testimony in the desert, just as He who spoke to Moses commanded him to make it according to the pattern he had seen. [45] Our forefathers in turn received it and with Joshua brought it in when they dispossessed the nations that God drove out before our fathers, until the days of David. [46] He found favor in God's sight and asked that he might provide a dwelling place for the God[e] of Jacob. [47] But it was Solomon who built Him a house. [48] However, the Most High does not dwell in sanctuaries made with hands, as the prophet says:

[49] Heaven is My throne,
and earth My footstool.
What sort of house will you build for Me?
says the Lord,
or what is My resting place?

[50] Did not My hand make all
these things?[f]

Resisting the Holy Spirit

[51] "You stiff-necked people with uncircumcised hearts and ears! You are always resisting the Holy Spirit; as your forefathers did, so do you. [52] Which of the prophets did your fathers not persecute? They even killed those who announced beforehand the coming of the Righteous One, whose betrayers and murderers you have now become. [53] You received the law under the direction of angels and yet have not kept it."

The First Christian Martyr

[54] When they heard these things, they were enraged in their hearts[g] and gnashed their teeth at him. [55] But Stephen, filled by the Holy Spirit, gazed into heaven. He saw God's glory, with[h] Jesus standing at the right hand of God, and he said, [56] "Look! I see the heavens opened and the •Son of Man standing at the right hand of God!"

[57] Then they screamed at the top of their voices, stopped their ears, and rushed together against him. [58] They threw him out of the city and began to stone him. And the witnesses laid their robes at the feet of a young man named Saul. [59] They were stoning Stephen as he called out: "Lord Jesus, receive my spirit!" [60] Then he knelt down and cried out with a loud voice, "Lord, do not charge them with this sin!" And saying this, he fell •asleep.[i]

Saul the Persecutor

8 Saul agreed with putting him to death.

On that day a severe persecution broke out against the church in Jerusalem, and all except the apostles were scattered throughout the land of Judea and Samaria. [2] But devout men buried Stephen and mourned deeply over him. [3] Saul, however, was ravaging the church, and he would enter house after house, drag off men and women, and put them in prison.

Philip in Samaria

[4] So those who were scattered went on their way proclaiming the message of good news. [5] Philip went down

---

[a]**7:40** Ex 32:1,23 [b]**7:43** Canaanite or Phoenician sky or sun god [c]**7:43** Perhaps an Assyrian star god—the planet Saturn [d]**7:42–43** Am 5:25–27 [e]**7:46** Other mss read *house* [f]**7:49–50** Is 66:1–2 [g]**7:54** Or *were cut to the quick* [h]**7:55** Lit *and* [i]**7:60** He died; see Jn 11:11; 1 Co 11:30; 1 Th 4:13–15

---

rection of angels. Jewish (and Christian) tradition taught the law was given through the mediation of angels (Gal. 3:19; Heb. 2:2), whereas the gospel is announced directly by the Messiah Himself.

7:58 threw him out of the city. John 18:31 indicates the Sanhedrin did not have the right to mete out capital punishment, so this may have been an act of mob violence. But Acts 26:10 indicates that perhaps by this time Pilate's ability to control the Sanhedrin had weakened and that it indeed took capital cases into its own hands. **Saul.** This is the person who was to become the great apostle to the Gentiles.

8:1–3 all except the apostles were scattered. That the apostles remained in Jerusalem indicates the persecution was directed mainly against the Greek-speaking converts who shared Stephen's views of the temple. The church's spread to Judea and Samaria shows that God used this persecution to show that He is not limited to Jerusalem (1:8).

8:5 Samaria. When the Northern Kingdom (Israel) was conquered by the Assyrians in 722 B.C., many of its people were deported while exiles from elsewhere in the vast Assyrian Empire were brought in to settle the land (2 Kings 17:23–41). These people intermarried with the remaining Israelites and adopted some of their religious practices. As a result, the Jews of the Southern Kingdom (Judah) considered the Samaritans as religious compromisers and racial half-breeds. By Jesus' day, strict Jews avoided Samaria and the word *Samaritan* was an insult (John 8:48). As a Greek-speaking Jew, Philip may have been less prejudiced against the Samaritans than the Palestinian Jews. This al-

lowed him to speak freely with them.

8:9–11 Simon. While biblical information about Simon is limited to this passage, church tradition is rich with stories (vv. 20–24). Superstition and the practice of the occult allow for the demonstration of supernatural powers, which were wrongly assumed to be done by God just because they were powerful.

8:12–13 even Simon himself believed. Philip's message and signs even attracted the attention of Simon. His initial interest appears to have been in the miraculous aspect of Philip's ministry more than in the message of the kingdom of God that he preached.

8:14–17 Upon hearing that faith in Jesus had broken out in Samaria, the apostles apparently decided they needed to check out the situation (see also 11:22–23). Thus, Peter and John were sent as representatives to investigate.

to a[a] city in Samaria and preached the •Messiah to them. [6] The crowds paid attention with one mind to what Philip said, as they heard and saw the signs he was performing. [7] For unclean spirits, crying out with a loud voice, came out of many who were possessed, and many who were paralyzed and lame were healed. [8] So there was great joy in that city.

The Response of Simon

[9] A man named Simon had previously practiced sorcery in that city and astounded the •Samaritan people, while claiming to be somebody great. [10] They all paid attention to him, from the least of them to the greatest, and they said, "This man is called the Great Power of God!"[b] [11] They were attentive to him because he had astounded them with his sorceries for a long time. [12] But when they believed Philip, as he proclaimed the good news about the kingdom of God and the name of Jesus Christ, both men and women were baptized. [13] Then even Simon himself believed. And after he was baptized, he went around constantly with[c] Philip and was astounded as he observed the signs and great miracles that were being performed.

Simon's Sin

[14] When the apostles who were at Jerusalem heard that Samaria had welcomed God's message, they sent Peter and John to them. [15] After they went down there, they prayed for them, that they might receive the Holy Spirit. [16] For He had not yet come down on[d] any of them; they had only been baptized in the name of the Lord Jesus. [17] Then Peter and John laid their hands on them, and they received the Holy Spirit.

[18] When Simon saw that the Holy[e] Spirit was given through the laying on of the apostles' hands, he offered them money, [19] saying, "Give me this power too, so that anyone I lay hands on may receive the Holy Spirit."

[20] But Peter told him, "May your silver be destroyed with you, because you thought the gift of God could be obtained with money! [21] You have no part or share in this matter, because your heart is not right before God. [22] Therefore repent of this wickedness of yours, and pray to the Lord that the intent of your heart may be forgiven you. [23] For I see you are poisoned by bitterness and bound by iniquity."

[24] "Please pray[f] to the Lord for me," Simon replied, "so that nothing you[f] have said may happen to me."

[25] Then, after they had testified and spoken the message of the Lord, they traveled back to Jerusalem, evangelizing many villages of the Samaritans.

Sharing Good News

1. When did you get your first Bible? Who gave it to you?

Acts 8:26-40

2. How much time do you spend reading the Bible? How did Bible reading change the Ethiopian's life?

3. What was required for Philip to baptize the Ethiopian (v. 37)?

4. Who, like Philip, helped you understand the Bible? What was the most important thing that person taught you?

5. What is "the good news about Jesus" (v. 35) that Philip described? How would you summarize that good news for someone who asked?

The Conversion of the Ethiopian Official

[26] An angel of the Lord spoke to Philip: "Get up and go south to the road that goes down from Jerusalem to desert Gaza."[g] [27] So he got up and went. There was an Ethiopian man, a eunuch and high official of Candace, queen of the Ethiopians, who was in charge of her

---

[a] **8:5** Other mss read *the*   [b] **8:10** Or *This is the power of God called Great*   [c] **8:13** Or *he kept close company with*   [d] **8:16** Or *yet fallen on*
[e] **8:18** Other mss omit *Holy*   [f] **8:24** Gk words *you* and *pray* are plural   [g] **8:26** Perhaps old *Gaza* or *the road near the desert*

There are various interpretations for the delay between the Samaritans' response of faith and their reception of the Spirit. But the one that best fits the context of Acts is that it occurred so the apostles would be convinced the Lord was including the Samaritans as full members of His church (1:8; see also 10:44–45 and 11:15).

8:27 eunuch. Eunuchs (men who were emasculated to protect a king's wives and concubines) were commonly employed as royal officials. Although attracted to Judaism, a eunuch would never be allowed to participate fully in the temple worship (Deut. 23:1). **Candace.** A title for the queens of Ethiopia.

8:32–33 He was led like a sheep. The eunuch was reading from Isaiah 53:7–8, a key Old Testament passage that describes Jesus as the "Suffering Servant" or "Servant of the Lord."

This passage underlines much of what Luke has already recorded about the apostles' preaching about the identity of Jesus (3:13; 4:27).

8:34 who is the prophet saying this about? The eunuch's question was a common one in Jewish circles. Some thought the prophet was speaking of his own sufferings as one rejected, while others thought he was speaking figuratively of Israel as a nation that suffered at the hands of its oppressors (Isa. 44:1–2). Still another view of the Servant's identity linked him with Cyrus the King of Persia (see Isa. 44:28–45:1–3.) The traditional rabbis had not made any connection between the Suffering Servant of Isaiah 53, the kingly Messiah of Isaiah 11, and the glorified Son of Man in Daniel 13. Only in Jesus' teachings did these concepts finally come together (Luke 24:26).

8:35 the good news about Jesus. Philip used this passage as a jumping-off point to explain the ministry of Jesus. He undoubtedly referred the eunuch to other verses in Isaiah 53 as well as the other references to the Servant in Isaiah that point out the Servant's suffering for the sake of others and how this Servant would be a light for the Gentiles. All of this would have been related to Jesus' ministry, death, and resurrection.

8:36–38 What would keep me from. The Greek word behind this expression may be part of a baptismal liturgy the early church used with candidates for baptism. Strict Jews would offer at least one reason why this man was ineligible to be considered part of God's people: he was a eunuch. He could never become a Jewish proselyte (v. 27), but he could become a full member of the church through Jesus Christ. This fulfills the prophecy of Isaiah

entire treasury. He had come to worship in Jerusalem [28] and was sitting in his chariot on his way home, reading the prophet Isaiah aloud.

[29] The Spirit told Philip, "Go and join that chariot."

[30] When Philip ran up to it, he heard him reading the prophet Isaiah, and said, "Do you understand what you're reading?"

[31] "How can I," he said, "unless someone guides me?" So he invited Philip to come up and sit with him. [32] Now the Scripture passage he was reading was this:

> He was led like a sheep to the slaughter,
> and as a lamb is silent before its shearer,
> so He does not open His mouth.
> [33] In His humiliation justice
>   was denied Him.
> Who will describe His generation?
> For His life is taken from the earth.[a]

[34] The eunuch replied to Philip, "I ask you, who is the prophet saying this about—himself or another person?" [35] So Philip proceeded[b] to tell him the good news about Jesus, beginning from that Scripture.

[36] As they were traveling down the road, they came to some water. The eunuch said, "Look, there's water! What would keep me from being baptized?" [[37] And Philip said, "If you believe with all your heart you may." And he replied, "I believe that Jesus Christ is the Son of God."][c] [38] Then he ordered the chariot to stop, and both Philip and the eunuch went down into the water, and he baptized him. [39] When they came up out of the water, the Spirit of the Lord carried Philip away, and the eunuch did not see him any longer. But he went on his way rejoicing. [40] Philip appeared in[d] Azotus,[e] and passing through, he was evangelizing all the towns until he came to Caesarea.

The Damascus Road

9 Meanwhile Saul, still breathing threats and murder against the disciples of the Lord, went to the high priest [2] and requested letters from him to the synagogues in Damascus, so that if he found any who belonged to the Way, either men or women, he might bring them as prisoners to Jerusalem. [3] As he traveled and was nearing Damascus, a light from heaven suddenly flashed around him. [4] Falling to the ground, he heard a voice saying to him, "Saul, Saul, why are you persecuting Me?"

Really? That Guy?

1. What's the most dramatic surprise you've had on a trip? Was it a good or bad surprise?

Acts 9:1-19

2. How was Saul persecuting Jesus, since Jesus had already ascended to heaven?

3. Saul asked, "Who are You, Lord?" (v. 5), while Ananias answered, "Here I am, Lord!" (v. 10). What was the difference in these men's lives?

4. Why was Ananias afraid to visit Saul? What does it show of his character that he went?

5. When did Saul become "Brother Saul" (v. 17)? (Consider verses 5-8.)

6. Is there someone God has sent for you to help mentor in the faith?

[5] "Who are You, Lord?" he said.

"I am Jesus, whom you are persecuting," He replied. [6] "But get up and go into the city, and you will be told what you must do."

[7] The men who were traveling with him stood speechless, hearing the sound but seeing no one. [8] Then Saul got up from the ground, and though his eyes were open, he could see nothing. So they took him by the hand and led him into Damascus. [9] He was unable to see for three days, and did not eat or drink.

---

[a] **8:32–33** Is 53:7–8 [b] **8:35** Lit *Philip opened his mouth* [c] **8:37** Other mss omit bracketed text [d] **8:40** Or *Philip was found at*, or *Philip found himself in* [e] **8:40** Or *Ashdod*

56:3–8, which anticipated a time when both foreigners and eunuchs would be welcomed into God's household.

9:1 breathing threats and murder. This reflects Paul's obsessive hatred toward the Christians.

9:2 letters. While the Sanhedrin had no formal authority outside of Judea, its prestige could influence elders in synagogues far from Jerusalem. In this case, the Sanhedrin asked the elders in Damascus to cooperate with Paul by allowing him to arrest as blasphemers those Christians who had fled from Jerusalem to Damascus, and bring them for trial in Jerusalem. **Damascus.** A city about 150 miles from Jerusalem. Luke has not told us how the church began among the sizable Jewish community in this important city, but Paul desired to expand his persecution there so it would not spread

any further. **the Way.** Unique to Acts as a name for Christianity (19:9,23; 22:4; 24:14,22). It may stem from Jesus' claim in John 14:6.

9:3 a light from heaven suddenly flashed around him. The term is often used of lightning, indicating the brilliance of the light (see also 26:13). Light (glory) is commonly connected with divine appearances (Luke 9:29; Rev. 1:14–16).

9:10 a disciple named Ananias. Apart from Paul's comment in 22:12, nothing is known of this Ananias.

9:11 the street called Straight. The "street called Straight" where Saul's host lived is still a main thoroughfare in Damascus, Syria. The house of Judas was traditionally located near the western end of the street. Nothing is known

of Judas.

9:15–16 this man is My chosen instrument to carry My name. The Lord overruled Ananias's objections with a final command to "Go!" and a description of what Paul's mission would be. **My chosen instrument.** Literally "a choice vessel." The Servant of Isaiah was God's chosen (Isa. 44:1). Paul would carry on the mission of the Servant by bringing Jesus' light to the Gentiles (Isa. 42:6; 49:6) and by sharing in His suffering.

9:17 Brother Saul. Without further question, Ananias affirms Paul as part of the family through the grace of Jesus. Paul's sight was restored; then he was baptized (presumably by Ananias) and was filled with the Holy Spirit.

9:20 he began proclaiming Jesus. That Paul,

Saul's Baptism

¹⁰ Now in Damascus there was a disciple named Ananias. And the Lord said to him in a vision, "Ananias!"

"Here I am, Lord!" he said.

¹¹ "Get up and go to the street called Straight," the Lord said to him, "to the house of Judas, and ask for a man from Tarsus named Saul, since he is praying there. ¹² In a visionᵃ he has seen a man named Ananias coming in and placing his hands on him so he may regain his sight."

¹³ "Lord," Ananias answered, "I have heard from many people about this man, how much harm he has done to Your saints in Jerusalem. ¹⁴ And he has authority here from the •chief priests to arrest all who call on Your name."

¹⁵ But the Lord said to him, "Go! For this man is My chosen instrument to carry My name before Gentiles, kings, and the sons of Israel. ¹⁶ I will certainly show him how much he must suffer for My name!"

¹⁷ So Ananias left and entered the house. Then he placed his hands on him and said, "Brother Saul, the Lord Jesus, who appeared to you on the road you were traveling, has sent me so you may regain your sight and be filled with the Holy Spirit."

¹⁸ At once something like scales fell from his eyes, and he regained his sight. Then he got up and was baptized. ¹⁹ And after taking some food, he regained his strength.

Saul Proclaiming the Messiah

Saulᵇ was with the disciples in Damascus for some days. ²⁰ Immediately he began proclaiming Jesus in the synagogues: "He is the Son of God."

²¹ But all who heard him were astounded and said, "Isn't this the man who, in Jerusalem, was destroying those who called on this name, and then came here for the purpose of taking them as prisoners to the chief priests?"

²² But Saul grew more capable, and kept confounding the Jews who lived in Damascus by proving that this One is the •Messiah.

²³ After many days had passed, the Jews conspired to kill him, ²⁴ but their plot became known to Saul. So they

Capable Christianity

1. What skill have you developed the most? What has helped you to improve?

Acts 9:20-31

2. Why did Saul immediately begin to proclaim, "[Jesus] is the Son of God" (v. 20)?

3. What does it mean that "Saul grew more capable, and kept confounding the Jews" (v. 22)? How was he "confounding" them? How did he grow "more capable"?

4. Why did the Jews want to kill him? Since they killed Jesus as well, what does this suggest about being a disciple of Christ?

5. How can you grow "more capable" in defending your faith?

were watching the gates day and night intending to kill him, ²⁵ but his disciples took him by night and lowered him in a large basket through ⌊an opening in⌋ the wall.

Saul in Jerusalem

²⁶ When he arrived in Jerusalem, he tried to associate with the disciples, but they were all afraid of him, since they did not believe he was a disciple. ²⁷ Barnabas, however, took him and brought him to the apostles and explained to them how, on the road, Saulᶜ had seen the Lord, and that He had talked to him, and how in Damascus he had spoken boldly in the name of Jesus. ²⁸ Saulᶜ was coming and going with them in Jerusalem, speaking boldly in the name of the Lord. ²⁹ He conversed and debated with the Hellenistic Jews,ᵈ but they attempted to kill him. ³⁰ When the brothers found out, they took him down to Caesarea and sent him off to Tarsus.

ᵃ9:12 Other mss omit *In a vision* ᵇ9:19 Lit *He* ᶜ9:27,28 Lit *he* ᵈ9:29 Lit *Hellenists*; that is, Gk-speaking Jews

---

as a representative from the Sanhedrin, would be invited to speak in the synagogues of Damascus is not unusual. What was unexpected was his message! **He is the Son of God.** This is one of Paul's favorite ways of describing Jesus in his letters.

9:21–22 astounded. The shocked reaction of the Jews in Damascus is understandable, given their previous understanding of why Paul came to the city. **proving that this One is the Messiah.** This was undoubtedly done by pointing out Old Testament passages about the Messiah that were fulfilled in the life and ministry of Jesus (see also 8:34–35).

9:23–25 After many days. When Paul returned to Damascus, the leaders of the synagogues were prepared for him. They drew upon the help of the governor of the city in a plot to capture and kill Paul (2 Cor. 11:32–33). The phrase

"the Jews" refers to the religious leaders of the Jewish community. **through [an opening in] the wall.** Ancient cities were surrounded by walls as a defense against enemies. Although the city gates were being closely observed, Paul escaped from the city by being lowered over the wall in a large basket.

9:27 Barnabas. See 4:36. Barnabas assumes an important role later on as Paul's companion on his missionary trips. Barnabas risked alienating himself from the church by befriending this former persecutor of the early believers.

9:31 increased in numbers. With the persecution over, and the uproar caused by Paul's preaching quieted down, the church throughout Palestine had a period of peace and growth. Perhaps its persecutors thought it would just go away on its own. With this summary, Luke prepares his readers to anticipate the next step of expansion for the church—to

the ends of the earth (1:8).

9:32 As Peter was traveling. Peter and the other apostles probably made many trips throughout Judea, Samaria, and Galilee to teach and encourage the Christian communities throughout the area (8:25). **Lydda.** A town about 25 miles west of Jerusalem.

9:33–35 Aeneas, Jesus Christ heals you. This healing of a paralyzed man is similar to Jesus' healing of a man with the same condition (Luke 5:17–26), affirming Peter as a representative of Jesus.

9:40–43 Tabitha, get up! Peter followed the pattern of Jesus when he raised Jairus's daughter. This miracle, like the healing of Aeneas, was seen as a sign that pointed to the power of Jesus as Lord. Peter stayed on for some time in Joppa. This sets the stage for his encounter with Cornelius (10:1–48).

³¹ So the church throughout all Judea, Galilee, and Samaria had peace, being built up and walking in the fear of the Lord and in the encouragement of the Holy Spirit, and it increased in numbers.

The Healing of Aeneas

³² As Peter was traveling from place to place,ᵃ he also came down to the saintsᵇ who lived in Lydda. ³³ There he found a man named Aeneas, who was paralyzed and had been bedridden for eight years. ³⁴ Peter said to him, "Aeneas, Jesus Christ heals you. Get up and make your own bed,"ᶜ and immediately he got up. ³⁵ So all who lived in Lydda and Sharon saw him and turned to the Lord.

Dorcas Restored to Life

³⁶ In Joppa there was a disciple named Tabitha, which is translated Dorcas.ᵈ She was always doing good works and acts of charity. ³⁷ In those days she became sick and died. After washing her, they placed her in a room upstairs. ³⁸ Since Lydda was near Joppa, the disciples heard that Peter was there and sent two men to him who begged him, "Don't delay in coming with us." ³⁹ So Peter got up and went with them. When he arrived, they led him to the room upstairs. And all the widows approached him, weeping and showing him the robes and clothes that Dorcas had made while she was with them. ⁴⁰ Then Peter sent them all out of the room. He knelt down, prayed, and turning toward the body said, "Tabitha, get up!" She opened her eyes, saw Peter, and sat up. ⁴¹ He gave her his hand and helped her stand up. Then he called the saints and widows and presented her alive. ⁴² This became known throughout all Joppa, and many believed in the Lord. ⁴³ And Peterᵉ stayed on many days in Joppa with Simon, a leather tanner.ᶠ

Cornelius' Vision

10 There was a man in Caesarea named Cornelius, a •centurion of what was called the Italian •Regiment. ² He was a devout man and feared God along with his whole household. He did many charitable deeds for the ⌐Jewish₁ people and always prayed to God. ³ At about three in the afternoonᵍ he distinctly saw in a vision an angel of God who came in and said to him, "Cornelius!"

Accepting One Another

1. Which of these foods would you refuse to eat: Snails? Pickled pigs' feet? Chocolate-covered ants?

Acts 10:1-23

2. The Old Testament forbids God's people from eating certain types of foods. How was Peter trying to obey God in this passage? What was God trying to teach him?

3. Cornelius was not a Jew. How did Peter treat him when they met (v. 23)? How did Peter's vision help him to behave this way?

4. What does verse 15 mean: "What God has made clean, you must not call common"? How does this principle apply to us today?

⁴ Looking intently at him, he became afraid and said, "What is it, Lord?"

And he told him, "Your prayers and your acts of charity have come up as a memorial offering before God. ⁵ Now send men to Joppa and call for Simon, who is also named Peter. ⁶ He is lodging with Simon, a tanner, whose house is by the sea."

⁷ When the angel who spoke to him had gone, he called two of his household slaves and a devout soldier, who was one of those who attended him. ⁸ After explaining everything to them, he sent them to Joppa.

ᵃ**9:32** Lit *Peter was passing through all* ᵇ**9:32** The believers ᶜ**9:34** Or *and get ready to eat* ᵈ**9:36** *Dorcas* = Gazelle ᵉ**9:43** Lit *he* ᶠ**9:43** Tanners were considered ritually unclean because of their occupation. ᵍ**10:3** Lit *about the ninth hour*

10:1 Cornelius. This was a popular name taken by the descendants of slaves who were released from slavery by the action of a P. Cornelius Sculla in 82 B.C. **a centurion.** Equivalent to the modern rank of army captain. **the Italian Regiment.** An auxiliary force stationed in the area that was composed of men recruited from Italy.

10:2 feared God. The distinction between Gentile God-fearers (who believed in the true God and obeyed His ethical commands) and proselytes (who fully converted to Judaism) lay in the hesitancy of God-fearers to submit to the Jewish ceremonial laws, especially circumcision.

10:4 Lord. Cornelius did not yet know about Jesus, so this is an expression of respect for what Cornelius recognized as a divine visitor. **as a memorial offering before God.** Although as a Gentile Cornelius would not have been al-

lowed to offer animal sacrifices in the temple, the angel lets him know that devotion to God is recognized as a sacrifice that is acceptable to God.

10:13 kill and eat. The voice invites Peter to partake of any of the animals in the sheet, but Peter protests because eating some of these animals would violate the dietary laws of the Jews.

10:15 What God has made clean. Peter soon understood that if God could pronounce that certain foods which were formerly unclean are now acceptable, He can do the same thing with people.

10:23 Peter then invited them in. While Jews offered Gentiles hospitality, they refused to accept it from Gentiles lest they violate dietary laws. Assuming the

messengers from Cornelius arrived in early afternoon (see 10:9), it would have been too late in the day for them to start the 30-mile journey back to Caesarea.

10:25–26 fell at his feet, and worshiped him. Cornelius was showing great deference to Peter whom he regarded as a special messenger from God. But Peter believed that such respect was to be shown only to God.

10:28 forbidden for a Jewish man. Jews would not associate with Gentiles partly because of the problems associated with their dietary laws. To have such associations rendered the Jew ceremonially unclean. **But God has shown me.** Although the dream Peter had was about food, he realized that it was also about people. He could no longer consider Gentiles unclean.

Peter's Vision

⁹ The next day, as they were traveling and nearing the city, Peter went up to pray on the housetop at about noon.ᵃ ¹⁰ Then he became hungry and wanted to eat, but while they were preparing something he went into a visionary state. ¹¹ He saw heaven opened and an object coming down that resembled a large sheet being lowered to the earth by its four corners. ¹² In it were all the four-footed animals and reptiles of the earth, and the birds of the sky. ¹³ Then a voice said to him, "Get up, Peter; kill and eat!"

¹⁴ "No, Lord!" Peter said. "For I have never eaten anything commonᵇ and unclean!"

¹⁵ Again, a second time, a voice said to him, "What God has made clean, you must not call common." ¹⁶ This happened three times, and then the object was taken up into heaven.

Peter Visits Cornelius

¹⁷ While Peter was deeply perplexed about what the vision he had seen might mean, the men who had been sent by Cornelius, having asked directions to Simon's house, stood at the gate. ¹⁸ They called out, asking if Simon, who was also named Peter, was lodging there.

¹⁹ While Peter was thinking about the vision, the Spirit told him, "Three men are here looking for you. ²⁰ Get up, go downstairs, and accompany them with no doubts at all, because I have sent them."

²¹ Then Peter went down to the men and said, "Here I am, the one you're looking for. What is the reason you're here?"

²² They said, "Cornelius, a centurion, an upright and God-fearing man, who has a good reputation with the whole Jewish nation, was divinely directed by a holy angel to call you to his house and to hear a message from you." ²³ Peterᶜ then invited them in and gave them lodging.

The next day he got up and set out with them, and some of the brothers from Joppa went with him. ²⁴ The following day he entered Caesarea. Now Cornelius was expecting them and had called together his relatives and close friends. ²⁵ When Peter entered, Cornelius met him, fell at his feet, and worshiped him.

²⁶ But Peter helped him up and said, "Stand up! I myself am also a man." ²⁷ While talking with him, he went on in and found that many had come together there. ²⁸ Peterᶜ said to them, "You know it's forbidden for a Jewish man to associate with or visit a foreigner. But God has shown me that I must not call any person common or unclean. ²⁹ That's why I came without any objection when I was sent for. So I ask, 'Why did you send for me?' "

³⁰ Cornelius replied, "Four days ago at this hour, at three in the afternoon,ᵈ I wasᵉ praying in my house. Just then a man in a dazzling robe stood before me ³¹ and said, 'Cornelius, your prayer has been heard, and your acts of charity have been remembered in God's sight. ³² Therefore send someone to Joppa and invite Simon here, who is also named Peter. He is lodging in Simon the tanner's house by the sea.'ᶠ ³³ Therefore I immediately sent for you, and you did the right thing in coming. So we are all present before God, to hear everything you have been commanded by the Lord."

Good News for Gentiles

³⁴ Then Peter began to speak: "In truth, I understand that God doesn't show favoritism, ³⁵ but in every nation the person who fears Him and does righteousness is acceptable to Him. ³⁶ He sent the message to the sons of Israel, proclaiming the good news of peace through Jesus Christ—He is Lord of all. ³⁷ You know the eventsᵍ that took place throughout all Judea, beginning from Galilee after the baptism that John preached: ³⁸ how God anointed Jesus of Nazareth with the Holy Spirit and with power, and how He went about doing good and curing all who were under the tyranny of the Devil, because God was with Him. ³⁹ We ourselves are witnesses of everything He did in both the Judean country and in Jerusalem; yet they

---

ᵃ**10:9** Lit *about the sixth hour*   ᵇ**10:14** Perhaps *profane,* or *non-sacred*; Jews ate distinctive food according to OT law and their traditions, similar to modern kosher or non-kosher foods.   ᶜ**10:23,28** Lit *He*   ᵈ**10:30** Lit *at the ninth hour*   ᵉ**10:30** Other mss add *fasting and*   ᶠ**10:32** Other mss add *When he arrives, he will speak to you.*   ᵍ**10:37** Lit *thing,* or *word*

10:34–35 God doesn't show favoritism. While this truth is firmly rooted in the Old Testament (Deut. 10:17; Mal. 2:9), the Jews did not apply it to Gentiles. **in every nation the person who fears Him and does righteousness is acceptable to Him.** A sense of humility before the Creator and a desire to live in love and justice toward others are the key signs of faith (Mic. 6:8; see also Rom. 2).

10:39 they killed Him. While it was the Jewish leaders who arranged for Jesus' death, the fact that He was crucified implied Roman involvement.

10:45 believers … with Peter. This phenomenon shocked Peter's companions because it violated all they had believed about relations between Jews and Gentiles. It meant that the Gentiles were on equal terms with Jews before God.

10:46 they heard them speaking in other languages. Luke's mention that these Gentiles spoke in languages or tongues showed the Jewish believers that the Gentiles' experience of the Spirit was no less than that of the apostles. This appears to relate to the outpouring of the Spirit at Pentecost (2:1–8).

10:47 baptized. Baptism with the Spirit usually accompanied (2:38) or followed (8:16–17) baptism with water, but in this groundbreaking situation the Spirit's baptism became the grounds on which water baptism could not be denied. Had the Spirit not come at this point, the Jewish believers may have insisted that before Cornelius and his friends could be baptized as genuine followers of the Messiah they must observe Jewish traditions about food, the Sabbath, etc.

10:48 they asked him to stay for a few days. Violating custom once again, Peter, a Jew, accepted Gentile hospitality. This was another indication of his acceptance of them as full members of God's family.

11:2 those who stressed circumcision. Since at this point all the believers (except Cornelius) were circumcised, Luke may be using a term popular at the time of his writing to describe those Jews who still insisted that Gentiles must first become Jews before they could be Christians.

11:17 gift. The gift of the Holy Spirit taking up residence in a person's heart is the indisputable mark of the Christian. Peter highlights that the Spirit is given to all (Jew or Gentile) who believe in the Lord Jesus (see also Gal. 3:2).

11:18 God has granted repentance. While

killed Him by hanging Him on a tree. [40] God raised up this man on the third day and permitted Him to be seen, [41] not by all the people, but by us, witnesses appointed beforehand by God, who ate and drank with Him after He rose from the dead. [42] He commanded us to preach to the people, and to solemnly testify that He is the One appointed by God to be the Judge of the living and the dead. [43] All the prophets testify about Him that through His name everyone who believes in Him will receive forgiveness of sins."

Gentile Conversion and Baptism

[44] While Peter was still speaking these words, the Holy Spirit came down on all those who heard the message. [45] The circumcised believers[a] who had come with Peter were astounded, because the gift of the Holy Spirit had been poured out on the Gentiles also. [46] For they heard them speaking in ₁other₁ languages and declaring the greatness of [b] God.

Then Peter responded, [47] "Can anyone withhold water and prevent these from being baptized, who have received the Holy Spirit just as we have?" [48] And he commanded them to be baptized in the name of Jesus Christ. Then they asked him to stay for a few days.

Gentile Salvation Defended

11 The apostles and the brothers who were throughout Judea heard that the Gentiles had welcomed God's message also. [2] When Peter went up to Jerusalem, those who stressed circumcision[c] argued with him, [3] saying, "You visited uncircumcised men and ate with them!"

[4] Peter began to explain to them in an orderly sequence, saying: [5] "I was in the town of Joppa praying, and I saw, in a visionary state, an object coming down that resembled a large sheet being lowered from heaven by its four corners, and it came to me. [6] When I looked closely and considered it, I saw the four-footed animals of the earth, the wild beasts, the reptiles, and the birds of the sky. [7] Then I also heard a voice telling me, 'Get up, Peter; kill and eat!'

[8] " 'No, Lord!' I said. 'For nothing common or unclean has ever entered my mouth!' [9] But a voice answered from heaven a second time, 'What God has made clean, you must not call common.'

[10] "Now this happened three times, and then everything was drawn up again into heaven. [11] At that very moment, three men who had been sent to me from Caesarea arrived at the house where we were. [12] Then the Spirit told me to go with them with no doubts at all. These six brothers accompanied me, and we went into the man's house. [13] He reported to us how he had seen the angel standing in his house and saying, 'Send[d] to Joppa, and call for Simon, who is also named Peter. [14] He will speak words[e] to you by which you and all your household will be saved.'

[15] "As I began to speak, the Holy Spirit came down on them, just as on us at the beginning. [16] Then I remembered the word of the Lord, how He said, 'John baptized with water, but you will be baptized with the Holy Spirit.' [17] Therefore, if God gave them the same gift that He also gave to us when we believed on the Lord Jesus Christ, how could I possibly hinder God?"

[18] When they heard this they became silent. Then they glorified God, saying, "So God has granted repentance resulting in life[f] to even the Gentiles!"

The Church in Antioch

[19] Those who had been scattered as a result of the persecution that started because of Stephen made their way as far as Phoenicia, Cyprus, and Antioch, speaking the message to no one except Jews. [20] But there were some of them, Cypriot and Cyrenian men, who came to Antioch and began speaking to the Hellenists,[g][h] proclaiming the good news about the Lord Jesus. [21] The Lord's hand was with them, and a large number who believed turned to the Lord. [22] Then the report about them reached the ears of the church in Jerusalem, and they sent out Barnabas to travel[i] as far as Antioch. [23] When he arrived and saw the grace of God, he was glad, and he encouraged all of them to remain true to the Lord with a firm resolve of

---

[a] **10:45** Jewish Christians who stressed circumcision; Ac 11:2; 15:5; Gl 2:12; Col 4:11; Ti 1:10   [b] **10:46** Or *and magnifying*   [c] **11:2** Lit *those of the circumcision*   [d] **11:13** Other mss add *men*   [e] **11:14** Or *speak a message*   [f] **11:18** Or *repentance to life*   [g] **11:20** Other mss read *Greeks*   [h] **11:20** In this context, a non-Jewish person who spoke Gk   [i] **11:22** Other mss omit *to travel*

---

the Jerusalem church realized that Gentiles were to be included in the church, tradition and prejudice prevented it from acting on that truth to any great extent (see Acts 15). Instead, it was the church at Antioch, to which Luke now turns his attention, that spearheaded the missionary movement among Gentiles.

11:19 had been scattered. Since there were Jewish communities through the Roman Empire, it is not unusual that the Jewish believers would have spread throughout such a large area.

11:20–21 came to Antioch and began speaking. The synagogues in Antioch were probably attended by Gentile God-fearers (like Cornelius). They were attracted to the ethics and values of Judaism, but did not accept its customs about food, circumcision, and Sabbath regulations. It is probably with

these Gentiles that the believers shared the gospel.

11:23 he arrived and saw the grace of God. Barnabas did not require the Gentile converts to submit to Jewish traditions, but he encouraged them to maintain loyalty to Jesus as Lord.

11:24 he was a good man. Barnabas is first mentioned in Acts 4:36 as one who sold a field and brought the money to the apostles. He is there said to have been a Levite, and it is noted that his name meant "Son of Encouragement." He encouraged the disciples to take a chance on Saul after Saul's conversion (9:26–27), and he encouraged Paul to take a chance on John Mark after John Mark's desertion on a missionary journey (15:36–41). The manner in which he is eulogized here ("he was a good man") may indicate that he had died by the time of this writing.

11:26 the disciples were first called Christians. By the time of Luke's writing, this Latin term was a widespread name for the believers. The only other places in the New Testament where this term is used are situations of ridicule and persecution (Acts 26:28; 1 Pet. 4:16). It may have originally been used to mock the believers.

11:28 severe famine. There were at least five localized famines during this period, including one that struck Judea around A.D. 46.

12:1 King Herod. This is Herod Agrippa I, the grandson of Herod the Great, who ruled when Jesus was born, and the nephew of Herod Antipas who governed Galilee during Jesus' ministry. Herod Agrippa I was popular with the Jews. To further cultivate this popularity, he resumed the persecution of the church that had come to a stop upon Paul's conversion (9:31).

12:7 a light shone. Peter was guarded by four

the heart— ²⁴ for he was a good man, full of the Holy Spirit and of faith—and large numbers of people were added to the Lord. ²⁵ Then heᵃ went to Tarsus to search for Saul, ²⁶ and when he found him he brought him to Antioch. For a whole year they met with the church and taught large numbers, and the disciples were first called Christians in Antioch.

Famine Relief

²⁷ In those days some prophets came down from Jerusalem to Antioch. ²⁸ Then one of them, named Agabus, stood up and predicted by the Spirit that there would be a severe famine throughout the Roman world.ᵇ This took place during the time of Claudius.ᶜ ²⁹ So each of the disciples, according to his ability, determined to send relief to the brothers who lived in Judea. ³⁰ This they did, sending it to the elders by means of Barnabas and Saul.

James Martyred and Peter Jailed

12 About that time King •Herod cruelly attacked some who belonged to the church, ² and he killed James, John's brother, with the sword. ³ When he saw that it pleased the Jews, he proceeded to arrest Peter too, during the days of •Unleavened Bread. ⁴ After the arrest, he put him in prison and assigned four squads of four soldiers each to guard him, intending to bring him out to the people after the •Passover. ⁵ So Peter was kept in prison, but prayer was being made earnestly to God for him by the church.

Peter Rescued

⁶ On the night before Herod was to bring him out for execution, Peter was sleeping between two soldiers, bound with two chains, while the sentries in front of the door guarded the prison. ⁷ Suddenly an angel of the Lord appeared, and a light shone in the cell. Striking Peter on the side, he woke him up and said, "Quick, get up!" Then the chains fell off his wrists. ⁸ "Get dressed," the angel told him, "and put on your sandals." And he did so. "Wrap your cloak around you," he told him, "and follow me." ⁹ So he went out and followed, and he did not know that what took place through the angel was real, but thought he was seeing a vision. ¹⁰ After they passed the first and second guard posts, they came to the iron gate that leads into the city, which opened to them by itself. They went outside and passed one street, and immediately the angel left him.

"Get Out of Jail Free" Card

1. What's your closest encounter with the police or other law-enforcement authority?

Acts 12:1-19

2. Why was Herod persecuting Christians? What were his motives?

3. The church was praying for Peter (vv. 5,12). Why didn't they believe Peter was at the door? When have you been surprised by an answer to prayer?

4. Herod and his guards expected to execute Peter. What happened instead? What does this show about God's control when His people are persecuted?

5. Have you ever faced persecution for your belief in Jesus? How did you respond? How can this passage give you courage?

¹¹ Then Peter came to himself and said, "Now I know for certain that the Lord has sent His angel and rescued me from Herod's grasp and from all that the Jewish people expected." ¹² When he realized this, he went to the house of Mary, the mother of John Mark,ᵈ where many had assembled and were praying. ¹³ He knocked at the door in the gateway, and a servant named Rhoda came to answer. ¹⁴ She recognized Peter's voice, and because of her joy she did not open the gate, but ran in and announced that Peter was standing at the gateway.

ᵃ**11:25** Other mss read *Barnabas*   ᵇ**11:28** Or *the whole world*   ᶜ**11:28** Emperor A.D. 41–54; there was a famine A.D. 47–48.   ᵈ**12:12** Lit *John who was called Mark*

---

soldiers on six-hour shifts (vv. 4,6). Such intense security measures may have been implemented to prevent any further "unexplainable" release such as that which happened when the Sanhedrin imprisoned him earlier (5:19ff). The description of the light underscores that this was a miraculous intervention of God.

12:11 the Lord ... rescued me from Herod's grasp. In Acts, there is no predictable pattern of how God might work. While Peter was released from prison, James, for whom the church undoubtedly prayed just as earnestly, was killed. The call to the church is to be faithful and take responsible action whether or not God chooses to act in a miraculous way.

12:12 Mary, the mother of John Mark. This is the Mark who later wrote the Gospel that bears his name (see v. 25; 13:5).

12:13–17 Luke recounts humorously how Peter was left standing at the gate of the courtyard while the disciples who were praying for just such a release could not believe he was there!

12:15 It's his angel! Assuming that Peter had been killed, the disciples could come up with only one solution—that Peter's angel had taken on the form of Peter.

12:17 James. This is a half brother of Jesus (Mark 6:3). James did not believe in Jesus as the Messiah during Jesus' ministry (John 7:5), but after the resurrection, Jesus appeared to James in a special way (1 Cor. 15:7), qualifying him to be an apostle. James became a leader in the Jerusalem church (15:13; 21:18; Gal. 2:9); his piety and devotion to God gained the respect of the Jewish community. When executed by the Sadducean high priest in

A.D. 61, his death was mourned by many Pharisaic Jews as well as Christians.

12:18–19 Herod ... interrogated the guards. The release of Peter threw the officials into confusion. Unable to explain how Peter could possibly escape without the cooperation of the guards, Herod ordered them to be executed. Under Roman law, a guard who allowed his prisoner to escape suffered the fate intended for the prisoner.

12:22 the voice of a god. The Gentiles listening to Herod probably intended this chant as nothing more than royal flattery. But Herod should have repudiated such a blasphemous gesture.

12:23 infected with worms and died. While this may refer to tapeworms or roundworms as the cause of death, this phrase also appears

15 "You're crazy!" they told her. But she kept insisting that it was true. Then they said, "It's his angel!" 16 Peter, however, kept on knocking, and when they opened the door and saw him, they were astounded. 17 Motioning to them with his hand to be silent, he explained to them how the Lord had brought him out of the prison. "Report these things to James[a] and the brothers," he said. Then he departed and went to a different place.

18 At daylight, there was a great commotion[b] among the soldiers as to what could have become of Peter. 19 After Herod had searched and did not find him, he interrogated the guards and ordered their execution. Then Herod went down from Judea to Caesarea and stayed there.

Herod's Death

20 He had been very angry with the Tyrians and Sidonians.[c] Together they presented themselves before him, and having won over Blastus, who was in charge of the king's bedroom, they asked for peace, because their country was supplied with food from the king's country. 21 So on an appointed day, dressed in royal robes and seated on the throne, Herod delivered a public address to them. 22 The populace began to shout, "It's the voice of a god and not of a man!" 23 At once an angel of the Lord struck him because he did not give the glory to God, and he became infected with worms and died. 24 Then God's message flourished and multiplied. 25 And Barnabas and Saul returned to[d] Jerusalem after they had completed their relief mission, on which they took John Mark.[e]

Preparing for the Mission Field

13 In the local church at Antioch there were prophets and teachers: Barnabas, Simeon who was called Niger, Lucius the Cyrenian, Manaen, a close friend of •Herod the tetrarch, and Saul. 2 As they were ministering to[f] the Lord and fasting, the Holy Spirit said, "Set apart for Me Barnabas and Saul for the work that I have called them to." 3 Then,

after they had fasted, prayed, and laid hands on them,[g] they sent them off.

False Prophets

1. Have you ever taken a sailing cruise? Where did you go? What was it like?

Acts 13:1-12

2. The name Bar-Jesus (v. 6) means "son of Jesus." What kind of false doctrine might this sorcerer have been preaching? What modern "prophets" do the same thing?

3. How did Paul react when he met the sorcerer (vv. 10-11)?

4. Who are the "false prophets" today who are trying to turn people "from the faith" (v. 8)?

5. How should a Christian respond to false teachers? When have you encountered a false teacher?

The Mission to Cyprus

4 Being sent out by the Holy Spirit, they came down to Seleucia, and from there they sailed to Cyprus. 5 Arriving in Salamis, they proclaimed God's message in the Jewish •synagogues. They also had John as their assistant. 6 When they had gone through the whole island as far as Paphos, they came across a sorcerer, a Jewish false prophet named Bar-Jesus. 7 He was with the •proconsul, Sergius Paulus, an intelligent man. This man summoned Barnabas and Saul and desired to hear God's message. 8 But Elymas, the sorcerer, which is how his name is translated, opposed them and tried to turn the proconsul away from the faith.

---

[a]12:17 This was James, the Lord's brother; see Mk 6:3. This was not James the apostle; see Ac 12:2. [b]12:18 Or was no small disturbance [c]12:20 The people of the area of modern Lebanon [d]12:25 Other mss read from [e]12:25 Lit John who [f]13:2 Or were worshiping [g]13:3 See note at Ac 6:6

---

to be a stock way for ancient writers to describe the death of disreputable leaders.

13:1 prophets and teachers. Teachers were church leaders who interpreted and applied the Old Testament Scriptures and the words of Jesus to the life of the church.

13:3 laid hands on them. The laying on of hands was a sign of solidarity between the church and the missionaries, as well as a sign that the church was committing them to God's grace.

13:5 Salamis. A Greek city with a substantial Jewish population on the island of Cyprus.

13:6 Paphos. The Roman seat of power on the island of Cyprus, about 90 miles from the port of Salamis.

13:10 son of the Devil. Although Elymas was also called Bar-Jesus (meaning "son of a savior"), Paul does not hesitate to clarify the reality of the situation. Elymas' opposition to the gospel meant he reflected the characteristics of Satan.

13:11–12 you are going to be blind. This was a temporary blindness meant as a warning for Elymas to repent.

13:13 set sail. A 160-mile boat trip followed by a difficult journey of over 100 miles across the Tarsus Mountains brought the missionaries to Antioch. **Paul and his companions.** Up to verse 7, Barnabas was regarded as the leader of this team; from here on Paul is given the leadership position. **John ... left them.** No reason is given, but Paul's reaction in 15:38 indicates that he at least viewed this as some sort of failure on John (Mark's) part.

13:20 450 years. This was approximately the period of time when the Israelites lived in Egypt, traveled in the desert, and conquered the land of Canaan.

13:24–25 John. Acts 18:24–25 and 19:3 hint that the influence of John the Baptist had spread among Jews throughout the Roman Empire, from North Africa through Asia Minor. It may be that at Pisidian Antioch there were those who acknowledged that John was a prophet sent by God.

13:26 sons of Abraham's race. The wall between Jew and Gentile was broken down as Paul proclaimed that the message of God's salvation was sent to the "the sons of Abraham's race, and those among you who fear God." These God-fearing Gentiles (10:2) would form a natural bridge from the synagogue to pagan Gentile society.

9 Then Saul—also called Paul—filled with the Holy Spirit, stared straight at the sorcerer[a] 10 and said, "You son of the Devil, full of all deceit and all fraud, enemy of all righteousness! Won't you ever stop perverting the straight paths of the Lord? 11 Now, look! The Lord's hand is against you: you are going to be blind, and will not see the sun for a time." Suddenly a mist and darkness fell on him, and he went around seeking someone to lead him by the hand.

12 Then the proconsul, seeing what happened, believed and was astonished at the teaching about the Lord.

Paul's Sermon in Antioch of Pisidia

13 Paul and his companions set sail from Paphos and came to Perga in Pamphylia. John, however, left them and went back to Jerusalem. 14 They continued their journey from Perga and reached Antioch in Pisidia. On the Sabbath day they went into the synagogue and sat down. 15 After the reading of the Law and the Prophets, the leaders of the synagogue sent ⌈word⌉ to them, saying, "Brothers, if you have any message of encouragement for the people, you can speak."

16 Then standing up, Paul motioned with his hand and spoke: "Men of Israel, and you who fear God, listen! 17 The God of this people Israel chose our forefathers, exalted the people during their stay in the land of Egypt, and led them out of it with a mighty[b] arm. 18 And for about 40 years He put up with them[c] in the desert; 19 then after destroying seven nations in the land of Canaan, He gave their land to them as an inheritance. 20 This all took about 450 years. After this, He gave them judges until Samuel the prophet. 21 Then they asked for a king, so God gave them Saul the son of Kish, a man of the tribe of Benjamin, for 40 years. 22 After removing him, He raised up David as their king, of whom He testified: 'I have found David the son of Jesse, a man after My heart,[d] who will carry out all My will.'

23 "From this man's descendants, according to the promise, God brought the Savior, Jesus,[e] to Israel.

24 Before He came to public attention,[f] John had previously proclaimed a baptism of repentance to all the people of Israel. 25 Then as John was completing his life work, he said, 'Who do you think I am? I am not the One. But look! Someone is coming after me, and I am not worthy to untie the sandals on His feet.'

26 "Brothers, sons of Abraham's race, and those among you who fear God, the message of this salvation has been sent to us. 27 For the residents of Jerusalem and their rulers, since they did not recognize Him or the voices of the prophets that are read every Sabbath, have fulfilled their words[g] by condemning Him. 28 Though they found no grounds for the death penalty, they asked •Pilate to have Him killed. 29 When they had fulfilled all that had been written about Him, they took Him down from the tree and put Him in a tomb. 30 But God raised Him from the dead, 31 and He appeared for many days to those who came up with Him from Galilee to Jerusalem, who are now His witnesses to the people. 32 And we ourselves proclaim to you the good news of the promise that was made to our forefathers. 33 God has fulfilled this to us their children by raising up Jesus, as it is written in the second Psalm:

You are My Son;
today I have become Your Father.[h] [i]

34 Since He raised Him from the dead, never to return to decay, He has spoken in this way, I will grant you the faithful covenant blessings[j] made to David.[k] 35 Therefore He also says in another passage, You will not allow Your Holy One to see decay.[l] 36 For David, after serving his own generation in God's plan, fell •asleep, was buried with his fathers, and decayed. 37 But the One whom God raised up did not decay. 38 Therefore, let it be known to you, brothers, that through this man forgiveness of sins is being proclaimed to you, 39 and everyone who believes in Him is justified from everything, which you could not be justified from through the law of Moses. 40 So beware that what is said in the prophets does not happen to you:

a13:9 Lit at him   b13:17 Lit with an uplifted   c13:18 Other mss read He cared for them   d13:22 1 Sm 13:14; Ps 89:20   e13:23 Other mss read brought salvation   f13:24 Lit Before the face of His entrance   g13:27 Lit fulfilled them   h13:33 Or I have begotten You   i13:33 Ps 2:7   j13:34 Lit faithful holy things   k13:34 Is 55:3   l13:35 Ps 16:10

13:36–37 David. Paul reminds his listeners that David's death and subsequent decay proves that the passages refer to one who would not be left to "rot in the grave" (GNB).

13:38 forgiveness of sins. This phrase sums up all that salvation involves. It means the believer's guilt is atoned for so that he enjoys a restored relationship with God, free from shame or anxiety over the past. It also means the believer is being freed from the power of sin as his desires conform more and more to God's will. Finally, it means the believer can experience a relationship of peace with God.

13:39 justified. This term brings to mind a courtroom scene in which a judge, after hearing the accusations against a defendant, declares that he is not guilty. Because Jesus' death was a sacrifice for sin, the be-

liever is set right before God and pronounced not guilty of sin.

13:43 devout proselytes. These were Gentiles who had submitted to the Jewish traditions on circumcision, dietary laws, and Sabbath observance.

13:48 all who had been appointed to eternal life believed. The fact that these Gentiles responded to the gospel with faith is evidence that their names had also been written in God's figurative book of life (Ex. 32:32; Rev. 13:8; 21:27).

13:50 religious women of high standing. Palestinian women were allowed little social mobility, but women in Gentile regions could hold official offices and run businesses.

13:51 shaking the dust off their feet. Jews

entering Palestine from a Gentile area wiped off their feet as a symbol that they were getting rid of Gentile contamination. Paul and Barnabas used this custom to indicate that they were exempt from the judgment to come upon the Jews at Antioch who had rejected the gospel.

14:5 an attempt ... to assault and stone them. Opposition to Paul and Barnabas in Antioch proceeded through official channels. But the fact that a stoning was planned here indicates that Jewish leaders were responsible for this plot. They intended to bypass the Roman court system to get rid of Paul and Barnabas.

14:6 the Lycaonian towns called Lystra and Derbe. Iconium had originally been a Phrygian settlement and was in the province of Lycaonia. Lystra was about 20 miles

⁴¹ Look, you scoffers,
marvel and vanish away,
because I am doing a work in your days,
a work that you will never believe,
even if someone were to explain it to you."ᵃ

Paul and Barnabas in Antioch

⁴² As theyᵇ were leaving, theyᶜ ᵈ begged that these matters be presented to them the following Sabbath. ⁴³ After the synagogue had been dismissed, many of the Jews and devout •proselytes followed Paul and Barnabas, who were speaking with them and persuading them to continue in the grace of God.

⁴⁴ The following Sabbath almost the whole town assembled to hear the message of the Lord.ᵉ ⁴⁵ But when the Jews saw the crowds, they were filled with jealousy and began to oppose what Paul was saying by insulting him.

⁴⁶ Then Paul and Barnabas boldly said: "It was necessary that God's message be spoken to you first. But since you reject it, and consider yourselves unworthy of eternal life, we now turn to the Gentiles! ⁴⁷ For this is what the Lord has commanded us:

I have appointed you as a light
for the Gentiles,
to bring salvation to the endsᶠ of the earth."ᵍ

⁴⁸ When the Gentiles heard this, they rejoiced and glorified the message of the Lord, and all who had been appointed to eternal life believed. ⁴⁹ So the message of the Lord spread through the whole region. ⁵⁰ But the Jews incited the religious women of high standing and the leading men of the city. They stirred up persecution against Paul and Barnabas and expelled them from their district. ⁵¹ But shaking the dust off their feet against them, they proceeded to Iconium. ⁵² And the disciples were filled with joy and the Holy Spirit.

Growth and Persecution in Iconium

14 The same thing happened in Iconium; they entered the Jewish •synagogue and spoke in

such a way that a great number of both Jews and Greeks believed. ² But the Jews who refused to believe stirred up and poisoned the mindsʰ of the Gentiles against the brothers. ³ So they stayed there for some time and spoke boldly, in reliance on the Lord, who testified to the message of His grace by granting that signs and wonders be performed through them. ⁴ But the people of the city were divided, some siding with the Jews and some with the apostles. ⁵ When an attempt was made by both the Gentiles and Jews, with their rulers, to assault and stone them, ⁶ they found out about it and fled to the Lycaonian towns called Lystra and Derbe, and to the surrounding countryside. ⁷ And there they kept evangelizing.

Mistaken for Gods in Lystra

⁸ In Lystra a man without strength in his feet, lame from birth,ⁱ and who had never walked, sat ⁹ and heard Paul speaking. After observing him closely and seeing that he had faith to be healed, ¹⁰ ₗPaulₗ said in a loud voice, "Stand up straight on your feet!" And he jumped up and started to walk around.

¹¹ When the crowds saw what Paul had done, they raised their voices, saying in the Lycaonian language, "The gods have come down to us in the form of men!" ¹² And they started to call Barnabas, Zeus, and Paul, Hermes, because he was the main speaker. ¹³ Then the priest of Zeus, whose temple was just outside the town, brought oxen and garlands to the gates. He, with the crowds, intended to offer sacrifice.

¹⁴ The apostles Barnabas and Paul tore their robes when they heard this and rushed into the crowd, shouting: ¹⁵ "Men! Why are you doing these things? We are men also, with the same nature as you, and we are proclaiming good news to you, that you should turn from these worthless things to the living God, **who made the heaven, the earth, the sea, and everything in them.**ʲ ¹⁶ In past generations He allowed all the nations to go their own way, ¹⁷ although He did not leave Himself without a wit-

ᵃ**13:41** Hab 1:5 ᵇ**13:42** Paul and Barnabas ᶜ**13:42** Other mss read *they were leaving the synagogue of the Jews, the Gentiles* ᵈ**13:42** The people ᵉ**13:44** Other mss read *of God* ᶠ**13:47** Lit *the end* ᵍ**13:47** Is 49:6 ʰ**14:2** Lit *and harmed the souls* ⁱ**14:8** Lit *from his mother's womb* ʲ**14:15** Ex 20:11; Ps 146:6

southwest of Iconium, and Derbe lay 60 miles further southeast.

14:8 Lystra. The small Jewish community in Lystra (16:1–3) apparently did not have a synagogue. Adopting a new strategy that brought the gospel directly to the Gentiles, Paul probably preached in the Greek forum, the site of the local marketplace and gathering place for public discussion.

14:12 Hermes ... the main speaker. Zeus was the chief god among the Greek deities while Hermes was the herald of the gods. The fact that Paul was identified with Hermes shows that he was the leading figure in this missionary enterprise. Paul was also of much smaller stature than Barnabas, who would have appeared more like the regal Zeus.

14:23 elders. This is the first mention of elders outside of Palestine. The early churches adopted the synagogue form of leadership in selecting leaders who were responsible for the spiritual oversight of the members. How Paul and Barnabas selected these leaders, or whether the entire church was involved in the process, is not clear.

14:27 reported. The tense of the Greek word implies they "kept on reporting" what had happened. This was probably because the church was actually a combination of small house groups that met throughout the city; at this point Christians had no common meeting places. **opened the door of faith to the Gentiles.** It is precisely the nature of this report that led to the conflict in chapter 15 and the important meeting of the church that resulted from it.

15:1–4 The controversy surrounding circumcision stirred up such a debate that the church felt it necessary to call together the church leaders from Jerusalem and Antioch to settle the issue.

15:5 the believers from the party of the Pharisees. The resistance to allowing Gentiles into the church originated with Jewish Christians who had formerly been Pharisees. This small but influential sect was widely respected for its adherence to the law and traditions. Their concern arose from a genuine desire to ensure that God's honor was not violated through disregard of His law. To them, the offer of the gospel apart from the law was inconceivable since for centuries their people had been taught to discern God's will by examining the law. Paul's ministry seemed like a slap in Israel's face—an unthinkable rejection of all the

ness, since He did good: giving you rain from heaven and fruitful seasons, and satisfying your[a] hearts with food and happiness." [18] Even though they said these things, they barely stopped the crowds from sacrificing to them.

[19] Then some Jews came from Antioch and Iconium, and when they had won over the crowds and stoned Paul, they dragged him out of the city, thinking he was dead. [20] After the disciples surrounded him, he got up and went into the town. The next day he left with Barnabas for Derbe.

Church Planting

[21] After they had evangelized that town and made many disciples, they returned to Lystra, to Iconium, and to Antioch, [22] strengthening the hearts[b] of the disciples by encouraging them to continue in the faith, and by telling them, "It is necessary to pass through many troubles on our way into the kingdom of God."

[23] When they had appointed elders in every church and prayed with fasting, they committed them to the Lord in whom they had believed. [24] Then they passed through Pisidia and came to Pamphylia. [25] After they spoke the message in Perga, they went down to Attalia. [26] From there they sailed back to Antioch where they had been entrusted to the grace of God for the work they had completed. [27] After they arrived and gathered the church together, they reported everything God had done with them, and that He had opened the door of faith to the Gentiles. [28] And they spent a considerable time[c] with the disciples.

Dispute in Antioch

15 Some men came down from Judea and began to teach the brothers: "Unless you are circumcised according to the custom prescribed by Moses, you cannot be saved!" [2] But after Paul and Barnabas had engaged them in serious argument and debate, they arranged for Paul and Barnabas and some others of them to go up to the apostles and elders in Jerusalem concerning this controversy. [3] When they had been sent on their way by the church, they passed

through both Phoenicia and Samaria, explaining in detail the conversion of the Gentiles, and they created great joy among all the brothers.

[4] When they arrived at Jerusalem, they were welcomed by the church, the apostles, and the elders, and they reported all that God had done with them. [5] But some of the believers from the party of the •Pharisees stood up and said, "It is necessary to circumcise them and to command them to keep the law of Moses!"

The Jerusalem Council

[6] Then the apostles and the elders assembled to consider this matter. [7] After there had been much debate, Peter stood up and said to them: "Brothers, you are aware that in the early days God made a choice among you,[d] that by my mouth the Gentiles would hear the gospel message and believe. [8] And God, who knows the heart, testified to them by giving[e] the Holy Spirit, just as He also did to us. [9] He made no distinction between us and them, cleansing their hearts by faith. [10] Why, then, are you now testing God by putting on the disciples' necks a yoke that neither our forefathers nor we have been able to bear? [11] On the contrary, we believe we are saved through the grace of the Lord Jesus, in the same way they are."

[12] Then the whole assembly fell silent and listened to Barnabas and Paul describing all the signs and wonders God had done through them among the Gentiles. [13] After they stopped speaking, James responded: "Brothers, listen to me! [14] Simeon[f] has reported how God first intervened to take from the Gentiles a people for His name. [15] And the words of the prophets agree with this, as it is written:

[16] **After these things I will return**
 and will rebuild David's tent,
 which has fallen down.
 I will rebuild its ruins and will set it up
 again,
[17] so that those who are left of mankind
 may seek the Lord—

---

[a]**14:17** Other mss read *our* [b]**14:22** Lit *souls* [c]**14:28** Or *spent no little time* [d]**15:7** Other mss read *us* [e]**15:8** Other mss add *them* [f]**15:14** Simon (Peter)

---

covenant responsibilities of God's chosen people throughout their history.

15:7–8 Peter … said to them. As part of the discussion, Peter recounted his experience with Cornelius (10:1–11:18). The fact that Cornelius experienced the presence of the Spirit in the same way the disciples did was proof that God accepted the Gentiles apart from the practice of Jewish law.

15:10 yoke. A reference to the Law of Moses. Peter declared that requiring Gentile converts to be circumcised would be like putting a yoke around the necks of these believers.

15:13–21 James was the leader of the Jerusalem church (see 12:17). The ultimate decision as to the position of the Jerusalem church was his to make. Since in Galatians

2:11–13, James appears to have represented those who believed that Gentiles could not be considered equal members of the church with Jews, it may be that this council was the turning point when he realized the scope of Jesus' mission. James's affirmation of God's plan to save all types of people through faith in Jesus is his last statement in the book of Acts.

15:16–18 rebuild its ruins. The original context of the prophecy was the anticipation of the destruction of Israel (722 B.C.) after which God, at a future time, would return the nation to its former glory that it had enjoyed in David's time.

15:20 things polluted by idols. In Gentile areas meat was sold only after the animal had been sacrificed as part of a worship service to an idol. The eating of such food later

became a source of controversy between Jewish and Gentile believers in Rome (Rom. 14:1–8) and Corinth (1 Cor. 8). **sexual immorality.** This may be related to "the pollution of idols", since idolatry sometimes involved ritual prostitution (1 Cor. 6:12–20). **eating anything that has been strangled, and from blood.** Jews were forbidden to eat meat that contained blood (Lev. 17:10,13). Gentiles would make the sharing of meals with Jewish believers easier if they would respect this tradition.

15:27 Judas. Probably a leader in the Jerusalem church, but nothing more is known about him. **Silas.** Probably also a leader, but one who played a prominent role in the rest of Acts (see also 1 Thess. 1:1; 2 Cor. 1:19; 1 Pet. 5:12).

15:28 put no greater burden on you. The

even all the Gentiles who are called
by My name,
says the Lord who does these things,
¹⁸ which have been known from long ago.ᵃ ᵇ

¹⁹ Therefore, in my judgment, we should not cause difficulties for those who turn to God from among the Gentiles, ²⁰ but instead we should write to them to abstain from things polluted by idols, from sexual immorality, from eating anything that has been strangled, and from blood. ²¹ For since ancient times, Moses has had in every city those who proclaim him, and he is read aloud in the •synagogues every Sabbath day."

The Letter to the Gentile Believers

²² Then the apostles and the elders, with the whole church, decided to select men from among them and to send them to Antioch with Paul and Barnabas: Judas, called Barsabbas, and Silas, both leading men among the brothers. ²³ They wrote this letter to be delivered by them:ᶜ

From the apostles and the elders, your brothers,
To the brothers from among the Gentiles in Antioch, Syria, and Cilicia:
Greetings.
²⁴ Because we have heard that some to whom we gave no authorization went out from us and troubled you with their words and unsettled your hearts,ᵈ ²⁵ we have unanimously decided to select men and send them to you along with our beloved Barnabas and Paul, ²⁶ who have risked their lives for the name of our Lord Jesus Christ. ²⁷ Therefore we have sent Judas and Silas, who will personally report the same things by word of mouth.ᵉ ²⁸ For it was the Holy Spirit's decision— and ours—to put no greater burden on you than these necessary things: ²⁹ that you abstain from food offered to idols, from blood, from eating anything that has been strangled, and from sexual immorality. If you keep yourselves from these things, you will do well. Farewell.

The Outcome of the Jerusalem Letter

³⁰ Then, being sent off, they went down to Antioch, and after gathering the assembly, they delivered the letter. ³¹ When they read it, they rejoiced because of its encouragement. ³² Both Judas and Silas, who were also prophets themselves, encouraged the brothers and strengthened them with a long message. ³³ After spending some time there, they were sent back in peace by the brothers to those who had sent them.ᶠ ᵍ ³⁵ But Paul and Barnabas, along with many others, remained in Antioch teaching and proclaiming the message of the Lord.

Parting Company

1. Who was your closest friend when you were 7 years old? Are you still friends?

Acts 15:36-41

2. Why did Paul and Barnabas part company? What were the strengths and weaknesses of each person's reasons?

3. John Mark may have written the gospel of Mark, and Paul later reunited with him. What does this suggest about Barnabas? About Paul's willingness to admit an error?

4. What good can you see coming out of Paul and Barnabas parting ways in this story?

5. How should you deal with a broken relationship with someone in the Christian community?

ᵃ**15:17-18** Other mss read *says the Lord who does all these things. Known to God from long ago are all His works.* ᵇ**15:16-18** Am 9:11-12; Is 45:21 ᶜ**15:23** Lit *Writing by their hand:* ᵈ**15:24** Other mss add *by saying, "Be circumcised and keep the law."* ᵉ**15:27** Lit *things through word* ᶠ**15:33** Other mss read *the brothers to the apostles* ᵍ**15:33** Other mss add v. 34: *But Silas decided to stay there.*

---

council of church leaders meeting in Jerusalem recognized that these regulations were over and above what was needed for salvation. It was not necessary that the Gentiles submit to these standards to be right with God, but it was important that they do so to avoid alienating Jews from the gospel.

15:29 If you keep yourselves from these things, you will do well. The implication is that no other requirement—especially circumcision (v. 5)—is to be imposed on Gentile believers.

15:32 encouraged ... and strengthened. The ministry involved in the prophetic gift of Silas and Judas is captured by the word *encouraged.*

15:38 who had deserted them. Luke does not tell us why Mark left Paul and Barnabas during the first missionary journey, but Paul viewed it as a serious problem and was unwilling to let Mark go with them again.

15:39-40 a sharp disagreement. Paul and Barnabas disagreed on whether Mark should be allowed to accompany them on this journey. Barnabas wanted him to join them, while Paul did not. Mark's earlier departure had placed increased demands on Paul and Barnabas, and Paul was unwilling to risk that again. This disagreement caused the missionaries to go their separate ways.

15:41-16:5 The limits of Paul's first journey were reached by an overland trek westward to the border of Cilicia. But this time he went east, going overland through the provinces until he came to Derbe.

16:1-3 circumcised him. This refers to Timothy, the son of a Jewish woman and a Gentile father. For Paul to allow Timothy, a Jew, to accompany him without first following the Jewish custom of circumcision would communicate to other Jews that Paul had no regard for their traditions. This shows Paul's willingness to accommodate himself to cultural sensitivities.

16:6-7 did not allow them. Why Jesus would not allow Paul and Silas to preach in Asia and Bithyna is not known.

16:8 Troas. An important seaport city on the Aegean Sea. While it appears that Paul did not conduct any evangelistic work here at this time, he did so later on (2 Cor. 2:12).

16:9-10 we. Verses 10-17 comprise the first of four passages written in the first person

Paul and Barnabas Part Company

36 After some time had passed, Paul said to Barnabas, "Let's go back and visit the brothers in every town where we have preached the message of the Lord, and see how they're doing." 37 Barnabas wanted to take along John Mark.[a] 38 But Paul did not think it appropriate to take along this man who had deserted them in Pamphylia and had not gone on with them to the work. 39 There was such a sharp disagreement that they parted company, and Barnabas took Mark with him and sailed off to Cyprus. 40 Then Paul chose Silas and departed, after being commended to the grace of the Lord by the brothers. 41 He traveled through Syria and Cilicia, strengthening the churches.

Paul Selects Timothy

16 Then he went on to Derbe and Lystra, where there was a disciple named Timothy, the son of a believing Jewish woman, but his father was a Greek. 2 The brothers at Lystra and Iconium spoke highly of him. 3 Paul wanted Timothy[b] to go with him, so he took him and circumcised him because of the Jews who were in those places, since they all knew that his father was a Greek. 4 As they traveled through the towns, they delivered the decisions reached by the apostles and elders at Jerusalem for them to observe. 5 So the churches were strengthened in the faith and were increased in number daily.

Evangelization of Europe

6 They went through the region of Phrygia and Galatia and were prevented by the Holy Spirit from speaking the message in the province of Asia. 7 When they came to Mysia, they tried to go into Bithynia, but the Spirit of Jesus did not allow them. 8 So, bypassing Mysia, they came down to Troas. 9 During the night a vision appeared to Paul: a Macedonian man was standing and pleading with him, "Cross over to Macedonia and help us!" 10 After he had seen the vision, we[c] immediately made efforts to set out for Macedonia, concluding that God had called us to evangelize them.

Closed Doors

1. If you could visit any country in the world, where would you visit?

Acts 16:6-10

2. Why did Paul not preach in Asia and Bithynia? What does it mean that the Holy Spirit prevented him from speaking (v. 6)?

3. How did this setback turn out to be a good thing?

4. When has God prevented you from pursuing a course of action, even when it seemed like a good choice? What was the result?

5. Do you struggle to pry open a door that God has closed? What closed doors are you struggling with right now?

Lydia's Conversion

11 Then, setting sail from Troas, we ran a straight course to Samothrace, the next day to Neapolis, 12 and from there to Philippi, a Roman colony, which is a leading city of that district of Macedonia. We stayed in that city for a number of days. 13 On the Sabbath day we went outside the city gate by the river, where we thought there was a place of prayer. We sat down and spoke to the women gathered there. 14 A woman named Lydia, a dealer in purple cloth from the city of Thyatira, who worshiped God, was listening. The Lord opened her heart to pay attention to what was spoken by Paul. 15 After she and her household were baptized, she urged us, "If you consider me a believer in the Lord, come and stay at my house." And she persuaded us.

---

[a]**15:37** Lit John who was called Mark [b]**16:3** Lit wanted this one [c]**16:10** The use of we in this passage probably indicates that the author Luke is joining Paul's missionary team here.

(20:1–15; 21:1–18; 27:1–28:16), indicating that Luke himself, the author of Acts, was accompanying Paul at these points.

16:13 a place of prayer. Ten men were required to form a synagogue. The fact that there was no synagogue in Philippi indicates the Jewish population in this city was small. **outside the city gate by the river.** The Jews may have been forbidden to meet inside the city limits, or they may have wanted to be near a river to perform their ceremonial washings.

16:14–15 Lydia. Lydia was a businesswoman who sold purple cloth, a luxury item indicating that she was a woman of wealth. **Thyatira.** A city in the province of Asia noted for its cloth-dyeing industry.

16:16 a spirit of prediction. Literally "a

spirit, a python." A snake was supposed to guard the oracle of Delphi, and thus the snake was a symbol of a fortuneteller.

16:18 come out of her. While the girl, who was a fortuneteller, uttered the truth, the spirit that motivated her was not what Paul desired as a collaborator in his mission. Proclamations from this girl attracted attention, but it made Paul and Silas appear more as magicians than as representatives of God. Therefore, Paul commanded the spirit to leave her.

16:19 their hope of profit was gone. The girl's worth to her masters was only in her gift of fortunetelling. To them, Paul had not delivered a girl from the power of evil, but had violated their property rights.

16:22 stripped ... beaten. The authorities

should have put Paul and Silas in custody to be formally tried, but they beat them publicly without a trial.

16:24 secured their feet in the stocks. The stocks were locked wooden boards that clamped about the ankles, making movement impossible.

16:27–28 he ... was going to kill himself. The penalty for a guard who allowed his prisoners to escape was the punishment the prisoner preferred to receive. The jailer preferred sudden death by his own hand rather than going through the humiliation of a trial and execution by the authorities.

16:31–32 Believe on the Lord Jesus, and you will be saved. Paul's statement to the jailer promised deliverance from divine judgment.

Paul and Silas in Prison

16 Once, as we were on our way to prayer, a slave girl met us who had a spirit of prediction[a] and made a large profit for her owners by fortune-telling. 17 As she followed Paul and us she cried out, "These men are the slaves of the Most High God, who are proclaiming to you[b] the way of salvation." 18 And she did this for many days.

But Paul was greatly aggravated, and turning to the spirit, said, "I command you in the name of Jesus Christ to come out of her!" And it came out right away.[c]

19 When her owners saw that their hope of profit was gone, they seized Paul and Silas and dragged them into the marketplace to the authorities. 20 And bringing them before the chief magistrates, they said, "These men are seriously disturbing our city. They are Jews, 21 and are promoting customs that are not legal for us as Romans to adopt or practice."

Singing in Prison

1. When you're down, what song or type of music lifts your spirits?

Acts 16:22-40

2. Why were Paul and Silas "praying and singing hymns to God" (v. 25) when they were in prison? What does this suggest about their attitude toward God?

3. Why did Paul and Silas stay when they could have left? What was the result?

4. If someone asked you, "What must I do to be saved?" (v. 30), what would you say?

5. How can this passage encourage you to trust more in God during times of trial?

22 Then the mob joined in the attack against them, and the chief magistrates stripped off their clothes and ordered them to be beaten with rods. 23 After they had inflicted many blows on them, they threw them in jail, ordering the jailer to keep them securely guarded. 24 Receiving such an order, he put them into the inner prison and secured their feet in the stocks.

A Midnight Deliverance

25 About midnight Paul and Silas were praying and singing hymns to God, and the prisoners were listening to them. 26 Suddenly there was such a violent earthquake that the foundations of the jail were shaken, and immediately all the doors were opened, and everyone's chains came loose. 27 When the jailer woke up and saw the doors of the prison open, he drew his sword and was going to kill himself, since he thought the prisoners had escaped. 28 But Paul called out in a loud voice, "Don't harm yourself, because all of us are here!"

29 Then the jailer[d] called for lights, rushed in, and fell down trembling before Paul and Silas. 30 Then he escorted them out and said, "Sirs, what must I do to be saved?" 31 So they said, "Believe on the Lord Jesus, and you will be saved—you and your household." 32 Then they spoke the message of the Lord to him along with everyone in his house. 33 He took them the same hour of the night and washed their wounds. Right away he and all his family were baptized. 34 He brought them up into his house, set a meal before them, and rejoiced because he had believed God with his entire household.

An Official Apology

35 When daylight came, the chief magistrates sent the police to say, "Release those men!"

36 The jailer reported these words to Paul: "The magistrates have sent orders for you to be released. So come out now and go in peace."

37 But Paul said to them, "They beat us in public without a trial, although we are Roman citizens, and threw us in jail. And now are they going to smuggle us out secretly? Certainly not! On the contrary, let them come themselves and escort us out!"

---

[a]**16:16** Or *a spirit by which she predicted the future* [b]**16:17** Other mss read *us* [c]**16:18** Lit *out this hour* [d]**16:29** Lit *Then he*

16:35–40 The magistrates wanted to expel Paul and Silas from Philippi to avoid any further trouble. But they refused to leave without a personal apology from the magistrates for their breach of justice. This was important for the protection of the young church in Philippi. By being escorted out of the prison by the magistrates, a signal would be communicated to the community that the charges against Paul and Silas had been false. Then the community would be more likely to leave the young church alone.

16:37 without a trial. While local magistrates could execute punishment upon troublemakers without a trial, this practice was never permitted in the case of a Roman citizen. The magistrates had overlooked the possibility that these two Jews might be Roman citizens.

17:5 the Jews became jealous. In Philippi economic interest had motivated the opposition against Paul and Silas. Here it was the jealousy of the Jews.

17:7 acting contrary to Caesar's decrees. In Philippi, the anger of the owner of the slave girl over his economic loss was masked by a charge of public disturbance. Here, the Jews' jealousy is masked by a charge of sedition against Rome.

17:9 taking a security bond. Since Paul could not be brought before the local officials, they insisted that Jason post a bond. This assured them that Jason would no longer be a host to Paul so he would have to leave the city.

17:17 he reasoned ... in the marketplace. Paul preached not only in the synagogue at Athens, but also in their marketplace where, three centuries before, Socrates had debated with anyone who would listen.

17:18 Epicurean and Stoic philosophers. Epicurus maintained that a tranquil life free from pain, passions, and fears was the highest good. This could be achieved only by detaching oneself from the world. The Epicureans were practical atheists since they believed the gods had no interest in everyday affairs. **this pseudo-intellectual.** A derisive term stemming from the actions of a bird that picks up seeds wherever it can find them. To the philosophers, Paul seemed like someone who picked up scraps of ideas here and there and then had the audacity to teach them to others.

17:19 Areopagus. Athens was a free city within the Roman Empire, so the Areopagus

[38] Then the police reported these words to the magistrates. And they were afraid when they heard that Paul and Silas[a] were Roman citizens. [39] So they came and apologized to them, and escorting them out, they urged them to leave town. [40] After leaving the jail, they came to Lydia's house where they saw and encouraged the brothers, and departed.

A Short Ministry in Thessalonica

17 Then they traveled through Amphipolis and Apollonia and came to Thessalonica, where there was a Jewish •synagogue. [2] As usual, Paul went to them, and on three Sabbath days reasoned with them from the Scriptures, [3] explaining and showing that the •Messiah had to suffer and rise from the dead, and saying: "This is the Messiah, Jesus, whom I am proclaiming to you." [4] Then some of them were persuaded and joined Paul and Silas, including a great number of God-fearing Greeks, as well as a number[b] of the leading women.

The Assault on Jason's House

[5] But the Jews became jealous, and when they had brought together some scoundrels from the marketplace and formed a mob, they set the city in an uproar. Attacking Jason's house, they searched for them to bring them out to the public assembly. [6] When they did not find them, they dragged Jason and some of the brothers before the city officials, shouting, "These men who have turned the world upside down have come here too, [7] and Jason has received them as guests! They are all acting contrary to Caesar's decrees, saying that there is another king—Jesus!" [8] The Jews[c] stirred up the crowd and the city officials who heard these things. [9] So taking a security bond from Jason and the others, they released them.

The Bereoans Search the Scriptures

[10] As soon as it was night, the brothers sent Paul and Silas off to Beroea. On arrival, they went into the synagogue of the Jews. [11] The people here were more open-minded than those in Thessalonica, since they welcomed the message with eagerness and examined the Scriptures daily to see if these things were so. [12] Consequently, many of them believed, including a number of the prominent Greek women as well as men. [13] But when the Jews from Thessalonica found out that God's message had been proclaimed by Paul at Beroea, they came there too, agitating and disturbing[d] the crowds. [14] Then the brothers immediately sent Paul away to go to the sea, but Silas and Timothy stayed on there. [15] Those who escorted Paul brought him as far as Athens, and after receiving instructions for Silas and Timothy to come to him as quickly as possible, they departed.

Paul in Athens

[16] While Paul was waiting for them in Athens, his spirit was troubled within him when he saw that the city was full of idols. [17] So he reasoned in the synagogue with the Jews and with those who worshiped God, and in the marketplace every day with those who happened to be there. [18] Then also, some of the Epicurean and Stoic philosophers argued with him. Some said, "What is this pseudo-intellectual[e] trying to say?"

Others replied, "He seems to be a preacher of foreign deities"—because he was telling the good news about Jesus and the resurrection.

[19] They took him and brought him to the Areopagus,[f] and said, "May we learn about this new teaching you're speaking of? [20] For what you say sounds strange to us, and we want to know what these ideas mean." [21] Now all the Athenians and the foreigners residing there spent their time on nothing else but telling or hearing something new.

The Areopagus Address

[22] Then Paul stood in the middle of the Areopagus and said: "Men of Athens! I see that you are extremely religious in every respect. [23] For as I was passing through and observing the objects of your worship, I even found an altar on which was inscribed:

> **TO AN UNKNOWN GOD**

---

[a] **16:38** Lit *heard they*   [b] **17:4** Lit *as well as not a few*   [c] **17:8** Lit *They*   [d] **17:13** Other mss omit *and disturbing*   [e] **17:18** Lit *this seed picker*; that is, one who picks up scraps   [f] **17:19** Or *Mars Hill*, the oldest and most famous court in Athens with jurisdiction in moral, religious, and civil matters

---

had legal and judicial authority over what went on in the city. It does not appear that Paul was on trial as much as his message was being evaluated on its credibility and worth.

17:21 something new. Luke's sarcastic observation about the nature of the Athenians in general is an echo of what the Greek orator Demosthenes had said 400 years earlier: "You are the best people at being deceived by something new that is said."

17:24 does not live in shrines. Euripides, a Greek philosopher, recognized this when he wrote, "What house built by craftsman could enclose the ... divine within enfolding walls?"

17:25 Neither is He served by human hands. With this observation of Paul, the philosophers would also agree. Plato had written, "What advantage accrues to the gods from what they get from us?"

17:27 He is not far from each one of us. Challenging the Epicurean assumption that God was unknowable, Paul says that God is knowable by those who seek Him.

17:28 your own poets. Paul supports his points by quoting two Greek authors, Epimenides and Aratus, indicating he recognized that God revealed truth about Himself even through other religions and philosophies.

17:32–34 some men joined him and believed. The converts in Athens included Dionysius, a member of the Athenian council. Nothing more is said in the New Testament about Athens, so it is unlikely that these believers established a church in this city.

18:2 Aquila ... Priscilla. This couple, apparently converted to Christianity in Rome prior to meeting Paul, became important coworkers with him (Rom. 16:3; 1 Cor. 16:19; 2 Tim. 4:19).

18:12 Gallio. A highly respected Roman official who served as proconsul in Archia for one year—from A.D. July 51 to A.D. June 52.

18:13 the law. The Jews probably did not expect that the proconsul could distinguish between Jews and Christians any better than the Emperor Claudius (v. 2). So it is probable that they accused Paul of violating the Roman laws against advocating religions that threatened the state.

18:18 Priscilla and Aquila were with him. It is significant that Priscilla's name is listed ahead of her husband's. This probably indi-

Therefore, what you worship in ignorance, this I proclaim to you. 24 The God who made the world and everything in it—He is Lord of heaven and earth and does not live in shrines made by hands. 25 Neither is He served by human hands, as though He needed anything, since He Himself gives everyone life and breath and all things. 26 From one man[a] He has made every nation of men to live all over the earth and has determined their appointed times and the boundaries of where they live, 27 so that they might seek God, and perhaps they might reach out and find Him, though He is not far from each one of us. 28 For in Him we live and move and exist, as even some of your own poets have said, 'For we are also His offspring.'[b] 29 Being God's offspring, then, we shouldn't think that the divine nature is like gold or silver or stone, an image fashioned by human art and imagination.

30 "Therefore, having overlooked the times of ignorance, God now commands all people everywhere to repent, 31 because He has set a day on which He is going to judge the world in righteousness by the Man He has appointed. He has provided proof of this to everyone by raising Him from the dead."

32 When they heard about resurrection of the dead, some began to ridicule him. But others said, "We will hear you about this again." 33 So Paul went out from their presence. 34 However, some men joined him and believed, among whom were Dionysius the Areopagite, a woman named Damaris, and others with them.

Founding the Corinthian Church

18 After this, he[c] left from Athens and went to Corinth, 2 where he found a Jewish man named Aquila, a native of Pontus, who had recently come from Italy with his wife Priscilla because Claudius[d] had ordered all the Jews to leave Rome. Paul[e] came to them, 3 and being of the same occupation, stayed with them and worked, for they were tentmakers by trade. 4 He reasoned in the •synagogue every Sabbath and tried to persuade both Jews and Greeks.

5 When Silas and Timothy came down from Macedonia, Paul was occupied with preaching the message[f] and solemnly testified to the Jews that the •Messiah is Jesus. 6 But when they resisted and blasphemed, he shook out his clothes[g] and told them, "Your blood is on your own heads! I am clean. From now on I will go to the Gentiles." 7 So he left there and went to the house of a man named Titius Justus, a worshiper of God, whose house was next door to the synagogue. 8 Crispus, the leader of the synagogue, believed the Lord, along with his whole household; and many of the Corinthians, when they heard, believed and were baptized.

9 Then the Lord said to Paul in a night vision, "Don't be afraid, but keep on speaking and don't be silent. 10 For I am with you, and no one will lay a hand on you to hurt you, because I have many people in this city." 11 And he stayed there a year and six months, teaching the word of God among them.

12 While Gallio was •proconsul of Achaia, the Jews made a united attack against Paul and brought him to the judge's bench. 13 "This man," they said, "persuades people to worship God contrary to the law!"

14 And as Paul was about to open his mouth, Gallio said to the Jews, "If it were a matter of a crime or of moral evil, it would be reasonable for me to put up with you Jews. 15 But if these are questions about words, names, and your own law, see to it yourselves. I don't want to be a judge of such things." 16 So he drove them from the judge's bench. 17 Then they all[h] seized Sosthenes, the leader of the synagogue, and beat him in front of the judge's bench. But none of these things concerned Gallio.

The Return Trip to Antioch

18 So Paul, having stayed on for many days, said goodbye to the brothers and sailed away to Syria. Priscilla and Aquila were with him. He shaved his head at Cenchreae, because he had taken a vow. 19 When they reached Ephesus he left them there, but he himself entered the synagogue and engaged in discussion with[i]

---

[a] **17:26** Other mss read *one blood* [b] **17:28** This citation is from Aratus, a third-century B.C. Gk poet. [c] **18:1** Other mss read *Paul* [d] **18:2** Roman emperor A.D. 41–54; he expelled all Jews from Rome in A.D. 49. [e] **18:2** Lit *He* [f] **18:5** Other mss read *was urged by the Spirit* [g] **18:6** A symbolic display of protest; see Ac 13:51; Mt 10:14 [h] **18:17** Other mss read *Then all the Greeks* [i] **18:19** Or *and addressed*

---

cates that Priscilla was the more influential and outspoken of the two. **He shaved his head ... because he had taken a vow.** Pious Jews would take vows, based on the pattern of the Nazarites (Num. 6:1–21), as an indication of their devotion to God. Since the cutting of one's hair indicated the termination of the vow, Paul may have made a vow of dedication to God for as long as he was in Corinth to express his thanks for God's promise of protection (v. 10). Vows normally were terminated by shaving one's head and offering a sacrifice in the temple at Jerusalem. People far from Jerusalem could shave their heads where they were and carry the trimmings to the temple to be presented along with a sacrifice. Luke may have included this incident as evidence that Paul did not abandon the traditions of his people.

18:25 he knew only John's baptism. While

Apollos was an articulate believer in Jesus, he had not received the full story of the gospel. Just what he was lacking is unclear, but, as the story in 19:1–7 indicates, he may not have heard of the coming of the Holy Spirit promised to those who are baptized in the name of Jesus.

19:2 Did you receive the Holy Spirit when you believed? As Paul talked with these men, something must have seemed out of place that led him to ask this question. Since John spoke of the coming of the Holy Spirit (Luke 3:16), it is likely that the intent of their response was more thast they were not aware that the Holy Spirit had been given. Or perhaps they had responded to some other teaching of John's and his words about the Spirit had not registered with them.

19:3 John's baptism. John baptized peo-

ple upon their repentance, symbolizing their cleansing from sin in anticipation of the coming of the Messiah. Jesus' baptism is a symbol of the pouring out of the Spirit in fulfillment of the Old Testament promises about the Messiah.

19:4 a baptism of repentance. John's baptism symbolized cleansing from sin. It may have been based on the baptism of the Essene sect at Qumran, a desert community where the Dead Sea Scrolls were found. Or it may have been a refinement of Jewish baptism of Gentile converts. Such were baptized to symbolize their turning away from their sinful Gentile ways. John taught that Jews also needed repentance and cleansing from sin. The baptism that Jesus practiced also involved repentance. But by itself a baptism of repentance focuses only on the past and finding forgiveness for one's sins. Christian

the Jews. 20 And though they asked him to stay for a longer time, he declined, 21 but said good-bye and stated,a "I'll come back to you again, if God wills." Then he set sail from Ephesus.

22 On landing at Caesarea, he went up and greeted the church,b and went down to Antioch. 23 He set out, traveling through one place after another in the Galatian territory and Phrygia, strengthening all the disciples.

The Eloquent Apollos

24 A Jew named Apollos, a native Alexandrian, an eloquent man who was powerful in the Scriptures, arrived in Ephesus. 25 This man had been instructed in the way of the Lord; and being fervent in spirit,c he spoke and taught the things about Jesus accurately, although he knew only John's baptism. 26 He began to speak boldly in the synagogue. After Priscilla and Aquila heard him, they took him homed and explained the way of God to him more accurately. 27 When he wanted to cross over to Achaia, the brothers wrote to the disciples urging them to welcome him. After he arrived, he greatly helped those who had believed through grace. 28 For he vigorously refuted the Jews in public, demonstrating through the Scriptures that Jesus is the Messiah.

Twelve Disciples of John the Baptist

19 While Apollos was in Corinth, Paul traveled through the interior regions and came to Ephesus. He found some disciples 2 and asked them, "Did you receive the Holy Spirit when you believed?"

"No," they told him, "we haven't even heard that there is a Holy Spirit."

3 "Then with what ⌊baptism⌋ were you baptized?" he asked them.

"With John's baptism," they replied.

4 Paul said, "John baptized with a baptism of repentance, telling the people that they should believe in the One who would come after him, that is, in Jesus."

5 On hearing this, they were baptized in the name of the Lord Jesus. 6 And when Paul had laid his hands on them, the Holy Spirit came on them, and they began to speak with ⌊other⌋ languages and to prophesy. 7 Now there were about 12 men in all.

In the Lecture Hall of Tyrannus

8 Then he entered the •synagogue and spoke boldly over a period of three months, engaging in discussion and trying to persuade them about the things related to the kingdom of God. 9 But when some became hardened and would not believe, slandering the Way in front of the crowd, he withdrew from them and met separately with the disciples, conducting discussions every day in the lecture hall of Tyrannus. 10 And this went on for two years, so that all the inhabitants of the province of Asia, both Jews and Greeks, heard the word of the Lord.

Demonism Defeated at Ephesus

11 God was performing extraordinary miracles by Paul's hands, 12 so that even facecloths or work apronse that had touched his skin were brought to the sick, and the diseases left them, and the evil spirits came out of them.

13 Then some of the itinerant Jewish exorcists attempted to pronounce the name of the Lord Jesus over those who had evil spirits, saying, "I command you by the Jesus whom Paul preaches!" 14 Seven sons of Sceva, a Jewish •chief priest, were doing this. 15 The evil spirit answered them, "Jesus I know, and Paul I recognize—but who are you?" 16 Then the man who had the evil spirit leaped on them, overpowered them all, and prevailed against them, so that they ran out of that house naked and wounded. 17 This became known to everyone who lived in Ephesus, both Jews and Greeks. Then fear fell on all of them, and the name of the Lord Jesus was magnified. 18 And many who had become believers came confessing and disclosing their practices, 19 while many of those who had practiced magic collected their books and burned them in front of everyone. So they calculated their value, and found it to be 50,000 pieces of silver. 20 In this way the Lord's message flourished and prevailed.

---

a**18:21** Other mss add *"By all means it is necessary to keep the coming festival in Jerusalem. But*   b**18:22** The church in Jerusalem   c**18:25** Or *in the Spirit*   d**18:26** Lit *they received him*   e**19:12** Or *that also sweatbands and sweatcloths or handkerchiefs*

---

baptism also includes the gift of the Spirit, which empowers believers for the future.

19:6 laid his hands on them. The last time this action was mentioned was when the gospel broke through into Samaria (see 8:17). The laying on of hands and the manifestation of tongues was reminiscent of Pentecost in Acts 2. The laying on of hands here may indicate an assurance that these people were now fully included in the church, and that Ephesus was to be a major new site for the proclamation of the gospel.

19:8–20 Ephesus became the hub of Paul's ministry for two years. During this time churches were founded in Colossae, Laodecia, and the cities mentioned in Revelation 1:11. It was also at Ephesus that Paul wrote 1 Corinthians.

19:11 extraordinary miracles. See the similar miracles wrought by Peter in 5:15. Ephesus was known for its magic arts. Some scrolls of magic spells from this ancient city can be seen today in museum collections. Perhaps for that reason, this type of evidence was necessary to convince people that the gospel was more powerful than magic.

19:14 Sceva, a Jewish chief priest. Other historical records never identify a high priest in Jerusalem by this name, although he may have been a member of the high priest's family. He was probably a successful exorcist who assumed the title to command respect (and business) from people in the area.

19:18 believers. The tense of the word implies that these were Christians who secretly practiced magic arts. The incident with Sceva's sons showed them that they needed to give up these practices.

19:19 calculated their value...50,000 pieces of silver. A piece of silver was called a drachma. This would have been an incredible amount of money, since a drachma was equal to a day's wages.

19:21 I must see Rome as well! Paul intended to visit Rome and then go on to Spain after delivering an offering from the Gentile churches he had founded to Jerusalem (Rom. 1:11; 15:23–25). The letter to the Romans was written from Corinth after Paul left Ephesus and just before his trip to Jerusalem (20:1–6).

19:24 a silversmith. Silversmiths in Ephesus made a great deal of money through the

The Riot in Ephesus

21 When these events were over, Paul resolved in the Spirit to pass through Macedonia and Achaia and go to Jerusalem. "After I've been there," he said, "I must see Rome as well!" 22 So after sending two of those who assisted him, Timothy and Erastus, to Macedonia, he himself stayed in the province of Asia for a while.

23 During that time there was a major[a] disturbance about the Way. 24 For a person named Demetrius, a silversmith who made silver shrines of Artemis,[b] provided a great deal of[c] business for the craftsmen. 25 When he had assembled them, as well as the workers engaged in this type of business, he said: "Men, you know that our prosperity is derived from this business. 26 You both see and hear that not only in Ephesus, but in almost the whole province of Asia, this man Paul has persuaded and misled a considerable number of people by saying that gods made by hand are not gods! 27 So not only do we run a risk that our business may be discredited, but also that the temple of the great goddess Artemis may be despised and her magnificence come to the verge of ruin—the very one whom the whole province of Asia and the world adore."

28 When they had heard this, they were filled with rage and began to cry out, "Great is Artemis of the Ephesians!" 29 So the city was filled with confusion; and they rushed all together into the amphitheater, dragging along Gaius and Aristarchus, Macedonians who were Paul's traveling companions. 30 Though Paul wanted to go in before the people, the disciples did not let him. 31 Even some of the provincial officials of Asia, who were his friends, sent word to him, pleading with him not to take a chance by going[d] into the amphitheater. 32 Meanwhile, some were shouting one thing and some another, because the assembly was in confusion, and most of them did not know why they had come together. 33 Then some of the crowd gave Alexander advice when the Jews pushed him to the front. So motioning with his hand, Alexander wanted to make his defense to the people. 34 But when they recognized

that he was a Jew, a united cry went up from all of them for about two hours: "Great is Artemis of the Ephesians!"

Anger Over the Gospel

1. Who is the best craftsman that you know? What does that person make? How did he or she become so skillful?

Acts 19:23-41

2. How did Demetrius and the other artisans make their living? Why were they upset about Paul?

3. What does verse 26 show about Demetrius' beliefs and priorities?

4. He described Artemis as the goddess that "the whole province of Asia and the world adore" (v. 27). What does this suggest about how the gospel or "good news" of Jesus affects the world?

5. How does the world today get angry over the gospel of Jesus Christ?

35 However, when the city clerk had calmed the crowd down, he said, "Men of Ephesus! What man is there who doesn't know that the city of the Ephesians is the temple guardian of the great[e] Artemis, and of the image that fell from heaven? 36 Therefore, since these things are undeniable, you must keep calm and not do anything rash. 37 For you have brought these men here who are not temple robbers or blasphemers of our[f] goddess. 38 So if Demetrius and the craftsmen who are with him have a case against anyone, the courts are in session, and there are •proconsuls. Let them bring charges against one another. 39 But if you want something else, it must be decided in a legal assembly. 40 In fact, we run a risk of being charged with rioting for what happened

---

[a]**19:23** Lit *was not a little*   [b]**19:24** Artemis was the ancient Gk mother goddess believed to control all fertility.   [c]**19:24** Lit *provided not a little*
[d]**19:31** Lit *not to give himself*   [e]**19:35** Other mss add *goddess*   [f]**19:37** Other mss read *your*

---

manufacture and sale of models of the goddess Artemis. This goddess combined belief in the Roman virgin goddess Diana with an Asian fertility goddess. The center for her worship was in Ephesus.

19:35 the city clerk. This was the highest-ranking official in the city. He was accountable to the Roman provincial government for keeping the peace in Ephesus.

19:39 legal assembly. The people could gather for meetings to discuss issues that concerned them, but these were to be held at scheduled times and with specific procedures. Such an irregular, chaotic meeting as this one could have led to Roman suppression of their right to assemble.

20:4 He was accompanied. Although Luke does not say why Paul was accompanied by

so many men from such different areas, it must be remembered that he was carrying the collection he had gathered for the church in Jerusalem from the churches in Macedonia, Achaia, and Asia (see 19:21–22). First Corinthians 16:3 indicates that some men from Corinth accompanied him as well. These men served as protection for Paul against robbers, and as a means of accountability to their home churches for Paul's deliverance of the offering as promised (2 Cor. 8:19–21).

20:7 the first day of the week. This meeting probably occurred on a Sunday evening. Meetings were held in the evenings because Sunday, like every day, was a work day for slaves, who made up a large percentage of the believers (Eph. 6:5). This also may have contributed to the weariness of Eutychus.

20:8 there were many lamps. These would have been oil lamps giving off fumes that would add to a sense of drowsiness.

20:19 humility. In the Greek world, humility was a weakness, a sign of a slave. For Paul, who saw himself as a slave for God (Rom. 1:1; Col. 3:24), humility was essential for being a disciple or follower of Jesus Christ (Phil. 2:3; Col. 3:12).

20:23 the Holy Spirit testifies to me that chains and afflictions are waiting for me. Paul was undertaking this journey in the conviction that God wanted him to go, but also with an awareness that it would lead to difficulty. All along the way, the Spirit was preparing him for the hardships he would face in Jerusalem. This sense of foreboding led him to ask the Roman church to pray for him as he went (Rom. 15:30–32).

today, since there is no justification that we can give as a reason for this disorderly gathering." 41 After saying this, he dismissed the assembly.

Paul in Macedonia

20 After the uproar was over, Paul sent for the disciples, encouraged them, and after saying good-bye, departed to go to Macedonia. 2 And when he had passed through those areas and exhorted them at length, he came to Greece 3 and stayed three months. When he was about to set sail for Syria, a plot was devised against him by the Jews, so a decision was made to go back through Macedonia. 4 He was accompanieda by Sopater, son of Pyrrhus,b from Beroea, Aristarchus and Secundus from Thessalonica, Gaius from Derbe, Timothy, and Tychicus and Trophimus from Asia. 5 These men went on ahead and waited for us in Troas, 6 but we sailed away from Philippi after the days of •Unleavened Bread. In five days we reached them at Troas, where we spent seven days.

Eutychus Revived at Troas

7 On the first day of the week,c wed assembled to break bread. Paul spoke to them, and since he was about to depart the next day, he extended his message until midnight. 8 There were many lamps in the room upstairs where we were assembled, 9 and a young man named Eutychus was sitting on a window sill and sank into a deep sleep as Paul kept on speaking. When he was overcome by sleep he fell down from the third story, and was picked up dead. 10 But Paul went down, threw himself on him, embraced him, and said, "Don't be alarmed, for his •life is in him!" 11 After going upstairs, breaking the bread, and eating, he conversed a considerable time until dawn. Then he left. 12 They brought the boy home alive and were greatly comforted.

From Troas to Miletus

13 Then we went on ahead to the ship and sailed for Assos, from there intending to take Paul on board. For these were his instructions, since he himself was going by land. 14 When he met us at Assos, we took him on board and came to Mitylene. 15 Sailing from there, the next day we arrived off Chios. The following day we crossed over to Samos, ande the day after, we came to Miletus. 16 For Paul had decided to sail past Ephesus so he would not have to spend time in the province of Asia, because he was hurrying to be in Jerusalem, if possible, for the day of Pentecost.

Farewell Address to the Ephesian Elders

17 Now from Miletus, he sent to Ephesus and called for the elders of the church. 18 And when they came to him, he said to them: "You know, from the first day I set foot in Asia, how I was with you the whole time— 19 serving the Lord with all humility, with tears, and with the trials that came to me through the plots of the Jews— 20 and that I did not shrink back from proclaiming to you anything that was profitable, or from teaching it to you in public and from house to house. 21 I testified to both Jews and Greeks about repentance toward God and faith in our Lord Jesus.

22 "And now I am on my way to Jerusalem, bound in my spirit, not knowing what I will encounter there, 23 except that in town after town the Holy Spirit testifies to me that chains and afflictions are waiting for me. 24 But I count my life of no value to myself, so that I may finish my coursef and the ministry I received from the Lord Jesus, to testify to the gospel of God's grace.

25 "And now I know that none of you, among whom I went about preaching the kingdom, will ever see my face again. 26 Therefore I testify to you this day that I am innocentg of everyone's blood, 27 for I did not shrink back from declaring to you the whole plan of God. 28 Be on guard for yourselves and for all the flock, among whom the Holy Spirit has appointed you as •overseers, to shepherd the church of God,h which He purchased with His own blood. 29 I know that after my departure savage wolves will come in among you, not sparing the flock. 30 And men from among yourselves will rise up with deviant doctrines to lure the disciples into follow-

---

a20:4 Other mss add to Asia b20:4 Other mss omit son of Pyrrhus c20:7 Lit On one between the Sabbaths; that is, Sunday d20:7 Other mss read the disciples e20:15 Other mss add after staying at Trogyllium f20:24 Other mss add with joy g20:26 Lit clean h20:28 Other mss read church of the Lord; other mss read church of the Lord and God

---

20:24 finish my course. Just before his death, Paul wrote to Timothy at Ephesus using this same metaphor to describe his ministry (2 Tim. 4:7). **the gospel of God's grace.** Just as repentance and faith sum up what it means to respond to God, so grace sums up the news of what God has done for us (Rom. 5:1–11; Eph. 2:8–9).

20:25 none of you ... will ever see my face again. A few weeks earlier, Paul wrote to the Romans that after he went to Jerusalem he hoped to visit them and proceed to Spain, since his work in Macedonia and Achaia (and presumably Asia) was finished (Rom. 15:23). Whether this is why he declared he would not see these people again or whether he felt that the warnings of the Spirit (v. 23) were to prepare him for death is uncertain.

20:35 keep in mind the words of the Lord

Jesus. This beatitude is not found in the Gospels. Paul quotes Jesus only two other times in his letters (1 Cor. 7:10; 1 Tim. 5:18).

21:2–3 Finding a ship crossing over to Phoenicia. Paul and his companions found a ship that was sailing directly to Phoenicia, an area in Syria of which Tyre was the chief city. Tyre was only about 100 miles from Jerusalem.

21:10–11 Agabus. Many years earlier, Paul had met Agabus in Antioch where he had prophesied about a coming famine that would affect Judea (11:28). Agabus acted out his prophecy to accent its impact. The form of this prophecy brings out the similarity between what happened to Jesus and what would happen to Paul.

21:16 Mnason. Nothing more is known of

this man who may have been one of the original converts at Pentecost. His home became the residence of Paul and his companions during their stay in Jerusalem.

21:17–19 the brothers. It was undoubtedly at this meeting with James (Jesus' half brother and the spokesperson for the church in Jerusalem) that Paul and his companions presented the offering from the Gentile churches. This meeting also allowed Paul an opportunity to update James and other church leaders on everything that had happened since his last visit to Jerusalem.

21:20–21 abandon Moses. If Jewish believers in Rome could still be rigid about the Jewish dietary and Sabbath laws (Rom. 14:2,4), how much more would these Judean believers, since they had lived all

ing them. ³¹ Therefore be on the alert, remembering that night and day for three years I did not stop warning each one of you with tears.

³² "And now ᵃ I commit you to God and to the message of His grace, which is able to build you up and to give you an inheritance among all who are sanctified. ³³ I have not coveted anyone's silver or gold or clothing. ³⁴ You yourselves know that these hands have provided for my needs, and for those who were with me. ³⁵ In every way I've shown you that by laboring like this, it is necessary to help the weak and to keep in mind the words of the Lord Jesus, for He said, 'It is more blessed to give than to receive.' "

³⁶ After he said this, he knelt down and prayed with all of them. ³⁷ There was a great deal of weeping by everyone. And embracing Paul, they kissed him, ³⁸ grieving most of all over his statement that they would never see his face again. Then they escorted him to the ship.

Warnings on the Journey to Jerusalem

21 After we tore ourselves away from them and set sail, we came by a direct route to Cos, the next day to Rhodes, and from there to Patara. ² Finding a ship crossing over to Phoenicia, we boarded and set sail. ³ After we sighted Cyprus, leaving it on the left, we sailed on to Syria and arrived at Tyre, because the ship was to unload its cargo there. ⁴ So we found some disciples and stayed there seven days. They said to Paul through the Spirit not to go to Jerusalem. ⁵ When our days there were over, we left to continue our journey, while all of them, with their wives and children, escorted us out of the city. After kneeling down on the beach to pray, ⁶ we said good-bye to one another. Then we boarded the ship, and they returned home.

⁷ When we completed our voyage from Tyre, we reached Ptolemais, where we greeted the brothers and stayed with them one day. ⁸ The next day we left and came to Caesarea, where we entered the house of Philip the evangelist, who was one of the Seven, and stayed with him. ⁹ This man had four virgin daughters who prophesied.

¹⁰ While we were staying there many days, a prophet named Agabus came down from Judea. ¹¹ He came to us, took Paul's belt, tied his own feet and hands, and said, "This is what the Holy Spirit says: 'In this way the Jews in Jerusalem will bind the man who owns this belt, and deliver him into Gentile hands.' " ¹² When we heard this, both we and the local people begged him not to go up to Jerusalem.

¹³ Then Paul replied, "What are you doing, weeping and breaking my heart? For I am ready not only to be bound, but also to die in Jerusalem for the name of the Lord Jesus."

¹⁴ Since he would not be persuaded, we stopped talking and simply said, "The Lord's will be done!"

Conflict over the Gentile Mission

¹⁵ After these days we got ready and went up to Jerusalem. ¹⁶ Some of the disciples from Caesarea also went with us and brought us to Mnason, a Cypriot and an early disciple, with whom we were to stay.

¹⁷ When we reached Jerusalem, the brothers welcomed us gladly. ¹⁸ The following day Paul went in with us to James, and all the elders were present. ¹⁹ After greeting them, he related one by one what God did among the Gentiles through his ministry.

²⁰ When they heard it, they glorified God and said, "You see, brother, how many thousands of Jews there are who have believed, and they are all zealous for the law. ²¹ But they have been told about you that you teach all the Jews who are among the Gentiles to abandon Moses, by telling them not to circumcise their children or to walk in our customs. ²² So what is to be done? ᵇ They will certainly hear that you've come. ²³ Therefore do what we tell you: We have four men who have obligated themselves with a vow. ²⁴ Take these men, purify yourself along with them, and pay for them to get their heads shaved. Then everyone will know that what they were told about you amounts to nothing, but that you yourself are also careful about observing the law. ²⁵ With regard to the Gentiles who have believed, we have written a letter containing our decision that ᶜ they

---

ᵃ20:32 Other mss add brothers, ᵇ21:22 Other mss add A multitude has to come together, since ᶜ21:25 Other mss add they should observe no such thing, except that

---

their lives in a strictly Jewish environment? Paul's letters reveal that even after the council's decision in Acts 15, he was consistently troubled by Palestinian believers who insisted that his gospel was deficient because he did not require Christian converts to observe Jewish laws (Col. 2:16; Phil. 3:2–3; Rom. 14:5).

21:22–24 a vow. To prove that Paul still honored Jewish customs, it was suggested that he participate in a vow that four of the local Jewish elders had made.

21:27–29 Jews from the province of Asia. These Jews assumed that Paul had brought Trophimus, a Gentile, into the temple. While Gentiles could enter the outermost court of the temple, they were banned from the inner courts.

21:31–32 all Jerusalem was in chaos. Paul was probably dragged outside the temple and beaten. A group of Roman soldiers was quartered on the northwest side of the temple. The commander of this squad and some of his soldiers raced through the crowd to the center of the action.

21:38 Aren't you the Egyptian? A notorious Egyptian had led a revolt against Rome a couple of years earlier. Josephus gives an account of a messianic Egyptian terrorist, who, in A.D. 54, led a movement against Rome to take the city of Jerusalem. **Assassins.** In Latin, the *sicarii*—so called because they carried the short dagger known as the *sica* under their robes. The sicarii were an anti-Roman guerilla group.

21:39–40 let me speak to the people. Paul spoke to the people who had assembled in

Aramaic, the common language of Jews in Palestine, but a language not widely spoken outside that area. This got the crowd's attention.

22:3 brought up in this city. Although a citizen of Tarsus, Paul spent most of his life in Jerusalem. Acts 23:16 implies that Paul's sister and her family lived in the city. **Gamaliel.** See 5:34. Gamaliel was a highly respected Pharisee. To study under him was to receive the best possible Jewish education.

22:4–5 this Way. This word is unique to Acts as a name for Christianity (19:9,23; 22:4; 24:14,22). It may stem from Jesus' claim in John 14:6. **to the death.** Although Stephen's death is the only one recorded in Acts, there may well have been other believers who suffered death as a result of the persecution instigated by Paul (see also 26:10).

should keep themselves from food sacrificed to idols, from blood, from what is strangled, and from sexual immorality."

The Riot in the Temple Complex

26 Then the next day, Paul took the men, having purified himself along with them, and entered the temple, announcing the completion of the purification days when the offering for each of them would be made. 27 As the seven days were about to end, the Jews from the province of Asia saw him in the •temple complex, stirred up the whole crowd, and seized him, 28 shouting, "Men of Israel, help! This is the man who teaches everyone everywhere against our people, our law, and this place. What's more, he also brought Greeks into the temple and has profaned this holy place." 29 For they had previously seen Trophimus the Ephesian in the city with him, and they supposed that Paul had brought him into the temple complex.ᵃ

30 The whole city was stirred up, and the people rushed together. They seized Paul, dragged him out of the temple complex, and at once the gates were shut. 31 As they were trying to kill him, word went up to the commander of the •regiment that all Jerusalem was in chaos. 32 Taking along soldiers and •centurions, he immediately ran down to them. Seeing the commander and the soldiers, they stopped beating Paul. 33 Then the commander came up, took him into custody, and ordered him to be bound with two chains. He asked who he was and what he had done. 34 Some in the mob were shouting one thing and some another. Since he was not able to get reliable information because of the uproar, he ordered him to be taken into the barracks. 35 When Paulᵇ got to the steps, he had to be carried by the soldiers because of the mob's violence, 36 for the mass of people were following and yelling, "Kill him!"

Paul's Defense before the Jerusalem Mob

37 As he was about to be brought into the barracks, Paul said to the commander, "Am I allowed to say something to you?"

He replied, "Do you know Greek? 38 Aren't you the Egyptian who raised a rebellion some time ago and led 4,000 Assassinsᶜ into the desert?"

39 Paul said, "I am a Jewish man from Tarsus of Cilicia, a citizen of an important city.ᵈ Now I ask you, let me speak to the people."

40 After he had given permission, Paul stood on the steps and motioned with his hand to the people. When there was a great hush, he addressed them in the Hebrew language: 1 "Brothers and fathers, listen now to my defense before you." 2 When they heard that he was addressing them in the Hebrew language, they became even quieter. 3 He continued, "I am a Jewish man, born in Tarsus of Cilicia, but brought up in this cityᵉ at the feet of Gamaliel, and educated according to the strict view of our patriarchal law. Being zealous for God, just as all of you are today, 4 I persecuted this Way to the death, binding and putting both men and women in jail, 5 as both the high priest and the whole council of elders can testify about me. Having received letters from them to the brothers, I was traveling to Damascus to bring those who were prisoners there to be punished in Jerusalem.

Paul's Testimony

6 "As I was traveling and near Damascus, about noon an intense light from heaven suddenly flashed around me. 7 I fell to the ground and heard a voice saying to me, 'Saul, Saul, why are you persecuting Me?'

8 "I answered, 'Who are You, Lord?'

"He said to me, 'I am Jesus the •Nazarene, whom you are persecuting!' 9 Now those who were with me saw the light,ᶠ but they did not hear the voice of the One who was speaking to me.

10 "Then I said, 'What should I do, Lord?'

ᵃ21:29 The inner temple court for Jewish men   ᵇ21:35 Lit he   ᶜ21:38 Lit 4,000 men of the Assassins; that is, Sicarii, a Lat loanword from sica, dagger; compare "cut-throats" or daggermen.   ᵈ21:39 Lit of no insignificant city   ᵉ22:3 Probably Jerusalem, but others think Tarsus   ᶠ22:9 Other mss add and were afraid

---

22:17–18 I went into a visionary state. This account of why Paul left Jerusalem differs from that in 9:19–30. Chapter 9 tells of the external opposition Paul faced; here Paul recounts the inner direction he received from the Lord. **praying in the temple.** The situation in chapter 9 leads us to assume Paul was praying for direction from God in light of the opposition he was facing. The mention of the temple would be a reminder to his audience that, far from defiling the temple, he considered it a refuge for prayer.

22:22 it's a disgrace for him to live. For Paul to claim that he was divinely inspired to minister among the Gentiles appeared as rank heresy—a slap in the face to God and the Jews. This was justification for their charges that he was anti-Jewish, lacked respect for the law, and would defile the temple.

22:25 a Roman citizen. Flogging was a severe punishment since leather thongs weighted with pieces of bone, metal, or rocks were used to administer a beating. Because Roman citizens were protected from punishment without trial and were sheltered from this form of punishment, Paul once again brought up his Roman citizenship (see also 16:37).

22:28 I bought this citizenship for a large amount of money. Citizenship was not supposedly a matter of money, but of birthright or notable service. But bribes and other means of influence were used to gain the privilege. **I myself was born a citizen.** Paul's response turns the table on the commander. His citizenship was not a matter of bribery, but of natural right. How Paul's family earned their Roman citizenship is unknown.

22:29–30 The commander too was alarmed. The fact that Paul, a Roman citizen, had been imprisoned without charge and had been almost flogged was a dangerous breach of policy that could have cost the commander his rank (and perhaps his life).

23:2 the high priest Ananias. Ananias was appointed to this office by Herod Agrippa II (25:13) in A.D. 47, and he held the position until A.D. 58 or 59. He had a reputation as a violent, greedy, and unscrupulous man. **ordered those who were standing next to him to strike him.** It was against Jewish law for a defendant to be treated like this.

23:3 God is going to strike you. Paul's word came true. In A.D. 66 Jews who were leading a revolt against Rome captured Ananias and murdered him for his pro-Roman policies. **you whitewashed wall!** The pic-

"And the Lord told me, 'Get up and go into Damascus, and there you will be told about everything that is assigned for you to do.'

¹¹ "Since I couldn't see because of the brightness of that light, I was led by the hand by those who were with me, and came into Damascus. ¹² Someone named Ananias, a devout man according to the law, having a good reputation with all the Jews residing there, ¹³ came to me, stood by me, and said, 'Brother Saul, regain your sight.' And in that very hour I looked up and saw him. ¹⁴ Then he said, 'The God of our fathers has appointed you to know His will, to see the Righteous One, and to hear the sound of His voice.ª ¹⁵ For you will be a witness for Him to all people of what you have seen and heard. ¹⁶ And now, why delay? Get up and be baptized, and wash away your sins by calling on His name.'

¹⁷ "After I came back to Jerusalem and was praying in the •temple complex, I went into a visionary state ¹⁸ and saw Him telling me, 'Hurry and get out of Jerusalem quickly, because they will not accept your testimony about Me!'

¹⁹ "But I said, 'Lord, they know that in •synagogue after synagogue I had those who believed in You imprisoned and beaten. ²⁰ And when the blood of Your witness Stephen was being shed, I myself was standing by and approving,ᵇ and I guarded the clothes of those who killed him.'

²¹ "Then He said to me, 'Go, because I will send you far away to the Gentiles.'"

Paul's Roman Protection

²² They listened to him up to this word. Then they raised their voices, shouting, "Wipe this person off the earth—it's a disgrace for him to live!"

²³ As they were yelling and flinging aside their robes and throwing dust into the air, ²⁴ the commander ordered him to be brought into the barracks, directing that he be examined with the scourge, so he could discover the reason they were shouting against him like this. ²⁵ As they stretched him out for the lash, Paul said to the •centurion standing by, "Is it legal for you to scourge a man who is a Roman citizen and is uncondemned?"

²⁶ When the centurion heard this, he went and reported to the commander, saying, "What are you going to do? For this man is a Roman citizen."

²⁷ The commander came and said to him, "Tell me—are you a Roman citizen?"

"Yes," he said.

²⁸ The commander replied, "I bought this citizenship for a large amount of money."

"But I myself was born a citizen," Paul said.

²⁹ Therefore, those who were about to examine him withdrew from him at once. The commander too was alarmed when he realized Paul was a Roman citizen and he had bound him.

Paul before the Sanhedrin

³⁰ The next day, since he wanted to find out exactly why Paul was being accused by the Jews, he released himᶜ and instructed the •chief priests and all the •Sanhedrin to convene. Then he brought Paul down and

23 placed him before them. ¹ Paul looked intently at the •Sanhedrin and said, "Brothers, I have lived my life before God in all good conscience until this day." ² But the high priest Ananias ordered those who were standing next to him to strike him on the mouth. ³ Then Paul said to him, "God is going to strike you, you whitewashed wall! You are sitting there judging me according to the law, and in violation of the law are you ordering me to be struck?"

⁴ And those standing nearby said, "Do you dare revile God's high priest?"

⁵ "I did not know, brothers," Paul said, "that it was the high priest. For it is written, **You must not speak evil of a ruler of your people.**ᵈ ⁶ When Paul realized that one part of them were •Sadducees and the other part were •Pharisees, he cried out in the Sanhedrin, "Brothers, I am a Pharisee, a son of Pharisees! I am being judged because of the hope of the resurrection of the dead!" ⁷ When he said this, a dispute broke out between the Pharisees and the Sadducees, and the assembly was divided. ⁸ For the Sadducees say there is no resurrection, and no angel or spirit, but the Pharisees affirm them all.

ª**22:14** Lit *to hear a voice from His mouth*   ᵇ**22:20** Other mss add *of his murder*   ᶜ**22:30** Other mss add *from his chains*   ᵈ**23:5** Ex 22:28

---

ture is of a person trying to fix up a wall about to collapse just by covering it with a thin coat of paint.

23:8 resurrection. The resurrection was rejected by the Sadducees.

23:11 the Lord stood by him. For the fourth and final time in Acts (see also 18:9), the Lord addresses Paul personally to encourage him in a time of crisis (an angel comforts him in the midst of a storm in 27:23). **testified about Me.** The issue at stake for Paul was speaking about Jesus, not defending himself against false charges.

23:12–13 until they had killed Paul. A group of radical Jewish nationalists decided Paul must die for his alleged anti-Jewish sentiments. **bound themselves under a curse.** If they failed to kill Paul, they ac-

knowledged by this curse that they ought to be struck down by God.

23:14–15 chief priests and elders. The would-be assassins drew at least some members of the Sanhedrin into the plot. Under pretense of wanting another hearing with Paul, they were to ask the Roman commander to bring Paul to them, at which time he would be ambushed. Since Paul was escorted by Roman soldiers, these men were willing to risk death to kill Paul.

23:16 the son of Paul's sister. This is the only glimpse the New Testament gives us about Paul's family. Perhaps his sister and her family lived in Jerusalem, or perhaps his nephew was sent there to receive his education as Paul had been (22:3). How his nephew got wind of the plot is not revealed. **entered the barracks and reported it to**

Paul. Paul was held in custody pending charges on the near-riot, but as a Roman citizen he was permitted visitors.

23:23 Get 200 soldiers ready with 70 cavalry and 200 spearmen. Having witnessed the severity of the reaction against Paul, the Roman commander was taking no chances with this radical group. He placed Paul under the protection of almost half his soldiers and sent him off under cover of darkness.

23:24 Felix the governor. The Roman historian Tacitus described Felix as a self-indulgent ruler who used forceful measures to put down Jewish uprisings and who was cruel toward the people he was supposed to govern. Once in Caesarea, Paul would be under the custody of Felix.

23:27 I arrived … and rescued him. The

⁹ The shouting grew loud, and some of the •scribes of the Pharisees' party got up and argued vehemently: "We find nothing evil in this man. What if a spirit or an angel has spoken to him?"ª ¹⁰ When the dispute became violent, the commander feared that Paul might be torn apart by them and ordered the troops to go down, rescue him from them, and bring him into the barracks.

The Plot against Paul

¹¹ The following night, the Lord stood by him and said, "Have courage! For as you have testified about Me in Jerusalem, so you must also testify in Rome."

¹² When it was day, the Jews formed a conspiracy and bound themselves under a curse: neither to eat nor to drink until they had killed Paul. ¹³ There were more than 40 who had formed this plot. ¹⁴ These men went to the •chief priests and elders and said, "We have bound ourselves under a solemn curse that we won't eat anything until we have killed Paul. ¹⁵ So now you, along with the Sanhedrin, make a request to the commander that he bring him down to youᵇ as if you were going to investigate his case more thoroughly. However, before he gets near, we are ready to kill him."

¹⁶ But the son of Paul's sister, hearing about their ambush, came and entered the barracks and reported it to Paul. ¹⁷ Then Paul called one of the •centurions and said, "Take this young man to the commander, because he has something to report to him."

¹⁸ So he took him, brought him to the commander, and said, "The prisoner Paul called me and asked me to bring this young man to you, because he has something to tell you."

¹⁹ Then the commander took him by the hand, led him aside, and inquired privately, "What is it you have to report to me?"

²⁰ "The Jews," he said, "have agreed to ask you to bring Paul down to the Sanhedrin tomorrow, as though they are going to hold a somewhat more careful inquiry about him. ²¹ Don't let them persuade you, because there are more than 40 of them arranging to ambush him, men who have bound themselves under a curse not to eat or drink until they kill him. Now they are ready, waiting for a commitment from you."

²² So the commander dismissed the young man and instructed him, "Don't tell anyone that you have informed me about this."

To Caesarea by Night

²³ He summoned two of his centurions and said, "Get 200 soldiers ready with 70 cavalry and 200 spearmen to go to Caesarea at nine tonight.ᶜ ²⁴ Also provide mounts so they can put Paul on them and bring him safely to Felix the governor."

²⁵ He wrote a letter of this kind:

²⁶ Claudius Lysias,

To the most excellent governor Felix:

Greetings.

²⁷ When this man had been seized by the Jews and was about to be killed by them, I arrived with my troops and rescued him because I learned that he is a Roman citizen. ²⁸ Wanting to know the charge for which they were accusing him, I brought him down before their Sanhedrin. ²⁹ I found out that the accusations were about disputed matters in their law, and that there was no charge that merited death or chains. ³⁰ When I was informed that there was a plot against the man,ᵈ I sent him to you right away. I also ordered his accusers to state their case against him in your presence.ᵉ

³¹ Therefore, during the night, the soldiers took Paul and brought him to Antipatris as they were ordered. ³² The next day, they returned to the barracks, allowing the cavalry to go on with him. ³³ When these men entered Caesarea and delivered the letter to the governor, they also presented Paul to him. ³⁴ After heᶠ read it, he asked what province he was from. So when he learned he was from Cilicia, ³⁵ he said, "I will give you a hearing whenever your accusers get here too." And

ª23:9 Other mss add Let us not fight God.   ᵇ23:15 Other mss add tomorrow   ᶜ23:23 Lit at the third hour tonight   ᵈ23:30 Other mss add by the Jews   ᵉ23:30 Other mss add Farewell   ᶠ23:34 Other mss read the governor

Roman commander Lysias may have inverted a couple of facts in order to save face. He did not find out about Paul's Roman citizenship until he was about to have him beaten (22:25), but here he says he rescued Paul from the mob because he learned that Paul was a Roman citizen.

23:34 asked what province he was from. By the second century A.D. prisoners were normally tried in the province they were from, regardless of where the crime was committed.

24:1 a lawyer. Literally, "an orator." Tertullus, who bears a Roman name, may have been a Greek-speaking Jew with more knowledge and experience in Roman law and customs than the Palestinian Jews had.

24:5 an agitator ... throughout the Roman world. Since Felix was known for his impatience with Jewish uprisings, Tertullus tried to present Paul as an instigator of such movements. **the sect of the Nazarenes.** Just as the name "Christian" appears to have been a derogatory term for early believers (see note on 11:26), so "the Nazarenes" was also used as an insult (see John 1:46; 7:41).

24:6 tried to desecrate the temple. The charge has been changed from the accusation in 21:28 that Paul had defiled the temple by bringing a Gentile into the inner court.

24:14–15 according to the Way ... I worship my fathers' God. While Paul denied the charges of insurrection and temple defilement, he agreed he was a follower of "the Way" but he did so as a Jew who was loyal to the God of his ancestors. There was nothing heretical about his views.

24:24 Drusilla. A daughter of Herod Agrippa, Drusilla was barely 20 years old at this time. She had divorced another man to become Felix's third wife. Since she was Jewish and in a position to hear a lot about the Christians, she may have been the source of Felix's information about their beliefs.

24:26 money would be given to him by Paul. The offering and acceptance of a bribe in such cases was illegal.

24:27 Porcius Festus. Felix's administration ended when he was found guilty of using excessive violence in crushing a civil strife between Jews and Greeks in Caesarea. Even when forced to leave office (probably about A.D. 58), he refused to dispense with Paul's case but left him imprisoned as a favor to the Jews. Festus replaced him and was governor of the area until his death two

he ordered that he be kept under guard in •Herod's palace.[a]

The Accusation against Paul

24 After five days Ananias the high priest came down with some elders and a lawyer[b] named Tertullus. These men presented their case against Paul to the governor. [2] When he was called in, Tertullus began to accuse him and said: "Since we enjoy great peace because of you, and reforms are taking place for the benefit of this nation by your foresight, [3] we gratefully receive them always and in all places, most excellent Felix, with all thankfulness. [4] However, so that I will not burden you any further, I beg you in your graciousness to give us a brief hearing. [5] For we have found this man to be a plague, an agitator among all the Jews throughout the Roman world, and a ringleader of the sect of the •Nazarenes! [6] He even tried to desecrate the temple, so we apprehended him [and wanted to judge him according to our law. [7] But Lysias the commander came and took him from our hands, commanding his accusers to come to you.][c] [8] By examining him yourself you will be able to discern all these things of which we accuse him." [9] The Jews also joined in the attack, alleging that these things were so.

Paul's Defense before Felix

[10] When the governor motioned to him to speak, Paul replied: "Because I know you have been a judge of this nation for many years, I am glad to offer my defense in what concerns me. [11] You are able to determine that it is no more than 12 days since I went up to worship in Jerusalem. [12] And they didn't find me disputing with anyone or causing a disturbance among the crowd, either in the •temple complex or in the •synagogues, or anywhere in the city. [13] Neither can they provide evidence to you of what they now bring against me. [14] But I confess this to you: that according to the Way, which they call a sect, so I worship my fathers' God, believing all the things that are written in the Law and in the Prophets. [15] And I have a hope in God, which these men themselves also accept, that there is going to be a resurrection,[d] both of the righteous and the unrighteous. [16] I always do my best to have a clear conscience toward God and men. [17] After many years, I came to bring charitable gifts and offerings to my nation, [18] and while I was doing this, some Jews from the province of Asia found me ritually purified in the temple, without a crowd and without any uproar. [19] It is they who ought to be here before you to bring charges, if they have anything against me. [20] Either let these men here state what wrongdoing they found in me when I stood before the •Sanhedrin, [21] or about this one statement I cried out while standing among them, 'Today I am being judged before you concerning the resurrection of the dead.' "

The Verdict Postponed

[22] Since Felix was accurately informed about the Way, he adjourned the hearing, saying, "When Lysias the commander comes down, I will decide your case." [23] He ordered that the •centurion keep Paul[e] under guard, though he could have some freedom, and that he should not prevent any of his friends from serving[f] him.

[24] After some days, when Felix came with his wife Drusilla, who was Jewish, he sent for Paul and listened to him on the subject of faith in Christ Jesus. [25] Now as he spoke about righteousness, self-control, and the judgment to come, Felix became afraid and replied, "Leave for now, but when I find time I'll call for you." [26] At the same time he was also hoping that money would be given to him by Paul.[g] For this reason he sent for him quite often and conversed with him.

[27] After two years had passed, Felix received a successor, Porcius Festus, and because he wished to do a favor for the Jews, Felix left Paul in prison.

Appeal to Caesar

25 Three days after Festus arrived in the province, he went up to Jerusalem from Caesarea. [2] Then

---

[a]**23:35** Lit *praetorium*, a Lat word that can also refer to a military headquarters, to the governor's palace, or to the emperor's imperial guard
[b]**24:1** Gk *rhetor*; compare the Eng "rhetoric," "rhetorician"—an orator skilled in public speaking. In this situation, skill in the Gk language was needed.
[c]**24:6–7** Other mss omit bracketed text   [d]**24:15** Other mss add *of the dead*   [e]**24:23** Lit *him*   [f]**24:23** Other mss add *or visiting*   [g]**24:26** Other mss add *so that he might release him*

---

or three years later in A.D. 61.

25:5 if there is any wrong in this man. Festus reopened Paul's case in an attempt to win the favor of the Jewish leaders.

25:8 Caesar. The first five emperors of Rome (from Octavian to Nero) were descendants of Julius Caesar and thus kept his name, although it was commonly used as a title. At the time of this trial, Nero was the emperor. The cruelties for which he is remembered would not occur until several years later.

25:9 a favor for the Jews. If Paul was sent to Jerusalem for trial, the Sanhedrin would be responsible for charging him on matters of Jewish law. Festus would have only to ratify a decision for capital punishment if that is what the Sanhedrin decided upon. This action was a tacit admission that Paul was innocent of having violated Roman law. Since that was the only reason Paul could be held in a Roman prison, this suggestion showed that Festus was willing to sacrifice Paul for the sake of some political advantage with the Sanhedrin.

25:10–11 I am standing at Caesar's tribunal. Paul knew there was no chance of a fair hearing in Jerusalem even if he could make it there alive. Recognizing that his only hope for justice lay in getting out of an area where the Sanhedrin exercised great influence, he exercised his right as a Roman citizen to appeal his case to the emperor in Rome.

25:13 King Agrippa. The son of Herod Agrippa I. Agrippa II had been appointed as a puppet king (under Roman authority) over some provinces northeast of Palestine. When Judea was returned to the control of Roman governors after the death of his father, Herod Agrippa was given the right to appoint the Jewish high priest. **Bernice.** Agrippa's sister. After her first husband died, she lived with her brother, prompting rumors of incest. She also maintained loyalty to Rome and later was the mistress of Titus, who became the emperor.

25:26–27 I have nothing definite to write. It would have been unreasonable for Festus to send on to Rome a prisoner with no statement of the charges against. It also would have made a travesty of Roman justice. He hoped that Agrippa might provide some insight that would allow him to better explain the nature of Paul's case to the Roman authorities.

26:4 among my own nation. This may refer to Paul's early childhood among the Jewish

the •chief priests and the leaders of the Jews presented their case against Paul to him; and they appealed, ³ asking him to do them a favor against Paul,ᵃ that he might summon him to Jerusalem. They were preparing an ambush along the road to kill him. ⁴ However, Festus answered that Paul should be kept at Caesarea, and that he himself was about to go there shortly. ⁵ "Therefore," he said, "let the men of authority among you go down with me and accuse him, if there is any wrong in this man."

⁶ When he had spent not more than eight or 10 days among them, he went down to Caesarea. The next day, seated at the judge's bench, he commanded Paul to be brought in. ⁷ When he arrived, the Jews who had come down from Jerusalem stood around him and brought many serious charges that they were not able to prove, ⁸ while Paul made the defense that, "Neither against the Jewish law, nor against the temple, nor against Caesar have I sinned at all."

⁹ Then Festus, wanting to do a favor for the Jews, replied to Paul, "Are you willing to go up to Jerusalem, there to be tried before me on these charges?"

¹⁰ But Paul said: "I am standing at Caesar's tribunal, where I ought to be tried. I have done no wrong to the Jews, as even you can see very well. ¹¹ If then I am doing wrong, or have done anything deserving of death, I do not refuse to die, but if there is nothing to what these men accuse me of, no one can give me up to them. I appeal to Caesar!"

¹² After Festus conferred with his council, he replied, "You have appealed to Caesar; to Caesar you will go!"

King Agrippa and Bernice Visit Festus

¹³ After some days had passed, King Agrippaᵇ and Bernice arrived in Caesarea and paid a courtesy call on Festus. ¹⁴ Since they stayed there many days, Festus presented Paul's case to the king, saying, "There's a man who was left as a prisoner by Felix. ¹⁵ When I was in Jerusalem, the chief priests and the elders of the Jews presented their case and asked for a judgment against him. ¹⁶ I answered them that it's not the Romans' custom to give any man upᶜ before the accused confronts

the accusers face to face and has an opportunity to give a defense concerning the charge. ¹⁷ Therefore, when they had assembled here, I did not delay. The next day I sat at the judge's bench and ordered the man to be brought in. ¹⁸ Concerning him, the accusers stood up and brought no charge of the sort I was expecting. ¹⁹ Instead they had some disagreements with him about their own religion and about a certain Jesus, a dead man whom Paul claimed to be alive. ²⁰ Since I was at a loss in a dispute over such things, I asked him if he wished to go to Jerusalem and be tried there concerning these matters. ²¹ But when Paul appealed to be held for trial by the Emperor, I ordered him to be kept in custody until I could send him to Caesar."

²² Then Agrippa said to Festus, "I would like to hear the man myself."

"Tomorrow," he said, "you will hear him."

Paul before Agrippa

²³ So the next day, Agrippa and Bernice came with great pomp and entered the auditorium with the commanders and prominent men of the city. When Festus gave the command, Paul was brought in. ²⁴ Then Festus said: "King Agrippa and all men present with us, you see this man about whom the whole Jewish community has appealed to me, both in Jerusalem and here, shouting that he should not live any longer. ²⁵ Now I realized that he had not done anything deserving of death, but when he himself appealed to the Emperor, I decided to send him. ²⁶ I have nothing definite to write to the Emperor about him. Therefore, I have brought him before all of you, and especially before you, King Agrippa, so that after this examination is over, I may have something to write. ²⁷ For it seems unreasonable to me to send a prisoner and not to indicate the charges against him."

Paul's Defense before Agrippa

26 Agrippa said to Paul, "It is permitted for you to speak for yourself."

Then Paul stretched out his hand and began his defense: ² "I consider myself fortunate, King Agrippa,

---

ᵃ**25:3** Lit *asking a favor against him*   ᵇ**25:13** Herod Agrippa II ruled Palestine A.D. 52–92.   ᶜ**25:16** Other mss add *to destruction*

---

community in Tarsus or to a family home somewhere in Judea. **in Jerusalem.** The fact that Paul was sent to Jerusalem as a boy to be educated by Gamaliel showed the commitment of his parents to his Jewish heritage (see 22:3).

26:6 promise made by God to our fathers. Paul identified with his own Jewish heritage. He believed in the promise of the Messiah that God had made to Israel.

26:7 our 12 tribes. While 10 of the original 12 tribes that formed the nation of Israel (Northern Kingdom) had been dispersed by the Assyrians seven centuries before, there were still traceable links to these tribes among the Jews in Paul's day (see also Luke 2:36; Jas. 1:1). **Because of this hope I am being accused.** The only point where Paul differed from his Jewish brothers was in the

conviction that the hope of the Messiah had already been fulfilled in the coming of Jesus.

26:10 I cast my vote against them. Taken literally, this may imply that Paul had been a member of the Sanhedrin. But the fact that he does not mention this affiliation in his writings makes that doubtful. It is more probable that he meant he approved of such actions (8:1).

26:14 It is hard for you to kick against the goads. There are several examples of this proverb in classical Greek literature. It expresses the difficulty involved in resisting one's destiny—the probable meaning here as well.

26:21–23 the Jews. Of course, Paul, Jesus and many other believers were also Jews. But by this phrase Luke probably means the

Jewish religious leaders.

26:24 driving you mad! Festus, probably bewildered by Paul's conviction that "a dead man named Jesus" (25:19) was alive, and by his talk of a vision that so radically changed his life, broke in with the exasperated cry that Paul must be out of his mind. This reaction was not very different than that of many Jews (John 10:20) and even Jesus' own family when He was beginning His ministry (see Mark 3:20–21). Jesus had come with such a radically different message than they were expecting—and such a radically different approach to life—that they saw it as madness.

26:32 This man could have been released if he had not appealed to Caesar. Once an appeal to the Roman emperor had been made, it was considered an insult against

that today I am going to make a defense before you about everything I am accused of by the Jews, [3] especially since you are an expert in all the Jewish customs and controversies. Therefore I beg you to listen to me patiently.

[4] "All the Jews know my way of life from my youth, which was spent from the beginning among my own nation and in Jerusalem. [5] They had previously known me for quite some time, if they were willing to testify, that according to the strictest party of our religion I lived as a •Pharisee. [6] And now I stand on trial for the hope of the promise made by God to our fathers, [7] [the promise] our 12 tribes hope to attain as they earnestly serve Him night and day. Because of this hope I am being accused by the Jews, O king! [8] Why is it considered incredible by any of you that God raises the dead? [9] In fact, I myself supposed it was necessary to do many things in opposition to the name of Jesus the •Nazarene. [10] This I actually did in Jerusalem, and I locked up many of the saints in prison, since I had received authority for that from the •chief priests. When they were put to death, I cast my vote against them. [11] In all the •synagogues I often tried to make them blaspheme by punishing them. Being greatly enraged at them, I even pursued them to foreign cities.

Paul's Account of His Conversion and Commission

[12] "Under these circumstances I was traveling to Damascus with authority and a commission from the chief priests. [13] At midday, while on the road, O king, I saw a light from heaven brighter than the sun, shining around me and those traveling with me. [14] When we had all fallen to the ground, I heard a voice speaking to me in the Hebrew language, 'Saul, Saul, why are you persecuting Me? It is hard for you to kick against the goads.'[a]

[15] "But I said, 'Who are You, Lord?'

"And the Lord replied: 'I am Jesus, whom you are persecuting. [16] But get up and stand on your feet. For I have appeared to you for this purpose, to appoint you as a servant and a witness of things you have seen,[b] and of things in which I will appear to you. [17] I will rescue you from the people and from the Gentiles, to whom I now send you, [18] to open their eyes that they may turn from darkness to light and from the power of Satan to God, that they may receive forgiveness of sins and a share among those who are sanctified by faith in Me.'

[19] "Therefore, King Agrippa, I was not disobedient to the heavenly vision. [20] Instead, I preached to those in Damascus first, and to those in Jerusalem and in all the region of Judea, and to the Gentiles, that they should repent and turn to God, and do works worthy of repentance. [21] For this reason the Jews seized me in the •temple complex and were trying to kill me. [22] Since I have obtained help that comes from God, to this day I stand and testify to both small and great, saying nothing else than what the prophets and Moses said would take place— [23] that the •Messiah must suffer, and that as the first to rise from the dead, He would proclaim light to our people and to the Gentiles."

Not Quite Persuaded

[24] As he was making his defense this way, Festus exclaimed in a loud voice, "You're out of your mind, Paul! Too much study is driving you mad!"

[25] But Paul replied, "I'm not out of my mind, most excellent Festus. On the contrary, I'm speaking words of truth and good judgment. [26] For the king knows about these matters. It is to him I am actually speaking boldly. For I'm not convinced that any of these things escapes his notice, since this was not done in a corner! [27] King Agrippa, do you believe the prophets? I know you believe."

[28] Then Agrippa said to Paul, "Are you going to persuade me to become a Christian so easily?"

[29] "I wish before God," replied Paul, "that whether easily or with difficulty, not only you but all who listen to me today might become as I am—except for these chains."

[30] So the king, the governor, Bernice, and those sitting with them got up, [31] and when they had left they talked with each other and said, "This man is doing nothing that deserves death or chains."

---

[a]**26:14** Sharp sticks used to prod animals, such as oxen in plowing [b]**26:16** Other mss read *things in which you have seen Me*

Roman law to short-circuit the process.

27:2 we. Luke is again in the picture. Some believe that he and Aristarchus may have come along on this journey to Rome as Paul's servants.

27:3 Sidon. A day's sail of about 70 nautical miles from Caesarea. Paul was allowed (probably under the supervision of a soldier) to visit the Christian community there.

27:5–6 we reached Myra. At Myra, Paul and the other prisoners were transferred to another ship heading to Italy because their original ship was continuing north to Adramyttium.

27:9 the voyage was already dangerous. According to one Roman military writer, sailing on the Mediterranean Sea was dangerous after

September 15, and it usually was halted from mid-November until at least early February.

27:10–11 this voyage is headed toward damage and heavy loss. It is unclear whether Paul's comment was in response to a prophetic word he had received or a foreboding based on the difficulties they had already experienced.

27:14 a fierce wind called the "northeaster." The Greek word behind this expression is the source of the English word *typhoon*.

27:16 Cauda. A small island, known today as Gavaho or Gozzo, about 20 miles south of Crete. **the skiff.** This small boat was normally towed, but in a storm it was brought on board.

27:17 girded the ship. Literally "they used helps to undergird the ship." The "helps" were block and tackle used to pull ropes or cables tightly around the ship to keep it from breaking apart. **the Syrtis.** A dangerous shoal off the coast of Africa. **lowered the drift-anchor.** Literally, "the tackle." This phrase may refer to taking down the mainsail or to dragging an anchor to slow the ship's speed.

27:21 without food. Much of the food on board was probably spoiled by seawater, and conditions were such that eating must have been impossible.

27:29 from the stern. If anchors had been dropped from the bow (which was the usual practice) the ship would have swung around and been facing the wrong way for the crew to attempt a beaching on shore in the morning.

[32] Then Agrippa said to Festus, "This man could have been released if he had not appealed to Caesar."

Sailing for Rome

27 When it was decided that we were to sail to Italy, they handed over Paul and some other prisoners to a •centurion named Julius, of the Imperial •Regiment. [2] So when we had boarded a ship of Adramyttium, we put to sea, intending to sail to ports along the coast of the province of Asia. Aristarchus, a Macedonian of Thessalonica, was with us. [3] The next day we put in at Sidon, and Julius treated Paul kindly and allowed him to go to his friends to receive their care. [4] When we had put out to sea from there, we sailed along the northern coast[a] of Cyprus because the winds were against us. [5] After sailing through the open sea off Cilicia and Pamphylia, we reached Myra in Lycia. [6] There the centurion found an Alexandrian ship sailing for Italy and put us on board. [7] Sailing slowly for many days, we came with difficulty as far as Cnidus. But since the wind did not allow us to approach it, we sailed along the south side[a] of Crete off Salmone. [8] With yet more difficulty we sailed along the coast, and came to a place called Fair Havens near the city of Lasea.

Paul's Advice Ignored

[9] By now much time had passed, and the voyage was already dangerous. Since the Fast[b] was already over, Paul gave his advice [10] and told them, "Men, I can see that this voyage is headed toward damage and heavy loss, not only of the cargo and the ship, but also of our lives." [11] But the centurion paid attention to the captain and the owner of the ship rather than to what Paul said. [12] Since the harbor was unsuitable to winter in, the majority decided to set sail from there, hoping somehow to reach Phoenix, a harbor on Crete open to the southwest and northwest, and to winter there.

Storm-Tossed Vessel

[13] When a gentle south wind sprang up, they thought they had achieved their purpose; they weighed anchor and sailed along the shore of Crete. [14] But not long afterwards, a fierce wind called the "northeaster"[c] rushed down from the island.[d] [15] Since the ship was caught and was unable to head into the wind, we gave way to it and were driven along. [16] After running under the shelter of a little island called Cauda,[e] we were barely able to get control of the skiff. [17] After hoisting it up, they used ropes and tackle and girded the ship. Then, fearing they would run aground on the Syrtis,[f] they lowered the drift-anchor, and in this way they were driven along. [18] Because we were being severely battered by the storm, they began to jettison the cargo the next day. [19] On the third day, they threw the ship's gear overboard with their own hands.

[20] For many days neither sun nor stars appeared, and the severe storm kept raging; finally all hope that we would be saved was disappearing. [21] Since many were going without food, Paul stood up among them and said, "You men should have followed my advice not to sail from Crete and sustain this damage and loss. [22] Now I urge you to take courage, because there will be no loss of any of your lives, but only of the ship. [23] For this night an angel of the God I belong to and serve stood by me, [24] saying, 'Don't be afraid, Paul. You must stand before Caesar. And, look! God has graciously given you all those who are sailing with you.' [25] Therefore, take courage, men, because I believe God that it will be just the way it was told to me. [26] However, we must run aground on a certain island."

[27] When the fourteenth night came, we were drifting in the Adriatic Sea,[g] and in the middle of the night the sailors thought they were approaching land.[h] [28] They took a sounding and found it to be 120 feet[i] deep; when they had sailed a little farther and sounded again, they found it to be 90 feet[j] deep. [29] Then, fearing we might run aground in some rocky place, they dropped four anchors from the stern and prayed for daylight to come.

---

[a]**27:4,7** Lit sailed under the lee   [b]**27:9** The Day of Atonement   [c]**27:14** Lit Euraquilo, a violent northeast wind   [d]**27:14** Lit from her   [e]**27:16** Or Clauda
[f]**27:17** Syrtis = sand banks or bars near North Africa   [g]**27:27** Part of the northern Mediterranean Sea; not the modern Adriatic Sea east of Italy
[h]**27:27** Lit thought there was land approaching them   [i]**27:28** Lit 20 fathoms   [j]**27:28** Lit 15 fathoms

---

27:30–32 tried to escape. At least some of the sailors planned to make a run for shore that night under pretense of securing the ship. Paul was concerned that the safety of the other passengers depended on the experience of the sailors.

27:38 throwing the grain … into the sea. All portable cargo had already been thrown overboard (v. 18), but now the main load was removed to lighten the ship for its approach to land.

27:41 bow jammed fast. The traditional site of St. Paul's Bay on the island of Malta is composed of mud and clay that would trap a stuck ship. The pounding of the waves soon began to break the ship apart.

27:42–43 kill the prisoners. Since the soldiers were responsible for making sure prisoners did not escape in transit, some of the soldiers planned to kill the prisoners on the spot rather than face the possibility that some might escape. Because of the centurion's respect for Paul, he prevented that from happening.

28:1–10 The ship's crew and passengers landed at Malta, a small island 60 miles south of Sicily.

28:4 does not allow him to live! The natives of the island thought that Paul, who had been spared by such a disaster as a shipwreck only to be bitten by a viper, must have committed a serious crime for which he was being punished by the gods.

28:11 After three months. The ship sailed again in February.

28:14 we found believers. At Puteoli, Paul and the others were able to spend a week with some Christians. **And so we came to Rome.** Rome was still about 140 miles away, but Paul's safe arrival in Italy marked the fulfillment of God's promise that Paul would preach the gospel in the imperial city.

28:15 had come to meet us. News of Paul's arrival reached the church at Rome. Some of the believers traveled to the Forum of Appius (about 43 miles from Rome) and others to the Three Taverns (33 miles from Rome) to accompany him into the city.

28:16 Paul was permitted to stay by himself. Paul was kept under guard in a type of house arrest while he awaited trial. He may have been able to work as a leather worker during this time, or gifts from the churches may have provided for his needs (Phil. 4:14–18).

30 Some sailors tried to escape from the ship; they had let down the skiff into the sea, pretending that they were going to put out anchors from the bow. 31 Paul said to the centurion and the soldiers, "Unless these men stay in the ship, you cannot be saved." 32 Then the soldiers cut the ropes holding the skiff and let it drop away.

33 When it was just about daylight, Paul urged them all to take food, saying, "Today is the fourteenth day that you have been waiting and going without food, having eaten nothing. 34 Therefore I urge you to take some food. For this has to do with your survival, since not a hair will be lost from the head of any of you." 35 After he said these things and had taken some bread, he gave thanks to God in the presence of them all, and when he had broken it, he began to eat. 36 They all became encouraged and took food themselves. 37 In all there were 276 of us on the ship. 38 And having eaten enough food, they began to lighten the ship by throwing the grain overboard into the sea.

Shipwreck

39 When daylight came, they did not recognize the land, but sighted a bay with a beach. They planned to run the ship ashore if they could. 40 After casting off the anchors, they left them in the sea, at the same time loosening the ropes that held the rudders. Then they hoisted the foresail to the wind and headed for the beach. 41 But they struck a sandbar and ran the ship aground. The bow jammed fast and remained immovable, but the stern began to break up with the pounding of the waves.

42 The soldiers' plan was to kill the prisoners so that no one could swim off and escape. 43 But the centurion kept them from carrying out their plan because he wanted to save Paul, so he ordered those who could swim to jump overboard first and get to land. 44 The rest were to follow, some on planks and some on debris from the ship. In this way, all got safely to land.

Malta's Hospitality

28 Safely ashore, we then learned that the island was called Malta. 2 The local people showed us extraordinary kindness, for they lit a fire and took us all in, since rain was falling and it was cold. 3 As Paul gathered a bundle of brushwood and put it on the fire, a viper came out because of the heat and fastened itself to his hand. 4 When the local people saw the creature hanging from his hand, they said to one another, "This man is probably a murderer, and though he has escaped the sea, Justice[a] does not allow him to live!" 5 However, he shook the creature off into the fire and suffered no harm. 6 They expected that he would swell up or suddenly drop dead. But after they waited a long time and saw nothing unusual happen to him, they changed their minds and said he was a god.

Ministry in Malta

7 Now in the area around that place was an estate belonging to the leading man of the island, named Publius, who welcomed us and entertained us hospitably for three days. 8 It happened that Publius' father was in bed suffering from fever and dysentery. Paul went to him, and praying and laying his hands on him, he healed him. 9 After this, the rest of those on the island who had diseases also came and were cured. 10 So they heaped many honors on us, and when we sailed, they gave us what we needed.

Rome at Last

11 After three months we set sail in an Alexandrian ship that had wintered at the island, with the Twin Brothers[b] as its figurehead. 12 Putting in at Syracuse, we stayed three days. 13 From there, after making a circuit along the coast,[c] we reached Rhegium. After one day a south wind sprang up, and the second day we came to Puteoli. 14 There we found believers[d] and were invited to stay with them for seven days.

And so we came to Rome. 15 Now the believers[d] from there had heard the news about us and had come to meet us as far as Forum of Appius and Three Taverns. When Paul saw them, he thanked God and took courage. 16 And when we entered Rome,[e] Paul was permitted to stay by himself with the soldier who guarded him.

---

a **28:4** Gk *Dike*, a goddess of justice b **28:11** Gk *Dioscuri*, twin sons of Zeus c **28:13** Other mss read *From there, casting off*, d **28:14,15** Lit brothers e **28:16** Other mss add *the centurion turned the prisoners over to the military commander; but*

28:19 my nation. Notice also "brothers" and "our people" (v. 17). Once again, Luke presents Paul as a faithful Jew. His commitment to Jesus as the Messiah was to be seen as a natural outgrowth of his trust in the Old Testament Scriptures and his loyalty to God (v. 20; 23:6; 24:15; 26:22–23). His appeal to Caesar was not an attempt to cause problems for the Jews in Rome or Jerusalem.

28:23 He persuaded them concerning Jesus. Examples of how Paul argued for the gospel from the Old Testament Scriptures are given in 13:16–41; 22:3–21; 26:4–27. **the kingdom of God** (see also v. 31). This phrase serves as summary of all that the gospel is about. It announces the present and coming reign of God in human affairs and calls people to affirm their loyalty to Jesus as God's appointed King.

28:30 welcomed all who visited him. Luke concludes Acts with the picture of Paul continuing his missionary activities with everyone who would listen.

28:31 full boldness and without hindrance. In this last statement in Acts, the emphasis in the Greek sentence falls on the boldness and freedom with which Paul preached the gospel. During this period of house arrest, Paul wrote the letter of Philippians and probably the letters of Ephesians, Colossians, and Philemon. Philippians 1:12–13 gives insight into his situation during this time as he carried on an extensive ministry to the soldiers assigned to guard him, undoubtedly resulting in the conversion of many. While some believe that Paul was executed at the end of these two years, other scholars contend that at the end of these two years, Luke was released and enjoyed freedom for another two years. During this time he traveled once again to Crete, Asia, and Macedonia. It was probably during this time that he wrote the letters of 1 Timothy and Titus. According to this second perspective, at some point after this, Paul was again arrested and imprisoned at Rome. The Roman emperor, Nero, widely suspected of starting the great fire of Rome in A.D. 64, needed to shift the blame from himself to others, and Christians were chosen as the scapegoats. This brought an outburst of cruel persecution against the church, resulting in the execution of both Paul and Peter by Roman authorities.

Paul's First Interview with Roman Jews

[17] After three days he called together the leaders of the Jews. And when they had gathered he said to them: "Brothers, although I have done nothing against our people or the customs of our forefathers, I was delivered as a prisoner from Jerusalem into the hands of the Romans [18] who, after examining me, wanted to release me, since I had not committed a capital offense. [19] Because the Jews objected, I was compelled to appeal to Caesar; it was not as though I had any accusation against my nation. [20] So, for this reason I've asked to see you and speak to you. In fact, it is for the hope of Israel that I'm wearing this chain."

[21] And they said to him, "We haven't received any letters about you from Judea; none of the brothers has come and reported or spoken anything evil about you. [22] But we consider it suitable to hear from you what you think. For concerning this sect, we are aware that it is spoken against everywhere."

The Response to Paul's Message

[23] After arranging a day with him, many came to him at his lodging. From dawn to dusk he expounded and witnessed about the kingdom of God. He persuaded them concerning Jesus from both the Law of Moses and the Prophets. [24] Some were persuaded by what he said, but others did not believe.

[25] Disagreeing among themselves, they began to leave after Paul made one statement: "The Holy Spirit correctly spoke through the prophet Isaiah to your[a] forefathers [26] when He said,

Go to this people and say:
'You will listen and listen,
   yet never understand;
and you will look and look, yet never perceive.
[27]   For this people's heart has grown callous,
   their ears are hard of hearing,
and they have shut their eyes; otherwise
   they might see with their eyes
and hear with their ears,
   understand with their heart,
   and be converted—and I would heal them.'[b]

[28] Therefore, let it be known to you that this saving work of God has been sent to the Gentiles; they will listen!" [[29] After he said these things, the Jews departed, while engaging in a prolonged debate among themselves.][c]

Paul's Ministry Unhindered

[30] Then he stayed two whole years in his own rented house. And he welcomed all who visited him, [31] proclaiming the kingdom of God and teaching the things concerning the Lord Jesus Christ with full boldness and without hindrance.

---

a28:25 Other mss read our   b28:26–27 Is 6:9–10   c28:29 Other mss omit bracketed text

INTRODUCTION TO
ROMANS

AUTHOR

The writer is the Apostle Paul.

DATE

Paul wrote his letter during a three-month period during the winter spent in Corinth at the home of his friend and convert Gaius (16:23). The time was probably A.D. 56-57 (though it was certainly sometime between A.D. 54-59).

THEME

Being right with God through faith in Christ.

HISTORICAL BACKGROUND

For nearly 10 years Paul evangelized the Gentile territories ringing the Aegean

Sea. Now that there were established churches throughout the region, he turns his eyes to fresh fields. He plans a trip to Spain, the oldest Roman colony in the West. But first there was unfinished business: he had taken up a collection to aid the poor in Jerusalem—a fine gesture on the part of the newer churches—and now he would deliver it to Jerusalem, though he did so with some misgiving (15:31).

After Jerusalem, he planned to travel to Spain, stopping en route to fulfill a long-held dream to visit Rome—the capital of the world. He wrote the letter to the Romans by way of introduction (the Roman Christians did not know him, though—as chapter 16 reveals—he had friends there). He was eager to assure the Roman Christians, contrary to false rumors they might have heard, that the gospel he was

preaching was, indeed, the gospel of Jesus Christ.

Paul's plan did not work as he intended. He did visit Rome, but not for three more years, and then he went not as a tourist, but as a prisoner. His misgivings about his Jerusalem trip proved accurate. Once there, he was quickly arrested and eventually sent to Rome for trial. Paul remained in Rome under house arrest for at least two years. Ultimately, according to reliable tradition, he was executed at a place just outside Rome. He never made it to Spain.

It is not known how the Roman church began. It is not unlikely that some Roman Jews, converted on the Day of Pentecost (Acts 2:10), began the church. The Roman historian, Suetonius, writes that Jews were expelled from Rome about A.D. 50 for rioting, probably as a result of preaching Jesus in synagogues. As for the Gentile Christians in Rome, it is known that other Christian missionaries besides Paul were active in founding churches.

CHARACTERISTICS

Romans is Paul's most complete theological statement—precise and painstakingly logical. This is not to say, that Romans is boring and burdensome; it is vibrant, colorful, and sweeping in scope. The magnitude of its themes makes Romans heavy going at times. Even the Apostle Peter sometimes found Paul's writing hard to understand (2 Peter 3:16)!

Paul's main focus is the question of how God will judge each of us on the final day. Will it be on the basis of how "good" we were and how well we kept the law? Acutely aware of repeated fail-

ure, we would never have any assurance of salvation, but this is not God intention. Thus, the great theme of Romans emerges that we can have assurance of right standing before God and a positive verdict on Judgment Day. Such confidence does not come because of what we have done; it comes because of what God does. Thanks to Christ's death in our place, He freely offers us grace.

Paul sets this theme against the teaching of certain Jewish Christians, legalists who would add circumcision to grace (thus nullifying grace). Salvation cannot be both the result of our works *and* a gracious gift, freely given by God. In the course of his argument, Paul sets up a series of opposites: faith versus works, Spirit versus flesh, and liberty versus bondage.

As to how we gain right standing before God, Paul argues first that both pagans and religious people stand condemned before God (1:18-3:20). Right standing comes only by God's grace shown in Christ's sacrificial death and accepted by faith (3:21-5:21). This righteousness leads to a whole new lifestyle (6:1-8:39). He then deals with the question of why Israel rejected Christ (9:1-11:36), ending with practical exhortations for a life of faith (12:1-15:13). The impact of Romans on the history of the church can hardly be overstated. From Augustine to Luther to Wesley, many lives were changed as the result of reflecting on this book.

PASSAGES FOR TOPICAL GROUP STUDY

PASSAGES FOR GENERAL GROUP STUDY

God's Good News for Rome

1 Paul, a slave of Christ Jesus, called as an apostle[a] and singled out for God's good news— [2] which He promised long ago through His prophets in the Holy Scriptures— [3] concerning His Son, Jesus Christ our Lord, who was a descendant of David[b] according to the flesh [4] and was established as the powerful Son of God by the resurrection from the dead according to the Spirit of holiness.[c] [5] We have received grace and apostleship through Him to bring about[d] the obedience of faith[e] among all the nations,[f] on behalf of His name, [6] including yourselves who are also Jesus Christ's by calling:

[7] To all who are in Rome, loved by God, called as saints.

Grace to you and peace from God our Father and the Lord Jesus Christ.

Serving Jesus

1. From whom do you look forward to getting letters or e-mails? What makes them worth waiting for?

Romans 1:1-7

2. Why does Paul refer to himself as "a slave of Christ Jesus" (v. 1)? What rights does a slave have? What role?

3. What is the calling of all Christians, according to this passage?

4. What facts do you learn about Jesus Christ in this passage?

5. Do you consider yourself a "slave" of Jesus Christ? How obedient are you to the faith (v. 5)?

Not Ashamed

1. What was the best piece of good news you heard this past week? The worst bad news?

Romans 1:8-17

2. Nero ruled the Christians in Rome, and he soon become famous for persecuting them. Why might the news of the Christians' faith be "reported in all the world" (v. 8)? Why might Paul want to travel there?

3. Why does Paul say, "I am not ashamed of the gospel" (v. 16)? How might the Christians in Rome have been "ashamed of the gospel"? How about you?

4. How can you learn to live more "by faith" (v. 17)?

The Apostle's Desire to Visit Rome

[8] First, I thank my God through Jesus Christ for all of you because the news of your faith[g] is being reported in all the world. [9] For God, whom I serve with my spirit in ⌊telling⌋ the good news about His Son, is my witness that I constantly mention you, [10] always asking in my prayers that if it is somehow in God's will, I may now at last succeed in coming to you. [11] For I want very much to see you, that I may impart to you some spiritual gift to strengthen you, [12] that is, to be mutually encouraged by each other's faith, both yours and mine.

[13] Now I want you to know,[h] brothers, that I often planned to come to you (but was prevented until now) in order that I might have a fruitful ministry[i] among you, just as among the rest of the Gentiles. [14] I am obligated both to Greeks and barbarians,[j] both to the wise

---

[a] **1:1** Or *Jesus, a called apostle* [b] **1:3** Lit *was of the seed of David* [c] **1:4** Or *the spirit of holiness*, or *the Holy Spirit* [d] **1:5** Lit *Him into*, or *Him for*
[e] **1:5** Or *the obedience that is faith*, or *the faithful obedience*, or *the obedience that comes from faith* [f] **1:5** Or *Gentiles* [g] **1:8** Or *because your faith*
[h] **1:13** Lit *I don't want you to be unaware* [i] **1:13** Lit *have some fruit* [j] **1:14** Or *non-Greeks*

1:1 Paul. In introducing himself, Paul uses his Roman name and not his Jewish name (Saul). **slave.** Or, bond servant. Paul states that he is choosing to be a servant of Jesus whom he identifies as "Lord" (v. 4), a Master in authority over all believers. **called.** Paul did not just decide to be an apostle and declare himself one. He is an apostle because God appointed him to this task. **apostle.** In the broad sense, an apostle is anyone sent on a mission with a message. **singled out.** In Galatians 1:15 Paul is set apart by God from birth for a special task, and in Acts 13:2 the church at Antioch appoints him, along with Barnabas, for a special mission of evangelization in the Gentile world.

1:2 promised long ago. Having defined the gospel (good news of salvation through Christ) as being from God in verse 1, Paul

further specifies that the gospel was a fulfillment of prophecy. It was not a new thought with God or an invention of man. God had always sought to bring man into fellowship with Him.

1:3-4 concerning His Son. A short, creedal statement of faith probably familiar to the Roman Christians (4:24-25; 10:8-10; 16:25-26). **Son, Jesus.** Jesus belongs to two spheres of existence: the human, in which He is the descendant of King David (from whose line the Messiah was to come); and the divine, in which He is God's Son (this having been verified through His resurrection).

1:5 grace. Grace is God's love reaching out to people who do not deserve it but are loved by God anyway. The gospel is the full expression of God's grace. Paul refers to

God's grace throughout Romans as well as his other epistles. **apostleship.** Paul did not earn his apostleship or deserve to be an apostle. Unlike other apostles, he had never seen Jesus in the flesh. He was one because of God's "undeserved favor" ("grace"). He considered the churches he founded a mark of his apostleship (1 Cor. 9:2). He also stated that he bore in his body the marks of Jesus that come through his apostolic suffering (1 Cor. 15:10). **all the nations.** Paul's apostolic commission is to evangelize the non-Jewish world. **obedience of faith.** This is active response to God—faith that shows itself in obedience (Gal. 5:6-8).

1:14 I am obligated. Paul was obligated to God for the price Christ paid for his salvation. Second, because he had been given this incalculable gift, he felt a strong

and the foolish. ¹⁵ So I am eager to preach the good news to you also who are in Rome.

The Righteous Will Live by Faith

¹⁶ For I am not ashamed of the gospel,ᵃ because it is God's power for salvation to everyone who believes, first to the Jew, and also to the Greek. ¹⁷ For in it God's righteousness is revealed from faith to faith,ᵇ just as it is written: **The righteous will live by faith.**ᶜ ᵈ

Homosexuality

1. What are some things you have observed in nature that confirm to you "there is a God"?

Romans 1:18-32

2. How does God reveal His wrath against unrighteousness (v. 18)?
3. Who suppresses the truth in today's culture?
4. Homosexuality is now known as an "alternative lifestyle." What does Paul say about that?
5. According to this passage, why does God permit homosexuality? Where does it come from? To what does it lead?
6. How do people today "not think it worthwhile to have God in their knowledge" (v. 28)?

The Guilt of the Gentile World

¹⁸ For God's wrath is revealed from heaven against all godlessness and unrighteousness of people who by their unrighteousness suppress the truth, ¹⁹ since what can be knownᵉ about God is evident among them, because God has shown it to them. ²⁰ From the creation of the world His invisible attributes, that is, His eternal power and divine nature, have been clearly seen, being understood through what He has made. As a result, peopleᶠ are without excuse. ²¹ For though they knew God, they did not glorify Him as God or show gratitude. Instead, their thinking became nonsense, and their senseless mindsᵍ were darkened. ²² Claiming to be wise, they became fools ²³ and exchanged the glory of the immortal God for images resembling mortal man, birds, four-footed animals, and reptiles.

²⁴ Therefore God delivered them over in the cravings of their hearts to sexual impurity, so that their bodies were degraded among themselves. ²⁵ They exchanged the truth of God for a lie, and worshiped and served something created instead of the Creator, who is blessed forever. •Amen.

From Idolatry to Depravity

²⁶ This is why God delivered them over to degrading passions. For even their females exchanged natural sexual intercourseʰ for what is unnatural. ²⁷ The males in the same way also left natural sexual intercourseʰ with females and were inflamed in their lust for one another. Males committed shameless acts with males and received in their own personsⁱ the appropriate penalty for their perversion.ʲ

²⁸ And because they did not think it worthwhile to have God in their knowledge, God delivered them over to a worthless mind to do what is morally wrong. ²⁹ They are filled with all unrighteousness,ᵏ evil, greed, and wickedness. They are full of envy, murder, disputes, deceit, and malice. They are gossips, ³⁰ slanderers, God-haters, arrogant, proud, boastful, inventors of evil, disobedient to parents, ³¹ undiscerning, untrustworthy, unloving,ˡ and unmerciful. ³² Although they know full well God's just sentence— that those who practice such things deserve to dieᵐ — they not only do them, but even applaudⁿ others who practice them.

God's Righteous Judgment

2 Therefore, anyone of youᵒ who judges is without excuse. For when you judge another, you con-

---

^a**1:16** Other mss add *of Christ*   ^b**1:17** Or *revealed out of faith into faith*   ^c**1:17** Or *The one who is righteous by faith will live*   ^d**1:17** Hab 2:4   ^e**1:19** Or *what is known*   ^f**1:20** Lit *they*   ^g**1:21** Lit *hearts*   ^h**1:26,27** Lit *natural use*   ⁱ**1:27** Or *in themselves*   ^j**1:27** Or *error*   ^k**1:29** Other mss add *sexual immorality*   ^l**1:31** Other mss add *unforgiving*   ^m**1:32** Lit *things are worthy of death*   ⁿ**1:32** Lit *even take pleasure in*   ^o**2:1** Lit *Therefore, O man, every one*

---

obligation to tell this good news to all mankind.

1:16 salvation. This word carries the Hebrew idea of salvation as wholeness and healing (in the here and now), as well as the idea of spiritual rescue (which will be realized in the future). **everyone who believes.** For those seeking a relationship with God, the required response to the good news of salvation is faith.

1:17 righteousness. In Hebrew thought, righteousness is not so much a moral quality as a legal judgment. The idea is not that a person is made righteous (in the ethical sense) or proved righteous (virtuous) by such a pronouncement. Rather, a person is counted or reckoned as righteous or pardoned, even though he is actually guilty. Then he has the right to stand before God and enter into a relationship with Him. **God's.** This declaration of righteousness comes from God to us—it is a reflection of His character. He is righteous, and this is proved by His saving activity. **from faith to faith.** What faith is becomes clear as the epistle unfolds, though in verse 5 its primary meaning has already been made clear—it is believing obedience. The person who has faith trusts in the life, death, and resurrection of Jesus Christ. In these actions He sees the power of God at work. He then responds to God by submitting to Christ and trusting solely in God's saving work. **The righteous will live by faith.** This citation from Habakkuk 2:4 is the first of many quotes that Paul uses from the Old Testament to demonstrate and prove his point.

1:18 God's wrath. The wrath of God is His anger toward evil, including human sin and rebellion.

1:24 God delivered them over. This phrase is used three times (see also vv. 26,28) to indicate that God allowed people to carry out their rebellion and experience the fruit of their choices.

1:24-27 degrading passions. Refusing to embrace and reverence the revealed nature of their Creator, those who rebel against God are not protected from evil assault. This lack of protection is expressed in a distorted sexuality. Greek and Roman writers agree with Paul's description; it was an age of unparalleled immorality.

1:29 unrighteousness. The opposite of jus-

Playing Judge

1. If you were a judge, what famous trial would you like to re-try? What would your verdict be, and why?

Romans 2:1-16

2. What is the difference between "judging" and identifying sin when it is present?

3. What does Paul mean in verse 11? What does this have to do with judging others?

4. In the last chapter, Paul discussed homosexuality. How can we stand up for what is true without judging others?

5. When have you assumed that God would "play favorites," giving you special grace? How can you guard against this?

demn yourself, since you, the judge, do the same things. ² We know that God's judgment on those who do such things is based on the truth. ³ Do you really think—anyone of you who judges those who do such things yet do the same—that you will escape God's judgment? ⁴ Or do you despise the riches of His kindness, restraint, and patience, not recognizingᵃ that God's kindness is intended to lead you to repentance? ⁵ But because of your hardness and unrepentant heart you are storing up wrath for yourself in the day of wrath, when God's righteous judgment is revealed. ⁶ He **will repay each one according to his works:**ᵇ ⁷ eternal life to those who by patiently doing good seek for glory, honor, and immortality; ⁸ but wrath and indignation to those who are self-seeking and disobey the truth, but are obeying unrighteousness; ⁹ affliction and distress for every human being who does evil, first

to the Jew, and also to the Greek; ¹⁰ but glory, honor, and peace for everyone who does good, first to the Jew, and also to the Greek. ¹¹ There is no favoritism with God.

¹² All those who sinned without the law will also perish without the law, and all those who sinned under the law will be judged by the law. ¹³ For the hearers of the law are not righteous before God, but the doers of the law will be declared righteous.ᶜ ¹⁴ So, when Gentiles, who do not have the law, instinctively do what the law demands, they are a law to themselves even though they do not have the law. ¹⁵ They show that the work of the lawᵈ is written on their hearts. Their consciences testify in support of this, and their competing thoughts either accuse or excuse themᵉ ¹⁶ on the day when God judges what people have kept secret, according to my gospel through Christ Jesus.

Bragging Rights

1. What accomplishment in your life are you most proud of? What are you most tempted to boast about?

Romans 2:17-29

2. What principle is Paul stating in verses 17-24?

3. What does it mean to "boast in the law" (v. 23)? What is the risk of doing so?

4. What does it mean in verse 29 that "a person is a Jew who is one inwardly"? That "circumcision is of the heart"?

5. How often do you boast or gloat when you "win" or accomplish something? How can you have a "purified heart"?

ᵃ**2:4** Or patience, because you do not recognize ᵇ**2:6** Ps 62:12; Pr 24:12 ᶜ**2:13** Or will be justified or acquitted ᵈ**2:15** The code of conduct required by the law ᵉ**2:15** Internal debate, either in a person or among the pagan moralists

tice: robbing God and others of their due. **evil.** The deliberate attempt to harm or to corrupt; such a person is not only intentionally bad, but he seeks to make others evil. **greed.** Taking whatever one wants without regard for the rights of others. **wickedness.** The most general term for badness; a vicious person devoid of any good quality. **envy.** Grudging resentment of (and desire for) another's accomplishments or possessions. **murder.** Jesus teaches that people must avoid the spirit of hatred, which causes such a deed (Matt. 5:21-26). **disputes.** Contention or disagreement born of envy. **deceit.** Underhanded, devious actions designed to get one's own way. **malice.** Literally "evil-nature"; always thinking the worst of another.

1:29-30 gossips, slanderers. The gossiper

spreads ill news about others secretly, while the slanderer openly accuses other people.

1:30 God-haters. These are people who hate God because they believe He suppresses pleasure. **arrogant.** A type of pride that defies God and hurts others, just for the delight in doing so. **inventors of evil.** People who create new ways of sinning.

1:31 undiscerning. One who does not learn from experience. **untrustworthy.** One who breaks agreements. **unloving.** One without love for others, even members of his own family. **unmerciful.** One without pity who harms or even kills without thought.

2:4 the riches of His kindness. Jews are presuming upon the mercy of God, taking

His kindness as a sign of their immunity from judgment (when, in fact, such kindness was meant to lead them to change their lives, not to serve as an excuse for continued sinning).

2:11 favoritism. This is the point of Paul's argument. The means by which a person gains "wrath and indignation" (v. 8) or "eternal life" (v. 7) has nothing to do with national or racial heritage.

2:12 All ... will be judged by the law. Everyone will be held accountable according to his or her particular awareness of God. The Jews had the written law; the Gentiles had their conscience (v. 15) and the revelation of nature (1:20).

2:14-15 the work of the law is written on

Jewish Violation of the Law

[17] Now if[a] you call yourself a Jew, and rest in the law, and boast in God, [18] and know His will, and approve the things that are superior, being instructed from the law, [19] and are convinced that you are a guide for the blind, a light to those in darkness, [20] an instructor of the ignorant, a teacher of the immature, having in the law the full expression[b] of knowledge and truth— [21] you then, who teach another, do you not teach yourself? You who preach, "You must not steal"—do you steal? [22] You who say, "You must not commit adultery"—do you commit adultery? You who detest idols, do you rob their temples? [23] You who boast in the law, do you dishonor God by breaking the law? [24] For, as it is written: **The name of God is blasphemed among the Gentiles because of you.[c]**

Circumcision of the Heart

[25] For circumcision benefits you if you observe the law, but if you are a lawbreaker, your circumcision has become uncircumcision. [26] Therefore if an uncircumcised man keeps the law's requirements, will his uncircumcision not be counted as circumcision? [27] A man who is physically uncircumcised, but who fulfills the law, will judge you who are a lawbreaker in spite of having the letter ⌊of the law⌋ and circumcision. [28] For a person is not a Jew who is one outwardly, and ⌊true⌋ circumcision is not something visible in the flesh. [29] On the contrary, a person is a Jew who is one inwardly, and circumcision is of the heart—by the Spirit, not the letter.[d] His praise[e] is not from men but from God.

Paul Answers an Objection

3 So what advantage does the Jew have? Or what is the benefit of circumcision? [2] Considerable in every way. First, they were entrusted with the spoken words of God. [3] What then? If some did not believe, will their unbelief cancel God's faithfulness? [4] Absolutely not! God must be true, but everyone is a liar, as it is written:

That You may be justified in Your words
and triumph when You judge.[f]

[5] But if our unrighteousness highlights[g] God's righteousness, what are we to say? I use a human argument:[h] Is God unrighteous to inflict wrath? [6] Absolutely not! Otherwise, how will God judge the world? [7] But if by my lie God's truth is amplified to His glory, why am I also still judged as a sinner? [8] And why not say, just as some people slanderously claim we say, "Let us do evil so that good may come"? Their condemnation is deserved!

We've All Blown It

1. What laws do you frequently ignore: Speed limits? School rules? Coach's demands? Other?

Romans 3:9-24

2. Who does Paul consider a sinner? Who has never sinned?

3. Who has been saved from sin? How?

4. In verse 20 Paul says, "For no flesh will be justified in His sight by the works of the law." How is a person justified (made right)?

5. Have you gotten right with God? Are you trying to earn your way into His favor through good works?

6. How does disregard for rules show the attitude of your heart?

The Whole World Guilty before God

[9] What then? Are we any better?[i] Not at all! For we have previously charged that both Jews and Gentiles[j] are all under sin,[k] [10] as it is written:[l]

---

[a]**2:17** Other mss read *Look—* [b]**2:20** Or *the embodiment* [c]**2:24** Is 52:5 [d]**2:29** Or *heart—spiritually, not literally* [e]**2:29** In Hb, the words *Jew, Judah,* and *praise* are related. [f]**3:4** Ps 51:4 [g]**3:5** Or *shows,* or *demonstrates* [h]**3:5** Lit *I speak as a man* [i]**3:9** Are we Jews any better than the Gentiles? [j]**3:9** Lit *Greeks* [k]**3:9** Under sin's power or dominion [l]**3:10** Paul constructs this charge from a chain of OT quotations, mainly from the Psalms.

---

their hearts. Gentiles not only know about God from His creation, but their conscience tells them that He is the judge of the difference between right and wrong.

2:17 Jew. To be a Jew was to be special— to be a child of God. Paul attacked this intense nationalistic pride, stating that it is not enough for salvation. **rest in the law.** Literally to "rest upon the law"; to believe that one is right with God because of his heritage and culture as a Jew.

2:25 circumcision. This was the sign of the covenant between the Jewish people and God (Gen. 17:1-14).

2:28-29 true circumcision. The Old Testament teaches in Deuteronomy 30:6 that true

circumcision is not an outward, physical mark, but an inward spiritual work by God. Paul teaches that it is possible to neglect circumcision and still be counted as obedient to God's law. This would be interpreted by Paul's Jewish readers as a radical new teaching.

3:1 what advantage. Paul raises a question he has heard or that he knows is on the minds of some readers: "Do you really mean that there is no significant difference between a Jew and a Gentile?" Questions like this arise out of an accurate understanding that God had set Israel apart from all other nations.

3:2 Considerable in every way. We might assume that Paul would reply: "Jews have no advantage." But this would not be accurate. They had an important place in God's

plan. It was through the Jewish people that God worked out the redemption of the world through His Son Jesus, who was a Jew. **words of God.** It is a great advantage to have known the mind and will of God.

3:20 in His sight. God's perspective is the only one that matters.

3:21 But now. Paul moves from the revelation of God's wrath (1:18) to the revelation of God's righteousness. **apart from the law.** God's righteousness as revealed in the law leads only to wrath (4:15), but God's righteousness as revealed in Jesus Christ leads to right standing before Him. **attested by the Law and the Prophets.** The Old Testament, if rightly understood, does contain such a message. Paul has already used Habakkuk 2:4 when describing the gospel (1:17).

There is no one righteous, not even one;
11 there is no one who understands,
there is no one who seeks God.
12 All have turned away,
together they have become useless;
there is no one who does good,
there is not even one.[a]
13 Their throat is an open grave;
they deceive with their tongues.[b]
Vipers' venom is under their lips.[c]
14 Their mouth is full of cursing and bitterness.[d]
15 Their feet are swift to shed blood;
16 ruin and wretchedness are in their paths,
17 and the path of peace they have not known.[e]
18 There is no fear of God before their eyes.[f]

19 Now we know that whatever the law says speaks to those who are subject to the law,[g] so that every mouth may be shut and the whole world may become subject to God's judgment.[h] 20 For no flesh will be justified[i] in His sight by the works of the law, for through the law ⌈comes⌉ the knowledge of sin.

God's Righteousness through Faith

21 But now, apart from the law, God's righteousness has been revealed—attested by the Law and the Prophets[j] 22—that is, God's righteousness through faith in Jesus Christ,[k] to all who believe, since there is no distinction. 23 For all have sinned and fall short of the[l] glory of God. 24 They are justified freely by His grace through the redemption that is in Christ Jesus. 25 God presented Him as a propitiation[m] through faith in His blood, to demonstrate His righteousness, because in His restraint God passed over the sins previously committed. 26 He presented Him to demonstrate His righteousness at the present time, so that He would be righteous and declare righteous[n] the one who has faith in Jesus.

Boasting Excluded

27 Where then is boasting? It is excluded. By what kind of law?[o] By one of works? No, on the contrary, by a law[p] of faith. 28 For we conclude that a man is justified by faith apart from works of law. 29 Or is God for Jews only? Is He not also for Gentiles? Yes, for Gentiles too, 30 since there is one God who will justify the circumcised by faith and the uncircumcised through faith. 31 Do we then cancel the law through faith? Absolutely not! On the contrary, we uphold the law.

Getting on God's Good Side

1. What was your first paying job outside of the house? How much did you make?

Romans 4:1-25
2. What is the distinction that Paul makes between something earned and something given as a gift? Which applies to salvation and forgiveness of sins?
3. Circumcision here refers to earning God's favor by works or outward obedience. How do we receive God's favor? What does God actually owe us?
4. Why do we need faith to receive God's forgiveness (v. 16)?
5. How did Abraham find favor with God? How can you?

Abraham Justified by Faith

4 What then can we say that Abraham, our forefather according to the flesh, has found? 2 If Abraham was justified[q] by works, then he has something to

[a]3:10–12 Ps 14:1-3; 53:1-3; see Ec 7:20   [b]3:13 Ps 5:9   [c]3:13 Ps 140:3   [d]3:14 Ps 10:7   [e]3:15–17 Is 59:7–8   [f]3:18 Ps 36:1   [g]3:19 Lit those in the law   [h]3:19 Or become guilty before God, or may be accountable to God   [i]3:20 Or will be declared righteous, or will be acquitted   [j]3:21 When capitalized, the Law and the Prophets = OT   [k]3:22 Or through the faithfulness of Jesus Christ   [l]3:23 Or and lack the   [m]3:25 Or as a propitiatory sacrifice, or as an offering of atonement, or as a mercy seat; see Heb 9:5. The word propitiation has to do with the removal of divine wrath. Jesus' death is the means that turns God's wrath from the sinner; see 2 Co 5:21.   [n]3:26 Or and justify, or and acquit   [o]3:27 Or what principle?   [p]3:27 Or a principle   [q]4:2 Or was declared righteous, or was acquitted

3:22 faith. Individuals are not counted as righteous because of faith, as if it were an attitude on their part that forces God to accept them. Rather, they are counted as righteous (justified) because of grace through faith (or on the basis of faith). Faith, then, is a profound trust and hope in God's work in Christ. It is the opposite of works. Works give people a sense of self-confidence. They assume that their religious and moral activities will cause God to pronounce them justified. **in Jesus Christ.** Paul writes not about faith in general but about faith in a specific person—Jesus Christ. **to all.** The gospel is for Jew and Gentile alike.

3:23 fall short. The picture is of arrows that have failed to reach their target. **glory of God.** This is God's divine splendor, which is reflected in the law.

3:24 justified. This is a word drawn from the law courts. The image is of humanity on trial before God. To be justified is to be granted acquittal on the day of judgment. That a guilty person would be reckoned as not guilty was shocking to the Jew (Ex. 23:7; Prov. 17:15). Such assurance of acquittal, coming as it does at the beginning of the Christian life (the Jew hoped for acquittal at the end of life), brings a sense of personal freedom, since a person is released from the nagging questions: Am I good enough? Will I merit heaven? Now, by grace, people are pronounced "righteous" and are free to do good works out of love for God, not out of fear of His wrath. **redemption.** This refers to the act of buying the freedom of a slave—in this case, a slave in bondage to sin (Mark 10:45; 1 Pet. 1:18-19).

3:25 propitiation. The removal of divine wrath. Christ's death is the ultimate, final, and complete sacrifice for sin. Christ is the victim who takes upon Himself the wrath intended for sinful humanity. **His blood.** In terms of atonement, the importance of Jesus' death is that His blood was offered to God as a sacrifice on our behalf.

3:26 demonstrate His righteousness at the present time. The sacrificial death of Christ exhibits God's justice in two ways: First, by vindicating Jesus—He has taken sin so seriously that He sent His own Son to die. Second, by showing a whole new way of living that Christ's sacrifice has opened up for humanity.

4:1 Abraham. As the first patriarch and thus the founder of the Jewish nation, Abraham was revered by all Jews.

brag about—but not before God.[a] 3 For what does the Scripture say?

Abraham believed God,
and it was credited to him for righteousness.[b]

4 Now to the one who works, pay is not considered as a gift, but as something owed. 5 But to the one who does not work, but believes on Him who declares righteous[c] the ungodly, his faith is credited for righteousness.

David Celebrating the Same Truth

6 Likewise, David also speaks of the blessing of the man to whom God credits righteousness apart from works:

7 How happy those whose lawless acts
   are forgiven
   and whose sins are covered!
8 How happy the man whom
   the Lord will never charge with sin![d]

Abraham Justified before Circumcision

9 Is this blessing only for the circumcised, then? Or is it also for the uncircumcised? For we say, Faith was credited to Abraham for righteousness.[b] 10 How then was it credited—while he was circumcised, or uncircumcised? Not while he was circumcised, but uncircumcised. 11 And he received the sign of circumcision as a seal of the righteousness that he had by faith[e] while still uncircumcised. This was to make him the father of all who believe but are not circumcised, so that righteousness may be credited to them also. 12 And he became the father of the circumcised, not only to those who are circumcised, but also to those who follow in the footsteps of the faith our father Abraham had while still uncircumcised.

The Promise Granted through Faith

13 For the promise to Abraham or to his descendants that he would inherit the world was not through the law, but through the righteousness that comes by faith.[e]

14 If those who are of the law are heirs, faith is made empty and the promise is canceled. 15 For the law produces wrath; but where there is no law, there is no transgression.

16 This is why the promise is by faith, so that it may be according to grace, to guarantee it to all the descendants—not only to those who are of the law,[f] but also to those who are of Abraham's faith. He is the father of us all 17 in God's sight. As it is written: I have made you the father of many nations.[g] He believed in God, who gives life to the dead and calls things into existence that do not exist. 18 Against hope, with hope he believed, so that he became the father of many nations,[g] according to what had been spoken: So will your descendants be.[h] 19 He considered[i] his own body to be already dead (since he was about a hundred years old), and the deadness of Sarah's womb, without weakening in the faith. 20 He did not waver in unbelief at God's promise, but was strengthened in his faith and gave glory to God, 21 because he was fully convinced that what He had promised He was also able to perform. 22 Therefore, it was credited to him for righteousness.[b] 23 Now it was credited to him was not written for Abraham alone, 24 but also for us. It will be credited to us who believe in Him who raised Jesus our Lord from the dead. 25 He was delivered up for[j] our trespasses and raised for[j] our justification.[k]

Faith Triumphs

5 Therefore, since we have been declared righteous by faith, we have peace[l] with God through our Lord Jesus Christ. 2 Also through Him, we have obtained access by faith[m] into this grace in which we stand, and we rejoice in the hope of the glory of God. 3 And not only that, but we also rejoice in our afflictions, because we know that affliction produces endurance, 4 endurance produces proven character, and proven character produces hope. 5 This hope does not disappoint, because God's love has been

---

[a]4:2 He has no reason for boasting in God's presence   [b]4:3,9,22 Gn 15:6   [c]4:5 Or who acquits, or who justifies   [d]4:7–8 Ps 32:1–2   [e]4:11,13 Lit righteousness of faith   [f]4:16 Or not to those who are of the law only   [g]4:17,18 Gn 17:5   [h]4:18 Gn 15:5   [i]4:19 Other mss read He did not consider   [j]4:25 Or because of   [k]4:25 Or acquittal   [l]5:1 Other mss read faith, let us have peace, which can also be translated faith, let us grasp the fact that we have peace   [m]5:2 Other mss omit by faith

---

4:3 Abraham believed God. It was the condition of Abraham's heart demonstrated through obedience that caught the favorable attention of God.

4:5 believes. The Jews saw faith as a definite activity, as faithful action in accordance with God's will. Thus, they understood that God responded to Abraham's faith by declaring him "righteous." In contrast, Paul understood faith as a person's response to God's action (1:17; 3:21-26). **declares righteous the ungodly.** That God would do this contradicts Jewish expectations. God was supposed to condemn the guilty (Ex. 23:7). Paul makes this point because everyone would agree that acquitting the guilty could only be seen as an act of grace, not as a response by God to good works. God was able to justify the wicked because of the fu-

ture sacrifice of the Messiah (Isa. 53:4-12).

4:9 Faith was credited to Abraham for righteousness. This is a financial reference communicating the idea that Abraham, in a sense, borrowed against the future atonement achieved through the death, burial, and resurrection of Jesus.

4:16 promise. The word Paul uses in this verse describes an unconditional promise made out of the generosity of a person's heart. God's promise is a gift of grace, not a contract with certain obligations. **by faith.** By the very nature of a promise, a person must wait for the fulfillment of a promised inheritance.

5:1-4 We have been declared righteous

by faith. Paul points out the fourfold fruit of justification: the past blessing of peace with God (v. 1), the present blessing of grace (v. 2), the future hope of glory (v. 2), and the redeeming value of affliction (v. 3).

5:1 peace. This is not some sort of inner experience of harmony, but the objective fact of a new relationship with God. The root image is of war. Those who were in rebellion against God, their rightful King, are now reconciled to Him through Christ. This is the basis for the Christian's access to God's grace and hope for the future. In the Bible the term peace often describes the total blessing of salvation.

5:2 access. This word is used to describe ushering someone into the presence of royalty. **grace.** To be at peace with God is to

Finding Joy in Troubles

1. When has someone sacrificed something costly for your benefit? When have you done that for someone else?

Romans 5:1-11

2. How does Paul describe humanity in verses 6, 8, and 10?
3. What does "reconciled" mean? How does it change things in our relationship with God?
4. What does it mean to "rejoice in our afflictions" (v. 3)? How does one do this?
5. How does this change the way a Christian is to look upon suffering and stress?
6. How do you view your present stresses and trials?

Justified by Jesus

1. Whom do you take after in your temperament, your mother or your father? How about in your body build? Your talents and abilities?

Romans 5:12-21

2. What does Paul mean when he says "sin entered the world through one man" (v. 12)? Why did sin enter through one man? Why not through Eve's sin?
3. What does "justification" mean? How does a person become "justified"?
4. Who is the "one man" who brought justification (v. 15)? What does this say about the worldview that there are many ways to God?
5. Have you been justified, "resulting in eternal life through Jesus Christ our Lord" (v. 21)?

poured out in our hearts through the Holy Spirit who was given to us.

Those Declared Righteous Are Reconciled

⁶ For while we were still helpless, at the appointed moment, Christ died for the ungodly. ⁷ For rarely will someone die for a just person—though for a good person perhaps someone might even dare to die. ⁸ But God proves His own love for us in that while we were still sinners Christ died for us! ⁹ Much more then, since we have now been declared righteous by His blood, we will be saved through Him from wrath. ¹⁰ For if, while we were enemies, we were reconciled to God through the death of His Son, ⌊then how⌋ much more, having been reconciled, will we be saved by His life! ¹¹ And not only that, but we also rejoice in God through our Lord Jesus Christ, through whom we have now received reconciliation.

Death through Adam and Life through Christ

¹² Therefore, just as sin entered the world through one man, and death through sin, in this way death spread to all men, because all sinned.ᵃ ¹³ In fact, sin was in the world before the law, but sin is not charged to one's account when there is no law. ¹⁴ Nevertheless, death reigned from Adam to Moses, even over those who did not sin in the likeness of Adam's transgression. He is a prototype of the Coming One.

¹⁵ But the gift is not like the trespass. For if by the one man's trespass the many died, how much more have the grace of God and the gift overflowed to the many by the grace of the one man, Jesus Christ. ¹⁶ And the gift is not like the one man's sin, because from one sin came the judgment, resulting in condemnation, but from many trespasses came the gift, resulting in justificationᵇ ¹⁷ Since by the one man's trespass, death reigned through that one man, how much more will those who

---

ᵃ**5:12** Or *have sinned* ᵇ**5:16** Or *acquittal*

---

come into the sphere of His grace and thus experience the new kind of life described in 5:12–8:39. **hope.** This is a sense of confidence based on the fact of justification. **glory of God.** That for which people were created and from which they have fallen, but which they will experience again someday.

5:3 afflictions. Literally, "pressure" or "tribulation." This is not sorrow or pain, but the negative reaction of an unbelieving world. In New Testament times, suffering was the normal and expected lot of Christians (Acts 14:22). Thus, suffering was seen as a sign of true Christianity (2 Thess. 1:4-5). **endurance.** This word describes positive action taken against misfortune rather than passive acceptance.

5:4 character. A word used of metal that has

been so heated by fire that all the impurities are removed. **hope.** The confidence born out of suffering that God is transforming a person's character, and that He will keep on doing so until he is glorified.

5:12 sin entered ... through one man. Jews thought of themselves not as isolated individuals, but as part of a family, a tribe, and a nation. The actions and consequences of one person were the actions and consequences of all. So when Adam sinned by doubting God and eating the forbidden fruit (Gen. 2–3), all humanity sinned. **death through sin.** Death is the consequence of sin (Gen. 2:17), and so all people die because Adam sinned.

5:14 death. More than the physical end of life is meant here, since the contrast is al-

ways with eternal life (v. 21). Death brings a person to judgment and to condemnation (v. 18)—since all have sinned—and thus to punishment. It is spiritual death as well as physical death that concerns Paul. **Adam's transgression.** Adam disobeyed God's clear instructions (Gen. 2:17). **prototype.** Literally, a mark or impression that has been left by something. Adam and his impact on humanity was a representation of Christ, who would also impact all people.

5:15 gift. This could refer to Christ and His work on behalf of humanity. But in light of verses 18, 20, and 21, it probably indicates the status conferred on people who are made righteous before God.

5:16 from one sin came the judgment ... justification. One act of disobedience by

receive the overflow of grace and the gift of righteous-ness reign in life through the one man, Jesus Christ.

[18] So then, as through one trespass there is condemnation for everyone, so also through one righteous act there is life-giving justification[a] for everyone. [19] For just as through one man's disobedience the many were made sinners, so also through the one man's obedience the many will be made righteous. [20] The law came along to multiply the trespass. But where sin multiplied, grace multiplied even more, [21] so that, just as sin reigned in death, so also grace will reign through righteousness, resulting in eternal life through Jesus Christ our Lord.

A New Way of Life

1. What is the closest you have come to losing your life? What happened? What did you learn from the experience?

Romans 6:1-14

2. What does Paul mean that "all of us who were baptized into Christ Jesus were baptized into His death" (v. 3)? How does this concept relate to sin and temptation?

3. What does it mean to "walk in a new way of life" (v. 4)? How does this relate to sin and temptation?

4. How are we "dead to sin" (v. 11)?

5. In practical terms, how can you "not let sin reign" (v. 12) in your life?

The New Life in Christ

6 What should we say then? Should we continue in sin in order that grace may multiply? [2] Absolutely

not! How can we who died to sin still live in it? [3] Or are you unaware that all of us who were baptized into Christ Jesus were baptized into His death? [4] Therefore we were buried with Him by baptism into death, in order that, just as Christ was raised from the dead by the glory of the Father, so we too may •walk in a new way[b] of life. [5] For if we have been joined with Him in the likeness of His death, we will certainly also be[c] in the likeness of His resurrection. [6] For we know that our old self[d] was crucified with Him in order that sin's dominion over the body[e] may be abolished, so that we may no longer be enslaved to sin, [7] since a person who has died is freed[f] from sin's claims.[g] [8] Now if we died with Christ, we believe that we will also live with Him, [9] because we know that Christ, having been raised from the dead, no longer dies. Death no longer rules over Him. [10] For in that He died, He died to sin once for all; but in that He lives, He lives to God. [11] So, you too consider yourselves dead to sin, but alive to God in Christ Jesus.[h]

[12] Therefore do not let sin reign in your mortal body, so that you obey[i] its desires. [13] And do not offer any parts[j] of it to sin as weapons for unrighteousness. But as those who are alive from the dead, offer yourselves to God, and all the parts[j] of yourselves to God as weapons for righteousness. [14] For sin will not rule over you, because you are not under law but under grace.

From Slaves of Sin to Slaves of God

[15] What then? Should we sin because we are not under law but under grace? Absolutely not! [16] Do you not know that if you offer yourselves to someone[k] as obedient slaves, you are slaves of that one you obey—either of sin leading to death or of obedience leading to righteousness? [17] But thank God that, although you used to be slaves of sin, you obeyed from the heart that pattern of teaching you were entrusted to, [18] and having been liberated from sin, you became enslaved to righteousness. [19] I am using a human analogy[l] because of the weakness of your flesh.[m] For just as you offered the

---

[a]5:18 Lit *is justification of life*   [b]6:4 Or *in newness*   [c]6:5 Be joined with Him   [d]6:6 Lit *man; that is, the person that one was in Adam*   [e]6:6 Lit *that the body of sin*   [f]6:7 Lit *acquitted,* or *justified*   [g]6:7 Lit *from sin*   [h]6:11 Other mss add *our Lord*   [i]6:12 Other mss add *sin* (lit *it*) in   [j]6:13 Or *members*   [k]6:16 Lit *that to whom you offer yourselves*   [l]6:19 Lit *I speak humanly*; Paul is personifying sin and righteousness as slave masters.   [m]6:19 Or *your human nature*

Adam brought judgment and condemnation to all people. But Christ's gift brings justification and forgiveness not only for that sin, but for all sins across the centuries.

5:18-19 one man's disobedience ... one man's obedience. With the lack of similarity between Adam and Christ established, Paul can return to the formal comparison he began in verse 12: One man's disobedience brought condemnation and death to all people, just as one man's obedience now brings justification to all who choose it. The only similarity between Christ and Adam is that by one deed, each had a great impact on humanity.

5:18 one righteous act. The obedience of Christ's entire life, which led to His sacrificial death on our behalf.

5:20 law. When the law came, it defined what was "sinful." It brought sin into clear view by functioning as a mirror.

6:1-2 Should we continue in sin. Paul's poses a rhetorical question, stating the typical cynical attitude of the day: "If grace is the most wonderful thing there is and if grace abounds in the presence of sin (5:20), then shouldn't we sin all the more in order to produce more grace?"

6:2 died to sin. Paul's point is that the question is absurd. To be a Christian is to have died to sin; therefore it is impossible to live in a state to which one has died!

6:3 baptized. Baptism was mostly an adult rite in the early church, occurring generally

at the moment when a person confessed faith in Christ. It served as a public declaration that a person was no longer an unbeliever but was now identified with Christ.

6:4 buried with Him. When family and friends bury a loved one, they acknowledge publicly the reality of that death. To be baptized provides an experience in a direct (though symbolic) way to the reality of Christ's death. The experience of baptism marks the end of the old way of life and acknowledges that a person has committed himself to follow the new way of life in Christ.

6:6 old self. This refers to the unregenerate life before salvation—what a person was before turning his life over to Christ. **dominion over the body.** This reference is to a person's lower self—the sinful nature that be-

The Perfect Offering

1. Who was your first "boss"? Was this person easy or hard to work for?

Romans 6:15-23

2. What does it mean to be a slave to sin? To righteousness?

3. What are the results of being a slave to sin? To righteousness?

4. Why does Paul say that sin pays wages, while Christ gives a gift (v. 23)? What does this suggest about working for one's salvation?

5. Slaves have no choice but to obey, but Paul speaks of "offering" ourselves (v. 19). To what things do you frequently offer yourself? How can you offer yourself more to God?

"It's Like Being Married"

1. Describe your ideal mate. What things are most important to you? What things are "negotiable"?

Romans 7:1-6

2. Put Paul's "marriage" analogy into your own words. What point is he making?

3. What does "the law" mean to us today: Working for God's favor? Earning our salvation? Following rules? Other?

4. What does it mean that we have been "released from the law" (v. 6)?

5. When do you get caught up "in the old letter of the law"? In practical terms, how can you "serve in the new way of the Spirit" (v. 6)?

parts[a] of yourselves as slaves to moral impurity, and to greater and greater lawlessness, so now offer them as slaves to righteousness, which results in sanctification. [20] For when you were slaves of sin, you were free from allegiance to righteousness.[b] [21] And what fruit was produced[c] then from the things you are now ashamed of? For the end of those things is death. [22] But now, since you have been liberated from sin and become enslaved to God, you have your fruit, which results in sanctification[d] — and the end is eternal life! [23] For the wages of sin is death, but the gift of God is eternal life in Christ Jesus our Lord.

An Illustration from Marriage

7 Since I am speaking to those who understand law, brothers, are you unaware that the law has authority over someone as long as he lives? [2] For example, a married woman is legally bound to her husband while he lives. But if her husband dies, she is released from the law regarding the husband. [3] So then, if she gives herself to another man while her husband is living, she will be called an adulteress. But if her husband dies, she is free from that law. Then, if she gives herself to another man, she is not an adulteress.

[4] Therefore, my brothers, you also were put to death in relation to the law through the ₍crucified₎ body of the •Messiah, so that you may belong to another—to Him who was raised from the dead—that we may bear fruit for God. [5] For when we were in the flesh,[e] the sinful passions operated through the law in every part of us[f] and bore fruit for death. [6] But now we have been released from the law, since we have died to what held us, so that we may serve in the new way[g] of the Spirit and not in the old letter of the law.

---

[a]**6:19** Or *members*   [b]**6:20** Lit *free to righteousness*   [c]**6:21** Lit *what fruit do you have*   [d]**6:22** Or *holiness*   [e]**7:5** *in the flesh* = a person's life before accepting Christ   [f]**7:5** Lit *of our members*   [g]**7:6** Lit *in newness*

---

longs to his body (v. 12). **may be abolished.** The Greek word means "to be defeated," not "to become extinct." The sinful part of a person's nature is not destroyed, but it is deprived of power; its domination is broken.

6:7 freed from sin's claims. The only way to be freed from sin (literally, "justified from sin") is by paying its penalty. But for the Christian, resurrection follows death, and a believer is freed to rise to new life in which sin cannot overpower and dominate.

6:18 liberated from sin. Freed in the sense of having a new master—God—in place of the old master—sin. Paul is not teaching that Christians do not sin, but that they have a greater capacity to commit themselves to following Christ.

6:19 slaves. In contrast to a servant, a slave was the absolute possession of his master. A slave's time was not his own. It was literally impossible for a slave to serve two masters. **sanctification.** The process by which a person is conformed to God's ways is the theme of chapters 5–8.

6:23 wages of sin. Literally, "wages with which to buy food"—a phrase used to describe the rations eaten by soldiers. **gift of God.** In contrast to the wage of death that sin pays, God does not pay wages. He is under obligation to no one. He gives eternal life freely.

7:2-3 a married woman. A wife is bound to her husband for the duration of his life. If she goes off ("consorts," NEB) with another man while her husband is living, she "incurs the

stigma of adultery" (J. B. Phillips). But if he dies, she is free to remarry without any fault or stigma.

7:5-6 But now we have been released from the law. Paul now contrasts life without Christ (v. 5) with the new life in Christ (v. 6) experienced by a believer.

7:5 in the flesh. That is, when a person's direction in life was determined by his fallen or sinful nature. **sinful passions operated.** Our sinful nature, inherited from Adam when he fell into sin, affects every area of our lives.

7:6 released from the law. The death of Christ has delivered us from the tyranny of the law. **serve.** A Christian is freed from the law to serve and not to sin—free for obedi-

Sin's Use of the Law

7 What should we say then? Is the law sin? Absolutely not! On the contrary, I would not have known sin if it were not for the law. For example, I would not have known what it is to covet if the law had not said, **Do not covet.**[a] 8 And sin, seizing an opportunity through the commandment, produced in me coveting of every kind. For apart from the law sin is dead. 9 Once I was alive apart from the law, but when the commandment came, sin sprang to life 10 and I died. The commandment that was meant for life resulted in death for me. 11 For sin, seizing an opportunity through the commandment, deceived me, and through it killed me. 12 So then, the law is holy, and the commandment is holy and just and good.

The Problem of Sin in Us

13 Therefore, did what is good cause my death?[b] Absolutely not! On the contrary, sin, in order to be recognized as sin, was producing death in me through what is good, so that through the commandment sin might become sinful beyond measure. 14 For we know that the law is spiritual; but I am made out of flesh,[c] sold into sin's power. 15 For I do not understand what I am doing, because I do not practice what I want to do, but I do what I hate. 16 And if I do what I do not want to do, I agree with the law that it is good. 17 So now I am no longer the one doing it, but it is sin living in me. 18.For I know that nothing good lives in me, that is, in my flesh. For the desire to do what is good is with me, but there is no ability to do it. 19 For I do not do the good that I want to do, but I practice the evil that I do not want to do. 20 Now if I do what I do not want, I am no longer the one doing it, but it is the sin that lives in me. 21 So I discover this principle:[d] when I want to do good, evil is with me. 22 For in my inner self[e] I joyfully agree with God's law. 23 But I see a different law in the parts of my body,[f] waging war against the law of my mind and taking me prisoner to the law of sin in the parts of my body.[f] 24 What a wretched man I am! Who will rescue

me from this body of death? 25 I thank God through Jesus Christ our Lord![g] So then, with my mind I myself am a slave to the law of God, but with my flesh, to the law of sin.

I Do What I Don't Want to Do

1. When have you been pressured into doing something that you didn't really want to do? Who or what pressured you? Why did you do it?

Romans 7:7-25

2. Explain in your own words what Paul is saying about how the law actually produces sin. How have you seen this happen in your own life?

3. What does Paul mean in verse 15, "I do not practice what I want to do, but I do what I hate"? How have you experienced this?

4. What is reigning in your life right now—sin or grace? How can you get on the right track?

The Life-Giving Spirit

8 Therefore, no condemnation now exists for those in Christ Jesus,[h] 2 because the Spirit's law of life in Christ Jesus has set you[i] free from the law of sin and of death. 3 What the law could not do since it was limited[j] by the flesh, God did. He condemned sin in the flesh by sending His own Son in flesh like ours under sin's domain,[k] and as a sin offering, 4 in order that the law's requirement would be accomplished in us who do not •walk according to the flesh but according to the Spirit. 5 For those whose lives are[l] according to the flesh think about the things of the flesh, but those

---

[a]**7:7** Ex 20:17   [b]**7:13** Lit good become death to me?   [c]**7:14** Other mss read I am carnal   [d]**7:21** Or law   [e]**7:22** Lit inner man   [f]**7:23** Lit my members   [g]**7:25** Or Thanks be to God—(it is done) through Jesus Christ our Lord!   [h]**8:1** Other mss add who do not walk according to the flesh but according to the Spirit   [i]**8:2** Other mss read me   [j]**8:3** Or weak   [k]**8:3** Lit in the likeness of sinful flesh   [l]**8:5** Or those who are

---

ence, but not license. **new way ... old letter of the law.** The Christian does not serve the law in its crippling and binding details, but he follows the liberating way of the Spirit.

7:8 opportunity. This word describes a military base or the bridgehead from which an assault is launched. **sin.** Paul personifies sin as a great power with an evil intention.

7:9 I died. Though living physically after the law came, Paul fell under its judgment—the sentence of death.

7:13 sin, was producing death in me. Sin reveals its true colors by bringing death through what is good. The law offered life if it was obeyed, but it lacked the power to enable people to overcome sin.

7:24 What a wretched man I am! The nearer people get to God, the more aware they are of how far short they fall. **Who will rescue me?** People are helpless to deliver themselves from sin. They need someone else to rescue them. This is precisely what God has done through Christ (v. 25).

8:1 no condemnation. Christians are free from the guilt that sin produces (and therefore have no anxiety being condemned on the future day of judgment), as well as the enslaving power of sin (so they can live in God's way in the here and now).

8:2 the Spirit's law. The Holy Spirit is the third person of the Trinity who indwells believers in power. In chapter 8, Paul will refer to the Spirit over 20 times—more references to the Spirit than in any other chapter

of the New Testament. **has set you free.** There is at work in believers a power greater than sin—a power that enables them to resist sin. They are no longer slaves of sin.

8:3 the flesh. Human nature was unable to keep God's law. Therefore, the law could not save anyone. In response to this plight, Christ, as God's representative, bore the punishment of sin in place of those who deserved it. **in flesh like ours.** Jesus took on weak human nature, but this did not take away His divine nature. He was fully God and fully man.

8:6 death ... life. The two outlooks lead to two patterns of conduct, which result in two spiritual states—death to God (because sin separates us from Him), or life in the Spirit.

Walking by the Spirit

1. When have you been set free from some rule that applied to others? How did you use your freedom?

Romans 8:1-17

2. What does it mean to "walk according to the flesh" (v. 4)? According to the Spirit?

3. What is the "mind-set of the flesh" (v. 6)? Of the Spirit?

4. What does it mean to "put to death the deeds of the body" (v. 13)? How does a person do this? What is the result?

5. Does the flesh or the Spirit govern your responses when you are facing stress? How can you more fully develop the mind-set of the Spirit?

whose lives are^a according to the Spirit, about the things of the Spirit. ⁶ For the mind-set of the flesh is death, but the mind-set of the Spirit is life and peace. ⁷ For the mind-set of the flesh is hostile to God because it does not submit itself to God's law, for it is unable to do so. ⁸ Those whose lives are^a in the flesh are unable to please God. ⁹ You, however, are not in the flesh, but in the Spirit, since^b the Spirit of God lives in you. But if anyone does not have the Spirit of Christ, he does not belong to Him. ¹⁰ Now if Christ is in you, the body is dead^c because of sin, but the Spirit^d is life because of righteousness. ¹¹ And if the Spirit of Him who raised Jesus from the dead lives in you, then He who raised Christ from the dead will also bring your mortal bodies to life through^e His Spirit who lives in you.

The Holy Spirit's Ministries

¹² So then, brothers, we are not obligated to the flesh to live according to the flesh, ¹³ for if you live according

to the flesh, you are going to die. But if by the Spirit you put to death the deeds of the body, you will live. ¹⁴ All those led by God's Spirit are God's sons. ¹⁵ For you did not receive a spirit of slavery to fall back into fear, but you received the Spirit of adoption, by whom we cry out, "•Abba, Father!" ¹⁶ The Spirit Himself testifies together with our spirit that we are God's children, ¹⁷ and if children, also heirs—heirs of God and co-heirs with Christ—seeing that^b we suffer with Him so that we may also be glorified with Him.

Suffering and Hoping

1. When have you endured suffering in order to gain something you wanted? What was the suffering? Did you get what you wanted?

Romans 8:18-27

2. What are "the sufferings of this present time" (v. 18)? What is "the glory that is going to be revealed to us"?

3. What is it that Christians "hope for" (v. 25)? Why must we wait with patience?

4. How does the Holy Spirit help us in waiting and hoping (v. 26)?

5. In what ways have you been "suffering" lately? How might these sufferings be leading to God's blessings?

From Groans to Glory

¹⁸ For I consider that the sufferings of this present time are not worth comparing with the glory that is going to be revealed to us. ¹⁹ For the creation eagerly waits with anticipation for God's sons to be revealed. ²⁰ For the creation was subjected to futility—not willingly, but because of Him who subjected it—in the hope ²¹ that the creation itself will also be set free from

---

^a**8:5** Or *those who are*   ^b**8:9,17** Or *provided that*   ^c**8:10** Or *the body will die*   ^d**8:10** Or *spirit*   ^e**8:11** Other mss read *because of*

8:13 put to death. In 7:4 Paul says that Christians are dead to the law through Christ's act of dying on the cross in their place. Believers are to "put to death"—the sinful practices they know to be wrong.

8:15 spirit of slavery. The Holy Spirit unites us with Christ, enabling us to share in His sonship. **you received.** The verb tense indicates that this is a one-time, past action—something that happened at conversion. **spirit of adoption.** For a child to be adopted into a new family, he was first symbolically "sold" by his father to the adopting father. Then the legal case for adoption was taken to the magistrate.

8:16 The Spirit Himself testifies. In the Roman adoptive proceedings, there were several witnesses to the ceremony who could

verify that the child had actually been adopted. The Holy Spirit verifies a person's adoption into the family of God.

8:17 heirs. If a person is a child of God, he is an heir, and he will share in God's riches. In fact, Jesus is God's true heir (v. 3). But since believers are "in Christ," they become sons and daughters of God by adoption and thus are joint-heirs with Christ.

8:18 sufferings of this present time. This refers to the persecutions (5:3) that Christians face in the time between Jesus' first coming and His return. These sufferings are minor in comparison with the glory we will experience.

8:19 eagerly waits with anticipation. The

image is of a person scanning the horizon for the first sign of the coming dawn of glory. The only other occurrence of this word in the New Testament is in Philippians 1:20. **for God's sons to be revealed.** Christians are sons and daughters of God in this life. What Paul refers to here is that believers are incognito. At the second coming of Jesus, those who are the children of God will be revealed for everyone to see.

8:20 futility. The inability of creation to achieve the goal for which it was created—glorifying God—because the key actor in this drama of praise (mankind) has fallen. **in hope.** There was divine judgment at the original fall of mankind in Eden, but this was not without hope. One day the woman's offspring would strike the serpent (Gen. 3:15).

the bondage of corruption into the glorious freedom of God's children. 22 For we know that the whole creation has been groaning together with labor pains until now. 23 And not only that, but we ourselves who have the Spirit as the •firstfruits—we also groan within ourselves, eagerly waiting for adoption, the redemption of our bodies. 24 Now in this hope we were saved, yet hope that is seen is not hope, because who hopes for what he sees? 25 But if we hope for what we do not see, we eagerly wait for it with patience.

The Point of Pain

1. When did you experience a painful separation from family or friends? How long did it take to get over it?

Romans 8:28-39

2. What does it mean to be "called according to His purpose" (v. 28)? What people are "called"?
3. According to verse 29, how do "all things work together for the good" (v. 28)? What is the purpose of suffering?
4. If God "did not even spare His own Son" (v. 32), what does that mean about His willingness to bring good into your life?
5. Read verses 38-39. What can separate you from God's love? Is anything left out of that list?

26 In the same way the Spirit also joins to help in our weakness, because we do not know what to pray for as we should, but the Spirit Himself intercedes for us[a] with unspoken groanings. 27 And He who searches the hearts knows the Spirit's mind-set, because He intercedes for the saints according to the will of God.

28 We know that all things work together[b] for the good[c] of those who love God: those who are called according to His purpose. 29 For those He foreknew[d] He also predestined to be conformed to the image of His Son, so that He would be the firstborn among many brothers. 30 And those He predestined, He also called; and those He called, He also justified; and those He justified, He also glorified.

The Believer's Triumph

31 What then are we to say about these things?
If God is for us, who is against us?
32 He did not even spare His own Son,
but offered Him up for us all;
how will He not also with Him grant us everything?
33 Who can bring an accusation
against God's elect?
God is the One who justifies.
34 Who is the one who condemns?
Christ Jesus is the One who died,
but even more, has been raised;
He also is at the right hand of God
and intercedes for us.
35 Who can separate us from the love of Christ?
Can affliction or anguish or persecution
or famine or nakedness or danger or sword?
36 As it is written:
**Because of You we are being put to death
all day long;
we are counted as sheep to be slaughtered.**[e]
37 No, in all these things we are
more than victorious
through Him who loved us.
38 For I am persuaded that neither death nor life,
nor angels nor rulers,
nor things present, nor things to come,
nor powers,
39 nor height, nor depth, nor any other
created thing
will have the power to separate us

---

[a]**8:26** Some mss omit *for us*   [b]**8:28** Other mss read *that God works together in all things*   [c]**8:28** The ultimate good   [d]**8:29** From eternity God knew His people and entered into a personal relationship with them   [e]**8:36** Ps 44:22; see Is 53:7; Zch 11:4,7

8:21 will also be set free. Creation will be freed from its bondage at the second coming of Christ when the children of God are freed from the last vestiges of sin.

8:22 labor pains. Such pain is intense, but it is only temporary. The image is not of the annihilation of the present universe, but of the emergence of a transformed order (Rev. 21:1). Childbirth was a Jewish metaphor for the suffering that would precede the coming of the new age (Isa. 26:17).

8:23 firstfruits. The experience by the believer of the work of the Holy Spirit is a pledge that God will one day grant all He has promised. **we ... groan within ourselves.** Believers' bodies are still subject to weakness, pain, and death. We long for the suffering to end and for the redemption of the body to be complete.

8:28 all things work together. God takes that which is painful (the groans, the persecution, and even death—vv. 35-36) and brings profit out of it. **for the good of those who love God.** This does not mean things work out so believers preserve their comfort and convenience. Rather, such action on God's part enables these difficult experiences to assist in the process of salvation and growth. **those who love God: who are called according to His purpose.** The love that people have for God is a reflection of the reality of God's love for them as expressed in His call to follow Christ.

8:29 foreknew. God knew even before the world was created who would have faith (Eph. 1:4; 2 Tim. 1:9). For God to know someone is for Him to love and have a purpose for that person. **predestined.** God puts into effect what He foreknew. **conformed to**

the image of His Son. While Paul has in mind that time of glorification (when believers will be brought into full conformity to the image of Christ), he is also thinking of sanctification. This is the process by which believers grow closer and closer to the image of Christ.

8:30 called. Foreknowledge and predestination are God's prerogatives. They enter the realm of history at the point of His calling or initiative with each person, bringing that person to hear the gospel and responds in faith. The end result is justification.

8:31 If God ... against us? Paul does not ask, "Who is against us?" In response, many enemies could be named: hostile society, Satan, sin, suffering, and death. Rather, he prefaces the question with an assertion that "God is for us" and then asks, "Who is

from the love of God that is in Christ Jesus our Lord!

Rage or Mercy?

1. When have you unexpectedly received mercy instead of punishment? What did you learn from that experience?

Romans 9:1-29

2. Paul says that not all Jews are children of God (vv. 6-7). Why? Who are the true children of God?

3. What does God mean when He says, "I will show mercy to whom I show mercy" (v. 15)?

4. What does it mean that God's mercy "does not depend on human will or effort" (v. 16)? What does it depend on?

5. Are you a child of God? How can you show mercy to others, as God has shown it to you?

Israel's Rejection of Christ

9 I speak the truth in Christ—I am not lying; my conscience is testifying to me with the Holy Spirit[a]— 2 that I have intense sorrow and continual anguish in my heart. 3 For I could wish that I myself were cursed and cut off[b] from the •Messiah for the benefit of my brothers, my countrymen by physical descent.[c] 4 They are Israelites, and to them belong the adoption, the glory, the covenants, the giving of the law, the temple service, and the promises. 5 The forefathers are theirs, and from them, by physical descent,[d] came the Messiah, who is God over all, blessed forever.[e] •Amen.

God's Gracious Election of Israel

6 But it is not as though the word of God has failed. For not all who are descended from Israel are Israel. 7 Neither are they all children because they are Abraham's descendants.[f] On the contrary, in Isaac your seed will be called.[g] 8 That is, it is not the children by physical descent[h] who are God's children, but the children of the promise are considered seed. 9 For this is the statement of the promise: At this time I will come, and Sarah will have a son.[i] 10 And not only that, but also when Rebekah became pregnant[j] by Isaac our forefather 11 (for though they had not been born yet or done anything good or bad, so that God's purpose according to election might stand, 12 not from works but from the One who calls) she was told: The older will serve the younger.[k] 13 As it is written: Jacob I have loved, but Esau I have hated.[l]

God's Selection Is Just

14 What should we say then? Is there injustice with God? Absolutely not! 15 For He tells Moses:

> I will show mercy to whom I show mercy,
> and I will have compassion on whom
> I have compassion.[m]

16 So then it does not depend on human will or effort,[n] but on God who shows mercy. 17 For the Scripture tells Pharaoh:

> For this reason I raised you up:
> so that I may display My power in you,
> and that My name may be proclaimed
> in all the earth.[o]

18 So then, He shows mercy to whom He wills, and He hardens whom He wills.

19 You will say to me, therefore, "Why then does He still find fault? For who can resist His will?" 20 But who are you—anyone[p] who talks back to God? Will what is formed say to the one who formed it, "Why did you

---

[a]9:1 Or testifying with me by the Holy Spirit [b]9:3 Lit were anathema [c]9:3 Lit countrymen according to the flesh [d]9:5 Lit them, according to the flesh [e]9:5 Or the Messiah, the One who is over all, the God who is blessed forever, or Messiah. God, who is over all, is blessed forever [f]9:7 Lit seed [g]9:7 Gn 21:12 [h]9:8 Lit children of the flesh [i]9:9 Gn 18:10,14 [j]9:10 Or Rebekah conceived by the one act of sexual intercourse [k]9:12 Gn 25:23 [l]9:13 Mal 1:2-3 [m]9:15 Ex 33:19 [n]9:16 Lit on the one willing, or on the one running [o]9:17 Ex 9:16 [p]9:20 Lit you, O man

---

against us?" All potential enemies fade into insignificance.

8:32 not even spare His own Son. Again Paul does not ask, "Will not God give us all things?" He indicates that God has already given the supreme gift—His Son who died on our behalf.

8:33-34 Who can. Paul's next two questions are set in the context of a law court. The point of these questions is that there is no charge that can be leveled against Christians to cause their condemnation, since God is the Judge who has already justified them.

8:35 Who can separate us. In response to this question, Paul names those enemies that might appear powerful enough to separate believers from God's love.

8:37 more than victorious. Literally, superconquerors.

8:38 death ... life. For Paul, to die was not a threat—it was to "be with Christ" (Phil. 1:21-23). Life is used here in the sense of trials, distractions, and enticements that could lead a person away from God. **angels ... rulers.** Continuing his pairing of opposites, Paul says that neither benevolent nor evil spiritual powers need be feared. **present ... to come.** Neither this age nor the events in the future age (after the end time) are to be feared.

8:39 height ... depth. The reference could also be to the influence of a star at the height or depth of its zenith. It may simply mean that neither heaven nor hell can separate Christians from God's love.

9:4 adoption. Israel has a special relationship with God. The word *adoption* emphasizes that this relationship is by grace—a product of God's action and not the result of natural succession. **temple service.** Through the sacrificial system, Israel had special access to God. **promises.** Old Testament prophecies, which emphasized that God had a great and noble task for Israel.

9:8 children of the promise. To be a physical descendant of Abraham is not necessarily to be a part of the true Israel. Paul will soon point out that there has always been a remnant of Jews within the larger nation of Israel who were true to God (11:1-15).

9:15-16 God who shows mercy. Paul used Exodus 33:19 to show the freedom of God's mercy. God is free to offer His mercy to whomever He chooses.

make me like this?" 21 Or has the potter no right over His clay, to make from the same lump one piece of pottery for honor and another for dishonor? 22 And what if God, desiring to display His wrath and to make His power known, endured with much patience objects of wrath ready for destruction? 23 And ₍what if₎ He did this to make known the riches of His glory on objects of mercy that He prepared beforehand for glory— 24 on us whom He also called, not only from the Jews but also from the Gentiles? 25 As He also says in Hosea:

I will call "Not-My-People," "My-People,"
and she who is "Unloved," "Beloved."ᵃ
26 And it will be in the place where
they were told,
you are not My people,
there they will be called
sons of the living God.ᵇ

27 But Isaiah cries out concerning Israel:

Though the number of Israel's sons is like
the sand of the sea,
only the remnant will be saved;
28 for the Lord will execute His sentence
completely and decisively on the earth.ᶜ ᵈ

29 And just as Isaiah predicted:

If the Lord of Hostsᵉ had not left us a seed,
we would have become like Sodom,
and we would have been made
like Gomorrah.ᶠ

Israel's Present State

30 What should we say then? Gentiles, who did not pursue righteousness, have obtained righteousness— namely the righteousness that comes from faith. 31 But Israel, pursuing the law for righteousness, has not achieved the law.ᵍ 32 Why is that? Because they did not pursue it by faith, but as if it were by works.ʰ They stumbled over the stumbling stone. 33 As it is written:

Look! I am putting a stone in Zion
to stumble over,
and a rock to trip over,
yet the one who believes on Him will not
be put to shame.ⁱ

Calling Heaven's Number

1. When have you called on someone in authority for help? Did you get the help you needed? Why did you need it in the first place?

Romans 9:30–10:21
2. What is the only way to be saved, according to Paul in 10:9-10? How does this compare with other religious teachings? With the teachings of the world around you?
3. What does it mean to "call on the name of the Lord" (10:13)?
4. What does verse 14 suggest about the importance of sharing Jesus with others? How often do you tell others about Jesus? How can you do this more often?

Righteousness by Faith Alone

10 Brothers, my heart's desire and prayer to God concerning themʲ is for their salvation! 2 I can testify about them that they have zeal for God, but not according to knowledge. 3 Because they disregarded the righteousness from God and attempted to establish their own righteousness, they have not submitted to God's righteousness. 4 For Christ is the endᵏ of the law for righteousness to everyone who believes. 5 For Moses writes about the righteousness that is from the law: **The one who does these things**

ᵃ**9:25** Hs 2:23 ᵇ**9:26** Hs 1:10 ᶜ**9:28** Or *land* ᵈ**9:27–28** Is 10:22–23; 28:22; Hs 1:10 ᵉ**9:29** Gk *Sabaoth*; this word is a transliteration of the Hb word for *Hosts*, or *Armies*. ᶠ**9:29** Is 1:9 ᵍ**9:31** Other mss read *the law for righteousness* ʰ**9:32** Other mss add *of the law* ⁱ**9:33** Is 8:14; 28:16 ʲ**10:1** Other mss read *God for Israel* ᵏ**10:4** Or *goal*

9:21 has the potter no right over his clay...? Paul draws on an image that both Isaiah and Jeremiah used in picturing the relationship of God to human beings. The clay is what it is. It doesn't argue with the potter about how it is shaped. One of the illusions that sin creates is that we can show that God is unjust. Even Job, whom God characterized as a man of perfect integrity (Job 1:1), thought he could bring God to court and demonstrate that God had treated him unfairly. Through an agonizing process Job learned what it means that God is God and we are not. As people whose minds and hearts have been corrupted by sin, we have difficulty grasping the infinite distance between God and ourselves. Only by God's mercy do we begin to recognize how totally dependent we are on Him for everything.

9:22 objects of wrath ready for destruc-

tion. The Greek verb translated "ready" carries the sense that destruction is the natural outcome for objects of wrath.

9:23 objects of mercy that He prepared beforehand for mercy. The Greek verb translated "prepared beforehand" is a different Greek work than is translated "ready" in v. 22. While v. 22 has the connotation that destruction is the natural course of objects of wrath, v. 23 gives the sense that for objects of mercy there has been an interruption to change the outcome from destruction to glory. In their commentary on Romans, Ken Boa and William Kruidenier ask us to "picture the flow of God's action, before any mercy is exercised, as a river. His justice sees that all people are flowing in the direction of judgment. That is his will because it is consistent with his justice. None in the flow of that river are resisting his will because there

are none who seek God. It is the flow (the purpose) of his will that is carrying them along, and all are acting in concert with his will, not resisting his will. God is not standing on the banks crying out for them to turn to him and be saved, only to discover that they are resisting his will. When his purpose for some changes, and his hand of mercy is extended to them, they are given a new heart, a clean heart, and are saved willingly. The not-chosen do not remain where they are against either their own will or God's will. Therefore, none resist his will."

9:27 only the remnant will be saved. Remnant is a key Bible concept. A remnant is something left over, especially the righteous people of God after divine judgment. Several activities of everyday life are associated with these words. Objects or people may be separated from a larger group by

will live by them.[a] 6 But the righteousness that comes from faith speaks like this: **Do not say in your heart, "Who will go up to heaven?"[b]** that is, to bring Christ down 7 or, **"Who will go down into the •abyss?"[c]** that is, to bring Christ up from the dead. 8 On the contrary, what does it say? **The message is near you, in your mouth and in your heart.[d]** This is the message of faith that we proclaim: 9 if you confess with your mouth, "Jesus is Lord," and believe in your heart that God raised Him from the dead, you will be saved. 10 With the heart one believes, resulting in righteousness, and with the mouth one confesses, resulting in salvation. 11 Now the Scripture says, **No one who believes on Him will be put to shame,[e]** 12 for there is no distinction between Jew and Greek, since the same Lord of all is rich to all who call on Him. 13 For **everyone who calls on the name of the Lord will be saved.[f]**

Israel's Rejection of the Message

14 But how can they call on Him in whom they have not believed? And how can they believe without hearing about Him? And how can they hear without a preacher? 15 And how can they preach unless they are sent? As it is written: **How welcome[g] are the feet of those[h] who announce the gospel of good things![i]** 16 But all did not obey the gospel. For Isaiah says, **Lord, who has believed our message?[j]** 17 So faith comes from what is heard, and what is heard comes through the message about Christ.[k] 18 But I ask, "Did they not hear?" Yes, they did:

> **Their voice has gone out to all the earth, and their words to the ends of the inhabited world.[l]**

19 But I ask, "Did Israel not understand?" First, Moses said:

> **I will make you jealous of those who are not a nation;**

I will make you angry by a nation that lacks understanding.[m]

20 And Isaiah says boldly:

> **I was found by those who were not looking for Me;**
> **I revealed Myself to those who were not asking for Me.[n]**

21 But to Israel he says: **All day long I have spread out My hands to a disobedient and defiant people.[o]**

Works vs. Faith

1. When have you fallen for a trap: In sports? From a friend or enemy? What did you learn?

Romans 11:1-36

2. How can good works "become a snare and a trap" (v. 9)?

3. How do you balance works and grace? What can good works never accomplish? In what ways are works still important?

4. Are you relying more on performance of rituals than on God's grace? Are you taking God's grace for granted?

5. What are you depending on for your own salvation? Are you obedient even though you've been saved by faith?

Israel's Rejection Not Total

11 I ask, then, has God rejected His people? Absolutely not! For I too am an Israelite, a descendant of Abraham, from the tribe of Benjamin. 2 God has not rejected His people whom He foreknew. Or do you

---

a**10:5** Lv 18:5   b**10:6** Dt 9:4; 30:12   c**10:7** Dt 30:13   d**10:8** Dt 30:14   e**10:11** Is 28:16   f**10:13** Jl 2:32   g**10:15** Or *timely, or beautiful*   h**10:15** Other mss read *feet of those who announce the gospel of peace, of those*   i**10:15** Is 52:7; Nah 1:15   j**10:16** Is 53:1   k**10:17** Other mss read *God*   l**10:18** Ps 19:4   m**10:19** Dt 32:21   n**10:20** Is 65:1   o**10:21** Is 65:2

---

selection, assignment, consumption (eating food), or by destruction. What is left over is the residue, or, in the case of people, those who remain after an epidemic, famine, drought, or war. One of the first cases of this in the Bible is God's saving Noah and his family from the flood. In this verse, Paul makes a distinction between Israel and the remnant who will be saved out of Israel.

9:32 stumbling stone. Jesus identifies Himself as "the stone that the builders rejected" (Ps. 118:22-23; Matt. 21:42). In not recognizing Jesus as the inner meaning of the law, Israel can do little else than stumble over Him.

10:6 Who will go up to heaven? This phrase means that Israel does not have to go all the way up to heaven to find God's law

(Deut. 30:12). The righteousness of the law is found in Christ—Christ had come to them. Now, righteousness is obtained only through our faith.

10:7 bring Christ up. There is no need to bring Christ up from the dead, since He has already been inside the abyss after His death on the cross. He conquered sin and death, and then was raised from the dead.

10:12 no distinction. In 3:23, when Jews and non-Jews are discussed, the emphasis is negative—all are sinners. Here, the positive comparison is given: The Lord is available to all people who call on Him.

10:15 preach. This means to proclaim like a herald. Proclamation or preaching came to refer to declaring the gospel message of Jesus' salvation to all who believe (16:28-

26).

11:1 I too am an Israelite. Paul, who remains a zealous Jew who happens to be a believing Christian, is proof that God has not cast off Israel. He is still using Israel, through Paul and others, to fulfill its God-given task of bearing God's redemptive message to the world.

11:5 remnant. There was always at least a small number of people who were true to God. Through history, God has preserved a faithful remnant of His people even in wicked times. They were like a nation within a nation.

11:7 Israel did not find what it was looking for. The nation of Israel was looking for righteousness, but they thought they earned righteous by keeping the law. The blood of

not know what the Scripture says in the Elijah section—how he pleads with God against Israel?

3 Lord, they have killed Your prophets,
  torn down Your altars;
and I am the only one left, and they are trying
  to take my life![a]

[4] But what was God's reply to him? I have left 7,000 men for Myself who have not bowed down to Baal.[b] [5] In the same way, then, there is also at the present time a remnant chosen by grace. [6] Now if by grace, then it is not by works; otherwise grace ceases to be grace.[c]

[7] What then? Israel did not find what it was looking for, but the elect did find it. The rest were hardened, [8] as it is written:

God gave them a spirit of stupor,
eyes that cannot see and ears
  that cannot hear, to this day.[d]

[9] And David says:

Let their feasting[e] become a snare and a trap,
  a pitfall and a retribution to them.
[10] Let their eyes be darkened
  so they cannot see,
and their backs be bent continually.[f]

Israel's Rejection Not Final

[11] I ask, then, have they stumbled so as to fall? Absolutely not! On the contrary, by their stumbling,[g] salvation has come to the Gentiles to make Israel[h] jealous. [12] Now if their stumbling[g] brings riches for the world, and their failure riches for the Gentiles, how much more will their full number bring!

[13] Now I am speaking to you Gentiles. In view of the fact that I am an apostle to the Gentiles, I magnify my ministry, [14] if I can somehow make my own people[i] jealous and save some of them. [15] For if their being rejected is world reconciliation, what will their acceptance mean but life from the dead? [16] Now if the •firstfruits

offered up are holy, so is the whole batch. And if the root is holy, so are the branches.

[17] Now if some of the branches were broken off, and you, though a wild olive branch, were grafted in among them, and have come to share in the rich root[j] of the cultivated olive tree, [18] do not brag that you are better than those branches. But if you do brag—you do not sustain the root, but the root sustains you. [19] Then you will say, "Branches were broken off so that I might be grafted in." [20] True enough; they were broken off by unbelief, but you stand by faith. Do not be arrogant, but be afraid. [21] For if God did not spare the natural branches, He will not spare you either. [22] Therefore, consider God's kindness and severity: severity toward those who have fallen, but God's kindness toward you—if you remain in His kindness. Otherwise you too will be cut off. [23] And even they, if they do not remain in unbelief, will be grafted in, because God has the power to graft them in again. [24] For if you were cut off from your native wild olive, and against nature were grafted into a cultivated olive tree, how much more will these—the natural branches—be grafted into their own olive tree?

[25] So that you will not be conceited, brothers, I do not want you to be unaware of this •mystery: a partial hardening has come to Israel until the full number of the Gentiles has come in. [26] And in this way all[k] Israel will be saved, as it is written:

The Liberator will come from Zion;
He will turn away godlessness from Jacob.
[27] And this will be My covenant with them,[l]
  when I take away their sins.[m]

[28] Regarding the gospel, they are enemies for your advantage, but regarding election, they are loved because of their forefathers, [29] since God's gracious gifts and calling are irrevocable.[n] [30] As you once disobeyed God, but now have received mercy through their disobedience, [31] so they too have now disobeyed, [resulting] in mercy to you, so that they also now[o] may

---

[a]11:3 1 Kg 19:10,14   [b]11:4 1 Kg 19:18   [c]11:6 Other mss add *But if of works it is no longer grace; otherwise work is no longer work.*   [d]11:8 Dt 29:4; Is 29:10   [e]11:9 Lit *table*   [f]11:9–10 Ps 69:22–23   [g]11:11,12 Or *transgression*   [h]11:11 Lit *them*   [i]11:14 Lit *flesh*   [j]11:17 Other mss read *the root and the richness*   [k]11:26 Or *And then all*   [l]11:26–27 Is 59:20–21   [m]11:27 Jr 31:31–34   [n]11:29 Or *are not taken back*   [o]11:31 Other mss omit *now*

Jesus is now the channel through which righteousness is obtained.

11:14 jealous. Jealousy or envy is usually something that is negative. In this case it brings about good. **save.** God's goal was to convert people to the Christian faith and redeem them.

11:17 branches ... broken off. Paul is referring here to unbelieving Israel. **a wild olive.** The Gentile (non-Jewish) Christians. **among them.** The Jewish Christians.

11:25 mystery. This is something that is hidden in the mind of God, but which He is now pleased to reveal to all who are willing to seek Him.

12:1 by the mercies of God. Paul has just declared God's amazing mercy (11:30-32).

A Christian's motivation to obedience is gratitude for God's mercy. **bodies.** The Christian lifestyle is not a matter of mystical spirituality that transcends one's bodily nature, but an everyday, practical exercise of love (6:13). The idea of "bodies" also emphasizes the metaphor of sacrifice, since animal bodies were put on the altar. **living ... holy ... pleasing to God.** In Greek, these three phrases are attached with equal weight as requirements for "sacrifices."

12:2 Do not be conformed. Literally, "stop allowing yourself to be conformed." Believers are no longer helpless victims of natural and supernatural forces that shape them into a distorted pattern; they now have the ability and help to resist such powers. **be transformed.** The force of the verb is "continue to let yourself be transformed"—a continuous action by the Holy Spirit that goes on for a

lifetime. A Christian's responsibility is to stay open to this sanctification process as the Spirit works to teach him or her to look at life from God's view of reality. **renewing of your mind.** Developing a spiritual sensitivity and perception—learning to look at life on the basis of God's view of reality. Paul emphasizes the need to develop understanding of God's ways. **so that you may discern.** Christians are called to a responsible freedom of choice and action, based on the inner renewing work of the Holy Spirit.

12:3 everyone among you. The truth about spiritual gifts applies to every believer. **think sensibly.** The command is to know oneself accurately rather than to have too high an opinion of oneself in comparison to others.

12:5 we who are many are one body in Christ. Paul is speaking here of believers in

receive mercy. ³² For God has imprisoned all in disobedience, so that He may have mercy on all.

A Hymn of Praise

³³ Oh, the depth of the riches
both of the wisdom and the knowledge of God!
How unsearchable His judgments
and untraceable His ways!

³⁴ **For who has known the mind of the Lord?**
Or who has been His counselor?

³⁵ **Or who has ever first given to Him,**
and has to be repaid?ᵃ

³⁶ For from Him and through Him and to Him
are all things.
To Him be the glory forever. •Amen.

A Living Sacrifice

12 Therefore, brothers, by the mercies of God, I urge you to present your bodies as a living sacrifice, holy and pleasing to God; this is your spiritual worship.ᵇ ² Do not be conformed to this age, but be transformed by the renewing of your mind, so that you may discern what is the good, pleasing, and perfect will of God.

Many Gifts but One Body

³ For by the grace given to me, I tell everyone among you not to think of himself more highly than he should think. Instead, think sensibly, as God has distributed a measure of faith to each one. ⁴ Now as we have many parts in one body, and all the parts do not have the same function, ⁵ in the same way we who are many are one body in Christ and individually members of one another. ⁶ According to the grace given to us, we have different gifts:

If prophecy, use it according to the standard of faith;

⁷ if service, in service; if teaching, in teaching;

⁸ if exhorting, in exhortation; giving,
with generosity;
leading, with diligence; showing mercy,
with cheerfulness.

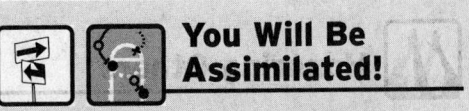

You Will Be Assimilated!

1. When have you thought of yourself more highly than you should have? How did you discover your error?

Romans 12:1-8

2. What does Paul mean in verse 2 when he says, "Do not be conformed to this age, but be transformed by the renewing of your mind"?

3. How can you offer your body "as a living sacrifice" (v. 1)?

4. According to this passage, what is required of you to discover God's will for your life?

5. How much are you conforming to the world's standards? Are you working to transform your mind to God's way of thinking?

Christian Ethics

⁹ Love must be without hypocrisy. Detest evil; cling to what is good. ¹⁰ Show family affection to one another with brotherly love. Outdo one another in showing honor. ¹¹ Do not lack diligence; be fervent in spirit; serve the Lord. ¹² Rejoice in hope; be patient in affliction; be persistent in prayer. ¹³ Share with the saints in their needs; pursue hospitality. ¹⁴ Bless those who persecute you; bless and do not curse. ¹⁵ Rejoice with those who rejoice; weep with those who weep. ¹⁶ Be in agreement with one another. Do not be proud; instead, associate with the humble. Do not be wise in your own estimation. ¹⁷ Do not repay anyone evil for evil. Try to do what is honorable in everyone's eyes. ¹⁸ If possible, on your part, live at peace with everyone. ¹⁹ Friends, do not avenge yourselves; instead, leave room for Hisᶜ wrath. For it is written: **Vengeance belongs to Me; I will repay,**ᵈ says the Lord. ²⁰ But

---

ᵃ**11:34-35** Is 40:13; Jb 41:11; Jr 23:18   ᵇ**12:1** Or *your reasonable service*   ᶜ**12:19** Lit *the*   ᵈ**12:19** Dt 32:35

---

the church, the body of Christ. The church is like a family. Although individual members of the family are distinct and different, they belong to one another because of the common Lord whom they serve.

12:6 gifts. Those endowments given by God to every believer by grace (the words *grace* and *gifts* come from the same root word) to be used in God's service. The gifts listed here (or elsewhere in the New Testament) are not meant to be exhaustive or absolute since no gift list overlaps completely. **prophecy.** Inspired utterances, distinguished from teaching by their immediacy and spontaneous nature, the source of which is direct revelation by God.

12:7 service. The special capacity for rendering practical service to the needy. **teaching.** In contrast to the prophet (with direct revelation from God), the teacher relied on

the Old Testament Scriptures and the teachings of Jesus to instruct others.

12:8 exhorting. This is supporting and assisting others to live a life of obedience to God. **giving.** A person with this gift takes delight in giving away his or her possessions. **leading.** Those with special ability to guide a congregation are called upon to do so with zeal. **showing mercy.** Serving those who need care with cheerfulness.

12:9 Love. The Greek word *agape*—self-giving love in action on behalf of others—which is made possible by God's Spirit. **without hypocrisy.** Genuine, not counterfeit or showy.

12:10 brotherly love. The word for love used here, *philadelphia*, denotes the tender affection expressed in families, now said to

be appropriate to those in the church—which is the believer's new family. **honor.** Since other Christians are in union with Christ, they are to be honored.

12:11 be fervent. This Greek word is also used of water when it has been brought to a boil (or of metal, like copper, which glows red-hot in the refining or shaping process).

13:1 Everyone. That is, every Christian in Rome; no one is exempt. **submit.** Submission must be understood in light of 12:10 (honoring others above oneself) and Philippians 2:3-4 (considering others as more important). Christians must recognize the God-given claim that the authorities have upon them.

13:3-4 government is God's servant. Paul,

Honoring Others

1. To whom do you find yourself showing real honor? Why do you honor that person? How do you express it?

Romans 12:9-21

2. How do we sometimes show love with hypocrisy (v. 9)? What does love without hypocrisy look like?

3. What does it mean to "outdo one another in showing honor" (v. 10)? How can we honor others in this way?

4. What can you do this week, in a practical way, to "live at peace" with someone who irritates you?

5. How are you sometimes "wise in your own estimation" (v. 16)? How can you avoid this?

> If your enemy is hungry, feed him.
> If he is thirsty, give him something to drink.
> For in so doing you will be heaping fiery coals on his head.ᵃ

21 Do not be conquered by evil, but conquer evil with good.

A Christian's Duties to the State

13 Everyone must submit to the governing authorities, for there is no authority except from God, and those that exist are instituted by God. 2 So then, the one who resists the authority is opposing God's command, and those who oppose it will bring judgment on themselves. 3 For rulers are not a terror to good conduct, but to bad. Do you want to be unafraid of the authority? Do good and you will have its approval. 4 For government is God's servant to you for good. But if you do wrong, be afraid, because it does not carry the sword for no reason.

For government is God's servant, an avenger that brings wrath on the one who does wrong. 5 Therefore, you must submit, not only because of wrath, but also because of your conscience. 6 And for this reason you pay taxes, since the ₍authorities₎ are God's public servants, continually attending to these tasks.ᵇ 7 Pay your obligations to everyone: taxes to those you owe taxes, tolls to those you owe tolls, respect to those you owe respect, and honor to those you owe honor.

God-given Authority

1. What is the closest you have come to having a "run-in" with the police?

Romans 13:1-7

2. What does it mean that all authorities "are instituted by God" (v. 1)? What about people who abuse their authority? Those who are incompetent?

3. According to this passage, what should our response be to all people in authority over us?

4. If a law passed by Congress was contrary to God's law, what would you do?

5. Do you ever try to cheat on taxes, tolls, and school or team rules? What does Paul say about this?

Love Our Primary Duty

8 Do not owe anyone anything,ᶜ except to love one another, for the one who loves another has fulfilled the law. 9 The commandments:

> Do not commit adultery,
> do not murder,
> do not steal,ᵈ
> do not covet,ᵉ

ᵃ**12:20** Pr 25:21–22   ᵇ**13:6** Lit to this very thing   ᶜ**13:8** Or Leave no debt outstanding to anyone   ᵈ**13:9** Other mss add you shall not bear false witness   ᵉ**13:9** Ex 20:13–17; Dt 5:17–21

---

both a Roman citizen and a Jew, was not being naïve when he wrote this. Although he grew up in Tarsus of Cilicia, he lived in Jerusalem as a student of Gamaliel. From his wide reading and first hand experience he knew the character of the Roman emperors and he was aware of the suffering of occupied peoples at the hands of Roman authorities. Christians had lived under Caligula (A.D. 37–41) and Claudius (A.D 41–54). As Paul wrote this letter (A.D. 57), Nero was 18 and had been Emperor for three years. How can these pagans be God's servant and why should Christians submit to them? The answer lies in the sovereignty of God. God brought the Roman emperors to power and he deposed of them. **an avenger that brings wrath.** Governments can't make bad people good but they can use force to restrain evil. That's what God has charged them to do whether they know it or not.

13:5 submit...because of wrath. Paul gives two motivations for submitting to the government. The first is to avoid punishment. **because of your conscience.** A higher motive for submission is to maintain a clear conscience. Although a clear conscience is not infallible, a bad conscience will adversely affect one's relationship with God, with fellow believers and with those outside the family of faith.

13:7 taxes. Local taxes such as duty, import and export taxes, taxes for the use of roads or for the right to drive a cart, etc.

13:10 love...the fulfillment of the law. Jesus summarized the law with two love-commands (Matt 22:37,39).

13:11 time. Although the distinction is not absolute, there are two words in the NT that

emphasize these two dimensions of time. Chronos is the Greek term usually referring simply to the chronological measurement of time, while kairos usually refers to the spiritual significance of an era (Rom. 5:6, 13:11; Titus 1:3; Rev. 1:3). Christians should be careful to discern the meaning and significance of their time, comprehending both the reality of evil and the movement of God in history. **salvation.** Here understood as a divine event that will take place at a particular time in the future. Although a person enters into salvation upon conversion, this is a state to be realized fully only when Christ returns at the second coming.

13:12 night. The present age. **daylight.** The coming age inaugurated by Christ's second coming, in which God's new order will appear. **the daylight is near.** The early church understood that the life, death, and

and if there is any other commandment—all are summed up by this: **You shall love your neighbor as yourself.**[a]

The Power of Love

1. Who supports you with their love?

Romans 13:8-14

2. How does love fulfill all of the other commandments (v. 9)?

3. The Bible teaches us to love others as we love ourselves. How does this compare with the world's teaching that we must love ourselves?

4. Paul says, "Love does no wrong to a neighbor" (v. 10). How does this compare with the world's teaching that we should look after our own interests?

5. What does it mean to "walk with decency" (v. 13)?

6. How can you work harder at loving others more than yourself?

[10] Love does no wrong to a neighbor. Love, therefore, is the fulfillment of the law.

Put On Christ

[11] Besides this, knowing the time, it is already the hour for you[b] to wake up from sleep, for now our salvation is nearer than when we first believed. [12] The night is nearly over, and the daylight is near, so let us discard the deeds of darkness and put on the armor of light. [13] Let us •walk with decency, as in the daylight: not in carousing and drunkenness; not in sexual impurity and promiscuity; not in quarreling and jealousy. [14] But put on the Lord Jesus Christ, and make no plans to satisfy the fleshly desires.

The Law of Liberty

14 Accept anyone who is weak in faith,[c] but don't argue about doubtful issues. [2] One person believes he may eat anything, but one who is weak eats only vegetables. [3] One who eats must not look down on one who does not eat; and one who does not eat must not criticize one who does, because God has accepted him. [4] Who are you to criticize another's household slave? Before his own Lord he stands or falls. And stand he will! For the Lord is able[d] to make him stand.

Doubtful Issues

1. What foods do you avoid eating? Why? What foods do you eat freely?

Romans 14:1-15:13

2. Why does Paul say, "don't argue about doubtful issues" (v. 1)? How do you know the difference between "doubtful issues" and important ones?

3. What are some issues that Christians have argued about in your church? Are any of those "doubtful issues"?

4. If someone disagrees with you about a "doubtful issue," what is the correct response: To argue back? To give up your rights for his or her benefit? Other?

5. Do you use Christian liberty as an excuse to do what you want? Why or why not?

[5] One person considers one day to be above another day. Someone else considers every day to be the same. Each one must be fully convinced in his own mind. [6] Whoever observes the day, observes it to the Lord.[e] Whoever eats, eats to the Lord, since he gives thanks to God; and whoever does not eat, it is to the Lord that he

---

---

resurrection of Jesus had ushered in the last days—the end time. But because of His patience, God had provided an interval before the culmination of the "night," in order to allow other people to come to faith. During this interval Christians are to remain alert and expectant, knowing that the second coming may occur at any time. **armor of light.** Character and behavior that a person obtains from God and which will also be appropriate to wear when the new age dawns (Eph. 6:11-12).

13:13 sexual impurity. In the first century, prior to Christianity, chastity or sexual purity was almost unknown and was not considered a virtue by most people. **promiscuity.** Public display, without shame, of immoral acts. **quarreling.** The desire for power and prestige demonstrated by a willingness to

stir up trouble if one is not in charge. **jealousy.** Envy that begrudges another's place or gifts.

14:1 Accept anyone. This is the basic imperative addressed to the "strong" majority in the church: receive the "weak" into fellowship. **anyone who is weak in faith.** Those who are not sure their faith is adequate to do certain things. The issue is not a lack of faith in Christ. Both the "weak" and the "strong" are authentically Christian. **doubtful issues.** Do not judge the principles of others that are not essential to following Christ.

14:3 look down ... criticize. Two forms of judgment: the tendency of the "strong" not to take seriously the moral convictions of the weak (to laugh at them or even to despise them); and the tendency of the "weak" to act

superior and become hypercritical (because they felt that not doing certain things made them better Christians). Both attitudes are wrong. **God has accepted him.** The person who abstains cannot condemn those who indulge, since no one should judge a person whom God has accepted.

14:13 stumbling block. A new theme is introduced into the discussion: the liberty of the strong can be detrimental to others. What appears to the strong as an innocent action may cause the more scrupulous or morally rigid people to suffer pain, shock, outrage, or even hurt.

14:14 I know and am persuaded. Paul comes down clearly on the side of the "strong" (see Mark 7:15). **unclean.** That is, in the ritual sense. There is no food that has power to harm a person's relationship with

does not eat, yet he thanks God. [7] For none of us lives to himself, and no one dies to himself. [8] If we live, we live to the Lord; and if we die, we die to the Lord. Therefore, whether we live or die, we belong to the Lord. [9] Christ died and came to life for this: that He might rule over both the dead and the living. [10] But you, why do you criticize your brother? Or you, why do you look down on your brother? For we will all stand before the judgment seat of God.[a] [11] For it is written:

As I live, says the Lord,
every knee will bow to Me,
and every tongue will give praise to God.[b]

[12] So then, each of us will give an account of himself to God.

The Law of Love

[13] Therefore, let us no longer criticize one another, but instead decide not to put a stumbling block or pitfall in your brother's way. [14] (I know and am persuaded by the Lord Jesus that nothing is unclean in itself. Still, to someone who considers a thing to be unclean, to that one it is unclean.) [15] For if your brother is hurt by what you eat, you are no longer •walking according to love. By what you eat, do not destroy that one for whom Christ died. [16] Therefore, do not let your good be slandered, [17] for the kingdom of God is not eating and drinking, but righteousness, peace, and joy in the Holy Spirit. [18] Whoever serves the •Messiah in this way is acceptable to God and approved by men.

[19] So then, we must pursue what promotes peace and what builds up one another. [20] Do not tear down God's work because of food. Everything is clean, but it is wrong for a man to cause stumbling by what he eats. [21] It is a noble thing not to eat meat, or drink wine, or do anything that makes your brother stumble.[c] [22] Do you have faith? Keep it to yourself before God. Blessed is the man who does not condemn himself by what he approves. [23] But whoever doubts stands condemned if he eats, because his eating is not from faith, and everything that is not from faith is sin.

Pleasing Others, Not Ourselves

15 Now we who are strong have an obligation to bear the weaknesses of those without strength, and not to please ourselves. [2] Each one of us must please his neighbor for his good, in order to build him up. [3] For even the •Messiah did not please Himself. On the contrary, as it is written, **The insults of those who insult You have fallen on Me.**[d] [4] For whatever was written before was written for our instruction, so that through our endurance and through the encouragement of the Scriptures we may have hope. [5] Now may the God of endurance and encouragement grant you agreement with one another, according to Christ Jesus, [6] so that you may glorify the God and Father of our Lord Jesus Christ with a united mind and voice.

Glorifying God Together

[7] Therefore accept one another, just as the Messiah also accepted you, to the glory of God. [8] Now I say that Christ has become a servant of the circumcised[e] on behalf of the truth of God, to confirm the promises to the fathers, [9] and so that Gentiles may glorify God for His mercy. As it is written:

Therefore I will praise You
among the Gentiles,
and I will sing psalms to Your name.[f]

[10] Again it says: Rejoice, you Gentiles, with His people![g] [11] And again:

Praise the Lord, all you Gentiles;
all the peoples should praise Him![h]

[12] And again, Isaiah says:

The root of Jesse will appear,
the One who rises to rule the Gentiles;
in Him the Gentiles will hope.[i]

[13] Now may the God of hope fill you with all joy and peace in believing, so that you may overflow with hope by the power of the Holy Spirit.

---

[a]**14:10** Other mss read *of Christ*   [b]**14:11** Is 45:23; 49:18   [c]**14:21** Other mss add *or offended or weakened*   [d]**15:3** Ps 69:9   [e]**15:8** The Jews
[f]**15:9** 2 Sm 22:50; Ps 18:49   [g]**15:10** Dt 32:43   [h]**15:11** Ps 117:1   [i]**15:12** Is 11:10

God. who considers a thing to be unclean. For those believers who have not been convinced that Christ abolished the ceremonial law of the Old Testament (even though the food is not objectively unclean), it is subjectively unclean for that person.

14:15 walking according to love. If the "strong" exercise their liberty even when they know such actions are considered sinful by the "weak," they are failing to act lovingly toward them. To do so jeopardizes the faith of the weak and disturbs the delicate harmony of the body of Christian believers. To act lovingly is more vital than exercising one's freedom. **destroy.** By exercising this liberty, it is possible that the weaker Christian could be caused great harm in his faith.

14:17-18 the kingdom of God is not eating. Such matters as eating or drinking are trivial in kingdom terms; to cause spiritual

ruin over such minor issues is scandalous.

14:19 builds up one another. Our pursuits must be focused on helping individual Christians and the church body to grow in faith and practice.

14:21 a noble thing. The "strong" are called on not to eat or drink when doing so would cause harm. **drink wine.** The Bible does not specifically forbid the drinking of wine except for priests on duty (Lev. 10:9) or for Nazirites (Num. 6:2-3), but drunkenness is clearly condemned. Wisdom suggests abstinence from strong drink as a logical precaution against falling into sin.

14:23 faith. Here faith signifies a sort of inner freedom or liberty that comes from knowing that what one is doing is in accord with Christian faith in general. **sin.** When a Christian acts without a sense of inner liberty, such

an act, even though in itself morally neutral (neither inherently bad or good), is sin to that believer.

15:1 we who are strong. Paul is not talking about physical strength but about conscience. Some believers' consciences allow them options on nonessential issues. Paul was such a believer. He was able to eat meat that had been offered to idols and then sold in the market place at Corinth (1 Cor. 8). Some believers, who were new to the faith or had worshiped idols, would feel guilty if they ate meat that had been offered to idols. The principle Paul articulates is that the strong need to be mindful of the weak and not flaunt their strong conscience before them.

15:3 the Messiah did not please Himself. Jesus is our model in these matters. He did

Future Plans

1. What things are you most tempted to boast about? What are you most likely not to boast about?

Romans 15:14-33

2. What motivates and inspires Paul (vv. 16-22)? What motivates and inspires you?

3. What is Paul's "aim" in life (v. 20)? What is your aim in life? How concerned are you about the needs of others?

4. How fully are you presently fulfilling God's will for your life? What can you do to be more fully obedient?

5. In your plans for the future, how much does God's will fit in? How much do your own desires fit in?

From Jerusalem to Illyricum

[14] Now, my brothers, I myself am convinced about you that you also are full of goodness, filled with all knowledge, and able to instruct one another. [15] Nevertheless, to remind you, I have written to you more boldly on some points[a] because of the grace given me by God [16] to be a minister of Christ Jesus to the Gentiles, serving as a priest of God's good news. My purpose is that the offering of the Gentiles may be acceptable, sanctified by the Holy Spirit. [17] Therefore I have reason to boast in Christ Jesus regarding what pertains to God. [18] For I would not dare say anything except what Christ has accomplished through me to make the Gentiles obedient by word and deed, [19] by the power of miraculous signs and wonders, and by the power of God's Spirit. As a result, I have fully proclaimed the good news about the Messiah from Jerusalem all the way around to Illyricum.[b] [20] So my aim is to evangelize where Christ has not been named, in order that I will not be building on someone else's foundation, [21] but, as it is written:

> Those who had no report of Him will see,
> and those who have not heard
> will understand.[c]

Paul's Travel Plans

[22] That is why I have been prevented many times from coming to you. [23] But now I no longer have any work to do in these provinces,[d] and I have strongly desired for many years to come to you [24] whenever I travel to Spain.[e] For I do hope to see you when I pass through, and to be sent on my way there by you, once I have first enjoyed your company for a while. [25] Now, however, I am traveling to Jerusalem to serve the saints; [26] for Macedonia and Achaia[f] were pleased to make a contribution to the poor among the saints in Jerusalem. [27] Yes, they were pleased, and they are indebted to them. For if the Gentiles have shared in their spiritual benefits, then they are obligated to minister to Jews[g] in material needs. [28] So when I have finished this and safely delivered the funds[h] to them, I will go by way of you to Spain. [29] But I know that when I come to you, I will come in the fullness of the blessing[i] of Christ.

[30] Now I implore you, brothers, through the Lord Jesus Christ and through the love of the Spirit, to agonize together with me in your prayers to God on my behalf: [31] that I may be rescued from the unbelievers in Judea, that my service for Jerusalem may be acceptable to the saints, [32] and that, by God's will, I may come to you with joy and be refreshed together with you.

[33] The God of peace be with all of you. •Amen.

Paul's Commendation of Phoebe

16 I commend to you our sister Phoebe, who is a servant[j] of the church in Cenchreae. [2] So you

---

[a]**15:15** Other mss add *brothers* [b]**15:19** A Roman province northwest of Greece on the eastern shore of the Adriatic Sea [c]**15:21** Is 52:15 [d]**15:23** Lit *now, having no longer a place in these parts* [e]**15:24** Other mss add *I will come to you.* [f]**15:26** The churches of these provinces [g]**15:27** Lit *to them* [h]**15:28** Lit *delivered this fruit* [i]**15:29** Other mss add *of the gospel* [j]**16:1** Others interpret this term in a technical sense: *deacon,* or *deaconess,* or *minister*

---

not come to be served but to be a servant. Paul quote Psalm 69 that foreshadows the Messiah. This is the second most frequently quoted psalm is in the New Testament.

15:14 you also are full. These are not words of flattery designed to win over a hostile audience. One sentence would hardly suffice in light of the preceding chapters. Paul seems to feel that writing such specific instructions for behavior (as he has done in 12:1–15:13) to a church he has never visited might seem overly bold (v. 15), even presumptuous. So he hastens to assure the Roman Christians that he does consider them to be mature Christians.

15:24 Spain. The Roman colony of Spain was situated at the edge of the civilized world—no doubt the reason why Paul's pioneering spirit was drawn there.

15:25-27 the poor among the saints. The collection for the poor in Jerusalem is like a debt in Paul's thinking. When he was commissioned by the church to serve as the apostle to the Gentiles, they requested that he remember the poor (Gal. 2:10).

15:26 Macedonia and Achaia. Two Roman provinces located south of Illyricum, on a peninsula bordering the Adriatic and Aegean Seas (in the region of modern Greece).

16:1-2 I commend ... Phoebe. Phoebe probably carried Paul's letter from Corinth to the church at Rome. Typical in letters of his day, Paul includes a note of commendation in which he makes two requests: that they receive Phoebe as a sister in the Lord, and that they assist her because she has helped many others. Phoebe was probably a woman of wealth and influence who had committed herself to God's kingdom.

16:3-16 Of the 26 people named in these verses, at least four are women. Thirteen of these names occur in manuscripts or inscriptions related to the imperial household, giving rise to speculation that the gospel of Christ had penetrated even into the royal palace (Phil. 4:22).

16:3-5 Prisca and Aquila. Aquila, a Jew born in Pontus in Asia Minor, and his wife Priscilla appear regularly in the New Testament. They are often involved in Paul's work of sharing Christ, planting new churches, and training new converts.

16:5 the church ... in their home. During the first two centuries, there were no special church buildings, so Christians met in the

Smooth Talkers

1. When have you seen someone causing problems with "bad mouthing" and negative talk: On you team? In your school? In your own life?

Romans 16:1-27

2. What does it mean to "cause dissensions and pitfalls" (v. 17)? How can a person cause such things just by talking?

3. What does it mean to serve "their own appetites" (v. 18)? Do you sometimes do this?

4. How can "smooth talk and flattering words" (v. 18) actually deceive people? When have you seen this happen? How can you guard against being deceived?

should welcome her in the Lord in a manner worthy of the saints, and assist her in whatever matter she may require your help. For indeed she has been a benefactor of many—and of me also.

Greeting to Roman Christians

3 Give my greetings to Prisca[a] and Aquila, my co-workers in Christ Jesus, 4 who risked their own necks for my life. Not only do I thank them, but so do all the Gentile churches.

5 Greet also the church that meets in their home. Greet my dear friend Epaenetus, who is the first convert[b] to Christ from Asia.[c]

6 Greet Mary,[d] who has worked very hard for you.[e]

7 Greet Andronicus and Junia,[f] my fellow countrymen and fellow prisoners. They are outstanding among the apostles, and they were also in Christ before me.

8 Greet Ampliatus, my dear friend in the Lord.

9 Greet Urbanus, our co-worker in Christ, and my dear friend Stachys.

10 Greet Apelles, who is approved in Christ. Greet those who belong to the household of Aristobulus.

11 Greet Herodion, my fellow countryman. Greet those who belong to the household of Narcissus who are in the Lord.

12 Greet Tryphaena and Tryphosa, who have worked hard in the Lord. Greet my dear friend Persis, who has worked very hard in the Lord.

13 Greet Rufus, chosen in the Lord; also his mother—and mine.

14 Greet Asyncritus, Phlegon, Hermes, Patrobas, Hermas, and the brothers who are with them.

15 Greet Philologus and Julia, Nereus and his sister, and Olympas, and all the saints who are with them.

16 Greet one another with a holy kiss. All the churches of Christ send you greetings.

Warning against Divisive People

17 Now I implore you, brothers, watch out for those who cause dissensions and pitfalls contrary to the doctrine you have learned. Avoid them; 18 for such people do not serve our Lord Christ but their own appetites,[g] and by smooth talk and flattering words they deceive the hearts of the unsuspecting.

Paul's Gracious Conclusion

19 The report of your obedience has reached everyone. Therefore I rejoice over you. But I want you to be wise about what is good, yet innocent about what is evil. 20 The God of peace will soon crush Satan under your feet. The grace of our Lord Jesus be with you.

21 Timothy, my co-worker, and Lucius, Jason, and Sosipater, my fellow countrymen, greet you.

22 I Tertius, who penned this epistle in the Lord, greet you.

homes of their members (1 Cor. 16:19; Col. 4:15; Philem. 2). The growth of these churches was overwhelming.

16:13 Rufus. Quite possibly the son of Simon of Cyrene, who carried Jesus' cross. Simon is identified (Mark 15:21) as the father of Alexander and Rufus.

16:17 watch out for those who cause dissensions. Paul must have heard that some troublemakers were causing a problem in the church at Rome. The nature of this problem is a mystery. Even at this early point in Christian history, the church was not perfect. Believers must act decisively to protect the

harmony and fellowship of the church.

16:22 Tertius. The only time the name of one of Paul's secretaries is revealed.

16:23 Gaius. This name is mentioned several times in the New Testament. It probably refers to the Gaius mentioned in 1 Corinthians 1:14, with whom Paul was staying in Corinth while he wrote this letter to the Romans.

16:25-27 to Him who has power. This closing doxology is a single, complex sentence in which God is praised for the salvation that He freely offers in Christ Jesus.

16:25 the sacred secret. In the New Testament, this refers to truths about God's plan that were unknown until God disclosed them. They are insights about God that could not be achieved through reasoning or deduction (1 Cor. 1:18-20), but are known solely because God has revealed them.

16:26 the obedience of faith among all nations. This is the goal of the gospel message: it is for all nations, not just for the Jews. Since Jesus' death and resurrection, people of all backgrounds and nationalities are invited to become the people of God.

23 Gaius, who is host to me and to the whole church, greets you. Erastus, the city treasurer, and our brother Quartus greet you.

[24 The grace of our Lord Jesus Christ be with you all.]ᵃ

Glory to God

25 Now to Him who has power to strengthen you according to my gospel and the proclamation of Jesus Christ, according to the revelation of the sacred secret kept silent for long ages, 26 but now revealed and made known through the prophetic Scriptures, according to the command of the eternal God, to advance the obedience of faith among all nations— 27 to the only wise God, through Jesus Christ—to Him be the glory forever!ᵇ •Amen.

ᵃ**16:24** Other mss omit bracketed text; see v. 20   ᵇ**16:25–27** Other mss have these vv. at the end of chap 14 or 15.

INTRODUCTION TO
1 CORINTHIANS

AUTHOR

The writer is the Apostle Paul.

DATE

Paul wrote 1 Corinthians sometime between A.D. 53-55.

THEME

Christian lifestyle in a pagan society.

PURPOSE

First Corinthians is a practical, issue-oriented letter in which Paul tells his readers what they ought or ought not to do. Paul's typical pattern in other letters is to begin with a strong theological statement and then to follow up by applying this insight to daily life. But that is not the case in the letter, which has come to be known as 1 Corinthians. Here we find little direct theological teaching. Rather Paul discusses, in turn, a number of practical life issues.

The problem was that these proud, materialistic, independent ex-pagans were having a most difficult time learning how to live as Christians. It was at this level of lifestyle that paganism directed its attack on the newly emerging Christian faith. Christian behavior was the underlying issue. Where were the lines to be drawn? How much of one's culture had to be abandoned to become a Christian? Residual paganism was mounting a frontal attack on Christianity. If Christianity lost in Corinth, its existence would be threatened throughout the Roman Empire.

So just as he did in Galatians, when residual Judaism attacked Christianity over the issue of whether or not one must keep the law, Paul struck back decisively and directly with this letter to the Corinthians.

HISTORICAL BACKGROUND

Paul visited Corinth during his second missionary journey, probably in A.D. 50. Having been in some peril in Macedonia, he fled by ship to Athens (Acts 17:1-15). Not meeting with great success there (Acts 17:16-34), he then journeyed the short distance to Corinth where he met Priscilla and Aquila (Acts 18:1-3). At first he preached in the synagogue with some success (even the ruler of the synagogue was won to Christ). But then the Jews forced him to leave, so he moved next door into the home of a Gentile. Hoping to silence him, the Jews eventually hauled Paul before the governor Gallio, but Gallio threw the case out of court as having no merit. After some 18 months (his longest stay anywhere except Ephesus), Paul left and continued his missionary work in Syria.

Two events sparked the writing of 1 Corinthians some three or four years later. First, Paul heard that a divisive spirit was loose in the church (1 Cor. 1:11). Second, he received a letter in which the Corinthians asked him questions about marriage and other matters (1 Cor. 7:1). In addition, a delegation from Corinth completed his knowledge of the problems there (1 Cor. 16:15-17). Being unable to visit Corinth personally, Paul sought to deal with the issues by letter. Thus the Corinthian correspondence was begun.

THE CITY OF CORINTH

Corinth was an unusual city. After its capture by the Roman legions in 146 B.C., the city was leveled. It lay in ruins for nearly 100 years until Julius Caesar rebuilt it in 44 B.C. Then it grew rapidly, thanks largely to its unique geographical location. Because it lay at the neck of a narrow isthmus connecting the Peloponnesus with central Greece, it controlled all north-south land traffic. To the east and the west of the city were two fine harbors. Both goods and ships were hauled across the four-mile-wide isthmus of Corinth. Thus Corinth also controlled most east-west sea routes. This strategic location commanded wealth and influence. By the time of Paul's visit some 100 years after its rebuilding, Corinth had become the capital of the province of Achaia and the third most important city in the Roman Empire, after Rome and Alexandria.

In this wealthy young city, excess seemed to be the norm. The city was stocked with art purchased from around the Roman Empire. It became a center of philosophy, though apparently few citizens were seriously interested in studying philosophy, preferring rather to listen to stirring orations on faddish topics delivered by the city's numerous itinerant philosophers. Even in religion, this excess was obvious. The Greek author Pausanias describes 26 pagan shrines and temples including the great temples of Apollo and Aphrodite. In Old Corinth, 1,000 temple prostitutes had served Aphrodite, the goddess of love, and New Corinth continued this tradition of sexual worship practices. The city developed a worldwide reputation for vice and debauchery.

Luxury was the hallmark of Corinth. Because storms in the Aegean Sea were frequent and treacherous, sailors preferred to put into one of the harbors and transport their ship overland to the other harbor, despite the exorbitant tolls charged by the Corinthians. Consequently, goods from around the world passed through Corinthian ports, and some 400,000 slaves were kept in the city to provide the labor for this arduous job.

Into Corinth flowed people from around the Roman Empire. There were "Greek adventurers and Roman bourgeois, with a tainting infusion of Phoenicians, a mass of Jews, ex-soldiers, philosophers, merchants, sailors, freed men, slaves, tradespeople, hucksters and agents of every form of vice" (Farrar, quoted by William Barclay, *The Letters to the Corinthians*, p. 4). Not surprisingly, it was in Corinth that Paul had to fight this battle to prevent Christianity from giving in to debilitating enticements offered by paganism.

PASSAGES FOR TOPICAL GROUP STUDY

1:10-17	CLIQUES and DIVISIONS	Divided We Fall
1:18–2:5	STANDING FOR YOUR FAITH	Looking Foolish
2:6-16	THE MIND OF CHRIST	Conflicting Spirits
4:1-21	TREATED BADLY	The World's Garbage
5:1-13	SEXUALITY	Sex and the Christian
6:1-11	HEAVEN OR HELL	Judging Others
6:12-20	SEXUAL TEMPTATION	Run From Sex
7:1-40	MARRIAGE and DIVORCE	The Question of Marriage
8:1-13	CHOICES and CHRISTIAN LIBERTY	Careful Choices
9:24-27	DISCIPLINE AND TRAINING	The Ultimate Qualification
10:1-13	SESUAL PURITY	Standing and falling
11:2-16	GENDER ROLES	Roles of Men and Women
11:17-34	THE LORD'S SUPPER	Evaluate Yourself
12:12-31	UNIQUENESS and TEAMWORK	All for One
13:1-13	LOVING OTHERS	True Love
14:26-40	ORDERLY WORSHIP	Order vs. Chaos
15:1-11	PEER PRESSURE and STAYING TRUE	Holding Firm
15:12-34	RESURRECTION	THE Vital Statistic
15:35-58	VICTORY OVER SIN AND DEATH	Victory Over Death
16:1-24	BRAVERY and PRESSURE	Bravery Under Fire

PASSAGES FOR GENERAL GROUP STUDY

3:1-23	Building with Gold (God's Co-workers in Building Eternity)	
10:14–11:1	Handling Our Freedom as Christians	
14:1-25	Gifted and Talented (Spiritual Gifts)	

Greeting

1 Paul, called as an apostle of Christ Jesus by God's will, and our brother Sosthenes:

² To God's church at Corinth, to those who are sanctified in Christ Jesus and called as saints, with all those in every place who call on the name of Jesus Christ our Lord—theirs and ours.

³ Grace to you and peace from God our Father and the Lord Jesus Christ.

Divided We Fall

1. When there is an argument, do you quickly take sides or do you try to stay out of it? How do you decide?

1 Corinthians 1:10-17

2. Reading between the lines, what would seem to be causing the arguments and division in the Corinthian church?

3. Why does Paul suggest (v. 12) that it's wrong to say, "I'm with so and so" ... even "I'm with Christ"?

4. Why are cliques and divisions, especially within the church, so damaging to the Christian community (vv. 10,13,17)?

5. What issues cause the biggest division between people in your school? Your church? Your group or team?

Thanksgiving

⁴ I always thank my God for you because of God's grace given to you in Christ Jesus, ⁵ that by Him you were made rich in everything—in all speaking and all knowledge— ⁶ as the testimony about Christ was confirmed among you, ⁷ so that you do not lack any spiritual gift as you eagerly wait for the revelation of our Lord Jesus Christ. ⁸ He will also confirm you to the end, blameless in the day of our Lord Jesus Christ. ⁹ God is faithful; by Him you were called into fellowship with His Son, Jesus Christ our Lord.

Divisions at Corinth

¹⁰ Now I urge you, brothers, in the name of our Lord Jesus Christ, that you all say the same thing, that there be no divisions among you, and that you be united with the same understanding and the same conviction. ¹¹ For it has been reported to me about you, my brothers, by members of Chloe's household, that there are quarrels among you. ¹² What I am saying is this: each of you says, "I'm with Paul," or "I'm with Apollos," or "I'm with •Cephas," or "I'm with Christ." ¹³ Is Christ divided? Was it Paul who was crucified for you? Or were you baptized in Paul's name? ¹⁴ I thank Godᵃ ᵇ that I baptized none of you except Crispus and Gaius, ¹⁵ so that no one can say you had been baptized in my name. ¹⁶ I did, in fact, baptize the household of Stephanas; beyond that, I don't know if I baptized anyone else. ¹⁷ For Christ did not send me to baptize, but to preach the gospel—not with clever words, so that the cross of Christ will not be emptied ₍of its effect₎.

Christ the Power and Wisdom of God

¹⁸ For to those who are perishing the message of the cross is foolishness, but to us who are being saved it is God's power. ¹⁹ For it is written:

> I will destroy the wisdom of the wise,
> and I will set aside the understanding
> of the experts.ᶜ

²⁰ Where is the philosopher?ᵈ Where is the scholar? Where is the debater of this age? Hasn't God made the world's wisdom foolish? ²¹ For since, in God's wisdom, the world did not know God through wisdom, God was pleased to save those who believe through the foolishness of the message preached. ²² For the Jews ask for

---

ᵃ**1:14** Other mss omit *God*   ᵇ**1:14** Or *I am thankful*   ᶜ**1:19** Is 29:14   ᵈ**1:20** Or *wise*

1:1 an apostle. Paul does not always identify himself an apostle: "one who is sent," an office held by those who witnessed the resurrected Christ (1 Thess. 1:1). He may have done so here because his authority as an apostle was an issue with the Corinthians. **Sosthenes.** Possibly mentioned in Acts 18:17.

1:2 sanctified. Dedicated to God's service. **as saints.** Set apart to serve God's purposes. All believers are saints, holy persons.

1:3 Grace to you. Grace is the unmerited gift of God by which a person receives salvation.

1:7 spiritual gift. *Charismata,* special gifts given by God to build up the church. **revelation.** Literally, the unveiling of Jesus Christ as He comes in glory.

1:10 divisions. *Schismata* ("schism"); a word often used to describe an incision in a piece of clothing. **united.** Their disunity is rooted in differing ideas (doctrines).

1:11 Chloe's household. Paul is writing from Ephesus. The slaves (or freedmen) of an Ephesian woman named Chloe had visited Corinth and brought back the story of disunity there.

1:12 I'm with Paul. Paul does not commend those "on his side." No better than any other faction, these people had probably exaggerated and falsified his actual viewpoints. (This was probably the Gentile party.) **I'm with Apollos.** After he had been instructed in the gospel by Priscilla and Aquila, Apollos, a bright, articulate Jew from Alexandria with great skill in debate (Acts 18:24-28), went to Corinth to assist the church there. A natural

leader for those who attempted to intellectualize Christianity. **I'm with Cephas.** Cephas is the Jewish form of the name Peter, who probably visited Corinth. This faction would have been oriented toward a more Jewish Christianity. **I'm with Christ.** Possibly those who look with disdain on the others who profess allegiance to the Christ preached by Paul, Apollos, or Cephas. In other words, "holier-than-thou." This may even be a mystical or Gnostic-like party, given to inner visions and revelations.

1:17 clever words. *Sophia,* the Greek word for "wisdom" is a key word in 1 Corinthians, which Paul uses in both positive and negative ways. Here the idea is the negative use of human reason with a view to convincing the hearer of a position. **the cross of Christ will not be emptied.** Paul is eager that people be persuaded by the actual truth and

Looking Foolish

1. When have you felt or looked foolish for believing something that others didn't believe? What was your belief? Was it true or false?

1 Corinthians 1:18-2:5

2. Who are those "who are being saved" (v. 18)? Why "being saved," rather than "saved"?

3. How has "God made the world's wisdom foolish" (v. 20)? What *is* the "world's wisdom"? What is God's wisdom?

4. How is "Christ crucified ... foolishness to the Gentiles" (v. 23)?

5. On what issue do you need to take a stand for your faith, even though you might look foolish?

signs and the Greeks seek wisdom, 23 but we preach Christ crucified, a stumbling block to the Jews and foolishness to the Gentiles.ª 24 Yet to those who are called, both Jews and Greeks, Christ is God's power and God's wisdom, 25 because God's foolishness is wiser than human wisdom, and God's weakness is stronger than human strength.

Boasting Only in the Lord

26 Brothers, consider your calling: not many are wise from a human perspective,ᵇ not many powerful, not many of noble birth. 27 Instead, God has chosen the world's foolish things to shame the wise, and God has chosen the world's weak things to shame the strong. 28 God has chosen the world's insignificant and despised things—the things viewed as nothing—so He might bring to nothing the things that are viewed as something, 29 so that no oneᶜ can boast in His presence.

30 But from Him you are in Christ Jesus, who for us became wisdom from God, as well as righteousness, sanctification, and redemption, 31 in order that, as it is written: **The one who boasts must boast in the Lord.**ᵈ

Paul's Proclamation

2 When I came to you, brothers, announcing the testimonyᵉ of God to you, I did not come with brilliance of speech or wisdom. 2 For I determined to know nothing among you except Jesus Christ and Him crucified. 3 And I was with you in weakness, in fear, and in much trembling. 4 My speech and my proclamation were not with persuasive words of wisdom,ᶠ but with a demonstration of the Spirit and power, 5 so that your faith might not be based on men's wisdom but on God's power.

Conflicting Spirits

1. What is your favorite mystery movie or book? Who is your favorite fictional detective?

1 Corinthians 2:6-16

2. What does it mean that "we speak God's hidden wisdom in a mystery" (v. 7)? What is the "mystery" to which Paul is referring?

3. What is the "spirit of the world" (v. 12)? How does it compare with the "Spirit who is from God"?

4. What is "the mind of Christ" (v. 16)? What do you need to do to have Christ's wisdom more fully in your life?

5. Whose spirit governs your decisions: the spirit of the world or of God? Why?

ª**1:23** Other mss read *Greeks*   ᵇ**1:26** Lit *wise according to the flesh*   ᶜ**1:29** Lit *that not all flesh*   ᵈ**1:31** Jr 9:24   ᵉ**2:1** Other mss read *mystery*
ᶠ**2:4** Other mss read *human wisdom*

---

not mere eloquence.

1:18 foolishness. It is absurd to many that God's redemptive activity involves death by crucifixion. **perishing.** Unless they repent (turn around and go the other way), they will not be acquitted on the Day of Judgment. **being saved.** Salvation is a process, begun at conversion, consummated at the second coming of Jesus, and fulfilled in heaven .

1:22 Jews ask for signs. The Jews expected a divine-warrior Messiah of megamiracles, not a Jesus executed by His enemies. **Greeks seek wisdom.** Their delight was in clever, cunning logic delivered with compelling persuasiveness.

1:23 stumbling block. Literally, a scandal. Jesus' crucifixion "proved" to the Jews that He could not be of God (Deut. 21:23 says

those hanging from a tree are cursed of God). A suffering, dying Messiah was totally outside first-century Jewish expectations. **foolishness.** Both Jesus' incarnation (human birth) and His crucifixion were actions that Greeks felt were unworthy of their gods.

1:26 consider your calling. In their own calling they see the paradox of the all-powerful God using the "weak things of the world." **not many.** The early church had special appeal to the poor and to those with little social standing. This was part of its offensiveness—the "wrong" people were attracted to it. **wise.** This refers to people with education or philosophical training. **powerful.** This means people in high positions politically or socially. **noble birth.** These were people of distinguished families who may have held Roman citizenship.

1:28 the things viewed as nothing ... the

things that are viewed as something. God chooses "nobodies" and thus exposes the foolishness of the way the world defines "somebodies."

1:30 But from Him. They owe the fact that they are related to God solely to Jesus Christ. **wisdom from God.** God's plan of salvation through Christ. **righteousness.** Christ is their righteousness in that He took upon Himself the guilt of human sin. On the Last Day when Christians stand before the Judge, they are viewed not in terms of their own failure and inadequacy but as being "in Christ." **sanctification.** Christ provides the holiness people lack enabling them to appear before God. **redemption.** It is by Christ's redeeming work on the cross that wisdom, righteousness, and holiness are mediated to humankind.

2:4 a demonstration of the Spirit and

Spiritual Wisdom

6 However, among the mature we do speak a wisdom, but not a wisdom of this age, or of the rulers of this age, who are coming to nothing. 7 On the contrary, we speak God's hidden wisdom in a •mystery, which God predestined before the ages for our glory. 8 None of the rulers of this age knew it, for if they had known it, they would not have crucified the Lord of glory. 9 But as it is written:

> What no eye has seen and no ear has heard,
> and what has never come into a man's heart,
> is what God has prepared for those
> who love Him.[a]

10 Now God has revealed them to us by the Spirit, for the Spirit searches everything, even the deep things of God. 11 For who among men knows the concerns[b] of a man except the spirit of the man that is in him? In the same way, no one knows the concerns[b] of God except the Spirit of God. 12 Now we have not received the spirit of the world, but the Spirit who is from God, in order to know what has been freely given to us by God. 13 We also speak these things, not in words taught by human wisdom, but in those taught by the Spirit, explaining spiritual things to spiritual people.[c] 14 But the natural man does not welcome what comes from God's Spirit, because it is foolishness to him; he is not able to know it since it is evaluated[d] spiritually. 15 The spiritual person, however, can evaluate[e] everything, yet he himself cannot be evaluated[d] by anyone. 16 For:

> who has known the Lord's mind,
> that he may instruct Him?[f]

But we have the mind of Christ.

The Problem of Immaturity

3 Brothers, I was not able to speak to you as spiritual people but as people of the flesh, as babies in Christ. 2 I fed you milk, not solid food, because you were not yet able to receive it. In fact, you are still not able, 3 because you are still fleshly. For since there is

envy and strife[g] among you, are you not fleshly and living like ordinary people?[h] 4 For whenever someone says, "I'm with Paul," and another, "I'm with Apollos," are you not typical men?[i]

Building with Gold

1. Did you ever plant a garden? What did you grow? Who did most of the weeding? Watering? Harvesting?

1 Corinthians 3:1-23

2. What is Paul saying about Christian workers in verses 5-8? How does this apply to different "jobs" and ministries in the church?

3. What does it mean that "we are God's co-workers" (v. 9)?

4. What kinds of work are like "gold, silver, costly stones" (v. 12)? What are like "wood, hay, or straw"?

5. Name one thing you can do this week to build "God's sanctuary" (you) with the gems of holiness (vv. 16-17).

The Role of God's Servants

5 So, what is Apollos? And what is Paul? They are servants through whom you believed, and each has the role the Lord has given. 6 I planted, Apollos watered, but God gave the growth. 7 So then neither the one who plants nor the one who waters is anything, but only God who gives the growth. 8 Now the one who plants and the one who waters are equal, and each will receive his own reward according to his own labor. 9 For we are God's co-workers. You are God's field, God's building. 10 According to God's grace that was given to me, as a skilled master builder I have laid a foundation, and another builds on it. But each one must

---

a 2:9 Is 52:15; 64:4   b 2:11 Lit things   c 2:13 Or things with spiritual words   d 2:14,15 Or judged, or discerned   e 2:15 Or judge, or discern
f 2:16 Is 40:13   g 3:3 Other mss add and divisions   h 3:3 Lit and walking according to man   i 3:4 Other mss read are you not carnal

---

power. People were moved by the convicting power of the Holy Spirit.

2:6 we do speak a wisdom. Not the false wisdom in 1:17. **mature.** A potential that all Christians have (Col. 1:28) though not all experience (3:1). **wisdom of this age.** "This age" is person-centered and corrupted by rebellion against God, while "the age to come" is when God's kingdom will be present and visible.

2:7 God's hidden wisdom. In contrast to the "wisdom of the world" no one could have guessed God's plan. Even when it was revealed, many shunned it as "foolish" and/or scandalous (1:23).

2:10 by the Spirit. Insight not by reasoning but as a result of revelation. **the Spirit searches everything.** In Corinth, people

believed one could discover the nature of God through philosophy. Paul indicates that only the Spirit communicates accurate knowledge about God.

2:12 the spirit of the world. An equivalent phrase to "the wisdom of this age" (v. 6). **has been freely given to us.** These gifts of God (v. 9) are not merely for the future, but are the present experience of Christians.

3:1 people of the flesh. Immature Christians who are molded more by the spirit of the age than by the Spirit of God.

3:3 ordinary people By exalting certain teachers, they betray their lack of understanding of the gospel. Paul's point is that although they have the Spirit, they are acting precisely like people without the Spirit.

3:6 Apollos watered. Paul preached salvation. Apollos gave instruction on holy living.

3:10 master builder. (In Greek, architekton.) The one who plans and supervises the construction of a building, not a laborer. **I have laid a foundation.** By preaching Christ the foundation (vv. 6, 11).

3:12 gold, silver, costly stones. These works or materials will survive the test of fire. **wood, hay, or straw.** These are inferior or inadequate materials: works that will burn up.

3:13 the day. On the Day of Judgment the quality of labor will be revealed. **revealed by fire.** The idea is not of fire as punishment, but as a means of testing the "quality of each one's work."

3:16 sanctuary. This reference is not to individual believers' bodies as the temple of the Spirit; that comes in 6:19. The sanctuary is the community they are becoming—wher-

be careful how he builds on it, [11] because no one can lay any other foundation than what has been laid—that is, Jesus Christ. [12] If anyone builds on the foundation with gold, silver, costly stones, wood, hay, or straw, [13] each one's work will become obvious, for the day[a] will disclose it, because it will be revealed by fire; the fire will test the quality of each one's work. [14] If anyone's work that he has built survives, he will receive a reward. [15] If anyone's work is burned up, it will be lost, but he will be saved; yet it will be like an escape through fire.[b]

[16] Don't you know that you are God's sanctuary and that the Spirit of God lives in you? [17] If anyone ruins God's sanctuary, God will ruin him; for God's sanctuary is holy, and that is what you are.

The Folly of Human Wisdom

[18] No one should deceive himself. If anyone among you thinks he is wise in this age, he must become foolish so that he can become wise. [19] For the wisdom of this world is foolishness with God, since it is written: **He catches the wise in their craftiness**[c] — [20] and again, **The Lord knows the reasonings of the wise, that they are futile.**[d] [21] So no one should boast in men, for all things are yours: [22] whether Paul or Apollos or •Cephas or the world or life or death or things present or things to come—all are yours, [23] and you belong to Christ, and Christ to God.

The Faithful Manager

4 A person should consider us in this way: as servants of Christ and managers of God's •mysteries. [2] In this regard, it is expected of managers that each one be found faithful. [3] It is of little importance that I should be evaluated by you or by a human court.[e] In fact, I don't even evaluate myself. [4] For I am not conscious of anything against myself, but I am not justified by this. The One who evaluates me is the Lord. [5] Therefore don't judge anything prematurely, before the Lord comes, who will both bring to light what is hidden in darkness and reveal the intentions of the hearts. And then praise will come to each one from God.

The World's Garbage

1. Are you a pack rat, or do you easily get rid of things? What item do you still have from your childhood?

1 Corinthians 4:1-21

2. What does Paul mean in verse 3? When are the opinions of other people unimportant? When are they important?

3. Why does Paul emphasize humility so often? How does the realization in verse 7 bring true humility?

4. In what way was Jesus treated "like the world's garbage, like the filth of all things" (v. 13)?

5. When have others treated you like "garbage" due to your faith? How did you react? How can Paul's counsel help you deal with this?

The Apostles' Example of Humility

[6] Now, brothers, I have applied these things to myself and Apollos for your benefit, so that you may learn from us the saying: "Nothing beyond what is written."[f] The purpose is that none of you will be inflated with pride in favor of one person over another. [7] For who makes you so superior? What do you have that you didn't receive? If, in fact, you did receive it, why do you boast as if you hadn't received it? [8] Already you are full! Already you are rich! You have begun to reign as kings without us—and I wish you did reign, so that we also could reign with you! [9] For I think God has displayed us, the apostles, in last place, like men condemned to die: we have become a spectacle to the world and to angels and to men. [10] We are fools for Christ, but you are wise in Christ! We are weak, but you are strong! You are distinguished, but we are dishonored! [11] Up to the present hour we are both hungry and thirsty; we are poorly

---

[a]3:13 The Day of Christ's judgment of believers [b]3:15 Lit *yet so as through fire* [c]3:19 Jb 5:13 [d]3:20 Ps 94:11 [e]4:3 Lit *a human day* [f]4:6 The words in quotation marks could refer to the OT, a Jewish maxim, or a popular proverb.

---

ever it gathered—a particularly vivid and exciting image for the Corinthians, surrounded as they were by pagan temples, because Paul shows them that God's Spirit is creating a new people.

3:17 ruins. The idea has shifted from losing one's pay for having used inferior building materials (vv. 12-15) to being punished for destroying the church.

4:1 A person should consider us in this way. How Christians should relate to their ministers or church leaders. **servants of Christ.** First and foremost, a minister who does the work given him or her under Christ's authority. **managers.** Literally, stewards. In a Greek household this was the slave who directed the staff, saw to securing supplies, and, in effect, ran the entire household for his master. **God's mysteries.** As in

2:7, these are the plans of God once known only by Him, but now revealed to all. It is the minister's task to share and coordinate work in accord with these mysteries.

4:3-4 evaluated. Neither the Corinthians nor Paul himself is fit to judge Paul's faithfulness as God's steward. Only God can; and Paul is content to rest in that knowledge and not let criticism bother him.

4:5 before the Lord comes. At the second coming of Christ, the Day of Judgment will occur. Paul cautions about making premature judgments. Let the Lord judge. He is the only one able to do it properly. **intentions.** Not just actions but also one's personal intentions will be made plain when Christ returns.

4:8 Already. The Corinthians are acting as if

the kingdom of God itself had already arrived. **we also could reign with you.** Paul wishes they were right because, in fact, his present experience was quite grim (vv. 11-12; 2 Cor. 6:4-10).

4:9 condemned to die. The image is of the triumphal return of a Roman general who parades before the people his trophies who will be taken into the arena to fight and die.

4:10 fools for Christ. By the standards of the world's wisdom, Paul is indeed foolish. This is the pathway to God's wisdom (3:18). **you are wise in Christ.** In ironic contrast Paul points out that the worldly Corinthians are acting as if they are wise and superior. **We are weak.** In fact, in God's economy, weakness is strength. Christ came not as a conquering hero, but to be crucified as a common criminal. In the suffering Savior one

clothed, roughly treated, homeless; ¹²we labor, working with our own hands. When we are reviled, we bless; when we are persecuted, we endure it; ¹³when we are slandered, we entreat. We are, even now, like the world's garbage, like the filth of all things.

Paul's Fatherly Care

¹⁴ I'm not writing this to shame you, but to warn you as my dear children. ¹⁵For you can have 10,000 instructors in Christ, but you can't have many fathers. Now I have fathered you in Christ Jesus through the gospel. ¹⁶Therefore I urge you, be imitators of me. ¹⁷This is why I have sent to you Timothy, who is my beloved and faithful child in the Lord. He will remind you about my ways in Christ Jesus, just as I teach everywhere in every church. ¹⁸Now some are inflated with pride, as though I were not coming to you. ¹⁹But I will come to you soon, if the Lord wills, and I will know not the talk but the power of those who are inflated with pride. ²⁰For the kingdom of God is not in talk but in power. ²¹What do you want? Should I come to you with a rod, or in love and a spirit of gentleness?

Immoral Church Members

5 It is widely reported that there is sexual immorality among you, and the kind of sexual immorality that is not even condoned[a] among the Gentiles—a man is living with his father's wife. ²And you are inflated with pride, instead of filled with grief so that he who has committed this act might be removed from among you. ³For though absent in body but present in spirit, I have already decided about him who has done this thing as though I were present. ⁴In the name of our Lord Jesus, when you are assembled, along with my spirit and with the power of our Lord Jesus, ⁵turn that one over to Satan for the destruction of the flesh, so that his spirit may be saved in the Day of the Lord.

⁶ Your boasting is not good. Don't you know that a little yeast permeates the whole batch of dough? ⁷Clean out the old yeast so that you may be a new batch, since you are unleavened. For Christ our •Passover has been sacrificed.[b] ⁸Therefore, let us observe the feast, not

Sex and the Christian

1. What do you think of the dress code at your school? What would you change?

1 Corinthians 5:1-13
2. How can handing someone over to Satan result in that person's salvation on the Day of the Lord (v. 5)?
3. What happens when Christians are more concerned with judging those around them than with evaluating their own behavior and motives?
4. What distinction does Paul draw between sexually immoral Christians and non-Christians? Why is the Christian treated more severely?
5. Are you examining your own life or comparing yourself with others, especially in the area of sexual morality?

with old yeast, or with the yeast of malice and evil, but with the unleavened bread of sincerity and truth.

Church Discipline

⁹ I wrote to you in a letter not to associate with sexually immoral people— ¹⁰by no means referring to this world's immoral people, or to the greedy and swindlers, or to idolaters; otherwise you would have to leave the world. ¹¹But now I am writing[c] you not to associate with anyone who bears the name of brother who is sexually immoral or greedy, an idolater or a reviler, a drunkard or a swindler. Do not even eat with such a person. ¹²For what is it to me to judge outsiders? Do you not judge those who are inside? ¹³But God judges outsiders. **Put away the evil person from among yourselves.**[d]

Lawsuits among Believers

6 Does any of you who has a complaint against someone dare go to law before the unrighteous,[e]

---

a**5:1** Other mss read *named*   b**5:7** Other mss add *for us*   c**5:11** Or *now I wrote*   d**5:13** Dt 17:7   e**6:1** Unbelievers; see v. 6

---

finds the model for the Christian life.

4:12 we labor. Covering all of his expenses by making tents, sometimes with the tent-making missionary couple Aquila and Priscilla (Acts 18:3; 20:34).

4:14-21 Paul ends the section begun in 1:10. The Corinthians preference for worldly wisdom has resulted in patronizing their missionaries and ministers and in attempting to play them off against one another. In this context, Paul uses the metaphor of a father correcting his children.

4:14 to shame you. Indeed, though Corinthians ought to be blushing in acute distress over their ungodliness, it is not shame Paul intends. **warn.** The word means, "to admonish" as a father might do, in hope that his children will see their error.

4:16 be imitators of me. They can look to Paul: a servant eager to do Christ's bidding and a man who walks in the footsteps of a despised, crucified Savior (vv. 11-12).

4:17 This is why. Since Paul himself cannot come yet (though he is planning a trip), he will send his convert and disciple Timothy who will model the Christian life for them.

5:1 sexual immorality. Literally, "fornication." Since Paul does not label this "adultery," the man's father was probably either dead or divorced from his wife. The Corinthians had been newly converted from a pagan environment that was notoriously lax regarding sexual standards. **not even condoned among the Gentiles.** Incest was also condemned by pagans (as well as by Jews: Lev. 18:8; 20:11), who were shocked at the idea of a father and a son having sexual re-

lations with the same woman. **his father's wife.** Probably not the man's actual mother, but rather his stepmother.

5:3-6 Clearly intending discipline, not destruction, Paul orders the church to cut off the man from fellowship.

5:4 when you are assembled. Such excommunication (removal from the church) should not be done by Paul or the leaders, but by the whole church gathered together under the guidance of Jesus (Matt. 18:17-18).

5:5 for the destruction of the flesh. He hopes that by exclusion from the church, the man may see clearly the enormity of his loss, and then repent (1 Tim. 1:20).

5:11 Do not even eat. Dining together was an important practice among early Chris-

Judging Others

1. If you could judge the whole world for one day, what crimes would you address?

1 Corinthians 6:1-11

2. Why should Christians "rather put up with injustice" and "be cheated" (v. 7) than take another Christian to court? Why is it so damaging for Christians to sue one another?

3. Look at the list of people in verses 9-10 who will not inherit God's kingdom. Why are "greedy people" listed with "thieves"? What does this suggest?

4. Why will homosexuals not inherit God's kingdom? How does this differ from the world's teachings? How do you deal with this issue?

 Run From Sex

1. What food would be the hardest for you to give up eating?

1 Corinthians 6:12-20

2. Explain in your own words what Paul means in verse 12. How does this apply to behaviors such as drinking or smoking?

3. How does a person "Flee from sexual immorality" (v. 18)? Why are we to do this, according to this passage?

4. In what way does a "person who is sexually immoral sin against his [or her] own body" (v. 18)?

5. How does this passage compare with the world's view of sex? With your view of sex?

and not before the saints? ²Or do you not know that the saints will judge the world? And if the world is judged by you, are you unworthy to judge the smallest cases? ³Do you not know that we will judge angels— not to speak of things pertaining to this life? ⁴So if you have cases pertaining to this life, do you select thoseª who have no standing in the church to judge? ⁵I say this to your shame! Can it be that there is not one wise person among you who will be able to arbitrate between his brothers? ⁶Instead, brother goes to law against brother, and that before unbelievers!

⁷Therefore, it is already a total defeat for you that you have lawsuits against one another. Why not rather put up with injustice? Why not rather be cheated? ⁸Instead, you act unjustly and cheat—and this to brothers! ⁹Do you not know that the unjust will not inherit God's kingdom? Do not be deceived: no sexually immoral

people, idolaters, adulterers, male prostitutes, homosexuals, ¹⁰thieves, greedy people, drunkards, revilers, or swindlers will inherit God's kingdom. ¹¹Some of you were like this; but you were washed, you were sanctified, you were justified in the name of the Lord Jesus Christ and by the Spirit of our God.

Glorifying God in Body and Spirit

¹²"Everything is permissible for me,"ᵇ but not everything is helpful. "Everything is permissible for me,"ᵇ but I will not be brought under the control of anything. ¹³"Foods for the stomach and the stomach for foods,"ᵇ but God will do away with both of them.ᶜ The body is not for sexual immorality but for the Lord, and the Lord for the body. ¹⁴God raised up the Lord and will also raise us up by His power. ¹⁵Do you not know that your bodies are the members of Christ? So

ª**6:4** Or *life, appoint those* (as a command)   ᵇ**6:12,13** The words in quotation marks are most likely slogans used by some Corinthian Christians. Paul evaluates and corrects these slogans.   ᶜ**6:13** Lit *both it and them*

tians (10:14-22; 11:17-34). In excommunication all contact is severed.

6:1 dare. The implication is that such action is an affront to God and to the church. **go to law.** The bench from which justice was dispensed was located in the market place at Corinth. In hauling a brother or sister into court, a Christian was not simply settling a dispute, but holding the church itself up to public scrutiny and ridicule. **the unrighteous.** Here this term simply means "non-Christian."

6:7 already a total defeat. A lawsuit is a clear sign that love in the church has been replaced by selfishness. **Why not rather put up with injustice?** Paul counsels non-retaliation, as Jesus had taught (Matt. 5:38-42; Rom. 12:17-21; 1 Thess. 5:15) because the Christian knows that his or her true life is

to be found in the coming age. **Why not rather be cheated?** An indication that Paul is writing about financial and property cases.

6:9 unjust. Paul illustrates typical destructive lifestyles in Corinth and elsewhere in the Greco-Roman world by the list that follows. **God's kingdom.** Paul continues with this idea of living out the ethic of the age to come when all evil is undone and God reigns visibly. **male prostitutes, homosexuals.** The passive and active partners in male homosexual activity (Lev 18:22; 20:13; Rom 1:27; 1 Tim 1:10). Homosexuality was widespread in the Greco-Roman world; 14 of the first 15 Roman emperors practiced it.

6:12 Everything is permissible for me. This was probably the slogan of a libertarian party at Corinth, which felt that since the body was insignificant (in comparison with

the "spirit"), it did not really matter what one did. **not everything is helpful ... I will not be brought under the control of anything.** Paul argues that while everything may be permissible, not everything is good. The principle of freedom must be guided by the principle of love. We should ask: (1) Is what I am doing beneficial for myself or others; and (2) What does my activity show about whom or what I honor as Lord? Without guiding principles, Christian freedom becomes a cover for self-indulgence. **under the control.** To indulge one's appetites in unsuitable ways opens the possibility of slavery to a harmful habit.

6:13 Foods for the stomach. Diet is a matter of indifference—especially in that it has no impact on one's salvation. **body.** The Corinthians fail to see that the body is the means by which one serves and honors the Lord.

should I take the members of Christ and make them members of a prostitute? Absolutely not! ¹⁶ Do you not know that anyone joined to a prostitute is one body with her? For it says, **The two will become one flesh.**ᵃ ¹⁷ But anyone joined to the Lord is one spirit with Him.

¹⁸ Flee from sexual immorality! "Every sin a person can commit is outside the body,"ᵇ but the person who is sexually immoral sins against his own body. ¹⁹ Do you not know that your body is a sanctuary of the Holy Spirit who is in you, whom you have from God? You are not your own, ²⁰ for you were bought at a price; therefore glorify God in your body.ᶜ

Principles of Marriage

7 About the things you wrote:ᵈ "It is good for a man not to have relations withᵉ a woman."ᶠ ² But because of sexual immorality,ᵍ each man should have his own wife, and each woman should have her own husband. ³ A husband should fulfill his marital duty to his wife, and likewise a wife to her husband. ⁴ A wife does not have authority over her own body, but her husband does. Equally, a husband does not have authority over his own body, but his wife does. ⁵ Do not deprive one another—except when you agree, for a time, to devote yourselves toʰ prayer. Then come together again; otherwise, Satan may tempt you because of your lack of self-control. ⁶ I say this as a concession, not as a command. ⁷ I wish that all people were just like me. But each has his own gift from God, one this and another that.

A Word to the Unmarried

⁸ I say to the unmarried and to widows: It is good for them if they remain as I am. ⁹ But if they do not have self-control, they should marry, for it is better to marry than to burn with desire.

Advice to Married People

¹⁰ I command the married—not I, but the Lord—a wife is not to leaveⁱ her husband. ¹¹ But if she does leave, she must remain unmarried or be reconciled to her husband—and a husband is not to leave his wife. ¹² But to the rest I, not the Lord, say: If any brother has an unbelieving wife, and she is willing to live with him, he must not leave her. ¹³ Also, if any woman has an unbelieving husband, and he is willing to live with her, she must not leave her husband. ¹⁴ For the unbelieving husband is sanctified by the wife, and the unbelieving wife is sanctified by the Christian husband. Otherwise your children would be unclean, but now they are holy. ¹⁵ But if the unbeliever leaves, let him leave.ⁱ A brother or a sister is not bound in such cases. God has called youʲ to peace. ¹⁶ For you, wife, how do you know whether you will save your husband? Or you, husband, how do you know whether you will save your wife?

 ## The Question of Marriage

1. Who do you know that has remained single? What do you admire about that person?

1 Corinthians 7:1-40

2. What does Paul mean that "A wife does not have authority over her own body, but her husband does" and vice versa (v. 4)? What does this say about marriage?

3. Why is it better for some people to remain unmarried? For others to marry?

4. What do verses 10-11 and 39 teach about divorce and remarriage? How does this compare with the world's beliefs?

5. How can you be sure to follow God's plan for your life regarding marriage?

ᵃ**6:16** Gn 2:24   ᵇ**6:18** See note at 1 Co 6:12   ᶜ**6:20** Other mss add *and in your spirit, which belong to God.*   ᵈ**7:1** Other mss add *to me*   ᵉ**7:1** Lit *not to touch*   ᶠ**7:1** The words in quotation marks are a principle that the Corinthians wrote to Paul and asked for his view about.   ᵍ**7:2** Lit *immoralities*   ʰ**7:5** Other mss add *fasting and to*   ⁱ**7:10,15** Or *separate from,* or *divorce*   ʲ**7:15** Other mss read *us*

6:18 Flee. Paul's counsel regarding sexual temptation is simple and direct.

7:5 Abstinence is allowed under two conditions: both partners agree, and it is for a limited time. **deprive.** Literally, "rob." For one partner to opt out of sexual relations under the guise of spirituality is a form of robbery. **prayer.** The purpose of such abstinence is prayer. **lack of self-control.** Paul assumes that a couple would not have married if they did not feel any legitimate sexual desire, which they ought to fulfill lest they be tempted to commit adultery.

7:7 were just like me. That is, celibate. Paul is not advocating celibacy as much as resistance against inappropriate sexual expression. **gift.** Celibacy is a spiritual gift that not everyone has.

7:8 remain as I am. Paul was more likely a

widower than a bachelor, since it was quite rare for a rabbi to be unmarried. In fact, marriage was virtually obligatory for a Jew. His point applies to unmarried and widowed people.

7:9 do not have self-control. Abstinence would be problematical for those who had once experienced an active married life. **burn.** It is difficult to lead a devoted Christian life when one is consumed with desire.

7:10 not I, but the Lord. Paul is probably referring to statements by Jesus, as in Mark 10:2-12. **a wife.** Paul writes (vv. 10-11) primarily to women, because they were probably advocating sexual abstinence in order to remain "spiritually pure." **not to leave her husband.** Despite preferring the single life, Paul does not encourage those who are already married to be divorced (see Mal. 2:16).

7:12-14 he must not leave ... she must not leave. A Christian must not take the initiative to divorce his or her non-believing spouse.

7:15 let him leave. But should the non-Christian partner leave, the prohibition against divorce does not apply.

7:16 you will save. Christians who remain in a mixed marriage may have the joy of seeing their spouses converted to Christ (see also 1 Pet. 3:1-2).

7:17-24 Paul now gives the general principle (stay as one was when called into service by God), repeated three times (vv. 17, 20, 24), upon which he based his arguments in verses 1-16 and then verses 25-40. He illustrates this principle by references to circumcision and slavery.

7:25 virgins. Those persons without sexual experience. Here Paul uses the word to refer

Various Situations of Life

[17] However, each one must live his life in the situation the Lord assigned when God called him.[a] This is what I command in all the churches. [18] Was anyone already circumcised when he was called? He should not undo his circumcision. Was anyone called while uncircumcised? He should not get circumcised. [19] Circumcision does not matter and uncircumcision does not matter, but keeping God's commandments does. [20] Each person should remain in the life situation[b] in which he was called. [21] Were you called while a slave? It should not be a concern to you. But if you can become free, by all means take the opportunity.[c] [22] For he who is called by the Lord as a slave is the Lord's freedman.[d] Likewise he who is called as a free man[e] is Christ's slave. [23] You were bought at a price; do not become slaves of men. [24] Brothers, each person should remain with God in whatever situation he was called.

About the Unmarried and Widows

[25] About virgins: I have no command from the Lord, but I do give an opinion as one who by the Lord's mercy is trustworthy. [26] Therefore I consider this to be good because of the present distress: it is fine for a man to stay as he is. [27] Are you bound to a wife? Do not seek to be loosed. Are you loosed from a wife? Do not seek a wife. [28] However, if you do get married, you have not sinned, and if a virgin marries, she has not sinned. But such people will have trouble in this life,[f] and I am trying to spare you. [29] And I say this, brothers: the time is limited, so from now on those who have wives should be as though they had none, [30] those who weep as though they did not weep, those who rejoice as though they did not rejoice, those who buy as though they did not possess, [31] and those who use the world as though they did not make full use of it. For this world in its current form is passing away.

[32] I want you to be without concerns. An unmarried man is concerned about the things of the Lord—how he may please the Lord. [33] But a married man is concerned about the things of the world—how he may please his wife— [34] and he is divided. An unmarried woman or a virgin is concerned about the things of the Lord, so that she may be holy both in body and in spirit. But a married woman is concerned about the things of the world—how she may please her husband. [35] Now I am saying this for your own benefit, not to put a restraint on you, but because of what is proper, and so that you may be devoted to the Lord without distraction.

[36] But if any man thinks he is acting improperly toward his virgin,[g] if she is past marriageable age,[h] and so it must be, he can do what he wants. He is not sinning; they can get married. [37] But he who stands firm in his heart (who is under no compulsion, but has control over his own will) and has decided in his heart to keep his own virgin, will do well. [38] So then he who marries[i] his virgin does well, but he who does not marry[j] will do better.

[39] A wife is bound[k] as long as her husband is living. But if her husband dies, she is free to be married to anyone she wants—only in the Lord.[l] [40] But she is happier if she remains as she is, in my opinion. And I think that I also have the Spirit of God.

Food Offered to Idols

8 About food offered to idols: We know that "we all have knowledge."[m] Knowledge inflates with pride, but love builds up. [2] If anyone thinks he knows anything, he does not yet know it as he ought to know it. [3] But if anyone loves God, he is known by Him.

[4] About eating food offered to idols, then, we know that "an idol is nothing in the world,"[m] and that "there is no God but one."[m] [5] For even if there are so-called gods, whether in heaven or on earth—as there are many "gods" and many "lords"—

[6] yet for us there is one God, the Father,
from whom are all things, and we for Him;
and one Lord, Jesus Christ,

---

[a]**7:17** Lit called each [b]**7:20** Lit in the calling [c]**7:21** Or But even though you can become free, make the most of your position as a slave. [d]**7:22** A former slave [e]**7:22** A man who was never a slave [f]**7:28** Lit in the flesh [g]**7:36** (1) a man's fiancée, or (2) his daughter, or (3) his Levirate wife, or (4) a celibate companion [h]**7:36** Or virgin, if his passions are strong, [i]**7:38** Or marries off [j]**7:38** Or marry her off [k]**7:39** Other mss add by law [l]**7:39** Only a believer [m]**8:1,4** See note at 1 Co 6:12

---

to women. **give an opinion.** Paul does not have a clear word from the Lord about whether single people ought to marry, but he does offer his Spirit-directed advice (v. 40).

7:26 the present distress. Written when the gospel was spreading rapidly, Christians were being persecuted for their faith, and they expected Christ's return would come very soon. In light of these circumstances, it was felt that it would be proper to put aside the responsibilities of marriage to devote oneself to furthering God's kingdom. **it is fine for a man to stay as he is.** Again Paul appears to be quoting a truism or maxim from Corinth.

7:28 have not sinned. The Corinthians have probably been insisting that unmarried men remain single. While Paul sees the wisdom of this, it is not a command, but good advice

that the Christian is free to accept or reject.

7:34 he is divided. The married man is rightly concerned about how to please the Lord and please his wife. This is the problem: how to be fully faithful to both legitimate commitments. **a married woman.** The same is true of a married woman: her attention is divided in a way that is not true of a single woman.

7:39 only in the Lord. It is also possible to translate this phrase, "remembering that she is a Christian." In any case, Christian widows (or widowers) may remarry other Christians.

8:1 food offered to idols. In ancient cities, most of the meat for sale came from the temples where it had first been offered to an idol, since only priests were allowed by the Romans to function as butchers. Jews were ab-

solutely forbidden to eat such idol-food, and the question is whether the same prohibition applied to Christians. **we all have knowledge.** Once again, Paul appears to be quoting from their letter which argued that eating such food should be all right in view of their new position in Christ. Paul agrees with the assertion, but then goes on to qualify it sharply. **Knowledge inflates with pride, but love builds up.** While knowledge is useful, the basic aim of the Christian must be love. When people feel "superior" because they have special insights, this attitude may make it hard to reach out in love to others.

8:9 Be careful. Love for others is the limitation placed upon one's freedom in Christ. **stumbling block.** If "strong" Christians exercise their right to eat idol-meat at a temple, this may induce "weak" Christians to violate their consciences to their detriment. **weak.**

Careful Choices

1. Do you think a Christian should ever drink alcohol? Why or why not?

1 Corinthians 8:1-13

2. Why might Christians in Paul's day have refrained from eating food offered to idols? Why might others have felt free to do so?
3. What sorts of choices today are like the choice to eat "food offered to idols"?
4. Put into your own words the principle of "Christian liberty" that Paul addresses here, and the principle of "dying to self."
5. Have you done anything lately to wound the conscience of a fellow Christian (v. 12)? How will you choose differently next time?

through whom are all things, and we through Him.

⁷ However, not everyone has this knowledge. In fact, some have been so used to idolatry up until now, that when they eat food offered to an idol, their conscience, being weak, is defiled. ⁸ Food will not make us acceptable to God. We are not inferior if we don't eat, and we are not better if we do eat. ⁹ But be careful that this right of yours in no way becomes a stumbling block to the weak. ¹⁰ For if somebody sees you, the one who has this knowledge, dining in an idol's temple, won't his weak conscience be encouraged to eat food offered to idols? ¹¹ Then the weak person, the brother for whom Christ died, is ruined by your knowledge. ¹² Now when you sin like this against the brothers and wound their weak conscience, you are sinning against Christ. ¹³ Therefore, if food causes my brother to fall, I will never again eat meat, so that I won't cause my brother to fall.

Paul's Example as an Apostle

9 Am I not free? Am I not an apostle? Have I not seen Jesus our Lord? Are you not my work in the Lord? ² If I am not an apostle to others, at least I am to you, for you are the seal of my apostleship in the Lord. ³ My defense to those who examine me is this: ⁴ Don't we have the right to eat and drink? ⁵ Don't we have the right to be accompanied by a Christian wife, like the other apostles, the Lord's brothers, and •Cephas? ⁶ Or is it only Barnabas and I who have no right to refrain from working? ⁷ Who ever goes to war at his own expense? Who plants a vineyard and does not eat its fruit? Or who shepherds a flock and does not drink the milk from the flock? ⁸ Am I saying this from a human perspective? Doesn't the law also say the same thing? ⁹ For it is written in the law of Moses, **Do not muzzle an ox while it treads out the grain.**[a] Is God really concerned with oxen? ¹⁰ Or isn't He really saying it for us? Yes, this is written for us, because he who plows ought to plow in hope, and he who threshes should do so in hope of sharing the crop. ¹¹ If we have sown spiritual things for you, is it too much if we reap material things from you? ¹² If others share this authority over you, don't we even more?

However, we have not used this authority; instead we endure everything so that we will not hinder the gospel of Christ. ¹³ Do you not know that those who perform the temple services eat the food from the temple, and those who serve at the altar share in the offerings of the altar? ¹⁴ In the same way, the Lord has commanded that those who preach the gospel should earn their living by the gospel.

¹⁵ But I have used none of these rights, and I have not written this to make it happen that way for me. For it would be better for me to die than for anyone to deprive me of my boast! ¹⁶ For if I preach the gospel, I have no reason to boast, because an obligation is placed on me. And woe to me if I do not preach the gospel! ¹⁷ For if I do this willingly, I have a reward; but if unwillingly, I am entrusted with a stewardship. ¹⁸ What then is my reward? To preach the gospel and

---

[a]**9:9** Dt 25:4

These are people whose faith is still relatively immature or ill-informed.

8:10 dining in an idol's temple. Temples were the "restaurants" of the time. Social life involved invitations to join friends at a temple for a meal held in honor of the god of that temple. Therefore, to eat at such a temple implied involvement with that god. If a Christian with "knowledge" that "an idol is nothing" (v. 4) exercised his or her knowledge by eating at such an occasion, this could induce weaker Christians who are not so informed to compromise or abandon their faith by again falling into idolatry and immorality.

8:12 sinning against Christ. Instead of proving oneself to be "strong" and "spiritual," a Christian who ignores the concerns of the "weak" has offended the more important law of love.

9:1 Am I not free? He is certainly as free as any Christian, but because of his commitment to the way of love he restricts his lifestyle (as he showed in ch. 8). **Have I not seen Jesus our Lord?** A person could not become an apostle unless he had witnessed firsthand the resurrected Christ (15:7-8; Acts 1:22). This was the primary evidence that he was a legitimate apostle (15:3-11; Gal. 1:11-24).

9:4 the right to eat and drink. Paul is certainly free to eat idol-food, but he refuses to exercise this right because it would harm the "weaker" Christians in the community.

9:5 accompanied by a Christian wife. All Christians have the right to a wife (ch. 7). Apparently the Christian community they were serving would support both an apostle and his wife. **Cephas.** Peter is singled out be-

cause he had probably visited Corinth along with his wife.

9:12 we have not used this authority. This is the point Paul wants to get across to the Corinthians so that they might follow his example. While he has the right to financial support (vv. 7-12), he has chosen not to exercise this right. **hinder the gospel.** If Paul had accepted financial reward, potential converts might have misunderstood this as the major motive for his ministry. Paul had the right to support; instead he supported himself making tents.

9:15 these rights Though Paul had the right to be supported just as priests were supported in temple service, he forwent these privileges so that it would not be perceived that he was rendering services for its material benefits or was under obligation to any-

The Ultimate Qualification

1. Who is your favorite Olympic athlete, and why?

1 Corinthians 9:24-27

2. What does it mean that athletes compete "to receive a perishable crown" (v. 25)? What is an "imperishable" crown?

3. What does Paul do to assure "that after preaching to others, I myself will not be disqualified" (v. 27)? How can we avoid being disqualified?

4. What kinds of discipline are required in your own sport? How costly is it for you to follow those disciplines?

5. What kinds of discipline are required in serving Christ? Do you follow those disciplines as faithfully as your sport's disciplines?

offer it free of charge, and not make full use of my authority in the gospel.

¹⁹ For although I am free from all people, I have made myself a slave to all, in order to win more people. ²⁰ To the Jews I became like a Jew, to win Jews; to those under the law, like one under the law—though I myself am not under the lawᵃ—to win those under the law. ²¹ To those who are outside the law, like one outside the law—not being outside God's law, but under the law of Christ—to win those outside the law. ²² To the weak I became weak, in order to win the weak. I have become all things to all people, so that I may by all means save some. ²³ Now I do all this because of the gospel, that I may become a partner in its benefits.ᵇ

²⁴ Do you not know that the runners in a stadium all race, but only one receives the prize? Run in such a way that you may win. ²⁵ Now everyone who competes exercises self-control in everything. However, they do it to receive a perishable crown, but we an imperish-

able one. ²⁶ Therefore I do not run like one who runs aimlessly, or box like one who beats the air. ²⁷ Instead, I discipline my body and bring it under strict control, so that after preaching to others, I myself will not be disqualified.

Standing and Falling

1. Have you ever been winning a competition only to lose at the very end? Did overconfidence play a part in that loss?

1 Corinthians 10:1-13

2. What is "sexual immorality" (v. 8)? How far is too far? What physical actions are appropriate?

3. Why would complaining (v. 10) bring the same punishment as sexual immorality?

4. What does Paul mean, "whoever thinks he stands must be careful not to fall" (v. 12)?

5. Are you being sexually pure? Uncomplaining? How can you avoid becoming overconfident in your own abilities and strength?

Warnings from Israel's Past

10 Now I want you to know, brothers, that our fathers were all under the cloud, all passed through the sea, ² and all were baptized into Moses in the cloud and in the sea. ³ They all ate the same spiritual food, ⁴ and all drank the same spiritual drink. For they drank from a spiritual rock that followed them, and that rock was Christ. ⁵ But God was not pleased with most of them, for they were struck down in the desert.

⁶ Now these things became examples for us, so that we will not desire evil as they did.ᶜ ⁷ Don't become idolaters as some of them were; as it is written, **The people sat down to eat and drink, and got up to play.**ᵈ ᵉ ⁸ Let

---

ᵃ**9:20** Other mss omit *though I myself am not under law* ᵇ**9:23** Lit *partner of it* ᶜ**10:6** Lit *they desired* ᵈ**10:7** Or *to dance* ᵉ**10:7** Ex 32:6

---

one. Thus, receiving no reward was his reward!

9:19 although I am free. In verse 1, this appears to have referred to Paul's freedom from dietary concerns based on religious principles. While it carries the same meaning here, it also includes the fact that since he refuses financial support from those he teaches, he is "owned" by no one (6:20). He is obligated to no system or group.

9:22 the weak. Those with weak consciences (8:7-13) who are not yet free from legalism or from the power of paganism.

9:26 runs aimlessly. Such a runner has no fixed goal. Paul's activities are not without a point. Everything he does is for the sake of the gospel. **beats the air.** In the same way that he pictured pointless running, now he

switches to the image of futile boxing.

10:1 Now I want you to know. They claimed to have "knowledge" (8:1-2), but the Corinthians had really misunderstood the meaning of baptism and Communion (the Eucharist). **our fathers.** Though his readers are largely Gentiles, Paul considers them to be the spiritual heirs of Israel. **cloud ... sea.** Paul reminds them of the Exodus (Ex. 13:21; 14:19-31), using the engulfing presence of the cloud of God and their passing through the sea as analogies to baptism.

10:3-4 spiritual food ... drink. Not only did these gifts from God nourish their physical bodies, they had an additional spiritual function (in that they were symbols that prefigured Christian Communion, and therefore, the benefits of Christ's death).

10:5 not pleased Paul gives an example of

those who were direct benefactors of God's grace but who ultimately proved themselves to be imposters. A stern warning to be sure of one's salvation.

10:8 sexual immorality. Paul now explicitly condemns the sexual vice associated with pagan religion (6:12-20). **23,000.** Paul is referring to the story of the Israelites' fornication with the Moabite women as recorded in Numbers 25:1-9 (the figure there is 24,000).

10:9 tempt Christ. The Corinthians (as had the Israelites before them) were testing God by these actions.

10:10 complain. They were also grumbling against Paul for telling them not to engage in temple feasts and ritual prostitution.

10:11 they were written as a warning. One

us not commit sexual immorality as some of them did,[a] and in a single day 23,000 people fell dead. 9 Let us not tempt Christ as some of them did,[b] and were destroyed by snakes. 10 Nor should we complain as some of them did,[c] and were killed by the destroyer.[d] 11 Now these things happened to them as examples, and they were written as a warning to us, on whom the ends of the ages have come. 12 Therefore, whoever thinks he stands must be careful not to fall! 13 No temptation has overtaken you except what is common to humanity. God is faithful and He will not allow you to be tempted beyond what you are able, but with the temptation He will also provide a way of escape, so that you are able to bear it.

Handling Our Freedom

1. What freedom would you like to have that your parents now deny you? From what are they protecting you?

1 Corinthians 10:14–11:1

2. What things does the world today "sacrifice to demons" (v. 20)? Consider popular music, entertainment, video games, and so forth.

3. What does Paul mean, "You cannot drink the cup of the Lord and the cup of demons" (v. 21)? How might we sometimes fall into that in the world today?

4. In what ways is a Christian free (vv. 23-24)? How can you exercise that freedom properly? What is the highest priority?

Warning against Idolatry

14 Therefore, my dear friends, flee from idolatry. 15 I am speaking as to wise people. Judge for yourselves

what I say. 16 The cup of blessing that we bless, is it not a sharing in the blood of Christ? The bread that we break, is it not a sharing in the body of Christ? 17 Because there is one bread, we who are many are one body, for all of us share that one bread. 18 Look at the people of Israel.[e] Are not those who eat the sacrifices partners in the altar? 19 What am I saying then? That food offered to idols is anything, or that an idol is anything? 20 No, but I do say that what they[f] sacrifice, they sacrifice to demons and not to God. I do not want you to be partners with demons! 21 You cannot drink the cup of the Lord and the cup of demons. You cannot share in the Lord's table and the table of demons. 22 Or are we provoking the Lord to jealousy? Are we stronger than He?

Christian Liberty

23 "Everything is permissible,"[g][h] but not everything is helpful. "Everything is permissible,"[g][h] but not everything builds up. 24 No one should seek his own good, but the good of the other person.

25 Eat everything that is sold in the meat market, asking no questions for conscience' sake, for 26 **the earth is the Lord's, and all that is in it.**[i] 27 If one of the unbelievers invites you over and you want to go, eat everything that is set before you, without raising questions of conscience. 28 But if someone says to you, "This is food offered to an idol," do not eat it, out of consideration for the one who told you, and for conscience' sake.[j] 29 I do not mean your own conscience, but the other person's. For why is my freedom judged by another person's conscience? 30 If I partake with thanks, why am I slandered because of something for which I give thanks?

31 Therefore, whether you eat or drink, or whatever you do, do everything for God's glory. 32 Give no offense to the Jews or the Greeks or the church of God, 33 just as I also try to please all people in all things, not seeking my own profit, but the profit of many, that they

11 may be saved. 1 Be imitators of me, as I also am of Christ.

---

[a]**10:8** Lit *them committed sexual immorality* [b]**10:9** Lit *them tempted* [c]**10:10** Lit *them complained* [d]**10:10** Or *the destroying angel* [e]**10:18** Lit *Look at Israel according to the flesh* [f]**10:20** Other mss read *Gentiles* [g]**10:23** Other mss add *for me* [h]**10:23** See note at 1 Co 6:12 [i]**10:26** Ps 24:1 [j]**10:28** Other mss add *"For the earth is the Lord's and all that is in it."*

---

of the great values of Scripture is to keep before us the danger and consequences of sin. One habit of the human heart is to keep hidden from itself the certain consequences of sin. God's Word is designed to remind us constantly of the danger than accompanies sinful attitudes and actions.

10:12 whoever thinks he stands. The person at greatest risk is the person who believes he is immune from danger.

10:13 Paul encourages the Corinthians to stand firm by reminding them that when Christians resist sin they do so in the knowledge that they will be able to endure. **temptation.** Paul has identified various temptations that Israel faced: idolatry, sexual immorality, the temptation to test God, and the temptation to grumble about where God led them. To be tempted is to be tested. Fac-

ing the choice of deserting God's will or doing God's will, the person must either resist or yield. Temptation is not sin. Yielding is. **a way of escape.** Temptation is not unusual or unexpected. Resisting temptation is not pleasant, but the Christian can do it with God's help.

10:14 Therefore. Paul will now draw the logical conclusions from his survey of Israel's past. **flee from idolatry.** In the same way that he unequivocally forbids fornication (6:18), he forbids Christians to participate in idol worship. While Paul urges Christians to "stand fast" in the face of evil (Eph. 6:10-18), he counsels flight (not a fight) when it comes to "sins of the flesh." Constant temptations are too strong to resist.

10:16 The cup of blessing. This refers to the cup of wine drunk at the conclusion of

the meal in a Jewish home, over which a blessing was spoken. During the Last Supper, Jesus made this cup a symbol of His soon-to-be-shed blood, to be drunk regularly in remembrance of Him.

10:18 eat the sacrifices. The priests were allowed to eat parts of the sacrificial offerings (Lev. 10:12-15), as were others in certain instances (1 Sam. 9:10-24).

10:20 partners with demons Just as Paul and Scripture (Exod. 22:20; 32:8; Deut. 28:64; 32:17; Ps. 106:36-37) are explicitly clear that the worship of pagan gods and the offering of sacrifices to them is condemned, so too must the Christian be extremely conscientious in avoiding divided loyalties.

10:23 permissible In 6:12, Paul addresses the correct attitude towards what is permis-

Roles of Husbands and Wives

1. What is your ideal for how you'd like to relate with your future spouse?

1 Corinthians 11:22-16

2. A husband can't properly love and lead his wife until Christ is "his head" (v.3). What can you do to make Christ your head?
3. As a wife follows the lead of her husband, is she any less valuable to God because she takes the role of a supportive and helping partner? (See Gal. 3:27-28.)
4. Is the husband of any more value to God because God it is his role to lead in marriage?
5. Should a wife follow her husband's lead if he is disobeying God?

Instructions about Head Coverings

2 Now I praise you[a] because you remember me in all things and keep the traditions just as I delivered them to you. 3 But I want you to know that Christ is the head of every man, and the man is the head of the woman,[b] and God is the head of Christ. 4 Every man who prays or prophesies with something on his head dishonors his head. 5 But every woman who prays or prophesies with her head uncovered dishonors her head, since that is one and the same as having her head shaved. 6 So if a woman's head[c] is not covered, her hair should be cut off. But if it is disgraceful for a woman to have her hair cut off or her head shaved, she should be covered. 7 A man, in fact, should not cover his head, because he is God's image and glory, but woman is man's glory. 8 For man did not come from woman, but woman came from man; 9 and man was not created for woman, but

woman for man. 10 This is why a woman should have [a symbol of] authority on her head: because of the angels. 11 However, in the Lord, woman is not independent of man, and man is not independent of woman. 12 For just as woman came from man, so man comes through woman, and all things come from God.

13 Judge for yourselves: Is it proper for a woman to pray to God with her head uncovered? 14 Does not even nature itself teach you that if a man has long hair it is a disgrace to him, 15 but that if a woman has long hair, it is her glory? For her hair is given to her[d] as a covering. 16 But if anyone wants to argue about this, we have no other[e] custom, nor do the churches of God.

Evaluate Yourself

1. How do you evaluate how well you are progressing in your sport, artistic pursuits, or job?

1 Corinthians 11:17-34

2. What is the purpose of the Lord's Supper? How does it "proclaim the Lord's death" (v. 26)?
3. What does it mean to "drink the cup of the Lord in an unworthy way" (v. 27)? What is the result of that? How does one guard against this?
4. In verses 31 and 32, Paul discusses the inescapable aspect of judgment from either God or ourselves. What area of your life do you need to "properly evaluate" so that God doesn't have to discipline you?

The Lord's Supper

17 Now in giving the following instruction I do not praise you, since you come together not for the better

---

a11:2 Other mss add brothers, b11:3 Or the husband is the head of the wife c11:6 Lit a woman d11:15 Other mss omit to her e11:16 Or no such

---

sible to each individual "body of Christ," that is, each individual member. Here, Paul explains what is permissible in view of the body of Christ as a whole, represented by the Corinthian church. First, Christians are not to defile themselves or the church in what they participate in publicly.

10:27 everything that is set before you. Paul shifts his focus to the related question of what one might eat or not eat at the home of a non-Christian friend. Christians can eat whatever is placed before them in such a setting, although the conscience of one's dinner companions must also be considered. It could be a greater evil to reject a host's food.

10:28 someone. It is probably a pagan who points out that what is being offered is idol-food. Pagans viewed Christianity as a Jew-

ish sect, and so assumed Christians followed the same dietary laws.

11:3 head of. Paul uses this metaphor and cites three examples: Christ as head of man, man as head of woman, and God as head of Christ. "Head of" has two different connotations. One is "source of." The other is "authority." There are times when "source" needs to be emphasized. At other times, "authority" should be emphasized. Paul's point in using this metaphor with these three examples is to point to a divine order—even between God the Father and God the Son. Father and Son are equal but they are distinct persons and have different roles. Husband and wife have equal worth before God. They both bear the image of God. The husband is charged with being head of that relationship as Christ is head of the church. A wife is to be submissive to the servant lead-

ership of her husband in the same way that the church submits to Christ, her head.

11:11 not independent. While verses 2-16 do not directly mention the context of marriage, the relationship between husband and wife is clearly in view here. Paul points out the mutual interdependence that exists between men and women and their equal dependence on God.

11:18 I hear. Paul had heard what was going on from other sources (1:11; 16:17). He's shocked that it is as bad as reported ("in part I believe it").

11:20 it is not really to eat the Lord's Supper. The Corinthians have so badly abused the Lord's Supper that it was more like a pagan temple celebration than a meal held in honor of the Lord.

but for the worse. 18 For, to begin with, I hear that when you come together as a church there are divisions among you, and in part I believe it. 19 There must, indeed, be factions among you, so that the approved among you may be recognized. 20 Therefore when you come together in one place, it is not really to eat the Lord's Supper. 21 For in eating, each one takes his own supper ahead of others, and one person is hungry while another is drunk! 22 Don't you have houses to eat and drink in? Or do you look down on the church of God and embarrass those who have nothing? What should I say to you? Should I praise you? I do not praise you for this!

23 For I received from the Lord what I also passed on to you: on the night when He was betrayed, the Lord Jesus took bread, 24 gave thanks, broke it, and said,a "This is My body, which isb for you. Do this in remembrance of Me."

25 In the same way ⌊He⌋ also ⌊took⌋ the cup, after supper, and said, "This cup is the new covenant in My blood. Do this, as often as you drink it, in remembrance of Me." 26 For as often as you eat this bread and drink the cup, you proclaim the Lord's death until He comes.

Self-Examination

27 Therefore, whoever eats the bread or drinks the cup of the Lord in an unworthy way will be guilty of sin against the bodyc and blood of the Lord. 28 So a man should examine himself; in this way he should eat of the bread and drink of the cup. 29 For whoever eats and drinks without recognizing the body,d eats and drinks judgment on himself. 30 This is why many are sick and ill among you, and many have fallen •asleep. 31 If we were properly evaluating ourselves, we would not be judged, 32 but when we are judged, we are disciplined by the Lord, so that we may not be condemned with the world.

33 Therefore, my brothers, when you come together to eat, wait for one another. 34 If anyone is hungry, he should eat at home, so that you can come together and not cause judgment. And I will give instructions about the other matters whenever I come.

Diversity of Spiritual Gifts

12 About matters of the spirit:e brothers, I do not want you to be unaware. 2 You know how, when you were pagans, you were led to dumb idols—being led astray. 3 Therefore I am informing you that no one speaking by the Spirit of God says, "Jesus is cursed," and no one can say, "Jesus is Lord," except by the Holy Spirit.

4 Now there are different gifts, but the same Spirit. 5 There are different ministries, but the same Lord. 6 And there are different activities, but the same God is active in everyone and everything.f 7 A manifestation of the Spirit is given to each person to produce what is beneficial:

8 to one is given a message of wisdom
  through the Spirit,
  to another, a message of knowledge
   by the same Spirit,
9 to another, faith by the same Spirit,
  to another, gifts of healing by the one Spirit,
10 to another, the performing of miracles,
  to another, prophecy,
  to another, distinguishing between spirits,
  to another, different kinds of languages,
  to another, interpretation of languages.

11 But one and the same Spirit is active in all these, distributing to each one as He wills.

Unity Yet Diversity in the Body

12 For as the body is one and has many parts, and all the parts of that body, though many, are one body—so also is Christ. 13 For we were all baptized by one Spirit into one body—whether Jews or Greeks, whether slaves or free—and we were all made to drink of one Spirit. 14 So the body is not one part but many. 15 If the foot should say, "Because I'm not a hand, I don't belong to the body," in spite of this it still belongs to the body.

---

a11:24 Other mss add "Take, eat. b11:24 Other mss add broken c11:27 Lit be guilty of the body d11:29 Other mss read drinks unworthily, not discerning the Lord's body e12:1 Lit About things spiritual f12:6 Lit God acts all things in all

---

11:21 takes his own supper ahead of others. The purpose of the meal was for the body of believers to remember the Lord and His victory over sin and death on the cross. **hungry ... drunk.** The contrast could not be more stark. The poor in the church went hungry during this meal, while others indulged themselves to the point of drunkenness.

11:22 Don't you have houses. If the rich can't wait to indulge in their food and drink, at least they should do this at home and not demean the common meal at church.

11:24 "This is My body." Jesus interprets for the disciples the new meaning He is giving to these ordinary acts. He himself will become the Passover lamb for them, to be slain for their sins. **in remembrance.** Paul repeats this phrase twice, to stress that the Lord's Supper is a memorial feast (Luke 22:19).

11:26 This cup is the new covenant. This statement is not found in the four Gospels. It is Paul's summary of the meaning of the Lord's Supper. **proclaim the Lord's death.** The Lord's Supper proclaims the fact and meaning of Jesus' death in several ways: the broken bread and outpoured wine symbolically proclaim His death; the words spoken at such a meal (formally and informally) recall the Jesus' crucifixion; and the whole event "proclaims" His atoning death.

11:29 without recognizing. When the meal turned into a time of drunkenness, division, and gluttony, people lost sight of the meaning of the event. **the body.** Here, "the body" in view is the body of the Lord remembered in the supper and secondarily the church (12:12), both of which the Corinthians were abusing.

12:8 wisdom ... knowledge. Exposition of biblical truth with practical, ethical application.

12:9 faith. To believe God for extraordinary results. Saving faith, which all Christians share, is not in view here. **healing.** The special ability to effect miraculous cures. Paul apparently had this gift (Acts 14:8-10).

12:10 the performing of miracles. This could refer to miraculous powers of kind witnessed in Acts (5:1-10; 9:40-41; 13:10-11; 16:8; 20:9-10). **prophecy.** Inspired utterances given in ordinary (not ecstatic) speech, distinguished from teaching and wisdom by its unprepared nature. **distinguishing between spirits.** Just because a person claimed to be inspired by the Holy Spirit did not make it true. Those who possessed this gift of discernment were able to identify the source of an utterance—the Holy

16 And if the ear should say, "Because I'm not an eye, I don't belong to the body," in spite of this it still belongs to the body. 17 If the whole body were an eye, where would the hearing be? If the whole were an ear, where would be the sense of smell? 18 But now God has placed the parts, each one of them, in the body just as He wanted. 19 And if they were all the same part, where would the body be? 20 Now there are many parts, yet one body.

All for One

1. Have you ever broken a bone? How did it affect the rest of your body?

1 Corinthians 12:12-31

2. Put into your own words what Paul is saying in this passage. Why does he use the analogy of a body?
3. What body part is the most "glamorous"? Which is most important to survival? Which is "weaker"?
4. Describe yourself as a "part" of the body of Christ (an eye, hand, etc.). Why did you select that part?
5. How do you treat some of your "weaker" or less desirable brothers and sisters in Christ? How can you make them feel more loved?

21 So the eye cannot say to the hand, "I don't need you!" nor again the head to the feet, "I don't need you!" 22 On the contrary, all the more, those parts of the body that seem to be weaker are necessary. 23 And those parts of the body that we think to be less honorable, we clothe these with greater honor, and our unpresentable parts have a better presentation. 24 But our presentable parts have no need ⌊of clothing⌋. Instead, God has put the body together, giving greater honor to the less hon-

orable, 25 so that there would be no division in the body, but that the members would have the same concern for each other. 26 So if one member suffers, all the members suffer with it; if one member is honored, all the members rejoice with it.

27 Now you are the body of Christ, and individual members of it. 28 And God has placed these in the church:

first apostles, second prophets, third teachers,
   next, miracles,
then gifts of healing, helping, managing,
   various kinds of languages.
29   Are all apostles? Are all prophets?
   Are all teachers? Do all do miracles?
30   Do all have gifts of healing?
   Do all speak in languages?
Do all interpret?

31 But desire the greater gifts. And I will show you an even better way.

Love: The Superior Way

13 If I speak the languages of men and of angels,
   but do not have love,
   I am a sounding gong or a clanging cymbal.
2   If I have ⌊the gift of⌋ prophecy,
   and understand all •mysteries and all knowledge,
   and if I have all faith,
      so that I can move mountains,
   but do not have love, I am nothing.
3   And if I donate all my goods to feed the poor,
   and if I give my body to be burned,[a]
   but do not have love, I gain nothing.
4   Love is patient; love is kind. Love does not envy;
   is not boastful; is not conceited;
5   does not act improperly; is not selfish;
   is not provoked; does not keep a record
      of wrongs;
6   finds no joy in unrighteousness, but rejoices
      in the truth;
7   bears all things, believes all things,
   hopes all things, endures all things.

---

a **13:3** Other mss read *to boast*

Spirit or another spirit. **different kinds of languages.** Some interpret this to be ecstatic speech, unintelligible except by those with the gift of interpretation of tongues. Others believe it refers to the supernatural ability to speak in real, known languages (as at Pentecost in Acts 2). **interpretation of languages.** This gift allowed a person to understand and explain to others what was being said by someone else in a different tongue or language.

12:28 Paul offers a second list of the types of gifts given by the Holy Spirit (see the parallel list in Eph. 4:11)—mixing together ministries (apostles) with spiritual gifts (the gift of healing). **apostles.** These individuals were responsible for founding new churches. **prophets.** Those who were inspired to speak God's Word to the church, in plain language. **teachers.** Those gifted to instruct

others in the meaning of the Christian faith. **next.** Having first focused on those gifts whereby the church is established and nurtured, Paul then shifts to other gifts. **helping.** The gift of support; those with this gift often function to aid the needy (e.g., the poor, the widow, the orphan). **managing.** The is gift of direction, literally, the process of steering a ship through the rocks and safely to shore.

13:1 languages of men and of angels. This seems to refer again to the gift of tongues (ecstatic speech or speaking in other languages)—highly prized in Corinth and an authentic gift of the Holy Spirit (see also note for 12:10).

13:2 prophecy. Such activity is highly commended by Paul (14:1), yet without love a prophet is really nothing. **understand all mysteries.** In Corinth, special and mysteri-

ous knowledge was highly valued (1:18—2:16). **faith, so that I can move mountains.** Paul refers to Jesus' words in Mark 11:23—even such massive faith is not enough to make a person significant without love.

13:8 Love never ends. It functions both now and in the age to come without ceasing or being held back. By contrast, spiritual gifts are relevant only to this age. **come to an end ... cease.** One day, when Christ comes again in fullness, the prophecy will be fulfilled (and so the gift of prophecy will come to an end), indirect communication with God through languages or tongues will no longer be needed (so they cease), and since all will be revealed and be evident, the gift of knowledge will be unnecessary (and so will come to an end).

13:12 now ... then. Paul is thinking of the

True Love

1. What is your favorite love story from a movie, book, TV show, or fairy tale? Why is it a favorite?

1 Corinthians 13:1-13

2. Why does Paul use the analogy of "a sounding gong or a clanging cymbal" (v. 1) to describe someone who is gifted but unloving?

3. How does verse 5 compare with our modern idea of "loving yourself"? What would Paul say about that concept in light of this passage?

4. Why is love greater than the virtues of faith and hope?

5. Name one specific thing you can do in the coming week to be more loving toward others.

Gifted and Talented

1. Do you speak any foreign languages? Which ones do you wish you could speak fluently?

1 Corinthians 14:1-25

2. What is the difference between speaking in tongues and prophesying (vv. 2-4)? What is the most important thing about such gifts?

3. What does it mean to "be childish in your thinking" (v. 20)? To "be infants in evil and adult in your thinking"?

4. What is the purpose of spiritual gifts, according to this passage? What is their most important function?

5. What do you think your main spiritual gift is? How can you develop it more?

---

8 Love never ends.
But as for prophecies, they will come to an end;
as for languages, they will cease;
as for knowledge, it will come to an end.
9 For we know in part, and we prophesy in part.
10 But when the perfect comes,
the partial will come to an end.
11 When I was a child, I spoke like a child,
I thought like a child, I reasoned like a child.
When I became a man, I put aside childish things.
12 For now we see indistinctly, as in a mirror,
but then face to face.
Now I know in part, but then I will know fully,
as I am fully known.
13 Now these three remain: faith, hope, and love.
But the greatest of these is love.

Prophecy: A Superior Gift

14 Pursue love and desire spiritual gifts, and above all that you may prophesy. 2 For the person who speaks in ₍another₎ language is not speaking to men but to God, since no one understands him; however, he speaks •mysteries in the Spirit.[a] 3 But the person who prophesies speaks to people for edification, encouragement, and consolation. 4 The person who speaks in ₍another₎ language builds himself up, but he who prophesies builds up the church. 5 I wish all of you spoke in other languages, but even more that you prophesied. The person who prophesies is greater than the person who speaks in languages, unless he interprets so that the church may be built up.

6 But now, brothers, if I come to you speaking in ₍other₎ languages, how will I benefit you unless I speak to you with a revelation or knowledge or prophecy or teaching? 7 Even inanimate things producing sounds—

---

a **14:2** Or *in spirit*, or *in his spirit*

---

second coming of Christ. The here-and-now experience is contrasted with the complete reality when Christ's kingdom is revealed in its fullness. **indistinctly.** Corinth was famous for the mirrors it made out of highly polished metal. Still, no mirror manufactured in the first century was without imperfections. All of them distorted the image somewhat, and so this is an apt metaphor for the present knowledge of God—it lacks clarity (until the day we see the Lord clearly in heaven).

13:13 remain. Many spiritual gifts will cease, because they bring only partial knowledge of God; but three things will carry over into the new age: faith, hope, and love. **the greatest of these is love.** Love is the greatest because God is love (1 John 4:8). After everything else is no longer necessary, love will still be the governing principle.

14:5 but even more. While affirming the value of both tongues and prophecy, Paul stresses prophecy because of its value when the church is gathered. **languages.** In verses 2-5, Paul gives insight into just what tongues are. They seem to be a gift from the Holy Spirit whereby an individual "utters mysteries" to God by (or in) the Spirit, from which great personal benefit is gained. Uninterpreted tongues, however, are meant to be part of private devotions, not public worship. **greater.** "Greater" in the sense that prophecy edifies, and is therefore an act of love. Interpreted tongues have the same use and value as prophecy.

14:6-12 Now the real issue comes out: intelligibility (v. 9). It appears that it is not just prophecy that Paul is commending (v. 6). Prophecy is just the example he has chosen of an intelligible gift. Paul examines the value of various gifts from the point of view of what

will build the body.

14:13 Therefore. Connects the previous sentence with what follows.

14:14-17 In the same way that Paul has described that spiritual gifts without love are useless, he goes on to explain that the exercise of the gift of tongues must always keep in mind the ultimate benefit for believers and non-believers alike. The amount of time Paul spends on this subject speaks to its potential abuse for the purpose of self-glory.

14:15 pray with the spirit. Paul adds another insight into tongues: this is prayer that bypasses the mind. It is, according to verse 15, one quite legitimate (and edifying—v. 4) means of prayer, but it is meant to be complemented with prayer that engages the mind.

whether flute or harp—if they don't make a distinction in the notes, how will what is played on the flute or harp be recognized? ⁸ In fact, if the trumpet makes an unclear sound, who will prepare for battle? ⁹ In the same way, unless you use your tongue for intelligible speech, how will what is spoken be known? For you will be speaking into the air. ¹⁰ There are doubtless many different kinds of languages in the world, and all have meaning.ᵃ ¹¹ Therefore, if I do not know the meaning of the language, I will be a foreignerᵇ to the speaker, and the speaker will be a foreigner to me. ¹² So also you—since you are zealous in matters of the spirit,ᶜ seek to excel in building up the church.

¹³ Therefore the person who speaks in ⌊another⌋ language should pray that he can interpret. ¹⁴ For if I pray in ⌊another⌋ language, my spirit prays, but my understanding is unfruitful. ¹⁵ What then? I will pray with the spirit, and I will also pray with my understanding. I will sing with the spirit, and I will also sing with my understanding. ¹⁶ Otherwise, if you bless with the spirit, how will the uninformed personᵈ say "•Amen" at your giving of thanks, since he does not know what you are saying? ¹⁷ For you may very well be giving thanks, but the other person is not being built up. ¹⁸ I thank God that I speak in ⌊other⌋ languages more than all of you; ¹⁹ yet in the church I would rather speak five words with my understanding, in order to teach others also, than 10,000 words in ⌊another⌋ language.

²⁰ Brothers, don't be childish in your thinking, but be infants in evil and adult in your thinking. ²¹ It is written in the law:

> By people of other languages
> and by the lips of foreigners,
> I will speak to this people;
> and even then, they will not listen to Me,ᵉ

says the Lord. ²² It follows that speaking in other languages is intended as a sign,ᶠ not to believers but to unbelievers. But prophecy is not for unbelievers but for believers. ²³ Therefore if the whole church assembles together, and all are speaking in ⌊other⌋ languages, and people who are uninformed or unbelievers come in, will they not say that you are out of your minds? ²⁴ But if all are prophesying, and some unbeliever or uninformed person comes in, he is convicted by all and is judged by all. ²⁵ The secrets of his heart will be revealed, and as a result he will fall down on his face and worship God, proclaiming, "God is really among you."

Order vs. Chaos

1. What was the most disciplined and organized team you've ever been on? The most disorderly and chaotic? Which team played better?

1 Corinthians 14:26-40

2. According to this passage, how should Christians properly use the gift of tongues? What are improper uses of that gift?

3. Why does Paul insist that worship times together be done in an orderly way (vv. 26, 31-33)?

4. When you gather as a group, how can you use your God-given gifts to build up one another?

Order in Church Meetings

²⁶ How is it then, brothers? Whenever you come together, each oneᵍ has a psalm, a teaching, a revelation, ⌊another⌋ language, or an interpretation. All things must be done for edification. ²⁷ If any person speaks in ⌊another⌋ language, there should be only two, or at the most three, each in turn, and someone must interpret. ²⁸ But if there is no interpreter, that person should keep

---

ᵃ**14:10** Lit *and none is without a sound*   ᵇ**14:11** Gk *barbaros* = in Eng *a barbarian*. To a Gk, a *barbaros* was anyone who did not speak Gk.
ᶜ**14:12** Lit *zealous of spirits; spirits* = human spirits, spiritual gifts or powers, or the Holy Spirit   ᵈ**14:16** Lit *the one filling the place of the uninformed*
ᵉ**14:21** Is 28:11–12   ᶠ**14:22** Lit *that tongues are for a sign*   ᵍ**14:26** Other mss add *of you*

14:18 rather speak five words Simply put, don't major on the minors. In line with the other imbalances manifested in the church at Corinth, far too much emphasis was being placed on the demonstration of languages. It may be that the Corinthians' familiarity with "mystery" religions and the ecstatic languages expressed in such meetings caused them to believe that the same should be the hallmark of Christianity as well. Paul is careful here to refocus their concentration on the message of the gospel. In 12:28-29 apostles, prophets, and teachers head the list of spiritual gifts and are indispensable to the establishment and continuance of the church. Many would say that, beyond these primary gifts, the other gifts are simply evidences of the words of the apostles, prophets, and teachers having been spoken and received. And that word directly revolved around the Word Himself, Jesus Christ (John

1:1-5). Therefore, it is understandable why Paul would declare that five intelligible words such as these outweigh the 10,000 words of ecstatic speech. As Paul says, ultimately all spiritual gifts will pass away (13:10), but the Word is eternal.

14:26 each one. Paul reiterates that each believer has a gift to offer during times when the church gathers, that there are a variety of gifts, and that gifts are to be used to build up other people in the body of believers. **a psalm.** Like church services today, worship begins with songs followed by teaching. Paul makes a point by placing these in such order.

14:29-33 Here Paul gives guidelines for prophecy: two or three speak, followed by discerning interpretation.

14:37-38 As to those who are teaching this,

if they are really inspired by the Holy Spirit, they cannot help but agree. God is the author of peace, not confusion.

15:1-3 received Paul uses the same word to describe what he received from the Lord when he gave the Corinthians the instruction on the Lord's Supper (11:23), as he does here to describe the instruction he is again reminding them of in regards to the Lord's resurrection. What he received, they in turn have received.

15:4 He was buried. Jesus was really dead, and so He really rose from the dead. It was a real resurrection, not just resuscitation. **He was raised.** Paul shifts the tense of the verb in Greek (completed past action—"died / buried") to the perfect tense in order to convey the idea that what once happened is even now still in force.

silent in the church and speak to himself and to God. [29] Two or three prophets should speak, and the others should evaluate. [30] But if something has been revealed to another person sitting there, the first prophet should be silent. [31] For you can all prophesy one by one, so that everyone may learn and everyone may be encouraged. [32] And the prophets' spirits are under the control of the prophets, [33] since God is not a God of disorder but of peace.

As in all the churches of the saints, [34] the women[a] should be silent in the churches, for they are not permitted to speak, but should be submissive, as the law also says. [35] And if they want to learn something, they should ask their own husbands at home, for it is disgraceful for a woman to speak in the church meeting. [36] Did the word of God originate from you, or did it come to you only?

[37] If anyone thinks he is a prophet or spiritual, he should recognize that what I write to you is the Lord's command. [38] But if anyone ignores this, he will be ignored.[b] [39] Therefore, my brothers, be eager to prophesy, and do not forbid speaking in ⌊other⌋ languages. [40] But everything must be done decently and in order.

Resurrection Essential to the Gospel

15 Now brothers, I want to clarify[c] for you the gospel I proclaimed to you; you received it and have taken your stand on it. [2] You are also saved by it, if you hold to the message I proclaimed to you—unless you believed to no purpose.[d] [3] For I passed on to you as most important what I also received:

> that Christ died for our sins
>   according to the Scriptures,
> [4] that He was buried,
> that He was raised on the third day
>   according to the Scriptures,
> [5] and that He appeared to •Cephas,
>   then to the Twelve.
> [6] Then He appeared to over 500 brothers
>   at one time,

Holding Firm

1. Who has best helped you to understand God's Word? How did that person effectively pass on God's message to you?

1 Corinthians 15:1-11

2. What does it means to "hold to the message I proclaimed to you" (v. 2)?
3. What does Paul list as the most important aspects of the gospel?
4. In previous passages, Paul has warned against divisions and disagreements. Why might the list in verses 3-8 be the things on which all Christians need to agree?
5. How are you holding firmly to the important things of God's Word when friends or teammates pressure you?

> most of whom remain to the present,
>   but some have fallen •asleep.
> [7] Then He appeared to James, then to all
>   the apostles.
> [8] Last of all, as to one abnormally born,
>   He also appeared to me.

[9] For I am the least of the apostles, unworthy to be called an apostle, because I persecuted the church of God. [10] But by God's grace I am what I am, and His grace toward me was not ineffective. However, I worked more than any of them, yet not I, but God's grace that was with me. [11] Therefore, whether it is I or they, so we preach and so you have believed.

Resurrection Essential to the Faith

[12] Now if Christ is preached as raised from the dead, how can some of you say, "There is no resurrection of the dead"? [13] But if there is no resurrection of the dead,

---

[a] **14:34** Other mss read *your women*   [b] **14:38** Other mss read *he should be ignored*   [c] **15:1** Or *I make known*   [d] **15:2** Or *believed in vain*

15:6 to over 500 brothers ... most of whom remain to the present. Paul is inviting people to check out for themselves the reality of Christ's resurrection. What he is saying is: "There are more than 500 people who some 20 years ago saw Jesus after His resurrection. Ask one of them."

15:8 Last of all ... to me. This appearance came several years after the resurrection of Christ (Acts 9:1-8). **abnormally born.** This probably refers to the fact that, unlike Peter and James, circumstances were such that Paul never knew Jesus during His earthly ministry.

15:9 I persecuted As the book of Acts records, Paul, a devout Pharisee, persecuted the Christians (Acts 8:1-3) immediately following the stoning of Stephen for preaching the gospel (Acts 7:54-60).

Through God's gracious sovereignty, Paul now finds himself preaching the very same gospel. For, on the Damascus Road, Lord Jesus Christ appeared to him and said, "Saul, Saul, Why are you persecuting Me?" Perhaps Paul says he is unworthy to be called an apostle because, by that time, other apostles were being put to death. Eventually, Paul too would seal his love of Christ with his life on the banks of the Tiber.

15:16 if the dead are not raised. This is the first of three times in this section (vv. 12-34) that Paul uses this phrase that summarizes the implications of their errant view about the resurrection of the body. If the dead are not raised, then: (a) Christ could not have been resurrected (and they believe He was); (b) there would be no point in baptizing people for the dead (as they were apparently doing—v. 29); and (c) believers might as well

"live it up," since they had no future (v. 32).

15:17-19 if Christ has note been raised. Relentlessly, Paul points out to his readers the implications of no resurrection: (a) they are still lost and dead in sin; (b) those who have died are lost; (c) their "hope" is groundless; and (d) they are pitiable people. Without the resurrection, Christianity crumbles.

15:20-28 The future resurrection of believers is the logical outcome of Christ's past resurrection. First Thessalonians 4:13-18 refers also to this future resurrection of believers. Paul returns to the metaphor of the "first-fruits," showing how it relates to the second coming. In order for the Corinthians to understand the future resurrection, Paul must place it in the context of the time when Christ returns.

15:27 put everything under His feet Psalm

THE Vital Statistic

1. What would your coach say is the single most important rule in your sport? What would happen if you broke that rule?

1 Corinthians 15:12-34

2. Why is Christ's resurrection so vitally important to the Christian faith? What would be the implications if He had *not* really risen again?
3. According to 15:1-8, how can we be assured that Jesus really did rise again?
4. Why would Paul suggest that "Let us eat and drink, for tomorrow we die" (v. 32) would be an appropriate attitude if there were no resurrection?
5. How should your own eternal life affect your behavior today in sports and in life?

so also in Christ all will be made alive. ²³ But each in his own order: Christ, the firstfruits; afterward, at His coming, the people of Christ. ²⁴ Then comes the end, when He hands over the kingdom to God the Father, when He abolishes all rule and all authority and power. ²⁵ For He must reign until He puts all His enemies under His feet. ²⁶ The last enemy to be abolished is death. ²⁷ For **He has put everything under His feet.**ᵇ But when it says "everything" is put under Him, it is obvious that He who puts everything under Him is the exception. ²⁸ And when everything is subject to Him, then the Son Himself will also be subject to Him who subjected everything to Him, so that God may be all in all.

Resurrection Supported by Christian Experience

²⁹ Otherwise what will they do who are being baptized for the dead? If the dead are not raised at all, then why are peopleᶜ baptized for them?ᵈ ³⁰ Why are we in danger every hour? ³¹ I affirm by the pride in you that I have in Christ Jesus our Lord: I die every day! ³² If I fought wild animals in Ephesus with only human hope,ᵉ what good does that do me?ᶠ If the dead are not raised, **Let us eat and drink, for tomorrow we die.**ᵍ ³³ Do not be deceived: "Bad company corrupts good morals."ʰ ³⁴ Become right-mindedⁱ and stop sinning, because some people are ignorant about God. I say this to your shame.

The Nature of the Resurrection Body

³⁵ But someone will say, "How are the dead raised? What kind of body will they have when they come?" ³⁶ Foolish one! What you sow does not come to life unless it dies. ³⁷ And as for what you sow—you are not sowing the future body, but only a seed,ʲ perhaps of wheat or another grain. ³⁸ But God gives it a body as He wants, and to each of the seeds its own body. ³⁹ Not all flesh is the same flesh; there is one flesh for humans, another for animals, another for birds, and another for fish. ⁴⁰ There are heavenly bodies and earthly bodies, but the splendor of the heavenly bodies is different

then Christ has not been raised; ¹⁴ and if Christ has not been raised, then our preaching is without foundation, and so is your faith.ᵃ ¹⁵ In addition, we are found to be false witnesses about God, because we have testified about God that He raised up Christ—whom He did not raise up if in fact the dead are not raised. ¹⁶ For if the dead are not raised, Christ has not been raised. ¹⁷ And if Christ has not been raised, your faith is worthless; you are still in your sins. ¹⁸ Therefore those who have fallen asleep in Christ have also perished. ¹⁹ If we have placed our hope in Christ for this life only, we should be pitied more than anyone.

Christ's Resurrection Guarantees Ours

²⁰ But now Christ has been raised from the dead, the •firstfruits of those who have fallen asleep. ²¹ For since death came through a man, the resurrection of the dead also comes through a man. ²² For just as in Adam all die,

---

ᵃ**15:14** Or *preaching is useless, and your faith also is useless,* or *preaching is empty, and your faith also is empty* ᵇ**15:27** Ps 8:6 ᶜ**15:29** Lit *they* ᵈ**15:29** Other mss read *for the dead* ᵉ**15:32** Lit *Ephesus according to man* ᶠ**15:32** Lit *what to me the profit?* ᵍ**15:32** Is 22:13 ʰ**15:33** A quotation from the poet Menander, *Thais,* 218 ⁱ**15:34** Lit *Sober up righteously* ʲ**15:37** Lit *but a naked seed*

8:6, quoted here, continues the allusion to Psalm 110:1 in verse 25. That the final obstacle, death (v. 26), is already considered a done deal still to be realized gives reason for the Corinthians to hope in resurrection.

15:29-34 Thus far, Paul has shown that there is a resurrection for believers in the future. Here he points out that both his actions and theirs demonstrate a belief in the resurrection of the dead.

15:29 baptized for the dead. It seems that among the strange things that happened at Corinth was the practice (by some) of vicarious baptism. A living person was immersed in water on behalf of a dead person to secure, as if by magic, the benefits of baptism for the departed friend. This practice may also have been for believers who died without first being baptized. In this case, it would

have been merely a symbolic act.

15:36-38 What you sow. Death brings transformation, not extinction. Here, Paul probes the nature of the transformation; his point being that what one plants is not what one gets in the end. A small grain of wheat grows mysteriously into a tall, grain-bearing stalk (John 12:24). So, too, with the bodies of believers.

15:39-41 heavenly bodies. A second analogy is used to show that there are a host of different kinds of bodies, and it is not unreasonable to expect the resurrection body to be quite different from the natural body.

15:42-44 resurrection of the dead. Paul reinforces the idea of verse 36: what is sown in one way is raised in another. He makes this point by means of a series of antithetical

comparisons: corruption/incorruption; dishonor/glory; weakness/power; natural/spiritual.

15:43 glory. Paul now describes the nature of the changed body. The resurrection body is characterized by glory (brightness, radiance, splendor). This is a quality ascribed to God, in which believers will somehow share (Phil. 3:21).

15:44 natural ... spiritual. The natural body is that which is animated by the soul of the person, while the spiritual body has as its animating source the Holy Spirit.

15:49 the heavenly man. This is Jesus, whose image Christians will reflect both in terms of character and glory.

15:50 flesh and blood. That is, living people

Victory Over Death

1. What is the sweetest victory you have experienced? How did you celebrate?

1 Corinthians 15:35-58

2. What does it mean that our bodies are "sown in corruption" and "raised in incorruption" (v. 42)?

3. Who is "the last Adam" (v. 45)? How did He become "a life-giving Spirit"?

4. Why can't "corruption ... inherit incorruption" (v. 50)? How should this affect the way we live?

5. How did Jesus win victory over death? How can you share in this victory (see John 5:24)?

---

from that of the earthly ones. ⁴¹ There is a splendor of the sun, another of the moon, and another of the stars; for star differs from star in splendor. ⁴² So it is with the resurrection of the dead:

Sown in corruption, raised in incorruption;
⁴³ sown in dishonor, raised in glory;
sown in weakness, raised in power;
⁴⁴ sown a natural body, raised a spiritual body.

If there is a natural body, there is also a spiritual body. ⁴⁵ So it is written: **The first man Adam became a living being;**ᵃ the last Adam became a life-giving Spirit. ⁴⁶ However, the spiritual is not first, but the natural; then the spiritual.

⁴⁷ The first man was from the earth and made of dust; the second man isᵇ from heaven.

⁴⁸ Like the man made of dust, so are those who are made of dust; like the heavenly man, so are those who are heavenly.

⁴⁹ And just as we have borne the image of the man made of dust, we will also bear the image of the heavenly man.

Victorious Resurrection

⁵⁰ Brothers, I tell you this: flesh and blood cannot inherit the kingdom of God, and corruption cannot inherit incorruption. ⁵¹ Listen! I am telling you a •mystery:

We will not all fall asleep,
but we will all be changed,
⁵² in a moment, in the twinkling of an eye,
at the last trumpet.
For the trumpet will sound, and the dead
will be raised incorruptible,
and we will be changed.
⁵³ Because this corruptible must be clothed
with incorruptibility,
and this mortal must be clothed
with immortality.
⁵⁴ Now when this corruptible is clothed
with incorruptibility,
and this mortal is clothed with immortality,
then the saying that is written will take place:
Death has been swallowed up in victory.ᶜ
⁵⁵ **O Death, where is your victory?**
O Death, where is your sting?ᵈ
⁵⁶ Now the sting of death is sin, and the power
of sin is the law.
⁵⁷ But thanks be to God, who gives us the victory
through our Lord Jesus Christ!

⁵⁸ Therefore, my dear brothers, be steadfast, immovable, always excelling in the Lord's work, knowing that your labor in the Lord is not in vain.

ᵃ15:45 Gn 2:7 ᵇ15:47 Other mss add *the Lord* ᶜ15:54 Is 25:8 ᵈ15:55 Hs 13:14

---

cannot inherit the kingdom. corruption. Nor can the unchanged dead inherit the kingdom. What Paul is saying is that at the second coming neither the living nor the dead can take part in the kingdom without being changed.

15:51 mystery. A truth about the end times, once hidden but now revealed. **We.** Paul expected to be alive at the Second Coming. **not all fall asleep.** Some Christians will be alive at the Second Coming. **all be changed.** Both the living and the dead will be changed.

15:52 in a moment. This change will occur instantaneously. **the trumpet will sound.** The sounding of the trumpet was used to rally an army for action. This image is used to describe God's calling of His people together (1 Thess. 4:16). **the dead will be**

raised. Those who are in the grave at the second coming will be transformed, as will the living.

15:56 the power of sin is the law. By this Paul means that the law of God has the unfortunate result of arousing sin within people. As he shows from his own example in Romans 7, the law's command not to covet did not put an end to his wanting what others had. The command, holy in itself, actually stirred him up to covet all the more.

15:57 victory. In great joy, Paul exults in the fact that sin and the law (that by which sin is made known) do not have the last word. Christ's death was a victory over sin and death.

15:58 be steadfast. His letter is at an end; his chastening is finished, and so it is appro-

priate that he challenge his readers to allow this same Christ who has won victories for them to win victories through them. **your labor in the Lord is not in vain.** Because the resurrection is real, the future is secure and magnificent.

16:1 the collection. When in Jerusalem, Paul had agreed to help support the poor there (Gal. 2:10). In this way, the Gentile and the Jewish wings of the church would be bound together in a new fashion.

16:2 On the first day. Sunday, when Christians typically met for worship (Jewish Christians often went to the worship with Jews in a Synagogue on Saturdays). **set something aside.** Paul is not calling for a collection to be taken each Sunday for his purpose. Rather, he asks individual Christians to set aside funds on their own. **no collections**

Collection for the Jerusalem Church

16 Now about the collection for the saints: you should do the same as I instructed the Galatian churches. ² On the first day of the week, each of you is to set something aside and save to the extent that he prospers, so that no collections will need to be made when I come. ³ And when I arrive, I will send those whom you recommend by letter to carry your gracious gift to Jerusalem. ⁴ If it is also suitable for me to go, they will travel with me.

Paul's Travel Plans

⁵ I will come to you after I pass through Macedonia— for I will be traveling through Macedonia— ⁶ and perhaps I will remain with you, or even spend the winter, that you may send me on my way wherever I go. ⁷ I don't want to see you now just in passing, for I hope to spend some time with you, if the Lord allows. ⁸ But I will stay in Ephesus until Pentecost, ⁹ because a wide door for effective ministry has opened for me[a] —yet many oppose me. ¹⁰ If Timothy comes, see that he has nothing to fear from you, because he is doing the Lord's work, just as I am. ¹¹ Therefore no one should look down on him; but you should send him on his way in peace so he can come to me, for I am expecting him with the brothers.[b]

¹² About our brother Apollos: I strongly urged him to come to you with the brothers, but he was not at all willing to come now. However, when he has time, he will come.

Final Exhortation

¹³ Be alert, stand firm in the faith, be brave and strong. ¹⁴ Your every ⌜action⌝ must be done with love.

¹⁵ Brothers, you know the household of Stephanas: they are the •firstfruits of Achaia and have devoted themselves to serving the saints. I urge you ¹⁶ also to submit to such people, and to everyone who works and

Bravery Under Fire

1. Who is the bravest person you know? What has that person done to show real courage?

1 Corinthians 16:1-24

2. What does it mean to "be alert" (v. 13)? To "stand firm in the faith"?

3. Why do Christians need to "be brave and strong" (v. 13)? When has obedience required that *you* be brave?

4. Are you spiritually alert? Brave? Strong? How can you improve in these areas?

5. When you get under fire—and pressure or competition heats up—how does your bravery stand up?

labors with them. ¹⁷ I am delighted over the presence of Stephanas, Fortunatus, and Achaicus, because these men have made up for your absence. ¹⁸ For they have refreshed my spirit and yours. Therefore recognize such people.

Conclusion

¹⁹ The churches of the Asian province greet you. Aquila and Priscilla greet you heartily in the Lord, along with the church that meets in their home. ²⁰ All the brothers greet you. Greet one another with a holy kiss.

²¹ This greeting is in my own hand[c] — Paul. ²² If anyone does not love the Lord, a curse be on him. *Maranatha!*[d] ²³ The grace of our Lord Jesus be with you. ²⁴ My love be with all of you in Christ Jesus.

---

[a]**16:9** Lit *for a door has opened to me, great and effective* [b]**16:11** *With the brothers* may connect with Paul or Timothy. [c]**16:21** Paul normally dictated his letters to a secretary, but signed the end of each letter himself; see Rm 16:22; Gl 6:11; Col 4:18; 2 Th 3:17. [d]**16:22** Aram expression meaning *Our Lord come!*, or *Our Lord has come!*

---

will need to be made. Paul hoped that each person would have a sum of money set aside, ready to hand over when he came, so that he would not have to bother with the time-consuming process of taking a collection.

16:20 a holy kiss. This was a custom used in the early church as part of the worship ser-

vice. Kisses were a common form of greeting in biblical times, especially in the Middle Eastern culture.

16:22 a curse be on him. Paul calls for God's judgment upon those who fail to love Jesus and, by implication, follow Him. The Lord is then invoked as a witness to the judgment. *Maranatha!* This is an Aramaic ex-

pression, translated *"Come, O Lord!"* transliterated by Paul into Greek (see also Rev. 22:20). This was an expression used by the early Christians referring to the fact that Christ would soon return. The Lord's return would mark the moment when the curse on those who had refused to love Him would be put into effect.

2 CORINTHIANS

AUTHOR

The Apostle Paul was the writer of 2 Corinthians.

DATE

Paul wrote this letter around A.D. 55-56.

THEME

The strength of weakness.

HISTORICAL BACKGROUND

Paul's founded a church on his first visit to Corinth during his second missionary journey. In 2 Corinthians 13:1, Paul proposes a third visit to the city. It seems that his second visit was the cause of much trouble and the reason he wrote 2 Corinthians.

This second visit had been promised in 1 Corinthians 16:1-9. Paul wrote that he would leave Ephesus, journey to Macedonia, and then come down to Corinth on his way to Jerusalem with the collection. But Paul traveled straight to Corinth, intending to go from there up to Macedonia and then back to Corinth once again. He anticipated visiting Corinth as mutual pleasure (1:15-16). But his unexpected visit proved so painful (due to conflict with false apostles), that he canceled his return trip from Macedonia. Instead he went back to Ephesus, then north again to Troas, and finally back once more to Macedonia. At Macedonia, he wrote 2 Corinthians to prepare them for a third visit.

Reconstructing the events surrounding the writing of 2 Corinthians is further complicated because it seems Paul wrote two other letters to the Corinthians that have not been preserved (see

1 Cor. 5:9; 2 Cor. 2:3-4,9; 7:8-13). Paul wrote one of these letters prior to 1 Corinthians and another (the "sorrowful" letter) in between 1 and 2 Corinthians, probably to explain why he was not returning to Corinth from Macedonia (1:23; 2:4).

Some believe that 2 Corinthians may be two letters. The fierce tone of chapters 10-13 stands in sharp contrast to the gentle, reconciling tone of chapters 1-9. According to this theory, the first nine chapters (Paul's fourth letter) seem to be based on the report of Titus (7:6-16) that the situation in Corinth had been rectified. But when Titus returned to Corinth with chapters 1-9, he found to his horror that the "super-apostles" were back in charge, so he quickly returned to Macedonia. Reacting to the new situation, Paul penned chapters 10-13 (his fifth letter). The fourth and fifth letters were later copied together, since they were so closely related in subject matter, and they became what we know as 2 Corinthians.

PAUL'S NEW OPPONENTS

Who then opposed Paul with such vigor during his second "painful" visit? The best guess is that the troublemakers were not from the Corinthian church itself. Rather, they were a band of outside "apostles" (called cynically by Paul "super-apostles" in 11:5 and 12:11), probably Jewish

Christians from Palestine, who sought to conform the Corinthian church to Jewish Law. They attacked Paul vigorously, calling him two-faced (10:1-11); they questioned his credentials as an apostle; and they criticized him for drawing no financial support from the Corinthians (the way a real apostle would). Apparently Paul's real pain came because the Corinthians did not rally to his support in this conflict.

PAUL'S PAIN

In many ways, 2 Corinthians is Paul's most personal letter. He reveals his pain and his joy, his outrage and his suffering, his love and his convictions. Second Corinthians is filled with profound feeling. As C. K. Barrett said: "Writing 2 Corinthians must have come near to breaking Paul, and ... a church that is prepared to read it with him and understand it, may find itself broken too" *(The Second Epistle to the Corinthians: Harper New Testament Commentaries).*

Not only is Paul's pain evident in this letter, but also his toughness. He was willing to fight to wrest the Corinthians from the corrupting influence of the false apostles. "It would have been natural for Paul simply to give up the ungrateful, unruly, unloving, unintelligent Corinthians and leave them to their destiny. There is no indication that this thought ever crossed his mind" (Barrett, *The Second Epistle to the Corinthians,* pp. 32-33). The reason for his tenacity is found in the strength of his calling. He was an apostle—called by God to bring men and women into the kingdom. No band of petty pretenders was going to defeat him in that God-given purpose.

PASSAGES FOR TOPICAL GROUP STUDY

1:3-11	HURTING and COMFORT	God's Comfort
1:12-2:11	GOD"S PROMISE and SIN	Yes, No, Maybe
3:7-18	THE LAW VS. GRACE	The Old and New Covenants
4:1-18	CHRIST-CONFIDENCE	Unwavering Confidence
5:1-10	TAKING CARE OR OURSELVES	Camping Out on Earth
5:11-6:2	DRAWING PEOPLE TO GOD	A Ministry of Reconciliation
6:3-13	ENDURING IN TRIALS	The Test of Faith
6:14-7:1	FRIENDSHIPS WITH UNBELIVERS	An Uneven Match
7:2-16	TURNING BACK TO GOD	Godly Grief
8:1-15	USING YOUR BLESINGS	Using What You Have
8:16-9:5	MONEY and GIVING	Generous Giving
9:6-15	GIVING	Cheerful Giving
10:1-18	SPIRTUAL WAR	Weapons of War
11:1-15	SATAN'S SCHEMES	Evil in Disguise
12:1-10	WEAKNESS AND PROBLEMS	Thorn in the Flesh
12:11-21	PERSISTING I LOVE	Unselfish Sacrifice
13:1-14	TESTING YOURSELF	Passing the Test

PASSAGES FOR GENERAL GROUP STUDY

2:12-3:6	Fragrant Letters (Scent of "Life" or of "Death")	
11:16-33	Tolerating Fools (Handling Foolish Teaching)	

Greeting

1 Paul, an apostle of Christ Jesus by God's will, and Timothy our[a] brother:

To God's church at Corinth, with all the saints who are throughout Achaia.

[2] Grace to you and peace from God our Father and the Lord Jesus Christ.

God's Comfort

1. What was your favorite "comforter" as a child: Teddy bear? Blanket? Thumb? Other?

2 Corinthians 1:3-11

2. From what "terrible death" (v. 10) has Jesus delivered us? How does that lead to the comfort and hope that Paul speaks of here?

3. What does it mean that the "sufferings of Christ overflow to us" (v. 5)? What does this suggest about suffering and the Christian life?

4. How does our "comfort overflow through Christ" (v. 5)?

5. Are you in need of God's comfort? Do you know someone else to whom you can show God's comfort?

The God of Comfort

[3] Blessed be the God and Father of our Lord Jesus Christ, the Father of mercies and the God of all comfort. [4] He comforts us in all our affliction,[b] so that we may be able to comfort those who are in any kind of affliction, through the comfort we ourselves receive from God. [5] For as the sufferings of Christ overflow to us, so our comfort overflows through Christ. [6] If we are afflicted, it is for your comfort and salvation; if we are comforted, it is for your comfort, which is experienced in the endurance of the same sufferings that we suffer. [7] And our hope for you is firm, because we know that as you share in the sufferings, so you will share in the comfort.

[8] For we don't want you to be unaware, brothers, of our affliction that took place in the province of Asia: we were completely overwhelmed—beyond our strength—so that we even despaired of life. [9] However, we personally had a death sentence within ourselves so that we would not trust in ourselves, but in God who raises the dead. [10] He has delivered us from such a terrible death, and He will deliver us; we have placed our hope in Him that He will deliver us again. [11] And you can join in helping with prayer for us, so that thanks may be given by many[c] on our[d] behalf for the gift that came to us through ⸤the prayers of⸥ many.

A Clear Conscience

[12] For our boast is this: the testimony of our conscience that we have conducted ourselves in the world, and especially toward you, with God-given sincerity and purity, not by fleshly[e] wisdom but by God's grace. [13] Now we are writing you nothing other than what you can read and also understand. I hope you will understand completely— [14] as you have partially understood us—that we are your reason for pride, as you are ours, in the day of our[f] Lord Jesus.

A Visit Postponed

[15] In this confidence, I planned to come to you first, so you could have a double benefit,[g] [16] and to go on to Macedonia with your help, then come to you again from Macedonia and be given a start by you on my journey to Judea. [17] So when I planned this, was I irresponsible? Or what I plan, do I plan in a purely human[h] way so that I say "Yes, yes" and "No, no" ⸤simultaneously⸥? [18] As God is faithful, our message to you is not "Yes and no." [19] For the Son of God, Jesus Christ, who was preached among you by us—by me and Silvanus[i] and

---

[a]**1:1** Lit *the* [b]**1:4** Or *trouble,* or *tribulation,* or *trials,* or *oppression*; the Gk word has a lit meaning of being under pressure. [c]**1:11** Lit *by many faces* [d]**1:11** Other mss read *your* [e]**1:12** The word *fleshly* (characterized by flesh) indicates that the wisdom is natural rather than spiritual. [f]**1:14** Other mss omit *our* [g]**1:15** Other mss read *a second joy* [h]**1:17** Or *a worldly,* or *a fleshly,* or *a selfish* [i]**1:19** Or *Silas*; see Ac 15:22–32; 16:19–40; 17:1–16

1:1 an apostle of Christ Jesus by God's will. While this is a stock phrase Paul often used to identify himself (1 Cor. 1:1; Eph. 1:1; Col. 1:1; 2 Tim. 1:1), in this letter the title takes on special force since it is precisely Paul's apostleship that is being called into question. **Timothy.** Timothy was Paul's co-worker and colleague who had also been involved with the Corinthian church (Acts 18:5; 1 Cor. 4:17; 16:10). **Achaia.** Roughly equivalent to what today is southern Greece, Achaia was the Roman province of which Corinth was the capital city.

1:4 our affliction. Literally, "our trials." This includes both the internal anguish and the physical hardships that Christians experience because of following Jesus. **so that we may be able to comfort.** The purpose of God's aid is to enable those so helped to aid others who are afflicted.

1:5 the sufferings of Christ. Those who follow Christ share in His sufferings. Rejection, injustice, and bearing the affliction of others are all common experiences for the Christian.

1:6 endurance. Not a grim, bleak acceptance of difficulties, but a hopeful steadfastness in the midst of trial.

1:8 affliction. The Book of Acts has no record of what was obviously an extremely difficult experience for Paul in Asia. Some commentators think it may refer to the imprisonment mentioned in Philippians 1:12-20 where Paul was not certain whether he would live or die. **Asia.** This was the Roman province located in the western part of modern Turkey. Ephesus was its leading city. **completely overwhelmed.** This is to be weighed down like an overloaded ship.

1:12 boast. Paul begins the defense of his integrity by pointing out that he has nothing to be ashamed of—despite this criticism of him. "Boast" literally means, "confidence." Paul uses this word (or a derivative of it) 29 times in this letter. This may be in response to the "boasting" done by the itinerant teachers who were promoting themselves over him. **especially toward you.** Paul had taken great pains to act with integrity toward the Corinthians: he took no payment from them (11:7-9); he also worked to ensure that the collection for the needy in Jerusalem was not misappropriated (1 Cor. 16:1-4). **sincerity.** The Corinthians have charged him with deception. On the contrary, he says, his actions were characterized throughout by sincerity. **fleshly wisdom.** Such "wisdom" guides one's actions in the ways of self-interest or self-promotion. In contrast, Paul focused on God and the needs of others.

Timothy—did not become "Yes and no"; on the contrary, "Yes" has come about in Him. ²⁰ For every one of God's promises is "Yes" in Him. Therefore the "•Amen" is also through Him for God's glory through us. ²¹ Now the One who confirms us with you in Christ, and has anointed us, is God; ²² He has also sealed us and given us the Spirit as a down payment in our hearts.

Yes, No, Maybe

1. From which parent can you rely on a "no" reply? A "yes" reply? Which one waffles? Why is that?

2 Corinthians 1:12-2:11

2. In what does Paul boast (1:12)? What is the basis for his integrity?

3. What does it mean that Jesus is the "Yes" of God's promise to us (1:20)?

4. Paraphrase the "business deal" of 1:22 in modern terms. How have you experienced this spiritual "new deal"?

5. What can we learn from 2:5-11 about dealing with fellow Christians in sin? How should they be corrected? What completes the restoration?

²³ I call on God as a witness against me:ᵃ it was to spare you that I did not come to Corinth. ²⁴ Not that we have control ofᵇ your faith, but we are workers with you for your joy, because you stand by faith. ¹ In fact, I made up my mind about this:ᶜ not to come to you on another painful visit.ᵈ ² For if I cause you pain, then who will cheer me other than the one hurt?ᵉ ³ I wrote this very thing so that when I came I wouldn't have pain from those who ought to give me joy, because I am confident about all of you that my joy is yours.ᶠ ⁴ For out

of an extremely troubled and anguished heart I wrote to you with many tears—not that you should be hurt, but that you should know the abundant love I have for you.

A Sinner Forgiven

⁵ If anyone has caused pain, he has not caused pain to me, but in some degree—not to exaggerate—to all of you. ⁶ The punishment by the majority is sufficient for such a person, ⁷ so now you should forgive and comfort him instead; otherwise, this one may be overwhelmed by excessive grief. ⁸ Therefore I urge you to confirm your love to him. ⁹ It was for this purpose I wrote: so I may know your proven character, if you are obedient in everything. ¹⁰ Now to whom you forgive anything, I do too. For what I have forgiven, if I have forgiven anything, it is for you in the presence of Christ, ¹¹ so that we may not be taken advantage of by Satan; for we are not ignorant of his intentions.ᵍ

A Trip to Macedonia

¹² When I came to Troas for the gospel of Christ, a door was opened to me by the Lord. ¹³ I had no rest in my spirit because I did not find my brother Titus, but I said good-bye to them and left for Macedonia.

A Ministry of Life or Death

¹⁴ But thanks be to God, who always puts us on displayʰ in Christ,ⁱ and spreads through us in every place the scent of knowing Him. ¹⁵ For to God we are the fragrance of Christ among those who are being saved and among those who are perishing. ¹⁶ To some we are a scent of death leading to death, but to others, a scent of life leading to life. And who is competent for this? ¹⁷ For we are not like the manyʲ who make a trade in God's message [for profit], but as those with sincerity, we speak in Christ, as from God and before God.

Living Letters

Are we beginning to commend ourselves again? Or like some, do we need letters of recommendation to you or from you? ² You yourselves are our letter,

---

ᵃ**1:23** Lit *against my soul*   ᵇ**1:24** Or *we lord it over, or we rule over*   ᶜ**2:1** Lit *I decided this for myself*   ᵈ**2:1** Lit *not again in sorrow to come to you*   ᵉ**2:2** Lit *the one pained*   ᶠ**2:3** Lit *is of you all*   ᵍ**2:11** Or *thoughts*   ʰ**2:14** Or *always leads us in a triumphal procession*, or less likely, *always causes us to triumph*   ⁱ**2:14** Lit *in the Christ*, or *in the Messiah*; see 1 Co 15:22; Eph 1:10,12,20; 3:11   ʲ**2:17** Other mss read *the rest*

1:15-16 I planned. Paul addresses the charge that he was unreliable. He had written that he intended to go to Macedonia and then to Corinth (1 Cor. 16:5-9). However, perhaps in response to a report from Timothy (1 Cor. 16:10-11), he changed his plans and visited Corinth first, sooner than expected. His intention at the time was to go from there to Macedonia and then return to Corinth again. However, since this unexpected visit was so difficult (2:1), it is thought that he returned to Ephesus and wrote another letter (now lost) to Corinth (2:1-4). Then he went to Macedonia and chose not to return to Corinth at all (v. 23). The changes in Paul's plans opened the way for him to be charged as being untrustworthy.

1:19 Silvanus and Timothy. Paul's coworkers in Corinth during his original trip

(Acts 18:5). **Yes.** The sending of Jesus, God's Son, is God's guarantee to humanity that He is for us; that He will fulfill all His promises; that He can be trusted absolutely.

2:3 I wrote. Paul was in a bind. If he came again as proposed, he would cause pain. If he didn't come, he would be charged with fickleness. **I wouldn't have pain.** Paul was concerned both that they would be grieved by another visit (vv. 1-2) and that he too would find it painful. His fear, perhaps, was that indeed they had been subverted by the false teachers and had embraced a false gospel.

2:12-13 When I came. Leaving Corinth as a result of the painful incident, Paul went to Macedonia, then to Ephesus, and then to Troas (a city 150 miles north of Ephesus).

Finally, he returned to Macedonia.

2:13 Titus. Although not mentioned in Acts, Titus traveled with Paul and was entrusted with several important missions.

2:14 puts us on display. This phrase may simply mean "displays us," or it may refer to the Roman practice of a military general leading a victory march with those he had conquered following behind.

3:1 letters of recommendation. It was common for itinerant teachers to get such letters as a means of introducing and validating their work in a new area.

3:6 new covenant. A covenant is an agreement initiated and defined by God between Himself and His people. This covenant is quite different from the old one. Jeremiah clearly

Fragrant Letters

1. What is your favorite fragrance? Favorite perfume or cologne? What smells always make you gag?

2 Corinthians 2:12-3:6

2. How can the same gospel be either the "scent of death" or the "scent of life" (2:16)?

3. Until Titus returns with "good news" (see 7:6-13), Paul has no rest in his spirit (2:13). What does that say about Paul's concern for this church?

4. What does Paul mean by "You yourselves are our letter" (3:2)? What sort of a "letter" are you?

5. How can you spread the aroma of Christ in the environment of your home? In your school?

written on our hearts, recognized and read by everyone, ³ since it is plain that you are Christ's letter, produced^a by us, not written with ink but with the Spirit of the living God; not on stone tablets but on tablets that are hearts of flesh.

Paul's Competence

⁴ We have this kind of confidence toward God through Christ: ⁵ not that we are competent in^b ourselves to consider anything as coming from ourselves, but our competence is from God. ⁶ He has made us competent to be ministers of a new covenant, not of the letter, but of the Spirit; for the letter kills, but the Spirit produces life.

New Covenant Ministry

⁷ Now if the ministry of death, chiseled in letters on stones, came with glory, so that the sons of Israel were not able to look directly at Moses' face because of the glory from his face—a fading ⌊glory⌋— ⁸ how will the ministry of the Spirit not be more glorious? ⁹ For if the ministry of condemnation had glory, the ministry of righteousness overflows with even more glory. ¹⁰ In fact, what had been glorious is not glorious in this case because of the glory that surpasses it. ¹¹ For if what was fading away was glorious, what endures will be even more glorious.

The Old and New Covenants

1. Who is the boldest person you know? What has that person done that is so bold? Was it a good boldness or just arrogance?

2 Corinthians 3:7-18

2. How does Paul contrast the old and new covenants (see also 3:3,6)?

3. Why did the everlasting covenant of Christ have to replace the once-glorious covenant of Moses?

4. What are the practical results of this new covenant (vv. 16-18)?

5. In what sense is the law (such as the Ten Commandments referred to in verse 7) "fading away" (v. 11)? In what sense does that law still apply today?

¹² Therefore having such a hope, we use great boldness— ¹³ not like Moses, who used to put a veil over his face so that the sons of Israel could not look at the end of what was fading away. ¹⁴ But their minds were closed.^c For to this day, at the reading of the old covenant, the same veil remains; it is not lifted, because it is set aside ⌊only⌋ in Christ. ¹⁵ However, to this day, whenever Moses is read, a veil lies over their hearts, ¹⁶ but whenever a person turns to the Lord, the veil is removed. ¹⁷ Now the Lord is the Spirit; and where the

^a**3:3** Lit *ministered to* ^b**3:5** Lit *from* ^c**3:14** Lit *their thoughts were hardened*

prophesied about this new covenant (Jer. 31:31-34). **letter ... Spirit.** "Letter" refers to the words of the Old Covenant law; "Spirit" is the Holy Spirit. The Old Covenant law kills because we are sinful. The law is good and spiritual but in itself it only shows that people don't measure up. The Old Covenant condemns. The New Covenant forgives and empowers.

3:7-11 Paul uses what we might call a "how much more" argument here. If there was great glory when the Law—an instrument of condemnation— was given, how much more or how much greater glory attends the ministry of the Spirit through which we are made righteous.

3:7 glory. This refers to the radiance in Moses' face that reflected God's presence when he came down from Mount Sinai.

3:12-13 boldness. Paul's point is not that he is superior to Moses. Rather, he simply uses the thought of Moses' veiling himself as a contrast with his open approach to ministry. While Moses hid the diminishing glory of the Old Covenant behind the veil, Paul hides nothing of the permanent glory of the New Covenant of the Spirit. This imagery serves to highlight the superiority and permanence of the New Covenant.

3:13 a veil. To cover one's face or head was to hide something, or a sign of shame; to unveil the head and face was to be completely open and bold.

3:14-16 But their minds were closed. Paul now uses the veil of Moses as an illustration to describe why those who hold to the Old Covenant are unable to see the glory of the new. Their minds and hearts are only un-

veiled (and thus able to see) when they turn to the Lord.

3:17 the Lord is the Spirit. The Holy Spirit is Jesus' Agent within us bringing to completion in us all that Jesus did for us in His death and resurrection. **Where the Spirit of the Lord...freedom**. We were slaves to sin. The law only made us acutely aware of that. Because of Jesus death, we are free from both the condemnation of the law and the power of sin. We are freed from our past and freed for our future, freed to be what God always intended us to be.

3:18 reflecting. As believers see the glory of God in Jesus (who is the image of God— 4:4,6), they are themselves continually being transformed by that encounter so that they will ultimately reflect the character and glory of Jesus (Rom. 8:29; Phil. 3:21).

Spirit of the Lord is, there is freedom. ¹⁸ We all, with unveiled faces, are reflectingᵃ the glory of the Lord and are being transformed into the same image from glory to glory;ᵇ this is from the Lord who is the Spirit.ᶜ

Unwavering Confidence

1. When have you accidentally broken something very valuable? How did it happen?

2 Corinthians 4:1-18

2. Why is it important to "renounce shameful secret things" (v. 2)?

3. Who is "the god of this age" (v. 4)? How has he "blinded the minds of the unbelievers so they cannot see the light of the gospel of the glory of Christ"?

4. In verse 7, what are the "clay jars"? What is the "treasure"?

5. Paul had unwavering confidence in the Lord and his work for the Lord (vv. 13-14). Where do you draw confidence in your life?

The Light of the Gospel

4 Therefore, since we have this ministry, as we have received mercy, we do not give up. ² Instead, we have renounced shameful secret things, not •walking in deceit or distorting God's message, but in God's sight we commend ourselves to every person's conscience by an open display of the truth. ³ But if, in fact, our gospel is veiled, it is veiled to those who are perishing. ⁴ Regarding them: the god of this age has blinded the minds of the unbelievers so they cannot see the light of the gospel of the glory of Christ,ᵈ who is the image of God. ⁵ For we are not proclaiming our-

selves but Jesus Christ as Lord, and ourselves as your slaves because of Jesus. ⁶ For God, who said, "Light shall shine out of darkness"—He has shone in our hearts to give the light of the knowledge of God's glory in the face of Jesus Christ.

Treasure in Clay Jars

⁷ Now we have this treasure in clay jars, so that this extraordinary power may be from God and not from us. ⁸ We are pressured in every way but not crushed; we are perplexed but not in despair; ⁹ we are persecuted but not abandoned; we are struck down but not destroyed. ¹⁰ We always carry the death of Jesus in our body, so that the life of Jesus may also be revealed in our body. ¹¹ For we who live are always given over to death because of Jesus, so that Jesus' life may also be revealed in our mortal flesh. ¹² So death works in us, but life in you. ¹³ And since we have the same spirit of faith in accordance with what is written, **I believed, therefore I spoke,**ᵉ we also believe, and therefore speak, ¹⁴ knowing that the One who raised the Lord Jesus will raise us also with Jesus, and present us with you. ¹⁵ For all this is because of you, so that grace, extended through more and more people, may cause thanksgiving to overflow to God's glory.

¹⁶ Therefore we do not give up; even though our outer person is being destroyed, our inner person is being renewed day by day. ¹⁷ For our momentary light afflictionᶠ is producing for us an absolutely incomparable eternal weight of glory. ¹⁸ So we do not focus on what is seen, but on what is unseen; for what is seen is temporary, but what is unseen is eternal.

Our Future after Death

5 For we know that if our earthly house, a tent,ᵍ is destroyed, we have a building from God, a houseʰ not made with hands, eternal in the heavens. ² And, in fact, we groan in this one, longing to put on our house from heaven, ³ since, when we are clothed,ⁱ we will not be found naked. ⁴ Indeed, we who are in this tent groan, burdened as we are, because we do not want to

---

ᵃ**3:18** Or *are looking as in a mirror at* ᵇ**3:18** Progressive glorification or sanctification ᶜ**3:18** Or *from the Spirit of the Lord*, or *from the Lord, the Spirit* ᵈ**4:4** Or *the gospel of the glorious Christ*, or *the glorious gospel of Christ* ᵉ**4:13** Ps 116:10 LXX ᶠ**4:17** See note at 2 Co 1:4 ᵍ**5:1** Our present physical body ʰ**5:1** *a building . . . a house* = our future body ⁱ**5:3** Other mss read *stripped*

4:8-10 We are pressured. God's power is seen, not in that Paul rides above suffering, but that in the midst of suffering he is continually sustained by God. The hardships experienced by the apostles reflect the opposition and, ultimately, the death (v. 10) experienced by Jesus (Rom. 8:17; Phil. 3:10). The ministry of the glory of the gospel requires all of its messengers—all of Christ's followers—to share in the suffering of Christ. These verses should bring us all hope in the midst of suffering.

4:8 pressured. The affliction (the idea behind this word) was real but not fatal (he was not "crushed").

4:9 persecuted. The opposition Paul faced—both from Jewish and Gentile sources—was very real and very intense, yet in it all, God enabled him to prevail. **struck**

down. Even when the blow was overwhelming, Paul was preserved by God.

4:12 in us. Paul absorbs the brunt of the persecution (as a key leader in the Christian movement) so that the church might be able to thrive (Col. 1:24).

4:16 we do not give up. Paul again states his confidence in his ministry (v. 1).

4:18 focus. This is a dedicated striving, like a runner pursuing the goal (Heb. 12:1-2). The prize for a race, in ancient times, was placed at the end of the race so the runners could focus upon it, motivating them to win. Paul is calling on Christians to focus on the unseen rewards of God's Kingdom. **seen ... unseen.** Christians are not to shape their lives on the basis of visible standards of success (5:12), but in light of Christ's Kingdom.

5:1 our earthly house, a tent. The tent, as a temporary home, is a metaphor for the mortal body which is destroyed by suffering, weakness, and, finally, death. **building ... house.** A heavenly building was a common end of the time image representing all the fullness of God's Kingdom (Rev. 21:2). In this case Paul refers to our resurrected, transformed bodies.

5:10 the judgment seat of Christ. This is the specific evaluation of believers in the end times during which rewards are given or withheld. The judgment of unbelievers is at the "great white throne" (Rev. 20:11-15).

5:11 knowing...the fear of the Lord. The word translated *fear*, can also be translated *terror*. Even when we come to know God's grace and love, God's awesomeness stirs a reverential awe within it. Contemplating judg-

be unclothed but clothed, so that mortality may be swallowed up by life. ⁵ And the One who prepared us for this very thing is God, who gave us the Spirit as a down payment.

Camping Out on Earth

1. Have you ever lived in a tent? For how long? Why? What was it like?

2 Corinthians 5:1-10

2. What is Paul referring to as "our earthly house" (v. 1)? Why does he call it a tent? What does this suggest about our earthly life?
3. What does it mean that we are "longing to put on our house from heaven" (v. 2)?
4. Why must we "all appear before the judgment seat of Christ" (v. 10)? How should this knowledge affect your daily life?
5. Are you disciplined in taking care of your earthly "tent"? How about your eternal "house"?

⁶ Therefore, though we are always confident and know that while we are at home in the body we are away from the Lord— ⁷ for we •walk by faith, not by sight— ⁸ yet we are confident and satisfied to be out of the body and at home with the Lord. ⁹ Therefore, whether we are at home or away, we make it our aim to be pleasing to Him. ¹⁰ For we must all appear before the judgment seat of Christ, so that each may be repaid for what he has done in the body, whether good or bad.

¹¹ Knowing, then, the fear of the Lord, we persuade people. We are completely open before God, and I hope we are completely open to your consciences as well. ¹² We are not commending ourselves to you again, but

giving you an opportunity to be proud of us, so that you may have a reply for those who take pride in the outward appearanceᵃ rather than in the heart. ¹³ For if we are out of our mind, it is for God; if we have a sound mind, it is for you. ¹⁴ For Christ's love compelsᵇ us, since we have reached this conclusion: if One died for all, then all died. ¹⁵ And He died for all so that those who live should no longer live for themselves, but for the One who died for them and was raised.

A Ministry of Reconciliation

1. Who is the most persuasive person you know? What does that person persuade people to do?

2 Corinthians 5:11-6:2

2. According to 5:15, what is the purpose of Christ's death? What does it mean, in practical terms, to live for ourselves? To live for Christ?
3. What does it mean to be reconciled (v. 18)? How does God reconcile us to Himself?
4. Why did God give us "the ministry of reconciliation" (v. 18)? How can you carry out this ministry in practical terms?

The Ministry of Reconciliation

¹⁶ From now on, then, we do not knowᶜ anyone in a purely human way.ᵈ Even if we have knownᵉ Christ in a purely human way,ᶠ yet now we no longer knowᶜ Him like that. ¹⁷ Therefore if anyone is in Christ, there is a new creation; old things have passed away, and look, new thingsᵍ have come. ¹⁸ Now everything is from God, who reconciled us to Himself through Christ and gave

---

---

ment before a Holy God, **we persuade men**.

5:14 One died for all. This (v. 15) is an adaptation of a creedal statement of belief (Rom. 5:8; 1 Cor. 15:3; 1 Thess. 5:10). They can no longer be evaluated on the basis of an old, worldly standard (1:12,17; 5:12,16). **all died.** In the sense that when Christ died, He opened up a new way of life to everyone. They could be free from the law of sin and death—and instead live for Christ. They could die to the old life of futility and self-centeredness.

5:17 in Christ. A favorite phrase of Paul's, signifying the union of the believer with Jesus Christ and hence with Jesus' death and resurrection; it is by this union that the believer enters into new life. **a new creation.** To be in Christ is to be new. A believer has died to the old life and is raised to a whole

new sphere of existence by this act of recreation.

5:19 the message of reconciliation. All the work of reconciliation—bringing us back into relationship with God—has been done. Now it is simply a matter of people accepting the finished work of Christ.

5:20 ambassadors. In Roman territories considered dangerous and not fully loyal, the key administrator was the ambassador. He was a direct representative of the emperor. Ambassadors were also those individuals who arranged the terms of peace between a hostile country and Rome. Paul, therefore, understands his role to be that of one acting on behalf of God to offer reconciliation and peace to a hostile, alienated people. **we plead.** Reconciliation will not take place until God's offer is accepted; thus the

urgency of Paul's appeal.

5:21 the One who did not know sin. A key to Christ's power to reconcile is His own lack of sin (John 8:46; Rom. 8:3; Heb. 4:15). **to be sin for us.** Because He had no sin of His own He could therefore bear the sins of others. He exchanged His righteousness for our sin. As He became the sins of humanity, He stood in relationship to God as we should have: cut off and the object of wrath. As He became sin for us, He cried out, "My God, My God, why have You forsaken Me?"

6:5 labors. Paul generally earned his own living, toiling to the point of exhaustion. **by sleepless nights, by times of hunger.** His hardships led to physical deprivation.

6:6 by the Holy Spirit. Paul demonstrated the presence of the Spirit in his life through

us the ministry of reconciliation: ¹⁹ that is, in Christ, God was reconciling the world to Himself, not counting their trespasses against them, and He has committed the message of reconciliation to us. ²⁰ Therefore, we are ambassadors for Christ; certain that God is appealing through us, we plead on Christ's behalf, "Be reconciled to God." ²¹ He made the One who did not know sin to be sin for us, so that we might become the righteousness of God in Him.

6 Working together[a] with Him, we also appeal to you: "Don't receive God's grace in vain." ² For He says:

In an acceptable time, I heard you,
and in the day of salvation, I helped you.[b]

Look, now is the acceptable time; look, now is the day of salvation.

The Test of Faith

1. What is the greatest physical hardship you've been through? What did it accomplish?

2 Corinthians 6:3-13

2. How does Paul defend the authenticity of his ministry?

3. By appealing to these things instead of his supernatural conversion or miracles (Acts 9:3-5; 19:11-12), what is he saying the real test of faith is?

4. What is Paul asking the Corinthians (and us) to do in verses 11-13 (see 3:2-3)?

5. What does it mean to be "having nothing yet possessing everything" (v. 10)? How did this attitude help Paul to endure all that is listed in verses 4-10? How could it help you?

The Character of Paul's Ministry

³ We give no opportunity for stumbling to anyone, so that the ministry will not be blamed. ⁴ But in everything, as God's ministers, we commend ourselves:

by great endurance, by afflictions, by hardship,
by pressures,
⁵ by beatings, by imprisonments, by riots, by labors,
by sleepless nights, by times of hunger,
⁶ by purity, by knowledge, by patience,
by kindness,
by the Holy Spirit, by sincere love,
⁷ by the message of truth, by the power of God;
through weapons of righteousness
on the right hand and the left,
⁸ through glory and dishonor, through slander
and good report;
as deceivers yet true;
⁹ as unknown yet recognized; as dying and look—
we live;
as being chastened yet not killed;
¹⁰ as grieving yet always rejoicing; as poor
yet enriching many;
as having nothing yet possessing everything.

¹¹ We have spoken openly[c] to you, Corinthians; our heart has been opened wide. ¹² You are not limited by us, but you are limited by your own affections. ¹³ Now in like response—I speak as to children—you also should be open to us.

Separation to God

¹⁴ Do not be mismatched with unbelievers. For what partnership is there between righteousness and lawlessness? Or what fellowship does light have with darkness? ¹⁵ What agreement does Christ have with Belial?[d] Or what does a believer have in common with an unbeliever? ¹⁶ And what agreement does God's sanctuary have with idols? For we[e] are the sanctuary of the living God, as God said:

ᵃ6:1 Or *As we work together* ᵇ6:2 Is 49:8 ᶜ6:11 Lit *Our mouths have been open* ᵈ6:15 Or *Beliar*, a name for the Devil or antichrist in extra-biblical Jewish writings ᵉ6:16 Other mss read *you*

---

the qualities of love, kindness, etc. (refer to Gal. 5:22-23). **sincere love.** This is an active goodwill toward others.

6:7 the message of truth. A shorthand way of referring to the gospel. **weapons.** A Roman soldier carried a spear or sword in his right hand and a shield in his left. Likewise, Paul was fully equipped with God's righteousness to reach out and minister to others.

6:8 glory and dishonor ... slander and good report. Neither rejection nor praise distracted him from his ministry (1 Cor. 4:12-13; 1 Thess. 2:2). **deceivers.** This begins a series of contrasts in which Paul renounces the charges that have been made against him.

6:9 as unknown yet recognized. While some did not recognize Paul as a legitimate apostle, God and the Corinthian church

knew his genuineness (5:11).

6:10 as poor yet enriching many. While financially poor, Paul gave others the gift of life in Christ. This too reflects the ministry of Jesus (8:9). **possessing everything.** Though in this life he may have nothing, the fullness of God's Kingdom is given to him (Luke 6:20; 1 Cor. 3:21-23).

6:14 mismatched. Or "yoked together," The idea of the double yoke has Old Testament roots, as in Deuteronomy 22:10 where it is forbidden to put an ox and a donkey in the same harness. The point is that the fundamental incompatibility of an ox and a donkey would make it very difficult to plow in a straight line, besides causing strain to both animals and their driver. This is also true for believers and unbelievers.

6:15 Belial. This name for Satan, not used elsewhere in the New Testament, is common in the writings from the ancient community of Qumran.

7:2 corrupted. Literally, "ruined." This may refer either to financial or moral ruin. **defrauded.** This implies taking advantage of someone.

7:3 I don't say this to condemn you. Paul is not interested in striking back at the church by accusing them of being in the wrong. He simply wants to clear himself of the suspicions that have been raised by his opponents.

7:5 afflicted in every way. Paul had already mentioned how he came near to death in the province of Asia (1:8-10). His troubles evidently followed him into Mace-

I will dwell among them and walk
    among them,
and I will be their God,
and they will be My people.[a]

17 Therefore, come out from among them
    and be separate, says the Lord;
    do not touch any unclean thing,
    and I will welcome you.[b]

18 I will be a Father to you,
    and you will be sons and daughters
        to Me,
    says the Lord Almighty.[c]

An Uneven Match

1. What's the dirtiest you've ever been? How did you get that way?

2 Corinthians 6:14–7:1

2. What does it mean to "be mismatched with unbelievers" (v. 14)? What relationships does this include?

3. What does it mean to "come out from among them and be separate" (v. 17)? How does a Christian "come out from among" non-Christians?

4. How can you be a friend to an unbeliever and still be "separate"?

5. What are "impurities of the flesh and spirit" (7:1)? How can you wash yourself from them?

7 Therefore dear friends, since we have such promises, we should wash ourselves clean from every impurity of the flesh and spirit, making our sanctification complete[d] in the fear of God.

Godly Grief

1. What finally gets your attention: Tough talk? Slammed door? Tears? Letter? Walkout? Give a recent example.

2 Corinthians 7:2-16

2. Why does Paul want this church to open up to him (vv. 2-4; see 6:11-13)?

3. What was the result of Paul's previous letter to them (vv. 8-13; see 2:3-4)?

4. In light of his previous hurtful letter, why would he underscore his present joy and confidence (v. 16)?

5. What is "godly grief" (v. 10)? What produces such grief? To what does it lead?

6. What grief in your life could be resolved with repentance (turning back to God)?

Joy and Repentance

2 Take us into your hearts.[e] We have wronged no one, corrupted no one, defrauded no one. 3 I don't say this to condemn you, for I have already said that you are in our hearts, to die together and to live together. 4 I have great confidence in you; I have great pride in you. I am filled with encouragement; I am overcome with joy in all our afflictions.

5 In fact, when we came into Macedonia, we[f] had no rest. Instead, we were afflicted in every way: struggles on the outside, fears inside. 6 But God, who comforts the humble, comforted us by the coming of Titus, 7 and not only by his coming, but also by the comfort he received from you. He announced to us your deep longing, your sorrow,[g] your zeal for me, so that I rejoiced even more. 8 For although I grieved you with my letter, I do not regret it—even though I did regret it since I

---

[a]6:16 Lv 26:12; Jr 31:33; 32:38; Ezk 37:26   [b]6:17 Is 52:11   [c]6:18 2 Sm 7:14; Is 43:6; 49:22; 60:4; Hs 1:10   [d]7:1 Or spirit, perfecting holiness
[e]7:2 Lit Make room for us.   [f]7:5 Lit our flesh   [g]7:7 Or lamentation, or mourning

---

donia. **struggles on the outside, fears inside.** He faced external pressures from his enemies as well as inner anxiety such as his concern over Titus and the situation in Corinth.

7:6 God, who comforts the humble. Paul returns to the description of God with which he began this letter (1:3-5; Isa. 49:13). To "comfort" does not mean simply to console, but to actively help, encourage, and strengthen someone undergoing trial. **comforted us by the coming of Titus.** Paul had a lot of confidence in Titus who had the ability to deal with tough situations. He was entrusted with the delicate task of delivering Paul's severe letter (2:1-4) to Corinth and correcting problems within the church there (7:13-15). Titus' genuine concern for and evenhanded dealing with the Corinthians (8:16-17; 12:18) no doubt contributed to his

success which he reported in person to Paul, anxiously awaiting word in Macedonia.

7:10 godly grief produces a repentance. Two different Greek words are translated repentance. Judas' repentance for betraying Jesus was more regret. The repentance produced by godly grief stems from a person's awareness of sin in their lives and an intention to change—to be in conformity with God's ways. The Corinthians became aware of how out of line their actions were, and this insight brought sorrow, which in turn led to a change of attitude and behavior. **worldly grief.** Worldly sorrow does not lead to the positive change of heart and life that repentance implies, but brings only bitterness and resentment.

7:11 diligence. Having realized their sin, the

Corinthians went to extreme lengths to clear themselves. **zeal.** They now took the problem seriously and passionately wanted to correct it.

8:1 the churches of Macedonia. Macedonia was the Roman province just north of the province of Achaia where Corinth was located. The churches in mind were probably those located at Philippi, Thessalonica, and Berea (Acts 16:6–17:15). These churches were planted by Paul, Silvanus, and Timothy on Paul's second missionary journey. At least two of the three churches began with severe persecution that didn't let up but intensified. The impact of the gospel in the Macedonia is seen in the fact that though they were experiencing persecution and poverty, they responded with great generosity. Difficult circumstances have the potential for bringing out the best in those in whom the

saw that the letter grieved you, though only for a little while. ⁹ Now I am rejoicing, not because you were grieved, but because your grief led to repentance. For you were grieved as God willed, so that you didn't experience any loss from us. ¹⁰ For godly grief produces a repentance not to be regretted and leading to salvation, but worldly grief produces death. ¹¹ For consider how much diligence this very thing—this grieving as God wills—has produced in you: what a desire to clear yourselves, what indignation, what fear, what deep longing, what zeal, what justice! In every way you have commended yourselves to be pure in this matter. ¹² So even though I wrote to you, it was not because of the one who did wrong, or because of the one who was wronged, but in order that your diligence for us might be made plain to you in the sight of God. ¹³ For this reason we have been comforted.

In addition to our comfort, we were made to rejoice even more over the joy Titus had,ᵃ because his spirit was refreshed by all of you. ¹⁴ For if I have made any boast to him about you, I have not been embarrassed; but as I have spoken everything to you in truth, so our boasting to Titus has also turned out to be the truth. ¹⁵ And his affection toward you is even greater as he remembers the obedience of all of you, and how you received him with fear and trembling. ¹⁶ I rejoice that I have complete confidence in you.

Appeal to Complete the Collection

8 We want you to know, brothers, about the grace of God granted to the churches of Macedonia: ² during a severe testing by affliction, their abundance of joy and their deep poverty overflowed into the wealth of their generosity. ³ I testify that, on their own, according to their ability and beyond their ability, ⁴ they begged us insistently for the privilege of sharing in the ministry to the saints, ⁵ and not just as we had hoped. Instead, they gave themselves especially to the Lord, then to us by God's will. ⁶ So we urged Titus that, just as he had begun, so he should also complete this grace to you. ⁷ Now as you excel in everything—in

Using What You Have

1. With what are you generous: Your money? Time? Talents? Toys? With what are you stingy?

2 Corinthians 8:1-15

2. What do we learn about the Macedonians from their giving?
3. How can the equality principle (vv. 13-15) help us decide what cause needs our immediate attention?
4. What does this principle say about getting our own needs met?
5. Verse 15 is a quotation from Exodus 16:18, where God provided manna in the desert. What does this principle show you about the blessings you enjoy? How should you use those blessings?

faith, in speech, in knowledge, in all diligence, and in your love for usᵇ — excel also in this grace.

⁸ I am not saying this as a command. Rather, by means of the diligence of others, I am testing the genuineness of your love. ⁹ For you know the grace of our Lord Jesus Christ: although He was rich, for your sake He became poor, so that by His poverty you might become rich. ¹⁰ Now I am giving an opinion on this because it is profitable for you, who a year ago began not only to do something but also to desire it.ᶜ ¹¹ But now finish the taskᵈ as well, that just as there was eagerness to desire it, so there may also be a completion from what you have. ¹² For if the eagerness is there, it is acceptable according to what one has, not according to what he does not have. ¹³ It is not that there may be relief for others and hardship for you, but it is a question of equalityᵉ—¹⁴ at the present time your surplus is ₍available₎ for their need, so that their abundance may

---

ᵃ**7:13** Lit *the joy of Titus*   ᵇ**8:7** Other mss read *in our love for you*   ᶜ**8:10** Lit *to will*   ᵈ**8:11** Lit *finish the doing*   ᵉ**8:13** Lit *but from equality*

Spirit of Christ dwells.

8:4 they begged us. This verse contains three words that show how the motivation for this offering sprang not only from humanitarian concerns, but from distinctly Christian convictions as well. **privilege.** Literally, "grace." **sharing.** The Greek word is *koinonia*, often translated as "fellowship." Giving is an expression of partnership in other believers in Christ. **ministry.** Giving is a way of serving and ministering to the needs of others, a Christian responsibility (5:15).

8:5 they gave themselves especially to the Lord. Here is the source of generosity. Seeing what God has done for us, we give ourselves to Him and consequently give to support His work here on earth. A person's priorities can be seen in his checkbook and his calendar.

8:7 excel. Paul exhorts the Corinthians to participate in giving as wholeheartedly as they participate in the exercise of other spiritual gifts (1 Cor. 12:7-11; 14:1) and as a reflection of their desire to affirm his apostleship (7:11).

8:11 now finish the task. This is reminiscent of Christ's parable of the two sons, one of whom said he was going to do something (work in the vineyard), but didn't, and the other of whom said he would not, but did (Matt. 21:28-32). Following through on good intentions is vital. **from what you have.** One reason the Corinthians may have stalled is that they felt they could not make a significant contribution. The issue is not how much one gives, but simply that one gives out of love for God and people.

8:13 equality. In their abundance the Corinthians share what they have with those who

are in need. Likewise, in the future, it could be the other way around and the Corinthians could expect aid if they needed it from Christians in Jerusalem and elsewhere.

8:18 the brother. An unnamed fellow worker known for acts of Christian service.

8:19 he was ... appointed. This brother comes not merely on his own initiative, but as a representative of the churches (probably in Macedonia).

8:22 We have also sent. There will also be a third traveling companion. Paul is going to great lengths to ensure his enemies and critics cannot charge him with profiting personally from this collection. Titus is his friend and fellow worker, so it is vital to have two other respected traveling companions appointed by the churches to accompany Titus.

also become ⟨available⟩ for your need, that there may be equality. ¹⁵ As it has been written:

> The person who gathered much did not have too much,
> and the person who gathered little did not have too little.ᵃ

Generous Giving

1. Do you like to save your money or spend it? Why?

2 Corinthians 8:16-9:5

2. Why did the churches choose Titus to deliver this offering to Jerusalem and ensure its use for mission-relief work?

3. Why does Paul expect the Corinthians to be generous (9:1-5)? In what ways?

4. If the Macedonians came to visit you, would they find your generosity lacking or overflowing? With what else besides money are you generous?

5. What is the difference between a "gift" and an "extortion" (9:5)? Which is more typical of your own generosity to others?

Administration of the Collection

¹⁶ Thanks be to God who put the same diligence for you into the heart of Titus. ¹⁷ For he accepted our urging and, being very diligent, went out to you by his own choice. ¹⁸ With him we have sent the brother who is praised throughout the churches for his gospel ministry.ᵇ ¹⁹ And not only that, but he was also appointed by the churches to accompany us with this giftᶜ that is being administered by us for the glory of the Lord Him-

self and to show our eagerness ⟨to help⟩. ²⁰ We are taking this precaution so no one can find fault with us concerning this large sum administered by us. ²¹ For we are making provision for what is honorable, not only before the Lord but also before men. ²² We have also sent with them our brother whom we have often tested, in many circumstances, and found diligent— and now even more diligent because of his great confidence in you. ²³ As for Titus, he is my partner and co-worker serving you; as for our brothers, they are the messengers of the churches, the glory of Christ. ²⁴ Therefore, before the churches, show them the proof of your love and of our boasting about you.

Motivations for Giving

9 Now concerning the ministry to the saints, it is unnecessary for me to write to you. ² For I know your eagerness, and I brag about you to the Macedonians:ᵈ "Achaiaᵉ has been prepared since last year," and your zeal has stirred up most of them. ³ But I sent the brothers so our boasting about you in the matter would not prove empty, and so you would be prepared just as I said. ⁴ For if any Macedonians should come with me and find you unprepared, we, not to mention you, would be embarrassed in that situation.ᶠ ⁵ Therefore I considered it necessary to urge the brothers to go on ahead to you and arrange in advance the generous gift you promised, so that it will be ready as a gift and not an extortion.

⁶ Remember this:ᵍ the person who sows sparingly will also reap sparingly, and the person who sows generously will also reap generously. ⁷ Each person should do as he has decided in his heart—not out of regret or out of necessity, for God loves a cheerful giver. ⁸ And God is able to make every grace overflow to you, so that in every way, always having everything you need, you may excel in every good work. ⁹ As it is written:

> He has scattered;
> He has given to the poor;
> His righteousness endures forever.ʰ

ᵃ8:15 Ex 16:18   ᵇ8:18 Lit *churches, in the gospel*   ᶜ8:19 Or *grace*   ᵈ9:2 Macedonia was a Roman province in the northern area of modern Greece.   ᵉ9:2 Achaia was the Roman province, south of Macedonia, where Corinth was located.   ᶠ9:4 Or *in this confidence*   ᵍ9:6 Lit *And this*   ʰ9:9 Ps 112:9

9:2 brag. Apparently in the same way that Paul used the Macedonians as examples to the Corinthians (8:1-5), so too he has used the readiness of the Corinthians to give as an example to the Macedonians. **Achaia.** Corinth was the largest city in the province of Achaia and probably the site of the largest church.

9:6 the person who sows ... will also reap. Paul may be quoting a proverb (similar sayings were known in both Jewish and Greek literature) as support for his encouragement for generous giving. It is not that a person can be assured of financial security by giving (and thus obligating God in some way), but rather that the exercise of giving leads to the growth in grace in the life of the giver.

9:7 not out of regret or out of necessity.

Unlike the temple tax, this voluntary offering required people to consider for themselves what they would contribute. **God loves a cheerful giver.** It is not that giving earns God's love, but that God "approves of" the character of a person who is generous.

9:8 every. The stress on "every" in this verse emphasizes God's lavish generosity.

9:11 you are enriched. The purpose of such riches is not to pamper personal indulgences but to facilitate generosity. **in every way.** God might not reward faithfulness with material wealth, but with a wealth of spiritual and emotional resources. James 2:5 reminds us, "Didn't God chose the poor in this world to be rich in faith and heirs the kingdom He has promised to those who love Him?"

9:12 service. Giving is a way of ministering

to the needs of others, a Christian responsibility (5:15). **needs of the saints.** The poor are actually helped. This is one fruit of generosity.

10:1 a personal appeal. This verse begins the final section of the letter. From his extravagant hope of what might be in the future as expressed in 9:12-15 (based probably on Titus' report mentioned in 7:6-16), Paul moves to what is happening in Corinth. Paul begins his case by defending himself against the charge that he has a weak character. Paul was charged with being unimpressive (v. 10) and thus not an authoritative apostle of Christ. The fact that Paul begins the final section of this letter by invoking the meekness and gentleness of Jesus (Matt. 11:29) immediately shows that he rejects authoritarianism and aggressive behavior as a sign of apostleship. His oppo-

Cheerful Giving

1. How much money do you have on you right now? Under what conditions would you give it all away?

2 Corinthians 9:6-15

2. What does Paul mean in verse 6? If you give $100, you will get $1,000 back? Why or why not?
3. Why do you think God cares about our attitudes when we give?
4. In what ways, other than money, can you give to your church?
5. What is something you are cheerfully willing to give to God?

---

¹⁰ Now the One who provides seed for the sower and bread for food will provide and multiply your seed and increase the harvest of your righteousness, ¹¹ as you are enriched in every way for all generosity, which produces thanksgiving to God through us. ¹² For the ministry of this service is not only supplying the needs of the saints, but is also overflowing in many acts of thanksgiving to God. ¹³ Through the proof of this service, they will glorify God for your obedience to the confession of ᵃ the gospel of Christ, and for your generosity in sharing with them and with others. ¹⁴ And in their prayers for you they will have deep affection for ᵇ you because of the surpassing grace of God on you. ¹⁵ Thanks be to God for His indescribable gift.

Paul's Apostolic Authority

10 Now I, Paul, make a personal appeal to you by the gentleness and graciousness of Christ—I

who am humble among you in person, but bold toward you when absent. ² I beg you that when I am present I will not need to be bold with the confidence by which I plan to challenge certain people who think we are walking in a fleshly way.ᶜ ³ For although we are walking in the flesh, we do not wage war in a fleshly way,ᵈ ⁴ since the weapons of our warfare are not fleshly, but are powerful through God for the demolition of strongholds. We demolish arguments ⁵ and every highminded thing that is raised up against the knowledge of God, taking every thought captive to the obedience of Christ. ⁶ And we are ready to punish any disobedience, once your obedience is complete.

Weapons of War

1. If you were to fight in a war, what weapons would you want to have? Why?

2 Corinthians 10:1-18

2. What does Paul mean when he says, "we are walking in the flesh" (v. 3)? What, in practical terms, does it mean to wage a spiritual war "in a fleshly way"?
3. What are the weapons of our warfare (v. 4)?
4. What "strongholds" does the Word of God demolish? What arguments? Give examples of modern "strongholds" and "arguments" that are contrary to the Word of God.
5. What would you say if you were to "boast in the Lord" (v. 17)?

---

⁷ Look at what is obvious.ᵉ If anyone is confident that he belongs to Christ, he should remind himself of this: just as he belongs to Christ, so do we. ⁸ For if I boast some more about our authority, which the Lord gave

---

ᵃ**9:13** Or your obedient confession to ᵇ**9:14** Or will long for ᶜ**10:2** Lit walking according to flesh ᵈ**10:3** Lit war according to flesh ᵉ**10:7** Or You are looking at things outwardly

---

nents saw this as weakness, not Christlikeness.

10:3 walking in the flesh. Paul acknowledges his humanity. **do not wage war in a fleshly way.** God's work can't be done just any way. We err if we think we can bring about God's kingdom using fleshly methods.

10:4 weapons of our warfare are not fleshly. Sheer intellect, cleverness, marketing savvy, organizational genius, and persuasive rhetoric in themselves can never accomplish God's purposes. He does not accept the self-oriented lifestyle of the world. He refuses to live life relying solely on his own resources and with an eye only to increasing his own power and prestige. **powerful through God for the demolition of strongholds.** In contrast to the weapons of

the world, Paul relies on Christ's extremely powerful spiritual weapons to bring about change. The picture is of a situation where a city attempts to protect itself from invasion by constructing various defensive barriers. The spiritual walls can only be breeched by divine weapons that seem weak to those who have a fleshly outlook. Spiritual warfare is real. Those who fully give themselves to Christ will experience opposition that is not merely human.

10:7 Look at what is obvious. Since they view what is happening on the basis of human wisdom, they misinterpret the situation. **belongs to Christ.** Quite possibly Paul's opponents in Corinth are claiming to be Christ's true apostles which, by inference or direct accusation, would make Paul a false apostle—a claim he rejects.

10:8 building you up. Paul's commission as an apostle was to preach the gospel and so to build churches. His commission is not to destroy churches (as his opponents were doing; 1 Cor. 3:17).

10:10 his public speaking is despicable. Paul was probably in ill health and he had long ago rejected the art of rhetoric (1 Cor. 2:1-5). But in Corinth, which had many educated citizens, both powerful speech and a persuasive personality were highly valued, which may account for why the church started to listen to these new teachers.

10:16 the regions beyond you. Paul had no desire to hang onto any power or position in Corinth. He wanted to resolve the difficulties in Corinth so he could get on with the business of preaching the gospel in the parts of the empire that had not yet

for building you up and not for tearing you down, I am not ashamed. ⁹ I don't want to seem as though I am trying to terrify you with my letters. ¹⁰ For it is said, "His letters are weighty and powerful, but his physical presence is weak, and his public speaking is despicable." ¹¹ Such a person should consider this: what we are in the words of our letters when absent, we will be in actions when present.

¹² For we don't dare classify or compare ourselves with some who commend themselves. But in measuring themselves by themselves and comparing themselves to themselves, they lack understanding. ¹³ We, however, will not boast beyond measure, but according to the measure of the area ₍of ministry₎ that God has assigned to us, ₍which₎ reaches even to you. ¹⁴ For we are not overextending ourselves, as if we had not reached you, since we have come to you with the gospel of Christ. ¹⁵ We are not bragging beyond measure about other people's labors. But we have the hope that as your faith increases, our area ₍of ministry₎ will be greatly enlarged, ¹⁶ so that we may preach the gospel to the regions beyond you, not boasting about what has already been done in someone else's area ₍of ministry₎. ¹⁷ So **the one who boasts must boast in the Lord.**ᵃ ¹⁸ For it is not the one commending himself who is approved, but the one the Lord commends.

Paul and the False Apostles

11 I wish you would put up with a little foolishness from me. Yes, do put up with me.ᵇ ² For I am jealous over you with a godly jealousy, because I have promised you in marriage to one husband—to present a pure virgin to Christ. ³ But I fear that, as the serpent deceived Eve by his cunning, your minds may be corrupted from a complete and pureᶜ devotion to Christ. ⁴ For if a person comes and preaches another Jesus, whom we did not preach, or you receive a different spirit, which you had not received, or a different gospel, which you had not accepted, you put up with it splendidly!

⁵ Now I consider myself in no way inferior to the "super-apostles." ⁶ Though untrained in public speak-

Evil in Disguise

1. What's the most memorable encounter you ever had with a snake?

2 Corinthians 11:1-15

2. Read Genesis 3. How did Satan (the serpent) deceive Eve? How does he use those same arguments to deceive people today?

3. What "different gospel" has pulled you away from Jesus in the past? How did you become aware of its deceitfulness?

4. How does Satan disguise himself as an "angel of light" today (v. 14)?

5. Sin rarely approaches us as evil, but as "virtue in disguise." From verses 2-4, how can you guard yourself against this satanic strategy?

ing, I am certainly not ₍untrained₎ in knowledge. Indeed, we have always made that clear to you in everything. ⁷ Or did I commit a sin by humbling myself so that you might be exalted, because I preached the gospel of God to you free of charge? ⁸ I robbed other churches by taking pay ₍from them₎ to minister to you. ⁹ When I was present with you and in need, I did not burden anyone, for the brothers who came from Macedonia supplied my needs. I have kept myself, and will keep myself, from burdening you in any way. ¹⁰ As the truth of Christ is in me, this boasting of mine will not be stoppedᵈ in the regions of Achaia. ¹¹ Why? Because I don't love you? God knows I do!

¹² But I will continue to do what I am doing, in order to cut off the opportunity of those who want an opportunity to be regarded just as we are in what they are boasting about. ¹³ For such people are false apostles, deceitful workers, disguising themselves as apostles of Christ. ¹⁴ And no wonder! For Satan himself is disguised

---

ᵃ**10:17** Jr 9:24　ᵇ**11:1** Or *Yes, you are putting up with me*　ᶜ**11:3** Other mss omit *and pure*　ᵈ**11:10** Or *silenced*

---

heard the good news of Jesus Christ. In fact, his plans were to leave the region around the Aegean Sea, to push on to Rome, and then head into Spain (Rom. 15:23-29).

11:5 "super-apostles." This is a sarcastic label for the false apostles.

11:6 untrained in public speaking. A popular style of rhetoric had developed among the Greeks that utilized rhetorical form as a means of manipulating people rather than communicating truth. It was this abuse of rhetoric that Paul rejected. **knowledge.** This was more than understanding information; Paul brought revelation from God with spiritual insight.

11:7 free of charge. In 1 Corinthians 9, Paul makes it clear that he believed it was appropriate for apostles to be supported by the

churches they served. He refused the support of the Corinthians so that he would not be a burden to them (v. 9).

11:14 angel of light. Paul has already referred to Satan as the arch-deceiver (v. 3), masquerading as something he is not.

11:16 accept me as a fool, so I too may boast a little. By comparison to the super apostles, the false teachers, Paul seemed incredibly weak and ineffective. The Corinthians came to this conclusion about Paul because they were judging by worldly standards. So Paul, with ironic sarcasm says, in the following section (11:22-33), if you want to play the game on this field I can do that. Paul takes this tact not to show how great he is but to show that worldly standards of measuring God's representatives collapse.

11:22 the seed of Abraham. Often a synonym for "Israelites." Paul points out that he shares all the ethnic, social, and religious claims of the false teachers regarding their background. **Israelites.** This emphasizes the religious and cultural dimension of their backgrounds. This was the nation God had chosen to be his representatives to the nations. Through Abraham's seed, the Messiah would come and the Scriptures were given. Paul was born into all the privileges of God's people and prior to his conversion had distinguished himself as a zealous Israelite of the tribe of Benjamin.

11:23-27 Paul reveals his weaknesses rather than his strengths .

11:25 beaten with rods. This was a common Roman punishment (Acts 16:22-23). **shipwrecked.** One shipwreck is described

as an angel of light. [15] So it is no great thing if his servants also disguise themselves as servants of righteousness. Their destiny[a] will be according to their works.

Tolerating Fools

1. When have you put up with someone's bullying or abuse? Why did you tolerate it? What would you do now if you had it to do over?

2 Corinthians 11:16-33

2. What does Paul mean in verse 19, "For you gladly put up with fools since you are so smart"? How do Christians do this today?

3. Why does Paul say this is a weakness (v. 21)? What should Christians do when confronted with foolish teaching?

4. How can you discern foolish teaching from sound, wise teaching?

Paul's Sufferings for Christ

[16] I repeat: no one should consider me a fool. But if ⌊you do⌋, at least accept me as a fool, so I too may boast a little. [17] What I say in this matter[b] of boasting, I don't speak as the Lord would, but foolishly. [18] Since many boast from a human perspective,[c] I will also boast. [19] For you gladly put up with fools since you are so smart![d] [20] In fact, you put up with it if someone enslaves you, if someone devours you, if someone captures you, if someone dominates you, or if someone hits you in the face. [21] I say this to ⌊our⌋ shame: we have been weak.

But in whatever anyone dares ⌊to boast⌋—I am talking foolishly—I also dare:

[22] Are they Hebrews? So am I.
Are they Israelites? So am I.
Are they the seed of Abraham? So am I.
[23] Are they servants of Christ?
I'm talking like a madman—I'm a better one:
with far more labors,
   many more imprisonments,
far worse beatings, near death[e] many times.
[24] Five times I received from the Jews 40 lashes
   minus one.
[25] Three times I was beaten with rods.[f]
Once I was stoned.[g]
Three times I was shipwrecked.
I have spent a night and a day in the depths
   of the sea.
[26] On frequent journeys, ⌊I faced⌋
dangers from rivers, dangers from robbers,
dangers from my own people,
   dangers from the Gentiles,
dangers in the city, dangers in the open country,
dangers on the sea, and dangers
   among false brothers;
[27] labor and hardship,
many sleepless nights, hunger and thirst,
   often without food, cold, and lacking clothing.

[28] Not to mention[h] other things, there is the daily pressure on me: my care for all the churches. [29] Who is weak, and I am not weak? Who is made to stumble, and I do not burn with indignation? [30] If boasting is necessary, I will boast about my weaknesses. [31] The eternally blessed One, the God and Father of the Lord Jesus, knows I am not lying. [32] In Damascus, the governor under King Aretas[i] guarded the city of the Damascenes in order to arrest me, [33] so I was let down in a basket through a window in the wall and escaped his hands.

Sufficient Grace

12 It is necessary to boast; it is not helpful, but I will move on to visions and revelations of the

---

[a]**11:15** Lit *end*   [b]**11:17** Or *business,* or *confidence*   [c]**11:18** Lit *boast according to the flesh*   [d]**11:19** Or *are wise*   [e]**11:23** Lit *and in deaths*
[f]**11:25** A specifically Roman punishment; see Ac 16:22   [g]**11:25** A common Jewish method of capital punishment; see Ac 14:5   [h]**11:28** Lit *Apart from*   [i]**11:32** Aretus IV (9 B.C.–A.D. 40), a Nabatean Arab king

---

in Acts 27:14-44, but that had not yet occurred when Paul wrote this letter. Since Paul traveled frequently by ship and since shipwrecks were by no means uncommon in those days, it appears that Paul endured several shipwrecks.

11:26 dangers from rivers. Not all rivers had bridges or safe ferries. **dangers from robbers.** This could have been a special problem when Paul was transporting collections taken in aid of poorer churches. **dangers from my own people.** Such danger came from mobs, from the courts, and from personal attacks (Acts 9:23,29; 13:6-8,45; 14:2,19; 17:5; 18:6,12; 20:3,19; 21:11,27). **dangers among false brothers.** Not only did he face the possibility of harm (bodily and otherwise) from Jews and Gentiles, but also from those claiming to be Christ-followers.

11:29 weak. In his "boasting" he now boasts of being weakest of all. **burn.** In his concern for the churches, Paul has a constant source of anguish over those who have been led astray from the faith.

11:30-33 Because it seems absurd that one could be both weak and be an apostle, Paul asserts that he has indeed been telling the truth (v. 31). To wrap-up the accounts of his weakness, he recounts a final incident that was especially humiliating (Acts 9:23-25). The mighty apostle, far from being heralded with glory, was reduced to hiding in a basket. **King Aretas.** This Arab king ruled from 9 BC to AD 39.

12:1 visions and revelations. It is difficult to distinguish between these two. Perhaps "vision" refers to what was seen in the experience while "revelation" refers to what was

heard (the content). These are ecstatic experiences of some sort, whereby for a brief time the limitations of space, time, and sense perception are removed so that one experiences firsthand, immediate, direct access to the supernatural.

12:2 14 years ago. This was probably around AD 42, well before he planted the Corinthian church. This is the only time in any letter that Paul mentions such an experience. While Paul doesn't indicate that this was his vision (so as not to draw the attention to himself), it seems clear that he is referring to himself. **caught up.** Visions were often spoken of in terms of a journey to another place. Whether Paul was literally transported to a new place or simply found himself in a new reality is impossible to know. **third heaven.** Jewish literature spoke of heaven having various levels, although the number

Thorn in the Flesh

1. What is the greatest weakness that you face in your sport? How do you compensate for it?

2 Corinthians 12:1-10

2. What does Paul mean by "a thorn in the flesh" (v. 7)? Why does he refer to it as "a messenger of Satan"?

3. How has Paul's "thorn" affected his life?

4. How do you react when God appears to be silent in answering your urgent requests? How do you feel about God's promise in verse 9? Why doesn't God simply take your problem away?

Lord. ² I know a man in Christ who was caught up into the third heaven 14 years ago. Whether he was in the body or out of the body, I don't know; God knows. ³ I know that this man—whether in the body or out of the body I do not know, God knows— ⁴ was caught up into paradise. He heard inexpressible words, which a man is not allowed to speak. ⁵ I will boast about this person, but not about myself, except of my weaknesses. ⁶ For if I want to boast, I will not be a fool, because I will be telling the truth. But I will spare you, so that no one can credit me with something beyond what he sees in me or hears from me, ⁷ especially because of the extraordinary revelations. Therefore, so that I would not exalt myself, a thorn in the flesh was given to me, a messenger[a] of Satan to torment me so I would not exalt myself. ⁸ Concerning this, I pleaded with the Lord three times to take it away from me. ⁹ But He said to me, "My grace is sufficient for you, for power[b] is

perfected in weakness." Therefore, I will most gladly boast all the more about my weaknesses, so that Christ's power may reside in me. ¹⁰ So because of Christ, I am pleased in weaknesses, in insults, in catastrophes, in persecutions, and in pressures. For when I am weak, then I am strong.

Signs of an Apostle

¹¹ I have become a fool; you forced it on me. I ought to have been recommended by you, since I am in no way inferior to the "super-apostles," even though I am nothing. ¹² The signs of an apostle were performed among you in all endurance—not only signs but also wonders and miracles. ¹³ So in what way were you treated worse than the other churches, except that I personally did not burden you? Forgive me this wrong!

Paul's Concern for the Corinthians

¹⁴ Look! I am ready to come to you this third time. I will not burden you, for I am not seeking what is yours, but you. For children are not obligated to save up for their parents, but parents for their children. ¹⁵ I will most gladly spend and be spent for you.[c] If I love you more, am I to be loved less? ¹⁶ Now granted, I have not burdened you; yet sly as I am, I took you in by deceit! ¹⁷ Did I take advantage of you by anyone I sent you? ¹⁸ I urged Titus ₍to come₎, and I sent the brother with him. Did Titus take advantage of you? Didn't we •walk in the same spirit and in the same footsteps?

¹⁹ You have thought all along that we were defending ourselves to you.[d] ₍No₎, in the sight of God we are speaking in Christ, and everything, dear friends, is for building you up. ²⁰ For I fear that perhaps when I come I will not find you to be what I want, and I may not be found by you to be what you want;[e] there may be quarreling, jealousy, outbursts of anger, selfish ambitions, slander, gossip, arrogance, and disorder. ²¹ I fear that when I come my God will again[f] humiliate me in your presence, and I will grieve for many who sinned before and have not repented of the uncleanness, sexual immorality, and promiscuity they practiced.

---

[a]12:7 Or angel. [b]12:9 Other mss read My power [c]12:15 Lit for your souls, or for your lives [d]12:19 Or Have you thought . . . to you? [e]12:20 Lit be as you want [f]12:21 Or come again my God will

---

of levels differs. **in the body or out of the body.** Paul refuses to speculate on how this experience occurred.

12:6 telling the truth. This may infer that his opponents had fabricated tales of their visions.

12:7 a thorn in the flesh. It is unknown what Paul means here, but the reference may be unclear so that we can all apply these truths to our won struggles. **messenger of Satan.** Sickness was thought to be caused by Satan, but the false apostles in Corinth are also referred to as servants of Satan (11:13-15). **torment me.** Literally, "to continually torment me." Whatever the problem was, it was chronic, though not debilitating.

12:8 three times. There are parallels between Paul's experience and that of Jesus in the Garden of Gethsemane. Like Jesus, Paul

was not delivered of the hardship that faced him, but received strength to remain faithful in the midst of the suffering.

12:9 My grace is sufficient for you. This sentence is the lens through which 2 Corinthians must be understood. It reflects the fundamental misunderstanding that the false teachers and the Corinthians had about the gospel. They thought the power of God meant that Christians should escape or avoid the experiences of weakness, vulnerability, suffering, and hardship that are common to life. Paul's emphasis has been that the power of God does not mean such trials are avoided, but that God empowers believers to love, bring healing, serve others, and remain faithful in the midst of such times (1:3-11).

12:11 you forced it on me. Paul is forced to

boast because the Corinthians refused to speak up on his behalf and stand with him.

12:12 signs ... wonders and miracles. While there is no record of Paul performing any miracles in Corinth, he did do so elsewhere (Acts 14:8-10; 20:9-12).

12:13-16 Since Paul's desire to minister without thought of profiteering was seen as a lack of love (11:9-11), he offers a mock apology. Yet he asserts that when he visits again he still will refuse their financial support because his intent is to serve them as a parent does a child.

12:13 did not burden you. Once again, it seems that what most rankled the Corinthians was Paul's refusal to allow them to support him.

12:21 God will again humiliate me. Paul is aware that this could be another very painful

Unselfish Sacrifice

1. What is one way your parents have sacrificed for you? How do you feel about that unselfish sacrifice?

2 Corinthians 12:11-21

2. What led Paul to write this letter (vv. 11-13)? How have the false "super-apostles" distorted his ministry (see 2:17; 11:7)?

3. How would you respond if fellow Christians you love were behaving like the Corinthians in verses 20-21? How persistent would you be in loving them?

4. To whom is God leading you to reach out and help? How can you show the spirit of verses 14-15 to this person?

Passing the Test

1. What do you do to prepare yourself for big exams?

2 Corinthians 13:1-14

2. Paul prefers to come to the Corinthians in "the gentleness and graciousness of Christ" (10:1), and as a loving parent (12:14-15). How will he come, instead, if repentance has not occurred? How does this relate to the ministry of Jesus?

3. What does Paul hope for as he considers his upcoming visit (vv. 10-11)?

4. In which area of your spiritual life will you be "strong" (13:9) this week? In which area will you be content with "weakness" (12:9-10)?

Final Warnings and Exhortations

13 This is the third time I am coming to you. **On the testimony**ᵃ **of two or three witnesses every word will be confirmed.**ᵇ ² I gave warning, and I give warning—as when I was present the second time, so now while I am absent—to those who sinned before and to all the rest: if I come again, I will not be lenient, ³ since you seek proof of Christ speaking in me. He is not weak toward you, but powerful among you. ⁴ In fact, He was crucified in weakness, but He lives by God's power. For we also are weak in Him, yet toward you we will live with Him by God's power.

⁵ Test yourselves ⌊to see⌋ if you are in the faith. Examine yourselves. Or do you not recognize for yourselves that Jesus Christ is in you?—unless you fail the test.ᶜ ⁶ And I hope you will recognize that we are not failing the test. ⁷ Now we pray to God that you do

nothing wrong, not that we may appear to pass the test, but that you may do what is right, even though we ⌊may appear⌋ to fail. ⁸ For we are not able to do anything against the truth, but only for the truth. ⁹ In fact, we rejoice when we are weak and you are strong. We also pray for this: your maturity.ᵈ ¹⁰ This is why I am writing these things while absent, that when I am there I will not use severity, in keeping with the authority the Lord gave me for building up and not for tearing down.

¹¹ Finally, brothers, rejoice. Be restored, be encouraged, be of the same mind, be at peace, and the God of love and peace will be with you. ¹² Greet one another with a holy kiss. All the saints greet you.

¹³ The grace of the Lord Jesus Christ, and the love of God, and the fellowship of the Holy Spirit be with all of you.ᵉ

ᵃ**13:1** Lit *mouth* ᵇ**13:1** Dt 17:6; 19:15 ᶜ**13:5** Or *you are disqualified*, or *you are counterfeit* ᵈ**13:9** Or *completion*, or *restoration* ᵉ**13:12–13** Some translations divide these 2 vv. into 3 vv. so that v. 13 begins with *All the saints . . .* and v. 14 begins with *The grace of . . .*

---

visit because he will see that the people will not have repented and his work has not been as effective as he would like. **uncleanness, sexual immorality and promiscuity.** These three terms describe sexual sin of all types. Sexual sins were an especially prevalent problem in Corinth (1Cor. 5:1; 6:12-20).

13:1-4 The Old Testament Law required that there be at least two witnesses before anyone could be accused of a crime (Deut. 19:15). Paul adapts this principle to justify the rightness of his coming with judgment on his next visit, since he has already

warned the people twice (through his second visit and his sorrowful letter—2:3-4) of their need to correct their ways.

13:2 those who sinned before and to all the rest. Paul intends to deal both with the long-standing problems in the Corinthian church (detailed in 1 Corinthians), and with the newer problems arising as a result of their seduction by false apostles (12:20-21).

13:3 powerful. Paul may have not been all they expected, but the resurrected Christ is. The power of Christ has been readily visible

to the Corinthians in miracles (12:12; Rom. 15:19; Gal. 3:5), in Paul's preaching (1 Cor. 2:4), and in the conversion of sinners to faith in Christ (1 Cor. 6:11).

13:4 in weakness. It is not that Christ was killed because He was powerless to prevent His crucifixion. Rather, He was killed because He allowed Himself to be weak for our sakes. He renounced the power that could have saved Him and so died to save us. **He lives by God's power.** God's power was displayed in Christ's resurrection from the dead.

GALATIANS

AUTHOR

The Apostle Paul was the author of Galatians.

DATE

The date of Paul's epistle depends on whether he was writing to churches in North or South Galatia. If Paul had been writing to congregations in North Galatia, the letter could not have been written before his third missionary expedition after the journey mentioned in Acts 16:6 and 18:23, around A.D. 55. On the other hand, if Paul were writing to the churches in the southern region, the epistle to the Galatians is his earliest letter–written in A.D. 48 or 49, possibly while he was in Syrian Antioch just prior to the Council in Jerusalem (Acts 15:6-21).

THEME

Justification by faith alone.

HISTORICAL BACKGROUND

Paul tells us he is writing "to the churches in Galatia" (1:2). But where are these churches located? This is unclear because in 25 B.C. the Romans created a new imperial province that they named Galatia. This new province was made up of the original kingdom of Galatia plus a new region to the south forged out of territory originally belonging to six other regions. So when a first-century writer speaks of Galatia, it is not always clear whether he is referring to the original territory in the north or the new province extending southward–which included the cities of Pisidian, Antioch, Iconium, Lystra, and Derbe that Paul visited during his first missionary journey described in Acts 13-14.

CHARACTERISTICS

Paul writes in anger: "You foolish Galatians! Who has hypnotized you?" (3:1). He felt it strongly because the issue he was addressing in this letter was not a minor matter of church policy; it struck right to the heart of the gospel.

Apparently some legalistic Jewish Christians (Judaizers) had been stirring up trouble. They had twisted the gospel into something Jesus never intended, and then they had made false charges against Paul. "Who is that fellow, anyway. He wasn't one of the Twelve. He is a self-appointed apostle. No wonder he left out some crucial parts of the message. Let us set you straight ..." And the Galatians seemingly believed their words against Paul. Paul wrote, "I am amazed that you are so quickly turning away from Him who called you by the grace of Christ, [and are turning] to a different gospel" (1:6).

What were the Judaizers saying? At first glance, they seemed to be adding only a little to the message. "Believe in Christ," they were saying (they were Christians), "but also be circumcised" (6:12 Paul saw the implications: if the Galatians let themselves be circumcised, it would be but the first step back to keeping the whole law (5:3) which Paul called slavery (4:9). This is not the gospel. The gospel asserts that salvation is a free gift, by grace. If you add anything else to grace, salvation is no longer free. It then becomes a matter of doing the "other thing."

The core issue in Galatians is justification. How does a person gain right standing before God? The Judaizers said that Christ (grace) plus circumcision (law-keeping) equals right standing.

Paul's equation was different; Christ (grace) plus *nothing else* equals right standing. Works are excluded from Paul's equation. "Yet we know that no one is justified by the works of the law but by faith in Jesus Christ. And we have believed in Christ Jesus, so that we might be justified by faith in Christ and not by the works of the law, because by the works of the law no human being will be justified" (2:16). This key verse sums up Paul's argument.

THE IMPLICATIONS

To the modern reader, it may sound as if Paul is getting worked up over a small issue. The important thing is to believe in Jesus, and all the parties agreed to that. But history demonstrated that Paul's concerns were valid. Was Christianity for all people in all cultures (as Paul was arguing), or was it only a Jewish sect? To be a Christian, did you have to accept Jewish customs and submit to Jewish laws? If the Judaizers had won, Christianity would probably have died out in the first century.

Instead, the church was able to expand into the Graeco-Roman world because the gospel was truly universal. It was not tied to temple sacrifice and the Law of Moses, about which most pagans neither knew nor cared. The Judaizers wanted a Christianity circumcised by Jewish exclusiveness, taboos, and customs—in which Gentile believers would always be second-class citizens. Paul fought this with vehemence and passion, as had other believers from Stephen onward; so Christianity became the transcultural world religion Christ intended (Matt. 28:19-20).

THE RELATIONSHIP BETWEEN GALATIANS AND ROMANS

It is obvious that there is a close thematic connection between Galatians and Romans. Galatians appears to be Paul's first attempt at

wrestling with the issue of justification by faith alone. Paul does so in the context of having to deal with a local problem. Romans, on the other hand, is a more studied consideration of the same issue. It is an eloquent, carefully stated, logical argument, which stands as one of the finest pieces of theological writing ever penned.

STRUCTURE

After a terse greeting (1:1-5) and pronouncement of condemnation against the troublemakers (1:6-10), Paul launches into his first major theme: his *personal defense,* in which he deals with the charge that he is not a real apostle (1:11-2:21). This is followed by a *doctrinal defense,* in which he shows that Christianity lived under the law is inferior to Christianity lived by faith (3:1-4:31). On the basis of these two arguments, he then shows what true Christian freedom is (5:1-6:10), ending with an unusual conclusion written in his own hand (6:11-18).

PASSAGES FOR TOPICAL GROUP STUDY

Greeting

1 Paul, an apostle—not from men or by man, but by Jesus Christ and God the Father who raised Him from the dead— ² and all the brothers who are with me:

To the churches of Galatia.ᵃ

³ Grace to you and peace from God the Father and our Lordᵇ Jesus Christ, ⁴ who gave Himself for our sins to rescue us from this present evil age, according to the will of our God and Father, ⁵ to whom be the glory forever and ever. •Amen.

A Different Gospel

1. What subject do you have the most trouble learning? What lessons do you find yourself forgetting soon after you leave class?

Galatians 1:1-10

2. What did Jesus voluntarily do for Paul, the Galatians, and us (v. 4)?
3. What does Paul say will happen to anyone who promotes a "gospel" other than that which Paul preached—the good news of grace (vv. 8-9)?
4. What are some modern teachings that promote a different "gospel"? How do some teachings claim to have special "authority" from enlightened teachers?

No Other Gospel

⁶ I am amazed that you are so quickly turning away from Him who called you by the grace of Christ, ⌐and are turning⌐ to a different gospel— ⁷ not that there is another ⌐gospel⌐, but there are some who are troubling

you and want to change the gospel of Christ. ⁸ But even if we or an angel from heaven should preach to you a gospel other than what we have preached to you, a curse be on him!ᶜ ⁹ As we have said before, I now say again: if anyone preaches to you a gospel contrary to what you received, a curse be on him!ᵈ

¹⁰ For am I now trying to win the favor of people, or God? Or am I striving to please people? If I were still trying to please people, I would not be a slave of Christ.

The Final Authority

1. Who is the "final authority" on your sport or hobby? Whose opinions carry the most weight? Why?

Galatians 1:11-24

2. What does Paul mean in verse 11, "the gospel preached by me is not based on a human point of view"? On what is the gospel based?
3. How does the gospel run counter to human logic and opinion? Why does the world react in anger to the gospel?
4. By whom (and what) was Paul called (v. 15)? What was he specifically called to do (v. 16)?
5. For what has God called you? Are you fulfilling His calling?

Paul Defends His Apostleship

¹¹ Now I want you to know, brothers, that the gospel preached by me is not based on a human point of view.ᵉ ¹² For I did not receive it from a human source and I was not taught it, but it came by a revelation from Jesus Christ.

ᵃ**1:2** A Roman province in what is now Turkey ᵇ**1:3** Other mss read *God our Father and the Lord* ᶜ**1:8** Or *you, let him be condemned*, or *you, let him be condemned to hell*; Gk *anathema* ᵈ**1:9** Or *received, let him be condemned*, or *received, let him be condemned to hell*; Gk *anathema* ᵉ**1:11** Lit. *not according to man*

1:1 Paul. Virtually everyone accepts that he was the author of Galatians. **apostle.** This New Testament word means "a special messenger." **not from men ... but by Jesus Christ.** Paul emphasizes that his apostleship derives not from any human intermediary. Rather, his commission and authority were received directly from the resurrected Christ on the Damascus road.

1:2 Galatia. The Roman province of Galatia was located in what is now the central part of Turkey (see a Bible map).

1:4 gave Himself. The idea is one of voluntary sacrifice for a specific purpose. **rescue.** To be rescued from bondage is a key idea in the letter.

1:6 amazed. Typically at this place in a letter, Paul would commend the church (e.g.

Rom. 1:8; Phil. 1:3). But here he launches straight into his remonstration, expressing indignation at the news that they have been persuaded by the teaching of people referred to as Judaizers. **turning away.** The word means, literally, a removal from one place to another. The word can also be used for those who "change sides"—for example, army deserters. **grace.** This pinpoints the nature of their turning—from a gospel of unmerited favor to a gospel of works. **gospel.** The proclamation of the good news that in the life, death, and resurrection of Jesus, the kingdom of God has been made clearly evident and is open to all who by faith trust in His atoning work on the cross.

1:8 a curse be on him! This stands as the direct opposite of God's grace, and is used by Paul as a solemn calling down of judg-

ment on the Judaizers, who insisted that to become a good Christian, one had to accept the demands of Jewish law.

1:12 revelation. It was only after Jesus Christ revealed the truth and meaning of these facts to him following the Damascus road experience that Paul accepted the gospel.

1:15 set me apart. Paul's experience is similar to that of Old Testament prophets (Isa. 49:1-6; Jer. 1:5). He could see the special calling and hand of God throughout his life.

1:16 among the Gentiles. With Paul's conversion came his commission to preach to the Gentiles (Acts 9:15). In encountering Christ, he came to the realization that the Law was bankrupt insofar as its ability to save anyone. There was no barrier to pre-

¹³ For you have heard about my former way of life in Judaism: I persecuted God's church to an extreme degree and tried to destroy it; ¹⁴ and I advanced in Judaism beyond many contemporaries among my people, because I was extremely zealous for the traditions of my ancestors. ¹⁵ But when God, who from my mother's womb set me apart and called me by His grace, was pleased ¹⁶ to reveal His Son in me, so that I could preach Him among the Gentiles, I did not immediately consult with anyone.^a ¹⁷ I did not go up to Jerusalem to those who had become apostles before me; instead I went to Arabia and came back to Damascus.

¹⁸ Then after three years I did go up to Jerusalem to get to know •Cephas,^b and I stayed with him 15 days. ¹⁹ But I didn't see any of the other apostles except James, the Lord's brother. ²⁰ Now in what I write to you, I'm not lying. God is my witness.^c

²¹ Afterwards, I went to the regions of Syria and Cilicia. ²² I remained personally unknown to the Judean churches in Christ; ²³ they simply kept hearing: "He who formerly persecuted us now preaches the faith he once tried to destroy." ²⁴ And they glorified God because of me.

Paul Defends His Gospel at Jerusalem

2 Then after 14 years I went up again to Jerusalem with Barnabas, taking Titus along also. ² I went up because of a revelation and presented to them the gospel I preach among the Gentiles—but privately to those recognized ⌊as leaders⌋—so that I might not be running, or have run, in vain. ³ But not even Titus who was with me, though he was a Greek, was compelled to be circumcised. ⁴ ⌊This issue arose⌋ because of false brothers smuggled in, who came in secretly to spy on our freedom that we have in Christ Jesus, in order to enslave us. ⁵ But we did not yield in submission to these people for even an hour, so that the truth of the gospel would remain for you.

⁶ But from those recognized as important (what they really were makes no difference to me; God does not show favoritism^d)—those recognized as important

Caring for All

1. Are you the type of person who usually "goes with the crowd" or "does your own thing"?

Galatians 2:1-10

2. If Paul's converts had to become Jews to be Christians, what would have happened to Paul's ministry to the Gentiles (v. 2)? What would be different about the church today?
3. What did the spiritual "pillars" of the Jerusalem church recognize about Paul (v. 9)?
4. How does caring for the poor (v. 10) relate to proclaiming the gospel of grace?
5. What can you do this week to help care for the poor?

added nothing to me. ⁷ On the contrary, they saw that I had been entrusted with the gospel for the uncircumcised, just as Peter was for the circumcised. ⁸ For He who was at work with Peter in the apostleship to the circumcised was also at work with me among the Gentiles. ⁹ When James, •Cephas, and John, recognized as pillars, acknowledged the grace that had been given to me, they gave the right hand of fellowship to me and Barnabas, ⌊agreeing⌋ that we should go to the Gentiles and they to the circumcised. ¹⁰ ⌊They asked⌋ only that we would remember the poor, which I made every effort to do.

Freedom from the Law

¹¹ But when Cephas^e came to Antioch, I opposed him to his face because he stood condemned.^f ¹² For he used to eat with the Gentiles before certain men came from James. However, when they came, he withdrew and

^a**1:16** Lit flesh and blood   ^b**1:18** Other mss read Peter   ^c**1:20** Lit Behold, before God   ^d**2:6** Or God is not a respecter of persons, lit God does not receive the face of man   ^e**2:11** Other mss read Peter   ^f**2:11** Or he was in the wrong

---

vent Gentiles from coming to the all-sufficient Christ for eternal salvation.

1:18 after three years. A significant interval of time elapsed between his conversion and his first visit to Jerusalem. **Jerusalem.** It was a courageous act by Paul to return here—to his former friends who might well try to harm him (because of his conversion to Christianity), and to new friends who might not even receive him (because of their suspicions about him). **15 days.** This was a short visit, and Paul spent much of his time preaching (Acts 9:28-29).

1:19 James. James, the brother of Jesus, eventually became the leader of the Jerusalem church (Mark 6:3; Acts 1:14; 15:13; 21:18).

1:21 Syria and Cilicia. After leaving Jerusa-

lem, Paul went north into Syria and then into the adjacent area of Cilicia to the city of Tarsus, his birthplace.

2:1 after 14 years. It is not clear whether Paul means 14 years after his conversion or after his first visit to Jerusalem. In any case, the significant factor is that Paul had little contact with the leaders in Jerusalem. He was not their missionary. He did not take orders from them. **I went up again.** In 14 years Paul made only two visits to Jerusalem. The first was for the purpose of meeting Peter. The second was necessary in order to deliver to the mother church a famine collection donated by Christians at Antioch. **Barnabas.** A Levite from Cyprus, whose name was actually Joseph but who had been nicknamed Barnabas (Son of Encouragement) by the apostles (Acts 4:36). When the church in Jerusalem heard that a

great number of people in Antioch had turned to Jesus, they sent Barnabas to verify what was happening. Barnabas in turn, having seen this to be an authentic work of God, sought out Paul in Tarsus and brought him back to Antioch, where the two of them labored together to establish the church (Acts 11:19-30). **Titus.** A Gentile Christian from Antioch. Titus became an important coworker with Paul, and later was the recipient of a pastoral letter.

2:2 in vain. Paul preached that Gentiles could become Christians without first becoming Jews, i.e., that there was one church made up of both Jews and Gentiles. If the leaders in Jerusalem disputed this, his 14 years of work would have been in vain.

2:11-14 I opposed him. Paul concludes his autobiographical sketch by recounting an

The Big "I" or JC?

1. Have you ever "told off" your parents, teacher, coach, or some other adult? Why? What was the outcome?

Galatians 2:11-21

2. Why did Paul confront Cephas? How was Cephas being a hypocrite?
3. What is the difference between "the works of the law" and "faith in Jesus Christ" (v. 16)?
4. In the Christian life, what dies and what gets resurrected (vv. 19-20)? How is that made possible?
5. Applying the spiritual concept of verse 20, who is "alive" in your life right now—the big "I" or "Christ in me"?

rebuild those things that I tore down, I show myself to be a lawbreaker. 19 For through the law I have died to the law, that I might live to God. I have been crucified with Christ; 20 and I no longer live, but Christ lives in me. The life I now live in the flesh,g I live by faith in the Son of God, who loved me and gave Himself for me. 21 I do not set aside the grace of God; for if righteousness comes through the law, then Christ died for nothing.

Grasping Grace

1. Have you ever seen someone hypnotized? What was it like? Was it real or fake?

Galatians 3:1-14

2. What is the answer to Paul's question in verse 2? Give some Scripture verses to support your answer.
3. According to verse 5, what is required of us to have God's Spirit doing miraculous things in our lives?
4. Did God consider Abraham righteous through his faith or through his works (vv. 5-9)?
5. Who are those "who rely on the works of the law" (v. 10)?
6. Do you rely on your own good works or on God's grace for your salvation?

separated himself, because he feared those from the circumcision party. 13 Then the rest of the Jews joined his hypocrisy, so that even Barnabas was carried away by their hypocrisy. 14 But when I saw that they were deviating from the truth of the gospel, I told Cephasa in front of everyone, "If you, who are a Jew, live like a Gentile and not like a Jew, how can you compel Gentiles to live like Jews?"b

15 We are Jews by birth and not "Gentile sinners"; 16 yet we know that no one is justified by the works of the law but by faith in Jesus Christ.c And we have believed in Christ Jesus, so that we might be justified by faith in Christd and not by the works of the law, because by the works of the law no human being wille be justified. 17 But if, while seeking to be justified by Christ, we ourselves are also found to be sinners, is Christ then a promoterf of sin? Absolutely not! 18 If I

Justification through Faith

3 You foolish Galatians! Who has hypnotized you,h before whose eyes Jesus Christ was vividly portrayedi as crucified? 2 I only want to learn this from you: Did you receive the Spirit by the works of the law or by hearing with faith?j 3 Are you so foolish? After beginning with the Spirit, are you now going to be made complete by the flesh?k 4 Did you suffer so much

---

a2:14 Other mss read *Peter*   b2:14 Some translations continue the quotation through v. 16 or v. 21.   c2:16 Or *by the faithfulness of Jesus Christ*
d2:16 Or *by the faithfulness of Christ*   e2:16 Lit *law all flesh will not*   f2:17 Or *servant*   g2:20 The physical body   h3:1 Other mss add *not to obey the truth*   i3:1 Other mss add *among you*   j3:2 Lit *by law works or faith hearing* or *hearing the message*   k3:3 By human effort

---

incident in which he had to rebuke the Apostle Peter for his inconsistency. This incident probably occurred after Paul's return to Antioch following his second visit to Jerusalem (vv. 1-10), but prior to his first missionary journey (Acts 13-14) during which he founded the Galatian churches.

2:15 "Gentile sinners." Jews did look down rather arrogantly on all Gentiles. But Paul's point is that both Jew and Gentile come to God by faith, not by works. Being "better" morally has nothing to do with justification before God.

2:16 justified. Behind this word stands the image of the Judgment Day. The Jew was preoccupied with how one obtained a positive verdict (justification) from God the Judge. The opposite of justification is condemnation—to be declared guilty—on

Judgment Day. This is the language of the courtroom where people are either found guilty or innocent. If you ask most people why God will let them into heaven, they will say He will do so because their good deeds outweighed the bad. This common understanding is dangerously wrong. Only God can justify people based on the work of Christ on the cross.

2:20 I no longer live. Paul died in relationship to the Law. **Christ lives in me.** That which now activates the believer is the resurrection life and power of Jesus. **I live by faith.** Faith is that which bonds together the believer and the risen Christ. Paul will also refers to this as living by the Spirit (5:25).

3:1 foolish. Paul's feelings of exasperation and indignation flare up. How could they have been so stupid (as the NEB translates

the word)? It is not that they were unable to understand what was happening. They simply failed to use their minds. **hypnotized.** Their actions were so bizarre it seemed that their minds were altered.

3:6-9 Scripture. Paul turns from his argument based on their experience to an argument based on Scripture. Here he shows that it has always been by faith that men and women became God's children.

3:6 believed God. God promised Abraham that he would have descendants as numerous as the stars, even though his wife Sarah was barren. Despite the improbability of this ever happening, Abraham still trusted God that it would be so. **credited ... for righteousness.** For Abraham, right standing before God came by faith, not by law-keeping.

for nothing—if in fact it was for nothing? [5] So then, does God[a] supply you with the Spirit and work miracles among you by the works of the law or by hearing with faith?[b]

[6] Just as Abraham **believed God, and it was credited to him for righteousness,**[c] [7] so understand that those who have faith are Abraham's sons. [8] Now the Scripture foresaw that God would justify the Gentiles by faith and foretold the good news to Abraham, saying, **All the nations will be blessed in you.**[d] [9] So those who have faith are blessed with Abraham, who had faith.[e]

Law and Promise

[10] For all who ⌊rely on⌋ the works of the law are under a curse, because it is written: **Cursed is everyone who does not continue doing everything written in the book of the law.**[f] [11] Now it is clear that no one is justified before God by the law, because **the righteous will live by faith.**[g] [12] But the law is not based on faith; instead, **the one who does these things will live by them.**[h] [13] Christ has redeemed us from the curse of the law by becoming a curse for us, because it is written: **Cursed is everyone who is hung on a tree.**[i] [14] The purpose was that the blessing of Abraham would come to the Gentiles in Christ Jesus, so that we could receive the promise of the Spirit through faith.

[15] Brothers, I'm using a human illustration.[j] No one sets aside even a human covenant that has been ratified, or makes additions to it. [16] Now the promises were spoken to Abraham and to his seed. He does not say "and to seeds," as though referring to many, but **and to your seed,**[k] referring to one, who is Christ. [17] And I say this: the law, which came 430 years later, does not revoke a covenant that was previously ratified by God,[l] so as to cancel the promise. [18] For if the inheritance is from the law, it is no longer from the promise; but God granted it to Abraham through the promise.

The Only Seed

1. Have you ever been inside a jail? What was it like? How did you feel there?

Galatians 3:15-26
2. Can the Old Testament Law give "life" (v. 21)? Who can? How (v. 22)?
3. Why does Paul make a distinction in verse 16 between one seed and many "seeds"?
4. If Christ is the only "seed" of God's salvation, what does that say about other world religions? How does this compare with what the world teaches us about religion?
5. How do you share your faith with someone from another religion?

The Purpose of the Law

[19] Why the law then? It was added because of transgressions until the Seed to whom the promise was made would come. ⌊The law⌋ was ordered through angels by means of a mediator. [20] Now a mediator is not for just one person, but God is one. [21] Is the law therefore contrary to God's promises? Absolutely not! For if a law had been given that was able to give life, then righteousness would certainly be by the law. [22] But the Scripture has imprisoned everything under sin's power,[m] so that the promise by faith in Jesus Christ might be given to those who believe. [23] Before this faith came, we were confined under the law, imprisoned until the coming faith was revealed. [24] The law, then, was our guardian[n] until Christ, so that we could be

---

[a]**3:5** Lit *He* [b]**3:5** Lit *by law works or faith hearing* or *hearing the message* [c]**3:6** Gn 15:6 [d]**3:8** Gn 12:3; 18:18 [e]**3:9** Or *with believing Abraham*
[f]**3:10** Dt 27:26 [g]**3:11** Hab 2:4 [h]**3:12** Lv 18:5 [i]**3:13** Dt 21:23 [j]**3:15** Lit *I speak according to man* [k]**3:16** Gn 12:7; 13:15; 17:8; 24:7 [l]**3:17** Other mss add *in Christ* [m]**3:22** Lit *under sin* [n]**3:24** The word translated *guardian* in vv. 24–25 is different from the word in Gl 4:2. In our culture, we do not have a slave who takes a child to and from school, protecting the child from harm or corruption. In Gk the word *paidogogos* described such a slave. This slave was not a teacher.

3:10-14 under a curse. Paul's next point is that law-keeping is ultimately futile, because no one is able to fulfill the whole Law—therefore no one is justified by the Law. Rather a curse hangs heavy upon them. Blessing comes by faith.

3:15-18 human illustration. Having argued from experience and from Scripture, Paul now argues the same point from human reason. He asks the Galatians to think about how wills are made. His point is that once established, no one can alter a will. Likewise, the covenant given by God to Abraham cannot be altered. The promised blessings came to Abraham's true children, not because they earned them through law-keeping, but because they came by grace without conditions.

3:16 to your seed. God's promises to Abra-

ham were not for all his many descendants, but more specifically, for his one crucial descendant: the Messiah. The blessings are then channeled outward to all who believe—Jew or Gentile—through Jesus the Messiah.

3:17 The prior Abrahamic covenant is unaffected by the later Law. **430 years later.** The Law was given much later, during the time of Moses.

3:18 inheritance. Promises, along with material possessions, given to a person's descendants. **promise.** God's promise to Abraham had nothing to do with law or obligations. It was a pure gift without conditions.

3:19 Why the law then? If the promises came by faith, what about the Law? What purpose did it have? This was a burning question to the Judaizers, because they felt

that it perfectly reflected God's will. **It was added ... until.** Paul answers that the Law was temporary. Its purpose was to make people aware of their sin, but when the Messiah came, its function would cease. **a mediator.** On the basis of Deuteronomy 33:2, it was concluded that the Law was given to Moses at Mount Sinai by the angels who accompanied God. Paul's point is that a word that came indirectly from God is of less significance than one that came directly, as did God's promise to Abraham.

3:24 our guardian. The Law is now pictured as a tutor. The same word is used for household slaves whose responsibility it was to look after the young men in the family until they reached the age of accountability.

3:27 baptized. A common water rite in Judaism. One of three acts by which a person be-

justified by faith. ²⁵ But since that faith has come, we are no longer under a guardian,ᵃ ²⁶ for you are all sons of God through faith in Christ Jesus.

Leveling the Field

1. In what ways does your sport make equals of all players? How does it bring out inequalities?

Galatians 3:27-4:7

2. What does it take to become a child of God?
3. What does it mean to "put on Christ" (3:27)? How does that happen on the field and off?
4. What does Paul mean that all are one in Christ Jesus (3:28)? What effect does being "in Christ" have on relationships among believers?
6. What is the difference between being a slave and an heir? Which have you felt more like lately?

Sons and Heirs

²⁷ For as many of you as have been baptized into Christ have put on Christ. ²⁸ There is no Jew or Greek, slave or free, male or female; for you are all one in Christ Jesus. ²⁹ And if you are Christ's, then you are Abraham's seed, heirs according to the promise. **4** Now I say that as long as the heir is a child, he differs in no way from a slave, though he is the owner of everything. ² Instead, he is under guardians and stewards until the time set by his father. ³ In the same way we also, when we were children, were in slavery under the elemental forces of the world. ⁴ But when the completion of the time came, God sent His Son, born of a

woman, born under the law, ⁵ to redeem those under the law, so that we might receive adoption as sons. ⁶ And because you are sons, God has sent the Spirit of His Son into ourᵇ hearts, crying, "•*Abba*, Father!" ⁷ So you are no longer a slave, but a son; and if a son, then an heir through God.

Enslaved

1. What is one of your most compulsive habits? How are you trying to break it?

Galatians 4:8-20

2. Overall, was Paul more concerned for himself or the Galatians? Why?
3. Do you show deep concern for the welfare of others, as Paul did for the Galatians?
4. In what ways does sin "enslave" us? How can a Christian break out of such slavery?
5. Like the Galatians, have you slipped back into any bad habits or old ways from which Christ once delivered you? Which ones? What can you do about it?

Paul's Concern for the Galatians

⁸ But in the past, when you didn't know God, you were enslaved to thingsᶜ that by nature are not gods. ⁹ But now, since you know God, or rather have become known by God, how can you turn back again to the weak and bankrupt elemental forces? Do you want to be enslaved to them all over again? ¹⁰ You observe special days, months, seasons, and years. ¹¹ I am fearful for you, that perhaps my labor for you has been wasted.

ᵃ**3:25** The word translated *guardian* in vv. 24–25 is different from the word in Gl 4:2. In our culture, we do not have a slave who takes a child to and from school, protecting the child from harm or corruption. In Gk the word *paidogogos* described such a slave. This slave was not a teacher.   ᵇ**4:6** Other mss read *your*   ᶜ**4:8** Or *beings*

---

came a Jew, it was picked up and given new meaning (repentance and remission of sins) by John the Baptist; and later used by the Christian church as the visible, outward sign of admission into the Christian community. **put on.** This image may spring from the practice by the early church of removing old garments prior to baptism and then donning a new white robe after baptism.

3:28 no Jew or Greek. The Jewish contempt for the non-Jew was immense. **slave or free.** Although some 60 million slaves virtually ran the Roman Empire, they were generally regarded as mere things, without rights. This was another barrier broken down by Christ. **male or female.** A woman had few if any rights in either first-century Judaism or Greco-Roman culture. She belonged to her husband and he could treat her as he chose, including divorcing her with ease. **one in**

Christ Jesus. In morning prayer, a Jewish man thanked God that he had not been made a Gentile, a slave, or a woman. The traditional distinctions are finished. In Christ all are one.

4:2 guardians and stewards. In his will, a Roman father appointed a guardian who looked after the child until he came of age at 14. Then a curator looked after the child's affairs until age 25. **until the time set.** The father had some discretion as to when the child received the inheritance.

4:4 elemental forces. This concept has been interpreted in two ways. (1) It could be basic religious and moral principles or (2) it may be spirits, spiritual powers that were thought to move the heavenly bodies. No matter which interpretation on favors, Paul was speaking of people who were enslaved

by some force other than the Holy Spirit of God, the Spirit of Christ.

4:4 when the completion of the time came. Finally, the long history of God's revelation reached the culminating point: Jesus was sent. From a human point of view, Jesus was born at a favorable time. Roman law, the wonderful system of Roman highways, the political stability maintained throughout the Mediterranean world by Rome, the widespread use of the Greek language by people of diverse cultures, and the growing interest in Jewish religious teaching all combined to create a situation in which the gospel could spread.

4:10 observe. Paul observed certain sacred events (Acts 20:16; 1 Cor. 16:8). It is one thing for a Jew to continue in his ethnic tradition in a nonbinding way, and another for a

¹² I beg you, brothers: become like me, for I also became like you. You have not wronged me; ¹³ you know that previously I preached the gospel to you in physical weakness, ¹⁴ and though my physical condition was a trial for you,ᵃ you did not despise or reject me. On the contrary, you received me as an angel of God, as Christ Jesus ⌊Himself⌋.

¹⁵ What happened to this blessedness of yours? For I testify to you that, if possible, you would have torn out your eyes and given them to me. ¹⁶ Have I now become your enemy by telling you the truth? ¹⁷ Theyᵇ are enthusiastic about you, but not for any good. Instead, they want to isolate you so you will be enthusiastic about them. ¹⁸ Now it is always good to be enthusiastic about good—and not just when I am with you. ¹⁹ My children, again I am in the pains of childbirth for you until Christ is formed in you. ²⁰ I'd like to be with you right now and change my tone of voice, because I don't know what to do about you.

Sarah and Hagar: Two Covenants

²¹ Tell me, you who want to be under the law, don't you hear the law? ²² For it is written that Abraham had two sons, one by a slave and the other by a free woman. ²³ But the one by the slave was born according to the flesh, while the one by the free woman was born as the result of a promise. ²⁴ These things are illustrations,ᶜ for the women represent the two covenants. One is from Mount Sinai and bears children into slavery—this is Hagar. ²⁵ Now Hagar is Mount Sinai in Arabia and corresponds to the present Jerusalem, for she is in slavery with her children. ²⁶ But the Jerusalem above is free, and she is our mother. ²⁷ For it is written:

> Rejoice, O barren woman
> who does not give birth.
> Break forth and shout,
> you who are not in labor,
> for the children of the desolate are many,
> more numerous than those
> of the woman who has a husband.ᵈ

Freedom vs. Obedience

1. Were you an obedient child? How did your parents discipline you?

Galatians 4:21-31

2. What was extraordinary about Isaac's birth (Gen. 21:1-7)?
3. Why does Paul turn the tables on this story and indicate that the Jews are actually the ones in slavery with Hagar—their slave mother (vv. 25-26)?
4. Read verse 29 and explain how it applies to the struggle between flesh (temptation) and spirit (obedience).
5. How can you live out your "freedom" in Christ and still please Him with your sacrificial obedience?

²⁸ Now you, brothers, like Isaac, are children of promise. ²⁹ But just as then the child born according to the flesh persecuted the one born according to the Spirit, so also now. ³⁰ But what does the Scripture say?

> Throw out the slave and her son, for the son of the slave will never inherit with the son of the free woman.ᵉ

³¹ Therefore, brothers, we are not children of the slave but of the free woman.

Freedom of the Christian

5 Christ has liberated us into freedom. Therefore stand firm and don't submit again to a yoke of slavery. ² Take note! I, Paul, tell you that if you get circumcised, Christ will not benefit you at all. ³ Again I testify to every man who gets circumcised that he is obligated to keep the entire law. ⁴ You who are trying to be justified by the law are alienated from Christ; you

ᵃ4:14 Other mss read *me* ᵇ4:17 The false teachers ᶜ4:24 Typology or allegory ᵈ4:27 Is 54:1 ᵉ4:30 Gn 21:10

---

group of Gentiles to be forced to adopt the Jewish calendar.

4:14 physical condition. While there has been speculation about malaria, epilepsy, and other ailments, there is no way to be certain about the exact nature of Paul's illness. **an angel.** Perhaps there is an allusion to the time when Paul and Barnabas went to Lystra and were mistaken for gods (Acts 14:11-13). In any case, the contrast is between the greeting given an angel or Christ Jesus and their present attitude toward Paul.

4:15 torn out your eyes. At that time there was nothing the Galatians would not have done for Paul.

4:19 pains of childbirth. Paul often refers to himself as the father of spiritual children (1 Cor. 4:15). Here he plays the mother role,

and expresses his deep love and concern. **My children.** Paul cannot mask his deep affection for them despite his distress over their actions. **again.** For the second time he must endure the pangs of childbirth—first, when he sought to bring them out of paganism and into new birth in Christ, and now as he seeks to bring them out of legalism. **Christ is formed in you.** The metaphor is mixed but the point is clear. Paul's desire is that they come to possess Christ-like characteristics.

4:25 the present Jerusalem. For Paul, this represents contemporary Judaism with all its legalism. **in slavery.** Just as Jerusalem was in slavery to Rome, the Jews were enslaved to the Law.

4:26 Jerusalem above. The heavenly city that was thought to provide the pattern for

the physical city. The heavenly Jerusalem is the real thing—uncorrupted, perfect (Heb. 12:22; Rev. 3:12; 21:2,9-27).

5:2 I, Paul. Paul speaks with the full weight of his apostolic authority.

5:4 grace. Grace is not grace (a freely given gift) if there is any requirement at all for receiving it. **trying to be justified.** Paul has said repeatedly that it is impossible to gain right standing through the Law (Rom. 11:5-7). The only thing the Law brings (in this context) is a curse (3:10-14).

5:5 Spirit. It is the Holy Spirit who fosters such assurances of acquittal. **hope.** The Christian can confidently expect a positive verdict on the Judgment Day. To have such a hope in advance of the event brings great liberty and rejoicing. This stands in contrast

Love, Not Slavery

1. How do you feel when others cut in front of you in line? What do you do?

Galatians 5:1-15

2. What does Paul mean by a "yoke of slavery" (v. 1)?
3. Since our own efforts and achievements aren't the way to God, what is (vv. 5-6)?
4. What does it mean to "love your neighbor as yourself" (v. 14)? Does "loving yourself" look more like verse 15 or 1 Corinthians 13?
5. How do we "serve one another through love" (v. 13)? What fellow Christian can you serve through love in the coming week?

self.[a] 15 But if you bite and devour one another, watch out, or you will be consumed by one another.

Fruit Inspection

1. What is your favorite fruit? What is your least favorite?

Galatians 5:16-26

2. How are the Spirit and the sinful nature in conflict (vv. 16-18)?
3. How does society today encourage the behaviors listed in verses 19-21?
4. Consider each item in the fruit of the Spirit list (vv. 22-23), and explain how they are opposite to those in 19-21. (For example, patience is opposite to anger; love is opposite to selfish ambition, etc.)
5. Are you allowing any of the behaviors from verses 19-21 in your own life? Does all the fruit of the Spirit does your life show? How about in the heat of competition?

have fallen from grace! 5 For by the Spirit we eagerly wait for the hope of righteousness from faith. 6 For in Christ Jesus neither circumcision nor uncircumcision accomplishes anything; what matters is faith working through love.

7 You were running well. Who prevented you from obeying the truth? 8 This persuasion did not come from Him who called you. 9 A little yeast leavens the whole lump of dough. 10 In the Lord I have confidence in you that you will not accept any other view. But whoever it is who is troubling you will pay the penalty. 11 Now brothers, if I still preach circumcision, why am I still persecuted? In that case the offense of the cross has been abolished. 12 I wish those who are disturbing you might also get themselves castrated!

13 For you are called to freedom, brothers; only don't use this freedom as an opportunity for the flesh, but serve one another through love. 14 For the entire law is fulfilled in one statement: **Love your neighbor as your-**

The Spirit versus the Flesh

16 I say then, •walk by the Spirit and you will not carry out the desire of the flesh. 17 For the flesh desires what is against the Spirit, and the Spirit desires what is against the flesh; these are opposed to each other, so that you don't do what you want. 18 But if you are led by the Spirit, you are not under the law.

19 Now the works of the flesh are obvious:[b] [c] sexual immorality, moral impurity, promiscuity, 20 idolatry, sorcery, hatreds, strife, jealousy, outbursts of anger, selfish ambitions, dissensions, factions, 21 envy,[d] drunkenness, carousing, and anything similar, about which I tell you in advance—as I told you before—that those who practice such things will not inherit the kingdom of God.

[a]5:14 Lv 19:18   [b]5:19 Other mss add *adultery*   [c]5:19 Lit *obvious, which are:*   [d]5:21 Other mss add *murders*

to the anxiety of one who is never sure if he or she has done quite enough "good works" or has been faithful to all points of the Law.

5:7 running well. Paul uses an athletic metaphor to describe what happened to the Galatians. **prevented you.** A word originally referring to the breaking up of roads by armies so as to hinder the progress of the enemy; it came to carry the idea of cutting in front of a runner to trip him up. **the truth.** The gospel (2:5,14-16).

5:13 freedom ... but. What Paul has written about freedom from the Law could be misunderstood to be a license to indulge in one's appetites, and certainly he does not mean that. He begins this new section on Christian living by examining the use of freedom.

5:20 idolatry. The worship of any idol, be it

a carved image of God (a statue) or an abstract substitute for God (a status symbol). An idol can be defined as anything that takes a person's time, attention, and devotion away from God, and influences a person to follow its leading first when faced with a choice. Money, for instance, becomes an idol when a person will do anything to gain it. **hatreds.** This is the underlying political, social and religious hostility which drives individuals and communities apart. **strife.** This is the type of contention which leads to factions. **selfish ambitions.** This word has come to refer to anyone who works only for his or her own good and not for the benefit of others. **factions.** This refers to the partisan spirit that leads people to regard those with whom they disagree as enemies.

5:21 drunkenness. In the first century, diluted wine was drunk, but drunkenness was

condemned. **anything similar.** The list is representative, not exhaustive—touching, in order, upon the sins of sensuality, idolatry, social dissension, and intemperance. **not inherit.** The issue here is not sins into which one falls, but sin as a lifestyle. These are evidence of a life not controlled by the Spirit.

5:22 fruit of the Spirit. These are the traits which characterize the child of God. The list is representative and not exhaustive. **love.** The Greek *agape* (self-giving, active benevolence); in contrast, there is *eros* (sexual love), *philos* (warm feelings to friends and family), and *storge* (family affection). **joy.** The Greek word is *chara*, and comes from the same root as "grace" (*charis*). It is not based on earthly things or human achievement; it is a gift from God based on a right relationship with Him. **peace.** The prime meaning of this word is not negative ("an ab-

22 But the fruit of the Spirit is love, joy, peace, patience, kindness, goodness, faith,ª 23 gentleness, self-control. Against such things there is no law. 24 Now those who belong to Christ Jesus have crucified the flesh with its passions and desires. 25 If we live by the Spirit, we must also follow the Spirit. 26 We must not become conceited, provoking one another, envying one another.

Carrying Your Load

1. What's the heaviest thing you've ever tried to lift? Did you need help to carry it? Did you succeed?

Galatians 6:1-10

2. How are we to help "restore" a brother or sister who is caught up in sin? Why must we take care about this?

3. What does it mean to "sow to the flesh" (v. 8)?

4. As outlined in this passage, what responsibilities do we have for our brothers and sisters in Christ?

5. Why does God also call us to be accountable for ourselves? How are you doing at carrying your "own load" (v. 5)?

Carry One Another's Burdens

6 Brothers, if someone is caught in any wrongdoing, you who are spiritual should restore such a person with a gentle spirit, watching out for yourselves so you won't be tempted also. 2 Carry one another's burdens; in this way you will fulfill the law of Christ. 3 For if anyone considers himself to be something when he is nothing, he is deceiving himself. 4 But each person should examine his own work, and then he will have a reason for boasting in himself alone, and not in respect to someone else. 5 For each person will have to carry his own load.

6 The one who is taught the message must share his goods with the teacher. 7 Don't be deceived: God is not mocked. For whatever a man sows he will also reap, 8 because the one who sows to his flesh will reap corruption from the flesh, but the one who sows to the Spirit will reap eternal life from the Spirit. 9 So we must not get tired of doing good, for we will reap at the proper time if we don't give up. 10 Therefore, as we have opportunity, we must work for the good of all, especially for those who belong to the household of faith.

Concluding Exhortation

11 Look at what large letters I have written to you in my own handwriting. 12 Those who want to make a good showing in the flesh are the ones who would compel you to be circumcised—but only to avoid being persecuted for the cross of Christ. 13 For even the circumcised don't keep the law themselves; however, they want you to be circumcised in order to boast about your flesh. 14 But as for me, I will never boast about anything except the cross of our Lord Jesus Christ, through whomᵇ the world has been crucified to me, and I to the world. 15 Forᶜ both circumcision and uncircumcision mean nothing; ⌊what matters⌋ instead is a new creation. 16 May peace be on all those who follow this standard, and mercy also be on the Israel of God!

17 From now on, let no one cause me trouble, because I carry the marks of Jesus on my body. 18 Brothers, the grace of our Lord Jesus Christ be with your spirit. •Amen.

ª5:22 Or *faithfulness* ᵇ6:14 Or *which* ᶜ6:15 Other mss add *in Christ Jesus*

---

sence of conflict"), but positive ("the presence of that which brings wholeness and well-being"). **patience.** This is the ability to be steadfast with people, refusing to give up on them. **kindness.** This is the compassionate use of strength for the good of another. **goodness.** This implies moral purity which reflects the character of God. **faith.** This refers to firm conviction, which leads to being reliable and trustworthy.

5:23 gentleness. According to Aristotle, this is the virtue that lies between excessive proneness to anger and the inability to be angry; it implies control of oneself. **self-control.** This is control of one's sensual passions, emotions, and physical desires.

6:1 any wrongdoing. A temporary lapse (as compared to an active lifestyle). **you who are spiritual.** Those whose lives bear the mark of the Spirit. This is not a clique of "special" Christians but is a call to all Christians (followers of Christ; 5:24-25). **restore.** A medical term, used to describe the resetting of a fractured bone. The verb tense (in Greek) implies that this is not a single act but a continuous action. **with a gentle spirit.** This is an evidence of control by the Spirit (5:23).

6:2 Carry one another's burdens. Mutual burden-bearing lies at the heart of Christian fellowship. **burdens.** A heavy, crushing weight, which a single individual cannot carry. **law of Christ.** The law of love (5:14), which stands in sharp contrast to the Jewish Law.

6:5 load. This is not the same as the crushing burden in verse 2. Rather, the word is used to describe the small individual pack a hiker or soldier carries. This is the same word used by Jesus in Matthew 11:30 to describe the burden (load) of His yoke, signifying that each of us has a burden (load) to carry.

INTRODUCTION TO
EPHESIANS

AUTHOR

The Apostle Paul was the writer of Ephesians.

DATE

Paul probably wrote this letter in the early A.D. 60s, some 30 years after Jesus' crucifixion and only a few years before Paul's death.

THEME

God's new society.

HISTORICAL BACKGROUND

Paul is in prison once again, and Epaphras has come to visit him bearing news about the church at Colosse that was disturbing. Paul sends a letter in which he addresses the Colossian heresy. Onesimus, (now converted), carries the letter and returns to his owner Philemon, in the Colossian Church, Paul also writes two more letters: one to Philemon and one to a neighboring area, the letter to the Ephesians. These three epistles form the core of what we now know as the Prison Epistles or the Captivity Letters. It is unclear which imprisonment produced these letters (see 2 Cor. 11:23), but most likely Paul was at Rome (Acts 28).

Ephesians and Colossians are more similar in language and content than any other two letters in the New Testament. Seventy-five of the 155 verses in Ephesians are found in parallel form in Colossians. It seems that Paul first developed those themes in Colossians while dealing with a local problem, and then expanded them, explained them and cast them into a universal setting in Ephesians.

CHARACTERISTICS

In Ephesians, Paul focuses on Jesus Christ who breaks down the wall between God and humanity. We see Jesus creating the church, a new social order of love and unity that transcends the racial, ethnic, and social distinctions between people. In conveying this vision, Paul reaches into eternity past and eternity future to demonstrate how God, out of his love and glory, calls people to be reconciled to himself and to one another through the cross of Christ. The cross provides forgiveness of sins, a new life and a new people. Between Paul's greeting (1:1-2) and salutation (6:21-24), the letter divides easily into two parts. Part one (chapters 1-3) focuses on *doctrine*, specifically, the new life and new society God has created through Jesus. Part two (chapters 4-6) focuses on *ethics*--specifically, the new standards and new relationships expected of believers.

THE CITY OF EPHESUS

The city of Ephesus was the capital of the Roman province of Asia. It was a large, bustling, secular city situated on the west coast of Asia Minor (modern Turkey) on the Aegean Sea. Originally a Greek colony, by Roman times it had become a center for international trade, largely as a result of its fine, natural harbor.

Its key architectural feature was the Temple of Artemis (of Diana), considered to be one of the seven wonders of the ancient world. The image of Artemis was thought to have descended from heaven (Acts 19:35). There was also a huge, outdoor Greek theatre, capable of holding 50,000 people as well as a stadium where fights, races and other athletic contests were held.

Paul's first visit to Ephesus was brief—little more than a reconnaissance trip (Acts 18:18-22). He later returned during his third missionary journey and spent over two years there. His ministry was both effective and controversial. After three months in the synagogue, he was forced out and took up residence in the lecture hall of Tyrannus (Acts 19:8-9). Paul probably worked as a tentmaker in the mornings and lecturer in the afternoons. News of his message spread throughout Asia Minor (Acts 19:10) and extraordinary things happened. Handkerchiefs touched by him were used to cure the sick (Acts 19:11-12). Demons were cast out in the name of Jesus, even by Jewish exorcists (Acts 19:13-17). Pagan converts burned their books of magic (Acts 19:18-20). Eventually, a riot broke out in Ephesus because of Paul. Demetrius, a silversmith, organized a citywide protest. He charged that Paul's success posed a threat to the economic well-being of craftsmen who made their living from the worshipers of Artemis (Acts 19:23-41). As a result, Paul moved on to Macedonia. But by this time the church was firmly established.

Paul never visited Ephesus again. He did, however, stop at the nearby port of Miletus on his return to Jerusalem. He called the Ephesian elders to him there and gave a moving farewell address (Acts 20:13-38). Later on, Paul would write 1 and 2 Timothy in an attempt to deal with false teaching that had arisen in Ephesus—as he had warned in his farewell address might happen (Acts 20:28-31). His words and Timothy's ministry were apparently successful. The apostle John's Book of Revelation records that the Ephesians resisted false teaching—though they had lost their first love (Rev. 2:1-7). Tradition says that John spent the final years of his life in Ephesus—as the beloved bishop and last surviving apostle.

PASSAGES FOR TOPICAL GROUP STUDY

Greeting

1 Paul, an apostle of Christ Jesus by God's will:
To the saints and believers in Christ Jesus at Ephesus.ᵃ

² Grace to you and peace from God our Father and the Lord Jesus Christ.

Picked for the Team

1. Under what circumstances would you be willing to adopt a child, and what qualities would you look for in that child?

Ephesians 1:3-14

2. What is the significance of God choosing us before the "foundation of the world" (v. 4)? How are we "holy and blameless in His sight"?

3. Who is the "agent" through which God adopts us (v. 5)? How did this "agent" accomplish our adoption (v. 7)?

4. With all that God has done for you, what do you think He expects in return?

God's Rich Blessings

³ Blessed be the God and Father of our Lord Jesus Christ, who has blessed us with every spiritual blessing in the heavens, in Christ; ⁴ for He chose us in Him, before the foundation of the world, to be holy and blameless in His sight.ᵇ In loveᶜ ⁵ He predestined us to be adopted through Jesus Christ for Himself, according to His favor and will, ⁶ to the praise of His glorious grace that He favored us with in the Beloved.

⁷ In Him we have redemption through His blood, the forgiveness of our trespasses, according to the riches of His grace ⁸ that He lavished on us with all wisdom and understanding. ⁹ He made known to us the •mystery of His will, according to His good pleasure that He planned in Him ¹⁰ for the administrationᵈ of the days of fulfillmentᵉ—to bring everything together in the •Messiah, both things in heaven and things on earth in Him.

¹¹ In Him we were also made His inheritance,ᶠ predestined according to the purpose of the One who works out everything in agreement with the decision of His will, ¹² so that we who had already put our hope in the Messiah might bring praise to His glory.

¹³ In Him you also, when you heard the word of truth, the gospel of your salvation—in Him when you believed—were sealed with the promised Holy Spirit.

Open Your Eyes!

1. What magic trick have you seen that left you speechless?

Ephesians 1:15-23

2. What major change does Paul include in his prayer for the Ephesians, and how would it benefit them?

3. What is the benefit of seeing more with our hearts (v. 18), and how can that happen for us?

4. If everything is "under His feet" and we are part of His body, the church, how should that affect our struggles (vv. 22-23)?

5. If God answered Paul's prayer completely in you, how would it change the way you live?

ᵃ**1:1** Other mss omit *at Ephesus*   ᵇ**1:4** Vv. 3–14 are 1 sentence in Gk.   ᶜ**1:4** Or *In His sight in love*   ᵈ**1:10** Or *dispensation*; lit *house law* (Gk *oikonomia*)   ᵉ**1:10** Lit *the fulfillment of times*   ᶠ**1:11** Or *we also were chosen as an inheritance*, or *we also received an inheritance*

1:1 apostle. Apostles are much like ambassadors. This was the title that was given to the original Twelve (Luke 6:13) and then later to Paul (Gal. 1:11-24). By using this title, Paul indicates that he is writing with the authority of the Lord Jesus Christ.

1:2 Grace to you and peace. Grace refers to the undeserved favor of God freely given as a gift. Peace refers to the reconciliation of sinners to God and others.

1:3 Blessed. The verb translated "bless" or "praise" can also be translated "to speak well of" and carries the idea of thanking, glorifying, and singing the praises of the one who is the object of this gratitude. **God.** God is the subject of virtually every main verb in this passage. **Jesus Christ.** It is in and through Jesus that God's work of love, grace, and redemption is performed.

has blessed us. The tense of the Greek verb indicates that what is in view here is a single, past action on God's part. **in the heavens.** The unseen world of spiritual reality.

1:5 predestined. Literally, "marked out beforehand." **adopted.** This was a common Roman custom, in which a child was given all the rights of the adoptive family by grace, not by birth. **His favor and will.** This phrase is also translated "pleasure and will," and carries with it the sense that God goes about such choosing with great joy.

1:7 redemption. The setting free (originally of prisoners or slaves) by payment of a ransom (in this case, Jesus' death in place of the sinner).

1:9 mystery. Contrary to the normal use of

the word (with its emphasis on a secret being kept), here the word focuses on the disclosure of what was once hidden but is now revealed by God.

1:13 sealed. A mark placed by an owner on a package, a cow, or even a slave. The cults in the first century sometimes tattooed a mark on their devotees. For the Jews, circumcision was such a seal (Rom. 4:11); the Holy Spirit is the Christian's seal.

1:14 down payment. A deposit, or "earnest money" that guarantees ultimate ownership by God.

1:17 wisdom and revelation. God must do a work within individuals to enable them to "see" and understand what is going on.

1:18 the eyes of your heart. Paul wants this

¹⁴ He is the down payment of our inheritance, for the redemption of the possession,ᵃ to the praise of His glory.

Prayer for Spiritual Insight

¹⁵ This is why, since I heard about your faith in the Lord Jesus and your love for all the saints, ¹⁶ I never stop giving thanks for you as I remember you in my prayers. ¹⁷ ⌊I pray⌋ that the God of our Lord Jesus Christ, the glorious Father,ᵇ would give you a spirit of wisdom and revelation in the knowledge of Him. ¹⁸ ⌊I pray⌋ that the eyes of your heart may be enlightened so you may know what is the hope of His calling, what are the glorious riches of His inheritance among the saints, ¹⁹ and what is the immeasurable greatness of His power to us who believe, according to the working of His vast strength.

God's Power in Christ

²⁰ He demonstrated ⌊this power⌋ in the Messiah by raising Him from the dead and seating Him at His right hand in the heavens— ²¹ far above every ruler and authority, power and dominion, and every title given,ᶜ not only in this age but also in the one to come. ²² And **He put everything under His feet**ᵈ and appointed Him as head over everything for the church, ²³ which is His body, the fullness of the One who fills all things in every way.

From Death to Life

2 And you were dead in your trespasses and sins ² in which you previously •walked according to this worldly age, according to the ruler of the atmospheric domain,ᵉ the spirit now working in the disobedient.ᶠ ³ We too all previously lived among them in our fleshly desires, carrying out the inclinations of our flesh and thoughts, and by nature we were children under wrath, as the others were also. ⁴ But God, who is abundant in mercy, because of His great love that He had for us,ᵍ ⁵ made us alive with the •Messiah even though we were dead in trespasses. By grace you are saved! ⁶ He also raised us up with Him and seated us with Him in the heavens, in Christ Jesus, ⁷ so that in

The Greatest Gift

1. What is a really great gift you've received? What did you do to deserve it? How did you express thanks to the giver?
2. What is the unpardonable sin in your family? At your school?

Ephesians 2:1-10

3. How does Paul describe the person who is "dead" in his or her trespasses (vv. 1-3)?
4. What does Paul want to make sure people understand about salvation (v. 9), and why is it so important to understand?
5. How is your life different now than it was before you became a Christian? What do you still need to change?

the coming ages He might display the immeasurable riches of His grace in ⌊His⌋ kindness to us in Christ Jesus. ⁸ For by grace you are saved through faith, and this is not from yourselves; it is God's gift— ⁹ not from works, so that no one can boast. ¹⁰ For we are His creation—created in Christ Jesus for good works, which God prepared ahead of time so that we should walk in them.

Unity in Christ

¹¹ So then, remember that at one time you were Gentiles in the flesh—called "the uncircumcised" by those called "the circumcised," done by hand in the flesh. ¹² At that time you were without the Messiah, excluded from the citizenship of Israel, and foreigners to the covenants of the promise, with no hope and without God in the world. ¹³ But now in Christ Jesus, you who were far away have been brought near by the

---

ᵃ**1:14** the possession could be either man's or God's   ᵇ**1:17** Or the Father of glory   ᶜ**1:21** Lit every name named   ᵈ**1:22** Ps 8:6   ᵉ**2:2** Lit ruler of the authority of the air   ᶠ**2:2** Lit sons of disobedience   ᵍ**2:4** Lit love with which He loved us

---

illumination to strike right to the core of a person's being.

1:19 immeasurable greatness of His power. Seeing this makes a world of difference in one's life as a Christian.

1:20 raising Him from the dead. Jesus was really dead and buried in a tomb. But so mighty is God's power that it burst the bonds of death. **seating Him at His right hand.** Jesus is now the King who reigns in absolute power. One day that reign will result in the bringing together of all things under him (1:10; Heb. 2:5-9).

1:21 ruler and authority, power and dominion, and every title given. Paul wants to be quite clear that there is no power by any name—be it angelic or demonic, natural or supernatural, from the past or in the future—that stands outside the scope of

Christ's powerful reign.

2:1 dead. They were spiritually dead. **trespasses and sins.** These two words refer, respectively, to active wrongdoing (sins of commission), and passive failure (sins of omission).

2:2 ruler of the atmospheric domain. This is the first of several references in Ephesians to Satan, the Devil. **now working.** Satan's activity is not only past, nor only in the future. It is here and now in this present evil age. **the disobedient.** They are, in fact, in active rebellion against God.

2:3 our fleshly desires. The word here is literally "the flesh," and it refers to self-centered human nature that expresses itself in destructive activities of both body and mind.

2:5 made us alive. Paul coins this phrase to describe exactly what happens to us when

we are "in Christ"; namely, we share in Christ's resurrection, ascension, and enthronement

2:8 For by grace you are saved. This is the second time Paul acclaims this amazing fact (v. 5). **through faith.** Salvation does not come about because of faith in and of itself. Salvation comes by grace (from God) through faith (from us).

2:8-9 not from yourselves ... not from works. Salvation is not a reward for being good or keeping the Law.

2:10 good works. Although good works do not save a person, they are a result of salvation.

2:11 remember. In verses 1-3, Paul reminded his Gentile readers that once they were trapped in their transgressions and sins, and so were spiritually dead and alienated from God.

Making Peace

1. What was your favorite wall, fence, or playground equipment to climb over when you were little?
2. Who is the peacemaker among your family or group, and how does this person do it?

Ephesians 2:11-22

3. Who do you think the two groups are in verse 14, and what barriers did they have to overcome?
4. How does Christ put "hostility to death" (v. 16)?
5. What role does the Holy Spirit play in helping us to be peacemakers (vv. 18-22)?
6. What relationship in your life still has walls that need knocking down? How can the Holy Spirit help?

The Power of Love

1. What is the hardest thing you have tried to teach another person?
2. What is the last thing you remember praying very hard about?

Ephesians 3:14-21

3. What does it look like when God strengthens our "inner man" (v. 16)?
4. What does Paul mean by a "love that surpasses knowledge," and what is the point of experiencing this love (v. 19)?
5. When have you felt overwhelmed by the love of God?
6. What needs to change in you to fully comprehend and experience God's love?

blood of the Messiah. [14] For He is our peace, who made both groups one and tore down the dividing wall of hostility. In His flesh, [15] He did away with the law of the commandments in regulations, so that He might create in Himself one new man from the two, resulting in peace. [16] ⌊He did this so⌋ that He might reconcile both to God in one body through the cross and put the hostility to death by it.[a] [17] When ⌊Christ⌋ came, He proclaimed the good news of peace to you who were far away and peace to those who were near. [18] For through Him we both have access by one Spirit to the Father. [19] So then you are no longer foreigners and strangers, but fellow citizens with the saints, and members of God's household, [20] built on the foundation of the apostles and prophets, with Christ Jesus Himself as the cornerstone. [21] The whole building is being fitted together in Him and is growing into a holy sanctuary in the Lord, [22] in whom you also are being built together for God's dwelling in the Spirit.

Paul's Ministry to the Gentiles

3 For this reason, I, Paul, the prisoner of Christ Jesus on behalf of you Gentiles— [2] you have heard, haven't you, about the administration of God's grace that He gave to me for you? [3] The •mystery was made known to me by revelation, as I have briefly written above. [4] By reading this you are able to understand my insight about the mystery of the •Messiah. [5] This was not made known to people[b] in other generations as it is now revealed to His holy apostles and prophets by the Spirit: [6] the Gentiles are co-heirs, members of the same body, and partners of the promise in Christ Jesus through the gospel. [7] I was made a servant of this ⌊gospel⌋ by the gift of God's grace that was given to me by the working of His power.

[8] This grace was given to me—the least of all the saints!—to proclaim to the Gentiles the incalculable riches of the Messiah, [9] and to shed light for all about the administration of the mystery hidden for ages in

---

[a] **2:16** Or *death in Himself*   [b] **3:5** Lit *to the sons of men*

2:14 our peace. Jesus brings peace between human beings and God. He also creates harmony in human relationships, bringing people into peace with one another. **the dividing wall of hostility.** Paul might have in mind an actual wall that existed in the temple in Jerusalem beyond which Gentiles could not go. They were cut off by a stone-wall ("the dividing wall")—a wall bearing signs that warned in Greek and Latin that trespassing foreigners would be killed.

2:17 He proclaimed the good news of peace. Christ's first words to the stunned apostles after His resurrection were, in fact, "Peace be with you!" (John 20:19).

2:19 foreigners. Nonresident aliens were disliked by the native population and often held in suspicion. **strangers.** These are residents in a foreign land. They pay taxes, but

have no legal standing and few rights. **fellow citizens.** Whereas once the Gentiles were "excluded from citizenship in Israel" (v. 12), now they are members of God's kingdom. **members of God's household.** In fact, their relationship is far more intimate.

2:20 cornerstone. The stone that rested firmly on the foundation and anchored two walls together, giving each its correct alignment.

2:21 fitted together. A term used by a mason to describe how two stones were prepared so that they would bond tightly together. **sanctuary.** The new temple is not like the old one, carved out of dead stone—beautiful, but forbidding and exclusive. Rather, it is alive all over the world, inclusive of all, and made up of the individuals in whom God dwells.

3:3 mystery. In Greek, a mystery is something that is beyond human reason to figure out, but once revealed by God, it is open and plain to all. **revelation.** This new reality was given by God.

3:9 to shed light. Paul's original commission, given by Jesus on the Damascus Road, carried this idea: "I am sending you to open their eyes and turn them from darkness to light..." (see also Acts 26:17-18)

3:10 rulers and authorities in the heavens. The supernatural powers see what God is doing in His church.

3:16 strengthened with power. Paul asks that Christians be fortified or invigorated within by the Holy Spirit. He asks that they experience this awesome power of God about which he has written so eloquently. **in-**

God who created all things. 10 This is so that God's multi-faceted wisdom may now be made known through the church to the rulers and authorities in the heavens. 11 This is according to the purpose of the ages, which He made in the Messiah, Jesus our Lord, 12 in whom we have boldness, access, and confidence through faith in Him.a 13 So then I ask you not to be discouraged over my afflictions on your behalf, for they are your glory.

Prayer for Spiritual Power

14 For this reason I bow my knees before the Fatherb 15 from whom every family in heaven and on earth is named. 16 ⌊I pray⌋ that He may grant you, according to the riches of His glory, to be strengthened with power through His Spirit in the inner man, 17 and that the Messiah may dwell in your hearts through faith. ⌊I pray that⌋ you, being rooted and firmly established in love, 18 may be able to comprehend with all the saints what is the length and width, height and depth ⌊of God's love⌋, 19 and to know the Messiah's love that surpasses knowledge, so you may be filled with all the fullness of God.

20 Now to Him who is able to do above and beyond all that we ask or think—according to the power that works in you— 21 to Him be glory in the church and in Christ Jesus to all generations, forever and ever. •Amen.

Unity and Diversity in the Body of Christ

4 I, therefore, the prisoner in the Lord, urge you to •walk worthy of the calling you have received, 2 with all humility and gentleness, with patience, acceptingc one another in love, 3 diligently keeping the unity of the Spirit with the peace that binds ⌊us⌋. 4 There is one body and one Spirit, just as you were called to one hoped at your calling; 5 one Lord, one faith, one baptism, 6 one God and Father of all, who is above all and through all and in all.

7 Now grace was given to each one of us according to the measure of the •Messiah's gift. 8 For it says:

> When He ascended on high,
> He took prisoners into captivity;e
> He gave gifts to peoplef

Building Up and Hanging Out

1. What activities can draw together a large crowd of your friends?
2. What problems can pull your friends apart?

Ephesians 4:1-16

3. What are the things that bind us together (vv. 4-6), and which one is most underutilized?
4. What is the ultimate purpose of having people in specific positions (v. 11), and how can that be abused?
5. What is keeping your church or team from modeling the church as it was meant to be? What can you do to help bring unity?

9 But what does "He ascended" mean except that Heg descended to the lower parts of the earth?h 10 The One who descended is the same as the One who ascended far above all the heavens, that He might filli all things. 11 And He personally gave some to be apostles, some prophets, some evangelists, some pastors and teachers, 12 for the training of the saints in the work of ministry, to build up the body of Christ, 13 until we all reach unity in the faith and in the knowledge of God's Son, ⌊growing⌋ into a mature man with a stature measured by Christ's fullness. 14 Then we will no longer be little children, tossed by the waves and blown around by every wind of teaching, by human cunning with cleverness in the techniques of deceit. 15 But speaking the truth in love, let us grow in every way into Him who is

a3:12 Or through His faithfulness b3:14 Other mss add of our Lord Jesus Christ c4:2 Or tolerating d4:4 Lit called in one hope e4:8 Or He led the captives f4:8 Ps 68:18 g4:9 Other mss add first h4:9 Or the lower parts, namely, the earth i4:10 Or fulfill; see Eph 1:23

ner man. By this term, Paul may be referring to the deepest part of the human personality, where a person's true essence lies.

3:17 dwell. This means "to settle down," and it implies a permanent residency (in a house), versus a temporary stopover (in a tent or hotel). In other words, Christ has come to stay. **love.** Agape love is selfless giving to others, regardless of how one feels. Such love is the foundation upon which the church will grow.

4:2 humility. Humility is an absence of pride and self-assertion, based upon accurate self-knowledge and on an understanding of the God-given worth of others. Humility is the key to the growth of healthy relationships between people. **gentleness.** Paul is not urging people to be timid and without convictions. Gentleness is the quality of

strength under control, like a thoroughbred horse. **patience.** Patience with others is also called long-suffering. **accepting one another.** This is tolerance of the faults of others that springs from humility, gentleness, and patience.

4:8 When He ascended. Paul quotes Psalm 68:18, which describes the triumphal procession of a conquering Jewish king up Mt. Zion and into Jerusalem. The king is followed by a procession of prisoners in chains. As he marches up the hill, he is given gifts of tribute and in turn disperses gifts of booty. Paul uses this verse to describe Christ's ascension into heaven.

4:9 descended. Paul is referring to Christ's incarnation, whereby He came down from heaven and into our space and time (Phil. 2:5-11).

4:11 He personally gave. This is one of several lists of gifts in the New Testament. The emphasis in this list is on teaching gifts. **apostles.** Paul probably had in mind the small group of individuals who had seen the resurrected Christ, and had been commissioned by Him to launch His church (Acts 1:21-22; 1 Cor. 9:1), but some take this to be a more general gift of "missions". **prophets.** In contrast to teachers who relied upon the Old Testament Scripture and the teaching of Jesus to instruct others, prophets offered words of instruction, exhortation, and admonition, which were immediate and unpremeditated. Their source was direct revelation from God. **evangelists.** Those with the special gift of making the gospel clear and convincing to others. **pastors and teachers.** The way in which this is expressed in Greek indicates that these two functions reside in one person.

the head—Christ. ¹⁶ From Him the whole body, fitted and knit together by every supporting ligament, promotes the growth of the body for building up itself in love by the proper working of each individual part.

A New Uniform

1. When it comes to getting angry, do you tend to have a short or long fuse?
2. How can someone tell when you are angry? When you are lying?

Ephesians 4:17-32

3. What do verses 22 and 24 mean by taking off "the old man" and putting on "the new man"?
4. What are some of the reasons we do not speak the truth?
5. How do you usually deal with anger? What do you learn about anger from verses 26-27?
6. Which attitude or behavior that grieves God (vv.31-32) do you struggle with most? How can you take off this old, smelly uniform?

Living the New Life

¹⁷ Therefore, I say this and testify in the Lord: You should no longer walk as the Gentiles walk, in the futility of their thoughts. ¹⁸ They are darkened in their understanding, excluded from the life of God, because of the ignorance that is in them and because of the hardness of their hearts. ¹⁹ They became callous and gave themselves over to promiscuity for the practice of every kind of impurity with a desire for more and more.ª

²⁰ But that is not how you learned about the Messiah, ²¹ assuming you heard Him and were taught by Him, because the truth is in Jesus: ²² you took offᵇ your former way of life, the old man that is corrupted by deceitful desires; ²³ you are being renewedᶜ in the spirit of your minds; ²⁴ you put onᵈ the new man, the one created according to God's ₗlikeness₎ in righteousness and purity of the truth.

²⁵ Since you put away lying, **Speak the truth, each one to his neighbor,**ᵉ because we are members of one another. ²⁶ **Be angry and do not sin.**ᶠ Don't let the sun go down on your anger, ²⁷ and don't give the Devil an opportunity. ²⁸ The thief must no longer steal. Instead, he must do honest work with his own hands, so that he has something to share with anyone in need. ²⁹ No rotten talk should come from your mouth, but only what is good for the building up of someone in need,ᵍ in order to give grace to those who hear. ³⁰ And don't grieve God's Holy Spirit, who sealed youʰ for the day of redemption. ³¹ All bitterness, anger and wrath, insult and slander must be removed from you, along with all wickedness. ³² And be kind and compassionate to one another, forgiving one another, just as God also forgave youⁱ in Christ.

5 Therefore, be imitators of God, as dearly loved children. ² And •walk in love, as the •Messiah also loved us and gave Himself for us, a sacrificial and fragrant offering to God. ³ But sexual immorality and any impurity or greed should not even be heard ofʲ among you, as is proper for saints. ⁴ And coarse and foolish talking or crude joking are not suitable, but rather giving thanks. ⁵ For know and recognize this: no sexually immoral or impure or greedy person, who is an idolater, has an inheritance in the kingdom of the Messiah and of God.

Light versus Darkness

⁶ Let no one deceive you with empty arguments, for because of these things God's wrath is coming on the disobedient.ᵏ ⁷ Therefore, do not become their part-

---

ª**4:19** Lit *with greediness*   ᵇ**4:21–22** Or *Jesus. This means: take off* (as a command)   ᶜ**4:22–23** Or *desires; renew* (as a command)   ᵈ**4:23–24** Or *minds; and put on* (as a command)   ᵉ**4:25** Zch 8:16   ᶠ**4:26** Ps 4:4   ᵍ**4:29** Lit *for the building up of the need*   ʰ**4:30** Or *Spirit, by whom you were sealed*   ⁱ**4:32** Other mss read *us*   ʲ**5:3** Or *be named*   ᵏ**5:6** Lit *sons of disobedience*

4:15 speaking the truth in love. Truth without love becomes harsh. Love without truth becomes weak.

4:18 hardness of their hearts. The center of their being (the heart) has become "stonelike."

4:26 Be angry. Paul recognizes that there is such a thing as legitimate anger. But once admitted, anger is to be dealt with, and so Paul identifies ways to deal with anger. Do not let anger develop into resentment.

4:29-30 No rotten talk. Paul turns to the use of one's mouth. The word "rotten" is elsewhere used to describe spoiled fruit (Matt. 12:33). Instead of rancid words that wound others, the words of Christians ought to edify ("building up"), be appropriate ("of someone in need"), bring grace (in other words, be of

benefit to those who hear), and not cause distress for the Holy Spirit (by unholy words).

4:31 must be removed. Paul identifies six negative attitudes that must be erased from the Christian life. **bitterness.** Spiteful, longstanding, resentment. **anger and wrath.** These two attitudes are related. Anger may be a quick flare up, or a longer term, sullen hostility. Wrath often carries the connotation of violence and punishment. **insult and slander.** Saying hurtful and untrue things about another person.

5:4 crude joking. Vulgar talk is out of place, because it demeans God's good gift of sex (which is a subject for thanksgiving, not joking).

5:5 greedy person. The reference is to the sexually greedy person. **idolater.** When vice

has become an obsession, it functions in a person's life as a "god" (or idol), drawing forth passionate commitment of time and energy.

5:8-14 Walk as children of light. A second reason why Christians should not get involved in immoral practices (v. 11) is that they have become "children of light" (v. 8). In fact, it is not just that they walk in the light; they "are light in the Lord" (v. 8). To be such a child of light implies a lifestyle of "goodness, righteousness, and truth" (v. 9).

5:18 be filled. This is a command, not an option. It means, "let the Spirit fill you."

5:21 submitting to one another. Another aspect of being filled with the Spirit involves mutual submission within the Christian community.

ners. [8] For you were once darkness, but now ⌊you are⌋ light in the Lord. Walk as children of light— [9] for the fruit of the light[a] ⌊results⌋ in all goodness, righteousness, and truth— [10] discerning what is pleasing to the Lord. [11] Don't participate in the fruitless works of darkness, but instead, expose them. [12] For it is shameful even to mention what is done by them in secret. [13] Everything exposed by the light is made clear, [14] for what makes everything clear is light. Therefore it is said:

Get up, sleeper, and rise up from the dead,
and the Messiah will shine on you.[b]

Follow the Light

1. Who is your best friend right now? What makes this person such a good friend?
2. Who has had the biggest influence on your life? What good advice did this person give you?

Ephesians 5:1-21

3. What kind of people and what kind of advice should we avoid, and how do we stay friends while avoiding the "partner" trap (vv. 5-7)?
4. When Paul says, "making the most of the time" (v. 16), what do you think he is talking about?
5. What have you found helpful in resisting pressure to do something you shouldn't?

Consistency in the Christian Life

[15] Pay careful attention, then, to how you walk—not as unwise people but as wise— [16] making the most of the time,[c] because the days are evil. [17] So don't be foolish, but understand what the Lord's will is. [18] And don't get drunk with wine, which ⌊leads to⌋ reckless actions, but be filled with the Spirit:

[19]   speaking to one another in psalms, hymns,
       and spiritual songs,
       singing and making music to the Lord
       in your heart,
[20]   giving thanks always for everything
       to God the Father in the name
       of our Lord Jesus Christ,
[21]   submitting to one another in the fear of Christ.

Marriage Matters

1. Who was your first "true love"?
2. Who has a marriage that you admire? What makes it work?

Ephesians 5:22-33

3. Guys: How do you feel about the standard for husbands in verses 25 and 28? Ladies: How do you feel about the standard for wives in verses 22 and 33?
4. As you look at the phrase "the two will become one flesh" (v. 31), what do you think it means and doesn't mean?
5. What is the best way to know if someone is right for you?
6. What is God saying to you about dating and marriage?

Wives and Husbands

[22] Wives, submit[d] to your own husbands as to the Lord, [23] for the husband is head of the wife as also Christ is head of the church. He is the Savior of the body. [24] Now as the church submits to Christ, so wives should ⌊submit⌋ to their husbands in everything. [25] Husbands, love your wives, just as also Christ loved

---

[a]**5:9** Other mss read *fruit of the Spirit*; see Gl 5:22, but compare Eph 5:11-14   [b]**5:14** This poem may have been an early Christian hymn based on several passages in Isaiah; see Is 9:2; 26:19; 40:1; 51:17; 52:1; 60:1.   [c]**5:16** Lit *buying back the time*   [d]**5:22** Other mss omit *submit*

5:22 submit to your own husbands. The verb in 5:21 ("submit") is linked grammatically both backward to 5:18 and forward to this verse. Looking backward, "submit" describes what is involved in being filled with the Spirit (speaking, singing, giving thanks, submitting). Looking forward, "submit" provides the verb for this verse, which has no verb of its own. Submitting goes against our sinful natures, but is specifically commanded by God, in this case of a wife to her husband and to the Lord.

5:23 Christ is head of the church. Paul has already described in 4:15-16 the way in which Christ is the head of the church. He is head in that the rest of the body derives from Him the health and strength that allows each part to play its own distinctive role. It is a headship of love, not of control; of nurture, not of suppression. The word "head" when used today has the sense of "ruler" or "authority." However, in Greek when "head" is used in a metaphorical sense as it is here, it also means "origin" as in the "source (head) of a river." Woman has her origins in man (Gen. 2:18-23) just as the church has its origins in Christ. **the Savior.** The emphasis in this analogy is not on Christ as Lord, but on Christ as Savior. Paul is not saying that husbands are to express "headship" through the exertion of authority (as befits a "lord"), but through the expression of sacrificial love (as characterized by the Savior).

5:25 love your wives. This is the main thing Paul says to husbands. It is so important that he repeats this injunction three times (vv. 25,28,33). In Greek culture, although certain philosophers such as Aristotle taught that men ought to love their wives, they used a mild word for love (*phileo*) signifying the sort of affection a person has for family and friends. Here, however, Paul urges a far stronger type of love: *agape*, which is characterized by sacrificial, self-giving action. **just as Christ loved the church and gave Himself for her.** Two actions characterize Christ's role for the church: love and sacrifice. The husband is called upon to act toward his wife in the same way. A husband is never instructed to force submission to his leadership of tyrannical authority, but to lead as Jesus did through sacrificial love. In the case of domestic abuse, it is role of the church and civil authorities to step with discipline.

5:28 their own bodies. The deep-rooted instinct to care for and protect oneself is to be carried over to the wife who has become one flesh with her husband.

the church and gave Himself for her, [26] to make her holy, cleansing[a] her in the washing of water by the word. [27] He did this to present the church to Himself in splendor, without spot or wrinkle or any such thing, but holy and blameless. [28] In the same way, husbands should love their wives as their own bodies. He who loves his wife loves himself. [29] For no one ever hates his own flesh, but provides and cares for it, just as Christ does for the church, [30] since we are members of His body.[b]

> [31] For this reason a man will leave his father
>   and mother
>   and be joined to his wife,
>   and the two will become one flesh.[c]

[32] This •mystery is profound, but I am talking about Christ and the church. [33] To sum up, each one of you is

Parental Expectations

1. Which TV family best reflects your family?
2. When you are away from home, how often do your parents expect you to check in? Do you feel this is a reasonable expectation?

Ephesians 6:1-4

3. What does God ask of children? What does the phrase "in the Lord" mean (v. 1)?
4. Do you look at verse 3 as a promise or a threat? Why?
5. If you have kids, how will you apply the lesson in verse 4?
6. In what way can you honor your parents this week?

to love his wife as himself, and the wife is to respect her husband.

Children and Parents

6 Children, obey your parents in the Lord, because this is right. [2] **Honor your father and mother—** which is the first commandment[d] with a promise— [3] **that it may go well with you and that you may have a long life in the land.**[e][f] [4] And fathers, don't stir up anger in your children, but bring them up in the training and instruction of the Lord.

Slaves and Masters

[5] Slaves, obey your human[g] masters with fear and trembling, in the sincerity of your heart, as to Christ. [6] Don't ⌊work only⌋ while being watched, in order to please men, but as slaves of Christ, do God's will from your heart.[h] [7] Render service with a good attitude, as to the Lord and not to men, [8] knowing that whatever good each one does, slave or free, he will receive this back from the Lord. [9] And masters, treat them the same way, without threatening them, because you know that both their and your Master is in heaven, and there is no favoritism with Him.

Christian Warfare

[10] Finally, be strengthened by the Lord and by His vast strength. [11] Put on the full armor of God so that you can stand against the tactics[i] of the Devil. [12] For our battle is not against flesh and blood, but against the rulers, against the authorities, against the world powers of this darkness, against the spiritual forces of evil in the heavens. [13] This is why you must take up the full armor of God, so that you may be able to resist in the evil day, and having prepared everything, to take your stand. [14] Stand, therefore,

> with truth like a belt around your waist,
> righteousness like armor on your chest,
> [15] and your feet sandaled with readiness
>   for the gospel of peace.[j]
> [16] In every situation take the shield of faith,

5:31 one flesh. Paul does not view marriage as some sort of spiritual covenant devoid of sexuality. His illustration of how a husband is to love his wife (vv. 28-31) revolves around their sexual union, as is made explicit here by his quotation of Genesis 2:24.

6:1 Children. That he addresses children in this public letter means that children were in attendance with their families at worship when such a letter would have been read. **obey.** Paul tells the children to "obey" ("follow," "be subject to," literally, "listen to").

6:4 Just as children have a duty to obey, parents have the duty to instruct children with gentleness and restraint. **fathers.** The ultimate model for a father is God, the "Father of all" (4:6). This view of fatherhood stands in sharp contrast to the harsh Roman father, who had the power of life and death over his children. **stir up anger.** Parents are

to be responsible for not provoking hostility on the part of their children, or exasperating them. By humiliating children, being cruel to them, over-indulging them, or being unreasonable, parents squash children, rather than encouraging them. **bring them up.** This verb is literally "nourish" or "feed" them. **training.** This word can be translated "discipline." **instruction.** The emphasis here is on what is said verbally to children.

6:10 be strengthened ... by His vast strength. In order to wage successful warfare against Satan, the Christian must draw upon God's own power.

6:11 Put on. It is not enough to rely passively on God's power. The Christian must do something. He or she must "put on" God's armor. **the tactics of the Devil.** Evil does not operate in the light. It lurks in shadows and strikes unexpectedly, with cleverness and

subtlety.

6:12 the rulers ... authorities ... world powers ... spiritual forces of evil. By these various titles, Paul names the diverse spiritual forces which rage against believers and which can't be fought by solely human means. **the world powers of this darkness.** It was no empty boast on Satan's part when during Jesus' temptations he claimed to be able to give Him "all the kingdoms of the world." These world rulers have real power, and even though Christ has defeated them, they refuse to concede their defeat.

6:13 the evil day. The immediate reference is to those special times of pressure and testing that come to all Christians. **take your stand.** Fully-equipped soldiers were virtually invulnerable to enemy onslaught—unless they panicked and broke ranks. As long as they "stood firm" when the enemy attacked,

and with it you will be able to extinguish the flaming arrows of the evil one.

¹⁷ Take the helmet of salvation,
and the sword of the Spirit, which is
God's word.

¹⁸ With every prayer and request, pray at all times in the Spirit, and stay alert in this, with all perseverance and intercession for all the saints. ¹⁹ Pray also for me, that the message may be given to me when I open my mouth to make known with boldness the •mystery of the gospel. ²⁰ For this I am an ambassador in chains. Pray that I might be bold enough in Him to speak as I should.

Paul's Farewell

²¹ Tychicus, our dearly loved brother and faithful servant[a] in the Lord, will tell you everything so that you also may know how I am and what I'm doing. ²² I am sending him to you for this very reason, to let you know how we are and to encourage your hearts.

²³ Peace to the brothers, and love with faith, from God the Father and the Lord Jesus Christ. ²⁴ Grace be with all who have undying love for our Lord Jesus Christ.[b][c]

Life on the Front Line

1. What is the scariest situation you have ever experienced?

2. What do you think the Devil's most successful strategy is right now in your team, your school, or the world in general?

Ephesians 6:10-20

3. What makes up the "armor of God" (vv. 14-17)? Which piece of armor are you most likely to forget to put on?

4. How important is prayer to the battle strategy (v. 18), and what makes this kind of prayer so effective?

5. What would you say to a friend who is losing the unseen battle? How would you explain this teaching in your own words?

---

a**6:21** Or *deacon*   b**6:24** Other mss add *Amen.*   c**6:24** Lit *all who love our Lord Jesus Christ in incorruption*

---

they would prevail in the long run.

6:14 truth like a belt. The leather belt on which the Roman soldier hung his sword, and by which he secured his tunic and armor (so he would be unimpeded in battle). The "truth" referred to is the inner integrity and sincerity by which the Christian fights evil. Lying and deceit are tactics of the enemy. **righteousness like armor on your chest.** The breastplate (or "mail") was the major piece of armor for the Roman soldier. Made of metal and leather, it protected his vital organs. "Righteousness" refers to the right standing before God that is the status of the Christian, out of which moral conduct and character emerges.

6:15 feet sandaled. These are the leather half-boots worn by the Roman legionnaire, with heavy studded soles that enabled him to dig in and resist being pushed out of place. **readiness.** This term can be translated as "firmness" or "steadfastness," in which case the "gospel of peace" is understood to provide the solid foundation on which the Christian stands in the fight against evil.

6:16 the shield of faith. A large, oblong shield constructed of layers of wood on an iron frame, which was then covered with linen and hide. When wet, such a shield could absorb "flaming arrows." **flaming arrows.** These were pitch-soaked arrows.

Their aim was not so much to kill a soldier as to set him aflame and cause him to break rank and create panic.

6:17 the helmet of salvation. A heavy, metal head covering lined with felt or sponge, which gave substantial protection to the soldier's head. **sword.** A short, stabbing sword used for personal combat. The sword is the only piece of offensive equipment in the armor.

6:18 pray. Paul does not consider prayer a seventh weapon. Rather, it underlies the whole process of spiritual warfare. **in the Spirit.** Prayer is guided by the Spirit. This is, after all, spiritual warfare.

INTRODUCTION TO
PHILIPPIANS

AUTHOR

The Apostle Paul was the writer of Philippians.

DATE

Philippians was probably written around A.D. 61-63, a dozen or so years after Paul had founded the church in Philippi (the first church in Europe; see Acts 16).

THEME

The joy of knowing Jesus.

HISTORICAL BACKGROUND

Paul founded the church at Philippi around A.D. 50 as the result of a vision during the night in which a "man of Macedonian man" pleaded with him to "Cross over to Macedonia and help us!" (Acts 16:9). He sailed immediately from Asia, thus launching Christianity in Europe. Paul's stay at Philippi was marked by joy and trial. Positive results were the conversion of Lydia, the dealer in purple cloth, as well as the conversion of the jailer and his family after an earthquake unexpectedly released Paul from prison. Unfortunately it was, in Philippi that the first recorded conflict between Christians and Gentiles occurred, and Paul was thrown in jail for casting out a demon from a fortuneteller's slave girl.

Paul is in prison (probably in Rome) when Epaphroditus, an old friend from Philippi, arrives bearing yet another gift from the church. Unfortunately, Epaphroditus falls gravely ill. His home church hears about it and is grieved. Eventually he recovers and Paul is anxious for him to return home and relieve their fears. This affords Paul an opportunity to send along a letter.

So he writes these old friends in the warmest and most personal of his epistles. There is no need for him to assert his authority as an apostle, like he usually does when beginning a letter. There is no formality in his outline either. Paul puts down ideas as they occur to him, interspersed with strong declarations of emotion.

Basically, Philippians is a letter of thanksgiving (1:3-11 and 4:14-20) and a report on his imprisonment (1:12-26; 2:19-30; 4:10-13). Philippians reads like a thank you for all that this, perhaps his favorite church, has done for him (particularly their gift, as seen in 4:10-19). Still, Paul has two concerns: a tendency in the church toward disunity (1:27-2:18 and 4:2-3) and potential dangers from Judaizers (3:2-16) and false teachers (3:17-21).

THE CITY OF PHILIPPI

Located in the Roman province of Macedonia (a territory corresponding to northern Greece and parts of several other Balkan countries), Philippi was an historic city founded by Alexander the Great's father in 360 B.C. so he could mine its gold to pay for his army. Philippi eventually came to prominence as the result of two battles. In 42 B.C. on the plains of Philippi, the Caesarean forces of Anthony and Octavian defeated the Republican forces led by the assassins of Julius Caesar– Brutus and Cassius. Then in 31 B.C., Octavian (who later became the Emperor Caesar Augustus) became sole ruler by defeating his former colleague, Anthony, who was in alliance with the Egyptian Queen Cleopatra. Veterans from these conflicts were given land in Philippi, and Octavian declared it to be a Roman colony with all the accompanying rights, tax breaks and privileges. To be in Philippi was to be in a miniature Rome.

CHARACTERISTICS

Joy permeates Philippians from start to finish. And yet this is not joy forged out of privilege and abundance. It is not the joy of people who have no problems. This is joy in the midst of hard situations. Paul is writing from prison where he faces the very real possibility of execution. The Philippian church is confronted with internal dissension and with false teachers who would seduce it away from the gospel. Furthermore, both Paul and the Philippians live with the sense that the world might end any day. The second coming of Jesus was a living reality for them.

How can you be joyful in that kind of world? How can you urge joy when you are in prison? How can you be joyful when the world is about to end? Since most of us are puzzled by the emphasis in this epistle, it is therefore important to listen carefully to Paul's words. The hardship would not go away for either Paul or the Philippians. Yet they could write Philippians, brimming with joy.

STRUCTURE

There is a question about whether the epistle to the Philippians is one letter or two. It opens in a traditional way: Paul talks about his imprisonment and about how the gospel is advancing. He makes an appeal for harmony among the members of the Philippian church. He tells them that he will be sending both Epaphroditus and Timothy to see them. And in 3:1 he says, "Finally, my brothers ..." as if he is about to close the letter. But then he abruptly launches into a warning about dangerous men who will harm the church (3:2-21). This is followed by more exhortations (4:1-9) and by thanks for their gifts (4:10-20), after which he actually concludes his letter.

Most commentators regard Philippians as a single letter, but it is instructive to note the two sections that could be separate letters. First, there is the warning about troublemakers that begins in 3:2 and goes to at least 4:1 (and possibly to 4:9). Then, second, there is Paul's note of thanks in 4:10-20.

PASSAGES FOR TOPICAL GROUP STUDY

Greeting

1 Paul and Timothy, slaves of Christ Jesus:

To all the saints in Christ Jesus who are in Philippi, including the •overseers and deacons.

² Grace to you and peace from God our Father and the Lord Jesus Christ.

A Work in Progress

1. When you care for someone, are you more likely to send a funny card or a touching one?

Philippians 1:1-11

2. What are Paul's feelings for this church? What does that show about his leadership style?

3. How is God at work in a Christian's life, according to verses 6 and 9-11? How does this make you feel about uncertainties in your life?

4. Who was the "Apostle Paul" in your spiritual life that introduced you to Jesus Christ and cared about your spiritual growth?

5. What is God saying to you about your identity in this passage?

Thanksgiving and Prayer

³ I give thanks to my God for every remembrance of you,ᵃ ⁴ always praying with joy for all of you in my every prayer, ⁵ because of your partnership in the gospel from the first day until now. ⁶ I am sure of this, that He who started a good work in youᵇ will carry it on to completion until the day of Christ Jesus. ⁷ It is right for me to think this way about all of you, because I have you in my heart,ᶜ and you are all partners with me in grace, both in my imprisonment and in the defense and estab-

lishment of the gospel. ⁸ For God is my witness, how I deeply miss all of you with the affection of Christ Jesus. ⁹ And I pray this: that your love will keep on growing in knowledge and every kind of discernment, ¹⁰ so that you can determine what really matters and can be pure and blameless inᵈ the day of Christ, ¹¹ filled with the fruit of righteousness that ₍comes₎ through Jesus Christ, to the glory and praise of God.

A Reason to Live

1. When you were little, what helped you get through the night: A flashlight? Teddy bear? Special blanket? Other?

2. Paul was in prison but joyful. What trying circumstances are you dealing with? What is your attitude toward them?

Philippians 1:12-30

3. What was Paul's reason for wanting to "live on in the flesh" (v. 22)? What does today's culture teach about the reason for living?

4. What do you think Paul would consider a life "worthy of the gospel" (v. 27)?

5. What is something that opposes you and your progress with Jesus right now?

Advance of the Gospel

¹² Now I want you to know, brothers, that what has happened to me has actually resulted in the advancement of the gospel, ¹³ so that it has become known throughout the whole imperial guard,ᵉ and to everyone else, that my imprisonment is for Christ.ᶠ ¹⁴ Most of the brothers in the Lord have gained confidence from my imprisonment and dare even more to speak the messageᵍ

ᵃ**1:3** Or *For your every remembrance of me* ᵇ**1:6** Or *work among you* ᶜ**1:7** Or *because you have me in your heart* ᵈ**1:10** Or *until* ᵉ**1:13** Lit *praetorium*, a Lat word that can also refer to a military headquarters, to the governor's palace, or to Herod's palace ᶠ**1:13** Lit *in Christ* ᵍ**1:14** Other mss add *of God*

1:1 Timothy. Timothy had long been a companion of Paul. Timothy was with Paul when he visited Philippi for the first time and was well-known there. Paul may have dictated this letter to Timothy.

1:3 for every remembrance of you. During times of prayer, Paul was compelled by love to mention his Philippian friends.

1:4 with joy. "Joy" is a theme that pervades Philippians. This is the first of 14 times that Paul will refer to "joy" or "rejoice" in this letter.

1:5 because of your partnership. The Greek word rendered here as "partnership" is the familiar word *koinonia*, translated elsewhere as "fellowship." It means, literally, "having something in common."

1:6 I am sure of this. This is confidence that

springs out of faith in who God is and what He is doing. **the day of Christ Jesus.** This is the moment when Christ will return in glory and triumph to establish His kingdom on earth.

1:7 defense and establishment of the gospel. This references Paul's defense before the Roman court. In court, he hopes not only to vindicate himself and the gospel from false charges, but also to proclaim the gospel and its life-changing power to those in the courtroom.

1:9 And I pray this. He prays that this love will increase (i.e., that it will go on developing) and that it will be regulated by knowledge and discernment. **knowledge and every kind of discernment.** This growing love is to be focused by intellectual, practical, and moral insight.

1:10 you can determine what really matters. The word translated "determine" is used to describe the process of testing coins in order to distinguish between those that are real and those that are counterfeit.

1:13 imperial guard. The elite soldiers in the Roman army; the bodyguards of the emperor.

1:18 false motives. The three words by which Paul characterizes the motivation of his rivals—envy, strife, and rivalry—are all words he has used in other contexts to describe those actions and attitudes that are to be shunned by Christians. They are "vices that always adversely affect, even endanger, the life of the church" (Hawthorne) .

1:20 with all boldness. Paul's desire is the courage to speak boldly during his trial.

fearlessly. ¹⁵ Some, to be sure, preach Christ out of envy and strife, but others out of good will.ᵃ ¹⁶ These do so out of love, knowing that I am appointed for the defense of the gospel; ¹⁷ the others proclaim Christ out of rivalry, not sincerely, seeking to cause ⌐me⌐ trouble in my imprisonment.ᵇ ¹⁸ What does it matter? Just that in every way, whether out of false motives or true, Christ is proclaimed. And in this I rejoice. Yes, and I will rejoice ¹⁹ because I know this will lead to my deliveranceᶜ through your prayers and help from the Spirit of Jesus Christ. ²⁰ My eager expectation and hope is that I will not be ashamed about anything, but that now as always, with all boldness, Christ will be highly honored in my body, whether by life or by death.

Living Is Christ

²¹ For me, living is Christ and dying is gain. ²² Now if I live on in the flesh, this means fruitful work for me; and I don't know which one I should choose. ²³ I am pressured by both. I have the desire to depart and be with Christ—which is far better— ²⁴ but to remain in the flesh is more necessary for you. ²⁵ Since I am persuaded of this, I know that I will remain and continue with all of you for your advancement and joy in the faith, ²⁶ so that, because of me, your confidence may grow in Christ Jesus when I come to you again.

²⁷ Just one thing: live your life in a manner worthy of the gospel of Christ. Then, whether I come and see you or am absent, I will hear about you that you are standing firm in one spirit, with one mind,ᵈ working side by side for the faith of the gospel, ²⁸ not being frightened in any way by your opponents. This is evidence of their destruction, but of your deliverance—and this is from God. ²⁹ For it has been given to you on Christ's behalf not only to believe in Him, but also to suffer for Him, ³⁰ having the same struggle that you saw I had and now hear about me.

Christian Humility

2 If then there is any encouragement in Christ, if any consolation of love, if any fellowship with the Spirit, if any affection and mercy, ² fulfill my joy by thinking the same way, having the same love, sharing the same feelings, focusing on one goal. ³ Do nothing out of rivalry or conceit, but in humility consider others as more important than yourselves. ⁴ Everyone should look out not ⌐only⌐ for his own interests, but also for the interests of others.

Who's Number One?

1. Growing up, who was your role model—someone you respected and wanted to be like?
2. When has another person put your needs before his or her own? How did you feel?

Philippians 2:1-11

3. What does verse 3 mean? Can that attitude go too far, resulting in others taking advantage of us?
4. What is Christ's attitude (vv. 6-11)? How does your attitude compare?
5. How would the relationships with your friends or teammates be different if you practiced the humility demonstrated by Jesus?

Christ's Humility and Exaltation

⁵ Make your own attitude that of Christ Jesus,

⁶ who, existing in the form of God,
did not consider equality with God
as something to be used for His own advantage.ᵉ
⁷ Instead He emptied Himself by assuming
the form of a slave,
taking on the likeness of men.
And when He had come as a man
in His external form,
⁸ He humbled Himself by becoming obedient

ᵃ**1:15** The good will of men, or God's good will or favor   ᵇ**1:17** Lit *sincerely, intending to raise tribulation to my bonds*   ᶜ**1:19** Or *salvation,* or *vindication*   ᵈ**1:27** Lit *soul*   ᵉ**2:6** Or *to be grasped,* or *to be held on to*

---

highly honored. This word means, literally, "to make something or someone large." **by life or by death.** By this phrase, Paul simply means that his single goal is to bring praise to Christ ... no matter what happens.

1:21 living is Christ. For Paul, his entire existence revolves around Christ. He is inspired by Christ; he works for Christ; his sole focus in life is Christ. He is a man with a single, all-consuming passion. **dying is gain.** Death is the door into the presence of Christ. Death is not so much escape from hardship as it is entrance into joy.

1:23 to depart and be with Christ. Death would be a gain for Paul since being with, in, and for Christ meant everything to him.

1:27 standing firm. This is a military term used for Roman soldiers standing back-to-back, protecting each other while resisting the enemy. **for the faith of the gospel.** The goal is not victory on the battlefield, but the preservation of the Christian faith.

1:28 not being frightened. The Greek word used here is rare, appearing only once in the Bible. Its original reference was to horses that were timid and shied easily. The Philippians must not let their opponents spook them into an uncontrolled stampede.

2:1 If. In Greek, this construction assumes a positive response, e.g., "If you have any encouragement in Christ, and of course you do so..."

2:3 rivalry. This is the second time in this letter that Paul has used this word (1:17). It means working to advance oneself without thought for others. **conceit.** This is the only occurrence of this word in the New Testament. Translated literally, it means "vain glory" (*kendoxia*), which is asserting oneself over God who alone is worthy of true glory (*doxa*). **humility.** This was not a virtue that was valued by the Greeks in the first century. They considered this to be the attitude of a slave (i.e., servility).

2:7 the likeness of men. The point is not that Jesus just seemed to be human. He assumed the identity of a person and was in actuality a human being.

2:8 He humbled Himself. Jesus is the ultimate model of One who lived a life of self-sacrifice, self-renunciation, and self-surrender. **death on a cross.** Crucifixion was a harsh, demeaning and utterly painful way to die. According to the Old Testament, those

to the point of death—even to death on a cross. ⁹ For this reason God also highly exalted Him and gave Him the name that is above every name, ¹⁰ so that at the name of Jesus every knee should bow— of those who are in heaven and on earth and under the earth— ¹¹ and every tongue should confess that Jesus Christ is Lord, to the glory of God the Father.

Working Out

1. Who demands the most from you: Your dad? Your mom? Your coach? A teacher?
2. What training do you find most difficult, and why: Physical? Spiritual? Academic? Other?

Philippians 2:12-18

3. Verse 12 says, "work out your own salvation," and verse 13 says, "it is God who is working in you." How does this apparent contradiction work?
4. Why do you think it is important that God works on the "will" and the "act" (v. 13)? Which one is harder for you?
5. What is God saying to you about your spiritual training in this passage?

Lights in the World

¹² So then, my dear friends, just as you have always obeyed, not only in my presence, but now even more in my absence, work out your own salvation with fear and trembling. ¹³ For it is God who is working in you, ₍enabling you₎ both to will and to act for His good purpose. ¹⁴ Do everything without grumbling and arguing,

ᵃ**2:16** Or *Offer*, or *Hold out*

¹⁵ so that you may be blameless and pure, children of God who are faultless in a crooked and perverted generation, among whom you shine like stars in the world. ¹⁶ Hold firmlyᵃ the message of life. Then I can boast in the day of Christ that I didn't run in vain or labor for nothing. ¹⁷ But even if I am poured out as a drink offering on the sacrifice and service of your faith, I am glad and rejoice with all of you. ¹⁸ In the same way you also should rejoice and share your joy with me.

Teaming Up

1. Are you more like your mother or father? In what way?
2. What is the most important message you have ever delivered?

Philippians 2:19-30

3. Consider verses 20-22 and 30. Give some examples of how verse 21 is true today.
4. Epaphroditus has five roles listed in verse 25. Which one do you think is best to have, and why?
5. Is it easy or hard for you to give praise? Where do you need to improve?
6. What does this passage teach about the importance of teamwork?

Timothy and Epaphroditus

¹⁹ Now I hope in the Lord Jesus to send Timothy to you soon so that I also may be encouraged when I hear news about you. ²⁰ For I have no one else like-minded who will genuinely care about your interests; ²¹ all seek their own interests, not those of Jesus Christ. ²² But you know his proven character, because he has served with me in the gospel ministry like a son with a father. ²³ Therefore, I hope to send him as soon as I see how

---

who died by hanging on a tree were considered to have been cursed by God.

2:11 Jesus Christ is Lord. This is the earliest and most basic confession of faith on the part of the church (Acts 2:36; Rom. 10:9; 1 Cor. 12:3). **Lord.** This is the name that was given to Jesus—the name that reflects who He really is (v. 9). This is the name of God. Jesus is the supreme Sovereign of the universe.

2:25 Epaphroditus. Epaphroditus had been sent by the Philippian church to convey a gift to Paul, and then to stay on as a member of Paul's apostolic group. However, he fell ill. The church heard about this and became quite anxious about him. In addition, Epaphroditus was homesick. For both reasons, Paul sensed that it was time for Epaphroditus to return to Philippi.

2:30 risking his life. A gambling term, it denotes one who risked everything on the roll of the dice.

3:2 those who mutilate the flesh. Paul is saying that their circumcision is really mutilation.

3:4 confidence in the flesh. This is what these Jews are promoting: a righteousness based on their heritage and many accomplishments.

3:5 eighth day. It was on the eighth day after birth that a Jewish child (as opposed to a proselyte) was circumcised. Paul was a true Jew right from the time of his birth. **the tribe of Benjamin.** The members of the tribe of Benjamin constituted an elite group within Israel. *a Pharisee.* He was one of the spiritual elite in Israel.

3:6 as to zeal, persecuting the church. Zeal was a highly prized virtue among the Jews. Paul had demonstrated his zeal for the Law by ferreting out Christians and bringing them to trial (Acts 22:4-5; 26:9-11). **blameless.** To the best of his ability, Paul tried to observe the whole Law. Taken together, all these attributes mean that Paul was in every way the match to his opponents in Philippi. He had lived at the very pinnacle of Judaism.

3:7 gain … loss. Paul describes his change in outlook in terms of a balance sheet. What was once on the "profit" side of the ledger (when he was a Pharisee) has been shifted over to the "loss" side (now that he is a Christian).

3:8 in view of the surpassing value. Paul discovered only one thing had any ultimate

things go with me. 24 And I am convinced in the Lord that I myself will also come quickly.

25 But I considered it necessary to send you Epaphroditus—my brother, co-worker, and fellow soldier, as well as your messenger and minister to my need— 26 since he has been longing for all of you and was distressed because you heard that he was sick. 27 Indeed, he was so sick that he nearly died. However, God had mercy on him, and not only on him but also on me, so that I would not have one grief on top of another. 28 For this reason, I am very eager to send him so that you may rejoice when you see him again and I may be less anxious. 29 Therefore, welcome him in the Lord with all joy and hold men like him in honor, 30 because he came close to death for the work of Christ, risking his life to make up what was lacking in your ministry to me.

The Secret to Success

1. What person in your school would you vote "most likely to succeed"? Why?
2. What is it going to take for you to be a success in the eyes of your parents? Your friends? God?

Philippians 3:1-11

3. According to Paul, what is the secret to success (v. 8)?
4. Paul desires to know Christ better by experiencing things He experienced (vv. 10-11). How does that change the way we look at suffering?
5. What "filth" (v. 8) do you need to give up to know Christ better?
6. How would you compare your life goals to the Apostle Paul's goals in this passage?

Knowing Christ

3 Finally, my brothers, rejoice in the Lord. To write to you again about this is no trouble for me and is a protection for you.

2 Watch out for "dogs,"a watch out for evil workers, watch out for those who mutilate the flesh. 3 For we are the circumcision, the ones who serve by the Spirit of God, boast in Christ Jesus, and do not put confidence in the flesh— 4 although I once had confidence in the flesh too. If anyone else thinks he has grounds for confidence in the flesh, I have more: 5 circumcised the eighth day; of the nation of Israel, of the tribe of Benjamin, a Hebrew born of Hebrews; as to the law, a •Pharisee; 6 as to zeal, persecuting the church; as to the righteousness that is in the law, blameless.

7 But everything that was a gain to me, I have considered to be a loss because of Christ. 8 More than that, I also consider everything to be a loss in view of the surpassing value of knowing Christ Jesus my Lord. Because of Him I have suffered the loss of all things and consider them filth, so that I may gain Christ 9 and be found in Him, not having a righteousness of my own from the law, but one that is through faith in Christb—the righteousness from God based on faith. 10 ⌊My goal⌋ is to know Him and the power of His resurrection and the fellowship of His sufferings, being conformed to His death, 11 assuming that I will somehow reach the resurrection from among the dead.

Reaching Forward to God's Goal

12 Not that I have already reached ⌊the goal⌋ or am already fully mature, but I make every effort to take hold of it because I also have been taken hold of by Christ Jesus. 13 Brothers, I do notc consider myself to have taken hold of it. But one thing I do: forgetting what is behind and reaching forward to what is ahead, 14 I pursue as my goal the prize promised by God's heavenlyd call in Christ Jesus. 15 Therefore, all who are mature should think this way. And if you think differently about anything, God will reveal this to you also. 16 In any case, we should live up to whatever ⌊truth⌋ we

---

a**3:2** An expression of contempt for the unclean, those outside the people of God   b**3:9** Or *through the faithfulness of Christ*   c**3:13** Other mss read *not yet*   d**3:14** Or *upward*

---

value—knowing Christ Jesus. Knowing Christ did not come as a result of any personal accomplishment.

3:10 know. The knowledge about which Paul speaks is personal knowledge and not just intellectual knowledge (i.e., not just knowing "about" someone). **the power of His resurrection.** Paul wants to personally experience the resurrected Christ in all His power (Eph. 1:18-21). **being conformed to His death.** Paul coins a new phrase by which he expresses that he wants to be obedient to God just as Christ was ... even to the point of death.

3:11 somehow reach. In humility, he expresses his sense that it is solely by God's grace that he would gain such a gift.

3:12 Not ... already reached. He has not gained full possession of what Christ has for him. **fully mature.** This is the only time in his letters that Paul uses this word. Paul indicates he has not yet fully understood Jesus Christ. There is simply too much to know of Christ ever to grasp it all this side of heaven. **make every effort.** In contrast to those groups that claim it is possible to attain spiritual perfection here and now, the Christian life is one of relentless striving to know Christ in His fullness. **to take hold of it.** Winning a prize, as for example, in a race, or also to understand or comprehend something. **I also have been taken hold of by Christ Jesus.** Paul refers here to his conversion experience on the Damascus Road.

3:13 forgetting what is behind. In order to

press on to a successful conclusion of his spiritual pilgrimage, Paul must first cease looking at what he has accomplished in the past. **what is ahead.** If the first movement in the spiritual pilgrimage is to forget the past, the second is to concentrate totally on what lies ahead—full comprehension of Jesus Christ.

3:14 goal. The mark on the track that signifies the end of the race. Paul had apparently experienced the Greek games first hand. He draws a number of parallels between the Christian life and athletic contests. Both require training, discipline, courage, endurance, concentration, and strong commitment. **the prize.** What Paul seems to have in mind is the moment at the end of the race, when the winner is called forward by the games master to receive the victory palm or wreath.

Reach for the Prize

1. If you could compete in the Olympics, what sport would you choose?
2. When have you had a hard time moving on and letting go of the past?

Philippians 3:12-21

3. What "prize" is Paul trying to win (v. 14)? How did this goal guide his life?
4. Why is it so hard to maintain the balance between "earthly things" and spiritual things (vv. 19-20)?
5. What might God be calling you to do for Him in your athletics or other interests? How about with your life?

Don't Worry—Be Happy!

1. What makes you anxious: A trip to the dentist? A big test? A date? Other?

Philippians 4:2-9

2. What makes Paul's challenge to rejoice so difficult (v. 4)?
3. What are some things people do to relieve stress from worry in their lives? What does Paul say to do (vv. 6,8)?
4. How does what you think about affect how you feel? How does it affect your relationship with God?
5. What is something you are anxious about right now? Present these worries to God in prayer.

have attained. ¹⁷ Join in imitating me, brothers, and observe those who live according to the example you have in us. ¹⁸ For I have often told you, and now say again with tears, that many live as enemies of the cross of Christ. ¹⁹ Their end is destruction; their god is their stomach; their glory is in their shame. They are focused on earthly things, ²⁰ but our citizenship is in heaven, from which we also eagerly wait for a Savior, the Lord Jesus Christ. ²¹ He will transform the body of our humble condition into the likeness of His glorious body, by the power that enables Him to subject everything to Himself.

Practical Counsel

4 So then, in this way, my dearly loved brothers, my joy and crown, stand firm in the Lord, dear friends. ² I urge Euodia and I urge Syntyche to agree in the Lord. ³ Yes, I also ask you, true partner,ᵃ to help

these women who have contended for the gospel at my side, along with Clement and the rest of my co-workers whose names are in the book of life. ⁴ Rejoice in the Lord always. I will say it again: Rejoice! ⁵ Let your graciousness be known to everyone. The Lord is near. ⁶ Don't worry about anything, but in everything, through prayer and petition with thanksgiving, let your requests be made known to God. ⁷ And the peace of God, which surpasses every thought, will guard your hearts and your minds in Christ Jesus.

⁸ Finally brothers, whatever is true, whatever is honorable, whatever is just, whatever is pure, whatever is lovely, whatever is commendable—if there is any moral excellence and if there is any praise—dwell on these things. ⁹ Do what you have learned and received and heard and seen in me, and the God of peace will be with you.

ᵃ4:3 Or *true Syzygus*, possibly a person's name

3:20 our citizenship is in heaven. This metaphor was especially meaningful to the Christians in Philippi. In 42 BC Philippi became a Roman colony and the Philippians could truly say and took pride in saying "our citizenship is in Rome" even though they were far removed from it geographically. In the same way as Christians their citizenship was not just on earth. Their true and lasting citizenship was in heaven. Paul captures the keen anticipation and happy expectation of the Christians who long for Christ's return.

3:21 the body of our humble condition. In contrast to those who taught that perfection was possible here and now, Christians knew that it was only at the second coming, by the work of Christ, that their frail, weak, and corrupt bodies would be transformed into a spiritual body akin to Christ's body.

4:2 urge. This is a strong verb, meaning "to exhort, to implore, to beg." **Euodia ... Syntyche.** Apparently these two women had carried their quarrel into the body, and it was threatening to split the church. Peace between them was crucial to the unity of the whole body. **in the Lord.** The only hope for this kind of unity to develop between these two women is found in the fact and power of their common commitment to Jesus.

4:3 true partner. Can be descriptive or it may be a proper name, *Syzgus* or *Suzuge.* Some commentators have speculated that it might be Lydia, the first convert in the church at Philippi (Acts 16:14,15,40). In any case, Paul had great confidence in this person and saw them as a peacemaker.

4:4 Rejoice in the Lord always. Paul em-

phasizes this command by repeating it. The object of their rejoicing is the Lord who is constant in an ever-changing world, faithfulness to His people.

4:5 graciousness. This word can also be translated *gentleness.* A person with this quality isn't a doormat but neither does he go around asserting his rights. He's able to see and care for not only his own interests but that of others.

4:6 Don't worry. They are to stop being anxious. To worry is to display a lack of confidence in God's care and in God's control over a situation (Matt. 6:25-34). **prayer ... petition ... requests.** Paul uses three synonyms in a row to describe the alternative to anxiety. Instead of worrying, a person ought to converse directly with God and lay out before Him all that is on his or

Carefree Contentment

1. What would you say causes the most stress among students at your school?

Philippians 4:10-20

2. What is the great value of Paul's complete contentment (vv. 11-13)?

3. What "account" do you think Paul is referring to in verse 17, and what is he really saying?

4. In what ways are you feeling insecure with your life? How do verses 13 and 19 help you?

5. What is Paul's secret to contentment? What needs to change in your life for you to find true contentment in all circumstances?

Appreciation of Support

¹⁰ I rejoiced in the Lord greatly that now at last you have renewed your care for me. You were, in fact, concerned about me, but lacked the opportunity ₁to show it₁. ¹¹ I don't say this out of need, for I have learned to be content in whatever circumstances I am. ¹² I know both how to have a little, and I know how to have a lot. In any and all circumstances I have learned the secret ₁of being content₁—whether well-fed or hungry, whether in abundance or in need. ¹³ I am able to do all things through Himª who strengthens me. ¹⁴ Still, you did well by sharing with me in my hardship.

¹⁵ And you, Philippians, know that in the early days of the gospel, when I left Macedonia, no church shared with me in the matter of giving and receiving except you alone. ¹⁶ For even in Thessalonica you sent ₁gifts₁ for my need several times. ¹⁷ Not that I seek the gift, but I seek the fruit that is increasing to your account. ¹⁸ But I have received everything in full, and I have an abundance. I am fully supplied, having received from Epaphroditus what you provided—a fragrant offering, a welcome sacrifice, pleasing to God. ¹⁹ And my God will supply all your needs according to His riches in glory in Christ Jesus. ²⁰ Now to our God and Father be glory forever and ever. •Amen.

Final Greetings

²¹ Greet every saint in Christ Jesus. Those brothers who are with me greet you. ²² All the saints greet you, but especially those from Caesar's household. ²³ The grace of the Lord Jesus Christ be with your spirit.ᵇ

ª**4:13** Other mss read *Christ* ᵇ**4:23** Other mss add *Amen.*

---

her mind, confident that God will hear and respond.

4:7 the peace of God. This is supernatural peace that comes from God and is focused on Him. **surpasses every thought.** Such peace can never fully be understood by human beings. **guard.** This is a military term. It describes a garrison of soldiers, such as those stationed at Philippi, whose job it is to stand watch over the city and protect it.

4:8 true. Sincerity and accuracy, not only in thought and word, but also in deed and attitude. **honorable.** Those majestic things that command respect and lift up one's mind from the mundane. **just.** Giving to God and others that which is their due. **pure.** In all

spheres of life—ideas, actions, motives, etc. **lovely.** A warmth that calls forth love from others. **commendable.** What people admire and think well of. **moral excellence.** The best; without fault. **praise.** Behavior that is universally praised.

4:12 a little. This word refers to the lowering of water in a river. As such, it is a reference to fundamental needs which are basic to life (such as food and water). Paul has learned to live even in the midst of abject poverty. **a lot.** This is the opposite state of "a little." It means literally, "to overflow," that is, to have enough for one's own daily needs plus something left over. **well-fed.** This describes force-fed animals that are stuffed to capacity in order to fatten them for slaughter. It is

used by Paul to define one of the extremes: having more than enough to eat. **in abundance or in need.** Another set of contrasting words. It is by the experience of these extremes that Paul has come to know the secret of coping with all circumstances.

4:13 all things. Paul is referring to what he has just described: his ability to live in all types of material circumstances—wealth or poverty, abundant food or no food, etc. **through Him who strengthens me.** The source of Paul's ability to live successfully in all circumstances is his union with Christ. This is his secret.

4:22 All the saints. The Christians in Rome are the third group that sends greetings.

COLOSSIANS

AUTHOR

The Apostle Paul was the writer of Colossians.

DATE

Tradition has it that Paul wrote Colossians, Ephesians and Philemon during his imprisonment in Rome. This would mean these letters were written in the early A.D. 60s. However, other sites including Caesarea and Ephesus have been proposed as the place of Paul's confinement, so that neither date nor place is certain.

THEME

Fullness and freedom in Christ.

HISTORICAL BACKGROUND

Paul did not found this church, at least not directly. It was probably established as a result of his ministry in Ephesus, since during Paul's two or three years in Ephesus the whole province of Asia was evangelized (Acts 19:10). Paul evidently never visited the churches at Colosse or Laodicea (2:1). Epaphras probably founded the Colossian church. A native of Colosse (4:12), he worked hard on behalf of the church there (4:13). In fact, in 1:6-7 Paul says: "the gospel that has come to you. It is bearing fruit and growing all over the world ... You learned this from Epaphras." Paul then commends Epaphras as his dear friend and a faithful minister of Christ. In fact, because of their friendship, Epaphras stayed with Paul during his imprisonment (Philem. 23) and so was unable to deliver the letter to the Colossians personally. We also meet the church at Colosse in Paul's letter to Philemon, where he requests that the runaway slave Onesimus (converted through Paul's ministry) be accepted back.

The church at Colosse was probably Gentile in composition. In 1:21 Paul speaks of the Colossian Christians as having once been "alienated" from God and "hostile in the minds"—phrases he uses elsewhere to describe those who are not part of God's covenant with Israel. Then in 1:27, he talks about making the mystery of God clear to the Gentiles; the reference is obviously to the Colossians. Finally in 3:5-7, Paul lists their past sins, which are characteristic of Gentiles rather than Jews.

RELIGION IN COLOSSE

A large number of Jews had lived in the region of Colosse, ever since the second century B.C. when Antiochus III brought 2,000 Jews from Mesopotamia and Babylon to settle there. By Paul's time there may have been as many as 50,000 Jews living in the region and practicing their religion. However, their synagogue had a "reputation for laxity and openness to speculation drifting in from the hellenistic world" (Ralph P. Martin, *Colossians and Philemon: New Century Bible Commentary*, p. 18).

But freethinking Judaism was not the major religious force in the Lycus Valley. The Greek religions also flourished there. The fertility cult of Cybele was highly popular; it was characterized by ecstasy and excessive enthusiasm Throughout the Roman Empire, the worship of Isis, Apollo, Dionysus, Asclepius and other gods was widespread. The cult of Mithras, a mystery religion based on astrology and sacrifice, abounded in Colosse. The church at Colosse, therefore, grew up in an atmosphere that blended a variety of religious traditions that may have been sources of heresy within the church.

CHARACTERISTICS

As Paul does so often, he begins his letter with a strong doctrinal statement and concludes with behavioral implications. Here his doctrinal emphasis is on the cosmic nature of Jesus Christ. Jesus is the divine Lord of the universe who reconciles all things to Himself through his death, not by rules and regulations. Paul sets this strong statement of Christ's deity (1:15-23) over against the mystical, ritualistic religion of the false teachers (2:8-23). (Apparently, these teachings had something to do with astrology. The "star-deities" could only be pleased by a life of abstinence and self-denial.) Once the truth about Christ is stated, Paul turns to the implications of Christ's lordship over all and describes how Christ's followers ought to live (3:1-4:6).

The epistle to the Colossians begins, like most of Paul's letters, with a lengthy introduction (1:1-14). In the first major division on doctrine, Paul establishes the preeminence of Christ (1:15-2:23). He follows this with an exhortation to the Colossians to live in union with Christ (3:1-4:6). He concludes with personal greetings (4:7-18).

THE CITY OF COLOSSE

About 100 miles west of Ephesus in the Lycus River Valley lay the city of Colosse. In Paul's time, it was located in the Roman province of Asia (in what today is Turkey). It was one of three major population centers that flourished in the region. Hierapolis and Laodicea (4:13) stood on opposite sides of the Lycus River, about six miles apart, while Colosse straddled the river 12 miles upstream.

Since it was located on a major trade route from Ephesus, Colosse was considered a great city in the days of Xerxes, the Persian king (fifth century B.C.). One hundred years later, it had developed into a prosperous commercial center on account of its weaving industry. In fact, "Colossian" came to mean a specific color of dyed wool.

By the time of Paul, however, Colosse's prominence had diminished; though its sister cities, Laodicea and Hierapolis, were still prospering. Laodicea had become the seat of Roman government in the region, and Hierapolis was famous for its healing waters. But Colosse, when Paul wrote, was no longer even a city. In fact, Colosse was the least important town to which Paul ever wrote.

PASSAGES FOR TOPICAL GROUP STUDY

PASSAGES FOR GENERAL GROUP STUDY

Greeting

1 Paul, an apostle of Christ Jesus by God's will, and Timothy our[a] brother:

[2] To the saints and faithful brothers in Christ in Colossae.

Grace to you and peace from God our Father.[b]

The Lasting Hope

1. What were you the most thankful for when you got up this morning?

Colossians 1:1-14

2. Why are faith and love the result of hope (vv. 4-5)? Why must hope exist first?

3. How does what Paul prays for (vv. 9-11) compare with what he thanks God for (vv. 12-14)?

4. Where is Paul saying real spiritual growth comes from (vv. 9-14)?

5. When did you first come to know the hope offered through Christ in the gospel (when He rescued you from darkness)? What life situation caused you to need hope?

Thanksgiving

[3] We always thank God, the Father of our Lord Jesus Christ, when we pray for you, [4] for we have heard of your faith in Christ Jesus and of the love you have for all the saints [5] because of the hope reserved for you in heaven. You have already heard about this hope in the message of truth, the gospel [6] that has come to you. It is bearing fruit and growing all over the world, just as it has among you since the day you heard it and recognized God's grace in the truth.[c] [7] You learned this from Epaphras, our much loved fellow slave. He is a faithful minister of the •Messiah on your[d] behalf, [8] and he has told us about your love in the Spirit.

Prayer for Spiritual Growth

[9] For this reason also, since the day we heard this, we haven't stopped praying for you. We are asking that you may be filled with the knowledge of His will in all wisdom and spiritual understanding, [10] so that you may •walk worthy of the Lord, fully pleasing to Him, bearing fruit in every good work and growing in the knowledge of God. [11] May you be strengthened with all power, according to His glorious might, for all endurance and patience, with joy [12] giving thanks to the Father, who has enabled you[e] to share in the saints'[f] inheritance in the light. [13] He has rescued us from the domain of darkness and transferred us into the kingdom of the Son He loves, [14] in whom we have redemption,[g] the forgiveness of sins.

The Centrality of Christ

[15] He is the image of the invisible God,
the firstborn over all creation;[h]

[16] because by Him everything was created,
in heaven and on earth, the visible
and the invisible,
whether thrones or dominions or rulers
or authorities—
all things have been created through Him
and for Him.

[17] He is before all things, and by Him all things
hold together.

[18] He is also the head of the body, the church;
He is the beginning, the firstborn from the dead,
so that He might come to have first place
in everything.

[19] For God was pleased to have all His fullness
dwell in Him,

[20] and through Him to reconcile everything
to Himself

---

a **1:1** Lit *the* b **1:2** Other mss add *and the Lord Jesus Christ* c **1:6** Or *and truly recognized God's grace* d **1:7** Other mss read *our* e **1:12** Other mss read *us* f **1:12** Or *holy ones'* g **1:14** Other mss add *through His blood* h **1:15** The One who is preeminent over all creation

---

1:2 Grace to you and peace. Right from the beginning, this letter highlights the reality of God's grace through Christ and the reconciliation (peace) that results.

1:4-5 faith ... love ... hope. This triad of Christian graces is arranged and expanded upon in various ways throughout the New Testament. The center of the Christian faith is Jesus Christ; the essence of its lifestyle is love; and the sure hope of a future with Christ is its motivation.

1:6 all over the world. Within 30 years after Jesus' resurrection, the gospel had spread from Palestine throughout the Roman Empire.

1:9 knowledge ... all wisdom and spiritual understanding. The false teachers (combining elements of Christianity, Greek mystery religions, and Judaism) defined salvation in terms of secret, divine knowledge and ecstatic experiences which could only be gained by following their regimen of ascetic disciplines and ceremonies.

1:10 walk worthy of the Lord. Rather than esoteric knowledge and experiences, true spirituality is seen in a lifestyle that reflects the love and holiness of Jesus. **growing in the knowledge of God.** Knowing and obeying God is the key to ongoing spiritual growth.

1:11 strengthened with all power. The false teachers taught that spiritual power was a matter of gaining control over the celestial forces that dominated human life (Eph. 2:2; 6:12). Paul teaches instead that true spiritual power is shown by patiently enduring life's hardships with a spirit of thankfulness to God (v. 12).

1:13 the domain of darkness. Darkness is an appropriate image for the influence of the hostile spiritual forces (v. 16) since their domination only leads to spiritual and moral blindness (Luke 22:53; John 1:5; Eph. 5:8-14). Paul reminds the Colossians that these astral powers are not a threat to the Christian because He has rescued us from their kingdom and transferred us into Jesus' eternal kingdom.

1:15 image of the invisible God. "Image" does not mean a second-hand representation (as a photograph is an image of a person), but rather a complete representation. All that God is, Jesus is (John 1:18; 14:9; 2 Cor. 4:4-6; Heb. 1:3). One need not look anywhere else but to Christ in order to fully know God.

1:16 thrones or dominions or rulers or authorities. Christ is Lord over all authorities, physical or spiritual.

Supernatural Hero

1. As a kid, who was your favorite superhero? What special power did he or she have?
2. Do you tend to think of Jesus as a superhero? Why or why not?

Colossians 1:15-23

3. How does Jesus hold all things together (vv. 16-17)? What does that mean for our lives, both now and in eternity?
4. How did Jesus reconcile us to God (v. 20)? Why was this necessary (v. 21)?
5. Considering who Jesus is (vv. 15-20) and what He did for you (vv. 21-23), how will you live your life? How can you give Him "first place in everything"?

by making peace through the blood
of His cross[a]—
whether things on earth or things in heaven.

[21] And you were once alienated and hostile in mind because of your evil actions. [22] But now He has reconciled you by His physical body[b] through His death, to present you holy, faultless, and blameless before Him— [23] if indeed you remain grounded and steadfast in the faith, and are not shifted away from the hope of the gospel that you heard. ⌊This gospel⌋ has been proclaimed in all creation under heaven, and I, Paul, have become a minister of it.

Paul's Ministry

[24] Now I rejoice in my sufferings for you, and I am completing in my flesh what is lacking in Christ's afflictions for His body, that is, the church. [25] I have

become its minister, according to God's administration that was given to me for you, to make God's message fully known, [26] the •mystery hidden for ages and generations but now revealed to His saints. [27] God wanted to make known to those among the Gentiles the glorious wealth of this mystery, which is Christ in you, the hope of glory. [28] We proclaim Him, warning and teaching everyone with all wisdom, so that we may present everyone mature in Christ. [29] I labor for this, striving with His strength that works powerfully in me.

No Pain ... No Gain

1. When have you worked very hard in sports or in school to achieve a goal? How did you feel when you were done?

Colossians 1:24-2:5

2. In what sense are Paul's sufferings a continuation of Jesus' sufferings? Why would this lead him to rejoice (see 2 Cor. 12:9-10)?
3. How can we make Paul's stated purpose (1:28; 2:2) a reality in our lives?
4. What "persuasive arguments" (2:4) from others or the world's system hinder you in following Jesus? How does Paul speak to your concerns?
5. What is God saying to you in this passage about the training necessary to achieve your spiritual goals?

2 For I want you to know how great a struggle I have for you, for those in Laodicea, and for all who have not seen me in person. [2] ⌊I want⌋ their hearts to be encouraged and joined together in love, so that they may have all the riches of assured understanding, and have the knowledge of God's •mystery—Christ.[c]

---

[a]**1:20** Other mss add *through Him*   [b]**1:22** His body of flesh on the cross   [c]**2:2** Other mss read *mystery of God, both of the Father and of Christ;* other ms variations exist on this v.

1:17 He is before all things. Christ's preexistence and preeminence means He is Lord over everything.

1:18 the head of the body. This emphasizes the organic, living relationship between Christ and His people. **firstborn.** As Jesus is Lord over the original creation, so also He is Lord over the new creation (v. 15).

1:19 fullness. Paul declares that Christ is fully God, and that there is nothing else other than Christ needed in our lives to have right standing before God.

1:20 reconcile everything to Himself. Jesus seeks the eventual goal of not only reconciling humanity to Himself but to creation, which has been thrown out of kilter by sin (Rom. 8:19-25). **the blood of His cross.** The irony of the gospel is that this work of re-

demption was completed through the gory, earthly act of crucifixion.

1:21 alienated. Jews viewed Gentile idolatry and immorality as the chief evidence that humanity was in revolt against God. Paul utilizes that idea to contrast the Colossians' "before" and "after" status in Christ.

1:22 His physical body. The stress here is on Jesus' actual body, which died, rather than the church as the expression of Christ's body (v. 18). **holy ... faultless ... blameless.** While the false teachers taught that the Colossians needed something more in order to be truly spiritual, Paul uses the language both of sacrifice and the law court to emphasize that believers are completely acceptable to God through Christ (Rom. 8:1ff).

1:24 what is lacking in Christ's afflictions.

Given Paul's stress on the once-for-all sufficiency of Christ's death as a sacrifice for sin (v. 22), he cannot mean that his sufferings add to the value of Christ's death. Rather, believers will continue to suffer as Christ would if He were still here. Paul's suffering results in the spread of the good news of redemption.

1:26 the mystery ... now revealed. The "mystery" of the gospel is revealed by God to all—including Gentiles—who believe. It is not a secret form of spiritual power as the false teachers claimed, but the hope for eternity guaranteed by the presence of Christ within the believer.

1:28 mature in Christ. Each Christian is perfect in Christ. Jesus stands wholly righteous on our behalf before God. We mature in our relationship with Him through obedi-

3 In Him all the treasures of wisdom and knowledge are hidden.

Christ versus the Colossian Heresy

4 I am saying this so that no one will deceive you with persuasive arguments. 5 For I may be absent in body, but I am with you in spirit, rejoicing to see your good order and the strength of your faith in Christ.

Victory over the Enemy

1. Do you consider your parents "permissive" or "strict"?

Colossians 2:6-23

2. What does walking "in Him" (v. 6) involve (see 1:10-12)?
3. What are "the elemental forces of this world" (vv. 8, 20) and the "rulers and authorities" (vv. 10,15)? How did Christ give the Colossians victory over these?
4. What is the result of trying to base one's relationship with God on rule-keeping or private visions, as the false teachers were doing?
5. What is God saying to you in this passage about the key to a victorious and growing faith?

---

6 Therefore as you have received Christ Jesus the Lord, •walk in Him, 7 rooted and built up in Him and established in the faith, just as you were taught, and overflowing with thankfulness.

8 Be careful that no one takes you captive through philosophy and empty deceit based on human tradition, based on the elemental forces of the world, and not based on Christ. 9 For in Him the entire fullness of God's naturea dwells bodily,b 10 and you have been filled by Him, who is the head over every ruler and authority.

11 In Him you were also circumcised with a circumcision not done with hands, by putting off the body of flesh, in the circumcision of the •Messiah. 12 Having been buried with Him in baptism, you were also raised with Him through faith in the working of God, who raised Him from the dead. 13 And when you were dead in trespasses and in the uncircumcision of your flesh, He made you alive with Him and forgave us all our trespasses. 14 He erased the certificate of debt, with its obligations, that was against us and opposed to us, and has taken it out of the way by nailing it to the cross. 15 He disarmed the rulers and authorities and disgraced them publicly; He triumphed over them by Him.c

16 Therefore don't let anyone judge you in regard to food and drink or in the matter of a festival or a new moon or a sabbath day.d 17 These are a shadow of what was to come; the substance ise the Messiah. 18 Let no one disqualify you,f insisting on ascetic practices and the worship of angels, claiming access to a visionary realm and inflated without cause by his fleshly mind. 19 He doesn't hold on to the head, from whom the whole body, nourished and held together by its ligaments and tendons, develops with growth from God.

20 If you died with Christ to the elemental forces of this world, why do you live as if you still belonged to the world? Why do you submit to regulations: 21 "Don't handle, don't taste, don't touch"? 22 All these ⌐regulations⌐ refer to what is destroyed by being used up; they are human commands and doctrines. 23 Although these have a reputation of wisdom by promoting ascetic practices, humility, and severe treatment of the body, they are not of any value against fleshly indulgence.

The Life of the New Man

3 So if you have been raised with the •Messiah, seek what is above, where the Messiah is, seated at the right hand of God. 2 Set your minds on what is above, not on what is on the earth. 3 For you have died, and your life is hidden with the Messiah in God. 4 When the Messiah, who is yourg life, is revealed, then you also will be revealed with Him in glory.

---

a2:9 Or the deity b2:9 Or nature lives in a human body c2:15 Or them through it; that is, through the cross d2:16 Or or sabbaths e2:17 Or substance belongs to f2:18 Or no one cheat us out of your prize g3:4 Other mss read our

---

ence, as we continue moving toward the goal of the completed work of Christ in us.

2:8 based on human tradition. The false teachings were not based on the teachings of Christ, but upon faulty ideas influenced by the "elemental forces" of the world, angelic beings that manipulated human affairs in opposition to God (1:16; 1 Cor. 2:6,8; Gal. 3:19; 4:3,9; Eph. 6:12).

2:10 filled by Him. Christ is fully God. **the head.** This stresses Christ's lordship over all creation (1:15-17). To go "beyond" Christ is to go backwards spiritually.

2:11 circumcised. True circumcision is through Christ spiritually, and not the removal of flesh.

2:14 the certificate of debt. This refers to a

written agreement to pay back a debt or to obey a law. When fulfilled, the document was blotted out and canceled.

2:16 a festival or a new moon or a sabbath day. While this serves as a summary of the annual, monthly, and weekly Jewish holy days (1 Chron. 23:31), pagans also observed cycles of worship determined by astrological practices. The false teachers probably used the Jewish traditions to support their astrological calendar.

2:17 a shadow ... the substance. Hebrews 8:3-13 and 10:1-18 compared the work of Christ to the Old Testament sacrificial system (1 Cor. 5:7). While the false teachers claimed their ascetic practices were the pathway that led to the reality of spiritual experience, Paul asserts they only lead to the shadow-lands and not to a true spiritual life found in Christ.

2:23 fleshly indulgence. Paul plays with the false teacher's fondness for spiritual fulfillment by pointing out that their ascetic rules about the body ironically only fill up the "body" or the "flesh" (v.18)"

3:1 raised with the Messiah. As the Christian's death-with-Christ cut the bonds to the old authorities (2:20), so one's life with Christ creates new bonds with God and others. **seek what is above.** This is not encouraging escapism from earthly affairs. The point is that Christians are to shape their lives by the values of the heavenly world in which Christ sits enthroned as King rather than heeding rules based on the elemental spirits.

3:3 hidden with the Messiah. What God did in the past is now a present reality in Christ.

3:5 put to death. Believers are to daily turn

⁵ Therefore, put to death whatever in you is worldly:ᵃ sexual immorality, impurity, lust, evil desire, and greed, which is idolatry. ⁶ Because of these, God's wrath comes on the disobedient,ᵇ ⁷ and you once •walked in these things when you were living in them. ⁸ But now you must also put away all the following: anger, wrath, malice, slander, and filthy language from your mouth. ⁹ Do not lie to one another, since you have put off the old man with his practices ¹⁰ and have put on the new man, who is being renewed in knowledge according to the image of his Creator. ¹¹ Here there is not Greek and Jew, circumcision and uncircumcision, barbarian, Scythian,ᶜ slave and free; but Christ is all and in all.

Take out the Trash

1. What did you really want as a child that you never got?

Colossians 3:1-25

2. How does God's forgiveness affect our willingness to forgive others (vv. 12-13)?

3. How does the message and truth from God help us to get along with others (vv.16-17)?

4. What do you need to "put away" (v. 8)? What should you "put on" instead (v. 12)?

5. Verse 13 says, "Just as the Lord has forgiven you." Whom do you need to forgive? How can you reach out to this person in the coming week?

The Christian Life

¹² Therefore, God's chosen ones, holy and loved, put on heartfelt compassion, kindness, humility, gentleness, and patience, ¹³ accepting one another and forgiving one another if anyone has a complaint against another. Just as the Lord has forgiven you, so also you must ₍forgive₎. ¹⁴ Above all, ₍put on₎ love—the perfect bond of unity. ¹⁵ And let the peace of the Messiah, to which you were also called in one body, control your hearts. Be thankful. ¹⁶ Let the message about the Messiah dwell richly among you, teaching and admonishing one another in all wisdom, and singing psalms, hymns, and spiritual songs, with gratitude in your hearts to God. ¹⁷ And whatever you do, in word or in deed, do everything in the name of the Lord Jesus, giving thanks to God the Father through Him.

Christ in Your Home

¹⁸ Wives, be submissive to your husbands, as is fitting in the Lord.

¹⁹ Husbands, love your wives and don't become bitter against them.

²⁰ Children, obey your parents in everything, for this is pleasing in the Lord.

²¹ Fathers, do not exasperate your children, so they won't become discouraged.

²² Slaves, obey your human masters in everything; don't work only while being watched, in order to please men, but ₍work₎ wholeheartedly, fearing the Lord.

²³ Whatever you do, do it enthusiastically,ᵈ as something done for the Lord and not for men, ²⁴ knowing that you will receive the reward of an inheritance from the Lord—you serve the Lord Christ. ²⁵ For the wrongdoer will be paid back for whatever wrong he has done, and there is no favoritism.

4 Masters, supply your slaves with what is right and fair, since you know that you too have a Master in heaven.

Speaking to God and Others

² Devote yourselves to prayer; stay alert in it with thanksgiving. ³ At the same time, pray also for us that God may open a door to us for the message, to speak the •mystery of the •Messiah—for which I am in prison—

---

away from attitudes and actions that reflect the old way of life. **sexual immorality ... greed.** This list of sins begins with external actions and proceeds to internal motives and attitudes (see also v. 8).

3:8 put away. Anger, slander, abusive talk, and the like have no place in the life of a Christian.

3:9 put off the old man. Literally, "to strip off." This phrase is also used to describe the putting off of the sinful nature through Christ's death (2:11), and Christ's victory over spiritual powers (2:15).

3:10 put on the new man. The lifestyle of Christians is patterned after the attitudes and actions of Christ who is at work within them (1 Cor. 15:45; Gal. 3:27). It's not enough to put off the old; the "new man"

must be put on to replace the old.

3:11 Scythian. The Greeks considered Scythians to be especially uncouth barbarians. Allegiance to Christ eradicates prideful divisions based on race, religion, culture, or social class (and gender—Gal. 3:28).

3:12-17 put on. Paul uses the image of putting on new clothes to show how true spirituality involves "wearing" the Christ-like qualities of love, peace, and thankfulness (Rom. 13:14).

3:16 the message about the Messiah. While the false teachers don't "hold on to the head" (2:19), the message that the Colossians teach must be centered on Jesus. **dwell richly among you.** Spiritual fullness is rooted in a commitment to Christ. **teaching ... one another.** The Christian faith is lived in

community, not held in as a solely personal faith. All the aspects of worship listed here are to be carried out to build one another up, as well as directing our hearts toward God.

3:18-22 be submissive. In Christ, this is transformed from a passive obedience to an authority to a specific, active application of Christ's call to put the needs and interest of others before one's own (Eph. 5:21-24; Phil. 2:4).

3:21 Fathers. This applies to both parents (Heb. 11:23).

4:2 Devote yourselves to prayer. See the example of the church in Acts 1:14, 2:42, and 6:4. **stay alert.** An allusion to Matthew 26:41 and Luke 18:1. This call to vigilance and spiritual alertness became part of the Apostles' teaching to Christians in general

1165

⁴ so that I may reveal it as I am required to speak. ⁵ •Walk in wisdom toward outsiders, making the most of the time. ⁶ Your speech should always be gracious, seasoned with salt, so that you may know how you should answer each person.

Christian Greetings

⁷ Tychicus, a loved brother, a faithful servant, and a fellow slave in the Lord, will tell you all the news about me. ⁸ I have sent him to you for this very purpose, so that you may know how we are,ᵃ and so that he may encourage your hearts. ⁹ He is with Onesimus, a faithful and loved brother, who is one of you. They will tell you about everything here.

¹⁰ Aristarchus, my fellow prisoner, greets you, as does Mark, Barnabas' cousin (concerning whom you have received instructions: if he comes to you, welcome him), ¹¹ and so does Jesus who is called Justus. These alone of the circumcision are my co-workers for the kingdom of God, and they have been a comfort to me. ¹² Epaphras, who is one of you, a slave of Christ Jesus, greets you. He is always contending for you in his prayers, so that you can stand mature and fully assuredᵇ in everything God wills. ¹³ For I testify about him that he works hardᶜ for you, for those in Laodicea, and for those in Hierapolis. ¹⁴ Luke, the loved physician, and Demas greet you. ¹⁵ Give my greetings to the brothers in Laodicea, and to Nympha and the church in her house. ¹⁶ And when this letter has been read among you, have it read also in the church of the Laodiceans; and see that you also read the letter from Laodicea. ¹⁷ And tell Archippus, "Pay attention to the ministry you have received in the Lord, so that you can accomplish it."

¹⁸ This greeting is in my own hand—Paul. Remember my imprisonment. Grace be with you.ᵈ

Open Doors

1. In elementary school, who were two of your best friends? What was one quality about each one that stands out to you?

Colossians 4:1-18

2. In "speaking the mystery" of Jesus with others (vv. 2-6), what is the role of prayer?
3. Why is thankfulness such a key ingredient in a Christian's life (see 2:7; 3:15,17)?
4. What has helped you to grow the most in your prayer life?
5. What would happen at school if you and some of your friends followed Paul's model in verses 2-6?

ᵃ**4:8** Other mss read *that he may know how you are*   ᵇ**4:12** Other mss read *and complete*   ᶜ**4:13** Other mss read *he has a great zeal*   ᵈ**4:18** Other mss add *Amen.*

(Acts 20:31; 1 Cor. 16:13; 1 Thess. 5:6; 1 Peter 5:8).

4:3 in prison. Paul, imprisoned several times because Jewish opponents considered his missionary activity as subversive to their interests, probably wrote this letter while under the house arrest described in Acts 28.

4:5 making the most of the time. An emphasis on being alert to God-given opportunities to bear witness to Christ in the course of daily life is in view.

4:7 Tychicus. Personal name meaning "fortunate." One of Paul's fellow workers in the ministry. A native of Asia Minor (Acts 20:4), he traveled with the apostle on the third missionary journey. Tychicus and Onesimus carried the Colossian letter from Paul (Col. 4:7-9) and were to relate to the church Paul's condition. Paul also sent Tychicus to Ephesus on one occasion (2 Tim. 4:12) and possibly to Crete on another (Titus 3:12). Tradition holds that he died a martyr.

4:9 Onesimus. The slave for whom Paul wrote his letter to Philemon. In his letter Paul pled with Philemon to free the servant because Onesimus had been so helpful to the apostle. Onesimus accompanied Tychicus in bearing Paul's letter to the church at Colossae.

4:12 Epaphras. Personal name meaning "lovely." A native Colossian who established the church there and throughout the Lycus valley (1:7; Philem. 23). Paul's commendation here and in Colossians 1:7 substantiates his claim that the church had already heard the gospel. His ministry also included the churches at Laodicea and Hierapolis.

4:13 Laodicea. A city near Colosse. **Hierapolis.** A city about 12 miles northwest of Colosse and six miles north of Laodicea.

4:14 Luke, the loved physician. It is from this reference that we learn of Luke's profession. The various "we" passages in the book of Acts (16:10-17; 20:5–21:18; 27:1–28:16)

indicate that Luke accompanied Paul at several points during his missionary work.

4:15 Nympha and the church in her house. The Laodicean church, or at least part of it, followed the custom of other early churches in meeting in the homes of members who could accommodate them. Philemon's home was one of the sites of the congregation in Colosse (Philem. 1-2).

4:17 Archippus. In Philemon 2 he is called a "fellow soldier."

4:18 This greeting is in my own hand—Paul. Typically, others actually wrote Paul's letters at his dictation (Rom. 16:22), while he penned the final greeting as a mark of the letter's genuineness (1 Cor. 16:21; Gal. 6:11; 2 Thess. 3:17; Philem. 19). 2 Thessalonians 2:2 hints at the possibility that forged letters had been circulated in Paul's name.

INTRODUCTION TO
1 THESSALONIANS

AUTHOR

The Apostle Paul wrote 1 Thessalonians.

DATE

First Thessalonians may well be the first document written in the New Testament. Many scholars believe that it is Paul's earliest letter, although a few say that Galatians has that honor. It is generally agreed that 1 Thessalonians was written about A.D. 50, during Paul's second missionary journey not long after the founding of the church in Thessalonica. Paul probably wrote from Corinth, where he went after he left Athens. Timothy had returned with news from Thessalonica, and this letter was Paul's response to his report.

THEME

Living in the light of the coming of Christ.

HISTORICAL BACKGROUND

When Paul crossed over into Macedonia in A.D. 50, a new era began for Christianity. Now the gospel had spread to Europe and from there it flowed west, through Greece, into Italy, on to Spain and the limits of the Roman Empire. After the vision that sent Paul across the Aegean Sea to Philippi, he came to Thessalonica, which turned out to be a key stop in his pioneering work in Europe.

His stay in Thessalonica was brief and stormy. After he preached in the synagogue three Sabbaths, the Jews were so jealous of his success that they organized a mob by rounding up "some bad characters from the marketplace" (Acts 17:5). The mob then rushed around looking for Paul and Silas. Failing to find them, they dragged Jason (at whose home Paul was staying) and a few other Christians before the city officials. They claimed that these men were associates of Paul who was preaching that Jesus, not Caesar, was king. That night after Jason and the others were released on bail, Paul and Silas slipped away to Berea.

PAUL'S CONCERNS ABOUT THE CHURCH AT THESSALONICA

Could three weeks of ministry produce a viable church at Thessalonica? Apparently this question troubled Paul. After ministering in Berea, Paul went on to Athens. He attempted to return to Thessalonica, but his efforts were frustrated (2:17-18). In his place he sent Timothy to see how they were doing and to give them what help he could (3:1-5).

What Timothy found was twofold. Generally the news was good. The converts were standing fast in their faith despite persecution and Paul's hasty departure from the city. In fact, they were even doing evangelistic work on their own. On the other hand, some of the converts had not fully understood the ethical implications of the gospel. In particular, there was laxity in sexual matters (4:3-8). Some felt it unnecessary to work and had become a burden to the others (4:11-12; 5:14). There was also misunderstanding about the second coming. They knew Christ would return again and rescue them from the "coming wrath" (1:9-10; 5:9-10). But some worried about those Christians who died prior to the Lord's return (4:13-14). Quite possibly Paul and the others had departed from Thessalonica before their teaching on this subject was complete. So Paul assures them that the dead in Christ were at no disadvantage. In fact, the first event of the second coming would be the resurrection of the dead (4:16).

In his letter to them, Paul expresses his relief and joy at their good progress in the gospel. He calls them "an example to all the believers in Macedonia and Achaia" (1:7). Paul explains why he never returned to them and ends his letter with further instruction about the life of holiness and about the second coming.

THE CONVERTS

Who were these believers? Luke says (in Acts 17:1-4) that the church had its roots in the Jewish community. Some members of the synagogue where Paul preached, along with a large number of God-fearing Greeks—Gentiles who worshiped at the synagogue—and several prominent women, had become convinced that Jesus was the Messiah and so became Christians. These included Jason who opened his home to Paul and his companions, and Aristarchus who was later Paul's traveling companion and prison mate (Acts 19:29; 20:4; 27:2; Col. 4:10; Philem. 24).

In fact, throughout Paul's ministry in Macedonia many prominent women were converted. Lydia, the businesswoman, was his first convert in Philippi (Acts 16:14). Many "prominent Greek women" were converted in Berea (Acts 17:12). Unlike most other women in the first century, the women in Macedonia were noted for their competence and the active role they played in society. As it turns out, they were crucial to the growth of the church in Europe.

The greater part of the church, however, consisted of converted pagans, as Paul's comment in 1:9 indicates: "You turned to God from idols."

THE CITY OF THESSALONICA

Thessalonica was a great city. Originally named Therme, its famous harbor became the base for the Persian fleet during Xerxes' invasion of Europe. In 315 B.C., Cassander, the Macedonian king, renamed the city Thessalonica after his wife, the half-sister of Alexander the Great. In 146 B.C. after Rome had taken over Greece, Thessalonica was made the capital of the Roman province of Macedonia. In 42 B.C., Rome granted it the status of a free city, which gave Thessalonica a high degree of autonomy.

The key to its importance was Thessalonica's location astride the famous *Via Egnatia*—the great Roman military road across northern Greece, which stretched from the Adriatic Sea on the west to Constantinople in the east. Hence trade between Rome and Asia Minor and points farther east flowed through Thessalonica, making it very wealthy. This was a crucial site for a church if Christianity were to spread throughout the world.

CHARACTERISTICS

First Thessalonians stands out from the four books that precede it because, unlike them, this letter does not emphasize theology and doctrine. Rather, it reflects the concern, gratitude, disappointment, and joy of a beloved missionary who can't stop thinking about the church he left behind.

PASSAGES FOR TOPICAL GROUP STUDY

1:1-10 . . . . . HOLY SPIRIT and MODEL OF FAITH . . . . Real-Life Power

2:1-16 . . . . OPPOSITION and PERSECUTION . . . . Misunderstood

2:17-3:13 . . ENCOURAGEMENT . . . . Encouragement to Press On

4:1-12 . . . . DESIRES and SEXUAL PURITY . . Choosing the Best Way

4:13-5:11 . . JESUS' RETURN . . . . Heaven's Gonna Be a Blast

PASSAGES FOR GENERAL GROUP STUDY

5:12-28 . . . God's Incredible Gifts to Us

Greeting

1 Paul, Silvanus,ª and Timothy:
To the church of the Thessalonians in God the Father and the Lord Jesus Christ.
Grace to you and peace.ᵇ

Real-Life Power

1. How do you stay motivated to improve in your chosen sport or field of study?

1 Thessalonians 1:1-10

2. What do you think Paul was referring to in verse 5 when he said, "For our gospel did not come to you in word only, but also in power"?

3. How did the Thessalonians first become imitators of, and then models for, the faith (vv. 6-10)? What does this demonstrate about their growth in Christ?

4. In a time without any mass media, how do you suppose their faith became so legendary?

5. How can you tap into and experience the power of the Holy Spirit in your life?

Thanksgiving

² We always thank God for all of you, remembering you constantly in our prayers. ³ We recall, in the presence of our God and Father, your work of faith, labor of love, and endurance of hope in our Lord Jesus Christ, ⁴ knowing your election, brothers loved by God. ⁵ For our gospel did not come to you in word only, but also in power, in the Holy Spirit, and with much assurance. You know what kind of men we were among you for your benefit, ⁶ and you became imitators of us and of the Lord when, in spite of severe persecution, you welcomed the message with the joy from the Holy Spirit.

⁷ As a result, you became an example to all the believers in Macedonia and Achaia. ⁸ For the Lord's message rang out from you, not only in Macedonia and Achaia, but in every place that your faithᶜ in God has gone out, so we don't need to say anything. ⁹ For they themselves report about us what kind of reception we had from you: how you turned to God from idols to serve the living and true God, ¹⁰ and to wait for His Son from heaven, whom He raised from the dead—Jesus, who rescues us from the coming wrath.

Misunderstood

1. When have you felt completely misunderstood or falsely accused?

1 Thessalonians 2:1-16

2. Judging from the way Paul was defending himself from the "opposition" (vv. 1-6), what was he most likely being accused of?

3. Why do you think it was so important for Paul to clear his name of these false accusations?

4. What difficulties were the Thessalonians facing (vv. 14-15)? How would Paul's example of "hanging in there" through persecution encourage them?

5. In what situation do you need to persevere—to press on? What person can be an example or help to get you through?

Paul's Conduct

2 For you yourselves know, brothers, that our visit with you was not without result. ² On the contrary, after we had previously suffered and been outrageously treated in Philippi, as you know, we were emboldened by our God to speak the gospel of God to you in spite of great opposition. ³ For our exhortation

---

ª **1:1** Or *Silas*; see Ac 15:22-32; 16:19-40; 17:1-16   ᵇ **1:1** Other mss add *from God our Father and the Lord Jesus Christ*   ᶜ **1:8** Or *in every place news of your faith*

1:1 Silvanus. Silvanus (also called Silas) was a representative of the Jerusalem church to the Christians at Antioch (Acts 15:22). He accompanied Paul on his second missionary journey during which they met Timothy, a young man highly spoken of by the Christians in his area (Acts 16:1-5). **Thessalonians.** Thessalonica was an important city in northern Greece, the capital of the province of Macedonia. Paul, Silvanus, and Timothy came to Thessalonica from Philippi where they planted the first church in Europe. As was Paul's custom, he went first to the Jewish synagogue where he reasoned with the Jews. He showed them from the Hebrew Scriptures that Messiah had to die and be raised from death. He further argued that this prophecy had been fulfilled in Jesus of Nazareth.

1:2 We always thank God for all of you.

Paul most often began his letters with an affirmation of the recipients (Rom. 1:8; 1 Cor. 1:4; Eph. 1:15-16; Phil. 1:3; Col. 1:3; 2 Thess. 1:3).

1:3 faith ... love ... hope. Paul and other New Testament writers use these words (or a combination of them) as a way of summing up the essentials of the Christian life (5:8; Rom. 5:1-5; 1 Cor. 13:13; Gal. 5:5-6; Eph. 4:2-5; Col. 1:4-5; Heb. 6:10-12; 10:22-24; 1 Peter 1:21-22). Faith in Christ, rooted in the promise (hope) of eternal life, is expressed by love to others. These are active concepts, the presence of which is evidenced by the tangible activities of sacrifice and service.

1:4 knowing your election. Paul's purpose in reminding them of God's initiative in their salvation is to strengthen their hope in light

of the pressures of external persecution (2:14) and internal uncertainty (4:13). **brothers loved by God.** This is a reminder of the intimacy with which "God the Father" relates to His people.

1:5 our gospel did not come to you in word only. Sometimes Paul's and the other apostles' preaching was accompanied by signs and miracles. That wasn't so in Thessalonica. But God's Spirit was strongly present with Paul and his listeners as he opened their Scriptures and showed them their Messiah had come.

2:2 we were emboldened by our God to speak the gospel of God to you. Paul was as susceptible to fear in difficult situations as anyone (Acts 18:9-10; Phil. 1:20). His strength, as he continually declares, is found in God.

didn't come from error or impurity or an intent to deceive. [4] Instead, just as we have been approved by God to be entrusted with the gospel, so we speak, not to please men, but rather God, who examines our hearts. [5] For we never used flattering speech, as you know, or had greedy motives—God is our witness— [6] and we didn't seek glory from people, either from you or from others. [7] Although we could have been a burden as Christ's apostles, instead we were gentle[a] among you, as a nursing mother nurtures her own children. [8] We cared so much for you that we were pleased to share with you not only the gospel of God but also our own lives, because you had become dear to us. [9] For you remember our labor and hardship, brothers. Working night and day so that we would not burden any of you, we preached God's gospel to you. [10] You are witnesses, and so is God, of how devoutly, righteously, and blamelessly we conducted ourselves with you believers. [11] As you know, like a father with his own children, [12] we encouraged, comforted, and implored each one of you to •walk worthy of God, who calls you into His own kingdom and glory.

Reception and Opposition to the Message

[13] Also, this is why we constantly thank God, because when you received the message about God that you heard from us, you welcomed it not as a human message, but as it truly is, the message of God, which also works effectively in you believers. [14] For you, brothers, became imitators of God's churches in Christ Jesus that are in Judea, since you have also suffered the same things from people of your own country, just as they did from the Jews. [15] They killed both the Lord Jesus and the prophets, and persecuted us; they displease God, and are hostile to everyone, [16] hindering us from speaking to the Gentiles so that they may be saved. As a result, they are always adding to the number of their sins, and wrath has overtaken them completely.[b]

Paul's Desire to See Them

[17] But as for us, brothers, after we were forced to leave you for a short time (in person, not in heart), we greatly desired and made every effort to return and see you face to face. [18] So we wanted to come to you—even I, Paul, time and again—but Satan hindered us. [19] For who is our hope, or joy, or crown of boasting in the presence of our Lord Jesus at His coming? Is it not you? [20] For you are our glory and joy!

Encouragement to Press On

1. What struggle, competitive situation, or worry has hit you recently? How did you deal with it?

1 Thessalonians 2:17-3:13

2. What do you think Paul meant when he called the Thessalonian church his "hope," "joy" and "crown" (2:19)?
3. What in Timothy's report particularly encouraged Paul?
4. In what specific ways have you been encouraged by someone else's faith? Have you told that person about it? 5. Where do you need some encouragement in your life right now? (Be sure to talk to God about it too.) How can you encourage someone in your group, team, or circle of friends?

Anxiety in Athens

3 Therefore, when we could no longer stand it, we thought it was better to be left alone in Athens. [2] And we sent Timothy, our brother and God's co-worker[c] in the gospel of Christ, to strengthen and encourage you concerning your faith, [3] so that no one will be shaken by these persecutions. For you yourselves know that we are appointed to[d] this. [4] In fact, when we were with you, we told you previously that we were going to suffer persecution, and as you know, it happened. [5] For this reason, when I could no longer stand it, I also sent to find out about your faith, fearing that

---

[a] **2:7** Other mss read *infants* [b] **2:16** Or *to the end* [c] **3:2** Other mss read *servant* [d] **3:3** Or *we are destined for*

2:7 gentle ... as a nursing mother. Paul eloquently described his love for his spiritual children.

2:11 like a father with his own children. In some respects Paul was what a single parent must be—both mother (v. 7) and father. In the ancient world, the father's role was to see that his children learned how to live as responsible citizens.

2:14 just as they did from the Jews. As in John's Gospel, Paul often uses the term "Jews" when referring to the entrenched opposition of the Jewish religious leaders to Christianity. While the prime opposition to Jesus and the early church came from these leaders, it must be remembered that the first church was almost entirely Jewish in makeup.

2:15-16 hostile to everyone, hindering us from speaking to the Gentiles. Prior to his visit to Thessalonica, Paul had encountered Jewish opposition in Antioch of Pisidia (Acts 13:50), Iconium (Acts 14:2), and Lystra, where he was stoned (Acts 14:19). The Thessalonian Jews forced Paul not only to leave that city, but also chased him out of Beroea (Acts 17:5,13). In Corinth, where he was probably living when he wrote this letter, he likewise suffered at the hands of Jewish opposition (Acts 18:12).

2:17 forced to leave you. Literally, this is "to be bereaved." It describes the anguish of a parent being forcibly separated from his or her children.

2:18 Satan hindered us. Whether Paul's forced change of plans was due to sickness, inability to make travel arrangements, or some other factor is unknown, but ultimately he attributes this frustration to Satan, God's adversary. At other times, Paul sees roadblocks to his plans as the leading of the Holy Spirit or the Spirit of Jesus (Acts 16:7). The difference may be that whereas one set of difficulties ends up in the spread of the gospel, at another time those difficulties would hinder that process and delay the mission that Paul was trying to accomplish.

3:10 complete what is lacking in your faith. The prayer that follows (vv. 11-13) and the final two chapters, which are full of both ethical and doctrinal instructions, give us hints about what Paul felt was lacking.

3:12 may the Lord cause you to increase and overflow with love. This petition highlights love as the defining element in a Christian's relationships with others.

the tempter had tempted you and that our labor might be for nothing.

Encouraged by Timothy

⁶ But now Timothy has come to us from you and brought us good news about your faith and love, and that you always have good memories of us, wanting to see us, as we also want to see you. ⁷ Therefore, brothers, in all our distress and persecution, we were encouraged about you through your faith. ⁸ For now we live, if you stand firm in the Lord. ⁹ How can we thank God for you in return for all the joy we experience because of you before our God, ¹⁰ as we pray earnestly night and day to see you face to face and to complete what is lacking in your faith?

Prayer for the Church

¹¹ Now may our God and Father Himself, and our Lord Jesus, direct our way to you. ¹² And may the Lord cause you to increase and overflow with love for one another and for everyone, just as we also do for you. ¹³ May He make your hearts blameless in holiness before our God and Father at the coming of our Lord Jesus with all His saints. •Amen.ᵃ

The Call to Sanctification

4 Finally then, brothers, we ask and encourage you in the Lord Jesus, that as you have received from us how you must •walk and please God—as you are doingᵇ —do so even more. ² For you know what commands we gave you through the Lord Jesus.

³ For this is God's will, your sanctification: that you abstain from sexual immorality, ⁴ so that each of you knows how to possess his own vesselᶜ in sanctification and honor, ⁵ not with lustful desires, like the Gentiles who don't know God. ⁶ This means one must not transgress against and defraud his brother in this matter, because the Lord is an avenger of all these offenses,ᵈ as we also previously told and warned you. ⁷ For God has not called us to impurity, but to sanctification. ⁸ Therefore, the person who rejects this does not reject man, but God, who also gives you His Holy Spirit.

Choosing the Best Way

1. What teacher, coach, or other person has really challenged you to live up to your best?

1 Thessalonians 4:1-12

2. What is "God's will" regarding sexual conduct (v. 3)?
3. How can we control our bodies in "sanctification and honor, not with lustful desires" (vv. 4-5)? What pressures at school and with your friends make it hard to maintain self-control?
4. What would you say to a Christian who tries to push physical intimacy of take advantage of you on a date? How about a non-Christian?
5. What lines have you drawn and what decisions have you made for yourself about sexual purity?

Loving and Working

⁹ About brotherly love: you don't need me to write you because you yourselves are taught by God to love one another. ¹⁰ In fact, you are doing this toward all the brothers in the entire region of Macedonia. But we encourage you, brothers, to do so even more, ¹¹ to seek to lead a quiet life, to mind your own business,ᵉ and to work with your own hands, as we commanded you, ¹² so that you may walk properlyᶠ in the presence of outsidersᵍ and not be dependent on anyone.ʰ

The Comfort of Christ's Coming

¹³ We do not want you to be uninformed, brothers, concerning those who are •asleep, so that you will not grieve like the rest, who have no hope. ¹⁴ Since we believe that Jesus died and rose again, in the same way God will bring with Him those who have fallen asleep throughⁱ Jesus.ʲ ¹⁵ For we say this to you by a revelation

---

ᵃ3:13 Other mss omit Amen.   ᵇ4:1 Lit walking   ᶜ4:4 Or to control his own body, or to acquire his own wife   ᵈ4:6 Lit things   ᵉ4:11 Lit to practice one's own things   ᶠ4:12 Or may live respectably   ᵍ4:12 Non-Christians   ʰ4:12 Or not need anything, or not be in need   ⁱ4:14 Or asleep in   ʲ4:14 those who have fallen asleep through Jesus = Christians who have died

---

4:1 walk and please God. Just as a spouse desires to please his or her mate, so the Christian's concern is how to please God.

4:3 sanctification. This is an act and a process of being set apart for God's use. The emphasis here is that Christians are not to passively wait for God to make them holy, but to pursue holiness in dependence upon the Spirit (Rom. 6:13; 8:13). **sexual immorality.** This term is an inclusive one for sexual sin—including fornication, adultery, prostitution, and homosexuality, all of which were routine realities in pagan life. New Christians from this environment did not automatically give up the sexual sins that were part of their previous life, but had to be instructed on the new way to live in Christ (1 Cor. 5:1-2; 6:9-18).

4:4 possess his own vessel. Paul insists on

sexual self-control in contrast to being controlled by lustful sexual impulses. He is saying that sexual activity must be only within marriage, and is to be carried out in a way that respects the dignity and worth of the woman and the man.

4:10 all the brothers in the entire region of Macedonia. At this time, churches had been established at least in Philippi and Beorea. **do so even more.** A Christian lifestyle grows out of a desire to please God and love others. Paul encourages these new believers to press on in that direction, unfolding the limitless possibilities within each directive.

4:13 asleep. This is simply a common metaphor for death and has no bearing on any doctrine of the intermediate state between the time of one's death and the resurrection of believers at Christ's return. **who have no**

hope. While Greek philosophy and some pagan cults speculated about the immortality of the soul and the afterlife, the rank and file among the people saw death as the end of everything.

4:14 we believe that Jesus died and rose again. This was probably a creedal statement Paul had passed on to this church earlier. He now draws out its implications for those who have died. **God will bring with Him those who have fallen asleep through Jesus.** Rather than being "left out" of the return of the Lord, those who have died in Christ will be the first to join the Lord in the air.

4:16 with a shout ... the archangel's voice ... the trumpet of God. These elements of a military advance are used throughout Scripture as a picture of the manifestation of

Heaven's Gonna Be a Blast!

1. Who do you look forward to seeing in heaven someday?
2. What question would you like to ask God when you get to heaven?

1 Thessalonians 4:13–5:11

3. How can we have hope when it comes to death (4:13-14)? What's the importance of Jesus' resurrection?
4. On a scale of 1 ("This can't be happening now!") to 10 ("Let's do it!"), how prepared are you if Christ returned right now?
5. What can you do to better prepare yourself for His return (5:6-10)? How can you help to prepare others?

---

from the Lord:[a] We who are still alive at the Lord's coming will certainly have no advantage over[b] those who have fallen asleep. [16] For the Lord Himself will descend from heaven with a shout,[c] with the archangel's voice, and with the trumpet of God, and the dead in Christ will rise first. [17] Then we who are still alive will be caught up together with them in the clouds to meet the Lord in the air; and so we will always be with the Lord. [18] Therefore encourage[d] one another with these words.

The Day of the Lord

5 About the times and the seasons: brothers, you do not need anything to be written to you. [2] For you yourselves know very well that the Day of the Lord will come just like a thief in the night. [3] When they say, "Peace and security," then sudden destruction comes on them, like labor pains on a pregnant woman, and they will not escape. [4] But you, brothers, are not in the dark, so that this day would overtake you like a thief.

[5] For you are all sons of light and sons of the day. We're not of the night or of darkness. [6] So then, we must not sleep, like the rest, but we must stay awake and be sober. [7] For those who sleep, sleep at night, and those who get drunk are drunk at night. [8] But since we are of the day, we must be sober and put on the armor of faith and love on our chests, and put on a helmet of the hope of salvation. [9] For God did not appoint us to wrath, but to obtain salvation through our Lord Jesus Christ, [10] who died for us, so that whether we are awake or •asleep, we will live together with Him. [11] Therefore encourage one another and build each other up as you are already doing.

God's Incredible Gifts

1. What people, things, and circumstances are you particularly thankful for now, and why?

1 Thessalonians 5:12-28

2. From this passage, what are the ways we should help one another, especially other Christians (vv. 14-15)?
3. What is the goal and hope of the Christian life (vv. 23-24)? What assurance do we have that we will receive these incredible gifts?
4. Which command from verses 16-22 will you work on this week? Give a specific example of what you will do.
5. God's gifts are so much better and lasting than the stuff of this life. Thank Him now for His incredible gifts!

Exhortations and Blessings

[12] Now we ask you, brothers, to give recognition to those who labor among you and lead you in the Lord and admonish you, [13] and to esteem them very highly in love because of their work. Be at peace among your-

---

[a]**4:15** Or *a word of the Lord*   [b]**4:15** Or *certainly not precede*   [c]**4:16** Or *command*   [d]**4:18** Or *comfort*

God's presence and glory when He comes to deliver His people and bring judgment upon their enemies (Ex. 19:13,16,19; Isa. 27:13; Zeph. 1:14-16; Matt. 24:31; 1 Cor. 15:52; Rev. 19:17).

4:17 we ... will be caught up together with them. When a royal figure came to a city, its inhabitants (or a delegation of them) went out of the city to greet this person and escort the royal procession into their town.

5:4 you, brothers, are not in the dark. The Apostle John as well as Paul often referred to people who lived with disregard to God as living in "darkness" (John 8:12; 2 Cor. 6:14; Eph. 6:12).

5:5 sons of light and sons of the day. In the Hebrew idiom, to be a "son of" someone or something meant to share in the charac-

teristics of that person or thing. Christians who believe in the One who is the "light of the world" share the characteristics of that light.

5:6 must not sleep. Continuing on with the metaphor of day and night, Christians, since they operate in "the day," must not "sleep" as are those who live in "the night." Whereas in 4:14, the metaphor of sleep meant death, here it refers to spiritual indifference and unawareness (Eph. 5:14).

5:7 those who get drunk. Paul is not talking about literal sobriety and drunkenness, but uses it as a metaphor of how the Christian life of purpose, awareness, and direction contrasts with the "worldly" life of excess, spiritual insensitivity, and folly.

5:8 put the armor of faith and love on our chests, and put on a helmet of the hope of

salvation. Elsewhere Paul uses other virtues to describe the various parts of the Christian's armor (Rom. 13:12; 2 Cor. 6:7; 10:4; Eph. 6:13-17). Here, faith, love, and hope are the primary pieces of the spiritual armor that Christians need in order to stand at watch for the Day of the Lord. The "hope of salvation" is not a wish, but a firm confidence and expectation that give courage in the face of struggle.

5:9 to obtain salvation. Salvation includes both the present experience of God's grace and the confident fulfillment of that grace in the future.

5:10 who died for us. The Christian's hope for life is rooted in Jesus' death on their behalf (Rom. 5:6-8; 2 Cor. 5:15; 1 Peter 2:21-24). **whether we are awake or asleep.** This most likely refers to the issue of whether we

selves. [14] And we exhort you, brothers: warn those who are lazy,[a] comfort the discouraged, help the weak, be patient with everyone. [15] See to it that no one repays evil for evil to anyone, but always pursue what is good for one another and for all.

[16] Rejoice always!

[17] Pray constantly.

[18] Give thanks in everything,
for this is God's will for you in Christ Jesus.

[19] Don't stifle the Spirit.

[20] Don't despise prophecies,

[21] but test all things.
Hold on to what is good.

[22] Stay away from every form of evil.

[23] Now may the God of peace Himself sanctify you completely. And may your spirit, soul, and body be kept sound and blameless for the coming of our Lord Jesus Christ. [24] He who calls you is faithful, who also will do it. [25] Brothers, pray for us also. [26] Greet all the brothers with a holy kiss. [27] I charge you by the Lord that this letter be read to all the brothers. [28] May the grace of our Lord Jesus Christ be with you!

---

[a] **5:14** Or who are disorderly, or who are undisciplined

---

are alive or dead at the time of Christ's coming.

5:14 lazy. Second Thessalonians 3:6-15 is a strong admonition against idleness that stemmed from a "watching" for the Lord's return, and which precluded doing anything else. Such people not only failed to pull their own weight, but became a nuisance and weight upon others.

5:15 See to it that no one repays evil for evil. The temptation to retaliate against persecution would have been strong, but is admonished in Scripture (Prov. 25:21; Matt. 5:43-44; Rom. 12:17-20; 1 Peter 3:9).

5:16 Rejoice always! Joy springs not from circumstances, but from the Holy Spirit giving believers a confidence of God's presence no matter what happens (Rom. 5:3-5; 2 Cor. 6:10; Gal. 5:22-23; Phil. 4:4; Col. 1:24).

5:17 Pray constantly. This does not mean one is literally to pray all the time in exclusion of other activities, but that one continually approaches life with the spirit of prayer; that is, with a sense of dependency upon God and thankfulness to Him.

5:18 Give thanks in everything. One has the confidence that all things are under the sovereign hand of God. **this is God's will.** God's will is not simply to get believers to do what is right, but to produce a spirit of joy, dependence, and thankfulness within them.

5:19 Don't stifle the Spirit. Fire is often used as an image of the Holy Spirit (Matt. 3:11; Acts 2:3). This "fire" can be dampened by disobedience (Eph. 4:30).

5:20 Don't despise prophecies. Whereas in Corinth the problem was an undiscerning obsession with spiritual gifts, perhaps here the problem was an undiscerning repression of them. Paul advocates a discerning acceptance instead (v. 21). It may be that "prophecies" about the Lord's return caused some of the anxiety in this church about this topic.

5:26 a holy kiss. Kissing on the cheek was a common greeting in this culture, and still is in many Mediterranean and Middle Eastern countries. This kiss is similar to a handshake in Western cultures.

INTRODUCTION TO
2 THESSALONIANS

AUTHOR

The Apostle Paul wrote 2 Thessalonians.

DATE

Paul probably wrote 2 Thessalonians around A.D. 51; 1 and 2 Thessalonians or Galatians are the earliest letters of Paul.

THEME

Living in the light of the coming of Christ.

HISTORICAL BACKGROUND

See the Introduction to 1 Thessalonians.

CHARACTERISTICS

First and Second Thessalonians are very much alike. In fact, 2 Thessalonians covers almost the same content as 1 Thessalonians. There is thanksgiving for the faith and love of the Thessalonians, encouragement to them in the midst of their persecution, teaching about the second coming, and a warning against idleness. Second Thessalonians was probably written within months, if not weeks, of 1 Thessalonians. Why was it necessary?

Perhaps Paul's first letter to these young, untaught Christians produced a serious misunderstanding that necessitated a second, clarifying letter. Specifically, his teaching that "the day of the Lord will come just like a thief in the night" (1 Thess. 5:2) may have encouraged people to abandon normal pursuits to prepare for the second coming. Thus, he wrote 2 Thessalonians 2:1-12, outlining the events that must take place *prior* to the return of Christ. "The second coming is imminent," he seems to be saying, "but not so imminent that you have to stop everything else." Then he goes on to reiterate what he said in his earlier letter: Stand firm and do not be idle.

In fact, 1 and 2 Thessalonians complement one another concerning the second coming. Paul's teaching in 1 Thessalonians is mainly on a personal level and it is given in response to questions about the lot of believers who have died before the second coming. In 2 Thessalonians believers are given further instructions on how they may be prepared for the great day. The ungodly will be taken by surprise, but believers will be awake and prepared for Christ's return.

PASSAGES FOR
TOPICAL GROUP STUDY

3:6-15 ... MANAGING OUR TIME .... Who's Responsible

PASSAGES FOR
GENERAL GROUP STUDY

1:1-12 .... Worthy of God's Kingdom

2:1-17 .... The Man of Lawlessness

Greeting

1 Paul, Silvanus,[a] and Timothy:
To the church of the Thessalonians in God our Father and the Lord Jesus Christ.
[2] Grace to you and peace from God our Father and the Lord Jesus Christ.

Worthy of God's Kingdom

1. What have your parents done right in raising you? What rewards and punishments worked best?

2 Thessalonians 1:1-12

2. What has happened to this church since Paul wrote 1 Thessalonians (v. 4)? How has persecution affected them?
3. Why is God waiting until the second coming to punish these persecutors? Who benefits from this delayed justice? How?
4. What quality do you think Paul admires most in these Christians?
5. Are your faith and endurance "worthy of God's Kingdom" right now? Why or why not?

God's Judgment and Glory

[3] We must always thank God for you, brothers, which is fitting, since your faith is flourishing, and the love of every one of you for one another is increasing. [4] Therefore we ourselves boast about you among God's churches—about your endurance and faith in all the persecutions and afflictions you endure. [5] It is a clear evidence of God's righteous judgment that you will be counted worthy of God's kingdom, for which you also are suffering, [6] since it is righteous for God to repay with affliction those who afflict you, [7] and ⌊to reward⌋ with rest you who are afflicted, along with us. ⌊This will

take place⌋ at the revelation of the Lord Jesus from heaven with His powerful angels, [8] taking vengeance with flaming fire on those who don't know God and on those who don't obey the gospel of our Lord Jesus. [9] These will pay the penalty of everlasting destruction, away from the Lord's presence and from His glorious strength, [10] in that day when He comes to be glorified by His saints and to be admired by all those who have believed, because our testimony among you was believed. [11] And in view of this, we always pray for you that our God will consider you worthy of His calling, and will, by His power, fulfill every desire for goodness and the work of faith, [12] so that the name of our Lord Jesus will be glorified by you, and you by Him, according to the grace of our God and the Lord Jesus Christ.

The Man of Lawlessness

1. Who is the worst bad guy or nasty woman that you've seen on TV or in the movies?

2 Thessalonians 2:1-17

2. What must have been happening in Thessalonica to lead Paul to write this passage?
3. What is God's ultimate purpose in allowing the "man of lawlessness" to deceive people? What signs will mark his appearing?
4. How and why will God save His people (vv. 13-14)? In response to God's initiative and Paul's ministry, what are the people to do?
5. When is it difficult for you to "stand firm" (v. 15)? How does knowing the end of the story encourage you?

The Man of Lawlessness

2 Now concerning the coming of our Lord Jesus Christ and our being gathered to Him: we ask

---

[a] **1:1** Or *Silas*; see Ac 15:22–32; 16:19–40; 17:1–16

1:1 Silvanus. Silvanus (also called Silas), was a representative of the Jerusalem church to the Christians at Antioch (Acts 15:22). He accompanied Paul on his second missionary journey. Silvanus is mentioned again in 1 Peter 5:12 as the one who penned that letter under the authority of the Apostle Peter. **church.** In the New Testament, "church" can refer either to the whole, worldwide Christian community (1 Cor. 10:32; Col. 1:18), or a gathering of believers that met in a house (Rom. 16:5), or all such gatherings within a given locality (Rom. 16:1; 1 Cor. 1:2). It is unlikely that this community had the time to develop a formal organizational structure. **Thessalonians.** Thessalonica was an important city in northern Greece, the capital of the province of Macedonia. Wealth, trade, and news flowed freely through this city between Rome on the west and Asia Minor on the east. **from God our**

Father and the Lord Jesus Christ. The terms "Father" and "Lord" highlight the relationship of God and Jesus to the believer.

1:3-10 persecutions and afflictions. This church is facing persecution and is unsure how to interpret its meaning: Is it a sign of God's disfavor? Or is it a sign of the nearness of the return of the Lord? Paul reassures them that their response to the suffering is notable, and comforts them with the thought that the Lord will one day make right all the wrongs and provide the strength to endure.

1:5 a clear evidence. Their faithfulness in suffering for Christ and Paul's sharing of it with others is an evidence of their new life in Christ.

1:7-8 the Lord Jesus. Paul uses this term more in the Thessalonian letters than he

does elsewhere. It stresses the royal authority of Jesus as the true King. It was this teaching that caused the original trouble in Thessalonica (Paul's opponents claimed he was proclaiming a rival king to Caesar—Acts 17:7) and may still have been the source of tension. **with His powerful angels ... with flaming fire.** Fire and angels are commonly associated with God's presence with His people in the Old Testament.

1:9 pay the penalty of everlasting destruction. *Paying the penalty* carries the sense of justice being done rather than that of vengeance. *Everlasting destruction* doesn't mean annihilation but rather eternal separation from God.

2:1-12 This passage, the heart of the letter, is meant to correct some erroneous ideas that had developed about the return of the Lord.

you, brothers, [2] not to be easily upset in mind or troubled, either by a spirit or by a message or by a letter as if from us, alleging that the Day of the Lord[a] has come. [3] Don't let anyone deceive you in any way. For ⌊that day⌋ will not come unless the apostasy[b] comes first and the man of lawlessness[c] is revealed, the son of destruction. [4] He opposes and exalts himself above every so-called god or object of worship, so that he sits[d] in God's sanctuary,[e] publicizing that he himself is God.

[5] Don't you remember that when I was still with you I told you about this? [6] And you know what currently restrains ⌊him⌋, so that he will be revealed in his time. [7] For the •mystery of lawlessness is already at work; but the one now restraining will do so until he is out of the way, [8] and then the lawless one will be revealed. The Lord Jesus will destroy him with the breath of His mouth and will bring him to nothing with the brightness of His coming. [9] The coming ⌊of the lawless one⌋ is based on Satan's working, with all kinds of false miracles, signs, and wonders, [10] and with every unrighteous deception among those who are perishing. ⌊They perish⌋ because they did not accept the love of the truth in order to be saved. [11] For this reason God sends them a strong delusion so that they will believe what is false, [12] so that all will be condemned—those who did not believe the truth but enjoyed unrighteousness.

Stand Firm

[13] But we must always thank God for you, brothers loved by the Lord, because from the beginning[f] God has chosen you for salvation through sanctification by the Spirit and through belief in the truth. [14] He called you to this through our gospel, so that you might obtain the glory of our Lord Jesus Christ. [15] Therefore, brothers, stand firm and hold to the traditions you were taught, either by our message or by our letter.

[16] May our Lord Jesus Christ Himself and God our Father, who has loved us and given us eternal encouragement and good hope by grace, [17] encourage your hearts and strengthen you in every good work and word.

Pray for Us

3 Finally, pray for us, brothers, that the Lord's message may spread rapidly and be honored, just as it was with you, [2] and that we may be delivered from wicked and evil men, for not all have faith. [3] But the Lord is faithful; He will strengthen and guard you from the evil one. [4] We have confidence in the Lord about you, that you are doing and will do what we command. [5] May the Lord direct your hearts to God's love and Christ's endurance.

Who's Responsible?

1. What was your first paying job?
2. How do you typically spend your free time?

2 Thessalonians 3:6-15

3. How does the "rule" in verse 10 apply to Christians today?
4. Why is the way we manage our time and energies important to God, according to this passage?
5. In light of the command in verse 6, what changes, if any, do you need to make regarding the people you hang out?
6. What's one thing you would like to change this week in how you spend your time?

Warning against Irresponsible Behavior

[6] Now we command you, brothers, in the name of our Lord Jesus Christ, to keep away from every brother who •walks irresponsibly and not according to the tradition received from us. [7] For you yourselves know how you must imitate us: we were not irresponsible among you; [8] we did not eat anyone's bread free of charge;

---

[a]**2:2** Other mss read *Christ* [b]**2:3** Or *rebellion* [c]**2:3** Other mss read *man of sin* [d]**2:4** Other mss add *as God* [e]**2:4** Or *temple* [f]**2:13** Other mss read *because as a firstfruit*

2:2 by a spirit ... message ... letter as if from us. The false teaching was being supported by either a mistaken view of what Paul had written or preached, or by a forged letter that distorted his views. **The Day of the Lord has come.** The nature of the false teaching here is not clear, but it apparently led some people to think the presence (*parousia*) of the Lord had already come in all its fullness. This led them to overlook the mundane issues of being a disciple, things such as work (3:6-15).

2:3 apostasy ... man of lawlessness. Other passages foresee a time when the powers of evil will rise up (Matt. 24; 1 Tim. 4:1-3), and this will be centered on the rise of an antichrist (1 John 4:3), or false prophets (Matt. 24:5; Rev. 16:13).

2:4 he sits in God's sanctuary. Paul's description of this figure here is steeped in Old Testament apocalyptic imagery (Ezek. 28:2; Dan. 7:25; 8:9-12; 11:36-37; Zech. 3:1). The "man of lawlessness" sets himself in total opposition to God by claiming the prerogatives of God (Mark 13:14).

2:6-7 you know what currently restrains him ... the one now restraining. God restrains sin and the man of lawlessness through the work of the Holy Spirit.

2:11 God sends them a strong delusion. Because people refuse to embrace the gospel, God acts in such a way as to confirm their disbelief. First Kings 22:23 and Ezekiel 14:9 tell of God sending a "lying spirit" into so-called prophets who only served to confirm the rebellion that was in the hearts of their listeners.

2:13 from the beginning God has chosen you. Paul often refers to God's initiative in bringing people to salvation as a way of reassuring Christians in times of suffering.

3:2 wicked and evil men. The Thessalonians would be well aware of the opposition that Paul encountered time and again, since he met with such resistance in their own city (Acts 17:1-9; 1 Thess. 2:1-2). In Corinth, where Paul was living when he wrote this letter, he faced such strong resistance that he needed a special word from the Lord to keep on (Acts 18:9). The news of their faithfulness was an encouragement (1 Thess. 3:7).

3:5 Christ's endurance. The prayer is that the Thessalonians realize the fullness of God's love for them so that they draw cour-

instead, we labored and toiled, working night and day, so that we would not be a burden to any of you. [9] It is not that we don't have the right ⌊to support⌋, but we did it to make ourselves an example to you so that you would imitate us. [10] In fact, when we were with you, this is what we commanded you: "If anyone isn't willing to work, he should not eat." [11] For we hear that there are some among you who walk irresponsibly, not working at all, but interfering with the work ⌊of others⌋. [12] Now we command and exhort such people, by the Lord Jesus Christ, that quietly working, they may eat their own bread.[a]

[13] Brothers, do not grow weary in doing good. [14] And if anyone does not obey our instruction in this letter, take note of that person; don't associate with him, so that he may be ashamed. [15] Yet don't treat him as an enemy, but warn him as a brother.

Final Greetings

[16] May the Lord of peace Himself give you peace always in every way. The Lord be with all of you. [17] This greeting is in my own hand—Paul. This is a sign in every letter; this is how I write. [18] The grace of our Lord Jesus Christ be with all of you.

---

[a] 3:12 Or food

---

age from Christ's perseverance as a model for their own.

3:6 keep away from every brother who walks irresponsibly. While these people are not to be considered as enemies of the gospel (v. 15), they need to be disciplined so they will give up their mistaken practice. The purpose of such discipline is a "tough love" approach to correcting a potentially serious problem, yet it is to be carried out in a way that communicates that the "family ties" are still strong.

3:11 not working at all, but interfering with the work of others. These people are bothering others with their false notions, probably trying to convince them to wait for

the Day of the Lord with them. Such action would also give a negative impression of the Christian community to outsiders, as it would appear that they are lazy and content to live off the income of others.

3:12 quietly working. Throughout church history there have been groups that have set the date for the return of the Lord, and responded by abandoning the normal pursuits of life in a feverish state of religious excitement. The end result is disenchantment and a discrediting of the gospel. In contrast, Paul wants them to live in peace, providing for their own needs (1 Thess. 4:11-12).

3:16 May the Lord of peace Himself give you peace always in every way. At times,

"peace" is used as a summary of all the benefits that Christ gives to His people (John 20:21,26; Rom. 15:33; Phil. 4:9). Paul prays that peace would mark their lives both personally and as a church.

3:17 This greeting is in my own hand—Paul. Paul typically used a secretary to write his letters. Tertius wrote Romans (Rom. 16:22). Tychicus, who delivered the letters of Ephesians and Colossians, may have penned those as well, and Silvanus (1 Peter 5:12) may have written the Thessalonian letters. Sometimes Paul calls attention to the fact that he has actually penned the final greeting (1 Cor. 16:21; Gal. 6:11), which may be to assure the recipients of the authenticity of the letter that he is sending them.

INTRODUCTION TO
1 TIMOTHY

PERSONAL READING PLAN

☐ 1 Timothy 1:1-2:15

☐ 1 Timothy 3:1-4:16

☐ 1 Timothy 5:1-6:2

☐ 1 Timothy 6:3-21

AUTHOR

The Apostle Paul was most likely the author of 1 Timothy. However, based on considerations of vocabulary and style, the Pauline authorship of the Pastoral Epistles (1 and 2 Timothy, and Titus) has been questioned by some scholars.

DATE

First Timothy was written about A.D. 63-65.

THEME

A faithful ministry.

HISTORICAL BACKGROUND

When Paul first met Timothy, he was living at Lystra in the Roman province of Galatia (modern Turkey). Timothy was the child of a mixed marriage. His father was a Gentile and his mother was Jewish (Acts 16:1). Timothy, along with his mother Eunice and his grandmother Lois, was probably converted during Paul's first missionary journey (Acts 14:8-25; compare 2 Tim. 3:10-11). By the time of Paul's second visit to the area a year or two later, Timothy had matured so quickly that the local church recommended Timothy to Paul as a helpful traveling companion (Acts 16:2). However, Paul decided that Timothy must be circumcised first to legitimize him in the eyes of Paul's Jewish critics. Without circumcision, they would have considered him a Gentile.

From this point on, Timothy works alongside Paul (Rom. 16:21; 1 Cor. 16:10; Phil. 2:22; 1 Thess. 3:2). He collaborated in the writing of six of Paul's letters (1 and 2 Thess., 2 Cor., Phil., Col. and Philem.). He was Paul's trusted representative on three missions before this one in Ephesus (to Thessalonica around A.D. 50; to Corinth

between A.D. 53 and 54; and to Philippi around A.D. 60-62).

Timothy was more than a colleague of Paul's. Paul called him "my beloved and faithful child in the Lord" (1 Cor. 4:17). In Philippians 2:20-22, the aging apostle says: "or I have no one else like-minded ... But you know his proven character, because he has served with me in the gospel ministry like a son with a father."

AUDIENCE

The three so-called Pastoral Epistles (plus Philemon) are set apart from the other letters written by Paul; they are addressed to persons, not churches. In 1 Timothy, Paul wrote his instructions to the church via Timothy, since the local church leadership was itself the problem. There are few personal remarks in 1 Timothy, and all of these are directed toward Timothy's commission to restore proper order in the church (see 1:18-19; 4:6-16; 6:11-21).

PURPOSE

Paul tells us why he wrote 1 Timothy: "As I urged you when I went to Macedonia, remain in Ephesus so that you may command certain people not to teach other doctrine (1:3).

"I write these things to you, hoping to come to you soon. But if I should be delayed, [I have written] so that you will know how people ought to act in God's household, which is the church of the living God, the pillar and foundation of the truth." (3:14-15).

Timothy had been left in Ephesus to prevent those who had "suffered the shipwreck of their faith" (1:19) from corrupting the rest of the church (see 2 Tim. 2:17-18). He was Paul's apos-

tolic delegate, taking temporary charge of the Ephesian church during the crises it was facing.

THE FALSE TEACHERS

Who were these false teachers who had so upset the Ephesian church? The best guess is that they were *elders* of that church! It is clear that the teaching in Ephesians was done by the elders (3:2; 5:17). Furthermore, Paul devotes considerable space to outlining qualifications for leaders in the church. These qualifications contrast sharply with what he says about the false teachers. For example, the false teachers "forbid marriage" (4:3). Paul says that an overseer (elder), in contrast, "must be ... the husband of but one wife" and he "manages his own household competently" (3:2,4-5; see also 3:12). The false teachers "imagine that godliness is a way to material gain" (6:5), whereas an elder must "not greedy" (3:3). In other words, Paul is saying: "Here is what true elders should be like, in contrast to your erring elders." Finally in 5:17-25, he outlines the process of selection and discipline of elders "who sin" (5:20).

Paul had a sense that this might happen in Ephesus. In his farewell address he said, "Even from your own number men will arise and distort the truth in order to draw away disciples after them" (Acts 20:30).

From various references (2:9-15; 5:11-15; 2 Tim. 3:6-7), it appears that these false teachers were listened to, supported and encouraged by some of the women in the church, especially younger widows. Also, it is likely that the church in Ephesus was not a single large body that met together on Sunday. Rather, it consisted of a number of house churches, some of which had been taken over by the false teachers.

THE NATURE OF THE FALSE TEACHING

Since we have only Paul's response to the problem, we are forced to figure out the nature of the false teaching. From the text, it appears that the false teachers were involved in questionable speculation rather than the teaching of accepted Christian doctrine. Furthermore, the teachers were proud, arrogant, argumentative, and greedy. They used religion to make money and gain power. Their false teaching was connected with the Old Testament, but it also had an aspect of self-denial and a strong Greek element. It sounds much like the false teaching in the Lycus Valley churches (see the Introduction to Colossians).

PASSAGES FOR TOPICAL GROUP STUDY

PASSAGES FOR GENERAL GROUP STUDY

Greeting

1 Paul, an apostle of Christ Jesus according to the command of God our Savior and of Christ Jesus, our hope:

² To Timothy, my true child in the faith.

Grace, mercy, and peace from God the^a Father and Christ Jesus our Lord.

Watch Out for False Teachers!

1. What is your favorite topic to debate? How often do you win?

1 Timothy 1:1-11

2. Why does Paul consider Timothy to be his "true child in the faith" (v. 2)?
3. What kind of problem is Timothy facing? What do you think is motivating the people causing the problem (vv. 4,7)?
4. What is the major contrast in motive between Paul and Timothy and these false teachers (v. 5)?
5. What does this passage teach you regarding the proper response to false teachers? How should your response be different in different situations, i.e., school vs. church?

False Doctrine and Misuse of the Law

³ As I urged you when I went to Macedonia, remain in Ephesus so that you may command certain people not to teach other doctrine ⁴ or to pay attention to myths and endless genealogies. These promote empty speculations rather than God's plan, which operates by faith. ⁵ Now the goal of our instruction is love from a pure heart, a good conscience, and a sincere faith. ⁶ Some have deviated from these and turned aside to fruitless discussion. ⁷ They want to be teachers of the law, although they don't understand what they are say-

ing or what they are insisting on. ⁸ Now we know that the law is good, provided one uses it legitimately. ⁹ We know that the law is not meant for a righteous person, but for the lawless and rebellious, for the ungodly and sinful, for the unholy and irreverent, for those who kill their fathers and mothers, for murderers, ¹⁰ for the sexually immoral and homosexuals, for kidnappers, liars, perjurers, and for whatever else is contrary to the sound teaching ¹¹ based on the glorious gospel of the blessed God that was entrusted to me.

Never Beyond God's Love

1. What is the worst thing you've gotten busted for by your parents or a teacher? What did you learn from it?
2. Who has shown you the most patience when you've failed?

1 Timothy 1:12-20

3. Why did Jesus come to this world (v. 15)? Why was Paul reminding Timothy about this belief?
4. What was causing Paul to talk about himself as he does in verses 13 and 15? Do you think it hurt the way the church thought about him as their leader, and why?
5. How can you let God use your failures the way He used Paul's (v. 16)?

Paul's Testimony

¹² I give thanks to Christ Jesus our Lord, who has strengthened me, because He considered me faithful, appointing me to the ministry— ¹³ one who was formerly a blasphemer, a persecutor, and an arrogant man. Since it was out of ignorance that I had acted in unbelief, I received mercy, ¹⁴ and the grace of our Lord overflowed, along with the faith and love that are in Christ

---

^a**1:2** Other mss read *our*

1:1 Paul, an apostle. When Paul uses the designation "an apostle" in his salutation, it is because his authority is in question, or because he has an "official" word for the recipients of the letter

1:3 remain in Ephesus. Paul had to go on to Macedonia, leaving Timothy behind in Ephesus. As he indicates in 3:15, the purpose of this letter is to instruct Timothy in his role while there, in case Paul is delayed in returning to Ephesus (which according to 2 Timothy is exactly what happened). **Ephesus.** The capital of the Roman Province of Asia. Ephesus was one of the largest and most impressive cities in the ancient world. The church in Ephesus apparently flourished. It was not a single congregation, but rather a collection of house churches (1 Cor. 16:19). Paul's ministry in Ephesus was strategic in the spread of

Christianity to the entire province of Asia (Acts 19:10).

1:10 sexually immoral and homosexuals. The seventh commandment was interpreted by the Jewish teachers (as well as Christian orthodoxy) to refer to all types of sexual sin.

1:13 formerly. Paul is utterly amazed that he of all people was chosen for this high calling, given his past record. **blasphemer.** Paul had denied Christ and tried to force others to do the same (Acts 26:11). **out of ignorance ... in unbelief.** Paul is clearly not saying that he had received mercy because he was without guilt. All he is saying is that he acted "unintentionally" instead of "defiantly," using a common Old Testament distinction (Num. 15:22-31, Luke 23:34).

1:20 Hymenaeus and Alexander. Hyme-

naeus is mentioned again in 2 Timothy 2:17 (along with Philetus) as one who taught that the resurrection was already past. An Alexander (a coppersmith) is also mentioned in 2 Timothy 4:14-15 as having done great harm to Paul. **delivered them to Satan.** Paul excommunicated them from the church; i.e., they were expelled from the fellowship of other followers of Christ and sent back into the world, which is Satan's realm (1 Cor. 5:5).

2:9 good sense. Also translated "propriety." This is the central issue for Paul in this area (vv. 10,15). He is concerned that the women in the church live in a way that is considered decent and modest by the culture.

2:12 I do not allow. The issue of the role of women in the church is complex, and often causes disagreements among believers. Scripture affirms that women functioned in

Jesus. [15] This saying is trustworthy and deserving of full acceptance: "Christ Jesus came into the world to save sinners"—and I am the worst of them. [16] But I received mercy because of this, so that in me, the worst ⌊of them⌋, Christ Jesus might demonstrate the utmost patience as an example to those who would believe in Him for eternal life. [17] Now to the King eternal, immortal, invisible, the only[a] God, be honor and glory forever and ever. •Amen.

Engage in Battle

[18] Timothy, my child, I am giving you this instruction in keeping with the prophecies previously made about you, so that by them you may strongly engage in battle, [19] having faith and a good conscience. Some have rejected these and have suffered the shipwreck of their faith. [20] Hymenaeus and Alexander are among them, and I have delivered them to Satan, so that they may be taught not to blaspheme.

Instructions on Prayer

2 First of all, then, I urge that petitions, prayers, intercessions, and thanksgivings be made for everyone, [2] for kings and all those who are in authority, so that we may lead a tranquil and quiet life in all godliness and dignity. [3] This is good, and it pleases God our Savior, [4] who wants everyone to be saved and to come to the knowledge of the truth.

[5] For there is one God
and one mediator between God and man,
a man, Christ Jesus,
[6] who gave Himself—a ransom for all,
a testimony at the proper time.

[7] For this I was appointed a herald, an apostle (I am telling the truth;[b] I am not lying), and a teacher of the Gentiles in faith and truth.

Instructions to Men and Women

[8] Therefore I want the men in every place to pray, lifting up holy hands without anger or argument. [9] Also, the women are to dress themselves in modest clothing, with decency and good sense; not with elaborate hairstyles, gold, pearls, or expensive apparel, [10] but with good works, as is proper for women who affirm that they worship God. [11] A woman should learn in silence with full submission. [12] I do not allow a woman to teach or to have authority over a man; instead, she is to be silent. [13] For Adam was created first, then Eve. [14] And Adam was not deceived, but the woman was deceived and transgressed. [15] But she will be saved through childbearing, if she continues[c] in faith, love, and holiness, with good sense.

Qualifications of Church Leaders

3 This saying is trustworthy:[d] "If anyone aspires to be an •overseer, he desires a noble work." [2] An overseer, therefore, must be above reproach, the husband of one wife, self-controlled, sensible, respectable, hospitable, an able teacher,[e] [3] not addicted to

[a]**1:17** Other mss add *wise* [b]**2:7** Other mss add *in Christ* [c]**2:15** Lit *if they continue* [d]**3:1** *This saying is trustworthy* could refer to 1 Tm 2:15. [e]**3:2** Or *hospitable, skillful in teaching*

the early church with service, influence, leadership, and teaching. Mark's mother Mary and Lydia of Thyatira opened their homes for meetings of believers and practiced hospitality (Acts 12:12; 16:14-15). Priscilla, with here husband Aquila instructed Apollos in individual ministry (Acts 18:26). Women offered themselves in special ministries to Jesus (John 12:1-11). Paul obviously did not feel that women could not engage in ministry, as evidenced by his statements in Romans 16:1-3 and Philippians 4:2-3. He encouraged women to work within the divinely given framework based on the natural order of creation and appropriateness of function. He commended women for learning (2:11) but didn't allow women to teach men or rule over men—and that within two spheres, the home and church.

3:1 overseer. Sometimes translated "bishop." The words "overseer" and "elder" were used interchangeably.

3:2 above reproach. Paul begins with an all-encompassing category: there should be no obvious defect in the character of the overseer that would cause people to question the appointment. **husband of one wife.** Literally, "a one-woman man." Paul could mean four things by this phrase. First, that church leaders must be married, in contrast to the false teachers who forbade marriage. Second, that polygamy was forbidden. Third, that second marriages were forbidden whether due to divorce or death of one's spouse. (Yet, he gives in 5:14 what amounts almost to a "command" to young widows to remarry.) Fourth, the most likely

meaning, that sexual faithfulness to one's spouse was demanded; that is, the married life of the overseer must be exemplary—in contrast to the widespread infidelity of that day. **sensible.** Temperate; free from excesses. **self-controlled/respectable.** These companion terms were considered in Greek literature to be great virtues. If people are self-controlled in their outer conduct, it is because they are respectable in their inner lives. **hospitable.** Overseers must be willing to open up their homes to guests. It was a common practice in the first century to offer hospitality to travelers since the inns were notorious for dirtiness and immorality, not to mention expense (5:10; Rom. 12:13; 1 Pet. 4:9). **an able teacher.** This is the one quality that implies a function. Paul says more about this in 5:17.

Stepping Up to Lead

1. When have you served as a leader (in school, athletics, a club, a job)? What did you enjoy about it?

1 Timothy 3:1-16

2. Why is this list of qualifications for leadership focused on the outward, as well as on inward character traits? How does this list line up with your idea of a good leader?

3. Verse 8 says leaders in the church must be "worthy of respect" and verse 10 says they must be "tested" before they can lead. In what areas do you need to step up so you can become a strong leader?

4. What can you do to prepare yourself to be a leader in God's work—both for the future and right now?

wine, not a bully but gentle, not quarrelsome, not greedy— 4 one who manages his own household competently, having his children under control with all dignity. 5 (If anyone does not know how to manage his own household, how will he take care of God's church?) 6 He must not be a new convert, or he might become conceited and fall into the condemnation of the Devil. 7 Furthermore, he must have a good reputation among outsiders, so that he does not fall into disgrace and the Devil's trap.

8 Deacons, likewise, should be worthy of respect, not hypocritical, not drinking a lot of wine, not greedy for money, 9 holding the •mystery of the faith with a clear conscience. 10 And they must also be tested first; if they prove blameless, then they can serve as deacons. 11 Wives, too, must be worthy of respect, not slanderers, self-controlled, faithful in everything. 12 Deacons must be husbands of one wife, managing their children and their own households competently. 13 For those

a**3:16** Other mss read *God*

who have served well as deacons acquire a good standing for themselves, and great boldness in the faith that is in Christ Jesus.

The Mystery of Godliness

14 I write these things to you, hoping to come to you soon. 15 But if I should be delayed, ⌊I have written⌋ so that you will know how people ought to act in God's household, which is the church of the living God, the pillar and foundation of the truth. 16 And most certainly, the mystery of godliness is great:

> Hea was manifested in the flesh,
> justified in the Spirit,
> seen by angels,
> preached among the Gentiles,
> believed on in the world,
> taken up in glory.

Demonic Influence

4 Now the Spirit explicitly says that in the latter times some will depart from the faith, paying attention to deceitful spirits and the teachings of demons, 2 through the hypocrisy of liars whose consciences are seared. 3 They forbid marriage and demand abstinence from foods that God created to be received with gratitude by those who believe and know the truth. 4 For everything created by God is good, and nothing should be rejected if it is received with thanksgiving, 5 since it is sanctified by the word of God and by prayer.

A Good Servant of Jesus Christ

6 If you point these things out to the brothers, you will be a good servant of Christ Jesus, nourished by the words of the faith and of the good teaching that you have followed. 7 But have nothing to do with irreverent and silly myths. Rather, train yourself in godliness, 8 for,

> the training of the body has a limited benefit,
> but godliness is beneficial in every way,
> since it holds promise for the present life
> and also for the life to come.

3:3 not addicted to wine. Paul is not forbidding all drinking of wine (which was widely used in his time, due to poor water supplies), but he is forbidding over-indulgence. **not a bully but gentle.** "Not a bully" means literally "not a giver of blows." "Gentle" refers to those who do not seek to apply the letter of the law in cases where to do so would bring injustice.

3:6 new convert. It is a temptation for a church to unwisely put into office people of worldly standing and influence who have been recently converted.

3:8 Deacons. Paul often describes himself and others as a *diakonos* ("deacon"), a word also translated as "servant" or "minister."

4:1 the Spirit explicitly says. Paul does not identify the specific prophecy he has in

mind. However, the idea that there will be apostasy in the last days is found at other places in Scripture (Mark 13:22; 2 Tim. 3:1-5). **deceitful spirits and ... demons.** This is the real source of the false doctrine. Satan (with his minions) is behind the chaos in the Ephesian church as he has been in other churches (2 Cor. 2:11).

4:2 consciences are seared. Their moral judgment has been cauterized so that they are no longer able to distinguish between truth and falsehood.

4:3 They forbid marriage. Paul identifies two specific errors in their teaching. They were saying that people ought not to get married, and that they should not eat certain foods.

4:4 everything created by God is good.

This is the theological basis on which Paul says what he does about food (v. 3).

4:6 point these things out. Paul's gentle tone is evident right from the beginning. He does not instruct Timothy to "order" or "command" the brothers and sisters in the church. What he is to do is more akin to "suggesting" and "persuading" than it is to "instructing."

4:7 train yourself in godliness. In contrast to the unchristian asceticism (v. 3), Paul now proposes a genuinely Christian form of self-discipline.

4:8 training of the body. While affirming the value of physical exercise, Paul's real interest is in spiritual exercise ("godliness"). **promise for the present life and also for the life to come.** The "life" Paul refers to is

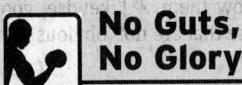

No Guts, No Glory

1. How often do you exercise? Are you in better physical or spiritual shape?
2. What is one bad habit you would like to break? What healthy habit would you like to start?

1 Timothy 4:1-16

3. What are some parallels between physical training and spiritual training (v. 8)? Why is training in godliness even more important than physical training alone?
4. When have you felt ignored or looked down on because you are young? How can you still influence others for Christ (v.12)?
5. What gifts (capacity for serving in His work) do you feel God has given you? How can you more fully use these gifts to please God?

Lending a Helping Hand

1. What kind of human suffering is hardest for you to look at? When have you been extremely moved to want to help?

1 Timothy 5:1-6:2

2. What possible abuses of care for the needy does Paul imply in verses 3-15? Is a different response to each person in need appropriate in today's world as well?
3. What should be the Christian's/church's response to the welfare issue?
4. According to Paul, how are we to treat our bosses or authorities (masters in 6:1-2)? Why is this important?
5. Who in your church needs some help that you or your group can provide?

⁹This saying is trustworthy and deserves full acceptance. ¹⁰In fact, we labor and strive[a] for this, because we have put our hope in the living God, who is the Savior of everyone, especially of those who believe.

Instructions for Ministry

¹¹Command and teach these things. ¹²No one should despise your youth; instead, you should be an example to the believers in speech, in conduct, in love,[b] in faith, in purity. ¹³Until I come, give your attention to public reading, exhortation, and teaching. ¹⁴Do not neglect the gift that is in you; it was given to you through prophecy, with the laying on of hands by the council of elders. ¹⁵Practice these things; be committed to them, so that your progress may be evident to all. ¹⁶Be conscientious about yourself and your teaching; persevere in these things, for by doing this you will save both yourself and your hearers.

5 Do not rebuke an older man, but exhort him as a father, younger men as brothers, ²older women as mothers, and with all propriety, the younger women as sisters.

The Support of Widows

³Support[c] widows who are genuinely widows. ⁴But if any widow has children or grandchildren, they should learn to practice their religion toward their own family first and to repay their parents, for this pleases God. ⁵The real widow, left all alone, has put her hope in God and continues night and day in her petitions and prayers; ⁶however, she who is self-indulgent is dead even while she lives. ⁷Command this, so that they won't be blamed. ⁸Now if anyone does not provide for his own relatives, and especially for his household, he has denied the faith and is worse than an unbeliever.

---

a**4:10** Other mss read *and suffer reproach* b**4:12** Other mss add *in spirit* c**5:3** Lit *Honor*

---

the "eternal life" one receives through belief in Jesus (1:16).

4:11 Command. Paul instructs that Timothy must speak with authority. The impression given here in verses 11-12 and elsewhere (1 Cor. 16:10-11; 2 Tim. 1:6-9) is that Timothy was a somewhat diffident, even timid, person.

4:12 youth. The problem may have to do with Timothy's age. He is probably only in his early 30s. Yet, he is living in a culture that respects age. **be an example.** There is little he can do about his age, but Timothy can lead by example. Paul identifies five areas in which he is to model Christian conduct. "Speech" and "conduct" refer to day-by-day conversation and behavior. "Love" (*agape*), "faith" (faithfulness), and "purity" (not only chastity but general integrity) refer to inner qualities that show themselves by an outer lifestyle.

4:13 public reading. This is the first reference to the use of Scripture in Christian worship, although this was common in Jewish worship. **teaching.** This is instruction in Christian doctrine.

4:14 laying on of hands. Appointment to office (ordination) was accompanied by the laying on of hands (literally, the "pressing of hands") by the commissioning body (here, the elders).

5:1 rebuke … exhort. Timothy will have to confront older men over the issue of false teaching. Paul tells him how to do it. It is not by means of harsh "rebuke"; instead, he is to appeal to them.

5:3 widows. The early church—following the pattern of the Jewish nation before them—was committed to caring for those

women who had lost their husbands (Deut. 24:17,19-21; Ps. 68:5; Isa. 1:17; Acts 6:1-6; 9:36-41; Jas. 1:27).

5:4 has children or grandchildren. The first group of widows who do not qualify for help are those who have family and friends that can care for them (vv. 8,16).

5:5-6 All alone … self-indulgent. Paul next contrasts two types of widows: those who put their hope in God (v. 5) and those who by their sensual living give no evidence of trusting God to meet their needs (v. 6). The first group is really "all alone" and so must trust God. The second group is "self-indulgent." It may be that Paul is contrasting those women who refuse to be compromised (and so put their trust in God) with those women who live by sensual means (whether in actual prostitution or by being involved with individual men).

⁹ No widow should be placed on the official support list[a] unless she is at least 60 years old, has been the wife of one husband, ¹⁰ and is well known for good works—that is, if she has brought up children, shown hospitality, washed the saints' feet, helped the afflicted, and devoted herself to every good work. ¹¹ But refuse to enroll younger widows; for when they are drawn away from Christ by desire, they want to marry, ¹² and will therefore receive condemnation because they have renounced their original pledge. ¹³ At the same time, they also learn to be idle, going from house to house; they are not only idle, but are also gossips and busybodies, saying things they shouldn't say. ¹⁴ Therefore, I want younger women to marry, have children, manage their households, and give the adversary no opportunity to accuse us. ¹⁵ For some have already turned away to follow Satan. ¹⁶ If any[b] believing woman has widows, she should help them, and the church should not be burdened, so that it can help those who are genuinely widows.

Honoring the Elders

¹⁷ The elders who are good leaders should be considered worthy of an ample honorarium,[c] especially those who work hard at preaching and teaching. ¹⁸ For the Scripture says:

> **You must not muzzle an ox**
> **that is threshing grain,**[d] and,
> The laborer is worthy of his wages.

¹⁹ Don't accept an accusation against an elder unless it is supported by two or three witnesses. ²⁰ Publicly rebuke[e] those who sin, so that the rest will also be afraid. ²¹ I solemnly charge you, before God and Christ Jesus and the elect angels, to observe these things without prejudice, doing nothing out of favoritism. ²² Don't be too quick to lay hands on[f] anyone, and don't share in the sins of others. Keep yourself pure. ²³ Don't continue drinking only water, but use a little wine because of your stomach and your frequent illnesses. ²⁴ Some people's sins are evident, going before them to judgment,

but ⌊the sins⌋ of others follow them. ²⁵ Likewise, good works are obvious, and those that are not ⌊obvious⌋ cannot remain hidden.

Honoring Masters

6 All who are under the yoke as slaves must regard their own masters to be worthy of all respect, so that God's name and His teaching will not be blasphemed. ² And those who have believing masters should not be disrespectful to them because they are brothers, but should serve them better, since those who benefit from their service are believers and dearly loved.

Money Issues

1. What was your first job where you made real money? Why were you working?
2. If you suddenly had lots of money, what is the first thing you would buy?

1 Timothy 6:3-21

3. Why does "godliness with contentment" lead to "great gain" (v. 6)?
4. What is dangerous about wanting to be rich (v. 9)? Why is it dangerous?
5. What should we focus on in life, instead of the pursuit of wealth (vv. 11-12)?
6. What is your biggest concern about money right now? How can you use your money for the good even now (vv. 17-19)?

False Doctrine and Human Greed

Teach and encourage these things. ³ If anyone teaches other doctrine and does not agree with the sound teaching of our Lord Jesus Christ and with the teaching that promotes godliness, ⁴ he is conceited, understanding nothing, but having a sick interest in dis-

---

[a]**5:9** Lit *be enrolled*   [b]**5:16** Other mss add *believing man* or   [c]**5:17** Lit *of double honor,* or possibly *of respect and remuneration*   [d]**5:18** Dt 25:4   [e]**5:20** Before the congregation   [f]**5:22** To ordain

---

5:9 60 years old. In the first century, 60 was considered the age of retirement and the point at which "old age" began. It was also considered to be the age beyond which remarriage was not a real possibility.

5:11-15 younger widows. Paul now comes to the real issue—the problematic younger widows. He gives two reasons for not putting them on the list for support. First, because their sexual desires are such that they do not want to remain widows (vv. 11-12), and second, because they are not really living according to the model of the godly widow that he has just sketched (v. 13). His advice is that they remarry (v. 14) lest they fall away from the faith (v. 15).

5:14 no opportunity to accuse. The younger widows' behavior had become the grounds on which others were speaking evil

of the church. Paul continues with his concern that the church not be judged negatively by the surrounding culture.

5:18 the Scripture says. Paul justifies his assertion that elders deserve remuneration from the community by means of two citations, one from the Old Testament (Deut. 25:4) and the other from Jesus (Luke 10:7).

5:19-20 Don't accept an accusation. Paul next addresses the matter of discipline with two points. First, no unsubstantiated charge is to be made about an elder. Second, if valid charges are made, those found guilty are to be rebuked publicly, serving as a warning to other elders who are in error, as well as the whole church.

5:23 use a little wine. Having told him to remain "pure," Paul quickly adds that what he

has in mind is not the sort of abstinence from food and drink taught by the false teachers (4:3). He recommends that Timothy follow the common medical practice of using wine as a treatment for his stomach problems.

6:4 he is conceited, understanding nothing. These teachers are swollen with pride despite the fact that they are really quite ignorant. **disputes.** This refers to a sort of idle speculation. **arguments.** This is literally a "battle of words," which Paul sharply criticizes. **from these come.** Paul identifies two negative results of this sick preoccupation with word battles. First, it produces strife within the church, and second, it brings about a kind of corruption or decay to the minds of the teachers themselves. **envy.** Controversy produces jealousy as people take up sides (see Romans 1:29, and Galatians 5:21, where envy is said to be one of

putes and arguments over words. From these come envy, quarreling, slanders, evil suspicions, [5] and constant disagreement among men whose minds are depraved and deprived of the truth, who imagine that godliness[a] is a way to material gain.[b] [6] But godliness with contentment is a great gain.

[7] For we brought nothing into the world,
and[c] we can take nothing out.
[8] But if we have food and clothing,[d]
we will be content with these.

[9] But those who want to be rich fall into temptation, a trap, and many foolish and harmful desires, which plunge people into ruin and destruction. [10] For the love of money is a root[e] of all kinds of evil, and by craving it, some have wandered away from the faith and pierced themselves with many pains.

Compete for the Faith

[11] Now you, man of God, run from these things;
but pursue righteousness, godliness, faith,
love, endurance, and gentleness.
[12] Fight the good fight for the faith;
take hold of eternal life,
to which you were called
and have made a good confession
before many witnesses.

[13] In the presence of God, who gives life to all, and before Christ Jesus, who gave a good confession before Pontius •Pilate, I charge you [14] to keep the commandment without spot or blame until the appearing of our Lord Jesus Christ, [15] which God[f] will bring about in His own time. ⌊He is⌋

the blessed and only Sovereign,
the King of kings,
and the Lord of lords,
[16] the only One who has immortality,
dwelling in unapproachable light,
whom none of mankind has seen or can see,
to whom be honor and eternal might.
•Amen.

Instructions to the Rich

[17] Instruct those who are rich in the present age not to be arrogant or to set their hope on the uncertainty of wealth, but on God,[g] who richly provides us with all things to enjoy. [18] ⌊Instruct them⌋ to do good, to be rich in good works, to be generous, willing to share, [19] storing up for themselves a good foundation for the age to come, so that they may take hold of life that is real.

Guard the Heritage

[20] Timothy, guard what has been entrusted to you, avoiding irreverent, empty speech and contradictions from the "knowledge" that falsely bears that name. [21] By professing it, some people have deviated from the faith.

Grace be with all of you.

---

[a] **6:5** Referring to religion as a means of financial gain   [b] **6:5** Other mss add *From such people withdraw yourself.*   [c] **6:7** Other mss add *it is clear that*   [d] **6:8** Or *food and shelter*   [e] **6:10** Or *is the root*   [f] **6:15** Lit *He*   [g] **6:17** Other mss read *on the living God*

---

the evidences of the sinful nature). **slanders, evil suspicions.** This quarreling drives people to tell lies about one another and question one another's motives.

6:5 minds are depraved. "Mind" refers to one's whole way of thinking.

6:6 contentment. This word refers to a person who is not impacted by circumstances. Such a person is self-contained and thus able to rise above all conditions. For Paul, however, this sort of contentment is derived from the Lord (Phil. 4:11).

6:7-8 brought nothing ... have food. There are two reasons why "godliness with contentment" is a great gain. First, at death peo-

ple can take nothing with them (so why worry about material gain that has to be given up in the end anyway?). Second, if people have the essentials in life, this should be enough.

6:9 temptation. Greed causes people to notice and desire what they might not otherwise have paid attention to.

6:10 For the love of money is a root of all kinds of evil. This verse is often misquoted as "money is the root of all evil." While Paul clearly sees the danger of money, he is not contending that all evil can be traced to avarice.

6:12 Fight the good fight. Paul again uses an athletic metaphor to encourage Timothy to persevere in the faith. The verb tense em-

phasizes the ongoing nature of the struggle. **take hold of eternal life.** The focus shifts from the contest to the prize. A person can grasp eternal life in a single act.

6:17 those who are rich. This is the only place in his letters that Paul addresses the wealthy directly. His consistent "command" is that the rich share their wealth with the poor (Rom. 12:8,13; 2 Cor. 9:6-15). **not to be arrogant or to set their hope on ... wealth.** These are the twin dangers of wealth—that it will cause people to think of themselves as better than others, and that they might put their trust in their riches (and not in God). **to enjoy.** But Paul is no ascetic. That the wealthy should not place confidence in their wealth does not carry with it an attitude of total rejection of wealth.

INTRODUCTION TO
2 TIMOTHY

PERSONAL READING PLAN

☐ 2 Timothy 1:1–2:13
☐ 2 Timothy 2:14–3:9

☐ 2 Timothy 3:10–4:8
☐ 2 Timothy 4:9-22

AUTHOR

The Apostle Paul was most likely the author of 2 Timothy. However, based on considerations of vocabulary and style, the Pauline authorship of the Pastoral Epistles (1 and 2 Timothy, and Titus) has been questioned by some scholars.

DATE

Second Timothy is probably the last epistle Paul ever wrote. The date is thought to be around A.D. 67-68. He is an old man now, in prison once again, deserted by most all of his friends, and facing the likely prospect of death. "For I am already being poured out as a drink offering, and the time for my departure is close. I have fought the good fight, I have finished the race, I have kept the faith. In the future, there is reserved for me the crown of righteousness" (4:6-8).

THEME

Guard the gospel.

PURPOSE

Second Timothy is deeply moving as Paul writes Timothy, imploring him to come and be with him in the last days of his life. In 2 Timothy, the urgency of the problem in Ephesus is in the background. Paul's more pressing need is to have Timothy at his side once again. Even more than personal comfort, Paul wants to pass on the torch of his ministry to Timothy.

Timothy was the logical choice for this new responsibility. He had been Paul's trusted colleague for over 15 years, and he really cared for the welfare of the churches (Phil. 2:20-22). This was a crucial time for the churches in Europe

and Asia. They seemed fragile in the face of their opposition. For one thing, Nero seemed bent on destroying the church. Furthermore, in the Roman province of Asia there had been widespread desertion (1:15). Only a generation after Christ's resurrection, Christianity appeared to be on the verge of annihilation. But Paul's ministry was over. No longer could he travel through the Roman Empire troubleshooting, correcting, or, establishing order. Now it was up to Timothy and the new leaders.

In many ways Timothy was an unlikely leader. He was relatively young by Roman standards, in his mid-thirties (1 Tim. 4:12; 2 Tim. 2:22). He was prone to illness (1 Tim. 5:23). And he was, apparently, somewhat shy and in need of encouragement (1 Cor. 16:10; 2 Tim. 1:7-8; 2:1,3; 3:12-14). To his credit, Timothy overcame his natural inclination and tackled risky assignments for Paul (for example, in Corinth).

If Timothy did not make it to Rome in time, these instructions in 2 Timothy would have to suffice. Paul's last letter was a crucial one.

HISTORICAL BACKGROUND

It is difficult to trace Paul's movements during the period when he wrote the Pastoral Epistles. The best guess is that after being released from the house arrest in Rome (described at the end of Acts), Paul went on another preaching tour taking with him Timothy and Titus. In the course of their travels, they came to Crete. When it came time to move on, Paul left Titus behind to appoint leaders for the new church there. Paul and Timothy went to Macedonia via Ephesus. At Ephesus, Paul discovered that heresy was rotting away the church. So he excommunicated Hymenaeus and Alexander, two of the erring leaders (1 Tim. 1:19-20), and he left Timothy

behind to help the church through its difficulties (1 Tim. 1:3-4). Paul himself went on to Macedonia. Once there he wrote 1 Timothy and Titus (hence the similarity between the two letters).

Paul wintered in the Adriatic seacoast town of Nicopolis where he was (presumably) joined by Titus. In the spring, Paul started back to Ephesus, only to be arrested along the way—probably at Troas—at the instigation of Alexander the metalworker (2 Tim. 4:14-15).

Paul was eventually taken back to Rome and thrown into prison. This time he was not allowed the relative comfort of a rented house with twenty-four-hour-a-day guards, as was the case during his first imprisonment. Instead he was chained and thrown into a dark, damp dungeon (1:16), "like a criminal" (2:9). Onesiphorus was able to find Paul only after a long search (1:17). Paul was cold ("bring the cloak," 4:13), bored ("bring ... the scrolls, especially the parchments," 4:13), and lonely ("only Luke is with me," 4:11). He had already had a preliminary hearing (4:16-17). His full trial was yet to come, and he did not expect to be acquitted. Nero's insane persecution of the Christians was at its height.

So Paul wrote Timothy to come to him in Rome. He sent this important letter (2 Timothy) via Tychicus, who was to replace Timothy in Ephesus.

CHARACTERISTICS

Although 2 Timothy is similar in content and focus to both 1 Timothy and Titus, there are some marked differences. Second Timothy is far more personal than 1 Timothy. First Timothy has the feel of a business letter containing important instructions to be heeded by the local congregation. But in 2 Timothy, Paul is writing to Timothy and not to the church, and he reminisces about the work he and Timothy did together. His primary purpose is not combating heresy (although that is a background concern), but to call Timothy to join him in Rome.

In fact, it is Paul's altered situation that gives 2 Timothy its distinct flavor. There is an urgency to his writing. His ministry is over. He tells Timothy to "keep ablaze the gift of God that is in you" (1:6). Timothy must not "be ashamed about the testimony of our Lord" (1:8). He must "guard ... the good thing entrusted" to him (1:14). "Proclaim the message" (4:2), Paul says, "whether convenient or not."

Second Timothy is also characterized, somewhat surprisingly, by a note of triumph. Paul knows that despite all the difficulties he is facing, despite the pressure on the church, the gospel will prevail. It cannot be chained even if he is chained (2:9). Nor will the church ultimately be hampered. It, too, will prevail (2:11-13; 4:8). Therefore, Paul writes to Timothy to carry on the work of the gospel despite persecution, despite Paul's death, because God's kingdom will prevail (3:10-4:8).

PASSAGES FOR TOPICAL GROUP STUDY

1:1-12 . . . . .POWER, LOVE, SOUND MIND . . . . .Fired Up

2:14-26 . . .REPENTANCE and RIGHT LIVING. . Positive Pursuits

4:9-18 . . . .LONELINESS and LOSING FRIENDS. . . . Never Alone

PASSAGES FOR GENERAL GROUP STUDY

3:1-9 . . . . .The Dark Side (False Teachers)

3:10-4:8 . .The Living Word (the Bible)

Greeting

1 Paul, an apostle of Christ Jesus by God's will, for the promise of life in Christ Jesus:

[2] To Timothy, my dearly loved child.

Grace, mercy, and peace from God the Father and Christ Jesus our Lord.

Fired Up

1. How does your team get ready for an important game or event?

2 Timothy 1:1-12

2. Judging by what Paul exhorts Timothy to keep doing in verse 6, what kinds of examples do you suppose Timothy's mother and grandmother demonstrated (v. 5)?

3. Verse 7 says that God gives us a spirit of power, not fearfulness. How do you think your life would be different if that really grabbed hold of that promise in your life?

4. What are you doing to "keep ablaze" the gift that God has given you?

5. In what area do you need to get "fired up"? Where do you most need God to give you power, love, and a sound mind?

Thanksgiving

[3] I thank God, whom I serve with a clear conscience as my forefathers did, when I constantly remember you in my prayers night and day. [4] Remembering your tears, I long to see you so that I may be filled with joy, [5] clearly recalling your sincere faith that first lived in your grandmother Lois, then in your mother Eunice, and that I am convinced is in you also.

[6] Therefore, I remind you to keep ablaze the gift of God that is in you through the laying on of my hands.

[7] For God has not given us a spirit[a] of fearfulness, but one of power, love, and sound judgment.

Not Ashamed of the Gospel

[8] So don't be ashamed of the testimony about our Lord, or of me His prisoner. Instead, share in suffering for the gospel, relying on the power of God,

[9]   who has saved us and called us
        with a holy calling,
    not according to our works,
        but according to His own purpose and grace,
    which was given to us in Christ Jesus
        before time began.
[10]   This has now been made evident
    through the appearing of our Savior Christ Jesus,
        who has abolished death
    and has brought life and immortality to light
        through the gospel.

[11] For this ⌊gospel⌋ I was appointed a herald, apostle, and teacher,[b] [12] and that is why I suffer these things. But I am not ashamed, because I know whom I have believed and am persuaded that He is able to guard what has been entrusted to me[c] until that day.

Be Loyal to the Faith

[13] Hold on to the pattern of sound teaching that you have heard from me, in the faith and love that are in Christ Jesus. [14] Guard, through the Holy Spirit who lives in us, that good thing entrusted to you. [15] This you know: all those in Asia have turned away from me, including Phygelus and Hermogenes. [16] May the Lord grant mercy to the household of Onesiphorus, because he often refreshed me and was not ashamed of my chains. [17] On the contrary, when he was in Rome, he diligently searched for me and found me. [18] May the Lord grant that he obtain mercy from the Lord on that day. And you know how much he ministered at Ephesus.

Be Strong in Grace

2 You, therefore, my child, be strong in the grace that is in Christ Jesus. [2] And what you have heard

---

1:4 Remembering your tears. Paul is probably recalling that when they parted the last time, he was to go on to Macedonia while Timothy stayed in Ephesus (see Acts 20:37 for a similar situation). **I long to see you.** This is the main reason he writes this letter: to urge Timothy to join him (4:9). **joy.** Once again, as he did in the Philippian letter, Paul sounds a note of joy even though he is in prison.

1:5 Eunice. Timothy's mother was a Jewish Christian (Acts 16:1). His father was a Gentile, probably not a believer.

1:6 keep ablaze. "Rekindle." Paul uses the image of a fire, not to suggest that his spiritual gift has "gone out," but that it needs constant stirring up so that it always burns brightly. **the gift of God.** Paul reminds Timothy not only of his spiritual roots (the faith of

his mother and grandmother), but also of the gift he has been given for ministry.

1:7 spirit of fearfulness. Paul makes this sort of appeal because Timothy is not a forceful person (1 Tim. 4:12).

1:8 ashamed of the testimony about our Lord. The gospel message about a dying Savior was not immediately popular in the first-century world. The Greeks laughed at the idea that the Messiah could be a convicted criminal, and that God was so weak He would allow His own Son to die. The Jews could not conceive of a Messiah (whom they knew to be all-powerful) dying on a cross (which they felt disqualified Him from acceptance by God). It was not easy to preach the gospel in the face of such scorn.

2:2 what you have heard from me. Just as

the gospel has been committed to Timothy (1:14; 1 Tim. 6:20), so he is to commit it to others who, in turn, teach it to still more people. This whole process of "committing" is made doubly important by the fact that Paul will soon call Timothy to join him in Rome (which means that others will have to take over his teaching ministry in Ephesus).

2:3-6 soldier ... athlete ... farmer. Paul uses three metaphors (drawn from the military, athletics, and agriculture) to encourage Timothy to work hard and endure suffering with the knowledge that he will be rewarded.

2:9 criminal. This is the term used for those who committed serious crimes (such as murder and theft).

2:10 the elect. God's chosen people; Christ-followers.

from me in the presence of many witnesses, commit to faithful men who will be able to teach others also.

³ Share in suffering as a good soldier of Christ Jesus. ⁴ To please the recruiter, no one serving as a soldier gets entangled in the concerns of everyday life. ⁵ Also, if anyone competes as an athlete, he is not crowned unless he competes according to the rules. ⁶ It is the hardworking farmer who ought to be the first to get a share of the crops. ⁷ Consider what I say, for the Lord will give you understanding in everything.

⁸ Keep in mind Jesus Christ, risen from the dead, descended from David, according to my gospel. ⁹ For this I suffer, to the point of being bound like a criminal; but God's message is not bound. ¹⁰ This is why I endure all things for the elect: so that they also may obtain salvation, which is in Christ Jesus, with eternal glory. ¹¹ This saying is trustworthy:

> For if we have died with Him,
> we will also live with Him;
> ¹² if we endure, we will also reign with Him;
> if we deny Him, He will also deny us;
> ¹³ if we are faithless, He remains faithful,
> for He cannot deny Himself.

An Approved Worker

¹⁴ Remind them of these things, charging them before God^a not to fight about words; this is in no way profitable and leads to the ruin of the hearers. ¹⁵ Be diligent to present yourself approved to God, a worker who doesn't need to be ashamed, correctly teaching the word of truth. ¹⁶ But avoid irreverent, empty speech, for this will produce an even greater measure of godlessness. ¹⁷ And their word will spread like gangrene, among whom are Hymenaeus and Philetus. ¹⁸ They have deviated from the truth, saying that the resurrection has already taken place, and are overturning the faith of some. ¹⁹ Nevertheless, God's solid foundation stands firm, having this inscription:

> The Lord knows those who are His,^b and
> Everyone who names the name of the Lord
> must turn away from unrighteousness.

²⁰ Now in a large house there are not only gold and silver bowls, but also those of wood and earthenware, some for special^c use, some for ordinary. ²¹ So if anyone purifies himself from these things, he will be a special^d instrument, set apart, useful to the Master, prepared for every good work.

Positive Pursuits

1. What happened the last time your coach changed game plans due to the opposing team's strategies?

2 Timothy 2:14-26

2. Looking over this passage, especially verses 15-16 and 22-24, what should we pursue? What should we run from?
3. Since repentance means "changing directions," how does repentance (v. 25) relate to fleeing and pursuing (v. 22)?
4. What seems to be the main goal of all of this righteous living (v.26)?
5. How do you need to change your strategies for pursuing "faith, love, and peace" (v. 22) and "escaping the Devil's trap" (v. 26) in the coming week?

²² Flee from youthful passions, and pursue righteousness, faith, love, and peace, along with those who call on the Lord from a pure heart. ²³ But reject foolish and ignorant disputes, knowing that they breed quarrels. ²⁴ The Lord's slave must not quarrel, but must be gentle to everyone, able to teach,^e and patient, ²⁵ instructing his opponents with gentleness. Perhaps God will grant them repentance to know the truth. ²⁶ Then they may come to their senses and escape the Devil's trap, having been captured by him to do his will.

^a**2:14** Other mss read *before the Lord*   ^b**2:19** Nm 16:5   ^c**2:20** Or *honorable*   ^d**2:21** Or *an honorable*   ^e**2:24** Or *everyone, skillful in teaching*

2:14 Remind them of these things. Timothy's first task is to keep people in touch with the truth of the gospel. The verb tense indicates that this is something he will have to do over and over again. **fight about words.** Literally, "word battle." This lies at the heart of the false teaching.

2:15 approved to God. Literally, "one who has stood the test." A word used to describe gold or silver that had been purified in fire, or a stone that has been cut without a flaw, (examined and then pronounced fit to be used in a building). **a worker.** The picture is of a farm laborer who has done a good job and is therefore not afraid to show his boss what he has accomplished. **correctly teaching the word of truth.** In contrast to the false teachers and their "word battles," Timothy is

called upon to teach and preach the gospel correctly. The phrase "word of truth" refers not to Scripture specifically, but to the gospel message as a whole.

2:17 gangrene. A disease that "gnaws away" at healthy tissue, causing its decay. Likewise, false teaching eats away at the healthy life in a church. **Hymenaeus and Philetus.** False teachers who have been a real problem. Paul had mentioned Hymenaeus in 1 Timothy 1:20 as one he had "delivered over to Satan." It appears he is still at work "overturning the faith of some" (v. 18).

2:18 the resurrection has already taken place. They were probably teaching that the resurrection of believers was a spiritual or mystical event that had already taken place

(1 Cor. 15:20-23; 2 Thess. 2:2).

2:19 solid foundation. Paul is probably referring to God's truth (Isa. 40:8). **having this inscription.** Paul has in mind the practice of placing an inscription on the foundation stone of a building to indicate the purpose of the building or the name of the owner.

2:22 Flee ... pursue. Simply trying to avoid evil desires isn't enough to keep us pure: we have to replace the evil desires, and strive for positive virtues. **youthful passions.** Part of what Paul has in mind is the impatience and arrogance of self-assertive youth, who love novelty and indulge in argument for argument's own sake.

The Dark Side

1. What crimes have you seen reported in the news that really made you angry?

2 Timothy 3:1-9

2. How are the sins listed in this passage a failure of the true love Jesus described in Matthew 22:37-39?

3. What does it mean to "hold to the form of religion but deny its power" (v. 5)? Why should we avoid people who do this?

4. According to verses 6-9, what is the character, danger, and fate of false teachers?

5. What do you think is the right thing to do with people like the ones described in this passage? Is there someone you need to avoid?

Difficult Times Ahead

3 But know this: difficult times will come in the last days. ² For people will be lovers of self, lovers of money, boastful, proud, blasphemers, disobedient to parents, ungrateful, unholy, ³ unloving, irreconcilable, slanderers, without self-control, brutal, without love for what is good, ⁴ traitors, reckless, conceited, lovers of pleasure rather than lovers of God, ⁵ holding to the form of religion but denying its power. Avoid these people!

⁶ For among them are those who worm their way into households and capture idle women burdened down with sins, led along by a variety of passions, ⁷ always learning and never able to come to a knowledge of the truth. ⁸ Just as Jannes and Jambres resisted Moses, so these also resist the truth, men who are corrupt in mind, worthless in regard to the faith. ⁹ But they

will not make further progress, for their lack of understanding will be clear to all, as theirs[a] was also.

The Sacred Scriptures

¹⁰ But you have followed my teaching, conduct, purpose, faith, patience, love, and endurance, ¹¹ along with the persecutions and sufferings that came to me in Antioch, Iconium, and Lystra. What persecutions I endured! Yet the Lord rescued me from them all. ¹² In fact, all those who want to live a godly life in Christ Jesus will be persecuted. ¹³ Evil people and imposters will become worse, deceiving and being deceived. ¹⁴ But as for you, continue in what you have learned and firmly believed, knowing those from whom you learned, ¹⁵ and that from childhood you have known the sacred Scriptures, which are able to instruct you for salvation through faith in Christ Jesus. ¹⁶ All Scripture is inspired by God[b]

The Living Word

1. What is your all-time favorite book?

2. How old were you when you first started learning about the Bible? Who taught you?

2 Timothy 3:10-4:8

3. What type of literature would the average student in your school call the Bible: Fiction? History? Mystery? Nonfiction?

4. In what ways has the Bible taught, rebuked, corrected, or encouraged you?

5. Comparing your spiritual life to a race, are you: Just getting out of the blocks? Really hitting your stride? Ready to drop?

6. What would you like to accomplish for God in the future? How can the Word of God help?

---

[a]**3:9** Referring to Jannes and Jambres   [b]**3:16** Lit *breathed out by God*; the Scripture is the product of God's Spirit working through men; see 2 Pt 1:20–21.

3:2 people. Although he casts this list into general terms ("people"), Paul implies that these vices characterize (at least in part) the false teachers. **lovers of money.** The path is short from love of self to love of money. Self-interest leads to self-indulgence. **boastful, proud.** These two terms are connected. The first refers to outward expressions of unrealistic pride, while the second to an inner attitude of superiority. These words can also be translated as "braggart" and "conceited." This second term has already been applied to the false teachers (1 Tim. 6:4). **disobedient to parents.** Duty to parents was considered obligatory by both Greeks and Jews. **ungrateful.** To be "ungrateful" is to refuse to honor the debt one owes to others. **unholy.** Such a person violates the unwritten laws that stand at the core of life.

3:3 unloving. The lack of natural, human af-

fection. **irreconcilable.** Such a person finds it impossible to forgive or to be reconciled to others. This sort of person is harsh and often bitter. **without self-control.** This is the person who is a slave to a habit or desire.

3:4 reckless. To be swept along by impulse or passion into bad decisions. **conceited.** Such people are swollen with pride at the sense of their own importance.

3:5 holding to the form of religion. These teachers missed out on the real power of God by substituting an outward religiosity for the inner reality of a relationship with God.

3:6 variety of passions. There may have been some sort of sexual involvement between the false teachers and the women they influenced.

3:8 Jannes and Jambres. These were Pharaoh's magicians, who by means of their secret arts duplicated the miracles of Moses and Aaron.

3:10 my teaching. This is the first of nine characteristics of Paul's life and ministry that Timothy is asked to note and reproduce. These nine make up a sort of "virtue list" that stands in sharp contrast to the "vice list" in verses 2-5 (2 Cor. 6:4-10).

3:15 instruct you for salvation through faith in Christ Jesus. The Old Testament Scriptures lead one to salvation; i.e., to an understanding of God's saving purpose.

3:16 All Scripture is inspired by God. Scripture has a divine origin. It comes from God (2 Peter 1:21). **is profitable for.** By means of two contrasting pairs of phrases,

and is profitable for teaching, for rebuking, for correcting, for training in righteousness, [17] so that the man of God may be complete, equipped for every good work.

Fulfill Your Ministry

4 Before God and Christ Jesus, who is going to judge the living and the dead, and by His appearing and His kingdom, I solemnly charge you: [2] proclaim the message; persist in it whether convenient or not; rebuke, correct, and encourage with great patience and teaching. [3] For the time will come when they will not tolerate sound doctrine, but according to their own desires, will accumulate teachers for themselves because they have an itch to hear something new.[a] [4] They will turn away from hearing the truth and will turn aside to myths. [5] But as for you, keep a clear head about everything, endure hardship, do the work of an evangelist, fulfill your ministry.

[6] For I am already being poured out as a drink offering, and the time for my departure is close. [7] I have fought the good fight, I have finished the race, I have kept the faith. [8] In the future, there is reserved for me the crown of righteousness, which the Lord, the righteous Judge, will give me on that day, and not only to me, but to all those who have loved His appearing.

Final Instructions

[9] Make every effort to come to me soon, [10] for Demas has deserted me, because he loved this present world, and has gone to Thessalonica. Crescens has gone to Galatia, Titus to Dalmatia. [11] Only Luke is with me. Bring Mark with you, for he is useful to me in the ministry. [12] I have sent Tychicus to Ephesus. [13] When you come, bring the cloak I left in Troas with Carpus, as well as the scrolls, especially the parchments. [14] Alexander the coppersmith did great harm to me. The Lord will repay him according to his works. [15] Watch out for him yourself, because he strongly opposed our words.

Never Alone

1. If you were in prison, who would come to visit you?
2. When have you been stranded somewhere? Who finally came to your rescue?

2 Timothy 4:9-18

3. What can we learn from Paul's attitude toward the coppersmith (v. 14)?
4. When everyone deserted Paul, to whom did he turn (vv. 17-18)?
5. In what ways are you feeling deserted? How can Paul's words in verses 17-18 help you the next time you feel all alone?
6. How can you help someone who is lonely and in need of a friend in the coming week?

[16] At my first defense, no one came to my assistance, but everyone deserted me. May it not be counted against them. [17] But the Lord stood with me and strengthened me, so that the proclamation might be fully made through me, and all the Gentiles might hear. So I was rescued from the lion's mouth. [18] The Lord will rescue me from every evil work and will bring me safely into His heavenly kingdom. To Him be the glory forever and ever! •Amen.

Benediction

[19] Greet Prisca and Aquila, and the household of Onesiphorus. [20] Erastus has remained at Corinth; Trophimus I left sick at Miletus. [21] Make every effort to come before winter. Eubulus greets you, as do Pudens, Linus, Claudia, and all the brothers.

[22] The Lord be with your spirit. Grace be with you!

---

[a] **4:3** Or *to hear what they want to hear*; lit *themselves, itching in the hearing*

Paul names four ministry tasks in which Scripture plays a vital part. **teaching.** Scripture is the source of what Timothy teaches, in contrast to the speculative nature of the erring elders' doctrine. **rebuking.** Not only does Scripture teach that which is true, it also reveals that which is in error. **correcting.** Scripture also defines how to live. It is thus a measuring stick against which to assess behavior and change what is found wanting. **training in righteousness.** This is the positive side of "correcting."

4:2 proclaim the message. Above all else, Timothy is to proclaim the message of the gospel. This is the main command and controls the next four. **persist in it whether convenient or not.** Probably Paul is encouraging Timothy to keep on preaching whether his hearers find it convenient or not, though he may be urging Timothy to continue with this task whether or not it is convenient to him. **rebuke, correct, and encourage.** In preaching the gospel he is to "correct" those who are in error, "rebuke" them if they fail to heed his correction, and "encourage" or "urge" them all to respond to what the gospel says.

4:9 come to me soon. Paul highlights his main request. He wants Timothy to leave his post at Ephesus and join him in Rome, journey of over 1,000 miles.

4:10-11 deserted ... gone. All his colleagues have left him (with the exception of Luke), either by reason of defection (Demas) or because of ministry needs (Crescens and Titus).

4:11 Bring Mark with you. It is a remarkable testimony to the power of the Holy Spirit that after the argument over Mark, which had resulted in the split between Paul and Barnabas (because Mark had deserted them in Perga—Acts 13:13; 15:36-41), reconciliation has taken place. Mark is now once again a valued coworker with Paul (Col. 4:10; Philem. 24).

4:13 cloak. A heavy wool cape that was worn in the cold and rain, consisting of a single piece of material with a hole in the middle for the head. Winter was coming and Paul needed his cloak to stay warm while in jail. **scrolls ... parchments.** Various suggestions have been made about what these were: portions of the Old Testament, blank writing materials, early copies of the Gospels, official documents (such as Paul's birth certificate).

TITUS

AUTHOR

The Apostle Paul was most likely the writer of Titus. However, based on considerations of vocabulary and style, the Pauline authorship of the Pastoral Epistles (1 and 2 Timothy, and Titus) has been questioned by some scholars.

DATE

Titus was written about A.D. 63-65 (at the same time 1 Timothy was written).

THEME

Be devoted to what is good.

HISTORICAL BACKGROUND

Paul and Titus, along with Timothy, went to Crete as part of a preaching tour following Paul's release from his first imprisonment in Rome. When Paul and Timothy left for Macedonia, Titus stayed behind to establish firmly the new church on Crete. When Paul reached Macedonia he wrote two letters—one to Timothy who had remained in Ephesus and the other to Titus.

In his letter to Titus, Paul reminds the younger man of his role: to appoint good leaders who will guide the church wisely. He also urges Titus to combat the false teachers found on the island. Finally, he tells him that either Artemas or Tychicus will come to relieve him (3:12), after which he is to join Paul for the winter. (See details of Paul's itinerary during this period in the Introduction to 2 Timothy.)

Titus was a Greek (Gal. 2:3) who was probably converted through Paul's ministry. He was a trusted colleague of Paul's and was often sent on difficult assignments. For example, when the conflict between Paul and the Corinthian church had reached a breaking point, it was Titus who delivered Paul's "harsh" letter and restored order in that community (2 Cor. 7:5-7). At some point, Titus was sent to Dalmatia (modern Yugoslavia) for yet another mission.

Titus is strikingly similar to 1 Timothy. Apart from the greeting and two pieces of theological writing in 2:11-14 and 3:3-7 (which appear to be creeds), all the material is parallel to 1 Timothy. The main difference is found in the contrasting situation of Titus and Timothy. Timothy had been left to straighten out a mess in an already established church. Titus, on the other hand, had the job of appointing elders in a new church. As a result, there is less intensity in Titus. There are few imperatives ("Do this"); there is no mention of endurance (as one finds in 1 Timothy); and there are no appeals to "keep the faith." Establishing order in a new church was quite different from restoring order to an established church.

PASSAGES FOR TOPICAL GROUP STUDY

PASSAGES FOR GENERAL GROUP STUDY

Greeting

1 Paul, a slave of God, and an apostle of Jesus Christ for the faith of God's elect and the knowledge of the truth that leads[a] to godliness, ² in the hope of eternal life that God, who cannot lie, promised before time began, ³ and has in His own time revealed His message in the proclamation that I was entrusted with by the command of God our Savior:

Powerful Knowledge

1. What subject or hobby would you like to learn more about?

Titus 1:1-4

2. In verse 1, Paul explains that God called him as an apostle to help people come to the "knowledge of the truth that leads to godliness." When did you come to the knowledge of the truth of Christ? What happened?
3. After coming to faith in Christ, did your new knowledge lead to godliness? In what ways?
4. When have you questioned your own "eternal life"? How does verse 2 speak to someone questioning his or her position with God?

⁴ To Titus, my true child in our common faith.

Grace and peace from God the Father and Christ Jesus our Savior.

Titus' Ministry in Crete

⁵ The reason I left you in Crete was to set right what was left undone and, as I directed you, to appoint elders in every town: ⁶ someone who is blameless, the husband of one wife, having faithful[b] children not accused of wildness or rebellion. ⁷ For an •overseer, as God's manager, must be blameless, not arrogant, not quick tempered, not addicted to wine, not a bully, not greedy for money, ⁸ but hospitable, loving what is good, sensible, righteous, holy, self-controlled, ⁹ holding to the faithful message as taught, so that he will be able both to encourage with sound teaching and to refute those who contradict it.

¹⁰ For there are also many rebellious people, idle talkers and deceivers, especially those from Judaism.[c] ¹¹ It is necessary to silence them; they overthrow whole households by teaching for dishonest gain what they should not. ¹² One of their very own prophets said,

> Cretans are always liars, evil beasts,
> lazy gluttons.[d]

¹³ This testimony is true. So, rebuke them sharply, that they may be sound in the faith ¹⁴ and may not pay attention to Jewish myths and the commandments of men who reject the truth.

Walking the Talk

1. Who in your family, group of friends, or team is the most disciplined?

Titus 1:5-16

2. Why is Paul's list of leadership qualifications focused mostly on "being" and not on "doing" (vv. 6-9)?
3. Which of the qualities in verses 7-9 do you feel you need to develop in your own life?
4. How, in the past or present, have your actions not fit with your profession "to know God" (v. 16)?
5. Are there some areas where you aren't truly living out your beliefs? How can you become more disciplined?

ᵃ**1:1** Or *corresponds*   ᵇ**1:6** Or *believing*   ᶜ**1:10** Lit *the circumcision*   ᵈ**1:12** This saying is from the Cretan poet Epimenides (6th century B.C.).

1:1-4 an apostle. The salutation that begins the letter to Titus is different from those that open 1 and 2 Timothy. The most notable difference is the way in which Paul defines the purpose of his apostleship.

1:5-16 Crete. The problem in Crete has to do with the erroneous teaching of the circumcision party (see note for 1:10), which Paul strenuously opposed in the Book of Galatians as well. Paul urges Titus to deal with this problem by appointing elders who will resist the false teachers.

1:5 set right ... appoint. The reason he left Titus behind was to complete the task of organizing the churches, specifically, to appoint and train up elders.

1:6 Paul begins this list of characteristics by focusing on the home life of the potential elder. **blameless.** This is a general term covering a variety of behaviors, some of which Paul will identify. **husband of one wife.** The most likely meaning is that sexual faithfulness to one's spouse was demanded.

1:7 overseer. Sometimes translated "bishop" (*episkopoi*), this title probably did not mean in the first century what "bishop" has come to mean today. It seems likely that in Paul's day the terms "overseers" and "elders" were interchangeable. **not greedy for money.** The Cretans had a reputation for making money in shady ways.

1:8 Paul follows the list of five vices (v. 7) with a list of six virtues. **hospitable.** Overseers must be willing to open up their homes to guests. It was a common practice in the first century to offer hospitality to travelers (Rom. 12:13; 1 Tim. 5:10; 1 Pet. 4:9). **sensible.** The

Greek word, *sophron*, is hard to translate into English, and has been variously rendered as "prudent," "of sound mind," and "chaste." **righteous.** Such a person acts justly toward others. **self-controlled.** Overseers must have worked to master their desires and behaviors.

1:10 For. Paul connects the character required of elders to the problem facing the church. **Judaism.** Literally, "of the circumcision." This group of Christian Jews was insisting that before Gentiles could become Christians they must first become Jews by undergoing the rite of circumcision.

1:13 rebuke them sharply. This is the only time in this letter that Paul calls upon Titus to directly confront the false teachers (v. 9 indicates the elders confronting them).

15 To the pure, everything is pure, but to those who are defiled and unbelieving nothing is pure; in fact, both their mind and conscience are defiled. 16 They profess to know God, but they deny Him by their works. They are detestable, disobedient, and disqualified for any good work.

Just Say No

1. In what area do you need to learn more self-control?

Titus 2:1-15
2. What one quality in each of the groups mentioned is most important for Christians in our society (see vv. 2-7)?
3. What is Paul implying about the importance of mentors (trusted guides or models)? How important have mentors been in your life?
4. What difference does our salvation make in our behavior in this "present age" (vv. 11-12)? What is it hardest for you to say "No" to?
5. How can you live in a "sensible, righteous, and godly way" (v. 12) in the coming week?

Sound Teaching

2 But you must speak what is consistent with sound teaching. 2 Older men are to be self-controlled, worthy of respect, sensible, and sound in faith, love, and endurance. 3 In the same way, older women are to be reverent in behavior, not slanderers, not addicted to much wine. ⌊They are⌋ to teach what is good, 4 so that they may encourage the young women to love their husbands and children, 5 to be sensible, pure, good homemakers, and submissive to their husbands, so that God's message will not be slandered.

6 Likewise, encourage the young men to be sensible 7 about everything. Set an example of good works yourself, with integrity and dignity[a] in your teaching. 8 Your message is to be sound beyond reproach, so that the opponent will be ashamed, having nothing bad to say about us.

9 Slaves are to be submissive to their masters in everything, and to be well-pleasing, not talking back 10 or stealing, but demonstrating utter faithfulness, so that they may adorn the teaching of God our Savior in everything.

11 For the grace of God has appeared, with salvation[b] for all people, 12 instructing us to deny godlessness and worldly lusts and to live in a sensible, righteous, and godly way in the present age, 13 while we wait for the blessed hope and the appearing of the glory of our great God and Savior, Jesus Christ. 14 He gave Himself for us to redeem us from all lawlessness and to cleanse for Himself a special people, eager to do good works.

15 Say these things, and encourage and rebuke with all authority. Let no one disregard[c] you.

The Importance of Good Works

3 Remind them to be submissive to rulers and authorities, to obey, to be ready for every good work, 2 to slander no one, to avoid fighting, and to be kind, always showing gentleness to all people. 3 For we too were once foolish, disobedient, deceived, captives of various passions and pleasures, living in malice and envy, hateful, detesting one another.

4 But when the goodness and love for man
   appeared from God our Savior,
5 He saved us—
   not by works of righteousness that we had done,
   but according to His mercy,
   through the washing of regeneration
   and renewal by the Holy Spirit.
6 This ⌊Spirit⌋ He poured out on us abundantly
   through Jesus Christ our Savior,
7 so that having been justified by His grace,

---

[a] 2:7 Other mss add *incorruptibility*   [b] 2:11 Or *appeared, bringing salvation*   [c] 2:15 Or *despise*

1:15-16 pure ... defiled. Food prohibitions, important to Jewish tradition, are probably in view here (1 Tim. 4:3).

1:15 everything is pure. This is a common New Testament theme. What people eat does not defile them (Mark 7:1-23; Rom. 14:20; 1 Tim. 4:4).

2:2 Older men. These would be men over 50. Paul's words to them parallel what he said to the potential elders (1:6-9), since most church leaders would be elders in age as well.

2:3 teach what is good. Formal instruction is probably not intended. Rather, the idea is that the older women would mentor, modeling "what is good" for younger women in terms of a woman's character and in her role as a wife and mother.

2:5 submissive to their husbands. Paul is not placing women under the authority of all men. Instead he has in mind submission to the woman's own husband.

2:7 integrity. This means "without corruption," "sincere." In contrast to the false teachers, Titus' motivation must not be mercenary. **in your teaching.** The focus is on the activity of teaching. The three words that Paul uses to describe how Titus should teach relate to the motive, demeanor, and content of his teaching.

2:8 message ... sound beyond reproach. Literally, "healthy" or "wholesome" speech—a medical metaphor that Paul probably borrowed from the itinerant philosophers of the day. By this, he refers to teaching that is in accord with the gospel proclaimed by the apostles (v. 2; 1:9,13; 1 Tim. 1:10; 6:3; 2 Tim. 1:13; 4:3).

2:9 Slaves are to be submissive to their masters. Slavery was widespread in the first century. To be a slave was to be at the bottom of the social system.

2:10 so they may adorn the teaching of God our Savior in everything. What Paul urges for slaves is, in fact, what he wants from all Christians in Crete, namely, the kind of behavior that honors the Lord and that society in general will count as respectable. This will make the Christian message attractive to those outside the church (v. 5).

2:13 the blessed hope. This refers to the second coming of Jesus. **our great God and Savior, Jesus Christ.** This is a clear statement of the deity of Christ.

2:14 to redeem us ... and to cleanse us. Paul identifies the connection between the

we may become heirs with the hope
of eternal life.

⁸ This saying is trustworthy. I want you to insist on these things, so that those who have believed God might be careful to devote themselves to good works. These are good and profitable for everyone. ⁹ But avoid foolish debates, genealogies, quarrels, and disputes about the law, for they are unprofitable and worthless. ¹⁰ Reject a divisive person after a first and second warning, ¹¹ knowing that such a person is perverted and sins, being self-condemned.

Final Instructions and Closing

¹² When I send Artemas to you, or Tychicus, make every effort to come to me in Nicopolis, for I have decided to spend the winter there. ¹³ Diligently help Zenas the lawyer and Apollos on their journey, so that they will lack nothing.

¹⁴ And our people must also learn to devote themselves to good works for cases of urgent need, so that they will not be unfruitful. ¹⁵ All those who are with me greet you. Greet those who love us in the faith. Grace be with all of you.

Doing Good

1. What memory comes to mind when you think of being disobedient as a child?

Titus 3:1-15

2. Why do you think Paul again stresses devotion to "good works" (vv. 1,8,14)? What is there about human nature that makes such reminders necessary (v. 3)?
3. When can doing "good works" become a problem?
4. What do verses 4-7 say about God's character? About His work in us?
5. Over the past year, where do you sense growth in doing "good works" for God in the key areas you give you life to (relationships, school, sports, activities, etc.)?

---

salvation Jesus brought and their lifestyle. Jesus died in order to: (1) rescue them from wickedness (therefore they ought not to live that way any longer); (2) make them a pure people (which defines how they are now to live). A godly lifestyle is, therefore, a response to the saving work of Jesus and a testimony to the power He has to change lives.

3:1-11 Remind them. Paul now returns to his main concern in the letter: the behavior of Christians. Previously, his focus was on the relationships between Christians and how this was viewed by the world (2:5,10). Now he turns to the question of how Christians are to behave to outsiders.

3:5 He saved us. This is the main focus of verses 4-7. The tense of the verb indicates that this is a once-for-all act. **according to**

His mercy. The mercy of God, not their character or works, is the basis for salvation. **regeneration.** This is the first of three metaphors that describe salvation. Believers become new persons; they are reborn. **renewal.** The second metaphor is similar to the first. It expresses the fact that they have been transformed into newness of life (2 Cor. 5:14-17).

3:7 justified. The third salvation metaphor emphasizes that believers are made right with God.

3:9 avoid. Paul contrasts the good deeds, to which they are to devote themselves, with the evil deeds, which they are to flee. **genealogies.** Some Jewish scholars took the family trees in the Old Testament and devoted great energy to constructing "biographies" for each character. **quarrels.** Literally, "word-battles,"

probably between those who disagree about genealogies and other such matters.

3:12 come to me. Titus is to be replaced as soon as Paul can send someone to take over his work. **Artemas.** Nothing is known about this individual. **Tychicus.** Tychicus was a trusted fellow worker, who often traveled with or for Paul (Acts 20:4; Eph. 6:21; Col. 4:7). **Nicopolis.** This city was located several hundred miles northwest of Athens near the Adriatic Sea.

3:13 Zenas the lawyer and Apollos. These men probably carried this letter to Titus. Zenas was an expert in Roman law. Apollos is probably the well-known orator from Alexandria (Acts 18:24– 19:1; 1 Cor. 1:12; 3:4,22; 16:12).

3:14 our people. These are the believers on Crete, as opposed to the false teachers.

INTRODUCTION TO
PHILEMON

PERSONAL READING PLAN

☐ Philemon 1-25

AUTHOR

The Apostle Paul wrote Philemon.

DATE

Paul probably wrote Philemon in the early A.D. 60s.

THEME

Radical forgiveness.

HISTORICAL BACKGROUND

At this point in history, the 60 million slaves in the Roman Empire made up a critical component of Rome's social and economic structure. Runaways were considered criminals who were punishable by severe measures, including death. Philemon, a member of the church at Colosse, was the owner of a slave (Onesimus) who had run away. Somehow Onesimus got to Rome, met Paul and became a Christian. We may wonder why Paul did not take this opportunity simply to condemn slavery. The reason is partially clear; conditions were not yet right for such a massive social upheaval. The Romans would never have voluntarily freed their slaves. Any revolt would have been savagely crushed. Also, Roman slavery was not a permanent condition based on race. This meant that slaves could purchase their freedom and enter the mainstream of society. Still, Paul did strike the first note for emancipation by his teaching on how Christians, regardless of race or economic condition, are one "family" in Christ (v. 16; Col. 3:11). This letter is Paul's attempt to persuade Philemon to forgive the crime and receive Onesimus as he would receive Paul himself. Onesimus carried this letter (and possibly Colossians and Ephesians) back to his home (Col. 4:9). The outcome of this story is not recorded in Scripture, but about A.D. 110 Bishop Ignatius of Antioch wrote a letter to the bishop of Ephesus, who was a man named Onesimus. In it, he used the same word-play on his name as Paul does here in verses 10-11. Since many scholars think that Paul's letters were first collected at Ephesus, Bishop Ignatius may have included this personal note as a vivid demonstration of how Christ can transform and use even a runaway slave.

CHARACTERISTICS

Philemon is the shortest of Paul's New Testament letters and it is his only private letter preserved in Scripture. All his other letters, whether to churches or to coworkers, relate to Paul's ministry. But Philemon is a personal plea written to a friend about a private matter—the fate of Onesimus, a runaway slave. As such, it gives us a valuable glimpse into Paul's personality. He is deeply sympathetic to the plight of Onesimus, so much so that he is willing to deprive himself of Onesimus' help and to pay Philemon for any loss Onesimus has caused him (vv. 18-19). This is certainly Christian compassion in action.

PASSAGES FOR TOPICAL GROUP STUDY

Greeting

Paul, a prisoner of Christ Jesus, and Timothy, our brother:

To Philemon, our dear friend and co-worker, ² to Apphia our sister,ᵃ to Archippus our fellow soldier, and to the church that meets in your house.

³ Grace to you and peace from God our Father and the Lord Jesus Christ.

Philemon's Love and Faith

⁴ I always thank my God when I mention you in my prayers, ⁵ because I hear of your love and faith towardᵇ the Lord Jesus and for all the saints. ⁶ ⌊I pray⌋ that your participation in the faith may become effective through knowing every good thing that is in usᶜ for ⌊the glory of⌋ Christ. ⁷ For I have great joy and encouragement from your love, because the hearts of the saints have been refreshed through you, brother.

An Appeal for Onesimus

⁸ For this reason, although I have great boldness in Christ to command you to do what is right, ⁹ I appeal, instead, on the basis of love. I, Paul, as an elderly manᵈ and now also as a prisoner of Christ Jesus, ¹⁰ appeal to you for my child, whom I fatheredᵉ while in chains—Onesimus.ᶠ ¹¹ Once he was useless to you, but now he is useful to both you and me. ¹² I am sending him—a part of myselfᵍ—back to you.ʰ ¹³ I wanted to keep him with me, so that in my imprisonment for the gospel he might serve me in your place. ¹⁴ But I didn't want to do anything without your consent, so that your good deed might not be out of obligation, but of your own free will. ¹⁵ For perhaps this is why he was separated ⌊from you⌋ for a brief time, so that you might get him back permanently, ¹⁶ no longer as a slave, but more than a slave—as a dearly loved brother. This is especially so to me, but even more to you, both in the flesh and in the Lord.ⁱ

¹⁷ So if you consider me a partner, accept him as you would me. ¹⁸ And if he has wronged you in any way, or owes you anything, charge that to my account. ¹⁹ I, Paul, write this with my own hand: I will repay it—not to mention to you that you owe me even your own self. ²⁰ Yes, brother, may I have joy from you in the Lord; refresh my heart in Christ. ²¹ Since I am confident of your obedience, I am writing to you, knowing that you will do even more than I say. ²² But meanwhile, also prepare a guest room for me, for I hope that through your prayers I will be restored to you.

Final Greetings

²³ Epaphras, my fellow prisoner in Christ Jesus, greets you, and so do ²⁴ Mark, Aristarchus, Demas, and Luke, my co-workers.

²⁵ The grace of the Lordʲ Jesus Christ be with your spirit.

Faithful Friendships

1. Who was your best friend in grade school? What made this person such a good friend?

Philemon 1-25

2. What qualities in Philemon does Paul commend (vv. 4-7)?

3. Does the fact that Onesimus has become a Christian lessen the seriousness of his crime? Why or why not?

4. Why does Paul take such a strong stand with Philemon about forgiving and accepting Onesimus (vv. 9-12)?

5. Have you had an opportunity to "stand" for someone with a troubled background, but who has been changed by Christ? Would you stand up for somebody like this?

ᵃ**2** Other mss read *our beloved*   ᵇ**5** Lit *faith that you have toward*   ᶜ**6** Other mss read *in you*   ᵈ**9** Or *an ambassador*   ᵉ**10** Referring to the fact that Paul led him to Christ; see 1 Co 4:15   ᶠ**10** The name *Onesimus* in Gk means "useful."   ᵍ**12** Lit *him—that is, my inward parts*   ʰ**12** Other mss read *him back. Receive him as a part of myself.*   ⁱ**16** Both physically and spiritually   ʲ**25** Other mss read *our Lord*

---

1 prisoner. Paul may have written this letter during his imprisonment in Rome (Acts 28) or from an unrecorded imprisonment somewhere closer to Colosse, perhaps in Ephesus. **Philemon.** This man, not mentioned anywhere else in the New Testament, was obviously someone close to Paul.

2 Apphia. It is assumed she was Philemon's wife. **the church that meets in your house.** How Philemon responded to Onesimus was a matter that would affect the life of the church to which both of them now belonged.

8-9 on the basis of love. Christian love, not a grudging obedience to Paul's command, was the only basis on which a true brotherly relationship could be built between Philemon and Onesimus. **elderly man ... prisoner.** While not appealing to his apostolic authority, Paul certainly appeals to the respect Philemon has for him.

11 useless ... useful. There is a play on words here. These two words, which sound very similar in Greek, share a root word that sounds like the word for "Christ" (*christos* means Christ; *euchrestos* means useful). Through Christ, Onesimus (whose name means useful), formerly a useless, disobedient slave, has now become truly useful as a brother in the Lord.

12 sending him ... back to you. In spite of his love, Paul had to send Onesimus back since harboring a runaway slave was a serious crime. The reality of his conversion would be seen in his willingness to return to Philemon and face up to the consequences of what he had done. Christian slaves were expected to view their work for their master as work done as unto the Lord (Col. 3:22-25).

16 both in the flesh and in the Lord. "In the flesh" Onesimus is just a slave, but "in the Lord" he is now Philemon's spiritual brother.

18 wronged you ... owes you. Onesimus may have stolen some money before running away. Besides that, his escape caused economic loss through lost services.

19 I will repay it. This first part of this verse is a promissory note whereby Paul obligates himself to carry out the pledge he made in verse 18. The latter half of the verse reminds Philemon of the spiritual debt that he owes to Paul for the treasure of the gospel to which Paul introduced him.

INTRODUCTION TO
HEBREWS

AUTHOR

No one knows who wrote the epistle to the Hebrews. The author is nowhere named within it, nor is there any strong external evidence pointing to a particular person. At least eight good candidates have been proposed.

Paul is listed as the author in the King James Version even though no evidence is found in any of the ancient manuscripts. It is unlikely that Paul wrote Hebrews Since the style and language is quite unlike Paul's. Hebrews is a polished piece of writing. Its transitions are neatly in place and its argument carefully spelled out. This sharply contrasts Paul's more expansive style.

Other suggested authors include Barnabas (Acts 4:36), Luke, Priscilla, Silas (1 Peter 5:12), Apollos (Acts 18:24), and Clement of Rome. Origen, a third-century Christian scholar, had the last word on this issue: saying that "only God knows certainly" (recorded in Eusebius, *Historia Ecclesiastica*).

DATE

It is difficult to be certain about its date as well. If the persecution referred to is that of Nero, then Hebrews was written after A.D. 64. Some believe it had to be written prior to the fall of Jerusalem and the destruction of the temple in A.D. 70, for such a dramatic event would have been mentioned as the end of the sacrificial system. Others argue for a later date nearer to the persecution by Emperor Domitian in A.D. 85, probably somewhere around A.D. 80.

THEME

The superiority of Jesus.

HISTORICAL BACKGROUND

This letter was probably written to a particular assembly of Jewish-Christian believers (perhaps a house church) that was part of a larger community, quite possibly in Rome. Whoever they were, it is clear that they had suffered great persecution (10:32-34) and that they were being tempted to abandon Christianity. What was weighing on them? Perhaps the constant injustices they suffered as Christians were beginning to take their toll. Or perhaps they were facing the prospect of severe persecution in the near future. Maybe they were being enticed away from Christ by false teaching that seemed to offer relief from their struggles. Whatever the temptation, Hebrews was written to encourage these beleaguered Christians to "hold on" (3:6), to "persevere" (10:36), and to "hold unswervingly to the hope we profess" (10:23) lest they compromise Christ and lose all the enormous blessings of the New Covenant.

CHARACTERISTICS

To modern readers, Hebrews is a strange book filled with references to ancient traditions of a foreign culture. It is true that to understand Hebrews, the reader must understand the Old Testament. Yet for all its strangeness, Hebrews contains compelling themes and images, stirring remembrances of the heroes of the faith, and a

breathtaking portrait of Jesus—the ultimate priest.

Hebrews has been called an epistle but in fact, it lacks several key features of a true letter: no introductory greeting, nor names of a sender or recipients. Its ending is typical of a letter, however, with personal greetings and a standard conclusion.

PURPOSE

How does one write to suffering Christians and tell them to stay faithful despite the price they are paying? The writer points them to Jesus, the only one who is worth such costly allegiance. As a result, in the book of Hebrews, we get a marvelous portrait of Christ—the prophet, priest and king whose New Covenant is so superior to the Old Covenant that to fall away from him would be unthinkable. The central theme of Hebrews, therefore, is the superiority of Christ. He is superior to the great religious leaders of the past such as Moses, Joshua, and Aaron. He is superior to the great supernatural powers like angels. The New Covenant he established and the new order he inaugurated are superior to the old beliefs and practices of the Jewish religion.

PASSAGES FOR TOPICAL GROUP STUDY

PASSAGES FOR GENERAL GROUP STUDY

The Nature of the Son

1 Long ago God spoke to the fathers by the prophets at different times and in different ways. [2] In these last days, He has spoken to us by ⌊His⌋ Son, whom He has appointed heir of all things and through whom He made the universe.[a] [3] He is the radiance[b] of His glory, the exact expression[c] of His nature, and He sustains all things by His powerful word. After making purification for sins,[d] He sat down at the right hand of the Majesty on high.[e] [4] So He became higher in rank than the angels, just as the name He inherited is superior to theirs.

The Role of Angels

1. What is your favorite movie, TV show, or story about an angel or angels?

Hebrews 1:1-14

2. What is this writer's main reason for bringing up angels (vv. 5-8)?

3. Why might someone be tempted to worship angels instead of Jesus?

4. What is the difference between the biblical view of angels and some modern ideas about angels?

5. What does verse 14 say about the purpose of angels? How does that make you feel?

6. How do you need one of God's angels to minister to you right now?

The Son Superior to Angels

[5] For to which of the angels did He ever say, **You are My Son; today I have become Your Father,**[f] [g] or again, **I will be His Father, and He will be My Son?**[h] [6] When He again brings His firstborn into the world,[i] He says, **And all God's angels must worship Him.**[j] [7] And about the angels He says:

> He makes His angels winds,[k]
> and His servants[l] a fiery flame;[m]

[8] but about the Son:

> Your throne, O God, is forever and ever,
> and the scepter of Your kingdom is a scepter
>   of justice.
> [9] You have loved righteousness and hated
>   lawlessness;
> this is why God, Your God, has anointed You,
> rather than Your companions,[n] [o] with the oil
>   of joy.

[10] And:

> In the beginning, Lord, You established
>   the earth,
> and the heavens are the works of Your hands;
> [11] they will perish, but You remain.
> They will all wear out like clothing;
> [12] You will roll them up like a cloak,[p]
> and they will be changed like a robe.
> But You are the same,
> and Your years will never end.[q]

[13] Now to which of the angels has He ever said:

> Sit at My right hand
> until I make Your enemies Your footstool?[r] [s]

[14] Are they not all ministering spirits sent out to serve those who are going to inherit salvation?

Warning against Neglect

2 We must therefore pay even more attention to what we have heard, so that we will not drift away. [2] For if the message spoken through angels was legally binding,[t] and every transgression and disobedience received a just punishment, [3] how will we escape

---

[a]**1:2** Lit *ages*   [b]**1:3** Or *reflection*   [c]**1:3** Or *representation,* or *copy,* or *reproduction*   [d]**1:3** Other mss read *for our sins by Himself*   [e]**1:3** Or *He sat down on high at the right hand of the Majesty*   [f]**1:5** Or *have begotten You*   [g]**1:5** Ps 2:7   [h]**1:5** 2 Sm 7:14; 1 Ch 17:13   [i]**1:6** Or *And again, when He brings His firstborn into the world*   [j]**1:6** Dt 32:43 LXX; Ps 97:7   [k]**1:7** Or *spirits*   [l]**1:7** Or *ministers*   [m]**1:7** Ps 104:4   [n]**1:9** Or *associates*   [o]**1:8–9** Ps 45:6–7   [p]**1:12** Other mss omit *like a cloak*   [q]**1:10–12** Ps 102:25–27   [r]**1:13** Or *enemies a footstool for Your feet*   [s]**1:13** Ps 110:1   [t]**2:2** Or *valid,* or *reliable*

1:1 by the prophets. God spoke to His people through his representatives at different times and in various ways.

1:2 He has spoken ... by His Son. In contrast to the partial, limited revelation of the prophets, the Son fully reveals God to the world. The author intends to show that Jesus is superior to all the forms of communication used in the past. **last days.** This term signifies the time after Jesus' resurrection.

1:3 the radiance of His glory. God's glory is like light that radiates from its source. Jesus' miracles revealed God's glory (John 2:11), and thus made God known to people (John 1:18). **exact expression.** The Greek word *charakter* was used to refer to an impression made by a stamping die (such as the inscription on the face of a coin). The image on a coin exactly matches the image engraved on

the die. **sustains all things.** The Son's role in creation was not limited to creation's origin or its future. It is His powerful word that keeps order and stability in creation (Col. 1:17).

1:14 ministering spirits. In contrast to the ruling authority of the Son, the function of the angels is to serve God's people at the Son's command. **ministering.** This word describes the priestly service at the tabernacle (8:4-6). In the New Testament, angels perform tasks such as interceding for children (Matt. 18:10), protecting the apostles (Acts 12:7-10), revealing God's will (Luke 1:11-38; Acts 8:26), and carrying out God's judgment (Rev. 7:1). **salvation.** Later passages indicate salvation as a deliverance (from the devil's power – 2:14; the fear of death – 2:15; and the power of sin – 9:26). Salvation also leads to holiness (10:10), forgiveness (10:18), free access to God (10:22), and the

eternal inheritance that God provides for those who have faith (9:15).

2:2-4 The author appeals to four things that show the divine origin of the message of the gospel: (1) it was the Lord, the Son, who first announced this message; (2) this message was supported by that of the apostles, men commissioned by the Son; (3) the signs, wonders, and various miracles that have come through the apostles (v. 4) show the divine authorization of the message; and (4) the gifts of the Holy Spirit, personally experienced by these people and given for their mutual encouragement (1 Cor. 12; Eph. 4), give God's confirmation to this message.

2:9 crowned ... because of the suffering of death. Jesus' death was not a denial of His glory, but the means through which this glory was revealed.

if we neglect such a great salvation? It was first spoken by the Lord and was confirmed to us by those who heard Him. ⁴ At the same time, God also testified by signs and wonders, various miracles, and distributions ₍of gifts₎ from the Holy Spirit according to His will.

Power of Shared Experiences

1. What is some good news you've recently had that you couldn't wait to share with someone else?

Hebrews 2:1-18

2. In what respects was Jesus "made lower than the angels" (v. 9)? What elevated Him above them?
3. Why did we need someone with flesh and blood like us—not an angel—to die in our place (vv. 14-18)? What is the goal of our salvation (vv. 10-11)?
4. What do you think Jesus gained from His earthbound experience that He didn't already have?
5. How can you use your own experiences to share Christ with others?

Jesus and Humanity

⁵ For He has not subjected to angels the world to come that we are talking about. ⁶ But one has somewhere testified:

What is man, that You remember him,
or the son of man, that You care for him?
⁷ You made him lower than the angels
for a short time;
You crowned him with glory and honor[a]
⁸ and subjected everything under his feet.[b]

For in **subjecting everything** to him, He left nothing not subject to him. As it is, we do not yet see **everything subjected** to him. ⁹ But we do see Jesus—**made lower than the angels for a short time** so that by God's grace He might taste death for everyone—crowned with glory and honor because of the suffering of death.

¹⁰ For it was fitting, in bringing many sons to glory, that He, for whom and through whom all things exist, should make the source[c] of their salvation perfect through sufferings. ¹¹ For the One who sanctifies and those who are sanctified all have one Father.[d] That is why He is not ashamed to call them brothers, ¹² saying:

I will proclaim Your name to My brothers;
I will sing hymns to You in the congregation.[e]

¹³ Again, **I will trust in Him.**[f] And again, **Here I am with the children God gave Me.**[g]

¹⁴ Now since the children have flesh and blood in common, He also shared in these, so that through His death He might destroy the one holding the power of death—that is, the Devil— ¹⁵ and free those who were held in slavery all their lives by the fear of death. ¹⁶ For it is clear that He does not reach out to help angels, but to help Abraham's offspring. ¹⁷ Therefore He had to be like His brothers in every way, so that He could become a merciful and faithful high priest in service[h] to God, to make propitiation[i] for the sins of the people. ¹⁸ For since He Himself was tested and has suffered, He is able to help those who are tested.

Our Apostle and High Priest

3 Therefore, holy brothers and companions in a heavenly calling, consider Jesus, the apostle and high priest of our confession; ² He was faithful to the One who appointed Him, just as Moses was in all God's[j] household. ³ For Jesus[k] is considered worthy of more glory than Moses, just as the builder has more honor than the house. ⁴ Now every house is built by someone, but the One who built everything is God. ⁵ Moses was faithful as

---

a**2:7** Other mss add *and set him over the works of your hands*   b**2:6–8** Ps 8:5–7 LXX   c**2:10** Or *pioneer,* or *leader*   d**2:11** Or *father,* or *origin,* or *all are of one*   e**2:12** Ps 22:22   f**2:13** Is 8:17 LXX; 12:2 LXX; 2 Sm 22:3 LXX   g**2:13** Is 8:18 LXX   h**2:17** Lit *things*   i**2:17** The word *propitiation* has to do with the removal of divine wrath. Jesus' death is the means that turns God's wrath from the sinner; see 2 Co 5:21.   j**3:2** Lit *His*   k**3:3** Lit *He*

2:10 it was fitting. While the idea of a suffering Messiah was unacceptable to the Jews, the author maintains that the idea is appropriate. **source.** Literally, "pioneer" (12:2). The image is of one who blazes the way, making it possible for others to follow. **make ... perfect.** This does not imply that Jesus had faults that needed to be purged.

2:16 Abraham's offspring. Since Jewish converts were the primary audience, the author points out that it is only through Jesus that the ancient promise to Abraham is fulfilled (Gen. 12:3; Rom. 2:28-29; 4:9,13-23; Gal. 3:6-14).

2:17 like His brothers. Because of God's choice of Israel to be His people, the Son became a flesh and blood Jew. Only in this way could He truly serve as a representative of the people before God. **a merciful and**

faithful high priest. The idea of the Messiah as a high priest is this author's unique way of communicating the identity of Jesus. This picture is found only in this New Testament book. **make propitiation.** A priest's main function was to offer the blood of a sacrifice in place of the blood of the sinner. Chapters 9–10 interpret Jesus' death in this framework.

2:18 since He Himself was tested. Jesus is more, not less, able to help those who are currently tempted. Jesus' humanity, rather than detracting from His elevated status, fully qualifies Him to enter into the struggles of His people. He can help them in a way angels never could (4:15).

3:1 consider Jesus. Two phrases are used to remind the readers of who they are in Christ. **holy brothers.** Not morally perfect

but "set apart" by God as His people (2:11-13). **companions in a heavenly calling.** Since the readers share together in God's call, they have special responsibilities toward God and one another. **consider Jesus.** This implies concentrated attention and reflection. While Jesus helps believers deal with temptations, they are to focus their attention on Him so they will not be distracted by temptations to follow another course (12:2). **the apostle.** One charged with the full authority of the one who sent him.

3:3-6 Two analogies substantiate the claim that Jesus is worthy of far more honor than even Moses: (1) In terms of a house (or dynasty), Jesus is the builder (God made the universe through Jesus as indicated in 1:2), whereas Moses is part of the house itself; and (2) Moses was faithful as a servant, but Jesus is the Son who owns the estate.

a servant in all God's[a] household, as a testimony to what would be said ⌈in the future⌉. 6 But Christ was faithful as a Son over His household, whose household we are if we hold on to the courage and the confidence of our hope.[b]

Help for the Heart

1. What or who can cheer you up when you are down or disappointed?

Hebrews 3:1-19

2. In what ways are Jesus and Moses similar (vv. 1-6)? In what ways is Jesus greater? Why is that important?

3. What does it mean to "enter [God's] rest" (vv. 11,18-19; 4:1-11; Matt. 11:28-30)?

4. What is the ultimate danger of allowing our hearts to be hardened?

5. What role does the Christian community play in keeping its fellow members true to God (v. 13)?

6. Are there any areas of your life where you are in danger of being "hardened by sin's deception"?

Warning against Unbelief

7 Therefore, as the Holy Spirit says:

Today, if you hear His voice,
8   do not harden your hearts as in the rebellion,
on the day of testing in the desert,
9   where your fathers tested Me, tried ⌈Me⌉,
and saw My works 10 for 40 years.
Therefore I was provoked with this generation
and said, "They always go astray
in their hearts,
and they have not known My ways."
11   So I swore in My anger,
"They will not enter My rest."[c]

12 Watch out, brothers, so that there won't be in any of you an evil, unbelieving heart that departs from the living God. 13 But encourage each other daily, while it is still called **today**, so that none of you is hardened by sin's deception. 14 For we have become companions of the •Messiah if we hold firmly until the end the reality[d] that we had at the start. 15 As it is said:

Today, if you hear His voice,
do not harden your hearts
as in the rebellion.[e]

16 For who heard and rebelled? Wasn't it really all who came out of Egypt under Moses? 17 And with whom was He "provoked for 40 years"? Was it not with those who sinned, whose bodies fell in the desert? 18 And to whom did He "swear that they would not enter His rest," if not those who disobeyed? 19 So we see that they were unable to enter because of unbelief.

The Promised Rest

4 Therefore, while the promise remains of entering His rest, let us fear so that none of you should miss it.[f] 2 For we also have received the good news just as they did; but the message they heard did not benefit them, since they were not united with those who heard it in faith[g] 3 (for we who have believed enter the rest), in keeping with what[h] He has said:

So I swore in My anger,
they will not enter My rest.[i]

And yet His works have been finished since the foundation of the world, 4 for somewhere He has spoken about the seventh day in this way:

And on the seventh day
God rested from all His works.[j]

5 Again, in that passage ⌈He says⌉, They will never enter My rest.[i] 6 Since it remains for some to enter it, and those who formerly received the good news did not enter because of disobedience, 7 again, He specifies

---

a3:5 Lit *His*   b3:6 Other mss add *firm to the end*   c3:7–11 Ps 95:7–11   d3:14 Or *confidence*   e3:15 Ps 95:7–8   f4:1 Or *should seem to miss it*   g4:2 Other mss read *since it was not united by faith in those who heard*   h4:3 Or *rest), just as*   i4:3,5 Ps 95:11   j4:4 Gn 2:2

3:6 our hope. Not a wish, but an expectation that is guaranteed to come about.

3:11 My rest. In the context of the Israelites, this meant the promised land of Canaan where they would have prosperity and peace (4:1).

3:12 departs. Literally, "abandons" or "defects." Whereas the warning in 2:1 was against "drifting" from the Lord, this is a deliberate turning from God's way.

3:16-19 Through the five questions based on events in Numbers 14:26-35, the author hammers home the importance of maintaining faith.

4:1 the promise. God's promise was to bring Israel into a "good and spacious land" where they would have peace (Ex. 3:8).

However, the generation who originally received this promise never experienced its fulfillment. **His rest.** Not a state of idleness, but a condition in which one is free to live in peace, joy, security, and freedom. Israel thought of rest in terms of dwelling securely in their own land in freedom and prosperity (Deut. 5:33; 8:6-9). Later on, this developed into the hope of an eternal kingdom under the wise, compassionate leadership of a Davidic king (Ezek. 34:24-31; Dan. 7:13-14). It is likely some of the original readers thought of this rest in such national, physical terms (Acts 1:6). **let us fear.** This is reverence that produces careful behavior.

4:9 Sabbath rest. This term, found only here in the New Testament, is a play on words—the Greek words for "sabbath" and "rest" sound alike. The term identifies this rest with the traditional Jewish Sabbath rest yet emphasizes that this rest fulfills the reality that the Jewish Sabbath only symbolized. Once again Jesus' superiority over all elements of traditional Jewish faith is evidenced. **God's people.** This includes all people, Jew or Gentile, who entrust themselves to Jesus.

4:11 make every effort. Literally, "strive." The life of faith is not a passive waiting for God but an urgent, determined resolve to push on in the pursuit of God.

4:12 the word of God is living and effective. The comparison of God's Word to a sword was first made by Isaiah (Isa. 49:2). It shows the piercing, discerning power of God's Word to cut through people's thoughts, intentions, and motivations (Eph. 6:17; Rev. 1:16). **penetrating as far as to divide soul, spirit, joints, and marrow ... the ideas and thoughts of the heart.** The

The Ultimate Reward

1. What is your favorite way to spend a Sunday afternoon?

Hebrews 4:1-13

2. What efforts (v. 11) can help us enter into God's rest (John 6:27-29)?

3. How would you explain the "promised rest" to someone who is not a Christian?

4. What does it mean that, "the word of God is living" (v. 12)? "Effective"? That it penetrates?

5. Is there anything in your life that you are trying to hide from God (v. 13)? If so, how do you think you can you break this "pattern of disobedience" (v. 11)?

a certain day—**today**—speaking through David after such a long time, as previously stated:

> **Today if you hear His voice, do not harden your hearts.**ᵃ

⁸ For if Joshua had given them rest, He would not have spoken later about another day. ⁹ A Sabbath rest remains, therefore, for God's people. ¹⁰ For the person who has entered His rest has rested from his own works, just as God did from His. ¹¹ Let us then make every effort to enter that rest, so that no one will fall into the same pattern of disobedience.

¹² For the word of God is living and effective and sharper than any two-edged sword, penetrating as far as to divide soul, spirit, joints, and marrow; it is a judge of the ideas and thoughts of the heart. ¹³ No creature is hidden from Him, but all things are naked and exposed to the eyes of Him to whom we must give an account.

ᵃ**4:7** Ps 95:7–8 ᵇ**5:1** Lit *things*

Our Great High Priest

¹⁴ Therefore since we have a great high priest who has passed through the heavens—Jesus the Son of God—let us hold fast to the confession. ¹⁵ For we do not have a high priest who is unable to sympathize with our weaknesses, but One who has been tested in every way as we are, yet without sin. ¹⁶ Therefore let us approach the throne of grace with boldness, so that we may receive mercy and find grace to help us at the proper time.

Bold Confessions

1. When you "blow it," how do you feel about the mistake? About yourself? About others involved?

Hebrews 4:14-5:10

2. What characteristic about Jesus' priesthood is most encouraging (4:14-15; see 2:17; 3:1)?

3. What are two qualities of Jesus that allow Him to be compared to Melchizedek (5:6,10; see chapter 7)?

4. What is the significance for our eternal salvation, as well as our current situations, that Jesus was fully human? That Jesus was without sin?

5. How does this passage affect your feelings about your relationship with Jesus? What sins do you need to confess to your "High Priest"?

The Messiah, a High Priest

5 For every high priest taken from men is appointed in serviceᵇ to God for the people, to offer both gifts and sacrifices for sins. ² He is able to deal gently with those who are ignorant and are going astray, since he himself is also subject to weakness. ³ Because of this, he must make a sin offering for himself as well as

whole person is spoken to by God's Word—spirit, body, and mind (the heart was referred to as the source of one's thought process, the core of a person's mental and moral activity).

4:13 naked and exposed. Three possibilities exist as to the meaning of this graphic image. It may refer to: (1) a wrestler whose head has been thrust back rendering him vulnerable to being pinned; (2) a soldier without armor to cover his throat; (3) a sacrificial animal whose neck is bared so that a knife can be drawn across its throat. All three images portray a frightening picture of being defenseless before an opponent.

4:14 a great high priest. The high priest served as the spiritual leader (and often as the civil leader) of the Jews. His most unique function was to bring a sacrifice to God in the Most Holy Place on the Day of Atonement (9:3,8; Lev. 16:17). **passed through heavens.** As the high priest would pass through a curtain into the Most Holy Place in the tabernacle, so Jesus entered into the presence of God as the representative of those who trust in Him. **heavens.** Heaven is often referred to in the plural form in the Old Testament.

4:15 tested in every way. Jesus was tempted in the desert by Satan (Luke 4:1-

13). Here we find that He experienced every kind of temptation that we face. **without sin.** Technically, every high priest was without sin before offering atonement for the people. This was achieved by offering a sacrifice for himself prior to offering those for the people (5:3). Jesus was superior to the Old Testament priesthood because He had no sin for which to offer sacrifice.

4:16 approach. the throne of grace. Jesus sits at the right hand of God, interceding for us. **with boldness.** The readers are urged to approach God, knowing they have a compassionate, perfect high priest who is gracious and merciful to the needy (6:20).

for the people. ⁴ No one takes this honor on himself; instead, a person is called by God, just as Aaron was. ⁵ In the same way, the •Messiah did not exalt Himself to become a high priest, but the One who said to Him, **You are My Son; today I have become Your Father,**ᵃ ⁶ also said in another passage, **You are a priest forever in the order of Melchizedek.**ᵇ

⁷ During His earthly life,ᶜ He offered prayers and appeals, with loud cries and tears, to the One who was able to save Him from death, and He was heard because of His reverence. ⁸ Though a Son, He learned obedience through what He suffered. ⁹ After He was perfected, He became the source of eternal salvation to all who obey Him, ¹⁰ and He was declared by God a high priest "in the order of Melchizedek."

The Problem of Immaturity

¹¹ We have a great deal to say about this, and it's difficult to explain, since you have become slow to understand. ¹² For though by this time you ought to be teachers, you need someone to teach you again the basic principles of God's revelation. You need milk, not solid food. ¹³ Now everyone who lives on milk is inexperienced with the message about righteousness, because he is an infant. ¹⁴ But solid food is for the mature—for those whose senses have been trained to distinguish between good and evil.

Warning against Regression

6 Therefore, leaving the elementary message about the •Messiah, let us go on to maturity, not laying again the foundation of repentance from dead works, faith in God, ² teaching about ritual washings,ᵈ laying on of hands, the resurrection of the dead, and eternal judgment. ³ And we will do this if God permits.

⁴ For it is impossible to renew to repentance those who were once enlightened, who tasted the heavenly gift, became companions with the Holy Spirit, ⁵ tasted God's good word and the powers of the coming age, ⁶ and who have fallen away, because,ᵉ to their own harm, they are recrucifying the Son of God and holding Him up to contempt. ⁷ For ground that has drunk the rain that has often fallen on it, and that produces vegetation useful to those it is cultivated for, receives a blessing from God. ⁸ But if it produces thorns and thistles, it is worthless and about to be cursed, and will be burned at the end.

Keep Moving Forward

1. What do you like hot out of the oven with a glass of cold milk: Chocolate chip cookies? Pound cake? Homemade bread? Apple pie?
2. What skill did you learn when you were younger that caused you to realize you were growing up?

Hebrews 5:11–6:12

3. What effect does "solid food" have on the believer (5:14)?
4. What is wrong with this prolonged immaturity (6:4-6)?
5. How and why does the author encourage his readers to do "better," to increase in maturity (6:9-12)?
6. What is the overarching warning you see here? How does it apply to your life?

⁹ Even though we are speaking this way, dear friends, in your case we are confident of the better things connected with salvation. ¹⁰ For God is not unjust; He will not forget your work and the loveᶠ you showed for His name when you served the saints—and you continue to serve them. ¹¹ Now we want each of you to demonstrate the same diligence for the final realization of your hope, ¹² so that you won't become lazy, but imitators of those who inherit the promises through faith and perseverance.

Inheriting the Promise

¹³ For when God made a promise to Abraham, since He had no one greater to swear by, He swore by Himself:

5:5-6 the Messiah. Jesus, the God-appointed priestly-king. Psalms 2:7 and 110:4 are linked to show that Jesus' priesthood can be traced to the mysterious Old Testament figure of Melchizedek, a king/priest who lived long before Aaron was born (Gen. 14:18-19). This connection between the Messiah and Melchizedek (first identified in Psalm 110) was unique to the author of Hebrews.

5:5 Messiah did not exalt Himself. For the second time (1:5) in Hebrews the author quotes Psalm 2 to show that Jesus did not on Himself the honor of being high priest but responded to God's call to that appointment.

5:6 a priest forever in the order of Melchizedek. The high priesthood in Israel was a hereditary office based on descent from Aaron who was of the tribe of Levi. The priesthood of Christ was of a different order—the order of Melchizedek who was both

king and priest. Jesus, too, is both king and priest. Unlike the Aaronic priesthood, Jesus was of the tribe of Judah. His priesthood is both perfect and will last always.

5:7 prayers and appeals. The two words overlap, but the latter most often indicates an intense pleading. **loud cries and tears.** Western culture does not typically associate such emotion with prayer, but this would be a normal part of sincere intercession by the faithful Jew. Jesus' prayer in Gethsemane may be in view (Matt. 26:36-42). **save Him from death.** In one sense Jesus was not "saved from death." He had to pass through it to experience resurrection and victory over death. **reverence.** Literally, "godly fear."

5:12 milk ... solid food. While these readers have been believers long enough to have become "teachers," their uncertain faithfulness is more akin to that of "babies" just be-

ginning to walk with Christ.

5:13-14 inexperienced ... those whose senses have been trained. Spiritual maturity, like emotional maturity, is developed through practicing that which leads to responsible development.

6:1-2 go on to maturity. The only way to become trained (5:14) is to start exercising. The author wants to move on to weightier matters. **repentance ... faith, ritual washings ... laying on of hands the resurrection of the dead ... judgment.** These three couplets focus on basic elements of the Christian life, church practices, and doctrine. All could be found in Judaism and the readers may have lost sight of how Jesus had changed their meaning. The themes that dominate the rest of the book; Jesus' role as high priest and sacrifice, will remind them. **dead works.** Acts that stem from sin

The Promise

1. What tries your patience more: Slow elevators? Slow food service? Traffic jams? How do you react?
2. What is one goal you would like to accomplish this year?

Hebrews 6:13-20
3. How does Abraham's example help these people understand God's promise (3:12; 6:6)?
4. What effect did God's promise and oath have on Abraham's descendants? How does this affect Christians now?
5. What is the source of our hope (vv. 17-19)?
6. Where in your life does trusting in God come hardest? Easiest? Why?

Jesus is #1

1. If you could live to be 100, but could retain either the body or the mind of a 30-year-old, which would you choose? Why?

Hebrews 7:1-28
2. From verses 1-10, what do we know about Melchizedek? How did Abraham regard him?
3. In what ways is Jesus like the Melchizedek portrayed here (vv. 12-17)?
4. In what ways is Jesus a better priest than those under the Old Testament system (vv. 20-28)?
5. Why is the writer emphasizing Jesus' superior qualifications as a priest?
6. How do you need Jesus to intercede for you (v. 25) this week?

---

¹⁴ I will most certainly bless you,
and I will greatly multiply you.^a

¹⁵ And so, after waiting patiently, Abraham^b obtained the promise. ¹⁶ For men swear by something greater than themselves, and for them a confirming oath ends every dispute. ¹⁷ Because God wanted to show His unchangeable purpose even more clearly to the heirs of the promise, He guaranteed it with an oath, ¹⁸ so that through two unchangeable things, in which it is impossible for God to lie, we who have fled for refuge might have strong encouragement to seize the hope set before us. ¹⁹ We have this ⌊hope⌋—like a sure and firm anchor of the soul—that enters the inner sanctuary behind the curtain. ²⁰ Jesus has entered there on our behalf as a forerunner, because He has become a "high priest forever in the order of Melchizedek."

The Greatness of Melchizedek

7 For this Melchizedek—

King of Salem, priest of the Most High God,
who met Abraham and blessed him
    as he returned from defeating the kings,
²   and Abraham gave him a tenth of everything;
first, his name means "king of righteousness,"
then also, "king of Salem,"
    meaning "king of peace";
³   without father, mother, or genealogy,
having neither beginning of days nor end of life,
but resembling the Son of God—

remains a priest forever.

⁴ Now consider how great this man was, to whom even Abraham the patriarch gave a tenth of the plunder! ⁵ The sons of Levi who receive the priestly office have a commandment according to the law to collect a

---

^a**6:14** Gn 22:17 ^b**6:15** Lit *he*

---

and lead to death. Repentance from sin was the first note of the gospel message (Mark 1:14-15). **ritual washings.** Some Jewish sects practiced ceremonies for cleansing far beyond what the Law required.

6:4-6 renew to repentance. Western Christians often think of the terms in this warning in a subjective, individual sense and wonder how someone who has been touched by God like this could give up faith. The author was likely not referring to subjective experiences at all but to "tasted the heavenly gift" as the Lord's Supper; "became companions with the Holy Spirit" as the laying on of hands (a sign that the person was included in the community of the Spirit); "tasted God's good word " as hearing gospel preaching; and "tasted the powers of the coming age" as observing the use of spiritual gifts within the church. Jewish Christians viewed these ritu-

als as vital expressions of faith. To partake in them and then deliberately choose not to live up to the obligations they represented was unthinkable. **impossible to renew to repentance.** Since to leave required a deliberate, conscious act, there could be no reasonable expectation that such people would ever return.

6:9-12 He will not forget your work. The warning gives way to encouragement. Their works of love indicate that they have not fallen away (v. 10). They are urged to stay on that course, following the example of others in the past who held on to God's promises (v. 12)

7:1 Melchizedek. Probably not as obscure a figure to the original readers as he is to readers today. **King of Salem.** This city was associated with the site of Jerusalem. **defeating the kings.** Abraham had fought against a coalition of tribal rulers.

7:2 gave him a tenth. The tribute may have been given as an acknowledgment of Melchizedek's relationship with Abraham's God. In any case Abraham recognized Melchizedek as a superior, worthy of a tithe (tenth) of all he owned. **king of Salem ... king of peace.** Since vowels were never written in Hebrew, both "Salem" and "peace [*shalom*]" were spelled *slm*— allowing for an easy identification of the two words.

7:4-10 Melchizedek's priesthood is compared to that of Levi (Num. 8). In the mindset of an Israelite, what my ancestor did was what I did—for I was part of him or her; what I did reflects what my ancestor did, since he or she lives on in me. Since Abraham paid tribute to Melchizedek, the Levitical priests, as Abraham's descendants, also paid tribute to him. Since tribute is paid from the lesser to the greater, Melchizedek's priest-

tenth from the people—that is, from their brothers—though they have ₎also₎ descended from Abraham.ᵃ ⁶ But one without thisᵇ lineage collected tithes from Abraham and blessed the one who had the promises. ⁷ Without a doubt,ᶜ the inferior is blessed by the superior. ⁸ In the one case, men who will die receive tithes; but in the other case, ₎Scripture₎ testifies that he lives. ⁹ And in a sense Levi himself, who receives tithes, has paid tithes through Abraham, ¹⁰ for he was still within his forefatherᵈ when Melchizedek met him.

A Superior Priesthood

¹¹ If, then, perfection came through the Levitical priesthood (for under it the people received the law), what further need was there for another priest to arise in the order of Melchizedek, and not to be described as being in the order of Aaron? ¹² For when there is a change of the priesthood, there must be a change of law as well. ¹³ For the One about whom these things are said belonged to a different tribe, from which no one has served at the altar. ¹⁴ Now it is evident that our Lord came from Judah, and about that tribe Moses said nothing concerning priests.

¹⁵ And this becomes clearer if another priest like Melchizedek arises, ¹⁶ who doesn't become a ₎priest₎ based on a legal command concerning physicalᵉ descent but based on the power of an indestructible life. ¹⁷ For it has been testified:

> You are a priest forever in the order
> of Melchizedek.ᶠ

¹⁸ So the previous commandment is annulled because it was weak and unprofitable ¹⁹ (for the law perfected nothing), but a better hope is introduced, through which we draw near to God. ²⁰ None of this ₎happened₎ without an oath. For others became priests without an oath, ²¹ but He with an oath made by the One who said to Him:

> The Lord has sworn, and He will not change
> His mind,
> You are a priest forever.ᶠ

ᵃ7:5 Lit have come out of Abraham's loins ᵇ7:6 Lit their ᶜ7:7 Or Beyond any dispute ᵈ7:10 Lit still in his father's loins ᵉ7:16 Or fleshly ᶠ7:17,21 Ps 110:4 ᵍ7:25 Or He is able to save completely ʰ8:4 Other mss read priests ⁱ8:5 Ex 25:40 ʲ8:6 Lit He ᵏ8:8 Lit with them ˡ8:8 Other mss read finding fault, He says to them

²² So Jesus has also become the guarantee of a better covenant.

²³ Now many have become ₎Levitical₎ priests, since they are prevented by death from remaining in office. ²⁴ But because He remains forever, He holds His priesthood permanently. ²⁵ Therefore He is always able to saveᵍ those who come to God through Him, since He always lives to intercede for them.

²⁶ For this is the kind of high priest we need: holy, innocent, undefiled, separated from sinners, and exalted above the heavens. ²⁷ He doesn't need to offer sacrifices every day, as high priests do—first for their own sins, then for those of the people. He did this once for all when He offered Himself. ²⁸ For the law appoints as high priests men who are weak, but the promise of the oath, which came after the law, ₎appoints₎ a Son, who has been perfected forever.

A Heavenly Priesthood

8 Now the main point of what is being said is this: we have this kind of high priest, who sat down at the right hand of the throne of the Majesty in the heavens, ² a minister of the sanctuary and the true tabernacle, which the Lord set up, and not man. ³ For every high priest is appointed to offer gifts and sacrifices; therefore it was necessary for this ₎priest₎ also to have something to offer. ⁴ Now if He were on earth, He wouldn't be a priest, since there are thoseʰ offering the gifts prescribed by the law. ⁵ These serve as a copy and shadow of the heavenly things, as Moses was warned when he was about to complete the tabernacle. For He said, **Be careful that you make everything according to the pattern that was shown to you on the mountain.**ⁱ ⁶ But Jesusʲ has now obtained a superior ministry, and to that degree He is the mediator of a better covenant, which has been legally enacted on better promises.

A Superior Covenant

⁷ For if that first ₎covenant₎ had been faultless, no opportunity would have been sought for a second one. ⁸ But finding fault with His people,ᵏ He says:ˡ

---

hood is superior to that of the Levites.

7:11-19 The need for a new high priest is the theme of this section.

7:16-17 physical descent. The Levitical priesthood was based solely on ancestry. The new priesthood is based on one's eternal nature. Jesus' resurrection thus qualified Him to be the better High Priest foretold in Psalm 110.

7:18-19 perfected. While the endless repetition of sacrifices served to remind people of their sin, it was powerless to change their condition (10:3-4; Rom. 3:20).

7:20-21 oath. The Levitical priests were appointed by divine command (Num. 8), but there was no oath involved. In contrast, as the full quote from Psalm 110:4 reveals, God's promise of a new high priest is sealed with an oath.

7:22 guarantee. This literally means "surety." Covenants were sealed with a pledge as a token that their terms would be carried out. Jesus' sacrifice is God's pledge of the New Covenant. **a better covenant.** A covenant was a binding commitment of mutual obligations between two parties. In the case of ancient kings, covenants were unilateral in that the king determined what both he and his subjects would do for one another.

7:23-24 He holds His priesthood permanently. Naturally, priests died, and so their service was only temporary; they had to be replaced. Jesus' superior priesthood is evidenced by the fact that His is permanent.

7:25 always able to save. One of this letter's main themes is that Jesus has the power to truly cleanse believers from sin and thus enable them to draw near to God.

8:1-6 This passage begins to consider the value of Jesus' priestly offering, a theme taken up in detail in chapters 9–10.

8:2 sanctuary. This refers to the Most Holy Place (9:3). **tabernacle.** God gave Moses a pattern for how to build a copy of the true heavenly tabernacle (Ex. 26). Jesus' greatness is seen in that He serves in this true tabernacle, not in an earthly copy. The tabernacle, an elaborate movable tent, gave way to Solomon's Temple, and later still, to the Herodian Temple destroyed by the Romans in A.D. 70. The fact that the author does not refer to its destruction as proof that the old order had passed away (v. 13) is a strong clue that the letter was written prior to that date. The focus on the tabernacle may have been because some Jewish sects considered the current administration of the temple services to be corrupted and invalid.

The Best Game Plan

1. What game plan has best helped your team to win? What game plan would you like your coach to try?
2. What are you best at forgetting: Names? Chores? Birthdays? Scripture references?

Hebrews 8:1-13

3. What is a covenant? What is the significance of the fact that God initiates and guarantees it?
4. What is the main difference between the Old and New Covenants (vv. 5-6)?
5. What four promises does this new covenant involve (vv. 10-12)?
6. Which aspect of the new covenant do you wish to experience more? Why?

"Look, the days are coming," says the Lord,
"when I will make a new covenant
with the house of Israel
and with the house of Judah—
⁹ not like the covenant
that I made with their fathers
on the day I took them by their hand
to lead them out of the land of Egypt.
Because they did not continue
in My covenant,
I disregarded them," says the Lord.
¹⁰ "But this is the covenant that I will make
with the house of Israel
after those days," says the Lord:
"I will put My laws into their minds,
and I will write them on their hearts,
and I will be their God,
and they will be My people.

¹¹ And each person will not teach
his fellow citizen,ᵃ
and each his brother, saying, 'Know the Lord,'
because they will all know Me,
from the least to the greatest of them.
¹² For I will be merciful to their wrongdoing,
and I will never again remember
their sins."ᵇ ᶜ

¹³ By saying, a new ₍covenant₎, He has declared that the first is old. And what is old and aging is about to disappear.

A Guilty Plea

1. How often were you told, "Don't touch!" when you were a little kid? What were you trying to touch?

Hebrews 9:1-10

2. How do you picture the earthly sanctuary described in verses 1-5?
3. Why were the gifts and sacrifices of the Old Testament worshipers not sufficient to clear their consciences (vv. 9-10)?
4. What is the "time of restoration" (v. 10)? Why do we have "physical regulations" prior to that time?
5. When you feel guilty, how do you try to clear your conscience and restore your peace of mind?

Old Covenant Ministry

9 Now the first ₍covenant₎ also had regulations for ministry and an earthly sanctuary. ² For a tabernacle was set up; and in the first room, which is called "the holy place," were the lampstand, the table, and the presentation loaves. ³ Behind the second curtain,

8:3 gifts and sacrifices. A primary function of the Old Testament high priests was to offer sacrifice on the Day of Atonement (Lev. 16). Jesus, as a priest, must likewise have a sacrifice to offer—namely, Himself (7:27).

8:5 copy and shadow. These words communicate the difference between the physical, visible nature of the old covenant and the spiritual, heavenly nature of the new. The quote, "Be careful..." is from Exodus 25:40.

8:6 a superior ministry. Jesus' ministry supersedes that of the old priests because the New Covenant accomplishes that which the old never could (vv. 7-13). **mediator.** Since a covenant involved two parties, the mediator

served as a go-between to work out the various terms of the covenant between the two parties. **better promises.** The New Covenant promises are "better" in that they promise far more than was ever promised in the old.

8:8-12 Jeremiah prophesied just prior to Babylon's conquest of Judah in 586 B.C. When the Jews were free to return to Jerusalem about 70 years later, expectations ran high that his prophecy quoted here was being fulfilled. Christians by contrast saw it fulfilled in the covenant established by Christ.

9:2 the holy place. The tabernacle, a flat-roofed tent about 15 by 45 feet, had two curtains forming separate rooms (Ex. 26).

Priests entering the tabernacle through the first curtain came into the "Holy Place" where they carried out their daily functions. **the lampstand.** A seven-branched lampstand (Ex. 25:31-40) provided the only light in the otherwise dark tent. **the table, and the presentation loaves.** Twelve loaves of fresh bread were placed daily upon this table (Ex. 25:30; Lev. 24:5-9).

9:3 the holy of holies. Behind the second curtain was a small (about 9 by 15 feet), dark, mysterious place reserved for God, and at special times, the high priest. Here God said He would meet Moses (Ex. 25:22).

the tabernacle was called "the holy of holies." ⁴ It contained the gold altar of incense and the ark of the covenant, covered with gold on all sides, in which there was a gold jar containing the manna, Aaron's rod that budded, and the tablets of the covenant. ⁵ The cherubim of glory were above it overshadowing the mercy seat. It is not possible to speak about these things in detail right now.

⁶ These things having been set up this way, the priests enter the first room repeatedly, performing their ministry. ⁷ But the high priest alone enters the second room, and that only once a year, and never without blood, which he offers for himself and for the sins of the people committed in ignorance. ⁸ The Holy Spirit was making it clear that the way into the holy of holies had not yet been disclosed while the first tabernacle was still standing. ⁹ This is a symbol for the present time, during which gifts and sacrifices are offered that cannot perfect the worshiper's conscience. ¹⁰ They are physical regulations and only deal with food, drink, and various washings imposed until the time of restoration.

New Covenant Ministry

¹¹ Now the •Messiah has appeared, high priest of the good things that have come.ᵃ In the greater and more perfect tabernacle not made with hands (that is, not of this creation), ¹² He entered the holy of holies once for all, not by the blood of goats and calves, but by His own blood, having obtained eternal redemption. ¹³ For if the blood of goats and bulls and the ashes of a heifer sprinkling those who are defiled, sanctify for the purification of the flesh, ¹⁴ how much more will the blood of the Messiah, who through the eternal Spirit offered Himself without blemish to God, cleanse ourᵇ consciences from dead works to serve the living God?

¹⁵ Therefore He is the mediator of a new covenant,ᶜ so that those who are called might receive the promise of the eternal inheritance, because a death has taken place for redemption from the transgressions ₗcommittedₗ under the first covenant. ¹⁶ Where a will exists, the death of the testator must be established. ¹⁷ For a will is

Passionate Sacrifice

1. Have you ever seen a movie with lots of blood and gore? Which one? How did you feel about watching it?

Hebrews 9:11-28

2. What distinguishes the priesthood of Christ from the old system (vv. 12-14)?
3. Why the emphasis on shed blood (vv. 19-22)? Whose blood? What for?
4. In verses 27-28, how is the once-and-for-all sacrifice of Christ's death illustrated?
5. How should this New Covenant affect the way we relate to Jesus on a daily basis?
6. What sacrifice is Jesus calling you to make to help others come to know Him?

valid only when people die, since it is never in force while the testator is living. ¹⁸ That is why even the first covenant was inaugurated with blood. ¹⁹ For when every commandment had been proclaimed by Moses to all the people according to the law, he took the blood of calves and goats, along with water, scarlet wool, and hyssop, and sprinkled the scroll itself and all the people, ²⁰ saying, **This is the blood of the covenant that God has commanded for you.**ᵈ ²¹ In the same way, he sprinkled the tabernacle and all the vessels of worship with blood. ²² According to the law almost everything is purified with blood, and without the shedding of blood there is no forgiveness.

²³ Therefore it was necessary for the copies of the things in the heavens to be purified with these ₗsacrificesₗ, but the heavenly things themselves ₗto be purifiedₗ with better sacrifices than these. ²⁴ For the Messiah did not enter a sanctuary made with hands

ᵃ**9:11** Other mss read *that are to come* ᵇ**9:14** Other mss read *your* ᶜ**9:15** The Gk word used here and in vv. 15–18 can be translated *covenant, will,* or *testament.* ᵈ**9:20** Ex 24:8

9:4 ark of the covenant. A box in which was placed: (1) the jar of manna—a reminder of God's care for the people during their time in the wilderness; (2) Aaron's staff—a reminder of God's election of his sons as priests; and (3) the stone tablets (the Ten Commandments)—a reminder of Israel's covenant responsibilities.

9:5 The cherubim. Two winged statues, representative of the angelic protection of God's honor, stood over the ark (Ex. 25:18). **glory.** A reverent way of referring to God (1:3). **the mercy seat.** Located on top of the ark (Ex. 25:17-22), and upon which the high priest sprinkled blood on the Day of Atonement.

9:7-8 the way ... had not yet been disclosed. The entire setup of the tabernacle reinforced this point. The altar for sacrifice, where the people brought their sacrifices, was outside the tabernacle. Directly in line

with that, but inside the first curtain of the tabernacle, was the altar where only priests could go. Behind that was the Most Holy Place into which only the high priest could enter, only on the Day of Atonement, and only if he first offered a sacrifice for himself (Lev. 16).

9:11 greater and more perfect tabernacle. In contrast to the temple worship, Jesus entered a "tabernacle" that is not a part of the sin-infected creation.

9:12 once for all. The finality of Christ's ministry stands in marked contrast with the ongoing cycle of sacrifices represented in the Old Covenant: Christ was sacrificed one time only (v. 26); He as the ultimate and eternal High Priest brought the blood of this sacrifice into God's presence (v. 21); His sacrifice secures the forgiveness of the sins of His people once and for all (10:10). **eternal redemption.** The liberation from sin that

Christ has secured, by contrast, is spiritual and permanent.

9:13 The blood of goats and bulls. A reference to the sacrifices on the Day of Atonement (Lev. 16). **ashes of a heifer.** Israelites who were ceremonially defiled through contact with a dead body were cleansed by being sprinkled with water mixed with the ashes of a burned heifer. Without this cleansing, they could not worship at the tabernacle (Num. 19). **purification of the flesh.** This is outward or bodily cleanness set in opposition to the cleanness of the spirit (v. 14).

9:14 how much more. If the sacrifice of an animal could effect some change in a person's standing with God, obviously the sacrifice of the royal Son of God would be far more effective. **the blood of the Messiah.** Blood represents sacrifice and death. **the eternal Spirit.** Literally, "an eternal spirit." This does not refer to the Holy Spirit, but to

(only a model[a] of the true one) but into heaven itself, that He might now appear in the presence of God for us. 25 He did not do this to offer Himself many times, as the high priest enters the sanctuary yearly with the blood of another. 26 Otherwise, He would have had to suffer many times since the foundation of the world. But now He has appeared one time, at the end of the ages, for the removal of sin by the sacrifice of Himself. 27 And just as it is appointed for people to die once— and after this, judgment— 28 so also the Messiah, having been offered once to bear the sins of many, will appear a second time, not to bear sin, but[b] to bring salvation to those who are waiting for Him.

Giving It Up

1. What part of your daily routine do you enjoy the most? The least?
2. During your teen or young adult years, who has inspired you to strive for holiness?

Hebrews 10:1-18

3. In what ways does Christ replace the inadequate sacrifices of the Law?
4. How does Jesus' obedience relate to our ability to be holy and "sanctified" (vv. 9-10)?
5. How would you define holiness to a person who doesn't know God but is interested?
6. Do you live your life as if you "are sanctified" (v. 14)? In what way is God calling you to practice greater holiness?

The Perfect Sacrifice

10 Since the law has ⌊only⌋ a shadow of the good things to come, and not the actual form of those realities, it can never perfect the worshipers by the same sacrifices they continually offer year after year. 2 Otherwise, wouldn't they have stopped being offered, since the worshipers, once purified, would no longer have any consciousness of sins? 3 But in the sacrifices[c] there is a reminder of sins every year. 4 For it is impossible for the blood of bulls and goats to take away sins.

5 Therefore, as He was coming into the world, He said:

> You did not want sacrifice and offering,
> but You prepared a body for Me.
> 6 You did not delight
> in whole burnt offerings and sin offerings.
> 7 Then I said, "See, I have come—
> it is written about Me
> in the volume of the scroll—
> to do Your will, O God!"[d]

8 After He says above, **You did not desire or delight in sacrifices and offerings, whole burnt offerings and sin offerings,** (which are offered according to the law), 9 He then says, **See, I have come to do Your will.**[e] He takes away the first to establish the second. 10 By this will, we have been sanctified through the offering of the body of Jesus Christ once and for all.

11 Now every priest stands day after day ministering and offering time after time the same sacrifices, which can never take away sins. 12 But this man, after offering one sacrifice for sins forever, sat down at the right hand of God. 13 He is now waiting until His enemies are made His footstool. 14 For by one offering He has perfected forever those who are sanctified. 15 The Holy Spirit also testifies to us about this. For after He had said:

> 16 **This is the covenant that I will make with them after those days, says the Lord:**
> **I will put My laws on their hearts,**
> **and I will write them on their minds,**

17 ⌊He adds⌋:

> **I will never again remember**
> **their sins and their lawless acts.**[f]

---

[a]**9:24** Or antitype, or figure [b]**9:28** Lit time, apart from sin, [c]**10:3** Lit in them [d]**10:5–7** Ps 40:6–8 [e]**10:9** Other mss add O God [f]**10:16–17** Jr 31:33–34

Christ's eternal nature. Because Christ Himself is eternal in nature, the redemption He secured is likewise everlasting (v. 12). The phrase also contrasts the spiritual nature of Christ's sacrifice to the fleshly nature of the old (v. 13). While they only ceremonially cleansed the body, the new sacrifice actually cleanses the conscience. **without blemish.** Sacrificial animals had to be of the best quality. What was true of them physically was true of Jesus morally.

9:20 This is the blood. This paraphrase of Exodus 24:8 would remind the readers of Jesus' words as He instituted the New Covenant (Matt. 26:28).

9:22 without the shedding of blood. This is the main point of the argument. Just as there is no inheritance from a will without a death, so the covenant promises cannot be fulfilled without a sacrifice. God accepts the death of the sinner (Lev. 17:11).

9:26 the removal of sin. Literally, "to effect an annulment." Christ not only brings forgiveness of sin, but also breaks its power.

9:28 appear a second time. Unlike the old high priests, Christ will not have to come again to bear sin. Instead, He will come to usher in the fullness of salvation.

10:2 once purified. The continuous repetition of the sacrifices indicated that the root problem of sin was never addressed, until Christ.

10:4 impossible. No amount of animal sacrifices could change the moral imperfection within people. The main purpose of the Old Covenant was to point out the need for One who is finally able to "take away sins" of believers forever.

10:9 takes away. Literally, "to abolish." The old sacrificial system, which could not accomplish God's will of making people holy (v. 10), was superseded by the Messiah who was devoted to doing God's will.

10:10 this will. That is, God's will (v. 9). **through the offering of the body of Jesus Christ.** Cleansing from sin is a matter of complete identification with Jesus, whose once-for-all sacrifice merits full redemption.

10:15-18 As the final proof that Jesus' sacrifice brings about the true cleansing God requires, Jeremiah's promise of the New Covenant is again considered (8:8-12). Since under this covenant the peoples' sins are forgiven (v. 18) and they now live according to the law embedded in their hearts, there is no longer any need for sacrifices (v. 18).

18 Now where there is forgiveness of these, there is no longer an offering for sin.

Exhortations to Godliness

19 Therefore, brothers, since we have boldness to enter the sanctuary through the blood of Jesus, 20 by the new and living way that He has inaugurated for us, through the curtain (that is, His flesh); 21 and since we have a great high priest over the house of God, 22 let us draw near with a true heart in full assurance of faith, our hearts sprinkled [clean] from an evil conscience and our bodies washed in pure water. 23 Let us hold on to the confession of our hope without wavering, for He who promised is faithful. 24 And let us be concerned about one another in order to promote love and good works, 25 not staying away from our meetings, as some habitually do, but encouraging each other, and all the more as you see the day drawing near.

Draw Near and Hold On

1. Which of your possessions would be the hardest for you to give away? Why?

Hebrews 10:19-39

2. Note the three "let us" statements in verses 22-25. What does each one mean? What incentives are given?

3. In rejecting Christ, what are the three big mistakes a person would be guilty of (v. 29)? What would the consequence be for these mistakes (v. 31)?

4. After such a dire warning, how does the author encourage the people to whom he is writing (vv. 32-39)? Which appeal do you find persuasive?

5. What encouragement do you need in order to hold on to your faith?

Warning against Willful Sin

26 For if we deliberately sin after receiving the knowledge of the truth, there no longer remains a sacrifice for sins, 27 but a terrifying expectation of judgment, and the fury of a fire about to consume the adversaries. 28 If anyone disregards Moses' law, he dies without mercy, based on the testimony of two or three witnesses. 29 How much worse punishment, do you think one will deserve who has trampled on the Son of God, regarded as profane[a] the blood of the covenant by which he was sanctified, and insulted the Spirit of grace? 30 For we know the One who has said, **Vengeance belongs to Me, I will repay,**[b][c] and again, **The Lord will judge His people.**[d] 31 It is a terrifying thing to fall into the hands of the living God!

32 Remember the earlier days when, after you had been enlightened, you endured a hard struggle with sufferings. 33 Sometimes you were publicly exposed to taunts and afflictions, and at other times you were companions of those who were treated that way. 34 For you sympathized with the prisoners[e] and accepted with joy the confiscation of your possessions, knowing that you yourselves have a better and enduring possession.[f] 35 So don't throw away your confidence, which has a great reward. 36 For you need endurance, so that after you have done God's will, you may receive what was promised.

37 For in yet a very little while,
   the Coming One will come and not delay.
38 But My righteous one[g] will live by faith;
   and if he draws back,
   My soul has no pleasure in him.[h]

39 But we are not those who draw back and are destroyed, but those who have faith and obtain life.

Heroes of Faith

11 Now faith is the reality[i] of what is hoped for, the proof[j] of what is not seen. 2 For by it our ancestors were approved.

---

a **10:29** Or *ordinary*   b **10:30** Other mss add *says the Lord*   c **10:30** Dt 32:35   d **10:30** Dt 32:36   e **10:34** Other mss read *sympathized with my imprisonment*   f **10:34** Other mss add *in heaven*   g **10:38** Other mss read *the righteous one*   h **10:37–38** Is 26:20 LXX; Hab 2:3–4   i **11:1** Or *assurance*   j **11:1** Or *conviction*

10:19 enter the sanctuary. In the Old Covenant only the high priest could draw near to God. In contrast, all Christians can do so with assurance.

10:20 new and living way. Not "new" as opposed to "old," but rather something fresh and alive.

10:22 hearts sprinkled. Priestly garments were consecrated for use by being sprinkled with the blood of a sacrifice (Ex. 29:19-21).

10:26 no longer remains a sacrifice for sins. The Levitical sacrifices covered ceremonial uncleanness, moral lapses for which one repented (Lev. 6:1-7), and sins of ignorance and passion (Lev. 5:17-19; 19:20-22). Sins that were a defiant rejection of the Law were not covered by the sacrifices (Num. 15:30). The author transfers this principle to the New Covenant as well. The God-appointed sacrifice must be met with an attitude of repentance and dedication. To reject Christ's sacrifice is to reject the only sacrifice for sins.

10:29 trampled on the Son of God, regarded as profane the blood of the covenant ... insulted the Spirit of grace. These three phrases amplify the nature of the sin warned against. It is a deliberate rejection of Jesus as the Messiah, a decision to abandon the covenant that comes through His sacrifice, and a resistance to the Spirit who applies God's grace to those who trust.

10:32 hard struggle. Jewish Christians (the most likely recipients of this letter) had suffered persecution from their fellow Jews. This ranged from harassment (Acts 18:17) to murder (Acts 7:59). Some experienced family rejection, economic boycotts, and physical abuse, which lead to forced relocation and the resultant loss of property.

Faith Hall of Fame

1. What is the riskiest thing you have done recently?

2. Who has inspired you the most by his or her example of faith?

Hebrews 11:1-16

3. How do you define faith? How does your answer compare with verse 1?

4. What is the essential ingredient in a life that is pleasing to God (v. 6)? Does this seem unreasonable to you?

5. What are some of the risks the heroes of faith took in order to follow God's will?

6. If you knew you could not fail, what big dream would you pursue? What is keeping you from going for this?

³ By faith we understand that the universe wasª created by the wordᵇ of God, so that what is seen has been made from things that are not visible.

⁴ By faith Abel offered to God a better sacrifice than Cain ⌊did⌋. By this he was approved as a righteous man, because God approved his gifts, and even though he is dead, he still speaks through this.

⁵ By faith, Enoch was taken away so that he did not experience death, and **he was not to be found because God took him away.**ᶜ For prior to his transformation he was approved, having pleased God. ⁶ Now without faith it is impossible to please God, for the one who draws near to Him must believe that He exists and rewards those who seek Him.

⁷ By faith Noah, after being warned about what was not yet seen, in reverence built an ark to deliver his

family. By this he condemned the world and became an heir of the righteousness that comes by faith.

⁸ By faith Abraham, when he was called, obeyed and went out to a place he was going to receive as an inheritance; he went out, not knowing where he was going. ⁹ By faith he stayed as a foreigner in the land of promise, living in tents with Isaac and Jacob, co-heirs of the same promise. ¹⁰ For he was looking forward to the city that has foundations, whose architect and builder is God.

¹¹ By faith even Sarah herself, when she was barren, received power to conceive offspring, even though she was past the age, since sheᵈ considered that the One who had promised was faithful. ¹² And therefore from one man—in fact, from one as good as dead—came offspring as numerous as the stars of heaven and as innumerable as the grains of sand by the seashore.

¹³ These all died in faith without having received the promises, but they saw them from a distance, greeted them, and confessed that they were foreigners and temporary residents on the earth. ¹⁴ Now those who say such things make it clear that they are seeking a homeland. ¹⁵ If they had been remembering that land they came from, they would have had opportunity to return. ¹⁶ But they now aspire to a better land—a heavenly one. Therefore God is not ashamed to be called their God, for He has prepared a city for them.

¹⁷ By faith Abraham, when he was tested, offered up Isaac; he who had received the promises was offering up his unique son, ¹⁸ about whom it had been said, **In Isaac your seed will be called.**ᵉ ¹⁹ He considered God to be able even to raise someone from the dead, from which he also got him back as an illustration.ᶠ

²⁰ By faith Isaac blessed Jacob and Esau concerning things to come. ²¹ By faith Jacob, when he was dying, blessed each of the sons of Joseph, and, **he worshiped, leaning on the top of his staff.**ᵍ ²² By faith Joseph, as he was nearing the end of his life, mentioned the exodus of the sons of Israel and gave instructions concerning his bones.

ª**11:3** Or *the worlds were,* or *the ages were* ᵇ**11:3** Or *voice,* or *utterance* ᶜ**11:5** Gn 5:21–24 ᵈ**11:11** Or *By faith Abraham, even though he was past age—and Sarah herself was barren—received the ability to procreate since he* ᵉ**11:18** Gn 21:12 ᶠ**11:19** Or *foreshadowing,* or *parable,* or *type* ᵍ**11:21** Gn 47:31

11:3 the universe was created by the word of God. The stories of faith begin with creation, which in itself dramatically exemplifies how God brought into being things that were unseen.

11:4 Abel. Abel's faith is not mentioned in Genesis, but it is clear that the reason God accepted his sacrifice and not Cain's had to do with a matter of attitude (Gen. 4:4-7).

11:5 Enoch. The main facts about Enoch were his mysterious disappearance and that "he pleased God" (Gen. 5:21-24, Septuagint). Enoch was a popular figure in Jewish legends, which taught that his purity was such that God "took him" because he had no sin.

11:7 Noah. Noah's faith is not mentioned in the Old Testament, but is seen in his obedience to God (Gen. 6:9–9:17). **not yet seen.** Acting upon that which God promises (or warns), even when unseen, is the essence of

faith (v. 1). **reverence.** Faith lives in recognition of the awesome power of God. **condemned the world.** In that he acted in obedience to God while others did not.

11:8-10 Abraham ... stayed as a foreigner. In contrast to his settled life in Ur, Abraham's nomadic life in Canaan showed that his eyes were fixed upon a vision of something greater than could be found in this world.

11:13 These all. Abraham, Sarah, Isaac, Jacob. **died in faith.** None of the patriarchs saw the fulfillment of God's promise regarding the land or the vast nation Abraham would father. **foreigners and temporary residents.** Both terms describe how believers are to view their lives in the world (John 17:14).

11:16 a heavenly one. In the New Covenant a superior territory to the land of Canaan is to be achieved (8:5). **called their God.** God

openly identifies with these people, pledging Himself to them (Ex. 3:6,15).

11:17 offered up Isaac. Since child sacrifice was part of the worship life of the surrounding cultures, this may not have seemed as outrageous to Abraham as it does to modern readers. That does not minimize his anxiety regarding the death of his son, however. It also would generate tension in Abraham in that it was through Isaac that God had said the promise would come true (v. 18; Gen. 21:12).

11:19 even to raise someone from the dead. Abraham believed God would keep His promise even if it meant resurrecting Isaac from the dead.

11:21 Jacob. Looking two generations ahead, the elderly Jacob passed on the blessing and promise to Ephraim and Manasseh (Gen. 48:20). **leaning on the top of**

23 By faith Moses, after he was born, was hidden by his parents for three months, because they saw that the child was beautiful, and they didn't fear the king's edict. 24 By faith Moses, when he had grown up, refused to be called the son of Pharaoh's daughter 25 and chose to suffer with the people of God rather than to enjoy the short-lived pleasure of sin. 26 For he considered reproach for the sake of the •Messiah to be greater wealth than the treasures of Egypt, since his attention was on the reward.

27 By faith he left Egypt behind, not being afraid of the king's anger, for he persevered, as one who sees Him who is invisible. 28 By faith he instituted the •Passover and the sprinkling of the blood, so that the destroyer of the firstborn might not touch them. 29 By faith they crossed the Red Sea as though they were on dry land. When the Egyptians attempted to do this, they were drowned.

30 By faith the walls of Jericho fell down after being encircled for seven days. 31 By faith Rahab the prostitute received the spies in peace and didn't perish with those who disobeyed.

32 And what more can I say? Time is too short for me to tell about Gideon, Barak, Samson, Jephthah, of David and Samuel and the prophets, 33 who by faith conquered kingdoms, administered justice, obtained promises, shut the mouths of lions, 34 quenched the raging of fire, escaped the edge of the sword, gained strength after being weak, became mighty in battle, and put foreign armies to flight. 35 Women received their dead raised to life again. Some men were tortured, not accepting release, so that they might gain a better resurrection, 36 and others experienced mockings and scourgings, as well as bonds and imprisonment. 37 They were stoned,[a] they were sawed in two, they died by the sword, they wandered about in sheepskins, in goatskins, destitute, afflicted, and mistreated. 38 The world was not worthy of them. They wandered in deserts, mountains, caves, and holes in the ground.

39 All these were approved through their faith, but they did not receive what was promised, 40 since God had provided something better for us, so that they would not be made perfect without us.

Running Wide Open

1. What discipline did you sometimes resent as a child that you appreciate now: Practicing? Turning in homework on time? Not overspending your allowance? Other?

Hebrews 12:1-13

2. How should Christians run the "race" (v. 1) in sports, in school, and in life?
3. What does it mean to keep "our eyes on Jesus" (v. 2)? Why is this often difficult?
4. How does Christ's discipline differ from human discipline? What benefits does discipline bring?
5. What is the hardest thing you're going through right now? How is God using this in your life?

The Call to Endurance

12 Therefore since we also have such a large cloud of witnesses surrounding us, let us lay aside every weight and the sin that so easily ensnares us, and run with endurance the race that lies before us, 2 keeping our eyes on Jesus,[b] the source and perfecter[c] of our faith, who for the joy that lay before Him[d] endured a cross and despised the shame, and has sat down at the right hand of God's throne.

Fatherly Discipline

3 For consider Him who endured such hostility from sinners against Himself, so that you won't grow weary and lose heart. 4 In struggling against sin, you have not yet resisted to the point of shedding your blood. 5 And you have forgotten the exhortation that addresses you as sons:

---

[a] **11:37** Other mss add *they were tempted*   [b] **12:2** Or *looking to Jesus*   [c] **12:2** Or *the founder and completer*   [d] **12:2** Or *who instead of the joy lying before Him,* that is, the joy of heaven

---

his staff. A reference back to Joseph's oath to Jacob in Genesis 47:31.

11:22 Joseph. His faith was evidenced by his belief in God's promise to one day deliver Israel from Egypt (Gen. 15:13-16).

11:24 refused to be called the son of Pharaoh's daughter. Moses was raised by the Pharaoh's daughter (Ex. 2:5-10), but he chose not to identify with the oppressor of his people, even though that would have been an easier, more comfortable option.

11:26 the sake of the Messiah. Literally, "the anointed." In the Old Testament, Israel as a nation was sometimes called "the anointed one" (Ps. 89:51). The author uses Moses' loyalty to "God's anointed" nation as a model for how the individual believer ought to be loyal to God's anointed Messiah, Jesus Christ.

11:28 Passover. This action demonstrated faith that God would keep the promise to "pass over" the homes of the Israelites as the destroying angel came through the land (Ex. 12). **sprinkling of the blood.** Blood from the Passover lamb was sprinkled on the doorframe of each Jewish home.

11:31 Rahab. All the previous examples of faith were men held in high esteem by the Jews. Rahab was a Gentile prostitute who had faith to see that the God of Israel was the God of the whole earth (Josh. 2:11).

11:39 did not receive what was promised. All that was included in the coming of the Messiah and His sacrifice occurred after their deaths.

12:1 witnesses. This is the same word used for "martyrs." It is probably a deliberate play on words in which both meanings are in-

tended. The heroes of faith are pictured as a cheering section of former runners in a race urging the contemporary readers to persevere as they did. **lay aside every weight.** In Greek games at the time, runners ran with no clothes so that they could move freely without hindrance. **the sin that so easily ensnares.** Just as a flowing robe makes it impossible to run well, so sin makes the Christian life difficult.

12:2 keeping our eyes on Jesus. In races of the time, the prize for the race was placed at the end to motivate the runners. Jesus is here described as the focus of the Christian life. **joy that lay before Him.** Jesus knew the joy His mission of reconciliation would bring, and so pursued it whatever the cost. **despised the shame.** Crucifixion was considered so degrading that no Roman citizen could be crucified, regardless of the crime committed.

JAGMES

PERSONAL READING PLAN

☐ James 1:1-27
☐ James 2:1-26

☐ James 3:1-4:12
☐ James 4:13-5:20

AUTHOR

In the New Testament there are apparently two men by the name of James, who might have written this epistle—either James the apostle, or James the brother of Jesus. Since it is almost certain that the Apostle James (the son of Zebedee) was killed by Herod in A.D. 44 (before the epistle could have been written), traditionally the author has been assigned to James, the leader of the church in Jerusalem and the brother of Jesus (Mark 6:3).

The pilgrimage of James to faith is fascinating. At first Jesus' family was hostile to his ministry (John 7:5) and, in fact, tried to stop it at one point (Mark 3:21). Yet after Jesus' ascension, Jesus' mother and brothers are listed among the early believers (Acts 1:14). For James, this coming to faith may have resulted from Jesus' post-resurrection appearance to him (1 Cor. 15:7).

James emerged as a leader of the church in Jerusalem, presiding over the first Jerusalem Council, which decided whether to admit Gentiles to the church (Acts 15, especially vv. 13-21). And it is to James that Paul later brought the collection for the poor in Jerusalem (Acts 21:17-25).

DATE

Some place it very early, around A.D. 45, making it the first New Testament book. Others date it quite late.

THEME

Christianity in action.

AUDIENCE

James is one of the General Epistles (along with 1 and 2 Peter, John's epistles and Jude), so called because it has no single destination. . It appears that he is writing to Jewish Christians dispersed around the Greek world: "to the temporary residents of the Dispersion" (1:1). But since Peter uses the same sort of inscription (1 Peter 1:1-2) James' destination remains unclear.

PURPOSE

While James clearly stands in the tradition of other Christian writers, he has some special concerns. The relationship between rich and poor crops up at various points (1:9-11; 5:1-6)—an issue of special significance to the modern affluent West. He is concerned about the use and abuse of speech (1:19,26; 2:12; 3:3-12; 5:12). He gives instruction on prayer (1:5-8; 4:2-3; 5:13-18). Above all, he is concerned with ethical behavior. How believers act, he says, has significance for the Day of Judgment; future reward or punishment depends on it. In this regard, James bemoans the inconsistency of human behavior (1:6-8,22-24; 2:14-17; 4:1,3). Human beings are "indecisive" or "double-minded" (1:8; 4:8) in sharp contrast to God who is one (2:19) and does not change (1:17).

James has been incorrectly understood by some to be contradicting Paul's doctrine of justification of faith (2:14-26). In fact if James had Paul in mind at all, he was addressing himself to those who had perverted Paul's message—insisting that it doesn't matter what you do, as long as you have faith. James responded by asserting that works are the outward evidence of inner faith. Works make faith visible to others. In contrast, Paul was concerned with our standing before God. As is evident from Romans 12-15,

Paul certainly agreed with James that faith in Christ has direct implications for how believers live.

ITS OMISSIONS

James contains no mention of the Holy Spirit and no reference to the redemptive work or resurrection of Christ. In fact, it contains only two references to the name Jesus Christ (1:1 and 2:1). Furthermore, examples are drawn from the lives of Old Testament prophets, not from the experiences of Jesus. Although the title *Lord* appears 11 times, it generally refers to the name of God (in Old Testament fashion) and not to the kingly authority of Jesus. Indeed, it is God the Father who is the focus of the book of James.

HISTORICAL BACKGROUND

James draws his language, images and ideas from three worlds: Judaism, Greek culture and early Christianity. From Christianity, he uses language referring to the second coming (5:7-9); common patterns of Christian ethical instruction, which parallel those in 1 Peter (1:2-4,21; 4:7-10); and especially the teachings of Jesus (1:5,17; 2:5,8,19; 4:3; 5:12). From Judaism, he draws his insistence on the unity of God, concern for keeping the Law and quotations from Jewish Scriptures (2:8,11,21-25; 4:6; 5:11,17-18) along with his use of Jewish terms (e.g., the word translated "hell" in 3:6 is the Hebrew word *gehenna*). Christianity and Judaism shared his concern for the poor and oppressed

STRUCTURE

Written in epistle (letter) form, James is loosely structured and rambling in style. James shares many characteristics of the sermonic style of both Greek philosophers and Jewish rabbis. James carries on a conversation with a hypothetical opponent (2:18-26; 5:13-16), switches subjects by means of a question (2:14; 4:1), uses many commands (60 of the 108 verses in James are imperatives), relies on vivid images from everyday life (3:3-6; 5:7), illustrates points by reference to famous people (2:21-23,25; 5:11,17), uses vivid opposites in which the right way is set alongside the wrong way (2:13,26). (James Hardy Ropes, *The International Critical Commentary*; William Barclay, *The Letters of James and Peter*). Jewish sermons had many of the same characteristics. But rabbis also had the habit, as did James, of constructing sermons that were deliberately disconnected—a series of moral truths and commands strung together like beads.

PASSAGES FOR TOPICAL GROUP STUDY

1:2-18 . . . . . TEMPTATIONS and TRIALS . . . . Passing the Test

1:19-27 . . . . DOER OF THE TRUTH . . . . Just Do It

2:1-13 . . . . . FAVORITICISM and ACCEPTANCE .Been Misjudged Lately?

2:14-26 . . . PERFECTING YOUR FAITH . . . . Talk is Cheap

3:1-18 . . . . . HARSH WORDS and GOSSIP . . . . . . Tongue Trouble

4:1-12 . . . . . FRIENDSHIPS and CHOICES . Favorable Friendship

4:13-17 . . . . FUTURE PLANS . . . . One Day at a Time

5:7-20 . . . . PATIENCE AND WAITING . . . . It's Tough to Wait

PASSAGES FOR GENERAL GROUP STUDY

5:1-6 . . . . Money Concerns (and Management)

Greeting

1 James, a slave of God and of the Lord Jesus Christ: To the 12 tribes in the Dispersion. Greetings.

Passing the Test

1. What is your usual approach to a test: Fear? Joy? Prayer? Study all night?

James 1:2-18

2. How is it that we can "consider it a great joy" when we are going through difficult times (v. 2)?

3. What reward comes with persevering in the faith (v. 12)?

4. What does James say is the origin of temptation, and why is it so important to understand this (vv. 13-15)?

5. How are you dealing with the trials and temptations in your life? Who or what can help you to persevere?

Trials and Maturity

² Consider it a great joy, my brothers, whenever you experience various trials, ³ knowing that the testing of your faith produces endurance. ⁴ But endurance must do its complete work, so that you may be mature and complete, lacking nothing.

⁵ Now if any of you lacks wisdom, he should ask God, who gives to all generously and without criticizing, and it will be given to him. ⁶ But let him ask in faith without doubting. For the doubter is like the surging sea, driven and tossed by the wind. ⁷ That person should not expect to receive anything from the Lord. ⁸ An indecisive man is unstable in all his ways.

⁹ The brother of humble circumstances should boast in his exaltation; ¹⁰ but the one who is rich ⌞should boast⌟ in his humiliation, because he will pass away like a flower of the field. ¹¹ For the sun rises with its scorching heat and dries up the grass; its flower falls off, and its beautiful appearance is destroyed. In the same way, the rich man will wither away while pursuing his activities.

¹² Blessed is a man who endures trials,ᵃ because when he passes the test he will receive the crown of life that Heᵇ has promised to those who love Him.

¹³ No one undergoing a trial should say, "I am being tempted by God." For God is not tempted by evil,ᶜ and He Himself doesn't tempt anyone. ¹⁴ But each person is tempted when he is drawn away and enticed by his own evil desires. ¹⁵ Then after desire has conceived, it gives birth to sin, and when sin is fully grown, it gives birth to death.

¹⁶ Don't be deceived, my dearly loved brothers. ¹⁷ Every generous act and every perfect gift is from above, coming down from the Father of lights; with Him there is no variation or shadow cast by turning. ¹⁸ By His own choice, He gave us a new birth by the message of truthᵈ so that we would be the •firstfruits of His creatures.

Hearing and Doing the Word

¹⁹ My dearly loved brothers, understand this: everyone must be quick to hear, slow to speak, and slow to anger, ²⁰ for man's anger does not accomplish God's righteousness. ²¹ Therefore, ridding yourselves of all moral filth and evil excess, humbly receive the implanted word, which is able to save you.ᵉ

²² But be doers of the word and not hearers only, deceiving yourselves. ²³ Because if anyone is a hearer of the word and not a doer, he is like a man looking at his own faceᶠ in a mirror; ²⁴ for he looks at himself, goes away, and right away forgets what kind of man he was. ²⁵ But the one who looks intently into the perfect law of freedom and perseveres in it, and is not a forgetful hearer but a doer who acts—this person will be blessed in what he does.

ᵃ**1:12** Lit *trial*, used as a collective   ᵇ**1:12** Other mss read *that the Lord*   ᶜ**1:13** Or *evil persons*, or *evil things*   ᵈ**1:18** *message of truth* = the gospel
ᵉ**1:21** Lit *save your souls*   ᶠ**1:23** Lit *at the face of his birth*

1:3 endurance. This could also be translated as "perseverance." It is used in the sense of active overcoming, rather than passive acceptance.

1:4 its complete work. Perfection is not automatic—it takes time and effort. **mature and complete.** What James has in mind here is wholeness of character. **lacking.** The opposite of mature and complete. This word is used of an army that has been defeated or a person who has failed to reach a standard.

1:5 wisdom. This is not just abstract knowledge, but God-given insight that leads to right living.

1:6 But. Both here and in 4:3, unanswered prayer is connected to the quality of our asking, not the unwillingness of God to give. **ask**

in faith. To be *single-minded* about God's ability to answer prayer.

1:8 indecisive. To doubt is to be double-minded—to both believe and disbelieve.

1:12 Blessed. Happy is the person who has withstood all the trials to the end. **endures.** Such a person is like metal that has been purged by fire and is purified of all foreign substances. **crown of life.** Crowns were worn at weddings and feasts (signifying joy); were given to winners of athletic competitions (signifying victory); and worn by royalty (as befits children of God the King).

1:13 tempted. The focus shifts from enduring outward trials (v. 12) to resisting inner temptations. **"I am being tempted by God."** The natural tendency is to blame others for our failure. In this case, God is blamed for

sending a test that is too hard to bear. **He Himself doesn't tempt anyone.** God does not lure anyone into a tempting situation just to see whether that person will stand or fall.

1:14 evil desires. The true source of evil is a person's own inner inclinations (Mark 7:21-23).

1:19 slow to speak. One needs to consider carefully what is to be said, rather than impulsively and carelessly launching into unwise words. **slow to anger.** James does not forbid anger. He does caution against responding in anger at every opportunity.

1:21 ridding yourselves. This verb means literally, "to lay aside" or "to strip off," as one would do with filthy clothing. **implanted word.** They are Christians already. They have the life of God in them. It is now up to them to act upon what is already theirs.

1217

Just Do It

1. When have you forgotten to do something important your parents, teacher, or coach asked you to do? What happened?

James 1:19-27

2. What would James recommend as a solution to conflicts in relationships (v. 19)?

3. How do we prepare ourselves to receive God's word fully in our lives (v. 21)? What do you need to "get rid of"?

4. What does the mirror illustration say about the importance of doing and not just hearing (vv. 22-25)?

5. What is one way this week that you can practice being a "doer" this week—a person who lives the way God says?

²⁶ If anyone[a] thinks he is religious, without controlling his tongue but deceiving his heart, his religion is useless. ²⁷ Pure and undefiled religion before our[b] God and Father is this: to look after orphans and widows in their distress and to keep oneself unstained by the world.

The Sin of Favoritism

2 My brothers, hold your faith in our glorious Lord Jesus Christ without showing favoritism. ² For suppose a man comes into your meeting wearing a gold ring, dressed in fine clothes, and a poor man dressed in dirty clothes also comes in. ³ If you look with favor on the man wearing the fine clothes so that you say, "Sit here in a good place," and yet you say to the poor man, "Stand over there," or, "Sit here on the floor by my footstool," ⁴ haven't you discriminated among yourselves and become judges with evil thoughts?

⁵ Listen, my dear brothers: Didn't God choose the poor in this world to be rich in faith and heirs of the kingdom that He has promised to those who love Him? ⁶ Yet you dishonored that poor man. Don't the rich oppress you and drag you into the courts? ⁷ Don't they blaspheme the noble name that you bear?

⁸ If you really carry out the royal law prescribed in Scripture, **Love your neighbor as yourself,**[c] you are doing well. ⁹ But if you show favoritism, you commit sin and are convicted by the law as transgressors. ¹⁰ For whoever keeps the entire law, yet fails in one point, is guilty of ⌊breaking it⌋ all. ¹¹ For He who said, **Do not commit adultery,**[d] also said, **Do not murder.**[e] So if you do not commit adultery, but you do murder, you are a lawbreaker.

Been Misjudged Lately?

1. Who are the kids at your school or on your team you have the hardest time accepting?

2. When have you either misjudged someone or been misjudged yourself, based on appearance?

James 2:1-13

3. What is the connection between being poor and being rich in verse 5?

4. How does God look upon favoritism (v. 9)?

5. What is the significance of James' statement, "Mercy triumphs over judgment" (v. 13), in the context of verses 8-11?

6. What can you do to be more accepting of others in the coming week?

¹² Speak and act as those who will be judged by the law of freedom. ¹³ For judgment is without mercy to the

---

a**1:26** Other mss add *among you*   b**1:27** Or *before the*   c**2:8** Lv 19:18   d**2:11** Ex 20:14; Dt 5:18   e**2:11** Ex 20:13; Dt 5:17

1:26 if anyone thinks. The focus is on a person's own self-assessment of his or her religious commitment. By contrast, in verse 27, James states what God considers as truly religious. **religious.** The emphasis here is probably on the overt acts of religion, such as scrupulous observance of the details of worship and personal piety. **controlling his tongue.** The inability to control one's speech (as in gossip and criticism) is the mark of the person who thinks he or she is religious, but really is not.

1:27 religion. True religion has more to do with acts of charity than acts of piety. It involves caring for others, and avoiding the corrupting influence of one's culture. **orphans and widows.** In the Old Testament, orphans and widows were the poor and oppressed, whom God's people were to care for because God cared for them (Deut.

10:17-18; 24:17-22). **unstained.** Unpolluted; pure; undefiled. **world.** This refers to the world system that is in opposition to God.

2:1 favoritism. The practice James addresses in these verses keeps one's religion from being pure and undefiled. The motive for this partiality to the rich is likely self-serving.

2:2 a gold ring. This is the mark of those who belonged to the equestrian order—the second level of Roman aristocracy. These noblemen were typically wealthy. Rings, in general, were signs of wealth. Early Christians were urged to wear only one ring, on the little finger, bearing the image of a dove, fish, or anchor. **fine clothes.** These are literally "bright and shining" garments, like those worn by the angels in Acts 10:30. **poor man.**

The word used here denotes a beggar, a person from the lowest level of society. **dirty clothes.** In contrast to the spotless garments of the rich man, the beggar wears filthy rags, probably because this is all he owns. Our treatment of others should not be based on outward appearances.

2:6 oppress you. In a day of abject poverty the poor were often forced to borrow money at exorbitant rates of interest just to survive. The rich profited from their need. **drag you into the courts.** This was probably over the issue of a debt.

2:7 the noble name. The early followers of Jesus were dubbed with the name "Christians" (Acts 11:26). At baptism they formally took upon themselves the name of Christ, knowing that they might well be vilified simply for bearing that name.

one who hasn't shown mercy. Mercy triumphs over judgment.

Talk Is Cheap

1. Are you a doer or a thinker? Are you more likely to act without thinking or think without acting?

James 2:14-26

2. Is James saying that faith or belief doesn't really matter? If not, why does it matter?

3. What is the significance of verse 22? In what way does faith need to be "perfected"?

4. What is God really saying with the Rahab example in verse 25? How would you apply this to your thoughts and actions in everyday life?

5. Give some examples of works you can do to help perfect your faith.

Faith and Works

¹⁴ What good is it, my brothers, if someone says he has faith, but does not have works? Can his faith^a save him?

¹⁵ If a brother or sister is without clothes and lacks daily food, ¹⁶ and one of you says to them, "Go in peace, keep warm, and eat well," but you don't give them what the body needs, what good is it? ¹⁷ In the same way faith, if it doesn't have works, is dead by itself.

¹⁸ But someone will say, "You have faith, and I have works."^b Show me your faith without works, and I will show you faith from my works.^c ¹⁹ You believe that God is one; you do well. The demons also believe—and they shudder.

²⁰ Foolish man! Are you willing to learn that faith without works is useless? ²¹ Wasn't Abraham our father justified by works when he offered Isaac his son on the altar? ²² You see that faith was active together with his works, and by works, faith was perfected. ²³ So the Scripture was fulfilled that says, **Abraham believed God, and it was credited to him for righteousness,**^d and he was called God's friend. ²⁴ You see that a man is justified by works and not by faith alone. ²⁵ And in the same way, wasn't Rahab the prostitute also justified by works when she received the messengers and sent them out by a different route? ²⁶ For just as the body without the spirit is dead, so also faith without works is dead.

Controlling the Tongue

3 Not many should become teachers, my brothers, knowing that we will receive a stricter judgment; ² for we all stumble in many ways. If anyone does not stumble in what he says,^e he is a mature man who is also able to control his whole body.^f

³ Now when we put bits into the mouths of horses to make them obey us, we also guide the whole animal.^g ⁴ And consider ships: though very large and driven by fierce winds, they are guided by a very small rudder wherever the will of the pilot directs. ⁵ So too, though the tongue is a small part ⌊of the body⌋, it boasts great things. Consider how large a forest a small fire ignites. ⁶ And the tongue is a fire. The tongue, a world of unrighteousness, is placed among the parts of our ⌊bodies⌋; it pollutes the whole body, sets the course of life on fire, and is set on fire by •hell.

⁷ For every creature—animal or bird, reptile or fish—is tamed and has been tamed by man, ⁸ but no man can tame the tongue. It is a restless evil, full of deadly poison. ⁹ With it we bless our^h Lord and Father, and with it we curse men who are made in God's likeness. ¹⁰ Out of the same mouth come blessing and cursing. My brothers, these things should not be this way. ¹¹ Does a spring pour out sweet and bitter water from the same

---

^a**2:14** Or *Can faith*, or *Can that faith*, or *Can such faith*   ^b**2:18** The quotation may end here or after v. 18b or v. 19.   ^c**2:18** Other mss read *Show me your faith from your works, and from my works I will show you my faith.*   ^d**2:23** Gn 15:6   ^e**3:2** Lit *in word*   ^f**3:2** Lit *to bridle the whole body*   ^g**3:3** Lit *whole body*   ^h**3:9** Or *bless the*

2:12 the law of freedom. Judaism had become encrusted with countless rules that bound people. Christians had only one key principle to follow: to love others freely as Christ freely loved them (v. 8; 1:25).

2:14 faith. James uses this word in a special way. The faith he speaks of here is mere intellectual affirmation. Such a mind-oriented profession stands in sharp contrast to the comprehensive, whole-life commitment that characterizes true New Testament faith. New Testament faith involves believing with one's full being: mind, emotions, body (behavior), and spirit. The people James has in mind differ from their pagan and Jewish neighbors only in what they *profess* to believe. **works.** Just as James uses the word "faith" in his own way, so too he uses "works" in a unique way. For James, works have to do with proper ethical behavior. **Can

his faith save him? The implied answer is "No," based on what James just said in verses 12-13. Intellectual faith cannot save one from judgment when one has not been merciful.

2:17 faith, if it doesn't have works, is dead. An inevitable result of faith is good works. Jesus said you can recognize a person by the fruit he's bearing. Grapes don't come from thornbushes nor do figs come from thistles. Good fruit comes from a good tree and bad fruit from a bad tree (Mt 7:15-20).

2:18 the demons also believe. James clinches his argument against faith as just intellectual assent by pointing out that even the demons believe in God. They shudder but they don't repent and have authentic faith from which good works flow.

2:21-25 Abraham ... Rahab. James concludes with two illustrations from the Old Testament, which contain the evidence demanded by the fruit in verse 20. In both cases, faith is demonstrated by means of concrete action. Abraham actually had the knife raised over his beloved son Isaac, and Rahab actually hid the spies. Without faith, Abraham would never have even considered sacrificing his only son, nor would Rahab have defied her king at great personal risk.

2:24 not by faith alone. James declares that saying you have faith isn't the same as sharing your faith. Real faith produces a changed life, which in turn, does good works.

opening? ¹²Can a fig tree produce olives, my brothers, or a grapevine ₁produce₁ figs? Neither can a saltwater spring yield fresh water.

The Wisdom from Above

¹³Who is wise and understanding among you? He should show his works by good conduct with wisdom's gentleness. ¹⁴But if you have bitter envy and selfish ambition in your heart, don't brag and lie in defiance of the truth. ¹⁵Such wisdom does not come down from above, but is earthly, sensual, demonic. ¹⁶For where envy and selfish ambition exist, there is disorder and every kind of evil. ¹⁷But the wisdom from above is first pure, then peace-loving, gentle, compliant, full of mercy and good fruits, without favoritism and hypocrisy. ¹⁸And the fruit of righteousness is sown in peace by those who make peace.

Tongue Trouble

1. In your family or group, are you more likely to tease or be teased? Whom do you tease or who teases you?

James 3:1-18

2. How does James illustrate the power of the tongue (vv. 3-6)? When have you been hurt by harsh words or gossip?

3. What is the ultimate solution for controlling our speech (vv. 10-12)? How does our heart need to change?

4. How does "the wisdom from above" (v. 17) guide us in how we talk to others?

5. When has your mouth gotten you into trouble lately? Competition or stress has a way of bringing that out. How can you correct this?

Favorable Friendship

1. When has a "friend" gotten you in trouble? What did you learn from that experience?

James 4:1-12

2. What are two reasons we don't get what we want (vv. 2-3)? What does this reveal about God's heart toward answered prayer?

3. How does the statement, "friendship with the world is hostility toward God" (v. 4), balance with, "For God loved the world" (John 3:16)? What is James trying to communicate?

4. Where do you need to submit yourself to God and resist the Devil this week (v. 7)? Are there any friends that are making it harder for you to resist temptation?

Proud or Humble

4 What is the source of the wars and the fights among you? Don't they come from the cravings that are at war within you?ᵃ ²You desire and do not have. You murder and covet and cannot obtain. You fight and war. You do not have because you do not ask. ³You ask and don't receive because you ask wrongly, so that you may spend it on your desires for pleasure.

⁴Adulteresses!ᵇ Do you not know that friendship with the world is hostility toward God? So whoever wants to be the world's friend becomes God's enemy. ⁵Or do you think it's without reason the Scripture says that the Spirit He has caused to live in us yearns jealously?ᶜ

⁶But He gives greater grace. Therefore He says:

> God resists the proud,
> but gives grace to the humble.ᵈ

ᵃ**4:1** Lit *war in your members* ᵇ**4:4** Other mss read *Adulterers and adulteresses* ᶜ**4:5** Or *He who caused the Spirit to live in us yearns jealously,* or *the spirit He caused to live in us yearns jealously,* or *He jealously yearns for the Spirit He made to live in us* ᵈ**4:6** Pr 3:34

3:14 bitter envy. The word "bitter" is the same word that was used in verse 12 to describe brackish water unfit for human consumption. It is now applied to zeal (the word translated "envy" is literally *zelos*). Zeal that has gone astray becomes jealousy. **in your heart.** This is the issue: What lies at the core of the person's being? **don't brag and lie in defiance of the truth.** Those whose hearts are filled with this sense of rivalry and party-spirit ought not to pretend they are speaking God's wisdom. This merely compounds the wrong that is taking place.

3:15 earthly, sensual, demonic. Wisdom that springs from envy is not of God but ultimately has its source in Satan.

3:16 disorder and every kind of evil. It was out of envy that Cain murdered his brother Abel. Many of the evils of this world can be traced to this spirit of envy that produces disorder.

3:17 peace-loving. This is the opposite of envy and ambition. True wisdom produces right relationships between people, and this is the root idea behind the word "peace" in the New Testament. **compliant.** True wisdom is willing to listen, learn, and then yield when persuaded. **full of mercy and good fruits.** True wisdom reaches out to the unfortunate in practical ways, a point James never tires of making. **without favoritism.** Literally, "undivided." True wisdom does not vacillate back and forth. It is the opposite of the wavering in 1:6-8. **hypocrisy.** True wisdom does not act or pretend. It is honest and genuine.

4:1 wars and fights. Literally, "wars and battles." These are long-term conflicts, not sudden explosions. **among you.** The struggle is within a believer—between the part of

him or her that is controlled by the Holy Spirit and that which is controlled by the flesh.

4:2 You desire. This is desire at work (1:14). **and do not have.** This is desire frustrated. **murder and covet.** This is how frustrated desire responds. It lashes out at others in anger and abuse. (This is "killing" in the sense of heart attitude—Matt. 5:21-22.) It responds in jealousy to those who have what it wants. **fight and war.** This mad desire-driven quest causes a person to disregard other people, trampling over them to get what they want. **you do not ask.** One reason for this frustrated desire is a lack of prayer.

4:3 you ask wrongly. Jesus teaches us to ask for our daily bread, for our earthly needs. But he doesn't stop there. We may ask wrongly failing to pray the other petitions in the Model Prayer (Mt 6:9-13).

⁷ Therefore, submit to God. But resist the Devil, and he will flee from you. ⁸ Draw near to God, and He will draw near to you. Cleanse your hands, sinners, and purify your hearts, double-minded people! ⁹ Be miserable and mourn and weep. Your laughter must change to mourning and your joy to sorrow. ¹⁰ Humble yourselves before the Lord, and He will exalt you.

¹¹ Don't criticize one another, brothers. He who criticizes a brother or judges his brother criticizes the law and judges the law. But if you judge the law, you are not a doer of the law but a judge. ¹² There is one lawgiver and judgeᵃ who is able to save and to destroy. But who are you to judge your neighbor?

One Day at a Time

1. What is your favorite way to spend a weekend?
2. How far into the future have you planned your life?

James 4:13-17

3. What attitude should you have toward planning (v. 15)? How do you balance having faith about the future and being presumptuous?
4. Whom do you admire for the way he or she lives one day at a time—making every day count for God?
5. Where do you need God's guidance in your plans for the future? How will you get this guidance?

Our Will and His Will

¹³ Come now, you who say, "Today or tomorrow we will travel to such and such a city and spend a year there and do business and make a profit." ¹⁴ You don't even know what tomorrow will bring—what your life will be! For you are a bit of smoke that appears for a little while, then vanishes.

¹⁵ Instead, you should say, "If the Lord wills, we will live and do this or that." ¹⁶ But as it is, you boast in your arrogance. All such boasting is evil. ¹⁷ So, for the person who knows to do good and doesn't do it, it is a sin.

Money Concerns

1. If you won the lottery, how would you spend your first $100,000?

James 5:1-6

2. How do you think the rich people reacted to this warning from James?
3. What are the abuses the rich committed (vv. 4-6)? How do these injustices happen in the world today? How should Christians respond and be involved?
4. What do you think James would say about the concerns most people have for saving money, preparing for retirement, estate planning, etc.?
5. How does this passage challenge you in the way you manage your money?

Warning to the Rich

5 Come now, you rich people! Weep and wail over the miseries that are coming on you. ² Your wealth is ruined: your clothes are moth-eaten; ³ your silver and gold are corroded, and their corrosion will be a witness against you and will eat your flesh like fire. You stored up treasure in the last days! ⁴ Look! The pay that you withheld from the workers who reaped your fields cries out, and the outcry of the harvesters has reached the ears of the Lord of Hosts.ᵇ ⁵ You have lived luxuriously on the land and have indulged yourselves. You have fattened your hearts forᶜ the day of

---

ᵃ**4:12** Other mss omit *and judge*   ᵇ**5:4** Gk *Sabaoth*; this word is a transliteration of the Hb word for *Hosts*, or *Armies*.   ᶜ**5:5** Or *hearts in*

4:7 Therefore, submit to God. His first and primary command is that they must submit to God. **resist the Devil.** Submission to God begins with resistance to Satan. Thus far they have been giving in to the Devil's enticements. **he will flee from you.** Since the Devil has no ultimate power over a Christian, when resisted he can do little but withdraw.

4:13 Boasting about the future is arrogant because God is the only One who knows what will happen in the future.

4:14 tomorrow. All such planning presupposes that tomorrow will unfold like any other day, when in fact, the future is anything but secure (Prov. 27:1). **what your life will be.** Hosea 13:3 says, "Therefore, they will be like the morning mist, like the early dew that vanishes."

4:15 If the Lord's wills. The uncertainty of the future ought not to be a terror to the Christian. Instead, it ought to force on him or her to an awareness of how vital dependence upon God is. **we will live and do this or that.** James is not ruling out planning. He says, "Go ahead and plan, but involve God in your plans and be flexible."

4:16 boast. The problem with this boasting is that they are claiming to have the future under control when, in fact, only God holds time in His hands. These are empty claims.

5:1 rich people. In the first century there was a great gulf between rich and poor. **wail.** This is a strong word meaning, "to shriek" or "howl," and is used to describe the terror that will be felt by the damned.

5:4 The pay that you withheld. The Old Testament insisted that it was wrong to withhold wages. A worker was to be paid immediately. **the workers.** In Palestine, day laborers were used to plant and harvest crops. They were cheaper than slaves. **fields.** The Greek word means "estates." These were large tracts of land owned by the very wealthy. **outcry.** This is a word used to describe the wild, incoherent cry of an animal.

5:5 luxuriously. In contrast to the hunger of the laborers is the soft and easy living of the landowners (Amos 6:1-7). **indulged yourselves.** Not just luxury, but also vice is in view here. **day of slaughter.** Cattle were pampered and fattened for one purpose only: to be slaughtered. On the day when this took place a great feast was held.

slaughter. [6] You have condemned—you have murdered—the righteous man; he does not resist you.

Waiting for the Lord

[7] Therefore, brothers, be patient until the Lord's coming. See how the farmer waits for the precious fruit of the earth and is patient with it until it receives the early and the late rains. [8] You also must be patient. Strengthen your hearts, because the Lord's coming is near.

[9] Brothers, do not complain about one another, so that you will not be judged. Look, the judge stands at the door!

[10] Brothers, take the prophets who spoke in the Lord's name as an example of suffering and patience. [11] See, we count as blessed those who have endured.[a] You have heard of Job's endurance and have seen the outcome from the Lord: the Lord is very compassionate and merciful.

Truthful Speech

[12] Now above all, my brothers, do not swear, either by heaven or by earth or with any other oath. Your "yes" must be "yes," and your "no" must be "no," so that you won't fall under judgment.[b]

Effective Prayer

[13] Is anyone among you suffering? He should pray. Is anyone cheerful? He should sing praises. [14] Is anyone among you sick? He should call for the elders of the church, and they should pray over him after anointing him with olive oil in the name of the Lord. [15] The prayer of faith will save the sick person, and the Lord will raise him up; and if he has committed sins, he will be forgiven. [16] Therefore, confess your sins to one another and pray for one another, so that you may be healed.

The intense prayer of the righteous is very powerful. [17] Elijah was a man with a nature like ours; yet he prayed earnestly that it would not rain, and for three years and six months it did not rain on the land. [18] Then he prayed again, and the sky gave rain and the land produced its fruit.

[19] My brothers, if any among you strays from the truth, and someone turns him back, [20] he should know that whoever turns a sinner from the error of his way will save his •life from death and cover a multitude of sins.

It's Tough to Wait

1. For what do you hate waiting?
2. Rate yourself on the patience meter from 1 (none) to 10 (plenty).

James 5:7-20

3. As Christians, for what are we waiting (vv. 7-8)? How easy is it to wait?
4. What do you think verse 12 is really saying about making promises? Why is swearing by heaven or earth a bad thing to do?
5. What is something in your life for which you've been waiting a long time? How do verses 13-18 encourage you?

---

[a]5:11 Or have persevered . . . [b]5:12 Other mss read fall into hypocrisy

---

5:12 swear. The issue is not that of using foul language but of taking an oath to guarantee a promise. **"yes" must be "yes."** Christians have no need for oaths. They are expected to speak only truth.

5:14 sick. Illness is not something anybody else does to you. Especially in the first century, when only a minimum of medical help was available, illness made one feel vulnerable. What could be done? Where could a believer go for help? **call for the elders.** Illness was to be dealt with in the context of the Christian community. The elders were to be called to minister to the ill person. They had

two things to do: pray over the person, and anoint him or her with oil. **anointing him with olive oil.** When a Jew was ill, he or she first went to a rabbi to be anointed with oil. Oil was used not only for ritual purposes, but also for cleaning wounds, for paralysis, and for toothaches. In this case, the olive oil is not being used as a medicine, but as a part of the healing prayer (Mark 6:13; Luke 10:34).

5:15 the Lord will raise him up. James is quite clear about the source of the healing. It is not the oil; it is not the laying on of hands by the elders; nor is it even prayer in some sort of magical sense. It is God who heals!

5:16 confess your sins. Confessing your sins to one another removes barriers between people and promotes honesty in the Christian community. Prayer is directed to God, who is all-powerful and who works in this world.

5:17 man with a nature like ours. Elijah knew depression, despair, and doubt, just as did the Christians (1 Kings 19). And yet, God answered his prayer in a mighty way. All Christians can pray like this, not just prophets.

1 PETER

PERSONAL READING PLAN

AUTHOR

Traditionally, the Apostle Peter is credited with writing this letter. Peter was one of the first disciples called by Jesus. From Galilee, he was by trade a fisherman. His father was Jonah. His brother was Andrew the apostle. He was married, and his wife accompanied him on some of his preaching tours. Peter quickly became one of the leaders among the 12 apostles; later, he was a leader of the church in Jerusalem. He was the apostle to the Jews, yet because of his response to a vision, the first Gentile convert, Cornelius, was admitted to the church (Acts 10). Tradition says that Peter was martyred in Rome, around A.D. 68, by crucifixion upside down.

DATE

First Peter was written sometime between the fire in Rome (A.D. 64) and Peter's death (A.D. 68).

THEME

Hope in the midst of suffering.

AUDIENCE

First Peter is a circular letter to Christians living in the northwest section of Asia Minor (in what is now modern Turkey). Pontus, Galatia, Cappadocia, Asia and Bithynia (1:1) are all Roman provinces. This area had a large population and the fact that Christians were living throughout the region testifies to the success of early Christian missionaries.

That these Christians were mainly Gentiles is clear from the way Peter describes their pre-conversion life; he uses categories and phrases typically applied to pagans but not to Jews (1:14; 2:9-10; 4:3-4). Peter also uses the Greek form of his name, Cephas, in this letter, and not Simon, his Jewish name.

HISTORICAL BACKGROUND

One hot July night in A.D. 64, Rome caught fire. For three days and nights the fire blazed out of control. Ancient temples and landmarks were swept away; homes were destroyed. Ten of the 14 city sections suffered damage; three sections were reduced to rubble. The people of Rome were distraught and angry, especially because certain of Nero's officers were caught with firebrands trying to rekindle the waning fire. Many felt that Nero's passion for building caused him to want the city destroyed so he might rebuild it. No matter what Nero did to refute this rumor—and he aided the homeless extensively—nothing reduced the suspicion that the fire was his doing. Clearly he needed a scapegoat on which to blame the fire.

The Christians were accused of setting fire to Rome. Up to this time, they were thought to be simply a Jewish sect and were hardly noticed by Roman authorities. In fact, the Roman courts protected Christians against the wrath of the synagogue and others. But now all this changed. Nero introduced the church to martyrdom. What began in Rome would soon burn across the Roman Empire.

Under Roman law there were two types of religious systems: those that were legal, such as Judaism, and those that were forbidden. Anyone who practiced a forbidden religion was considered a criminal and was subject to harsh penalties. After the great fire, Christianity was judged to be distinct from Judaism, and it was quickly prohibited. This meant that throughout the Roman Empire, Christians were now technically

outlaws and thus subject to persecution. Just such persecution was taking place in Asia Minor among the Christians to whom Peter writes (4:12).

PURPOSE

In the midst of the "fiery ordeal" (4:12) Peter writes to comfort and encourage. He says, "As you share in the sufferings of the Messiah rejoice. How can they rejoice at such a difficult time? Because of the great *hope* they have as Christians. Hope is the theme of Peter's letter to these suffering believers.

CHARACTERISTICS

When reading 1 Peter, one hears echoes from the Old Testament, particularly from Isaiah. For example in 1:24-25, he quotes Isaiah 40:6-8; in 2:6, Isaiah 28:16; in 2:8, Isaiah 8:14; and in 2:22, Isaiah 53:9. He also alludes to Old Testament ideas and stories.

Peter is also familiar with Paul's writings. This letter contains parallels to Romans and, in particular, Ephesians. For example, compare 1:3 with Ephesians 1:3 and 1:20 with Ephesians 1:4. Note also the similarity between Peter and Paul in their instructions to family members and slaves (-3:7; Eph. 5:21-6:9; Col. 3:18-25). In addition, there are parallels to Hebrews, James and, to Peter's own sermons in Acts.

First Peter is written in excellent Greek, which has caused scholars to question whether a Galilean fisherman like Peter could have had such a sophisticated command of the language. First Peter contains some of the best Greek in the New Testament. Its style is smoother even than Paul's with his years of training; its rhythmic structure is not unlike that of the Greek masters.

The answer to this question is found in 5:12: "Through Silvanus ... I have written briefly." Silas could well be the source of the excellent style as he helped Peter draft the letter and polish up the language.

PASSAGES FOR TOPICAL GROUP STUDY

Greeting

1 Peter, an apostle of Jesus Christ:

To the temporary residents of the Dispersion in the provinces of Pontus, Galatia, Cappadocia, Asia, and Bithynia, chosen [2] according to the foreknowledge of God the Father and set apart by the Spirit for obedience and [for the] sprinkling with the blood of Jesus Christ.

May grace and peace be multiplied to you.

Hanging Tough

1. What is the worst sport's injury you've had? How did you recover?
2. When have you felt like quitting the team or sport in which you participate? What kept you going?

1 Peter 1:3-12

2. What purpose do life's trials serve (v. 7)?
3. In what can we rejoice, despite the trials we face (vv. 3-5)?
4. What does verse 12 tell us about the place of humanity in God's grand design?
5. What have you found helpful when you are dealing with struggles?
6. What spiritual struggles are you going through right now?

A Living Hope

[3] Blessed be the God and Father of our Lord Jesus Christ. According to His great mercy, He has given us a new birth into a living hope through the resurrection of Jesus Christ from the dead, [4] and into an inheritance that is imperishable, uncorrupted, and unfading, kept in heaven for you, [5] who are being protected by God's power through faith for a salvation that is ready to be revealed in the last time. [6] You rejoice in this,[a] though now for a short time you have had to be distressed by various trials [7] so that the genuineness of your faith—more valuable than gold, which perishes though refined by fire—may result in[b] praise, glory, and honor at the revelation of Jesus Christ. [8] You love Him, though you have not seen Him. And though not seeing Him now, you believe in Him and rejoice with inexpressible and glorious joy, [9] because you are receiving the goal of your[c] faith, the salvation of your souls.[d]

[10] Concerning this salvation, the prophets who prophesied about the grace that would come to you searched and carefully investigated. [11] They inquired into what time or what circumstances[e] the Spirit of Christ within them was indicating when He testified in advance to the messianic sufferings[f] and the glories that would follow.[g] [12] It was revealed to them that they were not serving themselves but you concerning things that have now been announced to you through those who preached the gospel to you by the Holy Spirit sent from heaven. Angels desire to look into these things.

A Call to Holy Living

[13] Therefore, get your minds ready for action,[h] being self-disciplined, and set your hope completely on the grace to be brought to you at the revelation of Jesus Christ. [14] As obedient children, do not be conformed to the desires of your former ignorance [15] but, as the One who called you is holy, you also are to be holy in all your conduct; [16] for it is written, **Be holy, because I am holy.**[i]

[17] And if you address as Father the One who judges impartially based on each one's work, you are to conduct yourselves in reverence during this time of temporary residence. [18] For you know that you were redeemed from your empty way of life inherited from the fathers, not with perishable things, like silver or gold, [19] but with the precious blood of Christ, like that of a lamb without defect or blemish. [20] He was destined[j] before the foundation of the world, but was revealed at

---

[a]**1:6** Or *In this (fact) rejoice* [b]**1:7** Lit *may be found for* [c]**1:9** Other mss read *our*, or they omit the possessive pronoun [d]**1:9** Or *your lives* [e]**1:11** Or *inquired about the person or time* [f]**1:11** Or *the sufferings of Christ* [g]**1:11** Lit *the glories after that* [h]**1:13** Lit *Therefore, gird the loins of your minds* [i]**1:16** Lv 11:44–45; 19:2; 20:7 [j]**1:20** Or *was chosen*, or *was known*

1:1 Peter. Peter was the leader of the 12 apostles. Before joining Jesus' band of disciples he, along with his brother Andrew, was a fisherman on the Sea of Galilee. **an apostle.** This means, literally, "one who is sent." It is the term used in the New Testament to identify those who were selected for the special task of founding and guiding the new church. **Dispersion.** This word originally referred to the Jews who were scattered in exile throughout the world. **Pontus, Galatia, Cappadocia, Asia, and Bithynia.** These are Roman provinces located in Asia Minor (now modern Turkey). The order in which they are named is the order in which a traveler would visit each.

1:2 chosen according to the foreknowledge of God the Father. Israel knew itself to be chosen by God to be His people (Ezek.

20:5; Hos. 11:1). They were to be the people through whom He would reveal Himself to the rest of the world. The first Christians knew that they too had been chosen by God.

1:4 imperishable, uncorrupted, and unfading. The first word, "imperishable," means never to be overcome by an enemy. The second word, "uncorrupted," refers to a land that has not been polluted or defiled by a conquering army. The third word, "unfading," paints a picture of a land without change or decay. It refers especially to flowers that do not fade.

1:14 do not be conformed to the desires. They are not to allow themselves to be shaped by the sensuality of their pre-Christian existence. **ignorance.** Not only was their pre-Christian life dominated by physical de-

sires of all sorts, they also lived in ignorance of God. Pagans believed there was a god, but thought him to be unknowable and disinterested in human beings.

1:18 redeemed. To redeem someone is to rescue that person from bondage. This is a technical term for the money paid to buy freedom for a slave.

1:19 blood. In the Old Testament, the blood of the sacrificial animal was offered to God in place of the life of the sinner. In the New Testament, it is not the sacrifice of animals that secures forgiveness; it is the death of Jesus who gave Himself once for all. **without defect or blemish.** Jesus was able to be such a sacrifice because He was without sin.

the end of the times for you ²¹ who through Him are believers in God, who raised Him from the dead and gave Him glory, so that your faith and hope are in God.

Choosing to Do It Right

1. What do you do to keep in shape physically? Mentally? Emotionally?

1 Peter 1:13-2:3

2. According to Peter, what does it mean to be holy (vv. 13-16)?

3. Why does Peter talk about the mind first (vv. 13-16), and then about conduct (v. 17)?

4. What is a good test to see if a Christian really has "a pure heart" (v. 22)?

5. What makes loving others deeply and actively possible (vv. 22-23)?

6. Which of the characteristics of holy living listed in verses 13-16 is the greatest challenge for you?

²² By obedience to the truth,ª having purified yourselvesᵇ for sincere love of the brothers, love one another earnestly from a pureᶜ heart, ²³ since you have been born again—not of perishable seed but of imperishable—through the living and enduring word of God. ²⁴ For

> All flesh is like grass,
> and all its glory like a flower of the grass.
> The grass withers, and the flower drops off,
> ²⁵ but the word of the Lord endures forever.ᵈ

And this is the word that was preached as the gospel to you.

The Living Stone and a Holy People

2 So rid yourselves of all wickedness, all deceit, hypocrisy, envy, and all slander. ² Like newborn infants, desire the unadulterated spiritual milk, so that you may grow by it in ⌊your⌋ salvation,ᵉ ³ since **you have tasted that the Lord is good.**ᶠ ⁴ Coming to Him, a living stone—rejected by men but chosen and valuable to God— ⁵ you yourselves, as living stones, are being built into a spiritual house for a holy priesthood to offer spiritual sacrifices acceptable to God through Jesus Christ. ⁶ For it stands in Scripture:

> **Look! I lay a stone in Zion,**
> **a chosen and valuable cornerstone,**
> **and the one who believes in Him**
> **will never be put to shame!**ᵍ ʰ

Made for God

1. What is something you've made or built recently?

2. How does it make you feel to know you are chosen by God—that you belong to Him?

1 Peter 2:4-12

3. What kind of process is necessary to you to be "built into a spiritual house" (v. 5)? What is the wisdom of this strategy by God?

4. Peter talks about things "that war against you" (v. 11). What are you fighting against right now?

5. How can you "glorify God" (v. 12) and show others that you belong to Him?

ª**1:22** Other mss add *through the Spirit* ᵇ**1:22** Or *purified your souls* ᶜ **1:22** Other mss omit *pure* ᵈ**1:24–25** Is 40:6–8 ᵉ**2:2** Other mss omit *in your salvation* ᶠ**2:3** Ps 34:8 ᵍ**2:6** Or *be disappointed* ʰ**2:6** Is 28:16 LXX

1:22 obedience to the truth. In the context of Peter's writings this is a reference to one's conversion which involves repentance and faith in Christ. **love one another earnestly.** This command for love that is both earnest, sincere, and from a pure heart is possible because of the cleansing that comes through conversion. The word translated *earnestly* is used to describe the intense prayer of the church in Jerusalem when Peter was imprisoned (Acts 12:5). It is also used to describe Jesus' agonizing prayer in Gethsemane (Lk.22:44).

1:23 not of perishable seed. The seed of a human father is "perishable and earthly, and even if it produces children, they too will die eventually. The seed God uses to beget his people…is invincible and incorruptible " (Schreiner). **the living and enduring word of God.** God's Word is the agent that gives

us new birth. The result of our being born again is life that doesn't perish but continues forever.

2:1 rid yourselves. This verb was used to describe taking off one's clothes. Christians must strip off, like spoiled and dirty clothes, their old lifestyle. An essential practice in maintaining one's house is to regularly take out the trash. This is also true in our lives as Christians. This is the daily maintenance required to keep the command of loving one another earnestly and with a pure heart. **all wickedness, all deceit, hypocrisy.** Wickedness is an attitude of ill will toward others. Deceit and hypocrisy undermine trust between people and so disrupt community. **envy, and all slander.** Envy is divisive and robs love of the earnestness and purity of heart that come from a right relationship with Christ. It takes a dim view of someone having something that it lacks and is pleased with others fail. Slander may lie about people but it may also tell the truth in such a way that other people are placed in a bad light.

2:2 desire…spiritual milk. The word translated *desire* conveys the sense of craving nourishment. Milk has all the components infants need to help them grow and mature.

2:4 a living stone. He gets this metaphor from two Old Testament texts: Isaiah 28:16 (quoted in verse 6) speaks of "a chosen and valuable cornerstone" and Psalm 118:22 (quoted in verse 7) speaks of the rejection of that stone. Both verses point out the supreme value of the cornerstone. Peter's point is that, despite His rejection, Christ is the chosen One of God, and in the end He prevails.

2:5 being built into. Stones by themselves

[7] So the honor is for you who believe; but for the unbelieving,

The stone that the builders rejected—
this One has become the cornerstone,[a]

and

[8] A stone that causes men to stumble,[b]
and a rock that trips them up.[c] [d]

They stumble by disobeying the message; they were destined for this.

[9] But you are a chosen race,[e] [f]
a royal priesthood,[g]
a holy nation,[h] a people for His possession,[i]
so that you may proclaim the praises[j] [k]
of the One who called you out of darkness
into His marvelous light.

[10] Once you were not a people,
but now you are God's people;
you had not received mercy,
but now you have received mercy.

A Call to Good Works

[11] Dear friends, I urge you as aliens and temporary residents to abstain from fleshly desires that war against you.[l] [12] Conduct yourselves honorably among the Gentiles,[m] so that in a case where they speak against you as those who do evil, they may, by observing your good works, glorify God in a day of visitation.[n]

[13] Submit to every human institution because of the Lord, whether to the Emperor[o] as the supreme authority, [14] or to governors as those sent out by him to punish those who do evil and to praise those who do good. [15] For it is God's will that you, by doing good, silence the ignorance of foolish people. [16] As God's slaves, ⌊live⌋ as free people, but don't use your freedom as a way to conceal evil. [17] Honor everyone. Love the brotherhood. Fear God. Honor the Emperor.[o]

Facing Hardship

1. In what job or task have you felt like a slave?

1 Peter 2:13-25

2. How are Christians to act toward governmental authority, and why?
3. What kind of suffering "brings favor with God" (v. 20)?
4. How does Christ's death have both an ending and a beginning effect on our lives (v. 24)?
5. What example did Jesus give us to follow when we have to endure suffering (vv. 21-25)?
6. How can Jesus' example help you when you face hardships you cannot change?

Submission of Slaves to Masters

[18] Household slaves, submit yourselves to your masters with all respect, not only to the good and gentle but also to the cruel.[p] [19] For it ⌊brings⌋ favor[q] if, because of conscience toward God,[r] someone endures grief from suffering unjustly. [20] For what credit is there if you endure when you sin and are beaten? But when you do good and suffer, if you endure, it brings favor with God.

[21] For you were called to this,
because Christ also suffered for you,
leaving you an example,
so that you should follow in His steps.
[22] He did not commit sin,
and no deceit was found in His mouth;[s]

---

[a] **2:7** Ps 118:22 [b] **2:8** Or *a stone causing stumbling* [c] **2:8** Or *a rock to trip over* [d] **2:8** Is 8:14 [e] **2:9** Or *chosen generation,* or *chosen nation* [f] **2:9** Is 43:20 LXX; Dt 7:6; 10:15 [g] **2:9** Ex 19:6; 23:22 LXX; Is 61:6 [h] **2:9** Ex 19:6; 23:22 LXX [i] **2:9** Ex 19:5; 23:22 LXX; Dt 4:20; 7:6; Is 43:21 LXX [j] **2:9** Or *the mighty deeds* [k] **2:9** Is 42:12; 43:21 [l] **2:11** Lit *against the soul* [m] **2:12** Or *among the nations,* or *among the pagans* [n] **2:12** A day when God intervenes in human history, either in grace or in judgment [o] **2:13,17** Lit *king* [p] **2:18** Lit *crooked,* or *unscrupulous* [q] **2:19** Other mss add *with God* [r] **2:19** Other mss read *because of a good conscience* [s] **2:22** Is 53:9

---

serve no function. But shaped together into a structure by a master builder, they become something of use and importance. **a spiritual house.** The church is the temple of God, made up of a close-knit community of men and women. **a holy priesthood.** Not only are they a "spiritual house," they are the priests or ministers set apart to serve in it.

2:9 a people for His possession. The church is a community chosen by God. **that you may proclaim the praises of the One.** This is what our "spiritual sacrifices" are all about: making God known in the world.

2:11 aliens and temporary residents. They may be a chosen nation and a royal priesthood, but they are also outsiders in terms of the world and culture in which they live. **abstain from fleshly desires.** "Fleshly de-

sires" are literally "fleshly lusts." In the New Testament, "sins of the flesh" encompass a far wider sphere than just sexual sin, including pride, envy, hatred, greed, gluttony, etc. (see Gal. 5:19-21).

2:13 Submit. This is the key concept in the next two passages. What Peter urges is voluntary subordination in all spheres of human life.

2:13-14 Emperor ... governors. The first situation in which Peter applies this general principle is with civil authorities.

2:16 God's slaves. The paradox is that Christians are both free and bound. They are to "live as free people" while simultaneously they are "slaves of God."

2:18 slaves, submit yourselves. Slaves were the legal property of their masters. This fact, though inherently wrong, defined the reality within which they had to live. Peter does not counsel rebellion or even "passive resistance." What gave slaves the freedom to submit in this way was the sense that they as Christians were, in fact, members of a heavenly family and of a kingdom far more significant than the earthly reality within which they lived.

2:21 For you were called to this, because Christ also suffered for you. The example of Jesus, who gave His life for us, is the basis on which Peter says what he does about accepting unjust treatment. Christian slaves are to imitate Christ.

23 when reviled, He did not revile in return;
when suffering, He did not threaten,
but committed Himself to the One
who judges justly.
24 He Himself bore our sins
in His body on the tree,
so that, having died to sins,
we might live for righteousness;
by His wounding you have been healed.a
25 For you were like sheep going astray,b
but you have now returned
to the shepherd and guardianc of your souls.

Marriage that Works

1. How would you rate your parents' marriage?

1 Peter 3:1-7

2. How does Peter define beauty? When appreciating or striving for beauty, which kind do you tend to focus on—that in verses 3 or 4?

3. What does the fact that husband and wife are "co-heirs of the grace of life" (v. 7) say about their equality in the eyes of God?

4. How should men and women today follow the spirit of Peter's teaching on submission in this passage and in 2:13-15?

5. What does this passage tell you about the type of person you should look for in a spouse?

Wives and Husbands

3 Wives, in the same way, submit yourselves to your own husbands so that, even if some disobey the ⌊Christian⌋ message, they may be won overd without a message by the way their wives live, 2 when they observe your pure, reverent lives. 3 Your beauty should not consist of outward things ⌊like⌋ elaborate hairstyles and the wearing of gold ornamentse or fine clothes; 4 instead, ⌊it should consist of⌋ the hidden person of the heart with the imperishable quality of a gentle and quiet spirit, which is very valuable in God's eyes. 5 For in the past, the holy women who hoped in God also beautified themselves in this way, submitting to their own husbands, 6 just as Sarah obeyed Abraham, calling him lord. You have become her children when you do good and aren't frightened by anything alarming.

7 Husbands, in the same way, live with your wives with understanding of their weaker naturef yet showing them honor as co-heirs of the grace of life, so that your prayers will not be hindered.

Do No Evil

8 Now finally, all of you should be like-minded and sympathetic, should love believers,g and be compassionate and humble,h 9 not paying back evil for evil or insult for insult but, on the contrary, giving a blessing, since you were called for this, so that you can inherit a blessing.

10 For the one who wants to love life
and to see good days
must keep his tongue from evil
and his lips from speaking deceit,
11 and he must turn away from evil and do good.
He must seek peace and pursue it,
12 because the eyes of the Lord
are on the righteous
and His ears are open to their request.
But the face of the Lord is against those
who do evil.i

Undeserved Suffering

13 And who will harmj you if you are passionate for what is good?k 14 But even if you should suffer for righteousness, you are blessed. Do not fear what they

---

a2:24 Is 53:5 b2:25 Is 53:6 c2:25 Or *overseer* d3:1 Lit *may be gained* e3:3 Lit *and of putting around of gold items* f3:7 Lit *understanding as the weaker vessel* g3:8 Lit *brotherly-loving* h3:8 Other mss read *courteous* i3:10–12 Ps 34:12–16 j3:13 Or *will mistreat*, or *will do evil to* k3:13 Lit *you are zealots*, or *you are partisans for the good*, or *you are eager to do good*

2:24 bore our sins. In a key passage about Christ's saving work, Peter points out that Jesus was their substitute. He bore their sins. He took upon Himself the penalty, which they deserved because of their sin. **so that.** Peter points to two results of Jesus' death on the cross: (1) because of it they are able to be free of sin and (2) they can now live for righteousness. It is the moral impact of the cross which Peter chooses to highlight here. **healed.** Christ's wounds bring restoration to our sin-scarred lives.

3:1 Wives, in the same way. By this phrase Peter makes a transition from slaves to wives. Just as the behavior of Christ was the model for slaves, so too is it for women. **submit yourselves.** Again, as he did for slaves, Peter counsels submission to husbands, not rebellion. **won over.** Peter (like Paul) does not counsel Christian women to leave unbe-

lieving husbands. His desire is that the husbands be converted, perhaps by the example of their wives.

3:7 Husbands. In contrast to verses 1-2, where the focus is on Christian wives and unbelieving husbands, here Peter discusses how Christian husbands should relate to Christian wives. Peter reminds husbands that the respect they are to show to all people (2:17) is also due to their own wives. **in the same way.** As he did when he addressed wives (v. 1), Peter points back to the example of Christ who voluntarily gave Himself for the sake of others (2:21). **with understanding.** This phrase is literally "according to knowledge," it is also translated "treat them with respect." In other words, the husband is not supposed to ride rough shod over his wife's needs and desires, but rather he is supposed to know her, to understand

her, and to treat her with respect. The culture of the time, both pagan and Jewish, considered women to be inferior to men. The idea that the "superior" should show honor to the "inferior" by seeking to understand her was a strange teaching. **their weaker nature.** Literally, the "weaker vessel." There has been much debate as to what this means. It might refer to anatomical differences between men and women (this phrase was used in Greek to refer to the woman's body), to the inferior position of women in that society, or to the comparative lack of physical strength on the part of the woman. **co-heirs of the grace of life.** Literally, "joint heirs." Both husband and wife are equal participants in the grace of God, again reinforcing the idea that men and women have equal value in God's eyes (Gal. 3:26-29).

3:8 be like-minded. The phrase is literally

fear or be disturbed,[a] [15] but set apart the •Messiah[b] as Lord in your hearts, and always be ready to give a defense to anyone who asks you for a reason[c] for the hope that is in you. [16] However, do this with gentleness and respect, keeping your conscience clear,[d] so that when you are accused,[e] those who denounce your Christian life will be put to shame. [17] For it is better to suffer for doing good, if that should be God's will,[f] than for doing evil.

Changing Behavior

1. Was there ever a time you unfairly got "caught holding the bag"? What happened? Did justice prevail in the end?

1 Peter 3:8-22
2. How is it possible to live like verses 8-12: Prayer? Effort? Obedience no matter what? A deepening relationship with Christ? Other?
3. How can suffering for what is right be a means of blessing (v. 14)?
4. How does hope change your everyday behavior (v. 15)? What situation seemed hopeless to you until God brought hope?

[18] For Christ also suffered for sins once for all,[g]
the righteous for the unrighteous,[h]
that He might bring you[i] to God,
after being put to death in the fleshly realm[j]
but made alive in the spiritual realm.[k]

[19] In that state[l] He also went and made a proclamation to the spirits in prison[m] [20] who in the past were disobedient, when God patiently waited in the days of Noah while an ark was being prepared; in it, a few—that is, eight people[n]—were saved through water. [21] Baptism, which corresponds to this, now saves you (not the removal of the filth of the flesh, but the pledge[o] of a good conscience toward God) through the resurrection of Jesus Christ. [22] Now that He has gone into heaven, He is at God's right hand, with angels, authorities, and powers subjected to Him.

Changing Priorities

1. Where do the party kids in your school go after a ball game, and what do they do? Have they ever gotten in trouble?

1 Peter 4:1-11
2. When has someone "heaped abuse on you" (v. 4) because you didn't join them in something you considered wrong?
3. What are some priorities that a Christian should have in his or her life (vv. 7-10)?
4. How have your priorities changed since becoming a Christian or since you got serious about your faith?
5. Right now, are you living more for yourself or for God? In what ways?

Following Christ

4 Therefore, since Christ suffered[p] in the flesh,[q] arm yourselves also with the same resolve[r]—

---

[a]**3:14** Is 8:12   [b]**3:15** Other mss read *set God*   [c]**3:15** Or *who demands of you an accounting*   [d]**3:16** Lit *good*; or *keeping a clear conscience* [e]**3:16** Other mss read *when they speak against you as evildoers*   [f]**3:17** Lit *if the will of God should will*   [g]**3:18** Other mss read *died for sins on our behalf*; other mss read *died for our sins*; other mss read *died for sins on your behalf*   [h]**3:18** Or *the Righteous One in the place of the unrighteous many*   [i]**3:18** Other mss read *us*   [j]**3:18** Or *in the flesh*   [k]**3:18** Or *in the spirit*, or *in the Spirit*   [l]**3:19** Or *In whom*, or *At that time*, or *In which* [m]**3:19** The *spirits in prison* are most likely fallen supernatural beings or angels; see 2 Pt 2:4; Jd 6.   [n]**3:20** Lit *souls*   [o]**3:21** Or *the appeal*   [p]**4:1** Other mss read *suffered for us*   [q]**4:1** *In the flesh* probably means "in human existence"; see 1 Pt 3:18.   [r]**4:1** Or *perspective*, or *attitude*

"all of one mind." By it Peter encourages the kind of unity that is vital in a hostile environment. There must be no divisions within the church. **love believers.** Peter uses the verb related to *philadelphia* (love amongst family) instead of the verb related to *agape* (self-giving love).

3:15 set apart the Messiah. Literally, "sanctify" Christ. Christ is to be acknowledged as holy and worshiped as Lord. They are to open themselves to His inner presence. **in your hearts.** At the core of their being, Christ must reign. **be ready to give a defense.** Although this may refer to an official inquiry in which they are called upon to defend the fact they are Christians, it probably

is more general in reference. When anybody asks about the hope they have, they are to explain why they are followers of Jesus. **a reason.** Greeks valued a logical, intelligent statement as to why one held certain beliefs.

3:16 with gentleness and respect. This reply should not be given in a contentious or defensive way.

3:18 suffered for sins. Christ died—as have men and women down through the ages. But His death was different in that it was a full, sufficient, and adequate sacrifice that atones for the sins of all people. **once for all.** The sacrifices in the temple had to be repeated over and over again; Christ's sac-

rifice was the final and perfect sacrifice through which all people in all ages may obtain salvation (Heb. 10:14). **the righteous for the unrighteous.** His death was vicarious; He died in the place of others.

3:19 made a proclamation. The nature of Jesus' proclamation has been interpreted as: (1) The gospel which was proclaimed to those who lived before Christ came, or as (2) The announcement to the rebellious spirits that their power had been broken. **the spirits.** Who these spirits were is not clear. They have been variously identified as: (1) sinners who lived before the incarnation of Christ, or (2) the rebellious angels of Genesis 6:1-4.

No Big Surprise

1. What kind of pain affects you the most: physical or emotional?

2. How do you feel when you hear that your country is sending military troops into conflict around the world?

1 Peter 4:12-19

3. What false assumption does Peter set straight in verse 12? How often are you surprised at the trials of life?

4. What is the first and most important course of action amidst suffering (v. 19)? How will this lift some of the burden of suffering?

5. Our society does not physically persecute Christians. What form, then, does your suffering for Christ take?

---

because the One who suffered in the flesh^a has finished with sin^b— ² in order to live the remaining time in the flesh,^a no longer for human desires,^c but for God's will. ³ For there has already been enough time spent in doing the will of the pagans:^d carrying on in unrestrained behavior, evil desires, drunkenness, orgies, carousing, and lawless idolatry. ⁴ In regard to this, they are surprised that you don't plunge with them into the same flood^e of dissipation—and they slander you. ⁵ They will give an account to the One who stands ready to judge the living and the dead. ⁶ For this reason the gospel was also preached to ⌊those who are now⌋ dead, so that, although they might be judged by men in the fleshly realm,^f they might live by God in the spiritual realm.^g

End-Time Ethics

⁷ Now the end of all things is near; therefore, be clear-headed and disciplined for prayer. ⁸ Above all, keep your love for one another at full strength, since **love covers a multitude of sins.**^h ⁹ Be hospitable to one another without complaining. ¹⁰ Based on the gift they have received, everyone should use it to serve others, as good managers of the varied grace of God. ¹¹ If anyone speaks, ⌊his speech should be⌋ like the oracles of God; if anyone serves, ⌊his service should be⌋ from the strength God provides, so that in everything God may be glorified through Jesus Christ. To Him belong the glory and the power forever and ever. •Amen.

Christian Suffering

¹² Dear friends, when the fiery ordealⁱ arises among you to test you, don't be surprised by it, as if something unusual were happening to you. ¹³ Instead, as you share in the sufferings of the •Messiah rejoice, so that you may also rejoice with great joy at the revelation of His glory. ¹⁴ If you are ridiculed for the name of Christ, you are blessed, because the Spirit of glory and of God rests on you.^j ¹⁵ None of you, however, should suffer as a murderer, a thief, an evildoer, or as a meddler.^k ¹⁶ But if ⌊anyone suffers⌋ as a Christian, he should not be ashamed, but should glorify God with that name. ¹⁷ For the time has come for judgment to begin with God's household; and if it begins with us, what will the outcome be for those who disobey the gospel of God?

¹⁸ And **if the righteous is saved with difficulty,**
    what will become of the ungodly
       and the sinner?^l

¹⁹ So those who suffer according to God's will should, in doing good, entrust themselves to a faithful Creator.

About the Elders

5 Therefore, as a fellow elder and witness to the sufferings of the •Messiah, and also a participant

---

^a**4:1,2** *In the flesh* probably means "in human existence"; see 1 Pt 3:18.   ^b**4:1** Or *the one who has suffered in the flesh has ceased from sin*   ^c**4:2** Lit *for desires of human beings*   ^d**4:3** Or *Gentiles*   ^e**4:4** Lit *you don't run with them into the same pouring out*   ^f**4:6** Or *in the flesh*   ^g**4:6** Or *in the spirit*   ^h**4:8** Pr 10:12   ⁱ**4:12** Lit *the burning*   ^j**4:14** Other mss add *He is blasphemed because of them, but He is glorified because of you.*   ^k**4:15** Or *as one who defrauds others*   ^l**4:18** Pr 11:31 LXX

4:3 will of the pagans. The list of vices here parallels the lists in Romans 13:13 and Galatians 5:19-21. The picture it paints is of an out of control lifestyle characterized by sexual and alcoholic addictions and cultic practices. **time spent.** Christians have two views of time: (1) time past, in which they gave themselves over to a destructive lifestyle, and (2) "the remaining time" (v. 2)—that time following conversion in which they live in accord with God's will. **unrestrained behavior.** "Excesses;" "debauchery," "outrages against decency;" "living in sensualities." **drunkenness.** Literally, "overflowings of wine." **carousing.** Literally, "drinking bouts;" "drunken parties."

4:6 the gospel was also preached to [those who are now] dead. The meaning of this phrase is quite difficult and has been much debated. It probably refers to those members of the church who have heard and accepted the gospel but who have since died. Some scholars, however, connect this verse to 3:19-20 and conclude that this is a reference to Christ's descent into hell, during which He proclaimed the gospel to those who were there.

4:10 gift. This word is *charisma* and refers to the different gifts which the Holy Spirit gives to individual Christians for the sake of the whole body. **to serve others.** The point of

these gifts is to use them for the sake of others. **varied grace of God.** Each one has a gift, but not all have the same gift (see also Rom 12:6-8; 1 Cor. 12:7-10; and Eph. 4:11-12 for lists of various gifts).

4:16 Christian. Apart from two references in Acts (11:26; 26:28), this is the only other use of "Christian" in the New Testament.

4:19 entrust themselves. This is a technical term which refers to the act of depositing money with a trusted friend. This is the same word Jesus used in Luke 23:46: "Father, into Your hands I entrust My spirit."

in the glory about to be revealed, I exhort the elders among you: 2 shepherd God's flock among you, not overseeing[a] out of compulsion but freely, according to God's ⌊will⌋;[b] not for the money but eagerly; 3 not lording it over those entrusted to you, but being examples to the flock. 4 And when the chief Shepherd appears, you will receive the unfading crown of glory.

5 Likewise, you younger men, be subject to the elders. And all of you clothe yourselves with[c] humility toward one another, because

> God resists the proud,
> but gives grace to the humble.[d]

6 Humble yourselves therefore under the mighty hand of God, so that He may exalt you in due time,[e] 7 casting all your care upon Him, because He cares about you.

Conclusion

8 Be sober! Be on the alert! Your adversary the Devil is prowling around like a roaring lion, looking for anyone he can devour. 9 Resist him, firm in the faith, knowing that the same sufferings are being experienced by your brothers in the world.

10 Now the God of all grace, who called you to His eternal glory in Christ Jesus, will personally[f] restore, establish, strengthen, and support you after you have suffered a little.[g] 11 To Him be the dominion[h] forever.[i] •Amen.

12 Through Silvanus,[j] whom I consider a faithful brother, I have written briefly, encouraging you and testifying that this is the true grace of God. Take your stand in it! 13 She who is in Babylon, also chosen, sends you greetings, as does Mark, my son. 14 Greet one another with a kiss of love. Peace to all of you who are in Christ.[k]

Stressed Out

1. What do you do when you are anxious or stressed out: Bite your nails? Eat? Stop eating? Withdraw?
2. Where do you turn for help in times of stress: Friends? Teammates? Parents? Coach?

1 Peter 5:1-11

3. During storms in your life, what are some good things to do (vv. 6-9)?
4. What would the opposite teaching of verse 6 be?
5. Among your Christian friends, what is the greatest cause for spiritual collapse?
6. What anxiety in your life do you need to turn over to God?

---

[a]**5:2** Other mss omit *overseeing* [b]**5:2** Other mss omit *according to God's will* [c]**5:5** Lit *you tie around yourselves* [d]**5:5** Pr 3:34 LXX [e]**5:6** Lit *in time* [f]**5:10** Lit *Himself* [g]**5:10** Or *a little while;* or *to a small extent* [h]**5:11** Other mss read *dominion and glory;* other mss read *glory and dominion* [i]**5:11** Other mss read *forever and ever* [j]**5:12** Or *Silas;* Ac 15:22–32; 16:19–40; 17:1–16 [k]**5:14** Other mss read *Christ Jesus. Amen.*

5:3 not lording it over those entrusted to you, but being examples. Mutual respect, submission, humility, and love are attitudes that should characterize the Christian community. The elders would be expected to set an example in displaying these attitudes.

5:5 younger men. The Greek social order was such that young men were considered subordinate to older men. **be subject.** Submission and respect are called for once again. **clothe yourselves with humility.** This is a rare verb, meaning "wrap yourselves," or "gird yourselves." It is derived from the name for the apron which was worn by slaves when working.

5:6 Humble yourselves. The same humility that is owed to one another is owed to God as well. **that He may exalt you in due time.** This will happen when Christ returns and they experience His glory.

5:7 casting all your care upon Him. This is connected to the imperative "humble yourself." It is not a separate commandment.

5:8 Be sober! Be on the alert! That they are not to be passive in the face of trouble is seen in this command. Coupled with conscious reliance on God, there must also be diligent effort on their part. **the Devil.** Behind all their trials stands the Devil (*diabolos*). In the Old Testament he is known by the Hebrew name Satan. In the New Testament he is seen as the one who tempts (as he did with Jesus), as the prince of evil who rebels against God, and as the one who seeks to undo God's purposes.

5:9 Resist him. Peter's advice is plain: do not run away, but stand your ground and face him, refusing to give in to his purposes, and trusting in God (Eph. 6:10-13; James 4:7; Rev. 12:9-11). **the same sufferings are being experienced by your brothers in the world.** Solidarity with Christian brothers and sisters around the

world is a strong motivation for standing firm.

5:12 Silvanus. Like Paul (and others), Peter used an amanuensis (secretary/scribe) to write this letter. In this case, Silvanus seems to have had an active part in shaping the final form of the letter with its rather polished Greek. The Silvanus referred to here was probably Paul's companion on his second missionary trip (Acts 15:40–18:5), a minister of the gospel (2 Cor. 1:19), and the co-author with Paul of 1 and 2 Thessalonians.

5:13 She who is in Babylon ... sends you greetings. Peter is probably referring to the church (2 John 1,13) in Rome, where he was when he wrote this letter. **Mark, my son.** Tradition has it that Mark was another of Peter's secretaries; and, in writing the Gospel that bears his name, Mark was expressing Peter's experience of Jesus. Certainly this phrase reflects a warm relationship between the two.

INTRODUCTION TO
2 PETER

PERSONAL READING PLAN

☐ 2 Peter 1:1-21
☐ 2 Peter 2:1-22

☐ 2 Peter 3:1-18

AUTHOR

Traditionally, the Apostle Peter is thought to have authored this letter. However, questions about his authorship have existed since the earliest times. It was not uncommon in the first century to attribute pieces of writing to famous people. In fact, Peter's name is attached to several other books that clearly were not written by him (e.g., the Gospel of Peter, the Preaching of Peter and the Apocalypse of Peter).

So questions arise when the language and thought of 1 and 2 Peter are compared. In their original Greek form, these two books are strikingly different. Could the same man have written both? This difference in style, of course, may simply be the result of Peter's use of several different secretaries. Peter indicates in his first letter that Silas helped him write it (1 Peter 5:12), and it is known that Peter had other secretaries (e.g., Mark and Glaucias

DATE

Second Peter was probably written near the time of Peter's death in A.D. 68 (see 1:12-15).

THEME

Be eager and on your guard.

AUDIENCE

On the basis of 1:1, it appears that there were no specific recipients of the letter. It seems intended for all Christians everywhere (hence its description as a General Epistle). However, in the body of the letter it becomes clear that 2 Peter was sent to a church or group of churches that had previously received 1 Peter (3:1). This would make the recipients Gentile Christians in Asia Minor. Furthermore, the tone of the letter makes it clear that a specific problem and specific false teachers are in view--which implies that 2 Peter is written for a specific people living in a particular area.

PURPOSE

Second Peter is a very important book for today because it deals with similar issues confronting the modern church, such as a lax lifestyle based on weak theology. Some church members in Peter's time argued that the doctrine of the Second Coming needed to be reconsidered. "The plain fact is that Christ has not returned yet," they said, "and he probably won't" (see 3:4,9). In fact, they suggested that this doctrine may have been invented by the apostles rather than revealed by God (1:16). It was suggested that the doctrine of the Second Coming was a moral restriction used to inhibit one's lifestyle. In contrast, the false teachers were saying that behavior does not matter. "Freedom" was their catchword, and evidently they felt free to indulge in sexual immorality and drunkenness.

"Not so!" exclaims Peter in this letter. We, too, need to remain firmly established within the truth we received from the prophets and from our Lord (chapter 1). We, too, need to be warned against those who would lead people away from that truth (chapter 2

CHARACTERISTICS

Chapter 1 is an exhortation to grow in the Christian virtues. Chapter 2 is very similar to the epistle of Jude (see the Introduction to Jude). A marked contrast is drawn there between the character and teaching of true apostles (like Peter and Paul) and that of false teachers whose lives are marked by their denial of Jesus, immo-

rality, rejection of authority, enslavement to sin and misuse of Scripture. Chapter 3 addresses the second coming of Jesus Christ.

STRUCTURE

Second Peter begins like a typical first-century letter (1:1-2) by identifying sender and recipients and offering a Christian greeting. And then, in typical fashion, it announces its theme (1:3-11) and tells the occasion of writing (1:12-15). The only thing 2 Peter lacks is personal greetings at the end, but these were not characteristic of all first-century letters.

Second Peter is also a farewell speech. It sounds like the last words of a great leader. In the New Testament Paul's farewell speech to the Ephesian elders had this character (Acts 20:17-35), as does the book of 2 Timothy.

In 1:12-15, Peter says that his death is soon to take place, and the way he writes his letter is typical of testament literature in general. The letter contains ethical instructions in which the author summarizes his view, and then he makes predictions about the future.

THE EARLY CHURCH

Controversies abounded in the early church.

One group denied Jesus was God, and another theory declared him God but not fully man. The apostles denounced obtaining salvation by works, only to encounter those who took it to the extreme and assumed "anything goes." Members of one church quit working and gathered together to await Jesus' return, while others gave up on His coming again at all.

Second Peter was written in response to a young church's questioning and doubting tendencies. Where 1 Peter centered on dangers from outside the church, this letter speaks to dangers from within. False teachers were stirring up problems, casting doubt on doctrine, and leading Christians into immoral behavior.

PASSAGES FOR TOPICAL GROUP STUDY

1:1-11. . . . MUSIC and ENTERTAINMENT . . Maturing in the Faith

PASSAGES FOR GENERAL GROUP STUDY

1:12-21 . . . . Pay Attention to God and His Word

2:1-22 . . . . Dangerous Lies

3:1-18 . . . . Anticipation (of Jesus' Return)

Greeting

1 Simeon[a] Peter, a slave and an apostle of Jesus Christ:

To those who have obtained a faith of equal privilege with ours[b] through the righteousness of our God and Savior Jesus Christ.

[2] May grace and peace be multiplied to you through the knowledge of God and of Jesus our Lord.

Maturing in the Faith

1. How does music influence the lifestyle of kids in your school?

2 Peter 1:1-11

2. How much of today's music, movies, and entertainment emphasizes the qualities listed in verses 5-7?

3. Do you think there is any purpose to the progressive order in verses 5-7? Which one of these qualities are you adding to your faith currently? How? On which quality do you need to work?

4. How does your commitment to Christ affect your choice of movies and music? How difficult is it to avoid listening to or watching things that undermine your faith, and why?

Growth in the Faith

[3] For His[c] divine power has given us everything required for life and godliness, through the knowledge of Him who called us by[d] His own glory and goodness. [4] By these He has given us very great and precious promises, so that through them you may share in the divine nature, escaping the corruption that is in the world because of evil desires. [5] For this very reason, make every effort to supplement your faith with goodness, goodness with knowledge, [6] knowledge with self-control, self-control with endurance, endurance with godliness, [7] godliness with brotherly affection, and brotherly affection with love. [8] For if these qualities are yours and are increasing, they will keep you from being useless or unfruitful in the knowledge of our Lord Jesus Christ. [9] The person who lacks these things is blind and shortsighted, and has forgotten the cleansing from his past sins. [10] Therefore, brothers, make every effort to confirm your calling and election, because if you do these things you will never stumble. [11] For in this way, entry into the eternal kingdom of our Lord and Savior Jesus Christ will be richly supplied to you.

Pay Attention

1. What event in your life this past year was the most memorable?

2 Peter 1:12-21

2. What event of Jesus' life does Peter recall (vv. 16-18)?

3. Why do you think it was so important for Peter to emphasize the divine inspiration of God's Word in verses 20-21? How can this teaching be misused?

4. If you could have been with Jesus at one event in His life, which would you choose? Why?

5. What is God saying to you about His Word (the Bible) in this passage?

[12] Therefore I will always remind you about these things, even though you know them and are established in the truth you have. [13] I consider it right, as long as I am in this tent,[e] to wake you up with a reminder, [14] knowing that I will soon lay aside my tent, as our Lord Jesus Christ has also shown me. [15] And I will also make

---

[a]**1:1** Simon   [b]**1:1** Or *obtained a faith of the same kind as ours*   [c]**1:3** Lit *As His*   [d]**1:3** Or *to*   [e]**1:13** A euphemism for Peter's body

---

1:1 Simon Peter. Probably Peter wrote the letter shortly before his death in the mid 60s. The letter was most likely written to the same readers who received 1 Peter (cp. 3:2). In this letter, Peter allude to his being an eye witness of Jesus' transfiguration (1:16-18). **righteousness.** This refers to God's justice or fairness in that this second-generation audience of Christians had a faith that was in no way inferior ("of equal privilege") to that of the apostles.

1:3 everything needed. Nothing is more frustrating than setting to work on a project or an assignment and realizing that you don't have what you need to complete the task. Likewise, nothing is as encouraging as realizing that you have all that's needed to complete the project. For Christians, God's power has provided everything needed for living a godly life. **through the knowledge**

of Him. God's power is imparted to us through our knowledge of Christ. This knowledge refers to our initial encounter with Christ at conversion but it doesn't stop their. Knowledge increases and Peter will soon describe this process of growth (1:5).

1:4 great and precious promises. This refers to the many promises found in Scripture based on having Christ making His home within us (John 14:23). **share in the divine nature.** We are now new creations in Christ. We are being transformed into His image (2 Cor. 3:18).

1:5 make every effort. Peter's command is built on God's provision. This is no self help approach to the Christian life. God has provided all that is needed, therefore "make every effort." What follows is a chain of eight virtues that begins with faith, the root of

these virtues, and ends with love, the goal of the Christian life. It's doubtful that Peter is calling on believers to work on these virtues one at a time. **supplement your faith.** Faith in Christ, the starting point for the Christian life, must produce a new quality of life. **goodness.** Literally, "virtue," an ethical term meaning moral excellence. **knowledge.** This is the wisdom and discernment gained from life experiences.

1:6 self-control. This is the self-discipline that leads to the pursuit of a virtuous life. It was often used in regard to sexual behavior. **endurance.** This is steadiness and faithfulness in the face of suffering and trials.

1:7 brotherly affection. The Greek word here (*philadelphia*) refers to family affection. It was commonly used to describe how Christians should relate to other members of

every effort that after my departure[a] you may be able to recall these things at any time.

The Trustworthy Prophetic Word

16 For we did not follow cleverly contrived myths when we made known to you the power and coming of our Lord Jesus Christ; instead, we were eyewitnesses of His majesty. 17 For when He received honor and glory from God the Father, a voice came to Him from the Majestic Glory:

This is My beloved Son.[b]
I take delight in Him![c]

18 And we heard this voice when it came from heaven while we were with Him on the holy mountain. 19 So we have the prophetic word strongly confirmed. You will do well to pay attention to it, as to a lamp shining in a dismal place, until the day dawns and the morning star arises in your hearts. 20 First of all, you should know this: no prophecy of Scripture comes from one's own interpretation, 21 because no prophecy ever came by the will of man; instead, moved by the Holy Spirit, men spoke from God.

The Judgment of False Teachers

2 But there were also false prophets among the people, just as there will be false teachers among you. They will secretly bring in destructive heresies, even denying the Master who bought them, and will bring swift destruction on themselves. 2 Many will follow their unrestrained ways, and because of them the way of truth will be blasphemed. 3 In their greed they will exploit you with deceptive words. Their condemnation, ⌊pronounced⌋ long ago, is not idle, and their destruction does not sleep.

4 For if God didn't spare the angels who sinned, but threw them down into Tartarus[d] and delivered them to be kept in chains[e] of darkness until judgment; 5 and if He didn't spare the ancient world, but protected Noah, a preacher of righteousness, and seven others,[f] when He brought a flood on the world of the ungodly; 6 and if

He reduced the cities of Sodom and Gomorrah to ashes and condemned them to ruin,[g] making them an example to those who were going to be ungodly;[h] 7 and if He rescued righteous Lot, distressed by the unrestrained behavior of the immoral 8 (for as he lived among them, that righteous man tormented himself day by day with the lawless deeds he saw and heard)— 9 then the Lord knows how to rescue the godly from trials and to keep the unrighteous under punishment until the day of judgment, 10 especially those who follow the polluting desires of the flesh and despise authority.

Dangerous Lies

1. If people have pets that are like them in some way, what does your choice of pet say about you?

2 Peter 2:1-22

2. If it is so plain that judgment awaits these false teachers, why does anyone follow them (vv. 2-3,14,18-19)?
3. Who are the gross sinners in verses 13-16? What are they like? On what basis is Peter assured they will be paid back for what they've done?
4. How can you help a "brother" or "sister" in Christ who is "entangled" (v. 20) in the ways of the world?

Bold, arrogant people! They do not tremble when they blaspheme the glorious ones; 11 however, angels, who are greater in might and power, do not bring a slanderous charge against them before the Lord.[i] 12 But these people, like irrational animals—creatures of instinct born to be caught and destroyed—speak

---

[a]1:15 Or my death   [b]1:17 Other mss read My Son, My Beloved   [c]1:17 A reference to the transfiguration; see Mt 17:5   [d]2:4 Tartarus is a Gk name for a subterranean place of divine punishment lower than Hades.   [e]2:4 Other mss read in pits   [f]2:5 Lit righteousness, as the eighth   [g]2:6 Other mss omit to ruin   [h]2:6 Other mss read an example of what is going to happen to the ungodly   [i]2:11 Other mss read them from the Lord

---

the church, their spiritual family. **love.** Agape, which is the quality of showing loving actions toward even those who are one's enemies. This type of love is the chief aim of the Christian faith.

1:19 prophetic word. The whole Old Testament was seen as a prophetic anticipation of the Messiah. **strongly confirmed.** Rather than dismiss the prophecies as the false teachers did, the readers ought to consider them very seriously. **lamp shining in a dismal place.** God's Word was often compared to a light (Ps. 119:105). **the morning star arises.** This refers to Numbers 24:17, and is considered a prophecy of the Messiah. When the morning star (Venus) arises, daybreak is soon to come.

1:20-21 men spoke from God. While the false teachers claimed prophetic words of a

future judgment were made up, the Peter asserts that the prophets were empowered by the Holy Spirit (Jer. 20:9).

1:21 moved by the Holy Spirit. The same verb describes how God's voice came to the apostles at the transfiguration (v. 17). What they heard and what the Old Testament authors wrote came from God.

2:1 false prophets. The presence of Israel's lying prophets (Deut. 18:20; Jer. 14:13-16) is used to expose the presence of false teachers within the Christian community. The major problem of these teachers was their rejection of the Lord (1:16-21; 2:18-21; 3:3-11). **destructive heresies.** Literally, "teachings of destruction."

2:2 unrestrained ways. Since these false teachers denied accountability, they as-

sumed they had freedom (v. 19) to indulge in immorality.

2:3 greed. The motivation for these false teachers is to teach what people will pay to hear.

2:4 Tartarus. This was hell in Greek mythology.

2:5 preacher of righteousness. Noah's righteous living set against the backdrop of the sinful world was a strong statement about God's ways. Those around him were indifferent.

2:7 righteous. Lot was not willing to participate in the sin of Sodom and Gomorrah. Peter describes him three times here as righteous. Righteousness is not based on works.

blasphemies about things they don't understand, and in their destruction they too will be destroyed, [13] suffering harm as the payment for unrighteousness. They consider it a pleasure to carouse in the daytime. They are blots and blemishes, delighting in their deceptions[a] as they feast with you, [14] having eyes full of adultery and always looking for sin, seducing unstable people, and with hearts trained in greed. Accursed children! [15] By abandoning the straight path, they have gone astray and have followed the path of Balaam, the son of Bosor,[b] who loved the wages of unrighteousness, [16] but received a rebuke for his transgression: a speechless donkey spoke with a human voice and restrained the prophet's madness.

[17] These people are springs without water, mists driven by a whirlwind. The gloom of darkness has been reserved for them. [18] For uttering bombastic, empty words, they seduce, by fleshly desires and debauchery, people who have barely escaped[c] from those who live in error. [19] They promise them freedom, but they themselves are slaves of corruption, since people are enslaved to whatever defeats them. [20] For if, having escaped the world's impurity through the knowledge of our Lord and Savior Jesus Christ, they are again entangled in these things and defeated, the last state is worse for them than the first. [21] For it would have been better for them not to have known the way of righteousness than, after knowing it, to turn back from the holy commandment delivered to them. [22] It has happened to them according to the true proverb: **A dog returns to its own vomit,**[d] and, "a sow, after washing itself, wallows in the mud."

The Day of the Lord

3 Dear friends, this is now the second letter I've written you; in both, I awaken your pure understanding with a reminder, [2] so that you can remember the words previously spoken by the holy prophets, and the commandment of our Lord and Savior ₍given₎ through your apostles. [3] First, be aware of this: scoffers will come in the last days to scoff, following their own

lusts, [4] saying, "Where is the promise of His coming? For ever since the fathers fell •asleep, all things continue as they have been since the beginning of creation." [5] They willfully ignore this: long ago the heavens and the earth existed out of water and through water by the word of God. [6] Through these the world of that time perished when it was flooded by water. [7] But by the same word the present heavens and earth are held in store for fire, being kept until the day of judgment and destruction of ungodly men.

Anticipation

1. When did an important person in your life promise a fishing trip, a ball game, or a graduation present and then fail to deliver? How did that make you feel?

2 Peter 3:1-18

2. What frustrations are produced by God's patience in coming again? How is God's patience beneficial (vv. 9,15)?

3. In verses 10-16, is Peter addressing the certainty, the timing, or the manner of Christ's coming?

4. How can you best occupy your time while you await Jesus' coming (v. 14)?

[8] Dear friends, don't let this one thing escape you: with the Lord one day is like 1,000 years, and 1,000 years like one day. [9] The Lord does not delay His promise, as some understand delay, but is patient with you, not wanting any to perish, but all to come to repentance.

[10] But the Day of the Lord will come like a thief;[e] on that ₍day₎ the heavens will pass away with a loud noise,

---

[a]**2:13** Other mss read *delighting in the love feasts*   [b]**2:15** Other mss read *Beor*   [c]**2:18** Or *people who are barely escaping*   [d]**2:22** Pr 26:11   [e]**3:10** Other mss add *in the night*

2:10-12 Bold, arrogant people! Like those mentioned in verses 4-9, the false teachers follow the corrupt desire of the sinful nature and despise authority. This involves blatant sexual immorality (v. 14) and a wholesale rejection of Christ's lordship.

2:13 blots and blemishes. These people are like animals unfit to be offered in sacrifice to God. **their deceptions.** Literally, "deceits" or perversions of pleasure.

2:19 freedom. In light of the false teachers' denial of the second coming (3:4), this probably refers to the "freedom" from the moral implications of preparing for His imminent return. They may have used Paul's teaching on freedom in Christ (Rom. 6:1-18) to justify their position (3:15-16). **people are enslaved to whatever defeats them.** This was a common saying based on what actually

happened to people conquered in war (John 8:34; Rom. 6:16). Their supposed "freedom" is simply slavery to sin.

3:3 scoffers. In the book of 2 Peter, these are the teachers who mock the idea of the Lord's return (v. 4).

3:4 Where is the promise of His coming? Since Jesus stressed the imminence of His return (Matt. 24:34), the death of those followers of Jesus raised the critical problem of whether His promise could be trusted. **since the beginning of creation.** The scoffers argued that the world has always just gone on and on with no divine intervention or judgment, a belief shared by much of Greek philosophy as well.

3:6 flooded by water. In the flood, it was God who released the waters to deluge the earth.

3:10 like a thief. Like a thief, the Lord will come without warning (Matt. 24:43-44; 1 Thess. 5:4). **heavens will pass away with a loud noise.** The coming of God in judgment is always described in graphic images. The roar here may be the sound of the heavens being rolled up (Heb. 1:12), or the shout of God pronouncing judgment upon the cosmos. **elements ... dissolved ... earth ... disclosed.** There will be nothing to hide the wickedness of the earth from the eyes of the heavenly Judge (Isa. 2:19).

3:16 matters that are hard to understand. In the context of the problems at this church, this might refer either to Paul's teaching about Christian freedom (Gal. 5:1), or to passages in his letters that indicated the imminent return of Christ (Rom. 13:11-12; Phil. 4:5; 1 Thess. 4:15). Both may have been distorted to provide the false teachers with jus-

the elements will burn and be dissolved, and the earth and the works on it will be disclosed.[a] 11 Since all these things are to be destroyed in this way, ⌊it is clear⌋ what sort of people you should be in holy conduct and godliness 12 as you wait for and earnestly desire the coming of the day of God, because of which the heavens will be on fire and be dissolved, and the elements will melt with the heat. 13 But based on His promise, we wait for new heavens and a new earth, where righteousness will dwell.

Conclusion

14 Therefore, dear friends, while you wait for these things, make every effort to be found in peace without spot or blemish before Him. 15 Also, regard the patience of our Lord as ⌊an opportunity for⌋ salvation, just as our dear brother Paul, according to the wisdom given to him, has written to you. 16 He speaks about these things in all his letters, in which there are some matters that are hard to understand. The untaught and unstable twist them to their own destruction, as they also do with the rest of the Scriptures.

17 Therefore, dear friends, since you have been forewarned, be on your guard, so that you are not led away by the error of the immoral and fall from your own stability. 18 But grow in the grace and knowledge of our Lord and Savior Jesus Christ. To Him be the glory both now and to the day of eternity.[b] •Amen.[c]

---

[a]**3:10** Other mss read *will be burned up*   [b]**3:18** Or *now and forever*   [c]**3:18** Other mss omit *Amen.*

---

tification for their acceptance of immorality.

3:17 stability. A secure position, in contrast to the instability of the false teachers (v. 16).

3:18 Lord and Savior. In the New Testament, these two names are found together as titles for Jesus only in 2 Peter; and 2 Peter refers to Jesus as Savior more than any other New Testament book. **To Him.** Typically doxologies were ascribed to God, but this one is clearly ascribed to the Son. Second Peter stands out in the New Testament as a letter that clearly affirms

INTRODUCTION TO
1 JOHN

PERSONAL READING PLAN

☐ 1 John 1:1–2:17

☐ 1 John 2:18–3:24

☐ 1 John 4:1-21

☐ 1 John 5:1-21

AUTHOR

Although the author is nowhere named in the epistle, it is likely the beloved Apostle John, now an old man living in Asia Minor and pastoring the churches in and around Ephesus. There are a number of reasons for attributing this anonymous epistle to John:

1. A strong tradition dating back to the early days of the church holds that John is the author.

2. There are many similarities in style and content between the Gospel of John and this epistle. The same sharp contrasts appear in light and darkness, truth and falsehood, love and hate. The differences between them can be traced to differences in purpose and to the length of time that elapsed between the composition of each.

3. The internal information in the epistle points to John. For example, the author tells us that he was one of the original eyewitnesses of Jesus (1:1-2). Also, the author writes with the air of authority that would be expected of an apostle (4:6).

DATE

There is little clear evidence by which to date this letter accurately. Although it can be dated as early as A.D. 60, it was probably written toward the end of the New Testament era (A.D. 90-95), by which time many false teachings had flourished.

THEME

Walking in the light.

THE PROBLEM OF FALSE TEACHERS

Apparently a group of Christians got involved in false teaching, split off from the church (2:19), and were hassling their former friends, trying to convince them to accept their new views (2:26). This deeply troubled the church and thus John, as pastor, wrote to assure the Christians in and around Ephesus that they were, indeed, true Christians with the assurance of eternal life.

The nature of the false teaching is not completely clear. John does not describe it. The recipients of his letter knew well enough what was being taught. As John defends orthodox Christianity, certain features of the incorrect doctrine emerge.

In particular, the false teachers had a low view of Jesus. They did not believe he was the Messiah (2:22; 5:1). They did not believe he was the Son of God (5:5). They denied that Jesus had come in the flesh (4:2). They apparently claimed they did not need Jesus because they already knew God (2:4) and had fellowship with him (1:6). They did not believe that sin separated a person from God (1:6,8,10), and thus they had no need of Jesus' atoning death (5:6) to provide forgiveness and a way back to God. It is not by accident that John calls them "antichrists" (2:22).

SPIRITUAL "SUPERIORITY"

This group had come to think of themselves as some sort of spiritual elite, claiming that they had a "deeper" understanding of Christianity (4:1-6). As an antidote to such spiritual pride, John reminded his readers over and over that Christians are called to love one another, not to look down on their brothers and sisters.

It is not clear what to call this group of false teachers. They were probably related to what later became Gnosticism—a philosophy in which matter (including the body) was impure and spirit was all that counted. Therefore, these false teachers denied that Christ was fully human. They kept his deity, but at the expense of his humanity. To them, salvation came by illumination. Thus, secret "knowledge" was eagerly sought, often at the expense of apostolic doctrine.

PURPOSE

John's central concerns are quite clear. He wants to define the marks of a true Christian against the claims of the false teachers. He wants his congregation to have assurance that they have eternal life (5:13). He wants them to know the characteristics of a true Christian: right belief (the doctrinal test), righteousness (the moral test), and love (the social test).

CHARACTERISTICS

First John is written in the simplest Greek of all the New Testament. Although 5,437 different Greek words appear in the New Testament, only 303 are used in the three letters of John—less than six percent. This is not to say, however, that 1 John is a superficial book. On the contrary, the apostle John, now an old man, is writing a summary of all he has learned. "This is what Christianity is all about," he is saying. "This is what it all boils down to: God is light (1:5); God is love

(4:16); Jesus is the Messiah (2:22), the Son of God (4:15), who has come in the flesh (4:2). We are to be God's children (3:1); as such we have eternal life (2:25). We do not continue in sin (2:1), but we love one another (3:11). I repeat, we are to love one another (4:7-12)."

STRUCTURE

First John is not a letter like 2 and 3 John or most of Paul's writings. It lacks identification of writer and recipients, a salutation and a final greeting. Still, it is not a generalized document written to all Christians. John has a specific audience in mind, probably the churches in his charge in Asia Minor. Despite the lack of usual greetings, he writes in personal terms. Many see 1 John as a tract, perhaps intended to be read as a sermon, in which John deals with a specific problem.

PASSAGES FOR TOPICAL GROUP STUDY

Prologue

1 What was from the beginning,
what we have heard,
what we have seen with our eyes,
what we have observed,
and have touched with our hands,
concerning the Word of life—

2 that life was revealed,
and we have seen it
and we testify and declare to you
the eternal life that was with the Father
and was revealed to us—

On Jesus' Team

1. What is the most unbelievable thing you have personally witnessed?

1 John 1:1-4

2. John makes a point of saying that he has heard, seen, and touched Jesus. What were your "beginnings" with Jesus like? In what ways have you "seen," "heard," and "touched" Him?
3. Who has been like the Apostle John in your life—a person who has convinced you of Jesus' love and cared about your spiritual growth and maturity?
4. A key part of being on Jesus' team is revealing the truth about Him to others. How could you help someone else "see" Jesus?

3 what we have seen and heard
we also declare to you,
so that you may have fellowship along with us;
and indeed our fellowship is with the Father
and with His Son Jesus Christ.

4 We are writing these things[a]
so that our[b] joy may be complete.

Fellowship with God

5 Now this is the message we have heard from Him and declare to you: God is light, and there is absolutely no darkness in Him. 6 If we say, "We have fellowship with Him," and •walk in darkness, we are lying and are not practicing[c] the truth. 7 But if we walk in the light as He Himself is in the light, we have fellowship with one another, and the blood of Jesus His Son cleanses us from all sin. 8 If we say, "We have no sin," we are deceiving ourselves, and the truth is not in us. 9 If we confess our sins, He is faithful and righteous to forgive us our sins and to cleanse us from all unrighteousness. 10 If we say, "We have not sinned," we make Him a liar, and His word is not in us.

Living in the Light

1. When was the last time the lights went out in your house and you were plunged into darkness?

1 John 1:5-2:6

2. When you've blown it, what should you do to "clean up" (1:9)? Does that work for every sin?
3. How does it make you feel to know Jesus speaks to God "in our defense" (2:1)?
4. What are two ways you can tell if you are walking in the light (1:7; 2:3)?
5. Where have you been walking lately—in the light or in the darkness? How can you live more in the "light"?

---

a**1:4** Other mss add *to you*   b**1:4** Other mss read *your*   c**1:6** Or *not living according to*

1:1 from the beginning. The initial clause makes the assertion that this "Word of life" was pre-existent (John 1:1). Since only divine beings pre-existed, John affirms Jesus' deity.

1:2 testify. This is a legal term describing what an eyewitness does while in court. Such a person makes a public declaration of what he or she has experienced firsthand.

1:3 fellowship. This word has the dual sense of participation together in shared activity or outlook, and union together because of this shared experience.

1:5 God is light. Within the context of the Bible, "light" was connected to two basic ideas. First, on the intellectual level, it was a symbol of truth. John is saying that God is truth. Second, on the moral level, light is a symbol of purity.

1:6 If we say. Here is the first of three false

claims that John will refute. He will measure the validity of each claim against the apostolic proclamation that God is light and in Him is no darkness whatsoever. **have fellowship ... walk in darkness.** It is claimed by the false teachers that it is possible to be in union with God and yet habitually sin.

1:7 walk in the light. The image here is of a person confidently striding forth, illuminated by the light of God's truth, in contrast to the person who stumbles around in darkness. **cleanses.** If the first result of "walking in the light" is fellowship with one another. The second result is cleansing from sin.

1:8 If we say, "We have no sin." The second false claim is that they are sinless. It is one thing to deny that sin breaks fellowship with God (vv. 6-7). At least the existence of sin is admitted (even if its impact is denied); but it is another thing to deny the fact of sin

altogether. **we are deceiving ourselves.** This assertion goes beyond a mere lie (v. 6). This is self-deception. **the truth is not in us.** Not only do they not live by the truth (v. 6), but they demonstrate that they do not even know the truth.

1:9 If we confess our sins. Rather than denying their sinful natures, they need to admit their sin to God and so gain forgiveness. **faithful.** God will keep His promise to forgive (Mic. 7:18-20). **righteous.** The granting of forgiveness is not merely an act of unanticipated mercy but a response of justice, since the conditions for forgiveness have been fulfilled as a result of the death of Christ. **cleanse.** Sin makes a person unclean; Christ cleanses us of our sin (v. 7).

1:10 If we say, "We have not sinned." The third false claim: not only do they say that at the present moment they are without sin (v.

2 My little children, I am writing you these things so that you may not sin. But if anyone does sin, we have an •advocate with the Father—Jesus Christ the righteous One. ² He Himself is the propitiationᵃ for our sins, and not only for ours, but also for those of the whole world.

God's Commands

³ This is how we are sure that we have come to know Him: by keeping His commands. ⁴ The one who says, "I have come to know Him," without keeping His commands, is a liar, and the truth is not in him. ⁵ But whoever keeps His command, truly in him the love of God is perfected.ᵇ This is how we know we are in Him: ⁶ the one who says he remains in Him should •walk just as He walked.

The Test of Faith

1. What game did you play as a child where you were blindfolded? What was the experience like?

1 John 2:7-14

2. How can the command to love God and others be both old and new at the same time (vv. 7-8)?
3. John makes a very bold claim (vv. 9-11) about who really loves God. What is it about loving others that becomes such solid evidence? Does that seem like a fair test? Why or why not?
4. What three things does John stress again in verses 12-13? Which one of these do you most need to hear this week, and why?

⁷ Dear friends, I am not writing you a new command, but an old command that you have had from the beginning. The old command is the message you have heard.

⁸ Yet I am writing you a new command, which is true in Him and in you, because the darkness is passing away and the true light is already shining.

⁹ The one who says he is in the light but hates his brother is in the darkness until now. ¹⁰ The one who loves his brother remains in the light, and there is no cause for stumbling in him.ᶜ ¹¹ But the one who hates his brother is in the darkness, walks in the darkness, and doesn't know where he's going, because the darkness has blinded his eyes.

Love Is the Key

1. What do you love to do most with your free time?

1 John 2:15-27

2. What does John mean by "the world" (vv. 15-16)? Is it wrong to love the outdoors or our pets? Are all human desires contrary to God's will? Why?
3. Why can't love for the world and love for God coexist in our lives (v. 17)?
4. How can we be sure that we "remain" in the truth (vv. 24-27)?
5. In what areas of your life does love for the world compete with love for God: In your use of money? Time? Priorities? Relationships? Ambitions?

Reasons for Writing

¹² I am writing to you, little children,
    because your sins have been forgiven
        on account of His name.
¹³ I am writing to you, fathers,
    because you have come to know the One who is
        from the beginning.

ᵃ**2:2** The word *propitiation* has to do with the removal of divine wrath. Jesus' death is the means that turns God's wrath from the sinner; see 2 Co 5:21. ᵇ**2:5** Or *truly completed* ᶜ**2:10** Or *in it*

---

8), they actually claim never to have sinned! **we make Him a liar.** By claiming sinlessness they are, in essence, saying that God is lying about human nature and about His claim to forgive people. **His word is not in us.** Contrary to what they might claim, they are, in fact, alienated from God (Col. 1:21).

2:1 so that you may not sin. John quickly points out that sin is not compatible with Christian commitment. **if anyone does sin.** The provision for sin is found in Jesus, who is the Advocate, "the righteous One," and the atoning sacrifice for believers.

2:2 the propitiation. Jesus, the Advocate, bases His plea (that their sins should be forgiven) on the fact that His death legally and fully paid for their sin. Propitiation is one of

the key concepts in the New Testament. Propitiation is not just the removal of our sins and their effects. Propitiation is required because of God's wrath toward sin. God's wrath is not a whimsical, out-of-control outburst. Wrath is God's eternal opposition to sin and evil. We are strongly offended when someone in authority overlooks wrong. We say they are unjust. In order for God to be just and to offer mercy to those who had sinned, someone must take the punishment due. That someone is Jesus Christ.

2:3 by keeping His commands. The first test to determine whether a person knows God is moral in nature: Does that person keep God's commands?

2:5 the love of God. This is the reward for

obedience. God's love reaches its fulfillment in that person's life. **perfected.** The verb John uses here means ongoing fulfillment rather than sudden completion.

2:12 children ... have been forgiven. The verb tense indicates John is thinking of the forgiveness that comes at the time of conversion. In 1:9, his concern was with ongoing forgiveness for subsequent sins, based on the confession of sins.

2:12 children ... have been forgiven. The verb tense indicates John is thinking of the forgiveness that comes at the time of conversion. In 1:9, his concern was with ongoing forgiveness for subsequent sins, based on the confession of sins.

I am writing to you, young men,
because you have had victory over the evil one.
14 I have written to you, children,
because you have come to know the Father.
I have written to you, fathers,
because you have come to know the One who is
from the beginning.
I have written to you, young men,
because you are strong,
God's word remains in you,
and you have had victory over the evil one.

A Warning about the World

15 Do not love the world or the things that belong to[a] the world. If anyone loves the world, love for the Father is not in him. Because everything that belongs to[b] the world— 16 the lust of the flesh, the lust of the eyes, and the pride in one's lifestyle—is not from the Father, but is from the world. 17 And the world with its lust is passing away, but the one who does God's will remains forever.

The Last Hour

18 Children, it is the last hour. And as you have heard, "Antichrist is coming," even now many antichrists have come. We know from this that it is the last hour. 19 They went out from us, but they did not belong to us; for if they had belonged to us, they would have remained with us. However, they went out so that it might be made clear that none of them belongs to us.

20 But you have an anointing from the Holy One, and you all have knowledge.[c] 21 I have not written to you because you don't know the truth, but because you do know it, and because no lie comes from the truth. 22 Who is the liar, if not the one who denies that Jesus is the •Messiah? He is the antichrist, the one who denies the Father and the Son. 23 No one who denies the Son can have the Father; he who confesses the Son has the Father as well.

Remaining with God

24 What you have heard from the beginning must remain in you. If what you have heard from the beginning remains in you, then you will remain in the Son and in the Father. 25 And this is the promise that He Himself made to us: eternal life. 26 I have written these things to you about those who are trying to deceive you.

27 The anointing you received from Him remains in you, and you don't need anyone to teach you. Instead, His anointing teaches you about all things, and is true and is not a lie; just as it has taught you, remain in Him.

God is My Dad

1. How would you feel if Jesus returned right now: Excited? Relieved? Ashamed?

1 John 2:28-3:10

2. How easy is it for you to see God as your loving Father (3:1-2)? God is the perfect Father— far beyond any earthly father—and He loves you. How does that make you feel?

3. When John says, "Everyone who remains in Him does not sin" (3:6), do you think he's referring to occasional sins or a lifestyle of continuous sin?

4. How can you know you are a child of God (3:10)? When has it recently been difficult for you to love?

God's Children

28 So now, little children, remain in Him, so that when He appears we may have boldness and not be ashamed before Him at His coming. 29 If you know that He is righteous, you know this as well: everyone who does what is right has been born of Him.

3 1 Look at how great a love[d] the Father has given us, that we should be called God's children. And we are! The reason the world does not know us is that it didn't know Him. 2 Dear friends, we are God's children now, and

---

[a]**2:15** Lit *things in*   [b]**2:15** Lit *that is in*   [c]**2:20** Other mss read *and you know all things*   [d]**3:1** Or *at what sort of love*

2:15 world. The word John uses here is *kosmos* and in this context it means that which is alienated from God and is contrary to who God is. It refers to pagan culture which is alien to God.

2:16 lust of the flesh. That part of human nature which demands gratification—be it for sexual pleasure, for luxury, for possessions, for expensive food or for whatever. **lust of the eyes.** Greed, which is aroused by sight. A person sees something and wants it. (Gen. 3:6; Josh. 7:21; 2 Sam. 11:2-4.) **pride.** Pride in one's possessions; an attitude of arrogance because one has acquired so much.

2:18 the last hour. They knew that His second coming (the *parousia*) would bring to a

close the "last days" and usher in a new age in which God's rule would be visible and universal. **Antichrist.** In the last days an evil opponent will arise under the control of Satan. **antichrists.** John points out that the coming of the Antichrist was not just some future threat. Even at that moment the "spirit of the antichrist" (4:3) was loose in the world and active in those who denied Christ and His teachings (v. 22).

2:19 They went out from us. John now identifies those who are imbued with the spirit of the antichrist. They are none other than the secessionists who left the church and even now seek to win over their former friends and colleagues to their point of view (v. 26).

2:22 denies. John now reveals the master lie in the secessionists' false teaching: they deny that Jesus is the Messiah and the Son of God.

3:2 what we will be has not yet been revealed. The precise nature of what Christians will become when they meet Christ is not fully clear yet. However, they can get an idea of what they will be like by looking at Jesus ("we will be like Him"). In some way, Christians will become like Jesus when the process of glorification—which began at rebirth—is completed at Jesus' second coming.

what we will be has not yet been revealed. We know that when He appears, we will be like Him, because we will see Him as He is. ³ And everyone who has this hope in Him purifies himself just as He is pure.

⁴ Everyone who commits sin also breaks the law;ᵃ sin is the breaking of law. ⁵ You know that He was revealed so that He might take away sins,ᵇ and there is no sin in Him. ⁶ Everyone who remains in Him does not sin; everyone who sins has not seen Him or known Him.

⁷ Little children, let no one deceive you! The one who does what is right is righteous, just as He is righteous. ⁸ The one who commits sin is of the Devil, for the Devil has sinned from the beginning. The Son of God was revealed for this purpose: to destroy the Devil's works. ⁹ Everyone who has been born of God does not sin, because Hisᶜ seed remains in him; he is not able to sin, because he has been born of God. ¹⁰ This is how God's children—and the Devil's children—are made evident.

Love's Imperative

Whoever does not do what is right is not of God, especially the one who does not love his brother. ¹¹ For this is the message you have heard from the beginning: we should love one another, ¹² unlike Cain, who was of the evil one and murderedᵈ his brother. And why did he murder him? Because his works were evil, and his brother's were righteous. ¹³ Do not be surprised, brothers, if the world hates you. ¹⁴ We know that we have passed from death to life because we love our brothers. The one who does not love remains in death. ¹⁵ Everyone who hates his brother is a murderer, and you know that no murderer has eternal life residing in him.

Love in Action

¹⁶ This is how we have come to know love: He laid down His life for us. We should also lay down our lives for our brothers. ¹⁷ If anyone has this world's goods and sees his brother in need but shuts off his compassion from him—how can God's love reside in him?

 True Love

1. How do you know when someone really loves you?

1 John 3:11-24

2. What is the definition of love in this passage (vv. 16-18)? How does this compare with the definition of love at your school or among your friends?
3. What kind of comfort should we receive from verses 21 and 22?
4. How does the Spirit help us to have assurance that God remains in us and loves us (v. 24)?
5. What can you do to share God's love with someone this week: Visit someone who is lonely? Help your brother or sister with homework? Other?

¹⁸ Little children, we must not love in word or speech, but in deed and truth; ¹⁹ that is how we will know we are of the truth, and will convince our hearts in His presence, ²⁰ because if our hearts condemn us, God is greater than our hearts and knows all things.

²¹ Dear friends, if our hearts do not condemn ₍us₎ we have confidence before God, ²² and can receive whatever we ask from Him because we keep His commands and do what is pleasing in His sight. ²³ Now this is His command: that we believe in the name of His Son Jesus Christ, and love one another as He commanded us. ²⁴ The one who keeps His commands remains in Him, and He in him. And the way we know that He remains in us is from the Spirit He has given us.

The Spirit of Truth and the Spirit of Error

4 Dear friends, do not believe every spirit, but test the spirits to determine if they are from God,

---

ᵃ**3:4** Or *also commits iniquity*   ᵇ**3:5** Other mss read *our sins*   ᶜ**3:9** God's   ᵈ**3:12** Or *slaughtered*

3:6 does not sin. John appears to be saying here (and in vv. 8-10) that a Christian cannot sin. Yet in other passages, he points out that Christians can and do sin (1:8,10; 2:1; 5:16). Some scholars feel that what John has in mind here is willful and deliberate sin (as opposed to involuntary error). Other scholars stress the tense of the verb that John uses: a Christian does not keep on sinning. In other words, Christians do not habitually sin.

3:9 His seed. John probably is referring to the Word of God (Luke 8:11; Jas. 1:18; 1 Pet. 1:23), to the Holy Spirit (John 3:6) or to both, by which the Christian is kept from sin.

3:19-20 God is greater than our hearts. John seems to be saying that Christians can be at peace with themselves even when troubled by their consciences. But, as John points

out, the basis of their confidence is the fact that it is God who will judge them and not their own hearts. They can trust themselves to His all-knowing justice because they have sought and found His forgiveness (1 Cor. 4:3-5).

3:21 confidence. Confidence is necessary in order to come before God. Without confidence a person does not feel free to enter into prayer.

3:22 receive whatever we ask. Once again, John states a truth in a stark, unqualified way: if we ask, we will receive. **keep His commands.** Obedience does not cause prayer to be answered; it is a condition that motivates Christians to pray.

3:23-24 believe … love … keeps His commands. In these verses, John brings to-

gether the three issues underlying the three tests by which believers can know they are truly children of God. He shows the connection between obedience (the moral test), love (the social test), and belief (the doctrinal test) and how these relate to the question of union with God.

4:1 do not believe every spirit. It is dangerous to accept uncritically everything that is said "in the name of God." Not everyone claiming inner revelation is hearing God's voice. **test.** The test that John suggests by which to distinguish between spirits is doctrinal in nature. It has to do with who Jesus is. False spirits will not acknowledge that Jesus of Nazareth (a fully human man) is the incarnate Messiah (the divine Son of God).

Seeking Truth

1. What is the strangest story you have heard about a religious cult?
2. When you are unsure, how do you determine if someone is telling you the truth?

1 John 4:1-6

3. How are we to determine if a spirit is the "Spirit of God" or the "spirit of the antichrist" (vv. 2-3)?
4. What power equips us to overcome false teachings and prophets (v. 4)?
5. Why do you think some students are attracted to strange groups?
6. What have you found is the best strategy in resisting cults?

because many false prophets have gone out into the world.

² This is how you know the Spirit of God: Every spirit who confesses that Jesus Christ has come in the flesh[a] is from God. ³ But every spirit who does not confess Jesus[b] is not from God. This is the spirit of the antichrist; you have heard that he is coming, and he is already in the world now.

⁴ You are from God, little children, and you have conquered them, because the One who is in you is greater than the one who is in the world. ⁵ They are from the world. Therefore what they say is from the world, and the world listens to them. ⁶ We are from God. Anyone who knows God listens to us; anyone who is not from

God does not listen to us. From this we know the Spirit of truth and the spirit of deception.

Knowing God through Love

⁷ Dear friends, let us love one another, because love is from God, and everyone who loves has been born of God and knows God. ⁸ The one who does not love does not know God, because God is love. ⁹ God's love was revealed among us in this way:[c] God sent His •One and Only Son into the world so that we might live through Him. ¹⁰ Love consists in this: not that we loved God, but that He loved us and sent His Son to be the[d] propitiation[e] for our sins. ¹¹ Dear friends, if God loved us in this way, we also must love one another. ¹² No one has ever seen God.[f] If we love one another, God remains in[g] us and His love is perfected in us.

Fear vs. Love

1. When was the last time you were truly afraid? What happened?
2. How do you show your friends and family that you love them?

1 John 4:7-21

3. How has God demonstrated that He is love (vv. 9-10)? How can we know God and experience His love (vv. 15-17)?
4. In what way does God's love motivate us to love others (v. 11)? How big of a challenge is that?
5. What is some fear you need to trade in for love (v. 18)?

ᵃ**4:2** Or *confesses Jesus to be the Christ come in the flesh*   ᵇ**4:3** Other mss read *confess that Jesus has come in the flesh*   ᶜ**4:9** Or *revealed in us*   ᵈ**4:10** Or *a*   ᵉ**4:10** The word *propitiation* has to do with the removal of divine wrath. Jesus' death is the means that turns God's wrath from the sinner; see 2 Co 5:21.   ᶠ**4:12** Since God is an infinite being, no one can see Him in His absolute essential nature; see Ex 33:18–23.   ᵍ**4:12** Or *remains among*

4:2 This is how you know. By the strong claims Jesus made, He will not be one option among many. His assertion that "no one comes to the Father except through me (Jn 14:6) is clear and calls for a decision from each person who hears the claim. Knowing if a prophet has the Spirit of God can be tested by the content of what he confesses publicly.

4:3 antichrist. In this context, *antichrist* doesn't refer to a political ruler but to the spirit of evil that leads men to promote a religion contrary to God's revelation. In 2:18-27 John's concern was that believers not be led astray by those who are filled with the spirit of the antichrist.

4:10 the propitiation for our sins. By this phrase, John describes the saving work of Jesus. The idea of atonement is tied up with

the Old Testament concept of substitution and sacrifice. In the Old Testament, sin was dealt with when a person symbolically placed his sins on an animal that he had brought to the temple. This animal had to be perfect—without spot or blemish. It was then sacrificed in place of the sinful (imperfect) person. Such substitutionary sacrifices were a picture of the final sacrifice Jesus would one day make.

4:18 no fear in love. People cannot love and fear at the same moment. The love casts out the fear. **fear involves punishment.** This is the root of the fear: they think God is going to punish them. They forget that they are His forgiven children.

5:1 believes. Belief on the part of Christians is clear proof that they have been born of God.

5:3 burden. Obedience to the thousands of often picayune rules and regulations promulgated by the scribes and Pharisees was indeed a heavy burden. But obedience to God does not exasperate the Christian, since God enables the believer through the Holy Spirit to respond in obedience.

5:4 our faith. This is the source of the overcoming power of the Christian—confidence and trust that Jesus is the Son of God (v. 5).

5:6 by water and blood. By these two phrases, John is probably referring to Jesus' baptism and His death. These two events are crucial in understanding who Jesus really is. The secessionists felt that Jesus, the man, became the Christ at His baptism and that the Christ then departed prior to the death of Jesus. In contrast, the apostolic witness (as recorded in the New Testament) as-

[13] This is how we know that we remain in Him and He in us: He has given to us from His Spirit. [14] And we have seen and we testify that the Father has sent the Son as Savior of the world. [15] Whoever confesses[a] that Jesus is the Son of God—God remains in him and he in God. [16] And we have come to know and to believe the love that God has for us. God is love, and the one who remains in love remains in God, and God remains in him.

[17] In this, love is perfected with us so that we may have confidence in the day of judgment; for we are as He is in this world. [18] There is no fear in love; instead, perfect love drives out fear, because fear involves punishment.[b] So the one who fears has not reached perfection in love. [19] We love[c] because He first loved us.

Confidence in Eternity

1. What is one thing that you take for granted?
2. Which part of your church worship service helps to strengthen your faith the most?

1 John 5:1-15

3. Judging by the standard in verse 2, how loved would you say God feels by you?
4. What would you say to a friend who has doubts that he or she is really a Christian (vv. 11-12)?
5. With how much confidence can you say you *"know* that you have eternal life" (v. 13)? What would help you to increase your confidence level?

Keeping God's Commands

[20] If anyone says, "I love God," yet hates his brother, he is a liar. For the person who does not love his brother whom he has seen cannot love God whom he has not seen.[d] [21] And we have this command from Him: the one who loves God must also love his brother.

[5] Everyone who believes that Jesus is the •Messiah has been born of God, and everyone who loves the parent also loves his child. [2] This is how we know that we love God's children when we love God and obey[e] His commands. [3] For this is what love for God is: to keep His commands. Now His commands are not a burden, [4] because whatever has been born of God conquers the world. This is the victory that has conquered the world: our faith. [5] And who is the one who conquers the world but the one who believes that Jesus is the Son of God?

The Sureness of God's Testimony

[6] Jesus Christ—He is the One who came by water and blood; not by water only, but by water and by blood. And the Spirit is the One who testifies, because the Spirit is the truth. [7] For there are three that testify:[f] [8] the Spirit, the water, and the blood—and these three are in agreement. [9] If we accept the testimony of men, God's testimony is greater, because it is God's testimony that He has given about His Son. [10] (The one who believes in the Son of God has the testimony in himself. The one who does not believe God has made Him a liar, because he has not believed in the testimony that God has given about His Son.) [11] And this is the testimony: God has given us eternal life, and this life is in His Son.

[12] The one who has the Son has life. The one who doesn't have the Son of God does not have life. [13] I have written these things to you who believe in the name of the Son of God, so that you may know that you have eternal life.

---

a[4:15] Or *acknowledges*   b[4:18] Or *fear has its own punishment* or *torment*   c[4:19] Other mss add *Him*   d[4:20] Other mss read *seen, how is he able to love . . . seen?* (as a question)   e[5:2] Other mss read *keep*   f[5:7–8] Other mss (the Lat Vg and a few late Gk mss) read *testify in heaven, the Father, the Word, and the Holy Spirit, and these three are One.* 8 *And there are three who bear witness on earth:*

---

serts that at His baptism, Jesus publicly identified Himself with the sins of the people (even though He Himself was without sin). By His death, Jesus took away those sins. **not by water only.** The secessionists agreed that the baptism of Jesus was important. They felt it was then that the heavenly Christ infused the man Jesus. (In fact, it was the Holy Spirit who descended on Jesus at His baptism.) John is insistent that both the Jesus' baptism and crucifixion are crucial in understanding Him. **the Spirit is the truth.** The Holy Spirit is the third witness, and is qualified to be such because the Spirit is, in His essence, truth Himself.

5:7 three that testify. There are two kinds of testimony: the objective historical witnesses

of the water and the blood and the subjective, experiential witness of the Spirit (Christians experience within themselves the reality of these events). These two types of witness complement one another. Believers know in their hearts the truthfulness and power of the historical facts of Jesus' life and death.

5:10 believes in. It is one thing to believe Jesus. It is another to believe in Jesus. To believe Jesus is to accept what He says as true. To believe in Jesus is to accept who He is. It involves trusting him completely and committing one's life to Him.

5:11 eternal life. The Greek word that is here translated "eternal" means "that which

belongs to the coming age." But since that age has already broken into the present age, eternal life can be enjoyed even now (John 17:3).

5:13 so that you may know. This verse parallels John 20:31 which is the concluding verse of that Gospel. John wrote his Gospel in order to witness about Jesus and so inspire faith in those who did not yet know Christ. By believing in Jesus, they would discover "life." His purpose in the letter is similar, except that now his words are directed to those who have, in fact, come to believe in Jesus. His purpose is no longer to tell them how to find "life" but, instead, to assure them that they do have eternal life.

Effective Prayer

14 Now this is the confidence we have before Him: whenever we ask anything according to His will, He hears us. 15 And if we know that He hears whatever we ask, we know that we have what we have asked Him for.

16 If anyone sees his brother committing a sin that does not bring death, he should ask, and Goda will give life to him—to those who commit sin that doesn't bring death. There is sinb that brings death. I am not saying he should pray about that. 17 All unrighteousness is sin, and there is sin that does not bring death.

Conclusion

18 We know that everyone who has been born of God does not sin, but the Onec who is born of God keeps him,d e and the evil one does not touch him.

19 We know that we are of God, and the whole world is under the sway of the evil one.

20 And we know that the Son of God has come and has given us understanding so that we may know the true One.f We are in the true One—that is, in His Son Jesus Christ. He is the true God and eternal life.

21 Little children, guard yourselves from idols.

---

a5:16 Lit He b5:16 Or is a sin c5:18 Jesus Christ d5:18 Other mss read himself e5:18 Or the one who is born of God keeps himself f5:20 Other mss read the true God

---

5:14 confidence. Originally this word meant "freedom of speech." It was used to describe the right of all those in a democracy to speak their mind. By this word John refers to the bold confidence Christians have—that they can approach God in prayer and freely speak their minds. **according to His will.** In 3:22, John says that a condition for answered prayer is obedient behavior. Here John adds another condition: what we ask must be in accord with God's purposes (Matt. 26:39,42).

5:15 He hears. By this phrase John means, "He hears us favorably." To know that God

hears us is to know that "we have what we have asked for."

5:16 sin that brings death. Although John's readers probably understood what he was referring to, it is not at all clear to the modern reader just what this phrase means. A specific kind of sin is probably not in view here, but rather a lifestyle of habitual, willing, and persistent sinning.

5:18 We know. John concludes with a final list of assurances. The first affirmation relates to Christian behavior. The new birth results in new behavior. Sin and the child

of God are incompatible.

5:19 of God. The second affirmation that John makes is that they are, indeed, "children of God." They are part of the family of God and in relationship with the other children of God.

5:20 We are in the true One. The third affirmation is that they really do know what is true. **understanding.** This is the power or ability to know what is actually so. Specifically, Jesus gave Christians the power to perceive the one and only true God over and against false idols (v. 21).

INTRODUCTION TO
2 JOHN / 3 JOHN

PERSONAL READING PLAN

☐ 2 John 1-13

☐ 3 John 1-14

AUTHOR

There is much similarity of style and content between 2 and 3 John. For example, compare 2 John 1 with 3 John 1, 2 John 4 with 3 John 4; 2 John 12 with 3 John 13-14. Undoubtedly both were written by the same person. There is also a close connection between 1 John and these two shorter letters (compare, for example, 1 John 4:3 with 2 John 7). All three epistles seem to deal with the same situation. Therefore, it seems very likely that the "elder" who wrote 2 and 3 John is, indeed, the Apostle John.

DATE

The dates are uncertain, but both letters were probably written in the late A.D. 80s or early 90s, when the false doctrine that they rebuke began to flourish.

THEME

Hospitality for traveling missionaries.

PURPOSE

The issue addressed by 2 and 3 John is that of wandering missionaries. In a time when Roman inns were notorious for being dirty and flea-infested, visiting Christian teachers would turn to the local church for hospitality. The problem was that some of the people seeking room and board were false teachers, expounding erroneous doctrines; others were phony, pretending to be true prophets to get free hospitality. Even a pagan Greek author like Lucian noticed this sort of abuse. In his satirical work Peregrinus, he wrote about a religious charlatan who lived off the generosity of the church simply as a way to avoid working. In an attempt to cope with this problem, the Didache, an early church manual, laid down a series of regulations guiding the reception of itinerant ministers. It said, for example, that true prophets were indeed to be entertained—for a day or two. But if a prophet stayed three days, this was a sign that he was false. Likewise, if a prophet under the inspiration of the Spirit asked for money, he was a false prophet.

These concerns are found in 2 and 3 John. In 2 John, the author worries about false prophets who are teaching erroneous doctrine, such as Gnosticism (salvation is a product of special knowledge). "Do not receive him," he says (2 John 10). But in 3 John, he addresses the opposite problem: Christians who failed to provide hospitality for genuine teachers.

PASSAGES FOR TOPICAL GROUP STUDY

Greeting

The Elder:[a]

To the elect lady[b] and her children, whom I love in truth—and not only I, but also all who have come to know the truth— 2 because of the truth that remains in us and will be with us forever.

3 Grace, mercy, and peace will be with us from God the Father and from Jesus Christ, the Son of the Father, in truth and love.

Truth and Deception

4 I was very glad to find some of your children •walking in truth, in keeping with a command we have received from the Father. 5 So now I urge you, lady—not as if I were writing you a new command, but one we have had from the beginning—that we love one another. 6 And this is love: that we walk according to His commands. This is the command as you have heard it from the beginning: you must walk in love.[c]

7 Many deceivers have gone out into the world; they do not confess the coming of Jesus Christ in the flesh.[d] This is the deceiver and the antichrist. 8 Watch yourselves so that you don't lose what we[e] have worked for, but you may receive a full reward. 9 Anyone who does not remain in the teaching about Christ, but goes beyond it, does not have God. The one who remains in that teaching, this one has both the Father and the Son. 10 If anyone comes to you and does not bring this teaching, do not receive him into your home, and don't say, "Welcome," to him; 11 for the one who says, "Welcome," to him shares in his evil works.

Farewell

12 Though I have many things to write to you, I don't want to do so with paper and ink. Instead, I hope to be with you and talk face to face[f] so that our joy may be complete.

13 The children of your elect sister send you greetings.

 Truth or Consequences

1. Whose home could you drop in on unexpectedly and know that you would be welcome?

2 John 1-13

2. How do John's exhortations to true Christ-followers (vv. 4-6) help them resist the deception and wickedness of the religious frauds (vv. 7-11)?

3. Have you ever been involved in a deep relationship that had to end because of an overriding issue involving your faith? What happened?

4. When was the last time you spent time with someone who was hurting, lonely, or needing help (no names)? What is stopping you from doing this more often?

---

[a]1 Or *Presbyter*   [b]1 Or *Kyria*, a proper name; probably a literary figure for a local church known to John; the *children* would be its members.   [c]6 Lit *in it*   [d]7 Or *confess Jesus Christ as coming in the flesh*   [e]8 Other mss read *you*   [f]12 Lit *mouth to mouth*

1-3 The Elder. As was the custom in first-century letters, the writer of this letter first identifies himself, then names the recipients of the letter, and finally concludes his salutation by pronouncing a blessing.

4-11 your children. This is the heart of John's message. In verses 4-6 he focuses on the internal life of the local church. He points out its need to walk in truth, obedience, and love. In verses 7-11 he focuses on the external life of the local church, specifically the threat posed by false teachers who espouse erroneous doctrine. John makes a sharp distinction between what is true (vv. 4-6) and what is false (vv. 7-11).

7-11 deceivers. John now turns from true believers to false deceivers. He warns Christians not to be deceived (vv. 7-8). He tells

them not to encourage false teachers by giving them hospitality (vv. 10-11). If his exhortations in verses 4-6 to walk in truth, obedience, and love are followed, the believers will be able to resist the heresy being taught by these false teachers.

7 Many. In contrast to "some" children who walk in truth, there are the "many" who deceive. **have gone out.** John may be saying that these false teachers were once in the church but have now left (1 John 2:19). Or he may be saying that in the same way that the emissaries of God are sent out into the world (John 17:18; 20:21), Satan sends out his own emissaries. **do not confess the coming of Jesus Christ in the flesh.** John defines the deceivers' error. They deny His incarnation.

8. receive a full reward. The Greek word translated "reward" refers to "the wages of a workman." John's concern is not with the loss of salvation which one does not earn in any case (it is a free gift), but with the loss of reward due for faithful service.

10 do not receive him. John now issues his second warning: do not receive or welcome false teachers into your home. This injunction sounds harsh in the light of the New Testament's insistence upon hospitality—including John's own words on the subject (Rom. 12:13; 1 Tim. 3:2; Titus 1:8; Heb. 13:2; 1 Peter 4:8-10; 3 John 5-8). However, it is important to notice that John refers to teachers and not believers who might hold errant views.

Greeting

The Elder:

To my dear friend[a] Gaius, whom I love in truth. [2] Dear friend,[b] I pray that you may prosper in every way and be in good health, just as your soul prospers. [3] For I was very glad when some brothers came and testified to your ⌊faithfulness⌋ to the truth—how you are •walking in the truth. [4] I have no greater joy than this: to hear that my children are walking in the truth.

Gaius Commended

[5] Dear friend,[b] you are showing your faith[c] by whatever you do for the brothers, and this ⌊you are doing⌋ for strangers; [6] they have testified to your love before the church. You will do well to send them on their journey in a manner worthy of God, [7] since they set out for the sake of the name, accepting nothing from pagans. [8] Therefore, we ought to support such men, so that we can be co-workers with[d] the truth.

Diotrephes and Demetrius

[9] I wrote something to the church, but Diotrephes, who loves to have first place among them, does not receive us. [10] This is why, if I come, I will remind him of the works he is doing, slandering us with malicious words. And he is not satisfied with that! He not only refuses to welcome the brothers himself, but he even stops those who want to do so and expels them from the church.

[11] Dear friend,[b] do not imitate what is evil, but what is good. The one who does good is of God; the one who does evil has not seen God. [12] Demetrius has a ⌊good⌋ testimony from everyone, and from the truth itself. And we also testify for him, and you know that our testimony is true.

Farewell

[13] I have many things to write you, but I don't want to write to you with pen and ink. [14] I hope to see you soon, and we will talk face to face.[e]

Peace be with you. The friends send you greetings. Greet the friends by name.

Picking Your Friends

1. Did you ever run out of money when you were away from home? What happened?

3 John 1-14

2. Why is John urging that these teachers be cared for in their travels?
3. What is John's big problem with Diotrephes, and why does he take it so seriously?
4. How would you explain what John is saying in verse 11? Does this seem too black and white?
5. When picking close friends (as Gaius was to John), what do you look for? How can you be that kind of friend to others?

---

[a]**1** Or *my beloved*   [b]**2,5,11** Or *Beloved*   [c]**5** Lit *are doing faith*   [d]**8** Or *co-workers for*   [e]**14** Lit *mouth to mouth*

---

1 The Elder. Both 2 and 3 John were written by the same person, identified only as "the Elder"—the Apostle John. **To my dear friend.** This is one of only two personal letters in the New Testament (the other is Philemon). While other letters do bear the name of an individual recipient—Timothy and Titus, for example—they are, in fact, letters meant to be read publicly. **Gaius.** There are several men by this name mentioned in the New Testament (Acts 19:29; 20:4; Rom. 16:23; 1 Cor. 1:14). "Gaius" was one of the most common names in the Roman Empire. As a result, it is not possible to identify with certainty the Gaius to whom John writes with any other Gaius in the New Testament.

3 faithfulness to the truth. This was one of several characteristics of Gaius that John singled out for commendation.

4 my children. Paul used this phrase to describe those he assisted in converting to Christ. Perhaps, therefore, Gaius was John's spiritual son. **walking in the truth.** Gaius did not just know the truth; he lived what he believed. He let his theological convictions guide his moral behavior.

5-8 showing your faith. Here John commends Gaius for showing hospitality to the visiting teachers. John's words in verses 5-8 stand in sharp contrast to what he wrote in 2 John 10-11 where he warned against offering hospitality to certain teachers. The difference is that in 2 John he was concerned about false teachers and here he discusses "brothers" who went out "for the sake of the name" and who are "co-workers with the truth." Second and Third John must be read together to get a balanced picture of the sit-uation in the early church related to itinerant teachers.

9 Diotrephes. He and Gaius may have been members of the same congregation or, more likely, of neighboring congregations. In any case, they act in opposite ways when it comes to hospitality. Diotrephes refuses to receive them. This may have to do with his desire "to be first."

12 Demetrius. Demetrius probably delivered this letter to Gaius. Since he was unknown to Gaius, John wrote this threefold recommendation. Demetrius may himself have been a wandering missionary whom John wished the house-church to receive.

INTRODUCTION TO
JUDE

PERSONAL READING PLAN

☐ Jude 1-25

AUTHOR

Traditionally Jude, the brother of Jesus, is considered the author of Jude (see Matt. 13:55, Jude is a form of the name "Judas"). In the New Testament there are five people by the name of Jude or Judas (Mark 6:3; Luke 6:16; John 14:22; Acts 9:11; 15:22,27,32) but only the brother of Jesus is a serious candidate as author. Little is known about Jude other than that he was one of four brothers (Mark 6:3). He was probably not a follower of Jesus during the years of his brother's ministry (Mark 3:21,31-35; John 7:5). It was only after the Resurrection that Jude became a believer (Acts 1:14). The brothers of Jesus eventually became itinerant missionaries (1 Cor. 9:5). Tradition says they spread the gospel throughout Palestine. Jude's brother, James the Just, was leader of the church in Jerusalem. Jude gives us a view of the early church under Jesus' own brothers' leadership.

DATE

The date of Jude is hard to determine. If the author of 2 Peter made use of it, then it would be dated around A.D. 65; otherwise it could be dated as late as A.D. 80.

THEME

Contend for the faith.

PURPOSE

Jude gives an overview of his book in verses 3-4. He makes two points: Christians are "to contend for the faith"; and secondly, they are to contend with false Christians who "have come in by stealth." The rest of the book develops these two points. In verses 5-19, the nature of the false teachers is explained. Jude makes it clear that false teachers are not a new problem. In verses

20-23, Jude's main point is an appeal to the Christians to hold on to the Christian faith despite false teachers.

THE FALSE TEACHERS

Jude's opponents are a band of smooth-talking teachers who go from church to church, receiving hospitality in return for their instruction. Such itinerant teachers were often a source of trouble in the early church (Matt. 7:15; 2 Cor. 10-11; 1 John 4:1; 2 John 10). These teachers were antinomians, those who rejected all moral standards (since they misunderstood grace) and indulged in all manner of immoral behavior, particularly sexual. Their teaching was derived largely from individual subjective experiences.

CHARACTERISTICS

Most people know Jude only because of its benediction (vv. 24-25):

Now to Him who is able to protect you from stumbling and to make you stand in the presence of His glory, blameless and with great joy, to the only God our Savior, through Jesus Christ our Lord, be glory, majesty, power, and authority before all time, now, and forever. Amen.

Today, Jude is less frequently read than the other New Testament letters. To its first readers, however, Jude was anything but obscure. It was heard as a fiery call to defend the faith against the heretics who had wormed their way into the church (v. 4).

In true sermonic fashion, Jude quotes (or alludes to) various texts and then explains them. What sets Jude's sermon apart from contemporary Christian sermons is his choice of texts. His first references are to Old Testament stories (vv. 5-7,11), and his concluding reference is to "the

word foretold by the apostles of our Lord Jesus Christ" (v. 17). This is familiar material. But in between, Jude quotes 1 Enoch (vv. 14-15), a Jewish apocryphal book, and alludes to the Assumption of Moses (v. 9), probably to the Testament of Naphtali (v. 7) and to the Testament of Asher (v. 8).

The Apocryphal books Jude quotes were written during the time between the Old and New Testament. They were not accepted as orthodox and so never became part of the Bible itself.

Some of the church fathers concluded (wrongly) that any book that used apocryphal literature could not be genuine. But this view says more about the presuppositions of those theologians than it does about what can and cannot be included within Scripture.

Certainly, other New Testament authors used nonbiblical Jewish writing (such as 2 Tim. 3:8). Paul quotes the heathen poets in Acts 17:28; 1 Corinthians 15:32-33; and Titus 1:12. The author of Hebrews echoes the works of Philo; James makes reference to nonbiblical sources. The issue is not where the specific words came from but how the New Testament writer used these words to reveal God's truth.

RELATIONSHIP TO 2 PETER

It is clear that Jude and 2 Peter are somehow related. Of the 25 verses in Jude, 15 of them appear in whole or in part in 2 Peter. The question is: What is the nature of the relationship between Jude and 2 Peter? Did Jude quote from 2 Peter? Or was the reverse true? Or did they both quote from the same outside source?

OLD TESTAMENT LINK IN JUDE

1. The way of Cain (v. 11)–Adam and Eve's first son, Cain, consumed with jealousy and anger, murdered his brother, Abel (Gen. 4:3-8).

2. Balaam's error (v. 11)–Balaam was an ancient pagan sorcerer hired to curse God's people. Though God compelled him to bless Israel instead, his greed apparently motivated him to give advice that proved destructive to the Israelites (Num. 22-24; 31:16).

3. Korah's rebellion (v. 11)–Korah was a Levite who led a rebellion against the authority God had given to Moses and Aaron (Num. 16:1-3,11).

STRUCTURE

Jude is a genuine letter with a standard opening (vv. 1-2). Verses 3-4 develop the theme and occasion of the epistle are defined. But Jude is also a short sermon. The bulk of the book (vv. 5-25) consists of an exposition of certain texts as related to a particular problem facing the church. Thus, Jude is a sermon sent by mail to be read before the congregation(s).

The book of Jude is a painstakingly crafted document. Jude packs a lot of content into a few words by carefully choosing his words and images. Verses 11-13 are particularly vivid in imagery, evoking a wide range of thought in remarkably few words.

PASSAGES FOR TOPICAL GROUP STUDY

Greeting

Jude, a slave of Jesus Christ, and a brother of James: To those who are the called, loved[a] by God the Father and kept by Jesus Christ.

2 May mercy, peace, and love be multiplied to you.

Jude's Purpose in Writing

3 Dear friends, although I was eager to write you about our common salvation, I found it necessary to write and exhort you to contend for the faith that was delivered to the saints once for all. 4 For certain men, who were designated for this judgment long ago, have come in by stealth; they are ungodly, turning the grace of our God into promiscuity and denying our only Master and Lord, Jesus Christ.

Apostates: Past and Present

5 Now I want to remind you, though you know all these things: the Lord, having first of all[b] saved a people out of Egypt, later destroyed those who did not believe; 6 and He has kept, with eternal chains in darkness for the judgment of the great day, angels who did not keep their own position but deserted their proper dwelling. 7 In the same way, Sodom and Gomorrah and the cities around them committed sexual immorality and practiced perversions,[c] just as they did, and serve as an example by undergoing the punishment of eternal fire.

8 Nevertheless, these dreamers likewise defile their flesh, despise authority, and blaspheme glorious beings. 9 Yet Michael the archangel, when he was disputing with the Devil in a debate about Moses' body, did not dare bring an abusive condemnation against him, but said, "The Lord rebuke you!" 10 But these people blaspheme anything they don't understand, and what they know by instinct, like unreasoning animals—they destroy themselves with these things. 11 Woe to them! For they have traveled in the way of Cain, have abandoned themselves to the error of Balaam for profit, and have perished in Korah's rebellion.

The Apostates' Doom

12 These are the ones who are like dangerous reefs[d] at your love feasts. They feast with you, nurturing only themselves without fear. They are waterless clouds carried along by winds; trees in late autumn—fruitless, twice dead, pulled out by the roots; 13 wild waves of the sea, foaming up their shameful deeds; wandering stars for whom is reserved the blackness of darkness forever!

 Bad News, Good News

1. Share a time when you really fell for a lie or got "taken for a ride."

Jude 1-25

2. How does Jude describe himself and his fellow Christians (vv. 3-5)? From this description, what does it mean to be a Christian?

3. What is the challenge that these young Christians face (vv. 17-21)?

4. Which part of Jude's speech do people in your school, team, or community most need to hear?

5. In light of the warnings in Jude, what hope do you find in verses 24-25? How does that help as you struggle with sin in groups or teams, at home, or even when you're alone?

14 And Enoch, in the seventh ⌊generation⌋ from Adam, prophesied about them:

> Look! The Lord comes[e] with thousands
>   of His holy ones
> 15 to execute judgment on all,
>   and to convict them[f]

---

1 brother of James. James was the leader of the Jerusalem church (Acts 12:17; Gal. 2:9). **called, loved ... kept.** These terms, drawn from Isaiah 40–45, are a marked contrast to the description of the false teachers later on.

4 turning the grace of God. The critical problem with the false teachers is their manipulation of the gospel's emphasis on God's grace into an excuse for living an immoral lifestyle (Rom. 6:1,15; Gal. 5:13; Phil. 3:2; 2 Tim. 3:1-9; 1 Pet. 2:16; 1 John 1:6; Rev. 2:4).

7 Sodom and Gomorrah. These were two Old Testament towns whose wickedness was legendary (Gen. 18–19).

8 dreamers. This mocks the false teachers' claim to special revelations that justify their actions (v. 19; Col. 2:18). **defile their flesh.** Like the fallen angels, they indulge in illicit sexual activities. **despise authority.** Literally, "lordship." As in all the examples above, they defy Jesus' lordship over their lives (v. 4). **blaspheme glorious beings.** Jewish tradition taught that the Law was mediated through and guarded by angels (Gal. 3:19; Heb. 2:2). To justify their rejection of the Law, these people may have taught that the Law originated with the angels as well, and could be discarded by people like them who had special revelations from God.

11 Cain ... Balaam ... Korah. Their lifestyle reflects that of Cain (Gen. 4—the first murderer, viewed as a man full of lust, violence and greed); their motivations those of Balaam (Num. 31:16—he led Israel into idolatry and immorality by allowing his gift of prophecy to be bought by the highest bidder); and their future that of Korah (Num. 16—his rebellion against Moses was ended by God's judgment).

12 dangerous reefs. Just as a submerged reef endangers a ship, so these teachers threaten the church. **love feasts.** These were communal meals eaten by the church as a celebration of their unity and love in Christ. Six images from nature are used to accent how the immorality of the false teachers threatened the very meaning of that common meal.

of all their ungodly deeds that they have done
in an ungodly way,
and of all the harsh things ungodly sinners
have said against Him.

16 These people are discontented grumblers, •walking according to their desires; their mouths utter arrogant words, flattering people for their own advantage. 17 But you, dear friends, remember the words foretold by the apostles of our Lord Jesus Christ; 18 they told you, "In the end time there will be scoffers walking according to their own ungodly desires." 19 These people create divisions and are merely natural, not having the Spirit.

Exhortation and Benediction

20 But you, dear friends, building yourselves up in your most holy faith and praying in the Holy Spirit, 21 keep yourselves in the love of God, expecting the mercy of our Lord Jesus Christ for eternal life. 22 Have mercy on some who doubt; 23 save others by snatching ₊them₎ from the fire; on others have mercy in fear, hating even the garment defiled by the flesh.

24 Now to Him who is able to protect you from stumbling and to make you stand in the presence of His glory, blameless and with great joy, 25 to the only God our Savior, through Jesus Christ our Lord,[a] be glory, majesty, power, and authority before all time,[b] now, and forever. •Amen.

---

a25 Other mss omit *through Jesus Christ our Lord*   b25 Other mss omit *before all time*

INTRODUCTION TO
REVELATION

AUTHOR

The "John" of 1:4 has traditionally been interpreted as John the apostle. John writes in his own name, and only an apostle could expect to hold authority. Furthermore, the Gospel of John and the three letters of John contain striking similarities in ideas, theology, and language.

John wrote from the island of Patmos, a barren island in the Aegean Sea where he had been exiled because of his Christian witness. Tradition says that he was eventually released from Patmos and spent the remaining years of his long life in Ephesus.

DATE

Most scholars believe the book of Revelation was written near the end of the reign of Domitian, around A.D. 90-95. Evidence also exists for a date during the last years of Nero's reign (between A.D. 65 and 68) or possibly when Vespasian was emperor (A.D. 69-79).

THEME

Christ shall overcome!

HISTORICAL BACKGROUND

Rome is a central, negative image in the Book of Revelation. This view of the Roman government stands in sharp contrast to most of the rest of the New Testament, where Rome is seen as the protector of Christianity. In the early days of missionary activity, Roman judges protected Christians from Jewish mobs (Acts 18:1-17; 19:13-

41). Roman justice aided Paul on several occasions (Acts 23:12-35; 25:10-11). As a result, the apostles urged submission to Rome (Rom. 13:1-7; 1 Peter 2:13-17). But in Revelation, the attitude is quite different. Rome is seen as a whore, drunk with the blood of Christians (17:5-6), deserving nothing but destruction.

This shift in attitude was due to Caesar worship. Although Roman rulers were long considered divine, their centrality in Roman civil religion was not enforced until the end of the first century. Then Roman citizens were required to appear annually to burn a pinch of incense and declare, "Caesar is Lord." To Romans a mere formality, but Christians could not declare loyalty to anyone except Jesus. Thus, civil authorities hounded them mercilessly. Revelation reminds Christians they may suffer now, but ahead lies unimaginable glory when Jesus, the true Lord, comes in power.

APOCALYPTIC LITERATURE

The Book of Revelation is unique as the only apocalyptic book in the New Testament despite the fact that during the period between the Old and New Testaments, apocalyptic literature was the most common type of Jewish religious writing.

At the heart of apocalyptic literature was *hope*—hope that God would right wrongs, and rescue the righteous. The Jews, God's chosen people, had been subject to ungodly rulers for so long that they longed for God to intervene in history. Their hopes are clear in the apocalyptic writings (*apocalypse* is a Greek word meaning an "unveil-

ing" or "uncovering" of future events or hidden realms, like heaven).

Apocalyptic literature dealt with God's return: how He would burst into history, who He would destroy, and how He would set up His kingdom. These books were, of necessity, the products of dreams and visions. They were filled with swirling images and vivid pictures of death, supernatural creatures, destruction, and redemption. Since the events described were unlike anything ever seen, they could only be alluded to, often in cryptic language--thus our difficulty in interpreting the author's original meanings.

THE APOCALYPTIC WORLD VIEW

Underlying both Jewish and Christian apocalyptic literature was the view that history is divided into two ages: the present age of evil, which will be destroyed and the future that is characterized by God's presence and power. The turning point comes on the Day of the Lord, when the present age will give way to the new age.

Christian writers understood the Day of the Lord as Christ's second coming. When he came again, it would not be as an infant but as a king before whom the whole creation would bow. Christians must live in the in-between time.

The similarities in Christian and Jewish apocalyptic literature are striking. Beyond the obvious difference over the role of Christ, the same outline is found in Jewish literature as in Revelation. Specifically:

1. The Messiah will be the central figure in the Day of the Lord.

2. The coming of the new age will be preceded by a terrible time in history filled with war, famine, and calamity of all sorts.

3. The Day of the Lord will be the time when judgment is rendered.

4. After judgment will come a time of great peace and joy. The New Jerusalem will descend. The dead will rise and the Messiah will reign.

INTERPRETATON

There are widely varying interpretations for Revelation. Some limit its meaning to the first-century struggle between the church and Rome. Others see Revelation as a collection of symbols that predict future events (e.g., the locusts from the bottomless pit represents the invasion of Europe by Islam). Most likely Revelation speaks both to first-century struggle of Christians *and* also to the future when the Lord will return.

PASSAGES FOR TOPICAL GROUP STUDY

2:1-3:22 .... LUKEWARM FAITH.......... Letters of Warning

4:1-5:14 .... ONLY JESUS IS WORTHY ....Lion and Lamb

6:1-7:17 .... PROTECTION AT THE END.....Sealed by Jesus from Wrath

12:1-13:18 ... DEVIL CONQUERED............. Dragon Slayer

14:1-15:8 .... JOYS OF FOLLOWING GOD . Wrath and Rejoicing

18:1-19:1 ..... THE END OF EVIL...... Heaven's Marriage Feast

19:11-20:10 .. FINAL SPIRTUAL BATTLE....... The Last Battle

20:11-21:8 ... HEAVEN AND HELL .. Lake of Fire or Eternal Life

22:7-21 ..... PREPARE FOR CHRIST'S RETURN .... Come!

PASSAGES FOR GENERAL GROUP STUDY

1:1-20........ A Strange Vision (of the Risen Lord)

8:1-9:21..... Incense and Death (Final Judgments)

10:1-11:19.... Two Witnesses Persecuted

16:1-17:18 ... Plagues and Prostitutes (The Seven Bowl Judgments)

21:9-22:6 ... Heavenly Citizenship

Prologue

1 The revelation of[a] Jesus Christ that God gave Him to show His •slaves what must quickly[b] take place. He sent it and signified it[c] through His angel to His slave John, [2] who testified to God's word and to the testimony[d] about Jesus Christ, in all he saw.[e] [3] Blessed is the one who reads and blessed are those who hear the words of this prophecy and keep[f] what is written in it, because the time is near!

[4] John:

To the seven churches in the province of Asia.[g]

Grace and peace to you from[h] the One who is, who was, and who is coming; from the seven spirits[i] before His throne; [5] and from Jesus Christ, the faithful witness, the firstborn from the dead and the ruler of the kings of the earth.

To Him who loves us and has set us free[j] from our sins by His blood, [6] and made us a kingdom,[k] priests[l] to His God and Father—to Him be the glory and dominion forever and ever. •Amen.

[7] Look! He is coming with the clouds,
  and every eye will see Him,
  including those who pierced[m] Him.
  And all the families of the earth[n] [o]
  will mourn over Him.[p] [q]
  This is certain. Amen.

[8] "I am the •Alpha and the Omega," says the Lord God, "the One who is, who was, and who is coming, the Almighty."

John's Vision of the Risen Lord

[9] I, John, your brother and partner in the tribulation, kingdom, and perseverance in Jesus, was on the island called Patmos because of God's word and the testimony about Jesus.[r] [10] I was in the Spirit[s] [t] on the Lord's day,[u] and I heard behind me a loud voice like a trumpet [11] saying, "Write on a scroll[v] what you see and send it to the seven churches: Ephesus, Smyrna, Pergamum, Thyatira, Sardis, Philadelphia, and Laodicea."

[12] I turned to see the voice that was speaking to me. When I turned I saw seven gold lampstands, [13] and among the lampstands was One like the •Son of Man,[w] dressed in a long robe, and with a gold sash wrapped around His chest. [14] His head and hair were white like wool—white as snow, His eyes like a fiery flame, [15] His feet like fine bronze fired in a furnace, and His voice like the sound of cascading[x] waters. [16] In His right hand He had seven stars; from His mouth came a sharp two-edged sword; and His face was shining like the sun at midday.[y]

A Strange Vision

1. How often do you remember your dreams? What dream is most vivid in your memory right now?

Revelation 1:1-20

2. Alpha and Omega (v. 8) are the first and last letters of the Greek alphabet. Why does God describe Himself that way? What does this suggest about His character?

3. Look at the description of Jesus in verses 13-16 and consider each part individually. Why does He have "eyes like a fiery flame" (v. 15)? Feet like fine bronze? What does each thing tell us about Jesus?

4. How does this view of Jesus make you feel about Him?

[17] When I saw Him, I fell at His feet like a dead man. He laid His right hand on me, and said, "Don't be

---

[a]**1:1** Or *Revelation of,* or *A revelation of* [b]**1:1** Or *soon* [c]**1:1** Made it known through symbols [d]**1:2** Or *witness* [e]**1:2** Lit *as many as he saw* [f]**1:3** Or *follow,* or *obey* [g]**1:4** Lit *churches in Asia;* that is, the Roman province that is now a part of modern Turkey [h]**1:4** Other mss add *God* [i]**1:4** Or *the sevenfold Spirit* [j]**1:5** Other mss read *has washed us* [k]**1:6** Other mss read *kings and* [l]**1:6** Or *made us into* (or *to be*) *a kingdom of priests;* see Ex 19:6 [m]**1:7** Or *impaled* [n]**1:7** Or *All the tribes of the land* [o]**1:7** Gn 12:3; 28:14; Zch 14:17 [p]**1:7** Or *will wail because of Him* [q]**1:7** Dn 7:13; Zch 12:10 [r]**1:9** Lit *the witness of Jesus* [s]**1:10** Lit *I became in the Spirit* or *in spirit* [t]**1:10** John was brought by God's Spirit into a realm of spiritual vision. [u]**1:10** Sunday [v]**1:11** Or *book* [w]**1:13** Or *like a son of man* [x]**1:15** Lit *many* [y]**1:16** Lit *like the sun shines in its power*

1:1 The revelation. Literally, *apokalupsis*—an unveiling or uncovering of something that was hidden; supernatural truths that could not be known had God not spoken them.

1:4 seven churches. Those named in verse 11. There were other churches in this region, and (Acts 20:5-6; Col. 1:2; 4:13) why only these seven are addressed is not clear. They may have been the key churches in seven regions in Asia. Number seven is important (it represented perfection) and used often in Revelation. The seven churches were located 30 to 50 miles from each other on a circular road that connected them. **province of Asia.** Western half of Asia Minor (western part of modern Turkey). **the One who is, who was, and who is coming.** An elaboration of the name of God in Exodus 3:14-15. **the seven spirits.** This may be an unusual way of speaking about the Holy Spirit (num-

ber seven referring to a complete manifestation of the Holy Spirit). Or it could refer to seven angels who minister to the Lamb (4:5; 5:6).

1:8 the Alpha and the Omega. The first and last letters in the Greek alphabet. **says the Lord God.** One of the two places where God speaks directly (21:5-8)

1:9 Patmos. A small island in the Aegean Sea off the coast of modern Turkey; probably a Roman penal colony.

1:10 in the Spirit. A trance, an ecstatic experience; a type of mystical experience (Acts 10:10; 11:5; 22:17; 2 Cor. 12:2-4). **the Lord's day.** The first day of the week (Sunday) when Christians met to worship together.

1:12 seven gold lampstands. These stand for the seven churches (v. 20), a fitting symbol for the church, which is meant to be a light to the world (Matt. 5:14-16).

1:13 One like the Son of Man. See Daniel 7:13. **dressed in a long robe.** Jesus wore the full-length robe of a high priest. In verses 1-20, Jesus is presented in the threefold office of Prophet (v. 1), Priest (v. 13), and King (v. 5).

1:16 sword. The sword that came from the mouth of Jesus represents the fact of divine judgment.

1:20 angels. This word means "messengers." It is possible that this word refers to leaders of the seven congregations. However, because of the use of the word throughout the book, it probably refers to

afraid! I am the First and the Last, [18] and the Living One. I was dead, but look—I am alive forever and ever, and I hold the keys of death and •Hades. [19] Therefore write what you have seen, what is, and what will take place after this. [20] The secret[a] of the seven stars you saw in My right hand, and of the seven gold lampstands, is this: the seven stars are the angels[b] of the seven churches, and the seven lampstands[c] are the seven churches.

The Letters to the Seven Churches

The Letter to Ephesus

2 "To the angel[d] of the church in Ephesus write:
"The One who holds the seven stars in His right hand and who walks among the seven gold lampstands says: [2] I know your works, your labor, and your endurance, and that you cannot tolerate evil. You have tested those who call themselves apostles and are not, and you have found them to be liars. [3] You also possess endurance and have tolerated ⌊many things⌋ because of My name, and have not grown weary. [4] But I have this against you: you have abandoned the love ⌊you had⌋ at first. [5] Remember then how far you have fallen; repent, and do the works you did at first. Otherwise, I will come to you[e] and remove your lampstand from its place—unless you repent. [6] Yet you do have this: you hate the practices of the Nicolaitans, which I also hate.

[7] "Anyone who has an ear should listen to what the Spirit says to the churches. I will give the victor the right to eat from the tree of life, which is in[f] the paradise of God.

The Letter to Smyrna

[8] "To the angel of the church in Smyrna write:
"The First and the Last, the One who was dead and came to life, says: [9] I know your[g] tribulation and poverty, yet you are rich. ⌊I know⌋ the slander of those who say they are Jews and are not, but are a •synagogue of Satan. [10] Don't be afraid of what you are about to suffer. Look, the Devil is about to throw some of you into

prison to test you, and you will have tribulation for 10 days. Be faithful until death, and I will give you the crown[h] of life.

[11] "Anyone who has an ear should listen to what the Spirit says to the churches. The victor will never be harmed by the second death.

Letters of Warning

1. Do you write many letters or e-mails? To whom do you write, and about what?

Revelation 2:1-3:22

2. To whom is God talking in 2:7? What does He want us to learn from these letters to the churches?
3. What strengths did each church have? What weaknesses?
4. What does it mean that Laodicea was "neither cold nor hot" (3:15)? Why did this make God vomit them out of His mouth (3:16)?
5. Are you lukewarm about Jesus? What will you do to heat up your walk with the Lord?

The Letter to Pergamum

[12] "To the angel of the church in Pergamum write:
"The One who has the sharp, two-edged sword says: [13] I know[i] where you live—where Satan's throne is! And you are holding on to My name and did not deny your faith in Me,[j] even in the days of Antipas, My faithful witness, who was killed among you, where Satan lives. [14] But I have a few things against you. You have some there who hold to the teaching of Balaam, who taught Balak to place a stumbling block[k] in front of the

---

[a]**1:20** Or *mystery* [b]**1:20** Or *messengers* [c]**1:20** Other mss add *that you saw* [d]**2:1** Or *messenger* here and elsewhere [e]**2:5** Other mss add *quickly* [f]**2:7** Other mss read *in the midst of* [g]**2:9** Other mss add *works and* [h]**2:10** Or *wreath* [i]**2:13** Other mss add *your works and* [j]**2:13** Or *deny My faith* [k]**2:14** Or *to place a trap*

---

heavenly beings that are associated with the churches (compare Dan. 10:13,20-21; Matt. 18:10; Acts 12:15).

2:1 the seven stars ... the seven gold lampstands. Here Jesus is the One who holds control over the seven angels and He walks among the seven churches. He has come to inspect His church.

2:6 Nicolaitans. It is hard to say for certain who these individuals are. They are some sort of heretical sect who mixed Christianity with pagan practices such as idolatry and immorality.

2:7 churches. The plural is significant. These words are not intended only for the church at Ephesus, but as a challenge to all churches. **tree of life ... in the paradise of God.** This anticipates the New Jerusalem

(21:10-11; 22:1-5).

2:8 Smyrna. A beautiful city approximately 35 miles north of Ephesus on the eastern shore of the Aegean Sea. **The First and the Last.** Smyrna had strong ties to Rome. The imperial cult, with its emperor worship, was strong there. **was dead and came to life.** His second title assures them that they too can overcome death, an important promise given the persecution they faced.

2:9 tribulation. This is a church under siege. **rich.** Though they were experiencing material poverty, they were rich spiritually (Matt. 5:11-12). **say they are Jews.** These may be Jewish proselytes. But also, the New Testament sense is that being Jewish (a descendant of Abraham) has far more to do with sharing Abraham's faithfulness than it does with simply sharing his lineage (Rom. 2:28-29).

2:11 second death. The promised reward is that the victors will be unhurt by the second death, eternal death in the "lake of fire" (20:14-15).

2:12 Pergamum. Located approximately 40 miles north of Smyrna and 10 miles inland from the Aegean Sea. the city sat atop a thousand-foot high cone-shaped hill. It was the site of a famous library.

2:13 where Satan's throne is. Pagan religion flourished in Pergamum. Four gods were worshiped there—including Zeus, for whom a spectacular altar had been built jutting out from the top of the mountain (some identify this as Satan's throne).

2:14 Balaam. Reference to the Old Testament story where Balaam advised the Moabite women to seduce the Israelites into

sons of Israel: to eat meat sacrificed to idols and to commit sexual immorality.[a] [15] In the same way, you also have those who hold to the teaching of the Nicolaitans.[b] [16] Therefore repent! Otherwise, I will come to you quickly and fight against them with the sword of My mouth.

[17] "Anyone who has an ear should listen to what the Spirit says to the churches. I will give the victor some of the hidden manna.[c] I will also give him a white stone, and on the stone a new name is inscribed that no one knows except the one who receives it.

The Letter to Thyatira

[18] "To the angel of the church in Thyatira write:

"The Son of God, the One whose eyes are like a fiery flame, and whose feet are like fine bronze says: [19] I know your works—your love, faithfulness,[d] service, and endurance. Your last works are greater than the first. [20] But I have this against you: you tolerate the woman Jezebel, who calls herself a prophetess, and teaches and deceives My slaves to commit sexual immorality[a] and to eat meat sacrificed to idols. [21] I gave her time to repent, but she does not want to repent of her sexual immorality.[e] [22] Look! I will throw her into a sickbed, and those who commit adultery with her into great tribulation, unless they repent of her[f] practices. [23] I will kill her children with the plague.[g] Then all the churches will know that I am the One who examines minds[h] and hearts, and I will give to each of you according to your works. [24] I say to the rest of you in Thyatira, who do not hold this teaching, who haven't known the deep things[i] of Satan—as they say—I do not put any other burden on you. [25] But hold on to what you have until I come. [26] The victor and the one who keeps My works to the end: I will give him authority over the nations—

[27] and He will shepherd[j] them
  with an iron scepter;
He will shatter them like pottery[k]—

just as I have received [this] from My Father. [28] I will also give him the morning star.

[29] "Anyone who has an ear should listen to what the Spirit says to the churches.

The Letter to Sardis

3 "To the angel of the church in Sardis write:

"The One who has the seven spirits of God and the seven stars says: I know your works; you have a reputation[l] for being alive, but you are dead. [2] Be alert and strengthen[m] what remains, which is about to die, for I have not found your works complete before My God. [3] Remember therefore what you have received and heard; keep it, and repent. But if you are not alert, I will come[n] like a thief, and you have no idea at what hour I will come against you.[o] [4] But you have a few people[p] in Sardis who have not defiled[q] their clothes, and they will walk with Me in white, because they are worthy. [5] In the same way, the victor will be dressed in white clothes, and I will never erase his name from the book of life, but will acknowledge his name before My Father and before His angels.

[6] "Anyone who has an ear should listen to what the Spirit says to the churches.

The Letter to Philadelphia

[7] "To the angel of the church in Philadelphia write:

"The Holy One, the True One, the One who has the key of David, who opens and no one will close, and closes and no one opens says: [8] I know your works. Because you have limited strength, have kept My word, and have not denied My name, look, I have placed before you an open door that no one is able to close. [9] Take note! I will make those from the •synagogue of Satan, who claim to be Jews and are not, but are lying— note this—I will make them come and bow down at your feet, and they will know that I have loved you. [10] Because you have kept My command to endure,[r] I will also keep you from the hour of testing that is going to come over the whole world to test those who live on

---

[a] 2:14,20 Or commit fornication   [b] 2:15 Other mss add which I hate   [c] 2:17 Other mss add to eat   [d] 2:19 Or faith   [e] 2:21 Or her fornication   [f] 2:22 Other mss read their   [g] 2:23 Or I will surely kill her children   [h] 2:23 Lit kidneys   [i] 2:24 Or the secret things   [j] 2:27 Or rule; see 19:15   [k] 2:27 Ps 2:9   [l] 3:1 Lit have a name   [m] 3:2 Other mss read guard   [n] 3:3 Other mss add upon you   [o] 3:3 Or upon you   [p] 3:4 Lit few names   [q] 3:4 Or soiled   [r] 3:10 Lit My word of endurance

---

leaving their God (v. 20; Num. 25:1-3; 31:16).

2:17 hidden manna. Supernatural food given to the Israelites during their wanderings in the wilderness.

2:18 Thyatira. City southeast of Pergamum; a manufacturing and marketing center with numerous trade guilds. Lydia, a dealer of purple cloth, was from Thyatira (Acts 16:14).

2:20 tolerate ... Jezebel. The original Jezebel was the wicked wife of Israel's King Ahab who promoted the detestable worship of Baal (1 Kings 16:29-33; 2 Kings 9:30-37). Her first-century counterpart played the same role in the church, promoting false practices. **meat sacrificed to idols.** Trade guilds were pagan in orientation, requiring participation in meals involving meat dedicated to idols. To refuse to participate would

have great economic consequences, since it would have been difficult to work without being a member of one of the guilds.

2:28 the morning star. No clear understanding about what this refers to.

3:1 Sardis. Sardis, located 50 miles east of Ephesus atop a 1,500-foot citadel, had once been a powerful city, but by the first century had lost much of its influence. The temple in Sardis was dedicated to the goddess Cybele who was thought to have the power to bring dead people back to life—possibly the reason Jesus spoke to them about being dead and the need to be made alive again.

3:4 not defiled their clothes. In a place like Sardis, where making and dyeing wool cloth was a central occupation, the reference to clothing is appropriate. The image of defiled garments hints that sin of some sort had

been allowed to stain the church.

3:5 book of life. Some sort of divine ledger where the names of the people who have eternal life are written. This picture was first found in the Old Testament (Ex. 32:32-33; Ps. 69:28; Dan. 12:1). In the first century, the names of citizens were recorded in a register. To have your name removed was to lose your citizenship.

3:7 Philadelphia. This was the newest of the seven cities. It was located 28 miles southeast of Sardis in a region of severe earthquakes.

3:12 a pillar. This metaphor speaks of stability and permanence (Gal. 2:9; 1 Tim. 3:15).

3:14 Laodicea. A wealthy city, situated at the intersection of three major roads, known for its banking and industry. Paul wrote a letter to this church, which unfortunately has been lost

the earth. [11] I am coming quickly. Hold on to what you have, so that no one takes your crown. [12] The victor: I will make him a pillar in the sanctuary of My God, and he will never go out again. I will write on him the name of My God, and the name of the city of My God—the new Jerusalem, which comes down out of heaven from My God—and My new name.

[13] "Anyone who has an ear should listen to what the Spirit says to the churches.

The Letter to Laodicea

[14] "To the angel of the church in Laodicea write:

"The •Amen, the faithful and true Witness, the Originator[a] of God's creation says: [15] I know your works, that you are neither cold nor hot. I wish that you were cold or hot. [16] So, because you are lukewarm, and neither hot nor cold, I am going to vomit[b] you out of My mouth. [17] Because you say, 'I'm rich; I have become wealthy, and need nothing,' and you don't know that you are wretched, pitiful, poor, blind, and naked, [18] I advise you to buy from Me gold refined in the fire so that you may be rich, and white clothes so that you may be dressed and your shameful nakedness not be exposed, and ointment to spread on your eyes so that you may see. [19] As many as I love, I rebuke and discipline. So be committed[c] and repent. [20] Listen! I stand at the door and knock. If anyone hears My voice and opens the door, I will come in to him and have dinner with him, and he with Me. [21] The victor: I will give him the right to sit with Me on My throne, just as I also won the victory and sat down with My Father on His throne.

[22] "Anyone who has an ear should listen to what the Spirit says to the churches."

The Throne Room of Heaven

4 After this I looked, and there in heaven was an open door. The first voice that I had heard speaking to me like a trumpet said, "Come up here, and I will show you what must take place after this."

[2] Immediately I was in the Spirit,[d] and there in heaven a throne was set. One was seated on the throne,

Lion and Lamb

1. What wild animals have you seen up close: Lion? Bear? Eagle? Other?

Revelation 4:1-5:14

2. Jesus is pictured here as a victorious Lion (5:5). What does that suggest about His character?

3. Jesus is also pictured as a slaughtered Lamb (5:6). What does that suggest about His character? How can He be both a powerful Lion and a meek Lamb?

4. Why is Christ the only one worthy to open the scroll (5:4-9; see John 1:29)? What does this suggest about other religions in the world?

5. How can this passage help you to worship Jesus in a new way?

[3] and the One seated[e] looked like jasper[f] and carnelian[g] stone. A rainbow that looked like an emerald surrounded the throne. [4] Around that throne were 24 thrones, and on the thrones sat 24 elders dressed in white clothes, with gold crowns on their heads. [5] From the throne came flashes of lightning, rumblings, and thunder. Burning before the throne were seven fiery torches, which are the seven spirits of God. [6] Also before the throne was something like a sea of glass, similar to crystal. In the middle[h] and around the throne were four living creatures covered with eyes in front and in back. [7] The first living creature was like a lion; the second living creature was like a calf; the third living creature had a face like a man; and the fourth living creature was like a flying eagle. [8] Each of the four living creatures had six wings; they were covered with eyes around and inside. Day and night they never stop,[i] saying:

---

[a]**3:14** Or *Ruler*, or *Source*, or *Beginning* [b]**3:16** Or *spit* [c]**3:19** Or *be zealous* [d]**4:2** Lit *I became in the Spirit* or *in spirit* [e]**4:3** Other mss omit *and the One seated* [f]**4:3** A precious stone [g]**4:3** A translucent red gem [h]**4:6** Lit *In the middle of the throne* [i]**4:8** Or *they never rest*

(Col. 4:16). Like the church at Sardis, this church seems to be prosperous and without persecution or heresy. **Amen.** The word "amen" was used in the Old Testament as an acknowledgment that something was true.

3:18 gold. Thinking themselves "rich" (v. 17), they will become truly rich only with the spiritual gold they can get from Christ. **nakedness.** A startling image for a people who lived in a city famous for its textile industry. At Laodicea, they raised sheep with a glossy black wool that they made into a popular black fabric. What the church has need of, however, are the white garments of heaven. **ointment.** Laodicea was the site of a famous medical school. One of its well-known products was an eye ointment.

3:19 discipline. Rebuke and discipline are expressions not of hatred, but of love (Prov. 3:11-12; Heb. 12:5-6). **love.** The Greek word

used here is *phile_*, warm and tender affection, rather than *agapa_* that means to value unconditionally.

3:20 I stand at the door and knock. The call here is to those within the church to return to the Lord. **have dinner with him.** Sharing a meal was a sign that an intimate bond existed between people.

4:2 I was in the Spirit. John is caught up in an ecstatic vision. Such visions are not uncommon in Scripture (1 Kings 22:19). **in heaven ... One was seated on the throne.** John is granted a vision of God on His throne. The image of the throne pervades Revelation, occurring more than 40 times.

4:3 jasper. As it is known today, jasper is opaque, while this heavenly gem is described in 21:11 as a transparent crystal. **carnelian.** A fiery red mineral found in Sardis.

4:4 24 elders. There are various interpretations of these figures. Some say they represent the 24 orders of God's people of the Old and New Testament (the 12 patriarchs of Israel and the 12 apostles). Others hold that they are angels who assist in the ruling of the universe. In any case, they function to worship and serve God.

4:6 four living creatures. These are similar to the creatures ("seraphim," "cherubim") seen in the vision of Isaiah (Isa. 6:1-3) and Ezekiel (Ezek. 10:9-14). They are some sort of angelic order that serve God.

5:1 seals. The scroll is rolled up and sealed along its edge with seven wax seals (that ensure the secrecy of its contents), which must be broken in order for the contents to be read. As each seal is broken, a momentous event takes place.

Holy, holy, holy,[a]
Lord God, the Almighty,
who was, who is, and who is coming.

9 Whenever the living creatures give glory, honor, and thanks to the One seated on the throne, the One who lives forever and ever, 10 the 24 elders fall down before the One seated on the throne, worship the One who lives forever and ever, cast their crowns before the throne, and say:

11 Our Lord and God,[b]
You are worthy to receive
glory and honor and power,
because You have created all things,
and because of Your will
they exist and were created.

The Lamb Takes the Scroll

5 Then I saw in the right hand of the One seated on the throne a scroll with writing on the inside and on the back, sealed with seven seals. 2 I also saw a mighty angel proclaiming in a loud voice, "Who is worthy to open the scroll and break its seals?" 3 But no one in heaven or on earth or under the earth was able to open the scroll or even to look in it. 4 And I cried and cried because no one was found worthy to open[c] the scroll or even to look in it.

5 Then one of the elders said to me, "Stop crying. Look! The Lion from the tribe of Judah, the Root of David, has been victorious so that He may open the scroll and[d] its seven seals." 6 Then I saw one like a slaughtered lamb standing between[e] the throne and the four living creatures and among the elders. He had seven horns and seven eyes, which are the seven spirits of God sent into all the earth. 7 He came and took ⌊the scroll⌋[f] out of the right hand of the One seated on the throne.

The Lamb Is Worthy

8 When He took the scroll, the four living creatures and the 24 elders fell down before the Lamb. Each one had a harp and gold bowls filled with incense, which are the prayers of the saints. 9 And they sang a new song:

You are worthy to take the scroll
and to open its seals;
because You were slaughtered,
and You redeemed[g] ⌊people⌋[h] for God
by Your blood
from every tribe and language and people
and nation.
10 You made them a kingdom[i] and priests
to our God,
and they will reign on the earth.

11 Then I looked, and heard the voice of many angels around the throne, and also of the living creatures, and of the elders. Their number was countless thousands, plus thousands of thousands. 12 They said with a loud voice:

The Lamb who was slaughtered is worthy
to receive power and riches
and wisdom and strength
and honor and glory and blessing!

13 I heard every creature in heaven, on earth, under the earth, on the sea, and everything in them say:

Blessing and honor and glory and dominion
to the One seated on the throne,
and to the Lamb, forever and ever!

14 The four living creatures said, "•Amen," and the elders fell down and worshiped.

The First Seal on the Scroll

6 Then I saw[j] the Lamb open one of the seven[k] seals, and I heard one of the four living creatures say with a voice like thunder, "Come!"[l] [m] 2 I looked, and there was a white horse. The horseman on it had a bow; a crown was given to him, and he went out as a victor to conquer.[n]

---

[a] 4:8 Other mss read holy 9 times   [b] 4:11 Other mss add the Holy One; other mss read O Lord   [c] 5:4 Other mss add and read   [d] 5:5 Other mss add loose   [e] 5:6 Or standing in the middle of   [f] 5:7 Other mss include the scroll   [g] 5:9 Or purchased   [h] 5:9 Other mss read us   [i] 5:10 Other mss read them kings   [j] 6:1 Lit saw when   [k] 6:1 Other mss omit seven   [l] 6:1 Other mss add and see   [m] 6:1 Or Go!   [n] 6:2 Lit went out conquering and in order to conquer

---

5:5 The Lion from the tribe of Judah. An ancient title for the Messiah (Gen. 49:9-10) that was in use in the first century. The image is of a conquering King. **the Root of David.** Another messianic title, referring this time to the fact that the Messiah will come from the royal family of David (Isa. 11:1).

5:6 seven horns. A horn is a symbol of power in the Old Testament (Deut. 33:17; Ps. 18:2). **seven eyes.** He has fullness of vision, omniscience (Zech. 4:10). **the seven spirits.** The work of Christ on earth is done by the Holy Spirit Who is pictured by means of this symbol (4:5).

5:8 harp. The instrument of praise in the Psalms (Ps. 33:2). **incense.** Incense was used in Old Testament worship (Deut. 33:10). Here it stands for the prayers of God's people.

5:9 a new song. A special song praises the Lamb for His worthiness and His redemptive work. **redeemed.** Redeemed—a word used to describe the freeing of a slave from bondage by the payment of a price. The purchase price, in this case, was the blood of Christ. What it bought was the freedom of men and women from the bondage of sin. **from every tribe and language and people and nation.** Christ redeems believers from the whole of humankind—past, present, and future—by this great and terrible payment.

6:2 a white horse. There has been much debate about the identity of the rider on the white horse. One suggestion is that he symbolizes military conquest, an image in line with the identity of the other three riders. Another suggestion is that the rider on a white horse symbolizes the preaching of the gospel throughout the world prior to the end. The bow is used in the Old Testament as a symbol of divine victories (Hab. 3:9). In Revelation, white is generally a symbol of Christ (1:14; 14:14; 19:11,14). Furthermore, unlike the coming of the other three horsemen, no calamities follow after this rider.

6:3-4 second seal. The second seal is broken and a red horse and rider appear, a symbol of bloodshed and war.

6:5 third seal. The third seal is broken and a black horse and rider are called forth, symbolizing a time of great scarcity, verging on famine. **balance scale.** A device used for measuring out grain.

6:6 a quart of wheat for a denarius. Food is sold at inflated prices—over 10 times what it should cost. **do not harm the olive oil and**

Sealed by Jesus from Wrath

1. Have you ever been in an earthquake? What was it like? Where were you?

Revelation 6:1-7:17

2. Authority and instructions were given to each of the four horsemen (6:1-8). Who gave them their power and instructions? What does this suggest about suffering and death—who has control?

3. Who are "the slaves of our God" (7:3)? What does the seal on their foreheads mean?

4. Jesus was the only one who could open the seals on the scroll. What does this suggest about the seals on the slaves' foreheads? How does this bring comfort to you?

The Second Seal

3 When He opened the second seal, I heard the second living creature say, "Come!"[a][b] 4 Then another horse went out, a fiery red one, and its horseman was empowered[c] to take peace from the earth, so that people would slaughter one another. And a large sword was given to him.

The Third Seal

5 When He opened the third seal, I heard the third living creature say, "Come!"[a][b] And I looked, and there was a black horse. The horseman on it had a balance scale in his hand. 6 Then I heard something like a voice among the four living creatures say, "A quart of wheat for a •denarius, and three quarts of barley for a denarius—but do not harm the olive oil and the wine."

The Fourth Seal

7 When He opened the fourth seal, I heard the voice of the fourth living creature say, "Come!"[a][b] 8 And I looked, and there was a pale green[d] horse. The horseman on it was named Death, and •Hades was following after him. Authority was given to them[e] over a fourth of the earth, to kill by the sword, by famine, by plague, and by the wild animals of the earth.

The Fifth Seal

9 When He opened the fifth seal, I saw under the altar the souls of those slaughtered because of God's word and the testimony they had.[f] 10 They cried out with a loud voice: "O Lord,[g] holy and true, how long until You judge and avenge our blood from those who live on the earth?" 11 So a white robe was given to each of them, and they were told to rest a little while longer until ⸤the number of⸥ their fellow slaves and their brothers, who were going to be killed just as they had been, would be completed.

The Sixth Seal

12 Then I saw Him open[h] the sixth seal. A violent earthquake occurred; the sun turned black like sackcloth made of goat hair; the entire moon[i] became like blood; 13 the stars[j] of heaven fell to the earth as a fig tree drops its unripe figs when shaken by a high wind; 14 the sky separated like a scroll being rolled up; and every mountain and island was moved from its place.

15 Then the kings of the earth, the nobles, the military commanders, the rich, the powerful, and every slave and free person hid in the caves and among the rocks of the mountains. 16 And they said to the mountains and to the rocks, "Fall on us and hide us from the face of the One seated on the throne and from the wrath of the Lamb, 17 because the great day of Their[k] wrath has come! And who is able to stand?"

The Sealed of Israel

7 After this I saw four angels standing at the four corners of the earth, restraining the four winds of

---

a **6:3,5,7** Other mss add *and see*   b **6:3,5,7** Or *Go!*   c **6:4** Or *was granted;* lit *was given*   d **6:8** Or *a greenish gray*   e **6:8** Other mss read *him*   f **6:9** Other mss add *about the Lamb*   g **6:10** Or *Master*   h **6:12** Lit *I saw when He opened*   i **6:12** Or *the full moon*   j **6:13** Perhaps meteors   k **6:17** Other mss read *His*

---

the wine. A limitation is placed upon the rider of the black horse. Grain is easily destroyed by drought, but the drought is not to be so severe as to damage the deeper roots of the olive trees or grapevines.

6:7-8 fourth seal. The fourth horse and rider represent death from various causes. These are the "four devastating judgments" in Ezekiel 14:21.

6:8 a pale green horse. Pale greenish gray, the color of a corpse. **Hades.** It is not clear whether Hades is following behind Death on foot, on another horse, or on the same horse. Still, the image is clear. After Death comes the grave or the underworld. Hades was understood to be the place where the dead resided as they awaited the final judgment. **a fourth of the earth.** There is a limitation placed upon Death. It threat-

ens all of life, but is not permitted to totally do away with all of it. **kill by the sword.** This is death by murder, war, or violence. **famine.** The issue is no longer scarcity (as with the black horse), but a severe lack of food that leads to death.

6:9 fifth seal. A new scene unfolds with the breaking of the fifth seal. Those who have been martyred in the name of God are pictured under the altar.

6:12-14 sixth seal. The sixth seal is broken and John sees cosmic disturbances, which herald the coming of the last days.

6:12-13 earthquake. The very trembling of the earth is often associated with the presence of God (Ex. 19:18; Hag. 2:6). **sun ... moon ... stars.** Even the predictable, well-ordered movement of the heavenly bodies

goes awry (Isa. 34:4; Acts 2:20).

7:1-4 The earth is pictured as a great square, with an angel at each corner holding back a lethal wind until the 144,000 can be sealed.

7:3 seal ... on their foreheads. Probably similar to the signet ring that kings used to authenticate documents by its imprint. The purpose of this seal is to mark God's people so that they will be spared from the plagues that are to come (9:4).

7:5 12,000. This number is symbolic, as is the total number of 144,000 (12 squared times a thousand), and conveys the idea of completeness: 12,000 are sealed from each of the 12 tribes.

7:12 glory. A reference to the brightness of

the earth so that no wind could blow on the earth or on the sea or on any tree. 2 Then I saw another angel rise up from the east, who had the seal of the living God. He cried out in a loud voice to the four angels who were empowereda to harm the earth and the sea: 3 "Don't harm the earth or the sea or the trees until we seal the slaves of our God on their foreheads." 4 And I heard the number of those who were sealed:

144,000 sealed from every tribe of the sons of Israel:

5 12,000 sealed from the tribe of Judah,
12,000b from the tribe of Reuben,
12,000 from the tribe of Gad,
6 12,000 from the tribe of Asher,
12,000 from the tribe of Naphtali,
12,000 from the tribe of Manasseh,
7 12,000 from the tribe of Simeon,
12,000 from the tribe of Levi,
12,000 from the tribe of Issachar,
8 12,000 from the tribe of Zebulun,
12,000 from the tribe of Joseph,
12,000 sealed from the tribe of Benjamin.

A Multitude from the Great Tribulation

9 After this I looked, and there was a vast multitude from every nation, tribe, people, and language, which no one could number, standing before the throne and before the Lamb. They were robed in white with palm branches in their hands. 10 And they cried out in a loud voice:

Salvation belongs to our God,
who is seated on the throne,
and to the Lamb!

11 All the angels stood around the throne, the elders, and the four living creatures, and they fell on their faces before the throne and worshiped God, 12 saying:

•Amen! Blessing and glory and wisdom
and thanksgiving and honor
and power and strength,
be to our God forever and ever. Amen.

13 Then one of the elders asked me, "Who are these people robed in white, and where did they come from?"

14 I said to him, "Sir,c you know."

Then he told me:

These are the ones coming out
of the great tribulation.
They washed their robes and made them white
in the blood of the Lamb.
15 For this reason they are before the throne of God,
and they serve Him day and night
in His sanctuary.
The One seated on the throne will shelterd them:
16 no longer will they hunger; no longer
will they thirst;
no longer will the sun strike them, or any heat.
17 Because the Lamb who is at the center
of the throne will shepherd them;
He will guide them to springs of living waters,
and God will wipe away every tear
from their eyes.

The Seventh Seal

8 When He opened the seventh seal, there was silence in heaven for about half an hour. 2 Then I saw the seven angels who stand in the presence of God; seven trumpets were given to them. 3 Another angel, with a gold incense burner, came and stood at the altar. He was given a large amount of incense to offer with the prayers of all the saints on the gold altar in front of the throne. 4 The smoke of the incense, with the prayers of the saints, went up in the presence of God from the angel's hand. 5 The angel took the incense burner, filled it with fire from the altar, and hurled it to the earth; there were thunders, rumblings, lightnings, and an earthquake. 6 And the seven angels who had the seven trumpets prepared to blow them.

The First Trumpet

7 The first angele blew his trumpet, and hail and fire, mixed with blood, were hurled to the earth. So a

---

a7:2 Lit angels to whom it was given   b7:5–8 Other mss add sealed after each number   c7:14 Lit My lord   d7:15 Or will spread His tent over
e8:7 Other mss include angel

God, His divine luminous presence.

7:13-14 Who are these people? The question of the identity of the great multitude is raised and then answered, a process often used in prophetic literature when a vision is to be explained (Jer. 1:11,13; 24:3; Amos 7:8; 8:2; Zech. 4:4-14).

7:14 the ones coming out of. These are the martyrs from the great tribulation: those who maintained their faith to the point of death. **the great tribulation.** This event is mentioned in both the Old and New Testaments. Daniel 12:1 refers to the "time of distress" (literally, "tribulation" in Hebrew) that will come. See Matthew 24:21-22.

7:17 the Lamb ... will shepherd them. The Lamb becomes the shepherd (who tends the flock of lambs); Jesus is pictured as the

Good Shepherd (John 10:1-30; 21:15-17).

8:1 seventh seal. The breaking of the seventh seal opens the scroll so that the events of the end times can be revealed. Unlike the other seals (with the possible exception of the first seal), the breaking of this seal brings no judgment, simply silence.

8:2 trumpets. In the Old Testament, trumpets are used for various purposes: to signal various activities (Num. 10:1-10); as part of worship and celebration (Num. 10:10; 29:1); in war (Josh. 6); and at coronations (1 Kings 1:34). Here in Revelation, however, they have the more ominous purpose of announcing and loosing the plagues of the end times.

8:7 a third of the earth was burned up. The first plague destroys a third of the earth's vegetation. The fact that only a third of the

earth is pictured as being afflicted represents a severe, but limited, act of judgment. This is similar to the seventh Egyptian plague (Ex. 9:13-35).

8:8-9 second ... trumpet. The second plague is unique; it is impossible to parallel it with any known natural event, such as a volcano. It destroys a third of the sea, along with a third of the fish in the sea and a third of the boats in the sea. This plague is similar to what happened to the Nile in Exodus 7:20-21.

8:10-11 third ... trumpet. During the third plague, a great meteor falls from the sky and poisons a third of the fresh water.

8:12 fourth ... trumpet. The fourth plague strikes the heavenly bodies. A third of the sun, moon, and stars go dark. This is similar

Incense and Death

1. When have you experienced excruciating pain? What happened?

Revelation 8:1-9:21

2. What do we learn about prayer from the use of altars and incense (8:3-5)? When was the last time you cried for justice or mercy?

3. What events does the sixth trumpet begin? Why did this woe fail to bring the majority to repentance as originally intended?

4. What do you see in our society that fits with the actions listed in 9:20-21? Which of these actions do you see in your own life? In what way? What can you do about this in the coming week?

third of the earth was burned up, a third of the trees were burned up, and all the green grass was burned up.

The Second Trumpet

8 The second angel blew his trumpet, and something like a great mountain ablaze with fire was hurled into the sea. So a third of the sea became blood, 9 a third of the living creatures in the sea died, and a third of the ships were destroyed.

The Third Trumpet

10 The third angel blew his trumpet, and a great star, blazing like a torch, fell from heaven. It fell on a third of the rivers and springs of water. 11 The name of the star is Wormwood,a and a third of the waters became wormwood. So, many of the people died from the waters, because they had been made bitter.

The Fourth Trumpet

12 The fourth angel blew his trumpet, and a third of the sun was struck, a third of the moon, and a third of the stars, so that a third of them were darkened. A third of the day was without light, and the night as well.

13 I looked, and I heard an eagle,b flying in midheaven,c saying in a loud voice, "Woe! Woe! Woe to those who live on the earth, because of the remaining trumpet blasts that the three angels are about to sound!"

The Fifth Trumpet

9 The fifth angel blew his trumpet, and I saw a star that had fallen from heaven to earth. The key to the shaft of the •abyss was given to him. 2 He opened the shaft of the abyss, and smoke came up out of the shaft like smoke from a greatd furnace so that the sun and the air were darkened by the smoke from the shaft. 3 Then out of the smoke locusts came to the earth, and powere was given to them like the power that scorpions have on the earth. 4 They were told not to harm the grass of the earth, or any green plant, or any tree, but only people who do not have God's seal on their foreheads. 5 They were not permitted to kill them, but were to torment them, for five months; their torment is like the torment caused by a scorpion when it strikes a man. 6 In those days people will seek death and will not find it; they will long to die, but death will flee from them.

7 The appearance of the locusts was like horses equipped for battle. On their heads were something like gold crowns; their faces were like men's faces; 8 they had hair like women's hair; their teeth were like lions' teeth; 9 they had chests like iron breastplates; the sound of their wings was like the sound of chariots with many horses rushing into battle; 10 and they had tails with stingers, like scorpions, so that with their tails they had the powere to harm people for five months. 11 They had as their kingf the angel of the abyss; his name in Hebrew is Abaddon,g and in Greek he has the

---

a **8:11** Wormwood is absinthe, a bitter herb. b **8:13** Other mss read angel c **8:13** Very high d **9:2** Other mss omit great e **9:3,10** Or authority
f **9:11** Or as king over them g **9:11** Or destruction

---

to the ninth plague in Egypt (Ex. 10:21-23).

8:13 Woe! The triple "Woe" corresponds to the final three trumpets (9:12). **those who live on the earth.** These plagues will come upon those who are hostile to God.

9:1 a star. An angel, a demon, or Satan himself with the power to unlock the underworld. **the abyss.** In the way the Bible speaks of the cosmos, there are said to be three levels: the heavens, the earth, and the underworld (which is a huge, bottomless pit). It is the realm of the dead (Rom. 10:7); it is where the beast abides (11:7); it is the place of demons (Luke 8:31); it will be used as the prison of Satan during the millennium (20:3); and in this case, it is the home of the demon locusts.

9:3 locusts. These are not actual locusts,

but some sort of demonic entity. Their coming is similar to the plague of (real) locusts in Exodus 10:1-20.

9:4 harm ... only people. Real locusts consume plants, trees, and grass. These locusts lack that ability, attacking only humans.

9:8 hair like women's hair. Perhaps a reference to the antennae of locusts, or to the hair on their legs or bodies.

9:9 iron breastplates. The scales on the body of locusts are shaped like this. **the sound of their wings.** When locusts swarm into an area, they make a loud noise by beating their wings.

9:11 Abaddon. A Hebrew word meaning "destruction." In the Old Testament, this word is used along with "Sheol" for the place

of destruction and death (Job 26:6; 28:22; Prov. 15:11; 27:20).

9:12 first woe is passed. This refers back to 8:13. The first woe is passed. The second will be described in verses 13-21, when the sixth trumpet is sounded. The third woe will come when the seventh trumpet is sounded in 11:14-19.

9:13-21 The plague of the fifth trumpet brought pain and suffering; plague six brings death. The Old Testament parallel for such an invasion of horses is found in Ezekiel 38:14-16 (Isa. 5:26-30; Jer. 6:22-26).

9:17 the horses. The demon locusts in the previous plague are followed by demon horses in this plague. There is a difference. While the locusts had the power to torture, the horses have the power to kill. **fire,**

name Apollyon.[a] [12] The first woe has passed. There are still two more woes to come after this.

The Sixth Trumpet

[13] The sixth angel blew his trumpet. From the four[b] horns of the gold altar that is before God, I heard a voice [14] say to the sixth angel who had the trumpet, "Release the four angels bound at the great river Euphrates." [15] So the four angels who were prepared for the hour, day, month, and year were released to kill a third of the human race. [16] The number of mounted troops was 200 million;[c] I heard their number. [17] This is how I saw the horses in my vision: The horsemen had breastplates that were fiery red, hyacinth blue, and sulfur yellow. The heads of the horses were like lions' heads, and from their mouths came fire, smoke, and sulfur. [18] A third of the human race was killed by these three plagues—by the fire, the smoke, and the sulfur that came from their mouths. [19] For the power of the horses is in their mouths and in their tails, because their tails, like snakes, have heads, and they inflict injury with them.

[20] The rest of the people, who were not killed by these plagues, did not repent of the works of their hands to stop worshiping demons and idols of gold, silver, bronze, stone, and wood, which are not able to see, hear, or walk. [21] And they did not repent of their murders, their sorceries,[d] their sexual immorality, or their thefts.

The Mighty Angel and the Small Scroll

10 Then I saw another mighty angel coming down from heaven, surrounded by a cloud, with a rainbow over his head.[e] His face was like the sun, his legs[f] were like fiery pillars, [2] and he had a little scroll opened in his hand. He put his right foot on the sea, his left on the land, [3] and he cried out with a loud voice like a roaring lion. When he cried out, the seven thunders spoke with their voices. [4] And when the seven thunders spoke, I was about to write. Then I heard a voice from heaven, saying, "Seal up what the seven thunders said, and do not write it down!"

[5] Then the angel that I had seen standing on the sea and on the land raised his right hand to heaven. [6] He swore an oath by the One who lives forever and ever, who created heaven and what is in it, the earth and what is in it, and the sea and what is in it: "There will no longer be an interval of time,[g] [7] but in the days of the sound of the seventh angel, when he will blow his trumpet, then God's hidden plan[h] will be completed, as He announced to His servants[i] the prophets."

Two Witnesses Persecuted

1. Where would you least like to live: An area prone to earthquakes? Hurricanes? Floods?

Revelation 10:1-11:19
2. Why is God's Word "sweet as honey" in John's mouth, but bitter in his stomach (10:9)?
3. Why was this scroll lying open (10:2), instead of closed and sealed like other scrolls? What does this suggest about God's Word?
4. Why were the two witnesses dressed in "sackcloth" (11:3)? What does this suggest about those who preach God's Word?
5. Why did the world rejoice when the two witnesses had died? Have you seen this happen in the world today?

[8] Now the voice that I heard from heaven spoke to me again and said, "Go, take the scroll that lies open in the hand of the angel who is standing on the sea and on the land."

[9] So I went to the angel and asked him to give me the little scroll. He said to me, "Take and eat it; it will be bitter in your stomach, but it will be as sweet as honey in your mouth."

---

[a]9:11 Or *destroyer* [b]9:13 Other mss omit *four* [c]9:16 Other mss read *100 million* [d]9:21 Or *magic potions*, or *drugs*; Gk *pharmakon* [e]10:1 Or *a halo on his head* [f]10:1 Or *feet* [g]10:6 Or *be a delay* [h]10:7 Or *God's secret* or *mystery*; see Rv 1:20; 17:5,7 [i]10:7 Or *slaves*

---

smoke, and sulfur. Fire, smoke, and sulfur (brimstone) of this sort are straight out of hell (14:10-11; 19:20; 21:8).

9:20-21 did not repent. The intent of the plagues is not vengeance—it is to lead humankind to repentance. Despite the horror of the plagues, people still refuse to turn from their worship of demons and the lifestyle that such a commitment brings.

10:1 another mighty angel. The description of this angel is so similar to that of Christ in chapter 1 that some commentators have identified him as such. However, in verse 6 he shows himself to be a genuine angel by swearing by "the One who lives forever and ever." **surrounded by a cloud.** Celestial beings are often described as ascending and descending with clouds (Ps. 104:3; Dan. 7:13; Acts 1:9). **rainbow.** This can be under-

stood as a kind of crown or as the reflection of His brilliance ("His face was like the sun") through the clouds.

10:2 a little scroll. This is an unusual word, used nowhere else in Greek literature prior to this time. John probably coined it himself. Unlike the scroll of 5:1 that was a book, this scroll was more akin to a booklet.

10:4 seven thunders. John understood what the seven thunders communicated but he was told not to record them. What these thunders convey is unknown, but in the three other instances where there is thunder, it is the precursor to judgment (8:5; 11:19; 16:18).

10:7 in the days ... when. The sounding of the seventh trumpet is not a single act but a period of time. As will emerge, it includes the events of the seven bowls (16:1-21). **God's**

hidden plan. "Hidden plan" in the New Testament does not refer to something that is secret, but to the purpose of God that has been revealed.

10:8 the angel who is standing on the sea and on the land. For the third time the tremendous size of this angel is emphasized. His coming has something to do with all of the earth (vv. 2,5).

11:1 sanctuary. The Greek word refers to the temple building itself and not the outer courtyard. The temple itself consisted of a building at the center containing the Holy Place and the Holy of Holies, bordered by the court of the priests, the court of Israel, and the court of the women where the people of Israel assembled. This temple complex was surrounded by a huge outer court where Gentiles were allowed to come.

[10] Then I took the little scroll from the angel's hand and ate it. It was as sweet as honey in my mouth, but when I ate it, my stomach became bitter. [11] And I was told,[a] "You must prophesy again about[b] many peoples, nations, languages, and kings."

The Two Witnesses

11 Then I was given a measuring reed like a rod,[c] with these words: "Go[d] and measure God's sanctuary and the altar, and ⌊count⌋ those who worship there. [2] But exclude the courtyard outside the sanctuary. Don't measure it, because it is given to the nations,[e] and they will trample the holy city for 42 months. [3] I will empower[f] my two witnesses, and they will prophesy for 1,260 days,[g] dressed in sackcloth."[h] [4] These are the two olive trees and the two lampstands that stand before the Lord[i] of the earth. [5] If anyone wants to harm them, fire comes from their mouths and consumes their enemies; if anyone wants to harm them, he must be killed in this way. [6] These men have the power to close the sky so that it does not rain during the days of their prophecy. They also have power over the waters to turn them into blood, and to strike the earth with any plague whenever they want.

The Witnesses Martyred

[7] When they finish their testimony, the beast[j] that comes up out of the •abyss will make war with them, conquer them, and kill them. [8] Their dead bodies[k] will lie in the public square[l] of the great city, which is called, prophetically,[m] Sodom and Egypt, where also their Lord was crucified. [9] And representatives from[n] the peoples, tribes, languages, and nations will view their bodies for three and a half days and not permit their bodies to be put into a tomb. [10] Those who live on the earth will gloat over them and celebrate and send gifts to one another, because these two prophets tormented those who live on the earth.

The Witnesses Resurrected

[11] But after the three and a half days, the breath[o] of life from God entered them, and they stood on their feet. So great fear fell on those who saw them. [12] Then they heard[p] a loud voice from heaven saying to them, "Come up here." They went up to heaven in a cloud, while their enemies watched them. [13] At that moment a violent earthquake took place, a tenth of the city fell, and 7,000 people were killed in the earthquake. The survivors were terrified and gave glory to the God of heaven. [14] The second woe has passed. Take note: the third woe is coming quickly!

The Seventh Trumpet

[15] The seventh angel blew his trumpet, and there were loud voices in heaven saying:

The kingdom of the world has become
the ⌊kingdom⌋
of our Lord and of His •Messiah,
and He will reign forever and ever!

[16] The 24 elders, who were seated before God on their thrones, fell on their faces and worshiped God, [17] saying:

We thank You, Lord God, the Almighty, who is
and who was,[q]
because You have taken Your great power
and have begun to reign.
[18] The nations were angry, but Your wrath
has come.
The time has come for the dead to be judged,
and to give the reward to Your servants
the prophets,
to the saints, and to those who fear Your name,
both small and great,
and the time has come to destroy those
who destroy the earth.

---

[a]**10:11** Lit *And they said to me* [b]**10:11** Or *prophesy again against* [c]**11:1** Other mss add *and the angel stood up* [d]**11:1** Lit *Arise* [e]**11:2** Or *Gentiles* [f]**11:3** Lit *I will give to* [g]**11:3** Three and a half years of thirty-day months [h]**11:3** Mourning garment of coarse, often black, material [i]**11:4** Other mss read *God* [j]**11:7** Or *wild animal* [k]**11:8** Lit *Their corpse* [l]**11:8** Or *lie on the broad street* [m]**11:8** Or *spiritually*, or *symbolically* [n]**11:9** Lit *And from* [o]**11:11** Or *spirit* [p]**11:12** Other mss read *Then I heard* [q]**11:17** Other mss add *and who is to come*

11:2 42 months. Three and a half years, the length of time evil is allowed to dominate (Dan. 7:25; 12:6-7,11-12; Rev. 12:6,14; 13:5).

11:3 two witnesses. What is clear is that these two men are similar to Moses and Elijah (Ex. 7:14-18; 1 Kings 17:1; 2 Kings 1:10-12; Mal. 4:5; Mark 9:4). In this context, they may represent those who preach repentance during the tribulation. **1,260 days.** Three and a half years = 42 months = 1,260 days (a solar month had 30 days).

11:4 the two olive trees and the two lampstands. John's imagery comes from Zechariah 4:1-14, "two anointed ones" produced a united witness represented by one lampstand. John's witnesses have separate lampstands. The olive oil alludes to the power of the Holy Spirit (Zech. 4:6).

11:7 the beast. This is the first time that this figure appears. He will become the major threat in the last days. His origins are clear: he is a demon out of the abyss.

11:13 violent earthquake. This devastating earthquake that levels a tenth of the city can be linked to the prophecy in Ezekiel 38:19-20.

11:18 destroy those who destroy the earth. People were created to be the stewards of the earth (Gen. 1:26), but the results of human sin have led creation to groan (Rom. 8:19-22). God's final judgment will be a time when judgment is directed against those who have worked against Him.

11:19 the ark of His covenant. In the Old Testament the ark of the covenant was a wooden chest that stood in the Holy of Holies and symbolized the presence of God.

12:1 a woman. The first participant in this heavenly drama is introduced: the radiant woman who represents the church, Israel, or believing Jews (Isa. 54:1; 66:7-8; Gal. 4:26). The details of her dress indicate her magnificence. Psalm 104:2 describes God in such terms.

12:3 fiery red dragon. The second participant comes on stage: the great dragon, Satan (v. 9). **seven heads.** Indicating great intelligence. **seven diadems.** Seven is the number of completeness; a crown is the sign of power.

12:4 devour her child. The purpose of Satan is revealed: he wants to destroy the Messiah.

12:5 a Son. The third participant is the Mes-

[19] God's sanctuary in heaven was opened, and the ark of His covenant[a] appeared in His sanctuary. There were lightnings, rumblings, thunders, an earthquake,[b] and severe hail.

The Woman, the Child, and the Dragon

12 A great sign[c] appeared in heaven: a woman clothed with the sun, with the moon under her feet, and a crown of 12 stars on her head. [2] She was pregnant and cried out in labor and agony to give birth. [3] Then another sign[d] appeared in heaven: There was a great fiery red dragon having seven heads and 10 horns, and on his heads were seven diadems.[e] [4] His tail swept away a third of the stars in heaven and hurled them to the earth. And the dragon stood in front of the woman who was about to give birth, so that when she did give birth he might devour her child. [5] But she gave birth to a Son—a male who is going to shepherd[f] all nations with an iron scepter—and her child was caught up to God and to His throne. [6] The woman fled into the wilderness, where she had a place prepared by God, to be fed there[g] for 1,260 days.

The Dragon Thrown Out of Heaven

[7] Then war broke out in heaven: Michael and his angels fought against the dragon. The dragon and his angels also fought, [8] but he could not prevail, and there was no place for them in heaven any longer. [9] So the great dragon was thrown out—the ancient serpent, who is called the Devil[h] and Satan,[i] the one who deceives the whole world. He was thrown to earth, and his angels with him.

[10] Then I heard a loud voice in heaven say:

The salvation and the power and the kingdom
    of our God
and the authority of His •Messiah
    have now come,
because the accuser of our brothers
    has been thrown out:

the one who accuses them before our God
    day and night.
[11] They conquered him by the blood of the Lamb
    and by the word of their testimony,
for they did not love their lives in the face
    of death.
[12] Therefore rejoice, O heavens,
    and you who dwell in them!
Woe to the earth and the sea,
    for the Devil has come down to you
    with great fury,
because he knows he has a short time.

Dragon Slayer

1. What is your favorite book about dragons? Movie about monsters?

Revelation 12:1–13:18

2. Who or what does the dragon represent? The woman's Son (12:5)?
3. Why is the Devil in a "great fury" (12:12)? How is this bad news for humanity?
4. How was the Devil conquered (12:11)? How is this good news for humanity?
5. What does the description of the second beast refer to in 13:11? What real people or forces in history have appeared like a lamb but spoken like a dragon?
6. Is your name written in the Book of Life (13:8)? How do you know?

The Woman Persecuted

[13] When the dragon saw that he had been thrown to earth, he persecuted the woman who gave birth to the male. [14] The woman was given two wings of a great

---

[a] **11:19** Other mss read *ark of the covenant of the Lord*   [b] **11:19** Other mss omit *an earthquake*   [c] **12:1** Or *great symbolic display;* see Rv 12:3   [d] **12:3** Or *another symbolic display*   [e] **12:3** Or *crowns*   [f] **12:5** Or *rule*   [g] **12:6** Lit *God, that they might feed her there*   [h] **12:9** Gk *diabolos,* meaning slanderer   [i] **12:9** Hb word meaning adversary

---

siah (Ps. 2:9; Rev. 2:27; 19:15).

12:6 wilderness. Not a wasteland but a place of refuge (as it often was for the children of Israel). **1,260 days.** This is the period when evil is allowed to do its work upon earth.

12:9 the ancient serpent. An allusion to Genesis 3:1-5. **the Devil.** Literally, *diabolos,* a Greek term for Satan meaning "accuser," "adversary," or "slanderer" (Zech. 3:1-2; 1 Pet. 5:8). **Satan.** A Hebrew term meaning "accuser."

12:12 Woe to the earth. Some say this is the third woe announced in 8:13.

12:14 a time, times, and half a year. One year plus two years plus a half year. This phrase is taken from Daniel 7:25, the same

time period as three and a half years = 42 months = 1,260 days.

13:1 seven heads. On his horns were 10 diadems. Like the dragon, the beast has multiple heads and horns. There is a difference; the dragon has seven diadems on his heads, while the beast has 10 diadems on his horns. These 10 diadems represent 10 kings (17:12). **on his heads were blasphemous names.** The beast has taken to himself divine names. In verse 4 he is worshiped. This accords with Paul's description of "the man of lawlessness" (2 Thess. 2:3-4).

13:2 The beast. This beast has all the attributes of the four beasts in Daniel 7. He is the complete embodiment of evil, his power derived from Satan. In Daniel, these beasts represent four dominant kingdoms of the world that were hostile to God.

13:5 boasts and blasphemies. Thus the beast speaks as if he were God, in accord with Daniel 7:8,20,25.

13:8 All … will worship him. All are required to worship the beast. Those who belong to the Lamb will die as martyrs because of their refusal to worship.

13:11-18 A second beast arises who is a servant to the first beast. His purpose is to cause people to worship the first beast. He is probably meant to represent organized religion. He is later called "the false prophet" (16:13; 19:20; 20:10). With the coming of this beast, the evil trinity is complete. Satan, the antichrist, and the false prophet oppose God the Father, Son, and the Holy Spirit.

13:14 is permitted to perform. In verses 5-

eagle, so that she could fly from the serpent's presence to her place in the wilderness, where she was fed for a time, times, and half a time.[a] 15 From his mouth the serpent spewed water like a river after the woman, to sweep her away in a torrent. 16 But the earth helped the woman: the earth opened its mouth and swallowed up the river that the dragon had spewed from his mouth. 17 So the dragon was furious with the woman and left to wage war against the rest of her offspring[b]—those who keep the commandments of God and have the testimony about Jesus. 18 He[c] stood on the sand of the sea.[d]

The Beast from the Sea

13 And I saw a beast coming up out of the sea. He[e] had 10 horns and seven heads. On his horns were 10 diadems, and on his heads were blasphemous names.[f] 2 The beast I saw was like a leopard, his feet were like a bear's, and his mouth was like a lion's mouth. The dragon gave him his power, his throne, and great authority. 3 One of his heads appeared to be fatally wounded,[g] but his fatal wound was healed. The whole earth was amazed and followed the beast.[h] 4 They worshiped the dragon because he gave authority to the beast. And they worshiped the beast, saying, "Who is like the beast? Who is able to wage war against him?"

5 A mouth was given to him to speak boasts and blasphemies. He was also given authority to act[i][j] for 42 months. 6 He began to speak[k] blasphemies against God: to blaspheme His name and His dwelling—those who dwell in heaven. 7 And he was permitted to wage war against the saints and to conquer them. He was also given authority over every tribe, people, language, and nation. 8 All those who live on the earth will worship him, everyone whose name was not written from the foundation of the world in the book[l] of life of the Lamb who was slaughtered.[m]

9 If anyone has an ear, he should listen:

10   If anyone is destined for captivity,
        into captivity he goes.
      If anyone is to be killed[n] with a sword,
        with a sword he will be killed.

Here is the endurance and the faith of the saints.[o]

The Beast from the Earth

11 Then I saw another beast coming up out of the earth; he had two horns like a lamb,[p] but he sounded like a dragon. 12 He exercises all the authority of the first beast on his behalf and compels the earth and those who live on it to worship the first beast, whose fatal wound was healed. 13 He also performs great signs, even causing fire to come down from heaven to earth before people. 14 He deceives those who live on the earth because of the signs that he is permitted to perform on behalf of the beast, telling those who live on the earth to make an image[q] of the beast who had the sword wound yet lived. 15 He was permitted to give a spirit[r] to the image of the beast, so that the image of the beast could both speak and cause whoever would not worship the image of the beast to be killed. 16 And he requires everyone—small and great, rich and poor, free and slave—to be given a mark[s] on his[t] right hand or on his[t] forehead, 17 so that no one can buy or sell unless he has the mark: the beast's name or the number of his name.

18 Here is wisdom:[u] The one who has understanding must calculate[v] the number of the beast, because it is the number of a man.[w] His number is 666.[x]

The Lamb and the 144,000

14 Then I looked, and there on Mount Zion stood the Lamb, and with Him were 144,000 who had His name and His Father's name written on their

---

[a]12:14 An expression occurring in Dn 7:25; 12:7 that means 3½ years or 42 months (Rv 11:2; 13:5) or 1,260 days (Rv 11:3) [b]12:17 Or seed [c]12:18 Other mss read He is apparently a reference to the dragon. [d]12:18 Some translations put Rv 12:18 either in Rv 12:17 or Rv 13:1. [e]13:1 The beasts in Rv 13:1,11 are customarily referred to as "he" or "him" rather than "it." The Gk word for a beast (therion) is grammatically neuter. [f]13:1 Other mss read heads was a blasphemous name [g]13:3 Lit be slain to death [h]13:3 Lit amazed after the beast [i]13:5 Other mss read wage war [j]13:5 Or to rule [k]13:6 Lit He opened his mouth in [l]13:8 Or scroll [m]13:8 Or written in the book of life of the Lamb who was slaughtered from the foundation of the world [n]13:10 Other mss read anyone kills [o]13:10 Or This calls for the endurance and faith of the saints. [p]13:11 Or ram [q]13:14 Or statue, or likeness [r]13:15 Or give breath, or give life [s]13:16 Or stamp, or brand [t]13:16 Lit their [u]13:18 Or This calls for wisdom [v]13:18 Or count, or figure out [w]13:18 Or is a man's number, or is the number of a person [x]13:18 One Gk ms plus other ancient evidence read 616

---

7 (when speaking about the first beast) the passive "was given" is used four times (in the Greek text) to show that the first beast was a front for Satan. Here too the point is made that this second beast has no independent power. It also is controlled by Satan.

13:15 cause … to be killed. It is the statue that commands the death of those who will not worship it, in this battle between God and Satan.

13:16 mark. Satan causes people to be sealed with the name of the beast, just as God's people were sealed with God's mark in 7:3. Now there are people sealed for God and those sealed for Satan.

13:17 no one can buy or sell. There are severe economic consequences for failing to

have the mark of the beast. Such people cannot purchase anything or engage in trade.

13:18 666. Many attempts have been made to translate this number into a name. None really succeed, since all such translation is, in the end, guesswork. Some suggest that this is a symbol not a cryptogram; since 7 is the perfect number, each number in the mark falls short of such perfection.

14:1 Mount Zion. In the vision of Joel, this is the place of deliverance for those who call upon the name of the Lord (Joel 2:32). This is either the temple site in Jerusalem or the heavenly Zion, the Jerusalem that is above (Gal. 4:26; Heb. 12:22) since this whole scene takes place in a heavenly context.

14:4 who follow the Lamb. Many take this verse to mean that the 144,000 are a special class of people who enjoy a special relationship with God and who are characterized by three things: abstinence from marriage (celibacy); following of the Lamb; special consecration to God. **not defiled with women.** It is true that both Jesus and Paul spoke approvingly of those who abstained from marriage (Matt. 19:12; 1 Cor. 7:1, 32), but they also spoke approvingly of marriage (Matt. 19:4-6; Eph. 5:31-32). Furthermore, Israel was spoken of as a virgin in the Old Testament (Jer. 18:13; Lam. 2:13; Amos 5:2), as was the church in the New Testament (2 Cor. 11:2). **firstfruits.** Originally this was an offering to God of some of the fruit from the beginning of the harvest (Lev. 23:9-14).

14:8 second angel. This is another announcement of what is yet to come (11:15;

foreheads. ² I heard a sound[a] from heaven like the sound of cascading waters and like the rumbling of loud thunder. The sound I heard was also like harpists playing on their harps. ³ They sang[b] a new song before the throne and before the four living creatures and the elders, but no one could learn the song except the 144,000 who had been redeemed[c] from the earth. ⁴ These are the ones not defiled with women, for they have kept their virginity. These are the ones who follow the Lamb wherever He goes. They were redeemed[d][c] from the human race as the •firstfruits for God and the Lamb. ⁵ No lie was found in their mouths; they are blameless.

The Proclamation of Three Angels

⁶ Then I saw another angel flying in mid-heaven, having the eternal gospel to announce to the inhabitants of the earth—to every nation, tribe, language, and people. ⁷ He spoke with a loud voice: "Fear God and give Him glory, because the hour of His judgment has come. Worship the Maker of heaven and earth, the sea and springs of water."

⁸ A second angel[e] followed, saying: "It has fallen, Babylon the Great has fallen,[f] who made all nations drink the wine of her sexual immorality,[g] which brings wrath."

⁹ And a third angel[h] followed them and spoke with a loud voice: "If anyone worships the beast and his image and receives a mark on his forehead or on his hand, ¹⁰ he will also drink the wine of God's wrath, which is mixed full strength in the cup of His anger. He will be tormented with fire and sulfur in the sight of the holy angels and in the sight of the Lamb, ¹¹ and the smoke of their torment will go up forever and ever. There is no rest[i] day or night for those who worship the beast and his image, or anyone who receives the mark of his name. ¹² Here is the endurance[j][k] of the saints, who keep the commandments of God and the faith in Jesus."[l]

¹³ Then I heard a voice from heaven saying, "Write: Blessed are the dead who die in the Lord from now on."

"Yes," says the Spirit, "let them rest from their labors, for their works follow them!"

Wrath and Rejoicing

1. What is one of your favorite pop tunes? One of your favorite worship songs or hymns?

Revelation 14:1-15:8

2. Who is the Lamb? What has He done? Why are the people following Him?

3. What determines who will "drink the wine of God's wrath" (14:10) and who will "rest from their labors" (14:13)?

4. Look at the pictures used for God's wrath (strong wine, fire, sickles, etc.). What does each suggest about His anger? Why is He so angry about humanity's wickedness?

5. Are you following God with your whole heart? What can you praise God for today?

Reaping the Earth's Harvest

¹⁴ Then I looked, and there was a white cloud, and One like the Son of Man[m] was seated on the cloud, with a gold crown on His head and a sharp sickle in His hand. ¹⁵ Another angel came out of the sanctuary, crying out in a loud voice to the One who was seated on the cloud, "Use your sickle and reap, for the time to reap has come, since the harvest of the earth is ripe." ¹⁶ So the One seated on the cloud swung His sickle over the earth, and the earth was harvested.

¹⁷ Then another angel who also had a sharp sickle came out of the sanctuary in heaven. ¹⁸ Yet another angel, who had authority over fire, came from the altar, and he called with a loud voice to the one who had the

---

ª**14:2** Or *voice* ᵇ**14:3** Other mss add *as it were* ᶜ**14:3,4** Or *purchased* ᵈ**14:4** Other mss add *by Jesus* ᵉ**14:8** Lit *Another angel, a second* ᶠ**14:8** Other mss omit the second *has fallen* ᵍ**14:8** Or *wine of her passionate immorality* ʰ**14:9** Lit *Another angel, a third* ⁱ**14:11** Lit *They have no rest* ʲ**14:12** Or *This calls for the endurance of the saints* ᵏ**14:12** This is what the endurance of the saints means ˡ**14:12** Or *and faith in Jesus*, or *their faith in*, or *faithfulness to Jesus* ᵐ**14:14** Or *like a son of man*

12:10) as if it had just happened (17:1–18:24). **Babylon.** The original Babylon was a great city in Mesopotamia, renowned for its luxury and its corruption. It was also the traditional enemy of Israel.

14:9-11 third angel. The third angel discloses the fate of those who do not leave the beast and worship God. In contrast to 13:15-17, here those who worship the beast and bear his mark will be the objects of God's wrath.

14:10 fire and sulfur. The lake of fire and sulfur is the description used in Revelation for the final resting place of Satan, his cohorts, and followers (20:10,14-15).

14:14 One like the Son of Man. This title was also used in Daniel 7:13-14; it was used extensively by Jesus as a title for Himself (Mark 2:10).

14:15 the harvest. Harvest in the New Testament carries the idea both of gathering people into God's kingdom (Matt. 9:37-38) and gathering the wicked for divine judgment (Matt. 13:30,40-42).

14:18 gather the clusters of grapes. Harvesting grapes is used elsewhere in the Bible as an image for judgment (Isa. 63:2-6; Joel 3:13).

14:19 great winepress of God's wrath. Clearly judgment, not salvation, since the grapes are tossed into a huge winepress to be trampled on.

14:20 blood flowed out of the press. The image shifts from wine to blood. The amount of blood is enormous. **up to the horses' bridles.** About four feet deep. **about 180 miles.** The approximate length of Palestine.

15:1 another great and awe-inspiring sign. This is the third such sign. The first was of the radiant woman (12:1); the second was of the fiery red dragon (12:3). **the seven last plagues.** This is the third and final set of calamities.

15:2 those who had won the victory. They won over the demands of the beast (13:15-17) by refusing to disown the name of Christ, by remaining steadfast in their faith, and by refusing to worship the beast or receive his mark (14:12). They died instead, frustrating the purposes of the beast. What seemed like defeat became victory.

15:3 Lord God, the Almighty. God is called Almighty nine times in Revelation and only once in the rest of the New Testament (2 Cor. 6:18). This is appropriate, since His overwhelming power is a central feature in this book.

sharp sickle, "Use your sharp sickle and gather the clusters of grapes from earth's vineyard, because its grapes have ripened." [19] So the angel swung his sickle toward earth and gathered the grapes from earth's vineyard, and he threw them into the great winepress of God's wrath. [20] Then the press was trampled outside the city, and blood flowed out of the press up to the horses' bridles for about 180 miles.[a]

Preparation for the Bowl Judgments

15 Then I saw another great and awe-inspiring sign[b] in heaven: seven angels with the seven last plagues, for with them, God's wrath will be completed. [2] I also saw something like a sea of glass mixed with fire, and those who had won the victory from the beast, his image,[c] and the number of his name, were standing on the sea of glass with harps from God.[d] [3] They sang the song of God's servant Moses, and the song of the Lamb:

Great and awe-inspiring are Your works,
Lord God, the Almighty;
righteous and true are Your ways,
King of the Nations.
[4] Lord, who will not fear and glorify Your name?
Because You alone are holy,
because all the nations will come and worship before You,
because Your righteous acts have been revealed.

[5] After this I looked, and the heavenly sanctuary—the tabernacle of testimony—was opened. [6] Out of the sanctuary came the seven angels with the seven plagues, dressed in clean, bright linen, with gold sashes wrapped around their chests. [7] One of the four living creatures gave the seven angels seven gold bowls filled with the wrath of God who lives forever and ever. [8] Then the sanctuary was filled with smoke from God's glory and from His power, and no one could enter the sanctuary until the seven plagues of the seven angels were completed.

The First Bowl

16 Then I heard a loud voice from the sanctuary saying to the seven angels, "Go and pour out the seven[e] bowls of God's wrath on the earth." [2] The first went and poured out his bowl on the earth, and severely painful sores[f] broke out on the people who had the mark of the beast and who worshiped his image.

The Second Bowl

[3] The second[g] poured out his bowl into the sea. It turned to blood like a dead man's, and all life[h] in the sea died.

The Third Bowl

[4] The third[g] poured out his bowl into the rivers and the springs of water, and they became blood. [5] I heard the angel of the waters say:

You are righteous, who is and who was,
the Holy One,
for You have decided these things.
[6] Because they poured out the blood of the saints and the prophets,
You also gave them blood to drink;
they deserve it!

[7] Then I heard someone from the altar say:

Yes, Lord God, the Almighty,
true and righteous are Your judgments.

The Fourth Bowl

[8] The fourth[g] poured out his bowl on the sun. He[i] was given the power[j] to burn people with fire, [9] and people were burned by the intense heat. So they blasphemed the name of God who had the power[j] over these plagues, and they did not repent and give Him glory.

The Fifth Bowl

[10] The fifth[g] poured out his bowl on the throne of the beast, and his kingdom was plunged into

---

[a]**14:20** Lit *1,600 stadia*   [b]**15:1** Or *and awesome symbolic display*   [c]**15:2** Other mss add *his mark*   [d]**15:2** Or *harps of God;* that is, harps belonging to the service of God   [e]**16:1** Other mss omit *seven*   [f]**16:2** Lit *and a severely painful sore*   [g]**16:3,4,8,10** Other mss add *angel*   [h]**16:3** Lit *and every soul of life*   [i]**16:8** Or *It*   [j]**16:8,9** Or *authority*

15:8 filled with smoke. When God appeared in the Old Testament, there was often smoke (Ex. 19:18; Isa. 6:4). It signified God's power and His judgment.

16:2 first ... bowl. The first plague falls upon those who bear the mark of the beast, marking them with painful sores.

16:3 second ... bowl. The second plague turns the oceans and seas into blood, killing all the sea life.

16:4 third ... bowl. The third plague does the same to all the fresh water, thus no water to drink in the land.

16:8-9 fourth ... bowl. The fourth plague strikes the sun so that it flares up, scorching and searing people. The impact of the fourth trumpet (8:12) also fell on the sun, moon,

and stars but it brought the opposite effect (darkness, not intense light).

16:9 they blasphemed the name of God. They know full well who is behind these calamities. **they did not repent.** Even at this point, it seems, repentance is possible. Still, they will not turn to God. Like Pharaoh, who saw the plagues and yet would not change, their hearts are hard.

16:10-11 fifth ... bowl. The fifth plague directly attacks the heart of the problem. It assaults the throne of the beast and plunges his kingdom into darkness. This darkness parallels the ninth Egyptian plague (Ex. 10:21-29).

16:12-16 The sixth plague dries up the great river Euphrates. Since it is no longer a barrier, an invasion is planned (Ex. 14:21-22;

Josh. 3:14-17 for other examples of God drying up water). The sixth trumpet plague (9:13-14) was also centered on the Euphrates. This plague is different from the others in that it does not directly bring suffering to people. It does, however, pave the way for war.

16:14 sixth ... bowl. The frogs are identified as the "spirits of demons." In the sixth trumpet plague (9:16-19), demon locusts were loosed on the world. In this case, the demons cause people to follow the beast. These deceiving spirits go over to the kings of the world in anticipation of the final great battle.

16:16 Armageddon. In Hebrew, this word means "the mountain of Megiddo." However, in Palestine, Megiddo is a plain that stretches from the Sea of Galilee to the Mediterranean, so it is not clear where, precisely,

darkness. People[a] gnawed their tongues from pain [11] and blasphemed the God of heaven because of their pains and their sores, yet they did not repent of their actions.

The Sixth Bowl

[12] The sixth[b] poured out his bowl on the great river Euphrates, and its water was dried up to prepare the way for the kings from the east. [13] Then I saw three unclean spirits like frogs ₍coming₎ from the dragon's mouth, from the beast's mouth, and from the mouth of the false prophet. [14] For they are spirits of demons performing signs, who travel to the kings of the whole world to assemble them for the battle of the great day of God, the Almighty.

[15] "Look, I am coming like a thief. Blessed is the one who is alert and remains clothed[c] so that he may not go naked, and they see his shame."

[16] So they assembled them at the place called in Hebrew Armagedon.[d] [e]

The Seventh Bowl

[17] Then the seventh[b] poured out his bowl into the air,[f] and a loud voice came out of the sanctuary,[g] from the throne, saying, "It is done!" [18] There were lightnings, rumblings, and thunders. And a severe earthquake occurred like no other since man has been on the earth—so great was the quake. [19] The great city split into three parts, and the cities of the nations[h] fell. Babylon the Great was remembered in God's presence; He gave her the cup filled with the wine of His fierce anger. [20] Every island fled, and the mountains disappeared.[i] [21] Enormous hailstones, each weighing about 100 pounds,[j] fell from heaven on the people, and they[k] blasphemed God for the plague of hail because that plague was extremely severe.

The Woman and the Scarlet Beast

17 Then one of the seven angels who had the seven bowls came and spoke with me: "Come, I will show you the judgment of the notorious prostitute[l] who sits on many[m] waters. [2] The kings of the earth committed sexual immorality with her, and those who live on the earth became drunk on the wine of her sexual immorality." [3] So he carried me away in the Spirit[n] to a desert. I saw a woman sitting on a scarlet beast that was covered[o] with blasphemous names, having seven heads and 10 horns. [4] The woman was dressed in purple and scarlet, adorned with gold, precious stones, and pearls. She had a gold cup in her hand filled with everything vile and with the impurities of her[p] prostitution. [5] On her forehead a cryptic name was written:

> **BABYLON THE GREAT**
> **THE MOTHER OF PROSTITUTES**
> **AND OF THE VILE THINGS OF THE EARTH**

[6] Then I saw that the woman was drunk on the blood of the saints and on the blood of the witnesses to Jesus. When I saw her, I was utterly astounded.

The Meaning of the Woman and of the Beast

[7] Then the angel said to me, "Why are you astounded? I will tell you the secret meaning[q] of the woman and of the beast, with the seven heads and the 10 horns, that carries her. [8] The beast that you saw was, and is not, and is about to come up from the •abyss and go to destruction. Those who live on the earth whose names were not written in the book of life from the foundation of the world will be astounded when they see the beast that was, and is not, and will be present ₍again₎.

[9] "Here is the mind with wisdom:[r] the seven heads are seven mountains on which the woman is seated.

[a]**16:10** Lit *They* [b]**16:12,17** Other mss add *angel* [c]**16:15** Or *and guards his clothes* [d]**16:16** Other mss read *Armageddon*; other mss read *Harmegedon*; other mss read *Mageddon*; other mss read *Magedon* [e]**16:16** Traditionally *the hill of Megiddo*, a great city that guarded the pass between the coast and the valley of Jezreel or Esdraelon; see Jdg 5:19; 2 Kg 9:27 [f]**16:17** Or *on the air* [g]**16:17** Other mss add *of heaven* [h]**16:19** Or *the Gentile cities* [i]**16:20** Lit *mountains were not found* [j]**16:21** Lit *about a talent*; talents varied in weight upwards from 75 pounds [k]**16:21** Lit *people.* [l]**17:1** Traditionally, *the great whore* [m]**17:1** Or *by many* [n]**17:3** Or *in spirit* [o]**17:3** Lit *was filled* [p]**17:4** Other mss read *of earth's* [q]**17:7** Lit *the mystery* [r]**17:9** Or *This calls for the mind with wisdom*

---

this is. The region of Megiddo was the site of many battles in the history of Israel (Judg. 5:19; 2 Kings 9:27; 23:29; 2 Chron. 35:22).

16:17-21 seventh … bowl. The seventh and final plague brings about the overthrow of Babylon. This was announced in 14:8 and will be described in detail in chapters 17 and 18.

16:19 the great city. The city of the beast is undone, as are the cities of those who aligned themselves with the beast. **the cup filled with the wine of His fierce anger.** Babylon caused the nations to drink from the cup of her sexual immorality and they grew rich from this adultery (18:3). Now Babylon is forced to drink from another cup—the cup of God's wrath (14:8,10).

17:1 sits on many waters. The Babylon of

history was built on a network of canals (Jer. 51:13). John interprets the meaning of these "many waters" in verse 15 as "peoples, multitudes, nations, and languages."

17:2 sexual immorality. In this context, this term describes the corrupting influence of Babylon, which enticed the nations to prostitute everything for the sake of riches, luxury, and pleasure (Isa. 23:16-17; Jer. 51:7; Nah. 3:4).

17:3 carried me away. The angel then takes John to a desert. **in the Spirit.** John is in the midst of a vision (1:10; 4:2). **a scarlet beast.** The same beast as in 13:1—the antichrist. His scarlet color identifies him with his master, Satan, the fiery red dragon (12:3). It is the beast that has made the city (the prostitute) great.

17:4 purple and scarlet. The high cost of these dyes made clothing of this color expensive, so that it could only be worn by the wealthy.

17:5 On her forehead. Prostitutes in Rome wore headbands bearing the name of their owners. **THE MOTHER OF PROSTITUTES.** Not content simply to pursue her own adulteries, she made her daughters into prostitutes.

17:8 was, and is not, and is about to come up from the abyss. A description that mimics that of the Lamb (1:18; 2:8).

17:9 seven mountains. Rome was famed as a city built on seven hills along the east bank of the Tiber River.

17:10 seven kings. The identity of these kings has been hotly debated. Some schol-

[10] They are also seven kings:[a] five have fallen, one is, the other has not yet come, and when he comes, he must remain for a little while. [11] The beast that was and is not, is himself the eighth, yet is of the seven and goes to destruction. [12] The 10 horns you saw are 10 kings who have not yet received a kingdom, but they will receive authority as kings with the beast for one hour. [13] These have one purpose, and they give their power and authority to the beast. [14] These will make war against the Lamb, but the Lamb will conquer them because He is Lord of lords and King of kings. Those with Him are called and elect and faithful."

Plagues and Prostitutes

1. If you could rule the world for just one hour, what would you do?

Revelation 16:1–17:18

2. What might these plagues represent? If they turn out to be literal, how might they come about?

3. Who is in control of the plagues? Why is He pouring them out?

4. How did the world respond to the plagues? How might things have been different if the world's response had been different?

5. Who or what is like the "notorious prostitute" (17:1) in today's world? In your own life?

[15] He also said to me, "The waters you saw, where the prostitute was seated, are peoples, multitudes, nations, and languages. [16] The 10 horns you saw, and the beast, will hate the prostitute. They will make her desolate and naked, devour her flesh, and burn her up with fire. [17] For God has put it into their hearts to carry out His plan by having one purpose, and to give their kingdom[b] to the beast until God's words are accomplished. [18] And the woman you saw is the great city that has an empire[c] over the kings of the earth."

Heaven's Marriage Feast

1. What is the most romantic or unusual wedding proposal you've ever heard of? What was the most interesting wedding you've attended?

Revelation 18:1–19:10

2. Are there any cities or societies today that remind you of Babylon? How are they similar? How are they different?

3. Read the list of things bought and sold in Babylon (18:11-13). What sort of city is this? How might a city buy and sell "human bodies and souls"?

4. Who are the blessed people invited to the marriage feast of the Lamb? Are you one of the blessed?

The Fall of Babylon the Great

18 After this I saw another angel with great authority coming down from heaven, and the earth was illuminated by his splendor. [2] He cried in a mighty voice:

It has fallen,[d] Babylon the Great has fallen!
She has become a dwelling for demons,
a haunt[e] for every unclean spirit,
a haunt[e] for every unclean bird,
and a haunt[e] for every unclean
and despicable beast.[f]

---

[a] **17:10** Some editors or translators put *They are also seven kings:* in v. 9. [b] **17:17** Or *sovereignty* [c] **17:18** Or *has sovereignty* or *rulership* [d] **18:2** Other mss omit *It has fallen* [e] **18:2** Or *prison* [f] **18:2** Other mss omit the words *and a haunt for every unclean beast.* The words *and despicable* then refer to the *bird* of the previous line.

---

ars take the number seven to represent (as it often does in Revelation) the fullness of imperial power so that the seven kings stand for a succession of kingdoms.

17:11 the beast that was and is not. The eighth king is the Antichrist (Dan. 7:24). This is a difficult verse with complex symbolism. A best guess is that the seventh king with the short reign will reappear a second time as the eighth king (who is therefore one of the seven) and will be a particularly virulent manifestation of the beast.

17:14 make war against the Lamb. They are even willing to fight against the Lamb. This final conflict at Armageddon is discussed in 19:11-21. **because He is Lord of lords and King of kings.** Given the nature of the Messiah's sovereign power as captured in this title, the outcome of the battle is

certain (19:16; Deut. 10:17; Ps. 136:2-3; Dan. 2:47). His victory will be shared by those who have remained faithful to Him even to the point of death.

18:2 fallen, Babylon the Great has fallen. The language used to describe the fall of this Babylon is similar to the language used to describe the fall of Babylon in the Old Testament, as well as the fall of Edom and Nineveh (Isa. 34:11-15; Zeph. 2:15). This phrase (also in 14:8) echoes the words of Isaiah 21:9.

18:3 committed sexual immorality with her. Sexual promiscuity is used in the Old Testament as a metaphor for spiritual unfaithfulness on the part of the people of Israel (Isa. 1:21; Jer. 2:20-30; 3:1; Ezek. 16:15; Hos. 2:5; 4:15). She has seduced the nations to follow the beast. What she used was the

lure of riches and luxury.

18:7 I am not a widow, and I will never see grief. Babylon is so secure in her power and invincibility that she boasts. She denies that her armies will die on the battlefield. Others may experience loss, but she will not (Isa. 47:7-9). Her self-deception will end with her fall.

18:9-10 kings of the earth. Not the 10 kings of 17:12-14, who are utterly loyal to the beast and join with him in his war against the Lamb. These represent the nations who have allowed themselves to be seduced by the prostitute of Babylon into a life of excess.

18:12-13 merchandise. The 29 items are divided into seven types of merchandise: precious minerals, fabrics used for expensive clothing, ornamental decorations, aromatic substances, food, animals, and slaves. Fif-

3 For all the nations have drunk[a]
the wine of her sexual immorality,
    which brings wrath.
The kings of the earth have committed
    sexual immorality with her,
and the merchants of the earth
    have grown wealthy
    from her excessive luxury.

4 Then I heard another voice from heaven:

Come out of her, My people,
so that you will not share in her sins,
or receive any of her plagues.
5 For her sins are piled up[b] to heaven,
and God has remembered her crimes.
6 Pay her back the way she also paid,
and double it according to her works.
In the cup in which she mixed,
mix a double portion for her.
7 As much as she glorified herself
    and lived luxuriously,
give her that much torment and grief.
Because she says in her heart, 'I sit as queen;
I am not a widow, and I will never see grief,'
8 therefore her plagues will come in one day[c]—
death, and grief, and famine.
She will be burned up with fire,
because the Lord God who judges her is mighty.

The World Mourns Babylon's Fall

9 The kings of the earth who have committed sexual immorality and lived luxuriously with her will weep and mourn over her when they see the smoke of her burning. 10 They stand far off in fear of her torment, saying:

Woe, woe, the great city,
Babylon, the mighty city!
For in a single hour[c]
your judgment has come.

11 The merchants of the earth will also weep and mourn over her, because no one buys their merchandise any longer— 12 merchandise of gold, silver, precious stones, and pearls; fine fabrics of linen, purple, silk, and scarlet; all kinds of fragrant wood products; objects of ivory; objects of expensive wood, brass,[d] iron, and marble; 13 cinnamon, spice,[e][f] incense, myrrh,[g] and frankincense; wine, olive oil, fine wheat flour, and grain; cattle and sheep; horses and carriages; and human bodies and souls.[h][i]

14   The fruit you craved has left you.
All your splendid and glamorous things
    are gone;
they will never find them again.

15 The merchants of these things, who became rich from her, will stand far off in fear of her torment, weeping and mourning, 16 saying:

Woe, woe, the great city,
clothed in fine linen, purple, and scarlet,
adorned with gold, precious stones, and pearls;
17 because in a single hour[c] such fabulous wealth
    was destroyed!

And every shipmaster, seafarer, the sailors, and all who do business by sea, stood far off 18 as they watched the smoke from her burning and kept crying out: "Who is like the great city?" 19 They threw dust on their heads and kept crying out, weeping, and mourning:

Woe, woe, the great city,
where all those who have ships on the sea
became rich from her wealth;
because in a single hour[c] she was destroyed.
20   Rejoice over her, heaven, and you saints,
    apostles, and prophets,
because God has executed your judgment
    on her![j]

---

[a]18:3 Other mss read *have collapsed*; other mss read *have fallen*   [b]18:5 Or *sins have reached up*   [c]18:8,10,17,19 Suddenly   [d]18:12 Or *bronze*, or *copper*   [e]18:13 Other mss omit *spice*   [f]18:13 Or *amomum*, an aromatic plant   [g]18:13 Or *perfume*   [h]18:13 Or *carriages; and slaves, namely, human beings*   [i]18:13 Slaves; "bodies" was the Gk way of referring to slaves; "souls of men" was the Hb way.   [j]18:20 Or *God pronounced on her the judgment she passed on you*; see Rv 18:6

---

teen of the items in this catalog of imports are mentioned in the lament over the destruction of Tyre, another great trading nation (Ezek. 27).

18:15-17 the merchants. It is now the turn of the merchants to lament the loss of the great city in the same way as did the kings. This is the second dirge.

18:20 Rejoice over her. This song of praise from heaven stands in contrast to the lament that has just ended. The reason for such praise is that the judgment of God has come upon the city that persecuted His people.

18:21 mighty angel picked up a stone. It all happens so suddenly. Babylon was there in her arrogance and power and then she is gone, like a stone dropped into the sea. This is a large stone used for grinding wheat and weighing thousands of pounds.

18:22 The sound of harpists, musicians, flutists, and trumpeters. Babylon was known as a great patron of the arts. Flutes were used for festivals and funerals (Isa. 30:29; Matt. 9:23). Trumpets were sounded at the games and in the theater. **mill.** A small millstone used in the home to grind wheat into flour for bread, in contrast to the massive commercial millstone in verse 21.

19:1-5 The story of the destruction of Babylon is concluded by a shout of thanksgiving on the part of the heavenly company. The fall of Babylon and the removal of her corrupting influence is celebrated. This contrasts sharply with the preceding dirges of the kings, merchants, and seafarers who mourn their loss of income.

19:1 Hallelujah! An exclamation of praise derived from two Hebrew words meaning, "Praise the Lord." It is used frequently in the Psalms (Ps. 106; 111-113), though never in the New Testament apart from the four occurrences in this passage (vv. 1,3-4,6).

19:6-10 John announces the marriage of the Lamb, though he does not describe it. It is announced here and assumed in later chapters (21:2,3,9-10). The metaphor used here is based on Jewish wedding customs of the first century.

19:7 His wife. Israel was regularly spoken of as the wife of Yahweh (Isa. 54:5; 62:5; Jer. 31:32; Ezek. 16:8-14; Hos. 2:19-20). Jesus spoke of Himself as the bridegroom (Mark 2:19-20), and John the Baptist used this same language to describe Jesus (John 3:29). Jesus also used the idea of the wed-

The Finality of Babylon's Fall

21 Then a mighty angel picked up a stone like a large millstone and threw it into the sea, saying:

> In this way, Babylon the great city
>   will be thrown down violently
>   and never be found again.
22 The sound of harpists, musicians, flutists,
>   and trumpeters
>   will never be heard in you again;
> no craftsman of any trade
>   will ever be found in you again;
> the sound of a mill
>   will never be heard in you again;
23 the light of a lamp will never shine in you again;
> and the voice of a groom and bride
>   will never be heard in you again.
> ⌊All this will happen⌋
> because your merchants were the nobility
>   of the earth,
> because all the nations were deceived
>   by your sorcery,ᵃ
24 and the blood of prophets and saints,
>   and all those slaughtered on earth, was found
>   in you.ᵇ

Heaven Exults over Babylon

19 After this I heard something like the loud voice of a vast multitude in heaven, saying:

> Hallelujah!ᶜ
> Salvation, glory, and power belong to our God,
2   because His judgments are trueᵈ and righteous,
> because He has judged the notorious prostitute
>   who corrupted the earth
>   with her sexual immorality;
> and He has avenged the blood of His servants
>   that was on her hands.

3 A second time they said:

> Hallelujah!ᵉ
> Her smoke ascends forever and ever!

4 Then the 24 elders and the four living creatures fell down and worshiped God, who is seated on the throne, saying:

> •Amen! Hallelujah!ᵉ

5 A voice came from the throne, saying:

> Praise our God,
> all you His servants, you who fear Him,
> both small and great!

Marriage of the Lamb Announced

6 Then I heard something like the voice of a vast multitude, like the sound of cascading waters, and like the rumbling of loud thunder, saying:

> Hallelujahᵉ—because our Lord God,
>   the Almighty,
> has begun to reign!
7 Let us be glad, rejoice, and give Him glory,
> because the marriage of the Lamb has come,
> and His wife has prepared herself.
8 She was permitted to wear fine linen,
>   bright and pure.

For the fine linen represents the righteous acts of the saints.

9 Then heᶠ said to me, "Write: Blessed are those invited to the marriage feast of the Lamb!" He also said to me, "These words of God are true." 10 Then I fell at his feet to worship him, but he said to me, "Don't do that! I am a fellow •slave with you and your brothers who have the testimony aboutᵍ Jesus. Worship God, because the testimony aboutᵍ Jesus is the spirit of prophecy."

The Rider on a White Horse

11 Then I saw heaven opened, and there was a white horse! Its rider is called Faithful and True, and in righteousness He judges and makes war. 12 His eyes were like a fiery flame, and on His head were many crowns. He had a name written that no one knows except Himself. 13 He

---

ᵃ**18:23** Ancient sorcery or witchcraft often used spells and drugs. Here the term may be non-literal, that is, Babylon drugged the nations with her beauty and power.   ᵇ**18:24** Lit *in her*   ᶜ**19:1** Lit *Praise Yahweh*; the Gk word is transliterated *hallelujah* from a Hb expression of praise and is used in many places in the OT, such as Ps 106:1.   ᵈ**19:2** Valid; see Jn 8:16; 19:35   ᵉ**19:3,4,6** See note at Rv 19:1   ᶠ**19:9** Probably an angel; see Rv 17:1; 22:8–9   ᵍ**19:10** Or *testimony to*

---

ding feast in His parables (Matt. 22:1-14; 25:1-13). Paul picks up the idea of Israel as the bride of God and applies it to the church as the bride of Christ (Rom. 7:1-4; 1 Cor. 6:17; 2 Cor. 11:2; Eph. 5:25-27).

19:8 fine linen, bright and pure. This contrasts sharply to the gaudy robes of the prostitute (17:4). The wedding clothes of the bride are similar to the white robes of the martyrs washed in the blood of the Lamb (7:14).

19:9 The focus shifts to the wedding guests. In the fluid language of metaphor, the church is both bride and guests. This same fluidity is seen elsewhere in the New Testament. In Mark 2:19-20, the disciples are pictured as guests at the wedding. Likewise in the parable of the wedding banquet, the bride is not mentioned. The issue there has to do with who the guests will be. However,

in Ephesians 5:25-27 the church is spoken of as the bride who is made ready for her Husband, Christ. **the marriage feast.** This is the great messianic banquet about which Jesus spoke (Matt. 8:11; 26:29).

19:13 a robe stained with blood. Not His own blood. Here Jesus comes not as the Redeemer who dies for sins, but as the Warrior who conquers evil. This parallels Isaiah 63:1-6 where the Messiah has the blood of His enemies on His garments.

19:14 The armies that were in heaven. May be an army of angels or an army of the redeemed as 17:14 suggests (Zech. 14:5; Mark 8:38; 1 Thess. 3:13; 2 Thess. 1:7). The army does not engage in battle. That is left to Christ (v. 21).

19:15 sword ... iron scepter ... winepress.

Three symbols in this verse, all taken from the Old Testament, describe the actions of the Warrior. First, the weapon that He uses in this battle issues from His mouth, an image that is drawn from Isaiah 11:4 (1:16; 2:12,16). His sword is His Word; the same Word that was the source of all creation (John 1:1-3; Heb. 1:2). Second, He rules with a rod of iron, an image taken from Psalm 2:9, a rod not of governing but of destruction. Third, He treads the winepress, a familiar image in Revelation (14:19), drawn originally from Isaiah 63:3.

19:18 everyone. All who bear the mark of the beast, a number that includes all kinds of people who have not stood as a witness for God.

20:1-3 The meaning of this passage has been the subject of great debate in the

wore a robe stained with blood,[a] and His name is called the Word of God. 14 The armies that were in heaven followed Him on white horses, wearing pure white linen. 15 From His mouth came a sharp[b] sword, so that with it He might strike the nations. He will shepherd[c] them with an iron scepter. He will also trample the winepress of the fierce anger of God, the Almighty. 16 And on His robe and on His thigh He has a name written:

> ### KING OF KINGS
> ### AND LORD OF LORDS

The Beast and His Armies Defeated

17 Then I saw an angel standing in the sun, and he cried out in a loud voice, saying to all the birds flying in mid-heaven, "Come, gather together for the great supper of God, 18 so that you may eat the flesh of kings, the flesh of commanders, the flesh of mighty men, the flesh of horses and of their riders, and the flesh of everyone, both free and •slave, small and great."

19 Then I saw the beast, the kings of the earth, and their armies gathered together to wage war against the rider on the horse and against His army. 20 But the beast was taken prisoner, and along with him the false prophet, who had performed signs on his authority,[d] by which he deceived those who accepted the mark of the beast and those who worshiped his image. Both of them were thrown alive into the lake of fire that burns with sulfur. 21 The rest were killed with the sword that came from the mouth of the rider on the horse, and all the birds were filled with their flesh.

Satan Bound

20 Then I saw an angel coming down from heaven with the key to the •abyss and a great chain in his hand. 2 He seized the dragon, that ancient serpent who is the Devil and Satan,[e] and bound him for 1,000 years. 3 He threw him into the abyss, closed it, and put a seal on it so that he would no longer

deceive the nations until the 1,000 years were completed. After that, he must be released for a short time.

The Last Battle

The Saints Reign with the Messiah

4 Then I saw thrones, and people seated on them who were given authority to judge. ⌊I⌋ also ⌊saw⌋ the souls of those who had been beheaded[f] because of their testimony about Jesus and because of God's word, who had not worshiped the beast or his image, and who had not accepted the mark on their foreheads or their hands. They came to life and reigned with the •Messiah for 1,000 years. 5 The rest of the dead did not come to life until the 1,000 years were completed. This is the first resurrection. 6 Blessed and holy is the one who shares in the first resurrection! The second death has no power[g] over these, but they will be priests of God and the Messiah, and they will reign with Him for 1,000 years.

---

[a] **19:13** Or *a robe dipped in*   [b] **19:15** Other mss add *double-edged*   [c] **19:15** Or *rule*   [d] **19:20** Lit *signs before him*   [e] **20:2** Other mss add *who deceives the whole world*   [f] **20:4** All who had given their lives for their faith in Christ   [g] **20:6** Or *authority*

---

church. There are three main schools of thought when it comes to the Millennium (the thousand-year reign of Christ). Postmillennialists feel that the return of Christ will not occur until the kingdom of God has been established here on earth, in history as we know it. This will be the "golden age" of the church, a long reign of peace and prosperity. It will be followed by the second coming, the resurrection of the dead, the final judgment, and the eternal kingdom. Amillennialists do not believe there will be a literal thousand-year reign of Christ. They see it as a metaphor for the history of the church between the resurrection of Christ and His second coming, during which those believers who have died will reign with Christ in heaven. When Christ returns there will be a general resurrection, the final judgment, and the start of Christ's reign over the new heaven and earth. They consider the binding

of Satan to be what Christ did when He died on the cross (Matt. 12:29). Premillennialists believe that the events described in verses 1-6 will literally take place. Christ will remove believers from the earth before He returns. Christ will return, the first resurrection will occur, and there will be a thousand years of peace in which Christ reigns here on earth. Then will come the final resurrection, the last judgment, and the new heaven and earth. The millennial reign is seen (by some premillennialists) as a special reward to the martyrs of chapter 6 (6:9-11).

20:6 The second death. The first death is the death of the body; the second death involves being cast into the lake of fire (v. 14; 21:8).

20:8 Gog and Magog. In Ezekiel 38-39, there is an extended prophecy about "Gog,

of the land of Magog" (38:2). As in Ezekiel, the final battle follows the establishment of the messianic kingdom that Israel has looked forward to for centuries (Ezek. 36-37).

20:10 the lake of fire and sulfur. In the rest of the New Testament this is called *Gehenna* in Greek—translated "hell" in English (Matt. 5:22; Mark 9:43). The Valley of Hinnom, from which Gehenna is drawn, was a place where human sacrifice took place (2 Kings 16:3; 23:10; Jer. 7:31-32). It eventually became a kind of town dump where a fire perpetually smoldered, and thus it became a metaphor for hell.

20:13 Hades. This is not the same as Gehenna (v. 10). It is the place where departed souls go. It was thought of as an intermediate state (Luke 16:23; Acts 2:27).

Satanic Rebellion Crushed

⁷ When the 1,000 years are completed, Satan will be released from his prison ⁸ and will go out to deceive the nations at the four corners of the earth, Gog and Magog, to gather them for battle. Their number is like the sand of the sea. ⁹ They came up over the surface of the earth and surrounded the encampment of the saints, the beloved city. Then fire came down from heavenª and consumed them. ¹⁰ The Devil who deceived them was thrown into the lake of fire and sulfur where the beast and the false prophet are, and they will be tormented day and night forever and ever.

Lake of Fire or Eternal Life?

1. Have you ever been scuba diving? How deep did you go? What did you see?

Revelation 20:11–21:8

2. What is the "lake of fire" (20:14)? Who will be thrown into it? What will that be like?

3. What will life be like when "death will exist no longer" (21:4)?

4. Who is heaven reserved for (21:7)? Who is hell reserved for (21:8)?

5. How can the person described in 21:8 still find eternal life?

6. What must you do to overcome and share in God's eternal inheritance (see 1 John 5:5,11-12)?

The Great White Throne Judgment

¹¹ Then I saw a great white throne and One seated on it. Earth and heaven fled from His presence, and no place was found for them. ¹² I also saw the dead, the great and the small, standing before the throne, and books were opened. Another book was opened, which is the book of life, and the dead were judged according to their works by what was written in the books.

¹³ Then the sea gave up its dead, and Death and •Hades gave up their dead; allᵇ were judged according to their works. ¹⁴ Death and Hades were thrown into the lake of fire. This is the second death, the lake of fire.ᶜ ¹⁵ And anyone not found written in the book of life was thrown into the lake of fire.

The New Creation

21 Then I saw a new heaven and a new earth, for the first heaven and the first earth had passed away, and the sea existed no longer. ² I also saw the Holy City, new Jerusalem, coming down out of heaven from God, prepared like a bride adorned for her husband.

³ Then I heard a loud voice from the throne:ᵈ

Look! God's dwellingᵉ is with men,
and He will live with them.
They will be His people,
and God Himself will be with them
and be their God.ᶠ
⁴ He will wipe away every tear from their eyes.
Death will exist no longer;
grief, crying, and pain will exist no longer,
because the previous thingsᵍ have passed away.

⁵ Then the One seated on the throne said, "Look! I am making everything new." He also said, "Write, because these wordsʰ are faithful and true." ⁶ And He said to me, "It is done! I am the •Alpha and the Omega, the Beginning and the End. I will give to the thirsty from the spring of living water as a gift. ⁷ The victor will inherit these things, and I will be his God, and he will be My son. ⁸ But the cowards, unbelievers,ⁱ vile, murderers, sexually immoral, sorcerers, idolaters, and all liars—their share will be in the lake that burns with fire and sulfur, which is the second death."

ª**20:9** Other mss add *from God* ᵇ**20:13** Lit *each* ᶜ**20:14** Other mss omit *the lake of fire* ᵈ**21:3** Other mss read *from heaven* ᵉ**21:3** Or *tent,* or *tabernacle* ᶠ**21:3** Other mss omit *and be their God* ᵍ**21:4** Or *the first things* ʰ**21:5** Other mss add *of God* ⁱ**21:8** Other mss add *the sinful*

21:1 the first earth had passed away. This event occurred in 20:11, described by means of a few terse words. **the sea existed no longer.** In ancient times the sea was often pictured as dark and mysterious; it was an enemy not a friend. The lack of any seas in the new earth indicates how radically different the new will be.

21:6 the Alpha and the Omega. The first and last letters in the Greek alphabet. **the Beginning and the End.** God encompasses the whole of time. **I will give to the thirsty.** He satisfies the deepest needs—physical and spiritual—of humanity.

21:16 12,000 stadia. It is an enormous city, beyond what any earthly city will be or could be. Each of its four sides was approximately 1,400 miles long. John struggles to convey the vastness of the city. **length, width, and height are equal.** The new Jerusalem is a cube, as high as it is wide. The inner sanctuary of the temple was a perfect cube (1 Kings 6:20), a symbol of perfection.

21:17 144 cubits. The walls will be over 200 feet thick. Of course, such a city will not need walls which, in ancient days, were a defense against enemies. This is God's city, and all His enemies will have been destroyed.

21:18 building material. This city is built of materials unlike those used in any human city. **jasper.** A green, translucent crystal. This is the third time this mineral has been mentioned (vv. 11,19; 4:3). In verse 11, jasper was said to glow with the radiance of God. The whole city would be aglow with God. The word jasper was used for various gemstones. **pure gold like clear glass.** Gold has long been considered very precious, and here is a city of gold! This is unlike ordinary gold, however, since it is transparent.

21:19 sapphire. A deep blue, transparent gem. **chalcedony.** Green silicate of copper found near Chalcedon in Asia Minor. **emerald.** A green gemstone.

21:20 sardonyx. An agate made up of layers of a red mineral by the name of sard, and white onyx. **carnelian.** Blood red. **chrysolite.** Yellow topaz or golden jasper. **beryl.** A sea-green mineral. **topaz.** A greenish-gold or yellow mineral. **chrysoprase.** A type of quartz that was apple-green. **jacinth.** A bluish-purple mineral. **amethyst.** Another variety of quartz; it was purple and transparent.

21:21 12 gates. The gates of ancient cities were an important part of their defense. They

The New Jerusalem

⁹ Then one of the seven angels, who had held the seven bowls filled with the seven last plagues, came and spoke with me: "Come, I will show you the bride, the wife of the Lamb." ¹⁰ He then carried me away in the Spiritᵃ to a great and high mountain and showed me the holy city, Jerusalem, coming down out of heaven from God, ¹¹ arrayed with God's glory. Her radiance was like a very precious stone, like a jasper stone, bright as crystal. ¹² ₍The city₎ had a massive high wall, with 12 gates. Twelve angels were at the gates; ₍on the gates₎, names were inscribed, the names of the 12 tribes of the sons of Israel. ¹³ There were three gates on the east, three gates on the north, three gates on the south, and three gates on the west. ¹⁴ The city wall had 12 foundations, and on them were the 12 names of the Lamb's 12 apostles.

Heavenly Citizenship

1. What is the biggest city you've been in? Would you like to live there?

Revelation 21:9–22:6

2. What does the wealth and beauty of the city suggest?

3. What did John mean in 21:22 that he "did not see a sanctuary in it, because the Lord God the Almighty and the Lamb are its sanctuary"? Why would there be no "sanctuary"? How is the Lamb our sanctuary?

4. What does it mean that in heaven "there will no longer be any curse" (22:3)?

5. What will you like most about being a citizen in the New Jerusalem?

---

¹⁵ The one who spoke with me had a gold measuring rod to measure the city, its gates, and its wall. ¹⁶ The city is laid out in a square; its length and width are the same. He measured the city with the rod at 12,000 *stadia*.ᵇ Its length, width, and height are equal. ¹⁷ Then he measured its wall, 144 •cubits according to human measurement, which the angel used. ¹⁸ The building material of its wall was jasper, and the city was pure gold like clear glass.

¹⁹ The foundations of the city wall were adorned with every kind of precious stone:

the first foundation jasper,
the second sapphire,
the third chalcedony,
the fourth emerald,
20   the fifth sardonyx,
the sixth carnelian,
the seventh chrysolite,
the eighth beryl,
the ninth topaz,
the tenth chrysoprase,
the eleventh jacinth,
the twelfth amethyst.

²¹ The 12 gates are 12 pearls; each individual gate was made of a single pearl. The broad streetᶜ of the city was pure gold, like transparent glass.

²² I did not see a sanctuary in it, because the Lord God the Almighty and the Lamb are its sanctuary. ²³ The city does not need the sun or the moon to shine on it, because God's glory illuminates it, and its lamp is the Lamb. ²⁴ The nationsᵈ will walk in its light, and the kings of the earth will bring their glory into it.ᵉ ²⁵ Each day its gates will never close because it will never be night there. ²⁶ They will bring the glory and honor of the nations into it.ᶠ ²⁷ Nothing profane will ever enter it: no one who does what is vile or false, but only those written in the Lamb's book of life.

ᵃ**21:10** Or *in spirit* ᵇ**21:16** A *stadion* (sg) equals about 600 feet; the total is about 1,400 miles. ᶜ**21:21** Or *The public square* ᵈ**21:24** Other mss add *of those who are saved* ᵉ**21:24** Other mss read *will bring to Him the nations' glory and honor* ᶠ**21:26** Other mss add *in order that they might go in*

---

were built into the wall, often with a tower as part of their construction. **12 pearls.** Pearls were of great value in the ancient world (Matt. 13:45-46; 1 Tim. 2:9). The pearls from which these gates will be built will have to be enormous; again, quite beyond anything on this earth.

22:2 the tree of life. The great story ends where it began, with the tree of life. In Genesis the tree of life in the garden of Eden was lost to humanity by reason of sin (Gen. 2:9; 3:22). In Revelation it is restored.

22:7 Look! I am coming quickly. Jesus affirms that He said at the beginning of the book (2:16; 3:11). In light of this fact, His people must always be alert, always prepared for His return. **Blessed.** This is the

sixth of seven beatitudes. **keeps the prophetic words.** The important thing for believers is to realize that the aim of the book is not so much to inform the church about the details of the last days as it is to call the church to faithful living in the midst of the struggle it faces with evil in whatever historical context it finds itself.

22:14 wash their robes. An allusion to 3:4 and 7:14. Those who are blessed are those who, by faith, have benefited from the redeeming death of Jesus. **the right to the tree of life.** Those who are thus clad in the righteousness of Jesus have access to the very life of God (vv. 1-5). **enter the city by the gates.** Furthermore, they have access to the city of God, the new Jerusalem where they will live eternally.

22:16 the Root and the Offspring of David. He is the messianic King from the line of David (5:5; Matt. 1:1; 9:27; 15:22; 21:9; Rom. 1:3). The image of a shoot that grows out of the stump of David is taken from Isaiah 11:1. **the Bright Morning Star.** See Numbers 24:17, which is understood to be a prophecy about the Messiah.

22:18-19 plagues … take away his share. A warning is affixed to the book. No one is to tamper with its contents, either to add to or take away from it (Deut. 4:2). This would be a real temptation with a book like this, whose message is mysterious, harsh at times, and often hard to understand. The temptation would be to leave out or explain away the parts that do not conform to one's views.

The Source of Life

22 Then he showed me the river[a] of living water, sparkling like crystal, flowing from the throne of God and of the Lamb [2] down the middle of the broad street [of the city]. On both sides of the river was the tree of life[b] bearing 12 kinds of fruit, producing its fruit every month. The leaves of the tree are for healing the nations, [3] and there will no longer be any curse. The throne of God and of the Lamb will be in the city,[c] and His servants will serve Him. [4] They will see His face, and His name will be on their foreheads. [5] Night will no longer exist, and people will not need lamplight or sunlight, because the Lord God will give them light. And they will reign forever and ever.

The Time Is Near

[6] Then he said to me, "These words are faithful and true. And the Lord, the God of the spirits of the prophets,[d] has sent His angel to show His servants what must quickly take place."[e]

[7] "Look, I am coming quickly! Blessed is the one who keeps the prophetic words of this book."

[8] I, John, am the one who heard and saw these things. When I heard and saw them, I fell down to worship at the feet of the angel who had shown them to me. [9] But he said to me, "Don't do that! I am a fellow •slave with you, your brothers the prophets, and those who keep the words of this book. Worship God." [10] He also said to me, "Don't seal the prophetic words of this book, because the time is near. [11] Let the unrighteous go on in unrighteousness; let the filthy go on being made filthy; let the righteous go on in righteousness; and let the holy go on being made holy."

[12] "Look! I am coming quickly, and My reward is with Me to repay each person according to what he has done. [13] I am the •Alpha and the Omega, the First and the Last, the Beginning and the End.

[14] "Blessed are those who wash their robes,[f] so that they may have the right to the tree of life and may enter the city by the gates. [15] Outside are the dogs, the sorcerers, the sexually immoral, the murderers, the idolaters, and everyone who loves and practices lying.

[16] "I, Jesus, have sent My angel to attest these things to you[g] for the churches. I am the Root and the Offspring of David, the Bright Morning Star."

[17] Both the Spirit and the bride say, "Come!" Anyone who hears should say, "Come!" And the one who is thirsty should come. Whoever desires should take the living water as a gift.

[18] I testify to everyone who hears the prophetic words of this book: If anyone adds to them, God will add to him the plagues that are written in this book. [19] And if anyone takes away from the words of this prophetic book, God will take away his share of the tree of life and the holy city, written in this book.

[20] He who testifies about these things says, "Yes, I am coming quickly."

•Amen! Come, Lord Jesus!

[21] The grace of the Lord Jesus[h] be with all the saints.[i] Amen.[j]

Come!

1. When you see Jesus face-to-face, what is the one question you'd most like to ask Him?

Revelation 22:7-21

2. Regarding Jesus' claims in verses 12-17, how is the final state of humanity determined: By some arbitrary reward system, fixed from eternity? By what we have done in this present life? By our response to his universal and undeserved invitation to simply "come"?
3. Is it ever too late for people to change their ways and come to Christ? Why?
4. How have you prepared yourself for Christ's second coming? In what way has this study of Revelation helped to prepare you?

[a]**22:1** Other mss read *pure river* [b]**22:2** Or *was a tree of life*, or *was a tree that gives life* [c]**22:3** Lit *in it* [d]**22:6** Other mss read *God of the holy prophets* [e]**22:6** Or *soon* [f]**22:14** Other mss read *who keep His commandments* [g]**22:16** *you* (pl in Gk) [h]**22:21** Other mss add *Christ* [i]**22:21** Other mss omit *the saints* [j]**22:21** Other mss omit *Amen*.

22:20 Yes, I am coming quickly! For the third time in this epilogue, the reader is re-minded that Jesus is coming soon. **Amen! Come, Lord Jesus!** John's response to this declaration is enthusiastic: "So be it; let it happen; please come Lord Jesus."

HOLMAN CSB BULLET NOTES

Holman CSB Bullet Notes are one of the unique features of the Holman Christian Standard Bible®. These notes explain frequently used biblical words or terms. These "bullet" words (for example: •abyss) are normally marked with a bullet only on their first occurrence in a chapter of the biblical text. However, certain important or easily misunderstood terms, such as •Jews or •slaves, will have more than one bullet per chapter. Other frequently used words, like •gate, are marked with bullets only where the use of the word fits the definitions given below. A few words in footnotes, like •acrostic, also have a bullet.

Abaddon	Either the grave or the realm of the dead		Asherah pole(s)	(see "Asherah(s)")
Abba	The Aramaic word for "father"		Asherah(s)	A Canaanite fertility goddess, who was the mother of the god Baal; also the wooden poles associated with the worship of her
abyss	The *bottomless pit* or *the depths* (of the sea); the prison for Satan and the demons			
acrostic	A device in Hebrew poetry in which each verse begins with a successive letter of the Hebrew alphabet		Ashtoreth(s)	A Canaanite goddess of fertility, love, and war, who was the daughter of Asherah and consort of Baal; the plural form of her name in Hebrew is *Ashtaroth*.
advocate	(see "Counselor/advocate")			
Almighty	(see "God Almighty")		Asia	A Roman province that is now part of modern Turkey; it did not refer to the modern continent of Asia.
Alpha and Omega	The first and last letters of the Greek alphabet; it is used to refer to God the Father in Rv 1:8 and 21:6, and to Jesus, God the Son, in Rv 22:13.			
			asleep	A term used in reference to those who have died
Amen	The transliteration of a Hebrew word signifying that something is certain, valid, truthful, or faithful; it is often used at the end of biblical songs, hymns, and prayers.		atone/ atonement	A theological term for God's provision to deal with human sin. In the OT, it primarily means purification. In some contexts forgiveness, pardon, expiation, propitiation, or reconciliation is included. The basis of atonement is substitutionary sacrifice offered in faith. The OT sacrifices were types and shadows of the great and final sacrifice of Jesus on the cross.
Arabah	The section of the Great Rift in Palestine, extending from the Jordan Valley and the Dead Sea to the Gulf of Aqabah. The Hebrew word can also be translated as "plain," referring to any plain or to any part of the Arabah.			
			Baal	A fertility god who was the main god of the Canaanite religion and the god of rain and thunderstorms; also the Hebrew word meaning "lord," "master," "owner," or "husband"
Asaph	A musician appointed by David to oversee the music used in worship at the Temple; 12 psalms are attributed to Asaph.			

Beelzebul — A term of slander, which was variously interpreted "lord of flies," "lord of dung," or "ruler of demons"; 2 Kg 1:2; Mk 3:22

burnt offering(s) — Or *holocaust*, an offering completely burned to ashes; it was used in connection with worship, seeking God's favor, expiating sin, or averting judgment.

cause the downfall of/ causes to sin — The Greek word *skandalizo* has a root meaning of "snare" or "trap," but has no real English counterpart.

centurion — A Roman officer who commanded about 100 soldiers

Cephas — The Aramaic word for *rock*; it is parallel to the Greek word *petros* from which the English name Peter is derived; Jn 1:42; 1 Co 1:12.

cherubim — A class of winged angels, associated with the throne of God, who function as guardians and who prevented Adam and Eve from returning to the garden of Eden

chief priest(s) — A group of Jewish temple officers that included the highpriest, captain of the temple, temple overseers, and treasurers

company/ regiment — Or *cohort*, a Roman military unit that numbered as many as 600 men

completely destroy — (see "set apart for destruction/ completely destroy")

Counselor/ advocate — The Greek word *parakletos* means one called alongside to help, counsel, or protect; it is used of the Holy Spirit in Jn and in 1 Jn.

cubit — An OT measurement of distance that equaled about 18 inches

Cush/Cushite — The lands of the Nile in southern Egypt, including Nubia and Northern Sudan; the people who lived in that region

Decapolis — Originally a federation of 10 Gentile towns east of the Jordan River

denarius — A small silver Roman coin, which was equal to a day's wage for a common laborer

divination — An attempt to foresee future events or discover hidden knowledge by means of physical objects such as water, arrows, flying birds, or animal livers

engaged — Jewish engagement was a binding agreement that could only be broken by divorce.

ephod — A vestlike garment, extending below the waist and worn under the breastpiece, which was used by both the priests and the high priest

everyone/ human race — Literally, *sons of man* or *sons of Adam*

family redeemer — A family member who had certain obligations of marriage, redeeming an estate, and punishment of a wrongdoer

fear(s) God or the LORD/ the fear of the LORD — No single English word conveys every aspect of the word *fear* in this phrase. The meaning includes worshipful submission, reverential awe, and obedient respect to the covenant-keeping God of Israel.

firstfruits — The agricultural products harvested first and given to God as an offering; also the first of more products to come

fellowship sacrifice(s) or offering(s) — An animal offering was given to maintain and strengthen a person's relationship with God. It was not required as a remedy for impurity or sin but was an expression of thanksgiving for various blessings. An important function of this sacrifice was to provide meat for the priests and the participants in the sacrifice; it was also called the *peace offering* or the *sacrifice of well-being*.

gate(s) — The center for community discussions, political meetings, and trying of court cases

Gittith — Perhaps an instrument, musical term, tune from Gath, or song for the grape harvest

God Almighty — The Hebrew word is *El Shaddai*; *El* = "God," but the meaning of *Shaddai* is disputed; traditionally it is translated "Almighty".

grain offering(s) — An offering given along with animal sacrifices or given by itself. A portion was burnt and the priests and participant ate the remainder.

Hades — The Greek word for the place of the dead; it corresponds to the Hebrew word *Sheol*.

Hallelujah! — Or *Praise the LORD!*; it literally means *Praise Yah!* (a shortened form of Yahweh)

headquarters/ palace — The Latin word *Praetorium* was used by Greek writers for the residence of the Roman governor; it may also refer to military headquarters, the imperial court, or the emperor's guard.

Hebrew — Or *Aramaic*; the translation of this word is debated since some claim Aramaic was commonly spoken in Palestine during NT times. More recently others claim that Hebrew was the spoken language.

hell/hellfire — Greek *Gehenna*; Aramaic for Valley of Hinnom on the south side of Jerusalem; it was formerly a place of human sacrifice and in NT times a place for the burning of garbage; the place of final judgment for those rejecting Christ.

Herod — The name of the Idumean family ruling Palestine from 37 B.C. to A.D. 95; the main rulers from this family mentioned in the NT are:

Herod I — (37 B.C.–4 B.C.) also known as Herod the Great; built the great temple in Jerusalem and massacred the male babies in Bethlehem

Herod Antipas — (4 B.C.–A.D. 39) son of Herod the Great; ruled one-fourth of his father's kingdom (Galilee and Perea); killed John the Baptist and mocked Jesus

Agrippa I — (A.D. 37–44) grandson of Herod the Great; beheaded James the apostle and imprisoned Peter

Agrippa II — (A.D. 52–c. 95) great-grandson of Herod the Great; heard Paul's defense

Herodians — Political supporters of Herod the Great and his family

Higgaion — Perhaps a musical notation, a device denoting a pause in an instrumental interlude, or a murmuring harp tone

high place(s) — An ancient place of worship most often associated with pagan religions, usually built on an elevated location

horn — A symbol of power based on the strength of animal horns

Hosanna — A term of praise derived from the Hebrew word for *save*

Hosts/hosts — Military forces consisting of God's angels, sometimes including the sun, moon, and stars, and occasionally, Israel

human race — (see "everyone")

I assure you — This is a phrase used only by Jesus to testify to the certainty and importance of His words; in Mt, Mk and Lk it is literally *Amen, I say to you*, and in Jn it is literally *Amen, amen, I say to you.*

Jew(s) — In Jn the term *Jews* usually indicates those in Israel who were opposed to Jesus, particularly the Jewish authorities in Jerusalem who led the nation.

Leviathan — Or *twisting one*; a mythological sea serpent or dragon associated with the chaos at creation. Sometimes it is applied to an animal such as a crocodile.

life/soul	The Greek word *psyche* can be translated *life* or *soul*.
mankind	Literally *sons of man* or *sons of Adam*
Mary Magdalene	Or *Mary of Magdala*; Magdala was probably on the western shore of the Sea of Galilee, north of Tiberias.
Maskil	From a Hebrew word meaning *to be prudent* or *to have insight*; possibly a contemplative, instructive, or wisdom psalm
men	Literally *sons of man* or *sons of Adam*
mercy seat	Or *place of atonement*; the gold lid on the ark of the covenant, first used in the tabernacle and later in the temple
Messiah	Or *the Christ*; the Greek word *Christos* means "the anointed one".
Miktam	A musical term of uncertain meaning, possibly denoting a plaintive style
Milcom	An Ammonite god who was the equivalent of Baal, the Canaanite storm god
Molech	A Canaanite god associated with death and the underworld. The worship ritual of passing someone through the fire is connected with him. This ritual could have been either fire-walking or child sacrifice.
Most High	The Hebrew word is *Elyon*. It is often used with other names of God, such as *El (God)* or *Yahweh (LORD)*; it is used to refer to God as the supreme being.
Mount of Olives	A mountain east of Jerusalem, across the Kidron Valley
Mystery	Transliteration of the Greek word *mysterion*; a secret hidden in the past but now revealed
Nazarene	A person from Nazareth; growing up in Nazareth was an aspect of the Messiah's humble beginnings; Jn 1:46.

Negev	An arid region in the southern part of Israel; the Hebrew word means "south".
offend	(see "cause the downfall of/cause to sin")
offspring/seed	This term is used literally or metaphorically to refer to plants or grain, sowing or harvest, male reproductive seed, human children or physical descendants, and also to spiritual children or to Christ (Gl 3:16).
One and Only	Or *one of a kind*, or *incomparable*, or *only begotten*; the Greek word can refer to someone's only child such as in Lk 7:12; 8:42; 9:38. It can also refer to someone's special child as in Heb 11:17.
oracle	A prophetic speech of a threatening or menacing character, often against the nations
overseer(s)	Or *elder(s)*, or *bishop(s)*
palace	(see "headquarters/palace")
Passover	The Israelite festival celebrated on the fourteenth day of the first month in the early spring. It was a celebration of the deliverance of the Israelites from Egypt, commemorating the final plague on Egypt when the firstborn were killed.
people	Literally *sons of man* or *sons of Adam*
perverted men	(see "wicked men/perverted men")
Pharisee(s)	In Judaism a religious sect that followed the whole written and oral law
Pilate	Pontius Pilate was governor of the province of Judea A.D. 26–36.
Pit	Either the grave or the realm of the dead

proconsul The chief Roman government official in a senatorial province who presided over Roman court hearings

proselyte A person from another race or religion who went through a prescribed ritual to become a Jew

Rabbi The Hebrew word *Rabbi* means *my great one*; it is used of a recognized teacher of the Scriptures.

Rabshakeh The title of a high-ranking Assyrian official who was the chief cupbearer to the king

Rahab Or *boisterous one*, a mythological sea serpent or dragon defeated at the time of creation. Scripture sometimes uses the name metaphorically to describe Egypt.

Red Sea Literally *Sea of Reeds*

regiment (see "company/regiment")

restitution offering(s) An offering that was a penalty for unintentional sins, primarily in relation to the tabernacle or temple; traditionally *trespass* or *guilt offering*

sackcloth Garment made of poor quality material and worn as a sign of grief and mourning

sacred bread Literally *bread of presentation*; 12 loaves, representing the 12 tribes of Israel, put on the table in the holy place in the tabernacle, and later in the temple. The priests ate the previous week's loaves; Ex 25:30; 29:32; Lv 24:5-9.

Sadducee(s) In Judaism a religious sect that followed primarily the first 5 books of the OT (Torah or Pentateuch)

Samaritan(s) People of mixed, Gentile/Jewish ancestry who lived between Galilee and Judea and were hated by the Jews

Sanhedrin The supreme council of Judaism with 70 members, patterned after Moses' 70 elders

scribe(s) A professional group in Judaism that copied the law of Moses and interpreted it, especially in legal cases

seed (see "offspring/seed")

Selah A Hebrew word whose meaning is uncertain; various interpretations include: (1) a musical notation, (2) a pause for silence, (3) a signal for worshipers to fall prostrate on the ground, (4) a term for the worshipers to call out, and (5) a word meaning "forever"

set apart for destruction/ completely destroy In Canaan or its neighboring countries, this was the destruction during war of a city, its inhabitants, and their possessions, including livestock.

shekel(s) In the OT the *shekel* is a measurement of weight that came to be used as money, either gold or silver.

Sheminith A musical term meaning *instruments* or *on the instrument of eight strings*

Sheol A Hebrew word for either the grave or the realm of the dead

Shinar A land in Mesopotamia, including ancient Sumer and Babylon; modern Iraq

sin offering(s) Or *purification offering*, the *sin offering* was the most important OT sacrifice for cleansing from impurities. It provided purification from sin and certain forms of ceremonial uncleanness.

slave The strong Greek word *doulos* cannot be accurately translated in English by "servant" or "bond servant"; the HCSB translates this word as "slave," not out of insensitivity to the legitimate concerns of modern English speakers, but out of a commitment to accurately convey the brutal reality of the Roman empire's inhumane institution as well as the ownership called for by Christ.

Son of Man	The most frequent title Jesus used for Himself; Dn 7:13
song of ascents	Probably the songs pilgrims sang as they traveled the roads going up to worship in Jerusalem; Pss 120–134
soul	(see "life/soul")
stumble	(see "cause the downfall of/ cause to sin")
synagogue	A place where the Jewish people met for prayer, worship and teaching of the Scriptures
tabernacle	Or *tent*, or *shelter*, terms used for temporary housing
take offense	(see "cause the downfall of/ cause to sin")
tassel	Fringe put on the clothing of devout Jews to remind them to keep the law; Nm 15:37-41
temple complex	In the Jerusalem temple, the complex included the sanctuary (the holy place and the holy of holies), at least 4 courtyards (for priests, Jewish men, Jewish women, and Gentiles), numerous gates, and several covered walkways.
testimony	A reference to either the Mosaic law in general or to a specific section of the law, the Ten Commandments, which were written on stone tablets and placed in the ark of the covenant (also called the ark of the testimony)
Topheth	A place of human sacrifice outside Jerusalem in the Hinnom Valley; Jr 7:31-32; see "hell/ hellfire"
Unleavened Bread	A seven-day festival celebrated in conjunction with the Passover; Ex 12:1-20
Urim & Thummim	Two objects used by Israelite priests to determine God's will
wadi	A seasonal stream that flows only in the rainy season
walk	A term often used in a figurative way to mean "way of life" or "behavior"
wicked men/ perverted men	Literally *sons of Belial*; the basic meaning of *Belial* in Hebrew is "worthless".
wise men	The Greek word is *magoi*; the English word "Magi" is based on a Persian word. They were eastern sages who observed the heavens for signs and omens.
woman	When used in direct address, "Woman" was not a term of disrespect but of honor.
world	The organized Satanic system that is opposed to God and hostile to Jesus and His followers. The non-Christian culture including governments, educational systems, and businesses
wormwood	A small shrub used as a medicinal herb, noted for its bitter taste
Yah	(see "Yahweh")
Yahweh	Or *The LORD*; the personal name of God in Hebrew; "Yah" is the shortened form of the name.

SUBJECT INDEX

Page numbers in **bold** are Old Testament, in ***bold italics*** are New Testament.
For example: **55** Gen. 16:7-11; **61** Gen. 22:11,16; ***1115*** 1 Cor. 16:24; ***1141*** Gal. 6:18

A

Abraham
born Abram in Ur, married Sarai, lived in Haran
52 Gen. 11:27-31
called and given a promise
52 Gen. 12:1-3; **54** Gen. 13:14-17;
54 Gen. 15; **55** Gen. 17; **61** Gen. 22:15-18
lied to kings about his wife
53 Gen. 12:10-20; **59** Gen. 20
separated from his nephew Lot
53 Gen. 13
rescued Lot
54 Gen. 14:1-16
blessed by Melchizedek
54 Gen. 14:17-20; *1205* Heb. 7:1-10
declared righteous because of faith
55 Gen. 15:6; *1076* Rom. 4:3,20-22;
1137 Gal. 3:6; *1219* Jas. 2:23
name changed
55 Gen. 17:5
covenant and circumcision
56 Gen. 17:9-27; *1076* Rom. 4:9-12
promised a son with Sarah
56 Gen. 18:9-14
fathered Isaac
59 Gen. 21:1-7
sent Hagar away at Sarah's request
59 Gen. 21:8-14
tested by God concerning Isaac
60 Gen. 22; *1211* Heb. 11:17-19;
1219 Jas. 2:21-24
buried with Sarah at Machpelah
61 Gen. 23; **64** Gen. 25:7-11
God's covenant with him was the basis of future blessings
93 Exod. 2:24; **153** Lev. 26:42;
369 2 Kings 13:23; **555** Ps. 105:6-11;
1033 Acts 3:25
Also see *People and Places*.

Abstinence
from sexual immorality
1102 1 Cor. 6:18-20; *1140* Gal. 5:19-21;
1148 Eph. 5:3-5; *1171* 1 Thess. 4:3-5;
1277 Rev. 22:14-15

Adoption
465 Esth. 2:7,15; *1038* Acts 7:21;
1081 Rom. 8:15,23; *1138* Gal. 4:5;
1144 Eph. 1:5

Alcohol
beer cautioned against
594 Prov. 20:1; **603** Prov. 31:4,6
some idolize beer
622 Isa. 5:11,22; **838** Mic. 2:11
wine cautioned against
594 Prov. 20:1; *1149* Eph. 5:18
Nazirites abstain from
161 Num. 6; **258** Judg. 13:7; **823** Amos 2:12
church overseers not addicted
1181 1 Tim. 3:3; *1193* Titus 1:7
Timothy encouraged to use a little
1184 1 Tim. 5:23

Alien
61 Gen. 23:4; **67** Gen. 28:4; **686** Jer. 7:6;
1037 Acts 7:6; *1227* 1 Pet. 2:11

Angels
are ministering spirits
535 Ps. 68:17; *978* Luke 16:22;
1046 Acts 12:7-11; *1066* Acts 27:23;
1200 Heb. 1:7,14
not to be worshiped
1164 Col. 2:18; *1273* Rev. 19:10;
1277 Rev. 22:8-9
know and delight in the gospel
1182 1 Tim. 3:16; *1225* 1 Pet. 1:12
rejoice over every repentant sinner
976 Luke 15:7,10
will attend Christ at His second coming
896 Matt. 16:27; *909* Matt. 25:31;
931 Mark 8:38; *1175* 2 Thess. 1:7

Anger
be slow to
590 Prov. 15:18; **591** Prov. 16:32;
593 Prov. 19:11; *1193* Titus 1:7;
1217 Jas. 1:19
characteristic of fools
587 Prov. 12:16; **589** Prov. 14:29;
599 Prov. 27:3
children should not be stirred up to
1150 Eph. 6:4; *1165* Col. 3:21
pray without
1181 1 Tim. 2:8
a work of sinful nature
1140 Gal. 5:20

Antichrist
1242 1 John 2:18,22; *1244* 1 John 4:3;
1248 2 John 7

Anxiety
the cure for
882 Matt. 6:25-34; *1157* Phil. 2:28;
1231 1 Pet. 5:7
prevented
568 Ps. 121:4; *1231* 1 Pet. 5:7

Apostle
886 Matt. 10:2; *922* Mark 3:14;
1030 Acts 1:26; *1109* 1 Cor. 12:28;
1112 1 Cor. 15:9; *1146* Eph. 2:20;
1147 Eph. 4:11; *1201* Heb. 3:1;
1276 Rev. 21:14

Appearance
can be deceiving
906 Matt. 23:27-28
do not judge by
1218 Jas. 2:2-4
inner versus outward
286 1 Sam. 16:7; *1228* 1 Pet. 3:1-6

Arabs
429 2 Chron. 26:7; **452** Neh. 2:19;
454 Neh. 6:1; *1030* Acts 2:11

Ark of the Covenant
113 Exod. 25; **276** 1 Sam. 4:11;
335 1 Kings 8:9,21; *1266* Rev. 11:19

Ark, Noah's
49 Gen. 6:14; *907* Matt. 24:38;
1211 Heb. 11:7; *1229* 1 Pet. 3:20

Assurance
eternal life
1082 Rom. 8:28-39; *1169* 1 Thess. 1:5;
1245 1 John 5:13

Azazel
143 Lev. 16:8,10,26

B

Babylon
Mesopotamian city
52 Gen. 11:9; 635 Isa. 21:9
place of captivity
380 2 Kings 24; 441 Ezra 1:11; 572 Ps. 137:1;
703 Jer. 25:11; *792* Dan. 1:1-6
symbolic name of Rome
1231 1 Pet. 5:13
symbol of wickedness
1268 Rev. 14:8; *1270* Rev. 17:5
Also see *People and Places*.

Baptism
Jesus was baptized
877 Matt. 3:13-16
believers were baptized at Pentecost
1032 Acts 2:41
the Ethiopian eunuch
1041 Acts 8:36
Paul was baptized
1042 Acts 9:18
a sign of repentance and sins forgiven
919 Mark 1:4
shows identification with Jesus Christ
1078 Rom. 6:3-8; *1164* Col. 2:12
a command for all believers
916 Matt. 28:18-20

Beatitudes
879 Matt. 5:3-12; *959* Luke 6:20-23

Beer
see **Alcohol**

Bible
inspired by God
1190 2 Tim. 3:14-17
inspired by the Holy Spirit
1029 Acts 1:16; *1235* 2 Pet. 1:21
points to Christ
1002 John 5:39; *1056* Acts 18:28
learn about salvation from
1190 2 Tim. 3:15
an unerring guide
1235 2 Pet. 1:19
sharp as a sword
1151 Eph. 6:17; *1203* Heb. 4:12
hearing is not enough
1217 Jas. 1:22
received message, not from men, but from God
1170 1 Thess. 2:13
everything should be tested against
626 Isa. 8:20; *1054* Acts 17:11
warning against those who add to or take from
196 Deut. 4:2; *1277* Rev. 22:18-19

Blasphemy
664 Isa. 52:5; *890* Matt. 12:31; *921* Mark 2:7;
1074 Rom. 2:24

Bless
44 Gen. 1:22; 52 Gen. 12:2; 66 Gen. 27:34;
109 Exod. 20:11; 162 Num. 6:24;
202 Deut. 11:26; 211 Deut. 23:5;
563 Ps. 118:26; 596 Prov. 22:9;
604 Prov. 31:28; 776 Ezek. 34:26;
879 Matt. 5:3; *902* Matt. 21:9;
911 Matt. 26:26; *928* Mark 6:41;
934 Mark 10:16; *959* Luke 6:28;
1033 Acts 3:25; *1087* Rom. 12:14;
1144 Eph. 1:3

Blind
95 Exod. 4:11; 490 Job 29:15; 576 Ps. 146:8;
647 Isa. 35:5; *888* Matt. 11:5; *959* Luke 6:39;
1009 John 9:25; *1259* Rev. 3:17

Blood
50 Gen. 9:6; 113 Exod. 24:8; 144 Lev. 17:11;
191 Num. 35:33; *1051* Acts 15:20;
1208 Heb. 9:22

Blood of Christ
911 Matt. 26:28; *1004* John 6:53-56;
1075 Rom. 3:25; *1077* Rom. 5:9;
1106 1 Cor. 10:16; *1108* 1 Cor. 11:25;
1144 Eph. 1:7; *1145* Eph. 2:13;
1162 Col. 1:20; *1208* Heb. 9:12;
1225 1 Pet. 1:19; *1240* 1 John 1:7;
1256 Rev. 1:5; *1260* Rev. 5:9; *1262* Rev. 7:14;
1266 Rev. 12:11; *1274* Rev. 19:13

Body
is the temple of Holy Spirit
1102 1 Cor. 6:19
will be resurrected
1112 1 Cor. 15:12-58
Also see People and Places.

Boldness
600 Prov. 28:1; *1035* Acts 4:31;
1127 2 Cor. 10:1; *1147* Eph. 3:12;
1151 Eph. 6:19-20; *1203* Heb. 4:16

Branch
623 Isa. 4:2; 629 Isa. 11:1; 701 Jer. 23:5;
860 Zech. 3:8; 861 Zech. 6:12;
1018 John 15:5; *1086* Rom. 11:16;
1086 Rom. 11:17

Bread
114 Exod. 25:30; 199 Deut. 8:3; 458 Neh.
9:15; *878* Matt. 4:4; *882* Matt. 6:11;
911 Matt. 26:26; *1003* John 6:35;
1108 1 Cor. 11:23

Breath
45 Gen. 2:7; 477 Job 7:7; 778 Ezek. 37:10;
1055 Acts 17:25

Bribery
112 Exod. 23:8; 202 Deut. 10:17;
590 Prov. 15:27; 609 Eccl. 7:7

C

Celibacy
Jesus' teaching concerning
900 Matt. 19:10-12
Paul's teaching concerning
1102 1 Cor. 7:1-9,25-26,32-39
wrongly insisted on
1182 1 Tim. 4:1-3

Cherubim
46 Gen. 3:24; *113* Exod. 25:18-20;
322 2 Sam. 22:11; *333* 1 Kings 6:23;
543 Ps. 80:1; *751* Ezek. 10; *1208* Heb. 9:5

Chief Priest
381 2 Kings 25:18; *423* 2 Chron. 19:11;
911 Matt. 26:14; *931* Mark 8:31;
943 Mark 15:11
see also **High Priest**

Children
Christ taught
934 Mark 10:13-16
gifts from God
72 Gen. 33:5; *569* Ps. 127:3
should honor the aged
146 Lev. 19:32; *1231* 1 Pet. 5:5
should obey parents
109 Exod. 20:12; *583* Prov. 6:20;
1150 Eph. 6:1
should take care of parents
1183 1 Tim. 5:4
should be treated with respect
1150 Eph. 6:4

Christian
1046 Acts 11:26; *1065* Acts 26:28;
1230 1 Pet. 4:16

Church
Christ will build
896 Matt. 16:18
commission of
916 Matt. 28:18-20
is the bride of Christ
1273 Rev. 19:7-8
Christ is the head
1162 Col. 1:18
is like a body
1108 1 Cor. 12:12-13

Circumcision
56 Gen. 17:10; *59* Gen. 21:4;
202 Deut. 10:16; *950* Luke 1:59;
1005 John 7:22; *1050* Acts 15:1;
1074 Rom. 2:29; *1139* Gal. 5:2,11;
1141 Gal. 6:15; *1157* Phil. 3:3-5;
1164 Col. 2:11

Citizenship
1061 Acts 22:25-29; *1158* Phil. 3:20

Coming
advent of Jesus the Messiah
563 Ps. 118:26; *626* Isa. 9:1-7;
869 Mal. 3:1-3; *888* Matt. 11:3;
902 Matt. 21:9

return of Jesus the Lord
906 Matt. 24:3; *1029* Acts 1:11;
1171 1 Thess. 4:13-18; *1175* 2 Thess. 2:1;
1222 Jas. 5:7; *1236* 2 Pet. 3:4;
1277 Rev. 22:20

Commandments
given to Moses
109 Exod. 20; *123* Exod. 34:28;
196 Deut. 4:13; *510* Ps. 19:8;
566 Ps. 119:127
mentioned in the NT
879 Matt. 5:17-20; *900* Matt. 19:18;
1017 John 14:15; *1080* Rom. 7:12;
1150 Eph. 6:2; *1241* 1 John 2:3-6;
1268 Rev. 14:12
summarized in love
905 Matt. 22:34-40; *1088* Rom. 13:9
a new commandment
1016 John 13:34; *1241* 1 John 2:7-10

Commission
218 Deut. 31:23; *916* Matt. 28:16-20

Confession
of sin
132 Lev. 5:5; *143* Lev. 16:21; *152* Lev. 26:40;
160 Num. 5:7; *451* Neh. 1:6; *517* Ps. 32:5;
521 Ps. 38:18; *1222* Jas. 5:16;
1240 1 John 1:9
of faith
1085 Rom. 10:9; *1156* Phil. 2:11;
1185 1 Tim. 6:12; *1203* Heb. 4:14;
1242 1 John 2:23; *1244* 1 John 4:2

Conscience
507 Ps. 16:7; *1063* Acts 24:16;
1073 Rom. 2:15; *1088* Rom. 13:5;
1104 1 Cor. 8:7; *1182* 1 Tim. 4:2;
1208 Heb. 9:14; *1210* Heb. 10:22;
1229 1 Pet. 3:16

Contentment
with wages and possessions
953 Luke 3:14; *1159* Phil. 4:11;
1214 Heb. 13:5
with food and clothing
1185 1 Tim. 6:8
with godliness is great gain
520 Ps. 37:16; *1185* 1 Tim. 6:6

Cornerstone
563 Ps. 118:22; *641* Isa. 28:16;
863 Zech. 10:4; *904* Matt. 21:42;
1034 Acts 4:11; *1146* Eph. 2:20;
1226 1 Pet. 2:6

Counselor
627 Isa. 9:6; *1017* John 14:16,26;
1018 John 15:26; *1018* John 16:7

Covenant
with Noah
49 Gen. 6:18; *50* Gen. 9:9
with the patriarchs
55 Gen. 15:18; *93* Exod. 2:24;
153 Lev. 26:42; *369* 2 Kings 13:23;

397 1 Chron. 16:14-18; *1033* Acts 3:25; *1038* Acts 7:8; *1137* Gal. 3:16-17

with Phinehas
181 Num. 25:12-13

with David
306 2 Sam. 7

with the people of Israel
108 Exod. 19:5; **113** Exod. 24:8; **123** Exod. 34:27; **196** Deut. 4:23; **216** Deut. 29:1; **247** Judg. 2:1; **378** 2 Kings 23:2; **554** Ps. 103:18; *1083* Rom. 9:4; *1120* 2 Cor. 3:14; *1145* Eph. 2:12; *1207* Heb. 9:1,18

new covenant in Christ
671 Isa. 61:8; **711** Jer. 31:31; **757** Ezek. 16:60; **869** Mal. 3:1; *987* Luke 22:20; *1086* Rom. 11:27; *1108* 1 Cor. 11:25; *1120* 2 Cor. 3:6; *1139* Gal. 4:21-31; *1206* Heb. 7:22; *1208* Heb. 9:15

other
448 Ezra 10:3; **491** Job 31:1

Creation
44 Gen. 1–2; **54** Gen. 14:22; **528** Ps. 51:10; **573** Ps. 139:13; **577** Ps. 148:5; **612** Eccl. 12:1; **653** Isa. 42:5; *995* John 1:3; *1072* Rom. 1:25; *1081* Rom. 8:19; *1122* 2 Cor. 5:17; *1145* Eph. 2:10; *1162* Col. 1:16; *1230* 1 Pet. 4:19; *1260* Rev. 4:11

Cross
210 Deut. 21:23; *888* Matt. 10:38; *896* Matt. 16:24; *914* Matt. 27:31-50; *965* Luke 9:23; *1096* 1 Cor. 1:17-18; *1140* Gal. 5:11; *1141* Gal. 6:12,14; *1146* Eph. 2:16; *1155* Phil. 2:8; *1162* Col. 1:20; *1164* Col. 2:14; *1212* Heb. 12:2

Crowns
587 Prov. 12:4; **591** Prov. 16:31; **671** Isa. 61:3; *914* Matt. 27:29; *1105* 1 Cor. 9:25; *1158* Phil. 4:1; *1189* 2 Tim. 2:5; *1191* 2 Tim. 4:8; *1201* Heb. 2:7; *1217* Jas. 1:12; *1231* 1 Pet. 5:4; *1257* Rev. 2:10; *1260* Rev. 4:10; *1268* Rev. 14:14

Cursing
53 Gen. 12:3; **177** Num. 22:6; **202** Deut. 11:26; **210** Deut. 21:23; **214** Deut. 28:15; **559** Ps. 109:17; **599** Prov. 26:2; *937* Mark 11:21; *959* Luke 6:28; *1134* Gal. 1:8; *1137* Gal. 3:10,13; *1219* Jas. 3:10

D

Daniel
called Belteshazzar
792 Dan. 1:7

refused to eat the king's food
792 Dan. 1:8-20

interpreted the king's dreams
794 Dan. 3–4

interpreted writing on the wall
797 Dan. 5

thrown in the lion's den
798 Dan. 6

received visions
799 Dan. 7–12

Also see *People and Places*.

Darkness, Spiritual
322 2 Sam. 22:29; **626** Isa. 9:2; *882* Matt. 6:23; *995* John 1:5; *998* John 3:19; *1123* 2 Cor. 6:14; *1149* Eph. 5:8; *1227* 1 Pet. 2:9; *1240* 1 John 1:5; *1241* 1 John 2:9

David
son of Jesse, anointed by Samuel
271 Ruth 4:17-22; **286** 1 Sam. 16:1-13

sought God's heart
283 1 Sam. 13:14; *1048* Acts 13:22

killed Goliath
287 1 Sam. 17

friendship with Jonathan
289 1 Sam. 18:1-4; **290** 1 Sam. 19–20; **294** 1 Sam. 23:16-18

spared Saul's life
294 1 Sam. 24; **296** 1 Sam. 26

made king of Judah and Israel
302 2 Sam. 2:1-11; **305** 2 Sam. 5:1-4

conquered Jerusalem
305 2 Sam. 5:6-9

brought the ark there
306 2 Sam. 6

promised an eternal dynasty
306 2 Sam. 7

prepared for building the temple
401 1 Chron. 22–29

Psalmist, musician, and prophet
512 Ps. 23:1; *905* Matt. 22:43; *1029* Acts 1:16; *1034* Acts 4:25

adultery with Bathsheba
309 2 Sam. 11–12

family and political troubles:
—Amnon, Tamar, and Absalom
311 2 Sam. 13–18

—Sheba
320 2 Sam. 20

—military census
324 2 Sam. 24; **400** 1 Chron. 21

—Adonijah and Solomon
327 1 Kings 1–2

death
323 2 Sam. 23:1-7; **328** 1 Kings 2:10-12

ancestor of Jesus
875 Matt. 1:1,6

Jesus is heir to his throne forever
889 Matt. 12:23; *902* Matt. 21:9; *936* Mark 11:10; *949* Luke 1:32; *1277* Rev. 22:16

Also see *People and Places*.

Day of the Lord
621 Isa. 2:10-22; **630** Isa. 13:6,9; **750** Ezek. 7:19; **753** Ezek. 13:5; **817** Joel 1:15; **817** Joel 2:1-11,31;

along with prayer, when seeking God's grace
278 1 Sam. 7:5-6; **451** Neh. 1:4;
801 Dan. 9:3; *1047* Acts 13:3;
1050 Acts 14:23

wrong way and right way compared
668 Isa. 58:3-12; **861** Zech. 7:5-10;
882 Matt. 6:16-18

Father

God in heaven
881 Matt. 6:9; **905** Matt. 23:9

duties of godly
198 Deut. 6:6-7; *1150* Eph. 6:4

to be honored
109 Exod. 20:12; **597** Prov. 23:22;
1150 Eph. 6:2; *1165* Col. 3:17

Fear

of God, advantages of
585 Prov. 9:10; **590** Prov. 15:16;
593 Prov. 19:23; *1124* 2 Cor. 7:1

godly are delivered from
514 Ps. 27:1; **579** Prov. 1:33;
1245 1 John 4:16-18

Festivals

Sabbath and New Moon
402 1 Chron. 23:31; **410** 2 Chron. 2:4;
416 2 Chron. 8:13; **620** Isa. 1:13-14;
676 Isa. 66:23; **807** Hos. 2:11; **827** Amos 8:5;
1164 Col. 2:16

Unleavened Bread (Passover)
101 Exod. 12; **148** Lev. 23:5;
432 2 Chron. 30; **445** Ezra 6:22;
911 Matt. 26:17; **940** Mark 14:1,12;
986 Luke 22:1,7; *1046* Acts 12:3;
1058 Acts 20:6

Weeks (Pentecost, Harvest, Firstfruits)
112 Exod. 23:16; **122** Exod. 34:22;
149 Lev. 23:15-17; **184** Num. 28:26;
206 Deut. 16:10,13-16; **416** 2 Chron. 8:13;
1030 Acts 2:1-4

Booths (Tabernacles, Ingathering)
112 Exod. 23:16; **122** Exod. 34:22;
149 Lev. 23:36,41; **206** Deut. 16:13-14;
416 2 Chron. 8:13; **442** Ezra 3:4;
787 Ezek. 45:25; **865** Zech. 14:16;
1004 John 7:2

Trumpets (Rosh Hashanah)
149 Lev. 23:24; **184** Num. 29:1

Purim
470 Esth. 9:17-32

Dedication (Hanukkah, Lights)
1010 John 10:22

Flattery

beware of
503 Ps. 5:9; **506** Ps. 12:3; **601** Prov. 29:5;
1092 Rom. 16:18; *1253* Jude 16

Forgiveness

of sins, from God
122 Exod. 34:6-7; **554** Ps. 103:1-4;
802 Dan. 9:9

of sins, through Christ
1034 Acts 4:11-12; *1241* 1 John 2:12

of each other
882 Matt. 6:14-15; **899** Matt. 18:21-35;
937 Mark 11:25

Friends

constancy of
592 Prov. 17:17; **593** Prov. 18:24

David and Jonathan
289 1 Sam. 18:1-4; **291** 1 Sam. 20:1-29

Jesus called His disciples
1018 John 15:13-15

Fullness of God

995 John 1:16; *1145* Eph. 1:23;
1147 Eph. 3:19; *1162* Col. 1:19;
1164 Col. 2:9

G

Genealogy

47 Gen. 5; **51** Gen. 10; **52** Gen. 11:10-30;
64 Gen. 25:12-19; **74** Gen. 36;
271 Ruth 4:18-22; **383** 1 Chron. 1–9;
875 Matt. 1:1-17; **954** Luke 3:23-38;
1180 1 Tim. 1:4; *1205* Heb. 7:3

Gift

593 Prov. 18:16; **880** Matt. 5:24;
883 Matt. 7:11; **929** Mark 7:11;
1032 Acts 2:38; *1079* Rom. 6:23;
1087 Rom. 12:6; *1102* 1 Cor. 7:7;
1108 1 Cor. 12:4; *1127* 2 Cor. 9:15;
1217 Jas. 1:17

Giving

blessings connected with
522 Ps. 41:1; **596** Prov. 22:9;
601 Prov. 28:27; **611** Eccl. 11:1-2;
669 Isa. 58:10; *1059* Acts 20:35

encouraged
959 Luke 6:38; *1125* 2 Cor. 8:1-12

toward enemies
599 Prov. 25:21

God

is good
513 Ps. 25:8; **565** Ps. 119:68

unchanging
553 Ps. 102:26-27; *1217* Jas. 1:17

our Father
807 Hos. 1:10; **881** Matt. 6:9;
1081 Rom. 8:15

all powerful
712 Jer. 32:27; **949** Luke 1:37; *1256* Rev. 1:8

is spirit
1000 John 4:24

all knowing
666 Isa. 55:9; **793** Dan. 2:20;
1087 Rom. 11:33

is knowable
711 Jer. 31:34; *1145* Eph. 1:17

judges
505 Ps. 9:7; *1221* Jas. 4:12

is love
199 Deut. 7:8; **709** Jr 31:3; **813** Hos. 11:4;
1245 1 John 4:16

is kind
1073 Rom. 2:4

is holy
273 1 Sam. 2:2; **668** Isa. 57:15;
1225 1 Pet. 1:15-16
Also see *People and Places.*

Gospel
described
1112 1 Cor. 15:1-4
brings peace
951 Luke 2:10-14
veiled to the lost
1121 2 Cor. 4:3
there is only one
1134 Gal. 1:8
must be believed
919 Mark 1:15; *1202* Heb. 4:2
the power of God for salvation
1072 Rom. 1:16; *1096* 1 Cor. 1:18;
1169 1 Thess. 1:5
produces hope
1097 1 Cor. 1:23

Grace
came by Christ
995 John 1:17; *1077* Rom. 5:15
believers should grow in
1237 2 Pet. 3:18
God's work completed in believers by
1175 2 Thess. 1:11-12
justifies sinners
527 Ps. 51:1-12; *1076* Rom. 5:1-21
not to be abused
1074 Rom. 3:8; *1078* Rom. 6:1,15;
1252 Jude 4
salvation by
1050 Acts 15:11; *1145* Eph. 2:1-10;
1194 Titus 2:11

Greed
601 Prov. 28:22,25; *971* Luke 12:15;
1072 Rom. 1:29; *1100* 1 Cor. 5:9-11;
1101 1 Cor. 6:10; *1148* Eph. 5:3,5;
1165 Col. 3:5; *1181* 1 Tim. 3:3,8;
1193 Titus 1:7; *1235* 2 Pet. 2:3,14

H

Hate
embitters life
590 Prov. 15:17
of neighbors, prohibited
145 Lev. 19:17; *1243* 1 John 3:15
of evil, condoned
552 Ps. 97:10; **565** Ps. 119:104;
573 Ps. 139:21; **584** Prov. 8:13
believers should expect
887 Matt. 10:22; *1018* John 15:18-19
return good for
881 Matt. 5:44

Healing
comes from God
105 Exod. 15:26; **554** Ps. 103:3
proof that Jesus is the Messiah
888 Matt. 11:5
son of a royal official
1001 John 4:46-54

Heaven
believers rewarded in
674 Isa. 65:17-25; *879* Matt. 5:12;
1225 1 Pet. 1:4; *1275* Rev. 21:1-7
Jesus entered
1033 Acts 3:21; *1205* Heb. 6:20
God's dwelling place
506 Ps. 11:4; **561** Ps. 115:3; **675** Isa. 66:1;
881 Matt. 6:9
believers names are written in
967 Luke 10:20; *1213* Heb. 12:23
wicked are excluded from
1140 Gal. 5:21; *1148* Eph. 5:5;
1277 Rev. 22:15

Hell
the beast, false prophet, and the Devil thrown into
1274 Rev. 19:20; *1275* Rev. 20:10
body suffers in
880 Matt. 5:29; *887* Matt. 10:28
described as everlasting fire
621 Isa. 1:28-31; **676** Isa. 66:24;
877 Mt 3:12; *910* Mt 25:41,46
destruction, away from God's presence
1175 2 Thess. 1:9
strive to keep others from
898 Matt. 18:14; *1253* Jude 23

High Priest
147 Lev. 21:10-15; **190** Num. 35:25,28,32;
452 Neh. 3:1; **856** Hag 1:1,12,14;
860 Zech. 3:1; *912* Matt. 26:57-66;
1013 John 11:49-51; *1036* Acts 5:17;
1063 Acts 24:1; *1201* Heb. 2:17;
1206 Heb. 7:26; *1208* Heb. 9:7,25

Holy Spirit
believers receive
1242 1 John 2:20
guides into all truth
643 Isa. 30:21; **778** Ezek. 36:27;
1018 John 16:13; *1242* 1 John 2:27
baptism of, through Christ
1194 Titus 3:6
communicates joy
1090 Rom. 14:17; *1141* Gal. 5:22;
1169 1 Thess. 1:6
given by the Father
458 Neh. 9:20; **778** Ezek. 36:27;
819 Joel 2:28; *1017* John 14:15-18
gives the new birth
998 John 3:5-6
called God
1035 Acts 5:3-4
convinces of sin
459 Neh. 9:30; **838** Mic. 3:8;
1018 John 16:8-11
lives in believers
670 Isa. 59:21; **856** Hag. 2:5;
1017 John 14:16-17; *1099* 1 Cor. 3:16;
1102 1 Cor. 6:19; *1149* Eph. 5:18;
1230 1 Pet. 4:14
blasphemy against is unpardonable
861 Zech. 7:12-13; *890* Matt. 12:31-32;
1246 1 John 5:16

man's for Christ
1008 John 8:42; *1017* John 14:23;
1026 John 21:15-17; *1151* Eph. 6:24;
1197 Philem. 5
commanded
202 Deut. 11:13; *938* Mark 12:31;
1016 John 13:34; *1018* John 15:12,17;
1088 Rom. 13:9; *1243* 1 John 3:23;
1245 1 John 4:21; *1248* 2 John 5
marks the child of God
1016 John 13:35; *1242* 1 John 2:15;
1244 1 Jn 4:7
covers sin
585 Prov. 10:12
described
1109 1 Cor. 13:4-7
fulfills the law
1088 Rom. 13:8; *1140* Gal. 5:6

Loyalty
199 Deut. 7:9; 235 Josh. 14:8-9;
283 1 Sam. 13:14; 323 2 Sam. 22:51;
506 Ps. 12:1; 516 Ps. 31:23;
541 Ps. 78:8; 579 Prov. 2:8; 580 Prov. 3:3;
681 Jer. 3:15; 810 Hos. 6:6

Lust
must be controlled by God
1089 Rom. 13:14; *1140* Gal. 5:17
same as committing adultery
491 Job 31:1; *880* Matt. 5:27-28
leads to trouble
309 2 Sam. 11:2-5; 582 Prov. 5:3-5;
583 Prov. 6:25-35; *1242* 1 John 2:16-17
results in perverted sexual behavior
311 2 Sam. 13:1-18; *1072* Rom. 1:26-27

Lying
a characteristic of unbelief
1170 1 Thess. 2:9; *1182* 1 Tim. 4:2;
1241 1 John 2:4
God does not
179 Num. 23:19
the Devil is the father of
1008 John 8:44
forbidden
145 Lev. 19:11; 588 Prov. 12:22;
859 Zech. 1:16; *1165* Col. 3:9
punished
1035 Acts 5:1-5; *1275* Rev. 21:8

M

Male and Female
equally saved in Christ
1138 Gal. 3:28
mutual love
1102 1 Cor. 7:3-4; *1165* Col. 3:19;
1194 Titus 2:4
different roles
46 Gen. 3:16-19; *1112* 1 Cor. 14:34-35;
1149 Eph. 5:22-33; *1165* Col. 3:18-19;
1181 1 Tim. 2:11; *1194* Titus 2:2-5;
1228 1 Pet. 3:1-7

Mankind
made in God's image
44 Gen. 1:26-27; *1219* Jas. 3:9

more valuable than animals
44 Gen. 1:28; 50 Gen. 9:3-6; 504 Ps. 8:4-8;
887 Matt. 10:31; *889* Matt. 12:11-12
all have sinned
507 Ps. 14:1-3; *1075* Rom. 3:23
object of God's love
998 John 3:16

Manna
107 Exod. 16:31; 167 Num. 11:7;
227 Josh. 5:12; *1003* John 6:31,49

Manslaughter
197 Deut. 4:42; 240 Josh. 21:13-38

Marriage
Jesus blesses
997 John 2:1-11
honorable for all
1182 1 Tim. 4:3; *1214* Heb. 13:4
should be permanent
869 Mal. 2:14; *900* Matt. 19:6;
1103 1 Cor. 7:39
illustrates Christ and the church
1149 Eph. 5:22-32

Mary
1. mother of Jesus
875 Matt. 1:16; *948* Luke 1:26-56;
950 Luke 2:1-20,34-35
present at the cross
1023 John 19:25-27
among the believers
1029 Acts 1:14
2. Magdalene; delivered from demons
962 Luke 8:2
follower and supporter of Jesus
945 Mark 15:40-41
witness to the crucifixion and resurrection
915 Matt. 27:54-28:10; *945* Mark 16:1-10;
991 Luke 24:10; *1023* John 19:25-20:18
3. mother of James and Joseph/Joses; follower of
Jesus
945 Mark 15:40-41
witness to the crucifixion and resurrection
915 Matt. 27:54-28:10; *945* Mark 16:1-8;
991 Luke 24:10
4. sister of Martha and Lazarus
1011 John 11
anointed Jesus' feet
1013 John 12:1-3
Also see *People and Places.*

Maturity
1098 1 Cor. 2:6; *1157* Phil. 3:15;
1204 Heb. 5:14; *1204* Heb. 6:1

Mediator
1137 Gal. 3:19; *1181* 1 Tim. 2:5;
1206 Heb. 8:6

Meditation
502 Ps. 1:2; 510 Ps. 19:14;
563 Ps. 119:15,97; *951* Luke 2:19

Mercy
643 Isa. 30:18; 741 Lam. 3:22; 849 Hab. 3:2;
879 Matt. 5:7; *886* Matt. 9:13;
906 Matt. 23:23; *959* Luke 6:36;

1083 Rom. 9:15; *1087* Rom. 12:1;
1118 2 Cor. 1:3; *1145* Eph. 2:4;
1201 Heb. 2:17; *1218* Jas. 2:13;
1222 Jas. 5:11

Mind
love God with
905 Matt. 22:36-40
renewed, key to spirituality
1087 Rom. 12:2; *1148* Eph. 4:23
to be prepared before taking action
1225 1 Pet. 1:13
God puts law in believer's
1207 Heb. 8:10
have a sound
1188 2 Tim. 1:7
use while praying or singing
1111 1 Cor. 14:15-16

Ministry
397 1 Chron. 16:4; 671 Isa. 61:6;
1037 Acts 6:4; *1091* Rom. 15:16;
1122 2 Cor. 5:18; *1123* 2 Cor. 6:4;
1147 Eph. 4:12; *1191* 2 Tim. 4:5;
1206 Heb. 8:2,6

Miracles
purpose is to encourage belief
94 Exod. 4:1-5; *945* Mark 16:20;
1025 John 20:30-31
insufficient to produce conversion
556 Ps. 106:7; *978* Luke 16:31
Jesus proved to be the Messiah by
888 Matt. 11:4-6; *960* Luke 7:20-22;
1002 John 5:36
performed by false prophets
97 Exod. 7:12; 204 Deut. 13:1-3;
907 Matt. 24:24; *1176* 2 Thess. 2:9;
1274 Rev. 19:20

Miracles of Jesus
turning water into wine
997 John 2:1
cleansing a leper
884 Matt. 8:1-4; *920* Mark 1:40-45;
957 Luke 5:12-16
healing a centurion's slave
884 Matt. 8:5-13; *960* Luke 7:1-10
healing Peter's mother-in-law
884 Matt. 8:14-15; *920* Mark 1:29-31;
956 Luke 4:38-39
calming the storm
885 Matt. 8:23-27; *924* Mark 4:35-41;
962 Luke 8:22-25
driving out demons near the tombs
885 Matt. 8:28-34; *925* Mark 5:1-20;
963 Luke 8:26-39
healing a paralytic
885 Matt. 9:1-8; *920* Mark 2:1-12;
957 Luke 5:17-26
healing a bleeding woman
886 Matt. 9:20-22; *926* Mark 5:25-34;
963 Luke 8:43-48
raising Jairus' daughter from death
886 Matt. 9:18-19,23-26;
925 Mark 5:21-24,35-43;
963 Luke 8:40-42,49-56

healing two blind men
886 Matt. 9:27-31
healing a demon-possessed mute
886 Matt. 9:32-34
healing a man with a paralyzed hand
889 Matt. 12:9-14; *922* Mark 3:1-6;
958 Luke 6:6-11
healing a demon-possessed blind mute
889 Matt. 12:22-37; *923* Mark 3:20-30;
969 Luke 11:14-23
feeding 5,000 people
893 Matt. 14:13-23; *928* Mark 6:30-46;
964 Luke 9:10-17; *1002* John 6:1-15
walking on the water
893 Matt. 14:22-33; *928* Mark 6:45-51;
1003 John 6:16-21
healing a Gentile mother's daughter
895 Matt. 15:21-28; *929* Mark 7:24-30
feeding 4,000 people
895 Matt. 15:32-39; *930* Mark 8:1-9
healing an epileptic boy
897 Matt. 17:14-29; *932* Mark 9:14-29;
965 Luke 9:37-43
cursing the fig tree
903 Matt. 21:18-22; *936* Mark 11:12-14
healing a demon-possessed man in the synagogue
919 Mark 1:21-28; *956* Luke 4:31-37
healing a deaf mute
930 Mark 7:31-37
healing a blind man at Bethsaida
930 Mark 8:22-26
healing the blind at Jericho
902 Matt. 20:29-34; *935* Mark 10:46-52;
981 Luke 18:35-43
a miraculous catch of fish
956 Luke 5:1-11
a widow's son raised to life
960 Luke 7:11-17
healing a disabled woman
973 Luke 13:10-17
healing a man with edema
974 Luke 14:1-6
healing 10 lepers
978 Luke 17:11-19
healing Malchus' ear
987 Luke 22:49-51
healing an official's son
1001 John 4:46-54
healing the lame man at Bethesda
1001 John 5:1-9
healing a man born blind
1008 John 9:1-12
raising Lazarus from the dead
1011 John 11:1-46
a second miraculous catch of fish
1025 John 21:1-14

Miracles, Other
by Moses
94 Exod. 4:3-7; 97 Exod. 7—11;
104 Exod. 14:21-31; 105 Exod. 15:25;
106 Exod. 16:13-15; 107 Exod. 17:6;
173 Num. 16:28-35; 175 Num. 20:11;
176 Num. 21:8-9
by Joshua
225 Josh. 3; 227 Josh. 6; 231 Josh. 10:12-14

third missionary journey
1056 Acts 19–20
farewell in Ephesus
1058 Acts 20:17-38
arrested at riot in Jerusalem
1060 Acts 21:26-36
testified before the Sanhedrin
1061 Acts 23:1-10
before governors Felix and Festus
1063 Acts 24:10-21; *1063* Acts 25:1-12
before King Agrippa
1064 Acts 26
appealed to Caesar
1064 Acts 25:11
shipwrecked on the way to Rome
1066 Acts 27
ministered in Malta, then Rome
1067 Acts 28
Also see *People and Places*.

Peace
takes the place of worry
1158 Phil. 4:6-7
believers have
546 Ps. 85:8; **639** Isa. 26:3; **665** Isa. 53:5;
1076 Rom. 5:1; *1017* John 14:27;
1162 Col. 1:19-20
believers will have forever
667 Isa. 57:2; **776** Ezek. 34:25
wicked do not know
660 Isa. 48:22; **669** Isa. 59:8; **685** Jer. 6:14;
1075 Rom. 3:17

Pentecost
1030 Acts 2:1; *1058* Acts 20:16;
1115 1 Cor. 16:8

Persecution
Christ's followers will have
896 Matt. 16:21-26; *1190* 2 Tim. 3:12
God will deliver from
795 Dan. 3:25,28; *1118* 2 Cor. 1:10;
1121 2 Cor. 4:9; *1190* 2 Tim. 3:11

Perseverance
1151 Eph. 6:18; *1183* 1 Tim. 4:16

Persistence
968 Luke 11:8; *1087* Rom. 12:12;
1191 2 Tim. 4:2

Perversion
145 Lev. 18:23; **219** Deut. 32:20;
264 Judg. 19:22; **477** Job 8:3;
1072 Rom. 1:27; *1156* Phil. 2:15

Peter
former fisherman
956 Luke 5:2-3
apostle
878 Matt. 4:18-20; *886* Matt. 10:2
AKA Simon, Simeon, Cephas
922 Mark 3:16; *996* John 1:42;
1050 Acts 15:14
married, lived in Capernaum
919 Mark 1:21,29-30
walked on water
894 Matt. 14:28-31

confessed Jesus as Messiah
896 Matt. 16:13-20; *931* Mk 8:27-30;
965 Luke 9:18-21
at transfiguration
897 Matt. 17:1-9; *931* Mark 9:2-8;
965 Luke 9:28-36; *1235* 2 Pet. 1:16-18
Jesus predicted he would deny Him
911 Matt. 26:31-35; *941* Mark 14:27-31;
987 Luke 22:31-34; *1016* John 13:36-38
denial
913 Matt. 26:69-75; *943* Mark 14:66-72;
988 Luke 22:54-62;
1021 John 18:15-18,25-27
restoration to "feed My sheep"
1026 John 21:15-19
spoke at Pentecost
1030 Acts 2:14-40
healed people
1032 Acts 3:1-10; *1035* Acts 5:15;
1043 Acts 9:34
raised Tabitha from the dead
1043 Acts 9:36-43
arrested and forbidden to preach
1033 Acts 4:1-31; *1036* Acts 5:17-41
saw vision: sent to Cornelius
1043 Acts 10
reported Gentile conversions
1045 Acts 11; *1050* Acts 15
confronted by Paul for inconsistency
1135 Gal. 2:11-14
imprisoned by Herod; freed by angel
1046 Acts 12:1-19
focused on Jewish evangelism
1135 Gal. 2:7
wrote two letters
1225 1 Pet. 1:1; *1234* 2 Pet. 1:1
Also see *People and Places*.

Pharisees
880 Matt. 5:20; *904* Matt. 22:15;
905 Matt. 23:13; *969* Luke 11:37;
980 Luke 18:10; *996* John 1:24;
1036 Acts 5:34; *1061* Acts 23:6;
1157 Phil. 3:5
Also see *People and Places*.

Philistines
people of Philistia
51 Gen. 10:14; **65** Gen. 26:1
Casluhim from Caphtor
51 Gen. 10:14; **724** Jer. 47:4; **828** Amos 9:7
enemies of:
Moses and Joshua
103 Exod. 13:17; **234** Josh. 13:2;
247 Judg. 3:1-3
Shamgar and Samson
248 Judg. 3:31; **258** Judg. 13–16
Samuel
275 1 Sam. 4–7
Saul
282 1 Sam. 13–14; **287** 1 Sam. 17;
294 1 Sam. 23:27-28; **298** 1 Sam. 28:5,15;
300 1 Sam. 31:1-6
David
287 1 Sam. 17:20-57; **289** 1 Sam. 18:20-27;
290 1 Sam. 19:8; **293** 1 Sam. 23:1-5;

Propitiation
1075 Rom. 3:25; *1201* Heb. 2:17;
1241 1 John 2:2; *1244* 1 John 4:10

Proselytes
906 Matt. 23:15; *1030* Acts 2:10

Prosperity
217 Deut. 30:15; *502* Ps. 1:3; *538* Ps. 73:3

Prostitutes
224 Josh. 2:1; 601 Prov. 29:3; 807 Hos. 1:2;
903 Matt. 21:31; *1101* 1 Cor. 6:15

Punishment
47 Gen. 4:13; 521 Ps. 38:1; 665 Isa. 53:5;
759 Ezek. 18:20; *910* Matt. 25:46;
1213 Heb. 12:6; *1245* 1 John 4:18

Purity
desired
528 Ps. 51:7; 563 Ps. 119:9; *879* Matt. 5:8
commanded
603 Prov. 31:3; *1089* Rom. 13:13;
1158 Phil. 4:8; *1165* Col. 3:5
persuasiveness of
1228 1 Pet. 3:1-2
impurity is punished
1099 1 Cor. 3:16-17; *1148* Eph. 5:5-6;
1214 Heb. 13:4

Q

Quarreling
175 Num. 20:3; 593 Prov. 18:18;
599 Prov. 26:17; *1096* 1 Cor. 1:11;
1181 1 Tim. 3:3; *1189* 2 Tim. 2:24;
1195 Titus 3:9

Quiet
512 Ps. 23:2; *1181* 1 Tim. 2:2;
1228 1 Pet. 3:4

R

Racism
rejected since all are from one man
51 Gen. 9:18-19; *1055* Acts 17:26
no racial distinction in the law
150 Lev. 24:22; 212 Deut. 24:17
no racial distinction in Christ
1138 Gal. 3:28-29; *1146* Eph. 2:19;
1260 Rev. 5:9-10

Ransom
526 Ps. 49:7; 647 Isa. 35:10; 663 Isa. 51:11;
709 Jer. 31:11; 815 Hos. 13:14;
902 Matt. 20:28; *1181* 1 Tim. 2:6

Rebellion
170 Num. 14:9; 285 1 Sam. 15:23;
502 Ps. 2:1; 527 Ps. 51:1; 541 Ps. 78:8;
602 Prov. 29:16; 620 Isa. 1:2;
897 Matt. 17:17

Reconciliation
880 Matt. 5:24; *1077* Rom. 5:11;
1086 Rom. 11:15; *1122* 2 Cor. 5:18,20;
1146 Eph. 2:16; *1162* Col. 1:20

Redemption
96 Exod. 6:6; 307 2 Sam. 7:23;
484 Job 19:25; 510 Ps. 19:14; 526 Ps. 49:7-9;
554 Ps. 103:4; 558 Ps. 107:2;
596 Prov. 23:11; 653 Isa. 41:14;
985 Luke 21:28; *1082* Rom. 8:23;
1137 Gal. 3:13; *1138* Gal. 4:5; *1144* Eph. 1:7;
1162 Col. 1:14; *1208* Heb. 9:12;
1260 Rev. 5:9

Refuge
190 Num. 35:6; 270 Ruth 2:12; 525 Ps. 46:1;
602 Prov. 30:5; *1205* Heb. 6:18

Remnant
376 2 Kings 19:31; 448 Ezra 9:8;
628 Isa. 10:21; 701 Jer. 23:3; *1084* Rom. 9:27

Renewal
512 Ps. 23:3; 528 Ps. 51:10; 554 Ps. 103:5;
652 Isa. 40:31; *1087* Rom. 12:2;
1121 2 Cor. 4:16; *1194* Titus 3:5

Repentance
given by God
1045 Acts 11:18; *1189* 2 Tim. 2:25
godly grief produces
448 Ezra 9:6-9; 710 Jer. 31:19;
864 Zech. 12:10; *1125* 2 Cor. 7:10
commanded
759 Ezek. 18:30-32; *919* Mark 1:15;
1055 Acts 17:30
results are changed attitudes and behavior
414 2 Chron. 6:26; *953* Luke 3:7-14;
1125 2 Cor. 7:11

Respect
145 Lev. 19:3; *1088* Rom. 13:7;
1150 Eph. 5:33; *1184* 1 Tim. 6:1;
1229 1 Pet. 3:16

Rest
45 Gen. 2:2; 119 Exod. 31:15; 551 Ps. 95:11;
685 Jer. 6:16; *889* Matt. 11:28; *1203* Heb. 4:9

Resurrection
OT doctrine of
484 Job 19:26; 508 Ps. 16:10; 526 Ps. 49:15;
639 Isa. 26:19; 805 Dan. 12:2;
815 Hos. 13:14
of Jesus, the historical event
915 Matt. 28:5-10
preached by the Apostles
1033 Acts 4:2
of the body
639 Isa. 26:19; *1114* 1 Cor. 15:42-45
first principle of the gospel
1112 1 Cor. 15:1-19

Revenge
law of
110 Exod. 21:23-25
prohibited
145 Lev. 19:18; *1087* Rom. 12:17-19;
1173 1 Thess. 5:15; *1228* 1 Pet. 3:9
alternatives to
594 Prov. 20:22; *880* Matt. 5:38-42;
1087 Rom. 12:14

Reverence
1194 Titus 2:3; *1213* Heb. 12:28;
1228 1 Pet. 3:2

Rewards
531 Ps. 58:11; **569** Ps. 127:3; **651** Isa. 40:10;
879 Matt. 5:12; **881** Matt. 6:2,5,16;
1099 1 Cor. 3:14; *1211* Heb. 11:6,26

Riches
temporal
596 Prov. 23:4; **601** Prov. 28:20;
608 Eccl. 4:8; **689** Jer. 9:23; **900** Matt. 19:23;
959 Luke 6:24; *1185* 1 Tim. 6:9;
410 2 Chron. 1:11; *1217* Jas. 1:10
eternal
580 Prov. 3:16; *1084* Rom. 9:23;
1087 Rom. 11:33; *1144* Eph. 1:7

Righteousness
our own does not save
1194 Titus 3:5
God gives
513 Ps. 24:5; **671** Isa. 61:10
given through Christ
1075 Rom. 3:21-26; *1157* Phil. 3:4-11

Rivalry
145 Lev. 18:18; **273** 1 Sam. 1:6;
1155 Phil. 1:17; *1155* Phil. 2:3

Ruler
God and Christ as
534 Ps. 66:7; **839** Mic. 5:2
Satan as
1014 John 12:31
spiritual
1082 Rom. 8:38; *1150* Eph. 6:12;
1113 1 Cor. 15:24
earthly
502 Ps. 2:2; **901** Matt. 20:25; *1194* Titus 3:1

S

Sabbath
109 Exod. 20:8; **119** Exod. 31:12-17;
148 Lev. 23:1-3; **889** Matt. 12:1;
922 Mark 2:27-28; *922* Mark 3:2,4;
1203 Heb. 4:9

Salt
58 Gen. 19:26; **130** Lev. 2:13;
174 Num. 18:19; **879** Matt. 5:13;
1166 Col. 4:6

Salvation
from God
502 Ps. 3:8; **658** Isa. 45:21-22; **681** Jer. 3:23
in Jesus alone
1034 Acts 4:11-12; *1085* Rom. 10:9
gospel is power of God for
1072 Rom. 1:16; *1096* 1 Cor. 1:21

Samaritans
373 2 Kings 17:24-34; *967* Luke 10:33;
979 Luke 17:16; *999* John 4:9

Also see *People and Places*.

Sanctification
1020 John 17:17; *1078* Rom. 6:19,22;
1101 1 Cor. 6:11; *1171* 1 Thess. 4:3;
1173 1 Thess. 5:23; *1176* 2 Thess. 2:13

Sanctuary
113 Exod. 25:8; **514** Ps. 28:2; **577** Ps. 150:1;
779 Ezek. 37:26; *997* John 2:19;
1099 1 Cor. 3:16; *1102* 1 Cor. 6:19;
1208 Heb. 9:24; *1276* Rev. 21:22

Satan
see **Devil**
Also see *People and Places*.

Savior
557 Ps. 106:21; **655** Isa. 43:11;
814 Hos. 13:4; *951* Luke 2:11;
1183 1 Tim. 4:10; *1188* 2 Tim. 1:10;
1194 Titus 2:13; *1237* 2 Pet. 3:18

Second Coming of Christ
Jesus predicted
909 Matt. 25:31; *1016* John 14:3
in same way as He ascended into heaven
800 Dan. 7:13; *1029* Acts 1:9-11
will complete salvation of believers
1209 Heb. 9:28
time of, unknown and sudden
907 Matt. 24:36,44; *940* Mark 13:32-37;
972 Luke 12:40; *1172* 1 Thess. 5:1-11;
1175 2 Thess. 1:3-12; *1236* 2 Pet. 3:10-13

Security
based on God not works
1075 Rom. 3:21-26; *1082* Rom. 8:29-39;
1136 Gal. 3:1-5; *1154* Phil. 1:6;
1176 2 Thess. 3:3
sealed by the Holy Spirit
1017 John 14:16-18,25-26;
1018 John 16:8-15; *1119* 2 Cor. 1:22
assumes genuine faith
1242 1 John 2:19
does not preclude perseverance
1105 1 Cor. 10:1-14; *1200* Heb. 2:1-3;
1202 Heb. 3:12-19; *1204* Heb. 6:1-8;
1210 Heb. 10:26-31; *1222* Jas. 5:19-20

Self-control
1102 1 Cor. 7:5; *1141* Gal. 5:23;
1193 Titus 1:8; *1234* 2 Pet. 1:6

Sense
583 Prov. 6:32; **586** Prov. 10:21;
590 Prov. 15:5; *908* Matt. 25:2

Sermon on the Mount
879 Matt. 5-7; *959* Luke 6:20-49

Serpent
45 Gen. 3:1; **887** Matt. 10:16;
1128 2 Cor. 11:3; *1266* Rev. 12:9

Servant
275 1 Sam. 3:10; **571** Ps. 135:1;
664 Isa. 52:13; **889** Matt. 12:18;
902 Matt. 20:26; *933* Mark 9:35;
1014 John 12:26

Service
552 Ps. 100:2; *902* Matt. 20:28;
987 Luke 22:27; *1087* Rom. 12:7;
1140 Gal. 5:13; *1150* Eph. 6:7

Sex
prohibited outside marriage
615 Songs 2:7; *1101* 1 Cor. 6:15-20
blessed within marriage
615 Songs 4:1–5:1; *1214* Heb. 13:4
not to be withheld in marriage
1102 1 Cor. 7:3-5
lust is sin
880 Matt. 5:28
see also **Abstinence; Homosexuality**

Shame
45 Gen. 2:25; *662* Isa. 49:23; *805* Dan. 12:2;
1072 Rom. 1:27; *1084* Rom. 9:33;
1097 1 Cor. 1:27; *1101* 1 Cor. 6:5;
1149 Eph. 5:12; *1158* Phil. 3:19;
1212 Heb. 12:2; *1226* 1 Pet. 2:6

Sheep
353 1 Kings 22:17; *552* Ps. 100:3;
665 Isa. 53:6; *665* Isa. 53:7; *865* Zech. 13:7;
886 Matt. 9:36; *887* Matt. 10:6;
898 Matt. 18:12; *909* Matt. 25:32;
1010 John 10:3,15,27; *1026* John 21:17;
1041 Acts 8:32

Shepherd
305 2 Sam. 5:2; *353* 1 Kings 22:17;
512 Ps. 23:1; *651* Isa. 40:11; *775* Ezek. 34:2;
776 Ezek. 34:23; *865* Zech. 13:7;
886 Matt. 9:36; *911* Matt. 26:31;
951 Luke 2:8; *1010* John 10:11;
1058 Acts 20:28; *1214* Heb. 13:20;
1231 1 Pet. 5:2,4

Signs
625 Isa. 7:14; *890* Matt. 12:39;
906 Matt. 24:3; *945* Mark 16:17;
951 Luke 2:12; *997* John 2:11;
1025 John 20:30; *1049* Acts 14:3;
1096 1 Cor. 1:22; *1111* 1 Cor. 14:22

Sin
begins in the mind
880 Matt. 5:27-28; *1217* Jas. 1:14-15
all have committed
1075 Rom. 3:23
confession of followed by forgiveness
311 2 Sam. 12:13; *517* Ps. 32:5;
1240 1 John 1:9
God helps believers resist
563 Ps. 119:11; *1106* 1 Cor. 10:13
Christ's blood removes
911 Matt. 26:28; *1144* Eph. 1:7;
1240 1 John 1:7

Singing
commanded
397 1 Chron. 16:9; *552* Ps. 100:2;
1149 Eph. 5:19; *1165* Col. 3:16;
1222 Jas. 5:13

from God
522 Ps. 40:3
see also **Worship**

Singleness
1102 1 Cor. 7:8-9,25-40

Slander
507 Ps. 15:3; *585* Prov. 10:18;
602 Prov. 30:10; *1072* Rom. 1:30;
1074 Rom. 3:8; *1100* 1 Cor. 4:13;
1182 1 Tim. 3:11; *1194* Titus 2:3;
1194 Titus 3:2; *1226* 1 Pet. 2:1

Slavery
103 Exod. 13:3; *197* Deut. 5:15;
596 Prov. 22:7; *882* Matt. 6:24;
902 Matt. 20:27; *909* Matt. 25:21;
978 Luke 17:10; *1008* John 8:34;
1018 John 15:15; *1078* Rom. 6:17;
1081 Rom. 8:15; *1138* Gal. 3:28;
1139 Gal. 5:1; *1155* Phil. 2:7;
1227 1 Pet. 2:16

Snake
94 Exod. 4:3; *176* Num. 21:9;
597 Prov. 23:32; *883* Matt. 7:10;
906 Matt. 23:33; *945* Mark 16:18;
967 Luke 10:19; *998* John 3:14

Snare
113 Exod. 23:33; *243* Josh. 23:13;
581 Prov. 3:26; *602* Prov. 29:25

Son of David
875 Matt. 1:1; *886* Matt. 9:27;
889 Matt. 12:23; *895* Matt. 15:22;
902 Matt. 20:30-31; *902* Matt. 21:9,15;
935 Mark 10:47-48; *939* Mark 12:35;
954 Luke 3:31; *981* Luke 18:38-39;
984 Luke 20:41

Son of God
878 Matt. 4:3,6; *885* Matt. 8:29;
894 Matt. 14:33; *912* Matt. 26:63;
914 Matt. 27:40; *919* Mark 1:1;
949 Luke 1:35; *954* Luke 3:38;
988 Luke 22:70; *996* John 1:34,49;
998 John 3:18; *1011* John 10:36;
1012 John 11:27; *1022* John 19:7;
1025 John 20:31; *1041* Acts 8:37;
1042 Acts 9:20; *1071* Rom. 1:4;
1118 2 Cor. 1:19; *1136* Gal. 2:20;
1203 Heb. 4:14; *1204* Heb. 6:6;
1205 Heb. 7:3; *1210* Heb. 10:29;
1245 1 John 4:15; *1245* 1 John 5:5,9-13;
1258 Rev. 2:18

Son of Man
179 Num. 23:19; *488* Job 25:6; *504* Ps. 8:4;
746 Ezek. 2:1; *800* Dan. 7:13;
885 Matt. 8:20; *907* Matt. 24:27,30;
909 Matt. 25:31; *913* Matt. 26:64;
996 John 1:51; *998* John 3:14;
1039 Acts 7:56; *1256* Rev. 1:13;
1268 Rev. 14:14

Sorcery

207 Deut. 18:10; *1047* Acts 13:8;
1140 Gal. 5:20; *1273* Rev. 18:23

Sorrow

606 Eccl. 1:18; 647 Isa. 35:10;
911 Matt. 26:38; *1019* John 16:20;
1083 Rom. 9:2

Spirit of God

44 Gen. 1:2; 286 1 Sam. 16:13; 671 Isa. 61:1;
878 Matt. 3:16; *955* Luke 4:18;
1120 2 Cor. 3:17

Spirit, Evil

255 Judg. 9:23; 286 1 Sam. 16:14-16,23;
289 1 Sam. 18:10; 290 1 Sam. 19:9;
960 Luke 7:21; *962* Luke 8:2;
1056 Acts 19:12-13,15-16

Spiritual

1087 Rom. 12:1; *1098* 1 Cor. 2:13,14;
1114 1 Cor. 15:44; *1141* Gal. 6:1;
1144 Eph. 1:3; *1149* Eph. 5:19;
1165 Col. 3:16; *1226* 1 Pet. 2:2

Spirit, Unclean

865 Zech. 13:2; *886* Matt. 10:1;
890 Matt. 12:43; *919* Mark 1:23;
922 Mark 3:11,30; *925* Mark 5:2;
927 Mark 6:7; *929* Mark 7:25;
932 Mark 9:25; *1035* Acts 5:16;
1040 Acts 8:7; *1270* Rev. 16:13;
1271 Rev. 18:2

Stealing

prohibited
109 Exod. 20:15
from the poor, specially forbidden
596 Prov. 22:22
do honest work instead
1148 Eph. 4:28

Strength

105 Exod. 15:2; 198 Deut. 6:5;
274 1 Sam. 2:9; 515 Ps. 28:7; 525 Ps. 46:1;
652 Isa. 40:31; 860 Zech. 4:6;
938 Mark 12:30; *987* Luke 22:32;
1159 Phil. 4:13; *1180* 1 Tim. 1:12;
1230 1 Pet. 4:11

Strife

591 Prov. 17:1; *1098* 1 Cor. 3:3;
1140 Gal. 5:20

Striving

972 Luke 12:29; *1163* Col. 1:29

Stumbling

567 Ps. 119:165; 581 Prov. 4:12;
978 Luke 17:2; *1011* John 11:9;
1090 Rom. 14:20; *1097* 1 Cor. 1:23;
1123 2 Cor. 6:3; *1219* Jas. 3:2; *1253* Jude 24

Submission

665 Isa. 53:12; *1088* Rom. 13:1;
1139 Gal. 5:1; *1149* Eph. 5:22;
1165 Col. 3:18; *1181* 1 Tim. 2:11;

1194 Titus 3:1; *1221* Jas. 4:7;
1227 1 Pet. 2:13; *1228* 1 Pet. 3:1

Success

224 Josh. 1:7; 429 2 Chron. 26:5;
452 Neh. 2:20; 579 Prov. 2:7;
611 Eccl. 10:10; 657 Isa. 45:7

Suffering

of Jesus
665 Isa. 53:3; *931* Mark 8:31;
986 Luke 22:15; *992* Luke 24:46;
1033 Acts 3:18; *1157* Phil. 3:10;
1204 Heb. 5:8; *1227* 1 Pet. 2:21;
1229 1 Pet. 3:18; *1230* 1 Pet. 4:13
of Christians
1081 Rom. 8:17,18; *1188* 2 Tim. 1:8;
1222 Jas. 5:13; *1227* 1 Pet. 2:20;
1229 1 Pet. 3:17; *1230* 1 Pet. 4:13

Sustain

502 Ps. 3:5; 529 Ps. 54:4; 627 Isa. 9:7;
1086 Rom. 11:18; *1200* Heb. 1:3

Swearing (an Oath)

God
61 Gen. 22:16; 551 Ps. 95:11;
570 Ps. 132:11; *1202* Heb. 3:11;
1204 Heb. 6:13; *1206* Heb. 7:21
people cautioned about
132 Lev. 5:4; *880* Matt. 5:36; *1222* Jas. 5:12

Synagogue

878 Matt. 4:23; *955* Luke 4:16;
1018 John 16:2; *1021* John 18:20;
1055 Acts 18:4; *1257* Rev. 2:9

T

Tabernacle

113 Exod. 25:8-9; 114 Exod. 26–27;
128 Exod. 40:34; 165 Num. 9:15-23;
306 2 Sam. 7:6; *897* Matt. 17:4;
1039 Acts 7:44; *1208* Heb. 9:11;
1269 Rev. 15:5

Tattoos

146 Lev. 19:28

Tax

904 Matt. 22:17; *1088* Rom. 13:7

Tax Collectors

881 Matt. 5:46; *888* Matt. 11:19;
898 Matt. 18:17; *903* Matt. 21:31;
980 Luke 18:10; *981* Luke 19:2

Teachers

887 Matt. 10:24; *905* Matt. 23:8;
998 John 3:10; *1109* 1 Cor. 12:28;
1147 Eph. 4:11; *1181* 1 Tim. 3:2; *1204*
Heb. 5:12; *1235* 2 Pet. 2:1

Tears

523 Ps. 42:3; 688 Jer. 9:1; *961* Luke 7:38;
1275 Rev. 21:4

Temper

1193 Titus 1:7

Temple
332 1 Kings 6–8; 381 2 Kings 25:13-15;
443 Ezra 3:8-11; 445 Ezra 6:6-10;
856 Hag. 1–2; 506 Ps. 11:4; 869 Mal. 3:1;
889 Matt. 12:6; 953 Luke 2:46
see also **Sanctuary**

Temptation
878 Matt. 4:1-11; 882 Matt. 6:13;
911 Matt. 26:41; 1102 1 Cor. 7:5;
1106 1 Cor. 10:13; 1203 Heb. 4:15;
1217 Jas. 1:13

Ten Commandments
109 Exod. 20; 197 Deut. 5

Tenth
54 Gen. 14:20; 869 Mal. 3:10;
906 Matt. 23:23; 980 Luke 18:12

Thankfulness
commanded
527 Ps. 50:14; 1158 Phil. 4:6
accompanies prayer
1158 Phil. 4:6; 1165 Col. 4:2
in all things
1149 Eph. 5:20; 1173 1 Thess. 5:18;
1182 1 Tim. 4:4-5

Thoughts
550 Ps. 94:11; 572 Ps. 139:2; 666 Isa. 55:8;
885 Matt. 9:4; 1127 2 Cor. 10:5

Time
a moment, occasion, or season
467 Esth. 4:14; 607 Eccl. 3:1;
911 Matt. 26:18; 1005 John 7:6;
1166 Col. 4:5
a period or term
800 Dan. 7:25; 805 Dan. 12:7; 1029 Acts 1:7;
1172 1 Thess. 5:1; 1266 Rev. 12:14

Tongues
see **Languages, Other**

Tradition
929 Mark 7:13; 1164 Col. 2:8;
1176 2 Thess. 2:15

Treachery
365 2 Kings 9:23; 503 Ps. 5:6;
680 Jer. 3:6-11; 868 Mal. 2:10-16;
910 Matt. 26:4

Treasure
563 Ps. 119:11; 882 Matt. 6:19-21;
892 Matt. 13:44; 900 Matt. 19:21;
1121 2 Cor. 4:7

Trinity
reference to
1081 Rom. 8:9; 1108 1 Cor. 12:3-6;
1147 Eph. 4:4-6; 1176 2 Thess. 2:13-14;
1194 Titus 3:4-6; 1225 1 Pet. 1:2;
1253 Jude 20-21
evident at Jesus' baptism
878 Matt. 3:16-17
to be baptized in the name of
916 Matt. 28:18-20

the apostolic benediction
1131 2 Cor. 13:13

Trust
in God
503 Ps. 4:5; 530 Ps. 56:3; 530 Ps. 56:4,11;
580 Prov. 3:5; 652 Isa. 40:31; 1201 Heb. 2:13
in God's Word
510 Ps. 19:7; 1181 1 Tim. 1:15;
1181 1 Tim. 3:1; 1183 1 Tim. 4:9
not in other things
587 Prov. 11:28

Truth
567 Ps. 119:160; 995 John 1:17;
1000 John 4:23; 1008 John 8:32;
1016 John 14:6; 1072 Rom. 1:25;
1147 Eph. 4:15; 1189 2 Tim. 2:15;
1240 1 John 1:8

Turning
away from God
507 Ps. 14:3; 665 Isa. 53:6
away from evil
774 Ezek. 33:11; 1065 Acts 26:18;
1222 Jas. 5:20
toward God
564 Ps. 119:36; 625 Isa. 6:10; 818 Joel 2:12

U

Unbelief
is sin
1018 John 16:8-11
believers should not partner with unbelievers
1123 2 Cor. 6:14-18
questions truthfulness of God
372 2 Kings 17:13-15; 557 Ps. 106:24;
1245 1 John 5:10

Unclean
624 Isa. 6:5; 886 Matt. 10:1;
1044 Acts 10:14; 1090 Rom. 14:14

Understand
579 Prov. 2:5; 580 Prov. 3:5; 891 Matt. 13:15;
992 Luke 24:45; 1075 Rom. 3:11;
1237 2 Pet. 3:16

Unity
1010 John 10:16; 1020 John 17:21-22;
1147 Eph. 4:13; 1165 Col. 3:14

Unrighteousness
550 Ps. 92:15; 881 Matt. 5:45;
977 Luke 16:10; 1240 1 John 1:9

V

Vegetarian Diet
44 Gen. 1:29; 50 Gen. 9:3; 792 Dan. 1:8-20;
1089 Rom. 14:2-3

Victory
595 Prov. 21:31; 1082 Rom. 8:37;
1114 1 Cor. 15:54-57; 1245 1 John 5:4;
1257 Rev. 2:7

Vineyard
900 Matt. 20:1; 903 Matt. 21:33;
1017 John 15:1

Violence

48 Gen. 6:11; 665 Isa. 53:9; 750 Ezek. 7:23;
888 Matt. 11:12

Virgin

625 Isa. 7:14; 876 Matt. 1:23;
908 Matt. 25:1; 948 Luke 1:27;
1103 1 Cor. 7:28

Visions

819 Joel 2:28; 1031 Acts 2:17;
1044 Acts 10:10; 1129 2 Cor. 12:1

Vowing

161 Num. 6:2; 257 Judg. 11:30;
512 Ps. 22:25; 594 Prov. 20:25; 608 Eccl. 5:4

W

War

105 Exod. 15:3; 199 Deut. 7:1-6;
525 Ps. 46:9; 607 Eccl. 3:8; 621 Isa. 2:4;
907 Matt. 24:6; 1127 2 Cor. 10:3-4;
1220 Jas. 4:1

Weakness

885 Matt. 8:17; 911 Matt. 26:41;
1082 Rom. 8:26; 1089 Rom. 14:1;
1097 1 Cor. 1:27; 1114 1 Cor. 15:43;
1130 2 Cor. 12:9-10; 1203 Heb. 4:15

Wealth

worldly

526 Ps. 49:6; 586 Prov. 11:4;
600 Prov. 27:24; 602 Prov. 30:8;
891 Matt. 13:22; 934 Mark 10:23

spiritual

1163 Col. 1:27

Weeping

515 Ps. 30:5; 572 Ps. 137:1; 607 Eccl. 3:4;
884 Matt. 8:12; 983 Luke 19:41;
1012 John 11:35; 1087 Rom. 12:15;
1275 Rev. 21:4

Widows

111 Exod. 22:22; 202 Deut. 10:18;
347 1 Kings 17:9; 534 Ps. 68:5; 620 Isa. 1:17;
686 Jer. 7:6; 861 Zech. 7:10;
939 Mark 12:40,42-43; 979 Luke 18:3-5;
1036 Acts 6:1; 1102 1 Cor. 7:8;
1183 1 Tim. 5:3; 1218 Jas. 1:27

Wife

Adam's, a helper like him

45 Gen. 2:18-23

a capable

603 Prov. 31:10-31

a blessing to her husband

587 Prov. 12:4; 603 Prov. 31:10,12

submissive to her husband

1107 1 Cor. 11:3-12; 1149 Eph. 5:22-33

win unbelieving husband by her life

1228 1 Pet. 3:1-2

Wine see Alcohol

Wisdom

332 1 Kings 4:29; 585 Prov. 9:1,10;
889 Matt. 11:25; 961 Luke 7:35;
1087 Rom. 11:33; 1096 1 Cor. 1:19,27;
1164 Col. 2:3; 1217 Jas. 1:5; 1260 Rev. 5:12

Work

believers should

585 Prov. 10:4; 588 Prov. 13:4,11;
1150 Eph. 6:5-8; 1176 2 Thess. 3:7-15

Worry

882 Matt. 6:25; 1158 Phil. 4:6

Worship

with fear and reverence

503 Ps. 5:7; 551 Ps. 96:9; 624 Isa. 6:1-7

with music

530 Ps. 57:7-8; 577 Ps. 150

with a new song

517 Ps. 33:3; 551 Ps. 96:1; 552 Ps. 98:1;
577 Ps. 149:1; 654 Isa. 42:10; 1260 Rev. 5:9;
1268 Rev. 14:3

with dance

306 2 Sam. 6:14-16; 577 Ps. 149:3

bowing down

408 1 Chron. 29:20; 551 Ps. 95:6;
876 Matt. 2:11

authentic

1000 John 4:19-26

Wrath

503 Ps. 6:1; 540 Ps. 76:10; 586 Prov. 11:4;
589 Prov. 15:1; 877 Matt. 3:7;
1072 Rom. 1:18; 1145 Eph. 2:3;
1261 Rev. 6:16

Y

Youth

examples of

274 1 Sam. 2:11; 287 1 Sam. 17:1-54

depending on God

513 Ps. 25:7; 563 Ps. 119:9

should be an example

1183 1 Tim. 4:12

Z

Zeal

376 2 Kings 19:31; 536 Ps. 69:9;
593 Prov. 19:2; 627 Isa. 9:7; 997 John 2:17;
1084 Rom. 10:2; 1157 Phil. 3:6

PEOPLE AND PLACES

A

Aaron—Levite, brother of Moses (Exod. 4:14; 6:16-20). Spokesman for Moses (4:14-16; 7:1-2). Consecrated (Exod. 29) and ordained (Lev. 8) as priest (Exod. 28:1; 1 Chron. 6:49; Heb. 5:1-4; 7). Made golden calf (Exod. 32). Died outside the promised land (Num. 20:1-12,22-29; 33:38-39).

Abaddon—The Hb name of the angel of the bottomless pit whose Gk name was Apollyon.

Your faithfulness in **A**? . . . . Ps. 88:11

Sheol and **A** lie open . . . . Prov. 15:11

his name in Hebrew is **A**, ... Rev. 9:11

Abel—Shepherd, second son of Adam; brought acceptable sacrifice; was murdered (Gen. 4:2-8; Matt. 23:35; Heb. 11:4).

Abraham—Born Abram son of Terah in Ur, Mesopotamia, then lived in Haran (Gen. 11:31; Acts 7:2-4). Called to Canaan and given a promise of progeny and prosperity (Gen. 12:1-3). God declared him righteous because of his faith (15:6; Rom. 4:3,20-22; Gal. 3:6; Jas. 2:23). Fathered Ishmael by Hagar (Gen. 16). Promised a son with Sarah (18:9-14; cp. 17:15-19; 21:1-7). Tested by God concerning Isaac (Gen. 22; Heb. 11:17-19; Jas. 2:21-24). John and Paul showed that salvation does not come from descent from Abraham, but from emulating his faith (Matt. 3:9; Rom. 4; 9; Gal. 3). Also see *Subject Index*.

Adam and Eve—First man and woman; created by God (Gen. 1:26-2:25). Their failure in the Garden of Eden resulted in the fall (Gen. 3). The corruption that permeates our world and our lives is the direct result of Adam's decision to disobey God (Rom. 5:14; 1 Cor. 15:22).

Ahab—The seventh king of Israel, he married a foreigner, Jezebel, and incited God's anger more than any of Israel's previous kings by serving other gods (1 Kings 20:13-14,22,28; 22:8, 16; Mic. 6:16).

Amos—Prophet from Judah who ministered in Israel about 750 B.C. (Amos 7:14-15). He opposed the moral and religious evils of his day (5:24).

Ananias—**1.** Husband of Sapphira (Acts 5:1-6). They sold property, lied to the Holy Spirit about the amount they were contributing, and were both struck dead (5:5,10). **2.** Disciple who lived in Damascus (9:10-19; 22:12). He laid his hands on Paul, and he received the Holy Spirit. **3.** Jewish high priest and president of the Sanhedrin that tried Paul in Jerusalem (Acts 23).

Andrew—A fisherman and one of Jesus' first apostles, he led his brother Simon to Jesus (John 1:40-41; 6:8-9; 12:12; Acts 1:13).

Apollos—Jewish Christian who used the Scriptures to demonstrate that Jesus was the Christ (Acts 18:28; cp. 1 Cor. 1:12; 3:4-6,22; 4:6; 16:12; Titus 3:13).

Aquila and Priscilla—Married couple of Corinth who assisted Paul in his ministry (Acts 18; Rom. 16:3; 1 Cor. 16:19; 2 Tim. 4:19).

Arabah—Desert region with a hot climate and sparse rainfall.

Armagedon—Site of future final battle between forces of good and evil (Rev. 16:16).

Asherah—Phoenician and Canaanite fertility goddess represented by a wooden pole.

Ashtaroth, Ashtoreths—A Canaanite goddess of fertility, love, and war (1 Sam. 31:10).

Assyria—Nation in northern Mesopotamia north of Babylonia along the banks of the upper Tigris River (Gen. 10:11; Isa. 10:5; Jer. 50:18). Nineveh became its capital. The Assyrians conquered Samaria in 721 B.C. (2 Kings 18:11).

B

Baal—Canaanite false god of thunderstorms and fertility (Num. 25:3; 1 Kings 18:19; 19:18; Jer. 2:8).

Babel—A tower and city intended to be a monument of human pride, where people sought to "make a name" for themselves (Gen. 11:4-9); it is also the Hb word for Babylon.

Babylon—City-state in southern Mesopotamia on the Euphrates River. One of the largest and most magnificent cities that ever existed. Babylon became symbolic of man's decadence and God's judgment. "Babylon" in Rev. 14:8; 16:19; 17:5; 18:2 and probably in 1 Pet. 5:13 refers to Rome, the city which personified this idea for early Christians. Also see *Subject Index*.

from a distant country, from **B**. 2 Kings 20:14

serve the king of **B** for 70 years. . Jer. 25:11

It has fallen, **B** the Great . . . . Rev. 14:8

Balaam—Non-Israelite prophet whom Balak, king of Moab, hired to curse the invading Israelites (Num. 22:1-21; 2 Pet. 2:16). God made him bless Israel instead (Num. 23–24; Neh. 13:2). He was condemned for promoting Baal worship (2 Pet. 2:15-16; Jude 11; Rev. 2:14).

Barabbas—A murderer and insurrectionist. When Pilate offered to release Jesus or Barab-

bas, the crowd demanded Barabbas (Mark 15:6-15).

Barnabas—Co-worker with Paul on his first missionary journey (Acts 13–15; see also 4:36; 9:26-27; 11:19-30; 1 Cor. 9:6; Gal. 2:1,9,13; Col. 4:10).

Bartholomew—One of the 12 apostles (Mark 3:18).

Bathsheba—Wife of Uriah the Hittite (2 Sam. 11). David had an adulterous relationship with her then had arranged for the death of Uriah so he could take her as his wife. She was the mother of Solomon (1 Kings 1:11–2:19).

Beelzebul—Name for Satan based on Hb Baalzebub, "lord of the flies."

if I drive out demons by **B**, ... Matt. 12:27

Benjamin—The last son of Jacob, second by Rachel (Gen. 35:17-18,24). The tribe occupied the smallest territory (Josh. 18:11-20; 1 Sam. 9:21; see also Josh. 20–21; 1 Sam. 9:1; Rom. 11:1; Phil. 3:5).

Bethany— Home of Jesus' friends Mary, Martha, and Lazarus (Matt. 21:17; Mark 11:11-12).

Bethel—City in Ephraim where Abraham built an altar (Gen. 12:8; 13:3), Jacob spent the night (28:10-22; 35:1-16; Hos. 12:4-5), and Jeroboam I erected a golden calf (1 Kings 12:29-33).

Bethlehem—Hometown of David (1 Sam. 16:1-13; 17:12,15) and birthplace of Jesus the Messiah (Mic. 5:2; Matt. 2:1; Luke 2:4; John 7:42; see also Gen. 35:19; Ruth 1:22).

C

Caesar—Family name of Julius Caesar assumed as a title by the emperors who followed him.

Caiaphas—High Priest at the time of the trial and crucifixion of Jesus (Matt. 26:3,57; Luke 3:2; John 11:49-52; Acts 4:6).

Cain— Firstborn son of Adam and Eve. He murdered Abel (Gen. 4; Heb. 11:4; 1 John 3:12; Jude 11).

Caleb—The spy representing Judah sent by Moses to scout out the territory of Canaan (Num. 13:6). He brought back a positive report (13:30; Deut. 1:36; Josh. 14:13).

Canaan—The promised land, from the Mediterranean Sea to the Jordan River and from the Brook of Egypt to Syria or to the Euphrates. Named for a son of Ham (Gen. 9:18-27; 10:15-19).

Capernaum—City on the northwest shore of the Sea of Galilee where Jesus began His ministry.

Chaldeans—People who lived on the lower Tigris and Euphrates Rivers, central and southeastern Mesopotamia (Gen. 11:31; 2 Kings 25:10; Ezra 5:12).

Christ—The "anointed one," the Messiah, who is Jesus of Nazareth, the Son of God.

The birth of Jesus **C** came about . Matt. 1:18
I know that Messiah is coming
   (who is called **C**) . . . . John 4:25
God and Savior, Jesus **C**. . . . . Titus 2:13

Corinth—A city in Greece (Acts 18:1; 19:1; 1 Cor. 1:2; 2 Cor. 1:1,23; 2 Tim. 4:20).

Cornelius—Centurion in the Roman army who lived at Caesarea (Acts 10).

Cyrus—King of the Persians and Medes who permitted the Jews to return and rebuild the temple and city of Jerusalem (2 Chron. 36:22-23; Ezra 1:1-4; cp. Isa. 44:28-45:6; Dan. 6:28).

D

Daniel—A young man of nobility taken captive by the king of Babylon and elevated to high rank (Dan. 1). In addition to wisdom, he was gifted in dream interpretation (2:25-45; 4:19; cp. 5:25). Throughout his entire life he demonstrated an unshakable faith in his God (1:8; 6). Also see *Subject Index*.

David—Shepherd, musician, poet, warrior, and loyal subject of King Saul, David became Israel's second king. He received the promise of a royal Messiah in his line (2 Sam. 7:11-16). Though he was not perfect (2 Sam. 11), he was a man who pursued God's heart (1 Sam. 13:14; Acts 13:22). Also see *Subject Index*.

Dead Sea—Inland lake at the end of the Jordan Valley with no outlet. The surface is 1,292 feet below sea level.

Deborah—A prophetess and judge who delivered Israel (Judg. 4–5).

Devil—A personal being in direct opposition to God, His purposes, and His people. Also see *Subject Index*.

don't give the **D** an opportunity . . Eph. 4:27
against the tactics of the **D**. . . . . . . Eph. 6:11
But resist the **D**, and he will . . . . Jas. 4:7
adversary the **D** is prowling . . . . . 1 Pet. 5:8

E

Earth—The planet created by God for mankind. In the beginning God created the heavens and the **e**. Gen. 1:1

may know the **e** is the LORD's. . . . Exod. 9:29
The **e** and everything in it, ... Ps. 24:1
they will inherit the **e**. . . . . Matt. 5:5
new heavens and a new **e**, ... 2 Pet. 3:13

Eden—Garden of God, the idyllic place of creation (Gen. 2:8-15; 3:22-24; Isa. 51:3; Ezek.
28:13). Located somewhere near the source of
the Tigris and Euphrates rivers.

Edom—Another name for Esau, his descendants, and the land they lived in south of the
Dead Sea (Gen. 25:30; 32:3).

Egypt—Land in northeastern Africa, an important cultural and political influence on ancient
Israel (Gen. 12:10; 37:36; 46:6).

Israelites lived in **E** ... 430 years. Exod. 12:40
and out of **E** I called My son. . . . . Hos. 11:1;
Matt. 2:15

Elijah—A prophet of Israel who condemned
baalism (1 Kings 18), confronted kings prophetically, and passed his mantle to Elisha (19:19)
before he ascended to heaven in a whirlwind
(2 Kings 2:11). He was a forerunner to the Messiah, embodied in John the Baptist (Mal. 4:5;
Matt. 11:14; 17:10-13; Luke 1:17). He appeared
with Jesus (Matt. 17:3-4).

Elisha—An Israelite prophet, he completed the
assignment God had given Elijah (1 Kings
19:11-16; 2 Kings 8:7-15; 9:1-13). Elisha performed many miracles during his life (2:14, 19-
24; 3:13-22; 4–7) and one even after his death
(13:21).

Elizabeth—Descendant of Aaron and wife of
Zacharias the priest (Luke 1:5) and mother of
John the Baptist.

Emmaus—A village about seven miles from
Jerusalem (Luke 24:13).

Enoch—Methuselah's father, taken up to God
without dying (Gen. 5:24; Heb. 11:5; Jude 14).

Ephesus—One of the largest and most impressive cities in the ancient world, a political, religious, and commercial center in Asia Minor.
Associated with the ministries of Paul, Timothy,
and the Apostle John, the city played a significant
role in the spread of early Christianity (Acts 18:19;
19:1; 1 Cor. 16:8; Eph. 1:1). One of the seven
churches in Revelation (Rev. 1:11; 2:1).

Ephraim—A son of Joseph (Gen. 41:52) and
the tribe and territory named for him (Gen. 48;
Josh. 14:4; 16:4-5). Used as another name for
the Northern Kingdom of Israel (Isa. 11:13; Jer.
7:15; Ezek. 37:16; Hos. 5:13).

Esau—Son of Isaac and Rebekah; elder twin
brother of Jacob; father of the Edomites. Sold

his birthright (Gen. 25:30-34; Heb. 12:16) and
was tricked out of his blessing (Gen. 27;
Heb. 11:20).

Esther—Mordecai's niece who became queen
of Persia and was used by God to protect His
people from genocide.

Euphrates and Tigris Rivers—Two great rivers of Western Asia (Gen. 2:14; 15:18; Exod.
23:31; Mic. 7:12; Zech. 9:10; Rev. 9:14; 16:12).
They originate in the mountains of Armenia and
unite about 90 miles from the Persian Gulf.

Eve—See Adam and Eve.

Ezekiel—Prophet who ministered to Judean
exiles in Babylon. He related striking visions
(Ezek. 1; 8–11; 37:1-14; 40–48), crafted powerful word pictures (17:1-24; 19:1-14; 27:1-9),
and performed symbolic acts (4–5; 12:1-20;
37:15-28).

Ezra—Priest and scribe who was sent with a
large company of Israelites to Jerusalem by
King Artaxerxes of Persia in 458 b.c. (Ezra 7:1;
Neh. 8:1; 12:1). His mission was "to study the
law of the Lord, obey it, and teach its statutes
and ordinances in Israel" (Ezra 7:10).

G

Gabriel—Angel sent to Daniel (Dan. 8:15-27;
9:20-27), Zechariah (Luke 1:8-20), and Mary
(1:26-38).

Galilee—1. Northern part of Palestine. Jesus
devoted most of His earthly ministry to Galilee,
being known as the Galilean (Matt. 26:69). 2. A
freshwater sea along the Jordan River area
(Matt. 4:18; 15:29).

Gentiles—People who are not part of God's
chosen family by birth.

a light for revelation to the **G** . . . . Luke 2:32
full number of the **G** . . . . Rom. 11:25

Gideon—After God gave him a sign, he delivered the Israelites from the Midianites
and Amalekites and judged for 40 years
(Judg. 6:11–8:35; Heb. 11:32).

God—Personal Creator and Lord of the universe. When not capitalized or when plural, it
refers to other so-called gods. Also see *Subject
Index*.

In the beginning **G** created the . . . Gen. 1:1
Do not have other **g-s** . . . . Exod. 20:3
G is not a man who lies, or a . . . Num. 23:19
G is a consuming fire, ... Deut. 4:24
they had worshiped other **g-s**. . 2 Kings 17:7
I will be their **G**, and they will . . . . Jer. 31:33
was with **G**, and the Word was **G**. . John 1:1

For **G** loved the world in this way: John 3:16
G is spirit, and those who worship   John 4:24
I said, you are **g-s**? . . . .   John 10:34
We must obey **G** rather than men   . Acts 5:29
If **G** is for us, who is against . . . . .   Rom. 8:31
not know **G**, because **G** is love. . . 1 John 4:8

Goliath—The huge Philistine champion who baited the Israelite army and was slain by David (1 Sam. 17).

H

Habakkuk—Preexilic prophet who asked God for justice and praised His sovereignty.

Hades—A place of torment for wicked souls.
   forces of **H** will not overpower it.   Matt. 16:18
   I hold the keys of death and **H**.   . . . Rev. 1:18

Hagar—Sarah's personal servant, given as a concubine to Abraham and became the mother of Ishmael (Gen. 16:1-16; 25:12; Gal. 4:24-25).

Haggai—Postexilic prophet who roused the people of Judah to finish rebuilding the Temple (Ezra 5:1; 6:14; Hag. 1–2).

Ham—Youngest of Noah's three sons (Gen. 5:32). He discovered his father naked and reported it to Shem and Japheth, so Noah cursed Ham's son Canaan (9:20-29).

heaven—See *Subject Index*.

Hebrew—A designation for Israelites (Gen. 14:13; Jonah 1:9; Phil. 3:5) and the language they spoke and wrote (2 Kings 18:26; John 19:20).

hell—See *Subject Index*.

Herod—Name given to the family ruling Palestine around the time of Christ: Herod the Great (Matt. 2:1-19), Archelaus (2:22), Antipas (14:1-12), Philip (14:3), Agrippa I (Acts 12:20-23) and II (25:13).

Herodias—Wife of Herod Antipas; called for the head of John the Baptist (Matt. 14:3-11).

Hezekiah—King of Judah who promoted religious reforms, reopened the temple, and removed the idols from it. He fortified the city of Jerusalem and constructed a tunnel from the spring of Gihon to the Siloam pool (2 Kings 18–20; Matt. 1:9-10).

Holy Spirit—Third person of the Trinity through whom God acts, reveals His will, empowers individuals, and discloses His personal presence in the OT and NT. Also see *Subject Index*.
   or take Your **H** from me. . . . .   Ps. 51:11
   they were all filled with the **H** . . . . . .   Acts 2:4
   your body is a sanctuary of the **H**   1 Cor. 6:19

were sealed with the promised **H**.   Eph. 1:13
don't grieve God's **H**, ...   Eph. 4:30
moved by the **H**, men spoke   . . . . 2 Pet. 1:21

Hosea—Prophet who illustrated God's unfailing love for unfaithful Israel and called for repentance.

I

Isaac—Only son of Abraham by Sarah, he was the child of a promise from God, born when Abraham and Sarah were very old (Gen. 17:17; 21:5). God tested Abraham's faith by commanding him to sacrifice Isaac (22:1-19). Isaac married Rebekah (Gen. 24), who bore him twin sons, Esau and Jacob (25:21-28).

Isaiah—Prophet who predicted the exile of Judah because of their rebellion against God. He also predicted the Messiah as a branch (Isa. 11:1), a kingly figure (9:6-7), and a suffering servant (50:6; 53:3-6). Jesus fulfilled all of these.

Ishmael—Son of Abraham by the Egyptian concubine Hagar (Gen. 16:11).

Israel—Name that God gave Jacob after he wrestled with the divine messenger (Gen. 32:28). It was also the name of the nation made up of his descendants—chosen by God and delivered from slavery in Egypt—as well as the land they occupied. Later it was the name of the Northern Kingdom when they separated from Judah (1 Kings 12). Also see *Subject Index*.
   LORD saved **I** from the power of the Egyptians
      Exod. 14:30
   go to the lost sheep of the house
      of **I**. . . . .   Matt. 10:6
   not all who are descended from **I**
      are **I**. . . . .   Rom. 9:6

J

Jabez—Israelite who asked God for a blessing and received it (4:9-10).

Jacob—The son of Isaac and Rebekah, he cheated his older twin Esau out of the rights of the firstborn. At Peniel he wrestled with a stranger who gave him the name Israel, "he struggles with God." As father of the 12 ancestors of the 12 tribes of Israel, he was the progenitor of the nation (Gen. 25:26–Exod. 1:5).

James—**1.** An apostle, the son of Zebedee and brother of John the apostle (Matt. 4:21; 10:2). **2.** An apostle, Alphaeus's son (Matt. 10:3; Acts 1:13). **3.** The half brother of Jesus. He assumed

the leadership of the Jerusalem church (15:13) and is probably the author of the book of James.

Japheth—One of Noah's three sons (Gen. 5:32).

Jeremiah—Hilkiah's son, called to be a prophet in Judah (Jer. 1:2). He constantly proclaimed God's judgment upon Judah and Jerusalem, recommended surrender to Babylon, and called Nebuchadnezzar the "servant of the Lord" (25:9; 27:6). Yet he wrote aggressive oracles against Babylon (50–51).

Jericho—The first city Israel conquered in Canaan west of the Jordan (Josh. 6).

Jeroboam—First king of the Northern Kingdom Israel. Jeroboam previously had managed the laborers for Solomon (1 Kings 11:28). He became the example of evil kings in Israel because he set up idols in Dan and Bethel (12:25-33).

Jerusalem—A city set high on a plateau in the hills of Judah, Yahweh's chosen center of His divine kingship and of the human kingship of David and his sons. It was originally named Jebus and was also called "the City of David" and "Zion." Also see *Subject Index*.

J, the city I chose for Myself . 1 Kings 11:36
Pray for the peace of J: . . . . Ps. 122:6
you will be My witnesses in J, in all . . . Acts 1:8
the Holy City, new J, coming down Rev. 21:2

Jesse—Father of David (Ruth 4:17-22; 1 Sam. 16:1; Acts 13:22).

Jesus—The Son of God, the Messiah, the Savior; the only way to God (John 14:6; Acts 4:12). Also see *Subject Index*.

you are to name Him J, because . Matt. 1:21
confess with your mouth,
"J is Lord," . . . . Rom. 10:9
name of J every knee should bow . . . Phil. 2:10

Jew—Judahite, a person from the Southern Kingdom; Judean.

has been born King of the J-s? . . . Matt. 2:2
salvation is from the J-s. . . . . John 4:22
There is no J or Greek, slave or . . Gal. 3:28

Jezebel—Wife of King Ahab of Israel, she brought the worship of Baal from Sidon (1 Kings 16:31) and tried to destroy all God's prophets in Israel (18:4).

Job—A wealthy nomad (Job 1:3; 42:12) who was an example of patient and persistent faith in the face of hardships (Jas. 5:11). God allowed him to lose his possessions, his children, and his health, yet he did not turn away from God.

John—**1.** John the Baptist was a prophet who preached a message of repentance, announced the coming of the Messiah, baptized Jesus, and was beheaded by Herod Antipas (Matt. 3; 14). **2.** The apostle, brother of James, and leader in the early church (Gal. 2:9). He wrote a Gospel, three letters, and Revelation. Also see *Subject Index*.

John Mark—See Mark, John.

Jonah—A prophet, a reluctant messenger of God to Nineveh. Jesus said Jonah's three days in the belly of the fish was a sign concerning Jesus' death and resurrection (Matt. 12:39-41; 16:4; Luke 11:29-30, 32).

Jonathan—Eldest son of King Saul, friend of David (1 Sam. 18–20). When he was killed by the Philistines, David mourned (2 Sam. 1:17-27).

Joppa—City on the coast northwest of Jerusalem.

Jordan—The longest and most important river of Palestine, it flows south through the Sea of Galilee to the Dead Sea.

dry ground in the middle of the J . . . Josh. 3:17
Jesus came ... to John at the J . . . . . Matt. 3:13

Joseph—**1.** Son of Jacob by his favorite wife, Rachel, he became Jacob's favorite son. This and the dreams that showed his rule over his family inspired the envy of his brothers, who sold him into slavery (Gen. 37). In Egypt he eventually became second in command to the pharaoh (41:39-45). Later, Jacob moved the rest of his family to Egypt (46:1–47:12). **2.** Husband of Mary, mother of Jesus (Luke 2:8-33). **3.** Joseph of Arimathea, a rich member of the Sanhedrin and a disciple of Jesus, he requested Jesus' body from Pilate and laid it in his own unused tomb (Matt. 27:57-60; John 19:38-42).

Joshua—Moses' successor. He was on Matt. Sinai when Moses received the Law (Exod. 32:17). He was the spy representing Ephraim sent to investigate Canaan (Num. 13:8, 16). He and Caleb returned with a positive, minority report; of all the adults alive at that time, only the two of them were allowed to enter Canaan (14:28-30, 38). He led the Israelites to conquer the promised land (Josh. 1–12) and to divide it among the tribes (Josh. 13–22).

Josiah—Judah's king who led the people to renew their loyalty to the Lord (2 Kings 21:19–23:30).

Judah—**1.** Fourth son of Jacob (Gen. 29:35) and ancestor of David and Jesus (49:10; 1 Sam. 17:12; Matt. 1:3,6,16; Rev. 5:5). **2.** A tribe of

Israel. **3.** When the kingdom was divided, the Southern Kingdom, including Judah and Benjamin, was called Judah.

Judas—**1.** Half brother of Jesus (Matt. 13:55; Mark 6:3), also called Jude (Jude 1). **2.** An apostle, also called Lebbaeus or Thaddaeus (Matt. 10:3; Mark 3:18; John 14:22). **3.** Judas Iscariot, who betrayed Jesus (Matt. 26:21-25, 44-50; Luke 22:3-6; John 13:21-30). He acted as treasurer for the disciples but was known as a miser and a thief (12:4-6). Also see *Subject Index.*

Judea—Judah, from the area around Jerusalem and south to the Negev, was called Judea after the exile (Ezra 5:8).

> Jesus was born in Bethlehem of **J** . . . Matt. 2:1
> in Jerusalem, in all **J** and Samaria, . . . Acts 1:8

L

Lazarus—**1.** One of the principal characters in a parable Jesus told to warn the selfish rich that justice will eventually prevail (Luke 16:19-31). **2.** A personal friend of Jesus and the brother of Mary and Martha (John 11:1-3). Jesus raised him from the dead (11:38-44).

Leah—Older daughter of Laban (Gen. 29:16); Jacob's first wife. She bore six sons (Reuben, Simeon, Levi, Judah, Issachar, Zebulun) (29:31-35; 35:23) and a daughter (Dinah).

Levi—**1.** Son of Jacob and Leah (Gen. 29:34), ancestor of priestly tribe (Exod. 32:25-29; Num. 3:11-13; Deut. 10:6-9). **2.** Apostle, called Matthew (Mark 2:14; Luke 5:27-29; cp. Matt. 9:9).

Levites—Descendants of Levi, and assistants to the priests in Israel's sacrificial system (Num. 3:11-13; 2 Chron. 17:7-9; 29:12-21; Neh. 8:9-12). They did not receive a land allotment; God was their inheritance (Num. 18:20).

Lot—Nephew of Abraham (Gen. 11:27) who accompanied him to Canaan (12:5). Lot chose to live in the Jordan Valley in the city of Sodom (13:8-12).

Luke—Author of the Third Gospel and the Acts of the Apostles in the NT; Paul's traveling companion (Col. 4:14; 2 Tim. 4:11; Philem. 24).

M

Macedonia—A mountainous country north of Greece to which Paul was beckoned in a vision (Acts 16:9-10) and where he founded the first Christian community in Europe (19:21-22; 20:1,3; Rom. 15:26; 2 Cor. 1:16; 8:1; 11:9; Phil. 4:15; 1 Thess. 1:7-8; 4:10).

Malachi—Author of the last book of the OT; he calls the people to turn from their spiritual apathy, honor the Lord with tithes and offerings, and be faithful to covenants, especially marriage.

Manasseh—**1.** A son of Joseph (Gen. 41:50-51). Along with his brother Ephraim, he became one of the 12 tribes of Israel. **2.** King of Judah who led the people to worship false gods (2 Kings 21; 24:3).

Mark, John—Author of the Second Gospel. He was a cousin of Barnabas (Col. 4:10) and a companion of Barnabas and Paul on their first missionary journey (Acts 12:12,25). On the second journey, Paul refused to take Mark since he had left them on the first (15:37,39). Later, however, Mark was with Paul (Col. 4:10; Philem. 24).

Martha—Sister of Mary and Lazarus, she was concerned with being a hostess (Luke 10:38-42; John 11).

Mary—**1.** Mother of Jesus (Matt. 2; Luke 1–2; Acts 1:14). **2.** Magdalene, from whom seven demons were driven (Luke 8:2). She was a key witness to Jesus' death (Matt. 27:56), burial (Mark 15:47), the empty tomb (Luke 24:1-10), and was the first to encounter the risen Christ (John 20:1-18). **3.** Sister of Martha and Lazarus, she anointed the feet of Jesus with perfume (John 12:1-8). **4.** Mother of James the Younger and Joses (Mark 15:40–16:1). **5.** Wife of Clopas (John 19:25). **6.** Mother of Mark (Acts 12). **7.** A believer greeted by Paul (Rom. 16:6). Also see *Subject Index.*

Matthew—A tax collector who became an apostle of Jesus (Matt. 9:9; 10:3). Also called Levi (Luke 5:27).

Melchizedek—Priest and king of Salem who blessed Abraham in the name of "God Most High" (Gen. 14:18-20), he symbolized the undying priesthood fulfilled by Jesus (Ps. 110:4; Heb. 5–7).

Mesopotamia—The area between the Tigris and Euphrates rivers (Acts 2:9; 7:2).

Messiah—The anointed one, Christ. This title carried overtones of political power. Only after the resurrection did the disciples see how Jesus was truly a royal Messiah (Luke 24:45-46).

> until **M** the Prince will be seven . . . Dan. 9:25
> You are the **M**, the Son of the . . . Matt. 16:16
> proving that this One is the **M.** . . . Acts 9:22
> who denies that Jesus is the **M**? 1 John 2:22

Methuselah—Noah's grandfather who died at the age of 969 (Gen. 5:25-29).

Michael—Archangel who served as the guardian of the nation of Israel (Dan. 12:1; Jude 9; Rev. 12:7).

Miriam—Sister of Moses and Aaron (Num. 20:1; 26:59). After crossing the Red Sea, she led the women in singing a song of victory (Exod. 15:20-21). When she rebelled against Moses, God struck her with leprosy but healed her after Moses' intercession (Num. 12:1, 4-5, 10, 15; Deut. 24:8-9).

Moses—Son of Amram and Jochabed, and brother of Miriam and Aaron; leader of the Israelites in their exodus from Egyptian slavery and in their journey toward the promised land. He was the author of the Pentateuch and Ps. 90. Also see *Subject Index*.

N

Naaman—Syrian general cured of leprosy under the direction of the prophet Elisha (2 Kings 5).

Naomi—Mother-in-law to Orpah and Ruth (Ruth 1–4). Her matchmaking between Ruth and Boaz was successful, and she became a forebear of David (4:21-22).

Naphtali—Sixth son of Jacob and second son by Rachel's slave Bilhah (Gen. 30:7-8).

Nathan—Prophet in David's court, he confronted David about Uriah and Bathsheba (2 Sam. 12).

Nathanael—Possibly another name for the apostle Bartholomew, he was an Israelite whom Jesus complimented as being guileless and who, in turn, confessed Jesus as the Son of God and King of Israel (John 1:45-49).

Nazarene—A person from Nazareth, the hometown of Jesus. It is in lower Galilee about halfway between the Sea of Galilee and the Mediterranean.

that He will be called a **N** . . . . . . Matt. 2:23
of the sect of the **N-s**! . . . . Acts 24:5

Nazirite—An individual especially devoted to God by taking a vow. Lifelong Nazirites included Samson (Judg. 13:5, 7; 16:17), Samuel (1 Sam. 1), and John the Baptist (Luke 1:15-17). The essential elements of the Nazirite vow were abstention from wine or any other product of grapes, not touching a dead body, and not cutting one's hair (Num. 6). Also see *Subject Index*.

Nebuchadnezzar—King of Babylon who conquered Jerusalem and exiled its inhabitants (1 Chron. 6:15; 2 Chron. 36; Neh. 7:6; Esth. 2:6).

Negev—An arid region in southern Palestine.

Nehemiah—Cupbearer to Artaxerxes, king of Persia (Neh. 1:11). He repaired the walls of Jerusalem then led a revival.

Nicodemus—A "ruler of the Jews" who came to Jesus at night and was told he must be born again (John 3:1-20; 7:50-51; 19:39).

Nile—The major river considered the "life" of ancient Egypt. Also see *Subject Index*.

Nineveh—The capital of the ancient Assyrian Empire, it was the enemy city to which God called the reluctant Prophet Jonah (Gen. 10:11-12; 2 Kings 19:36; Isa. 37:37; Jonah 3:2-7; Nah. 1:1; Zeph. 2:13; Matt. 12:41; Luke 11:30-32).

Noah—A righteous man, God gave him specific instructions for building the ark by which he and his family survived the flood (Gen. 5:28–10:1; Ezek. 14:14; Matt. 24:37-38; Heb. 11:7; 1 Pet. 3:20; 2 Pet. 2:5). His sons were Shem, Ham, and Japheth.

P

Palestine—The land west of Jordan River that God allotted to Israel for an inheritance (Josh. 13–19).

Paul—His Jewish name was Saul. He was educated in the Jewish religion and became a Pharisee (23:6; 26:5). Initially he rejected Jesus and persecuted Christians, but he was converted when the resurrected Christ appeared to him. He became an outstanding missionary, theologian, and writer of the early church; he wrote 13 letters that comprise the most important theological interpretation of the teachings of Christ and of the significance of His life, death, and resurrection. Also see *Subject Index*.

Persia—In ancient times, a vast collection of states and kingdoms reaching from Asia Minor to India and from Russia to Egypt and the Persian Gulf.

Peter—Simon was his given name; he was called Peter, Gk for "rock," by Jesus (Matt. 16:18); also called Simeon and Cephas (Aramaic for "rock"). He was a leader among the 12 disciples. He confessed "You are the Messiah" (Matt. 16:16) but later said "I don't know this man" (Mark 14:71). After Pentecost (Acts 2:1) he was a bold evangelist even when persecuted. Also see *Subject Index*.

Pharaoh—1. Of Abraham (Gen. 12:10-20). 2. Of Joseph (Gen. 39–50). 3. Of the oppression (Exod. 1). 4. Of the exodus (2:23–15:19). 5. Of Solomon (1 Kings 3–11). 6. Of Rehoboam, called Shishak (14:25). 7. Of Hezekiah and

Isaiah (2 Kings 18:21; Isa. 36). 8. Of Josiah (2 Kings 23:29). 9. Other (1 Chron. 4:18; Jer. 44:30; Ezek. 29:1-16).

Pharisees—Religious group that insisted on obedience to the law and numerous strict rules. Also see *Subject Index*.

> unless your righteousness surpasses
> that of the scribes and **P-s** . . . . Matt. 5:20
> I am a **P**, a son of **P-s**! . . . . Acts 23:6

Philip—1. One of 12 apostles (Matt. 10:3). 2. One of first seven deacons (Acts 6:5), and an evangelist (8:5-13,26-39). 3. Philip Herod, a tetrarch.

Philistines—Enemies of Israel from Joshua's conquest to the time of David and beyond. Also see *Subject Index*.

Pilate, Pontius—Roman governor of Judea under whom Christ "suffered" (Mark 15:1-15; 1 Tim. 6:13).

R

Rachel—Laban's younger daughter, second wife and cousin of Jacob, and mother of Joseph and Benjamin (Gen. 29–31; 33:1-2,7; 35:16-25).

Rahab—Prostitute in Jericho who hid the Israelite spies (Josh. 2; 6:17,22-25; Heb. 11:31); mother of Boaz (Matt. 1:5).

Rebekah—Isaac's wife and mother of Jacob and Esau (Gen. 24; 25:25-26).

Red Sea—Body of water God divided in the exodus (Exod. 13:18; 14:15-31; Deut. 11:4; Josh. 2:10; 4:23; 24:6; Neh. 9:9; Ps. 106:9-11; Acts 7:36; Heb. 11:29). The Hb *yam suph* means "sea of reeds."

Reuben—Eldest son of Jacob and the tribe descended from him.

Rome—The name of the empire in control of Europe and the Near East at the time of Christ, and the name of its capital city in Italy.

Ruth—Moabite widow who pledged loyalty to her mother-in-law, Naomi, and her people (Ruth 1:16-17). There she "happened to" end up in the field of Boaz (2:3). Boaz married Ruth and provided Naomi with a family heir, and an ancestor of David and Jesus.

S

Sadducees—A Jewish group that took the Pentateuch as their authority. They did not believe in the afterlife (Matt. 22:23), so were focused on temporal rewards.

Samaritans—The few Israelites that remained after the fall of Samaria intermarried with the Assyrian captives from distant places who were settled there (2 Kings 17:23-24) becoming hated half-breeds who did not worship in the same manner as the Jews. In the days of Christ, the animosity was so great that the Jews bypassed Samaria as they traveled between Galilee and Judea. Also see *Subject Index*.

> But a **S** on his journey came up . Luke 10:33
> Jews do not associate with **S-s**. . . . John 4:9

Samson—Last of the major judges; a lifelong Nazirite (Judg. 13:3-7). Samson's legendary strength came from the Spirit of the LORD (14:6, 19; 15:14; Heb. 11:32,34). Delilah betrayed him (Judg. 16).

Samuel—Priest and prophet who linked the period of the judges with the monarchy. He was raised by the priest Eli (1 Sam. 2:11). Israel appealed to Samuel to appoint a king (8:3,5,20). He warned Israel of the dangers of a monarchy before anointing Saul (10:1). After God rejected Saul, Samuel anointed David (16:13).

Sarah—Abraham's wife (1 Pet. 3:6). Originally named Sarai, when she was almost 90 years old God changed her name to Sarah and promised her a son (Gen. 17:15-16; cp. 18:10; Rom. 9:9). A year later, she bore Isaac (Gen. 21:1-7; Heb. 11:11).

Satan—Adversary or accuser; the Devil.

> told Peter, "Get behind Me, **S**! . . Matt. 16:23
> For **S** himself is disguised . . . . 2 Cor. 11:14
> messenger of **S** to torment me . . . . 2 Cor. 12:7
> I watched **S** fall from heaven . . . Luke 10:18

Saul—1. First king of Israel. His presumptuous offering (1 Sam. 13:8-14) and violation of a holy war ban led to his rejection by God (15:7-23). 2. Paul's Hebrew name.

Shem—Noah's oldest son and ancestor of the Semitic peoples, including the Israelites.

Sheol—Abode of the unrighteous dead.

> You will not abandon me to **S** . . . . . Ps. 16:10
> make my bed in **S**, You are there. . . Ps. 139:8

Silas—A leader in the Jerusalem church, he traveled with Paul and also served as Peter's scribe (Acts 15:22,32,40-41; 16:19-40; 17:10-15; 18:5; 2 Cor. 1:19; 1 Thess. 1:1; 2 Thess. 1:1; 1 Pet. 5:12).

Simon—1. The father of Judas Iscariot. 2. See Peter. 3. Pharisee who hosted Jesus. 4. Native of Cyrene forced to carry Jesus' cross (Mark 15:21). 5. Tanner who lived in Joppa. 6. One of Jesus' twelve apostles, also called

"the Canaanite" (Matt. 10:4) or the Zealot (Luke 6:15). **7.** Half brother of Jesus (Matt. 13:55). **8.** Leper who hosted Jesus. **9.** Sorcerer from Samaria who believed Philip's preaching, was baptized, and then tried to buy the power of the gospel (Acts 8:9-24).

Sinai, Mount—Mountain on the Sinai Peninsula where God gave the Ten Commandments to Moses (Exod. 19:1-3,20; 31:18; Lev. 25:1; Acts 7:38; Gal. 4:25).

Sodom and Gomorrah—Two cities destroyed by God because of their wickedness (Gen. 19).

Solomon—David's son and successor as king of Israel (1 Kings 1–2). He was granted wisdom and wealth from God (3:12-13), and he built the temple (1 Kings 5–8). But his "700 wives who were princesses and 300 concubines ... turned his heart away from the LORD" (11:3).

Stephen—One of seven men chosen to serve in the Jerusalem church (Acts 6:5), and the first Christian martyr (7:54-60).

T

Thaddaeus—Another name for the Apostle Judas, not Iscariot (Matt. 10:3; Mark 3:18).

Thomas—One of the apostles (Mark 3:18). He sought evidence of Jesus' resurrection, and when shown, expressed faith (John 20:25-28).

Tigris—See Euphrates and Tigris Rivers.

Timothy—Paul's friend and trusted coworker. He may have been converted on Paul's first missionary journey (Acts 14:6-23). When Paul came to Lystra on his second journey, Timothy was a disciple who was well respected by the believers (Acts 16:1-2). Timothy not only accompanied Paul but also was sent on many crucial missions (17:14-15; 18:5; 19:22; 20:4; Rom. 16:21; 1 Cor. 16:10; 2 Cor. 1:19; 1 Thess. 3:2,6).

Titus—Gentile companion of Paul (Gal. 2:3). Paul spoke highly of Titus and entrusted him with ministry (2 Cor. 2:13; 7:6,13-14; 8:6,16,23; 12:18; cp. Gal. 2:1; 2 Tim. 4:10).

Y

Yahweh—God's name that He revealed to Moses. In most English translations it is represented by LORD in small caps.

Y, the God of your fathers . . . . Exod. 3:15

I am Y, that is My name . . . . Isa. 42:8

Z

Zacchaeus—Corrupt tax collector whom Jesus visited in Jericho (Luke 19:2-9).

Zealot—Member of the Jewish group that wanted to liberate Judea from Rome by force.

Zechariah—**1.** Prophet who urged the people of Judah to rebuild the temple. **2.** Father of John the Baptist (Luke 1:5-64).

Zion—Originally, the fortified hill of Jebus, also called the City of David; Jerusalem (2 Sam. 5:7; Ps. 48:2; Ps. 137:3; Joel 2:1; Zech. 9:9; Matt. 21:5; Rom. 9:33).

I have consecrated My King on Z . . . . Ps. 2:6

laid a stone in Z, a tested stone . . Isa. 28:16

The Liberator will come from Z . . . Rom. 11:26

DICTIONARY-CONCORDANCE

A

Abba—Aramaic word for "father" used by Jesus and Paul to speak an intimate relationship with God.

> He said, "**A**, Father! . . . . Mark 14:36
> we cry out, "**A**, Father!" . . . . Rom. 8:15
> crying, "**A**, Father!" . . . . Gal. 4:6

abomination—That which is detestable to God.

> Milcom, the **a** of the Ammonites. 2 Kings 23:13
> and set up the **a** of desolation. . . . Dan. 11:31
> see the **a** that causes desolation, Matt. 24:15

abortion—Induced miscarriage. Prohibited by implication from God's dealings with the unborn (Judg. 13:7; Isa.. 49:1; Jer. 1:5; Luke 1:15,41).

abstinence—Voluntarily refraining from some action, such as sexual relations, eating certain foods, or drinking alcoholic beverages.

abyss—The dark abode of the dead (Ps. 140:10; Luke 8:31; Rom. 10:7).

acrostic—Literary device by which each section of a literary work begins with the succeeding letter of a certain word or of the alphabet. Pss. 9–10; 25; 34; 37; 111–112; 119; 145; Prov. 31:10-31; Lam. 1–4 are alphabetic acrostics.

adoption—Legal process whereby one person receives another into his family and confers upon that person familial privileges and advantages (Rom. 8:15,23; 9:4).

adultery—Act of unfaithfulness in marriage. The Bible addresses literal adultery—both actual (Exod. 20:14; Deut. 5:18) and in the thought life of a person (Matt. 5:28)—and also uses adultery figuratively for unfaithfulness to God (Ezek. 16:32; Matt. 12:39; 16:4; Jas. 4:4).

adversary—Enemy; one who is against another. The devil is the greatest adversary (1 Pet. 5:8-9).

advocate—One who intercedes in behalf of another. Abraham (Gen. 18:23-33), Moses (Exod. 32:11-14), and Samuel interceded with God on behalf of Israel (1 Sam. 7:8-9), and Christ intercedes with the Father on behalf of sinners (1 John 2:1).

affliction—Condition of physical or mental distress. It ultimately shows the power of God (Rom. 5:3; 2 Cor. 4:17).

alien—Person living in a society other than his own. The patriarchs (Abraham, Isaac, Jacob) were aliens in Canaan but owned large material resources (20:1; 26:3; 32:5). God loves aliens (Deut. 10:19). They could observe Passover (Num. 9:14) and offer sacrifices (Lev. 17:8) just as any Israelite.

> the land where you live as an **a**, . Gen. 28:4
> if you no longer oppress the **a**, ... Jer. 7:6
> I urge you as **a-s** . . . . 1 Pet. 2:11

allotment—Land allocation either by God directly or by casting lots. Num. 32; Josh. 13–19; Ezek. 48.

Almighty—Title of God expressing His power.

> I am God **A**. . . . . Gen. 17:1
> Can … discover the limits of the **A**? Job 11:7

Alpha and Omega—First and last letters of the Greek alphabet, used in Revelation to describe God or Christ (Rev. 1:8; 21:6; 22:13).

altar—Structure used in worship as the place for presenting sacrifices to God or gods (Exod. 20:25; 27:1-4; 30:1-6; 1 Kings 7:48-50; 2 Chron. 4:1).

ambassador—Representative of one government to another.

> we are **a-s** for Christ; . . . . 2 Cor. 5:20
> For this I am an **a** in chains. . . . . . . Eph. 6:20

amen—Transliteration of Hb word signifying something as certain, truthful, or faithful.

> The **A**, the faithful and true . . . . . . Rev. 3:14

Ancient of Days—Phrase used to describe the everlasting God, implying age, dignity, endurance, and wisdom (Dan. 7:9,13,22).

angel—Created being whose primary function is to serve and worship God.

> He will send His **a** before you, . . . Gen. 24:7
> the **a** Gabriel was sent . . . . Luke 1:26
> we will judge **a-s** . . . . 1 Cor. 6:3
> disguised as an **a** of light. . . . . 2 Cor. 11:14

anoint, anointed—Procedure of rubbing or smearing a person or thing, usually with olive oil, for the purpose of grooming, healing, setting apart, or embalming (Exod. 30:30; 1 Sam. 15:1; Matt. 6:17; Mark 16:1; Luke 10:34).

antichrist—One who opposes God and His purpose (1 John 2:18,22; 4:3; 2 John 7).

anxiety—State of mind ranging from genuine, legitimate concern (Phil. 2:28) to obsessions that originate from a distorted perspective of life (Prov. 12:25; Luke 12:22-31).

apostle—**1**. One of the Twelve whom Jesus chose. Paul was also an apostle because he had seen the risen Christ. **2**. A person sent to perform a task.

> 12—He also named them **a-s** . . . Mark 3:14
> received grace and **a-ship** . . . . Rom. 1:5

I am an **a** to the Gentiles, ... Rom. 11:13

unworthy to be called an **a**, ... 1 Cor. 15:9

Aramaic—North Semitic language similar to Phoenician and Hebrew; the language of the Arameans of northwestern Mesopotamia, used widely in commerce and diplomacy (2 Kings 18:26). Jesus and the Apostles probably spoke in Aramaic.

archangel—Chief angel; functions as a messenger on God's spiritual business (1 Thess. 4:16; Jude 9).

ark—Water vessel (Gen. 6–9; Matt. 24:38; Luke 17:27; Heb. 11:7; 1 Pet. 3:20).

ark of the covenant—Also called ark of the LORD and ark of the testimony. Original container for the Ten Commandments (Deut. 10:1-5; Exod. 25:10-22; Jer. 3:16-17; Ps. 132:7-8; Heb. 9:1-10).

armor—Defensive tools of warfare (Eph. 6:10-17; cp. Isa. 59:16-17).

ascents—Word used in the titles of 15 psalms (Ps. 120–134); probably a reference to pilgrims going up to Jerusalem for the festivals.

ascribe—To consider something as coming from or belonging to somebody (Ps. 96:7-8).

assay—To test ore for its silver and gold content (Jer. 6:27).

assembly—Official gathering of the people of Israel or of the church; congregation.

atonement—God's reconciling of sinners to Himself through the sacrificial work of Jesus Christ (Ps. 79:9; Prov. 16:6; 2 Cor. 5:20).

priest will make **a** on their behalf, . Lev. 4:20

is the Day of **A**. . . . . Lev. 23:27

authority—The rightful and legitimate exercise of power by virtue of position. Delegated authority is given from one who has intrinsic authority to one serving in an office or carrying out a function.

Son of Man has **a** on earth . . . . . . Matt. 9:6

gave them **a** over unclean spirits . Matt. 10:1

All **a** has been given to Me . . . . . Matt. 28:18

submit to the governing **a-ies**, . . . Rom. 13:1

teach or to have **a** over a man; . 1 Tim. 2:12

be submissive to rulers and **a-ies**, . Titus 3:1

avenger—Person with the legal responsibility to punish a wrongdoer (Num. 35:12,19; Rom. 12:19; 13:4).

awe—Honor, fear, and respect for a superior.

the great, mighty, and **a-some** God, Deut. 10:17

stand in **a** of the God of Israel, . . . Isa. 29:23

Azazel—A "scapegoat" or a desert demon (Lev. 16:8,10,26).

B

balance—A type of scale for weighing.

You are to have honest **b-s**, ... Lev. 19:36

b-s and scales are the LORD's; . Prov. 16:11

weighed the mountains in a **b** . . . Isa. 40:12

balm—Aromatic resin or gum used for cosmetic and medical purposes.

Is there no **b** in Gilead? . . . . Jer. 8:22

banner—Sign carried to identify a group, to give it a rallying point, and to make signals.

baptism—Immersion in water as a symbol of cleansing from sin and as a public confession of faith in Jesus the Savior.

preaching a **b** of repentance . . . . . Mark 1:4

we were buried with Him by **b** . . . . Rom. 6:4

barren—Unable to bear children (Gen. 11:30; 25:21; 29:31; Judg. 13:2; 1 Sam. 1:5; Luke 1:7, 36).

beasts—Symbolic enemies of God's people in Daniel and Revelation.

Four huge **b-s** came up . . . . Dan. 7:3

b that comes up out of the abyss . . Rev. 11:7

a **b** coming up out of the sea. . . . . . Rev. 13:1

beer—Intoxicating drink made from grain, traditionally called "strong drink."

he is to abstain from wine and **b**. . . Num. 6:3

Wine is a mocker, **b** is a brawler, . Prov. 20:1

besiege—To apply a military siege.

birthright—Special privileges that belonged to the firstborn male child in a family, including a double portion of the inheritance and the father's major blessing (Gen. 27:36; Deut. 21:17; cp. 2 Kings 2:9).

First sell me your **b**. . . . . Gen. 25:31

b in exchange for one meal. . . . . Heb. 12:16

blasphemy—Speech or actions that show disrespect for God (Lev. 24:11-16). Jesus was regarded by the Jewish leaders as a blasphemer (Matt. 9:3; 26:65; Mark 2:7; 14:64; Luke 5:21; John 10:33).

b against the Spirit will not . . . . . Matt. 12:31

blemish—Deformity or defect that disqualifies an animal as a sacrifice (Lev. 22:17-25) or a man from priestly service (21:17-24).

Messiah who ... offered Himself
without **b** to God, ... Heb. 9:14

bless—To fill with benefits; or to "praise," as if filling something with honor and good words.

I will **b** you, ... Gen. 12:2

has **b-ed** us with every spiritual . . . Eph. 1:3

blind—Unable to see. The Bible addresses spiritual blindness as the great human problem.

the eyes of the **b** will be opened, ... Isa. 35:5

Woe to you, **b** guides, ... Matt. 23:16

are wretched, pitiful, poor, **b**, ... Rev. 3:17

blood—In OT it was intimately associated with physical life (Lev. 17:11,14; Deut. 12:23; Acts 15:20). The blood of Christ represents atonement in His death (Heb. 9:12-14, 22; 13:20; 1 Pet. 1:1-2, 19).

this is My **b** ... the covenant; ... Matt. 26:28

through faith in His **b**, ... Rom. 3:25

redemption through His **b**, ... Eph. 1:7

by making peace through the **b** ... Col. 1:20

b of Jesus His Son cleanses us ... 1 John 1:7

book of life—Heavenly record (Luke 10:20; Phil. 4:3; Heb. 12:23; Rev. 3:5) written by God before the foundation of the world (13:8; 17:8) containing names of those who are destined because of God's grace and their faithfulness to participate in God's heavenly kingdom (cp. Exod. 32:32; Ps. 69:28; Isa. 4:3; Dan. 12:1; Mal. 3:16).

booth—Temporary shelter constructed for cattle (Gen. 33:17) and people (Lev. 23:40-43; 2 Sam. 11:11; 1 Kings 20:12,16; Neh. 8:15; Isa. 1:8; Jonah 4:5).

boundary marker—Pillar or heap of stones indicating the edge of a field (Deut. 19:14; 27:17; Job 24:2; Hos. 5:10).

bread—A cake or loaf made from wheat or barley flour, the basic food of most people in Bible times.

man does not live on **b** alone ..... Deut. 8:3

Give us today our daily **b**. .... Matt. 6:11

I am the **b** of life, ... John 6:35

breastpiece—Piece of elaborate embroidery about nine inches square worn by the high priest upon his breast (Exod. 28; Lev. 8:8).

breath—Source and evidence of life.

breathed the **b** of life into ...... Gen. 2:7

gives everyone life and **b** ..... Acts 17:25

bride—A woman getting married; an image of the church and its relationship to Christ (John 3:29).

brother—This usually refers to siblings (Exod. 4:14; Judg. 9:5) but is also used to signify kinsmen, allies, and members of the same country or community.

Am I my **b**-'s guardian? ...... Gen. 4:9

a **b** is born for a difficult time. .. Prov. 17:17

Whoever does the will of God is My **b** and sister and mother. .... Mark 3:35

buckler—Small, round shield.

burden—A heavy weight to carry.

My yoke is easy and My **b** is light. ...... Matt. 11:30

C

camel—Large hump-backed mammal of Asia and Africa used for desert travel to bear burdens or passengers.

it is easier for a **c** to go through the eye of a needle .... Matt. 19:24

gulp down a **c**! .... Matt. 23:24

censer—Vessel used for offering incense before the Lord (Lev. 10:1).

census—A count of population for the purpose of taxation or for the determination of manpower for war (Num. 1:2; 2 Sam. 24:10).

centurion—Officer in the Roman army, nominally in command of 100 soldiers.

chaff—Husks and other materials separated from the kernel of grain during the threshing and winnowing process.

But the **c** He will burn up with fire Matt. 3:12

chariot—Two-wheeled, horse-drawn vehicle.

even though they have iron **c-s** .. Josh. 17:18

Some take pride in a **c**, ... Ps. 20:7

cherub, plural **cherubim**—A class of winged angels who functioned primarily as guards (Gen. 3:24) or attendants (Ezek. 10:1-22).

chosen people—The group God has selected in order to bless them (Deut. 7:6; 1 Pet. 2:9).

Christian—Slave or follower of Christ (Acts 11:26).

chronicle—A written report of events in chronological order, such as that written by the court historian (1 Kings 14:19).

church—A local group of people who believe in Christ (Matt. 18:17; Rom. 16:5; Rev. 2:1) or the universal body of all believers (Matt. 16:18; 1 Cor. 15:9). The description of the church as the body of Christ (Eph. 5:23; Col. 1:18,24) designates Jesus' rule over the community.

circumcision—Removal of the foreskin of the penis as a sign of the covenant between God and mankind (Gen. 17:11). The Jerusalem Council determined that circumcision was not essential to Christian faith (Acts 15:1-12; cp. Gal. 5:2).

and **c** is of the heart .... Rom. 2:29

cistern—A well or a reservoir into which water could drain from a roof, tunnel, or courtyard.

city of refuge—Safe place to flee for a person who had accidentally killed another (Num. 35:11; Josh. 20). The city provided asylum until a trial could be held to determine his guilt or innocence.

citizen—Officially recognized status in political state bringing certain rights and responsibilities (Acts 16:37; 22:26-28).

city of David—In the OT the phrase refers to Jerusalem; its original reference may have been only to the southeastern hill and the Jebusites' military fortress there (2 Sam. 5:6-10). In Luke 2:4,11 the reference is to Bethlehem, the birthplace of David (John 7:42).

clan—A kinship group more extensive than "household" or "family" but smaller than "tribe."

clean—Ceremonially acceptable to God. People must be clean to participate in worship (Lev. 22:2-9; Num. 8:15; Ps. 24:3-4). Certain animals were considered clean and therefore suitable for food or for sacrifice (Lev. 11; Deut. 14:3-21). Jesus cleansed His people by His blood (1 John 1:7,9; cp. John 15:3; Titus 2:14).

common—In the context of the law, it means profane, the opposite of holy (Lev. 10:10; Acts 10:14-15).

compassion—Deep sympathy for one who is in sorrow and pain. Jesus had compassion for people (Matt. 9:36; 14:14; 15:32; 20:34). Compassion is evidence that one is a child of God (1 John 3:17).

the LORD your God is a **c-ate** God.　Deut. 4:31

concubine—A wife of lower status than a primary wife.

He had 700 wives ... and 300 **c-s**,　1 Kings 11:3

condemn—To pronounce someone guilty after weighing the evidence.

He **c-s** a man who schemes.　.　Prov. 12:2
who believes in Him is not **c-ed**,　John 3:18

confess—1. To admit sin (Lev. 16:21; 1 Sam. 7:6; Neh. 1:6; 9:2-3; Ps. 32:5; Dan. 9:4-5; Matt. 3:6). **2.** To acknowledge faith and commitment to God (Rom. 10:9-10; 1 Tim. 6:12-13; Heb. 13:15; 1 John 4:15; 2 John 7). One's public acknowledgment of Jesus is the basis for Jesus' own acknowledgment of that believer to God (Matt. 10:32-33; cp. 1 John 4:2-3; Rev. 3:5).

c that Jesus Christ is Lord,　Phil. 2:11
c your sins to one another　.　Jas. 5:16
If we **c** our sins, He is faithful　.1 John 1:9
he who **c-es** the Son has
the Father as well.　.1 John 2:23

conscience—The capacity to know whether one's behavior is good or bad, right or wrong.

at night my **c** instructs me.　.　Ps. 16:7
a clear **c** toward God and men.　.　Acts 24:16
of liars whose **c-s** are seared.　.　1 Tim. 4:2

consecrate—Give to God or set apart for the service of God.

C every firstborn male to Me,　.　Exod. 13:2
C yourselves and be holy, for I　.　Lev. 20:7

convert—Turn or return to God.

c-ed and become like　.　Matt. 18:3
be **c-ed**　.　John 12:40; Acts 28:27

convict—Cause a sense of guilt and shame leading to repentance.

He will **c** the world about sin,　.　John 16:8

corban—Gift particularly designated for the Lord, and so forbidden for any other use.

might have received from me is **C**　Mark 7:11

cornerstone—Stone laid at the corner to bind two walls together, symbolic of strength and prominence. Christ is the only sure foundation of faith.

rejected has become the **c**.　.　Ps. 118:22
a precious **c**, a sure foundation; .　Isa. 28:16
This Jesus ... has become the **c**.　.　Acts 4:11
Christ Jesus Himself as the **c**.　.　Eph. 2:20

Counselor—John used this word to describe the Holy Spirit as one who teaches (John 14:16), reminds the disciples of what Jesus taught (14:26), testifies (15:26), and convicts of sin (16:7-8). Jesus was the first Counselor (14:16) and is for the Christian an Advocate in heaven (1 John 2:1).

court historian—Person in the palace who wrote down the king's daily business.

covenant—Oath-bound promise whereby one party solemnly pledges to bless or serve another party in some specified way.

the LORD made a **c** with Abram,　.　Gen. 15:18
will never break My **c** with you.　.　Judg. 2:1
I will make a new **c** with　.　Jer. 31:31
This cup is the new **c**　.　Luke 22:20
He is the mediator of a new **c**,　.　Heb. 9:15

covet—To inordinately desire to possess what belongs to another.

Do not **c** your neighbor's　.　Exod. 20:17

creation—The act of God in bringing the world and everything in it into existence (Gen. 1–2; John 1:1-3; Heb. 11:3) and the result of that act (Col. 1:15, 23), which proclaims the glory of God (Ps. 8; 19:1-4).

From the **c** of the world His　.　Rom. 1:20

For the **c** eagerly waits with . . . . . Rom. 8:19

For we are His **c**—created in . . . . . Eph. 2:10

cross—Method the Romans used to execute Jesus Christ. It was seen by the Jews as a curse (Deut. 21:23; Gal. 3:13). For Paul the message of the cross is the heart of the gospel (1 Cor. 1:17-18, 23; 2:2). Jesus Himself established the primary figurative interpretation of the cross as a call to complete surrender to God (Matt. 10:38; 16:24; cp. Rom. 12:1; Gal. 6:14).

crown—Special headdress worn by royalty and other persons of high merit and honor.

A capable wife is her husband's **c**, Prov. 12:4

twisted together a **c** of thorns, . . . Matt. 27:29

do it to receive a perishable **c**, . . . 1 Cor. 9:25

for me the **c** of righteousness, . . . 2 Tim. 4:8

will receive the unfading **c** of glory. 1 Pet. 5:4

cast their **c-s** before the throne, . . Rev. 4:10

crucible—Melting pot used in the refining of silver, a figure for testing of people (Prov. 17:3; 27:21).

cubit—The distance from a person's elbow to the tip of the middle finger, approximately 18 inches.

cupbearer—An officer of the royal court who had charge of wines and other beverages and who helped prevent the poisoning of the king.

king of Egypt's **c** and his baker . . Gen. 40:1

I was the king's **c**. . . . . Neh. 1:11

curse—To predict, pray for, or cause misfortune on someone. Since belonging to God and His people meant blessing, being cursed often meant separation from God and the community of faith.

come and put a **c** on these people . Num. 22:6

an undeserved **c** goes nowhere. . Prov. 26:2

D

day—1. The time of daylight from sunrise to sunset. 2. The 24-hour period, usually defined as one sunset to the next, but also as starting at sunrise. 3. An undetermined time period or era associated with a particular person, event, or characteristic.

God called the light "**d**," . . . . Gen. 1:5

can endure the **d** of His coming? . . . Mal. 3:2

Give us each **d** our daily bread. . . Luke 11:3

now is the **d** of salvation. . . . . 2 Cor. 6:2

one **d** is like 1,000 years, ... 2 Pet. 3:8

Day of the Lord—Time when God reveals His sovereignty; day of divine judgment (Joel 2:31; Amos 5:18; 1 Thess. 5:2).

deacon—Title for an office in the local church (Phil. 1:1; 1 Tim. 3:8-13). The events of Acts 6:1-6 may be the origin of the office.

death—The cessation of life. The Bible talks about physical, spiritual, and eternal death.

He will destroy **d** forever. . . . . Isa. 25:8

he will never see **d**—ever! . . . . . . John 8:51

For the wages of sin is **d**, ... Rom. 6:23

that neither **d** nor life, ... Rom. 8:38

O **D**, where is your victory? . . . . 1 Cor. 15:55

D will exist no longer; . . . . Rev. 21:4

decree—Command or decision made by someone of authority.

dedicate—To set apart for special purposes.

defile—To make something unclean or impure.

things that **d** a man, ... Matt. 15:20

deliver—To rescue from danger.

deluge—A great flood (Gen. 6–9).

demons—Fallen angels who joined Satan in his rebellion.

drive out **d** in Your name . . . . Matt. 7:22

d also believe—and they shudder. . .Jas. 2:19

denarius—Coin representing a day's wage for a soldier or an ordinary laborer (Matt. 20:2).

desecrate—To take away sacredness, or to treat something as if it were not sacred (Dan. 11:31; Acts 24:6).

devoted—Set apart for something, such as God's use.

devout—Careful in fulfilling religious duties.

This man was righteous and **d**, . . Luke 2:25

die—To become lifeless. To die to something is to give up any association to it.

you eat from it, you will certainly **d**. Gen. 2:17

eat and drink, for tomorrow we **d**! Isa. 22:13

will never **d**—ever. . . . . John 11:26

moment, Christ **d-d** for the ungodly Rom. 5:6

How can we who **d-d** to sin still . . . Rom. 6:2

living is Christ and **dying** is gain. . . Phil. 1:21

appointed for people to **d** once . . . Heb. 9:27

discern—The ability to see differences and make choices (Rom. 12:2; Eph. 5:10; Phil. 1:9). One of the spiritual gifts (1 Cor. 12:10).

and to **d** between good and evil. 1 Kings 3:9

disciple—An adherent of a particular teacher or school. The primary reference is to followers of Jesus Christ (Matt. 10:1; 27:57; 28:19; Acts 6:7).

and make **d-s** of all nations, . . . Matt. 28:19

He summoned His **d-s**, and

He chose 12 of them . . . . Luke 6:13

discipline—Moral training, and the punishment inflicted to effect it. God disciplines His children for their own good in love (Deut. 8:5).

happy is the man You **d** and teach ... Ps. 94:12
for the LORD **d-s** the one He loves   Prov. 3:12
What son is there whom a father
  does not **d**? .... Heb. 12:7

dispossess—To drive residents out.

dissipation—Recklessness; lack of discipline (1 Pet. 4:4).

dissension—Contention; quarreling; discord (Rom. 16:17; Gal. 5:20).

distaff—Either part of the spindle or a stick used to hold the unspun fibers, used in spinning thread (Prov. 31:19).

divination—The practice of making decisions or telling the future by means of reading signs and omens (Lev. 19:26; Ezek. 21:21).

divine—Having to do with God.

His eternal power and **d** nature, . Rom. 1:20
For His **d** power has given us .... 2 Pet. 1:3
you may share in the **d** nature, ... 2 Pet. 1:4

divorce—Breaking of the marriage covenant.

may write her a **d** certificate, ... Deut. 24:1
If he hates and **d-s** {his wife}, ... Mal. 2:16
Permitted you to **d** your wives ... Matt. 19:8

doctrine—Christian truth and teaching passed on from generation to generation.

teaching as **d-s** the commands .... Matt. 15:9
they will not tolerate sound **d**, ... 2 Tim. 4:3

dominion—Political authority.

His **d** is an everlasting **d**, ... Dan. 4:34; 7:14
power and **d**, and every title ...... Eph. 1:21

door—Opening into a house or room.

and the **d** will be opened to you ... Matt. 7:7
to enter through the narrow **d**, .. Luke 13:24
a **d** was opened to me .... 2 Cor. 2:12
I stand at the **d** and knock. .... Rev. 3:20

double-minded—Lacking purity of heart or failing to trust only God (Ps. 119:113; Jas. 4:8).

doubt—Uncertainty; failure to believe.

of little faith, why did you **d**? .... Matt. 14:31
whoever **d-s** stands condemned   Rom. 14:23
let him ask in faith without **d-ing**. ... Jas. 1:6

dreams—One of the ways people sought to know God's will, see the future, and make decisions. Interpretation was often necessary (Gen. 40:8; 41:8; Dan. 2:3), and dreams could be false (Deut. 13:1-3).

your old men will have **d-s**, and ... Joel 2:28
appeared to Joseph in a **d**, ... Matt. 2:13

dross—Waste products that float to the top of molten metal in the refining process.

Israel has become **d** into Me. .... Ezek. 22:18

dust—Fine, loose earth.

man out of the **d** from the ground . Gen. 2:7
remembering that we are **d**. ..... Ps. 103:14
and all return to **d**. .... Eccl. 3:20

E

edification—Encouragement and consolation with the goal of establishment in the faith.

speaks to people for **e**, ... 1 Cor. 14:3

elder—Title for a leader in both Jewish and early Christian communities.

to appoint **e-s** in every town: ..... Titus 1:5
thrones sat 24 **e-s** dressed in ..... Rev. 4:4

election—The plan of God whereby He chooses certain individuals and groups through whom He fulfills His purpose of salvation.

God's purpose according to **e** ... Rom. 9:11
knowing your **e**, brothers loved   1 Thess. 1:4
to confirm your calling and **e**, ... 2 Pet. 1:10

elements, elemental forces—1. The primary or elementary points of learning, especially for a religion or philosophy (Heb. 6:1). 2. The four basic elements: fire, air, water, and earth (2 Pet. 3:10, 12). 3. Spirits who were thought by some to exercise a certain amount of control over the heavenly bodies (Gal. 4:3, 9; Col. 2:8, 20).

endure—To bear something difficult and keep on going.

the one who **e-s** to the end will . Matt. 10:22
hopes all things, **e-s** all things. .. 1 Cor. 13:7
if we **e**, we will also reign .... 2 Tim. 2:12
joy that lay before Him **e-d** a cross Heb. 12:2
testing of your faith produces **e-ance** . Jas. 1:3

enemy—An opponent.

me in the presence of my **e-ies**; .... Ps. 23:5
love your **e-ies** and pray for those   Matt. 5:44
The last **e** He abolishes is death 1 Cor. 15:26

engagement—Solemn promise to marry; in Bible times, engagement was as binding as marriage.

envoy—Representative; ambassador.

envy—To resent another's perceived advantage.

Don't **e** evil men .... Prov. 24:1
Love does not **e**; is not boastful . 1 Cor. 13:4

ephod—Priestly garment, possibly a short apron or loincloth (Exod. 28; 1 Sam. 2:18; 2 Sam. 6:14).

eternal life—Life at its best, having infinite duration, characterized by abiding fellowship with God.

will awake, some to **e**. . . . . Dan. 12:2
what good must I do to have **e**? Matt. 19:16
will not perish but have **e**. . . . . . . John 3:16
the gift of God is **e** in Christ Jesus Rom. 6:23

eunuch—A castrated male; the term came to be used of officials without regard to emasculation.

The **e** replied to Philip, "I ask . . . . . Acts 8:34

everlasting—Unending; eternal.

Yahweh is the **e** God, the Creator Isa. 40:28
the penalty of **e** destruction, . . . 2 Thess. 1:9

evil—Wicked, immoral; malevolent, malicious, harmful; contrary to the goodness of God.

tree of the knowledge of good and **e**. Gen. 2:9
To fear the LORD is to hate **e**. . . . Prov. 8:13
but deliver us from the **e** one. . . . Matt. 6:13
Do not repay anyone **e** for **e**. . . Rom. 12:17
from every form of **e**. . . . . 1 Thess. 5:22
root of all kinds of **e**, ... 1 Tim. 6:10
For God is not tempted by **e**, ... Jas. 1:13

exalt—To elevate in rank, honor, or power; to praise.

let us **e** His name together. . . . . . Ps. 34:3
Righteousness **e-s** a nation, but Prov. 14:34
humbles himself will be **e-ed**. . . . Matt. 23:12

execration—Cursing (Jer. 42:18; 44:12).

exhortation—Argument or advice intended to incite hearers to action (1 Tim. 5:1).

with many other **e-s**, he
proclaimed the good news . . . . Luke 3:18

exile—Forced deportation from one's homeland (2 Kings 17; 24–25).

exodus—The departure or emigration of a large number of people. The book of Exodus tells about Israel's escape from slavery in Egypt.

exorcism—Expelling demons by means of some ritual act (Acts 19:13).

expanse—A way the ancients described the sky or atmosphere (Gen. 1; Ps. 19:1; 150:1; Ezek. 1:22-26; 10:1; Dan. 12:3).

exploit—To take unfair advantage of (Exod. 22:21).

extortion—Obtaining something by force, threat, or abuse of authority.

F

fable—Short, fictitious story that uses animals or inanimate objects as characters to teach ethical or practical lessons. There are only two fables in the Bible (Judg. 9:8-15; 2 Kings 14:8-10; 2 Chron. 25:17-19).

fairness—Justice with integrity and without bias (Ps. 96:10; Ezek. 18:25; 33:17; Col. 4:1).

faith—Trust or dependence on a person or thing.

righteous one will live by his **f**. . . . . Hab. 2:4
f the size of a mustard seed, . . . Matt. 17:20
is justified by **f** apart from works . . . Rom. 3:28
So **f** comes from what is heard, . . Rom. 10:17
is not from **f** is sin. . . . . Rom. 14:23
if I have all **f**, so that I can move 1 Cor. 13:2
for we walk by **f**, not by sight . . . . 2 Cor. 5:7
by grace you are saved through **f**, . . Eph. 2:8
one Lord, one **f**, one baptism, ... Eph. 4:5
finished the race, I have kept the **f**. 2 Tim. 4:7
Now **f** is the reality of what is . . . . Heb. 11:1
Now without **f** it is impossible . . . . Heb. 11:6
source and perfecter of our **f**, . . . Heb. 12:2
f, if it doesn't have works, is dead . . . Jas. 2:17

faithful—Constant; true to one's word.

great is Your **f-ness**! . . . . Lam. 3:23
Well done, good and **f** slave! . . . Matt. 25:21
God is **f** and He will not allow . . 1 Cor. 10:13
He who calls you is **f**, who also 1 Thess. 5:24
commit to **f** men who will be able . 2 Tim. 2:2
for He who promised is **f**. . . . . . . Heb. 10:23
He is **f** and righteous to forgive . . 1 John 1:9
Its rider is called **F** and True, ... Rev. 19:11

faithless—Having distrusted or stopped trusting; without faith.

if we are **f**, He remains faithful, . 2 Tim. 2:13

false—Deceptive, misleading; phony, fake.

Do not give **f** testimony against . . . Exod. 20:16
F messiahs and **f** prophets will . . . Matt. 24:24
there will be **f** teachers . . . . 2 Pet. 2:1

famine—Extreme shortage of food (Amos 4:6).

There was a **f** in the land, ... Gen. 12:10
not a **f** of bread or a thirst for . . . Amos 8:11
or persecution or **f** or nakedness . Rom. 8:35

fast—To refrain from eating food (Ezra 8:23; Isa. 58; Joel 2:12; Zech. 7:5; Acts 13:2-3).

Whenever you **f**, don't be sad-faced like the hypocrites. . . . . Matt. 6:16

fate—That which must necessarily happen.

father—Male parent; progenitor, provider, and person of responsibility and authority. Sometimes it means "ancestor" (Deut. 26:5). One of the titles of God, the first person in the Trinity, expressing kinship, compassion, and loving discipline.

Honor your **f** and your mother . . . Exod. 20:12
You are my **F**, my God, the rock . . Ps. 89:26
Our **F** in heaven, Your name be . . . Matt. 6:9
What **f** among you, if his son . . . Luke 11:11

The **F** and I are one. . . . . John 10:30

F-s, do not exasperate your . . . . . . Col. 3:21

son is there whom a **f** does not . . Heb. 12:7

fear—**1**. Natural emotional response of terror when facing a perceived threat. **2**. Respect, honor; awe, reverence.

F the LORD your God, worship Him   Deut. 6:13

The **f** of the LORD is the beginning . Prov. 1:7

Do not **f**, for I am with you; . . . . . Isa. 41:10

f Him who is able to destroy both   Matt. 10:28

salvation with **f** and trembling. . . . . Phil. 2:12

There is no **f** in love; instead,

perfect love drives out **f**, ... 1 John 4:18

feast—A meal given to celebrate a joyous event, either a singular event such as a wedding (Judg. 14:10) or periodic events such as harvest or sheep-shearing (1 Sam. 25:7-8) or the Jewish festivals.

to the marriage **f** of the Lamb!   . . . . Rev. 19:9

fellowship—A bond of common purpose and devotion, a close association, a good relationship.

teaching, to **f**, to the breaking   . . . . Acts 2:42

Or what **f** does light have with . . 2 Cor. 6:14

we say, "We have **f** with Him," . . . 1 John 1:6

fertile—Able to produce fruit.

festival—Regular religious celebration remembering God's great acts of salvation.

a **f** in My honor three times a year.   Exod. 23:14

fetter—A constraint, especially a foot shackle (Jer. 2:20; 5:5; 27:2; 30:8).

fig—Important fruit and tree of the Holy Land. Fruits could be eaten fresh (Isa. 28:4; Jer. 24:2) or dried and stored as cakes (1 Sam. 25:18; 30:12).

At once the **f** tree withered. . . . . Matt. 21:19

firstborn—The first son born to a newly married couple. In memory of the death of Egypt's first-born, all the firstborn of Israel belonged to Yahweh (Exod. 13:2). The birthright of a first-born included a double portion of the estate and leadership of the family.

she gave birth to her **f** Son, ... Luke 2:7

the **f** from the dead and the ruler . . . Rev. 1:5

firstfruits—Choice portions of a crop harvested first and dedicated to God (Exod. 23:19). Used figuratively of the Spirit as the beginning of our salvation (Rom. 8:23), of Christ as the first man to rise from the dead (1 Cor. 15:20, 23), and of certain Christians as the first of humanity to enter the kingdom (16:15; Jas. 1:18; Rev. 14:4).

flesh—The skin, meat, or the body as a whole of humans or animals. It can also mean all mankind, or one's relatives. In the NT, especially in Paul's writings, it stands for the fallen human nature, which is incapable of conforming to God's holy expectations.

spirit is willing, but the **f** is weak.   Matt. 26:41

The Word became **f** . . . . John 1:14

are not in the **f**, but in the Spirit, . . . Rom. 8:9

the works of the **f** are obvious: . . . . Gal. 5:19

flock—A group of sheep, goats, or both. Figuratively, people in need of care and guidance.

sheep of the **f** will be scattered. . Matt. 26:31

watch at night over their **f**. . . . . . . Luke 2:8

flog—Punish by repeated blows of a whip or rod.

after having Jesus **f-ged**, ...Matt. 27:26

fodder—Feed for domestic animals (Job 6:5; 24:6; Isa. 30:24).

folly, foolishness—Lack of wisdom.

answer a fool according to his **f**,   Prov. 26:4,5

the message of the cross is **f**, . . 1 Cor. 1:18

wisdom of this world is **f**, ... 1 Cor. 3:19

fool—Unwise and ungodly person.

The **f** says in his heart, "God . . . Ps. 14:1; 53:1

whoever says to his brother, 'F!' . . Matt. 5:22

Claiming to be wise,

they became **f-s** . . . . Rom. 1:22

foreknowledge—God's omniscience with regard to the future (Isa. 42:9; 46:10; Rom. 8:29; 11:2; 1 Pet. 1:2).

forgive—Pardon a fault or offense; excuse payment for a debt owed.

f their sin, and heal their land.   2 Chron. 7:14

And **f** us our debts, as we also

have **f-n** our debtors. . . . . Matt. 6:12

f-ing one another, just as God

also **f-gave** you in Christ. . . . . . Eph. 4:32

the **f-ness** of sins. . . . . Col. 1:14

forsake—Abandon.

I will not leave you or **f** you. . . . . . . Josh. 1:5

My God, why have You **f-n** Me? . Matt. 27:46

fortified cities—Strategically located walled cities guarding travel routes or borders (Josh. 19:35-38; 2 Chron. 11:5-12).

fowler—One who traps birds (Prov. 6:5; Jer. 5:26; Hos. 9:8).

frankincense—A resinous substance derived from certain trees in the balsam family (Matt. 2:11).

free—Not captive or enslaved.

and the truth will set you **f**. . . . . . John 8:32

Jesus has set you **f** from the law . . Rom. 8:2
slave or **f**, male or female; . . . . Gal. 3:28
Christ has liberated us into **f-dom**. . Gal. 5:1

freedmen—Former slaves (Acts 6:9;
1 Cor. 7:22).

freewill offering—Gift given at the impulse of
the giver.

friend—Person with a close, trusting relationship with another. The "king's friend" was his
adviser (1 Kings 4:5 KJV).

Now when Job's three **f-s**—Eliphaz   Job 2:11
A **f** loves at all times, ... Prov. 17:17
a **f** of tax collectors and . . . . Matt. 11:19
I have called you **f-s**, ... John 15:15
the world's **f** becomes God's enemy.   Jas. 4:4

fruit—Literally, the useful product of a plant;
figuratively, the product of anything.

recognize them by their **f**. . . . . . . Matt. 7:16
But the **f** of the Spirit is love, joy, . . Gal. 5:22

fulfill—To bring about what was promised,
predicted, or foreshadowed.

F what you vow. . . . . Eccl. 5:4
not come to destroy but to **f**. . . . . Matt. 5:17
this Scripture has been **f-ed**. . . . . Luke 4:21
entire law is **f-ed** in one statement   Gal. 5:14

fullness—Completeness; the entire essence.
filled with all the **f** of God. . . . . . . Eph. 3:19

G

gall—Bitter, poisonous herb (Ps. 69:21; Matt.
27:34).

garrison—Body of troops stationed for defense, often in the sense of occupying forces.

gate—Point of access to a walled town. The
space near the gate was used for public
proceedings.

genealogy—A family tree, sometimes selective.
to myths and endless **g-ies**. . . . . 1 Tim. 1:4

gift—Favor, item, or ability bestowed on someone.

but the **g** of God is eternal life . . . Rom. 6:23
Now there are different **g-s**, ... 1 Cor. 12:4
every perfect **g** is from above, ... Jas. 1:17

glean—Gather remnants of grain or fruit.
you must not **g** what is left. . . . . Deut. 24:21
saw what she had **g-ed**. . . . . Ruth 2:18

glorify—Praise, recognize the honor or importance of another.

the Son of Man is **g-ied**, and
   God is **g-ied** in Him. . . . . John 13:31
those He justified, He also **g-ied**.   Rom. 8:30

glory—Weighty importance and shining
majesty that accompany God's presence.

Declare His **g** among ...nations   1 Chron. 16:24
ascribe to the LORD **g** and strength. . Ps. 96:7
observed His **g**, the **g** as the One   John 1:14
and fall short of the **g** of God. . . . Rom. 3:23
do everything for God's **g**. . . . . 1 Cor. 10:31
Christ in you, the hope of **g**. . . . . . Col. 1:27

gnash—Grate (one's teeth) together as an
expression of anger or despair.

they **g-ed** their teeth at me. . . . . . . Ps. 35:16
weeping and **g-ing** of teeth. . . . . . Matt. 8:12

goad—Rod with a pointed end used to control
oxen (Eccl. 12:11; Acts 26:14).

goat—Hollow-horned, cud-chewing mammal
with long, floppy ears. Milk, meat, skin, and hair
were utilized, and it was used as a sacrifice.

God-fearers—Gentiles who were drawn to the
Jewish religion and practices.

godless—Excluding God from thought and
ignoring or deliberately violating God's laws.

godly—Respecting God, resulting in obedience
and piety.

But **g-iness** with contentment is a   1 Tim. 6:6

gospel—The good news about salvation
provided for all through the life, death, and
resurrection of Jesus the Messiah.

and preach the **g** to the whole . . Mark 16:15
For I am not ashamed of the **g**, . . Rom. 1:16

Gospels—The first four books of the NT.

grace—Undeserved acceptance and love,
usually from a superior to an inferior. In the
Bible, the favor of God in providing salvation in
Christ for those who deserve condemnation.

g and truth came through Jesus . John 1:17
For by **g** you are saved through . . . . Eph. 2:8
having been justified by His **g**, ... Titus 3:7

grieve—To express or to cause sorrow.

And don't **g** God's Holy Spirit, ... Eph. 4:30
you will not **g** like the rest, . . . 1 Thess. 4:13

guardian—Adult responsible for the person and
property of a minor.

law, then, was our **g** until Christ, . . Gal. 3:24

guilt—Responsibility for an offense or wrongdoing; guilt requires either punishment or expiation.

You took away the **g** of my sin. . . . . Ps. 32:5

H

half tribe—Part of Manasseh, usually the part
dwelling east of the Jordan (Num. 32:33; Deut.
3:13; Josh. 1:12; 4:12; 22:1).

hallelujah—Exclamation meaning "Praise Yahweh!"

    H! My soul, praise the LORD. ...... Ps. 146:1
    multitude in heaven, saying: **H**! ... Rev. 19:1

hardness of heart—Resistance to and rejection of the Word and will of God.

    He rebuked their unbelief and **h**, Mark 16:14

harp—Musical instrument with strings.

    who knows how to play the **h**. . 1 Sam. 16:16
    praise Him with **h** and lyre. .... Ps. 150:3

hate—Strong negative reaction implying volatile hostility. Sometimes hate means to love less than something better (Matt. 10:37; Luke 14:26; John 12:26).

    To fear the LORD is to **h** evil. ...... Prov. 8:13
    I loved Jacob, but I **h-d** Esau. ..... Mal. 1:3
    does not **h** his own .... Luke 14:26
    want to do, but I do what I **h**. ..... Rom. 7:15

haughty—Proud.

    You humble those with **h** eyes. ..... Ps. 18:27

head—The uppermost part of the body; the first, top, or chief.

    Christ is the **h** of every man, the
      man is the **h** of the woman, ... 1 Cor. 11:3
    He is also **h** of the body, ... Col. 1:18

heal—Bring health to persons who are sick physically, emotionally, and spiritually.

    For I am the LORD who **h-s** you. . Exod. 15:26
    gifts of **h-ing** by the one Spirit, . 1 Cor. 12:9
    by His wounding
      you have been **h-ed** .... 1 Pet. 2:24

heart—Center of intellectual, moral, emotional, and spiritual life.

    LORD your God with all your **h**, ... Deut. 6:5
    but the LORD sees the **h**. ...... 1 Sam. 16:7
    create a clean **h** for me and ..... Ps. 51:10
    Your word in my **h** so that I may . . Ps. 119:11
    Search me, God, and know my **h**; Ps. 139:23
    them and write it on their **h-s**. ... Jer. 31:33
    I will give you a new **h** .... Ezek. 36:26
    there your **h** will be also. .... Matt. 6:21

heaven—The part of God's creation above the earth, including air and space, serving as the home of God and the final abode of the righteous.

    God created the **h-s** and the earth. Gen. 1:1
    The **h-s** declare the glory of God, . . Ps. 19:1
    for yourselves treasures in **h**, ... Matt. 6:20
    but our citizenship is in **h**, ... Phil. 3:20
    I saw a new **h** and a new earth ... Rev. 21:1

heifer—Young cow, especially one that has not yet calved (Heb. 9:13).

heir—One who inherits the property, blessing, or position of a predecessor.

    if children, also **h-s**—**h-s** of God . Rom. 8:17
    h-s according to the promise. .... Gal. 3:29
    the Gentiles are co-**h-s**, members . Eph. 3:6

hell—The final abode of the unrighteous dead wherein they suffer eternal punishment.

    to have two hands and go to **h** ... Mark 9:43
    authority to throw {people} into **h** . Luke 12:5

high place—Elevated site, usually on the top of a mountain or hill. Most high places were places of pagan worship and idolatry, and God commanded that they be destroyed.

high priest—One in charge of the temple (or tabernacle) worship, a hereditary office based on descent from Aaron.

    led Him away to Caiaphas the **h**, Matt. 26:57
    become a merciful and faithful **h** . Heb. 2:17
    this is the kind of **h** we need: .... Heb. 7:26

hill country—High ground west of the Jordan Valley, differentiated from the Shephelah (foot-hills) and coastal plain on the west and the Negev on the south.

holy—Separated from the world and dedicated to God; separated from worldliness.

    you are standing is **h** ground. ...... Exod. 3:5
    and be **h** because I am **h**. ...... Lev. 11:44
    H, h, h is the LORD of Hosts; ...... Isa. 6:3
    and called us with a **h** calling, ... 2 Tim. 1:9

holy of holies—Innermost sanctuary of the temple (Heb. 9:3), also called the most holy place.

holy place—Courts, inner room, and outer room of the tabernacle (Exod. 26:33).

honor—Respect, recognition.

    H your father and your mother . . Exod. 20:12
    Your name be **h-ed** as holy. .... Matt. 6:9
    is not without **h** except in his .... Matt. 13:57

hope—Trustful expectation, particularly with reference to the fulfillment of God's promises.

    Put your **h** in God, for I will .... Ps. 42:5
    This **h** does not disappoint, ... Rom. 5:5
    Christ in you, the **h** of glory. ...... Col. 1:27
    the rest, who have no **h**. ...... 1 Thess. 4:13
    the reality of what is **h-d** for, ... Heb. 11:1
    reason for the **h** that is in you ... 1 Pet. 3:15

horn—Metaphorically, strength and honor.

    My shield, the **h** of my salvation 2 Sam. 22:3

hosanna—A Hb or Aramaic word originally meaning "Save now," or "Save, we plead of You," used as an exclamation of praise.

    H in the highest heaven! .... Matt. 21:9

hostile—Opposed, antagonistic, against.
   I will put **h-ity** between you and the   Gen. 3:15
   mind-set of the flesh is **h** to God . .   Rom. 8:7
   tore down the dividing wall of **h-ity**.   Eph. 2:14

humanity—Humankind, male and female,
created in the image of God (Gen. 1:27), having
a body and soul (2:7).

humble—Free from arrogance and pride.
   Moses was a very **h** man, ...   Num. 12:3
   and to walk **h-y** with your God. . . . .   Mic. 6:8
   whoever **h-s** himself like this child   Matt. 18:4
   He **h-d** Himself by becoming . . . . . .   Phil. 2:8
   but gives grace to the **h**. . . . .   Jas. 4:6

humility—Absence of pride.
   and **h** comes before honor. . . . . . .   Prov. 15:33
   but in **h** consider others as more . . .   Phil. 2:3

hunger—Literally, a desire for food (Gen.
41:55). Figuratively, any strong desire (Mic.
6:14; Matt. 5:6).

hymns—Songs of praise.
   singing psalms, **h**, and . . . .   Col. 3:16

hypocrite—One who pretends to be better than
he really is.
   you must not be like the **h-s**, ...   Matt. 6:5
   H! First take the log out of . . . .   Matt. 7:5

hyssop—Small bushy plant used to apply
ritually cleansing blood.
   Purify me with **h**, and I will be clean;   Ps. 51:7

I

I Am—The way God identified or described
Himself to Moses (Exod. 3:13-14). Jesus spoke
the same phrase, claiming equality with God
(John 8:58).

idol—Image or form representing a divine being
and thus an object of worship in place of God.
   Do not make an **i** for yourself, . . .   Exod. 20:4
   we know that "an **i** is nothing . . . . .   1 Cor. 8:4
   and greed, which is **i-atry**. . . . .   Col. 3:5

image—Likeness.
   Let Us make man in Our **i**, ...   Gen. 1:26
   He is the **i** of the invisible God . . . .   Col. 1:15

Immanuel—"God with us"; name of a son to be
born in Isaiah's prophecy to King Ahaz (Isa. 7:14;
cp. 8:8), fulfilled in the birth of Jesus (Matt. 1:23).

immorality—Wickedness; what is not right.
   Flee from sexual **i**! . . . .   1 Cor. 6:18

immortal—Exempt from death: the gift of God
to mankind.
   mortal must be clothed
       with **i-ity**. . . . .   1 Cor. 15:53
   the King eternal, **i**, invisible . . . . .   1 Tim. 1:17

imperishable—Not subject to decay.
   into an inheritance that is **i**, ...   1 Pet. 1:4

impurity—Uncleanness; imperfection.
   I will remove all your **i-ies**. . . . . . .   Isa. 1:25
   God has not called us to **i**, ...   1 Thess. 4:7

incense—Mixture of aromatic spices burned
during sacrificial worship (Exod. 30:1-10, 34-38).
   prayer be set before You as **i**, ...   Ps. 141:2

indignation—Displeasure at something offensive; righteous, justified anger.

inherit—Receive assets from someone who
died.
   they will **i** the earth. . . . .   Matt. 5:5
   must I do to **i** eternal life?   Luke 10:25; 18:18

inheritance—Assets received from someone
who died.
   to be a people for His **i**, ...   Deut. 4:20
   Levi has no **i** among his brothers,
       the LORD is his **i**, ...   Deut. 18:2
   In Him we were also made His **i**, . .   Eph. 1:11

iniquity—Sin.
   crushed because of our **i-ies**; . . . .   Isa. 53:5

inquire of God—Seek God's guidance and will
regarding such things as battles (1 Sam. 23:2),
illness (2 Kings 1:2-3, 16), and other decisions
(2 Sam. 2:1).

inscription—Words or letters carved,
engraved, or printed on a surface (Exod. 31:18;
Dan. 5:8; Mark 15:26).

instruct—Teach or exhort; disciple.
   Your good Spirit to **i** them. . . . . . .   Neh. 9:20
   are able to **i** you for salvation . . .   2 Tim. 3:15

instruction—The act or content of teaching or
exhortation; discipleship.
   This book of **i** must not depart . . . .   Josh. 1:8
   Listen to **i** and be wise; . . . .   Prov. 8:33

integrity—Unwavering support of a standard of
values; singleness of heart or mind.
   if you walk before Me ... with **i** . .   1 Kings 9:4
   You desire **i** in the inner self . . . . . .   Ps. 51:6

intercede—Intervene or mediate between
differing parties, particularly to pray to God on
behalf of another person.
   But Moses **i-d** with the LORD his   Exod. 32:11
   the Spirit Himself **i-s** for us with . .   Rom. 8:26
   He always lives to **i** for them. . . . .   Heb. 7:25

intercession—Act of interceding.
   perseverance and **i** for all the . . . .   Eph. 6:18
   prayers, **i-s**, and thanksgivings . . .   1 Tim. 2:1

intermarry—Marry someone from another
culture or religion.
   Do not **i** with them. . . . .   Deut. 7:3

interpret—Explain the meaning of something.
and the ability to **i** dreams, ... Dan. 5:12
Do all speak in languages?
Do all **i**? . . . . 1 Cor. 12:30

invoke—To call on by name for help.
must not **i** the names of other gods; Exod. 23:13

J

jealousy—1. Intolerance of rivalry or unfaithfulness. God is jealous for His people Israel in this first sense: He is intolerant of rival gods (Deut. 4:24; 5:9; Ezek. 8:3). **2.** A disposition suspicious of rivalry or unfaithfulness (Num. 5:11-31). **3.** Hostility toward a rival or one believed to enjoy an advantage; envy (Acts 5:17; 13:45).
provoked His **j** with foreign gods   Deut. 32:16

Judaism—Religion and way of life of the Jews.

judge—1. An official with authority to administer justice by trying cases (Exod. 2:14) and condemning the guilty (Ps. 1:5). **2.** A military deliverer in the period between Joshua and David (Judg. 2:16).
He **j-s** the world with righteousness; . Ps. 9:8
Do not **j**, so that you won't be **j-d**. . Matt. 7:1
I did not come to **j** the world but . John 12:47
before the **j-ment** seat of Christ,   2 Cor. 5:10
who is going to **j** the living and . . . 2 Tim. 4:1
die once—and after this, **j-ment**—   Heb. 9:27

just—Fair, impartial, legally correct.
Won't the Judge of all the earth
do what is **j**? . . . . Gen. 18:25
Only to act **j-ly**, to love . . . . Mic. 6:8
whatever is **j**, whatever is pure . . . . . . Phil. 4:8

justice—Fair and impartial treatment.
He will bring **j** to the nations. . . . . . . Isa. 42:1
But let **j** flow like water, ... Amos 5:24
will proclaim **j** to the nations. . . . Matt. 12:18

justification—Divine, forensic act of God whereby a sinner is pronounced righteous by the imputation of the righteousness of Christ.
and raised for our **j**. . . . . Rom. 4:25

justified—Pronounced righteous.
who believes in Him is **j** . . . . Acts 13:39
They are **j** freely by His grace . . . Rom. 3:24
no one is **j** by the works of the law . Gal. 2:16

K

key—Instrument for gaining access.
give you the **k-s** of the kingdom . Matt. 16:19
and I hold the **k-s** of death and . . . Rev. 1:18
the One who has the **k** of David, . . . Rev. 3:7

kind—Compassionate, gentle, gracious.

with ropes of **k-ness**. . . . . Hos. 11:4
God's **k-ness** is intended to lead . . Rom. 2:4
Love is patient; love is **k**. . . . . . 1 Cor. 13:4
And be **k** and compassionate . . . . Eph. 4:32

king—Male monarch of a country.
said, "Give us a **k** to judge us . . . 1 Sam. 8:6
who has been born **K** of the Jews?   Matt. 2:2
K OF **K-S** AND LORD OF . . . . Rev. 19:16

kingdom—The realm over which rule is exerted and the exercise of authority to reign. Jesus preached that God's kingdom was at hand (Matt. 11:12). Jesus' miracles, preaching, forgiving sins, and resurrection were an inbreaking of God's sovereign rule in this dark, evil age.
you will be My **k** of priests and . . . Exod. 19:6
But seek first the **k** of God . . . . . . Matt. 6:33
I will give you the keys of the **k** . Matt. 16:19
the **k** of God is among you. . . . . Luke 17:21
My **k** is not of this world, ... John 18:36
transferred us into the **k** of the Son   Col. 1:13

kiss—The touching of the lips to another person's lips, cheeks, shoulders, hands, or feet as a gesture of friendship, acceptance, respect, and reverence.
betraying the Son of Man with a **k**?   Luke 22:48
Greet one another with a holy **k**.   Rom. 16:16

knowledge—Awareness of facts, truths, and principles. Right knowledge gives direction, conviction, and assurance to faith (2 Cor. 4:14).
fear of the LORD is the beginning
of **k**; . . . . Prov. 1:7
K inflates with pride, but love . . . 1 Cor. 8:1

L

lamb—Young sheep, used for sacrifice during Passover (Exod. 12:1-36) as well as in the daily sacrifices of Israel (Lev. 14:12-21). Christ was the Lamb of God who provided salvation for the world.
God Himself will provide the **l** . . . . Gen. 22:8
Like a **l** led to the slaughter . . . . . . Isa. 53:7
L of God, who takes away the sin   John 1:29
L who was slaughtered is worthy . . Rev. 5:12

lament, lamentation—Expression of grief and mourning.

lamp—An open bowl for oil with a pinched spout to support a wick.
Your word is a **l** for my feet and . Ps. 119:105
No one lights a **l** and puts it . . . . Matt. 5:15
like 10 virgins who took their **l-s** . . Matt. 25:1

language—System of communication.
the whole earth had the same **l** . . Gen. 11:1
began to speak in different **l-s**, ... Acts 2:4

different kinds of **l-s**, to another,
interpretation of **l-s**. . . . . 1 Cor. 12:10
do not forbid speaking
in {other} **l-s**. . . . . 1 Cor. 14:39
every tribe and **l** and people . . . . . . Rev. 5:9

lattice—Structure of crisscrossed strips used as window covering to allow some light to penetrate while keeping heat and rain to a minimum.

law—Term used for commandments, customs, legal judgments, collections of regulations and ordinances, the book of Deuteronomy (which means "second law"), the entire complex of regulations revealed at Sinai, the first five books of the OT, and the OT as a whole as opposed to the NT.

Moses wrote down this **l** . . . . Deut. 31:9
l will place My **l** within them . . . . . Jer. 31:33
All the **L** and the Prophets
depend on these . . . . Matt. 22:40
are not under **l** but under grace . . Rom. 6:14
The **l**, then, was our guardian until Gal. 3:24
sin is the breaking of **l**. . . . . 1 John 3:4

leaven—Natural yeast used to make dough rise.

lewdness—Lust; sexual unchastity (Mark 7:22).

life—The animating force in both animals and humans (Gen. 1:20). Just as physical life is the gift of God, so is eternal life (Rom. 6:23).

breathed the breath of **l** into his . . . Gen. 2:7
the **l** of a creature is in the blood, Lev. 17:11
gains the whole world yet
loses his **l**? . . . . Matt. 16:26
l am the resurrection and the **l**. . John 11:25
l am the way, the truth, and the **l**. . John 14:6

light—Radiant energy, illumination. Symbolic of instruction (Ps. 119:105,130), truth (43:3), good (Isa. 5:20), salvation (49:6), life (Job 33:28,30), peace (Isa. 45:7), rejoicing (Ps. 97:11), covenant (Isa. 42:6), justice and righteousness (59:9), God's presence and favor (Ps. 89:15; 1 John 1:5), and the glory of Yahweh (Isa. 60:1-3; Rev. 21:23).

"Let there be **l**," and there was **l**. . . Gen. 1:3
in darkness have seen a great **l**; . . . Isa. 9:2
You are the **l** of the world. . . . . . . Matt. 5:14
l am the **l** of the world. . . . . John 8:12

linen—Common fabric spun from the flax plant.

lion—Large meat-eating cat.
and the **l** will eat straw like an ox. . Isa. 11:7
prowling around like a roaring **l**, . . 1 Pet. 5:8
The **L** from the tribe of Judah, ... Rev. 5:5

live—Be physically or spiritually alive.

for no one can see Me and **l**. . . . Exod. 33:20
man does not **l** on bread alone . . . Deut. 8:3
The one who believes in Me,
even if he dies, will **l**. . . . . John 11:25
The righteous will **l** by faith. . . . . . Rom. 1:17
l no longer **l**, but Christ **l-s** in me. The
life **l** now **l** in the flesh, **l l** by faith Gal. 2:20

locust—An insect, similar to the grasshopper, that periodically multiplies to astronomical numbers devouring vegetation.

What the devouring **l** has left, the . . Joel 1:4
his food was **l-s** and wild honey. . . Matt. 3:4

Lord—A title of God. Yahweh is the name of God (Exod. 3:15), commonly represented by LORD (in small caps; "LD" below). 'Adonai is another important Hb designation for God as Lord and master in the OT. In the NT, the Gk word *kurios* is used of God as well as Jesus. 'Adonai and *kurios* are also used of humans (Gen. 18:12; 39:2; Num. 21:28; Isa. 26:13; Matt. 13:27; 21:30; 27:63; Luke 14:22).

The **LD** is my shepherd; . . . . Ps. 23:1
The **LD** declared to my **L**: . . . . Ps. 110:1
who says to Me, '**L**, **L**!' will enter . Matt. 7:21
to Him, "My **L** and my God!" . . . . John 20:28
crucified, both **L** and Messiah! . . . . Acts 2:36
with your mouth, "Jesus is **L**," . . . Rom. 10:9
one can say, "Jesus is **L**," except 1 Cor. 12:3
confess that Jesus Christ is **L**, ... Phil. 2:11
King of kings, and the **L** of **l-s**, . . 1 Tim. 6:15
obeyed Abraham, calling him **l**. . . . 1 Pet. 3:6
but set apart the Messiah as **L** . . 1 Pet. 3:15

lot—Object used to discover God's will. Person casting lots would first pray to God asking for a correct answer (1 Sam. 14:41; Acts 1:26).

The land must be divided by **l**; . . . Num. 26:55
The **l** is cast into the lap, ... Prov. 16:33
His clothes by casting **l-s**. . . . . . Matt. 27:35

love—Unselfish, loyal, and benevolent intention and commitment toward another person. Gk word *agape* was used in the NT to denote the unconditional love of God (John 3:16; Rom. 5:8).

showing faithful **l** to a thousand . . Exod. 20:6
but **l** your neighbor as yourself; . . Lev. 19:18
L the LORD your God with all your . Deut. 6:5
A friend **l-s** at all times, ... Prov. 17:17
l your enemies and pray for . . . Matt. 5:44
For God **l-d** the world in this way . John 3:16
give you a new commandment:
l one another. . . . . John 13:34
No one has greater **l** than this, . John 15:13
God proves His own **l** for us in that Rom. 5:8
L is patient; **l** is kind. **L** does not 1 Cor. 13:4
Husbands, **l** your wives, just as . . . Eph. 5:25

For the **l** of money is a root of .. 1 Tim. 6:10
Do not **l** the world or the things . 1 John 2:15
l one another, because **l** is
   from God .... 1 John 4:7
God is **l**, ... 1 John 4:16

lust—Strong craving or desire for something wrong, especially illicit sexual desire.
   looks at a woman to **l** for her has . Matt. 5:28
   the **l** of the flesh, the **l** of
   the eyes .... 1 John 2:16

lyre—A stringed instrument similar to a harp.

M

magic—The manipulation of natural or super-natural events through incantation or other means (Exod. 7:22; Prov. 17:8; Acts 19:19).

majesty—Imposing, regal dignity.
   Splendor and **m** are before Him; 1 Chron. 16:27
   He is robed in **m**; .... Ps. 93:1
   right hand of the **M** on high. ...... Heb. 1:3
   we were eyewitnesses of His **m**. . 2 Pet. 1:16

malice—Hatred; harmful intentions.
   put away ... wrath, **m**, slander, ... Col. 3:8

manna—Food from heaven that sustained the Israelites in the wilderness.
   Israel named the substance **m**. . Exod. 16:31
   fathers ate the **m** in the desert, John 6:31,49

mantle—Robe worn as an outer garment (1 Kings 19:19; 2 Kings 2:13-14).

marriage—The covenantal union of one man and one woman enacted with an oath before God of lifelong loyalty and love for each other.
   nor are given in **m** but are like .. Matt. 22:30
   M must be respected by all, ... Heb. 13:4
   the **m** of the Lamb has come, ... Rev. 19:7

marry—Form a marriage.
   it is better to **m** than to burn ..... 1 Cor. 7:9

master—One in authority over others (Mark 13:35; Luke 13:25; 14:21; 16:13; Eph. 6:9).
   if I am a **m**, where is {your} fear .... Mal. 1:6
   No one can be a slave of two **m-s** Matt. 6:24
   slave is not greater than his **m**, . John 13:16

mattock—Tool used for digging (1 Sam. 13:20-21).

mediator—One who stands between two or more parties to negotiate and reconcile. Jesus was the perfect mediator between God and man.
   one God and one **m** between God 1 Tim. 2:5

meditate—Think deeply or reflect upon some truth or supposition.
   he **m-s** on it day and night. .... Ps. 1:2

mouth and the **m-ion** of my heart . Ps. 19:14

medium—A person possessed by (Lev. 20:6) or consulting (Deut. 18:11) a ghost or spirit of the dead.
   Do not turn to **m-s** or consult .... Lev. 19:31
   a woman at Endor who is a **m**. . 1 Sam. 28:7

mercy—Compassionate action towards some-one over whom one has the advantage.
   for His **m-ies** never end......... Lam. 3:22
   I desire **m** and not sacrifice. ..... Matt. 9:13
   I will show **m** to whom I show **m**, . Rom. 9:15
   M triumphs over judgment. .... Jas. 2:13

mercy seat—Slab of pure gold that sat atop the ark of the covenant, it symbolized the throne from which God ruled Israel (Lev. 16:2; Num. 7:89; Heb. 9:5).

midwife—Woman who assisted in the delivery of a baby (Gen. 35:17; 38:28; Exod. 1:15-21).

millstone—Either of a pair of circular stones used to grind grain.
   or an upper **m** as security for a .. Deut. 24:6
   better for him if a heavy **m** were .. Matt. 18:6

miracle—Event which involves an immediate and powerful action of God designed to reveal His character or purposes.
   and do many **m-s** in Your name? . Matt. 7:22
   testified by signs ... various **m-s**, .. Heb. 2:4

money—Medium of exchange.
   loves **m** is never satisfied with **m** . Eccl. 5:10
   without **m**, come, buy, and eat! ... Isa. 55:1
   cannot be slaves of God
   and of **m**. .... Matt. 6:24
   For the love of **m** is a root of ... 1 Tim. 6:10

mortal—Human; susceptible to death.
   this **m** must be clothed
   with immortality. .... 1 Cor. 15:53

mourn—Express sorrow and grief.
   a time to **m** and a time to dance; .. Eccl. 3:4
   Blessed are those who **m**, because Matt. 5:4

murder—Intentional, illegal taking of human life.
   Do not **m**. .... Exod. 20:13
   who hates his brother is a **m-er** . 1 John 3:15

mute—Unable to speak.
   Who makes him **m** or deaf, seeing Exod. 4:11

myrrh—Aromatic resin used as an ingredient in anointing oil (Exod. 30:23), applied as perfume (Esth. 2:12; Prov. 7:17; Songs 1:13; 3–5), given as a gift (Matt. 2:11; cp. Rev. 18:13), and used in embalming (John 19:39; cp. Mark 15:23).

mystery—A revealed secret that could not have been understood apart from divine revelation.

The **m** was then revealed
to Daniel .... Dan. 2:19
the **m** hidden for ages .... Col. 1:26
the **m** of godliness is great: .... 1 Tim. 3:16

myth—An unproven but popular belief; a
contrived tale that does not adhere to facts.
 not ... to pay attention to **m-s** ..... 1 Tim. 1:4

N

nard—Expensive fragrance (Songs 4:13-14;
Mark 14:3; John 12:3).

neighbor—A nearby person. Jesus
expanded the definition to any person in need
(Luke 10:29-37).
 but love your **n** as yourself; ..... Lev. 19:18

O

oath—Invoking of God's name or something
else of value to promise that a vow will be kept
or that a statement is true.

offense—That which causes indignation or
disgust (Gen. 31:36; Matt. 18:7; Gal. 5:11).

offering—A gift to God as an act of worship.
 LORD had regard for Abel and his **o**, Gen. 4:4
 and fragrant **o** to God. .... Eph. 5:2
 You did not want sacrifice and **o**, ... Heb. 10:5

oil—A product of olives, it had many uses
including the treatment of wounds (Isa. 1:6;
Luke 10:34) and anointing (Exod. 29:7; 30:25;
cp. Matt. 26:7, 12).
 You anoint my head with **o**; .... Ps. 23:5
 sensible ones took **o**
 in their flasks .... Matt. 25:4
 anointing him with olive **o**
 in the name of the Lord. .... Jas. 5:14

oppress—Burden with unjust restraints.
 raises up those who are **o-ed** ..... Ps. 146:8
 He was **o-ed** and afflicted, ... Isa. 53:7

oracle—A communication from God.

ordain—1. Determine ahead of time what will
happen. 2. Commission a person for special
service to the Lord and His people.

ordinance—A law, especially one from God.

overseer—1. Secular superintendent or super-
visor (Exod. 5:10). 2. A church office (Acts
20:28; Phil. 1:1; 1 Tim. 3:1-2; Titus 1:7;
1 Pet. 5:2).

ox—Large bovine used as a work animal, as
food, and as a sacrifice.
 Do not muzzle an **o** while it .... Deut. 25:4;
 1 Cor. 9:9

P

pagan—One who worships a god or gods other
than Yahweh.

parable—A story that puts one thing alongside
another for purposes of comparison and new
insight (cp. John 10:6).
 He told them many things in **p-s**. Matt. 13:3

paradise—Literally a garden (Songs 4:13);
another word for heaven (Rev. 2:7).
 you will be with Me in **p** .... Luke 23:43
 was caught up into **p**. .... 2 Cor. 12:4

paralytic—One who has lost use of a body part.
 brought to Him a **p** lying on a ..... Matt. 9:2

parents—Fathers and mothers.
 who sinned, this man or his **p**, ... John 9:2
 Children, obey your **p** in the Lord, .. Eph. 6:1

Passover—Israelite festival commemorating
deliverance from Egyptian bondage (Exod. 12:11).
 Christ our **P** has been sacrificed. .. 1 Cor. 5:7

patience—Endurance of opposition; perseverance, steadfastness, forbearance.
 endured with much **p** objects of .. Rom. 9:22
 love, joy, peace, **p**, kindness, ... Gal. 5:22

patient—Displaying patience.
 Love is **p**; love is kind. .... 1 Cor. 13:4

patriarch—An ancestor, the founding father of
a family, clan, or nation.

peace—A condition or sense of security,
harmony, well-being, and prosperity.
 who proclaims **p**, who brings news Isa. 52:7
 P, **p**, when there is no **p**. ..... Jer. 6:14; 8:11
 P I leave with you. My **p** I give ... John 14:27
 And the **p** of God, which surpasses . Phil. 4:7
 by making **p** through the blood .... Col. 1:20

Pentecost—A Jewish festival fifty days after
Passover. The Holy Spirit came to dwell with the
disciples on this day (Acts 2:1-4).

people—1. Human beings. 2. Persons in a particular ethnic, cultural, or geographical group.
 your **p** will be my **p**, ... Ruth 1:16
 My **p** who are called by
 My name .... 2 Chron. 7:14
 a holy nation, a **p** for
 His possession, ... 1 Pet. 2:9
 and language and **p** and nation. .... Rev. 5:9

perfect—Whole or complete, without defect
and lacking nothing; also mature.
 Be **p**, therefore, as your heavenly Matt. 5:48

perish—Die, disappear, cease to exist, be
destroyed.

and they will never **p**—ever! . . . . John 10:28

not wanting any to **p**, but all to . . . . 2 Pet. 3:9

persecute—Harass and cause suffering for being different in faith, culture, or race.

Princes have **p-d** me without . . . Ps. 119:161

and pray for those who **p** you, . . . Matt. 5:44

they **p-d** Me, they will also **p** you. John 15:20

in Christ Jesus will be **p-d**. . . . . . 2 Tim. 3:12

persevere—Maintain Christian faith through the trying times of life.

p in these things, for by doing . . . . 1 Tim. 4:16

perverted—Bent, crooked, twisted; inverted.

p men of the city surrounded . . . Judg. 19:22

in a crooked and **p** generation, . . . Phil. 2:15

pestilence—Devastating epidemic sent by God.

or the **p** that ravages at noon. . . . . . Ps. 91:6

petition—Formal request.

Pharaoh—Title for the ancient kings of Egypt. See *People and Places*.

plague—Widespread disease or calamity implying divine judgment.

to send all My **p-s** against you, . . Exod. 9:14

angels with the seven last **p-s** . . . . Rev. 15:1

pledge—Something given as a deposit or guarantee of a debt. The Holy Spirit is a down payment or pledge on our souls guaranteeing Jesus' "purchase" of our souls (2 Cor. 1:22; 5:5; Eph. 1:14).

plowshare—A metal tip for a wooden plow (1 Sam. 13:20-21; Isa. 2:4; Joel 4:10; Mic. 4:3).

plumb line—Weighted cord that assures vertical accuracy (Amos 7:8).

plunder—Loot after victory in battle.

So you will **p** the Egyptians. . . . . . Exod. 3:22

pomegranate—A fruit with many seeds and juicy, red pulp.

poor—People with little or no money.

there will never cease to be **p** . . Deut. 15:11

Me to bring good news to the **p** . . . . Isa. 61:1

Blessed are the **p** in spirit, ... Matt. 5:3

if I donate all my goods

to feed the **p**. . . . . 1 Cor. 13:3

portico—Covered entrance; porch or vestibule.

p in front of the temple sanctuary . 1 Kings 6:3

praise—Proclaim the merit or worth of someone or something in worship and thanksgiving.

This is my God, and I will **p** Him, . Exod. 15:2

and His courts with **p**. . . . . Ps. 100:4

have prepared **p** from

the mouths . . . . Matt. 21:16

up to God a sacrifice of **p**, ... Heb. 13:15

pray—Engage in dialogue with God.

I will not sin against the LORD

by ceasing to **p** for you. . . . . 1 Sam. 12:23

humble themselves, **p** and

seek My . . . . 2 Chron. 7:14

p for those who persecute you, . . Matt. 5:44

you should **p** like this: . . . . Matt. 6:9

know what to **p** for as we should . Rom. 8:26

P constantly. . . . . 1 Thess. 5:17

preach—Tell about God's acts of salvation through Jesus Christ.

Go into all the world and

p the gospel . . . . Mark 16:15

but we **p** Christ crucified, ... 1 Cor. 1:23

precept—Command, decree.

How I long for Your **p-s**! . . . . Ps. 119:40

precious—Valuable, costly; dear.

their lives are **p** in his sight. . . . . . Ps. 72:14

but with the **p** blood of Christ, . . . 1 Pet. 1:19

predestine—Determine or decree ahead of time.

Your plan had **p-d** to take place. . . Acts 4:28

He also **p-d** to be conformed to . . Rom. 8:29

He **p-d** us to be adopted through . . Eph. 1:5

preparation day—Sixth day of the week, in which Jews prepared life's necessities in order to avoid work on the Sabbath (John 19:31).

prevail—Succeed; conquer.

pride—Undue confidence in and attention to one's own skills, accomplishments, possessions, or position.

P comes before destruction, ... Prov. 16:18

Knowledge inflates with **p**, ... 1 Cor. 8:1

priest—Person who represented God to human beings and human beings to God (1 Tim. 2:5).

you will be My kingdom of **p-s** . . . Exod. 19:6

you are a chosen race,

a royal **p-hood**, ... 1 Pet. 2:9

proclaim—Declare, announce.

P His salvation from

day to day. . . . . 1 Chron. 16:23

and the sky **p-s** the work of His . . . . Ps. 19:1

to **p** the year of the LORD's favor, . . . Isa. 61:2

you **p** the Lord's death until He . 1 Cor. 11:26

profane—Treat what is holy as if it were common.

they **p-d** My holy name . . . . Ezek. 36:20

promise—A declaration of the gifts and deeds that God will bestow. All the promises of God were fulfilled in Jesus Christ.
 of God's **p-s** is "Yes" in Him. . . . . 2 Cor. 1:20

prophecy—A message from the Lord through the Holy Spirit.
 p-ies, they will come to an end; . . 1 Cor. 13:8
 no **p** of Scripture comes from . . . 2 Pet. 1:20

prophesy—Deliver a prophecy.
 your sons and your daughters
  will **p**, ... Joel 2:28
 and above all that you may **p**. . . . 1 Cor. 14:1

prophet, prophetess—A person who receives a prophecy.
 God will raise up for you a **p** like Deut. 18:15
 A **p** is not without honor except . Matt. 13:57
 some to be apostles, some **p-s**, . . Eph. 4:11

propitiation—The satisfaction of an offended party—in this case, God (Rom. 3:25; Heb. 2:17; 1 John 2:2; 4:10).

proselyte—Convert to a religion, especially a non-Jew who accepted the Jewish faith.
 over land and sea to make
  one **p**, ... Matt. 23:15

prostitute—One who trades sexual services for pay.
 who consorts with **p-s**
  destroys his . . . . Prov. 29:3

proud—Having pride.
 God resists the **p**, but gives grace to Jas. 4:6

proverb—A wise observation.
 Solomon composed 3,000 **p-s**, 1 Kings 4:32

provoke—Arouse anger or exasperation.
 tested God and **p-d** the Holy One . Ps. 78:41

prudent—Wise and practical.

prune—To remove branches from a plant in order to improve its health or productivity.

psalm—A hymn or poem of praise.
 speaking to one another in **p-s**, . . . Eph. 5:19

punishment—Penalty for wrongdoing.
 p for our peace was on Him, ... Isa. 53:5
 they will go away into eternal **p**, . Matt. 25:46

pure—Clean; without fault or contamination.
 eyes are too **p** to look on evil, ... Hab. 1:13
 whatever is just, whatever is **p**, ... Phil. 4:8

purge—To cleanse from impurity.

purify—Make pure.
 P me with hyssop,
  and I will be clean; . . . . Ps. 51:7

Purim—A Jewish holiday celebrating Esther's rescue of Israel from destruction (Esth. 9:26).

purple—Color often designating luxury or royalty.

pursue—Follow in order to capture or obtain.
 seek peace and **p** it. . . . . Ps. 34:14
 who did not **p** righteousness,
  have . . . . Rom. 9:30

R

Rabbi—One learned in the law of Moses.

ram—Male sheep.

ransom—The price paid to gain the freedom of a captive or slave.
 to give His life—a **r** for many. . . . Matt. 20:28
 gave Himself—a **r** for all, ... 1 Tim. 2:6

reap—To harvest grain; figuratively, to receive the product of one's actions.
 who sows injustice will **r** disaster, Prov. 22:8
 whatever a man sows he will also **r**, Gal. 6:7

rebuke—Reprimand, admonish.
 profitable for teaching, for **r-ing**, 2 Tim. 3:16
 many as I love, I **r** and discipline. . . Rev. 3:19

reconcile—Bring together two parties that are estranged or in dispute. Jesus Christ brings together God and man.
 First go and be **r-d** with
  your brother, ... Matt. 5:24
 on Christ's behalf, "Be **r-d**
  to God." . . . . 2 Cor. 5:20

redeem—Pay a price in order to secure the release of something or someone.
 He **r-s** your life from the Pit; . . . . . . Ps. 103:4
 Christ has **r-ed** us from the curse . Gal. 3:13

redemption—The act or result of redeeming.
 In Him we have **r** through His . . . . . Eph. 1:7

refuge—Place of safety.
 God is our **r** and strength, ... Ps. 46:1

regard—Notice, consider, pay attention.

regeneration—Rebirth, renewal (Titus 3:5).

regulation—Rule dictating procedure.
 Why do you submit to **r-s**: . . . . Col. 2:20

reign—Rule, exercise sovereign authority.
 do not let sin **r** in your
  mortal body, ... Rom. 6:12
 and He will **r** forever and ever! . . . Rev. 11:15

rejoice—Express joy.
 let us **r** and be glad in it. . . . . Ps. 118:24
 but **r** that your names are written Luke 10:20
 I will say it again: **R**! . . . . Phil. 4:4

remnant—Something left over, especially the people who remain after divine judgment.
 only the **r** will be saved; . . . . Rom. 9:27

repent—Change one's mind; turn to God and away from sin.

R, because the kingdom of heaven   Matt. 3:2

R ... and be baptized, ... Acts 2:38

repentance—Turning from sin to God.

fruit consistent with **r**. . . . . Matt. 3:8

godly grief produces a **r** . . . . 2 Cor. 7:10

reproach—Disgrace, dishonor, discredit.

require—Demand, deem as necessary.

what it is the Lord **r-s** of you: . . . . . Mic. 6:8

given us everything **r-d** for life . . . . 2 Pet. 1:3

rescue—Save, free, liberate.

He has **r-d** us from the domain of . Col. 1:13

restore—Reinstate, rectify; return something to its former state.

R the joy of Your salvation to me, . . Ps. 51:12

resurrection—Bodily rising and returning to life after being dead.

the **r** of life ... the **r** of judgment. . . John 5:29

I am the **r** and the life. . . . . John 11:25

if there is no **r** of the dead, ... 1 Cor. 15:13

retribution—Punishment for evil.

revelation—Act of disclosing, making known.

light for **r** to the Gentiles . . . . Luke 2:32

was made known to me by **r**, ... Eph. 3:3

revere—Show respect and awe.

revile—Speak abusively.

When we are **r-d**, we bless; . . . . 1 Cor. 4:12

when **r-d**, He did not **r** in return; . . 1 Pet. 2:23

reward—Compensation for goodness.

your **r** is great in heaven. . . . . Matt. 5:12

righteousness—Justice and rightness; conformity to divine law and morality.

He credited it to him as **r**. . . . . . . Gen. 15:6

R exalts a nation, but sin is . . . . Prov. 14:34

apart from the law, God's **r** has . . Rom. 3:21

reserved for me the crown of **r**, . . 2 Tim. 4:8

rod—A short stick used for walking or defense.

S

Sabbath—Day of rest, a time for sacred assembly and worship (Lev. 23:1-3), and a symbol of Israel's covenant with God (Exod. 31:12-17).

Remember to dedicate the **S** day: Exod. 20:8

The **S** was made for man and not Mark 2:27

sackcloth—Garment of coarse material made from goat or camel hair and worn as a sign of mourning (Isa. 15:3) or repentance (58:5; Jonah 3:5-8).

sacred—Holy; set apart for God.

sacrifice—A slaughtered animal given to God during worship to express devotion, thanksgiving, or the need for forgiveness (Lev. 1–7). Christ fulfilled the law as the sinless high priest who offered Himself up as a sacrifice for sinners (Heb. 7:27).

to obey is better than **s**, ... 1 Sam. 15:22

present your bodies as a living **s**, Rom. 12:1

removal of sin by the **s** of Himself. Heb. 9:26

offer up to God a **s** of praise, . . . Heb. 13:15

saints—Holy people; a title for all believers in Christ. In the Book of Revelation, saints are faithful and true witnesses for Jesus.

He intercedes for the **s-s** . . . . Rom. 8:27

Greet every **s** in Christ Jesus. . . . . Phil. 4:21

salvation—Rescue from danger or death. Biblical salvation is a free gift from God through Jesus Christ that rescues the believer from sin and its consequences.

He has become my **s**. . . . . Ps. 118:14

For my eyes have seen Your **s**. . . Luke 2:30

There is **s** in no one else, ... Acts 4:12

work out your own **s** with fear and . Phil. 2:12

escape if we neglect such

a great **s**? . . . . Heb. 2:3

sanctification—Process of being made holy and growing into the likeness of Jesus Christ through the work of the Holy Spirit.

For this is God's will, your **s**: . . . 1 Thess. 4:3

sanctuary—Place set aside as sacred and holy, especially a place of worship (Exod. 25:8).

your body is a **s** of the Holy Spirit 1 Cor. 6:19

Sanhedrin—Highest Jewish council in NT times. The Great Sanhedrin at the Jerusalem temple had 71 members and was presided over by the high priest. They did not have the authority to condemn people to death (John 18:31).

satrap—Political official who governed a province of the Persian Empire.

save—Rescue from danger.

come to seek and to **s** the lost. . . Luke 19:10

everyone who calls on the

name of the Lord will be **s-d**. . . Rom. 10:13

by grace you are **s-d** through faith, Eph. 2:8

Savior—God is the only true Savior (Ps. 106:21; Isa. 45:15, 21-22). Jesus is also the Savior because He is God incarnate.

a **S**, who is Messiah the Lord. . . . Luke 2:11

our great God and **S**, Jesus Christ. . . . . Titus 2:13

scepter—Official staff or baton of a king that symbolized his authority (Isa. 14:5).

The **s** will not depart from Judah, Gen. 49:10

scoff—Show contempt or disrespect for others.

scorn—Consider something to be of low value.
s-ed by men
and despised by people. . . . . Ps. 22:6

scourge—An affliction (Isa. 28:15, 18), or a severe form of corporal punishment involving whipping and beating (Josh. 23:13; Acts 22:24-25; Heb. 11:36).

scribe—Person trained in writing skills (Jer. 36:32). During the exile in Babylon, scribes apparently copied, preserved, and taught the law.

Scripture—Sacred writings that reveal God's redemption. For the NT authors, "Scripture" was the OT. Now the NT is also Scripture (2 Pet. 3:15-16).
concerning Himself in all the **S-s.** Luke 24:27
All **S** is inspired by God and is . . 2 Tim. 3:16
no prophecy of **S** comes
from one's own interpretation. . . 2 Pet. 1:20

seal—Ring, stamp, or small cylinder containing a distinctive engraving. An object marked with a seal implied ownership. A letter marked with a seal was considered an official dispatch.
s-ed with the promised Holy Spirit. Eph. 1:13
to open the scroll and break
its **s-s**?" . . . . Rev. 5:2

seer—Prophet; one whom God has enabled to see the future.

selah—Term of unknown meaning appearing in Psalms and Hab. 3:3,9,13. The word probably called for a pause or an intensification of instruments or voices in worship.

self-control—Mastery of personal desires and passions.
gentleness, **s**. Against such . . . . . Gal. 5:23
knowledge with **s**,
s with endurance, ... 2 Pet. 1:6

selfish—Concerned with one's own needs rather than the needs of others and the purpose of God.
is not **s**; is not provoked; . . . . 1 Cor. 13:5

sexual immorality—Sexual activity outside the context of the marital covenant, including premarital sex (fornication) and adultery (Exod. 20:14, 1 Cor. 6:9-10).
Flee from **s**! . . . . 1 Cor. 6:18
works of the flesh are obvious: **s**, . Gal. 5:19

shame—Painful emotion arising from the consciousness of improper conduct.
on Him will not be put to **s**. . . . . . Rom. 9:33
a cross and despised the **s**, ... Heb. 12:2

sheep—A prominent animal in the sacrificial system of Israel, also a source for food and clothing.
His people, the **s** of His pasture. . . Ps. 100:3
separates the **s** from the goats. . Matt. 25:32
I lay down My life for the **s**. . . . . . John 10:15

shekel—A weight of about four-tenths of an ounce; a coin of that weight.

shepherd—Keeper of sheep. Used figuratively for kings (2 Sam. 5:2), other political and religious leaders (Ezek. 34), and God Himself (Ps. 23:1).
like sheep without a **s**. . . . . . . 1 Kings 22:17;
Matt. 9:36
The LORD is my **s**; there is . . . . Ps. 23:1
I am the good **s**. The good **s** lays John 10:11

shield—Protective devise used in battle.
LORD is my strength and my **s**; . . . Ps. 28:7
In every situation take the
s of faith, ... Eph. 6:16

shrine—Small building or part of a building devoted to the worship of a god.

sickle—Curved blade of flint or metal used to cut down stalks of grain (Joel 3:13; Rev. 14:14).

siege—Battle tactic in which an army surrounds an objective and cuts off all supplies.

signet—A ring used as a seal.

sin—Rebellion against God; a violation of the righteous nature of God; unbelief.
forgive their **s**, and heal
their land. . . . . 2 Chron. 7:14
so that I may not **s** against You. . . Ps. 119:11
yet He bore the **s** of many . . . . . . Isa. 53:12
authority on earth to forgive **s-s** . . Matt. 9:6
takes away the **s** of the world! . . . John 1:29
For all have **s-ned** and fall short . . Rom. 3:23
For the wages of **s** is death, ... Rom. 6:23
Christ died for our **s-s** . . . . 1 Cor. 15:3
as we are, yet without **s**. . . . . Heb. 4:15
If we confess our **s-s**, . . .
forgive us . . . . 1 John 1:9
If we say, "We have not **s-ned**,"
we make Him a liar, ... 1 John 1:10

sinner—Person who sins.
or take the path of **s-s**, ... Ps. 1:1
Don't be jealous of **s-s**; . . . . Prov. 23:17
joy in heaven over one **s**
who repents . . . . Luke 15:7
while we were still **s-s** Christ died . Rom. 5:8
came into the world to save **s-s** . 1 Tim. 1:15

slacker—Lazy person.
Go to the ant, you **s**! . . . . Prov. 6:6

slander—To speak critically and maliciously of another person (Lev. 19:16). In a court of law, it means to accuse another person falsely (Deut. 5:20).

Don't **s** a servant to his master, . . Prov. 30:10
to **s** no one, to avoid fighting, ... Titus 3:2

slave—A person bonded to work for another and dependent on that other for daily needs.

No one can be a **s** of two masters   Matt. 6:24
be first among you must be
    your **s**; . . . . Matt. 20:27
Well done, good and faithful **s**! . Matt. 25:21
who commits sin is a **s** of sin. . . . John 8:34
you used to be **s-s** of sin, ... Rom. 6:17
no Jew or Greek, **s** or free, male . . Gal. 3:28
by assuming the form of a **s**, ... Phil. 2:7

slay, slain—Kill violently.

sling—Weapon consisting of two long straps with a pouch at the end to hold a stone.

defeated the Philistine with a **s** 1 Sam. 17:50

slumber—Sleep, doze, nod off.

your Protector will not **s**. . . . . Ps. 121:3
A little sleep, a little **s**, ... Prov. 6:10; 24:33

snare—Trap that lures birds and animals.

son—Male descendant.

This man really was God's **S**! . . Matt. 27:54
will be called **s-s** of
    the living God. . . . . Rom. 9:26
slave, but a **s**; and if a **s**, then
    an heir . . . . Gal. 4:7
The one who has the **S** has life. . . 1 John 5:12

Son of Man—1. A poetic synonym for "human." Jesus sometimes used the title in the context of His humanity. 2. In Dan. 7:13 it was a reference to the Messiah (Matt. 24:27; 25:31).

S did not come to be served, but   Mark 10:45
the **S** seated at the right hand of   Mark 14:62

sons of the prophets—Members of a band or guild of prophets (2 Kings 2:3, 5, 7, 15; Amos 7:14).

sorcery—Magic by appeal to evil spirits.

interpret omens, practice **s**, ... Deut. 18:10

soul—The inner part of the person; the non-physical aspect of being that does not die.

all your **s**, and with all your strength.   Deut. 6:5
Him who is able to destroy
    both **s** and body in hell. . . . . . . Matt. 10:28
as far as to divide **s**, spirit, joints, . Heb. 4:12
the salvation of your **s-s**. . . . . 1 Pet. 1:9

sovereign—Possessing all power and authority.

{He is} the blessed and only **S**, . 1 Tim. 6:15

sow—To scatter seeds on the ground.

As he was **s-ing**, some seeds fell   Matt. 13:4
One **s-s** and another reaps. . . . . . John 4:37
whatever a man **s-s** he will also . . . . Gal. 6:7

spirit—1. The animating force from God in a living being. 2. The part of a human being associated with thinking and understanding, emotions; a compelling notion or tendency in a person. 3. The Spirit of God. 4. An evil spirit or demon.

renew a steadfast **s** within me. . . . . Ps. 51:10
pour out My **S** on all humanity . . . . Joel 2:28
The **s** is willing, but the flesh . . . Matt. 26:41
God is **s**, and those who worship Him
    must worship in **s** and truth. . . . John 4:24
distinguishing between **s-s**, ... 1 Cor. 12:10
Don't stifle the **S**. . . . . 1 Thess. 5:19

splendor—Brilliant or magnificent appearance.

spoils—Items taken by a victorious army.

staff—A long stick used for walking, defense, or herding sheep, or as a symbol of office.

rod and Your **s**—they comfort me. . . Ps. 23:4

stag—Adult male deer.

statute—Law or commandment.

steadfast—Immovable and patient.

me and renew a **s** spirit within . . . . Ps. 51:10
grounded and **s** in the faith, ... Col. 1:23

steal—Take someone's property without permission. Seize illegally.

Do not **s**. . . . . Exod. 20:15
The thief must no longer **s**. . . . . . . Eph. 4:28

stewardship—Management of resources on behalf of someone else (1 Cor. 9:17).

stiff-necked—Stubborn, obstinate.

stoning—Capital punishment carried out by throwing stones at a person.

strength—Power, potency.

The LORD is my **s** and my song; . . Exod. 15:2
with all your soul, and with all your **s**.   Deut. 6:5
in the LORD will renew their **s**; . . . Isa. 40:31
Not by **s** or by might, but by My . . . Zech. 4:6

strife—Conflict, lack of harmony.

than a house full of feasting
    with **s**. . . . . Prov. 17:1

stronghold—Secure place.

the God of Jacob is our **s**. . . . . . Ps. 46:7,11

submission—Voluntary placement of oneself under the authority and leadership of another.

learn in silence with full **s**. . . . . . 1 Tim. 2:11

submit—Voluntarily yield to another.

s to the governing authorities, . . . Rom. 13:1
Wives, **s** to your own husbands . . . Eph. 5:22

DICTIONARY- CONCORDANCE

Therefore, **s** to God. But resist .... Jas. 4:7
S to every human institution .... 1 Pet. 2:13

suffer—Go through something difficult or painful.
He was ... a man of **s-ing** .... Isa. 53:3
Son of Man must **s** many things, . Mark 8:31
we **s** with Him so that we
 also may .... Rom. 8:17
one member **s-s**, all ... **s** with it; . 1 Cor. 12:26
it is better to **s** for doing good, ... 1 Pet. 3:17

sustain—Provide what is needed to carry on.
wake again because the LORD **s-s** me Ps. 3:5
and He **s-s** all things by His .... Heb. 1:3

swear—Take an oath.
Neither should you **s**
 by your head, ... Matt. 5:36

symbol—Token or sign; a thing that represents something else.
a **s** on your forehead Exod. 13:16; Deut. 6:8

synagogue—Local meeting place and assembly of the Jewish people.
He entered the **s** on the Sabbath Luke 4:16
reasoned in the **s** every Sabbath .. Acts 18:4

T

tabernacle—Sacred tent, portable and provisional sanctuary, where the God of Israel revealed Himself to and dwelled among His people. It was built in accordance with directions given to Moses by God on Sinai (Exod. 25–40).
glory of the LORD filled the **t**. ... Exod. 40:34

talent—In the OT, a weight of about 75 pounds; in the NT, a coin worth that much in gold.
one who owed 10,000 **t-s** ..... Matt. 18:24
To one he gave five **t-s**; .... Matt. 25:15

taxes—Regular payments to a government.
lawful to pay **t** to Caesar or not? Matt. 22:17
t to those you owe **t**, ... Rom. 13:7

teach—Instruct, pass on knowledge or skill.
T them to your children .... Deut. 4:9; 11:19
t us to pray .... Luke 11:1
Holy Spirit ... will **t** you all things John 14:26
who will be able to **t** others also. . 2 Tim. 2:2

tempest—Violent storm.

temple—Place of worship, especially the temple Solomon built in Jerusalem.
But the LORD is in His holy **t**; ..... Hab. 2:20
something greater than
 the **t** is here! .... Matt. 12:6

temptation—The enticement to do evil.
And do not bring us into **t**, ... Matt. 6:13
No **t** has overtaken you except . 1 Cor. 10:13

tenant—Person who rents land or other property.

testimony—Solemn affirmation of fact; statement of a witness.
Do not give false **t** against your . Exod. 20:16

tetrarch—Roman political office, originally over the "fourth part" of a territory.

thanks—Expression of gratitude.
Give **t** to the LORD, for He is good. . Ps. 136:1
and after giving **t**, He gave it ... Matt. 26:27
But **t** be to God, who gives us . 1 Cor. 15:57
Give **t** in everything, for this .. 1 Thess. 5:18

thanksgiving—Acknowledgement of a benefactor.
Enter His gates with **t** and .... Ps. 100:4
through prayer and petition with **t**, .. Phil. 4:6

thresh—Separate seeds from plants by beating or dragging something across the stalks.

Thummim—See Urim and Thummim.

tithe—Tenth part.

tomb—Natural or man-made cave, with a stone door, used for burial.
You are like whitewashed **t-s**, .. Matt. 23:27
stone rolled away from the **t**. .... Luke 24:2

tongue—1. Organ of speech. 2. See language.
and a gentle **t** can break a bone. Prov. 25:15
and every **t** should confess that ... Phil. 2:11
but no man can tame the **t**. .... Jas. 3:8

torment—Persecute with injurious intent.
come here to **t** us before
 the time? .... Matt. 8:29

tradition—Doctrine or ritual which is handed down from generation to generation.
You revoke God's word by your **t** . Mark 7:13

transform—Change in appearance or nature.
He was **t-ed** in front of them, ... Matt. 17:2
be **t-ed** by the renewing of your .. Rom. 12:2

transgression—Sin; overstepping the limits of God's law.
How happy is the one whose **t**
 is forgiven, ... Ps. 32:1
was pierced because of our **t-s**, .. Isa. 53:5

treacherous—Faithless, untrustworthy; unreliable with the result that harm may result.

treasure—Something highly esteemed or valued.
I have **t-d** Your word in my heart . Ps. 119:11
For where your **t** is, there your ... Matt. 6:21

treaty—Agreement between two nations.
Make no **t** with them .... Deut. 7:2

trespass—Sin.
He was delivered up for our **t-es** . Rom. 4:25
when you were dead in **t-es** ..... Col. 2:13

1340

tribe—Group of people of common ancestry.
These are the **t-s** of Israel, 12 .. Gen. 49:28

tribulation—1. Suffering; affliction; distress.
2. The eschatological time of trouble that will usher in the second coming of Christ (Matt. 24:15-22; Rev. 2:22; 7:14; cp. Dan. 12:1).

tribute—Any payment exacted by a superior power, usually a country, from an inferior one.

triumph—Decisive and exultant victory.
He **t-ed** over them by Him. . . . . Col. 2:15
Mercy **t-s** over judgment. . . . . Jas. 2:13

true—Conforming to fact, standard, or reality.
He is righteous and **t**. . . . . Deut. 32:4
God must be **t**, but everyone
is a liar, ... Rom. 3:4
whatever is **t**, whatever is . . . . Phil. 4:8
these words are faithful and **t** . Rev. 21:5; 22:6

trust—Have faith in, rely on, believe.
in God I **t**; ... What can man do . Ps. 56:4,11
T in the LORD with all your . . . . . . Prov. 3:5
those who **t** in the LORD
will renew their strength; . . . . . . Isa. 40:31

truth—That which accurately reflects facts or reality.
The entirety of Your word is **t**, .. Ps. 119:160
worship the Father in spirit and **t**. . John 4:23
the **t**, and the **t** will set you free. . . John 8:32
am the way, the **t**, and the life. . . . John 14:6
exchanged the **t** of God for a lie .. Rom. 1:25
But speaking the **t** in love, ... Eph. 4:15
teaching the word of **t**. . . . . 2 Tim. 2:15
and the **t** is not in us. . . . . 1 John 1:8

tunic—Loose-fitting, knee-length garment worn next to the skin (John 19:23).

turban—Headdress formed by wrapping long strips of cloth around the head.

U

unbelief—Skepticism or doubt.
I do believe! Help my **u**. . . . . Mark 9:24

unbeliever—Skeptic; one who does not believe the gospel of Jesus.
he has denied the faith
and is worse than an **u**. . . . . . . 1 Tim. 5:8

uncircumcised—Not Jewish.
called "the **u**" by those called . . . . . Eph. 2:11

unclean—Not ceremonially clean; food not acceptable to eat, or a person not admissible for worship.
I have never eaten anything ... **u**! . Acts 10:14
nothing is **u** in itself. . . . . Rom. 14:14

unity—Full and perfect agreement.

until we all reach **u** in the faith . . . Eph. 4:13
love—the perfect bond of **u**. . . . . . Col. 3:14

unleavened bread—Bread prepared without a substance such as yeast that produces fermentation and rising in dough.
observe the {Festival of} **U** Bread Exod. 12:17

upright—Doing what is morally right.
The **u** will see His face. . . . . Ps. 11:7

Urim and Thummim—Objects Israel, and especially the high priest, used to determine God's will (Num. 27:21; Deut. 33:8; 1 Sam. 28:6; Ezra 2:63; Neh. 7:65). They were kept by the high priest in a "breastplate of judgment" (Exod. 28:15-30; Lev. 8:8).

V

vain—Without value or significance; "in vain" means without a worthwhile result.
and the peoples plot in **v**? . . . . Ps. 2:1
its builders labor over it in **v**; . . . . . Ps. 127:1
They worship Me in **v**, ... Matt. 15:9
labor in the Lord is not in **v**. . . . 1 Cor. 15:58
be running, or have run, in **v**. . . . . . Gal. 2:2
I didn't run in **v** or labor for . . . . . . Phil. 2:16

valiant—Fearless, courageous.

vengeance—Retaliation or punishment of crime for the sake of justice and deliverance.
V belongs to Me; I will repay. . . . Deut. 32:35

vigor—Strength, as in one's prime.

vindicate—Justify, clear; defend.
wisdom is **v-ed** by all her children. Luke 7:35

viper—Poisonous snake.
he said to them, "Brood of **v-s**! . . . Matt. 3:7

virgin—Person who has not had sexual intercourse.
The **v** will conceive, have a son, .. Isa. 7:14
The **v-'s** name was Mary. . . . . Luke 1:27

vision—One method that God used to communicate with mankind, either literally through one's eyes, in a dream, or by prophetic inspiration.
your young men will
see **v-s** . . . . Joel 2:28; Acts 2:17

vow—Voluntary promise, as an expression of devotion, usually fulfilled after some condition had been met.
I will fulfill my **v-s** before those . . . . Ps. 22:25
Fulfill what you **v**. . . . . Eccl. 5:4

W

wadi—A rocky watercourse that is dry except during rainy seasons.

wages—Terms of employment or compensation for services rendered.

For the **w** of sin is death, ... Rom. 6:23

walk—To travel at a normal pace on foot. Used figuratively for a person's conduct or way of life (Gen. 5:24; Rom. 8:4; Eph. 5:15; 1 John 1:6-7).

and to **w** humbly with your God. .... Mic. 6:8

we too may **w** in a new way of life... Rom. 6:4

we **w** by faith, not by sight .... 2 Cor. 5:7

But if we **w** in the light as He ..... 1 John 1:7

wander—Travel aimlessly and without a plan.

will be a restless **w-er** on the earth. Gen. 4:12

have **w-ed** away from the faith .... 1 Tim. 6:10

wash—Cleanse.

but you were **w-ed**, you were ... 1 Cor. 6:11

the **w-ing** of water by the word. .... Eph. 5:26

watch—1. Division of time during which soldiers or others were on duty (1 Chron. 26:16; Ps. 63:6; 119:148; Jer. 51:12; Luke 2:8). 2. Be vigilant, alert.

unless the LORD **w-es** over a city, . Ps. 127:1

W! Be alert! For you don't know Mark 13:33

watchman—One who stands guard to sound a warning if trouble approaches (Ezek. 3; 33).

way—Path, route; manner of conduct.

See if there is any offensive **w** in me;
lead me in the everlasting **w**. .. Ps. 139:24

There is a **w** that seems right .. Prov. 14:12

we all have turned to our own **w**; .. Isa. 53:6

I am the **w**, the truth, and the life. John 14:6

will show you an even better **w**. . 1 Cor. 12:31

weapon—Device used in battle.

No **w** formed against you will .... Isa. 54:17

the **w-s** of our warfare are not .... 2 Cor. 10:4

weary—Being drained of strength or of patience.

they will run and not grow **w**; ..... Isa. 40:31

Come to Me, all of you who
are **w** .... Matt. 11:28

welcome—Greet; invite in, accept.

whoever **w-s** one child like this .. Matt. 18:5

wholehearted—Genuine and without reservation or hesitation.

wicked—Immoral, sinful.

does not follow the advice of the **w**, .. Ps. 1:1

no pleasure in the death
of the **w**, ... Ezek. 33:11

widow—Woman whose husband has died.

wilderness—Area with little rainfall and sparse population.

will—Desire.

I delight to do Your **w**, my God; .... Ps. 40:8

Your **w** be done on earth as it is . Matt. 6:10

My food is to do the **w** of Him ... John 4:34

and He hardens whom He **w-s**. ... Rom. 9:18

say, "If the Lord **w-s**, we will ..... Jas. 4:15

ask anything according to His **w**, 1 John 5:14

winepress—Place for squeezing or treading grapes, usually a pit or vat.

wineskin—Animal skin formed into a bag by sewing, made to contain wine.

wisdom—Insight, discernment, understanding.

The fear of the LORD
is the beginning of **w**, ... Prov. 9:10

depth of the riches both of the **w** Rom. 11:33

wise men—Astrologers from Arabia, Persia, or Babylon whose interpretation of the stars led them to visit the baby Jesus (Matt. 2:1-12).

wither—Dry up and wilt, as from a lack of moisture.

witness—One that bears testimony to things seen, heard, transacted, or experienced.

the testimony of two or three **w-es**. Deut. 19:15

will be My **w-es** in Jerusalem, ... Acts 1:8

woe—Anguish, misery, wretchedness.

W is me, for I am ruined, ... Isa. 6:5

w to you, scribes and Pharisees, Matt. 23:13

womb—Uterus, where a baby develops before birth.

You knit me together in my
mother's **w**. .... Ps. 139:13

before I formed you in the **w**; ...... Jer. 1:5

word—1. A single term. 2. A short statement. 3. A message or prophecy or command. 4. A speech or story. 5. The entire law. 6. The gospel message. 7. Scripture. 8. Christ.

My **w** ... will not return to Me
empty .... Isa. 55:11

In the beginning was the **W**,
and the **W** was with God,
and the **W** was God. .... John 1:1

the **w** of God is living and effective Heb. 4:12

work—Act, deed, accomplishment, effort.

six days and do all your **w**, ... Exod. 20:9

do even greater **w-s** than these, John 14:12

by faith apart from **w-s** of law. ... Rom. 3:28

test the quality of each one's **w**. . 1 Cor. 3:13

w out your own salvation with .... Phil. 2:12

isn't willing to **w**, he should not
eat. .... 2 Thess. 3:10

has faith, but does not have **w-s**? Jas. 2:14

judged according to their **w-s**. Rev. 20:13

world—**1**. The planet earth. **2**. All mankind. **3**. The environment or spirit of evil and enmity toward God.

the **w** and everything in it is Mine. . Ps. 50:12
For God loved the **w** in this way: . John 3:16
Do not love the **w** or the things . 1 John 2:15

wormwood—Nonpoisonous but bitter plant.

worry—Be anxious or burdened.

Don't **w** about anything, but . . . . Phil. 4:6

worship—Attribute honor or value to someone or something.

W the LORD in the
splendor of . . . . 1 Chron. 16:29
who **w** Him must **w** in spirit
and truth . . . . John 4:24

worthy—Deserving; having sufficient merit.

the LORD, who is **w** of praise, . . . 2 Sam. 22:4
urge you to walk **w** of the calling . . . Eph. 4:1
Lamb who was slaughtered is **w** . . Rev. 5:12

wrath—Anger, indignation, and fury. The punitive righteousness of God by which He maintains His moral order.

but a harsh word stirs up **w**. . . . . . Prov. 15:1
God's **w** is revealed from heaven . . Rom. 1:18
by nature we were children under **w** . . Eph. 2:3

Y

Yahweh—God's name that He revealed to Moses. In most English translations it is represented by LORD in small caps.

Y, the God of your fathers, ... Exod. 3:15
I am **Y**, that is My name; . . . . Isa. 42:8

yearn—Want very much, desire earnestly.

yeast—A fungus that permeates dough and makes it rise.

beware of the **y** of the Pharisees . Matt. 16:6
know that a little **y** permeates . . . 1 Cor. 5:6

yoke—Wooden frame placed on the backs of draft animals to make them pull in tandem.

take up My **y** and learn from Me, Matt. 11:29
don't submit again to a **y** of slavery. . Gal. 5:1

youth—Period between childhood and maturity, characterized by freshness and vigor.

y is renewed like the eagle. . . . . . . Ps. 103:5
Teach a **y** about the way
he should go . . . . Prov. 22:6

Z

zeal—Intense eagerness that compels action.

Z for Your house will consume Me. John 2:17
that they have **z** for God, but not . . Rom. 10:2

FOR THE
GLORY™
NOW & FOREVER
JUDE 24-25

FCA'S GAME PLAN

INDEX

"Now to Him who is able to protect you from stumbling and to make you stand in the presence of His glory, blameless and with great joy, to the only God our Savior, through Jesus Christ our Lord, be glory, majesty, power, and authority before all time, now, and forever. Amen." – Jude 24-25

DAY 1: HIS GLORY – "IT'S NOT ABOUT ME!"

As an athlete, I need to understand God's definition of glory and why He deserves it all. Competition is not about me. Life is not about me. I must die to myself and fully understand the power, majesty, and authority of God.

Warm-Up

If you could make the headline in the sports section of a local newspaper, what would the headline read? Write a headline and description or draw a picture with a caption.

Workout

1. Up to this point in life what would you say is your "crowning glory" or your most headline-worthy accomplishment? How did you feel? What are some ways people give you glory? When you receive glory, how does it make you feel? What emotions do you experience?

2. We are going to experience what "For the Glory" means. When you hear the phrase "For the Glory," what comes to your mind? How would you complete the following sentence? I am living for the glory of _____. We must look at ourselves differently in order to give Him the glory.

Read Jude 24-25

"Now to Him who is able to protect you from stumbling and to make you stand in the presence of His glory, blameless and with great joy, to the only God our Savior, through Jesus Christ our Lord, be glory, majesty, power, and authority before all time, now, and forever. Amen."

3. If you could define glory in one word, what would it be? Now, building from that word, write a short definition for glory.

The *Holman Christian Standard Bible* gives the following definition for glory. Glory is the "weighty importance and shining majesty that accompany God's presence." (Page 1238)

4. How did your definition differ? What were some similarities?

As competitors, many times we want recognition. It's difficult to watch others receive the glory. Why should we give God glory?

Read Revelation 4:11
"Our Lord and God, You are worthy to receive glory and honor and power, because You have created all things, and because of Your will they exist and were created."

5. What does this verse say about glory? Why is this hard to live out as an athlete?

Below is a great glory illustration. Sponges soak up glory for themselves and rob God of the glory that He is due. On the other hand, a mirror reflects. We should be like the mirror and reflect God's glory. When God looks at us He should see a reflection of His Son, Jesus.

6. When it comes to glory, which one are you? Explain.

Cool-Down

1 Corinthians 10:31 reads, "Therefore, whether you eat or drink, or whatever you do, do everything for God's glory." It is hard to live every day glorifying God when there is no one paying attention to us, no spotlight or recognition. We want people to see how great we are. Our goal is not to be successful, but to be faithful. Our focus is to show the glory of God in every aspect of our life – even competing.

It's all about God. It's not about me.

DAY 2: HIS GOAL – "IT'S ABOUT SERVING!"

God's goals for me as a competitor are to play to honor Him and to live to honor Him. I am to bring Him joy in all I do – on and off the field of competition. That is the challenge.

Warm-Up

What do you need to do in order to become the best athlete you can be? What specific goals would you need to set in order to achieve this? In order to play at your best, you need to set goals in areas of your life other than sports. List some goals in the following areas of your life: athletics, academics, and spirituality.

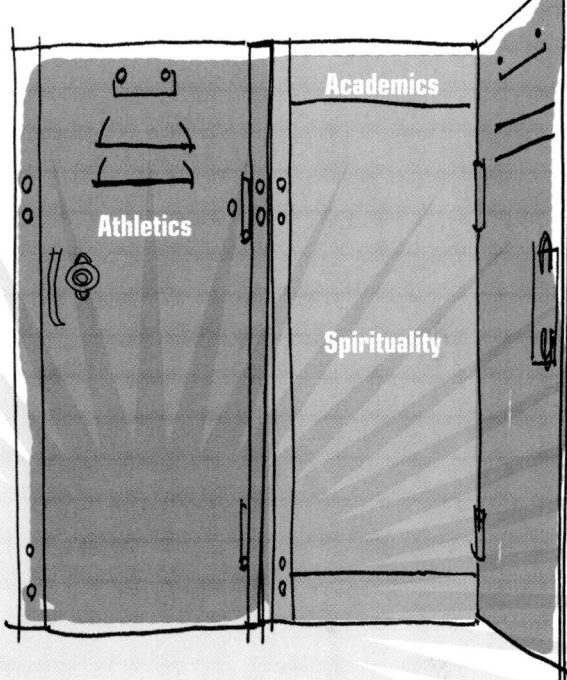

Workout

1. Have you ever experienced setbacks in reaching any of these goals? Have you experienced victory in reaching your goals? What sacrifices have you made in order to draw closer to your goals? You've heard the phrase "No guts, no glory." There are sacrifices to be made if you want to accomplish great things.

2. Have you ever sought a position of status (class president, team captain, valedictorian, etc.)? Why are these positions of status so important to you? Did you go down in a "blaze of glory," or did you accomplish what you set out to achieve?

FCA GAME PLAN

Read Matthew 20:20-28

"Then the mother of Zebedee's sons approached Him with her sons. She knelt down to ask Him for something. 'What do you want?' He asked her.
'Promise,' she said to Him, 'that these two sons of mine may sit, one on Your right and the other on Your left, in Your kingdom.'
But Jesus answered, 'You don't know what you're asking. Are you able to drink the cup that I am about to drink?'
'We are able,' they said to Him.
He told them, 'You will indeed drink My cup. But to sit at My right and left is not Mine to give; instead, it belongs to those for whom it has been prepared by My Father.' When the 10 disciples heard this, they became indignant with the two brothers. But Jesus called them over and said, 'You know that the rulers of the Gentiles dominate them, and the men of high position exercise power over them. It must not be like that among you. On the contrary, whoever wants to become great among you must be your servant, and whoever wants to be first among you must be your slave; just as the Son of Man did not come to be served, but to serve, and to give His life—a ransom for many.' "

3. What goal did the mother have in mind for her sons? Would you have wanted to be one of her sons at that moment? Why or why not?

Mom wanted her sons to have favor and greatness with Jesus. As athletes we get sucked into the same agenda, striving for favor and greatness. The competitor in each of us wants to be greater than our team-mates and opponents. In verse 26, Jesus reveals to us how to become great: "whoever wants to become great among you must be your servant."

4. How can we find favor with Jesus? Verses 27 and 28 tell us that "whoever wants to be first among you must be your slave; just as the Son of Man did not come to be served, but to serve, and to give His life—a ransom for many."

5. How do we become great, on and off the field, in His eyes? How can we serve Jesus today? What does the passage reveal about His goal for each of us? How can His goals for you bring Him glory?

6. What do you really enjoy doing? When are you "in your glory"? Why? How do you feel in these situations?

Read Luke 10:38-40

"While they were traveling, He entered a village, and a woman named Martha welcomed Him into her home. She had a sister named Mary, who also sat at the Lord's feet and was listening to what He said. But Martha was distracted by her many tasks, and she came up and asked, 'Lord, don't You care that my sister has left me to serve alone? So tell her to give me a hand.' "

Mary and Martha were both serving, but Martha became distracted from His goal. On the other hand, Mary was serving through simply spending time with Jesus.

7. Which can you relate to more, Mary or Martha? Why? Which one brought more glory to Jesus? When it comes to your regular, daily life, how can you bring glory to God? How can you bring glory to God when you practice? In competition? In your relationships with family and friends?

Cool-Down

FCA's Competitor's Creed states:

I compete for the pleasure of
my Heavenly Father, the honor of Christ
and the reputation of the Holy Spirit.

It's about God. It's all about serving.

DAY 3: HIS GRIP – "IT'S ABOUT LOVE!"

God loves me and desires to protect me. His grip on my life will guide, shape, and mold me.

Warm-Up

List three times when you felt you were placed on the bench or you faced adversity within your sport. (The situations do not need to be physical. Examples: The time you were yelled at by a coach or parent, or the time you questioned whether the Bible is the true word of God.)

Sports Adversity

1.

2.

3.

Workout

1. Share with everyone in your group how these adverse situations made you feel.

Read 2 Corinthians 4:8-9

"We are pressured in every way but not crushed; we are perplexed but not in despair; we are persecuted but not abandoned; we are struck down but not destroyed."

2. We mentioned the phrase "No guts, no glory" on Day 2. Life is going to be tough. You'll be knocked around. We all are pressured every day. What are some pressures you face in your life? How have you responded? Explain a time in your life when you felt crushed or destroyed. What got you through?

Read 2 Corinthians 4:15-18

"For all this is because of you, so that grace, extended through more and more people, may cause thanksgiving to overflow to God's glory. Therefore we do not give up; even though our outer person is being destroyed, our inner person is being renewed day by day. For our momentary light affliction is producing for us an absolutely incomparable eternal weight of glory. So we do not focus on what is seen, but on what is unseen; for what is seen is temporary, but what is unseen is eternal."

3. What does this passage say about getting through tough times?

God sent us the Holy Spirit as an internal Guide to help us stay in His grip.

Read John 14:16-18 and John 14:25-26

"And I will ask the Father, and He will give you another Counselor to be with you forever. He is the Spirit of truth. The world is unable to receive Him because it doesn't see Him or know Him. But you do know Him, because He remains with you and will be in you. I will not leave you as orphans; I am coming to you." (John 14:16-18)

"I have spoken these things to you while I remain with you. But the Counselor, the Holy Spirit – the Father will send Him in My name – will teach you all things and remind you of everything I have told you." (John 14:25-26)

4. Based on these scriptures, describe in your own words one thing the Holy Spirit does. Are there parts of your life that are totally in His grip? Are there any areas of your life that you try to hide from His grip? What's holding you back? How can the Holy Spirit help you bring glory to God on and off the field?

Read Ephesians 3:17-19

"I pray that you, being rooted and firmly established in love, may be able to comprehend with all the saints what is the length and width, height and depth of God's love, and to know the Messiah's love that surpasses knowledge, so you may be filled with all the fullness of God."

5. What does this passage say about God's love? Can you escape His grip? Explain your answer. How does His grip on our lives demonstrate His love for us?

FCA GAME PLAN

Cool-Down

God loves me and desires to protect me. His grip on my life will guide, shape and mold me.

FCA's Competitor's Creed states:

I give my all – all of the time.
I do not give up. I do not give in.
I do not give out. I am the Lord's warrior –
a competitor by conviction
and a disciple of determination.
I am confident beyond reason
because my confidence lies in Christ.

My confidence comes from knowing the love He has for me.

It's about God. It's about serving. It's about love.

DAY 4: HIS GROUND — "IT'S ABOUT POWER!"

When I step onto His field, there is power. Power comes through Jesus Christ. We can experience this power when we play and live on His ground. Everything I do should start on His ground.

Warm-Up

Identify and describe your favorite place to compete (field, court, pool, arena, track, etc.).

Workout

1. Share why this is your favorite place for competition. What makes it so special? Did you find victory here? Did you receive encouragement or support from your coach or fans? Did it give you confidence?

Read Exodus 3:2-6

"Then the Angel of the LORD appeared to him in a flame of fire within a bush. As Moses looked, he saw that the bush was on fire but was not consumed. So Moses thought: I must go over and look at this remarkable sight. Why isn't the bush burning up?
When the LORD saw that he had gone over to look, God called out to him from the bush, 'Moses, Moses!'
'Here I am,' he answered.
'Do not come closer,' He said. 'Take your sandals off your feet, for the place where you are standing is holy ground.' Then He continued, 'I am the God of your father, the God of Abraham, the God of Isaac, and the God of Jacob.' Moses hid his face because he was afraid to look at God."

2. What did God tell Moses to do? Why? Why was it holy ground? When have you felt like you were on holy ground? Moses was on holy ground because God was present. As followers of Christ, why are we always on holy ground?

Psalm 84:1-2 states, *"How lovely is Your dwelling place, LORD of Hosts. I long and yearn for the courts of the LORD; my heart and flesh cry out for the living God."*

3. When you are fully committed to Christ, you are always on holy ground. What does a life fully committed to Christ look like?

4. What are some things you've fully committed to God?

FCA GAME PLAN

A total commitment involves spiritual training. Read 1 Timothy 4:7-8

"But have nothing to do with irreverent and silly myths. Rather, train yourself in godliness, for, the training of the body has a limited benefit, but godliness is beneficial in every way, since it holds promise for the present life and also for the life to come."

5. Spiritual training is the way we access God's power. His power is on His ground. In the same way you have physical training for your sport, spiritual disciplines bring power and strength to your life. Take a few minutes to read the Scripture passages below and then discuss.

Disciplines:

Read His Word..........................John 14:23

Pray...................................Ephesians 3:16

Fellowship............................Hebrews 3:13

Talk with friends about Jesus...........Acts 5:42

Read Psalm 68:34-35

"Ascribe power to God. His majesty is over Israel, His power among the clouds. God, You are awe-inspiring in Your sanctuaries. The God of Israel gives power and strength to His people. May God be praised!"

Cool-Down

While God is working and doing the unthinkable, we must step back and say, "God did it!" At that moment, He receives the glory. Bringing God the greatest amount of glory is the goal. We need to be warriors for God's glory. Are you ready to be different so that God's power and goodness will be made clear to all? Take that step.

It's about God. It's about serving. It's about love. It's about the power we receive by playing on His ground.

Every morning, set aside a special time called "Quiet Time" or spiritual "Training Time." During this time you can talk to God and let him talk to you through the Bible. There are many effective methods that can be used for your daily time with God. The **PRESS** method is the one we suggest.

When a Child of God reads the Word of God, he or she sees the Son of God and is transformed by the Spirit of God into the Image of God for the Glory of God!

PRAY ...

Begin by thanking God for the new day, and then ask Him to help you learn from what you read. Prepare yourself by:

- Clearing your mind and being quiet before the Lord
- Asking God to settle your heart
- Listening to worship music to prepare your spirit
- Asking God for a teachable heart

READ ...

A great way to start is to read each day a proverb (there are 31 chapters in Proverbs, so you have one per day), a psalm, and a chapter out of the New Testament or Old Testament. Another way is to begin with one of the Gospels such as John; or one of the shorter letters such as Ephesians or James; or even just one chapter from the Book of Proverbs or a psalm. You might also start with the first four "training times":

Bound for Glory – page 1360

Get the Guarantee – page 1361

The Right Race or the Rat Race – page 1362

And Now for Your ... – page 1363

EXAMINE ...

Ask yourself the following questions in regards to the passage:

Teaching: What I need to **KNOW** about God, myself, and others?

Rebuking: What I need to **STOP** doing – sins, habits, selfish patterns?

Correcting: What I need to **CHANGE** in my thoughts, attitudes, or actions?

Training: What I need to **DO** in obedience to God's leading?

FCA GAME PLAN

FCA GAME PLAN

SUMMARIZE ...

Do one of the following:

- Discover what the passage reveals about God and His character, what it says or promises about me, and what it says or promises about others—my parents, friends, teammates, etc. Write this in a personal journal.

- Rewrite one or two key verses in your own words.

- Outline what each verse is saying.

- Give each verse a one-word title that summarizes what it is saying.

SHARE ...

Talk with God about what you've learned. Also, take time each day to share with someone from your group what you learned in "Training Time."

Having a daily "Training Time" is extremely important. It is the key to developing spiritually.

This is why we have prepared 31 devotions for you. If you commit to doing these over the next month, you will have established this habit which is a key to your spiritual development.

I will commit to establishing this daily habit.

Signed _____

Today's Date _____

TIME-OUT

FCA is excited to present devotions that will challenge you to play and live for the Glory of God. Each is written from the athletic perspective to encourage you to be like Christ in your life on and off the field. In life and sport, there is always the need to take a TIME-OUT to think about your purpose in living and playing for God.

WRITERS ...

There are many writers and editors who have contributed time, talents, and experience to writing these devotions. Writers include representatives from the sports of baseball, soccer, basketball, football, lacrosse, and track and field. Our writing team consists of coaches, athletes, team chaplains, and FCA staff. The writers come from very diverse backgrounds.

TOPICS ...

High school, college, and pro athletes along with coaches, a club team coach, and FCA staff submitted the topics covered in the following devotions.

FORMAT ...

READY Focus (a verse, passage, quote, or thought to direct your heart and mind). Please turn to Scripture reference in your Bible so you can read it within the overall context of the passage.

SET Teaching point (a story, training point, or thought taken from a sports perspective)

GO Application (a prayer, question, thought, or action to direct you to be like Christ)

OVERTIME Additional Bible reading to help you dig deeper and develop as a champion.

To receive a daily e-mail devotional called FCA's Peptalk, go to www.FCA.org.

BOUND FOR GLORY

Jere Johnson

Ready:

¹ Therefore since we also have such a large cloud of witnesses surrounding us, let us lay aside every weight and the sin that so easily ensnares us, and run with endurance the race that lies before us, ² keeping our eyes on Jesus, the source and perfecter of our faith.

Hebrews 12:1-2a

Set:

Every team sets goals before the season. They work, strive, and stretch to reach those goals, but the reality is only one team wins it all in the end. Does that mean all the other teams were failures in their seasons? Not by any means. Most teams reach their goals each season. The key is to be focused on the established team goals as players pursue each game and contest. In this way each team is bound to end their season in glory.

What is your goal spiritually? Are you bound for glory? Are you unsure what road you are traveling on? It can be easy to get sidetracked in life. Struggles at home, difficult school work, your coach not playing you enough, and many other things can get you sidetracked and focused on things besides your actual goals. Things in life can so easily trip us up and push us off course. As we pursue our goals, we need to ask whether we are keeping first things first. Where does Christ fit into your goals? Is He your goal? Is heaven your goal? If so, are you preparing yourself daily to get there?

Winning championships and accomplishing season goals are great things but do not compared to what heaven has in store for us. If we are truly bound for glory we will be so focused that all our decisions will be "Cross-eyed." We will be focused on Jesus and His glory and the home He is getting ready for us. All our choices should be made with that in mind: from the movies we see to the music we hear, from the shows we watch to the things we do online. We must remember to take it day-by-day. Endure for eternity. Now that's a good goal!

Go:

1. What are some of your team or personal goals for this coming year?

2. What deters you from reaching your goals?

3. Today, how can you be "Cross-eyed" and bound for glory?

Overtime:

Philippians 3:12-15
John 14:1-6

GET THE GUARANTEE

Clay Elliott

Ready:

And when the chief Shepherd appears, you will receive the unfading crown of glory.

1 Peter 5:4

Set:

Years ago Hall of Fame quarterback Joe Namath guaranteed that his underdog New York Jets were going to beat the powerful Baltimore Colts in the Super Bowl … and wouldn't you know … they did it! But since that time there have been many athletes and coaches who have guaranteed a win and it didn't turn out that way. Why? Nothing on this planet is truly guaranteed. As a matter of fact, there are very few real guarantees in life. Even when you purchase something that is guaranteed, that doesn't mean it's going to work forever. It just means that when it breaks, the guarantor will fix or replace it.

God has an exceptional guarantee. What He gives us doesn't ever need to be fixed or replaced because it lasts forever. The verse above calls it the "unfading crown of glory." But what exactly is this guarantee?

During Bible times there were many athletic competitions, usually track-type events such as running, throwing, or jumping. The winners were given "a crown of glory" made of laurel leaves. It was like a trophy. But this crown always withered and faded. Peter is contrasting this crown with the unfading crown. The unfading crown is given to everybody who gives his or her life to Jesus Christ. This includes you if you have asked Jesus to become your Savior and Lord. You are then a permanent winner! You win the trophy! And your unfading crown is eternity with the chief Shepherd in heaven! Get the guarantee!

Go:

1. Going after the "unfading crown of glory" is not selfish; it's smart. Do you have it? Do you want it? Read "More than Winning" in the Life Playbook section in this FCA Bible and find out how.

2. Have you already won the unfading crown but still struggle? Spend time feeding your soul by reading the Bible. Start by reading all about Jesus in any of the four Gospels—Matthew, Mark, Luke, or John.

Overtime:

Revelation 21:1-5

THE RIGHT RACE OR THE RAT RACE?

Dan Britton

Ready:

¹ Therefore since we also have such a large cloud of witnesses surrounding us, let us lay aside every weight and the sin that so easily ensnares us, and run with endurance the race that lies before us, ² keeping our eyes on Jesus, the source and perfecter of our faith, who for the joy that lay before Him endured a cross and despised the shame, and has sat down at the right hand of God's throne.

Hebrews 12:1-2

Set:

The first race I ever ran was a marathon. Talk about starting with a bang! I always played team sports and raced until I ran the dreaded 26.2-miler. It was an incredible experience my body will never forget. I learned firsthand the four key aspects to every race, and they all can be related to our spiritual life.

The race is against the competition. There were thousands of competitors I wanted to beat and who wanted to beat me. In the same way, when we run the race for Christ, we have three main competitors: the world, the flesh, and the devil. Each one intends to prevent us from crossing the finish line.

The race is against the clock. The clock at every mile marker was a constant reminder that the race was coming to an end. Praise God! People say that since you only go around once, you should live it up. Christ says that since you only go around once, you should make it count. James 4:14 compares our lives to "a bit of smoke." Gone in seconds! The great missionary Amy Carmichael said, "We have all eternity to celebrate our victories, but only a few short years to win them."

The race is for the prize. I received a medallion suspended by a ribbon for completing the marathon. Not much of a prize. But as Christians, our prize is heaven and a life with God that lasts for eternity!

The race is for the praise. It was awesome to have hundreds of people cheering for me as I finally crossed the finish line, but it won't compare to one day hearing the words from Jesus: "Well done, good and faithful servant!" (Matthew 25:21 NIV). That is the ultimate praise!

My pastor asked, "Are you running the right race or the rat race?" Even if you win the rat race, you're still a rat. The rat race is anything that gets our eyes off Jesus. Run the right race – the race of Christ.

Go:

1. What race are you running – the right race or the rat race? How do you reach that conclusion?

2. Which one of the three competitors – the world, the flesh, or the devil – do you battle most? Why?

3. How can you be reminded daily that your life is "a bit of smoke"?

4. What needs to change in your life for you to run the right race every day? What are some things that hold you back?

Overtime: 1 Corinthians 9:24-26   Philippians 2:16

AND NOW FOR YOUR ...

Jere Johnson

Ready:

24 Now to Him who is able to protect you from stumbling and to make you stand in the presence of His glory, blameless and with great joy, 25 to the only God our Savior, through Jesus Christ our Lord, be glory, majesty, power, and authority before all time, now, and forever. Amen.

Jude 24-25

Set:

It is copied in gyms all over the country. It started back in the 80's in an old beat-up stadium in downtown Chicago. Basketball fans all over can still hear these words in their heads, "And now the starting line up for your Chicago Bulls." These words echoed as Pippen, Grant, Cartwright, Armstrong, and Michael Jordan were announced. High schools and colleges today still imitate these now-famous words.

Our theme verses for camp this year are basically a prayer and some closing thoughts, but I wonder how they would sound blaring from the loud speakers of heaven down to earth when the Lord returns and we enter heaven. Who might get the job of announcing it to all? It might sound something like this ...

And now coming down from His glorious throne to take back His own, the One who picks you up when you are down, who puts a smile in place of that frown, the One who won't let you fall and is Savior of All. He is King of Kings. He is Lord of Lords. He is Alpha and Omega. He IS the MAN. He became man to save all men. You know Him in prayer. We know Him in person. He is not One, or Two, but the Trinity Himself. Let's rise to our feet to give Him all glory, majesty, power, and authority now, tomorrow, and forever more ... you know who I'm talking about ... give it up for OUR KING ... Jesus Christ!

What a wonderful announcement that would be. Jesus Christ desires to be the King of your kingdom, the Savior of your situation, and the Lord of your life. Will you let Him? So who is your Lord, your Jesus today? What is keeping you back from giving the real King complete control of your life? He desires not only to be a part of your life, but to be your life. Paul knew this quite well. He felt that if he lived he could keep on sharing about Christ, but if he died, he would join Him in glory! What a win-win situation. Are you ready to hear your name called by the PA announcer in heaven? And now for your new heavenly teammate, please give it up for ... Will your name be said?

Go:

1. What do you enjoy about listening to the starting line ups before a ball game? How does your local PA announcer do it?

2. Who's Number One in your life – Jesus or you? What difference does that make?

3. Today, how can you know for sure that your name will be spoken all over heaven when it is your time to go?

Overtime: Jude 20-21   Philippians 1:21-22   Romans 8:10

DO OVER

Michael Hill

Ready:

Therefore if anyone is in Christ, there is a new creation; old things have passed away, and look, new things have come.

2 Corinthians 5:17

Set:

I don't know about your neighborhood, but when I was younger we had the "do over." Remember? You took a swing and your foot went out from under you. You mis-kicked the ball in a kickball game because you slipped on some wet grass. What were the first words to come out of your mouth? "Do over!!"

Did you know that God gave us a "do over"? Paul wrote the church in Corinth that when they accepted Christ they became a new creation. Well, thousands of years later, the same is still true for us. When we accept Christ as Savior and Lord, we become a new creation.

This means that no matter how many times you slip trying to hit or kick the ball you get a chance to do it again, completely free of charge. This means that no matter how our life was before we asked Christ to come in, we get a chance to do it all again.

God does not keep a list of our mistakes, no matter how awful we may think they are. What an amazing thing. Our life is radically changed when we give it over to Jesus. The old is gone, and we are a new creation.

Go:

1. When did you accept Jesus as Savior and Lord? If you haven't, are you ready to become a new creation?

2. What new things have come into your life because you are new creation?

3. If you are not living your new life, what is holding you back? What are some areas you are not allowing God's forgiveness to cleanse?

4. What are you doing with your new life so that people know you are a new creation?

Overtime:

John 1:12; 14:6   Acts 15:11
Galatians 2:20   Colossians 2:6-7
2 Timothy 1:9

CARE CASTING
Clay Elliott

Ready:
... casting all your care upon Him, because He cares about you.

1 Peter 5:7

Set:
As an athlete your job is fairly simple in some ways – just listen to the coach and do what he or she tells you to do. But this doesn't guarantee success because the coach does make mistakes and will at times fall short in his or her instruction.

Of course a driven athlete would never be completely satisfied with what only one coach has to say. The driven athlete may go to a better coach and seek advice or read a book for additional input, or even watch a video to gain some direction.

God, on the other hand, is the perfect Coach. You can go to Him and get the perfect advice, input, or direction anytime. And you can go to Him with all of your cares too! If you are having an issue or problem, take it to God – He wants to hear about it. He will give you some great coaching, and He will give you perfect answers.

Go:
1. What cares do you have that you haven't given to God yet?

2. Take some time today and write out descriptions of a few of these cares and give all these details to God. Then pray that you don't take them back!

Overtime:
Psalm 46

LITTLE THINGS
Jere Johnson

Ready:
Then He said to them all, "If anyone wants to come with Me, he must deny himself, take up his cross daily, and follow Me."

Luke 9:23

Set:
There are about a million things I loved about John Wooden's coaching, but one of my favorite things was that he taught his players each year how to put on their socks and tie their shoes properly. Now, you would think that college-aged men could do this on their own, but Wooden took nothing for granted. He paid attention to the little things of the game. I believe this is what made the big things come easier for his teams over the years. He always took care of the little things.

Sometimes, in walking with the Lord, we try to go right to the big things and neglect the little things that are so important. What are some examples of these little things? Spending time daily with God as we read His Word and pray, serving our loved ones, and reaching out to help someone in need. Sure, we can do the big things for God and not care for these little things, but these little things make a huge difference in the way we handle the big things. To serve the Lord in the big things of life, we need to put aside our own selfish desires and follow Christ in the little things.

Of course Wooden knew his players could put on their socks and tie their shoes, but he wanted to teach them a lesson: If they were going to play in his program, they would have to put aside what they wanted to do and follow his plans for the team. It was the simple discipline in the small things that gave his teams great results in the big things (namely, winning 10 NCAA National Championships). Coach Wooden shows us a great example of how the little things make the biggest difference.

Go:
1. What are some little things you need to do better as an athlete to help your team?

2. Why do you think it is important to do the little things well in your spiritual walk?

3. Today, how can you start to do the little things better in every area of your life?

Overtime:
Ephesians 6:13-18
1 Thessalonians 5:14-18

ON FIRE

Michael Hill

Ready:

²⁸ Therefore, since we are receiving a kingdom that cannot be shaken, let us hold on to grace. By it, we may serve God acceptably, with reverence and awe; ²⁹ for our God is a consuming fire.

Hebrews 12:28-29

FCA GAME PLAN

Set:

As coaches we want players who are "on fire" for our team. We want players who "live" our sport and don't just "play" from time to time. As athletes we should want to excel to the highest level possible. We should not be satisfied with less than our total "sold out" effort. That is exactly what God wants from us.

Look at the verses above. The author of Hebrews tells how to reach that "sold out" level. We are receiving a kingdom that cannot be shaken. No matter what happens in our lives, as children of God and believers in Jesus, the kingdom cannot be shaken. How hard would we compete if we believed with all our being that the outcome would be the biggest victory in the history of sports and we would be on the winning team?

That is what God promises us. "Our God is a consuming fire." This power is in each of us as believers. There is a big difference between a flickering candle and a raging forest fire. The power of our God is like a raging forest fire. Nothing can stand in its way. That is how we are called to approach life – with a "sold out, burning fire" attitude.

Go:

1. What do you think an "on fire" life for God would look like?

2. How can you start to catch that fire and burn for God?

3. Who is one person that can help you live the life God calls you to?

Overtime:

Deuteronomy 4:24
1 Chronicles 16:23-30a
Psalm 29
Psalm 114
Colossians 3:23-24

HIS GLORY—IT'S NOT ABOUT ME!
Carmen Foster

Ready:
For all have sinned and fall short of the glory of God.

Romans 3:23

Set:
At the end of the game, the win or the loss falls on the coach. The coach receives the glory or the blame associated with the game. In the game of life, Jesus is our Coach. But, unlike in sports, Jesus can only receive glory. No blame is associated with Him because He is perfect. He is holy. He is everything that we are not.

The blame is associated with us. Each day we sin. Each day we fall short of God's glory because He is perfect. Jesus stepped into our place and became our substitute. Because of His love for us, He chose to die on the cross to make us perfect. Only when we realize that He died so we could be free and have a relationship with God, do we truly begin to understand His glory. Only then do we realize our need for Him and that He deserves all of our glory.

Go:
1. Think of a time when you have fallen short in practice or during a game, and your teammate or coach was there to cover your mistake.

2. In what ways do you fall short of God's glory?

3. Why does Christ deserve all the glory in your life?

Overtime:
John 14:1-6
John 8:34-38
Romans 6:17-20

TRUE HUMILITY
Clay Elliott

Ready:
Likewise, you younger men, be subject to the elders. And all of you clothe yourselves with humility toward one another.

1 Peter 5:5

Set:
Louis Garza moved into our neighborhood when he was in the sixth grade. He was big and strong and fast … and humble. He was easily the best athlete in our whole group, and we had a lot of really good athletes. But Louis was different; he willingly did anything for the good of the team.

It's always tough trying to fit into a new group, but Louis slipped into ours easily. He didn't demand anything special. As a matter of fact, Louis was so humble that he always tried to get his weaker team-mates to experience the more glamorous positions. He wanted others to feel special and succeed.

Most of us don't strive to be humble. Most of us don't desire to be subject to others. Most of us don't want to serve anybody, especially those who are inferior to us in intelligence, athletic ability, or whatever. But God tells us not only to live in humility, but also to clothe ourselves in it. But what does that mean?

Clothing ourselves is something we do every day. And when we clothe ourselves, we do it for the entire day. Clothing ourselves with humility means we have to put humility on, because it doesn't come natu-rally. It takes effort. It takes willpower. It takes stamina. And it takes God.

True humility means to choose to think of others as more important than ourselves. It means that we need to remove our selfish desires. It means we need to willingly let others get the first choice. It means to be of service to others and God for God's glory.

We need a lot of Louis Garzas on our teams and in our schools. Why don't you be one of them?

Go:
1. How can you show humility today?

2. Who will you serve when you go back to school, and how will you do it?

Overtime:
Philippians 2:5-11

PAGE **1369**

GET FIT

Jere Johnson

Ready:

⁷ Rather, train yourself in godliness, ⁸ for, the training of the body has a limited benefit, but godliness is beneficial in every way, since it holds promise for the present life and also for the life to come.

1 Timothy 4:7b-8

Set:

As an athlete, your goal is to get in the best possible physical shape. Many athletes will cross train to stay fit for their sport. Running, biking, swimming, and other training programs will get any athlete into great shape to compete.

I am sure the Apostle Paul knew what it took to be in shape. We have to remember he did not just hop into his Hummer and take off on his missionary journeys. He hoofed it, boated it, and even thumbed a ride here and there in order to get from place to place. I don't doubt that he was in pretty good shape. He talked many times in his books about athletes and staying fit, and one thing he fully understood was the need for spiritual fitness. Paul knew in order to battle his spiritual opponents he had to be in the best shape spiritually he could be. He studied God's Word, prayed without ceasing, and lived in real community with countless other believers. He knew good spiritual fitness would draw him closer to his heavenly goal.

Are you in good shape? Physically? Spiritually? Hopefully, both! Physical fitness and conditioning is great for sure, but spiritual fitness will get us farther in life. Are you doing the things necessary to get yourself in better shape spiritually? We cannot expect to get spiritually fit without taking the steps to make it happen. Going to church or a group huddle once a week won't get us in the proper fitness we need for Christ. We need to work out seven days a week for Him … time in His Word, time in prayer, and time with other believers. Getting fit in Christ takes time and effort. Trust me, your effort will pay off in the end.

Go:

1. Are you in good shape physically? What is your workout routine?

2. Are you fit spiritually? What is your spiritual routine?

3. Today, what can you start doing to get in better shape for God's glory?

Overtime:

Psalm 119:11, 105
1 Corinthians 9:24-27
Colossians 2:7

IN EVERYTHING
Carmen Foster

Ready:
Therefore, whether you eat or drink, or whatever you do, do everything for God's glory.
1 Corinthians 10:31

Set:
The debate over steroid use on the college, professional, and Olympic levels is growing. Allegations of steroid use have cost many athletes their jobs and their lives. When their first priority is to honor and glorify self, some athletes will go to extreme measures. Their hope is in themselves and in pursuing their own glory. If they fail, they feel worthless. Their worth is tied up in being the best no matter what the cost.

In the 2004 Olympic games, Meb Keflezighi became the first American man since 1976 to win an Olympic medal in the marathon. What was Meb's motivation? He wanted to honor and glorify God. Meb told Christianity Today, "I have goals, but God has a plan. Whatever plan he has, whether I finish first place, third or twelfth, I do everything I can to satisfy God."

Meb's focus was not on glorifying self, but on glorifying God. Meb's hope is not in himself, but in Christ. Meb has a hope that does not disappoint because, win or lose, he is a child of God. He has a relationship with Christ. His life is secure in Jesus. So, no matter the cost, he chooses to be faithful to Christ.

Go:
1. As a competitor, is your attitude like that of Meb or of self-centered athletes?

2. Have you ever tried something illegal because you wanted to win? How did you feel afterwards? Did it bring you joy?

3. Why is it important to honor and glorify Christ in all that we do?

4. In what ways can you begin to honor and glorify Christ while you compete?

Overtime:
Colossians 3:17
John 14:12-17
John 17:1-4

FOR THE GLORY

Dan Britton

Ready:

26 The king said in reply to Daniel, whose name was Belteshazzar, "Are you able to tell me the dream I had and its interpretation?" 27 Daniel answered the king: "No wise man, medium, diviner-priest, or astrologer is able to make known to the king the mystery he asked about. 28 But there is a God in heaven who reveals mysteries, and He has let the King Nebuchadnezzar know what will happen in the last day."

Daniel 2:26-28

Set:

As a competitor, it is hard to give glory where glory is due, when others deserve it more than we do. Training, discipline, perseverance, and drive are all characteristics that can propel an athlete to the next level, making good athletes into great athletes. But often after achieving a goal, we feel that it is our hard work that got us to that point. The praise, honor, and glory are focused on us as individual athletes.

Part of FCA's Competitor's Creed states:

> "I do not trust in myself.
> I do not boast in my abilities
> or believe in my own strength.
> I rely solely on the power of God.
> I compete for the pleasure of
> my Heavenly Father, the honor of Christ
> and the reputation of the Holy Spirit."

Bottom line: the results of my efforts must result in His glory. To accept it for myself would be to rob God of His glory. Daniel had the perfect chance to take the glory from God the King, but he chose to give it to Him instead.

Go:

1. As an athlete, how much confidence do you have in your own abilities?

2. What does it mean to compete for the joy of the Heavenly Father?

3. If Daniel had scored the winning goal or was awarded the team MVP, what do you think would have been his response?

Overtime:

2 Corinthians 5:1-10

COLD FEET
Michael Hill

Ready:
Don't worry about anything, but in everything, through prayer and petition with thanksgiving, let your requests be known to God.

Philippians 4:6

Set:
How many times as athletes, or coaches, have we been nervous before a big game? Maybe we were getting ready to play the big school rivalry game. Maybe it was a playoff game. Maybe that boyfriend or girlfriend was in the stands. Maybe we just get nervous in front of big crowds.

We all handle these situations differently. Some of us get sick to our stomachs. Some cannot stop talking or moving around. Others come across as unfazed. These athletes seem to know the secret to remaining calm under pressure.

God not only tells us how to remain calm, He gives us a command in Philippians. We are not to be anxious about anything. If we worry about what is about to happen, we are going against His direct command. Worrying shows a lack of confidence in God's sovereignty. But God doesn't tell just to get rid of the nervousness on our own; He tells us that He cares and He wants us to bring our worries to Him, being thankful that He will do what's best for us now and in the long haul.

Pray and talk to Him. In the pressure of the big game, or in any life situation that makes us anxious, we need to take a minute and pray to the Father who has everything under control.

Go:
1. What do you do when you are nervous?

2. What are we called to do when we are nervous? What attitude does this require from us about life, ourselves, and God?

3. What steps can we take to turn to God when we are nervous?

Overtime:
Matthew 6:25-34
Luke 12:22-26

NO COMPROMISE

Kyle Shultz

Ready:

² Happy are those who keep His decrees and seek Him with all their heart. ³ They do nothing wrong; they follow His ways. ⁴ You have commanded that Your precepts be diligently kept.

Psalm 119.2-4

Set:

On February 16, 2005, NHL commissioner Gary Bettman cancelled what little was left of the 2004–2005 hockey season exactly five months after the NHL lockout began. No compromise was reached between players and owners, and the NHL received the shameful distinction of becoming the first professional sports league in North America to miss an entire season due to a labor dispute.

Check out the verses above. "No compromise" is a philosophy we should use when dealing with sin and disobedience to God's commands for us. Compromise is something we encounter every day in our normal course of life, and it's plainly necessary in many of life's dealings. But when addressing sin against obedience to God, we should never let pride lead us to compromise. We should choose obedience every time. If we take an honest look, we might be surprised at how often we're tempted to compromise what we know is right. We say things like "Only this one time," "Everybody else is fine with it," "It's normal. What does it matter?" or "Surely there's no harm in this." But if we know something to be contrary to God's will for us, then we must not steer off course, but rather walk straight ahead doing what's right. When we compromise with sin, we reach an agreement with it, and the outcome will be dreadful and dangerous.

I've said it before, and I'll say it again. God's ideas for how we should live aren't simply rules to follow. They're guidelines that protect us and help us live the best life we can live. There's no better place to be than in the center of God's will.

Go:

1. In what areas of your life are you tempted to compromise today?

2. What do you think God is asking you to do instead?

3. How can you fortify your life so you are more likely to make the right decision?

Overtime:

Joshua 24:15
Proverbs 25:26
1 Corinthians 10:13
James 1:13-15

LEAVE IT ON THE FIELD
David Hermes

Ready:
[21] *"If you want to be perfect,"* Jesus said to him, *"go, sell your belongings and give to the poor, and you will have treasure in heaven. Then come, follow Me."* [22] *When the young man heard that command, he went away grieving, because he had many possessions.*

Matthew 19:21-22

Set:
It was my freshman year of high school, and I decided to try cross-country running. The only problems were my seven-minute miles and the thirty extra pounds that chased me everywhere I ran. If I were going to be competitive in this sport, it was going to take everything I had. Riding my bike to practice and then riding home after practice only to pass out in my parents' kitchen became my morning routine for the entire summer vacation.

Two months later, after knocking two minutes off of my mile time and all thirty of those extra pounds off of my body, it was time for my first race. At the first mile marker I was in the front half of the pack. By the second marker I was feeling sick, but I was edging toward the front. By the third marker I was sweating profusely, choking down my breakfast, and my body was ready to quit. With the finish line in my sight, there was nothing that could stop me from winning the race. I had to cross! I never saw the last 15 yards of the race, but according to my coaches and teammates I made it far enough to pass out over the finish line.

I placed in the top 10 in that race, and though I would go on to race in the regional competition that season my greatest race was the one where I left it all out on the field. That first race was where I learned how to win. In Matthew 19, the young man essentially asked Jesus, "How do I win in life?" Jesus responded to the young man by instructing him to, "Give up all your possessions and follow Me." Jesus was outlining what was and still is the cost of becoming a disciple and victor in the race of life.

Go:
1. What do you think it means to "leave it on the field" for Christ?

2. What might Jesus be asking you to give up to live wholeheartedly for Him?

3. What would it cost you to leave it all on the field for Christ? How much courage would it take for you to do it?

Overtime:
Mark 12:41-44

TRAINING TIME
Carmen Foster

Ready:
^{11} Put on the full armor of God so that you can stand against the tactics of the Devil. ^{12} For our battle is not against flesh and blood, but against the rulers, against the authorities, against the world powers of this darkness, against the spiritual forces of evil in the heavens. ^{13} This is why you must take up the full armor of God, so that you may be able to resist in the evil day, and having prepared everything, to take your stand.

Ephesians 6:11-13

Set:
"Some of my vivid images of Jerry Rice are him working out at the Pro Bowl. Here you are, after he wins the Super Bowl, he's played in front of 500 million people. Less than a week later, he's out there running wind sprints to play in what is our only exhibition game,' says NFL Commissioner Paul Tagliabue on ESPN Classic's SportsCentury series.

Jerry Rice is arguably the best wide receiver in the history of football. Rice had a reputation for training hard. He understood the benefits of taking care of his physical body so that on the field he could perform at a level that surpassed everyone else. He understood the power of training.

In our Christian life, we can gain power from training. God has given us the power tools of prayer, daily reading of the Scriptures, and joining together in fellowship with other believers. If we do not exercise these tools daily, then we will not grow in our relationship with Christ. Jerry Rice knew that if he did not stick to a strict training regimen, then he would not be the best wide receiver that he could be.

Recognize that there is power in training. In order to draw closer to Christ, you must be disciplined and faithful.

Go:
1. When you do not properly train for your sport, how is your game affected?

2. Why is it important to read the Scriptures daily? To pray without ceasing? Fellowship with other believers?

3. How can you increase your desire to have a deeper relationship with Christ?

4. In what ways do you need to train harder spiritually?

Overtime:
1 Timothy 4:7-10
Ephesians 6:14-18
Acts 2:42

TAKING A STAND

Josh Carter

Ready:

Stand, therefore, with truth like a belt around your waist, righteousness like armor on your chest.

Ephesians 6:14

Set:

The Indianapolis Colts battled back from a 21-point deficit against the New England Patriots in their November 30, 2003, game. The Colts found themselves down by four points with less than three minutes to play and moved the ball deep inside Patriots' territory. They had a first down and goal at the two-yard line. However, without their goal-line offense, the Colts were stopped short on four straight plays, preserving the eighth straight win for New England. It was an impressive goal-line stand by the Patriots' defense.

Sometimes the challenge of standing firm in our faith in Jesus Christ can be like a goal-line stand. It is tough to stand our ground in a world that is constantly pushing us in the direction opposite to Jesus' teaching. Others perceive that we somehow think we are better than everyone else if we don't go along with the crowd. Also, believing that Jesus Christ is the ONLY way to a right relationship with God (John 14:6) is widely criticized as intolerant.

We must daily take a stand for Christ and His message. This message deals with the truth and the righteousness that Paul wrote about to the Ephesians. Truth comes from knowing God's Word and righteousness comes from living out truth. Taking a stand for truth and righteousness is a formidable task, just like facing first and goal from the two-yard line. But now is the time to step up and make a goal-line stand. Are you ready?

"Be alert, stand firm in the faith, be brave and strong" (1 Corinthians 16:13).

Go:

1. What do you think is the hardest part about taking a stand for Christ?

2. What does it mean to you to stand firm in the faith?

3. How are you taking a stand for the Lord on your team? How can you do better?

Overtime:

1 Corinthians 15:58
Galatians 5:1
2 Thessalonians 2:15

WAITING ... NOT AN EASY JOB

Jere Johnson

FCA GAME PLAN

Ready:

But those who trust in the LORD will renew their strength; they will soar on wings like eagles; they will run and not grow weary; they will walk and not faint.

Isaiah 40:31

Set:

"The wait is finally over. The White Sox have won the pennant." Many people in the organization have had to wait a long time to get to the World Series. Every person on the team and each fan would say it has been worth the wait, but it wasn't easy in the process. Waiting is one tough job! In sports today, players and teams are waiting ... waiting patiently for their time to shine.

In God's Word, Isaiah wrote in chapter 40 that waiting is a good thing. The word "wait" does not measure time spent, but rather it is a process of strengthening until fulfillment. Let me suggest three reasons why we must wait on the Lord:

1. Waiting creates time during which we can trust God more (Psalm 27).
2. Waiting prepares us to have our real needs met (Psalm 40).
3. Waiting encourages us to always be prepared for Christ's return (Matthew 24).

What do you find yourself waiting for? Unanswered prayers? A loved one to come to Christ? An opportunity to play for your team? Regardless of the reason, we know through God's promises that waiting will be worth it in the end.

I am sure it was not easy for the White Sox to be patient while they waited. But as they look back at all the hard work they put in to get to this point, the waiting has paid off in tremendous satisfaction. Are you trusting God during your season of waiting? Are you leaning on Him or are you blaming Him for the things you are waiting on? Let Him give you strength during your wait so you will soar, walk, and run in HIM when His time of success for you comes.

Go:

1. What don't you like to wait on?

2. How do you know when you are growing weary of waiting on God to act in your life?

3. Today, how do you think you can find strength and patience to wait on the Lord?

Overtime: Hebrews 12:1-2   Philippians 1:6   Proverbs 20:22

UNAWARE
Michael Hill

Ready:
For You are our glory and joy!   1 Thessalonians 2:20

Set:
Glory – it is such a simple word. It is what all of us play the game for. We want the glory associated with being an athlete. We want to be recognized for our skill. Who doesn't want to win a championship this year? How many times have you put your goals for the season down and listed "To NOT be remembered"?

At first glance, we have it all messed up. We should not want to get the entire spotlight. We should want to be a team player. We should not want to be so focused that we "win at all costs." It's in the nature of a competitor to "go for it." Shouldn't we want to be that focused?

The answer is we should be that focused, but not on a game. God wants us to be that focused on Him. The singing group Mercy Me has a song entitled "Unaware." In it they say, "Nothing else matters here but glorifying Your name. I am unaware that I still breathe. Unaware of everything, knowing You're aware of me."

That is the focus God wants us to have. Let's be honest for a minute. What else is there except God? Regardless of our background, or how bad we were and still are at times, He STILL loved us enough to die for us.

Go:
1. How can you strengthen your focus on God in the way you live your daily life?

2. What things in your life cause you to lose your focus on God?

3. What satisfaction will you get from focusing on giving God glory?

Overtime:
Mark 1:34-38
Luke 5:16
Matthew 28:18-20
Acts 2:42-47

LACED UP

Jere Johnson

Ready:

Protect me, LORD, from the clutches of the wicked. Keep me safe from violent men who plan to make me stumble.

Psalm 140:4

Set:

Fred was a very good player in my high school program. He could run, jump, dunk, and shoot. He had all the tools he needed in order to be successful. But Fred made a big mistake one day. He came out to practice late, and I did not see him until "it" happened. We were doing our warm-up drill involving lay-ups when Fred came down after a lay-up and turned his ankle badly. When I looked at his feet, I realized he was not prepared for the drill. Fred's shoes were untied and not laced up tight for practice. He tripped over his laces, tore up his ankle, and missed the remainder of our season.

Are you properly "laced up" spiritually? What does that mean? When we become relaxed spiritually and do not make sure we are ready to compete against Satan and his schemes, it is easy to be tripped up by the world and all it offers. Let's take a look at how the world wants to trip us up ...

Look at slogans today. Burger King®: "Have it YOUR way." The Army: "Be all YOU can be." Sprite®: "Obey YOUR thirst." And it goes on and on. These slogans and products themselves are not bad, but the world tells us we can do it on our own and that YOU are all you need. Jesus Christ offers us a different way. He wants us to be laced up in Him, ready in Him. You need to be in God's Word, talking with Him all the time, and laced up spiritually so that you are ready to battle the enemy.

Fred could have hurt his ankle even with properly laced shoes, but it would have been a sports injury rather than a careless one. He wouldn't be kicking himself for neglecting to do something as simple as tying his shoes. In your life with Christ are you leaving your spiritual shoes untied, hoping not to be tripped up by the evil one? Don't get spiritually sloppy. Take time each day to make sure you're ready to compete for Christ. Spend time in prayer and in His Word, and focus on Him throughout the day. Do this and I know you will be less likely to be tripped up.

Before you go out into the world today, ask yourself if you are ready to compete against what it offers. If not, get laced up in Christ right now! You won't regret it!

Go:

1. What appeals of the world tend to trip you up most easily?

2. How can you "lace up" to resist those worldly appeals?

3. What could you do even today to "lace up" tighter to play the "game" of life better?

Overtime: Job 18:7   Psalm 36:11, 37:24, 119:165   Ephesians 6:10-18

BEYOND OURSELVES

Josh Carter

Ready:

Everyone should look out not only for his own interests, but also for the interests of others.

Philippians 2:4

Set:

Due to Hurricane Katrina, the New Orleans Saints began the 2005 NFL season with more on their minds than winning football games. Katrina caused devastation not only in the lives of many Saints fans, players and families, but also to the whole city of New Orleans. In the season opener, kicker John Carney hit a 47-yard field goal with three seconds left to give the saints a 23-20 victory over the Carolina Panthers. "You don't want to attach too much importance to it, you know, because it's still just a football game," Carney said. "But, sure, there was a sense that we were playing for more than ourselves today."

In one sense, John Carney was right in that it was "just a football game," but for many of those Saints fans it was more than a football game. It meant another opportunity to come together as a community to continue picking up the pieces of their lives and to heal their brokenness. It was obvious that the Saints players wanted to play their hearts out to help bring some encouragement to their fans.

If you're like me, you may often find yourself going through life focused solely on meeting your needs and doing what is best for you. However, this is not an appropriate attitude for a follower of Jesus Christ. Paul addressed self-centeredness in the church at Philippi and challenged them to humbly consider the needs of others before their own (Philippians 2:3-4).

I encourage you to live and compete today not for your own personal glory, but for the glory of God and for the encouragement, support, and strengthening of those around you.

Go:

1. When has someone put your needs above his or her own? How did you feel about that?

2. Why does God call us to put others first?

3. As a competitor, how can you put the needs of others before your own?

No one should seek his own good, but the good of the other person (1 Corinthians 10:24).

Overtime:

Romans 15:2
Philippians 2:19-22
Hebrews 13:16

THE ONLY NEED

Michael Hill

Ready:

LORD, You are my portion and my cup of blessing; You hold my future.

Psalm 16:5

Set:

In athletics we do a good job of misusing the verb "need." We need a win. We need new uniforms. We need this player to play well. We need to raise this much with our fund-raiser. We need to have everyone at workouts.

The only problem is we are not looking at the verb "need" right. When we use "need" we use it to mean something we would like to have ... a lot. All of the situations above are things any coach would like to have. Who would not like new uniforms every season? We should use "need" a little differently.

What would our life look like if we substituted a different definition for "need"? Maybe something like, "A need is something we must get or we will die." Then we would go from needing new uniforms to needing air, food, water, and the water of life—Jesus Christ.

Go:

1. What does it mean to say, "God is my only true need"?

2. How would your life change if you took this truth to heart more than you have before?

3. In what areas of life do you need to believe that God will provide for you in spite of your circumstances?

Overtime:

Isaiah 40:11
Psalms 13:6; 55:22
Luke 1:37
2 Corinthians 1:9-10; 2:10
1 Peter 5:7

HUMILITY TO GOD?
Clay Elliott

Ready:
Humble yourselves therefore under the mighty hand of God, so that He may exalt you in due time.
1 Peter 5:6

Set:
On the surface it sounds pretty easy to humble yourself before God, but in reality it's tough. To humble ourselves before Him means to be subject to Him. But we can't see Him, so we forget He's watching. Sometimes we can't hear Him, so we forget He's speaking. We can't always feel Him close, so we forget He never leaves or forsakes us. So you can see why it is tough to humble ourselves before Him. Just because we can't always see, hear, or touch God doesn't mean He isn't mighty. God is mighty. He is able to destroy entire nations if He so desires, as illustrated in many Old Testament stories like the one in which He gave the Israelites the highly fortified city of Jericho. (Read more about it in Joshua 6.)

God is all-powerful. When we live in accordance with His will, we get to experience the full effects of His abundant blessing. And as the 1 Peter 5:8 states, He will exalt us in due time if we remain humble before Him.

How can you humble yourself before God? Well, a start is to listen willingly to His advice. Go to His Word and discover His ideas. Spend time with Him. He would enjoy hanging out with you!

OK, so what if you do humble yourself under the mighty hand of God? Are there any real benefits? Yes! He tells us that He will exalt us in due time. This means you will be raised or lifted up out of a trial or trouble. If you have been faithful with your finances, He will bless them. If you are faithful to remain pure, He will bless you with an amazing spouse. In other words, God loves you so much that He will step in and take you out of the tough situation when He knows you need it ... but probably not until then!

God does not give us more than we are able to handle (1 Corinthians 10:13). Even though at times our circumstances seem impossible to survive, He uses these tough times to grow us in our relationship with Him. Humble yourself before God and He will exalt and carry you through – ultimately for His glory.

Go:
1. On what occasions have you been humble before God? Why were you humble then?

2. Think about an area in your life that you need to give to God and be subject to Him. Offer this up to Him right now.

3. Be looking for God to step in and carry you through a tough time. When it happens and you see it, be sure to thank Him for intervening!

Overtime: Philippians 2   Psalm 84:11   Proverbs 3:34

WHAT WILL YOU GIVE?

Josh Carter

Ready:

And whatever you do, in word or in deed, do everything in the name of the Lord Jesus, giving thanks to God the Father through Him.

Colossians 3:17

Set:

The 2005 Northwestern College football schedule appeared to have a misprint on it, showing two games scheduled for October 8. It was no mistake, though, and the Division III school became the first to play two football games in one day, knocking off Trinity Bible College and Macalester College 59-0 and 47-14 respectively.

Prior to the first game, one group of players was asked to come up to the chalkboard and answer the question, "What will you give?" Players wrote things like intensity, love, respect, etc. Then senior defensive back Dan Pazurek approached the board and wrote, "All the glory to Jesus Christ."

How many times do you go into competition asking, "What can I give today?" I have to be honest and say that I can be a pretty selfish competitor, often thinking about what I hope to GET out of competition (victory, praise, self-satisfaction), not what I can give.

In Colossians 3:1-17, Paul described what the conduct of a Christian should look like, and he wrapped up the passage with the all inclusive "whatever you do ... do everything in the name of the Lord Jesus." The "whatever" includes competition, which we should approach with the attitude and goal of giving glory to Jesus Christ.

"Therefore, whether you eat or drink, or whatever you do, do everything for God's glory" (1 Corinthians 10:31).

Go:

1. In competition, do you focus more on what you can get or what you can give? Explain.

2. How can you give "all the glory to Jesus Christ" today? The next time you're in competition? (Be specific.)

Overtime:

1 Peter 4:11
Revelation 14:7
Revelation 19:7

JUST SAY IT!

Dan Britton

Ready:

15 But one of them, seeing that he was healed, returned and, with a loud voice, gave glory to God. 16 He fell facedown at His feet, thanking Him. And he was a Samaritan.

Luke 17:15-16

Set:

Athletes love to be called great. At least I do. It has been a while since I've heard those words on the field of competition. I do hear them from my kids every once in a while; so I've got that going for me. If you truly are the best, then you are called the greatest of all time. Only a few have reached that level of success, and they are certainly in their respective halls of fame.

I think every true competitor has a secret desire to be great, and that is okay. That shows drive and passion. My question is not whether or not you are great, or even if you have that desire. My question is this: would you rather be great or grateful?

In Luke 17, out of the 10 lepers healed by Jesus, only one guy scrambled back to say, "Thanks." I am sure that the other nine wanted to say it, but they just didn't. But that one guy understood the power of saying, "Thank you." It is a simple thing, but simple isn't the same as easy. Expressing gratitude can be very hard to do, but it's important. Unexpressed gratitude can be taken for arrogance or ignorance!

I love to meet athletes or coaches who are truly thankful. Their hearts are full of God's goodness, and it pours out. It shows in everything – their speech, attitude, and actions. It's a blessing to be around them. They are thankful for the gifts and talents that God has blessed them with. They are thankful for their coaches and teams. They are even thankful for the tough times. But the best part is that they express it.

Every day, we should first thank God, and then we should thank the people whom God has put in our lives. The one thing that prevents me from saying, "Thanks," is that I sometimes feel like I deserve what I should be thankful for. The best way to defeat that mentality is to practice being grateful or thankful.

So go ahead and just say it! What are you waiting for? Be known as an athlete with a thankful heart.

Go:

1. Do you think people who know you say you have a heart of thankfulness? Why or why not?

2. List five people you are thankful for and why.

3. What are some things that God has done for you for which you are thankful?

4. What tends to hinder you from freely expressing your thanks?

Overtime: Psalm 100   Psalm 138:1   Philippians 4:6   Colossians 3:15

JUMP

Jere Johnson

Ready:

²⁹ *And climbing out of the boat, Peter started walking on the water and came toward Jesus.* ³⁰ *But when he saw the strength of the wind, he was afraid. And beginning to sink he cried out, "Lord, save me!"* ³¹ *Immediately Jesus reached out His hand, caught hold of him, and said to him, "You of little faith, why did you doubt?"* ³² *When they got into the boat, the wind ceased.* ³³ *Then those in the boat worshiped Him and said, "Truly You are the Son of God!"*

Matthew 14:29b-33

Set:

Last night after getting my two-year-old Evan ready for bed, he bounced right up in a playful mood. Seeing this, I encouraged him to jump off the bed to me, but I did not put my hands out … yet. His face went from joy to fear and looked at the elements. The bed was high; the floor was low. The end table was close, but not close enough. I could see total indecision in his eyes.

As an athlete, we are filled with indecision at times. We want to step up and step out to help the team, but fear and doubt hold us back. I see this most often in basketball. A coach will put a player on the floor for his or her ability to shoot the ball, but when the player does not take advantage of the opportunity, the opportunity passes away. Why do we fear and why do we doubt when the coach has full confidence that we can do it and get the job done?

Peter was just the same. When he saw Christ walking on the water, he wanted to be with Him but was afraid. Jesus simply said to Peter, "Come." Peter tried, but started to flounder because he failed to believe in his Coach, Jesus Christ, and had to be helped out of his disbelief.

Evan had a decision to make. Would he trust his father or would he let fear and doubt hold him back. He started, and then stopped. He would not move until I finally held out my arms, and he readily jumped into them (with eyes closed, I might add). In his mind, he was saying, "Daddy, catch me," but in his heart he had fear until he saw his father's open arms waiting to catch him willingly. Maybe it's time for you to jump into action as a player or coach. But more importantly, now is the time to jump into your heavenly Father's arms with confidence and trust because He will always catch you! It's okay … go for it and JUMP!

Go:

1. When, as an athlete, do you tend to have doubts?

2. How can you draw confidence from your coach and teammates?

3. How confident do you feel about jumping into your heavenly Father's arms today?
   If you have questions, contact your local FCA staff member.

Overtime: Matthew 6:25-34; 7:7-12   Romans 10:11, 15:13   Proverbs 3:5-6

HALL OF FAME

Michael Hill

Ready:

[God says:] "Look, I have inscribed you on the palms of My hands; your walls are continually before Me."

Isaiah 49:16

Set:

What athlete doesn't want to be in a hall of fame? What little kid playing t-ball doesn't dream of hitting the winning home run in the World Series? What sixth grader playing touch football at recess doesn't dream of playing in the Super Bowl?

It is our nature to be driven competitors. We are wired to work to be the best we can be. Our society has a special place of honor for those who are above average. Whether a person dreams of being inducted in Canton, Ohio, as a gridiron great or making it to Cooperstown, New York, as a hero of the diamond, everybody wants to be the best. The thing some Christian athletes don't realize is that they are already in God's Hall of Fame.

The prophet Isaiah relayed some critical information to us from the Head Coach. God has already written our names on His hands. When Jesus comes back for His church, spending eternity with God as part of that group of people will be so much more than just going to services in a church building that will come to ruins in the end.

We are wired to push ourselves to the limit to be the best. That is what God wants. He wants us to compete at the highest level in whatever we do. The amazing thing is, when we ask Him to take over our lives, we get automatic induction into the ultimate Hall of Fame!

Go:

1. What do you think of the idea of competing for God?

2. What are you doing to build His Kingdom?

3. If you are not competing for God, why not?

Overtime:

Jeremiah 1:5
Colossians 3:23
2 Corinthians 5:11,14,18-20
Matthew 28:16-20

IT'S ABOUT LOVE

Josh Carter

FCA GAME PLAN

Ready:
Now this is His command: that we believe in the name of His Son Jesus Christ, and love one another as He commanded us.

1 John 3:23

Set:
Rulon Gardner and Dremiel Byers were both vying for one spot on the 2004 U.S. Olympic wrestling team. Gardner was the 2000 Olympic gold medalist and 2001 World Champion and Byers the 2002 World Champion. Gardner won a pair of 2-1 overtime matches at the Olympic trials, and Byers laid down his pride and went to Athens to help prepare his friend for another gold medal run by serving as his training partner. Gardner came home with the bronze medal and a gold medal friend. Would he have done the same for Byers? No doubt about it!

God's Word is unmistakably clear in its command for us to love one another. But how is this biblical love fleshed out in the sports world? By putting the needs of others (the team) ahead of our own, as Dremiel Byers did for Rulon Gardner. I believe there are many ways that we can practically show love toward one another in sport. Sacrifice-bunting your teammate into scoring position, taking on two blockers so your teammate can make the tackle, moving over to take a charge when your teammate got beat, or staying after practice to help a teammate with a drill are all examples of loving others the way Jesus calls us to.

I encourage you to proactively find ways today to love one another with the love God has given us.

"Dear friends, if God loved us in this way, we also must love one another" (1 John 4:11).

Go:
1. How do you know when someone truly loves and cares about you?

2. When you show love to your teammates, how does that strengthen your team?

3. What is one thing you could do today that would show someone on your team that you love him or her?

Overtime:
John 13:34-35
Romans 13:8
1 Peter 1:22
1 John 4:7

TRUE GLORY

Clay Elliott

Ready:

Now the God of all grace, who called you to His eternal glory in Christ Jesus, will personally restore, establish, strengthen, and support you after you have suffered a little.

1 Peter 5:10

Set:

Have you ever been on a team that has won it all? Winning a championship title is truly a position of glory. Really it is the only position of true glory in sports because you received the highest honor possible! No other team could make that claim.

Now, while we are on the earth, we can get a position of glory if we give our lives to Jesus Christ by receiving Him as Savior and Lord. God restores us when we give our sins to Him. God establishes us when we willingly say, "Here I am Lord ... use me." God strengthens us when we come to Him and ask Him for His care. God supports us when we face our enemies or problems.

Peter tells us here that we will suffer a little, which is a drag ... but that's what is cool about God; He never lies or tells us that life will be smooth sailing. You may suffer through physical problems or mental issues or emotional dark times, but stand firm because true glory is still coming. But when?

True glory comes when we live by faith. Don't bail out on God when the tough times come. Live by faith. Don't stop walking with God because you can't feel Him with you. Live by faith. Don't stop praying because it doesn't seem like He's hearing you. Live by faith. Living by faith will bring true glory ... now ... and later!

Go:

1. In the space below, list a few tough things you are currently dealing with.

2. Take some time and pray for restoration, establishment, strength, and support during these tough times.

3. How does your distance from God feel now? Keep on praying in faith.

Overtime:

Hebrews 11
John 16:33

ONE FOR THE TEAM

Jere Johnson

Ready:

Jesus spoke these things, looked up to heaven, and said: "Father, the hour has come. Glorify Your Son so that the Son may glorify You."

John 17:1

Set:

Baseball is a great team sport. Every player works together on the field to make his or her team successful. One of my favorite plays in baseball is not what most would think. I love to see players give up their at bat for the advancement of the team. They sacrifice their turn at bat so their team might win in the end. This is an important play in baseball. The home run hitters get all the glory, but these role players do just as much to help the team win.

Jesus knew as soon as He came to earth He had a role to carry out for His team (people who followed Him). He lived His life day-to-day to make sure the plan would be completed in the end. He knew what He had to do. Jesus prayed while preparing His heart for the task ahead of Him. Jesus knew it was time to take one for His team. He knew He was born to be the sacrifice for all that we might enjoy eternity with Him. This selfless act was the greatest act of love in all mankind. Christ knew the plan had to be complete for ultimate victory and the win in the end. Christ went to the cross to be the sacrifice for our sin and with that act we have life with Him forever. Now that is a glory-filled event.

Just as in baseball, where one play can change the whole course of a game, Jesus' glorious sacrifice changed the course for all mankind. When you are asked to do something, or give yourself up for the team, remember what Christ did for you on the cross. Surely, we can be Christ-like in making a sacrifice for victory, because He Himself showed us by His example the ultimate sacrifice for all eternity. Thank You, Lord, for taking one (going to the cross) for me!

Go:

1. What is your reaction when you have to give yourself up for the sake of the team?

2. What does the sacrifice Christ made on the cross mean to you personally?

3. Today, how can you make sacrifices in your life to show a Christ-like attitude?

Overtime:

Romans 5:6
1 Thessalonians 5:9-10
Romans 8:34

WARM-UPS

Team-Building Exercises to Connect Your Group

The Warm-ups on the following pages have icons that match the icons on the front of the Bible for the Student Studies. You can also choose one of the Team-Builders that would work as Warm-Ups for the Athlete Studies.

There are 4 basic group types for more effective activities:

 **TWOSOMES**

 **FOURSOMES**

 **CIRCLE OF EIGHT**

 **WHOLE HUDDLE**

WARM-UPS TABLE OF CONTENTS

WARM-UPS   **Page**   **Page**

GROUP WARM-UPS

BIBLICAL INVENTORIES

SPECIAL TOPICS

SCRIPTURE REFLECTIONS

AFFIRMATION EXERCISES

EVALUATION

GROUP WARM-UPS

WHAT IS YOUR DREAM ... ?

Begin by having a member of the group read the first dream and its possible answers. Before that person chooses an answer, allow others in the group to guess what answer he or she might select. Then have that person reveal his or her answer, and give anyone who guessed correctly 10 points. Allow the next person to continue with dream 2. Move through the questions going around the group, starting over from dream 1 again if you have more than 4 people.

1. What is your dream vacation?
    ❏ Surfing in Hawaii
    ❏ Working on a deep-sea fishing boat
    ❏ Floating in space at the Space Station
    ❏ Staying home to read, watch TV, or dive into my computer
    ❏ Traveling around Europe
    ❏ Other: _____

2. What is your dream job?
    ❏ Professional athlete
    ❏ Lawyer or doctor
    ❏ Flavor tester for Coca-Cola
    ❏ Farmer
    ❏ Airline pilot
    ❏ Other: _____

3. What is your dream date?
    ❏ Dinner with a supermodel or movie celebrity
    ❏ Picnic with the girl or guy next door
    ❏ Going to a sold-out concert
    ❏ Attending a spiritual retreat
    ❏ Going to a movie with a group of friends
    ❏ Other: _____

4. What is your dream home?
    ❏ Country cottage in the woods
    ❏ Huge mansion in Beverly Hills
    ❏ Average house in a subdivision
    ❏ Mobile home in a mobile-home park
    ❏ Cave in the mountains
    ❏ Other: _____

MY PARTNER

Pair off into groups of 2 and have one person guess what his or her partner would do in each of the following situations. Check "yes," "no," or "maybe." Give 10 points for every correct guess. Then reverse the roles and let the other person guess. Total the scores to find the winner.

My partner is someone who would:

	YES	NO	MAYBE
1. Yell at a referee	❑	❑	❑
2. Enjoy horror movies	❑	❑	❑
3. Spend most of his or her money on video games	❑	❑	❑
4. Skip school to do something fun	❑	❑	❑
5. Buy only brand-name clothes	❑	❑	❑
6. Rather participate in a sport than watch one	❑	❑	❑
7. Choose vanilla ice cream instead of a wild flavor	❑	❑	❑
8. Prefer to walk than drive	❑	❑	❑
9. Choose ESPN over MTV	❑	❑	❑
10. Buy an old, used car instead of a new BMW	❑	❑	❑

MY TEMPERAMENT

Get together in groups of 2 to 4 and explain how you see yourself in the seven categories below. In each category, circle which statement is closest to the way you think or act. Go down the list one item at a time letting everyone share his or her response for each category.

ON SHOWING MY FEELINGS:
Big boys (girls) don't cry. _____ I love you, man!

ON INTENSITY:
Chill out. _____ Just do it.

ON BEING GENTLE AND KIND:
Nice guys finish last. _____ You say "Jump"; I say, "How high?"

ON SPIRITUAL DESIRE:
Don't go overboard. _____ Full speed ahead.

ON CARING FOR OTHER PEOPLE:
Not my problem. _____ How can I serve you?

ON BEING OPEN AND HONEST:
Mind your own business. _____ Lay it on the line.

ON HANDLING CONFLICT:
Peace at any price. _____ I don't get mad; I get even.

 **KWIZ**

Form groups of 4 to 8 people. Everyone in the group chooses one of the categories. One person at a time will read aloud the questions in his or her category—pausing to let others guess before revealing the answer. For each correct answer, the correct guesser receives the dollar amount for that question. After everyone is finished, add up your winnings and see who has the most money.

GROUP WARM-UPS

SPORTING EVENTS

For $1—I would prefer:
- ❏ to watch a sports event
- ❏ to play a sport

For $2—At a sporting event, I am more likely to:
- ❏ yell at the ref
- ❏ do the wave
- ❏ paint my face and act crazy

For $3—My favorite ballpark food is:
- ❏ hot dogs
- ❏ nachos
- ❏ peanuts
- ❏ pretzels

For $4—One sport I would never try is:
- ❏ parasailing
- ❏ ski jumping
- ❏ motocross racing
- ❏ sky surfing
- ❏ scuba diving
- ❏ snowboarding

DRIVING

For $1—I could best be described as:
- ❏ Cautious Casey
- ❏ Racey Randy

For $2—I am probably more likely to:
- ❏ speed
- ❏ roll through a stop sign
- ❏ zoom through a yellow light

For $3—I got my last speeding ticket:
- ❏ within the last month
- ❏ within the last six months
- ❏ over a year ago
- ❏ never

For $4—My pet peeve when driving is:
- ❏ people who don't use a turn signal
- ❏ rush hour traffic
- ❏ speeders in residential neighborhoods
- ❏ slow traffic in the left lane
- ❏ Sunday drivers

OUTDOORS

For $1—I would rather go to the:
- ❏ mountains
- ❏ beach

For $2—I would rather stay in a:
- ❏ tent
- ❏ motor home
- ❏ cabin
- ❏ hotel

For $3—When I go camping I prefer to:
- ❏ go hiking
- ❏ go swimming
- ❏ take photographs
- ❏ do nothing

For $4—My favorite camping food is:
- ❏ hot chocolate
- ❏ trail mix
- ❏ hot dogs cooked over a campfire
- ❏ roasted marshmallows
- ❏ hot, spicy chili

PETS

For $1—In my opinion, the cutest animal is:
- ❏ a puppy
- ❏ a kitten

For $2—If I could choose a dog, I'd select:
- ❏ a frisky, little dog
- ❏ a big, playful dog
- ❏ a lovable, lazy dog

For $3—What bugs me most about having a pet is:
- ❏ cleaning up the mess
- ❏ when they are noisy
- ❏ finding hair or feathers everywhere
- ❏ when they scratch things

For $4—My favorite unusual type of pet is:
- ❏ a snake
- ❏ a parrot
- ❏ a pot-bellied pig
- ❏ a gerbil
- ❏ a lizard
- ❏ a monkey

HABITS

For $1—I'm more likely to squeeze the tooth-paste:
- ❏ in the middle
- ❏ from the end

For $2—If I am lost, I will probably
- ❏ stop and ask directions
- ❏ check the map
- ❏ find the way by driving around

For $3—I read the newspaper starting with the:
- ❏ front page
- ❏ entertainment
- ❏ comics
- ❏ sports

For $4—When I undress at night, I put my clothes:
- ❏ on a hanger in the closet
- ❏ folded neatly over a chair
- ❏ into a hamper or clothes basket
- ❏ on the floor

FOOD

For $1—I prefer to eat at a:
- ❏ fast-food restaurant
- ❏ fancy restaurant

For $2—On the menu, I look for something:
- ❏ familiar
- ❏ different
- ❏ way-out

For $3—When eating chicken, my preference is a:
- ❏ drumstick
- ❏ wing
- ❏ breast
- ❏ gizzard

For $4—I draw the line when it comes to eating:
- ❏ frog legs
- ❏ sushi
- ❏ Rocky Mountain oysters

SHOWS

For $1—I am more likely to:
- ❏ go see a first-run movie
- ❏ rent a video at home

For $2—On TV, my first choice is:
- ❏ news
- ❏ sports
- ❏ sitcoms

For $3—If a show gets scary, I will usually:
- ❏ go to the restroom
- ❏ close my eyes
- ❏ clutch a friend
- ❏ love it

For $4—In movies, I prefer:
- ❏ comedies
- ❏ serious drama
- ❏ action films
- ❏ animations

CLOTHES

For $1—I'm more likely to shop at:
- ❏ Wal-Mart
- ❏ Neiman Marcus

For $2—I feel more comfortable wearing:
- ❏ formal clothes
- ❏ sport clothes
- ❏ casual clothes
- ❏ grubbies

For $3—In buying clothes, I look first for:
- ❏ fashion/style
- ❏ price
- ❏ name brand
- ❏ quality

For $4—In buying clothes, I usually:
- ❏ shop all day for a bargain
- ❏ choose one store but try on everything
- ❏ buy the first thing I try on
- ❏ buy without trying it on

THE BEST OF TIMES, THE WORST OF TIMES

Go around the group and have each person choose an aspect of his or her life in the past week that could be described as "the best of times." It's okay to choose more than one category, such as "spiritually" and "emotionally." Be sure each person briefly explains why he or she chose each answer. Then, go around the group again for each of the other categories.

The Best of Times

❏ Spiritually

❏ Physically

❏ Athletically

❏ Emotionally

❏ Intellectually

❏ Other: _____

Not Bad, Could Have Been Better

❏ Spiritually

❏ Physically

❏ Athletically

❏ Emotionally

❏ Intellectually

❏ Other: _____

The Worst of Times

❏ Spiritually

❏ Physically

❏ Athletically

❏ Emotionally

❏ Intellectually

❏ Other: _____

SCOUTING REPORT

Get together with 2 or 3 people and work together on the scouting report below. Taking one category at a time (Mental, Emotional, Spiritual), check one or two points that are your greatest strengths. See if the others agree with you … and let them add one more that you did not mention. Then do the next person's list.

MENTAL

___intelligence
___creativity
___good judgment
___self-confidence
___common sense
___determination
___sense of humor
___perception
___comprehension
___good memory

EMOTIONAL

___warmth
___sensitivity
___consistency
___enthusiasm
___patience
___self-control
___cheerfulness
___dependability
___balance
___peacefulness

SPIRITUAL

___compassion
___joyfulness
___serenity
___dedication
___gentleness
___generosity
___humility
___discipline
___faith
___courage

LIFESTYLE CHECKUP

How healthy is your lifestyle? Taking one line at a time, mark an "X" where you would rate yourself for each of the areas. Share the results of your checkup with your group.

DIET / NUTRITION
health food   junk food

EXERCISE / PHYSICAL ACTIVITY
marathon runner   couch potato

SLEEPING HABITS
"Good morning, Lord!"   "O Lord, it's morning!"

TOBACCO
Mr. Clean   Joe Camel

STRESS / HYPERACTIVITY
Garfield   Tazmanian Devil

MENTAL ALERTNESS
Road Runner   Wile E. Coyote

OVERALL FITNESS / VITALITY
Energizer Bunny   dead battery

THE GRAND TOTAL

Fill each box with the correct number and then total your score. When everyone is finished, go around the group and explain how you got your total. You can also determine who has the highest and lowest totals.

☐ X ☐ = ☐

Number of hours
you sleep

Number of push-ups
you can do

☐ − ☐ = ☐

Number of times sent
to principal's office

Number of speeding
tickets you've received

☐ ÷ ☐ = ☐

Number of hours spent
watching TV daily

Number of books you
read this year for fun

☐ + ☐ = ☐

Number of states you
have lived in

Number of brothers and sisters
you have (including stepbrothers
and stepsisters)

☐

Grand Total

MY DAILY ROUTINE

Everybody gets 24 hours a day. It's how you use those hours that counts. Get together with 1 to 3 people and finish the sentences below. Take turns explaining to each other your daily routine. "In a usual day …"

1. I get up around …
2. It takes me about _____ minutes to dress and get ready.
3. For breakfast I usually have …
4. I leave for school around …
5. The way I usually get to school is by …
6. For lunch, I usually have …
7. After school, I usually …
8. If I have some free time before supper, I usually …
9. It usually takes me about _____ hour(s) to do my homework.
10. If I have a test the next day, I usually start studying around …
11. If I don't have any homework, I usually …
12. In a typical day, I watch about _____ hour(s) of TV.
13. In a typical day, I spend about _____ minutes on the computer.
14. In a typical day, I check my look in the mirror _____ times.
15. I usually go to bed around …
16. It takes me about _____ minutes to fall asleep.

  # YOU ARE WHAT YOU EAT

Get together in groups of 8, sitting in the shape of a wagon wheel—4 people back to back in the center and 4 people across from them on the outside of the circle. Everyone shares with the person across from them the answer to the first three questions about your eating habits. After 2 minutes, the four people on the outside move left (clockwise) to form new pairs. Now everyone answers the next three questions. Shift again to answer questions 7 to 9, and again to answer 10 to 12. Keep it moving—spending only about 2 minutes with each partner.

1. My favorite food is …
2. My favorite place to eat out is …
3. My favorite dessert is …
4. I draw the line when it comes to eating …
5. If I could visit another part of the world to taste their food, I would go to …
6. My idea of a midnight snack is …
7. On a first date, I would probably eat at …
8. If this were a really special occasion, I might take this person to …
9. My favorite meal of the year with my family is …
10. If I could order something "way out" at a restaurant, I might order …
11. The most bizarre thing I ever ate was …
12. The food that best describes my personality in the morning is …

 # MY COAT OF ARMS

In Medieval times, families had colorful symbols, usually in the shape of a shield, that represented their family heritage—a Coat of Arms. Get together with a partner and share your family strengths, using the Coat of Arms below (Part 1). Explain how you would fill in the Coat of Arms with five things about your parents and yourself. Then use the half-finished sentences that follow (Part 2) to comment on what your partner said.

Part 1:

Part 2: FEEDBACK FROM YOUR PARTNER:

1. I really like what you said about ...

2. If I could add one more strength that I have seen in you, it would be ...

 # FOUR FACTS ... ONE LIE

Here's a chance to share some significant facts about yourself and have fun doing it. In groups of 4 to 8, ask one person to finish the five sentences below—making one of the five a lie. (Try to keep a straight face.) Then let the others in the group try to guess which fact is a lie. When everyone has guessed, ask the person to explain which fact was the lie ... and what would be an honest answer. Continue around the group until everyone has had a chance to share.

1. At age 7, my favorite TV show was ...

2. At age 9, my hero was ...

3. At age 10, I wanted to be a ...

4. At age 12, my favorite music was ...

5. Right now, my favorite pastime is ...

(Sidebar, left margin:) GROUP WARM-UPS

 # FAMILY EXPECTATIONS

Our family background is an important factor determining who we are. Take turns answering the following questions about your family and share them in groups of 2 to 4.

I feel that my parents look upon me as ...
- ❏ a troublesome kid
- ❏ a helpless baby
- ❏ a scapegoat
- ❏ glue
- ❏ a security blanket
- ❏ a capable adult
- ❏ their pride and joy
- ❏ a liability
- ❏ a disappointment
- ❏ invisible
- ❏ good stock
- ❏ a continuation of themselves
- ❏ the family name

I feel that my parents expect me to be ...
- ❏ the next president
- ❏ a doctor
- ❏ an incredible success
- ❏ a minister
- ❏ completely obedient
- ❏ just like them
- ❏ the next Albert Einstein
- ❏ perfect
- ❏ a great athlete
- ❏ independent
- ❏ self-sufficient
- ❏ a compensation for their failures
- ❏ whatever makes me happy

 # TAKE YOUR CHOICE

Get together with 1 to 3 people and do this quiz together. Take one question at a time, letting the others try to guess your answer before you share.

In my free time, I would rather:
- a. read
- b. watch TV
- c. listen to music

At night, I put my clothes:
- a. on the floor
- b. on a hanger
- c. folded over a chair

When I relax, I like to:
- a. be alone
- b. be in a crowd
- c. be with friends

For an award, I would rather get:
- a. a Nobel prize
- b. an Oscar
- c. an Olympic gold medal

In buying clothes, I look for:
- a. cost
- b. fashion / style
- c. quality

When eating chicken, I prefer:
- a. white meat
- b. dark meat
- c. the gizzard

For transportation, I prefer:
- a. a sports car
- b. a truck
- c. anything that runs

For a vacation, I would choose:
- a. a Caribbean cruise
- b. going to Europe
- c. going to Disney World

For a movie, I would choose:
- a. comedy
- b. drama
- c. action adventure

I would like to marry someone:
- a. rich
- b. attractive
- c. with a good personality

  # MR./MISS WORLD CONTEST

Get together with 1 to 3 people from your group and discuss the exercise below. Taking one category at a time, put an "X" somewhere in between the two extremes to indicate how you see yourself. For instance, on ATHLETICISM you might put the "X" in the middle because you are in between the two extremes.

ATHLETICISM
Most Valuable Player _____ Bench Warmer

MANNERS
Mr. / Miss Manners_____ Rude Dude

FITNESS
Mr. / Miss Universe _____ Couch Potato

SENSITIVITY
I'm listening _____ I can't hear you

FASHION
All dressed up _____ Grubbies

NEATNESS
Mr. / Miss Clean _____ Mr. / Miss Messy

SEX APPEAL
Homecoming king / queen _____ Home alone on Friday night

911 PHONE NUMBERS

Get together with one other person and work on this exercise together. Read the five situations below and think of the telephone number or the person you would call for each situation.

CRISIS SITUATION: **PERSON/PHONE NUMBER TO CALL:**

1. You just received a break-up letter. You need someone to talk to.   _____

2. You are at a crossroads in your life. You need good counsel.   _____

3. You had a big fight with your parents. You need to talk to someone who understands.   _____

4. You just found out that you have a serious disease. You need someone to pray for you.   _____

5. Someone you thought was your friend has been spreading rumors about you. You need advice about what to do.   _____

 # MY FAVORITE THINGS

Pair off with one other person (preferably someone that you do NOT know very well) and work together on this exercise. Read over the list below and choose the top five things you like to do. Then, compare your list with your partner's list.

MY TOP FIVE

_____ Playing sports
_____ Watching TV
_____ Hiking / biking
_____ Listening to music
_____ Shopping
_____ Talking on the phone or chatting online
_____ Working out
_____ Spending time alone
_____ Spending time with friends
_____ Playing on my computer

_____ Reading
_____ Working on my car / bike
_____ Going to the beach / mountains
_____ Going to the movies
_____ Going to parties
_____ Working on my hobby
_____ Playing a musical instrument
_____ Playing with my pet
_____ Going on vacation
_____ Going to sporting events

  # MEDICAL HISTORY

Have everyone in your group stay together for this ice-breaker. Here are some "highly scientific" but not so rare "diseases." As someone reads the descriptions one at a time, raise your hand if that's part of your "medical history"!

CHATROOM-ITIS—staring at a monitor for hours while typing messages to people you've never met.

JOYSTICKY-ELBOW—spending hours … or days … playing computer games until your arm won't move.

CHOCO-HOLISM—snarling when people suggest that you share your "chocolate decadence" dessert.

MALL-ITIS—a strong compulsion to spend many hours (and many dollars!) at the mall.

ESPN DEFICIENCY SYNDROME—going into convulsions when you haven't heard the sports scores in too long a time.

HAVEIGOTAGREATPERSONFORYOU-APHOBIA—fear of friends who are anxious to set you up with a member of the opposite sex.

CHANNELSURF-EOSIS—cramps in your index finger from having to push the remote control buttons so much—often makes you bed or couch-ridden.

INVOLUNTARY LEADFOOT REFLEX—a physiological phenomenon that results in "keeping the pedal to the metal" while driving.

ATTABOY-APHOBIA—fear of the motives of parents when they compliment you.

WALLET SCAVENGER HUNT

Get together with 1 to 3 people and work on this exercise together. If you have a wallet or purse, use the first set of questions below. If you do not have your wallet or purse with you, use the second set of questions below.

This is run like a scavenger hunt. You get 2 minutes in silence to go through your possessions or think about your answers. Then you break the silence and "show and tell" what you have found. For instance, "the thing I have had for the LONGEST TIME is ... this picture of me when I was a baby." Now, take 2 minutes in silence to find the items on this scavenger hunt.

WALLET OR PURSE LIST OF ITEMS (finish each sentence):

1. The thing I have had for the LONGEST TIME is ...
2. The thing that has SENTIMENTAL VALUE is ...
3. The thing that reminds me of a FUN TIME is ...
4. The most REVEALING thing about me is ...

IF YOU DON'T HAVE YOUR WALLET OR PURSE (finish each sentence):

1. The most EXPENSIVE thing I am wearing is ...
2. The CHEAPEST thing I am wearing is ...
3. The one thing that I CARRY with me all the time is ...
4. The thing I wear that has SENTIMENTAL VALUE is ...

A BUNCH OF BESTS

Get together in groups of about 4. Think of the "bests" in your life using the following suggestions. Choose two or three items from the list below to talk about the highlights from your past.

1. The best friend I ever had was ...
2. The best teacher I ever had was ...
3. The best concert I ever went to was ...
4. The best game I ever went to was ...
5. The best babysitter I ever had was ...
6. The best class in school I ever had was ...
7. The best pet I ever had was ...
8. The best birthday I ever had was ...
9. The best vacation I ever had was ...
10. The best book I ever read or movie I ever saw was ...

 # PLACES IN MY LIFE

On the map below, place the corresponding letter to indicate these five significant places in your life journey. Gather in groups of 2 to 4. Then go around and have everyone explain their selections.

B = Where I was born

C = Where I spent most of my childhood

V = My favorite vacation

H = Where I would like to go on my honeymoon

G = Where God became real to me—more than just a name

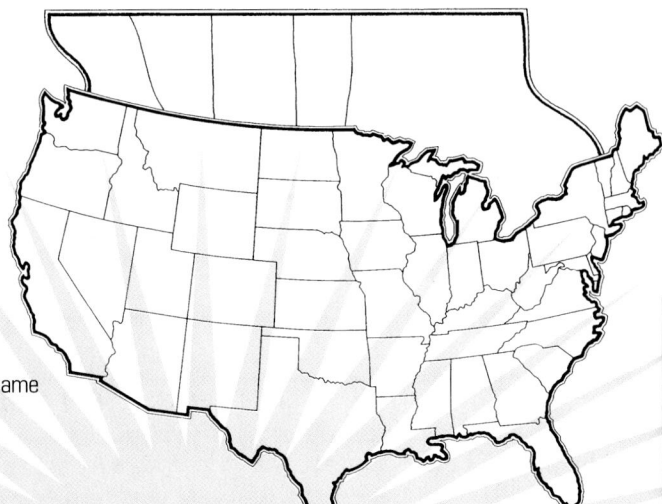

 # THE DATING GAME

Get together with one other person and interview each other for a feature story about your attitudes about dating for *People* magazine. The interview questions to ask are below.

1. What is your "nickname"? What do your friends call you?

2. When you were 7 years old, who was your hero?

3. Who was your first "true love"?

4. What TV show or movie did you like because it showed a dating relationship that you admired?

5. What TV show or movie did you not like because it showed dating relationships that were not attractive to you?

6. When it comes to dating, what do you look for in a date?

7. When it comes to going with someone, what do you look for in that person?

8. When it comes to marriage, what would you look for in a mate?

  # HOW'S THE WEATHER?

Consider all the different areas of your life. Choose two or three areas and assign a month of the year to each one. Get together in groups of 2 to 4 and share what season it is in each of the following areas of your life. Feel free to explain why you chose what you did.

- ❏ health
- ❏ social life
- ❏ school
- ❏ spiritual
- ❏ future outlook
- ❏ emotional
- ❏ family life
- ❏ friendships

JANUARY: Cold and snowy, but at least we're starting a new year

FEBRUARY: The bleakest time of the year; I'm getting tired of the color gray

MARCH: Cold and blustery, but there is a sniff of spring in the air

APRIL: Tumultuous and stormy, but life is breaking out everywhere

MAY: Spring has sprung! The flowers are blooming, and the skies are full of sunlight and cool breezes

JUNE: It's pleasantly warm, things are growing, and life is good

JULY: Boy, it's hot—everything is smoldering and oppressive

AUGUST: The heat has settled in; we sure could use some rain

SEPTEMBER: The first cool breezes of fall can be felt; there is change in the air

OCTOBER: Autumn has arrived; life is beginning to hibernate, but the colors are still beautiful

NOVEMBER: The leaves have fallen and it's getting cold

DECEMBER: Even though it's cold and desolate-looking outside, the holidays keep things festive

 # COMFORT ZONES

There are people in the world who go for all the adventure they can find. Others simply try to keep their waters as calm as possible. Where are you on the risk scale? Taking one line at a time, place an "X" on the following lines and share your responses with each other.

go skysurfing _____ go bowling

spend my inheritance _____ put the money in the bank

take a lap around the track
with an Indy driver _____ sit in the stands

lead a group _____ go with the crowd

study hard for a test _____ wing it

say what I think _____ keep my opinions to myself

explore the city _____ stay close to home

watch a suspense thriller _____ watch an animated feature

God has full control _____ I'm scared to death to
of my future _____ think of my future

  # FRIENDSHIP SURVEY

Get into groups of 2 to 4 and discuss your preferences in choosing friends. On the first category—PERSONALITY—put an "X" on the line somewhere in between the two extremes and explain why. Then let your partners explain where they marked themselves and why. Move to the next category and continue on through the list.

PERSONALITY
similar to mine_____ different from mine

COMMUNICATION
motormouth_____ quiet as a mouse

TEMPERAMENT
laid-back_____ intense

COMPATIBILITY
like doing the same things _____ not afraid to disagree and go their own way

LOYALTY
go along with me through thick and thin _____ challenge me when I need it

SELF-ESTEEM
put themselves down all the time _____ brag about themselves all the time

RELATIONSHIP TO THEIR FAMILY
speak highly of their parents _____ always complaining about their parents

MORAL STANDARDS
wild and free _____ stick to the rules

RELATIONSHIP TO A CHURCH
couldn't care less_____ very committed

ATTITUDE ABOUT LIFE
optimistic_____ pessimistic

CHOOSING FRIENDS

Get together with 1 to 3 people from your group and look over the list of qualities that you look for in a friend. See if you can agree on the top five.

___ right clothes	___ nice smile	___ honesty
___ generosity	___ spiritual depth	___ shares personally
___ good looks	___ solid family	___ plenty of money
___ plenty of time for me	___ cool car or truck	___ same music taste
___ good personality	___ big house	___ great sense of humor
___ popularity	___ laid-back	___ loyalty
___ common interests	___ strong morals	___ athletic interest
___ similar background	___ academic interest	___ fun to be with

 # MY RISK QUOTIENT

Gather with 1 to 3 people from your group and discuss your "risk quotient." The test below is a fun way to figure out how much of a risk-taker you really are. First, complete the questionnaire. Then figure out your score.

1. In playing Monopoly, I usually:
   a. play it safe / stash my cash
   b. stay cool and hold back a little
   c. go for broke—gambling everything

2. With my parents, I usually:
   a. do exactly as I'm asked
   b. test my boundaries a little
   c. do my own thing despite the cost

3. On a menu, I usually pick:
   a. something familiar that I know I like
   b. something that's a little different
   c. something way out that I've never tried

4. At a party, I usually:
   a. stick with my friends
   b. mingle with some strangers
   c. see how many new people I can meet

5. In starting a relationship, I usually:
   a. let the other person do the talking
   b. meet the other person halfway
   c. take the initiative

6. I would prefer my life to have:
   a. no risks and lots of safety
   b. some risks and some safety
   c. lots of risks and little safety

Scoring: Give yourself 1 point for every "a," 2 points for every "b," and 3 points for every "c." Then circle the total on the line below to get your risk quotient.

PLAY IT SAFE   TAKE A CHANCE

6   7   8   9   10   11   12   13   14   15   16   17   18

 # A SLICE OF LIFE

Get together in groups of 2 to 4. As you think about all the different things you do in your life, do you consider your time well managed? How much of your time is spent in activities such as:

- **school**
- **sleep**
- **leisure**
- **church**
- **work**
- **household duties**
- **homework**
- **extracurricular activities**
- **etc.**

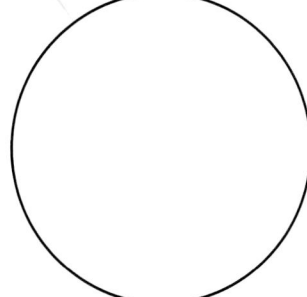

Draw a pie chart which shows how your time is spent right now. Then share your chart with your group.

GROUP WARM-UPS

 # WOW, SO-SO, OR HO-HUM

Rank each of the following activities as WOW ... SO-SO ... or HO-HUM. Then get together with 1 to 3 other people and go over your lists together.

		WOW	SO-SO	HO-HUM
1.	Spending a day with the President of the United States	___	___	___
2.	Having a date with the best-looking person in school	___	___	___
3.	Having $1,000 to spend on clothes	___	___	___
4.	Having a computer do all my homework	___	___	___
5.	Owning the latest hot car	___	___	___
6.	Having a continual supply of junk food at my disposal	___	___	___
7.	Getting the lead in a movie	___	___	___
8.	Making the Olympic team	___	___	___
9.	Being the lead singer in a rock group	___	___	___
10.	Getting two seats on the 50-yard line at the Super Bowl	___	___	___

  # DOWN MEMORY LANE

Have groups of 8 get in the shape of a Wagon wheel—4 people back to back in the center and 4 people across from them on the outside of the circle. The four who are on the inside finish statement #1, and the four who are on the outside finish statement #2. Then the four on the outside move left (clockwise) to form new pairs. Those on the inside answer #3, and those on the outside answer #4. Then shift again ... and keep rotating until you've completed all the statements. Each time you rotate, the inside person goes first, answering the odd-numbered statements; then the outside partner answers the even-numbered statements. Keep it moving—spending less than one minute on each rotation. Here's your chance to take a walk down memory lane—to your elementary school years.

I REMEMBER ...

1. My favorite subject in grade school:
2. The person I went to when I got hurt:
3. My first pet:
4. The chore I hated to do:
5. My first big trip or vacation:
6. My favorite room in the house:
7. The adult who took time to play with me:
8. The fun thing we often did as a family:
9. My favorite thing to do on a summer day:
10. The person who helped me with homework:
11. The first thing I can remember wanting to be when I grew up:
12. My favorite thing to eat:
13. My favorite uncle or aunt:
14. The first person of the opposite sex I thought was cute:
15. The best Christmas present I received:
16. The friend who got in trouble with me:

MY CHILDHOOD SUPPER TABLE

Get together with 1 to 3 people and share some things in your life at age 7. Focus on your supper table—the place where you ate your nightly meal. Let your partner interview you like a talk show host—*The Tonight Show*. Switch roles until everyone has been interviewed.

1. When you were 7 years old, where were you living?

2. What was the shape of the table where you ate your evening meal? Round? Square? Rectangle?

3. How often did you eat together as a family? All of the time? Most of the time? About half of the time? Seldom? Almost never?

4. Where did you sit? Who else was at the table and where did they sit?

5. Who did most of the talking? About what usually?

6. How would you describe the typical atmosphere at the table? Relaxed? Tense? Quiet? Exciting? Crazy? Rushed? Dull? Peaceful?

7. Did anyone say the "blessing"? If so, who?

8. Who reached out to you and always included you in the conversation?

9. What is your favorite or best memory of your childhood supper table?

Imagine that a rich aunt or uncle just gave you $5,000. Decide how much you would spend in each of the following categories. Get together in groups of up to 8 and compare your results. To make it more fun, see if the others can guess which category you spent the most in before you share your answers.

_____ clothes
_____ sports equipment
_____ gas
_____ going out with friends
_____ dates
_____ savings
_____ concert tickets

_____ my hobby
_____ video games
_____ my family
_____ sporting events tickets
_____ music
_____ skiing
_____ church

THINGS THAT DRIVE YOU CRAZY

Here's a list of things that drive a lot of people crazy. Do they drive you crazy, too? Take turns reading the different lines (person #1 reads line 1, person #2 reads line 2, and so on). Let others guess your answer before sharing your response.

	yes	no	sometimes
people who constantly channel-surf	❏	❏	❏
an annoying song that gets stuck in your head	❏	❏	❏
dripping faucet	❏	❏	❏
someone talking during a movie	❏	❏	❏
losing one sock	❏	❏	❏
not enough toilet paper	❏	❏	❏
someone who is always late	❏	❏	❏
someone who sings in the car	❏	❏	❏
boring teacher	❏	❏	❏
a motormouth	❏	❏	❏
preempting of a television program	❏	❏	❏
an itch you can't reach	❏	❏	❏
screeching chalk on a chalkboard	❏	❏	❏
people who smack their gum	❏	❏	❏
people who crack their knuckles	❏	❏	❏
backseat drivers	❏	❏	❏
people who chew with their mouths open	❏	❏	❏
someone leaving the toilet seat up	❏	❏	❏

ASSESSING THE FUTURE

Get together with 1 or 2 others and take turns interviewing each other about the future.

1. Which phrase would best describe your philosophy about facing the future?
   - ❏ "I don't want to grow up!"
   - ❏ "Back to the future!"
   - ❏ "You can't go home again."
   - ❏ "One day at a time, Sweet Jesus."
   - ❏ "Sometimes you're the bug; sometimes you're the windshield."
   - ❏ "He who isn't busy being born is busy dying."
   - ❏ "The future belongs to those who plan for it."
   - ❏ "I don't know what the future holds, but I know who holds the future."
   - ❏ "Every day in every way, things are getting better."
   - ❏ "The future's so bright that I've got to wear shades!"

2. What would you like to be doing when you're 40 years old?

3. What is one thing you expect to have in the future which you do not have now?

PREFERENCES

Divide into groups of up to 4 people each. Go down this exercise, one line at a time. Share your preferences with each other by choosing one of the two options on each line. For more fun, let your group guess your answer first.

I PREFER:

spending the day inside . . . . spending the day outside
one-topping pizza . . . . pizza with the works
a home-cooked meal . . . . eating out
playing sports . . . . watching sports
skiing in the mountains . . . . sunning by the sea
going to the movies . . . . renting a video
lots of friends . . . . one close friend

I WOULD CHOOSE:

traveling by plane . . . . traveling by car
a leisurely life . . . . daily challenges
sitting on the bench on a winning team . . . . playing every game on a losing team
a stand-up roller coaster . . . . the carousel
a challenging job with no security . . . . a boring job with lots of security
living in the city . . . . living in the country

LIVING UNDER THE INFLUENCE

Form groups of up to 4. Before sharing your answers, silently read over the list and check on the left side the three most important things in your life right now. Then jot down on the right side one of three codes to indicate how much influence your relationship with Jesus has on these three areas of your life.

D =   My relationship with Jesus DIRECTLY influences this.

I =   My relationship with Jesus INDIRECTLY influences this.

N =   My relationship with Jesus has NOTHING to do with this.

CHOICES (check three):   INFLUENCE

_____ Being accepted by my peers and friends . . . . _____
_____ Getting along at home . . . . _____
_____ Feeling good about myself . . . . _____
_____ Dating . . . . _____
_____ Going to heaven . . . . _____
_____ Getting good grades . . . . _____
_____ Knowing what is right . . . . _____
_____ Having a job or car . . . . _____
_____ Knowing who I am and what I want to do in life . . . . _____

SOME OF MY FEELINGS

Get together with 1 to 3 people in your group and explain how you would finish each of the half-finished sentences below. Do one sentence at a time.

1. For me, school is going ...
2. If I am bored at a party, I will usually ...
3. At halftime in a basketball game when my team is way behind, I would probably ...
4. My outlook on life right now is ...
5. When I get frustrated at home, I usually ...
6. When I see a handsome guy or beautiful girl, I usually say ...
7. The best thing happening in my life right now is ...
8. My biggest concern or worry right now is ...

HEADACHE SURVEY

In groups of about 4, work on the headache survey below. For each headache, decide together whether the situation is a 1-aspirin, 2-aspirin, or a 3-aspirin headache.

	1 aspirin	2 aspirin	3 aspirin
not having enough money	❏	❏	❏
curfew / rules at home	❏	❏	❏
braces	❏	❏	❏
Sunday School / religion class	❏	❏	❏
girls / guys	❏	❏	❏
losing my driver's license	❏	❏	❏
getting into college	❏	❏	❏
arguing with my parents	❏	❏	❏
sitting alone in school cafeteria	❏	❏	❏
people I don't get along with at school	❏	❏	❏
death of a friend	❏	❏	❏
worrying about my parents getting divorced	❏	❏	❏
grades	❏	❏	❏
getting a job	❏	❏	❏
getting up in the morning	❏	❏	❏
violence at school	❏	❏	❏

 # LAY IT ON THE LINE

Get together with 1 to 3 people and explain where you stand on these issues. For instance, on FEMINISM you might put yourself in the middle, because you are equal distance between the two positions on feminism. Go through the categories one at a time by placing an "X" on the lines, with each person sharing his or her answer.

ON FEMINISM
in the home. _____ of Representatives!
ON LAW AND ORDER
Lock the "losers" up. _____ Educate and rehabilitate them.
ON DRUGS
Just say no. _____ Make them legal.
ON ABORTION
People should have a choice. _____ Babies have rights, too.
ON CONDOMS
Kids have got to learn to protect themselves. _____ They encourage promiscuity.
ON PORNOGRAPHY
It's a first amendment freedom. _____ We can't let such "freedom" destroy society.
ON SMOKING
It's my right._____ Your right to smoke stops at my
nose.

OUR UN-CALLING

Get together in groups of about 8 and have fun discussing your future. To recognize your calling in life, perhaps it might help to eliminate some lines of work that you would not like to do. Look over the list below and choose the three WORST options for a future career.

- ❏ crowd control officer at a rock concert
- ❏ organizer of paperwork for Congress
- ❏ day care center director
- ❏ researcher studying the spawning habits of Alaskan salmon
- ❏ toy assembler for a local toy store over the holidays
- ❏ middle / high school principal
- ❏ nurse's aide at a home for retired Sumo wrestlers
- ❏ referee at a mud wrestling match
- ❏ official physician for the National Association of Hypochondriacs
- ❏ chief animal control officer at a reptile zoo
- ❏ pump operator for portable toilet company
- ❏ other:_____

GROUP WARM-UPS

RELATING TO OBNOXIOUS PEOPLE

Have a group member read the first selection and briefly describe how he or she tends to respond to item 1: "a cashier who talks on the phone while waiting on me." Then work through the group, each person reading the next selection and sharing how he or she tends to interact with these different types of people.

When I encounter ...   I tend to ...

a cashier who talks on the phone while waiting on me ...

a waiter or waitress who gets my order all wrong ...

a driver who cuts me off on the highway ...

a telemarketer who won't take "no" for an answer ...

a person of the opposite sex who flirts with me ...

someone who chews with his or her mouth open ...

someone who is boring me with endless conversation ...

a homeless person begging for money ...

a person who cuts ahead in a long line ...

someone who is being rude to an elderly person ...

someone whose political views are the opposite of mine ...

a person who seems very shallow or very arrogant ...

GROUP WARM-UPS

ROBINSON CRUSOE

Imagine that you are going to be Robinson Crusoe for a year and live on a deserted tropical island. Get together in groups of up to 8 and discuss the question below.

Besides adequate food and clothing, you can choose three of the following items to take with you. Which will you choose?

- ❏ lots of novels
- ❏ a CD player and lots of CDs
- ❏ a Jeep Grand Cherokee
- ❏ a solar-powered curling iron
- ❏ exercise equipment
- ❏ a cellular phone
- ❏ a rifle

- ❏ a bed
- ❏ a Bible
- ❏ a surfboard
- ❏ a battery-powered TV and satellite dish
- ❏ a pet
- ❏ a first-aid kit
- ❏ a deck of cards

 # WHO INFLUENCES YOU?

Get together with 1 to 3 people and discuss who influences you most in making decisions in your life. In each category, check one or two columns—either parents, brother / sister, friends, teachers, church / youth group or TV / movies / music. Take one category at a time

GROUP WARM-UPS

Who influences ...	my parents	my brother / sister	my friends	my teachers	my church or youth group	TV / Movies / Music
How I spend my time						
How I spend my money						
What I feed my mind						
What I wear						
Where I draw the line						
What I believe						
What I want out of life						
How I see myself						
How I handle fear, failure, and guilt						

  # THE LIFE RAFT

Get together in groups of up to 8 and work together on the exercise below. Here are the instructions. There is a group of 12 people stranded on a deserted island. A raft is available, but it can only accommodate 8. Four people will have to stay. Your group has been asked to choose the 8 who get the life raft. Read over the list below and decide who you will choose.

___ Pop musician on drugs (sleeps around)
___ Playboy centerfold model (divorced twice)
___ Medical doctor, Protestant (performs abortions)
___ Environmental engineer (single mother)
___ Police officer, Irish Catholic (father of six)
___ All-Pro football player (helps inner city kids)
___ Millionaire (generous giver in your church)
___ Scientist (Black man, specializing in AIDS research)
___ Teacher (American Indian, working on a reservation)
___ Communist student (devoted to revolution in South America)
___ Black Muslim (outspoken against "white imperialism")
___ Roman Catholic priest (started home for unwed mothers)

See what God has to say on some of these issues. Consider 1 Corinthians 5:9-11 about sleeping around. Your group leader may suggest other Scripture references or check the indices in the back of the Bible.

 **PRECIOUS TIME**

God has given us a precious gift: the time to live. Maybe that's why *now* is called "the present." Answer the following questions about precious time and share your answers in your group of 4.

My idea of a great time is:
- ❏ going to a party
- ❏ going to a cool concert
- ❏ hanging out at the mall
- ❏ watching a good movie or TV show
- ❏ watching an exciting sports event
- ❏ fishing or hiking
- ❏ going out on a date
- ❏ playing my favorite sport
- ❏ eating my favorite food
- ❏ playing video or computer games
- ❏ curling up with a good book

These things make a bad day for me:
- ❏ crummy weather
- ❏ Mondays
- ❏ bad hair
- ❏ being broke
- ❏ getting a bad grade
- ❏ when my team loses
- ❏ boring classes or work
- ❏ hassles with parents
- ❏ conflict with a friend
- ❏ dating problems

If I knew I had three months to live, I would:
- ❏ do exactly what I'm doing now
- ❏ party, party, party
- ❏ see the world
- ❏ spend all my money
- ❏ give everything away
- ❏ be very angry
- ❏ love everyone more
- ❏ climb Mt. Everest
- ❏ spend more time with friends
- ❏ spend more time with family
- ❏ do all I can for God

 # STRESSING ME OUT

Get into groups of 2 (guys with guys and girls with girls) and go through the following list of situations. Share with each other what really stresses you out in each situation. The suggestions offered help to get you started, but they may not be the right answers for you, so be honest about your own experiences. Then describe what you do to relieve that stress.

School exams:
- The feeling of doom that hangs over me
- Procrastinating when I'm really trying to study
- Drawing a blank on an answer that I should know
- Other: _____

Important athletic competitions:
- Sitting on the sidelines waiting to get in the game
- Wondering if I can play my best
- Seeing a teammate make a really bad play
- Other: _____

Relationships with the opposite sex:
- Fear of rejection
- Trying to understand the way they think
- Being ignored by someone I really like
- Other: _____

Family interactions:
- Dealing with my parents' divorce
- Getting along with my siblings
- Having very strict rules and restrictions
- Other: _____

Daily frustrations:
- Having unreliable or nonexistent transportation
- Feeling that I don't have enough time to do everything
- Feeling that I have no direction in life
- Other: _____

Athletic training:
- Having a coach who is way too demanding
- Feeling that I'm just not good enough to compete
- Being disciplined to stay in training
- Other: _____

MONEY AND SUCCESS

The Apostle Paul said that "the love of money is a root of all kinds of evil" (1 Tim. 6:10). There is no doubt that money can play a powerful role in our life. The same is true for success. Get in groups of 4 and share your answers to the three questions below.

Your group members can learn a lot about each other by discussing your answers to these questions about money and success.

My attitude toward money is:
- ❏ It should be saved.
- ❏ Spend, spend, spend!
- ❏ It's something I need more of.
- ❏ It's a necessary evil.
- ❏ It's a source of arguments.
- ❏ It's a source of fun.
- ❏ It's a resource for freedom.

My feelings about "getting ahead" are:
- ❏ Look out for # 1.
- ❏ What else is there in life?
- ❏ It's a high priority.
- ❏ Keep a balanced life instead.
- ❏ Don't neglect your family.
- ❏ It's not worth it.

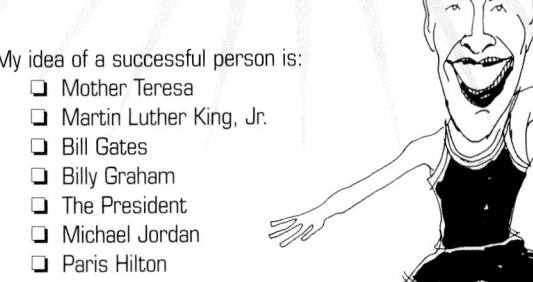

My idea of a successful person is:
- ❏ Mother Teresa
- ❏ Martin Luther King, Jr.
- ❏ Bill Gates
- ❏ Billy Graham
- ❏ The President
- ❏ Michael Jordan
- ❏ Paris Hilton
- ❏ Other:_____

 # PROBLEM SURVEY

Get together with one other person and discuss how you would rank the problems young people face today—from 1 (greatest) to 15 (least). Put your ranking in the left column and your partner's ranking in the right column. If you would like, share with your partner the greatest problem you face, so he or she can pray for you.

YOUR RANKING   YOUR PARTNER'S

_____ Conflict with teachers at school . . . . _____
_____ Gangs and violence. . . . . _____
_____ Parents splitting up . . . . _____
_____ Use of alcohol or drugs . . . . _____
_____ Feelings of loneliness and need for friendship . . . . _____
_____ TV programs and movies that promote lousy morals . . . . _____
_____ Family problems. . . . . _____
_____ Uncertain future and goals . . . . _____
_____ Cliques in school . . . . _____
_____ Teen pregnancy and the threat of sexual diseases such as AIDS . . . . _____
_____ Not knowing how to handle anger . . . . _____
_____ Peer pressure . . . . _____
_____ Disillusionment with or apathy toward church or faith . . . . _____
_____ Grades in school . . . . _____
_____ Abusive relationships . . . . _____

 # SHARING DREAMS

Here's your chance to dream about your future. Get together in groups of 4 and interview each other on your future plans. Below is a list of interview questions. Each person in the group can choose one or two questions from the list below to ask the person being interviewed.

1. What would you like to be doing five years from now?
2. Where would you like to be living in five years?
3. In 10 years, how much money would you like to be making?
4. What is it going to take for you to get to where you want to be in 10 years?
5. What values would you look for in the person you will marry?
6. What kind of spiritual commitment would you want the person you marry to have?
7. How many children would you like to have? Boys or girls?
8. When are you going to allow your children to start dating?
9. Are you going to send your children to a private school or a public school?
10. Are you going to be more or less strict with your kids than your parents have been with you?
11. Will it be easier to get along with your parent(s) when you have a family of your own?

 # STRESS TEST

This is one test where everyone would like to have a low score! Circle the events you have experienced within the past year. Total your score. If it's more than 150 points, you're probably living under a lot of stress. Get together in groups of about 4 to share your scores and compare the types of stress you're each under.

EVENT	STRESS POINTS
Death of parent	100
Death of family member	75
Death of friend	65
Divorce of parents	60
Breakup with girlfriend or boyfriend	55
Major personal injury or illness	53
Failed a class	50
Got in trouble at school	45
Lost your driver's license	40
Moved to a new community	37
Failed a big test	35
Conflict with parents	33
Changed schools	30
Got in a fight with a friend	27
Health or financial problem in family	23
Forgot to do your homework	20
Had a "bad hair day"	10
Found a zit on your nose	5

Your Total _____

  # WARM MEMORIES

Get together in groups of up to 4. Each of you answer the first question. Then go around again on question #2, and work your way through the four questions.

1. Where were you living between the ages of 7 and 12, and what was your favorite thing to do on a warm summer day?

2. What is the worst storm you can remember? Where was your favorite place to hide during bad storms?

3. What was the center of warmth in your life when you were a child? (It could be a place in the house, a time of year, a person, etc.)

4. When did God become a "warm" person to you, and how did that happen?

 # OLD-FASHIONED AUCTION

Get together in groups of 8 or more. Just like an old-fashioned farm auction, conduct an auction in your group—starting each item at $50. Everybody starts out with $1,000. Select an auctioneer. This person can also get in on the bidding. Start the bidding on each item at $50. Then, write the winning bid in the left column and the winner's name in the right column. Remember, you only have $1,000 to spend for the whole game.

Auctioneer, start off by asking: "Who will give me $50 for two Super Bowl tickets on the 50-yard line?" ... and keep going until you have a winner. Have fun!

WINNING BID   WINNER'S NAME

$_____Two Super Bowl tickets on the 50-yard line . . . . _____

$_____All-expense-paid vacation for four to Disney World . . . . _____

$_____Big screen TV with surround sound. . . . . _____

$_____Date with your favorite celebrity . . . . _____

$_____Freedom from household chores for one year . . . . _____

$_____Complete new wardrobe of latest fashions . . . . _____

$_____A guaranteed college degree . . . . _____

$_____Backstage passes with your favorite band . . . . _____

$_____Season pass to ski resort of my choice. . . . . _____

$_____A role in a major motion picture . . . . _____

$_____Six months of no hassles with your parents. . . . . _____

$_____A brand new, shiny red Corvette . . . . _____

$_____Five-minute shopping spree in a music or electronics store . . . . _____

$_____One year off to do anything you want. . . . . _____

WILD PREDICTIONS

Get in groups of 8 or more. Try to match the people in your group to the crazy forecasts below. (Don't take it too seriously; it's meant to be fun!) Read out loud the first item and ask everyone to call out the name of the person who is most likely to accomplish this feat. Then, read the next item and ask everyone to make a new prediction, etc.

THE PERSON IN OUR GROUP MOST LIKELY TO ...

rollerblade across the country

become most famous pet psychologist in Beverly Hills

win the *MAD* Magazine award for worst jokes

become the first woman to win the Indianapolis 500

appear on the cover of *Muscle & Fitness* Magazine

become the host of a popular national talkshow

become a superstar or supermodel

win the tattoo contest at the Harley-Davidson National Convention

win the Iditarod dogsled race in Alaska

become a stunt expert for Mountain Dew commercials

make a fortune on portable toilet rentals

become the sales associate of the year for athletic shoes

write a best-selling novel based on his or her love life

set a world record for marathon dancing

get listed in the *Guinness Book of World Records* for the messiest car

become a millionaire by age 30

 # CHRISTIAN BASICS

How do you view the Christian faith? Get in groups of about 4 people. Answer these questions—one topic at a time. Feel free to discuss your answers with your group. You may check more than one answer on each question.

This ice-breaker is intended to let people talk freely about their feelings on these religious subjects without worrying about "right or wrong" answers.

I see prayer as:
- ❑ wishful thinking
- ❑ a psychological exercise
- ❑ a direct line to God
- ❑ powerful
- ❑ magic
- ❑ a daily practice
- ❑ a life saver
- ❑ positive thinking
- ❑ the key to my sanity

I think of Jesus as:
- ❑ a great guy
- ❑ a courageous rabbi
- ❑ a wise teacher
- ❑ one of many teachers
- ❑ a miracle worker
- ❑ a great example
- ❑ a Jewish rebel
- ❑ confused
- ❑ my Savior
- ❑ my best friend

I view the church as:
- ❑ scary
- ❑ too traditional
- ❑ boring
- ❑ hard to relate to
- ❑ friendly
- ❑ uplifting
- ❑ fun
- ❑ always asking for money
- ❑ a safe place
- ❑ confusing because of the different denominations

I see the Bible as:
- ❑ hard to understand
- ❑ old-fashioned
- ❑ inspiring
- ❑ the Word of God
- ❑ full of promises
- ❑ hard to apply
- ❑ the secret to life
- ❑ full of violence
- ❑ having too many pages
- ❑ too far removed from our culture

I view Christians as:
- ❑ the salt of the earth
- ❑ hypocrites
- ❑ fanatics
- ❑ too conservative
- ❑ just like everyone else
- ❑ world changers
- ❑ God's people
- ❑ more loving
- ❑ goody-two-shoes

When I think about the cross I feel:
- ❑ squeamish
- ❑ relieved
- ❑ skeptical
- ❑ unsure
- ❑ angry
- ❑ grateful
- ❑ inspired
- ❑ humbled
- ❑ hopeful
- ❑ nothing

GROUP WARM-UPS

MY LAST WILL AND TESTAMENT

Get together with 1 to 3 people from your group and discuss the funeral arrangements below, choosing from the multiple-choice options. Let your partners interview you.

HOW WOULD YOU CHOOSE TO DIE?
- ❏ prolong life as long as possible with support systems
- ❏ die naturally in a hospital, with pain relievers if needed
- ❏ die at home without medical care, but with family

WHAT FUNERAL WOULD YOU CHOOSE?
- ❏ big funeral with lots of flowers
- ❏ small funeral, money to charity
- ❏ no funeral, just family at grave

WHAT WOULD YOU WANT ON YOUR TOMBSTONE?
- ❏ the words from my favorite song
- ❏ something about my life
- ❏ just my date of birth and death

HOW WOULD YOU LIKE TO BE REMEMBERED?
- ❏ someone who cared for people
- ❏ someone who loved God
- ❏ someone who lived life to the fullest

HOW WOULD YOU WANT YOUR BODY TREATED?
- ❏ cremated
- ❏ given to science / organ donation
- ❏ buried intact

IF YOU HAD ANY MONEY, WHERE WOULD YOU LIKE IT TO GO?
- ❏ to my family
- ❏ to a charity
- ❏ to a memorial in my honor

PARENT PROBLEMS

Gather in groups of about 4. Have each person answer the first question. Then go around on the second question and the third question.

1. What was the funniest thing you ever did that got you in trouble with your parents?

2. What important thing have you learned in conflicts with your parents?
   - ❏ Always apologize (even if you're right!).
   - ❏ It's best to talk it out.
   - ❏ Even parents can be wrong sometimes.
   - ❏ What your parents don't know won't hurt them (or you either!).
   - ❏ Listening to each other clears up many conflicts.
   - ❏ It's better to face a conflict and get it over with than to try to hide or ignore it.
   - ❏ Other:_____

3. In your normal style of handling conflict, which are you more like?
   - ❏ An ostrich—I hide my head in the sand until it goes away.
   - ❏ A cat—I timidly slip away, then scratch up the couch when no one's looking.
   - ❏ A hawk—I fly above it all and pick my targets.
   - ❏ A fox—I use my brains to win.
   - ❏ A dolphin—I can fight if necessary, but would rather swim away.
   - ❏ Other:_____

WHAT TO DO, WHAT TO DO?

Imagine that you're in one of the following situations. What would you do? Begin by having one group member take the first situation and briefly explain what he or she would do and why. Then have the next person take the second situation, and so on until each person in the group has had a turn. Circle back to the first situation again if you have more than 8 in your group.

What would you do if you ...

saw a house on fire?
- Call 911 and wait for the fire department
- Run inside and help people get out
- Keep going and hope for the best
- Other: _____

lost your wallet or purse?
- Panic!
- Retrace my steps for the past 12 hours—over and over again
- Relax—there was nothing in it!
- Other: _____

found someone else's wallet or purse?
- Check the identification and contact the owner
- Take some time to browse through the contents
- Take the money and drop the rest into a mailbox
- Other: _____

hit a dog while driving on a dark street late at night?
- Look for its owner in nearby homes
- Put him in the car and rush to the nearest vet
- Call the police
- Other: _____

saw a friend cheating on an exam?
- Confront my friend in private later on
- Turn my friend in on the spot
- Ignore it and hope I was wrong
- Other: _____

heard someone calling for help down a dark alley?
- Call 911 and wait for the police
- Rush down the alley to see what's happening
- Walk faster in the other direction
- Other: _____

were given too much change from a cashier?
- Give back the extra
- Keep the extra, figuring it all evens out in the long run
- Assume that I counted wrong
- Other: _____

happened to find a "juicy" letter or e-mail?
- Quickly trash it
- Return it to the owner
- Use it to my best advantage
- Other: _____

 # HALLOWED INHIBITIONS

Pair off with someone else and take turns sharing your answer to each question below. Try to guess your partner's answer before he or she tells you what it is. For every right guess, give yourself 10 points.

"I am someone who would ..."

	Yes	No	Maybe
pig out on chocolate	❏	❏	❏
go to the 10-item express lane with 14 items	❏	❏	❏
come home after curfew	❏	❏	❏
blush at the mention of sex	❏	❏	❏
cry at the movies	❏	❏	❏
lie about my age	❏	❏	❏
forge my parent's signature	❏	❏	❏
roll a friend's house with toilet paper	❏	❏	❏
try skydiving	❏	❏	❏
go to a ballet or opera	❏	❏	❏
forget my gym clothes ... on purpose	❏	❏	❏
go on a blind date	❏	❏	❏
sneak into a movie or concert without paying	❏	❏	❏
belch in public	❏	❏	❏

GROUP WARM-UPS

 # THE OLD NEIGHBORHOOD

Get together with 1 to 3 people and share about your "old neighborhood." If you have moved a lot, talk about the neighborhood where you spent the most time, or the one which was your favorite. On the other hand, you may still be living in your "old neighborhood." Take turns sharing with your group where your "old neighborhood" is located, and your responses to the following.

1. My "old neighborhood" was more like:
    ❏ Manhattan—urban and multicultural
    ❏ New Delhi—distinctively ethnic
    ❏ Anywhere in Ohio—suburban housing with a common cultural background
    ❏ Great Plains, Kansas—spread out but close-knit

2. Share your responses to as many of the following questions as you have time for:
    ❏ Where did the kids gather in your neighborhood?
    ❏ What were your favorite things to do together?
    ❏ What were the special places—the best places to climb trees, skateboard or rollerblade, hide from adults, etc.?
    ❏ Where were the "danger spots"—the yards with mean dogs, the "grumpy old Mr. Wilson" who didn't like kids, the "haunted" houses or boarded-up buildings?
    ❏ Who was the Dennis the Menace who always got into trouble or got you into trouble?
    ❏ Who was the "one-of-a-kind"—the kid who really stood out from the rest of the crowd?

 # LIKE MUSIC TO MY EARS

Have everyone in your group stay together for this ice-breaker. In each of the following pairs, which sound is more likely to be "music to your ears"? For each pair, circle one of the choices. Then have one person read the first pair. Everyone who circled "the crackling of a campfire" gets up and moves to the left side of the room. All of those who circled "the sounds of city traffic at night" move to the right side of the room. Have fun going down the list this way.

the crackling of a campfire _____ the sounds of city traffic at night

the cry of "play ball!" _____ waves crashing against the shore

the clatter of a roller coaster _____ the beat coming through the stereo

the ring of the telephone _____ the ring of a cash register

the gurgling of a mountain stream _____ the buzz of a crowd just before a concert

the purr of a kitten _____ the hum of a well-tuned engine

the school lunch bell _____ the school dismissal bell

 # COMPETITION VS. COOPERATION

Are you more likely to compete or cooperate in each of the situations below? Gather in groups of about 4 and take turns going first as you go down this list:

	compete	cooperate
playing a game of pick-up ball with friends	❏	❏
playing on a school sports team	❏	❏
working with a group at school on a project	❏	❏
playing a board game	❏	❏
taking the lead with a group of friends	❏	❏
discussing an issue in class	❏	❏
driving the family car	❏	❏
using the telephone	❏	❏
making a decision as a family	❏	❏

EMOTIONAL DASHBOARD

How are you feeling today? Check your gauges on your emotional dashboard. Use the drawing below to mark where you are emotionally. How high are your stress, frustration, and friendship levels? Is your love tank full or empty? How many miles per hour is your enthusiasm running? What gear is your optimism transmission in?

Fill in the gauges and take turns sharing in groups of about 4 how you are feeling.

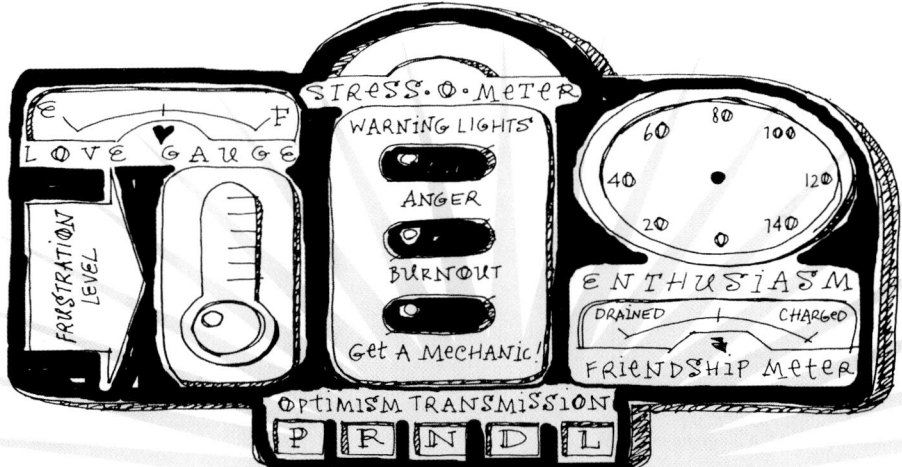

TV GAME SHOW

Imagine that you're a contestant on a TV game show, and you're down to the final round. The following categories are the topics you have to choose from, and you need to get more right answers than your opponents do in order to win. Which categories will be "winners" for you? Which categories will you most likely lose? Go around the group and have each person share his or her best and worst category. If time permits, see who can list the most answers in each category.

- ❏ Current music groups
- ❏ Movie stars from the '40s and '50s
- ❏ Names in the Old Testament
- ❏ Teams that won the Super Bowl
- ❏ Presidents of the United States
- ❏ Capitals of European countries
- ❏ Internet search sites
- ❏ Song titles with the word "Love"

 # POWER PEOPLE

Some people in your life have a powerful effect on you. Different kinds of "power people" are listed below. Fill in the names of at least three of the "power people" in your life. Then get together in groups of about 4 and share your answers with each other.

_____ **LISTENER**: the person who will always hear what I have to say without trying to change me

_____ **ENCOURAGER**: someone who helps me look on the bright side of things

_____ **MENTOR**: someone willing to take me under his or her wing and guide me on my life's journey

_____ **INSPIRER**: the person who reminds me that God has everything under control

_____ **CONSOLER**: the person who can calm me down when life gets out of control

_____ **CONFRONTER**: a person who loves me enough to tell me things I might not want to hear

_____ **PRAYER PARTNER**: someone I trust enough to come with me when I go to God in prayer

_____ **ROLE MODEL**: the person I want to be like in my actions, character, and reputation

_____ **CRAZY FRIEND**: someone I can count on to do something fun and bring out my fun side

_____ **DREAMER**: that special person who will listen to and appreciate my dreams

 # I DREAM OF GENIE

If you could have three wishes, which three would you choose from the list below? Get together with 1 to 3 people and share your choices with the group.

- ❏ **WIN THE LOTTERY**: never have to work
- ❏ **ROMANCE**: an active and exciting love life
- ❏ **SECURE AND REWARDING JOB**: lifetime guarantee with benefits
- ❏ **PERFECT BODY:** appearance that stands out in a crowd
- ❏ **STRESS-FREE LIFE**: no pain, no struggle, no tension
- ❏ **POPULARITY**: everybody knocking at my door to spend time with me
- ❏ **CLOSE FAMILY**: no hassles, lots of love and support
- ❏ **GOOD HEALTH**: long life, full of vigor and vitality
- ❏ **ONE DEEP, ABIDING FRIENDSHIP**: someone who will always be there
- ❏ **SUCCESS**: fame and recognition in your chosen field
- ❏ **STRONG, SPIRITUAL FAITH**: a deep, satisfying relationship with God

  # LIFE SIGNS

Get together in groups of about 4 and spend some time thinking about your lives in terms of traffic signs. One at a time share your responses to the first question. Then go around on the second question and the third question.

1. If you were to select a traffic sign to tell how you've been trying to live your life, what sign would it be?
    ❏ "Merge"—because I've been trying to get along with everyone
    ❏ "Slow"—because I've been seeking to slow down and experience more of life
    ❏ "Keep Right"—because I'm trying to keep my life on the right track
    ❏ "One Way"—because I'm seeking to be more decisive in my life
    ❏ "Yield"—because I'm seeking to yield my life to God
    ❏ "Children Playing"—because I'm trying to let out the "little kid" in me
    ❏ "Under Construction"—because I'm changing so much

2. What sign are you displaying in your relationship with others?
    ❏ "No Trespassing!"—because I keep people at a distance
    ❏ "Help Wanted"—because I'm reaching out for support
    ❏ "One Way"—because I'm not always tolerant of differences
    ❏ "Open 24 Hours"—because I'm always available to others
    ❏ "Keep Right"—because I encourage others to do what is right
    ❏ "No Vacancy"—because there's no room in my life for anyone else right now

3. If God were to give you a "traffic ticket" right now for how you are living your life, what would it be for?
    ❏ "Speeding"—not slowing down enough to really live
    ❏ "Failing to Yield"—trying to do things my own way
    ❏ "Blocking Traffic"—I feel I've gotten in the way of others who are doing more.
    ❏ "Illegal U-Turn"—I have been trying to live in the past.
    ❏ "Driving the Wrong Way on a One-Way Street"—I need to turn my life around.

  # MY ROLES

Get together in groups of about 4. From the list below, check the different roles you fill in your life. After sharing your answers with the group, take turns answering the questions below.

I am a / an ...

- ❏ Brother
- ❏ Sister
- ❏ Student
- ❏ Friend
- ❏ Employee
- ❏ Singer
- ❏ Athlete
- ❏ Sports fan

- ❏ Writer
- ❏ Boyfriend
- ❏ Girlfriend
- ❏ Babysitter
- ❏ Youth group member
- ❏ Volunteer
- ❏ Automobile operator
- ❏ Musician

- ❏ Skier
- ❏ Actor / Actress
- ❏ Rollerblader
- ❏ Pet owner
- ❏ Club member
- ❏ Hobbyist
- ❏ Health nut
- ❏ Computer whiz

Which of these is the most fun?
    ... the most challenging?   ... the most rewarding?   ... the most frustrating?

MUSIC IN MY LIFE

Get together with 1 to 3 people. Put an "X" on the first line below—somewhere between the two extremes—to indicate how you are feeling right now. Share your answers with each other, and then repeat this process down the list. If you feel comfortable, briefly explain why you put the "X" where you did.

1. In my emotional life, I'm feeling like ...
   "Blues in the Night" _____ "Celebrate!"

2. In my family life, I'm feeling like ...
   "Love Stinks"_____ "Ain't Life Grand?"

3. In my attitude toward school or work, I'm feeling like ...
   "Take This Job and Shove It"_____ "Be True to Your School"

4. In my spiritual life, I'm feeling like ...
   "Sounds of Silence"_____ "Hallelujah Chorus"

5. In my close relationships, I'm feeling like ...
   "Love Is a Battlefield" _____ "I'll Be There for You"

6. As I look toward the future, I'm feeling like ...
   "Help!"_____ "The Future's So Bright
                                                      I Gotta Wear Shades"

 # GOOD STUFF

Move into groups of 4 and read the Beatitudes in Matthew 5:3-10. Then discuss each type of "blessed" person and the positive results of being that kind of person. Talk about what each one means in real, day-to-day life. For example, "What does it mean to be 'poor in spirit' when I'm trying to get along with my family?" or "What does it mean to me to be given 'the kingdom of heaven'?" After the discussion time, have each group member rate how he or she is doing with living out that Beatitude. Use a scoring system of 1 ("I'm having a hard time") to 5 ("I think I've got this one down"). Finish by sharing examples of people who live up to each type of "blessedness."

1. "the poor in spirit"
- means: _____
- results in: _____
- my score: _____
- a great example is: _____

2. "those who mourn"
- means: _____
- results in: _____
- my score: _____
- a great example is: _____

3. "the gentle"
- means: _____
- results in: _____
- my score: _____
- a great example is: _____

4. "those who hunger and thirst for righteousness"
- means: _____
- results in: _____
- my score: _____
- a great example is: _____

5. "the merciful"
- means: _____
- results in: _____
- my score: _____
- a great example is: _____

6. "the pure in heart"
- means: _____
- results in: _____
- my score: _____
- a great example is: _____

7. "the peacemakers"
- means: _____
- results in: _____
- my score: _____
- a great example is: _____

8. "those who are persecuted for righteousness"
- means: _____
- results in: _____
- my score: _____
- a great example is: _____

 **LIP POWER**

The Bible teaches us that our thoughts are important, because they influence what we say and do. What we say is important because our words can greatly influence the people around us. Take turns reading the following verses from Proverbs 15. After reading each verse and paraphrase below, go around the group and have each person share how he or she rates in that category from 1 (low) to 10 (very high). Encourage group members who rate themselves too low by telling them how they are doing better than they think.

Speaking gentle answers, not harsh words (Proverbs 15:1): I don't say mean things when someone hurts me, and I try to be kind even when I'm treated badly.

1	2	3	4	5	6	7	8	9	1 0
very low									very high

Encouraging knowledge, not foolishness (Proverbs 15:2): I talk about things that help others to know God's will, rather than chattering about silly things.

1   2   3   4   5   6   7   8   9   1 0

Bringing healing, not crushing others (Proverbs 15:4): I try to heal the wounds of others, rather than adding to their hurts and troubles.

1   2   3   4   5   6   7   8   9   1 0

Spreading knowledge (Proverbs 15:7): I am able to teach others about the truths of Scripture, and my actions are consistent with my words.

1   2   3   4   5   6   7   8   9   1 0

Seeking knowledge (Proverbs 15:14): I am teachable, always wanting to know more about God's truth, and I avoid spending time discussing foolish things.

1   2   3   4   5   6   7   8   9   1 0

Being patient (Proverbs 15:18): I control my temper, choosing to be patient and calm even when I'm feeling angry.

1   2   3   4   5   6   7   8   9   1 0

Giving good answers (Proverbs 15:23): I always try to speak the truth and be encouraging to those around me.

1   2   3   4   5   6   7   8   9   1 0

Having pure thoughts (Proverbs 15:26): I try not to dwell on thoughts that are displeasing to God by deliberately changing my thinking when impure thoughts enter my mind.

1   2   3   4   5   6   7   8   9   1 0

Weighing my answers (Proverbs 15:28): I try to think before I speak, considering how my words might affect the people around me.

1   2   3   4   5   6   7   8   9   1 0

Accepting correction (Proverbs 15:31): I don't get angry or defensive when someone rebukes me, trying instead to learn from criticism and improve my character.

1   2   3   4   5   6   7   8   9   1 0

 # HOW'S YOUR LOVE LIFE?

The best-known passage in the Bible about love is 1 Corinthians 13—the "love chapter." The personal inventory below is taken from this passage. Get into groups of about 4. Turn to 1 Corinthians 13:4-7 and have someone read the verses out loud. Then, let one person read the first phrase. Go around the group and have everyone pick a number between 1 (failure) and 10 (success) to rate their own personal love inventory. Have someone else read the next phrase, as you take turns through the inventory.

Love is patient: I don't take out my frustrations on those I love. I am calm under pressure and careful with my tongue.

1   2   3   4   5   6   7   8   9   10

Love is kind: I go out of my way to say nice words and do thoughtful things for others.

1   2   3   4   5   6   7   8   9   10

Love does not envy: I am not envious of others' gifts and abilities or of what they have. Neither am I jealous with my time toward those who need me.

1   2   3   4   5   6   7   8   9   10

Love is not boastful: I don't consider my role any more important than those I love—or talk like "I know better."

1   2   3   4   5   6   7   8   9   10

Love is not conceited: I don't think of myself as better than those I love; or better at skills or activities.

1   2   3   4   5   6   7   8   9   10

Love does not act improperly: I don't make cutting or crude remarks when I don't get my way—or become silent and withdrawn.

1   2   3   4   5   6   7   8   9   10

Love is not selfish: I don't put myself first. I try to give those I love spiritual and emotional support.

1   2   3   4   5   6   7   8   9   10

Love is not provoked: I don't let little things bother me, especially with those I love. I control my mouth.

1   2   3   4   5   6   7   8   9   10

Love does not keep a record of wrongs: I don't keep score of the number of times those I love have said something or done something that upset me, and I don't bring it up when we have conflict.

1   2   3   4   5   6   7   8   9   10

Love finds no joy in unrighteousness: I accept those I love, but I don't have to approve of everything they do.

1   2   3   4   5   6   7   8   9   10

Love rejoices in the truth: With a compassionate spirit, I will say what needs to be said to someone, even if it might be difficult. I seek the truth in my own life and encourage others to do the same.

1   2   3   4   5   6   7   8   9   10

Love bears all things: I am always there for those I love—even when they upset me—seeking to comfort and care as Christ would.

1   2   3   4   5   6   7   8   9   10

Love believes all things: I believe in those I love, and I believe in God. And I am willing to let God do the shaping and molding.

1   2   3   4   5   6   7   8   9   10

Love hopes all things: I am good at expecting the best and thinking the best about those I love. I always give those I love the benefit of the doubt.

1   2   3   4   5   6   7   8   9   10

Love endures all things: I am committed to those I love, and I am prepared to see that commitment through to the end.

1   2   3   4   5   6   7   8   9   10

 # THE ARMOR OF GOD

Scripture doesn't promise Christians an easy life. In Ephesians 6, the Apostle Paul calls the Christian life a struggle and compares the spiritual equipment of a Christian to a Roman soldier fully dressed for battle.

Get into groups of about 4 to take the personal inventory below. Turn to Ephesians 6:10-18 and have someone read the Scripture out loud. Then, let one person read the first piece of equipment and its application. Go around the group and have everyone give a number from 1 (very low) to 10 (very high), and explain why you gave yourself this number. Have someone else read the next piece of equipment and application, etc. until you've completed the inventory.

Truth like a belt: I am prepared to stake my life on the fact that Jesus Christ is the Son of God. I have thought through what I believe, and I am willing to take a stand.

    1   2   3   4   5   6   7   8   9   10

Righteousness like armor on your chest: I am prepared to put my life where my mouth is—in clean and right living—with genuine integrity—as Christ did. I am serious about being God's man or God's woman.

    1   2   3   4   5   6   7   8   9   10

Feet sandaled with readiness for the gospel of peace: I am willing to publicly affirm my faith in Christ—at school, work or wherever. I find it easy to talk about my personal faith.

    1   2   3   4   5   6   7   8   9   10

Shield of faith: I am prepared to step out with Christ—to risk my life, my fortune and my future for Him whatever the cost or consequences. And through faith, I am taking a stand against the "evil one."

    1   2   3   4   5   6   7   8   9   10

Helmet of salvation: I know that I am part of the family of God because of Jesus Christ. I have a strong inner peace because I am at peace with God.

    1   2   3   4   5   6   7   8   9   10

Sword of the Spirit, which is God's Word: I actively seek to know more about God and His will for my life through an ongoing study of his guidebook, the Bible. I discipline myself to reflect on it daily.

    1   2   3   4   5   6   7   8   9   10

Prayer: I set aside time regularly to talk with God and to let Him speak to me. I consciously try to submit every decision in my life to God.

    1   2   3   4   5   6   7   8   9   10

GROUP WARM-UPS

A HIGH STANDARD

Gather in groups of about 4 to take the personal inventory below. Turn to Romans 12:9-21 and have someone read the Scripture out loud. Then, let one person read the phrase and the paraphrase. Go around the group and have everyone give a number from 1 (very low) to 10 (very high) to indicate how they measure themselves in that area. Have someone else read the next phrase, and continue on until you've completed the inventory.

Love must be without hypocrisy: I am able to give myself to others; not in a phony way but with real meaning.

1   2   3   4   5   6   7   8   9   10

Detest evil; cling to what is good: I am learning to stand up for my convictions, to say "no" to something I know is wrong and "yes" to God.

1   2   3   4   5   6   7   8   9   10

Show family affection to one another with brotherly love: I am learning how to reach out and hug my Christian brothers and sisters warmly—in the right way—and for purely spiritual reasons.

1   2   3   4   5   6   7   8   9   10

Be fervent in spirit; serve the Lord: I am eager and enthusiastic to do anything I can for Christ because my heart is full of gratitude for what He has done for me.

1   2   3   4   5   6   7   8   9   10

Rejoice in hope: I am experiencing a new freedom that overflows in praise because I know God is in control.

1   2   3   4   5   6   7   8   9   10

Patient in affliction: Problems don't always get me down. I can take the heat. Under pressure I can stay cool.

1   2   3   4   5   6   7   8   9   10

Persistent in prayer: I have learned to turn over every need to Christ and to share every decision I have to make with Him. I have learned to "wait on God" and let Him work things out.

1   2   3   4   5   6   7   8   9   10

Share with the saints in their needs; pursue hospitality: I have learned that my possessions, my time, my whole being belongs to God—to be shared with those in need.

1   2   3   4   5   6   7   8   9   10

Bless those who persecute you: I have learned to respond with kindness to those who put me down—and to pray on their behalf. I am no longer defensive about my life.

1   2   3   4   5   6   7   8   9   10

Rejoice with those who rejoice; weep with those who weep: I celebrate when others are rejoicing, and grieve openly when others are hurting. I am not afraid to show my feelings.

1   2   3   4   5   6   7   8   9   10

 # EVIL ON THE PROWL

Provide newspapers and news magazines for student to use. Instruct your group to look for articles or headlines that are evidence that evil and injustice are everywhere in our society today.

Allow a brief time for each person to share some of what he or she finds and then discuss the following questions about how evil affects us.

1. List some of the headlines and topics you found.

2. When I see evil or injustice happen I typically …

- ❏ Get mad
- ❏ Want to do something to stop it
- ❏ Try to ignore it
- ❏ Pray for God to intervene
- ❏ Jump in the middle and try to help
- ❏ Hope someone else decides to do something
- ❏ Feel helpless
- ❏ Other:

3. Share an example of an injustice you have seen recently.

4. When someone wrongs you, how do you usually respond?

 # LIVE LIKE YOU WERE DYING

In 2004, country singer Tim McGraw had a crossover radio hit entitled, "Live Like You Were Dying." In the song, a man is diagnosed with a condition that gives him only a few months to live. As a result, he experiences things he never dreamed of doing. He goes skydiving, tries bull riding, and chooses to forgive those who he'd long refused to pardon.

This powerful song was written in memory of his famous baseball star father, "Tug" McGraw. "Tug," whom Tim didn't meet until he was 11, died of brain cancer at the age of 59. For the last several months of his life, Tug moved in with Tim and his family in their Tennessee home. They shared stories and experiences, knowing Tug's time on this earth was coming to an end." (Accessed 9/19/05 from http://archive.parade. com/2004/0822_tim_mcgraw.html.)

Optional: Play the Tim McGraw's song, "Live Like You Were Dying" for the group.

1. As a small group, brainstorm 10 things you'd want to be sure to do if you were told your lives were going to suddenly end within six months. Write your lists on a poster or tear sheet.

2. If everyone will die someday, what's the purpose of living?

3. What keeps us from doing the things we listed in question 1? How would our feelings change if we really did find out we have a limited time to live?

4. What from this life can we take into the next? How should that knowledge affect what we do while here on earth?

GROUP WARM-UPS

 **TEMPATION SAYS ...**

Bring individually wrapped candies to award as prizes.

Tell the group they are going to play a unique version of Simon Says. The catch is that instead of having to listen for the catch phrase "Simon Says" in order to know which orders to follow or skip, they must evaluate whether or not each command given is right or wrong. In other words, the instructions you give that are in no way rude, wrong, or inappropriate should be acted upon. Anything that isn't fully acceptable should be avoided. (The point is that some students will be tempted—largely for the sake of humor—to act on the "wrong" instructions just because they can. Or, they may fall prey to acting on a "wrong" instruction simply because they aren't paying attention.)

Ask your group to stand in a close circle, and then give the following commands. Should anyone act on a "wrong" request, ask him or her to sit down. Give the commands quickly.

· Compliment the person to your left   (OK)
· Smile and wave at the person directly across from you   (OK)
· Politely cover your mouth and cough   (OK)
· Tell the person across from you that his or her real name is "Stinky"   (WRONG)
· Gently tug the hair of the person to your right   (WRONG)
· Quickly blink three times at anyone in the group   (OK)
· Politely cover your mouth and belch loudly   (WRONG)
· Slowly turn in a circle while humming The Star Spangled Banner   (OK)
· Shout, "You are a warthog!" to the person to your left.   (WRONG)

After the activity, give a piece of candy to everyone still standing, and then discuss the following questions:

1. For some of you, it was very tempting to follow the "wrong" instructions just for the sake of getting a laugh or livening things up. In the real world, we are often tempted to do the wrong thing for the sake of covering up mistakes or making ourselves look better. Can you think of some examples of how this is true?

2. Even if you managed to do all of the "right" things and none of the "wrong" in our game, you will some-times mess up in life. Think about how you felt when a group member had to sit down for having done a "wrong" thing. How did you feel toward that person in their "failure"? How do you feel when a friend makes a poor moral choice?

3. How do you think God feels when we give into the temptation to rebel against Him? Why do you think He gave us the free will to make mistakes and poor choices?

 # THANKS A BUNCH!

Giving thanks is a great thing to do, even if there's no turkey in front of us. This exercise provides an opportunity for you to say "thank you" to God. Get together in groups of 8 or more. Looking at the list below, choose those things you are thankful for and share your answers with the group.

I AM THANKFUL FOR MY ...

family	neighborhood	sense of purpose
church	home	calling
school	nationality	mind
heritage	pets	emotions
faith	accomplishments	education
spiritual gifts	creativity	job
friends	health	reputation
talents	appearance	car
hobby	character	memories
wisdom	courage	future

Next choose a Bible verse from the list below. Then go around the circle and have everyone read the verse they selected.

Give thanks to the LORD; call on His name; proclaim His deeds among the peoples. ... Give thanks to the LORD, for He is good; His faithful love endures forever.
1 Chronicles 16:8,34

I will thank the LORD for His righteousness; I will sing about the name of the LORD, the Most High.
Psalm 7:17

I will thank the LORD with all my heart; I will declare all Your wonderful works ... I will rejoice and boast about You; I will sing about Your name, Most High.
Psalm 9:1-2

Enter His gates with thanksgiving and His courts with praise. Give thanks to Him and praise His name.
Psalm 100:4

Let them give thanks to the LORD for His faithful love and His wonderful works for the human race. Let them offer sacrifices of thanksgiving and announce His works with shouts of joy.
Psalm 107:21-22

Don't worry about anything, but in everything, through prayer and petition with thanksgiving, let your requests be made known to God.
Philippians 4:6

After everyone has shared what they are thankful for and a Bible verse, close with a prayer of thanksgiving.

GROUP WARM-UPS

PICK A PROMISE

Gather in groups of 8 or more. Take your pick of the Scripture promises listed below. Tell the group why you chose the one you did.

You can also personalize the promise. After you have chosen a verse, restate it in first-person language. For example, if you personalized the first verse listed below, it would sound like this: "Therefore, if I am in Christ, I am a new creation; my old things have passed away, and look new things have come to me."

Therefore if anyone is in Christ, there is a new creation; old things have passed away, and look, new things have come.   *2 Corinthians 5:17*

I am sure of this, that He who started a good work in you will carry it on to completion until the day of Christ Jesus.   *Philippians 1:6*

Call to Me and I will answer you and tell you great and wondrous things you do not know.   *Jeremiah 33:3*

And God is able to make every grace overflow to you, so that in every way, always having everything you need, you may excel in every good work.   *2 Corinthians 9:8*

I am able to do all things through Him who strengthens me.   *Philippians 4:13*

We know that all things work together for the good of those who love God: those who are called according to His purpose.   *Romans 8:28*

"Keep asking, and it will be given to you. Keep searching, and you will find. Keep knocking, and the door will be opened to you. For everyone who asks receives, and the one who searches finds, and to the one who knocks, the door will be opened."   *Matthew 7:7–8*

No temptation has overtaken you except what is common to humanity. God is faithful and He will not allow you to be tempted beyond what you are able, but with the temptation He will also provide a way of escape, so that you are able to bear it.   *1 Corinthians 10:13*

"Listen! I stand at the door and knock. If anyone hears My voice and opens the door, I will come in to him and have dinner with him, and he with Me."   *Revelation 3:20*

"Peace I leave with you. My peace I give to you. I do not give to you as the world gives. Your heart must not be troubled or fearful."   *John 14:27*

Trust in the Lᴏʀᴅ with all your heart, and do not rely on your own understanding; think about Him in all your ways, and He will guide you on the right paths.   *Proverbs 3:5–6*

The Lᴏʀᴅ will protect you from all harm; He will protect your life. The Lᴏʀᴅ will protect your coming and going both now and forever.   *Psalm 121:7–8*

 # YOU AND ME, PARTNER

Get in groups of 8 or more. Think of the people in your group as you read over the list of activities below. If you had to choose someone from your group to be your partner, who would you choose to do these activities with? Jot down each person's name beside the activity you have chosen for him or her. You can use each person's name only once and you have to use everyone's name once (therefore, you won't be writing a name in every blank). Then, let one person listen to what the others chose for him or her. Move to the next person, and continue through the list around your group.

WHO WOULD YOU CHOOSE FOR THE FOLLOWING?

_____**ENDURANCE DANCE** contest partner

_____**BOBSLED** race partner for the Olympics

_____**MONDAY NIGHT FOOTBALL ANNOUNCER** teammate

_____**TRAPEZE ACT** partner

_____**MY UNDERSTUDY** for my debut in a Broadway musical

_____**TAG-TEAM** partner for a professional wrestling match

_____**BEST MAN** or **MAID OF HONOR** at my wedding

_____**SECRET UNDERCOVER** agent partner

_____**BODYGUARD** for me when I strike it rich

_____**MOUNTAIN CLIMBING** partner in climbing Mt. Everest

_____**ASTRONAUT** to fly the space shuttle while I walk in space

_____**SAND CASTLE** tournament building partner

_____**PIT CREW** foreman for entry in Indianapolis 500

_____**AUTHOR** of a book about my love life

_____**SURGEON** to operate on me for a life-threatening cancer

_____**TWO-ON-TWO BEACH VOLLEYBALL** teammate

_____**NEW BUSINESS START-UP** partner

_____**HEAVY-DUTY PRAYER** partner

 # VALUED VALUES

Get together in groups of 8 or more. Below is a list of qualities based on positive values. Think about the members of your group and jot down their names next to the value that describes them best. You can use each person's name only once, and you have to use everyone's name once (therefore, you won't be writing a name in every blank). Ask one person to listen while the others explain which value they selected for that individual. Then go to the next person and do the same until everyone is affirmed.

_____**PURE IN HEART:** Your life is marked with integrity before God and other people.

_____**PEACEMAKER:** You have a gift from God to help people overcome their differences.

_____**TRANSPARENT:** You can be yourself without any pretenses and let the light of Christ shine through you.

_____**FAITHFUL:** You are faithful to uphold God's morality even under pressure.

_____**MERCIFUL / COMPASSIONATE:** You have the ability to feel what others feel—to be happy or to hurt with them.

_____**MEEK / GENTLE**: You can be outwardly tender because you are inwardly strong.

_____**SPIRITUALLY HUNGRY:** I admire the longing in your heart for a growing, genuine relationship with God.

_____**ALWAYS LOVING:** You have a Christlike capacity to love others unconditionally—no matter what.

_____**COMMUNITY BUILDER:** God uses you as a bond to bring people together in unity.

_____**HUMBLE**: I admire the quiet way you demonstrate what humility is all about.

_____**GENEROUS**: You give freely, not for attention or praise—but for the simple joy of giving.

_____**CONTENTED**: You know that your worth is based on who you are rather than on what you have.

_____**JOYFUL**: Regardless of the circumstances, you have a smile on your face and a positive outlook about life.

_____**PATIENT**: You never seem to be in a hurry or to get irritated by others.

GROUP WARM-UPS

BROADWAY JOBS

Get together in groups of 8 or more. Imagine for a moment that your group has been chosen to produce a Broadway show, and you had to choose people from your group for all of the jobs for this production. Have someone read out loud the job description for the first job below—PRODUCER. Then, let everyone in your group call out the name of the person in your group who would best fit this job. (You don't have to agree.) Then read the job description for the next job and let everyone nominate another person. Repeat this process through the list.

PRODUCER: Typical Hollywood business tycoon; extravagant, big-spender, big-production magnate.

DIRECTOR: Creative, imaginative brain who coordinates the production and draws the best out of others.

HEROINE: Beautiful, captivating, everybody's heartthrob; defenseless when men are around, but nobody's fool.

HERO: Tough, macho, champion of the underdog, knight in shining armor, defender of truth.

COMEDIAN: Childlike, happy-go-lucky, outrageously funny, keeps everyone laughing.

CHARACTER ACTOR: Rugged individualist, outrageously different, colorful, adds spice to any surrounding.

FALL GUY: Easy-going, nonchalant character who wins the hearts of everyone by being the "foil" of the heavy characters.

TECHNICAL DIRECTOR: The genius for "sound and lights"; creates the perfect atmosphere.

COMPOSER OF LYRICS: Communicates in music what everybody understands; heavy into feelings, moods, outbursts of energy.

PUBLICITY AGENT: Advertising and public relations expert; knows all the angles, good at one-liners, a flair for "hot" news.

VILLAIN: The "bad guy" who really is the heavy for the plot, forces others to think, challenges traditional values; out to destroy anything artificial or hypocritical.

AUTHOR: Shy, aloof; very much in touch with feelings, sensitive to people, puts into words what others only feel.

STAGEHAND: Supportive, behind-the-scenes person who makes things run smoothly; patient and tolerant.

 # BRAIN FOOD

Congratulations! You have won a gift certificate for a free class at a local junior college. You get to take any course they offer! Form groups of 4 to 8 people. Have someone read out loud the first course description, and then ask those who would be interested in that class to raise their hands. Take turns reading the courses down through the list. When you're done, have everyone choose their FIRST and LAST choices for a course.

Archaeology 714: "Bones Down Under: The study of aboriginal fossils in Australia." Professor: C. Dundee. Prerequisite: Archaeology 602, "Providing Data for Your Professor's Latest Book." Shovels provided.

Bird-Watching 101: "Birds Are Our Friends." In this introductory course you will learn what a bird looks like, how many wings it has, and how to identify a feather. BYOB (Bring your own binoculars). Prerequisite: none. Tests: none. Term papers: none. Professor: none.

Political Science 403: "The Management of a Bureaucracy." An introduction to bureaucratic language, form making, and standing in line. Special segments will include "How to get a driver's license" and "You can't fight city hall until you can find a parking place." Professor: Ann R. Kay. Prerequisite: Surviving enrollment or equivalent.

Calculus 555: "The Mathematics of Chaos." This class meets in several different locations at several different times and is taught by several different professors. Prerequisites: Literature 101, Ceramics, and Physical Education.

Creative Writing 201: "The Limerick." There once was a student in school/Who thought he was totally cool/Then he took this class/And he did not pass/Now everyone thinks he's a fool. Professor: Dr. Seuss. Prerequisite: Creative Writing 121, "The Food Label."

Sociology 313: "TV Viewing in America." A fascinating sociological study of television viewing at its finest. Special sections will focus on becoming an expert couch potato, snacking and viewing habits, and channel surfing. The art of reciting lines from classic reruns will also be addressed. Professor: Mr. Potato Head. Prerequisite: Sociology 213: "Relating to Your Nintendo."

Radio, Television, and Film 202: "Movie Snacks." This class is a serious investigation of popcorn, Goo-Goo clusters, Whoppers, and Good 'n Fruity in the 20th century American film experience. Professor: Dr. Hitchcock. Prerequisite: Radio, Television and Film 132, "Finding a Seat at the Theatre."

Car Repair 401: "Automotive Electronics." This course is for serious students only. The first part of the semester will be devoted to setting the buttons on your car radio. The second part of the course will focus on how to use intermittent wipers. Professor: Tim "The Tool Man" Taylor. Prerequisite: Home Repair 401, "Setting the Clock on Your VCR" or equivalent.

YOU REMIND ME OF JESUS

Get together in groups of 8 or more. Every Christian reflects the character of Jesus in some way. As your group has gotten to know each other, you can begin to see how each person demonstrates Christ in his or her own personality. Go around the circle and have each person listen while others take turns telling that person what they notice in him or her that reminds them of Jesus. You may also want to tell them why you selected what you did.

YOU REMIND ME OF:

JESUS THE HEALER: You seem to be able to touch someone's life with your compassion and help make them whole.

JESUS THE SERVANT: There's nothing that you wouldn't do for someone.

JESUS THE PREACHER: You share your faith in a way that challenges and inspires people.

JESUS THE LEADER: As Jesus had a plan for the disciples, you are able to lead others in a way that honors God.

JESUS THE REBEL: By doing the unexpected, you remind me of Jesus' way of revealing God in unique, surprising ways.

JESUS THE RECONCILER: Like Jesus, you have the ability to be a peacemaker between others.

JESUS THE TEACHER: You have a gift for bringing light and understanding to God's Word.

JESUS THE CRITIC: You have the courage to say what needs to be said, even if it isn't always popular.

JESUS THE SACRIFICE: Like Jesus, you seem to be willing to sacrifice anything to glorify God.

DREAM CAREER

What would you do if you could choose any career? Look at the list below and choose two: (1) your first choice and (2) your last choice. Feel free to choose a career that is not listed. Get in groups of up to 8, and let other group members take turns guessing what you have selected.

Police Officer:
A brave upholder of the law in an exciting fight against criminals.

Actor / Actress:
A glamorous movie star who gets big money to appear on the silver screen.

High-Powered Attorney:
An eloquent, intelligent spokesman of the law who defends the innocent in the courtroom.

Politician:
A high-profile public servant who can whip out a clever deal or an inspiring speech at the drop of a hat.

Fashion Model:
A jet-setting career for those with charm and an alluring smile.

Teacher:
The educator who inspires students to expand their horizons and appreciate the world.

Banker:
The respected lender who can help people fulfill their greatest dreams.

Missionary:
The bold preacher who is willing to travel the world to share the gospel.

Psychologist:
The trusted counselor who helps people come to peace with God and themselves.

Astronaut:
A daring outer space pilot and extraterrestrial scientist.

Minister:
A beloved servant who takes care of a congregation's spiritual needs.

Race Car Driver:
A courageous competitor who tears around the track at 200 mph.

Veterinarian:
The beloved animal doctor everyone trusts with his pets and livestock.

Novelist:
The fiction writer who can produce best-sellers that everyone talks about.

Social Worker:
The steward of government resources who strives to help the unfortunate get back on their feet.

Doctor:
The family physician who is a trusted healer, devoted listener, and close friend.

Jet Pilot:
A courageous aviator who streaks across the sky in a screaming jet, ready to defend the nation.

Computer Jockey:
The computer whiz who boldly writes software programs that no one has written before.

 # AUTOMOTIVE AFFIRMATION

Get together in groups of 8 or more. Use this list of automotive items to affirm the contribution of each person in your group. Have someone read out loud the first item—BATTERY. Then, let everyone in the group call out the name of the person in your group who best fits this description. (You don't all have to agree.) Then read the next item, etc., down through the list.

BATTERY: A dependable "die-hard"—provides the "juice" for everything to happen.

SPARK PLUG: Gets things started. Makes sure there is "fire," even on cold mornings.

OIL: "The lubricant" to protect against engine wear-out, provide longer mileage, and reduce friction for fast-moving parts.

SHOCK ABSORBER: Cushions heavy bumps. Provides an easy, comfortable ride.

RADIO: The "music machine," making the trip fun and enjoyable. Adds a little "rock 'n' roll" for a good time.

MUFFLER: Reduces the engine's roar to a cat's "purr," even at high speeds over rough terrain.

CUP HOLDER: The servant, always meeting a need.

SUBWOOFER: The strong voice in the crowd. When they talk, people listen.

TRANSMISSION: Converts the energy into motion, enables the engine to slip from one speed to another without stripping the gears.

SEAT BELT / AIR BAG: Restrains or protects others when there is a possibility of them getting hurt.

GASOLINE: Liquid fuel that is consumed, giving away its own life for the energy to keep things moving.

WINDSHIELD: Keeps the vision clear, protects from debris and flying objects.

  # WHAT ARE YOUR VALUES?

GROUP WARM-UPS

How do your values affect the decisions you make? Get together with 1 to 3 people and share your answers with each other—going through the questions one at a time.

1. When it comes to making a tough decision, I generally:
   - ❏ struggle for days
   - ❏ wait to see what someone else will do
   - ❏ never ask for advice
   - ❏ take myself on a long walk
   - ❏ make a snap decision
   - ❏ ask for advice
   - ❏ hope it will go away

2. The hardest decisions for me are usually when (rank top three):
   - ___ money is involved
   - ___ my reputation is on the line
   - ___ my moral values are involved
   - ___ friendship is involved
   - ___ my popularity is at stake

3. The biggest fear I have to deal with in standing up for what I believe is:
   - ❏ being laughed at
   - ❏ getting someone else in trouble
   - ❏ losing my friends
   - ❏ standing alone
   - ❏ being wrong
   - ❏ other:_____

4. In my home, my parents have stressed that morality is:
   - ❏ a very individual thing
   - ❏ the mark of a gentleman / lady
   - ❏ dependent upon the circumstances
   - ❏ a matter of black and white
   - ❏ a byproduct of Christianity
   - ❏ other:_____

There are many tough situations in life that call for decisions. You may take one of a variety of actions or do nothing. What would you do in each situation below?

1. You don't agree with the behavior of a friend. What do you do?
   - ❏ ignore it
   - ❏ stop running around with him or her
   - ❏ confront him or her about it
   - ❏ talk to someone else about it

2. You are the friend of someone who has been deliberately omitted from a party. What do you do?
   - ❏ ignore the offense and go
   - ❏ refuse to go
   - ❏ call and ask why

3. Your friends are going to a beer party and you're invited. What do you do?
   - ❏ tell them I don't drink
   - ❏ go along but don't drink
   - ❏ tell their parents
   - ❏ make some excuse
   - ❏ join the party

4. Your best friend never studies. It's exam time and he wants to cheat off your paper. He'll flunk if you don't let him. What do you do?
   - ❏ let him copy
   - ❏ quietly explain my feelings about cheating
   - ❏ refuse him, but offer to help him study for the next exam
   - ❏ tell the teacher
   - ❏ cover my paper

THIS LITTLE LIGHT OF YOURS

Get together in groups of 8 or more. What kind of light best describes each of the members of your group? Focus on one group member at a time and share what light you would choose for him or her.

FLASHLIGHT: You showed insight that brought light into an area that has been dark for me.

SUNLIGHT: You bring warmth and life to others.

WARNING LIGHT: You gave some needed cautions, without which I or the group may have gotten into trouble.

CANDLELIGHT: You help provide a relaxed, gentle mood.

LIGHTHOUSE BEAM: You showed us the way when we got "lost in the fog."

NEON LIGHT: You bring color and personality to the group.

PORCH LIGHT: You were the light that said, "You are welcome here!"

NIGHT-LIGHT: You made some scary things seem less scary.

FIREPLACE LIGHT: You bring people together around your warmth and crackling flames.

MOONLIGHT: You reflect well the light of the Son.

THE GIVING GAME

Get together in groups of about 4. This game is a beautiful way to express your love and appreciation for one another. Follow the three steps below.

1. Ask everyone to sit in silence and ask themselves this question: "If I could give something of myself to each person in this group that expresses my feelings right now for them, what would I want to give each person that they could keep for the rest of their lives?" (This is for keeps.)

2. Still in silence, take out your purse or wallet ... or things in your pockets ... and try to find symbols or tokens of the real thing you would like to give this person. For instance:

   ❏ picture of my family—to remember the times we have shared together
   ❏ a ticket stub to a concert—to remember the music that we enjoy in Christ
   ❏ a Band-Aid—for the "little hurts" that come along in life

   Remember, you need ONE gift (a different gift) for each person—a token or symbol of the real gift.

3. Ask one person to listen while the others go around and explain their gift and hand it to this person. The person who receives the gift is to say "Thanks." Nothing more.

Repeat this procedure until everyone in your group has been given their gifts. In the giving and receiving of gifts, you are able to say two things: (1) What I have appreciated most about you and (2) What I want you to keep as a token of our friendship—for the rest of your life.

GROUP EVALUATION

Get together in groups of 8 or more. Sometimes a group needs to stop and give themselves a checkup. Go down this list one question at a time, and let everyone share their response.

Mark each question by circling a number:

      1 = never
      2 = rarely
      3 = sometimes
      4 = most of the time
      5 = always

After everyone has answered the questions, the group could have an open discussion about their opinions of the group. Keep in mind that no group is perfect, and every group needs time to grow and mature.

Generally speaking, I feel that this group:

understands what I am trying to say	1 2 3 4 5
encourages my comments and opinions	1 2 3 4 5
accepts me for who I am	1 2 3 4 5
feels free to let me know when I'm bugging them	1 2 3 4 5
helps me understand God better	1 2 3 4 5
includes me in what's going on	1 2 3 4 5
can tell when something is bothering me	1 2 3 4 5
gives me support	1 2 3 4 5
encourages me to grow in my Christian faith	1 2 3 4 5
succeeds with problem solving	1 2 3 4 5
is fulfilling its total potential	1 2 3 4 5

ATHLETE STUDIES

Welcome to the Athlete Studies section of your FCA Bible! In the following pages, you will have many selections from Scripture to choose from to use for your personal Bible reading time, team Bible studies, small-group meetings, or chapels. We encourage you to read the Scripture passages carefully, and take some time to meditate on the questions that follow. This will help you to understand what the Bible has to say, and learn to apply God's truths in your own life.

TABLE OF CONTENTS

FUNDAMENTALS

MAXIMIZING YOUR TALENTS

Warm-up

1. List some of the athletic talents you possess. What about non-athletic talents?

2. Where did the talents come from? What are some things you do to develop these talents?

Workout

Matthew 25:14-30

3. In this parable, who does the master represent? How about the slaves? What can the talents represent?

4. Why is it so important to develop what we have been given? (vv. 21,23)

5. For whom are you using your talents? How and why? How will you use these talents differently in the future?

FUNDAMENTALS

BEYOND EXPECTATION

Warm-up

1. What is expected of you by your teammates? What does your coach expect of you?

2. Describe a time when you or someone else did something in a game that was unexpected. What was the response from others?

Workout

Romans 12:9-21

3. In the Romans passage, how are love and life described? (vv. 9-16)

4. How are we to deal with wrongs in life? (vv. 17-21)

5. Which description seems most difficult to you?

THE INSIDE TRACK

Warm-up

1. Who on your team or league seems to have it all? What makes you think so?

2. What is one thing that someone said or showed you that improved your game? Who said it to you?

Workout

Psalm 1:1-6

3. According to this passage, what is the importance of knowing what is right and focusing on it? (vv. 2-3, 6)

4. What happens to those who do not listen to good advice and do wrong? (vv. 4-6)

5. Think of one time when you followed "the advice of the wicked" or took the "path of sinners" or joined with a "group of mockers" (hung with the wrong group). How did it impact you and others? (v. 1)

FUNDAMENTALS

PERSEVERANCE

Warm-up

1. In the last year, what have been some of the most difficult things you have endured to compete in your sport?

2. What is most helpful to you as you persevere through hard situations?

3. Who has been an example of perseverance to you?

Workout

Genesis 37:18-24; 39:7-10,19-21; 40:2-4,20-23; 41:14-16,37-40

4. Through what sorts of things did Joseph have to persevere in these pieces of his story?

5. What impact would an attitude like Joseph's make upon your circumstances?

PRESSING ON

Warm-up

1. What's the last athletic achievement you had that made all the practice worthwhile? How long did that sense of accomplishment last?

2. What training or lessons have you had in your sport which you would consider "foundational" to your performance?

Workout

Matthew 7:24-27

3. In this passage, what are the four things for which these two builders needed to prepare? What could these things represent? What was the difference between their "technique"?

4. How does someone know what builds a firm foundation for his or her life? What are two things that have recently tested you in your desire to press on and have a firm foundation?

5. How important is this foundation when your athletic accomplishments/failures fade? How about when you find success?

FUNDAMENTALS

POTENTIAL

Warm-up

1. Describe the perfect day. How does it start? How does it end? Did that day involve a practice or game? The perfect day should be free of what?

2. What would be the most "fearful" day you could imagine? What would make it so fearful?

Workout

Psalm 34:1-10

3. What three things does King David describe in verse 4? What could a king fear? From how many of these fears does God deliver him?

4. How does someone taste and see that the Lord is good (v. 8)? How do you suppose a king would take refuge in the Lord? According to verse 10, certain people lack something. Who and what do they lack? To you, what is "any good thing?"

5. What are the conditions for you to receive each of the benefits listed in this passage? Are you willing to do these things?

PREPARING FOR COMPETITION

Warm-up

1. What do you do in the hours before a competition to prepare yourself mentally?

2. Have you ever been so nervous before a competition that the fear made you freeze up? How did this affect your performance?

Workout

Joshua 2:1-24

3. In this passage, how is Joshua preparing for his big battle? How is Rahab preparing?

4. What is Rahab's motivation?
   a. Fear
   b. Desire for safety
   c. Respect for God's power
   d. Other:

5. How can God help you to prepare for your next competition?

COMPETITION

COMPETITION

In this section of Sport Focused Huddles, we will consider the topic of competition. If Christians are supposed to be servants of others, where does the concept of competing with others come in? Can a Christian athlete really be fully competitive? Where does the balance lie?

We will consider these and other pertinent questions in the following Bible studies, designed for your own personal Bible times.

IS COMPETITION CHRISTIAN?

Warm-up

1. What has been your greatest athletic accomplishment? Did it involve defeating an opponent, as opposed to performing a personal best?

Workout

2 Timothy 2:3-11

2. In what ways would you say God is competitive? (v. 10)

3. If competition has a healthy expression, how can competitiveness be abused?

4. How can you channel your competitiveness to use it properly off the field (in your school work or in a job)?

5. What is your biggest struggle as it pertains to competitiveness?

6. What can you do that will please God while you are competing?

![COMPETITION logo] COMPETITION

IN THE ZONE

Warm-up

1. Have you ever played "In the Zone?" Briefly describe the experience.

2. What sports figure do you find yourself imitating most often?

Workout

Ephesians 5:1-10

3. Paul says to be an imitator of God. What does it mean to imitate someone? Is it more than just talking and acting like them (v. 1)?

4. What things does Paul say that someone should do to imitate God (vv. 3-7)?

5. Ask God to show you what it means to play "In the Zone" for Christ. Pray as a group that you find out more ways to please Him and not please yourself.

COURAGE

Warm-up

1. Tell us about a time when you showed courage in competition.

2. How have you seen other players demonstrate courage through sports?

Workout

1 Samuel 17:20-24,31-37,39-51

3. What are the most striking features of David's courage in this story?

4. How much is your experience with courage like his?

COMPETITION

COMPETITIVE DRIVE

1. Tell us about a time when your competitive drive was critical to your performance.

2. Is that drive to compete something you've always had or was it developed over time? Please explain.

Workout

1 Kings 18:20-40

3. What is some evidence of competitive drive in Elijah from this story?

4. How much did his competitive spirit cause him to risk?

5. What risks might your drive to compete lead you to take?

SELF-CONTROL

Warm-up

1. What part of your sport requires the most self-control?

2. What happens if you play in an out-of-control way?

Workout

Matthew 4:1-11

3. How is Jesus' self-control evident in this story? Over what factors does He exercise self-control?

4. In what situations in your game do you struggle to maintain self-control?

5. How might Jesus' example here affect your how you approach games with respect to self-control?

 **COMPETITION**

RULING YOUR SPORT

Warm-up

1. Tell about a time when you experienced good sportsmanship from an opponent. Do the same regarding bad sportsmanship.

2. Who has the best sportsmanship you know?

3. How can you want to beat an opponent and still show sportsmanship?

Workout

Genesis 1:26

4. What does God command us to do in this verse? How is our desire to "rule" a part of God's character?

5. What is the difference between this "ruling" and bullying?

STUMBLING

Warm-up

1. When was the last time you knew you were only human in competition or practice? How did you feel? What were the circumstances?

2. How did you regain your drive to excel after a time of failure?

Workout

Isaiah 64:5-9

3. How does Isaiah describe humans in verses 5 and 6? How does Isaiah describe our best efforts and intentions? How is this possible, if our hearts are in the right place?

4. Even though all of us fall down, verses 8 and 9 open the door for hope. What are two possible aspects of this hope? What can someone do so that their sins are not remembered forever? How could this effect you during competition the next time you "fall down"?

COMPETITION

CELEBRATION

Warm-up

1. What do you love about your favorite sport?

2. Have you ever experienced an accomplishment or victory that made you, your teammates, coach, fans, or parents leap up and down for joy? What were the circumstances?

Workout

2 Samuel 6:1-5,12-15

3. Describe the picture of what is happening in verses 1-5. Verse 12 describes how the ark of God blessed a family. What do you suppose this "blessing" looked like? Using your own words, describe what happened in verses 14 and 15.

4. Into what area of your team's "life" could God bring His presence and blessing? Do you think God really wants to do this?

5. Into what area of your life could God bring His presence and blessing that would cause you to leap for joy?

PLAYING IN THE ZONE

Warm-up

1. Have you ever experienced someone being "in the Zone," who had a career game? What were the results?

2. How did that person feel before, during, and after the game? How did people view that person during and after the game?

3. How easy is it to get "in the Zone"?

Workout

2 Corinthians 5:16-20

4. What does it mean to be "in Christ"? What parts of this "new creation" are changed? When did you become a new creation?

5. How do you represent your team or school in some formal way? How is this like being God's ambassador? What kind of appeal does God want to make through you?

⚡ COMPETITION

ENTHUSIASM

Warm-up

1. When was the last time you and your team were really pumped up for a game? How did it happen? What was the result?

2. How did this make you ready for the competition?

Workout

Ephesians 6:10-18

3. How does verse 12 describe the battles of our lives? Using your own words, describe what this verse is saying.

4. Why do you suppose truth is described as a belt? Why do you suppose that righteousness was to be positioned over our chests? What is in the chest that would need righteousness?

5. A shield is a very defensive weapon. How could faith be effectively used defensively? Why would salvation be best protecting the head? The word of God is the only offensive weapon described in this armor. Why? How do you suppose we could use it offensively?

PLAYING OVER YOUR HEAD

Warm-up

1. How do you feel when you compete against someone who is equally matched with you? Do you prefer a quick victory or a close competition?

2. When you compete against someone who is equally matched, what is your response? Does it push you to improve, or just frustrate you?

Workout

Genesis 32:22-32

3. Why does God wrestle with Jacob here? If God is almighty or omnipotent, why does He not just pin Jacob to the ground?

4. Why does Jacob ask God for His name? Why does God change Jacob's name to Israel?

5. In what area of your life are you wrestling with God?

COMPETITION

SPORTS ETHICS

Warm-up

1. When have you been faced with either losing a competition or doing something unethical? What did you do?

2. What "price" are you willing to pay in order to win? What "prices" are you not willing to pay?

Workout

1 Samuel 24:1-22

3. Why does David choose not to kill Saul? What "price" would he have paid if he'd done so?

4. David eventually becomes Israel's greatest human king. How might his reign have been different if he'd killed Saul to become king?

5. How might God bless you if you choose to make His priorities more important than winning?

VICTORY GLOATING

Warm-up

1. When you or your team win a great victory, how do you react?

2. When is it okay to do a "victory dance," and when is it prideful gloating?

Workout

1 Chronicles 15:25–16:3

3. Which do you think David is doing here: a joyful victory dance, or a prideful gloating? Why?

4. Who is responsible for David's victory in this passage? Who is responsible for your own victories? How might this distinction help you keep from gloating?

COMPETITION

TRASH TALK

Warm-up

1. How does it make you feel when an opponent mocks you or ridicules your team?

2. When others have ridiculed you and threatened to humiliate you in competition, how have you or your teammates responded? Did you respond with similar taunts, or did you ignore them?

Workout

Nehemiah 4:1-23

3. What types of opposition is Nehemiah faced with in this passage?

4. How does Nehemiah respond to the verbal taunts? How does he respond to the threats of physical harm?

5. How can you adapt Nehemiah's attitude toward verbal abuse? Toward legitimate threats of defeat?

JEALOUSY AND HATRED

Warm-up

1. How do your competitors think about you? Do they respect you or dislike you? Why?

2. When a competitor tries to cheat against you, how do you respond?

Workout

Daniel 6:1-24

3. Why do the people in this passage set a trap for Daniel, hoping to kill him?

4. Why do they resort to having the king write such a decree? How do you compare with Daniel's faultless record?

ATHLETE STUDIES

TEAMWORK

Being a good teammate is critical to most athlete's performance; each of us must learn how to cooperate with others, working together and sharing together all our wins and losses. This is vitally true of the Christian life, as well. Nobody is a superstar, we are all just part of God's team.

Spend some time reflecting on this idea as you go through the following Scripture passages, considering the questions that we have provided.

ARE YOU THE GREATEST?

Warm-up

1. Who is the greatest player you ever played against?

2. How does someone become great in sports? What does it take to become great in God's eyes? (v. 43)

Workout

Mark 10:35-45

3. What did Jesus come to the earth to do? (v. 45)

4. How would your team be different if you all had a servant attitude? How would your family be different?

5. Are there things you need to change to become a better servant? What are they?

 # TEAMWORK

TEAMWORK

Warm-up

1. Who has been a great teammate to you?

2. What were the most important factors in such teamwork?

Workout

Luke 9:10-17

3. Where do you see teamwork happening in this story?

4. What was Jesus' role in the team effort?

5. What can we learn from how He promoted teamwork with His disciples?

COURAGE

Warm-up

1. Who are some players you've known who showed real humility?

2. Why were they so humble?

Workout

Mark 1:4-11

3. In this passage what are some indicators of humility you see in John the Baptist?

4. Why do you think John acts and speaks so humbly?

5. What are some ways that we can express true humility in the world of sports?

TEAMWORK

ACCOUNTABILITY

Warm-up

1. How much is accountability an issue within your team: None, little, some or very much?

2. How do your team leaders or coaches call others to account for their actions?

Workout

Galatians 2:11-21

3. For what issue did Paul call Peter into accountability? How did he do it? Have you ever had a similar experience? Tell us about it.

4. For what issues is it important to be accountable?

5. How can we build team relationships with this important factor?

LOYALTY

Warm-up

1. Who has shown you loyalty during your career in sports? Tell us about it.

2. How do people express loyalty at various levels of sport?

Workout

Ruth 1:11-18

3. How did Ruth demonstrate loyalty to her mother-in-law, Naomi?

4. Do you find such loyalty among your teammates and coaches? What factors contribute to that situation?

5. How will you help to build more of a sense of loyalty on your team?

⚡ TEAMWORK

FAITH

Warm-up

1. What is the most consistent way you have to trust in your favorite sport?

2. In whom do you see faith at work in sports? What or who seems to be the object of that faith?

Workout

Luke 7:1-10

3. What did this man want from Jesus? How did he express trust in Christ Jesus?

4. Why would Jesus be surprised by his great faith?

5. How similar is your faith to this man's trust?

FORGIVE?

Warm-up

1. What nickname do your teammates call you? How did you get that name? If you could have any nickname, what would you want it to be?

2. How have you reacted when someone on your team has done something detrimental to the team? How did that person's attitude determine your reaction?

Workout

Philemon 1-16

3. Do you ever see the qualities that Paul talks about (sharing your faith, deep understanding of Christ, full of love, giving others joy and encouragement, refreshing people's hearts) in those around you, on your team or in school (vv. 6-7)?

4. Paul was asking Philemon to forgive his run-away slave, Onesimus (v.10), who had come to know Christ personally since he ran away. What do you think Philemon should do? Why (vv. 8-16)?

5. Do Paul's words offer any new solution for you in dealing with this kind of situation? Why or why not?

TEAMWORK

IS IT REAL?

Warm-up

1. What's the last thing your coach told you that was hard to believe? Was it about you? A teammate? An opponent? What did you do with what he said?

2. Describe a time when a coach or teacher "opened your mind" to some idea or technique that you had struggled to understand. How did this understanding come about finally?

Workout

Luke 24:36-45

3. What are the circumstances around Jesus' appearance? Why do you think He said those first words? Why is verse 45 important?

4. What area of your life would you like to have your mind opened to, so you can experience what is for real? How do you think this could effect your relationships with teammates? Friends? Family?

MORE GRACE

Warm-up

1. When was the last time a teammate or coach gave you a second chance? What were the circumstances? How did you react?

2. Describe a time when someone said something that calmed you down from fear or anger. What was the situation? What did the person say?

Workout

Zephaniah 3:17

3. According to this passage, how does God take delight in you? How could His love for someone quiet his or her spirit? What do you suppose some of the words in His song would be, for someone in your group right now? At practice tomorrow, how could He quiet you with His love?

4. Close by starting your prayer with "Lord, thank you for giving me more than I deserve. I will remember to be quiet because of your love when ... "

 **TEAMWORK**

FAITHFUL SUPPORTERS

Warm-up

1. Who supports you the most: your teammates, coach, fans, parents? What effect do they have on your desire to play your sport?

2. Which group supports you the least?

Workout

John 4:7-24

3. What would cause the Jews not to talk to the Samaritans? Are there any groups at your school that people don't talk too? How about on your team?

4. In verse 10, do you think that the woman understood what Jesus meant at first? What did he really mean (look at verses 13 and 14)? Why would Jesus ask her to get her husband before he gave her this "water"?

5. How could worship of God meet this woman's real needs? What do you suppose it looks like to worship in "spirit"? How about in "truth"?

WHERE IS YOUR HEART?

Warm-up

1. When was the last time your team had a "heart to heart" talk? Who did the talking? Who did the listening? Was it just your coach that was talking? Was it during practice or after practice? What was the talk about?

2. Has your team ever been scolded for not putting into practice the strategies that you've worked so hard to master?

Workout

Habakkuk 1:2-5

3. What are the things (there are at least seven) Habakkuk complains about? Have you seen strife and conflict abound in situations like this?

4. Why would Habakkuk be concerned that the law (God's heart and command for His people) was paralyzed? What happened in Habakkuk's heart when he heard the Lord's answer? What do you suppose happened in Habakkuk's mind when God answered by saying "you will not believe when you hear about it"?

LAY IT DOWN

Warm-up

1. Has a teammate or coach ever given you a break you didn't deserve or given you a start when you really didn't deserve it? How did this make you feel?

Workout

Acts 7:57–8:1; 9:1-9

2. In chapter 7 of Acts, what was Saul's (Paul's) track record with Jesus? What do you suppose motivated him?

3. In chapter 9, why was he going to Damascus? Describe in your own words how you think Paul might have reacted. Do you think Paul would have been on the disciple's top 10 list of people who will come to know Jesus? Why or why not?

4. Who do you know on your team or in your school that really needs to know Jesus? List 10 people you pray for.

JEALOUSY

Warm-up

1. When has your team been affected by jealousy?

2. What caused the jealousy? What effect did it have on the team? On you?

Workout

Genesis 16:1-16

3. What is the cause of Sarai's jealousy in this passage? Whose fault is it?

4. How might this jealousy have been avoided in the first place? How can you or your team work to avoid jealousy?

5. What is the proper response when faced with jealousy, according to this passage? What should be your own response?

TEAMWORK

RECONCILIATION

Warm-up

1.   When someone on your team offends you or hurts you, how do you respond?

2.   When there is disagreement among your team members, how does that affect your game? How do you bring about team unity after a disagreement?

Workout

Genesis 45:1-28

3.   What had Joseph's brothers done to him in the past?

4.   If you had been Joseph, how would you have responded?

5.   How can Joseph's attitude help you to bring reconciliation to teammates or family?

TEAMMATES/FAMILY

ATHLETE STUDIES

Warm-up

1.   Have you ever had a teammate or partner who seemed closer to you than your own family? What made that relationship so close?

2.   Give some examples of how you and your friend made sacrifices for one another. How did this friendship affect your sports performance?

Workout

1 Samuel 20:1-18

3.   How did the friendship of Jonathan and David affect the lives of these two men? What sacrifices or risks did Jonathan take for David?

4.   How has Jesus been this kind of friend to you? What sacrifices or risks would you be willing to take for Him?

TRAINING

Any sport requires time spent in training. An athlete needs training to learn the basic rules and skills of a new sport, to teach the body how to adapt to new moves and techniques. It is the same in the Christian life: we need to master the basics (such as those in the Fundamentals section), teach our bodies, minds, and spirits how to think and act in new ways so we can live and compete as Jesus would have us.

Spend some time reflecting on this idea as you go through the following Scripture passages, considering the questions that we have provided.

COMMITMENT

Warm-up

1. How have you recently demonstrated commitment to someone or something in your sport?

2. Who is the most highly committed player you've ever known? To what or to whom was he committed?

Workout

1 Kings 19:19-21

3. What did Elisha do that looks like commitment to you?

4. To what or whom does it seem that Elisha is committed?

5. How are you affected when a player shows commitment like Elisha's? How can you best demonstrate commitment in your life as a competitor?

SACRIFICE

Warm-up

1. What does it cost you to be a competitive athlete?

2. What do you regularly sacrifice to compete in your sport?

3. What sacrifices have you seen others make to achieve highly in their sport?

Workout

Luke 23:32-46

4. What was it that Jesus sacrificed in this story? Why would He do that? Why do you make the sacrifices that you do?

5. For what and for whom will you make sacrifices today and in the coming days?

ATHLETE STUDIES

HARD WORK

Warm-up

1. How important is your work ethic to your performance? How important is it to your competitor?

2. Who is an example of someone with a strong work ethic? How is it seen in his approach to sports?

Workout

Proverbs 10:4; 12:2; 14:2; 22:29

3. Which one of these Proverbs best illustrates your thoughts about hard work?

4. Why would this be such an important factor for success in competition?

5. How do we lead others to build a stronger work ethic for their sport?

TRAINING

SUPERSTAR OR BENCHWARMER?

Warm-up

1. What parts of your athletic ability would you describe as a "winning season?" "Losing season?" Why?

2. On a scale of 1 to 10, how much time do you spend thinking about the good points in your game or the bad points? (1=constantly, 10=never)

3. Describe a time when you felt like a superstar. Describe a time when you felt like a benchwarmer.

Workout

Romans 12:3

4. What do you think viewing yourself soberly means? Who is the best example of this? On a scale of 1 to 10, do you believe you view yourself soberly? (1=no, 5=maybe, 10=definitely)

5. How does Romans 12:3 affect your view of your game, practice, and competition and how you interact with your teammates and opponents?

RADICALLY CHANGED

Warm-up

1. What is the last thing your coach, teammate or parent told you to give up or quit doing? Why did they tell you this? Did you do it? What were the results?

Workout

Exodus 24:15-18; 34:29-35

2. What do you suppose Moses did for the first six days on the mountain?

3. In chapter 34, what were the physical effects on Moses from being in the Lord's presence? Who recognized what the glory of the Lord looked like? Where were they?

4. If you could ask the Lord's consuming fire to burn up one thing in your life, what would it be? How would the 10 Commandments influence your response (Ex. 20:2-17)? If these things were consumed, how could their absence make you a better athlete?

TRAINING

DOING THE IMPOSSIBLE

Warm-up

1. When have you been asked to do the "impossible" for your team or your coach?

2. Were you successful in doing it? If so, how did you accomplish it? If not, what prevented you?

Workout

Exodus 3:1-22

3. What "impossible" things are happening in this passage? What "impossible" task does God command Moses to fulfill?

4. What "impossible" task might God be asking you to fulfill? What makes it seem impossible?

5. How might the "God of the burning bush" be able to make the impossible come true in your life?

ATHLETE STUDIES

TRUE CONFIDENCE

Warm-up

1. When have you been defeated because you lacked confidence?

2. What do you do before a competition to increase your confidence of victory?

Workout

Numbers 13:1-16

3. Why does Joshua send 12 spies in before doing battle? What distinguishes lack of confidence from good preparations?

4. Why do 10 spies lack confidence? Why do 2 have confidence?

5. Where does your true confidence come from?

REAL TRUST

Warm-up

1. What coach or trainer has helped you the most? In what ways?

2. If that coach had asked you to do something very difficult, would you have done it? Why?

Workout

Job 1:1-2:13

3. Why does Job trust God in this passage?

4. In what ways is God like your greatest coach? In what ways is He greater?

WEAKNESS

Warm-up

1. When have you tried to force your body to do something in your sport which it just couldn't do? What was the result?

2. What weaknesses do you have the greatest struggle with in your sport?

3. How do you train your body to get beyond such limitations?

Workout

Romans 7:7-28

4. What weaknesses does Paul address in this passage? Do you see these weaknesses in your own life?

5. What does Paul say is the answer to these limitations? How can you push yourself past your own spiritual weaknesses?

 **TRAINING**

MORE THAN CONQUERORS

Warm-up

1. In what competition have you ever won a very dramatic, decisive victory?

2. What factors contributed to that tremendous victory? How did you feel afterwards?

Workout

Romans 8:28-39

3. What brings tremendous victory in the Christian life? How does one attain such victory?

4. According to this passage, in what areas of your life can you actually attain complete victory?

5. How can you be confident this week of obtaining real spiritual victory?

WEAKNESS AND STRENGTH

Warm-up

1. When you were just starting out in your sport, was there a more advanced player who helped you?

2. Is there someone on your team who is a weaker player than you? How can you help that person to improve?

3. How might a stronger player actually harm or hinder a weaker player?

Workout

Romans 14:1-9

4. In what ways might a stronger Christian help a weaker one? How might the stronger Christian harm or hinder the weaker believer?

5. What stronger Christian can you turn to for help and encouragement this week? What weaker believer can you be a strong friend to?

ATHLETE STUDIES

TRAINING

STRIVING FOR THE GOAL

Warm-up

1. What goal has been, or still is, the most difficult to reach in your sport?

2. What costs have you paid in striving toward that goal? What reward have you or will you receive upon attaining it?

Workout

Philippians 3:12-4:1

3. What goal is Paul striving toward in this passage?

4. What costs did Paul pay in attaining that goal? What reward did he receive?

5. What is the most important goal in your whole life? How will you work to attain it?

CRITICAL EQUIPMENT

Warm-up

1. What single piece of clothing or equipment is most important to you in your sport?

2. If you had to go without that equipment, how would it affect your game?

Workout

Colossians 3:1-17

3. What pieces of "equipment" does Paul discuss in this passage? Why is each important?

4. Which of the areas in this passage do you need to work on in the coming week?

TRAINING

GOOD TECHNIQUE

Warm-up

1. Have you ever watched a video of yourself in competition, or worked out in front of a mirror? How did these things help you improve your technique?

2. After watching your own technique, how long does it take to catch yourself before slipping back into poor form? Do you improve from one video session, or does it take repeated viewings?

Workout

James 1:19-27

3. How is the Word of God like a mirror or personal training video?

4. What steps are necessary if you are to improve your spiritual technique?

5. What are some practical ways which James lists here of improving one's spiritual technique?

BEING A TEAM

Warm-up

1. What would happen to your team if you lost just one member? Is there anyone on your team that you feel is expendable? Completely irreplaceable?

2. What happens to the team's performance if one player feels himself to be of no value? To be irreplaceable?

3. How do you and your teammates maintain team spirit and loyalty? How do you encourage all team members to feel valuable?

Workout

Ephesians 4:1-16

4. According to this passage, what is the secret for maintaining unity on Jesus' "team"? Why is it vitally important?

5. How are you doing lately at demonstrating "all humility and gentleness"?

ATHLETE STUDIES

PERFORMANCE

Any athlete knows that all the training and practice in the world is only as good as one's performance in competition. Taking one's training and putting it into practice is the athlete's ultimate goal: to keep improving one's skills by using them on the field of play. It is the same in the Christian life: all the book-learning and preaching in the world is of no value unless one takes those truths and puts them into practice in daily life. We call the study part "learning," and the practice part we call "wisdom." In these studies we will learn how to perform on and off the field for God.

Spend some time reflecting on this idea as you go through the following Scripture passages, considering the questions that we have provided.

TEAMMATES' KEEPER

Warm-up

1. Who is the most helpful member of your team? In what ways is that person helpful to the rest of the team?

2. What professional athlete do you think of as a real team player? Which one seems like a real self-promoter?

Workout

Genesis 4:1-12

3. What motivates Cain to murder his brother? What motivates an athlete to hog the glory for himself?

4. What could Cain have done differently?

5. Why is it important for an athlete to care about his or her teammates? How can you look out for your teammates' interests more?

STUBBORNNESS

Warm-up

1. When has someone's stubbornness caused problems on your team? When has your stubbornness been a problem?

2. What motivates a person to be stubborn?

Workout

Exodus 7:14-24; 12:28-30

3. What motivates Pharaoh in this passage to be so stubborn?

4. What affect does his stubbornness have on the entire nation of Egypt? How would things have been different for everybody if Pharaoh had not been stubborn?

5. How is the attitude of the Israelites in this passage different from that of Pharaoh? How can you be like the Israelites this week?

SPEECH HAS POWER

Warm-up

1. What member of your team tends to be the most encouraging? The most discouraging?

2. When have you seen how words can have a negative effect on your sports performance?

Workout

James 3:1-12

3. Why does James use the analogies here of the ship and the horse? What is he trying to teach us about the power of words?

4. Do your words tend to encourage or discourage others?

5. How can you use the power of your words this week to glorify God?

PERFORMANCE

OBEY

Warm-up

1. What would you consider to be the greatest sacrifice you've made for your sport or team?

2. Which do you consider more important: to sacrifice your all for your team, or to do exactly what the coach tells you? Why?

Workout

1 Samuel 15:1-23

3. What was Saul commanded to do in this passage? What does he actually do?

4. What is Saul's logic for not obeying God's exact command? What is the result of his compromise?

5. What is your true motivation when you "fudge" on your coach's instruction? What should be your attitude toward God's instruction?

DO IT FOR GOD'S GLORY

Warm-up

1. When you or your team wins a competition, who gets the glory?

2. What might be some things that are permissible on your team, yet not helpful to the members of the team?

Workout

1 Corinthians 10:23–11:1

3. What sorts of things might Paul be referring to in this passage as "permissible" but not "helpful"?

4. What "permissible" things might you do which could cause someone else to struggle with conscience?

5. How can you pursue all areas of your life for God's glory?

PERFORMANCE

GOD'S UNIFORM

Warm-up

1. Which piece of your team uniform or sports equipment do you consider the most important? What piece, if any, could you do without?

2. Imagine if your opponents were invisible. How would that alter the competition? What special equipment might you need to win?

Workout

Ephesians 6:10-20

3. Paul tells us that our real opponents are invisible (v. 12). What does this mean?

4. Examine each piece of equipment in this list. How does each item (helmet, shield, etc.) help the Christian in daily life? What would happen to a Christian if any item were missing?

5. What is needed for you to put on the full armor of God this week?

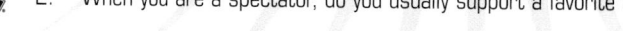

VICTORY OF THE UNDERDOG

Warm-up

1. Have you ever beaten a competitor despite overwhelming odds against you? Describe the victory, or one that you remember seeing.

2. When you are a spectator, do you usually support a favorite team or the underdog?

Workout

Judges 7:1-25

3. Why did God have Gideon reduce his forces to the point that they were so severely outnumbered?

4. How did God accomplish this victory?

5. How has God demonstrated his miraculous power in your life? How might he be asking you now to rely on his strength instead of your own?

PERFORMANCE

OFF THE BENCH

Warm-up

1. Have you ever spent an entire game sitting on the bench? What did it feel like the very first time you were called into the game?

2. When you are waiting to be called into competition, what do you think about? What do you do to be ready to go at a moment's notice?

Workout

1 Samuel 3:1-21

3. Samuel may have been only 12 years old when the Lord called him. How does he demonstrate a readiness to answer God's call?

4. How does Samuel continue as he grows up to be always ready for God's call?

5. How can you make yourself more ready for God's call in the coming week?

TRIED BY FIRE

Warm-up

1. Eric Liddell once gave up a chance at an Olympic gold medal because he refused to race on Sunday. Have you ever been confronted with a choice between serving God and playing your sport?

2. What did you do in that situation? What would you have done if you'd been Eric Liddell?

Workout

Daniel 3:1-30

3. Shadrach and friends were successful government officials. What does this suggest about their characters and work ethic?

4. Why do they refuse to obey the king in this one law? Would you feel differently about their decision if they'd died in the furnace?

5. In what area of life might God be calling you to obey Him above all else?

GO FOR THE REAL PRIZE

Warm-up

1. Have you ever competed in a game for which you were unprepared? What was—or might be—the outcome?

2. What was the greatest award or trophy you've ever won? What would you most like to win someday?

Workout

1 Corinthians 9:24-27

3. What prize does Paul most desire? Why?

4. How is this prize won? How does a Christian prepare for this contest?

5. How can you prepare for the prize this week?

PERSEVERE

Warm-up

1. When have you been pushed beyond your own expectations by the encouragement of a friend or coach?

2. If you've been pursuing your sport for a few years, have you noticed your enthusiasm decreasing any? Do you know any athletes who have lost the joy of their sport?

Workout

Hebrews 10:19-39

3. Why do you think the Christians being addressed here might have been losing their determination to persevere?

4. List three ways that the author gives in this passage for strengthening our confidence and perseverance.

5. How can you strengthen your own perseverance this week? That of a friend?

PERFORMANCE

MOMENTUM

Warm-up

1. Have you ever suffered through a bad call from a ref or decision from a judge? How did you respond?

2. How do you respond when the crowd becomes hostile to you or your team?

Workout

1 Peter 3:8-17

3. What does Peter say are the secrets to "see good days" in life? What, in practical terms, does each of these things mean?

4. What does it mean to "always be prepared to give a defense ... for the hope that is in you"? How would you answer such a question if asked by a stranger?

5. How can you become better prepared this week to see good days and to give an answer?

SELF-CONTROL

Warm-up

1. What aspect of your sport requires the greatest amount of physical control?

2. What have you done to teach yourself this area of control?

Workout

1 Thessalonians 4:1-12

3. In what specific ways does Paul call us to control our own bodies in this passage?

4. What reasons does Paul give for this self-control? Why?

5. How will you strengthen control of your sexual passions this week?

PERFORMANCE

SACRIFICES

Warm-up

1. What is the greatest sacrifice you've ever made for your sport or your team? Was it worthwhile?

2. Who has made great sacrifices to help you in your sports career?

Workout

Genesis 22:1-19

3. Why is the sacrifice of Isaac so costly to Abraham?

4. Why is Abraham willing to obey God here? What would you have done?

5. What person or thing or goal is most important in your life? Would you be willing to sacrifice that if God asked you to?

HONOR AND PRIVILEGE

Warm-up

1. Has someone ever stolen the praise or glory which was rightfully yours? What happened? How did you react?

2. If you were about to become the world champion in your sport, would you give up that title in exchange for a bowl of soup? What would you think of someone who did that?

Workout

Genesis 25:19-34

3. Why is Jacob so determined to steal Esau's birthright here? Why is Esau so careless about keeping it?

4. Whose sin was worse: Jacob's for stealing the birthright, or Esau's for treating it with contempt?

5. What is your birthright as a Christian? Are you treating it as a precious gift, or selling it for quick pleasures?

GAME PLAN

GAME PLAN

No athletic endeavor is complete without a detailed game plan... one made well in advance of the game! So it is with the Christian life: it is important for each of us to know in advance what we will do when faced with temptations or trials. In this section we will address that topic, helping you to know what to do whether you're in the middle of a big match or on a night out with friends.

Spend some time reflecting on this idea as you go through the following Scripture passages, considering the questions that we have provided.

GAME PLAN

Warm-up

1. When your coach comes up with a plan that seems strange to you, what is your response?

2. When have you felt that your team won a victory, not because of you, but in spite of you?

Workout

Exodus 13:17–14:31

3. Imagine yourself with the Israelites, seeing Pharaoh's army marching toward you. How would you have reacted?

4. What lessons did the Israelites learn from this experience?

5. Is God asking you to trust him in some area? How will you respond?

 **GAME PLAN**

BLIND SPOTS

Warm-up

1. Have you ever gotten upset with a coach or teammate who was trying to help you? How did you feel afterwards?

2. Who are the people who have helped you most to discover and fix your "blind spots" in your game? What are those blind spots?

Workout

Numbers 22:21-41

3. What is suggested by the fact that Balaam couldn't see the angel but his donkey could?

4. Why is the Lord angry with Balaam here?

5. What is the Lord trying to make you see in your own life? What "donkeys" is he using to open your eyes?

MIRACLE GAME

Warm-up

1. What game have you seen or participated in that was won or lost because of unusual weather conditions?

2. Which game have you participated in that took the longest or had most overtime?

Workout

Joshua 10:1-14

3. According to this passage, what is the great miracle which God performed for the Israelites? How could this have happened?

4. Why does God choose to do this?

5. What great miracle do you need in your life? Do you believe that the God who makes the sun stand still can answer your prayers?

GAME PLAN

TEAMWORK

Warm-up

1. When have you spent time to help a weaker teammate? Who has done that for you?

2. What athlete do you know of who has overcome physical disability in his sport?

Workout

2 Samuel 9:1-13

3. Why does David treat Mephibosheth with such honor? What does this reveal of David's character?

4. Who do you know who needs special mercy or grace? How can you be merciful and gracious to others this week?

POWER GAME

Warm-up

1. When have you seen a team or an athlete that exhibited great power? What was your reaction as you watched?

2. Have you ever been at a game with players or spectators from all over the world? What was it like?

Workout

Acts 2:1-13

3. If you had been present for this scene, how would you have reacted?

4. Why do you think the Holy Spirit appeared as tongues like flames?

5. How can the power of the Holy Spirit change your life this week?

GAME PLAN

BROTHERS IN SPORT

Warm-up

1. Have you or a friend ever experienced racial or ethnic bigotry in sports? What happened?

2. How have people of various races contributed to your sport?

Workout

Acts 10:9-48

3. What is God trying to tell Peter through his strange vision?

4. How does Peter immediately put this lesson into practice?

5. In what areas do you need to become more accepting of people from different racial or ethnic backgrounds?

ATHLETE STUDIES

WEAKNESS

Warm-up

1. How have you experienced or witnessed the frailty of the human body? What happened?

2. When have you felt during a competition as though your team were being hopelessly crushed?

Workout

2 Corinthians 4:1-18

3. What does Paul mean when he says "we have this treasure in clay jars" (v.7)? What is the treasure? What are the jars of clay?

4. Where does Paul find encouragement in this passage?

5. How can you focus on "what is unseen" this week?

GAME PLAN

GOD'S GAMEPLAN

Warm-up

1. When has your coach or trainer made a gameplan that seemed doomed to fail?

2. Did you follow that gameplan? Did it work?

Workout

Genesis 6:9-22

3. What is God's game plan in this passage? Why is He doing it?

4. It may be that it had never rained on earth prior to the flood (see 2:5). What sort of mockery and abuse might Noah have endured while building the ark?

5. Are you willing to follow God's game plan, even if it seems difficult or strange?

TOUGH CHOICES

Warm-up

1. Which is more important: good players or a good plan? Why?

2. If God allowed you to have one request fulfilled, what would you ask for?

Workout

1 Kings 3:4-14

3. Why does Solomon ask for wisdom?

4. Why do you think God gave Solomon riches and honor along with his wisdom?

5. Ask God for wisdom and He will grant it (see James 1:5).

 **GAME PLAN**

RISK IT ALL

Warm-up

1. What is the greatest risk you have ever taken for your sport?

2. What athlete do you know of who sacrificed his all for his team?

Workout

Esther 4:1-17

3. What is Esther's danger in this passage? What danger do the Jews face?

4. How might Esther have avoided danger if she'd chosen to? What would have been the outcome then?

5. Would you be willing to risk your life for Christ? Is he calling you to take some risks for his sake this week?

POWER OR SKILL?

Warm-up

1. Who is the most powerful athlete you know? What has he accomplished?

2. When have you seen a team or an athlete greatly affected by something that seemed insignificant?

 ### Workout

Zechariah 4:6-10

3. What does the Lord mean by his question in verse 10, "who scorns the day of small things?"

4. What does he mean in verse 6, "not by strength or by might, but by My Spirit"?

5. In what ways have you tried to live by your own power rather than by the Spirit's power? How can you change this?

GAME PLAN

TEAM PARTS

Warm-up

1. What person or job on your team is the least "significant?" What impact would it have on the team if that person were not there?

2. What person or job on your team is most glamorous? What impact would it have on the team if that person were not there?

3. What part of your body is least "significant?" What would your life be like if that part were missing?

Workout

1 Corinthians 12:12-31

4. What part of the Christian body are you? What service do you provide to the rest of the body?

5. Does your attitude need to change toward your teammates, based on the passage? Toward yourself?

TEAM UNITY

Warm-up

1. How do you treat teammates when you see ways that they can improve? How well do you receive such criticism from others?

2. How do you feel about your coach or trainer? Do you show respect and appreciation, or do you resent the hard work and criticism?

Workout

Galatians 6:1-10

3. According to this passage, how are we to approach fellow Christians who need to improve their walk with God? How should we react when others approach us?

4. What should be our attitude toward those who teach and lead us in our Christian walk? How can you apply this practically?

GAME PLAN

SWEAT AND HUMILITY

Warm-up

1. Do you know any athletes who view themselves as "shining stars?" How do you view yourself?

2. Do you give 100 percent at every game and practice? Or do you try to avoid excessive work and sweat?

Workout

Philippians 2:1-18

3. What does Paul mean in verses 12 and 13, "work out your own salvation with fear and trembling"?

4. In practical terms, how can you be more humble, considering others better than yourself?

5. How will you implement these things in your life this week?

OBEDIENCE

Warm-up

1. What discipline, exercise, or training for your sport do you find unpleasant?

2. When your coach or trainer tells you to do something that you really don't want to do, how do you generally react? What has happened in the past when you have disregarded the coach's advice?

3. What have you found to be helpful in working through the pain or fatigue of practice?

Workout

Jonah 1:1-17

4. What lessons on obedience did Jonah learn? How would his life have been different if he had not run away from the Lord?

5. Is there an area of your life where you are running away from God or disobeying Him? How can you change that in the coming week?

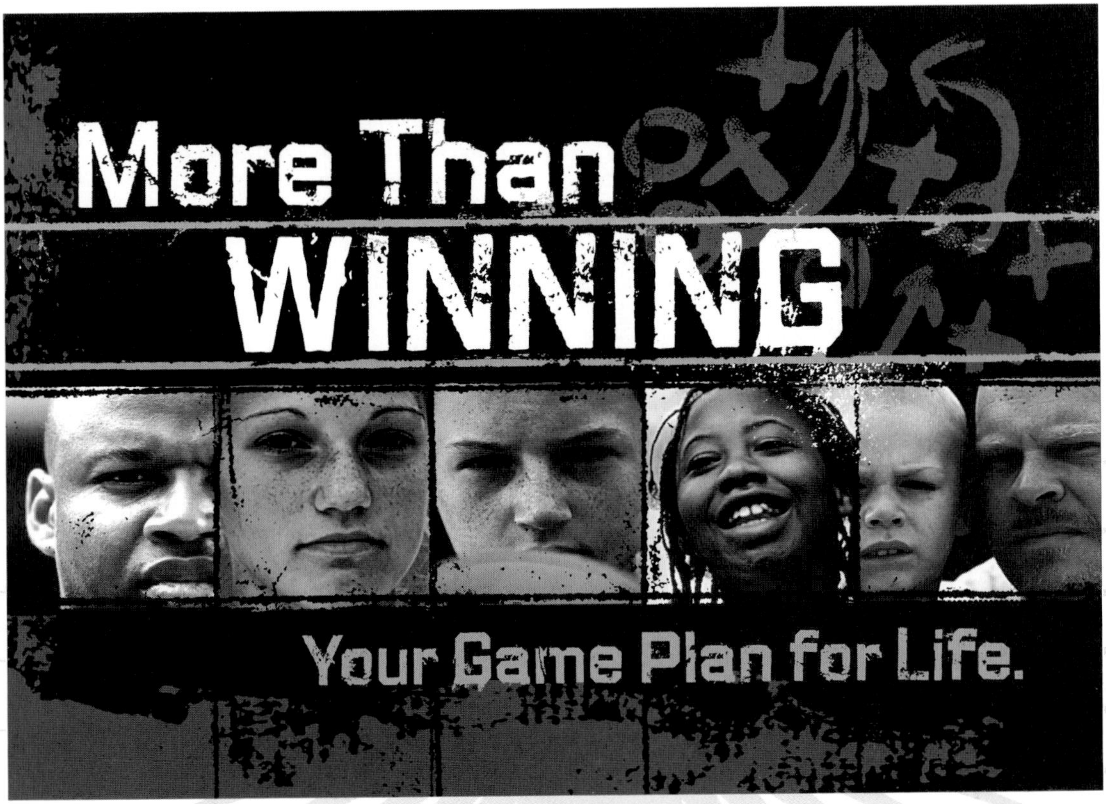

More Than **WINNING**

Your Game Plan for Life.

GOD'S PLAN

In most athletic contests a coach prepares a game plan ahead of time. God designed a plan for our lives before the world began.

God is holy and perfect. He created us to love him, glorify him, and enjoy him forever.

WHAT IS GOD'S STANDARD?

The Bible, God's playbook, says that the standard for being on his team is to:

Be holy.
"Be holy because I am holy"-1 Peter 1:16

Be perfect.
"Be perfect, therefore, as your heavenly Father is perfect"-Matthew 5:48

WHAT IS GOD'S PLAN?

God created us to:

Love Him.
"He said to him, 'Love the Lord your God with all your heart, with all your soul, and with all your mind.'"-Matthew 22:37

Glorify (honor) Him.
"Our Lord and God, You are worthy to receive glory and honor and power, because You have created all things, and because of Your will they exist and were created."-Revelation 4:11

Enjoy Him forever.
Jesus said, *"...I have come that they may have life and have it in abundance"*
                                        -John 10:10

Why is it that we cannot live up to God's standard of holiness and perfection and fulfill God's plan for our lives?
Because of...

Love Him
Glorify Him
Enjoy Him forever

HOLY GOD

LIFE PLAYBOOK

MAN'S PROBLEM

Man is sinful and is separated from God.

WHAT IS SIN?

Sin means missing the mark, falling short of God's standard. It is not only doing wrong and failing to do what God wants (lying, gossip, losing our temper, lustful thoughts, etc.), but it is also an attitude of ignoring or rejecting God which is a result of our sinful nature.

"Indeed, I was guilty when I was born..."
-Psalm 51:5

WHO HAS SINNED?

"For all have sinned and fall short of the glory of God."-Romans 3:23

WHAT'S THE RESULT OF SIN?

Separation from God.
"But your iniquities have built barriers between you and your God..."-Isaiah 59:2

Death.
"For the wages of sin is death"
-Romans 6:23

Judgment.
"...just as it is appointed for people to die once—and after this, judgment"
-Hebrews 9:27

This illustration shows that God is holy and we are sinful and separated from him. Man continually tries to reach God through his own efforts (being good, religious activities, philosophy, etc.) but, while these can be good things, they all fall short of God's standard.

"All of us have become like something unclean, and all our righteous acts are like a polluted garment"-Isaiah 64:6

There is only one way to bridge this gap between God and man...

GOD'S SUBSTITUTE

God provided the only way to be on His team by sending His son, Jesus Christ, as the holy and perfect substitute to die in our place.

WHO IS JESUS CHRIST?

He is God.
Jesus said, *"The Father and I are one"*
-John 10:30

He is Man.
"...the Word (Jesus) was God...The Word became flesh and took up residence among us"-John 1:1,14

WHAT HAS JESUS DONE?

He died as our substitute.
"God proves His own love for us in that while we were still sinners Christ died for us"-Romans 5:8

He rose from the dead.
"...Christ died for our sins..he was buried...he was raised on the third day according to the Scriptures and...he appeared to Cephas, then to the Twelve. Then He appeared to over 500 brothers at one time..."-1 Corinthians 15:3-6

He is the only way to God.
"I am the way, the truth, and the life. No one comes to the Father except through Me"-John 14:6

This diagram shows that God has bridged the gap between himself and man by sending Jesus Christ to die in our place as our substitute. Jesus defeated sin and death and rose from the grave. Yet, it isn't enough just to know these facts. *The following page tells how to become part of God's team and experience His plan...*

MAN'S RESPONSE

Knowing a lot about a sport and "talking the game" doesn't make you a member of a team. The same is true in becoming a Christian. It takes more than just knowing about Jesus Christ; it requires a total commitment by faith in Him.

FAITH IS NOT:

Just knowing the facts.
"You believe that God is one; you do well. The demons also believe—and they shudder."-James 2:19

Just an emotional experience.
Raising your hand or repeating a prayer is not enough.

FAITH IS:

Repenting.
Turning to God from sin.
"godly grief produces a repentance not to be regretted and leading to salvation..."
-2 Corinthians 7:10

Receiving Jesus Christ.
Trusting in Christ alone for salvation.
"But to all who did receive Him, He gave them the right to be children of God, to those who believe in His name..."
-John 1:12,13

Look at the diagram-
On which side do you see yourself? Where would you like to be?

Jesus said, "I assure you: Anyone who hears My word and believes Him who sent Me has eternal life and will not come under judgment but has passed from death to life."-John 5:24

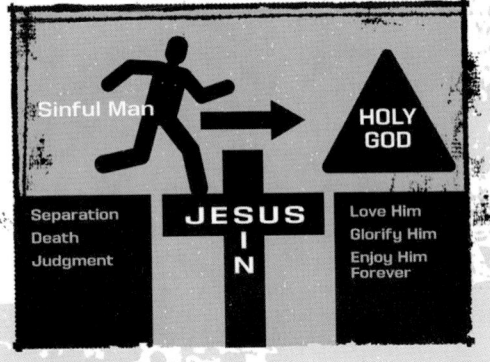

LIFE PLAYBOOK

REPLAY OF GOD'S PLAN

 REalize God is holy and perfect; we are sinners and cannot save ourselves.

 REcognize who Jesus is and what He's done as our substitute.

 REceive Jesus Christ by faith as Savior and Lord.
"But to all who did receive Him, He gave them the right to become children of God, to those who believe in His name..."-John 1:12,13

 REspond to Jesus Christ in a life of obedience.
"If anyone wants to come with me, he must deny himself, take up his cross daily, and follow Me."-Jesus, Luke 9:23

Does God's plan make sense to you? Are you willing to repent and receive Jesus Christ?

If so, express to God your need for him. Consider the "Suggested Prayer of Commitment" on the next page. Remember that God is more concerned with your attitude than with the words you say.

Suggested
PRAYER OF COMMITMENT

"Lord Jesus, I need you. I realize I'm a sinner and I can't save myself. I need your forgiveness. I believe that you loved me so much that you died on the cross for my sins and rose from the dead. I repent of my sins and put my faith in you as Savior and Lord. Take control of my life and help me to follow you in obedience. I love you Jesus. In Jesus' name, Amen."

"...If you confess with your mouth, 'Jesus is Lord', and believe in your heart that God raised Him from the dead, you will be saved...for 'Everyone who calls on the name of the Lord will be saved'"
-Romans 10:9,10,13

Once you have committed your life to Jesus Christ, it is important to understand what your position is on this team...

KNOW YOUR POSITION

Too many people make the mistake of measuring the certainty of their salvation by their feelings instead of the facts of God's Word. In Jesus Christ you have a new life. See what God's Word says about your new position on his team...

N I am a New Creation in Christ.
2 Corinthians 5:17; Galatians 2:20

E I have Everything I need for life and godliness.
2 Peter 1:3; Ephesians 1:3

W I am a Witness for Christ and am His Workmanship, created for good works.
Acts 1:8; Ephesians 2:10

L I am Loved and accepted completely in Christ.
Ephesians 1:6; Romans 8:39

I I am Indwelt by the Holy Spirit.
1 Corinthians 6:19, 20; 1 John 4:4

F I am Forgiven and Free from condemnation.
1 John 1:9; Romans 8:1-2

E I have Eternal Life in Christ.
John 5:24; 1 John 5:11-13

Trust God! Put your faith in His Word, not in your feelings: *"I have written these things to you who believe in the name of the Son of God, so that you may know that you have eternal life."*
-1 John 5:13

4 DAILY EXERCISES

Just as physical growth demands physical exercise, spiritual growth as a Christian demands spiritual exercise. To build spiritual muscle here are four daily exercises.

1. Daily Seek Christ.
Spend time every day reading God's Word and devoting time in prayer.

"...they welcomed the message with eagerness and examined the Scriptures daily to see if these things were so."-Acts 17:11

"I praise You seven times a day..."-Psalms 119:164

2. Daily Share Christ.

Share Jesus every day through your words and actions.

"Every day in the temple complex, and in various homes, they continued teaching and proclaiming the good news that the Messiah is Jesus."
                                                    -Acts 5:42

"Therefore, we are ambassadors for Christ; certain that God is appealing through us."
                                        -2 Corinthians 5:20

3. Daily Lead Others.

Lead others by serving as Christ did. Every day die to self and yield complete control of your life to Jesus Christ.

"The greatest among you will be your servant."
                                                -Matt 23:11

"If anyone wants to come with Me, he must deny himself, take up his cross daily, and follow Me."
                                                -Luke 9:23

4. Daily Love Others.

Take every opportunity to show others around you that you love them.

"...love your neighbor as yourself..."-Mark 12:33

"But encourage each other daily, while it is still called today..."-Heb 3:13

Do these exercises and you will grow strong in your Christian life and be an effective member of God's team.

FELLOWSHIP OF CHRISTIAN ATHLETES

☐ I just received Jesus Christ into my life. Please send me information on how to grow in my new relationship with Him.

☐ I rededicated my life to Jesus Christ. Please send me information that will strengthen me as a Christian.

☐ I've read this booklet, and still have questions about what it means to receive Christ and live for Him. Please send me information that will give me answers I need.

My Name:_____ Grad.Year: _____

Address:_____

City/State/Zip:_____

Phone #: _____ Email: _____

Complete and mail today to:
FCA • 8701 Leeds Road • Kansas City, MO 64129-1680

TO ORDER *MORE THAN WINNING* BOOKLETS OR OTHER GREAT FCA RESOURCES, GO TO FCAGEAR.COM

LIFE PLAYBOOK

FOR THE GLORY™
NOW & FOREVER
JUDE 24-25

THE STARTING LINE
MY NEW LIFE IN CHRIST

THE FIRST STEPS IN BUILDING A STRONG FOUNDATION FOR YOUR FAITH

LIFE PLAYBOOK

READY

Remember the day that Coach was going to post the list of those who made the team. You were pretty sure you had a good tryout. You worked extremely hard in the off-season. But as you drove to school with your friends, you just wondered ...

What were the emotions you felt ... **if you made the team**?
What did this mean to you, your friends, and your family?

What were the emotions you felt ... **if you didn't make the team**? What did this mean to you, your friends, and your family?

As athletes, we have a strong desire to compete—whether we are trying to make the team, make the cut, or help put our team in the tournament. God puts that desire in our hearts, because the athlete's heart is never satisfied until the contest is won. That is one of the greatest things God uses to draw us to Himself.

God is the "ultimate prize," the only thing that really satisfies our desires. When God moves into our hearts, we are launched from death into new life.

SET

There are some major differences between striving to win a competition and gaining the prize of becoming alive in a relationship with Jesus Christ.

Read Ephesians 2:1-10.

Here are the **three points** related to the "ultimate prize" that God has given to us.

To be added to His roster demands simply trusting in the work done by Jesus Christ on the cross (on our behalf). God even gives us the faith to respond to the gift that He has offered.

1. The "ultimate prize" was based solely on **GOD'S LOVE** for us (verses 1-4).

   The opportunity for salvation is based in God's character. Fill in the following blanks about God.

   a. Because of His great _____ that He had for _____

   b. God, who is abundant (or rich) in _____

   c. A definition of mercy is

   We have not earned this special privilege. We have not accomplished any great feats to make us worthy of God's gift. He gives out of the goodness of His heart and the mystery of His will.

2. We have been saved by **GRACE** (verses 4-5).

   What was our condition before this grace?

   If grace means "a free, undeserved gift," rewrite verses 4 and 5 in your own words.

   God chose us to be on His team, providing salvation as a gift because He is a loving God who chose to make us the recipients of His love. We play and serve on His team, even though we can never develop the skills or talent to make it on our own.

3. We need to respond to His gift with **FAITH** (verses 8-9).

   How does someone receive salvation?

What is true of this salvation? What is not true?

Now write Ephesians 2:8-9 in your own words.

GO

We were born sinful—objects of God's wrath. Yet, it was God who provided the ultimate prize of a right relationship with Him. We can enjoy the benefits of being on God's team and being part of His family because of His love for us.

Read Romans 8:14-17.

List the incredible privileges that accompany this new relationship of being on God's team.

List the responsibilities too.

How will the confidence of knowing your Heavenly Father affect you at home? In school? At practice? Hanging out with your teammates?

READY

Time is a factor in every sport. There are 60-minute games, 30-second time-outs, three-second lane violations, two outs in the bottom of the ninth, two-minute warnings. In all sports the clock controls the movement, as well as the end, of the game or match.

Have you ever had the clock run out on you or your team when all you needed was a little more time to win? List three emotions that you felt and how they did or could have affected your performance.

Describe a game or match where you or your team made changes based upon being up or down on the scoreboard with little time to play. What were the adjustments you had to make?

You may never have thought about it, but someday you will see the end of life. During that time, you may even think back to the days of your sport when you were facing the end of some competition. As an athlete, God can use those times now to prepare you to handle real-life issues where a real end is coming.

SET

It is true that time controls competitions and our lives. Death is the end of this game we call life. All of us will experience it. It buzzes as the ultimate time clock. But we only see life within the constraints of time. But, Jesus died so that even when we pass from this life, we can live with Him forever. God grants eternal life to those who accept Jesus Christ as Savior and Lord! Imagine that!

Read John 3:16, Romans 6:23, and 1 John 5:11. What does the Bible say that God promises us?

Read 1 Corinthians 15:42-58. What does this passage say about our bodies now and in the future?

When will this change happen?

Read Revelation 21:1-5. List at least five cool things about this eternal life.

GO

2 Peter 3:10-15 reveals to us how knowing that we have eternal life should affect our life on earth.

What will be destroyed?

Considering what will be destroyed and what will last, how should we live? How will this affect who we are on and off the field of competition when it comes to:

Being without spot or blemish?

Living in peace with Him?

God had no beginning nor will He ever end. He does not need air, food, or water to exist. He created them for us. How does that thought make you feel? Take a minute to write your thoughts to God about His greatness, and about spending eternity with Him.

It is because God is eternal that we can have eternal life. We cannot create eternal life on our own. Praise Him today as you practice, play, and live!

READY

Have you been in a situation with the game on the line when your number is called? You make the free throw or you don't. You make the penalty kick or your don't. You make the hole big enough so the four yards can be gained or you don't. You make a birdie or you don't. If you succeed, you win; if you don't, you lose. You either become the hero or the goat.

Describe a time when you made the shot or were very important to the success of your team. What were the emotions you felt? What preparation went into that success?

Describe a time when you did not come through and how you felt. What did it feel like to be the goat? What broke down?

God puts the desire to not be the "goat" in our hearts as athletes so we can understand how our relationship with Him works. If you blow the free-throw, you are not off the team, but it may affect your relationship with your teammates and coach. If you blow it in life with God, it could affect your communication with Him and effectiveness in life.

SET

In living for God, it may seem we drop the ball a lot. In critical times, when we need to love someone, we treat him or her badly. When our thoughts need to be pure, we lust. When we should tell the truth, we lie. When we should honor our parents by listening to their advice, we do our own thing. When we should give our all during practice, we give in to comfort and "dog it." When we should love God and our neighbor, we ignore them. It doesn't have to be this way, but it sure seems to happen too often.

Before Christ was in our lives, even our best efforts were sinful. But because Christ has taken care of our sin before God, we have a chance to lead a holy life. Our sinful nature has been covered, now we spend the rest of our lives growing to be more like Christ.

Sin is missing the mark, like shooting for a bull's eye and missing. God has a bull's eye that we miss regularly. Those who do not have Christ in their lives will never have the opportunity to hit the mark, but those who do know Christ have the chance to do things right … even when we miss!

LIFE PLAYBOOK

FORGIVENESS

The thought of missing God's mark could leave you in despair and feeling like you should get off of God's team. But, God is a forgiving God. Once we have asked Christ into our lives, He releases us from the guilt of our sin and cancels the debt we owe. Now it is just a matter of having an open communication with Him who is without sin. Our salvation is secure, but our communication can be clouded and our effectiveness weakened when we miss the mark.

Let's look at the forgiveness of God in the Bible.

Before forgiveness our best efforts are sinful. Read Romans 3:23. What does it say about our sinful nature?

With a relationship with Christ, things change. Read 2 Corinthians 5:17. Once we are in Christ, how are things different?

Our relationship with God is kept open through confession. Rephrase 1 John 1:9 in your own words.

Unforgiveness toward others can be a trap of the devil and hinder God's work in your life. Read 2 Corinthians 2:5-11, Matthew 6:14-15, and Matthew 18:21-35. Why is forgiving others so important to God?

LIFE PLAYBOOK

GO

What does God require of us? How do we receive His forgiveness?

The Answer: Confession and Repentance.

Read 1 John 1:9 again. To confess means "to agree with."

Read Romans 2:4-6. Repent means "to change our mind or purpose" and to "turn and go the other way." So we are to agree with God that what we did was wrong. We are to turn from our way and to go His way.

How will you remember to confess your sins today?

We are to forgive as we have been forgiven. Read Ephesians 4:32-5:2. Who on your team do you need to forgive? Who in your family do you need to forgive? Which of your friends do you need to forgive?

Warning: Ask God to help you forgive those who have hurt you. Unforgiveness will make us bitter and angry. It will deeply affect us on and off the field.

LIFE PLAYBOOK

THE HOLY SPIRIT

READY

Have you ever been given bad advice on the field? What about good advice? When and what was it?

If you ever have taken bad advice or counsel, what was the outcome for you or your team?

What was the best advice you ever have taken?

The understanding that we don't know everything is one of the most important lessons in life. We spend hours in practice—hopefully those hours are spent listening and trying to figure out how to get better. The fact that an athlete listens to a coach prepares the athlete to listen to God in a unique way.

LIFE PLAYBOOK

SET

Wouldn't it be nice if Jesus walked the earth today! What if we got to hang out with Him all the time? What if we could ask Him about how to handle the strains in life? What if He could go to practice with us, help us with homework or even hang out with us and our friends?

Sometimes it might be a bit uncomfortable to have Him around because of bad choices we or the people around us make. But that discomfort is good, because that is Him reminding us to keep our lives on the right track.

Jesus knew that He needed to be around because without Him it would be impossible for His disciples and for us. In fact, Jesus knew that without His power in our lives, we were doomed in trying to walk with Him.

Read John 1:12 and Romans 8:12-17. Whose child does that make us?

Read John 14:16-18, 24-25 and John 16:7-14. Who did Jesus say was coming after Him as His representative?

What are some words used by Jesus in these passages to describe the Holy Spirit?

GO

What a list! Because God loves us so much, we have been given the Holy Spirit! The Holy Spirit is with us 24/7. The role of the Holy Spirit is to be our Counselor, Comforter, and Guide. Describe a time in the past week when you were with the team where you could have relied more on the Holy Spirit in His role as:

Counselor

Comforter

Guide

Describe a time in the past week when you were with friends or family where you could have relied more on the Holy Spirit in His role as:

Counselor

Comforter

Guide

The greatest encouragement in the Christian life is that whatever God is asking us to do, He enables us to do it through the power of the Holy Spirit!

Coaches want us to stop, listen, and then do what they taught us. This is called being "led by" the coach. When we obey, we have a much better chance at being successful. The Holy Spirit serves as our coach and trainer in every area of life. He speaks to us through His Spirit. Our response to Him needs to be to stop, listen, and then do what He teaches us. When we listen and obey, we will have success in God's game of life.

Read Galatians 5:16-23. What does it mean to "walk by the Spirit" or "in the Spirit"?

According to Galatians, what can we accomplish if we do?

Which desires of your sinful flesh (or sinful nature) do you need to overcome on the field and in life?

How are wrong desires affecting you in your performance on the field?

How are wrong desires affecting you in life with your teammates? Friends? Family?

Take a moment to ask the Holy Spirit to do the following:
> Teach me once again in these areas that I have listed.
> Lead me in the right direction.
> Give me your strength and peace today as I obey.

READY

Every sport has its basic fundamentals to learn. The basic fundamentals sometimes can be unexciting and difficult to master. But, mastering the basics is vital for success in every sport.

What are three or four of the basic fundamentals of your position and/or sport that you have mastered?

Why do you want to master the basics?

How has learning a basic helped you in your performance?

SET

Your desire as an athlete to master the fundamentals of your sport can be used by God in a perfect way to develop a growing relationship with Him. Just like in sports, the Christian life has its basics to learn. Below are three Christian basics that will be essential for your Christian life.

Bible Study

To gain all the benefits of your new life in Christ, you need to know God (Father, Son, and Holy Spirit). That means spending time getting to know God and learning from Him. To know Him is to be intimately acquainted with Him. We spend time with Him through His Word, the Bible. When we study in His Word and obey it, He reveals Himself to us. That is a promise from Christ Himself.

Read John 14:21-23. What did Jesus say would happen to those who obey His commandments (in the Bible)?

Read 2 Timothy 3:16-17 and list the four benefits the Bible will add to your life.

Which of these do you need most and why?

Studying the Bible can be like studying a complicated playbook. The book looks overwhelming and almost impossible to understand. But, if you learn the basic principles that cause each play to work, then the plays become easier to understand and to execute. The same applies to the Bible. When you learn the basics you will be surprised at how much more you will understand.

LIFE PLAYBOOK

Now turn to page 73 in this Game Plan section for How to Read and Study the Bible, plus page 13 of this section for doing a Quiet Time. Using this PRESS method will make your study of the Bible more effective. To practice these steps turn to John 15:1-11 and write what you learned and what you will apply to your life.

Prayer

In Bible study, we get to know God and listen to Him, but prayer is our opportunity to communicate with God. When we approach God, we should approach Him as our King AND as our friend. God knows everything about you, so there should be no holding back. It makes no sense to attempt to hide things from Him. When you pray to be real, be relaxed, and be revealing (tell Him all). Remember to listen to what He wants to tell you too.

Jesus gave us a model for prayer in His Sermon on the Mount. This prayer is not to be repeated to "get on His good side" or to show that we are "religious," but it should reflect the attitude of our hearts.

Read Matthew 6:5-15. Rephrase the prayer (verses 9-13) in your own words.

What things did Jesus pray for? How can you pray in the same way for your life?

Start recording the things you learn and pray in a journal. All you need is a pad of paper, a pen, and an open heart. The journal will help keep you focused, plus allow you to look back to see how you have grown and how God has worked in your life.

Church

Not being an active member of a local church is like playing on a soccer or volleyball team all by yourself. You will get killed spiritually if you try to play a team game without a team. God never meant for us to play the game of life by ourselves and you certainly can't stand alone in the Christian life. Never forget that Christianity is a team sport. We need the help, talent, and encouragement of our teammates to withstand the offensive of our enemy—the devil of Hell (Hades). Jesus told Peter, "on this rock (Peter's confession of faith in Jesus as the promised Savior, the Messiah) I will build My church, and the forces of Hades will not overcome it." (Matthew 16:18)

Read Matthew 16:13-18. What insights do you see in this passage about faith or the church?

Anyone who has trusted Christ as Savior and Lord is part of the church. The church crosses denomina-

tional lines and encompasses all true believers in Christ. As a master builder of churches, the apostle Paul addressed his team at Corinth about playing and working together. Read his instruction to that team in 1 Corinthians 12:12-31. What important truths do you see about teamwork in the church?

What gifts, talents, and resources has God blessed you with that you will contribute to your church?

Church involvement is vital to spiritual growth. In fact, the Bible directs us to become involved in a local church. Read Hebrews 10:24-25. What does this passage say about meeting together and what should we do when we meet?

GO

Pick a time each day that you will set aside to pray and read your Bible. As you have certain routines for stretching, weightlifting, and sports practice, so you will need a routine to grow in Bible study and prayer.

What will be your regular time set aside for time with the Lord?

How will this make you a better athlete? Student? Friend? Son or daughter?

If you do not have a church to attend, find somebody on your team who goes to church regularly. Who are some solid church attenders you know?

Ask them if the church talks about the Bible a lot and if there is a good youth group. Then, see if you can go with them.

If you do attend a church, what will you do to be more involved? Be sure to consider the unique gifts God has given you to use.

Be proactive! Go to the leaders of your church and tell them you want to be involved. Ask them to suggest some areas and give them some of your ideas too.

LIFE PLAYBOOK

A LIFE OF VICTORY

READY

Athletes always are striving for perfection. The perfecting of a skill and the attaining of a goal motivates any athlete. Blood, sweat, and tears are essential for success.

What has been the hardest technique for you to learn and why has it been so hard? Explain what it took to learn it.

What did it feel like when you finally learned the technique?

Once you have learned a technique, what does it take to maintain the high level of effectiveness you have achieved?

SET

Victory over sin in your life will be a lot like the perfecting of a skill and the maintaining of that skill. It will take blood, sweat and tears in faith, commitment, prayer, and obedience.

List the sin(s) that are affecting your athletic performance. Sin can be laziness, fear, lack of respect for a coach, abusing your body with drugs or alcohol, etc. Are there additional sins in your life off the field?

Here are three things you can do in order to have victory over sin in your life. Like a muscle that needs constant work to stay strong, these things will need constant exercise or you will become weak spiritually.

Trust in what God has done on your behalf.

Read 2 Peter 1:3-4. What has been given to us as believers in Christ?

LIFE PLAYBOOK

What two things is this power provided for?

What do we get to share or participate in? What do we get to escape or avoid?

Pray for your heart and mind to be pure toward God.

Read James 5:13-16. What are the results of prayer?

Do what the Bible tells you. Action is necessary. What you know in your head has got to get to your feet and hands. The goal in athletics is to learn a skill so well that when the game is being played you do naturally what you learned. Doing is necessary in gaining victory over sin.

Read Romans 6:11-13. What does this passage in Romans tell us not to do? What does it tell to do?

What does it mean to you to have your body as a "weapon (or instrument) for righteousness"?

GO

Psalm 19:14 encourages us to ask God to make our words and thoughts acceptable to Him. Write a prayer to God about the words of your mouth and the meditations of your heart. Consider your mouth and heart in all aspects of your life: school, practice, friends, games/competition, family, etc.

Confide in a trusted friend or teammate about the struggles you have and the areas of sin you want to gain victory over. Accountability will be very helpful toward success. Even more important than the earthly friend is God. Remember that God is with you wherever you are, so lean on Him for strength.

Which of your friends and teammates could you ask to help you be accountable for the way you talk and live?

1.

2.

3.

OW2P! COMMITMENT

I'VE MADE THE COMMITMENT!

I've accepted the challenge to strive for excellence as a student athlete by choosing the **One Way 2 Play—Drug Free!** lifestyle!

Faith in Jesus Christ.

We believe Christ forgives us, gives us the wisdom to make good decisions, and the strength to carry them out.

Commitment to say NO! to alcohol and drugs.

We pledge to be strong in our commitment and to help others be strong, too.

Accountability to one another.

We will regularly ask each other the five hard questions.

The Five Hard Questions:

1. Are you living and playing alcohol and drug free?
2. Are you encouraging others to live and play that way?
3. Are you being honest with at least one mature person about your feelings and temptations?
4. Are you trusting Christ to meet your needs?
5. Are you honoring Him in your thoughts, words, and actions?

I, _____ MADE MY
   (name)

ONE WAY 2 PLAY—DRUG FREE!

COMMITMENT ON _____.
                    (date)

HOW TO READ AND STUDY THE BIBLE

The Bible is God's living Word. It's alive and will come alive in your life as you read it.

The Bible is divided into two sections:

THE OLD TESTAMENT
These are 39 books written before Jesus walked on Earth as a man.

17   historical books (creation of man and Israel's history)
5   poetic & wisdom books
17   prophetic books

THE NEW TESTAMENT
These 27 books were written after Jesus died and rose from the dead.

5   historical books (life and teach of Jesus and His disciples)
13   books known as Paul's Epistles (or lLetters)
9   books that are called the General Epistles (or Letters)

A good way to study the Bible is to keep a notebook, and as you read, ask these questions:

1. Who is speaking?
2. What's the setting?
3. What's happening?
4. What are the main points?
5. How does it apply to me?

If you are just beginning to study the Bible, Matthew, Mark, Luke, and John are good books to start with. These four books begin the New Testament and are known as the Gospels. They were written by men who knew Jesus personally.

On pages 1531-1532 of this Life Playbook section, you'll find two reference lists that will help you locate some topics covered in the Bible. You can also search for Bible passages using the Study Plans in the front of this Bible or the Subject/People and Places/Dictionary-Concordance indices that begin on page 1284. These lists can be very helpful as you seek out what God has to say on a particular issue.

LIFE PLAYBOOK

MY NEW IDENTITY IN CHRIST!

Therefore if anyone is in Christ, there is a new creation; old things have passed away, and look, new things have come.—2 Corinthians 5:17

What good news! If you're a believer in Christ, you've become new, spiritually, and the following is already true of you:

You are a new creation ...

- You were crucified with Christ. You no longer live, spiritually, but Christ lives in you. The life you are now living is Christ's life (Galatians 2:20).
- You died with Christ, spiritually, and died to the power of sin's rule over your life (Romans 6:1-7).
- You've been given the mind of Christ (1 Corinthians 2:16).
- Christ Himself is in you (Colossians 1:27).
- You've been forgiven of all your sins. The debt of sin against you has been canceled (Colossians 1:13-14).
- You've already been made complete in Christ (Colossians 2:10).
- You've been given a spirit of power, love and self-discipline (2 Timothy 1:7).

You are accepted ...

- You are God's child (John 1:12).
- You are Christ's friend (John 15:15).
- You are united with Christ, and one with Him in spirit (1 Corinthians 6:17).
- You've been bought with a price. You belong to God (1 Corinthians 6:19-20).
- You are a member of Christ's body (1 Corinthians 12:27).
- You are holy and blameless (Ephesians 1:4).
- You've been adopted as God's child (Ephesians 1:5).
- You have direct access to God through the Holy Spirit (Ephesians 2:18).
- You may approach God with freedom and confidence (Ephesians 3:12).

You are secure ...

- You are free forever from condemnation (Romans 8:1).
- You can be assured that all things in your life will work together for good (Romans 8:28).
- You can never be separated from the love of God (Romans 8:35-39).
- You are hidden with Christ in God (Colossians 3:3).
- The good work that God has begun in you will be completed (Philippians 1:6).
- You are a citizen of heaven (Philippians 3:20).
- You will find grace and mercy in time of need (Hebrews 4:16).
- You are born of God, and the Evil One cannot touch you (1 John 5:18).

You are significant ...

- You are the salt and light of the earth (Matthew 5:13-16).
- You are a branch of the true vine, a channel of His life (John 15:5).
- You have been chosen and appointed to bear fruit (John 15:16).
- You are a personal witness of Christ's (Acts 1:8).
- You are God's temple (1 Corinthians 3:16).
- You are seated with Christ in the heavenly realm (Ephesians 2:6).
- You are God's "work of art," created to do good works (Ephesians 2:10).
- You can do all things through Christ who will give you strength (Philippians 4:13).

Adapted from Living Free In Christ and Victory Over The Darkness

WHERE TO FIND HELP WHEN YOU ...

... face a superior opponent—**Proverbs 21:31; 2 Timothy 1:7**

... worry about being eligible to play—**Proverbs 22:29; Colossians 3:23**

... just won a championship—**Ephesians 5:20; Hebrews 13:15; James 1:17**

... have everything all figured out—**Proverbs 27:1; James 4:13-16**

... want to brag—**Proverbs 11:2; 16:18-19; 27:2; Luke 14:11; 1 Peter 5:5-6**

... made a mistake that cost the ballgame—**Philippians 3:13,14; 4:4-7**

... know your favorite girl/guy dated someone else—**Psalm 34; Proverbs 14:30; 1 Corinthians 13:4-5**

... are invited to drink—**Psalm 1; Proverbs 12:26; 20:1; 23:29-35; 1 Corinthians 5:11; 6:10; Ephesians 5:18**

... need to decide where to go to school—**Psalm 32:8; Proverbs 3:5-6; Matthew 6:33**

... keep having impure thoughts—**Psalm 1:2; 1 Corinthians 6:18-20; Philippians 4:8**

... feel like the only Christian on the team—**Psalm 23; Romans 8:31-39**

... find out your parents are splitting up—**Psalm 27:10; 55:22; 68:5**

... are at your summer job—**Ephesians 6:5-8; 1 Peter 2:13-21**

... disagree with your coach—**Ephesians 6:5-8; 1 Peter 2:13-21**

... have a misunderstanding with your parents—**Ephesians 6:1-3; Colossians 3:20**

... lose your temper with a roommate—**Proverbs 17:14; Matthew 18:15-35; James 1:19-26**

... wonder if God cares about your game—**Matthew 6:25-34; 1 Peter 5:7**

... are injured and unable to play—**2 Corinthians 1:3-5; 12:9-10**

... are too tired to play another quarter.—**Psalm 90; Romans 5:3-5**

... your teammate dies—**John 11:25-26; 1 Thessalonians 4:13-18**

... wanted to win so badly and didn't—**Matthew 26:39**

... want to take it easy rather than practice—**Proverbs 10:4-5**

... are tempted to cheat to get ahead—**Proverbs 20:17**

... don't know what to say to God—**Romans 8:26**

... feel as though nothing is going right—**Romans 8:28-29; Hebrews 13:5-6**

... are discouraged because you keep blowing it—**Psalm 37:23,34; Philippians 3:7-14**

... know what is wrong—**1 Corinthians 10:13; 2 Corinthians 5:10; Hebrews 4:15-16; 1 John 1:6**

... are propositioned—**Proverbs 5; 7:6-27**

... want to marry (or date) an unbeliever—**2 Corinthians 6:14-16**

LIFE PLAYBOOK

WHAT THE BIBLE SAYS ABOUT ...

... Abortion—**Mark 10:19; Luke 18:20; James 2:11**
... Bible Study—**Psalm 119:9,11; 2 Timothy 2:15**
... Cleanliness—**2 Corinthians 7:1**
... Complaining—**Philippians 2:14; Hebrews 13:5**
... Crime—**Matthew 15:17-20**
... Criticism—**Matthew 7:1-5; Eph. 4:29**
... Death (physical)—**Luke 16:19-26; Romans 5:12; Hebrews 9:27**
... Death (spiritual)—**Genesis 2:17; John 5:24; Romans 5:12; 6:23**
... Divorce—**Matt. 19:3-12; Mark 10:2-12; 1 Corinthians 7**
... Final judgment—**Revelation 20:11-15**
... Forgiveness—**Matthew 18:21-35**
... Giving—**2 Corinthians 8:7-12; 9:6-11**
... Goals—**Matthew 6:33; Romans 8:29**
... Gossip—**Ephesians 4:29; Colossians 3:8; James 4:11**
... Heaven—**Matthew 6:20; Luke 10:20; John 14:2-3**
... Hell—**Matthew 13:41-42; 25:41; Revelation 20:10**
... Homosexuality—**Romans 1:24-27**
... Hypocrisy—**Matthew 15:7-9; 23:1-38**
... Love—**1 Corinthians 13**
... Making money—**Proverbs 30:7-9; Matthew 6:25-33; 1 Timothy 6:6-10**
... Older people—**1 Peter 5:5**
... Parents—**Ephesians 6:1-3**
... Patience—**Psalm 40:1**
... Physical fitness—**1 Corinthians 6:19-20**
... Popularity—**John 12:43; Colossians 3:22**
... Pride—**Psalm 119:21; Proverbs 8:13; 11:2; 16:18; 29:23**
... Revenge—**Matthew 5:43-48**
... Salvation—**John 3:16; Romans 10:9-13; Ephesians 2:8-10**
... Satisfaction in God—**Psalm 17:15; 107:9**
... Sex outside marriage—**Matthew 5:27-32; 1 Corinthians 6:15-20**
... Sex within marriage—**1 Corinthians 7:3-5; Hebrews 13:4**
... Sin and confession—**Proverbs 28:13; 1 John 1:9**
... Swearing—**Matthew 5:34-37; Ephesians 4:29; James 5:12**
... Witnessing—**2 Corinthians 5:11-20**
... Worry—**Matthew 6:25-34**
... Worship—**John 4:21-24; Revelation 19:1,5-8**

CHOOSING A CHURCH

Here are some guidelines for choosing a church:

1) Look for a church where the Bible is taken seriously, taught clearly, and applied practically. (See 2 Timothy 3:14-17.)

2) Look for a church that welcomes youth and even has a great youth group. A strong youth group can give you the encouragement that you need, and can help you grow in your relationship with Christ.

3) Look for people who are responsive to the claims Christ makes upon them in His Word. Christianity shouldn't be something we put on and take off with our Sunday clothes. Ask yourself if the people in this church live in continuous repentance and faith. Are they maturing in character? Most of all, do they love one another? (See John 14:15 and James 1:22-25.)

4) Look for a church that will train you to serve. A good church should treat you as a responsible person that is capable of ministering, and it should hold you accountable for that ministry. (See 1 Timothy 4:6-8.)

5) Look for a church that's reaching out. Ask yourself, "Do they sacrifice their time, money, and talents to see that others at home and abroad experience the good news of Jesus Christ?" (See Matthew 28:18-20.)

6) Beware of the ever-present cults. These false churches take from, add to, or twist the meaning of the Bible.

7) Find a church that's a "house of prayer for all people" (see Mark 11:17). The early church brought together in one community the young and old, rich and poor, black and white, and new converts.

GETTING INVOLVED WITH FCA

VISION:

To see the world impacted for Jesus Christ through the influence of athletes and coaches.

MISSION:

To present to athletes and coaches, and all whom they influence, the challenge and adventure of receiving Jesus Christ as Savior and Lord, serving Him in their relationships and in the fellowship of the church.

VALUES:

Our relationships will demonstrate a steadfast commitment to Jesus Christ and His Word through Integrity, Serving, Teamwork, and Excellence.

COACHES MINISTRY:

The very first and most important ministry we have in FCA is ministry to coaches. Coaches are the heart of FCA. Our role is to minister to them by encouraging and equipping them to know and serve Christ. FCA ministers to coaches through Bible studies, staff contacts, prayer support, discipleship, and mentoring, resources, outreach events, and retreats. We believe that coaches are incredibly valued by God first for who they are and then for what God has created for them to do.

CAMPUS MINISTRY:

The Campus Ministry is initiated and led by student-athletes and coaches on junior high, high school, and college campuses across this country. It is important for you to know that Campus Ministry has many different expressions. For many years we simply had Huddles, but as God has blessed FCA the Campus Ministry has expanded to include Huddles, Team Bible studies, Chapel Programs, One Way 2 Play—Drug Free, and Special Events, even networking with other campus Bible clubs.

CAMPS MINISTRY:

Camps are a time of "inspiration and perspiration" for coaches and athletes to reach their potential by offering comprehensive athletic, spiritual, and leadership training. In FCA we offer different types of Camps: Sports Camps, Leadership Camps, Coaches' Camps, Youth Camps, and Partnership Camps.

COMMUNITY MINISTRY:

FCA Ministries has ministries that reach the community through partnerships with the local churches, businesses, parents, and volunteers. These ministries not only reach out to the community but also allow the community to invest in athletes and coaches. Stewardship Ministries, Adult Ministries, Sport-Specific Ministries, Clinics, Resources, and Professional Athlete Ministries are our main areas of ministry in the area of Community.

Visit FCA.org or call 800-289-0909 for more info.

THE COMPETITOR'S CREED

I am a Christian first and last.
I am created in the likeness of
God Almighty to bring Him glory.
I am a member of Team Jesus Christ.
I wear the colors of the cross.

I am a Competitor now and forever.
I am made to strive, to strain,
to stretch and to succeed
in the arena of competition.
I am a Christian Competitor
and as such, I face my challenger
with the face of Christ.

I do not trust in myself.
I do not boast in my abilities
or believe in my own strength.
I rely solely on the power of God.
I compete for the pleasure of
my Heavenly Father, the honor of Christ
and the reputation of the Holy Spirit.

My attitude on and off
the field is above reproach -
my conduct beyond criticism.
Whether I am preparing,
practicing or playing;
I submit to God's authority
and those He has put over me.
I respect my coaches, officials,
teammates and competitors
out of respect for the Lord.

My body is the temple of Jesus Christ.
I protect it from within and without.
Nothing enters my body that
does not honor the Living God.
My sweat is an offering to my Master.
My soreness is a sacrifice to my Savior.

I give my all - all of the time.
I do not give up. I do not give in.
I do not give out. I am the Lord's warrior -
a competitor by conviction
and a disciple of determination.
I am confident beyond reason
because my confidence lies in Christ.
The results of my efforts
must result in His glory.

LET THE COMPETITION BEGIN.
LET THE GLORY BE GOD'S.

JOIN TEAMFCA:

As a competitor-athlete, coach, or fan, you are a skilled person. You have talents and abilities. You have expectations and deliver results. But for a Christian competitor, being skilled is just the beginning. A Christian competitor aims to become like Jesus Christ—the greatest competitor of all time. He is the greatest competitor for the souls of men, the greatest champion to hang on the cross, the greatest teammate to lift up those around him, the greatest captain to build a lasting team. If you want to play like Christ every time you put on your uniform, lace up your shoes, or walk out of the locker room, then you are ready to join TeamFCA. To find out more visit our Web page today.

Join TeamFCA today at FCA.org

FELLOWSHIP OF CHRISTIAN ATHLETES